The Norton Anthology
of Western Literature

Eighth Edition

VOLUME 1

The Norton Anthology
of Western Literature

Eighth Edition

Sarah Lawall, *General Editor*

PROFESSOR EMERITA OF COMPARATIVE LITERATURE,
UNIVERSITY OF MASSACHUSETTS, AMHERST

VOLUME 1
The Ancient World through the Renaissance

W · W · NORTON & COMPANY · *New York · London*

W. W. Norton & Company has been independent since its founding in 1923, when William Warder Norton and Mary D. Herter Norton first published lectures delivered at the People's Institute, the adult education division of New York City's Cooper Union. The Nortons soon expanded their program beyond the Institute, publishing books by celebrated academics from America and abroad. By mid-century, the two major pillars of Norton's publishing program—trade books and college texts—were firmly established. In the 1950s, the Norton family transferred control of the company to its employees, and today—with a staff of four hundred and a comparable number of trade, college, and professional titles published each year—W. W. Norton & Company stands as the largest and oldest publishing house owned wholly by its employees.

Editor: Peter Simon
Managing Editor, College: Marian Johnson
Developmental Editor: Carol Flechner
Electronic Media and Ancillaries Editor: Eileen Connell
Editorial Assistants: Robert Bellinger, Simone Gubar, Birgit Larsson
Permission Manager: Nancy Rodwan
Production Manager: Diane O'Connor
Book Designer: Antonina Krass
Art Research: Neil Ryder Hoos

The text of this book is composed in Fairfield Medium
with the display set in Bernhard Modern.
Composition by Binghamton Valley Composition.
Manufacturing by R. R. Donnelley & Sons.

Cover illustration: Benozzo Gozzoli (1420–1497), *Lorenzo the Magnificent (Medici)*, detail from *Procession of the Magi*. Palazzo Medici Riccardi, Florence, Italy. Photo: Erich Lessing/Art Resource, NY.

ISBN 0-393-92572-2 (pbk.)

W. W. Norton & Company, Inc., 500 Fifth Avenue, New York, NY 10110
www.wwnorton.com

W. W. Norton & Company Ltd., Castle House, 75/76 Wells Street, London W1T 3QT

1 2 3 4 5 6 7 8 9 0

Contents

The Middle Ages

The Renaissance

Preface to the Eighth Edition

The literature of the Western tradition is a celebrated stream of rich and diverse texts that have brought enjoyment and wisdom to readers for—in some cases—thousands of years. As the tradition has evolved and expanded over time, certain authors have been read and reread with remarkable continuity, even as perspectives on their work have changed with changing cultural attitudes. These authors—such as Homer, Sappho, and the Greek dramatists; Virgil and Dante; Cervantes, Shakespeare, and Molière; Goethe, Tolstoy, Flaubert, and Proust—and dozens of others still appear in *The Norton Anthology of Western Literature*, many with additional selections and in vivid new translations. As we have done in the past, the editors have made a number of additions to the list of celebrated authors in the anthology. New authors to this edition include Hesiod, Apuleius, Chrétien de Troyes, Jean de la Fontaine, Lord Byron, Mikhail Lermontov, Nikolai Gogol, Giovanni Verga, Guy de Maupassant, Joseph Conrad, Constantine Cavafy, Alfonsina Storni, Pablo Neruda, Italo Calvino, and Derek Walcott, among others.

This edition improves upon its predecessors in an important new dimension as well: the presence of numerous texts—historical, philosophical, political, and religious—that provide cultural contexts and illuminate patterns of thought. Grouped in thematic clusters for ease of reference and as points of departure for classroom discussion, these texts are more than mere historical documentation. They show how different thinkers viewed the events and central issues of their times. These events and issues resonate with, and sometimes even appear within, the literary works that surround each thematic cluster. Together, the documents reprinted in these clusters comprise a polyphonic tradition of different voices and concepts of reality: they display divergent images of social, political, ethnic, and gendered identity as well as competing concepts of human nature, the nature of the universe, ethical values, and the proper organization of society. Some of the authors are famous: Herodotus, Thucydides, Joan of Arc, Christopher Columbus, Charles Darwin, Karl Marx, and Jean-Paul Sartre, for example. Others—Lucretius, Theophrastus, Christine de Pizan, Madame de Staël, Mona Caird, Giuseppe Garibaldi, Sol T. Plaatje, and Frantz Fanon—are significant but less widely known figures. Reading these cultural texts in conjunction with texts ruled by the artistic imagination richly illuminates a shared world of experience and brings alive the complex reality of a literary-cultural tradition in which all are embedded. Complementing the written texts are sixteen colored plates in each volume, each with a caption situating its subject in cultural history.

Throughout *The Norton Anthology of Western Literature*, you will recognize many other changes, both large and small. What follows is a section-by-section overview of these changes.

The Ancient World. The epic of *Gilgamesh* is brought into sharp focus by the juxtaposition of two differing translations of Tablet XI (the story of the Flood and Gilgamesh's return home), one by noted Near Eastern scholar Benjamin Foster and the other by contemporary poet and translator Stephen Mitchell. The passages from Genesis and Exodus in the Hebrew Bible are newly translated by Robert Alter and now include the story of Abraham and Sarah, and of Moses receiving the Law. Job is newly translated by Raymond Scheindlin. The familiar and influential cadence of the King James Version is retained in our selections from the Psalms and the Song of Songs. Aeschylus's trilogy the *Oresteia* now appears complete with the inclusion of *The Libation Bearers*. *Antigone* has been added to Sophocles' *Oedipus the King*, and a new author, the Carthaginian writer Apuleius, is represented by selections from his comic masterpiece *The Golden Ass*. Book I of Virgil's *Aeneid* is now included, as is the creation myth in Ovid's *Metamorphoses*—and Ovid is newly translated by Charles Martin. Other new translations appear throughout. Homer is represented by Stanley Lombardo's *Iliad*, a realistic rendering that has been enormously successful in the classroom, and by Robert Fagles's well-known translation of the *Odyssey*. Sappho's lyrics are translated by Anne Carson, and Plato's *Apology* by C. D. C. Reeve. Classicist Jeffrey Henderson gives us a new translation of Aristophanes' unforgettable *Lysistrata*. Richmond Lattimore translates the selections from the New Testament. Complementing these and other works in this section is a cluster that describes the competing belief systems in Greece and Rome, ranging from a traditional faith in the Olympian gods to various secular, scientific, and philosophical inquiries. Plato, Aristotle, and Aeschylus, as well as five new authors—Hesiod, Herodotus, Thucydides, Lucretius, and Seneca—contribute their perspectives in a span that ranges over eight centuries.

The Middle Ages. The Middle Ages are not known for their charitable view of women, and another cluster, "Medieval Women," explores this reputation in ten selections, all new to this volume, and concludes that the period was far more divided on the issue than is generally recognized. Passages from Tertullian, St. John Chrysostom, Theophrastus, Heloise, Andreas Capellanus, Guillaume de Mailly, the anonymous Southern Passion, Christine de Pizan, legal records in England, and a transcript of the trial of Joan of Arc furnish passionate arguments on both sides of a debate that reaches back into the ancient world and has not yet disappeared. Echoes of these attitudes appear throughout the most popular works of the period—for example, in Boccaccio's *Decameron*, Chaucer's *Canterbury Tales*, the *lais* of Marie de France, Dante's *Divine Comedy*, and many of the lyric poems printed here. Several new works appear in this section: *The Story of the Grail* by Chrétien de Troyes, "The Story of the Fisherman and the Demon" in *The Thousand and One Nights*, the Prologue to Boccaccio's *Decameron*, and seven new suras added to the existing selections from the Koran. There are also two new translations of note: Seamus Heaney's acclaimed rendering of *Beowulf*, and Mark Musa's *Divine Comedy*.

The Renaissance. Shakespeare's *Hamlet*, found indispensable by many of our readers, returns to the Renaissance section, joined by a group of poems by John Donne, three new stories from *The Heptameron* of Marguerite de Navarre, and additional passages from Cervantes's *Don Quixote* and Milton's *Paradise Lost*. Lope de Vega's *Fuente Ovejuna* appears in a new translation by Gwynne Edwards, and several new translations by Mark Musa round out the selection of Petrarch's sonnets. A major addition to this section consists in an eminently teachable set of three thematically organized clusters of lyric poetry: love poetry in the Petrarchan tradition, "carpe diem" poetry, and a wider range of metaphysical poetry. Leading poets of several national traditions are reunited in these groupings, which demonstrate the power of artistic ideas to cross national boundaries and reinvent themselves in a new setting. For lyric poetry after Petrarch, we have Michelangelo Buonarroti, Francesco Berni, Maurice Scève, Sir Thomas Wyatt, Veronica Franco, Edmund Spenser, Sir Philip Sidney, and Giambattista Marino; for those trying to persuade their loved one to "seize the day," there is Lorenzo de' Medici, Angelo Poliziano, Torquato Tasso, Christopher Marlowe, Sir Walter Raleigh, Edmund Spenser, Sir Philip Sidney, John Donne, Ben Jonson, Robert Herrick, Martin Opitz, and Andrew Marvell. The other metaphysicals are represented by Guy Le Fèvre de la Boderie, San Juan de la Cruz, Agrippa d'Aubigné, George Herbert, Francisco de Queveda, and Constantijn Huygens. Finally, a cluster of prose texts in "Travel and Discovery" run the gamut from fantastic voyages to tales of conquest and subsequently a bleak critique of that conquest, setting side by side the voyagers' assumed (European) norms for human behavior and the challenging reality of contact with other cultures. The spirit of inquiry and self-interrogation shown variously in the writings of Sir John Mandeville, Christopher Columbus, Hernán Cortés, Bernal Díaz, Hans Staden, Bartolomé de Las Casas, and Captain John Smith recur throughout Renaissance writings (notably in Montaigne's celebrated essay *On Cannibals*) and take on new life in nineteenth- and twentieth-century debates over colonization and globalization.

   The Enlightenment. The situation of women is the subject of our Enlightenment cluster, with energetic testimony from Judith Drake, Theodor Gottlieb von Hippel, Mary Robinson, Hannah More, and Olympe de Gouges as well as a passage from Jean-Jacques Rousseau's narrative treatise on education, *Émile.* One of the most passionately sought rights for women was the opportunity to receive a full (and not merely "practical") education, and the debate initiated so forcefully here continues well into the nineteenth and twentieth centuries (see Mona Caird and Virginia Woolf, later in this anthology). Also new to this section is a series of celebrated fables by the French classical author Jean de La Fontaine.

   The Nineteenth Century: Romanticism. Rousseau, although living in the eighteenth century, is usually discussed as a precursor of nineteenth-century Romanticism, and the new translation of his *Confessions* by J. M. Cohen launches the next section. We are pleased to be able to offer, in addition, Martin Greenberg's remarkable new translation of *Faust*, Part I. Poems by Lord Byron have been added to current selections from Blake, Wordsworth, Coleridge, Shelley, and Keats to form an overview of English Romantic lyrics that corresponds to the section on Continental Romantic lyrics, which itself has expanded to include the Frenchman Gérard de Nerval and the Russian Mikhail Lermontov. The cluster "Revolutionary Moments" focuses on a contrast of American and French figures in the revolutionary period: Governor

Thomas Hutchinson of the Massachusetts Bay Colony, John and Abigail Adams, Mercy Otis Warren, Madame de Staël, Thomas Paine, Jean-Paul Marat (whose death is depicted by Jacques-Louis David in the color insert), and various participants in the French Revolution.

The Nineteenth Century: Realism and Symbolism. This section adds short stories by three celebrated and influential authors who have been claimed at different times for both realism and naturalism: Guy de Maupassant, with *Hautot and His Son*; Giovanni Verga, co-founder of the Italian movement of *verismo* (truthful representation), with *Freedom*; and Nikolai Gogol (paradoxically, also a master of the grotesque) with his tragicomic *The Overcoat*. A new translation of Ibsen's *Hedda Gabler*, by Rick Davis and Brian Johnston, is also offered. To the selections of Symbolist poetry we have added short prose works by Baudelaire, Mallarmé, and Rimbaud that clarify crucial aspects of their poetry: Baudelaire's *The Queen of Faculties* from his *Salon of 1859*; Mallarmé, in passages from an interview and in *Crisis in Poetry*; and Rimbaud, in his letter to Paul Demeny known as the *Letter of the Seer*. Two clusters—"Revolutionary Principles" and "Perspectives on European Empire"—present major texts in intellectual and political history. The former focuses on influential ideas that challenged accepted wisdom and structures of authority: Charles Darwin's evolutionary theory in *The Origin of Species* and *The Descent of Man*; Karl Marx and Friedrich Engels's definitions of "Bourgeois and Proletarians" from the *Manifesto of the Communist Party*; Émile Zola's famous letter *J'Accuse,* denouncing governmental corruption and anti-Semitism in the Dreyfus case; Friedrich Nietzsche's attack on the West's moral decay in *The Gay Science*; and Mona Caird's description of patriarchal marriage as a system of legalized slavery in *The Emancipation of the Family.* "Perspectives on European Empire," focusing especially on the history of colonialism and racist policies, cites documents from various positions of power or vulnerability: Thomas Babington Macaulay's influential *Minute on Indian Education*, prescribing English as the language of instruction in India; the Yao chief Machemba, protesting invasions by German soldiers; the British imperialist Cecil Rhodes, urging the exploitation of Africa for the benefit of Europe; the South African Olive Schreiner, urging a similar development for the benefit of colonists; a fascinating account of her travels in West Africa by the intrepid Victorian ethnologist Mary Kingsley; the diary of an African civil servant, Sol T. Plaatje, set in the siege of Mafeking during the Boer War; and a surprising (and unsuccessful) proposal by international revolutionary Giuseppe Garibaldi to restructure European government in a way that foreshadows the next century's European Union.

The Twentieth Century. The first of many new works in the twentieth-century section is Joseph Conrad's *Heart of Darkness*, which echoes themes of the preceding cluster and can profitably be read in conjunction with it. Other new entries include evocative lyrics by the chief modern Greek poet Constantine Cavafy; the short story *Flowering Judas* by Katherine Anne Porter; poems by the Argentinian writer Alfonsina Storni; selections from the Chilean poet Pablo Neruda, including sections VI through XII of his epic *The Heights of Macchu Picchu* from *General Song*; an intriguing chapter from *Invisible Cities* by the Italian fantasist Italo Calvino; and selections from *Omeros* by the Caribbean poet Derek Walcott. Virginia Woolf's *A Room of One's Own* now contains the addition of Chapter One and is appropriately accompanied by the short story *An Unwritten Novel*. William Faulkner is represented by two favorite short stories: *Barn Burning* and *Spotted Horses*. *The Hollow Men* has been added to the selections by T. S. Eliot. *Borges and I*, Borges's short meditation on textual and personal identity, now accompanies the author's *The Garden of Forking Paths*. The Proust selection from *Swann's Way* appears in a celebrated new translation by Lydia Davis, and Kafka's *Metamorphosis* is now offered in a translation by J. A. Underwood.

Three thematic clusters—"Civilization on Trial," "Freedom and Responsibility at Mid-Century," and "On Being a Cultural Other"—document important issues in twentieth-century thought. Doubts about the status of European civilization begin to be aired at the turn of the century and strengthen after World War I, as is shown in the first cluster with Max Weber's *The Protestant Ethic and the Spirit of Capitalism*, the entry *Civilization* from the famous eleventh edition of the *Encyclopaedia Britannica*, Oswald Spengler's bleak assessment in *The Decline of the West*, Paul Valéry's letter-essay *The Crisis of the Mind*, and two works by Sigmund Freud: *The Future of an Illusion* and *Civilization and Its Discontents*. By mid-century, directly following World War II, attention turned to the role played by individual choice in human affairs, and our second cluster presents analyses by the existentialist philosopher Jean-Paul Sartre (*Being and Nothingness*), the social philosopher Hannah Arendt (*Organized Guilt and Universal Responsibility*), and the novelist and essayist George Orwell (*The Prevention of Literature*). Finally, recapitulating the emphasis on cultural identity that has, in one or another form, permeated the century, the third cluster invokes a range of speakers who remind us—from their own experience—that easy definitions have little validity in real life. Included are selections from René Ménil, *Concerning Colonial Exoticism*; Simone de Beauvoir, *The Second Sex*; Frantz Fanon, *The Wretched of the Earth*; Chinua Achebe, *Named for Victoria, Queen of England*; Audre Lorde, *Age, Race, Class, and Sex: Women Redefining Difference*; Edward Said, *Orientalism*; Trinh T. Minh-ha, *Woman, Native, Other: Writing Postcoloniality and Feminism*; and Salman Rushdie's recent *Step across This Line*.

The new Eighth Edition contains all of the pedagogical support to which our users are accustomed: maps, time lines, pronunciation glossaries, and, of course, the informative introductions and notes, written by editors who are themselves experienced teachers and who often incorporate suggestions from our users. The sixteen color plates new to this volume are captioned and broadly coordinated with each period. In addition, *The Norton Anthology of Western Literature* now provides students and teachers access to a new online resource for students of literature—Norton Literature Online. More information about Norton Literature Online can be found inside the back cover of this anthology.

Each section of *The Norton Anthology of Western Literature* has added new material to old favorites, allowing the teacher to keep tried-and-true works and also to experiment with different contexts and combinations. Some links are suggested by the organization of the table of contents, but there is no prescribed way of using the anthology, and we are confident that the materials presented here offer a wealth of viable options to support customized syllabi geared to specific student needs. A separate *Instructor's Guide*, with further suggestions and helpful guidance for new and experienced instructors alike, is available from the publisher on request.

In closing, we want to pay tribute to Jerome Wright Clinton, professor of Near Eastern Studies at Princeton University, who died in 2003. Professor Clinton, a translator of classical Persian literature and a scholar of great learning and humanity, was the Near Eastern editor for the *Norton Anthology of World Literature* and edited the entries for the Koran and *The Thousand and One Nights* in this edition. A generous colleague and friend, he will be missed.

Acknowledgments

In preparing the texts and contextual clusters of this Eighth Edition, we have called on many colleagues and friends for expert advice in matters that range from linguistic subtleties to cultural expectations at a given place or time. For special help, which has often included related remarks on classroom experience, we are pleased to thank Clifford Ando (University of Southern California); Anthony Boyle (University of Southern California); Jenny Strauss Clay (University of Virginia); Anthony Edwards (University of California, San Diego); Lori Ann Ferrell (Claremont Graduate University); Elizabeth Fitzpatrick (University of Massachusetts); Karen Polinger Foster (Yale University); Andrea Frisch (University of Maryland, Baltimore County); Thomas Habinek (University of Southern California); Peter Mancall (University of Southern California); Richard Martin (Stanford University); Nicholas Moschovakis (Reed College); Anthony Parr (University of the Western Cape); Steven Reece (St. Olaf College); Kathryn Ridenour (University of Massachusetts); Robert Rothstein (University of Massachusetts); Seth Schein (University of California, Davis); Eva Schiffer (University of Massachusetts); Laura Slatkin (New York University); and Robert Sullivan (University of Massachusetts).

In addition, we wish to recognize the contribution of a team of undergraduates at the University of Southern California who reviewed and commented on various editorial introductions and annotations: Phil Taylor (project coordinator), Anne Aubert-Santelli, Monika Lind, and Bryce McFerran. Their perspective as student readers and respondents was invaluable and much appreciated.

In the spring of 2003, W. W. Norton & Company solicited advice from instructors who had contacted the publisher over the years with suggestions for improvement. We are especially grateful to the following, who replied with helpful and thought-provoking responses: Susan Ahern (University of Houston); Heidi E. Ajrami (Victoria College); Allison Alison (Southeastern Community College); Elaine Ancekewicz (Long Island University, C. W. Post Campus); Chris Anderson (Oregon State University); Francis Auld (University of South Florida); Warren G. Babilot (Pueblo Community College); Jim Barnes (Truman State University); Juluette F. Bartlett-Pack (Texas Southern University); Martha Bartter (Truman State University); Patti Bates (California Polytechnic State University); Bridget Beaver (Connors State College); Lee Bedell (Cuesta College); James Bednarz (Long Island University, C. W. Post Campus); Albert J. Bekus (Austin Peay State University); Deb Belt (Hillsdale College); Craig Bennett (Valley Forge Military Academy and College); Paul Benson (Dallas County Community College); Boyd M. Berry (Virginia Commonwealth University); Barbara Bird (St. Petersburg College); Angela Bisong (Texas Southern University); Raymond J. Biziorek (Baker College); Kristin Bluemel (Monmouth University); Richard Bodek

(College of Charleston); Scott Boltwood (Emory & Henry College); David Bordelon (Ocean County College); Marilyn Boutwell (Long Island University); Terence Bowers (College of Charleston); Stephen Boyer (Camden County College); Deborah E. Brassard (Marywood University); John Brinegar (Virginia Commonwealth University); Dan Brooks (Aquinas College); Addison Bross (Lehigh University); Devin Brown (Asbury College); Gayle Brown (University of Florida); Sarah Brown (Schreiner University); Dana Burbank (University of North Alabama); John Burke (University of Alabama); Ann M. Bush (Marywood University); A. Thorpe Butler (Texas Southern University); Lynn Butler (University of Northern Alabama); Catherine Calloway (Arkansas State University); Joseph F. Caputo (Marywood University); Thomas Carabas (Community College of Southern Nevada); Terri Carine; Peter J. Casagrande (University of Kansas); Allen J. Christenson (Brigham Young University); Patricia Cleary-Miller (Rockhurst University); Debra Rae Cohen (University of Arkansas); Adrienne Condon (University of South Florida); William Conlogue (Marywood University); Sharon Coolidge (Wheaton College); Stephen Cooper (Troy State University); Thomas A. Copeland (Youngstown State University); Connie Corbett-Whittier (Friends University); Peter Cortland (Quinnipiac University); Robert Cosgrove (Saddleback College); Catherine Cox (Texas A&M University—Corpus Christi); Sandra Coyle (College of St. Joseph in Vermont); Marcel M. Crespil (Texas Southern University); Phyllis S. Dallas (Georgia Southern University); Dennis Danvers (Virginia Commonwealth University); Lesley Danziger (Orange Coast College); James Davis (Troy State University); James Day (Troy State University); Andrew P. Debicki (University of Kansas); Dorothy Deering (Purdue University); Margaret Del Guercio (Monmouth University); John A. Dern (Gwynedd-Mercy College); Thomas Deveny (McDaniel College); Emily Dial-Driver (Rogers State University); Christopher Dick (Tabor College); Donald R. Dickson (Texas A&M University); Sheila Diecidue (University of South Florida); John DiGaetani (Hofstra University); Joseph M. Ditta (Dakota Wesleyan University); Sharon S. Drake (Texarkana College); David L. Dudley (Georgia Southern University); Alexander Dunlop (Auburn University); Alice T. Duxbury (Palm Beach Community College); Michael Dzanko (College Misericordia); Marilyn Edelstein (Santa Clara University); William Edinger (University of Maryland); Christina Elvidge (Marywood University); Ann W. Engar (University of Utah); Chad Engbers (Calvin College); Renee Epstein (Baruch College, CUNY); Heide Estes (Monmouth University); Prescott Evarts (Monmouth University); Alex Fagan (Virginia Commonwealth University); Chris Fahy (Boston University); Tom Fahy (California Polytechnic State University); Gerald Farber (San Diego State University); Thomas J. Farrell (University of Minnesota, Duluth); Joan Ferrell (Southeastern Illinois College); Shelly Fischer (Community College of Southern Nevada); Randy Fisher (Chapman University, Coachella Valley); Irene Fizer (Hofstra University); Robert Forman (St. John's University); Beverly Forsyth (Odessa College); Marjorie Francoeur (Rivier College); Bruce Gans (Wilbur Wright College); Maria Garcia (Texas Southern University); Elaine Gardiner (William Paterson University); Brian Garvey (Monmouth University); Julie Gates (Angelo State University); Mary Geer (Monmouth University); Jerry D. Gibbens (Williams Baptist College); Virginia Gilbert (Alabama A&M University); John Gillen (Vermont State College, Castleton);

Haydn Gilmore (Marywood University); Janice Glor (University of Northern Alabama); Al Glover (Troy State University); Carolyn Gordon (Mineral Area College); Jonna Gormely Semeiks (Long Island University, C. W. Post Campus); Susan Goulding (Monmouth University); Genie Greavu-Comley (Gainesville College); David Greene (Long Island University, C. W. Post Campus); Ronald Greene (Guilford Technical Community College); Julia B. Griffin (Georgia Southern University); David Gross (University of Oklahoma); Loren C. Gruber (Missouri Valley College); Susan A. Hagedorn (Virginia Polytechnic Institute and State University); Joyce Haines (Friends University); Keith Hale (South Texas Community College); Mary Theresa Hall (Thiel College); Margaret Hallissy (Long Island University, C. W. Post Campus); Jan Haluska (Southern Adventist University); Carol E. Harding (Western Oregon University); Mary Ellen Harje (Angelo State University); Allison Harl (University of Arkansas Community College); Donna Harmon (Texas Southern University); Kent Harrelson (Dalton State College); Charles Harrison (San Jacinto College South); Sarah H. Harrison (Tyler Junior College); Thomas Harrison (Macon State College); John Heath (Santa Clara University); Gloria Henderson (Gordon College); John Henderson (Central Texas College); Dennis E. Hensley (Taylor University Fort Wayne); Deborah Hicks (Troy State University); Adam Hill (California Polytechnic State University); Jack Himmelblau (University of Texas at San Antonio); Susanna Hoeness-Krupsaw (University of Southern Indiana); Michael Holden (Delaware State University); Gail Holian (Georgian Court College); Thomasita Homan (Benedictine College); Glenn Hopp (Howard Payne University); Greg Horn (Southwest Virginia Community College); Barbara Horwitz (Long Island University, C. W. Post Campus); Carolina Hospital (Miami Dade College); Alan Howell (California Polytechnic State University); Dennis J. Humphrey (Arkansas State University—Beebe); John Hussey (Fairmont State Community & Technical College); Collin Hutchison (San Jacinto College South); Ursula Irwin (Mount Hood Community College); Nalini Iyer (Seattle University); Scott Jarvis (Hofstra University); Arbolina L. Jennings (Texas Southern University); Melba M. Johnson (Texas Southern University); Eileen Johnston (United States Naval Academy); Lars R. Jones (Florida Institute of Technology); Debbie Jones (Maranatha Baptist Bible College); Julie Kane (Northwestern State University); Veena Kasbekar (Ohio University—Chillicothe); Robert Keane (Hofstra University); Jill Keller (Middlesex Community College); Joseph Khoury; Geoffrey Kimball (Our Lady of Holy Cross College); Donna K. Kimble (Texas Southern University); John Kingsbury (University of North Alabama); Pam Kingsbury (University of North Alabama); Mark Knoernschild (Fullerton College); Neal Kramer (Brigham Young University); Norbert Krapf (Long Island University, C. W. Post Campus); Richard Krause (Somerset Community College); Bob Kroll (Luzerne County Community College); Ken Kuzmich (Albertus Magnus College); Barb Laman (Dickinson State University); Roger Lathbury (George Mason University); Michael Leddy (Eastern Illinois University); Anthony Leuzzi (Monroe Community College); Lan Lipscomb (Troy State University Montgomery); John Thomas Lloyd (Georgia Southern University); Jon Loessin (Wharton County Junior College); Laura Long (Sul Ross State University); Thomas L. Long (Thomas Nelson Community College); Susan Lorsch (Hofstra University); Gerald Lucas (Macon State College); Scott Lucas (The Citadel); Rob Luscher (University of Nebraska at Kearney); Gary McAllister (Central Baptist College); Patrick A. McCarthy (University of Miami); John L. McCraney (Georgia Military College, Augusta Community College); Sheila McDonald (Long Island University, C. W. Post Campus); Ruth McDowell (Milligan College); Joyce J. McEwing (Texas Southern University); Maria McGarrity (Long Island University); Sherry McGuire (Boise State University); Judith S. McKay (Arkansas State University—Beebe); Rebecca McNeer (Ohio University Southern Campus); William N. Mac-Pherson (Essex County College); Kelley Mahoney (Dalton State College); Dominic Manganiello (University of Ottowa); Kelly Marsh (Mississippi State University); Timothy Martin (Rutgers University); Delinda X. Marzette (Texas Southern University); Jim Matthews (Fairmont State Community & Technical College); David Mead (Texas A&M University, Corpus Christi); Lewis Meyers (Hunter College, CUNY); Brett Millan (South Texas Community College); Arthur Miller (New College of Florida); Edmund Miller (Long Island University, C. W. Post Campus); Nelson Miller (Macon State College); Edward Milowicki (Mills College); Rob Modica (Pima Community College); Todd Moffett (Community College of Southern Nevada); Michael Montgomery (Life University); Theron Montgomery (Troy State University); Janice Townley Moore (Young Harris College); Shirley W. Moore (Texas Southern University); Ken Moss (Marist College); Eric R. Nelson (Georgia Southern University); John H. Newell (College of Charleston); Ronald Newman (University of Miami); Laura K. Noell (Northern Virginia Community College); Michael O'Donnell (United States Naval Academy); Louis J. Oldani (Rockhurst University); Catherine Olson (Tomball College); Jill Onega (University of Alabama in Huntsville); Sherry Organ (Harding University); Michael Orlofsky (Troy State University); Sam Overstreet (Maryville College); John Pagano (Barnard College; Manhattan School of Music); Richard Paris (Monmouth University); Jane Parks (Dalton State College); David Partenheimer (Truman State University); Craig Payne (Indian Hills Community College); S. L. Pearce; Meg F. Pearson (University of Maryland); Allene Phy-Olsen (Austin Peay State University); David Pinault (Santa Clara University); Bruce Plourde (Temple University); Michael W. Price (Grove City College); Richard Priebe (Virginia Commonwealth University); Nichelle Puder (Texas Southern University); Maria A. Quintana (Texas Southern University); Diane Rayor (Grand Valley State University); Lana L. Reese (Texas Southern University); Thomas J. Reiter (Monmouth University); Stuart Richman (Cheney University); Mark Roberts (California Polytechnic State University); David Wayne Robinson (Georgia Southern University); David M. Rogers (Seton Hall University); Clifford Ronan (Southwest Texas State University); Sherry Rosenthal (Community College of Southern Nevada); Alan M. Rosiene (Florida Institute of Technology); Jennifer Rosti (Roanoke College); Lance Rubin (Arapahoe Community College); Ted Ruml (California State University, San Bernardino); Carl Runyon (Owensboro Community College); Craig Rustici (Hofstra University); Robert Ryan (Rutgers University); Steven Ryan (Austin Peay State University); Rhonda Saldivar (Texas Southern University); Ronald C. Samples (Texas Southern University); Frederick K. Sanders (Georgia Southern University); Mark Sandona (Hood College); Rhonda Sanford (Fairmont State Community & Technical College); Tom Sauret (Gainsville College); Rita Saylors (Texas Southern University);

Bill Scalia (Hillsdale College); Tracy Schaelen (Southwestern College); John Scheckter (Long Island University, C. W. Post Campus); Mary Jane Schenck (University of Tampa); James D. Schiavoni (Tennessee Wesleyan College); Owen Schur (Seton Hall University); John Scott (Western Baptist College); Evan Seymour (Community College of Philadelphia); Nick Sharp (Virginia Commonwealth University); Sandra D. Shattuck (Alabama A&M University); Lisa Shoemaker (State Fair Community College); Ellen S. Silber (Marymount College of Fordham University); B. D. Sinclair (University of Nebraska at Kearney); Deborah Sinnreich-Levi (Stevens Institute of Technology); Lynn Siracusa (Monmouth University); Tim Sistrunk (California State University, Chico); Diane Smith (Farmingdale State University of New York); Myrna Smith (Raritan Valley Community College); Wendy Smith (Miramar College); Michael D. Sollars (Texas Southern University); Karen Soreson (Austin Peay State University); David Southmayd (Vanier College); Julie Sparks (University of Arkansas—Monticello); Betty Spitzmiller (Rochester Community and Technical College); James R. Sprouse (Pensacola Christian College); Scott T. Starbuck (San Diego Mesa College); Matthew Stewart (Boston University); Ron Stormer (Culver-Stockton College); David T. Stout (Luzerne County Community College); Chris Sullivan (San Diego Mesa College); John Sweeney (Seton Hall University); Jenny Tabb (Pace University); Phyllis Talmadge (Troy State University); Philip J. Tama (Marywood University); Betty Taylor-Thompson (Texas Southern University); Joan Templeton (Long Island University, Brooklyn Campus); Colette Tennant (Western Baptist College); Burt Thorp (University of North Dakota); John Tucker (Nassau Community College); Billy J. Turner (Texas Southern University); W. Ulmer (University of Alabama); Paul Varner (Oklahoma Christian University); Patricia Vazquez (Community College of Southern Nevada); Beert Verstraete (Acadia University); Cory Wade (Santa Clara University); Joyce S. Walker (Everett Community College); Patricia Ward (College of Charleston); Ward Welty (Alabama A&M University); Marian Wernicke (Pensacola Junior College); Bryan West (Spokane Falls Community College); David Whalen (Hillsdale College); Timothy D. Whelan (Georgia Southern University); Toby Widdicombe (University of Alaska Anchorage); Katherine Ann Wildt (Missouri Valley College); Benjamin Wiley (St. Petersburg College); Dan M. Wiley (Hastings College); Ned Williams (Brigham Young University—Hawaii); Thomas L. Wilmeth (Concordia University Wisconsin); Jean Wilson (McMaster University); Carol Y. Wilson (Lander University); Rodney Wilson (Community College of Southern Nevada); Leigh Winser (Seton Hall University); Timothy Winters (Austin Peay State University); Carl Wooton (California Polytechnic State University); Alok Yadav (George Mason University); Linda Yakle (St. Petersburg College); James Yard (Delaware Valley College); Martha Zamorano (Miami-Dade Community College); David Zehr (Santa Monica College); John Ziebell (Community College of Southern Nevada); Jeffrey Zorn (Santa Clara University).

Phonetic Equivalents

For use with the Pronouncing Glossaries preceding
most selections in this volume.

a as in *cat*
ah as in *father*
ai as in *light*
aw as in *raw*
ay as in *day*
e as in *pet*
ee as in *street*
ehr as in *air*
er as in *bird*
eu as in *lurk*
g as in *good*
i as in *sit*
j as in *joke*
nh a nasal sound (as in French *vin, vẽ*)
o as in *pot*
oh as in *no*
oo as in *boot*
or as in *bore*
ow as in *now*
oy as in *toy*
s as in *mess*
ts as in *ants*
u as in *us*
zh as in *vision*

The Norton Anthology
of Western Literature

Eighth Edition

VOLUME 1

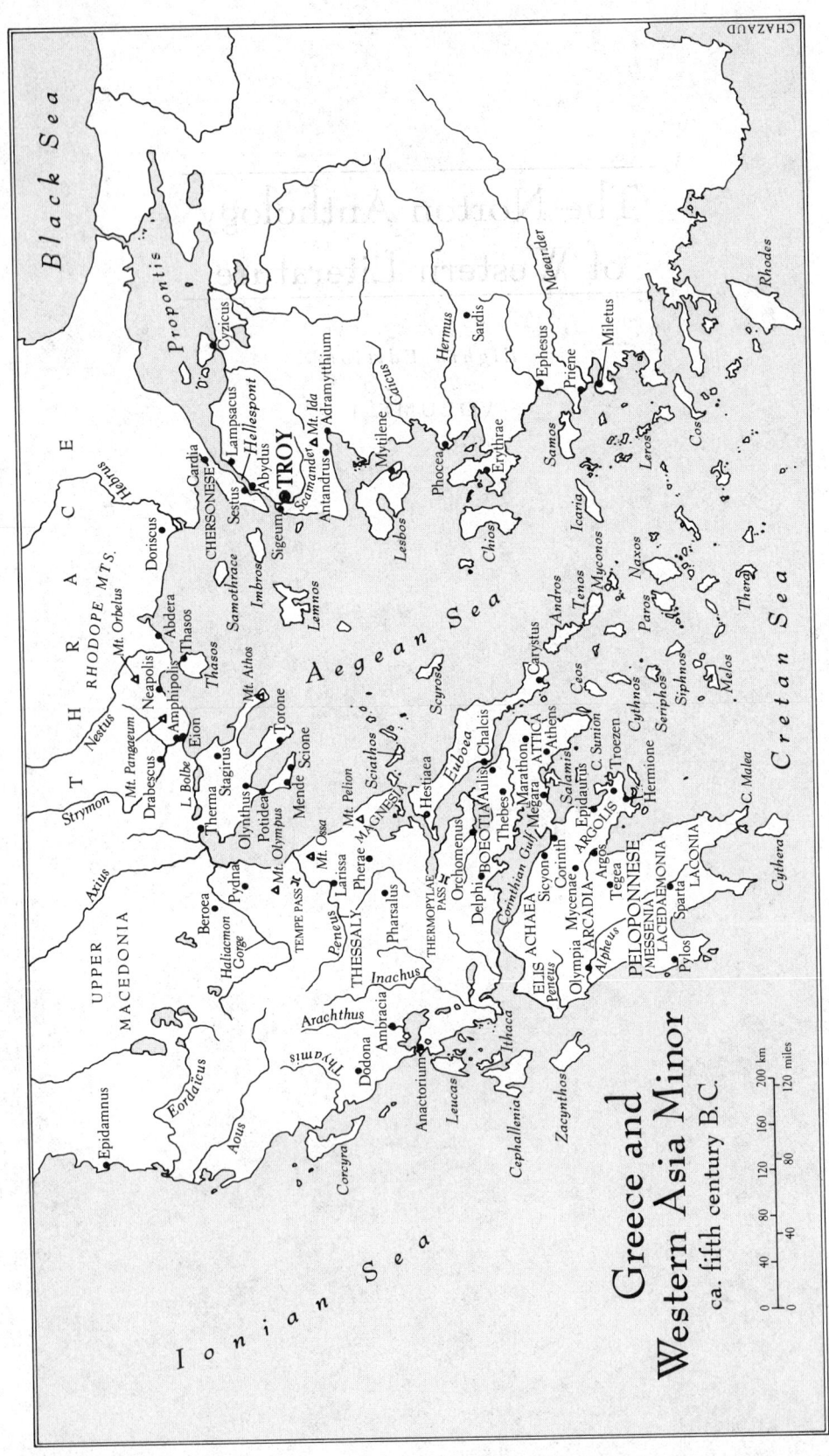

Greece and
Western Asia Minor
ca. fifth century B.C.

CHAZAUD

The Ancient World

This section represents not the ancient world as a whole but a particularly significant area and period. The area is the Mediterranean basin, and the period the twelve hundred years from, roughly, 800 B.C.E. to 400 C.E. In this place and time the intellectual and religious foundations of the modern Western outlook were laid.

The literature that was to help shape that outlook was written in three languages—Hebrew, Greek, and Latin. The peoples who spoke these languages created their civilizations independently in place and time, but the development of the Mediterranean area into one economic and political unit as the result of the Roman conquest brought them into contact with one another and produced a fusion of their typical attitudes that formed the basis of later European thought. This process of independent development, interaction, and final fusion is represented in the tripartite arrangement of this section. As the three separate lines converge, they finally meet in the figure of St. Augustine, who had the intellectual honesty and curiosity of the Greeks at their best, the social seriousness and sense of order of the Romans, and the Hebrews' feeling of human inadequacy and God's omnipotent justice.

THE ANCIENT WORLD

Although Rome at the height of her power was to extend her rule northward through France as far as Britain and eastward to the Euphrates, the ancient world was centered on the Mediterranean Sea. "We live around the sea," said the Greek philosopher Socrates, "like frogs around a pond." Climate and basic crops were (and still are) similar over most of the area: a dry hot summer and a comparatively mild winter, more favorable to sheep and goats than cattle, to vine and olive rather than cereal crops. Though metal was mined and worked, what we know as heavy industry did not exist. Coal and oil were not exploited for energy; the war galleys were propelled by sail and human oarsmen; and the armies moved on foot. All the advanced civilizations of the ancient world depended for their existence on slaves to do their heavy work on the land, in the mines, and in the house. The system of dependent labor, widely varied in its forms—peasants tied to the land as in Egypt, bought slaves as in Greece and Rome, or people enslaved for debt as in Greece and Israel—lasted until the end of the ancient world, to be gradually replaced in Europe by the feudal system with a peasantry technically free but in practice working the land for the benefit of an overlord.

Mediterranean civilization began not on the coasts but east and south of the sea: in Babylon and Egypt. Ancient civilization was based on agriculture, and it flourished first in regions where the soil gave rich rewards: in the valley of the Nile, where annual floods left large tracts of land moist and fertile under the Egyptian sun, and in the valleys of the Euphrates and Tigris rivers, which flowed through the "Fertile Crescent," the land now known as Iraq and Iran. Great cities—Thebes and Memphis in Egypt, Babylon and Nineveh in the Fertile Crescent—came into being as centers for the complicated administration of the irrigated fields. Supported by the surplus the land produced, they became centers also for government, religion, and the emerging cultures. As far back as 3000 B.C.E., the pharaohs of Egypt began to build their splendid temples and gigantic pyramids, as well as to record their political acts and

1

religious beliefs in hieroglyphic script. The Sumerians, Babylonians, and Assyrians began to build the palaces and temples of Babylon, as well as to record their laws in cuneiform script on clay tablets.

From the second millennium B.C.E. onward a number of splendid and sophisticated cultures flourished around the Mediterranean Sea and in Asia Minor. That three in particular so heavily influenced later European culture is largely the result of empire: first those of Alexander and his successors, which spread Greek culture to the cities of Asia Minor and Egypt, and then that of Rome. Many indigenous cultures within these empires continued to exist, especially outside the urban centers, but in the transmission to later ages they were crowded out by the dominant Greco-Roman and Judeo-Christian traditions. Since the nineteenth century, archaeology has slowly, and of course incompletely, restored knowledge to us of the ancient Persians, Egyptians, Carthaginians, and many others, and it is becoming possible to see the Greeks, Romans, and Hebrews within a broader Mediterranean context. We are beginning to understand that for thousands of years the Mediterranean has been the scene of intercultural exchanges on a large scale, the result of trade, colonization, and impe-rialism. Greek sculpture and architecture of the seventh century B.C.E., for instance, show heavy debts to Egypt, and striking similarities between Greek and Near Eastern myths are probably the result of Anatolian and Mesopotamian influence, perhaps in the Bronze Age. The Greek and Roman alphabets (and therefore our own) are derived from a script used by the Phoenicians, who were extremely active in trade all over the Medi-terranean from a very early period. The selective process of transmission to Europe in later periods has obscured for us the diversity of the ancient Mediterranean. In any case, the cultural history of the ancient world came to medieval and Renaissance Europe not in the languages of Babylon and Egypt but in Hebrew, Greek, and Latin.

THE HEBREWS

In their period of independence, the Hebrews progressed from their beginnings as a pastoral tribe to their high point as a kingdom with a splendid capital in Jerusalem. Their later history was a bitter and unsuccessful struggle for freedom against a series of foreign masters—Babylonian, Greek, and Roman.

After the period of expansion and prosperity under the great kings David and Sol-omon (1005–925 B.C.E.), the kingdom fell apart again into warring factions, which called in outside powers. The melancholy end of a long period of internal and external struggle was the destruction of the cities and the deportation of the population to Babylon (586 B.C.E.). This period of exile (which ended in 539 B.C.E. when Cyrus, the Persian conqueror of Babylon, released the Hebrews from bondage) was a for-mative period for Hebrew religious thought, which was enriched and refined by the teachings of the prophet Ezekiel and the anonymous prophet known as the Second Isaiah. The return to Palestine was crowned by the rebuilding of the Temple and the creation of the canonical version of the Pentateuch or Torah, the first five books of the Hebrew Bible. The religious legacy of the Hebrew people was now codified for future generations.

Foreign domination, however, continued for the next several centuries. After encroachments by the Macedonian successors of Alexander the Great around 300 B.C.E., Palestine became part of a Hellenistic Greek-speaking kingdom. In 63 B.C.E., after a short period of independence, it was absorbed by the Roman Empire. A des-perate revolt against Rome was crushed in 70 C.E. by the emperor Titus (on the arch of Titus in Rome a relief shows the legionaries carrying the menorah, a seven-branched candelabrum, in Titus's triumph). A second revolt, against the emperor Hadrian (131–34 C.E.) resulted in the *diaspora*, the "scattering" of the Hebrew people. Religious communities in the great cities of the ancient world maintained local cohe-sion and universal religious solidarity but remained stateless, as they were to be all through the centuries until the creation, in 1948, of the state of Israel.

The ancient Hebrews left us a religious literature, written down probably between the eighth and second centuries B.C.E., which is informed by an attitude different from that of any other nation of the ancient world. It is founded on the idea of one God, the creator of all things, all-powerful and just—a conception revolutionary in its time.

THE GREEKS

The origin of the peoples who eventually called themselves Hellenes is still a mystery. The language they spoke belongs clearly to the Indo-European family (which includes the Germanic, Celtic, Italic, and Sanskrit language groups), but many of the ancient Greek words and place names have terminations that are definitely not Indo-European—the word for sea (thalassa), for example. The Greeks of historic times were presumably a blend of the native tribes and the Indo-European invaders, en route from the European landmass.

In the last hundred years archaeology has given us a clearer picture than our forebears had of the level of civilization in early Greece. The second millennium B.C.E. saw a brilliant culture, called Minoan after the mythical king Minos, flourishing on the large island of Crete; and the citadel of Mycenae and the palace at Pylos show that mainland Greece, in that same period, had centers of wealth and power unsuspected before the excavators discovered the gold masks of the buried kings and clay tablets covered with strange signs. The decipherment of these signs (published in 1953) revealed that the language of these Myceneans was an early form of Greek. It must have been the memory of these rich kingdoms that inspired Homer's vision of "Mycenae rich in gold" and the splendid armed hosts that assembled for the attack on Troy.

It was a blurred memory (Homer does not remember the writing, for example, or the detailed bureaucratic accounting recorded on the tablets), and this is easy to understand: some time in the last century of the millennium the great palaces were destroyed by fire. With them disappeared not only the arts and skills that had created Mycenean wealth but even the system of writing. For the next few hundred years the Greeks were illiterate and so no written evidence survives for what, in view of our ignorance about so many aspects of it, we call the Dark Age of Greece.

One thing we do know about it: it produced a body of oral epic poetry that was the raw material Homer shaped into two great poems, the *Iliad* and *Odyssey*. These Homeric poems seem from internal evidence to date from the eighth century B.C.E.— which is incidentally, or perhaps not incidentally, the century in which the Greeks learned how to write again. They played in the subsequent development of Greek civilization the same role that the Torah had played in Palestine: they became the basis of an education and therefore of a whole culture. Not only did the great characters of the epic serve as models of conduct for later generations of Greeks, but the figures of the Olympian gods retained, in the prayers, poems, and sculpture of the succeeding centuries, the shapes and attributes set down by Homer. The difference between the Greek and the Hebrew hero, between Achilles and Joseph, for example, is remarkable, but the difference between "the God of Abraham and of Isaac" and the Olympians who interfere capriciously in the lives of Hector or Achilles or Helen is an unbridgeable chasm. The two conceptions of the power that governs the universe are irreconcilable; and in fact the struggle between them ended not in synthesis but in the complete victory of the one and the disappearance of the other. The Greek conception of the nature of the gods and of their relation to humanity is so alien to us that it is difficult for the modern reader to take it seriously. The Hebrew basis of European religious thought has made it almost impossible for us to imagine a god who can be feared and laughed at, blamed and admired, and still sincerely worshiped.

Yet all these are proper attitudes toward the gods on Olympus; they are all implicit in Homer's poems.

The Hebrew conception of God emphasizes those aspects of the universe that imply a harmonious order. Just as clearly, the Greeks conceived their gods, in one of their aspects, as an expression of the disorder of the world in which they lived. This view is especially prominent in Homer, although in the *Odyssey* and in some later texts the gods are also seen as upholders of justice and punishers of wrongdoing. Their arbitrary tendencies were never lost sight of for long, however. Particularly (but not only) in the *Iliad*, the Olympian gods, like the natural forces of sea and sky, follow their own will even to the extreme of conflict with each other, and always with a sublime disregard for the human beings who may be affected by the results of their actions. It is true that they are all subjects of a single more powerful god, Zeus. But his authority over them is based only on superior strength; though he cannot be openly resisted, he can be temporarily deceived by his fellow Olympians. And Zeus, although by virtue of his superior power his will is finally accomplished in the matter of Achilles' wrath, knows limits to his power too. He cannot save the life of his son the Lycian hero Sarpedon. Behind Zeus stands the mysterious power of Fate, to which even he must bow.

Such gods as these, representing as they do the blind forces of the universe that humans cannot control, are not always thought of as connected with morality. Morality is a human creation, and though the gods may approve of it, and even enforce it, they are not bound by it. And violent as they are, they cannot feel the ultimate consequence of violence: death is a human fear, just as the courage to face it is a human quality. There is a double standard, one for gods and one for mortals, and the inevitable consequence is that our real admiration and sympathy are directed not toward the gods but toward the mortals. With Hector and Andromache, and even with Achilles at his worst, we can sympathize; but the gods, though they may excite terror or laughter, can never have our sympathy. We could as easily sympathize with a blizzard or the force of gravity. Homer imposed on Greek literature the anthropocentric emphasis that is its distinguishing mark and its great contribution to the Western mind. Though the gods are ever-present characters in the incidents of his poems, his true concern, first and last, is with men and women.

THE CITY-STATES OF GREECE

The stories told in the Homeric poems are set in the age of the Trojan War, which archaeologists (those, that is, who believe that it happened at all) date to the twelfth century B.C.E. Though the poems do preserve some faded memories of the Mycenaean Age, as we have them they probably are the creation of later centuries, the tenth to the eighth B.C.E.—the so-called Dark Age that succeeded the collapse (or destruction) of Mycenaean civilization. This was the time of the final settlement of the Greek peoples, an age of invasion perhaps and migration certainly, which saw the foundation and growth of many small independent cities. The geography of Greece—a land of mountain barriers and scattered islands—encouraged this fragmentation. The Greek cities never lost sight of their common Hellenic heritage, but it was not enough to unite them except in the face of unmistakable and overwhelming danger, and even then they came together only partially and for a short time. They differed from each other in custom, political constitution, and even dialect: their relations with each other were those of rivals and fierce competitors.

These cities, constantly at war in the pursuit of more productive land for growing populations, were dominated from the late eighth century B.C.E. by aristocratic oligarchies, which maintained a stranglehold on the land and the economy of which it was the base. At the same time, cultural horizons were expanding. In the eighth and seventh centuries B.C.E. Greeks (perhaps including the landless) founded new cities (always near the sea and generally owing little or no allegiance to the home base) all over the Mediterranean coast—in Spain, southern France (Marseilles, Nice, and Antibes were all Greek cities), South Italy (Naples), Sicily (Syracuse), North Africa (Cyrene), all along the coast of Asia Minor (Smyrna, Miletus), and even on the Black Sea as far as Russian Crimea. Many of these new outposts of Greek civilization experienced a faster economic and cultural development than the older cities of the mainland. It was in the cities founded on the Asian coast that the Greeks adapted to their own language the Phoenician system of writing, adding signs for the vowels to create their alphabet. Its first use was probably for commercial records and transactions, but as literacy became a general condition all over the Greek world in the course of the seventh century B.C.E., treaties and political decrees were inscribed on stone and literary works written on rolls of paper made from the Egyptian papyrus plant.

ATHENS AND SPARTA

By the beginning of the fifth century B.C.E. the two most prominent city-states were Athens and Sparta. These two cities led the combined Greek resistance to the Persian invasion of Europe in the years 490 to 479 B.C.E. The defeat of the solid Persian power by the divided and insignificant Greek cities surprised the world and inspired in Greece, particularly in Athens, a confidence that knew no bounds.

Athens was at this time a democracy, the first in Western history. It was a direct, not a representative, democracy, for the number of free citizens was small enough to permit the exercise of power by a meeting of the citizens as a body in assembly. Athens's power lay in the fleet with which it had played its decisive part in the struggle against Persia, and with this fleet it rapidly became the leader of a naval alliance that included most of the islands of the Aegean Sea and many Greek cities on the coast of Asia Minor. This alliance, originally for defense against Persia, soon became an empire; the "allies" paid an annual tribute to Athens, with its formidable navy. Sparta, on the other hand, was rigidly conservative in government and policy. Because the individual citizen was reared and trained by the state for the state's business, war, the Spartan land army was superior to any other in Greece, and the Spartans controlled, by direct rule or by alliance, a majority of the city-states of the Peloponnese.

These two cities, allies for the war of liberation against Persia, became enemies when the external danger was eliminated. The middle years of the fifth century were disturbed by indecisive hostilities between them and haunted by the probability of full-scale war to come. As the years went by, this war came to be accepted as "inevitable" by both sides, and in 431 B.C.E. it began. It was to end in 404 B.C.E. with the total defeat of Athens.

Before the beginning of this disastrous war, known as the Peloponnesian War, Athenian democracy provided its citizens with a cultural and political environment that was without precedent in the ancient world. The institutions of Athens encouraged the maximum development of the individual's capacities and at the same time inspired the maximum devotion to the interests of the community. It was a moment in history of delicate and precarious balance between the freedom of the individual and the demands of the state. It was the proud boast of the Athenians that without sacrificing the cultural amenities of civilized life they could yet when called upon surpass in policy and war their adversary, Sparta, whose citizen body was an army in constant training. The Athenians were, in this respect as in others, a nation of amateurs. "The individual Athenian," said Pericles, Athens's great statesman at this time, "in his own person seems to have the power of adapting himself to the most varied forms of action with the utmost versatility and grace." But the freedom of the individual did not, in Athens's great days, produce anarchy. "While we are . . . unconstrained in our private intercourse," Pericles had observed earlier in his speech, "a spirit of reverence pervades our public acts."

There were limits on who could participate in the democracy. The "individual Athenian" of whom Pericles spoke was the adult male citizen. In his speech, he mentioned women only once, to tell them that the way for them to obtain glory was not to be worse than their nature made them, and to be least talked of among males for either praise or blame. Women could not own property, hold office, or vote. Peasant women may have had to work in the fields with their husbands, but affluent women were expected to remain inside the house except for funerals and religious festivals, rarely seen by men other than their husbands or male relatives. Their reputations for sexual chastity were fiercely protected, for it was necessary to keep any suspicion of illegitimacy from falling on the sons they were expected to produce: future Athenian citizens, heirs to the family property and continuators of the family line (which was traced through the male side). There were, in addition, a number of men from other cities who settled in Athens, often for business reasons—*metics*, or "resident aliens." These could not own land or take part in civic affairs. A great deal of labor—in the houses and fields, in craftsmen's shops, in the silver mines that underlay Athens's wealth—was performed by slaves, who of course had no rights at all. And finally, even among citizens who participated in civic life on a footing of equality, there were marked divisions between the elite and the poorer classes and thus tensions between them. Still, although it was exclusionary in all these ways, and although it pursued a ruthless imperialist policy abroad, Athenian democracy represented a bold achievement of civic equality for those who belonged.

This democracy came under strain as the Peloponnesian War progressed. Under the mounting pressure of the long conflict, the Athenians lost the "spirit of reverence" that Pericles saw as the stabilizing factor in Athenian democracy. They subordinated all considerations to the immediate interest of the city and surpassed their enemy in the logical ferocity of their actions. They finally fell victim to leaders who carried the process one step further and subordinated all considerations to their own private interest. The war years saw the decay of that freedom in unity which is celebrated in Pericles' speech. By the end of the fifth century Athens was divided internally as well as defeated externally. The individual citizen no longer thought of himself and Athens as one and the same; the balance was gone forever.

One of the solvents of traditional values was an intellectual revolution that was taking place in the advanced Athenian democracy of the last half of the fifth century, a critical reevaluation of accepted ideas in every sphere of thought and action. It stemmed from innovations in education. Democratic institutions had created a demand for an education that would prepare men for public life, especially by training them in the art of public speaking. The demand was met by the appearance of the professional teacher, the Sophist, as he was called, who taught, for a handsome fee, not only the techniques of public speaking but also the subjects that gave a man something to talk about—government, ethics, literary criticism, even astronomy. The curriculum of the Sophists, in fact, marks the first appearance in European civilization of liberal education (for affluent males), just as they themselves were the first professors.

The Sophists were great teachers, but like most teachers they had little or no control over the results of their teaching. Their methods placed an inevitable emphasis on effective presentation of a point of view, to the detriment, and if necessary the exclusion, of anything that might make it less convincing. They produced a generation that had been trained to see both sides of any question and to argue the weaker side as effectively as the stronger, the false as effectively as the true. They taught how to argue inferentially from probability in the absence of concrete evidence, to appeal to the audience's sense of its own advantage rather than to accepted moral standards, and to justify individual defiance of general prejudice and even of law by making a distinction between "nature" and "convention." These methods dominated the thinking of the Athenians of the late fifth and fourth centuries B.C.E. Emphasis on the technique of effective presentation of both sides of any case encouraged a relativistic point of view. The canon of probability (which implies an appeal to human reason as the supreme authority) became a critical weapon for an attack on myth and on traditional conceptions of the gods, though it had its constructive side, too, for it was the base for historical reconstruction of the unrecorded past and of the stages of human progress from savagery to civilization. The rhetorical appeal to the self-interest of the audience, to expediency, became the method of the political leaders of the wartime democracy and the fundamental doctrine of new theories of power politics. These theories served to justify the increasing severity of the measures Athens took to terrorize her rebellious subjects. The new spirit in Athens had magnificent achievements to its credit, but it undermined traditional moral convictions. At its roots was a supreme confidence in human intelligence and a secular view of humanity's position in the universe that is best expressed in the statement of Protagoras, the most famous of the Sophists: "Man is the measure of all things." These shifts in worldview and moral beliefs led to new forms of creativity in art, literature, and thought, although they also caused bitter debates, and sometimes conflicts, between traditionalists and proponents of the new ideas and traditionalists.

THE TRANSFORMATION OF THE CITY-STATE

In the last quarter of the fifth century the whole traditional basis of individual conduct, which had been concern for the unity and cohesion of the city-state, was undermined—gradually at first by the critical approach of the Sophists and their pupils, and then rapidly, as the war accelerated the loosening of the old standards. "In peace and prosperity," says Thucydides, "both states and individuals are actuated by higher motives; . . . but war, which takes away the comfortable provision of daily life, is a hard master, and tends to assimilate men's characters to their conditions." The war brought to Athens the rule of new politicians who were schooled in the doctrine of power politics and initiated savage reprisals against Athens's rebellious subject-allies, launching the city on an expansionist course that ended in disaster in Sicily (413 B.C.E.) and a short-lived oligarchic revolution at home (411 B.C.E.). Seven years later Athens, her last fleet gone, surrendered to the Spartans. A pro-Spartan antidemocratic regime, the Thirty Tyrants, was installed, but soon overthrown. Athens became a democracy again but the confidence and unity of its great age were gone forever. Community and individual were no longer one. Yet despite a perceptible retreat into privacy, Athenian democracy continued to work through most of the fourth century, until the conquest of Philip (see below). That same century witnessed, in addition to continued creativity in poetry, painting, and sculpture, two new developments. It saw the flowering of Athenian rhetoric, a legacy of the Sophists and one of Greek culture's greatest contributions to Rome in turn. During the same time, Plato and Aristotle revolutionized philosophy and laid the foundations for later ancient and European philosophical thought. But they had a predecessor in Plato's great teacher, Socrates.

In the wake of their defeat by Sparta, Athenians began to feel more and more exasperation with a voice they had been listening to for many years. This was the voice of Socrates, a stonemason who for most of his adult life had made it his business to discuss with his fellow citizens such great issues as the nature of justice, of truth, of piety. Unlike the Sophists, he did not lecture nor did he charge a fee: his method was dialectic, a search for truth through questions and answers, and his dedication to his mission had kept him poor. But the initial results of his discussions were often infuriatingly like the results of sophistic teaching. By questions and answers he exposed the illogicality of his opponent's position, but did not often provide a substitute for the belief he had destroyed. Yet it is clear that he did believe in absolute standards—and what is more, he believed they could be discovered by a process of logical inquiry and supported by logical proof. His ethics rested on an intellectual basis. The resentment against him, which came to a head in 399 B.C.E., is partly explained by his questioning of the old standards in order to establish new, and by his refusal to let the Athenians live in peace, for he preached that it was every person's duty to think through to the truth. In this last respect he was the prophet of the new age. For him, the city and the accepted code were no substitute for the task of individual self-examination. The characteristic statement of the old Athens was public, in the assembly or the theater; Socrates proclaimed the responsibility of each individual to work out a means to fulfillment and happiness and made clear his distrust of public life: "he who will fight for the right . . . must have a private station and not a public one."

The Athenians sentenced him to death on a charge of impiety. They hoped, no doubt, that he would go into exile to escape execution, but he remained, as he put it himself, at his post, and they were forced to have the sentence carried out. If they thought they were finished with him, they were sadly mistaken. In the next century Athens became the center for a large group of philosophical schools, all of them claiming to develop and interpret the ideas of Socrates.

The century that followed his death saw the exhaustion of the Greek city-states in constant internecine warfare. Politically and economically bankrupt, they fell under the power of Macedon in the north, whose king, Philip, combined a ferocious energy with a cynicism that enabled him to take full advantage of the disunity of the city-states. Greek liberty ended at the battle of Chaeronea in 338 B.C.E., and Philip's son Alexander inherited a powerful army and the political control of all Greece. He led his Macedonian and Greek armies against Persia, and in a few brilliant campaigns became master of an empire that extended into Egypt in the south and to the borders of India in the east. He died at Babylon in 323 B.C.E., and his empire broke up into a number of independent kingdoms ruled by his generals; modern scholars refer to this period (323–31 B.C.E.) as the Hellenistic age. One of these generals, Ptolemy, founded a Greek dynasty that ruled Egypt until after the Roman conquest and ended only with the death of the famous Cleopatra. The results of Alexander's fantastic achievements were more durable than might have been expected. Into the newly conquered territories came thousands of Greeks who wished to escape from the political futility and economic crisis of the homeland. Wherever they went they took with them their language, their culture, and their typical buildings, the gymnasium and the theater. The great Hellenistic cities, though now part of kingdoms, grew out of the earlier city-state and continued many of its civic and political institutions. At Alexandria in Egypt, the Ptolemies formed a Greek library to preserve the texts of Greek literature for the scholars who edited them, a school of Greek poetry flourished, and Greek mathematicians and geographers made new advances in science. The Middle East became, as far as the cities were concerned, a Greek-speaking area; and when, some two or three centuries later, the first accounts of the life and teaching of Jesus of Nazareth were written down, they were written in Greek, the language on which the cultural homogeneity of the whole area was based.

ROME

When Alexander died in 323 B.C.E., the city of Rome, situated on the Tiber in the western coastal plain of Italy, was engaged in a struggle for the control of the surrounding areas. By the middle of the third century B.C.E., it dominated most of the Italian peninsula. Expansion southward brought Rome into collision with Carthage, a city in North Africa that was then the greatest power in the western Mediterranean. Two protracted wars resulted (264–241 and 218–201 B.C.E.), and it was only at the end of a third, shorter war (149–146 B.C.E.) that the Romans destroyed their great

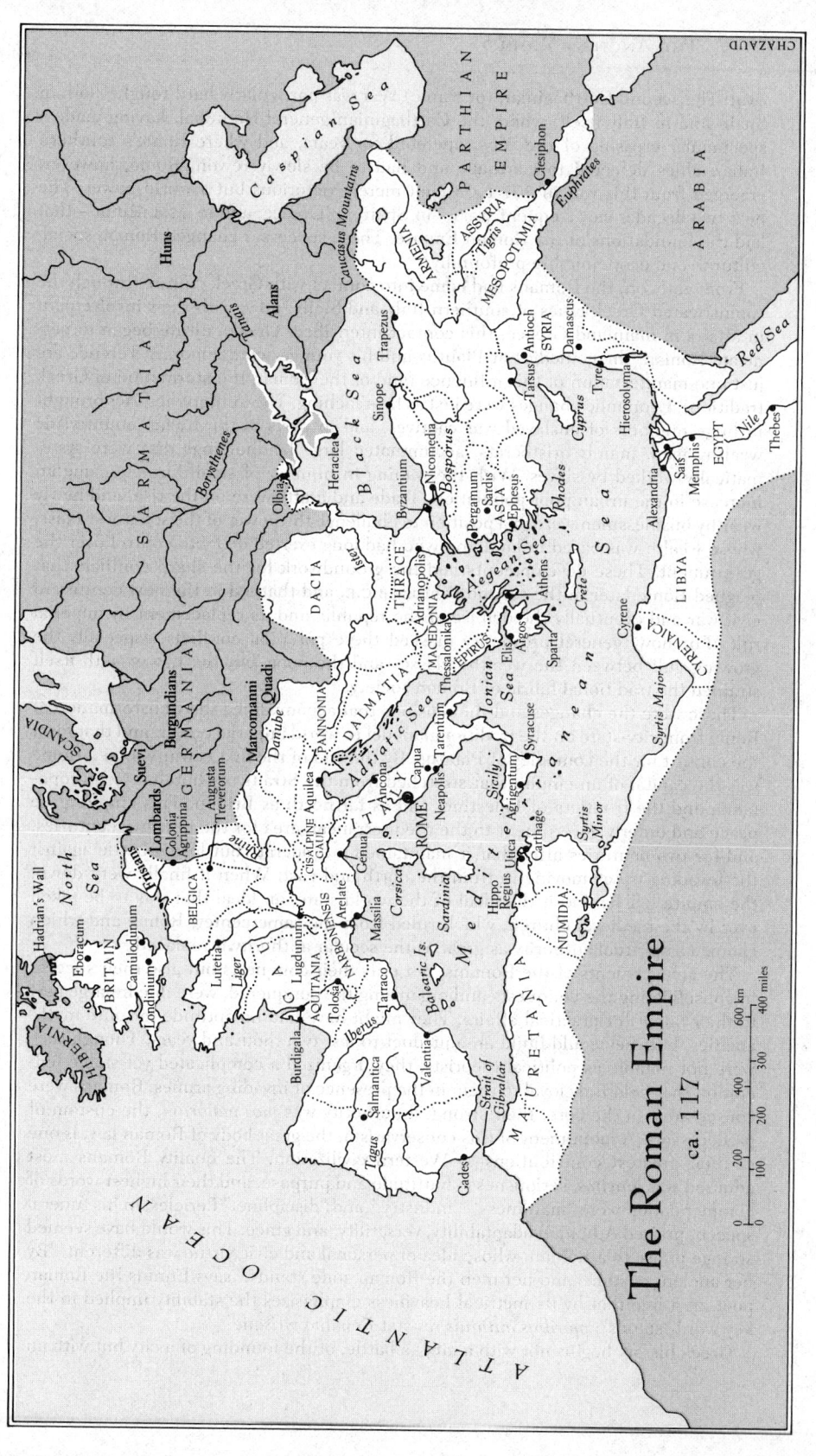

The Roman Empire
ca. 117

ATLANTIC OCEAN

HIBERNIA

BRITAN
Hadrian's Wall
Eboracum
Camulodunum
Londinium

North Sea

SCANDIA

Frisians
Lombards
Suevi
Burgundians
GERMANIA
Colonia Agrippina
Augusta Treverorum
Rhine
BELGICA
Lutetia
Liger
Lugdunum
GAUL
AQUITANIA
Tolosa
NARBONENSIS
Tarraco
Burdigala
Salmantica
Valentia
Iberus
Tagus
Gades
Strait of Gibraltar

Marcomanni
Quadi
Danube
PANNONIA
DALMATIA
Aquilea
CISALPINE GAUL
Genua
Massilia
Arelate
Corsica
Sardinia
Balearic Is.
Mediter

MAURETANIA

NUMIDIA
Hippo Regius
Utica
Carthage
Syrtis Minor

Ister
DACIA
THRACE
Adrianopolis
MACEDONIA
Thessalonika
EPIRUS
Ancona
ITALY
ROME
Capua
Neapolis
Tarentum
Ionian Sea
Sicily
Agrigentum
Syracuse
Carthage
Syrtis Major

Adriatic Sea

Elis
Argos
Sparta
Athens
Aegean Sea
Crete
Cyrene
CYRENAICA

ranean Sea
LIBYA

SARMATIA
Huns
Alans
Tanais
Borysthenes
Olbia
Heraclea
Black Sea
Sinope
Trapezus

Caspian Sea
Caucasus Mountains
ARMENIA
ASSYRIA
Tigris
Euphrates
Ctesiphon
PARTHIAN EMPIRE
MESOPOTAMIA

Byzantium
Nicomedia
Bosporus
Pergamum
Sardis
ASIA
Ephesus
Rhodes
Cyprus
Antioch
SYRIA
Tarsus
Tyre
Damascus
Hierosolyma

Red Sea
Nile
EGYPT
Saïs
Memphis
Alexandria
Thebes

ARABIA

0   100   200   300   400 miles
0   200   400   600 km

rival. The second Carthaginian (or Punic) War was particularly hard-fought, both in Spain and in Italy itself, where the Carthaginian general Hannibal, having made a spectacular crossing of the Alps, operated for years, and where Rome's southern Italian allies defected to Carthage and had to be slowly rewon. Rome, however, emerged from this war in 201 B.C.E. not merely victorious but a world power. The next two decades saw frequent wars—in Spain, in Greece, and in Asia Minor—that laid the foundations of the Roman Empire. These successes changed Roman social, cultural, and economic life profoundly.

From early on, the Romans had come into contact with Greek culture through the sophisticated Greek cities of southern Italy and Sicily; now, with their involvement in affairs in mainland Greece, this contact intensified. Greek culture began to permeate Roman; the comedies of Plautus and his younger contemporary Terence are just one manifestation of this influence (and of the Roman transformation of Greek tradition). Economic changes were just as far-reaching. The military victories brought in huge numbers of enslaved war captives, and in parts of the Italian countryside wealthy men, mainly aristocrats, accumulated large landholdings that were systematically worked by slaves. With the waning in number of small farmers came an increase in the urban poor population. Trade and crafts were on the rise, and newly wealthy businessmen were in a position to challenge the power of the senatorial class, whose wealth was based in land and who had long exerted de facto control over the government. These developments laid the groundwork for the sharp conflicts that plagued Rome later in the second century B.C.E. and that led in the next century to civil war and eventually the demise of the republic and its replacement by imperial rule. For now, general prosperity masked these potential conflicts, especially the growing gulf between the wealthy classes and the poor, but the new wealth itself strained the traditional fabric of Roman society.

These were the changes and the tensions that accompanied the transformation of Rome from city-state on the traditional model to world imperial power, and that form the context for the comedies of Plautus. By the end of the first century B.C.E., Rome was the capital of an empire that stretched from the Straits of Gibraltar to Mesopotamia and the frontiers of Palestine, and as far north as Britain. This empire gave peace and orderly government to the Mediterranean area for the next two centuries, and for two centuries after that it maintained a desperate but losing battle against the invading tribes moving in from the north and east. When it finally went down, the empire left behind it the ideal of the world-state, an ideal that was to be taken over by the medieval church, which ruled from the same center, Rome, and which claimed a spiritual authority as great as the secular authority it replaced.

The achievements of the Romans, not only their conquests but also their success in consolidating the conquests and organizing the conquered, were due in large part to their talent for practical affairs. They might have had no aptitude for pure mathematics, but they could build an aqueduct to last two thousand years. Though they were not notable as political theorists, they organized a complicated yet stable federation that held Italy loyal to them in the presence of invading armies. Romans were conservative to the core; their strongest authority was *mos maiorum,* the custom of predecessors. A monument of this conservatism, the great body of Roman law, is one of their greatest contributions to Western civilization. The quality Romans most admired was *gravitas,* seriousness of attitude and purpose, and their highest words of commendation were "manliness," "industry," and "discipline." Pericles, in his funeral speech, praised Athenian adaptability, versatility, and grace. This would have seemed strange praise to a Roman, whose idea of personal and civic virtue was different. "By her ancient customs and her men the Roman state stands," says Ennius the Roman poet, in a line that by its metrical heaviness emphasizes the stability implied in the key word "stands": *moribus antiquis res stat Romana virisque.*

Greek history begins not with a king, a battle, or the founding of a city but with an epic poem. The Romans, on the other hand, had conquered half the world before they began to write. The stimulus to the creation of Latin literature was the Greek literature that the Romans discovered when, in the second century B.C.E., they assumed political responsibility for Greece and the Near East. Latin literature began with a translation of the *Odyssey*, made by a Greek prisoner of war; and with the exception of satire, until Latin literature became Christian the model was always Greek. The Latin writer (especially the poet) borrowed wholesale from his Greek original, not furtively but openly and proudly, as a tribute to the master from whom he had learned. But this frank acknowledgment of indebtedness should not blind us to the fact that Latin literature is original, and sometimes profoundly so. This is true above all of Virgil, who based his epic on Homer but chose as his theme the coming of the Trojan prince Aeneas to Italy, where he was to found a city from which, in the fullness of time, would come "the Latin race . . . and the high walls of Rome."

When Virgil was born in 70 B.C.E. the Roman republic, which had conquered and now governed the Mediterranean world, had barely recovered from one civil war and was drifting inexorably toward another. The institutions of the city-state proved inadequate for world government. The civil conflict that had disrupted the republic for more than a hundred years ended finally in the establishment of a powerful executive. Although the Senate, which had been the controlling body of the republic, retained an impressive share of the power, the new arrangement developed inevitably toward autocracy, the rule of the executive—the emperor, as he was called once the system was stabilized. The first of the long line of Roman emperors who gave stable government to the Roman world during the first two centuries C.E. was Octavius, known generally by his title, Augustus. He had made his way cautiously through the intrigues and bloodshed that followed the murder of his uncle Julius Caesar in 44 B.C.E. until by 31 B.C.E. he controlled the western half of the empire. In that year he fought a decisive battle with the ruler of the eastern half of the empire, Mark Antony, who was supported by Cleopatra, queen of Egypt. Octavius's victory at Actium united the empire under one authority and ushered in an age of peace and reconstruction.

For the next two hundred years the successors of Augustus, the Roman emperors, ruled the ancient world with only occasional disturbances, most of them confined to Rome, where emperors who flagrantly abused their immense power—Nero, for example—were overthrown by force. The second half of this period was described by Edward Gibbon, the great historian of imperial Rome, as the period "in the history of the world during which the condition of the human race was most happy and prosperous." The years 96–180 C.E., those of the "five good emperors," were in fact remarkable: this was the longest period of peace that has ever been enjoyed by the inhabitants of an area that included Britain, France, all southern Europe, the Middle East, and the whole of North Africa. Trade and agriculture flourished, and the cities with their public baths, theaters, and libraries offered all the amenities of civilized life. Yet there was apparent, especially in the literature of the second century, a spiritual emptiness. Petronius's *Satyricon* paints a sardonic portrait of the vulgar display and intellectual poverty of the newly rich who can think only in terms of money and possessions. The old religion offered no comfort to those who looked beyond mere material ends; it had been too closely knit into the fabric of the independent city-state and was inadequate for a time in which men were citizens of the world. New religions arose or were imported from the East, universal religions that made their appeal to all nations and classes: the worship of the Egyptian goddess Isis; of the Persian god Mithras, who offered bliss in the life to come; and of the Hebrew prophet Jesus, crucified in Jerusalem and believed risen from the dead. This was the religion that, working underground and often suppressed (there was a persecution of the Christians under Nero in the first century and another under the last of the "good emperors," Marcus Aurelius, in the second), finally triumphed and became the official and later the exclusive religion of the Roman world. As the empire in the third and fourth centuries disintegrated under the never-ending invasions by peoples from the north, the church, with its center and spiritual head in Rome, converted the new inhabitants and so made possible the preservation of much of that Latin and Greek literature that was to serve the European Middle Ages and, later, the Renaissance as a model and a basis for their own great achievements in the arts and letters.

THE ANCIENT WORLD

TEXTS	CONTEXTS
	2200–1450 B.C.E. Minoan civilization flourishes on Crete
	ca. 1450 Mycenaeans from mainland Greece occupy Crete
	ca. 1250 Troy destroyed by the Achaeans
	776 Olympic Games founded in Greece
late 8th century B.C.E. Greek alphabetic scripts	
ca. 700 Homer, the *Iliad* and the *Odyssey*; Hesiod, *Theogony* and *Works and Days*	
600 Sappho writing her **lyrics** on the island of Lesbos	
	594 Solon reforms laws at Athens, which becomes the world's first democracy (508) and defeats a Persian invasion at Marathon (490)
	480–479 Greece turns back a massive Persian invasion by sea at Salamis and by land at Plataea
472 Aeschylus, *The Persians*	
458 Aeschylus's dramatic trilogy, *The Oresteia*, produced in Athens	
ca. 441 Sophocles, *Antigone*	
431 Euripides, *Medea*	**431–404** Peloponnesian War between **Athens and Sparta**; Athens surrenders (404)
ca. 430 Herodotus, *The Histories*	
429–347 Plato, author of *The Apology of Socrates*, *Phaedo*, and *The Republic*	
426? Sophocles, *Oedipus the King*	
424–404 Thucydides, *The Peloponnesian War*	
411 Aristophanes, *Lysistrata*	
	399 Trial and execution of Socrates
	ca. 385 Plato founds the Academy
384–322 Aristotle, author of *Poetics*	
	ca. 350 Greek amphitheater built at Epidauros
	338 United Greeks defeated by Philip II of Macedon at Chaeronea

Boldface titles indicate works in the anthology

THE ANCIENT WORLD

TEXTS	CONTEXTS
	335 Aristocle founds Peripatetic school of philosophy and lectures in the Lyceum
	334 Alexander of Macedon, Philip's son, conquers Persian empire
	323 Euclid writes *Elements*, the first work of geometry
	307 Library and museum established at Alexandria, Egypt
ca. 254–184 Plautus, author of *Pseudolus*	
	148 Macedonia becomes a Roman province
ca. 94–55 Lucretius, author of *On the Nature of Things*	
ca. 84–54 Catullus	
70–19 Virgil, author of the *Aeneid*	
	47 Julius Caesar dictator; murdered in 44
43 B.C.E.–ca. 17 C.E. Ovid, author of *Metamorphoses*	
	31 At Actium, Octavian (later called Augustus Caesar) defeats Antony and Cleopatra
	ca. 6 Birth of Jesus
	ca. 33 C.E. Crucifixion of Jesus
	ca. 35 Conversion of Paul
	47–58 Paul's missionary journeys
	64 Persecution of Christians under Nero
65 Seneca, author of moral epistles and essays (including *On Anger*), dies	
66 Petronius, author of the *Satyricon*, dies	**66–70** Jewish revolt against Roman rule; Roman emperor Titus captures Jerusalem
ca. 75 Luke, **Gospels** and Acts of the Apostles	
ca. 80 Matthew, **Gospels**	
ca. 120–90 Lucian, author of *A True Story*	
ca. 125–after 170 Apuleius, author of *The Golden Ass*	
354–430 Augustine, author of *Confessions*	

GILGAMESH
ca. 2500–1500 B.C.E.

Gilgamesh is a poem of unparalleled antiquity, the first great heroic narrative of world literature. Its origins stretch back to the margins of prehistory, and its evolution spans millennia. When it was known, it was widely known. Tablets containing portions of *Gilgamesh* have been found at sites throughout the Middle East and in all the languages written in cuneiform characters (wedge-shaped characters incised in clay or stone). But then, at a time when the civilizations of the Hebrews, Greeks, and Romans had only just developed beyond their infancy, *Gilgamesh* vanished from memory. For reasons that scholars have not yet fathomed, the literature of the cuneiform languages—whether Akkadian, Sumerian, or Hittite—was not translated into the new alphabets that replaced them. Some portions of this once-famous work survived in subsequent traditions, but they did so as scattered and anonymous fragments. They became an invisible substratum buried under what was for a long time believed to be the earliest level of our common tradition. Until Utanapistim's "The Story of the Flood," a portion of *Gilgamesh,* was accidentally rediscovered and published in 1872, no one suspected that the biblical story of Noah and the Great Flood was neither original nor unique.

The epic of *Gilgamesh* developed over a period of nearly a thousand years, and its precarious survival illustrates the complex history of ancient texts reread in modern times. The historical Gilgamesh ruled in Uruk, a city in ancient Mesopotamia, in roughly 2700 B.C.E. Tales both mythical and legendary grew up around him, and were repeated and copied for centuries. Their earliest written versions date from roughly 2100 B.C.E., but oral variants both preceded these and continued on, parallel with the written tradition. The history of the epic itself begins before 1600 B.C.E., some eight centuries before Homer, when a Babylonian author (Mesopotamian tradition identifies a scholar-priest named Sîn-leqi-unninni) created a single connected work by selecting and recasting some of the early Sumerian narratives. This first version of the epic continued to develop for the next few centuries, but its text was essentially stabilized by the time of Assurbanipal, the last great king of the Assyrian Empire (668–627 B.C.E.) and the founder of the royal library at Nineveh. The epic poem was written on hardened-clay tablets in Akkadian, a Semitic language like Hebrew and Arabic and one of the principal languages of Babylonia and Assyria. Both *Gilgamesh* and Nineveh disappeared, however, and were forgotten when the ancient empires fell. Only in 1844 were ruins of the palaces and library uncovered through chance excavations, and thousands of tablets in cuneiform—a language that would not be deciphered until 1857—shipped to the British Museum. Only in 1872 did a curator at the museum realize that one of the tablets contained the story of the Flood. Excitement mounted, and renewed searches at Nineveh turned up other fragments.

Assurbanipal's text is known to modern scholars as the Standard Version, and it covers eleven tablets (in modern terms, eleven books or chapters). Of these, some are heavily damaged, although a few, such as Tablet XI printed here, are nearly complete. As in many ancient manuscripts, there are gaps, missing passages, and places where individual words are damaged and illegible; sometimes their meaning can be established from other fragments and sometimes it is still uncertain, a subject of ongoing debate among linguists. Incomplete or not, in one or another translation, the story of Gilgamesh has fascinated generations of modern readers, including the poet Rainer Maria Rilke for whom it was "one of the greatest things that can happen to a person." *Gilgamesh* has been translated into prose and poetry, in scholarly and poetic modes, in versions that respect the gaps in the transmitted ancient text and in those that aim to recapture the continuity of the original narrative by filling in those gaps according to the perceived spirit of the tale. Each is an attempt to convey the richness and beauty of an epic four thousand years old, written in a long-dead language whose cuneiform clay tablets are only one indication of the vast distance between our own civilization and that in which the poem is rooted. We print here the final tablet, containing, "The Story of the Flood" and Gilgamesh's return home, in two different translations—two re-creations of the same ancient text.

Most of Tablet XI is taken up with the tale told by Utanapishtim, the sage who responds to Gilgamesh's request for the secret of immortality by telling how he survived the Flood and received immortality himself as a gift of the gods. Utanapishtim's story is at once an independent narrative, similar to the biblical story of the Flood (Genesis 6–9), and an important part of the plot of *Gilgamesh*. It marks the frustrating end to Gilgamesh's search: the sage demonstrates that the king is not qualified for everlasting life and sends him back to take up his mortal destiny. Yet, as the prologue in Tablet I makes clear, that the hero has made his arduous journey and "brought back tidings from before the Flood" has brought him understanding and even peace. The final seven lines of Tablet XI, which invite the hearer to inspect the great walls, gardens, and temple of Uruk, echo identical lines in the prologue; together they frame the larger narrative of human striving and passion that is the story of *Gilgamesh*.

Despite its enormous differences in setting and cultural expectations, the story of King Gilgamesh and his companion, Enkidu, speaks to contemporary readers with astonishing immediacy. Its moving depiction of the bonds of friendship, of the quest for worldly renown, of the bitterness of death, and of a tragic struggle to go beyond human limits has a timeless resonance and appeal. Gilgamesh's reputation for wisdom, celebrated in the prologue, is achieved only after a difficult, long journey, during which he is transformed from a confident and semidivine king whose only concern is to gain a hero's fame to a mere mortal appalled at the transience of life and the uncertain results of heroic action. The Gilgamesh who questions Utnapishtim in the last book and hears the story of the Flood has not yet relinquished his hopes of personal immortality or learned to serve his people—not yet become the ruler whose inspired rebuilding of the city of Uruk will be remembered for thousands of years.

In the course of the epic, Gilgamesh changes from an arrogant, oppressive ruler whose people complain to the gods to a person who has experienced friendship, love, and loss, and who has been humbled by grief and the fear of death. This transformation occurs largely through the coming of Enkidu, created by the gods as a counterweight to Gilgamesh's unchecked excesses. Where Gilgamesh is a mixture of human and divine, Enkidu, who also appears godlike, is a blend of human and wild animal, and at first the animal predominates. He is raised by wild beasts, lives as they do (eating only uncooked food), and embodies the conflict between animal and human natures that is a recurrent theme in Mesopotamian literature and myth. His coming has been announced to Gilgamesh in one of the many dreams that play such an important role in the poem. Although Enkidu and Gilgamesh are initially bent on destroying each other, their encounter results, as it was meant to, in a deep bond of friendship. Each finds in the other the true companion he has sought. The consequence of their union is that their prodigious energies are directed outward toward heroic achievements.

Gilgamesh proposes that they go to the great Cedar Forest and there slay its guardian, the terrible giant Humbaba, and cut down a massive tree as a sign of strength. With the help of the sun god Shamash they succeed, but their victory is not a simple, glorious triumph. Humbaba pleads for his life and curses them before he dies. Enlil, the god of wind and storm, who had appointed Humbaba to guard the forest, is enraged by his slaying and he also curses them. The heroes' second adventure is not of their choosing and it too leads to an ambiguous success. Gilgamesh and Enkidu destroy the Bull of Heaven, which was wreaking havoc among the people of Uruk, but that victory brings about the slow and painful death of Enkidu.

The death of his companion shocks Gilgamesh into questioning the heroic ideal by which he has lived; moreover, he is terrified by this sudden evidence of his own mortality. Unable to believe that Enkidu is dead, he refuses him burial and mourns his friend for six days and seven nights "until a worm fell out of his nose. / I was frightened." No longer the splendid, dauntless hero of the beginning, Gilgamesh fears for his own life and sets off on a journey to discover the secret of eternal life. Filthy, emaciated, dressed in wild animal skins when his clothes fall apart, he wanders through the steppes seeking the one man who lives forever: Utanapishtim, who survived the Flood. Although he at last finds Utanapishtim, his goal eludes him: Gilgamesh fails a simple test of his potential for immortality when he cannot remain awake for six days and seven nights. He fails a second test as well when he is directed to a plant that ensures eternal rejuvenation and then, in a moment of carelessness, loses it to a serpent. Discouraged and defeated, Gilgamesh returns at last to Uruk, finally accepting his fate and learning to value mortal accomplishments. He builds the colossal walls of the city of Uruk, dedicates a shining treasury to the goddess Ishtar, and inscribes his hardships on stone for future generations to read.

The different translations of Tablet XI printed here are both poetic versions based on the same Standard Version of *Gilgamesh* with some interpolations from older manuscripts; they are fundamentally similar, despite differing in style and occasionally in their interpretation of specific lines. Each translator has supplied notes that reflect his opinions. Benjamin R. Foster is a professor and translator of ancient Near Eastern languages and literature, an anthologist of ancient Mesopotamian literature, and a scholar experienced in the verbal intricacies and stylistic peculiarities of Akkadian texts; his aim is to provide, in readable English, a close approximation of the ancient epic. Foster preserves the repetitions that charmed the Babylonian audience, reproduces patterns of diction (e.g., Utanapishtim's elevated, sagelike speech), does not ease the difficulty of problematic passages, and tries whenever possible to re-create the characteristic wordplay—humorous or serious—permeating the text. His text recaptures the pattern of traditional Mesopotamian poetry, in which each line offers a complete sentence or idea. Insofar as it is possible, his translation offers a word-for-word rendition of the Akkadian text. Like other modern editors of ancient manuscripts, he leaves gaps when passages are missing and uses various symbols to identify textual problems. Square brackets enclose important words that are visible in the text and whose meaning seems clear—though that meaning has not been established in other manuscripts. Square brackets enclosing ellipses mark places where the characters are clear but the translator cannot guess their meaning. Question marks within parentheses indicate uncertain restorations, and simple parentheses set off explanatory additions by the translator. While Tablet XI is largely complete and such symbols occur infrequently, they signify a reliable, scholarly translation that presents a *Gilgamesh* of its own time and cultural context, consciously preserving much of its strangeness and mystery for today's readers.

A different approach is taken by Stephen Mitchell, a poet and acclaimed translator of the twentieth-century German poet Rainer Maria Rilke who has also translated texts in Spanish, Chinese, and modern Hebrew as well as selections from the Bible (both the Hebrew Bible and the Greek New Testament). Mitchell, who does not read Akkadian, prepared for his translation by studying Andrew George's authoritative critical edition of the Babylonian texts and by reading numerous translations in several languages. His aim is not to reconstruct an ancient text but rather to transpose the epic of *Gilgamesh* into a fluent modern narrative that keeps the spirit of the original poem. Contemporary terms are employed, descriptions simplified, and explanations inserted: gallons, feet, and miles replace measures, cubits, and leagues; the lengthy description of birds and fish, bread cakes and rice raining from heaven is pruned to "they will have all they want, and more"; and Gilgamesh's error in his second trial is spelled out ("He left the plant on the ground") rather than simply implied. The translator is aware of manuscript problems but relegates them to the notes: for example, when there is a jarring inconsistency between the first and second accounts of Ea's warning, he provides narrative consistency by repeating the first account. Mitchell's translation (or version, as he prefers to call it) was a two-stage project: he first composed a rough prose version based on his understanding of other texts, and then "began the real work of raising the language to the level of English verse." Literal when he can be, he does not hesitate to fill in gaps, change images that seem unclear, add lines to provide transitions or to elaborate on a dramatic episode, or cut repetitive or fragmentary passages. The result is a strikingly vivid, complete, and readable retelling of the ancient poem by a modern bard.

Gilgamesh

TABLET XI[1]

Gilgamesh said to him, to Utanapishtim the Distant One:[2]

As I look upon you, Utanapishtim,
Your limbs are not different, you are just as I am.
Indeed, you are not different at all, you are just as I am!
Yet your heart is drained of battle spirit,   5
You lie flat on your back, your arm [idle].
You then, how did you join the ranks of the gods and find eternal life?

Utanapishtim said to him, to Gilgamesh:

I will reveal to you, O Gilgamesh, a secret matter,
And a mystery of the gods I will tell you.   10
The city Shuruppak, a city you yourself have knowledge of,
Which once was set on the [bank] of the Euphrates,[3]
That aforesaid city was ancient and gods once were within it.
The great gods resolved to send the deluge,
Their father Anu was sworn,   15
The counselor the valiant Enlil,
Their throne-bearer Ninurta
Their canal-officer Ennugi,[4]
Their leader Ea[5] was sworn with them.
He repeated their plans to the reed fence:[6]   20
"Reed fence, reed fence, wall, wall!
Listen, O reed fence! Pay attention, O wall!
O Man of Shuruppak, son of Ubar-Tutu,
Wreck house, build boat,
Forsake possessions and seek life,   25
Belongings reject and life save!

1. Translated and edited in 2001 by Benjamin R. Foster. Tablet XI is the last installment of the *Gilgamesh* epic; a twelfth tablet found with the others contains a Sumerian poem about Gilgamesh and is not part of the epic.   2. An epithet for Utanapishtim, who lives "far distant at the source of the rivers" (Tablet I, line 208).   3. One of two great rivers flowing in ancient Mesopotamia (the other was the Tigris); Gilgamesh's city of Uruk lay on its banks. *Shuruppak:* city in Babylonia that supposedly flourished before the Flood (near modern Tell Fara); it was abandoned by the time the epic was written.   4. Anu, supreme among the gods, was the god of the sky; Enlil was the chief god on earth, and usually an enemy of humanity; Ninurta, the god of agriculture and of war, was the son of Enlil; Ennugi was a minor deity in charge of water courses.   5. The god of wisdom, magic, and clever solutions to problems (named Enki in the Sumerian poems). Also the god of fresh water, Ea lived in the great subterranean ocean (see lines 31, 42) and was friendly to humanity.   6. Ea's subterfuge enables him to inform Utanapishtim of the gods' plans without visibly breaking his oath to the group.

Take aboard the boat seed of all living things.
The boat you shall build,
Let her dimensions be measured out:
Let her width and length be equal,   30
Roof her over like the watery depths."[7]
I understood full well, I said to Ea, my lord:
"Your command, my lord, exactly as you said it,
I shall faithfully execute.
What shall I answer the city, the populace, and the elders?"   35
Ea made ready to speak,
Saying to me, his servant:
"So, you shall speak to them thus:
'No doubt Enlil dislikes me,
I shall not dwell in your city.   40
I shall not set my foot on the dry land of Enlil,
I shall descend to the watery depths and dwell with my lord Ea.
Upon you he shall shower down in abundance,
A windfall of birds, a surprise of fishes,
He shall pour upon you a harvest of riches,   45
In the morning cakes in spates,
In the evening grains in rains.' "[8]
At the first glimmer of dawn,
The land was assembling at the gate of Atrahasis:[9]
The carpenter carried his axe,   50
The reed cutter carried his stone,
The old men brought cordage(?),[1]
The young men ran around [. . .],
The wealthy carried the pitch,
The poor brought what was needed of [. . .].   55
In five days I had planked her hull:
One full acre was her deck space,
Ten dozen cubits,[2] the height of each of her sides,
Ten dozen cubits square, her outer dimensions.
I laid out her structure, I planned her design: 60
I decked her in six,
I divided her in seven,
Her interior I divided in nine.
I drove the water plugs into her,[3]
I saw to the spars and laid in what was needful.   65
Thrice thirty-six hundred measures[4] of pitch I poured in the
    oven,

7. The Mesopotamians believed that the freshwater sea under the earth was covered in order to hold in
the waters; the cubical ark will also be roofed, but in this case to keep out the water.   8. Foster suggests
that these lines foreshadow but also deceive the listeners about the coming deluge, observing a punning
play on words: "*cakes* suggesting *darkness*, *grains* suggesting something like *grievous*, and *rains* suggesting
provide for." (See lines 92–95, in which the storm descends.)   9. Another name for Utanapishtim. A
Babylonian poem called "The Myth of Atrahasis" described the creation of the human race and the coming
of the Flood.   1. The hull of an ancient boat was the first part to be built, even before the interior
framework, and its planks were sewn together with cordage.   2. I.e., about 180 feet (a cubit was about
18 inches).   3. The "water plugs" have been explained in various ways, for example, as caulking, stabi-
lizers, depth markers, water taps, bilge drains, and drains to let out rainwater when the boat was beached.
None of these suggestions is supported by Mesopotamian evidence [Translator's note].   4. The repeated
"thrice thirty-six hundred measures" illustrates the epic's use of fantastic numbers. The precise amount
here is left to the imagination, but it is unquestionably large.

Thrice thirty-six hundred measures of tar [I poured out] inside
    her.
Thrice thirty-six hundred measures basket-bearers brought
    aboard for oil,
Not counting the thirty-six hundred measures of oil that the
    offering consumed,
And the twice thirty-six hundred measures of oil that the
    boatbuilders made off with.   70
For the [builders] I slaughtered bullocks,
I killed sheep upon sheep every day,
Beer, ale, oil, and wine
[I gave out] to the workers like river water,
They made a feast as on New Year's Day,   75
[. . .] I dispensed ointment with my own hand.
By the setting of Shamash,[5] the ship was completed.
[Since boarding was(?)] very difficult,
They brought up gangplanks(?), fore and aft,
They came up her sides(?) two-thirds (of her height).[6]   80
[Whatever I had] I loaded upon her:
What silver I had I loaded upon her,
What gold I had I loaded upon her,
What living creatures I had I loaded upon her,
I sent up on board all my family and kin,   85
Beasts of the steppe, wild animals of the steppe, all types of
    skilled craftsmen I sent up on board.
Shamash set for me the appointed time:
"In the morning, cakes in spates,
In the evening, grains in rains,
Go into your boat and caulk the door!"   90
That appointed time arrived,
In the morning cakes in spates,
In the evening grains in rains,
I gazed upon the face of the storm,
The weather was dreadful to behold!   95
I went into the boat and caulked the door.
To the caulker of the boat, to Puzur-Amurri the boatman,
I gave over the edifice, with all it contained.

At the first glimmer of dawn,
A black cloud rose above the horizon.   100
Inside it Adad was thundering,
While the destroying gods Shullat and Hanish[7] went in front,
Moving as an advance force over hill and plain.
Errakal[8] tore out the mooring posts (of the world),
Ninurta came and made the dikes overflow.   105
The supreme gods held torches aloft,
Setting the land ablaze with their glow.

---

5. The sun god and god of oracles, Gilgamesh's protector throughout the epic. The reference to Shamash here and in line 87 may show that in earlier versions of the story, it was Shamash who warned of the flood. **6.** Plays on numbers and mathematical riddles were popular with Mesopotamians. Gilgamesh is two-thirds divine, one-third human; and Ur-Shanabi, the name of the boatman who ferries him to Utanapishtim, means "Servant of Two-Thirds." **7.** Adad was god of thunderstorms; Shullat and Hanish were gods of destructive storms. **8.** Another name for the Sumerian Nergal, god of the underworld.

Adad's awesome power passed over the heavens,
Whatever was light was turned into darkness,
[He flooded] the land, he smashed it like a [clay pot]! 110
For one day the storm wind [blew],
Swiftly it blew, [the flood came forth],
It passed over the people like a battle,
No one could see the one next to him,
The people could not recognize one another in the downpour. 115
The gods became frightened of the deluge,
They shrank back, went up to Anu's highest heaven.
The gods cowered like dogs, crouching outside.
Ishtar screamed like a woman in childbirth,
And sweet-voiced Belet-ili[9] wailed aloud: 120
"Would that day had come to naught,
When I spoke up for evil in the assembly of the gods!
How could I have spoken up for evil in the assembly of the gods,
And spoken up for battle to destroy my people?
It was I myself who brought my people into the world, 125
Now, like a school of fish, they choke up the sea!"
The supreme gods were weeping with her,
The gods sat where they were, weeping,
Their lips were parched, taking on a crust.
Six days and seven nights 130
The wind continued, the deluge and windstorm leveled the land.
When the seventh day arrived,
The windstorm and deluge left off their battle,
Which had struggled, like a woman in labor.
The sea grew calm, the tempest stilled, the deluge ceased. 135

I looked at the weather, stillness reigned,
And the whole human race had turned into clay.
The landscape was flat as a rooftop.
I opened the hatch, sunlight fell upon my face.
Falling to my knees, I sat down weeping, 140
Tears running down my face.
I looked at the edges of the world, the borders of the sea,
At twelve times sixty double leagues the periphery emerged.
The boat had come to rest on Mount Nimush,
Mount Nimush held the boat fast, not letting it move.[1]
One day, a second day Mount Nimush held the boat fast, not
    letting it move.
A third day, a fourth day Mount Nimush held the boat fast, not
    letting it move.
A fifth day, a sixth day Mount Nimush held the boat fast, not
    letting it move.

When the seventh day arrived,
I brought out a dove and set it free. 150
The dove went off and returned,

---

9. Ishtar was the chief goddess of Mesopotamian religion, associated with sex, love, and warfare. Belet-ili was goddess of birth; in the Atrahasis myth, she and Enki created the human race.   1. The boat has run aground.

No landing place came to its view, so it turned back.
I brought out a swallow and set it free,
The swallow went off and returned,
No landing place came to its view, so it turned back.   155
I brought out a raven and set it free,
The raven went off and saw the ebbing of the waters.
It ate, preened, left droppings, did not turn back.
I released all to the four directions,
I brought out an offering and offered it to the four directions,   160
I set up an incense offering on the summit of the mountain,
I arranged seven and seven cult vessels,
I heaped reeds, cedar, and myrtle in their bowls.[2]
The gods smelled the savor,
The gods smelled the sweet savor,   165
The gods crowded round the sacrificer like flies.[3]

As soon as Belet-ili arrived,
She held up the great fly-ornaments that Anu had made in his
    ardor:
"O gods, these shall be my lapis[4] necklace, lest I forget,
I shall be mindful of these days and not forget, not ever!   170
The gods should come to the incense offering,
But Enlil should not come to the incense offering,
For he, irrationally, brought on the flood,
And marked my people for destruction!"
As soon as Enlil arrived,   175
He saw the boat, Enlil flew into a rage,
He was filled with fury at the gods:
"Who came through alive? No man was to survive destruction!"
Ninurta made ready to speak,
Said to the valiant Enlil: 180
"Who but Ea could contrive such a thing?
For Ea alone knows every artifice."

Ea made ready to speak,
Said to the valiant Enlil:
"You, O valiant one, are the wisest of the gods,   185
How could you, irrationally, have brought on the flood?
Punish the wrongdoer for his wrongdoing,
Punish the transgressor for his transgression,
But be lenient, lest he be cut off,
Bear with him, lest he [. . .].   190
Instead of your bringing on a flood,
Let the lion rise up to diminish the human race!
Instead of your bringing on a flood,
Let the wolf rise up to diminish the human race!
Instead of your bringing on a flood,   195

2. The Mesopotamians sometimes burned various plants and branches in order to produce an attractive
odor when making *offerings* to the gods [Translator's note].   3. The gods miss the nourishment of their
regular offerings.   4. Lapis lazuli, a hard blue semiprecious stone. In the prologue, Gilgamesh's story is
carved on a lapis tablet (Tablet I, line 28). *Fly-ornaments*: the goddess's necklace of fly-shaped beads has
been taken to represent the rainbow.

Let famine rise up to wreak havoc in the land!
Instead of your bringing on a flood,
Let pestilence rise up to wreak havoc in the land!
It was not I who disclosed the secret of the great gods,
I made Atrahasis have a dream and so he heard the secret of the
    gods.   200
Now then, make some plan for him."
Then Enlil came up into the boat,
Leading me by the hand, he brought me up too.
He brought my wife up and had her kneel beside me.
He touched our brows, stood between us to bless us: 205
"Hitherto Utanapishtim and his wife shall become like us gods.
Utanapishtim shall dwell far distant at the source of the rivers."
Thus it was that they took me far distant and had me dwell at
    the source of the rivers.
Now then, who will convene the gods for your sake,   210
That you may find the eternal life you seek?
Come, come, try not to sleep for six days and seven nights.[5]

As he sat there on his haunches,
Sleep was swirling over him like a mist.
Utanapishtim said to her, to his wife: 215

    Behold this fellow who seeks eternal life!
    Sleep swirls over him like a mist.

His wife said to him, to Utanapishtim the Distant One:

    Do touch him that the man may wake up,
    That he may return safe on the way whence he came,   220
    That through the gate he came forth he may return to his land.

Utanapishtim said to her, to his wife:

    Since the human race is duplicitous, he'll endeavor to dupe you.
    Come, come, bake his daily loaves, put them one after another
        by his head,
    Then mark the wall for each day he has slept.   225

She baked his daily loaves for him, put them one after another by his
    head,
Then dated the wall for each day he slept.
The first loaf was dried hard,
The second was leathery, the third soggy,
The crust of the fourth turned white,   230
The fifth was gray with mold, the sixth was fresh,
The seventh was still on the coals when he touched him, the man
    woke up.

---

5. At the beginning of the epic, in the fullness of his godlike strength, Gilgamesh is described as "never resting by day or night" (Tablet I, line 239). Utanapishtim now challenges him to stay awake for a week.

Gilgamesh said to him, to Utanapishtim the Distant One:

> Scarcely had sleep stolen over me,
> When straightaway you touched me and roused me.   235

Utanapishtim said to him, to Gilgamesh:

> [Up with you], Gilgamesh, count your daily loaves,
> [That the days you have slept] may be known to you.
> The first loaf is dried hard,
> The second is leathery, the third soggy,   240
> The crust of the fourth has turned white,
> The fifth is gray with mold,
> The sixth is fresh,
> The seventh was still in the coals when I touched you and you
>   woke up.

Gilgamesh said to him, to Utanapishtim the Distant One: 245

> What then should I do, Utanapishtim, whither should I go,
> Now that the Bereaver[6] has seized my [flesh]?
> Death lurks in my bedchamber,
> And wherever I turn, there is death!

Utanapishtim said to him, to Ur-Shanabi the boatman: 250

> Ur-Shanabi, may the harbor [offer] you no [haven],
> May the crossing point reject you,
> Be banished from the shore you shuttled to.[7]
> The man you brought here,
> His body is matted with filthy hair,   255
> Hides have marred the beauty of his flesh.
> Take him away, Ur-Shanabi, bring him to the washing place.
> Have him wash out his filthy hair with water, clean as snow,
> Have him throw away his hides, let the sea carry them off,
> Let his body be rinsed clean.   260
> Let his headband be new,
> Have him put on raiment worthy of him.
> Until he reaches his city,[8]
> Until he completes his journey,
> Let his garments stay spotless, fresh and new.   265

Ur-Shanabi took him away and brought him to the washing place.
He washed out his filthy hair with water, clean as snow,
He threw away his hides, the sea carried them off,
His body was rinsed clean.
He renewed his headband,   270
He put on raiment worthy of him.
Until he reached his city,

---

6. Death.   7. Ur-Shanabi has lost his job as ferryman for bringing Gilgamesh to Utanapishtim.
8. Uruk, the largest city of Mesopotamia.

Until he completed his journey,
His garments would stay spotless, fresh and new.

Gilgamesh and Ur-Shanabi embarked on the boat,   275
They launched the boat, they embarked upon it.
His wife said to him, to Utanapishtim the Distant One:

> Gilgamesh has come here, spent with exertion,
> What will you give him for his homeward journey?

At that he, Gilgamesh, lifted the pole,   280
Bringing the boat back by the shore.
Utanapishtim said to him, to Gilgamesh:

> Gilgamesh, you have come here, spent with exertion,
> What shall I give you for your homeward journey?
> I will reveal to you, O Gilgamesh, a secret matter,   285
> And a mystery of the gods I will tell you.
> There is a certain plant, its stem is like a thornbush,
> Its thorns, like the wild rose, will prick [your hand].
> If you can secure this plant, [. . .]
> [. . .]   290

No sooner had Gilgamesh heard this,
He opened a shaft, [flung away his tools].
He tied heavy stones [to his feet],
They pulled him down into the watery depths [. . .].
He took the plant though it pricked [his hand].   295
He cut the heavy stones [from his feet],
The sea cast him up on his home shore.[9]

Gilgamesh said to him, to Ur-Shanabi the boatman:

> Ur-Shanabi, this plant is cure for heartache,
> Whereby a man will regain his stamina.   300
> I will take it to ramparted Uruk,
> I will have an old man eat some and so test the plant.
> His name shall be "Old Man Has Become Young-Again-Man."
> I myself will eat it and so return to my carefree youth.

At twenty double leagues they took a bite to eat,   305
At thirty double leagues they made their camp.

Gilgamesh saw a pond whose water was cool,
He went down into it to bathe in the water.
A snake caught the scent of the plant,
[Stealthily] it came up and carried the plant away,   310
On its way back it shed its skin.

9. Gilgamesh digs a shaft through the earth to reach the underground ocean. Tying stones to his feet (like a pearl diver), he is drawn down through the water and picks the plant of rejuvenation. Removing the stones, he rises to the surface and finds himself on the opposite side of the ocean.

Thereupon Gilgamesh sat down weeping,
His tears flowed down his face,
He said to Ur-Shanabi the boatman:

> For whom, Ur-Shanabi, have my hands been toiling?   315
> For whom has my heart's blood been poured out?
> For myself I have obtained no benefit,
> I have done a good deed for a reptile!
> Now, floodwaters rise against me for twenty double leagues,[1]
> When I opened the shaft, I flung away the tools.   320
> How shall I find my bearings?
> I have come much too far to go back, and I abandoned the boat
>   on the shore.

At twenty double leagues they took a bite to eat,
At thirty double leagues they made their camp.
When they arrived in ramparted Uruk,   325
Gilgamesh said to him, to Ur-Shanabi the boatman:

> Go up, Ur-Shanabi, pace out the walls of Uruk.
> Study the foundation terrace and examine the brickwork.
> Is not its masonry of kiln-fired brick?
> And did not seven masters lay its foundations?   330
> One square mile of city, one square mile of gardens,
> One square mile of clay pits, a half square mile of Ishtar's dwell-
>   ing,
> Three and a half square miles is the measure of Uruk![2]

Gilgamesh

BOOK XI[1]

Gilgamesh said to Utnapishtim,[2]
"I imagined that you would look like a god.   1
But you look like me, you are not any different.
I intended to fight you, yet now that I stand
before you, now that I see who you are,
I can't fight, something is holding me back.   5
Tell me, how is it that you, a mortal,
overcame death and joined the assembly
of the gods and were granted eternal life?"

Utnapishtim said, "I will tell you   10
a mystery, a secret of the gods.
You know Shuruppak, that ancient city

---

1. Gilgamesh left his tools on the other shore after digging the shaft, which the ocean has filled in the meantime.   2. 333 (Uruk) Lines 327–33 repeat lines 18–24 of the prologue (Tablet I).   1. Translated and edited in 2004 by Stephen Mitchell. Book XI is the last installment of the *Gilgamesh* epic; a twelfth book found with the others contains a Sumerian poem about Gilgamesh and is not part of the epic. 2. The sage who survived the Great Flood and whom the gods gave the gift of immortality. Gilgamesh has journeyed to meet him and learn the secret of eternal life.

on the Euphrates.[3] I lived there once.
I was its king once, a long time ago,
when the great gods decided to send the Flood.   15
Five gods decided, and they took an oath
to keep the plan secret: Anu their father,
the counselor Enlil, Ninurta the gods'
chamberlain, and Ennugi[4] the sheriff.
Ea[5] also, the cleverest of the gods,   20
had taken the oath, but I heard him whisper
the secret to the reed fence around my house.
'Reed fence, reed fence, listen to my words.
King of Shuruppak, quickly, quickly
tear down your house and build a great ship,   25
leave your possessions, save your life.
The ship must be square, so that its length
equals its width. Build a roof over it,
just as the Great Deep is covered by the earth.[6]
Then gather and take aboard the ship   30
examples of every living creature.

"I understood Ea's words, and I said,
'My lord, I will obey your command,
exactly as you have spoken it.
But what shall I say when the people ask me   35
why I am building such a large ship?'

"Ea said, 'Tell them that Enlil hates you,
that you can no longer live in their city
or walk on the earth, which belongs to Enlil,
that it is your fate to go down into   40
the Great Deep and live with Ea your lord,
and that Ea will rain abundance upon them.
They will all have all that they want, and more.'

"I laid out the structure, I drafted plans.
At the first glow of dawn, everyone gathered—   45
carpenters brought their saws and axes,
reed workers brought their flattening-stones,
rope makers brought their ropes, and children
carried the tar. The poor helped also,
however they could—some carried timber,   50
some hammered nails, some cut wood.
By the end of the fifth day the hull had been built:[7]
the decks were an acre large, the sides

---

3. One of two great rivers flowing in ancient Mesopotamia; the other is the Tigris. *Shuruppak:* a city in central southeastern Mesopotamia (near modern Tell Fara); it was abandoned by the time the epic was written.   4. Anu is god of the sky and father of the gods, specifically Enlil and Aruru; Enlil, an irritable and capricious god, governs the universe with Anu, Ea, and Aruru. Ninurta, the son of Enlil, is the god of agriculture and a war god; Ennugi is the gods' constable.   5. The god of wisdom, magic, and clever solutions to problems (named Enki in the Sumerian poems), as well as the god of the freshwater subterranean ocean (see lines 29, 41). He is friendly to humanity, and finds a way to warn Utnapishtim without openly breaking his oath.   6. Just as earth covers the Great Deep (the subterranean ocean), so Utnapishtim is to put a roof on his boat.   7. The hull of an ancient boat was the first part to be built, even before the interior framework.

two hundred feet high. I built six decks,
so that the ship's height was divided in seven.[8]   55
I divided each deck into nine compartments,
drove water plugs into all the holes,
brought aboard spars and other equipment,
had three thousand gallons of tar poured into
the furnace, and three thousand gallons of pitch   60
poured out. The bucket carriers brought
three thousand gallons of oil—a thousand
were used for the caulking, two thousand were left,
which the boatman stored. Each day I slaughtered
bulls for my workmen, I slaughtered sheep,   65
I gave them barrels of beer and ale
and wine, and they drank it like river water.
When all our work on the ship was finished,
we feasted as though it were New Year's Day.
At sunrise I handed out oil for the ritual,   70
by sunset the ship was ready. The launching
was difficult. We rolled her on logs
down to the river and eased her in
until two-thirds was under the water.
I loaded onto her everything precious   75
that I owned: all my silver and gold,
all my family, all my kinfolk,
all kinds of animals, wild and tame,
craftsmen and artisans of every kind.

"Then Shamash[9] announced that the time had come.   80
'Enter the ship now. Seal the hatch.'
I gazed at the sky—it was terrifying.
I entered the ship. To Puzur-amurri
the shipwright, the man who sealed the hatch,
I gave my palace, with all its contents.   85

"At the first glow of dawn, an immense black cloud
rose on the horizon and crossed the sky.
Inside it the storm god Adad was thundering,
while Shullat and Hanish, twin gods of destruction,
went first, tearing through mountains and valleys.   90
Nergal, the god of pestilence, ripped out
the dams of the Great Deep, Ninurta opened
the floodgates of heaven, the infernal gods
blazed and set the whole land on fire.
A deadly silence spread through the sky   95
and what had been bright now turned to darkness.
The land was shattered like a clay pot.
All day, ceaselessly, the storm winds blew,
the rain fell, then the flood burst forth,
overwhelming the people like war.   100

8. The ship is shaped like a cube, possible in an allusion to the Mesopotamian ziggurat—a massive cubical construction, with four to seven levels, that served as base for a temple.   9. The sun god, god of justice and patron of travelers; he is Gilgamesh's protector throughout the epic.

No one could see through the rain, it fell
harder and harder, so thick that you couldn't
see your own hand before your eyes.
Even the gods were afraid. The water
rose higher and higher until the gods fled   105
to Anu's palace in the highest heaven.
But Anu had shut the gates. The gods
cowered by the palace wall, like dogs.

"Sweet-voiced Aruru,[1] mother of men,
screamed out, like a woman in childbirth: 110
'If only that day had never been,
when I spoke up for evil in the council of the gods!
How could I have agreed to destroy
my children by sending the Great Flood upon them?
I have given birth to the human race, only   115
to see them fill the ocean like fish.'
The other gods were lamenting with her.
They sat and listened to her and wept.
Their lips were parched, crusted with scabs.[2]

"For six days and seven nights, the storm   120
demolished the earth. On the seventh day,
the downpour stopped. The ocean grew calm.
No land could be seen, just water on all sides,
as flat as a roof.[3] There was no life at all.
The human race had turned into clay.   125
I opened a hatch and the blessed sunlight
streamed upon me, I fell to my knees
and wept. When I got up and looked around,
a coastline appeared, a half mile away.
On Mount Nimush the ship ran aground,   130
the mountain held it and would not release it.
For six days and seven nights, the mountain
would not release it. On the seventh day,
I brought out a dove and set it free.
The dove flew off, then flew back to the ship,   135
because there was no place to land. I waited,
then I brought out a swallow and set it free.
The swallow flew off, then flew back to the ship,
because there was no place to land. I waited,
then I brought out a raven and set it free.   140
The raven flew off, and because the water
had receded, it found a branch, it sat there,
it ate, it flew off and didn't return.

"When the waters had dried up and land appeared,
I set free the animals I had taken,   145

1. The mother goddess who created the human race with Ea's help (also called Belet-ili).   2. The gods
are starving without their regular offerings from human beings. When Utnapishtim sets out sacrifices after
the flood, they gather like flies to the feast (line 151).   3. Flat roofs, often used as patios or terraces, are
common in hot, dry countries.

I slaughtered a sheep on the mountaintop
and offered it to the gods, I arranged
two rows of seven ritual vases,
I burned reeds, cedar, and myrtle branches.
The gods smelled the fragrance, they smelled the sweet fragrance   150
and clustered around the offering like flies.

"When Aruru came, she held up in the air
her necklace of lapis lazuli,[4]
Anu's gift when their love was new.
'I swear by this precious ornament   155
that never will I forget these days.
Let all the gods come to the sacrifice,
except for Enlil, because he recklessly
sent the Great Flood and destroyed my children.'

"Then Enlil arrived. When he saw the ship,   160
he was angry, he raged at the other gods.
'Who helped these humans escape? Wasn't
the Flood supposed to destroy them all?'

"Ninurta answered, 'Who else but Ea,
the cleverest of us, could devise such a thing?'   165

"Ea said to the counselor Enlil,
'You, the wisest and bravest of the gods,
how did it happen that you so recklessly
sent the Great Flood to destroy mankind?
It is right to punish the sinner for his sins,   170
to punish the criminal for his crime,
but be merciful, do not allow all men
to die because of the sins of some.
Instead of a flood, you should have sent
lions to decimate the human race,   175
or wolves, or a famine, or a deadly plague.
As for my taking the solemn oath,
I didn't reveal the secret of the gods,
I only whispered it to a fence
and Utnapishtim happened to hear.[5]   180
Now *you* must decide what his fate will be.'

"Then Enlil boarded, he took my hand,
he led me out, then he led out my wife.
He had us kneel down in front of him,
he touched our foreheads and, standing between us,   185
he blessed us. 'Hear me, you gods: Until now,
Utnapishtim was a mortal man.
But from now on, he and his wife shall be

---

4. A hard blue semiprecious stone. In the prologue, Gilgamesh's story is carved on a lapis tablet (book I, line 21). The goddess's necklace is made of fly-shaped beads that have possible symbolic meaning.   5. Ea says literally "I made a dream appear to Atrahasis, and thus he heard the secret of the gods." The name Atrahasis and the mention of a dream seem to be taken from an earlier poem.

gods like us, they shall live forever,
at the source of the rivers, far away.' 190
Then they brought us to this distant place
at the source of the rivers. Here we live.

"Now then, Gilgamesh, who will assemble
the gods for *your* sake? Who will convince them
to grant you the eternal life that you seek? 195
How would they know that you deserve it?
First pass this test: Just stay awake
for seven days.[6] Prevail against sleep,
and perhaps you will prevail against death."

So Gilgamesh sat down against a wall 200
to begin the test. The moment he sat down,
sleep swirled over him, like a fog.

Utnapishtim said to his wife,
"Look at this fellow! He wanted to live
forever, but the very moment he sat down, 205
sleep swirled over him, like a fog."

His wife said, "Touch him on the shoulder, wake him,
let him depart and go back safely
to his own land, by the gate he came through."

Utnapishtim said, "All men are liars. 210
When he wakes up, watch how he tries to deceive us.
So bake a loaf for each day he sleeps,
put them in a row beside him, and make
a mark on the wall for every loaf."

She baked the loaves and put them beside him, 215
she made a mark for each day he slept.
The first loaf was rock-hard, the second loaf
was dried out like leather, the third had shrunk,
the fourth had a whitish covering, the fifth
was spotted with mold, the sixth was stale, 220
the seventh loaf was still on the coals
when he reached out and touched him. Gilgamesh
woke with a start and said, "I was almost
falling asleep when I felt your touch."

Utnapishtim said, "Look down, friend, 225
count these loaves that my wife baked and put here
while you sat sleeping. This first one, rock-hard,

---

6. At the beginning of the epic, in the fullness of his godlike strength, Gilgamesh is described as "so full of life-force that he never needs sleep" (book I, line 199).

was baked seven days ago, this leathery one
was baked six days ago, and so on for all
the rest of the days you sat here sleeping.   230
Look. They are marked on the wall behind you."

Gilgamesh cried out, "What shall I do,
where shall I go now? Death has caught me,
it lurks in my bedroom, and everywhere I look,
everywhere I turn, there is only death."   235

Utnapishtim said to the boatman,
"This is the last time, Urshanabi,
that you are allowed to cross the vast ocean
and reach these shores. As for this man,
he is filthy and tired, his hair is matted,   240
animal skins have obscured his beauty.
Bring him to the tub and wash out his hair,
take off his animal skin and let
the waves of the ocean carry it away,
moisten his body with sweet-smelling oil,   245
bind his hair in a bright new headband,
dress him in fine robes fit for a king.
Until he comes to the end of his journey
let his robes be spotless, as though they were new."

He brought him to the tub, he washed out his hair,   250
he took off his animal skin and let
the waves of the ocean carry it away,
he moistened his body with sweet-smelling oil,
he bound his hair in a bright new headband,
he dressed him in fine robes fit for a king.   255
Then Gilgamesh and Urshanabi
boarded, pushed off, and the little boat
began to move away from the shore.

But the wife of Utnapishtim said, "Wait,
this man came a very long way, he endured   260
many hardships to get here. Won't you
give him something for his journey home?"

When he heard this, Gilgamesh turned the boat
around, and he brought it back to the shore.
Utnapishtim said, "Gilgamesh,   265
you came a very long way, you endured
many hardships to get here. Now
I will give you something for your journey home,
a mystery, a secret of the gods.
There is a small spiny bush that grows   270
in the waters of the Great Deep, it has sharp spikes
that will prick your fingers like a rose's thorns.
If you find this plant and bring it to the surface,
you will have found the secret of youth."

Gilgamesh dug a pit on the shore   275
that led down into the Great Deep. He tied
two heavy stones to his feet, they pulled him
downward into the water's depths.
He found the plant, he grasped it, it tore
his fingers, they bled, he cut off the stones,   280
his body shot up to the surface, and the waves
cast him back, gasping, onto the shore.[7]

Gilgamesh said to Urshanabi,
"Come here, look at this marvelous plant,
the antidote to the fear of death.   285
With it we return to the youth we once had.
I will take it to Uruk,[8] I will test its power
by seeing what happens when an old man eats it.
If that succeeds, I will eat some myself
and become a carefree young man again."   290

At four hundred miles they stopped to eat,
at a thousand miles they pitched their camp.
Gilgamesh saw a pond of cool water.
He left the plant on the ground and bathed.
A snake smelled its fragrance, stealthily   295
it crawled up and carried the plant away.
As it disappeared, it cast off its skin.

When Gilgamesh saw what the snake had done,
he sat down and wept. He said to the boatman,
"What shall I do now? All my hardships   300
have been for nothing. O Urshanabi,
was it for this that my hands have labored,
was it for this that I gave my heart's blood?
I have gained no benefit for myself
but have lost the marvelous plant to a reptile.   305
I plucked it from the depths, and how could I ever
manage to find that place again?
And our little boat—we left it on the shore."

At four hundred miles they stopped to eat,
at a thousand miles they pitched their camp.   310

When at last they arrived, Gilgamesh
said to Urshanabi, "This is
the wall of Uruk, which no city on earth can equal.
See how its ramparts gleam like copper in the sun.
Climb the stone staircase, more ancient than the mind can imagine 315
approach the Eanna Temple, sacred to Ishtar,[9]
a temple that no king has equaled in size or beauty,

---

7. Gilgamesh rises the surface of the ocean rather than emerging from the pit that took him into the Great Deep. He now finds himself on the opposite shore, ready to begin his journey home in the company of Urshanabi, the exiled boatman.   8. The largest city of Mesopotamia, where Gilgamesh is king.   9. The chief goddess of Mesopotamian religion, associated with sex, love, and warfare.

walk on the wall of Uruk, follow its course
around the city, inspect its mighty foundations,
examine its brickwork, how masterfully it is built,   320
observe the land it encloses: the palm trees, the gardens,
the orchards, the glorious palaces and temples, the shops
and marketplaces, the houses, the public squares."[1]

1. Lines 312–23 repeat lines 8–18 of the prologue (book I).

THE HEBREW BIBLE
ca. 1000–300 B.C.E.

The sacred writings of the Jews encompass a rich variety of texts from different periods composed in poetry and prose, and sometimes in a mixture of both. They represent a striking mixture of literary types; an only partial list includes historical narrative, short story, genealogy, proverbs, laws, visionary narrative (prophecy), and many kinds of lyric poetry. Together they tell the story of the Jewish people in different modes and from various perspectives. This history is filled with risks and trials, but it is given meaning by the Jews' relation to their god, who rewards righteousness and punishes wrongdoing and who, it is believed, works through that history to fulfill his covenant or agreement with the people he has chosen.

GENESIS

The book of Genesis forms the first part of an interconnected group of writings that are central to Jewish belief and are known collectively in Hebrew as the Torah (a word meaning "instruction" or "guidance," but also with the specific sense of "law"); they are also often called the Pentateuch ("five scrolls"), a name derived from Greek. The division into five books was artificial, and probably was determined by how much would fit on individual papyrus rolls. The narrative parts of the Torah told a continuous story, from the creation of the world to the sojourn in Egypt, the Israelites' exodus from Egypt, their subsequent wandering led by Moses, and finally Moses' death just before the entry into the Promised Land. Embedded within this narrative, however, and occupying a considerable amount of the Torah, are laws given by God to Moses, and passed on by Moses to his people. The core experience of the exodus was the interlude at Mount Sinai, which occupies Exodus from chapter 19 on, the whole book of Leviticus, and the first part of Numbers (to 10.11). Here God reveals to Moses laws of various kinds, especially those, including the Ten Commandments, meant to guide individual life (Exodus) and those concerned with cult and ritual (all of Leviticus). The selection from Exodus printed here describes Moses receiving the Ten Commandments. Much of the final book of the Torah, Deuteronomy, consists of Moses' address to his people on the last day of his life, in which (among other things) he partly repeats and partly elaborates on the laws delivered at Sinai to give guidance for life in Canaan, which the Israelites are about to enter. Just as the story of the exodus is essential to Jewish faith because it tells of God's deliverance of his people in the execution of his plan for them, so the law is central because it defines the Jews' relation to God; and Moses dominates the Torah and Jewish tradition as the intermediary through whom God gave the law to his people.
    The narratives in Genesis give background to these later events, not just by telling

what happened before them but also by providing a framework through which to understand their importance and by characterizing the relation between God and his people through a series of exemplary stories. The book falls into two distinct parts. The first (chapters 1–11) recounts "creation history"—God's creation of the world and of humankind, and the evolution of early human society. Human beings occupy center stage in this account of the world's origin, as they do not in, for example, Mesopotamian and Greek creation stories. This early age is marked especially by human wrongdoing and God's punishment, from the disobedience of Adam and Eve and their expulsion from Eden to the construction of the Tower of Babel, which results in God scattering human beings and dividing their single language into many languages. Because this view of the world is human-centered (when God blesses man and woman after he creates them in chapter 1, he gives them all the plants and animals that fill the world), it is fitting that when he decides to destroy humanity he reverses his original act of creation. The flood mixes together again the waters that were separated on the second day of creation, and it destroys all the different kinds of animal created on the fifth and sixth days, together with all humans.

Not quite all, of course. The world is not destroyed. Noah and his family, and the pairs of animals taken onto the ark, are spared, because Noah is righteous and has found favor in God's eyes. With this dramatic demonstration of God's justice, and its pendant in the story of the Tower of Babel, there is a new beginning. In this second part of Genesis (chapters 12–50) the focus shifts from humanity in general to four generations of ancestors of the people of Israel: Abraham and Sarah; Isaac and Rebekah; Jacob and his wives, Leah and Rachel; and Joseph and his brothers. In the transition between the two sections, a passage at the beginning of chapter 12 plays a pivotal role. When God tells Noah's descendant Abram (who will be renamed Abraham) to leave his home in Mesopotamia, he says, "Go forth from your land and your birthplace and your father's house to the land I will show you. And I will make you a great nation and I will bless you and make your name great, and you shall be a blessing. And I will bless those who bless you, and those who damn you I will curse, and all the clans of the earth through you shall be blessed." This is the first statement of God's covenant with Israel, which is repeated a number of times throughout the Torah. After the flood God made a covenant with humanity in general, but it was essentially negative: he would never again destroy the world by flood (chapter 9). This new covenant implies a positive purpose in history: other peoples will be blessed through the people of Israel, who are chosen for a particularly close relation with God. This destiny, viewed as the ultimate goal of history, gives that history meaning. But two other pledges made as part of that destiny are more immediately relevant to the narrative of Genesis: a land to dwell in and a multitude of descendants (implied here in the phrase "a great nation" and made more explicit in God's subsequent promises to Abraham in chapters 17 and 22 and to Jacob in chapter 35).

The emphasis on posterity as part of God's covenant gives significance to the genealogical lists that are scattered throughout Genesis, as well as to the generational structure of the main story, and the Promised Land figures not just in the story of Moses but in the narrative of every generation of the ancestors. But complications arise in respect to both the family and the land that seem to threaten the fulfillment of the covenant. Abraham's wife Sarah is barren, and they are childless into their nineties. Though both understandably laugh when God promises them a son, Isaac is born to them. God then demands, but at the last moment forestalls, Abraham's sacrifice of Isaac. Jacob and Esau, Isaac's sons, are rivals and struggle with each other even in the womb. When Jacob tricks Esau out of his patrimony, Esau intends to kill him, and their mother Rebekah saves him by sending him to live with her brother Laban. Jacob's sons renew the pattern: their jealous resentment of their brother Joseph leads to Joseph's being sold into slavery in Egypt after their plot to kill him is frustrated. This strife between brothers, with the threat of fratricide, recalls the story of Cain and Abel. The land is involved in these tensions, because as a result of them

Jacob as a young man and later Joseph, followed eventually by his brothers and the aged Jacob, leave it and go to live somewhere else. In the first generation too Abraham leaves the land to which God has led him and goes to Egypt to avoid a famine, in a clear anticipation of the story of Joseph (chapter 12). In Genesis, this land is left again and again, and the attainment of a settled home in it is deferred beyond the end of the Torah.

In the end, God fulfills his purpose and shapes events according to his covenant, and he does so in unexpected ways. Aged parents beget a son, and in the next two generations it is the younger branch of the family (Jacob, Joseph) that serves as the vehicle for carrying out God's purpose (according to the rule of primogeniture in Hebrew society, primacy would be given to the oldest son). In addition, fraternal strife and exile, which at first seem to derail God's plan, turn out to be the means for carrying it out. Jacob brings back from refuge with his uncle Laban the latter's two daughters, Leah and Rachel, as his wives, and the line is perpetuated through them. Joseph's servitude in Egypt becomes the means of preserving his father and brothers from famine in Canaan and leads, generations later, to the exodus from Egypt and the giving of the law to Moses. This pattern of near-disaster turned to a positive outcome reveals God's power and his surpassing of merely human expectations. It is also excellent narrative technique.

JOB

Genesis depicts a world in which people get exactly what they deserve: goodness is rewarded and sin is punished. This is a world that makes sense. All one has to do in order to live well is to obey God and conform to his law. It is in this sense that the stories in Genesis and the law of Moses in the rest of the Torah give guidance on how to live. Even apparently arbitrary events, such as the younger brother being favored over the elder (Jacob and Esau), can be referred to God's plan.

The book of Job challenges this sense of coherence and intelligibility because it shows a good and upright man who nevertheless suffers horribly—who even is selected for suffering *because* of his goodness. It raises the question not only of why the innocent suffer but more generally of why there is misfortune and unhappiness in the world. "Have you taken note of my servant Job," God asks the Accuser, "for there is no one like him on earth: innocent, upright, and God-fearing, and keeping himself apart from evil." But Job loses his family and wealth in a series of calamities that strike one on the other like hammer blows, and is then plagued with a loathsome disease. In a series of magnificent speeches, he expresses his sense of his own innocence and demands one thing: to understand the reason for his suffering.

From the beginning, we can see a little farther into the problem than Job. The verse speeches of Job and his comforters, which fill most of the book, are framed by a prologue and epilogue in prose. In the prologue, the Accuser challenges God's praise of Job by pointing out that Job's goodness has never been tested; it is easy to be righteous in prosperity. Because we see that Job's afflictions originate in a test, we know that there is a reason for his suffering. We may think it not much of a reason, and feel that Job is the object of sport for higher powers. If so, what we know from the prologue only makes the problem of innocent suffering worse. We may, however, want to take the explanation more seriously. In his wager with the Adversary, God is putting his trust in Job, and trust is a very important and wonderful aspect of his relation with humankind. In some ways too it seems to be not just Job who is being tested but humanity through him, and the question is whether people can have and retain their faith in God, and remain good, independently of circumstances. Should we expect to be rewarded for goodness with material and physical well-being, and are we good only because of these rewards? These are not trivial questions.

This line of thought puts the problem in some perspective but does not solve it. The fact remains that Job is innocent, and he still suffers. What kind of order can we find in a world where that can happen? The prologue in no way cancels the profundity with which Job seeks to probe the reasons for his suffering, or his need for understanding.

For Job's comforters, there is no problem. They are anchored solidly within the world of goodness rewarded and wickedness punished. They can account for suffering easily. If Job is suffering, he must have done something wrong. All he has to do, then, is to repent his sin and be reconciled with God. All their speeches essentially express and elaborate this one thought. Their pious formula, however, will not cover Job's situation. As we know from the prologue, their mistake is to confuse moral goodness with outward circumstance. Despite or because of their conventional piety, they do not understand Job's suffering, and they get God wrong. In the epilogue, God says to Eliphaz, "I am very angry at you and your two friends, for you have not spoken rightly about me as did my servant Job." Job has spoken rightly by insisting on his innocence and not reducing God's ways to a formula. He also avoids identifying goodness with his fortune in life; it is their disparity, in fact, that appalls him. But he fulfills God's expectations because he does not curse or in any way repudiate him. Instead, Job wants God to meet him on his own terms and explain:

> You can call, and I will answer,
> or I will speak and You can answer me.
> How many are my sins and my offenses?
> Advise me of my crimes and sins.
> Why do You hide Your face,
> regard me as Your enemy?

Far from cursing God, he is speaking from within an assumed relationship with him. But he is mistaken to think that he and God can meet on such equal terms that he merits an explanation. In the end, God does speak to him; he gets that much. But God addresses him with a series of questions, not answers:

> Cinch your waist like a fighter.
> I will put questions, and you will inform me:
> Where were you when I founded the earth?
> Speak, if you have any wisdom:
> Who set its measurements, if you know,
> laid out the building lot, stretching the plumb line?
> Where was the ground where He sank its foundations?

There is no reciprocal conversation; Job has no answers, and is silent except to confess his error.

God's magnificent speech from the storm ranges over all of creation and its animal life. The contrast with the account of creation in the first chapter of Genesis, which puts human beings at the center, is dramatic. Here there are beasts whose might far surpasses that of humans, who seem just a part of the created world, and the poetry of this speech conveys the awe and mystery that are attributes of God. The book of Job does not succeed in explaining innocent suffering, if that is its purpose, but it does leave us with a sense of what we cannot understand.

THE SONG OF SONGS

In this great dialogue between lovers, a man and a woman, frankly and in detail, express their appreciation of each other's bodies. The Song of Songs (or Song of Solomon) celebrates human sexuality and love in all their sensual splendor, as well as human life itself: "for love," it says, "is strong as death." Each of the lovers, again and again, takes inventory of the other's body, describing each part and comparing it to an animal, some feature of the natural landscape, or an aspect of the built human environment, so that we not only feel the power of physical desire but also appreciate the human body and love as harmonious parts of the world. Some of these comparisons are of great natural beauty ("thy belly is like a heap of wheat set about with lilies"); others are extravagant, fantastic ("thy hair is as a flock of goats," "thy teeth are like a flock of sheep," "thy neck is like the tower of David," "thy nose is as the tower of Lebanon"). The concreteness of the imagery and the piling of image upon image make the pair of bodies a figure of the world itself, to be contemplated in wonder.

But the incorporation of this poem in sacred scripture raises the possibility of further meanings, although what these might be is an open question. This challenging and beautiful text has had a long history of divergent interpretations; a medieval Jewish commentator described it as "locks to which the key has been lost." Is it an allegory, and if so, is it religious or is it historical? If the former, does the allegory concern the love between God and his chosen people? Christians later understood the poem to describe the love between Christ and his church, or between God or Christ and the individual soul. The question of allegory is complicated by other uncertainties. Is the text as we have it a single composition, or is it a collection of poems? How are passages to be divided between the pair of lovers? Are there other speakers as well? In addition, many words and phrases in the Hebrew text are ambiguous and obscure. For this reason, English translations differ markedly. The King James version is given here because of its beauty as an English poem and because of its influence on Anglophone literature and music, but readers should be aware that it is less accurate than modern translations.

Many scholars today consider the Song of Songs to be one or several love poems, similar in important ways to Middle Eastern marriage songs that were collected early in the twentieth century, and perhaps rooted in ancient fertility rituals of the great pagan religions of Asia Minor. But we may want to ask if there are not also aspects of this text that invite an allegorical reading, and if we must choose between sensual and more abstract meanings. Where do we draw the line between the literal and figurative meanings of words? Would we always want to? If the Song of Songs is an allegory, it is one that is wonderfully in touch with the world of the senses, as Dante's *Divine Comedy*, another great allegorical poem, is in a different way.

A NOTE ON THESE TRANSLATIONS

Genesis and Job are given here in clear, readable modern English translations in order to make the narrative of the former and the arguments of the latter accessible to contemporary readers. The other selections from the Hebrew Bible are from the King James or authorized version of 1611, so called because it was the work of a team of fifty-four scholars named by King James I of England to produce a new translation "appointed to be read in churches." Since that time advances in biblical scholarship have corrected some of the translators' mistakes and substituted clearer versions where their prose is obscure. Yet the King James version remains one of the greatest literary texts in the history of the English language. The echoes of its magnificent rhythms and cadences can be heard in the verse of English poets from John Milton to T. S. Eliot, in the prose of John Bunyan, and in the speeches of Abraham Lincoln.

PRONOUNCING GLOSSARY

The following list uses common English syllables and stress accents to provide rough equivalents of selected words whose pronunciation may be unfamiliar to the general reader.

Baalhamon: *bahl-ha'-mon*	Euphrates: *yoo-fray'-teez*
Canaan: *kay'-nuhn*	Job: *johb*
Esau: *ee'-saw*	Tirzah: *teer'-zah*

The Hebrew Bible

From Genesis[1]

GENESIS 1–3

[*The Creation—The Fall*]

1. When God[2] began to create heaven and earth, and the earth then was welter and waste and darkness over the deep and God's breath hovering over the waters, God said, "Let there be light." And there was light. And God saw the light, that it was good, and God divided the light from the darkness. And God called the light Day, and the darkness He called Night. And it was evening and it was morning, first day. And God said, "Let there be a vault in the midst of the waters,[3] and let it divide water from water." And God made the vault and it divided the water beneath the vault from the water above the vault, and so it was. And God called the vault Heavens, and it was evening and it was morning, second day. And God said, "Let the waters under the heavens be gathered in one place so that the dry land will appear," and so it was. And God called the dry land Earth and the gathering of waters He called Seas, and God saw that it was good. And God said, "Let the earth grow grass, plants yielding seed of each kind and trees bearing fruit of each kind, that has its seed within it." And so it was. And the earth put forth grass, plants yielding seed of each kind, and trees bearing fruit that has its seed within it of each kind, and God saw that it was good. And it was evening and it was morning, third day. And God said, "Let there be lights in the vault of the heavens to divide the day from the night, and they shall be signs for the fixed times[4] and for days and years, and they shall be lights in the vault of the heavens to light up the earth." And so it was. And God made the two great lights, the great light for dominion of day and the small light for dominion of night, and the stars. And God placed them in the vault of the heavens to light up the earth and to have dominion over day and night and to divide the light from the darkness. And God saw that it was good. And it was evening and it was morning, fourth day. And God said, "Let the waters swarm with the swarm of living creatures and let fowl fly over the earth across the vault of the heavens." And God created the great sea monsters and every living creature that crawls, which the water had swarmed forth of each kind, and the winged fowl of each kind, and God saw that it was good. And God blessed them, saying, "Be fruitful and multiply and fill the water in the seas and let the fowl multiply in the earth." And it was evening and it was morning, fifth day. And God said, "Let the earth bring forth living creatures of each kind, cattle and crawling things and wild beasts of each kind. And so it was. And God made wild beasts of each kind and cattle of every kind and crawling things on the ground of each kind, and God saw that it was good.

And God said, "Let us make a human in our image, by our likeness, to

---

1. Translated by Robert Alter.   2. This translates *Elohim*, one of the two most common names for God in the Torah. The other is *Yhwh*, probably pronounced "Yahweh"; it is used, for example, in the story of Adam and Eve in chapter 2 of Genesis (signified in the translation by "Lord").   3. The sky, which seen from below has the appearance of a ceiling. The waters above are those that come down in the form of rain.   4. Probably the seasons, but possibly the days and years that follow (the word translated by "and" would then mean "that is").

hold sway over the fish of the sea and the fowl of the heavens and the cattle and the wild beasts and all the crawling things that crawl upon the earth."

And God created the human in his image,
in the image of God He created him,
male and female He created them.

And God blessed them, and God said to them, "Be fruitful and multiply and fill the earth and conquer it, and hold sway over the fish of the sea and the fowl of the heavens and every beast that crawls upon the earth." And God said, "Look, I have given you every seed-bearing plant on the face of all the earth and every tree that has fruit bearing seed, yours they will be for food. And to all the beasts of the earth and to all the fowl of the heavens and to all that crawls on the earth, which has the breath of life within it, the green plants for food." And so it was. And God saw all that He had done, and, look, it was very good. And it was evening and it was morning, the sixth day.

2. Then the heavens and the earth were completed, and all their array. And God completed on the seventh day the work He had done, and He ceased on the seventh day from all the work He had done. And God blessed the seventh day and hallowed it, for on it He had ceased from all His work that He had done. This is the tale of the heavens and the earth when they were created.

On the day the LORD God made earth and heavens,[5] no shrub of the field being yet on the earth and no plant of the field yet sprouted, for the LORD God had not caused rain to fall on the earth and there was no human to till the soil, and wetness would well from the earth to water all the surface of the soil, then the LORD God fashioned the human, humus[6] from the soil, and blew into his nostrils the breath of life, and the human became a living creature. And the LORD God planted a garden in Eden, to the east, and He placed there the human He had fashioned. And the LORD God caused to sprout from the soil every tree lovely to look at and good for food, and the tree of life was in the midst of the garden, and the tree of knowledge, good and evil. Now a river runs out of Eden to water the garden and from there splits off into four streams. The name of the first is Pishon, the one that winds through the whole land of Havilah, where there is gold. And the gold of that land is goodly, bdellium is there, and lapis lazuli. And the name of the second river is Gihon, the one that winds through all the land of Cush. And the name of the third river is Tigris, the one that goes to the east of Ashur. And the fourth river is Euphrates. And the LORD God took the human and set him down in the garden of Eden to till it and watch it. And the LORD God commanded the human, saying, "From every fruit of the garden you may surely eat. But from the tree of knowledge, good and evil, you shall not eat, for on the day you eat from it, you are doomed to die."

And the LORD God said, "It is not good for the human to be alone, I shall make him a sustainer beside him." And the LORD God fashioned from the

---

5. A very different account of the creation begins here.   6. The Hebrew text makes a pun on the words for *human* and *soil*, which are similar in sound.

soil each beast of the field and each fowl of the heavens and brought each to the human to see what he would call it, and whatever the human called a living creature, that was its name. And the human called names to all the cattle and to the fowl of the heavens and to all the beasts of the field, but for the human no sustainer beside him was found. And the LORD God cast a deep slumber on the human, and he slept, and He took one of his ribs and closed over the flesh where it had been, and the LORD God built the rib He had taken from the human into a woman and He brought her to the human. And the human said:

> This one at last, bone of my bones
> and flesh of my flesh,
> This one shall be called Woman,
> for from man was this one taken.

Therefore does a man leave his father and his mother and cling to his wife and they become one flesh. And the two of them were naked, the human and his woman, and they were not ashamed.

3. Now the serpent was most cunning of all the beasts of the field that the LORD God had made. And he said to the woman, "Though God said, you shall not eat from any tree of the garden—" And the woman said to the serpent, "From the fruit of the garden's trees we may eat, but from the fruit of the tree in the midst of the garden God has said, 'You shall not eat from it and you shall not touch it, lest you die.'" And the serpent said to the woman, "You shall not be doomed to die. For God knows that on the day you eat of it your eyes will be opened and you will become as gods knowing good and evil." And the woman saw that the tree was good for eating and that it was lust to the eyes and the tree was lovely to look at,[7] and she took of its fruit and ate, and she also gave to her man, and he ate. And the eyes of the two were opened, and they knew they were naked, and they sewed fig leaves and made themselves loincloths.

And they heard the sound of the LORD God walking about in the garden in the evening breeze, and the human and his woman hid from the LORD God in the midst of the trees of the garden. And the LORD God called to the human and said to him, "Where are you?" And he said, "I heard your sound in the garden and I was afraid, for I was naked, and I hid." And He said, "Who told you that you were naked? From the tree I commanded you not to eat have you eaten?" And the human said, "The woman whom you gave by me, she gave me from the tree, and I ate." And the LORD God said to the woman, "What is this you have done?" And the woman said, "The serpent beguiled me and I ate." And the LORD God said to the serpent, "Because you have done this,

> Cursed be you
> of all cattle and all beasts of the field.
> On your belly shall you go
> and dust shall you eat all the days of your life.

---

7. The Hebrew verb translated "to look at" may also imply gaining wisdom.

> Enmity will I set between you and the woman,
> > between your seed and hers.
> He will boot[8] your head
> > and you will bite his heel."

To the woman He said,

> > "I will terribly sharpen your birth pangs,
> > > in pain shall you bear children.
> > And for your man shall be your longing,
> > > and he shall rule over you."

And to the human he said, "Because you listened to the voice of your wife and ate from the tree that I commanded you, 'You shall not eat from it,'

> Cursed be the soil for your sake,
> > with pangs shall you eat from it all the days of your life.
> Thorn and thistle shall it sprout for you
> > and you shall eat the plants of the field.
> By the sweat of your brow shall you eat bread
> > till you return to the soil,
> > > for from there were you taken,
> for dust you are
> > and to dust shall you return."

And the human called his woman's name Eve, for she was the mother of all that lives.[9] And the Lord God made skin coats for the human and his woman, and He clothed them. And the Lord God said, "Now that the human has become like one of us, knowing good and evil, he may reach out and take as well from the tree of life and live forever." And the Lord God sent him from the garden of Eden to till the soil from which he had been taken. And he drove out the human and set up east of the garden of Eden the cherubim and the flame of the whirling sword to guard the way to the tree of life.

FROM GENESIS 4

[*The First Murder*]

4. And the human knew Eve his woman and she conceived and bore Cain, and she said, "I have got me a man with the Lord." And she bore as well his brother, Abel, and Abel became a herder of sheep while Cain was a tiller of the soil. And it happened in the course of time that Cain brought from the fruit of the soil an offering to the Lord. And Abel too had brought from the choice firstlings of his flock, and the Lord regarded Abel and his offering but He did not regard Cain and his offering, and Cain was very incensed, and his face fell. And the Lord said to Cain.

---

8. Trample. The translation reproduces the pun in Hebrew between this word and the word for "bite" in the next line. 9. The name Eve resembles the word for *to live* in Hebrew.

"Why are you incensed,
      and why is your face fallen?
For whether you offer well,
      or whether you do not,
at the tent flap sin crouches
and for you is its longing
      but you will rule over it."

And Cain said to Abel his brother, "Let us go out to the field." And when they were in the field, Cain rose against Abel his brother and killed him. And the LORD said to Cain, "Where is Abel your brother?" And he said, "I do not know. Am I my brother's keeper?" And He said, "What have you done? Listen! your brother's blood cries out to me from the soil. And so, cursed shall you be by the soil that gaped with its mouth to take your brother's blood from your hand. If you till the soil, it will no longer give you its strength. A restless wanderer shall you be on the earth." And Cain said to the LORD, "My punishment is too great to bear. Now that You have driven me this day from the soil and I must hide from Your presence, I shall be a restless wanderer on the earth and whoever finds me will kill me." And the LORD said to him, "Therefore whoever kills Cain shall suffer sevenfold vengeance." And the LORD set a mark upon Cain so that whoever found him would not slay him.

*   *   *

FROM GENESIS 6–9

[The Flood]

6. * * * And the LORD saw that the evil of the human creature was great on the earth and that every scheme of his heart's devising was only perpetually evil. And the LORD regretted having made the human on earth and was grieved to the heart. And the LORD said, "I will wipe out the human race I created from the face of the earth, from human to cattle to crawling thing to the fowl of the heavens, for I regret that I have made them." But Noah found favor in the eyes of the LORD. This is the lineage of Noah—Noah was a righteous man, he was blameless in his time, Noah walked with God—and Noah begot three sons, Shem and Ham and Japheth. And the earth was corrupt before God and the earth was filled with outrage. And God saw the earth and, look, it was corrupt, for all flesh had corrupted its ways on the earth. And God said to Noah, "The end of all flesh is come before me, for the earth is filled with outrage by them, and I am now about to destroy them, with the earth. Make yourself an ark of cypress wood, with cells you shall make the ark, and caulk it inside and out with pitch. This is how you shall make it: three hundred cubits,[1] the ark's length; fifty cubits, its width; thirty cubits, its height. Make a skylight in the ark, within a cubit of the top you shall finish it, and put an entrance in the ark on one side. With lower and middle and upper decks you shall make it. As for me, I am about to bring the Flood, water upon the earth, to destroy all flesh that has within it the breath of life from under the heavens, everything on the earth shall perish. And I will set up my covenant with you, and you shall enter the ark, you and

1. I.e., about 450 feet (a cubit was about 18 inches).

your sons and your wife and the wives of your sons, with you. And from all that lives, from all flesh, two of each thing you shall bring to the ark to keep alive with you, male and female they shall be. From the fowl of each kind and from the cattle of each kind and from all that crawls on the earth of each kind, two of each thing shall come to you to be kept alive. As for you, take you from every food that is eaten and store it by you, to serve for you and for them as food." And this Noah did; as all that God commanded him, so he did.

7. * * * Noah was six hundred years old when the Flood came, water over the earth. And Noah and his sons and his wife and his sons' wives came into the ark because of the waters of the Flood. Of the clean[2] animals and of the animals that were not clean and of the fowl and of all that crawls upon the ground two each came to Noah into the ark, male and female, as God had commanded Noah. And it happened after seven days, that the waters of the Flood were over the earth. In the six hundredth year of Noah's life, in the second month, on the seventeenth day of the month, on that day,

> All the wellsprings of the great deep burst
>   and the casements of the heavens were opened.

And the rain was over the earth forty days and forty nights. That very day, Noah and Shem and Ham and Japheth, the sons of Noah, and Noah's wife, and the three wives of his sons together with them, came into the ark, they as well as beasts of each kind and cattle of each kind and each kind of crawling thing that crawls on the earth and each kind of bird, each winged thing. They came to Noah into the ark, two by two of all flesh that has the breath of life within it. And those that came in, male and female of all flesh they came, as God had commanded him, and the LORD shut him in. And the Flood was forty days over the earth, and the waters multiplied and bore the ark upward and it rose above the earth. And the waters surged and multiplied mightily over the earth, and the ark went on the surface of the water. And the waters surged most mightily over the earth, and all the high mountains under the heavens were covered. Fifteen cubits above them the waters surged as the mountains were covered. And all flesh that stirs on the earth perished, the fowl and the cattle and the beasts and all swarming things that swarm upon the earth, and all humankind. All that had the quickening breath of life in its nostrils, of all that was on dry land, died. And He wiped out all existing things from the face of the earth, from humans to cattle to crawling things to the fowl of the heavens, they were wiped out from the earth. And Noah alone remained, and those with him in the ark. And the waters surged over the earth one hundred and fifty days.

8. And God remembered Noah and all the beasts and all the cattle that were with him in the ark. And God sent a wind over the earth and the waters subsided. And the wellsprings of the deep were dammed up, and the casements of the heavens, the rain from the heavens held back. And the waters receded from the earth little by little, and the waters ebbed. At the end of a hundred and fifty days the ark came to rest, on the seventeenth day of the

---

2. Ritually pure, and probably thus fit for sacrifice.

seventh month, on the mountains of Ararat. The waters continued to ebb, until the tenth month, on the first day of the tenth month, the mountaintops appeared. And it happened, at the end of forty days, that Noah opened the window of the ark he had made. And he let out the raven and it went forth to and fro until the waters should dry up from the earth. And he let out the dove to see whether the waters had abated from the surface of the ground. But the dove found no resting place for its foot and it returned to him to the ark, for the waters were over all the earth. And he reached out and took it and brought it back to him into the ark. Then he waited another seven days and again let the dove out of the ark. And the dove came back to him at eventide and, look, a plucked olive leaf was in its bill, and Noah knew that the waters had abated from the earth. Then he waited still another seven days and let out the dove, and it did not return to him again. And it happened in the six hundred and first year, in the first month, on the first day of the month, the waters dried up from the earth, and Noah took off the covering of the ark and he saw and, look, the surface of the ground was dry. And in the second month, on the twenty-seventh day of the month, the earth was completely dry. And God spoke to Noah, saying, "Go out of the ark, you and your wife and your sons and your sons' wives, with you. All the animals that are with you of all flesh, fowl and cattle and every crawling thing that crawls on the earth, take out with you, and let them swarm through the earth and be fruitful and multiply on the earth." And Noah went out, his sons and his wife and his sons' wives with him. Every beast, every crawling thing, and every fowl, everything that stirs on the earth, by families, came out of the ark. And Noah built an altar to the LORD and he took from every clean cattle and every clean fowl and offered burnt offerings on the altar. And the LORD smelled the fragrant odor and the LORD said in His heart, "I will not again damn the soil on humankind's score. For the devisings of the human heart are evil from youth. And I will not again strike down all living things as I did. As long as all the days of the earth—

> seedtime and harvest
> and cold and heat
> and summer and winter
> and day and night
> shall not cease."

9. And God blessed Noah and his sons and He said to them, "Be fruitful and multiply and fill the earth. And the dread and fear of you shall be upon all the beasts of the field and all the fowl of the heavens, in all that crawls on the ground and in all the fish of the sea. In your hand they are given. All stirring things that are alive, yours shall be for food, like the green plants, I have given all to you. But flesh with its lifeblood still in it you shall not eat.[3] And just so, your lifeblood I will requite, from every beast I will requite it, and from humankind, from every man's brother, I will requite human life.

> He who sheds human blood
> by humans his blood shall be shed,
> for in the image of God

---

3. A reference to the biblical dietary laws: blood was supposed to be drained from a slaughtered animal.

He made humankind.
As for you, be fruitful and multiply,
  swarm through the earth, and hold sway over it."

And God said to Noah and to his sons with him, "And I, I am about to establish My covenant with you and with your seed after you, and with every living creature that is with you, the fowl and the cattle and every beast of the earth with you, all that have come out of the ark, every beast of the earth. And I will establish My covenant with you, that never again shall all flesh be cut off by the waters of the Flood, and never again shall there be a Flood to destroy the earth." And God said, "This is the sign of the covenant that I set between Me and you and every living creature that is with you, for everlasting generations: My bow[4] I have set in the clouds to be a sign of the covenant between Me and the earth, and so, when I send clouds over the earth, the bow will appear in the cloud. Then I will remember My covenant, between Me and you and every living creature of all flesh, and the waters will no more become a Flood to destroy all flesh. And the bow shall be in the cloud and I will see it, to remember the everlasting covenant between God and all living creatures, all flesh that is on the earth." And God said to Noah, "This is the sign of the covenant I have established between Me and all flesh that is on the earth."

* * *

FROM GENESIS 11

[The Origin of Languages]

11. And all the earth was one language, one set of words. And it happened as they journeyed from the east that they found a valley in the land of Shinar[5] and settled there. And they said to each other, "Come, let us bake bricks and burn them hard." And the brick served them as stone and bitumen served them as mortar. And they said, "Come, let us build us a city and a tower[6] with its top in the heavens, that we may make us a name, lest we be scattered over all the earth." And the LORD came down to see the city and the tower that the human creatures had built. And the LORD said, "As one people with one language for all, if this is what they have begun to do, nothing they plot will elude them. Come, let us go down and baffle their language there so that they will not understand each other's language." And the LORD scattered them from there over all the earth and they left off building the city. Therefore it is called Babel, for there the LORD made the language of all the earth babble. And from there the LORD scattered them over all the earth.

* * *

---

4. The rainbow.   5. In Mesopotamia. *They:* humankind.   6. This story is based on the Babylonian practice of building temples in the form of terraced pyramids (ziggurats).

FROM GENESIS 17–19

[*Abraham and Sarah*]

17. And Abram[7] was ninety-nine years old and the LORD appeared to Abram and said to him, "I am El Shaddai.[8] Walk with Me and be blameless, and I will grant My covenant between Me and you and I will multiply you very greatly." And Abram flung himself on his face, and God spoke to him, saying, "As for Me, this is My covenant with you: you shall be father to a multitude of nations. And no longer shall your name be called Abram but your name shall be Abraham,[9] for I have made you father to a multitude of nations. And I will make you most abundantly fruitful and turn you into nations, and kings shall come forth from you. And I will establish My covenant between Me and you and your seed after you through their generations as an everlasting covenant to be God to you and to your seed after you. And I will give unto you and your seed after you the land in which you sojourn, the whole land of Canaan, as an everlasting holding, and I will be their God."

And God said to Abraham, "As for you, you shall keep My commandment, you and your seed after you through their generations. This is My covenant which you shall keep, between Me and you and your seed after you: every male among you must be circumcised. You shall circumcise the flesh of your foreskin and it shall be the sign of the covenant between Me and you. Eight days old every male among you shall be circumcised through your generations, even slaves born in the household and those purchased with silver from any foreigner who is not of your seed. Those born in your household and those purchased with silver must be circumcised, and My covenant in your flesh shall be an everlasting covenant. And a male with a foreskin, who has not circumcised the flesh of his foreskin, that person shall be cut off from his folk. My covenant he has broken." And God said to Abraham, "Sarai your wife shall no longer call her name Sarai, for Sarah is her name." And I will bless her and I will also give you from her a son and I will bless him, and she shall become nations, kings of peoples shall issue from her." And Abraham flung himself on his face and he laughed, saying to himself,

"To a hundred-year-old will a child be born,
    will ninety-nine-year-old Sarah give birth?"

And Abraham said to God, "Would that Ishmael[1] might live in Your favor!" And God said, "Yet Sarah your wife is to bear you a son and you shall call his name Isaac[2] and I will establish My covenant with him as an everlasting covenant, for his seed after him. As for Ishmael, I have heard you. Look, I will bless him and make him fruitful and will multiply him most abundantly, twelve chieftains he shall beget, and I will make him a great nation. But My covenant I will establish with Isaac whom Sarah will bear you by this season next year." And He finished speaking with him, and God ascended from Abraham.

7. Soon to be renamed Abraham: the descendant, in the tenth generation, of Noah's son Shem, and the first great patriarch.   8. Another name for God.   9. Both names mean "exalted father," and there is little difference between them. Abraham undergoes a change of name to indicate his new status under the covenant that God now announces. The same holds for the change of his wife's name from Sarai to Sarah (both mean "princess").   1. The son Abraham has had with the slave woman Hagar.   2. The name plays on the word translated "he laughed" above.

And Abraham took Ishmael his son and all the slaves born in his household and those purchased with silver, every male among the people of Abraham's household, and he circumcised the flesh of their foreskin on that very day as God had spoken to him. And Abraham was ninety-nine years old when the flesh of his foreskin was circumcised. And Ishmael was thirteen years old when the flesh of his foreskin was circumcised. On that very day Abraham was circumcised, and Ishmael his son, and all the men of his household, those born in the household and those purchased with silver from the foreigners, were circumcised with him.

18. And the LORD appeared to him in the Terebinths of Mamre when he was sitting by the tent flap in the heat of the day. And he raised his eyes and saw, and, look, three men were standing before him. He saw, and he ran toward them from the tent flap and bowed to the ground. And he said, "My lord, if I have found favor in your eyes, please do not go on past your servant. Let a little water be fetched and bathe your feet and stretch out under the tree, and let me fetch a morsel of bread, and refresh yourselves. Then you may go on, for have you not come by your servant?" And they said, "Do as you have spoken." And Abraham hurried to the tent to Sarah and he said, "Hurry! Knead three *seahs*[3] of choice flour and make loaves." And to the herd Abraham ran and fetched a tender and goodly calf and gave it to the lad, who hurried to prepare it. And he fetched curds and milk and the calf that had been prepared and he set these before them, he standing over them under the tree, and they ate. And they said to him, "Where is Sarah your wife?" And he said, "There, in the tent." And he[4] said, "I will surely return to you at this very season and, look, a son shall Sarah your wife have," and Sarah was listening at the tent flap, which was behind him. And Abraham and Sarah were old, advanced in years, Sarah no longer had her woman's flow. And Sarah laughed inwardly, saying, "After being shriveled, shall I have pleasure, and my husband is old?" And the LORD said to Abraham, "Why is it that Sarah laughed, saying, 'Shall I really give birth, old as I am?' Is anything beyond the LORD? In due time I will return to you, at this very season, and Sarah shall have a son." And Sarah dissembled, saying, "I did not laugh," for she was afraid. And He said, "Yes, you did laugh."

And the men arose from there and looked out over Sodom, Abraham walking along with them to see them off. And the LORD had thought, "Shall I conceal from Abraham what I am about to do? For Abraham will surely be a great and mighty nation, and all the nations of the earth will be blessed through him. For I have embraced him so that he will charge his sons and his household after him to keep the way of the LORD to do righteousness and justice, that the LORD may bring upon Abraham all that He spoke concerning him." And the LORD said,

> "The outcry of Sodom and Gomorrah, how great!
> Their offense is very grave.

Let Me go down and see whether as the outcry that has come to me they have dealt destruction, and if not, I shall know." And the men turned from

---

3. A dry measure; estimates of its size vary, but this was a very generous amount.   4. One of the visitors.

there and went on toward Sodom while the LORD was still standing before Abraham. And Abraham stepped forward and said, "Will you really wipe out the innocent with the guilty? Perhaps there may be fifty innocent within the city. Will you really really wipe out the place and not spare it for the sake of the fifty innocent within it? Far be it from You to do such a thing, to put to death the innocent with the guilty, making innocent and guilty the same. Far be it from You! Will not the Judge of all the earth do justice?" And the LORD said, "Should I find in Sodom fifty innocent within the city, I will forgive the whole place for their sake." And Abraham spoke up and said, "Here, pray, I have presumed to speak to my Lord when I am but dust and ashes. Perhaps the fifty innocent will lack five. Would you destroy the whole city for the five?" And He said, "I will not destroy if I find there forty-five." And he spoke to Him still again and he said, "Perhaps there will be found forty." And He said, "I will not do it on account of the forty." And he said, "Please, let not my Lord be incensed and let me speak, perhaps there will be found thirty." And He said, "I will not do it if I find there thirty." And he said, "Here, pray, I have presumed to speak to my Lord. Perhaps there will be found twenty." And He said, "I will not destroy for the sake of the twenty." And he said, "Please, let not my Lord be incensed and let me speak just this time. Perhaps there will be found ten." And He said, "I will not destroy for the sake of the ten." And the LORD went off when He finished speaking with Abraham, and Abraham returned to his place.

19. And the two messengers came into Sodom at evening, when Lot[5] was sitting in the gate of Sodom. And Lot saw, and he rose to greet them and bowed, with his face to the ground. And he said, "O please, my lords, turn aside to your servant's house to spend the night, and bathe your feet, and you can set off early on your way." And they said, "No. We will spend the night in the square." And he pressed them hard, and they turned aside to him and came into his house, and he prepared them a feast and baked flat bread, and they ate. They had not yet lain down when the men of the city, the men of Sodom, surrounded the house, from lads to elders, every last man of them. And they called out to Lot and said, "Where are the men who came to you tonight? Bring them out to us so that we may know them!" And Lot went out to them at the entrance, closing the door behind him, and he said, "Please, my brothers, do no harm. Look, I have two daughters who have known no man. Let me bring them out to you and do to them whatever you want.[6] Only to these men do nothing, for have they not come under the shadow of my roof-beam?" And they said, "Step aside." And they said, "This person came as a sojourner and he sets himself up to judge! Now we'll do more harm to you than to them," and they pressed hard against the man Lot and moved forward to break down the door. And the men[7] reached out their hands and drew Lot to them into the house and closed the door. And the men at the entrance of the house they struck with blinding light, from the smallest to the biggest, and they could not find the entrance. And the men said to Lot, "Whom do you still have here? Your sons and your daughters and whomever you have in the city take out of the place. For we are about

---

5. Abraham's nephew.   6. One possible explanation for this extraordinary offer is that the code of hospitality prevalent in the Near East and elsewhere required Lot to protect his guests at all costs.   7. Lot's guests.

to destroy this place because the outcry against them has grown great before the LORD and the LORD has sent us to destroy it."

And Lot went out and spoke to his sons-in-law who had married his daughters and he said, "Rise, get out of this place, for the LORD is about to destroy the city." And he seemed to be joking to his sons-in-law. And as dawn was breaking the messengers urged Lot, saying, "Rise, take your wife and your two daughters who remain with you, lest you be wiped out in the punishment of the city." And he lingered, and the men seized his hand and his wife's hand and the hands of his two daughters in the LORD's compassion for him and led them outside the city. And as they were bringing them out, he said, "Flee for your life. Don't look behind you and don't stop anywhere on the plain. Flee to the high country lest you be wiped out." And Lot said to them, "Oh, no, my lord. Look, pray, your servant has found favor in your eyes, and you have shown such great kindness in what you have done for me in saving my life, but I cannot flee to the high country, lest evil overtake me and I die. Here, pray, this town is nearby to escape there, and it is a small place. Let me flee there, for it is but a small place, and my life will be saved." And he said, "I grant you a favor in this matter as well, and I will not overthrow the town of which you spoke. Hurry, flee there, for I can do nothing before you arrive there." Thus is the name of the town called Zoar. The sun had just come out over the earth when Lot arrived at Zoar. And the LORD rained upon Sodom and Gomorrah brimstone and fire from the LORD from the heavens. And He overthrew all those cities and all the plain and all the inhabitants of the cities and what grew in the soil. And his wife looked back and she became a pillar of salt. And Abraham hastened early in the morning to the place where he had stood in the presence of the LORD. And he looked out over Sodom and Gomorrah and over all the land of the plain, and he saw and, look, smoke was rising like the smoke from a kiln.

* * *

FROM GENESIS 22

[Abraham and Isaac]

22. And it happened after these things that God tested Abraham. And He said to him, "Abraham!" and he said, "Here I am." And He said, "Take, pray, your son, your only one, whom you love, Isaac, and go forth to the land of Moriah and offer him up as a burnt offering on one of the mountains which I shall say to you." And Abraham rose early in the morning and saddled his donkey and took his two lads with him, and Isaac his son, and he split wood for the offering, and rose and went to the place that God had said to him. On the third day Abraham raised his eyes and saw the place from afar. And Abraham said to his lads, "Sit you here with the donkey and let me and the lad walk ahead and let us worship and return to you." And Abraham took the wood for the offering and put it on Isaac his son and he took in his hand the fire and the cleaver, and the two of them went together. And Isaac said to Abraham his father, "Father!" and he said, "Here I am, my son." And he said, "Here is the fire and the wood but where is the sheep for the offering?" And Abraham said, "God will see to the sheep for the offering, my son." And the two of them went together. And they came to the place that God had said to him, and Abraham built there an altar and laid out the wood and

bound Isaac his son and placed him on the altar on top of the wood. And Abraham reached out his hand and took the cleaver to slaughter his son. And the LORD's messenger called out to him from the heavens and said, "Abraham, Abraham!" and he said, "Here I am." And he said, "Do not reach out your hand against the lad, and do nothing to him, for now I know that you fear God and you have not held back your son, your only one, from Me." And Abraham raised his eyes and saw and, look, a ram was caught in the thicket by its horns, and Abraham went and took the ram and offered him up as a burnt offering instead of his son. And Abraham called the name of that place YHWH-yireh, as is said to this day, "On the mount of the LORD there is sight."[8] And the LORD's messenger called out to Abraham once again from the heavens, and He said, "By my own Self I swear, declares the LORD, that because you have done this thing and have not held back your son, your only one, I will greatly bless you and will greatly multiply your seed, as the stars in the heavens and as the sand on the shore of the sea, and your seed shall take hold of its enemies' gate. And all the nations of the earth will be blessed through your seed because you have listened to my voice." And Abraham returned to his lads, and they rose and went together to Beer-sheba, and Abraham dwelled in Beer-sheba.

* * *

FROM GENESIS 25, 27

[Jacob and Esau]

25. * * * And Isaac pleaded with the LORD on behalf of his wife, for she was barren, and the LORD granted his plea, and Rebekah his wife conceived. And the children clashed together within her, and she said, "Then why me?" and she went to inquire of the LORD. And the LORD said to her:

> "Two nations—in your womb,
> two peoples from your loins shall issue.
> People over people shall prevail,
> the elder, the younger's slave."

And when her time was come to give birth, look, there were twins in her womb. And the first one came out ruddy, like a hairy mantle all over, and they called his name Esau. Then his brother came out, his hand grasping Esau's heel, and they called his name Jacob. And Isaac was sixty years old when they were born.

And the lads grew up, and Esau was a man skilled in hunting, a man of the field, and Jacob was a simple man, a dweller in tents. And Isaac loved Esau for the game that he brought him, but Rebekah loved Jacob. And Jacob prepared a stew and Esau came from the field, and he was famished. And Esau said to Jacob, "Let me gulp down some of this red red stuff, for I am famished." Therefore is his name called Edom.[9] And Jacob said, "Sell now your birthright to me." And Esau said, "Look, I am at the point of death, so why do I need a birthright?"

And Jacob said, "Swear to me now," and he swore to him, and he sold his

---

8. Either "he sees" or "he is seen (appears)."   9. From a semitic root meaning "red."

birthright to Jacob. Then Jacob gave Esau bread and lentil stew, and he ate and he drank and he rose and he went off, and Esau spurned the birthright.

27. And it happened when Isaac was old, that his eyes grew too bleary to see, and he called to Esau his elder son and said to him, "My son!" and he said, "Here I am." And he said, "Look, I have grown old; I know not how soon I shall die. So now, take up, pray, your gear, your quiver and your bow, and go out to the field, and hunt me some game, and make me a dish of the kind that I love and bring it to me that I may eat, so that I may solemnly bless you before I die." And Rebekah was listening as Isaac spoke to Esau his son, and Esau went off to the field to hunt game to bring.

And Rebekah said to Jacob her son, "Look, I have heard your father speaking to Esau your brother, saying, 'Bring me some game and make me a dish that I may eat, and I shall bless you in the LORD's presence before I die.' So now, my son, listen to my voice, to what I command you. Go, pray, to the flock, and fetch me from there two choice kids that I may make them into a dish for your father of the kind he loves. And you shall bring it to your father and he shall eat, so that he may bless you before he dies." And Jacob said to Rebekah his mother, "Look, Esau my brother is a hairy man and I am a smooth-skinned man. What if my father feels me and I seem a cheat to him and bring on myself a curse and not a blessing?" And his mother said, "Upon me your curse, my son. Just listen to my voice and go, fetch them for me." And he went and he fetched and he brought to his mother, and his mother made a dish of the kind his father loved. And Rebekah took the garments of Esau her elder son, the finery that was with her in the house, and put them on Jacob her younger son, and the skins of the kids she put on his hands and on the smooth part of his neck. And she placed the dish, and the bread she had made, in the hand of Jacob her son. And he came to his father and said, "Father!" And he said, "Here I am. Who are you, my son?" And Jacob said to his father, "I am Esau your firstborn. I have done as you have spoken to me. Rise, pray, sit up, and eat of my game so that you may solemnly bless me." And Isaac said to his son, "How is it you found it this soon, my son?" And he said, "Because the LORD your God gave me good luck." And Isaac said to Jacob, "Come close, pray, that I may feel you, my son, whether you are my son Esau or not." And Jacob came close to Isaac his father and he felt him and he said, "The voice is the voice of Jacob and the hands are Esau's hands." But he did not recognize him for his hands were, like Esau's hands, hairy, and he blessed him. And he said, "Are you my son Esau? "And he said, "I am." And he said, "Serve me, that I may eat of the game of my son, so that I may solemnly bless you." And he served him and he ate, and he brought him wine and he drank. And Isaac his father said to him, "Come close, pray, and kiss me, my son." And he came close and kissed him, and he smelled his garments and he blessed him and he said, "See, the smell of my son is like the smell of the field that the LORD has blessed.

> May God grant you
>> from the dew of the heavens and the fat of the earth.
> May peoples serve you,
>> and nations bow before you.
> Be overlord to your brothers,

may your mother's sons bow before you.
Those who curse you be cursed,
and those who bless you, blessed."

And it happened as soon as Isaac finished blessing Jacob, and Jacob barely
had left the presence of Isaac his father, that Esau his brother came back
from the hunt. And he, too, made a dish and brought it to his father and he
said to his father, "Let my father rise and eat of the game of his son so that
you may solemnly bless me." And his father Isaac said, "Who are you?" And
he said, "I am your son, your firstborn, Esau." And Isaac was seized with a
very great trembling and he said, "Who is it, then, who caught game and
brought it to me and I ate everything before you came and blessed him? Now
blessed he stays." When Esau heard his father's words, he cried out with a
great and very bitter outcry and he said to his father, "Bless me, too, Father!"
And he said, "Your brother has come in deceit and has taken your blessing."
And he said,

"Was his name called Jacob
        that he should trip me now twice by the heels?[1]
My birthright he took,
        and look, now, he's taken my blessing."

And he said, "Have you not kept back a blessing for me?"
And Isaac answered and said to Esau, "Look, I made him overlord to you,
and all his brothers I gave him as slaves, and with grain and wine I endowed
him. For you, then, what can I do, my son?" And Esau said to his father,
"Do you have but one blessing, my father? Bless me, too, Father." And Esau
raised his voice and he wept. And Isaac his father answered and said to him,

"Look, from the fat of the earth be your dwelling
        and from the dew of the heavens above.
By your sword shall you live
        and your brother you'll serve.
And when you rebel
        you shall break off his yoke from your neck."

* * *

GENESIS 37, 39–46

[The Story of Joseph]

37. And Jacob dwelled in the land of his father's sojournings, in the land
of Canaan. This is the lineage of Jacob—Joseph, seventeen years old, was
tending the flock with his brothers, assisting the sons of Bilhah and the sons
of Zilpah, the wives of his father. And Joseph brought ill report of them to
their father. And Israel loved Joseph more than all his sons, for he was the
child of his old age, and he made him an ornamented tunic.[2] And his brothers

---

1. There is a pun on the name Jacob (which means something like "God protects") and the word for *heel*,
which is set up earlier when Jacob grasps Esau's heel at birth.   2. This is the "coat of many colors" made
famous by the King James translation. A parallel in a cuneiform text suggests a garment with ornaments
sewn on.

saw it was he their father loved more than all his brothers, and they hated him and could not speak a kind word to him. And Joseph dreamed a dream and told it to his brothers and they hated him all the more. And he said to them, "Listen, pray, to this dream that I dreamed. And, look, we were binding sheaves in the field, and, look, my sheaf arose and actually stood up, and, look, your sheaves drew round and bowed to my sheaf." And his brothers said to him, "Do you mean to reign over us, do you mean to rule us?" And they hated him all the more, for his dreams and for his words. And he dreamed yet another dream and recounted it to his brothers, and he said, "Look, I dreamed a dream again, and, look, the sun and the moon and eleven stars were bowing to me." And he recounted it to his father and to his brothers, and his father rebuked him and said to him, "What is this dream that you have dreamed? Shall we really come, I and your mother and your brothers, to bow before you to the ground?" And his brothers were jealous of him, while his father kept the thing in mind.

And his brothers went to graze their father's flock at Shechem. And Israel said to Joseph, "You know, your brothers are pasturing at Shechem. Come, let me send you to them," and he said to him, "Here I am." And he said to him, "Go, pray, to see how your brothers fare, and how the flock fares, and bring me back word." And he sent him from the valley of Hebron and he came to Shechem. And a man found him and, look, he was wandering in the field, and the man asked him, saying, "What is it you seek?" And he said, "My brothers I seek. Tell me, pray, where are they pasturing?" And the man said, "They have journeyed on from here, for I heard them say, 'Let us go to Dothan.'" And Joseph went after his brothers and found them at Dothan. And they saw him from afar before he drew near them and they plotted against him to put him to death. And they said to each other, "Here comes that dream-master! And so now, let us kill him and fling him into one of the pits and we can say, a vicious beast has devoured him, and we shall see what will come of his dreams." And Reuben heard and came to his rescue and said, "We must not take his life." And Reuben said to them, "Shed no blood! Fling him into this pit in the wilderness and do not raise a hand against him"—that he might rescue him from their hands to bring him back to his father. And it happened when Joseph came to his brothers that they stripped Joseph of his tunic, the ornamented tunic that he had on him. And they took him and flung him into the pit, and the pit was empty, there was no water in it. And they sat down to eat bread, and they raised their eyes and saw and, look, a caravan of Ishmaelites was coming from Gilead, their camels bearing gum and balm and ladanum on their way to take down to Egypt. And Judah said to his brothers, "What gain is there if we kill our brother and cover up his blood?[3] Come, let us sell him to the Ishmaelites and our hand will not be against him, for he is our brother, our own flesh." And his brothers agreed. And Midianite merchantmen passed by and pulled Joseph up out of the pit and sold Joseph to the Ishmaelites for twenty pieces of silver.[4] And Reuben came back to the pit and, look, Joseph was not in the pit, and he rent his garments, and he came back to his brothers, and he said, "The boy is gone,

---

3. I.e., the fact that we have killed him.   4. The text at this point seems to combine two different versions of the story: (1) Joseph's brothers took him out of the pit and sold him to the Ishmaelites; (2) Midianite merchants passing by discovered Joseph in the pit and sold him to the Ishmaelites. Reuben then returned to the pit and discovered that Joseph was gone.

and I, where can I turn?" And they took Joseph's tunic and slaughtered a kid and dipped the tunic in the blood, and they sent the ornamented tunic and had it brought to their father, and they said, "Recognize, pray, is it your son's tunic or not?" And he recognized it, and he said, "It is my son's tunic.

> A vicious beast has devoured him,
> Joseph's been torn to shreds!"

And Jacob rent his clothes and put sackcloth round his waist and mourned for his son many days. And all his sons and all his daughters rose to console him and he refused to be consoled and he said, "Rather I will go down to my son in Sheol[5] mourning," and his father bewailed him.

But the Midianites had sold him into Egypt to Potiphar, Pharoah's courtier, the high chamberlain.

39. And Joseph was brought down to Egypt, and Potiphar, courtier of Pharaoh, the high chamberlain, an Egyptian man, bought him from the hands of the Ishmaelites who had brought him down there. And the LORD was with Joseph and he was a successful man, and he was in the house of his Egyptian master. And his master saw that the LORD was with him, and all that he did the LORD made succeed in his hand, and Joseph found favor in his eyes and he ministered to him, and he put him in charge of his house, and all that he had he placed in his hands. And it happened from the time he put him in charge of his house that the LORD blessed the Egyptian's house for Joseph's sake and the LORD's blessing was on all that he had in house and field. And he left all that he had in Joseph's hands, and he gave no thought to anything with him there save the bread he ate. And Joseph was comely in features and comely to look at.

And it happened after these things that his master's wife raised her eyes to Joseph and said, "Lie with me." And he refused. And he said to his master's wife, "Look, my master has given no thought with me here to what is in the house, and all that he has he has placed in my hands. He is not greater in this house than I, and he has held back nothing from me except you, as you are his wife, and how could I do this great evil and give offense to God?" And so she spoke to Joseph day after day, and he would not listen to her, to lie by her, to be with her. And it happened, on one such day, that he came into the house to perform his task, and there was no man of the men of the house there in the house. And she seized him by his garment, saying, "Lie with me." And he left his garment in her hand and he fled and went out. And so, when she saw that he had left his garment in her hand and fled outside, she called out to the people of the house and said to them, "See, he has brought us a Hebrew man to play with us. He came into me to lie with me and I called out in a loud voice, and so, when he heard me raise my voice and call out, he left his garment by me and fled and went out." And she laid out his garment by her until his master returned to his house. And she spoke to him things of this sort, saying, "The Hebrew slave came into me, whom you brought us, to play with me. And so, when I raised my voice and called out, he left his garment by me and fled outside." And it happened, when his

5. The dwelling place of the dead.

master heard his wife's words which she spoke to him, saying, "Things of this sort your slave has done to me," he became incensed. And Joseph's master took him and placed him in the prison-house, the place where the king's prisoners were held.

And he was there in the prison-house, and God was with Joseph and extended kindness to him, and granted him favor in the eyes of the prison-house warden. And the prison-house warden placed in Joseph's hands all the prisoners who were in the prison-house, and all that they were to do there, it was he who did it. The prison-house warden had to see to nothing that was in his hands, as the Lord was with him, and whatever he did, the Lord made succeed.

40. And it happened after these things that the cupbearer of the king of Egypt and his baker gave offense to their lord, the king of Egypt. And Pharaoh was furious with his two courtiers, the chief cupbearer and the chief baker. And he put them under guard in the house of the high chamberlain, the prison-house, the place where Joseph was held. And the high chamberlain assigned Joseph to them and he ministered to them, and they stayed a good while under guard.

And the two of them dreamed a dream, each his own dream, on a single night, each a dream with its own solution—the cupbearer and the baker to the king of Egypt who were held in the prison-house. And Joseph came to them in the morning and saw them and, look, they were frowning. And he asked Pharaoh's courtiers who were with him under guard in his lord's house, saying, "Why are your faces downcast today?" And they said to him, "We dreamed a dream and there is no one to solve it." And Joseph said to them, "Are not solutions from God? Pray, recount them to me." And the chief cupbearer recounted his dream to Joseph and said to him, "In my dream— and look, a vine was before me. And on the vine were three tendrils, and as it was budding, its blossom shot up, its clusters ripened to grapes. And Pharaoh's cup was in my hand. And I took the grapes and crushed them into Pharaoh's cup and I placed the cup in Pharaoh's palm." And Joseph said, "This is its solution. The three tendrils are three days. Three days hence Pharaoh will lift up your head and restore you to your place, and you will put Pharaoh's cup in his hand, as you used to do when you were his cup-bearer. But if you remember I was with you once it goes well for you, do me the kindness, pray, to mention me to Pharaoh and bring me out of this house. For indeed I was stolen from the land of the Hebrews, and here, too, I have done nothing that I should have been put in the pit." And the chief baker saw that he had solved well, and he said to Joseph, "I, too, in my dream— and look, there were three openwork baskets on my head, and in the topmost were all sorts of food for Pharaoh, baker's ware, and birds were eating from the basket over my head." And Joseph answered and said, "This is its solution. The three baskets are three days. Three days hence Pharaoh will lift up your head from upon you and impale you on a pole and the birds will eat your flesh from upon you."

And it happened on the third day, Pharaoh's birthday, that he made a feast for all his servants, and he lifted up the head of the chief cupbearer and the head of the chief baker in the midst of his servants. And he restored the chief cupbearer to his cupbearing, and he put the cup in Pharaoh's hand;

and the chief baker he impaled—just as Joseph had solved it for them. But the chief cupbearer did not remember Joseph, no, he forgot him.

41. And it happened at the end of two full years that Pharaoh dreamed, and, look, he was standing by the Nile. And, look, out of the Nile came up seven cows, fair to look at and fat in flesh, and they grazed in the rushes. And, look, another seven cows came up after them out of the Nile, foul to look at and meager in flesh, and stood by the cows on the bank of the Nile. And the foul-looking meager-fleshed cows ate up the seven fair-looking fat cows, and Pharaoh awoke. And he slept and dreamed a second time, and, look, seven ears of grain came up on a single stalk, fat and goodly. And, look, seven meager ears, blasted by the east wind, sprouted after them. And the meager ears swallowed the fat and full ears, and Pharaoh awoke, and, look, it was a dream. And it happened in the morning that his heart pounded, and he sent and called in all the soothsayers of Egypt and all its wise men, and Pharaoh recounted to them his dreams, but none could solve them for Pharaoh. And the chief cupbearer spoke to Pharaoh, saying, "My offenses I recall today. Pharaoh had been furious with his servants and he placed me under guard in the house of the high chamberlain—me and the chief baker. And we dreamed a dream on the same night, he and I, each of us dreamed a dream with its own solution.

And there with us was a Hebrew lad, a slave of the high chamberlain, and we recounted to him and he solved our dreams, each of us according to his dream he solved it. And it happened just as he had solved it for us, so it came about—me he restored to my post and him he impaled."

And Pharaoh sent and called for Joseph, and they hurried him from the pit, and he shaved and changed his garments and came before Pharaoh. And Pharaoh said to Joseph, "I dreamed a dream and none can solve it, and I have heard about you that you can understand a dream to solve it." And Joseph answered Pharaoh, saying, "Not I! God will answer for Pharaoh's well-being." And Pharaoh spoke to Joseph: "In my dream, here I was standing on the bank of the Nile, and, look, out of the Nile came up seven cows fat in flesh and fair in feature, and they grazed in the rushes. And, look, another seven cows came up after them, gaunt and very foul-featured and meager in flesh, I had not seen their like in all the land of Egypt for foulness. And the meager, foul cows ate up the first seven fat cows, and they were taken into their bellies and you could not tell that they had come into their bellies, for their looks were as foul as before, and I woke. And I saw in my dream, and, look, seven ears of grain came up on a single stalk, full and goodly. And, look, seven shriveled, meager ears, blasted by the east wind, sprouted after them. And the meager ears swallowed the seven goodly ears, and I spoke to my soothsayers and none could tell me the meaning." And Joseph said to Pharaoh, "Pharaoh's dream is one. What God is about to do He has told Pharaoh. The seven goodly cows are seven years, and the seven ears of grain are seven years. The dream is one. And the seven meager and foul cows who came up after them are seven years, and the seven meager ears of grain, blasted by the east wind, will be seven years of famine. It is just as I said to Pharaoh: what God is about to do He has shown Pharaoh. Look, seven years are coming of great plenty through all the land of Egypt. And seven years of famine will arise after them and all the plenty will be forgotten in the land of Egypt, and the famine will ravage the land, and you will not be able to tell there was plenty in the land because of that famine afterward, for it will be very grave. And the repeating of the dream to Pharaoh two times, this means that the thing has been fixed by God and God is hastening to do it. And so, let Pharaoh look out for a discerning, wise man and set him over the land of Egypt. Let Pharaoh do this: appoint overseers for the land and muster the land of Egypt in the seven years of plenty. And let them collect all the food of these good years that are coming and let them pile up grain under Pharaoh's hand; food in the cities, to keep under guard. And the food will be a reserve for the land for the seven years of famine which will be in the land of Egypt, that the land may not perish in the famine." And the thing seemed good in Pharaoh's eyes and in the eyes of his servants. And Pharaoh said to his servants, "Could we find a man like him, in whom is the spirit of God?" And Pharaoh said to Joseph, "After God has made known to you all this, there is none as discerning and wise as you. You shall be over my house, and by your lips all my folk shall be guided. By the throne alone shall I be greater than you." And Pharaoh said to Joseph, "See, I have set you over all the land of Egypt." And Pharaoh took off his ring from his hand and put it on Joseph's hand and had him clothed in fine linen clothes and placed the golden collar round his neck. And he had him ride in the chariot of his viceroy, and they called out before him *Abrekh*,[6] setting him over all the land of Egypt. And Pharaoh said to Joseph, "I am Pharaoh! Without you no man shall raise hand or foot in all the land of Egypt." And Pharaoh called Joseph's name Zaphenath-paneah, and he gave him Asenath daughter of Poti-phera, priest of On, as wife, and Joseph went out over the land of Egypt.

And Joseph was thirty years old when he stood before Pharaoh king of Egypt, and Joseph went out from Pharaoh's presence and passed through all the land of Egypt. And the land in the seven years of plenty made gatherings. And he collected all the food of the seven years that were in the land of Egypt and he placed food in the cities, the food from the fields round each city he placed within it. And Joseph piled up grain like the sand of the sea, very much, until he ceased counting, for it was beyond count.

And to Joseph two sons were born before the coming of the year of famine, whom Asenath daughter of Poti-phera priest of On bore him. And Joseph called the name of the firstborn Manasseh, meaning, God has released me from all the debt of my hardship, and of all my father's house. And the name of the second he called Ephraim, meaning, God has made me fruitful in the land of my affliction.

And the seven years of the plenty that had been in the land of Egypt came to an end. And the seven years of famine began to come, as Joseph had said, and there was famine in all the lands, but in the land of Egypt there was bread. And all the land of Egypt was hungry and the people cried out to Pharaoh for bread, and Pharaoh said to all of Egypt, "Go to Joseph. What he says to you, you must do." And the famine was over all the land. And Joseph laid open whatever had grain within and sold provisions to Egypt. And the famine grew harsh in the land of Egypt. And all the earth came to Egypt, to Joseph, to get provisions, for the famine had grown harsh in all the earth.

6. Probably "Make way!" (evidently an Egyptian word).

42. And Jacob saw that there were provisions in Egypt, and Jacob said to his sons, "Why are you fearful?" And he said, "Look, I have heard that there are provisions in Egypt. Go down there, and get us provisions from there that we may live and not die." And the ten brothers of Joseph went down to buy grain from Egypt. But Benjamin, Joseph's brother,[7] Jacob did not send with his brothers, for he thought, Lest harm befall him.

And the sons of Israel came to buy provisions among those who came, for there was famine in the land of Canaan. As for Joseph, he was the regent of the land, he was the provider to all the people of the land. And Joseph's brothers came and bowed down to him, their faces to the ground. And Joseph saw his brothers and recognized them, and he played the stranger to them and spoke harshly to them, and said to them, "Where have you come from?" And they said, "From the land of Canaan, to buy food." And Joseph recognized his brothers but they did not recognize him. And Joseph remembered the dreams he had dreamed about them, and he said to them, "You are spies! To see the land's nakedness you have come." And they said to him, "No, my lord, for your servants have come to buy food. We are all the sons of one man. We are honest. Your servants would never be spies." He said to them, "No! For the land's nakedness you have come to see." And they said, "Your twelve servants are brothers, we are the sons of one man in the land of Canaan, and, look, the youngest is now with our father, and one is no more." And Joseph said to them, "That's just what I told you, you are spies. In this shall you be tested—by Pharaoh! You shall not leave this place unless your youngest brother comes here. Send one of you to bring your brother, and as for the rest of you, you will be detained, and your words will be tested as to whether the truth is with you, and if not, by Pharaoh, you must be spies!" And he put them under guard for three days. And Joseph said to them on the third day, "Do this and live, for I fear God. If you are honest, let one of your brothers be detained in this very guardhouse, and the rest of you go forth and bring back provisions to stave off the famine in your homes. And your youngest brother you shall bring to me, that your words may be confirmed and you need not die." And so they did. And they said each to his brother, "Alas, we are guilty for our brother, whose mortal distress we saw when he pleaded with us and we did not listen. That is why this distress has overtaken us." Then Reuben spoke out to them in these words: "Didn't I say to you, 'Do not sin against the boy,' and you would not listen? And now, look, his blood is requited." And they did not know that Joseph understood, for there was an interpreter between them. And he turned away from them and wept and returned to them and spoke to them, and he took Simeon from them and placed him in fetters before their eyes.

And Joseph gave orders to fill their baggage with grain and to put back their silver into each one's pack and to give them supplies for the way, and so he did for them. And they loaded their provisions on their donkeys and they set out. Then one of them opened his pack to give provender to his donkey at the encampment, and he saw his silver and, look, it was in the mouth of his bag. And he said to his brothers, "My silver has been put back and, look, it's actually in my bag." And they were dumbfounded and trembled

---

7. Only Benjamin is Joseph's full brother; both are sons of Jacob and Rachel. The other ten are his half-brothers, sons of Jacob by other women.

each before his brother, saying, "What is this that God has done to us?" And they came to Jacob their father, to the land of Canaan, and they told him all that had befallen them, saying, "The man who is lord of the land spoke harshly to us and made us out to be spies in the land. And we said to him, 'We are honest. We would never be spies. Twelve brothers we are, the sons of our father. One is no more and the youngest is now with our father in the land of Canaan.' And the man who is lord of the land said to us, 'By this shall I know if you are honest: one of your brothers leave with me and provisions against the famine in your homes take, and go. And bring your youngest brother to me that I may know you are not spies but are honest. I shall give you back your brother and you can trade in the land.' " And just as they were emptying their packs, look, each one's bundle of silver was in his pack. And they saw their bundles, both they and their father, and were afraid. And Jacob their father said to them, "Me you have bereaved. Joseph is no more and Simeon is no more, and Benjamin you would take! It is I who bear it all." And Reuben spoke to his father, saying, "My two sons you may put to death if I do not bring him back to you. Place him in my hands and I will return him to you." And he said, "My son shall not go down with you, for his brother is dead, and he alone remains, and should harm befall him on the way you are going, you would bring down my gray head in sorrow to Sheol."

43. And the famine grew grave in the land. And it happened when they had eaten up the provisions they had brought from Egypt, that their father said to them, "Go back, buy us some food." And Judah said to him, saying, "The man firmly warned us, saying, 'You shall not see my face unless your brother is with you.' If you are going to send our brother with us, we may go down and buy you food, but if you are not going to send him, we will not go down, for the man said to us, 'You shall not see my face unless your brother is with you.' " And Israel said, "Why have you done me this harm to tell the man you had another brother?" And they said, "The man firmly asked us about ourselves and our kindred, saying, 'Is your father still living? Do you have a brother?' And we told him, in response to these words. Could we know he would say, 'Bring down your brother?' " And Judah said to Israel his father, "Send the lad with me, and let us rise and go, that we may live and not die, neither we, nor you, nor our little ones. I will be his pledge, from my hand you may seek him: if I do not bring him to you and set him before you, I will bear the blame to you for all time. For had we not tarried, by now we could have come back twice." And Israel their father said to them, "If it must be so, do this: take of the best yield of the land in your baggage and bring down to the man as tribute, some balm and some honey, gum and ladanum, pistachio nuts and almonds. And double the silver take in your hand, and the silver that was put back in the mouths of your bags bring back in your hand. Perhaps it was a mistake. And your brother take, and rise and go back to the man. And may El Shaddai grant you mercy before the man, that he discharge to you your other brother, and Benjamin. As for me, if I must be bereaved, I will be bereaved."

And the men took this tribute and double the silver they took in their hand, and Benjamin, and they rose and went down to Egypt and stood in Joseph's presence. And Joseph saw Benjamin with them and he said to the one who was over his house, "Bring the men into the house, and slaughter an animal and prepare it, for with me the men shall eat at noon." And the man did as Joseph had said, and the man brought the men to Joseph's house. And the men were afraid at being brought to Joseph's house, and they said, "Because of the silver put back in our bags the first time we've been brought, in order to fall upon us, to attack us, and to take us as slaves, and our donkeys." And they approached the man who was over Joseph's house, and they spoke to him by the entrance of the house. And they said, "Please, my lord, we indeed came down the first time to buy food, and it happened when we came to the encampment that we opened our bags and, look, each man's silver was in the mouth of his bag, our silver in full weight, and we have brought it back in our hand, and we have brought down more silver to buy food. We do not know who put our silver in our bags." And he said, "All is well with you, do not fear. Your God and the God of your father has placed treasure for you in your bags. Your silver has come to me."[8] And he brought Simeon out to them. And the man brought the men into Joseph's house, and he gave them water and they bathed their feet, and he gave provender to their donkeys. And they prepared the tribute against Joseph's arrival at noon, for they had heard that there they would eat bread. And Joseph came into the house, and they brought him the tribute that was in their hand, into the house, and they bowed down to him to the ground. And he asked how they were, and he said, "Is all well with your aged father of whom you spoke? Is he still alive?" And they said, "All is well with your servant, our father. He is still alive." And they did obeisance and bowed down. And he raised his eyes and saw Benjamin his brother, his mother's son, and he said, "Is this your youngest brother of whom you spoke to me?" And he said, "God be gracious to you, my son." And Joseph hurried out, for his feelings for his brother overwhelmed him and he wanted to weep, and he went into the chamber and wept there. And he bathed his face and came out and held himself in check and said, "Serve bread." And they served him and them separately and the Egyptians that were eating with him separately, for the Egyptians would not eat bread with the Hebrews, as it was abhorrent to Egypt. And they were seated before him, the firstborn according to his birthright, the youngest according to his youth, and the men marvelled to each other. And he had portions passed to them from before him, and Benjamin's portion was five times more than the portion of all the rest, and they drank, and they got drunk with him.

44. And he commanded the one who was over his house, saying, "Fill the men's bags with as much food as they can carry, and put each man's silver in the mouth of his bag. And my goblet, the silver goblet, put in the mouth of the bag of the youngest, with the silver for his provisions." And he did as Joseph had spoken. The morning had just brightened when the men were sent off, they and their donkeys. They had come out of the city, they were not far off, when Joseph said to the one who was over his house, "Rise, pursue the men, and when you overtake them, say to them, 'Why have you paid back evil for good? Is not this the one from which my lord drinks, and in which he always divines?[9] You have wrought evil in what you did.' " And he overtook

8. I.e., "I have been paid." 9. Predicts the future from the appearance of a liquid in the cup.

them and spoke to them these words. And they said to him, "Why should our lord speak words like these? Far be it from your servants to do such a thing! Why, the silver we found in the mouth of our bags we brought back to you from the land of Canaan. How then could we steal from your master's house silver or gold? He of your servants with whom it be found shall die, and, what's more, we shall become slaves to our lord." And he said, "Even so, as by your words, let it be: he with whom it be found shall become a slave to me, and you shall be clear." And they hurried and each man set down his bag on the ground and each opened his bag. And he searched, beginning with the oldest and ending with the youngest, and he found the goblet in Benjamin's bag. And they rent their garments, and each loaded his donkey and they returned to the city.

And Judah with his brothers came into Joseph's house, for he was still there, and they threw themselves before him to the ground. And Joseph said to them, "What is this deed you have done? Did you not know that a man like me would surely divine?" And Judah said, "What shall we say to my lord? What shall we speak and how shall we prove ourselves right? God has found out your servants' crime. Here we are, slaves to my lord, both we and the one in whose hand the goblet was found." And he said, "Far be it from me to do this! The man in whose hand the goblet was found, he shall become my slave, and you, go up in peace to your father." And Judah approached him and said, "Please, my lord, let your servant speak a word in my lord's hearing and let your wrath not kindle against your servant, for you are like Pharaoh. My lord had asked his servants, saying, 'Do you have a father or brother?' And we said to my lord, 'We have an aged father and a young child of his old age, and his brother being dead, he alone is left of his mother, and his father loves him.' And you said to your servants, 'Bring him down to me, that I may set my eyes on him.' And we said to my lord, 'The lad cannot leave his father. Should he leave his father, he would die.' And you said to your servants, 'If your youngest brother does not come down with you, you shall not see my face again.' And it happened when we went up to your servant, my father, that we told him the words of my lord. And our father said, 'Go back, buy us some food.' And we said, 'We cannot go down. If our youngest brother is with us, we shall go down. For we cannot see the face of the man if our youngest brother is not with us.' And your servant, our father, said to us, 'You know that two did my wife bear me.[1] And one went out from me and I thought, O, he's been torn to shreds, and I have not seen him since. And should you take this one, too, from my presence and harm befall him, you would bring down my gray head in evil to Sheol.' And so, should I come to your servant, my father, and the lad be not with us, for his life is bound to the lad's, when he saw the lad was not with us, he would die, and your servants would bring down the gray head of your servant, our father, in sorrow to Sheol. For your servant became pledge for the lad to my father, saying, 'If I do not bring him to you, I will bear the blame to my father for all time.' And so, let your servant, pray, stay instead of the lad as a slave to my lord, and let the lad go up with his brothers. For how shall I go up to my father, if the lad be not with us? Let me see not the evil that would find out my father!"

---

1. Rachel. His other wife was Rachel's sister Leah, who bore him six sons. Jacob also had two sons each by two slave girls (one of Rachel, the other of Leah).

45. And Joseph could no longer hold himself in check before all who stood attendance upon him, and he cried, "Clear out everyone around me!" And no man stood with him when Joseph made himself known to his brothers. And he wept aloud and the Egyptians heard and the house of Pharaoh heard. And Joseph said to his brothers, "I am Joseph. Is my father still alive?" But his brothers could not answer him, for they were dismayed before him. And Joseph said to his brothers, "Come close to me, pray," and they came close, and he said, "I am Joseph your brother whom you sold into Egypt. And now, do not be pained and do not be incensed with yourselves that you sold me down here, because for sustenance God has sent me before you. Two years now there has been famine in the heart of the land, and there are yet five years without plowing and harvest. And God has sent me before you to make you a remnant on earth[2] and to preserve life, for you to be a great surviving group. And so, it is not you who sent me here but God, and he has made me father to Pharaoh and lord to all his house and ruler over all the land of Egypt. Hurry and go up to my father and say to him, 'Thus says your son Joseph: God has made me lord to all Egypt. Come down to me, do not delay. And you shall dwell in the land of Goshen[3] and shall be close to me, you and your sons and the sons of your sons and your flocks and your cattle and all that is yours. And I will sustain you there, for yet five years of famine remain—lest you lose all, you and your household and all that is yours.' And, look, your own eyes can see, and the eyes of my brother Benjamin, that it is my very mouth that speaks to you. And you must tell my father all my glory in Egypt and all that you have seen, and hurry and bring down my father here." And he fell upon the neck of his brother Benjamin and he wept, and Benjamin wept on his neck. And he kissed all his brothers and wept over them. And after that, his brothers spoke with him.

And the news was heard in the house of Pharaoh, saying, "Joseph's brothers have come." And it was good in Pharaoh's eyes and in his servants' eyes. And Pharaoh said to Joseph, "Say to your brothers: This now do. Load up your beasts and go, return to the land of Canaan. And take your father and your households and come back to me, that I may give you the best of the land of Egypt, and you shall live off the fat of the land.' And you, command them: 'This now do. Take you from the land of Egypt wagons for your little ones and for your wives, and convey your father, and come. And regret not your belongings, for the best of all the land of Egypt is yours.' "

And so the sons of Israel did, and Joseph gave them wagons, as Pharaoh had ordered, and he gave them supplies for the journey. To all of them, each one, he gave changes of garments, and to Benjamin he gave three hundred pieces of silver and five changes of garments. And to his father he sent as follows: ten donkeys conveying from the best of Egypt, and ten she-asses conveying grain and bread and food for his father for the journey. And he sent off his brothers and they went, and he said to them, "Do not be perturbed on the journey."

And they went up from Egypt and they came to the land of Canaan to Jacob their father. And they told him, saying, "Joseph is still alive," and that he was ruler in all the land of Egypt. And his heart stopped, for he did not believe them. And they spoke to him all the words of Joseph that he had spoken to them, and he saw the wagons that Joseph had sent to convey him,

2. I.e., "to ensure a posterity for you."   3. Probably the Nile Delta.

and the spirit of Jacob their father revived. And Israel said, "Enough! Joseph my son is still alive. Let me go see him before I die."

46. And Israel journeyed onward, with all that was his, and he came to Beer-sheba, and he offered sacrifices to the God of his father Isaac. And God said to Israel through visions of the night, "Jacob, Jacob," and he said, "Here I am." And He said, "I am the god, God of your father. Fear not to go down to Egypt, for a great nation I will make you there. I Myself will go down with you to Egypt and I Myself will surely bring you back up as well, and Joseph shall lay his hand on your eyes." And Jacob arose from Beer-sheba, and the sons of Israel conveyed Jacob their father and their little ones and their wives in the wagons Pharaoh had sent to convey him. And they took their cattle and their substance that they had got in the land of Canaan and they came to Egypt, Jacob and all his seed with him. His sons, and the sons of his sons with him, his daughters and the daughters of his sons, and all his seed, he brought with him to Egypt.

* * *

From Exodus[1]

FROM EXODUS 19–20

[Moses Receives the Law]

19. On the third new moon of the Israelites' going out from Egypt, on this day did they come to the Wilderness of Sinai.[2] And they journeyed onward from Rephidim and they came to the Wilderness of Sinai, and Israel camped there over against the mountain. And Moses had gone up to God, and the LORD called out to him from the mountain, saying, "Thus shall you say to the house of Jacob, and shall you tell to the Israelites: 'You yourselves saw what I did to Egypt, and I bore you on the wings of eagles[3] and I brought you to Me. And now, if you will truly heed My voice and keep My covenant, you will become for Me a treasure among all the peoples, for Mine is all the earth. And as for you, you will become for Me a kingdom of priests and a holy nation.' These are the words that you shall speak to the Israelites."

And Moses came and he called to the elders of the people, and he set before them all these words that the LORD had charged him. And all the people answered together and said, "Everything that the LORD has spoken we shall do." And Moses brought back the people's words to the LORD. And the LORD said to Moses, "Look, I am about to come to you in the utmost cloud, so that the people may hear as I speak to you, and you as well they will trust for all time." And Moses told the people's words to the LORD. And the LORD said to Moses, "Go to the people and consecrate them today and tomorrow, and they shall wash their cloaks. And they shall ready themselves

---

1. Translated by Robert Alter, to whose notes some of the following annotations are indebted.   2. The peninsula, shaped like an inverted triangle, that lies between Egypt and Palestine. The mountain was called either Sinai or Horeb.   3. A metaphor for salvation. "What I did unto the Egyptians" refers to the plagues that afflicted Egypt and to the destruction of the Egyptian army, as it pursued the departing Israelites, at the Red Sea.

for the third day, for on the third day the LORD will come down before the eyes of all the people on Mount Sinai. And you shall set bounds for the people all around, saying, 'Watch yourselves not to go up on the mountain or to touch its edge. Whosoever touches the mountain is doomed to die. No hand shall touch him,[4] but He shall surely be stoned or be shot, whether beast or man, he shall not live. When the ram's horn blasts long, they[5] it is who will go up the mountain.' " And Moses came down from the mountain to the people, and he consecrated the people, and they washed their cloaks. And he said to the people, "Ready yourselves for three days. Do not go near a woman."[6] And it happened on the third day as it turned morning, that there was thunder and lightning and a heavy cloud on the mountain and the sound of the ram's horn, very strong, and all the people who were in the camp trembled. And Moses brought out the people toward God from the camp and they stationed themselves at the bottom of the mountain. And Mount Sinai was all in smoke because the LORD had come down on it in fire, and its smoke went up like the smoke from a kiln, and the whole mountain trembled greatly. And the sound of the ram's horn grew stronger and stronger. Moses would speak, and God would answer him with voice.[7] And the LORD came down on Mount Sinai, to the mountaintop, and the LORD called Moses to the mountaintop, and Moses went up. And the LORD said to Moses, "Go down, warn the people, lest they break through to the LORD to see and many of them perish.[8] And the priests, too, who come near to the LORD, shall consecrate themselves,[9] lest the LORD burst forth against them." And Moses said to the Lord, "The people will not be able to come up to Mount Sinai, for You Yourself warned us, saying, 'Set bounds to the mountain and consecrate it.' " And the LORD said to him, "Go down, and you shall come up, you and Aaron[1] with you, and the priests and the people shall not break through to go up to the LORD, lest He burst forth against them." And Moses went down to the people and said it to them.

20. And God spoke all these words, saying: "I am the LORD your God Who brought you out of the land of Egypt, out of the house of slaves. You[2] shall have no other gods beside Me. You shall make you no carved likeness and no image of what is in the heavens above or what is on the earth below or what is in the waters beneath the earth.[3] You shall not bow to them and you shall not worship them, for I am the LORD your God, a jealous god, reckoning the crime of fathers with sons, with the third generation and with the fourth, for My foes,[4] and doing kindness to the thousandth generation for My friends and for those who keep My commands. You shall not take the name of the

---

4. Whoever violates the ban on touching the mountain will be impure and an outcast from the community. Therefore he has to be killed at a distance, with stones or arrows.   5. I.e., Moses and Aaron, as the end of chapter 19 shows.   6. Sexual abstinence and the washing of clothes were methods of ritual purification.   7. I.e., with words, as two mortals might communicate with one another.   8. Moses has already delivered this warning. The repetition emphasizes both the solemnity of the ban and Moses' role as intermediary between God and the people of Israel.   9. I.e., they are to purify themselves and remain at the bottom of the mountain as the rest of the people do.   1. Moses' closest companion and in an early tradition his brother; Aaron was Israel's first High Priest.   2. Here and throughout this passage, the Hebrew text uses the singular of "you" (formulations of law elsewhere in the Hebrew Bible use the plural). The commandments are thus addressed to each person individually.   3. In ancient polytheistic religions, statues of gods and of personified natural powers were worshipped.   4. This can be read in at least two ways. Limiting vengeance to the fourth generation of the transgressor's family may be a sign of mercy (by contrast with extending blessings on the righteous to the thousandth generation). Or it may be a statement of the severity of God's punishment, and in particular a reference to the common belief that if someone did wrong and seemed to go unpunished, vengeance would fall on his or her posterity.

LORD your God in vain,[5] for the LORD will not acquit whosoever takes His name in vain. Remember the sabbath day to hallow it. Six days you shall work and you shall do your tasks, but the seventh day is a sabbath to the LORD your God. You shall do no task, you and your son and your daughter, your male slave and your slavegirl and your beast and your sojourner who is within your gates. For six days did the LORD make the heavens and the earth, the sea and all that is in it, and He rested on the seventh day.[6] Therefore did the LORD bless the sabbath day and hallow it. Honor your father and your mother, so that your days may be long on the soil that the LORD your God has given you. You shall not murder. You shall not commit adultery. You shall not steal. You shall not bear false witness against your fellow man.[7] You shall not covet your fellow man's wife, or his male slave, or his slavegirl, or his ox, or his donkey, or anything that your fellow man has."

And all the people were seeing the thunder and the flashes and the sound of the ram's horn and the mountain in smoke, and the people saw and they drew back and stood at a distance. And they said to Moses, "Speak you with us that we may hear, and let not God speak with us lest we die." And Moses said to the people, "Do not fear, for in order to test you God has come and in order that His fear be upon you, so that you do not offend." And the people stood at a distance, and Moses drew near the thick cloud where God was.

* * *

From Job[1]

1. A man once lived in the land of Utz. His name was Job. This man was innocent, upright, and God-fearing, and kept himself apart from evil. Seven sons and three daughters were born to him. His flock consisted of seven thousand sheep, three thousand camels, five hundred yoke of oxen, five hundred female donkeys, and a large staff of servants. He was the greatest of the men of the East.

His sons would make a feast each year, each one in his own house by turns, and they would invite their three sisters to eat and drink with them. When the days of the feast would come round, Job would send to purify them, rising early in the morning to offer wholeburnt offerings, one for each. For Job thought, "Perhaps my sons have sinned by cursing God in their hearts." Job did this every year.

One day, the lesser gods came to attend upon Yahweh, and the Accuser[2] came among them. Yahweh said to the Accuser, "Where are you coming from?" and the Accuser answered Yahweh, "From roving and roaming about the world." Yahweh said to the Accuser, "Have you taken note of my servant Job, for there is no one like him on earth: innocent, upright, and God-fearing, and keeping himself apart from evil." The Accuser answered Yahweh, "Is Job

---

5. I.e., falsely—in the taking of oaths, for example.   6. See Genesis 2.   7. Testify falsely in a lawsuit.
1. Translated by Raymond P. Scheindlin.   2. "The Satan" in the original. But here he is not the principle of evil that the name conjures up for us. He is a member of Yahweh's court and seems to have the job of roaming the world to keep watch on humankind for Yahweh (his name sounds like the Hebrew word for roam).

God-fearing for nothing? Look how You have sheltered him on all sides, him and his household and everything he has, and have blessed everything he does, so that his cattle have spread out all over the land. But reach out with Your hand and strike his property, and watch him curse You to Your face!"

Yahweh said to the Accuser, "Everything he has is in your power, but do not harm his person."

The Accuser took his leave of Yahweh.

One day, when his sons and daughters were feasting and drinking wine in the house of the eldest brother, a messenger came to Job and said, "The cattle were plowing and the donkeys were grazing by their side and Sabeans fell on them and seized them and killed the servants with their swords, and only I got away to tell you!"

While he was speaking, another came and said, "A fearful fire fell from heaven and burned up the sheep and the servants and consumed them, and only I got away to tell you!"

While he was speaking, another came and said, "The Chaldeans formed into three companies and came at the camels from all directions and took them and killed the servants with their swords, and only I got away to tell you!"

While he was speaking, another came and said, "Your sons and daughters were eating and drinking wine in the house of the eldest brother and a great wind came from across the desert and struck the four corners of the house and it fell on the young people and they died, and only I got away to tell you!"

Job got up and tore his robe and shaved his head and flung himself to the ground and lay there prostrate and said,

> "Naked I came from my mother's womb
> and naked I return there.
> Yahweh has given and Yahweh has taken.
> Blessed be the name of Yahweh."

In spite of everything, Job did not sin and did not attach blame to God.

2. One day, the lesser gods came to attend upon Yahweh, and among them came the Accuser to attend upon Yahweh. Yahweh said to the Accuser, "Where are you coming from?" and the Accuser answered Yahweh, "From roving and roaming about the world." Yahweh said to the Accuser, "Have you taken note of my servant Job, for there is no one like him on earth: innocent, upright, and God-fearing, and keeping himself apart from evil; he even persists in his innocence, though you prevailed upon me to ruin him for no reason!" The Accuser answered Yahweh,

"Skin protecting skin![3] A man will give whatever he has for the sake of his own life. But reach out with Your hand and strike his person, his flesh, and watch him curse You to Your face!"

Yahweh said to the Accuser, "He is in your power, but see that you preserve his life."

The Accuser took his leave of Yahweh and smote Job with sickening erup-

---

3. Perhaps "Job's wounds are only superficial" (an outer layer of skin protects the inner layers). Job has not yet been injured in his own person, or had his life threatened.

tions from the soles of his feet to the crown of his head. Job took a shard to scrape himself with and sat down in ashes.[4] His wife said to him, "Are you still persisting in your innocence? Curse God and die!"

He said to her, "You are speaking like a disgraceful woman! Should we accept the good from God and not accept the bad?" In spite of everything, Job did not sin with his lips.

Job's three friends heard about all the trouble that had come upon him, and each one came from his own place: Eliphaz the Temanite, Bildad the Shuhite, and Zophar the Naamatite. They agreed to meet to go and to mourn with him and comfort him. Peering from the distance, they could not recognize him. They raised their voices and wept, and each tore his robe, and all put dirt on their heads, throwing it heavenward. Seven days and seven nights they sat with him on the ground, none saying a word to him, for they saw that his pain was very great.

3. Then Job spoke and cursed his day and raised his voice and said:

Blot out the day when I was born
    and the night that said, "A male has been conceived!"
Make that day dark!
    No god look after it from above,
    no light flood it.
Foul it, darkness, deathgloom;
    rain-clouds settle on it;
    heat-winds turn it to horror.
Black take that night!
    May it not count in the days of the year,
    may it not come in the round of the months.
That night be barren! That night!
    No joy ever come in it!
Curse it, men who spell the day,[5]
    men skilled to stir Leviathan.[6]
May its morning stars stay dark,
    may it wait for light in vain,
    never look on the eyelids of dawn—
because it did not lock the belly's gates[7]
    and curtain off my eyes from suffering.

Why did I not die inside the womb,
    or, having left it, give up breath at once?
Why did knees advance to greet me,
    or breasts, for me to suck?
Now I would be lying quietly;
    I would be sleeping then, at rest,
with kings and counselors of the earth,
    men who build rubble heaps for themselves,
or with princes, men with gold,
    men who fill their tombs with silver.
Why was I not like a stillbirth, hidden,
    like infants who never saw the light?

---

4. Gestures of mourning.   5. Sorcerers. *Spell:* cast spells on.   6. A sea monster, the embodiment of the forces of chaos. *Stir:* summon forth.   7. I.e., prevent my birth.

There the wicked cease their troubling,
    there the weary are at rest,
where the captives have repose,
    and need not heed the foreman's voice;
where the humble and the great are,
    the slave, now free, beside his lord.

Why is the sufferer given light?
    Why life, to men who gag on bile,
who wait for a death that never comes,
    though they would rather dig for it than gold;
whose joy exceeds mere happiness,
    thrill to find the grave?
Why, to a man whose way is hidden,
    because a god has blocked his path?
For my sighs are brought to me for bread,
    and my cries poured out for water.
One thing I feared, and it befell,
    and what I dreaded came to me.
No peace had I, nor calm, nor rest;
    but torment came.

4. Eliphaz the Temanite then took up the argument and said:

Might one try a word with you, or would you tire?—
    But who could hold back words now?
You were always the one to instruct the many,
    to strengthen failing hands;
your words would pick up men who had fallen
    and firm up buckling knees;
yet now it is your turn, and you go faint;
    it has reached you, and you are undone.

Isn't your innocence some reassurance?
    Doesn't your righteousness offer you hope?
Think: What really guiltless man has gone under?
    Where have the upright perished?
I see men plowing wickedness,
    seeding, harvesting trouble—
one breath from God and they perish;
    one snort from Him and they're gone.
The lion roars! Listen! The lion!—
    The lion's teeth are cracked.
The lion wanders, finds no prey.
    Young lions scatter.

Now, word has reached me in stealth—
    my ear caught only a snatch of it—
in wisps of thought, night visions,
    when slumber drifts down upon men.
Fear came over me, fear and a shudder,
    every bone in me shook.

Then—a gust crossing my face,
bristling the hairs on my skin,
and there he was standing—I could not make him out—
a shape before my eyes—
Hush! I hear his voice:
    "Can man be more righteous than God,
      or purer than He who made him?
    God does not trust His own courtiers,
      sees folly in His own angels;
    what then of dwellers in houses of clay,
      their foundations sunk in the dirt,
    that crumble before the moth,
        crack into shards between morning and evening,
          perish forever, not even aware of their fate?
    See how their wealth wanders away with them,
      how they die without wisdom.

5.   Go, cry out your rage—but who will answer?
      Which of the angels would you implore?
    Remember: Only fools are killed by anger,
      only simpletons by jealous fury.

I have seen a fool strike roots;
snap! I cursed his house:
Now his sons are far from help,
    crushed in the public square;
    no one came to their rescue.
Now the hungry dine on his harvest,
while he has to scrabble for it among thorns,
and thirsty men gulp his wealth.
Remember: Evil does not emerge from the soil,
    or trouble sprout from the ground.
Man was born to trouble
as sparks dart to the sky."

No, I look to El,[8]
    entrust my affairs to the care of a god
who makes things great beyond man's grasp,
    and wonders beyond any numbering;
who puts the rain on the face of the earth,
    sends water to the countryside;
raises the humble to the heights,
    lifts gloomy men to rescue;
spoils the plans of cunning men,
    so their hands can do nothing clever;
traps the shrewd in their own cunning,
    makes the schemer's plotting seem like rashness
(by day they stumble against the darkness,
    grope in midday as if it were night);
who saves the poor from the knife,

8. God.

from the maw, from the mighty,
so that the humble have hope,
    and evil has to shut its mouth.

Yes, happy the man whom God reproves!
Do not reject Shaddai's[9] correction.
    He may give pain, but He binds the wound;
    He strikes, but His hands bring healing.
In six-times-trouble He will save you;
in seven, no harm will touch you.
    He will rescue you from death in dearth,
    from sword in war.
When the tongue's lash snaps, you will be well hidden,
have nothing to fear when raiders arrive.
    Raiders and famine will make you smile,
    wild beasts give you nothing to fear.
The stones in the field will be your allies;
predators will yield to you.
    You will be sure of peace in your household;
    visit it when you like—you will not fail!
Then, be assured of plentiful seed,
of offspring like the earth's green shoots.
    Still robust you will reach the grave,
    like sheaves heaped high in their season.
All this we have studied and know it is so.
Think it over; take it to heart!

6. Job answered:

If there were some way to weigh my rage,
    if my disaster would fit in a balance,
they would drag down the ocean's sands;
that is why my speech is clumsy.
For Shaddai's arrows are all around me—
    my breath absorbs their venom—
    terror of the god invests me.

Is that a wild ass braying over his grass?—
    an ox bellowing over his feed?[1]
Who can eat unsalted food?[2]
What flavor is there in the drool of mallows?
I have no appetite to touch them;
    they are as nauseous as my flesh!

If only what I ask would happen—
if some god would grant my hope—
if that god would consent to crush me,
loose his hand and crack me open—

9. Another name for God.   1. Animals do not complain without reason; therefore, when a rational person complains, he or she must have some justification for it.   2. This and the next sentence may either refer to Job's situation or express his opinion of Eliphaz's arguments.

even that would comfort me
(though I writhed in pain unsparing),
for never have I suppressed the Holy One's commands.

What strength have I to go on hoping?
How far off is my end,
even if I live long?
Have I the bearing-strength of rock? Is my flesh bronze?
Is there no help within myself?
Has common sense been driven from me
to one who holds back kindnesses from friends,
to one who has lost the fear of Shaddai?

As for my friends—
they failed me like a riverbed,
wandered off, like water in a wadi.[3]
Gloomy on an icy day,
covered up with snow;
they flow one moment, then are gone;
when it is hot, they flicker away.
Their dry courses twist,
wander into wasteland, vanish.
Caravans from Tema peer;
Sebean trains move toward them, hoping:[4]
Disappointment for their trust—
they reach them, find frustration.
That is how you are to me:
You see terror, take fright yourselves.

When have I said to you, "Give me, give"?
"Bribe someone for me with your wealth"?
"Save me from my enemy"?
"Pay my ransom to some tyrant"?
All I ask is that you teach me—
I will listen quietly:
Tell me what I have done wrong!
How eloquent are honest words—
How then can you teach effectively?
Do you think you can teach me with words?
Is a speech of despair just wind?
Would you also divide an orphan's goods by lot
and haggle over your neighbor's property?

And now, be good enough to turn toward me—
See if I lie to your faces.
Come back! You'll find no evil here—
Come back!—only my vindication.
Is there error on my tongue?
What am I speaking of except disaster?

---

3. A streambed in the desert. Because it cheats the traveler's longing for water by being dry for most of
the year or by emptying itself quickly of the water that flows through it, it can serve as an image for treachery.
4. I.e., for water, as the caravans from Tema also look for it.

7. Man's life on earth is a term of indenture;
        his days are like a laborer's,
    a slave, who pants for a little shade,
        a day laborer, who only wants his wages.
    I too am granted blank moons;[5]
        troubled nights have been my lot.
    When I lie down, I say,
        "How soon can I get up?"
            The night time stretches,
    and I have tossing and turning enough to last till dawn.
    My flesh is covered with worms and dirty scabs;
        my skin is cracked and oozing.
    My days are swifter than a weaver's shuttle;
        they end when the thread of hope gives out.
    Remember: My life is just a breath;
    my eye will never again see pleasure.
    The questing eye will not detect me;
    Your eye will catch me—just!—
        and I'll be gone.

    A cloud dissipates, vanishes,
    and once below the ground
    no man comes up again;
    he never goes back to his home;
        his place no longer knows him.

    Why should I restrain my mouth?—
        I speak from a dejected spirit,
        complain out of sheer bitterness:
    Am I Yamm-ocean or the Serpent,[6]
    that You post a guard over me?
    I tell myself, "My couch will comfort me,
        my bed will bear a part of my complaint,"
    only to have You frighten me with nightmares,
        panic me with visions of the night;
            I'd rather choke—
    death is better than this misery.
    I've had enough! I will not live forever!
    Let me alone; my life is just a breath.
    What is man that You make so much of him,
        and think about him so,
    examine him each morning,
        appraise him every moment?
    How long till You turn away from me
    long enough for me to swallow my own spit?[7]
    I have sinned: But what have I done to You,
    keeper, jailer of men?
    Why should You make me Your target,

---

5. Empty (i.e., morally and materially unprofitable) months.   **6.** Job, now addressing God directly, compares his situation with that of the sea monster whom the weather god Baal fought against in Babylonian myth. He reproves God for exerting his power against anything as small as Job himself.   **7.** I.e., even for a moment.

a burden to myself?
Why not forgive my crimes,
    and pardon me my sin?
In no time, I'll be lying in the earth;
    when You come looking for me, I'll be gone.

8. Bildad the Shuhite then took up the argument and said:

How long will you go on like this?
    What a great wind are the words from your mouth!
Would El pervert judgment?
    Would Shaddai pervert what is right?
Your sons have sinned against Him, that is all,
    and He got rid of them
    on account of their own crimes.
If you would now seek out the god,
    beseech Shaddai,
      be pure and true—
He would rouse Himself for you,
    restore your righteous home.
Your former life will seem a paltry thing,
    so greatly will you prosper in the end.

Just ask the older generation,
    and set your mind to questioning *their* fathers
(for we are no older than yesterday
    and do not really know;
    our days on earth are only shadows):
They will teach you,
    they will tell you,
      they will bring words up from memory.
Can papyrus grow tall without a marsh
    or reeds flourish without water?
    Still in flower,
    not yet cut,
    even before the grass,
    it withers.
Such is the fate of all who put God out of mind;
    thus the hope of the wicked man fades,
    whatever he trusts in fails.
He puts his trust in a spider's web,
    leans on his house, but it does not stand;
    grasps at it, but it does not hold.

Juicy green before the sun,
    his suckers creep over his planting bed,
    his roots tangle-twist a rock heap,
    he clutches a house of stones.
But let him be snatched from his place,
    and his place denies him: "I know you not!"
    Such is his happy lot—
    others sprout from that dirt. . . .

No, God would not reject the innocent,
 would not take hold of a bad man's hand.
He will yet fill your mouth with laughter,
 fill your lips with cries of joy.
Your foe will yet be clothed in shame,
 the wicked untented.

9. Job answered:

True, I know that this is so;
but can a mortal beat a god at law?
If someone chose to challenge Him,
He would not answer even the thousandth part!
Shrewd or powerful one may be,
but who has faced Him hard and come out whole?
He moves the mountains and they are unaware,
 overturns them in His rage.
He shakes the earth from its place;
 its pillars totter.
He orders the sun not to rise,
 seals up the stars.
He stretches out the heavens all alone,
 and treads Yamm's back.
He makes the Pleiades, Orion, and the Bear,
 the South Wind's chambers.
He makes things great beyond man's grasp,
 and wonders beyond any numbering.
Yet when He comes my way, I do not notice;
 He passes on, and I am unaware.

If He should seize a thing, who could restore it?
 Who could say to Him, "What are You doing?"
A god could not avert His anger—
 Rahab's[8] cohorts bent beneath Him—
how then could I raise my voice at Him,
 or choose to match my words with His?
Even if I were right, I could not answer,
 could only plead with my opponent;
and if I summoned Him, and if He answered me,
 I doubt that He would listen to my voice,
since He crushes me for just a hair,
 and bruises me for nothing,
will not let me catch my breath,
 feeds me full of poison.
Is it power? He is mighty!
Is it judgment? Who can summon Him?
I may be righteous, but my mouth convicts me;
 innocent, yet it makes me seem corrupt.
I *am* good.

---

8. Another name for the sea monster conquered by the god in Near Eastern myth.

I do not know myself.
I hate my life.
It is all one; and so I say,
"The good and the guilty He destroys alike."
If some scourge brings sudden death,
    He mocks the guiltless for their melting hearts;
some land falls under a tyrant's sway—
    He veils its judges' faces;
if not He, then who?

But I—
my days are lighter than a courier's feet;
they flee and never see a moment's joy;
they dart away as if on skiffs of reed,[9]
swift as a vulture swooping to his food.

I tell myself to give up my complaining,
    put aside my sullenness and breathe a while;
but still I fear my suffering,
knowing You will never count me innocent.
I am always the one in the wrong—
why should I struggle in vain?
Even if I bathed in liquid snow
    and purified my palms with lye,
You would just dip me in a ditch—
    my very clothes would find me sickening.

For a man like me cannot just challenge Him,
"Let's go to court together!"
Now if there were an arbiter between us
to lay his hand on both of us,
    to make Him take His rod away,
        so that His terror would not cow me,
then I could speak without this fear of Him;
    for now I am not steady in His presence.

10. I am fed up with my life;
    I might as well complain with all abandon,
        and put my bitter spirit into words.
So to the god I say, "Do not condemn me!
Just tell me what the accusation is!
Do You get pleasure from harassing,
    spurning what You wore Yourself out making,
        shining on the councils of the wicked?
Do You have eyes of flesh?
    Do You see as mortals do?
Is Your life span the same as any human's,
    Your years like those of ordinary men,
that You come seeking out my every sin

9. Papyrus. Boats made from it were fast.

and leave no fault of mine unpunished—
knowing I've done nothing truly wicked,
   that nothing can be rescued from Your hands?

Your hands shaped me, kneaded me
together, round about—
   and now would You devour me?
Remember, You kneaded me like clay;
   will You turn me back to dirt?
Just look:
You poured me out like milk,
   You curdled me like cheese;
You covered me with flesh and skin,
   wove me a tangle of sinews and bones,
gave me life, a gift,
   sustained my breath with Your command.
Yet all these things You stored up in Your heart—
I know how Your mind works!
When I do sin, You keep Your eye on me,
and You would never clear me of my guilt.
If I do wrong, too bad for me!
But even when I'm good I cannot raise my head,
so filled with shame,
   so drenched with my own misery.
Proud as a lion You stalk me
and then withdraw,
   pleased with Yourself for what You've done to me.
You keep Your enmity toward me fresh,
   work up Your anger at me;
so my travail is constantly renewed.

Why did You ever take me from the womb?
I could have died, and no eye had to see.
I could have been as if I never were,
hauled from belly to grave.
But as it is, my days are few, so stop!
Let me alone so I can catch my breath
before I go my way, not to return,
into a land of dark and deathgloom,
land obscure as any darkness,
land of deathgloom, land of chaos,
where You blaze forth in rays of black!"

11. Zophar the Naamatite then took up the argument and said:

Should a speech go unanswered just because it is long?
   Is someone with ready lips always right?
You want to silence people with your bluster,
   cow them with sarcasm, no one restrains you.
You say, "My teaching's perfect," "I was pious"—
Yes, in *your* eyes.

But how I wish the god would speak,
   open His lips when you are present,
   tell you some of wisdom's mysteries
(for wisdom comes wrapped up in double folds)—
then you would realize:
The god is punishing you less than you deserve.

Can you find out God's depths,
   or find the outer limits of Shaddai?
What can you do at the heavens' height?
    What can you know that is deeper than Sheol,[1]
   greater than the earth's extension, wider than the sea?
Should He pass by, confine, or confiscate,
who could restore?
He knows which men are false;
could He see wrong and look the other way?
Yet hollow-core man thinks he has some wisdom—
man, born no better than a saddle-ass or onager.[2]

If you would only set your mind,
   stretch out your hands to Him,
get rid of anything you own through crime,
   and harbor nothing wrongly gotten in your home—
then you could hold your head up, blameless,
   be rock-solid, fearing nothing.
Then you would put your troubles out of mind,
   remember them no more than water
   vanished from a wadi.
Your earthbound days would rise as high as noon,
   and darkness turn to morning.
You'd live in confidence, with hope,
   dig your burrow, lie secure,
   crouch there, fearing no one.
Multitudes would seek your favor,
while the wicked gaze with longing eyes,
all refuge lost to them,
   their hopes all spent in sighs.

12. Job answered:

What a distinguished tribe you are!
   All wisdom dies with you!
But I too have a mind.
I am no less a man than you;
   and who does *not* have such ideas as these?
I am one who gives his neighbors cause to smile:
   "He calls to God and He answers him!"—
   a laughingstock—righteous, innocent.
Smug men's minds hold scorn for disaster,
   ready for anyone who stumbles.

---

1. The dwelling place of the dead.   2. A wild ass.

Highway robbers' families lie tranquil;
    men who anger El are confident
      of what the god has brought into their hands.

But just ask the animals—they will instruct you;
    the birds of heaven—they will tell.
Or speak to the earth and it will instruct you,
    the fish of the ocean will tell you the tale:
Who of all these is not aware
that Yahweh's hand has done all this,[3]
the hand that controls every living soul,
    the breath of every man made of flesh?

"The ear," they say, "is the best judge of speech,
    the palate knows what food is tasty."
    "Wisdom," they say, "belongs to elders;
    length of years makes a man perspicacious."
He has wisdom and power;
    He has counsel and insight.
If He tears down, there is no rebuilding;
    if He confines, there is no release.
If He blocks the water, the water dries up;
    but if He lets it loose,
    if overturns the earth.
Both skill and might are with Him;
    He owns both those who do wrong
    and those who lead others astray.
He makes counselors go mad and judges rave,
    unties the bonds of kings,
    (though He Himself had bound the sash about their waists).
He makes the priests go mad,
    and gives eternal truths the lie.
He strips the ready counselors of speech,
    makes off with the elders' reason,
heaps scorn on nobles,
    weakens the pride of the mighty.
He discloses deep things out of darkness,
    brings deathdark to the light.
He elevates some nations, then destroys them,
    spreads traps for other nations,
    but guides them safely through.
He strips the peoples' leaders of their judgment,
    sends them off-course in a trackless wasteland,
    groping in the darkness, lightless,
    wandering crazily like drunken men.

13. Look, there is nothing my eye hasn't seen,
    nothing my ear hasn't heard and taken in,
    nothing that you know that I do not.

---

3. If "this" refers to Job's suffering, the meaning is that even animals know that God acts arbitrarily, whereas "smug men" (above) think that if a man suffers he has done something to deserve it.

I am no less a man than you.
But I would speak to Shaddai,
    I want to dispute with El,
while you are merely smearers, liars,
    mountebanks, every one of you.
If only you would just be quiet!—
    In you, that would be wisdom!

Listen to my accusation,
    pay heed to my lips' complaint.
Will you speak falsehood for the sake of El,
    and speak deceit on His account?
Will you show partiality to Him,
    argue on El's behalf?
How would it be if He questioned you?
    Could you play Him for a fool, as you do with people?
He is sure to reprimand you,
    if you behave with secret partiality.
Think how you would panic if He were to loom,
    and all His fearsomeness came down on you:
    Your memory would turn to ashes,
    your bodies, into lumps of clay.

Be silent in my presence! I will speak,
    and let whatever happens to me happen.
Why am I carrying my body in my teeth,
    my life-breath in my hands?[4]
Let Him kill me!—I will never flinch,
    but will protest His conduct to His face,
and He Himself will be my vindication,
    for flatterers can never come before Him.

Listen, all who hear me, to my speech,
    my declaration in your ears:
I am laying out my case,
knowing I am in the right.
Who would contend with me?—
I will shut my mouth at once and die.
Only two things do not do to me,
and then I will not hide from You:
Take Your palm away from me,
    and do not cow me with the fear of You.
Then You can call, and I will answer,
or I will speak and You can answer me.
How many are my sins and my offenses?
    Advise me of my crimes and sins.
Why do You hide Your face,
    regard me as Your enemy?
Would You tyrannize a driven leaf
    or hound a shriveled straw,

---

4. Like a wild beast at bay, defending its life with its teeth.

that You record my every bitter deed,
    charge me with my boyhood sins?
Is that why You put my feet in stocks,
    watch my every step,
    mark the roots of my feet?[5]

14. Man born of woman:
  His days are few, his belly full of rage.
  He blooms and withers like a blossom,
    flees, unlingering, like a shadow,
    wears out like a rotten thing,
    a cloth moth-eaten.
  Do You really keep a watch on such a thing?
    Do You call a man like me
    to judgement against You?

Who can purify a thing impure?
No one!
If his years are predetermined,
    and You control the number of his months,
    and You have set him bounds he cannot cross—
just turn away from him and let him be!
Let him work off his contract,
day laborer that he is.

Even a tree has hope:
If you cut it, it sprouts again.
Its suckers never fail.
Its roots may grow old in the earth,
    its stumps may die in the ground,
but just the smell of water makes it bud
and put out branches like a sapling.
But man, when he wearies and dies,
    when a human gives out—where is he then?
Water vanishes from a lake,
    rivers dry up parched,
and man lies down and does not rise;
they will not wake till the skies disappear;
    they will not rise from their sleep.

If You would only hide me in Sheol,
    conceal me till Your anger passes,
    set me a term and then remember me
    (but if a person dies, how can he live?),
I could endure my term in hope,
until my time came round to sprout again.
Then You would call, and I would answer,
    when You longed to see Your handiwork.
But as it is, You count my every step,
    see nothing but my sins.

---

5. The meaning here is obscure.

My sin is sealed up in a bundle,
    and You attached the seal.

Yes, the mountain collapses and wears away;
    the cliff is dislodged from its place;
stones are scoured by water into dust,
    torrents wash away earth's soil—
    and You destroy man's hopes.
You assault him and he vanishes forever;
    You turn his face dark and send him away.
His sons become great and he never knows,
    or else they fail, and he never finds out.
All he knows is his own body's ache;
he mourns himself alone.

          *   *   *

29. Job went on with his poem:

If only I could be under the moons of old again,
back in the days when the god watched over me!
When He held His lamp so it shone above my head,
and I could walk by the light in darkness.
If I could be again as I was in my daring days,
with the god above my tent, protecting;
when Shaddai was still with me—
    my men around me too!—
my feet washed with butter,
    the rocks pouring oil out for me in streams!

When I would stride out to the gate of the town,
    and take my place in the city square,[6]
young men would see me and hide in the crowd,
    elders would rise and stand still in their places;
chieftains would dam their words' flow,
    putting their hands to their lips;
commanders' voices were muffled;
    tongues stuck to the roofs of mouths;
but ears would hear and admire;
    eyes would see and bear witness to me:
how I rescued poor men when they cried,
    and orphans, people none would help.

Desperate, ruined men would bless me,
    and I brought song to the widow's heart.
I put on justice and it suited me;
    my decree was my turban and robe.
I was the blind man's eyes;
I was feet for the lame;
I was father to the poor.
I studied the stranger's complaint.
I cracked the fangs of villains,

---

6. Towns were walled, and the town's meeting place and law court were just inside the gate.

ripped the prey from their teeth.
So I said:
I will die in my nest,
   live as long as the phoenix,[7]
my roots open to water,
   my shoots night-moistened by dew.
My pride constantly renewed for me,
   my bow blooming in my hand. . . .

They would listen to me, waiting
silently for my advice;
when I had spoken they would not ask again,
once my word had dripped over them.
They would look to me as if for rain,
   their mouths wide to the spring showers.
When I smiled at them, they were uneasy;
   they took care not to make my face fall.
I chose their paths;
I sat at their head;
I dwelt among them like a king with his troops,
   or like one who comforts men who mourn.

30. And now I find myself mocked by men younger than myself, men whose fathers I rejected from working alongside my sheepdogs!

Even their manual labor, what good was it to me?
Their vigor was long gone
in dearth and famine, barren,
fleeing to the wilderness,
a horror-night of ruin;
plucking saltwort from scrub-brush,
burning broom-root to get warm,
driven from society,
shouted at like thieves;
squatting in the wadi-channels,
dust-caves, cliff-hollows;
braying in the bushes,
keeping company among thorns;
louts' brood, no one's children,
ousted from the world of men—
now I am their mocking song,
   the topic of their gossip!
They scorn me, they shun me,
   they spare my face no spit.

For He undid my cord, tormented me,
and they shake loose my reins.
Young bullies crop up on my right,
range anywhere they like,
pave right up to me their highways of destruction,

7. The King James version's "multiply my days as the sand" is more literal (sand is a common biblical image for a quantity past counting). The phoenix was a fabulous bird that lived for several hundred years and then burned to death in its nest. A young phoenix arose from the ashes.

ruin my own paths.
They work effectively to bring me down,
  they need no help.
They come on like a wide rush of water,
  downward, ravaging, rolling.

Horror has rolled over me,
and driven off my dignity like wind;
my wealth has vanished like a cloud,
and now my life is spilling out of me.
Days of suffering have seized me;
  by night my bones are hacked from me,
  my sinews cannot rest.
Just to dress takes all my strength;
my collar fits my waist.

He conceived me as clay,
and I have come to be like dust and ashes.

I cry to You—no answer;
  I stand—You stare at me,
You harden Yourself to me,
  spurn me with Your mighty hand.
You lift me up and mount me on a wind,
  dissolve my cunning,
and I know that You will send me back to death,
  to the house awaiting every living creature.
But why this violence to a pile of rubble?
  In his disaster is there some salvation?
Did I not weep for the hapless?
  Did my soul not grieve for the poor?
Yes—
I hoped for good, got only wrong;
  I hoped for light, got only darkness.
My insides seethe and never stop,
  I face days of suffering,
I go about in sunless gloom.
In assembly I stand up and wail,
changed to a jackal's brother,
  fellow to the ostrich.[8]
My skin has blackened on my body,
  my bones are charred with fever.
My lyre has gone to mourning,
  my pipe to the sound of sobs.

31. Then what does the god above have in store,
  what lot from Shaddai in the heavens?
Only disaster for doers of evil,
  estrangement for men who do wrong.
Does He not see my ways,

---

8. Both animals are known for their loud, mournful cries.

count all my steps?
Have I walked the way of falsehood?
    Was my foot fleet to deceit?
Let God weigh me in an honest balance—
    He will have to see my innocence.

If my step has left the path,
if my heart has obeyed my eye,
if anyone's goods have stuck to my palms,
    may I sow for another to eat;
    may my offspring be uprooted.
If I have let a woman beguile me,
if I have lurked at my neighbor's door,
    may my own wife grind for another,
    may other men crouch over her;
    for that would be indecent, foul,
    that would be a crime for the judges.
    For it is fire
    raging down to Abaddon[9]
and would uproot my increase.
I have made a pact with my eyes
never to gaze at young women.
If I deny my men-slaves or women-slaves justice
when they raise complaints to me,
    what will I do when God comes forward,
    to demand accounting?
    What will I answer Him?
    Did not my maker make him[1] in the selfsame belly,
    form us in a single womb?
If I have refused the poor their wants,
    or made the eyes of widows languish,
if I have eaten my bread alone,
without an orphan sharing it
    (for since I was a boy, I raised him like a father,
    and from my mother's womb I guided her)[2]—
If ever I saw someone dying naked,
or a poor man with no clothing,
    I swear, his very loins would bless me,
    as he warmed himself in the wool of my sheep.
If ever I raised my hand to an orphan,
seeing I had support in the gate,[3]
    may my shoulder fall out of its socket,
    and my forearm break off at the elbow;
    for disaster from El is terror to me;
    I cannot bear His awesome looming.
If ever I put my hope in gold,
    or thought to place my trust in it;
if I was smug because my wealth was great,
    because my hand had acquired so much—

---

9. The underworld.   1. The slave.   2. The widow. *Him:* the orphan.   3. I.e., when I had influence in the court and other public places.

If I have ever looked at the sun as it beamed,
or at the moon coming on in splendor,
and my heart was secretly beguiled,
and my hand crept up to touch my mouth,[4]
    that too would be a crime for judges,
    for it would mean denying God on high.
If ever I rejoiced in my enemy's downfall,
or felt a rush of joy when trouble found him,
    never did I let my mouth taste sin,
    asking for his life by execration.[5]
If the men of my household ever failed to say,
"Why did we consume his flesh?"—
    No stranger ever spent the night in the street;
    for I would open my doors to the wanderer.
If, as men will, I hid my crimes,
    concealed my sin inside me,
    fearing public scandal,
    frightened by the scorn of clans,
    kept silent, never setting foot outdoors—
If my land cries out because of me,
    and its furrows weep together,
if I consumed its produce without paying,
    made its workers sigh their souls out,
may it sprout up thorns instead of wheat,
    stinkweed instead of barley.

If only I had someone to hear me!

Here is my desire: that Shaddai answer me,
    that my opponent write a brief;
I swear that I would wear it on my shoulder,
    bind it on me like a crown.
I would tell my steps to Him by number,
    come before Him as before a prince.

Here Job's speeches ended.

*   *   *

38. Yahweh answered Job from the storm:

Who dares speak darkly words with no sense?

Cinch your waist like a fighter.
I will put questions, and you will inform me:
Where were you when I founded the earth?
Speak, if you have any wisdom:
Who set its measurements, if you know,
    laid out the building lot, stretching the plumb line?
Where was the ground where He sank its foundations?
Who was setting the cornerstone

---

4. Idolatrous acts of worship of the sun and moon.   5. A formal curse.

when the morning stars were all singing,
   when the gods were all shouting, triumphant?
Who barred the sea behind double gates
as it was gushing out of the womb?
When I made the clouds its covering, fog its swaddling,
broke its will with my decree,
set bar and double gate,
and said, "This far, no farther!
   Here stops your breakers' surge."
When did you ever give dawn his orders,
   assign the rising sun his post,
to grasp the corners of the world
   and shake the wicked out of it,[6]
make the world heave, break like a seal of clay:
   They stand up naked.
The wicked are denied their light,
   the haughty arm is broken.

Have you ever reached the depths of the sea
   and walked around there, exploring the abyss?
Have you been shown behind the Gates of Death,
   or seen the Gates of Deathdark?
Have you beheld the earth's expanses?
Tell me, if you know everything!—
Where is the path to where light dwells,
   and darkness, where does it belong?
Can you conduct them to their regions,
   or even imagine their homeward paths?
You must know, you were born long ago!
   So many years you have counted!

Have you reached the stores of snow,
   or seen the stock of hailstones
that I have laid up for times of trouble,
   days of battle, days of war?

Where is the path to where lightning forks,
   when an east wind scatters it over the ground?
Who cracked open a channel for the torrent,
   clove the path for the thundershower,
to rain on lands where no man lives,
   on wildernesses uninhabited,
to feed a wasteland, fill a desolation,
   make it flower, sprout grass?
Does the shower have a father?
   Who begot the drops of dew?
From whose womb did the ice come forth?
Who gave birth to the sky-frost—
   water clotting as to stone,
     the abyss congeals.

---

6. I.e., the sun exposes the wicked, who commit their crimes in the darkness of night.

Do you tie the Sky-Sisters[7] with ropes
    or undo Orion's bonds?
Do you bring out the stars as they are due,
    guide the Great Bear and her young?
Do you know the laws that rule the sky,
    and can you make it control the earth?
Can you thunder at the clouds
    so that a flood of water covers you?
Can you loose the lightning,
    and have it say, as it goes, "Your servant!"?
Who gave wisdom to the ibis,
    gave the cock its knowledge?
Who is wise enough to count the clouds,
    pour out the jars of heaven,
when the soil is fused solid
    and clods stick thickly?

Do you hunt prey for the lioness?
    Do you satisfy her young,
when they are crouching in their lair,
    sitting in ambush in the covert?
Who puts prey in the raven's way,
    when her fledglings cry to God,
        wandering, aimless, without food?

39. Do you know when the antelope gives birth,
    watch for the calving of the deer?
Do you count the months they have to pass,
    know how, when their time has come,
    they crouch, split open for their young,
    release their newborns?
The calves thrive, grow in the wild,
    then leave them, never return.

Who gave the wild ass his freedom,
    undid his bonds—
the beast I made to live in wasteland,
    gave the salt flat as a home,
so that he might laugh at crowded cities
    and never hear the driver's call,
but scour the hills for pasturage,
    hunting for any bit of green?

Does the buffalo deign to serve you?
    Will he sleep by your feeding trough?
Can you tie him to a furrow with a rope?
    Will he harrow the plain behind you?
Can you rely on him, for all his power,
    and leave your work to him?
Can you trust him to bring in your produce
    and heap it up for threshing?

7. The Pleiades.

Delightful is the ostrich wing—
　　but is it a pinion, like stork or vulture?
Does the eagle soar at your bidding,
　　building his nest up high?—
He dwells, shelters on cliffs,
　　on rock crags and fastnesses.
From there he seeks food,
　　and his eyes peer far;
　　his chicks lap gore.
Where there's a corpse you will find him.

40. Yahweh turned back to Job:

One who brings Shaddai to court should fight!
　　He who charges a god should speak.

But Job answered Yahweh:

I see how little I am.
I will not answer You.
I am putting my hand to my lips:
　　One time I spoke;
　　　　I will not speak again;
　　two times I spoke,
　　　　and I will not go on.

Yahweh answered Job from the storm:

Cinch your waist like a fighter.
　　I will put questions, and you will inform me.
Would you really annul my judgment,
　　make me out to be guilty, and put yourself in the right?
Is your arm as mighty as God's?
　　Does your voice thunder like His?
Just dress up in majesty, greatness!
　　Try wearing splendor and glory!
Snort rage in every direction!
　　Seek out the proud, bring him down!
Seek out the proud man, subdue him,
　　crush cruel men where they stand,
hide them together in dirt,
　　bind them in the Hidden Place:
Then even I would concede to you,
　　when your right hand had gained you a triumph.

Just look at the River Beast[8] that I put alongside you:
He eats grass like cattle.
Look at his thighs: What power!
　　The might in his belly muscles!

---

8. The Hebrew word is *behemot* (rendered in English "behemoth"), a general term for animals; but the description seems to be modeled on the hippopotamus.

He wills his tail into cedar—
  his thigh-thews twist tight.
His bones are unyielding bronze,
  his limbs are like iron bars.
He is the first of God's ways.
  Let none but his maker bring forth his sword![9]

For the hills bring their yield, their tribute to him,
  the hills where the wild beasts play—
to him, who lies under the lotus,
  in a marsh, in a covert of reeds.

Sheltered, shaded by lotus,
  surrounded by droop-leaf willows.
Look: He gulps a whole river, but languidly,
  calm, as the Jordan surges into his mouth!

    Can you catch him by the eye?
    Can you pierce his nose with thorns?

Can you draw the River Coiler[1] with a hook?
  Bind down his tongue with a rope?
String him through the nose with a reed?
  Bore his cheek with a thistle?
Would he beg you for mercy,
  gentle you with words?
Would he deign to be your ally?
  Could you make him a slave for life?
Could you pet him like a bird,
  leash him for your girls to play with?
Will partners haggle over him
  or cut him into lots for mongers?
Can you fill his skin with darts,
  get his head into a fishnet?
Just put your hand on him—
you will remember the battle, you will not do it again!

41. Look: Hope of him is delusion;
    even to glance at him is to fall.
      Is he not fierce when aroused?
Who could stand ground in his presence?
  Who could address him unscathed?
Under all the heavens, that man would be mine!
  I would not silence his boasting,
  his talk of feats,
    his grace in battle.
Who could strip away the surface that covers him,
  get him into the folds of his bridle?
Who could throw open the gates of his countenance?—
  his teeth cast terror all round.

9. I.e., to kill him.   1. Leviathan (referred to also in chapter 3). The description here seems modeled on the crocodile.

Haughty, his mighty shields,[2]
   shut, sealed tight;
each comes right up to the other,
   no air gets between them;
each clings to each,
    untied, unparting.

His sneezes make the light shimmer;
   his eyes are like the eyelids of dawn.
From his mouth come torches,
   fire-sparks fleeting.

His nostrils smoke
   like a pot that seethes over reeds.
His throat blazes like coals;
   his mouth emits flame.

Might resides in his neck;
   misery dances before him.
The cascades of his flesh cling,
   like cast metal on him, immovable.
Solid as rock is his heart,
   millstone-solid.
When he erupts, the gods cower,
   shrink from the waves.

Reach him with a sword and it fails,
   far-traveling spear or arrow.
Iron to him is straw;
   bronze, a rotten tree.
Arrows cannot repel him,
   fling-stones he turns to chaff;
   stubble to him, the shaft.
    He laughs at the lances' whir.

His underside is sharp shards;
   he drags a threshing sledge on the mud.
He makes the deep boil,
   the sea like soup.
Behind him gleams his wake,
   the abyss, white as an old man's head.

Nothing on dusty earth is like him,
   made not to fear.
He gazes at lofty creatures,
   king of the haughtiest beings!

42. Job answered Yahweh:

I know that You are all-powerful,
and that no plan is beyond You.

---

2. I.e., scales.

"Who dares to speak hidden words with no sense?"[3]

I see that I spoke with no wisdom
   of things beyond me I did not know.

"Listen now and I will speak,
I will put questions, and you will inform me. . . ."

I knew You, but only by rumor;
   my eye has beheld You today.
I retract. I even take comfort
   for dust and ashes.[4]

After Yahweh had said these things to Job, He said to Eliphaz the Temanite, "I am very angry at you and your two friends, for you have not spoken rightly about me as did my servant Job. So take seven bulls and seven rams and go to my servant Job and offer them as wholeburnt offerings for yourselves. And make sure that Job my servant prays for you; for only him will I heed not to treat you with the disgrace you deserve for not speaking rightly of me as did my servant Job." Eliphaz the Temanite and Bildad the Shuhite and Zophar the Naamatite went and did exactly what Yahweh told them to do, and Yahweh accepted Job's prayer.

Yahweh restored Job's fortunes after he prayed for his friends, doubling everything Job had.

All his brothers and sisters and all his former acquaintances came and ate bread with him in his house and mourned with him and comforted him for all the harm that Yahweh had brought upon him. Each one gave him a qesita coin[5] and a gold ring.

Yahweh made Job more prosperous in the latter part of his life than in the former. He had fourteen thousand sheep, six thousand camels, a thousand yoke of cattle, and a thousand female donkeys, besides seven sons and three daughters. He named the first daughter Dove, and the second daughter Cinnamon, and the third daughter Horn-of-Kohl[6]—there were no women as beautiful as Job's daughters in all the land—and he gave them an inheritance alongside their brothers.

Afterward, Job lived one hundred forty years; he lived to see his sons and grandsons to the fourth generation and died in old age after a full life span.

Psalm 8[1]

  1. O Lord our Lord, how excellent is thy name in all the earth! who hast set thy glory above the heavens.

  2. Out of the mouth of babes and sucklings hast thou ordained strength because of thine enemies, that thou mightest still the enemy and the avenger.

---

3. Here and in the next quotation, Job repeats Yahweh's words from the beginning of his first speech and responds to them from the perspective of his new understanding. **4.** Mortality. **5.** Value unknown. **6.** Kohl is a powdered cosmetic often stored in animal horns. The name thus suggests feminine beauty. **1.** The text of the Psalms and the Song of Songs is that of the King James version (see "A Note on These Translations," above).

3. When I consider thy heavens, the work of thy fingers, the moon and the stars, which thou hast ordained;

4. What is man, that thou art mindful of him? and the son of man, that thou visitest him?

5. For thou hast made him a little lower than the angels, and hast crowned him with glory and honour.

6. Thou madest him to have dominion over the works of thy hands; thou hast put all things under his feet:

7. All sheep and oxen, yea, and the beasts of the field;

8. The fowl of the air, and the fish of the sea, and whatsoever passeth through the paths of the seas.

9. O Lord our Lord, how excellent is thy name in all the earth!

Psalm 19

1. The heavens declare the glory of God; and the firmament sheweth his handywork.

2. Day unto day uttereth speech, and night unto night sheweth knowledge.

3. There is no speech nor language, where their voice is not heard.

4. Their line is gone out through all the earth, and their words to the end of the world. In them hath he set a tabernacle for the sun,

5. Which is as a bridegroom coming out of his chamber, and rejoiceth as a strong man to run a race.

6. His going forth is from the end of the heaven, and his circuit unto the ends of it: and there is nothing hid from the heat thereof.

7. The law of the Lord is perfect, converting the soul: the testimony of the Lord is sure, making wise the simple.

8. The statutes of the Lord are right, rejoicing the heart: the commandment of the Lord is pure, enlightening the eyes.

9. The fear of the Lord is clean, enduring for ever: the judgments of the Lord are true and righteous altogether.

10. More to be desired are they than gold, yea, than much fine gold: sweeter also than honey and the honeycomb.

11. Moreover by them is thy servant warned: and in keeping of them there is great reward.

12. Who can understand his errors? cleanse thou me from secret faults.

13. Keep back thy servant also from presumptuous sins; let them not have dominion over me: then shall I be upright, and I shall be innocent from the great transgression.

14. Let the words of my mouth, and the meditation of my heart, be acceptable in thy sight, O Lord, my strength, and my redeemer.

Psalm 23

1. The Lord is my shepherd; I shall not want.

2. He maketh me to lie down in green pastures: he leadeth me beside the still waters.

3. He restoreth my soul: he leadeth me in the paths of righteousness for his name's sake.

4. Yea, though I walk through the valley of the shadow of death, I will fear no evil: for thou art with me; thy rod and thy staff they comfort me.

5. Thou preparest a table before me in the presence of mine enemies: thou anointest my head with oil; my cup runneth over.

6. Surely goodness and mercy shall follow me all the days of my life: and I will dwell in the house of the Lord for ever.

Psalm 104

1. Bless the Lord, O my soul. O Lord my God, thou art very great; thou art clothed with honour and majesty.

2. Who coverest thyself with light as with a garment: who stretchest out the heavens like a curtain:

3. Who layeth the beams of his chambers in the waters: who maketh the clouds his chariot: who walketh upon the wings of the wind:

4. Who maketh his angels spirits; his ministers a flaming fire:

5. Who laid the foundations of the earth, that it should not be removed for ever.

6. Thou coveredst it with the deep as with a garment: the waters stood above the mountains.

7. At thy rebuke they fled; at the voice of thy thunder they hasted away.

8. They go up by the mountains; they go down by the valleys unto the place which thou hast founded for them.

9. Thou hast set a bound that they may not pass over; that they turn not again to cover the earth.

10. He sendeth the springs into the valleys, which run among the hills.

11. They give drink to every beast of the field: the wild asses quench their thirst.

12. By them shall the fowls of the heaven have their habitation, which sing among the branches.

13. He watereth the hills from his chambers: the earth is satisfied with the fruit of thy works.

14. He causeth the grass to grow for the cattle, and herb for the service of man: that he may bring forth food out of the earth;

15. And wine that maketh glad the heart of man, and oil to make his face to shine, and bread which strengtheneth man's heart.

16. The trees of the Lord are full of sap; the cedars of Lebanon, which he hath planted;

17. Where the birds make their nests: as for the stork, the fir trees are her house.

18. The high hills are a refuge for the wild goats; and the rocks for the conies.

19. He appointed the moon for seasons: the sun knoweth his going down.

20. Thou makest darkness, and it is night: wherein all the beasts of the forest do creep forth.

21. The young lions roar after their prey, and seek their meat from God.

22. The sun ariseth, they gather themselves together, and lay them down in their dens.

23. Man goeth forth unto his work and to his labour until the evening.

24. O Lord, how manifold are thy works! in wisdom hast thou made them all: the earth is full of thy riches.

25. So is this great and wide sea, wherein are things creeping innumerable, both small and great beasts.

26. There go the ships: there is that leviathan, whom thou hast made to play therein.

27. These wait all upon thee; that thou mayest give them their meat in due season.

28. That thou givest them they gather: thou openest thine hand, they are filled with good.

29. Thou hidest thy face, they are troubled: thou takest away their breath, they die, and return to their dust.

30. Thou sendest forth thy spirit, they are created: and thou renewest the face of the earth.

31. The glory of the Lord shall endure for ever: the Lord shall rejoice in his works.

32. He looketh on the earth, and it trembleth: he toucheth the hills, and they smoke.

33. I will sing unto the Lord as long as I live: I will sing praise to my God while I have my being.

34. My meditation of him shall be sweet: I will be glad in the Lord.

35. Let the sinners be consumed out of the earth, and let the wicked be no more. Bless thou the Lord, O my soul. Praise ye the Lord.

Psalm 137

1. By the rivers of Babylon,[1] there we sat down, yea, we wept, when we remembered Zion.

2. We hanged our harps upon the willows in the midst thereof.

3. For there they that carried us away captive required of us a song; and they that wasted us required of us mirth, saying, Sing us one of the songs of Zion.

4. How shall we sing the Lord's song in a strange land?

5. If I forget thee, O Jerusalem, let my right hand forget her cunning.

6. If I do not remember thee, let my tongue cleave to the roof of my mouth; if I prefer not Jerusalem above my chief joy.

7. Remember, O Lord, the children of Edom[2] in the day of Jerusalem; who said, Rase it, rase it, even to the foundation thereof.

8. O daughter of Babylon, who art to be destroyed; happy shall he be, that rewardeth thee as thou hast served us.

9. Happy shall he be, that taketh and dasheth thy little ones against the stones.

1. On the Euphrates River. Jerusalem was captured and sacked by the Babylonians in 586 B.C.E. The Hebrews were taken away into captivity in Babylon.   2. The Edomites helped the Babylonians capture Jerusalem.

The Song of Songs

1. The song of songs, which is Solomon's.

Let him kiss me with the kisses of his mouth: for thy love is better than wine. Because of the savor of thy good ointments thy name is as ointment poured forth, therefore do the virgins love thee. Draw me, we will run after thee: the King hath brought me into his chambers: we will be glad and rejoice in thee, we will remember thy love more than wine: the upright love thee. I am black,[1] but comely, O ye daughters of Jerusalem, as the tents of Kedar,[2] as the curtains of Solomon. Look[3] not upon me, because I am black, because the sun hath looked upon me: my mother's children were angry with me; they made me the keeper of the vineyards; but mine own vineyard have I not kept. Tell me, O thou whom my soul loveth, where thou feedest, where thou makest thy flock to rest at noon: for why should I be as one that turneth aside by the flocks of thy companions?

If thou know not, O thou fairest among women, go thy way forth by the footsteps of the flock, and feed thy kids beside the shepherds' tents. I have compared thee, O my love, to a company of horses in Pharaoh's chariots. Thy cheeks are comely with rows of jewels, thy neck with chains of gold. We will make thee borders of gold with studs of silver.

While the King sitteth at his table, my spikenard[4] sendeth forth the smell thereof. A bundle of myrrh is my well-beloved unto me; he shall lie all night betwixt my breasts. My beloved is unto me as a cluster of camphire in the vineyards of En-gedi.[5] Behold, thou art fair, my love; behold, thou art fair; thou hast doves' eyes. Behold, thou art fair, my beloved, yea, pleasant: also our bed is green. The beams of our house are cedar, and our rafters of fir.

2. I am the rose of Sharon,[6] and the lily of the valleys. As the lily among thorns, so is my love among the daughters. As the apple tree among the trees of the wood, so is my beloved among the sons. I sat down under his shadow with great delight, and his fruit was sweet to my taste. He brought me to the banqueting house, and his banner over me was love. Stay me with flagons, comfort me with apples: for I am sick of love. His left hand is under my head, and his right hand doth embrace me. I charge you, O ye daughters of Jerusalem, by the roes, and by the hinds of the field, that ye stir not up, nor awake my love, till he please. The voice of my beloved! behold he cometh leaping upon the mountains skipping upon the hills. My beloved is like a roe or a young hart: behold, he standeth behind our wall, he looketh forth at the windows, showing himself through the lattice. My beloved spake, and said unto me, Rise up, my love, my fair one, and come away. For, lo, the winter is past, the rain is over and gone; the flowers appear on the earth; the time of the singing of birds is come, and the voice of the turtle[7] is heard in our land; the fig tree putteth forth her green figs, and the vines with the tender grape give a good smell. Arise, my love, my fair one, and come away.

---

1. Tanned from sun and weather; feminine beauty required a protected and fair skin. 2. A nomadic people of northern Arabia, living east of Palestine. 3. Better, *gaze* or *stare* (with fascination). 4. Fragrant oil made from an Indian plant. 5. An oasis on the western shore of the Dead Sea, a source of fragrant oil made from the camphire (henna) plant. 6. A plain on the coast of Palestine, notable for its wildflowers. 7. The turtledove.

O my dove, that art in the clefts of the rock, in the secret places of the stairs, let me see thy countenance, let me hear thy voice; for sweet is thy voice, and thy countenance is comely. Take us the foxes, the little foxes, that spoil the vines: for our vines have tender grapes.

My beloved is mine, and I am his: he feedeth among the lilies. Until the day break, and the shadows flee away, turn, my beloved, and be thou like a roe or a young hart upon the mountains of Bether.[8]

3. By night on my bed I sought him whom my soul loveth: I sought him, but I found him not. I will rise now, and go about the city in the streets, and in the broad ways I will seek him whom my soul loveth: I sought him, but I found him not. The watchmen that go about the city found me: to whom I said, Saw ye him whom my soul loveth? It was but a little that I passed from them, but I found him whom my soul loveth: I held him, and would not let him go, until I had brought him into my mother's house, and into the chamber of her that conceived me. I charge you, O ye daughters of Jerusalem, by the roes, and by the hinds of the field, that ye stir not up, nor wake my love, till he please.

Who is this that cometh out of the wilderness like pillars of smoke, perfumed with myrrh and frankincense, with all powders of the merchant? Behold his bed, which is Solomon's; threescore valiant men are about it, of the valiant of Israel. They all hold swords, being expert in war: every man hath his sword upon his thigh because of fear in the night. King Solomon made himself a chariot of the wood of Lebanon. He made the pillars thereof of silver, the bottom thereof of gold, the covering of it of purple, the midst thereof being paved with love, for the daughters of Jerusalem. Go forth, O ye daughters of Zion, and behold king Solomon with the crown wherewith his mother crowned him in the day of his espousals, and in the day of the gladness of his heart.

4. Behold, thou art fair, my love; behold, thou art fair; thou hast doves' eyes within thy locks: thy hair is as a flock of goats, that appear from mount Gilead.[9] Thy teeth are like a flock of sheep that are even shorn, which came up from the washing; whereof every one bear twins, and none is barren among them. Thy lips are like a thread of scarlet, and thy speech is comely: thy temples are like a piece of a pomegranate within thy locks. Thy neck is like the tower of David builded for an armory, whereon there hang a thousand bucklers, all shields of mighty men. Thy two breasts are like two young roes that are twins, which feed among the lilies. Until the day break, and the shadows flee away, I will get me to the mountain of myrrh, and to the hill of frankincense. Thou art all fair, my love; there is no spot in thee.

Come with me from Lebanon, my spouse, with me from Lebanon: look from the top of Amana, from the top of Shenir and Hermon,[1] from the lions' dens, from the mountains of the leopards. Thou hast ravished my heart, my sister, my spouse; thou hast ravished my heart with one of thine eyes, with one chain of thy neck. How fair is thy love, my sister, my spouse! how much better is thy love than wine! and the smell of thine ointments than all spices!

8. Name of a city of Judah, southwest of Jerusalem; the phrase may also mean "the cleft mountains" (a reference to female breasts or genitals). 9. Location uncertain; perhaps a high inland plateau. 1. Mountains in the Antilebanon range of Syria.

Thy lips, O my spouse, drop as the honeycomb: honey and milk are under thy tongue; and the smell of thy garments is like the smell of Lebanon. A garden inclosed is my sister, my spouse; a spring shut up, a fountain sealed. Thy plants are an orchard of pomegranates, with pleasant fruits; camphire, with spikenard, spikenard and saffron; calamus[2] and cinnamon, with all trees of frankincense; myrrh and aloes, with all the chief spices: a fountain of gardens, a well of living waters, and streams from Lebanon.

Awake, O north wind; and come, thou south; blow upon my garden, that the spices thereof may flow out. Let my beloved come into his garden, and eat his pleasant fruits.

5. I am come into my garden, my sister, my spouse: I have gathered my myrrh with my spice; I have eaten my honeycomb with my honey; I have drunk my wine with my milk: eat, O friends; drink, yea, drink abundantly, O beloved.

I sleep, but my heart waketh: it is the voice of my beloved that knocketh, saying, Open to me, my sister, my love, my dove, my undefiled: for my head is filled with dew, and my locks with the drops of the night. I have put off my coat; how shall I put it on? I have washed my feet; how shall I defile them? My beloved put in his hand[3] by the hole of the door, and my bowels[4] were moved for him. I rose up to open to my beloved; and my hands dropped with myrrh, and my fingers with sweet smelling myrrh, upon the handles of the lock. I opened to my beloved; but my beloved had withdrawn himself, and was gone: my soul failed when he spake: I sought him, but I could not find him; I called him, but he gave me no answer. The watchmen that went about the city found me, they smote me, they wounded me; the keepers of the walls took away my veil from me. I charge you, O daughters of Jerusalem, if ye find my beloved, that ye tell him, that I am sick of love. What is thy beloved more than another beloved, O thou fairest among women? what is thy beloved more than another beloved, that thou dost so charge us? My beloved is white and ruddy, the chiefest among ten thousand. His head is as the most fine gold; his locks are bushy, and black as a raven: his eyes are as the eyes of doves by the rivers of waters, washed with milk, and fitly set: his cheeks are as a bed of spices, as sweet flowers: his lips like lilies, dropping sweet smelling myrrh: his hands are as gold rings set with the beryl: his belly is as bright ivory overlaid with sapphires: his legs are as pillars of marble, set upon sockets of fine gold: his countenance is as Lebanon, excellent as the cedars: his mouth is most sweet: yea, he is altogether lovely. This is my beloved, and this is my friend, O daughters of Jerusalem.

6. Whither is thy beloved gone, O thou fairest among women? whither is thy beloved turned aside? that we may seek him with thee. My beloved is gone down into his garden, to the beds of spices, to feed in the gardens, and to gather lilies. I am my beloved's, and my beloved is mine: he feedeth among the lilies.

Thou art beautiful, O my love, as Tirzah,[5] comely as Jerusalem, terrible as an army with banners. Turn away thine eyes from me, for they have overcome

---

2. Cane, an aromatic spice. 3. Possibly a euphemism for *phallus*. 4. Entrails, considered the seat of tender emotions. 5. A Canaanite city.

me: thy hair is as a flock of goats that appear from Gilead: thy teeth are as a flock of sheep which go up from the washing, whereof every one beareth twins, and there is not one barren among them. As a piece of a pomegranate are thy temples within thy locks. There are threescore queens, and fourscore concubines, and virgins without number. My dove, my undefiled, is but one; she is the only one of her mother, she is the choice one of her that bare her. The daughters saw her, and blessed her; yea, the queens and the concubines, and they praised her. Who is she that looketh forth as the morning, fair as the moon, clear as the sun, and terrible as an army with banners? I went down into the garden of nuts to see the fruits of the valley, and to see whether the vine flourished, and the pomegranates budded. Or ever I was aware, my soul made me like the chariots of Amminadib. Return, return, O Shulamite;[6] return, return, that we may look upon thee. What will ye see in the Shulamite? As it were the company of two armies.

7. How beautiful are thy feet with shoes, O prince's daughter! the joints of thy thighs are like jewels, the work of the hands of a cunning workman. Thy navel is like a round goblet, which wanteth not liquor: thy belly is like a heap of wheat set about with lilies. Thy two breasts are like two young roes that are twins. Thy neck is as a tower of ivory; thine eyes like the fishpools in Heshbon, by the gate of Bathrabbim:[7] thy nose is as the tower of Lebanon which looketh toward Damascus. Thine head upon thee is like Carmel,[8] and the hair of thine head like purple; the King is held in the galleries. How fair and how pleasant art thou, O love, for delights! This thy stature is like to a palm tree, and thy breasts to clusters of grapes. I said, I will go up to the palm tree, I will take hold of the boughs thereof: now also thy breasts shall be as clusters of the vine, and the smell of thy nose like apples: and the roof of thy mouth like the best wine for my beloved, that goeth down sweetly, causing the lips of those that are asleep to speak.

I am my beloved's, and his desire is toward me. Come, my beloved, let us go forth into the field; let us lodge in the villages. Let us get up early to the vineyards; let us see if the vine flourish, whether the tender grape appear, and the pomegranates bud forth: there will I give thee my loves. The mandrakes[9] give a smell, and at our gates are all manner of pleasant fruits, new and old, which I have laid up for thee, O my beloved.

8. O that thou wert as my brother, that sucked the breasts of my mother! when I should find thee without, I would kiss thee; yea, I should not be despised. I would lead thee, and bring thee into my mother's house, who would instruct me: I would cause thee to drink of spiced wine of the juice of my pomegranate. His left hand should be under my head, and his right hand should embrace me. I charge you, O daughters of Jerusalem, that ye stir not up, nor awake my love, until he please. Who is this that cometh up from the wilderness, leaning upon her beloved? I raised thee up under the apple tree: there thy mother brought thee forth; there she brought thee forth

6. The name, often taken as the feminine counterpart to Solomon, may also be the name or epithet of a Near Eastern goddess or a reference to the town Shunem. 7. Another name for Heshbon, a city east of the northern end of the Dead Sea; or one of its gates. 8. A high promontory on the seacoast of Palestine. 9. A common plant in Palestine, known for its narcotic or aphrodisiac effect, whose root was thought to look like the male genitalia.

that bare thee. Set me as a seal upon thine heart, as a seal upon thine arm: for love is strong as death; jealousy is cruel as the grave: the coals thereof are coals of fire, which hath a most vehement flame. Many waters cannot quench love, neither can the floods drown it: if a man would give all the substance of his house for love, it would utterly be contemned.

We have a little sister, and she hath no breasts: what shall we do for our sister in the day when she shall be spoken for? If she be a wall, we will build upon her a palace of silver: and if she be a door, we will inclose her with boards of cedar. I am a wall, and my breasts like towers: then was I in his eyes as one that found favor. Solomon had a vineyard at Baalhamon;[1] he let out the vineyard unto keepers; every one for the fruit thereof was to bring a thousand pieces of silver. My vineyard, which is mine, is before me: thou, O Solomon, must have a thousand, and those that keep the fruit thereof two hundred. Thou that dwellest in the gardens, the companions hearken to thy voice: cause me to hear it. Make haste, my beloved, and be thou like to a roe or to a young hart upon the mountains of spices.

---

1. Otherwise unknown. The name means "lord of a crowd."

HOMER
eighth century B.C.E.

Greek literature begins with two masterpieces, the *Iliad* and *Odyssey,* which cannot be accurately dated (the conjectural dates range over three centuries) and which are attributed to the poet Homer, about whom nothing is known except his name. The Greeks believed that he was blind, perhaps because the bard Demodocus in the *Odyssey* was blind (see pp. 206–495), and seven different cities put forward claims to be his birthplace. They are all in what the Greeks called Ionia, the western coast of Asia Minor, which was heavily settled by Greek colonists. It does seem likely that he came from this area; the *Iliad* contains several accurate descriptions of natural features of the Ionian landscape, but Homer's grasp of the geography of mainland, especially western, Greece is unsure. But even this is a guess, and all the other stories the Greeks told about him are obvious inventions.

The two great epics that have made his name supreme among poets may have been fixed in something like their present form before the art of writing was in general use in Greece; it is certain that they were intended not for reading but for oral recitation. The earliest stages of their composition date from around the beginnings of Greek literacy—the late eighth century B.C.E. The poems exhibit the unmistakable characteristics of oral composition.

The oral poet had at his disposal not reading and writing but a vast and intricate system of metrical formulas—phrases that would fit in at different places in the line—and a repertoire of standard scenes (the arming of the warrior, the battle of two champions), as well as the known outline of the story. Of course he could and did invent new phrases and scenes as he recited—but his base was the immense poetic reserve created by many generations of singers who lived before him. When he told again for his hearers the old story of Achilles and his wrath, he was re-creating a traditional story that had been recited, with variations, additions, and improvements, by a long line of predecessors. The poem was not, in the modern sense, the poet's creation, still less an expression of his personality. Consequently, there is no trace of individual identity to be found in it; the poet remains as hidden behind the action and speech of his characters as if he were a dramatist.

The *Iliad* and *Odyssey* as we have them, however, are unlike most of the oral literature we know from other times and places. The poetic organization of each of these two epics—the subtle interrelationship of the parts, which creates their structural and emotional unity—has suggested to many that they owe their present form to the shaping hand of a single poet, the architect who selected from the enormous wealth of the oral tradition and fused what he took with original material to create, perhaps with the aid of the new medium of writing, the two magnificently ordered poems known as the *Iliad* and *Odyssey*. Others imagine the texts becoming more and more fixed over centuries of oral performance.

THE ILIAD

Of the two poems the *Iliad* is perhaps the earlier. Its subject is war; its characters are men in battle and women whose fate depends on the outcome. The war is fought by the Achaeans against the Trojans for the recovery of Helen, the wife of the Achaean chieftain Menelaus; the combatants are heroes who engage in individual duels before the supporting lines of infantry and archers. There is no sentimentality in Homer's descriptions of these battles.

> Patrolcus eased up
> Alongside him and shattered his right jaw
> With his spear, driving the point through his teeth,
> Then, gripping the shaft, levered him up
> And over his chariot rail, the way a man
> Sitting on a jutting rock with a fishing rod
> Flips a flounder he has hooked out of the sea.
> So Thestor was prised gaping from his chariot
> And left flat on his face. His soul crawled off.

This is meticulously accurate; there is no attempt to suppress the ugliness of Thestor's death. The bare, careful description creates the true nightmare quality of battle, in which men perform monstrous actions with the same matter-of-fact efficiency they display in their normal occupations, and the simile reproduces the grotesque appearance of violent death—the simple spear thrust takes away Thestor's dignity as a human being even before it takes his life. He is gaping, like a fish on the hook.

The simile also does something else. It glorifies Patroclus. He skewers Thestor and flips him from the chariot as easily as a fisherman lands a fish. Thestor is simply no match for him; his ignominy is Patroclus's honor. This function of the simile is important because, shortly afterward and in the same battle, Patroclus himself will die, killed by Hector (who will later be killed in revenge by Achilles). Patroclus will fall at the height of his exploits and abilities as a warrior; that is how he will be remembered and commemorated in epic poetry like the *Iliad*. This simile, like so many other passages in the poem, displays the two aspects of war: it is destructive but it also calls forth the warriors' highest efforts and achievements. The *Iliad* shows us people constantly faced with death and yet managing to find meaning in that death: their survival in the memory of future generations for what they did. More generally, we see men and women placed in a situation in which violence always threatens to spiral out of control and not only destroy them but also force them to act in ways that de-humanize them. They have to find ways to claim their humanity. The *Iliad* raises profound questions about violence but also faces it directly, without sentimentality, as a basic aspect of human life. After three thousand years, Homer is still one of war's greatest interpreters.

The story of Achilles greatly complicates these issues. The *Iliad* describes the events of a few weeks near the end of the ten-year siege of Troy. The particular subject of the poem, as its first line announces, is the anger of Achilles, the bravest of the Achaean chieftains encamped outside the city. Achilles is a man who comes to live by and for violence. His anger cuts him off from his commander and his fellow princes; to spite them he withdraws from the fighting. He is brought back into it at last by the death of his closest friend, Patroclus; the consequences of his wrath and withdrawal fall heavily on the Achaeans but most heavily on himself.

The great champion of the Trojans, Hector, fights bravely but reluctantly. War, for him, is a necessary evil, and he thinks nostalgically of the peaceful past, though he has little hope of peace to come. His preeminence in peace is emphasized by the tenderness of his relations with his wife and child and also by his kindness to Helen, the cause of the war that he knows in his heart will bring his city to destruction. We see Hector, as we do not see Achilles, against the background of the patterns of civilized life—the rich city with its temples and palaces, the continuity of the family. The duel between these two men is the inevitable crisis of the poem, and just as inevitable is Hector's defeat and death.

At the climactic moment of Hector's death, as everywhere in the poem, Homer's firm control of his material preserves the balance in which our contrary emotions are held; pity for Hector does not entirely rob us of sympathy for Achilles. His brutal words to the dying Hector and the insults he inflicts on Hector's corpse are truly savage, but we are never allowed to forget that this inflexible hatred is the expression of his love for Patroclus. And the final book of the poem shows us an Achilles whose iron heart is moved at last; he is touched by the sight of Hector's father clasping in supplication the terrible hands that have killed so many of his sons. He remembers that he has a father and that he will never see him again; Achilles and Priam, the slayer and the father of the slain, weep together. Achilles gives Hector's body to Priam for honorable burial. His anger has run its full course and been appeased. It has brought death, first to the Achaeans and then to the Trojans, to Patroclus and to Hector, and so to Achilles himself, for his death is fated to come soon after Hector's.

This tragic action is the center of the poem, but it is surrounded by scenes that remind us that the organized destruction of war, though an integral part of human life, is still only a part of it. The yearning for peace and its creative possibilities is never far below the surface. This is most poignantly expressed by the scenes that take place in Troy, especially the farewell between Hector and Andromache, but it is made clear that the Achaeans too are conscious of what they have sacrificed. Early in the poem, when Agamemnon, the Achaean commander, tests the morale of his troops by suggesting that the war be abandoned, they rush for the ships so eagerly and with such heartfelt relief that their commanders are hard put to stop them. These two poles of the human condition—war and peace, with their corresponding aspects of human nature, the destructive and the creative—are implicit in every situation and statement of the poem, and they are put before us, in symbolic form, in the shield that the god Hephaestus makes for Achilles, with its scenes of human life in both peace and war. Whether these two sides of life can ever be integrated, or even reconciled, is a question that the *Iliad* raises but cannot answer.

Yet the poem leaves us with a vision that is not entirely bleak. War puts human values under stress but it also clarifies them, a point made clear especially in the final book. Achilles has killed Priam's son Hector, but because of the grief he feels for Patroclus, he understands and shares Priam's grief. And it is because he knows that he himself will soon die that he can see his father, Peleus, in the aged king of Troy, his enemy.

THE ODYSSEY

The other Homeric epic, the *Odyssey*, is concerned with the peace that followed the war and in particular with the return of the heroes who survived. Its subject is the long, drawn-out return of one of the heroes, Odysseus of Ithaca, who was destined to spend ten years wandering in unknown seas before he returned to his rocky kingdom. When Odysseus's wanderings began, Achilles had already received, at the hands of Apollo, the death that he had chosen. Odysseus struggles for life, and his outstanding quality is a probing and versatile intelligence that, combined with long experience, keeps him safe and alive through the trials and dangers of twenty years of war and seafaring. To stay alive he has to do things that Achilles would never have done and use an ingenuity and experience that Achilles did not possess, but his life is just as much a struggle.

Although Odysseus has become for us the archetypal adventurer, the *Odyssey* gives us a hero whose one goal is to get home. He struggles not simply for his own and his shipmates' personal survival but also to preserve and complete the heroic reputation that he won in war at Troy. It may seem ironic that Odysseus succeeds by concealing his name, as when he tricks the Cyclops by presenting himself as "Nobody," or when, at home on Ithaca, he tricks his wife's suitors by disguising himself as a beggar. But Odysseus's shiftiness, his talent for disguise, deception, and plain lying, is part of his versatility. It complements his strength and courage in battle—qualities he demonstrated at Troy as he will do again when he fights the suitors in his own hall. It makes this complex hero dangerous to his enemies, and sometimes to his friends, as the Phaeacians discover when Poseidon punishes them for helping him.

The adventures on the voyage home test these mental qualities, as well as Odysseus's physical endurance, by tempting him to lapse from the struggle homeward. The Lotus flower offers forgetfulness of home and family. Circe gives him a life of ease and self-indulgence on an enchanted island. In Phaeacia, Odysseus is offered the love of a young princess and her hand in marriage. The Sirens tempt him to live in the memory of the glorious past. Calypso, the goddess with whom he spends seven years, offers him the greatest temptation of all: immortality. In refusing, Odysseus chooses the human condition, with all its struggle, its disappointments, and its inevitable end. And the end, death, is ever-present. But he hangs on tenaciously and, in the midst of his ordeals, he is sent living to the world of the dead to see for himself what death means. Dark and comfortless, Homer's land of the dead is the most frightening picture of the afterlife in European literature. Odysseus talks to the dead, and when he consoles the shade of Achilles with talk of everlasting glory Achilles replies that it is better to be the most insignificant person on Earth than lord of the dead. Here the heroes of the two great epics confront one another over the chasm of death. Through them, the *Odyssey* defines its values by contrast with those of the *Iliad*. Against the dark background of Achilles' regret for life, Odysseus's dedication to life— his acceptance of its limitations and his ability to seize its possibilities—shines out. His death, Tiresias assures him in this same episode, will come late and gently. Odysseus gets both long life and glory; Achilles could have only either one.

The *Odyssey* celebrates return to ordinary life and makes it seem a worthy prize after excitement, toil, and danger. The adventures occupy only four of twenty-four books (or eight if we include Calypso and the Phaeacians). For the entire second half of the poem, Odysseus is back on Ithaca, winning his way, by deceit that only paves the way for force, from the swineherd Eumaeus's hut to the center of his own house. There, and in books 1–4, we see the social disorder on Ithaca that Odysseus's return is to set right. We also see Telemachus, his son, emerging from adolescence and impatient with all that keeps him from assuming a man's role (his mother as well as her suitors). In his aspirations a foil to Odysseus's mature wisdom, he is his father's potential rival, though in the end his willing subordinate. And we see Penelope's dealings with her son, with her suitors, and with the beggar who is really her husband in disguise. Penelope is a challenging figure, because the narrative does not give us full access to her thoughts and motives. But she seems, with a cunning that matches Odysseus's, to keep in balance two contradictory requirements of her situation. First, she has a duty to herself. If Odysseus, absent twenty years now, is lost for good, then she ought to remarry instead of devoting herself to a house without a head (and in Homeric and later Greek culture, a woman as head of a household was unthinkable). More immediately, she seems to take a natural pleasure in being wooed. On the other hand, she has a duty to her former marriage. If she remarries and Odysseus then returns, she will seem to have betrayed him and, in his and society's eyes, she will be classed with those other adulterers Helen and Clytemnestra. In its ambivalence, Penelope's trick of the web (she promised the suitors to choose one of them when she had finished a shroud for Odysseus's father, Laertes, and for three years she unwove each night what she had woven by day) perfectly encapsulates the way she is forced to play loyal wife and available bride at the same time; it is both a delaying tactic and a way of stringing the suitors along. Odysseus evidently interprets the trick simply as an expression of Penelope's faithfulness to him, and so have readers over the ages. But that only shows how Penelope's interests are folded into his at the end, how his restoration to home and authority retrospectively arranges potentially disorderly elements within a patriarchal order. That is not to say that Penelope lacks autonomy or initiative, at least in the shorter term. To a large extent she controls the timing and means of Odysseus's final homecoming (and therefore she controls key stages in the plot of the poem), not only by her famous trick of the marriage bed in book 23 but also by deciding in book 19 to set the contest of the bow, which will ultimately get a weapon into the beggar's hands (book 21). Why she does so, after the beggar has assured her that Odysseus is about to return, is one of the poem's mysteries. Has she recognized this beggar as her husband, consciously or not, so that she helps him against the suitors? Does she neither recognize nor believe the beggar, so that she acts in despair? Or is she again calculating probabilities to her best advantage?

The period in which the *Iliad* and the *Odyssey* probably took shape, 750–700 B.C.E. or a little after, saw enormous cultural, political, and social developments in Greece, especially the formation, in many areas, of the *polis*, or "city-state" (see pp. 4–5, above). As often happens, these changes occurred amid sharp conflicts and debates, in which the Homeric epics, publicly performed as they were, must have taken part. Along with the issue of peace and war, for instance, a central conflict of the *Iliad* concerns the nature of political authority. Which has the stronger claim, acknowledged position (Agamemnon) or merit (Achilles)? It is difficult to tell which side wins in the end, if either does, but the poem examines the ramifications of this debate, even while showing, paradoxically, the Greeks maintaining enough unity to destroy a tightly knit and orderly city. The problems of violence and order in this poem are as much political as individual. They involve profound questions about the nature of a political community.

The *Odyssey* offers a more positive meditation on the nature of civilization and of the structures of daily political life as the Greeks experienced it. It does so by showing what a community has to lose by the absence of those structures and to gain by their affirmation, as we see in the contrast between the disorder created by the suitors and Odysseus's restoration of hierarchical and patriarchal order in house and polity. In addition, Odysseus's adventures explore alternatives to "ordinary" (that is, Greek) civilization. Odysseus experiences nature itself as the threatening antithesis to human culture, and he encounters other cultural forms that seem defective or excessive when measured against Ithaca. The richest contrast is provided by the Cyclopes, who lack many of the features of the evolving Greek civilization: houses (they live in caves), agriculture (they are herders), ships for trade and colonization, political integration (their highest political unit is the family), and the key institution of hospitality. (This episode is complex, however, since the Cyclopes enjoy a golden-age existence on which Odysseus intrudes, and Polyphemus has the last word, his curse on Odysseus.) The Laestrygonians are organized as a community and not just by families—they have a ruler and an assembly place—but they share the Cyclopes' unfortunate habit of eating guests. Aeolus, like the Phaeacians, offers Odysseus flawless hospitality, but he lives isolated with his family and marries his daughters to his sons (in contrast to the Greek practice of knitting households together by exchanging women in marriage). Calypso lives in a cave, Circe in a house (she weaves like Penelope), but both live alone. Both are heads of households without husbands, and this, besides the fact that they are sexually threatening to males, makes them "strong" female figures intended to show the need for women's subordination. The Phaeacians, on the other hand, represent an idealized form of "normal" culture but are isolated from other communities and excessively civilized, with no opportunity for heroic achievement. When Odysseus finally is restored to Ithaca, he, and his Greek audience, can appreciate the familiar for having explored alternatives to it in these and many other ways. This self-fashioning by reference to the foreign, which was to have a long history among the Greeks, must have been especially important during this formative period of their culture.

But the *Odyssey* is a much more complex poem than this account suggests, its resolution of issues anything but tidy. One enormous contradiction underlies the final books: Odysseus restores order by killing men from his own community, within his house, and he is prepared to prolong internal warfare by killing the suitors' relatives in the final book. In fact, this struggle recapitulates the Trojan War and resembles the dispute between Achilles and Agamemnon in book 1 of the *Iliad*. In all three cases, men compete for honor over a woman. What is more, Odysseus kills the suitors within his own house, which should be exempt from competition and conflict, as the *Odyssey*'s many scenes of feasting in this same hall show. The *Odyssey* is no more successful than the *Iliad*, then, in resolving the problem of violence. Both poems leave us with questions. How can human aggression be controlled, if not eliminated? Can violence within the community be channeled into safe, perhaps even socially creative, forms? Can it be successfully controlled by being turned outward, against other communities? If so, does that justify the human suffering and waste that external wars cause? And what about the more refined forms of violence at the heart of social hierarchies that create asymmetries of gender and class? Such are the issues raised by the epics amid the formation of the polis, which was to lead, through a long process, to the modern state. Thousands of years later, we cannot claim to have solved them.

NOTE ON THESE TRANSLATIONS

By re-creating the *Iliad* as a war poem in English, Stanley Lombardo has been faithful to what the *Iliad* essentially is. Using a spare language that attempts to reproduce the rhythms and idioms of ordinary spoken English, he gets the essential meanings of the Greek into a flexible line of four or five beats. In this way, he conveys Homer's rapidity and flow, as well as the range of his narrative: the anger of the quarrel between Achilles and Agamemnon (book 1), the excitement and pathos of the battle scenes, the tenderness of Hector's scene with Andromache (book 6), the savagery of Hector's death (book 22), and the sorrowing pity that Achilles and Priam feel in the poem's final book. His language shows a corresponding wide variety of registers, from the fairly standard and perhaps somewhat literary diction at moments of high intensity to informal, and even occasionally colloquial, English in circumstances that seem to call for plain speaking (for example, the speech of soldiers on the battlefield). He takes an equally flexible approach to Homer's highly formulaic language; whereas Homer repeats phrases, lines, and groups of lines with few or no changes, Lombardo usually varies his translations of them to bring out different meanings according to context. But whenever it matters that the same formula is used in different places, the reader can rely on him to convey that faithfully. Lombardo has also found a unique way to convey the effect of one of Homer's most wonderful devices, his many similes—for example, extended comparisons of warriors in battle to animals (e.g., lions) stalking and killing their prey. These similes can do many things, but what they have in common is that they interrupt the action, drawing the reader or listener out of the immediate situation and relating it to typical events in the world beyond the battlefield. Lombardo reproduces this effect of interruption, of fading out from and back into the action of the poem, by printing the similes in italics. In all these ways, Lombardo gives us an *Iliad* that is immediately accessible to modern readers *and* puts them firmly in touch with Homer's world and his poetry.

Robert Fagles's *Odyssey* in its own way creates for English readers the excitement, suspense, and deep emotion of this poem about a homecoming and its difficulties. Fagles translates into an English that is recognizably literary: a little more formal than day-to-day language but always as readable and clear in its meanings. He uses a somewhat longer line than Lombardo (five or six beats), occasionally with longer lines to slow the pace for emphasis or weight, and a shorter line here and there for particular emphasis. Like Lombardo, he varies his translations of formulas according to context. He uses this method especially with epithets and lines introducing speeches; by contrast, there is little variation in his translation of typical scenes (such as feasting, setting sail, going to bed), so that the reader gets a full sense of recurring action. Fagles's style of translating is an excellent match for the depth and sophistication of the *Odyssey's* narrative.

Both of these translations succeed as English poems and as versions of Homer. They superbly meet the challenge of rendering poetry that was orally performed (if not orally composed) into a written medium. To see how good they are, read them— not just silently, but out loud.

PRONOUNCING GLOSSARY

The following list uses common English syllables and stress accents to provide rough equivalents of selected words whose pronunciation may be unfamiliar to the general reader.

Achaeans: *a-kee'-anz / a-kai'-ans*

Achelous: *a-ke-loh'-us*

Achilles: *a-kil'-eez*

Aeantes: *ee-an'-teez / ai-an'-teez*

Aepea: *ee-pee'-a / ai-pay'-a*

Alcinous: *al-sin'-oh-uhs / al-kin'-oh-uhs*

Andromache: *an-dro'-ma-kee*

Atreus: *ay'-tree-uhs / ay'-troos*

Atrides: *a-trai'-deez / ah'-tri-deez*

Caeneus: *seen'-yoos / cai'-nyoos*

Chiron: *kai'-ron / ki'-ron*

Chryseis *krai-se'-is / kri-say'-is*

Chryses: *krai'-seez / Kri'-seez*

Circe: *ser'-see / keer-kay*

Danaans: *da'-nay-unz*

Deiphobus: *dee-i'-foh-bus / day-i'-foh-bus*

Demodocus: *de-mo'-do-kuhs*

Eetion: *ee-e'-tee-on*

Eurystheus: *yoo-ris'-thyoos*

Glaucus: *glow'-kus*

Helios: *hee'-lee-os / hay'-lee-os*

Hephaestus: *he-fess'-tus / hay-fais'-tus*

Hermes: *her'-meez*

Idaeus: *ai-dee'-us / i-dai'us*

Idomeneus: *i-do'-men-yoos*

Laertes: *lay-er'-teez*

Laodice: *lay-o'-di-see / lay-o'-di-kay*

Laothoë: *lay-o'-thoh-ee*

Menelaus: *me-ne-lay'-us / me-ne-lah'-us*

Myrmidons: *mer'-mi-donz*

Mysians: *mee'-shunz / mi'-see-unz*

Nausicaa: *naw-si'-kay-ah / now-si'-ka-ah*

Odysseus: *oh-dis'-yoos*

Oeneus: *een'-yoos / oi'-nyoos*

Orestes: *o-res'-teez*

Panthous: *pan'-tho-us*

Patroclus: *pa-troh'-klus*

Peleus: *peel'-yoos*

Phaeacians: *fee-ay'-shunz / fai-ah'-ki-ans*

Pherae: *fee'-ree / fay'-rai*

Phoebus: *fee'-bus / foy'-bus*

Phthia: *fthai'-uh / fthee'-uh*

Polyphemus: *po-li-fee'-mus*

Pirithous: *pai-ri'-tho-us / pi-ri'-thoh-us*

Priam: *prai'-am*

Sarpedon: *sar-pee'-don*

Scaean: *see'-an / skai'-an*

Scylla: *si'-lah / skil'-ah*

Scyros: *skai'-ros / ski'-ros*   Theseus: *thee'-see-uhs / thee'-syoos*

Smintheus: *smin'-thyoos*   Xanthus: *zan'-thus / ksan'-thus*

Telemachus: *te-le'-ma-kus*

The Iliad[1]

BOOK I

[The Rage of Achilles]

Rage:
        Sing; Goddess,[2] Achilles' rage,
Black and murderous, that cost the Greeks
Incalculable pain, pitched countless souls
Of heroes into Hades' dark,
And left their bodies to rot as feasts   5
For dogs and birds, as Zeus' will was done.
    Begin with the clash between Agamemnon—
The Greek warlord—and godlike Achilles.

    Which of the immortals set these two
At each other's throats?   10
                  Apollo,
Zeus' son and Leto's, offended
By the warlord. Agamemnon had dishonored
Chryses,[3] Apollo's priest, so the god
Struck the Greek camp with plague,   15
And the soldiers were dying of it.
                 Chryses
Had come to the Greek beachhead camp
Hauling a fortune for his daughter's ransom.
Displaying Apollo's sacral ribbons   20
On a golden staff, he made a formal plea
To the entire Greek army, but especially
The commanders, Atreus' two sons:

"Sons of Atreus and Greek heroes all:
May the gods on Olympus grant you plunder   25
Of Priam's city[4] and a safe return home.
But give me my daughter back and accept
This ransom out of respect for Zeus' son,
Lord Apollo, who deals death from afar."

A murmur rippled through the ranks: 30
"Respect the priest and take the ransom."

---

1. Translated by Stanley Lombardo.   2. The Muse, inspiration for epic poetry.   3. Chryses is from the town of Chryse near Troy. The Greeks had captured his daughter when they sacked Thebes (see below) and had given her to Agamemnon as his share of the booty.   4. Troy; Priam is its king. Olympus is the mountain in northern Greece that was supposed to be the home of the gods.

But Agamemnon was not pleased
And dismissed Chryses with a rough speech:

"Don't let me ever catch you, old man, by these ships again,
Skulking around now or sneaking back later.   35
The god's staff and ribbons won't save you next time.
The girl is mine, and she'll be an old woman in Argos[5]
Before I let her go, working the loom in my house
And coming to my bed, far from her homeland.
Now clear out of here before you make me angry!"   40

The old man was afraid and did as he was told.
He walked in silence along the whispering surf line,
And when he had gone some distance the priest
Prayed to Lord Apollo, son of silken-haired Leto:

"Hear me, Silverbow, Protector of Chryse,   45
Lord of Holy Cilla, Master of Tenedos,[6]
And Sminthian[7] God of Plague!
If ever I've built a temple that pleased you
Or burnt fat thighbones of bulls and goats[8]—
    Grant me this prayer: 50
Let the Danaans[9] pay for my tears with your arrows!"

Apollo heard his prayer and descended Olympus' crags
Pulsing with fury, bow slung over one shoulder,
The arrows rattling in their case on his back
As the angry god moved like night down the mountain.   55

He settled near the ships and let loose an arrow.
Reverberation from his silver bow hung in the air.
He picked off the pack animals first, and the lean hounds,
But then aimed his needle-tipped arrows at the men
And shot until the death-fires crowded the beach.   60

   Nine days the god's arrows rained death on the camp.
On the tenth day Achilles called an assembly.
Hera,[1] the white-armed goddess, planted the thought in him
Because she cared for the Greeks and it pained her
To see them dying. When the troops had all mustered,   65
Up stood the great runner Achilles, and said:

"Well, Agamemnon, it looks as if we'd better give up
And sail home—assuming any of us are left alive—
If we have to fight both the war and this plague.
But why not consult some prophet or priest   70
Or a dream interpreter, since dreams too come from Zeus,

---

5. Agamemnon's home in the northeastern Peloponnesus, the southern part of mainland Greece.   6. An
island off the Trojan coast. Like Chryse, Cilla is a town near Troy.   7. A cult epithet of Apollo, probably
a reference to his role as the destroyer of field mice (the Greek *sminthos* means "mouse").   8. In sacrifice
to Apollo.   9. The Greeks. Homer also calls them Achaeans and Argives.   1. Sister and wife of Zeus;
she was hostile to the Trojans and therefore favored the Greeks.

Who could tell us why Apollo is so angry,
If it's for a vow or a sacrifice he holds us at fault.
Maybe he'd be willing to lift this plague from us
If he savored the smoke from lambs and prime goats."   75

Achilles had his say and sat down. Then up rose
Calchas, son of Thestor, bird-reader supreme,
Who knew what is, what will be, and what has been.
He had guided the Greek ships to Troy
Through the prophetic power Apollo   80
Had given him, and he spoke out now:

"Achilles, beloved of Zeus, you want me to tell you
About the rage of Lord Apollo, the Arch-Destroyer.
And I will tell you. But you have to promise me and swear
You will support me and protect me in word and deed.   85
I have a feeling I might offend a person of some authority
Among the Greeks, and you know how it is when a king
Is angry with an underling. He might swallow his temper
For a day, but he holds it in his heart until later
And it all comes out. Will you guarantee my security?"   90

Achilles, the great runner, responded:

"Don't worry. Prophesy to the best of your knowledge.
I swear by Apollo, to whom you pray when you reveal
The gods' secrets to the Greeks, Calchas, that while I live
And look upon this earth, no one will lay a hand   95
On you here beside these hollow ships, no, not even
Agamemnon, who boasts he is the best of the Achaeans."

And Calchas, the perfect prophet, taking courage:

"The god finds no fault with vow or sacrifice.
It is for his priest, whom Agamemnon dishonored   100
And would not allow to ransom his daughter,
That Apollo deals and will deal death from afar.
He will not lift this foul plague from the Greeks
Until we return the dancing-eyed girl to her father
Unransomed, unbought, and make formal sacrifice   105
On Chryse. Only then might we appease the god."

He finished speaking and sat down. Then up rose
Atreus' son, the warlord Agamemnon,
Furious, anger like twin black thunderheads seething
In his lungs, and his eyes flickered with fire   110
As he looked Calchas up and down, and said:

                    "You damn soothsayer!
You've never given me a good omen yet.
You take some kind of perverse pleasure in prophesying
Doom, don't you? Not a single favorable omen ever!   115

Nothing good ever happens! And now you stand here
Uttering oracles before the Greeks, telling us
That your great ballistic god is giving us all this trouble
Because I was unwilling to accept the ransom
For Chryses' daughter but preferred instead to keep her   120
In my tent! And why shouldn't I? I like her better than
My wife Clytemnestra. She's no worse than her
When it comes to looks, body, mind, or ability.
Still, I'll give her back, if that's what's best.
I don't want to see the army destroyed like this.   125
But I want another prize ready for me right away.
I'm not going to be the only Greek without a prize,
It wouldn't be right. And you all see where mine is going."

And Achilles, strong, swift, and godlike:

"And where do you think, son of Atreus,   130
You greedy glory-hound, the magnanimous Greeks
Are going to get another prize for you?
Do you think we have some kind of stockpile in reserve?
Every town in the area has been sacked and the stuff all divided.
You want the men to count it all back and redistribute it?   135
All right, you give the girl back to the god. The army
Will repay you three and four times over—when and if
Zeus allows us to rip Troy down to its foundations."

The warlord Agamemnon responded:

"You may be a good man in a fight, Achilles,   140
And look like a god, but don't try to put one over on me—
It won't work. So while you have your prize,
You want me to sit tight and do without?
Give the girl back, just like that? Now maybe
If the army, in a generous spirit, voted me   145
Some suitable prize of their own choice, something fair—
But if it doesn't, I'll just go take something myself,
Your prize perhaps, or Ajax's, or Odysseus',[2]
And whoever she belongs to, it'll stick in his throat.

But we can think about that later.   150
                          Right now we launch
A black ship on the bright salt water, get a crew aboard,
Load on a hundred bulls, and have Chryseis[3] board her too,
My girl with her lovely cheeks. And we'll want a good man
For captain, Ajax or Idomeneus[4] or godlike Odysseus—   155
Or maybe you, son of Peleus, our most formidable hero—
To offer sacrifice and appease the Arch-Destroyer for us."

Achilles looked him up and down and said:

---

2. Ajax, son of Telamon, was the bravest of the Greeks after Achilles, Odysseus the most crafty of the
Greeks.   3. Daughter of Chryses.   4. King of Crete and a prominent leader on the Greek side.

"You shameless, profiteering excuse for a commander!
How are you going to get any Greek warrior   160
To follow you into battle again? You know,
I don't have any quarrel with the Trojans,
They didn't do anything to *me* to make me
Come over here and fight, didn't run off *my* cattle or horses
Or ruin *my* farmland back home in Phthia,[5] not with all   165
The shadowy mountains and moaning seas between.
It's for *you*, dogface, for your precious pleasure—
And Menelaus'[6] honor—that we came here,
A fact you don't have the decency even to mention!
And now you're threatening to take away the prize   170
That I sweated for and the Greeks gave me.
I never get a prize equal to yours when the army
Captures one of the Trojan strongholds.
No, I do all the dirty work with my own hands,
And when the battle's over and we divide the loot   175
You get the lion's share and I go back to the ships
With some pitiful little thing, so worn out from fighting
I don't have the strength left even to complain.
Well, I'm going back to Phthia now. Far better
To head home with my curved ships than stay here,   180
Unhonored myself and piling up a fortune for you."

The warlord Agamemnon responded:

"Go ahead and desert, if that's what you want!
I'm not going to beg you to stay. There are plenty of others
Who will honor me, not least of all Zeus the Counselor.   185
To me, you're the most hateful king under heaven,
A born troublemaker. You actually *like* fighting and war.
If you're all that strong, it's just a gift from some god.
So why don't you go home with your ships and lord it over
Your precious Myrmidons.[7] I couldn't care less about you   190
Or your famous temper. But I'll tell you this:
Since Phoebus Apollo is taking away my Chryseis,
Whom I'm sending back aboard ship with my friends,
I'm coming to your hut and taking Briseis,[8]
Your own beautiful prize, so that you will see just how much   195
Stronger I am than you, and the next person will wince
At the thought of opposing me as an equal."

Achilles' chest was a rough knot of pain
Twisting around his heart: should he
Draw the sharp sword that hung by his thigh,   200
Scatter the ranks and gut Agamemnon,
Or control his temper, repress his rage?
He was mulling it over, inching the great sword
From its sheath, when out of the blue

---

5. Achilles' home in northern Greece.   **6.** Agamemnon's brother. The aim of the expedition against Troy was to recover his wife, Helen, who had run off with Paris, a son of Priam.   **7.** The contingent led by Achilles.   **8.** A captive woman who had been awarded to Achilles.

Athena[9] came, sent by the white-armed goddess   205
Hera, who loved and watched over both men.
She stood behind Achilles and grabbed his sandy hair,
Visible only to him: not another soul saw her.
Awestruck, Achilles turned around, recognizing
Pallas Athena at once—it was her eyes—   210
And words flew from his mouth like winging birds:

"Daughter of Zeus! Why have you come here?
To see Agamemnon's arrogance, no doubt.
I'll tell you where I place my bets, Goddess:
Sudden death for this outrageous behavior."   215

Athena's eyes glared through the sea's salt haze.

"I came to see if I could check this temper of yours,
Sent from heaven by the white-armed goddess
Hera, who loves and watches over both of you men.
Now come on, drop this quarrel, don't draw your sword.   220
Tell him off instead. And I'll tell you,
Achilles, how things will be: You're going to get
Three times as many magnificent gifts
Because of his arrogance. Just listen to us and be patient."

Achilles, the great runner, responded: 225

"When you two speak, Goddess, a man has to listen
No matter how angry. It's better that way.
Obey the gods and they hear you when you pray."

With that he ground his heavy hand
Onto the silver hilt and pushed the great sword   230
Back into its sheath. Athena's speech
Had been well-timed. She was on her way
To Olympus by now, to the halls of Zeus
And the other immortals, while Achilles
Tore into Agamemnon again: 235

                              "You bloated drunk,
With a dog's eyes and a rabbit's heart!
You've never had the guts to buckle on armor in battle
Or come out with the best fighting Greeks
On any campaign! Afraid to look Death in the eye,   240
Agamemnon? It's far more profitable
To hang back in the army's rear—isn't it?—
Confiscating prizes from any Greek who talks back
And bleeding your people dry. There's not a real man
Under your command, or this latest atrocity   245
Would be your last, son of Atreus.

---

9. A goddess, daughter of Zeus, and a patron of human ingenuity and resourcefulness, whether exemplified
by handicrafts (such as carpentry or weaving) or cunning in dealing with others. One of her epithets is
Pallas. Like Hera, she sided with the Greeks in the war.

Now get this straight. I swear a formal oath:
   By this scepter,[1] which will never sprout leaf
Or branch again since it was cut from its stock
In the mountains, which will bloom no more   250
Now that bronze has pared off leaf and bark,
And which now the sons of the Greeks hold in their hands
At council, upholding Zeus' laws—
                 By this scepter I swear:
When every last Greek desperately misses Achilles,   255
Your remorse won't do any good then,
When Hector[2] the man-killer swats you down like flies.
And you will eat your heart out
Because you failed to honor the best Greek of all."

Those were his words, and he slammed the scepter,   260
Studded with gold, to the ground and sat down.

Opposite him, Agamemnon fumed.
              Then Nestor
Stood up, sweet-worded Nestor, the orator from Pylos[3]
With a voice high-toned and liquid as honey.   265
He had seen two generations of men pass away
In sandy Pylos and was now king in the third.
He was full of good will in the speech he made:

"It's a sad day for Greece, a sad day.
Priam and Priam's sons would be happy indeed,   270
And the rest of the Trojans too, glad in their hearts,
If they learned all this about you two fighting,
Our two best men in council and in battle.
Now you listen to me, both of you. You are both
Younger than I am, and I've associated with men   275
Better than you, and they didn't treat me lightly.
I've never seen men like those, and never will,
The likes of Peirithous and Dryas, a shepherd to his people,
Caineus and Exadius and godlike Polyphemus,
And Aegeus' son, Theseus,[4] who could have passed for a god,   280
The strongest men who ever lived on earth, the strongest,
And they fought with the strongest, with wild things
From the mountains, and beat the daylights out of them.
I was their companion, although I came from Pylos,
From the ends of the earth—they sent for me themselves.   285
And I held my own fighting with them. You couldn't find
A mortal on earth who could fight with them now.
And when I talked in council, they took my advice.
So should you two now: taking advice is a good thing.
   Agamemnon, for all your nobility, don't take his girl.   290

1. A wooden staff that symbolized authority. It was handed by a herald to whichever leader rose to speak in an assembly as a sign of his authority to speak.   2. Son of Priam; he was the foremost warrior among the Trojans.   3. A territory on the western shore of the Peloponnesus.   4. Heroes of an earlier generation. Except for the Athenian Theseus, these are the Lapiths from Thessaly in northern Greece. At the wedding of Peirithous, the mountain-dwelling centaurs (half human, half horse) got drunk and tried to rape the women who were present. The Lapiths killed them after a fierce fight.

Leave her be: the army originally gave her to him as a prize.
Nor should you, son of Peleus, want to lock horns with a king.
A scepter-holding king has honor beyond the rest of men,
Power and glory given by Zeus himself.
You are stronger, and it is a goddess[5] who bore you.   295
But he is more powerful, since he rules over more.
Son of Atreus, cease your anger. And I appeal
Personally to Achilles to control his temper, since he is,
For all Greeks, a mighty bulwark in this evil war."

And Agamemnon, the warlord: 300

"Yes, old man, everything you've said is absolutely right.
But this man wants to be ahead of everyone else,
He wants to rule everyone, give orders to everyone,
Lord it over everyone, and he's not going to get away with it.
If the gods eternal made him a spearman, does that mean   305
They gave him permission to be insolent as well?"

And Achilles, breaking in on him:

"Ha, and think of the names people would call me
If I bowed and scraped every time you opened your mouth.
Try that on somebody else, but not on me.   310
I'll tell you this, and you can stick it in your gut:
I'm not going to put up a fight on account of the girl.
You, all of you, gave her and you can all take her back.
But anything else of mine in my black sailing ship
You keep your goddamn hands off, you hear?   315
Try it. Let everybody here see how fast
Your black blood boils up around my spear."

    So it was a stand-off, their battle of words,
And the assembly beside the Greek ships dissolved.
Achilles went back to the huts by his ships   320
With Patroclus[6] and his men. Agamemnon had a fast ship
Hauled down to the sea, picked twenty oarsmen,
Loaded on a hundred bulls due to the god, and had Chryses' daughter,
His fair-cheeked girl, go aboard also. Odysseus captained,
And when they were all on board, the ship headed out to sea.   325

Onshore, Agamemnon ordered a purification.
The troops scrubbed down and poured the filth
Into the sea. Then they sacrificed to Apollo
Oxen and goats by the hundreds on the barren shore.
The smoky savor swirled up to the sky.   330

That was the order of the day. But Agamemnon
Did not forget his spiteful threat against Achilles.

---

5. The sea nymph Thetis, who was married to the mortal Peleus (Achilles' father). She later left him and
went to live with her father, Nereus, in the depths of the Aegean Sea.   6. Achilles' closest friend.

He summoned Talthybius and Eurybates,
Faithful retainers who served as his heralds:

"Go to the hut of Achilles, son of Peleus;   335
Bring back the girl, fair-cheeked Briseis.
If he won't give her up, I'll come myself
With my men and take her—and freeze his heart cold."

It was not the sort of mission a herald would relish.
The pair trailed along the barren seashore   340
Until they came to the Myrmidons' ships and encampment.
They found Achilles sitting outside his hut
Beside his black ship. He was not glad to see them.
They stood respectfully silent, in awe of this king,
And it was Achilles who was moved to address them first: 345

"Welcome, heralds, the gods' messengers and men's.
Come closer. You're not to blame, Agamemnon is,
Who sent you here for the girl, Briseis.

                             Patroclus,
Bring the girl out and give her to these gentlemen.   350
You two are witnesses before the blessed gods,
Before mortal men and that hard-hearted king,
If ever I'm needed to protect the others
From being hacked to bits. His mind is murky with anger,
And he doesn't have the sense to look ahead and behind   355
To see how the Greeks might defend their ships."

Thus Achilles.
              Patroclus obeyed his beloved friend
And brought Briseis, cheeks flushed, out of the tent
And gave her to the heralds, who led her away.   360
She went unwillingly.

                    Then Achilles, in tears,
Withdrew from his friends and sat down far away
On the foaming white seashore, staring out
At the endless sea. Stretching out his hands,   365
He prayed over and over to his beloved mother:

"Mother, since you bore me for a short life only,
Olympian Zeus was supposed to grant me honor.
Well, he hasn't given me any at all. Agamemnon
Has taken away my prize and dishonored me."   370

His voice, choked with tears, was heard by his mother
As she sat in the sea-depths beside her old father.
She rose up from the white-capped sea like a mist,
And settling herself beside her weeping child
She stroked him with her hand and talked to him: 375

"Why are you crying, son? What's wrong?
Don't keep it inside. Tell me so we'll both know."

And Achilles, with a deep groan:

"You already know. Why do I have to tell you?
We went after Thebes, Eëtion's[7] sacred town,   380
Sacked it and brought the plunder back here.
The army divided everything up and chose
For Agamemnon fair-cheeked Chryseis.
Then her father, Chryses, a priest of Apollo,
Came to our army's ships on the beachhead,   385
Hauling a fortune for his daughter's ransom.
He displayed Apollo's sacral ribbons
On a golden staff and made a formal plea
To the entire Greek army, but especially
The commanders, Atreus' two sons.   390
You could hear the troops murmuring,
'Respect the priest and take the ransom.'
But Agamemnon wouldn't hear of it
And dismissed Chryses with a rough speech.
The old man went back angry, and Apollo   395
Heard his beloved priest's prayer.
He hit the Greeks hard, and the troops
Were falling over dead, the god's arrows
Raining down all through the Greek camp.
A prophet told us the Arch-Destroyer's will,   400
And I demanded the god be appeased.
Agamemnon got angry, stood up
And threatened me, and made good his threat.
The high command sent the girl on a fast ship
Back to Chryse with gifts for Apollo,   405
And heralds led away my girl, Briseis,
Whom the army had given to me.
Now you have to help me, if you can.
    Go to Olympus
And call in the debt that Zeus owes you.   410
I remember often hearing you tell
In my father's house how you alone managed,
Of all the immortals, to save Zeus' neck
When the other Olympians wanted to bind him—
Hera and Poseidon[8] and Pallas Athena.   415
You came and loosened him from his chains,
And you lured to Olympus' summit the giant
With a hundred hands whom the gods call
Briareus but men call Aegaeon, stronger
Even than his own father Uranus,[9] and he   420
Sat hulking in front of cloud-black Zeus,
Proud of his prowess, and scared all the gods
Who were trying to put the son of Cronus in chains.
    Remind Zeus of this, sit holding his knees,

---

7. King of the Cilicians in Asia Minor and father of Hector's wife, Andromache. *Thebes* (or Thebe): the Cilicians' capital city, not the Greek or Egyptian city of the same name.   8. Brother of Zeus and god of the sea.   9. The Sky, husband of Earth and the first divine ruler. He was overthrown by his son Cronus, who in turn was overthrown by his son Zeus.

See if he is willing to help the Trojans   425
Hem the Greeks in between the fleet and the sea.
Once they start being killed, the Greeks may
Appreciate Agamemnon for what he is,
And the wide-ruling son of Atreus will see
What a fool he's been because he did not honor   430
The best of all the fighting Achaeans."

And Thetis, now weeping herself:

   "O my poor child. I bore you for sorrow,
Nursed you for grief. Why? You should be
Spending your time here by your ships   435
Happily and untroubled by tears,
Since life is short for you, all too brief.
Now you're destined for both an early death
And misery beyond compare. It was for this
I gave birth to you in your father's palace   440
Under an evil star.
                    I'll go to snow-bound Olympus
And tell all this to the Lord of Lightning.
I hope he listens. You stay here, though,
Beside your ships and let the Greeks feel   445
Your spite; withdraw completely from the war.
Zeus left yesterday for the River Ocean
On his way to a feast with the Ethiopians.[1]
All the gods went with him. He'll return
To Olympus twelve days from now,   450
And I'll go then to his bronze threshold
And plead with him. I think I'll persuade him."

And she left him there, angry and heartsick
At being forced to give up the silken-waisted girl.

   Meanwhile, Odysseus was putting in   455
At Chryse with his sacred cargo on board.
When they were well within the deepwater harbor
They furled the sail and stowed it in the ship's hold,
Slackened the forestays and lowered the mast,
Working quickly, then rowed her to a mooring, where   460
They dropped anchor and made the stern cables fast.
The crew disembarked on the seabeach
And unloaded the bulls for Apollo the Archer.
Then Chryses' daughter stepped off the seagoing vessel,
And Odysseus led her to an altar   465
And placed her in her father's hands, saying:

"Chryses, King Agamemnon has sent me here
To return your child and offer to Phoebus

---

1. A people believed to live at the extreme edges of the world. Ocean was thought of as a river that encircled the earth.

Formal sacrifice on behalf of the Greeks.
So may we appease Lord Apollo, and may he   470
Lift the afflictions he has sent upon us."

Chryses received his daughter tenderly.

Moving quickly, they lined the hundred oxen
Round the massive altar, a glorious offering,
Washed their hands and sprinkled on the victims   475
Sacrificial barley. On behalf of the Greeks
Chryses lifted his hands and prayed aloud:

"Hear me, Silverbow, Protector of Chryse,
Lord of Holy Cilla, Master of Tenedos,
As once before you heard my prayer,   480
Did me honor, and smote the Greeks mightily,
So now also grant me this prayer:
                        Lift the plague
From the Greeks and save them from death."

Thus the old priest, and Apollo heard him.   485

After the prayers and the strewing of barley
They slaughtered and flayed the oxen,
Jointed the thighbones and wrapped them
In a layer of fat with cuts of meat on top.
The old man roasted them over charcoal   490
And doused them with wine. Younger men
Stood by with five-tined forks in their hands.
When the thigh pieces were charred and they had
Tasted the tripe, they cut the rest into strips,
Skewered it on spits and roasted it skillfully.   495
When they were done and the feast was ready,
Feast they did, and no one lacked an equal share.
When they had all had enough to eat and drink,
The young men topped off mixing bowls with wine
And served it in goblets to all the guests.   500
All day long these young Greeks propitiated
The god with dancing, singing to Apollo
A paean[2] as they danced, and the god was pleased.
When the sun went down and darkness came on,
They went to sleep by the ship's stern-cables.   505

Dawn came early, a palmetto of rose,
Time to make sail for the wide beachhead camp.
They set up mast and spread the white canvas,
And the following wind, sent by Apollo,
Boomed in the mainsail. An indigo wave   510
Hissed off the bow as the ship surged on,
Leaving a wake as she held on course through the billows.

---

2. A song of praise to Apollo.

When they reached the beachhead they hauled the black ship
High on the sand and jammed in the long chocks;
Then the crew scattered to their own huts and ships.   515

All this time Achilles, the son of Peleus in the line of Zeus,[3]
Nursed his anger, the great runner idle by his fleet's fast hulls.
He was not to be seen in council, that arena for glory,
Nor in combat. He sat tight in camp consumed with grief,
His great heart yearning for the battle cry and war.   520

        Twelve days went by. Dawn.
The gods returned to Olympus,
Zeus at their head.
                    Thetis did not forget
Her son's requests. She rose from the sea   525
And up through the air to the great sky
And found Cronus' wide-seeing son
Sitting in isolation on the highest peak
Of the rugged Olympic massif.
She settled beside him, and touched his knees   530
With her left hand, his beard with her right,[4]
And made her plea to the Lord of Sky:

"Father Zeus, if I have ever helped you
In word or deed among the immortals,
    Grant me this prayer: 535
Honor my son, doomed to die young
And yet dishonored by King Agamemnon,
Who stole his prize, a personal affront.
Do justice by him, Lord of Olympus.
Give the Trojans the upper hand until the Greeks   540
Grant my son the honor he deserves."

Zeus made no reply but sat a long time
In silence, clouds scudding around him.
Thetis held fast to his knees and asked again:

"Give me a clear yes or no. Either nod in assent   545
Or refuse me. Why should you care if I know
How negligible a goddess I am in your eyes."

This provoked a troubled, gloomy response:

"This is disastrous. You're going to force me
Into conflict with Hera. I can just hear her now,   550
Cursing me and bawling me out. As it is,
She already accuses me of favoring the Trojans.
Please go back the way you came. Maybe
Hera won't notice. I'll take care of this.

---

3. Peleus was the son of Aeacus, son of Zeus.   4. She takes on the posture of the suppliant, which
physically emphasizes the desperation and urgency of her request. Zeus was, above all other gods, the
protector of suppliants.

And so you can have some peace of mind,   555
I'll say yes to you by nodding my head,
The ultimate pledge. Unambiguous,
Irreversible, and absolutely fulfilled,
Whatever I say yes to with a nod of my head."

And the Son of Cronus nodded. Black brows   560
Lowered, a glory of hair cascaded down from the Lord's
Immortal head, and the holy mountain trembled.

    Their conference over, the two parted. The goddess
Dove into the deep sea from Olympus' snow-glare
And Zeus went to his home. The gods all   565
Rose from their seats at their father's entrance. Not one
Dared watch him enter without standing to greet him.
And so the god entered and took his high seat.
                                        But Hera
Had noticed his private conversation with Thetis,   570
The silver-footed daughter of the Old Man of the Sea,
And flew at him with cutting words:

"Who was that you were scheming with just now?
You just love devising secret plots behind my back,
Don't you? You can't bear to tell me what you're thinking,   575
Or you don't dare. Never have and never will."

The Father of Gods and Men answered:

"Hera, don't hope to know all my secret thoughts.
It would strain your mind even though you are my wife.
What it is proper to hear, no one, human or divine,   580
Will hear before you. But what I wish to conceive
Apart from the other gods, don't pry into that."

And Lady Hera, with her oxen eyes wide:

"Oh my. The awesome son of Cronus has spoken.
Pry? You know that I never pry. And you always   585
Cheerfully volunteer—whatever information you please.
It's just that I have this feeling that somehow
The silver-footed daughter of the Old Man of the Sea
May have won you over. She *was* sitting beside you
Up there in the mists, and she did touch your knees.   590
And I'm pretty sure that you agreed to honor Achilles
And destroy Greeks by the thousands beside their ships."

And Zeus, the master of cloud and storm:

"You witch! Your intuitions are always right.
But what does it get you? Nothing, except that   595
I like you less than ever. And so you're worse off.
If it's as you think it is, it's my business, not yours.

So sit down and shut up and do as I say.
You see these hands? All the gods on Olympus
Won't be able to help you if I ever lay them on you."   600

Hera lost her nerve when she heard this.
She sat down in silence, fear cramping her heart,
And gloom settled over the gods in Zeus' hall.
Hephaestus,[5] the master artisan, broke the silence,
Out of concern for his ivory-armed mother: 605

"This is terrible; it's going to ruin us all.
If you two quarrel like this over mortals
It's bound to affect us gods. There'll be no more
Pleasure in our feasts if we let things turn ugly.
Mother, please, I don't have to tell you,   610
You have to be pleasant to our father Zeus
So he won't be angry and ruin our feast.
If the Lord of Lightning want to blast us from our seats,
He can—that's how much stronger he is.
So apologize to him with silken-soft words,   615
And the Olympian in turn will be gracious to us."

He whisked up a two-handled cup, offered it
To his dear mother, and said to her:

"I know it's hard, mother, but you have to endure it.
I don't want to see you getting beat up, and me   620
Unable to help you. The Olympian can be rough.
Once before when I tried to rescue you
He flipped me by my foot off our balcony.
I fell all day and came down when the sun did
On the island of Lemnos[6] scarcely alive.   625
The Sintians had to nurse me back to health."

By the time he finished, the ivory-armed goddess
Was smiling at her son. She accepted the cup from him.
Then the lame god turned serving boy, siphoning nectar[7]
From the mixing bowl and pouring the sweet liquor   630
For all of the gods, who couldn't stop laughing
At the sight of Hephaestus hustling through the halls.

And so all day long until the sun went down
They feasted to their hearts' content,
Apollo playing beautiful melodies on the lyre,   635
The Muses singing responsively in lovely voices.
And when the last gleams of sunset had faded,
They turned in for the night, each to a house
Built by Hephaestus, the renowned master craftsman,
The burly blacksmith with the soul of an artist.   640

---

5. The lame god of fire and the patron of craftspeople, especially metalworkers.   6. An island in the
Aegean Sea, inhabited by the Sintians.   7. The drink of the gods.

And the Lord of Lightning, Olympian Zeus, went to his bed,
The bed he always slept in when sweet sleep overcame him.
He climbed in and slept, next to golden-throned Hera.

[The Greeks, in spite of Achilles' withdrawal, continued to fight. They did not suffer
immoderately from Achilles' absence; on the contrary, they pressed the Trojans so
hard that Hector, the Trojan leader, after rallying his men, returned to the city to
urge the Trojans to offer special prayers and sacrifices to the gods.]

FROM BOOK VI

[Hector Returns to Troy]

And Hector left, helmet collecting light
Above the black-hide shield whose rim tapped
His ankles and neck with each step he took.

Then Glaucus, son of Hippolochus,   120
Met Diomedes[8] in no-man's-land.
Both were eager to fight, but first Tydeus' son
Made his voice heard above the battle noise:

"And which mortal hero are you? I've never seen you
Out here before on the fields of glory,   125
And now here you are ahead of everyone,
Ready to face my spear. Pretty bold.
I feel sorry for your parents. Of course,
You may be an immortal, down from heaven.
Far be it from me to fight an immortal god.   130
Not even mighty Lycurgus[9] lived long
After he tangled with the immortals,
Driving the nurses of Dionysus[1]
Down over the Mountain of Nysa
And making them drop their wands   135
As he beat them with an ox-goad. Dionysus
Was terrified and plunged into the sea,
Where Thetis received him into her bosom,
Trembling with fear at the human's threats.
Then the gods, who live easy, grew angry   140
With Lycurgus, and the Son of Cronus
Made him go blind, and he did not live long,
Hated as he was by the immortal gods.
No, I wouldn't want to fight an immortal.
But if you are human, and shed blood,   145
Step right up for a quick end to your life."

And Glaucus, Hippolochus' son:

"Great son of Tydeus, why ask about my lineage?
Human generations are like leaves in their seasons.

8. One of the foremost Greek leaders, son of Tydeus. *Glaucus*: a Trojan ally, from Lycia in Asia Minor.
9. King of Thrace, a half-wild region along the north shore of the Aegean Sea.   1. God of the vine.

The wind blows them to the ground, but the tree 150
Sprouts new ones when spring comes again.
Men too. Their generations come and go.
But if you really do want to hear my story,
You're welcome to listen. Many men know it.
  Ephyra,[2] in the heart of Argive horse country, 155
Was home to Sisyphus, the shrewdest man alive,
Sisyphus son of Aeolus. He had a son, Glaucus,
Who was the father of faultless Bellerophon,
A man of grace and courage by gift of the gods.
But Proetus, whom Zeus had made king of Argos, 160
Came to hate Bellerophon
And drove him out. It happened this way.
Proetus' wife, the beautiful Anteia,
Was madly in love with Bellerophon
And wanted to have him in her bed. 165
But she couldn't persuade him, not at all,
Because he was so virtuous and wise.
So she made up lies and spoke to the king:
'Either die yourself, Proetus, or kill Bellerophon.
He wanted to sleep with me against my will.' 170
The king was furious when he heard her say this.
He did not kill him—he had scruples about that—
But he sent him to Lycia with a folding tablet
On which he had scratched many evil signs, 175
And told him to give it to Anteia's father,
To get him killed. So off he went to Lycia,
With an immortal escort, and when he reached
The river Xanthus,[3] the king there welcomed him
And honored him with entertainment
For nine solid days, killing an ox each day. 180
But when the tenth dawn spread her rosy light,
He questioned him and asked to see the tokens
He brought from Proetus, his daughter's husband.
And when he saw the evil tokens from Proetus,
He ordered him, first, to kill the Chimaera, 185
A raging monster, divine, inhuman—
A lion in the front, a serpent in the rear,
In the middle a goat—and breathing fire.
Bellerophon killed her, trusting signs from the gods.
Next he had to fight the glorious Solymi, 190
The hardest battle, he said, he ever fought,
And, third, the Amazons, women the peers of men.
As he journeyed back the king wove another wile.
He chose the best men in all wide Lycia
And laid an ambush. Not one returned home; 195
Blameless Bellerophon killed them all.
When the king realized his guest had divine blood,
He kept him there and gave him his daughter
And half of all his royal honor. Moreover,

2. An old name for Corinth, a city in the northeast Peloponnesus. 3. A river in Lycia.

The Lycians cut out for him a superb   200
Tract of land, plow-land and orchard.
His wife, the princess, bore him three children,
Isander, Hippolochus, and Laodameia.
Zeus in his wisdom slept with Laodameia,
And she bore him the godlike warrior Sarpedon.   205
But even Bellerophon lost the gods' favor
And went wandering alone over the Aleian plain.
His son Isander was slain by Ares
As he fought against the glorious Solymi,
And his daughter was killed by Artemis.   210
Of the golden reins. But Hippolochus
Bore me, and I am proud he is my father.
He sent me to Troy with strict instructions
To be the best ever, better than all the rest,
And not to bring shame on the race of my fathers,   215
The noblest men in Ephyra and Lycia.
This, I am proud to say, is my lineage."

Diomedes grinned when he heard all this.
He planted his spear in the bounteous earth
And spoke gently to the Lycian prince: 220

"We have old ties of hospitality!
My grandfather Oeneus long ago
Entertained Bellerophon in his halls
For twenty days, and they gave each other
Gifts of friendship.[4] Oeneus gave   225
A belt bright with scarlet, and Bellerophon
A golden cup, which I left at home.
I don't remember my father Tydeus,
Since I was very small when he left for Thebes
In the war that killed so many Achaeans.[5]   230
But that makes me your friend and you my guest
If ever you come to Argos, as you are my friend
And I your guest whenever I travel to Lycia.
So we can't cross spears with each other
Even in the thick of battle. There are enough   235
Trojans and allies for me to kill, whomever
A god gives me and I can run down myself.
And enough Greeks for you to kill as you can.
And let's exchange armor, so everyone will know
That we are friends from our fathers' days."   240

With this said, they vaulted from their chariots,
Clasped hands, and pledged their friendship.
But Zeus took away Glaucus' good sense,
For he exchanged his golden armor for bronze,
The worth of one hundred oxen for nine.   245

4. It was customary for guest-friends to exchange gifts.   5. Tydeus was one of the seven heroes who attacked Thebes. They were led by Oedipus's son Polynices, who was attempting to dislodge his brother, Eteocles, from the kingship. The brothers killed each other, and the rest of the seven also perished. Diomedes, along with the sons of the other champions, later sacked Thebes.

When Hector reached the oak tree by the Western Gate,
Trojan wives and daughters ran up to him,
Asking about their children, their brothers,
Their kinsmen, their husbands. He told them all,
Each woman in turn, to pray to the gods. 250
Sorrow clung to their heads like mist.

Then he came to Priam's palace, a beautiful
Building made of polished stone with a central courtyard
Flanked by porticoes, upon which opened fifty
Adjoining rooms, where Priam's sons 255
Slept with their wives. Across the court
A suite of twelve more bedrooms housed
His modest daughters and their husbands.
It was here that Hector's mother[6] met him,
A gracious woman, with Laodice, 260
Her most beautiful daughter, in tow.
Hecuba took his hand in hers and said:

"Hector, my son, why have you left the war
And come here? Are those abominable Greeks
Wearing you down in the fighting outside, 265
And does your heart lead you to our acropolis
To stretch your hands upward to Zeus?
But stay here while I get you
Some honey-sweet wine, so you can pour a libation
To Father Zeus first and the other immortals, 270
Then enjoy some yourself, if you will drink.
Wine greatly bolsters a weary man's spirits,
And you are weary from defending your kinsmen."

Sunlight shimmered on great Hector's helmet.

"Mother, don't offer me any wine. 275
It would drain the power out of my limbs.
I have too much reverence to pour a libation
With unwashed hands to Zeus almighty,
Or to pray to Cronion[7] in the black cloudbanks
Spattered with blood and the filth of battle. 280
But you must go to the War Goddess's[8] temple
To make sacrifice with a band of old women.
Choose the largest and loveliest robe in the house,
The one that is dearest of all to you,
And place it on the knees of braided Athena. 285
And promise twelve heifers to her in her temple,
Unblemished yearlings, if she will pity
The town of Troy, its wives, and its children,
And if she will keep from holy Ilion[9]
Wild Diomedes, who's raging with his spear. 290
Go then to the temple of Athena the War Goddess,

6. Hecuba.   7. The son of Cronus (i.e., Zeus).   8. Athena.   9. Another name for Troy.

And I will go over to summon Paris,[1]
If he will listen to what I have to say.
I wish the earth would gape open beneath him.
Olympian Zeus has bred him as a curse   295
To Troy, to Priam, and all Priam's children.
If I could see him dead and gone to Hades,
I think my heart might be eased of its sorrow."

Thus Hector. Hecuba went to the great hall
And called to her handmaidens, and they   300
Gathered together the city's old women.
She went herself to a fragrant storeroom
Which held her robes, the exquisite work
Of Sidonian[2] women whom godlike Paris
Brought from Phoenicia when he sailed the sea   305
On the voyage he made for high-born Helen.
Hecuba chose the robe that lay at the bottom,
The most beautiful of all, woven of starlight,
And bore it away as a gift for Athena.
A stream of old women followed behind.   310

They came to the temple of Pallas Athena
On the city's high rock, and the doors were opened
By fair-cheeked Theano, daughter of Cisseus
And wife of Antenor, breaker of horses.
The Trojans had made her Athena's priestess.   315
With ritual cries they all lifted their hands
To Pallas Athena. Theano took the robe
And laid it on the knees of the rich-haired goddess,
Then prayed in supplication to Zeus' daughter:

"Lady Athena who defends our city,   320
Brightest of goddesses, hear our prayer.
Break now the spear of Diomedes
And grant that he fall before the Western Gate,
That we may now offer twelve heifers in this temple,
Unblemished yearlings. Only do thou pity   325
The town of Troy, its wives and its children."

But Pallas Athena denied her prayer.

    While they prayed to great Zeus' daughter,
Hector came to Paris' beautiful house,
Which he had built himself with the aid   330
Of the best craftsmen in all wide Troy:
Sleeping quarters, a hall, and a central courtyard
Near to Priam's and Hector's on the city's high rock.
Hector entered, Zeus' light upon him,
A spear sixteen feet long cradled in his hand,   335

---

1. Hector's brother, whose seduction and abduction of Helen, the wife of Menelaus, caused the war.
2. From the Phoenician city Sidon, on the coast of what is now Lebanon.

The bronze point gleaming, and the ferrule gold.
He found Paris in the bedroom, busy with his weapons,
Fondling his curved bow, his fine shield, and breastplate.
Helen of Argos sat with her household women
Directing their exquisite handicraft.   340

Hector meant to shame Paris and provoke him:[3]

"This is a fine time to be nursing your anger,
You idiot! We're dying out there defending the walls.
It's because of you the city is in this hellish war.
If you saw someone else holding back from combat   345
You'd pick a fight with him yourself. Now get up
Before the whole city goes up in flames!"

And Paris, handsome as a god:

"That's no more than just, Hector,
But listen now to what I have to say.   350
It's not out of anger or spite toward the Trojans
I've been here in my room. I only wanted
To recover from my pain. My wife was just now
Encouraging me to get up and fight,
And that seems the better thing to do.   355
Victory takes turns with men. Wait for me
While I put on my armor, or go on ahead—
I'm pretty sure I'll catch up with you."

To which Hector said nothing.

But Helen said to him softly: 360
                    "Brother-in-law
Of a scheming, cold-blooded bitch,
I wish that on the day my mother bore me
A windstorm had swept me away to a mountain
Or into the waves of the restless sea,
Swept me away before all this could happen.   365
But since the gods have ordained these evils,
Why couldn't I be the wife of a better man,
One sensitive at least to repeated reproaches?
Paris has never had an ounce of good sense
And never will. He'll pay for it someday.   370
But come inside and sit down on this chair,
Dear brother-in-law. You bear such a burden
For my wanton ways and Paris' witlessness.
Zeus has placed this evil fate on us so that   375
In time to come poets will sing of us."

And Hector, in his burnished helmet:

3. In book 3, Paris fought with Menelaus in single combat to settle the war. He was about to lose when
Aphrodite spirited him off to his house in Troy, where she then persuaded Helen to join him. In book 4,
fighting broke out again when the Trojan archer Pandarus, on Athena's advice, wounded Menelaus.

"Don't ask me to sit, Helen, even though
You love me. You will never persuade me.
My heart is out there with our fighting men.   380
They already feel my absence from battle.
Just get Paris moving, and have him hurry
So he can catch up with me while I'm still
Inside the city. I'm going to my house now
To see my family, my wife and my boy. I don't know   385
Whether I'll ever be back to see them again, or if
The gods will destroy me at the hands of the Greeks."

And Hector turned and left. He came to his house
But did not find white-armed Andromache there.
She had taken the child and a robed attendant   390
And stood on the tower, lamenting and weeping—
His blameless wife. When Hector didn't find her inside,
He paused on his way out and called to the servants:

"Can any of you women tell me exactly
Where Andromache went when she left the house?   395
To one of my sisters or one of my brothers' wives?
Or to the temple of Athena along with the other
Trojan women to beseech the dread goddess?"

The spry old housekeeper answered him:

"Hector, if you want the exact truth, she didn't go   400
To any of your sisters, or any of your brothers' wives,
Or to the temple of Athena along with the other
Trojan women to beseech the dread goddess.
She went to Ilion's great tower, because she heard
The Trojans were pressed and the Greeks were strong.   405
She ran off to the wall like a madwoman,
And the nurse went with her, carrying the child."

Thus the housekeeper, but Hector was gone,
Retracing his steps through the stone and tile streets
Of the great city, until he came to the Western Gate.   410
He was passing through it out onto the plain
When his wife came running up to meet him,
His beautiful wife, Andromache,
A gracious woman, daughter of great Eëtion,
Eëtion, who lived in the forests of Plakos   415
And ruled the Cilicians from Thebes-under-Plakos—
His daughter was wed to bronze-helmeted Hector.
She came up to him now, and the nurse with her
Held to her bosom their baby boy,
Hector's beloved son, beautiful as starlight,   420
Whom Hector had named Scamandrius[4]
But everyone else called Astyanax, Lord of the City,

---

4. After the Trojan river Scamander.

For Hector alone could save Ilion now.
He looked at his son and smiled in silence.
Andromache stood close to him, shedding tears,   425
Clinging to his arm as she spoke these words:

"Possessed is what you are, Hector. Your courage
Is going to kill you, and you have no feeling left
For your little boy or for me, the luckless woman
Who will soon be your widow. It won't be long   430
Before the whole Greek army swarms and kills you.
And when they do, it will be better for me
To sink into the earth. When I lose you, Hector,
There will be nothing left, no one to turn to,
Only pain. My father and mother are dead.   435
Achilles killed my father when he destroyed
Our city, Thebes with its high gates,
But had too much respect to despoil his body.
He burned it instead with all his armor
And heaped up a barrow. And the spirit women[5]   440
Came down from the mountain, daughters
Of the storm god, and planted elm trees around it.
I had seven brothers once in that great house.
All seven went down to Hades on a single day,
Cut down by Achilles in one blinding sprint   445
Through their shambling cattle and silver sheep.
Mother, who was queen in the forests of Plakos,
He took back as prisoner, with all her possessions,
Then released her for a fortune in ransom.
She died in our house, shot by Artemis'[6] arrows.   450
Hector, you are my father, you are my mother,
You are my brother and my blossoming husband.
But show some pity and stay here by the tower,
Don't make your child an orphan, your wife a widow.
Station your men here by the fig tree, where the city   455
Is weakest because the wall can be scaled.
Three times their elite have tried an attack here
Rallying around Ajax or glorious Idomeneus
Or Atreus' sons or mighty Diomedes,
Whether someone in on the prophecy told them   460
Or they are driven here by something in their heart."

And great Hector, helmet shining, answered her:

"Yes, Andromache, I worry about all this myself,
But my shame before the Trojans and their wives,
With their long robes trailing, would be too terrible   465
If I hung back from battle like a coward.
And my heart won't let me. I have learned to be
One of the best, to fight in Troy's first ranks,

---

5. Mountain nymphs.   6. The virgin goddess of the hunt, dispenser of natural and painless death to women.

Defending my father's honor and my own.
Deep in my heart I know too well   470
There will come a day when holy Ilion will perish,
And Priam and the people under Priam's ash spear.
But the pain I will feel for the Trojans then,
For Hecuba herself and for Priam king,
For my many fine brothers who will have by then   475
Fallen in the dust behind enemy lines—
All that pain is nothing to what I will feel
For you, when some bronze-armored Greek
Leads you away in tears, on your first day of slavery.
And you will work some other woman's loom   480
In Argos or carry water from a Spartan spring,
All against your will, under great duress.
And someone, seeing you crying, will say,
'That is the wife of Hector, the best of all
The Trojans when they fought around Ilion.'   485
Someday someone will say that, renewing your pain
At having lost such a man to fight off the day
Of your enslavement. But may I be dead
And the earth heaped up above me
Before I hear your cry as you are dragged away."   490

With these words, resplendent Hector
Reached for his child, who shrank back screaming
Into his nurse's bosom, terrified of his father's
Bronze-encased face and the horsehair plume
He saw nodding down from the helmet's crest.   495
This forced a laugh from his father and mother,
And Hector removed the helmet from his head
And set it on the ground all shimmering with light.
Then he kissed his dear son and swung him up gently
And said a prayer to Zeus and the other immortals: 500

"Zeus and all gods: grant that this my son
Become, as I am, foremost among Trojans,
Brave and strong, and ruling Ilion with might.
And may men say he is far better than his father
When he returns from war, bearing bloody spoils,   505
Having killed his man. And may his mother rejoice."

And he put his son in the arms of his wife,
And she enfolded him in her fragrant bosom
Laughing through her tears. Hector pitied her
And stroked her with his hand and said to her: 510

"You worry too much about me, Andromache.
No one is going to send me to Hades before my time,
And no man has ever escaped his fate, rich or poor,
Coward or hero, once born into this world.
Go back to the house now and take care of your work,   515
The loom and the shuttle, and tell the servants

To get on with their jobs. War is the work of men,
Of all the Trojan men, and mine especially."

With these words, Hector picked up
His plumed helmet, and his wife went back home,   520
Turning around often, her cheeks flowered with tears.
When she came to the house of man-slaying Hector,
She found a throng of servants inside,
And raised among these women the ritual lament.
And so they mourned for Hector in his house   525
Although he was still alive, for they did not think
He would ever again come back from the war,
Or escape the murderous hands of the Greeks.

    Paris meanwhile
Did not dally long in his high halls.   530
He put on his magnificent bronze-inlaid gear
And sprinted with assurance out through the city.

Picture a horse that has fed on barley in his stall
Breaking his halter and galloping across the plain,
Making for his accustomed swim in the river,   535
A glorious animal, head held high, mane streaming
Like wind on his shoulders. Sure of his splendor
He prances by the horse-runs and the mares in pasture.

That was how Paris, son of Priam, came down
From the high rock of Pergamum,[7]   540
Gleaming like amber and laughing in his armor,
And his feet were fast.
           He caught up quickly
With Hector just as he turned from the spot
Where he'd talked with his wife, and called out: 545

"Well, dear brother, have I delayed you too much?
Am I not here in time, just as you asked?"

Hector turned, his helmet flashing light:

"I don't understand you, Paris.
No one could slight your work in battle.   550
You're a strong fighter, but you slack off—
You don't have the will. It breaks my heart
To hear what the Trojans say about you.
It's on your account they have all this trouble.
Come on, let's go. We can settle this later,   555
If Zeus ever allows us to offer in our halls
The wine bowl of freedom to the gods above,
After we drive these bronze-kneed[8] Greeks from Troy."

---

7. The citadel of Troy.   **8.** I.e., with bronze greaves (the shin protectors of Homeric warriors).

[The Trojans rallied successfully and went over to the offensive. They drove the Greeks back to the light fortifications they had built around their beached ships. The Trojans lit their watchfires on the plain, ready to deliver the attack in the morning.]

[The Tide of Battle Turns]

But the Trojans had great notions that night,
Sitting on the bridge of war by their watchfires.

> Stars: crowds of them in the sky, sharp   565
> In the moonglow when the wind falls
> And all the cliffs and hills and peaks
> Stand out and the air shears down
> From heaven, and all the stars are visible
> And the watching shepherd smiles.   570

So the bonfires between the Greek ships
And the banks of the Xanthus,[9] burning
On the plain before Ilion.
           And fifty men
Warmed their hands by the flames of each fire.   575

And the horses champed white barley,
Standing by their chariots, waiting for Dawn
To take her seat on brocaded cushions.

BOOK IX

[The Embassy to Achilles]

So the Trojans kept watch. But Panic,
Fear's sister, had wrapped her icy fingers
Around the Greeks, and all their best
Were stricken with unendurable grief.

> When two winds rise on the swarming deep,   5
> Boreas and Zephyr,[1] blowing from Thrace
> In a sudden squall, the startled black waves
> Will crest and tangle the surf with seaweed.

The Greeks felt like that, pummeled and torn.

Agamemnon's heart was bruised with pain   10
As he went around to the clear-toned criers
Ordering them to call each man to assembly,
But not to shout. He pitched in himself.
It was a dispirited assembly. Agamemnon
Stood up, weeping, his face like a sheer cliff   15
With dark springwater washing down the stone.
Groaning heavily he addressed the troops:

---

9. One of the rivers of the Trojan plain.   1. The north and west winds, respectively.

"Friends, Argive commanders and counsellors:
Great Zeus, son of Cronus,
Is a hard god, friends. He's kept me in the dark   20
After all his promises, all his nods my way
That I'd raze Ilion's walls before sailing home.
It was all a lie, and I see now that his orders
Are for me to return to Argos in disgrace,
And this after all the armies I've destroyed.   25
I have no doubt that this is the high will
Of the god who has toppled so many cities
And will in the future, all glory to his power.
So this is my command for the entire army:
Clear out with our ships and head for home.   30
There's no hope we will take Troy's tall town."

He spoke, and they were all stunned to silence,
The silence of an army too grieved to speak,
Until at last Diomedes' voice boomed out:

"I'm going to oppose you if you talk foolishness—   35
As is my right in assembly, lord. Keep your temper.
First of all, you insulted me, saying in public
I was unwarlike and weak.[2] Every Greek here,
Young and old alike, knows all about this.
The son of crooked Cronus split the difference   40
When he gave you gifts. He gave you a scepter
And honor with it, but he didn't give you
Strength to stand in battle, which is real power.
Are you out of your mind? Do you really think
The sons of the Achaeans are unwarlike and weak?   45
If you yourself are anxious to go home,
Then go. You know the way. Your ships are here
Right by the sea, and a whole fleet will follow you
Back to Mycenae.[3] But many a long-haired Achaean
Will stay, too, until we conquer Troy. And if they won't—   50
Well, let them all sail back to their own native land.
The two of us, Sthenelus[4] and I, will fight on
Until we take Ilion. We came here with Zeus."

He spoke, and all the Greeks cheered
The speech of Diomedes, breaker of horses.   55
Then up stood Nestor, the old charioteer:

"Son of Tydeus, you are our mainstay in battle
And the best of your age in council as well.
No Greek will find fault with your speech
Or contradict it. But it is not the whole story.   60
You are still young. You might be my son,
My youngest. Yet you have given prudent advice

2. This insult was voiced during Agamemnon's review of his forces before the battle (book 4).   3. The
city near Argos that Agamemnon ruled.   4. Diomedes' companion.

To the Argive kings, since you have spoken aright.
But I, who am privileged to be your senior,
Will speak to all points. Nor will anyone   65
Scorn my words, not even King Agamemnon.
Only outlaws and exiles favor civil strife.
For the present, however, let us yield to night
And have our dinner. Guards should be posted
Outside the wall along the trench. I leave   70
This assignment to the younger men. But you,
Son of Atreus, take charge. You are King.
Serve the elders a feast. It is not unseemly.
Your huts are filled with wine which our ships
Transport daily over the sea from Thrace.   75
You have the means to entertain us and the men.
Then choose the best counsel your assembled guests
Can offer. The Achaeans are in great need
Of good counsel. The enemies' campfires
Are close to our ships. Can this gladden any heart?   80
This night will either destroy the army or save it."

They all heard him out and did as he said.
The guard details got their gear and filed out
On the double under their commanders:
Thrasymedes, Nestor's son; Ascalaphus   85
And Ialmenus, sons of Ares; Meriones,
Aphareus, and Diphyrus; and Creion,
The son of Lycomedes. Each of these seven
Had a hundred men under his command.
Spears in hand, they took up their positions   90
In a long line between the wall and the trench,[5]
Where they lit fires and prepared their supper.

Agamemnon meanwhile gathered the elders
Into his hut and served them a hearty meal.
They helped themselves to the dishes before them,   95
And when they had enough of food and drink,
The first to spin out his plan for them was Nestor,
Whose advice had always seemed best before,
And who spoke with their best interests at heart:

"Son of Atreus, most glorious lord,   100
I begin and end with you, since you are
King of a great people, with authority
To rule and right of judgment from Zeus.
It is yours to speak as well as to listen,
And to stand behind others whenever they speak   105
To our good. The final word is yours.
But I will speak as seems best to me.
No one will have a better idea

---

5. In book 7, the Greeks built this wall and dug the trench in front of it to protect their ships, which were
threatened by the Trojans.

Than I have now, nor has anyone ever,
From the time, divine prince, you wrested away   110
The girl Briseis from Achilles' shelter,
Defying his anger and my opposition.
I tried to dissuade you, but you gave in
To your pride and dishonored a great man
Whom the immortals esteem. You took his prize   115
And keep it still. But it is not too late. Even now
We must think of how to win him back
With appeasing gifts and soothing words."

And the warlord Agamemnon responded:

"Yes, old man, you were right on the mark   120
When you said I was mad. I will not deny it.
Zeus' favor multiplies a man's worth,
As it has here, and the army has suffered for it.
But since I did succumb to a fit of madness,
I want to make substantial amends.   125
I hereby announce my reparations:
Seven unfired tripods,[6] ten gold bars,
Twenty burnished cauldrons, a dozen horses—
Solid, prizewinning racehorses
Who have won me a small fortune—   130
And seven women who do impeccable work,
Surpassingly beautiful women from Lesbos[7]
I chose for myself when Achilles captured the town.
And with them will be the woman I took,
Briseus's daughter, and I will solemnly swear   135
I never went to her bed and lay with her
Or did what is natural between women and men.
All this he may have at once. And if it happens
That the gods allow us to sack Priam's city,
He may when the Greeks are dividing the spoils   140
Load a ship to the brim with gold and bronze,
And choose for himself the twenty Trojan women
Who are next in beauty to Argive Helen.
And if we return to the rich land of Argos,
He will marry my daughter, and I will honor him   145
As I do Orestes,[8] who is being reared in luxury.
I have three daughters in my fortress palace,
Chrysothemis, Laodice, and Iphianassa.
He may lead whichever he likes as his bride
Back to Peleus' house, without paying anything,   150
And I will give her a dowry richer than any
A father has ever given his daughter.
And I will give him seven populous cities,
Cardamyle, Enope, grassy Hire,
Sacred Pherae, Antheia with its meadowlands,   155

6. Three-footed kettles; such metal equipment was rare and highly valued.   7. A large island off the coast of present-day Turkey.   8. Agamemnon's son.

Beautiful Aepeia, and Pedasus, wine country.
They are all near the sea, on sandy Pylos' frontier,
And cattlemen live there, rich in herds and flocks,
Who will pay him tribute as if he were a god
And fulfill the shining decrees of his scepter.   160
I will do all this if he will give up his grudge.
And he should. Only Hades cannot be appeased,
Which is why of all gods mortals hate him most.
And he should submit to me, inasmuch as I
Am more of a king and can claim to be elder."   165

And then spoke Nestor, the Gerenian rider:

"Son of Atreus, most glorious Agamemnon,
Your gifts for Achilles are beyond reproach.
But come, we must dispatch envoys
As soon as possible to Achilles' tent,   170
And I see before me who should volunteer.
Phoenix,[9] dear to Zeus, should lead the way,
Followed by Ajax and brilliant Odysseus.
Odius and Eurybates can attend them as heralds.
Now bring water for our hands and observe silence,   175
That we may beseech Zeus to have mercy on us."

Nestor spoke, and his speech pleased them all.
Heralds poured water over their hands,
And then youths filled bowls to the brim with drink
And served it all around, first tipping the cups.   180
Having made their libations and drunk their fill,
They went out in a body from Agamemnon's hut.
Gerenian Nestor filled their ears with advice,
Glancing at each, but especially at Odysseus,
On how to persuade Peleus' peerless son.   185

They went in tandem along the seething shore,
Praying over and over to the god in the surf[1]
For an easy time in convincing Achilles.
They came to the Myrmidons' ships and huts
And found him plucking clear notes on a lyre—   190
A beautiful instrument with a silver bridge
He had taken when he ransacked Eëtion's[2] town—
Accompanying himself as he sang the glories
Of heroes in war. He was alone with Patroclus,
Who sat in silence waiting for him to finish.   195
His visitors came forward, Odysseus first,
And stood before him. Surprised, Achilles
Rose from his chair still holding his lyre.
Patroclus, when he saw them, also rose,
And Achilles, swift and sure, received them: 200

9. He is especially suited for this embassy because he was tutor to the young Achilles.   1. Poseidon, god of the sea.   2. Andromache's father. In book 6, she recalls his death at Achilles' hands.

"Welcome. Things must be bad to bring you here,
The Greeks I love best, even in my rage."

With these words Achilles led them in
And had them sit on couches and rugs
Dyed purple, and he called to Patroclus: 205

"A larger bowl, son of Menoetius,
And stronger wine, and cups all around.
My dearest friends are beneath my roof."

Patroclus obliged his beloved companion.
Then he cast a carving block down in the firelight   210
And set on it a sheep's back and a goat's,
And a hog chine too, marbled with fat.
Automedon[3] held the meat while Achilles
Carved it carefully and spitted the pieces.
Patroclus, godlike in the fire's glare,   215
Fed the blaze. When the flames died down
He laid the spits over the scattered embers,
Resting them on stones, and sprinkled the morsels
With holy salt. When the meat was roasted
He laid it on platters and set out bread   220
In exquisite baskets. Achilles served the meat,
Then sat down by the wall opposite Odysseus
And asked Patroclus to offer sacrifice.
After he threw the offerings[4] in the fire,
They helped themselves to the meal before them,   225
And when they had enough of food and drink,
Ajax nodded to Phoenix. Odysseus saw this,
And filling a cup he lifted it to Achilles:

"To your health, Achilles, for a generous feast.
There is no shortage in Agamemnon's hut,   230
Or now here in yours, of satisfying food.
But the pleasures of the table are not on our minds.
We fear the worst. It is doubtful
That we can save the ships without your strength.
The Trojans and their allies are encamped   235
Close to the wall that surrounds our black ships
And are betting that we can't keep them
From breaking through. They may be right.
Zeus has been encouraging them with signs,
Lightning on the right. Hector trusts this—   240
And his own strength—and has been raging
Recklessly, like a man possessed.
He is praying for dawn to come early
So he can fulfill his threat to lop the horns
From the ships' sterns, burn the hulls to ash,   245
And slaughter the Achaeans dazed in the smoke.

3. Achilles' charioteer.   4. The portion of meat reserved for the gods.

This is my great fear, that the gods make good
Hector's threats, dooming us to die in Troy
Far from the fields of home. Up with you, then,
If you intend at all, even at this late hour,   250
To save our army from these howling Trojans.
Think of yourself, of the regret you will feel
For harm that will prove irreparable.
This is the last chance to save your countrymen.
Is it not true, my friend, that your father Peleus   255
Told you as he sent you off with Agamemnon:
'My son, as for strength, Hera and Athena
Will bless you if they wish, but it is up to you
To control your proud spirit. A friendly heart
Is far better. Steer clear of scheming strife,   260
So that Greeks young and old will honor you.'
You have forgotten what the old man said,
But you can still let go of your anger, right now.
Agamemnon is offering you worthy gifts
If you will give up your grudge. Hear me   265
While I list the gifts he proposed in his hut:
Seven unfired tripods, ten gold bars,
Twenty burnished cauldrons, a dozen horses—
Solid, prizewinning racehorses
Who have won him a small fortune—   270
And seven women who do impeccable work,
Surpassingly beautiful women from Lesbos
He chose for himself when you captured the town.
And with them will be the woman he took from you,
Briseus' daughter, and he will solemnly swear   275
He never went to her bed and lay with her
Or did what is natural between women and men.
All this you may have at once. And if it happens
That the gods allow us to sack Priam's city,
You may when the Greeks are dividing the spoils   280
Load a ship to the brim with gold and bronze,
And choose for yourself the twenty Trojan women
Who are next in beauty to Argive Helen.
And if we return to the rich land of Argos,
You would marry his daughter, and he would honor you   285
As he does Orestes, who is being reared in luxury.
He has three daughters in his fortress palace,
Chrysothemis, Laodice, and Iphianassa.
You may lead whichever you like as your bride
Back to Peleus' house, without paying anything,   290
And he would give her a dowry richer than any
A father has ever given his daughter.
And he will give you seven populous cities,
Cardamyle, Enope, grassy Hire,
Sacred Pherae, Antheia with its meadowlands,   295
Beautiful Aepeia, and Pedasus, wine country.
They are all near the sea, on sandy Pylos' frontier,
And cattlemen live there, rich in herds and flocks,

Who will pay you tribute as if you were a god
And fulfill the shining decrees of your scepter.   300
All this he will do if you give up your grudge.
But if Agamemnon is too hateful to you,
Himself and his gifts, think of all the others
Suffering up and down the line, and of the glory
You will win from them. They will honor you   305
Like a god.
          And don't forget Hector.
You just might get him now. He's coming in close,
Deluded into thinking that he has no match
In the Greek army that has landed on his beach."   310

And Achilles, strong, swift, and godlike:

"Son of Laertes in the line of Zeus,
Odysseus the strategist—I can see
That I have no choice but to speak my mind
And tell you exactly how things are going to be.   315
Either that or sit through endless sessions
Of people whining at me. I hate like hell
The man who says one thing and thinks another.
So this is how I see it.
I cannot imagine Agamemnon,   320
Or any other Greek, persuading me,
Not after the thanks I got for fighting this war,
Going up against the enemy day after day.
It doesn't matter if you stay in camp or fight—
In the end, everybody comes out the same.   325
Coward and hero get the same reward:
You die whether you slack off or work.
And what do I have for all my suffering,
Constantly putting my life on the line?
Like a bird who feeds her chicks   330
Whatever she finds, and goes without herself,
That's what I've been like, lying awake
Through sleepless nights, in battle for days
Soaked in blood, fighting men for their wives.
I've raided twelve cities with our ships   335
And eleven on foot in the fertile Troad,
Looted them all, brought back heirlooms
By the ton, and handed it all over
To Atreus' son, who hung back in camp
Raking it in and distributing damn little.   340
What the others did get they at least got to keep.
They all have their prizes, everyone but me—
I'm the only Greek from whom he took something back.
He should be happy with the woman he has.
Why do the Greeks have to fight the Trojans?   345
Why did Agamemnon lead the army to Troy
If not for the sake of fair-haired Helen?
Do you have to be descended from Atreus

To love your mate? Every decent, sane man
Loves his woman and cares for her, as I did,   350
Loved her from my heart. It doesn't matter
That I won her with my spear. He took her,
Took her right out of my hands, cheated me,
And now he thinks he's going to win me back?
He can forget it. I know how things stand.   355
It's up to you, Odysseus, and the other kings
To find a way to keep the fire from the ships.
He's been pretty busy without me, hasn't he,
Building a wall, digging a moat around it,
Pounding in stakes for a palisade.   360
None of that stuff will hold Hector back.
When I used to fight for the Greeks,
Hector wouldn't come out farther from his wall
Than the oak tree by the Western Gate.
He waited for me there once, and barely escaped.   365
Now that I don't want to fight him anymore,
I will sacrifice to Zeus and all gods tomorrow,
Load my ships, and launch them on the sea.
Take a look if you want, if you give a damn,
And you'll see my fleet on the Hellespont   370
In the early light, my men rowing hard.
With good weather from the sea god,
I'll reach Phthia after a three-day sail.
I left a lot behind when I hauled myself here,
And I'll bring back more, gold and bronze,   375
Silken-waisted women, grey iron—
Everything except the prize of honor
The warlord Agamemnon gave me
And in his insulting arrogance took back.
So report back to him everything I say,   380
And report it publicly—get the Greeks angry,
In case the shameless bastard still thinks
He can steal us blind. He doesn't dare
Show his dogface here. Fine. I don't want
To have anything to do with him either.   385
He cheated me, wronged me. Never again.
He's had it. He can go to hell in peace,
The half-wit that Zeus has made him.
His gifts? His gifts mean nothing to me.
Not even if he offered me ten or twenty times   390
His present gross worth and added to it
All the trade Orchomenus[5] does in a year,
All the wealth laid up in Egyptian Thebes,
The wealthiest city in all the world,
Where they drive two hundred teams of horses   395
Out through each of its hundred gates.
Not even if Agamemnon gave me gifts

---

5. A city in central Greece, northwest of Thebes; it was one of the most important Greek cities from the
Bronze Age onward.

As numberless as grains of sand or dust,
Would he persuade me or touch my heart—
Not until he's paid in full for all my grief.   400
His daughter? I would not marry
The daughter of Agamemnon son of Atreus
If she were as lovely as golden Aphrodite
Or could weave like owl-eyed Athena.
Let him choose some other Achaean   405
More to his lordly taste. If the gods
Preserve me and I get home safe
Peleus will find me a wife himself.
There are many Greek girls in Hellas[6] and Phthia,
Daughters of chieftains who rule the cities.   410
I can have my pick of any of them.
I've always wanted to take a wife there,
A woman to have and to hold, someone with whom
I can enjoy all the goods old Peleus has won.
Nothing is worth my life, not all the riches   415
They say Troy held before the Greeks came,
Not all the wealth in Phoebus Apollo's
Marble shrine up in craggy Pytho.[7]
Cattle and flocks are there for the taking;
You can always get tripods and chestnut horses.   420
But a man's life cannot be won back
Once his breath has passed beyond his clenched teeth.
My mother Thetis, a moving silver grace,
Tells me two fates sweep me on to my death.
If I stay here and fight, I'll never return home,   425
But my glory will be undying forever.
If I return home to my dear fatherland
My glory is lost but my life will be long,
And death that ends all will not catch me soon.
As for the rest of you, I would advise you too   430
To sail back home, since there's no chance now
Of storming Ilion's height. Zeus has stretched
His hand above her, making her people bold.
What's left for you now is to go back to the council
And announce my message. It's up to them   435
To come up with another plan to save the ships
And the army with them, since this one,
Based on appeasing my anger, won't work.
Phoenix can spend the night here. Tomorrow
He sails with me on our voyage home,   440
If he wants to, that is. I won't force him to come."

He spoke, and they were hushed in silence,
Shocked by his speech and his stark refusal.
Finally the old horseman Phoenix spoke,
Bursting into tears. He felt the ships were lost.   445

---

6. Although Hellas later became the name for all of Greece, in Homer it refers to a region next to Achilles'
home district of Phthia. Both are in northern Greece.   7. Apollo's oracular shrine at Delphi. Its wealth
consisted of offerings made to the god by grateful worshippers.

"If you have set your mind on going home,
Achilles, and will do nothing to save the ships
From being burnt, if your heart is that angry,
How could I stay here without you, my boy,
All by myself? Peleus sent me with you   450
On that day you left Phthia to go to Agamemnon,
A child still, knowing nothing of warfare
Or assemblies where men distinguish themselves.
He sent me to you to teach you this—
To be a speaker of words and a doer of deeds.   455
I could not bear to be left behind now
Apart from you, child, not even if a god
Promised to smooth my wrinkles and make me
As young and strong as I was when I first left
The land of Hellas and its beautiful women.   460
I was running away from a quarrel with Amyntor,
My father, who was angry with me
Over his concubine, a fair-haired woman
Whom he loved as much as he scorned his wife,
My mother. She implored me constantly   465
To make love to his concubine so that this woman
Would learn to hate the old man. I did as she asked.
My father found out and cursed me roundly,
Calling on the Furies[8] to ensure that never
Would a child of mine sit on his knees.   470
The gods answered his prayers, Underworld Zeus
And dread Persephone.[9] I decided to kill him
With a sharp sword, but some god calmed me down—
Putting in my mind what people would say,
The names they would call me—so that in fact   475
I would not be known as a parricide.
From then on I could not bear to linger
In my father's house, although my friends
And my family tried to get me to stay,
Entreating me, slaughtering sheep and cattle,   480
Roasting whole pigs on spits, and drinking
Jar after jar of the old man's wine.
For nine solid days they kept watch on me,
Working in shifts, staying up all night.
The fires stayed lit, one under the portico   485
Of the main courtyard, one on the porch
In front of my bedroom door. On the tenth night,
When it got dark, I broke through the latches
And vaulted over the courtyard fence,
Eluding the watchmen and servant women.   490
I was on the run through wide Hellas
And made it to Phthia's black soil, her flocks,
And to Lord Peleus. He welcomed me kindly
And loved me as a father loves his only son,

8. Avenging spirits, particularly concerned with crimes committed by kin against kin.   9. Wife of Hades
(the "Underworld Zeus").

A grown son who will inherit great wealth.   495
He made me rich and settled me on the border,
Where I lived as king of the Dolopians.
I made you what you are, my godlike Achilles,
And loved you from my heart. You wouldn't eat,
Whether it was at a feast or a meal in the house,   500
Unless I set you on my lap and cut your food up
And fed it to you and held the wine to your lips.
Many a time you wet the tunic on my chest,
Burping up wine when you were colicky.
I went through a lot for you, because I knew   505
The gods would never let me have a child
Of my own. No, I tried to make you my child,
Achilles, so you would save me from ruin.
But you have to master your proud spirit.
It's not right for you to have a pitiless heart.   510
Even the gods can bend. Superior as they are
In honor, power, and every excellence,
They can be turned aside from wrath
When humans who have transgressed
Supplicate them with incense and prayers,   515
With libations and savor of sacrifice.
Yes, for Prayers are daughters of great Zeus.
Lame and wrinkled and with eyes averted,
They are careful to follow in Folly's footsteps,
But Folly is strong and fleet, and outruns them all,   520
Beating them everywhere and plaguing humans,
Who are cured by the Prayers when they come behind.
Revere the daughters of Zeus when they come,
And they will bless you and hear your cry.
Reject them and refuse them stubbornly,   525
And they will ask Zeus, Cronus' son, to have
Folly plague you,[1] so you will pay in pain.
No, Achilles, grant these daughters of Zeus
The respect that bends all upright men's minds.
If the son of Atreus were not offering gifts   530
And promising more, if he were still raging mad,
I would not ask you to shrug off your grudge
And help the Greeks, no matter how sore their need.
But he is offering gifts and promising more,
And he has sent to you a delegation   535
Of the best men in the army, your dearest friends.
Don't scorn their words or their mission here.
    No one could blame you for being angry before.
We all know stories about heroes of old,
How they were furiously angry, but later on   540
Were won over with gifts or appeased with words.
I remember a very old story like this, and since
We are all friends here, I will tell it to you now.
    The Curetes were fighting the Aetolians

---

1. A serious curse, since the Greek word for "folly" can also mean "destruction."

In a bloody war around Calydon town.[2]   545
The Aetolians were defending their city
And the Curetes meant to burn it down.
This was all because gold-throned Artemis
Had cursed the Curetes,[3] angry that Oeneus
Had not offered her his orchard's first fruits.   550
The other gods feasted on bulls by the hundred,
But Oeneus forgot somehow or other
Only the sacrifice to great Zeus' daughter.
So the Archer Goddess, angry at heart,
Roused a savage boar, with gleaming white tusks,   555
And sent him to destroy Oeneus' orchard.
The boar did a good job, uprooting trees
And littering the ground with apples and blossoms.
But Oeneus' son, Meleager, killed it
After getting up a party of hunters and hounds   560
From many towns: it took more than a few men
To kill this huge boar, and not before
It set many a hunter on the funeral pyre.
But the goddess caused a bitter argument
About the boar's head and shaggy hide   565
Between the Curetes and Aetolians.
They went to war. While Meleager still fought
The Curetes had the worst of it
And could not remain outside Calydon's wall.[4]
But when wrath swelled Meleager's heart,   570
As it swells even the hearts of the wise,
And his anger rose against Althaea his mother,
He lay in bed with his wife, Cleopatra,
Child of Marpessa and the warrior Idas.
Idas once took up his bow against Apollo   575
To win lissome Marpessa. Her parents
Called the girl Halcyone back then
Because her mother wept like a halcyon,
The bird of sorrows, because the Archer God,
Phoebus Apollo, had stolen her daughter.   580
Meleager nursed his anger at Cleopatra's side,
Furious because his mother had cursed him,
Cursed him to the gods for murdering his uncle,[5]
Her brother, that is, and she beat the earth,
The nurturing earth, with her hands, and called   585
Upon Hades and Persephone the dread,
As she knelt and wet her bosom with tears,
To bring death to her son. And the Fury
Who walks in darkness heard her

---

2. A city in northwestern Greece. The Curetes and Aetolians were the local tribes, once allied but at odds in this story.   3. The Greek says, ambiguously, "had cursed them." Possibly Artemis cursed both Aetolians and Curetes, since Oeneus was king of the Aetolian city Calydon.   4. The Greek text says only "the wall"—probably not Calydon's wall, since the Curetes should be attacking that city. It may be the wall of Pleuron, the Curetes' city. Or, as one commentator has suggested, the wall could be one built by the besieging Curetes around their encampment outside Calydon, as the Greeks have done at Troy.   5. In the course of the battles Meleager had killed one of his mother's brothers.

From the pit of Erebus,[6] and her heart was iron.   590
Soon the enemy was heard at the walls again,
Battering the gates. The Aetolian elders
Sent the city's high priests to pray to Meleager
To come out and defend them, offering him
Fifty acres of Calydon's richest land   595
Wherever he chose, half in vineyard,
Half in clear plowland, to be cut from the plain.
And the old horseman Oeneus shook his doors,
Standing on the threshold of his gabled room,
And recited a litany of prayers to his son,   600
As did his sisters and his queenly mother.
He refused them all, and refused his friends,
His very best friends and boon companions.
No one could move his heart or persuade him
Until the Curetes, having scaled the walls   605
Were burning the city and beating down
His bedroom door. Then his wife wailed
And listed for him all the woes that befall
A captured people—the men killed,
The town itself burnt, the women and children   610
Led into slavery. This roused his spirit.
He clapped on armor and went out to fight.
And so he saved the Aetolians from doom
Of his own accord, and they paid him none
Of those lovely gifts, savior or not.   615
    Don't be like that. Don't think that way,
And don't let your spirit turn that way.
The ships will be harder to save when they're burning.
Come while there are gifts, while the Achaeans
Will still honor you as if you were a god.   620
But if you go into battle without any gifts,
Your honor will be less, save us or not."

And strong, swift-footed Achilles answered:

"I don't need that kind of honor, Phoenix.
My honor comes from Zeus, and I will have it   625
Among these beaked ships as long as my breath
Still remains and my knees still move.
Now listen to this. You're listening? Good.
Don't try to confuse me with your pleading
On Agamemnon's behalf. If you're his friend   630
You're no longer mine, although I love you.
Hate him because I hate him. It's as simple as that.
You're like a second father to me. Stay here,
Be king with me and share half the honor.
These others can take my message. Lie down   635
And spend the night on a soft couch. At daybreak
We will decide whether to set sail or stay."

6. The underworld.

And he made a silent nod to Patroclus
To spread a thick bed for Phoenix. It was time
For the others to think about leaving. Big Ajax,   640
Telamon's godlike son, said as much:

"Son of Laertes in the line of Zeus,
Resourceful Odysseus—it's time we go.
I do not think we will accomplish
What we were sent here to do. Our job now   645
Is to report this news quickly, bad as it is.
They will be waiting to hear. Achilles
Has made his great heart savage.
He is a cruel man, and has no regard
For the love that his friends honored him with,   650
Beyond anyone else who camps with the ships.
Pitiless. A man accepts compensation
For a murdered brother, a dead son.
The killer goes on living in the same town
After paying blood money, and the bereaved   655
Restrains his proud spirit and broken heart
Because he has received payment. But you,
The gods have replaced your heart
With flint and malice, because of one girl,
One single girl, while we are offering you   660
Seven of the finest women to be found
And many other gifts. Show some generosity
And some respect. We have come under your roof,
We few out of the entire army, trying hard
To be the friends you care for most of all."   665

And Achilles, the great runner, answered him:

"Ajax, son of Telamon in the line of Zeus,
Everything you say is after my own heart.
But I swell with rage when I think of how
The son of Atreus treated me like dirt   670
In public, as if I were some worthless tramp.
Now go, and take back this message:
I won't lift a finger in this bloody war
Until Priam's illustrious son Hector
Comes to the Myrmidons' ships and huts   675
Killing Greeks as he goes and torching the fleet.
But when he comes to my hut and my black ship
I think Hector will stop, for all his battle lust."

He spoke. They poured their libations
And headed for the ships, Odysseus leading.   680
Patroclus ordered a bed made ready
For Phoenix, and the old man lay down
On fleeces and rugs covered with linen
And waited for bright dawn. Achilles slept
In an inner alcove, and by his side   685

Lay a woman he had brought from Lesbos
With high, lovely cheekbones, Diomede her name,
Phorbas' daughter. Patroclus lay down
In the opposite corner, and with him lay Iphis,
A silken girl Achilles had given him   690
When he took steep Scyrus, Enyeus' city.

By now Odysseus and Ajax
Were in Agamemnon's quarters,
Surrounded by officers drinking their health
From gold cups and shouting questions.   695
Agamemnon, the warlord, had priority:

"Odysseus, pride of the Achaeans, tell me,
Is he willing to repel the enemy fire
And save the ships, or does he refuse,
His great heart still in the grip of wrath?"   700

Odysseus, who endured all, answered:

"Son of Atreus, most glorious Agamemnon,
Far from quenching his wrath, Achilles
Is filled with even more. He spurns you
And your gifts, and suggests that you   705
Think of a way to save the ships and the army.
He himself threatens, at dawn's first light,
To get his own ships onto the water,
And he said he would advise the others as well
To sail for home, since there is no chance now   710
You will storm Ilion's height. Zeus has stretched
His hand above her, making her people bold.
This is what he said, as these men here
Who came with me will tell you, Ajax
And the two heralds, prudent men both.   715
Phoenix will spend the night there. Tomorrow
He sails with Achilles on his voyage home,
If he wants to. He will not be forced to go."

They were stunned by the force of his words
And fell silent for a long time, hushed in grief,   720
Until at last Diomedes said in his booming voice:

"Son of Atreus, glorious Agamemnon,
You should never have pleaded with him
Or offered all those gifts. Achilles
Was arrogant enough without your help.   725
Let him do what he wants, stay here
Or get the hell out. He'll fight later, all right,
When he is ready or a god tells him to.
Now I want everyone to do as I say.
Enjoy some food and wine to keep up   730
Your strength, and then get some sleep.

When the rosy light first streaks the sky
Get your troops and horses into formation
Before the ships. Fight in the front yourselves."

The warlords assented, taken aback   735
By the authority of Diomedes' speech.
Each man poured libation and went to his hut,
Where he lay down and took the gift of sleep.

[After Achilles' refusal, the situation of the Greeks worsened rapidly. Agamemnon,
Diomedes, and Odysseus were all wounded. The Trojans breached the stockade and
fought beside the ships. Patroclus tried to bring Achilles to the aid of the Greeks, but
the most he could obtain was permission for himself to fight, clad in Achilles' armor,
at the head of the Myrmidons.]

FROM BOOK XVI

[Patroclus Fights and Dies]

    Sarpedon[7] saw his comrades running   455
With their tunics flapping loose around their waists
And being swatted down like flies by Patroclus.
He called out, appealing to their sense of shame:

"Why this sudden burst of speed, Lycian heroes?
Slow down a little, while I make the acquaintance   460
Of this nuisance of a Greek[8] who seems by now
To have hamstrung half the Trojan army."

And he stepped down from his chariot in his bronze
As Patroclus, seeing him, stepped down from his.

    High above a cliff vultures are screaming   465
In the air as they savage each other's craws
With their hooked beaks and talons.

    And higher still,
Zeus watched with pity as the two heroes closed
And said to his wife Hera, who is his sister too: 470

"Fate has it that Sarpedon, whom I love more
Than any man, is to be killed by Patroclus.
Shall I take him out of battle while he still lives
And set him down in the rich land of Lycia,
Or shall I let him die under Patroclus' hands?"   475

And Hera, his lady, her eyes soft and wide:

"Son of Cronus, what a thing to say!
A mortal man, whose fate has long been fixed,

---

7. King of Lycia in Asia Minor, son of Zeus and a mortal woman; he is a Trojan ally (for his genealogy, see
his cousin Glaucus's account in his speech to Diomedes in book 6, pp. 122–24, esp. line 205).   8. He
is referring to Patroclus, who has returned to the battle wearing Achilles' armor.

And you want to save him from rattling death?
Do it. But don't expect all of us to approve. 480
Listen to me. If you send Sarpedon home alive,
You will have to expect other gods to do the same
And save their own sons—and there are many of them
In this war around Priam's great city.
Think of the resentment you will create. 485
But if you love him and are filled with grief,
Let him fall in battle at Patroclus' hands,
And when his soul and life have left him,
Send Sleep[9] and Death to bear him away
To Lycia, where his people will give him burial 490
With mound and stone, as befits the dead."

The Father of Gods and Men agreed
Reluctantly, but shed drops of blood as rain
Upon the earth in honor of his own dear son
Whom Patroclus was about to kill 495
On Ilion's rich soil, far from his native land.

When they were close, Patroclus cast, and hit
Not Prince Sarpedon, but his lieutenant
Thrasymelus, a good man—a hard throw
Into the pit of his belly. He collapsed in a heap. 500
Sarpedon countered and missed. His bright spear
Sliced instead through the right shoulder
Of Pedasus,[1] who gave one pained, rasping whinny,
Then fell in the dust. His spirit fluttered off.
With the trace horse down, the remaining two 505
Struggled in the creaking yoke, tangling the reins.
Automedon[2] remedied this by drawing his sword
And cutting loose the trace horse. The other two
Righted themselves and pulled hard at the reins,
And the two warriors closed again in mortal combat. 510
Sarpedon cast again. Another miss. The spearpoint
Glinted as it sailed over Patroclus' left shoulder
Without touching him at all. Patroclus came back,
Leaning into his throw, and the bronze point
Caught Sarpedon just below the rib cage 515
Where it protects the beating heart. Sarpedon fell

    As a tree falls, oak, or poplar, or spreading pine,
    When carpenters cut it down in the forest
    With their bright axes, to be the beam of a ship,

And he lay before his horses and chariot, 520
Groaning heavily and clawing the bloody dust,

---

9. The brother of Death, according to the Greeks. 1. The third or trace horse that ran alongside the
pair pulling Patroclus's chariot to help it maneuver. The other two horses are immortal, given by the gods
to Achilles' father Peleus. In the next lines, they shy away from contact with death. 2. Patroclus's charioteer.

Like some tawny, spirited bull a lion has killed
In the middle of the shambling herd, groaning
As it dies beneath the predator's jaws.

Thus beneath Patroclus the Lycian commander   525
Struggled in death. And he called his friend:

"Glaucus, it's time to show what you're made of
And be the warrior you've always been,
Heart set on evil war—if you're fast enough.
Hurry, rally our best to fight for my body,   530
All the Lycian leaders. Shame on you,
Glaucus, until your dying day, if the Greeks
Strip my body bare beside their ships.
Be strong and keep the others going."

The end came as he spoke, and death settled   535
On his nostrils and eyes. Patroclus put his heel
On Sarpedon's chest and pulled out his spear.
The lungs came out with it, and Sarpedon's life.
The Myrmidons steadied his snorting horses.
They did not want to leave their master's chariot.   540

Glaucus could hardly bear to hear Sarpedon's voice,
He was so grieved that he could not save him.
He pressed his arm with his hand. His wound
Tormented him, the wound he got when Teucer
Shot him with an arrow as he attacked the wall.[3]   545
He prayed to Apollo, lord of bright distances:

"Hear me, O Lord, wherever you are
In Lycia or Troy, for everywhere you hear
Men in their grief, and grief has come to me.
I am wounded, Lord, my arm is on fire,   550
And the blood can't be staunched. My shoulder
Is so sore I cannot hold a steady spear
And fight the enemy. Sarpedon is dead,
My Lord, and Zeus will not save his own son.
Heal my wound and deaden my pain,[4]   555
And give me the strength to call the Lycians
And urge them on to fight, and do battle myself
About the body of my fallen comrade."

Thus Glaucus' prayer, and Apollo heard him.
He stilled his pain and staunched the dark blood   560
That flowed from his wound. Glaucus felt
The god's strength pulsing through him,
Glad that his prayers were so quickly answered.
He rounded up the Lycian leaders
And urged them to fight for Sarpedon's body,   565

---

3. The wall erected by the Greeks to protect their ships and breached by the Trojans. *Teucer:* an archer on the Greek side, half-brother of Ajax.   4. Apollo, who inflicted the plague in book 1, is also the god of healing.

Then went with long strides to the Trojans,
To Polydamas, Agenor, Aeneas,
And then saw Hector's bronze-strapped face,
Went up to him and said levelly:

"Hector, you have abandoned your allies.   570
We have been putting our lives on the line for you
Far from our homes and loved ones,
And you don't care enough to lend us aid.
Sarpedon is down, our great warlord,
Whose word in Lycia was Lycia's law,   575
Killed by Patroclus under Ares' prodding.
Show some pride and fight for his body,
Or the Myrmidons will strip off the armor
And defile his corpse, in recompense
For all the Greeks we have killed by the ships."   580

This was almost too much for the Trojans.
Sarpedon, though a foreigner, had been
A mainstay of their city, the leader
Of a large force and its best fighter.
Hector led them straight at the Greeks, "For Sarpedon!"   585
And Patroclus, seeing them coming,
Urged on the already eager two Ajaxes:[5]

"Let me see you push these Trojans back
With everything you've ever had and more.   590
Sarpedon is down, first to breach our wall.
He's ours, to carve up his body and strip
The armor off. And all his little saviors
Are ours to massacre with cold bronze."

They heard this as if hearing their own words.   595
The lines on both sides hardened to steel.
Then Trojans and Lycians, Myrmidons and Greeks
Began fighting for the corpse, howling and cursing
As they threw themselves into the grinding battle.
And Zeus stretched hellish night over the armies   600
So they might do their lethal work over his son.

The Trojans at first pushed back the Greeks
When Epeigeus was hit, Agacles' son.
This man was far from the worst of the Myrmidons.
He once lived in Boudeum, but having killed   605
A cousin of his, came as a suppliant
To Peleus and silver-footed Thetis,
Who sent him with Achilles to fight at Troy.
He had his hand on the corpse when Hector
Brought down a stone on his head, splitting his skull   610
In two inside his heavy helmet. He collapsed

5. Of the two Greek warriors with this name, the son of Telamon was among the most outstanding fighters
at Troy; the less distinguished son of Oïleus still played a prominent role in battle (and, according to poetry
outside the *Iliad*, in the sack of Troy). They are sometimes found fighting together.

On Sarpedon's body, and death drifted over him.
Patroclus ached for his friend and swooped
Into the front like a hawk after sparrows—
Yes, my Patroclus—and they scattered like birds   615
Before your anger for your fallen comrade.
Sthenelaos, Ithaemenes' beloved son,
Never knew what hit him. The stone Patroclus threw
Severed the tendons at the nape of his neck.
The Trojan champions, including Hector,   620
Now withdrew, about as far as a javelin flies
When a man who knows how throws it hard
In competition or in mortal combat.

The Greeks pressed after them, and Glaucus,
The Lycian commander now, wheeled around   625
And killed Bathycles, a native of Hellas
And the wealthiest of the Myrmidons.
He was just catching up with Glaucus
When the Lycian suddenly pivoted on his heel
And put his spear straight into Bathycles' chest.   630
He fell hard, and the Greeks winced.
A good man was down, much to the pleasure
Of the Trojans, who thronged around his body.

But the Greeks took the offensive again,
And Meriones[6] killed Laogonus,   635
A priest of Idaean[7] Zeus who was himself
Honored as a god. Meriones thrust hard
Into his jaw, just beneath the ear,
And he was dead, in the hated dark.
Aeneas launched his spear at Meriones,   640
Hoping to hit him as he advanced
Under cover of his shield, but Meriones
Saw the spear coming and ducked forward,
Leaving it to punch into the ground and stand there
Quivering, as if Ares had twanged it   645
So it could spend its fury. Aeneas fumed:

"That would have been your last dance,[8] Meriones,
Your last dance, if only my spear had hit you!"

And Meriones, himself famed for his spear:

"Do you think you can kill everyone   650
Who comes up against you, Aeneas,
And defends himself? You're mortal stuff too.
If I got a solid hit on you with my spear
You'd be down in no time, for all your strength.
You'd give me the glory, and your life to Hades."   655

6. A warrior from Crete on the Greek side.   7. Of Ida, a high mountain near Troy where Zeus had a
cult (and from which he watches the fighting on the plain).   8. In Homer, the opposite of warfare.

Patroclus would have none of this, and yelled:

"Cut the chatter, Meriones. You're a good man,
But don't think the Trojans are going to retreat
From the corpse because you make fun of them.
Use hands in war, words in council.   660
Save your big speeches; we've got fighting to do."

And he moved ahead, with Meriones,
Who himself moved like a god, in his wake.

  Woodcutters are working in a distant valley,
  But the sound of their axes, and of trees falling,   665
  Can be heard for miles around in the mountains.

The plain of Troy thrummed with the sound
Of bronze and hide stretched into shields,
And of swords and spears knifing into these.
Sarpedon's body was indistinguishable   670
From the blood and grime and splintered spears
That littered his body from head to foot.

  But if you have ever seen how flies
  Cluster about the brimming milk pails
  On a dairy farm in early summer,   675

You will have some idea of the throng
Around Sarpedon's corpse.
                              And not once did Zeus
Avert his luminous eyes from the combatants.
All this time he looked down at them and pondered   680
When Patroclus should die, whether
Shining Hector should kill him then and there
In the conflict over godlike Sarpedon
And strip the armor from his body, or whether
He should live to destroy even more Trojans.   685
And as he pondered it seemed preferable
That Achilles' splendid surrogate should once more
Drive the Trojans and bronze-helmed Hector
Back to the city, and take many lives.
And Hector felt it, felt his blood turn milky,   690
And mounted his chariot, calling to the others
To begin the retreat, that Zeus' scales were tipping.
Not even the Lycians stayed, not with Sarpedon
Lying at the bottom of a pile of bodies
That had fallen upon him in this node of war.   695

The Greek stripped at last the glowing bronze
From Sarpedon's shoulders, and Patroclus gave it
To some of his comrades to take back to the ships.

Then Zeus turned to Apollo and said:

"Sun God, take our Sarpedon out of range.   700
Cleanse his wounds of all the clotted blood,
And wash him in the river far away
And anoint him with our holy chrism
And wrap the body in a deathless shroud
And give him over to be taken swiftly   705
By Sleep and Death to Lycia,
Where his people shall give him burial
With mound and stone, as befits the dead."

And Apollo went down from Ida
Into the howling dust of war,   710
And cleansed Sarpedon's wounds of all the blood,
And washed him in the river far away
And anointed him with holy chrism
And wrapped the body in a deathless shroud
And gave him over to be taken swiftly   715
By Sleep and Death to Lycia.

Patroclus called to his horses and charioteer
And pressed on after the Trojans and Lycians,
Forgetting everything Achilles had said[9]
And mindless of the black fates gathering above.   720
Even then you might have escaped them,
Patroclus, but Zeus' mind is stronger than men's,
And Zeus now put fury in your heart.

Do you remember it, Patroclus, all the Trojans
You killed as the gods called you to your death?   725
Adrastus was first, then Autonous, and Echeclus,
Perimas, son of Megas, Epistor, Melanippus,
Elasus, Mulius, and last, Pylartes,
And it would have been more, but the others ran,
Back to Troy, which would have fallen that day   730
By Patroclus' hands.

            But Phoebus Apollo
Had taken his stand on top of Troy's wall.

            Three times Patroclus
Reached the parapet, and three times   735
Apollo's fingers flicked against the human's shield
And pushed him off. But when he came back
A fourth time, like a spirit from beyond,
Apollo's voice split the daylight in two:

"Get back, Patroclus, back where you belong.   740
Troy is fated to fall, but not to you,
Nor even to Achilles, a better man by far."

---

9. In sending Patroclus into battle, Achilles told him only to chase the Trojans from the Greek ships and
not to pursue them all the way back to Troy.

And Patroclus was off, putting distance
Between himself and that wrathful voice.

Hector had halted his horses at the Western Gate   745
And was deciding whether to drive back into battle
Or call for a retreat to within the walls.
While he pondered this, Phoebus Apollo
Came up to him in the guise of Asius.
This man was Hector's uncle on his mother's side,   750
And Apollo looked just like him as he spoke:

"Why are you out of action, Hector? It's not right.
If I were as much stronger than you as I am weaker,
You'd pay dearly for withdrawing from battle.
Get in that chariot and go after Patroclus.   755
Who knows? Apollo may give you the glory."

Hector commanded Cebriones, his charioteer,
To whip the horses into battle. Apollo melted
Into the throng, a god into the toil of men.
The Greeks felt a sudden chill,   760
While Hector and the Trojans felt their spirits lift.
Hector was not interested in the other Greeks.
He drove through them and straight for Patroclus,
Who leapt down from his own chariot
With a spear in one hand and in the other   765
A jagged piece of granite he had scooped up
And now cupped in his palm. He got set,
And without more than a moment of awe
For who his opponent was, hurled the stone.
The throw was not wasted. He hit Hector's   770
Charioteer, Cebriones, Priam's bastard son,
As he stood there holding the reins. The sharp stone
Caught him right in the forehead, smashing
His brows together and shattering the skull.
So that his eyeballs spurted out and dropped   775
Into the dirt before his feet. He flipped backward
From the chariot like a diver, and his soul
Dribbled away from his bones. And you,
Patroclus, you, my horseman, mocked him:

"What a spring the man has! Nice dive!   780
Think of the oysters he could come up with
If he were out at sea, jumping off the boat
In all sorts of weather, to judge by the dive
He just took from his chariot onto the plain."

And with that he rushed at the fallen warrior   785

Like a lion who has been wounded in the chest
As he ravages a farmstead, and his own valor
Destroys him.

Yes, Patroclus, that is how you leapt
Upon Cebriones. 790
Hector vaulted from his chariot,
And the two of them fought over Cebriones

Like a pair of lions fighting over a slain deer
In the high mountains, both of them ravenous,
Both high of heart, 795

very much like these two
Human heroes hacking at each other with bronze.
Hector held Cebriones' head and would not let go.
Patroclus had hold of a foot, and around them
Greeks and Trojans squared off and fought. 800

Winds sometimes rise in a deep mountain wood
From different directions, and the trees—
Beech, ash, and cornelian cherry—
Batter each other with their long, tapered branches,
And you can hear the sound from a long way off, 805
The unnerving splintering of hardwood limbs.

The Trojans and Greeks collided in battle,
And neither side thought of yielding ground.

Around Cebriones many spears were stuck,
Many arrows flew singing from the string, 810
And many stones thudded onto the shields
Of men fighting around him. But there he lay
In the whirling dust, one of the great,
Forgetful of his horsemanship.

While the sun still straddled heaven's meridian, 815
Soldiers on both sides were hit and fell.
But when the sun moved down the sky and men
All over earth were unyoking their oxen,
The Greeks' success exceeded their destiny.
They pulled Cebriones from the Trojan lines 820
And out of range, and stripped his armor.

And then Patroclus unleashed himself.

Three times he charged into the Trojan ranks
With the raw power of Ares, yelling coldly,
And on each charge he killed nine men. 825
But when you made your fourth, demonic charge,
Then—did you feel it, Patroclus?—out of the mist,
Your death coming to meet you. It was
Apollo, whom you did not see in the thick of battle,
Standing behind you, and the flat of his hand 830
Found the space between your shoulder blades.

The sky's blue disk went spinning in your eyes
As Achilles' helmet rang beneath the horses' hooves,
And rolled in the dust—no, that couldn't be right[1]—
Those handsome horsehair plumes grimed with blood,   835
The gods would never let that happen to the helmet
That had protected the head and graceful brow
Of divine Achilles. But the gods did
Let it happen, and Zeus would now give the helmet
To Hector, whose own death was not far off.   840

Nothing was left of Patroclus' heavy battle spear
But splintered wood, his tasselled shield and baldric
Fell to the ground, and Apollo, Prince of the Sky,
Split loose his breastplate. And he stood there, naked,
Astounded, his silvery limbs floating away,   845
Until one of the Trojans slipped up behind him
And put his spear through, a boy named Euphorbus,
The best his age with a spear, mounted or on foot.
He had already distinguished himself in this war
By knocking twenty warriors out of their cars   850
The first time he went out for chariot lessons.
It was this boy who took his chance at you,
Patroclus, but instead of finishing you off,
He pulled his spear out and ran back where he belonged,
Unwilling to face even an unarmed Patroclus,   855
Who staggered back toward his comrades, still alive,
But overcome by the god's stroke, and the spear.

Hector was watching this, and when he saw
Patroclus withdrawing with a wound, he muscled
His way through to him and rammed his spearhead   860
Into the pit of his belly and all the way through.
Patroclus fell heavily. You could hear the Greeks wince.

   A boar does not wear out easily, but a lion
   Will overpower it when the two face off
   Over a trickling spring up in the mountains   865
   They both want to drink from. The boar
   Pants hard, but the lion comes out on top.

So too did Hector, whose spear was draining the life
From Menoetius' son, who had himself killed many.

His words beat down on Patroclus like dark wings: 870

"So, Patroclus, you thought you could ransack my city
And ship our women back to Greece to be your slaves.
You little fool. They are defended by me,
By Hector, by my horses and my spear. I am the one,
Troy's best, who keeps their doom at bay. But you,   875

---

1. Because it was divinely made, part of the armor given by the gods to Peleus on his marriage to Thetis.

Patroclus, the vultures will eat you
On this very spot. Your marvelous Achilles.
Has done you no good at all. I can just see it,
Him sitting in his tent and telling you as you left:
'Don't bother coming back to the ships,   880
Patroclus, until you have ripped Hector's heart out
Through his bloody shirt.[2] That's what he said,
Isn't it? And you were stupid enough to listen."

And Patroclus, barely able to shake the words out:

"Brag while you can, Hector. Zeus and Apollo   885
Have given you an easy victory this time.
If they hadn't knocked off my armor,
I could have made mincemeat of twenty like you.
It was Fate, and Leto's son, who killed me.
Of men, Euphorbus. You came in third at best.   890
And one more thing for you to think over.
You're not going to live long. I see Death
Standing at your shoulder, and you going down
Under the hands of Peleus' perfect son."

Death's veil covered him as he said these things;   895
And his soul, bound for Hades, fluttered out
Resentfully, forsaking manhood's bloom.
He was dead when Hector said to him:

"Why prophesy my death, Patroclus?
Who knows? Achilles, son of Thetis,   900
May go down first under my spear."

And propping his heel against the body,
He extracted his bronze spear and took off
After Automedon. But Automedon was gone,
Pulled by immortal horses, the splendid gifts   905
    The gods once gave to Peleus.

[Hector stripped Achilles' divine armor from Patroclus's corpse. A fierce fight for the
body itself ended in partial success for the Greeks; they took Patroclus's body but had
to retreat to their camp, with the Trojans at their heels.]

BOOK XVIII

[The Shield of Achilles]

The fight went on, like wildfire burning.
Antilochus,[3] running hard like a herald,
Found Achilles close to his upswept hulls,
His great heart brooding with premonitions
Of what had indeed already happened.   5

2. Hector is, of course, wrong.   3. A son of Nestor. He has been sent to tell Achilles that Patroclus is
dead.

"This looks bad,
All these Greeks with their hair in the wind
Stampeding off the plain and back to the ships.
God forbid that what my mother told me
Has now come true, that while I'm still alive   10
Trojan hands would steal the sunlight
From the best of all the Myrmidons.
Patroclus, Menoetius' brave son, is dead.
Damn him! I told him only to repel
The enemy fire from our ships,   15
And not to take on Hector in a fight."

Antilochus was in tears when he reached him
And delivered his unendurable message:

"Son of wise Peleus, this is painful news
For you to hear, and I wish it were not true.   20
Patroclus is down, and they are fighting
For his naked corpse. Hector has the armor."

A mist of black grief enveloped Achilles.
He scooped up fistfuls of sunburnt dust
And poured it on his head, fouling   25
His beautiful face. Black ash grimed
His fine-spun cloak as he stretched his huge body
Out in the dust and lay there,
Tearing out his hair with his hands.
The women, whom Achilles and Patroclus   30
Had taken in raids, ran shrieking out of the tent
To be with Achilles, and they beat their breasts
Until their knees gave out beneath them.
Antilochus, sobbing himself, stayed with Achilles
And held his hands—he was groaning   35
From the depths of his soul—for fear
He would lay open his own throat with steel.

The sound of Achilles' grief stung the air.

Down in the water his mother heard him,
Sitting in the sea depths beside her old father,   40
And she began to wail.
                        And the saltwater women
Gathered around her, all the deep-sea Nereids,
Glaucē and Thaleia and Cymodocē,
Neseia and Speio, Thoē and ox-eyed Haliē,   45
Cymothoē, Actaeē, and Limnoeira,
Melitē and Iaera, Amphithoē and Agauē,
Doris, Panopē, and milk-white Galateia,
Nemertes, Apseudes, and Callianassa,
Clymenē, Ianeira, Ianassa, and Maera,   50
Oreithyia and Amatheia, hair streaming behind her,
And all of the other deep-sea Nereids.

They filled the silver, shimmering cave,
And they all beat their breasts.

Thetis led the lament: 55

"Hear me, sisters, hear the pain in my heart.
I gave birth to a son, and that is my sorrow,
My perfect son, the best of heroes.
He grew like a sapling, and I nursed him
As I would a plant on the hill in my garden,   60
And I sent him to Ilion on a sailing ship
To fight the Trojans. And now I will never
Welcome him home again to Peleus' house.
As long as he lives and sees the sunlight
He will be in pain, and I cannot help him.   65
But I'll go now to see and hear my dear son,
Since he is suffering while he waits out the war."

She left the cave, and they went with her,
Weeping, and around them a wave
Broke through the sea, and they came to Troy.   70
They emerged on the beach where the Myrmidons' ships
Formed an encampment around Achilles.
He was groaning deeply, and his mother
Stood next to him and held her son's head.
Her lamentation hung sharp in the air,   75
And then she spoke in low, sorrowful tones:

"Child, why are you crying? What pain
Has come to your heart? Speak, don't hide it.
Zeus has granted your prayer. The Greeks
Have all been beaten back to their ships   80
And suffered horribly. They can't do without you."

Achilles answered her:

"Mother, Zeus may have done all this for me,
But how can I rejoice? My friend is dead,
Patroclus, my dearest friend of all. I loved him,   85
And I killed him. And the armor—
Hector cut him down and took off his body
The heavy, splendid armor, beautiful to see,
That the gods gave to Peleus as a gift
On the day they put you to bed with a mortal.   90
You should have stayed with the saltwater women,
And Peleus should have married a mortal.
But now—it was all so you would suffer pain
For your ravaged son. You will never again
Welcome me home, since I no longer have the will   95
To remain alive among men, not unless Hector
Loses his life on the point of my spear
And pays for despoiling Menoetius' son."

And Thetis, in tears, said to him:

"I won't have you with me for long, my child,   100
If you say such things. Hector's death means yours."

From under a great weight, Achilles answered:

"Then let me die now. I was no help
To him when he was killed out there. He died
Far from home, and he needed me to protect him.   105
But now, since I'm not going home, and wasn't
A light for Patroclus or any of the rest
Of my friends who have been beaten by Hector,
But just squatted by my ships, a dead weight on the earth . . .
I stand alone in the whole Greek army   110
When it comes to war—though some do speak better.
I wish all strife could stop, among gods
And among men, and anger too—it sends
Sensible men into fits of temper,
It drips down our throats sweeter than honey   115
And mushrooms up in our bellies like smoke.
Yes, the warlord Agamemnon angered me.
But we'll let that be, no matter how it hurts,
And conquer our pride, because we must.
But I'm going now to find the man who destroyed   120
My beloved—Hector.
                        As for my own fate,
I'll accept it whenever it pleases Zeus
And the other immortal gods to send it.
Not even Heracles[4] could escape his doom.   125
He was dearest of all to Lord Zeus, but fate
And Hera's hard anger destroyed him.
If it is true that I have a fate like his, then I too
Will lie down in death.
                        But now to win glory   130
And make some Trojan woman or deep-breasted
Dardanian[5] matron wipe the tears
From her soft cheeks, make her sob and groan.
Let them feel how long I've been out of the war.
Don't try, out of love, to stop me. I won't listen."   135

And Thetis, her feet silver on the sand:

"Yes, child. It's not wrong to save your friends
When they are beaten to the brink of death.
But your beautiful armor is in the hands of the Trojans,
The mirrored bronze. Hector himself   140
Has it on his shoulders. He glories in it.
Not for long, though. I see his death is near.

---

4. The greatest of Greek hereos, the son of Zeus by a mortal woman; pursued by the jealousy of Hera, he
was forced to undertake twelve great labors and finally died in agony from the effects of a poisoned garment.
5. Trojan.

But you, don't dive into the red dust of war
Until with your own eyes you see me returning.
Tomorrow I will come with the rising sun   145
Bearing beautiful armor from Lord Hephaestus."

Thetis spoke, turned away
From her son, and said to her saltwater sisters:

"Sink now into the sea's wide lap
And go down to our old father's house   150
And tell him all this. I am on my way
Up to Olympus to visit Hephaestus,
The glorious smith, to see if for my sake
He will give my son glorious armor."

As she spoke they dove into the waves,   155
And the silver-footed goddess was gone
Off to Olympus to fetch arms for her child.

   And while her feet carried her off to Olympus,
Hector yelled, a yell so bloodcurdling and loud
It stampeded the Greeks all the way back   160
To their ships beached on the Hellespont's shore.
They could not pull the body of Patroclus
Out of javelin range, and soon Hector,
With his horses and men, stood over it again.
Three times Priam's resplendent son   165
Took hold of the corpse's heels and tried
To drag it off, bawling commands to his men.
Three times the two Ajaxes put their heads down,
Charged, and beat him back. Unshaken, Hector
Sidestepped, cut ahead, or held his ground   170
With a shout, but never yielded an inch.

       It was like shepherds against a starving lion,
          Helpless to beat it back from a carcass,

The two Ajaxes unable to rout
The son of Priam from Patroclus' corpse.   175
And Hector would have, to his eternal glory,
Dragged the body off, had not Iris[6] stormed
Down from Olympus with a message for Achilles,
Unbeknownst to Zeus and the other gods.
Hera had sent her, and this was her message: 180

"Rise, son of Peleus, most formidable of men.
Rescue Patroclus, for whom a terrible battle
Is pitched by the ships, men killing each other,
Some fighting to save the dead man's body,
The Trojans trying to drag it back   185
To windy Ilion. Hector's mind especially

---

6. Goddess of the rainbow and the usual messenger of the gods in the *Iliad*.

Is bent on this. He means to impale the head
On Troy's palisade after he strips off its skin.
And you just lie there? Think of Patroclus
Becoming a ragbone for Trojan dogs. Shame   190
To your dying day if his corpse is defiled."

The shining sprinter Achilles answered her:

"Iris, which god sent you here?"

And Iris, whose feet are wind, responded:

"None other than Hera, Zeus' glorious wife.   195
But Zeus on high does not know this, nor do
Any of the immortals on snow-capped Olympus."

And Achilles, the great runner:

"How can I go to war? They have my armor.
And my mother told me not to arm myself   200
Until with my own eyes I see her come back
With fine weapons from Hephaestus.
I don't know any other armor that would fit,
Unless maybe the shield of Telamonian Ajax.⁷
But he's out there in the front ranks, I hope,   205
Fighting with his spear over Patroclus dead."

Windfoot Iris responded:

"We know very well that they have your armor.
Just go to the trench and let the Trojans see you.
One look will be enough. The Trojans will back off   210
Out of fear of you, and this will give the Greeks
Some breathing space, what little there is in war."

Iris spoke and was gone. And Achilles,
Whom the gods loved, rose. Around
His mighty shoulders Athena threw   215
Her tasselled aegis,⁸ and the shining goddess
Haloed his head with a golden cloud
That shot flames from its incandescent glow.

    Smoke is rising through the pure upper air
    From a besieged city on a distant island.   220
    Its soldiers have fought hard all day,
    But at sunset they light innumerable fires
    So that their neighbors in other cities
    Might see the glare reflected off the sky
    And sail to their help as allies in war.   225

7. The son of Telemon, the more famous of the two heroes named Ajax. His distinctive attribute in the *Iliad* is a huge shield that covers his whole body.   8. A tasseled garment or piece of armor that belonged to Zeus but was often carried by Athena in poetry and art. It induced panic when shaken at an enemy.

So too the radiance that flared
From Achilles' head and up to the sky.
He went to the trench—away from the wall
And the other Greeks, out of respect
For his mother's tense command. Standing there, 230
He yelled, and behind him Pallas Athena
Amplified his voice, and shock waves
Reverberated through the Trojan ranks.

> *You have heard the piercing sound of horns*
> *When squadrons come to destroy a city.* 235

The Greek's voice was like that,
Speaking bronze that made each Trojan heart
Wince with pain.
                    And the combed horses
Shied from their chariots, eyes wide with fear, 240
And their drivers went numb when they saw
The fire above Achilles' head
Burned into the sky by the Grey-Eyed One.[9]
Three times Achilles shouted from the trench;
Three times the Trojans and their confederates 245
Staggered and reeled, twelve of their best
Lost in the crush of chariots and spears.
But the Greeks were glad to pull Patroclus' body
Out of range and placed it on a litter. His comrades
Gathered around, weeping, and with them Achilles, 250
Shedding hot tears when he saw his loyal friend
Stretched out on the litter, cut with sharp bronze.
He had sent him off to war with horses and chariot,
But he never welcomed him back home again.

And now the ox-eyed Lady Hera 255
Sent the tireless, reluctant sun
Under the horizon into Ocean's streams,
Its last rays touching the departing Greeks with gold.
It had been a day of brutal warfare.

    After the Trojans withdrew from battle, 260
They unhitched their horses from the chariots
And held an assembly before thinking of supper.
They remained on their feet, too agitated to sit,
Terrified, in fact, that Achilles,
After a long absence, was back. 265
Polydamas was the first to speak, prudent
Son of Panthous, the only Trojan who looked
Both ahead and behind.[1] This man was born
The same night as Hector, and was his comrade,
As good with words as Hector was with a spear. 270
He had their best interests at heart when he spoke:

---

9. Athena.   1. I.e., he was a prophet; he knew the past and foresaw the future.

"Take a good look around, my friends. My advice
Is to return to the city and not wait for daylight
On the plain by the ships. We are far from our wall.
As long as this man raged against Agamemnon,   275
The Greeks were easier to fight against.
I too was glad when I spent the night by the ships,
Hoping we would capture their upswept hulls.
That hope has given way to a terrible fear
Of Peleus' swift son. He is a violent man   280
And will not be content to fight on the plain
Where Greeks and Trojans engage in combat.
It is for our city he will fight, and our wives.
We must go back. Trust me, this is how it will be:
Night is holding him back now, immortal night.   285
But if he finds us here tomorrow
When he comes out in his armor in daylight,
Then you will know what Achilles is,
And you will be glad to be back in sacred Ilion—
If you make it back, and are not one   290
Of the many Trojans the dogs and vultures
Will feast upon. I hope I'm not within earshot.
But if we trust my words, as much as it may gall,
We will camp tonight in the marketplace, where
The city is protected by its towers, walls,   295
And high gates closed with bolted, polished doors.
At dawn we take our positions on the wall
In full armor, and so much the worse for him
If he wants to come out from the ships and fight us
For our wall. He will go back to the ships   300
After he has had enough of parading
His high-necked prancers in front of the city.
He will not have the will to force his way in.
Dogs will eat him before he takes our town."

And Hector, glaring at him under his helmet: 305

"Polydamas, I don't like this talk
About a retreat and holing up in the city.
Aren't you sick of being penned inside our walls?
People everywhere used to talk about how rich
Priam's city was, all the gold, all the bronze.   310
Now the great houses are empty, their heirlooms
Sold away to Phrygia, to Maeonia,[2] since Zeus
Has turned wrathful. But now—when the great god,
Son of Cronus, has vouchsafed me the glory
Of hemming the Greeks in beside the sea—   315
Now is no time for you to talk like a fool.
Not a Trojan here will listen. I won't let them.
  Now hear this! All troops will mess tonight
With guards posted and on general alert.

2. Countries in Asia Minor allied with Troy.

If any of you are worried about your effects,   320
You can hand them over for distribution!
Better our men should have them than the Greeks.
At first light we strap on our armor
And start fighting hard by the ships.
If Achilles really has risen up again   325
And wants to come out, he'll find it tough going,
For I will be there. I, for one,
Am not retreating. Maybe he'll win, maybe I will.
The War God doesn't care which one he kills."

Thus Hector, and the Trojans cheered,   330
The fools, their wits dulled by Pallas Athena.
Hector's poor counsel won all the applause,
And not a man praised Polydamas' good sense.
Then the troops started supper.

                    But the Greeks   335
Mourned Patroclus the whole night through.
Achilles began the incessant lamentation,
Laying his man-slaying hands on Patroclus' chest
And groaning over and over like a bearded lion

   Whose cubs some deer hunter has smuggled out   340
   Of the dense woods. When the lion returns,
   It tracks the human from valley to valley,
   Growling low the whole time. Sometimes it finds him.

Achilles' deep voice sounded among the Myrmidons:

"It was all for nothing, what I said that day   345
When I tried to hearten the hero Menoetius,
Telling him I would bring his glorious son
Home to Opoeis[3] with his share of the spoils
After I had sacked Ilion. Zeus does not fulfill
A man's every thought. We two are fated   350
To redden the selfsame earth with our blood,
Right here in Troy. I will never return home
To be welcomed by my old father, Peleus,
Or Thetis, my mother. The earth here will hold me.
And since I will pass under the earth after you,   355
Patroclus, I will not bury you until
I have brought here the armor and head of Hector,
Who killed you, great soul. And I will cut
The throats of twelve Trojan princes
Before your pyre in my wrath. Until then,   360
You will lie here beside our upswept hulls
Just as you are, and round about you
Deep-bosomed Trojan and Dardanian women

---

3. An ancient city near the eastern coast of the central Greek mainland and home of Menoetius, father of
Patroclus.

Will lament you day and night, weeping,
Women we won with blood, sweat and tears,   365
Women we cut through rich cities to get."

With that, he ordered his companions
To put a great cauldron on the fire,
So they could wash the gore
From Patroclus' body without further delay.   370
They put a cauldron used for heating baths
Over a blazing fire and poured in the water,
Then stoked the fire with extra wood.
The flames licked the cauldron's belly
And the water grew warm. When it was boiling   375
In the glowing bronze, they washed the body,
Anointed it with rich olive oil,
And filled the wounds with a seasoned ointment.
Then they laid him on his bed, covered him
From head to foot with a soft linen cloth,   380
And spread a white mantle above it.
Then the whole night through the Myrmidons
Stood with Achilles, mourning Patroclus.

Zeus said to Hera, his wife and sister:

"So you have had your way, my ox-eyed lady.   385
You have roused Achilles, swift of foot. Truly,
The long-haired Greeks must be from your womb."

And the ox-eyed lady Hera replied:

"Awesome son of Cronus, what a thing to say!
Even a mortal man, without my wisdom,   390
Will succeed in his efforts for another man.
How then was I—the highest of goddesses
Both by my own birth and by marriage to you,
The lord and ruler of all the immortals—
Not to cobble up evil for Troy in my wrath?"   395

   While they spoke to each other this way,
Thetis' silver feet took her to Hephaestus' house,
A mansion the lame god had built himself
Out of starlight and bronze, and beyond all time.
She found him at his bellows, glazed with sweat   400
As he hurried to complete his latest project,
Twenty cauldrons on tripods to line his hall,
With golden wheels at the base of each tripod
So they could move by themselves to the gods' parties
And return to his house—a wonder to see.   405
They were almost done. The intricate handles
Still had to be attached. He was getting these ready,
Forging the rivets with inspired artistry,
When the silver-footed goddess came up to him.

And Charis,[4] Hephaestus' wife, lovely   410
In her shimmering veil, saw her, and running up,
She clasped her hand and said to her:

"My dear Thetis, so grave in your long, robe,
What brings you here now? You almost never visit.
Do come inside so I can offer you something."   415

And the shining goddess led her along
And had her sit down in a graceful
Silver-studded chair with a footstool.
Then she called to Hephaestus, and said:

"Hephaestus, come here.   420
Thetis needs you for something."

And the renowned smith called back:

"Thetis? Then the dread goddess I revere
Is inside. She saved me when I lay suffering
From my long fall, after my shameless mother   425
Threw me out, wanting to hide my infirmity.
And I really would have suffered, had not Thetis
And Eurynome, a daughter of Ocean Stream,
Taken me into their bosom. I stayed with them
Nine years, forging all kinds of jewelry,   430
Brooches and bracelets and necklaces and pins,
In their hollow cave, while the Ocean's tides,
Murmuring with foam, flowed endlessly around.
No one knew I was there, neither god nor mortal,
Except my rescuers, Eurynome and Thetis.   435
Now the goddess has come to our house.
I owe her my life and would repay her in full.
Set out our finest for her, Charis,
While I put away my bellows and tools."

He spoke and raised his panting bulk   440
Up from his anvil, limping along quickly
On his spindly shanks. He set the bellows
Away from the fire, gathered up the tools
He had been using, and put them away
In a silver chest. Then he took a sponge   445
And wiped his face and hands, his thick neck,
And his shaggy chest. He put on a tunic,
Grabbed a stout staff, and as he went out
Limping, attendants rushed up to support him,
Attendants made of gold who looked like real girls,   450
With a mind within, and a voice, and strength,
And knowledge of crafts from the immortal gods.
These busily moved to support their lord,

---

4. Literally, "Grace" or "Beauty."

And he came hobbling up to where Thetis was,
Sat himself down on a polished chair,   455
And clasping her hand in his, he said:

"My dear Thetis, so grave in your long robe,
What brings you here now? You almost never visit.
Tell me what you have in mind, and I will do it
If it is anything that is at all possible to do."   460

And Thetis, shedding tears as she spoke:

"Hephaestus, is there a goddess on Olympus
Who has suffered as I have? Zeus son of Cronus
Has given me suffering beyond all the others.
Of all the saltwater women he singled me out   465
To be subject to a man, Aeacus' son Peleus.
I endured a man's bed, much against my will.
He lies in his halls forspent with old age,
But I have other griefs now. He gave me a son
To bear and to rear, the finest of heroes.   470
He grew like a sapling, and I nursed him
As I would nurse a plant in my hillside garden,
And I sent him to Ilion on a sailing ship
To fight the Trojans. And now I will never
Welcome him home again to Peleus' house.   475
As long as he lives and sees the sunlight
He will be in pain, and I cannot help him.
The girl that the army chose as his prize
Lord Agamemnon took out of his arms.
He was wasting his heart out of grief for her,   480
But now the Trojans have penned the Greeks
In their beachhead camp, and the Argive elders
Have petitioned him with a long list of gifts.
He refused to beat off the enemy himself,
But he let Patroclus wear his armor,   485
And sent him into battle with many men.
All day long they fought by the Scaean Gates
And would have sacked the city that very day,
But after Menoetius' valiant son
Had done much harm, Apollo killed him   490
In the front ranks and gave Hector the glory.
So I have come to your knees, to see if you
Will give my son, doomed to die young,
A shield and helmet, a fine set of greaves,
And a corselet too. His old armor was lost   495
When the Trojans killed his faithful companion,
And now he lies on the ground in anguish."

And the renowned smith answered her:

"Take heart, Thetis, and do not be distressed.
I only regret I do not have the power   500

To hide your son from death when it comes.
But armor he will have, forged to a wonder,
And its terrible beauty will be a marvel to men."

Hephaestus left her there and went to his bellows,
Turned them toward the fire and ordered them to work.   505
And the bellows, all twenty, blew on the crucibles,
Blasting out waves of heat in whatever direction
Hephaestus wanted as he hustled here and there
Around his forge and the work progressed.
He cast durable bronze onto the fire, and tin,   510
Precious gold and silver. Then he positioned
His enormous anvil up on its block
And grasped his mighty hammer
In one hand, and in the other his tongs.

He made a shield first, heavy and huge,   515
Every inch of it intricately designed.
He threw a triple rim around it, glittering
Like lightning, and he made the strap silver.
The shield itself was five layers thick, and he
Crafted its surface with all of his genius.   520

    On it he made the earth, the sky, the sea,
The unwearied sun, and the moon near full,
And all the signs that garland the sky,
Pleiades, Hyades, mighty Orion,
And the Bear[5] they also call the Wagon,   525
Which pivots in place and looks back at Orion
    And alone is aloof from the wash of Ocean.

    On it he made two cities, peopled
And beautiful. Weddings in one, festivals,
Brides led from their rooms by torchlight   530
Up through the town, bridal song rising,
Young men reeling in dance to the tune
Of lyres and flutes, and the women
Standing in their doorways admiring them.
There was a crowd in the market-place   535
And a quarrel arising between two men
Over blood money for a murder,
One claiming the right to make restitution,
The other refusing to accept any terms.
They were heading for an arbitrator   540
And the people were shouting, taking sides,
But heralds restrained them. The elders sat
On polished stone seats in the sacred circle
And held in their hands the staves of heralds.
The pair rushed up and pleaded their cases,   545

---

5. Ursa Major, or the Big Dipper, which never descends below the horizon (i.e., into Ocean). The Pleiades,
Hyades, and Orion are all clusters of stars or constellations. Orion was a giant hunter of Greek mythology.

And between them lay two ingots of gold
   For whoever spoke straightest in judgment.

   Around the other city two armies
Of glittering soldiery were encamped.
Their leaders were at odds—should they   550
Move in for the kill or settle for a division
Of all the lovely wealth the citadel held fast?
The citizens wouldn't surrender, and armed
For an ambush. Their wives and little children
Were stationed on the wall, and with the old men   555
Held it against attack. The citizens moved out,
Led by Ares and Pallas Athena,
Both of them gold, and their clothing was gold,
Beautiful and larger than life in their armor, as befits
Gods in their glory, and all the people were smaller.   560
They came to a position perfect for an ambush,
A spot on the river where stock came to water,
And took their places, concealed by fiery bronze.
Farther up they had two lookouts posted
Waiting to sight shambling cattle and sheep,   565
Which soon came along, trailed by two herdsmen
Playing their panpipes, completely unsuspecting.
When the townsmen lying in ambush saw this
They ran up, cut off the herds of cattle and fleecy
Silver sheep, and killed the two herdsmen.   570
When the armies sitting in council got wind
Of the ruckus with the cattle, they mounted
Their high-stepping horses and galloped to the scene.
They took their stand and fought along the river banks,
Throwing bronze-tipped javelins against each other.   575
Among them were Hate and Din and the Angel of Death,
Holding a man just wounded, another unwounded,
And dragging one dead by his heels from the fray,
And the cloak on her shoulders was red with human blood.
They swayed in battle and fought like living men,   580
   And each side salvaged the bodies of their dead.

   On it he put a soft field, rich farmland
Wide and thrice-tilled, with many plowmen
Driving their teams up and down rows.
Whenever they came to the end of the field   585
And turned, a man would run up and hand them
A cup of sweet wine. Then they turned again
Back up the furrow pushing on through deep soil
To reach the other end. The field was black
Behind them, just as if plowed, and yet   590
   It was gold, all gold, forged to a wonder.

   On it he put land sectioned off for a king,
Where reapers with sharp sickles were working.
Cut grain lay deep where it fell in the furrow,

And binders made sheaves bound with straw bands.   595
Three sheaf-binders stood by, and behind them children
Gathered up armfuls and kept passing them on.
The king stood in silence near the line of reapers,
Holding his staff, and his heart was happy.
Under an oaktree nearby heralds were busy   600
Preparing a feast from an ox they had slaughtered
In sacrifice, and women were sprinkling it
   With abundant white barley for the reapers' dinner.

   On it he put a vineyard loaded with grapes,
Beautiful in gold. The clusters were dark,   605
And the vines were set everywhere on silver poles.
Around he inlaid a blue enamel ditch
And a fence of tin. A solitary path led to it,
And vintagers filed along it to harvest the grapes.
Girls, all grown up, and light-hearted boys   610
Carried the honey-sweet fruit in wicker baskets.
Among them a boy picked out on a lyre
A beguiling tune and sang the Linos song[6]
In a low, light voice, and the harvesters
   Skipped in time and shouted the refrain.   615

   On it he made a herd of straight-horn cattle.
The cows were wrought of gold and tin
And rushed out mooing from the farmyard dung
To a pasture by the banks of a roaring river,
Making their way through swaying reeds.   620
Four golden herdsmen tended the cattle,
And nine nimble dogs followed along.
Two terrifying lions at the front of the herd
Were pulling down an ox. Its long bellows alerted
The dogs and the lads, who were running on up,   625
But the two lions had ripped the bull's hide apart
And were gulping down the guts and black blood.
The shepherds kept trying to set on the dogs,
But they shied away from biting the lions
   And stood there barking just out of harm's way.   630

   On it the renowned lame god made a pasture
In a lovely valley, wide, with silvery sheep in it,
   And stables, roofed huts, and stone animal pens.

   On it the renowned lame god embellished
A dancing ground, like the one Daedalus   635
Made for ringleted Ariadne[7] in wide Cnossus.
Young men and girls in the prime of their beauty
Were dancing there, hands clasped around wrists.

6. I.e., a dirge for Linos, a fabled musician. It may originally have been associated in Near Eastern cult with the annual "death" of vegetation.   7. Daughter of Minos, king of Crete. Daedalus was the prototypical craftsman who built the labyrinth to house the Minotaur and who escaped from Crete on wings with his son Icarus. Cnossus was the site of Minos's great palace.

The girls wore delicate linens, and the men
Finespun tunics glistening softly with oil.   640
Flowers crowned the girls' heads, and the men
Had golden knives hung from silver straps.
They ran on feet that knew how to run
With the greatest ease, like a potter's wheel
When he stoops to cup it in the palms of his hands   645
And gives it a spin to see how it runs. Then they
Would run in lines that weaved in and out.
A large crowd stood round the beguiling dance,
Enjoying themselves, and two acrobats
    Somersaulted among them on cue to the music.   650

On it he put the great strength of the River Ocean,
Lapping the outermost rim of the massive shield.

And when he had wrought the shield, huge and heavy,
He made a breastplate gleaming brighter than fire
And a durable helmet that fit close at the temples,   655
Lovely and intricate, and crested with gold.
And he wrought leg-armor out of pliant tin.
And when the renowned lame god had finished this gear,
He set it down before Achilles' mother,
And she took off like a hawk from snow-capped Olympus,   660
Carrying armor through the sky like summer lightning.

[Achilles finally accepted gifts of restitution from Agamemnon, as he had refused to
do earlier. His return to the fighting brought terror to the Trojans and turned the
battle into a rout in which Achilles killed every Trojan that crossed his path. As he
pursued Agenor, Apollo tricked him by rescuing his intended victim (he spirited him
away in a mist) and assumed Agenor's shape to lead Achilles away from the walls of
Troy. The Trojans took refuge in the city, all except Hector.]

BOOK XXII

[The Death of Hector]

   Everywhere you looked in Troy, exhausted
Soldiers, glazed with sweat like winded deer,
Leaned on the walls, cooling down
And slaking their thirst.
             Outside, the Greeks   5
Formed up close to the wall, locking their shields.
In the dead air between the Greeks
And Troy's Western Gate, Destiny
Had Hector pinned, waiting for death.

Then Apollo called back to Achilles: 10

"Son of Peleus, you're fast on your feet,
But you'll never catch me, man chasing god.
Or are you too raging mad to notice
I'm a god? Don't you care about fighting

The Trojans anymore? You've chased them back   15
Into their town, but now you've veered off here.
You'll never kill me. You don't hold my doom."

And the shining sprinter, Achilles:

"That was a dirty trick, Apollo,
Turning me away from the wall like that!   20
I could have ground half of Troy face down
In the dirt! Now you've robbed me
Of my glory and saved them easily
Because you have no retribution to fear.
I swear, I'd make you pay if I could!"   25

His mind opened to the clear space before him,
And he was off toward the town, moving

　　Like a thoroughbred stretching it out
　　Over the plain for the final sprint home—

Achilles, lifting his knees as he lengthened his stride.   30

Priam saw him first, with his old man's eyes,
A single point of light on Troy's dusty plain.

　　Sirius[8] *rises late in the dark, liquid sky*
　　On summer nights, star of stars,
　　Orion's Dog they call it, brightest   35
　　Of all, but an evil portent, bringing heat
　　And fevers to suffering humanity.

Achilles' bronze gleamed like this as he ran.

And the old man groaned, and beat his head
With his hands, and stretched out his arms   40
To his beloved son, Hector, who had
Taken his stand before the Western Gate,
Determined to meet Achilles in combat.

Priam's voice cracked as he pleaded:

"Hector, my boy, you can't face Achilles   45
Alone like that, without any support—
You'll go down in a minute. He's too much
For you, son, he won't stop at anything!
O, if only the gods loved him as I do:
Vultures and dogs would be gnawing his corpse.   50
Then some grief might pass from my heart.

---

8. The Dog Star, the brightest star in the constellation Canis Major. In Greece it rises in late summer, the
hottest time of the year.

So many fine sons he's taken from me,
Killed or sold them as slaves in the islands.
Two of them now, Lycaon and Polydorus,
I can't see with the Trojans safe in town,   55
Laothoë's boys.[9] If the Greeks have them
We'll ransom them with the gold and silver
Old Altes gave us.[1] But if they're dead
And gone down to Hades, there will be grief
For myself and the mother who bore them.   60
The rest of the people won't mourn so much
Unless *you* go down at Achilles' hands.
So come inside the wall, my boy.
Live to save the men and women of Troy.
Don't just hand Achilles the glory   65
And throw your life away. Show some pity for me
Before I go out of my mind with grief
And Zeus finally destroys me in my old age,
After I have seen all the horrors of war—
My sons butchered, my daughters dragged off,   70
Raped, bedchambers plundered, infants
Dashed to the ground in this terrible war,
My sons' wives abused by murderous Greeks.
And one day some Greek soldier will stick me
With cold bronze and draw the life from my limbs,   75
And the dogs that I fed at my table,
My watchdogs, will drag me outside and eat
My flesh raw, crouched in my doorway, lapping
My blood.
        When a young man is killed in war,   80
Even though his body is slashed with bronze,
He lies there beautiful in death, noble.
But when the dogs maraud an old man's head,
Griming his white hair and beard and private parts,
There's no human fate more pitiable."   85

And the old man pulled the white hair from his head,
But did not persuade Hector.
           His mother then,
Wailing, sobbing, laid open her bosom
And holding out a breast spoke through her tears: 90

"Hector, my child, if ever I've soothed you
With this breast, remember it now, son, and
Have pity on me. Don't pit yourself
Against that madman. Come inside the wall.
If Achilles kills you I will never   95
Get to mourn you laid out on a bier, O
My sweet blossom, nor will Andromache,

---

9. Priam had more than one wife. Achilles killed Polydorus and Lycaon in the fighting outside the city
(books 20 and 21).   1. The dowry of Laothoë, Altes' daughter.

Your beautiful wife, but far from us both
Dogs will eat your body by the Greek ships."

So the two of them pleaded with their son,   100
But did not persuade him or touch his heart.
Hector held his ground as Achilles' bulk
Loomed larger. He waited as a snake waits,

   Tense and coiled
   As a man approaches
   Its lair in the mountains,   105
   Venom in its fangs
   And poison in its heart,
   Glittering eyes
   Glaring from the rocks: 110

So Hector waited, leaning his polished shield
Against one of the towers in Troy's bulging wall,
But his heart was troubled with brooding thoughts:

"Now what? If I take cover inside,
Polydamas will be the first to reproach me.   115
He begged me to lead the Trojans back
To the city on that black night when Achilles rose.
But I wouldn't listen, and now I've destroyed
Half the army through my recklessness.
I can't face the Trojan men and women now,   120
Can't bear to hear some lesser man say,
'Hector trusted his strength and lost the army.'
That's what they'll say. I'll be much better off
Facing Achilles, either killing him
Or dying honorably before the city.   125
   But what if I lay down all my weapons,
Bossed shield, heavy helmet, prop my spear
Against the wall, and go meet Achilles,
Promise him we'll surrender Helen
And everything Paris brought back with her   130
In his ships' holds to Troy—that was the beginning
Of this war—give all of it back
To the sons of Atreus and divide
Everything else in the town with the Greeks,
And swear a great oath not to hold   135
Anything back, but share it all equally,
All the treasure in Troy's citadel.
   But why am I talking to myself like this?
I can't go out there unarmed. Achilles
Will cut me down in cold blood if I take off   140
My armor and go out to meet him
Naked like a woman. This is no time
For talking, the way a boy and a girl
Whisper to each other from oak tree or rock,
A boy and a girl with all their sweet talk.   145

Better to lock up in mortal combat
As soon as possible and see to whom
God on Olympus grants the victory."

Thus spoke Hector.
        And Achilles closed in 150
Like the helmeted God of War himself,
The ash-wood spear above his right shoulder
Rocking in the light that played from his bronze
In gleams of fire and the rising sun.
And when Hector saw it he lost his nerve, 155
Panicked, and ran, leaving the gates behind,
With Achilles on his tail, confident in his speed.

   You have seen a falcon
   In a long, smooth dive
   Attack a fluttering dove 160
   Far below in the hills.
   The falcon screams,
   Swoops, and plunges
   In its lust for prey.

So Achilles swooped and Hector trembled 165
In the shadow of Troy's wall.
                Running hard,
They passed Lookout Rock and the windy fig tree,
Following the loop of the wagon road.
They came to the wellsprings of eddying 170
Scamander,[2] two beautiful pools, one
Boiling hot with steam rising up,
The other flowing cold even in summer,
Cold as freezing sleet, cold as tundra snow.
There were broad basins there, lined with stone, 175
Where the Trojan women used to wash their silky clothes
In the days of peace, before the Greeks came.

They ran by these springs, pursuer and pursued—
A great man out front, a far greater behind—
And they ran all out. This was not a race 180
For such a prize as athletes compete for,
An oxhide or animal for sacrifice, but a race
For the lifeblood of Hector, breaker of horses.

   But champion horses wheeling round the course,
   Hooves flying, pouring it on in a race for a prize— 185
   A woman or tripod—at a hero's funeral games

Will give you some idea of how these heroes looked
As they circled Priam's town three times running
   While all the gods looked on.

---

2. One of the two rivers in the plain of Troy.

Zeus, the gods' father and ours, spoke: 190

"I do not like what I see, a man close
To my heart chased down around Troy's wall.
Hector has burned many an ox's thigh
To me, both on Ida's peaks and in the city's
High holy places, and now Achilles   195
Is running him down around Priam's town.
Think you now, gods, and take counsel whether
We should save him from death or deliver him
Into Achilles' hands, good man though he be."

The grey-eyed goddess Athena answered: 200

     "O Father,
You may be the Lord of Lightning and the Dark Cloud,
But what a thing to say, to save a mortal man,
With his fate already fixed, from rattling death!
Do it. But don't expect us all to approve."   205

Zeus loomed like a thunderhead, but answered gently:

"There, there, daughter, my heart wasn't in it.
I did not mean to displease you, my child. Go now,
Do what you have in mind without delay."

Athena had been longing for action   210
And at his word shot down from Olympus,

As Achilles bore down on Hector.

     A hunting hound starts a fawn in the hills,
     Follows it through brakes and hollows,
     And if it hides in a thicket, circles,   215
     Picks up the trail, and renews the chase.

No more could Hector elude Achilles.
Every time Hector surged for the Western Gate
Under the massive towers, hoping for
Trojan archers to give him some cover,   220
Achilles cut him off and turned him back
Toward the plain, keeping the inside track.

     Running in a dream, you can't catch up,
     You can't catch up and you can't get away.

No more could Achilles catch Hector   225
Or Hector escape.
                    And how could Hector
Have ever escaped death's black birds
If Apollo had not stood by his side
This one last time and put life in his knees?   230

Achilles shook his head at his soldiers:
He would not allow anyone to shoot
At Hector and win glory with a hit,
Leaving him only to finish him off.

But when they reached the springs the fourth time,   235
Father Zeus stretched out his golden scales
And placed on them two agonizing deaths,
One for Achilles and one for Hector.
When he held the beam, Hector's doom sank down
Toward Hades. And Phoebus Apollo left him.   240

By now the grey-eyed goddess Athena
Was at Achilles' side, and her words flew fast:

"There's nothing but glory on the beachhead
For us now, my splendid Achilles,
Once we take Hector out of action, and   245
There's no way he can escape us now,
Not even if my brother Apollo has a fit
And rolls on the ground before the Almighty.
You stay here and catch your breath while I go
To persuade the man to put up a fight."   250

Welcome words for Achilles. He rested,
Leaning on his heavy ash and bronze spear,
While the goddess made her way to Hector,
The spitting image of Deïphobus.[3]
And her voice sounded like his as she said: 255

"Achilles is pushing you hard, brother,
In this long footrace around Priam's town.
Why don't we stand here and give him a fight?"

Hector's helmet flashed as he turned and said:

"Deïphobus, you've always been my favorite   260
Brother, and again you've shown me why,
Having the courage to come out for me,
Leaving the safety of the wall, while all
Priam's other sons are cowering inside."

And Athena, her eyes as grey as winter moons: 265

"Mother and father begged me by my knees
To stay inside, and so did all my friends.
That's how frightened they are, Hector. But I
Could not bear the pain in my heart, brother.

3. Hector's brother.

Now let's get tough and fight and not spare   270
Any spears. Either Achilles kills us both
And drags our blood-soaked gear to the ships,
Or he goes down with your spear in his guts."

That's how Athena led him on, with guile.
And when the two heroes faced each other,   275
Great Hector, helmet shining, spoke first:

"I'm not running any more, Achilles.
Three times around the city was enough.
I've got my nerve back. It's me or you now.
But first we should swear a solemn oath.   280
With all the gods as witnesses, I swear:
If Zeus gives me the victory over you,
I will not dishonor your corpse, only
Strip the armor and give the body back
To the Greeks. Promise you'll do the same."   285

And Achilles, fixing his eyes on him:

"Don't try to cut any deals with me, Hector.
Do lions make peace treaties with men?
Do wolves and lambs agree to get along?
No, they hate each other to the core,   290
And that's how it is between you and me,
No talk of agreements until one of us
Falls and gluts Ares with his blood.
By God, you'd better remember everything
You ever knew about fighting with spears.   295
But you're as good as dead. Pallas Athena
And my spear will make you pay in a lump
For the agony you've caused by killing my friends."

With that he pumped his spear arm and let fly.
Hector saw the long flare the javelin made, and ducked.   300
The bronze point sheared the air over his head
And rammed into the earth. But Athena
Pulled it out and gave it back to Achilles
Without Hector noticing. And Hector,
Prince of Troy, taunted Achilles: 305

"Ha! You missed! Godlike Achilles! It looks like
You didn't have my number after all.
You said you did, but you were just trying
To scare me with big words and empty talk.
Did you think I'd run and you'd plant a spear   310
In my back? It'll take a direct hit in my chest,
Coming right at you, that and a god's help too.
Now see if you can dodge this piece of bronze.
Swallow it whole! The war will be much easier
On the Trojans with you dead and gone."   315

And Hector let his heavy javelin fly,
A good throw, too, hitting Achilles' shield
Dead center, but it only rebounded away.
Angry that his throw was wasted, Hector
Fumbled about for a moment, reaching   320
For another spear. He shouted to Deïphobus,
But Deïphobus was nowhere in sight.
It was then that Hector knew in his heart
What had happened, and said to himself:

"I hear the gods calling me to my death.   325
I thought I had a good man here with me,
Deïphobus, but he's still on the wall.
Athena tricked me. Death is closing in
And there's no escape. Zeus and Apollo
Must have chosen this long ago, even though   330
They used to be on my side. My fate is here,
But I will not perish without some great deed
That future generations will remember."

And he drew the sharp broadsword that hung
By his side and gathered himself for a charge.   335

    A high-flying eagle dives
    Through ebony clouds down
    To the sun-scutched[4] *plain to claw*
    A lamb or a quivering hare

Thus Hector's charge, and the light   340
That played from his blade's honed edge.

Opposite him, Achilles exploded forward, fury
Incarnate behind the curve of his shield,
A glory of metalwork, and the plumes
Nodded and rippled on his helmet's crest,   345
Thick golden horsehair set by Hephaestus,
And his spearpoint glinted like the Evening Star

    In the gloom of night
    Star of perfect splendor,

A gleam in the air as Achilles poised   350
His spear with murderous aim at Hector,
Eyes boring into the beautiful skin,
Searching for the weak spot. Hector's body
Was encased in the glowing bronze armor
He had stripped from the fallen Patroclus,   355
But where the collarbones join at the neck
The gullet offered swift and certain death.

4. Sun-beaten.

It was there Achilles drove his spear through
As Hector charged. The heavy bronze apex
Pierced the soft neck but did not slit the windpipe,   360
So that Hector could speak still.

He fell back in the dust.

                              And Achilles exulted:

"So you thought you could get away with it
Didn't you, Hector? Killing Patroclus   365
And ripping off his armor, *my* armor,
Thinking I was too far away to matter.
You fool. His avenger was far greater—
And far closer—than you could imagine,
Biding his time back in our beachhead camp.   370
And now I have laid you out on the ground.
Dogs and birds are going to draw out your guts
While the Greeks give Patroclus burial."

And Hector, barely able to shake the words out:

"I beg you, Achilles, by your own soul   375
And by your parents, do not
Allow the dogs to mutilate my body
By the Greek ships. Accept the gold and bronze
Ransom my father and mother will give you
And send my body back home to be burned   380
In honor by the Trojans and their wives."

And Achilles, fixing him with a stare:

"Don't whine to me about my parents,
You dog! I wish my stomach would let me
Cut off your flesh in strips and eat it raw   385
For what you've done to me. There is no one
And no way to keep the dogs off your head,
Not even if they bring ten or twenty
Ransoms, pile them up here and promise more,
Not even if Dardanian Priam weighs your body   390
Out in gold, not even then will your mother
Ever get to mourn you laid out on a bier.
No, dogs and birds will eat every last scrap."

Helmet shining, Hector spoke his last words:

"So this is Achilles. There was no way   395
To persuade you. Your heart is a lump
Of iron. But the gods will not forget this,
And I will have my vengeance on that day
When Paris and Apollo destroy you
In the long shadow of Troy's Western Gate."   400

Death's veil covered him as he said these things,
And his soul, bound for Hades, fluttered out
Resentfully, forsaking manhood's bloom.

He was dead when Achilles spoke to him:

"Die and be done with it. As for my fate,   405
I'll accept it whenever Zeus sends it."

And he drew the bronze spear out of the corpse,
Laid it aside, then stripped off the blood-stained armor.
The other Greeks crowded around
And could not help but admire Hector's   410
Beautiful body, but still they stood there
Stabbing their spears into him, smirking.

"Hector's a lot softer to the touch now
Than he was when he was burning our ships,"

One of them would say, pulling out his spear.   415

After Achilles had stripped the body
He rose like a god and addressed the Greeks:

"Friends, Argive commanders and councillors,
The gods have granted us this man's defeat,
Who did us more harm than all the rest   420
Put together. What do you say we try
Laying a close siege on the city now
So we can see what the Trojans intend—
Whether they will give up the citadel
With Hector dead, or resolve to fight on?   425
   But what am I thinking of? Patroclus' body
Still lies by the ships, unmourned, unburied,
Patroclus, whom I will never forget
As long as I am among the living,
Until I rise no more; and even if   430
In Hades the dead do not remember,
Even there I will remember my dear friend.
   Now let us chant the victory paean, sons
Of the Achaeans, and march back to our ships
With this hero in tow. The power and the glory   435
Are ours. We have killed great Hector,
Whom all the Trojans honored as a god."

But it was shame and defilement Achilles
Had in mind for Hector. He pierced the tendons
Above the heels and cinched them with leather thongs   440
To his chariot, letting Hector's head drag.
He mounted, hoisted up the prize armor,
And whipped his team to a willing gallop
Across the plain. A cloud of dust rose

Where Hector was hauled, and the long black hair   445
Fanned out from his head, so beautiful once,
As it trailed in the dust. In this way Zeus
Delivered Hector into his enemies' hands
To be defiled in his own native land.

Watching this from the wall, Hector's mother   450
Tore off her shining veil and screamed,
And his old father groaned pitifully,
And all through town the people were convulsed
With lamentation, as if Troy itself,
The whole towering city, were in flames.   455
They were barely able to restrain
The old man, frantic to run through the gates,
Imploring them all, rolling in the dung,
And finally making this desperate appeal:

"Please let me go, alone, to the Greek ships.   460
I don't care if you're worried. I want to see
If that monster will respect my age, pity me
For the sake of his own father, Peleus,
Who is about my age, old Peleus
Who bore him and bred him to be a curse   465
For the Trojans, but he's caused me more pain
Than anyone, so many of my sons,
Beautiful boys, he's killed. I miss them all,
But I miss Hector more than all of them.
My grief for him will lay me in the earth.   470
Hector! You should have died in my arms, son!
Then we could have satisfied our sorrow,
Mourning and weeping, your mother and I."

The townsmen moaned as Priam was speaking.
Then Hecuba raised the women's lament: 475

"Hector, my son, I am desolate!
How can I live with suffering like this,
With you dead? You were the only comfort
I had, day and night, wherever you were
In the town, and you were the only hope   480
For Troy's men and women. They honored you
As a god when you were alive, Hector.
Now death and doom have overtaken you."

    And all this time Andromache had heard
Nothing about Hector—news had not reached her   485
That her husband was caught outside the walls.
She was working the loom in an alcove
Of the great hall, embroidering flowers
Into a purple cloak, and had just called
To her serving women, ordering them   490
To put a large cauldron on the fire, so

A steaming bath would be ready for Hector
When he came home from battle. Poor woman,
She had little idea how far from warm baths
Hector was, undone by the Grey-Eyed One   495
And delivered into the hands of the Greeks.

Then she heard the lamentation from the tower.

She trembled, and the shuttle fell
To the floor. Again she called her women:

"Two of you come with me. I must see   500
What has happened. That was Hecuba's voice.
My heart is in my throat, my knees are like ice.
Something terrible has happened to one
Of Priam's sons. O God, I'm afraid
Achilles has cut off my brave Hector   505
Alone on the plain outside the city
And has put an end to my husband's
Cruel courage. Hector never held back
Safe in the ranks; he always charged ahead,
Second to no one in fighting spirit."   510

With these words on her lips Andromache
Ran outdoors like a madwoman, heart racing,
Her two waiting-women following behind.
She reached the tower, pushed through the crowd,
And looking out from the wall saw her husband   515
As the horses dragged him disdainfully
Away from the city to the hollow Greek ships.

Black night swept over her eyes.
She reeled backward, gasping, and her veil
And glittering headbands flew off,   520
And the diadem golden Aphrodite
Gave her on that day when tall-helmed Hector
Led her from her father's house in marriage.
And now her womenfolk were around her,
Hector's sisters and his brother's wives,   525
Holding her as she raved madly for death,
Until she caught her breath and her distraught
Spirit returned to her breast. She moaned then
And, surrounded by Trojan women, spoke:

"Hector, you and I have come to the grief   530
We were both born for, you in Priam's Troy
And I in Thebes in the house of Eëtion
Who raised me there beneath wooded Plakos
Under an evil star. Better never to have been born.
And now you are going to Hades' dark world,   535
Underground, leaving me in sorrow,
A widow in the halls, with an infant,

The son you and I bore but cannot bless.
You can't help him now you are dead, Hector,
And he can never help you. Even if   540
He lives through this unbearable war,
There's nothing left for him in life but pain
And deprivation, all his property
Lost to others. An orphan has no friends.
He hangs his head, his cheeks are wet with tears.   545
He has to beg from his dead father's friends,
Tugging on one man's cloak, another's tunic,
And if they pity him he gets to sip
From someone's cup, just enough to moisten
His lips but not enough to quench his thirst.   550
Or a child with both parents still alive
Will push him away from a feast, taunting him,
'Go away, your father doesn't eat with us.'
And the boy will go to his widowed mother
In tears, Astyanax, who used to sit   555
In his father's lap and eat nothing, but
Mutton and marrow. When he got sleepy
And tired of playing he would take a nap
In a soft bed nestled in his nurse's arms
His dreaming head filled with blossoming joy.   560
But now he'll suffer, now he's lost his father.
The Trojans called him Astyanax
Because you alone were Troy's defender,
You alone protected their walls and gates.
Now you lie by the curved prows of the ships,   565
Far from your parents. The dogs will glut
On your naked body, and shiny maggots
Will eat what's left.
                    Your clothes are stored away,
Beautiful, fine clothes made by women's hands—   570
I'll burn them all now in a blazing fire.
They're no use to you, you'll never lie
On the pyre in them. Burning them will be
Your glory before Trojan men and women."

And the women's moans came in over her lament.   575

[Achilles buried Patroclus, and the Greeks celebrated the dead hero's fame with athletic games, for which Achilles gave the prizes.]

BOOK XXIV

[Achilles and Priam]

   The funeral games were over.
The troops dispersed and went to their ships,
Where they turned their attention to supper
And a good night's sleep. But sleep
That masters all had no hold on Achilles.   5
Tears wet his face as he remembered his friend.

He tossed and turned, yearning for Patroclus,
For his manhood and his noble heart,
And all they had done together, the shared pain,
The battles fought, the hard times at sea.
Thinking on all this, he would weep softly,   10
Lying now on his side, now on his back,
And now face down. Then he would rise
To his feet and wander in a daze along the shore.
Dawn never escaped him. As soon as she appeared   15
Over the sea and the dunes, he would hitch
Horses to his chariot and drag Hector behind.
When he had hauled him three times around
Patroclus' tomb, he would rest again in his hut,
Leaving Hector stretched face down in the dust.   20
But Apollo kept Hector's flesh undefiled,
Pitying the man even in death. He kept him
Wrapped in his golden aegis, so that Achilles
Would not scour the skin as he dragged him.

So Achilles defiled Hector in his rage.   25
The gods, looking on, pitied Hector,
And urged Hermes to steal the body,
A plan that pleased all but Hera,
Poseidon, and the Grey-Eyed One,
Who were steady in their hatred   30
For sacred Ilion and Priam's people
Ever since Paris in his blindness
Offended these two goddesses
And honored the one who fed his fatal lust.[5]

    Twelve days went by. Dawn.   35
Phoebus Apollo addressed the immortals:

"How callous can you get? Has Hector
Never burned for you thighs of bulls and goats?
Of course he has. But now you cannot
Bring yourselves to save even his bare corpse   40
For his wife to look upon, and his mother,
And child, and Priam, and his people, who would
Burn him in fire and perform his funeral rites.
No, it's the dread Achilles that you prefer.
His twisted mind is set on what he wants,   45
As savage as a lion bristling with pride,
Attacking men's flocks to make himself a feast.
Achilles has lost all pity and has no shame left.
Shame sometimes hurts men, but it helps them too.
A man may lose someone dearer than Achilles has,   50
A brother from the same womb, or a son,
But when he has wept and mourned, he lets go.

---

5. Aphrodite, whom Paris judged more beautiful than Athena and Hera because he found the bribe that she offered him—Helen—the most attractive.

The Fates have given men an enduring heart.
But this man? After he kills Hector,
He ties him behind his chariot   55
And drags him around his dear friend's tomb.
Does this make him a better or nobler man?
He should fear our wrath, good as he may be,
For he defiles the dumb earth in his rage."

This provoked an angry response from Hera: 60

"What you say might be true, Silverbow,
If we valued Achilles and Hector equally.
But Hector is mortal and suckled at a woman's breast,
While Achilles is born of a goddess whom I
Nourished and reared myself, and gave to a man,   65
Peleus, beloved of the gods, to be his wife.
All of you gods came to her wedding,
And you too were at the feast, lyre in hand,
Our forever faithless and fair-weather friend."

And Zeus, who masses the thunderheads: 70

"Calm down, Hera, and don't be so indignant.
Their honor will not be the same. But Hector
Was dearest to the gods of all in Ilion,
At least to me. He never failed to offer
A pleasing sacrifice. My altar never lacked   75
Libation or burnt savor, our worship due.
But we will not allow his body to be stolen—
Achilles would notice in any case. His mother
Visits him continually night and day.
But I would have one of you summon Thetis   80
So that I might have a word with her. Achilles
Must agree to let Priam ransom Hector."

    Thus spoke Zeus,
And Iris stormed down to deliver his message.
Midway between Samos[6] and rocky Imbros,   85
She dove into the dark sea. The water moaned
As it closed above her, and she sank into the deep

    Like a lead sinker on a line
    That takes a hook of sharpened horn
    Down to deal death to nibbling fish.   90

She found Thetis in a cave's hollow, surrounded
By her saltwater women and wailing
The fate of her faultless son, who would die
On Trojan soil, far from his homeland.
Iris, whose feet are like wind, stood near her: 95

---

6. I.e., Samothrace. It and Imbros are islands in the northeast Aegean Sea.

"Rise, Thetis. Zeus in his wisdom commands you."

And the silver-footed goddess answered her:

"Why would the great god want me? I am ashamed
To mingle with the immortals, distraught as I am.
But I will go, and he will not speak in vain."   100

And she veiled her brightness in a shawl.
Of midnight blue and set out with Iris before her.
The sea parted around them in waves.
They stepped forth on the beach
And sped up the sky, and found themselves   105
Before the face of Zeus. Around him
Were seated all the gods, blessed, eternal.
Thetis sat next to him, and Athena gave place.
Hera put in her hand a fine golden cup
And said some comforting words. Thetis drank   110
And handed the cup back. Then Zeus,
The father of gods and men, began to speak:

"You have come to Olympus, Thetis,
For all your incurable sorrow. I know.
Even so, I will tell you why I have called you.   115
For nine days the gods have argued
About Hector's corpse and about Achilles.
Some want Hermes to steal the body away,
But I accord Achilles the honor in this, hoping
To retain your friendship along with your respect.   120
Go quickly now and tell your son our will.
The gods are indignant, and I, above all,
Am angry that in his heart's fury
He holds Hector by the beaked ships
And will not give him up. He may perhaps fear me   125
And so release the body. Meanwhile,
I will send Iris to great-souled Priam
To have him ransom his son, going to the ships
With gifts that will warm Achilles' heart."

Zeus had spoken, and the silver-footed goddess   130
Streaked down from the peaks of Olympus
And came to her son's hut. She found him there
Lost in grief. His friends were all around,
Busily preparing their morning meal,
For which a great, shaggy ram had been slaughtered.   135
Settling herself beside her weeping child,
She stroked him with her hand and talked to him:

"My son, how long will you let this grief
Eat at your heart, mindless of food and rest?
It would be good to make love to a woman.   140
It hurts me to say it, but you will not live

Much longer. Death and Doom are beside you.
Listen now, I have a message from Zeus.
The gods are indignant, and he, above all,
Is angry that in your heart's fury   145
You hold Hector by these beaked ships
And will not give him up. Come now,
Release the body and take ransom for the dead."

And Achilles, swift of foot, answered her:

"So be it. Let them ransom the dead,   150
If the god on Olympus wills it so."

So mother and son spoke many words
To each other, with the Greek ships all around.

Meanwhile, Zeus dispatched Iris to Troy:

"Up now, swift Iris, leave Olympus   155
For sacred Ilion and tell Priam
He must go to the Greek ships to ransom his son
With gifts that will soften Achilles' heart.
Alone he must go, with only one attendant,
An elder, to drive the mule cart and bear the man   160
Slain by Achilles back to the city.
He need have no fear. We will send
As his guide and escort Hermes himself,
Who will lead him all the way to Achilles.
And when he is inside Achilles' hut,   165
Achilles will not kill him, but will protect him
From all the rest, for he is not a fool,
Nor hardened, nor past awe for the gods.[7]
He will in kindness spare a suppliant."

Iris stormed down to deliver this message.   170
She came to the house of Priam and found there
Mourning and lamentation. Priam's sons
Sat in the courtyard around their father,
Fouling their clothes with tears. The old man,
Wrapped in his mantle, sat like graven stone.   175
His head and neck were covered with dung
He had rolled in and scraped up with his hands.
His daughters and sons' wives were wailing
Throughout the house, remembering their men,
So many and fine, dead by Greek hands.   180
Zeus' messenger stood near Priam,
Who trembled all over as she whispered:

"Courage, Priam, son of Dardanus,
And have no fear. I have come to you

7. Suppliants were under the protection of the gods, especially of Zeus.

Not to announce evil, but good.
I am a messenger from Zeus, who
Cares for you greatly and pities you.
You must go to the Greek ships to ransom Hector
With gifts that will soften Achilles' heart.
You must go alone, with only one attendant,
An elder, to drive the mule cart and bear the man
Slain by Achilles back to the city.
You need have no fear. We will send
As your guide and escort Hermes himself,
Who will lead you all the way to Achilles.
And when you are inside Achilles' hut,
Achilles will not kill you, but will protect you
From all the rest, for he is not a fool,
Nor hardened, nor past awe for the gods.
He will in kindness spare a suppliant."

Iris spoke and was gone, a blur in the air.
Priam ordered his sons to ready the mule cart
And fasten onto it the wicker trunk.
He himself went down to a high-vaulted chamber,
Fragrant with cedar, that glittered with jewels.
And he called to Hecuba, his wife, and said:

"A messenger has come from Olympian Zeus.
I am to go to the ships to ransom our son
And bring gifts that will soften Achilles' heart.
What do you make of this, Lady? For myself,
I have a strange compulsion to go over there,
Into the wide camp of the Achaean ships."

Her first response was a shrill cry, and then:

"This is madness. Where is the wisdom
You were once respected for at home and abroad?
How can you want to go to the Greek ships alone
And look into the eyes of the man who has killed
So many of your fine sons? Your heart is iron.
If he catches you, or even sees you,
He will not pity you or respect you,
Savage and faithless as he is. No, we must mourn
From afar, sitting in our hall. This is how Fate
Spun her stern thread[8] for him in my womb,
That he would glut lean hounds far from his parents,
With that violent man close by. I could rip
His liver bleeding from his guts and eat it whole.
That would be at least some vengeance
For my son. He was no coward, but died
Protecting the men and women of Troy
Without a thought of shelter or flight."

185

190

195

200

205

210

215

220

225

230

8. Fate or the Fates were often pictured as spinning the thread of a person's life.

And the old man, godlike Priam:

"Don't hold me back when I want to go,
And don't be a bird of ill omen
In my halls. You will not persuade me!
If anyone else on earth told me to do this,   235
A seer, diviner, or priest, we would
Set it aside and count it false.
But I heard the goddess myself and saw her face.
I will go, and her word will not be in vain.
If I am fated to die by the Achaean ships,   240
It must be so. Let Achilles cut me down
As soon as I have taken my son in my arms
And have satisfied my desire for grief."

He began to lift up the lids of chests
And took out a dozen beautiful robes,   245
A dozen single-fold cloaks, as many rugs,
And added as many white mantles and tunics.
He weighed and brought out ten talents of gold,
Two glowing tripods and four cauldrons with them,
And an exquisite cup, a state gift from the Thracians   250
And a great treasure. The old man spared nothing
In his house, not even this, in his passion
To ransom his son. Once out in the portico,
He drove off the men there with bitter words:

"Get out, you sorry excuses for Trojans!   255
Don't you have enough grief at home that you
Have to come here and plague me? Isn't it enough
That Zeus has given me the pain and sorrow
Of losing my finest son? You'll feel it yourselves
Soon enough. With him dead you'll be much easier   260
For the Greeks to pick off. But may I be dead and gone
Before I see my city plundered and destroyed."

And he waded through them, scattering them
With his staff. Then he called to his sons
In a harsh voice—Helenus and Paris,   265
Agathon, Pammon, Antiphonus, Polites,
Deïphobus, Hippothous, and noble Dius—
These nine, and shouted at them:

"Come here, you miserable brats. I wish
All of you had been killed by the ships   270
Instead of Hector. I have no luck at all.
I have fathered the best sons in all wide Troy,
And not one, not one I say, is left. Not Mestor,
Godlike Mestor, not Troilus, the charioteer,
Not Hector, who was like a god among men,   275
Like the son of a god, not of a mortal.
Ares killed them, and now all I have left

Are these petty delinquents, pretty boys, and cheats,
These dancers, toe-tapping champions,
Renowned throughout the neighborhood for filching goats!   280
Now will you please get the wagon ready
And load all this on, so I can leave?"

They cringed under their father's rebuke
And brought out the smooth-rolling wagon,
A beauty, just joinered,[9] and clamped on   285
The wicker trunk. They took the mule yoke
Down from its peg, a knobbed boxwood yoke
Fitted with guide rings, and the yoke-band with it,
A rope fifteen feet long. They set the yoke with care
Upon the upturned end of the polished pole,   290
Placing the ring on the thole-pin, and lashed it
Tight to the knob with three turns each way,
Then tied the ends to the hitch under the hook.
This done, they brought from the treasure chamber
The lavish ransom for Hector's head and heaped it   295
On the hand-rubbed wagon. Then they yoked the mules,
Strong-hooved animals that pull in harness,
Splendid gifts of the Mysians[1] to Priam.
And for Priam they yoked to a chariot horses
Reared by the king's hand at their polished stall.   300

So Priam and his herald, their minds racing,
Were having their rigs yoked in the high palace
When Hecuba approached them sorrowfully.
She held in her right hand a golden cup
Of honeyed wine for them to pour libation   305
Before they went. Standing by the horses she said:

"Here, pour libation to Father Zeus, and pray
For your safe return from the enemy camp,
Since you are set on going there against my will.
Pray to Cronion, the Dark Cloud of Ida,   310
Who watches over the whole land of Troy,
And ask for an omen, that swiftest of birds
That is his messenger, the king of birds,
To appear on the right before your own eyes,
Something to trust in as you go to the ships.   315
But if Zeus will not grant his own messenger,
I would not advise or encourage you
To go to the ships, however eager you are."

And Priam, with grave dignity:

"I will not disregard your advice, my wife.   320
It is good to lift hands to Zeus for mercy."

9. I.e., new-made.   1. A people of central Asia Minor.

And he nodded to the handmaid to pour
Pure water over his hands, and she came up
With basin and pitcher. Hands washed,
He took the cup from his wife and prayed,   325
Standing in the middle of the courtyard
And pouring out wine as he looked up to heaven:

"Father Zeus, who rules from Ida,
Most glorious, most great,
Send me to Achilles welcome and pitied.   330
And send me an omen, that swiftest of birds
That is your messenger, the king of birds,
To appear on the right before my own eyes,
That I may trust it as I go to the ships."

Zeus heard his prayer and sent an eagle,   335
The surest omen in the sky, a dusky hunter
Men call the dark eagle, a bird as large
As a doorway, with a wingspan as wide
As the folding doors to a vaulted chamber
In a rich man's house. It flashed on the right   340
As it soared through the city, and when they saw it
Their mood brightened.

                    Hurrying now, the old man
Stepped into his chariot and drove off
From the gateway and echoing portico.   345
In front of him the mules pulled the wagon
With Idaeus at the reins. Priam
Kept urging his horses with the lash
As they drove quickly through the city.
His kinsmen trailed behind, all of them   350
Wailing as if he were going to his death.
When they had gone down from the city
And onto the plain, his sons and sons-in-law
Turned back to Troy. But Zeus saw them
As they entered the plain, and he pitied   355
The old man, and said to his son, Hermes:

"Hermes, there's nothing you like more
Than being a companion to men,[2] and you do obey—
When you have a mind to. So go now
And lead Priam to the Achaean ships, unseen   360
And unnoticed, until he comes to Achilles."

Thus Zeus, and the quicksilver courier complied,
Lacing on his feet the beautiful sandals,
Immortal and golden, that carry him over
Landscape and seascape in a rush of wind.   365

2. Among his many functions, Hermes is an escort to travelers (in particular, he guides the souls of the
dead to the underworld). He is also a trickster and will put the guards at the Greek wall to sleep so that
Priam can pass through.

And he took the wand he uses to charm
Mortal eyes asleep and make sleepers awake.
Holding this wand, the tough quicksilver god
Flew down to Troy on the Hellespont,
And walked off as a young prince whose beard   370
Was just darkening, youth at its loveliest.

Priam and Idaeus had just driven past
The barrow of Ilus[3] and had halted
The mules and horses in the river to drink.
By now it was dusk. Idaeus looked up   375
And was aware of Hermes close by.
He turned to Priam and said:

"Beware, son of Dardanus, there's someone here,
And if we're not careful we'll be cut to bits.
Should we escape in the chariot   380
Or clasp his knees and see if he will pity us?"

But the old man's mind had melted with fear.
The hair bristled on his gnarled limbs,
And he stood frozen with fear. But the Helper came up
And took the old man's hand and said to him: 385

"Sir, where are you driving your horses and mules
At this hour of the night, when all else is asleep?
Don't you fear the fury of the Achaeans,
Your ruthless enemies, who are close at hand?
If one of them should see you bearing such treasure   390
Through the black night, what would you do?
You are not young, sir, and your companion is old,
Unable to defend you if someone starts a fight.
But I will do you no harm and will protect you
From others. You remind me of my own dear father."   395

And the old man, godlike Priam, answered:

"Yes, dear son, it is just as you say.
But some god has stretched out his hand
And sent an auspicious wayfarer to meet me.
You have an impressive build, good looks,   400
And intelligence. Blessed are your parents."

And the Guide, limned in silver light:

"A very good way to put it, old sir.
But tell me this now, and tell me the truth:
Are you taking all of this valuable treasure   405
For safekeeping abroad or are you
All forsaking sacred Ilion in fear?

---

3. Priam's grandfather. The tomb was a landmark on the Trojan plain.

You have lost such a great warrior, the noblest,
Your son. He never let up against the Achaeans."

And the old man, godlike Priam, answered: 410

"Who are you, and from what parents born,
That you speak so well about my ill-fated son?"

And Hermes, limned in silver, answered:

"Ah, a test! And a question about Hector.
I have often seen him win glory in battle   415
He would drive the Argives back to their ships
And carve them to pieces with his bronze blade.
And we stood there and marvelled, for Achilles,
Angry with Agamemnon, would not let us fight.
I am his comrade in arms, from the same ship,   420
A Myrmidon. My father is Polyctor,
A wealthy man, and about as old as you.
He has six other sons, seven, counting me.
We cast lots, and I was chosen to come here.
Now I have come out to the plain from the ships   425
Because at dawn the Achaeans
Will lay siege to the city. They are restless,
And their lords cannot restrain them from battle."

And the old man, godlike Priam, answered him:

"If you really are one of Achilles' men,   430
Tell me this, and I want the whole truth.
Is my son still by the ships, or has Achilles
Cut him up by now and thrown him to the dogs?"

And Hermes, limned in silver light:

"Not yet, old sir. The dogs and birds have not   435
Devoured him. He lies beside Achilles' ship
Amid the huts just as he was at first. This is now
The twelfth day he has been lying there,
But his flesh has not decayed at all, nor is it
Consumed by worms that eat the battle-slain.   440
Achilles does drag him around his dear friend's tomb,
And ruthlessly, every morning at dawn,
But he stays unmarred. You would marvel, if you came,
To see him lie as fresh as dew, washed clean of blood,
And uncorrupted. All the wounds he had are closed,   445
And there were many who drove their bronze in him.
This is how the blessed gods care for your son,
Corpse though he be, for he was dear to their hearts."

And the old man was glad, and answered:

"Yes, my boy. It is good to offer   450
The immortals their due. If ever
There was anyone in my house
Who never forgot the Olympian gods,
It was my son. And so now they have
Remembered him, even in death.   455
But come, accept from me this fine cup,
And give me safe escort with the gods
Until I come to the hut of Peleus' son."

And Hermes, glimmering in the dark:

"Ah, an old man testing a young one.   460
But you will not get me to take gifts from you
Without Achilles' knowledge. I respect him
And fear him too much to defraud him.
I shudder to think of the consequences.
But I would escort you all the way to Argos,   465
With attentive care, by ship or on foot,
And no one would fight you for scorn of your escort."

And he leapt onto the chariot,
Took the reins and whip, and breathed
Great power into the horses and mules.   470
When they came to the palisade and trench
Surrounding the ships, the guards were at supper.
Hermes sprinkled them with drowsiness,
Then opened the gates, pushed back the bars,
And led in Priam and the cart piled with ransom.   475
They came to the hut of the son of Peleus
That the Myrmidons had built for their lord.
They built it high, out of hewn fir beams,
And roofed it with thatch reaped from the meadows.
Around it they made him a great courtyard   480
With thick-set staves. A single bar of fir
Held the gate shut. It took three men
To drive this bar home and three to pull it back,
But Achilles could work it easily alone.
Hermes opened the gate for Priam   485
And brought in the gifts for Peleus' swift son.
As he stepped to the ground he said:

"I am one of the immortals, old sir—the god
Hermes. My father sent me to escort you here.
I will go back now and not come before   490
Achilles' eyes. It would be offensive
For a god to greet a mortal face to face.
You go in, though, and clasp the knees
Of the son of Peleus, and entreat him
By his father and rich-haired mother   495
And by his son, so you will stir his soul."

And with that Hermes left and returned
To high Olympus. Priam jumped down
And left Idaeus to hold the horses and mules.
The old man went straight to the house   500
Where Achilles, dear to Zeus, sat and waited.

He found him inside. His companions sat
Apart from him, and a solitary pair,
Automedon and Alcimus, warriors both,
Were busy at his side. He had just finished   505
His evening meal. The table was still set up.
Great Priam entered unnoticed. He stood
Close to Achilles, and touching his knees,
He kissed the dread and murderous hands
That had killed so many of his sons.   510

Passion sometimes blinds a man so completely
That he kills one of his own countrymen.
In exile, he comes into a wealthy house,
And everyone stares at him with wonder.

So Achilles stared in wonder at Priam.   515
Was he a god?
                    And the others there stared
And wondered and looked at each other.
But Priam spoke, a prayer of entreaty:

"Remember your father, godlike Achilles.   520
He and I both are on the doorstep
Of old age. He may well be now
Surrounded by enemies wearing him down
And have no one to protect him from harm.
But then he hears that you are still alive   525
And his heart rejoices, and he hopes all his days
To see his dear son come back from Troy.
But what is left for me? I had the finest sons
In all wide Troy, and not one of them is left.
Fifty I had when the Greeks came over,   530
Nineteen out of one belly, and the rest
The women in my house bore to me.
It doesn't matter how many they were,
The god of war has cut them down at the knees.
And the only one who could save the city   535
You've just now killed as he fought for his country,
My Hector. It is for him I have come to the Greek ships,
To get him back from you. I've brought
A fortune in ransom. Respect the gods, Achilles.
Think of your own father, and pity me.   540
I am more pitiable. I have borne what no man
Who has walked this earth has ever yet borne.
I have kissed the hand of the man who killed my son."

He spoke, and sorrow for his own father
Welled up in Achilles. He took Priam's hand   545
And gently pushed the old man away.
The two of them remembered. Priam,
Huddled in grief at Achilles' feet, cried
And moaned softly for his man-slaying Hector.
And Achilles cried for his father and   550
For Patroclus. The sound filled the room.

When Achilles had his fill of grief
And the aching sorrow left his heart,
He rose from his chair and lifted the old man
By his hand, pitying his white hair and beard.   555
And his words enfolded him like wings:

"Ah, the suffering you've had, and the courage.
To come here alone to the Greek ships
And meet my eye, the man who slaughtered
Your many fine sons! You have a heart of iron.   560
But come, sit on this chair. Let our pain
Lie at rest a while, no matter how much we hurt.
There's nothing to be gained from cold grief.
Yes, the gods have woven pain into mortal lives,
While they are free from care.   565
               Two jars
Sit at the doorstep of Zeus, filled with gifts
That he gives, one full of good things,
The other of evil. If Zeus gives a man
A mixture from both jars, sometimes   570
Life is good for him, sometimes not.
But if all he gives you is from the jar of woe,
You become a pariah, and hunger drives you
Over the bright earth, dishonored by gods and men.
Now take Peleus. The gods gave him splendid gifts   575
From the day he was born. He was the happiest
And richest man on earth, king of the Myrmidons,
And although he was a mortal, the gods gave him
An immortal goddess to be his wife.
But even to Peleus the god gave some evil: 580
He would not leave offspring to succeed him in power,
Just one child, all out of season. I can't be with him
To take care of him now that he's old, since I'm far
From my fatherland, squatting here in Troy,
Tormenting you and your children. And you, old sir,   585
We hear that you were prosperous once.
From Lesbos down south clear over to Phrygia
And up to the Hellespont's boundary,
No one could match you in wealth or in sons.
But then the gods have brought you trouble,   590
This constant fighting and killing around your town.
You must endure this grief and not constantly grieve.

You will not gain anything by torturing yourself
Over the good son you lost, not bring him back.
Sooner you will suffer some other sorrow."   595

And Priam, old and godlike, answered him:

"Don't sit me in a chair, prince, while Hector
Lies uncared for in your hut. Deliver him now
So I can see him with my own eyes, and you—
Take all this ransom we bring, take pleasure in it,   600
And go back home to your own fatherland,
Since you've taken this first step and allowed me
To live and see the light of day."

Achilles glowered at him and said:

"Don't provoke me, old man. It's my own decision   605
To release Hector to you. A messenger came to me
From Zeus—my own natural mother,
Daughter of the old sea god. And I know you,
Priam, inside out. You don't fool me one bit.
Some god escorted you to the Greek ships.   610
No mortal would have dared come into our camp,
Not even your best young hero. He couldn't have
Gotten past the guards or muscled open the gate.
So just stop stirring up grief in my heart,
Or I might not let you out of here alive, old man—   615
Suppliant though you are—and sin against Zeus."

The old man was afraid and did as he was told.

The son of Peleus leapt out the door like a lion,
Followed by Automedon and Alcimus, whom Achilles
Honored most now that Patroclus was dead.   620
They unyoked the horses and mules, and led
The old man's herald inside and seated him on a chair.
Then they unloaded from the strong-wheeled cart
The endless ransom that was Hector's blood price,
Leaving behind two robes and a fine-spun tunic   625
For the body to be wrapped in and brought inside.
Achilles called the women and ordered them
To wash the body well and anoint it with oil,
Removing it first for fear that Priam might see his son
And in his grief be unable to control his anger   630
At the sight of his child, and that this would arouse
Achilles' passion and he would kill the old man
And so sin against the commandments of Zeus.

After the female slaves had bathed Hector's body
And anointed it with olive, they wrapped it 'round   635
With a beautiful robe and tunic, and Achilles himself
Lifted him up and placed him on a pallet

And with his friends raised it onto the polished cart.
Then he groaned and called out to Patroclus:

"Don't be angry with me, dear friend, if somehow   640
You find out, even in Hades, that I have released
Hector to his father. He paid a handsome price,
And I will share it with you, as much as is right."

Achilles reentered his hut and sat down again
In his ornately decorated chair   645
Across the room from Priam, and said to him:

"Your son is released, sir, as you ordered.
He is lying on a pallet. At dawn's first light
You will go see him yourself.
     Now let's think about supper.   650
Even Niobe[4] remembered to eat
Although her twelve children were dead in her house,
Six daughters and six sturdy sons.
Apollo killed them with his silver bow,
And Artemis, showering arrows, angry with Niobe   655
Because she compared herself to beautiful Leto.
Leto, she said, had borne only two, while she
Had borne many. Well, these two killed them all.
Nine days they lay in their gore, with no one
To bury them, because Zeus had turned   660
The people to stone. On the tenth day
The gods buried them. But Niobe remembered
She had to eat, exhausted from weeping.
Now she is one of the rocks in the lonely hills
Somewhere in Sipylos, a place they say is haunted   665
By nymphs who dance on the Achelous' banks,
And although she is stone she broods on the sorrows
The gods gave her.[5]
                    Well, so should we, old sir,
Remember to eat. You can mourn your son later   670
When you bring him to Troy. You owe him many tears."

A moment later Achilles was up and had slain
A silvery sheep. His companions flayed it
And prepared it for a meal, sliced it, spitted it,
Roasted the morsels and drew them off the spits.   675
Automedon set out bread in exquisite baskets
While Achilles served the meat. They helped themselves
And satisfied their desire for food and drink.
Then Priam, son of Dardanus, gazed for a while
At Achilles, so big, so much like one of the gods,   680

---

4. Wife of Amphion, one of the two founders of the great Greek city of Thebes.   5. The legend of Niobe being turned into stone is thought to have had its origin in a rock face of Mount Sipylus (in Asia Minor) that resembled a woman who wept inconsolably for the loss of her children. The Achelous River runs near Mount Sipylus.

And Achilles returned his gaze, admiring
Priam's face, his words echoing in his mind.
When they had their fill of gazing at each other,
Priam, old and godlike, broke the silence:

"Show me to my bed now, prince, and quickly,   685
So that at long last I can have the pleasure of sleep.
My eyes have not closed since my son lost his life
Under your hands. I have done nothing but groan
And brood over my countless sorrows,
Rolling in the dung of my courtyard stables.   690
Finally I have tasted food and let flaming wine
Pass down my throat. I had eaten nothing till now."

Achilles ordered his companions and women
To set bedsteads on the porch and pad them
With fine, dyed rugs, spread blankets on top,   695
And cover them over with fleecy cloaks.
The women went out with torches in their hands
And quickly made up two beds. And Achilles,
The great sprinter, said in a bitter tone:

"You will have to sleep outside, dear Priam.   700
One of the Achaean counselors may come in,
As they always do, to sit and talk with me,
As well they should. If one of them saw you here
In the dead of night, he would tell Agamemnon,
And that would delay releasing the body.   705
But tell me this, as precisely as you can.
How many days do you need for the funeral?
I will wait that long and hold back the army."

And the old man, godlike Priam, answered:

"If you really want me to bury my Hector,   710
Then you could do this for me, Achilles.
You know how we are penned in the city,
Far from any timber, and the Trojans are afraid.
We would mourn him for nine days in our halls,
And bury him on the tenth, and feast the people.   715
On the eleventh we would heap a barrow over him,
And on the twelfth day fight, if fight we must."

And Achilles, strong, swift, and godlike:

"You will have your armistice."

And he clasped the old man's wrist   720
So he would not be afraid.
                    And so they slept,
Priam and his herald, in the covered courtyard,
Each with a wealth of thoughts in his breast.

But Achilles slept inside his well-built hut,   725
And by his side lay lovely Briseis.

Gods and heroes slept the night through,
Wrapped in soft slumber. Only Hermes
Lay awake in the dark, pondering how
To spirit King Priam away from the ships   730
And elude the strong watchmen at the camp's gates.
He hovered above Priam's head and spoke:

"Well, old man, you seem to think it's safe
To sleep on and on in the enemy camp
Since Achilles spared you. Think what it cost you   735
To ransom your son. Your own life will cost
Three times that much to the sons you have left
If Agamemnon and the Greeks know you are here."

Suddenly the old man was afraid. He woke up the herald.
Hermes harnessed the horses and mules   740
And drove them through the camp. No one noticed.
And when they reached the ford of the Xanthus,
The beautiful, swirling river that Zeus begot,
Hermes left for the long peaks of Olympus.

    Dawn spread her saffron light over earth,   745
And they drove the horses into the city
With great lamentation. The mules pulled the corpse.
No one in Troy, man or woman, saw them before
Cassandra, who stood like golden Aphrodite
On Pergamon's height. Looking out she saw   750
Her dear father standing in the chariot
With the herald, and then she saw Hector
Lying on the stretcher in the mule cart.
And her cry went out through all the city:

"Come look upon Hector, Trojan men and women,   755
If ever you rejoiced when he came home alive
From battle, a joy to the city and all its people."

She spoke. And there was not a man or woman
Left in the city, for an unbearable sorrow
Had come upon them. They met Priam by the gates   760
As he brought the body through, and in the front
Hector's dear wife and queenly mother threw themselves
On the rolling cart and pulled out their hair
As they clasped his head amid the grieving crowd.
They would have mourned Hector outside the gates   765
All the long day until the sun went down,
Had not the old man spoken from his chariot:

"Let the mules come through. Later you will have
Your fill of grieving, after I have brought him home."

He spoke, and the crowd made way for the cart.   770
And they brought him home and laid him
On a corded bed, and set around him singers
To lead the dirge and chant the death song.
They chanted the dirge, and the women with them.
White-armed Andromache led the lamentation   775
As she cradled the head of her man-slaying Hector:

"You have died young, husband, and left me
A widow in the halls. Our son is still an infant,
Doomed when we bore him. I do not think
He will ever reach manhood. No, this city   780
Will topple and fall first. You were its savior,
And now you are lost. All the solemn wives
And children you guarded will go off soon
In the hollow ships, and I will go with them.
And you, my son, you will either come with me   785
And do menial labor for a cruel master,
Or some Greek will lead you by the hand
And throw you from the tower, a hideous death,[6]
Angry because Hector killed his brother,
Or his father, or son. Many, many Greeks   790
Fell in battle under Hector's hands.
Your father was never gentle in combat.
And so all the townspeople mourn for him,
And you have caused your parents unspeakable
Sorrow, Hector, and left me endless pain.   795
You did not stretch your hand out to me
As you lay dying in bed, nor did you whisper
A final word I could remember as I weep
All the days and nights of my life."

The women's moans washed over her lament,   800
And from the sobbing came Hecuba's voice:

"Hector, my heart, dearest of all my children,
The gods loved you when you were alive for me,
And they have cared for you also in death.
My other children Achilles sold as slaves   805
When he captured them, shipped them overseas
To Samos, Imbros, and barren Lemnos.
After he took your life with tapered bronze
He dragged you around Patroclus' tomb, his friend
Whom you killed, but still could not bring him back.   810
And now you lie here for me as fresh as dew,
Although you have been slain, like one whom Apollo
Has killed softly with his silver arrows."

The third woman to lament was Helen.

---

6. Astyanax was, in fact, hurled from Troy's walls after the city fell.

"Oh, Hector, you were the dearest to me by far 815
Of all my husband's brothers. Yes, Paris
Is my husband, the godlike prince
Who led me to Troy. I should have died first.
This is now the twentieth year
Since I went away and left my home, 820
And I have never had an unkind word from you.
If anyone in the house ever taunted me,
Any of my husband's brothers or sisters,
Or his mother—my father-in-law was kind always—
You would draw them aside and calm them 825
With your gentle heart and gentle words.
And so I weep for you and for myself,
And my heart is heavy, because there is no one left
In all wide Troy who will pity me
Or be my friend. Everyone shudders at me." 830

And the people's moan came in over her voice.

Then the old man, Priam, spoke to his people:

"Men of Troy, start bringing wood to the city,
And have no fear of an Argive ambush.
When Achilles sent me from the black ships, 835
He gave his word he would not trouble us
Until the twelfth day should dawn."

He spoke, and they yoked oxen and mules
To wagons, and gathered outside the city.
For nine days they hauled in loads of timber. 840
When the tenth dawn showed her mortal light,
They brought out their brave Hector
And all in tears lifted the body high
Onto the bier, and threw on the fire.

Light blossomed like roses in the eastern sky. 845

The people gathered around Hector's pyre,
And when all of Troy was assembled there
They drowned the last flames with glinting wine.
Hector's brothers and friends collected
His white bones, their cheeks flowered with tears. 850
They wrapped the bones in soft purple robes
And placed them in a golden casket, and laid it
In the hollow of the grave, and heaped above it
A mantle of stones. They built the tomb
Quickly, with lookouts posted all around 855
In case the Greeks should attack early.
When the tomb was built, they all returned
To the city and assembled for a glorious feast
In the house of Priam, Zeus' cherished king.

That was the funeral of Hector, breaker of horses. 860

The Odyssey[1]

BOOK I

[Athena Inspires the Prince]

Sing to me of the man, Muse, the man of twists and turns
driven time and again off course, once he had plundered
the hallowed heights of Troy.
Many cities of men he saw and learned their minds,
many pains he suffered, heartsick on the open sea,   5
fighting to save his life and bring his comrades home.
But he could not save them from disaster, hard as he strove—
the recklessness of their own ways destroyed them all,
the blind fools, they devoured the cattle of the Sun
and the Sungod blotted out the day of their return.   10
Launch out on his story, Muse, daughter of Zeus,
start from where you will—sing for our time too.

                                         By now,
all the survivors, all who avoided headlong death
were safe at home, escaped the wars and waves.
But one man alone . . .   15
his heart set on his wife and his return—Calypso,[2]
the bewitching nymph, the lustrous goddess, held him back,
deep in her arching caverns, craving him for a husband.
But then, when the wheeling seasons brought the year around,
that year spun out by the gods when he should reach his home, 20
Ithaca[3]—though not even there would he be free of trials,
even among his loved ones—then every god took pity,
all except Poseidon.[4] He raged on, seething against
the great Odysseus till he reached his native land.

                                          But now
Poseidon had gone to visit the Ethiopians worlds away,   25
Ethiopians off at the farthest limits of mankind,
a people split in two, one part where the Sungod sets
and part where the Sungod rises. There Poseidon went
to receive an offering, bulls and rams by the hundred—
far away at the feast the Sea-lord sat and took his pleasure.   30
But the other gods, at home in Olympian Zeus's halls,
met for full assembly there, and among them now
the father of men and gods was first to speak,
sorely troubled, remembering handsome Aegisthus,[5]
the man Agamemnon's son, renowned Orestes, killed.   35
Recalling Aegisthus, Zeus harangued the immortal powers:
"Ah how shameless—the way these mortals blame the gods.
From us alone, they say, come all their miseries, yes,
but they themselves, with their own reckless ways,

---

1. Translated by Robert Fagles.   2. Her name suggests the Greek verb that means "cover, hide."
3. An island off the northwest coast of Greece.   4. God of the sea.   5. The cousin of Agamemnon.
While Agamemnon was away at Troy, Aegisthus seduced his wife, Clytemnestra; the two of them murdered
Agamemnon when he returned. Orestes, Agamemnon's son, later avenged his father. The story is told or
alluded to several times in the Odyssey, notably in books 3 and 11.

compound their pains beyond their proper share.   40
Look at Aegisthus now . . .
above and beyond *his* share he stole Atrides'[6] wife,
he murdered the warlord coming home from Troy
though he knew it meant his own total ruin.
Far in advance we told him so ourselves,   45
dispatching the guide, the giant-killer Hermes.
'Don't murder the man,' he said, 'don't court his wife.
Beware, revenge will come from Orestes, Agamemnon's son,
that day he comes of age and longs for his native land.'
So Hermes warned, with all the good will in the world,   50
but would Aegisthus' hardened heart give way?
Now he pays the price—all at a single stroke."

   And sparkling-eyed Athena[7] drove the matter home:
"Father, son of Cronus, our high and mighty king,
surely he goes down to a death he earned in full!   55
Let them all die so, all who do such things.
But my heart breaks for Odysseus,
that seasoned veteran cursed by fate so long—
far from his loved ones still, he suffers torments
off on a wave-washed island rising at the center of the seas.   60
A dark wooded island, and there a goddess makes her home,
a daughter of Atlas, wicked Titan[8] who sounds the deep
in all its depths, whose shoulders lift on high
the colossal pillars thrusting earth and sky apart.
Atlas' daughter it is who holds Odysseus captive,   65
luckless man—despite his tears, forever trying
to spellbind his heart with suave, seductive words
and wipe all thought of Ithaca from his mind.
But he, straining for no more than a glimpse
of hearth-smoke drifting up from his own land,   70
Odysseus longs to die . . .
                   Olympian Zeus,
have you no care for *him* in your lofty heart?
Did he never win your favor with sacrifices
burned beside the ships on the broad plain of Troy?
Why, Zeus, why so dead set against Odysseus?"   75

   "My child," Zeus who marshals the thunderheads replied,
"what nonsense you let slip through your teeth. Now,
how on earth could I forget Odysseus? Great Odysseus
who excels all men in wisdom, excels in offerings too
he gives the immortal gods who rule the vaulting skies?   80
No, it's the Earth-Shaker, Poseidon, unappeased,
forever fuming against him for the Cyclops
whose giant eye he blinded: godlike Polyphemus,
towering over all the Cyclops' clans in power.

---

6. The son of Atreus (i.e., Agamemnon).   7. The warrior goddess, also patroness of handicraft and intelligence. She is often given the epithet *Pallas.*   8. The Titans were the generation of gods ruled by Cronus, who were deposed by Zeus and the other Olympians. One of them, Atlas, was condemned to hold up the sky on his shoulders, perhaps in punishment for his part in their war against Zeus.

The nymph Thoosa bore him, daughter of Phorcys,   85
lord of the barren salt sea—she met Poseidon
once in his vaulted caves and they made love.
And now for his blinded son the earthquake god—
though he won't quite kill Odysseus—
drives him far off course from native land.   90
But come, all of us here put heads together now,
work out his journey home so Odysseus can return.
Lord Poseidon, I trust, will let his anger go.
How can he stand his ground against the will
of all the gods at once—one god alone?"   95

    Athena, her eyes flashing bright, exulted,
"Father, son of Cronus, our high and mighty king!
If now it really pleases the blissful gods
that wise Odysseus shall return—home at last—
let us dispatch the guide and giant-killer Hermes   100
down to Ogygia Island,[9] down to announce at once
to the nymph with lovely braids our fixed decree:
Odysseus journeys home—the exile must return!
While I myself go down to Ithaca, rouse his son
to a braver pitch, inspire his heart with courage   105
to summon the flowing-haired Achaeans[1] to full assembly,
speak his mind to all those suitors, slaughtering on and on
his droves of sheep and shambling longhorn cattle.
Next I will send him off to Sparta and sandy Pylos,[2]
there to learn of his dear father's journey home.   110
Perhaps he will hear some news and make his name
throughout the mortal world."
                So Athena vowed
and under her feet she fastened the supple sandals,
ever-glowing gold, that wing her over the waves
and boundless earth with the rush of gusting winds.   115
She seized the rugged spear tipped with a bronze point—
weighted, heavy, the massive shaft she wields to break the lines
of heroes the mighty Father's daughter storms against.
And down she swept from Olympus' craggy peaks
and lit on Ithaca, standing tall at Odysseus' gates,   120
the threshold of his court. Gripping her bronze spear,
she looked for all the world like a stranger now,
like Mentes, lord of the Taphians.[3]
There she found the swaggering suitors, just then
amusing themselves with rolling dice before the doors,   125
lounging on hides of oxen they had killed themselves.
While heralds and brisk attendants bustled round them,
some at the mixing-bowls, mulling wine and water,
others wiping the tables down with sopping sponges,
setting them out in place, still other servants   130
jointed and carved the great sides of meat.

---

9. Calypso's home.   1. Greeks (who have a number of collective names in Homer).   2. Either in the
northwest Peloponnesus, as some hints in the *Odyssey* seem to suggest, or a region in the southwest Peloponnesus later known as Pylos, where a great Mycenaean palace has been excavated. Sparta is in the south-
central Peloponnesus.   3. A nearby seafaring people.

First by far to see her was Prince Telemachus,
sitting among the suitors, heart obsessed with grief.
He could almost see his magnificent father, here . . .
in the mind's eye—if only *he* might drop from the clouds   135
and drive these suitors all in a rout throughout the halls
and regain his pride of place and rule his own domains!
Daydreaming so as he sat among the suitors,
he glimpsed Athena now
and straight to the porch he went, mortified   140
that a guest might still be standing at the doors.
Pausing beside her there, he clasped her right hand
and relieving her at once of her long bronze spear,
met her with winged words: "Greetings, stranger!
Here in our house you'll find a royal welcome.   145
Have supper first, then tell us what you need."

He led the way and Pallas Athena followed.
Once in the high-roofed hall, he took her lance
and fixed it firm in a burnished rack against
a sturdy pillar, there where row on row of spears,   150
embattled Odysseus' spears, stood stacked and waiting.
Then he escorted her to a high, elaborate chair of honor,
over it draped a cloth, and here he placed his guest
with a stool to rest her feet. But for himself
he drew up a low reclining chair beside her,   155
richly painted, clear of the press of suitors,
concerned his guest, offended by their uproar,
might shrink from food in the midst of such a mob.
He hoped, what's more, to ask him about his long-lost father.
A maid brought water soon in a graceful golden pitcher   160
and over a silver basin tipped it out
so they might rinse their hands,
then pulled a gleaming table to their side.
A staid housekeeper brought on bread to serve them,
appetizers aplenty too, lavish with her bounty.   165
A carver lifted platters of meat toward them,
meats of every sort, and set beside them golden cups
and time and again a page came round and poured them wine.

But now the suitors trooped in with all their swagger
and took their seats on low and high-backed chairs.   170
Heralds poured water over their hands for rinsing,
serving maids brought bread heaped high in trays
and the young men brimmed the mixing-bowls with wine.
They reached out for the good things that lay at hand,
and when they'd put aside desire for food and drink   175
the suitors set their minds on other pleasures,
song and dancing, all that crowns a feast.
A herald placed an ornate lyre in Phemius'[4] hands,

---

4. Literally, "One Who Spreads Fame." Phemius is a poet-singer who seems to have some kind of association with Odysseus's household. In Homer, poetry (including epic poetry) is always referred to as song, and it is performed to the accompaniment of a four-stringed instrument (the forerunner of the later seven-stringed lyre).

the bard who always performed among them there;
they forced the man to sing.
                              A rippling prelude—   180
and no sooner had he struck up his rousing song
than Telemachus, head close to Athena's sparkling eyes,
spoke low to his guest so no one else could hear:
"Dear stranger, would you be shocked by what I say?
Look at them over there. Not a care in the world,   185
just lyres and tunes! It's easy for them, all right,
they feed on another's goods and go scot-free—
a man whose white bones lie strewn in the rain somewhere,
rotting away on land or rolling down the ocean's salty swells.
But that man—if they caught sight of him home in Ithaca,   190
by god, they'd all pray to be faster on their feet
than richer in bars of gold and heavy robes.
But now, no use, he's died a wretched death.
No comfort's left for us . . . not even if
someone, somewhere, says he's coming home.   195
The day of his return will never dawn.
                              Enough.
Tell me about yourself now, clearly, point by point.
Who are you? where are you from? your city? your parents?
What sort of vessel brought you? Why did the sailors
land you here in Ithaca? Who did they say they are?   200
I hardly think you came this way on foot!
And tell me this for a fact—I need to know—
is this your first time here? Or are you a friend of father's,
a guest from the old days? Once, crowds of other men
would come to our house on visits—visitor that he was,   205
when he walked among the living."
                              Her eyes glinting,
goddess Athena answered, "My whole story, of course,
I'll tell it point by point. Wise old Anchialus
was my father. My own name is Mentes,
lord of the Taphian men who love their oars.   210
And here I've come, just now, with ship and crew,
sailing the wine-dark sea to foreign ports of call,
to Temese, out for bronze—our cargo gleaming iron.
Our ship lies moored off farmlands far from town,
riding in Rithron Cove, beneath Mount Nion's woods.   215
As for the ties between your father and myself,
we've been friends forever, I'm proud to say,
and he would bear me out
if you went and questioned old lord Laertes.[5]
He, I gather, no longer ventures into town   220
but lives a life of hardship, all to himself,
off on his farmstead with an aged serving-woman
who tends him well, who gives him food and drink
when weariness has taken hold of his withered limbs
from hauling himself along his vineyard's steep slopes.   225

---

5. Odysseus's father.

And now I've come—and why? I heard that he was back . . .
your father, that is. But no, the gods thwart his passage.
Yet I tell you great Odysseus is not dead. He's still alive,
somewhere in this wide world, held captive, out at sea
on a wave-washed island, and hard men, savages,   230
somehow hold him back against his will.
                                        Wait,
I'll make you a prophecy, one the immortal gods
have planted in my mind—it will come true, I think,
though I am hardly a seer or know the flights of birds.
He won't be gone long from the native land he loves,   235
not even if iron shackles bind your father down.
He's plotting a way to journey home at last;
he's never at a loss.
                      But come, please,
tell me about yourself now, point by point.
You're truly Odysseus' son? You've sprung up so!   240
Uncanny resemblance . . . the head, and the fine eyes—
I see him now. How often we used to meet in the old days
before he embarked for Troy, where other Argive[6] captains,
all the best men, sailed in the long curved ships.
From then to this very day   245
I've not set eyes on Odysseus or he on me."

And young Telemachus cautiously replied,
"I'll try, my friend, to give you a frank answer.
Mother has always told me I'm his son, it's true,
but I am not so certain. Who, on his own,   250
has ever really known who gave him life?
Would to god I'd been the son of a happy man
whom old age overtook in the midst of his possessions!
Now, think of the most unlucky mortal ever born—
since you ask me, yes, they say I am his son."   255

    "Still," the clear-eyed goddess reassured him,
"trust me, the gods have not marked out your house
for such an unsung future,
not if Penelope has borne a son like you.
But tell me about all this and spare me nothing.   260
What's this banqueting, this crowd carousing here?
And what part do you play yourself? Some wedding-feast,
some festival? Hardly a potluck supper, I would say.
How obscenely they lounge and swagger here, look,
gorging in your house. Why, any man of sense   265
who chanced among them would be outraged,
seeing such behavior."
                      Ready Telemachus
took her up at once: "Well, my friend,
seeing you want to probe and press the question,
once this house was rich, no doubt, beyond reproach   270

6. Greek.

when the man you mentioned still lived here, at home.
Now the gods have reversed our fortunes with a vengeance—
wiped that man from the earth like no one else before.
I would never have grieved so much about his death
if he'd gone down with comrades off in Troy   275
or died in the arms of loved ones,
once he had wound down the long coil of war.
Then all united Achaea would have raised his tomb
and he'd have won his son great fame for years to come.
But now the whirlwinds have ripped him away, no fame for him!   280
He's lost and gone now—out of sight, out of mind—and I . . .
he's left me tears and grief. Nor do I rack my heart
and grieve for him alone. No longer. Now the gods
have invented other miseries to plague me.
                                                  Listen.
All the nobles who rule the islands round about,   285
Dulichion, and Same, and wooded Zacynthus too,
and all who lord it in rocky Ithaca as well—
down to the last man they court my mother,
they lay waste my house! And mother . . .
she neither rejects a marriage she despises   290
nor can she bear to bring the courting to an end—
while they continue to bleed my household white.
Soon—you wait—they'll grind *me* down as well."
                                        "Shameful!"—
brimming with indignation, Pallas Athena broke out.
"Oh how much you need Odysseus, gone so long—   295
how *he'd* lay hands on all these brazen suitors!
If only he would appear, now,
at his house's outer gates and take his stand,
armed with his helmet, shield and pair of spears,
as strong as the man I glimpsed that first time   300
in our own house, drinking wine and reveling there . . .
just come in from Ephyra,[7] visiting Ilus, Mermerus' son.
Odysseus sailed that way, you see, in his swift trim ship,
hunting deadly poison to smear on his arrows' bronze heads.
Ilus refused—he feared the wrath of the everlasting gods—   305
but father, so fond of him, gave him all he wanted.
If only *that* Odysseus sported with these suitors,
a blood wedding, a quick death would take the lot!
True, but all lies in the lap of the great gods,
whether or not he'll come and pay them back,   310
here, in his own house.
                        But you, I urge you,
think how to drive these suitors from your halls.
Come now, listen closely. Take my words to heart.
At daybreak summon the island's lords to full assembly,
give your orders to all and call the gods to witness: 315
tell the suitors to scatter, each to his own place.
As for your mother, if the spirit moves her to marry,

---

7. Probably a town on the northwest coast of mainland Greece.

let her go back to her father's house, a man of power.
Her kin will arrange the wedding, provide the gifts,
the array that goes with a daughter dearly loved.
                            For you,   320
I have some good advice, if only you will accept it.
Fit out a ship with twenty oars, the best in sight,
sail in quest of news of your long-lost father.
Someone may tell you something
or you may catch a rumor straight from Zeus,   325
rumor that carries news to men like nothing else.
First go down to Pylos, question old King Nestor,
then cross over to Sparta, to red-haired Menelaus,
of all the bronze-armored Achaeans the last man back.
Now, if you hear your father's alive and heading home,   330
hard-pressed as you are, brave out one more year.
If you hear he's dead, no longer among the living,
then back you come to the native land you love,
raise his grave-mound, build his honors high
with the full funeral rites that he deserves—   335
and give your mother to another husband.
                              Then,
once you've sealed those matters, seen them through,
think hard, reach down deep in your heart and soul
for a way to kill these suitors in your house,
by stealth or in open combat.   340
You must not cling to your boyhood any longer—
it's time you were a man. Haven't you heard
what glory Prince Orestes won throughout the world
when he killed that cunning, murderous Aegisthus,
who'd killed his famous father?
                        And you, my friend—   345
how tall and handsome I see you now—be brave, you too,
so men to come will sing your praises down the years.
But now I must go back to my swift trim ship
and all my shipmates, chafing there, I'm sure,
waiting for my return. It all rests with you.   350
Take my words to heart."
                  "Oh stranger,"
heedful Telemachus replied, "indeed I will.
You've counseled me with so much kindness now,
like a father to a son. I won't forget a word.
But come, stay longer, keen as you are to sail,   355
so you can bathe and rest and lift your spirits,
then go back to your ship, delighted with a gift,
a prize of honor, something rare and fine
as a keepsake from myself. The kind of gift
a host will give a stranger, friend to friend."   360

    Her eyes glinting, Pallas declined in haste:
"Not now. Don't hold me here. I long to be on my way.
As for the gift—whatever you'd give in kindness—
save it for my return so I can take it home.

Choose something rare and fine, and a good reward   365
that gift is going to bring you."
       With that promise,
off and away Athena the bright-eyed goddess flew
like a bird in soaring flight
but left his spirit filled with nerve and courage,
charged with his father's memory more than ever now.   370
He felt his senses quicken, overwhelmed with wonder—
this was a god, he knew it well and made at once
for the suitors, a man like a god himself.
         Amidst them still
the famous bard sang on, and they sat in silence, listening
as he performed The Achaeans' Journey Home from Troy: 375
all the blows Athena doomed them to endure.
          And now,
from high above in her room and deep in thought,
she caught his inspired strains . . .
Icarius' daughter Penelope, wary and reserved,
and down the steep stair from her chamber she descended, 380
not alone: two of her women followed close behind.
That radiant woman, once she reached her suitors,
drawing her glistening veil across her cheeks,
paused now where a column propped the sturdy roof,
with one of her loyal handmaids stationed either side.   385
Suddenly, dissolving in tears and bursting through
the bard's inspired voice, she cried out, "Phemius!
So many other songs you know to hold us spellbound,
works of the gods and men that singers celebrate.
Sing one of those as you sit beside them here   390
and they drink their wine in silence.
        But break off this song—
the unendurable song that always rends the heart inside me . . .
the unforgettable grief, it wounds me most of all!
How I long for my husband—alive in memory, always,
that great man whose fame resounds through Hellas   395
right to the depths of Argos!"
       "Why, mother,"
poised Telemachus put in sharply, "why deny
our devoted bard the chance to entertain us
any way the spirit stirs him on?
Bards are not to blame—   400
Zeus is to blame. He deals to each and every
laborer on this earth whatever doom he pleases.
Why fault the bard if he sings the Argives' harsh fate?
It's always the latest song, the one that echoes last
in the listeners' ears, that people praise the most.   405
Courage, mother. Harden your heart, and listen.
Odysseus was scarcely the only one, you know,
whose journey home was blotted out at Troy.
Others, so many others, died there too.
       So, mother,
go back to your quarters. Tend to your own tasks,   410

the distaff and the loom, and keep the women
working hard as well. As for giving orders,
men will see to that, but I most of all:
I hold the reins of power in this house."
                                   Astonished,
she withdrew to her own room. She took to heart   415
the clear good sense in what her son had said.
Climbing up to the lofty chamber with her women,
she fell to weeping for Odysseus, her beloved husband,
till watchful Athena sealed her eyes with welcome sleep.

    But the suitors broke into uproar through the shadowed halls,   420
all of them lifting prayers to lie beside her, share her bed,
until discreet Telemachus took command: "You suitors
who plague my mother, you, you insolent, overweening . . .
for this evening let us dine and take our pleasure,
no more shouting now. What a fine thing it is   425
to listen to such a bard as we have here—
the man sings like a god.
                        But at first light
we all march forth to assembly, take our seats
so I can give my orders and say to you straight out:
You must leave my palace! See to your feasting elsewhere,   430
devour your own possessions, house to house by turns.
But if you decide the fare is better, richer here,
destroying one man's goods and going scot-free,
all right then, carve away!
But I'll cry out to the everlasting gods in hopes   435
that Zeus will pay you back with a vengeance—all of you
destroyed in0 my house while I go scot-free myself!"

    So Telemachus declared. And they all bit their lips,
amazed the prince could speak with so much daring.

    Eupithes' son Antinous broke their silence: 440
"Well, Telemachus, only the gods could teach you
to sound so high and mighty! Such brave talk.
I pray that Zeus will never make *you* king of Ithaca,
though your father's crown is no doubt yours by birth."

    But cool-headed Telemachus countered firmly: 445
"Antinous, even though my words may offend you,
I'd be happy to take the crown if Zeus presents it.
You think that nothing worse could befall a man?
It's really not so bad to be a king. All at once
your palace grows in wealth, your honors grow as well.   450
But there are hosts of other Achaean princes, look—
young and old, crowds of them on our island here—
and any one of the lot might hold the throne,
now great Odysseus is dead . . .
But I'll be lord of my own house and servants,   455
all that King Odysseus won for me by force."

And now Eurymachus, Polybus' son, stepped in:
"Surely this must lie in the gods' lap, Telemachus—
which Achaean will lord it over seagirt Ithaca.
Do hold on to your own possessions, rule your house.   460
God forbid that anyone tear your holdings from your hands
while men still live in Ithaca.

                    But about your guest,
dear boy, I have some questions. Where does he come from?
Where's his country, his birth, his father's old estates?
Did he bring some news of your father, his return?   465
Or did he come on business of his own?
How he leapt to his feet and off he went!
No waiting around for proper introductions.
And no mean man, not by the looks of him, I'd say."

   "Eurymachus," Telemachus answered shrewdly,   470
"clearly my father's journey home is lost forever.
I no longer trust in rumors—rumors from the blue—
nor bother with any prophecy, when mother calls
some wizard into the house to ask him questions.
As for the stranger though,   475
the man's an old family friend, from Taphos,
wise Anchialus' son. He says his name is Mentes,
lord of the Taphian men who love their oars."

                       So he said
but deep in his mind he knew the immortal goddess.
Now the suitors turned to dance and song,   480
to the lovely beat and sway,
waiting for dusk to come upon them there . . .
and the dark night came upon them, lost in pleasure.
Finally, to bed. Each to his own house.

                     Telemachus,
off to his bedroom built in the fine courtyard—   485
a commanding, lofty room set well apart—
retired too, his spirit swarming with misgivings.
His devoted nurse attended him, bearing a glowing torch,
Eurycleia the daughter of Ops, Pisenor's son.
Laertes had paid a price for the woman years ago,   490
still in the bloom of youth. He traded twenty oxen,
honored her on a par with his own loyal wife at home
but fearing the queen's anger, never shared her bed.
She was his grandson's escort now and bore a torch,
for she was the one of all the maids who loved   495
the prince the most—she'd nursed him as a baby.
He spread the doors of his snug, well-made room,
sat down on the bed and pulled his soft shirt off,
tossed it into the old woman's conscientious hands,
and after folding it neatly, patting it smooth,   500
she hung it up on a peg beside his corded bed,
then padded from the bedroom,
drawing the door shut with the silver hook,
sliding the doorbolt home with its rawhide strap.

There all night long, wrapped in a sheep's warm fleece,   505
he weighed in his mind the course Athena charted.

BOOK II

[Telemachus Sets Sail]

When young Dawn with her rose-red fingers shone once more
the true son of Odysseus sprang from bed and dressed,
over his shoulder he slung his well-honed sword,
fastened rawhide sandals under his smooth feet
and stepped from his bedroom, handsome as a god.   5
At once he ordered heralds to cry out loud and clear
and summon the flowing-haired Achaeans to full assembly.
Their cries rang out. The people filed in quickly.
When they'd grouped, crowding the meeting grounds,
Telemachus strode in too, a bronze spear in his grip   10
and not alone: two sleek hounds went trotting at his heels.
And Athena lavished a marvelous splendor on the prince
so the people all gazed in wonder as he came forward,
the elders making way as he took his father's seat.
The first to speak was an old lord, Aegyptius,   15
stooped with age, who knew the world by heart.
For one dear son had sailed with King Odysseus,
bound in the hollow ships to the stallion-land of Troy—
the spearman Antiphus—but the brutal Cyclops killed him,
trapped in his vaulted cave, the last man the monster ate.   20
Three other sons he had: one who mixed with the suitors,
Eurynomus, and two kept working their father's farms.
Still, he never forgot the soldier, desolate in his grief.
In tears for the son he lost, he rose and said among them,
"Hear me, men of Ithaca. Hear what I have to say.   25
Not once have we held assembly, met in session
since King Odysseus sailed away in the hollow ships.
Who has summoned us now—one of the young men,
one of the old-timers? What crisis spurs him on?
Some news he's heard of an army on the march,   30
word he's caught firsthand so he can warn us now?
Or some other public matter he'll disclose and argue?
He's a brave man, I'd say. God be with him, too!
May Zeus speed him on to a happy end,
whatever his heart desires!"   35
                    Winning words
with a lucky ring. Odysseus' son rejoiced;
the boy could sit no longer—fired up to speak,
he took his stand among the gathered men.
The herald Pisenor, skilled in custom's ways,
put the staff in his hand,[8] and then the prince,   40
addressing old Aegyptius first, led off with, "Sir,
that man is not far off—you'll soon see for yourself—

---

8. As in the assembly in book 1 of the *Iliad*, the herald hands the person who is given the floor a staff, the symbol of authority.

I was the one who called us all together.
Something wounds me deeply . . .
not news I've heard of an army on the march,   45
word I've caught firsthand so I can warn you now,
or some other public matter I'll disclose and argue.
No, the crisis is my own. Trouble has struck my house—
a double blow. First, I have lost my noble father
who ruled among you years ago, each of you here,   50
and kindly as a father to his children.
                But now this,
a worse disaster that soon will grind my house down,
ruin it all, and all my worldly goods in the bargain.
Suitors plague my mother—against her will—
sons of the very men who are your finest here!   55
They'd sooner die than approach her father's house
so Icarius himself might see to his daughter's bridal,
hand her to whom he likes, whoever meets his fancy.
Not they—they infest our palace day and night,
they butcher our cattle, our sheep, our fat goats,   60
feasting themselves sick, swilling our glowing wine
as if there's no tomorrow—all of it, squandered.
Now we have no man like Odysseus in command
to drive this curse from the house. We ourselves?
We're hardly the ones to fight them off. All we'd do   65
is parade our wretched weakness. A boy inept at battle.
Oh I'd swing to attack if I had the power in me.
By god, it's intolerable, what they do—disgrace,
my house a shambles!
             You should be ashamed yourselves,
mortified in the face of neighbors living round about!   70
Fear the gods' wrath—before they wheel in outrage
and make these crimes recoil on your heads.
I beg you by Olympian Zeus, by Themis[9] too,
who sets assemblies free and calls us into session—
stop, my friends! Leave me alone to pine away in anguish . . . 75
Unless, of course, you think my noble father Odysseus
did the Achaean army damage, deliberate harm,
and to pay me back you'd do me harm, deliberately
setting these parasites against me. Better for me
if *you* were devouring all my treasure, all my cattle—   80
if you were the ones, we'd make amends in no time.
We'd approach you for reparations round the town,
demanding our goods till you'd returned the lot.
But now, look, you load my heart with grief—
there's nothing I can do!"
               Filled with anger,   85
down on the ground he dashed the speaker's scepter—
bursting into tears. Pity seized the assembly.
All just sat there, silent . . . .

---

9. A daughter of Zeus. She embodies the principle of what is right and proper, both in the natural world
and in human society.

no one had the heart to reply with harshness.
Only Antinous, who found it in himself to say,
"So high and mighty, Telemachus—such unbridled rage!
Well now, fling your accusations at *us*?
Think to pin the blame on *us*? You think again.
It's not the suitors here who deserve the blame,
it's your own dear mother, the matchless queen of cunning.
Look here. For three years now, getting on to four,
she's played it fast and loose with all our hearts,
building each man's hopes—
dangling promises, dropping hints to each—
but all the while with something else in mind.
This was her latest masterpiece of guile:
she set up a great loom in the royal halls
and she began to weave, and the weaving finespun,
the yarns endless, and she would lead us on: 'Young men,
my suitors, now that King Odysseus is no more,
go slowly, keen as you are to marry me, until
I can finish off this web . . .
so my weaving won't all fray and come to nothing.
This is a shroud for old lord Laertes, for that day
when the deadly fate that lays us out at last will take him down.
I dread the shame my countrywomen would heap upon me,
yes, if a man of such wealth should lie in state
without a shroud for cover.'
     Her very words,
and despite our pride and passion we believed her.
So by day she'd weave at her great and growing web—
by night, by the light of torches set beside her,
she would unravel all she'd done. Three whole years
she deceived us blind, seduced us with this scheme . . .
Then, when the wheeling seasons brought the fourth year on,
one of her women, in on the queen's secret, told the truth
and we caught her in the act—unweaving her gorgeous web.
So she finished it off. Against her will. We forced her.

  Now Telemachus, here is how the suitors answer *you*—
you burn it in your mind, you and all our people:
send your mother back! Direct her to marry
whomever her father picks, whoever pleases her.
So long as she persists in tormenting us,
quick to exploit the gifts Athena gave her—
a skilled hand for elegant work, a fine mind
and subtle wiles too—we've never heard the like,
not even in old stories sung of all Achaea's
well-coifed queens who graced the years gone by:
Mycenae crowned with garlands, Tyro and Alcmena[1] . . .
Not one could equal Penelope for intrigue
but in this case she intrigued beyond all limits.

  90

  95

  100

  105

  110

  115

  120

  125

  130

  135

---

1. Famous heroines of earlier legend who bore heroes to gods; Alcmena was the mother of Heracles. Odysseus sees the ghosts of Tyro and Alcmena in book 11.

So, we will devour your worldly goods and wealth
as long as *she* holds out, holds to that course
the gods have charted deep inside her heart.
Great renown she wins for herself, no doubt,
great loss for you in treasure. We'll not go back   140
to our old estates or leave for other parts,
not till she weds the Argive man she fancies."

But with calm good sense Telemachus replied:
"Antinous, how can I drive my mother from our house
against her will, the one who bore me, reared me too?   145
My father is worlds away, dead or alive, who knows?
Imagine the high price I'd have to pay Icarius
if all on my own I send my mother home.
Oh what I would suffer from her father—
and some dark god would hurt me even more   150
when mother, leaving her own house behind,
calls down her withering Furies[2] on my head,
and our people's cries of shame would hound my heels.
I will never issue that ultimatum to my mother.
And you, if you have any shame in your own hearts,   155
you must leave my palace! See to your feasting elsewhere,
devour your own possessions, house to house by turns.
But if you decide the fare is better, richer here,
destroying one man's goods and going scot-free,
all right then, carve away!   160
But I'll cry out to the everlasting gods in hopes
that Zeus will pay you back with a vengeance—all of you
destroyed in my house while I go scot-free myself!"

And to seal his prayer, farseeing Zeus sent down a sign.
He launched two eagles[3] soaring high from a mountain ridge   165
and down they glided, borne on the wind's draft a moment,
wing to wingtip, pinions straining taut till just
above the assembly's throbbing hum they whirled,
suddenly, wings thrashing, wild onslaught of wings
and banking down at the crowd's heads—a glaring, fatal sign—   170
talons slashing each other, tearing cheeks and throats
they swooped away on the right through homes and city.
All were dumbstruck, watching the eagles trail from sight,
people brooding, deeply, what might come to pass . . .
Until the old warrior Halitherses,   175
Mastor's son, broke the silence for them—
the one who outperformed all men of his time
at reading bird-signs, sounding out the omens,
rose and spoke, distraught for each man there:
"Hear me, men of Ithaca! Hear what I have to say,   180
though my revelations strike the suitors first of all—
a great disaster is rolling like a breaker toward their heads.

2. Avenging spirits, particularly concerned with crimes committed by kin against kin. 3. The royal bird, emblem of Zeus.

Clearly Odysseus won't be far from loved ones any longer—
now, right now, he's somewhere near, I tell you,
breeding bloody death for all these suitors here,   185
pains aplenty too for the rest of us who live
in Ithaca's sunlit air.
                    Long before that,
we must put heads together, find some way
to stop these men, or let them stop themselves.
Better for them that way, by far, I myself   190
am no stranger to prophecy—I can see it now!
Odysseus . . . all is working out for him, I say,
just as I said it would that day the Argives sailed
for Troy and the mastermind of battle boarded with them.
I said then: after many blows, and all his shipmates lost,   195
after twenty years had wheeled by, he would come home,
unrecognized by all . . .
and now, look, it all comes to pass!"
                         "Stop, old man!"
Eurymachus, Polybus' son, rose up to take him on.
"Go home and babble your omens to your children—   200
save *them* from some catastrophe coming soon.
I'm a better hand than you at reading portents.
Flocks of birds go fluttering under the sun's rays,
not all are fraught with meaning. Odysseus?
He's dead now, far from home—   205
would to god that you'd died with him too.
We'd have escaped your droning prophecies then
and the way you've loosed the dogs of this boy's anger—
your eyes peeled for a house-gift he might give you.
Here's *my* prophecy, bound to come to pass.   210
If you, you old codger, wise as the ages,
talk him round, incite the boy to riot,
he'll be the first to suffer, let me tell you.
And you, old man, we'll clap some fine on you
you'll weep to pay, a fine to crush your spirit!
                        Telemachus?   215
Here in front of you all, here's my advice for him.
Let him urge his mother back to her father's house—
her kin will arrange the wedding, provide the gifts,
the array that goes with a daughter dearly loved.[4]
Not till then, I'd say, will the island princes quit   220
their taxing courtship. Who's there to fear? I ask you.
Surely not Telemachus, with all his tiresome threats.
Nor do we balk, old man, at the prophecies you mouth—
they'll come to grief, they'll make us hate you more.
The prince's wealth will be devoured as always,   225
mercilessly—no reparations, ever . . . not
while the queen drags out our hopes to wed her,
waiting, day after day, all of us striving hard

---

4. A dowry. In other passages, it is the suitors who offer gifts to the bride's father. Such mixing of customs
from different periods or places is characteristic of oral epic traditions.

to win one matchless beauty. Never courting others,
bevies of brides who'd suit each noble here." 230

Telemachus answered, firm in his resolve:
"Eurymachus—the rest of you fine, brazen suitors—
I have done with appeals to you about these matters.
I'll say no more. The gods know how things stand
and so do all the Achaeans. And now all I ask 235
is a good swift ship and a crew of twenty men
to speed me through my passage out and back.
I'm sailing off to Sparta, sandy Pylos too,
for news of my long-lost father's journey home.
Someone may tell me something 240
or I may catch a rumor straight from Zeus,
rumor that carries news to men like nothing else.
Now, if I hear my father's alive and heading home,
hard-pressed as I am, I'll brave out one more year.
If I hear he's dead, no longer among the living, 245
then back I'll come to the native land I love,
raise his grave-mound, build his honors high
with the full funeral rites that he deserves—
and give my mother to another husband."

                                     A declaration,
and the prince sat down as Mentor took the floor, 250
Odysseus' friend-in-arms to whom the king,
sailing off to Troy, committed his household,
ordering one and all to obey the old man
and he would keep things steadfast and secure.
With deep concern for the realm, he rose and warned, 255
"Hear me, men of Ithaca. Hear what I have to say.
Never let any sceptered king be kind and gentle now,
not with all his heart, or set his mind on justice—
no, let him be cruel and always practice outrage.
Think: not one of the people whom he ruled 260
remembers Odysseus now, that godlike man,
and kindly as a father to his children!
I don't grudge these arrogant suitors for a moment,
weaving their violent work with all their wicked hearts—
they lay their lives on the line when they consume 265
Odysseus' worldly goods, blind in their violence,
telling themselves that he'll come home no more.
But all the rest of you, how you rouse my fury!
Sitting here in silence . . .
never a word put forth to curb these suitors, 270
paltry few as they are and you so many."

                        "Mentor!"
Euenor's son Leocritus rounded on him, shouting,
"Rabble-rousing fool, now what's this talk?
Goading them on to try and hold us back!
It's uphill work, I warn you, 275
fighting a force like ours—for just a meal.
Even if Odysseus of Ithaca did arrive in person,

to find us well-bred suitors feasting in his halls,
and the man were hell-bent on routing us from the palace—
little joy would his wife derive from his return,   280
for all her yearning. Here on the spot he'd meet
a humiliating end if he fought against such odds.
You're talking nonsense—idiocy.
                              No more. Come,
dissolve the assembly. Each man return to his holdings.
Mentor and Halitherses can speed our young prince on,   285
his father's doddering friends since time began.
He'll sit tight a good long while, I trust,
scrabbling for news right here in Ithaca—
he'll never make that trip."

     This broke up the assembly, keen to leave.   290
The people scattered quickly, each to his own house,
while the suitors strolled back to King Odysseus' palace.

     Telemachus, walking the beach now, far from others,
washed his hands in the foaming surf and prayed to Pallas:
"Dear god, hear me! Yesterday you came to my house,   295
you told me to ship out on the misty sea and learn
if father, gone so long, is ever coming home . . .
Look how my countrymen—the suitors most of all,
the pernicious bullies—foil each move I make."

     Athena came to his prayer from close at hand,   300
for all the world with Mentor's build and voice,
and she urged him on with winging words: "Telemachus,
you'll lack neither courage nor sense from this day on,
not if your father's spirit courses through your veins—
now there was a man, I'd say, in words and action both!   305
So how can your journey end in shipwreck or defeat?
Only if you were not his stock, Penelope's too,
then I'd fear your hopes might come to grief.
Few sons are the equals of their fathers;
most fall short, all too few surpass them.   310
But you, brave and adept from this day on—
Odysseus' cunning has hardly given out in you—
there's every hope that you will reach your goal.
Put them out of your mind, these suitors' schemes and plots.
They're madmen. Not a shred of sense or decency in the crowd.   315
Nor can they glimpse the death and black doom hovering
just at their heads to crush them all in one short day.
But you, the journey that stirs you now is not far off,
not with the likes of me, your father's friend and yours,
to rig you a swift ship and be your shipmate too.   320
Now home you go and mix with the suitors there.
But get your rations ready,
pack them all in vessels, the wine in jars,
and barley-meal—the marrow of men's bones—
in durable skins, while I make rounds in town   325

and quickly enlist your crew of volunteers.
Lots of ships in seagirt Ithaca, old and new.
I'll look them over, choose the best in sight,
we'll fit her out and launch her into the sea at once!"

And so Athena, daughter of Zeus, assured him.   330
No lingering now—he heard the goddess voice—
but back he went to his house with aching heart
and there at the palace found the brazen suitors
skinning goats in the courtyard, singeing pigs for roasting.
Antinous, smiling warmly, sauntered up to the prince,   335
grasped his hand and coaxed him, savoring his name:
"Telemachus, my high and mighty, fierce young friend,
no more nursing those violent words and actions now.
Come, eat and drink with us, just like the old days.
Whatever you want our people will provide. A ship   340
and a picked crew to speed you to holy Pylos,
out for the news about your noble father."

But self-possessed Telemachus drew the line:
"Antinous, now how could I dine with you in peace
and take my pleasure? You ruffians carousing here!   345
Isn't it quite enough that you, my mother's suitors,
have ravaged it all, my very best, these many years,
while I was still a boy? But now that I'm full-grown
and can hear the truth from others, absorb it too—
now, yes, that the anger seethes inside me . . .   350
I'll stop at nothing to hurl destruction at your heads,
whether I go to Pylos or sit tight here at home.
But the trip I speak of will not end in failure.
Go I will, as a passenger, nothing more,
since I don't seem to command my own crew.   355
That, I'm sure, is the way that suits you best."

                                        With this
he nonchalantly drew his hand from Antinous' hand
while the suitors, busy feasting in the halls,
mocked and taunted him, flinging insults now.
"God help us," one young buck kept shouting,   360
"he wants to slaughter us all!
He's off to sandy Pylos to hire cutthroats,
even Sparta perhaps, so hot to have our heads.
Why, he'd rove as far as Ephyra's dark rich soil
and run back home with lethal poison, slip it   365
into the bowl and wipe us out with drink!"

"Who knows?" another young blade up and ventured.
"Off in that hollow ship of his, he just might drown,
far from his friends, a drifter like his father.
What a bore! He'd double our work for us,   370
splitting up his goods, parceling out his house
to his mother and the man who weds the queen."

                                        So they scoffed

but Telemachus headed down to his father's storeroom,
broad and vaulted, piled high with gold and bronze,
chests packed with clothing, vats of redolent oil.   375
And there, standing in close ranks against the wall,
were jars of seasoned, mellow wine, holding the drink
unmixed inside them, fit for a god, waiting the day
Odysseus, worn by hardship, might come home again.
Doors, snugly fitted, doubly hung, were bolted shut   380
and a housekeeper was in charge by night and day—
her care, her vigilance, guarding all those treasures—
Eurycleia the daughter of Ops, Pisenor's son.
Telemachus called her into the storeroom: "Come, nurse,
draw me off some wine in smaller traveling jars,   385
mellow, the finest vintage you've been keeping,
next to what you reserve for our unlucky king—
in case Odysseus might drop in from the blue
and cheat the deadly spirits, make it home.
Fill me an even dozen, seal them tightly.   390
Pour me barley in well-stitched leather bags,
twenty measures of meal, your stone-ground best.
But no one else must know. These rations now,
put them all together. I'll pick them up myself,
toward evening, just about the time that mother   395
climbs to her room and thinks of turning in.
I'm sailing off to Sparta, sandy Pylos too,
for news of my dear father's journey home.
Perhaps I'll catch some rumor."
                          A wail of grief—
and his fond old nurse burst out in protest, sobbing: 400
"Why, dear child, what craziness got into your head?
Why bent on rambling over the face of the earth?—
a darling only son! Your father's worlds away,
god's own Odysseus, dead in some strange land.
And these brutes here, just wait, the moment you're gone   405
they'll all be scheming against you. Kill you by guile,
they will, and carve your birthright up in pieces.
No, sit tight here, guard your own things here.
Don't go roving over the barren salt sea—
no need to suffer so!"
                          "Courage, old woman,"   410
thoughtful Telemachus tried to reassure her,
"there's a god who made this plan.
But swear you won't say anything to my mother.
Not till ten or a dozen days have passed
or she misses me herself and learns I'm gone.   415
She mustn't mar her lovely face with tears."

   The old one swore a solemn oath to the gods
and vowing she would never breathe a word,
quickly drew off wine in two-eared jars
and poured barley in well-stitched leather bags.   420
Telemachus returned to the hall and joined the suitors.

Then bright-eyed Pallas thought of one more step.
Disguised as the prince, the goddess roamed through town,
pausing beside each likely crewman, giving orders:
"Gather beside our ship at nightfall—be there."   425
She asked Noëmon, Phronius' generous son,
to lend her a swift ship. He gladly volunteered.

The sun sank and the roads of the world grew dark.
Now the goddess hauled the swift ship down to the water,
stowed in her all the tackle well-rigged vessels carry,   430
moored her well away at the harbor's very mouth
and once the crew had gathered, rallying round,
she heartened every man.

Then bright-eyed Pallas thought of one last thing.
Back she went to King Odysseus' halls and there   435
she showered sweet oblivion over the suitors,
dazing them as they drank, knocking cups from hands.
No more loitering now, their eyes weighed down with sleep,
they rose and groped through town to find their beds.
But calling the prince outside his timbered halls,   440
taking the build and voice of Mentor once again,
flashing-eyed Athena urged him on: "Telemachus,
your comrades-at-arms are ready at the oars,
waiting for your command to launch. So come,
on with our voyage now, we're wasting time."   445

And Pallas Athena sped away in the lead
as he followed in her footsteps, man and goddess.
Once they reached the ship at the water's edge
they found their long-haired shipmates on the beach.
The prince, inspired, gave his first commands: 450
"Come, friends, get the rations aboard!
They're piled in the palace now.
My mother knows nothing of this. No servants either.
Only one has heard our plan."
                              He led them back
and the men fell in and fetched down all the stores   455
and stowed them briskly, deep in the well-ribbed holds
as Odysseus' son directed. Telemachus climbed aboard.
Athena led the way, assuming the pilot's seat
reserved astern, and he sat close beside her.
Cables cast off, the crew swung to the oarlocks.   460
Bright-eyed Athena sent them a stiff following wind
rippling out of the west, ruffling over the wine-dark sea
as Telemachus shouted out commands to all his shipmates:
"All lay hands to tackle!" They sprang to orders,
hoisting the pinewood mast, they stepped it firm   465
in its block amidships, lashed it fast with stays
and with braided rawhide halyards hauled the white sail high.
Suddenly wind hit full and the canvas bellied out
and a dark blue wave, foaming up at the bow,

sang out loud and strong as the ship made way, 470
skimming the whitecaps, cutting toward her goal.
All running gear secure in the swift black craft,
they set up bowls and brimmed them high with wine
and poured libations out to the everlasting gods
who never die—to Athena first of all, 475
the daughter of Zeus with flashing sea-gray eyes—
and the ship went plunging all night long and through the dawn.

BOOK III

[King Nestor Remembers]

As the sun sprang up, leaving the brilliant waters in its wake,
climbing the bronze sky to shower light on immortal gods
and mortal men across the plowlands ripe with grain—
the ship pulled into Pylos, Neleus'[5] storied citadel,
where the people lined the beaches, 5
sacrificing sleek black bulls to Poseidon,
god of the sea-blue mane who shakes the earth.
They sat in nine divisions, each five hundred strong,
each division offering up nine bulls, and while the people
tasted the innards, burned the thighbones for the god, 10
the craft and crew came heading straight to shore.
Striking sail, furling it in the balanced ship,
they moored her well and men swung down on land.
Telemachus climbed out last, with Athena far in front
and the bright-eyed goddess urged the prince along: 15
"Telemachus, no more shyness, this is not the time!
We sailed the seas for this, for news of your father—
where does he lie buried? what fate did he meet?
So go right up to Nestor,[6] breaker of horses.
We'll make him yield the secrets of his heart. 20
Press him yourself to tell the whole truth:
he'll never lie—the man is far too wise."

The prince replied, wise in his own way too,
"How can I greet him, Mentor, even approach the king?
I'm hardly adept at subtle conversation. 25
Someone my age *might* feel shy, what's more.
interrogating an older man."
                              "Telemachus,"
the bright-eyed goddess Athena reassured him,
"some of the words you'll find within yourself,
the rest some power will inspire you to say. 30
You least of all—I know—
were born and reared without the gods' good will."

And Pallas Athena sped away in the lead
as he followed in her footsteps—man and goddess
gained the place where the Pylians met and massed. 35

5. Father of Nestor and mortal son of Poseidon.   6. The oldest of the warriors at the siege of Troy.

There sat Nestor among his sons as friends around them
decked the banquet, roasted meats and skewered strips for broiling.
As soon as they saw the strangers, all came crowding down,
waving them on in welcome, urging them to sit.
Nestor's son Pisistratus, first to reach them,   40
grasped their hands and sat them down at the feast
on fleecy throws spread out along the sandbanks,
flanking his brother Thrasymedes and his father.
He gave them a share of innards, poured some wine
in a golden cup and, lifting it warmly toward Athena,   45
daughter of Zeus whose shield is storm and thunder,
greeted the goddess now with an invitation:
"Say a prayer to lord Poseidon, stranger,
his is the feast you've found on your arrival.
But once you've made your libation and your prayer—   50
all according to ancient custom—hand this cup
of hearty, seasoned wine to your comrade here
so he can pour forth too. He too, I think,
should pray to the deathless ones himself.
All men need the gods . . .   55
but the man is younger, just about my age.
That's why I give the gold cup first to you."
                                        With that
Pisistratus placed in her hand the cup of mellow wine
and Pallas rejoiced at the prince's sense of tact
in giving the golden winecup first to her.   60
At once she prayed intensely to Poseidon:
"Hear me, Sea-lord, you who embrace the earth—
don't deny our wishes, bring our prayers to pass!
First, then, to Nestor and all his sons grant glory.
Then to all these Pylians, for their splendid rites   65
grant a reward that warms their gracious hearts.
And last, Poseidon, grant Telemachus and myself
safe passage home, the mission accomplished
that sped us here in our rapid black ship."

    So she prayed, and brought it all to pass.   70
She offered the rich two-handled cup to Telemachus,
Odysseus' son, who echoed back her prayer word for word.
They roasted the prime cuts, pulled them off the spits
and sharing out the portions, fell to the royal feast.
Once they'd put aside desire for food and drink,   75
old Nestor the noble charioteer began, at last:
"Now's the time, now they've enjoyed their meal,
to probe our guests and find out who they are.
Strangers—friends, who are you?
Where did you sail from, over the running sea-lanes?   80
Out on a trading spree or roving the waves like pirates,
sea-wolves raiding at will, who risk their lives
to plunder other men?"
                        Poised Telemachus answered,
filled with heart, the heart Athena herself inspired,

to ask for the news about his father, gone so long,   85
and make his name throughout the mortal world.
"Nestor, son of Neleus, Achaea's pride and glory—
where are we from, you ask? I will tell you all.
We hail from Ithaca, under the heights of Nion.
Our mission here is personal, nothing public now.   90
I am on the trail of my father's widespread fame,
you see, searching the earth to catch some news
of great-hearted King Odysseus who, they say,
fought with you to demolish Troy some years ago.
About all the rest who fought the Trojans there,   95
we know where each one died his wretched death,
but father . . . even his death—
the son of Cronus shrouds it all in mystery.
No one can say for certain where he died,
whether he went down on land at enemy hands   100
or out on the open sea in Amphitrite's[7] breakers.
That's why I've come to plead before you now,
if you can tell me about his cruel death:
perhaps you saw him die with your own eyes
or heard the wanderer's end from someone else.   105
More than all other men, that man was born for pain.
Don't soften a thing, from pity, respect for me—
tell me, clearly, all your eyes have witnessed.
I beg you—if ever my father, lord Odysseus,
pledged you his word and made it good in action   110
once on the fields of Troy where you Achaeans suffered,
remember his story now, tell me the truth."

    Nestor the noble charioteer replied at length:
"Ah dear boy, since you call back such memories,
such living hell we endured in distant Troy—   115
we headstrong fighting forces of Achaea—
so many raids from shipboard down the foggy sea,
cruising for plunder, wherever Achilles led the way;
so many battles round King Priam's walls we fought,
so many gone, our best and bravest fell.   120
There Ajax lies, the great man of war.
There lies Achilles too.
There Patroclus, skilled as the gods in counsel.[8]
And there my own dear son, both strong and staunch,
Antilochus—lightning on his feet and every inch a fighter!   125
But so many other things we suffered, past that count—
what mortal in this wide world could tell it all?
Not if you sat and probed his memory, five, six years,
delving for all the pains our brave Achaeans bore there.
Your patience would fray, you'd soon head for home . . .   130

7. A sea nymph; here she personifies the sea.   8. Nestor lists the great Greek heroes who fell at Troy.
Achilles was the bravest of the Greeks and the central hero of the *Iliad*. Priam, king of Troy, was killed
when the city fell. Ajax committed suicide when the dead Achilles' armor, which was to go to the best
warrior after Achilles, was awarded to Odysseus. Patroclus was Achilles' closest friend. Odysseus will meet
the ghosts of Achilles and Ajax when he visits the land of the dead in book 11.

Nine years we wove a web of disaster for those Trojans,
pressing them hard with every tactic known to man,
and only after we slaved did Zeus award us victory.
And no one there could hope to rival Odysseus,
not for sheer cunning—   135
at every twist of strategy he excelled us all.
Your father, yes, if you are in fact his son . . .
I look at you and a sense of wonder takes me.
Your way with words—it's just like his—I'd swear
no youngster could ever speak like you, so apt, so telling.   140
As long as I and great Odysseus soldiered there,
why, never once did we speak out at odds,
neither in open muster nor in royal council:
forever one in mind, in judgment balanced, shrewd,
we mapped our armies' plans so things might turn out best.   145
But then, once we'd sacked King Priam's craggy city,
Zeus contrived in his heart a fatal homeward run
for all the Achaeans who were fools, at least,
dishonest too, so many met a disastrous end,
thanks to the lethal rage   150
of the mighty Father's daughter.[9] Eye afire,
Athena set them feuding, Atreus' two sons[1] . . .
They summoned all the Achaean ranks to muster,
rashly, just at sunset—no hour to rally troops—
and in they straggled, sodden with wine, our heroes.   155
The brothers harangued them, told them why they'd met:
a crisis—Menelaus urging the men to fix their minds
on the voyage home across the sea's broad back,
but it brought no joy to Agamemnon, not at all.
He meant to detain us there and offer victims,   160
anything to appease Athena's dreadful wrath—
poor fool, he never dreamed Athena would not comply.
The minds of the everlasting gods don't change so quickly.
So the two of them stood there, wrangling, back and forth
till the armies sprang up, their armor clashing, ungodly uproar—   165
the two plans split the ranks. That night we barely slept,
seething with hard feelings against our own comrades,
for Zeus was brooding over us, poised to seal our doom . . .
At dawn, half of us hauled our vessels down to sea,
we stowed our plunder, our sashed and lovely women.   170
But half the men held back, camped on the beach,
waiting it out for Agamemnon's next commands
while our contingent embarked—
we pushed off and sailed at a fast clip
as a god smoothed out the huge troughing swells.   175
We reached Tenedos[2] quickly, sacrificed to the gods,
the crews keen for home, but a quick return was not

9. Athena. She was on the Greeks' side in the war, but her wrath was aroused when Ajax, son of Oïleus,
raped the Trojan princess Cassandra, who had taken refuge in Athena's temple during the sack of Troy.
Athena's anger included the whole Greek army because they did not punish Ajax.   1. Agamemnon and
Menelaus, the leaders of the Greeks.   2. An island off the coast of present-day Turkey, southwest of
Troy.

in Zeus's plans, not yet: that cruel power
loosed a cursed feud on us once again.
Some swung their rolling warships hard about—   180
Odysseus sailed them back, the flexible, wily king,
veering over to Agamemnon now to shore his fortunes up.
But not I. Massing the ships that came in my flotilla,
I sped away as the god's mischief kept on brewing,
dawning on me now. And Tydeus' fighting son   185
Diomedes[3] fled too, rousing all his comrades.
Late in the day the red-haired Menelaus joined us,
overtook us at Lesbos,[4] debating the long route home:
whether to head north, over the top of rocky Chios,
skirting Psyrie, keeping that island off to port   190
or run south of Chios, by Mimas' gusty cape.
We asked the god for a sign. He showed us one,
he urged us to cut out on the middle passage,
straight to Euboea now,
escape a catastrophe, fast as we could sail!   195
A shrilling wind came up, stiff, driving us on
and on we raced, over the sea-lanes rife with fish
and we made Geraestus Point in the dead of night.[5]
Many thighs of bulls we offered Poseidon there—
thank god we'd crossed that endless reach of sea.   200
Then on the fourth day out the crews of Diomedes,
breaker of horses, moored their balanced ships
at Argos port, but I held course for Pylos, yes,
and never once did the good strong wind go limp
from the first day the good unleashed its blast.   205

    And so, dear boy, I made it home from Troy,
in total ignorance, knowing nothing of their fates,
the ones who stayed behind:
who escaped with their lives and who went down.
But still, all I've gathered by hearsay, sitting here   210
in my own house—that you'll learn, it's only right,
I'll hide nothing now.
                    They say the Myrmidons,[6]
those savage spearmen led by the shining son
of lionhearted Achilles, traveled home unharmed.   215
Philoctetes[7] the gallant son of Poias, safe as well.
Idomeneus[8] brought his whole contingent back to Crete,
all who'd escaped the war—the sea snatched none from him.
But Atreus' son Agamemnon . . . you yourselves, even

---

3. One of the greatest Greek warriors at Troy; his home was Argos.   4. A large island off the coast of
Asia Minor, south of Troy and Tenedos.   5. Sailing frail ships and lacking compasses, Greek sailors
preferred to hug the shore. The normal route would have been east and then south of the island of Chios,
past the headland of Mimas on the shore of Asia Minor, and across the Aegean Sea along the island chain
of the Cyclades. But Nestor, in a hurry, went north of Chios and directly across the northern Aegean to
Cape Geraistos, on the tip of the long island of Euboea, which hugs the eastern coast of the Greek mainland.
6. The contingent led by Achilles. His son, Neoptolemus, came to Troy to avenge his father; he killed the
Trojan king Priam on the altar in his house.   7. A great archer, abandoned on a desert island by the
Greeks on their way to Troy because he fell sick as a result of a snake bite. Because it was prophesied that
the city could be captured only with his bow, he was brought to Troy for the final assault.   8. Leader of
the Greek troops from Crete.

in far-off Ithaca, must have heard how he returned,
how Aegisthus hatched the king's horrendous death. 220
But what a price he paid, in blood, in suffering.
Ah how fine it is, when a man is brought down,
to leave a son behind! Orestes took revenge,
he killed that cunning, murderous Aegisthus,
who'd killed his famous father. 225
            And you, my friend—
how tall and handsome I see you now—be brave, you too,
so men to come will sing your praises down the years."

Telemachus, weighing the challenge closely, answered,
"Oh Nestor, son of Neleus, Achaea's pride and glory,
what a stroke of revenge that was! All Achaeans 230
will spread Orestes' fame across the world,
a song for those to come.
If only the gods would arm me in such power
I'd take revenge on the lawless, brazen suitors
riding roughshod over me, plotting reckless outrage. 235
But for me the gods have spun out no such joy,
for my father or myself. I must bear up,
that's all."
            And the old charioteer replied,
"Now that you mention it, dear boy, I do recall
a mob of suitors, they say, besets your mother 240
there in your own house, against your will,
and plots your ruin. Tell me, though, do you
let yourself be so abused, or do people round about,
stirred up by the prompting of some god, despise you now?
Who knows if he will return someday to take revenge 245
on all their violence? Single-handed perhaps
or with an Argive army at his back? If only
the bright-eyed goddess chose to love you just
as she lavished care on brave Odysseus, years ago
in the land of Troy where we Achaeans struggled! 250
I've never seen the immortals show so much affection
as Pallas openly showed *him*, standing by your father—
if only she'd favor you, tend you with all her heart,
many a suitor then would lose all thought of marriage,
blotted out forever."
            "Never, your majesty," 255
Telemachus countered gravely, "that will never
come to pass, I know. What you say dumbfounds me,
staggers imagination! Hope, hope as I will
that day will never dawn . . .
not even if the gods should will it so."
            "Telemachus!" 260
Pallas Athena broke in sharply, her eyes afire—
"What's this nonsense slipping through your teeth?
It's light work for a willing god to save a mortal
even half the world away. Myself, I'd rather
sail through years of trouble and labor home 265

and see that blessed day, than hurry home
to die at my own hearth like Agamemnon,
killed by Aegisthus' cunning—by his own wife.
But the great leveler, Death: not even the gods
can defend a man, not even one they love, that day   270
when fate takes hold and lays him out at last."

                         "Mentor,"
wise Telemachus said, "distraught as we are for him,
let's speak of this no more. My father's return?
It's inconceivable now. Long ago the undying gods
have sealed his death, his black doom. But now   275
there's another question I would put to Nestor:
Nestor excels all men for sense and justice,
his knowledge of the world.
Three generations he has ruled, they say,
and to my young eyes he seems a deathless god!   280
Nestor, son of Neleus, tell me the whole story—
how did the great king Agamemnon meet his death?
Where was Menelaus? What fatal trap did he set,
that treacherous Aegisthus, to bring down a man
far stronger than himself? Was Menelaus gone   285
from Achaean Argos,[9] roving the world somewhere,
so the coward found the nerve to kill the king?"

    And old Nestor the noble charioteer replied:
"Gladly, my boy, I'll tell you the story first to last . . .
Right you are, you guess what would have happened   290
if red-haired Menelaus, arriving back from Troy,
had found Aegisthus alive in Agamemnon's palace.
No barrow piled high on the earth for *his* dead body,
no, the dogs and birds would have feasted on his corpse,
sprawled on the plain outside the city gates, and no one,   295
no woman in all Achaea, would have wept a moment,
such a monstrous crime the man contrived!
But there we were, camped at Troy, battling out
the long hard campaign while he at his ease at home,
in the depths of Argos, stallion-country—he lay siege   300
to the wife of Agamemnon, luring, enticing her with talk.
At first, true, she spurned the idea of such an outrage,
Clytemnestra the queen, her will was faithful still.
And there was a man, what's more, a bard close by,
to whom Agamemnon, setting sail for Troy,   305
gave strict commands to guard his wife. But then,
that day the doom of the gods had bound her to surrender,
Aegisthus shipped the bard away to a desert island,
marooned him there, sweet prize for the birds of prey,
and swept her off to his own house, lover lusting for lover.   310
And many thighbones he burned on the gods' holy altars,
many gifts he hung on the temple walls—gold, brocades—

9. In a broad sense, the realm of Agamemnon, who ruled Mycenae.

in thanks for a conquest past his maddest hopes.
                              Now we,
you see, were sailing home from Troy in the same squadron,
Menelaus and I, comrades-in-arms from years of war.   315
But as we rounded holy Sounion, Athens' headland,
lord Apollo attacked Atrides' helmsman, aye,
with his gentle shafts he shot the man to death—[1]
an iron grip on the tiller, the craft scudding fast—
Phrontis, Onetor's son, who excelled all men alive   320
at steering ships when gales bore down in fury.
So Menelaus, straining to sail on, was held back
till he could bury his mate with fitting rites.
But once he'd got off too, plowing the wine-dark sea
in his ribbed ships, and made a run to Malea's beetling cape,[2]   325
farseeing Zeus decided to give the man rough sailing,
poured a hurricane down upon him, shrilling winds,
giant, rearing whitecaps, monstrous, mountains high.
There at a stroke he cut the fleet in half and drove
one wing to Crete, where Cydonians make their homes   330
along the Iardanus River. Now, there's a sheer cliff
plunging steep to the surf at the farthest edge of Gortyn,
out on the mist-bound sea, where the South Wind piles breakers,
huge breakers, left of the headland's horn, toward Phaestos,[3]
with only a low reef to block the crushing tides.   335
In they sailed, and barely escaped their death—
the ships' crews, that is—
the rollers smashed their hulls against the rocks.
But as for the other five[4] with pitch-black prows,
the wind and current swept them on toward Egypt.   340

    So Menelaus, amassing a hoard of stores and gold,
was off cruising his ships to foreign ports of call
while Aegisthus hatched his vicious work at home.
Seven years he lorded over Mycenae rich in gold,
once he'd killed Agamemnon—he ground the people down.   345
But the eighth year ushered in his ruin, Prince Orestes
home from Athens, yes, he cut him down, that cunning,
murderous Aegisthus, who'd killed his famous father.
Vengeance done, he held a feast for the Argives,
to bury his hated mother, craven Aegisthus too,   350
the very day Menelaus arrived, lord of the warcry,
freighted with all the wealth his ships could carry.
                              So you,
dear boy, take care. Don't rove from home too long,
too far, leaving your own holdings unprotected—
crowds in your palace so brazen   355
they'll carve up all your wealth, devour it all,
and then your journey here will come to nothing.

---

1. A formula for a sudden death that has no obvious explanation; for women the arrows come from Artemis, Apollo's sister.   2. The easternmost of the three capes in which the Peloponnesus ends, still a place of storms. Menelaus would have to round it to reach a harbor for Sparta.   3. Gortyn and Phaestos are inland from the south coast of Crete.   4. Including Menelaus's ship.

Still I advise you, urge you to visit Menelaus.
He's back from abroad at last, from people so removed
you might abandon hope of ever returning home,   360
once the winds had driven you that far off course,
into a sea so vast not even cranes could wing their way
in one year's flight—so vast it is, so awesome . . .

        So, off you go with your ships and shipmates now.
Or if you'd rather go by land, there's team and chariot,   365
my sons at your service too, and they'll escort you
to sunny Lacedaemon,[5] home of the red-haired king.
Press him yourself to tell the whole truth:
he'll never lie—the man is far too wise."
                                So he closed
as the sun set and darkness swept across the earth   370
and the bright-eyed goddess Pallas spoke for all:
"There was a tale, old soldier, so well told.
Come, cut out the victims' tongues[6] and mix the wine,
so once we've poured libations out to the Sea-lord
and every other god, we'll think of sleep. High time—   375
the light's already sunk in the western shadows.
It's wrong to linger long at the gods' feast;
we must be on our way."
                        Zeus's daughter—
they all hung closely on every word she said.
Heralds sprinkled water over their hands for rinsing,   380
the young men brimmed the mixing bowls with wine,
they tipped first drops for the god in every cup
then poured full rounds for all. They rose and flung
the victims' tongues on the fire and poured libations out.
When they'd poured, and drunk to their hearts' content,   385
Athena and Prince Telemachus both started up
to head for their ship at once.
But Nestor held them there, objecting strongly:
"Zeus forbid—and the other deathless gods as well—
that you resort to your ship and put my house behind   390
like a rank pauper's without a stitch of clothing,
no piles of rugs, no blankets in his place
for host and guests to slumber soft in comfort.
Why, I've plenty of fine rugs and blankets here.
No, by god, the true son of my good friend Odysseus   395
won't bed down on a ship's deck, not while I'm alive
or my sons are left at home to host our guests,
whoever comes to our palace, newfound friends."
                                "Dear old man,
you're right," Athena exclaimed, her eyes brightening now.
"Telemachus should oblige you. Much the better way.   400
Let him follow you now, sleep in your halls,
but I'll go back to our trim black ship,

---

5. Sparta, Menelaus's home.   6. The tongue was one of the parts of the meat reserved for the gods; it
was thrown on the fire.

hearten the crew and give each man his orders.
I'm the only veteran in their ranks, I tell you.
All the rest, of an age with brave Telemachus,   405
are younger men who sailed with him as friends.
I'll bed down there by the dark hull tonight,
at dawn push off for the proud Cauconians.[7]
Those people owe me a debt long overdue,
and no mean sum, believe me.   410
But you, seeing my friend is now your guest,
speed him on his way with a chariot and your son
and give him the finest horses that you have,
bred for stamina, trained to race the wind."

    With that the bright-eyed goddess winged away   415
in an eagle's form and flight.
Amazement fell on all the Achaeans there.
The old king, astonished by what he'd seen,
grasped Telemachus' hand and cried out to the prince,
"Dear boy—never fear you'll be a coward or defenseless, 420
not if at your young age the gods will guard you so.
Of all who dwell on Olympus, this was none but she,
Zeus's daughter, the glorious one, his third born,
who prized your gallant father among the Argives.
Now, O Queen, be gracious! Give us high renown,   425
myself, my children, my loyal wife and queen.
And I will make you a sacrifice, a yearling heifer
broad in the brow, unbroken, never yoked by men.
I'll offer it up to you—I'll sheathe its horns in gold."

    So he prayed, and Pallas Athena heard his prayer.   430
And Nestor the noble chariot-driver led them on,
his sons and sons-in-law, back to his regal palace.
Once they reached the storied halls of the aged king
they sat on rows of low and high-backed chairs.
As they arrived the old man mixed them all a bowl,   435
stirring the hearty wine, seasoned eleven years
before a servant broached it, loosed its seal.
Mulling it in the bowl, old Nestor poured
a libation out, praying hard to Pallas Athena,
daughter of Zeus whose shield is storm and thunder.   440

    Once they had poured their offerings, drunk their fill,
the Pylians went to rest, each in his own house.
But the noble chariot-driver let Telemachus,
King Odysseus' son, sleep at the palace now,
on a corded bed inside the echoing colonnade,   445
with Prince Pisistratus close beside him there,
the young spearman, already captain of armies,
though the last son still unwed within the halls.

7. A people in the western Peloponnesus.

The king retired to chambers deep in his lofty house
where the queen his wife arranged and shared their bed.   450

When young Dawn with her rose-red fingers shone once more
old Nestor the noble chariot-driver climbed from bed,
went out and took his seat on the polished stones,
a bench glistening white, rubbed with glossy oil,
placed for the king before his looming doors.   455
There Neleus held his sessions years ago,
a match for the gods in counsel,
but his fate had long since forced him down to Death.
Now royal Nestor in turn, Achaea's watch and ward,
sat there holding the scepter while his sons,   460
coming out of their chambers, clustered round him,
hovering near: Echephron, Stratius, Perseus
and Aretus, Thrasymedes like a god, and sixth,
young lord Pisistratus came to join their ranks.
They escorted Prince Telemachus in to sit beside them.   465
Nestor, noble charioteer, began the celebration:
"Quickly, my children, carry out my wishes now
so I may please the gods, Athena first of all—
she came to me at Poseidon's flowing feast,
Athena in all her glory!   470
Now someone go to the fields to fetch a heifer,
lead her here at once—a herdsman drive her in.
Someone hurry down to Prince Telemachus' black ship
and bring up all his crewmen, leave just two behind.
And another tell our goldsmith, skilled Laerces,   475
to come and sheathe the heifer's horns in gold.
The rest stay here together. Tell the maids
inside the hall to prepare a sumptuous feast—
bring seats and firewood, bring pure water too."

They all pitched in to carry out his orders.   480
The heifer came from the fields, the crewmen came
from brave Telemachus' ship, and the smith came in
with all his gear in hand, the tools of his trade,
the anvil, hammer and well-wrought tongs he used
for working gold. And Athena came as well   485
to attend her sacred rites.
The old horseman passed the gold to the smith,
and twining the foil, he sheathed the heifer's horns
so the goddess' eyes might dazzle, delighted with the gift.
Next Stratius and Echephron led the beast by the horns.   490
Aretus, coming up from the storeroom, brought them
lustral water filling a flower-braided bowl,
in his other hand, the barley in a basket.[8]
Thrasymedes, staunch in combat, stood ready,
whetted ax in his grasp to cut the heifer down,   495
and Perseus held the basin for the blood.

8. Barley was sprinkled on the sacrificial victim.

Now Nestor the old charioteer began the rite.
Pouring the lustral water, scattering barley-meal,
he lifted up his ardent prayers to Pallas Athena,
launching the sacrifice, flinging onto the fire   500
the first tufts of hair from the victim's head.

    Prayers said, the scattering barley strewn,
suddenly Nestor's son impetuous Thrasymedes
strode up close and struck—the ax chopped
the neck tendons through—
                and the blow stunned   505
the heifer's strength—
               The women shrilled their cry,[9]
Nestor's daughters, sons' wives and his own loyal wife
Eurydice, Clymenus' eldest daughter. Then, hoisting up
the victim's head from the trampled earth, they held her fast
as the captain of men Pisistratus slashed her throat.   510
Dark blood gushed forth, life ebbed from her limbs—
they quartered her quickly, cut the thighbones out
and all according to custom wrapped them round in fat,
a double fold sliced clean and topped with strips of flesh.[1]
And the old king burned these over dried split wood   515
and over the fire poured out glistening wine
while young men at his side held five-pronged forks.
Once they'd burned the bones and tasted the organs,
they sliced the rest into pieces, spitted them on skewers
and raising points to the fire, broiled all the meats.   520

    During the ritual lovely Polycaste, youngest daughter
of Nestor, Neleus' son, had bathed Telemachus.
Rinsing him off now, rubbing him down with oil,
she drew a shirt and handsome cape around him.
Out of his bath he stepped, glistening like a god,   525
strode in and sat by the old commander Nestor.

    They roasted the prime cuts, pulled them off the spits
and sat down to the feast while ready stewards saw
to rounds of wine and kept the gold cups flowing.
When they'd put aside desire for food and drink,   530
Nestor the noble chariot-driver issued orders:
"Hurry, my boys! Bring Telemachus horses,
a good full-maned team—
hitch them to a chariot—he must be off at once."

    They listened closely, snapped to his commands   535
and hitched a rapid team to a chariot's yoke in haste.
A housekeeper stowed some bread and wine aboard
and meats too, food fit for the sons of kings.
Telemachus vaulted onto the splendid chariot—

9. The ritual cry uttered at the moment of sacrifice.   1. The bones wrapped in fat are burned as the
gods' portion of the sacrificial meal; the humans roast and eat the meat.

right beside him Nestor's son Pisistratus,   540
captain of armies, boarded, seized the reins,
whipped the team to a run and on the horses flew,
holding nothing back, out into open country,
leaving the heights of Pylos fading in their trail,
shaking the yoke across their shoulders all day long.   545

    The sun sank and the roads of the world grew dark
as they reached Phera, pulling up to Diocles' halls,
the son of Ortilochus, son of the Alpheus River.
He gave them a royal welcome; there they slept the night.

    When young Dawn with her rose-red fingers shone once more   550
they yoked their pair again, mounted the blazoned car
and out through the gates and echoing colonnade
they whipped the team to a run and on they flew,
holding nothing back—and the princes reached
the wheatlands, straining now for journey's end,   555
so fast those purebred stallions raced them on
as the sun sank and the roads of the world grew dark.

BOOK IV

[The King and Queen of Sparta]

At last they gained the ravines of Lacedaemon ringed by hills
and drove up to the halls of Menelaus in his glory.
They found the king inside his palace, celebrating
with throngs of kinsmen a double wedding-feast
for his son and lovely daughter. The princess   5
he was sending on to the son of great Achilles,[2]
breaker of armies. Years ago Menelaus vowed,
he nodded assent at Troy and pledged her hand
and now the gods were sealing firm the marriage.
So he was sending her on her way with team and chariot,   10
north to the Myrmidons' famous city governed by her groom.
From Sparta he brought Alector's daughter as the bride
for his own full-grown son, the hardy Megapenthes,[3]
born to him by a slave. To Helen the gods had granted
no more offspring once she had borne her first child,   15
the breathtaking Hermione,
a luminous beauty gold as Aphrodite.
          So now
they feasted within the grand, high-roofed palace,
all the kin and clansmen of Menelaus in his glory,
reveling warmly here as in their midst   20
an inspired bard sang out and struck his lyre—
and through them a pair of tumblers dashed and sprang,
whirling in leaping handsprings, leading on the dance.

---

2. Neoptolemus.   3. Literally, "Great Grief." In Homer, sons are often named for characteristics of their fathers. Compare Telemachus: either "One Who Fights Far Away" or "Fighter from Afar" (i.e., with the bow).

The travelers, Nestor's shining son and Prince Telemachus,
had brought themselves and their horses to a standstill   25
just outside the court when good lord Eteoneus,
passing through the gates now, saw them there,
and the ready aide-in-arms of Menelaus
took the message through his sovereign's halls
and stepping close to his master broke the news: 30
"Strangers have just arrived, your majesty, Menelaus.
Two men, but they look like kin of mighty Zeus himself.
Tell me, should we unhitch their team for them
or send them to someone free to host them well?"

    The red-haired king took great offense at that: 35
"Never a fool before, Eteoneus, son of Boëthous,
now I see you're babbling like a child!
Just think of all the hospitality *we* enjoyed
at the hands of other men before we made it home,
and god save us from such hard treks in years to come.   40
Quick, unhitch their team. And bring them in,
strangers, guests, to share our flowing feast."

    Back through the halls he hurried, calling out
to other brisk attendants to follow quickly.
They loosed the sweating team from under the yoke,   45
tethered them fast by reins inside the horse-stalls,
tossing feed at their hoofs, white barley mixed with wheat,
and canted the chariot up against the polished walls,
shimmering in the sun, then ushered in their guests,
into that magnificent place. Both struck by the sight,   50
they marveled up and down the house of the warlord dear to Zeus—
a radiance strong as the moon or rising sun came flooding
through the high-roofed halls of illustrious Menelaus.
Once they'd feasted their eyes with gazing at it all,
into the burnished tubs they climbed and bathed.   55
When women had washed them, rubbed them down with oil
and drawn warm fleece and shirts around their shoulders,
they took up seats of honor next to Atrides Menelaus.
A maid brought water soon in a graceful golden pitcher
and over a silver basin tipped it out   60
so they might rinse their hands,
then pulled a gleaming table to their side.
A staid housekeeper brought on bread to serve them,
appetizers aplenty too, lavish with her bounty.
As a carver lifted platters of meat toward them,   65
meats of every sort, and set before them golden cups,
the red-haired king Menelaus greeted both guests warmly:
"Help yourselves to food, and welcome! Once you've dined
we'll ask you who you are. But your parents' blood
is hardly lost in you. You must be born of kings,   70
bred by the gods to wield the royal scepter.
No mean men could sire sons like you."
                                        With those words

he passed them a fat rich loin with his own hands,
the choicest part, that he'd been served himself.
They reached for the good things that lay outspread 75
and when they'd put aside desire for food and drink,
Telemachus, leaning his head close to Nestor's son,
spoke low to the prince so no one else could hear:
"Look, Pisistratus—joy of my heart, my friend—
the sheen of bronze, the blaze of gold and amber, 80
silver, ivory too, through all this echoing mansion!
Surely Zeus's court on Olympus must be just like this,
the boundless glory of all this wealth inside!
My eyes dazzle . . . I am struck with wonder."

   But the red-haired warlord overheard his guest 85
and cut in quickly with winged words for both:
"No man alive could rival Zeus, dear boys,
with his everlasting palace and possessions.
But among men, I must say, few if any
could rival *me* in riches. Believe me, 90
much I suffered, many a mile I roved to haul
such treasures home in my ships. Eight years out,
wandering off as far as Cyprus, Phoenicia, even Egypt,
I reached the Ethiopians, Sidonians, Erembians—Libya too,
where lambs no sooner spring from the womb than they grow horns. 95
Three times in the circling year the ewes give birth.
So no one, neither king nor shepherd could want
for cheese or mutton, or sweet milk either,
udders swell for the sucklings round the year.

   But while I roamed those lands, amassing a fortune, 100
a stranger killed my brother, blind to the danger, duped blind—
thanks to the cunning of his cursed, murderous queen!
So I rule all this wealth with no great joy.
You must have heard my story from your fathers,
whoever they are—what hardships I endured, 105
how I lost this handsome palace built for the ages,
filled to its depths with hoards of gorgeous things.
Well, would to god I'd stayed right here in my own house
with a third of all that wealth and they were still alive,
all who died on the wide plain of Troy those years ago, 110
far from the stallion-land of Argos.
                              And still,
much as I weep for all my men, grieving sorely,
time and again, sitting here in the royal halls,
now indulging myself in tears, now brushing tears away—
the grief that numbs the spirit gluts us quickly— 115
for none of all those comrades, pained as I am,
do I grieve as much for one . . .
that man who makes sleep hateful, even food,
as I pore over his memory. No one, no Achaean
labored hard as Odysseus labored or achieved so much. 120
And how did his struggles end? In suffering for that man;

for me, in relentless, heartbreaking grief for him,
lost and gone so long now—dead or alive, who knows?
How they must mourn him too, Laertes, the old man,
and self-possessed Penelope. Telemachus as well,   125
the boy he left a babe in arms at home."
                              Such memories
stirred in the young prince a deep desire to grieve
for Odysseus. Tears streamed down his cheeks
and wet the ground when he heard his father's name,
both hands clutching his purple robe before his eyes.   130
Menelaus recognized him at once but pondered
whether to let him state his father's name
or probe him first and prompt him step by step.

    While he debated all this now within himself,
Helen emerged from her scented, lofty chamber—   135
striking as Artemis[4] with her golden shafts—
and a train of women followed . . .
Adreste drew up her carved reclining-chair,
Alcippe brought a carpet of soft-piled fleece,
Phylo carried her silver basket given by Alcandre,   140
King Polybus' wife, who made his home in Egyptian Thebes
where the houses overflow with the greatest troves of treasure.
The king gave Menelaus a pair of bathing-tubs in silver,
two tripods, ten bars of gold, and apart from these
his wife presented Helen her own precious gifts: 145
a golden spindle, a basket that ran on casters,
solid silver polished off with rims of gold.
Now Phylo her servant rolled it in beside her,
heaped to the brim with yarn prepared for weaving;
the spindle swathed in violet wool lay tipped across it. 150
Helen leaned back in her chair, a stool beneath her feet,
and pressed her husband at once for each detail:
"Do we know, my lord Menelaus, who our visitors
claim to be, our welcome new arrivals?
Right or wrong, what can I say? My heart tells me   155
to come right out and say I've never seen such a likeness,
neither in man nor woman—I'm amazed at the sight.
To the life he's like the son of great Odysseus,
surely he's Telemachus! The boy that hero left
a babe in arms at home when all you Achaeans   160
fought at Troy, launching your headlong battles
just for *my* sake, shameless whore that I was."

    "My dear, my dear," the red-haired king assured her,
"now that you mention it, I see the likeness too . . .
Odysseus' feet were like the boy's, his hands as well,   165
his glancing eyes, his head, and the fine shock of hair.
Yes, and just now, as I was talking about Odysseus,

---

4. A virgin goddess, Apollo's sister, she is associated with wild animals and childbirth. Helen, Menelaus's
wife, was the daughter of Leda and Zeus. Her elopement with Paris was the cause of the Trojan War.

remembering how he struggled, suffered, all for me,
a flood of tears came streaming down his face
and he clutched his purple robe before his eyes."   170

    "Right you are"—Pisistratus stepped in quickly—
"son of Atreus, King Menelaus, captain of armies:
here is the son of that great hero, as you say.
But the man is modest, he would be ashamed
to make a show of himself, his first time here,   175
and interrupt you. We delight in your voice
as if some god were speaking!
The noble horseman Nestor sent me along
to be his escort. Telemachus yearned to see you,
so you could give him some advice or urge some action.   180
When a father's gone, his son takes much abuse
in a house where no one comes to his defense.
So with Telemachus now. His father's gone.
No men at home will shield him from the worst."

    "Wonderful!" the red-haired king cried out.   185
"The son of my dearest friend, here in my own house!
That man who performed a hundred feats of arms for me.
And I swore that when he came I'd give him a hero's welcome,
him above all my comrades—if only Olympian Zeus,
farseeing Zeus, had granted us both safe passage   190
home across the sea in our swift trim ships.
Why, I'd have settled a city in Argos for him,
built him a palace, shipped him over from Ithaca,
him and all his wealth, his son, his people too—
emptied one of the cities nestling round about us,   195
one I rule myself. Both fellow-countrymen then,
how often we'd have mingled side-by-side!
Nothing could have parted us,
bound by love for each other, mutual delight . . .
till death's dark cloud came shrouding round us both.   200
But god himself, jealous of all this, no doubt,
robbed that unlucky man, him and him alone,
of the day of his return."

                    So Menelaus mused
and stirred in them all a deep desire to grieve.
Helen of Argos, daughter of Zeus, dissolved in tears,   205
Telemachus wept too, and so did Atreus' son Menelaus.
Nor could Nestor's son Pisistratus stay dry-eyed,
remembering now his gallant brother Antilochus,
cut down by Memnon[5] splendid son of the Morning.
Thinking of him, the young prince broke out: 210
"Old Nestor always spoke of you, son of Atreus,
as the wisest man of all the men he knew,
whenever we talked about you there at home,

---

5. The son of the goddess Dawn. After the events recounted in the *Iliad*, Memnon arrived as an ally of Troy and killed Nestor's son Antilochus in battle. Achilles took his life in revenge, drove the Trojans back to the city, and was then killed himself by Paris and Apollo.

questioning back and forth. So now, please,
if it isn't out of place, indulge me, won't you? 215
Myself, I take no joy in weeping over supper.
Morning will soon bring time enough for that.
Not that I'd grudge a tear
for any man gone down to meet his fate.
What other tribute can we pay to wretched men 220
than to cut a lock,[6] let tears roll down our cheeks?
And I have a brother of my own among the dead,
and hardly the poorest soldier in our ranks.
You probably knew him. I never met him, never
saw him myself. But they say he outdid our best, 225
Antilochus—lightning on his feet and every inch a fighter!"

    "Well said, my friend," the red-haired king replied.
"Not even an older man could speak and do as well.
Your father's son you are—your words have all his wisdom.
It's easy to spot the breed of a man whom Zeus 230
has marked for joy in birth and marriage both.
Take great King Nestor now:
Zeus has blessed him, all his livelong days,
growing rich and sleek in his old age at home,
his sons expert with spears and full of sense. 235
Well, so much for the tears that caught us just now;
let's think again of supper. Come, rinse our hands.
Tomorrow, at dawn, will offer me and Telemachus
time to talk and trade our thoughts in full."

    Asphalion quickly rinsed their hands with water, 240
another of King Menelaus' ready aides-in-arms.
Again they reached for the good things set before them.

    Then Zeus's daughter Helen thought of something else.
Into the mixing-bowl from which they drank their wine
she slipped a drug, heart's-ease, dissolving anger, 245
magic to make us all forget our pains . . .
No one who drank it deeply, mulled in wine,
could let a tear roll down his cheeks that day,
not even if his mother should die, his father die,
not even if right before his eyes some enemy brought down 250
a brother or darling son with a sharp bronze blade.
So cunning the drugs that Zeus's daughter plied,
potent gifts from Polydamna the wife of Thon,
a woman of Egypt,[7] land where the teeming soil
bears the richest yield of herbs in all the world: 255
many health itself when mixed in the wine,
and many deadly poison.
Every man is a healer there, more skilled
than any other men on earth—Egyptians born

---

6. Dedicating a lock of hair at the tomb was a gesture to mourn and commemorate the dead.   7. The Greeks had great respect for Egyptian doctors; surviving papyri document their skill as surgeons and their expertise with drugs.

of the healing god himself. So now Helen, once   260
she had drugged the wine and ordered winecups filled,
resuming the conversation, entertained the group:
"My royal king Menelaus—welcome guests here,
sons of the great as well! Zeus can present us
times of joy and times of grief in turn: 265
all lies within his power.
So come, let's sit back in the palace now,
dine and warm our hearts with the old stories.
I will tell something perfect for the occasion.
Surely I can't describe or even list them all,   270
the exploits crowding fearless Odysseus' record,
but what a feat that hero dared and carried off
in the land of Troy where you Achaeans suffered!
Scarring his own body with mortifying strokes,
throwing filthy rags on his back like any slave,   275
he slipped into the enemy's city, roamed its streets—
all disguised, a totally different man, a beggar,
hardly the figure he cut among Achaea's ships.
That's how Odysseus infiltrated Troy,
and no one knew him at all . . .   280
I alone, I spotted him for the man he was,
kept questioning him—the crafty one kept dodging.
But after I'd bathed him, rubbed him down with oil,
given him clothes to wear and sworn a binding oath
not to reveal him as Odysseus to the Trojans, not   285
till he was back at his swift ships and shelters,
then at last he revealed to me, step by step,
the whole Achaean strategy. And once he'd cut
a troop of Trojans down with his long bronze sword,
back he went to his comrades, filled with information.   290
The rest of the Trojan women shrilled their grief. Not I:
my heart leapt up—
                    my heart had changed by now—
                                                I yearned
to sail back home again! I grieved too late for the madness
Aphrodite sent me,[8] luring me there, far from my dear land,
forsaking my own child, my bridal bed, my husband too,   295
a man who lacked for neither brains nor beauty."

    And the red-haired Menelaus answered Helen:
"There was a tale, my lady. So well told.
Now then, I have studied, in my time,
the plans and minds of great ones by the score.   300
And I have traveled over a good part of the world
but never once have I laid eyes on a man like him—
what a heart that fearless Odysseus had inside him!
What a piece of work the hero dared and carried off
in the wooden horse where all our best encamped,   305

---

8. By promising him Helen's love, Aphrodite bribed Paris to judge her more beautiful than Hera or Athena.
Her flight with Paris from Menelaus's house ignited the Trojan War.

our champions armed with bloody death for Troy . . .
when along you came, Helen—roused, no doubt,
by a dark power bent on giving Troy some glory,
and dashing Prince Deiphobus[9] squired your every step.
Three times you sauntered round our hollow ambush,   310
feeling, stroking its flanks,
challenging all our fighters, calling each by name—
yours was the voice of all our long-lost wives!
And Diomedes and I, crouched tight in the midst
with great Odysseus, hearing you singing out,   315
were both keen to spring up and sally forth
or give you a sudden answer from inside,
but Odysseus damped our ardor, reined us back.
Then all the rest of the troops kept stock-still,
all but Anticlus. He was hot to salute you now   320
but Odysseus clamped his great hands on the man's mouth
and shut it, brutally—yes, he saved us all,
holding on grim-set till Pallas Athena
lured you off at last."

    But clear-sighted Telemachus ventured,   325
"Son of Atreus, King Menelaus, captain of armies,
so much the worse, for not one bit of that
saved *him* from grisly death . . .
not even a heart of iron could have helped.
But come, send us off to bed. It's time to rest,   330
time to enjoy the sweet relief of sleep."

    And Helen briskly told her serving-women
to make beds in the porch's shelter, lay down
some heavy purple throws for the beds themselves,
and over them spread some blankets, thick woolly robes,   335
a warm covering laid on top. Torches in hand,
they left the hall and made up beds at once.
The herald led the two guests on and so they slept
outside the palace under the forecourt's colonnade,
young Prince Telemachus and Nestor's shining son.   340
Menelaus retired to chambers deep in his lofty house
with Helen the pearl of women loosely gowned beside him.

    When young Dawn with her rose-red fingers shone once more
the lord of the warcry climbed from bed and dressed,
over his shoulder he slung his well-honed sword,   345
fastened rawhide sandals under his smooth feet,
stepped from his bedroom, handsome as a god,
and sat beside Telemachus, asking, kindly,
"Now, my young prince, tell me what brings you here
to sunny Lacedaemon, sailing over the sea's broad back.   350
A public matter or private? Tell me the truth now."

---

9. A son of Priam and thus brother of Hector and Paris. Helen married him after Paris's death.

And with all the poise he had, Telemachus replied,
"Son of Atreus, King Menelaus, captain of armies,
I came in the hope that you can tell me now
some news about my father.   355
My house is being devoured, my rich farms destroyed,
my palace crammed with enemies, slaughtering on and on
my droves of sheep and shambling longhorn cattle.
Suitors plague my mother—the insolent, overweening . . .
That's why I've come to plead before you now,   360
if you can tell me about his cruel death:
perhaps you saw him die with your own eyes
or heard the wanderer's end from someone else.
More than all other men, that man was born for pain.
Don't soften a thing, from pity, respect for me—   365
tell me, clearly, all your eyes have witnessed.
I beg you—if ever my father, lord Odysseus,
I pledged you his word and made it good in action
once on the fields of Troy where you Achaeans suffered,
remember his story now, tell me the truth."

                                    "How shameful!"   370
the red-haired king burst out in anger. "That's the bed
of a brave man of war they'd like to crawl inside,
those spineless, craven cowards!
Weak as the doe that beds down her fawns
in a mighty lion's den—her newborn sucklings—   375
then trails off to the mountain spurs and grassy bends
to graze her fill, but back the lion comes to his own lair
and the master deals both fawns a ghastly bloody death,
just what Odysseus will deal that mob—ghastly death.
Ah if only—Father Zeus, Athena and lord Apollo—   380
that man who years ago in the games at Lesbos
rose to Philomelides'[1] challenge, wrestled him,
pinned him down with one tremendous throw
and the Argives roared with joy . . .
if only that Odysseus sported with those suitors,   385
a blood wedding, a quick death would take the lot!
But about the things you've asked me, so intently,
I'll skew and sidestep nothing, not deceive you, ever.
Of all he told me—the Old Man of the Sea who never lies—
I'll hide or hold back nothing, not a single word.   390

    It was in Egypt, where the gods still marooned me,[2]
eager as I was to voyage home . . . I'd failed,
you see, to render them full, flawless victims,
and gods are always keen to see their rules obeyed.
Now, there's an island out in the ocean's heavy surge,   395
well off the Egyptian coast—they call it Pharos—

---

1. A king of Lesbos who challenged all comers to wrestle with him.   2. On the way home from Troy,
Menelaus had been blown off course and ended up in Egypt, as Nestor tells Telemachus in book 3.

far as a deep-sea ship can go in one day's sail
with a whistling wind astern to drive her on.
There's a snug harbor there, good landing beach
where crews pull in, draw water up from the dark wells   400
then push their vessels off for passage out.
But here the gods becalmed me twenty days . . .
not a breath of the breezes ruffling out to sea
that speed a ship across the ocean's broad back.
Now our rations would all have been consumed,   405
our crews' stamina too, if one of the gods
had not felt sorry for me, shown me mercy,
Eidothea, a daughter of Proteus,
that great power, the Old Man of the Sea.
My troubles must have moved her to the heart   410
when she met me trudging by myself without my men.
They kept roaming around the beach, day in, day out,
fishing with twisted hooks, their bellies racked by hunger.
Well, she came right up to me, filled with questions:
'Are you a fool, stranger—soft in the head and lazy too?   415
Or do you let things slide because you *like* your pain?
Here you are, cooped up on an island far too long,
with no way out of it, none that you can find,
while all your shipmates' spirit ebbs away.'

So she prodded and I replied at once,   420
'Let me tell you, goddess—whoever you are—
I'm hardly landlocked here of my own free will.
So I must have angered one of the deathless gods
who rule the skies up there. But you tell *me*—
you immortals know it all—which one of you   425
blocks my way here, keeps me from my voyage?
How can I cross the swarming sea and reach home at last?'

And the glistening goddess reassured me warmly,
'Of course, my friend, I'll answer all your questions.
Who haunts these parts? Proteus of Egypt does,   430
the immortal Old Man of the Sea who never lies,
who sounds the deep in all its depths, Poseidon's servant.
He's my father, they say, he gave me life. And he,
if only you ambush him somehow and pin him down,
will tell you the way to go, the stages of your voyage,   435
how you can cross the swarming sea and reach home at last.
And he can tell you too, if you want to press him—
you are a king, it seems—
all that's occurred within your palace, good and bad,
while you've been gone your long and painful way.'   440

'Then you are the one'—I quickly took her up.
'Show me the trick to trap this ancient power,
or he'll see or sense me first and slip away.
It's hard for a mortal man to force a god.'

'True, my friend,' the glistening one agreed,   445
'and again I'll tell you all you need to know.
When the sun stands striding at high noon,
then up from the waves he comes—
the Old Man of the Sea who never lies—
under a West Wind's gust that shrouds him round   450
in shuddering dark swells, and once he's out on land
he heads for his bed of rest in deep hollow caves
and around him droves of seals—sleek pups bred
by his lovely ocean-lady—bed down too
in a huddle, flopping up from the gray surf,   455
giving off the sour reek of the salty ocean depths.
I'll lead you there myself at the break of day
and couch you all for attack, side-by-side.
Choose three men from your crew, choose well,
the best you've got aboard the good decked hulls.   460
Now I will tell you all the old wizard's tricks . . .
First he will make his rounds and count the seals
and once he's checked their number, reviewed them all,
down in their midst he'll lie, like a shepherd with his flock.
That's your moment. Soon as you see him bedded down,   465
muster your heart and strength and hold him fast,
wildly as he writhes and fights you to escape.
He'll try all kinds of escape—twist and turn
into every beast that moves across the earth,
transforming himself into water, superhuman fire,   470
but you hold on for dear life, hug him all the harder!
And when, at last, he begins to ask you questions—
back in the shape you saw him sleep at first—
relax your grip and set the old god free
and ask him outright, hero,   475
which of the gods is up in arms against you?
How can you cross the swarming sea and reach home at last?'

    So she urged and under the breaking surf she dove
as I went back to our squadron beached in sand,
my heart a heaving storm at every step . . .   480
Once I reached my ship hauled up on shore
we made our meal and the godsent night came down
and then we slept at the sea's smooth shelving edge.
When young Dawn with her rose-red fingers shone once more
I set out down the coast of the wide-ranging sea,   485
praying hard to the gods for all their help,
taking with me the three men I trusted most
on every kind of mission.
                      Eidothea, now,
had slipped beneath the sea's engulfing folds
but back from the waves she came with four sealskins,   490
all freshly stripped, to deceive her father blind.
She scooped out lurking-places deep in the sand
and sat there waiting as we approached her post,

then couching us side-by-side she flung a sealskin
over each man's back. Now there was an ambush   495
that would have overpowered us all—overpowering,
true, the awful reek of all those sea-fed brutes!
Who'd dream of bedding down with a monster of the deep?
But the goddess sped to our rescue, found the cure
with ambrosia, daubing it under each man's nose—   500
that lovely scent, it drowned the creatures' stench.
So all morning we lay there waiting, spirits steeled,
while seals came crowding, jostling out of the sea
and flopped down in rows, basking along the surf.
At high noon the old man emerged from the waves   505
and found his fat-fed seals and made his rounds,
counting them off, counting *us* the first four,
but he had no inkling of all the fraud afoot.
Then down he lay and slept, but we with a battle-cry,
we rushed him, flung our arms around him—he'd lost nothing,   510
the old rascal, none of his cunning quick techniques!
First he shifted into a great bearded lion
and then a serpent—
                    a panther—
                              a ramping wild boar—
a torrent of water—
                    a tree with soaring branchtops—
but we held on for dear life, braving it out   515
until, at last, that quick-change artist,
the old wizard, began to weary of all this
and burst out into rapid-fire questions:
'Which god, Menelaus, conspired with you
to trap me in ambush? seize me against my will?   520
What on earth do you want?'
                          'You know, old man,'
I countered now. 'Why put me off with questions?
Here I am, cooped up on an island far too long,
with no way out of it, none that I can find,
while my spirit ebbs away. But you tell *me*—   525
you immortals know it all—which one of you
blocks my way here, keeps me from my voyage?
How can I cross the swarming sea and reach home at last?'

    'How wrong you were!' the seer shot back at once.
'You should have offered Zeus and the other gods   530
a handsome sacrifice, *then* embarked, if you ever hoped
for a rapid journey home across the wine-dark sea.
It's not your destiny yet to see your loved ones,
reach your own grand house, your native land at last,
not till you sail back through Egyptian waters—   535
the great Nile swelled by the rains of Zeus—
and make a splendid rite to the deathless gods
who rule the vaulting skies. Then, only then
will the gods grant you the voyage you desire.'

So he urged, and broke the heart inside me,   540
having to double back on the mist-bound seas,
back to Egypt, that, that long and painful way . . .
Nevertheless I caught my breath and answered,
'That I will do, old man, as you command.
But tell me this as well, and leave out nothing: 545
Did all the Achaeans reach home in the ships unharmed,
all we left behind, Nestor and I, en route from Troy?
Or did any die some cruel death by shipwreck
or die in the arms of loved ones,
once they'd wound down the long coil of war?'   550

And he lost no time in saying, 'Son of Atreus,
why do you ask me that? Why do you need to know?
Why probe my mind? You won't stay dry-eyed long,
I warn you, once you have heard the whole story.
Many of them were killed, many survived as well,   555
but only two who captained your bronze-armored units
died on the way home—you know who died in the fighting,
you were there yourself.
            And one is still alive,
held captive, somewhere, off in the endless seas . . .

    Ajax,[3] now, went down with his long-oared fleet.   560
First Poseidon drove him onto the cliffs of Gyrae,[4]
looming cliffs, then saved him from the breakers—
he'd have escaped his doom, too, despite Athena's hate,
if he hadn't flung that brazen boast, the mad blind fool.
"In the teeth of the gods," he bragged, "I have escaped   565
the ocean's sheer abyss!" Poseidon heard that frantic vaunt
and the god grasped his trident in both his massive hands
and struck the Gyraean headland, hacked the rock in two,
and the giant stump stood fast but the jagged spur
where Ajax perched at first, the raving madman—   570
toppling into the sea, it plunged him down, down
in the vast, seething depths. And so he died,
having drunk his fill of brine.
            Your brother?
He somehow escaped that fate; Agamemnon got away
in his beaked ships. Queen Hera[5] pulled him through.   575
But just as he came abreast of Malea's beetling cape
a hurricane snatched him up and swept him way off course—
groaning, desperate—driving him over the fish-infested sea
to the wild borderland where Thyestes[6] made his home
in the days of old and his son Aegisthus lived now.   580
But even from there a safe return seemed likely,

3. The lesser of the two heroes named Ajax, who had enraged Athena by raping Cassandra in the goddess's temple.   4. Located by ancient writers on Tenos or Mykonos (both islands in the Cyclades group) or at the western tip of Euboea, the long island that stretches along the north coast of Attica.   5. Wife of Zeus and a partisan of the Greeks in the Trojan War.   6. Brother of Atreus, Agamemnon's father. In a tradition drawn on by Aeschylus's *Oresteia* but ignored by or unknown to Homer, the brothers were bitter rivals over the kingship of Argos.

yes, the immortals swung the wind around to fair
and the victors sailed home. How he rejoiced,
Atrides setting foot on his fatherland once more—
he took that native earth in his hands and kissed it,   585
hot tears flooding his eyes, so thrilled to see his land!
But a watchman saw him too—from a lookout high above—
a spy that cunning Aegisthus stationed there,
luring the man with two gold bars in payment.
One whole year he'd watched . . .   590
so the great king would not get past unseen,
his fighting power intact for self-defense.
The spy ran the news to his master's halls
and Aegisthus quickly set his stealthy trap.
Picking the twenty best recruits from town   595
he packed them in ambush at one end of the house,
at the other he ordered a banquet dressed and spread
and went to welcome the conquering hero, Agamemnon,
went with team and chariot, and a mind aswarm with evil.
Up from the shore he led the king, he ushered him in—   600
suspecting nothing of all his doom—he feasted him well
then cut him down as a man cuts down some ox at the trough!
Not one of your brother's men-at-arms was left alive,
none of Aegisthus' either. All, killed in the palace.'

So Proteus said, and his story crushed my heart.   605
I knelt down in the sand and wept. I'd no desire
to go on living and see the rising light of day.
But once I'd had my fill of tears and writhing there,
the Old Man of the Sea who never lies continued,
'No more now, Menelaus. How long must you weep?   610
Withering tears, what good can come of tears?
None I know of. Strive instead to return
to your native country—hurry home at once!
Either you'll find the murderer still alive
or Orestes will have beaten you to the kill.   615
You'll be in time to share the funeral feast.'

So he pressed, and I felt my heart, my old pride,
for all my grieving, glow once more in my chest
and I asked the seer in a rush of winging words,
'Those two I know now. Tell me the third man's name.   620
Who is still alive, held captive off in the endless seas?
Unless he's dead by now. I want to know the truth
though it grieves me all the more.'
                                  'Odysseus'—
the old prophet named the third at once—
'Laertes' son, who makes his home in Ithaca . . .   625
I saw him once on an island, weeping live warm tears
in the nymph Calypso's house—she holds him there by force.
He has no way to voyage home to his own native land,
no trim ships in reach, no crew to ply the oars
and send him scudding over the sea's broad back.   630

But about your own destiny, Menelaus,
dear to Zeus, it's not for you to die
and meet your fate in the stallion-land of Argos,
no, the deathless ones will sweep you off to the world's end,
the Elysian Fields, where gold-haired Rhadamanthys[7] waits,   635
where life glides on in immortal ease for mortal man;
no snow, no winter onslaught, never a downpour there
but night and day the Ocean River sends up breezes,
singing winds of the West refreshing all mankind.
All this because you are Helen's husband now—   640
the gods count *you* the son-in-law of Zeus.'

So he divined and down the breaking surf he dove
as I went back to the ships with my brave men,
my heart a rising tide at every step.
Once I reached my craft hauled up on shore   645
we made our meal and the godsent night came down
and then we slept at the sea's smooth shelving edge.
When young Dawn with her rose-red fingers shone once more
we hauled the vessels down to the sunlit breakers first
then stepped the masts amidships, canvas brailed—   650
the crews swung aboard, they sat to the oars in ranks
and in rhythm churned the water white with stroke on stroke.
Back we went to the Nile swelled by the rains of Zeus,
I moored the ships and sacrificed in a splendid rite,
and once I'd slaked the wrath of the everlasting gods   655
I raised a mound for Agamemnon, his undying glory.
All this done, I set sail and the gods sent me
a stiff following wind that sped me home,
home to the native land I love.
                                But come,
my boy, stay on in my palace now with me,   660
at least till ten or a dozen days have passed.
Then I'll give you a princely send-off—shining gifts,
three stallions and a chariot burnished bright—
and I'll add a gorgeous cup so you can pour
libations out to the deathless gods on high   665
and remember Menelaus all your days."
                                Telemachus,
summoning up his newfound tact, replied,
"Please, Menelaus, don't keep me quite so long.
True, I'd gladly sit beside you one whole year
without a twinge of longing for home or parents.   670
It's wonderful how you tell your stories, all you say—
I delight to listen! Yes, but now, I'm afraid,
my comrades must be restless in sacred Pylos,
and here you'd hold me just a little longer.
As for the gift you give me, let it be a keepsake.   675
Those horses I really cannot take to Ithaca;

---

7. A son of Zeus by the mortal Europa, and brother to King Minos of Crete. Elysium is the paradise reserved
for a few mortal relatives of the gods.

better to leave them here to be your glory.
You rule a wide level plain
where the fields of clover roll and galingale
and wheat and oats and glistening full-grain barley.   680
No running-room for mares in Ithaca though, no meadows.
Goat, not stallion, land, yet it means the world to me.
None of the rugged islands slanting down to sea
is good for pasture or good for bridle paths,
but Ithaca, best of islands, crowns them all!"   685

      So he declared. The lord of the warcry smiled,
patted him with his hand and praised his guest, concluding,
"Good blood runs in you, dear boy, your words are proof.
Certainly I'll exchange the gifts. The power's mine.
Of all the treasures lying heaped in my palace   690
you shall have the finest, most esteemed. Why,
I'll give you a mixing-bowl, forged to perfection—
it's solid silver finished off with a lip of gold.
Hephaestus[8] made it himself. And a royal friend,
Phaedimus, king of Sidon,[9] lavished it on me   695
when his palace welcomed me on passage home.
How pleased I'd be if you took it as a gift!"

      And now as the two confided in each other,
banqueters arrived at the great king's palace,
leading their own sheep, bearing their hearty wine,   700
and their wives in lovely headbands sent along the food.
And so they bustled about the halls preparing dinner . . .
But all the while the suitors, before Odysseus' palace,
amused themselves with discus and long throwing spears,
out on the leveled grounds, free and easy as always,   705
full of swagger. But lord Antinous sat apart,
dashing Eurymachus beside him, ringleaders,
head and shoulders the strongest of the lot.
Phronius' son Noëmon approached them now,
quick to press Antinous with a question: 710
"Antinous, have we any notion or not
when Telemachus will return from sandy Pylos?
He sailed in a ship of mine and now I need her back
to cross over to Elis[1] Plain where I keep a dozen horses,
brood-mares suckling some heavy-duty mules, unbroken.   715
I'd like to drive one home and break him in."

      That dumbfounded them both. They never dreamed
the prince had gone to Pylos, Neleus' city—
certain the boy was still nearby somewhere,
out on his farm with flocks or with the swineherd.   720

      "Tell me the truth!" Antinous wheeled on Noëmon.
"When did he go? And what young crew went with him?

---

8. God of the forge and patron of metal workers, married to the goddess Aphrodite; in the *Iliad* (book 18)
he made Achilles' armor.   9. A wealthy and powerful city on the coast of Phoenicia (present-day Lebanon).   1. A region in the northwestern Peloponnesus, slightly southeast of Ithaca.

Ithaca's best? Or his own slaves and servants?
Surely he has enough to man a ship.
Tell me this—be clear—I've got to know: 725
did he commandeer your ship against your will
or did you volunteer it once he'd won you over?"

    "I volunteered it, of course," Noëmon said.
"What else could anyone do, when such a man,
a prince weighed down with troubles,   730
asked a favor? Hard to deny him anything.
And the young crew that formed his escort? Well,
they're the finest men on the island, next to us.
And Mentor took command—I saw him climb aboard—
or a god who looked like Mentor head to foot,   735
and that's what I find strange. I saw good Mentor
yesterday, just at sunup, here. But clearly
he boarded ship for Pylos days ago."

    With that he headed back to his father's house,
leaving the two lords stiff with indignation.   740
They made the suitors sit down in a group
and stop their games at once. Eupithes' son
Antinous rose up in their midst to speak,
his dark heart filled with fury,
blazing with anger—eyes like searing fire: 745
"By god, what a fine piece of work he's carried off!
Telemachus—what insolence—and we thought his little jaunt
would come to grief. But in spite of us all, look,
the young cub slips away, just like that—
picks the best crew in the land and off he sails.   750
And this is just the start of the trouble he can make.
Zeus kill that brazen boy before he hits his prime!
Quick, fetch me a swift ship and twenty men—
I'll waylay him from ambush, board him coming back
in the straits between Ithaca and rocky Same.[2]   755
This gallant voyage of his to find his father
will find *him* wrecked at last!"

    They all roared approval, urged him on,
rose at once and retired to Odysseus' palace.

    But not for long was Penelope unaware   760
of the grim plots her suitors planned in secret.
The herald Medon told her. He'd overheard their schemes,
listening in outside the court while they wove on within.
He rushed the news through the halls to tell the queen
who greeted him as he crossed her chamber's threshold: 765
"Herald, why have the young blades sent you now?
To order King Odysseus' serving-women
to stop their work and slave to fix their feast?
I hate their courting, their running riot here—

---

2. An island close to Ithaca (probably the modern Cephallenia).

would to god that this meal, here and now,   770
were their last meal on earth!
                  Day after day,
all of you swarming, draining our life's blood,
my wary son's estate. What, didn't you listen
to your fathers—when you were children, years ago—
telling you how Odysseus treated them, your parents?   775
Never an unfair word, never an unfair action
among his people here, though that's the way
of our god-appointed kings,
hating one man, loving the next, with luck.
Not Odysseus. Never an outrage done to any man alive.   780
But you, you and your ugly outbursts, shameful acts,
they're plain to see. Look at the thanks he gets
for all past acts of kindness!"
                  Medon replied,
sure of his own discretion, "Ah my queen,
if only *that* were the worst of all you face.   785
Now your suitors are plotting something worse,
harsher, crueler. God forbid they bring it off!
They're poised to cut Telemachus down with bronze swords
on his way back home. He's sailed off, you see . . .
for news of his father—to sacred Pylos first,   790
then out to the sunny hills of Lacedaemon."

   Her knees gave way on the spot, her heart too.
She stood there speechless a while, struck dumb,
tears filling her eyes, her warm voice choked.
At last she found some words to make reply: 795
"Oh herald, why has my child gone and left me?
No need in the world for him to board the ships,
those chariots of the sea that sweep men on,
driving across the ocean's endless wastes . . .
Does he want his very name wiped off the earth?"   800

   Medon, the soul of thoughtfulness, responded,
"I don't know if a god inspired your son
or the boy's own impulse led him down to Pylos,
but he went to learn of his father's journey home,
or whatever fate he's met."   805

   Back through King Odysseus' house he went
but a cloud of heartbreak overwhelmed the queen.
She could bear no longer sitting on a chair
though her room had chairs aplenty.
Down she sank on her well-built chamber's floor,   810
weeping, pitifully, as the women whimpered round her,
all the women, young and old, who served her house.
Penelope, sobbing uncontrollably, cried out to them,
"Hear me, dear ones! Zeus has given me torment—
me above all the others born and bred in *my* day.   815
My lionhearted husband, lost, long years ago,

who excelled the Argives all in every strength—
that great man whose fame resounds through Hellas
right to the depths of Argos!
                        But now my son,
my darling boy—the whirlwinds have ripped him   820
out of the halls without a trace! I never heard
he'd gone—not even from you, you hard, heartless . . .
not one of you even thought to rouse me from my bed,
though well you knew when he boarded that black ship.
Oh if only I had learned he was planning such a journey,   825
he would have stayed, by god, keen as he was to sail—
or left me dead right here within our palace.
Go, someone, quickly! Call old Dolius now,
the servant my father gave me when I came,
the man who tends my orchard green with trees,   830
so he can run to Laertes, sit beside him,
tell him the whole story, point by point.
Perhaps—who knows?—he'll weave some plan,
he'll come out of hiding, plead with all these people
mad to destroy his line, his son's line of kings!"   835

   "Oh dear girl," Eurycleia the fond old nurse replied,
"kill me then with a bronze knife—no mercy—or let me live,
here in the palace—I'll hide nothing from you now!
I knew it all, I gave him all he asked for,
bread and mellow wine, but he made me take   840
a binding oath that I, I wouldn't tell you,
no, not till ten or a dozen days had passed
or you missed the lad yourself and learned he'd gone,
so tears would never mar your lovely face . . .
Come, bathe now, put on some fresh clothes,   845
climb to the upper rooms with all your women
and pray to Pallas, daughter of storming Zeus—
she may save Telemachus yet, even at death's door.
Don't worry an old man, worried enough by now.
I can't believe the blessed gods so hate   850
the heirs of King Arcesius,[3] through and through.
One will still live on—I know it—born to rule
this lofty house and the green fields far and wide."
                             With that
she lulled Penelope's grief and dried her eyes of tears.
And the queen bathed and put fresh clothing on,   855
climbed to the upper rooms with all her women
and sifting barley into a basket, prayed to Pallas,
"Hear me, daughter of Zeus whose shield is thunder—
tireless one, Athena! If ever, here in his halls,
resourceful King Odysseus   860
burned rich thighs of sheep or oxen in your honor,
oh remember it now for *my* sake, save my darling son,
defend him from these outrageous, overbearing suitors!"

---

3. Laertes' father (thus Odysseus's grandfather).

She shrilled a high cry and the goddess heard her prayer
as the suitors burst into uproar through the shadowed halls   865
and one of the lusty young men began to brag, "Listen,
our long-courted queen's preparing us all a marriage—
with no glimmer at all
how the murder of her son has been decreed."
                                        Boasting so,
with no glimmer at all of what had been decreed.   870
But Antinous took the floor and issued orders:
"Stupid fools! Muzzle your bragging now—
before someone slips inside and reports us.
Up now, not a sound, drive home our plan—
it suits us well, we approved it one and all."   875

   With that he picked out twenty first-rate men
and down they went to the swift ship at the sea's edge.
First they hauled the craft into deeper water,
stepped the mast amidships, canvas brailed,
made oars fast in the leather oarlock straps   880
while zealous aides-in-arms brought weapons on.
They moored her well out in the channel, disembarked
and took their meal on shore, waiting for dusk to fall.

   But there in her upper rooms she lay, Penelope
lost in thought, fasting, shunning food and drink,   885
brooding now . . . would her fine son escape his death
or go down at her overweening suitors' hands?
Her mind in torment, wheeling
like some lion at bay, dreading gangs of hunters
closing their cunning ring around him for the finish.   890
Harried so she was, when a deep kind sleep overcame her,
back she sank and slept, her limbs fell limp and still.

   And again the bright-eyed goddess Pallas thought
of one more way to help. She made a phantom now,
its build like a woman's build, Iphthime's,[4] yes,   895
another daughter of generous Lord Icarius,
Eumelus' bride, who made her home in Pherae.[5]
Athena sped her on to King Odysseus' house
to spare Penelope, worn with pain and sobbing,
further spells of grief and storms of tears.   900
The phantom entered her bedroom,
passing quickly in through the doorbolt slit[6]
and hovering at her head she rose and spoke now:
"Sleeping, Penelope, your heart so wrung with sorrow?
No need, I tell you, no, the gods who live at ease   905
can't bear to let you weep and rack your spirit.
Your son will still come home—it is decreed.
He's never wronged the gods in any way."

---

4. Penelope's sister.   5. A town in Thessaly, far from Ithaca in north-central Greece. Eumelus, who has
a minor role in the *Iliad*, was of very distinguished ancestry.   6. We would say "through the keyhole."
The inside bolt could be closed from outside by means of a strap that came through a slit in the door.

And Penelope murmured back, still cautious,
drifting softly now at the gate of dreams,   910
"Why have you come, my sister?
Your visits all too rare in the past,
for you make your home so very far away.
You tell me to lay to rest the grief and tears
that overwhelm me now, torment me, heart and soul?   915
With my lionhearted husband lost long years ago,
who excelled the Argives all in every strength?
That great man whose fame resounds through Hellas
right to the depths of Argos . . .
                                        And now my darling boy,
he's off and gone in a hollow ship! Just a youngster,   920
still untrained for war or stiff debate.
Him I mourn even more than I do my husband—
I quake in terror for all that he might suffer
either on open sea or shores he goes to visit.
Hordes of enemies scheme against him now,   925
keen to kill him off
before he can reach his native land again."

   "Courage!" the shadowy phantom reassured her.
"Don't be overwhelmed by all your direst fears.
He travels with such an escort, one that others   930
would pray to stand beside them. She has power—
Pallas Athena. She pities you in your tears.
She wings me here to tell you all these things."

   But the circumspect Penelope replied,
"If you *are* a god and have heard a god's own voice,   935
come, tell me about that luckless man as well.
Is he still alive? does he see the light of day?
Or is he dead already, lost in the House of Death?"

   "About that man," the shadowy phantom answered,
"I cannot tell you the story start to finish,   940
whether he's dead or alive.
It's wrong to lead you on with idle words."
                                        At that
she glided off by the doorpost past the bolt—
gone on a lifting breeze. Icarius' daughter
started up from sleep, her spirit warmed now   945
that a dream so clear had come to her in darkest night.

   But the suitors boarded now and sailed the sea-lanes,
plotting in their hearts Telemachus' plunge to death.
Off in the middle channel lies a rocky island,
just between Ithaca and Same's rugged cliffs—   950
Asteris—not large, but it has a cove,
a harbor with two mouths where ships can hide.
Here the Achaeans lurked in ambush for the prince.

BOOK V

[Odysseus—Nymph and Shipwreck]

As Dawn rose up from bed by her lordly mate Tithonus,[7]
bringing light to immortal gods and mortal men,
the gods sat down in council, circling Zeus
the thunder king whose power rules the world.
Athena began, recalling Odysseus to their thoughts,   5
the goddess deeply moved by the man's long ordeal,
held captive still in the nymph Calypso's house:
"Father Zeus—you other happy gods who never die—
never let any sceptered king be kind and gentle now,
not with all his heart, or set his mind on justice—   10
no, let him be cruel and always practice outrage.
Think: not one of the people whom he ruled
remembers Odysseus now, that godlike man,
and kindly as a father to his children.
                      Now.
he's left to pine on an island, racked with grief   15
in the nymph Calypso's house—she holds him there by force.
He has no way to voyage home to his own native land,
no trim ships in reach, no crew to ply the oars
and send him scudding over the sea's broad back.
And now his dear son . . . they plot to kill the boy   20
on his way back home. Yes, he has sailed off
for news of his father, to holy Pylos first,
then out to the sunny hills of Lacedaemon."

    "My child," Zeus who marshals the thunderheads replied,
"what nonsense you let slip through your teeth. Come now,   25
wasn't the plan your own? You conceived it yourself:
Odysseus shall return and pay the traitors back.
Telemachus? Sail him home with all your skill—
the power is yours, no doubt—
home to his native country all unharmed   30
while the suitors limp to port, defeated, baffled men."

    With those words, Zeus turned to his own son Hermes.
"You are our messenger, Hermes, sent on all our missions.
Announce to the nymph with lovely braids our fixed decree:
Odysseus journeys home—the exile must return.   35
But not in the convoy of the gods or mortal men.
No, on a lashed, makeshift raft and wrung with pains,
on the twentieth day he will make his landfall, fertile Scheria,
the land of Phaeacians, close kin to the gods themselves,
who with all their hearts will prize him like a god   40
and send him off in a ship to his own beloved land,
giving him bronze and hoards of gold and robes—
more plunder than he could ever have won from Troy

---

7. A mortal man, given immortality (but not youth) by Zeus at the request of Dawn (Eos).

if Odysseus had returned intact with his fair share.
So his destiny ordains. He shall see his loved ones,   45
reach his high-roofed house, his native land at last."

    So Zeus decreed and the giant-killing guide obeyed at once.
Quickly under his feet he fastened the supple sandals,
ever-glowing gold, that wing him over the waves
and boundless earth with the rush of gusting winds.   50
He seized the wand that enchants the eyes of men
whenever Hermes wants, or wakes us up from sleep.
That wand in his grip, the powerful giant-killer,
swooping down from Pieria,[8] down the high clear air,
plunged to the sea and skimmed the waves like a tern   55
that down the deadly gulfs of the barren salt swells
glides and dives for fish,
dipping its beating wings in bursts of spray—
so Hermes skimmed the crests on endless crests.
But once he gained that island worlds apart,   60
up from the deep-blue sea he climbed to dry land
and strode on till he reached the spacious cave
where the nymph with lovely braids had made her home,
and he found her there inside . . . .
                            A great fire
blazed on the hearth and the smell of cedar   65
cleanly split and sweetwood burning bright
wafted a cloud of fragrance down the island.
Deep inside she sang, the goddess Calypso, lifting
her breathtaking voice as she glided back and forth
before her loom, her golden shuttle weaving.   70
Thick, luxuriant woods grew round the cave,
alders and black poplars, pungent cypress too,
and there birds roosted, folding their long wings,
owls and hawks and the spread-beaked ravens of the sea,
black skimmers who make their living off the waves.   75
And round the mouth of the cavern trailed a vine
laden with clusters, bursting with ripe grapes.
Four springs in a row, bubbling clear and cold,
running side-by-side, took channels left and right.
Soft meadows spreading round were starred with violets,   80
lush with beds of parsley. Why, even a deathless god
who came upon that place would gaze in wonder,
heart entranced with pleasure. Hermes the guide,
the mighty giant-killer, stood there, spellbound . . .
But once he'd had his fill of marveling at it all   85
he briskly entered the deep vaulted cavern.
Calypso, lustrous goddess, knew him at once,
as soon as she saw his features face-to-face.
Immortals are never strangers to each other,
no matter how distant one may make her home.   90
But as for great Odysseus—

8. Region in northern Greece, just north of the gods' home on Mount Olympus.

Hermes could not find him within the cave.
Off he sat on a headland, weeping there as always,
wrenching his heart with sobs and groans and anguish,
gazing out over the barren sea through blinding tears.   95
But Calypso, lustrous goddess, questioned Hermes,
seating him on a glistening, polished chair.
"God of the golden wand, why have you come?
A beloved, honored friend,
but it's been so long, your visits much too rare.   100
Tell me what's on your mind. I'm eager to do it,
whatever I *can* do . . . whatever can be done."

   And the goddess drew a table up beside him,
heaped with ambrosia, mixed him deep-red nectar.[9]
Hermes the guide and giant-killer ate and drank.   105
Once he had dined and fortified himself with food
he launched right in, replying to her questions:
"As one god to another, you ask me why I've come.
I'll tell you the whole story, mince no words—
your wish is my command.   110
It was Zeus who made me come, no choice of mine.
Who would willingly roam across a salty waste so vast,
so endless? Think: no city of men in sight, and not a soul
to offer the gods a sacrifice and burn the fattest victims.
But there is no way, you know, for another god to thwart   115
the will of storming Zeus and make it come to nothing.
Zeus claims you keep beside you a most unlucky man,
most harried of all who fought for Priam's Troy
nine years, sacking the city in the tenth,
and then set sail for home.   120
But voyaging back they outraged Queen Athena
who loosed the gales and pounding seas against them.
There all the rest of his loyal shipmates died
but the wind drove him on, the current bore him here.
Now Zeus commands you to send him off with all good speed: 125
it is not his fate to die here, far from his own people.
Destiny still ordains that he shall see his loved ones,
reach his high-roofed house, his native land at last."

   But lustrous Calypso shuddered at those words
and burst into a flight of indignation. "Hard-hearted   130
you are, you gods! You unrivaled lords of jealousy—
scandalized when goddesses sleep with mortals,
openly, even when one has made the man her husband.
So when Dawn with her rose-red fingers took Orion,[1]
you gods in your everlasting ease were horrified   135
till chaste Artemis throned in gold attacked him,
out on Delos,[2] shot him to death with gentle shafts.

---

9. Ambrosia (which literally means "immortality") and nectar are the food and drink of the gods.   1. A
legendary mighty hunter; after death, he became a constellation.   2. A small island in the middle of the
Aegean Sea, the birthplace of Apollo and Artemis and a center of their worship.

And so when Demeter[3] the graceful one with lovely braids
gave way to her passion and made love with Iasion,
bedding down in a furrow plowed three times—   140
Zeus got wind of it soon enough, I'd say,
and blasted the man to death with flashing bolts.
So now at last, you gods, you train your spite on *me*
for keeping a mortal man beside me. The man I saved,
riding astride his keel-board, all alone, when Zeus   145
with one hurl of a white-hot bolt had crushed
his racing warship down the wine-dark sea.
There all the rest of his loyal shipmates died
but the wind drove him on, the current bore him here.
And I welcomed him warmly, cherished him, even vowed   150
to make the man immortal, ageless, all his days . . .
But since there is no way for another god to thwart
the will of storming Zeus and make it come to nothing,
let the man go—if the Almighty insists, commands—
and destroy himself on the barren salt sea!   155
I'll send him off, but not with any escort.
I have no ships in reach, no crew to ply the oars
and send him scudding over the sea's broad back.
But I will gladly advise him—I'll hide nothing—
so he can reach his native country all unharmed."   160

     And the guide and giant-killer reinforced her words:
"Release him at once, just so. Steer clear of the rage of Zeus!
Or down the years he'll fume and make your life a hell."

     With that the powerful giant-killer sped away.
The queenly nymph sought out the great Odysseus—   165
the commands of Zeus still ringing in her ears—
and found him there on the headland, sitting, still,
weeping, his eyes never dry, his sweet life flowing away
with the tears he wept for his foiled journey home,
since the nymph no longer pleased. In the nights, true,   170
he'd sleep with her in the arching cave—he had no choice—
unwilling lover alongside lover all too willing . . .
But all his days he'd sit on the rocks and beaches,
wrenching his heart with sobs and groans and anguish,
gazing out over the barren sea through blinding tears.   175
So coming up to him now, the lustrous goddess ventured,
"No need, my unlucky one, to grieve here any longer,
no, don't waste your life away. Now I am willing,
heart and soul, to send you off at last. Come,
take bronze tools, cut your lengthy timbers,   180
make them into a broad-beamed raft
and top it off with a half-deck high enough
to sweep you free and clear on the misty seas.

---

3. Goddess associated with the growth of crops, especially wheat. Iasion was evidently a vegetation god, and his intercourse with Demeter "in a furrow plowed three times" seems to allude to a fertility ritual.

And I myself will stock her with food and water,
ruddy wine to your taste—all to stave off hunger—   185
give you clothing, send you a stiff following wind
so you can reach your native country all unharmed.
If only the gods are willing. They rule the vaulting skies.
They're stronger than I to plan and drive things home."

    Long-enduring Odysseus shuddered at that   190
and broke out in a sharp flight of protest.
"Passage home? Never. Surely you're plotting
something else, goddess, urging me—in a raft—
to cross the ocean's mighty gulfs. So vast, so full
of danger not even deep-sea ships can make it through,   195
swift as they are and buoyed up by the winds of Zeus himself.
I won't set foot on a raft until you show good faith,
until you consent to swear, goddess, a binding oath
you'll never plot some new intrigue to harm me!"

    He was so intense the lustrous goddess smiled,   200
stroked him with her hand, savored his name and chided,
"Ah what a wicked man you are, and never at a loss.
What a thing to imagine, what a thing to say!
Earth be my witness now, the vaulting Sky above
and the dark cascading waters of the Styx[4]—I swear   205
by the greatest, grimmest oath that binds the happy gods:
I will never plot some new intrigue to harm you.
Never. All I have in mind and devise for *you*
are the very plans I'd fashion for myself
if I were in your straits. My every impulse   210
bends to what is right. Not iron, trust me,
the heart within *my* breast. I am all compassion."

    And lustrous Calypso quickly led the way
as he followed in the footsteps of the goddess.
They reached the arching cavern, man and god as one,   215
and Odysseus took the seat that Hermes just left,
while the nymph set out before him every kind
of food and drink that mortal men will take.
Calypso sat down face-to-face with the king
and the women served her nectar and ambrosia.   220
They reached out for the good things that lay at hand
and when they'd had their fill of food and drink
the lustrous one took up a new approach. "So then,
royal son of Laertes, Odysseus, man of exploits,
still eager to leave at once and hurry back   225
to your own home, your beloved native land?
Good luck to you, even so. Farewell!
But if you only knew, down deep, what pains
are fated to fill your cup before you reach that shore,
you'd stay right here, preside in our house with me   230

---

4. One of the rivers of the underworld, by which gods regularly swore oaths.

and be immortal. Much as you long to see your wife,
the one you pine for all your days . . . and yet
I just might claim to be nothing less than she,
neither in face nor figure. Hardly right, is it,
for mortal woman to rival immortal goddess?   235
How, in build? in beauty?"

       "Ah great goddess,"
worldly Odysseus answered, "don't be angry with me,
please. All that you say is true, how well I know.
Look at my wise Penelope. She falls far short of you,
your beauty, stature. She is mortal after all   240
and you, you never age or die . . .
Nevertheless I long—I pine, all my days—
to travel home and see the dawn of my return.
And if a god will wreck me yet again on the wine-dark sea,
I can bear that too, with a spirit tempered to endure.   245
Much have I suffered, labored long and hard by now
in the waves and wars. Add this to the total—
bring the trial on!"

     Even as he spoke
the sun set and the darkness swept the earth.
And now, withdrawing into the cavern's deep recesses,   250
long in each other's arms they lost themselves in love.

 When young Dawn with her rose-red fingers shone once more
Odysseus quickly dressed himself in cloak and shirt
while the nymph slipped on a loose, glistening robe,
filmy, a joy to the eye, and round her waist   255
she ran a brocaded golden belt
and over her head a scarf to shield her brow,
then turned to plan the great man's voyage home.
She gave him a heavy bronze ax that fit his grip,
both blades well-honed, with a fine olive haft   260
lashed firm to its head. She gave him a polished
smoothing-adze as well and then she led the way
to the island's outer edge where trees grew tall,
alders, black poplars and firs that shot sky-high,
seasoned, drying for years, ideal for easy floating.   265
Once she'd shown her guest where the tall timber stood,
Calypso the lustrous goddess headed home again.
He set to cutting trunks—the work was done in no time.
Twenty in all he felled, he trimmed them clean with his ax
and split them deftly, trued them straight to the line.   270
Meanwhile the radiant goddess brought him drills—
he bored through all his planks and wedged them snugly,
knocking them home together, locked with pegs and joints.
Broad in the beam and bottom flat as a merchantman
when a master shipwright turns out her hull,   275
so broad the craft Odysseus made himself.
Working away at speed
he put up half-decks pinned to close-set ribs
and a sweep of gunwales rounded off the sides.

He fashioned the mast next and sank its yard in deep   280
and added a steering-oar to hold her right on course,
then he fenced her stem to stern with twigs and wicker,
bulwark against the sea-surge, floored with heaps of brush.
And lustrous Calypso came again, now with bolts of cloth
to make the sail, and he finished that off too, expertly.   285
Braces, sheets and brails—he rigged all fast on board,
then eased her down with levers into the sunlit sea.

    That was the fourth day and all his work was done.
On the fifth, the lovely goddess launched him from her island,
once she had bathed and decked him out in fragrant clothes.   290
And Calypso stowed two skins aboard—dark wine in one,
the larger one held water—added a sack of rations,
filled with her choicest meats to build his strength,
and summoned a wind to bear him onward, fair and warm.
The wind lifting his spirits high, royal Odysseus   295
spread sail—gripping the tiller, seated astern—
and now the master mariner steered his craft,
sleep never closing his eyes, forever scanning
the stars, the Pleiades and the Plowman⁵ late to set
and the Great Bear that mankind also calls the Wagon:⁶   300
she wheels on her axis always fixed, watching the Hunter,
and she alone is denied a plunge in the Ocean's baths.⁷
Hers were the stars the lustrous goddess told him
to keep hard to port as he cut across the sea.
And seventeen days he sailed, making headway well;   305
on the eighteenth, shadowy mountains slowly loomed . . .
the Phaeacians' island⁸ reaching toward him now,
over the misty breakers, rising like a shield.

    But now Poseidon, god of the earthquake, saw him—
just returning home from his Ethiopian friends,   310
from miles away on the Solymi mountain-range⁹
he spied Odysseus sailing down the sea
and it made his fury boil even more.
He shook his head and rumbled to himself,
"Outrageous! Look how the gods have changed their minds   315
about Odysseus—while I was off with my Ethiopians.
Just look at him there, nearing Phaeacia's shores
where he's fated to escape his noose of pain
that's held him until now. Still my hopes ride high—
I'll give that man his swamping fill of trouble!"   320

    With that he rammed the clouds together—both hands
clutching his trident—churned the waves into chaos, whipping
all the gales from every quarter, shrouding over in thunderheads
the earth and sea at once—and night swept down from the sky—

---

5. Another name for the constellation Boötes. *The Pleiades*: a cluster of stars in the constellation Taurus.
6. The Big Dipper.   7. I.e., it never sets. *The Hunter*: Orion, also a constellation.   8. Identified by later Greeks with Corcyra (modern Corfu), an island off the northwest coast of mainland Greece.   9. In Lycia in Asia Minor—a very long distance from Odysseus, sailing far to the west of Greece.

East and South Winds clashed and the raging West and North,   325
sprung from the heavens, roiled heaving breakers up—
and Odysseus' knees quaked, his spirit too;
numb with fear he spoke to his own great heart:
"Wretched man—what becomes of me now, at last?
I fear the nymph foretold it all too well—   330
on the high seas, she said, before I can reach
my native land I'll fill my cup of pain! And now,
look, it all comes to pass. What monstrous clouds—
King Zeus crowning the whole wide heaven black—
churning the seas in chaos, gales blasting,   335
raging around my head from every quarter—
my death-plunge in a flash, it's certain now!
Three, four times blessed, my friends-in-arms
who died on the plains of Troy those years ago,
serving the sons of Atreus to the end. Would to god   340
I'd died there too and met my fate that day the Trojans,
swarms of them, hurled at *me* with bronze spears,
fighting over the corpse of proud Achilles!
A hero's funeral then, my glory spread by comrades—
now what a wretched death I'm doomed to die!"   345

    At that a massive wave came crashing down on his head,
a terrific onslaught spinning his craft round and round—
he was thrown clear of the decks—
                       the steering-oar wrenched
from his grasp—
             and in one lightning attack the brawling
galewinds struck full-force, snapping the mast mid-shaft   350
and hurling the sail and sailyard far across the sea.
He went under a good long while, no fast way out,
no struggling up from under the giant wave's assault,
his clothing dragged him down—divine Calypso's gifts—
but at last he fought his way to the surface spewing   355
bitter brine, streams of it pouring down his head.
But half-drowned as he was, he'd not forget his craft—
he lunged after her through the breakers, laying hold
and huddling amidships, fled the stroke of death.
Pell-mell the rollers tossed her along down-current,   360
wild as the North Wind tossing thistle along the fields
at high harvest—dry stalks clutching each other tightly—
so the galewinds tumbled her down the sea, this way, that way,
now the South Wind flinging her over to North to sport with,
now the East Wind giving her up to West to harry on and on.   365

    But someone saw him—Cadmus' daughter with lovely ankles,
Ino, a mortal woman once with human voice and called
Leucothea now she lives in the sea's salt depths,
esteemed by all the gods as she deserves.[1]

---

1. Pursued by her insane husband, Ino leaped into the sea with her infant son and was made immortal.
Cadmus was founder and king of Thebes.

She pitied Odysseus, tossed, tormented so— 370
she broke from the waves like a shearwater on the wing,
lit on the wreck and asked him kindly, "Ah poor man,
why is the god of earthquakes so dead set against you?
Strewing your way with such a crop of troubles!
But he can't destroy you, not for all his anger. 375
Just do as I say. You seem no fool to me.
Strip off those clothes and leave your craft
for the winds to hurl, and swim for it now, you must,
strike out with your arms for landfall there,
Phaeacian land where destined safety waits. 380
Here, take this scarf,
tie it around your waist—it is immortal.
Nothing to fear now, neither pain nor death.
But once you grasp the mainland with your hands
untie it quickly, throw it into the wine-dark sea, 385
far from the shore, but you, you turn your head away!"

    With that the goddess handed him the scarf
and slipped back in the heavy breaking seas
like a shearwater once again
and a dark heaving billow closed above her. 390
But battle-weary Odysseus weighed two courses,
deeply torn, probing his fighting spirit: "Oh no—
I fear another immortal weaves a snare to trap me,
urging me to abandon ship! I won't. Not yet.
That shore's too far away— 395
I glimpsed it myself—where she says refuge waits.
No, here's what I'll do, it's what seems best to *me*.
As long as the timbers cling and joints stand fast,
I'll hold out aboard her and take a whipping—
once the breakers smash my craft to pieces, 400
then I'll swim—no better plan for now."

    But just as great Odysseus thrashed things out,
Poseidon god of the earthquake launched a colossal wave,
terrible, murderous, arching over him, pounding down on him,
hard as a windstorm blasting piles of dry parched chaff, 405
scattering flying husks—so the long planks of his boat
were scattered far and wide. But Odysseus leapt aboard
one timber and riding it like a plunging racehorse
stripped away his clothes, divine Calypso's gifts,
and quickly tying the scarf around his waist 410
he dove headfirst in the sea,
stretched his arms and stroked for life itself.
But again the mighty god of earthquakes spied him,
shook his head and grumbled deep in his spirit, "Go, go,
after all you've suffered—rove your miles of sea— 415
till you fall in the arms of people loved by Zeus.[2]
Even so I can hardly think you'll find

2. I.e., the Phaeacians.

your punishments too light!"
                          With that threat
he lashed his team with their long flowing manes,
gaining Aegae[3] port where his famous palace stands.   420

But Zeus's daughter Athena countered him at once.
The rest of the winds she stopped right in their tracks,
commanding them all to hush now, go to sleep.
All but the boisterous North—she whipped him up
and the goddess beat the breakers flat before Odysseus,   425
dear to Zeus, so he could reach the Phaeacians,
mingle with men who love their long oars
and escape his death at last.
                              Yes, but now,
adrift on the heaving swells two nights, two days—
quite lost—again and again the man foresaw his death.   430
Then when Dawn with her lovely locks brought on
the third day, the wind fell in an instant,
all glazed to a dead calm, and Odysseus,
scanning sharply, raised high by a groundswell,
looked up and saw it—landfall, just ahead.   435
Joy . . . warm as the joy that children feel
when they see their father's life dawn again,
one who's lain on a sickbed racked with torment,
wasting away, slowly, under some angry power's onslaught—
then what joy when the gods deliver him from his pains!   440
So warm, Odysseus' joy when he saw that shore, those trees,
as he swam on, anxious to plant his feet on solid ground again.
But just offshore, as far as a man's shout can carry,
he caught the boom of a heavy surf on jagged reefs—
roaring breakers crashing down on an ironbound coast,   445
exploding in fury—
                   the whole sea shrouded—
                                          sheets of spray—
no harbors to hold ships, no roadstead where they'd ride,
nothing but jutting headlands, riptooth reefs, cliffs.
Odysseus' knees quaked and the heart inside him sank;
he spoke to his fighting spirit, desperate: "Worse and worse!   450
Now that Zeus has granted a glimpse of land beyond my hopes,
now I've crossed this waste of water, the end in sight,
there's no way out of the boiling surf—I see no way!
Rugged reefs offshore, around them breakers roaring,
above them a smooth rock face, rising steeply, look,   455
and the surge too deep inshore, no spot to stand
on my own two legs and battle free of death.
If I clamber out, some big comber will hoist me,
dash me against that cliff—my struggles all a waste!
If I keep on swimming down the coast, trying to find   460
a seabeach shelving against the waves, a sheltered cove—
I dread it—another gale will snatch me up and haul me

---

3. Several places share this name. Homer mentions Poseidon's cult at Aegae several times.

back to the fish-infested sea, retching in despair.
Or a dark power will loose some monster at me,
rearing out of the waves—one of the thousands   465
Amphitrite's breakers teem with. Well I know
the famous god of earthquakes hates my very name!"

   Just as that fear went churning through his mind
a tremendous roller swept him toward the rocky coast
where he'd have been flayed alive, his bones crushed   470
if the bright-eyed goddess Pallas had not inspired him now.
He lunged for a reef, he seized it with both hands and clung
for dear life, groaning until the giant wave surged past
and so he escaped its force, but the breaker's backwash
charged into him full fury and hurled him out to sea.   475
Like pebbles stuck in the suckers of some octopus
dragged from its lair—so strips of skin torn
from his clawing hands stuck to the rock face.
A heavy sea covered him over, then and there
unlucky Odysseus would have met his death—   480
against the will of Fate—
but the bright-eyed one inspired him yet again.
Fighting out from the breakers pounding toward the coast,
out of danger he swam on, scanning the land, trying to find
a seabeach shelving against the waves, a sheltered cove,   485
and stroking hard he came abreast of a river's mouth,
running calmly, the perfect spot, he thought . . .
free of rocks, with a windbreak from the gales.
As the current flowed he felt the river's god and
prayed to him in spirit: "Hear me, lord, whoever you are,   490
I've come to you, the answer to all my prayers—
rescue me from the sea, the Sea-lord's curse!
Even immortal gods will show a man respect,
whatever wanderer seeks their help—like me—
I throw myself on your mercy, on your current now—   495
I have suffered greatly. Pity me, lord,
your suppliant cries for help!"
                              So the man prayed
and the god stemmed his current, held his surge at once
and smoothing out the swells before Odysseus now,
drew him safe to shore at the river's mouth.   500
His knees buckled, massive arms fell limp,
the sea had beaten down his striving heart.
His whole body swollen, brine aplenty gushing
out of his mouth and nostrils—breathless, speechless,
there he lay, with only a little strength left in him,   505
deathly waves of exhaustion overwhelmed him now . . .
But once he regained his breath and rallied back to life,
at last he loosed the goddess' scarf from his body,
dropped it into the river flowing out to sea
and a swift current bore it far downstream   510
and suddenly Ino caught it in her hands.
Struggling up from the banks, he flung himself

in the deep reeds, he kissed the good green earth
and addressed his fighting spirit, desperate still:
"Man of misery, what next? Is this the end?   515
If I wait out a long tense night by the banks,
I fear the sharp frost and the soaking dew together
will do me in—I'm bone-weary, about to breathe my last,
and a cold wind blows from a river on toward morning.
But what if I climb that slope, go for the dark woods   520
and bed down in the thick brush? What if I'm spared
the chill, fatigue, and a sweet sleep comes my way?
I fear wild beasts will drag me off as quarry."

　　But this was the better course, it struck him now.
He set out for the woods and not far from the water   525
found a grove with a clearing all around and crawled
beneath two bushy olives sprung from the same root,
one olive wild, the other well-bred stock.
No sodden gusty winds could ever pierce them,
nor could the sun's sharp rays invade their depths,   530
nor could a downpour drench them through and through,
so dense they grew together, tangling side-by-side.
Odysseus crept beneath them, scraping up at once
a good wide bed for himself with both hands.
A fine litter of dead leaves had drifted in,   535
enough to cover two men over, even three,
in the wildest kind of winter known to man.
Long-enduring great Odysseus, overjoyed at the sight,
bedded down in the midst and heaped the leaves around him.
As a man will bury his glowing brand in black ashes,   540
off on a lonely farmstead, no neighbors near,
to keep a spark alive—no need to kindle fire
from somewhere else—so great Odysseus buried
himself in leaves and Athena showered sleep
upon his eyes . . . sleep in a swift wave   545
delivering him from all his pains and labors,
blessed sleep that sealed his eyes at last.

BOOK VI

[The Princess and the Stranger]

So there he lay at rest, the storm-tossed great Odysseus,
borne down by his hard labors first and now deep sleep
as Athena traveled through the countryside
and reached the Phaeacians' city. Years ago
they lived in a land of spacious dancing-circles,   5
Hyperia,[4] all too close to the overbearing Cyclops,
stronger, violent brutes who harried them without end.
So their godlike king, Nausithous, led the people off
in a vast migration, settled them in Scheria,

---

4. Probably an imaginary place; however, the description of migration under pressure and the founding of a new city suggests the atmosphere of the great age of Greek colonization (8th century B.C.E.).

far from the men who toil on this earth—   10
he flung up walls around the city, built the houses,
raised the gods' temples and shared the land for plowing.
But his fate had long since forced him down to Death
and now Alcinous ruled, and the gods made him wise.
Straight to his house the clear-eyed Pallas went,   15
full of plans for great Odysseus' journey home.
She made her way to the gaily painted room
where a young girl lay asleep . . .
a match for the deathless gods in build and beauty,
Nausicaa, the daughter of generous King Alcinous.   20
Two handmaids fair as the Graces[5] slept beside her,
flanking the two posts, with the gleaming doors closed.
But the goddess drifted through like a breath of fresh air,
rushed to the girl's bed and hovering close she spoke,
in face and form like the shipman Dymas' daughter,   25
a girl the princess' age, and dearest to her heart.
Disguised, the bright-eyed goddess chided, "Nausicaa,
how could your mother bear a careless girl like you?
Look at your fine clothes, lying here neglected—
with your marriage not far off,   30
the day you should be decked in all your glory
and offer elegant dress to those who form your escort.
That's how a bride's good name goes out across the world
and it brings her father and queenly mother joy. Come,
let's go wash these clothes at the break of day—   35
I'll help you, lend a hand, and the work will fly!
You won't stay unwed long. The noblest men
in the country court you now, all Phaeacians
just like you, Phaeacia-born and raised. So come,
the first thing in the morning press your kingly father   40
to harness the mules and wagon for you, all to carry
your sashes, dresses, glossy spreads for your bed.
It's so much nicer for you to ride than go on foot.
The washing-pools are just too far from town."
                                    With that   45
the bright-eyed goddess sped away to Olympus, where,
they say, the gods' eternal mansion stands unmoved,
never rocked by galewinds, never drenched by rains,
nor do the drifting snows assail it, no, the clear air
stretches away without a cloud, and a great radiance
plays across that world where the blithe gods   50
live all their days in bliss. There Athena went,
once the bright-eyed one had urged the princess on.

Dawn soon rose on her splendid throne and woke
Nausicaa finely gowned. Still beguiled by her dream,
down she went through the house to tell her parents now,   65
her beloved father and mother. She found them both inside.
Her mother sat at the hearth with several waiting-women,

5. Goddesses (usually three) personifying charm and beauty.

spinning yarn on a spindle, lustrous sea-blue wool.
Her father she met as he left to join the lords
at a council island nobles asked him to attend.   60
She stepped up close to him, confiding, "Daddy dear,
I wonder, won't you have them harness a wagon for me,
the tall one with the good smooth wheels . . . so I
can take our clothes to the river for a washing?
Lovely things, but lying before me all soiled.   65
And you yourself, sitting among the princes,
debating points at your council,
you really should be wearing spotless linen.
Then you have five sons, full-grown in the palace,
two of them married, but three are lusty bachelors   70
always demanding crisp shirts fresh from the wash
when they go out to dance. Look at my duties—
that all rests on me."
                    So she coaxed, too shy
to touch on her hopes for marriage, young warm hopes,
in her father's presence. But he saw through it all   75
and answered quickly, "I won't deny you the mules,
my darling girl . . . I won't deny you anything.
Off you go, and the men will harness a wagon,
the tall one with the good smooth wheels,
fitted out with a cradle on the top."
                    With that   80
he called to the stablemen and they complied.
They trundled the wagon out now, rolling smoothly,
backed the mule-team into the traces, hitched them up,
while the princess brought her finery from the room
and piled it into the wagon's polished cradle.   85
Her mother packed a hamper—treats of all kinds,
favorite things to refresh her daughter's spirits—
poured wine in a skin, and as Nausicaa climbed aboard,
the queen gave her a golden flask of suppling olive oil
for her and her maids to smooth on after bathing.   90
Then, taking the whip in hand and glistening reins,
she touched the mules to a start and out they clattered,
trotting on at a clip, bearing the princess and her clothes
and not alone: her maids went with her, stepping briskly too.

    Once they reached the banks of the river flowing strong   95
where the pools would never fail, with plenty of water
cool and clear, bubbling up and rushing through
to scour the darkest stains—they loosed the mules,
out from under the wagon yoke, and chased them down
the river's rippling banks to graze on luscious clover.   100
Down from the cradle they lifted clothes by the armload,
plunged them into the dark pools and stamped them down
in the hollows, one girl racing the next to finish first
until they'd scoured and rinsed off all the grime,
then they spread them out in a line along the beach   105
where the surf had washed a pebbly scree ashore.

And once they'd bathed and smoothed their skin with oil,
they took their picnic, sitting along the river's banks
and waiting for all the clothes to dry in the hot noon sun.
Now fed to their hearts' content, the princess and her retinue   110
threw their veils to the wind, struck up a game of ball.
White-armed Nausicaa led their singing, dancing beat . . .
as lithe as Artemis with her arrows striding down
from a high peak—Taygetus' towering ridge or Erymanthus[6]—
thrilled to race with the wild boar or bounding deer,   115
and nymphs of the hills race with her,
daughters of Zeus whose shield is storm and thunder,
ranging the hills in sport, and Leto's[7] heart exults
as head and shoulders over the rest her daughter rises,
unmistakable—she outshines them all, though all are lovely.   120
So Nausicaa shone among her maids, a virgin, still unwed.

   But now, as she was about to fold her clothes
and yoke the mules and turn for home again,
now clear-eyed Pallas thought of what came next,
to make Odysseus wake and see this young beauty   125
and she would lead him to the Phaeacians' town.
The ball—
          the princess suddenly tossed it to a maid
but it missed the girl, splashed in a deep swirling pool
and they all shouted out—
             and that woke great Odysseus.
He sat up with a start, puzzling, his heart pounding: 130
"Man of misery, whose land have I lit on now?
What *are* they here—violent, savage, lawless?
or friendly to strangers, god-fearing men?
Listen: shouting, echoing round me—women, girls—
or the nymphs who haunt the rugged mountaintops   135
and the river springs and meadows lush with grass!
Or am I really close to people who speak my language?
Up with you, see how the land lies, see for yourself now . . ."

   Muttering so, great Odysseus crept out of the bushes,
stripping off with his massive hand a leafy branch   140
from the tangled olive growth to shield his body,
hide his private parts. And out he stalked
as a mountain lion exultant in his power
strides through wind and rain and his eyes blaze
and he charges sheep or oxen or chases wild deer   145
but his hunger drives him on to go for flocks,
even to raid the best-defended homestead.
So Odysseus moved out . . .
about to mingle with all those lovely girls,
naked now as he was, for the need drove him on,   150
a terrible sight, all crusted, caked with brine—

---

6. A mountain in Arcadia. *Taygetus:* the mountain range west of Sparta.   7. Mother of Artemis and Apollo.

they scattered in panic down the jutting beaches.
Only Alcinous' daughter held fast, for Athena planted
courage within her heart, dissolved the trembling in her limbs,
and she firmly stood her ground and faced Odysseus, torn now— 155
Should he fling his arms around her knees,[8] the young beauty,
plead for help, or stand back, plead with a winning word,
beg her to lead him to the town and lend him clothing?
This was the better way, he thought. Plead now
with a subtle, winning word and stand well back, 160
don't clasp her knees, the girl might bridle, yes.
He launched in at once, endearing, sly and suave:
"Here I am at your mercy, princess—
are you a goddess or a mortal? If one of the gods
who rule the skies up there, you're Artemis to the life, 165
the daughter of mighty Zeus—I see her now—just look
at your build, your bearing, your lithe flowing grace . . .
But if you're one of the mortals living here on earth,
three times blest are your father, your queenly mother,
three times over your brothers too. How often their hearts 170
must warm with joy to see you striding into the dances—
such a bloom of beauty. True, but he is the one
more blest than all other men alive, that man
who sways you with gifts and leads you home, his bride!
I have never laid eyes on anyone like you, 175
neither man nor woman . . .
I look at you and a sense of wonder takes me.

                                     Wait,
once I saw the like—in Delos, beside Apollo's altar—
the young slip of a palm-tree springing into the light.
There I'd sailed, you see, with a great army in my wake, 180
out on the long campaign that doomed my life to hardship.
That vision! Just as I stood there gazing, rapt, for hours . . .
no shaft like that had ever risen up from the earth—
so now I marvel at *you*, my lady: rapt, enthralled,
too struck with awe to grasp you by the knees 185
though pain has ground me down.

                          Only yesterday,
the twentieth day, did I escape the wine-dark sea.
Till then the waves and the rushing gales had swept me on
from the island of Ogygia. Now some power has tossed me here,
doubtless to suffer still more torments on your shores. 190
I can't believe they'll stop. Long before that
the gods will give me more, still more.

                             Compassion—
princess, please! You, after all that I have suffered,
you are the first I've come to. I know no one else,
none in your city, no one in your land. 200
Show me the way to town, give me a rag for cover,
just some cloth, some wrapper you carried with you here.

---

8. In the typical suppliant's posture.

And may the good gods give you all your heart desires:
husband, and house, and lasting harmony too.
No finer, greater gift in the world than that . . .   200
when man and woman possess their home, two minds,
two hearts that work as one. Despair to their enemies,
a joy to all their friends. Their own best claim to glory."

      "Stranger," the white-armed princess answered staunchly,
"friend, you're hardly a wicked man, and no fool, I'd say—   205
it's Olympian Zeus himself who hands our fortunes out,
to each of us in turn, to the good and bad,
however Zeus prefers . . .
He gave you pain, it seems. You simply have to bear it.
But now, seeing you've reached our city and our land,   210
you'll never lack for clothing or any other gift,
the right of worn-out suppliants come our way.
I'll show you our town, tell you our people's name.
Phaeacians we are, who hold this city and this land,
and I am the daughter of generous King Alcinous.   215
All our people's power stems from him."

      She called out to her girls with lovely braids:
"Stop, my friends! Why run when you see a man?
Surely you don't think *him* an enemy, do you?
There's no one alive, there never will be one,   220
who'd reach Phaeacian soil and lay it waste.
The immortals love us far too much for that.
We live too far apart, out in the surging sea,
off at the world's end—
no other mortals come to mingle with us.   225
But here's an unlucky wanderer strayed our way
and we must tend him well. Every stranger and beggar
comes from Zeus, and whatever scrap we give him
he'll be glad to get. So, quick, my girls,
give our newfound friend some food and drink   230
and bathe the man in the river,
wherever you find some shelter from the wind."
                                                                      At that
they came to a halt and teased each other on
and led Odysseus down to a sheltered spot
where he could find a seat,   235
just as great Alcinous' daughter told them.
They laid out cloak and shirt for him to wear,
they gave him the golden flask of suppling olive oil
and pressed him to bathe himself in the river's stream.
Then thoughtful Odysseus reassured the handmaids,   240
"Stand where you are, dear girls, a good way off,
so I can rinse the brine from my shoulders now
and rub myself with oil . . .
how long it's been since oil touched my skin!
But I won't bathe in front of you. I would be embarrassed—   245
stark naked before young girls with lovely braids."

The handmaids scurried off to tell their mistress.
Great Odysseus bathed in the river, scrubbed his body
clean of brine that clung to his back and broad shoulders,
scoured away the brackish scurf that caked his head.   250
And then, once he had bathed all over, rubbed in oil
and donned the clothes the virgin princess gave him,
Zeus's daughter Athena made him taller to all eyes,
his build more massive now, and down from his brow
she ran his curls like thick hyacinth clusters   255
full of blooms. As a master craftsman washes
gold over beaten silver—a man the god of fire[9]
and Queen Athena trained in every fine technique—
and finishes off his latest effort, handsome work,
so she lavished splendor over his head and shoulders now.   260
And down to the beach he walked and sat apart,
glistening in his glory, breathtaking, yes,
and the princess gazed in wonder . . .
then turned to her maids with lovely braided hair:
"Listen, my white-armed girls, to what I tell you.   265
The gods of Olympus can't be all against this man
who's come to mingle among our noble people.
At first he seemed appalling, I must say—
now he seems like a god who rules the skies up there!
Ah, if only a man like *that* were called my husband,   270
lived right here, pleased to stay forever . . .
                                        Enough.
Give the stranger food and drink, my girls."

        They hung on her words and did her will at once,
set before Odysseus food and drink, and he ate and drank,
the great Odysseus, long deprived, so ravenous now—   275
it seemed like years since he had tasted food.

        The white-armed princess thought of one last thing.
Folding the clothes, she packed them into her painted wagon,
hitched the sharp-hoofed mules, and climbing up herself,
Nausicaa urged Odysseus, warmly urged her guest,   280
"Up with you now, my friend, and off to town we go.
I'll see you into my wise father's palace where,
I promise you, you'll meet all the best Phaeacians.
Wait, let's do it this way. You seem no fool to me.
While we're passing along the fields and plowlands,   285
you follow the mules and wagon, stepping briskly
with all my maids. I'll lead the way myself.
But once we reach our city, ringed by walls
and strong high towers too, with a fine harbor either side . . .
and the causeway in is narrow; along the road the rolling ships 290
are all hauled up, with a slipway cleared for every vessel.
There's our assembly, round Poseidon's royal precinct,
built of quarried slabs planted deep in the earth.

9. Hephaestus.

Here the sailors tend their black ships' tackle,
cables and sails, and plane their oarblades down.   295
Phaeacians, you see, care nothing for bow or quiver,
only for masts and oars and good trim ships themselves—
we glory in our ships, crossing the foaming seas!
But I shrink from all our sea-dogs' nasty gossip.
Some old salt might mock us behind our backs—   300
we have our share of insolent types in town
and one of the coarser sort, spying us, might say,
'Now who's that tall, handsome stranger Nausicaa has in tow?
Where'd she light on *him*? Her husband-to-be, just wait!
But who—some shipwrecked stray she's taken up with,   305
some alien from abroad? Since nobody lives nearby.
Unless it's really a god come down from the blue
to answer all her prayers, and to have her all his days.
Good riddance! Let the girl go roving to find herself
a man from foreign parts. She only spurns her own—   310
countless Phaeacians round about who court her,
nothing but our best.'
                  So they'll scoff . . .
just think of the scandal that would face me then.
I'd find fault with a girl who carried on that way,
flouting her parents' wishes—father, mother, still alive—   315
consorting with men before she'd tied the knot in public.
No, stranger, listen closely to what I say, the sooner
to win your swift voyage home at my father's hands.
Now, you'll find a splendid grove along the road—
poplars, sacred to Pallas—   320
a bubbling spring's inside and meadows run around it.
There lies my father's estate, his blossoming orchard too,
as far from town as a man's strong shout can carry.
Take a seat there, wait a while, and give us time
to make it into town and reach my father's house.   325
Then, when you think we're home, walk on yourself
to the city, ask the way to my father's palace,
generous King Alcinous. You cannot miss it,
even an innocent child could guide you there.
No other Phaeacian's house is built like that: 330
so grand, the palace of Alcinous, our great hero.
Once the mansion and courtyard have enclosed you, go,
quickly, across the hall until you reach my mother.
Beside the hearth she sits in the fire's glare,
spinning yarn on a spindle, sea-blue wool—   335
a stirring sight, you'll see . . .
she leans against a pillar, her ladies sit behind.
And my father's throne is drawn up close beside her;
there he sits and takes his wine, a mortal like a god.
Go past him, grasp my mother's knees—if you want   340
to see the day of your return, rejoicing, soon,
even if your home's a world away.
If only the queen will take you to her heart,
then there's hope that you will see your loved ones,
reach your own grand house, your native land at last."   345

At that she touched the mules with her shining whip
and they quickly left the running stream behind.
The team trotted on, their hoofs wove in and out.
She drove them back with care so all the rest,
maids and Odysseus, could keep the pace on foot,   350
and she used the whip discreetly.
The sun sank as they reached the hallowed grove,
sacred to Athena, where Odysseus stopped and sat
and said a prayer at once to mighty Zeus's daughter:
"Hear me, daughter of Zeus whose shield is thunder—   355
tireless one, Athena! Now hear my prayer at last,
for you never heard me then, when I was shattered,
when the famous god of earthquakes wrecked my craft.
Grant that here among the Phaeacian people
I may find some mercy and some love!"   360

So he prayed and Athena heard his prayer
but would not yet appear to him undisguised.
She stood in awe of her Father's brother, lord of the sea
who still seethed on, still churning with rage against
the great Odysseus till he reached his native land.   365

BOOK VII

[Phaeacia's Halls and Gardens]

Now as Odysseus, long an exile, prayed in Athena's grove,
the hardy mule-team drew the princess toward the city.
Reaching her father's splendid halls, she reined in,
just at the gates—her brothers clustering round her,
men like gods, released the mules from the yoke   5
and brought the clothes indoors
as Nausicaa made her way toward her bedroom.
There her chambermaid lit a fire for her—
Eurymedusa, the old woman who'd come from Apiraea
years ago, when the rolling ships had sailed her in   10
and the country picked her out as King Alcinous' prize,
for he ruled all the Phaeacians, they obeyed him like a god.
Once, she had nursed the white-armed princess in the palace.
Now she lit a fire and made her supper in the room.

At the same time, Odysseus set off toward the city.   15
Pallas Athena, harboring kindness for the hero,
drifted a heavy mist around him, shielding him
from any swaggering islander who'd cross his path,
provoke him with taunts and search out who he was.
Instead, as he was about to enter the welcome city,   20
the bright-eyed goddess herself came up to greet him there,
for all the world like a young girl, holding a pitcher,
standing face-to-face with the visitor, who asked,
"Little girl, now wouldn't you be my guide
to the palace of the one they call Alcinous?   25
The king who rules the people of these parts.

I am a stranger, you see, weighed down with troubles,
come this way from a distant, far-off shore.
So I know no one here, none at all
in your city and the farmlands round about."

                                 "Oh yes, sir,   30
good old stranger," the bright-eyed goddess said,
"I'll show you the very palace that you're after—
the king lives right beside my noble father.
Come, quietly too, and I will lead the way.
Now not a glance at anyone, not a question.   35
The men here never suffer strangers gladly,
have no love for hosting a man from foreign lands.
All they really trust are their fast, flying ships
that cross the mighty ocean. Gifts of Poseidon,
ah what ships they are—   40
quick as a bird, quick as a darting thought!"

   And Pallas Athena sped away in the lead
as he followed in her footsteps, man and goddess.
But the famed Phaeacian sailors never saw him,
right in their midst, striding down their streets.   45
Athena the one with lovely braids would not permit it,
the awesome goddess poured an enchanted mist around him,
harboring kindness for Odysseus in her heart.
And he marveled now at the balanced ships and havens,
the meeting grounds of the great lords and the long ramparts   50
looming, coped and crowned with palisades of stakes—
an amazing sight to see . . .
And once they reached the king's resplendent halls
the bright-eyed goddess cried out, "Good old stranger,
here, here is the very palace that you're after—   55
I've guided you all the way. Here you'll find
our princes dear to the gods, busy feasting.
You go on inside. Be bold, nothing to fear.
In every venture the bold man comes off best,
even the wanderer, bound from distant shores.   60
The queen is the first you'll light on in the halls.
Arete, she is called, and earns the name:
she answers all our prayers:[1] She comes, in fact,
from the same stock that bred our King Alcinous.
First came Nausithous, son of the earthquake god   65
Poseidon and Periboea, the lovely, matchless beauty,
the youngest daughter of iron-willed Eurymedon,
king of the overweening Giants[2] years ago.
He led that reckless clan to its own ruin,
killed himself in the bargain, but the Sea-lord   70
lay in love with Periboea and she produced a son,
Nausithous, that lionheart who ruled Phaeacia well.
Now, Nausithous had two sons, Rhexenor and Alcinous,

---

1. Her name is related to Greek *araomai*, "pray."   **2.** A monstrous race, born of Earth; they were defeated
in battle by the Olympian gods.

but the lord of the silver bow, Apollo, shot Rhexenor down—
married, true, yet still without a son in the halls,   75
he left one child behind, a daughter named Arete.
Alcinous made the girl his wife and honors her
as no woman is honored on this earth, of all the wives
now keeping households under their husbands' sway.
Such is her pride of place, and always will be so: 80
dear to her loving children, to Alcinous himself
and all our people. They gaze on her as a god,
saluting her warmly on her walks through town.
She lacks nothing in good sense and judgment—
she can dissolve quarrels, even among men,   85
whoever wins her sympathies.
If only our queen will take you to her heart,
then there's hope that you will see your loved ones,
reach your high-roofed house, your native land at last."

    And with that vow the bright-eyed goddess sped away,   90
over the barren sea, leaving welcome Scheria far behind,
and reaching Marathon and the spacious streets of Athens,
entered Erechtheus[3] sturdy halls, Athena's stronghold.
Now as Odysseus approached Alcinous' famous house
a rush of feelings stirred within his heart,   95
bringing him to a standstill,
even before he crossed the bronze threshold . . .
A radiance strong as the moon or rising sun came flooding
through the high-roofed halls of generous King Alcinous.
Walls plated in bronze, crowned with a circling frieze   100
glazed as blue as lapis, ran to left and right
from outer gates to the deepest court recess
And solid golden doors enclosed the palace.
Up from the bronze threshold silver doorposts rose
with silver lintel above, and golden handle hooks.   105
And dogs of gold and silver were stationed either side,
forged by the god of fire with all his cunning craft
to keep watch on generous King Alcinous' palace,
his immortal guard-dogs, ageless, all their days.
Inside to left and right, in a long unbroken row   110
from farthest outer gate to the inmost chamber,
thrones stood backed against the wall, each draped
with a finely spun brocade, women's handsome work.
Here the Phaeacian lords would sit enthroned,
dining, drinking—the feast flowed on forever.   115
And young boys, molded of gold, set on pedestals
standing firm, were lifting torches high in their hands
to flare through the nights and light the feasters down the hall.
And Alcinous has some fifty serving-women in his house:
some, turning the handmill, grind the apple-yellow grain,   120
some weave at their webs or sit and spin their yarn,
fingers flickering quick as aspen leaves in the wind

---

3. Legendary king of Athens. *Marathon:* a village north of Athens on the coast of Attica.

and the densely woven woolens dripping oil droplets.
Just as Phaeacian men excel the world at sailing,
driving their swift ships on the open seas,   125
so the women excel at all the arts of weaving.
That is Athena's gift to them beyond all others—
a genius for lovely work, and a fine mind too.

    Outside the courtyard, fronting the high gates,
a magnificent orchard stretches four acres deep   130
with a strong fence running round it side-to-side.
Here luxuriant trees are always in their prime,
pomegranates and pears, and apples glowing red,
succulent figs and olives swelling sleek and dark.
And the yield of all these trees will never flag or die,   135
neither in winter nor in summer, a harvest all year round
for the West Wind always breathing through will bring
some fruits to the bud and others warm to ripeness—
pear mellowing ripe on pear, apple on apple,
cluster of grapes on cluster, fig crowding fig.   140
And here is a teeming vineyard planted for the kings,
beyond it an open level bank where the vintage grapes
lie baking to raisins in the sun while pickers gather others;
some they trample down in vats, and here in the front rows
bunches of unripe grapes have hardly shed their blooms   145
while others under the sunlight slowly darken purple.
And there by the last rows are beds of greens,
bordered and plotted, greens of every kind,
glistening fresh, year in, year out. And last,
there are two springs, one rippling in channels   150
over the whole orchard—the other, flanking it,
rushes under the palace gates
to bubble up in front of the lofty roofs
where the city people come and draw their water.
                                            Such
were the gifts, the glories showered down by the gods   155
on King Alcinous' realm.
                    And there Odysseus stood,
gazing at all this bounty, a man who'd borne so much . . .
Once he'd had his fill of marveling at it all,
he crossed the threshold quickly,
strode inside the palace. Here he found   160
the Phaeacian lords and captains tipping out
libations now to the guide and giant-killer Hermes,
the god to whom they would always pour the final cup
before they sought their beds. Odysseus went on
striding down the hall, the man of many struggles   165
shrouded still in the mist Athena drifted round him,
till he reached Arete and Alcinous the king. And then,
the moment he flung his arms around Arete's knees,
the godsent mist rolled back to reveal the great man.
And silence seized the feasters all along the hall—   170
seeing him right before their eyes, they marveled,

gazing on him now as Odysseus pleaded, "Queen,
Arete, daughter of godlike King Rhexenor!
Here after many trials I come to beg for mercy,
your husband's, yours, and all these feasters' here.   175
May the gods endow them with fortune all their lives,
may each hand down to his sons the riches in his house
and the pride of place the realm has granted *him*.
But as for myself, grant me a rapid convoy home
to my own native land. How far away I've been   180
from all my loved ones—how long I have suffered!"

   Pleading so, the man sank down in the ashes,
just at the hearth beside the blazing fire,[4]
while all the rest stayed hushed, stock-still.
At last the old revered Echeneus broke the spell,   185
the eldest lord in Phaeacia, finest speaker too,
a past master at all the island's ancient ways.
Impelled by kindness now, he rose and said,
"This is no way, Alcinous. How indecent, look,
our guest on the ground, in the ashes by the fire!   190
Your people are holding back, waiting for your signal.
Come, raise him up and seat the stranger now,
in a silver-studded chair,
and tell the heralds to mix more wine for all
so we can pour out cups to Zeus who loves the lightning,   195
champion of suppliants—suppliants' rights are sacred.
And let the housekeeper give our guest his supper,
unstinting with her stores."
              Hearing that,
Alcinous, poised in all his majesty, took the hand
of the seasoned, worldly-wise Odysseus, raised him up   200
from the hearth and sat him down in a burnished chair,
displacing his own son, the courtly Lord Laodamas
who had sat beside him, the son he loved the most.
A maid brought water soon in a graceful golden pitcher
and over a silver basin tipped it out   205
so the guest might rinse his hands,
then pulled a gleaming table to his side.
A staid housekeeper brought on bread to serve him,
appetizers aplenty too, lavish with her bounty.
As long-suffering great Odysseus ate and drank,   210
the hallowed King Alcinous called his herald:
"Come, Pontonous! Mix the wine in the bowl,
pour rounds to all our banqueters in the house
so we can pour out cups to Zeus who loves the lightning,
champion of suppliants—suppliants' rights are sacred."   215

   At that Pontonous mixed the heady, honeyed wine
and tipped first drops for the god in every cup,

---

4. The fire, or hearth, was the sacred center of the home; the suppliant who sat there could not be forcibly
removed without offending the gods.

then poured full rounds for all. And once they'd poured
libations out and drunk to their hearts' content,
Alcinous rose and addressed his island people: 220
"Hear me, lords and captains of Phaeacia,
hear what the heart inside me has to say.
Now, our feast finished, home you go to sleep.
But at dawn we call the elders in to full assembly,
host our guest in the palace, sacrifice to the gods   225
and then we turn our minds to his passage home,
so under our convoy our new friend can travel back
to his own land—no toil, no troubles—soon,
rejoicing, even if his home's a world away.
And on the way no pain or hardship suffered,   230
not till he sets foot on native ground again.
There in the future he must suffer all that Fate
and the overbearing Spinners spun out on his life line
the very day his mother gave him birth . . . But if
he's one of the deathless powers, out of the blue,   235
the gods are working now in strange, new ways.
Always, up to now, they came to us face-to-face
whenever we'd give them grand, glorious sacrifices—
they always sat beside us here and shared our feasts.
Even when some lonely traveler meets them on the roads,   240
they never disguise themselves. We're too close kin for that,
close as the wild Giants are, the Cyclops too."
                              "Alcinous!"
wary Odysseus countered, "cross that thought from your mind.
I'm nothing like the immortal gods who rule the skies,
either in build or breeding. I'm just a mortal man.   245
Whom do you know most saddled down with sorrow?
They are the ones I'd equal, grief for grief.
And I could tell a tale of still more hardship,
all I've suffered, thanks to the gods' will.
But despite my misery, let me finish dinner.   250
The belly's a shameless dog, there's nothing worse.
Always insisting, pressing, it never lets us forget—
destroyed as I am, my heart racked with sadness,
sick with anguish, still it keeps demanding,
'Eat, drink!' It blots out all the memory   255
of my pain, commanding, 'Fill me up!'
                              But you,
at the first light of day, hurry, please,
to set your unlucky guest on his own home soil.
How much I have suffered . . . Oh just let me see
my lands, my serving-men and the grand high-roofed house—   260
then I can die in peace."
                              All burst into applause,
urging passage home for their newfound friend,
his pleading rang so true. And once they'd poured
libations out and drunk to their hearts' content,
each one made his way to rest in his own house.   265
But King Odysseus still remained at hall,

seated beside the royal Alcinous and Arete
as servants cleared the cups and plates away.
The white-armed Queen Arete took the lead;
she'd spotted the cape and shirt Odysseus wore,   270
fine clothes she'd made herself with all her women,
so now her words flew brusquely, sharply: "Stranger,
I'll be the first to question you—myself.
Who are you? Where are you from?
Who gave you the clothes you're wearing now?   275
Didn't you say you reached us roving on the sea?"

   "What hard labor, queen," the man of craft replied,
"to tell you the story of my troubles start to finish.
The gods on high have given me my share.
Still, this much I will tell you . . .   280
seeing you probe and press me so intently.
There is an island, Ogygia, lying far at sea,
where the daughter of Atlas, Calypso, has her home,
the seductive nymph with lovely braids—a danger too,
and no one, god or mortal, dares approach her there. But I,   285
cursed as I am, some power brought me to her hearth,
alone, when Zeus with a white-hot bolt had crushed
my racing warship down the wine-dark sea.
There all the rest of my loyal shipmates died
but I, locking my arms around my good ship's keel,   290
drifted along nine days. On the tenth, at dead of night,
the gods cast me up on Ogygia, Calypso's island,
home of the dangerous nymph with glossy braids,
and the goddess took me in in all her kindness,
welcomed me warmly, cherished me, even vowed   295
to make me immortal, ageless, all my days—
but she never won the heart inside me, never.
Seven endless years I remained there, always drenching
with my tears the immortal clothes Calypso gave me.
Then, at last, when the eighth came wheeling round,   300
she insisted that I sail—inspired by warnings sent
from Zeus, perhaps, or her own mind had changed.
She saw me on my way in a solid craft.
tight and trim, and gave me full provisions,
food and mellow wine, immortal clothes to wear   305
and summoned a wind to bear me onward, fair and warm.
And seventeen days I sailed, making headway well;
on the eighteenth, shadowy mountains slowly loomed . . .
your land! My heart leapt up, unlucky as I am,
doomed to be comrade still to many hardships.   310
Many pains the god of earthquakes piled upon me,
loosing the winds against me, blocking passage through,
heaving up a terrific sea, beyond belief—nor did the whitecaps
let me cling to my craft, for all my desperate groaning.
No, the squalls shattered her stem to stern, but I,   315
I swam hard, I plowed my way through those dark gulfs
till at last the wind and current bore me to your shores.

But here, had I tried to land, the breakers would have hurled me,
smashed me against the jagged cliffs of that grim coast,
so I pulled away, swam back till I reached a river,   320
the perfect spot at last, or so it struck me,
free of rocks, with a windbreak from the gales.
So, fighting for life, I flung myself ashore
and the godsent, bracing night came on at once.
Clambering up from the river, big with Zeus's rains,   325
I bedded down in the brush, my body heaped with leaves,
and a god poured down a boundless sleep upon me, yes,
and there in the leaves, exhausted, sick at heart,
I slept the whole night through
and on to the break of day and on into high noon   330
and the sun was wheeling down when sweet sleep set me free.
And I looked up, and there were your daughter's maids
at play on the beach, and she, she moved among them
like a deathless goddess! I begged her for help
and not once did her sense of tact desert her;   335
she behaved as you'd never hope to find
in one so young, not in a random meeting—
time and again the youngsters prove so flighty.
Not she. She gave me food aplenty and shining wine,
a bath in the river too, and gave me all this clothing.   340
That's my whole story. Wrenching to tell, but true."

    "Ah, but in one regard, my friend," the king replied,
"her good sense missed the mark, this daughter of mine.
She never escorted you to our house with all her maids
but she was the first you asked for care and shelter."   345

    "Your majesty," diplomatic Odysseus answered,
"don't find fault with a flawless daughter now,
not for my sake, please.
She urged me herself to follow with her maids.
I chose not to, fearing embarrassment in fact—   350
what if you took offense, seeing us both together?
Suspicious we are, we men who walk the earth."

    "Oh no, my friend," Alcinous stated flatly,
"I'm hardly a man for reckless, idle anger.
Balance is best in all things. et   355
Father Zeus, Athena and lord Apollo! if only—
seeing the man you are, seeing we think as one—
you could wed my daughter and be my son-in-law
and stay right here with us. I'd give you a house
and great wealth—if you chose to stay, that is.   360
No Phaeacian would hold you back by force.
The curse of Father Zeus on such a thing!
And about your convoy home, you rest assured:
I have chosen the day and I decree it is tomorrow.
And all that voyage long you'll lie in a deep sleep   365
while my people sail you on through calm and gentle tides

till you reach your land and house, or any place you please.
True, even if landfall lies more distant than Euboea,[5]
off at the edge of the world . . .
So say our crews, at least, who saw it once,   370
that time they carried the gold-haired Rhadamanthys
out to visit Tityus,[6] son of Mother Earth. Imagine,
there they sailed and back they came in the same day,
they finished the homeward run with no strain at all.
You'll see for yourself how far they top the best—   375
my ships and their young shipmates
tossing up the whitecaps with their oars!"
                              So he vowed
and the long-enduring great Odysseus glowed with joy
and raised a prayer and called the god by name:
"Father Zeus on high—   380
may the king fulfill his promises one and all!
Then his fame would ring through the fertile earth
and never die—and I should reach my native land at last!"

    And now as the two men exchanged their hopes,
the white-armed queen instructed her palace maids   385
to make a bed in the porch's shelter, lay down
some heavy purple throws for the bed itself,
and over it spread some blankets, thick woolly robes,
a warm covering laid on top. Torches in hand,
they left the hall and fell to work at once,   390
briskly prepared a good snug resting-place
and then returned to Odysseus, urged the guest,
"Up, friend, time for sleep. Your bed is made."
How welcome the thought of sleep to that man now . . .
So there after many trials Odysseus lay at rest   395
on a corded bed inside the echoing colonnade.
Alcinous slept in chambers deep in his lofty house
where the queen his wife arranged and shared their bed.

BOOK VIII

[A Day for Songs and Contests]

When young Dawn with her rose-red fingers shone once more
royal Alcinous, hallowed island king, rose from bed
and great Odysseus, raider of cities, rose too.
Poised in his majesty, Alcinous led the way
to Phaeacia's meeting grounds, built for all   5
beside the harbored ships. Both men sat down
on the polished stone benches side-by-side
as Athena started roaming up and down the town,
in build and voice the wise Alcinous' herald,
furthering plans for Odysseus' journey home,   10

5. For many in the *Odyssey*'s Greek audiences, Euboea—the large island that stretches along the northern coast of Attica—would have been close by and familiar.   6. A giant who tried to rape Leto. In book 11 Odysseus sees him in the underworld, eternally punished for his crime. Why Rhadymanthus—renowned for justice and in later tradition one of the judges in the underworld—went to visit Tityus we have no idea.

and stopped beside each citizen, urged them all,
"Come this way, you lords and captains of Phaeacia,
come to the meeting grounds and learn about the stranger!
A new arrival! Here at our wise king's palace now,
he's here from roving the ocean, driven far off course—   15
he looks like a deathless god!"
                                          Rousing their zeal,
their curiosity, each and every man, and soon enough
the assembly seats were filled with people thronging,
gazing in wonder at the seasoned man of war . . .
Over Odysseus' head and shoulders now   20
Athena lavished a marvelous splendor, yes,
making him taller, more massive to all eyes,
so Phaeacians might regard the man with kindness,
awe and respect as well, and he might win through
the many trials they'd pose to test the hero's strength.   25
Once they'd grouped, crowding the meeting grounds,
Alcinous rose and addressed his island people:
"Hear me, lords and captains of Phaeacia,
hear what the heart inside me has to say.
This stranger here, our guest—   30
I don't know who he is, or whether he comes
from sunrise lands or the western lands of evening,
but he has come in his wanderings to my palace;
he pleads for passage, he begs we guarantee it.
So now, as in years gone by, let us press on   35
and grant him escort. No one, I tell you, no one
who comes to *my* house will languish long here,
heartsick for convoy home.
                                  Come, my people!
Haul a black ship down to the bright sea,
rigged for her maiden voyage—   40
enlist a crew of fifty-two young sailors,
the best in town, who've proved their strength before.
Let all hands lash their oars to the thwarts then disembark,
come to my house and fall in for a banquet, quickly.
I'll lay on a princely feast for all. So then,   45
these are the orders I issue to our crews.
For the rest, you sceptered princes here,
you come to my royal halls so we can give
this stranger a hero's welcome in our palace—
no one here refuse. Call in the inspired bard   50
Demodocus. God has given the man the gift of song,
to him beyond all others, the power to please,
however the spirit stirs him on to sing."

     With those commands Alcinous led the way
and a file of sceptered princes took his lead   55
while the herald went to find the gifted bard.
And the fifty-two young sailors, duly chosen,
briskly following orders,
went down to the shore of the barren salt sea.

And once they reached the ship at the surf's edge,   60
first they hauled the craft into deeper water,
stepped the mast amidships, canvas brailed,
they made oars fast in the leather oarlock straps,
moored her riding high on the swell, then disembarked
and made their way to wise Alcinous' high-roofed halls.   65
There colonnades and courts and rooms were overflowing
with crowds, a mounting host of people young and old.
The king slaughtered a dozen sheep to feed his guests,
eight boars with shining tusks and a pair of shambling oxen.
These they skinned and dressed, and then laid out a feast   70
to fill the heart with savor.
                              In came the herald now,
leading along the faithful bard the Muse adored
above all others, true, but her gifts were mixed
with good and evil both: she stripped him of sight
but gave the man the power of stirring, rapturous song.   75
Pontonous brought the bard a silver-studded chair,
right amid the feasters, leaning it up against
a central column—hung his high clear lyre
on a peg above his head and showed him how
to reach up with his hands and lift it down.   80
And the herald placed a table by his side
with a basket full of bread and cup of wine
for him to sip when his spirit craved refreshment.
All reached out for the good things that lay at hand
and when they'd put aside desire for food and drink,   85
the Muse inspired the bard
to sing the famous deeds of fighting heroes—
the song whose fame had reached the skies those days:
The Strife Between Odysseus and Achilles, Peleus' Son . . .
how once at the gods' flowing feast the captains clashed   90
in a savage war of words, while Agamemnon, lord of armies,
rejoiced at heart that Achaea's bravest men were battling so.
For this was the victory sign that Apollo prophesied
at his shrine in Pytho[7] when Agamemnon strode across
the rocky threshold, asking the oracle for advice—   95
the start of the tidal waves of ruin tumbling down
on Troy's and Achaea's forces, both at once,
thanks to the will of Zeus who rules the world.

    That was the song the famous harper sang
but Odysseus, clutching his flaring sea-blue cape   100
in both powerful hands, drew it over his head
and buried his handsome face,
ashamed his hosts might see him shedding tears.
Whenever the rapt bard would pause in the song,
he'd lift the cape from his head, wipe off his tears   105
and hoisting his double-handled cup, pour it out to the gods.
But soon as the bard would start again, impelled to sing

---

7. Delphi, on the southern slopes of Mount Parnassus, on the Greek mainland.

by Phaeacia's lords, who reveled in his tale,
again Odysseus hid his face and wept.
His weeping went unmarked by all the others;   110
only Alcinous, sitting close beside him,
noticed his guest's tears,
heard the groan in the man's labored breathing
and said at once to the master mariners around him,
"Hear me, my lords and captains of Phaeacia!   115
By now we've had our fill of food well-shared
and the lyre too, our loyal friend at banquets.
Now out we go again and test ourselves in contests,
games of every kind—so our guest can tell his friends,
when he reaches home, how far we excel the world   120
at boxing, wrestling, jumping, speed of foot."

      He forged ahead and the rest fell in behind.
The herald hung the ringing lyre back on its peg
and taking Demodocus by the hand, led him from the palace,
guiding him down the same path the island lords   125
had just pursued, keen to watch the contests.
They reached the meeting grounds
with throngs of people streaming in their trail
as a press of young champions rose for competition.
Topsail and Riptide rose, the helmsman Rowhard too   130
and Seaman and Sternman, Surf-at-the-Beach and Stroke-Oar,
Breaker and Bowsprit, Racing-the-Wind and Swing-Aboard
and Seagirt the son of Greatfleet, Shipwrightson
and the son of Launcher, Broadsea, rose up too,
a match for murderous Ares,[8] death to men—   135
in looks and build the best of all Phaeacians
after gallant Laodamas, the Captain of the People.
Laodamas rose with two more sons of great Alcinous,
Halius bred to the sea and Clytoneus famed for ships.
And now the games began, the first event a footrace . . .   140
They toed the line—
                    and broke flat out from the start
with a fast pack flying down the field in a whirl of dust
and Clytoneus the prince outstripped them all by far,
flashing ahead the length two mules will plow a furrow
before he turned for home, leaving the pack behind   145
and raced to reach the crowds.
                              Next the wrestling,
grueling sport. They grappled, locked, and Broadsea,
pinning the strongest champions, won the bouts.
Next, in the jumping, Seagirt leapt and beat the field.
In the discus Rowhard up and outhurled them all by far.   150
And the king's good son Laodamas boxed them to their knees.
When all had enjoyed the games to their hearts' content
Alcinous' son Laodamas spurred them: "Come, my friends,
let's ask our guest if he knows the ropes of any sport.

8. God of war.

He's no mean man, not with a build like that . . .
Look at his thighs, his legs, and what a pair of arms—
his massive neck, his big, rippling strength!
Nor is he past his prime,
just beaten down by one too many blows.
Nothing worse than the sea, I always say,   160
to crush a man, the strongest man alive."

   And Broadsea put in quickly,
"Well said, Laodamas, right to the point.
Go up to the fellow, challenge him yourself."

   On that cue, the noble prince strode up   165
before Odysseus, front and center, asking,
"Come, stranger, sir, won't you try your hand
at our contests now? If you have skill in any.
It's fit and proper for you to know your sports.
What greater glory attends a man, while he's alive,   170
than what he wins with his racing feet and striving hands?
Come and compete then, throw your cares to the wind!
It won't be long, your journey's not far off—
your ship's already hauled down to the sea,
your crew is set to sail."
           "Laodamas,"   175
quick to the mark Odysseus countered sharply,
"why do you taunt me so with such a challenge?
Pains weigh on my spirit now, not your sports—
I've suffered much already, struggled hard.
But here I sit amid your assembly still,   180
starved for passage home, begging your king,
begging all your people."
           "Oh I knew it!"
Broadsea broke in, mocking him to his face.
"I never took you for someone skilled in games,
the kind that real men play throughout the world.   185
Not a chance. You're some skipper of profiteers,
roving the high seas in his scudding craft,
reckoning up his freight with a keen eye out
for home-cargo, grabbing the gold he can!
You're no athlete. I see that."
              With a dark glance   190
wily Odysseus shot back, "Indecent talk, my friend.
You, you're a reckless fool—I see *that*. So,
the gods don't hand out all their gifts at once,
not build and brains and flowing speech to all.
One man may fail to impress us with his looks   195
but a god can crown his words with beauty, charm,
and men look on with delight when he speaks out.
Never faltering, filled with winning self-control,
he shines forth at assembly grounds and people gaze
at him like a god when he walks through the streets.   200
Another man may look like a deathless one on high

but there's not a bit of grace to crown his words.
Just like you, my fine, handsome friend. Not even
a god could improve those lovely looks of yours
but the mind inside is worthless.   205
Your slander fans the anger in my heart!
I'm no stranger to sports—for all your taunts—
I've held my place in the front ranks, I tell you,
long as I could trust to my youth and striving hands.
But now I'm wrestled down by pain and hardship, look,   210
I've borne my share of struggles, cleaving my way
through wars of men and pounding waves at sea.
Nevertheless, despite so many blows,
I'll compete in your games, just watch. Your insults
cut to the quick—you rouse my fighting blood!"   215

    Up he sprang, cloak and all, and seized a discus,
huge and heavy, more weighty by far than those
the Phaeacians used to hurl and test each other.
Wheeling round, he let loose with his great hand
and the stone whirred on—and down to ground they went,   220
those lords of the long oars and master mariners cringing
under the rock's onrush, soaring lightly out of his grip,
flying away past all the other marks, and Queen Athena,
built like a man, staked out the spot and cried
with a voice of triumph, "Even a blind man,   225
friend, could find your mark by groping round—
it's not mixed up in the crowd, it's far in front!
There's nothing to fear in *this* event—
no one can touch you, much less beat your distance!"

    At that the heart of the long-suffering hero laughed,   230
so glad to find a ready friend in the crowd that,
lighter in mood, he challenged all Phaeacia's best:
"Now go match *that*, you young pups, and straightaway
I'll hurl you another just as far, I swear, or even farther!
All the rest of you, anyone with the spine and spirit,   235
step right up and try me—you've incensed me so—
at boxing, wrestling, racing; nothing daunts me.
Any Phaeacian here except Laodamas himself.
The man's my host. Who would fight his friend?
He'd have to be good-for-nothing, senseless, yes,   240
to challenge his host and come to grips in games,
in a far-off land at that. He'd cut his own legs short.
But there are no others I'd deny or think beneath me—
I'll take on all contenders, gladly, test them head-to-head!
I'm no disgrace in the world of games where men compete.   245
Well I know how to handle a fine polished bow,
the first to hit my man in a mass of enemies,
even with rows of comrades pressing near me,
taking aim with our shafts to hit our targets.
Philoctetes[9] alone outshot me there at Troy   250

9. Inheritor of the bow of Heracles, which never missed its mark.

when ranks of Achaean archers bent their bows.
Of the rest I'd say that I outclass them all—
men still alive, who eat their bread on earth.
But I'd never vie with the men of days gone by,
not Heracles, not Eurytus[1] of Oechalia—archers   255
who rivaled immortal powers with their bows.
That's why noble Eurytus died a sudden death:
no old age, creeping upon him in his halls . . .
Apollo shot him down, enraged that the man
had challenged *him*, the Archer God.

                                    As for spears,   260
I can fling a spear as far as the next man wings an arrow!
Only at sprinting I fear you'd leave me in the dust.
I've taken a shameful beating out on heavy seas,
no conditioning there on shipboard day by day.
My legs have lost their spring."   265

     He finished. All stood silent, hushed.
Only Alcinous found a way to answer. "Stranger,
friend—nothing you say among us seems ungracious.
You simply want to display the gifts you're born with,
stung that a youngster marched up to you in the games,   270
mocking, ridiculing your prowess as no one would
who had some sense of fit and proper speech.
But come now, hear me out,
so you can tell our story to other lords
as you sit and feast in your own halls someday,   275
your own wife and your children by your side,
remembering there our island prowess here:
what skills great Zeus has given *us* as well,
down all the years from our fathers' days till now.
We're hardly world-class boxers or wrestlers, I admit,   280
but we can race like the wind, we're champion sailors too,
and always dear to our hearts, the feast, the lyre and dance
and changes of fresh clothes, our warm baths and beds.
So come—all you Phaeacian masters of the dance—
now dance away! So our guest can tell his friends,   285
when he reaches home, how far we excel the world
in sailing, nimble footwork, dance and song.

                                    Go, someone,
quickly, fetch Demodocus now his ringing lyre.
It must be hanging somewhere in the palace."

     At the king's word the herald sprang to his feet   290
and ran to fetch the ringing lyre from the house.
And stewards rose, nine in all, picked from the realm
to set the stage for contests: masters-at-arms who
leveled the dancing-floor to make a fine broad ring.
The herald returned and placed the vibrant lyre now   295
in Demodocus' hands, and the bard moved toward the center,

---

1. King of Oechalia (several towns had this name, and it is uncertain which is his). Eurytus's bow was given by his son Iphitus to Odysseus, and it is with this bow that Odysseus will kill the suitors in book 22. The bow's history is given at the beginning of book 21.

flanked by boys in the flush of youth, skilled dancers
who stamped the ground with marvelous pulsing steps
as Odysseus gazed at their flying, flashing feet,
his heart aglow with wonder.
           A rippling prelude—   300
now the bard struck up an irresistible song:
The Love of Ares and Aphrodite Crowned with Flowers . . .
how the two had first made love in Hephaestus' mansion,
all in secret. Ares had showered her with gifts
and showered Hephaestus' marriage bed with shame   305
but a messenger ran to tell the god of fire—
Helios, lord of the sun,[2] who'd spied the couple
lost in each other's arms and making love.
Hephaestus, hearing the heart-wounding story,
bustled toward his forge, brooding on his revenge—   310
planted the huge anvil on its block and beat out chains,
not to be slipped or broken, all to pin the lovers on the spot.
This snare the Firegod forged, ablaze with his rage at War,
then limped to the room where the bed of love stood firm
and round the posts he poured the chains in a sweeping net   315
with streams of others flowing down from the roofbeam,
gossamer-fine as spider webs no man could see,
not even a blissful god—
the Smith had forged a masterwork of guile.
Once he'd spun that cunning trap around his bed   320
he feigned a trip to the well-built town of Lemnos,[3]
dearest to him by far of all the towns on earth.
But the god of battle kept no blind man's watch.
As soon as he saw the Master Craftsman leave
he plied his golden reins and arrived at once   325
and entered the famous god of fire's mansion,
chafing with lust for Aphrodite crowned with flowers.
She'd just returned from her father's palace, mighty Zeus,
and now she sat in her rooms as Ares strode right in
and grasped her hand with a warm, seductive urging: 330
"Quick, my darling, come, let's go to bed
and lose ourselves in love! Your husband's away—
by now he must be off in the wilds of Lemnos,
consorting with his raucous Sintian friends."
           So he pressed
and her heart raced with joy to sleep with War   335
and off they went to bed and down they lay—
and down around them came those cunning chains
of the crafty god of fire, showering down now
till the couple could not move a limb or lift a finger—
then they knew at last: there was no way out, not now.   340
But now the glorious crippled Smith was drawing near . . .
he'd turned around, miles short of the Lemnos coast,

---

2. As the sun, Helios sees everything.   3. Island in the northeastern Aegean, where there was a cult of
Hephaestus. When Zeus in anger threw him off Olympus, Hephaestus landed on Lemnos and was cared
for by its inhabitants, the Sintians (*Iliad* 1.622–26).

for the Sungod kept *his* watch and told Hephaestus all,
so back he rushed to his house, his heart consumed with anguish.
Halting there at the gates, seized with savage rage   345
he howled a terrible cry, imploring all the gods,
"Father Zeus, look here—
the rest of you happy gods who live forever—
here is a sight to make you laugh, revolt you too!
Just because I am crippled, Zeus's daughter Aphrodite   350
will always spurn me and love that devastating Ares,
just because of his stunning looks and racer's legs
while I am a weakling, lame from birth, and who's to blame?
Both my parents—who else? If only they'd never bred me!
Just look at the two lovers . . . crawled inside my bed,   355
locked in each other's arms—the sight makes me burn!
But I doubt they'll want to lie that way much longer,
not a moment more—mad as they are for each other.
No, they'll soon tire of bedding down together,
but then my cunning chains will bind them fast   360
till our Father pays my bride-gifts back in full,
all I handed *him* for that shameless bitch his daughter,
irresistible beauty—all unbridled too!"
                              So Hephaestus wailed
as the gods came crowding up to his bronze-floored house.   365
Poseidon god of the earthquake came, and Hermes came,
the running god of luck, and the Archer, lord Apollo,
while modesty kept each goddess to her mansion.
The immortals, givers of all good things, stood at the gates,
and uncontrollable laughter burst from the happy gods
when they saw the god of fire's subtle, cunning work.   370
One would glance at his neighbor, laughing out,
"A bad day for adultery! Slow outstrips the Swift."

     "Look how limping Hephaestus conquers War,
the quickest of all the gods who rule Olympus!"

     "The cripple wins by craft."
                              "The adulterer,   375
he will pay the price!"
                    So the gods would banter
among themselves but lord Apollo goaded Hermes on:
"Tell me, Quicksilver, giver of all good things—
even with those unwieldy shackles wrapped around you,
how would you like to bed the golden Aphrodite?"   380

     "Oh Apollo, if only!" the giant-killer cried.
"Archer, bind me down with triple those endless chains!
Let all you gods look on, and all you goddesses too—
how I'd love to bed that golden Aphrodite!"

     A peal of laughter broke from the deathless ones   385
but not Poseidon, not a smile from him; he kept on
begging the famous Smith to loose the god of war,

pleading, his words flying, "Let him go!
I guarantee you Ares will pay the price,
whatever you ask, Hephaestus,   390
whatever's right in the eyes of all the gods."

But the famous crippled Smith appealed in turn,
"God of the earthquake, please don't urge this on me.
A pledge for a worthless man is a worthless pledge indeed.
What if he slips out of his chains—his debts as well?   395
How could I shackle *you* while all the gods look on?"

But the god of earthquakes reassured the Smith,
"Look, Hephaestus, if Ares scuttles off and away,
squirming out of his debt, I'll pay the fine myself."

And the famous crippled Smith complied at last: 400
"Now *there's* an offer I really can't refuse!"

With all his force the god of fire loosed the chains
and the two lovers, free of the bonds that overwhelmed them so,
sprang up and away at once, and the Wargod sped to Thrace[4]
while Love with her telltale laughter sped to Paphos,[5]   405
Cyprus Isle, where her grove and scented altar stand.
There the Graces bathed and anointed her with oil,
ambrosial oil, the bloom that clings to the gods
who never die, and swathed her round in gowns
to stop the heart . . . an ecstasy—a vision.   410

That was the song the famous harper sang
and Odysseus relished every note as the islanders,
the lords of the long oars and master mariners rejoiced.

Next the king asked Halius and Laodamas to dance,
the two alone, since none could match that pair.   415
So taking in hand a gleaming sea-blue ball,
made by the craftsman Polybus—arching back,
one prince would hurl it toward the shadowy clouds
as the other leaping high into the air would catch it
quickly, nimbly, before his feet hit ground again.   420
Once they'd vied at throwing the ball straight up,
they tossed it back and forth in a blur of hands
as they danced across the earth that feeds us all,
while boys around the ring stamped out the beat
and a splendid rhythmic drumming sound arose   425
and good Odysseus looked at his host, exclaiming,
"King Alcinous, shining among your island people,
you boasted Phaeacia's dancers are the best—
they prove your point—I watch and I'm amazed!"

---

4. Non-Greek territory to the north; it was thought to be Ares' home.   5. A town on the island of Cyprus
(in the eastern Mediterranean, opposite Syria), where an important cult of Aphrodite was located.

His praises cheered the hallowed island king   430
who spoke at once to the master mariners around him:
"Hear me, my lords and captains of Phaeacia,
our guest is a man of real taste, I'd say. Come,
let's give him the parting gifts a guest deserves.
There are twelve peers of the realm who rule our land,   435
thirteen, counting myself. Let each of us contribute
a fresh cloak and shirt and a bar of precious gold.
Gather the gifts together, hurry, so our guest
can have them all in hand when he goes to dine,
his spirit filled with joy.   440
As for Broadsea, let him make amends,
man-to-man, with his words as well as gifts.
His first remarks were hardly fit to hear."

    All assented and gave their own commands,
each noble sent a page to fetch his gifts.   445
And Broadsea volunteered in turn, obliging:
"Great Alcinous, shining among our island people,
of course I'll make amends to our newfound friend
as you request. I'll give the man this sword.
It's solid bronze and the hilt has silver studs,   450
the sheath around it ivory freshly carved.
Here's a gift our guest will value highly."

    He placed the silver-studded sword in Odysseus' hands
with a burst of warm words: "Farewell, stranger, sir—
if any remark of mine gave you offense,   455
may stormwinds snatch it up and sweep it off!
May the gods grant *you* safe passage home to see your wife—
you've been so far from loved ones, suffered so!"

    Tactful Odysseus answered him in kind:
"And a warm farewell to you, too, my friend.   460
May the gods grant *you* good fortune—
may you never miss this sword, this gift you give
with such salutes. You've made amends in full."

                                          With that
he slung the silver-studded sword across his shoulder.
As the sun sank, his glittering gifts arrived   465
and proud heralds bore them into the hall
where sons of King Alcinous took them over,
spread them out before their noble mother's feet—
a grand array of gifts. The king in all his majesty
led the rest of his peers inside, following in a file   470
and down they sat on rows of high-backed chairs.
The king turned to the queen and urged her, "Come,
my dear, bring in an elegant chest, the best you have,
and lay inside it a fresh cloak and shirt, your own gifts.
Then heat a bronze cauldron over the fire, boil water,   475
so once our guest has bathed and reviewed his gifts—
all neatly stacked for sailing,

gifts our Phaeacian lords have brought him now—
he'll feast in peace and hear the harper's songs.
And I will give him this gorgeous golden cup of mine,   480
so he'll remember Alcinous all his days to come
when he pours libations out in his own house
to Father Zeus and the other gods on high."

    And at that Arete told her serving-women,
"Set a great three-legged cauldron over the fire—   485
do it right away!"
             And hoisting over the blaze
a cauldron, filling it brimful with bathing water,
they piled fresh logs beneath and lit them quickly.
The fire lapped at the vessel's belly, the water warmed.
Meanwhile the queen had a polished chest brought forth   490
from an inner room and laid the priceless gifts inside,
the clothes and gold the Phaeacian lords had brought,
and added her own gifts, a cloak and a fine shirt,
and gave her guest instructions quick and clear:
"Now look to the lid yourself and bind it fast   495
with a good tight knot, so no one can rob you
on your voyage—drifting into a sweet sleep
as the black ship sails you home."
                Hearing that,
the storm-tossed man secured the lid straightway,
he battened it fast with a swift, intricate knot   500
the lady Circe[6] had taught him long ago.
And the housekeeper invited him at once
to climb into a waiting tub and bathe—
a hot, steaming bath . . .
what a welcome sight to Odysseus' eyes!   505
He'd been a stranger to comforts such as these
since he left the lovely-haired Calypso's house,
yet all those years he enjoyed such comforts there,
never-ending, as if he were a god . . . And now,
when maids had washed him, rubbed him down with oil   510
and drawn warm fleece and a shirt around his shoulders,
he stepped from the bath to join the nobles at their wine.
And there stood Nausicaa as he passed. Beside a column
that propped the sturdy roof she paused, endowed
by the gods with all her beauty, gazing at   515
Odysseus right before her eyes. Wonderstruck,
she hailed her guest with a winning flight of words:
"Farewell, my friend! And when you are at home,
home in your own land, remember me at times.
Mainly to me you owe the gift of life."   520

    Odysseus rose to the moment deftly, gently:
"Nausicaa, daughter of generous King Alcinous,
may Zeus the Thunderer, Hera's husband, grant it so—

---

6. A divine sorceress. Odysseus stayed for a year on her island as her lover (book 10).

that I travel home and see the dawn of my return.
Even at home I'll pray to you as a deathless goddess   525
all my days to come. You saved my life, dear girl."

    And he went and took his seat beside the king.
By now they were serving out the portions, mixing wine,
and the herald soon approached, leading the faithful bard
Demodocus, prized by all the people—seated him in a chair   530
amid the feasters, leaning it against a central column.
At once alert Odysseus carved a strip of loin,
rich and crisp with fat, from the white-tusked boar
that still had much meat left, and called the herald over:
"Here, herald, take this choice cut to Demodocus   535
so he can eat his fill—with warm regards
from a man who knows what suffering is . . .
From all who walk the earth our bards deserve
esteem and awe, for the Muse herself has taught them
paths of song. She loves the breed of harpers."   540

    The herald placed the gift in Demodocus' hands
and the famous blind bard received it, overjoyed.
They reached for the good things that lay outspread
and when they'd put aside desire for food and drink,
Odysseus, master of many exploits, praised the singer: 545
"I respect you, Demodocus, more than any man alive—
surely the Muse has taught you, Zeus's daughter,
or god Apollo himself. How true to life,
all too true . . . you sing the Achaeans' fate,
all they did and suffered, all they soldiered through,   550
as if you were there yourself or heard from one who was.
But come now, shift your ground. Sing of the wooden horse
Epeus built with Athena's help, the cunning trap that
good Odysseus brought one day to the heights of Troy,
filled with fighting men who laid the city waste.   555
Sing that for me—true to life as it deserves—
and I will tell the world at once how freely
the Muse gave *you* the gods' own gift of song."

    Stirred now by the Muse, the bard launched out
in a fine blaze of song, starting at just the point   560
where the main Achaean force, setting their camps afire,
had boarded the oarswept ships and sailed for home
but famed Odysseus' men already crouched in hiding—
in the heart of Troy's assembly—dark in that horse
the Trojans dragged themselves to the city heights.   565
Now it stood there, looming . . .
and round its bulk the Trojans sat debating,
clashing, days on end. Three plans split their ranks:
either to hack open the hollow vault with ruthless bronze
or haul it up to the highest ridge and pitch it down the cliffs   570
or let it stand—a glorious offering made to pacify the gods—
and that, that final plan, was bound to win the day.
For Troy was fated to perish once the city lodged

inside her walls the monstrous wooden horse
where the prime of Argive power lay in wait   575
with death and slaughter bearing down on Troy.
And he sang how troops of Achaeans broke from cover,
streaming out of the horse's hollow flanks to plunder Troy—
he sang how left and right they ravaged the steep city,
sang how Odysseus marched right up to Deiphobus' house   580
like the god of war on attack with diehard Menelaus.
There, he sang, Odysseus fought the grimmest fight
he had ever braved but he won through at last,
thanks to Athena's superhuman power.

    That was the song the famous harper sang   585
but great Odysseus melted into tears,
running down from his eyes to wet his cheeks . . .
as a woman weeps, her arms flung round her darling husband,
a man who fell in battle, fighting for town and townsmen,
trying to beat the day of doom from home and children.   590
Seeing the man go down, dying, gasping for breath,
she clings for dear life, screams and shrills—
but the victors, just behind her,
digging spear-butts into her back and shoulders,
drag her off in bondage, yoked to hard labor, pain,   595
and the most heartbreaking torment wastes her cheeks.
So from Odysseus' eyes ran tears of heartbreak now.
But his weeping went unmarked by all the others;
only Alcinous, sitting close beside him,
noticed his guest's tears,   600
heard the groan in the man's labored breathing
and said at once to the master mariners around him,
"Hear me, my lords and captains of Phaeacia!
Let Demodocus rest his ringing lyre now—
this song he sings can hardly please us all.   605
Ever since our meal began and the stirring bard
launched his song, our guest has never paused
in his tears and throbbing sorrow.
Clearly grief has overpowered his heart.
Break off this song! Let us all enjoy ourselves,   610
the hosts and guest together. Much the warmer way.
All these things are performed for him, our honored guest,
the royal send-off here and gifts we give in love.
Treat your guest and suppliant like a brother:
anyone with a touch of sense knows that.   615
So don't be crafty now, my friend, don't hide
the truth I'm after. Fair is fair, speak out!
Come, tell us the name they call you there at home—
your mother, father, townsmen, neighbors round about.
Surely no man in the world is nameless, all told.   620
Born high, born low, as soon as he sees the light
his parents always name him, once he's born.
And tell me your land, your people, your city too,
so our ships can sail you home—their wits will speed them there.

For we have no steersmen here among Phaeacia's crews   625
or steering-oars that guide your common craft.
Our ships know in a flash their mates' intentions,
know all ports of call and all the rich green fields.
With wings of the wind they cross the sea's huge gulfs,
shrouded in mist and cloud—no fear in the world of foundering,   630
fatal shipwreck.
                    True, there's an old tale I heard
my father telling once. Nausithous used to say
that lord Poseidon was vexed with us because
we escorted all mankind and never came to grief.
He said that one day, as a well-built ship of ours   635
sailed home on the misty sea from such a convoy,
the god would crush it, yes,
and pile a huge mountain round about our port.
So the old king foretold . . . And as for the god, well,
he can do his worst or leave it quite undone,   640
whatever warms his heart.
                         But come, my friend,
tell us your own story now, and tell it truly.
Where have your rovings forced you?
What lands of men have you seen, what sturdy towns,
what men themselves? Who were wild, savage, lawless?   645
Who were friendly to strangers, god-fearing men? Tell me,
why do you weep and grieve so sorely when you hear
the fate of the Argives, hear the fall of Troy?
That is the gods' work, spinning threads of death
through the lives of mortal men,   650
and all to make a song for those to come . . .
Did one of your kinsmen die before the walls of Troy,
some brave man—a son by marriage? father by marriage?
Next to our own blood kin, our nearest, dearest ties.
Or a friend perhaps, someone close to your heart,   655
staunch and loyal? No less dear than a brother,
the brother-in-arms who shares our inmost thoughts."

BOOK IX

[In the One-Eyed Giant's Cave]

Odysseus, the great teller of tales, launched out on his story:
"Alcinous, majesty, shining among your island people,
what a fine thing it is to listen to such a bard
as we have here—the man sings like a god.
The crown of life, I'd say. There's nothing better   5
than when deep joy holds sway throughout the realm
and banqueters up and down the palace sit in ranks,
enthralled to hear the bard, and before them all, the tables
heaped with bread and meats, and drawing wine from a mixing-bowl
the steward makes his rounds and keeps the winecups flowing.   10
This, to my mind, is the best that life can offer.
                                        But now
you're set on probing the bitter pains I've borne,

so I'm to weep and grieve, it seems, still more.
Well then, what shall I go through first,
what shall I save for last?   15
What pains—the gods have given me my share.
Now let me begin by telling you my name . . .
so you may know it well and I in times to come,
if I can escape the fatal day, will be your host,
your sworn friend, though my home is far from here.   20
I am Odysseus, son of Laertes, known to the world
for every kind of craft—my fame has reached the skies.
Sunny Ithaca is my home. Atop her stands our seamark,
Mount Neriton's leafy ridges shimmering in the wind.
Around her a ring of islands circle side-by-side,   25
Dulichion, Same, wooded Zacynthus too, but mine
lies low and away, the farthest out to sea,
rearing into the western dusk
while the others face the east and breaking day.
Mine is a rugged land but good for raising sons—   30
and I myself, I know no sweeter sight on earth
than a man's own native country.
                                    True enough,
Calypso the lustrous goddess tried to hold me back,
deep in her arching caverns, craving me for a husband.
So did Circe, holding me just as warmly in her halls,   35
the bewitching queen of Aeaea keen to have me too.
But they never won the heart inside me, never.
So nothing is as sweet as a man's own country,
his own parents, even though he's settled down
in some luxurious house, off in a foreign land   40
and far from those who bore him.
                                    No more. Come,
let me tell you about the voyage fraught with hardship
Zeus inflicted on me, homeward bound from Troy . . .

    The wind drove me out of Ilium on to Ismarus,[7]
the Cicones' stronghold. There I sacked the city,   45
killed the men, but as for the wives and plunder,
that rich haul we dragged away from the place—
we shared it round so no one, not on my account,
would go deprived of his fair share of spoils.
Then I urged them to cut and run, set sail,   50
but would they listen? Not those mutinous fools;
there was too much wine to swill, too many sheep to slaughter
down along the beach, and shambling longhorn cattle.
And all the while the Cicones sought out other Cicones,
called for help from their neighbors living inland: 55
a larger force, and stronger soldiers too,
skilled hands at fighting men from chariots,
skilled, when a crisis broke, to fight on foot.

---

7. In Thrace, on the north of the Aegean Sea. This alone of Odysseus's adventures in books 9 to 12 is set
in the known world. The Cicones were allies of Troy, but Odysseus evidently does not think any justification
of the piratical raid is necessary. *Ilium:* Troy.

Out of the morning mist they came against us—
packed as the leaves and spears that flower forth in spring— 60
and Zeus presented us with disaster, me and my comrades
doomed to suffer blow on mortal blow. Lining up,
both armies battled it out against our swift ships,
both raked each other with hurtling bronze lances.
Long as morning rose and the blessed day grew stronger 65
we stood and fought them off, massed as they were, but then,
when the sun wheeled past the hour for unyoking oxen,
the Cicones broke our lines and beat us down at last.
Out of each ship, six men-at-arms were killed;
the rest of us rowed away from certain doom. 70

From there we sailed on, glad to escape our death
yet sick at heart for the dear companions we had lost.
But I would not let our rolling ships set sail until the crews
had raised the triple cry, saluting each poor comrade
cut down by the fierce Cicones on that plain. 75
Now Zeus who masses the stormclouds hit the fleet
with the North Wind—
                a howling, demonic gale, shrouding over
in thunderheads the earth and sea at once—
                        and night swept down
from the sky and the ships went plunging headlong on,
our sails slashed to rags by the hurricane's blast! 80
We struck them—cringing at death we rowed our ships
to the nearest shoreline, pulled with all our power.
There, for two nights, two days, we lay by, no letup,
eating our hearts out, bent with pain and bone-tired.
When Dawn with her lovely locks brought on the third day, 85
then stepping the masts and hoisting white sails high,
we lounged at the oarlocks, letting wind and helmsmen
keep us true on course . . .
                And now, at long last,
I might have reached my native land unscathed,
but just as I doubled Malea's cape, a tide-rip 90
and the North Wind drove me way off course
careering past Cythera.[8]
                Nine whole days
I was borne along by rough, deadly winds
on the fish-infested sea. Then on the tenth
our squadron reached the land of the Lotus-eaters,[9] 95
people who eat the lotus, mellow fruit and flower.
We disembarked on the coast, drew water there
and crewmen snatched a meal by the swift ships.
Once we'd had our fill of food and drink I sent
a detail ahead, two picked men and a third, a runner, 100
to scout out who might live there—men like us perhaps,

8. A large island off Malea, the southeastern tip of the Peloponnesus.   9. It is generally thought that
this story contains some memory of early Greek contact with North Africa. The north wind Odysseus
describes would have taken him to the area of Cyrenaica, or modern Libya. The lotus has been variously
identified (suggestions range from dates to hashish).

who live on bread? So off they went and soon enough
they mingled among the natives, Lotus-eaters, Lotus-eaters
who had no notion of killing my companions, not at all,
they simply gave them the lotus to taste instead . . .   105
Any crewmen who ate the lotus, the honey-sweet fruit,
lost all desire to send a message back, much less return,
their only wish to linger there with the Lotus-eaters,
grazing on lotus, all memory of the journey home
dissolved forever. But I brought them back, back   110
to the hollow ships, and streaming tears—I forced them,
hauled them under the rowing benches, lashed them fast
and shouted out commands to my other, steady comrades:
'Quick, no time to lose, embark in the racing ships!'—
so none could eat the lotus, forget the voyage home.   115
They swung aboard at once, they sat to the oars in ranks
and in rhythm churned the water white with stroke on stroke.

　　　From there we sailed on, our spirits now at a low ebb,
and reached the land of the high and mighty Cyclops,[1]
lawless brutes, who trust so to the everlasting gods   120
they never plant with their own hands or plow the soil.
Unsown, unplowed, the earth teems with all they need,
wheat, barley and vines, swelled by the rains of Zeus
to yield a big full-bodied wine from clustered grapes.
They have no meeting place for council, no laws either,   125
no, up on the mountain peaks they live in arching caverns—
each a law to himself, ruling his wives and children,
not a care in the world for any neighbor.
　　　　　　　　　　　　　　　　Now,
a level island stretches flat across the harbor,
not close inshore to the Cyclops' coast, not too far out,   130
thick with woods where the wild goats breed by hundreds.
No trampling of men to start them from their lairs,
no hunters roughing it out on the woody ridges,
stalking quarry, ever raid their haven.
No flocks browse, no plowlands roll with wheat;   135
unplowed, unsown forever—empty of humankind—
the island just feeds droves of bleating goats.
For the Cyclops have no ships with crimson prows,[2]
no shipwrights there to build them good trim craft
that could sail them out to foreign ports of call   140
as most men risk the seas to trade with other men.
Such artisans would have made this island too
a decent place to live in . . . No mean spot,
it could bear you any crop you like in season.
The water-meadows along the low foaming shore   145
run soft and moist, and your vines would never flag.
The land's clear for plowing. Harvest on harvest,

---

1. Sicily, according to post-Homeric tradition.　　2. Greek ships were painted red on the bows and could
be decorated with an emblem (often shown on vase paintings as a huge eye).

a man could reap a healthy stand of grain—
the subsoil's dark and rich.
There's a snug deep-water harbor there, what's more, 150
no need for mooring-gear, no anchor-stones to heave,
no cables to make fast. Just beach your keels, ride out
the days till your shipmates' spirit stirs for open sea
and a fair wind blows. And last, at the harbor's head
there's a spring that rushes fresh from beneath a cave 155
and black poplars flourish round its mouth.
                                        Well,
here we landed, and surely a god steered us in
through the pitch-black night.
Not that he ever showed himself, with thick fog
swirling around the ships, the moon wrapped in clouds 160
and not a glimmer stealing through that gloom.
Not one of us glimpsed the island—scanning hard—
or the long combers rolling us slowly toward the coast,
not till our ships had run their keels ashore.
Beaching our vessels smoothly, striking sail, 165
the crews swung out on the low shelving sand
and there we fell asleep, awaiting Dawn's first light.

        When young Dawn with her rose-red fingers shone once more
we all turned out, intrigued to tour the island.
The local nymphs, the daughters of Zeus himself, 170
flushed mountain-goats so the crews could make their meal.
Quickly we fetched our curved bows and hunting spears
from the ships and, splitting up into three bands,
we started shooting, and soon enough some god
had sent us bags of game to warm our hearts. 175
A dozen vessels sailed in my command
and to each crew nine goats were shared out
and mine alone took ten. Then all day long
till the sun went down we sat and feasted well
on sides of meat and rounds of heady wine. 180
The good red stock in our vessels' holds
had not run out, there was still plenty left;
the men had carried off a generous store in jars
when we stormed and sacked the Cicones' holy city.
Now we stared across at the Cyclops' shore, so near 185
we could even see their smoke, hear their voices,
their bleating sheep and goats . . .
And then when the sun had set and night came on
we lay down and slept at the water's shelving edge.
When young Dawn with her rose-red fingers shone once more 190
I called a muster briskly, commanding all the hands,
'The rest of you stay here, my friends-in-arms.
I'll go across with my own ship and crew
and probe the natives living over there.
What *are* they—violent, savage, lawless? 195
or friendly to strangers, god-fearing men?'

With that I boarded ship and told the crew
to embark at once and cast off cables quickly.
They swung aboard, they sat to the oars in ranks
and in rhythm churned the water white with stroke on stroke.   200
But as soon as we reached the coast I mentioned—no long trip—
we spied a cavern just at the shore, gaping above the surf,
towering, overgrown with laurel. And here big flocks,
sheep and goats, were stalled to spend the nights,
and around its mouth a yard was walled up   205
with quarried boulders sunk deep in the earth
and enormous pines and oak-trees looming darkly . . .
Here was a giant's lair, in fact, who always pastured
his sheepflocks far afield and never mixed with others.
A grim loner, dead set in his own lawless ways.   210
Here was a piece of work, by god, a monster
built like no mortal who ever supped on bread,
no, like a shaggy peak, I'd say—a man-mountain
rearing head and shoulders over the world.

                                      Now then,
I told most of my good trusty crew to wait,   215
to sit tight by the ship and guard her well
while I picked out my dozen finest fighters
and off I went. But I took a skin of wine along,
the ruddy, irresistible wine that Maron gave me once,
Euanthes' son, a priest of Apollo, lord of Ismarus,   220
because we'd rescued him, his wife and children,
reverent as we were;
he lived, you see, in Apollo's holy grove.
And so in return he gave me splendid gifts,
he handed me seven bars of well-wrought gold,   225
a mixing-bowl of solid silver, then this wine . . .
He drew it off in generous wine-jars, twelve in all,
all unmixed—and such a bouquet, a drink fit for the gods!
No maid or man of his household knew that secret store,
only himself, his loving wife and a single servant.   230
Whenever they'd drink the deep-red mellow vintage,
twenty cups of water he'd stir in one of wine[3]
and what an aroma wafted from the bowl—
what magic, what a godsend—
no joy in holding back when *that* was poured!   235
Filling a great goatskin now, I took this wine,
provisions too in a leather sack. A sudden foreboding
told my fighting spirit I'd soon come up against
some giant clad in power like armor-plate—
a savage deaf to justice, blind to law.   240

    Our party quickly made its way to his cave
but we failed to find our host himself inside;
he was off in his pasture, ranging his sleek flocks.

---

3. The Greeks regularly mixed water with their wine, but the extraordinarily high ratio of water to wine
mentioned here (20:1) shows how strong this wine is.

So we explored his den, gazing wide-eyed at it all,
the large flat racks loaded with drying cheeses,   245
the folds crowded with young lambs and kids,
split into three groups—here the spring-born,
here mid-yearlings, here the fresh sucklings
off to the side—each sort was penned apart.
And all his vessels, pails and hammered buckets   250
he used for milking, were brimming full with whey.
From the start my comrades pressed me, pleading hard,
'Let's make away with the cheeses, then come back—
hurry, drive the lambs and kids from the pens
to our swift ship, put out to sea at once!'   255
But I would not give way—
and how much better it would have been—
not till I saw him, saw what gifts he'd give.
But he proved no lovely sight to my companions.

There we built a fire, set our hands on the cheeses,   260
offered some to the gods and ate the bulk ourselves
and settled down inside, awaiting his return . . .
And back he came from pasture, late in the day,
herding his flocks home, and lugging a huge load
of good dry logs to fuel his fire at supper.   265
He flung them down in the cave—a jolting crash—
we scuttled in panic into the deepest dark recess.
And next he drove his sleek flocks into the open vault,
all he'd milk at least, but he left the males outside,
rams and billy goats out in the high-walled yard.   270
Then to close his door he hoisted overhead
a tremendous, massive slab—
no twenty-two wagons, rugged and four-wheeled,
could budge that boulder off the ground, I tell you,
such an immense stone the monster wedged to block his cave!   275
Then down he squatted to milk his sheep and bleating goats,
each in order, and put a suckling underneath each dam.
And half of the fresh white milk he curdled quickly,
set it aside in wicker racks to press for cheese,
the other half let stand in pails and buckets,   280
ready at hand to wash his supper down.
As soon as he'd briskly finished all his chores
he lit his fire and spied us in the blaze and
'Strangers!' he thundered out, 'now who are you?
Where did you sail from, over the running sea-lanes?   285
Out on a trading spree or roving the waves like pirates,
sea-wolves raiding at will, who risk their lives
to plunder other men?'
                        The hearts inside us shook,
terrified by his rumbling voice and monstrous hulk.
Nevertheless I found the nerve to answer, firmly,   290
'Men of Achaea we are and bound now from Troy!
Driven far off course by the warring winds,
over the vast gulf of the sea—battling home

on a strange tack, a route that's off the map,
and so we've come to you . . .   295
so it must please King Zeus's plotting heart.
We're glad to say we're men of Atrides Agamemnon,
whose fame is the proudest thing on earth these days,
so great a city he sacked, such multitudes he killed!
But since we've chanced on you, we're at your knees   300
in hopes of a warm welcome, even a guest-gift,
the sort that hosts give strangers. That's the custom.
Respect the gods, my friend. We're suppliants—at your mercy!⁴
Zeus of the Strangers guards all guests and suppliants:
strangers are sacred—Zeus will avenge their rights!'   305

  'Stranger,' he grumbled back from his brutal heart,
'you must be a fool, stranger, or come from nowhere,
telling *me* to fear the gods or avoid their wrath!
We Cyclops never blink at Zeus and Zeus's shield
of storm and thunder, or any other blessed god—   310
we've got more force by far.
I'd never spare you in fear of Zeus's hatred,
you or your comrades here, unless I had the urge.
But tell me, where did you moor your sturdy ship
when you arrived? Up the coast or close in?   315
I'd just like to know.'
                    So he laid his trap
but he never caught me, no, wise to the world
I shot back in my crafty way, 'My ship?
Poseidon god of the earthquake smashed my ship,
he drove it against the rocks at your island's far cape,   320
he dashed it against a cliff as the winds rode us in.
I and the men you see escaped a sudden death.'

  Not a word in reply to that, the ruthless brute.
Lurching up, he lunged out with his hands toward my men
and snatching two at once, rapping them on the ground   325
he knocked them dead like pups—
their brains gushed out all over, soaked the floor—
and ripping them limb from limb to fix his meal
he bolted them down like a mountain-lion, left no scrap,
devoured entrails, flesh and bones, marrow and all!   330
We flung our arms to Zeus, we wept and cried aloud,
looking on at his grisly work—paralyzed, appalled.
But once the Cyclops had stuffed his enormous gut
with human flesh, washing it down with raw milk,
he slept in his cave, stretched out along his flocks.   335
And I with my fighting heart, I thought at first
to steal up to him, draw the sharp sword at my hip
and stab his chest where the midriff packs the liver—
I groped for the fatal spot but a fresh thought held me back.

---

4. In the *Odyssey*, the civilized (such as Menelaus and Alcinous) welcome strangers and send them on their way with gifts. In fact, as Odysseus says to the Cyclops, hospitality is a religious duty.

There at a stroke we'd finish off ourselves as well—   340
how could *we* with our bare hands heave back
that slab he set to block his cavern's gaping maw?
So we lay there groaning, waiting Dawn's first light.

When young Dawn with her rose-red fingers shone once more
the monster relit his fire and milked his handsome ewes,   345
each in order, putting a suckling underneath each dam,
and as soon as he'd briskly finished all his chores
he snatched up two more men and fixed his meal.
Well-fed, he drove his fat sheep from the cave,
lightly lifting the huge doorslab up and away,   350
then slipped it back in place
as a hunter flips the lid of his quiver shut.
Piercing whistles—turning his flocks to the hills
he left me there, the heart inside me brooding on revenge:
how could I pay him back? would Athena give me glory?   355
Here was the plan that struck my mind as best . . .
the Cyclops' great club: there it lay by the pens,
olivewood, full of sap. He'd lopped it off to brandish
once it dried. Looking it over, we judged it big enough
to be the mast of a pitch-black ship with her twenty oars,   360
a freighter broad in the beam that plows through miles of sea—
so long, so thick it bulked before our eyes. Well,
flanking it now, I chopped off a fathom's length,
rolled it to comrades, told them to plane it down,
and they made the club smooth as I bent and shaved   365
the tip to a stabbing point. I turned it over
the blazing fire to char it good and hard,
then hid it well, buried deep under the dung
that littered the cavern's floor in thick wet clumps.
And now I ordered my shipmates all to cast lots—   370
who'd brave it out with me
to hoist our stake and grind it into his eye
when sleep had overcome him? Luck of the draw:
I got the very ones I would have picked myself,
four good men, and I in the lead made five . . .   375

Nightfall brought him back, herding his woolly sheep
and he quickly drove the sleek flock into the vaulted cavern,
rams and all—none left outside in the walled yard—
his own idea, perhaps, or a god led him on.
Then he hoisted the huge slab to block the door   380
and squatted to milk his sheep and bleating goats,
each in order, putting a suckling underneath each dam,
and as soon as he'd briskly finished all his chores
he snatched up two more men and fixed his meal.
But this time I lifted a carved wooden bowl,   385
brimful of my ruddy wine,
and went right up to the Cyclops, enticing,
'Here, Cyclops, try this wine—to top off
the banquet of human flesh you've bolted down!

Judge for yourself what stock our ship had stored.   390
I brought it here to make you a fine libation,
hoping you would pity me, Cyclops, send me home,
but your rages are insufferable. You barbarian—
how can any man on earth come visit you after *this*?
What you've done outrages all that's right!'   395

    At that he seized the bowl and tossed it off⁵
and the heady wine pleased him immensely—'More'—
he demanded a second bowl—'a hearty helping!
And tell me your name now, quickly,
so I can hand my guest a gift to warm *his* heart.   400
Our soil yields the Cyclops powerful, full-bodied wine
and the rains from Zeus build its strength. But this,
this is nectar, ambrosia—this flows from heaven!'

    So he declared. I poured him another fiery bowl—
three bowls I brimmed and three he drank to the last drop,   405
the fool, and then, when the wine was swirling round his brain,
I approached my host with a cordial, winning word:
'So, you ask me the name I'm known by, Cyclops?
I will tell you. But you must give me a guest-gift
as you've promised. Nobody—that's my name. Nobody—   410
so my mother and father call me all, my friends.'

    But he boomed back at me from his ruthless heart,
'Nobody? I'll eat Nobody last of all his friends—
I'll eat the others first! That's my gift to *you*!'
                                        With that
he toppled over, sprawled full-length, flat on his back   415
and lay there, his massive neck slumping to one side,
and sleep that conquers all overwhelmed him now
as wine came spurting, flooding up from his gullet
with chunks of human flesh—he vomited, blind drunk.
Now, at last, I thrust our stake in a bed of embers   420
to get it red-hot and rallied all my comrades:
'Courage—no panic, no one hang back now!'
And green as it was, just as the olive stake
was about to catch fire—the glow terrific, yes—
I dragged it from the flames, my men clustering round   425
as some god breathed enormous courage through us all.
Hoisting high that olive stake with its stabbing point,
straight into the monster's eye they rammed it hard—
I drove my weight on it from above and bored it home
as a shipwright bores his beam with a shipwright's drill   430
that men below, whipping the strap back and forth, whirl
and the drill keeps twisting faster, never stopping—
So we seized our stake with its fiery tip
and bored it round and round in the giant's eye
till blood came boiling up around that smoking shaft   435

5. That the Cyclops drinks this strong wine neat both conveniently gets him drunk and marks him as a savage (in the Greek view, drinking undiluted wine demonstrated a lack of the self-restraint they prized).

and the hot blast singed his brow and eyelids round the core
and the broiling eyeball burst—
                                     its crackling roots blazed
and hissed—
                  as a blacksmith plunges a glowing ax or adze
in an ice-cold bath and the metal screeches steam
and its temper hardens—that's the iron's strength—
so the eye of the Cyclops sizzled round that stake!   440
He loosed a hideous roar, the rock walls echoed round
and we scuttled back in terror. The monster wrenched the spike
from his eye and out it came with a red geyser of blood—
he flung it aside with frantic hands, and mad with pain   445
he bellowed out for help from his neighbor Cyclops
living round about in caves on windswept crags.
Hearing his cries, they lumbered up from every side
and hulking round his cavern, asked what ailed him:
'What, Polyphemus, what in the world's the trouble?   450
Roaring out in the godsent night to rob us of our sleep.
Surely no one's rustling your flocks against your will—
surely no one's trying to kill you now by fraud or force!'

     'Nobody, friends'—Polyphemus bellowed back from his cave—
'Nobody's killing me now by fraud and not by force!'   455

     'If you're alone,' his friends boomed back at once,
'and nobody's trying to overpower you now—look,
it must be a plague sent here by mighty Zeus
and there's no escape from that.
You'd better pray to your father, Lord Poseidon.'   460

     They lumbered off, but laughter filled my heart
to think how nobody's name—my great cunning stroke—
had duped them one and all.[6] But the Cyclops there,
still groaning, racked with agony, groped around
for the huge slab, and heaving it from the doorway,   465
down he sat in the cave's mouth, his arms spread wide,
hoping to catch a comrade stealing out with sheep—
such a blithering fool he took me for!
But I was already plotting . . .
what was the best way out? how could I find   470
escape from death for my crew, myself as well?
My wits kept weaving, weaving cunning schemes—
life at stake, monstrous death staring us in the face—
till this plan struck my mind as best. That flock,
those well-fed rams with their splendid thick fleece,   475
sturdy, handsome beasts sporting their dark weight of wool:
I lashed them abreast, quietly, twisting the willow-twigs

6. In the Greek, an elaborate pun comes to fruition here. Odysseus has told the Cyclops that his name is
Outis, identical to the word for "nobody" except for a difference in the pitch at which the first syllable was
pronounced. The other Cyclops, misunderstanding, reply to Polyphemus using another term for "nobody,"
mē tis, which Odysseus echoes in referring to his "great cunning stroke," or *mētis* (again, differing only in
the pitch of the first syllable). This word, which means "craft" in senses that range from guile to skill at
craftsmanship, is persistently associated with Odysseus.

the Cyclops slept on—giant, lawless brute—I took them
three by three; each ram in the middle bore a man
while the two rams either side would shield him well.   480
So three beasts to bear each man, but as for myself?
There was one bellwether ram, the prize of all the flock,
and clutching him by his back, tucked up under
his shaggy belly, there I hung, face upward,
both hands locked in his marvelous deep fleece,   485
clinging for dear life, my spirit steeled, enduring . . .
So we held on, desperate, waiting Dawn's first light.
                                        As soon
as young Dawn with her rose-red fingers shone once more
the rams went rumbling out of the cave toward pasture,
the ewes kept bleating round the pens, unmilked,   490
their udders about to burst. Their master now,
heaving in torment, felt the back of each animal
halting before him here, but the idiot never sensed
my men were trussed up under their thick fleecy ribs.
And last of them all came my great ram now, striding out,   495
weighed down with his dense wool and my deep plots.
Stroking him gently, powerful Polyphemus murmured,
'Dear old ram, why last of the flock to quit the cave?
In the good old days you'd never lag behind the rest—
you with your long marching strides, first by far   500
of the flock to graze the fresh young grasses,
first by far to reach the rippling streams,
first to turn back home, keen for your fold
when night comes on—but now you're last of all.
And why? Sick at heart for your master's eye   505
that coward gouged out with his wicked crew?—
only after he'd stunned my wits with wine—
that, that Nobody . . .
who's not escaped his death, I swear, not yet.
Oh if only you thought like *me*, had words like *me*   510
to tell me where that scoundrel is cringing from my rage!
I'd smash him against the ground, I'd spill his brains—
flooding across my cave—and that would ease my heart
of the pains that good-for-nothing Nobody made me suffer!'

    And with that threat he let my ram go free outside.   515
But soon as we'd got one foot past cave and courtyard,
first I loosed myself from the ram, then loosed my men,
then quickly, glancing back again and again we drove
our flock, good plump beasts with their long shanks,
straight to the ship, and a welcome sight we were   520
to loyal comrades—we who'd escaped our deaths—
but for all the rest they broke down and wailed.
I cut it short, I stopped each shipmate's cries,
my head tossing, brows frowning, silent signals
to hurry, tumble our fleecy herd on board,   525
launch out on the open sea!
They swung aboard, they sat to the oars in ranks

and in rhythm churned the water white with stroke on stroke.
But once offshore as far as a man's shout can carry,
I called back to the Cyclops, stinging taunts: 530
'So, Cyclops, no weak coward it was whose crew
you bent to devour there in your vaulted cave—
you with your brute force! Your filthy crimes
came down on your own head, you shameless cannibal,
daring to eat your guests in your own house—   535
so Zeus and the other gods have paid you back!'

    That made the rage of the monster boil over.
Ripping off the peak of a towering crag, he heaved it
so hard the boulder landed just in front of our dark prow
and a huge swell reared up as the rock went plunging under—   540
a tidal wave from the open sea. The sudden backwash
drove us landward again, forcing us close inshore
but grabbing a long pole, I thrust us off and away,
tossing my head for dear life, signaling crews
to put their backs in the oars, escape grim death.   545
They threw themselves in the labor, rowed on fast
but once we'd plowed the breakers twice as far,
again I began to taunt the Cyclops—men around me
trying to check me, calm me, left and right:
'So headstrong—why? Why rile the beast again?'   550

   'That rock he flung in the sea just now, hurling our ship
to shore once more—we thought we'd die on the spot!'

   'If he'd caught a sound from one of us, just a moan,
he would have crushed our heads and ship timbers
with one heave of another flashing, jagged rock!'   555

   'Good god, the brute can throw!'
                   So they begged
but they could not bring my fighting spirit round.
I called back with another burst of anger, 'Cyclops—
if any man on the face of the earth should ask you
who blinded you, shamed you so—say Odysseus,   560
raider of cities, *he* gouged out your eye,
Laertes' son who makes his home in Ithaca!'

   So I vaunted and he groaned back in answer,
'Oh no, no—that prophecy years ago . . .
it all comes home to me with a vengeance now!   565
We once had a prophet here, a great tall man,
Telemus, Eurymus' son, a master at reading signs,
who grew old in his trade among his fellow-Cyclops.
All this, he warned me, would come to pass someday—
that I'd be blinded here at the hands of one Odysseus.   570
But I always looked for a handsome giant man to cross my path,
some fighter clad in power like armor-plate, but now,
look what a dwarf, a spineless good-for-nothing,

stuns me with wine, then gouges out my eye!
Come here, Odysseus, let me give you a guest-gift   575
and urge Poseidon the earthquake god to speed you home.
I am his son and he claims to be my father, true,
and he himself will heal me if he pleases—
no other blessed god, no man can do the work!'

                'Heal you!'—
here was my parting shot—'Would to god I could strip you   580
of life and breath and ship you down to the House of Death
as surely as no one will ever heal your eye,
not even your earthquake god himself!'

   But at that he bellowed out to lord Poseidon,
thrusting his arms to the starry skies, and prayed, 'Hear me—   585
Poseidon, god of the sea-blue mane who rocks the earth!
If I really am your son and you claim to be my father—
come, grant that Odysseus, raider of cities,
Laertes' son who makes his home in Ithaca,
never reaches home. Or if he's fated to see   590
his people once again and reach his well-built house
and his own native country, let him come home late
and come a broken man—all shipmates lost,
alone in a stranger's ship—
and let him find a world of pain at home!'

                   So he prayed   595
and the god of the sea-blue mane Poseidon heard his prayer.
The monster suddenly hoisted a boulder—far larger—
wheeled and heaved it, putting his weight behind it,
massive strength, and the boulder crashed close,
landing just in the wake of our dark stern,   600
just failing to graze the rudder's bladed edge.
A huge swell reared up as the rock went plunging under,
yes, and the tidal breaker drove us out to our island's
far shore where all my well-decked ships lay moored,
clustered, waiting, and huddled round them, crewmen   605
sat in anguish, waiting, chafing for our return.
We beached our vessel hard ashore on the sand,
we swung out in the frothing surf ourselves,
and herding Cyclops' sheep from our deep holds
we shared them round so no one, not on my account,   610
would go deprived of his fair share of spoils.
But the splendid ram—as we meted out the flocks
my friends-in-arms made him my prize of honor,
mine alone, and I slaughtered him on the beach
and burnt his thighs to Cronus' mighty son,   615
Zeus of the thundercloud who rules the world.
But my sacrifices failed to move the god:
Zeus was still obsessed with plans to destroy
my entire oarswept fleet and loyal crew of comrades.
Now all day long till the sun went down we sat   620
and feasted on sides of meat and heady wine.
Then when the sun had set and night came on

THE ODYSSEY / 315

we lay down and slept at the water's shelving edge.
When young Dawn with her rose-red fingers shone once more
I roused the men straightway, ordering all crews   625
to man the ships and cast off cables quickly.
They swung aboard at once, they sat to the oars in ranks
and in rhythm churned the water white with stroke on stroke.
And from there we sailed on, glad to escape our death
yet sick at heart for the comrades we had lost."   630

BOOK X

[The Bewitching Queen of Aeaea]

"We reached the Aeolian island next, the home of Aeolus,[7]
Hippotas' son, beloved by the gods who never die—
a great floating island it was, and round it all
huge ramparts rise of indestructible bronze
and sheer rock cliffs shoot up from sea to sky.   5
The king had sired twelve children within his halls,
six daughters and six sons in the lusty prime of youth,
so he gave his daughters as wives to his six sons.
Seated beside their dear father and doting mother,
with delicacies aplenty spread before them,   10
they feast on forever . . . All day long
the halls breathe the savor of roasted meats
and echo round to the low moan of blowing pipes,
and all night long, each one by his faithful mate,
they sleep under soft-piled rugs on corded bedsteads.   15
To this city of theirs we came, their splendid palace,
and Aeolus hosted me one entire month, he pressed me for news
of Troy and the Argive ships and how we sailed for home,
and I told him the whole long story, first to last.
And then, when I begged him to send me on my way,   20
he denied me nothing, he went about my passage.
He gave me a sack, the skin of a full-grown ox,
binding inside the winds that howl from every quarter,
for Zeus had made that king the master of all the winds,
with power to calm them down or rouse them as he pleased.   25
Aeolus stowed the sack inside my holds, lashed so fast
with a burnished silver cord
not even a slight puff could slip past that knot.
Yet he set the West Wind free to blow us on our way
and waft our squadron home. But his plan was bound to fail,   30
yes, our own reckless folly swept us on to ruin . . .

    Nine whole days we sailed, nine nights, nonstop.
On the tenth our own land hove into sight at last—
we were so close we could see men tending fires.
But now an enticing sleep came on me, bone-weary   35

---

7. King of the winds; his name in Greek means "shifting, changeable." Aeolia has been placed by modern geographers in the Lipari Islands off the Sicilian coast, but the great ancient geographer Eratosthenes observed that we would know exactly where Odysseus wandered after we had traced the leatherworker who made the bag in which the winds were contained.

from working the vessel's sheet myself, no letup,
never trusting the ropes to any other mate,
the faster to journey back to native land.
But the crews began to mutter among themselves,
sure I was hauling troves of gold and silver home,   40
the gifts of open-hearted Aeolus, Hippotas' son.
'The old story!' One man glanced at another, grumbling.
'Look at our captain's luck—so loved by the world,
so prized at every landfall, every port of call.'

'Heaps of lovely plunder he hauls home from Troy,   45
while we who went through slogging just as hard,
we go home empty-handed.'
                    'Now this Aeolus loads him
down with treasure. Favoritism, friend to friend!'

'Hurry, let's see what loot is in that sack,
how much gold and silver. Break it open—now!'   50

A fatal plan, but it won my shipmates over.
They loosed the sack and all the winds burst out
and a sudden squall struck and swept us back to sea,
wailing, in tears, far from our own native land.
And I woke up with a start, my spirit churning—   55
should I leap over the side and drown at once or
grit my teeth and bear it, stay among the living?
I bore it all, held firm, hiding my face,
clinging tight to the decks
while heavy squalls blasted our squadron back   60
again to Aeolus' island, shipmates groaning hard.

We disembarked on the coast, drew water there
and crewmen snatched a meal by the swift ships.
Once we'd had our fill of food and drink
I took a shipmate along with me, a herald too,   65
and approached King Aeolus' famous halls and here
we found him feasting beside his wife and many children.
Reaching the doorposts at the threshold, down we sat
but our hosts, amazed to see us, only shouted questions:
'Back again, Odysseus—why? Some blustering god attacked you? 70
Surely we launched you well, we sped you on your way
to your own land and house, or any place you pleased.'

So they taunted, and I replied in deep despair,
'A mutinous crew undid me—that and a cruel sleep.
Set it to rights, my friends. You have the power!'   75

So I pleaded—gentle, humble appeals—
but our hosts turned silent, hushed . . .
and the father broke forth with an ultimatum:
'Away from my island—fast—most cursed man alive!
It's a crime to host a man or speed him on his way   80

when the blessed deathless gods despise him so.
Crawling back like this—
it proves the immortals hate you! Out—get out!'

    Groan as I did, his curses drove me from his halls
and from there we pulled away with heavy hearts,   85
with the crews' spirit broken under the oars' labor,
thanks to our own folly . . . no favoring wind in sight.

    Six whole days we rowed, six nights, nonstop.
On the seventh day we raised the Laestrygonian land,
Telepylus heights where the craggy fort of Lamus[8] rises.   90
Where shepherd calls to shepherd as one drives in his flocks
and the other drives his out and he calls back in answer,
where a man who never sleeps could rake in double wages,
one for herding cattle, one for pasturing fleecy sheep,
the nightfall and the sunrise march so close together.[9]   95
We entered a fine harbor there, all walled around
by a great unbroken sweep of sky-scraping cliff
and two steep headlands, fronting each other, close
around the mouth so the passage in is cramped.
Here the rest of my rolling squadron steered,   100
right into the gaping cove and moored tightly,
prow by prow. Never a swell there, big or small;
a milk-white calm spreads all around the place.
But I alone anchored my black ship outside,
well clear of the harbor's jaws   105
I tied her fast to a cliffside with a cable.
I scaled its rock face to a lookout on its crest
but glimpsed no trace of the work of man or beast from there;
all I spied was a plume of smoke, drifting off the land.
So I sent some crew ahead to learn who lived there—   110
men like us perhaps, who live on bread?
Two good mates I chose and a third to run the news.
They disembarked and set out on a beaten trail
the wagons used for hauling timber down to town
from the mountain heights above . . .   115
and before the walls they met a girl, drawing water,
Antiphates' strapping daughter—king of the Laestrygonians.
She'd come down to a clear running spring, Artacia,
where the local people came to fill their pails.
My shipmates clustered round her, asking questions: 120
who was king of the realm? who ruled the natives here?
She waved at once to her father's high-roofed halls.
They entered the sumptuous palace, found his wife inside—
a woman huge as a mountain crag who filled them all with horror.
Straightaway she summoned royal Antiphates from assembly,   125
her husband, who prepared my crew a barbarous welcome.
Snatching one of my men, he tore him up for dinner—

8. Presumably the founder of the city of the Laestrygonians.   9. Generally thought to be a confused reference to the short summer nights of the far north.

the other two sprang free and reached the ships.
But the king let loose a howling through the town
that brought tremendous Laestrygonians swarming up   130
from every side—hundreds, not like men, like Giants!
Down from the cliffs they flung great rocks a man could hardly hoist
and a ghastly shattering din rose up from all the ships—
men in their death-cries, hulls smashed to splinters—
They speared the crews like fish   135
and whisked them home to make their grisly meal.
But while they killed them off in the harbor depths
I pulled the sword from beside my hip and hacked away
at the ropes that moored my blue-prowed ship of war
and shouted rapid orders at my shipmates: 140
'Put your backs in the oars—now row or die!'
In terror of death they ripped the swells—all as one—
and what a joy as we darted out toward open sea,
clear of those beetling cliffs . . . my ship alone.
But the rest went down en masse. Our squadron sank.   145

    From there we sailed on, glad to escape our death
yet sick at heart for the dear companions we had lost.
We reached the Aeaean island next, the home of Circe
the nymph with lovely braids, an awesome power too
who can speak with human voice,   150
the true sister of murderous-minded Aeetes.[1]
Both were bred by the Sun who lights our lives;
their mother was Perse, a child the Ocean bore.
We brought our ship to port without a sound
as a god eased her into a harbor safe and snug,   155
and for two days and two nights we lay by there,
eating our hearts out, bent with pain and bone-tired.
When Dawn with her lovely locks brought on the third day,
at last I took my spear and my sharp sword again,
rushed up from the ship to find a lookout point,   160
hoping to glimpse some sign of human labor,
catch some human voices . . .
I scaled a commanding crag and, scanning hard,
I could just make out some smoke from Circe's halls,
drifting up from the broad terrain through brush and woods.   165
Mulling it over, I thought I'd scout the ground—
that fire aglow in the smoke, I saw it, true,
but soon enough this seemed the better plan:
I'd go back to shore and the swift ship first,
feed the men, then send *them* out for scouting.   170
I was well on my way down, nearing our ship
when a god took pity on me, wandering all alone;
he sent me a big stag with high branching antlers,
right across my path—the sun's heat forced him down

---

1. King of Colchis, on the Black Sea, and owner of the Golden Fleece. It is widely believed that Odysseus's wanderings in the *Odyssey* were patterned after the voyage of Jason and the Argonauts, heroes of an earlier generation, in quest of the fleece.

from his forest range to drink at a river's banks— 175
just bounding out of the timber when I hit him
square in the backbone, halfway down the spine
and my bronze spear went punching clean through—
he dropped in the dust, groaning, gasping out his breath.
Treading on him, I wrenched my bronze spear from the wound, 180
left it there on the ground, and snapping off some twigs
and creepers, twisted a rope about a fathom long,
I braided it tight, hand over hand, then lashed
the four hocks of that magnificent beast.
Loaded round my neck I lugged him toward the ship, 185
trudging, propped on my spear—no way to sling him
over a shoulder, steadying him with one free arm—
the kill was so immense!
I flung him down by the hull and roused the men,
going up to them all with a word to lift their spirits: 190
'Listen to me, my comrades, brothers in hardship—
we won't go down to the House of Death, not yet,
not till our day arrives. Up with you, look,
there's still some meat and drink in our good ship.
Put our minds on food—why die of hunger here?' 195

   My hardy urging brought them round at once.
Heads came up from cloaks and there by the barren sea
they gazed at the stag, their eyes wide—my noble trophy.
But once they'd looked their fill and warmed their hearts,
they washed their hands and prepared a splendid meal. 200
Now all day long till the sun went down we sat
and feasted on sides of meat and seasoned wine.
Then when the sun had set and night came on
we lay down and slept at the water's shelving edge.
When young Dawn with her rose-red fingers shone once more 205
I called a muster quickly, informing all the crew,
'Listen to me, my comrades, brothers in hardship,
we can't tell east from west, the dawn from the dusk,
nor where the sun that lights our lives goes under earth
nor where it rises. We must think of a plan at once, 210
some cunning stroke. I doubt there's one still left.
I scaled a commanding crag and from that height
surveyed an entire island
ringed like a crown by endless wastes of sea.
But the land itself lies low, and I did see smoke 215
drifting up from its heart through thick brush and woods.'

   My message broke their spirit as they recalled
the gruesome work of the Laestrygonian king Antiphates
and the hearty cannibal Cyclops thirsting for our blood.
They burst into cries, wailing, streaming live tears 220
that gained us nothing—what good can come of grief?

   And so, numbering off my band of men-at-arms
into two platoons, I assigned them each a leader:

I took one and lord Eurylochus the other.
We quickly shook lots in a bronze helmet—   225
the lot of brave Eurylochus leapt out first.
So he moved off with his two and twenty comrades,
weeping, leaving us behind in tears as well . . .
Deep in the wooded glens they came on Circe's palace
built of dressed stone on a cleared rise of land.   230
Mountain wolves and lions were roaming round the grounds—
she'd bewitched them herself, she gave them magic drugs.
But they wouldn't attack my men; they just came pawing
up around them, fawning, swishing their long tails—
eager as hounds that fawn around their master,   235
coming home from a feast,
who always brings back scraps to calm them down.
So they came nuzzling round my men—lions, wolves
with big powerful claws—and the men cringed in fear
at the sight of those strange, ferocious beasts . . . But still   240
they paused at her doors, the nymph with lovely braids,
Circe—and deep inside they heard her singing, lifting
her spellbinding voice as she glided back and forth
at her great immortal loom, her enchanting web
a shimmering glory only goddesses can weave.   245
Polites, captain of armies, took command,
the closest, most devoted man I had: 'Friends,
there's someone inside, plying a great loom,
and how she sings—enthralling!
The whole house is echoing to her song.   250
Goddess or woman—let's call out to her now!'

So he urged and the men called out and hailed her.
She opened her gleaming doors at once and stepped forth,
inviting them all in, and in they went, all innocence.
Only Eurylochus stayed behind—he sensed a trap . . .   255
She ushered them in to sit on high-backed chairs,
then she mixed them a potion—cheese, barley
and pale honey mulled in Pramnian wine—[2]
but into the brew she stirred her wicked drugs
to wipe from their memories any thought of home.   260
Once they'd drained the bowls she filled, suddenly
she struck with her wand, drove them into her pigsties,
all of them bristling into swine—with grunts,
snouts—even their bodies, yes, and only
the men's minds stayed steadfast as before.   265
So off they went to their pens, sobbing, squealing
as Circe flung them acorns, cornel nuts and mast,
common fodder for hogs that root and roll in mud.

Back Eurylochus ran to our swift black ship
to tell the disaster our poor friends had faced.   270
But try as he might, he couldn't get a word out.

---

2. A wine also mentioned by later writers; one of then calls it harsh and dark.

Numbing sorrow had stunned the man to silence—
tears welled in his eyes, his heart possessed by grief.
We assailed him with questions—all at our wits' end—
till at last he could recount the fate our friends had met: 275
'Off we went through the brush, captain, as you commanded.
Deep in the wooded glens we came on Circe's palace
built of dressed stone on a cleared rise of land.
Someone inside was plying a great loom,
and how she sang—in a high clear voice!   280
Goddess or woman—we called out and hailed her . . .
She opened her gleaming doors at once and stepped forth,
inviting us all in, and in we went, all innocence.
But *I* stayed behind—I sensed a trap. Suddenly
all vanished—blotted out—not one face showed again,   285
though I sat there keeping watch a good long time.'

 At that report I slung the hefty bronze blade
of my silver-studded sword around my shoulder,
slung my bow on too and told our comrade,
'Lead me back by the same way that you came.'   290
But he flung both arms around my knees and pleaded,
begging me with his tears and winging words:
'Don't force me back there, captain, king—
leave me here on the spot.
You will never return yourself, I swear,   295
you'll never bring back a single man alive.
Quick, cut and run with the rest of us here—
we can still escape the fatal day!'

But I shot back, 'Eurylochus, stay right here,
eating, drinking, safe by the black ship.   300
I must be off. Necessity drives me on.'

 Leaving the ship and shore, I headed inland,
clambering up through hushed, entrancing glades until,
as I was nearing the halls of Circe skilled in spells,
approaching her palace—Hermes god of the golden wand   305
crossed my path, and he looked for all the world
like a young man sporting his first beard,
just in the prime and warm pride of youth,
and grasped me by the hand and asked me kindly,
'Where are you going now, my unlucky friend—   310
trekking over the hills alone in unfamiliar country?
And your men are all in there, in Circe's palace,
cooped like swine, hock by jowl in the sties.
Have you come to set them free?
Well, I warn you, you won't get home yourself,   315
you'll stay right there, trapped with all the rest.
But wait, I can save you, free you from that great danger.
Look, here is a potent drug. Take it to Circe's halls—
its power alone will shield you from the fatal day.
Let me tell you of all the witch's subtle craft . . .

She'll mix you a potion, lace the brew with drugs
but she'll be powerless to bewitch you, even so—
this magic herb I give will fight her spells.
Now here's your plan of action, step by step.
The moment Circe strikes with her long thin wand,   325
you draw your sharp sword sheathed at your hip
and rush her fast as if to run her through!
She'll cower in fear and coax you to her bed—
but don't refuse the goddess' bed, not then, not if
she's to release your friends and treat you well yourself.   330
But have her swear the binding oath of the blessed gods
she'll never plot some new intrigue to harm you,
once you lie there naked—
never unman you, strip away your courage!'
                                        With that
the giant-killer handed over the magic herb,   335
pulling it from the earth,
and Hermes showed me all its name and nature.
Its root is black and its flower white as milk
and the gods call it moly. Dangerous for a mortal man
to pluck from the soil but not for deathless gods.   340
All lies within their power.
                        Now Hermes went his way
to the steep heights of Olympus, over the island's woods
while I, just approaching the halls of Circe,
my heart a heaving storm at every step,
paused at her doors, the nymph with lovely braids—   345
I stood and shouted to her there. She heard my voice,
she opened her gleaming doors at once and stepped forth,
inviting me in, and in I went, all anguish now . . .
She led me in to sit on a silver-studded chair,
ornately carved, with a stool to rest my feet.   350
In a golden bowl she mixed a potion for me to drink,
stirring her poison in, her heart aswirl with evil.
And then she passed it on, I drank it down
but it never worked its spell—
she struck with her wand and 'Now,' she cried,   355
'off to your sty, you swine, and wallow with your friends!'
But I, I drew my sharp sword sheathed at my hip
and rushed her fast as if to run her through—
She screamed, slid under my blade, hugged my knees
with a flood of warm tears and a burst of winging words: 360
'Who are you? where are you from? your city? your parents?
I'm wonderstruck—you drank my drugs, you're not bewitched!
Never has any other man withstood my potion, never,
once it's past his lips and he has drunk it down.
You have a mind in *you* no magic can enchant!   365
You must be Odysseus, man of twists and turns—
Hermes the giant-killer, god of the golden wand,
he always said you'd come,
homeward bound from Troy in your swift black ship.

Come, sheathe your sword, let's go to bed together,   370
mount my bed and mix in the magic work of love—
we'll breed deep trust between us.'
                              So she enticed
but I fought back, still wary. 'Circe, Circe,
how dare you tell me to treat you with any warmth?
You who turned my men to swine in your own house and now   375
you hold me here as well—teeming with treachery
you lure me to your room to mount your bed,
so once I lie there naked
you'll unman me, strip away my courage!
Mount your bed? Not for all the world. Not   380
until you consent to swear, goddess, a binding oath
you'll never plot some new intrigue to harm me!'
                              Straightaway
she began to swear the oath that I required—never,
she'd never do me harm—and when she'd finished,
then, at last, I mounted Circe's gorgeous bed . . .   385

    At the same time her handmaids bustled through the halls,
four in all who perform the goddess' household tasks:
nymphs, daughters born of the springs and groves
and the sacred rivers running down to open sea.
One draped the chairs with fine crimson covers   390
over the seats she'd spread with linen cloths below.
A second drew up silver tables before the chairs
and laid out golden trays to hold the bread.
A third mulled heady, heart-warming wine
in a silver bowl and set out golden cups.   395
A fourth brought water and lit a blazing fire
beneath a massive cauldron. The water heated soon,
and once it reached the boil in the glowing bronze
she eased me into a tub and bathed me from the cauldron,
mixing the hot and cold to suit my taste, showering   400
head and shoulders down until she'd washed away
the spirit-numbing exhaustion from my body.
The bathing finished, rubbing me sleek with oil,
throwing warm fleece and a shirt around my shoulders,
she led me in to sit on a silver-studded chair,   405
ornately carved, with a stool to rest my feet.
A maid brought water soon in a graceful golden pitcher
and over a silver basin tipped it out
so I might rinse my hands,
then pulled a gleaming table to my side.   410
A staid housekeeper brought on bread to serve me,
appetizers aplenty too, lavish with her bounty.
She pressed me to eat. I had no taste for food.
I just sat there, mind wandering, far away . . .
lost in grim forebodings.
                              As soon as Circe saw me,   415
huddled, not touching my food, immersed in sorrow,

she sidled near with a coaxing, winged word:
'Odysseus, why just sit there, struck dumb,
eating your heart out, not touching food or drink?
Suspect me of still more treachery? Nothing to fear.   420
Haven't I just sworn my solemn, binding oath?'

    So she asked, but I protested, 'Circe—
how could any man in his right mind endure
the taste of food and drink before he'd freed
his comrades-in-arms and looked them in the eyes?   425
If you, you really want me to eat and drink,
set them free, all my beloved comrades—
let me feast my eyes.'
              So I demanded.
Circe strode on through the halls and out,
her wand held high in hand and, flinging open the pens,   430
drove forth my men, who looked like full-grown swine.
Facing her, there they stood as she went along the ranks,
anointing them one by one with some new magic oil—
and look, the bristles grown by the first wicked drug
that Circe gave them slipped away from their limbs   435
and they turned men again: younger than ever,
taller by far, more handsome to the eye, and yes,
they knew me at once and each man grasped my hands
and a painful longing for tears overcame us all,
a terrible sobbing echoed through the house . . .   440
The goddess herself was moved and, standing by me,
warmly urged me on—a lustrous goddess now:
'Royal son of Laertes, Odysseus, tried and true,
go at once to your ship at the water's edge,
haul her straight up on the shore first   445
and stow your cargo and running gear in caves,
then back you come and bring your trusty crew.'

    Her urging won my stubborn spirit over.
Down I went to the swift ship at the water's edge,
and there on the decks I found my loyal crew   450
consumed with grief and weeping live warm tears.
But now, as calves in stalls when cows come home,
droves of them herded back from field to farmyard
once they've grazed their fill—as all their young calves
come frisking out to meet them, bucking out of their pens,   455
lowing nonstop, jostling, rushing round their mothers—
so my shipmates there at the sight of my return
came pressing round me now, streaming tears,
so deeply moved in their hearts they felt as if
they'd made it back to their own land, their city,   460
Ithaca's rocky soil where they were bred and reared.
And through their tears their words went winging home:
'You're back again, my king! How thrilled we are—
as if we'd reached our country, Ithaca, at last!
But come, tell us about the fate our comrades met.'   465

Still I replied with a timely word of comfort:
'Let's haul our ship straight up on the shore first
and stow our cargo and running gear in caves.
Then hurry, all of you, come along with me
to see our friends in the magic halls of Circe,   470
eating and drinking—the feast flows on forever.'

    So I said and they jumped to do my bidding.
Only Eurylochus tried to hold my shipmates back,
his mutinous outburst aimed at one and all:
'Poor fools, where are we running now?   475
Why are we tempting fate?—
why stumble blindly down to Circe's halls?
She'll turn us all into pigs or wolves or lions
made to guard that palace of hers—by force, I tell you—
just as the Cyclops trapped our comrades in his lair   480
with hotheaded Odysseus right beside them all—
thanks to this man's rashness they died too!'

So he declared and I had half a mind
to draw the sharp sword from beside my hip
and slice his head off, tumbling down in the dust,   485
close kin[3] that he was. But comrades checked me,
each man trying to calm me, left and right:
'Captain, we'll leave him here if you command,
just where he is, to sit and guard the ship.
Lead us on to the magic halls of Circe.'
                                    With that,   490
up from the ship and shore they headed inland.
Nor did Eurylochus malinger by the hull;
he straggled behind the rest,
dreading the sharp blast of my rebuke.
                        All the while
Circe had bathed my other comrades in her palace,   495
caring and kindly, rubbed them sleek with oil
and decked them out in fleecy cloaks and shirts.
We found them all together, feasting in her halls.
Once we had recognized each other, gazing face-to-face,
we all broke down and wept—and the house resounded now   500
and Circe the lustrous one came toward me, pleading,
'Royal son of Laertes, Odysseus, man of action,
no more tears now, calm these tides of sorrow.
Well I know what pains you bore on the swarming sea,
what punishment you endured from hostile men on land.   505
But come now, eat your food and drink your wine
till the same courage fills your chests, now as then,
when you first set sail from native land, from rocky Ithaca!
Now you are burnt-out husks, your spirits haggard, sere,
always brooding over your wanderings long and hard,   510

---

3. The Greek word suggests a relation by marriage. This is the only mention in the poem of such a tie
between Odysseus and Eurylochus, who opposes Odysseus here and in the episode of the Sun's cattle in
book 12.

your hearts never lifting with any joy—
you've suffered far too much.'
                              So she enticed
and won our battle-hardened spirits over.
And there we sat at ease,
day in, day out, till a year had run its course,   515
feasting on sides of meat and drafts of heady wine . . .
But then, when the year was through and the seasons wheeled by
and the months waned and the long days came round again,
my loyal comrades took me aside and prodded,
'Captain, this is madness!   520
High time you thought of your own home at last,
if it really is your fate to make it back alive
and reach your well-built house and native land.'

    Their urging brought my stubborn spirit round.
So all that day till the sun went down we sat   525
and feasted on sides of meat and heady wine.
Then when the sun had set and night came on
the men lay down to sleep in the shadowed halls
but I went up to that luxurious bed of Circe's,
hugged her by the knees   530
and the goddess heard my winging supplication:
'Circe, now make good a promise you gave me once—
it's time to help me home. My heart longs to be home,
my comrades' hearts as well. They wear me down,
pleading with me whenever you're away.'
                              So I pressed   535
and the lustrous goddess answered me in turn:
'Royal son of Laertes, Odysseus, old campaigner,
stay on no more in my house against your will.
But first another journey calls. You must travel down
to the House of Death and the awesome one, Persephone,[4]   540
there to consult the ghost of Tiresias,[5] seer of Thebes,
the great blind prophet whose mind remains unshaken.
Even in death—Persephone has given him wisdom,
everlasting vision to him and him alone . . .
the rest of the dead are empty, flitting shades.'   545

    So she said and crushed the heart inside me.
I knelt in her bed and wept. I'd no desire
to go on living and see the rising light of day.
But once I'd had my fill of tears and writhing there,
at last I found the words to venture, 'Circe, Circe,   550
who can pilot us on that journey? Who has ever
reached the House of Death in a black ship?'

The lustrous goddess answered, never pausing,
'Royal son of Laertes, Odysseus, born for exploits,

---

4. Queen of the dead.   5. A blind prophet who figures prominently in the legends of Thebes (he is a character in Sophocles' Oedipus the King and Antigone).

let no lack of a pilot at the helm concern you, no,   555
just step your mast and spread your white sail wide—
sit back and the North Wind will speed you on your way.
But once your vessel has cut across the Ocean River
you will raise a desolate coast and Persephone's Grove,
her tall black poplars, willows whose fruit dies young.   560
Beach your vessel hard by the Ocean's churning shore
and make your own way down to the moldering House of Death.
And there into Acheron, the Flood of Grief, two rivers flow,
the torrent River of Fire, the wailing River of Tears
that branches off from Styx, the Stream of Hate,   565
and a stark crag looms
where the two rivers thunder down and meet.
Once there, go forward, hero. Do as I say now.
Dig a trench of about a forearm's depth and length
and around it pour libations out to all the dead—   570
first with milk and honey, and then with mellow wine,
then water third and last, and sprinkle glistening barley
over it all, and vow again and again to all the dead,
to the drifting, listless spirits of their ghosts,
that once you return to Ithaca you will slaughter   575
a barren heifer in your halls, the best you have,
and load a pyre with treasures—and to Tiresias,
alone, apart, you will offer a sleek black ram,
the pride of all your herds. And once your prayers
have invoked the nations of the dead in their dim glory,   580
slaughter a ram and a black ewe, turning both their heads
toward Erebus,[6] but turn your head away, looking toward
the Ocean River. Suddenly then the countless shades
of the dead and gone will surge around you there.
But order your men at once to flay the sheep   585
that lie before you, killed by your ruthless blade,
and burn them both, and then say prayers to the gods,
to the almighty god of death and dread Persephone.
But you—draw your sharp sword from beside your hip,
sit down on alert there, and never let the ghosts   590
of the shambling, shiftless dead come near that blood
till you have questioned Tiresias yourself. Soon, soon
the great seer will appear before you, captain of armies:
he will tell you the way to go, the stages of your voyage,
how you can cross the swarming sea and reach home at last.'   595

    And with those words Dawn rose on her golden throne
and Circe dressed me quickly in sea-cloak and shirt
while the queen slipped on a loose, glistening robe,
filmy, a joy to the eye, and round her waist
she ran a brocaded golden belt   600
and over her head a scarf to shield her brow.
And I strode on through the halls to stir my men,
hovering over each with a winning word: 'Up now!

6. Here the innermost and darkest region of the land of the dead.

No more lazing away in sleep, we must set sail—
Queen Circe has shown the way.'
               I brought them round,   605
my hardy friends-in-arms, but not even from there
could I get them safely off without a loss . . .
There was a man, Elpenor, the youngest in our ranks,
none too brave in battle, none too sound in mind.
He'd strayed from his mates in Circe's magic halls   610
and keen for the cool night air,
sodden with wine he'd bedded down on her roofs.[7]
But roused by the shouts and tread of marching men,
he leapt up with a start at dawn but still so dazed
he forgot to climb back down again by the long ladder—   615
headfirst from the roof he plunged, his neck snapped
from the backbone, his soul flew down to Death.

Once on our way, I gave the men their orders:
'You think we are headed home, our own dear land?
Well, Circe sets us a rather different course . . .   620
down to the House of Death and the awesome one, Persephone,
there to consult the ghost of Tiresias, seer of Thebes.'

So I said, and it broke my shipmates' hearts.
They sank down on the ground, moaning, tore their hair.
But it gained us nothing—what good can come of grief?   625

Back to the swift ship at the water's edge we went,
our spirits deep in anguish, faces wet with tears.
But Circe got to the dark hull before us,
tethered a ram and black ewe close by—
slipping past unseen. Who can glimpse a god   630
who wants to be invisible gliding here and there?"

BOOK XI

[The Kingdom of the Dead]

"Now down we came to the ship at the water's edge,
we hauled and launched her into the sunlit breakers first,
stepped the mast in the black craft and set our sail
and loaded the sheep aboard, the ram and ewe,
then we ourselves embarked, streaming tears,   5
our hearts weighed down with anguish . . .
But Circe the awesome nymph with lovely braids
who speaks with human voice, sent us a hardy shipmate,
yes, a fresh following wind ruffling up in our wake,
bellying out our sail to drive our blue prow on as we,   10
securing the running gear from stem to stern, sat back
while the wind and helmsman kept her true on course.
The sail stretched taut as she cut the sea all day
and the sun sank and the roads of the world grew dark.

7. The flat roof was the coolest place to sleep.

And she made the outer limits, the Ocean River's bounds   15
where Cimmerian people have their homes—their realm and city
shrouded in mist and cloud.[8] The eye of the Sun can never
flash his rays through the dark and bring them light,
not when he climbs the starry skies or when he wheels
back down from the heights to touch the earth once more—   20
an endless, deadly night overhangs those wretched men.
There, gaining that point, we beached our craft
and herding out the sheep, we picked our way
by the Ocean's banks until we gained the place
that Circe made our goal.   Here at the spot   25
Perimedes and Eurylochus held the victims fast,
and I, drawing my sharp sword from beside my hip,
dug a trench of about a forearm's depth and length
and around it poured libations out to all the dead,
first with milk and honey, and then with mellow wine,   30
then water third and last, and sprinkled glistening barley
over it all, and time and again I vowed to all the dead,
to the drifting, listless spirits of their ghosts,
that once I returned to Ithaca I would slaughter
a barren heifer in my halls, the best I had,   35
and load a pyre with treasures—and to Tiresias,
alone, apart, I would offer a sleek black ram,
the pride of all my herds. And once my vows
and prayers had invoked the nations of the dead,
I took the victims, over the trench I cut their throats   40
and the dark blood flowed in—and up out of Erebus they came,
flocking toward me now, the ghosts of the dead and gone . . .
Brides and unwed youths and old men who had suffered much
and girls with their tender hearts freshly scarred by sorrow
and great armies of battle dead, stabbed by bronze spears,   45
men of war still wrapped in bloody armor—thousands
swarming around the trench from every side—
unearthly cries—blanching terror gripped me!
I ordered the men at once to flay the sheep
that lay before us, killed by my ruthless blade,   50
and burn them both, and then say prayers to the gods,
to the almighty god of death and dread Persephone.
But I, the sharp sword drawn from beside my hip,
sat down on alert there and never let the ghosts
of the shambling, shiftless dead come near that blood   55
till I had questioned Tiresias myself.
                              But first
the ghost of Elpenor, my companion, came toward me.
He'd not been buried under the wide ways of earth,
not yet, we'd left his body in Circe's house,
unwept, unburied—this other labor pressed us.   60

---

8. Although Homer usually places the land of the dead below the earth, here it is across a great expanse
of sea—apparently in the far west (some think north), on the shore of Ocean, the great river that encircles
the earth. Homer's Cimmerians are probably a mythical people.

But I wept to see him now, pity touched my heart
and I called out a winged word to him there: 'Elpenor,
how did you travel down to the world of darkness?
Faster on foot, I see, than I in my black ship.'

My comrade groaned as he offered me an answer: 65
'Royal son of Laertes, Odysseus, old campaigner,
the doom of an angry god, and god knows how much wine—
they were my ruin, captain . . . I'd bedded down
on the roof of Circe's house but never thought
to climb back down again by the long ladder—   70
headfirst from the roof I plunged, my neck snapped
from the backbone, my soul flew down to Death. Now,
I beg you by those you left behind, so far from here,
your wife, your father who bred and reared you as a boy,
and Telemachus, left at home in your halls, your only son.   75
Well I know when you leave this lodging of the dead
that you and your ship will put ashore again
at the island of Aeaea—then and there,
my lord, remember me, I beg you! Don't sail off
and desert me, left behind unwept, unburied, don't,   80
or my curse may draw god's fury on your head.
No, burn me in full armor, all my harness,
heap my mound by the churning gray surf—
a man whose luck ran out—
so even men to come will learn my story.   85
Perform my rites, and plant on my tomb that oar
I swung with mates when I rowed among the living.'

   'All this, my unlucky friend,' I reassured him,
'I will do for you. I won't forget a thing.'
                          So we sat
and faced each other, trading our bleak parting words,   90
I on my side, holding my sword above the blood,
he across from me there, my comrade's phantom
dragging out his story.
                     But look, the ghost
of my mother came! My mother, dead and gone now . . .
Anticleia—daughter of that great heart Autolycus—   95
whom I had left alive when I sailed for sacred Troy.
I broke into tears to see her here, but filled with pity,
even throbbing with grief, I would not let her ghost
approach the blood till I had questioned Tiresias myself.

   At last he came. The shade of the famous Theban prophet,   100
holding a golden scepter, knew me at once and hailed me:
'Royal son of Laertes, Odysseus, master of exploits,
man of pain, what now, what brings you here,
forsaking the light of day
to see this joyless kingdom of the dead?   105
Stand back from the trench—put up your sharp sword
so I can drink the blood and tell you all the truth.'

Moving back, I thrust my silver-studded sword
deep in its sheath, and once he had drunk the dark blood
the words came ringing from the prophet in his power:[9]   110
'A sweet smooth journey home, renowned Odysseus,
that is what you seek
but a god will make it hard for you—I know—
you will never escape the one who shakes the earth,
quaking with anger at you still, still enraged   115
because you blinded the Cyclops, his dear son.
Even so, you and your crew may still reach home,
suffering all the way, if you only have the power
to curb their wild desire and curb your own, what's more,
from the day your good trim vessel first puts in   120
at Thrinacia Island, flees the cruel blue sea.
There you will find them grazing,
herds and fat flocks, the cattle of Helios,
god of the sun who sees all, hears all things.
Leave the beasts unharmed, your mind set on home,   125
and you all may still reach Ithaca—bent with hardship,
true—but harm them in any way, and I can see it now:
your ship destroyed, your men destroyed as well.
And even if *you* escape, you'll come home late
and come a broken man—all shipmates lost,   130
alone in a stranger's ship—
and you will find a world of pain at home,
crude, arrogant men devouring all your goods,
courting your noble wife, offering gifts to win her.
No doubt you will pay them back in blood when you come home!   135
But once you have killed those suitors in your halls—
by stealth or in open fight with slashing bronze—
go forth once more, you must . . .
carry your well-planed oar until you come
to a race of people who know nothing of the sea,   140
whose food is never seasoned with salt, strangers all
to ships with their crimson prows and long slim oars,
wings that make ships fly. And here is your sign—
unmistakable, clear, so clear you cannot miss it:
When another traveler falls in with you and calls   145
that weight across your shoulder a fan to winnow grain,[1]
then plant your bladed, balanced oar in the earth
and sacrifice fine beasts to the lord god of the sea,
Poseidon—a ram, a bull and a ramping wild boar—
then journey home and render noble offerings up   150
to the deathless gods who rule the vaulting skies,
to all the gods in order.
And at last your own death will steal upon you . . .
a gentle, painless death, far from the sea it comes

---

9. Tiresias here predicts the future of Odysseus. Like many Greek prophecies, this one contains alternatives: leave the cattle of the Sun alone or harm them.   1. A pole with a broad blade at the end, used to scoop up ears of wheat and toss them in the air so that the wind can separate the lighter chaff from the heavy kernels. People who mistake an oar for a winnowing fan have never seen the sea, and evidently Odysseus will appease the sea god Poseidon by spreading his cult to those who do not know him.

to take you down, borne down with the years in ripe old age   155
with all your people there in blessed peace around you.
All that I have told you will come true.'
                                        'Oh Tiresias,'
I replied as the prophet finished, 'surely the gods
have spun this out as fate, the gods themselves.
But tell me one thing more, and tell me clearly.   160
I see the ghost of my long-lost mother here before me.
Dead, crouching close to the blood in silence,
she cannot bear to look me in the eyes—
her own son—or speak a word to me. How,
lord, can I make her know me for the man I am?'   165

    'One rule there is,' the famous seer explained,
'and simple for me to say and you to learn.
Any one of the ghosts you let approach the blood
will speak the truth to you. Anyone you refuse
will turn and fade away.'
                        And with those words,   170
now that his prophecies had closed, the awesome shade
of lord Tiresias strode back to the House of Death.
But I kept watch there, steadfast till my mother
approached and drank the dark, clouding blood.
She knew me at once and wailed out in grief   175
and her words came winging toward me, flying home:
'Oh my son—what brings you down to the world
of death and darkness? You are still alive!
It's hard for the living to catch a glimpse of this . . .
Great rivers flow between us, terrible waters,   180
the Ocean first of all—no one could ever ford
that stream on foot, only aboard some sturdy craft.
Have you just come from Troy, wandering long years
with your men and ship? Not yet returned to Ithaca?
You've still not seen your wife inside your halls?'
                                        'Mother,'   185
I replied, 'I had to venture down to the House of Death,
to consult the shade of Tiresias, seer of Thebes.
Never yet have I neared Achaea, never once
set foot on native ground,
always wandering—endless hardship from that day   190
I first set sail with King Agamemnon bound for Troy,
the stallion-land, to fight the Trojans there.
But tell me about yourself and spare me nothing.
What form of death overcame you, what laid you low,
some long slow illness? Or did Artemis showering arrows   195
come with her painless shafts and bring you down?
Tell me of father, tell of the son I left behind:
do my royal rights still lie in their safekeeping?
Or does some stranger hold the throne by now
because men think that I'll come home no more?   200
Please, tell me about my wife, her turn of mind,
her thoughts . . . still standing fast beside our son,

still guarding our great estates, secure as ever now?
Or has she wed some other countryman at last,
the finest prince among them?'
                                                    'Surely, surely,'   205
my noble mother answered quickly, 'she's still waiting
there in your halls, poor woman, suffering so,
her life an endless hardship like your own . . .
wasting away the nights, weeping away the days.
No one has taken over your royal rights, not yet.   210
Telemachus still holds your great estates in peace,
he attends the public banquets shared with all,
the feasts a man of justice should enjoy,
for every lord invites him. As for your father,
he keeps to his own farm—he never goes to town—   215
with no bed for him there, no blankets, glossy throws;
all winter long he sleeps in the lodge with servants,
in the ashes by the fire, his body wrapped in rags.
But when summer comes and the bumper crops of harvest,
any spot on the rising ground of his vineyard rows   220
he makes his bed, heaped high with fallen leaves,
and there he lies in anguish . . .
with his old age bearing hard upon him, too,
and his grief grows as he longs for your return.
And I with the same grief I died and met my fate.   225
No sharp-eyed Huntress[2] showering arrows through the halls
approached and brought me down with painless shafts,
nor did some hateful illness strike me, that so often
devastates the body, drains our limbs of power.
No, it was my longing for *you*, my shining Odysseus—   230
you and your quickness, you and your gentle ways—
that tore away my life that had been sweet.'

    And I, my mind in turmoil, how I longed
to embrace my mother's spirit, dead as she was!
Three times I rushed toward her, desperate to hold her,   235
three times she fluttered through my fingers, sifting away
like a shadow, dissolving like a dream, and each time
the grief cut to the heart, sharper, yes, and I,
I cried out to her, words winging into the darkness:
'Mother—why not wait for me? How I long to hold you!—   240
so even here, in the House of Death, we can fling
our loving arms around each other, take some joy
in the tears that numb the heart. Or is this just
some wraith that great Persephone sends my way
to make me ache with sorrow all the more?'   245

    My noble mother answered me at once:
'My son, my son, the unluckiest man alive!
This is no deception sent by Queen Persephone,
this is just the way of mortals when we die.

2. Artemis.

Sinews no longer bind the flesh and bones together— 250
the fire in all its fury burns the body down to ashes
once life slips from the white bones, and the spirit,
rustling, flitters away . . . flown like a dream.
But you must long for the daylight. Go, quickly.
Remember all these things 255
so one day you can tell them to your wife.'

    And so we both confided, trading parting words,
and there slowly came a grand array of women,
all sent before me now by august Persephone,
and all were wives and daughters once of princes.[3] 260
They swarmed in a flock around the dark blood
while I searched for a way to question each alone,
and the more I thought, the more this seemed the best:
Drawing forth the long sharp sword from beside my hip,
I would not let them drink the dark blood, all in a rush, 265
and so they waited, coming forward one after another.
Each declared her lineage, and I explored them all.

    And the first I saw there? Tyro, born of kings,
who said her father was that great lord Salmoneus,
said that she was the wife of Cretheus, Aeolus' son. 270
And once she fell in love with the river god, Enipeus,
far the clearest river flowing across the earth,
and so she'd haunt Enipeus' glinting streams,
till taking his shape one day
the god who girds the earth and makes it tremble 275
bedded her where the swirling river rushes out to sea,
and a surging wave reared up, high as a mountain, dark,
arching over to hide the god and mortal girl together.
Loosing her virgin belt, he lapped her round in sleep
and when the god had consummated his work of love 280
he took her by the hand and hailed her warmly:
'Rejoice in our love, my lady! And when this year
has run its course you will give birth to glorious children—
bedding down with the gods is never barren, futile—
and you must tend them, breed and rear them well. 285
Now home you go, and restrain yourself, I say,
never breathe your lover's name but know—
I am Poseidon, god who rocks the earth!'

    With that he dove back in the heaving waves
and she conceived for the god and bore him Pelias, Neleus,[4] 290
and both grew up to be stalwart aides of Zeus almighty,
both men alike. Pelias lived on the plains of Iolcos,
rich in sheepflocks, Neleus lived in sandy Pylos.
And the noble queen bore sons to Cretheus too:
Aeson[5] Pheres and Amythaon, exultant charioteer. 295

3. The famous and beautiful legendary women who follow helped establish some of the most important
lineages in Greek legend through the sons they bore. **4.** Father of Nestor of Pylos (book 3). *Pelias:*
Jason's uncle, who sent him on the quest for the Golden Fleece. **5.** Father of Jason the Argonaut.

And after Tyro I saw Asopus'[6] daughter Antiope,
proud she'd spent a night in the arms of Zeus himself
and borne the god twin sons, Amphion and Zethus,
the first to build the footings of seven-gated Thebes,
her bastions too, for lacking ramparts none could live   300
in a place so vast, so open—strong as both men were.

    And I saw Alcmena next, Amphitryon's wife,
who slept in the clasp of Zeus and merged in love
and brought forth Heracles, rugged will and lion heart.
And I saw Megara too, magnanimous Creon's daughter   305
wed to the stalwart Heracles, the hero never daunted.

    And I saw the mother of Oedipus, beautiful Epicaste.[7]
What a monstrous thing she did, in all innocence—
she married her own son . . .
who'd killed his father, then he married *her*!   310
But the gods soon made it known to all mankind.
So he in growing pain ruled on in beloved Thebes,
lording Cadmus' people—thanks to the gods' brutal plan—
while she went down to Death who guards the massive gates.
Lashing a noose to a steep rafter, there she hanged aloft,   315
strangling in all her anguish, leaving her son to bear
the world of horror a mother's Furies bring to life.

    And I saw magnificent Chloris, the one whom Neleus
wooed and won with a hoard of splendid gifts,
so dazzled by her beauty years ago . . .   320
the youngest daughter of Iasus' son Amphion,
the great Minyan king who ruled Orchomenos[8] once.
She was his queen in Pylos, she bore him shining sons,
Nestor and Chromius, Periclymenus too, good prince.
And after her sons she bore a daughter, majestic Pero,   325
the marvel of her time, courted by all the young lords
round about. But Neleus would not give her to any suitor,
none but the man who might drive home the herds
that powerful Iphiclus had stolen. Lurching,
broad in the brow, those longhorned beasts,   330
and no small task to round them up from Phylace.
Only the valiant seer Melampus volunteered—
he would drive them home—
but a god's iron sentence bound him fast:
barbarous herdsmen dragged him off in chains.   335
Yet when the months and days had run their course
and the year wheeled round and the seasons came again,
then mighty Iphiclus loosed the prophet's shackles,
once he had told him all the gods' decrees.
And so the will of Zeus was done at last.   340

---

6. A river in Boeotia, the region in which Thebes is located.   7. More often known as Jocasta.   8. A very ancient city in Boeotia, northwest of Thebes. This is not the same Amphion who built the walls of Thebes (line 298).

And I saw Leda next, Tyndareus' wife,
who'd borne the king two sons, intrepid twins,[9]
Castor, breaker of horses, and the hardy boxer Polydeuces,
both buried now in the life-giving earth though still alive.
Even under the earth Zeus grants them that distinction: 345
one day alive, the next day dead, each twin by turns,
they both hold honors equal to the gods'.

And I saw Iphimedeia next, Aloeus' wife,
who claimed she lay in the Sea-lord's loving waves
and gave the god two sons, but they did not live long,   350
Otus staunch as a god and far-famed Ephialtes.
They were the tallest men the fertile earth has borne,
the handsomest too, by far, aside from renowned Orion.
Nine yards across they measured, even at nine years old,
nine fathoms tall they towered. They even threatened   355
the deathless gods they'd storm Olympus' heights
with the pounding rush and grinding shock of battle.
They were wild to pile Ossa upon Olympus, then on Ossa
Pelion dense with timber—their toeholds up the heavens.[1]
And they'd have won the day if they had reached peak strength   360
but Apollo the son of Zeus, whom sleek-haired Leto bore,
laid both giants low before their beards had sprouted,
covering cheek and chin with a fresh crop of down.

Phaedra and Procris too I saw, and lovely Ariadne,
daughter of Minos,[2] that harsh king. One day Theseus tried   365
to spirit her off from Crete to Athens' sacred heights
but he got no joy from her. Artemis killed her first
on wave-washed Dia's shores, accused by Dionysus.[3]

And I saw Clymene, Maera and loathsome Eriphyle—[4]
bribed with a golden necklace   370
to lure her lawful husband to his death . . .
But the whole cortege I could never tally, never name,
not all the daughters and wives of great men I saw there.
Long before that, the godsent night would ebb away.
But the time has come for sleep, either with friends   375
aboard your swift ship or here in your own house.
My passage home will rest with the gods and you."

Odysseus paused . . . They all fell silent, hushed,
his story holding them spellbound down the shadowed halls

---

9. She also bore him Clytemnestra, wife of Agamemnon, and she bore Helen, wife of Menelaus, to Zeus. Tyndareus was king of Sparta. **1.** Two mountains in Thessaly, near Olympus. **2.** King of Crete and father of Phaedra and Ariadne, who helped Theseus of Athens kill the Minotaur and left Crete with him. Phaedra, who married Theseus, fell in love with her stepson Hippolytus; when he rejected her advances, she killed herself and contrived his death. Procris was the unfaithful wife of Cephalus, king of Athens. **3.** God of the vine. His motive is unknown. In the usual later version of this story, Dionysus carried Ariadne off to be his bride after Theseus abandoned her on the island of Dia (or Naxos). **4.** Bribed by Polynices, son of Oedipus, she persuaded her husband, Amphiaraus, to take part in the attack on Thebes in which he was killed. Maira was a nymph of Artemis who broke her vow of chastity and was killed by the goddess. There were several legendary women named Clymene; perhaps Homer is referring to the mother of Iphiclus (line 329 above).

till the white-armed queen Arete suddenly burst out,   380
"Phaeacians! How does this man impress you now,
his looks, his build, the balanced mind inside him?
The stranger is my guest
but each of you princes shares the honor here.
So let's not be too hasty to send him on his way,   385
and don't scrimp on his gifts. His need is great,
great as the riches piled up in your houses,
thanks to the gods' good will."
                      Following her,
the old revered Echeneus added his support,
the eldest lord on the island of Phaeacia: 390
"Friends, the words of our considerate queen—
they never miss the mark or fail our expectations.
So do as Arete says, though on Alcinous here
depend all words and action."
                   "And so it will be"—
Alcinous stepped in grandly—"sure as I am alive   395
and rule our island men who love their oars!
Our guest, much as he longs for passage home,
must stay and wait it out here till tomorrow,
till I can collect his whole array of parting gifts.
His send-off rests with every noble here   400
but with me most of all:
I hold the reins of power in the realm."

    Odysseus, deft and tactful, echoed back,
"Alcinous, majesty, shining among your island people,
if you would urge me now to stay here one whole year   405
then speed me home weighed down with lordly gifts,
I'd gladly have it so. Better by far, that way.
The fuller my arms on landing there at home,
the more respected, well received I'd be
by all who saw me sailing back to Ithaca."   410

    "Ah Odysseus," Alcinous replied, "one look at you
and we know that you are no one who would cheat us—
no fraud, such as the dark soil breeds and spreads
across the face of the earth these days. Crowds of vagabonds
frame their lies so tightly none can test them. But you,   415
what grace you give your words, and what good sense within!
You have told your story with all a singer's skill,
the miseries you endured, your great Achaeans too.
But come now, tell me truly: your godlike comrades—
did you see any heroes down in the House of Death,   420
any who sailed with you and met their doom at Troy?
The night's still young, I'd say the night is endless.
For us in the palace now, it's hardly time for sleep.
Keep telling us your adventures—they are wonderful.
I could hold out here till Dawn's first light   425
if only you could bear, here in our halls,
to tell the tale of all the pains you suffered."

So the man of countless exploits carried on:
"Alcinous, majesty, shining among your island people,
there is a time for many words, a time for sleep as well.   430
But if you insist on hearing more, I'd never stint
on telling my own tale and those more painful still,
the griefs of my comrades, dead in the war's wake,
who escaped the battle-cries of Trojan armies
only to die in blood at journey's end—   435
thanks to a vicious woman's will.
                                        Now then,
no sooner had Queen Persephone driven off
the ghosts of lovely women, scattering left and right,
than forward marched the shade of Atreus' son Agamemnon,
fraught with grief and flanked by all his comrades,   440
troops of his men-at-arms who died beside him,
who met their fate in lord Aegisthus' halls.
He knew me at once, as soon as he drank the blood,
and wailed out, shrilly; tears sprang to his eyes,
he thrust his arms toward me, keen to embrace me there—   445
no use—the great force was gone, the strength lost forever,
now, that filled his rippling limbs in the old days.
I wept at the sight, my heart went out to the man,
my words too, in a winging flight of pity:
'Famous Atrides, lord of men Agamemnon!   450
What fatal stroke of destiny brought you down?
Wrecked in the ships when lord Poseidon roused
some punishing blast of stormwinds, gust on gust?
Or did ranks of enemies mow you down on land
as you tried to raid and cut off herds and flocks   455
or fought to win their city, take their women?'

    The field marshal's ghost replied at once:
'Royal son of Laertes, Odysseus, mastermind of war,
I was not wrecked in the ships when lord Poseidon
roused some punishing blast of stormwinds gust on gust,   460
nor did ranks of enemies mow me down on land—
Aegisthus hatched my doom and my destruction,
he killed me, he with my own accursed wife . . .
he invited me to his palace, sat me down to feast
then cut me down as a man cuts down some ox at the trough!   465
So I died—a wretched, ignominious death—and round me
all my comrades killed, no mercy, one after another,
just like white-tusked boars
butchered in some rich lord of power's halls
for a wedding, banquet or groaning public feast.   470
You in your day have witnessed hundreds slaughtered,
killed in single combat or killed in pitched battle, true,
but if you'd laid eyes on this it would have wrenched your heart—
how we sprawled by the mixing-bowl and loaded tables there,
throughout the palace, the whole floor awash with blood.   475
But the death-cry of Cassandra, Priam's daughter[5]—

5. Part of Agamemnon's share of the booty at Troy.

the most pitiful thing I heard! My treacherous queen,
Clytemnestra, killed her over my body, yes, and I,
lifting my fists, beat them down on the ground,
dying, dying, writhing around the sword.   480
But she, that whore, she turned her back on me,
well on my way to Death—she even lacked the heart
to seal my eyes with her hand or close my jaws.[6]
                                                        So
there's nothing more deadly, bestial than a woman
set on works like these—what a monstrous thing   485
she plotted, slaughtered her own lawful husband!
Why, I expected, at least, some welcome home
from all my children, all my household slaves
when I came sailing back again . . . . But she—
the queen hell-bent on outrage—bathes in shame   490
not only herself but the whole breed of womankind,
even the honest ones to come, forever down the years!'

    So he declared and I cried out, 'How terrible!
Zeus from the very start, the thunder king
has hated the race of Atreus with a vengeance—   495
his trustiest weapon women's twisted wiles.
What armies of us died for the sake of Helen . . .
Clytemnestra schemed your death while you were worlds away!'

    'True, true,' Agamemnon's ghost kept pressing on,
'so even your own wife—never indulge her too far.   500
Never reveal the whole truth, whatever you may know;
just tell her a part of it, be sure to hide the rest.
Not that you, Odysseus, will be murdered by your wife.
She's much too steady, her feelings run too deep,
Icarius' daughter Penelope, that wise woman.   505
She was a young bride, I well remember . . .
we left her behind when we went off to war,
with an infant boy she nestled at her breast.
That boy must sit and be counted with the men now—
happy man! His beloved father will come sailing home   510
and see his son, and he will embrace his father,
that is only right. But my wife—she never
even let me feast my eyes on my own son;
she killed me first, his father!
I tell you this—bear it in mind, you must—   515
when you reach your homeland steer your ship
into port in secret, never out in the open . . .
the time for trusting women's gone forever!

    Enough. Come, tell me this, and be precise.
Have you heard news of my son? Where's he living now?   520
Perhaps in Orchomenos, perhaps in sandy Pylos
or off in the Spartan plains with Menelaus?
He's not dead yet, my Prince Orestes, no,

6. I.e., to give him a proper burial.

he's somewhere on the earth.'
                            So he probed
but I cut it short: 'Atrides, why ask me that?   525
I know nothing, whether he's dead or alive.
It's wrong to lead you on with idle words.'

    So we stood there, trading heartsick stories,
deep in grief, as the tears streamed down our faces.
But now there came the ghosts of Peleus' son Achilles,   530
Patroclus, fearless Antilochus[7]—and Great Ajax too,
the first in stature, first in build and bearing
of all the Argives after Peleus' matchless son.
The ghost of the splendid runner knew me at once
and hailed me with a flight of mournful questions: 535
'Royal son of Laertes, Odysseus, man of tactics,
reckless friend, what next?
What greater feat can that cunning head contrive?
What daring brought you down to the House of Death?—
where the senseless, burnt-out wraiths of mortals make their home.' 540

    The voice of his spirit paused, and I was quick to answer:
'Achilles, son of Peleus, greatest of the Achaeans,
I had to consult Tiresias, driven here by hopes
he would help me journey home to rocky Ithaca.   545
Never yet have I neared Achaea, never once
set foot on native ground . . .
my life is endless trouble.
                        But you, Achilles,
there's not a man in the world more blest than you—
there never has been, never will be one.
Time was, when you were alive, we Argives   550
honored you as a god, and now down here, I see,
you lord it over the dead in all your power.
So grieve no more at dying, great Achilles.'

    I reassured the ghost, but he broke out, protesting,
'No winning words about death to *me*, shining Odysseus!   555
By god, I'd rather slave on earth for another man—
some dirt-poor tenant farmer who scrapes to keep alive—
than rule down here over all the breathless dead.
But come, tell me the news about my gallant son.
Did he make his way to the wars,   560
did the boy become a champion—yes or no?
Tell me of noble Peleus, any word you've heard—
still holding pride of place among his Myrmidon hordes,
or do they despise the man in Hellas and in Phthia
because old age has lamed his arms and legs?   565
For I no longer stand in the light of day—
the man I was—comrade-in-arms to help my father
as once I helped our armies, killing the best fighters

---

7. Nestor's son; he was Achilles' closest friend after Patroclus.

Troy could field in the wide world up there . . .
Oh to arrive at father's house—the man I was,   570
for one brief day—I'd make my fury and my hands,
invincible hands, a thing of terror to all those men
who abuse the king with force and wrest away his honor!'

     So he grieved but I tried to lend him heart:
'About noble Peleus I can tell you nothing,   575
but about your own dear son, Neoptolemus,
I can report the whole story, as you wish.
I myself, in my trim ship, I brought him
out of Scyros to join the Argives under arms.[8]
And dug in around Troy, debating battle-tactics,   580
he always spoke up first, and always on the mark—
godlike Nestor and I alone excelled the boy. Yes,
and when our armies fought on the plain of Troy
he'd never hang back with the main force of men—
he'd always charge ahead,   585
giving ground to no one in his fury,
and scores of men he killed in bloody combat.
How could I list them all, name them all, now,
the fighting ranks he leveled, battling for the Argives?
But what a soldier he laid low with a bronze sword: 590
the hero Eurypylus, Telephus' son, and round him
troops of his own Cetean comrades[9] slaughtered,
lured to war by the bribe his mother took.
The only man I saw to put Eurypylus
in the shade was Memnon,[1] son of the Morning.   595
Again, when our champions climbed inside the horse
that Epeus built with labor, and I held full command
to spring our packed ambush open or keep it sealed,
all our lords and captains were wiping off their tears,
knees shaking beneath each man—but not your son.   600
Never once did I see his glowing skin go pale;
he never flicked a tear from his cheeks, no,
he kept on begging me there to let him burst
from the horse, kept gripping his hilted sword,
his heavy bronze-tipped javelin, keen to loose   605
his fighting fury against the Trojans. Then,
once we'd sacked King Priam's craggy city,
laden with his fair share and princely prize
he boarded his own ship, his body all unscarred.
Not a wound from a flying spear or a sharp sword,   610
cut-and-thrust close up—the common marks of war.
Random, raging Ares plays no favorites.'
                                        So I said and
off he went, the ghost of the great runner, Aeacus'[2] grandson
loping with long strides across the fields of asphodel,

---

8. The Greeks were told by a prophet that Troy would fall only to Achilles' son Neoptolemus, who was
living on the island of Scyros.   9. Eurypylus's people (from Asia Minor), who came to the aid of the
Trojans.   1. King of the Ethiopians, a Trojan ally; his mother was the goddess Dawn.   2. A son of
Zeus.

triumphant in all I had told him of his son,   615
his gallant, glorious son.

   Now the rest of the ghosts, the dead and gone
came swarming up around me—deep in sorrow there,
each asking about the grief that touched him most.
Only the ghost of Great Ajax, son of Telamon,   620
kept his distance, blazing with anger at me still
for the victory I had won by the ships that time
I pressed my claim for the arms of Prince Achilles.
His queenly mother[3] had set them up as prizes,
Pallas and captive Trojans served as judges.   625
Would to god I'd never won such trophies!
All for them the earth closed over Ajax,
that proud hero Ajax . . .
greatest in build, greatest in works of war
of all the Argives after Peleus' matchless son.   630
I cried out to him now, I tried to win him over:
'Ajax, son of noble Telamon, still determined,
even in death, not once to forget that rage
you train on me for those accursed arms?
The gods set up that prize to plague the Achaeans—   635
so great a tower of strength we lost when you went down!
For *your* death we grieved as we did for Achilles' death—
we grieved incessantly, true, and none's to blame
but Zeus, who hated Achaea's fighting spearmen
so intensely, Zeus sealed your doom.   640
Come closer, king, and listen to my story.
Conquer your rage, your blazing, headstrong pride!'

   So I cried out but Ajax answered not a word.
He stalked off toward Erebus, into the dark
to join the other lost, departed dead.   645
Yet now, despite his anger,
he might have spoken to me, or I to him,
but the heart inside me stirred with some desire
to see the ghosts of others dead and gone.

   And I saw Minos there, illustrious son of Zeus,   650
firmly enthroned, holding his golden scepter,
judging all the dead . . .
Some on their feet, some seated, all clustering
round the king of justice, pleading for his verdicts
reached in the House of Death with its all-embracing gates.   655

   I next caught sight of Orion,[4] that huge hunter,
rounding up on the fields of asphodel those wild beasts
the man in life cut down on the lonely mountain-slopes,
brandishing in his hands the bronze-studded club

---

3. Thetis   4. In other legends, transformed after death into a constellation.

that time can never shatter.
     I saw Tityus too,   660
son of the mighty goddess Earth—sprawling there
on the ground, spread over nine acres—two vultures
hunched on either side of him, digging into his liver,
beaking deep in the blood-sac, and he with his frantic hands
could never beat them off, for he had once dragged off   665
the famous consort of Zeus in all her glory,
Leto, threading her way toward Pytho's ridge,
over the lovely dancing-rings of Panopeus.

  And I saw Tantalus[5] too, bearing endless torture.
He stood erect in a pool as the water lapped his chin—   670
parched, he tried to drink, but he could not reach the surface,
no, time and again the old man stooped, craving a sip,
time and again the water vanished, swallowed down,
laying bare the caked black earth at his feet—
some spirit drank it dry. And over his head   675
leafy trees dangled their fruit from high aloft,
pomegranates and pears, and apples glowing red,
succulent figs and olives swelling sleek and dark,
but as soon as the old man would strain to clutch them fast
a gust would toss them up to the lowering dark clouds.   680

  And I saw Sisyphus[6] too, bound to his own torture,
grappling his monstrous boulder with both arms working,
heaving, hands struggling, legs driving, he kept on
thrusting the rock uphill toward the brink, but just
as it teetered, set to topple over—
       time and again   685
the immense weight of the thing would wheel it back and
the ruthless boulder would bound and tumble down to the plain
  again—
so once again he would heave, would struggle to thrust it up,
sweat drenching his body, dust swirling above his head.

  And next I caught a glimpse of powerful Heracles—   690
his ghost, I mean: the man himself delights
in the grand feasts of the deathless gods on high,
wed to Hebe,[7] famed for her lithe, alluring ankles,
the daughter of mighty Zeus and Hera shod in gold.
Around him cries of the dead rang out like cries of birds,   695
scattering left and right in horror as on he came like night,
naked bow in his grip, an arrow grooved on the bowstring,
glaring round him fiercely, forever poised to shoot.
A terror too, that sword-belt sweeping across his chest,

---

5. A king in Asia Minor, a confidant of the gods who ate at their table but abused their hospitality (accounts differ as to how). 6. King of Corinth, the archetype of the liar and trickster; we do not know what crime he is being punished for in this passage. 7. Literally, "Youth." Heracles was made immortal after his death, and so he lives among the gods while only his image remains with the dead (the word translated here as "ghost" literally means "likeness").

a baldric of solid gold emblazoned with awesome work . . .   700
bears and ramping boars and lions with wild, fiery eyes,
and wars, routs and battles, massacres, butchered men.
May the craftsman who forged that masterpiece—
whose skills could conjure up a belt like that—
never forge another!   705
Heracles knew me at once, at first glance,
and hailed me with a winging burst of pity:
'Royal son of Laertes, Odysseus famed for exploits,
luckless man, you too? Braving out a fate as harsh
as the fate I bore, alive in the light of day?   710
Son of Zeus that I was, my torments never ended,
forced to slave for a man not half the man I was:
he saddled me with the worst heartbreaking labors.[8]
Why, he sent me down here once, to retrieve the hound
that guards the dead[9]—no harder task for me, he thought—   715
but I dragged the great beast up from the underworld to earth
and Hermes and gleaming-eyed Athena blazed the way!'

    With that he turned and back he went to the House of Death
but I held fast in place, hoping that others might still come,
shades of famous heroes, men who died in the old days   720
and ghosts of an even older age I longed to see,
Theseus and Pirithous,[1] the gods' own radiant sons.
But before I could, the dead came surging round me,
hordes of them, thousands raising unearthly cries,
and blanching terror gripped me—panicked now   725
that Queen Persephone might send up from Death
some monstrous head, some Gorgon's staring face![2]
I rushed back to my ship, commanded all hands
to take to the decks and cast off cables quickly.
They swung aboard at once, they sat to the oars in ranks   730
and a strong tide of the Ocean River swept her on downstream,
sped by our rowing first, then by a fresh fair wind."

BOOK XII

[The Cattle of the Sun]

"Now when our ship had left the Ocean River rolling in her wake
and launched out into open sea with its long swells to reach
the island of Aeaea—east where the Dawn forever young
has home and dancing-rings and the Sun his risings[3]—
heading in we beached our craft on the sands,   5
the crews swung out on the low sloping shore
and there we fell asleep, awaiting Dawn's first light.

8. Because of Hera's enmity, Heracles was forced to obey Eurystheus of Argos, who ordered him to perform
his twelve famous labors.   9. Cerberus.   1. After his adventures in Crete, Theseus went with his friend
Pirithous to Hades to kidnap Persephone. The venture failed, and the two heroes, imprisoned in Hades,
were rescued by Heracles.   2. Looking at the face of a Gorgon, a female snake-headed monster, turned
the viewer to stone.   3. This description places Circe's island to the east of Greece, though Odysseus's
ship, when it was blown past Cape Malea, was headed west (one more indication that Odyssean geography
is highly imaginative).

As soon as Dawn with her rose-red fingers shone again
I dispatched some men to Circe's halls to bring
the dead Elpenor's body. We cut logs in haste   10
and out on the island's sharpest jutting headland
held his funeral rites in sorrow, streaming tears.
Once we'd burned the dead man and the dead man's armor,
heaping his grave-mound, hauling a stone that coped it well,
we planted his balanced oar aloft to crown his tomb.   15

    And so we saw to his rites, each step in turn.
Nor did our coming back from Death escape Circe—
she hurried toward us, decked in rich regalia,
handmaids following close with trays of bread
and meats galore and glinting ruddy wine.   20
And the lustrous goddess, standing in our midst,
hailed us warmly: 'Ah my daring, reckless friends!
You who ventured down to the House of Death alive,
doomed to die twice over—others die just once.
Come, take some food and drink some wine,   25
rest here the livelong day
and then, tomorrow at daybreak, you must sail.
But I will set you a course and chart each seamark,
so neither on sea nor land will some new trap
ensnare you in trouble, make you suffer more.'   30

    Her foresight won our fighting spirits over.
So all that day till the sun went down we sat
and feasted on sides of meat and heady wine,
and then when the sun had set and night came on
the men lay down to sleep by the ship's stern-cables.   35
But Circe, taking me by the hand, drew me away
from all my shipmates there and sat me down
and lying beside me probed me for details.
I told her the whole story, start to finish,
then the queenly goddess laid my course: 40
'Your descent to the dead is over, true,
but listen closely to what I tell you now
and god himself will bring it back to mind.
First you will raise the island of the Sirens,
those creatures who spellbind any man alive,   45
whoever comes their way. Whoever draws too close,
off guard, and catches the Sirens' voices in the air—
no sailing home for him, no wife rising to meet him,
no happy children beaming up at their father's face.
The high, thrilling song of the Sirens will transfix him,   50
lolling there in their meadow, round them heaps of corpses
rotting away, rags of skin shriveling on their bones . . .
Race straight past that coast! Soften some beeswax
and stop your shipmates' ears so none can hear,
none of the crew, but if *you* are bent on hearing,   55
have them tie you hand and foot in the swift ship,
erect at the mast-block, lashed by ropes to the mast

so you can hear the Sirens' song to your heart's content.
But if you plead, commanding your men to set you free,
then they must lash you faster, rope on rope.   60

But once your crew has rowed you past the Sirens
a choice of routes is yours. I cannot advise you
which to take, or lead you through it all—
you must decide for yourself—
but I can tell you the ways of either course.   65
On one side beetling cliffs shoot up, and against them
pound the huge roaring breakers of blue-eyed Amphitrite—
the Clashing Rocks[4] they're called by all the blissful gods.
Not even birds can escape them, no, not even the doves
that veer and fly ambrosia home to Father Zeus: 70
even of those the sheer Rocks always pick off one
and Father wings one more to keep the number up.
No ship of men has ever approached and slipped past—
always some disaster—big timbers and sailors' corpses
whirled away by the waves and lethal blasts of fire.   75
One ship alone, one deep-sea craft sailed clear,
the *Argo*,[5] sung by the world, when heading home
from Aeetes' shores. And *she* would have crashed
against those giant rocks and sunk at once if Hera,
for love of Jason, had not sped her through.   80

On the other side loom two enormous crags . . .
One thrusts into the vaulting sky its jagged peak,
hooded round with a dark cloud that never leaves—
no clear bright air can ever bathe its crown,
not even in summer's heat or harvest-time.   85
No man on earth could scale it, mount its crest,
not even with twenty hands and twenty feet for climbing,
the rock's so smooth, like dressed and burnished stone.
And halfway up that cliffside stands a fog-bound cavern
gaping west toward Erebus, realm of death and darkness—   90
past it, great Odysseus, you should steer your ship.
No rugged young archer could hit that yawning cave
with a winged arrow shot from off the decks.
Scylla lurks inside it—the yelping horror,
yelping, no louder than any suckling pup   95
but she's a grisly monster, I assure you.
No one could look on her with any joy,
not even a god who meets her face-to-face . . .
She has twelve legs, all writhing, dangling down
and six long swaying necks, a hideous head on each,   100
each head barbed with a triple row of fangs, thickset,

4. These Wandering Rocks (*Planctae*) may or may not be the Symplegades, the Clashing Rocks (thought to be located at the entrance to the Black Sea) that came together to crush whatever tried to pass between them. Homer puts them near Scylla and Charybdis, which later tradition placed in the straits between Italy and Sicily. Once again the text seems to be creating imaginative geography that fuses landmarks of the east and west.   5. The ship of the Argonauts, who brought the Golden Fleece back to Greece from King Aeetes. This line suggests that epic poetry about the Argonauts' voyage preceded the *Odyssey* and may have provided the model for some of Odysseus's wanderings.

packed tight—and armed to the hilt with black death!
Holed up in the cavern's bowels from her waist down
she shoots out her heads, out of that terrifying pit,
angling right from her nest, wildly sweeping the reefs   105
for dolphins, dogfish or any bigger quarry she can drag
from the thousands Amphitrite spawns in groaning seas.
No mariners yet can boast they've raced their ship
past Scylla's lair without some mortal blow—
with each of her six heads she snatches up   110
a man from the dark-prowed craft and whisks him off.

　　The other crag is lower—you will see, Odysseus—
though both lie side-by-side, an arrow-shot apart.
Atop it a great fig-tree rises, shaggy with leaves,
beneath it awesome Charybdis gulps the dark water down.   115
Three times a day she vomits it up, three times she gulps it down,
that terror! Don't be there when the whirlpool swallows down—
not even the earthquake god could save you from disaster.
No, hug Scylla's crag—sail on past her—top speed!
Better by far to lose six men and keep your ship   120
than lose your entire crew.'
　　　　　　　　　　　'Yes, yes,
but tell me the truth now, goddess,' I protested.
'Deadly Charybdis—can't I possibly cut and run from *her*
and still fight Scylla off when Scylla strikes my men?'

　　'So stubborn!' the lovely goddess countered.   125
'Hell-bent yet again on battle and feats of arms?
Can't you bow to the deathless gods themselves?
Scylla's no mortal, she's an immortal devastation,
terrible, savage, wild, no fighting her, no defense—
just flee the creature, that's the only way.   130
Waste any time, arming for battle beside her rock,
I fear she'll lunge out again with all of her six heads
and seize as many men. No, row for your lives,
invoke Brute Force, I tell you, Scylla's mother—
she spawned her to scourge mankind,   135
she can stop the monster's next attack!

　　Then you will make the island of Thrinacia[6] . . .
where herds of the Sungod's cattle graze, and fat sheep
and seven herds of oxen, as many sheepflocks, rich and woolly,
fifty head in each. No breeding swells their number,   140
nor do they ever die. And goddesses herd them on,
nymphs with glinting hair, Phaëthousa, Lampetie,
born to the Sungod Helios by radiant Neaera.
Their queenly mother bred and reared them both
then settled them on the island of Thrinacia—   145
their homeland seas away—
to guard their father's sheep and longhorn cattle.

6. Later Greeks identified this island as Sicily.

Leave the beasts unharmed, your mind set on home,
and you all may still reach Ithaca—bent with hardship,
true—but harm them in any way, and I can see it now:　　150
your ship destroyed, your men destroyed as well!
And even if *you* escape, you'll come home late,
all shipmates lost, and come a broken man.'

At those words Dawn rose on her golden throne
and lustrous Circe made her way back up the island.　　155
I went straight to my ship, commanding all hands
to take to the decks and cast off cables quickly.
They swung aboard at once, they sat to the oars in ranks
and in rhythm churned the water white with stroke on stroke.
And Circe the nymph with glossy braids, the awesome one　　160
who speaks with human voice, sent us a hardy shipmate,
yes, a fresh following wind ruffling up in our wake,
bellying out our sail to drive our blue prow on as we,
securing the running gear from stem to stern, sat back
while the wind and helmsman kept her true on course.　　165
At last, and sore at heart, I told my shipmates,
'Friends . . . it's wrong for only one or two
to know the revelations that lovely Circe
made to me alone. I'll tell you all,
so we can die with our eyes wide open now　　170
or escape our fate and certain death together.
First, she warns, we must steer clear of the Sirens,
their enchanting song, their meadow starred with flowers.
I alone was to hear their voices, so she said,
but you must bind me with tight chafing ropes　　175
so I cannot move a muscle, bound to the spot,
erect at the mast-block, lashed by ropes to the mast.
And if I plead, commanding you to set me free,
then lash me faster, rope on pressing rope.'

So I informed my shipmates point by point,　　180
all the while our trim ship was speeding toward
the Sirens' island, driven on by the brisk wind.
But then—the wind fell in an instant,
all glazed to a dead calm . . .
a mysterious power hushed the heaving swells.　　185
The oarsmen leapt to their feet, struck the sail,
stowed it deep in the hold and sat to the oarlocks,
thrashing with polished oars, frothing the water white.
Now with a sharp sword I sliced an ample wheel of beeswax
down into pieces, kneaded them in my two strong hands　　190
and the wax soon grew soft, worked by my strength
and Helios' burning rays, the sun at high noon,
and I stopped the ears of my comrades one by one.
They bound me hand and foot in the tight ship—
erect at the mast-block, lashed by ropes to the mast—　　195
and rowed and churned the whitecaps stroke on stroke.
We were just offshore as far as a man's shout can carry,

scudding close, when the Sirens sensed at once a ship
was racing past and burst into their high, thrilling song:
'Come closer, famous Odysseus—Achaea's pride and glory—   200
moor your ship on our coast so you can hear our song!
Never has any sailor passed our shores in his black craft
until he has heard the honeyed voices pouring from our lips,
and once he hears to his heart's content sails on, a wiser man.
We know all the pains that the Greeks and Trojans once endured   205
on the spreading plain of Troy when the gods willed it so—
all that comes to pass on the fertile earth, we know it all!'

   So they sent their ravishing voices out across the air
and the heart inside me throbbed to listen longer.
I signaled the crew with frowns to set me free—   210
they flung themselves at the oars and rowed on harder,
Perimedes and Eurylochus springing up at once
to bind me faster with rope on chafing rope.
But once we'd left the Sirens fading in our wake,
once we could hear their song no more, their urgent call—   215
my steadfast crew was quick to remove the wax I'd used
to seal their ears and loosed the bonds that lashed me.

   We'd scarcely put that island astern when suddenly
I saw smoke and heavy breakers, heard their booming thunder.
The men were terrified—oarblades flew from their grip,   220
clattering down to splash in the vessel's wash.
She lay there, dead in the water . . .
no hands to tug the blades that drove her on.
But I strode down the decks to rouse my crewmen,
halting beside each one with a bracing, winning word: 225
'Friends, we're hardly strangers at meeting danger—
and this danger is no worse than what we faced
when Cyclops penned us up in his vaulted cave
with crushing force! But even from there my courage,
my presence of mind and tactics saved us all,   230
and we will live to remember *this* someday,
I have no doubt. Up now, follow my orders,
all of us work as one! You men at the thwarts—
lay on with your oars and strike the heaving swells,
trusting that Zeus will pull us through these straits alive.   235
You, helmsman, here's your order—burn it in your mind—
the steering-oar of our rolling ship is in your hands.
Keep her clear of that smoke and surging breakers,
head for those crags or she'll catch you off guard,
she'll yaw over there—you'll plunge us all in ruin!'   240

   So I shouted. They snapped to each command.
No mention of Scylla—how to fight that nightmare?—
for fear the men would panic, desert their oars
and huddle down and stow themselves away.
But now I cleared my mind of Circe's orders—   245
cramping my style, urging me not to arm at all.

I donned my heroic armor, seized long spears
in both my hands and marched out on the half-deck,
forward, hoping from there to catch the first glimpse
of Scylla, ghoul of the cliffs, swooping to kill my men. 250
But nowhere could I make her out—and my eyes ached,
scanning that mist-bound rock face top to bottom.

Now wailing in fear, we rowed on up those straits,
Scylla to starboard, dreaded Charybdis off to port,
her horrible whirlpool gulping the sea-surge down, down 255
but when she spewed it up—like a cauldron over a raging fire—
all her churning depths would seethe and heave—exploding spray
showering down to splatter the peaks of both crags at once!
But when she swallowed the sea-surge down her gaping maw
the whole abyss lay bare and the rocks around her roared, 260
terrible, deafening—
                    bedrock showed down deep, boiling
black with sand—
                    and ashen terror gripped the men.
But now, fearing death, all eyes fixed on Charybdis—
now Scylla snatched six men from our hollow ship,
the toughest, strongest hands I had, and glancing 265
backward over the decks, searching for my crew
I could see their hands and feet already hoisted,
flailing, high, higher, over my head, look—
wailing down at me, comrades riven in agony,
shrieking out my name for one last time! 270
Just as an angler poised on a jutting rock
flings his treacherous bait in the offshore swell,
whips his long rod—hook sheathed in an oxhorn lure—
and whisks up little fish he flips on the beach-break,
writhing, gasping out their lives . . . so now they writhed, 275
gasping as Scylla swung them up her cliff and there
at her cavern's mouth she bolted them down raw—
screaming out, flinging their arms toward me,
lost in that mortal struggle . . .
Of all the pitiful things I've had to witness, 280
suffering, searching out the pathways of the sea,
this wrenched my heart the most.
                              But now, at last,
putting the Rocks, Scylla and dread Charybdis far astern,
we quickly reached the good green island of the Sun
where Helios, lord Hyperion, keeps his fine cattle, 285
broad in the brow, and flocks of purebred sheep.
Still aboard my black ship in the open sea
I could hear the lowing cattle driven home,
the bleating sheep. And I was struck once more
by the words of the blind Theban prophet, Tiresias, 290
and Aeaean Circe too: time and again they told me
to shun this island of the Sun, the joy of man.
So I warned my shipmates gravely, sick at heart,

'Listen to me, my comrades, brothers in hardship,
let me tell you the dire prophecies of Tiresias   295
and Aeaean Circe too: time and again they told me
to shun this island of the Sun, the joy of man.
Here, they warned, the worst disaster awaits us.
Row straight past these shores—race our black ship on!'

   So I said, and the warnings broke their hearts.   300
But Eurylochus waded in at once—with mutiny on his mind:
'You're a hard man, Odysseus. Your fighting spirit's
stronger than ours, your stamina never fails.
You must be made of iron head to foot. Look,
your crew's half-dead with labor, starved for sleep,   305
and you forbid us to set foot on land, this island here,
washed by the waves, where we might catch a decent meal again.
Drained as we are, night falling fast, you'd have us desert
this haven and blunder off, into the mist-bound seas?
Out of the night come winds that shatter vessels—   310
how can a man escape his headlong death
if suddenly, out of nowhere, a cyclone hits,
bred by the South or stormy West Wind? They're the gales
that tear a ship to splinters—the gods, our masters,
willing or not, it seems. No, let's give way   315
to the dark night, set out our supper here.
Sit tight by our swift ship and then at daybreak
board and launch her, make for open sea!'

   So Eurylochus urged, and shipmates cheered.
Then I knew some power was brewing trouble for us,   320
so I let fly with an anxious plea: 'Eurylochus,
I'm one against all—the upper hand is yours.
But swear me a binding oath, all here, that if
we come on a herd of cattle or fine flock of sheep,
not one man among us—blind in his reckless ways—   325
will slaughter an ox or ram. Just eat in peace,
content with the food immortal Circe gave us.'

   They quickly swore the oath that I required
and once they had vowed they'd never harm the herds,
they moored our sturdy ship in the deep narrow harbor,   330
close to a fresh spring, and all hands disembarked
and adeptly set about the evening meal.
Once they'd put aside desire for food and drink,
they recalled our dear companions, wept for the men
that Scylla plucked from the hollow ship and ate alive,   335
and a welcome sleep came on them in their tears.
                                        But then,
at the night's third watch, the stars just wheeling down,
Zeus who marshals the stormclouds loosed a ripping wind,
a howling, demonic gale, shrouding over in thunderheads
the earth and sea at once—and night swept down from the sky.   340

When young Dawn with her rose-red fingers shone once more
we hauled our craft ashore, securing her in a vaulted cave
where nymphs have lovely dancing-rings and hold their sessions.
There I called a muster, warning my shipmates yet again,
'Friends, we've food and drink aplenty aboard the ship—   345
keep your hands off all these herds or we will pay the price!
The cattle, the sleek flocks, belong to an awesome master,
Helios, god of the sun who sees all, hears all things.'

    So I warned, and my headstrong men complied.
But for one whole month the South Wind blew nonstop,   350
no other wind came up, none but the South, Southeast.
As long as our food and ruddy wine held out, the crew,
eager to save their lives, kept hands off the herds.
But then, when supplies aboard had all run dry,
when the men turned to hunting, forced to range   355
for quarry with twisted hooks: for fish, birds,
anything they could lay their hands on—
hunger racked their bellies—I struck inland,
up the island, there to pray to the gods.
If only one might show me some way home!   360
Crossing into the heartland, clear of the crew,
I rinsed my hands in a sheltered spot, a windbreak,
but soon as I'd prayed to all the gods who rule Olympus,
down on my eyes they poured a sweet, sound sleep . . .
as Eurylochus opened up his fatal plan to friends: 365
'Listen to me, my comrades, brothers in hardship.
All ways of dying are hateful to us poor mortals,
true, but to die of hunger, starve to death—
that's the worst of all. So up with you now,
let's drive off the pick of Helios' sleek herds,   370
slaughter them to the gods who rule the skies up there.
If we ever make it home to Ithaca, native ground,
erect at once a glorious temple to the Sungod,
line the walls with hoards of dazzling gifts!
But if the Sun, inflamed for his longhorn cattle,   375
means to wreck our ship and the other gods pitch in—
I'd rather die at sea, with one deep gulp of death,
than die by inches on this desolate island here!'

    So he urged, and shipmates cheered again.
At once they drove off the Sungod's finest cattle—   380
close at hand, not far from the blue-prowed ship they grazed,
those splendid beasts with their broad brows and curving horns.
Surrounding them in a ring, they lifted prayers to the gods,
plucking fresh green leaves from a tall oak for the rite,
since white strewing-barley was long gone in the ship.   385
Once they'd prayed, slaughtered and skinned the cattle,
they cut the thighbones out, they wrapped them round in fat,
a double fold sliced clean and topped with strips of flesh.
And since they had no wine to anoint the glowing victims,
they made libations with water, broiling all the innards,   390

and once they'd burned the bones and tasted the organs—
hacked the rest into pieces, piercing them with spits.[7]

That moment soothing slumber fell from my eyes
and down I went to our ship at the water's edge
but on my way, nearing the long beaked craft,   395
the smoky savor of roasts came floating up around me . . .
I groaned in anguish, crying out to the deathless gods:
'Father Zeus! the rest of you blissful gods who never die—
you with your fatal sleep, you lulled me into disaster.
Left on their own, look what a monstrous thing   400
my crew concocted!'

                    Quick as a flash
with her flaring robes Lampetie sped the news
to the Sun on high that we had killed his herds
and Helios burst out in rage to all the immortals:
'Father Zeus! the rest of you blissful gods who never die—   405
punish them all, that crew of Laertes' son Odysseus—
what an outrage! They, they killed my cattle,
the great joy of my heart . . . day in, day out,
when I climbed the starry skies and when I wheeled
back down from the heights to touch the earth once more.   410
Unless they pay me back in blood for the butchery of my herds,
down I go to the House of Death and blaze among the dead!'

But Zeus who marshals the thunderheads insisted,
'Sun, you keep on shining among the deathless gods
and mortal men across the good green earth.   415
And as for the guilty ones, why, soon enough
on the wine-dark sea I'll hit their racing ship
with a white-hot bolt, I'll tear it into splinters.'

        —Or so I heard from the lovely nymph Calypso,
who heard it herself, she said, from Hermes, god of guides.   420

As soon as I reached our ship at the water's edge
I took the men to task, upbraiding each in turn,
but how to set things right? We couldn't find a way.
The cattle were dead already . . .
and the gods soon showed us all some fateful signs—   425
the hides began to crawl, the meat, both raw and roasted,
bellowed out on the spits, and we heard a noise
like the moan of lowing oxen.
                    Yet six more days
my eager companions feasted on the cattle of the Sun,
the pick of the herds they'd driven off, but then,   430

---

7. The killing and cooking of the victims follow the usual Homeric pattern of sacrifice, with two exceptions
that are conspicuous because sacrifice scenes in Homer are formulaic: the sailors sprinkle the victims with
leaves instead of barley, and they pour libations with water instead of wine. These departures from the
usual ritual make the sacrifice defective, with ominous implications for Odysseus's companions.

when Cronian Zeus brought on the seventh day,
the wind in its ceaseless raging dropped at last,
and stepping the mast at once, hoisting the white sail
we boarded ship and launched her, made for open sea.

But once we'd left that island in our wake—   435
no land at all in sight, nothing but sea and sky—
then Zeus the son of Cronus mounted a thunderhead
above our hollow ship and the deep went black beneath it.
Nor did the craft scud on much longer. All of a sudden
killer-squalls attacked us, screaming out of the west,   440
a murderous blast shearing the two forestays off
so the mast toppled backward, its running tackle spilling
into the bilge. The mast itself went crashing into the stern,
it struck the helmsman's head and crushed his skull to pulp
and down from his deck the man flipped like a diver—   445
his hardy life spirit left his bones behind.
Then, then in the same breath Zeus hit the craft
with a lightning-bolt and thunder. Round she spun,
reeling under the impact, filled with reeking brimstone,
shipmates pitching out of her, bobbing round like seahawks   450
swept along by the whitecaps past the trim black hull—
and the god cut short their journey home forever.

But I went lurching along our battered hulk
till the sea-surge ripped the plankings from the keel
and the waves swirled it away, stripped bare, and snapped   455
the mast from the decks—but a backstay[8] made of bull's-hide
still held fast, and with this I lashed the mast and keel
together, made them one, riding my makeshift raft
as the wretched galewinds bore me on and on.

At last the West Wind quit its wild rage   460
but the South came on at once to hound me even more,
making me double back my route toward cruel Charybdis.
All night long I was rushed back and then at break of day
I reached the crag of Scylla and dire Charybdis' vortex
right when the dreadful whirlpool gulped the salt sea down.   465
But heaving myself aloft to clutch at the fig-tree's height,
like a bat I clung to its trunk for dear life—not a chance
for a good firm foothold there, no clambering up it either,
the roots too far to reach, the boughs too high overhead,
huge swaying branches that overshadowed Charybdis.   470
But I held on, dead set . . . waiting for her
to vomit my mast and keel back up again—
Oh how I ached for both! and back they came,
late but at last, at just the hour a judge at court,
who's settled the countless suits of brash young claimants,   475
rises, the day's work done, and turns home for supper—

---

8. A rope stretched from the top of the mast to a side or the stern of a ship that, with other ropes fastened
fore and aft, supports the mast.

that's when the timbers reared back up from Charybdis.
I let go—I plunged with my hands and feet flailing,
crashing into the waves beside those great beams
and scrambling aboard them fast   480
I rowed hard with my hands right through the straits . . .
And the father of men and gods did not let Scylla see me,
else I'd have died on the spot—no escape from death.

    I drifted along nine days. On the tenth, at night,
the gods cast me up on Ogygia, Calypso's island,   485
home of the dangerous nymph with glossy braids
who speaks with human voice, and she took me in,
she loved me . . . Why cover the same ground again?
Just yesterday, here at hall, I told you all the rest,
you and your gracious wife. It goes against my grain   490
to repeat a tale told once, and told so clearly."

BOOK XIII

[Ithaca at Last]

His tale was over now. The Phaeacians all fell silent, hushed,
his story holding them spellbound down the shadowed halls
until Alcinous found the poise to say, "Odysseus,
now that you have come to my bronze-floored house,
my vaulted roofs, I know you won't be driven   5
off your course, nothing can hold you back—
however much you've suffered, you'll sail home.
Here, friends, here's a command for one and all,
you who frequent my palace day and night and drink
the shining wine of kings and enjoy the harper's songs.   10
The robes and hammered gold and a haul of other gifts
you lords of our island council brought our guest—
all lie packed in his polished sea-chest now. Come,
each of us add a sumptuous tripod, add a cauldron!
Then recover our costs with levies on the people: 15
it's hard to afford such bounty man by man."

    The king's instructions met with warm applause
and home they went to sleep, each in his own house.
When young Dawn with her rose-red fingers shone once more
they hurried down to the ship with handsome bronze gifts,   20
and striding along the decks, the ardent King Alcinous
stowed them under the benches, shipshape, so nothing
could foul the crewmen tugging at their oars.
Then back the party went to Alcinous' house
and shared a royal feast.
                    The majestic king   25
slaughtered an ox for them to Cronus' mighty son,
Zeus of the thundercloud, whose power rules the world.
They burned the thighs and fell to the lordly banquet,
reveling there, while in their midst the inspired bard
struck up a song, Demodocus, prized by all the people.   30

True, but time and again Odysseus turned his face
toward the radiant sun, anxious for it to set,
yearning now to be gone and home once more . . .
As a man aches for his evening meal when all day long
his brace of wine-dark oxen have dragged the bolted plowshare   35
down a fallow field—how welcome the setting sun to him,
the going home to supper, yes, though his knees buckle,
struggling home at last. So welcome now to Odysseus
the setting light of day, and he lost no time
as he pressed Phaeacia's men who love their oars,   40
addressing his host, Alcinous, first and foremost:
"Alcinous, majesty, shining among your island people,
make your libations, launch me safely on my way—
to one and all, farewell!
All is now made good, my heart's desire,   45
your convoy home, your precious, loving gifts,
and may the gods of Olympus bless them for me!
May I find an unswerving wife when I reach home,
and loved ones hale, unharmed! And you, my friends
remaining here in your kingdom now, may you delight   50
in your loyal wives and children! May the gods
rain down all kinds of fortune on your lives,
misfortune never harbor in your homeland!"

    All burst into applause, urging passage home
for their parting guest, his farewell rang so true.   55
Hallowed King Alcinous briskly called his herald:
"Come, Pontonous! Mix the wine in the bowl,
pour rounds to all our banqueters in the house,
so we, with a prayer to mighty Zeus the Father,
can sail our new friend home to native land."   60

    Pontonous mixed the heady, honeyed wine
and hovering closely, poured full rounds for all.
And from where they sat they tipped libations out
to the happy gods who rule the vaulting skies.
Then King Odysseus rose up from his seat   65
and placing his two-eared cup in Arete's hands,
addressed the queen with parting wishes on the wing:
"Your health, my queen, through all your days to come—
until old age and death, that visit all mankind,
pay you a visit too. Now I am on my way   70
but you, may you take joy in this house of yours,
in your children, your people, in Alcinous the king!"

    With that the great Odysseus strode across the threshold.
And King Alcinous sent the herald off with the guest
to lead him down to the swift ship and foaming surf.   75
And Arete sent her serving-women, one to carry
a sea-cloak, washed and fresh, a shirt as well,
another assigned to bear the sturdy chest
and a third to take the bread and ruddy wine.

When they reached the ship at the water's edge   80
the royal escorts took charge of the gifts at once
and stores of food and wine, stowed them deep in the holds,
and then for their guest they spread out rug and sheets
on the half-deck, clear astern on the ship's hull
so he might sleep there soundly, undisturbed.   85
And last, Odysseus climbed aboard himself
and down he lay, all quiet
as crewmen sat to the oarlocks, each in line.
They slipped the cable free of the drilled stone post
and soon as they swung back and the blades tossed up the spray   90
an irresistible sleep fell deeply on his eyes, the sweetest,
soundest oblivion, still as the sleep of death itself . . .
And the ship like a four-horse team careering down the plain,
all breaking as one with the whiplash cracking smartly,
leaping with hoofs high to run the course in no time—   95
so the stern hove high and plunged with the seething rollers
crashing dark in her wake as on she surged unwavering,
never flagging, no, not even a darting hawk,
the quickest thing on wings, could keep her pace
as on she ran, cutting the swells at top speed,   100
bearing a man endowed with the gods' own wisdom,
one who had suffered twenty years of torment, sick at heart,
cleaving his way through wars of men and pounding waves at sea
but now he slept in peace, the memory of his struggles
laid to rest.
          And then, that hour the star rose up,   105
the clearest, brightest star, that always heralds
the newborn light of day, the deep-sea-going ship
made landfall on the island . . . Ithaca, at last.

There on the coast a haven lies, named for Phorcys,
the old god of the deep—with two jutting headlands,   110
sheared off at the seaward side but shelving toward the bay,
that break the great waves whipped by the gales outside
so within the harbor ships can ride unmoored
whenever they come in mooring range of shore.
At the harbor's head a branching olive stands   115
with a welcome cave nearby it, dank with sea-mist,
sacred to nymphs of the springs we call the Naiads.
There are mixing-bowls inside and double-handled jars,
crafted of stone, and bees store up their honey in the hollows.
There are long stone looms as well, where the nymphs weave out   120
their webs from clouds of sea-blue wool—a marvelous sight—
and a wellspring flows forever. The cave has two ways in,
one facing the North Wind, a pathway down for mortals;
the other, facing the South, belongs to the gods,
no man may go that way . . .   125
it is the path for all the deathless powers.

Here at this bay the Phaeacian crew put in—
they'd known it long before—driving the ship so hard

she ran up onto the beach for a good half her length,
such way the oarsmen's brawny arms had made.   130
Up from the benches, swinging down to land,
first they lifted Odysseus off the decks—
linen and lustrous carpet too—and laid him
down on the sand asleep, still dead to the world,
then hoisted out the treasures proud Phaeacians,   135
urged by open-hearted Pallas, had lavished on him,
setting out for home. They heaped them all
by the olive's trunk, in a neat pile, clear
of the road for fear some passerby might spot
and steal Odysseus' hoard before he could awaken.   140
Then pushing off, they pulled for home themselves.

     But now Poseidon, god of the earthquake, never once
forgetting the first threats he leveled at the hero,
probed almighty Zeus to learn his plans in full:
"Zeus, Father, I will lose all my honor now   145
among the immortals, now there are mortal men
who show me no respect—Phaeacians, too,
born of my own loins! I said myself
that Odysseus would suffer long and hard
before he made it home, but I never dreamed   150
of blocking his return, not absolutely at least,
once *you* had pledged your word and bowed your head.
But now they've swept him across the sea in their swift ship,
they've set him down in Ithaca, sound asleep, and loaded the man
with boundless gifts—bronze and hoards of gold and robes—   155
aye, more plunder than he could ever have won from Troy
if Odysseus had returned intact with his fair share!"

     "Incredible," Zeus who marshals the thunderheads replied.
"Earth-shaker, you with your massive power, why moaning so?
The gods don't disrespect you. What a stir there'd be   160
if they flung abuse at the oldest, noblest of them all.
Those mortals? If any man, so lost in his strength
and prowess, pays you no respect—just pay him back.
The power is always yours.
Do what you like. Whatever warms your heart."   165

     "King of the dark cloud," the earthquake god agreed,
"I'd like to avenge myself at once, as you advise,
but I've always feared your wrath and shied away.
But now I'll crush that fine Phaeacian cutter
out on the misty sea, now on her homeward run   170
from the latest convoy. They will learn at last
to cease and desist from escorting every man alive—
I'll pile a huge mountain round about their port!"

     "Wait, dear brother," Zeus who collects the clouds
had second thoughts. "Here's what seems best to *me*.   175
As the people all lean down from the city heights

to watch her speeding home, strike her into a rock
that looks like a racing vessel, just offshore—
amaze all men with a marvel for the ages.
Then pile your huge mountain round about their port."[9]   180

Hearing that from Zeus, the god of the earthquake
sped to Scheria now, the Phaeacians' island home,
and waited there till the ship came sweeping in,
scudding lightly along—and surging close abreast,
the earthquake god with one flat stroke of his hand   185
struck her to stone, rooted her to the ocean floor
and made for open sea.
                            The Phaeacians, aghast,
those lords of the long oars, the master mariners
traded startled glances, sudden outcries:
"Look—who's pinned our swift ship to the sea?"   190

"Just racing for home!"
                            "Just hove into plain view!"

They might well wonder, blind to what had happened,
till Alcinous rose and made things all too clear:
"Oh no—my father's prophecy years ago . . .
it all comes home to me with a vengeance now!   195
He used to say Poseidon was vexed with us because
we escorted all mankind and never came to grief.
He said that one day, as a well-built ship of ours
sailed home on the misty sea from such a convoy,
the god would crush it, yes,   200
and pile a huge mountain round about our port.
So the old king foretold. Now, look, it all comes true!
Hurry, friends, do as I say, let us all comply:
stop our convoys home for every castaway
chancing on our city! As for Poseidon,   205
sacrifice twelve bulls to the god at once—
the pick of the herds. Perhaps he'll pity us,
pile no looming mountain ridge around our port."

The people, terrified, prepared the bulls at once.
So all of Phaeacia's island lords and captains,   210
milling round the altar, lifted prayers
to Poseidon, master of the sea . . .
                            That very moment
great Odysseus woke from sleep on native ground at last—
he'd been away for years—but failed to know the land
for the goddess Pallas Athena, Zeus's daughter,   215
showered mist over all, so under cover

9. In the manuscripts, as translated here, Zeus agrees with Poseidon's intention to cut the Phaeacians off
from the sea altogether by surrounding their city with a mountain but suggests that instead of wrecking
the returning ship he turn it into a rock. But already in antiquity the great Alexandrian scholar Aristophanes
of Byzantium (ca. 257–180 B.C.E.) proposed emending the text to read "but *do not* pile your huge mountain
around their port." The Phaeacians' ultimate fate is not revealed, and the line has been much discussed
since antiquity, since questions of divine justice seem to be at stake.

she might change his appearance head to foot
as she told him every peril he'd meet at home—
keep him from being known by wife, townsmen, friends,
till the suitors paid the price for all their outrage.   220
And so to the king himself all Ithaca looked strange . . .
the winding beaten paths, the coves where ships can ride,
the steep rock face of the cliffs and the tall leafy trees.
He sprang to his feet and, scanning his own native country,
groaned, slapped his thighs with his flat palms   225
and Odysseus cried in anguish:
"Man of misery, whose land have I lit on now?
What *are* they here—violent, savage, lawless?
or friendly to strangers, god-fearing men?
Where can I take this heap of treasure now   230
and where in the world do I wander off myself?
If only the trove had stayed among the Phaeacians there
and I had made my way to some other mighty king
who would have hosted me well and sent me home!
But now I don't know where to stow all this,   235
and I can't leave it here, inviting any bandit
to rob me blind.
                            So damn those lords and captains,
those Phaeacians! Not entirely honest or upright, were they?
Sweeping me off to this, this no-man's-land, and they,
they swore they'd sail me home to sunny Ithaca—well,   240
they never kept their word. Zeus of the Suppliants
pay them back—he keeps an eye on the world of men
and punishes all transgressors!
                            Come, quickly,
I'll inspect my treasure and count it up myself.
Did they make off with anything in their ship?"   245

   With that he counted up the gorgeous tripods,
cauldrons, bars of gold and the lovely woven robes.
Not a stitch was missing from the lot. But still
he wept for his native country, trailing down the shore
where the wash of sea on shingle ebbs and flows,   250
his homesick heart in turmoil.
But now Athena appeared and came toward him.
She looked like a young man . . . a shepherd boy
yet elegant too, with all the gifts that grace the sons of kings,
with a well-cut cloak falling in folds across her shoulders,   255
sandals under her shining feet, a hunting spear in hand.
Odysseus, overjoyed at the sight, went up to meet her,
joining her now with salutations on the wing:
"Greetings, friend! Since you are the first
I've come on in this harbor, treat me kindly—   260
no cruelty, please. Save these treasures,
save me too. I pray to you like a god,
I fall before your knees and ask your mercy!
And tell me this for a fact—I need to know—
where on earth am I? what land? who lives here?   265

Is it one of the sunny islands or some jutting shore
of the good green mainland slanting down to sea?"

    Athena answered, her eyes brightening now,
"You must be a fool, stranger, or come from nowhere,
if you really have to ask what land this is.   270
Trust me, it's not so nameless after all.
It's known the world around,
to all who live to the east and rising sun
and to all who face the western mists and darkness.
It's a rugged land, too cramped for driving horses,   275
but though it's far from broad, it's hardly poor.
There's plenty of grain for bread, grapes for wine,
the rains never fail and the dewfall's healthy.
Good country for goats, good for cattle too—
there's stand on stand of timber   280
and water runs in streambeds through the year.
                      So,
stranger, the name of Ithaca's reached as far as Troy,
and Troy, they say, is a long hard sail from Greece."

    Ithaca . . . Heart racing, Odysseus that great exile
filled with joy to hear Athena, daughter of storming Zeus,   285
pronounce that name. He stood on native ground at last
and he replied with a winging word to Pallas,
not with a word of truth—he choked it back,
always invoking the cunning in his heart:
"Ithaca . . . yes, I seem to have heard of Ithaca,   290
even on Crete's broad island far across the sea,
and now I've reached it myself, with all this loot,
but I left behind an equal measure for my children.
I'm a fugitive now, you see. I killed Idomeneus'[1] son,
Orsilochus, lightning on his legs, a man who beat   295
all runners alive on that long island—what a racer!
He tried to rob me of all the spoil I'd won at Troy,
the plunder I went to hell and back to capture, true,
cleaving my way through wars of men and waves at sea—
and just because I refused to please his father,   300
serve under *him* at Troy. I led my own command.
So now with a friend I lay in wait by the road,
I killed him just loping in from the fields—
with one quick stroke of my bronze spear
in the dead of night, the heavens pitch-black . . .   305
no one could see us, spot me tearing out his life
with a weapon honed for action. Once I'd cut him down
I made for a ship and begged the Phoenician crew[2] for mercy,
paying those decent hands a hearty share of plunder—
asked them to take me on and land me down in Pylos,   310

---

1. A prominent Greek warrior in the *Iliad* and king of Crete (the "long island" of line 296).   2. The
Phoenicians figure as (sometimes unreliable) traders in several stories told in the second half of the *Odyssey*.
Their trading ships in fact reached many parts of the Mediterranean in Homer's time.

there or lovely Elis, where Epeans rule in power.
But a heavy galewind blew them way off course,
much against their will—
they'd no desire to cheat me. Driven afar,
we reached this island here at the midnight hour,   315
rowing for dear life, we made it into your harbor—
not a thought of supper, much as we all craved food,
we dropped from the decks and lay down, just like that!
A welcome sleep came over my weary bones at once,
while the crew hoisted up my loot from the holds   320
and set it down on the sand near where I slept.
They reembarked, now homeward bound for Sidon,
their own noble city, leaving me here behind,
homesick in my heart . . ."

　　　　　　　　　　As his story ended,
goddess Athena, gray eyes gleaming, broke into a smile   325
and stroked him with her hand, and now she appeared a woman,
beautiful, tall and skilled at weaving lovely things.
Her words went flying straight toward Odysseus:
"Any man—any god who met you—would have to be
some champion lying cheat to get past *you*   330
for all-round craft and guile! You terrible man,
foxy, ingenious, never tired of twists and tricks—
so, not even here, on native soil, would you give up
those wily tales that warm the cockles of your heart!
Come, enough of this now. We're both old hands   335
at the arts of intrigue. Here among mortal men
you're far the best at tactics, spinning yarns,
and I am famous among the gods for wisdom,
cunning wiles, too.
Ah, but you never recognized me, did you?   340
Pallas Athena, daughter of Zeus—who always
stands beside you, shields you in every exploit:
thanks to me the Phaeacians all embraced you warmly.
And now I am here once more, to weave a scheme with you
and to hide the treasure-trove Phaeacia's nobles   345
lavished on you then—I willed it, planned it so
when you set out for home—and to tell you all
the trials you must suffer in your palace . . .
Endure them all. You must. You have no choice.
And to no one—no man, no woman, not a soul—   350
reveal that you are the wanderer home at last.
No, in silence you must bear a world of pain,
subject yourself to the cruel abuse of men."

　　"Ah goddess," the cool tactician countered,
"you're so hard for a mortal man to know on sight,   355
however shrewd he is—the shapes you take are endless!
But I do know this: you were kind to me in the war years,
so long as we men of Achaea soldiered on at Troy.
But once we'd sacked King Priam's craggy city,
boarded ship, and a god dispersed the fleet,   360

from then on, daughter of Zeus, I never saw you,
never glimpsed you striding along my decks
to ward off some disaster. No, I wandered on,
my heart forever torn to pieces inside my chest
till the gods released me from my miseries at last,   365
that day in the fertile kingdom of Phaeacia when
you cheered me with words, in person, led me to their city.
But now I beg you by your almighty Father's name . . .
for I can't believe I've reached my sunny Ithaca,
I must be roaming around one more exotic land—   370
you're mocking me, I know it, telling me tales
to make me lose my way. Tell me the truth now,
have I really reached the land I love?"

　　"Always the same, your wary turn of mind,"
Athena exclaimed, her glances flashing warmly.   375
"That's why I can't forsake you in your troubles—
you are so winning, so worldly-wise, so self-possessed!
Anyone else, come back from wandering long and hard,
would have hurried home at once, delighted to see
his children and his wife. Oh, but not you,   380
it's not your pleasure to probe for news of them—
you must put your wife to the proof yourself!
But she, she waits in your halls, as always,
her life an endless hardship . . .
wasting away the nights, weeping away the days.   385
I never had doubts myself, no, I knew down deep
that you would return at last, with all your shipmates lost.
But I could not bring myself to fight my Father's brother,
Poseidon, quaking with anger at you, still enraged
because you blinded the Cyclops, his dear son.   390
But come, let me show you Ithaca's setting,
I'll convince you. This haven—look around—
it's named for Phorcys, the old god of the deep,
and here at the harbor's head the branching olive stands
with the welcome cave nearby it, dank with sea-mist,   395
sacred to nymphs of the springs we call the Naiads.
Here, under its arching vault, time and again
you'd offer the nymphs a generous sacrifice
to bring success! And the slopes above you, look,
Mount Neriton decked in forests!"

　　　　　　　　　　　　At those words   400
the goddess scattered the mist and the country stood out clear
and the great man who had borne so much rejoiced at last,
thrilled to see his Ithaca—he kissed the good green earth
and raised his hands to the nymphs and prayed at once,
"Nymphs of the springs, Naiads, daughters of Zeus,   405
I never dreamed I would see you yet again . . .
Now rejoice in my loving prayers—and later,
just like the old days, I will give you gifts
if Athena, Zeus's daughter, Queen of Armies
comes to my rescue, grants this fighter life   410

and brings my son to manhood!"
                                    "Courage!"—
goddess Athena answered, eyes afire—
"Free your mind of all that anguish now.
Come, quick, let's bury your treasures here
in some recess of this haunted hallowed cave   415
where they'll be safe and sound,
then we'll make plans so we can win the day."
                                    With that
the goddess swept into the cavern's shadowed vault,
searching for hiding-places far inside its depths
while Odysseus hauled his treasures closer up,   420
the gold, durable bronze and finespun robes,
the Phaeacians' parting gifts.
Once he'd stowed them well away, the goddess,
Pallas Athena, daughter of storming Zeus,
sealed the mouth of the cavern with a stone.   425

Then down they sat by the sacred olive's trunk
to plot the death of the high and mighty suitors.
The bright-eyed goddess Athena led the way:
"Royal son of Laertes, Odysseus, old campaigner,
think how to lay your hands on all those brazen suitors,   430
lording it over your house now, three whole years,
courting your noble wife, offering gifts to win her.
But she, forever broken-hearted for your return,
builds up each man's hopes—
dangling promises, dropping hints to each—   435
but all the while with something else in mind."

    "God help me!" the man of intrigue broke out:
"Clearly I might have died the same ignoble death
as Agamemnon, bled white in my own house too,
if you had never revealed this to me now,   440
goddess, point by point.
Come, weave us a scheme so I can pay them back!
Stand beside me, Athena, fire me with daring, fierce
as the day we ripped Troy's glittering crown of towers down.
Stand by me—furious now as then, my bright-eyed one—   445
and I would fight three hundred men, great goddess,
with you to brace me, comrade-in-arms in battle!"

    Gray eyes ablaze, the goddess urged him on:
"Surely I'll stand beside you, not forget you,
not when the day arrives for us to do our work.   450
Those men who court your wife and waste your goods?
I have a feeling some will splatter your ample floors
with all their blood and brains. Up now, quickly.
First I will transform you—no one must know you.
I will shrivel the supple skin on your lithe limbs,   455
strip the russet curls from your head and deck you out

in rags you'd hate to see some other mortal wear;
I'll dim the fire in your eyes, so shining once—
until you seem appalling to all those suitors,
even your wife and son you left behind at home.   460
But you, you make your way to the swineherd first,
in charge of your pigs, and true to you as always,
loyal friend to your son, to Penelope, so self-possessed.
You'll find him posted beside his swine, grubbing round
by Raven's Rock and the spring called Arethusa,   465
rooting for feed that makes pigs sleek and fat,
the nuts they love, the dark pools they drink.
Wait there, sit with him, ask him all he knows.
I'm off to Sparta, where the women are a wonder,
to call Telemachus home, your own dear son, Odysseus.   470
He's journeyed to Lacedaemon's rolling hills
to see Menelaus, searching for news of you,
hoping to learn if you are still alive."

    Shrewd Odysseus answered her at once:
"Why not tell him the truth? You know it all.   475
Or is *he* too—like father, like son—condemned
to hardship, roving over the barren salt sea
while strangers devour our livelihood right here?"

    But the bright-eyed goddess reassured him firmly:
"No need for anguish, trust me, not for him—   480
I escorted your son myself
so he might make his name by sailing there.
Nor is he saddled down with any troubles now.
He sits at ease in the halls of Menelaus,
bathed in endless bounty . . . True enough,   485
some young lords in a black cutter lurk in ambush,
poised to kill the prince before he reaches home,
but I have my doubts they will. Sooner the earth
will swallow down a few of those young gallants
who eat you out of house and home these days!"   490

    No more words, not now—
Athena stroked Odysseus with her wand.
She shriveled the supple skin on his lithe limbs,
stripped the russet curls from his head, covered his body
top to toe with the wrinkled hide of an old man   495
and dimmed the fire in his eyes, so shining once.
She turned his shirt and cloak into squalid rags,
ripped and filthy, smeared with grime and soot.
She flung over this the long pelt of a bounding deer,
rubbed bare, and gave him a staff and beggar's sack,   500
torn and tattered, slung from a fraying rope.
               All plans made,
they went their separate ways—Athena setting off
to bring Telemachus home from hallowed Lacedaemon.

BOOK XIV

[The Loyal Swineherd]

So up from the haven now Odysseus climbed a rugged path
through timber along high ground—Athena had shown the way—
to reach the swineherd's place, that fine loyal man
who of all the household hands Odysseus ever had
cared the most for his master's worldly goods.   5

   Sitting at the door of his lodge he found him,
there in his farmstead, high-walled, broad and large,
with its long view on its cleared rise of ground . . .
The swineherd made those walls with his own hands
to enclose the pigs of his master gone for years.   10
Alone, apart from his queen or old Laertes,
he'd built them up of quarried blocks of stone
and coped them well with a fence of wild pear.
Outside he'd driven stakes in a long-line stockade,
a ring of thickset palings split from an oak's dark heart.   15
Within the yard he'd built twelve sties, side-by-side,
to bed his pigs, and in each one fifty brood-sows
slept aground, penned and kept for breeding.
The boars slept outside, but far fewer of them,
thanks to the lordly suitors' feasts that kept on   20
thinning the herd and kept the swineherd stepping,
sending to town each day the best fat hog in sight.
By now they were down to three hundred and sixty head.
But guarding them all the time were dogs like savage beasts,
a pack of four, reared by the swineherd, foreman of men.   25
The man himself was fitting sandals to his feet,
carving away at an oxhide, dark and supple.
As for his men, three were off with their pigs,
herding them here or there. Under orders he'd sent
a fourth to town, with hog in tow for the gorging suitors   30
to slaughter off and glut themselves with pork.

   Suddenly—those snarling dogs spotted Odysseus,
charged him fast—a shatter of barks—but Odysseus
sank to the ground at once, he knew the trick:
the staff dropped from his hand but here and now,   35
on his own farm, he might have taken a shameful mauling.
Yes, but the swineherd, quick to move, dashed for the gate,
flinging his oxhide down, rushed the dogs with curses,
scattered them left and right with flying rocks
and warned his master, "Lucky to be alive, old man—   40
a moment more, my pack would have torn you limb from limb!
Then you'd have covered me with shame. As if the gods
had never given me blows and groans aplenty . . .
Here I sit, my heart aching, broken for *him*,
my master, my great king—fattening up   45
his own hogs for other men to eat, while he,

starving for food, I wager, wanders the earth,
a beggar adrift in strangers' cities, foreign-speaking lands,
if he's still alive, that is, still sees the rising sun.
Come, follow me into my place, old man, so you,   50
at least, can eat your fill of bread and wine.
Then you can tell me where you're from
and all the pains you've weathered."
                              On that note
the loyal swineherd led the way to his shelter,
showed his guest inside and sat Odysseus down   55
on brush and twigs he piled up for the visitor,
flinging over these the skin of a shaggy wild goat,
broad and soft, the swineherd's own good bedding.
The king, delighted to be so well received,
thanked the man at once: "My host—may Zeus   60
and the other gods give *you* your heart's desire
for the royal welcome you have shown me here!"

   And you[3] replied, Eumaeus, loyal swineherd,
"It's wrong, my friend, to send any stranger packing—
even one who arrives in worse shape than you.   65
Every stranger and beggar comes from Zeus
and whatever scrap they get from the likes of us,
they'll find it welcome. That's the best we can do,
we servants, always cowed by our high and mighty masters,
especially our young lords . . . But my old king?   70
The gods, they must have blocked his journey home.
He'd have treated me well, he would, with a house,
a plot of land and a wife you'd gladly prize.
Goods that a kind lord will give a household hand
who labors for him, hard, whose work the gods have sped,   75
just as they speed the work I labor at all day.
My master, I tell you, would have repaid me well
if he'd grown old right here. But now he's dead . . .
If only Helen and all her kind had died out too,
brought to her knees, just as she cut the legs   80
from under troops of men! My king among them,
he went off to the stallion-land of Troy
to fight the Trojans, save Agamemnon's honor!"
                              Enough—
he brusquely cinched his belt around his shirt,
strode out to the pens, crammed with droves of pigs,   85
picked out two, bundled them in and slaughtered both,
singed them, sliced them down, skewered them through
and roasting all to a turn, set them before Odysseus,
sizzling hot on the spits.
Then coating the meat with white barley groats   90
and mixing honeyed wine in a carved wooden bowl,

---

3. This form of direct address by poet to character is confined to Eumaeus in the *Odyssey*, but in the *Iliad* it is used with five different characters (among them the god Apollo and the obscure Melanippus). What special effect was intended, if any, is unknown.

he sat down across from his guest, inviting warmly,
"Eat up now, my friend. It's all we slaves have got,
scrawny pork, while the suitors eat the fatted hogs—
no fear of the gods in their hard hearts, no mercy!   95
Trust me, the blessed gods have no love for crime.
They honor justice, honor the decent acts of men.
Even cutthroat bandits who raid foreign parts—
and Zeus grants them a healthy share of plunder,
ships filled to the brim, and back they head for home—   100
even their dark hearts are stalked by the dread of vengeance.
But the suitors know, they've caught some godsent rumor
of master's grisly death! That's why they have no mind
to do their courting fairly or go back home in peace.
No, at their royal ease they devour all his goods,   105
those brazen rascals never spare a scrap!
Not a day or a night goes by, sent down by Zeus,
but they butcher victims, never stopping at one or two,
and drain his wine as if there's no tomorrow—
swilling the last drop . . .   110
Believe me, my master's wealth was vast!
No other prince on earth could match his riches,
not on the loamy mainland or here at home in Ithaca—
no twenty men in the world could equal his great treasures!
Let me count them off for you. A dozen herds of cattle   115
back on the mainland, just as many head of sheep,
as many droves of pigs and goatflocks ranging free;
hired hands or his own herdsmen keep them grazing there.
Here in Ithaca, goatflocks, eleven in all, scatter
to graze the island, out at the wild end,   120
and trusty goatherds watch their every move.
And each herdsman, day after day, it never ends,
drives in a beast for the suitors—best in sight,
a sheep or well-fed goat. While I tend to these pigs,
I guard them, pick the best for those carousers   125
and send it to the slaughter!"
                                    His voice rose
while the stranger ate his meat and drank his wine,
ravenous, bolting it all down in silence . . .
brooding on ways to serve the suitors right.
But once he'd supped and refreshed himself with food,   130
he filled the wooden bowl he'd been drinking from,
brimmed it with wine and passed it to his host
who received the offer gladly, spirit cheered
as the stranger probed him now with winging words:
"Friend, who was the man who bought you with his goods,   135
the master of such vast riches, powerful as you say?
You tell me he died defending Agamemnon's honor?
What's his name? I just might know such a man . . .
Zeus would know, and the other deathless gods,
if I ever saw him, if I bring you any news,   140
I've roamed the whole earth over."

And the good swineherd answered, foreman of men,
"Old friend, no wanderer landing here with news of *him*
is likely to win his wife and dear son over.
Random drifters, hungry for bed and board,
lie through their teeth and swallow back the truth.   145
Why, any tramp washed up on Ithaca's shores
scurries right to my mistress, babbling lies,
and she ushers him in, kindly, pressing for details,
and the warm tears of grief come trickling down her cheeks,   150
the loyal wife's way when her husband's died abroad.
Even you, old codger, could rig up some fine tale—
and soon enough, I'd say,
if they gave you shirt and clothing for your pains.
My master? Well, no doubt the dogs and wheeling birds   155
have ripped the skin from his ribs by now, his life is through—
or fish have picked him clean at sea, and the man's bones
lie piled up on the mainland, buried deep in sand . . .
he's dead and gone. Aye, leaving a broken heart
for loved ones left behind, for *me* most of all.   160
Never another master kind as he!
I'll never find one—no matter where I go,
not even if I went back to mother and father,
the house where I was born and my parents reared me once.
Ah, but much as I grieve for them, much as I long   165
to lay my eyes on them, set foot on the old soil,
it's longing for him, him that wrings my heart—
Odysseus, lost and gone!
That man, old friend, far away as he is . . .
I can scarcely bear to say his name aloud,   170
so deeply he loved me, cared for me, so deeply.
Worlds away as he is, I call him Master, Brother!"

    "My friend," the great Odysseus, long in exile, answered,
"since you are dead certain, since you still insist
he's never coming back, still the soul of denial,   175
I won't simply say it—on my oath I swear
Odysseus is on his way!
Reward for such good news? Let me have it
the moment he sets foot in his own house,
dress me in shirt and cloak, in handsome clothes.   180
Before then, poor as I am, I wouldn't take a thing.
I hate that man like the very Gates of Death who,
ground down by poverty, stoops to peddling lies.
I swear by Zeus, the first of all the gods,
by this table of hospitality here, my host,   185
by Odysseus' hearth where I have come for help:
all will come to pass, I swear, exactly as I say.
True, this very month—just as the old moon dies
and the new moon rises into life—Odysseus will return!
He will come home and take revenge on any man   190
who offends his wedded wife and princely son!"

"Good news," you replied, Eumaeus, loyal swineherd,
"but I will never pay a reward for *that*, old friend—
Odysseus, he'll never come home again. Never . . .
Drink your wine, sit back, let's talk of other things.   195
Don't remind me of all this. The heart inside me
breaks when anyone mentions my dear master.
That oath of yours, we'll let it pass—
                                          Odysseus,
oh come back!—
                Just as *I* wish, I and Penelope,
old Laertes too, Telemachus too, the godlike boy.   200
How I grieve for *him* now, I can't stop—Odysseus' son,
Telemachus. The gods reared him up like a fine young tree
and I often said, 'In the ranks of men he'll match his father,
his own dear father—amazing in build and looks, that boy!'
But all of a sudden a god wrecks his sense of balance—   205
god or man, no matter—off he's gone to catch
some news of his father, down to holy Pylos.
And now those gallant suitors lie in wait for him,
sailing home, to tear the royal line of Arcesius
out of Ithaca, root and branch, good name and all!   210
Enough. Let *him* pass too—whether he's trapped
or the hand of Zeus will pull him through alive.
                                          Come,
old soldier, tell me the story of your troubles,
tell me truly, too, I'd like to know it well . . .
Who are you? where are you from? your city? your parents?   215
What sort of vessel brought you? Why did the sailors
land you here in Ithaca? Who did they say they are?
I hardly think you came this way on foot."

     The great teller of tales returned at length,
"My story—the whole truth—I'm glad to tell it all.   220
If only the two of us had food and mellow wine
to last us long, here in your shelter now,
for us to sup on, undisturbed,
while others take the work of the world in hand,
I could easily spend all year and never reach the end   225
of my endless story, all the heartbreaking trials
I struggled through. The gods willed it so . . .

     I hail from Crete's broad land, I'm proud to say,
and I am a rich man's son. And many other sons
he brought up in his palace, born in wedlock,   230
sprung of his lawful wife. Unlike my mother.
She was a slave, a concubine he'd purchased, yes,
but he treated me on a par with all his true-born sons—
Castor, Hylax' son. I'm proud to boast his blood, that man
revered like a god throughout all Crete those days,   235
for wealth, power and all his glorious offspring.
But the deadly spirits soon swept him down
to the House of Death, and his high and mighty sons

carved up his lands and then cast lots for the parts
and gave me just a pittance, a paltry house as well.   240
But I won myself a wife from wealthy, landed people,
thanks to my own strong points. I was no fool
and never shirked a fight.
                But now my heyday's gone—
I've had my share of blows. Yet look hard at the husk
and you'll still see, I think, the grain that gave it life.   245
By heaven, Ares gave me courage, Athena too, to break
the ranks of men wide open, once, in the old days,
whenever I picked my troops and formed an ambush,
plotting attacks to spring against our foes—
no hint of death could daunt my fighting spirit!   250
Far out of the front I'd charge and spear my man,
I'd cut down any enemy soldier backing off.
Such was I in battle, true, but I had no love
for working the land, the chores of households either,
the labor that raises crops of shining children. No,   255
it was always oarswept ships that thrilled my heart,
and wars, and the long polished spears and arrows,
dreadful gear that makes the next man cringe.
I loved them all—god planted that love inside me.
Each man delights in the work that suits him best.   260
Why, long before we Achaeans ever camped at Troy,
nine commands I led in our deep-sea-going ships,
raiding foreign men, and a fine haul reached my hands.
I helped myself to the lion's share and still more spoils
came by lot. And my house grew by leaps and bounds,   265
I walked among the Cretans, honored, feared as well.

    But then, when thundering Zeus contrived that expedition—
that disaster that brought so many fighters to their knees—
and men kept pressing me and renowned Idomeneus
to head a fleet to Troy,   270
there was no way out, no denying them then,
the voice of the people bore down much too hard.
So nine whole years we Achaeans soldiered on at Troy,
in the tenth we sacked King Priam's city, then embarked
for home in the long ships, and a god dispersed the fleet.   275
Unlucky me. Shrewd old Zeus was plotting still more pain.
No more than a month I stayed at home, taking joy
in my children, loyal wife and lovely plunder.
But a spirit in me urged, 'Set sail for Egypt—
fit out ships, take crews of seasoned heroes!'   280
Nine I fitted out, the men joined up at once
and then six days my shipmates feasted well,
while I provided a flock of sheep to offer up
to the gods and keep the feasters' table groaning.
On the seventh we launched out from the plains of Crete   285
with a stiff North Wind fair astern—smooth sailing,
aye, like coasting on downstream . . .
And not one craft in our squadron foundered;

all shipshape, and all hands sound, we sat back
while the wind and helmsmen kept us true on course.   290

Five days out and we raised the great river Nile
and there in the Nile delta moored our ships of war.
God knows I ordered my trusty crews to stand by,
just where they were, and guard the anchored fleet
and I sent a patrol to scout things out from higher ground.   295
But swept away by their own reckless fury, the crew went berserk—
they promptly began to plunder the lush Egyptian farms,
dragged off the women and children, killed the men.
Outcries reached the city in no time—stirred by shouts
the entire town came streaming down at the break of day,   300
filling the river plain with chariots, ranks of infantry
and the gleam of bronze. Zeus who loves the lightning
flung down murderous panic on all my men-at-arms—
no one dared to stand his ground and fight,
disaster ringed us round from every quarter.   305
Droves of my men they hacked down with swords,
led off the rest alive, to labor for them as slaves.
And I? Zeus flashed an inspiration through my mind,
though I wish I'd died a soldier down in Egypt then!
A world of pain, you see, still lay in wait for me . . .   310
Quickly I wrenched the skullcap helmet off my head,
I tore the shield from my back and dropped my spear
and ran right into the path of the king's chariot,
hugged and kissed his knees. He pitied me, spared me,
hoisted me onto his war-car, took me home in tears.   315
Troops of his men came rushing after, shaking javelins,
mad to kill me—their fighting blood at the boil—
but their master drove them off.
He feared the wrath of Zeus, the god of guests,
the first of the gods to pay back acts of outrage.
                                                  So,   320
there I lingered for seven years, amassing a fortune
from all the Egyptian people loading me with gifts.
Then, at last, when the eighth had come full turn,
along comes this Phoenician one fine day . . .
a scoundrel, swindler, an old hand at lies   325
who'd already done the world a lot of damage.
Well, he smoothly talked me round and off we sailed,
Phoenicia-bound, where his house and holdings lay.
There in his care I stayed till the year was out.
Then, when the months and days had run their course   330
and the year wheeled round and the seasons came again,
he conned me aboard his freighter bound for Libya,
pretending I'd help him ship a cargo there for sale
but in fact he'd sell *me* there and make a killing!
I suspected as much, of course, but had no choice,   335
so I boarded with him, yes, and the ship ran on
with a good strong North Wind gusting—
fast on the middle passage clear of Crete—

but Zeus was brewing mischief for that crew . . .
Once we'd left the island in our wake—   340
no land at all in sight, nothing but sea and sky—
then Zeus the son of Cronus mounted a thunderhead
above our hollow ship and the deep went black beneath it.
Then, then in the same breath Zeus hit the craft
with a lightning-bolt and thunder. Round she spun,   345
reeling under the impact, filled with reeking brimstone,
shipmates pitching out of her, bobbing round like seahawks
swept along by the breakers past the trim black hull—
and the god cut short their journey home forever.
                                                Not mine.
Zeus himself—when I was just at the final gasp—   350
thrust the huge mast of my dark-prowed vessel
right into my arms so I might flee disaster
one more time. Wrapping myself around it,
I was borne along by the wretched galewinds,
rushed along nine days—on the tenth, at dead of night,   355
a shouldering breaker rolled me up along Thesprotia's beaches[4]
There the king of Thesprotia, Phidon, my salvation,
treated me kindly, asked for no reward at all.
His own good son had found me, half-dead
from exhaustion and the cold. He raised me up   360
by the hand and led me home to his father's house
and dressed me in cloak and shirt and decent clothes.
That's where I first got wind of *him*—Odysseus . . .
The king told me he'd hosted the man in style,
befriended him on his way home to native land,   365
and showed me all the treasure Odysseus had amassed.
Bronze and gold and plenty of hard wrought iron,
enough to last a man and ten generations of his heirs—
so great the wealth stored up for *him* in the king's vaults!
But Odysseus, he made clear, was off at Dodona[5] then   370
to hear the will of Zeus that rustles forth
from the god's tall leafy oak: how should he return,
after all the years away, to his own green land of Ithaca—
openly or in secret? Phidon swore to me, what's more,
as the princely man poured out libations in his house,   375
'The ship's hauled down and the crew set to sail,
to take Odysseus home to native land.'
                                        But I . . .
he shipped me off before. A Thesprotian cutter
chanced to be heading for Dulichion[6] rich in wheat,
so he told the crew to take me to the king, Acastus,   380
treat me kindly, too, but it pleased them more
to scheme foul play against me,
sink me into the very depths of pain. As soon
as the ship was far off land, scudding in mid-sea,

---

4. Region on the west coast of the Greek mainland, north of Ithaca. The name of its king, Phidon, means "he who spares" or "saves." **5.** Site of an oracle of Zeus in the northwest of the Greek mainland. The god's message was supposed to come from a sacred oak in the sanctuary, perhaps from the rustling of leaves in the wind. **6.** An island evidently near Ithaca (its exact location is unknown)

they sprang their trap—my day of slavery then and there!   385
They stripped from my back the shirt and cloak I wore,
decked me out in a new suit of clothes, all rags,
ripped and filthy—the rags you see right now.
But then, once they'd gained the fields of Ithaca,
still clear in the evening light, they lashed me fast   390
to the rowing-benches, twisting a cable round me;
all hands went ashore
and rushed to catch their supper on the beach.
But the gods themselves unhitched my knots at once
with the gods' own ease. I wrapped my head in rags,   395
slid down the gangplank polished smooth, slipped my body
into the water, not a splash, chest-high, then quick,
launched out with both my arms and swam away—
out of the surf in no time, clear of the crew.
I clambered upland, into a flowery, fragrant brush   400
and crouched there, huddling low. They raised a hue and cry,
wildly beat the bushes, but when it seemed no use
to pursue the hunt, back they trudged again and
boarded their empty ship.
                              The gods hid me themselves—
it's light work for them—and brought me here,   405
the homestead of a man who knows the world.
So it seems to be my lot that I'll live on.'

   And you replied, Eumaeus, loyal swineherd,
"So much misery, friend! You've moved my heart,
deeply, with your long tale . . . such blows, such roving.   410
But one part's off the mark, I know—you'll never persuade me—
what you say about Odysseus. A man in your condition,
who are *you*, I ask you, to lie for no good reason?
Well I know the truth of my good lord's return,
how the gods detested him, with a vengeance—   415
never letting him go under, fighting Trojans,
or die in the arms of loved ones,
once he'd wound down the long coil of war.
Then all united Achaea would have raised his tomb
and he'd have won his son great fame for years to come.   420
But now the whirlwinds have ripped him away—no fame for him!
And I live here, cut off from the world, with all my pigs.
I never go into town unless, perhaps, wise Penelope
calls me back, when news drops in from nowhere.
There they crowd the messenger, cross-examine him,   425
heartsick for their long-lost lord or all too glad
to eat him out of house and home, scot-free.
But I've no love for all that probing, prying,
not since some Aetolian[7] fooled me with his yarn.
He'd killed a man, wandered over the face of the earth,   430
stumbled onto my hut, and I received him warmly.

---

7. Aetolia is on the mainland, east of Ithaca.

He told me he'd seen Odysseus
lodged with King Idomeneus down in Crete—
refitting his ships, hard-hit by the gales,
but he'd be home, he said, by summer or harvest-time, 435
his hulls freighted with treasure, manned by fighting crews.
So you, old misery, seeing a god has led you here to me,
don't try to charm me now, don't spellbind me with lies!
Never for *that* will I respect you, treat you kindly;
no, it's my fear of Zeus, the god of guests, 440
and because I pity you . . ."

    "Good god," the crafty man pressed on,
"what a dark, suspicious heart you have inside you!
Not even my oath can win you over, make you see the light.
Come, strike a bargain—all the gods of Olympus 445
witness now our pact!
If your master returns, here to your house,
dress me in shirt and cloak and send me off
to Dulichion at once, the place I long to be.
But if your master doesn't return as I predict, 450
set your men on me—fling me off some rocky crag
so the next beggar here may just think twice
before he peddles lies."

               "Surely, friend!"—
the swineherd shook his head—"and just think
of the praise and fame I'd win among mankind, 455
now and for all time to come, if first I took you
under my roof, I treated you kindly as my guest
then cut you down and robbed you of your life—
how keen I'd be to say my prayers to Zeus!
But it's high time for a meal. 460
I hope the men will be home at any moment
so we can fix a tasty supper in the lodge."

    As host and guest confided back and forth
the herdsmen came in, driving their hogs up close,
penning sows in their proper sties for the night, 465
squealing for all they're worth, shut inside their yard,
and the good swineherd shouted to his men,
"Bring in your fattest hog!
I'll slaughter it for our guest from far abroad.
We'll savor it ourselves. All too long we've sweated 470
over these white-tusked boars—our wretched labor—
while others wolf our work down free of charge!"

                     Calling out
as he split up kindling now with a good sharp ax
and his men hauled in a tusker five years old,
rippling fat, and stood him steady by the hearth. 475
The swineherd, soul of virtue, did not forget the gods.
He began the rite by plucking tufts from the porker's head,
threw them into the fire and prayed to all the powers,
"Bring him home, our wise Odysseus, home at last!"

Then raising himself full-length, with an oak log   480
he'd left unsplit he clubbed and stunned the beast
and it gasped out its life . . .
The men slashed its throat, singed the carcass,
quickly quartered it all, and then the swineherd,
cutting first strips for the gods from every limb,   485
spread them across the thighs, wrapped in sleek fat,
and sprinkling barley over them, flung them on the fire.
They sliced the rest into pieces, pierced them with skewers,
broiled them all to a turn and, pulling them off the spits,
piled the platters high. The swineherd, standing up   490
to share the meat—his sense of fairness perfect—
carved it all out into seven equal portions.
One he set aside, lifting up a prayer
to the forest nymphs and Hermes, Maia's son,
and the rest he handed on to each man in turn.   495
But to Odysseus he presented the boar's long loin
and the cut of honor cheered his master's heart.
The man for all occasions thanked his host:
"I pray, Eumaeus, you'll be as dear to Father Zeus
as you are to me—a man in my condition—   500
you honor me by giving me your best."

    You replied in kind, Eumaeus, swineherd:
"Eat, my strange new friend . . . enjoy it now,
it's all we have to offer. As for Father Zeus,
one thing he will give and another he'll hold back,   505
whatever his pleasure. All things are in his power."

    He burned choice parts for the gods who never die
and pouring glistening wine in a full libation,
placed the cup in his guest's hands—Odysseus,
raider of cities—and down he sat to his own share.   510
Mesaulius served them bread, a man the swineherd
purchased for himself in his master's absence—
alone, apart from his queen or old Laertes—
bought him from Taphians, bartered his own goods.
They reached out for the spread that lay at hand   515
and when they'd put aside desire for food and drink,
Mesaulius cleared the things away. And now, content
with bread and meat, they made for bed at once.

    A foul night came on—the dark of the moon—and Zeus
rained from dusk to dawn and a sodden West Wind raged.   520
Odysseus spoke up now, keen to test the swineherd.
Would he take his cloak off, hand it to his guest
or at least tell one of his men to do the same?
He cared for the stranger so, who ventured now,
"Listen, Eumaeus, and all you comrades here,   525
allow me to sing my praises for a moment.
Say it's the wine that leads me on, the wild wine
that sets the wisest man to sing at the top of his lungs,

laugh like a fool—it drives the man to dancing . . . it even
tempts him to blurt out stories better never told.   530
But now that I'm sounding off, I can't hold back.
Oh make me young again, and the strength inside me
steady as a rock! Just as I was that day
we sprang a sudden ambush against the Trojans.
Odysseus led the raid with Atreus' son Menelaus.   535
I was third in command—they'd chosen me themselves.
Once we'd edged up under the city's steep ramparts,
crowding the walls but sinking into the thick brake,
the reeds and marshy flats, huddling under our armor
there we lay, and a foul night came on, the North Wind struck,   540
freezing cold, and down from the skies the snow fell like frost,
packed hard—the rims of our shields armored round with ice.
There all the rest of the men wore shirts and cloaks and,
hunching shields over their shoulders, slept at ease.
Not I. I'd left my cloak at camp when I set out—   545
idiot—never thinking it might turn cold,
so I joined in with just the shield on my back
and a shining waist-guard . . . But then at last,
the night's third watch, the stars just wheeling down—
I muttered into his ear, Odysseus, right beside me,   550
nudging him with an elbow—he perked up at once—
'Royal son of Laertes, Odysseus, full of tactics,
I'm not long for the living. The cold will do me in.
See, I've got no cloak. Some spirit's fooled me—
I came out half-dressed. Now there's no escape!'   555
I hadn't finished—a thought flashed in his mind;
no one could touch the man at plots or battles.
'Shhh!' he hissed back—Odysseus had a plan—
'One of our fighters over there might hear you.'
Then he propped his head on his forearm, calling out,   560
'Friends, wake up. I slept and a god sent down a dream.
It warned that we're too far from the ships, exposed.
Go, someone, tell Agamemnon, our field marshal—
he might rush reinforcements from the beach.'
Thoas, son of Andraemon, sprang up at once,   565
flung off his purple cloak and ran to the ships
while I, bundling into his wrap, was glad at heart
till Dawn rose on her golden throne once more.
Oh make me young again
and the strength inside me steady as a rock!
One of the swineherds here would lend a wrap   570
for love of a good soldier, respect as well.
Now they spurn me, dressed in filthy rags."

   And you replied, Eumaeus, loyal swineherd,
"Now that was a fine yarn you told, old-timer,
not without point, not without profit either.   575
You won't want for clothes or whatever else
is due a worn-out traveler come for help—
not for tonight at least. Tomorrow morning

you'll have to flap around in rags again. 580
Here we've got no store of shirts and cloaks,
no changes. Just one wrap per man, that's all.
But just you wait till Odysseus' dear son comes back—
that boy will deck you out in a cloak and shirt
and send you off, wherever your heart desires!"
                                            With that 585
he rose to his feet and laid out a bed by the fire,
throwing over it skins of sheep and goats and
down Odysseus lay. Eumaeus flung on his guest
the heavy flaring cloak he kept in reserve
to wear when winter brought some wild storm.
                                            So here 590
Odysseus slept and the young hands slept beside him.
Not the swineherd. Not his style to bed indoors,
apart from his pigs. He geared up to go outside
and it warmed Odysseus' heart,
Eumaeus cared so much for his absent master's goods. 595
First, over his broad shoulders he slung a whetted sword,
wrapped himself in a cloak stitched tight to block the wind,
and adding a cape, the pelt of a shaggy well-fed goat,
he took a good sharp lance to fight off men and dogs.
Then out he went to sleep where his white-tusked boars 600
had settled down for the night . . . just under
a jutting crag that broke the North Wind's blast.

BOOK XV

[The Prince Sets Sail for Home]

Now south through the spacious dancing-rings of Lacedaemon
Athena went to remind the hero's princely son
of his journey home and spur him on his way.
She found him there with Nestor's gallant son,
bedded down in the porch of illustrious Menelaus— 5
Pisistratus, at least, overcome with deep sound sleep,
but not Telemachus. Welcome sleep could not hold him.
All through the godsent night he lay awake . . .
tossing with anxious thoughts about his father.
Hovering over him, eyes ablaze, Athena said, 10
"It's wrong, Telemachus, wrong to rove so far,
so long from home, leaving your own holdings
unprotected—crowds in your palace so brazen
they'll carve up all your wealth, devour it all,
and then your journey here will come to nothing. 15
Quickly, press Menelaus, lord of the warcry,
to speed you home at once, if you want to find
your irreproachable mother still inside your house.
Even now her father and brothers urge Penelope
to marry Eurymachus, who excels all other suitors 20
at giving gifts and drives the bride-price higher.
She must not carry anything off against your will!

You know how the heart of a woman always works:
she likes to build the wealth of her new groom—
of the sons she bore, of her dear, departed husband,
not a memory of the dead, no questions asked.
So sail for home, I say! 25
With your own hands turn over all your goods
to the one serving-woman you can trust the most,
till the gods bring to light your own noble bride. 30

    And another thing. Take it to heart, I tell you.
Picked men of the suitors lie in ambush, grim-set
in the straits between Ithaca and rocky Same,
poised to kill you before you can reach home,
but I have my doubts they will. Sooner the earth 35
will swallow down a few of those young gallants
who eat you out of house and home these days!
Just give the channel islands a wide berth,
push on in your trim ship, sail night and day,
and the deathless god who guards and pulls you through 40
will send you a fresh fair wind from hard astern.
At your first landfall, Ithaca's outer banks,
speed ship and shipmates round to the city side.
But you—you make your way to the swineherd first,
in charge of your pigs, and true to you as always. 45
Sleep the night there, send him to town at once
to tell the news to your mother, wise Penelope—
you've made it back from Pylos safe and sound."

    Mission accomplished, back she went to Olympus' heights
as Telemachus woke Nestor's son from his sweet sleep; 50
he dug a heel in his ribs and roused him briskly:
"Up, Pisistratus. Hitch the team to the chariot—
let's head for home at once!"

                    "No, Telemachus,"
Nestor's son objected, "much as we long to go,
we cannot drive a team in the dead of night. 55
Morning will soon be here. So wait, I say,
wait till he loads our chariot down with gifts—
the hero Atrides, Menelaus, the great spearman—
and gives us warm salutes and sees us off like princes.
That's the man a guest will remember all his days: 60
the lavish host who showers him with kindness."

    At those words Dawn rose on her golden throne
and Menelaus, lord of the warcry, rising up from bed
by the side of Helen with her loose and lovely hair,
walked toward his guests. As soon as he saw him, 65
Telemachus rushed to pull a shimmering tunic on,
over his broad shoulders threw his flaring cape
and the young prince, son of King Odysseus,
strode out to meet his host: "Menelaus,

royal son of Atreus, captain of armies,   70
let me go back to my own country now.
The heart inside me longs for home at last."

   The lord of the warcry reassured the prince,
"I'd never detain you here too long, Telemachus,
not if your heart is set on going home.   75
I'd find fault with another host, I'm sure,
too warm to his guests, too pressing or too cold.
Balance is best in all things. It's bad either way,
spurring the stranger home who wants to linger,
holding the one who longs to leave—you know,   80
'Welcome the coming, speed the parting guest!'
But wait till I load your chariot down with gifts—
fine ones, too, you'll see with your own eyes—
and tell the maids to serve a meal at hall.
We have god's plenty here.   85
It's honor and glory to us, a help to you as well
if you dine in style first, then leave to see the world.
And if you're keen for the grand tour of all Hellas,
right to the depths of Argos, I'll escort you myself,
harness the horses, guide you through the towns.   90
And no host will turn us away with empty hands,
each will give us at least one gift to prize—
a handsome tripod, cauldron forged in bronze,
a brace of mules or a solid golden cup."

   Firmly resolved, Telemachus replied,   95
"Menelaus, royal Atrides, captain of armies,
I must go back to my own home at once.
When I started out I left no one behind
to guard my own possessions. God forbid,
searching for my great father, I lose my life   100
or lose some priceless treasure from my house!"

   As soon as the lord of the warcry heard *that*,
he told his wife and serving-women to lay out a meal
in the hall at once. They'd stores aplenty there.
Eteoneus, son of Boëthous, came to join them—   105
fresh from bed, he lived close by the palace.
The warlord Menelaus told him to build a fire
and broil some meat. He quickly did his bidding.
Down Atrides walked to a storeroom filled with scent,
and not alone: Helen and Megapenthes went along.   110
Reaching the spot where all the heirlooms lay,
Menelaus chose a generous two-handled cup;
he told his son Megapenthes to take a mixing-bowl,
solid silver, while Helen lingered beside the chests,
and there they were, brocaded, beautiful robes   115
her own hands hand woven. Queenly Helen,
radiance of women, lifted one from the lot,
the largest, loveliest robe, and richly worked

and like a star it glistened, deep beneath the others.
Then all three went up and on through the halls until   120
they found Telemachus. The red-haired king spoke out:
"Oh my boy, may Zeus the Thunderer, Hera's lord,
grant you the journey home your heart desires!
Of all the treasures lying heaped in my palace
you shall have the finest, most esteemed. Look,   125
I'll give you this mixing-bowl, forged to perfection—
it's solid silver finished off with a lip of gold.
Hephaestus made it himself. And a royal friend,
Phaedimus, king of Sidon, lavished it on *me*
when his palace welcomed me on passage home.   130
How pleased I'd be if you took it as a gift!"

     And the warlord placed the two-eared cup
in his hands while stalwart Megapenthes carried in
the glittering silver bowl and set it down before him.
Helen, her cheeks flushed with beauty, moved beside him,   135
holding the robe in her arms, and offered, warmly,
"Here, dear boy, I too have a gift to give you,
a keepsake of Helen—I wove it with my hands—
for your own bride to wear
when the blissful day of marriage dawns . . .   140
Until then, let it rest in your mother's room.
And may you return in joy—my parting wish—
to your own grand house, your native land at last."
                              With that
she laid the robe in his arms, and he received it gladly.   145
Prince Pisistratus, taking the gifts, stowed them deep
in the chariot cradle, viewed them all with wonder.
The red-haired warlord led them back to his house
and the guests took seats on low and high-backed chairs.
A maid brought water soon in a graceful golden pitcher
and over a silver basin tipped it out   150
so they might rinse their hands,
then pulled a gleaming table to their side.
A staid housekeeper brought on bread to serve them,
appetizers aplenty too, lavish with her bounty.
Ready Eteoneus carved and passed the meat,   155
the son of illustrious Menelaus poured their wine.
They reached out for the good things that lay at hand
and once they'd put aside desire for food and drink,
Prince Telemachus and the gallant son of Nestor
yoked their team, mounted the blazoned car   160
and drove through the gates and echoing colonnade.
The red-haired King Menelaus followed both boys out,
his right hand holding a golden cup of honeyed wine
so the two might pour libations forth at parting.
Just in front of the straining team he strode,   165
lifting his cup and pledging both his guests:
"Farewell, my princes! Give my warm greetings
to Nestor, the great commander,

always kind to me as a father, long ago
when we young men of Achaea fought at Troy."   170

    And tactful Telemachus replied at once,
"Surely, my royal host, we'll tell him all,
as soon as we reach old Nestor—all you say.
I wish I were just as sure I'd find Odysseus
waiting there at home when I reach Ithaca.   175
I'd tell him I come from you,
treated with so much kindness at your hands,
loaded down with all these priceless gifts!"

    At his last words a bird flew past on the right,
an eagle clutching a huge white goose in its talons,   180
plucked from the household yards. And all rushed after,
shouting, men and women, and swooping toward the chariot now
the bird veered off to the right again before the horses.
All looked up, overjoyed—people's spirits lifted.
Nestor's son Pisistratus spoke out first: 185
"Look there! King Menelaus, captain of armies,
what, did the god send down that sign for you
or the two of us?"
                        The warlord fell to thinking—
how to read the omen rightly, how to reply? . . .
But long-robed Helen stepped in well before him: 190
"Listen to me and I will be your prophet,
sure as the gods have flashed it in my mind
and it will come to pass, I know it will.
Just as the eagle swooped down from the crags
where it was born and bred, just as it snatched   195
that goose fattened up for the kill inside the house,
just so, after many trials and roving long and hard,
Odysseus will descend on his house and take revenge—
unless he's home already, sowing seeds of ruin
for that whole crowd of suitors!"
                        "Oh if only,"   200
pensive Telemachus burst out in thanks to Helen,
"Zeus the thundering lord of Hera makes it so—
even at home I'll pray to you as a deathless goddess!"

    He cracked the lash and the horses broke quickly,
careering through the city out into open country,   205
shaking the yoke across their shoulders all day long.

    The sun sank and the roads of the world grew dark
as they reached Phera, pulling up to Diocles' halls,
the son of Ortilochus, son of the Alpheus River.
He gave them a royal welcome; there they slept the night.   210

    When young Dawn with her rose-red fingers shone once more
they yoked their pair again, mounted the blazoned car
and out through the gates and echoing colonnade
they whipped the team to a run and on they flew,

holding nothing back, approaching Pylos soon, 215
the craggy citadel. That was when Telemachus
turned to Pisistratus, saying, "Son of Nestor,
won't you do as I ask you, see it through?
We're friends for all our days now, so we claim,
thanks to our fathers' friendship. We're the same age as well 220
and this tour of ours has made us more like brothers.
Prince, don't drive me past my vessel, drop me there.
Your father's old, in love with his hospitality;
I fear he'll hold me, chafing in his palace—
I must hurry home!"

            The son of Nestor pondered . . . 225
how to do it properly, see it through?
Pausing a moment, then this way seemed best.
Swerving his team, he drove down to the ship
tied up on shore and loaded into her stern
the splendid gifts, the robes and gold Menelaus gave, 230
and sped his friend with a flight of winging words:
"Climb aboard now—fast! Muster all your men
before I get home and break the news to father.
With that man's overbearing spirit—I know it,
know it all too well—he'll never let you go, 235
he'll come down here and summon you himself.
He won't return without you, believe me—
in any case he'll fly into a rage."

   With that warning he whipped his sleek horses
back to Pylos city and reached his house in no time. 240
Telemachus shouted out commands to all his shipmates:
"Stow our gear, my comrades, deep in the holds
and board at once—we must be on our way!"

   His shipmates snapped to orders,
swung aboard and sat to the oars in ranks. 245
But just as Telemachus prepared to launch,
praying, sacrificing to Pallas by the stern,
a man from a far-off country came toward him now,
a fugitive out of Argos: he had killed a man . . .
He was a prophet, sprung of Melampus' line of seers, 250
Melampus who lived in Pylos, mother of flocks, some years ago,
rich among his Pylians, at home in his great high house.[8]
But then he was made to go abroad to foreign parts,
fleeing his native land and hot-blooded Neleus—
most imperious man alive—who'd commandeered 255
his vast estate and held it down by force

8. Melampus's brother (who lived in Pylos under King Neleus, Nestor's father) asked for the hand of Neleus's daughter Pero (whose shade Odysseus sees in the land of the dead in book 11). Neleus demanded as bride-price the herds of cattle of a neighboring lord, Phylacus. Attempting to steal the cattle for his brother, Melampus was caught and imprisoned. In prison he heard the worms in the roof beams announce that the wood was almost eaten through, and he predicted the collapse of the roof. Phylacus, impressed, released him and gave him the cattle; his brother was given the bride. Melampus then settled in Argos and prospered. The prophet Amphiaraus, one of Melampus's great-grandsons, foresaw that if he joined the champions who went to besiege Thebes he would lose his life. Melampus's son Mantius had a son named Polyphides, and it is his son Theoclymenus who now begs Telemachus for a place in his ship.

for one entire year. That year Melampus,
bound by cruel chains in the halls of Phylacus,
suffered agonies—all for Neleus' daughter Pero,
that and the mad spell a Fury, murderous spirit,   260
cast upon his mind. But the seer worked free of death
and drove the lusty, bellowing cattle out of Phylace,
back to Pylos. There he avenged himself on Neleus
for the shameful thing the king had done to him,
and escorted Pero home as his brother's bride.   265
But he himself went off to a distant country,
Argos, land of stallions—his destined home
where he would live and rule the Argive nation.
Here he married a wife and built a high-roofed house
and sired Antiphates and Mantius, two staunch sons.   270
Antiphates fathered Oicles, gallant heart,
Oicles fathered Amphiaraus, driver of armies,
whom storming Zeus and Apollo loved intensely,
showering him with every form of kindness,
But he never reached the threshold of old age,   275
he died at Thebes—undone by a bribe his wife[9] accepted—
leaving behind his two sons, Alcmaeon and Amphilochus.
On his side Mantius sired Polyphides and Clitus both
but Dawn of the golden throne whisked Clitus away,
overwhelmed by his beauty,   280
so the boy would live among the deathless gods.
Yet Apollo made magnanimous Polyphides a prophet—
after Amphiaraus' death—the greatest seer on earth.
But a feud with his father drove him off to Hyperesia[1]
where he made his home and prophesied to the world . . .   285

   This prophet's son it was—Theoclymenus his name—
who approached Telemachus now and found him pouring
wine to a god and saying prayers beside his ship.
"Friend," he said in a winging supplication,
"since I find you burning offerings here,   290
I beg you by these rites and the god you pray to,
then by your own life and the lives of all the men
who travel with you—tell me truly, don't hold back,
who are you? where are you from? your city? your parents?"

"Of course, stranger," the forthright prince responded,   295
"I will tell you everything, clearly as I can.
Ithaca is my country. Odysseus is my father—
there was a man, or was he all a dream? . . .
but he's surely died a wretched death by now.
Yet here I've come with my crew and black ship,   300
out for news of my father, lost and gone so long."

   And the godlike seer Theoclymenus replied,
Just like you, I too have left my land—

---

9. Eriphyle, whose shade Odysseus sees in book 11.   1. Near Argos.

I because I killed a man of my own tribe.
But he has many brothers and kin in Argos,
stallion-land, who rule the plains in force.   305
Fleeing death at their hands, a dismal fate,
I am a fugitive now,
doomed to wander across this mortal world.
So take me aboard, hear a fugitive's prayer:
don't let them kill me—they're after me, well I know!"   310

    "So desperate!" thoughtful Telemachus exclaimed.
"How could I drive you from my ship? Come sail with us,
we'll tend you at home, with all we can provide."

    And he took the prophet's honed bronze spear,   315
laid it down full-length on the rolling deck,
swung aboard the deep-sea craft himself,
assuming the pilot's seat reserved astern
and put the seer beside him. Cables cast off,
Telemachus shouted out commands to all his shipmates: 320
"All lay hands to tackle!" They sprang to orders,
hoisting the pinewood mast, they stepped it firm
in its block amidships, lashed it fast with stays
and with braided rawhide halyards hauled the white sail high.
Now bright-eyed Athena sent them a stiff following wind   325
blustering out of a clear sky, gusting on so the ship
might run its course through the salt sea at top speed—
and past the Springs she raced and the Chalcis' rushing stream
as the sun sank and the roads of the world grew dark and
on she pressed for Pheae, driven on by a wind from Zeus   330
and flew past lovely Elis, where Epeans rule in power,
and then Telemachus veered for the Jagged Islands,[2]
wondering all the way—
would he sweep clear of death or be cut down?

    The King and loyal swineherd, just that night,   335
were supping with other fieldhands in the lodge.
And once they'd put aside desire for food and drink,
Odysseus spoke up, eager to test the swineherd,
see if he'd stretch out his warm welcome now,
invite him to stay on in the farmstead here   340
or send him off to town. "Listen, Eumaeus,
all you comrades here—at the crack of dawn
I mean to go to town and do my begging,
not be a drain on you and all your men.
But advise me well, give me a trusty guide   345
to see me there. And then I'm on my own
to roam the streets—I must, I have no choice—
hoping to find a handout, just a crust or cupful.
I'd really like to go to the house of King Odysseus

---

2. The precise location of these places is uncertain, but the mention of Elis in line 331 suggests that all
are on the west coast of the Peloponnesus, south of the Gulf of Corinth.

and give my news to his cautious queen, Penelope.   350
Why, I'd even mix with those overweening suitors—
would they spare me a plateful? Look at all they have!
I'd do good work for them, promptly, anything they want.
Let me tell you, listen closely, catch my drift . . .
Thanks to Hermes the guide, who gives all work   355
of our hands the grace and fame that it deserves,
no one alive can match me at household chores:
building a good fire, splitting kindling neatly,
carving, roasting meat and pouring rounds of wine . . .
anything menials do to serve their noble masters."   360

   "God's sake, my friend!" you broke in now,
Eumaeus, loyal swineherd, deeply troubled.
"What's got into your head, what crazy plan?
You must be hell-bent on destruction, on the spot,
if you're keen to mingle with that mob of suitors—   365
their pride and violence hit the iron skies!
They're a far cry from you,
the men who do their bidding. Young bucks,
all rigged out in their fine robes and shirts,
hair sleeked down with oil, faces always beaming,   370
the ones who slave for *them!* The tables polished,
sagging under the bread and meat and wine.
No, stay here. No one finds you a burden,
surely not I, not any comrade here.
You wait till Odysseus' dear son comes back—   375
that boy will deck you out in a cloak and shirt
and send you off, wherever your heart desires!"

   "If only, Eumaeus," the wayworn exile said,
"you were as dear to Father Zeus as you are to me!
You who stopped my pain, my endless, homesick roving.   380
Tramping about the world—there's nothing worse for a man.
But the fact is that men put up with misery
to stuff their cursed bellies.
But seeing you hold me here, urging me now
to wait for *him*, the prince who's on his way,   385
tell me about the mother of King Odysseus, please,
the father he left as well—on the threshold of old age—
when he sailed off to war. Are they still alive,
perhaps, still looking into the light of day?
Or dead by now, and down in Death's long house?"

                                       "Friend,"   390
the swineherd, foreman of men, assured his guest,
"I'll tell you the whole story, point by point.
Laertes is still alive, but night and day
he prays to Zeus, waiting there in his house,
for the life breath to slip away and leave his body.   395
His heart's so racked for his son, lost and gone these years,
for his wife so fine, so wise—*her* death is the worst blow

he's had to suffer—it made him old before his time.
She died of grief for her boy, her glorious boy,
it wore her down, a wretched way to go.   400
I pray that no one I love dies such a death,
no island neighbor of mine who treats me kindly!
While she was still alive, heartsick as she was,
it always moved me to ask about her, learn the news.
She'd reared me herself, and right beside her daughter,   405
Ctimene, graceful girl with her long light gown,
the youngest one she'd borne . . .
Just the two of us, growing up together,
the woman tending me almost like her child,
till we both reached the lovely flush of youth   410
and then her parents gave her away in marriage, yes,
to a Samian[3] man, and a haul of gifts they got.
But her mother decked me out in cloak and shirt,
good clothing she wrapped about me—gave me sandals,
sent me here, this farm. She loved me from the heart.   415
Oh how I miss her kindness now! The happy gods
speed the work that I labor at, that gives me
food and drink to spare for the ones I value.
But from Queen Penelope I never get a thing,
never a winning word, no friendly gesture,   420
not since this, this plague has hit the house—
these high and mighty suitors. Servants miss it,
terribly, gossiping back and forth with the mistress,
gathering scraps of news, a snack and a cup or two,
then taking home to the fields some little gift.   425
It never fails to cheer a servant's heart."

    "Imagine that," his canny master said,
"you must have been just a little fellow, Eumaeus,
when you were swept so far from home and parents.
Come, tell me the whole story, truly too.   430
Was your city sacked?—
some city filled with people and wide streets
where your father and your mother made their home?
Or were you all alone, herding your sheep and cattle,
when pirates kidnapped, shipped and sold you off   435
to this man's house, who paid a healthy price?"

    "My friend," the swineherd answered, foreman of men,
"you really want my story? So many questions—well,
listen in quiet, then, and take your ease, sit back
and drink your wine. The nights are endless now.   440
We've plenty of time to sleep or savor a long tale.
No need, you know, to turn in before the hour.
Even too much sleep can be a bore.
But anyone else who feels the urge

---

3. From Same, a nearby island or town.

can go to bed and then, at the crack of dawn,   445
break bread, turn out and tend our master's pigs.
We two will keep to the shelter here, eat and drink
and take some joy in each other's heartbreaking sorrows,
sharing each other's memories. Over the years, you know,
a man finds solace even in old sorrows, true, a man   450
who's weathered many blows and wandered many miles.
My own story? This will answer all your questions . . .

    There's an island, Syrie—you may have heard of it—
off above Ortygia,[4] out where the sun wheels around.
Not so packed with people, still a good place, though,   455
fine for sheep and cattle, rich in wine and wheat.
Hunger never attacks the land, no sickness either,
that always stalks the lives of us poor men.
No, as each generation grows old on the island,
down Apollo comes with his silver bow, with Artemis,   460
and they shoot them all to death with gentle arrows.
Two cities there are, that split the land in half,
and over them both my father ruled in force—
Ormenus' son Ctesius, a man like a deathless god.
                                                   One day
a band of Phoenicians landed there. The famous sea-dogs,   465
sharp bargainers too, the holds of their black ship
brimful with a hoard of flashy baubles. Now,
my father kept a Phoenician woman in his house,
beautiful, tall and skilled at weaving lovely things,
and her rascal countrymen lusted to seduce her, yes,   470
and lost no time—she was washing clothes when one of them
waylaid her beside their ship, in a long deep embrace
that can break a woman's will, even the best alive.
And then he asked her questions . . .
her name, who was she, where did she come from?   475
She waved at once to my father's high-roofed house—
'But I'm proud to hail from Sidon paved in bronze,' she said,
'and Arybas was my father, a man who rolled in wealth.
I was heading home from the fields when Taphian pirates
snatched me away, and they shipped and sold me here   480
to this man's house. He paid a good stiff price!'

    The sailor, her secret lover, lured her on:
'Well then, why don't you sail back home with us?—
see your own high house, your father and mother there.
They're still alive, and people say they're rich!'   485

    'Now there's a tempting offer,' she said in haste,
'if only you sailors here would swear an oath
you'll land me safe at home without a scratch.'

---

4. The Greeks knew several islands named Ortygia, but the absence of disease and hunger suggests that this one, like Phaeacia, is in fantasyland.

Those were her terms, and once they vowed to keep them,
swore their oaths they'd never do her harm,   490
the woman hatched a plan: 'Now not a word!
Let none of your shipmates say a thing to me,
meeting me on the street or at the springs.
Someone might go running off to the house
and tell the old king—he'd think the worst,   495
clap me in cruel chains and find a way to kill you.
So keep it a secret, down deep, get on with buying
your home cargo, quickly. But once your holds
are loaded up with goods, then fast as you can
you send the word to me over there at the palace.   500
I'll bring you all the gold I can lay my hands on
and something else I'll give you in the bargain,
fare for passage home . . .
I'm nurse to my master's son in the palace now—
such a precious toddler, scampering round outside,   505
always at my heels. I'll bring him aboard as well.
Wherever you sell him off, whatever foreign parts,
he'll fetch you quite a price!'
                              Bargain struck,
back the woman went to our lofty halls
and the rovers stayed on with us one whole year,   510
bartering, piling up big hoards in their hollow ship,
and once their holds were loaded full for sailing
they sent a messenger, fast, to alert the woman.
This crafty bandit came to my father's house,
dangling a golden choker linked with amber beads,   515
and while the maids at hall and my noble mother
kept on fondling it—dazzled, feasting their eyes
and making bids—he gave a quiet nod to my nurse,
he gave her the nod and slunk back to his ship.
Grabbing my hand, she swept me through the house   520
and there in the porch she came on cups and tables
left by the latest feasters, father's men of council
just gone off to the meeting grounds for full debate—
and quick as a flash she snatched up three goblets,
tucked them into her bosom, whisked them off   525
and I tagged along, lost in all my innocence!
The sun sank, the roads of the world grew dark
and both on the run, we reached the bay at once
where the swift Phoenician ship lay set to sail.
Handing us up on board, the crewmen launched out   530
on the foaming lanes and Zeus sent wind astern.
Six whole days we sailed, six nights, nonstop
and then, when the god brought on the seventh day,
Artemis showering arrows came and shot the woman—
headfirst into the bilge she splashed like a diving tern   535
and the crewmen heaved her body over, a nice treat
for the seals and fish, but left me all alone,
cowering, sick at heart . . .
                    Until, at last,

the wind and current bore us on to Ithaca,
here where Laertes bought me with his wealth.   540
And so I first laid eyes on this good land."

    And royal King Odysseus answered warmly,
"Eumaeus, so much misery! You've moved my heart,
deeply, with your long tale—such pain, such sorrow.
True, but look at the good fortune Zeus sends you,   545
hand-in-hand with the bad. After all your toil
you reached the house of a decent, kindly man
who gives you all you need in meat and drink—
he's seen to that, I'd say—
it's a fine life you lead! Better than mine . . .   550
I've been drifting through cities up and down the earth
and now I've landed here."
                                So guest and host
confided through the night until they slept,
a little at least, not long.
Dawn soon rose and took her golden throne.
                                              That hour   555
Telemachus and his shipmates raised the coasts of home,
they struck sail and lowered the mast, smartly,
rowed her into a mooring under oars.
Out went the bow-stones, cables fast astern,
the crew themselves swung out in the breaking surf,   560
they got a meal together and mixed some ruddy wine.
And once they'd put aside desire for food and drink,
clear-headed Telemachus gave the men commands:
"Pull our black ship round to the city now—
I'm off to my herdsmen and my farms. By nightfall,   565
once I've seen to my holdings, I'll be down in town.
In the morning I'll give you wages for the voyage,
a handsome feast of meat and hearty wine."

    The seer Theoclymenus broke in quickly,
"Where shall I go, dear boy? Of all the lords   570
in rocky Ithaca, whose house shall I head for now?
Or do I go straight to your mother's house and yours?"

    "Surely in better times," discreet Telemachus replied,
"I would invite you home. Our hospitality never fails
but now, I fear, it could only serve you poorly.   575
I'll be away, and mother would never see you.
She rarely appears these days,
what with those suitors milling in the hall;
she keeps to her upper story, weaving at her loom.
But I'll mention someone else you might just visit: 580
Eurymachus, wise Polybus' fine, upstanding son.
He's the man of the hour! Our island people
look on him like a god—the prince of suitors,
hottest to wed my mother, seize my father's powers.
But god knows—Zeus up there in his bright Olympus—   585

whether or not before that wedding day arrives
he'll bring the day of death on all their heads!"

    At his last words a bird flew past on the right,
a hawk, Apollo's wind-swift herald—tight in his claws
a struggling dove, and he ripped its feathers out   590
and they drifted down to earth between the ship
and the young prince himself . . .
The prophet called him aside, clear of his men,
and grasped his hand, exclaiming, "Look, Telemachus,
the will of god just winged that bird on your right!   595
Why, the moment I saw it, here before my eyes,
I knew it was a sign. No line more kingly than yours
in all of Ithaca—yours will reign forever!"
                        "If only, friend,"
alert Telemachus answered, "all you say comes true!
You'd soon know my affection, know my gifts.   600
Any man you meet would call you blest."

    He turned to a trusted friend and said, "Piraeus,
son of Clytius, you are the one who's done my bidding,
more than all other friends who sailed with me to Pylos.
Please, take this guest of mine to your own house,   605
treat him kindly, host him with all good will
till I can come myself."
                 "Of course, Telemachus,"
Piraeus the gallant spearman offered warmly:
"Stay up-country just as long as you like.
I'll tend the man, he'll never lack a lodging."   610

    Piraeus boarded ship and told the crew
to embark at once and cast off cables quickly—
they swung aboard and sat to the oars in ranks.
Telemachus fastened rawhide sandals on his feet
and took from the decks his rugged bronze-tipped spear.   615
The men cast off, pushed out and pulled for town
as Telemachus ordered, King Odysseus' son.
The prince strode out briskly,
legs speeding him on till he reached the farm
where his great droves of pigs crowded their pens   620
and the loyal swineherd often slept beside them,
always the man to serve his masters well.

BOOK XVI

[Father and Son]

As dawn came into the lodge, the king and loyal swineherd
set out breakfast, once they had raked the fire up
and got the herdsmen off with droves of pigs.
And now Telemachus . . .
the howling dogs went nuzzling up around him,   5
not a growl as he approached. From inside

Odysseus noticed the pack's quiet welcome,
noticed the light tread of footsteps too
and turned to Eumaeus quickly, winged a word:
"Eumaeus, here comes a friend of yours, I'd say. 10
Someone you know, at least. The pack's not barking,
must be fawning around him. I can hear his footfall."

The words were still on his lips when his own son
stood in the doorway, there. The swineherd started up,
amazed, he dropped the bowls with a clatter—he'd been busy 15
mixing ruddy wine. Straight to the prince he rushed
and kissed his face and kissed his shining eyes,
both hands, as the tears rolled down his cheeks.
As a father, brimming with love, welcomes home
his darling only son in a warm embrace— 20
what pain he's borne for him and him alone!—
home now, in the tenth year from far abroad,
so the loyal swineherd hugged the beaming prince,
he clung for dear life, covering him with kisses, yes,
like one escaped from death. Eumaeus wept and sobbed, 25
his words flew from the heart: "You're home, Telemachus,
sweet light of my eyes! I never thought I'd see you again,
once you'd shipped to Pylos! Quick, dear boy, come in,
let me look at you, look to my heart's content—
under my own roof, the rover home at last. 30
You rarely visit the farm and men these days,
always keeping to town, as if it *cheered* you
to see them there, that infernal crowd of suitors!"

    "Have it your way," thoughtful Telemachus replied.
"Dear old man, it's all for you that I've come, 35
to see you for myself and learn the news—
whether mother still holds out in the halls
or some other man has married her at last,
and Odysseus' bed, I suppose, is lying empty,
blanketed now with filthy cobwebs."

                            "Surely," 40
the foreman of men responded, "she's still waiting
there in your halls, poor woman, suffering so,
her life an endless hardship . . .
wasting away the nights, weeping away the days."

                        With that
he took the bronze spear from the boy, and Telemachus, 45
crossing the stone doorsill, went inside the lodge.
As he approached, his father, Odysseus, rose
to yield his seat, but the son on his part
waved him back: "Stay where you are, stranger.
I know we can find another seat somewhere,
here on our farm, and here's the man to fetch it." 50

    So Odysseus, moving back, sat down once more,
and now for the prince the swineherd strewed a bundle

of fresh green brushwood, topped it off with sheepskin
and there the true son of Odysseus took his place.   55
Eumaeus set before them platters of roast meat
left from the meal he'd had the day before;
he promptly served them bread, heaped in baskets,
mixed their hearty wine in a wooden bowl
and then sat down himself to face the king.   60
They reached for the good things that lay at hand,
and when they'd put aside desire for food and drink
Telemachus asked his loyal serving-man at last,
"Old friend, where does this stranger come from?
Why did the sailors land him here in Ithaca?   65
Who did they say they are?
I hardly think he came this way on foot."

     You answered him, Eumaeus, loyal swineherd,
"Here, my boy, I'll tell you the whole true story.
He hails from Crete's broad land, he's proud to say,   70
but he claims he's drifted round through countless towns of men,
roaming the earth . . . and so a god's spun out his fate.
He just now broke away from some Thesprotian ship
and came to my farm. I'll put him in *your* hands,
you tend to him as you like.   75
He counts on you, he says, for care and shelter."

     "Shelter? Oh Eumaeus," Telemachus replied,
"that word of yours, it cuts me to the quick!
How can I lend the stranger refuge in my house?
I'm young myself. I can hardly trust my hands   80
to fight off any man who rises up against me.
Then my mother's wavering, always torn two ways:
whether to stay with me and care for the household,
true to her husband's bed, the people's voice as well,
or leave at long last with the best man in Achaea   85
who courts her in the halls, who offers her the most.
But our new guest, since he's arrived at your house,
I'll give him a shirt and cloak to wear, good clothing,
give him a two-edged sword and sandals for his feet
and send him off, wherever his heart desires.   90
Or if you'd rather, keep him here at the farmstead,
tend to him here, and I'll send up the clothes
and full rations to keep the man in food;
he'll be no drain on you and all your men.
But I can't let him go down and join the suitors.   95
They're far too abusive, reckless, know no limits:
they'll make a mockery of him—that would break my heart.
It's hard for a man to win his way against a mob,
even a man of iron. They are much too strong."

     "Friend"—the long-enduring Odysseus stepped in—   100
"surely it's right for *me* to say a word at this point.
My heart, by god, is torn to pieces hearing this,

both of you telling how these reckless suitors,
there in your own house, against your will,
plot your ruin—a fine young prince like you. 105
Tell me, though, do you let yourself be so abused
or do people round about, stirred up by the prompting
of some god, despise you? Or are your brothers at fault?
Brothers a man can trust to fight beside him, true,
no matter what deadly blood-feud rages on. 110
Would I were young as you, to match my spirit now,
or I were the son of great Odysseus, or the king himself
returned from all his roving—there's still room for hope!
Then let some foreigner lop my head off if I failed
to march right into Odysseus' royal halls 115
and kill them all. And what if I went down,
crushed by their numbers—I, fighting alone?
I'd rather die, cut down in my own house
than have to look on at their outrage day by day.
Guests treated to blows, men dragging the serving-women 120
through the noble house, exploiting them all, no shame,
and the gushing wine swilled, the food squandered—
gorging for gorging's sake—
and the courting game goes on, no end in sight!"

    "You're right, my friend," sober Telemachus agreed. 125
"Now let me tell you the whole story, first to last.
It's not that all our people have turned against me,
keen for a showdown. Nor have I any brothers at fault,
brothers a man can trust to fight beside him, true,
no matter what deadly blood-feud rages on . . . 130
Zeus made our line a line of only sons.
Arcesius had only one son, Laertes,
and Laertes had only one son, Odysseus,
and I am Odysseus' only son. He fathered me,
he left me behind at home, and from me he got no joy. 135
So now our house is plagued by swarms of enemies.
All the nobles who rule the islands round about,
Dulichion, and Same, and wooded Zacynthus too,
and all who lord it in rocky Ithaca as well—
down to the last man they court my mother, 140
they lay waste my house! And mother . . .
she neither rejects a marriage she despises
nor can she bear to bring the courting to an end—
while they continue to bleed my household white.
Soon—you wait—they'll grind *me* down as well! 145
But all lies in the lap of the great gods.
                Eumaeus,
good old friend, go, quickly, to wise Penelope.
Tell her I'm home from Pylos safe and sound.
I'll stay on right here. But you come back
as soon as you've told the news to her alone. 150
No other Achaean must hear—

all too many plot to take my life."
                              "I know."
you assured your prince, Eumaeus, loyal swineherd.
"I see your point—there's sense in this old head.
One thing more, and make your orders clear.   155
On the same trip do I go and give the news
to King Laertes too? For many years, poor man,
heartsick for his son, he'd always keep an eye
on the farm and take his meals with the hired hands
whenever he felt the urge to. Now, from the day   160
you sailed away to Pylos, not a sip or a bite
he's touched, they say, not as he did before,
and his eyes are shut to all the farmyard labors.
Huddled over, groaning in grief and tears,
he wastes away—the man's all skin and bones."   165

   "So much the worse," Telemachus answered firmly.
"Leave him alone; though it hurts us now, we must.
If men could have all they want, free for the taking,
I'd take first my father's journey home. So,
you go and give the message, then come back,   170
no roaming over the fields to find Laertes.
Tell my mother to send her housekeeper,
fast as she can, in secret—
she can give the poor old man the news."

   That roused Eumaeus. The swineherd grasped his sandals,   175
strapped them onto his feet and made for town.
His exit did not escape Athena's notice . . .
Approaching, closer, now she appeared a woman,
beautiful, tall and skilled at weaving lovely things.
Just at the shelter's door she stopped, visible to Odysseus   180
but Telemachus could not see her, sense her there—
the gods don't show themselves to every man alive.
Odysseus saw her, so did the dogs; no barking now,
they whimpered, cringing away in terror through the yard.
She gave a sign with her brows, Odysseus caught it,   185
out of the lodge he went and past the high stockade
and stood before the goddess. Athena urged him on:
"Royal son of Laertes, Odysseus, old campaigner,
now is the time, now tell your son the truth.
Hold nothing back, so the two of you can plot   190
the suitors' doom and then set out for town.
I myself won't lag behind you long—
I'm blazing for a battle!"

   Athena stroked him with her golden wand.
First she made the cloak and shirt on his body   195
fresh and clean, then made him him taller, supple, young,
his ruddy tan came back, the cut of his jawline firmed
and the dark beard clustered black around his chin.

Her work complete, she went her way once more
and Odysseus returned to the lodge. His own son   200
gazed at him, wonderstruck, terrified too, turning
his eyes away, suddenly—
                          this must be some god—
and he let fly with a burst of exclamations:
"Friend, you're a new man—not what I saw before!
Your clothes, they've changed, even your skin has changed—   205
surely you are some god who rules the vaulting skies!
Oh be kind, and we will give you offerings,
gifts of hammered gold to warm your heart—
spare us, please, I beg you!"
                          "No, I am not a god,"
the long-enduring, great Odysseus returned.
"Why confuse me with one who never dies?   210
No, I am your father—
the Odysseus you wept for all your days,
you bore a world of pain, the cruel abuse of men."

    And with those words Odysseus kissed his son   215
and the tears streamed down his cheeks and wet the ground,
though before he'd always reined his emotions back.
But still not convinced that it was his father,
Telemachus broke out, wild with disbelief,
"No, you're not Odysseus! Not my father!   220
Just some spirit spellbinding me now—
to make me ache with sorrow all the more.
Impossible for a mortal to work such marvels,
not with his own devices, not unless some god
comes down in person, eager to make that mortal   225
young or old—like that! Why, just now
you were old, and wrapped in rags, but *now*, look,
you seem like a god who rules the skies up there!"

    "Telemachus," Odysseus, man of exploits, urged his son,
"It's wrong to marvel, carried away in wonder so   230
to see your father here before your eyes.
No other Odysseus will ever return to you.
That man and I are one, the man you see . . .
here after many hardships,
endless wanderings, after twenty years   235
I have come home to native ground at last.
My changing so? Athena's work, the Fighter's Queen[5]—
she has that power, she makes me look as she likes,
now like a beggar, the next moment a young man,
decked out in handsome clothes about my body.   240
It's light work for the gods who rule the skies
to exalt a mortal man or bring him low."
                          At that

5. Athena was a warrior goddess.

Odysseus sat down again, and Telemachus threw his arms
around his great father, sobbing uncontrollably
as the deep desire for tears welled up in both.   245
They cried out, shrilling cries, pulsing sharper
than birds of prey—eagles, vultures with hooked claws—
when farmers plunder their nest of young too young to fly.
Both men so filled with compassion, eyes streaming tears,
that now the sunlight would have set upon their cries   250
if Telemachus had not asked his father, all at once,
"What sort of ship, dear father, brought you here?—
Ithaca, at last. Who did the sailors say they are?
I hardly think you came back home on foot!"

    So long an exile, great Odysseus replied,   255
"Surely, my son, I'll tell you the whole story now.
Phaeacians brought me here, the famous sailors
who ferry home all men who reach their shores.
They sailed me across the sea in their swift ship,
they set me down in Ithaca, sound asleep, and gave me   260
glittering gifts—bronze and hoards of gold and robes.
All lie stowed in a cave, thanks to the gods' help,
and Athena's inspiration spurred me here, now,
so we could plan the slaughter of our foes.
Come, give me the full tally of these suitors—   265
I must know their numbers, gauge their strength.
Then I'll deploy this old tactician's wits,
decide if the two of us can take them on,
alone, without allies,
or we should hunt reserves to back us up."

                                    "Father,"   270
clear-headed Telemachus countered quickly,
"all my life I've heard of your great fame—
a brave man in war and a deep mind in counsel—
but what you say dumbfounds me, staggers imagination!
How on earth could two men fight so many and so strong?   275
These suitors are not just ten or twenty, they're far more—
you count them up for yourself now, take a moment . . .
From Dulichion, fifty-two of them, picked young men,
six servants in their troop; from Same, twenty-four,
from Zacynthus, twenty Achaeans, nobles all,   280
and the twelve best lords from Ithaca itself.
Medon the herald's with them, a gifted bard,
and two henchmen, skilled to carve their meat.
If we pit ourselves against all these in the house,
I fear the revenge you come back home to take   285
will recoil on our heads—a bitter, deadly blow.
Think: can you come up with a friend-in-arms?
Some man to fight beside us, some brave heart?"

    "Let me tell you," the old soldier said,
"bear it in mind now, listen to me closely.   290
Think: will Athena flanked by Father Zeus

do for the two of us?
Or shall I rack my brains for another champion?"

   Telemachus answered shrewdly, full of poise,
"Two great champions, those you name, it's true.   295
Off in the clouds they sit
and they lord it over gods and mortal men."

   "Trust me," his seasoned father reassured him,
"they won't hold off long from the cries and clash of battle,
not when we and the suitors put our fighting strength   300
to proof in my own halls! But now, with daybreak,
home you go and mix with that overbearing crowd.
The swineherd will lead me into the city later,
looking old and broken, a beggar once again.
If they abuse me in the palace, steel yourself,   305
no matter what outrage I must suffer, even
if they drag me through our house by the heels
and throw me out or pelt me with things they hurl—
you just look on, endure it. Prompt them to quit
their wild reckless ways, try to win them over   310
with friendly words. Those men will never listen,
now the day of doom is hovering at their heads.
One more thing. Take it to heart, I urge you.
When Athena, Queen of Tactics, tells me it is time,
I'll give you a nod, and when you catch that signal   315
round up all the deadly weapons kept in the hall,
stow them away upstairs in a storeroom's deep recess—
all the arms and armor—and when the suitors miss them
and ask you questions, put them off with a winning story:
'I stowed them away, clear of the smoke. A far cry   320
from the arms Odysseus left when he went to Troy,
fire-damaged equipment, black with reeking fumes.
And a god reminded me of something darker too.
When you're in your cups a quarrel might break out,
you'd wound each other, shame your feasting here   325
and cast a pall on your courting.
Iron has powers to draw a man to ruin.'
                    Just you leave
a pair of swords for the two of us, a pair of spears
and a pair of oxhide bucklers, right at hand so we
can break for the weapons, seize them! Then Athena,   330
Zeus in his wisdom—they will daze the suitors' wits.
Now one last thing. Bear it in mind. You must.
If you are my own true son, born of my blood,
let no one hear that Odysseus has come home.
Don't let Laertes know, not Eumaeus either,   335
none in the household, not Penelope herself.
You and I alone will assess the women's mood
and we might test a few of the serving-men as well:
where are the ones who still respect us both,
who hold us in awe? And who shirk their duties?—   340
slighting you because you are so young."

"Soon enough, father," his gallant son replied,
"you'll sense the courage inside me, that I know—
I'm hardly a flighty, weak-willed boy these days.
But I think your last plan would gain us nothing.   345
Reconsider, I urge you.
You'll waste time, roaming around our holdings,
probing the fieldhands man by man, while the suitors
sit at ease in our house, devouring all our goods—
those brazen rascals never spare a scrap!   350
But I do advise you to sound the women out:
who are disloyal to you, who are guiltless?
The men—I say no to testing them farm by farm.
That's work for later, if you have really seen
a sign from Zeus whose shield is storm and thunder."   355

   Now as father and son conspired, shaping plans,
the ship that brought the prince and shipmates back
from Pylos was just approaching Ithaca, home port.
As soon as they put in to the harbor's deep bay
they hauled the black vessel up onto dry land   360
and eager deckhands bore away their gear
and rushed the priceless gifts to Clytius'[6] house.
But they sent a herald on to Odysseus' halls at once
to give the news to thoughtful, cautious Penelope
that Telemachus was home—just up-country now   365
but he'd told his mates to sail across to port—
so the noble queen would not be seized with fright
and break down in tears. And now those two men met,
herald and swineherd, both out on the same errand,
to give the queen the news. But once they reached   370
the house of the royal king the herald strode up,
into the serving-women's midst, and burst out,
"Your beloved son, my queen, is home at last!"
Eumaeus though, bending close to Penelope,
whispered every word that her dear son   375
entrusted him to say. Message told in full,
he left the halls and precincts, heading for his pigs.

   But the news shook the suitors, dashed their spirits.
Out of the halls they crowded, past the high-walled court
and there before the gates they sat in council.   380
Polybus' son Eurymachus opened up among them:
"Friends, what a fine piece of work he's carried off!
Telemachus—what insolence—and we thought his little jaunt
would come to grief! Up now, launch a black ship,
the best we can find—muster a crew of oarsmen,   385
row the news to our friends in ambush, fast,
bring them back at once."
                         And just then—
he'd not quite finished when Amphinomus,

---

6. The father of Piraeus, to whom Telemachus entrusted Theoclymenus (15.602–7).

wheeling round in his seat,
saw their vessel moored in the deep harbor,   390
their comrades striking sail and hoisting oars.
He broke into heady laughter, called his friends:
"No need for a message now. They're home, look there!
Some god gave them the news, or they saw the prince's ship
go sailing past and failed to overtake her."   395

    Rising, all trooped down to the water's edge
as the crew hauled the vessel up onto dry land
and the hot-blooded hands bore off their gear.
Then in a pack they went to the meeting grounds,
suffering no one else, young or old, to sit among them.   400
Eupithes' son Antinous rose and harangued them all:
"What a blow! See how the gods have saved this boy
from bloody death? And our lookouts all day long,
stationed atop the windy heights, kept watch,
shift on shift; and once the sun went down   405
we'd never sleep the night ashore, never,
always aboard our swift ship, cruising till dawn,
patrolling to catch Telemachus, kill him on the spot,
and all the while some spirit whisked him home!
So here at home we'll plot his certain death: 410
he must never slip through our hands again,
that boy—while he still lives,
I swear we'll never bring our venture off.
The clever little schemer, he does have his skills,
and the crowds no longer show us favor, not at all.   415
So act! before he can gather his people in assembly.
He'll never give in an inch, I know, he'll rise
and rage away, shouting out to them all how we,
we schemed his sudden death but never caught him.
Hearing of our foul play, they'll hardly sing our praises.   420
Why, they might do us damage, run us off our lands,
drive us abroad to hunt for strangers' shores.
Strike first, I say, and kill him!—
clear of town, in the fields or on the road.
Then we'll seize his estates and worldly goods,   425
carve them up between us, share and share alike.
But as for his palace, let his mother keep it,
she and the man she weds.
                    There's my plan.
If you find it offensive, if you want him
living on—in full command of his patrimony—   430
gather here no more then, living the life of kings,
consuming all his wealth. Each from his own house
must try to win her, showering her with gifts.
Then she can marry the one who offers most,
the man marked out by fate to be her husband."   435

    That brought them all to a hushed, stunned silence
till Amphinomus rose to have his say among them—

the noted son of Nisus, King Aretias' grandson,
the chief who led the suitors from Dulichion,
land of grass and grains,   440
and the man who pleased Penelope the most,
thanks to his timely words and good clear sense.
Concerned for their welfare now, he stood and argued:
"Friends, I've no desire to kill Telemachus, not I—
it's a terrible thing to shed the blood of kings.   445
Wait, sound out the will of the gods—that first.
If the decrees of mighty Zeus commend the work,
I'll kill the prince myself and spur on all the rest.
If the gods are against it, then I say hold back!"

So Amphinomus urged, and won them over.   450
They rose at once, returned to Odysseus' palace,
entered and took their seats on burnished chairs.

But now an inspiration took the discreet Penelope
to face her suitors, brutal, reckless men.   455
The queen had heard it all . . .
how they plotted inside the house to kill her son.
The herald Medon told her—he'd overheard their schemes.
And so, flanked by her ladies, she descended to the hall.
That luster of women, once she reached her suitors,
drawing her glistening veil across her cheeks,   460
paused now where a column propped the sturdy roof
and wheeling on Antinous, cried out against him:
"You Antinous! Violent, vicious, scheming—
you, they say, are the best man your age in Ithaca,
best for eloquence, counsel. You're nothing of the sort!   465
Madman, why do you weave destruction for Telemachus?—
show no pity to those who need it?—those over whom
almighty Zeus stands guard. It's wrong, unholy, yes,
weaving death for those who deserve your mercy!
Don't you know how your father fled here once?   470
A fugitive, terrified of the people, up in arms
against him because he'd joined some Taphian pirates
out to attack Thesprotians, sworn allies of ours.
The mobs were set to destroy him, rip his life out,
devour his vast wealth to their heart's content,   475
but Odysseus held them back, he kept their fury down.
And this is the man whose house you waste, scot-free,
whose wife you court, whose son you mean to kill—
you make my life an agony! Stop, I tell you,
stop all this, and make the rest stop too!"   480

But Polybus' son Eurymachus tried to calm her:
"Wise Penelope, daughter of Icarius, courage!
Disabuse yourself of all these worries now.
That man is not alive—
he never will be, he never can be born—   485
who'll lift a hand against Telemachus, your son,

not while *I* walk the land and I can see the light.
I tell you this—so help me, it will all come true—
in an instant that man's blood will spurt around my spear!
My spear, since time and again Odysseus dandled me   490
on his knees, the great raider of cities fed me
roasted meat and held the red wine to my lips.
So to *me* your son is the dearest man alive,
and I urge the boy to have no fear of death,   495
not from the suitors at least.
What comes from the gods—there's no escaping that."

Encouraging, all the way, but all the while
plotting the prince's murder in his mind . . .
The queen, going up to her lofty well-lit room,
fell to weeping for Odysseus, her beloved husband,   500
till watchful Athena sealed her eyes with welcome sleep.

Returning just at dusk to Odysseus and his son,
the loyal swineherd found they'd killed a yearling pig
and standing over it now were busy fixing supper.
But Athena had approached Laertes' son Odysseus,   505
tapped him with her wand and made him old again.
She dressed him in filthy rags too, for fear Eumaeus,
recognizing his master face-to-face, might hurry
back to shrewd Penelope, blurting out the news
and never hide the secret in his heart.   510

Telemachus was the first to greet the swineherd:
"Welcome home, my friend! What's the talk in town?
Are the swaggering suitors back from ambush yet—
or still waiting to catch me coming home?"

You answered the prince, Eumaeus, loyal swineherd,   515
"I had no time to go roaming all through town,
digging round for that. My heart raced me on
to get my message told and rush back here.
But I met up with a fast runner there,
sent by your crew, a herald,   520
first to tell your mother all the news.
And this I know, I saw with my own eyes—
I was just above the city, heading home,
clambering over Hermes' Ridge, when I caught sight
of a trim ship pulling into the harbor, loaded down   525
with a crowd aboard her, shields and two-edged spears.
I *think* they're the men you're after—I'm not sure."

At that the young prince Telemachus smiled,
glancing toward his father, avoiding Eumaeus' eyes.
          And now,
with the roasting done, the meal set out, they ate well   530
and no one's hunger lacked a proper share of supper.

When they'd put aside desire for food and drink,
they remembered bed and took the gift of sleep.

BOOK XVII

[Stranger at the Gates]

When young Dawn with her rose-red fingers shone once more
Telemachus strapped his rawhide sandals to his feet
and the young prince, the son of King Odysseus,
picked up the rugged spear that fit his grip
and striking out for the city, told his swineherd,   5
"I'm off to town, old friend, to present myself to mother.
She'll never stop her bitter tears and mourning,
well I know, till she sees me face-to-face.
And for you I have some orders—
take this luckless stranger to town, so he can beg   10
his supper there, and whoever wants can give the man
some crumbs and a cup to drink. How can I put up with
every passerby? My mind's weighed down with troubles.
If the stranger resents it, all the worse for him.
I like to tell the truth and tell it straight."   15

                                         "My friend,"
subtle Odysseus broke in, "I've no desire, myself,
to linger here. Better that beggars cadge their meals
in town than in the fields. Some willing soul
will see to my needs. I'm hardly fit, at my age,
to keep to a farm and jump to a foreman's every order.   20
Go on then. This man will take me, as you've told him,
once I'm warm from the fire and the sun's good and strong.
Look at the clothing on my back—all rags and tatters.
I'm afraid the frost at dawn could do me in,
and town, you say, is a long hard way from here."   25

    At that Telemachus strode down through the farm
in quick, firm strides, brooding death for the suitors.
And once he reached his well-constructed palace,
propping his spear against a sturdy pillar
and crossing the stone threshold, in he went.   30

    His old nurse was the first to see him, Euryclea,
just spreading fleeces over the carved, inlaid chairs.
Tears sprang to her eyes, she rushed straight to the prince
as the other maids of great Odysseus flocked around him,
hugged him warmly, kissed his head and shoulders.   35

    Now down from her chamber came discreet Penelope,
looking for all the world like Artemis or golden Aphrodite—
bursting into tears as she flung her arms around her darling son
and kissed his face and kissed his shining eyes and sobbed,
"You're home, Telemachus!"—words flew from her heart—   40

"sweet light of my eyes! I never thought I'd see you again,
once you shipped to Pylos—against my will, so secret,
out for news of your dear father. Quick tell me,
did you catch sight of the man—meet him—what?"

    "Please, mother," steady Telemachus replied,   45
"don't move me to tears, don't stir the heart inside me.
I've just escaped from death. Sudden death.
No. Bathe now, put on some fresh clothes,
go up to your own room with your serving-women,
pray, and promise the gods a generous sacrifice   50
to bring success, if Zeus will ever grant us
the hour of our revenge. I myself am off
to the meeting grounds to summon up a guest
who came with me from abroad when I sailed home.
I sent him on ahead with my trusted crew.   55
I told Piraeus to take him to his house,
treat him well, host him with all good will
till I could come myself."
                    Words to the mark
that left his mother silent . . .
She bathed now, put on some fresh clothes,   60
prayed, and promised the gods a generous sacrifice
to bring success, if Zeus would ever grant
the hour of their revenge.
                    Spear in hand,
Telemachus strode on through the hall and out,
and a pair of sleek hounds went trotting at his heels.   65
And Athena lavished a marvelous splendor on the prince
so the people all gazed in wonder as he came forward.
The swaggering suitors clustered, milling round him,
welcome words on their lips, and murder in their hearts.
But he gave them a wide berth as they came crowding in   70
and there where Mentor sat, Antiphus, Halitherses too—
his father's loyal friends from days gone by—
he took his seat as they pressed him with their questions.
And just then Piraeus the gallant spearman approached,
leading the stranger through the town and out onto   75
the meeting grounds. Telemachus, not hanging back,
went right up to greet Theoclymenus, his guest,
but Piraeus spoke out first: "Quickly now,
Telemachus, send some women to my house
to retrieve the gifts that Menelaus gave you."   80

    "Wait, Piraeus," wary Telemachus cautioned,
"we've no idea how all of this will go.
If the brazen suitors cut me down in the palace—
off guard—and carve apart my father's whole estate,
I'd rather you yourself, or one of his friends here,   85
keep those gifts and get some pleasure from them.
But if I can bring down slaughter on that crew,
you send the gifts to my house—we'll share the joy."

Their plans made, he led the wayworn stranger home
and once they reached the well-constructed palace,   90
spreading out their cloaks on a chair or bench,
into the burnished tubs they climbed and bathed.
When women had washed them, rubbed them down with oil
and drawn warm fleece and shirts around their shoulders,
out of the baths they stepped and sat on high-backed chairs.   95
A maid brought water soon in a graceful golden pitcher
and over a silver basin tipped it out
so they might rinse their hands,
then pulled a gleaming table to their side.
A staid housekeeper brought on bread to serve them,   100
appetizers aplenty too, lavish with her bounty.
Penelope sat across from her son, beside a pillar,
leaning back on a low chair and winding finespun yarn.
They reached out for the good things that lay at hand
and when they'd put aside desire for food and drink,   105
the queen, for all her composure, said at last,
"Telemachus, I'm going back to my room upstairs
and lie down on my bed . . .
that bed of pain my tears have streaked, year in,
year out, from the day Odysseus sailed away to Troy   110
with Atreus' two sons.[7]
                    But you, you never had the heart—
before those insolent suitors crowd back to the house—
to tell me clearly about your father's journey home,
if you've heard any news."
                    "Of course, mother,"
thoughtful Telemachus reassured her quickly,   115
"I will tell you the whole true story now.
We sailed to Pylos, to Nestor, the great king,
and he received me there in his lofty palace,
treated me well and warmly, yes, as a father treats
a long-lost son just home from voyaging, years abroad: 120
such care he showered on me, he and his noble sons.
But of strong, enduring Odysseus, dead or alive,
he's heard no news, he said, from any man on earth.
He sent me on to the famous spearman Atrides Menelaus,
on with a team of horses drawing a bolted chariot.   125
And there I saw her, Helen of Argos—all for her
Achaeans and Trojans suffered so much hardship,
thanks to the gods' decree . . .
The lord of the warcry, Menelaus, asked at once
what pressing need had brought me to lovely Lacedaemon,   130
and when I told him the whole story, first to last,
the king burst out, 'How shameful! That's the bed
of a brave man of war they'd like to crawl inside,
those spineless, craven cowards!
Weak as the doe that beds down her fawns   135
in a mighty lion's den—her newborn sucklings—

---

7. Agamemnon and Menelaus.

then trails off to the mountain spurs and grassy bends
to graze her fill, but back the lion comes to his own lair
and the master deals both fawns a ghastly bloody death,
just what Odysseus will deal that mob—ghastly death. 140
Ah if only—Father Zeus, Athena and lord Apollo—
that man who years ago in the games at Lesbos
rose to Philomelides' challenge, wrestled him,
pinned him down with one tremendous throw
and the Argives roared with joy . . . 145
if only *that* Odysseus sported with those suitors,
a blood wedding, a quick death would take the lot!
But about the things you've asked me, so intently,
I'll skew and sidestep nothing, not deceive you, ever.
Of all he told me—the Old Man of the Sea who never lies— 150
I'll hide or hold back nothing, not a single word.
He said he'd seen Odysseus on an island,
ground down in misery, off in a goddess' house,
the nymph Calypso, who holds him there by force.
He has no way to voyage home to his own native land, 155
no trim ships in reach, no crew to ply the oars
and send him scudding over the sea's broad back.'

    So Menelaus, the famous spearman, told me.
My mission accomplished, back I came at once,
and the gods sent me a stiff following wind 160
that sped me home to the native land I love."

    His reassurance stirred the queen to her depths
and the godlike seer Theoclymenus added firmly,
"Noble lady, wife of Laertes' son, Odysseus,
Menelaus can have no perfect revelations; 165
mark *my* words—I will make you a prophecy,
quite precise, and *I'll* hold nothing back.
I swear by Zeus, the first of all the gods,
by this table of hospitality here, my host,
by Odysseus' hearth where I have come for help— 170
I swear Odysseus *is* on native soil, here and now!
Poised or on the prowl, learning of these rank crimes
he's sowing seeds of ruin for all your suitors.
So clear, so true, that bird-sign I saw
as I sat on the benched ship 175
and sounded out the future to the prince!"

    "If only, my friend," reserved Penelope exclaimed,
"everything you say would come to pass!
You'd soon know my affection, know my gifts.
Any man you meet would call you blest." 180

    And so the three confided in the halls
while all the suitors, before Odysseus' palace,
amused themselves with discus and long throwing spears,
out on the leveled grounds, free and easy as always,

full of swagger. When the dinner-hour approached   185
and sheep came home from pastures near and far,
driven in by familiar drovers,
Medon called them all, their favorite herald,
always present at their meals: "My young lords,
now you've played your games to your hearts' content,   190
come back to the halls so we can fix your supper.
Nothing's better than dining well on time!"

    They came at his summons, rising from the games
and now, bustling into the well-constructed palace,
flinging down their cloaks on a chair or bench,   195
they butchered hulking sheep and fatted goats,
full-grown hogs and a young cow from the herd,
preparing for their feast.
                  At the same time
the king and his loyal swineherd geared to leave
the country for the town. Eumaeus, foreman of men,   200
set things in motion: "Friend, I know you're keen
on going down to town today, just as my master bid,
though I'd rather you stay here to guard the farm.
But I prize the boy, I fear he'll blame me later—
a dressing-down from your master's hard to bear.   205
So off we go now. The shank of the day is past.[8]
You'll find it colder with nightfall coming on."

    "I know, I see your point," the crafty man replied.
"There's sense in this old head. So let's be off.
And from now on, you lead me all the way.   210
Just give me a stick to lean on,
if you have one ready-cut. You say the road
is treacherous, full of slips and slides."
                    With that
he flung his beggar's sack across his shoulders—
torn and tattered, slung from a fraying rope.   215
Eumaeus gave him a staff that met his needs.
Then the two moved out, leaving behind them
dogs and herdsmen to stay and guard the farm.
And so the servant led his master toward the city,
looking for all the world like an old and broken beggar   220
hunched on a stick, his body wrapped in shameful rags . . .

    Down over the rugged road they went till hard by town
they reached the stone-rimmed fountain running clear
where the city people came and drew their water.
Ithacus built it once, with Neritus and Polyctor.[9]   225
Round it a stand of poplar thrived on the dank soil,
all in a nestling ring, and down from a rock-ledge overhead
the cold water splashed, and crowning the fountain

8. I.e., much of the day is gone.   9. Presumably the first rulers of Ithaca. Ithacus gave the island its
name; Neritus's name was given to the most prominent mountain on Ithaca; the name Polyctor may mean
"having great possessions."

rose an altar-stone erected to the nymphs,
where every traveler paused and left an offering. 230
Here Dolius' son, Melanthius, crossed their path,
herding his goats with a pair, of drovers' help,
the pick of his flocks to make the suitors' meal.
As soon as he saw them there he broke into a flood
of brutal, foul abuse that made Odysseus' blood boil. 235
"Look!"—he sneered—"one scum nosing another scum along,
dirt finds dirt by the will of god—it never fails!
Wretched pig-boy, where do you take your filthy swine,
this sickening beggar who licks the pots at feasts?
Hanging round the doorposts, rubbing his back, 240
scavenging after scraps,
no hero's swords and cauldrons, not for *him*.
Hand him over to me—I'll teach him to work a farm,
muck out my stalls, pitch feed to the young goats;
whey to drink will put some muscle on his hams! 245
Oh no, he's learned his lazy ways too well,
he's got no itch to stick to good hard work,
he'd rather go scrounging round the countryside,
begging for crusts to stuff his greedy gut!
Let me tell you—so help me it's the truth— 250
if he sets foot in King Odysseus' royal palace,
salvos of footstools flung at his head by all the lords
will crack his ribs as he runs the line of fire through the house!"

Wild, reckless taunts—and just as he passed Odysseus
the idiot lurched out with a heel and kicked his hip 255
but he couldn't knock the beggar off the path,
he stood his ground so staunchly. Odysseus was torn . . .
should he wheel with his staff and beat the scoundrel senseless?—
or hoist him by the midriff, split his skull on the rocks?
He steeled himself instead, his mind in full control. 260
But Eumaeus glared at the goatherd, cursed him to his face,
then lifted up his hands and prayed his heart out:
"O nymphs of the fountain, daughters of Zeus—
if Odysseus ever burned you the long thighs
of lambs or kids, covered with rich fat, 265
now bring my prayer to pass!
Let that man come back—some god guide him now!
He'd toss to the winds the flashy show you make,
Melanthius, so cocksure—always strutting round the town
while worthless fieldhands leave your flocks a shambles!" 270

"Listen to him!" the goatherd shouted back.
"All bark and no bite from the vicious mutt!
One fine day I'll ship him out in a black lugger,
miles from Ithaca—sell him off for a good stiff price!
Just let Apollo shoot Telemachus down with his silver bow, 275
today in the halls, or the suitors snuff his life out—
as sure as I know the day of the king's return
is blotted out, the king is worlds away!"

With his parting shot he left them trudging on
and went and reached the royal house in no time.   280
Slipping in, he took his seat among the suitors,
facing Eurymachus, who favored him the most.
The carvers set before him his plate of meat,
a staid housekeeper brought the man his bread.

And now at last the king and loyal swineherd,   285
drawing near the palace, halted just outside
as the lyre's rippling music drifted round them—
Phemius, striking up a song for assembled guests—
and the master seized his servant's hand, exclaiming,
"Friend, what a noble house! Odysseus' house, it must be! 290
No mistaking it—you could tell it among a townful, look.
One building linked to the next, and the courtyard wall
is finished off with a fine coping, the double doors
are battle-proof—no man could break them down!
I can tell a crowd is feasting there in force—   295
smell the savor of roasts . . . the ringing lyre, listen,
the lyre that god has made the friend of feasts."

"An easy guess," you said, Eumaeus, swineherd,
"for a man as keen as you at every turn.
Put heads together. What do we do next?   300
Either you're the first one into the palace—
mix with the suitors, leave me where I am.
Or if you like, stay put, and I'll go first myself.
Don't linger long. Someone might spot you here outside,
knock you down or pelt you. Mark my words. Take care."   305

The man who'd borne long years abroad replied,
"Well I know. Remember? There's sense in this old head.
You go in, you first, while I stay here behind.
Stones and blows and I are hardly strangers.
My heart is steeled by now,   310
I've had my share of pain in the waves and wars.
Add this to the total. Bring the trial on.
But there's no way to hide the belly's hungers—
what a curse, what mischief it brews in all our lives!
Just for hunger we rig and ride our long benched ships   315
on the barren salt sea, speeding death to enemies."

Now, as they talked on, a dog that lay there
lifted up his muzzle, pricked his ears . . .
It was Argos, long-enduring Odysseus' dog
he trained as a puppy once, but little joy he got   320
since all too soon he shipped to sacred Troy.
In the old days young hunters loved to set him
coursing after the wild goats and deer and hares.
But now with his master gone he lay there, castaway,
on piles of dung from mules and cattle, heaps collecting   325
out before the gates till Odysseus' serving-men

could cart it off to manure the king's estates.
Infested with ticks, half-dead from neglect,
here lay the hound, old Argos.
But the moment he sensed Odysseus standing by   330
he thumped his tail, nuzzling low, and his ears dropped,
though he had no strength to drag himself an inch
toward his master. Odysseus glanced to the side
and flicked away a tear, hiding it from Eumaeus,
diverting his friend in a hasty, offhand way: 335
"Strange, Eumaeus, look, a dog like this,
lying here on a dung-hill . . .
what handsome lines! But I can't say for sure
if he had the running speed to match his looks
or he was only the sort that gentry spoil at table,   340
show-dogs masters pamper for their points."

You told the stranger, Eumaeus, loyal swineherd,
"Here—it's all too true—here's the dog of a man
who died in foreign parts. But if he had now
the form and flair he had in his glory days—   345
as Odysseus left him, sailing off to Troy—
you'd be amazed to see such speed, such strength.
No quarry he chased in the deepest, darkest woods
could ever slip this hound. A champion tracker too!
Ah, but he's run out of luck now, poor fellow . . .   350
his master's dead and gone, so far from home,
and the heartless women tend him not at all. Slaves,
with their lords no longer there to crack the whip,
lose all zest to perform their duties well. Zeus,
the Old Thunderer, robs a man of half his virtue   355
the day the yoke clamps down around his neck."

With that he entered the well-constructed palace,
strode through the halls and joined the proud suitors.
But the dark shadow of death closed down on Argos' eyes
the instant he saw Odysseus, twenty years away.   360

Now Prince Telemachus, first by far to note
the swineherd coming down the hall, nodded briskly,
called and waved him on. Eumaeus, glancing about,
picked up a handy stool where the carver always sat,
slicing meat for the suitors feasting through the house.   365
He took and put it beside the prince's table, facing him,
straddled it himself as a steward set a plate of meat
before the man and served him bread from trays.

Right behind him came Odysseus, into his own house,
looking for all the world like an old and broken beggar   370
hunched on a stick, his body wrapped in shameful rags.
Just in the doorway, just at the ashwood threshold,
there he settled down . . .

leaning against the cypress post a master joiner
planed smooth and hung with a plumb line years ago. 375
Telemachus motioned the swineherd over now,
and choosing a whole loaf from a fine wicker tray
and as much meat as his outstretched hands could hold,
he said, "Now take these to the stranger, tell him too
to make the rounds of the suitors, beg from one and all. 380
Bashfulness, for a man in need, is no great friend."

  And Eumaeus did his bidding, went straight up
to the guest and winged a greeting: "Here, stranger,
Prince Telemachus sends you these, and tells you too
to make the rounds of the suitors, beg from one and all. 385
Bashfulness for a beggar, he says, is no great friend."

  "Powerful Zeus!" the crafty king responded,
"grant that your prince be blest among mankind—
and all his heart's desires come to pass!"

  Taking the food in both hands, setting it down, 390
spread out on his filthy sack before his feet,
the beggar fell to his meal
as the singer raised a song throughout the house.
Once he'd supped and the stirring bard had closed,
the suitors broke into uproar down along the hall. 395
And now Athena came to the side of Laertes' royal son
and urged him, "Go now, gather crusts from all the suitors,
test them, so we can tell the innocent from the guilty."
But not even so would Athena save one man from death.
Still, off he went, begging from each in turn, 400
circling left to right, reaching out his hand
like a beggar from the day that he was born.
They pitied him, gave him scraps, were puzzled too,
asking each other, "Who is this?" "Where's he from?"
Till the goatherd Melanthius shouted out in their midst, 405
"Listen to me, you lords who court our noble queen—
I'll tell you about the stranger. I've seen him before.
I know for a fact the swineherd led him in,
though I have no idea who the fellow is
or where he thinks he comes from."
                              At that 410
Antinous wheeled on Eumaeus, lashing out at him:
"Your highness, swineherd—why drag *this* to town?
Haven't we got our share of vagabonds to deal with,
disgusting beggars who lick the feasters' plates?
Isn't it quite enough, these swarming crowds 415
consuming your master's bounty—
must you invite this rascal in the bargain?"
                        "Antinous,
highborn as you are," you told the man, Eumaeus,
"that was a mean low speech!

Now who'd go out, who on his own hook—   420
not I—and ask a stranger in from nowhere
unless he had some skills to serve the house?
A prophet, a healer who cures disease, a worker in wood
or even a god-inspired bard whose singing warms the heart—
they're the ones asked in around the world. A beggar?   425
Who'd invite a beggar to bleed his household white?
You, you of all the suitors are always roughest
on the servants of our king, on me most of all.
Not that I care, no, so long as his queen,
his wise queen, is still alive in the palace,   430
Prince Telemachus too."
                          "Stop, Eumaeus,"
poised Telemachus broke in quickly now,
"don't waste so much breath on Antinous here.
It's just his habit to bait a man with abuse
and spur the rest as well."
                          He wheeled on the suitor,   435
letting loose: "How kind you are to me, Antinous,
kind as a father to his son! Encouraging me
to send this stranger packing from my house
with a harsh command! I'd never do it. God forbid.
Take and give to the beggar. I don't grudge it—   440
I'd even urge you on. No scruples now,
never fear your gifts will upset my mother
or any servant in King Odysseus' royal house.
But no such qualm could enter that head of yours,
bent on feeding your own face, not feeding strangers!"   445

     Antinous countered the young prince in kind:
"So high and mighty, Telemachus—such unbridled rage!
If all the suitors gave him the sort of gift I'll give,
the house would be rid of *him* for three whole months!"
With that, from under his table he seized the stool   450
that propped his smooth feet as he reveled on—
just lifting it into view . . .
                          But as for the rest,
all gave to the beggar, filled his sack with handouts,
bread and meat. And Odysseus seemed at the point
of getting back to his doorsill,   455
done with testing suitors, home free himself
when he stopped beside Antinous, begging face-to-face:
"Give me a morsel, friend. You're hardly the worst
Achaean here, it seems. The noblest one, in fact.
You look like a king to me!   460
So you should give a bigger crust than the rest
and I will sing your praises all across the earth.
I too once lived in a lofty house that men admired;
rolling in wealth, I'd often give to a vagabond like myself,
whoever he was, whatever need had brought him to my door.   465
And crowds of servants I had, and lots of all it takes
to live the life of ease, to make men call you rich.

But Zeus ruined it all—god's will, no doubt—
when he shipped me off with a roving band of pirates
bound for Egypt, a long hard sail, to wreck my life.   470
There in the Nile delta I moored our ships of war.
God knows I ordered my trusty crews to stand by,
just where they were, and guard the anchored fleet
and I sent a patrol to scout things out from higher ground.
But swept away by their own reckless fury, the crew went berserk—   475
they promptly began to plunder the lush Egyptian farms,
dragged off the women and children, killed the men.
Outcries reached the city in no time—stirred by shouts
the entire town came streaming down at the break of day,
filling the river plain with chariots, ranks of infantry   480
and the gleam of bronze. Zeus who loves the lightning
flung down murderous panic on all my men-at-arms—
no one dared to stand his ground and fight,
disaster ringed us round from every quarter.
Droves of my men they hacked down with swords,   485
led off the rest alive, to labor for them as slaves.
Myself? They passed me on to a stranger come their way,
to ship me to Cyprus—Iasus' son Dmetor it was,
who ruled Cyprus then with an iron fist.
And from there I sailed to Ithaca,   490
just as you see me now, ground down by pain and sorrow—"

    "Good god almighty!" Antinous cut the beggar short.
"What spirit brought this pest to plague our feast?
Back off! Into the open, clear of my table, or you,
you'll soon land in an Egypt, Cyprus, to break your heart!   495
What a brazen, shameless beggar! Scrounging food
from each man in turn, and look at their handouts,
reckless, never a qualm, no holding back, not
when making free with the next man's goods—
each one's got plenty here."
                                    "Pity, pity,"   500
the wry Odysseus countered, drawing away.
"No sense in your head to match your handsome looks.
You'd grudge your servant a pinch of salt from your own larder,
you who lounge at the next man's board but lack the heart
to tear a crust of bread and hand it on to me,   505
though there's god's plenty here."
                                    Boiling over
Antinous gave him a scathing look and let fly,
"Now you won't get out of the hall unscarred, I swear,
not after such a filthy string of insults!"
                                    With that
he seized the stool and hurled it—
                                    Square in the back   510
it struck Odysseus, just under the right shoulder
but he stood up against it—steady as a rock,
unstaggered by Antinous' blow—just shook his head,
silent, his mind churning with thoughts of bloody work.

Back he went to the doorsill, crouched, and setting down   515
his sack about to burst, he faced the suitors, saying,
"Hear me out, you lords who court the noble queen,
I must say what the heart inside me urges.
There's nothing to groan about, no hurt, when a man
takes a blow as he fights to save his own possessions,   520
cattle or shining flocks. But Antinous struck me
all because of my good-for-nothing belly—that,
that curse that makes such pain for us poor men.
But if beggars have their gods and Furies too,
let Antinous meet his death before he meets his bride!"   525

      "Enough, stranger!" Antinous volleyed back.
"Sit there and eat in peace—or go get lost! Or else,
for the way you talk, these young men will hale you
up and down the halls by your hands or feet
until you're skinned alive!"
                              Naked threats—   530
but the rest were outraged, even those brash suitors.
One would say to another, "Look, Antinous,
that was a crime, to strike the luckless beggar!"

      "Your fate is sealed if he's some god from the blue."

      "And the gods do take on the look of strangers   535
dropping in from abroad—"
                              "Disguised in every way
as they roam and haunt our cities, watching over us—"

      "All our foul play, all our fair play too!"

      So they warned, but Antinous paid no heed.
And the anguish welled up in Telemachus' breast   540
for the blow his father took, yet he let no tears
go rolling down his face—he just shook his head,
silent, his mind churning with thoughts of bloody work.

      But then, when cautious Queen Penelope heard
how Antinous struck the stranger, there in the halls,   545
she cried out, with her serving-women round her,
"May Apollo the Archer strike you just as hard!"
And her housekeeper Eurynome added quickly,
"If only our prayers were granted—
then not one of the lot would live to see   550
Dawn climb her throne tomorrow!"
                              "Dear old woman,"
alert Penelope replied, "they're all hateful,
plotting their vicious plots. But Antinous
is the worst of all—he's black death itself.
Here's this luckless stranger, wandering down   555
the halls and begging scraps—hard-pressed by need—
and the rest all give the man his fill of food

but that one gives him a footstool
hurled at his right shoulder, hits his back!"

While she exclaimed among her household women,   560
sitting there in her room, Odysseus bent to supper.
Penelope called the swineherd in and gave instructions:
"Go, good Eumaeus, tell the stranger to come at once.
I'd like to give him a warm welcome, ask the man
if he's heard some news about my gallant husband   565
or seen him in the flesh . . .
He seems like one who's roved around the world."

"My queen," you answered, Eumaeus, loyal swineherd,
"if only the lords would hold their peace a moment!
Such stories he tells—he'd charm you to your depths.   570
Three nights, three days I kept him in my shelter;
I was the first the fellow stumbled onto,
fleeing from some ship. But not even so
could he bring his tale of troubles to an end.
You know how you can stare at a bard in wonder—   575
trained by the gods to sing and hold men spellbound—
how you can long to sit there, listening, all your life
when the man begins to sing. So he charmed my heart,
I tell you, huddling there beside me at my fire.
He and Odysseus' father go way back, he says,   580
sworn friends, and the stranger hails from Crete
where the stock of old King Minos still lives on,
and from Crete he made his way, racked by hardship,
tumbling on like a rolling stone until he turned up here.
He swears he's heard of Odysseus—just in reach,   585
in rich Thesprotian country—still alive,
laden with treasure, heading home at last!"

                                        "Go,"
the cautious queen responded, "call him here
so he can tell me his own tale face-to-face.
Our friends can sit at the gates or down the halls   590
and play their games, debauched to their hearts' content.
Why not? Their own stores, their bread and seasoned wine,
lie intact at home; food for their serving-men alone.
But they, they infest our palace day and night,
they butcher our cattle, our sheep, our fat goats,   595
feasting themselves sick, swilling our glowing wine
as if there's no tomorrow—all of it, squandered.
No, there is no man like Odysseus in command
to drive this curse from the house. Dear god,
if only Odysseus came back home to native soil now,   600
he and his son would avenge the outrage of these men—like that!"

At her last words Telemachus shook with a lusty sneeze
and the sudden outburst echoed up and down the halls.
The queen was seized with laughter, calling out
to Eumaeus winged words: "Quickly, go!   605

Bring me this stranger now, face-to-face!
You hear how my son sealed all I said with a sneeze?[1]
So let death come down with grim finality on these suitors—
one and all—not a single man escape his sudden doom!
And another thing. Mark my words, I tell you.   610
If I'm convinced that all he says is true,
I'll dress him in shirt and cloak, in handsome clothes."

    Off the swineherd went, following her instructions,
made his way to the stranger's side and winged a word:
"Old friend—our queen, wise Penelope, summons you,   615
the prince's mother! The spirit moves her now,
heartsick as she is,
to ask a question or two about her husband.
And if she's convinced that all you say is true,
she'll dress you in shirt and cloak. That's what you need,   620
that most of all now. Bread you can always beg
around the country, fill your belly well—
they'll give you food, whoever has a mind to."

    "Gladly, Eumaeus," the patient man replied,
"I'll tell her the whole truth and nothing but,   625
Icarius' daughter, your wise queen Penelope.
I know all about that man . . .
it's been my lot to suffer what he's suffered.
But I fear the mob's abuse, those rough young bucks,
their pride and violence hit the iron skies!   630
Just now that scoundrel—as I went down the halls,
harming no one—up and dealt me a jolting blow,
and who would raise a hand to save me? Telemachus?
Anyone else? No one. So tell Penelope now,
anxious as she may be, to wait in the halls   635
until the sun goes down. Then she can ask me
all she likes about her husband's journey home.
But let her give me a seat close by the fire.
The clothes on my back are tatters. Well you know—
you are the first I begged for care and shelter."   640

    Back the swineherd went, following his instructions.
Penelope, just as he crossed her threshold, broke out,
"Didn't you bring him? What's in the vagrant's mind?
Fear of someone? Embarrassed by something else,
here in the house? Is the fellow bashful?   645
A bashful man will make a sorry beggar."

    You answered your queen, Eumaeus, loyal swineherd,
"He talks to the point—he thinks as the next man would
who wants to dodge their blows, that brutal crew.
He tells you to wait here till the sun goes down.   650
It's better for you, my queen. Then you can talk
with the man in private, hear the stranger's news."

1. A sneeze was considered an omen that words just uttered would be fulfilled.

"Nobody's fool, that stranger," wise Penelope said,
"he sees how things could go. Surely no men on earth
can match that gang for reckless, deadly schemes."   655

So she agreed, and now, mission accomplished,
back the loyal swineherd went to mix with the suitors.
Moving next to the prince, he whispered a parting word,
their heads close together so no one else could hear.
"Dear boy, I must be off, to see to the pigs   660
and the whole farm—your living, mine as well.
You're the one to tend to all things here.
Look out for your own skin first,
do take care, you mustn't come to grief.
Crowds of your own countrymen plot your death—   665
let Zeus wipe out the lot before they kill us all!"

"Right you are, old friend," the canny prince replied.
"Now off you go, once you've had your supper.
But come back bright and early,
bring some good sound boars for slaughter. Yes,   670
I'll tend to all things here, I and the deathless gods."

And the swineherd sat down again on his polished stool
and once he'd supped and drunk to his heart's content,
back he went to his pigs, leaving the royal precincts
still filled with feasters, all indulging now   675
in the joys of dance and song.
The day was over. Dusk was falling fast.

BOOK XVIII

[The Beggar-King of Ithaca]

Now along came this tramp, this public nuisance
who used to scrounge a living round the streets of Ithaca—
notorious for his belly, a ravenous, bottomless pit
for food and drink, but he had no pith, no brawn,
despite the looming hulk that met your eyes.   5
Arnaeus was his name,
so his worthy mother called him at birth,
but all the young men called him Irus[2] for short
because he'd hustle messages at any beck and call.
Well *he* came by to rout the king from his own house   10
and met Odysseus now with a rough, abusive burst:
"Get off the porch, you old goat, before I haul you
off by the leg! Can't you see them give me the wink,
all of them here, to drag you out—and so I would
but I've got some pangs of conscience. Up with you, man,   15
or before you know it, we'll be trading blows!"
                                          A killing look,

2. A pun on Iris, the name of the goddess who often served as the gods' messenger.

and the wily old soldier countered, "Out of your mind?
What damage have I done *you*? What have I said?
I don't grudge you anything,
not if the next man up and gives you plenty.   20
This doorsill is big enough for the both of us—
you've got no call to grudge me what's not yours.
You're another vagrant, just like me, I'd say,
and it lies with the gods to make us rich or poor. So,
keep your fists to yourself, don't press your luck, don't rile me,   25
or old as I am, I'll bloody your lip, splatter your chest
and buy myself some peace and quiet for tomorrow.
I doubt you'll ever come lumbering back again
to the halls of Laertes' royal son Odysseus."

   "Look who's talking!" the beggar rumbled in anger.   30
"How this pot-bellied pig runs off at the mouth—
like an old crone at her oven!
Well *I've* got a knock-out blow in store for *him*—
I'll batter the tramp with both fists, crack every tooth
from his jaws, I'll litter the ground with teeth   35
like a rogue sow's, punished for rooting corn!
Belt up—so the lords can see us fight it out.
How can you beat a champion half your age?"

   Tongue-lashing each other, tempers flaring,
there on the polished sill before the lofty doors.   40
And Antinous, that grand prince, hearing them wrangle,
broke into gloating laughter, calling out to the suitors,
"Friends, nothing like this has come our way before—
what sport some god has brought the palace now!
The stranger and Irus, look,   45
they'd battle it out together, fists flying.
Come, let's pit them against each other—fast!"

   All leapt from their seats with whoops of laughter,
clustering round the pair of ragged beggars there
as Eupithes' son Antinous planned the contest.   50
"Quiet, my fine friends. Here's what I propose.
These goat sausages[3] sizzling here in the fire—
we packed them with fat and blood to have for supper.
Now, whoever wins this bout and proves the stronger,
let that man step up and take his pick of the lot!   55
What's more, from this day on he feasts among us—
no other beggar will we allow inside
to cadge his meals from us!"
                              They all cheered
but Odysseus, foxy veteran, plotted on . . .
"Friends, how can an old man, worn down with pain,   60

---

3. In Greek these are literally "bellies"—that is, the stomach or intestine used as the membrane for the sausage. As Odysseus says in lines 61–62 (and has said several times before), the belly is what drives beggars and outcasts. The two beggars, under the belly's compulsion, thus compete for a belly as prize.

stand up to a young buck? It's just this belly of mine,
this trouble-maker, tempts me to take a licking.
So first, all of you swear me a binding oath:
come, not one of you steps in for Irus here,
strikes me a foul blow to pull him through   65
and lays me in the dust."
                    And at that
they all mouthed the oath that he required,
and once they vowed they'd never interfere,
Prince Telemachus drove the matter home:
"Stranger, if your spine and fighting pride   70
prompt you to go against this fellow now,
have no fear of any suitor in the pack—
whoever fouls you will have to face a crowd.
Count on *me*, your host. And two lords back me up,
Antinous and Eurymachus—both are men of sense."   75

    They all shouted approval of the prince
as Odysseus belted up, roping his rags around his loins,
baring his big rippling thighs—his boxer's broad shoulders,
his massive chest and burly arms on full display
as Athena stood beside him,   80
fleshing out the limbs of the great commander . . .
Despite their swagger, the suitors were amazed,
gaping at one another, trading forecasts:
"Irus will soon be ironed out for good!"

    "He's in for the beating he begged for all along."   85

    "Look at the hams on that old-timer—"
                              "Just under his rags!"

    Each outcry jolted Irus to the core—too late.
The servants trussed his clothes up, dragged him on,
the flesh on his body quaking now with terror.
Antinous rounded on him, flinging insults: 90
"You, you clumsy ox, you're better off dead
or never born at all, if you cringe at *him*,
paralyzed with fear of an old, broken hulk,
ground down by the pains that hound his steps.
Mark my word—so help me I'll make it good—   95
if that old relic whips you and wins the day,
I'll toss you into a black ship and sail you off
to Echetus,[4] the mainland king who wrecks all men alive!
He'll lop your nose and ears with his ruthless blade,
he'll rip your privates out by the roots, he will,   100
and serve them up to his dogs to bolt down raw!"

    That threat shook his knees with a stronger fit
but they hauled him into the ring. Both men put up their fists—

---

4. Probably imaginary; at least, we know nothing more of him than Homer tells us here.

with the seasoned fighter Odysseus deeply torn now . . .
should he knock him senseless, leave him dead where he dropped   105
or just stretch him out on the ground with a light jab?
As he mulled things over, that way seemed the best:
a glancing blow, the suitors would not detect him.
The two men squared off—
                              and Irus hurled a fist
at Odysseus' right shoulder as *he* came through   110
with a hook below the ear, pounding Irus' neck,
smashing the bones inside—
                          Suddenly red blood
came spurting out of his mouth, and headlong down
he pitched in the dust, howling, teeth locked in a grin,
feet beating the ground—
                        And the princely suitors,   115
flinging their hands in the air, died laughing.
Grabbing him by the leg, Odysseus hauled him
through the porch, across the yard to the outer gate,
heaped him against the courtyard wall, sitting slumped,
stuck his stick in his hand and gave him a parting shot: 120
"Now hold your post—play the scarecrow to all the pigs and dogs!
But no more lording it over strangers, no more playing
the beggar-king for you, you loathsome fool,
or you'll bring down something worse around your neck!"

     He threw his beggar's sack across his shoulders—   125
torn and tattered, slung from a fraying rope—
then back he went to the sill and took his seat.
The suitors ambled back as well, laughing jauntily,
toasting the beggar warmly now, those proud young blades,
one man egging the other on: "Stranger, friend, may Zeus   130
and the other deathless gods fill up your sack with blessings!"

     "All your heart desires!"
                         "You've knocked him out of action,
that insatiable tramp—"
                         "That parasite on the land!"

     "Ship him off to Echetus, fast—the mainland king
who wrecks all men alive!"
                         Welcome words   135
and a lucky omen too—Odysseus' heart leapt up.
Antinous laid before him a generous goat sausage,
bubbling fat and blood. Amphinomus took two loaves
from the wicker tray and set them down beside him,
drank his health in a golden cup and said,   140
"Cheers, old friend, old father,
saddled now as you are with so much trouble—
here's to your luck, great days from this day on!"

     And the one who knew the world replied at length,
"Amphinomus, you seem like a man of good sense to me.   145

Just like your father—at least I've heard his praises,
Nisus of Dulichion, a righteous man, and rich.
You're his son, they say, you seem well-spoken, too.
So I will tell you something. Listen. Listen closely.
Of all that breathes and crawls across the earth,   150
our mother earth breeds nothing feebler than a man.
So long as the gods grant him power, spring in his knees,
he thinks he will never suffer affliction down the years.
But then, when the happy gods bring on the long hard times,
bear them he must, against his will, and steel his heart.   155
Our lives, our mood and mind as we pass across the earth,
turn as the days turn . . .
as the father of men and gods makes each day dawn.
I too seemed destined to be a man of fortune once
and a wild wicked swath I cut, indulged my lust for violence,   160
staking all on my father and my brothers.
                                        Look at me now.
And so, I say, let no man ever be lawless all his life,
just take in peace what gifts the gods will send.
                                            True,
but here I see you suitors plotting your reckless work,
carving away at the wealth, affronting the loyal wife   165
of a man who won't be gone from kin and country long.
I say he's right at hand—and may some power save you,
spirit you home before you meet him face-to-face
the moment he returns to native ground!
Once under his own roof, he and your friends,   170
believe you me, won't part till blood has flowed."
                                        With that
he poured out honeyed wine to the gods and drank deeply,
then restored the cup to the young prince's hands.
Amphinomus made his way back through the hall,
his heart sick with anguish, shaking his head,   175
fraught with grave forebodings . . .
but not even so could he escape his fate.
Even then Athena had bound him fast to death
at the hands of Prince Telemachus and his spear.
Now back he went to the seat that he'd left empty.   180

    But now the goddess Athena with her glinting eyes
inspired Penelope, Icarius' daughter, wary, poised,
to display herself to her suitors, fan their hearts,
inflame them more, and make her even more esteemed
by her husband and her son than she had been before.   185
Forcing a laugh, she called her maid: "Eurynome,
my spirit longs—though it never did till now—
to appear before my suitors, loathe them as I do.
I'd say a word to my son too, for his own good,
not to mix so much with that pernicious crowd,   190
so glib with their friendly talk
but plotting wicked plots they'll hatch tomorrow."

"Well said, my child," the old woman answered,
"all to the point. Go to the boy and warn him now,
hold nothing back. But first you should bathe yourself,   195
give a gloss to your face. Don't go down like that—
your eyes dimmed, your cheeks streaked with tears.
It makes things worse, this grieving on and on.
Your son's now come of age—your fondest prayer
to the deathless gods, to see him wear a beard."   200

    "Eurynome," discreet Penelope objected,
"don't try to coax me, care for me as you do,
to bathe myself, refresh my face with oils.
Whatever glow I had died long ago . . .
the gods of Olympus snuffed it out that day   205
my husband sailed away in the hollow ships.
But please, have Autonoë and Hippodamia come
and support me in the hall. I'll never brave
those men alone. I'd be too embarrassed."

    Now as the old nurse bustled through the house   210
to give the women orders, call them to the queen,
the bright-eyed goddess thought of one more thing.
She drifted a sound slumber over Icarius' daughter,
back she sank and slept, her limbs fell limp and still,
reclining there on her couch, all the while Athena,   215
luminous goddess, lavished immortal gifts on her
to make her suitors lose themselves in wonder . . .
The divine unguent first. She cleansed her cheeks,
her brow and fine eyes with ambrosia smooth as the oils
the goddess Love[5] applies, donning her crown of flowers   220
whenever she joins the Graces' captivating dances.
She made her taller, fuller in form to all men's eyes,
her skin whiter than ivory freshly carved, and now,
Athena's mission accomplished, off the bright one went
as bare-armed maids came in from their own quarters,   225
chattering all the way, and sleep released the queen.
She woke, touched her cheek with a hand, and mused,
"Ah, what a marvelous gentle sleep, enfolding me
in the midst of all my anguish! Now if only
blessed Artemis sent me a death as gentle, now,   230
this instant—no more wasting away my life,
my heart broken in longing for my husband . . .
He had every strength,
rising over his countrymen, head and shoulders."

    Then, leaving her well-lit chamber, she descended,   235
not alone: two of her women followed close behind.
That radiant woman, once she reached her suitors,
drawing her glistening veil across her cheeks,
paused now where a column propped the sturdy roof,

5. Aphrodite.

with one of her loyal handmaids stationed either side. 240
The suitors' knees went slack, their hearts dissolved in lust—
all of them lifted prayers to lie beside her, share her bed.
But turning toward her son, she warned, "Telemachus,
your sense of balance is not what it used to be.
When you were a boy you had much better judgment. 245
Now that you've grown and reached your young prime
and any stranger, seeing how tall and handsome you are,
would think you the son of some great man of wealth—
now your sense of fairness seems to fail you.
Consider the dreadful thing just done in our halls— 250
how you let the stranger be so abused! Why,
suppose our guest, sitting here at peace,
here in our own house,
were hauled and badly hurt by such cruel treatment?
You'd be shamed, disgraced in all men's eyes!" 255

    "Mother . . ." Telemachus paused, then answered.
"I cannot fault your anger at all this.
My heart takes note of everything, feels it, too,
both the good and the bad—the boy you knew is gone.
But how can I plan my world in a sane, thoughtful way? 260
These men drive me mad, hedging me round, right and left,
plotting their lethal plots, and no one takes my side.
Still, this battle between the stranger and Irus
hardly went as the suitors might have hoped:
the stranger beat him down! 265
If only—Father Zeus, Athena and lord Apollo—
these gallants, now, this moment, here in our house,
were battered senseless, heads lolling, knees unstrung,
some sprawled in the courtyard, some sprawled outside!
Slumped like Irus down at the front gates now, 270
whipped, and his head rolling like some drunk.
He can't stand up on his feet and stagger home,
whatever home he's got—the man's demolished."

    So Penelope and her son exchanged their hopes
as Eurymachus stepped in to praise the queen. 275
"Ah, daughter of Icarius, wise Penelope,
if all the princes in Ionian Argos saw you now!
What a troop of suitors would banquet in your halls
tomorrow at sunrise! You surpass all women
in build and beauty, refined and steady mind." 280

    "Oh no, Eurymachus," wise Penelope demurred,
"whatever form and feature I had, what praise I'd won,
the deathless gods destroyed that day the Achaeans
sailed away to Troy, my husband in their ships,
Odysseus—if *he* could return to tend my life 285
the renown I had would only grow in glory.
Now my life is torment . . .
look at the griefs some god has loosed against me!

I'll never forget the day he left this land of ours;
he caught my right hand by the wrist and said, gently, 290
'Dear woman, I doubt that every Achaean under arms
will make it home from Troy, all safe and sound.
The Trojans, they say, are fine soldiers too,
hurling javelins, shooting flights of arrows,
charioteers who can turn the tide—like that!— 295
when the great leveler, War, brings on some deadlock.
So I cannot tell if the gods will sail me home again
or I'll go down out there, on the fields of Troy,
but all things here must rest in your control.
Watch over my father and mother in the palace, 300
just as now, or perhaps a little more,
when I am far from home.
But once you see the beard on the boy's cheek,
you wed the man you like, and leave your house behind.'
So my husband advised me then. Now it all comes true . . . 305
a night will come when a hateful marriage falls my lot—
this cursed life of mine! Zeus has torn away my joy.
But there's something else that mortifies me now.
Your way is a far cry from the time-honored way
of suitors locked in rivalry, striving to win 310
some noble woman, a wealthy man's daughter.
They bring in their own calves and lambs
to feast the friends of the bride-to-be, yes,
and shower her with gleaming gifts as well.
They don't devour the woman's goods scot-free." 315

Staunch Odysseus glowed with joy to hear all this—
his wife's trickery luring gifts from her suitors now,
enchanting their hearts with suave seductive words
but all the while with something else in mind.
Eupithes' son Antinous took her point at once. 320
"Daughter of Icarius, sensible Penelope,
whatever gifts your suitors would like to bring,
accept them. How ungracious to turn those gifts away!
We won't go back to our own estates, or anywhere else,
till you have wed the man you find the best." 325

So he proposed, and all the rest agreed.
Each suitor sent a page to go and get a gift.
Antinous' man brought in a grand, resplendent robe,
stiff with embroidery, clasped with twelve gold brooches,
long pins that clipped into sheathing loops with ease. 330
Eurymachus' man brought in a necklace richly wrought,
gilded, strung with amber and glowing like the sun.
Eurydamas' two men came with a pair of earrings,
mulberry clusters dangling in triple drops
with a glint to catch the heart. 335
From the halls of lord Pisander, Polyctor's son,
a servant brought a choker, a fine, gleaming treasure.

And so each suitor in turn laid on a handsome gift.
Then the noble queen withdrew to her upper room,
her file of waiting ladies close behind her,   340
bearing the gorgeous presents in their arms.

   Now the suitors turned to dance and song,
to the lovely beat and sway,
waiting for dusk to come upon them there . . .
and the dark night came upon them, lost in pleasure.   345
They rushed to set up three braziers along the walls
to give them light, piled them high with kindling,
sere, well-seasoned, just split with an ax,
and mixed in chips to keep the torches flaring.
The maids of Odysseus, steady man, took turns   350
to keep the fires up, but the king himself,
dear to the gods and cunning to the core,
gave them orders brusquely: "Maids of Odysseus,
your master gone so long—quick now, off you go
to the room where your queen and mistress waits.   355
Sit with her there and try to lift her spirits,
combing wool in your hands or spinning yarn.
But I will trim the torches for all her suitors,
even if they would like to revel on till Morning
mounts her throne. They'll never wear me down.   360
I have a name for lasting out the worst."
                                        At that
the women burst into laughter, glancing back and forth.
Flushed with beauty, Melantho[6] mocked him shamelessly—
Dolius was her father but Penelope brought her up;
she treated her like her own child and gave her toys   365
to cheer her heart. But despite that, her heart
felt nothing for all her mistress' anguish now.
She was Eurymachus' lover, always slept with him.
She was the one who mocked her king and taunted,
"Cock of the walk, did someone beat your brains out?   370
Why not go bed down at the blacksmith's cozy forge?
Or a public place where tramps collect? Why here—
blithering on, nonstop,
bold as brass in the face of all these lords?
No fear in your heart? Wine's got to your wits?—   375
or do you always play the fool and babble nonsense?
Lost your head, have you, because you drubbed that hobo Irus?
You wait—a better man than Irus will take you on,
he'll box both sides of your skull with heavy fists
and cart you out the palace gushing blood!"
                                        "You wait,   380
you bitch"—the hardened veteran flashed a killing look.
"I'll go straight to the prince with your foul talk.
The prince will chop you to pieces here and now!"

6. The sister of Melanthius, the goatherd who abuses Odysseus in book 17.

His fury sent the women fluttering off, scattering
down the hall with panic shaking every limb—   385
they knew he spoke the truth.
But he took up his post by the flaring braziers,
tending the fires closely, looking after them all,
though the heart inside him stirred with other things,
ranging ahead, now, to all that must be done . . .   390

But Athena had no mind to let the brazen suitors
hold back now from their heart-rending insults—
she meant to make the anguish cut still deeper
into the core of Laertes' son Odysseus.
Polybus' son Eurymachus launched in first,   395
baiting the king to give his friends a laugh:
"Listen to me, you lords who court our noble queen!
I simply have to say what's on my mind. Look,
surely the gods have fetched this beggar here
to Odysseus' house. At least our torchlight *seems*   400
to come from the sheen of the man's own head—
there's not a hair on his bald pate, not a wisp!"

Then he wheeled on Odysseus, raider of cities:
"Stranger, how would you like to work for me
if I took you on—I'd give you decent wages—   405
picking the stones to lay a tight dry wall
or planting tall trees on the edge of my estate?
I'd give you rations to last you year-round,
clothes for your body, sandals for your feet.
Oh no, you've learned your lazy ways too well,   410
you've got no itch to stick to good hard work,
you'd rather go scrounging round the countryside,
begging for crusts to stuff your greedy gut!"

"Ah, Eurymachus," Odysseus, master of many exploits,
answered firmly, "if only the two of us *could* go   415
man-to-man in the labors of the field . . .
In the late spring, when the long days come round,
out in the meadow, I swinging a well-curved scythe
and you swinging yours—we'd test our strength for work,
fasting right till dusk with lots of hay to mow.   420
Or give us a team of oxen to drive, purebreds,
hulking, ruddy beasts, both lusty with fodder,
paired for age and pulling-power that never flags—
with four acres to work, the loam churning under the plow—
you'd see what a straight unbroken furrow I could cut you then.   425
Or if Zeus would bring some battle on—out of the blue,
this very day—and give me a shield and two spears
and a bronze helmet to fit this soldier's temples,
then you'd see me fight where front ranks clash—
no more mocking this belly of mine, not then.   430
Enough. You're sick with pride, you brutal fool.
No doubt you count yourself a great, powerful man

because you sport with a puny crowd, ill-bred to boot.
If only Odysseus came back home and stood right here,
in a flash you'd find those doors—broad as they are— 435
too cramped for your race to safety through the porch!"

That made Eurymachus' fury seethe and burst—
he gave the beggar a dark look and let fly, "You,
you odious—I'll make you pay for your ugly rant!
Bold as brass in the face of all these lords? 440
No fear in your heart? Wine's got to your wits?—
or do you always play the fool and babble nonsense?
Lost your head, have you, because you drubbed that hobo Irus?"

As he shouted out he seized a stool, but Odysseus,
fearing the blow, crouched at Amphinomus' knees 445
as Eurymachus hurled and hit the wine-steward,
clipping his right hand—
his cup dropped, clattered along the floor
and flat on his back he went, groaning in the dust.
The suitors broke into uproar through the shadowed halls, 450
glancing at one another, trading angry outcries:
"Would to god this drifter had dropped dead—"

"Anywhere else before he landed here!"

"Then he'd never have loosed such pandemonium."

"Now we're squabbling over *beggars!*"
                                        "No more joy 455
in the sumptuous feast . . ."
                        "Now riot rules the day!"

But now Prince Telemachus dressed them down:
"Fools, you're out of your minds! No hiding it,
food and wine have gone to your heads. Some god
has got your blood up. Come, now you've eaten well 460
go home to bed—when the spirit moves, that is.
I, for one, I'll drive no guest away."

So he declared. And they all bit their lips,
amazed the prince could speak with so much daring.
At last Amphinomus rose to take the floor, 465
the noted son of Nisus, King Aretias' grandson.
"Fair enough, my friends; when a man speaks well
we have no grounds for wrangling, no cause for abuse.
Hands off the stranger! And any other servant
in King Odysseus' palace. Come, steward, 470
pour first drops for the god in every cup;
let's make libations, then go home to bed.
The stranger? Leave him here in Odysseus' halls
and have his host, Telemachus, tend him well—
it's the prince's royal house the man has reached." 475

So he said. His proposal pleased them all.
And gallant Mulius, a herald of Dulichion,
a friend-in-arms of lord Amphinomus too,
mixed the men a bowl and, hovering closely,
poured full rounds for all. They tipped cups   480
to the blissful gods and then, libations made,
they drank the heady wine to their hearts' content
and went their ways to bed, each suitor to his house.

BOOK XIX

[Penelope and Her Guest]

That left the great Odysseus waiting in his hall
as Athena helped him plot the slaughter of the suitors.
He turned at once to Telemachus, brisk with orders:
"Now we must stow the weapons out of reach, my boy,
all the arms and armor—and when the suitors miss them   5
and ask you questions, put them off with a winning story:
'I stowed them away, clear of the smoke. A far cry
from the arms Odysseus left when he went to Troy,
fire-damaged equipment, black with reeking fumes.
And a god reminded me of something darker too.   10
When you're in your cups a quarrel might break out,
you'd wound each other, shame your feasting here
and cast a pall on your courting.
Iron has powers to draw a man to ruin.'"

Telemachus did his father's will at once,   15
calling out to his old nurse Eurycleia: "Quick,
dear one, close the women up in their own quarters,
till I can stow my father's weapons in the storeroom.
Splendid gear, lying about, neglected, black with soot
since father sailed away. I was only a boy then.   20
Now I must safeguard them from the smoke."

"High time, child," the loving nurse replied.
"If only you'd bother to tend your whole house
and safeguard all your treasures. Tell me,
who's to fetch and carry the torch for you?   25
You won't let out the maids who'd light your way."

"Our friend here will," Telemachus answered coolly.
"I won't put up with a man who shirks his work,
not if he takes his ration from my stores,
even if he's miles away from home."   30

That silenced the old nurse.
She barred the doors that led from the long hall—
and up they sprang, Odysseus and his princely son,
and began to carry off the helmets, studded shields
and pointed spears, and Pallas Athena strode before them,   35

lifting a golden lamp that cast a dazzling radiance round about.
"Father," Telemachus suddenly burst out to Odysseus,
"oh what a marvel fills my eyes! Look, look there—
all the sides of the hall, the handsome crossbeams,
pinewood rafters, the tall columns towering— 40
all glow in my eyes like flaming fire!
Surely a god is here—
one of those who rule the vaulting skies!"

    "Quiet," his father, the old soldier, warned him.
"Get a grip on yourself. No more questions now. 45
It's just the way of the gods who rule Olympus.
Off you go to bed. I'll stay here behind
to test the women, test your mother too.
She in her grief will ask me everything I know."

    Under the flaring torchlight, through the hall 50
Telemachus made his way to his own bedroom now,
where he always went when welcome sleep came on him.
There he lay tonight as well, till Dawn's first light.
That left the great king still waiting in his hall
as Athena helped him plot the slaughter of the suitors . . . 55

    Now down from her chamber came reserved Penelope,
looking for all the world like Artemis or golden Aphrodite.
Close to the fire her women drew her favorite chair
with its whorls of silver and ivory, inlaid rings.
The craftsman who made it years ago, Icmalius, 60
added a footrest under the seat itself,
mortised into the frame,
and over it all was draped a heavy fleece.
Here Penelope took her place, discreet, observant.
The women, arms bared, pressing in from their quarters, 65
cleared away the tables, the heaped remains of the feast
and the cups from which the raucous lords had drunk.
Raking embers from the braziers onto the ground,
they piled them high again with seasoned wood,
providing light and warmth.
          And yet again 70
Melantho lashed out at Odysseus: "You still here?—
you pest, slinking around the house all night,
leering up at the women?
Get out, you tramp—be glad of the food you got—
or we'll sling a torch at you, rout you out at once!" 75

    A killing glance, and the old trooper countered,
"What's possessed you, woman? Why lay into me? Such abuse!
Just because I'm filthy, because I wear such rags,
roving round the country, living hand-to-mouth.
But it's fate that drives me on: 80
that's the lot of beggars, homeless drifters.
I too once lived in a lofty house that men admired;

rolling in wealth, I'd often give to a vagabond like myself,
whoever he was, whatever need had brought him to my door.
And crowds of servants I had, and lots of all it takes   85
to live the life of ease, to make men call you rich.
But Zeus ruined it all—god's will, no doubt.
So beware, woman, or one day you may lose it all,
all your glitter that puts your work-mates in the shade.
Or your mistress may just fly in a rage and dress you down   90
or Odysseus may return—there's still room for hope!
Or if he's dead as you think and never coming home,
well there's his son, Telemachus . . .
like father, like son—thanks to god Apollo.
No women's wildness here in the house escapes   95
the prince's eye. He's come of age at last."

    So he warned, and alert Penelope heard him,
wheeled on the maid and tongue-lashed her smartly:
"Make no mistake, you brazen, shameless bitch,
none of your ugly work escapes me either—   100
you will pay for it with your life, you will!
How well you knew—you heard from my own lips—
that I meant to probe this stranger in our house
and ask about my husband . . . my heart breaks for him."

    She turned to her housekeeper Eurynome and said,   105
"Now bring us a chair and spread it soft with fleece,
so our guest can sit and tell me his whole story
and hear me out as well.
I'd like to ask him questions, point by point."

    Eurynome bustled off to fetch a polished chair   110
and set it down and spread it soft with fleece.
Here Odysseus sat, the man of many trials,
as cautious Penelope began the conversation:
"Stranger, let me start our questioning myself. . . .
Who are you? where are you from? your city? your parents?"   115

    "My good woman," Odysseus, master of craft, replied,
"no man on the face of the earth could find fault with *you*.
Your fame, believe me, has reached the vaulting skies.
Fame like a flawless king's who dreads the gods,
who governs a kingdom vast, proud and strong—   120
who upholds justice, true, and the black earth
bears wheat and barley, trees bow down with fruit
and the sheep drop lambs and never fail and the sea
teems with fish—thanks to his decent, upright rule,
and under his sovereign sway the people flourish.   125
So then, here in your house, ask me anything else
but don't, please, search out my birth, my land,
or you'll fill my heart to overflowing even more
as I bring back the past . . .
I am a man who's had his share of sorrows.   130

It's wrong for me, in someone else's house,
to sit here moaning and groaning, sobbing so—
it makes things worse, this grieving on and on.
One of your maids, or you yourself, might scold me,
think it's just the wine that had doused my wits
and made me drown in tears." 135

"No, no, stranger," wise Penelope demurred,
"whatever form and feature I had, what praise I'd won,
the deathless gods destroyed that day the Achaeans
sailed away to Troy, my husband in their ships, 140
Odysseus—if he could return to tend my life
the renown I had would only grow in glory.
Now my life is torment . . .
look at the griefs some god has loosed against me!
All the nobles who rule the islands round about, 145
Dulichion, Same, and wooded Zacynthus too,
and all who lord it in sunny Ithaca itself—
they court me against my will, they lay waste my house.
So I pay no heed to strangers, suppliants at my door,
not even heralds out on their public errands here— 150
I yearn for Odysseus, always, my heart pines away.
They rush the marriage on, and I spin out my wiles.
A god from the blue it was inspired me first
to set up a great loom in our royal halls
and I began to weave, and the weaving finespun, 155
the yarns endless, and I would lead them on: 'Young men,
my suitors, now that King Odysseus is no more,
go slowly, keen as you are to marry me, until
I can finish off this web . . .
so my weaving won't all fray and come to nothing. 160
This is a shroud for old lord Laertes, for that day
when the deadly fate that lays us out at last will take him down.
I dread the shame my countrywomen would heap upon me,
yes, if a man of such wealth should lie in state
without a shroud for cover.'
                              My very words, 165
and despite their pride and passion they believed me.
So by day I'd weave at my great and growing web—
by night, by the light of torches set beside me,
I would unravel all I'd done. Three whole years
I deceived them blind, seduced them with this scheme. 170
Then, when the wheeling seasons brought the fourth year on
and the months waned and the long days came round once more,
then, thanks to my maids—the shameless, reckless creatures—
the suitors caught me in the act, denounced me harshly.
So I finished it off. Against my will. They forced me. 175
And now I cannot escape a marriage, nor can I contrive
a deft way out. My parents urge me to tie the knot
and my son is galled as they squander his estate—
he sees it all. He's a grown man by now, equipped
to tend to his own royal house and tend it well: 180

Zeus grants my son that honor . . .
But for all that—now tell me who you are.
Where do you come from? You've hardly sprung
from a rock or oak like some old man of legend."

The master improviser answered, slowly,   185
"My lady . . . wife of Laertes' son, Odysseus,
will your questions about my family never end?
All right then. Here's my story. Even though
it plunges me into deeper grief than I feel now.
But that's the way of the world, when one has been   190
so far from home, so long away as I, roving over
many cities of men, enduring many hardships.
                                                    Still,
my story will tell you all you need to know.

    There is a land called Crete[7] . . .
ringed by the wine-dark sea with rolling whitecaps—   195
handsome country, fertile, thronged with people
well past counting—boasting ninety cities,
language mixing with language side-by-side.
First come the Achaeans, then the native Cretans,
hardy, gallant in action, then Cydonian clansmen,   200
Dorians living in three tribes, and proud Pelasgians last.
Central to all their cities is magnificent Cnossos,
the site where Minos ruled and each ninth year
conferred with almighty Zeus himself. Minos,
father of my father, Deucalion, that bold heart.   205
Besides myself Deucalion sired Prince Idomeneus,
who set sail for Troy in his beaked ships of war,
escorting Atreus' sons. My own name is Aethon.
I am the younger-born;
my older brother's a better man than I am.   210
Now, it was there in Cnossos that I saw him . . .
Odysseus—and we traded gifts of friendship.
A heavy gale had landed him on our coast,
driven him way off course, rounding Malea's cape
when he was bound for Troy. He anchored in Amnisus,   215
hard by the goddess'[8] cave of childbirth and labor,
that rough harbor—barely riding out the storm.
He came into town at once, asking for Idomeneus,
claiming to be my brother's close, respected friend.
Too late. Ten or eleven days had already passed   220
since he set sail for Troy in his beaked ships.
So I took Odysseus back to my own house,
gave him a hero's welcome, treated him in style—
stores in our palace made for princely entertainment.

---

7. It is impossible to extract historical fact from the following confused account of Crete. Cydonians may
be the inhabitants of the western end of the island; Dorians were the people who, according to Greek belief
(debated by modern scholars), invaded Greece and destroyed the Mycenaean civilization of the second
millennium B.C.E.; Pelasgians were what Greeks often called the pre-Hellenic inhabitants of the area.
Cnossos is the site of a Bronze Age palace.   8. The goddess Eileithyia. The cave where she was worshipped from very early times has been excavated at Amnisus, which is on the coast near Cnossos.

As for his comrades, all who'd shipped with him,   225
I dipped into public stock to give them barley,
ruddy wine and fine cattle for slaughter,
beef to their hearts' content. A dozen days
they stayed with me there, those brave Achaeans,
penned up by a North Wind so stiff that a man,   230
even on dry land, could never keep his feet—
some angry spirit raised that blast, I'd say.
Then on the thirteenth day the wind died down
and they set sail for Troy."

                    Falsehoods all,
but he gave his falsehoods all the ring of truth.   235
As she listened on, her tears flowed and soaked her cheeks
as the heavy snow melts down from the high mountain ridges,
snow the West Wind piles there and the warm East Wind thaws
and the snow, melting, swells the rivers to overflow their banks—
so she dissolved in tears, streaming down her lovely cheeks,   240
weeping for him, her husband, sitting there beside her.
Odysseus' heart went out to his grief-stricken wife
but under his lids his eyes remained stock-still—
they might have been horn or iron—
his guile fought back his tears. And she,   245
once she'd had her fill of grief and weeping,
turned again to her guest with this reply:
"Now, stranger, I think I'll test you, just to see
if there in your house, with all his friends-in-arms,
you actually entertained my husband as you say.   250
Come, tell me what sort of clothing he wore,
what cut of man was he?
What of the men who followed in his train?"

                                  "Ah good woman,"
Odysseus, the great master of subtlety, returned,
"how hard it is to speak, after so much time   255
apart . . . why, some twenty years have passed
since he left my house and put my land behind him.
Even so, imagine the man as I portray him—
I can see him now.

                King Odysseus . . .
he was wearing a heavy woolen cape, sea-purple   260
in double folds, with a golden brooch to clasp it,
twin sheaths for the pins, on the face a work of art:
a hound clenching a dappled fawn in its front paws,
slashing it as it writhed. All marveled to see it,
solid gold as it was, the hound slashing, throttling   265
the fawn in its death-throes, hoofs flailing to break free.
I noticed his glossy tunic too, clinging to his skin
like the thin glistening skin of a dried onion,
silky, soft, the glint of the sun itself.
Women galore would gaze on it with relish.   270
And this too. Bear it in mind, won't you?
I've no idea if Odysseus wore these things at home
or a comrade gave him them as he boarded ship,

or a host perhaps—the man was loved by many.
There were few Achaeans to equal him . . . and I?   275
I gave him a bronze sword myself, a lined cloak,
elegant, deep red, and a fringed shirt as well,
and I saw him off in his long benched ship of war
in lordly style.
        Something else. He kept a herald
beside him, a man a little older than himself.   280
I'll try to describe him to you, best I can.
Round-shouldered he was, swarthy, curly-haired.
His name? Eurybates. And Odysseus prized him
most of all his men. Their minds worked as one."

His words renewed her deep desire to weep,   285
recognizing the strong clear signs Odysseus offered.
But as soon as she'd had her fill of tears and grief,
Penelope turned again to her guest and said,
"Now, stranger, much as I pitied you before,
now in my house you'll be my special friend,   290
my honored guest. I am the one, myself,
who gave him the very clothes that you describe.
I brought them up from the storeroom, folded them neatly,
fastened the golden brooch to adorn my husband,
Odysseus—never again will I embrace him,   295
striding home to his own native land.
A black day it was
when he took ship to see that cursed city . . .
Destroy,[9] I call it—I hate to say its name!"

    "Ah my queen," the man of craft assured her,   300
"noble wife of Laertes' son, Odysseus,
ravage no more your lovely face with tears
or consume your heart with grieving for your husband.
Not that I'd blame you, ever. Any woman will mourn
the bridegroom she has lost, lain with in love   305
and borne his children too. Even though he
was no Odysseus—a man like a god, they say.
But dry your tears and take my words to heart.
I will tell you the whole truth and hide nothing:
I have heard that Odysseus now, at last, is on his way,   310
he's just in reach, in rich Thesprotian country—
the man is still alive
and he's bringing home a royal hoard of treasure,
gifts he won from the people of those parts.
His crew? He's lost his crew and hollow ship   315
on the wine-dark waters off Thrinacia Island.
Zeus and Helios raged, dead set against Odysseus
for his men-at-arms had killed the cattle of the Sun,
so down to the last hand they drowned in crashing seas.
But not Odysseus, clinging tight to his ship's keel—   320

9. Literally, "Evil-Ilium."

the breakers flung him out onto dry land, on Scheria,
the land of Phaeacians, close kin to the gods themselves,
and with all their hearts they prized him like a god,
showered the man with gifts, and they'd have gladly
sailed him home unscathed. In fact Odysseus   325
would have been here beside you long ago
but he thought it the better, shrewder course
to recoup his fortunes roving through the world.
At sly profit-turning there's not a man alive
to touch Odysseus. He's got no rival there.   330
So I learned from Phidon, king of Thesprotia,
who swore to me as he poured libations in his house,
'The ship's hauled down and the shipmates set to sail,
to take Odysseus home to native land.'
                    But I . . .
he shipped me off before. A Thesprotian cutter   335
chanced to be heading for Dulichion rich in wheat.
But he showed me all the treasure Odysseus had amassed,
enough to last a man and ten generations of his heirs—
so great the wealth stored up for *him* in the king's vaults!
But Odysseus, he made clear, was off at Dodona then   340
to hear the will of Zeus that rustles forth
from the god's tall leafy oak: how should he return,
after all the years away, to his own beloved Ithaca,
openly or in secret?
                    And so the man is safe,
as you can see, and he's coming home, soon,   345
he's close, close at hand—
he won't be severed long from kin and country,
no, not now. I give you my solemn, binding oath.
I swear by Zeus, the first, the greatest god—
by Odysseus' hearth, where I have come for help: 350
all will come to pass, I swear, exactly as I say.
True, this very month—just as the old moon dies
and the new moon rises into life—Odysseus will return!"

     "If only, my friend," reserved Penelope exclaimed,
"everything you say would come to pass!   355
You'd soon know my affection, know my gifts.
Any man you meet would call you blest.
But my heart can sense the way it all will go.
Odysseus, I tell you, is never coming back,
nor will you ever gain your passage home,   360
for we have no masters in our house like him
at welcoming in or sending off an honored guest.
Odysseus. There was a man, or was he all a dream?
But come, women, wash the stranger and make his bed,
with bedding, blankets and lustrous spreads to keep him warm   365
till Dawn comes up and takes her golden throne.
Then, tomorrow at daybreak, bathe him well
and rub him down with oil, so he can sit beside
Telemachus in the hall, enjoy his breakfast there.

And anyone who offends our guest beyond endurance— 370
he defeats himself; he's doomed to failure here,
no matter how raucously he raves and blusters on.
For how can you know, my friend, if I surpass
all women in thoughtfulness and shrewd good sense,
if I'd allow you to take your meals at hall 375
so weatherbeaten, clad in rags and tatters?
Our lives are much too brief . . .
If a man is cruel by nature, cruel in action,
the mortal world will call down curses on his head
while he is alive, and all will mock his memory after death. 380
But then if a man is kind by nature, kind in action,
his guests will carry his fame across the earth
and people all will praise him from the heart."

   "Wait, my queen," the crafty man objected,
"noble wife of Laertes' son, Odysseus— 385
blankets and glossy spreads? They're not my style.
Not from the day I launched out in my long-oared ship
and the snowy peaks of Crete went fading far astern.
I'll lie as I've done through sleepless nights before.
Many a night I've spent on rugged beds afield, 390
waiting for Dawn to mount her lovely throne.
Nor do I pine for any footbaths either.
Of all the women who serve your household here,
not one will touch my feet. Unless, perhaps,
there is some old retainer, the soul of trust, 395
someone who's borne as much as I have borne . . .
I wouldn't mind if she would touch my feet."
                                   "Dear friend,"
the discreet Penelope replied, "never has any man
so thoughtful—of all the guests in my palace
come from foreign parts—been as welcome as you . . . 400
so sensible, so apt, is every word you say.
I have just such an old woman, seasoned, wise,
who carefully tended my unlucky husband, reared him,
took him into her arms the day his mother bore him—
frail as the woman is, she'll wash your feet. 405
Up with you now, my good old Eurycleia,
come and wash your master's . . . equal in years.
Odysseus must have feet and hands like his by now—
hardship can age a person overnight."
                        At that name
the old retainer buried her face in both hands, 410
burst into warm tears and wailed out in grief,
"Oh my child, how helpless I am to help you now!
How Zeus despised you, more than all other men,
god-fearing man that you were . . .
Never did any mortal burn the Old Thunderer 415
such rich thighbones—offerings charred and choice—
never as many as you did, praying always to reach
a ripe old age and raise a son to glory. Now,

you alone he's robbed of your home-coming day!
Just so, the women must have mocked my king,   420
far away, when he'd stopped at some fine house—
just as all these bitches, stranger, mock you here.
And because you shrink from their taunts, their wicked barbs,
you will not let them wash you. The work is mine—
Icarius' daughter, wise Penelope, bids me now   425
and I am all too glad. I will wash your feet,
both for my own dear queen and for yourself—
your sorrows wring my heart . . . and why?
Listen to me closely, mark my words.
Many a wayworn guest has landed here   430
but never, I swear, has one so struck my eyes—
your build, your voice, your feet—you're like Odysseus . . .
to the life!"

        "Old woman," wily Odysseus countered,
"that's what they all say who've seen us both.
We bear a striking resemblance to each other,   435
as you have had the wit to say yourself."

    The old woman took up a burnished basin
she used for washing feet and poured in bowls
of fresh cold water before she stirred in hot.
Odysseus, sitting full in the firelight, suddenly   440
swerved round to the dark, gripped by a quick misgiving—
soon as she touched him she might spot the scar!
The truth would all come out.
               Bending closer
she started to bathe her master . . . then,
in a flash, she knew the scar—
               that old wound   445
made years ago by a boar's white tusk when Odysseus
went to Parnassus,[1] out to see Autolycus and his sons.
The man was his mother's noble father, one who excelled
the world at thievery, that and subtle, shifty oaths.
Hermes[2] gave him the gift, overjoyed by the thighs   450
of lambs and kids he burned in the god's honor—
Hermes the ready partner in his crimes. Now,
Autolycus once visited Ithaca's fertile land,
to find his daughter's son had just been born.
Eurycleia set him down on the old man's knees   455
as he finished dinner, urging him, "Autolycus,
you must find a name for your daughter's darling son.
The baby comes as the answer to her prayers."
                  "You,
my daughter, and you, my son-in-law," Autolycus replied,
"give the boy the name I tell you now. Just as I   460

---

1. The mountain range above Apollo's oracular shrine at Delphi, on the Greek mainland.   2. Not only
the messenger of the gods and the god who guided the dead down to the lower world but also the god of
the marketplace and so of trickery and swindling.

have come from afar, creating pain[3] for many—
men and women across the good green earth—
so let his name be *Odysseus* . . .
the Son of Pain, a name he'll earn in full.
And when he has come of age and pays his visit   465
to Parnassus—the great estate of his mother's line
where all my treasures lie—I will give him enough
to cheer his heart, then speed him home to you."

And so,

in time, Odysseus went to collect the splendid gifts.
Autolycus and the sons of Autolycus warmed him in   470
with eager handclasps, hearty words of welcome.
His mother's mother, Amphithea, hugged the boy
and kissed his face and kissed his shining eyes.
Autolycus told his well-bred sons to prepare
a princely feast. They followed orders gladly,   475
herded an ox inside at once, five years old,
skinned it and split the carcass into quarters,
deftly cut it in pieces, skewered these on spits,
roasted all to a turn and served the portions out.
So all day long till the sun went down they feasted,   480
consuming equal shares to their hearts' content.
Then when the sun had set and night came on
they turned to bed and took the gift of sleep.

As soon

as young Dawn with her rose-red fingers shone once more
they all moved out for the hunt, hounds in the lead,   485
Autolycus' sons and Prince Odysseus in their ranks.
Climbing Parnassus' ridges, thick with timber,
they quickly reached the mountain's windy folds
and just as the sun began to strike the plowlands,
rising out of the deep calm flow of the Ocean River,   490
the beaters came to a wooded glen, the hounds broke,
hot on a trail, and right behind the pack they came,
Autolycus' sons—Odysseus out in front now,
pressing the dogs, brandishing high his spear
with its long shadow waving. Then and there   495
a great boar lay in wait, in a thicket lair so dense
that the sodden gusty winds could never pierce it,
nor could the sun's sharp rays invade its depths
nor a downpour drench it through and through,
so dense, so dark, and piled with fallen leaves.   500
Here, as the hunters closed in for the kill,
crowding the hounds, the tramp of men and dogs
came drumming round the boar—he crashed from his lair,
his razor back bristling, his eyes flashing fire
and charging up to the hunt he stopped, at bay—   505
and Odysseus rushed him first,
shaking his long spear in a sturdy hand,

---

3. In Greek, *odyssamenos* (one who is angry and gives cause for anger), close in sound to the name Odysseus. In book 1 (line 75), Athena uses a different form of the same word when she asks Zeus why he is so hostile to Odysseus. Giving and receiving anger, and therefore pain, is thus one of Odysseus's essential qualities.

wild to strike but the boar struck faster,
lunging in on the slant, a tusk thrusting up
over the boy's knee, gouging a deep strip of flesh   510
but it never hit the bone—
                              Odysseus thrust and struck,
stabbing the beast's right shoulder—
                              a glint of bronze—
the point ripped clean through and down in the dust he dropped,
grunting out his breath as his life winged away.
The sons of Autolycus, working over Odysseus,   515
skillfully binding up his open wound—
the gallant, godlike prince—
chanted an old spell that stanched the blood
and quickly bore him home to their father's palace.
There, in no time, Autolycus and the sons of Autolycus   520
healed him well and, showering him with splendid gifts,
sped Odysseus back to his native land, to Ithaca,
a young man filled with joy. His happy parents,
his father and noble mother, welcomed him home
and asked him of all his exploits, blow-by-blow: 525
how did he get that wound? He told his tale with style,
how the white tusk of a wild boar had gashed his leg,
hunting on Parnassus with Autolycus and his sons[4] . . .
                              That scar—
as the old nurse cradled his leg and her hands passed down
she felt it, knew it, suddenly let his foot fall—   530
down it dropped in the basin—the bronze clanged,
tipping over, spilling water across the floor.
Joy and torment gripped her heart at once,
tears rushed to her eyes—voice choked in her throat
she reached for Odysseus' chin and whispered quickly,   535
"Yes, yes! you are *Odysseus*—oh dear boy—
I couldn't know you before . . .
not till I touched the body of my king!"

  She glanced at Penelope, keen to signal her
that here was her own dear husband, here and now,   540
but she could not catch the glance, she took no heed,
Athena turned her attention elsewhere. But Odysseus—
his right hand shot out, clutching the nurse's throat,
with his left he hugged her to himself and muttered,
"Nurse, you want to kill me? You suckled me yourself   545
at your own breast—and now I'm home, at last,
after bearing twenty years of brutal hardship,
home, on native ground. But now you know,
now that a god has flashed it in your mind,
quiet! not a word to anyone in the house.   550
Or else, I warn you—and I mean business too—
if a god beats down these brazen suitors at my hands,

---

4. Leaving human society for nature, hunting and killing a fierce animal, and receiving a wound conform to the pattern of male initiation rituals that helped boys make the transition to adulthood. Odysseus's scar seems to commemorate his surmounting of such an initiatory ordeal.

I will not spare you—my old nurse that you are—
when I kill the other women in my house."

"Child," shrewd old Eurycleia protested,   555
"what nonsense you let slip through your teeth!
You know *me*—I'm stubborn, never give an inch—
I'll keep still as solid rock or iron.
One more thing. Take it to heart, I tell you.
If a god beats down these brazen suitors at your hands,   560
I'll report in full on the women in your house:
who are disloyal to you, who are guiltless."

"Nurse," the cool tactician Odysseus said,
"why bother to count them off? A waste of breath.   565
I'll observe them, judge each one myself.
Just be quiet. Keep your tales to yourself.
Leave the rest to the gods."
                                        Hushed so,
the old nurse went padding along the halls
to fetch more water—her basin had all spilled—
and once she'd bathed and rubbed him down with oil,   570
Odysseus drew his chair up near the fire again,
trying to keep warm,
but he hid his scar beneath his beggar's rags
as cautious Penelope resumed their conversation:
"My friend, I have only one more question for you,   575
something slight, now the hour draws on for welcome sleep—
for those who can yield to sweet repose, that is,
heartsick as they are. As for myself, though,
some god has sent me pain that knows no bounds.
All day long I indulge myself in sighs and tears   580
as I see to my tasks, direct the household women.
When night falls and the world lies lost in sleep,
I take to my bed, my heart throbbing, about to break,
anxieties swarming, piercing—I may go mad with grief.
Like Pandareus' daughter,[5] the nightingale in the green woods   585
lifting her lovely song at the first warm rush of spring,
perched in the treetops' rustling leaves and pouring forth
her music shifting, trilling and sinking, rippling high to burst
in grief for Itylus, her beloved boy, King Zethus' son
whom she in innocence once cut down with bronze . . .   590
so my wavering heart goes shuttling, back and forth:
Do I stay beside my son and keep all things secure—
my lands, my serving-women, the grand high-roofed house—
true to my husband's bed, the people's voice as well?
Or do I follow, at last, the best man who courts me   595
here in the halls, who gives the greatest gifts?
My son—when he was a boy and lighthearted—

5. The reference is to one of several stories the Greeks told to explain the nightingale's song. The daughter of Pandareus, a Cretan king, was married to Zethus, king of Thebes. Envying the many children of her sister-in-law Niobe, she tried to kill Niobe's eldest son but by mistake killed her only child, Itylus, instead. Zeus changed her into a nightingale, who sings in mourning for her son.

urged me not to marry and leave my husband's house.
But now he has grown and reached his young prime,
he begs me to leave our palace, travel home. 600
Telemachus, so obsessed with his own estate,
the wealth my princely suitors bleed away.
                                    But please,
read this dream for me, won't you? Listen closely . . .
I keep twenty geese in the house, from the water trough
they come and peck their wheat—I love to watch them all. 605
But down from a mountain swooped this great hook-beaked eagle,
yes, and he snapped their necks and killed them one and all
and they lay in heaps throughout the halls while he,
back to the clear blue sky he soared at once.
But I wept and wailed—only a dream, of course— 610
and our well-groomed ladies came and clustered round me,
sobbing, stricken: the eagle killed my geese. But down
he swooped again and settling onto a jutting rafter
called out in a human voice that dried my tears,
'Courage, daughter of famous King Icarius! 615
This is no dream but a happy waking vision,
real as day, that will come true for you.
The geese were your suitors—I was once the eagle
but now I am your husband, back again at last,
about to launch a terrible fate against them all!' 620
So he vowed, and the soothing sleep released me.
I peered around and saw my geese in the house,
pecking at their wheat, at the same trough
where they always took their meal."
                                    "Dear woman,"
quick Odysseus answered, "twist it however you like, 625
your dream can only mean one thing. Odysseus
told you himself—he'll make it come to pass.
Destruction is clear for each and every suitor;
not a soul escapes his death and doom."

"Ah my friend," seasoned Penelope dissented, 630
"dreams are hard to unravel, wayward, drifting things—
not all we glimpse in them will come to pass . . .
Two gates there are for our evanescent dreams,
one is made of ivory, the other made of horn.
Those that pass through the ivory cleanly carved 635
are will-o'-the-wisps, their message bears no fruit.
The dreams that pass through the gates of polished horn
are fraught with truth, for the dreamer who can see them.
But I can't believe my strange dream has come that way,
much as my son and I would love to have it so. 640
One more thing I'll tell you—weigh it well.
The day that dawns today, this cursed day,
will cut me off from Odysseus' house. Now,
I mean to announce a contest with those axes,
the ones he would often line up here inside the hall, 645
twelve in a straight unbroken row like blocks to shore a keel,

then stand well back and whip an arrow through the lot.[6]
Now I will bring them on as a trial for my suitors.
The hand that can string the bow with greatest ease,
that shoots an arrow clean through all twelve axes— 650
he's the man I follow, yes, forsaking this house
where I was once a bride, this gracious house
so filled with the best that life can offer—
I shall always remember it, that I know . . .
even in my dreams." 655
                          "Oh my queen,"
Odysseus, man of exploits, urged her on,
"royal wife of Laertes' son, Odysseus, now,
don't put off this test in the halls a moment.
Before that crew can handle the polished bow,
string it taut and shoot through all those axes— 660
Odysseus, man of exploits, will be home with you!"

    "If only, my friend," the wise Penelope replied,
"you were willing to sit beside me in the house,
indulging me in the comfort of your presence,
sleep would never drift across my eyes. 665
But one can't go without his sleep forever.
The immortals give each thing its proper place
in our mortal lives throughout the good green earth.
So now I'm going back to my room upstairs
and lie down on my bed, 670
that bed of pain my tears have streaked, year in,
year out, from the day Odysseus sailed away to see . . .
Destroy, I call it—I hate to say its name!
There I'll rest, while you lie here in the hall,
spreading your blankets somewhere on the floor, 675
or the women will prepare a decent bed."
                                    With that
the queen went up to her lofty well-lit room
and not alone: her women followed close behind.
Penelope, once they reached the upper story,
fell to weeping for Odysseus, her beloved husband, 680
till watchful Athena sealed her eyes with welcome sleep.

BOOK XX

[Portents Gather]

Off in the entrance-hall the great king made his bed,
spreading out on the ground the raw hide of an ox,
heaping over it fleece from sheep the suitors
butchered day and night, then Eurynome threw
a blanket over him, once he'd nestled down. 5

---

6. The nature of this archery contest has never been satisfactorily explained. The axes were probably double-headed; the aperture through which the arrow passed must have been the socket in which the wood handle fit. If the twelve ax heads were fixed in the ground (Telemachus later digs a trench for them) so that the empty sockets were perfectly aligned, an arrow might pass through them—although it would take an extremely powerful shot to make an arrow fly in such a perfectly horizontal line.

And there Odysseus lay . . .
plotting within himself the suitors' death—
awake, alert, as the women slipped from the house,
the maids who whored in the suitors' beds each night,
tittering, linking arms and frisking as before.   10
The master's anger rose inside his chest,
torn in thought, debating, head and heart—
should he up and rush them, kill them one and all
or let them rut with their lovers one last time?
The heart inside him growled low with rage,   15
as a bitch mounting over her weak, defenseless puppies
growls, facing a stranger, bristling for a showdown—
so he growled from his depths, hackles rising at their outrage.
But he struck his chest and curbed his fighting heart:
"Bear up, old heart! You've borne worse, far worse,   20
that day when the Cyclops, man-mountain, bolted
your hardy comrades down. But you held fast—
Nobody but your cunning pulled you through
the monster's cave you thought would be your death."

    So he forced his spirit into submission,   25
the rage in his breast reined back—unswerving,
all endurance. But he himself kept tossing, turning,
intent as a cook before some white-hot blazing fire
who rolls his sizzling sausage back and forth,
packed with fat and blood—keen to broil it quickly,   30
tossing, turning it, this way, that way—so he cast about:
how could he get these shameless suitors in his clutches,
one man facing a mob? . . . when close to his side she came,
Athena sweeping down from the sky in a woman's build
and hovering at his head, the goddess spoke: 35
"Why still awake? The unluckiest man alive!
Here is your house, your wife at home, your son,
as fine a boy as one could hope to have."
                                        "True,"
the wily fighter replied, "how right you are, goddess,
but still this worry haunts me, heart and soul—   40
how can I get these shameless suitors in my clutches?
Single-handed, braving an army always camped inside.
There's another worry, that haunts me even more.
What if I kill them—thanks to you and Zeus—
how do I run from under their avengers?   45
Show me the way, I ask you."
                                        "Impossible man!"
Athena bantered, the goddess' eyes ablaze.
"Others are quick to trust a weaker comrade,
some poor mortal, far less cunning than I.
But I am a goddess, look, the very one who   50
guards you in all your trials to the last.
I tell you this straight out:
even if fifty bands of mortal fighters
closed around us, hot to kill us off in battle,

still you could drive away their herds and sleek flocks!   55
So, surrender to sleep at last. What a misery,
keeping watch through the night, wide awake—
you'll soon come up from under all your troubles."

   With that she showered sleep across his eyes
and back to Olympus went the lustrous goddess.   60
As soon as sleep came on him, loosing his limbs,
slipping the toils of anguish from his mind,
his devoted wife awoke and,
sitting up in her soft bed, returned to tears.
When the queen had wept to her heart's content   65
she prayed to the Huntress, Artemis, first of all:
"Artemis—goddess, noble daughter of Zeus, if only
you'd whip an arrow through my breast and tear my life out,
now, at once! Or let some whirlwind pluck me up
and sweep me away along those murky paths and   70
fling me down where the Ocean River running
round the world rolls back upon itself!
                                 Quick
as the whirlwinds swept away Pandareus' daughters[7]
years ago, when the gods destroyed their parents,
leaving the young girls orphans in their house.   75
But radiant Aphrodite nursed them well
on cheese and luscious honey and heady wine,
and Hera gave them beauty and sound good sense,
more than all other women—virgin Artemis made them tall
and Athena honed their skills to fashion lovely work.   80
But then, when Aphrodite approached Olympus' peaks
to ask for the girls their crowning day as brides
from Zeus who loves the lightning—Zeus who knows all,
all that's fated, all not fated, for mortal man—
then the storm spirits snatched them away   85
and passed them on to the hateful Furies,
yes, for all their loving care.
                        Just so
may the gods who rule Olympus blot me out!
Artemis with your glossy braids, come shoot me dead—
so I can plunge beneath this loathsome earth   90
with the image of Odysseus vivid in my mind.
Never let me warm the heart of a weaker man!
Even grief is bearable, true, when someone weeps
through the days, sobbing, heart convulsed with pain
yet embraced by sleep all night—sweet oblivion, sleep   95
dissolving all, the good and the bad, once it seals our eyes—
but even my dreams torment me, sent by wicked spirits.
Again—just this night—someone lay beside me . . .
like Odysseus to the life, when he embarked

---

7. The fate of these daughters of Pandareus was different from that of the one who married Zethus and
became a nightingale (alluded to in book 19). They paid for the wrongdoing of their father, who stole a
golden image from the temple of Hephaestus. Though the gods showered gifts on them, in the end they
were swept away to their deaths by the stormwinds.

with his men-at-arms. My heart raced with joy. 100
No dream, I thought, the waking truth at last!"
                                        At those words
Dawn rose on her golden throne in a sudden gleam of light.
And great Odysseus caught the sound of his wife's cry
and began to daydream—deep in his heart it seemed
she stood beside him, knew him, now, at last . . . 105
Gathering up the fleece and blankets where he'd slept,
he laid them on a chair in the hall, he took the oxhide out
and spread it down, lifted his hands and prayed to Zeus:
"Father Zeus, if you really willed it so—to bring me
home over land and sea-lanes, home to native ground 110
after all the pain you brought me—show me a sign,
a good omen voiced by someone awake indoors,
another sign, outside, from Zeus himself!"

    And Zeus in all his wisdom heard that prayer.
He thundered at once, out of his clear blue heavens 115
high above the clouds, and Odysseus' spirit lifted.
Then from within the halls a woman grinding grain
let fly a lucky word. Close at hand she was,
where the good commander set the handmills once
and now twelve women in all performed their tasks, 120
grinding the wheat and barley, marrow of men's bones.
The rest were abed by now—they'd milled their stint—
this one alone, the frailest of all, kept working on.
Stopping her mill, she spoke an omen for her master:
"Zeus, Father! King of gods and men, now *there* 125
was a crack of thunder out of the starry sky—
and not a cloud in sight!
Sure it's a sign you're showing someone now.
So, poor as I am, grant *me* my prayer as well:
let this day be the last, the last these suitors 130
bolt their groaning feasts in King Odysseus' house!
These brutes who break my knees—heart-wrenching labor,
grinding their grain—now let them eat their last!"

    A lucky omen, linked with Zeus's thunder.
Odysseus' heart leapt up, the man convinced 135
he'd grind the scoundrels' lives out in revenge.
                                        By now
the other maids were gathering in Odysseus' royal palace,
raking up on the hearth the fire still going strong.
Telemachus climbed from bed and dressed at once,
brisk as a young god—
over his shoulder he slung his well-honed sword, 140
he fastened rawhide sandals under his smooth feet,
he seized his tough spear tipped with a bronze point
and took his stand at the threshold, calling Eurycleia:
"Dear nurse, how did you treat the stranger in our house? 145
With bed and board? Or leave him to lie untended?
That would be mother's way—sensible as she is—

all impulse, doting over some worthless stranger,
turning a good man out to face the worst."

"Please, child," his calm old nurse replied,   150
"don't blame *her*—your mother's blameless this time.
He sat and drank his wine till he'd had his fill.
Food? He'd lost his hunger. But she asked him.
And when it was time to think of turning in,
she told the maids to spread a decent bed, but he—   155
so down-and-out, poor soul, so dogged by fate—
said no to snuggling into a bed, between covers.
No sir, the man lay down in the entrance-hall,
on the raw hide of an ox and sheep's fleece,
and we threw a blanket over him, so we did."
                                              Hearing that,   160
Telemachus strode out through the palace, spear in hand,
and a pair of sleek hounds went trotting at his heels.
He made for the meeting grounds to join the island lords
while Eurycleia the daughter of Ops, Pisenor's son,
that best of women, gave the maids their orders: 165
"Quick now, look alive, sweep out the house,
wet down the floors!
                       You, those purple coverlets,
fling them over the fancy chairs!
                                   All those tables,
sponge them down—scour the winebowls, burnished cups!
The rest—now off you go to the spring and fetch some water,   170
fast as your legs can run!
Our young gallants won't be long from the palace,
they'll be bright and early—today's a public feast."

   They hung on her words and ran to do her bidding.
Full twenty scurried off to the spring's dark water,   175
others bent to the housework, all good hands.
Then in they trooped, the strutting serving-men,
who split the firewood cleanly now as the women
bustled in from the spring, the swineherd at their heels,
driving three fat porkers, the best of all his herds.   180
And leaving them to root in the broad courtyard,
up he went to Odysseus, hailed him warmly:
"Friend, do the suitors show you more respect
or treat you like the dregs of the earth as always?"

   "Good Eumaeus," the crafty man replied,   185
"if only the gods would pay back their outrage!
Wild and reckless young cubs, conniving here
in another's house. They've got no sense of shame."

   And now as the two confided in each other,
the goatherd Melanthius sauntered toward them,   190
herding his goats with a pair of drovers' help,
the pick of his flocks to make the suitors' meal.

Under the echoing porch he tethered these, then turned
on Odysseus once again with cutting insults: "Still alive?
Still hounding your betters, begging round the house?   195
Why don't you cart yourself away? Get out!
We'll never part, I swear,
till we taste each other's fists. Riffraff,
you and your begging make us sick! Get out—
we're hardly the only banquet on the island."   200

    No reply. The wily one just shook his head,
silent, his mind churning with thoughts of bloody work . . .

    Third to arrive was Philoetius, that good cowherd,
prodding in for the crowd a heifer and fat goats.
Boatmen had brought them over from the mainland,   205
crews who ferry across all travelers too,
whoever comes for passage.
Under the echoing porch he tethered all heads well
and then approached the swineherd, full of questions:
"Who's this stranger, Eumaeus, just come to the house?   210
What roots does the man claim—who are his people?
Where are his blood kin? his father's fields?
Poor beggar. But what a build—a royal king's!
Ah, once the gods weave trouble into our lives
they drive us across the earth, they drown us all in pain,   215
even kings of the realm."

               And with that thought
he walked up to Odysseus, gave him his right hand
and winged a greeting: "Cheers, old friend, old father,
here's to your luck, great days from this day on—
saddled now as you are with so much trouble.   220
Father Zeus, no god's more deadly than you!
No mercy for men, you give them life yourself
then plunge them into misery, brutal hardship.
I broke into sweat, my friend, when I first saw you—
see, my eyes still brim with tears, remembering *him*,   225
Odysseus . . . He must wear such rags, I know it,
knocking about, drifting through the world
if he's still alive and sees the light of day.
If he's dead already, lost in the House of Death,
my heart aches for Odysseus, my great lord and master.   230
He set me in charge of his herds, in Cephallenian country,
when I was just a youngster. How they've grown by now,
past counting! No mortal on earth could breed
a finer stock of oxen—broad in the brow,
they thrive like ears of corn. But just look,   235
these interlopers tell me to drive them in
for their own private feasts. Not a thought
for the young prince in the house, they never flinch—
no regard for the gods' wrath—in their mad rush
to carve up his goods, my master gone so long!   240
I'm tossed from horn to horn in my own mind . . .

What a traitor I'd be, with the prince still alive,
if I'd run off to some other country, herds and all,
to a new set of strangers. Ah, but isn't it worse
to hold out here, tending the herds for upstarts,   245
not their owners—suffering all the pains of hell?
I could have fled, ages ago, to some great king
who'd give me shelter. It's unbearable here.
True, but I still dream of my old master,
unlucky man—if only *he*'d drop in from the blue   250
and drive these suitors all in a rout throughout the halls!"

　　"Cowherd," the cool tactician Odysseus answered,
"you're no coward, and nobody's fool, I'd say.
Even I can see there's sense in that old head.
So I tell you this on my solemn, binding oath: 255
I swear by Zeus, the first of all the gods—
by the table of hospitality waiting for us,
by Odysseus' hearth where I have come for help,
Odysseus will come home while you're still here.
You'll see with your own eyes, if you have the heart,   260
these suitors who lord it here cut down in blood."

　　"Stranger, if only," the cowherd cried aloud,
"if only Zeus would make that oath come true—
you'd see my power, my fighting arms in action!"

　　Eumaeus echoed his prayer to all the gods   265
that their wise king would soon come home again.

　　Now as they spoke and urged each other on,
and once more the suitors were plotting certain doom
for the young prince—suddenly, banking high on the left
an omen flew past, an eagle clutching a trembling dove.   270
And Amphinomus rose in haste to warn them all,
"My friends, we'll never carry off this plot
to kill the prince. Let's concentrate on feasting."

　　His timely invitation pleased them all.
The suitors ambled into Odysseus' royal house   275
and flinging down their cloaks on a chair or bench,
they butchered hulking sheep and fatted goats,
full-grown hogs and a young cow from the herd.
They roasted all the innards, served them round
and filled the bowls with wine and mixed it well.   280
Eumaeus passed out cups; Philoetius, trusty herdsman,
brought on loaves of bread in ample wicker trays;
Melanthius poured the wine. The whole company
reached out for the good things that lay at hand.

　　Telemachus, maneuvering shrewdly, sat his father down   285
on the stone threshold, just inside the timbered hall,
and set a rickety stool and cramped table there.

He gave him a share of innards, poured his wine
in a golden cup and added a bracing invitation:
"Now sit right there. Drink your wine with the crowd.   290
I'll defend you from all their taunts and blows,
these young bucks. This is no public place,
this is *Odysseus'* house—
my father won it for me, so it's mine.
You suitors, control yourselves. No insults now,   295
no brawling, no, or it's war between us all."

   So he declared. And they all bit their lips,
amazed the prince could speak with so much daring.
Only Eupithes' son Antinous ventured,
"Fighting words, but do let's knuckle under—   300
to our *prince*. Such abuse, such naked threats!
But clearly Zeus had foiled us. Or long before
we would have shut his mouth for him in the halls,
fluent and flowing as he is."
                  So he mocked.
Telemachus paid no heed.
                  And now through the streets   305
the heralds passed, leading the beasts marked out
for sacrifice on Apollo's grand festal day,
and the islanders with their long hair were filing
into the god's shady grove—the distant deadly Archer.

   Those in the palace, once they'd roasted the prime cuts,   310
pulled them off the spits and, sharing out the portions,
fell to the royal feast . . .
The men who served them gave Odysseus his share,
as fair as the helping they received themselves.
So Telemachus ordered, the king's own son.   315

   But Athena had no mind to let the brazen suitors
hold back now from their heart-rending insults—
she meant to make the anguish cut still deeper
into the core of Laertes' son Odysseus.
There was one among them, a lawless boor—   320
Ctesippus was his name, he made his home in Same,
a fellow so impressed with his own astounding wealth
he courted the wife of Odysseus, gone for years.
Now the man harangued his swaggering comrades:
"Listen to me, my fine friends, here's what I say!   325
From the start our guest has had his fair share—
it's only right, you know.
How impolite it would be, how wrong to scant
whatever guest Telemachus welcomes to his house.
Look here, I'll give him a proper guest-gift too,   330
a prize he can hand the crone who bathes his feet
or a tip for another slave who haunts the halls
of our great king Odysseus!"
              On that note,

grabbing an oxhoof out of a basket where it lay,
with a brawny hand he flung it straight at the king— 335
but Odysseus ducked his head a little, dodging the blow,
and seething just as the oxhoof hit the solid wall
he clenched his teeth in a wry sardonic grin.
Telemachus dressed Ctesippus down at once: 340
"Ctesippus, you can thank your lucky stars
you missed our guest—he ducked your blow, by god!
Else I would have planted my sharp spear in your bowels—
your father would have been busy with your funeral,
not your wedding here. Enough.
Don't let me see more offenses in my house, 345
not from anyone! I'm alive to it all, now,
the good and the bad—the boy you knew is gone.
But I still must bear with this, this lovely sight . . .
sheepflocks butchered, wine swilled, food squandered—
how can a man fight off so many single-handed? 350
But no more of your crimes against me, please!
Unless you're bent on cutting me down, now,
and I'd rather die, yes, better that by far
than have to look on at your outrage day by day:
guests treated to blows, men dragging the serving-women 355
through our noble house, exploiting them all, no shame!"

    Dead quiet. The suitors all fell silent, hushed.
At last Damastor's son Agelaus rose and said,
"Fair enough, my friends; when a man speaks well
we have no grounds for wrangling, no cause for abuse. 360
Hands off this stranger! Or any other servant
in King Odysseus' palace. But now a word
of friendly advice for Telemachus and his mother—
here's hoping it proves congenial to them both.
So long as your hearts still kept a spark alive 365
that Odysseus would return—that great, deep man—
who could blame you, playing the waiting game at home
and holding off the suitors? The better course, it's true.
What if Odysseus had returned, had made it home at last?
But now it's clear as day—the man will come no more. 370
So go, Telemachus, sit with your mother, coax her
to wed the best man here, the one who offers most,
so you can have and hold your father's estate,
eating and drinking here, your mind at peace 375
while mother plays the wife in another's house."

    The young prince, keeping his poise, replied,
"I swear by Zeus, Agelaus, by all my father suffered—
dead, no doubt, or wandering far from Ithaca these days—
I don't delay my mother's marriage, not a moment,
I press her to wed the man who takes her heart. 380
I'll shower her myself with boundless gifts.
But I shrink from driving mother from our house,
issuing harsh commands against her will.

God forbid it ever comes to that!"
                    So he vowed
and Athena set off uncontrollable laughter in the suitors,   385
crazed them out of their minds—mad, hysterical laughter
seemed to break from the jaws of strangers, not their own,
and the meat they were eating oozed red with blood—
tears flooded their eyes, hearts possessed by grief.
The inspired seer Theoclymenus wailed out in their midst,   390
"Poor men, what terror is this that overwhelms you so?
Night shrouds your heads, your faces, down to your knees—
cries of mourning are bursting into fire—cheeks rivering tears—
the walls and the handsome crossbeams dripping dank with blood!
Ghosts, look, thronging the entrance, thronging the court,   395
go trooping down to the world of death and darkness!
The sun is blotted out of the sky—look there—
a lethal mist spreads all across the earth!"
                     At that
they all broke into peals of laughter aimed at the seer—
Polybus' son Eurymachus braying first and foremost,   400
"Our guest just in from abroad, the man is raving!
Quick, my boys, hustle him out of the house,
into the meeting grounds, the light of day—
everything *here* he thinks is dark as night!"

   "Eurymachus," the inspired prophet countered,   405
"when I want your escort, I'll ask for it myself.
I have eyes and ears, and both my feet, still,
and a head that's fairly sound,
nothing to be ashamed of. These will do
to take me past those doors . . .
                Oh I can see it now—   410
the disaster closing on you all! There's no escaping it,
no way out—not for a single one of you suitors,
wild reckless fools, plotting outrage here,
the halls of Odysseus, great and strong as a god!"

   With that he marched out of the sturdy house   415
and went home to Piraeus, the host who warmed him in.
Now all the suitors, trading their snide glances, started
heckling Telemachus, made a mockery of his guests.
One or another brash young gallant scoffed,
"Telemachus, no one's more unlucky with his guests!"   420

   "Look what your man dragged in—this mangy tramp
scraping for bread and wine!"
               "Not fit for good hard work,
the bag of bones—"
          "A useless dead weight on the land!"

   "And then this charlatan up and apes the prophet."

   "Take it from me—you'll be better off by far—   425

toss your friends in a slave-ship—"
                                    "Pack them off
to Sicily, fast—they'll fetch you one sweet price!"

    So they jeered, but the prince paid no attention . . .
silent, eyes riveted on his father, always waiting
the moment he'd lay hands on that outrageous mob.   430

    And all the while Icarius' daughter, wise Penelope,
had placed her carved chair within earshot, at the door,
so she could catch each word they uttered in the hall.
Laughing rowdily, men prepared their noonday meal,
succulent, rich—they'd butchered quite a herd.   435
But as for supper, what could be less enticing
than what a goddess and a powerful man
would spread before them soon? A groaning feast—
for they'd been first to plot their vicious crimes.

BOOK XXI

[Odysseus Strings His Bow]

The time had come. The goddess Athena with her blazing eyes
inspired Penelope, Icarius' daughter, wary, poised,
to set the bow and the gleaming iron axes out
before her suitors waiting in Odysseus' hall—
to test their skill and bring their slaughter on.   5
Up the steep stairs to her room she climbed
and grasped in a steady hand the curved key—
fine bronze, with ivory haft attached—
and then with her chamber-women made her way
to a hidden storeroom, far in the palace depths,   10
and there they lay, the royal master's treasures:
bronze, gold and a wealth of hard wrought iron
and there it lay as well . . . his backsprung bow
with its quiver bristling arrows, shafts of pain.
Gifts from the old days, from a friend he'd met   15
in Lacedaemon—Iphitus, Eurytus' gallant son.[8]
Once in Messene the two struck up together,
in sly Ortilochus'[9] house, that time Odysseus
went to collect a debt the whole realm owed him,
for Messenian raiders had lifted flocks from Ithaca,   20
three hundred head in their oarswept ships, the herdsmen too.
So his father and island elders sent Odysseus off,
a young boy on a mission,
a distant embassy made to right that wrong.
Iphitus went there hunting the stock that he had lost,   25
a dozen mares still nursing their hardy suckling mules.
The same mares that would prove his certain death
when he reached the son of Zeus, that iron heart,

---

8. Eurytus was king of Oechalia, a city in Thessaly. According to another story, Heracles sacked his city, killed him, and took his daughter Iole captive.   9. King of Pherae in the southern Peloponnesus.

Heracles—the past master of monstrous works—
who killed the man, a guest in his own house.   30
Brutal. Not a care for the wrathful eyes of god
or rites of hospitality he had spread before him,
no, he dined him, then he murdered him, commandeered
those hard-hoofed mares for the hero's own grange.
Still on the trail of these when he met Odysseus,   35
Iphitus gave him the bow his father, mighty Eurytus,
used to wield as a young man, but when he died
in his lofty house he left it to his son.
In turn, Odysseus gave his friend a sharp sword
and a rugged spear to mark the start of friendship,   40
treasured ties that bind. But before they got to know
the warmth of each other's board, the son of Zeus
had murdered Iphitus, Eurytus' magnificent son
who gave the prince the bow.
                            That great weapon—
King Odysseus never took it abroad with him   45
when he sailed off to war in his long black ships.
He kept it stored away in his stately house,
guarding the memory of a cherished friend,
and only took that bow on hunts at home.
                                      Now,
the lustrous queen soon reached the hidden vault   50
and stopped at the oaken doorsill, work an expert
sanded smooth and trued to the line some years ago,
planting the doorjambs snugly, hanging shining doors.
At once she loosed the thong from around its hook,
inserted the key and aiming straight and true,   55
shot back the bolts—and the rasping doors groaned
as loud as a bull will bellow, champing grass at pasture.
So as the key went home those handsome double doors
rang out now and sprang wide before her.
She stepped onto a plank where chests stood tall,   60
brimming with clothing scented sweet with cedar.
Reaching, tiptoe, lifting the bow down off its peg,
still secure in the burnished case that held it,
down she sank, laying the case across her knees,
and dissolved in tears with a high thin wail   65
as she drew her husband's weapon from its sheath . . .
Then, having wept and sobbed to her heart's content,
off she went to the hall to meet her proud admirers,
cradling her husband's backsprung bow in her arms,
its quiver bristling arrows, shafts of pain.   70
Her women followed, bringing a chest that held
the bronze and the iron axes, trophies won by the master.
That radiant woman, once she reached her suitors,
drawing her glistening veil across her cheeks,
paused now where a column propped the sturdy roof,   75
with one of her loyal handmaids stationed either side,
and delivered an ultimatum to her suitors:
"Listen to me, my overbearing friends!

You who plague this palace night and day,
drinking, eating us out of house and home   80
with the lord and master absent, gone so long—
the only excuse that you can offer is your zest
to win me as your bride. So, to arms, my gallants!
Here is the prize at issue, right before you, look—
I set before you the great bow of King Odysseus now!   85
The hand that can string this bow with greatest ease,
that shoots an arrow clean through all twelve axes—
he is the man I follow, yes, forsaking this house
where I was once a bride, this gracious house
so filled with the best that life can offer—   90
I shall always remember it, that I know . . .
even in my dreams."
      She turned to Eumaeus,
ordered the good swineherd now to set the bow
and the gleaming iron axes out before the suitors.
He broke into tears as he received them, laid them down.   95
The cowherd wept too, when he saw his master's bow.
But Antinous wheeled on both and let them have it:
"Yokels, fools—you can't tell night from day!
You mawkish idiots, why are you sniveling here?
You're stirring up your mistress! Isn't she drowned   100
in grief already? She's lost her darling husband.
Sit down. Eat in peace, or take your snuffling
out of doors! But leave that bow right here—
our crucial test that makes or breaks us all.
No easy game, I wager, to string *his* polished bow.   105
Not a soul in the crowd can match Odysseus—
what a man he was . . .
I saw him once, remember him to this day,
though I was young and foolish way back then."
         Smooth talk,
but deep in the suitor's heart his hopes were bent   110
on stringing the bow and shooting through the axes.
Antinous—fated to be the first man to taste
an arrow whipped from great Odysseus' hands,
the king he mocked, at ease in the king's house,
egging comrades on to mock him too.
        "Amazing!"   115
Prince Telemachus waded in with a laugh:
"Zeus up there has robbed me of my wits.
My own dear mother, sensible as she is,
says she'll marry again, forsake our house,
and look at *me*—laughing for all I'm worth,   120
giggling like some fool. Step up, my friends!
Here is the prize at issue, right before you, look—
a woman who has no equal now in all Achaean country,
neither in holy Pylos, nor in Argos or Mycenae,
not even Ithaca itself or the loamy mainland.   125
You know it well. Why sing my mother's praises?
Come, let the games begin! No dodges, no delays,

no turning back from the stringing of the bow—
we'll see who wins, we will.
I'd even take a crack at the bow myself . . .   130
If I string it and shoot through all the axes,
I'd worry less if my noble mother left our house
with another man and left me here behind—man enough
at last to win my father's splendid prizes!"
                              With that   135
he leapt to his feet and dropped his bright red cloak,
slipping the sword and sword-belt off his shoulders.
First he planted the axes, digging a long trench,
one for all, and trued them all to a line
then tamped the earth to bed them. Wonder took
the revelers looking on: his work so firm, precise,   140
though he'd never seen the axes ranged before.
He stood at the threshold, poised to try the bow . . .
Three times he made it shudder, straining to bend it,
three times his power flagged—but his hopes ran high
he'd string his father's bow and shoot through every iron   145
and now, struggling with all his might for the fourth time,
he would have strung the bow, but Odysseus shook his head
and stopped him short despite his tensing zeal.
"God help me," the inspired prince cried out,
"must I be a weakling, a failure all my life?   150
Unless I'm just too young to trust my hands
to fight off any man who rises up against me.
Come, my betters, so much stronger than I am—
try the bow and finish off the contest."

    He propped his father's weapon on the ground,   155
tilting it up against the polished well-hung doors
and resting a shaft aslant the bow's fine horn,
then back he went to the seat that he had left.
"Up, friends!" Antinous called, taking over.
"One man after another, left to right,   160
starting from where the steward pours the wine."

    So Antinous urged and all agreed.
The first man up was Leodes, Oenops' son,
a seer who could see their futures in the smoke,
who always sat by the glowing winebowl, well back,   165
the one man in the group who loathed their reckless ways,
appalled by all their outrage. His turn first . . .
Picking up the weapon now and the swift arrow,
he stood at the threshold, poised to try the bow
but failed to bend it. As soon as he tugged the string   170
his hands went slack, his soft, uncallused hands,
and he called back to the suitors, "Friends,
I can't bend it. Take it, someone—try.
Here is a bow to rob our best of life and breath,
all our best contenders! Still, better be dead   175
than live on here, never winning the prize

that tempts us all—forever in pursuit,
burning with expectation every day.
If there's still a suitor here who hopes,
who aches to marry Penelope, Odysseus' wife,   180
just let him try the bow; he'll see the truth!
He'll soon lay siege to another Argive woman
trailing her long robes, and shower her with gifts—
and then our queen can marry the one who offers most,
the man marked out by fate to be her husband."   185

　　With those words he thrust the bow aside,
tilting it up against the polished well-hung doors
and resting a shaft aslant the bow's fine horn,
then back he went to the seat that he had left.
But Antinous turned on the seer, abuses flying: 190
"Leodes! what are you saying? what's got past your lips?
What awful, grisly nonsense—it shocks me to hear it—
'here is a bow to rob our best of life and breath!'
Just because *you* can't string it, you're so weak?
Clearly your genteel mother never bred her boy   195
for the work of bending bows and shooting arrows.
We have champions in our ranks to string it quickly.
Hop to it, Melanthius!"—he barked at the goatherd—
"Rake the fire in the hall, pull up a big stool,
heap it with fleece and fetch that hefty ball   200
of lard from the stores inside. So we young lords
can heat and limber the bow and rub it down with grease
before we try again and finish off the contest!"

　　The goatherd bustled about to rake the fire
still going strong. He pulled up a big stool,   205
heaped it with fleece and fetched the hefty ball
of lard from the stores inside. And the young men
limbered the bow, rubbing it down with hot grease,
then struggled to bend it back but failed. No use—
they fell far short of the strength the bow required. 210
Antinous still held off, dashing Eurymachus too,
the ringleaders of all the suitors,
head and shoulders the strongest of the lot.
　　　　　　　　　　　　　　　But now
the king's two men, the cowherd and the swineherd,
had slipped out of the palace side-by-side   215
and great Odysseus left the house to join them.
Once they were past the courtyard and the gates
he probed them deftly, surely: "Cowherd, swineherd,
what, shall I blurt this out or keep it to myself?
No, speak out. The heart inside me says so.   220
How far would you go to fight beside Odysseus?
Say he dropped like *that* from a clear blue sky
and a god brought him back—
would you fight for the suitors or your king?
Tell me how you feel inside your hearts."   225

"Father Zeus," the trusty cowherd shouted,
"bring my prayer to pass! Let the master come—
some god guide him now! You'd see my power,
my fighting arms in action!"

Eumaeus echoed his prayer to all the gods   230
that their wise king would soon come home again.
Certain at least these two were loyal to the death,
Odysseus reassured them quickly: "I'm right here,
here in the flesh—myself—and home at last,
after bearing twenty years of brutal hardship.   235
Now I know that of all my men you two alone
longed for my return. From the rest I've heard
not one real prayer that I come back again.
So now I'll tell you what's in store for *you*.
If a god beats down the lofty suitors at my hands,   240
I'll find you wives, both of you, grant you property,
sturdy houses beside my own, and in my eyes you'll be
comrades to Prince Telemachus, brothers from then on.
Come, I'll show you something—living proof—
know me for certain, put your minds at rest.   245
                                        This scar,
look, where a boar's white tusk gored me, years ago,
hunting on Parnassus, Autolycus' sons and I."
                                        With that,
pushing back his rags, he revealed the great scar . . .
And the men gazed at it, scanned it, knew it well,
broke into tears and threw their arms around their master—   250
lost in affection, kissing his head and shoulders,
and so Odysseus kissed their heads and hands.
Now the sun would have set upon their tears
if Odysseus had not called a halt himself.
"No more weeping. Coming out of the house   255
a man might see us, tell the men inside.
Let's slip back in—singly, not in a pack.
I'll go first. You're next. Here's our signal.
When all the rest in there, our lordly friends,
are dead against my having the bow and quiver,   260
good Eumaeus, carry the weapon down the hall
and put it in my hands. Then tell the serving-women
to lock the snugly fitted doors to their own rooms.
If anyone hears from there the jolting blows
and groans of men, caught in our huge net,   265
not one of them show her face—
sit tight, keep to her weaving, not a sound.
You, my good Philoetius, here are your orders.
Shoot the bolt of the courtyard's outer gate,
lock it, lash it fast."
                                With that command   270
the master entered his well-constructed house
and back he went to the stool that he had left.
The king's two men, in turn, slipped in as well.

Just now Eurymachus held the bow in his hands,
turning it over, tip to tip, before the blazing fire   275
to heat the weapon. But he failed to bend it even so
and the suitor's high heart groaned to bursting.
"A black day," he exclaimed in wounded pride,
"a blow to myself, a blow to each man here!
It's less the marriage that mortifies me now—   280
that's galling too, but lots of women are left,
some in seagirt Ithaca, some in other cities.
What breaks my heart is the fact we fall so short
of great Odysseus' strength we cannot string his bow.
A disgrace to ring in the ears of men to come."   285

    "Eurymachus," Eupithes' son Antinous countered,
"it will never come to that, as you well know.
Today is a feast-day up and down the island
in honor of the Archer God. Who flexes bows today?
Set it aside. Rest easy now. And all the axes,   290
let's just leave them planted where they are.
Trust me, no one's about to crash the gates
of Laertes' son and carry off these trophies.
Steward, pour some drops for the god in every cup,
we'll tip the wine, then put the bow to bed.   295
And first thing in the morning have Melanthius
bring the pick of his goats from all his herds
so we can burn the thighs to Apollo, god of archers—
then try the bow and finish off the contest."

    Welcome advice. And again they all agreed.   300
Heralds sprinkled water over their hands for rinsing,
the young men brimmed the mixing bowls with wine,
they tipped first drops for the god in every cup,
then poured full rounds for all. And now, once
they'd tipped libations out and drunk their fill,   305
the king of craft, Odysseus, said with all his cunning,
"Listen to me, you lords who court the noble queen.
I have to say what the heart inside me urges.
I appeal especially to Eurymachus, and you,
brilliant Antinous, who spoke so shrewdly now.   310
Give the bow a rest for today, leave it to the gods—
at dawn the Archer God will grant a victory
to the man he favors most.
                        For the moment,
give me the polished bow now, won't you? So,
to amuse you all, I can try my hand, my strength . . .   315
is the old force still alive inside these gnarled limbs?
Or has a life of roaming, years of rough neglect,
destroyed it long ago?"
                    Modest words
that sent them all into hot, indignant rage,
fearing he just might string the polished bow.   320

So Antinous rounded on him, dressed him down:
"Not a shred of sense in your head, you filthy drifter!
Not content to feast at your ease with us, the island's pride?
Never denied your full share of the banquet, never,
you can listen in on our secrets. No one else   325
can eavesdrop on our talk, no tramp, no beggar.
The wine has overpowered you, heady wine—
the ruin of many another man, whoever
gulps it down and drinks beyond his limit.
Wine—it drove the Centaur,[1] famous Eurytion,   330
mad in the halls of lionhearted Pirithous.
There to visit the Lapiths, crazed with wine
the headlong Centaur bent to his ugly work
in the prince's own house! His hosts sprang up,
seized with fury, dragged him across the forecourt,   335
flung him out of doors, hacking his nose and ears off
with their knives, no mercy. The creature reeled away,
still blind with drink, his heart like a wild storm,
loaded with all the frenzy in his mind!
                              And so
the feud between mortal men and Centaurs had its start.   340
But the drunk was first to bring disaster on himself
by drowning in his cups. You too, I promise you
no end of trouble if you should string that bow.
You'll meet no kindness in our part of the world—
we'll sail you off in a black ship to Echetus,   345
the mainland king who wrecks all men alive.
Nothing can save you from his royal grip!
So drink, but hold your peace,
don't take on the younger, stronger men."

    "Antinous," watchful Penelope stepped in,   350
"how impolite it would be, how wrong, to scant
whatever guest Telemachus welcomes to his house.
You really think—if the stranger trusts so to his hands
and strength that he strings Odysseus' great bow—
he'll take me home and claim me as his bride?   355
He never dreamed of such a thing, I'm sure.
Don't let that ruin the feast for any reveler here.
Unthinkable—nothing, nothing could be worse."

    Polybus' son Eurymachus had an answer:
"Wise Penelope, daughter of Icarius, do we really   360
expect the man to wed you? Unthinkable, I know.
But we do recoil at the talk of men and women.
One of the island's meaner sort will mutter,

---

1. Half horse, half human. At the wedding of Pirithous, king of the Lapiths (their human neighbors), the centaurs got drunk and tried to rape the women who were present. The Lapiths killed them after a fierce fight.

'Look at the riffraff courting a king's wife.
Weaklings, look, they can't even string his bow. 365
But along came this beggar, drifting out of the blue—
strung his bow with ease and shot through all the axes!'
Gossip will fly. We'll hang our heads in shame."

"Shame?" alert Penelope protested—
"How can you hope for any public fame at all? 370
You who disgrace, devour a great man's house and home!
Why hang your heads in shame over next to nothing?
Our friend here is a strapping, well-built man
and claims to be the son of a noble father.
Come, hand him the bow now, let's just see . . . 375
I tell you this—and I'll make good my word—
if he strings the bow and Apollo grants him glory,
I'll dress him in shirt and cloak, in handsome clothes,
I'll give him a good sharp lance to fight off men and dogs,
give him a two-edged sword and sandals for his feet 380
and send him off, wherever his heart desires."

                                        "Mother,"
poised Telemachus broke in now, "my father's bow—
no Achaean on earth has more right than I
to give it or withhold it, as I please.
Of all the lords in Ithaca's rocky heights 385
or the islands facing Elis grazed by horses,
not a single one will force or thwart my will,
even if I decide to give our guest this bow—
a gift outright—to carry off himself.

                                So, mother,
go back to your quarters. Tend to your own tasks, 390
the distaff and the loom, and keep the women
working hard as well. As for the bow now,
men will see to that, but I most of all:
I hold the reins of power in this house."

                                        Astonished,
she withdrew to her own room. She took to heart 395
the clear good sense in what her son had said.
Climbing up to the lofty chamber with her women,
she fell to weeping for Odysseus, her beloved husband,
till watchful Athena sealed her eyes with welcome sleep.

And now the loyal swineherd had lifted up the bow, 400
was taking it toward the king, when all the suitors
burst out in an ugly uproar through the palace—
brash young bullies, this or that one heckling,
"Where on earth are you going with that bow?"

"You, you grubby swineherd, are you crazy? 405

"The speedy dogs you reared will eat your corpse—"

"Out there with your pigs, out in the cold, alone!"

"If only Apollo and all the gods shine down on us!"

Eumaeus froze in his tracks, put down the bow,
panicked by every outcry in the hall.   410
Telemachus shouted too, from the other side,
and full of threats: "Carry on with the bow, old boy!
If you serve too many masters, you'll soon suffer.
Look sharp, or I'll pelt you back to your farm
with flying rocks. I may be younger than you   415
but I'm much stronger. If only I had that edge
in fists and brawn over all this courting crowd,
I'd soon dispatch them—licking their wounds at last—
clear of our palace where they plot their vicious plots!"

His outburst sent them all into gales of laughter,   420
blithe and oblivious, that dissolved their pique
against the prince. The swineherd took the bow,
carried it down the hall to his ready, waiting king
and standing by him, placed it in his hands,
then he called the nurse aside and whispered,   425
"Good Eurycleia—Telemachus commands you now
to lock the snugly fitted doors to your own rooms.
If anyone hears from there the jolting blows
and groans of men, caught in our huge net,
not one of you show your face—   430
sit tight, keep to your weaving, not a sound."

That silenced the old nurse—
she barred the doors that led from the long hall.
The cowherd quietly bounded out of the house
to lock the gates of the high-stockaded court.   435
Under the portico lay a cable, ship's tough gear:
he lashed the gates with this, then slipped back in
and ran and sat on the stool that he'd just left,
eyes riveted on Odysseus.
                        Now *he* held the bow
in his own hands, turning it over, tip to tip,   440
testing it, this way, that way . . . fearing worms
had bored through the weapon's horn with the master gone abroad.
A suitor would glance at his neighbor, jeering, taunting,
"Look at our connoisseur of bows!"
                              "Sly old fox—
maybe he's got bows like it, stored in *his* house."   445

"That or he's bent on making one himself."

"Look how he twists and turns it in his hands!"

"The clever tramp means trouble—"

"I wish him luck," some cocksure lord chimed in,
"as good as his luck in bending back that weapon!"   450

So they mocked, but Odysseus, mastermind in action,
once he'd handled the great bow and scanned every inch,
then, like an expert singer skilled at lyre and song—
who strains a string to a new peg with ease,
making the pliant sheep-gut fast at either end—   455
so with his virtuoso ease Odysseus strung his mighty bow.
Quickly his right hand plucked the string to test its pitch
and under his touch it sang out clear and sharp as a swallow's cry.
Horror swept through the suitors, faces blanching white,
and Zeus cracked the sky with a bolt, his blazing sign,   460
and the great man who had borne so much rejoiced at last
that the son of cunning Cronus flung that omen down for *him.*
He snatched a winged arrow lying bare on the board—
the rest still bristled deep inside the quiver,
soon to be tasted by all the feasters there.   465
Setting shaft on the handgrip, drawing the notch
and bowstring back, back . . . right from his stool,
just as he sat but aiming straight and true, he let fly—
and never missing an ax from the first ax-handle
clean on through to the last and out   470
the shaft with its weighted brazen head shot free!
                                                    "My son,"
Odysseus looked to Telemachus and said, "your guest,
sitting here in your house, has not disgraced you.
No missing the mark, look, and no long labor spent
to string the bow. My strength's not broken yet,   475
not quite so frail as the mocking suitors thought.
But the hour has come to serve our masters right—
supper in broad daylight—then to other revels,
song and dancing, all that crowns a feast."

    He paused with a warning nod, and at that sign   480
Prince Telemachus, son of King Odysseus,
girding his sharp sword on, clamping hand to spear,
took his stand by a chair that flanked his father—
his bronze spearpoint glinting now like fire . . .

BOOK XXII

[Slaughter in the Hall]

Now stripping back his rags Odysseus master of craft and battle
vaulted onto the great threshold, gripping his bow and quiver
bristling arrows, and poured his flashing shafts before him,
loose at his feet, and thundered out to all the suitors:
"Look—your crucial test is finished, now, at last!   5
But another target's left that no one's hit before—
we'll see if *I* can hit it—Apollo give me glory!"

    With that he trained a stabbing arrow on Antinous . . .
just lifting a gorgeous golden loving-cup in his hands,
just tilting the two-handled goblet back to his lips,   10
about to drain the wine—and slaughter the last thing

on the suitor's mind: who could dream that one foe
in that crowd of feasters, however great his power,
would bring down death on himself, and black doom?
But Odysseus aimed and shot Antinous square in the throat   15
and the point went stabbing clean through the soft neck and out—
and off to the side he pitched, the cup dropped from his grasp
as the shaft sank home, and the man's life-blood came spurting
out his nostrils—
                    thick red jets—
                                    a sudden thrust of his foot—
he kicked away the table—
                            food showered across the floor,   20
the bread and meats soaked in a swirl of bloody filth.
The suitors burst into uproar all throughout the house
when they saw their leader down. They leapt from their seats,
milling about, desperate, scanning the stone walls—
not a shield in sight, no rugged spear to seize.   25
They wheeled on Odysseus, lashing out in fury:
"Stranger, shooting at men will cost your life!"

    "Your game is over—you, you've shot your last!"

    "You'll never escape your own headlong death!"

    "You killed the best in Ithaca—our fine prince!"   30

    "Vultures will eat your corpse!"
                            Groping, frantic—
each one persuading himself the guest had killed
the man by chance. Poor fools, blind to the fact
that all their necks were in the noose, their doom sealed.
With a dark look, the wily fighter Odysseus shouted back,   35
"You dogs! you never imagined I'd return from Troy—
so cocksure that you bled my house to death,
ravished my serving-women—wooed my wife
behind my back while I was still alive!
No fear of the gods who rule the skies up there,   40
no fear that men's revenge might arrive someday—
now all your necks are in the noose—your doom is sealed!"

    Terror gripped them all, blanched their faces white,
each man glancing wildly—how to escape his instant death?
Only Eurymachus had the breath to venture, "If you,   45
you're truly Odysseus of Ithaca, home at last,
you're right to accuse these men of what they've done—
so much reckless outrage here in your palace,
so much on your lands. But here he lies,
quite dead, and he incited it all—Antinous—   50
look, the man who drove us all to crime!
Not that he needed marriage, craved it so;
he'd bigger game in mind—though Zeus barred his way—
he'd lord it over Ithaca's handsome country, king himself,

once he'd lain in wait for your son and cut him down!   55
But now he's received the death that he deserved.
So spare your own people! Later we'll recoup
your costs with a tax laid down upon the land,
covering all we ate and drank inside your halls,
and each of us here will pay full measure too—   60
twenty oxen in value, bronze and gold we'll give
until we melt your heart. Before we've settled,
who on earth could blame you for your rage?"

But the battle-master kept on glaring, seething.
"No, Eurymachus! Not if you paid me all your father's wealth—   65
all you possess now, and all that could pour in from the world's end—
no, not even then would I stay my hands from slaughter
till all you suitors had paid for all your crimes!
Now life or death—your choice—fight me or flee
if you hope to escape your sudden bloody doom!   70
I doubt one man in the lot will save his skin!"

His menace shook their knees, their hearts too
but Eurymachus spoke again, now to the suitors: "Friends!
This man will never restrain his hands, invincible hands—
now that he's seized that polished bow and quiver, look,   75
he'll shoot from the sill until he's killed us all!
So fight—call up the joy of battle! Swords out!
Tables lifted—block his arrows winging death!
Charge him, charge in a pack—
try to rout the man from the sill, the doors,   80
race through town and sound an alarm at once—
our friend would soon see he's shot his bolt!"
                                        Brave talk—
he drew his two-edged sword, bronze, honed for the kill
and hurled himself at the king with a raw savage cry
in the same breath that Odysseus loosed an arrow   85
ripping his breast beside the nipple so hard
it lodged in the man's liver—
Out of his grasp the sword dropped to the ground—
over his table, head over heels he tumbled, doubled up,
flinging his food and his two-handled cup across the floor—   90
he smashed the ground with his forehead, writhing in pain,
both feet flailing out, and his high seat tottered—
the mist of death came swirling down his eyes.

Amphinomus rushed the king in all his glory,
charging him face-to-face, a slashing sword drawn—   95
if only he could force him clear of the doorway, now,
but Telemachus—too quick—stabbed the man from behind,
plunging his bronze spear between the suitor's shoulders
and straight on through his chest the point came jutting out—
down he went with a thud, his forehead slammed the ground.   100
Telemachus swerved aside, leaving his long spearshaft
lodged in Amphinomus—fearing some suitor just might

lunge in from behind as he tugged the shaft,
impale him with a sword or hack him down,
crouching over the corpse.   105
He went on the run, reached his father at once
and halting right beside him, let fly, "Father—
now I'll get you a shield and a pair of spears,
a helmet of solid bronze to fit your temples!
I'll arm myself on the way back and hand out   110
arms to the swineherd, arm the cowherd too—
we'd better fight equipped!"
                                 "Run, fetch them,"
the wily captain urged, "while I've got arrows left
to defend me—or they'll force me from the doors
while I fight on alone!"   115

    Telemachus moved to his father's orders smartly.
Off he ran to the room where the famous arms lay stored,
took up four shields, eight spears, four bronze helmets
ridged with horsehair crests and, loaded with these,
ran back to reach his father's side in no time.   120
The prince was first to case himself in bronze
and his servants followed suit—both harnessed up
and all three flanked Odysseus, mastermind of war,
and he, as long as he'd arrows left to defend himself,
kept picking suitors off in the palace, one by one   125
and down they went, corpse on corpse in droves.
Then, when the royal archer's shafts ran out,
he leaned his bow on a post of the massive doors—
where walls of the hallway catch the light—and armed:
across his shoulder he slung a buckler four plies thick,   130
over his powerful head he set a well-forged helmet,
the horsehair crest atop it tossing, bristling terror,
and grasped two rugged lances tipped with fiery bronze.

    Now a side-door was fitted into the main wall—
right at the edge of the great hall's stone sill—   135
and led to a passage always shut by good tight boards.
But Odysseus gave the swineherd strict commands
to stand hard by the side-door, guard it well—
the only way the suitors might break out.
Agelaus called to his comrades with a plan: 140
"Friends, can't someone climb through the hatch?—
tell men outside to sound the alarm, be quick—
our guest would soon see he'd shot his last!"

    The goatherd Melanthius answered, "Not a chance,
my lord—the door to the courtyard's much too near,   145
dangerous too, the mouth of the passage cramped.
One strong man could block us, one and all!
No, I'll fetch you some armor to harness on,
out of the storeroom—there, nowhere else, I'm sure,
the king and his gallant son have stowed their arms!"   150

With that the goatherd clambered up through smoke-ducts
high on the wall and scurried into Odysseus' storeroom,
bundled a dozen shields, as many spears and helmets
ridged with horsehair crests and, loaded with these,
rushed back down to the suitors, quickly issued arms.   155
Odysseus' knees shook, his heart too, when he saw them
buckling on their armor, brandishing long spears—
here was a battle looming, well he knew.
He turned at once to Telemachus, warnings flying:
"A bad break in the fight, my boy! One of the women's   160
tipped the odds against us—or could it be the goatherd?"

    "My fault, father," the cool clear prince replied,
"the blame's all mine. That snug door to the vault,
I left it ajar—they've kept a better watch than I.   165
Go, Eumaeus, shut the door to the storeroom,
check and see if it's one of the women's tricks
or Dolius' son Melanthius. He's our man, I'd say."

    And even as they conspired, back the goatherd
climbed to the room to fetch more burnished arms,
but Eumaeus spotted him, quickly told his king   170
who stood close by: "Odysseus, wily captain,
there he goes again, the infernal nuisance—
just as we suspected—back to the storeroom.
Give me a clear command!
Do I kill the man—if I can take him down—   175
or drag him back to you, here, to pay in full
for the vicious work he's plotted in your house?"

    Odysseus, master of tactics, answered briskly,
"I and the prince will keep these brazen suitors
crammed in the hall, for all their battle-fury.   180
You two wrench Melanthius' arms and legs behind him,
fling him down in the storeroom—lash his back to a plank
and strap a twisted cable fast to the scoundrel's body,
hoist him up a column until he hits the rafters—
let him dangle in agony, still alive,   185
for a good long time!"

    They hung on his orders, keen to do his will.
Off they ran to the storeroom, unseen by him inside—
Melanthius, rummaging after arms, deep in a dark recess
as the two men took their stand, either side the doorposts,   190
poised till the goatherd tried to cross the doorsill . . .
one hand clutching a crested helmet, the other
an ample old buckler blotched with mildew,
the shield Laertes bore as a young soldier once
but there it lay for ages, seams on the handstraps split—   195
Quick, they rushed him, seized him, haled him back by the hair,
flung him down on the floor, writhing with terror, bound him
hand and foot with a chafing cord, wrenched his limbs

back, back till the joints locked tight—
just as Laertes' cunning son commanded—   200
they strapped a twisted cable round his body,
hoisted him up a column until he hit the rafters,
then you mocked him, Eumaeus, my good swineherd:
"Now stand guard through the whole night, Melanthius—
stretched out on a soft bed fit for *you*, your highness!   205
You're bound to see the Morning rising up from the Ocean,
mounting her golden throne—at just the hour you always
drive in goats to feast the suitors in the hall!"

So they left him, trussed in his agonizing sling;
they clapped on armor again, shut the gleaming doors   210
and ran to rejoin Odysseus, mastermind of war.
And now as the ranks squared off, breathing fury—
four at the sill confronting a larger, stronger force
arrayed inside the hall—now Zeus's daughter Athena,
taking the build and voice of Mentor, swept in   215
and Odysseus, thrilled to see her, cried out,
"Rescue us, Mentor, now it's life or death!
Remember your old comrade—all the service
I offered you! We were boys together!"
                                        So he cried
yet knew in his bones it was Athena, Driver of Armies.   220
But across the hall the suitors brayed against her,
Agelaus first, his outburst full of threats:
"Mentor, never let Odysseus trick you into
siding with *him* to fight against the suitors.
Here's our plan of action, and we will see it through!   225
Once we've killed them both, the father and the son,
we'll kill you too, for all you're bent on doing
here in the halls—you'll pay with your own head!
And once our swords have stopped your violence cold—
all your property, all in your house, your fields,   230
we'll lump it all with Odysseus' rich estate
and never let your sons live on in your halls
or free your wife and daughters to walk through town!"

Naked threats—and Athena hit new heights of rage,
she lashed out at Odysseus now with blazing accusations: 235
"Where's it gone, Odysseus—your power, your fighting heart?
The great soldier who fought for famous white-armed Helen,
battling Trojans nine long years—nonstop, no mercy,
mowing their armies down in grueling battle—
you who seized the broad streets of Troy   240
with your fine strategic stroke! How can you—
now you've returned to your own house, your own wealth—
bewail the loss of your combat strength in a war with *suitors*?
Come, old friend, stand by me! You'll see action now,
see how Mentor the son of Alcimus, that brave fighter,   245
kills your enemies, pays you back for service!"
                                        Rousing words—

but she gave no all-out turning of the tide, not yet,
she kept on testing Odysseus and his gallant son,
putting their force and fighting heart to proof.
For all the world like a swallow in their sight   250
she flew on high to perch
on the great hall's central roofbeam black with smoke.

But the suitors closed ranks, commanded now by Damastor's son
Agelaus, flanked by Eurynomus, Demoptolemus and Amphimedon,
Pisander, Polyctor's son, and Polybus ready, waiting—   255
head and shoulders the best and bravest of the lot
still left to fight for their lives,
now that the pelting shafts had killed the rest.
Agelaus spurred his comrades on with battle-plans:
"Friends, at last the man's invincible hands are useless!   260
Mentor has mouthed some empty boasts and flitted off—
just four are left to fight at the front doors. So now,
no wasting your long spears—all at a single hurl,
just six of us launch out in the first wave!
If Zeus is willing, we may hit Odysseus,   265
carry off the glory! The rest are nothing
once the captain's down!"
                           At his command,
concentrating their shots, all six hurled as one
but Athena sent the whole salvo wide of the mark—
one of them hit the jamb of the great hall's doors,   270
another the massive door itself, and the heavy bronze point
of a third ashen javelin crashed against the wall.
Seeing his men untouched by the suitors' flurry,
steady Odysseus leapt to take command:
"Friends! now it's for *us* to hurl at them, I say,   275
into this ruck of suitors! Topping all their crimes
they're mad to strip the armor off our bodies!"

Taking aim at the ranks, all four let fly as one
and the lances struck home—Odysseus killed Demoptolemus,
Telemachus killed Euryades—the swineherd, Elatus—   280
and the cowherd cut Pisander down in blood.
They bit the dust of the broad floor, all as one.
Back to the great hall's far recess the others shrank
as the four rushed in and plucked up spears from corpses.

And again the suitors hurled their whetted shafts   285
but Athena sent the better part of the salvo wide—
one of them hit the jamb of the great hall's doors,
another the massive door itself, and the heavy bronze point
of a third ashen javelin crashed against the wall.
True, Amphimedon nicked Telemachus on the wrist—   290
the glancing blade just barely broke his skin.
Ctesippus sent a long spear sailing over
Eumaeus' buckler, grazing his shoulder blade

but the weapon skittered off and hit the ground.
And again those led by the brilliant battle-master   295
hurled their razor spears at the suitors' ranks—
and now Odysseus raider of cities hit Eurydamas,
Telemachus hit Amphimedon—Eumaeus, Polybus—
and the cowherd stabbed Ctesippus
right in the man's chest and triumphed over his body: 300
"Love your mockery, do you? Son of that blowhard Polytherses!
No more shooting off your mouth, you idiot, such big talk—
leave the last word to the gods—they're much stronger!
Take this spear, this guest-gift, for the cow's hoof
you once gave King Odysseus begging in his house!"   305

     So the master of longhorn cattle had his say—
as Odysseus, fighting at close quarters, ran Agelaus
through with a long lance—Telemachus speared Leocritus
so deep in the groin the bronze came punching out his back
and the man crashed headfirst, slamming the ground full-face.   310
And now Athena, looming out of the rafters high above them,
brandished her man-destroying shield of thunder, terrifying
the suitors out of their minds, and down the hall they panicked—
wild, like herds stampeding, driven mad as the darting gadfly
strikes in the late spring when the long days come round.   315
The attackers struck like eagles, crook-clawed, hook-beaked,
swooping down from a mountain ridge to harry smaller birds
that skim across the flatland, cringing under the clouds
but the eagles plunge in fury, rip their lives out—hopeless,
never a chance of flight or rescue—and people love the sport—   320
so the attackers routed suitors headlong down the hall,
wheeling into the slaughter, slashing left and right
and grisly screams broke from skulls cracked open—
the whole floor awash with blood.
                                     Leodes now—
he flung himself at Odysseus, clutched his knees,   325
crying out to the king with a sudden, winging prayer:
"I hug your knees, Odysseus—mercy! spare my life!
Never, I swear, did I harass any woman in your house—
never a word, a gesture—nothing, no, I tried
to restrain the suitors, whoever did such things.   330
They wouldn't listen, keep their hands to themselves—
so reckless, so they earn their shameful fate.
But I was just their prophet—
my hands are clean—and I'm to die their death!
Look at the thanks I get for years of service!"   335

     A killing look, and the wry soldier answered,
"Only a priest, a prophet for this mob, you say?
How hard you must have prayed in my own house
that the heady day of my return would never dawn—
my dear wife would be yours, would bear your children!   340
For that there's no escape from grueling death—you die!"

And snatching up in one powerful hand a sword
left on the ground—Agelaus dropped it when he fell—
Odysseus hacked the prophet square across the neck
and the praying head went tumbling in the dust.
                                         Now one was left,   345
trying still to escape black death. Phemius, Terpis' son,
the bard who always performed among the suitors—
they forced the man to sing . . .
There he stood, backing into the side-door,
still clutching his ringing lyre in his hands,   350
his mind in turmoil, torn—what should he do?
Steal from the hall and crouch at the altar-stone
of Zeus who Guards the Court,[2] where time and again
Odysseus and Laertes burned the long thighs of oxen?
Or throw himself on the master's mercy, clasp his knees?   355
That was the better way—or so it struck him, yes,
grasp the knees of Laertes' royal son. And so,
cradling his hollow lyre, he laid it on the ground
between the mixing-bowl and the silver-studded throne,
then rushed up to Odysseus, yes, and clutched his knees,   360
singing out to his king with a stirring, winged prayer:
"I hug your knees, Odysseus—mercy! spare my life!
What a grief it will be to you for all the years to come
if you kill the singer now, who sings for gods and men.
I taught myself the craft, but a god has planted   365
deep in my spirit all the paths of song—
songs I'm fit to sing for you as for a god.
Calm your bloodlust now—don't take my head!
He'd bear me out, your own dear son Telemachus—
never of *my* own will, never for any gain did I   370
perform in your house, singing after the suitors
had their feasts. They were too strong, too many—
they forced me to come and sing—I had no choice!"

        The inspired Prince Telemachus heard his pleas
and quickly said to his father close beside him,   375
"Stop, don't cut him down! This one's innocent.
So is the herald Medon—the one who always
tended me in the house when I was little—
spare him too. Unless he's dead by now,
killed by Philoetius or Eumaeus here—   380
or ran into *you* rampaging through the halls."

        The herald pricked up his anxious ears at that . . .
cautious soul, he cowered, trembling, under a chair—
wrapped in an oxhide freshly stripped—to dodge black death.
He jumped in a flash from there, threw off the smelly hide   385
and scuttling up to Telemachus, clutching his knees,
the herald begged for life in words that fluttered:
"Here I am, dear boy—spare me! Tell your father,

---

2. Zeus Herkeios, who had an altar in the courtyard of the house.

flushed with victory, not to kill me with his sword—
enraged as he is with these young lords who bled   390
his palace white and showed you no respect,
the reckless fools!"
                              Breaking into a smile
the canny Odysseus reassured him, "Courage!
The prince has pulled you through, he's saved you now
so you can take it to heart and tell the next man too: 395
clearly doing good puts doing bad to shame.
Now leave the palace, go and sit outside—
out in the courtyard, clear of the slaughter—
you and the bard with all his many songs.
Wait till I've done some household chores   400
that call for my attention."

    The two men scurried out of the house at once
and crouched at the altar-stone of mighty Zeus—
glancing left and right,
fearing death would strike at any moment.   405

    Odysseus scanned his house to see if any man
still skulked alive, still hoped to avoid black death.
But he found them one and all in blood and dust . . .
great hauls of them down and out like fish that fishermen
drag from the churning gray surf in looped and coiling nets   410
and fling ashore on a sweeping hook of beach—some noble catch
heaped on the sand, twitching, lusting for fresh salt sea
but the Sungod hammers down and burns their lives out . . .
so the suitors lay in heaps, corpse covering corpse.
At last the seasoned fighter turned to his son: 415
"Telemachus, go, call the old nurse here—
I must tell her all that's on my mind."

    Telemachus ran to do his father's bidding,
shook the women's doors, calling Eurycleia:
"Come out now! Up with you, good old woman!   420
You who watch over all the household hands—
quick, my father wants you, needs to have a word!"

    Crisp command that left the old nurse hushed—
she spread the doors to the well-constructed hall,
slipped out in haste, and the prince led her on . . .   425
She found Odysseus in the thick of slaughtered corpses,
splattered with bloody filth like a lion that's devoured
some ox of the field and lopes home, covered with blood,
his chest streaked, both jaws glistening, dripping red—
a sight to strike terror. So Odysseus looked now,   430
splattered with gore, his thighs, his fighting hands,
and she, when she saw the corpses, all the pooling blood,
was about to lift a cry of triumph—here was a great exploit,
look—but the soldier held her back and checked her zeal
with warnings winging home: "Rejoice in your heart,   435

old woman—peace! No cries of triumph now.
It's unholy to glory over the bodies of the dead.
These men the doom of the gods has brought low,
and their own indecent acts. They'd no regard
for any man on earth—good or bad—   440
who chanced to come their way. And so, thanks
to their reckless work, they met this shameful fate.
Quick, report in full on the women in my halls—
who are disloyal to me, who are guiltless?"

                               "Surely, child,"
his fond old nurse replied, "now here's the truth.   445
Fifty women you have inside your house,
women we've trained to do their duties well,
to card the wool and bear the yoke of service.
Some dozen in all went tramping to their shame,
thumbing their noses at me, at the queen herself!   450
And Telemachus, just now come of age—his mother
would never let the boy take charge of the maids.
But let me climb to her well-lit room upstairs
and tell your wife the news—
some god has put the woman fast asleep."   455

    "Don't wake her yet," the crafty man returned,
"you tell those women to hurry here at once—
just the ones who've shamed us all along."

    Away the old nurse bustled through the house
to give the women orders, rush them to the king.   460
Odysseus called Telemachus over, both herdsmen too,
with strict commands: "Start clearing away the bodies.
Make the women pitch in too. Chairs and tables—
scrub them down with sponges, rinse them clean.
And once you've put the entire house in order,   465
march the women out of the great hall—between
the roundhouse and the courtyard's strong stockade—
and hack them with your swords, slash out all their lives—
blot out of their minds the joys of love they relished
under the suitors' bodies, rutting on the sly!"   470

    The women crowded in, huddling all together . . .
wailing convulsively, streaming live warm tears.
First they carried out the bodies of the dead
and propped them under the courtyard colonnade,
standing them one against another. Odysseus   475
shouted commands himself, moving things along
and they kept bearing out the bodies—they were forced.
Next they scrubbed down the elegant chairs and tables,
washed them with sopping sponges, rinsed them clean.
Then Telemachus and the herdsmen scraped smooth   480
the packed earth floor of the royal house with spades
as the women gathered up the filth and piled it outside.
And then, at last, once the entire house was put in order,

they marched the women out of the great hall—between
the roundhouse and the courtyard's strong stockade—   485
crammed them into a dead end, no way out from there,
and stern Telemachus gave the men their orders:
"No clean death[3] for the likes of them, by god!
Not from me—they showered abuse on my head,
my mother's too!
                           You sluts—the suitors' whores!"   490

    With that, taking a cable used on a dark-prowed ship
he coiled it over the roundhouse, lashed it fast to a tall column,
hoisting it up so high no toes could touch the ground.
Then, as doves or thrushes beating their spread wings
against some snare rigged up in thickets—flying in   495
for a cozy nest but a grisly bed receives them—
so the women's heads were trapped in a line,
nooses yanking their necks up, one by one
so all might die a pitiful, ghastly death . . .
they kicked up heels for a little—not for long.
                           Melanthius?   500
They hauled him out through the doorway, into the court,
lopped his nose and ears with a ruthless knife,
tore his genitals out for the dogs to eat raw
and in manic fury hacked off hands and feet.
                           Then,
once they'd washed their own hands and feet,   505
they went inside again to join Odysseus.
Their work was done with now.
But the king turned to devoted Eurycleia, saying,
"Bring sulfur, nurse, to scour all this pollution—
bring me fire too, so I can fumigate the house.   510
And call Penelope here with all her women—
tell all the maids to come back in at once."

    "Well said, my boy," his old nurse replied,
"right to the point. But wait,
let me fetch you a shirt and cloak to wrap you.   515
No more dawdling round the palace, nothing but rags
to cover those broad shoulders—it's a scandal!"

    "Fire first," the good soldier answered.
"Light me a fire to purify this house."

    The devoted nurse snapped to his command,   520
brought her master fire and brimstone. Odysseus
purged his palace, halls and court, with cleansing fumes.

    Then back through the royal house the old nurse went
to tell the women the news and bring them in at once.
They came crowding out of their quarters, torch in hand,   525

3. I.e., by sword or spear. Hanging was considered an ignominious way to die.

flung their arms around Odysseus, hugged him, home at last,
and kissed his head and shoulders, seized his hands, and he,
overcome by a lovely longing, broke down and wept . . .
deep in his heart he knew them one and all.

BOOK XXIII

[The Great Rooted Bed]

Up to the rooms the old nurse clambered, chuckling all the way,
to tell the queen her husband was here now, home at last.
Her knees bustling, feet shuffling over each other,
till hovering at her mistress' head she spoke:
"Penelope—child—wake up and see for yourself,   5
with your own eyes, all you dreamed of, all your days!
He's here—Odysseus—he's come home, at long last!
He's killed the suitors, swaggering young brutes
who plagued his house, wolfed his cattle down,
rode roughshod over his son!"   10

        "Dear old nurse," wary Penelope replied,
"the gods have made you mad. They have that power,
putting lunacy into the clearest head around
or setting a half-wit on the path to sense.
They've unhinged you, and you were once so sane.   15
Why do you mock me?—haven't I wept enough?—
telling such wild stories, interrupting my sleep,
sweet sleep that held me, sealed my eyes just now.
Not once have I slept so soundly since the day
Odysseus sailed away to see that cursed city . . .   20
Destroy, I call it—I hate to say its name!
Now down you go. Back to your own quarters.
If any other woman of mine had come to me,
rousing me out of sleep with such a tale,
I'd have her bundled back to her room in pain.   25
It's only your old gray head that spares you that!"

        "Never"—the fond old nurse kept pressing on—
"dear child, I'd never mock you! No, it's all true,
he's here—Odysseus—he's come home, just as I tell you!
He's the stranger they all manhandled in the hall.   30
Telemachus knew he was here, for days and days,
but he knew enough to hide his father's plans
so he could pay those vipers back in kind!"

        Penelope's heart burst in joy, she leapt from bed,
her eyes streaming tears, she hugged the old nurse   35
and cried out with an eager, winging word,
"Please, dear one, give me the whole story.
If he's really home again, just as you tell me,
how did he get those shameless suitors in his clutches?—
single-handed, braving an army always camped inside."   40

"I have no idea," the devoted nurse replied.
"I didn't see it, I didn't ask—all I heard
was the choking groans of men cut down in blood.
We crouched in terror—a dark nook of our quarters—
all of us locked tight behind those snug doors   45
till your boy Telemachus came and called me out—
his father rushed him there to do just that. And then
I found Odysseus in the thick of slaughtered corpses;
there he stood and all around him, over the beaten floor,
the bodies sprawled in heaps, lying one on another . . .   50
How it would have thrilled your heart to see him—
splattered with bloody filth, a lion with his kill!
And now they're all stacked at the courtyard gates—
he's lit a roaring fire,
he's purifying the house with cleansing fumes   55
and he's sent me here to bring you back to him.
Follow me down! So now, after all the years of grief,
you two can embark, loving hearts, along the road to joy.
Look, your dreams, put off so long, come true at last—
he's back alive, home at his hearth, and found you,   60
found his son still here. And all those suitors
who did him wrong, he's paid them back, he has,
right in his own house!"
                    "Hush, dear woman,"
guarded Penelope cautioned her at once.
"Don't laugh, don't cry in triumph—not yet.   65
You know how welcome the sight of him would be
to all in the house, and to me most of all
and the son we bore together.
But the story can't be true, not as you tell it,
no, it must be a god who's killed our brazen friends—   70
up in arms at their outrage, heartbreaking crimes.
They'd no regard for any man on earth—
good or bad—who chanced to come their way. So,
thanks to their reckless work they die their deaths.
Odysseus? Far from Achaea now, he's lost all hope   75
of coming home . . . he's lost and gone himself."

    "Child," the devoted old nurse protested,
"what nonsense you let slip through your teeth.
Here's your husband, warming his hands at his own hearth,
here—and you, you say he'll never come home again,   80
always the soul of trust! All right, this too—
I'll give you a sign, a proof that's plain as day.
That scar, made years ago by a boar's white tusk—
I spotted the scar myself, when I washed his feet,
and I tried to tell you, ah, but he, the crafty rascal,   85
clamped his hand on my mouth—I couldn't say a word.
Follow me down now. I'll stake my life on it:
if I am lying to *you*—
kill me with a thousand knives of pain!"

"Dear old nurse," composed Penelope responded,   90
"deep as you are, my friend, you'll find it hard
to plumb the plans of the everlasting gods.
All the same, let's go and join my son
so I can see the suitors lying dead
and see . . . the one who killed them."
                  With that thought   95
Penelope started down from her lofty room, her heart
in turmoil, torn . . . should she keep her distance,
probe her husband? Or rush up to the man at once
and kiss his head and cling to both his hands?
As soon as she stepped across the stone threshold,   100
slipping in, she took a seat at the closest wall
and radiant in the firelight, faced Odysseus now.
There he sat, leaning against the great central column,
eyes fixed on the ground, waiting, poised for whatever words
his hardy wife might say when she caught sight of him.   105
A long while she sat in silence . . . numbing wonder
filled her heart as her eyes explored his face.
One moment he seemed . . . Odysseus, to the life—
the next, no, he was not the man she knew,
a huddled mass of rags was all she saw.   110

"Oh mother," Telemachus reproached her,
"cruel mother, you with your hard heart!
Why do you spurn my father so—why don't you
sit beside him, engage him, ask him questions?
What other wife could have a spirit so unbending?   115
Holding back from her husband, home at last for *her*
after bearing twenty years of brutal struggle—
your heart was always harder than a rock!"
                      "My child,"
Penelope, well-aware, explained, "I'm stunned with wonder,
powerless. Cannot speak to him ask him questions,   120
look him in the eyes . . . But if he is truly
Odysseus, home at last, make no mistake:
we two will know each other, even better—
we two have secret signs,
known to us both but hidden from the world."   125

Odysseus, long-enduring, broke into a smile
and turned to his son with pointed, winging words:
"Leave your mother here in the hall to test me
as she will. She soon will know me better.
Now because I am filthy, wear such grimy rags,   130
she spurns me—your mother still can't bring herself
to believe I am her husband.
               But you and I,
put heads together. What's our best defense?
When someone kills a lone man in the realm
who leaves behind him no great band of avengers,   135
still the killer flees, goodbye to kin and country.

But *we* brought down the best of the island's princes,
the pillars of Ithaca. Weigh it well, I urge you."

"Look to it all yourself now, father," his son
deferred at once. "You are the best on earth,   140
they say, when it comes to mapping tactics.
No one, no mortal man, can touch you there.
But we're behind you, hearts intent on battle,
nor do I think you'll find us short on courage,
long as our strength will last."
      "Then here's our plan,"   145
the master of tactics said. "I think it's best.
First go and wash, and pull fresh tunics on
and tell the maids in the hall to dress well too.
And let the inspired bard take up his ringing lyre
and lead off for us all a dance so full of heart   150
that whoever hears the strains outside the gates—
a passerby on the road, a neighbor round about—
will think it's a wedding-feast that's under way.
No news of the suitors' death must spread through town
till we have slipped away to our own estates,   155
our orchard green with trees. There we'll see
what winning strategy Zeus will hand us then."

 They hung on his words and moved to orders smartly.
First they washed and pulled fresh tunics on,
the women arrayed themselves—the inspired bard   160
struck up his resounding lyre and stirred in all
a desire for dance and song, the lovely lilting beat,
till the great house echoed round to the measured tread
of dancing men in motion, women sashed and lithe.
And whoever heard the strains outside would say,   165
"A miracle—someone's married the queen at last!"

"One of her hundred suitors."
      "That callous woman,
too faithless to keep her lord and master's house
to the bitter end—"
     "Till he came sailing home."

 So they'd say, blind to what had happened: 170
the great-hearted Odysseus was home again at last.
The maid Eurynome bathed him, rubbed him down with oil
and drew around him a royal cape and choice tunic too.
And Athena crowned the man with beauty, head to foot,
made him taller to all eyes, his build more massive,   175
yes, and down from his brow the great goddess
ran his curls like thick hyacinth clusters
full of blooms. As a master craftsman washes
gold over beaten silver—a man the god of fire
and Queen Athena trained in every fine technique—   180
and finishes off his latest effort, handsome work . . .

so she lavished splendor over his head and shoulders now.
He stepped from his bath, glistening like a god,
and back he went to the seat that he had left
and facing his wife, declared,
"Strange woman! So hard—the gods of Olympus   185
made you harder than any other woman in the world!
What other wife could have a spirit so unbending?
Holding back from her husband, home at last for *her*
after bearing twenty years of brutal struggle.   190
Come, nurse, make me a bed, I'll sleep alone.
She has a heart of iron in her breast."

                               "Strange *man*,"
wary Penelope said. "I'm not so proud, so scornful,
nor am I overwhelmed by your quick change . . .
You look—how well I know—the way he looked,   195
setting sail from Ithaca years ago
aboard the long-oared ship.

                     Come, Eurycleia,
move the sturdy bedstead out of our bridal chamber—
that room the master built with his own hands.
Take it out now, sturdy bed that it is,   200
and spread it deep with fleece,
blankets and lustrous throws to keep him warm."

     Putting her husband to the proof—but Odysseus
blazed up in fury, lashing out at his loyal wife:
"Woman—your words, they cut me to the core!   205
Who could move my bed? Impossible task,
even for some skilled craftsman—unless a god
came down in person, quick to lend a hand,
lifted it out with ease and moved it elsewhere.
Not a man on earth, not even at peak strength,   210
would find it easy to prise it up and shift it, no,
a great sign, a hallmark lies in its construction.
I know, I built it myself—no one else . . .
There was a branching olive-tree inside our court,
grown to its full prime, the bole like a column, thickset.   215
Around it I built my bedroom, finished off the walls
with good tight stonework, roofed it over soundly
and added doors, hung well and snugly wedged.
Then I lopped the leafy crown of the olive,
clean-cutting the stump bare from roots up,   220
planing it round with a bronze smoothing-adze—
I had the skill—I shaped it plumb to the line to make
my bedpost, bored the holes it needed with an auger.
Working from there I built my bed, start to finish,
I gave it ivory inlays, gold and silver fittings,   225
wove the straps across it, oxhide gleaming red.
There's our secret sign, I tell you, our life story!
Does the bed, my lady, still stand planted firm?—
I don't know—or has someone chopped away

that olive-trunk and hauled our bedstead off?"

Living proof— 230

Penelope felt her knees go slack, her heart surrender,
recognizing the strong clear signs Odysseus offered.
She dissolved in tears, rushed to Odysseus, flung her arms
around his neck and kissed his head and cried out,
"Odysseus—don't flare up at me now, not you, 235
always the most understanding man alive!
The gods, it was the gods who sent us sorrow—
they grudged us both a life in each other's arms
from the heady zest of youth to the stoop of old age.
But don't fault me, angry with me now because I failed, 240
at the first glimpse, to greet you, hold you, so . . .
In my heart of hearts I always cringed with fear
some fraud might come, beguile me with his talk;
the world is full of the sort,
cunning ones who plot their own dark ends. 245
Remember Helen of Argos, Zeus's daughter—
would *she* have sported so in a stranger's bed
if she had dreamed that Achaea's sons were doomed
to fight and die to bring her home again?
Some god spurred her to do her shameless work. 250
Not till then did her mind conceive that madness,
blinding madness that caused her anguish, ours as well.
But now, since you have revealed such overwhelming proof—
the secret sign of our bed, which no one's ever seen
but you and I and a single handmaid, Actoris, 255
the servant my father gave me when I came,
who kept the doors of our room you built so well . . .
you've conquered my heart, my hard heart, at last!"

The more she spoke, the more a deep desire for tears
welled up inside his breast—he wept as he held the wife 260
he loved, the soul of loyalty, in his arms at last.
Joy, warm as the joy that shipwrecked sailors feel
when they catch sight of land—Poseidon has struck
their well-rigged ship on the open sea with gale winds
and crushing walls of waves, and only a few escape, swimming, 265
struggling out of the frothing surf to reach the shore,
their bodies crusted with salt but buoyed up with joy
as they plant their feet on solid ground again,
spared a deadly fate. So joyous now to her
the sight of her husband, vivid in her gaze, 270
that her white arms, embracing his neck
would never for a moment let him go . . .
Dawn with her rose-red fingers might have shone
upon their tears, if with her glinting eyes
Athena had not thought of one more thing. 275
She held back the night, and night lingered long
at the western edge of the earth, while in the east
she reined in Dawn of the golden throne at Ocean's banks,

commanding her not to yoke the windswift team that brings men
    light,
Blaze and Aurora, the young colts that race the Morning on.   280
Yet now Odysseus, seasoned veteran, said to his wife,
"Dear woman . . . we have still not reached the end
of all our trials. One more labor lies in store—
boundless, laden with danger, great and long,
and I must brave it out from start to finish.   285
So the ghost of Tiresias prophesied to me,
the day that I went down to the House of Death
to learn our best route home, my comrades' and my own.
But come, let's go to bed, dear woman—at long last
delight in sleep, delight in each other, come!"   290

    "If it's bed you want," reserved Penelope replied,
"it's bed you'll have, whenever the spirit moves,
now that the gods have brought you home again
to native land, your grand and gracious house.
But since you've alluded to it,   295
since a god has put it in your mind,
please, tell me about this trial still to come.
I'm bound to learn of it later, I am sure—
what's the harm if I hear of it tonight?"
                           "Still so strange,"
Odysseus, the old master of stories, answered.   300
"Why again, why force me to tell you all?
Well, tell I shall. I'll hide nothing now.
But little joy it will bring you, I'm afraid,
as little joy for me.
               The prophet said
that I must rove through towns on towns of men,   305
that I must carry a well-planed oar until
I come to a people who know nothing of the sea,
whose food is never seasoned with salt, strangers all
to ships with their crimson prows and long slim oars,
wings that make ships fly. And here is my sign,   310
he told me, clear, so clear I cannot miss it,
and I will share it with you now . . .
When another traveler falls in with me and calls
that weight across my shoulder a fan to winnow grain,
then, he told me, I must plant my oar in the earth   315
and sacrifice fine beasts to the lord god of the sea,
Poseidon—a ram, a bull and a ramping wild boar—
then journey home and render noble offerings up
to the deathless gods who rule the vaulting skies,
to all the gods in order.   320
And at last my own death will steal upon me . . .
a gentle, painless death, far from the sea it comes
to take me down, borne down with the years in ripe old age
with all my people here in blessed peace around me.
All this, the prophet said, will come to pass."   325

"And so," Penelope said, in her great wisdom,
"if the gods will really grant a happier old age,
there's hope that we'll escape our trials at last."

So husband and wife confided in each other,
while nurse and Eurynome, under the flaring brands,   330
were making up the bed with coverings deep and soft.
And working briskly, soon as they'd made it snug,
back to her room the old nurse went to sleep
as Eurynome, their attendant, torch in hand,
lighted the royal couple's way to bed and,   335
leading them to their chamber, slipped away.
Rejoicing in each other, they returned to their bed,
the old familiar place they loved so well.[4]

Now Telemachus, the cowherd and the swineherd
rested their dancing feet and had the women do the same,   340
and across the shadowed hall the men lay down to sleep.

But the royal couple, once they'd reveled in all
the longed-for joys of love, reveled in each other's stories,
the radiant woman telling of all she'd borne at home,
watching them there, the infernal crowd of suitors   345
slaughtering herds of cattle and good fat sheep—
while keen to win her hand—
draining the broached vats dry of vintage wine.
And great Odysseus told his wife of all the pains
he had dealt out to other men and all the hardships   350
he'd endured himself—his story first to last—
and she listened on, enchanted . . .
Sleep never sealed her eyes till all was told.

He launched in with how he fought the Cicones down,
then how he came to the Lotus-eaters' lush green land.   355
Then all the crimes of the Cyclops and how he paid him back
for the gallant men the monster ate without a qualm—
then how he visited Aeolus, who gave him a hero's welcome
then he sent him off, but the homeward run was not his fate,
not yet—some sudden squalls snatched him away once more   360
and drove him over the swarming sea, groaning in despair.
Then how he moored at Telepylus, where Laestrygonians
wrecked his fleet and killed his men-at-arms.
He told her of Circe's cunning magic wiles
and how he voyaged down in his long benched ship   365
to the moldering House of Death, to consult Tiresias,
ghostly seer of Thebes, and he saw old comrades there

---

4. Two great Alexandrian critics said that this line was the "end" of the *Odyssey* (though one of the words they are said to have used could mean simply "culmination"). Modern critics are divided; some find the rest of the poem banal, unartistic, full of linguistic anomalies, and so on. But if the poem stops here we are left in suspense about many important themes that have been developed—notably, the question of reprisals for the slaughter in the hall.

and he saw his mother, who bore and reared him as a child.
He told how he caught the Sirens' voices throbbing in the wind
and how he had scudded past the Clashing Rocks, past grim
    Charybdis,   370
past Scylla—whom no rover had ever coasted by, home free—
and how his shipmates slaughtered the cattle of the Sun
and Zeus the king of thunder split his racing ship
with a reeking bolt and killed his hardy comrades,
all his fighting men at a stroke, but he alone   375
escaped their death at sea. He told how he reached
Ogygia's shores and the nymph Calypso held him back,
deep in her arching caverns, craving him for a husband—
cherished him, vowed to make him immortal, ageless, all his days,
yes, but she never won the heart inside him, never . . .   380
then how he reached the Phaeacians—heavy sailing there—
who with all their hearts had prized him like a god
and sent him off in a ship to his own beloved land,
giving him bronze and hoards of gold and robes . . .
and that was the last he told her, just as sleep   385
overcame him . . . sleep loosing his limbs,
slipping the toils of anguish from his mind.

    Athena, her eyes afire, had fresh plans.
Once she thought he'd had his heart's content
of love and sleep at his wife's side, straightaway   390
she roused young Dawn from Ocean's banks to her golden throne
to bring men light and roused Odysseus too, who rose
from his soft bed and advised his wife in parting,
"Dear woman, we both have had our fill of trials.
You in our house, weeping over my journey home,   395
fraught with storms and torment, true, and I,
pinned down in pain by Zeus and other gods,
for all my desire, blocked from reaching home.
But now that we've arrived at our bed together—
the reunion that we yearned for all those years—   400
look after the things still left me in our house.
But as for the flocks those brazen suitors plundered,
much I'll recoup myself, making many raids;
the rest our fellow-Ithacans will supply
till all my folds are full of sheep again.   405
But now I must be off to the upland farm,
our orchard green with trees, to see my father,
good old man weighed down with so much grief for me.
And you, dear woman, sensible as you are,
I would advise you, still . . .   410
quick as the rising sun the news will spread
of the suitors that I killed inside the house.
So climb to your lofty chamber with your women.
Sit tight there. See no one. Question no one."

    He strapped his burnished armor round his shoulders,   415
roused Telemachus, the cowherd and the swineherd,

and told them to take up weapons honed for battle.
They snapped to commands, harnessed up in bronze,
opened the doors and strode out, Odysseus in the lead.
By now the daylight covered the land, but Pallas,   420
shrouding them all in darkness,
quickly led the four men out of town.

BOOK XXIV

[Peace]

Now Cyllenian[5] Hermes called away the suitors' ghosts,
holding firm in his hand the wand of fine pure gold
that enchants the eyes of men whenever Hermes wants
or wakes us up from sleep.
With a wave of this he stirred and led them on[6]   5
and the ghosts trailed after with high thin cries
as bats cry in the depths of a dark haunted cavern,
shrilling, flittering, wild when one drops from the chain—
slipped from the rock face, while the rest cling tight . . .
So with their high thin cries the ghosts flocked now   10
and Hermes the Healer led them on, and down the dank
moldering paths and past the Ocean's streams they went
and past the White Rock and the Sun's Western Gates and past
the Land of Dreams, and they soon reached the fields of asphodel
where the dead, the burnt-out wraiths of mortals, make their home.   15

    There they found the ghosts of Peleus' son Achilles,
Patroclus, fearless Antilochus—and Great Ajax too,
the first in stature, first in build and bearing
of all the Argives after Peleus' matchless son.
They had grouped around Achilles' ghost, and now   20
the shade of Atreus' son Agamemnon marched toward them—
fraught with grief and flanked by all his comrades,
troops of his men-at-arms who died beside him,
who met their fate in lord Aegisthus' halls.
Achilles' ghost was first to greet him: "Agamemnon,   25
you were the one, we thought, of all our fighting princes
Zeus who loves the lightning favored most, all your days,
because you commanded such a powerful host of men
on the fields of Troy where we Achaeans suffered.
But you were doomed to encounter fate so early,   30
you too, yet no one born escapes its deadly force.
If only you had died your death in the full flush
of the glory you had mastered—died on Trojan soil!
Then all united Achaea would have raised your tomb
and you'd have won your son great fame for years to come.   35
Not so. You were fated to die a wretched death."

    And the ghost of Atrides Agamemnon answered,
"Son of Peleus, great godlike Achilles! Happy man,

---

5. Cyllene, a mountain in Arcadia (near the center of the Peloponnesus), was Hermes' birthplace.
6. One of Hermes' many functions is to guide the souls of the dead to the underworld.

you died on the fields of Troy, a world away from home,
and the best of Trojan and Argive champions died around you, 40
fighting for your corpse. And you . . . there you lay
in the whirling dust, overpowered in all your power
and wiped from memory all your horseman's skills.
That whole day we fought, we'd never have stopped
if Zeus had not stopped *us* with sudden gales. 45
Then we bore you out of the fighting, onto the ships,
we laid you down on a litter, cleansed your handsome flesh
with warm water and soothing oils, and round your body
troops of Danaans wept hot tears and cut their locks.
Hearing the news, your mother, Thetis, rose from the sea, 50
immortal sea-nymphs in her wake, and a strange unearthly cry
came throbbing over the ocean. Terror gripped Achaea's armies,
they would have leapt in panic, boarded the long hollow ships
if one man, deep in his age-old wisdom, had not checked them:
Nestor—from the first his counsel always seemed the best, 55
and now, concerned for the ranks, he rose and shouted,
'Hold fast, Argives! Sons of Achaea, don't run now!
This is Achilles' mother rising from the sea
with all her immortal sea-nymphs—
she longs to join her son who died in battle!' 60
That stopped our panicked forces in their tracks
as the Old Man of the Sea's daughters gathered round you—
wailing, heartsick—dressed you in ambrosial, deathless robes
and the Muses, nine in all, voice-to-voice in choirs,
their vibrant music rising, raised your dirge. 65
Not one soldier would you have seen dry-eyed,
the Muses' song so pierced us to the heart.
For seventeen days unbroken, days and nights
we mourned you—immortal gods and mortal men.
At the eighteenth dawn we gave you to the flames 70
and slaughtered around your body droves of fat sheep
and shambling longhorn cattle, and you were burned
in the garments of the gods and laved with soothing oils
and honey running sweet, and a long cortege of Argive heroes
paraded in review, in battle armor round your blazing pyre, 75
men in chariots, men on foot—a resounding roar went up.
And once the god of fire had burned your corpse to ash,
at first light we gathered your white bones, Achilles,
cured them in strong neat wine and seasoned oils.
Your mother gave us a gold two-handled urn, 80
a gift from Dionysus, she said,
a masterwork of the famous Smith, the god of fire.
Your white bones rest in that, my brilliant Achilles,
mixed with the bones of dead Patroclus, Menoetius' son,
apart from those of Antilochus, whom you treasured 85
more than all other comrades once Patroclus died.
Over your bones we reared a grand, noble tomb—
devoted veterans all, Achaea's combat forces—
high on its jutting headland over the Hellespont's[7]

---

7. The strait separating Asia Minor from Europe, visible from Troy.

broad reach, a landmark glimpsed from far out at sea   90
by men of our own day and men of days to come.
                                               And then
your mother, begging the gods for priceless trophies,
set them out in the ring for all our champions.
You in your day have witnessed funeral games
for many heroes, games to honor the death of kings,   95
when young men cinch their belts, tense to win some prize—
but if you'd laid eyes on these it would have thrilled your heart,
magnificent trophies the goddess, glistening-footed Thetis,
held out in your honor. You were dear to the gods,
so even in death your name will never die . . .   100
Great glory is yours, Achilles,
for all time, in the eyes of all mankind!
                                     But I?
What joy for *me* when the coil of war had wound down?
For my return Zeus hatched a pitiful death
at the hands of Aegisthus—and my accursed wife."   105

    As they exchanged the stories of their fates,
Hermes the guide and giant-killer drew up close to both,
leading down the ghosts of the suitors King Odysseus killed.
Struck by the sight, the two went up to them right away
and the ghost of Atreus' son Agamemnon recognized   110
the noted prince Amphimedon, Melaneus' dear son
who received him once in Ithaca, at his home,
and Atrides' ghost called out to his old friend now,
"Amphimedon, what disaster brings you down to the dark world?
All of you, good picked men, and all in your prime—   115
no captain out to recruit the best in any city
could have chosen better. What laid you low?
Wrecked in the ships when lord Poseidon roused
some punishing blast of gales and heavy breakers?
Or did ranks of enemies mow you down on land   120
as you tried to raid and cut off herds and flocks
or fought to win their city, take their women?
Answer me, tell me. I was once your guest.
Don't you recall the day I came to visit
your house in Ithaca—King Menelaus came too—   125
to urge Odysseus to sail with us in the ships
on our campaign to Troy? And the long slow voyage,
crossing wastes of ocean, cost us one whole month.
That's how hard it was to bring him round,
Odysseus, raider of cities."
                         "Famous Atrides!"   130
Amphimedon's ghost called back. "Lord of men, Agamemnon,
I remember it all, your majesty, as you say,
and I will tell you, start to finish now,
the story of our death,
the brutal end contrived to take us off.   135
We were courting the wife of Odysseus, gone so long.
She neither spurned nor embraced a marriage she despised,
no, she simply planned our death, our black doom!

This was her latest masterpiece of guile:
she set up a great loom in the royal halls   140
and she began to weave, and the weaving finespun,
the yarns endless, and she would lead us on: 'Young men,
my suitors, now that King Odysseus is no more,
go slowly, keen as you are to marry me, until
I can finish off this web . . .   145
so my weaving won't all fray and come to nothing.
This is a shroud for old lord Laertes, for that day
when the deadly fate that lays us out at last will take him down.
I dread the shame my countrywomen would heap upon me,
yes, if a man of such wealth should lie in state   150
without a shroud for cover.'
                          Her very words,
and despite our pride and passion we believed her.
So by day she'd weave at her great and growing web—
by night, by the light of torches set beside her,
she would unravel all she'd done. Three whole years   155
she deceived us blind, seduced us with this scheme . . .
Then, when the wheeling seasons brought the fourth year on
and the months waned and the long days came round once more,
one of her women, in on the queen's secret, told the truth
and we caught her in the act—unweaving her gorgeous web.   160
So she finished it off. Against her will. We forced her.
But just as she bound off that great shroud and washed it,
spread it out—glistening like the sunlight or the moon—
just then some wicked spirit brought Odysseus back,
from god knows where, to the edge of his estate   165
where the swineherd kept his pigs. And back too,
to the same place, came Odysseus' own dear son,
scudding home in his black ship from sandy Pylos.
The pair of them schemed our doom, our deathtrap,
then lit out for town—   170
Telemachus first in fact, Odysseus followed,
later, led by the swineherd, and clad in tatters,
looking for all the world like an old and broken beggar
hunched on a stick, his body wrapped in shameful rags.
Disguised so none of us, not even the older ones,   175
could spot that tramp for the man he really was,
bursting in on us there, out of the blue. No,
we attacked him, blows and insults flying fast,
and he took it all for a time, in his own house,
all the taunts and blows—he had a heart of iron.   180
But once the will of thundering Zeus had roused his blood,
he and Telemachus bore the burnished weapons off
and stowed them deep in a storeroom, shot the bolts
and he—the soul of cunning—told his wife to set
the great bow and the gleaming iron axes out   185
before the suitors—all of us doomed now—
to test our skill and bring our slaughter on . . .
Not one of us had the strength to string that powerful weapon,
all of us fell far short of what it took. But then,

when the bow was coming round to Odysseus' hands,   190
we raised a hue and cry—he must not have it,
no matter how he begged! Only Telemachus
urged him to take it up, and once he got it
in his clutches, long-suffering great Odysseus
strung his bow with ease and shot through all the axes,   195
then, vaulting onto the threshold, stood there poised, and pouring
his flashing arrows out before him, glaring for the kill,
he cut Antinous down, then shot his painful arrows
into the rest of us, aiming straight and true,
and down we went, corpse on corpse in droves.   200
Clearly a god was driving him and all his henchmen,
routing us headlong in their fury down the hall,
wheeling into the slaughter, slashing left and right
and grisly screams broke from skulls cracked open—
the whole floor awash with blood.
                       So we died,   205
Agamemnon . . . our bodies lie untended even now,
strewn in Odysseus' palace. They know nothing yet,
the kin in our houses who might wash our wounds
of clotted gore and lay us out and mourn us.
These are the solemn honors owed the dead."
                         "Happy Odysseus!"   210
Agamemnon's ghost cried out. "Son of old Laertes—
mastermind—what a fine, faithful wife you won!
What good sense resided in your Penelope—
how well Icarius' daughter remembered you,
Odysseus, the man she married once!   215
The fame of her great virtue will never die.
The immortal gods will lift a song for all mankind,
a glorious song in praise of self-possessed Penelope.
A far cry from the daughter of Tyndareus, Clytemnestra—
what outrage she committed, killing the man *she* married once!—   220
yes, and the song men sing of her will ring with loathing.
She brands with a foul name the breed of womankind,
even the honest ones to come!"
                    So they traded stories,
the two ghosts standing there in the House of Death,   225
far in the hidden depths below the earth.

    Odysseus and his men had stridden down from town
and quickly reached Laertes' large, well-tended farm
that the old king himself had wrested from the wilds,
years ago, laboring long and hard. His lodge was here
and around it stretched a row of sheds where fieldhands,   230
bondsmen who did his bidding, sat and ate and slept.
And an old Sicilian woman was in charge,
who faithfully looked after her aged master
out on his good estate remote from town.
Odysseus told his servants and his son,   235
"Into the timbered lodge now, go, quickly,
kill us the fattest porker, fix our meal.

And I will put my father to the test,
see if the old man knows me now, on sight,
or fails to, after twenty years apart." 240

    With that he passed his armor to his men
and in they went at once, his son as well. Odysseus
wandered off, approaching the thriving vineyard, searching,
picking his way down to the great orchard, searching,
but found neither Dolius nor his sons nor any hand. 245
They'd just gone off, old Dolius in the lead,
to gather stones for a dry retaining wall
to shore the vineyard up. But he did find
his father, alone, on that well-worked plot,
spading round a sapling—clad in filthy rags, 250
in a patched, unseemly shirt, and round his shins
he had some oxhide leggings strapped, patched too,
to keep from getting scraped, and gloves on his hands
to fight against the thorns, and on his head
he wore a goatskin skullcap 255
to cultivate his misery that much more . . .
Long-enduring Odysseus, catching sight of him now—
a man worn down with years, his heart racked with sorrow—
halted under a branching pear-tree, paused and wept.
Debating, head and heart, what should he do now? 260
Kiss and embrace his father, pour out the long tale—
how he had made the journey home to native land—
or probe him first and test him every way?
Torn, mulling it over, this seemed better:
test the old man first, 265
reproach him with words that cut him to the core.
Convinced, Odysseus went right up to his father.
Laertes was digging round the sapling, head bent low
as his famous offspring hovered over him and began,
"You want no skill, old man, at tending a garden. 270
All's well-kept here; not one thing in the plot,
no plant, no fig, no pear, no olive, no vine,
not a vegetable, lacks your tender, loving care.
But I must say—and don't be offended now—
your plants are doing better than yourself. 275
Enough to be stooped with age
but look how squalid you are, those shabby rags.
Surely it's not for sloth your master lets you go to seed.
There's nothing of slave about your build or bearing.
I have eyes: you look like a king to me. The sort 280
entitled to bathe, sup well, then sleep in a soft bed.
That's the right and pride of you old-timers.
Come now, tell me—in no uncertain terms—
whose slave are you? whose orchard are you tending?
And tell me this—I must be absolutely sure— 285
this place I've reached, is it truly Ithaca?
Just as that fellow told me, just now . . .
I fell in with him on the road here. Clumsy,

none too friendly, couldn't trouble himself
to hear me out or give me a decent answer   290
when I asked about a long-lost friend of mine,
whether he's still alive, somewhere in Ithaca,
or dead and gone already, lost in the House of Death.
Do you want to hear his story? Listen. Catch my drift.
I once played host to a man in my own country;   295
he'd come to my door, the most welcome guest
from foreign parts I ever entertained.
He claimed he came of good Ithacan stock,
said his father was Arcesius' son, Laertes.
So I took the new arrival under my own roof,   300
I gave him a hero's welcome, treated him in style—
stores in our palace made for princely entertainment.
And I gave my friend some gifts to fit his station,
handed him seven bars of well-wrought gold,
a mixing-bowl of solid silver, etched with flowers,   305
a dozen cloaks, unlined and light, a dozen rugs
and as many full-cut capes and shirts as well,
and to top it off, four women, perfect beauties
skilled in crafts—he could pick them out himself."

     "Stranger," his father answered, weeping softly,   310
"the land you've reached is the very one you're after,
true, but it's in the grip of reckless, lawless men.
And as for the gifts you showered on your guest,
you gave them all for nothing.
But if you'd found him alive, here in Ithaca,   315
he would have replied in kind, with gift for gift,
and entertained you warmly before he sent you off.
That's the old custom, when one has led the way.
But tell me, please—in no uncertain terms—
how many years ago did you host the man,   320
that unfortunate guest of yours, my son . . .
there was a son, or was he all a dream?
That most unlucky man, whom now, I fear,
far from his own soil and those he loves,
the fish have swallowed down on the high seas   325
or birds and beasts on land have made their meal.
Nor could the ones who bore him—mother, father—
wrap his corpse in a shroud and mourn him deeply.
Nor could his warm, generous wife, so self-possessed,
Penelope, ever keen for her husband on his deathbed,   330
the fit and proper way, or close his eyes at last.
These are the solemn honors owed the dead.
But tell me your own story—that I'd like to know:
Who are you? where are you from? your city? your parents?
Where does the ship lie moored that brought you here,   335
your hardy shipmates too? Or did you arrive
as a passenger aboard some stranger's craft
and men who put you ashore have pulled away?"
                                                  "The whole tale,"

his crafty son replied, "I'll tell you start to finish.
I come from Roamer-Town, my home's a famous place,   340
my father's Unsparing, son of old King Pain,
and my name's Man of Strife . . .
I sailed from Sicily, aye, but some ill wind
blew me here, off course—much against my will—
and my ship lies moored off farmlands far from town.   345
As for Odysseus, well, five years have passed
since he left my house and put my land behind him,
luckless man! But the birds were good as he launched out,
all on the right, and I rejoiced as I sent him off
and he rejoiced in sailing. We had high hopes   350
we'd meet again as guests, as old friends,
and trade some shining gifts."
                        At those words
a black cloud of grief came shrouding over Laertes.
Both hands clawing the ground for dirt and grime,
he poured it over his grizzled head, sobbing, in spasms.   355
Odysseus' heart shuddered, a sudden twinge went shooting up
through his nostrils, watching his dear father struggle . . .
He sprang toward him, kissed him, hugged him, crying,
"Father—I am your son—myself, the man you're seeking,
home after twenty years, on native ground at last!   360
Hold back your tears, your grief.
Let me tell you the news, but we must hurry—
I've cut the suitors down in our own house,
I've paid them back their outrage, vicious crimes!"
                                    "Odysseus . . ."
Laertes, catching his breath, found words to answer.   365
"You—you're truly my son, Odysseus, home at last?
Give me a sign, some proof—I must be sure."
                        "This scar first,"
quick to the mark, his son said, "look at this—
the wound I took from the boar's white tusk
on Mount Parnassus. There you'd sent me, you   370
and mother, to see her fond old father, Autolycus,
and collect the gifts he vowed to give me, once,
when he came to see us here.
                    Or these, these trees—
let me tell you the trees you gave me years ago,
here on this well-worked plot . . .   375
I begged you for everything I saw, a little boy
trailing you through the orchard, picking our way
among these trees, and you named them one by one.
You gave me thirteen pear, ten apple trees
and forty figs—and promised to give me, look,   380
fifty vinerows, bearing hard on each other's heels,
clusters of grapes year-round at every grade of ripeness,
mellowed as Zeus's seasons weigh them down."
                            Living proof—
and Laertes' knees went slack, his heart surrendered,

recognizing the strong clear signs Odysseus offered.   385
He threw his arms around his own dear son, fainting
as hardy great Odysseus hugged him to his heart
until he regained his breath, came back to life
and cried out, "Father Zeus—
you gods of Olympus, you still rule on high   390
if those suitors have truly paid in blood
for all their reckless outrage! Oh, but now
my heart quakes with fear that all the Ithacans
will come down on us in a pack, at any time,   395
and rush the alarm through every island town!"

    "There's nothing to fear," his canny son replied,
"put it from your mind. Let's make for your lodge
beside the orchard here. I sent Telemachus on ahead,
the cowherd, swineherd too, to fix a hasty meal."

    So the two went home, confiding all the way   400
and arriving at the ample, timbered lodge,
they found Telemachus with the two herdsmen
carving sides of meat and mixing ruddy wine.
Before they ate, the Sicilian serving-woman
bathed her master, Laertes—his spirits high   405
in his own room—and rubbed him down with oil
and round his shoulders drew a fresh new cloak.
And Athena stood beside him, fleshing out the limbs
of the old commander, made him taller to all eyes,
his build more massive, stepping from his bath,   410
so his own son gazed at him, wonderstruck—
face-to-face he seemed a deathless god . . .
"Father"—Odysseus' words had wings—"surely
one of the everlasting gods has made you   415
taller, stronger, shining in my eyes!"

    Facing his son, the wise old man returned,
"If only—Father Zeus, Athena and lord Apollo—
I were the man I was, king of the Cephallenians
when I sacked the city of Nericus[8] sturdy fortress
out on its jutting cape! If I'd been young in arms   420
last night in our house with harness on my back,
standing beside you, fighting off the suitors,
how many I would have cut the knees from under—
the heart inside you would have leapt for joy!"

    So father and son confirmed each other's spirits.   425
And then, with the roasting done, the meal set out,
the others took their seats on chairs and stools,
were just putting their hands to bread and meat

---

8. On the mainland. Its exact location is unknown.

when old Dolius trudged in with his sons,
worn out from the fieldwork.   430
The old Sicilian had gone and fetched them home,
the mother who reared the boys and tended Dolius well,
now that the years had ground the old man down . . .
When they saw Odysseus—knew him in their bones—
they stopped in their tracks, staring, struck dumb,   435
but the king waved them on with a warm and easy air:
"Sit down to your food, old friend. Snap out of your wonder.
We've been cooling our heels here long enough,
eager to get our hands on all this pork,
hoping you'd all troop in at any moment."   440

     Spreading his arms, Dolius rushed up to him,
clutched Odysseus by the wrist and kissed his hand,
greeting his king now with a burst of winging words:
"Dear master, you're back—the answer to our prayers!
We'd lost all hope but the gods have brought you home!   445
Welcome—health! The skies rain blessings on you!
But tell me the truth now—this I'd like to know—
shrewd Penelope, has she heard you're home?
Or should we send a messenger?"
                              "She knows by now,
old man," his wily master answered brusquely.   450
"Why busy yourself with that?"

     So Dolius went back to his sanded stool.
His sons too, pressing around the famous king,
greeted Odysseus warmly, grasped him by the hand
then took their seats in order by their father.   455

     But now, as they fell to supper in the lodge,
Rumor the herald sped like wildfire through the city,
crying out the news of the suitors' bloody death and doom,
and massing from every quarter as they listened, kinsmen milled
with wails and moans of grief before Odysseus' palace.   460
And then they carried out the bodies, every family
buried their own, and the dead from other towns
they loaded onto the rapid ships for crews
to ferry back again, each to his own home . . .
Then in a long, mourning file they moved to assembly   465
where, once they'd grouped, crowding the meeting grounds,
old lord Eupithes rose in their midst to speak out.
Unforgettable sorrow wrung his heart for his son,
Antinous, the first that great Odysseus killed.
In tears for the one he lost, he stood and cried,   470
"My friends, what a mortal blow this man has dealt
to all our island people! Those fighters, many and brave,
he led away in his curved ships—he lost the ships
and he lost the men and back he comes again
to kill the best of our Cephallenian princes.   475

Quick, after him! Before he flees to Pylos
or holy Elis, where Epeans rule in power—
up, attack! Or we'll hang our heads forever,
all disgraced, even by generations down the years,
if we don't punish the murderers of our brothers and our sons!   480
Why, life would lose its relish—for me, at least—
I'd rather die at once and go among the dead.
Attack!—before the assassins cross the sea
and leave us in their wake."
                              He closed in tears
and compassion ran through every Achaean there.   485
Suddenly Medon and the inspired bard approached them,
fresh from Odysseus' house, where they had just awakened.
They strode into the crowds; amazement took each man
but the herald Medon spoke in all his wisdom:
"Hear me, men of Ithaca. Not without the hand   490
of the deathless gods did Odysseus do these things!
Myself, I saw an immortal fighting at his side—
like Mentor to the life. I saw the same god,
now in front of Odysseus, spurring him on,
now stampeding the suitors through the hall,   495
crazed with fear, and down they went in droves!"

   Terror gripped them all, their faces ashen white.
At last the old warrior Halitherses, Mastor's son—
who alone could see the days behind and days ahead—
rose up and spoke, distraught for each man there: 500
"Hear me, men of Ithaca. Hear what I have to say.
Thanks to your own craven hearts these things were done!
You never listened to me or the good commander Mentor,
you never put a stop to your sons' senseless folly.
What fine work they did, so blind, so reckless,   505
carving away the wealth, affronting the wife
of a great and famous man, telling themselves
that he'd return no more! So let things rest now.
Listen to me for once—I say don't attack!
Else some will draw the lightning on their necks."

                                    So he urged   510
and some held fast to their seats, but more than half
sprang up with warcries now. They had no taste
for the prophet's sane plan—winning Eupithes[9]
quickly won them over. They ran for armor
and once they'd harnessed up in burnished bronze   515
they grouped in ranks before the terraced city.
Eupithes led them on in their foolish, mad campaign,
certain he would avenge the slaughter of his son
but the father was not destined to return—
he'd meet his death in battle then and there.   520

9. Literally, "Good at Persuading."

Athena at this point made appeals to Zeus:
"Father, son of Cronus, our high and mighty king,
now let me ask you a question . . .
tell me the secrets hidden in your mind.
Will you prolong the pain, the cruel fighting here   425
or hand down pacts of peace between both sides?"

"My child," Zeus who marshals the thunderheads replied,
"why do you pry and probe me so intently? Come now,
wasn't the plan your own? You conceived it yourself:
Odysseus should return and pay the traitors back.   530
Do as your heart desires—
but let me tell you how it should be done.
Now that royal Odysseus has taken his revenge,
let both sides seal their pacts that he shall reign for life,
and let us purge their memories of the bloody slaughter   535
of their brothers and their sons. Let them be friends,
devoted as in the old days. Let peace and wealth
come cresting through the land."
                                        So Zeus decreed
and launched Athena already poised for action—
down she swept from Olympus' craggy peaks.   540

By then Odysseus' men had had their fill
of hearty fare, and the seasoned captain said,
"One of you go outside—see if they're closing in."
A son of Dolius snapped to his command,
ran to the door and saw them all too close   545
and shouted back to Odysseus,
"They're on top of us! To arms—and fast!"
Up they sprang and strapped themselves in armor,
the three men with Odysseus, Dolius' six sons
and Dolius and Laertes clapped on armor too,   550
gray as they were, but they would fight if forced.
Once they had all harnessed up in burnished bronze
they opened the doors and strode out, Odysseus in the lead.

And now, taking the build and voice of Mentor,
Zeus's daughter Athena marched right in.   555
The good soldier Odysseus thrilled to see her,
turned to his son and said in haste, "Telemachus,
you'll learn soon enough—as you move up to fight
where champions strive to prove themselves the best—
not to disgrace your father's line a moment.   560
In battle prowess we've excelled for ages
all across the world."
                        Telemachus reassured him,
"Now you'll see, if you care to watch, father,
now I'm fired up. Disgrace, you say?   565
I won't disgrace your line!"

Laertes called out in deep delight,
"What a day for me, dear gods! What joy—
my son and my grandson vying over courage!"

                                        "Laertes!"
Goddess Athena rushed beside him, eyes ablaze:
"Son of Arcesius, dearest of all my comrades,   570
say a prayer to the bright-eyed girl and Father Zeus,
then brandish your long spear and wing it fast!"

    Athena breathed enormous strength in the old man.
He lifted a prayer to mighty Zeus's daughter,
brandished his spear a moment, winged it fast   575
and hit Eupithes, pierced his bronze-sided helmet
that failed to block the bronze point tearing through—
down Eupithes crashed, his armor clanging against his chest.
Odysseus and his gallant son charged straight at the front lines,
slashing away with swords, with two-edged spears and now   580
they would have killed them all, cut them off from home
if Athena, daughter of storming Zeus, had not cried out
in a piercing voice that stopped all fighters cold,
"Hold back, you men of Ithaca, back from brutal war!
Break off—shed no more blood—make peace at once!"   585

    So Athena commanded. Terror blanched their faces,
they went limp with fear, weapons slipped from their hands
and strewed the ground at the goddess' ringing voice.
They spun in flight to the city, wild to save their lives,
but loosing a savage cry, the long-enduring great Odysseus,   590
gathering all his force, swooped like a soaring eagle—
just as the son of Cronus hurled a reeking bolt
that fell at her feet, the mighty Father's daughter,
and blazing-eyed Athena wheeled on Odysseus, crying,
"Royal son of Laertes, Odysseus, master of exploits,   595
hold back now! Call a halt to the great leveler, War—
don't court the rage of Zeus who rules the world!"

    So she commanded. He obeyed her, glad at heart.
And Athena handed down her pacts of peace
between both sides for all the years to come—   600
the daughter of Zeus whose shield is storm and thunder,
yes, but the goddess still kept Mentor's build and voice.

SAPPHO OF LESBOS
born ca. 630 B.C.E.

About Sappho's life we know very little: she was born about 630 B.C.E. on the fertile island of Lesbos off the coast of Asia Minor and spent most of her life there; she was married and had a daughter. Her lyric poems (poems sung to the accompaniment of the lyre) were so admired in the ancient world that a later poet called her the tenth Muse. In the third century B.C.E. scholars at the great library in Alexandria arranged her poems in nine books, of which the first contained more than a thousand lines. But what we have now is a pitiful remnant: one (or possibly two) complete short poems, and a collection of quotations from her work by ancient writers, supplemented by bits and pieces written on ancient scraps of papyrus found in excavations in Egypt. Yet these remnants fully justify the enthusiasm of the ancient critics; Sappho's poems (insofar as we can guess at their nature from the fragments) give us the most vivid evocation of the joys and sorrows of love in all Greek literature.

Her themes are those of a Greek woman's world—girlhood, marriage, and love, especially the love of young women for each other and the poignancy of their parting as they leave to assume the responsibilities of a wife. About the social context of these songs we can only guess; all that can be said is that they reflect a world in which women, at least women of the aristocracy, lived an intense communal life of their own, one of female occasions, functions, and festivities, in which they were fully engaged with each other; to most of them, presumably, this was a stage preliminary to their later career in that world as wife and mother.

The first two poems printed here were quoted in their entirety by ancient critics (though it is possible that there was another stanza at the end of the second); their text is not a problem. But the important recent additions to our knowledge of Sappho's poetry, the pieces of ancient books found in Egypt, are difficult to read and usually full of gaps. Our third selection, in fact, comes from the municipal rubbish heap of the Egyptian village Oxyrhyncus, and several others also survive only on papyrus. Most of the gaps in these texts are due to holes or tears in the papyrus and can often be filled in from our knowledge of Sappho's dialect and the strict meter in which she wrote. In "Some Men Say an Army of Horse," for instance, at the end of the third stanza and the beginning of the fourth, the mutilated papyrus tells us that someone or something led Helen astray, and there are traces of a word that seems to have described Helen. The name Cypris (the Cyprian One, the love-goddess Aphrodite) and phrases like "against her will" or "as soon as she saw him [Paris]" to refer to Helen would fit the spaces and the meter. Uncertain as these supplements are, they could help determine our understanding of the poem. Rather than give possibly misleading reconstructions here and in similar cases, the translator, Anne Carson, has marked gaps in the text with square brackets, so that the reader can decide what Sappho might have meant.

PRONOUNCING GLOSSARY

The following list uses common English syllables and stress accents to provide rough equivalents of selected words whose pronunciation may be unfamiliar to the general reader.

Anaktoria: *an-a-k-toh'-ree-ah*	Geraiston: *gay-rai'-stee-on*
Aphrodite: *a-froh-dai'-teeh*	Pleiades: *plee'-a-deez / play'-a-deez*
Eros: *ay'-rohs*	Sappho: *saf'-foh*

[Deathless Aphrodite of the Spangled Mind][1]

Deathless Aphrodite of the spangled mind,[2]
child of Zeus, who twists lures, I beg you
do not break with hard pains,
    O lady, my heart

but come here if ever before   5
you caught my voice far off
and listening left your father's
    golden house and came,

yoking your car. And fine birds brought you,
quick sparrows[3] over the black earth   10
whipping their wings down the sky
    through midair—

they arrived. But you. O blessed one,
smiled in your deathless face
and asked what (now again) I have suffered and why   15
    (now again) I am calling out

and what I want to happen most of all
in my crazy heart. Whom should I persuade (now again)
to lead you back into her love? Who, O
    Sappho, is wronging you?   20

For if she flees, soon she will pursue.
If she refuses gifts, rather will she give them.
If she does not love, soon she will love
    even unwilling.

Come to me now: loose me from hard   25
care and all my heart longs
to accomplish, accomplish. You
    be my ally.

[Some Men Say an Army of Horse]

Some men say an army of horse and some men say an army on foot
and some men say an army of ships is the most beautiful thing
on the black earth. But I say it is
    what you love.

1. All selections translated by Anne Carson.   2. Or "of the spangled throne"; the manuscripts preserve both readings (in the Greek there is a single letter's difference between them). The word translated here as "spangled" usually refers to a surface shimmering with bright contrasting colors. The reader should choose whether to imagine a goddess seated in splendor on a highly wrought throne or a love goddess whose mind is shifting and fickle.   3. Aphrodite's sacred birds.

Easy to make this understood by all.   5
For she who overcame everyone
in beauty (Helen)
        left her fine husband

behind and went sailing to Troy.
Not for her children nor her dear parents   10
had she a thought, no—
        ]¹led her astray

                ]for
                ]lightly
        ]reminded me now of Anaktoria   15
        who is gone.

I would rather see her lovely step
and the motion of light on her face
than chariots of Lydians² or ranks
        of footsoldiers in arms.³

[He Seems to Me Equal to Gods]

He seems to me equal to gods that man
whoever he is who opposite you
sits and listens close
        to your sweet speaking

and lovely laughing—oh it   5
puts the heart in my chest on wings
for when I look at you, even a moment, no speaking
        is left in me

no: tongue breaks and thin
fire is racing under skin   10
and in eyes no sight and drumming
        fills ears

and cold sweat holds me and shaking
grips me all, greener than grass
I am and dead—or almost   15
        I seem to me.

But all is to be dared, because even a person of poverty

---

1. Square brackets indicate where the papyrus on which the poem is preserved is torn and words or whole lines are missing.   2. A wealthy and powerful non-Greek people in Asia Minor, with whom Sappho, living on Lesbos just off the coast, shows herself familiar. A generation or so later the Lydians would be absorbed into the expanding Persian Empire, but in Sappho's time they were near the height of their prosperity. 3. The poem may have ended here. The papyrus preserves scraps of three more stanzas that may have belonged either to this or to a different poem.

[Stars around the Beautiful Moon]

stars around the beautiful moon
hide back their luminous form
whenever all full she shines
    on the earth

    silvery

[Eros Shook My Mind]

Eros[1] shook my
mind like a mountain wind falling on oak trees

[You Came and I Was Crazy for You]

you came and I was crazy for you
and you cooled my mind that burned with longing

[I Simply Want to Be Dead]

I simply want to be dead.[1]
Weeping she left me

with many tears and said this:
Oh how badly things have turned out for us.
Sappho, I swear, against my will I leave you.   5

And I answered her:
Rejoice, go and
remember me. For you know how we cherished you.

But if not, I want
to remind you
        ]and beautiful times we had.   10

For many crowns of violets
and roses
        ]at my side you put on

and many woven garlands   15

1. God of love.   1. What we have of this poem (on papyrus) begins here, with the last line of a speech addressed to Sappho or spoken by her.

made of flowers
around your soft throat.

And with sweet oil
costly
you anointed yourself

and on a soft bed
delicate
you would let loose your longing

and neither any[   ]nor any
holy place nor
was there from which we were absent

no grove[   ]no dance
          ]no sound
          [

20

25

[Often Turning Her Thoughts Here]

]Sardis[1]
often turning her thoughts here

]
you like a goddess
          and in your song most of all she rejoiced.

But now she is conspicuous among Lydian women
          as sometimes at sunset
                    the rosyfingered moon

surpasses all the stars. And her light
          stretches over salt sea
                    equally and flowerdeep fields.

And the beautiful dew is poured out
          and roses bloom and frail
                    chervil and flowering sweetclover.

But she goes back and forth remembering
          gentle Atthis and in longing
                    she bites her tender mind

But to go there
]much
          talks[

5

10

15

20

1. The capital city of Lydia. This poem too has survived as a fragment on papyrus, and we do not have the beginning or the end. Most or all of the fragment seems to be part of a speech addressed by one woman to another about a third woman who is absent in Lydia.

Not easy for us
    to equal goddesses in lovely form
]

]
          ]desire   25
        and[   ]Aphrodite
]nectar poured from
    gold
       ]with hands Persuasion
]
       ]   30
           ]
]into the Geraiston[2]
]beloveds
       ]of none   35

]into desire I shall come

[As the Sweetapple Reddens on a High Branch]

as the sweetapple reddens on a high branch[1]
  high on the highest branch and the applepickers forgot—
no, not forgot: were unable to reach

[Like the Hyacinth in the Mountains]

like the hyacinth in the mountains that shepherd men[1]
with their feet trample down and on the ground the purple
  flower

[Moon Has Set]

Moon has set[1]
and Pleiades: middle
night, the hour goes by,
alone I lie.

2. The reference is uncertain.   1. This fragment may be from an epithalamium, or wedding song. If so, it is probably the bride, who was virgin and inaccessible to men until marriage, who is compared to the sweetapple.   1. Possibly also from an epithalamium.   1. It is not certain that this fragment is by Sappho. In the Greek, the form of the word for "alone" shows that the speaker is female.

AESCHYLUS

524?–456 B.C.E.

The earliest documents in the history of the Western theater are the seven plays of Aeschylus that have come down to us through the more than two thousand years since his death. When he produced his first play in the opening years of the fifth century B.C.E., the performance that we know as drama was still less than half a century old, still open to innovation—and Aeschylus, in fact, made such significant contributions to its development that he has been called "the creator of tragedy."

The origins of the theatrical contests in Athens are obscure; they were a puzzle even for Aristotle, who in the fourth century B.C.E. wrote a famous treatise on tragedy. All that we know for certain is that the drama began as a religious celebration that took the form of song and dance. Such ceremonies are of course to be found in the communal life of many early cultures, but it was in Athens, and in Athens alone, that the ceremony gave rise to what we know as tragedy and comedy and produced dramatic masterpieces that are still admired, read, and performed. At some time in the late sixth century B.C.E. the Athenians converted what seems to have been a rural celebration of Dionysus, a vegetation deity especially associated with the vine, into an annual city festival at which dancing choruses, competing for prizes, sang hymns of praise to the god. It was from this choral performance that tragedy and comedy developed. Some unknown innovator (his name was probably Thespis) combined the choral song with the speech of a masked actor who, playing a god or hero, engaged the chorus in dialogue. It was Aeschylus who added a second actor and so created the possibility of conflict and the prototype of the drama as we know it.

After the defeat of the Persian invaders (480–479 B.C.E.), as Athens with its fleets and empire moved toward supremacy in the Greek world, this spring festival became a splendid occasion. The Dionysia, as it was now called, lasted for four or five days, during which public business (except in emergencies) was suspended and prisoners were released on bail for the duration of the festival. In an open-air theater that could seat seventeen thousand spectators, tragic and comic poets competed for the prizes offered by the city. Poets in each genre had been selected by the magistrates for the year. On each of three days of the festival, a tragic poet presented three tragedies and a satyr play (a burlesque on a mythic theme), and a comic poet produced one comedy.

The three tragedies could deal with quite separate stories or, as in the case of Aeschylus's *Oresteia*, with the successive stages of one extended action. By the time this trilogy was produced (458 B.C.E.) the number of actors had been raised to three; the spoken part of the performance became steadily more important. In the *Oresteia* an equilibrium between the two elements of the performance has been established. The actors, with their speeches, create the dramatic situation and its movement, the plot; the chorus, while contributing to dramatic suspense and illusion, ranges free of the immediate situation in its odes, which extend and amplify the significance of the action.

In 458 B.C.E. Aeschylus was at the end of a great career; he died two years later in Gela, a Greek city in Sicily. He had begun his career as a dramatist before the Persian Wars, in the first days of the new Athenian democracy. He fought against the Persians at Marathon (where his brother was killed) and almost certainly also in the great sea fight at Salamis in 480 B.C.E. (his play the *Persians*, produced in 472 B.C.E., contains what sounds like an eyewitness account of that battle). Only six or seven of his plays survive (we know that he produced ninety); besides the *Persians* and the three plays of the *Oresteia*, we have the text of *Suppliants* (sometime in the 460s), *The Seven against Thebes* (467), and the famous and influential play *Prometheus Bound* (date unknown, and many scholars think it was not written by Aeschylus).

The *Oresteia* is a trilogy. The first play, *Agamemnon*, was followed at its performance by two more plays, *The Libation Bearers* and *The Eumenides*, which carried on its story and theme to a conclusion. The theme of the trilogy is justice, and its story, like that of almost all Greek tragedies, is a legend that was already well known to the audience that saw the first performance of the play. This legend, the story of the house of Atreus, is rich in dramatic potential, for it deals with a series of retributive murders that stained the hands of three generations of a royal family, and it has also a larger significance, social and historical, of which Aeschylus took full advantage. The legend preserves the memory of an important historical process through which the Greeks had passed: the transition from a tradition that demanded that a murdered person's next of kin avenge the death to a system requiring settlement of the private quarrel by a court of law (the typical institution of the city-state). When Agamemnon returns victorious from Troy, he is killed by his wife, Clytaemnestra, and her lover, Aegisthus, who is Agamemnon's cousin. Clytaemnestra kills her husband to avenge her daughter Iphigenia, whom Agamemnon sacrificed to the goddess Artemis when he had to choose between his daughter's life and his ambition to conquer Troy. Aegisthus avenges the crime of a previous generation, the hideous murder of his brothers by Agamemnon's father, Atreus. The killing of Agamemnon is, by the standards of the old system, justice; but it is the nature of this justice that the process can never be arrested, that one act of violence must give rise to another. Agamemnon's murder must be avenged too, as it is in the second play of the trilogy by Orestes, his son, who kills both Aegisthus and Clytaemnestra, his own mother. Orestes has acted justly according to the old code, but in doing so he has violated the most sacred blood relationship of all, the bond between mother and son. The old system of justice has produced an insoluble dilemma.

At the end of *The Libation Bearers*, Orestes sees a vision of the Furies. They are serpent-haired female hunters, the avengers of blood. Agamemnon had a son to avenge him, but for Clytaemnestra there was no one to exact payment. This task is taken up by the Furies, who are the guardians of the ancient sanctities; they enforce the old dispensation when no earthly agent is at hand to do so. Female themselves, they assert the claim of the mother against the son who killed her to avenge his father. At the end of the second play they are only a vision in Orestes' mind—"You can't see them," he says to the chorus. "I can, they drive me on! I must move on." But in the final play we see them too; they are the chorus of that play, and they have pursued Orestes to the great shrine of Apollo at Delphi where he has come to seek refuge.

Apollo can save him from immediate destruction at the Furies' hands, but he cannot resolve the dilemma. Orestes must go to Athens, where Athena, the patron goddess of the city, will set up the first court of law to try his case. At Athens, before the ancient court of the Areopagus, the Furies argue eloquently, but Apollo himself arrives to testify that he ordered Orestes to act. Athena tilts the judges' vote in Orestes' favor by either creating or breaking a tie with her own vote, and Orestes, acquitted, goes home to Argos. The Furies threaten to turn their dreadful wrath against Athens itself, but the goddess persuades them to accept a home deep in Athenian earth, to act as protectors of the court and of the land.

The arguments employed in the trial may not strike us as compelling, and may appear disappointing as an answer to the problems of guilt and justice raised by the trilogy. A possible reply is the "progressivist" argument. According to this argument, the fact of the court's establishment is more important than the particular judgment in Orestes' case. This is the end of an old era and the beginning of a new. The court institutes a system of communal justice, which punishes impersonally and has at last replaced the inconclusive anarchy of individual revenge. Besides, the trilogy not only is concerned with the history of human institutions but also makes a religious statement. The sequence of murderous acts and counter-acts over three generations, leading to an important advance in human understanding and civilization, can be seen as the working out of the will of Zeus. The chorus of *Agamemnon*, celebrating the power of Zeus, tells us that he

　　　　　　　has led us on to know,
　　　　　　　the Helmsman lays it down as law
　　　　　　　that we must suffer, suffer into truth.

From suffering come understanding and progress. That is Zeus's design in the trilogy, whereas in the *Iliad*, where events also are guided by a plan of Zeus, nothing at all comes out of the suffering except the certainty of more suffering. The ending of the *Eumenides*, then, when the Furies call blessings down on Athens, gives a vision of a city ruled by law and living in harmony with its land and its gods. In this story of progress painfully won, Aeschylus offers Athenian democracy its charter myth just as it is entering the era of its greatest achievements and its greatest risks.

　　This "progressivist" reading of the *Oresteia* has considerable force, but it does not account for everything. It leaves out, for example, one of the costs of this progress that the trilogy also shows clearly: gender asymmetry. In *Agamemnon*, Clytaemnestra is a powerful and transgressive figure, a woman who "maneuvers like a man," as the Watchman says the first time she is mentioned in the play. Her murder of her husband is, in Greek terms, only an intensified form of this self-assertion; and by raising the specter of a woman out of control, it justifies women's normal subjugation in Greek culture. But in avenging Iphigeneia, Clytaemnestra also defends the integrity of the family, and particularly the parent-child bond, against her husband's public ambition, to which he has sacrificed their daughter. She asserts this bond again in her last moments, when she bares her breast to Orestes to dissuade him from killing her. In murdering her husband in the name of her child, she has struck at the basis of marriage, but she does have a measure of justice on her side, not to mention a claim of vengeance against her son. Orestes' acquittal in the third play leaves her claims unsatisfied. Athena, the virgin warrior-goddess who represents the female as an ally of patriarchal order, declares as she casts her vote for Orestes, "no mother gave me birth. / I honor the male, in all things but marriage." From this point of view, the Furies' incorporation into Athens represents the appropriation and taming of female power, and it validates the exclusion of women from the civic processes of the democracy—a fact of Athenian daily life. On the other hand, in celebrating the Furies' roles of maintaining obedience to law through inspiring fear and of promoting natural fertility, the text acknowledges the power of the female, which it associates with the Earth's natural processes, "primitive" and prior to the male-centered rationality of the city but vital still. The female is given a role in the city, even though she is excluded from its official public life, and that role is celebrated. There is no doubt, however, about the dominance of the patriarchal principle under the authority of the Olympian gods.

　　The full scope of these events, however we interpret them, is apparent only to the audience, which follows the pattern of its execution through the three plays of the trilogy. The characters who act and suffer are in the dark. They claim a knowledge of Zeus's will and boast that their actions are its fulfillment (it is in these terms that Agamemnon speaks of the sack of Troy, and Clytaemnestra of Agamemnon's murder), and they are, of course, in one sense, right. But their knowledge is limited; Agamemnon does not realize that Zeus's will includes his death at the hands of Clytaemnestra, nor Clytaemnestra that it demands her death at the hands of her son. The chorus has, at times, a deeper understanding, but its knowledge of Zeus's laws is an abstraction that it cannot relate to the terrible facts.

　　In this murky atmosphere (made all the more terrible by the beacon fire of the opening lines, which brings not light but deeper darkness), one human being sees clear; she possesses the concrete vision of the future, which complements the chorus's abstract knowledge of the law. This is the prophet Cassandra, Priam's daughter, brought from Troy as Agamemnon's share of the spoils. She has been given the power of true prophecy by the god Apollo, but the gift is nullified by the condition that her prophecies will never be believed. She sees reality—past, present, and future—so plainly that she is cut off from ordinary human beings (represented by the chorus) by the clarity of her vision and the terrible burden of her knowledge. The great scene in which she sings her prophecies delays the action for which everything has been prepared—the death of Agamemnon. Before we hear his famous cry offstage, Cassandra presents us with a mysterious vision that combines cause, effect, and result: the murders that have led to this terrible moment, the death of Agamemnon, and the murders that will follow. The past, present, and future of Clytaemnestra's action and Agamemnon's suffering are fused into a timeless unity in Cassandra's great lines, an unearthly unity that is dissolved only when Agamemnon, in the real world of time and space, screams in mortal agony.

The tremendous statement of the trilogy is made in a style that for magnificence and richness of suggestion can be compared only with the style of Shakespeare at the height of his poetic power, the Shakespeare of *King Lear* and *Antony and Cleopatra*. The language of the *Oresteia* is an intricate tapestry of imagery in which combinations of metaphor, which at first seem bombastic in their violence, take their place in the ordered pattern of the poem as a whole. An image, once introduced, recurs and reappears again, to run its course verbally and visually through the whole length of the trilogy, richer in meaning with each fresh appearance. In the second choral ode, for example, the chorus, welcoming the news of Agamemnon's victory at Troy, sings of the net that Zeus and Night threw over the city, trapping the inhabitants like animals. The net is here an image of Zeus's justice, a retributive justice, since Troy is paying for the crime of taking Helen, and the image identifies Zeus's justice with Agamemnon's action in sacking the city. This image occurs again, with a different emphasis, in the hypocritical speech of welcome that Clytaemnestra makes to her husband on his return. She tells how she feared for his safety at Troy, how she trembled at the rumors of his death:

> and the rumors spread and fester,
> a runner comes with something dreadful,
> close on his heels the next and his news worse,
> and they shout it out and the whole house can hear;
> and wounds—if he took one wound for each report
> to penetrate these walls, he's gashed like a dragnet.

This vision of Agamemnon dead she speaks of as her fear, but we know that it represents her deepest desire and, more, the purpose that she is now preparing to execute. When, later, she stands in triumph over her husband's corpse, she uses the same image to describe the robe that she threw over his limbs to blind and baffle him before she stabbed him—"our never-ending, all embracing net, I cast it / wide for the royal haul, I coil him round and round / in the wealth, the robes of doom"—and this time the image materializes into an object visible on stage. We can see the net, the gashed robe still folded round Agamemnon's body. We see it again, for in the second play Orestes, standing over his mother's body as she now stands over his father's, will display the robe before us, with its holes and bloodstains, as a justification for what he has just done. Elsewhere in *Agamemnon* the chorus compares Cassandra to a wild animal caught in the net, and later Aegisthus exults to see Agamemnon's body lying "in the nets of Justice." For each speaker the image has a different meaning, but not one realizes the terrible sense in which it applies to them all. They are all caught in the net, the system of justice by vengeance that only binds tighter the more its captives struggle to free themselves. Clytaemnestra attempts to escape, to arrest the process of the chain of murders and the working out of the will of Zeus. "But I will swear a pact with the spirit / born within us," she says, but Agamemnon's body and the net she threw over him are there on the stage to remind us that her appeal will not be

heard; one more generation must act and suffer before the net will vanish, never to
be seen again.

PRONOUNCING GLOSSARY

The following list uses common English syllables and stress accents to provide rough equivalents of selected words whose pronunciation may be unfamiliar to the general reader.

Aegisthus: *ee-jis'-thus / ai-gis'-thus*

Aeschylus: *ess'-kel-us / ees'-kel-us*

Areopagus: *a-ree-op'-aguhs*

Aulis: *ow'-lis*

Calchas: *kal'-kahs*

Clytaemnestra: *klai-tem-nes'-truh /
kloo-tai-mnay'-stra*

Dionysus: *dai-oh-nai'-sus*

Erechtheus: *e-rek'-thee-us /
e-rek'-thyoos*

Eumenides: *yoo-me'-ni-deez*

Hermes: *her'-meez*

Iphigeneia: *i-fe-jen-ai'-uh*

Menelaus: *me-ne-lay'-us /
me-ne-lah'-us*

Oresteia: *o-res-tai'-uh / o-res-tay'-uh*

Orestes: *o-res'-teez*

Perseus: *per'-see-us / per'-syoos*

Scylla: *si'-lah/skil-ah*

Thyestes: *thai-es'-teez*

THE ORESTEIA[1]

Agamemnon

CHARACTERS

WATCHMAN
CLYTAEMNESTRA
HERALD
AGAMEMNON
CASSANDRA

AEGISTHUS
CHORUS, *the Old Men of Argos and
their* LEADER
*Attendants of Clytaemnestra and of
Agamemnon, bodyguard of
Aegisthus*

[TIME AND SCENE: *A night in the tenth and final autumn of the Trojan war. The
house of Atreus in Argos. Before it, an altar stands unlit; a* WATCHMAN *on the
high roofs fights to stay awake.*]

WATCHMAN   Dear gods, set me free from all the pain,
    the long watch I keep, one whole year awake . . .
    propped on my arms, crouched on the roofs of Atreus
    like a dog.
        I know the stars by heart,
    the armies of the night, and there in the lead   5
    the ones that bring us snow or the crops of summer,
    bring us all we have—
    our great blazing kings of the sky,
    I know them, when they rise and when they fall . . .

1. Translated by Robert Fagles.

and now I watch for the light, the signal-fire[2]   10
breaking out of Troy, shouting Troy is taken.
So she commands, full of her high hopes.
That woman[3]—she maneuvers like a man.

And when I keep to my bed, soaked in dew,
and the thoughts go groping through the night   15
and the good dreams that used to guard my sleep . . .
not here, it's the old comrade, terror, at my neck.
I mustn't sleep, no—
        [Shaking himself awake.]
                                Look alive, sentry.
And I try to pick out tunes, I hum a little,
a good cure for sleep, and the tears start,   20
I cry for the hard times come to the house,
no longer run like the great place of old.

Oh for a blessed end to all our pain,
some godsend burning through the dark—
        [Light appears slowly in the east; he struggles to his feet and scans it.]
                                I salute you!   25
You dawn of the darkness, you turn night to day—
I see the light at last.
They'll be dancing in the streets of Argos[4]
thanks to you, thanks to this new stroke of—
                                Aieeeeee!
There's your signal clear and true, my queen!
Rise up from bed—hurry, lift a cry of triumph   30
through the house, praise the gods for the beacon,
if they've taken Troy . . .
                        But there it burns,
fire all the way. I'm for the morning dances.
Master's luck is mine. A throw of the torch
has brought us triple-sixes[5]—we have won!   35
My move now—
        [Beginning to dance, then breaking off, lost in thought.]
                Just bring him home. My king,
I'll take your loving hand in mine and then . . .
the rest is silence. The ox is on my tongue.[6]
Aye, but the house and these old stones,
give them a voice and what a tale they'd tell.   40
And so would I, gladly . . .
I speak to those who know; to those who don't

---

2. I.e., the bonfire nearest to Argos, the last in a chain extending all the way to Troy, each one visible from the next when fired at night.   3. Clytaemnestra.   4. In Homer, Agamemnon, son of Atreus, is king of Mycenae. Later Greek poets, however, referred to his kingdom as Argos or Mycenae, perhaps because the Achaeans in Homer are sometimes called Argives. In 463 B.C.E., just five years before the production of the play, Argos had defeated Mycenae in battle and put an end to the city, displacing the inhabitants or selling them into slavery. Soon after, Argos and Athens entered into an alliance, aimed at Sparta. Since this alliance will be alluded to in the last play of the trilogy, it is important for Aeschylus to establish the un-Homeric location of the action right at the beginning.   5. The highest throw in the ancient Greek dice game.   6. A proverbial phrase for enforced silence.

my mind's a blank. I never say a word.
> [*He climbs down from the roof and disappears into the palace through a side entrance. A* CHORUS, *the old men of Argos who have not learned the news of victory, enters and marches round the altar.*]

CHORUS   Ten years gone, ten to the day
    our great avenger went for Priam—   45
        Menelaus[7] and lord Agamemnon,
two kings with the power of Zeus,
the twin throne, twin sceptre,
Atreus' sturdy yoke of sons
launched Greece in a thousand ships,   50
armadas cutting loose from the land,
armies massed for the cause, the rescue—
> [*From within the palace* CLYTAEMNESTRA *raises a cry of triumph.*]

the heart within them screamed for all-out war!
Like vultures robbed of their young,
    the agony sends them frenzied,   55
soaring high from the nest, round and
round they wheel, they row their wings,
stroke upon churning thrashing stroke,
but all the labor, the bed of pain,
    the young are lost forever.   60
Yet someone hears on high—Apollo,
Pan or Zeus[8]—the piercing wail
these guests of heaven raise,
and drives at the outlaws, late
but true to revenge, a stabbing Fury![9]   65
> [CLYTAEMNESTRA *appears at the doors and pauses with her entourage.*][1]

So towering Zeus the god of guests[2]
drives Atreus' sons at Paris,
all for a woman manned by many
the generations wrestle, knees
grinding the dust, the manhood drains,   70
the spear snaps in the first blood rites
    that marry Greece and Troy.
And now it goes as it goes
and where it ends is Fate.
And neither by singeing flesh   75
nor tipping cups of wine[3]
nor shedding burning tears can you
enchant away the rigid Fury.

---

7. Another son of Atreus, also a king of Argos and commander of the Greek expedition against Troy. Priam was the king of Troy. His son Paris abducted (or seduced) Menelaus's wife, Helen.   8. The movements of birds are regarded as prophetic signs. Apollo is mentioned perhaps as a prophetic god, Pan as a god of the wild places, Zeus because eagles and vultures were symbolic of his power.   9. This is the first mention of one of these avenging spirits, who will actually appear on stage as the chorus of the final play. Furies are called Erinyes in Greek.   1. There are no stage directions on the manuscript copies of the plays that have come down to us. Here the translator had the queen enter so that she will be visible on stage when the chorus addresses her by name in line 93. Other scholars, pointing out that in Greek tragedy characters who are offstage are often addressed, disagree, and bring Clytaemnestra on stage only at line 256. 2. Zeus was thought to be particularly interested in punishing those who violated the code of hospitality. Paris had been a guest in Menelaus's house.   3. Neither by burnt sacrifice nor by pouring libations.

[CLYTAEMNESTRA *lights the altar-fires.*]
We are the old, dishonoured ones,[4]
the broken husks of men.
Even then they cast us off,
the rescue mission left us here
to prop a child's strength upon a stick.
What if the new sap rises in his chest?
He has no soldiery in him,
   no more than we,
and we are aged past aging,
gloss of the leaf shriveled,
three legs at a time[5] we falter on.
Old men are children once again,
   a dream that sways and wavers
into the hard light of day.
                But you,
daughter of Leda, queen Clytaemnestra,
what now, what news, what message
drives you through the citadel
   burning victims?[6] Look,
the city gods, the gods of Olympus,
gods of the earth and public markets—
all the altars blazing with your gifts!
   Argos blazes! Torches
race the sunrise up her skies—
drugged by the lulling holy oils,
   unadulterated,
run from the dark vaults of kings.
   Tell us the news!
What you can, what is right—
Heal us, soothe our fears!
Now the darkness comes to the fore,
now the hope glows through your victims,
beating back this raw, relentless anguish
   gnawing at the heart.

    [CLYTAEMNESTRA *ignores them and pursues her rituals; they assemble for*
    the opening chorus.]
O but I still have power to sound the god's command at the roads
that launched the kings. The gods breathe power through my song,
   my fighting strength, Persuasion grows with the years—
I sing how the flight of fury hurled the twin command,
   one will that hurled young Greece
and winged the spear of vengeance straight for Troy!
The kings of birds to kings of the beaking prows, one black,
   one with a blaze of silver
      skimmed the palace spearhand right

80

85

90

95

100

105

110

115

120

---

4. The general sense of the passage is that only two classes of the male population are left in Argos: those who are too young to fight and those who, like the chorus, are too old.   5. I.e., using a stick, or cane, to support them when they walk.   6. Clytaemnestra is sacrificing in thanksgiving for the news of Troy's fall; the chorus does not know that the news has come via the signal fires.

and swooping lower, all could see,
    plunged their claws in a hare, a mother
bursting with unborn young—the babies spilling,
quick spurts of blood—cut off the race just dashing into life!
Cry, cry for death, but good win out in glory in the end.   125

But the loyal seer of the armies studied Atreus' sons,
two sons with warring hearts—he saw two eagle-kings
    devour the hare and spoke the things to come,[7]
"Years pass, and the long hunt nets the city of Priam,
    the flocks beyond the walls,   130
a kingdom's life and soul—Fate stamps them out.
Just let no curse of the gods lour on us first,
    shatter our giant armor
        forged to strangle Troy. I see
            pure Artemis bristle in pity—   135
                yes, the flying hounds of the Father
slaughter for armies . . . their own victim . . . a woman
trembling young, all born to die—She[8] loathes the eagles' feast!"
Cry, cry for death, but good win out in glory in the end.
    "Artemis, lovely Artemis, so kind   140
to the ravening lion's tender, helpless cubs,
the suckling young of beasts that stalk the wilds—
    bring this sign for all its fortune,
        all its brutal torment home to birth!
I beg you, Healing Apollo, soothe her before   145
her crosswinds hold us down and moor the ships too long,[9]
pressing us on to another victim . . .
    nothing sacred, no
        no feast to be eaten[1]
            the architect of vengeance   150
    [*Turning to the palace.*]
        growing strong in the house
    with no fear of the husband
here she waits
the terror raging back and back in the future
    the stealth, the law of the hearth, the mother—   155
        Memory womb of Fury child-avenging Fury!"
So as the eagles wheeled at the crossroads,

7. The seer Calchas identified the two eagles ("kings of birds") as symbolic of the two kings and their action as a symbolic prophecy of the destruction of Troy. The two eagles seized and tore a pregnant hare, which meant that the two kings would destroy Troy, thus killing not only the living Trojans but the Trojan generations yet unborn.   8. Artemis, a virgin goddess, patron of hunting, and protectress of wildlife, is angry that the eagles ("the flying hounds") have destroyed a pregnant animal. The prophet fears that she may turn her wrath against the kings whom the eagles represent. *A woman trembling young*: just as the eagles kill the hare, the kings will kill Agamemnon's daughter Iphigenia. The Greek text refers only to the hare, but the translator has made the allusion clear.   9. Calchas foresees the future. Artemis will send unfavorable winds to prevent the sailing of the Greek expedition from Aulis, the port of embarkation. She will demand the sacrifice of Agamemnon's daughter Iphigenia as the price of the fleet's release. He prays that in spite of its bad aspects, the omen will be truly prophetic—that is, that the Achaeans will capture Troy. He goes on to anticipate and try to avert some of the evils it portends.   1. At an ordinary sacrifice the celebrants gave the gods their due portion and then feasted on the animal's flesh. The word *sacrifice* comes to have the connotation of "feast." There will be no feast at this sacrifice, since the victim will be a human being. The ominous phrase reminds us of a feast of human flesh that has already taken place, Thyestes' feasting on his own children.

Calchas clashed out the great good blessings mixed with doom
  for the halls of kings, and singing with our fate   160
we cry, cry for death, but good win out in glory in the end.

      Zeus, great nameless all in all,
      if that name will gain his favor,
        I will call him Zeus.[2]
      I have no words to do him justice,
        weighing all in the balance,   165
        all I have is Zeus, Zeus—
  lift this weight, this torment from my spirit,
        cast it once for all.

      He who was so mighty once,[3]
      storming for the wars of heaven,   170
        he has had his day.
  And then his son[4] who came to power
      met his match in the third fall
      and he is gone. Zeus, Zeus—
  raise your cries and sing him Zeus the Victor!   175
      You will reach the truth:

      Zeus has led us on to know,
      the Helmsman lays it down as law
      that we must suffer, suffer into truth.
We cannot sleep, and drop by drop at the heart   180
  the pain of pain remembered comes again,
    and we resist, but ripeness comes as well.
From the gods enthroned on the awesome rowing-bench[5]
      there comes a violent love.

      So it was that day the king,   185
    the steersman at the helm of Greece,
  would never blame a word the prophet said—
  swept away by the wrenching winds of fortune
he conspired! Weatherbound we could not sail,
  our stores exhausted, fighting strength hard-pressed,   190
  and the squadrons rode in the shallows off Chalkis[6]
    where the riptide crashes, drags,

and winds from the north pinned down our hulls at Aulis,
  port of anguish . . . head winds starving,

2. It was important, in prayer, to address the divinity by his or her right name: here the chorus uses an
inclusive formula—they call on Zeus by whatever name pleases him.   3. Uranus, father of Cronus and
grandfather of Zeus, the first lord of heaven. This whole passage refers to a primitive legend that told how
Uranus was violently supplanted by his son, Cronus, who was in his turn overthrown by his son, Zeus. This
legend is made to bear new meaning by Aeschylus, for he suggests that it is not a meaningless series of acts
of violence but a progression to the rule of Zeus, who stands for order and justice. Thus the law of human
life that Zeus proclaims and administers—that wisdom comes through suffering—has its counterpart in
the history of the establishment of the divine rule.   4. Cronus.   5. The bench of the ship where the
helmsman sat.   6. The unruly water of the narrows between Aulis on the mainland and Chalkis on the
island of Euboea.

sheets and the cables snapped 195
   and the men's minds strayed,
      the pride, the bloom of Greece
  was raked as time ground on,
ground down, and then the cure for the storm
and it was harsher—Calchas cried, 200
"My captains, Artemis must have blood!"—
   so harsh the sons of Atreus
     dashed their scepters on the rocks,
   could not hold back the tears,

and I still can hear the older warlord saying, 205
"Obey, obey, or a heavy doom will crush me!—
Oh but doom *will* crush me
  once I rend my child,
    the glory of my house—
  a father's hands are stained, 210
blood of a young girl streaks the altar.
Pain both ways and what is worse?
Desert the fleets, fail the alliance?
  No, but stop the winds with a virgin's blood,
    feed their lust, their fury?—feed their fury!— 215
  Law is law!—
        Let all go well."

And once he slipped his neck in the strap of Fate,
his spirit veering black, impure, unholy,
once he turned he stopped at nothing,
   seized with the frenzy 220
     blinding driving to outrage—
wretched frenzy, cause of all our grief!
Yes, he had the heart
   to sacrifice his daughter!—
  to bless the war that avenged a woman's loss, 225
   a bridal rite that sped the men-of-war.

"My father, father!"—she might pray to the winds;
no innocence moves her judges mad for war.
Her father called his henchmen on,
   on with a prayer, 230
    "Hoist her over the altar
like a yearling, give it all your strength!
She's fainting—lift her,
  sweep her robes around her,
but slip this strap in her gentle curving lips . . . 235
  here, gag her hard, a sound will curse the house"—

and the bridle chokes her voice . . . her saffron robes
pouring over the sand
          her glance like arrows showering

wounding every murderer through with pity
     clear as a picture, live,
she strains to call their names   240
I remember often the days with father's guests
when over the feast her voice unbroken,
     pure as the hymn her loving father
bearing third libations,[7] sang to Saving Zeus—   245
transfixed with joy, Atreus' offspring
     throbbing out their love.

What comes next? I cannot see it, cannot say.
The strong techniques of Calchas do their work.[8]
But Justice turns the balance scales,   250
     sees that we suffer
and we suffer and we learn.
And we will know the future when it comes.
Greet it too early, weep too soon.
     It all comes clear in the light of day.   255
Let all go well today, well as she could want,
       [*Turning to* CLYTAEMNESTRA.]
our midnight watch, our lone defender,
     single-minded queen.
LEADER   We've come,
Clytaemnestra. We respect your power.
Right it is to honor the warlord's woman   260
once he leaves the throne.
                  But why these fires?
Good news, or more good hopes? We're loyal,
we want to hear, but never blame your silence.
CLYTAEMNESTRA   Let the new day shine, as the proverb says,
     glorious from the womb of Mother Night.   265
       [*Lost in prayer, then turning to the* CHORUS.]
You will hear a joy beyond your hopes.
Priam's citadel—the Greeks have taken Troy!
LEADER   No, what do you mean? I can't believe it.
CLYTAEMNESTRA   Troy is ours. Is that clear enough?
LEADER   The joy of it,
stealing over me, calling up my tears—   270
CLYTAEMNESTRA   Yes, your eyes expose your loyal hearts.
LEADER   And you have proof?
CLYTAEMNESTRA   I do,
I must. Unless the god is lying.
LEADER   That,
or a phantom spirit sends you into raptures.
CLYTAEMNESTRA   No one takes me in with visions—senseless dreams.   275
LEADER   Or giddy rumor, you haven't indulged yourself—
CLYTAEMNESTRA   You treat me like a child, you mock me?

---

7. Offerings of wine. At a banquet three libations were poured, the third and last to Zeus the savior; the last libation was accompanied by a hymn of praise.   8. This seems to refer to the sacrifice of Iphigenia. Some scholars take the Greek words to refer to the fulfillment of Calchas's prophecies.

LEADER   Then when did they storm the city?
CLYTAEMNESTRA   Last night, I say, the mother of this morning.
LEADER   And who on earth could run the news so fast?   280
CLYTAEMNESTRA   The god of fire—rushing fire from Ida![9]
    And beacon to beacon rushed it on to me,
    my couriers riding home the torch.
                                        From Troy
    to the bare rock of Lemnos, Hermes' Spur,[1]
    and the Escort winged the great light west   285
    to the Saving Father's face, Mount Athos[2] hurled it
    third in the chain and leaping Ocean's back
    the blaze went dancing on to ecstasy—pitch-pine
    streaming gold like a new-born sun—and brought
    the word in flame to Mount Makistos'[3] brow.   290
    No time to waste, straining, fighting sleep,
    that lookout heaved a torch glowing over
    the murderous straits of Euripos to reach
    Messapion's[4] watchmen craning for the signal.
    Fire for word of fire! tense with the heather   295
    withered gray, they stack it, set it ablaze—
    the hot force of the beacon never flags,
    it springs the Plain of Asôpos, rears
    like a harvest moon to hit Kithairon's[5] crest
    and drives new men to drive the fire on.   300
    That relay pants for the far-flung torch,
    they swell its strength outstripping my commands
    and the light inflames the marsh, the Gorgon's Eye,[6]
    it strikes the peak where the wild goats range[7]—
    my laws, my fire whips that camp!   305
    They spare nothing, eager to build its heat,
    and a huge beard of flame overcomes the headland
    beetling down the Saronic Gulf,[8] and flaring south
    it brings the dawn to the Black Widow's[9] face—
    the watch that looms above your heads—and now   310
    the true son of the burning flanks of Ida
    crashes on the roofs of Atreus' sons!

    And I ordained it all.
    Torch to torch, running for their lives,
    one long succession racing home my fire.
                                        One,   315
    first in the laps and last,[1] wins out in triumph.
    There you have my proof, *my* burning sign, I tell you—

9. The mountain range near Troy. The names that follow in this speech designate the places where beacon
fires flashed the message of Troy's fall to Argos. The chain began at Ida.   1. Hermes' cliff is on the island
of Lemnos (off the coast of Asia Minor).   2. On a rocky peninsula in north Greece.   3. On the island
of Euboea off the coast of central Greece.   4. A mountain on the mainland.   5. A mountain near
Thebes.   6. Lake Gorgopis.   7. Mount Aegiplanctus on the Isthmus of Corinth.   8. The sea.
9. Mount Arachnaeus ("spider") in Argive territory. This is the fire seen by the watchman at the beginning
of the play.   1. The chain of beacons is compared to a relay race in which the runners carry torches; the
last runner (who runs the final lap) comes in first to win.

the power my lord passed on from Troy to me![2]

LEADER   We'll thank the gods, my lady—first this story,
let me lose myself in the wonder of it all!   320
Tell it start to finish, tell us all.

CLYTAEMNESTRA   The city's ours—in our hands this very day!
I can hear the cries in crossfire rock the walls.
Pour oil and wine in the same bowl,
what have you, friendship? A struggle to the end.   325
So with the victors and the victims—outcries,
you can hear them clashing like their fates.

They are kneeling by the bodies of the dead,
embracing men and brothers, infants over
the aged loins that gave them life, and sobbing,   330
as the yoke constricts their last free breath,
for every dear one lost.
                        And the others,
there, plunging breakneck through the night—
the labor of battle sets them down, ravenous;
to breakfast on the last remains of Troy.   335
Not by rank but the lots of chance they draw,
they lodge in the houses captured by the spear,
settling in so soon, released from the open sky,
the frost and dew. Lucky men, off guard at last,
they sleep away their first good night in years.   340

If only they are revering the city's gods,
the shrines of the gods who love the conquered land,
no plunderer will be plundered in return.
Just let no lust, no mad desire seize the armies[3]
to ravish what they must not touch—   345
overwhelmed by all they've won!
                        The run for home
and safety waits, the swerve at the post,[4]
the final lap of the gruelling two-lap race.
And even if the men come back with no offense
to the gods, the avenging dead may never rest—   350
Oh let no new disaster strike! And here

2. This speech has often been criticized as discursive, but it has great poetic importance. The image of the light that will dispel the darkness, first introduced by the watchman, is one of the dominant images of the trilogy and is here developed with magnificent ambiguous effect. For the watchman the light means the safe return of Agamemnon and the restoration of order in the house; for Clytaemnestra it means the return of Agamemnon to his death at her hands. Each swift jump of the racing light is one step nearer home and death for Agamemnon. The light the watchman longs for brings only greater darkness, but eventually it brings darkness for Clytaemnestra too. The final emergence of the true light comes in the glare of the torchlight procession that ends the last play of the trilogy, a procession that symbolizes perfect reconciliation on both the human and the divine levels and the working out of the will of Zeus in the substitution of justice for vengeance. The conception of the beacons as a chain of descendants (compare line 311) is also important; the fire at Argos that announces Agamemnon's imminent death is a direct descendant of the fire on Ida that announces the sack of Troy and Agamemnon's sacrilegious conduct there. The metaphor thus reminds us of the sequence of crimes from generation to generation that is the history of the house of Pelops.   3. She, of course, hopes for the opposite of what she prays for here. The audience was familiar with the traditional account, according to which Agamemnon and his army failed signally to respect the gods and temples of Troy.   4. Greek runners turned at a post and came back on a parallel track.

you have it, what a woman has to say.
Let the best win out, clear to see.
A small desire but all that I could want.
LEADER   Spoken like a man, my lady, loyal,   355
full of self-command. I've heard your sign
and now your vision.

> [*Reaching towards her as she turns and re-enters the palace.*]
>
> Now to praise the gods.

The joy is worth the labor.
CHORUS   O Zeus my king and Night, dear Night,[5]
queen of the house who covers us with glories,[6]   360
you slung your net on the towers of Troy,
neither young nor strong could leap
the giant dredge net of slavery,
   all-embracing ruin.
I adore you, iron Zeus of the guests   365
and your revenge—you drew your longbow
year by year to a taut full draw
till one bolt, not falling short
or arching over the stars,
   could split the mark of Paris!   370

The sky stroke of god!—it is all Troy's to tell,
but even I can trace it to its cause:
god does as god decrees.
   And still some say
that heaven would never stoop to punish men   375
who trample the lovely grace of things
untouchable. How wrong they are!
   A curse burns bright on crime—
      full-blown, the father's crimes will blossom,
         burst into the son's.[7]   380
Let there be less suffering . . .
give us the sense to live on what we need.

> Bastions of wealth
> are no defense for the man
> who treads the grand altar of Justice   385
> down and out of sight.

Persuasion, maddening child of Ruin
overpowers him—Ruin plans it all.
And the wound will smolder on,
   there is no cure,   390

5. Troy fell to a night attack.   6. Probably the moon and stars; an obscure expression in the original.
7. The language throughout this passage is significantly general. The chorus refers to Paris, but everything
it says is equally applicable to Agamemnon, who sacrificed his daughter for his ambitions. The original
Greek is corrupt (that is, has been garbled in the handwritten tradition) but seems to proclaim the doctrine
that the sins of the fathers are visited on the children. So Paris and Agamemnon pay for the misdeeds of
their ancestors (as well as their own).

a terrible brilliance kindles on the night.
He is bad bronze scraped on a touchstone:
put to the test, the man goes black.[8]
    Like the boy who chases
      a bird on the wing, brands his city,   395
        brings it down and prays,
but the gods are deaf
to the one who turns to crime, they tear him down.

            So Paris learned:
            he came to Atreus' house   400
            and shamed the tables spread for guests,
              he stole away the queen.

And she left her land *chaos,* clanging shields,
companions tramping, bronze prows, men in bronze,
    and she came to Troy with a dowry, death,   405
strode through the gates
      defiant in every stride,
as prophets of the house[9] looked on and wept,
"Oh the halls and the lords of war,
    the bed and the fresh prints of love.   410
I *see* him, unavenging, unavenged,
the stun of his desolation is so clear—
    he longs for the one who lies across the sea
until her phantom seems to sway the house.

            Her curving images,   415
            her beauty hurts her lord,
            the eyes starve and the touch
              of love is gone,

and radiant dreams are passing in the night,
the memories throb with sorrow, joy with pain . . .   420
    it is pain to dream and see desires
slip through the arms,
      a vision lost forever
winging down the moving drifts of sleep."
So he grieves at the royal hearth   425
    yet others' grief is worse, far worse.
All through Greece for those who flocked to war
they are holding back the anguish now,
    you can feel it rising now in every house;
I tell you there is much to tear the heart.   430

            They knew the men they sent,
            but now in place of men

---

8. Inferior bronze, adulterated with lead, turns black with use.   **9.** Menelaus's.

ashes and urns come back
to every hearth.[1]

War, War, the great gold-broker of corpses   435
holds the balance of the battle on his spear!
Home from the pyres he sends them,
    home from Troy to the loved ones,
weighted with tears, the urns brimmed full,
    the heroes return in gold-dust,[2]   440
dear, light ash for men; and they weep,
they praise them, "He had skill in the swordplay,"
    "He went down so tall in the onslaught,"
"All for another's woman." So they mutter
in secret and the rancor steals   445
toward our staunch defenders, Atreus' sons.

            And there they ring the walls, the young,
            the lithe, the handsome hold the graves
            they won in Troy; the enemy earth
                rides over those who conquered.   450

The people's voice is heavy with hatred,
now the curses of the people must be paid,
and now I wait, I listen . . .
    there—there is something breathing
under the night's shroud. God takes aim   455
    at the ones who murder many;
the swarthy Furies stalk the man
gone rich beyond all rights—with a twist
    of fortune grind him down, dissolve him
into the blurring dead—there is no help.   460
The reach for power can recoil,
the bolt of god can strike you at a glance.

            Make me rich with no man's envy,
            neither a raider of cities, no,
            nor slave come face to face with life   465
                overpowered by another.

    [Speaking singly.]
—Fire comes and the news is good,
    it races through the streets
but is it true? Who knows?
Or just another lie from heaven?[3]   470

---

1. This strikes a contemporary note. In Homer the fallen Achaeans are buried at Troy, but in Aeschylus's Athens the dead were cremated on the battlefield, and their ashes were brought home for burial.   2. I.e., in ashes. The war god is a broker who gives, in exchange for bodies, gold dust (the word used for *bodies* could mean living bodies or corpses).   3. Later we will see Agamemnon come on stage with Cassandra (his Trojan captive) and the spoils of Troy. The chorus, which started out to sing a hymn of praise for the fall of Troy (line 359), ends in fear and despondency. It now questions the truth of Clytaemnestra's announcement; perhaps Troy has not fallen after all (line 469).

—Show us the man so childish, wonderstruck,
   he's fired up with the first torch,
then when the message shifts
he's sick at heart.

        —Just like a woman
to fill with thanks before the truth is clear.   475

—So gullible. Their stories spread like wildfire,
   they fly fast and die faster;
rumors voiced by women come to nothing.
LEADER   Soon we'll know her fires for what they are,
her relay race of torches hand-to-hand—   480
know if they're real or just a dream,
the hope of a morning here to take our senses.
I see a herald running from the beach
and a victor's spray of olive shades his eyes
and the dust he kicks, twin to the mud of Troy,   485
shows he has a voice—no kindling timber
on the cliffs, no signal-fires for him.
He can shout the news and give us joy,
or else . . . please, not that.
               Bring it on,
good fuel to build the first good fires.   490
And if anyone calls down the worst on Argos
let him reap the rotten harvest of his mind.
    [*The* HERALD *rushes in and kneels on the ground.*]
HERALD   Good Greek earth, the soil of my fathers!
Ten years out, and a morning brings me back.
All hopes snapped but one—I'm home at last.   495
Never dreamed I'd die in Greece, assigned
the narrow plot I love the best.
               And now
I salute the land, the light of the sun,
our high lord Zeus and the king of Pytho[4]—
no more arrows, master, raining on our heads!   500
At Scamander's banks we took our share,
your longbow brought us down like plague.[5]
Now come, deliver us, heal us—lord Apollo!
Gods of the market, here, take my salute.
And you, my Hermes,[6] Escort,   505
loving Herald, the herald's shield and prayer!—
And the shining dead[7] of the land who launched the armies,
warm us home . . . we're all the spear has left.

You halls of the kings, you roofs I cherish,
sacred seats—you gods that catch the sun,   510

4. Apollo.   5. Compare the opening scene of the *Iliad* 1 (p. 107), where Apollo punishes the Greeks
with his arrows (a metaphor for plague).   6. The gods' messenger and patron deity of heralds.   7. The
heroes of the past, who are buried in Argos and worshipped.

if your glances ever shone on him in the old days,
greet him well—so many years are lost.
He comes, he brings us light in the darkness,
free for every comrade, Agamemnon lord of men.

Give him the royal welcome he deserves!   515
He hoisted the pickax of Zeus who brings revenge,
he dug Troy down, he worked her soil down,
the shrines of her gods and the high altars, gone!—
and the seed of her wide earth he ground to bits.
That's the yoke he claps on Troy. The king,   520
the son of Atreus comes. The man is blest,
the one man alive to merit such rewards.

Neither Paris nor Troy, partners to the end,
can say their work outweighs their wages now.
Convicted of rapine, stripped of all his spoils,   525
and his father's house and the land that gave it life—
he's scythed them to the roots. The sons of Priam
pay the price twice over.
LEADER   Welcome home
from the wars, herald, long live your joy.
HERALD   Our joy—
now I could die gladly. Say the word, dear gods.   530
LEADER   Longing for your country left you raw?
HERALD   The tears fill my eyes, for joy.
LEADER   You too,
down the sweet disease that kills a man
with kindness . . .
HERALD   Go on, I don't see what you—
LEADER   Love
for the ones who love you—that's what took you.
HERALD   You mean   535
the land and the armies hungered for each other?
LEADER   There were times I thought I'd faint with longing.
HERALD   So anxious for the armies, why?
LEADER   For years now,
only my silence kept me free from harm.
HERALD   What,
with the kings gone did someone threaten you?
LEADER   So much . . . .[8]   540
now as you say, it would be good to die.
HERALD   True, we *have* done well.
Think back in the years and what have you?
A few runs of luck, a lot that's bad.
Who but a god can go through life unmarked?   545

---

8. Throughout this dialogue the chorus has been gearing itself up to warn the herald that there may be
danger for Agamemnon at home; at this point its nerve fails, and it abandons the attempt.

A long, hard pull we had, if I would tell it all.
The iron rations, penned in the gangways
hock by jowl like sheep. Whatever miseries
break a man, our quota, every sunstarved day.

Then on the beaches it was worse. Dug in   550
under the enemy ramparts—deadly going.
Out of the sky, out of the marshy flats
the dews soaked us, turned the ruts we fought from
into gullies, made our gear, our scalps
crawl with lice.

          And talk of the cold,   555
the sleet to freeze the gulls, and the big snows
come avalanching down from Ida. Oh but the heat,
the sea and the windless noons, the swells asleep,
dropped to a dead calm . . .

But why weep now?   560
It's over for us, over for them.
The dead can rest and never rise again;
no need to call their muster. We're alive,
do we have to go on raking up old wounds?
Good-by to all that. Glad I am to say it.   565

For us, the remains of the Greek contingents,
the good wins out, no pain can tip the scales,
not now. So shout this boast to the bright sun—
fitting it is—wing it over the seas and rolling earth:

"Once when an Argive expedition captured Troy   570
they hauled these spoils back to the gods of Greece,
they bolted them high across the temple doors,
the glory of the past!"

          And hearing that,
men will applaud our city and our chiefs,
and Zeus will have the hero's share of fame—   575
he did the work.

          That's all I have to say.
LEADER   I'm convinced, glad that I was wrong.
Never too old to learn; it keeps me young.
   [CLYTAEMNESTRA *enters with her women.*]
First the house and the queen, it's their affair,
but I can taste the riches.
CLYTAEMNESTRA   I cried out long ago!⁹—   580
for joy, when the first herald came burning
through the night and told the city's fall.
And there were some who smiled and said,

---

9. As the watchman had told her to (line 30).

"A few fires persuade you Troy's in ashes.
Women, women, elated over nothing."   585

You made me seem deranged.
For all that I sacrificed—a woman's way,
you'll say—station to station on the walls
we lifted cries of triumph that resounded
in the temples of the gods. We lulled and blessed   590
the fires with myrrh and they consumed our victims.
      [*Turning to the* HERALD.]
But enough. Why prolong the story?
From the king himself I'll gather all I need.
Now for the best way to welcome home
my lord, my good lord . . .
              No time to lose!   595
What dawn can feast a woman's eyes like this?
I can see the light, the husband plucked from war
by the Saving God and open wide the gates.

Tell him that, and have him come with speed,
the people's darling—how they long for him.   600
And for his wife,
may he return and find her true at hall,
just as the day he left her, faithful to the last.
A watchdog gentle to him alone,
      [*Glancing towards the palace.*]
                 savage
to those who cross his path. I have not changed.   605
The strains of time can never break our seal.
In love with a new lord, in ill repute I am
as practiced as I am in dyeing bronze.[1]

That is my boast, teeming with the truth.
I am proud, a woman of my nobility—   610
I'd hurl it from the roofs!
      [*She turns sharply, enters the palace.*]
LEADER She speaks well, but it takes no seer to know
  she only says what's right.
      [*The* HERALD *attempts to leave; the* LEADER *takes him by the arm.*]
              Wait, one thing.
Menelaus, is he home too, safe with the men?[2]
The power of the land—dear king.   615
HERALD I doubt that lies will help my friends,
  in the lean months to come.
LEADER Help us somehow, tell the truth as well.

---

1. She claims she is no more capable of adultery than she is of dyeing bronze; but she will later kill Agamemnon with a bronze weapon. 2. The relevance of this question and the following speeches lies in the fact that Menelaus's absence makes Agamemnon's murder easier (his presence might have made it impossible) and in the fact that Menelaus is bringing Helen home.

But when the two conflict it's hard to hide—
out with it.
HERALD   He's lost, gone from the fleets!³   620
He and his ship, it's true.
LEADER   After you watched him
pull away from Troy? Or did some storm
attack you all and tear him off the line?
HERALD   There,
like a marksman, the whole disaster cut to a word.
LEADER   How do the escorts give him out—dead or alive?   625
HERALD   No clear report. No one knows . . .
only the wheeling sun that heats the earth to life.
LEADER   But then the storm—how did it reach the ships?
How did it end? Were the angry gods on hand?
HERALD   This blessed day, ruin it with *them*?   630
Better to keep their trophies far apart.

When a runner comes, his face in tears,
saddled with what his city dreaded most,⁴
the armies routed, two wounds in one,
one to the city, one to hearth and home . . .   635
our best men, droves of them, victims
herded from every house by the two-barb whip
that Ares⁵ likes to crack,
                        that charioteer
who packs destruction shaft by shaft,
careening on with his brace of bloody mares—   640
When he comes in, I tell you, dragging that much pain,
wail your battle-hymn to the Furies, and high time!

But when he brings salvation home to a city
singing out her heart—
how can I mix the good with so much bad   645
and blurt out this?—
                        "Storms swept the Greeks,
and not without the anger of the gods!"

Those enemies for ages, fire⁶ and water,
sealed a pact and showed it to the world—
they crushed our wretched squadrons.
                              Night looming,   650
breakers lunging in for the kill
and the black gales come brawling out of the north—
ships ramming, prow into hooking prow, gored
by the rush-and-buck of hurricane pounding rain

---

3. For what happened to Menelaus, see the *Odyssey* 4 (pp. 247 ff.).   4. The herald creates a vivid picture
of a messenger bringing news of disaster to his city—a role he wishes to avoid.   5. The war god.
6. Lightning.

by the cloudburst—
ships stampeding into the darkness,   655
lashed and spun by the savage shepherd's hand![7]

But when the sun comes up to light the skies
I see the Aegean heaving into a great bloom
of corpses . . . Greeks, the pick of a generation
scattered through the wrecks and broken spars.   660

But not us, not our ship, our hull untouched.
Someone stole us away or begged us off.
No mortal—a god, death grip on the tiller,
or lady luck herself, perched on the helm,
she pulled us through, she saved us. Aye,   665
we'll never battle the heavy surf at anchor,
never shipwreck up some rocky coast.

But once we cleared that sea-hell, not even
trusting luck in the cold light of day,
we battened on our troubles, they were fresh—   670
the armada punished, bludgeoned into nothing.

And now if one of them still has the breath
he's saying *we* are lost. Why not?
We say the same of him. Well,
here's to the best.
                    And Menelaus?   675
Look to it, he's come back, and yet . . .
if a shaft of the sun can track him down,
alive, and his eyes full of the old fire—
thanks to the strategies of Zeus, Zeus
would never tear the house out by the roots—   680
then there's hope our man will make it home.

You've heard it all. Now you have the truth.
        [*Rushing out.*]
CHORUS   Who—what power named the name[8] that drove your fate?—
what hidden brain could divine your future,
steer that word to the mark,   685
to the bride of spears,
    the whirlpool churning armies,
        Oh for all the world a Helen!
Hell at the prows, hell at the gates
hell on the men-of-war,   690
from her lair's sheer veils she drifted
    launched by the giant western wind,
        and the long tall waves of men in armor,

---

7. The ships were scattered like sheep dispersed by a cruel shepherd.   8. Helen. The name contains the
Greek root *hele-*, which means "destroy." The chorus is so obsessed with Helen's guilt that it fails to
recognize the true responsibility for the war and the imminence of disaster.

huntsmen[9] trailing the oar-blades' dying spoor
slipped into her moorings,   695
    Simois'[1] mouth that chokes with foliage,
        bayed for bloody strife,

for Troy's Blood Wedding Day—she drives her word,
her burning will to the birth, the Fury
late but true to the cause,   700
to the tables shamed
    and Zeus who guards the hearth[2]—
        the Fury makes the Trojans pay!
Shouting their hymns, hymns for the bride
hymns for the kinsmen doomed   705
to the wedding march of Fate.
    Troy changed her tune in her late age,
        and I think I hear the dirges mourning
"Paris, born and groomed for the bed of Fate!"
They mourn with their life breath,   710
    they sing their last, the sons of Priam
        born for bloody slaughter.

    So a man once reared
a lion cub at hall, snatched
from the breast, still craving milk   715
    in the first flush of life.
A captivating pet for the young,
and the old men adored it, pampered it
    in their arms, day in, day out,
like an infant just born.   720
Its eyes on fire, little beggar,
fawning for its belly, slave to food.

    But it came of age
and the parent strain broke out
and it paid its breeders back.   725
    Grateful it was, it went
through the flock to prepare a feast,
an illicit orgy—the house swam with blood,
    one could resist that agony—
        massacre vast and raw!   730
From god there came a priest of ruin,
adopted by the house to lend it warmth.

And the first sensation Helen brought to Troy . . .
call it a spirit
    shimmer of winds dying   735
        glory light as gold
        shaft of the eyes dissolving, open bloom

---

9. The Achaean army, which came after her.   1. A river in Troy.   2. I.e., protects the host and guest.

that wounds the heart with love.
But veering wild in mid-flight
she whirled her wedding on to a stabbing end,   740
slashed at the sons of Priam—hearthmate, friend to the death,
    sped by Zeus who speeds the guest,
a bride of tears, a Fury.

There's an ancient saying, old as man himself:
men's prosperity   745
    never will die childless,
        once full-grown it breeds.
    Sprung from the great good fortune in the race
comes bloom on bloom of pain—
insatiable wealth. But not I,   750
I alone say this. Only the reckless act
can breed impiety, multiplying crime on crime,
    while the house kept straight and just
is blessed with radiant children.[3]

        ut ancient Violence longs to breed,   755
        new Violence comes
        when its fatal hour comes, the demon comes
        to take her toll—no war, no force, no prayer
        can hinder the midnight Fury stamped
        with parent Fury moving through the house.   760

        But Justice shines in sooty hovels,[4]
        loves the decent life.
        From proud halls crusted with gilt by filthy hands
        she turns her eyes to find the pure in spirit—
        spurning the wealth stamped counterfeit with praise,   765
        she steers all things toward their destined end.[5]

[AGAMEMNON *enters in his chariot, his plunder borne before him by his entourage; behind him, half hidden, stands* CASSANDRA. *The old men press toward him.*]

Come, my king, the scourge of Troy,
    the true son of Atreus—
How to salute you, how to praise you
neither too high nor low, but hit   770
the note of praise that suits the hour?
So many prize some brave display,
they prefer some flaunt of honor
    once they break the bounds.
When a man fails they share his grief,
but the pain can never cut them to the quick.   775

---

3. These lines begin with the traditional Greek view that immoderate good fortune (or excellence of any kind beyond the average) is itself the cause of disaster. The chorus, however, rejects this view and states that only an act of evil produces evil consequences. **4.** The homes of the poor. **5.** Here the chorus admits, by implication, that the poor are less likely to commit evil acts.

When a man succeeds they share his glory,
torturing their faces into smiles.
But the good shepherd knows his flock.
When the eyes seem to brim with love   780
    and it is only unction,
he will know, better than we can know.
That day you marshaled the armies
all for Helen—no hiding it now—
I drew you in my mind in black;   785
you seemed a menace at the helm,
    sending men to the grave
to bring her home, that hell on earth.
But now from the depths of trust and love
I say Well fought, well won—   790
    the end is worth the labor!
Search, my king, and learn at last
who stayed at home and kept their faith
and who betrayed the city.[6]

AGAMEMNON   First,
with justice I salute my Argos and my gods,   795
my accomplices who brought me home and won
my rights from Priam's Troy—the just gods.
No need to hear our pleas. Once for all
they consigned their lots to the urn of blood,[7]
they pitched on death for men, annihilation   800
for the city. Hope's hand, hovering
over the urn of mercy, left it empty.
Look for the smoke—it is the city's seamark,
building even now.
                    The storms of ruin live!
Her last dying breath, rising up from the ashes   805
sends us gales of incense rich in gold.

For that we must thank the gods with a sacrifice
our sons will long remember. For their mad outrage
of a queen we raped their city—we were right.
The beast of Argos, foals of the wild mare,[8]   810
thousands massed in armor rose on the night
the Pleiades went down,[9] and crashing through
their walls our bloody lion lapped its fill,
gorging on the blood of kings.
                    Our thanks to the gods,
long drawn out, but it is just the prelude.   815

    [CLYTAEMNESTRA approaches with her women; they are carrying dark red
    tapestries. AGAMEMNON turns to the LEADER.]

---

6. The chorus tries to warn Agamemnon against flatterers and dissemblers, but he misses its drift.   7. In
an Athenian law court there were two urns—one for acquittal, one for condemnation—into which the
jurors dropped their pebbles. (The audience will see them on stage in the final play of the trilogy.)   8. The
wooden horse, the stratagem with which the Greeks captured the city.   9. The setting of a group of stars
in the constellation Taurus, late in the fall.

And your concern, old man, is on my mind.
I hear you and agree, I will support you.
How rare, men with the character to praise
a friend's success without a trace of envy,
poison to the heart—it deals a double blow.   820
Your own losses weigh you down but then,
look at your neighbor's fortune and you weep.
Well I know. I understand society,
the fawning mirror of the proud.

                    My comrades . . .
they're shadows, I tell you, ghosts of men   825
who swore they'd die for me. Only Odysseus:
I dragged that man to the wars[1] but once in harness
he was a trace-horse,[2] he gave his all for me.
Dead or alive, no matter, I can praise him.

And now this cause involving men and gods.   830
We must summon the city for a trial,
found a national tribunal. Whatever's healthy,
shore it up with law and help it flourish.
Wherever something calls for drastic cures
we make our noblest effort: amputate or wield   835
the healing iron, burn the cancer at the roots.

Now I go to my father's house—
I give the gods my right hand, my first salute.
The ones who sent me forth have brought me home.
[*He starts down from the chariot, looks at* CLYTAEMNESTRA, *stops, and
offers up a prayer.*]
Victory, you have sped my way before,   840
now speed me to the last.
    [CLYTAEMNESTRA *turns from the king to the* CHORUS.]
CLYTAEMNESTRA   Old nobility of Argos
gathered here, I am not ashamed to tell you
how I love the man. I am older,
and the fear dies away . . . I am human.
Nothing I say was learned from others.   845
This is my life, my ordeal, long as the siege
he laid at Troy and more demanding.
                    First,
when a woman sits at home and the man is gone,
the loneliness is terrible,
unconscionable . . .   850
and the rumors spread and fester,
a runner comes with something dreadful,

---

1. Feigning madness to escape going to Troy, Odysseus was tricked into demonstrating his sanity. Agamemnon's remark shows that the truth is far from his mind; he has no thought that his danger comes from
a woman.   2. A third horse that ran beside the team that pulled a chariot; it lent help when special
maneuvering was needed, particularly in making tight turns.

close on his heels the next and his news worse,
and they shout it out and the whole house can hear;
and wounds—if he took one wound for each report 855
to penetrate these walls, he's gashed like a dragnet,
more, if he had only died . . .
for each death that swelled his record, he could boast
like a triple-bodied Geryon[3] risen from the grave,
"Three shrouds I dug from the earth, one for every body 860
that went down!"
            The rumors broke like fever,
broke and then rose higher. There were times
they cut me down and eased my throat from the noose.
I wavered between the living and the dead.

    [*Turning to* AGAMEMNON.]

                        And so
our child is gone, not standing by our side, 865
the bond of our dearest pledges, mine and yours;
by all rights our child should be here . . .
Orestes. You seem startled.
You needn't be. Our loyal brother-in-arms
will take good care of him, Strophios[4] the Phocian. 870
He warned from the start we court two griefs in one.
You risk all on the wars—and what if the people
rise up howling for the king, and anarchy
should dash our plans?
             Men, it is their nature,
trampling on the fighter once he's down. 875
Our child is gone. That is my self-defense
and it is true.
            For me, the tears that welled
like springs are dry. I have no tears to spare.
I'd watch till late at night, my eyes still burn,
I sobbed by the torch I lit for you alone. 880

    [*Glancing towards the palace.*]

I never let it die . . . but in my dreams
the high thin wail of a gnat would rouse me,
piercing like a trumpet—I could see you
suffer more than all
the hours that slept with me could ever bear. 885

I endured it all. And now, free of grief,
I would salute that man the watchdog of the fold,
the mainroyal,[5] saving stay of the vessel,
rooted oak that thrusts the roof sky-high,
the father's one true heir. 890
Land at dawn to the shipwrecked past all hope,

---

3. A monster (eventually killed by Heracles) who had three bodies and three heads.   4. King of Phocis, a mountainous region near Delphi. His son, Pylades, accompanies Orestes when he returns to avenge Agamemnon's death.   5. Upper section of the mainmast.

light of the morning burning off the night of storm,
the cold clear spring to the parched horseman—
O the ecstasy, to flee the yoke of Fate!

It is right to use the titles he deserves.   895
Let envy keep her distance. We have suffered
long enough.
        [*Reaching toward* AGAMEMNON.]
            Come to me now, my dearest,
down from the car of war, but never set the foot
that stamped out Troy on earth again, my great one.

Women, why delay? You have your orders.   900
Pave his way with tapestries.⁶
        [*They begin to spread the crimson tapestries between the king and the
        palace doors.*]
                        Quickly.
Let the red stream flow and bear him home
to the home he never hoped to see—Justice,
lead him in!
        Leave all the rest to me.
The spirit within me never yields to sleep.   905
We will set things right, with the god's help.
We will do whatever Fate requires.
AGAMEMNON   There
    is Leda's daughter,⁷ the keeper of my house.
And the speech to suit my absence, much too long.
But the praise that does us justice,   910
let it come from others, then we prize it.
                        This—
You treat me like a woman. Groveling, gaping up at me!
What am I, some barbarian⁸ peacocking out of Asia?
Never cross my path with robes and draw the lightning.
Never—only the gods deserve the pomps of honor   915
and the stiff brocades of fame. To walk on them . . .
I am human, and it makes my pulses stir
with dread.
        Give me the tributes of a man
and not a god, a little earth to walk on,
not this gorgeous work.   920
There is no need to sound my reputation.
I have a sense of right and wrong, what's more—
heaven's proudest gift. Call no man blest
until he ends his life in peace, fulfilled.
If I can live by what I say, I have no fear.   925

---

6. To walk on those tapestries, wall hangings dyed with the expensive crimson, would be an act of extravagant pride. Pride is the keynote of Agamemnon's character, and it suits Clytaemnestra's sense of fitness that he should go into his death in godlike state, "trampling royal crimson" (line 957), the color of blood.
7. Clytaemnestra. Helen is also a daughter of Leda.   8. Foreigner, especially Asiatic. Aeschylus is thinking of the pomp and servility of the contemporary Persian court.

CLYTAEMNESTRA   One thing more. Be true to your ideals and tell me—

AGAMEMNON   True to my ideals? Once I violate them I am lost.

CLYTAEMNESTRA   Would you have sworn this act to god in a time of
terror?

AGAMEMNON   Yes, if a prophet called for a last, drastic rite.

CLYTAEMNESTRA   But Priam—can you see him if he had your
success?   930

AGAMEMNON   Striding on the tapestries of God, I see him now.

CLYTAEMNESTRA   And *you* fear the reproach of common men?

AGAMEMNON   The voice of the people—aye, they have enormous power.

CLYTAEMNESTRA   Perhaps, but where's the glory without a little gall?

AGAMEMNON   And where's the woman in all this lust for glory?   935

CLYTAEMNESTRA   But the great victor—it becomes him to give way.

AGAMEMNON   Victory in this . . . war of ours, it means so much to you?

CLYTAEMNESTRA   O give way! The power is yours if you surrender
all of your own free will to me.

AGAMEMNON   Enough.
If you are so determined—   940
   [*Turning to the women, pointing to his boots.*]
Let someone help me off with these at least.
Old slaves, they've stood me well.
                                                       Hurry,
and while I tread his splendors dyed red in the sea,[9]
may no god watch and strike me down with envy
from on high. I feel such shame—   945
to tread the life of the house, a kingdom's worth
of silver in the weaving.
   [*He steps down from the chariot to the tapestries and reveals* CASSANDRA,
   dressed in the sacred regalia, the fillets, robes and scepter of Apollo.]
                             Done is done.
Escort this stranger[1] in, be gentle.
Conquer with compassion. Then the gods
shine down upon you, gently. No one chooses   950
the yoke of slavery, not of one's free will—
and she least of all. The gift of the armies,
flower and pride of all the wealth we won,
she follows me from Troy.
                             And now,
since you have brought me down with your insistence,   955
just this once I enter my father's house,
trampling royal crimson as I go.
   [*He takes his first steps and pauses.*]
CLYTAEMNESTRA   There is the sea
and who will drain it dry? Precious as silver,
inexhaustible, ever-new, it breeds the more we reap it—
tides on tides of crimson dye our robes blood-red.   960

9. The dye was made from shellfish.   1. Cassandra, daughter of Priam, Agamemnon's share of the
human booty of the sack of Troy. She was loved by Apollo, who gave her the gift of prophecy; but when
she refused her love to the god, he saw to it that her prophecies, though true, would never be believed until
it was too late.

Our lives are based on wealth, my king,
the gods have seen to that.
Destitution, our house has never heard the word.
I would have sworn to tread on legacies of robes,
at one command from an oracle, deplete the house—   965
suffer the worst to bring that dear life back!

[*Encouraged,* AGAMEMNON *strides to the entrance.*]

When the root lives on, the new leaves come back,
spreading a dense shroud of shade across the house
to thwart the Dog Star's² fury. So you return
to the father's hearth, you bring us warmth in winter   970
like the sun—

　　　　　And you are Zeus when Zeus
tramples the bitter virgin grape for new wine
and the welcome chill steals through the halls, at last
the master moves among the shadows of his house, fulfilled.

[AGAMEMNON *goes over the threshold; the women gather up the tapestries
while* CLYTAEMNESTRA *prays.*]

Zeus, Zeus, master of all fullfillment, now fulfill our prayers—   975
speed our rites to their fulfillment once for all!

[*She enters the palace, the doors close, the old men huddle in terror.*]

CHORUS　Why, why does it rock me, never stops,
this terror beating down my heart,
　　this seer that sees it all—
it beats its wings, uncalled unpaid   980
thrust on the lungs
the mercenary song beats on and on
singing a prophet's strain—
　and I can't throw it off
like dreams that make no sense,   985
and the strength drains
that filled the mind with trust,
and the years drift by and the driven sand
　　　has buried the mooring lines
that churned when the armored squadrons cut for Troy . . .   990
and now I believe it, I can prove he's home,
　　my own clear eyes for witness—
　　　　　　　　　　　　Agamemnon!
Still it's chanting, beating deep so deep in the heart
this dirge of the Furies, oh dear god,
not fit for the lyre,³ its own master   995
　it kills our spirit
kills our hopes
and it's real, true, no fantasy—
　　stark terror whirls the brain
　　　and the end is coming   1000
　　　　Justice comes to birth—

---

2. Sirius; its appearance in the summer sky marked the beginning of the hot season (the "dog days" of summer).　3. A stringed instrument played on joyful occasions (hence "lyric" poetry).

I pray my fears prove false and fall
and die and never come to birth!
Even exultant health, well we know,
 exceeds its limits,[4] comes so near disease   1005
it can breach the wall between them.

Even a man's fate, held true on course,
 in a blinding flash rams some hidden reef;
but if caution only casts the pick of the cargo—
one well-balanced cast—   1010
the house will not go down, not outright;[5]
laboring under its wealth of grief
the ship of state rides on.

Yes, and the great green bounty of god,
sown in the furrows year by year and reaped each fall   1015
can end the plague of famine.

But a man's lifeblood
 is dark and mortal.
Once it wets the earth
what song can sing it back?   1020
Not even the master-healer[6]
 who brought the dead to life—
Zeus stopped the man before he did more harm.

Oh, if only the gods had never forged
the chain that curbs our excess,   1025
 one man's fate curbing the next man's fate,
my heart would outrace my song, I'd pour out all I feel—
 but no, I choke with anguish,
  mutter through the nights.
Never to ravel out a hope in time   1030
and the brain is swarming, burning—

  [CLYTAEMNESTRA *emerges from the palace and goes to* CASSANDRA, *impassive in the chariot.*]

CLYTAEMNESTRA   Won't you come inside? I mean you, Cassandra.
Zeus in all his mercy wants you to share
some victory libations with the house.
The slaves are flocking. Come, lead them   1035
up to the altar of the god who guards
our dearest treasures.
        Down from the chariot,
no time for pride. Why even Heracles,[7]
they say, was sold into bondage long ago,

---

4. Excess, even in blessings like health, is always dangerous. The chorus fears that Agamemnon's triumphant success may threaten his safety.   **5.** These lines refer to a traditional Greek belief that the fortunate person could avert the envy of heaven by deliberately getting rid of some precious possession.   **6.** Asclepius, the great physician who was so skilled that he finally succeeded in restoring a dead man to life. Zeus struck him with a thunderbolt for going too far.   **7.** The Greek hero, famous for his twelve labors that rid the Earth of monsters, was at one time forced to be the slave to Omphale, an Eastern queen.

he had to endure the bitter bread of slaves. 1040
But if the yoke descends on you, be grateful
for a master born and reared in ancient wealth.
Those who reap a harvest past their hopes
are merciless to their slaves.
                                    From us
you will receive what custom says is right. 1045
        [CASSANDRA *remains impassive.*]
LEADER   It's *you* she is speaking to, it's all too clear.
    You're caught in the nets of doom—obey
    if you can obey, unless you cannot bear to.
CLYTAEMNESTRA   Unless she's like a swallow, possessed
    of her own barbaric song,[8] strange, dark. 1050
    I speak directly as I can—she must obey.
LEADER   Go with her. Make the best of it, she's right.
    Step down from the seat, obey her.
CLYTAEMNESTRA   Do it *now*—
    I have no time to spend outside. Already
    the victims crowd the hearth, the Navelstone,[9] 1055
    to bless this day of joy I never hoped to see!—
    our victims waiting for the fire and the knife,
    and you,
    if you want to taste our mystic rites, come now.
    If my words can't reach you—
        [*Turning to the* LEADER.]
                                    Give her a sign, 1060
    one of her exotic handsigns.
LEADER   I think
    the stranger needs an interpreter, someone clear.
    She's like a wild creature, fresh caught.
CLYTAEMNESTRA   She's mad,
    her evil genius murmuring in her ears.
    She comes from a *city* fresh caught. 1065
    She must learn to take the cutting bridle
    before she foams her spirit off in blood—
    and that's the last I waste on her contempt!
        [*Wheeling, re-entering the palace. The* LEADER *turns to* CASSANDRA, *who
        remains transfixed.*]
LEADER   Not I, I pity her. I will be gentle.
    Come, poor thing. Leave the empty chariot— 1070
    Of your own free will try on the yoke of Fate.
CASSANDRA   Aieeeeee! Earth—Mother—
                        Curse of the Earth—Apollo Apollo!
LEADER   Why cry to Apollo?
    He's not the god to call with sounds of mourning.
CASSANDRA   Aieeeeee! Earth—Mother— 1075
                        Rape of the Earth—Apollo Apollo!

8. The comparison of foreign speech to the twittering of a swallow was a Greek commonplace.   9. An
altar of Zeus Herkeios, guardian of the hearth, which was the religious center of the home.

LEADER   Again, it's a bad omen.
  She cries for the god who wants no part of grief.[1]
    [CASSANDRA *steps from the chariot, looks slowly towards the rooftops of*
    the palace.]
CASSANDRA   God of the long road,
  Apollo *Apollo* my destroyer—
you destroy me once,[2] destroy me twice—   1080
LEADER   She's about to sense her own ordeal, I think.
  Slave that she is, the god lives on inside her.
CASSANDRA   God of the iron marches,
  Apollo *Apollo* my destroyer—
where, where have you led[3] me now? what house—   1085
LEADER   The house of Atreus and his sons. Really—
  don't you know? It's true, see for yourself.
CASSANDRA   No . . . the house that hates god,
    an echoing womb of guilt, kinsmen
      torturing kinsmen, severed heads,   1090
slaughterhouse of heroes, soil streaming blood—
LEADER   A keen hound, this stranger.
  Trailing murder, and murder she will find.
CASSANDRA   See, my witnesses—
    I trust to them, to the babies   1095
      wailing, skewered on the sword,
their flesh charred, the father gorging on their parts[4]—
LEADER   We'd heard your fame as a seer,
  but no one looks for seers in Argos.
CASSANDRA   Oh no, what horror, what new plot,[5]   1100
new agony this?—
  it's growing, massing, deep in the house,
    a plot, a monstrous—*thing*
      to crush the loved ones, no,
there is no cure, and rescue's far away[6] and—   1105
LEADER   I can't read these signs; I knew the first,
  the city rings with them.
CASSANDRA   You, you godforsaken—you'd do *this*?
  The lord of your bed,
you bathe him . . . his body glistens, then—   1110
  how to tell the climax?—
      comes so quickly, see,
  hand over hand shoots out, hauling ropes—
                                          then lunge!
LEADER   Still lost. Her riddles, her dark words of god—
  I'm groping, helpless.

1. Apollo (and the Olympian gods in general) was not invoked in mourning or lamentation.   2. The
name *Apollo* suggests the Greek word *apollumi*, "destroy." He destroyed her the first time when he saw to
it that no one would believe her prophecies. *God of the long road*: Apollo Agyieus. This statue, a conical
pillar, was set up outside the door of the house; no doubt there was one onstage.   3. The Greek word (a
form of the verb *agō*) suggests the god's title Agyieus.   4. The feast of Thyestes, who was tricked by his
brother, Atreus, into eating his own children. The story is told by Aegisthus below (lines 1606–43).
5. Clytaemnestra's murder of Agamemnon.   6. A reference to Menelaus (distant in space) and Orestes
(distant in time).

CASSANDRA   No no, look *there!*—   1115
   what's that? some net flung out of hell—
     No, *she* is the snare,
   the bedmate, deathmate, murder's strong right arm!
     Let the insatiate discord in the race
   rear up and shriek "Avenge the victim—stone them dead!"   1120
LEADER   What Fury is this? Why rouse it, lift its wailing
   through the house? I hear you and lose hope.
CHORUS   Drop by drop at the heart, the gold of life ebbs out.
     We are the old soldiers . . . wounds will come
   with the crushing sunset of our lives.   1125
   Death is close, and quick.
CASSANDRA   Look out! *look out!*—
   Ai, drag the great bull from the mate!—
   a thrash of robes, she traps him—
   writhing—
         black horn glints, twists—
                    she gores him through!
     And now he buckles, look, the bath swirls red—   1130
   There's stealth and murder in the cauldron, do you hear?
LEADER   I'm no judge, I've little skill with the oracles,
   but even I know danger when I hear it.
CHORUS   What good are the oracles to men? Words, more words,
     and the hurt comes on us, endless words   1135
   and a seer's techniques have brought us
   terror and the truth.
CASSANDRA   The agony—O I am breaking!—Fate's so hard,
   and the pain that floods my voice is mine alone.
   Why have you brought me here, tormented as I am?   1140
   Why, unless to die with him, why else?
LEADER AND CHORUS   Mad with the rapture—god speeds you on
     to the song, the deathsong,
   like the nightingale[7] that broods on sorrow,
     mourns her son, her son,   1145
   her life inspired with grief for him,
   she lilts and shrills, dark bird that lives for night.
CASSANDRA   The nightingale—O for a song, a fate like hers!
     The gods gave her a life of ease, swathed her in wings,
   no tears, no wailing. The knife waits for me.   1150
   They'll splay me on the iron's double edge.
LEADER AND CHORUS   Why?—what god hurls you on, stroke on stroke
     to the long dying fall?
   Why the horror clashing through your music,
     terror struck to song?—   1155
   why the anguish, the wild dance?
   Where do your words of god and grief begin?
CASSANDRA   Ai, the wedding, wedding of Paris,

---

7. Philomela was raped by Tereus, the husband of her sister Procne. The two sisters avenged themselves by killing Tereus's son, Itys, and serving up his flesh to Tereus to eat. Procne was changed into a nightingale mourning for Itys (the name is an imitation of the sound of the nightingale's song).

death to the loved ones. Oh Scamander,[8]
you nursed my father . . . once at your banks   1160
    I nursed and grew, and now at the banks
of Acheron,[9] the stream that carries sorrow,
it seems I'll chant my prophecies too soon.
LEADER AND CHORUS   What are you saying? Wait, it's clear,
a child could see the truth, it wounds within,   1165
    Like a bloody fang it tears—
    I hear your destiny—breaking sobs,
        cries that stab the ears.
CASSANDRA   Oh the grief, the grief of the city
ripped to oblivion. Oh the victims,   1170
the flocks my father burned at the wall,
    rich herds in flames . . . no cure for the doom
that took the city after all, and I,
her last ember, I go down with her.
LEADER AND CHORUS   You cannot stop, your song goes on—   1175
some spirit drops from the heights and treads you down
    and the brutal strain grows—
    your death-throes come and come and
        I cannot see the end!
CASSANDRA   Then off with the veils that hid the fresh young
    bride[1]—   1180
we will see the truth.
Flare up once more, my oracle! Clear and sharp
as the wind that blows toward the rising sun,
I can feel a deeper swell now, gathering head
to break at last and bring the dawn of grief.   1185

No more riddles. I will teach you.
Come, bear witness, run and hunt with me.
We trail the old barbaric works of slaughter.

These roofs—look up—there is a dancing troupe
that never leaves. And they have their harmony   1190
but it is harsh, their words are harsh, they drink
beyond the limit. Flushed on the blood of men
their spirit grows and none can turn away
their revel breeding in the veins—the Furies!
They cling to the house for life. They sing,   1195
sing of the frenzy that began it all,
strain rising on strain, showering curses
on the man who tramples on his brother's bed.[2]

There. Have I hit the mark or not? Am I a fraud,
a fortune-teller babbling lies from door to door?   1200
Swear how well I know the ancient crimes

8. A Trojan river.   9. One of the rivers of the underworld.   1. At this point, as the meter indicates,
Cassandra changes from lyric song, the medium of emotion, to spoken iambic lines, the medium of rational
discourse.   2. Thyestes, who seduced the wife of his brother, Atreus.

that live within this house.

LEADER   And if I did?
Would an oath bind the wounds and heal us?
But you amaze me. Bred across the sea,
your language strange, and still you sense the truth   1205
as if you had been here.

CASSANDRA   Apollo the Prophet
introduced me to his gift.

LEADER   A *god*—and moved with love?

CASSANDRA   I was ashamed to tell this once,
but now . . .

LEADER   We spoil ourselves with scruples,   1210
long as things go well.

CASSANDRA   He came like a wrestler,
magnificent, took me down and breathed his fire
through me and—

LEADER   You bore him a child?

CASSANDRA   I yielded,
then at the climax I recoiled—I deceived Apollo!

LEADER   But the god's skills—they seized you even then?   1215

CASSANDRA   Even then I told my people all the grief to come.

LEADER   And Apollo's anger never touched you?—is it possible?

CASSANDRA   Once I betrayed him I could never be believed.

LEADER   We believe you. Your visions seem so true.

CASSANDRA   Aieeeee!—
the pain, the terror! the birth-pang of the seer   1220
who tells the truth—
                   it whirls me, oh,
the storm comes again, the crashing chords!
Look, you see them nestling at the threshold?
Young, young in the darkness like a dream,
like children really, yes, and their loved ones   1225
brought them down . . .
             their hands, they fill their hands
with their own flesh, they are serving it like food,
holding out their entrails . . . now it's clear,
I can see the armfuls of compassion, see the father
reach to taste and—
               For so much suffering,   1230
I tell you, someone plots revenge.
A lion[3] who lacks a lion's heart,
he sprawled at home in the royal lair
and set a trap for the lord on his return.
My lord . . . I must wear his yoke, I am his slave.   1235
The lord of the men-of-war, he obliterated Troy—
he is so blind, so lost to that detestable hellhound
who pricks her ears and fawns and her tongue draws out
her glittering words of welcome—
               No, he cannot see

---

3. Aegisthus.

the stroke that Fury's hiding, stealth, murder.   1240
What outrage—the woman kills the man!
                              What to call
that . . . monster of Greece, and bring my quarry down?
Viper coiling back and forth?
                         Some sea-witch?—
Scylla⁴ crouched in her rocky nest—nightmare of sailors?
Raging mother of death, storming deathless war against   1245
the ones she loves!
                   And how she howled in triumph,
boundless outrage. Just as the tide of battle
broke her way, she seems to rejoice that he
is safe at home from war, saved for her.

Believe me if you will. What will it matter   1250
if you won't? It comes when it comes,
and soon you'll see it face to face
and say the seer was all too true.
You will be moved with pity.
LEADER   Thyestes' feast,
the children's flesh—that I know,   1255
and the fear shudders through me. It's true,
real, no dark signs about it. I hear the rest
but it throws me off the scent.
CASSANDRA   Agamemnon.
You will see him dead.
LEADER   Peace, poor girl!
Put those words to sleep.
CASSANDRA   No use,   1260
the Healer⁵ has no hand in this affair.
LEADER   Not if it's true—but god forbid it is!
CASSANDRA   You pray, and they close in to kill!
LEADER   What man prepares this, this dreadful—
CASSANDRA   Man?
You *are* lost, to every word I've said.
LEADER   Yes—   1265
I don't see who can bring the evil off.
CASSANDRA   And yet I know my Greek, too well.
LEADER   So does the Delphic oracle,⁶
but he's hard to understand.
CASSANDRA   His *fire!*—
sears me, sweeps me again—the torture!   1270
Apollo Lord of the Light, you burn,
you blind me—
             Agony!
             She is the lioness,
she rears on her hind legs, she beds with the wolf

---

4. A human-eating sea monster (see *Odyssey* 12, pp. 349–50).   5. Apollo.   6. Apollo's oracle; its
replies were celebrated for their obscurity and ambiguity.

when her lion king goes ranging—
                              she will kill me—
Ai, the torture!
                    She is mixing her drugs,   1275
adding a measure more of hate for me.
She gloats as she whets the sword for him.
He brought me home and we will pay in carnage.

Why mock yourself with these—trappings, the rod,
the god's wreath, his yoke around my throat?   1280
Before I die I'll tread you—
          [*Ripping off her regalia, stamping it into the ground.*]
                              Down, out,
die die die!
Now you're down. I've paid you back.
Look for another victim—I am free at last—
make her rich in all your curse and doom.
          [*Staggering backwards as if wrestling with a spirit tearing at her robes.*]
                              See,   1285
Apollo himself, his fiery hands—I feel him again,
he's stripping off my robes, the Seer's robes!
And after he looked down and saw me mocked,
even in these, his glories, mortified by friends
I loved, and they hated me, they were so blind   1290
to their own demise—
                    I went from door to door,
I was wild with the god, I heard them call me
"Beggar! Wretch! Starve for bread in hell!"

And I endured it all, and now he will
extort me as his due. A seer for the Seer.   1295
He brings me here to die like this,
not to serve at my father's altar. No,
the block is waiting. The cleaver steams
with my life blood, the first blood drawn
for the king's last rites.
          [*Regaining her composure and moving to the altar.*]
                              We will die,   1300
but not without some honor from the gods.
There will come another[7] to avenge us,
born to kill his mother, born
his father's champion. A wanderer, a fugitive
driven off his native land, he will come home   1305
to cope the stones of hate that menace all he loves.
The gods have sworn a monumental oath: as his father lies
upon the ground he draws him home with power like a prayer.

Then why so pitiful, why so many tears?
I have seen my city faring as she fared,   1310

---

7. Orestes.

and those who took her, judged by the gods,
faring as they fare. I must be brave.
It is my turn to die.
    [*Approaching the doors.*]
I address you as the Gates of Death.
I pray it comes with one clear stroke,   1315
no convulsions, the pulses ebbing out
in gentle death. I'll close my eyes and sleep.
LEADER   So much pain, poor girl, and so much truth,
   you've told so much. But if you *see* it coming,
   clearly—how can you go to your own death,   1320
   like a beast to the altar driven on by god,
   and hold your head so high?
CASSANDRA   No escape, my friends,
   not now.
LEADER   But the last hour should be savored.
CASSANDRA   My time has come. Little to gain from flight.
LEADER   You're brave, believe me, full of gallant heart.   1325
CASSANDRA   Only the wretched go with praise like that.
LEADER   But to go nobly lends a man some grace.
CASSANDRA   My noble father—you and your noble children.
    [*She nears the threshold and recoils, groaning in revulsion.*]
LEADER   What now? what terror flings you back?
   Why? Unless some horror in the brain—
CASSANDRA   Murder.   1330
   The house breathes with murder—bloody shambles![8]
LEADER   No, no, only the victims at the hearth.
CASSANDRA   I know that odor. I smell the open grave.
LEADER   But the Syrian myrrh,[9] it fills the halls with splendor,
   can't you sense it?
CASSANDRA   Well, I must go in now,   1335
   mourning Agamemnon's death and mine.
   Enough of life!
    [*Approaching the doors again and crying out.*]
          Friends—I cried out,
   not from fear like a bird fresh caught,
   but that you will testify to *how* I died.
   When the queen, woman for woman, dies for me,   1340
   and a man falls for the man who married grief.
   That's all I ask, my friends. A stranger's gift
   for one about to die.
LEADER   Poor creature, you
   and the end you see so clearly. I pity you.
CASSANDRA   I'd like a few words more, a kind of dirge,   1345
   it is my own. I pray to the sun,
   the last light I'll see,
   that when the avengers cut the assassins down
   they will avenge me too, a slave who died,

---

8. A slaughterhouse.   9. Incense burned at the sacrifice. Another interpretation of this line runs, "What you speak of (that is, the smell of the open grave) is no Syrian incense, giving splendor to the palace."

an easy conquest.
                               Oh men, your destiny.   1350
When all is well a shadow can overturn it.
When trouble comes a stroke of the wet sponge,
and the picture's blotted out. And that,
I think that breaks the heart.
            [*She goes through the doors.*]
CHORUS   But the lust for power never dies—   1355
       men cannot have enough.
No one will lift a hand to send it
from his door, to give it warning,
"Power, never come again!"
Take this man: the gods in glory   1360
gave him Priam's city to plunder,
brought him home in splendor like a god.
But now if he must pay for the blood
his fathers shed, and die for the deaths
he brought to pass, and bring more death   1365
to avenge his dying, show us one
       who boasts himself born free
of the raging angel, once he hears—
            [*Cries break out within the palace.*]
AGAMEMNON   Aagh!
Struck deep—the death-blow, deep—
LEADER   Quiet. Cries,
but who? Someone's stabbed—
AGAMEMNON   Aaagh, again . . .   1370
second blow—struck home.
LEADER   The work is done,
you can feel it. The king, and the great cries—
Close ranks now, find the right way out.
            [*But the old men scatter, each speaks singly.*]
CHORUS   —I say send out heralds, muster the guard,
       they'll save the house.

                               —And I say rush in now,   1375
catch them red-handed—butchery running on their blades.

—Right with you, do something—now or never!

—Look at them, beating the drum for insurrection.

                                               —Yes,
we're wasting time. They rape the name of caution,
their hands will never sleep.

                               —Not a plan in sight.   1380
Let men of action do the planning, too.

—I'm helpless. Who can raise the dead with words?

—What, drag out our lives? bow down to the tyrants,
the ruin of the house?

    —Never, better to die
on your feet than live on your knees.

      —Wait,   1385
do we take the cries for signs, prophesy like seers
and give him up for dead?

     —No more suspicions,
not another word till we have proof.

      —Confusion
on all sides—one thing to do. See how it stands
with Agamemnon, once and for all we'll see—   1390
  [*He rushes at the doors. They open and reveal a silver cauldron that holds
  the body of* AGAMEMNON *shrouded in bloody robes, with the body of* CAS-
  SANDRA *to his left and* CLYTAEMNESTRA *standing to his right, sword in
  hand. She strides towards the* CHORUS.]

CLYTAEMNESTRA Words, endless words I've said to serve the moment—
Now it makes me proud to tell the truth.
How else to prepare a death for deadly men
who seem to love you? How to rig the nets
of pain so high no man can overleap them?   1395

I brooded on this trial, this ancient blood feud
year by year. At last my hour came.
Here I stand and here I struck
and here my work is done.
I did it all. I don't deny it, no.   1400
He had no way to flee or fight his destiny—
  [*Unwinding the robes from* AGAMEMNON's *body, spreading them before
  the altar where the old men cluster around them, unified as a chorus
  once again.*]
our never-ending, all embracing net, I cast it
wide for the royal haul, I coil him round and round
in the wealth, the robes of doom, and then I strike him
once, twice, and at each stroke he cries in agony—   1405
he buckles at the knees and crashes here!
And when he's down I add the third, last blow,
to the Zeus who saves the dead beneath the ground
I send that third blow home in homage like a prayer.[1]

So he goes down, and the life is bursting out of him—   1410
great sprays of blood, and the murderous shower
wounds me, dyes me black and I, I revel
like the Earth when the spring rains come down,

---

1. Like the third libation to Zeus (see n. 7, p. 513).

the blessed gifts of god, and the new green spear
splits the sheath and rips to birth in glory!   1415

So it stands, elders of Argos gathered here.
Rejoice if you can rejoice—I glory.
And if I'd pour upon his body the libation
it deserves, what wine could match my words?
It is right and more than right. He flooded   1420
the vessel of our proud house with misery,
with the vintage of the curse and now
he drains the dregs. My lord is home at last.

LEADER   You appall me, you, your brazen words—
exulting over your fallen king.

CLYTAEMNESTRA   And you,   1425
you try me like some desperate woman.
My heart is steel, well you know. Praise me,
blame me as you choose. It's all one.
Here is Agamemnon, my husband made a corpse
by this right hand—a masterpiece of Justice.   1430
Done is done.

CHORUS   Woman!—what poison cropped from the soil
or strained from the heaving sea, what nursed you,
drove you insane? You brave the curse of Greece.
    You have cut away and flung away and now
the people cast you off to exile,   1435
broken with our hate.

CLYTAEMNESTRA   And now you sentence me?—
you banish *me* from the city, curses breathing
down my neck? But *he*—
name one charge you brought against him then.
He thought no more of it than killing a beast,   1440
and his flocks were rich, teeming in their fleece,
but he sacrificed his own child, our daughter,
the agony I labored into love,
to charm away the savage winds of Thrace.[2]

Didn't the law demand you banish him?—   1445
hunt him from the land for all his guilt?
But now you witness what I've done
and you are ruthless judges.
                    Threaten away!
I'll meet you blow for blow. And if I fall
the throne is yours. If god decrees the reverse,   1450
late as it is, old men, you'll learn your place.

CHORUS   Mad with ambition,
        shrilling pride!—some Fury
crazed with the carnage rages through your brain—
    I can see the flecks of blood inflame your eyes!   1455

2. Winds from the North (at Aulis).

But vengeance comes—you'll lose your loved ones,
   stroke for painful stroke.
CLYTAEMNESTRA   Then learn this, too, the power of my oaths.
   By the child's Rights I brought to birth,
   by Ruin, by Fury—the three gods to whom   1460
   I sacrificed this man—I swear my hopes
   will never walk the halls of fear so long
   as Aegisthus lights the fire on my hearth.
   Loyal to me as always, no small shield
   to buttress my defiance.
                     Here he lies.   1465
   He brutalized me. The darling of all
   the golden girls[3] who spread the gates of Troy.
   And here his spearprize . . . what wonders she beheld!—
   the seer of Apollo shared my husband's bed,
   his faithful mate who knelt at the rowing-benches,   1470
   worked by every hand.
                They have their rewards.
   He as you know. And she, the swan of the gods
   who lived to sing her latest, dying song—
   his lover lies beside him.
   She brings a fresh, voluptuous relish to my bed!   1475
CHORUS   Oh quickly, let me die—
   no bed of labor, no, no wasting illness . . .
   bear me off in the sleep that never ends,
      now that he has fallen,
   now that our dearest shield lies battered—   1480
     Woman made him suffer,
      woman struck him down.
     Helen the wild, maddening Helen,
     one for the many, the thousand lives
     you murdered under Troy. Now you are crowned   1485
     with this consummate wreath, the blood
     that lives in memory, glistens age to age.
     Once in the halls she walked and she was war,
     angel of war, angel of agony, lighting men to death.

CLYTAEMNESTRA   Pray no more for death, broken   1490
   as you are. And never turn
     your wrath on her, call her
   the scourge of men, the one alone
   who destroyed a myriad Greek lives—
   Helen the grief that never heals.   1495
CHORUS   The *spirit!*—you who tread
   the house and the twinborn sons of Tantalus[4]—
   you empower the sisters, Fury's twins
     whose power tears the heart!

3. In Greek *chryseïdōn*, which recalls the girl in the first book of the *Iliad* (1.119–22), Chryseis, whom
Agamemnon said he preferred to Clytaemnestra.   4. Father of Pelops, grandfather of Atreus. *Sons:*
descendants—that is, Agamemnon and Menelaus.

Perched on the corpse your carrion raven   1500
   glories in her hymn,
      her screaming hymn of pride.
CLYTAEMNESTRA   Now you set your judgment straight,
   you summon *him*! Three generations
      feed the spirit in the race.   1505
Deep in the veins he feeds our bloodlust—
aye, before the old wound dies
it ripens in another flow of blood.
CHORUS   The great curse of the house, the spirit,
      dead weight wrath—and you can praise it!   1510
Praise the insatiate doom that feeds
relentless on our future and our sons.
Oh all through the will of Zeus,
the cause of all, the one who works it all.
   What comes to birth that is not Zeus?   1515
   Our lives are pain, what part not come from god?

     Oh, my king, my captain,
     how to salute you, how to mourn you?
     What can I say with all my warmth and love?
     Here in the black widow's web you lie,   1520
     gasping out your life
     in a sacrilegious death, dear god,
     reduced to a slave's bed,
     my king of men, yoked by stealth and Fate,
     by the wife's hand that thrust the two-edged sword.   1525

CLYTAEMNESTRA   You claim the work is mine, call me
   Agamemnon's wife—you are so wrong.
Fleshed in the wife of this dead man,
   the spirit lives within me,
our savage ancient spirit of revenge.   1530
In return for Atreus' brutal feast
he kills his perfect son—for every
murdered child, a crowning sacrifice.
CHORUS   And *you*, innocent of his murder?
     And who could swear to that? and how? . . .   1535
and still an avenger could arise,
bred by the fathers' crimes, and lend a hand.
He wades in the blood of brothers,
stream on mounting stream—black war erupts
   and where he strides revenge will stride,   1540
clots will mass for the young who were devoured.

     Oh my king, my captain,
     how to salute you, how to mourn you?
     What can I say with all my warmth and love?
     Here in the black widow's web you lie,   1545
     gasping out your life

in a sacrilegious death, dear god,
reduced to a slave's bed,
my king of men, yoked by stealth and Fate,
by the wife's hand that thrust the two-edged sword.   1550

CLYTAEMNESTRA   No slave's death, I think—
no stealthier than the death he dealt
our house and the offspring of our loins,
   Iphigeneia, girl of tears.
Act for act, wound for wound!   1555
Never exult in Hades, swordsman,
here you are repaid. By the sword
you did your work and by the sword you die.

CHORUS   The mind reels—where to turn?
   All plans dashed, all hope! I cannot think . . .   1560
   the roofs are toppling, I dread the drumbeat thunder
   the heavy rains of blood will crush the house
   the first light rains are over—
   Justice brings new acts of agony, yes,
on new grindstones Fate is grinding sharp the sword of Justice.   1565

Earth, dear Earth,
if only you'd drawn me under
long before I saw him huddled
in the beaten silver bath.
Who will bury him, lift his dirge?   1570
   [*Turning to* CLYTAEMNESTRA.]
You, can you dare *this*?
To kill your lord with your own hand
then mourn his soul with tributes, terrible tributes—
do his enormous works a great dishonor.
This godlike man, this hero. Who at the grave   1575
will sing his praises, pour the wine of tears?
Who will labor there with truth of heart?
CLYTAEMNESTRA   This is no concern of yours.
The hand that bore and cut him down
will hand him down to Mother Earth.   1580
This house will never mourn for him.
   Only our daughter Iphigeneia,
by all rights, will rush to meet him
first at the churning straits,[5]
the ferry over tears—   1585
she'll fling her arms around her father,
pierce him with her love.

CHORUS   Each charge meets counter-charge.
   one can judge between them. Justice.

---

5. The river of the underworld over which the dead were ferried.

The plunderer plundered, the killer pays the price.   1590
The truth still holds while Zeus still holds the throne:
       the one who acts must suffer—
    that is law. Who, who can tear from the veins
   the bad seed, the curse? The race is welded to its ruin.

CLYTAEMNESTRA   At last you see the future and the truth!   1595
But I will swear a pact with the spirit
born within us. I embrace his works,
cruel as they are but done at last,
   if he will leave our house
in the future, bleed another line   1600
with kinsmen murdering kinsmen.
Whatever he may ask. A few things
are all I need, once I have purged
our fury to destroy each other—
    purged it from our halls.
      [AEGISTHUS *has emerged from the palace with his bodyguard and stands*
      triumphant over the body of AGAMEMNON.]
AEGISTHUS   O what a brilliant day   1605
it is for vengeance! Now I can say once more
there are gods in heaven avenging men,
blazing down on all the crimes of earth.
Now at last I see this man brought down
in the Furies' tangling robes. It feasts my eyes—   1610
he pays for the plot his father's hand contrived.

Atreus, this man's father, was king of Argos.
My father, Thyestes—let me make this clear—
Atreus' brother challenged him for the crown,
and Atreus drove him out of house and home   1615
then lured him back, and home Thyestes came,
poor man, a suppliant to his own hearth,
to pray that Fate might save him.
               So it did.
There was no dying, no staining our native ground
with *his* blood. Thyestes was the guest,   1620
and this man's godless father—
   [*Pointing to* AGAMEMNON.]
the zeal of the host outstripping a brother's love,
made my father a feast that seemed a feast for gods,
a love feast of his children's flesh.
               He cuts
the extremities, feet and delicate hands   1625
into small pieces, scatters them over the dish
and serves it to Thyestes throned on high.
He picks at the flesh he cannot recognize,
the soul of innocence eating the food of ruin—
look,
    [*Pointing to the bodies at his feet.*]

that feeds upon the house! And then,   1630
when he sees the monstrous thing he's done, he shrieks,
he reels back head first and vomits up that butchery,
tramples the feast—brings down the curse of Justice:
"Crash to ruin, all the race of Pleisthenes,[6] crash down!"

So you see him, down. And I, the weaver of Justice,   1635
plotted out the kill. Atreus drove us into exile,
my struggling father and I, a babe-in-arms,
his last son, but I became a man
and Justice brought me home. I was abroad
but I reached out and seized my man,   1640
link by link I clamped the fatal scheme
together. Now I could die gladly, even I—
now I see this monster in the nets of Justice.

LEADER   Aegisthus, you revel in pain—you sicken me.
You say you killed the king in cold blood,   1645
singlehanded planned his pitiful death?
I say there's no escape. In the hour of judgment,
trust to this, your head will meet the people's
rocks and curses.

AEGISTHUS   You say! you slaves at the oars—
while the master of the benches cracks the whip?   1650
You'll learn, in your late age, how much it hurts
to teach old bones their place. We have techniques—
chains and the pangs of hunger,
two effective teachers, excellent healers.
They can even cure old men of pride and gall.   1655
Look—can't you see? The more you kick
against the pricks, the more you suffer.

LEADER   You, pathetic—
the king had just returned from battle.
You waited out the war and fouled his lair,   1660
you planned my great commander's fall.

AEGISTHUS   Talk on—
you'll scream for every word, my little Orpheus.[7]
We'll see if the world comes dancing to your song,
your absurd barking—snarl your breath away!
I'll make you dance, I'll bring you all to heel.   1665

LEADER   You rule Argos? You who schemed his death
but cringed to cut him down with your own hand?

AEGISTHUS   The treachery was the woman's work, clearly.
I was a marked man, his enemy for ages.
But I will use his riches, stop at nothing   1670
to civilize his people. All but the rebel:
him I'll yoke and break—
no cornfed colt, running free in the traces.

---

6. A name sometimes inserted into the genealogy of the house of Tantalus.   7. A mythical singer who charmed all nature with his music.

Hunger, ruthless mate of the dark torture-chamber,
trains her eyes upon him till he drops!   1675
LEADER   Coward, why not kill the man yourself?
Why did the woman, the corruption of Greece
and the gods of Greece, have to bring him down?
Orestes—If he still sees the light of day,
bring him home, good Fates, home to kill   1680
this pair at last. Our champion in slaughter!
AEGISTHUS   Bent on insolence? Well, you'll learn, quickly.
At them, men—you have your work at hand!
        [*His men draw swords; the old men take up their sticks.*]
LEADER   At them, fist at the hilt, to the last man—
AEGISTHUS   Fist at the hilt, I'm not afraid to die.   1685
LEADER   It's death you want and death you'll have—
we'll make that word your last.
        [CLYTAEMNESTRA *moves between them, restraining* AEGISTHUS.]
CLYTAEMNESTRA   No more, my dearest,
no more grief. We have too much to reap
right here, our mighty harvest of despair.
Our lives are based on pain. No bloodshed now.   1690

Fathers of Argos, turn for home before you act
and suffer for it. What we did was destiny.
If we could end the suffering, how we would rejoice.
The spirit's brutal hoof has struck our heart.
And that is what a woman has to say.   1695
Can you accept the truth?
        [CLYTAEMNESTRA *turns to leave.*]
AEGISTHUS   But these . . . mouths
that bloom in filth—spitting insults in my teeth.
You tempt your fates, you insubordinate dogs—
to hurl abuse at me, your master!
LEADER   No Greek
worth his salt would grovel at your feet.   1700
AEGISTHUS   I—I'll stalk you all your days!
LEADER   Not if the spirit brings Orestes home.
AEGISTHUS   Exiles feed on hope—well I know.
LEADER   More,
gorge yourself to bursting—soil justice, while you can.
AEGISTHUS   I promise you, you'll pay, old fools—in good time, too!   1705
LEADER   Strut on your own dunghill, you cock beside your mate.
CLYTAEMNESTRA   Let them howl—they're impotent. You and I have
    power now.
We will set the house in order once for all.
        [*They enter the palace; the great doors close behind them; the old men
        disband and wander off.*]

The Libation Bearers

CHARACTERS

ORESTES, *son of Agamemnon and Clytaemnestra*
PYLADES, *his companion*
ELECTRA, *his sister*
CHORUS *of Slavewomen and their* LEADER

CLYTAEMNESTRA
CILISSA, *Orestes' old nurse*
AEGISTHUS
A SERVANT *of Aegisthus*
Attendants of Orestes, bodyguard of Aegisthus

[TIME AND SCENE: *Several years have passed since Agamemnon's death. At Argos, before the tomb of the king and his fathers, stands an altar; behind it looms the house of Atreus.* ORESTES *and* PYLADES *enter, dressed as travelers.* ORESTES *kneels and prays.*[1]]

ORESTES Hermes, lord of the dead,[2] look down and guard
the fathers' power. Be my savior, I beg you,
be my comrade now.
                 I have come home
to my own soil, an exile home at last.
Here at the mounded grave I call my father,   5
Hear me—I am crying out to you . . .
[*He cuts two locks of hair and lays them on the grave.*]
There is a lock for Inachos[3] who nursed me
into manhood, there is one for death.
I was not here to mourn you when you died,
my father, never gave the last salute   10
when they bore your corpse away.
      [ELECTRA *and a chorus of slave-women enter in procession. They are dressed in black and bear libations, moving toward* ORESTES *at the grave.*]
                What's this?
Look, a company moving toward us. Women,
robed in black . . . so clear in the early light.

I wonder what they mean, what turn of fate?—
some new wound to the house?   15
Or perhaps they come to honor you, my father,
bearing cups[4] to soothe and still the dead.
That's right, it must be . . .
Electra, I think I see *her* coming, there,
my own sister, worn, radiant in her grief—   20
Dear god, let me avenge my father's murder—
fight beside me now with all your might!

---

1. The beginning of the play (perhaps as many as thirty lines) is missing in our manuscripts. Nine lines have been assembled from other ancient authors who quoted them.   2. Hermes conducts souls to the underworld; more generally, he crosses the boundary between the living and the dead. He is also a god of deception and is invoked as such later in the play.   3. The river of Argos. Greek youths, on coming to manhood, offered a lock of their hair to the river of their country as thanks for the nurture it had helped to provide. Locks of hair were also offered on the graves of the dead.   4. Libations, drink offerings to pour on the grave.

Out of their way, Pylades.[5] I must know
what they mean, these women turning towards us,
what their prayers call forth.   25
  [*They withdraw behind the tomb.*]
CHORUS   Rushed from the house we come
    escorting cups for the dead,
in step with the hands' hard beat,
      our cheeks glistening,
flushed where the nails have raked new furrows running blood,[6]   30
and life beats on, and through it all
we nurse our lives with tears,
to the sound of ripping linen beat our robes in sorrow,
    close to the breast the beats throb
and laughter's gone and fortune throbs and throbs.   35

Aie!—bristling Terror struck—
    Terror the seer of the house,
the nightmare ringing clear
      breathed its wrath in sleep,
in the midnight watch a cry!—the voice of Terror   40
deep in the house, bursting down
on the women's darkened chambers, yes,
and the old ones, skilled at dreams, swore oaths to god and called,
    "The proud dead stir under earth,
they rage against the ones who took their lives."   45

But the gifts,[7] the empty gifts
    she hopes will ward them off—
good Mother Earth!—that godless woman sends me here . . .
    I dread to say her prayer.
What can redeem the blood that wets the soil?   50
Oh for the hearthfire banked with grief,
    the rampart's down, a fine house down—
dark, dark, and the sun, the life is curst,
    and mist enshrouds the halls
      where the lords of war went down.   55

And the ancient pride no war,
      no storm, no force could tame,
ringing in all men's ears, in all men's hearts is gone.
    They are afraid. Success,
    they bow to success, more god than god himself.   60
But justice waits and turns the scales:
    a sudden blow for some at dawn,
    for some in the no man's land of dusk

---

5. Son of Strophios, who was Orestes' host in his kingdom of Phocis.   6. This and the following lines
list the semiritual actions of mourning for the dead: scratching the cheek, beating the head and breast,
ripping clothes.   7. Clytaemnestra's nightmare is interpreted by the "old ones, skilled at dreams": the
dead are angry with their killers. The gifts are the libations poured on the grave to appease the wrathful
dead. They were a mixture of honey, oil, wine, milk, and water.

her torments grow with time,
    and the lethal night takes others.   65

And the blood that Mother Earth consumes
clots hard, it won't seep through, it breeds revenge
    and frenzy goes through the guilty,
seething like infection, swarming through the brain.

For the one who treads a virgin's bed   70
there is no cure. All the streams of the world,
    all channels run into one
to cleanse a man's red hands will swell the bloody tide.[8]

And I . . . Fate and the gods brought down their yoke,
they ringed our city, out of our fathers' halls   75
    they led us here as slaves.[9]
And the will breaks, we kneel at their command—
    our masters right or wrong!
    And we beat the tearing hatred down,
    behind our veils we weep for her,   80
        [Turning to ELECTRA.]
her senseless fate.
Sorrow turns the secret heart to ice.
ELECTRA   Dear women,
you keep the house in order, best you can;
and now you've come to the grave to say a prayer
with me, my escorts. I'll need your help with this.   85
What to say when I pour the cup of sorrow?
    [Lifting her libation cup.]
What kindness, what prayer can touch my father?
Shall I say I bring him love for love, a woman's
love for husband? My mother, love from her?
I've no taste for that, no words to say   90
as I run the honeyed oil on father's tomb.

Or try the salute we often use at graves?
"A wreath for a wreath. Now bring the givers
gifts to match" . . . no, give them pain for pain.

Or silent, dishonored, just as father died,   95
empty it out for the soil to drink and then
retrace my steps, like a slave sent out with scourings
left from the purging of the halls, and throw
the cup behind me, looking straight ahead.[1]
Help me decide, my friends. Join me here.   100
We nurse a common hatred in the house.

8. Bloodguilt cannot be washed away.   9. The chorus consists of women enslaved when their city was
captured. It is not so stated in the text, but they are probably Trojan captives brought home by Agamemnon.
1. After throwing away refuse, an ancient Greek left without looking back, as if afraid that the action might
have provoked some hostile powers.

Don't hide your feelings—no, fear no one.
Destiny waits us all,
   [*Looking toward the tomb.*]
           born free,
or slaves who labor under another's hand.
Speak to me, please. Perhaps you've had   105
a glimpse of something better.

LEADER   I revere
your father's death-mound like an altar.
I'll say a word, now that you ask,
that comes from deep within me.

ELECTRA   Speak on,
with everything you feel for father's grave.   110

LEADER   Say a blessing as you pour, for those who love you.

ELECTRA   And of the loved ones, whom to call my friends?

LEADER   First yourself, then all who hate Aegisthus.

ELECTRA   I and you. I can say a prayer for us and then for—

LEADER   You know,
   try to say it.   115

ELECTRA   There is someone else to rally to our side?

LEADER   Remember Orestes, even abroad and gone.

ELECTRA   Well said, the best advice I've had.

LEADER   Now for the murderers. Remember them and—

ELECTRA   What?
I'm so unseasoned, teach me what to say.   120

LEADER   Let some god or man come down upon them.

ELECTRA   Judge or avenger, which?

LEADER   Just say "the one who murders in return!"

ELECTRA   How can I ask the gods for that and keep my conscience
   clear?

LEADER
              How not,[2] and pay the enemy back in kind?   125
   [ELECTRA *kneels at the grave in prayer.*]

ELECTRA   —Herald king
of the world above and the quiet world below,
lord of the dead, my Hermes, help me now.
Tell the spirits underground to hear my prayers,
and the high watch hovering over father's roofs,   130
and have her listen too, the Earth herself
who brings all things to life and makes them strong,
then gathers in the rising tide once more.

And I will tip libations to the dead.
I call out to my father. Pity me,   135
dear Orestes too.
Rekindle the light that saves our house!
We're auctioned off, drift like vagrants now.

---

2. Common Greek morality saw nothing wrong in individual vengeance. But it will lead, in this play, to a son's murder of a mother, and in the last play it will be superseded by communal justice.

Mother has pawned us for a husband, Aegisthus,
her partner in her murdering.
            I go like a slave,   140
and Orestes driven from his estates while they,
they roll in the fruits of all your labors,
magnificent and sleek. O bring Orestes home,
with a happy twist of fate, my father. Hear me,
make me far more self-possessed than mother,   145
make this hand more pure.

These prayers for us. For our enemies I say,
Raise up your avenger, into the light, my father—
kill the killers in return, with justice!
So in the midst of prayers for good I place   150
this curse for them.
            Bring up your blessings,
up into the air, led by the gods and Earth
and all the rights that bring us triumph.
   [*Pouring libations on the tomb and turning to the women.*]
These are my prayers. Over them I pour libations.
Yours to adorn them with laments, to make them bloom,   155
so custom says—sing out and praise the dead.
CHORUS   Let the tears fall, ring out and die,
     die with the warlord at this bank,
this bulwark of the good, defense against the bad,
the guilt, the curse we ward away   160
with prayer and all we pour. Hear me, majesty, hear me,
   lord of glory, from the darkness of your heart.
                    Ohhhhhh!—
Dear god, let him come! Some man
with a strong spear, born to free the house,
   with the torsion bow of Scythia[3] bent for slaughter,   165
splattering shafts like a god of war—sword in fist
   for the slash-and-hack of battle!
   [ELECTRA *remains at the grave, staring at the ground.*]
ELECTRA   Father,
and have it now, the earth has drunk your wine.
Wait, friends, here's news. Come share it.
LEADER   Speak on,
my heart's a dance of fear.
ELECTRA   A lock of hair,   170
here on the grave . . .
LEADER   Whose? A man's?
A growing girl's?
ELECTRA   And it has the marks,
and anyone would think—
LEADER   What?

---

3. The Scythians, who lived far to the north and east of Greece, were famous archers.

We're old. You're young, now you teach us.

ELECTRA   No one could have cut this lock but I and—   175

LEADER   Callous they are, the ones who ought to shear
the hair and mourn.

ELECTRA   Look at the texture, just like—

LEADER   Whose? I want to know.

ELECTRA   Like mine, identical,
can't you see?

LEADER   Orestes . . . he brought a gift
in secret?

ELECTRA   It's *his*—I can see his curls.   180

LEADER   And how could he risk the journey here?

ELECTRA   He sent it, true, a lock to honor father.

LEADER   All the more cause for tears. You mean
he'll never set foot on native ground again.

ELECTRA   Yes!
It's sweeping over me too—anguish   185
like a breaker—a sword ripping through my heart!
Tears come like the winter rains that flood the gates—
can't hold them back, when I see this lock of hair.
How could I think another Greek[4] could play
the prince with this?
                    She'd never cut it,   190
the murderess, my mother. She insults the name,
she and her godless spirit preying on her children.

But how, how can I come right out and say it *is*
the glory of the dearest man I know—Orestes?
Stop, I'm fawning on hope.
                    Oh, if only   195
it had a herald's voice, kind and human—
I'm so shaken, torn—and told me clearly
to throw it away, they severed it from a head
that I detest. Or it could sorrow with me
like a brother, aye,   200
this splendor come to honor father's grave.

We call on the gods, and the gods well know
what storms torment us, sailors whirled to nothing.
But if we are to live and reach the haven,
one small seed could grow a mighty tree—   205
Look, tracks.
                    A new sign to tell us more.
Footmarks . . . pairs of them, like mine.
Two outlines, two prints, his own, and there,
a fellow traveler's.

[*Putting her foot into* ORESTES' *print.*]

---

4. Only a close relative would have done it.

The heel, the curve of the arch
like twins.[5]
    [*While* ORESTES *emerges from behind the grave, she follows cautiously
in his steps until they come together.*]
Step by step, my step in his . . .
               we meet—   210
Oh the pain, like pangs of labor—this is madness!

ORESTES   Pray for the future. Tell the gods they've brought
your prayers to birth, and pray that we succeed.
    [ELECTRA *draws back, struggling for composure.*]

ELECTRA   The gods—why now? What have I ever won from them?

ORESTES   The sight you prayed to see for many years.   215

ELECTRA   And you know the one I call?

ORESTES   I know Orestes,
know he moves you deeply.

ELECTRA   Yes,
but now what's come to fill my prayers?

ORESTES   Here I am. Look no further.
No one loves you more than I.

ELECTRA   No,   220
it's a trap, stranger . . . a net you tie around me?

ORESTES   Then I tie myself as well.

ELECTRA   But the pain,
you're laughing at all—

ORESTES   Your pain is mine.
If I laugh at yours, I only laugh at mine.

ELECTRA   Orestes—
can I call you?—are you really—   225

ORESTES   I am!
Open your eyes. So slow to learn.
You saw the lock of hair I cut in mourning.
You scanned my tracks, you could see my marks,
your breath leapt, you all but saw me in the flesh—   230
Look—
    [*Holding the lock to his temple, then to* ELECTRA's.]
    put it where I cut it.
It's your brother's. Try, it matches yours.
    [*Removing a strip of weaving from his clothing.*]
Work of your own hand, you tamped the loom,
look, there are wild creatures in the weaving.
    [*She kneels beside him, weeping; he lifts her to her feet and they
embrace.*]
No, no, control yourself—don't lose yourself in joy!   235
Our loved ones, well I know, would slit our throats.

LEADER   Dearest, the darling of your father's house,
hope of the seed we nursed with tears—you save us.
Trust to your power, win your father's house once more!

---

5. Since Greeks wore open sandals they were much more conscious than we are of the shape of each
other's feet. Cf. *Odyssey* 4.165, where Menelaus sees a resemblance between the feet of Telemachus and
Odysseus.

ELECTRA   You light to my eyes, four loves in one!   240
   I have to call you father, it is fate;
   and I turn to you the love I gave my mother—
   I despise her, she deserves it, yes.
   and the love I gave my sister, sacrificed
   on the cruel sword, I turn to you.   245
   You were my faith, my brother—
   you alone restore my self-respect.
      [Praying.]
   Power and Justice, Saving Zeus, Third Zeus,[6]
   almighty all in all, be with us now.
ORESTES   Zeus, Zeus, watch over all we do,   250
   fledglings reft of the noble eagle father.
   He died in the coils, the viper's dark embrace.
   We are his orphans worn down with hunger,
   weak, too young to haul the father's quarry
   home to shelter.
                  Look down on us!   255
   I and Electra too, I tell you, children
   robbed of our father, both of us bound
   in exile from our house.
                  And what a father—
   a priest at sacrifice, he showered you
   with honors. Put an end to his nestlings now   260
   and who will serve you banquets rich as his?
   Destroy the eagle's brood, you can never
   send a sign that wins all men's belief.
   Rot the stock of a proud dynastic tree—
   it can never shore your altar steaming   265
   with the oxen in the mornings.
                  Tend us—
   we seem in ruins now, I know. Up from nothing
   rear a house to greatness.
   LEADER   Softly, children,
   white hopes of your father's hearth. Someone
   might hear you, children, charmed with his own voice   270
   blurt all this out to the masters. Oh, just once
   to see them—live bones crackling in the fire
   spitting pitch!
ORESTES   Apollo will never fail me, no,
   his tremendous power, his oracle charges me
   to see this trial through.
                  I can still hear the god—   275
   a high voice ringing with winters of disaster,
   piercing the heart within me, warm and strong,
   unless I hunt my father's murderers, cut them down
   in their own style—they destroyed my birthright.

---

6. Zeus is called on as savior when the third libation is poured at the feast (see *Agamemnon*, line 245, and note): Zeus was third in the succession of the rulers of the gods (see *Agamemnon*, note to 169).

"Gore them like a bull!" he called, "or pay their debt   280
with your own life, one long career of grief."

He revealed so much about us,
told how the dead take root beneath the soil,
they grow with hate and plague the lives of men.
He told of the leprous boils that ride the flesh,[7]   285
their wild teeth gnawing the mother tissue, aye,
and a white scurf spreads like cancer over these,
and worse, he told how assaults of Furies spring
to life on the father's blood . . .
      You can *see* them—
the eyes burning, grim brows working over you in the dark—   290
the dark sword of the dead—you murdered kinsmen
pleading for revenge. And the madness haunts
the midnight watch, the empty terror shakes you,
harries, drives you on—an exile from your city—
a brazen whip will mutilate your back.   295
For such as us, no share in the winebowl,
no libations poured in love. You never see
your father's wrath but it pulls you from the altars.
There is no refuge, none to take you in.
A pariah, reviled, at long last you die,   300
withered in the grip of all this dying.

Such oracles are persuasive,
don't you think? And even if I am not convinced,
the rough work of the world is still to do.
So many yearnings meet and urge me on.   305
The god's commands. Mounting sorrow for father.
Besides, the lack of patrimony presses hard;
and my compatriots, the glory of men
who toppled Troy with nerves of singing steel,
go at the beck and call of a brace of women.   310
Womanhearted he is[8]—if not, we'll soon see.
  [*The* LEADER *lights the altar fires.* ORESTES, ELECTRA, *and the* CHORUS
  gather for the invocation at the grave.]
CHORUS Powers of destiny, mighty queens of Fate!—
by the will of Zeus your will be done,
press on to the end now,
  Justice turns the wheel.   315
"Word for word, curse for curse
be born now," Justice thunders,
  hungry for retribution,
"stroke for bloody stroke be paid.
  The one who acts must suffer."   320
Three generations strong the word resounds.

7. This list of the loathsome afflictions that await the man who fails to avenge his murdered father moves from disease to social ostracism; the man who fails in his duty dies cut off from society and the gods.
8. I.e., Aegisthus is a coward; Argos is ruled by a "brace of women."

ORESTES   Dear father, father of dread,
 what can I do or say to reach you now?
  What breath can reach from here
 to the bank where you lie moored at anchor?   325
What light can match your darkness? None,
but there is a kind of grace that comes
 when the tears revive a proud old house
and Atreus' sons, the warlords lost and gone.
LEADER   The ruthless jaws of the fire,   330
 my child, can never tame the dead,
  his rage inflames his sons.
Men die and the voices rise, they light the guilty, true—
 cries raised for the fathers, clear and just,
  will hunt their killers harried to the end. 335
ELECTRA   Then hear me now, my father,
 it is my turn, my tears are welling now,
  as child by child we come
 to the tomb and raise the dirge, my father.
Your grave receives a girl in prayer   340
and a man in flight, and we are one,
 and the pain is equal, whose is worse?
And who outwrestles death—what third last fall?[9]
CHORUS   But still some god, if he desires,
 may work our strains to a song of joy,   345
from the dirges chanted over the grave
 may lift a hymn in the kings' halls
and warm the loving cup you stir this morning.
ORESTES[1]   If only at Troy
 a Lycian[2] cut you down, my father—   350
gone, with an aura left at home behind you,
 children to go their ways
and the eyes look on them bright with awe,
and the tomb you win on headlands seas away
 would buoy up the house . . .   355
LEADER   And loved by the men you loved
 who died in glory, there you'd rule
  beneath the earth—lord, prince,
stern aide to the giant kings who judge the shadows there.
You were a king of kings when you drew breath; 360
 the mace you held could make men kneel or die.
ELECTRA   No, not under Troy!—
not dead and gone with them, my father,
hordes pierced by the spear Scamander[3] washes down.
 Sooner the killers die   365
as they killed you—at the hands of friends,
 and the news of death would come from far away,
  we'd never know this grief.

---

9. There were three falls in a Greek wrestling match.   1. Compare this and the next stanza with the speech of Achilles in Hades (*Odyssey* 24.25 ff).   2. Allies of the Trojans; their kings were the famous warriors Glaucus and Sarpedon.   3. One of the rivers in the Trojan plain.

CHORUS   You are dreaming, children,
 dreams dearer than gold, more blest   370
than the Blest beyond the Northwind's raging.[4]
 Dreams are easy, oh,
but the double lash is striking home.
 Now our comrades group underground.
 Our masters' reeking hands are doomed—   375
 the children take the day!
ORESTES   That thrills his ear,
  that arrow lands!
   Zeus, Zeus, force up from the earth
 destruction, late but true to the mark,
to the reckless heart, the killing hand—   380
 for parents of revenge revenge be done.
LEADER   And the ripping cries of triumph mine
 to sing when the man is stabbed,
  the woman dies[5]—   385
 why, why hide what's deep inside me,
 black wings beating, storming the spirit's prow—
  hurricane, slashing hatred!
ELECTRA   Both fists at once
 come down, come down—
  Zeus, *crush* their skulls! Kill! kill!   390
Now give the land some faith, I beg you,
from these ancient wrongs bring forth our rights.
 Hear me, Earth, and all you lords of death.
CHORUS   It is the law: when the blood of slaughter
 wets the ground it wants more blood.   395
 Slaughter cries for the Fury
of those long dead to bring destruction
on destruction churning in its wake!
ORESTES   Sweet Earth, how long?—great lords of death, look on,
 you mighty curses of the dead. Look on   400
the last of Atreus' children, here, the remnant
 helpless, cast from home . . . god, where to turn?
LEADER   And again my pulses race and leap,
 I can feel your sobs, and hope
  becomes despair   405
 and the heart goes dark to hear you—
 then the anguish ebbs, I see you stronger,
  hope and the light come on me.
ELECTRA   *What* hope?—what force to summon, what can help?
 What but the pain we suffer, bred by her?   410
So let her fawn. She can never soothe her young wolves—
 Mother dear, you bred our wolves' raw fury.
LEADER AND CHORUS   I beat and beat the dirge like a Persian mourner,[6]
 hands clenched tight and the blows are coming thick and fast,

---

4. The land of the Hyperboreans, a legendary race of worshippers of Apollo who lived a paradisal life in
the far North.   5. For the first time, the killing of Clytaemnestra is mentioned.   6. Oriental mourning
was thought to be even more wild and extravagant than Greek.

you can see the hands shoot out, 415
    now hand over hand and down—the head pulsates,
      blood at the temples pounding to explode!
ELECTRA   Reckless, brutal mother—oh dear god!—
  the brutal, cruel cortège,
the warlord stripped of his honor guard 420
  and stripped of mourning rites—
you dared entomb your lord unwept, unsung.
ORESTES   Shamed for all the world, you mean—
dear god, my father degraded so!
Oh she'll pay, 425
she'll pay, by the gods and these bare hands—
  just let me take her life and *die*!⁷
LEADER AND CHORUS   Shamed? *Butchered*, I tell you—hands lopped,
strung to shackle his neck and arms!⁸
So she worked, 430
she buried him, made your life a hell.
  Your father mutilated—do you hear?
ELECTRA   You tell him of father's death, but I was an outcast,
worthless, leashed like a vicious dog in a dark cell.
  I wept—laughter died that day . . . 435
    I wept, pouring out the tears behind my veils.
      Hear *that*, my brother, carve it on your heart!
LEADER AND CHORUS   Let it ring in your ears
  but let your heart stand firm.
The outrage stands as it stands, 440
  you burn to know the end,
but first be strong, be steel, then down and fight.
ORESTES   I am calling you, my father—be with all you love!
ELECTRA   I am with you, calling through my tears.
LEADER AND CHORUS   We band together now, the call resounds— 445
  hear us now, come back into the light.
Be with us, battle all you hate.
ORESTES   Now force *clash* with force—right with right!
ELECTRA   Dear gods, be just—win back our rights.
LEADER AND CHORUS   The flesh crawls to hear them pray. 450
  the hour of doom has waited long . . .
pray for it once, and oh my god, it comes.
CHORUS   Oh, the torment bred in the race,
  the grinding scream of death
    and the stroke that hits the vein, 455
  the hemorrhage none can staunch, the grief,
the curse no man can bear.

But there is a cure in the house
  and not outside it, no,

---

7. This is not, as might appear from the translation, an expression of despair. The Greek phrase is an example of a fairly common formula that has the force: "I'd be willing to *die*, if I could only . . ." 8. This practice was supposed to prevent the dead man from rising from the grave to haunt his murderer.

not from others but from *them*,[9]   460
their bloody strife. We sing to you,
dark gods beneath the earth.

Now hear, you blissful powers underground—
answer the call, send help.
Bless the children, give them triumph now.   465
    [*They withdraw, while* ELECTRA *and* ORESTES *come to the altar.*]
ORESTES   Father, king, no royal death you died—
give me the power now to rule our house.
ELECTRA   I need you too, my father.
Help me kill her lover, then go free.
ORESTES   Then men will extend the sacred feast to you.   470
Or else, when the steam and the rich savor burn
for Mother Earth, you will starve for honor.
ELECTRA   And I will pour my birthright out to you—
the wine of the fathers' house, my bridal wine,
and first of all the shrines revere your tomb.   475
ORESTES   O Earth, bring father up to watch me fight.
ELECTRA   O Persephone,[1] give us power—lovely, gorgeous power!
ORESTES   Remember the bath—they stripped away your life, my father.
ELECTRA   Remember the all-embracing net—they made it first for you.
ORESTES   Chained like a beast—chains of hate, not bronze, my father! 480
ELECTRA   Shamed in the schemes, the hoods they slung around you!
ORESTES   Does our taunting wake you, oh my father?
ELECTRA   Do you lift your beloved head?
ORESTES   Send us justice, fight for all you love,
or help us pin them grip for grip. They threw you—   485
don't you long to throw them down in turn?
ELECTRA   One last cry, father. Look at your nestlings
stationed at your tomb—pity
your son and daughter. We are all you have.
ORESTES   Never blot out the seed of Pelops[2] here.   490
Then in the face of death you cannot die.
    [*The* LEADER *comes forward again.*]
LEADER   The voices of children—salvation to the dead!
Corks to the net, they rescue the linen meshes
from the depths. This line will never drown!
ELECTRA   Hear us—the long wail we raise is all for you.   495
Honor our call and you will save yourself.
LEADER   And a fine thing it is to lengthen out the dirge;
you adore a grave and fate they never mourned.
But now for action—now you're set on action,
put your stars to proof.
ORESTES   So we will.   500
One thing first, I think it's on the track.
Why did she send libations? What possessed her,
so late, to salve a wound past healing?

9. That is, from members of the family.   1. Queen of the underworld.   2. Ancestor of Agamemnon.

To the unforgiving dead she sends this sop,
this . . . who am I to appreciate her gifts? 505
They fall so short of all her failings. True,
"pour out your all to atone an act of blood,
you work for nothing." So the saying goes.
I'm ready. Tell me what you know.

LEADER   I know, my boy,
I was there. She had bad dreams. Some terror 510
came groping through the night, it shook her,
and she sent these cups, unholy woman.

ORESTES   And you know the dream, you can tell it clearly?

LEADER   She dreamed she bore a snake, said so herself and . . .

ORESTES   Come to the point—where does the story end? 515

LEADER   . . . she swaddled it like a baby, laid it to rest.

ORESTES   And food, what did the little monster want?

LEADER   She gave it her breast to suck—she was dreaming.

ORESTES   And didn't it tear her nipple, the brute inhuman—

LEADER   Blood curdled the milk with each sharp tug . . . 520

ORESTES   No empty dream. The vision of a man.

LEADER   . . . and she woke with a scream, appalled,
and rows of torches, burning out of the blind dark,
flared across the halls to soothe the queen,
and then she sent the libations for the dead, 525
an easy cure she hopes will cut the pain.

ORESTES   No,
I pray to the Earth and father's grave to bring
that dream to life in me. I'll play the seer—
it all fits together, watch!
If the serpent came from the same place as I, 530
and slept in the bands that swaddled me, and its jaws
spread wide for the breast that nursed me into life
and clots stained the milk, mother's milk,
and she cried in fear and agony—so be it.
As she bred this sign, this violent prodigy, 535
so she dies by violence. I turn serpent,
I kill her. So the vision says.

LEADER   You are the seer for me, I like your reading.
Let it come! But now rehearse your friends.
Say do this, or don't do that— 540

ORESTES   The plan is simple. My sister goes inside.
And I'd have her keep the bond with me a secret.
They killed an honored man by cunning, so
they die by cunning, caught in the same noose.
So he commands, 545
Apollo the Seer who's never lied before.
And I like a stranger, equipped for all events,
go to the outer gates with this man here,
Pylades, a friend, the house's friend-in-arms.
And we both will speak Parnassian, both try 550

for the native tones of Delphi.[3]
                Now, say none
at the doors will give us a royal welcome
(after all the house is ridden by a curse),
well then we wait . . . till a passer-by will stop
and puzzle and make insinuations at the house,   555
"Aegisthus shuts his door on the man who needs him.
Why, I wonder—does he know? Is he home?"

But once through the gates, across the threshold,
once I find that man on *my* father's throne,
or returning late to meet me face to face,   560
and his eyes shift and fall—
                I promise you,
before he can ask me, "Stranger, who are you?"—
I drop him dead, a thrust of the sword, and twist!
Our Fury never wants for blood. *His* she drinks unmixed,
our third libation poured to Saving Zeus.   565
     [*Turning to* ELECTRA.]
Keep a close watch inside, dear, be careful.
We must work together step by step.
     [*To the* CHORUS.]
                And you,
better hold your tongues, religiously.
Silence, friends, or speak when it will help.
     [*Looking towards* PYLADES *and the death-mound and beyond.*]
For the rest, watch over me, I need you—   570
guide my sword through struggle, guide me home!
     [*As* ORESTES, PYLADES, *and* ELECTRA *leave, the women reassemble for the*
     CHORUS.]

CHORUS   Marvels, the Earth breeds many marvels,
              terrible marvels overwhelm us.
          The heaving arms of the sea embrace and swarm
       with savage life. And high in the no man's land of night   575
          torches[4] hang like swords. The hawk on the wing,
             the beast astride the fields
          can tell of the whirlwind's fury roaring strong.

Oh but a man's high daring spirit,
       who can account for that? Or woman's   580
desperate passion daring past all bounds?
She couples with every form of ruin known to mortals.
Woman, frenzied, driven wild with lust,
       twists the dark, warm harness
     of wedded love—tortures man and beast!   585

---

3. Delphi is on the slopes of Mount Parnassus; the inhabitants of the area spoke a dialect that differed
from that of Argos (and Athens). Of course, the actors playing Orestes and Pylades do not, in fact, switch
to Parnassian dialect.   4. Comets, meteors, etc.

Well you know, you with a sense of truth
    recall Althaia,[5]
the heartless mother
who killed her son,
ai! what a scheme she had—   590
    she rushed his destiny,
        lit the bloody torch
preserved from the day he left her loins with a cry—
        the life of the torch paced his,
burning on till Fate burned out his life.   595

There is one more in the tales of hate:
    remember Scylla,[6]
the girl of slaughter
seduced by foes
to take her father's life.   600
    The gift of Minos,
        a choker forged in gold
turned her head and Nisos' immortal lock she cut
        as he slept away his breath . . .
ruthless bitch, now Hermes takes her down.   605

Now that I call to mind old wounds that never heal—
    Stop, it's time for the wedded love-in-hate,[7]
for the curse of the halls,
    the woman's brazen cunning
        bent on her lord in arms,   610
her warlord's power—
    Do you respect such things?
I prize the hearthstone warmed by faith,
a woman's temper nothing bends to outrage.

First at the head of legendary crime stands Lemnos.[8]
    People shudder and moan, and can't forget—   615
each new horror that comes
we call the hells of Lemnos.
    Loathed by the gods for guilt,
        cast off by men, disgraced, their line dies out.
Who could respect what god detests?   620
What of these tales have I not picked with justice?

        The sword's at the lungs!—it stabs deep,
            the edge cuts through and through

5. Mother of the hero Meleager. At his birth she was given a prophecy that his life would be no longer than that of a piece of wood then burning on the fire. She extinguished it and hid it away. But when, as a young man, Meleager killed her brother in a quarrel, she took it and threw it back on the fire, thus ending her son's life. 6. Daughter of Nisos, king of Megara, who had a purple lock of hair that made it impossible for him to die. When Megara was besieged by Minos, king of Crete, Scylla, bribed with a golden necklace, cut off her father's lock of hair. He died, and Scylla was changed into the sea monster of the *Odyssey*. 7. This stanza refers to Clytaemnestra. 8. An island off the coast of Asia Minor. The men of Lemnos brought back slave women from a war in neighboring Thrace; their wives, angry and jealous because of their husbands' affection for these women, massacred all the men on the island.

and Justice drives it—Outrage still lives on,
   not trodden to pieces underfoot, not yet,   625
   though the laws lie trampled down,
      the majesty of Zeus.

    The anvil of Justice stands fast
    and Fate beats out her sword.
    Tempered for glory, a child will wipe clean   630
    the inveterate stain of blood shed long ago—
      Fury brings him home at last,
      the brooding mother Fury!

[*The women leave.* ORESTES *and* PYLADES *approach the house of Atreus.*]

ORESTES   Slave, the slave!—
where is he? Hear me pounding the gates?
Is there a man inside the house?
For the third time, come out of the halls!   635
If Aegisthus has them welcome friendly guests.

[*A voice from inside.*]

PORTER   All right, I hear you . . .
Where do you come from, stranger? Who are you?

ORESTES   Announce me to the masters of the house.   640
I've come for them, I bring them news.
                       Hurry,
the chariot of the night is rushing on the dark!
The hour falls, the traveler casts his anchor
in an inn where every stranger feels at home.
                    Come out!
Whoever rules the house. The woman in charge.   645
No, the man, better that way.
No scruples then. Say what you mean,
man to man launch in and prove your point,
make it clear, strong.

[CLYTAEMNESTRA *emerges from the palace, attended by* ELECTRA.]

CLYTAEMNESTRA   Strangers, please,
tell me what you would like and it is yours.
We've all you might expect in a house like ours.   650
We have warm baths and beds to charm away your pains
and the eyes of Justice look on all we do.
But if you come for higher things, affairs
that touch the state, that is the men's concern   655
and I will stir them on.

ORESTES   I am a stranger,
from Daulis, close to Delphi, I'd just set out,
packing my own burden bound for Argos
(here I'd put my burden down and rest),
when I met a perfect stranger, out of the blue,   660
who asks about my way and tells me his.
                   Strophios,
a Phocian, so I gathered in conversation.
"Well, my friend," he says, "out for Argos

in any case? Remember to tell the parents
he is dead, Orestes . . .

                promise me please   665
(it's only right), it will not slip your mind.
Then whatever his people want, to bring him home
or bury him here, an alien, all outcast here
forever, won't you ferry back their wishes?
As it is, a bronze urn is armor to his embers   670
The man's been mourned so well . . ."

                            I only tell you
what I heard. And am I speaking now
with guardians, kinsmen who will care?
It's hard to say. But a parent ought to know.

CLYTAEMNESTRA   I, I—   675
  your words, you storm us, raze us to the roots,
you curse of the house so hard to wrestle down!
How you range—targets at peace, miles away,
and a shaft from your lookout brings them down.
You strip me bare of all I love, destroy me,
now—Orestes.   680

And he was trained so well, we'd been so careful,
kept his footsteps clear of the quicksand of death.
Just now, the hope of the halls, the surgeon to cure
our Furies' lovely revel—he seemed so close,
he's written off the rolls.

ORESTES   If only I were . . .   685
  my friends, with hosts as fortunate as you
if only I *could* be known for better news
and welcomed like a brother. The tie between
the host and stranger, what is kinder?
But what an impiety, so it seemed to me,   690
not to bring this to a head for loved ones.
I was bound by honor, bound by the rights
of hospitality.

CLYTAEMNESTRA   Nothing has changed.
  For all that you receive what you deserve,
as welcome in these halls as one of us.   695
Wouldn't another bear the message just as well?
But you must be worn from the long day's journey—
time for your rewards.

    [*To* ELECTRA.]

                   Escort him in,
where the men who come are made to feel at home.
He and his retinue, and fellow travelers.   700
Let them taste the bounty of our house.
Do it, as if you depended on his welfare.

And we will rouse the powers in the house
and share the news. We never lack for loved ones,

we will probe this turn of fortune every way.   705

[ELECTRA *leads* ORESTES, PYLADES, *and their retinue into the halls;*
CLYTAEMNESTRA *follows, while the* CHORUS *reassembles.*]

LEADER   Oh dear friends who serve the house,
   when can we speak out, when
can the vigor of our voices serve Orestes?

CHORUS   Queen of the Earth, rich mounded Earth,
  breasting over the lord of ships,
  the king's corpse at rest,   710
hear us now, now help us,
   now the time is ripe—
Down to the pit Persuasion goes
with all her cunning. Hermes of Death,
  the great shade patrols the ring   715
to guide the struggles, drive the tearing sword.

LEADER   And I think our new friend is at his mischief.
  Look, Orestes' nurse in tears.

[*Enter* CILISSA.[9]]

Where now, old-timer, padding along the gates?   720
With pain a volunteer to go your way.

NURSE   "Aegisthus,"
  your mistress calling, "hurry and meet your guests.
There's news. It's clearer man to man, you'll see."

And she looks at the maids and pulls that long face
and down deep her eyes are laughing over the work   725
that's done. Well and good for her. For the house
it's the curse all over—the strangers make that plain.
But let *him* hear, he'll revel once he knows.

                        Oh god,
the life is hard. The old griefs, the memories
mixing, cups of pain, so much pain in the halls,   730
the house of Atreus . . . I suffered, the heart within me
always breaking, oh, but I never shouldered
misery like this. So many blows, good slave,
I took my blows.

           Now dear Orestes—
the sweetest, dearest plague of all our lives!   735

Red from your mother's womb I took you, reared you . . .
nights, the endless nights I paced, your wailing
kept me moving—led me a life of labor,
all for what?

           And such care I gave it . . .
baby can't think for itself, poor creature.   740
You have to nurse it, don't you? Read its mind,
little devil's got no words, it's still swaddled.
Maybe it wants a bite or a sip of something,

---

9. The nurse's name means simply "a woman from Cilicia" (in Asia Minor); she is a slave.

or its bladder pinches—a baby's soft insides
have a will of their own. I had to be a prophet.   745
Oh I tried, and missed, believe you me, I missed,
and I'd scrub its pretty things until they sparkled.
Washerwoman and wet-nurse shared the shop.
A jack of two trades, that's me,
and an old hand at both . . .
            and so I nursed Orestes,   750
yes, from his father's arms I took him once,
and now they say he's dead,
I've suffered it all, and now I'll fetch that man,
the ruination of the house—give him the news,
he'll relish every word.

LEADER   She tells him to come,   755
but how, prepared?

NURSE   Prepared, how else?
I don't see . . .

LEADER   With his men, I mean, or all alone?

NURSE   Oh, she says to bring his bodyguard, his cutthroats.

LEADER   No, not now, not if you hate our master—
tell him to come alone.   760
Nothing for him to fear then, when he hears.
Have him come quickly too, rejoicing all the way!
The teller sets the crooked message straight.

NURSE   What,
you're *glad* for the news that's come?

LEADER   Why not,
if Zeus will turn the evil wind to good?   765

NURSE   But how? Orestes, the hope of the house is gone.

LEADER   Not yet. It's a poor seer who'd say so.

NURSE   What are you saying?—something I don't know?

LEADER   Go in with your message. Do as you're told.
May the gods take care of cares that come from them.   770

NURSE   Well, I'm off. Do as I'm told.
And here's to the best . . .
some help, dear gods, some help.
     [*Exit.*]

CHORUS   O now bend to my prayer, Father Zeus,
lord of the gods astride the sky—   775
grant them all good fortune,
the lords of the house who strain to see
    strict discipline return.
Our cry is the cry of Justice,
    Zeus, safeguard it well.
              Zeus,   780
set him against his enemies in the halls!
  Do it, rear him to greatness—two, threefold
    he will repay you freely, gladly.

Look now—watch the colt of a man you loved,
  yoked to the chariot of pain.   785

Now the orphan needs you—
harness his racing, rein him in,
   preserve his stride so we
can watch him surge at the last turn,
     storming for the goal.   790

   And you who haunt the vaults[1]
where the gold glows in the darkness,
hear us now, good spirits of the house,
   conspire with us—come,
    and wash old works of blood   795
in the fresh-drawn blood of Justice.
Let the gray retainer, murder, breed no more.

And you, Apollo, lord of the glorious masoned cavern,[2]
   grant that this man's house lift up its head,
     that we may see with loving eyes   800
the light of freedom burst from its dark veil!

   And lend a hand and scheme
for the rights, my Hermes,[3] help us,
sail the action on with all your breath.
   Reveal what's hidden, please,
or say a baffling word   805
in the night and blind men's eyes—
when the morning comes your word is just as dark.

Soon, at last, in the dawn that frees the house,
   we sea-widows wed to the winds   810
    will beat our mourning looms of song
     and sing, "Our ship's come in!
    Mine, mine is the wealth that swells her holds—
those I love are home and free of death."

But you, when your turn in the action comes, be strong.   815
When she cries "Son!" cry out "My *father's* son!"
   Go through with the murder—innocent at last.

Raise up the heart of Perseus[4] in your breast!
   And for all you love under earth
    and all above its rim, now scarf your eyes
     against the Gorgon's fury—   820
   In, go in for the slaughter now!
    [*Enter* AEGISTHUS, *alone.*]
The butcher comes. Wipe out death with death.
AEGISTHUS   Coming, coming. Yes, I have my summons.

1. The gods of the house—Hestia (the hearth), Zeus Ktesios (the storeroom), etc.   2. The temple of Apollo at Delphi. It was believed that his prophetess, the Pythia, was inspired by emanations from subterranean caves.   3. In his capacity of god of the marketplace and of thieves: he is the appropriate divinity to steer a murder plan that is based on deceit.   4. The hero who killed the Gorgon Medusa. Anyone who looked at her face was turned to stone; Perseus used a shield given him by Athena as a mirror.

There's news, I gather, travelers here to tell it.   825
No joy in the telling, though—Orestes dead.
Saddle the house with a bloody thing like that
and it might just collapse. It's still raw
from the last murders, galled and raw.

But how to take the story, for living truth?   830
Or work of a woman's panic, gossip starting up
in the night to flicker out and die?
     [*Turning to the* LEADER.]
                        Do you know?
Tell me, clear my mind.
LEADER   We've heard a little.
  But get it from the strangers, go inside.
Messengers have no power. Nothing like   835
a face-to-face encounter with the source.
AEGISTHUS —Must see him, test the messenger. Where was he
  when the boy died, standing on the spot?
Or is he dazed with rumor, mouthing hearsay?
No, he'll never trap me open-eyed!   840
     [*Striding through the doors.*]
CHORUS Zeus, Zeus, what can I say?—
  how to begin this prayer, call down
    the gods for help? what words
can reach the depth of all I feel?
Now they swing to the work,   845
  the red edge of the cleaver
hacks at flesh and men go down.
Agamemnon's house goes down—
  all-out disaster now,
or a son ignites the torch of freedom,   850
wins the throne, the citadel,
  the fathers' realms of gold.
The last man on the bench, a challenger
must come to grips with two. Up,
like a young god, Orestes, wrestle—   855
  let it be to win.
    [*A scream inside the palace.*]
—Listen!
     —What's happening?
                 —The house,
what have they done to the house?
LEADER   Back,
  till the work is over! Stand back—
they'll count us clean of the dreadful business.   860
    [*The women scatter; a wounded* SERVANT *of* AEGISTHUS *enters.*]
Look, the die is cast, the battle's done.
SERVANT   Ai,
  Ai, all over, master's dead—Aie,
a third, last salute. Aegisthus is no more.

[*Rushing at a side door, struggling to work it open.*]
Open up, wrench the bolts on the women's doors.
Faster! A strong young arm it takes, 865
but not to save him now, he's finished.
What's the use?
                    Look—wake up!
                              No good,
I call to the deaf, to sleepers . . . a waste of breath.
Where are you, Clytaemnestra? What are you doing?
LEADER Her head is ripe for lopping on the block. 870
She's next, and justice wields the ax.

[*The door opens, and* CLYTAEMNESTRA *comes forth.*]
CLYTAEMNESTRA   What now?
Why this shouting up and down the halls?
SERVANT The dead are killing the living, I tell you!
CLYTAEMNESTRA Ah, a riddle. I do well at riddles.
By cunning we die, precisely as we killed. 875
Hand me the man-ax, someone, hurry!

[*The* SERVANT *dashes out.*]
Now we will see. Win all or lose all,
we have come to this—the crisis of our lives.

[*The main doors open;* ORESTES, *sword in hand, is standing over the body*
      of AEGISTHUS, *with* PYLADES *close behind him.*]
ORESTES It's you I want. This one's had enough.
CLYTAEMNESTRA Gone, my violent one—Aegisthus, very dear. 880
ORESTES You love your man? Then lie in the same grave.
You can never be unfaithful to the dead.

[*Pulling her towards* AEGISTHUS' *body.*]
CLYTAEMNESTRA Wait, son—no feeling for this, my child?
The breast you held, drowsing away the hours,
soft gums tugging the milk that made you grow? 885

[ORESTES *turns to* PYLADES.]
ORESTES What will I do, Pylades?—I dread to kill my mother!
PYLADES What of the future? What of the Prophet God Apollo,
the Delphic voice, the faith and oaths we swear?
Make all mankind your enemy, not the gods.[5]
ORESTES O you win me over—good advice.

[*Wheeling on* CLYTAEMNESTRA, *thrusting her towards* AEGISTHUS.]
                              This way— 890
I want to butcher you—right across his body!
In life you thought he dwarfed my father—*Die!*—
go down with him forever!
                              You love this man,
the man you should have loved you hated.
CLYTAEMNESTRA I gave you life. Let me grow old with you. 895
ORESTES What—kill my father, then you'd live with me?
CLYTAEMNESTRA Destiny had a hand in that, my child.
ORESTES This too: destiny is handing you your death.

5. These are the only lines Pylades speaks in the play.

CLYTAEMNESTRA   You have no fear of a mother's curse, my son?
ORESTES   Mother? You flung me to a life of pain.   900
CLYTAEMNESTRA   Never flung you, placed you in a comrade's house.
ORESTES   —Disgraced me, sold me, a freeborn father's son.
CLYTAEMNESTRA   Oh? then name the price I took for you.
ORESTES   I am ashamed to mention it[6] in public.
CLYTAEMNESTRA   Please, and tell your father's failings, too.   905
ORESTES   Never judge him—he suffered, you sat here at home.
CLYTAEMNESTRA   It hurts women, being kept from men, my son.[7]
ORESTES   Perhaps . . . but the man slaves to keep them safe at home.
CLYTAEMNESTRA   —I see murder in your eyes, my child—mother's
    murder!
ORESTES   You are the murderer, not I—and you will kill yourself.   910
CLYTAEMNESTRA   Watch out—the hounds of a mother's curse will hunt
    you down.
ORESTES   But how to escape a father's if I fail?
CLYTAEMNESTRA   I must be spilling live tears on a tomb of stone.[8]
ORESTES   Yes, my father's destiny—it decrees your death.
CLYTAEMNESTRA   Ai—you are the snake I bore[9]—I gave you life!
ORESTES   *Yes!*   915
    That was the great seer, that terror in your dreams.
    You killed and it was outrage—suffer outrage now.
        [*He draws her over the threshold; the doors close behind them, and the*
        CHORUS *gathers at the altar.*]
LEADER   I even mourn the victims' double fates.
    But Orestes fought, he reached the summit
    of bloodshed here—we'd rather have it so.   920
    The bright eye of the halls must never die.
CHORUS   Justice came at last to the sons of Priam,
    late but crushing vengeance, yes,
    but to Agamemnon's house returned
        the double lion,[1]   925
            the double onslaught
    drove to the hilt—the exile sped by god,
    by Delphi's just command that drove him home.

    Lift the cry of triumph O! the master's house
    wins free of grief, free of the ones   930
    who bled its wealth, the couple stained with murder,
        free of Fate's rough path.

    He came back with a lust for secret combat,
    stealthy, cunning vengeance, yes,
    but his hand was steered in open fight   935
        by god's true daughter,
            Right, Right we call her,

6. Her adulterous liaison with Aegisthus.   7. A reflection of Greek gender attitudes: men were supposed
capable of controlling their appetites, but women were said to lack self-control.   8. This echoes a proverbial expression for futile action—"pleading with a tomb."   9. Clytaemnestra remembers her dream
(lines 514 ff.)   1. Orestes and Pylades.

we and our mortal voices aiming well—
she breathes her fury, shatters all she hates.

Lift the cry of triumph O! the master's house   940
   wins free of grief, free of the ones
who bled its wealth, the couple stained with murder,
   free of Fate's rough path.

Apollo wills it so!—
Apollo, clear from the Earth's deep cleft   945
   his voice came shrill, "Now stealth will master stealth!"
And the pure god came down and healed our ancient wounds,
   the heavens come, somehow to lift our yoke of grief—
      Now to praise the heavens' just command.

Look, the light is breaking!   950
The huge chain that curbed the halls gives way.
   Rise up, proud house, long, too long
your walls lay fallen, strewn along the earth.
   Time brings all to birth—
soon Time will stride through the gates with blessings,   955
   once the hearth burns off corruption, once
the house drives off the Furies. Look, the dice of Fate
   fall well for all to see. We sing how fortune smiles—
      the aliens in the house are routed out at last!

Look, the light is breaking!   960
The huge chain that curbed the halls gives way.
   Rise up, proud house, long, too long
your walls lay fallen, strewn along the earth.
   [*The doors open. Torches light* PYLADES *and* ORESTES, *sword in hand,*
   standing over the bodies of CLYTAEMNESTRA *and* AEGISTHUS, *as* CLYTAEM-
   NESTRA *stood over the bodies of* AGAMEMNON *and* CASSANDRA.]
ORESTES   Behold the double tyranny of our land!
They killed my father, stormed my father's house.   965
They had their power when they held the throne.
Great lovers still, as you may read their fate.
True to their oath, hand in hand they swore
to kill my father, hand in hand to die.
Now they keep their word.
   [*Unwinding from the bodies on the bier the robes that entangled* AGA-
   MEMNON, *he displays them, as* CLYTAEMNESTRA *had displayed them, to*
   the chorus at the altar.]
                  Look once more on this,   970
you who gather here to attend our crimes—
the master-plot that bound my wretched father,
shackled his ankles, manacled his hands.
Spread it out! Stand in a ring around it,
a grand shroud for a man.

                  Here, unfurl it   975

so the Father—no, not mine but the One
who watches over all, the Sun can behold
my mother's godless work. So he may come,
my witness when the day of judgment comes,
that I pursued this bloody death with justice,   980
mother's death.
                              Aegisthus, why mention him?
The adulterer dies. An old custom, justice.[2]

But she who plotted this horror against her husband,
she carried his children, growing in her womb
and she—I loved her once   985
and now I loathe, I have to loathe—
                              what is she?
[*Kneeling by the body of his mother.*]
Some moray eel, some viper born to rot her mate
with a single touch, no fang to strike him,
just the wrong, the reckless fury in her heart!
          [*Glancing back and forth from* CLYTAEMNESTRA *to the robes.*]
This—how can I dignify this . . . snare for a beast?—   990
sheath for a corpse's feet?
                    This winding-sheet,
This tent for the bath of death!
                              No, a hunting net,
a coiling—what to call—?
                    Foot-trap—

woven of robes . . .
why, this is perfect gear for the highwayman   995
who entices guests and robs them blind and plies
the trade of thieves. With a sweet lure like this
he'd hoist a hundred lives and warm his heart.

Live with such a woman, marry *her?* Sooner
the gods destroy me—die without an heir!   1000
CHORUS   Oh the dreadful work . . .
Death calls and she is gone.
     But oh, for you, the survivor,
suffering is just about to bloom.
ORESTES   Did she do the work or not?—Here, come close—   1005
This shroud's my witness, dyed with Aegisthus' blade—
Look, the blood ran here, conspired with time to blot
the swirling dyes, the handsome old brocade.
          [*Clutching* AGAMEMNON'S *robes, burying his face in them and weeping.*]
Now I can praise you, now I am here to mourn.
You were my father's death, great robe, I hail you!   1010
Even if I must suffer the work and the agony

---

2. An Athenian had the right to kill a man taken in adultery with his wife.

and all the race of man—
                                I embrace you . . . you,
my victory, are my guilt, my curse, and still—
CHORUS   No man can go through life
and reach the end unharmed.   1015
    Aye, trouble is now,
and trouble still to come.
ORESTES   But *still*,
that you may know—
                                I see no end in sight,
I am a charioteer—the reins are flying, look,
the mares plunge off the track³—
                                my bolting heart,   1020
it beats me down and terror beats the drum,
my dance-and-singing master pitched to fury—
And still, while I still have some self-control,
I say to my friends in public: I killed my mother,
not with a little justice. She was stained   1025
with father's murder, she was cursed by god.
And the magic spells that fired up my daring?
One comes first. The Seer of Delphi who declared,
"Go through with this and you go free of guilt.
Fail and—"
                        I can't repeat the punishment.   1030
What bow could hit the crest of so much pain?
    [PYLADES *gives* ORESTES *a branch of olive and invests him in the robes of*
    APOLLO, *the wreath and insignia of suppliants to* DELPHI.]
Now look on me, armed with the branch and wreath,
a suppliant bound for the Navelstone of Earth,
Apollo's sacred heights
where they say the fire of heaven⁴ can never die.   1035
    [*Looking at his hand that still retains the sword.*]
I must escape this blood . . . it is my own.
—Must turn toward his hearth,
none but his, the Prophet God decreed.

I ask you, Argos and all my generations,
remember how these brutal things were done.   1040
Be my witness to Menelaus when he comes.
And now I go, an outcast driven off the land,
in life, in death, I leave behind a name for—
LEADER   But you've done well. Don't burden yourself
with bad omens, lash yourself with guilt.   1045

---

3. Orestes feels himself going mad under the influence of the Furies. As stampeding horses pull a chariot off the race track and wreck it, so Orestes' thoughts whirl out of control.   4. A sacred fire was permanently maintained at Delphi: from it other fires, which had gone out through natural calamities or the sack of a city, could be renewed. *Navelstone*: Delphi claimed to be the center of the Earth: in the temple was a stone called the "navel."

You've set us free, the whole city of Argos,
lopped the heads of these two serpents once for all.

[*Staring at the women and beyond,* ORESTES *screams in terror.*]

ORESTES   No, no! Women—look—like Gorgons,
   shrouded in black, their heads wreathed,
   swarming serpents!⁵

                                    —Cannot stay, I must move on.   1050

LEADER   What dreams can whirl you so? You of all men,
   you have your father's love. Steady,
   nothing to fear with all you've won.

ORESTES   No dreams,
   these torments, not to me, they're clear, real—the hounds
   of mother's hate.

LEADER   The blood's still wet on your hands.   1055
   It puts a kind of frenzy in you . . .

ORESTES   *God Apollo!*
   Here they come, thick and fast,
   their eyes dripping hate—

LEADER   One thing
   will purge you. Apollo's touch will set you free
   from all your . . . torments.

ORESTES   You can't see them—   1060
   I can, they drive me on! I must move on—

      [*He rushes out;* PYLADES *follows close behind.*]

LEADER   Farewell then. God look down on you with kindness,
   guard you, grant you fortune.

CHORUS   Here once more, for the third time,
   the tempest in the race has struck   1065
   the house of kings and run its course.
      First the children eaten,
   the cause of all our pain, the curse,
   And next the kingly man's ordeal,
   the bath where the proud commander,   1070
   lord of Achaea's armies lost his life.
   And now a third has come, but who?
      A third like Saving Zeus?
   Or should we call him death?
   Where will it end?—   1075
   where will it sink to sleep and rest,
      this murderous hate, this Fury?

5. Orestes sees the Furies, come to hound him for his matricide.

The Eumenides

CHARACTERS

The PYTHIA, *the priestess of Apollo*   CHORUS OF FURIES *and their* LEADER
APOLLO   ATHENA
HERMES   *Escorting* CHORUS *of Athenian women*
ORESTES   *Men of the jury, herald, citizens*
THE GHOST OF CLYTAEMNESTRA

[TIME AND SCENE: *The* FURIES *have pursued* ORESTES *to the temple of* APOLLO *at
Delphi. It is morning. The priestess of the god appears at the great doors and
offers up her prayer.*]

PYTHIA   First of the gods I honor in my prayer is Mother Earth,
　　the first of the gods to prophesy,[1] and next I praise
　　Tradition, second to hold her Mother's mantic seat,
　　so legend says, and third by the lots of destiny,
　　by Tradition's free will—no force to bear her down—   5
　　another Titan, child of the Earth, took her seat
　　and Phoebe passed it on as a birthday gift to Phoebus,
　　Phoebus a name for clear pure light derived from hers.
　　Leaving the marsh and razorback of Delos, landing
　　at Pallas' headlands flocked by ships, here he came   10
　　to make his home Parnassus and the heights.[2]
　　And an escort filled with reverence brought him on,
　　the highway-builders, sons of the god of fire[3] who tamed
　　the savage country, civilized the wilds—on he marched
　　and the people lined his way to cover him with praise,   15
　　led by Delphos, lord, helm of the land, and Zeus
　　inspired his mind with the prophet's skill, with godhead,
　　made him fourth in the dynasty of seers to mount this throne,
　　but it is Zeus that Apollo speaks for, Father Zeus.
　　These I honor in the prelude of my prayers—these gods.   20
　　But Athena at the Forefront of the Temple crowns our legends.
　　I revere the nymphs who keep the Corycian rock's deep hollows,[4]
　　loving haunt of birds where the spirits drift and hover.
　　And Great Dionysus rules the land. I never forget that day
　　he marshaled his wild women in arms—he was all god,   25
　　he ripped Pentheus[5] down like a hare in the nets of doom.

1. The priestess of Apollo's oracle (Pythia) traces the peaceful succession of powers that controlled the
great prophetic site of Delphi. First Mother Earth; then Tradition (*Themis* in the Greek); and then Phoebe,
grandmother of Apollo, who handed it over to him as a birthday gift. This is a myth that stresses orderly,
peaceful succession; in other versions Apollo fights and kills the great serpent Pytho to gain possession.
2. The oracular site is situated on the lower slopes of the Parnassus mountain range (8,060 feet at its
summit). Delos is a small rocky island in the Cyclades and Apollo's birthplace. *Pallas' headlands*: the coast
of Attica.   3. Athenians, whose legendary ancestor Erichthonius was a son of Hephaestus, the smith god.
4. A capacious cave high above the site of Delphi, sacred to Pan and the nymphs. *The Temple*: Pronaia,
the temple of Athena situated at the entrance to the sacred precinct.   5. A king of Thebes who resisted
the establishment of Dionysiac rites in his domains. Dionysus, giver of wine and ecstasy, was thought to
inhabit Delphi in the winter months, when Apollo left for the land of the Hyperboreans (the happy people
who lived, as their name indicates, beyond the North Wind). Dionysiac festivals at which women danced
on the hills at night were held at Delphi in historical times.

And the rushing springs of Pleistos,[6] Poseidon's force I call,
and the king of the sky, the king of all fulfillment, Zeus.
Now the prophet goes to take her seat. God speed me—
grant me a vision greater than all my embarkations past!   30
    [*Turning to the audience.*]
Where are the Greeks among you? Draw your lots and enter.
It is the custom here. I will tell the future
only as the god will lead the way.
    [*She goes through the doors and reappears in a moment, shaken, thrown
    to her knees by some terrific force.*]
                           Terrors—
terrors to tell, terrors all can see!—
they send me reeling back from Apollo's house.   35
The strength drains, it's very hard to stand,
crawling on all fours, no spring in the legs . . .
an old woman, gripped by fear, is nothing,
a child, nothing more.
    [*Struggling to her feet, trying to compose herself.*]
I'm on my way to the vault,   40
it's green with wreaths, and there at the Navelstone[7]
I see a man—an abomination to god—
he holds the seat where suppliants sit for purging;
his hands dripping blood, and his sword just drawn,
and he holds a branch (it must have topped an olive)   45
wreathed with a fine tuft of wool,[8] all piety,
fleece gleaming white. So far it's clear, I tell you.
But there in a ring around the man, an amazing company—
women, sleeping, nestling against the benches . . .
women? No,   50
Gorgons I'd call them; but then with Gorgons
you'd see the grim, inhuman . . .
                      I saw a picture
years ago, the creatures tearing the feast
away from Phineus[9]—
              These have no wings,
I looked. But black they are, and so repulsive.   55
Their heavy, rasping breathing makes me cringe.
And their eyes ooze a discharge, sickening,
and what they wear[1]—to flaunt *that* at the gods,
the idols, sacrilege! even in the homes of men.
The tribe that produced that brood I never saw,   60
or a plot of ground to boast it nursed their kind
without some tears, some pain for all its labor.

Now for the outcome. This is his concern,
Apollo the master of this house, the mighty power.

6. The river (dry in summer) in the bottom of the deep gorge below Delphi.   7. A sacred stone that was
supposed to mark the center of the Earth.   8. Suppliants usually carried a branch of olive, hung with
small woolen wreaths.   9. Whenever he spread the table for a meal, the food was carried off by loathsome
creatures—half bird, half woman—called Harpies. The Pythia first thinks the Furies (Erinyes) are Gorgons,
but then rejects that theory (we are not told why); her next guess, Harpies, has to be abandoned because
the Furies have no wings.   1. Long black robes.

Healer, prophet, diviner of signs, he purges   65
the halls of others—He must purge his own.
    [*She leaves. The doors of the temple open and reveal* APOLLO *rising over*
    ORESTES; *he kneels in prayer at the Navelstone, surrounded by the* FURIES
    who are sleeping. HERMES *waits in the background.*]

APOLLO   No, I will never fail you, through to the end
your guardian standing by your side or worlds away!
I will show no mercy to your enemies! Now
look at these—
    [*Pointing to the* FURIES,]
        these obscenities!—I've caught them,   70
beaten them down with sleep.
                   They disgust me.
These gray, ancient children never touched
by god, man, or beast—the eternal virgins.
Born for destruction only, the dark pit,
they range the bowels of Earth, the world of death,   75
loathed by men and the gods who hold Olympus.

Nevertheless keep racing on and never yield.
Deep in the endless heartland they will drive you,
striding horizons, feet pounding the earth forever,
on, on over seas and cities swept by tides!   80
Never surrender, never brood on the labor.
And once you reach the citadel of Pallas, kneel
and embrace her ancient idol[2] in your arms and there,
with judges of your case, with a magic spell—
with words—we will devise the master-stroke   85
that sets you free from torment once for all.
I persuaded you to take your mother's life.

ORESTES   Lord Apollo, you know the rules of justice,
know them well. Now learn compassion, too.
No one doubts your power to do great things.   90

APOLLO   Remember that. No fear will overcome you.
    [*Summoning* HERMES *from the shadows.*]
You, my brother, blood of our common Father,
Hermes, guard him well. Live up to your name,
good Escort. Shepherd him well, he is my suppliant,
and outlaws have their rights that Zeus reveres.   95
Lead him back to the world of men with all good speed.
    [APOLLO *withdraws to his inner sanctuary;* ORESTES *leaves with* HERMES
    in the lead. THE GHOST[3] OF CLYTAEMNESTRA *appears at the Navelstone,*
    hovering over the FURIES *as they sleep.*]

THE GHOST OF CLYTAEMNESTRA   You—how can you *sleep*?
Awake, awake—what use are sleepers now?
I go stripped of honor, thanks to you,
alone among the dead. And for those I killed   100
the charges of the dead will never cease, never—

---

2. An ancient wooden statue of Athena in a temple on the Acropolis at Athens. *Citadel of Pallas:* Athens.
3. She is not really a ghost. In line 121 she tells us that she is a dream in the head of the Furies.

I wander in disgrace, I feel the guilt, I tell you,
withering guilt from all the outraged dead!

But I suffered too, terribly, from dear ones,
and none of my spirits rages to avenge me.   105
I was slaughtered by his matricidal hand.
See these gashes—

       [*Seizing one of the* FURIES *weak with sleep.*]
               Carve them in your heart!
The sleeping brain has eyes that give us light;
we can never see our destiny by day.

And after all my libations . . . how you lapped   110
the honey, the sober offerings poured to soothe you,
awesome midnight feasts[4] I burned at the hearthfire,
your dread hour never shared with gods.
All those rites, I see them trampled down.
And he springs free like a fawn, one light leap   115
at that—he's through the thick of your nets,
he breaks away!
Mocking laughter twists across his face.
Hear me, I am pleading for my life.
Awake, my Furies, goddesses of the Earth!   120
A dream is calling—Clytaemnestra calls you now.

       [*The* FURIES *mutter in their sleep.*]
Mutter on. Your man is gone, fled far away.
My son has friends to defend him, not like mine.

       [*They mutter again.*]
You sleep too much, no pity for my ordeal.
Orestes murdered his mother—he is gone.   125

       [*They begin to moan.*]
Moaning, sleeping—onto your feet, quickly.
What is your work? What but causing pain?
Sleep and toil, the two strong conspirators,
they sap the mother dragon's deadly fury—

       [*The* FURIES *utter a sharp moan and moan again, but they are still
       asleep.*]
FURIES   Get him, get him, get him, get him—   130
   there he goes.
THE GHOST OF CLYTAEMNESTRA   The prey you hunt is just a dream—
like hounds mad for the sport you bay him on,
you never leave the kill.
               But what are you *doing?*
Up! don't yield to the labor, limp with sleep.
Never forget my anguish.   135
Let my charges hurt you, they are just;
deep in the righteous heart they prod like spurs.

---

4. Offerings to the Furies were made only at night. *Sober offerings:* no wine was included in offerings to
them.

You, blast him on with your gory breath,
the fire of your vitals—wither him, after him,
one last foray—waste him, burn him out!
    [*She vanishes. The lead* FURY *urges on the pack.*]
LEADER   Wake up!   140
I rouse you, you rouse her. Still asleep?
Onto your feet, kick off your stupor.
See if this prelude has some grain of truth.
    [*The* FURIES *circle, pursuing the scent with hunting calls, and cry out
    singly when they find* ORESTES *gone.*]
FURIES   —Aieeeeee—no, no, *no,* they do us wrong, dear sisters.

—The miles of pain, the pain I suffer . . .   145
and all for nothing, all for pain, more pain,
    the anguish, oh, the grief too much to bear.

—The quarry's slipped from the nets, our quarry lost and gone.

—Sleep defeats me . . . I have lost the prey.

—You—child of Zeus[5]—*you,* a common thief!   150

—Young god, you have ridden down the powers
proud with age. You worship the suppliant,
    the godless man who tears his parent's heart—

—The matricide, you steal him away, and you a god!

—Guilt both ways, and who can call it justice?   155

—Not I: her charges stalk my dreams,
    yes, the charioteer rides hard,
        her spurs digging the vitals,
        under the heart, under the heaving breast—

—I can feel the executioner's lash, it's searing   160
    deeper, sharper, the knives of burning ice—

—Such is your triumph, you young gods,
    world dominion past all rights.
        Your throne is streaming blood,
        blood at the foot, blood at the crowning head—   165

—I can see the Navelstone of the Earth, it's bleeding,
    bristling corruption, oh, the guilt it has to bear—

Stains on the hearth! The Prophet stains the vault,
    he cries it on, drives on the crime himself.

5. Apollo.

      Breaking the god's first law, he rates men first,   170
        destroys the old dominions of the Fates.

  He wounds me too, yet *him* he'll never free,
    plunging under the earth, no freedom then:
      curst as he comes for purging, at his neck
      he feels new murder springing from his blood.   175
        [APOLLO *strides from his sanctuary in full armor, brandishing his bow*
        and driving back the FURIES.]
APOLLO   Out, I tell you, out of these halls—fast!—
   set the Prophet's chamber free!
        [*Seizing one of the* FURIES, *shaking an arrow across her face.*]
                    Or take
  the flash and stab of this, this flying viper
  whipped from the golden cord that strings my bow!

  Heave in torment, black froth erupting from your lungs,   180
  vomit the clots of all the murders you have drained.
  But never touch my halls, you have no right.

  Go where heads are severed, eyes gouged out,
  where Justice and bloody slaughter are the same . . .
  castrations, wasted seed, young men's glories butchered,   185
  extremities maimed, and huge stones at the chest,
  and the victims wail for pity—
  spikes inching up the spine, torsos stuck on spikes.[6]
        [*The* FURIES *close in on him.*]
  So, you hear your love feast, yearn to have it all?
  You revolt the gods. Your look,   190
  your whole regalia gives you away—your kind
  should infest a lion's cavern reeking blood.
  But never rub your filth on the Prophet's shrine.
  Out, you flock without a herdsman—out!
  No god will ever shepherd you with love.   195
LEADER   Lord Apollo, now it is your turn to listen.
  You are no mere accomplice in this crime.
  You did it all, and all the guilt is yours.
APOLLO   No, how? Enlarge on that, and only that.
LEADER   You commanded the guest to kill his mother.   200
APOLLO   —Commanded him to avenge his father, what of it?
LEADER   And then you dared embrace him, fresh from bloodshed.
APOLLO   Yes, I ordered him on, to my house, for purging.[7]
LEADER   And we sped him on, and you revile us?
APOLLO   Indeed, you are not fit to approach this house.   205
LEADER   And yet we have our mission and our—
APOLLO   Authority—you? Sound out your splendid power.

6. The methods of torture and execution listed by Apollo are what the Greeks saw as typically Eastern, and indeed, castration and impalement were Persian, not Greek, customs. But Apollo's dismissal of the Furies as non-Greek has no basis in fact; the Furies are not only Greek but much older than he is.   7. Ritual purification.

LEADER   Matricides: we drive them from their houses.
APOLLO   And what of the wife who strikes her husband down?
LEADER   That murder would not destroy one's flesh and blood.[8]   210
APOLLO   Why, you'd disgrace—obliterate the bonds of Zeus
   and Hera queen of brides! And the queen of love[9]
   you'd throw to the winds at a word, disgrace love,
   the source of mankind's nearest, dearest ties.
   Marriage of man and wife is Fate itself,   215
   stronger than oaths, and Justice guards its life.
   But if one destroys the other and you relent—
   no revenge, not a glance in anger—then
   I say your manhunt of Orestes is unjust.
   Some things stir your rage, I see. Others,   220
   atrocious crimes, lull your will to act.
                                                       Pallas
   will oversee this trial. She is one of us.
LEADER   I will never let that man go free, never.
APOLLO   Hound him then, and multiply your pains.
LEADER   Never try to cut my power with your logic.   225
APOLLO   I'd never touch it, not as a gift—your power.
LEADER   Of course,
   great as you are, they say, throned on high with Zeus.
   But blood of the mother draws me on—must hunt
   the man for Justice. Now I'm on his trail!
      [*Rushing out, with the* FURIES *in full cry.*]
APOLLO   And I will defend my suppliant and save him.   230
   A terror to gods and men, the outcast's anger,
   once I fail him, all of my own free will.
      [APOLLO *leaves. The scene changes to the Acropolis in Athens. Escorted*
      by HERMES, ORESTES *enters and kneels, exhausted, before the ancient*
      shrine and idol of ATHENA.]
ORESTES   Queen Athena,
   under Apollo's orders I have come.
   Receive me kindly. Curst and an outcast,
   no suppliant for purging . . . my hands are clean.
   My murderous edge is blunted now, worn down at last   235
   on the outland homesteads, beaten paths of men.[1]
   On and out over seas and dry frontiers,
   I kept alive the Prophet's strong commands.
   Struggling toward your house, your idol—
      [*Taking the knees of* ATHENA's *idol in his arms.*]
                                             Goddess,   240

8. Crimes of blood relations against each other are the most heinous kind. But husband and wife are, and must be, of different blood. The Furies would have pursued Orestes if he had not avenged his father, and they pursue him now because he killed his mother, but the killing of a husband by a wife seems to them a lesser crime. They think and feel in tribal terms, those of a society that has not yet developed the city-state, the *polis,* in which the institution of marriage (which Apollo champions in his reply, lines 215 ff.) was the guarantee of the legitimacy of male heirs for the transmittal of property from generation to generation. 9. Aphrodite. The marriage of Zeus and Hera was the divine model of earthly marriages, and Hera was the goddess who presided over marriage ceremonies.   1. Orestes has been given ritual purification by Apollo, but he also claims that the blood guilt is now "worn down" by his travels and contacts with men (compare lines 278–85).

here I keep my watch,
I await the consummation of my trial.

[*The* FURIES *enter in pursuit but cannot find* ORESTES *who is entwined
around* ATHENA's *idol. The* LEADER *sees the footprints.*]

LEADER   At last!
The clear trail of the man. After it, silent
but it tracks his guilt to light. He's wounded—
go for the fawn, my hounds, the splash of blood,
hunt him, rake him down.   245
                        Oh, the labor,
the man-killing labor. My lungs are bursting . . .
over the wide rolling earth we've ranged in flock,
hurdling the waves in wingless flight and now we come,
all hot pursuit, outracing ships astern—and now   250
he's here, somewhere, cowering like a hare . . .
the reek of human blood[2]—it's laughter to my heart!

[*Inciting a pair of* FURIES.]

Look, look again, you two,
scour the ground before he escapes—one dodge
and the matricide slips free.

[*Seeing* ORESTES, *one by one they press around him and* ATHENA's *idol.*]

FURIES   —There he is!   255
Clutching the knees of power once again,
    twined in the deathless goddess' idol,[3] look,
he wants to go on trial for his crimes.

                                    —Never . . .
    the mother's blood that wets the ground,
    you can never bring it back, dear god,   260
the Earth drinks, and the running life is gone.

                                        —No,
you'll give me blood for blood, you must!
    Out of your living marrow I will drain
    my red libation, out of your veins I suck my food,
    my raw, brutal cups—

                                        —Wither you alive,   265
    drag you down and there you pay, agony
for mother-killing agony!

                                —And there you will see them all.
Every mortal who outraged god or guest or loving parent:
each receives the pain his pains exact.

    —A mighty god is Hades. There   270
at the last reckoning underneath the earth

---

2. The Furies track him down by scent of the blood he shed, as if he were a wounded animal leaving a
trace behind him.   3. Orestes is still clinging to the statue of Pallas Athena.

   he scans all, he squares all men's accounts
and graves them on the tablets of his mind.
       [ORESTES *remains impassive.*]
ORESTES   I have suffered into truth. Well I know
the countless arts of purging, where to speak,   275
where silence is the rule. In this ordeal
a compelling master urges me to speak.
       [*Looking at his hands.*]
The blood sleeps, it is fading on my hands,
the stain of mother's murder washing clean.
It was still fresh at the god's hearth. Apollo   280
killed the swine and the purges drove it off.
Mine is a long story
if I'd start with the many hosts I met,
I lived with, and I left them all unharmed.
Time refines all things that age with time.   285

And now with pure, reverent lips I call
the queen of the land. Athena, help me!
Come without your spear—without a battle
you will win myself, my land, the Argive people[4]
true and just, your friends-in-arms forever.   290
Where are you now? The scorching wilds of Libya,
bathed by the Triton pool where you were born?[5]
Robes shrouding your feet
or shod and on the march to aid allies?
Or striding the Giants' Plain, marshal of armies,[6]   295
hero scanning, flashing through the ranks?
                                        Come—
you can hear me from afar, you are a god.
Set me free from this!
LEADER   Never—neither
Apollo's nor Athena's strength can save you.
Down you go, abandoned,   300
searching your soul for joy but joy is gone.
Bled white, gnawed by demons, a husk, a wraith—
       [*She breaks off, waiting for reply, but* ORESTES *prays in silence.*]
No reply? you spit my challenge back?
You'll feast me alive, my fatted calf,
not cut on the altar first. Now hear my spell,   305
the chains of song I sing to bind you tight.
FURIES   Come, Furies, dance!—
link arms for the dancing hand-to-hand,
now we long to reveal our art,
our terror, now to declare our right

---

4. This is the first clear reference to the alliance that Athens had concluded with Argos in 459 B.C.E., the year before the production of the trilogy.   5. One of Athena's titles, Tritogeneia, was thought to derive from Lake Tritonis, in Libya, where some said she was born. There may be a contemporary allusion here; Athens was backing, with ships and troops, the Libyan ruler Inaros, who was fighting the Persian rulers of Egypt.   6. Athena, a warrior goddess, took a prominent part in the battle between the gods and the giants, in which Zeus and the Olympians won a decisive victory.

to steer the lives of men,⁣   310
we all conspire, we dance! we are
the just and upright, we maintain.
Hold out your hands, if they are clean
   no fury of ours will stalk you,
you will go through life unscathed.   315
But show us the guilty—one like this
   who hides his reeking hands,
and up from the outraged dead we rise,
witness bound to avenge their blood
we rise in flames against him to the end!   320

Mother who bore me,
   O dear Mother Night,
to avenge the blinded dead
and those who see by day,
     now hear me! The whelp Apollo   325
spurns my rights, he tears this trembling victim
    from my grasp—the one to bleed,
    to atone away the mother-blood at last.

     Over the victim's burning head
this chant this frenzy striking frenzy   330
    lightning crazing the mind
     this hymn of Fury
chaining the senses, ripping cross the lyre,[7]
    withering lives of men!

This, this is our right,   335
   spun for us by the Fates,
the ones who bind the world,
and none can shake our hold.
   Show us the mortals overcome,
insane to murder kin—we track them down   340
    till they go beneath the earth,
and the dead find little freedom in the end.

     Over the victim's burning head
this chant this frenzy striking frenzy
    lightning crazing the mind   345
     this hymn of Fury
chaining the senses, ripping cross the lyre,
    withering lives of men!

Even at birth, I say, our rights were so ordained.
   The deathless gods must keep their hands far off—   350
no god may share our cups, our solemn feasts.
We want no part of their pious white robes—
   the Fates who gave us power made us free.

---

7. I.e., not accompanied by the lyre, an instrument associated with joyous occasions.

Mine is the overthrow of houses, yes,
 when warlust reared like a tame beast   355
  seizes near and dear—
   down on the man we swoop, aie!
    for all his power black him out!—
for the blood still fresh from slaughter on his hands.

So now, striving to wrench our mandate from the gods, 360
 we make ourselves exempt from their control,
we brook no trial—no god can be our judge.
  [*Reaching toward* ORESTES.]
His breed, worthy of loathing, streaked with blood,
 Zeus slights, unworthy his contempt.

Mine is the overthrow of houses, yes,   365
 when warlust reared like a tame beast
  seizes near and dear—
   down on the man we swoop, aie!
    for all his power black him out!—
for the blood still fresh from slaughter on his hands. 370

And all men's dreams of grandeur,
  tempting the heavens,
all melt down, under earth their pride goes down—
 lost in our onslaught, black robes swarming,
  Furies throbbing, dancing out our rage. 375

Yes! leaping down from the heights,
 dead weight in the crashing footfall
  down we hurl on the runner
   breakneck for the finish—
cut him down, our fury stamps him down! 380

Down he goes, sensing nothing,
 blind with defilement . . .
darkness hovers over the man, dark guilt,
 and a dense pall overhangs his house,
  legend tells the story through her tears. 385

Yes! leaping down from the heights,
 dead weight in the crashing footfall
  down we hurl on the runner
   breakneck for the finish—
cut him down, our fury stamps him down! 390

   So the center holds.
  We are the skilled, the masterful,
   we the great fulfillers,
  memories of grief, we awesome spirits
    stern, unappeasable to man, 395
  disgraced, degraded, drive our powers through;

banished far from god to a sunless, torchlit dusk,
we drive men through their rugged passage,
blinded dead and those who see by day.

Then where is the man   400
not stirred with awe, not gripped by fear
to hear us tell the law that
Fate ordains, the gods concede the Furies,
absolute till the end of time?
And so it holds, our ancient power still holds.   405
We are not without our pride, though beneath the earth
our strict battalions form their lines,
groping through the mist and sunstarved night.

[*Enter* ATHENA, *armed for combat with her aegis and her spear.*]
ATHENA   From another world I heard a call for help.
I was on the Scamander's banks, just claiming Troy.   410
The Achaean warlords chose the hero's share
of what their spear had won—they decreed that land,
root and branch all mine, for all time to be,
for Theseus' sons[8] a rare, matchless gift.

Home from the wars I come, my pace unflagging,   415
wingless, flown on the whirring, breasting cape[9]
that yokes my racing spirit in her prime.
[*Unfurling the aegis, seeing* ORESTES *and the* FURIES *at her shrine.*]
And I see some new companions on the land.
Not fear, a sense of wonder fills my eyes.

Who are you? I address you all as one: 420
you, the stranger seated at my idol,
and you, like no one born of the sown seed,
no goddess watched by the gods, no mortal either,
not to judge by your look at least, your features . . .
Wait, I call my neighbors into question.   425
They've done nothing wrong. It offends the rights,
it violates tradition.
LEADER   You will learn it all,
young daughter of Zeus, cut to a few words.
We are the everlasting children of the Night.
Deep in the halls of Earth they call us Curses.   430
ATHENA   Now I know your birth, your rightful name—
LEADER   But not our powers, and you will learn them quickly.

8. Homer does not mention it, but in later Athenian tradition the two sons of Theseus, the national hero who unified the whole of Attica under Athens, fought at Troy. This reference to Athenian participation in the war may be another allusion to contemporary reality; Athenians had won a foothold in the Troad, the region around Troy, under the tyrant Pisistratus at the end of the 6th century B.C.E., and in Aeschylus's day cities in and near the Troad, along the vital route for grain of the Black Sea area, were part of the Athenian empire. But there is another reason for introducing the subject of the Trojan War. In *Agamemnon* the audience is given an almost unrelievedly critical view of the war. But now Orestes is to be tried and acquitted, and Agamemnon's good name restored. The war has now to be presented in a favorable light (compare lines 470 ff.).   9. The aegis, a cloak worn by Athena: it has the face of the Gorgon Medusa on it. Here Athena uses it to fly; at other times it is used as a shield to produce terror, as in *Odyssey* 22.

ATHENA   I can accept the facts, just tell them clearly.
LEADER   Destroyers of life: we drive them from their houses.
ATHENA   And the murderer's flight, where does it all end?   435
LEADER   Where there is no joy, the word is never used.
ATHENA   Such flight for him? You shriek him on to that?
LEADER   Yes,
he murdered his mother—called that murder just.
ATHENA   And nothing forced him on, no fear of someone's anger?
LEADER   What spur would force a man to kill his mother?   440
ATHENA   Two sides are here, and only half is heard.
LEADER   But the oath—he will neither take the oath nor give it,
no, his will is set.
ATHENA   And you are set
on the name of justice rather than the act.
LEADER   How? Teach us. You have a genius for refinements.   445
ATHENA   Injustice, I mean, should never triumph thanks to oaths.
LEADER   Then examine him yourself, judge him fairly.
ATHENA   You would turn over responsibility to me,
to reach the final verdict?
LEADER   Certainly.
We respect you. You show us respect.   450
         [ATHENA *turns to* ORESTES.]
ATHENA   Your turn, stranger. What do you say to this?
Tell us your land, your birth, your fortunes.
Then defend yourself against their charge,
if trust in your rights has brought you here to guard
my hearth and idol, a suppliant for purging   455
like Ixion,[1] sacred. Speak to all this clearly,
speak to me.
ORESTES   Queen Athena, first,
the misgiving in your final words is strong.
Let me remove it. I haven't come for purging.
Look, not a stain on the hands that touch your idol.   460
I have proof for all I say, and it is strong.

The law condemns the man of the violent hand
to silence, till a master trained at purging
slits the throat of a young suckling victim,
blood absolves his blood. Long ago   465
at the halls of others I was fully cleansed
in the cleansing springs, the blood of many victims.
Threat of pollution—sweep it from your mind.
Now for my birth. You will know at once.
I am from Argos. My father, well you ask,   470
was Agamemnon, sea-lord of the men-of-war,
your partisan when you made the city Troy
a city of the dead.

---

1. The Greek Cain, the first murderer. He killed his father-in-law; coming to Zeus as a suppliant, he was purified by the great god himself.

What an ignoble death he died
when he came home—Ai! my blackhearted mother
cut him down, enveloped him in her handsome net— 475
it still attests his murder in the bath.
But I came back, my years of exile weathered—
killed the one who bore me, I won't deny it,
killed her in revenge. I loved my father,
fiercely.

And Apollo shares the guilt— 480
he spurred me on, he warned of the pains I'd feel
unless I acted, brought the guilty down.
But were we just or not? Judge us now.
My fate is in your hands. Stand or fall
I shall accept your verdict.

ATHENA   Too large a matter, 485
some may think, for mortal men to judge.
But by all rights not even I should decide
a case of murder—murder whets the passions.
Above all, the rites have tamed your wildness.
A suppliant, cleansed, you bring my house no harm. 490
If you are innocent, I'd adopt you for my city.

[Turning to the FURIES.]

But they have their destiny too, hard to dismiss,
and if they fail to win their day in court—
how it will spread, the venom of their pride,
plague everlasting blights our land, our future . . . 495

So it stands. A crisis either way.

[Looking back and forth from ORESTES to the FURIES.]

Embrace the one? expel the other? It defeats me.

But since the matter comes to rest on us,
I will appoint the judges of manslaughter,
swear them in, and found a tribunal here 500
for all time to come.[2]

[To ORESTES and the FURIES.]

My contestants,
summon your trusted witnesses and proofs,
your defenders under oath to help your cause.
And I will pick the finest men of Athens,
return and decide the issue fairly, truly— 505
bound to our oaths, our spirits bent on justice.

[ATHENA leaves. The FURIES form their chorus.]

FURIES   Here, now, is the overthrow
of every binding law—once his appeal,
    his outrage wins the day,
his matricide! One act links all mankind, 510
hand to desperate hand in bloody license.

---

2. The Areopagus, which in Aeschylus's lifetime was the court that tried homicide cases.

Over and over deathstrokes
     dealt by children wait their parents,
mortal generations still unborn.
  We are the Furies still, yes,   515
but now our rage that patrolled the crimes of men,
  that stalked their rage dissolves—
we loose a lethal tide to sweep the world!
Man to man foresees his neighbor's torments,
  groping to cure his own—   520
     poor wretch, there is no cure, no use,
the drugs that ease him speed the next attack.

  Now when the sudden blows come down,
let no one sound the call that once brought help,
"Justice, hear me—Furies throned in power!"   525
  Oh I can hear the father now
  or the mother sob with pain
    at the pain's onset . . . hopeless now,
  the house of Justice falls.[3]

  There is a time when terror helps,   530
the watchman must stand guard upon the heart.
It helps, at times, to suffer into truth.
  Is there a man who knows no fear
  in the brightness of his heart,
    or a man's city, both are one,   535
  that still reveres the rights?

      Neither the life of anarchy
       nor the life enslaved by tyrants, no,
         worship neither.
  Strike the balance all in all and god will give you power;   540
    the laws of god may veer from north to south—
      we Furies plead for Measure.
    Violence is Impiety's child, true to its roots,
  but the spirit's great good health breeds all we love
      and all our prayers call down,   545
       prosperity and peace.

      All in all I tell you people,
    bow before the altar of the rights,
       revere it well.
  Never trample it underfoot, your eyes set on spoils;   550
    revenge will hunt the godless day and night—
      the destined end awaits.
  So honor your parents first with reverence, I say,
    and the stranger guest you welcome to your house,

---

3. The Furies argue that the acquittal of Orestes will be a precedent for universal crime. Furthermore, they will no longer, in that case, continue to see that vengeance is exacted; appeals to the Furies for justice will be disregarded (lines 523 ff.).

turn to attend his needs,   555
respect his sacred rights.

All of your own free will, all uncompelled,
be just and you will never want for joy,
you and your kin can never be uprooted from the earth.
But the reckless one—I warn the marauder   560
dragging plunder, chaotic, rich beyond all rights:
he'll strike his sails,
harried at long last,
stunned when the squalls of torment break his spars to bits.

He cries to the deaf, he wrestles walls of sea   565
sheer whirlpools down, down, with the gods' laughter
breaking over the man's hot heart—they see him flailing, crushed.
The one who boasted never to shipwreck
now will never clear the cape and steer for home;
who lived for wealth,   570
golden his life long—
he rams on the reef of law and drowns unwept, unseen.

[*The scene has shifted to the Areopagus, the tribunal on the Crag of Ares.*[4]
ATHENA *enters in procession with a herald and ten Citizens she has chosen to be judges.*]

ATHENA   Call for order, herald, marshal our good people.
Lift the Etruscan battle-trumpet,[5]
strain it to full pitch with human breath,   575
crash out a stabbing blast along the ranks.

[*The trumpet sounds. The judges take up positions between the audience
and the actors.* ATHENA *separates the* FURIES *and* ORESTES, *directing him
to the Stone of Outrage and the* LEADER *to the Stone of Unmercifulness,*[6]
where the FURIES *form their chorus. Then* ATHENA *takes her stand
between two urns that will receive the ballots.*]

And while this court of judgment fills, my city,
silence will be best. So that you can learn
my everlasting laws. And you too,

[*To* ORESTES *and the* FURIES.]

that our verdict may be well observed by all.   580

[APOLLO *enters suddenly and looms behind* ORESTES.]

Lord Apollo—rule it over your own sphere!
What part have you in this? Tell us.[7]

APOLLO   I come
as a witness. This man, according to custom,
this suppliant sought out my house and hearth.
I am the one who purged his bloody hands.   585
His champion too, I share responsibility

---

4. A literal translation of the word *Areopagus*.   5. The Etruscans, a people living in central Italy, were
supposed to have invented the trumpet.   6. Though Aeschylus does not mention them, we know that
there were two stone bases on the Areopagus where prosecutor and defendant took their places for the
trial; naturally, the Stone of Unmercifulness was reserved for the prosecutor.   7. The manuscripts
assign lines 581–82 to the leader of the chorus; the peremptory tone certainly sounds more suitable to the
Furies than to Athena.

for his mother's execution.
                              Bring on the trial.
You know the rules, now turn them into justice.
        [ATHENA *turns to the* FURIES.]
ATHENA   The trial begins! Yours is the first word—
    the prosecution opens. Start to finish,   590
    set the facts before us, make them clear.
LEADER   Numerous as we are, we will be brief.
        [*To* ORESTES.]
    Answer count for count, charge for charge.
    First, tell us, did you kill your mother?
ORESTES   I killed her. There's no denying that.   595
LEADER   Three falls in the match.[8] One is ours already.
ORESTES   You exult before your man is on his back.
LEADER   But *how* did you kill her? You must tell us that.
ORESTES   I will. I drew my sword—more, I cut her throat.
LEADER   And who persuaded you? who led you on?   600
ORESTES   This god and his command.
        [*Indicating* APOLLO.]
                                      He bears me witness.
LEADER   The Seer? He drove you on to matricide?
ORESTES   Yes,
    and to this hour I have no regrets.
LEADER   If the verdict
    brings you down, you'll change your story quickly.
ORESTES   I have my trust; my father will help me from the grave.   605
LEADER   Trust to corpses now! You made your mother one.
ORESTES   I do. She had two counts against her, deadly crimes.
LEADER   How? Explain that to your judges.
ORESTES   She killed her husband—killed my father too.
LEADER   But murder set her free, and you live on for trial.   610
ORESTES   She lived on. You never drove *her* into exile—why?
LEADER   The blood of the man she killed was not her own.
ORESTES   And I? Does mother's blood run in my veins?
LEADER   How could she breed you in her body, murderer?
    Disclaim your mother's blood? She gave you life.   615
        [ORESTES *turns to* APOLLO.]
ORESTES   Bear me witness—show me the way, Apollo!
    Did I strike her down with justice?
    Strike I did, I don't deny it, no.
    But how does our bloody work impress you now?—
    Just or not? Decide.   620
    I must make my case to them.
APOLLO [*Looking to the judges.*]   Just,
    I say, to you and your high court, Athena.
    Seer that I am, I never lie. Not once
    from the Prophet's thrones have I declared
    a word that bears on man, woman or city   625

8. As in a Greek wrestling match.

that Zeus did not command, the Olympian Father.
This is *his* justice—omnipotent, I warn you.
Bend to the will of Zeus. No oath can match
the power of the Father.

LEADER   Zeus, you say,
gave that command to your oracle? He charged   630
Orestes here to avenge his father's death
and spurn his mother's rights?[9]

APOLLO   —Not the same
for a noble man to die, covered with praise,
his scepter the gift of god—murdered, at that,
by a woman's hand, no arrows whipping in   635
from a distance as an Amazon[1] would fight.
But as you will hear, Athena, and your people
poised to cast their lots and judge the case.

Home from the long campaign he came, more won
than lost on balance, home to her loyal, waiting arms,   640
the welcome bath . . .
                          he was just emerging at the edge,
and there she pitched her tent, her circling shroud—
she shackled her man in robes,
in her gorgeous never-ending web she chopped him down!

Such was the outrage of his death, I tell you,   645
the lord of the squadrons, that magnificent man.
Her I draw to the life to lash your people,
marshaled to reach a verdict.

LEADER   Zeus, you say,
sets more store by a father's death? He shackled
his own father, Kronos proud with age.   650
Doesn't that contradict you?
        [*To the judges.*]
Mark it well. I call you all to witness.

APOLLO   You grotesque, loathsome—the gods detest you!
Zeus can break chains, we've cures for that,
countless ingenious ways to set us free.   655
But once the dust drinks down a man's blood,
he is gone, once for all. No rising back,
no spell sung over the grave can sing him back—
not even Father can. Though all things else
he can overturn and never strain for breath.[2]

LEADER   So   660
you'd force this man's acquittal? Behold, Justice!
        [*Exhibiting* APOLLO *and* ORESTES.]

9. The chorus wants Apollo to state clearly that Zeus gave him the specific instructions for Orestes to kill his mother. When they have that assurance, they will face Apollo with a flagrant contradiction of his claim that Zeus is the champion of the father's rights (lines 648–51).   1. A member of a mythical tribe of female warriors, skilled archers, who were thought to have lived in Asia Minor on the Black Sea and to have once invaded Attica.   2. Apollo walks into the trap. Zeus only bound Cronus, he did not kill him, says Apollo. But Orestes did kill his mother.

Can a son spill his mother's blood on the ground,
then settle into his father's halls in Argos?
Where are the public altars he can use?
Can the kinsmen's holy water touch his hands?   665
APOLLO   Here is the truth, I tell you—see how right I am.
The woman you call the mother of the child
is not the parent, just a nurse to the seed,
the new-sown seed that grows and swells inside her.
The *man* is the source of life—the one who mounts.   670
She, like a stranger for a stranger, keeps
the shoot alive unless god hurts the roots.

I give you proof that all I say is true.
The father can father forth without a mother.
Here she stands, our living witness. Look—   675
        [*Exhibiting* ATHENA.]
Child sprung full-blown from Olympian Zeus,
never bred in the darkness of the womb
but such a stock no goddess could conceive![3]

And I, Pallas, with all my strong techniques
will rear your host and battlements to glory.   680
So I dispatched this suppliant to your hearth
that he might be your trusted friend forever,
that you might win a new ally, dear goddess.
He and his generations arm-in-arm with yours,
your bonds stand firm for all posterity[4]—
ATHENA   Now   685
have we heard enough? May I have them cast
their honest lots as conscience may decide?
LEADER   For us, we have shot our arrows, every one.
I wait to hear how this ordeal will end.
ATHENA   Of course.
And what can I do to merit your respect?   690
APOLLO   You have heard what you have heard.
        [*To the judges.*]
Cast your lots, my friends,
strict to the oath that you have sworn.
ATHENA   And now
if you would hear my law, you men of Greece,
you who will judge the first trial of bloodshed.   695

Now and forever more, for Aegeus' people[5]
this will be the court where judges reign.
This is the Crag of Ares, where the Amazons

---

3. The doctrine that the woman is not really a parent of the child but merely a sort of receptacle and nurse also appears elsewhere in Greek literature. It was a comforting formula for a society that, like the goddess Athena (see line 753), honored the male. Apollo appeals for confirmation to the birth of the goddess herself; she had no mother but was born from the head of Zeus.   **4.** Another reference to the Athenian alliance with Argos.   **5.** The Athenians. Aegeus was the father of Theseus.

pitched their tents when they came marching down
on Theseus, full tilt in their fury, erecting 700
a new city to overarch his city, towers thrust
against his towers—they sacrificed to Ares,
named this rock from that day onward Ares' Crag.

Here from the heights, terror and reverence,
my people's kindred powers 705
will hold them from injustice through the day
and through the mild night. Never pollute
our law with innovations. No, my citizens,
foul a clear well and you will suffer thirst.

Neither anarchy nor tyranny,[6] my people. 710
Worship the Mean, I urge you,
shore it up with reverence and never
banish terror from the gates, not outright.
Where is the righteous man who knows no fear?
The stronger your fear, your reverence for the just, 715
the stronger your country's wall and city's safety,
stronger by far than all men else possess
in Scythia's rugged steppes or Pelops' level plain.[7]
Untouched by lust for spoil, this court of law
majestic, swift to fury, rising above you 720
as you sleep, our night watch always wakeful,
guardian of our land—I found it here and now.

So I urge you, Athens. I have drawn this out
to rouse you to your future. You must rise,
each man must cast his lot and judge the case, 725
reverent to his oath. Now I have finished.
    [*The judges come forward, pass between the urns and cast their lots.*]
LEADER   Beware. Our united force can break your land.
Never wound our pride, I tell you, never.
APOLLO   The oracles, not mine alone but Zeus', too—
dread them, I warn you, never spoil their fruit. 730
    [*The* LEADER *turns to* APOLLO.]
LEADER   You dabble in works of blood beyond your depth.
Oracles, your oracles will be stained forever.
APOLLO   Oh, so the Father's judgment faltered when Ixion,
the first man-slayer, came to him for purging?
LEADER   Talk on, talk on. But if I lose this trial 735
I will return in force to crush the land.
APOLLO   Never—among the gods, young and old,
you go disgraced. I will triumph over you!
LEADER   Just as you triumphed in the house of Pheres,

6. Athena repeats the advice and even the words of the Furies in lines 537 ff.   7. The Peloponnesus in
central Greece. Scythia is in southern Russia. The expression may signify just geographical expanse, but
the choice of the two locations is possibly more pointed. The Scythians were famous for their good laws,
and the Peloponnesus was the territory of Sparta, famous for its stable constitution.

luring the Fates to set men free from death.   740
APOLLO   What?—is it a crime to help the pious man,
above all, when his hour of need has come?[8]
LEADER   You brought them down, the oldest realms of order,
seduced the ancient goddesses with wine.[9]
APOLLO   *You* will fail this trial—in just a moment   745
spew your venom and never harm your enemies.
LEADER   You'd ride me down, young god, for all my years?
Well here I stand, waiting to learn the verdict.
Torn with doubt . . . to rage against the city or—
ATHENA   My work is here, to render the final judgment.   750
Orestes,
        [*Raising her arm, her hand clenched as if holding a ballot-stone.*]
            I will cast my lot for you.
No mother gave me birth.
I honor the male, in all things but marriage.
Yes, with all my heart I am my Father's child.
I cannot set more store by the woman's death—   755
she killed her husband, guardian of their house.
Even if the vote is equal, Orestes wins.[1]

Shake the lots from the urns. Quickly,
you of the jury charged to make the count.
        [*Judges come forward, empty the urns, and count the ballot-stones.*]
ORESTES   O God of the Light, Apollo, how will the verdict go?   760
LEADER   O Night, dark mother, are you watching now?
ORESTES   Now for the goal—the noose, or the new day!
LEADER   Now we go down, or forge ahead in power.
APOLLO   Shake out the lots and count them fairly, friends
Honor Justice. An error in judgment now   765
can mean disaster. The cast of a single lot
restores a house to greatness.
        [*Receiving the judges' count,* ATHENA *lifts her arm once more.*]
ATHENA   The man goes free,
cleared of the charge of blood. The lots are equal.
ORESTES   O Pallas Athena—you, you save my house!
I was shorn of the fatherland but you   770
reclaim it for me. Now any Greek will say,
"He lives again, the man of Argos lives
on his fathers' great estates. Thanks to Pallas,
Apollo, and Zeus, the lord of all fulfillment,
Third, Saving Zeus." He respected father's death,   775
looked down on mother's advocates—
        [*Indicating the* FURIES.]
                              he saved me.

8. Pheres was the father of Admetus, king of Thessaly. Apollo repaid kindness shown him by Admetus by
persuading the fates to let Admetus avoid an early death if he could find someone willing to die in his stead.
(His wife, Alcestis, was willing; this is the subject of Euripides' play *Alcestis*, 438 B.C.E.)   9. According
to the Furies, Apollo got the Fates drunk.   1. So, in Athenian courts, a split jury meant acquittal. Athena
announces that if the votes are equal, she will give a casting vote for acquittal. (At the real court of the
Areopagus, if the votes were equal, the defendant was declared acquitted by "the vote of Athena.")

And now I journey home. But first I swear
to you, your land and assembled host, I swear
by the future years that bring their growing yield
that no man, no helmsman of Argos wars on Athens, 780
spears in the vanguard moving out for conquest.
We ourselves, even if we must rise up from the grave,
will deal with those who break the oath I take[2]—
baffle them with disasters, curse their marches,
send them hawks aloft on the left[3] at every crossing— 785
make their pains recoil upon their heads.
But all who keep our oath, who uphold your rights
and citadel forever, comrades spear to spear,
we bless with all the kindness of our heart.

Now farewell, you and the people of your city. 790
Good wrestling—a grip no foe can break.
A saving hope, a spear to bring you triumph!
> [*Exit* ORESTES, *followed by* APOLLO. *The* FURIES *reel in wild confusion*
> *around* ATHENA.]

FURIES   You, you younger gods!—you have ridden down
   the ancient laws, wrenched them from my grasp—
and I, robbed of my birthright, suffering, great with wrath, 795
   I loose my poison over the soil, aieee!—
poison to match my grief comes pouring out my heart,
     cursing the land to burn it sterile and now
rising up from its roots a cancer blasting leaf and child,
     now for Justice, Justice!—cross the face of the earth 800
the bloody tide comes hurling, all mankind destroyed.
   . . . Moaning, only moaning? What will I do?
   The mockery of it, Oh unbearable,
mortified by Athens,
we the daughters of Night, 805
our power stripped, cast down.

ATHENA   Yield to me.
No more heavy spirits. You were not defeated—
the vote was tied, a verdict fairly reached
with no disgrace to you, no, Zeus brought
luminous proof before us. He who spoke 810
god's oracle, he bore witness that Orestes
did the work but should not suffer harm.

And now you'd vent your anger, hurt the land?
Consider a moment. Calm yourself. Never
render us barren, raining your potent showers 815
down like spears, consuming every seed.
By all my rights I promise you your seat
in the depths of earth, yours by all rights—

---

2. Orestes will be a "hero" in the Greek sense: a protecting spirit for the land.   3. Birds seen on the left
were a portent of an evil to come.

stationed at hearths equipped with glistening thrones,
covered with praise! My people will revere you.   820
FURIES You, you younger gods!—you have ridden down
    the ancient laws, wrenched them from my grasp—
and I, robbed of my birthright, suffering, great with wrath,
    I loose my poison over the soil, aieee!—
poison to match my grief comes pouring out my heart,   825
      cursing the land to burn it sterile and now
rising up from its roots a cancer blasting leaf and child,
      now for Justice, Justice!—cross the face of the earth
the bloody tide comes hurling, all mankind destroyed.
    . . . Moaning, only moaning? What will I do?   830
    The mockery of it, Oh unbearable,
mortified by Athens,
we the daughters of Night,
our power stripped, cast down.
ATHENA   You have your power,
    you are goddesses—but not to turn   835
on the world of men and ravage it past cure.
I put my trust in Zeus and . . . must I add this?
I am the only god who knows the keys
to the armory where his lightning-bolt is sealed.
No need of that, not here.
                 Let me persuade you.   840
The lethal spell of your voice, never cast it
down on the land and blight its harvest home.
Lull asleep that salt black wave of anger—
awesome, proud with reverence, live with me.
The land is rich, and more, when its first fruits,   845
offered for heirs and the marriage rites, are yours[4]
to hold forever, you will praise my words.
FURIES But for me to suffer such disgrace . . . I,
    the proud heart of the past, driven under the earth,
condemned, like so much filth,   850
    and the fury in me breathing hatred—
O good Earth,
      what is this stealing under the breast,
what agony racks the spirit? . . . Night, dear Mother Night!
All's lost, our ancient powers torn away by their cunning,   855
ruthless hands, the gods so hard to wrestle down
obliterate us all.
ATHENA   I will bear with your anger.
You are older. The years have taught you more,
much more than I can know. But Zeus, I think,
gave me some insight too, that has its merits.   860
If you leave for an alien land and alien people,
you will come to love this land, I promise you.

---

4. The Furies, as spirits of the Earth, did in fact receive in Athens offerings for children born and marriages made.

As time flows on, the honors flow through all
my citizens, and you, throned in honor
before the house of Erechtheus,[5] will harvest   865
more from men and women moving in solemn file
than you can win throughout the mortal world.

Here in our homeland never cast the stones
that whet our bloodlust. Never waste our youth,
inflaming them with the burning wine of strife.   870
Never pluck the heart of the battle cock
and plant it in our people—intestine war
seething against themselves. Let our wars
rage on abroad,[6] with all their force, to satisfy
our powerful lust for fame. But as for the bird   875
that fights at home—my curse on civil war.

This is the life I offer, it is yours to take.
Do great things, feel greatness, greatly honored.
Share this country cherished by the gods.
FURIES   But for me to suffer such disgrace . . . I,   880
the proud heart of the past, driven under the earth,
condemned, like so much filth,
    and the fury in me breathing hatred—
O good Earth,
        what is this stealing under the breast,   885
what agony racks the spirit? . . . Night, dear Mother Night!
All's lost, our ancient powers torn away by their cunning,
ruthless hands, the gods so hard to wrestle down
obliterate us all.
ATHENA   No, I will never tire
of telling you your gifts. So that you,   890
the older gods, can never say that I,
a young god and the mortals of my city
drove you outcast, outlawed from the land.

But if you have any reverence for Persuasion,
the majesty of Persuasion,   895
the spell of my voice that would appease your fury—
Oh please stay . . . .
                    and if you refuse to stay,
it would be wrong, unjust to afflict this city
with wrath, hatred, populations routed. Look,
it is all yours, a royal share of our land—   900
justly entitled, glorified forever.
LEADER   Queen Athena,
where is the home you say is mine to hold?
ATHENA   Where all the pain and anguish end. Accept it.

---

5. The old shrine of Erechtheus on the Acropolis had been destroyed by the Persians in 480 B.C.E.; in 421
B.C.E. the Athenians began the construction of the new Erechtheum, which, much damaged, still stands.
6. Athens was at this time at war with Sparta, and its forces may still have been engaged in Egypt.

LEADER   And if I do, what honor waits for me?
ATHENA   No house can thrive without you.
LEADER   You would do that—   905
grant me that much power?
ATHENA   Whoever reveres us—
we will raise the fortunes of their lives.
LEADER   And you will pledge me that, for all time to come?
ATHENA   *Yes*—I must never promise things I cannot do.
LEADER   Your magic is working . . . I can feel the hate,   910
the fury slip away.
ATHENA   At last! And now take root
in the land and win yourself new friends.
LEADER   A spell—
what spell to sing? to bind the land forever? Tell us.
ATHENA   Nothing that strikes a note of brutal conquest. Only peace—
blessings, rising up from the earth and the heaving sea,   915
and down the vaulting sky let the wind-gods breathe
a wash of sunlight streaming through the land,
and the yield of soil and grazing cattle flood
our city's life with power and never flag
with time. Make the seed of men live on,   920
the more they worship you the more they thrive.
I love them as a gardener loves his plants,
these upright men, this breed fought free of grief.
All that is yours to give.
                    And I,
in the trials of war where fighters burn for fame,   925
will never endure the overthrow of Athens—
all will praise her, victor city, pride of man.
        [*The* FURIES *assemble, dancing around* ATHENA, *who becomes their
        leader.*]
FURIES   I will embrace
                one home with you, Athena,
                    never fail the city   930
        you and Zeus almighty, you and Ares
        hold as the fortress of the gods, the shield
        of the high Greek altars, glory of the powers.
        Spirit of Athens, hear my words, my prayer
            like a prophet's warm and kind,   935
            that the rare good things of life
                come rising crest on crest,
            sprung from the rich black earth and
            gleaming with the bursting flash of sun.
ATHENA   These blessings I bestow on you, my people, gladly.   940
I enthrone these strong, implacable spirits here
and root them in our soil.
                    Theirs,
    theirs to rule the lives of men,
        it is their fated power.
But he who has never felt their weight,   945

or known the blows of life and how they fall,
the crimes of his fathers hale him toward their bar,
and there for all his boasts—destruction,
   silent, majestic in anger,
crushes him to dust.

FURIES   Yes and I ban   950
         the winds that rock the olive—
            hear my love, my blessing—
      thwart their scorching heat that blinds the buds,
         hold from our shores the killing icy gales,
      and I ban the blight that creeps on fruit and withers—   955
      God of creation, Pan, make flocks increase
            and the ewes drop fine twin lambs
            when the hour of labor falls.
               And silver,[7] child of Earth,
               secret treasure of Hermes,   960
         come to light and praise the gifts of god.

ATHENA   Blessings—now do you hear, you guards of Athens,
   all that she will do?
Fury the mighty queen, the dread
of the deathless gods and those beneath the earth,   965
deals with mortals clearly, once for all.
She delivers songs to some, to others
   a blinding life of tears—
Fury works her will.

FURIES   And the lightning stroke
         that cuts men down before their prime, I curse,   970
            but the lovely girl who finds a mate's embrace,
      the deep joy of wedded life—O grant that gift, that prize,
         you gods of wedlock, grant it, goddesses of Fate!
         Sisters born of the Night our mother,
               spirits steering law,   975
            sharing at all our hearths,
            at all times bearing down
               to make our lives more just,
            all realms exalt you highest of the gods.

ATHENA   Behold, my land, what blessings Fury kindly,   980
   gladly brings to pass—
I am in my glory! Yes, I love Persuasion;
she watched my words, she met their wild refusals.
Thanks to Zeus of the Councils who can turn
dispute to peace—he won the day.   985
   [To the FURIES.]
Thanks to our duel for blessings;
we win through it all.

FURIES   And the brutal strife,
         the civil war devouring men, I pray

---

7. At Laurion (in southeast Attica) silver had been mined for many years when, sometime before 480
B.C.E., rich new veins were discovered. The Athenians used the money to build the fleet that defeated the
Persians at Salamis.

that it never rages through our city, no,
that the good Greek soil never drinks the blood of Greeks,   990
shed in an orgy of reprisal life for life—
that Fury like a beast will never
rampage through the land.
Give joy in return for joy,
one common will for love,   995
and hate with one strong heart:
such union heals a thousand ills of man.

ATHENA   Do you *hear* how Fury sounds her blessings forth,
how Fury finds the way?
Shining out of the terror of their faces   1000
I can see great gains for you, my people.
Hold them kindly, kind as they are to you.
Exalt them always, you exalt your land,
your city straight and just—
its light goes through the world.

FURIES   Rejoice   1005
rejoice in destined wealth,
rejoice, Athena's people—
poised by the side of Zeus,
loved by the loving virgin girl,
achieve humanity at last,   1010
nestling under Pallas' wings
and blessed with Father's love.

ATHENA   You too rejoice! and I must lead the way
to your chambers by the holy light of these,
your escorts bearing fire.   1015

[*Enter* ATHENA's *entourage of women, bearing offerings and
victims and torches still unlit.*]

Come, and sped beneath the earth
by our awesome sacrifices,
keep destruction from the country,
bring prosperity home to Athens,
triumph sailing in its wake.
                                And you,   1020
my people born of the Rock King,[8]
lead on our guests for life, my city—
May they treat you with compassion,
compassionate as you will be to them.

FURIES   Rejoice!—
rejoice—the joy resounds—   1025
all those who dwell in Athens,
spirits and mortals, come,
govern Athena's city well,
revere us well, we are your guests;
you will learn to praise your Furies,   1030
you will praise the fortunes of your lives.

---

8. The legendary ancestor Cranaos, whose name means "rocky." The soil of Attica is not rich.

ATHENA My thanks! And I will speed your prayers, your blessings—
lit by the torches breaking into flame
I send you home, home to the core of Earth,
escorted by these friends who guard my idol
duty-bound.   1035
          [ATHENA's *entourage comes forward, bearing crimson robes.*]
          Bright eye of the land of Theseus,
come forth, my splendid troupe. Girls and mothers,
trains of aged women grave in movement,
dress our Furies now in blood-red robes.[9]
Praise them—let the torch move on!   1040
So the love this family bears toward our land
will bloom in human strength from age to age.
          [*The women invest the* FURIES *and sing the final chorus. Torches blaze;
          a procession forms, including the actors and the judges.* ATHENA *leads
          them from the theater and escorts them through the city.*]
THE WOMEN OF THE CITY On, on, good spirits born for glory,
Daughters of Night, her children always young,
          now under loyal escort—   1045
Blessings, people of Athens, sing your blessings out.

          Deep, deep in the first dark vaults of Earth,
sped by the praise and victims we will bring,
          reverence will attend you—
Blessings now, all people, sing your blessings out.   1050

You great good Furies, bless the land with kindly hearts,
you Awesome Spirits,[1] come—exult in the blazing torch,
          exultant in our fires, journey on.
Cry, cry in triumph, carry on the dancing on and on!

This peace between Athena's people and their guests   1055
must never end. All-seeing Zeus and Fate embrace,
          down they come to urge our union on—
Cry, cry in triumph, carry on the dancing on and on!

---

9. At the Great Panathenea, the principal festival of Athens, resident aliens as well as full citizens took
part in the procession to the Acropolis. The resident aliens, *metics* as they were called, wore crimson cloaks
on this occasion. The Furies are thus given residential status in Attic soil.   1. *Semnai* in Greek, a favorable
formula for the Furies, like the term *Eumenides* (kindly ones), the title of the play.

SOPHOCLES

ca. 496–406 B.C.E.

Aeschylus belonged to the generation that fought at Marathon; his manhood and his old age were passed in the heroic period of the Persian defeat on Greek soil and the war that Athens fought to liberate its kin in the islands of the Aegean and on the Asiatic coast. Sophocles, his younger contemporary, lived to see an Athens that had advanced in power and prosperity far beyond the city that Aeschylus knew. The league of free Greek cities against Persia that Athens had led to victory in the Aegean had become an empire, in which Athens taxed and coerced the subject cities that had once been its free allies. Sophocles, born around 496 B.C.E., played his part—a prominent one—in the city's affairs. In 443 B.C.E. he served as one of the treasurers of the imperial league and, with Pericles, as one of the ten generals elected for the war against the island of Samos, which tried to secede from the Athenian league a few years later. When the Athenian expedition to Sicily ended in disaster, Sophocles was appointed to a special committee set up in 411 B.C.E. to deal with the emergency. He died two years before Athens surrendered to Sparta.

His career as a brilliantly successful dramatist began in 468; in that year he won first prize at the Dionysia, competing against Aeschylus. Over the next sixty-two years he produced more than 120 plays. He won first prize no fewer than twenty-four times, and when he was not first, he came in second, never third.

Aeschylus had been an actor as well as a playwright and director, but Sophocles, early in his career, gave up acting. It was he who added a third actor to the team; the early Aeschylean plays (*Persians, Seven against Thebes,* and *Suppliants*) can be played by two actors (who of course can change masks to extend the range of dramatis personae). In the *Oresteia,* Aeschylus has taken advantage of the Sophoclean third actor; this makes possible the role of Cassandra, the one three-line speech of Pylades in *The Libation Bearers,* and the trial scene in *The Eumenides.* But Sophocles used his third actor to create complex triangular scenes like the dialogue between Oedipus and the Corinthian messenger, which reveals to a listening Jocasta the ghastly truth that Oedipus will not discover until the next scene.

We have only seven of his plays, and not many of them can be accurately dated. *Ajax* (which deals with the suicide of the hero whose shade turns silently away from Odysseus in *Odyssey* 11) and *Trachiniae* (the story of the death of Heracles) are both generally thought to be early productions. *Antigone* is fairly securely fixed in the late 440s, and *Oedipus the King* was probably staged during the early years of the Peloponnesian War (431–404 B.C.E.). For *Electra* we have no date, but it is probably later than *Oedipus the King. Philoctetes,* a tale of the Trojan War, was staged in 409 B.C.E. and *Oedipus at Colonus,* which presents Oedipus's strangely triumphant death on Athenian soil, was produced after Sophocles' death.

Most of these plays date from the last half of the fifth century B.C.E.; they were written in and for an Athens that, since the days of Aeschylus, had undergone an intellectual revolution. It was in a time of critical reevaluation of accepted standards and traditions that Sophocles produced his masterpiece, *Oedipus the King,* and the problems of the time are reflected in the play.

OEDIPUS THE KING

Oedipus the King, which deals with a man of high principles and probing intelligence who follows the prompting of that intelligence to the final consequence of true self-knowledge—which makes him put out his eyes—was as full of significance for Sophocles' contemporaries as it is for us. Unlike a modern dramatist, Sophocles used for his tragedy a story well known to the audience and as old as their own history, a legend told by parent to child, handed down from generation to generation because of its implicit wealth of meaning, learned in childhood, and rooted deep in the consciousness of every member of the community. Such a story the Greeks called a *myth*; the use of it presented Sophocles, as it did Aeschylus in his trilogy, with material that, apart from its great inherent dramatic potential, already possessed the significance and authority that modern dramatists must create for themselves. It had the authority of history, for the history of ages that leave no records is myth—that is to say, the significant event of the past, stripped of irrelevancies and imaginatively shaped by the oral tradition. It had a religious authority, for the Oedipus story, like the story of the house of Atreus, is concerned with the relation between humanity and gods. Last, and this is especially true of the Oedipus myth, it had the power, because of its subject matter, to arouse the irrational hopes and fears that lie deep and secret in the human consciousness.

The use of the familiar myth enabled the dramatist to draw on all its wealth of unformulated meaning, but it did not prevent him from striking a contemporary note. Oedipus, in Sophocles' play, is at one and the same time the mysterious figure of the past who broke the most fundamental human taboos and a typical fifth-century Athenian. His character contains all the virtues for which the Athenians were famous and the vices for which they were notorious. The best commentary on Oedipus's character is the speech that Thucydides, the contemporary historian of the Peloponnesian War, attributed to a Corinthian spokesman at Sparta; it is a hostile but admiring assessment of the Athenian genius. "Athenians . . . [are] equally quick in the conception and in the execution of every new plan"—so Oedipus has already sent to Delphi when the priest advises him to do so and has already sent for Tiresias when the chorus suggests this course of action. "They are bold beyond their strength; they run risks that prudence would condemn"—as Oedipus risked his life to answer the riddle of the Sphinx and later, in spite of the oracle about his marriage, accepted the hand of the queen. "In the midst of misfortune they are full of hope"—so Oedipus, when he is told that he is not the son of Polybus and Merope, and Jocasta has already realized whose son he is, claims that he is the "child of Fortune." "When they do not carry out an intention that they have formed, they seem to have sustained a personal bereavement"—so Oedipus, shamed by Jocasta and the chorus into sparing Creon's life, yields sullenly and petulantly.

The Athenian devotion to the city, which received the main emphasis in Pericles' praise of Athens, is strong in Oedipus; his answer to the priest at the beginning of the play shows that he is a conscientious and patriotic ruler. His quick rage is the characteristic fault of Athenian democracy, which in 406 B.C.E., to give only one instance, condemned and executed the generals who had failed, in the stress of weather and battle, to pick up the drowned bodies of their own men killed in the naval engagement at Arginusae. Oedipus is like the fifth-century Athenian most of all in his confidence in the human intelligence, especially his own. This confidence takes him in the play through the whole cycle of the critical, rationalist movement of the century—from the piety and orthodoxy he displays in the opening scene, through his taunts at oracles when he hears that Polybus is dead, to the despairing courage with which he accepts the consequences when he sees the abyss opening at his feet. "I'm right at the edge, the horrible truth—I've got to say it!" says the herdsman from whom he is dragging the truth. "And I'm at the edge of hearing horrors, yes," Oedipus replies, "but I must hear!" And hear he does. He learns that the oracle he had first fought against and then laughed at has been fulfilled, that every step his intelligence prompted took him one step nearer to disaster, that his knowledge was ignorance and his clear vision blindness. Faced with the reality that his determined probing finally reveals, he puts out his eyes.

The relation of Oedipus's character to the development of the action is the basis of the most famous attempt to define the nature of the tragic process. Aristotle, writing his *Poetics* in the next century, developed the theory that pity and terror are aroused most effectively by the spectacle of a man who is "not pre-eminent in virtue and justice, and yet on the other hand does not fall into misfortune through vice or depravity, but falls because of some mistake; one among the number of the highly renowned and prosperous, such as Oedipus." Other references by Aristotle to this play make it clear that this influential doctrine of the fall of the tragic hero was based particularly on Sophocles' masterpiece, and it has been universally applied to the play. But the great influence (and validity) of the Aristotelian theory should not be allowed to obscure the fact that Sophocles' *Oedipus the King* is more highly organized and economical than Aristotle implies. The fact that the critics have differed about the nature of Oedipus's mistake or frailty (his errors are many, and his frailties include anger, impiety, and self-confidence) is a clue to the real situation. Oedipus falls not through "some vicious mole of nature" or some "particular fault" (to use Hamlet's terms) but because he is the man he is, because of all aspects of his character, good and bad alike; and the development of the action right through to the catastrophe shows us every aspect of his character at work in the process of self-revelation and self-destruction. His first decision in the play, to hear Creon's message from Delphi in public rather than, as Creon suggests, in private, is evidence of his kingly solicitude for his people and his trust in them, but it makes certain the full publication of the truth. His proclamation of a curse on the murderer of Laius, although prompted by his civic zeal, makes his final situation worse than it otherwise would have been. His anger at Tiresias forces a revelation that drives him on to accuse Creon; this in turn provokes Jocasta's revelations. And throughout the play his confidence in the efficacy of his own action, his hopefulness as the situation darkens, and his passion for discovering the truth guide the steps of the investigation that is to reveal the detective as the criminal. All aspects of his character, good and bad alike, are equally involved; it is no frailty or error that leads him to the terrible truth, but his total personality.

The character of Oedipus as revealed in the play does something more than explain the present action; it also explains his past. In Oedipus's speeches and actions on stage we can see the man who, given the circumstances in which Oedipus was involved, would inevitably do just what Oedipus has done. Each action on stage shows us the mood in which he committed some action in the past; his angry death sentence on Creon reveals the man who killed Laius because of an insult on the highway; his proclamation of total excommunication for the unknown murderer shows us the man who, without forethought, accepted the hand of Jocasta; his intelligent, persistent search for the truth shows us the brain and the courage that solved the riddle of the Sphinx. The revelation of his character in the play is at once a re-creation of his past and an interpretation of the oracle that predicted his future.

This organization of the material is what makes it possible for us to accept the story as tragedy at all, for it emphasizes Oedipus's independence of the oracle. When we first see Oedipus, he has already committed the actions for which he is to suffer— actions prophesied, before his birth, by Apollo. But the dramatist's emphasis on Oedipus's character suggests that although Apollo has predicted what Oedipus will do, he does not determine it; Oedipus determines his own conduct, by being the man he is. The relationship between Apollo's prophecy and Oedipus's actions is not that of cause and effect. It is the relationship of two independent entities that are equated.

This correspondence between his character and his fate removes the obstacle to our full acceptance of the play that an external fate governing his action would set up. Nevertheless, we feel that he suffers more than he deserves. He has served as an example of the inadequacy of the human intellect and a warning that there is a power in the universe that humanity cannot control or even fully understand, but Oedipus the man still has our sympathy. Sophocles felt this too, and in his last play, *Oedipus at Colonus,* he dealt with the reward that finally balanced Oedipus's suffering. In *Oedipus the King* itself there is a foreshadowing of this final development: the last scene shows us a man already beginning to recover from the shock of the catastrophe and reasserting a natural superiority.

"I am going—you know on what condition?" he says to Creon when ordered back into the house, and a few lines later Creon has to say bluntly to him: "Still the king, the master of all things? / No more: here your power ends." This renewed imperiousness is the first expression of a feeling on his part that he is not entirely guilty, a beginning of the reconstitution of the magnificent man of the opening scenes; it reaches its fulfillment in the final Oedipus play, *Oedipus at Colonus*, in which he is a titanic figure, confident of his innocence and more masterful than he has ever been.

ANTIGONE

Though *Antigone* was almost certainly produced before *Oedipus the King*, it deals with mythological events that, in the story, come after the exposure of Oedipus's identity and his self-blinding. Creon eventually expelled Oedipus from Thebes to wander as a blind beggar, accompanied only by his daughter Antigone. His sons, Eteocles and Polynices, raised no hand to help him; when he died at Colonus, near Athens, Antigone returned to Thebes. Eteocles and Polynices, who had agreed to rule jointly, soon quarreled; they fought each other for the throne of Thebes. Eteocles expelled his brother, who recruited supporters in Argos; and seven champions attacked the seven gates of Thebes. The assault was beaten off, but Polynices and Eteocles killed each other in the battle. As the play opens, the rule of Thebes has fallen to Creon. His first decision is to forbid burial to the corpse of Polynices, the traitor who brought foreign troops against his own city. Antigone disobeys the decree by scattering dust on the body; captured and brought before Creon, she defies him in the name of the eternal unwritten laws. In the struggle between them it is the king who in the end surrenders; he buries the body of Polynices and orders Antigone's release. But she has already killed herself in her underground prison, thus bringing about the two deaths that crush her enemy—the suicides of his son Haemon and of his wife, Eurydice.

Antigone, as a hero of the resistance to tyrannical power, has deservedly become one of the Western world's great symbolic figures; she is clearly presented, in her famous speech, as a champion of a higher morality against the overriding claims of state necessity, which the Sophist intellectuals of Sophocles' time had begun to formulate in philosophical terms. But Creon, too, is given his due; he is not a mere tyrant of melodrama but a ruler whose action stems from political and religious attitudes that were probably shared by many in the audience. Antigone and Creon clash not only as individuals, shaped with all Sophocles' dramatic genius (the ancient anonymous biography of Sophocles says truly that he could "match the moment with the action so as to create a whole character out of half a line or even a single word"), but also as representatives of two irreconcilable social and religious positions.

Antigone's chief loyalty is clearly to the family. She makes no distinction between the brothers, though one was a patriot and the other a traitor; and when her sister, Ismene, refuses to help her defy the state to bury a brother, she harshly disowns her. The denial of burial to Polynices strikes directly at her family loyalty, for it was the immemorial privilege and duty of the women of the house to mourn the dead man in unrestrained sorrow, sing his praises, wash his body, and consign him to the earth. Creon, on the other hand, sees loyalty to the state as the only valid criterion and, in his opening speech, expressly repudiates one who "places a friend above the good of his own country" (the Greek word for "friend" also means "relative"). This inaugural address of Creon repeats many concepts and even phrases that are to be found in the speeches of the democratic leader Pericles, and in fact, there was an ancient antagonism between the new democratic institutions that stressed the equal rights and obligations of all citizens and the old powerful families that through their wide influence had acted as separate factions in the body politic. The nature of Creon's assertion of state against family, refusal of burial to a corpse, is repellent, but the principle behind it was one that many Athenians would have accepted as valid.

These opposing social viewpoints have their corresponding religious sanctions. For

Antigone, the gods, especially the gods below, demand equality for all the dead, the common inalienable right of burial. But Creon's gods are the gods who protect the city; how, he asks, could those gods have any feeling for Polynices, a traitor who raised and led a foreign army against the city they protect and that contains their temples? Here again, there must have been many in the audience who saw merit in this argument.

The tension between household and civic institutions, between city gods and those who protect the more fundamental duties to the dead, can also be viewed from the perspective of gender. A socially effective male citizen, as Creon makes clear, was expected to be the unquestioned head of the household; but participation in the various aspects of the Athenian democracy was also his right. Athenian women, on the other hand, lacked citizen rights and therefore concentrated their activities and their emotional life on house and family. If the house, in fifth-century-B.C.E. Athens, could be viewed as a site of potential disorder that threatened the city's stability, it was easy to identify women with that disorder—for example, in their lamentation for dead relatives. From the sixth century B.C.E. on, periodic legislation in Athens attempted to curtail public display at funerals, and many scholars believe that this included women's laments. Thus when Creon insists, "never let some woman triumph over us," he is not only jealously guarding male prerogatives but is also speaking from a concern for civic order intelligible to the audience and widely shared among them.

Viewing *Antigone* within the Athenian context, however, does not force us to conclude that in the terms of the play Creon is right and Antigone wrong. Antigone speaks for religious values that the Athenians revered, and she does so in superbly powerful language. Furthermore, as the action develops, whatever validity Creon's initial position may have had is destroyed, and by Creon himself. For like all holders of absolute power, he proceeds, when challenged, to equate loyalty to the community with loyalty to himself—"the city *is* the king's—that's the law!" he tells his son Haemon. And in the end the prophet Tiresias tells him plainly that Antigone was right—the gods are on her side. He swallows his pride and surrenders, but too late. Antigone's suicide brings him to disaster in that institution, the family, that he subordinated to reasons of state; his son spits in his face before killing himself, and his wife dies cursing him as the murderer of his son.

Creon is punished, but Antigone is dead. As the play ends, the chorus points out a moral: the "mighty blows of fate . . . at long last . . . will teach us wisdom." But the price of wisdom is high; *Antigone*, like many of the Shakespearean tragedies, leaves us with a poignant sense of loss.

PRONOUNCING GLOSSARY

The following list uses common English syllables and stress accents to provide rough equivalents of selected words whose pronunciation may be unfamiliar to the general reader.

Antigone: *an-ti'-go-nee*

Ismene: *iz-mee'-nee*

Cithaeron: *ki-thai'-ron*

Laius: *lay'-us / lai-us*

Dionysus: *dai-oh-nai'-sus*

Oedipus: *ee'-di-pus* or *e'-di-pus*

Eteocles: *ee-tee'-ok-leez*

Polynices: *po-li-nai'-seez*

Eurydice: *yoo-ri'-di-see / yoo-ri'-d-kee*

Tiresias: *tai-ree'-see-uhs / ti-ray'-see-uhs*

Haemon: *hai'-mown*

Oedipus the King[1]

Characters

OEDIPUS, *king of Thebes*

A PRIEST *of Zeus*

CREON, *brother of Jocasta*

A CHORUS *of Theban citizens and their* LEADER

TIRESIAS, *a blind prophet*

JOCASTA, *the queen, wife of Oedipus*

A MESSENGER *from Corinth*

A SHEPHERD

A MESSENGER *from inside the palace*

ANTIGONE, ISMENE, *daughters of Oedipus and Jocasta*

GUARDS *and attendants*

PRIESTS *of Thebes*

[TIME AND SCENE: *The royal house of Thebes. Double doors dominate the façade; a stone altar stands at the center of the stage.*

Many years have passed since OEDIPUS *solved the riddle of the Sphinx and ascended the throne of Thebes, and now a plague has struck the city. A procession of priests enters; suppliants, broken and despondent, they carry branches wound in wool and lay them on the altar.*

The doors open. Guards assemble. OEDIPUS *comes forward, majestic but for a telltale limp, and slowly views the condition of his people.*]

OEDIPUS   Oh my children, the new blood of ancient Thebes,
   why are you here? Huddling at my altar,
   praying before me, your branches wound in wool.[2]
   Our city reeks with the smoke of burning incense,
   rings with cries for the Healer[3] and wailing for the dead.   5
   I thought it wrong, my children, to hear the truth
   from others, messengers. Here I am myself—
   you all know me, the world knows my fame:
   I am Oedipus.
        [*Helping a* PRIEST *to his feet.*]
                Speak up, old man. Your years,
   your dignity—you should speak for the others.   10
   Why here and kneeling, what preys upon you so?
   Some sudden fear? some strong desire?
   You can trust me. I am ready to help,
   I'll do anything. I would be blind to misery
   not to pity my people kneeling at my feet.   15
PRIEST   Oh Oedipus, king of the land, our greatest power!
   You see us before you now, men of all ages
   clinging to your altars. Here are boys,
   still too weak to fly from the nest,
   and here the old, bowed down with the years,   20
   the holy ones—a priest of Zeus myself—and here
   the picked, unmarried men, the young hope of Thebes.
   And all the rest, your great family gathers now,

---

1. Translated by Robert Fagles.   2. The insignia of suppliants, laid on the altar and left there until the suppliant's request was granted. At the end of the scene, when Oedipus promises action, he will tell them to take the branches away.   3. Apollo.

branches wreathed, massing in the squares,
kneeling before the two temples of queen Athena   25
or the river-shrine where the embers glow and die
and Apollo sees the future in the ashes.[4]
                              Our city—
look around you, see with your own eyes—
our ship pitches wildly, cannot lift her head
from the depths, the red waves of death . . .   30
Thebes is dying. A blight on the fresh crops
and the rich pastures, cattle sicken and die,
and the women die in labor, children stillborn,
and the plague, the fiery god of fever hurls down
on the city, his lightning slashing through us—   35
raging plague in all its vengeance, devastating
the house of Cadmus![5] And black Death luxuriates
in the raw, wailing miseries of Thebes.
Now we pray to you. You cannot equal the gods,
your children know that, bending at your altar.   40
But we do rate you first of men,
both in the common crises of our lives
and face-to-face encounters with the gods.
You freed us from the Sphinx, you came to Thebes
and cut us loose from the bloody tribute we had paid   45
that harsh, brutal singer.[6] We taught you nothing,
no skill, no extra knowledge, still you triumphed.
A god was with you, so they say, and we believe it—
you lifted up our lives.
                         So now again,
Oedipus, king, we bend to you, your power—   50
we implore you, all of us on our knees:
find us strength, rescue! Perhaps you've heard
the voice of a god or something from other men,
Oedipus . . . what do you know?
The man of experience—you see it every day—   55
his plans will work in a crisis, his first of all.

Act now—we beg you, best of men, raise up our city!
Act, defend yourself, your former glory!
Your country calls you savior now
for your zeal, your action years ago.   60
Never let us remember of your reign:
you helped us stand, only to fall once more.
Oh raise up our city, set us on our feet.
The omens were good that day you brought us joy—

---

4. At a temple of Apollo in Thebes the priests foretold the future according to patterns they saw in the ashes of the burned flesh of sacrificial victims.   5. Mythical founder of Thebes and its first king. 6. The Sphinx was the winged female monster that terrorized the city of Thebes until her riddle was finally answered by Oedipus. The riddle was "What is it that walks on four feet and two feet and three feet and has only one voice; when it walks on most feet, it is weakest?" Oedipus's answer was "Man." (We have four feet as children crawling on all fours and three feet in old age when we walk with the aid of a stick.) Many young men of Thebes had tried to answer the riddle, failed, and been killed.

be the same man today!   65
Rule our land, you know you have the power,
but rule a land of the living, not a wasteland.
Ship and towered city are nothing, stripped of men
alive within it, living all as one.

OEDIPUS   My children,
I pity you. I see—how could I fail to see   70
what longings bring you here? Well I know
you are sick to death, all of you,
but sick as you are, not one is sick as I.
Your pain strikes each of you alone, each
in the confines of himself, no other. But my spirit   75
grieves for the city, for myself and all of you.
I wasn't asleep, dreaming. You haven't wakened me—
I've wept through the nights, you must know that,
groping, laboring over many paths of thought.
After a painful search I found one cure: 80
I acted at once. I sent Creon,
my wife's own brother, to Delphi—
Apollo the Prophet's oracle[7]—to learn
what I might do or say to save our city.

Today's the day. When I count the days gone by   85
it torments me . . . what is he doing?
Strange, he's late, he's gone too long.
But once he returns, then, then I'll be a traitor
if I do not do all the god makes clear.

PRIEST   Timely words. The men over there   90
are signaling—Creon's just arriving.

OEDIPUS [*Sighting* CREON, *then turning to the altar.*]
                                  Lord Apollo,
let him come with a lucky word of rescue,
shining like his eyes!

PRIEST   Welcome news, I think—he's crowned, look,
and the laurel wreath is bright with berries.[8]   95

OEDIPUS   We'll soon see. He's close enough to hear—
        [*Enter* CREON *from the side; his face is shaded with a wreath.*]
Creon, prince, my kinsman, what do you bring us?
What message from the god?

CREON   Good news.
I tell you even the hardest things to bear,
if they should turn out well, all would be well.   100

OEDIPUS   Of course, but what were the god's *words*? There's no hope
and nothing to fear in what you've said so far.

CREON   If you want my report in the presence of these . . .
        [*Pointing to the priests while drawing* OEDIPUS *toward the palace.*]
I'm ready now, or we might go inside.

---

7. On the southern slopes of Mount Parnassus in central Greece.   8. Creon is wearing a crown of laurel
as a sign that he brings good news.

OEDIPUS   Speak out,
  speak to us all. I grieve for these, my people,   105
  far more than I fear for my own life.
CREON   Very well,
  I will tell you what I heard from the god.
  Apollo commands us—he was quite clear—
  "Drive the corruption from the land,
  don't harbor it any longer, past all cure,   110
  don't nurse it in your soil—root it out!"
OEDIPUS   How can we cleanse ourselves—what rites?
  What's the source of the trouble?
CREON   Banish the man, or pay back blood with blood.
  Murder sets the plague-storm on the city.
OEDIPUS   Whose murder?   115
  Whose fate does Apollo bring to light?
CREON   Our leader,
  my lord, was once a man named Laius,
  before you came and put us straight on course.
OEDIPUS   I know—
  or so I've heard. I never saw the man myself.
CREON   Well, he was killed, and Apollo commands us now—   120
  he could not be more clear,
  "Pay the killers back—whoever is responsible."
OEDIPUS   Where on earth are they? Where to find it now,
  the trail of the ancient guilt so hard to trace?
CREON   "Here in Thebes," he said.   125
  Whatever is sought for can be caught, you know,
  whatever is neglected slips away.
OEDIPUS   But where,
  in the palace, the fields or foreign soil,
  where did Laius meet his bloody death?
CREON   He went to consult an oracle, Apollo said,   130
  and he set out and never came home again.
OEDIPUS   No messenger, no fellow-traveler saw what happened?
  Someone to cross-examine?
CREON   No,
  they were all killed but one. He escaped,
  terrified, he could tell us nothing clearly,   135
  nothing of what he saw—just one thing.
OEDIPUS   What's that?
  one thing could hold the key to it all,
  a small beginning give us grounds for hope.
CREON   He said thieves attacked them—a whole band,
  not single-handed, cut King Laius down.
OEDIPUS   A thief,   140
  so daring, so wild, he'd kill a king? Impossible,
  unless conspirators paid him off in Thebes.
CREON   We suspected as much. But with Laius dead
  no leader appeared to help us in our troubles.
OEDIPUS   Trouble? Your *king* was murdered—royal blood!   145

What stopped you from tracking down the killer
then and there?
CREON   The singing, riddling Sphinx.
  She . . . persuaded us to let the mystery go
  and concentrate on what lay at our feet.
OEDIPUS   No,
  I'll start again—I'll bring it all to light myself!   150
  Apollo is right, and so are you, Creon,
  to turn our attention back to the murdered man.
  Now you have *me* to fight for you, you'll see:
  I am the land's avenger by all rights,
  and Apollo's champion too.   155
  But not to assist some distant kinsman, no,
  for my own sake I'll rid us of this corruption.
  Whoever killed the king may decide to kill me too,
  with the same violent hand—by avenging Laius
  I defend myself.
        [*To the priests.*]
                        Quickly, my children.   160
  Up from the steps, take up your branches now.
        [*To the guards.*]
  One of you summon the city[9] here before us,
  tell them I'll do everything. God help us,
  we will see our triumph—or our fall.
        [OEDIPUS *and* CREON *enter the palace, followed by the guards.*]
PRIEST   Rise, my sons. The kindness we came for   165
  Oedipus volunteers himself.
  Apollo has sent his word, his oracle—
  Come down, Apollo, save us, stop the plague.
        [*The priests rise, remove their branches and exit to the side. Enter a*
        CHORUS, *the citizens of Thebes, who have not heard the news that* CREON
        brings. They march around the altar, chanting.]
CHORUS   Zeus!
  Great welcome voice of Zeus, what do you bring?
  What word from the gold vaults of Delphi   170
  comes to brilliant Thebes? Racked with terror—
        terror shakes my heart
  and I cry your wild cries, Apollo, Healer of Delos[2]
  I worship you in dread . . . what now, what is your price?
  some new sacrifice? some ancient rite from the past   175
  come round again each spring?—
        what will you bring to birth?
  Tell me, child of golden Hope
        warm voice that never dies!

  You are the first I call, daughter of Zeus   180
  deathless Athena—I call your sister Artemis,[3]

9. Represented by the chorus, which comes on to the circular dancing floor immediately after this scene.
1. Apollo was his son and spoke for him.   2. A sacred island, Apollo's birthplace.   3. Apollo's sister,
a goddess associated with hunting and also a protector of women in childbirth.

heart of the market place enthroned in glory,
    guardian of our earth—
I call Apollo, Archer astride the thunderheads of heaven—
O triple shield against death, shine before me now!   185
If ever, once in the past, you stopped some ruin
launched against our walls
    you hurled the flame of pain
far, far from Thebes—you gods
    come now, come down once more!
                             No, no   190
the miseries numberless, grief on grief, no end—
too much to bear, we are all dying
O my people . . .
    Thebes like a great army dying
and there is no sword of thought to save us, no   195
and the fruits of our famous earth, they will not ripen
no and the women cannot scream their pangs to birth—
screams for the Healer, children dead in the womb
    and life on life goes down
        you can watch them go   200
    like seabirds winging west, outracing the day's fire
down the horizon, irresistibly
    streaking on to the shores of Evening
                                  Death
so many deaths, numberless deaths on deaths, no end—
Thebes is dying, look, her children   205
stripped of pity . . .
    generations strewn on the ground
unburied, unwept, the dead spreading death
and the young wives and gray-haired mothers with them
cling to the altars, trailing in from all over the city—   210
Thebes, city of death, one long cortege
    and the suffering rises
        wails for mercy rise
    and the wild hymn for the Healer blazes out
clashing with our sobs our cries of mourning—   215
    O golden daughter of god,[4] send rescue
    radiant as the kindness in your eyes!

Drive him back!—the fever, the god of death
    that raging god of war
not armored in bronze, not shielded now, he burns me,[5]   220
battle cries in the onslaught burning on—
O rout him from our borders!
Sail him, blast him out to the Sea-queen's chamber
    the black Atlantic gulfs

---

4. Athena, daughter of Zeus.   5. The plague is identified with Ares, the war god, though he comes now without armor and shield. Ares is not elsewhere connected with plague; this passage may be an allusion to the early years of the Peloponnesian War, when Spartan troops threatened the city from outside and the plague raged inside the walls.

or the northern harbor, death to all   225
where the Thracian[6] surf comes crashing.
Now what the night spares he comes by day and kills—
the god of death.

        O lord of the stormcloud,
you who twirl the lightning, Zeus, Father,
thunder Death to nothing!   230

Apollo, lord of the light, I beg you—
    whip your longbow's golden cord
showering arrows on our enemies—shafts of power
champions strong before us rushing on!

Artemis, Huntress,   235
torches flaring over the eastern ridges—
    ride Death down in pain!

God of the headdress gleaming gold, I cry to you—
your name and ours are one, Dionysus—
    come with your face aflame with wine   240
        your raving women's[7] cries
   your army on the march! Come with the lightning
come with torches blazing, eyes ablaze with glory!
Burn that god of death that all gods hate!

    [OEDIPUS *enters from the palace to address the* CHORUS, *as if addressing*
    the entire city of Thebes.]

OEDIPUS   You pray to the gods? Let me grant your prayers.   245
Come, listen to me—do what the plague demands:
you'll find relief and lift your head from the depths.
I will speak out now as a stranger to the story,
a stranger to the crime. If I'd been present then,
there would have been no mystery, no long hunt   250
without a clue in hand. So now, counted
a native Theban years after the murder,
to all of Thebes I make this proclamation:
if any one of you knows who murdered Laius,
the son of Labdacus, I order him to reveal   255
the whole truth to me. Nothing to fear,
even if he must denounce himself,
let him speak up
and so escape the brunt of the charge—
he will suffer no unbearable punishment,   260
nothing worse than exile, totally unharmed.

    [OEDIPUS *pauses, waiting for a reply.*]

                    Next,
if anyone knows the murderer is a stranger,

---

6. Ares was thought to be at home among the savages of Thrace, to the northeast of Greece proper. *Sea-
queen:* Amphitrite, consort of the sea god Poseidon.   7. The Bacchantes, nymphs or human female
votaries of the god Dionysus (Bacchus) who celebrated him with wild dancing rites.

a man from alien soil, come, speak up.
I will give him a handsome reward, and lay up
gratitude in my heart for him besides.   265
    [Silence again, no reply.]
But if you keep silent, if anyone panicking,
trying to shield himself or friend or kin,
rejects my offer, then hear what I will do.
I order you, every citizen of the state
where I hold throne and power: banish this man—   270
whoever he may be—never shelter him, never
speak a word to him, never make him partner
to your prayers, your victims burned to the gods.
Never let the holy water touch his hands
Drive him out, each of you, from every home.   275
He is the plague, the heart of our corruption,
as Apollo's oracle has just revealed to me.
So I honor my obligations:
I fight for the god and for the murdered man.

Now my curse on the murderer. Whoever he is,   280
a lone man unknown in his crime
or one among many, let that man drag out
his life in agony, step by painful step—
I curse myself as well . . . if by any chance
he proves to be an intimate of our house,   285
here at my hearth, with my full knowledge,
may the curse I just called down on him strike me!

These are your orders: perform them to the last.
I command you, for my sake, for Apollo's, for this country
blasted root and branch by the angry heavens.   290
Even if god had never urged you on to act,
how could you leave the crime uncleansed so long?
A man so noble—your king, brought down in blood—
you should have searched. But I am the king now,
I hold the throne that he held then, possess his bed   295
and a wife who shares our seed . . . why, our seed
might be the same, children born of the same mother
might have created blood-bonds between us
if his hope of offspring hadn't met disaster—
but fate swooped at his head and cut him short.   300
So I will fight for him as if he were my father,
stop at nothing, search the world
to lay my hands on the man who shed his blood,
the son of Labdacus descended of Polydorus,
Cadmus of old and Agenor, founder of the line: 305
their power and mine are one.   Oh dear gods,
my curse on those who disobey these orders!
Let no crops grow out of the earth for them—

shrivel their women, kill their sons,
burn them to nothing in this plague   310
that hits us now, or something even worse.
But you, loyal men of Thebes who approve my actions,
may our champion, Justice, may all the gods
be with us, fight beside us to the end!

LEADER   In the grip of your curse, my king, I swear   315
I'm not the murderer, I cannot point him out.
As for the search, Apollo pressed it on us—
he should name the killer.

OEDIPUS   Quite right,
but to force the gods to act against their will—
no man has the power.

LEADER   Then if I might mention   320
the next best thing . . .

OEDIPUS   The third best too—
don't hold back, say it.

LEADER   I still believe . . .
Lord Tiresias[8] sees with the eyes of Lord Apollo.
Anyone searching for the truth, my king,
might learn it from the prophet, clear as day.   325

OEDIPUS   I've not been slow with that. On Creon's cue
I sent the escorts, twice, within the hour.
I'm surprised he isn't here.

LEADER   We need him—
without him we have nothing but old, useless rumors.

OEDIPUS   Which rumors? I'll search out every word.   330

LEADER   Laius was killed, they say, by certain travelers.

OEDIPUS   I know—but no one can find the murderer.

LEADER   If the man has a trace of fear in him
he won't stay silent long,
not with your curses ringing in his ears.   335

OEDIPUS   He didn't flinch at murder,
he'll never flinch at words.

        [*Enter* TIRESIAS, *the blind prophet, led by a boy with escorts in atten-*
        dance. He remains at a distance.]

LEADER   Here is the one who will convict him, look,
they bring him on at last, the seer, the man of god.
The truth lives inside him, him alone.

OEDIPUS   O Tiresias,   340
master of all the mysteries of our life,
all you teach and all you dare not tell,
signs in the heavens, signs that walk the earth!
Blind as you are, you can feel all the more
what sickness haunts our city. You, my lord,   345
are the one shield, the one savior we can find.

We asked Apollo—perhaps the messengers
haven't told you—he sent his answer back:

---

8. The blind prophet of Thebes (whose ghost Odysseus goes to Hades to consult in *Odyssey* 11).

"Relief from the plague can only come one way.
Uncover the murderers of Laius,   350
put them to death or drive them into exile."
So I beg you, grudge us nothing now, no voice,
no message plucked from the birds, the embers
or the other mantic ways within your grasp.
Rescue yourself, your city, rescue me—   355
rescue everything infected by the dead.
We are in your hands. For a man to help others
with all his gifts and native strength:
that is the noblest work.

TIRESIAS   How terrible—to see the truth
when the truth is only pain to him who sees!   360
I knew it well, but I put it from my mind,
else I never would have come.

OEDIPUS   What's this? Why so grim, so dire?

TIRESIAS   Just send me home. You bear your burdens,
I'll bear mine. It's better that way,   365
please believe me.

OEDIPUS   Strange response . . . unlawful,
unfriendly too to the state that bred and reared you—
you withhold the word of god.

TIRESIAS   I fail to see
that your own words are so well-timed.
I'd rather not have the same thing said of me . . .   370

OEDIPUS   For the love of god, don't turn away,
not if you know something. We beg you,
all of us on our knees.

TIRESIAS   None of you knows—
and I will never reveal my dreadful secrets,
not to say your own.   375

OEDIPUS   What? You know and you won't tell?
You're bent on betraying us, destroying Thebes?

TIRESIAS   I'd rather not cause pain for you or me.
So why this . . . useless interrogation?
You'll get nothing from me.

OEDIPUS   Nothing! You,   380
you scum of the earth, you'd enrage a heart of stone!
You won't talk? Nothing moves you?
Out with it, once and for all!

TIRESIAS   You criticize my temper . . . unaware
of the one[9] *you* live with, you revile me.   385

OEDIPUS   Who could restrain his anger hearing you?
What outrage—you spurn the city!

TIRESIAS   What will come will come.
Even if I shroud it all in silence.

OEDIPUS   What will come? You're bound to *tell* me that.   390

TIRESIAS   I'll say no more. Do as you like, build your anger

---

9. In the Greek the veiled reference to Jocasta is more forceful, because the word translated "the one" has
a feminine ending (agreeing with the feminine noun *orgē*, "temper").

to whatever pitch you please, rage your worst—
OEDIPUS   Oh I'll let loose, I have such fury in me—   395
now I see it all. You helped hatch the plot,
you did the work, yes, short of killing him
with your own hands—and given eyes I'd say
you did the killing single-handed!
TIRESIAS   Is that so!
I charge you, then, submit to that decree
you just laid down: from this day onward
speak to no one, not these citizens, not myself.   400
You are the curse, the corruption of the land!
OEDIPUS   You, shameless—
aren't you appalled to start up such a story?
You think you can get away with this?
TIRESIAS   I have already.
The truth with all its power lives inside me.   405
OEDIPUS   Who primed you for this? Not your prophet's trade.
TIRESIAS   You did, you forced me, twisted it out of me.
OEDIPUS   What? Say it again—I'll understand it better.
TIRESIAS   Didn't you understand, just now?
Or are you tempting me to talk?   410
OEDIPUS   No, I can't say I grasped your meaning.
Out with it, again!
TIRESIAS   I say you are the murderer you hunt.
OEDIPUS   That obscenity, twice—by god, you'll pay.
TIRESIAS   Shall I say more, so you can really rage?   415
OEDIPUS   Much as you want. Your words are nothing—futile.
TIRESIAS   You cannot imagine . . . I tell you,
you and your loved ones live together in infamy,
you cannot see how far you've gone in guilt.
OEDIPUS   You think you can keep this up and never suffer?   420
TIRESIAS   Indeed, if the truth has any power.
OEDIPUS   It does
but not for you, old man. You've lost your power,
stone-blind, stone-deaf—senses, eyes blind as stone!
TIRESIAS   I pity you, flinging at me the very insults
each man here will fling at you so soon.
OEDIPUS   Blind,   425
lost in the night, endless night that cursed you!
You can't hurt me or anyone else who sees the light—
you can never touch me.
TIRESIAS   True, it is not your fate
to fall at my hands. Apollo is quite enough,
and he will take some pains to work this out.   430
OEDIPUS   Creon! Is this conspiracy his or yours?
TIRESIAS   Creon is not your downfall, no, you are your own.
OEDIPUS   O power—
wealth and empire, skill outstripping skill
in the heady rivalries of life,
what envy lurks inside you! Just for this,   435
the crown the city gave me—I never sought it,

they laid it in my hands—for this alone, Creon,
the soul of trust, my loyal friend from the start
steals against me . . . so hungry to overthrow me
he sets this wizard on me, this scheming quack,   440
this fortune-teller peddling lies, eyes peeled
for his own profit—seer blind in his craft!

Come here, you pious fraud. Tell me,
when did you ever prove yourself a prophet?
When the Sphinx, that chanting Fury kept her deathwatch here,   445
why silent then, not a word to set our people free?
There was a riddle, not for some passer-by to solve—
it cried out for a prophet. Where were you?
Did you rise to the crisis? Not a word,
you and your birds, your gods—nothing.   450
No, but I came by, Oedipus the ignorant,
I stopped the Sphinx! With no help from the birds,
the flight of my own intelligence hit the mark.

And this is the man you'd try to overthrow?
You think you'll stand by Creon when he's king?   455
You and the great mastermind—
you'll pay in tears, I promise you, for this,
this witch-hunt. If you didn't look so senile
the lash would teach you what your scheming means!
LEADER   I would suggest his words were spoken in anger,   460
  Oedipus . . . yours too, and it isn't what we need.
  The best solution to the oracle, the riddle
  posed by god—we should look for that.
TIRESIAS   You are the king no doubt, but in one respect,
  at least, I am your equal: the right to reply.   465
  I claim that privilege too.
  I am not your slave. I serve Apollo.
  I don't need Creon to speak for me in public.
                                    So,
  you mock my blindness? Let me tell you this.
  You with your precious eyes,   470
  you're blind to the corruption of your life,
  to the house you live in, those you live with—
  who *are* your parents? Do you know? All unknowing
  you are the scourge of your own flesh and blood,
  the dead below the earth and the living here above,   475
  and the double lash of your mother and your father's curse
  will whip you from this land one day, their footfall
  treading you down in terror, darkness shrouding
  your eyes that now can see the light!
                            Soon, soon
  you'll scream aloud—what haven won't reverberate?   480
  What rock of Cithaeron[1] won't scream back in echo?

---

1. The mountain range near Thebes, on which Oedipus was left to die when an infant.

That day you learn the truth about your marriage,
the wedding-march that sang you into your halls,
the lusty voyage home to the fatal harbor!
And a crowd of other horrors you'd never dream   485
will level you with yourself and all your children.

There. Now smear us with insults—Creon, myself,
and every word I've said. No man will ever
be rooted from the earth as brutally as you.
OEDIPUS Enough! Such filth from him? Insufferable—   490
what, still alive? Get out—
faster, back where you came from—vanish!
TIRESIAS I would never have come if you hadn't called me here.
OEDIPUS If I thought you would blurt out such absurdities,
you'd have died waiting before I'd had you summoned.   495
TIRESIAS Absurd, am I! To you, not to your parents:
the ones who bore you found me sane enough.
OEDIPUS Parents—who? Wait . . . who is my father?
TIRESIAS This day will bring your birth and your destruction.
OEDIPUS Riddles—all you can say are riddles, murk and darkness.   500
TIRESIAS Ah, but aren't you the best man alive at solving riddles?
OEDIPUS Mock me for that, go on, and you'll reveal my greatness.
TIRESIAS Your great good fortune, true, it was your ruin.
OEDIPUS Not if I saved the city—what do I care?
TIRESIAS Well then, I'll be going.   505
        [To his attendant.]
                                Take me home, boy.
OEDIPUS Yes, take him away. You're a nuisance here.
   Out of the way, the irritation's gone.
        [Turning his back on TIRESIAS, moving toward the palace.][2]
TIRESIAS   I will go,
once I have said what I came here to say.
I'll never shrink from the anger in your eyes—
you can't destroy me. Listen to me closely: 510
the man you've sought so long, proclaiming,
cursing up and down, the murderer of Laius—
he is here. A stranger,
you may think, who lives among you,
he soon will be revealed a native Theban   515
but he will take no joy in the revelation.
Blind who now has eyes, beggar who now is rich,
he will grope his way toward a foreign soil,
a stick tapping before him step by step.
        [OEDIPUS enters the palace.]
Revealed at last, brother and father both   520
to the children he embraces, to his mother
son and husband both—he sowed the loins
his father sowed, he spilled his father's blood!

---

2. There are no stage directions in the texts. It is suggested here that Oedipus moves offstage and does
not hear the critical section of Tiresias's speech (lines 520 ff.), which he could hardly fail to connect with
the prophecy made to him by Apollo many years ago.

Go in and reflect on that, solve that.
And if you find I've lied   525
from this day onward call the prophet blind.
        [TIRESIAS *and the boy exit to the side.*]
CHORUS   Who—
    who is the man the voice of god denounces
    resounding out of the rocky gorge of Delphi?
        The horror too dark to tell,
    whose ruthless bloody hands have done the work?   530
    His time has come to fly
        to outrace the stallions of the storm
            his feet a streak of speed—
    Cased in armor, Apollo son of the Father
    lunges on him, lightning-bolts afire!   535
    And the grim unerring Furies[3]
        closing for the kill.
                        Look,
    the word of god has just come blazing
    flashing off Parnassus' snowy heights!
        That man who left no trace—   540
    after him, hunt him down with all our strength!
    Now under bristling timber
        up through rocks and caves he stalks
            like the wild mountain bull—
    cut off from men, each step an agony, frenzied, racing blind   545
    but he cannot outrace the dread voices of Delphi
    ringing out of the heart of Earth,
        the dark wings beating around him shrieking doom
            the doom that never dies, the terror—
    The skilled prophet scans the birds and shatters me with terror!   550
    I can't accept him, can't deny him, don't know what to say,
    I'm lost, and the wings of dark foreboding beating—
    I cannot see what's come, what's still to come . . .
    and what could breed a blood feud between
        Laius' house and the son of Polybus?[4]   555
    I know of nothing, not in the past and not now,
    no charge to bring against our king, no cause
    to attack his fame that rings throughout Thebes—
        not without proof—not for the ghost of Laius,
        not to avenge a murder gone without a trace.   560

    Zeus and Apollo know, they know, the great masters
        of all the dark and depth of human life.
    But whether a mere man can know the truth,
    whether a seer can fathom more than I—
    there is no test, no certain proof   565
        though matching skill for skill
    a man can outstrip a rival. No, not till I see

3. Avenging spirits who pursued a murderer when no earthly avenger was at hand.   4. King of Corinth
and, so far as anyone except Tiresias knows, the father of Oedipus.

these charges proved will I side with his accusers.
We saw him then, when the she-hawk⁵ swept against him,
saw with our own eyes his skill, his brilliant triumph—   570
there was the test—he was the joy of Thebes!
Never will I convict my king, never in my heart.
　　　　[Enter CREON from the side.]
CREON　My fellow-citizens, I hear King Oedipus
levels terrible charges at me. I had to come.
I resent it deeply. If, in the present crisis   575
he thinks he suffers any abuse from me,
anything I've done or said that offers him
the slightest injury, why, I've no desire
to linger out this life, my reputation in ruins.
The damage I'd face from such an accusation   580
is nothing simple. No, there's nothing worse:
branded a traitor in the city, a traitor
to all of you and my good friends.
LEADER　　　　　　　　　　　　True,
but a slur might have been forced out of him,
by anger perhaps, not any firm conviction.   585
CREON　The charge was made in public, wasn't it?
I put the prophet up to spreading lies?
LEADER　Such things were said . . .
I don't know with what intent, if any.
CREON　Was his glance steady, his mind right   590
when the charge was brought against me?
LEADER　I really couldn't say. I never look
to judge the ones in power.
　　　　[The doors open. OEDIPUS enters.]
　　　　　　　　　　　　　　Wait,
here's Oedipus now.
OEDIPUS　　　　　　　　You—here? You have the gall
to show your face before the palace gates?   595
You, plotting to kill me, kill the king—
I see it all, the marauding thief himself
scheming to steal my crown and power!
　　　　　　　　　　　　　　　Tell me,
in god's name, what did you take me for,
coward or fool, when you spun out your plot?   600
Your treachery—you think I'd never detect it
creeping against me in the dark? Or sensing it,
not defend myself? Aren't you the fool,
you and your high adventure. Lacking numbers,
powerful friends, out for the big game of empire—   605
you need riches, armies to bring that quarry down!
CREON　Are you quite finished? It's your turn to listen
for just as long as you've . . . instructed me.
Hear me out, then judge me on the facts.

5. The Sphinx.

OEDIPUS You've a wicked way with words, Creon,   610
   but I'll be slow to learn—from you.
   I find you a menace, a great burden to me.
CREON Just one thing, hear me out in this.
OEDIPUS   Just one thing,
   don't tell *me* you're not the enemy, the traitor.
CREON Look, if you think crude, mindless stubbornness   615
   such a gift, you've lost your sense of balance.
OEDIPUS If you think you can abuse a kinsman,
   then escape the penalty, you're insane.
CREON Fair enough, I grant you. But this injury
   you say I've done you, what is it?   620
OEDIPUS Did you induce me, yes or no,
   to send for that sanctimonious prophet?
CREON I did. And I'd do the same again.
OEDIPUS All right then, tell me, how long is it now
   since Laius . . .
CREON   Laius—what did *he* do?
OEDIPUS   Vanished,   625
   swept from sight, murdered in his tracks.
CREON The count of the years would run you far back . . .
OEDIPUS And that far back, was the prophet at his trade?
CREON Skilled as he is today, and just as honored.
OEDIPUS Did he ever refer to me then, at that time?
CREON   No,   630
   never, at least, when I was in his presence.
OEDIPUS But you did investigate the murder, didn't you?
CREON We did our best, of course, discovered nothing.
OEDIPUS But the great seer never accused me then—why not?
CREON I don't know. And when I don't, *I* keep quiet.   635
OEDIPUS You do know this, you'd tell it too—
   if you had a shred of decency.
CREON   What?
   If I know, I won't hold back.
OEDIPUS   Simply this:
   if the two of you had never put heads together,
   we would never have heard about *my* killing Laius.   640
CREON If that's what he says . . . well, you know best.
   But now I have a right to learn from you
   as you just learned from me.
OEDIPUS   Learn your fill,
   you never will convict me of the murder.
CREON Tell me, you're married to my sister, aren't you?   645
OEDIPUS A genuine discovery—there's no denying that.
CREON And you rule the land with her, with equal power?
OEDIPUS She receives from me whatever she desires.
CREON And I am the third, all of us are equals?
OEDIPUS Yes, and it's there you show your stripes—   650
   you betray a kinsman.
CREON   Not at all.

Not if you see things calmly, rationally,
as I do. Look at it this way first:
who in his right mind would rather rule
and live in anxiety than sleep in peace? 655
Particularly if he enjoys the same authority.
Not I, I'm not the man to yearn for kingship,
not with a king's power in my hands. Who would?
No one with any sense of self-control.
Now, as it is, you offer me all I need, 660
not a fear in the world. But if I wore the crown . . .
there'd be many painful duties to perform,
hardly to my taste.

           How could kingship
please me more than influence, power
without a qualm? I'm not that deluded yet, 665
to reach for anything but privilege outright,
profit free and clear.
Now all men sing my praises, all salute me,
now all who request your favors curry mine.
I am their best hope: success rests in me. 670
Why give up that, I ask you, and borrow trouble?
A man of sense, someone who sees things clearly
would never resort to treason.
No, I've no lust for conspiracy in me,
nor could I ever suffer one who does. 675

Do you want proof? Go to Delphi yourself,
examine the oracle and see if I've reported
the message word-for-word. This too:
if you detect that I and the clairvoyant
have plotted anything in common, arrest me, 680
execute me. Not on the strength of one vote,
two in this case, mine as well as yours.
But don't convict me on sheer unverified surmise.
How wrong it is to take the good for bad,
purely at random, or take the bad for good. 685
But reject a friend, a kinsman? I would as soon
tear out the life within us, priceless life itself.
You'll learn this well, without fail, in time.
Time alone can bring the just man to light—
the criminal you can spot in one short day.

LEADER   Good advice, 690
my lord, for anyone who wants to avoid disaster.
Those who jump to conclusions may go wrong.

OEDIPUS   When my enemy moves against me quickly,
plots in secret, I move quickly too, I must,
I plot and pay him back. Relax my guard a moment, 695
waiting his next move—he wins his objective,
I lose mine.

CREON   What do you want?

You want me banished?
OEDIPUS   No, I want you dead.
CREON   Just to show how ugly a grudge can . . .
OEDIPUS   So,
  still stubborn? you don't think I'm serious?   700
CREON   I think you're insane.
OEDIPUS   Quite sane—in my behalf.
CREON   Not just as much in mine?
OEDIPUS   You—my mortal enemy?
CREON   What if you're wholly wrong?
OEDIPUS   No matter—I must rule.
CREON   Not if you rule unjustly.
OEDIPUS   Hear him, Thebes, my city!
CREON   My city too, not yours alone!   705
LEADER   Please, my lords.
         [Enter JOCASTA from the palace.]
                              Look, Jocasta's coming,
  and just in time too. With her help
  you must put this fighting of yours to rest.
JOCASTA   Have you no sense? Poor misguided men,
  such shouting—why this public outburst?   710
  Aren't you ashamed, with the land so sick,
  to stir up private quarrels?
         [To OEDIPUS.]
  Into the palace now. And Creon, you go home.
  Why make such a furor over nothing?
CREON   My sister, it's dreadful . . . Oedipus, your husband,   715
  he's bent on a choice of punishments for me,
  banishment from the fatherland or death.
OEDIPUS   Precisely. I caught him in the act, Jocasta,
  plotting, about to stab me in the back.
CREON   Never—curse me, let me die and be damned   720
  if I've done you any wrong you charge me with.
JOCASTA   Oh god, believe it, Oedipus,
  honor the solemn oath he swears to heaven.
  Do it for me, for the sake of all your people.
         [The CHORUS begins to chant.]
CHORUS   Believe it, be sensible   725
    give way, my king, I beg you!
OEDIPUS   What do you want from me, concessions?
CHORUS   Respect him—he's been no fool in the past
  and now he's strong with the oath he swears to god.
OEDIPUS   You know what you're asking?
CHORUS   I do.
OEDIPUS   Then out with it!   730
CHORUS   The man's your friend, your kin, he's under oath—
  don't cast him out, disgraced
  branded with guilt on the strength of hearsay only.
OEDIPUS   Know full well, if that is what you want
  you want me dead or banished from the land.

CHORUS   Never—   735
  no, by the blazing Sun, first god of the heavens!
    Stripped of the gods, stripped of loved ones,
  let me die by inches if that ever crossed my mind.
  But the heart inside me sickens, dies as the land dies
  and now on top of the old griefs you pile this,   740
  your fury—both of you!
OEDIPUS   Then let him go,
  even if it does lead to my ruin, my death
  or my disgrace, driven from Thebes for life.
  It's you, not him I pity—your words move me.
  He, wherever he goes, my hate goes with him.   745
CREON   Look at you, sullen in yielding, brutal in your rage—
  you'll go too far. It's perfect justice:
  natures like yours are hardest on themselves.
OEDIPUS   Then leave me alone—get out!
CREON   I'm going.
  You're wrong, so wrong. These men know I'm right.   750
     [Exit to the side. The CHORUS turns to JOCASTA.]
CHORUS   Why do you hesitate, my lady
  why not help him in?
JOCASTA   Tell me what's happened first.
CHORUS   Loose, ignorant talk started dark suspicions
  and a sense of injustice cut deeply too.   755
JOCASTA   On both sides?
CHORUS   Oh yes.
JOCASTA   What did they say?
CHORUS   Enough, please, enough! The land's so racked already
  or so it seems to me . . .
  End the trouble here, just where they left it.
OEDIPUS   You see what comes of your good intentions now?   760
  And all because you tried to blunt my anger.
CHORUS   My king,
  I've said it once, I'll say it time and again—
    I'd be insane, you know it, bereft,
  senseless, ever to turn my back on you.
  You who set our beloved land—storm-tossed, shattered—   765
  straight on course. Now again, good helmsman,
  steer us through the storm!
    [The CHORUS draws away, leaving OEDIPUS and JOCASTA side by side.]
JOCASTA   For the love of god,
  Oedipus, tell me too, what is it?
  Why this rage? You're so unbending.
OEDIPUS   I will tell you. I respect you, Jocasta,   770
  much more than these . . .
    [Glancing at the CHORUS.]
  Creon's to blame, Creon schemes against me.
JOCASTA   Tell me clearly, how did the quarrel start?
OEDIPUS   He says I murdered Laius—I am guilty.
JOCASTA   How does he know? Some secret knowledge   775

or simple hearsay?

OEDIPUS   Oh, he sent his prophet in
to do his dirty work. You know Creon,
Creon keeps his own lips clean.

JOCASTA   A prophet?
Well then, free yourself of every charge!
Listen to me and learn some peace of mind: 780
no skill in the world,
nothing human can penetrate the future.
Here is proof, quick and to the point.

An oracle came to Laius one fine day
(I won't say from Apollo himself   785
but his underlings, his priests) and it said
that doom would strike him down at the hands of a son,
our son, to be born of our own flesh and blood. But Laius,
so the report goes at least, was killed by strangers,
thieves, at a place where three roads meet . . . my son— 790
he wasn't three days old and the boy's father
fastened his ankles, had a henchman fling him away
on a barren, trackless mountain.
                              There, you see?
Apollo brought neither thing to pass. My baby
no more murdered his father than Laius suffered—   795
his wildest fear—death at his own son's hands.
That's how the seers and all their revelations
mapped out the future. Brush them from your mind.
Whatever the god needs and seeks
he'll bring to light himself, with ease.

OEDIPUS   Strange,   800
hearing you just now . . . my mind wandered,
my thoughts racing back and forth.

JOCASTA   What do you mean? Why so anxious, startled?

OEDIPUS   I thought I heard you say that Laius
was cut down at a place where three roads meet.   805

JOCASTA   That was the story. It hasn't died out yet.

OEDIPUS   Where did this thing happen? Be precise.

JOCASTA   A place called Phocis, where two branching roads,
one from Daulia, one from Delphi,
come together—a crossroads.   810

OEDIPUS   When? How long ago?

JOCASTA   The heralds no sooner reported Laius dead
than you appeared and they hailed you king of Thebes.

OEDIPUS   My god, my god—what have you planned to do to me?

JOCASTA   What, Oedipus? What haunts you so?

OEDIPUS   Not yet.   815
Laius—how did he look? Describe him.
Had he reached his prime?

JOCASTA   He was swarthy,
and the gray had just begun to streak his temples,

and his build . . . wasn't far from yours.

OEDIPUS   Oh no no,
  I think I've just called down a dreadful curse   820
  upon myself—I simply didn't know!

JOCASTA   What are you saying? I shudder to look at you.

OEDIPUS   I have a terrible fear the blind seer can see.
  I'll know in a moment. One thing more—

JOCASTA   Anything,
  afraid as I am—ask, I'll answer, all I can.   825

OEDIPUS   Did he go with a light or heavy escort,
  several men-at-arms, like a lord, a king?

JOCASTA   There were five in the party, a herald among them,
  and a single wagon carrying Laius.

OEDIPUS   Ai—
  now I can see it all, clear as day.   830
  Who told you all this at the time, Jocasta?

JOCASTA   A servant who reached home, the lone survivor.

OEDIPUS   So, could he still be in the palace—even now?

JOCASTA   No indeed. Soon as he returned from the scene
  and saw you on the throne with Laius dead and gone,   835
  he knelt and clutched my hand, pleading with me
  to send him into the hinterlands, to pasture,
  far as possible, out of sight of Thebes.
  I sent him away. Slave though he was,
  he'd earned that favor—and much more.   840

OEDIPUS   Can we bring him back, quickly?

JOCASTA   Easily. Why do you want him so?

OEDIPUS   I'm afraid,
  Jocasta, I have said too much already.
  That man—I've got to see him.

JOCASTA   Then he'll come.
  But even I have a right, I'd like to think,   845
  to know what's torturing you, my lord.

OEDIPUS   And so you shall—I can hold nothing back from you,
  now I've reached this pitch of dark foreboding.
  Who means more to me than you? Tell me,
  whom would I turn toward but you   850
  as I go through all this?

  My father was Polybus, king of Corinth.
  My mother, a Dorian, Merope. And I was held
  the prince of the realm among the people there,
  till something struck me out of nowhere,   855
  something strange . . . worth remarking perhaps,
  hardly worth the anxiety I gave it.
  Some man at a banquet who had drunk too much
  shouted out—he was far gone, mind you—
  that I am not my father's son. Fighting words!   860
  I barely restrained myself that day
  but early the next I went to mother and father,

questioned them closely, and they were enraged
at the accusation and the fool who let it fly.
So as for my parents I was satisfied,   865
but still this thing kept gnawing at me,
the slander spread—I had to make my move.

                            And so,
unknown to mother and father I set out for Delphi,
and the god Apollo spurned me, sent me away
denied the facts I came for,   870
but first he flashed before my eyes a future
great with pain, terror, disaster—I can hear him cry,
"You are fated to couple with your mother, you will bring
a breed of children into the light no man can bear to see—
you will kill your father, the one who gave you life!"   875
I heard all that and ran. I abandoned Corinth,
from that day on I gauged its landfall only
by the stars, running, always running
toward some place where I would never see
the shame of all those oracles come true.   880
And as I fled I reached that very spot
where the great king, you say, met his death.

Now, Jocasta, I will tell you all.
Making my way toward this triple crossroad
I began to see a herald, then a brace of colts   885
drawing a wagon, and mounted on the bench . . . a man,
just as you've described him, coming face-to-face,
and the one in the lead and the old man himself
were about to thrust me off the road—brute force—
and the one shouldering me aside, the driver,   890
I strike him in anger!—and the old man, watching me
coming up along his wheels—he brings down
his prod, two prongs straight at my head!
I paid him back with interest!
Short work, by god—with one blow of the staff   895
in this right hand I knock him out of his high seat,
roll him out of the wagon, sprawling headlong—
I killed them all—every mother's son!

Oh, but if there is any blood-tie
between Laius and this stranger . . .   900
what man alive more miserable than I?
More hated by the gods? I am the man
no alien, no citizen welcomes to his house,
law forbids it—not a word to me in public,
driven out of every hearth and home.   905
And all these curses I—no one but I
brought down these piling curses on myself!
And you, his wife, I've touched your body with these,
the hands that killed your husband cover you with blood.

Wasn't I born for torment? Look me in the eyes!   910
I am abomination—heart and soul!
I must be exiled, and even in exile
never see my parents, never set foot
on native ground again. Else I am doomed
to couple with my mother and cut my father down . . .   915
Polybus who reared me, gave me life.

                        But why, why?
Wouldn't a man of judgment say—and wouldn't he be right—
some savage power has brought this down upon my head?

Oh no, not that, you pure and awesome gods,
never let me see that day! Let me slip   920
from the world of men, vanish without a trace
before I see myself stained with such corruption,
stained to the heart.
LEADER   My lord, you fill our hearts with fear.
    But at least until you question the witness,   925
    do take hope.
OEDIPUS   Exactly. He is my last hope—
    I am waiting for the shepherd. He is crucial.
JOCASTA   And once he appears, what then? Why so urgent?
OEDIPUS   I will tell you. If it turns out that his story
    matches yours, I've escaped the worst.   930
JOCASTA   What did I say? What struck you so?
OEDIPUS   You said *thieves*—
    he told you a whole band of them murdered Laius.
    So, if he still holds to the same number,
    I cannot be the killer. One can't equal many.
    But if he refers to one man, one alone,   935
    clearly the scales come down on me:
    I am guilty.
JOCASTA   Impossible. Trust me,
    I told you precisely what he said,
    and he can't retract it now;
    the whole city heard it, not just I.   940
    And even if he should vary his first report
    by one man more or less, still, my lord,
    he could never make the murder of Laius
    truly fit the prophecy. Apollo was explicit:
    my son was doomed to kill my husband . . . my son,   945
    poor defenseless thing, he never had a chance
    to kill his father. They destroyed him first.

    So much for prophecy. It's neither here nor there.
    From this day on, I wouldn't look right or left.
OEDIPUS   True, true. Still, that shepherd,   950
    someone fetch him—now!
JOCASTA   I'll send at once. But do let's go inside.
    I'd never displease you, least of all in this.
    [OEDIPUS *and* JOCASTA *enter the palace.*]

CHORUS   Destiny guide me always
 Destiny find me filled with reverence   955
 pure in word and deed.
Great laws tower above us, reared on high
born for the brilliant vault of heaven—
 Olympian Sky their only father,
nothing mortal, no man gave them birth,   960
their memory deathless, never lost in sleep:
within them lives a mighty god, the god does not grow old.

Pride breeds the tyrant
violent pride, gorging, crammed to bursting
 with all that is overripe and rich with ruin—   965
clawing up to the heights, headlong pride
crashes down the abyss—sheer doom!
 No footing helps, all foothold lost and gone.
But the healthy strife that makes the city strong—
I pray that god will never end that wrestling: 970
god, my champion, I will never let you go.

But if any man comes striding, high and mighty
 in all he says and does,
no fear of justice, no reverence
for the temples of the gods—   975
 let a rough doom tear him down,
repay his pride, breakneck, ruinous pride!
If he cannot reap his profits fairly
 cannot restrain himself from outrage—
mad, laying hands on the holy things untouchable! 980

  Can such a man, so desperate, still boast
   he can save his life from the flashing bolts of god?
   If all such violence goes with honor now
    why join the sacred dance?

Never again will I go reverent to Delphi,   985
 the inviolate heart of Earth
or Apollo's ancient oracle at Abae
or Olympia[6] of the fires—
 unless these prophecies all come true
for all mankind to point toward in wonder.   990
King of kings, if you deserve your titles
 Zeus, remember, never forget!
You and your deathless, everlasting reign.

  They are dying, the old oracles sent to Laius,
  now our masters strike them off the rolls.   995

---

6. Site of a sanctuary of Zeus in the western Peloponnesus; divination by means of burnt offerings was practiced there. Abae is a city in central Greece.

Nowhere Apollo's golden glory now—
    the gods, the gods go down.
    [*Enter* JOCASTA *from the palace, carrying a suppliant's branch wound in wool.*]

JOCASTA   Lords of the realm,[7] it occurred to me,
just now, to visit the temples of the gods,
so I have my branch in hand and incense too.   1000

Oedipus is beside himself. Racked with anguish,
no longer a man of sense, he won't admit
the latest prophecies are hollow as the old—
he's at the mercy of every passing voice
if the voice tells of terror.   1005
I urge him gently, nothing seems to help,
so I turn to you, Apollo, you are nearest.
    [*Placing her branch on the altar, while an old herdsman enters from the side, not the one just summoned by the King but an unexpected* MES-
    SENGER *from Corinth.*]
I come with prayers and offerings . . . . I beg you,
cleanse us, set us free of defilement!
Look at us, passengers in the grip of fear,   1010
watching the pilot of the vessel go to pieces.

MESSENGER   [*Approaching* JOCASTA *and the* CHORUS.]
Strangers, please, I wonder if you could lead us
to the palace of the king . . . I think it's Oedipus.
Better, the man himself—you know where he is?

LEADER   This is his palace, stranger. He's inside.   1015
But here is his queen, his wife and mother
of his children.

MESSENGER   Blessings on you, noble queen,
queen of Oedipus crowned with all your family—
blessings on you always!

JOCASTA   And the same to you, stranger, you deserve it . . .   1020
such a greeting. But what have you come for?
Have you brought us news?

MESSENGER   Wonderful news—
for the house, my lady, for your husband too.

JOCASTA   Really, what? Who sent you?

MESSENGER   Corinth.
I'll give you the message in a moment.   1025
You'll be glad of it—how could you help it?—
though it costs a little sorrow in the bargain.

JOCASTA   What can it be, with such a double edge?

MESSENGER   The people there, they want to make your Oedipus
king of Corinth, so they're saying now.   1030

JOCASTA   Why? Isn't old Polybus still in power?

MESSENGER   No more. Death has got him in the tomb.

JOCASTA   What are you saying? Polybus, dead?—dead?

MESSENGER   If not,

---

7. The chorus.

if I'm not telling the truth, strike me dead too.

JOCASTA [*To a servant.*] Quickly, go to your master, tell him this! 1035
You prophecies of the gods, where are you now?
This is the man that Oedipus feared for years,
he fled him, not to kill him—and now he's dead,
quite by chance, a normal, natural death,
not murdered by his son.

OEDIPUS [*Emerging from the palace.*]
　　　　　　　　　　　Dearest, 1040
what now? Why call me from the palace?

JOCASTA [*Bringing the* MESSENGER *closer.*]
Listen to *him*, see for yourself what all
those awful prophecies of god have come to.

OEDIPUS And who is he? What can he have for me?

JOCASTA He's from Corinth, he's come to tell you 1045
your father is no more—Polybus—he's dead!

OEDIPUS [*Wheeling on the* MESSENGER.]
What? Let me have it from your lips.

MESSENGER 　　　　　　　　　Well,
if that's what you want first, then here it is:
Abae is a city in central Greece.
make no mistake, Polybus is dead and gone.

OEDIPUS How—murder? sickness?—what? what killed him? 1050

MESSENGER A light tip of the scales can put old bones to rest.

OEDIPUS Sickness then—poor man, it wore him down.

MESSENGER 　　　　　　　　　　　　　That,
and the long count of years he'd measured out.

OEDIPUS 　　　　　　　　　　　　　So!
Jocasta, why, why look to the Prophet's hearth,
the fires of the future? Why scan the birds 1055
that scream above our heads? They winged me on
to the murder of my father, did they? That was my doom?
Well look, he's dead and buried, hidden under the earth,
and here I am in Thebes, I never put hand to sword—
unless some longing for me wasted him away, 1060
then in a sense you'd say I caused his death.
But now, all those prophecies I feared—Polybus
packs them off to sleep with him in hell!
They're nothing, worthless.

JOCASTA 　　　　　　　　There.
Didn't I tell you from the start? 1065

OEDIPUS So you did. I was lost in fear.

JOCASTA No more, sweep it from your mind forever.

OEDIPUS But my mother's bed, surely I must fear—

JOCASTA 　　　　　　　　　　　　Fear?
What should a man fear? It's all chance,
chance rules our lives. Not a man on earth 1070
can see a day ahead, groping through the dark.
Better to live at random, best we can.
And as for this marriage with your mother—
have no fear. Many a man before you,

in his dreams, has shared his mother's bed.   1075
Take such things for shadows, nothing at all—
Live, Oedipus,
   as if there's no tomorrow!

OEDIPUS   Brave words,
and you'd persuade me if mother weren't alive.
But mother lives, so for all your reassurances   1080
I live in fear, I must.

JOCASTA   But your father's death,
that, at least, is a great blessing, joy to the eyes!

OEDIPUS   Great, I know . . . but I fear *her*—she's still alive.

MESSENGER   Wait, who is this woman, makes you so afraid?

OEDIPUS   Merope, old man. The wife of Polybus.   1085

MESSENGER   The queen? What's there to fear in her?

OEDIPUS   A dreadful prophecy, stranger, sent by the gods.

MESSENGER   Tell me, could you? Unless it's forbidden
other ears to hear.

OEDIPUS   Not at all.
Apollo told me once—it is my fate—   1090
I must make love with my own mother,
shed my father's blood with my own hands.
So for years I've given Corinth a wide berth,
and it's been my good fortune too. But still,
to see one's parents and look into their eyes   1095
is the greatest joy I know.

MESSENGER   You're afraid of that?
That kept you out of Corinth?

OEDIPUS   My *father*, old man—
so I wouldn't kill my father.

MESSENGER   So that's it.
Well then, seeing I came with such good will, my king,
why don't I rid you of that old worry now?   1100

OEDIPUS   What a rich reward you'd have for that!

MESSENGER   What do you think I came for, majesty?
So you'd come home and I'd be better off.

OEDIPUS   Never, I will never go near my parents.

MESSENGER   My boy, it's clear, you don't know what you're doing.   1105

OEDIPUS   What do you mean, old man? For god's sake, explain.

MESSENGER   If you ran from *them*, always dodging home . . .

OEDIPUS   Always, terrified Apollo's oracle might come true—

MESSENGER   And you'd be covered with guilt, from both your parents.

OEDIPUS   That's right, old man, that fear is always with me.   1110

MESSENGER   Don't you know? You've really nothing to fear.

OEDIPUS   But why? If I'm their son—Merope, Polybus?

MESSENGER   Polybus was nothing to you, that's why, not in blood.

OEDIPUS   What are you saying—Polybus was not my father?

MESSENGER   No more than I am. He and I are equals.

OEDIPUS   My father—   1115
how can my father equal nothing? You're nothing to me!

MESSENGER   Neither was he, no more your father than I am.

OEDIPUS Then why did he call me his son?

MESSENGER You were a gift,
years ago—know for a fact he took you
from my hands.

OEDIPUS No, from another's hands?
Then how could he love me so? He loved me, deeply . . .

MESSENGER True, and his early years without a child
made him love you all the more.

OEDIPUS And you, did you . . .
buy me? find me by accident?

MESSENGER I stumbled on you,
down the woody flanks of Mount Cithaeron.

OEDIPUS So close,
what were you doing here, just passing through?

MESSENGER Watching over my flocks, grazing them on the slopes.

OEDIPUS A herdsman, were you? A vagabond, scraping for wages?

MESSENGER Your savior too, my son, in your worst hour.

OEDIPUS Oh—
when you picked me up, was I in pain? What exactly?

MESSENGER Your ankles . . . they tell the story. Look at them.

OEDIPUS Why remind me of that, that old affliction?

MESSENGER Your ankles were pinned together. I set you free.

OEDIPUS That dreadful mark—I've had it from the cradle.

MESSENGER And you got your name[8] from that misfortune too,
the name's still with you.

OEDIPUS Dear god, who did it?—
mother? father? Tell me.

MESSENGER I don't know.
The one who gave you to me, he'd know more.

OEDIPUS What? You took me from someone else?
You didn't find me yourself?

MESSENGER No sir,
another shepherd passed you on to me.

OEDIPUS Who? Do you know? Describe him.

MESSENGER He called himself a servant of . . .
if I remember rightly—Laius.

[JOCASTA turns sharply.]

OEDIPUS The king of the land who ruled here long ago?

MESSENGER That's the one. That herdsman was *his* man.

OEDIPUS Is he still alive? Can I see him?

MESSENGER They'd know best, the people of these parts.

[OEDIPUS and the MESSENGER turn to the CHORUS.]

OEDIPUS Does anyone know that herdsman,
the one he mentioned? Anyone seen him
in the fields, in the city? Out with it!
The time has come to reveal this once for all.

LEADER I think he's the very shepherd you wanted to see,

---

8. In Greek the name *Oidipous* suggests "swollen foot."

a moment ago. But the queen, Jocasta,
she's the one to say.

OEDIPUS   Jocasta,   1155
you remember the man we just sent for?
Is *that* the one he means?

JOCASTA   That man . . .
why ask? Old shepherd, talk, empty nonsense,
don't give it another thought, don't even think—

OEDIPUS What—give up now, with a clue like this?   1160
Fail to solve the mystery of my birth?
Not for all the world!

JOCASTA   Stop—in the name of god,
if you love your own life, call off this search!
My suffering is enough.

OEDIPUS   Courage!
Even if my mother turns out to be a slave,   1165
and I a slave, three generations back,
you would not seem common.

JOCASTA   Oh no,
listen to me, I beg you, don't do this.

OEDIPUS Listen to you? No more. I must know it all,
must see the truth at last.

JOCASTA   No, please—   1170
for your sake—I want the best for you!

OEDIPUS Your best is more than I can bear.

JOCASTA   You're doomed—
may you never fathom who you are!

OEDIPUS [*To a servant.*] Hurry, fetch me the herdsman, now!
Leave her to glory in her royal birth.   1175

JOCASTA Aieeeeee—
                    man of agony—
that is the only name I have for you,
that, no other—ever, ever, ever!
        [*Flinging through the palace doors. A long, tense silence follows.*]

LEADER Where's she gone, Oedipus?
Rushing off, such wild grief . . .   1180
I'm afraid that from this silence
something monstrous may come bursting forth.

OEDIPUS Let it burst! Whatever will, whatever must!
I must know my birth, no matter how common
it may be—I must see my origins face-to-face.   1185
She perhaps, she with her woman's pride
may well be mortified by my birth,
but I, I count myself the son of Chance,
the great goddess, giver of all good things—
I'll never see myself disgraced. She is my mother!   1190
And the moons have marked me out, my blood-brothers,
one moon on the wane, the next moon great with power.
That is my blood, my nature—I will never betray it,
never fail to search and learn my birth!

CHORUS Yes—if I am a true prophet   1195
    if I can grasp the truth,
  by the boundless skies of Olympus,
at the full moon of tomorrow, Mount Cithaeron
you will know how Oedipus glories in you—
you, his birthplace, nurse, his mountain-mother!   1200
And we will sing you, dancing out your praise—
  you lift our monarch's heart!
    Apollo, Apollo, god of the wild cry
      may our dancing please you!
                        Oedipus—
    son, dear child, who bore you?   1205
Who of the nymphs who seem to live forever[9]
mated with Pan,[1] the mountain-striding Father?
Who was your mother? who, some bride of Apollo
the god who loves the pastures spreading toward the sun?
    Or was it Hermes, king of the lightning ridges?   1210
Or Dionysus,[2] lord of frenzy, lord of the barren peaks—
did he seize you in his hands, dearest of all his lucky finds?—
    found by the nymphs, their warm eyes dancing, gift
to the lord who loves them dancing out his joy!

      [OEDIPUS *strains to see a figure coming from the distance. Attended by*
      palace guards, an old SHEPHERD *enters slowly, reluctant to approach the*
      king.]

OEDIPUS I never met the man, my friends . . . still,   1215
if I had to guess, I'd say that's the shepherd,
the very one we've looked for all along.
Brothers in old age, two of a kind,
he and our guest here. At any rate
the ones who bring him in are my own men,   1220
I recognize them.
    [*Turning to the* LEADER.]
               But you know more than I,
you should, you've seen the man before.
LEADER I know him, definitely. One of Laius' men,
a trusty shepherd, if there ever was one.
OEDIPUS You, I ask you first, stranger,   1225
you from Corinth—is this the one you mean?
MESSENGER You're looking at him. He's your man.
OEDIPUS [*To the* SHEPHERD.] You, old man, come over here—
look at me. Answer all my questions.
Did you ever serve King Laius?
SHEPHERD   So I did . . .   1230
a slave, not bought on the block though,
born and reared in the palace.
OEDIPUS Your duties, your kind of work?
SHEPHERD   Herding the flocks, the better part of my life.

9. Though nymphs, unlike the gods, were not immortal, they lived much longer than mortals. 1. A
woodland god, patron of shepherds and flocks. 2. Dionysus, like Pan and Hermes, haunted the wild
country, woods, and mountains. Hermes was born on Mount Kyllene in Arcadia.

OEDIPUS   Where, mostly? Where did you do your grazing?

SHEPHERD   Well,   1235
Cithaeron sometimes, or the foothills round about.

OEDIPUS   This man—you know him? ever see him there?

SHEPHERD [Confused, glancing from the MESSENGER to the King.]
Doing what?—what man do you mean?

OEDIPUS [Pointing to the MESSENGER.]   This one here—ever have
dealings with him?

SHEPHERD   Not so I could say, but give me a chance,   1240
my memory's bad . . .

MESSENGER   No wonder he doesn't know me, master.
But let me refresh his memory for him.
I'm sure he recalls old times we had
on the slopes of Mount Cithaeron;   1245
he and I, grazing our flocks, he with two
and I with one—we both struck up together,
three whole seasons, six months at a stretch
from spring to the rising of Arcturus[3] in the fall,
then with winter coming on I'd drive my herds   1250
to my own pens, and back he'd go with his
to Laius' folds.
[To the SHEPHERD.]
Now that's how it was,
wasn't it—yes or no?

SHEPHERD   Yes, I suppose . . .
it's all so long ago.

MESSENGER   Come, tell me,
you gave me a child back then, a boy, remember?   1255
A little fellow to rear, my very own.

SHEPHERD   What? Why rake up that again?

MESSENGER   Look, here he is, my fine old friend—
the same man who was just a baby then.

SHEPHERD   Damn you, shut your mouth—quiet!   1260

OEDIPUS   Don't lash out at him, old man—
you need lashing more than he does.

SHEPHERD   Why,
master, majesty—what have I done wrong?

OEDIPUS   You won't answer his question about the boy.

SHEPHERD   He's talking nonsense, wasting his breath.   1265

OEDIPUS   So, you won't talk willingly—
then you'll talk with pain.
[The guards seize the SHEPHERD.]

SHEPHERD   No, dear god, don't torture an old man!

OEDIPUS   Twist his arms back, quickly!

SHEPHERD   God help us, why?—
what more do you need to know?   1270

OEDIPUS   Did you give him that child? He's asking.

---

3. The principal star in the constellation Boötes; its appearance in the sky ("rising") just before dawn in
September signals the end of summer.

SHEPHERD   I did . . . I wish to god I'd died that day.

OEDIPUS   You've got your wish if you don't tell the truth.

SHEPHERD   The more I tell, the worse the death I'll die.

OEDIPUS   Our friend here wants to stretch things out, does he?   1275
      [*Motioning to his men for torture.*]

SHEPHERD   No, no, I gave it to him—I just said so.

OEDIPUS   Where did you get it? Your house? Someone else's?

SHEPHERD   It wasn't mine, no, I got it from . . . someone.

OEDIPUS   Which one of them?
      [*Looking at the citizens.*]

OEDIPUS   Whose house?

SHEPHERD   No—
   god's sake, master, no more questions!   1280

OEDIPUS   You're a dead man if I have to ask again.

SHEPHERD   Then—the child came from the house . . . of Laius.

OEDIPUS   A slave? or born of his own blood?

SHEPHERD   Oh no,
   I'm right at the edge, the horrible truth—I've got to say it!

OEDIPUS   And I'm at the edge of hearing horrors, yes, but I must
      hear!   1285

SHEPHERD   All right! His son, they said it was—his son!
   But the one inside, your wife,
   she'd tell it best.

OEDIPUS   My wife—
   she gave it to you?   1290

SHEPHERD   Yes, yes, my king.

OEDIPUS   Why, what for?

SHEPHERD   To kill it.

OEDIPUS   Her own child,
   how could she?   1295

SHEPHERD   She was afraid—
   frightening prophecies.

OEDIPUS   What?

SHEPHERD   They said—
   he'd kill his parents.   1300

OEDIPUS   But you gave him to this old man—why?

SHEPHERD   I pitied the little baby, master,
   hoped he'd take him off to his own country,
   far away, but he saved him for this, this fate.
   If you are the man he says you are, believe me,   1305
   you were born for pain.

OEDIPUS   O god—
   all come true, all burst to light!
   O light—now let me look my last on you!
   I stand revealed at last—
   cursed in my birth, cursed in marriage,   1310
   cursed in the lives I cut down with these hands!
      [*Rushing through the doors with a great cry. The Corinthian* MESSENGER,
      the SHEPHERD *and attendants exit slowly to the side.*]

CHORUS   O the generations of men

the dying generations—adding the total
of all your lives I find they come to nothing . . .
   does there exist, is there a man on earth 1315
who seizes more joy than just a dream, a vision?
And the vision no sooner dawns than dies
blazing into oblivion.
You are my great example, you, your life
your destiny, Oedipus, man of misery—   1320
I count no man blest.

     You outranged all men!
  Bending your bow to the breaking-point
you captured priceless glory, O dear god,
and the Sphinx came crashing down,
    the virgin, claws hooked   1325
like a bird of omen singing, shrieking death—
like a fortress reared in the face of death
you rose and saved our land.

From that day on we called you king
we crowned you with honors, Oedipus, towering over all— 1330
mighty king of the seven gates of Thebes.

But now to hear your story—is there a man more agonized?
More wed to pain and frenzy? Not a man on earth,
the joy of your life ground down to nothing
O Oedipus, name for the ages—   1335
  one and the same wide harbor served you
    son and father both
son and father came to rest in the same bridal chamber.
How, how could the furrows your father plowed
bear you, your agony, harrowing on   1340
in silence O so long?

    But now for all your power
Time, all-seeing Time has dragged you to the light,
judged your marriage monstrous from the start—
the son and the father tangling, both one—
O child of Laius, would to god   1345
  I'd never seen you, never never!
  Now I weep like a man who wails the dead
and the dirge comes pouring forth with all my heart!
I tell you the truth, you gave me life
my breath leapt up in you   1350
and now you bring down night upon my eyes.

   [*Enter a* MESSENGER *from the palace.*]

MESSENGER: Men of Thebes, always first in honor,
 what horrors you will hear, what you will see,
 what a heavy weight of sorrow you will shoulder . . .
 if you are true to your birth, if you still have 1355

some feeling for the royal house of Thebes.
I tell you neither the waters of the Danube
nor the Nile[4] can wash this palace clean.
Such things it hides, it soon will bring to light—
terrible things, and none done blindly now,   1360
all done with a will. The pains
we inflict upon ourselves hurt most of all.
LEADER   God knows we have pains enough already.
     What can you add to them?
MESSENGER   The queen is dead.
LEADER   Poor lady—how?   1365
MESSENGER   By her own hand. But you are spared the worst,
     you never had to watch . . . I saw it all,
     and with all the memory that's in me
     you will learn what that poor woman suffered.

Once she'd broken in through the gates,   1370
dashing past us, frantic, whipped to fury,
ripping her hair out with both hands—
straight to her rooms she rushed, flinging herself
across the bridal-bed, doors slamming behind her—
once inside, she wailed for Laius, dead so long,   1375
remembering how she bore his child long ago,
the life that rose up to destroy him, leaving
its mother to mother living creatures
with the very son she'd borne.
Oh how she wept, mourning the marriage-bed   1380
where she let loose that double brood—monsters—
husband by her husband, children by her child.
                                                  And then—
but how she died is more than I can say. Suddenly
Oedipus burst in, screaming, he stunned us so
we couldn't watch her agony to the end,   1385
our eyes were fixed on him. Circling
like a maddened beast, stalking, here, there,
crying out to us—
                    Give him a sword![5] His wife,
no wife, his mother, where can he find the mother earth
that cropped two crops at once, himself and all his children?   1390
He was raging—one of the dark powers pointing the way,
none of us mortals crowding around him, no,
with a great shattering cry—someone, something leading him on—
he hurled at the twin doors and bending the bolts back
out of their sockets, crashed through the chamber.   1395
And there we saw the woman hanging by the neck,
cradled high in a woven noose, spinning,
swinging back and forth. And when he saw her,

4. The Greek reads "Phasis," a river in Asia Minor. The translator has substituted a big river more familiar
to modern readers.   5. Presumably so that he could kill himself.

giving a low, wrenching sob that broke our hearts,
slipping the halter from her throat, he eased her down,   1400
in a slow embrace he laid her down, poor thing . . .
then, what came next, what horror we beheld!

He rips off her brooches, the long gold pins
holding her robes—and lifting them high,
looking straight up into the points,   1405
he digs them down the sockets of his eyes, crying, "You,
you'll see no more the pain I suffered, all the pain I caused!
Too long you looked on the ones you never should have seen,
blind to the ones you longed to see, to know! Blind
from this hour on! Blind in the darkness—blind!"   1410
His voice like a dirge, rising, over and over
raising the pins, raking them down his eyes.
And at each stroke blood spurts from the roots,
splashing his beard, a swirl of it, nerves and clots—
black hail of blood pulsing, gushing down.   1415

These are the griefs that burst upon them both,
coupling man and woman. The joy they had so lately,
the fortune of their old ancestral house
was deep joy indeed. Now, in this one day,
wailing, madness and doom, death, disgrace   1420
all the griefs in the world that you can name,
all are theirs forever.

LEADER   Oh poor man, the misery—
has he any rest from pain now?
        [A voice within, in torment.]
MESSENGER   He's shouting,
"Loose the bolts, someone, show me to all of Thebes!
My father's murderer, my mother's—"   1425
No, I can't repeat it, it's unholy.
Now he'll tear himself from his native earth,
not linger, curse the house with his own curse.
But he needs strength, and a guide to lead him on.
This is sickness more than he can bear.
        [The palace doors open.]
                                Look,   1430
he'll show you himself. The great doors are opening—
you are about to see a sight, a horror
even his mortal enemy would pity.
        [Enter OEDIPUS, blinded, led by a boy. He stands at the palace steps, as
        if surveying his people once again.]
CHORUS   O the terror—
the suffering, for all the world to see,
the worst terror that ever met my eyes.   1435
What madness swept over you? What god,
what dark power leapt beyond all bounds,
beyond belief, to crush your wretched life?—

godforsaken, cursed by the gods!
I pity you but I can't bear to look.   1440
I've much to ask, so much to learn,
so much fascinates my eyes,
but you . . . I shudder at the sight.
OEDIPUS   Oh, Ohh—
the agony! I am agony—
where am I going? where on earth?   1445
    where does all this agony hurl me?
where's my voice?—
        winging, swept away on a dark tide—
    My destiny, my dark power, what a leap you made!
CHORUS   To the depths of terror, too dark to hear, to see.   1450
OEDIPUS   Dark, horror of darkness
    my darkness, drowning, swirling around me
    crashing wave on wave—unspeakable, irresistible
        headwind, fatal harbor! Oh again,
    the misery, all at once, over and over   1455
    the stabbing daggers, stab of memory
raking me insane.
CHORUS   No wonder you suffer
    twice over, the pain of your wounds,
    the lasting grief of pain.
OEDIPUS   Dear friend, still here?
    Standing by me, still with a care for me,   1460
    the blind man? Such compassion,
        loyal to the last. Oh it's you,
    I know you're here, dark as it is
    I'd know you anywhere, your voice—
it's yours, clearly yours.
CHORUS   Dreadful, what you've done . . .   1465
    how could you bear it, gouging out your eyes?
    What superhuman power drove you on?
OEDIPUS   Apollo, friends, Apollo—
    he ordained my agonies—these, my pains on pains!
    But the hand that struck my eyes was mine,   1470
    mine alone—no one else—
        I did it all myself!
    What good were eyes to me?
    Nothing I could see could bring me joy.
CHORUS   No, no, exactly as you say.
OEDIPUS   What can I ever see?   1475
    What love, what call of the heart
    can touch my ears with joy? Nothing, friends.
        Take me away, far, far from Thebes,
        quickly, cast me away, my friends—
    this great murderous ruin, this man cursed to heaven,   1480
        the man the deathless gods hate most of all!
CHORUS   Pitiful, you suffer so, you understand so much . . .
    I wish you'd never known.

OEDIPUS   Die, die—
    whoever he was that day in the wilds
  who cut my ankles free of the ruthless pins, 1485
    he pulled me clear of death, he saved my life
    for this, this kindness—
        Curse him, kill him!
    If I'd died then, I'd never have dragged myself,
    my loved ones through such hell. 1490
CHORUS Oh if only . . . would to god.
OEDIPUS   I'd never have come to this,
    my father's murderer—never been branded
    mother's husband, all men see me now! Now,
    loathed by the gods, son of the mother I defiled
    coupling in my father's bed, spawning lives in the loins 1495
  that spawned my wretched life. What grief can crown this grief?
       It's mine alone, my destiny—I am Oedipus!
CHORUS How can I say you've chosen for the best?
  Better to die than be alive and blind.
OEDIPUS What I did was best—don't lecture me, 1500
  no more advice. I, with *my* eyes,
  how could I look my father in the eyes
  when I go down to death? Or mother, so abused . . .
  I have done such things to the two of them,
  crimes too huge for hanging.
           Worse yet, 1505
  the sight of my children, born as they were born,
  how could I long to look into their eyes?
  No, not with these eyes of mine, never.
  Not this city either, her high towers,
  the sacred glittering images of her gods— 1510
  I am misery! I, her best son, reared
  as no other son of Thebes was ever reared,
  I've stripped myself, I gave the command myself.
  All men must cast away the great blasphemer,
  the curse now brought to light by the gods, 1515
  the son of Laius—I, my father's son!

  Now I've exposed my guilt, horrendous guilt,
  could I train a level glance on you, my countrymen?
  Impossible! No, if I could just block off my ears,
  the springs of hearing, I would stop at nothing— 1520
  I'd wall up my loathsome body like a prison,
  blind to the sound of life, not just the sight.
  Oblivion—what a blessing . . .
  for the mind to dwell a world away from pain.

  O Cithaeron, why did you give me shelter? 1525
  Why didn't you take me, crush my life out on the spot?
  I'd never have revealed my birth to all mankind.

O Polybus, Corinth, the old house of my fathers,
so I believed—what a handsome prince you raised—
under the skin, what sickness to the core.   1530
Look at me! Born of outrage, outrage to the core.
O triple roads—it all comes back, the secret,
dark ravine, and the oaks closing in
where the three roads join . . .
You drank my father's blood, my own blood   1535
spilled by my own hands—you still remember me?
What things you saw me do? Then I came here
and did them all once more!

                                        Marriages! O marriage,
you gave me birth, and once you brought me into the world
you brought my sperm rising back, springing to light   1540
fathers, brothers, sons—one murderous breed—
brides, wives, mothers. The blackest things
a man can do, I have done them all!

                                        No more—
it's wrong to name what's wrong to do. Quickly,
for the love of god, hide me somewhere,   1545
kill me, hurl me into the sea
where you can never look on me again.
        [Beckoning to the CHORUS as they shrink away.]
                                        Closer,
it's all right. Touch the man of grief.
Do. Don't be afraid. My troubles are mine
and I am the only man alive who can sustain them.   1550
        [Enter CREON from the palace, attended by palace guards.]
LEADER   Put your requests to Creon. Here he is,
    just when we need him. He'll have a plan, he'll act.
    Now that he's the sole defense of the country
    in your place.
OEDIPUS   Oh no, what can I say to him?
    How can I ever hope to win his trust?   1555
    I wronged him so, just now, in every way.
    You must see that—I was so wrong, so wrong.
CREON   I haven't come to mock you, Oedipus,
    or to criticize your former failings.
        [Turning to the guards.]
                                        You there,
    have you lost all respect for human feelings?   1560
    At least revere the Sun, the holy fire
    that keeps us all alive. Never expose a thing
    of guilt and holy dread so great it appalls
    the earth, the rain from heaven, the light of day!
    Get him into the halls—quickly as you can.   1565
    Piety demands no less. Kindred alone
    should see a kinsman's shame. This is obscene.
OEDIPUS   Please, in god's name . . . you wipe my fears away,

coming so generously to me, the worst of men.
Do one thing more, for your sake, not mine. 1570
CREON What do you want? Why so insistent?
OEDIPUS Drive me out of the land at once, far from sight,
where I can never hear a human voice.
CREON I'd have done that already, I promise you.
First I wanted the god to clarify my duties. 1575
OEDIPUS The god? His command was clear, every word:
death for the father-killer, the curse—
he said destroy me!
CREON So he did. Still, in such a crisis
it's better to ask precisely what to do.
OEDIPUS   So miserable— 1580
you'd consult the god about a man like me?
CREON By all means. And this time, I assume,
even you will obey the god's decrees.
OEDIPUS   I will,
I will. And you, I command you—I beg you . . .
the woman inside, bury her as you see fit. 1585
It's the only decent thing,
to give your own the last rites. As for me,
never condemn the city of my fathers
to house my body, not while I'm alive, no,
let me live on the mountains, on Cithaeron, 1590
my favorite haunt, I have made it famous.
Mother and father marked out that rock
to be my everlasting tomb—buried alive.
Let me die there, where they tried to kill me.

Oh but this I know: no sickness can destroy me, 1595
nothing can. I would never have been saved
from death—I have been saved
for something great and terrible, something strange.
Well let my destiny come and take me on its way!
About my children, Creon, the boys at least, 1600
don't burden yourself. They're men,
wherever they go, they'll find the means to live.
But my two daughters, my poor helpless girls,
clustering at our table, never without me
hovering near them . . . whatever I touched, 1605
they always had their share. Take care of them,
I beg you. Wait, better—permit me, would you?
Just to touch them with my hands and take
our fill of tears. Please . . . my king.
Grant it, with all your noble heart. 1610
If I could hold them, just once, I'd think
I had them with me, like the early days
when I could see their eyes.

[ANTIGONE and ISMENE, two small children, are led in from the palace
by a nurse.]

What's that
O god! Do I really hear you sobbing?—
my two children. Creon, you've pitied me?   1615
Sent me my darling girls, my own flesh and blood!
Am I right?
CREON   Yes, it's my doing.
I know the joy they gave you all these years,
the joy you must feel now.
OEDIPUS   Bless you, Creon!
May god watch over you for this kindness,   1620
better than he ever guarded me.
                         Children, where are you?
Here, come quickly—
        [*Groping for* ANTIGONE *and* ISMENE, *who approach their father cautiously, then embrace him.*]
                    Come to these hands of mine,
your brother's hands, your own father's hands
that served his once bright eyes so well—
that made them blind. Seeing nothing, children,   1625
knowing nothing, I became your father,
I fathered you in the soil that gave me life.
How I weep for you—I cannot see you now . . .
just thinking of all your days to come, the bitterness,
the life that rough mankind will thrust upon you.   1630
Where are the public gatherings you can join,
the banquets of the clans? Home you'll come,
in tears, cut off from the sight of it all,
the brilliant rites unfinished.
And when you reach perfection, ripe for marriage,   1635
who will he be, my dear ones? Risking all
to shoulder the curse that weighs down my parents,
yes and you too—that wounds us all together.
What more misery could you want?
Your father killed his father, sowed his mother,   1640
one, one and the selfsame womb sprang you—
he cropped the very roots of his existence.

Such disgrace, and you must bear it all!
Who will marry you then? Not a man on earth.
Your doom is clear: you'll wither away to nothing,   1645
single, without a child.
        [*Turning to* CREON.]
                    Oh Creon,
you are the only father they have now . . .
we who brought them into the world
are gone, both gone at a stroke—
Don't let them go begging, abandoned,   1650
men without men. Your own flesh and blood!
Never bring them down to the level of my pains.
Pity them. Look at them, so young, so vulnerable,

shorn of everything—you're their only hope.
Promise me, noble Creon, touch my hand!   1655
   [*Reaching toward* CREON, *who draws back.*]
You, little ones, if you were old enough
to understand, there is much I'd tell you.
Now, as it is, I'd have you say a prayer.
Pray for life, my children,
live where you are free to grow and season.   1660
Pray god you find a better life than mine,
the father who begot you.

CREON   Enough.
You've wept enough. Into the palace now.

OEDIPUS   I must, but I find it very hard.

CREON   Time is the great healer, you will see.   1665

OEDIPUS   I am going—you know on what condition?

CREON   Tell me. I'm listening.

OEDIPUS   Drive me out of Thebes, in exile.

CREON   Not I. Only the gods can give you that.

OEDIPUS   Surely the gods hate me so much—   1670

CREON   You'll get your wish at once.

OEDIPUS   You consent?

CREON   I try to say what I mean; it's my habit.

OEDIPUS   Then take me away. It's time.

CREON   Come along, let go of the children.

OEDIPUS   No—
don't take them away from me, not now! No no no!   1675
   [*Clutching his daughters as the guards wrench them loose and take them
   through the palace doors.*]

CREON   Still the king, the master of all things?
No more: here your power ends.
None of your power follows you through life.
   [*Exit* OEDIPUS *and* CREON *to the palace. The* CHORUS *comes forward to
   address the audience directly.*]

CHORUS   People of Thebes, my countrymen, look on Oedipus.
He solved the famous riddle with his brilliance,   1680
he rose to power, a man beyond all power.
Who could behold his greatness without envy?
Now what a black sea of terror has overwhelmed him.
Now as we keep our watch and wait the final day,
count no man happy till he dies, free of pain at last.   1685
   [*Exit in procession.*]

Antigone[1]

CHARACTERS

ANTIGONE, *daughter of Oedipus and*
    Jocasta
ISMENE, *sister of Antigone*
A CHORUS *of old Theban citizens*
    and their LEADER
CREON, *king of Thebes, uncle of*
    Antigone and Ismene

A SENTRY
HAEMON, *son of Creon and Eurydice*
TIRESIAS, *a blind prophet*
A MESSENGER
EURYDICE, *wife of Creon*
Guards, attendants, and a boy

[TIME AND SCENE: *The royal house of Thebes. It is still night, and the invading armies of Argos have just been driven from the city. Fighting on opposite sides, the sons of Oedipus, Eteocles and Polynices, have killed each other in combat. Their uncle,* CREON, *is now king of Thebes.*

    Enter ANTIGONE, *slipping through the central doors of the palace. She motions to her sister,* ISMENE, *who follows her cautiously toward an altar at the center of the stage.*]]

ANTIGONE   My own flesh and blood—dear sister, dear Ismene,
   how many griefs our father Oedipus handed down!
   Do you know one, I ask you, one grief
   that Zeus will not perfect for the two of us
   while we still live and breathe? There's nothing,   5
   no pain—our lives are pain—no private shame,
   no public disgrace, nothing I haven't seen
   in your griefs and mine. And now this:
   an emergency decree, they say, the Commander[2]
   has just now declared for all of Thebes.   10
   What, haven't you heard? Don't you see?
   The doom reserved for enemies
   marches on the ones we love the most.
ISMENE   Not I, I haven't heard a word, Antigone.
   Nothing of loved ones,   15
   no joy or pain has come my way, not since
   the two of us were robbed of our two brothers,
   both gone in a day, a double blow—
   not since the armies of Argos vanished,
   just this very night. I know nothing more,   20
   whether our luck's improved or ruin's still to come.
ANTIGONE   I thought so. That's why I brought you out here,
   past the gates, so you could hear in private.
ISMENE   What's the matter? Trouble, clearly . . .
   you sound so dark, so grim.   25
ANTIGONE   Why not? Our own brothers' burial!
   Hasn't Creon graced one with all the rites,
   disgraced the other? Eteocles, they say,

---

1. Translated by Robert Fagles.   2. Creon. In the original he is given a military title; Antigone will not refer to him as king.

has been given full military honors,
rightly so—Creon has laid him in the earth   30
and he goes with glory down among the dead.
But the body of Polynices, who died miserably—
why, a city-wide proclamation, rumor has it,
forbids anyone to bury him, even mourn him.
He's to be left unwept, unburied, a lovely treasure   35
for birds that scan the field and feast to their heart's content.
Such, I hear, is the martial law our good Creon

lays down for you and me—yes, me, I tell you—
and he's coming here to alert the uninformed
in no uncertain terms,   40
and he won't treat the matter lightly. Whoever
disobeys in the least will die, his doom is sealed:
stoning to death inside the city walls!

There you have it. You'll soon show what you are,
worth your breeding, Ismene, or a coward—   45
for all your royal blood.
ISMENE   My poor sister, if things have come to this,
who am I to make or mend them, tell me,
what good am I to you?
ANTIGONE   Decide.
Will you share the labor, share the work?   50
ISMENE   What work, what's the risk? What do you mean?
ANTIGONE   [Raising her hands.]
Will you lift up his body with these bare hands
and lower it with me?
ISMENE   What? You'd bury him—
when a law forbids the city?
ANTIGONE   Yes!
He is my brother and—deny it as you will—   55
your brother too.
No one will ever convict me for a traitor.
ISMENE   So desperate, and Creon has expressly—
ANTIGONE   No,
he has no right to keep me from my own.
ISMENE   Oh my sister, think—   60
think how our own father died, hated,[3]
his reputation in ruins, driven on
by the crimes he brought to light himself
to gouge out his eyes with his own hands—
then mother . . . his mother and wife, both in one,   65
mutilating her life in the twisted noose—
and last, our two brothers dead in a single day,
both shedding their own blood, poor suffering boys,
battling out their common destiny hand-to-hand.

---

3. This play was written before *Oedipus the King* and *Oedipus at Colonus*; the latter gives us a different
picture of Oedipus's end.

Now look at the two of us left so alone . . .   70
think what a death we'll die, the worst of all
if we violate the laws and override
the fixed decree of the throne, its power—
we must be sensible. Remember we are women,
we're not born to contend with men. Then too,   75
we're underlings, ruled by much stronger hands,
so we must submit in this, and things still worse.

I, for one, I'll beg the dead to forgive me—
I'm forced, I have no choice—I must obey
the ones who stand in power. Why rush to extremes?   80
It's madness, madness.
ANTIGONE   I won't insist,
no, even if you should have a change of heart,
I'd never welcome you in the labor, not with me.
So, do as you like, whatever suits you best—
I will bury him myself.   85
And even if I die in the act, that death will be a glory.
I will lie with the one I love and loved by him—
an outrage sacred to the gods! I have longer
to please the dead than please the living here:
in the kingdom down below I'll lie forever.   90
Do as you like, dishonor the laws
the gods hold in honor.
ISMENE   I'd do them no dishonor . . .
but defy the city? I have no strength for that.
ANTIGONE   You have your excuses. I am on my way,
I'll raise a mound for him, for my dear brother.   95
ISMENE   Oh Antigone, you're so rash—I'm so afraid for you!
ANTIGONE   Don't fear for me. Set your own life in order.
ISMENE   Then don't, at least, blurt this out to anyone.
Keep it a secret. I'll join you in that, I promise.
ANTIGONE   Dear god, shout it from the rooftops. I'll hate you   100
all the more for silence—tell the world!
ISMENE   So fiery—and it ought to chill your heart.
ANTIGONE   I know I please where I must please the most.
ISMENE   Yes, if you can, but you're in love with impossibility.
ANTIGONE   Very well then, once my strength gives out   105
I will be done at last.
ISMENE   You're wrong from the start,
you're off on a hopeless quest.
ANTIGONE   If you say so you will make me hate you,
and the hatred of the dead, by all rights,
will haunt you night and day.   110
But leave me to my own absurdity, leave me
to suffer this—dreadful thing. I will suffer
nothing as great as death without glory.
        [Exit to the side.]
ISMENE   Then go if you must, but rest assured,
wild, irrational as you are, my sister,   115

you are truly dear to the ones who love you.

[*Withdrawing to the palace. Enter a* CHORUS,[4] *the old citizens of Thebes chanting as the sun begins to rise.*]

CHORUS   Glory!—great beam of the sun, brightest of all
that ever rose on the seven gates of Thebes,
   you burn through night at last!
      Great eye of the golden day,   120
mounting the Dirce's[5] banks you throw him back—
the enemy out of Argos, the white shield,[6] the man of bronze—
he's flying headlong now
   the bridle of fate stampeding him with pain!

      And he had driven against our borders,   125
      launched by the warring claims of Polynices—
      like an eagle screaming, winging havoc
      over the land, wings of armor
      shielded white as snow,
      a huge army massing,   130
      crested helmets bristling for assault.

He hovered above our roofs, his vast maw gaping
closing down around our seven gates,
   his spears thirsting for the kill
      but now he's gone, look,   135
before he could glut his jaws with Theban blood
or the god of fire put our crown of towers to the torch.
He grappled the Dragon[7] none can master—Thebes—
   the clang of our arms like thunder at his back!

      Zeus hates with a vengeance all bravado,   140
      the mighty boasts of men. He watched them
      coming on in a rising flood, the pride
      of their golden armor ringing shrill—
      and brandishing his lightning
      blasted the fighter[8] just at the goal,   145
      rushing to shout his triumph from our walls.

Down from the heights he crashed, pounding down on the earth!
And a moment ago, blazing torch in hand—
   mad for attack, ecstatic
he breathed his rage, the storm   150
   of his fury hurling at our heads!
But now his high hopes have laid him low
and down the enemy ranks the iron god of war

---

4. The chorus of old men celebrates the victory won over the Argive forces and Polynices.   5. A river of the Theban plain.   6. The Argive soldiers' shields were painted white.   7. According to legend the Thebans sprang from the dragon's teeth sown by Cadmus.   8. Capaneus, the most violent of the Seven against Thebes. He had almost scaled the wall when the lightning of Zeus threw him down.

deals his rewards, his stunning blows—Ares[9]
rapture of battle, our right arm in the crisis.   155

    Seven captains marshaled at seven gates
seven against their equals, gave
their brazen trophies[1] up to Zeus
god of the breaking rout of battle,
all but two: those blood brothers,   160
one father, one mother—matched in rage,
spears matched for the twin conquest—
clashed and won the common prize of death.

But now for Victory! glorious in the morning,
joy in her eyes to meet our joy   165
  she is winging[2] down to Thebes,
our fleets of chariots wheeling in her wake—
    Now let us win oblivion from the wars,
thronging the temples of the gods
in singing, dancing choirs through the night!   170
    Lord Dionysus,[3] god of the dance
    that shakes the land of Thebes, now lead the way!
[*Enter* CREON *from the palace, attended by his guard.*]

    But look, the king of the realm is coming
Creon, the new man for the new day,
whatever the gods are sending now . . .   175
what new plan will he launch?
Why this, this special session?
Why this sudden call to the old men
summoned at one command?

CREON   My countrymen,
the ship of state is safe. The gods who rocked her,   180
after a long, merciless pounding in the storm,
have righted her once more.
                Out of the whole city
I have called you here alone. Well I know,
first, your undeviating respect
for the throne and royal power of King Laius.   185
Next, while Oedipus steered the land of Thebes,
and even after he died, your loyalty was unshakable,
you still stood by their children. Now then,
since the two sons are dead—two blows of fate
in the same day, cut down by each other's hands,   190

---

9. Not only the god of war but also one of the patron deities of Thebes.   **1.** The victors in Greek battle set up a trophy consisting of the armor of one of the enemy dead, fixed to a post and set up at the place where the enemy turned to run away.   **2.** Victory is portrayed in Greek painting and sculpture as a winged young woman.   **3.** A god of the vine and of revel; his father was Zeus, and his mother, Semele, was a Theban princess.

both killers, both brothers stained with blood—
as I am next in kin to the dead,
I now possess the throne and all its powers.

Of course you cannot know a man completely,
his character, his principles, sense of judgment,   195
not till he's shown his colors, ruling the people,
making laws. Experience, there's the test.
As I see it, whoever assumes the task,
the awesome task of setting the city's course,
and refuses to adopt the soundest policies   200
but fearing someone, keeps his lips locked tight,
he's utterly worthless. So I rate him now,
I always have. And whoever places a friend
above the good of his own country, he is nothing:
I have no use for him. Zeus my witness,   205
Zeus who sees all things, always—
I could never stand by silent, watching destruction
march against our city, putting safety to rout,
nor could I ever make that man a friend of mine
who menaces our country. Remember this: 210
our country *is* our safety.
Only while she voyages true on course
can we establish friendships, truer than blood itself.
Such are my standards. They make our city great.

Closely akin to them I have proclaimed,   215
just now, the following decree to our people
concerning the two sons of Oedipus.
Eteocles, who died fighting for Thebes,
excelling all in arms: he shall be buried,
crowned with a hero's honors, the cups we pour[4]   220
to soak the earth and reach the famous dead.

But as for his blood brother, Polynices,
who returned from exile, home to his father-city
and the gods of his race, consumed with one desire—
to burn them roof to roots—who thirsted to drink   225
his kinsmen's blood and sell the rest to slavery:
that man—a proclamation has forbidden the city
to dignify him with burial, mourn him at all.
No, he must be left unburied, his corpse
carrion for the birds and dogs to tear,   230
an obscenity for the citizens to behold!

These are my principles. Never at my hands
will the traitor be honored above the patriot.
But whoever proves his loyalty to the state—

---

4. Libations (liquid offerings—wine, honey, etc.) poured on the grave.

I'll prize that man in death as well as life. 235
LEADER   If this is your pleasure, Creon, treating
  our city's enemy and our friend this way . . .
  The power is yours, I suppose, to enforce it
  with the laws, both for the dead and all of us,
  the living.
CREON   Follow my orders closely then, 240
  be on your guard.
LEADER   We're too old.
  Lay that burden on younger shoulders.
CREON   No, no,
  I don't mean the body—I've posted guards already.
LEADER   What commands for us then? What other service?
CREON   See that you never side with those who break my orders. 245
LEADER   Never. Only a fool could be in love with death.
CREON   Death is the price—you're right. But all too often
  the mere hope of money has ruined many men.
        [A SENTRY enters from the side.]
SENTRY   My lord,
  I can't say I'm winded from running, or set out
  with any spring in my legs either—no sir, 250
  I was lost in thought, and it made me stop, often,
  dead in my track, heeling, turning back,
  and all the time a voice inside me muttering,
  "Idiot, why? You're going straight to your death."
  Then muttering, "Stopped again, poor fool? 255
  If somebody gets the news to Creon first,
  what's to save your neck?"
                            And so,
  mulling it over, on I trudge, dragging my feet,
  you can make a short road take forever . . .
  but at last, look, common sense won out, 260
  I'm here, and I'm all yours,
  and even though I come empty-handed
  I'll tell my story just the same, because
  I've come with a good grip on one hope,
  what will come will come, whatever fate— 265
CREON   Come to the point!
  What's wrong—why so afraid?
SENTRY   First, myself, I've got to tell you,
  I didn't do it, didn't see who did—
  Be fair, don't take it out on me. 270
CREON   You're playing it safe, soldier,
  barricading yourself from any trouble.
  It's obvious, you've something strange to tell.
SENTRY   Dangerous too, and danger makes you delay
  for all you're worth. 275
CREON   Out with it—then dismiss!
SENTRY   All right, here it comes. The body—
  someone's just buried it, then run off . . .

sprinkled some dry dust on the flesh,[5]
given it proper rites.

CREON   What?   280
What man alive would dare—

SENTRY   I've no idea, I swear it.
There was no mark of a spade, no pickaxe there,
no earth turned up, the ground packed hard and dry,
unbroken, no tracks, no wheelruts, nothing,
the workman left no trace. Just at sunup   285
the first watch of the day points it out—
it was a wonder! We were stunned . . .
a terrific burden too, for all of us, listen:
you can't see the corpse, not that it's buried,
really, just a light cover of road-dust on it,   290
as if someone meant to lay the dead to rest
and keep from getting cursed.
Not a sign in sight that dogs or wild beasts
had worried the body, even torn the skin.

But what came next! Rough talk flew thick and fast,   295
guard grilling guard—we'd have come to blows
at last, nothing to stop it; each man for himself
and each the culprit, no one caught red-handed,
all of us pleading ignorance, dodging the charges,
ready to take up red-hot iron in our fists,   300
go through fire,[6] swear oaths to the gods—
"I didn't do it, I had no hand in it either,
not in the plotting, not the work itself!"

Finally, after all this wrangling came to nothing,
one man spoke out and made us stare at the ground,   305
hanging our heads in fear. No way to counter him,
no way to take his advice and come through
safe and sound. Here's what he said:
"Look, we've got to report the facts to Creon,
we can't keep this hidden." Well, that won out,   310
and the lot fell to me, condemned me,
unlucky as ever, I got the prize. So here I am,
against my will and yours too, well I know—
no one wants the man who brings bad news.

LEADER   My king,
ever since he began I've been debating in my mind,   315
could this possibly be the work of the gods?

CREON   Stop—
before you make me choke with anger—the gods!
You, you're senile, must you be insane?

---

5. A symbolic burial, all Antigone could do alone, without Ismene's help.   **6.** Both traditional assertions of truthfulness, derived perhaps from some primitive ritual of ordeal—only the liar would get burned.

You say—why it's intolerable—say the gods
could have the slightest concern for the corpse?   320
Tell me, was it for meritorious service
they proceeded to bury him, prized him so? The hero
who came to burn their temples ringed with pillars,
their golden treasures—scorch their hallowed earth
and fling their laws to the winds.   325
Exactly when did you last see the gods
celebrating traitors? Inconceivable!
No, from the first there were certain citizens
who could hardly stand the spirit of my regime,
grumbling against me in the dark, heads together,   330
tossing wildly, never keeping their necks beneath
the yoke, loyally submitting to their king.
These are the instigators, I'm convinced—
they've perverted my own guard, bribed them
to do their work.

             Money! Nothing worse   335
in our lives, so current, rampant, so corrupting.
Money—you demolish cities, rot men from their homes,
you train and twist good minds and set them on
to the most atrocious schemes. No limit,
you make them adept at every kind of outrage,   340
every godless crime—money!

                   Everyone—
the whole crew bribed to commit this crime,
they've made one thing sure at least:
sooner or later they will pay the price.

    [*Wheeling on the* SENTRY.]
                    You—
I swear to Zeus as I still believe in Zeus,   345
if you don't find the man who buried that corpse,
the very man, and produce him before my eyes,
simple death won't be enough for you,
not till we string you up alive
and wring the immorality out of you.   350
Then you can steal the rest of our days,
better informed about where to make a killing.
You'll have learned, at last, it doesn't pay
to itch for rewards from every hand that beckons.
Filthy profits wreck most men, you'll see—   355
they'll never save your life.

SENTRY   Please,
may I say a word or two, or just turn and go?

CREON   Can't you tell? Everything you say offends me.

SENTRY   Where does it hurt you, in the ears or in the heart?

CREON   And who are you to pinpoint my displeasure?   360

SENTRY   The culprit grates on your feelings,
I just annoy your ears.

CREON   Still talking?

You talk too much! a born nuisance—

SENTRY   Maybe so,
but I never did this thing, so help me!

CREON   Yes you did— 365
what's more, you squandered your life for silver!

SENTRY   Oh it's terrible when the one who does the judging
judges things all wrong.

CREON   Well now,
you just be clever about your judgments—
if you fail to produce the criminals for me,
you'll swear your dirty money brought you pain. 370

          [*Turning sharply, reentering the palace.*]

SENTRY   I hope he's found. Best thing by far.
But caught or not, that's in the lap of fortune:
I'll never come back, you've seen the last of me.
I'm saved, even now, and I never thought,
I never hoped— 375
dear gods, I owe you all my thanks!

          [*Rushing out.*]

CHORUS   Numberless wonders
terrible wonders walk the world but none the match for man—
that great wonder crossing the heaving gray sea,
          driven on by the blasts of winter
on through breakers crashing left and right, 380
          holds his steady course
and the oldest of the gods he wears away—
the Earth, the immortal, the inexhaustible—
as his powers go back and forth, year in, year out
          with the breed of stallions[7] turning up the furrows. 385

And the blithe, lightheaded race of birds he snares,
the tribes of savage beasts, the life that swarms the depths—
          with one fling of his nets
woven and coiled tight, he takes them all,
          man the skilled, the brilliant! 390
He conquers all, taming with his techniques
the prey that roams the cliffs and wild lairs,
training the stallion, clamping the yoke across
          his shaggy neck, and the tireless mountain bull.
And speech and thought, quick as the wind
and the mood and mind for law that rules the city—
          all these he has taught himself
and shelter from the arrows of the frost
when there's rough lodging under the cold clear sky
and the shafts of lashing rain— 400
          ready, resourceful man!
          Never without resources
never an impasse as he marches on the future—

7. Mules, the working animal of a Greek farmer.

only Death, from Death alone he will find no rescue
but from desperate plagues he has plotted his escapes. 405

Man the master, ingenious past all measure
past all dreams, the skills within his grasp—
 he forges on, now to destruction
now again to greatness. When he weaves in
the laws of the land, and the justice of the gods 410
that binds his oaths together
 he and his city rise high—
  but the city casts out
that man who weds himself to inhumanity
thanks to reckless daring. Never share my hearth 415
never think my thoughts, whoever does such things.

 [*Enter* ANTIGONE *from the side, accompanied by the* SENTRY.]
Here is a dark sign from the gods—
what to make of this? I know her,
how can I deny it? That young girl's Antigone!
Wretched, child of a wretched father, 420
Oedipus. Look, is it possible?
They bring you in like a prisoner—
why? did you break the king's laws?
Did they take you in some act of mad defiance?
SENTRY She's the one, she did it single-handed— 425
we caught her burying the body. Where's Creon?

 [*Enter* CREON *from the palace.*]
LEADER Back again, just in time when you need him.
CREON In time for what? What is it?
SENTRY   My king,
there's nothing you can swear you'll never do—
second thoughts make liars of us all. 430
I could have sworn I wouldn't hurry back
(what with your threats, the buffeting I just took),
but a stroke of luck beyond our wildest hopes,
what a joy, there's nothing like it. So,
back I've come, breaking my oath, who cares? 435
I'm bringing in our prisoner—this young girl—
we took her giving the dead the last rites.
But no casting lots this time; this is *my* luck,
my prize, no one else's.
      Now, my lord,
here she is. Take her, question her, 440
cross-examine her to your heart's content.
But set me free, it's only right—
I'm rid of this dreadful business once for all.
CREON Prisoner! Her? You took her—where, doing what?
SENTRY Burying the man. That's the whole story.
CREON   What? 445
You mean what you say, you're telling me the truth?
SENTRY She's the one. With my own eyes I saw her

bury the body, just what you've forbidden.
There. Is that plain and clear?
CREON   What did you see? Did you catch her in the act?   450
SENTRY   Here's what happened. We went back to our post,
those threats of yours breathing down our necks—
we brushed the corpse clean of the dust that covered it,
stripped it bare . . . it was slimy, going soft,
and we took to high ground, backs to the wind   455
so the stink of him couldn't hit us;
jostling, baiting each other to keep awake,
shouting back and forth—no napping on the job,
not this time. And so the hours dragged by
until the sun stood dead above our heads,   460
a huge white ball in the noon sky, beating,
blazing down, and then it happened—
suddenly, a whirlwind!
Twisting a great dust-storm up from the earth,
a black plague of the heavens, filling the plain,   465
ripping the leaves off every tree in sight,
choking the air and sky. We squinted hard
and took our whipping from the gods.

And after the storm passed—it seemed endless—
there, we saw the girl!   470
And she cried out a sharp, piercing cry,
like a bird come back to an empty nest,
peering into its bed, and all the babies gone . . .
Just so, when she sees the corpse bare
she bursts into a long, shattering wail   475
and calls down withering curses on the heads
of all who did the work. And she scoops up dry dust,
handfuls, quickly, and lifting a fine bronze urn,
lifting it high and pouring, she crowns the dead
with three full libations.
                                              Soon as we saw   480
we rushed her, closed on the kill like hunters,
and she, she didn't flinch. We interrogated her,
charging her with offenses past and present—
she stood up to it all, denied nothing. I tell you,
it made me ache and laugh in the same breath.   485
It's pure joy to escape the worst yourself,
it hurts a man to bring down his friends.
But all that, I'm afraid, means less to me
than my own skin. That's the way I'm made.
CREON [*Wheeling on* ANTIGONE.]   You,
with your eyes fixed on the ground—speak up.   490
Do you deny you did this, yes or no?
ANTIGONE   I did it. I don't deny a thing.
CREON [*To the* SENTRY.]   You, get out, wherever you please—
you're clear of a very heavy charge.

[*He leaves;* CREON *turns back to* ANTIGONE.]
You, tell me briefly, no long speeches— 495
were you aware a decree had forbidden this?
ANTIGONE   Well aware. How could I avoid it? It was public.
CREON   And still you had the gall to break this law?
ANTIGONE   Of course I did. It wasn't Zeus, not in the least,
who made this proclamation—not to me. 500
Nor did that Justice, dwelling with the gods
beneath the earth, ordain such laws for men.
Nor did I think your edict had such force
that you, a mere mortal, could override the gods,
the great unwritten, unshakable traditions. 505
They are alive, not just today or yesterday:
they live forever, from the first of time,
and no one knows when they first saw the light.

These laws—I was not about to break them,
not out of fear of some man's wounded pride, 510
and face the retribution of the gods.
Die I must, I've known it all my life—
how could I keep from knowing?—even without
your death-sentence ringing in my ears.
And if I am to die before my time 515
I consider that a gain. Who on earth
alive in the midst of so much grief as I,
could fail to find his death a rich reward?
So for me, at least, to meet this doom of yours
is precious little pain. But if I had allowed 520
my own mother's son to rot, an unburied corpse—
that would have been an agony! This is nothing.
And if my present actions strike you as foolish,
let's just say I've been accused of folly
by a fool.
LEADER
              Like father like daughter, 525
passionate, wild . . .
she hasn't learned to bend before adversity.
CREON   No? Believe me, the stiffest stubborn wills
fall the hardest; the toughest iron,
tempered strong in the white-hot fire, 530
you'll see it crack and shatter first of all.
And I've known spirited horses you can break
with a light bit—proud, rebellious horses.
There's no room for pride, not in a slave,
not with the lord and master standing by. 535

This girl was an old hand at insolence
when she overrode the edicts we made public.
But once she'd done it—the insolence,
twice over—to glory in it, laughing,

mocking us to our face with what she'd done.   540
I am not the man, not now: she is the man
if this victory goes to her and she goes free.

Never! Sister's child or closer in blood
than all my family clustered at my altar
worshiping Guardian Zeus—she'll never escape,   545
she and her blood sister, the most barbaric death.
Yes, I accuse her sister of an equal part
in scheming this, this burial.
    [*To his attendants.*]
                        Bring her here!
I just saw her inside, hysterical, gone to pieces.
It never fails: the mind convicts itself   550
in advance, when scoundrels are up to no good,
plotting in the dark. Oh but I hate it more
when a traitor, caught red-handed,
tries to glorify his crimes.

ANTIGONE   Creon, what more do you want   555
than my arrest and execution?
CREON   Nothing. Then I have it all.
ANTIGONE   Then why delay? Your moralizing repels me,
every word you say—pray god it always will.
So naturally all I say repels you too.
                             Enough.   560
Give me glory! What greater glory could I win
than to give my own brother decent burial?
These citizens here would all agree,
    [*To the* CHORUS.]
they would praise me too
if their lips weren't locked in fear.   565
    [*Pointing to* CREON.]
Lucky tyrants—the perquisites of power!
Ruthless power to do and say whatever pleases *them*.
CREON   You alone, of all the people in Thebes,
see things that way.
ANTIGONE   They see it just that way
but defer to you and keep their tongues in leash.   570
CREON   And you, aren't you ashamed to differ so from them?
So disloyal!
ANTIGONE   Not ashamed for a moment,
not to honor my brother, my own flesh and blood.
CREON   Wasn't Eteocles a brother too—cut down, facing him?
ANTIGONE   Brother, yes, by the same mother, the same father.   575
CREON   Then how can you render his enemy such honors,
such impieties in his eyes?
ANTIGONE   He'll never testify to that,
Eteocles dead and buried.
CREON   He will—
if you honor the traitor just as much as him.   580
ANTIGONE   But it was his brother, not some slave that died—

CREON Ravaging our country!—
   but Eteocles died fighting in our behalf.
ANTIGONE No matter—Death longs for the same rites for all.
CREON Never the same for the patriot and the traitor.   585
ANTIGONE Who, Creon, who on earth can say the ones below
   don't find this pure and uncorrupt?
CREON Never. Once an enemy, never a friend,
   not even after death.
ANTIGONE I was born to join in love, not hate—   590
   that is my nature.
CREON   Go down below and love,
   if love you must—love the dead! while I'm alive,
   no woman is going to lord it over me.
      [*Enter* ISMENE *from the palace, under guard.*]
CHORUS   Look,
   Ismene's coming, weeping a sister's tears,
   loving sister, under a cloud . . .   595
   her face is flushed, her cheeks streaming.
   Sorrow puts her lovely radiance in the dark.
CREON   You—
   in my own house, you viper, slinking undetected,
   sucking my life-blood! I never knew
   I was breeding twin disasters, the two of you   600
   rising up against my throne. Come, tell me,
   will you confess your part in the crime or not?
   Answer me. Swear to me.
ISMENE   I did it, yes—
   if only she consents—I share the guilt,
   the consequences too.
ANTIGONE   No,   605
   Justice will never suffer that—not you,
   you were unwilling. I never brought you in.
ISMENE But now you face such dangers . . . I'm not ashamed
   to sail through trouble with you,
   make your troubles mine.
ANTIGONE   Who did the work?   610
   Let the dead and the god of death bear witness!
   I have no love for a friend who loves in words alone.
ISMENE Oh no, my sister, don't reject me, please,
   let me die beside you, consecrating
   the dead together.
ANTIGONE   Never share my dying,   615
   don't lay claim to what you never touched.
   My death will be enough.
ISMENE What do I care for life, cut off from you?
ANTIGONE Ask Creon. Your concern is all for him.
ISMENE Why abuse me so? It doesn't help you now.
ANTIGONE   You're right—   620
   if I mock you, I get no pleasure from it,
   only pain.
ISMENE Tell me, dear one,

what can I do to help you, even now?
ANTIGONE   Save yourself. I don't grudge you your survival.
ISMENE   Oh no, no, denied my portion in your death?   625
ANTIGONE   You chose to live, I chose to die.
ISMENE   Not, at least,
    without every kind of caution I could voice.
ANTIGONE   Your wisdom appealed to one world—mine, another.
ISMENE   But look, we're both guilty, both condemned to death.
ANTIGONE   Courage! Live your life. I gave myself to death,   630
    long ago, so I might serve the dead.
CREON   They're both mad, I tell you, the two of them.
    One's just shown it, the other's been that way
    since she was born.
ISMENE   True, my king,
    the sense we were born with cannot last forever . . .   635
    commit cruelty on a person long enough
    and the mind begins to go.
CREON   Yours did,
    when you chose to commit your crimes with her.
ISMENE   How can I live alone, without her?
CREON   Her?
    Don't even mention her—she no longer exists.   640
ISMENE   What? You'd kill your own son's bride?
CREON   Absolutely:
    there are other fields for him to plow.
ISMENE   Perhaps,
    but never as true, as close a bond as theirs.
CREON   A worthless woman for my son? It repels me.
ISMENE   Dearest Haemon, your father wrongs you so!   645
CREON   Enough, enough—you and your talk of marriage!
ISMENE   Creon—you're really going to rob your son of Antigone?
CREON   Death will do it for me—break their marriage off.
LEADER   So, it's settled then? Antigone must die?
CREON   Settled, yes—we both know that.   650
    [To the guards.]
    Stop wasting time. Take them in.
    From now on they'll act like women.
    Tie them up, no more running loose;
    even the bravest will cut and run,
    once they see Death coming for their lives.   655
    [The guards escort ANTIGONE and ISMENE into the palace. CREON remains
    while the old citizens form their CHORUS.]
CHORUS   Blest, they are the truly blest who all their lives
    have never tasted devastation. For others, once
    the gods have rocked a house to its foundations
        the ruin will never cease, cresting on and on
    from one generation on throughout the race—   660
    like a great mounting tide
    driven on by savage northern gales,
        surging over the dead black depths

rolling up from the bottom dark heaves of sand
and the headlands, taking the storm's onslaught full-force,   665
roar, and the low moaning
                  echoes on and on
                            and now
as in ancient times I see the sorrows of the house,
the living heirs of the old ancestral kings,
piling on the sorrows of the dead
    and one generation cannot free the next—   670
some god will bring them crashing down,
the race finds no release.
And now the light, the hope
        springing up from the late last root
in the house of Oedipus, that hope's cut down in turn   675
by the long, bloody knife swung by the gods of death
by a senseless word
                by fury at the heart.
                        Zeus,
yours is the power, Zeus, what man on earth
can override it, who can hold it back?
Power that neither Sleep, the all-ensnaring   680
    no, nor the tireless months of heaven
can ever overmaster—young through all time,
mighty lord of power, you hold fast
    the dazzling crystal mansions of Olympus.
And throughout the future, late and soon   685
as through the past, your law prevails:
no towering form of greatness
    enters into the lives of mortals
        free and clear of ruin.
                      True,
our dreams, our high hopes voyaging far and wide   690
bring sheer delight to many, to many others
    delusion, blithe, mindless lusts
and the fraud steals on one slowly . . . unaware
till he trips and puts his foot into the fire.
    He was a wise old man who coined   695
the famous saying: "Sooner or later
foul is fair, fair is foul
to the man the gods will ruin"—
    He goes his way for a moment only
        free of blinding ruin.   700
    [*Enter* HAEMON *from the palace.*]
    Here's Haemon now, the last of all your sons.
    Does he come in tears for his bride,
    his doomed bride, Antigone—
    bitter at being cheated of their marriage?
CREON We'll soon know, better than seer could tell us.   705
    [*Turning to* HAEMON.]
Son, you've heard the final verdict on your bride?

Are you coming now, raving against your father?
Or do you love me, no matter what I do?
HAEMON   Father, I'm your *son* . . . you in your wisdom
set my bearings for me—I obey you.   710
No marriage could ever mean more to me than you,
whatever good direction you may offer.
CREON   Fine, Haemon.
That's how you ought to feel within your heart,
subordinate to your father's will in every way.
That's what a man prays for: to produce good sons—   715
a household full of them, dutiful and attentive,
so they can pay his enemy back with interest
and match the respect their father shows his friend.
But the man who rears a brood of useless children,
what has he brought into the world, I ask you?   720
Nothing but trouble for himself, and mockery
from his enemies laughing in his face.
                                    Oh Haemon,
never lose your sense of judgment over a woman.
The warmth, the rush of pleasure, it all goes cold
in your arms, I warn you . . . a worthless woman   725
in your house, a misery in your bed.
What wound cuts deeper than a loved one
turned against you? Spit her out,
like a mortal enemy—let the girl go.
Let her find a husband down among the dead.   730
Imagine it: I caught her in naked rebellion,
the traitor, the only one in the whole city.
I'm not about to prove myself a liar,
not to my people, no, I'm going to kill her!
That's right—so let her cry for mercy, sing her hymns   735
to Zeus who defends all bonds of kindred blood.
Why, if I bring up my own kin to be rebels,
think what I'd suffer from the world at large.
Show me the man who rules his household well:
I'll show you someone fit to rule the state.   740
That good man, my son,
I have every confidence he and he alone
can give commands and take them too. Staunch
in the storm of spears he'll stand his ground,
a loyal, unflinching comrade at your side.   745

But whoever steps out of line, violates the laws
or presumes to hand out orders to his superiors,
he'll win no praise from me. But that man
the city places in authority, his orders
must be obeyed, large and small,   750
right and wrong.
                    Anarchy—
show me a greater crime in all the earth!

She, she destroys cities, rips up houses,
breaks the ranks of spearmen into headlong rout.
But the ones who last it out, the great mass of them   755
owe their lives to discipline. Therefore
we must defend the men who live by law,
never let some woman triumph over us.
Better to fall from power, if fall we must,
at the hands of a man—never be rated   760
inferior to a woman, never.

LEADER   To us,
    unless old age has robbed us of our wits,
    you seem to say what you have to say with sense.

HAEMON   Father, only the gods endow a man with reason,
    the finest of all their gifts, a treasure.   765
    Far be it from me—I haven't the skill,
    and certainly no desire, to tell you when,
    if ever, you make a slip in speech . . . though
    someone else might have a good suggestion.

    Of course it's not for you,   770
    in the normal run of things, to watch
    whatever men say or do, or find to criticize.
    The man in the street, you know, dreads your glance,
    he'd never say anything displeasing to your face.
    But it's for me to catch the murmurs in the dark,   775
    the way the city mourns for this young girl.
    "No woman," they say, "ever deserved death less,
    and such a brutal death for such a glorious action.
    She, with her own dear brother lying in his blood—
    she couldn't bear to leave him dead, unburied,   780
    food for the wild dogs or wheeling vultures.
    Death? She deserves a glowing crown of gold!"
    So they say, and the rumor spreads in secret,
    darkly . . .
                    I rejoice in your success, father—
    nothing more precious to me in the world.   785
    What medal of honor brighter to his children
    than a father's glowing glory? Or a child's
    to his proud father? Now don't, please,
    be quite so single-minded, self-involved,
    or assume the world is wrong and you are right.   790
    Whoever thinks that he alone possesses intelligence,
    the gift of eloquence, he and no one else,
    and character too . . . such men, I tell you,
    spread them open—you will find them empty.
                                             No,
    it's no disgrace for a man, even a wise man,   795
    to learn many things and not to be too rigid.
    You've seen trees by a raging winter torrent,
    how many sway with the flood and salvage every twig,

but not the stubborn—they're ripped out, roots and all.
Bend or break. The same when a man is sailing: 800
haul your sheets too taut, never give an inch,
you'll capsize, and go the rest of the voyage
keel up and the rowing-benches under.

Oh give way. Relax your anger—change!
I'm young, I know, but let me offer this: 805
it would be best by far, I admit,
if a man were born infallible, right by nature.
If not—and things don't often go that way,
it's best to learn from those with good advice.
LEADER   You'd do well, my lord, if he's speaking to the point,   810
to learn from him,
        [*Turning to* HAEMON.]
                    and you, my boy, from him.
You both are talking sense.
CREON   So,
men our age, we're to be lectured, are we?—
schooled by a boy his age?
HAEMON   Only in what is right. But if I seem young,   815
look less to my years and more to what I do.
CREON   Do? Is admiring rebels an achievement?
HAEMON   I'd never suggest that you admire treason.
CREON   Oh?—
isn't that just the sickness that's attacked her?
HAEMON   The whole city of Thebes denies it, to a man.   820
CREON   And is Thebes about to tell me how to rule?
HAEMON   Now, you see? Who's talking like a child?
CREON   Am I to rule this land for others—or myself?
HAEMON   It's no city at all, owned by one man alone.
CREON   What? The city *is* the king's—that's the law!   825
HAEMON   What a splendid king you'd make of a desert island—
you and you alone.
CREON [*To the* CHORUS.]   This boy, I do believe,
is fighting on her side, the woman's side.
HAEMON   If you are a woman, yes—
my concern is all for you.   830
CREON   Why, you degenerate—bandying accusations,
threatening me with justice, your own father!
HAEMON   I see my father offending justice—wrong.
CREON   Wrong?
To protect my royal rights?
HAEMON   Protect your rights?   835
When you trample down the honors of the gods?
CREON   You, you soul of corruption, rotten through—
woman's accomplice!
HAEMON   That may be,
but you'll never find me accomplice to a criminal.

CREON   That's what *she* is,   840
   and every word you say is a blatant appeal for her—
HAEMON   And you, and me, and the gods beneath the earth.
CREON   You will never marry her, not while she's alive.
HAEMON   Then she'll die . . . but her death will kill another.
CREON   What, brazen threats? You go too far!
HAEMON   What threat?   845
   Combating your empty, mindless judgments with a word?
CREON   You'll suffer for your sermons, you and your empty wisdom!
HAEMON   If you weren't my father, I'd say you were insane.
CREON   Don't flatter me with Father—you woman's slave!
HAEMON   You really expect to fling abuse at me   850
   and not receive the same?
CREON   Is that so!
   Now, by heaven, I promise you, you'll pay—
   taunting, insulting me! Bring her out,
   that hateful—she'll die now, here,
   in front of his eyes, beside her groom!   855
HAEMON   No, no, she will never die beside me—
   don't delude yourself. And you will never
   see me, never set eyes on my face again.
   Rage your heart out, rage with friends
   who can stand the sight of you.   860
        [*Rushing out.*]
LEADER   Gone, my king, in a burst of anger.
   A temper young as his . . . hurt him once,
   he may do something violent.
CREON   Let him do—
   dream up something desperate, past all human limit!
   Good riddance. Rest assured,   865
   he'll never save those two young girls from death.
LEADER   Both of them, you really intend to kill them both?
CREON   No, not her, the one whose hands are clean—
   you're quite right.
LEADER   But Antigone—
   what sort of death do you have in mind for her?   870
CREON   I'll take her down some wild, desolate path
   never trod by men, and wall her up alive
   in a rocky vault, and set out short rations,
   just the measure piety demands
   to keep the entire city free of defilement.[8]   875
   There let her pray to the one god she worships:
   Death—who knows?—may just reprieve her from death.
   Or she may learn at last, better late than never,
   what a waste of breath it is to worship Death.

---

8. The penalty originally proclaimed was death by stoning. But this demands the participation of the citizens, and it may be that Creon, after listening to Haemon's remarks, is not as sure as he once was of popular support. Creon proposed imprisonment in a tomb with a ration of food. Since Antigone would die of starvation but not actually by anyone's hand, Creon seems to think that the city will not be "defiled," that is, will not incur blood guilt.

[*Exit to the palace.*]

CHORUS   Love, never conquered in battle   880
  Love the plunderer laying waste the rich!
  Love standing the night-watch
    guarding a girl's soft cheek,
  you range the seas, the shepherds' steadings off in the wilds—
  not even the deathless gods can flee your onset,   885
  nothing human born for a day—
  whoever feels your grip is driven mad.
                    Love!—
  you wrench the minds of the righteous into outrage,
  swerve them to their ruin—you have ignited this,
  this kindred strife, father and son at war   890
    and Love alone the victor—
  warm glance of the bride triumphant, burning with desire!
  Throned in power, side-by-side with the mighty laws!
  Irresistible Aphrodite,[9] never conquered—
  Love, you mock us for your sport.   895

    [ANTIGONE *is brought from the palace under guard.*]

    But now, even I'd rebel against the king,
    I'd break all bounds when I see this—
    I fill with tears, I cannot hold them back,
    not any more . . . I see Antigone make her way
    to the bridal vault where all are laid to rest.   900

ANTIGONE   Look at me, men of my fatherland,
  setting out on the last road
  looking into the last light of day
  the last I'll ever see . . .
  the god of death who puts us all to bed   905
  takes me down to the banks of Acheron[1] alive—
    denied my part in the wedding-songs,
  no wedding-song in the dusk has crowned my marriage—
  I go to wed the lord of the dark waters.

CHORUS   Not crowned with glory,[2] or with a dirge,   910
  you leave for the deep pit of the dead.
  No withering illness laid you low,
  no strokes of the sword—a law to yourself,
  alone, no mortal like you, ever, you go down
  to the halls of Death alive and breathing.   915

ANTIGONE   But think of Niobe[3]—well I know her story—
  think what a living death she died,

9. Goddess of sexual love.   1. A river in the underworld.   2. The usual version of this line is "crowned with glory." The Greek word *oukoun* can be negative or positive, depending on the accent, which determines the pronunciation; because written accents were not yet in use in Sophocles' time, no one will ever know for sure which meaning he intended. The present version is based on the belief that the chorus is expressing pity for Antigone's ignominious and abnormal death; she has no funeral at which her fame and praise are recited; she will not die by either of the usual causes—violence and disease—but by a living death. It is, as they say, her own choice: she is "a law to [herself]" (line 913).   3. A Phrygian princess married to Amphion, king of Thebes. She boasted that she had borne more children than Leto, mother of Apollo and Artemis. As vengeance, Apollo and Artemis killed all of Niobe's children. She fled to Phrygia, where she was turned into a rock on Mount Sipylus; the melting of the snow on the mountain caused "tears" to flow down the rock formation, which resembles a woman's face. See *Iliad* 24.651–69.

Tantalus' daughter, stranger queen from the east:
there on the mountain heights, growing stone
binding as ivy, slowly walled her round   920
and the rains will never cease, the legends say
the snows will never leave her . . .
   wasting away, under her brows the tears
showering down her breasting ridge and slopes—
a rocky death like hers puts me to sleep.   925
CHORUS   But she was a god, born of gods,
       and we are only mortals born to die.
       And yet, of course, it's a great thing
       for a dying girl to hear, just to hear
       she shares a destiny equal to the gods,   930
       during life and later, once she's dead.
ANTIGONE   O you mock me!
Why, in the name of all my fathers' gods
   why can't you wait till I am gone—
     must you abuse me to my face?
O my city, all your fine rich sons!   935
And you, you springs of the Dirce,
holy grove of Thebes where the chariots gather,
   you at least, you'll bear me witness, look,
unmourned by friend and forced by such crude laws
I go to my rockbound prison, strange new tomb—   940
   always a stranger, O dear god,
   I have no home on earth and none below,
     not with the living, not with the breathless dead.
CHORUS   You went too far, the last limits of daring—
     smashing against the high throne of Justice!   945
     Your life's in ruins, child—I wonder . . .
     do you pay for your father's terrible ordeal?
ANTIGONE   There—at last you've touched it, the worst pain
   the worst anguish! Raking up the grief for father
     three times over, for all the doom   950
that's struck us down, the brilliant house of Laius.
O mother, your marriage-bed
   the coiling horrors, the coupling there—
   you with your own son, my father—doomstruck mother!
Such, such were my parents, and I their wretched child.   955
I go to them now, cursed, unwed, to share their home—
   I am a stranger! O dear brother, doomed
   in your marriage—your marriage murders mine,[4]
     your dying drags me down to death alive!
     [*Enter* creon.]
CHORUS   Reverence asks some reverence in return—   960
   but attacks on power never go unchecked,
     not by the man who holds the reins of power.

---

4. Polynices had married the daughter of Adrastus of Argos, to seal the alliance that enabled him to march
against Thebes.

Your own blind will, your passion has destroyed you.

ANTIGONE   No one to weep for me, my friends,
no wedding-song—they take me away   965
in all my pain . . . the road lies open, waiting.
Never again, the law forbids me to see
the sacred eye of day. I am agony!
No tears for the destiny that's mine,
no loved one mourns my death.

CREON   Can't you see?   970
If a man could wail his own dirge *before* he dies,
he'd never finish.

         [*To the guards.*]

                        Take her away, quickly!
Wall her up in the tomb, you have your orders.
Abandon her there, alone, and let her choose—
death or a buried life with a good roof for shelter.   975
As for myself, my hands are clean. This young girl—
dead or alive, she will be stripped of her rights,
her stranger's rights,[5] here in the world above.

ANTIGONE   O tomb, my bridal-bed—my house, my prison
cut in the hollow rock, my everlasting watch!   980
I'll soon be there, soon embrace my own,
the great growing family of our dead
Persephone[6] has received among her ghosts.

                                              I,
the last of them all, the most reviled by far,
go down before my destined time's run out.   985
But still I go, cherishing one good hope:
my arrival may be dear to father,
dear to you, my mother,
dear to you, my loving brother, Eteocles—
When you died I washed you with my hands,   990
I dressed you all, I poured the sacred cups
across your tombs. But now, Polynices,
because I laid your body out as well,
this, this is my reward. Nevertheless
I honored you—the decent will admit it—   995
well and wisely too.

                        Never, I tell you,
if I had been the mother of children
or if my husband died, exposed and rotting—
I'd never have taken this ordeal upon myself,
never defied our people's will. What law,   1000
you ask, do I satisfy with what I say?
A husband dead, there might have been another.
A child by another too, if I had lost the first.
But mother and father both lost in the halls of Death,

---

5. The Greek words suggest that he sees her not as a citizen but as a resident alien; by her action she has forfeited citizenship. But now she will be deprived even of that inferior status.   6. Queen of the underworld.

no brother could ever spring to light again.[7]   1005
For this law alone I held you first in honor.
For this, Creon, the king, judges me a criminal
guilty of dreadful outrage, my dear brother!
And now he leads me off, a captive in his hands,
with no part in the bridal-song, the bridal-bed,   1010
denied all joy of marriage, raising childen—
deserted so by loved ones, struck by fate,
I descend alive to the caverns of the dead.

What law of the mighty gods have I transgressed?
Why look to the heavens any more, tormented as I am?   1015
Whom to call, what comrades now? Just think,
my reverence only brands me for irreverence!
Very well: if this is the pleasure of the gods,
once I suffer I will know that I was wrong.
But if these men are wrong, let them suffer   1020
nothing worse than they mete out to me—
these masters of injustice!
LEADER   Still the same rough winds, the wild passion
raging through the girl.
CREON [To the guards.]   Take her away.
You're wasting time—you'll pay for it too.   1025
ANTIGONE   Oh god, the voice of death. Its come, it's here.
CREON   True. Not a word of hope—your doom is sealed.
ANTIGONE   Land of Thebes, city of all my fathers—
O you gods, the first gods of the race![8]
They drag me away, now, no more delay.   1030
Look on me, you noble sons of Thebes—
the last of a great line of kings,
I alone, see what I suffer now
at the hands of what breed of men—
all for reverence, my reverence for the gods!   1035
          [She leaves under guard: the CHORUS gathers.]
CHORUS   Danaë,[9] Danaë—
even she endured a fate like yours,
    in all her lovely strength she traded
the light of day for the bolted brazen vault—
buried within her tomb, her bridal-chamber,   1040
wed to the yoke and broken.
    But she was of glorious birth
        my child, my child

7. This strange justification for her action has been considered unacceptable by many critics, and they
have suspected that it was an interpolation by some later producer of the play. But Aristotle quotes it in
the next century and appears to have no doubt of its authenticity. If genuine, it means that Antigone
momentarily abandons the law she championed against Creon—that all people have a right to burial—and
sees her motive as exclusive devotion to her dead brother. For someone facing the prospect of a slow and
hideous death such a self-examination and realization is not impossible. And it makes no difference to the
courage and tenacity of her defiance of state power.   8. The Theban royal house traced its ancestry
through Harmonia, wife of Cadmus, to Aphrodite and Ares, her parents. Cadmus's daughter was Semele.
9. Daughter of Acrisius, king of Argos. It was prophesied that he would be killed by his daughter's son; so
he shut her up in a bronze tower. But Zeus came to her in the form of a golden rain shower and she bore
a son, Perseus, who did in the end accidentally kill his grandfather.

and treasured the seed of Zeus within her womb,
the cloudburst streaming gold!   1045
   The power of fate is a wonder,
   dark, terrible wonder—
   neither wealth nor armies
   towered walls nor ships
   black hulls lashed by the salt   1050
   can save us from that force.

The yoke tamed him too
   young Lycurgus flaming in anger
king of Edonia,[1] all for his mad taunts
Dionysus clamped him down, encased   1055
in the chain-mail of rock
   and there his rage
   his terrible flowering rage burst—
sobbing, dying away . . . at last that madman
came to know his god—   1060
   the power he mocked, the power
   he taunted in all his frenzy
   trying to stamp out
   the women strong with the god—
   the torch, the raving sacred cries—   1065
   enraging the Muses who adore the flute.

And far north[2] where the Black Rocks
   cut the sea in half
and murderous straits
split the coast of Thrace   1070
   a forbidding city stands
where once, hard by the walls
the savage Ares thrilled to watch
a king's new queen, a Fury rearing in rage
   against his two royal sons—   1075
     her bloody hands, her dagger-shuttle
stabbing out their eyes—cursed, blinding wounds—
their eyes blind sockets screaming for revenge!

They wailed in agony cries echoing cries
   the princes doomed at birth . . .   1080
and their mother doomed to chains,
walled up in a tomb of stone[3]—

1. Thrace. Lycurgus opposed the introduction of Dionysiac religion into his kingdom and was imprisoned by the god.   2. The whole story is difficult to follow, and its application to the case of Antigone is obscure. Cleopatra, the daughter of the Athenian princess Orithyia (whom Boreas, the North Wind, carried off to his home in Thrace), was married to Phineus, the Thracian king, and bore him two sons. He tired of her, abandoned her, and married Eidothea ("a king's new queen," line 1074), who put out the eyes of Cleopatra's two sons. Ares watched the savage act.   3. Lines 1081–82 have no equivalent in the Greek text. They represent a belief that Sophocles' audience knew a version of the legend in which Cleopatra was imprisoned in a stone tomb (which is found in a later source). This would give a point of comparison to Antigone as did the imprisonment of Danaë and Lycurgus.—

but she traced her own birth back
to a proud Athenian line and the high gods
and off in caverns half the world away,   1085
born of the wild North Wind
  she sprang on her father's gales,
   racing stallions up the leaping cliffs—
child of the heavens. But even on her the Fates
the gray everlasting Fates rode hard   1090
my child, my child.
   [*Enter* tiresias, *the blind prophet, led by a boy.*]
TIRESIAS   Lord of Thebes,
 I and the boy have come together,
 hand in hand. Two see with the eyes of one . . .
 so the blind must go, with a guide to lead the way.
CREON What is it, old Tiresias? What news now?
TIRESIAS I will teach you. And you obey the seer.
CREON   I will,   1095
 I've never wavered from your advice before.
TIRESIAS And so you kept the city straight on course.
CREON I owe you a great deal, I swear to that.
TIRESIAS Then reflect, my son: you are poised,   1100
 once more, on the razor-edge of fate.
CREON What is it? I shudder to hear you.
TIRESIAS   You will learn
 when you listen to the warnings of my craft.
 As I sat on the ancient seat of augury,
 in the sanctuary where every bird I know   1105
 will hover at my hands[4]—suddenly I hear it,
 a strange voice in the wingbeats, unintelligible,
 barbaric, a mad scream! Talons flashing, ripping,
 they were killing each other—that much I knew—
 the murderous fury whirring in those wings   1110
 made that much clear!
       I was afraid,
 I turned quickly, tasted the burnt-sacrifice,
 ignited the altar at all points—but no fire,
 the god in the fire never blazed.
 Not from those offerings . . . over the embers   1115
 slid a heavy ooze from the long thighbones,
 smoking, sputtering out, and the bladder
 puffed and burst—spraying gall into the air—
 and the fat wrapping the bones slithered off
 and left them glistening white. No fire!   1120
 The rites failed that might have blazed the future
 with a sign. So I learned from the boy here:
 he is my guide, as I am guide to others.
        And it is you—
 your high resolve that sets this plague on Thebes.

---

4. A place where the birds gathered and Tiresias waited for omens.

The public altars and sacred hearths are fouled,   1125
one and all, by the birds and dogs with carrion
torn from the corpse, the doomstruck son of Oedipus!
and so the gods are deaf to our prayers, they spurn
the offerings in our hands, the flame of holy flesh.
No birds cry out an omen clear and true—   1130
they're gorged with the murdered victim's blood and fat.
Take these things to heart, my son, I warn you.
All men make mistakes, it is only human.
But once the wrong is done, a man
can turn his back on folly, misfortune too,   1135
if he tries to make amends, however low he's fallen,
and stops his bullnecked ways. Stubbornness
brands you for stupidity—pride is a crime.
No, yield to the dead!
Never stab the fighter when he's down.   1140

Where's the glory, killing the dead twice over?
I mean you well. I give you sound advice.
It's best to learn from a good adviser
when he speaks for your own good:
it's pure gain.
CREON   Old man—all of you! So,   1145
you shoot your arrows at my head like archers at the target—
I even have *him* loosed on me, this fortune-teller.
Oh his ilk has tried to sell me short
and ship me off for years. Well,
drive your bargains, traffic—much as you like—   1150
in the gold of India, silver-gold of Sardis.[5]
You'll never bury that body in the grave,
not even if Zeus' eagles rip the corpse
and wing their rotten pickings off to the throne of god!
Never, not even in fear of such defilement   1155
will I tolerate his burial, that traitor.
Well I know, we can't defile the gods—
no mortal has the power.
                        No,
reverend old Tiresias, all men fall,
it's only human, but the wisest fall obscenely   1160
when they glorify obscene advice with rhetoric—
all for their own gain.
TIRESIAS   Oh god, is there a man alive
who knows, who actually believes . . .
CREON   What now?
What earth-shattering truth are you about to utter?   1165
TIRESIAS   . . . just how much a sense of judgment, wisdom
is the greatest gift we have?
CREON   Just as much, I'd say,

---

5. In Asia Minor. Electrum, a natural alloy of gold and silver, was found in a nearby river.

as a twisted mind is the worst affliction known.
TIRESIAS   You are the one who's sick, Creon, sick to death.
CREON   I am in no mood to trade insults with a seer.   1170
TIRESIAS   You have already, calling my prophecies a lie.
CREON   Why not?
You and the whole breed of seers are mad for money!
TIRESIAS   And the whole race of tyrants lusts for filthy gain.
CREON   This slander of yours—
are you aware you're speaking to the king?   1175
TIRESIAS   Well aware. Who helped you save the city?
CREON   You—
you have your skills, old seer, but you lust for injustice!
TIRESIAS   You will drive me to utter the dreadful secret in my heart.
CREON   Spit it out! Just don't speak it out for profit.
TIRESIAS   Profit? No, not a bit of profit, not for you.   1180
CREON   Know full well, you'll never buy off my resolve.
TIRESIAS   Then know this too, learn this by heart!
The chariot of the sun will not race through
so many circuits more, before you have surrendered
one born of your own loins, your own flesh and blood,   1185
a corpse for corpses given in return, since you have thrust
to the world below a child sprung for the world above,
ruthlessly lodged a living soul within the grave—
then you've robbed the gods below the earth,
keeping a dead body here in the bright air,   1190
unburied, unsung, unhallowed by the rites.

You, you have no business with the dead,
nor do the gods above—this is violence
you have forced upon the heavens.
And so the avengers, the dark destroyers late   1195
but true to the mark, now lie in wait for you,
the Furies sent by the gods and the god of death
to strike you down with the pains that you perfected!

There. Reflect on that, tell me I've been bribed.
The day comes soon, no long test of time, not now,   1200
when the mourning cries for men and women break
throughout your halls. Great hatred rises against you—
cities in tumult, all whose mutilated sons
the dogs have graced with burial, or the wild beasts
or a wheeling crow that wings the ungodly stench of carrion   1205
back to each city, each warrior's hearth and home.

These arrows for your heart! Since you've raked me
I loose them like an archer in my anger,
arrows deadly true. You'll never escape
their burning, searing force.   1210
    [Motioning to his escort.]
Come, boy, take me home.

So he can vent his rage on younger men,
and learn to keep a gentler tongue in his head
and better sense than what he carries now.
    [*Exit to the side.*]
LEADER   The old man's gone, my king—   1215
terrible prophecies. Well I know,
since the hair on this old head went gray,
he's never lied to Thebes.
CREON   I know it myself—I'm shaken, torn.
It's a dreadful thing to yield . . . but resist now?   1220
Lay my pride bare to the blows of ruin?
That's dreadful too.
LEADER   But good advice,
Creon, take it now, you must.
CREON   What should I do? Tell me . . . I'll obey.
LEADER   Go! Free the girl from the rocky vault   1225
and raise a mound for the body you exposed.
CREON   That's your advice? You think I should give in?
LEADER   Yes, my king, quickly. Disasters sent by the gods
cut short our follies in a flash.
CREON   Oh it's hard,
giving up the heart's desire . . . but I will do it—   1230
no more fighting a losing battle with necessity.
LEADER   Do it now, go, don't leave it to others.
CREON   Now—I'm on my way! Come, each of you,
take up axes, make for the high ground,
over there, quickly! I and my better judgment   1235
have come round to this—I shackled her,
I'll set her free myself. I am afraid . . .
it's best to keep the established laws
to the very day we die.
    [*Rushing out, followed by his entourage. The* CHORUS *clusters around
    the altar.*]
CHORUS   God of a hundred names!
                           Great Dionysus—   1240
    Son and glory of Semele! Pride of Thebes—
Child of Zeus whose thunder rocks the clouds—
Lord of the famous lands of evening—
King of the Mysteries!
                  King of Eleusis, Demeter's[6] plain
her breasting hills that welcome in the world—   1245
Great Dionysus!
              Bacchus, living in Thebes
the mother-city of all your frenzied women—
                         Bacchus
living along the Ismenus'[7] rippling waters
standing over the field sown with the Dragon's teeth!

---

6. The grain and harvest goddess. Eleusis, the site of the mysteries and the worship of Demeter, is near
Athens.   7. A river at Thebes. Dionysus (or Bacchus) was among the divinities worshipped by the initiates.

You—we have seen you through the flaring smoky fires,   1250
   your torches blazing over the twin peaks[8]
where nymphs of the hallowed cave climb onward
      fired with you, your sacred rage—
we have seen you at Castalia's running spring
and down from the heights of Nysa[9] crowned with ivy   1255
the greening shore rioting vines and grapes
   down you come in your storm of wild women
      ecstatic, mystic cries—
                Dionysus—
down to watch and ward the roads of Thebes!

First of all cities, Thebes you honor first   1260
you and your mother, bride of the lightning—
come, Dionysus! now your people lie
in the iron grip of plague,
come in your racing, healing stride
      down Parnassus'[1] slopes   1265
or across the moaning straits.
            Lord of the dancing—
dance, dance the constellations breathing fire!
Great master of the voices of the night!
Child of Zeus, God's offspring, come, come forth!
Lord, king, dance with your nymphs, swirling, raving   1270
arm-in-arm in frenzy through the night
   they dance you, Iacchus[2]—
           Dance, Dionysus
giver of all good things!
   [*Enter a* MESSENGER *from the side.*]
MESSENGER   Neighbors,
friends of the house of Cadmus and the kings,
there's not a thing in this mortal life of ours   1275
I'd praise or blame as settled once for all.
Fortune lifts and Fortune fells the lucky
and unlucky every day. No prophet on earth
can tell a man his fate. Take Creon:
there was a man to rouse your envy once,   1280
as I see it. He saved the realm from enemies,
taking power, he alone, the lord of the fatherland,
he set us true on course—he flourished like a tree
with the noble line of sons he bred and reared . . .
and now it's lost, all gone.
              Believe me,   1285
when a man has squandered his true joys,
he's good as dead, I tell you, a living corpse.

---

8. The two cliffs above Delphi, where Dionysus was thought to reside in the winter months.   9. A mountain associated with Dionysiac worship; several mountains are so named, but the reference here is probably to the one on the island of Euboea, off the Attic coast.   1. Mountain in central Greece just north of the Gulf of Corinth; an important cult of Dionysus was located there, as was Apollo's oracle at Delphi.   2. Dionysus.

Pile up riches in your house, as much as you like—
live like a king with a huge show of pomp,
but if real delight is missing from the lot,   1290
I wouldn't give you a wisp of smoke for it,
not compared with joy.

LEADER   What now?
What new grief do you bring the house of kings?

MESSENGER   Dead, dead—and the living are guilty of their death!

LEADER   Who's the murderer? Who is dead? Tell us.   1295

MESSENGER   Haemon's gone, his blood spilled by the very hand—

LEADER   His father's or his own?

MESSENGER   His own . . .
raging mad with his father for the death—

LEADER   Oh great seer,
you saw it all, you brought your word to birth!

MESSENGER   Those are the facts. Deal with them as you will.   1300

[As he turns to go, EURYDICE enters from the palace.]

LEADER   Look, Eurydice. Poor woman, Creon's wife,
so close at hand. By chance perhaps,
unless she's heard the news about her son.

EURYDICE   My countrymen,
all of you—I caught the sound of your words
as I was leaving to do my part,   1305
to appeal to queen Athena with my prayers.
I was just loosing the bolts, opening the doors,
when a voice filled with sorrow, family sorrow,
struck my ears, and I fell back, terrified,
into the women's arms—everything went black.   1310
Tell me the news, again, whatever it is . . .
sorrow and I are hardly strangers.
I can bear the worst.

MESSENGER   I—dear lady,
I'll speak as an eye-witness. I was there.
And I won't pass over one word of the truth.   1315
Why should I try to soothe you with a story,
only to prove a liar in a moment?
Truth is always best.

                              So,
I escorted your lord, I guided him
to the edge of the plain where the body lay,   1320
Polynices, torn by the dogs and still unmourned.
And saying a prayer to Hecate of the Crossroads,
Pluto[3] too, to hold their anger and be kind,
we washed the dead in a bath of holy water
and plucking some fresh branches, gathering . . .   1325
what was left of him, we burned them all together
and raised a high mound of native earth, and then

---

3. Or Hades, god of the underworld. Hecate is a goddess associated with darkness and burial grounds; offerings to her were left at crossroads.

we turned and made for that rocky vault of hers,
the hollow, empty bed of the bride of Death.
And far off one of us heard a voice,   1330
a long wail rising, echoing
out of that unhallowed wedding-chamber,
he ran to alert the master and Creon pressed on,
closer—the strange, inscrutable cry came sharper,
throbbing around him now, and he let loose   1335
a cry of his own, enough to wrench the heart,
"Oh god, am I the prophet now? going down
the darkest road I've ever gone? My son—
it's *his* dear voice, he greets me! Go, men,
closer, quickly! Go through the gap,   1340
the rocks are dragged back—
right to the tomb's very mouth—and look,
see if it's Haemon's voice I think I hear,
or the gods have robbed me of my senses."

The king was shattered. We took his orders,   1345
went and searched, and there in the deepest,
dark recesses of the tomb we found her . . .
hanged by the neck in a fine linen noose,
strangled in her veils—and the boy,
his arms flung around her waist,   1350
clinging to her, wailing for his bride,
dead and down below, for his father's crimes
and the bed of his marriage blighted by misfortune.
When Creon saw him, he gave a deep sob,
he ran in, shouting, crying out to him,   1355
"Oh my child—what have you done? what seized you,
what insanity? what disaster drove you mad?
Come out, my son! I beg you on my knees!"
But the boy gave him a wild burning glance,
spat in his face, not a word in reply,   1360
he drew his sword—his father rushed out,
running as Haemon lunged and missed!—
and then, doomed, desperate with himself,
suddenly leaning his full weight on the blade,
he buried it in his body, halfway to the hilt.   1365
And still in his senses, pouring his arms around her,
he embraced the girl and breathing hard,
released a quick rush of blood,
bright red on her cheek glistening white.
And there he lies, body enfolding body . . .   1370
he has won his bride at last, poor boy,
not here but in the houses of the dead.

Creon shows the world that of all the ills
afflicting men the worst is lack of judgment.

[EURYDICE *turns and reenters the palace.*]

LEADER   What do you make of that? The lady's gone,   1375
   without a word, good or bad.

MESSENGER   I'm alarmed too
   but here's my hope—faced with her son's death
   she finds it unbecoming to mourn in public.
   Inside, under her roof, she'll set her women
   to the task and wail the sorrow of the house.   1380
   She's too discreet. She won't do something rash.

LEADER   I'm not so sure. To me, at least,
   a long heavy silence promises danger,
   just as much as a lot of empty outcries.

MESSENGER   We'll see if she's holding something back,   1385
   hiding some passion in her heart.
   I'm going in. You may be right—who knows?
   Even too much silence has its dangers.

     [*Exit to the palace. Enter* CREON *from the side, escorted by attendants
     carrying* HAEMON's *body on a bier.*]

LEADER   The king himself! Coming toward us,
   look, holding the boy's head in his hands.   1390
   Clear, damning proof, if it's right to say so—
   proof of his own madness, no one else's,
     no, his own blind wrongs.

CREON   Ohhh,
   so senseless, so insane . . . my crimes,
   my stubborn, deadly—   1395
   Look at us, the killer, the killed,
   father and son, the same blood—the misery!
   My plans, my mad fanatic heart,
   my son, cut off so young!
   Ai, dead, lost to the world,   1400
   not through your stupidity, no, my own.

LEADER   Too late,
   too late, you see what justice means.

CREON   Oh I've learned
   through blood and tears! Then, it was then,
   when the god came down and struck me—a great weight
   shattering, driving me down that wild savage path,   1405
   ruining, trampling down my joy. Oh the agony,
     the heartbreaking agonies of our lives.

     [*Enter the* MESSENGER *from the palace.*]

MESSENGER   Master,
   what a hoard of grief you have, and you'll have more.
   The grief that lies to hand you've brought yourself—

     [*Pointing to* HAEMON's *body.*]

   the rest, in the house, you'll see it all too soon.   1410

CREON   What now? What's worse than this?

MESSENGER   The queen is dead.
   The mother of this dead boy . . . mother to the end—
   poor thing, her wounds are fresh.

CREON   No, no,

harbor of Death, so choked, so hard to cleanse!—
why me? why are you killing me?   1415
Herald of pain, more words, more grief?
I died once, you kill me again and again!
What's the report, boy . . . some news for me?
My wife dead? O dear god!
Slaughter heaped on slaughter?
　　　　[*The doors open; the body of* EURYDICE *is brought out on her bier.*]
MESSENGER　　　　　　　　　　See for yourself: 1420
now they bring her body from the palace.
CREON　　　　　　　　　　　　　　　　Oh no,
another, a second loss to break the heart.
What next, what fate still waits for me?
I just held my son in my arms and now,
look, a new corpse rising before my eyes—   1425
wretched, helpless mother—O my son!
MESSENGER　　She stabbed herself at the altar,
then her eyes went dark, after she'd raised
a cry for the noble fate of Megareus,[4] the hero
killed in the first assault, then for Haemon,   1430
then with her dying breath she called down
torments on your head—you killed her sons.
CREON　　　　　　　　　　　　　　Oh the dread,
I shudder with dread! Why not kill me too?—
run me through with a good sharp sword?
Oh god, the misery, anguish—   1435
I, I'm churning with it, going under.
MESSENGER　　Yes, and the dead, the woman lying there,
piles the guilt of all their deaths on you.
CREON　　How did she end her life, what bloody stroke?
MESSENGER　　She drove home to the heart with her own hand,   1440
once she learned her son was dead . . . that agony.
CREON　　And the guilt is all mine—
can never be fixed on another man,
no escape for me. I killed you,
I, god help me, I admit it all!   1445
　　　　[*To his attendants.*]
Take me away, quickly, out of sight.
I don't even exist—I'm no one. Nothing.
LEADER　　Good advice, if there's any good in suffering.
Quickest is best when troubles block the way.
CREON　　[*Kneeling in prayer.*]
Come, let it come—that best of fates for me   1450
that brings the final day, best fate of all.
Oh quickly, now—
so I never have to see another sunrise.
LEADER　　That will come when it comes;

---

4. Another son of Creon and Eurydice; he was killed during the siege of the city. Tiresias had prophesied that his death would save Thebes.

we must deal with all that lies before us.   1455
The future rests with the ones who tend the future.
CREON   That prayer—I poured my heart into that prayer!
LEADER   No more prayers now. For mortal men
there is no escape from the doom we must endure.
CREON   Take me away, I beg you, out of sight.   1460
A rash, indiscriminate fool!
I murdered you, my son, against my will—
you too, my wife . . .
                    Wailing wreck of a man,
whom to look to? where to lean for support?
[Desperately turning from HAEMON to EURYDICE on their biers.]
Whatever I touch goes wrong—once more   1465
a crushing fate's come down upon my head!
[The MESSENGER and attendants lead CREON into the palace.]
CHORUS   Wisdom is by far the greatest part of joy,
and reverence toward the gods must be safeguarded.
The mighty words of the proud are paid in full
with mighty blows of fate, and at long last   1470
those blows will teach us wisdom.
[The old citizens exit to the side.]

EURIPIDES
480–406 B.C.E.

Euripides' *Medea*, produced in 431 B.C.E., the year that brought the beginning of the Peloponnesian War, appeared earlier than Sophocles' *Oedipus the King*, but it has a bitterness that is more in keeping with the spirit of a later age. If *Oedipus* is, in one sense, a warning to a generation that has embarked on an intellectual revolution, *Medea* is the ironic expression of the disillusion that comes after the shipwreck. In this play we are conscious for the first time of an attitude characteristic of modern literature, the artist's feeling of separation from the audience, the isolation of the poet. "Often previously," says Medea to the king,

> Through being considered clever I have suffered much. . . .
> If you put new ideas before the eyes of fools
> They'll think you foolish and worthless into the bargain;
> And if you are thought superior to those who have
> Some reputation for learning, you will become hated.

The common background of audience and poet is disappearing, the old certainties are being undermined, the city divided. Euripides is the first Greek poet to suffer the fate of so many of the great modern writers: rejected by most of his contemporaries (he rarely won first prize and was the favorite target for the scurrilous humor of the comic poets), he was universally admired and revered by the Greeks of the centuries that followed his death.

It is significant that what little biographical information we have for Euripides makes no mention of military service or political office; unlike Aeschylus, who fought in the ranks at Marathon, and Sophocles, who took an active part in public affairs from youth to advanced old age, Euripides seems to have lived a private, an intellectual life. Younger than Sophocles (though they died in the same year), he was more receptive to the critical theories and the rhetorical techniques offered by the Sophist teachers; his plays often subject received ideas to fundamental questioning, expressed in vivid dramatic debate. His *Medea* is typical of his iconoclastic approach; his choice of subject and central characters is in itself a challenge to established canons. He still dramatizes myth, but the myth he chooses is exotic and disturbing, and the protagonist is not a man but a woman. Medea is both woman and foreigner—that is, in terms of the audience's prejudice and practice she is a representative of the two freeborn groups in Athenian society that had almost no rights at all (though the male foreign resident had more rights than the native woman). The tragic hero is no longer a king, "one among the . . . highly renowned and prosperous, such as Oedipus," but a woman who, because she finds no redress for her wrongs in society, is driven by her passion to violate that society's most sacred laws in a rebellion against its typical representative, Jason, her husband. She is not just a woman and a foreigner, she is also a person of great intellectual power. Compared with her the credulous king and her complacent husband are children; and once her mind is made up, she moves them like pawns to their proper places in her barbaric game. The myth is used for new purposes, to shock the members of the audience, attack their deepest prejudices, and shake them out of their complacent pride in the superiority of Greek masculinity.

But the play is more compelling than that. Before it is over, our sympathies have come full circle; the contempt with which we regard the Jason of the opening scenes turns to pity as we feel the measure of his loss and the ferocity of Medea's revenge. Medea's passion has carried her too far; the death of Kreon (Creon) and his daughter we might have accepted, but the murder of the children is too much. It was, of course, meant to be. Euripides' theme, like Homer's, is violence, but this is the unspeakable violence of the oppressed, which is greater than the violence of the oppressor and which, because it has been long pent up, cannot be controlled.

In this, as in the other Greek plays, the gods have their place. In the *Oresteia* the will of Zeus is manifested in every action and implied in every word. In *Oedipus the King* the gods bide their time and watch Oedipus fulfill the truth of their prophecy; but in *Medea,* the divine will, which is revealed at the end, is enigmatic and, far from bringing harmony, concludes the play with a terrifying discord. All through *Medea* the human beings involved call on the gods, and two especially are singled out for attention: Earth and Sun. It is by these two gods that Medea makes Aegeus swear to give her refuge in Athens, the chorus invokes them to prevent Medea's violence against her sons, and Jason wonders how Medea can look on Earth and Sun after she has killed her own children. These emphatic appeals clearly raise the question of the attitude of the gods, and the answer to the question is a shock. We are not told what Earth does, but Sun sends the magic chariot on which Medea makes her escape. His reason, too, is stated: it is not any concern for justice but the fact that Medea is his granddaughter. Euripides is here using the letter of the myth for his own purposes. This jarring detail emphasizes the significance of the whole. The play creates a world in which there is no relation whatsoever between the powers that rule the universe and the fundamental laws of human morality. It dramatizes disorder, not just the disorder of the family of Jason and Medea but the disorder of the universe as a whole. It is the nightmare in which the dream of the fifth century B.C.E. was to end, the senseless fury and degradation of permanent violence. "Flow backward to your sources, sacred rivers," the chorus sings. "And let the world's great order be reversed."

The following list uses common English syllables and stress accents to provide rough equivalents of selected words whose pronunciation may be unfamiliar to the general reader.

Aigeus: *ai'-jioos / ai-gyoos*

Aphrodite: *a-froh-dai'-tee*

Cypris: *sai'-pris / koo'-pris*

Erechtheus: *e-rek'-thee-us /
e-rek-thyoos*

Hecate: *he'-kah-tee*

Helios: *hee-lee-os / hay-lee-os*

Iolcos: *yol'-kuhs / ee-ol'-kuhs*

Medea: *me-dee'-uh*

Orpheus: *or'-fee-us / or'-fyoos*

Pelias: *pee'-lee-as*

Pieria: *pai-ee'-ree-uh / pee-ehr'-ee-uh*

Pittheus: *pit'-thee-us / pit'-thyoos*

Scylla: *si'-lah / ski'-lah*

Troezen: *troy'-zen*

Medea[1]

CHARACTERS

MEDEA, *princess of Colchis and wife
of Jason*
JASON, *son of Aeson, king of Iolcos*
Two CHILDREN *of Medea and Jason*
KREON, *king of Corinth*

AIGEUS, *king of Athens*
NURSE *to Medea*
TUTOR *to Medea's children*
MESSENGER
CHORUS *of Corinthian women*

[SCENE—*In front of* MEDEA's *house in Corinth. Enter from the house* MEDEA's
NURSE.]

NURSE   How I wish the Argo[2] never had reached the land
Of Colchis, skimming through the blue Symplegades,[3]
Nor ever had fallen in the glades of Pelion[3]
The smitten fir-tree to furnish oars for the hands
Of heroes who in Pelias'[4] name attempted   5
The Golden Fleece! For then my mistress Medea[5]
Would not have sailed for the towers of the land of Iolcos,
Her heart on fire with passionate love for Jason;
Nor would she have persuaded the daughters of Pelias
To kill their father,[6] and now be living here   10
In Corinth[7] with her husband and children. She gave
Pleasure to the people of her land of exile,
And she herself helped Jason in every way.

1. Translated by Rex Warner.   2. The ship in which Jason and his companions sailed on the quest for the Golden Fleece.   3. A mountain in northern Greece near Iolcos, the place from which Jason sailed. The Symplegades were clashing rocks that crushed ships endeavoring to pass between them. They were supposed to be located at the Hellespont, the passage between the Mediterranean and Black seas.   4. He seized the kingdom of Iolcos, expelling Aeson, Jason's father. When Jason came to claim his rights, Pelias sent him to get the Golden Fleece.   5. Daughter of the king of Colchis who fell in love with Jason and helped him take the Golden Fleece away from her own country.   6. After Jason and Medea returned to Iolcos, Medea (who had a reputation as a sorceress) persuaded Pelias's daughters to cut Pelias up and boil the pieces, which would restore him to youth. The experiment was, of course, unsuccessful, and Pelias's son banished Jason and Medea from the kingdom.   7. On the isthmus between the Peloponnesus and Attica, where they took refuge. In Euripides' time it was a wealthy trading city, a commercial rival of Athens.

This is indeed the greatest salvation of all,—
For the wife not to stand apart from the husband. 15
But now there's hatred everywhere. Love is diseased.
For, deserting his own children and my mistress,
Jason has taken a royal wife to his bed,
The daughter of the ruler of this land, Kreon.
And poor Medea is slighted, and cries aloud on the 20
Vows they made to each other, the right hands clasped
In eternal promise. She calls upon the gods to witness
What sort of return Jason has made to her love.
She lies without food and gives herself up to suffering,
Wasting away every moment of the day in tears. 25
So it has gone since she knew herself slighted by him.
Not stirring an eye, not moving her face from the ground,
No more than either a rock or surging sea water
She listens when she is given friendly advice.
Except that sometimes she twists back her white neck and 30
Moans to herself, calling out on her father's name,
And her land, and her home betrayed when she came away with
A man who now is determined to dishonor her.
Poor creature, she has discovered by her sufferings
What it means to one not to have lost one's own country. 35
She has turned from the children and does not like to see them.
I am afraid she may think of some dreadful thing,
For her heart is violent. She will never put up with
The treatment she is getting. I know and fear her
Lest she may sharpen a sword and thrust to the heart, 40
Stealing into the palace where the bed is made,
Or even kill the king and the new-wedded groom,
And thus bring a greater misfortune on herself.
She's a strange woman. I know it won't be easy
To make an enemy of her and come off best. 45
But here the children come. They have finished playing.
They have no thought at all of their mother's trouble.
Indeed it is not usual for the young to grieve.

[Enter from the right the slave who is the TUTOR to MEDEA's two small CHILDREN. The CHILDREN follow him.]

TUTOR   You old retainer of my mistress's household,
Why are you standing here all alone in front of the 50
Gates and moaning to yourself over your misfortune?
Medea could not wish you to leave her alone.
NURSE   Old man, and guardian of the children of Jason,
If one is a good servant, it's a terrible thing
When one's master's luck is out; it goes to one's heart. 55
So I myself have got into such a state of grief
That a longing stole over me to come outside here
And tell the earth and air of my mistress's sorrows.
TUTOR   Has the poor lady not yet given up her crying?
NURSE   Given up? She's at the start, not halfway through her tears. 60
TUTOR   Poor fool,—if I may call my mistress such a name,—

How ignorant she is of trouble more to come.
NURSE   What do you mean, old man? You needn't fear to speak.
TUTOR   Nothing. I take back the words which I used just now.
NURSE   Don't, by your beard, hide this from me, your fellow-servant.   65
    If need be, I'll keep quiet about what you tell me.
TUTOR   I heard a person saying, while I myself seemed
    Not to be paying attention, when I was at the place
    Where the old draught-players[8] sit, by the holy fountain,
    That Kreon, ruler of the land, intends to drive   70
    These children and their mother in exile from Corinth.
    But whether what he said is really true or not
    I do not know. I pray that it may not be true.
NURSE   And will Jason put up with it that his children
    Should suffer so, though he's no friend to their mother?   75
TUTOR   Old ties give place to new ones. As for Jason, he
    No longer has a feeling for this house of ours.
NURSE   It's black indeed for us, when we add new to old
    Sorrows before even the present sky has cleared.
TUTOR   But you be silent, and keep all this to yourself.   80
    It is not the right time to tell our mistress of it.
NURSE   Do you hear, children, what a father he is to you?
    I wish he were dead,—but no, he is still my master.
    Yet certainly he has proved unkind to his dear ones.
TUTOR   What's strange in that? Have you only just discovered   85
    That everyone loves himself more than his neighbor?
    Some have good reason, others get something out of it.
    So Jason neglects his children for the new bride.
NURSE   Go indoors, children. That will be the best thing.
    And you, keep them to themselves as much as possible.   90
    Don't bring them near their mother in her angry mood.
    For I've seen her already blazing her eyes at them
    As though she meant some mischief and I am sure that
    She'll not stop raging until she has struck at someone.
    May it be an enemy and not a friend she hurts!   95
        [MEDEA is heard inside the house.]
MEDEA   Ah, wretch! Ah, lost in my sufferings,
    I wish, I wish I might die.
NURSE   What did I say, dear children? Your mother
    Frets her heart and frets it to anger.
    Run away quickly into the house,   100
    And keep well out of her sight.
    Don't go anywhere near, but be careful
    Of the wildness and bitter nature
    Of that proud mind.
    Go now! Run quickly indoors.   105
    It is clear that she soon will put lightning
    In that cloud of her cries that is rising

---

8. Checkers players.

With a passion increasing. Oh, what will she do,
Proud-hearted and not to be checked on her course,
A soul bitten into with wrong?   110

[*The* TUTOR *takes the* CHILDREN *into the house.*]

MEDEA   Ah, I have suffered
What should be wept for bitterly. I hate you,
Children of a hateful mother. I curse you
And your father. Let the whole house crash.

NURSE   Ah, I pity you, you poor creature.   115
How can your children share in their father's
Wickedness? Why do you hate them? Oh children,
How much I fear that something may happen!
Great people's tempers are terrible, always
Having their own way, seldom checked,   120
Dangerous they shift from mood to mood.
How much better to have been accustomed
To live on equal terms with one's neighbors.
I would like to be safe and grow old in a
Humble way. What is moderate sounds best,   125
Also in practice *is* best for everyone.
Greatness brings no profit to people.
God indeed, when in anger, brings
Greater ruin to great men's houses.

[*Enter, on the right, a* CHORUS *of Corinthian women. They have come
to inquire about* MEDEA *and to attempt to console her.*]

CHORUS   I heard the voice, I heard the cry   130
Of Colchis' wretched daughter.
Tell me, mother, is she not yet
At rest? Within the double gates
Of the court I heard her cry. I am sorry
For the sorrow of this home. O, say, what has happened?   135

NURSE   There is no home. It's over and done with.
Her husband holds fast to his royal wedding,
While she, my mistress, cries out her eyes
There in her room, and takes no warmth from
Any word of any friend.   140

MEDEA   Oh, I wish
That lightning from heaven would split my head open.
Oh, what use have I now for life?
I would find my release in death
And leave hateful existence behind me.   145

CHORUS   O God and Earth and Heaven!
Did you hear what a cry was that
Which the sad wife sings?
Poor foolish one, why should you long
For that appalling rest?   150
The final end of death comes fast.
No need to pray for that.
Suppose your man gives honor
To another woman's bed.

It often happens. Don't be hurt.   155
God will be your friend in this.
You must not waste away
Grieving too much for him who shared your bed.
MEDEA   Great Themis, lady Artemis,[9] behold
The things I suffer, though I made him promise,   160
My hateful husband. I pray that I may see him,
Him and his bride and all their palace shattered
For the wrong they dare to do me without cause.
Oh, my father! Oh, my country! In what dishonor
I left you, killing my own brother for it.[1]   165
NURSE   Do you hear what she says, and how she cries
On Themis, the goddess of Promises, and on Zeus,
Whom we believe to be the Keeper of Oaths?
Of this I am sure, that no small thing
Will appease my mistress's anger.   170
CHORUS   Will she come into our presence?
Will she listen when we are speaking
To the words we say?
I wish she might relax her rage
And temper of her heart.   175
My willingness to help will never
Be wanting to my friends.
But go inside and bring her
Out of the house to us,
And speak kindly to her: hurry,   180
Before she wrongs her own.
This passion of hers moves to something great.
NURSE   I will, but I doubt if I'll manage
To win my mistress over.
But still I'll attempt it to please you.   185
Such a look she will flash on her servants
If any comes near with a message,
Like a lioness guarding her cubs.
It is right, I think, to consider
Both stupid and lacking in foresight   190
Those poets of old who wrote songs
For revels and dinners and banquets,
Pleasant sounds for men living at ease;
But none of them all has discovered
How to put an end with their singing   195
Or musical instruments grief,
Bitter grief, from which death and disaster
Cheat the hopes of a house. Yet how good
If music could cure men of this! But why raise
To no purpose the voice at a banquet? For *there* is   200
Already abundance of pleasure for men

---

9. The protector of women in pain and distress. Themis, a Titan, was justice personified.   1. Medea killed him to delay the pursuit when she escaped with Jason.

With a joy of its own.

[*The* NURSE *goes into the house.*]

CHORUS   I heard a shriek that is laden with sorrow.
Shrilling out her hard grief she cries out
Upon him who betrayed both her bed and her marriage.   205
Wronged, she calls on the gods,
On the justice of Zeus, the oath sworn,
Which brought her away
To the opposite shore of the Greeks
Through the gloomy salt straits to the gateway   210
Of the salty unlimited sea.

[MEDEA, *attended by servants, comes out of the house.*]

MEDEA   Women of Corinth, I have come outside to you
Lest you should be indignant with me; for I know
That many people are overproud, some when alone,
And others when in company. And those who live   215
Quietly, as I do, get a bad reputation.
For a just judgment is not evident in the eyes
When a man at first sight hates another, before
Learning his character, being in no way injured;
And a foreigner[2] especially must adapt himself.   220
I'd not approve of even a fellow-countryman
Who by pride and want of manners offends his neighbors.
But on me this thing has fallen so unexpectedly,
It has broken my heart. I am finished. I let go
All my life's joy. My friends, I only want to die.   225
It was everything to me to think well of one man,
And he, my own husband, has turned out wholly vile.
Of all things which are living and can form a judgment
We women are the most unfortunate creatures.[3]
Firstly, with an excess of wealth it is required   230
For us to buy a husband and take for our bodies
A master; for not to take one is even worse.
And now the question is serious whether we take
A good or bad one; for there is no easy escape
For a woman, nor can she say no to her marriage.   235
She arrives among new modes of behavior and manners,
And needs prophetic power, unless she has learnt at home,
How best to manage him who shares the bed with her.
And if we work out all this well and carefully,
And the husband lives with us and lightly bears his yoke,   240
Then life is enviable. If not, I'd rather die.
A man, when he's tired of the company in his home,
Goes out of the house and puts an end to his boredom
And turns to a friend or companion of his own age.
But we are forced to keep our eyes on one alone.   245

2. Foreign residents were encouraged to come to Athens but were rarely admitted to the rights of full citizenship, which was a jealously guarded privilege.   3. Athenian rights and institutions were made for men; the women had few privileges and almost no legal rights. Lines 230–31 refer to the dowry that the bride's family had to provide.

What they say of us is that we have a peaceful time
Living at home, while they do the fighting in war.
How wrong they are! I would very much rather stand
Three times in the front of battle than bear one child.
Yet what applies to me does not apply to you. 250
You have a country. Your family home is here.
You enjoy life and the company of your friends.
But I am deserted, a refugee, thought nothing of
By my husband,—something he won in a foreign land.
I have no mother or brother, nor any relation 255
With whom I can take refuge in this sea of woe.
This much then is the service I would beg from you:
If I can find the means or devise any scheme
To pay my husband back for what he has done to me,—
Him and his father-in-law and the girl who married him,— 260
Just to keep silent. For in other ways a woman
Is full of fear, defenseless, dreads the sight of cold
Steel; but, when once she is wronged in the matter of love,
No other soul can hold so many thoughts of blood.

CHORUS   This I will promise. You are in the right, Medea, 265
In paying your husband back. I am not surprised at you
For being sad. But look! I see our king Kreon
Approaching. He will tell us of some new plan.
    [*Enter, from the right,* KREON, *with attendants.*]

KREON   You, with that angry look, so set against your husband,
Medea, I order you to leave my territories 270
An exile, and take along with you your two children,
And not to waste time doing it. It is my decree,
And I will see it done. I will not return home
Until you are cast from the boundaries of my land.

MEDEA   Oh, this is the end for me. I am utterly lost. 275
Now I am in the full force of the storm of hate
And have no harbor from ruin to reach easily.
Yet still, in spite of it all, I'll ask the question:
What is your reason, Kreon, for banishing me?

KREON   I am afraid of you,—why should I dissemble it?— 280
Afraid that you may injure my daughter mortally.
Many things accumulate to support my feeling.
You are a clever woman, versed in evil arts,
And are angry at having lost your husband's love.
I hear that you are threatening, so they tell me, 285
To do something against my daughter and Jason
And me, too. I shall take my precautions first.
I tell you, I prefer to earn your hatred now
Than to be soft-hearted and afterwards regret it.

MEDEA   This is not the first time, Kreon. Often previously 290
Through being considered clever I have suffered much.
A person of sense ought never to have his children
Brought up to be more clever than the average.
For, apart from cleverness bringing them no profit,

It will make them objects of envy and ill-will. 295
If you put new ideas before the eyes of fools
They'll think you foolish and worthless into the bargain;
And if you are thought superior to those who have
Some reputation for learning, you will become hated.
I have some knowledge myself of how this happens; 300
For being clever, I find that some will envy me,
Others object to me. Yet all my cleverness
Is not so much. Well, then, are you frightened, Kreon,
That I should harm you? There is no need. It is not
My way to transgress the authority of a king. 305
How have you injured me? You gave your daughter away
To the man you wanted. O, certainly I hate
My husband, but you, I think, have acted wisely;
Nor do I grudge it you that your affairs go well.
May the marriage be a lucky one! Only let me 310
Live in this land. For even though I have been wronged,
I will not raise my voice, but submit to my betters.
KREON   What you say sounds gentle enough. Still in my heart
I greatly dread that you are plotting some evil,
And therefore I trust you even less than before. 315
A sharp-tempered woman, or for that matter a man,
Is easier to deal with than the clever type
Who holds her tongue. No. You must go. No need for more
Speeches. The thing is fixed. By no manner of means
Shall you, an enemy of mine, stay in my country. 320
MEDEA   I beg you. By your knees, by your new-wedded girl.
KREON   Your words are wasted. You will never persuade me.
MEDEA   Will you drive me out, and give no heed to my prayers?
KREON   I will, for I love my family more than you.
MEDEA   O my country! How bitterly now I remember you! 325
KREON   I love my country too,—next after my children.
MEDEA   O what an evil to men is passionate love!
KREON   That would depend on the luck that goes along with it.
MEDEA   O God, do not forget who is the cause of this!
KREON   Go. It is no use. Spare me the pain of forcing you. 330
MEDEA   I'm spared no pain. I lack no pain to be spared me.
KREON   Then you'll be removed by force by one of my men.
MEDEA   No, Kreon, not that! But do listen, I beg you.
KREON   Woman, you seem to want to create a disturbance.
MEDEA   I *will* go into exile. *This* is not what I beg for. 335
KREON   Why then this violence and clinging to my hand?
MEDEA   Allow me to remain here just for this one day,
So I may consider where to live in my exile,
And look for support for my children, since their father
Chooses to make no kind of provision for them. 340
Have pity on them! You have children of your own.
It is natural for you to look kindly on them.
For myself I do not mind if I go into exile.
It is the children being in trouble that I mind.

KREON   There is nothing tyrannical about my nature,   345
    And by showing mercy I have often been the loser.
    Even now I know that I am making a mistake.
    All the same you shall have your will. But this I tell you,
    That if the light of heaven tomorrow shall see you,
    You and your children in the confines of my land,   350
    You die. This word I have spoken is firmly fixed.
    But now, if you must stay, stay for this day alone.
    For in it you can do none of the things I fear.
        [Exit KREON with his attendants.]
CHORUS   Oh, unfortunate one! Oh, cruel!
    Where will you turn? Who will help you?   355
    What house or what land to preserve you
    From ill can you find?
    Medea, a god has thrown suffering
    Upon you in waves of despair.
MEDEA   Things have gone badly every way. No doubt of that.   360
    But not these things this far, and don't imagine so.
    There are still trials to come for the new-wedded pair,
    And for their relations pain that will mean something.
    Do you think that I would ever have fawned on that man
    Unless I had some end to gain or profit in it?   365
    I would not even have spoken or touched him with my hands.
    But he has got to such a pitch of foolishness
    That, though he could have made nothing of all my plans
    By exiling me, he has given me this one day
    To stay here, and in this I will make dead bodies   370
    Of three of my enemies,—father, the girl and my husband.
    I have many ways of death which I might suit to them,
    And do not know, friends, which one to take in hand;
    Whether to set fire underneath their bridal mansion,
    Or sharpen a sword and thrust it to the heart,   375
    Stealing into the palace where the bed is made.
    There is just one obstacle to this. If I am caught
    Breaking into the house and scheming against it,
    I shall die, and give my enemies cause for laughter.
    It is best to go by the straight road, the one in which   380
    I am most skilled, and make away with them by poison.
    So be it then.
    And now suppose them dead. What town will receive me?
    What friend will offer me a refuge in his land,
    Or the guarantee of his house and save my own life?   385
    There is none. So I must wait a little time yet,
    And if some sure defense should then appear for me,
    In craft and silence I will set about this murder.
    But if my fate should drive me on without help,
    Even though death is certain, I will take the sword   390
    Myself and kill, and steadfastly advance to crime.
    It shall not be,—I swear it by her, my mistress,
    Whom most I honor and have chosen as partner,

Hecate,[4] who dwells in the recesses of my hearth,—
That any man shall be glad to have injured me. 395
Bitter I will make their marriage for them and mournful,
Bitter the alliance and the driving me out of the land.
Ah, come, Medea, in your plotting and scheming
Leave nothing untried of all those things which you know.
Go forward to the dreadful act. The test has come 400
For resolution. You see how you are treated. Never
Shall you be mocked by Jason's Corinthian wedding,
Whose father was noble, whose grandfather Helios.[5]
You have the skill. What is more, you were born a woman,
And women, though most helpless in doing good deeds, 405
Are of every evil the cleverest of contrivers.

CHORUS   Flow backward to your sources, sacred rivers,
And let the world's great order be reversed.
It is the thoughts of *men* that are deceitful,
Their pledges that are loose. 410
Story shall now turn my condition to a fair one,
Women are paid their due.
No more shall evil-sounding fame be theirs.

Cease now, you muses of the ancient singers,
To tell the tale of my unfaithfulness; 415
For not on us did Phoebus,[6] lord of music,
Bestow the lyre's divine
Power, for otherwise I should have sung an answer
To the other sex. Long time
Has much to tell of us, and much of them. 420

You sailed away from your father's home,
With a heart on fire you passed
The double rocks of the sea.
And now in a foreign country
You have lost your rest in a widowed bed, 425
And are driven forth, a refugee
In dishonor from the land.

Good faith has gone, and no more remains
In great Greece a sense of shame.
It has flown away to the sky. 430
No father's house for a haven
Is at hand for you now, and another queen
Of your bed has dispossessed you and
Is mistress of your home.

    [*Enter* JASON, *with attendants.*]

JASON   This is not the first occasion that I have noticed 435
How hopeless it is to deal with a stubborn temper.

---

4. The patron of witchcraft, sometimes identified with Artemis; Medea has a statue and shrine of her in the house.   5. The Sun, father of Medea's father, Aeëtes.   6. Apollo.

For, with reasonable submission to our ruler's will,
You might have lived in this land and kept your home.
As it is you are going to be exiled for your loose speaking.
Not that I mind myself. You are free to continue   440
Telling everyone that Jason is a worthless man.
But as to your talk about the king, consider
Yourself most lucky that exile is your punishment.
I, for my part, have always tried to calm down
The anger of the king, and wished you to remain.   445
But you will not give up your folly, continually
Speaking ill of him, and so you are going to be banished.
All the same, and in spite of your conduct, I'll not desert
My friends, but have come to make some provision for you,
So that you and the children may not be penniless   450
Or in need of anything in exile. Certainly
Exile brings many troubles with it. And even
If you hate me, I cannot think badly of you.

MEDEA   O coward in every way,—that is what I call you,
With bitterest reproach for your lack of manliness,   455
You have come, you, my worst enemy, have come to me!
It is not an example of over-confidence
Or of boldness thus to look your friends in the face,
Friends you have injured,—no, it is the worst of all
Human diseases, shamelessness. But you did well   460
To come, for I can speak ill of you and lighten
My heart, and you will suffer while you are listening.
And first I will begin from what happened first.
I saved your life, and every Greek knows I saved it
Who was a ship-mate of yours aboard the Argo,   465
When you were sent to control the bulls that breathed fire
And yoke them, and when you would sow that deadly field.
Also that snake, who encircled with his many folds
The Golden Fleece and guarded it and never slept,[7]
I killed, and so gave you the safety of the light.   470
And I myself betrayed my father and my home,
And came with you to Pelias' land of Iolcos.
And then, showing more willingness to help than wisdom,
I killed him, Pelias, with a most dreadful death
At his own daughters' hands, and took away your fear.   475
This is how I behaved to you, you wretched man,
And you forsook me, took another bride to bed
Though you had children; for, if that had not been,
You would have had an excuse for another wedding.
Faith in your word has gone. Indeed I cannot tell   480
Whether you think the gods whose names you swore by then
Have ceased to rule and that new standards are set up,
Since you must know you have broken your word to me.

---

7. These lines refer to ordeals through which Jason had to pass to win the fleece and in which Medea helped him. He had to yoke a team of fire-breathing bulls, then sow a field that immediately sprouted armed warriors, and then deal with the snake that guarded the fleece.

O my right hand, and the knees which you often clasped
In supplication, how senselessly I am treated   485
By this bad man, and how my hopes have missed their mark!
Come, I will share my thoughts as though you were a friend,—
You! Can I think that you would ever treat me well?
But I will do it, and these questions will make you
Appear the baser. Where am I to go? To my father's?   490
Him I betrayed and his land when I came with you.
To Pelias' wretched daughters? What a fine welcome
They would prepare for me who murdered their father!
For this is my position,—hated by my friends
At home, I have, in kindness to you, made enemies   495
Of others whom there was no need to have injured.
And how happy among Greek women you have made me
On your side for all this! A distinguished husband
I have,—for breaking promises. When in misery
I am cast out of the land and go into exile,   500
Quite without friends and all alone with my children,
That will be a fine shame for the new-wedded groom,
For his children to wander as beggars and she who saved him.
O God, you have given to mortals a sure method
Of telling the gold that is pure from the counterfeit;   505
Why is there no mark engraved upon men's bodies,
By which we could know the true ones from the false ones?
CHORUS   It is a strange form of anger, difficult to cure
When two friends turn upon each other in hatred.
JASON   As for me, it seems I must be no bad speaker.   510
But, like a man who has a good grip of the tiller,
Reef up his sail, and so run away from under
This mouthing tempest, woman, of your bitter tongue.
Since you insist on building up your kindness to me,
My view is that Cypris[8] was alone responsible   515
Of men and gods for the preserving of my life.
You are clever enough,—but really I need not enter
Into the story of how it was love's inescapable
Power that compelled you to keep my person safe.
On this I will not go into too much detail.   520
In so far as you helped me, you did well enough.
But on this question of saving me, I can prove
You have certainly got from me more than you gave.
Firstly, instead of living among barbarians,
You inhabit a Greek land and understand our ways,   525
How to live by law instead of the sweet will of force.
And all the Greeks considered you a clever woman.
You were honored for it; while, if you were living at
The ends of the earth, nobody would have heard of you.
For my part, rather than stores of gold in my house   530
Or power to sing even sweeter songs than Orpheus,[9]

8. Aphrodite, goddess of love.   9. Legendary musician whose songs charmed animals and made trees
and rocks leave their places to come and listen.

I'd choose the fate that made me a distinguished man.
There is my reply to your story of my labors.
Remember it was you who started the argument.
Next for your attack on my wedding with the princess: 535
Here I will prove that, first, it was a clever move,
Secondly, a wise one, and, finally, that I made it
In your best interests and the children's. Please keep calm.
When I arrived here from the land of Iolcos,
Involved, as I was, in every kind of difficulty,   540
What luckier chance could I have come across than this,
An exile to marry the daughter of the king?
It was not,—the point that seems to upset you—that I
Grew tired of your bed and felt the need of a new bride;
Nor with any wish to outdo your number of children.   545
We have enough already. I am quite content.
But,—this was the main reason—that we might live well,
And not be short of anything. I know that all
A man's friends leave him stone-cold if he becomes poor.
Also that I might bring my children up worthy   550
Of my position, and, by producing more of them
To be brothers of yours, we would draw the families
Together and all be happy. You need no children.
And it pays me to do good to those I have now
By having others. Do you think this a bad plan?   555
You wouldn't if the love question hadn't upset you.
But you women have got into such a state of mind
That, if your life at night is good, you think you have
Everything; but, if in that quarter things go wrong,
You will consider your best and truest interests   560
Most hateful. It would have been better far for men
To have got their children in some other way, and women
Not to have existed. Then life would have been good.
CHORUS   Jason, though you have made this speech of yours look well,
Still I think, even though others do not agree,   565
You have betrayed your wife and are acting badly.
MEDEA   Surely in many ways I hold different views
From others, for I think that the plausible speaker
Who is a villain deserves the greatest punishment.
Confident in his tongue's power to adorn evil,   570
He stops at nothing. Yet he is not really wise.
As in your case. There is no need to put on the airs
Of a clever speaker, for one word will lay you flat.
If you were not a coward, you would not have married
Behind my back, but discussed it with me first.   575
JASON   And you, no doubt, would have furthered the proposal,
If I had told you of it, you who even now
Are incapable of controlling your bitter temper.
MEDEA   It was not that. No, you thought it was not respectable
As you got on in years to have a foreign wife.   580
JASON   Make sure of this: it was not because of a woman

I made the royal alliance in which I now live,
But, as I said before, I wished to preserve you
And breed a royal progeny to be brothers
To the children I have now, a sure defense to us.   585
MEDEA   Let me have no happy fortune that brings pain with it,
Or prosperity which is upsetting to the mind!
JASON   Change your ideas of what you want, and show more sense.
Do not consider painful what is good for you,
Nor, when you are lucky, think yourself unfortunate.   590
MEDEA   You can insult me. You have somewhere to turn to.
But I shall go from this land into exile, friendless.
JASON   It was what you chose yourself. Don't blame others for it.
MEDEA   And how did I choose it? Did I betray my husband?
JASON   You called down wicked curses on the king's family.   595
MEDEA   A curse, that is what I am become to your house too.
JASON   I do not propose to go into all the rest of it;
But, if you wish for the children or for yourself
In exile to have some of my money to help you,
Say so, for I am prepared to give with open hand,   600
Or to provide you with introductions to my friends
Who will treat you well. You are a fool if you do not
Accept this. Cease your anger and you will profit.
MEDEA   I shall never accept the favors of friends of yours,
Nor take a thing from you, so you need not offer it.   605
There is no benefit in the gifts of a bad man.
JASON   Then, in any case, I call the gods to witness that
I wish to help you and the children in every way,
But you refuse what is good for you. Obstinately
You push away your friends. You are sure to suffer for it.   610
MEDEA   Go! No doubt you hanker for your virginal bride,
And are guilty of lingering too long out of her house.
Enjoy your wedding. But perhaps,—with the help of God—
You will make the kind of marriage that you will regret.

[JASON *goes out with his attendants.*]

CHORUS   When love is in excess   615
It brings a man no honor
Nor any worthiness.
But if in moderation Cypris comes,
There is no other power at all so gracious.
O goddess, never on me let loose the unerring   620
Shaft of your bow in the poison of desire.

Let my heart be wise.
It is the gods' best gift.
On me let mighty Cypris
Inflict no wordy wars or restless anger   625
To urge my passion to a different love.
But with discernment may she guide women's weddings,
Honoring most what is peaceful in the bed.

O country and home,
Never, never may I be without you,   630
Living the hopeless life,
Hard to pass through and painful,
Most pitiable of all.
Let death first lay me low and death
Free me from this daylight.   635
There is no sorrow above
The loss of a native land.

I have seen it myself,
Do not tell of a secondhand story.
Neither city nor friend   640
Pitied you when you suffered
The worst of sufferings.
O let him die ungraced whose heart
Will not reward his friends,
Who cannot open an honest mind   645
No friend will he be of mine.

[*Enter* AIGEUS, *king of Athens, an old friend of* MEDEA.]

AIGEUS   Medea, greeting! This is the best introduction
    Of which men know for conversation between friends.
MEDEA   Greeting to you too, Aigeus, son of King Pandion,
    Where have you come from to visit this country's soil?   650
AIGEUS   I have just left the ancient oracle of Phoebus.[1]
MEDEA   And why did you go to earth's prophetic center?
AIGEUS   I went to inquire how children might be born to me.
MEDEA   Is it so? Your life still up to this point childless?
AIGEUS   Yes. By the fate of some power we have no children.   655
MEDEA   Have you a wife, or is there none to share your bed?
AIGEUS   There is. Yes, I am joined to my wife in marriage.
MEDEA   And what did Phoebus say to you about children?
AIGEUS   Words too wise for a mere man to guess their meaning.
MEDEA   Is it proper for me to be told the God's reply?   660
AIGEUS   It is. For sure what is needed is cleverness.
MEDEA   Then what was his message? Tell me, if I may hear.
AIGEUS   I am not to loosen the hanging foot of the wine-skin[2] . . .
MEDEA   Until you have done something, or reached some country?
AIGEUS   Until I return again to my hearth and house.   665
MEDEA   And for what purpose have you journeyed to this land?
AIGEUS   There is a man called Pittheus, king of Troezen.[3]
MEDEA   A son of Pelops, they say, a most righteous man.
AIGEUS   With him I wish to discuss the reply of the god.
MEDEA   Yes. He is wise and experienced in such matters.   670
AIGEUS   And to me also the dearest of all my spear-friends.[4]
MEDEA   Well, I hope you have good luck, and achieve your will.

---

1. Apollo. Delphi, the site of his oracle on the southern slopes of Mount Parnassus, was thought to be the
center or "navel" of the earth.   2. Cryptic; probably not to have intercourse.   3. In the Peloponnesus.
Pittheus was Aigeus's father-in-law. Corinth was on the way from Delphi to Troezen.   4. Allies in war,
companions in fighting.

AIGEUS   But why this downcast eye of yours, and this pale cheek?
MEDEA   O Aigeus, my husband has been the worst of all to me.
AIGEUS   What do you mean? Say clearly what has caused this grief.   675
MEDEA   Jason wrongs me, though I have never injured him.
AIGEUS   What has he done? Tell me about it in clearer words.
MEDEA   He has taken a wife to his house, supplanting me.
AIGEUS   Surely he would not dare to do a thing like that.
MEDEA   Be sure he has. Once dear, I now am slighted by him.   680
AIGEUS   Did he fall in love? Or is he tired of your love?
MEDEA   He was greatly in love, this traitor to his friends.
AIGEUS   Then let him go, if, as you say, he is so bad.
MEDEA   A passionate love,—for an alliance with the king.
AIGEUS   And who gave him his wife? Tell me the rest of it.   685
MEDEA   It was Kreon, he who rules this land of Corinth.
AIGEUS   Indeed, Medea, your grief was understandable.
MEDEA   I am ruined. And there is more to come: I am banished.
AIGEUS   Banished? By whom? Here you tell me of a new wrong.
MEDEA   Kreon drives me an exile from the land of Corinth.   690
AIGEUS   Does Jason consent? I cannot approve of this.
MEDEA   He pretends not to, but he will put up with it.
  Ah, Aigeus, I beg and beseech you, by your beard
  And by your knees I am making myself your suppliant,
  Have pity on me, have pity on your poor friend,   695
  And do not let me go into exile desolate,
  But receive me in your land and at your very hearth.
  So may your love, with God's help, lead to the bearing
  Of children, and so may you yourself die happy.
  You do not know what a chance you have come on here.   700
  I will end your childlessness, and I will make you able
  To beget children. The drugs I know can do this.
AIGEUS   For many reasons, woman, I am anxious to do
  This favor for you. First, for the sake of the gods,
  And then for the birth of children which you promise,   705
  For in that respect I am entirely at my wits' end.
  But this is my position: if you reach my land,
  I, being in my rights, will try to befriend you.
  But this much I must warn you of beforehand:
  I shall not agree to take you out of this country;   710
  But if you by yourself can reach my house, then you
  Shall stay there safely. To none will I give you up.
  But from this land you must make your escape yourself,
  For I do not wish to incur blame from my friends.
MEDEA   It shall be so. But, if I might have a pledge from you   715
  For this, then I would have from you all I desire.
AIGEUS   Do you not trust me? What is it rankles with you?
MEDEA   I trust you, yes. But the house of Pelias hates me,
  And so does Kreon. If you are bound by this oath,
  When they try to drag me from your land, you will not   720
  Abandon me; but if our pact is only words,
  With no oath to the gods, you will be lightly armed,

Unable to resist their summons. I am weak,
While they have wealth to help them and a royal house.
AIGEUS   You show much foresight for such negotiations.   725
Well, if you will have it so, I will not refuse.
For, both on my side this will be the safest way
To have some excuse to put forward to your enemies,
And for you it is more certain. You may name the gods.
MEDEA   Swear by the plain of Earth, and Helios, father   730
Of my father, and name together all the gods . . .
AIGEUS   That I will act or not act in what way? Speak.
MEDEA   That you yourself will never cast me from your land,
Nor, if any of my enemies should demand me,
Will you, in your life, willingly hand me over.   735
AIGEUS   I swear by the Earth, by the holy light of Helios,
By all the gods, I will abide by this you say.
MEDEA   Enough. And, if you fail, what shall happen to you?
AIGEUS   What comes to those who have no regard for heaven.
MEDEA   Go on your way. Farewell. For I am satisfied,   740
And I will reach your city as soon as I can,
Having done the deed I have to do and gained my end.
        [AIGEUS goes out.]
CHORUS   May Hermes, god of travelers,
Escort you, Aigeus, to your home!
And may you have the things you wish   745
So eagerly; for you
Appear to me to be a generous man.
MEDEA   God, and God's daughter, justice, and light of Helios!
Now, friends, has come the time of my triumph over
My enemies, and now my foot is on the road.   750
Now I am confident they will pay the penalty.
For this man, Aigeus, has been like a harbor to me
In all my plans just where I was most distressed.
To him I can fasten the cable of my safety
When I have reached the town and fortress of Pallas.[5]   755
And now I shall tell to you the whole of my plan.
Listen to these words that are not spoken idly.
I shall send one of my servants to find Jason
And request him to come once more into my sight.
And when he comes, the words I'll say will be soft ones.   760
I'll say that I agree with him, that I approve
The royal wedding he has made, betraying me.
I'll say it was profitable, an excellent idea.
But I shall beg that my children may remain here:
Not that I would leave in a country that hates me   765
Children of mine to feel their enemies' insults,
But that by a trick I may kill the king's daughter.
For I will send the children with gifts in their hands

5. Athens, city of Pallas Athena.

To carry to the bride, so as not to be banished,—
A finely woven dress and a golden diadem. 770
And if she takes them and wears them upon her skin
She and all who touch the girl will die in agony;
Such poison will I lay upon the gifts I send.
But there, however, I must leave that account paid.
I weep to think of what a deed I have to do 775
Next after that; for I shall kill my own children.
My children, there is none who can give them safety.
And when I have ruined the whole of Jason's house,
I shall leave the land and flee from the murder of my
Dear children, and I shall have done a dreadful deed. 780
For it is not bearable to be mocked by enemies.
So it must happen. What profit have I in life?
I have no land, no home, no refuge from my pain.
My mistake was made the time I left behind me
My father's house, and trusted the words of a Greek, 785
Who, with heaven's help, will pay me the price for that.
For those children he had from me he will never
See alive again, nor will he on his new bride
Beget another child, for she is to be forced
To die a most terrible death by these my poisons. 790
Let no one think me a weak one, feeble-spirited,
A stay-at-home, but rather just the opposite,
One who can hurt my enemies and help my friends;
For the lives of such persons are most remembered.
CHORUS   Since you have shared the knowledge of your plan with us, 795
I both wish to help you and support the normal
Ways of mankind, and tell you not to do this thing.
MEDEA   I can do no other thing. It is understandable
For you to speak thus. You have not suffered as I have.
CHORUS   But can you have the heart to kill your flesh and blood? 800
MEDEA   Yes, for this is the best way to wound my husband.
CHORUS   And you too. Of women you will be most unhappy.
MEDEA   So it must be. No compromise is possible.
[*She turns to the* NURSE.]
Go, you, at once, and tell Jason to come to me.
You I employ on all affairs of greatest trust. 805
Say nothing of these decisions which I have made,
If you love your mistress, if you were born a woman.
CHORUS   From of old the children of Erechtheus[6] are
Splendid, the sons of blessed gods. They dwell
In Athens' holy and unconquered land,[7] 810
Where famous Wisdom feeds them and they pass gaily
Always through that most brilliant air where once, they say,

6. An early king of Athens, a son of Hephaestus.   7. It was the Athenians' boast that their descent from the original settlers was uninterrupted by an invasion. There is a topical reference here, for the play was produced in 431 B.C.E., in a time of imminent war.

That golden Harmony gave birth to the nine
Pure Muses of Pieria.[8]

And beside the sweet flow of Cephisos' stream,   815
Where Cypris[9] sailed, they say, to draw the water,
And mild soft breezes breathed along her path,
And on her hair were flung the sweet-smelling garlands
Of flowers of roses by the Lovers, the companions
Of Wisdom, her escort, the helpers of men   820
In every kind of excellence.

How then can these holy rivers
Or this holy land love you,
Or the city find you a home,
You, who will kill your children,   825
You, not pure with the rest?
O think of the blow at your children
And think of the blood that you shed.
O, over and over I beg you,
By your knees[1] I beg you do not   830
Be the murderess of your babes!
O where will you find the courage
Or the skill of hand and heart,
When you set yourself to attempt
A deed so dreadful to do?   835
How, when you look upon them,
Can you tearlessly hold the decision
For murder? You will not be able,
When your children fall down and implore you,
You will not be able to dip   840
Steadfast your hand in their blood.

    [Enter JASON with attendants.]

JASON   I have come at your request. Indeed, although you are
    Bitter against me, this you shall have: I will listen
    To what new thing you want, woman, to get from me.

MEDEA   Jason, I beg you to be forgiving towards me   845
    For what I said. It is natural for you to bear with
    My temper, since we have had much love together.
    I have talked with myself about this and I have
    Reproached myself. "Fool" I said, "why am I so mad?
    Why am I set against those who have planned wisely?   850
    Why make myself an enemy of the authorities
    And of my husband, who does the best thing for me
    By marrying royalty and having children who
    Will be as brothers to my own? What is wrong with me?

---

8. A fountain in Boeotia where the Muses were supposed to live. The sentence means that the fortunate balance ("Harmony") of the elements and the genius of the people produced the cultivation of the arts ("the nine Pure Muses").   9. The goddess of love and, therefore, of the principle of fertility. Cephisos is an Athenian river.   1. Because clasping the other person's knees was a formal gesture of supplication, the knees could be invoked to add force to entreaties.

Let me give up anger, for the gods are kind to me.   855
Have I not children, and do I not know that we
In exile from our country must be short of friends?"
When I considered this I saw that I had shown
Great lack of sense, and that my anger was foolish.
Now I agree with you. I think that you are wise   860
In having this other wife as well as me, and I
Was mad. I should have helped you in these plans of yours,
Have joined in the wedding, stood by the marriage bed,
Have taken pleasure in attendance on your bride.
But we women are what we are,—perhaps a little   865
Worthless; and you men must not be like us in this,
Nor be foolish in return when we are foolish.
Now I give in, and admit that then I was wrong.
I have come to a better understanding now.
          [*She turns towards the house.*]
Children, come here, my children, come outdoors to us!   870
Welcome your father with me, and say goodbye to him,
And with your mother, who just now was his enemy,
Join again in making friends with him who loves us.
          [*Enter the* CHILDREN, *attended by the* TUTOR.]
We have made peace, and all our anger is over.
Take hold of his right hand,—O God, I am thinking   875
Of something which may happen in the secret future.
O children, will you just so, after a long life,
Hold out your loving arms at the grave? O children,
How ready to cry I am, how full of foreboding!
I am ending at last this quarrel with your father,   880
And, look, my soft eyes have suddenly filled with tears.
CHORUS   And the pale tears have started also in my eyes.
          O may the trouble not grow worse than now it is!
JASON   I approve of what you say. And I cannot blame you
          Even for what you said before. It is natural   885
          For a woman to be wild with her husband when he
          Goes in for secret love. But now your mind has turned
          To better reasoning. In the end you have come to
          The right decision, like the clever woman you are.
          And of you, children, your father is taking care.   890
          He has made, with God's help, ample provision for you.
          For I think that a time will come when you will be
          The leading people in Corinth with your brothers.
          You must grow up. As to the future, your father
          And those of the gods who love him will deal with that.   895
          I want to see you, when you have become young men,
          Healthy and strong, better men than my enemies.
          Medea, why are your eyes all wet with pale tears?
          Why is your cheek so white and turned away from me?
          Are not these words of mine pleasing for you to hear?   900
MEDEA   It is nothing. I was thinking about these children.
JASON   You must be cheerful. I shall look after them well.

MEDEA   I will be. It is not that I distrust your words,
  But a woman is a frail thing, prone to crying.
JASON   But why then should you grieve so much for these children?   905
MEDEA   I am their mother. When you prayed that they might live
  I felt unhappy to think that these things will be.
  But come, I have said something of the things I meant
  To say to you, and now I will tell you the rest.
  Since it is the king's will to banish me from here,—   910
  And for me too I know that this is the best thing,
  Not to be in your way by living here or in
  The king's way, since they think me ill-disposed to them,—
  I then am going into exile from this land;
  But do you, so that you may have the care of them,   915
  Beg Kreon that the children may not be banished.
JASON   I doubt if I'll succeed, but still I'll attempt it.
MEDEA   Then you must tell your wife to beg from her father
  That the children may be reprieved from banishment.
JASON   I will, and with her I shall certainly succeed.   920
MEDEA   If she is like the rest of us women, you will.
  And I too will take a hand with you in this business,
  For I will send her some gifts which are far fairer,
  I am sure of it, than those which now are in fashion,
  A finely-woven dress and a golden diadem,   925
  And the children shall present them. Quick, let one of you
  Servants bring here to me that beautiful dress.
       [One of her attendants goes into the house.]
  She will be happy not in one way, but in a hundred,
  Having so fine a man as you to share her bed,
  And with this beautiful dress which Helios of old,   930
  My father's father, bestowed on his descendants.
       [Enter attendant carrying the poisoned dress and diadem.]
  There, children, take these wedding presents in your hands.
  Take them to the royal princess, the happy bride,
  And give them to her. She will not think little of them.
JASON   No, don't be foolish, and empty your hands of these.   935
  Do you think the palace is short of dresses to wear?
  Do you think there is no gold there? Keep them, don't give them
  Away. If my wife considers me of any value,
  She will think more of me than money, I am sure of it.
MEDEA   No, let me have my way. They say the gods themselves   940
  Are moved by gifts, and gold does more with men than words.
  Hers is the luck, her fortune that which god blesses;
  She is young and a princess; but for my children's reprieve
  I would give my very life, and not gold only.
  Go children, go together to that rich palace,   945
  Be suppliants to the new wife of your father,
  My lady, beg her not to let you be banished.
  And give her the dress,—for this is of great importance,
  That she should take the gift into her hand from yours.
  Go, quick as you can. And bring your mother good news   950

By your success of those things which she longs to gain.

[JASON *goes out with his attendants, followed by the* TUTOR *and the*
CHILDREN *carrying the poisoned gifts.*]

CHORUS Now there is no hope left for the children's lives.
  Now there is none. They are walking already to murder.
  The bride, poor bride, will accept the curse of the gold,
  Will accept the bright diadem.   955
  Around her yellow hair she will set that dress
  Of death with her own hands.
  The grace and the perfume and glow of the golden robe
  Will charm her to put them upon her and wear the wreath,
  And now her wedding will be with the dead below,   960
  Into such a trap she will fall,
  Poor thing, into such a fate of death and never
  Escape from under that curse.
  You too, O wretched bridegroom, making your match with kings,
  You do not see that you bring   965
  Destruction on your children and on her,
  Your wife, a fearful death.
  Poor soul, what a fall is yours!

  In your grief too I weep, mother of little children,
  You who will murder your own,   970
  In vengeance for the loss of married love
  Which Jason has betrayed
  As he lives with another wife.

[*Enter the* TUTOR *with the* CHILDREN.]

TUTOR Mistress, I tell you that these children are reprieved,
  And the royal bride has been pleased to take in her hands   975
  Your gifts. In that quarter the children are secure.
  But come,
  Why do you stand confused when you are fortunate?
  Why have you turned round with your cheek away from me?
  Are not these words of mine pleasing for you to hear?   980
MEDEA Oh! I am lost!
TUTOR That word is not in harmony with my tidings.
MEDEA I am lost, I am lost!
TUTOR   Am I in ignorance telling you
  Of some disaster, and not the good news I thought?
MEDEA You have told what you have told. I do not blame you.   985
TUTOR Why then this downcast eye, and this weeping of tears?
MEDEA Oh, I am forced to weep, old man. The gods and I,
  I in a kind of madness have contrived all this.
TUTOR Courage! You too will be brought home by your children.
MEDEA Ah, before that happens I shall bring others home.   990
TUTOR Others before you have been parted from their children.
  Mortals must bear in resignation their ill luck.
MEDEA That is what I shall do. But go inside the house,
  And do for the children your usual daily work.

[*The* TUTOR *goes into the house.* MEDEA *turns to her* CHILDREN.]

O children, O my children, you have a city,   995
You have a home, and you can leave me behind you,
And without your mother you may live there for ever.
But I am going in exile to another land
Before I have seen you happy and taken pleasure in you,
Before I have dressed your brides and made your marriage beds   1000
And held up the torch at the ceremony of wedding.
Oh, what a wretch I am in this my self-willed thought!
What was the purpose, children, for which I reared you?
For all my travail and wearing myself away?
They were sterile, those pains I had in the bearing of you.   1005
O surely once the hopes in you I had, poor me,
Were high ones: you would look after me in old age,
And when I died would deck me well with your own hands;
A thing which all would have done. O but now it is gone,
That lovely thought. For, once I am left without you,   1010
Sad will be the life I'll lead and sorrowful for me.
And you will never see your mother again with
Your dear eyes, gone to another mode of living.
Why, children, do you look upon me with your eyes?
Why do you smile so sweetly that last smile of all?   1015
Oh, Oh, what can I do? My spirit has gone from me,
Friends, when I saw that bright look in the children's eyes.
I cannot bear to do it. I renounce my plans
I had before. I'll take my children away from
This land. Why should I hurt their father with the pain   1020
They feel, and suffer twice as much of pain myself?
No, no, I will not do it. I renounce my plans.
Ah, what is wrong with me? Do I want to let go
My enemies unhurt and be laughed at for it?
I must face this thing. Oh, but what a weak woman   1025
Even to admit to my mind these soft arguments.
Children, go into the house. And he whom law forbids
To stand in attendance at my sacrifices,
Let him see to it. I shall not mar my handiwork.
Oh! Oh!   1030
Do not, O my heart, you must not do these things!
Poor heart, let them go, have pity upon the children.
If they live with you in Athens they will cheer you.
No! By Hell's avenging furies it shall not be,—
This shall never be, that I should suffer my children   1035
To be the prey of my enemies' insolence.
Every way is it fixed. The bride will not escape.
No, the diadem is now upon her head, and she,
The royal princess, is dying in the dress, I know it.
But,—for it is the most dreadful of roads for me   1040
To tread, and them I shall send on a more dreadful still—
I wish to speak to the children.
        [*She calls the* CHILDREN *to her.*]
                            Come, children, give

Me your hands, give your mother your hands to kiss them.
O the dear hands, and O how dear are these lips to me,
And the generous eyes and the bearing of my children! 1045
I wish you happiness, but not here in this world.
What is here your father took. O how good to hold you!
How delicate the skin, how sweet the breath of children!
Go, go! I am no longer able, no longer
To look upon you. I am overcome by sorrow. 1050
    [*The* CHILDREN *go into the house.*]
I know indeed what evil I intend to do,
But stronger than all my afterthoughts is my fury,
Fury that brings upon mortals the greatest evils.
    [*She goes out to the right, towards the royal palace.*]
CHORUS Often before
I have gone through more subtle reasons,
And have come upon questionings greater 1055
Than a woman should strive to search out.
But we too have a goddess to help us
And accompany us into wisdom.
Not all of us. Still you will find 1060
Among many women a few,
And our sex is not without learning.
This I say, that those who have never
Had children, who know nothing of it,
In happiness have the advantage 1065
Over those who are parents.
The childless, who never discover
Whether children turn out as a good thing
Or as something to cause pain, are spared
Many troubles in lacking this knowledge. 1070
And those who have in their homes
The sweet presence of children, I see that their lives
Are all wasted away by their worries.
First they must think how to bring them up well and
How to leave them something to live on. 1075
And then after this whether all their toil
Is for those who will turn out good or bad,
Is still an unanswered question.
And of one more trouble, the last of all,
That is common to mortals I tell. 1080
For suppose you have found them enough for their living,
Suppose that the children have grown into youth
And have turned out good, still, if God so wills it,
Death will away with your children's bodies,
And carry them off into Hades. 1085
What is our profit, then, that for the sake of
Children the gods should pile upon mortals
After all else
This most terrible grief of all?
    [*Enter* MEDEA, *from the spectators' right.*]

MEDEA   Friends, I can tell you that for long I have waited   1090
  For the event. I stare towards the place from where
  The news will come. And now, see one of Jason's servants
  Is on his way here, and that labored breath of his
  Shows he has tidings for us, and evil tidings.
    [*Enter, also from the right, the* MESSENGER.]
MESSENGER   Medea, you who have done such a dreadful thing,   1095
  So outrageous, run for your life, take what you can,
  A ship to bear you hence or chariot on land.
MEDEA   And what is the reason deserves such flight as this?
MESSENGER   She is dead, only just now, the royal princess,
  And Kreon dead too, her father, by your poisons.   1100
MEDEA   The finest words you have spoken. Now and hereafter
  I shall count you among my benefactors and friends.
MESSENGER   What! Are you right in the mind? Are you not mad,
  Woman? The house of the king is outraged by you.
  Do you enjoy it? Not afraid of such doings?   1105
MEDEA   To what you say I on my side have something too
  To say in answer. Do not be in a hurry, friend,
  But speak. How did they die? You will delight me twice
  As much again if you say they died in agony.
MESSENGER   When those two children, born of you, had entered in,   1110
  Their father with them, and passed into the bride's house,
  We were pleased, we slaves who were distressed by your wrongs.
  All through the house we were talking of but one thing,
  How you and your husband had made up your quarrel.
  Some kissed the children's hands and some their yellow hair,   1115
  And I myself was so full of my joy that I
  Followed the children into the women's quarters.
  Our mistress, whom we honor now instead of you,
  Before she noticed that your two children were there,
  Was keeping her eye fixed eagerly on Jason.   1120
  Afterwards however she covered up her eyes,
  Her cheek paled and she turned herself away from him,
  So disgusted was she at the children's coming there.
  But your husband tried to end the girl's bad temper,
  And said "You must not look unkindly on your friends.   1125
  Cease to be angry. Turn your head to me again.
  Have as your friends the same ones as your husband has.
  And take these gifts, and beg your father to reprieve
  These children from their exile. Do it for my sake."
  She, when she saw the dress, could not restrain herself.   1130
  She agreed with all her husband said, and before
  He and the children had gone far from the palace,
  She took the gorgeous robe and dressed herself in it,
  And put the golden crown around her curly locks,
  And arranged the set of the hair in a shining mirror,   1135
  And smiled at the lifeless image of herself in it.
  Then she rose from her chair and walked about the room,
  With her gleaming feet stepping most soft and delicate,

All overjoyed with the present. Often and often
She would stretch her foot out straight and look along it.　　　　1140
But after that it was a fearful thing to see.
The color of her face changed, and she staggered back,
She ran, and her legs trembled, and she only just
Managed to reach a chair without falling flat down.
An aged woman servant who, I take it, thought　　　　1145
This was some seizure of Pan[2] or another god,
Cried out "God bless us," but that was before she saw
The white foam breaking through her lips and her rolling
The pupils of her eyes and her face all bloodless.
Then she raised a different cry from that "God bless us,"　　　　1150
A huge shriek, and the women ran, one to the king,
One to the newly wedded husband to tell him
What had happened to his bride; and with frequent sound
The whole of the palace rang as they went running.
One walking quickly round the course of a race-track　　　　1155
Would now have turned the bend and be close to the goal,
When she, poor girl, opened her shut and speechless eye,
And with a terrible groan she came to herself.
For a two-fold pain was moving up against her.
The wreath of gold that was resting around her head　　　　1160
Let forth a fearful stream of all-devouring fire,
And the finely-woven dress your children gave to her,
Was fastening on the unhappy girl's fine flesh.
She leapt up from the chair, and all on fire she ran,
Shaking her hair now this way and now that, trying　　　　1165
To hurl the diadem away; but fixedly
The gold preserved its grip, and, when she shook her hair,
Then more and twice as fiercely the fire blazed out.
Till, beaten by her fate, she fell down to the ground,
Hard to be recognized except by a parent.　　　　1170
Neither the setting of her eyes was plain to see,
Nor the shapeliness of her face. From the top of
Her head there oozed out blood and fire mixed together.
Like the drops on pine-bark, so the flesh from her bones
Dropped away, torn by the hidden fang of the poison.　　　　1175
It was a fearful sight; and terror held us all
From touching the corpse. We had learned from what had happened.
But her wretched father, knowing nothing of the event,
Came suddenly to the house, and fell upon the corpse,
And at once cried out and folded his arms about her,　　　　1180
And kissed her and spoke to her, saying, "O my poor child,
What heavenly power has so shamefully destroyed you?
And who has set me here like an ancient sepulchre,
Deprived of you? O let me die with you, my child!"
And when he had made an end of his wailing and crying,　　　　1185

2. As the god of wild nature he was supposed to be the source of the sudden, apparently causeless terror that solitude in wild surroundings may produce and hence of all kinds of sudden madness (compare the English word *panic*).

Then the old man wished to raise himself to his feet;
But, as the ivy clings to the twigs of the laurel,
So he stuck to the fine dress, and he struggled fearfully.
For he was trying to lift himself to his knee,
And she was pulling him down, and when he tugged hard   1190
He would be ripping his aged flesh from his bones.
At last his life was quenched and the unhappy man
Gave up the ghost, no longer could hold up his head.
There they lie close, the daughter and the old father,
Dead bodies, an event he prayed for in his tears.   1195
As for your interests, I will say nothing of them,
For you will find your own escape from punishment.
Our human life I think and have thought a shadow,
And I do not fear to say that those who are held
Wise amongst men and who search the reasons of things   1200
Are those who bring the most sorrow on themselves.
For of mortals there is no one who is happy.
If wealth flows in upon one, one may be perhaps
Luckier than one's neighbor, but still not happy.
            [Exit.]

CHORUS   Heaven, it seems, on this day has fastened many   1205
Evils on Jason, and Jason has deserved them.
Poor girl, the daughter of Kreon, how I pity you
And your misfortunes, you who have gone quite away
To the house of Hades because of marrying Jason.

MEDEA   Women, my task is fixed: as quickly as I may   1210
To kill my children, and start away from this land,
And not, by wasting time, to suffer my children
To be slain by another hand less kindly to them.
Force every way will have it they must die, and since
This must be so, then I, their mother, shall kill them.   1215
O arm yourself in steel, my heart! Do not hang back
From doing this fearful and necessary wrong.
O come, my hand, poor wretched hand, and take the sword,
Take it, step forward to this bitter starting point,
And do not be a coward, do not think of them,   1220
How sweet they are, and how you are their mother. Just for
This one short day be forgetful of your children,
Afterwards weep; for even though you will kill them,
They were very dear,—O, I am an unhappy woman!
            [With a cry she rushes into the house.]

CHORUS   O Earth, and the far shining   1225
Ray of the sun, look down, look down upon
This poor lost woman, look, before she raises
The hand of murder against her flesh and blood.
Yours was the golden birth from which
She sprang, and now I fear divine   1230
Blood may be shed by men.
O heavenly light, hold back her hand,
Check her, and drive from out the house
The bloody Fury raised by fiends of Hell.

Vain waste, your care of children;   1235
Was it in vain you bore the babes you loved,
After you passed the inhospitable strait
Between the dark blue rocks, Symplegades?
O wretched one, how has it come,
This heavy anger on your heart,   1240
This cruel bloody mind?
For God from mortals asks a stern
Price for the stain of kindred blood
In like disaster falling on their homes.
     [*A cry from one of the* CHILDREN *is heard.*]
CHORUS   Do you hear the cry, do you hear the children's cry?   1245
    O you hard heart, O woman fated for evil!
ONE OF THE CHILDREN [*From within.*]   What can I do and how escape
    my mother's hands?
ONE OF THE CHILDREN [*From within.*]   O my dear brother, I cannot tell.
    We are lost.
CHORUS   Shall I enter the house? O surely I should   1250
    Defend the children from murder.
A CHILD [*From within.*]   O help us, in God's name, for now we need
    your help.
    Now, now we are close to it. We are trapped by the sword.
CHORUS   O your heart must have been made of rock or steel,
    You who can kill   1255
    With your own hand the fruit of your own womb.
    Of one alone I have heard, one woman alone
    Of those of old who laid her hands on her children,
    Ino, sent mad by heaven when the wife of Zeus
    Drove her out from her home and made her wander;   1260
    And because of the wicked shedding of blood
    Of her own children she threw
    Herself, poor wretch, into the sea and stepped away
    Over the sea-cliff to die with her two children.
    What horror more can be? O women's love,   1265
    So full of trouble,
    How many evils have you caused already!
     [*Enter* JASON, *with attendants.*]
JASON   You women, standing close in front of this dwelling,
    Is she, Medea, she who did this dreadful deed,
    Still in the house, or has she run away in flight?   1270
    For she will have to hide herself beneath the earth,
    Or raise herself on wings into the height of air,
    If she wishes to escape the royal vengeance.
    Does she imagine that, having killed our rulers,
    She will herself escape uninjured from this house?   1275
    But I am thinking not so much of her as for
    The children,—her the king's friends will make to suffer
    For what she did. So I have come to save the lives
    Of my boys, in case the royal house should harm them
    While taking vengeance for their mother's wicked deed.   1280
CHORUS   Jason, if you but knew how deeply you are

Involved in sorrow, you would not have spoken so.
JASON   What is it? That she is planning to kill me also?
CHORUS   Your children are dead, and by their own mother's hand.
JASON   What! This is it? O woman, you have destroyed me.   1285
CHORUS   You must make up your mind your children are no more.
JASON   Where did she kill them? Was it here or in the house?
CHORUS   Open the gates and there you will see them murdered.
JASON   Quick as you can unlock the doors, men, and undo
The fastenings and let me see this double evil,   1290
My children dead and her,—O her I will repay.

[His attendants rush to the door. MEDEA appears above the house in a
chariot drawn by dragons. She has the dead bodies of the CHILDREN with
her.]

MEDEA   Why do you batter these gates and try to unbar them,
Seeking the corpses and for me who did the deed?
You may cease your trouble, and, if you have need of me,
Speak, if you wish. You will never touch me with your hand,   1295
Such a chariot has Helios, my father's father,
Given me to defend me from my enemies.

JASON   You hateful thing, you woman most utterly loathed
By the gods and me and by all the race of mankind,
You who have had the heart to raise a sword against   1300
Your children, you, their mother, and left me childless,—
You have done this, and do you still look at the sun
And at the earth, after these most fearful doings?
I wish you dead. Now I see it plain, though at that time
I did not, when I took you from your foreign home   1305
And brought you to a Greek house, you, an evil thing,
A traitress to your father and your native land.
The gods hurled the avenging curse of yours on me.
For your own brother you slew at your own hearthside,
And then came aboard that beautiful ship, the Argo.   1310
And that was your beginning. When you were married
To me, your husband, and had borne children to me,
For the sake of pleasure in the bed you killed them.
There is no Greek woman who would have dared such deeds,
Out of all those whom I passed over and chose you   1315
To marry instead, a bitter destructive match,
A monster not a woman, having a nature
Wilder than that of Scylla[3] in the Tuscan sea.
Ah! no, not if I had ten thousand words of shame
Could I sting you. You are naturally so brazen.   1320
Go, worker in evil, stained with your children's blood.
For me remains to cry aloud upon my fate,
Who will get no pleasure from my newly-wedded love,
And the boys whom I begot and brought up, never
Shall I speak to them alive. Oh, my life is over!   1325

---

3. A monster located in the straits between Italy and Sicily, who snatched sailors off passing ships and
devoured them. See *Odyssey* 12.

MEDEA Long would be the answer which I might have made to
    These words of yours, if Zeus the father did not know
    How I have treated you and what you did to me.
    No, it was not to be that you should scorn my love,
    And pleasantly live your life through, laughing at me;   1330
    Nor would the princess, nor he who offered the match,
    Kreon, drive me away without paying for it.
    So now you may call me a monster, if you wish,
    Or Scylla housed in the caves of the Tuscan sea
    I too, as I had to, have taken hold of your heart.   1335
JASON   You feel the pain yourself. You share in my sorrow.
MEDEA   Yes, and my grief is gain when you cannot mock it.
JASON   O children, what a wicked mother she was to you!
MEDEA   They died from a disease they caught from their father.
JASON   I tell you it was not my hand that destroyed them.   1340
MEDEA   But it was your insolence, and your virgin wedding.
JASON   And just for the sake of that you chose to kill them.
MEDEA   Is love so small a pain, do you think, for a woman?
JASON   For a wise one, certainly. But you are wholly evil.
MEDEA   The children are dead. I say this to make you suffer.   1345
JASON   The children, I think, will bring down curses on you.
MEDEA   The gods know who was the author of this sorrow.
JASON   Yes, the gods know indeed, they know your loathsome heart.
MEDEA   Hate me. But I tire of your barking bitterness.
JASON   And I of yours. It is easier to leave you.   1350
MEDEA   How then? What shall I do? I long to leave you too.
JASON   Give me the bodies to bury and to mourn them.
MEDEA   No, that I will not. I will bury them myself,
    Bearing them to Hera's temple on the promontory;
    So that no enemy may evilly treat them   1355
    By tearing up their grave. In this land of Corinth
    I shall establish a holy feast and sacrifice[4]
    Each year for ever to atone for the blood guilt.
    And I myself go to the land of Erechtheus
    To dwell in Aigeus' house, the son of Pandion.   1360
    While you, as is right, will die without distinction,
    Struck on the head by a piece of the Argo's timber,
    And you will have seen the bitter end of my love.
JASON   May a Fury for the children's sake destroy you,
    And justice, requitor of blood.   1365
MEDEA   What heavenly power lends an ear
    To a breaker of oaths, a deceiver?
JASON   O, I hate you, murderess of children.
MEDEA   Go to your palace. Bury your bride.
JASON   I go, with two children to mourn for.   1370
MEDEA   Not yet do you feel it. Wait for the future.
JASON   Oh, children I loved!
MEDEA   I loved them, you did not.

4. Some such ceremony was still performed at Corinth in Euripides' time.

JASON   You loved them, and killed them.

MEDEA   To make you feel pain.

JASON   Oh, wretch that I am, how I long
To kiss the dear lips of my children!   1375

MEDEA   Now you would speak to them, now you would kiss them.
Then you rejected them.

JASON   Let me, I beg you,
Touch my boys' delicate flesh.

MEDEA   I will not. Your words are all wasted.

JASON   O God, do you hear it, this persecution,   1380
These my sufferings from this hateful
Woman, this monster, murderess of children?
Still what I can do that I will do:
I will lament and cry upon heaven,
Calling the gods to bear me witness   1385
How you have killed my boys and prevent me from
Touching their bodies or giving them burial.
I wish I had never begot them to see them
Afterwards slaughtered by you.

CHORUS   Zeus in Olympus is the overseer   1390
Of many doings. Many things the gods
Achieve beyond our judgment. What we thought
Is not confirmed and what we thought not god
Contrives. And so it happens in this story.

ARISTOPHANES
450?–385? B.C.E.

By the fifth century B.C.E. both tragedy and comedy were regularly produced at the winter festivals of the god Dionysus in Athens. Comedy, like tragedy, employed a chorus—that is, a group of dancers (who also sang)—and actors, who wore masks; its tone was burlesque and parodic, though there was often a serious theme emphasized by the crude clowning and the free play of wit. The only comic poet of the fifth century B.C.E. whose work has survived is Aristophanes; in his thirteen extant comedies, produced over the years 425–388 B.C.E., the institutions and personalities of his time are caricatured and criticized in a brilliant combination of poetry and obscenity, of farce and wit that can be described only in terms of itself, by the adjective *Aristophanic.*

He was born sometime in the middle of the fifth century B.C.E. and died in the next, around 385 B.C.E. The earliest of his plays to survive, *The Acharnians,* was produced in 425 B.C.E., and the bulk of his extant work dates from the years of the Peloponnesian War (431–404 B.C.E.). The war, in fact, is one of his comic targets; in *The Acharnians,* an Athenian citizen, fed up with the privations caused by the Spartan invasions that shut the Athenians inside their walls, makes a separate peace for himself and his family, defends his decision against an irate chorus of patriots (the Acharnians of the title), and proceeds to enjoy all the benefits of peace while his fellow citizens suffer as before. In *Peace* (421 B.C.E.), another Athenian flies up to heaven on a gigantic dung beetle (a parody of a Euripidean play in which a hero flew up on a winged horse); once arrived, he petitions Zeus to stop the war. Euripides is another favorite target and was held up to ridicule in play after play; and Socrates was the "hero" of a play, *Clouds* (423 B.C.E.), that held him up to ridicule as a Sophistic charlatan. (Socrates refers to this play in his speech in court, p. 760.) In *Birds* (414 B.C.E.), two Athenians, tired of the war and taxes, go off to found a new city; they organize the birds, who cut off the smoke of sacrifice that the gods live on, and force Zeus to surrender the government of the universe to the birds. These plays are all very funny, with plenty of sexual and scatological wit. But coarse humor and exquisite wit combine with lyric poetry of a high quality and comic plots of startling audacity to produce a mixture unlike anything that went before or has come after it.

Lysistrata, which is outstanding among the Aristophanic comedies in its coherence of structure and broad humor, was first produced in 411 B.C.E. In 413 the news of the total destruction of the Athenian fleet in Sicily had reached Athens, and though heroic efforts to carry on the war were under way, the confidence in victory with which Athens had begun the war had disappeared forever. In Aristophanic comedy, the comic hero typically upsets the status quo to produce a series of extraordinary results and a wish-fulfilling ending. In this play the Athenian women, who have no political rights, seize the Acropolis, the repository of the city's treasury, and leave the men without sex or the money to carry on the war. At the same time similar revolutions take place in all the Greek cities according to a coordinated plan. The men are eventually "starved" into submission, and the Spartans come to Athens to end the war.

Aristophanes does not miss any chance to exploit the possibilities for ribald humor inherent in this female sex-strike against war; Myrrhine's teasing game with her husband, Kinesias, for example, is rare fooling, and the final appearance of the uncomfortably rigid Spartan ambassadors and their equally tense Athenian hosts is a visual and verbal climax of astonishing brilliance. But underneath all the fooling, real issues are pursued, and they come to the surface with telling effect in the argument between Lysistrata and the magistrate who has been sent to suppress the revolt. Reversing the words of Hector to Andromache, which had become proverbial, Lysistrata claims that "war shall be the business of womenfolk!" It is too important a matter to be left to men, for women are its real victims. When asked what the women will do, she explains that they will treat politics just as they do wool in their household tasks: "We hold it this way, and carefully wind out the strands on our spindles, now this way, now that way."

Women, who spent a great deal of their time weaving indoors, might be expected to express themselves this way, if they ever got a chance to talk politics. The magistrate replies, "You really think your way with wool and yarnballs and spindles can stop a terrible crisis? How brainless!" These words, of course, say as much about his own prejudices as they do about women's supposed incapacities. Aristophanes can scarcely have meant Lysistrata's words as a serious formula for peace, and yet there is a lucid simplicity to them. Men have botched affairs, as the prolonged war shows. Why *not* simply declare peace and work out the snarls amicably? Here and throughout the play, Aristophanes works through gender stereotypes, both inviting us to see the world through them and holding them up to good-natured ridicule. Women are addicted to wine and sex. They are tricky and deceitful, always probing for men's weaknesses, and an obstacle to the conduct of serious political business. So men say, and the women in this play admit it. But these characteristics are here enlisted in the service of peace (to see them viewed as destructive, compare Euripides' *Medea.*) As for men, Aristophanes suggests that the dirty secret of imperialism is that war and territorial aggression are a substitute for sex, and vice versa. The great expression of this diagnosis is the scene in which the Athenian and Spartan ambassadors divide up the naked body of Reconciliation, personified as a beautiful woman; they relate her various anatomical features to territories of Greece over which their cities were fighting. This suggestion is at once devastatingly accurate and an oversimplification. But this sort of reductiveness is characteristic of comedy, which offers us the reassurance that the world is not always as complicated as our daily experience and the rival genre, tragedy, would seem to suggest, that there is room in the world for wish-fulfilling fantasies—in this case, that a sex-strike might actually end war. Well, why not?

We do not know how the Athenians welcomed the play. All we know is that they were not impressed by its serious undertone; the war continued for seven more exhausting years, until Athens' last fleet was defeated, the city laid open to the enemy, the empire lost.

PRONOUNCING GLOSSARY

The following list uses common English syllables and stress accents to provide rough equivalents of selected words whose pronunciation may be unfamiliar to the general reader.

Andromache: *an-dro'-ma-kee*

Aristophanes: *a-ri-sto'-fa-neez*

Kalonike: *kal-oh-nee'-kay*

Kinesias: *kin-ay'-see-as*

Lysistrata: *lai-sis'-trah-tuh / li-sis-trah'-tuh*

Myrrhine: *meer-ree'-nay*

Lysistrata[1]

CHARACTERS[2]

LYSISTRATA, *an Athenian woman*
KALONIKE, *Lysistrata's friend*
MYRRHINE, *an Athenian wife*
LAMPITO, *a Spartan wife*
MAGISTRATE, *one of the ten Probouloi*
OLD WOMEN (three), *allies of Lysistrata*

WIVES (four), *Lysistrata's conspirators*
KINESIAS, *Myrrhine's husband*
BABY, *son of Kinesias and Myrrhine*
SPARTAN HERALD
SPARTAN AMBASSADOR
ATHENIAN AMBASSADORS (two)

MUTE CHARACTERS

ATHENIAN WOMEN
ISMENIA, *a Theban woman*
KORINTHIAN WOMAN
SPARTAN WOMEN
SKYTHIAN GIRL, *Lysistrata's slave*
MAGISTRATE'S SLAVES
SKYTHIAN POLICEMEN
OLD WOMEN, *allies of Lysistrata*

MANES, *Kinesias' slave*
SPARTAN DELEGATES
SPARTAN SLAVES, *with the Spartan delegation*
ATHENIAN DELEGATES
RECONCILIATION
DOORKEEPER

CHORUS

OLD ATHENIAN MEN (twelve)

OLD ATHENIAN WOMEN (twelve)

1. Translated by Jeffrey Henderson.   2. The leading characters have significant names. *Lysistrata:* "disbander of the armies." *Kalonike:* "beautiful victory." *Lampito:* a typical upper-class Spartan name. *Kinesias* suggests the verb *kinein,* "to move," a common slang term for "copulate." *Myrrhine,* though a common Athenian name, in association with *Kinesias* would suggest "myrtle," a slang term for the female genitals.

PROLOGUE

[SCENE: *A neighborhood street in Athens, after dawn. The stage-building has a large central door and two smaller, flanking doors. From one of these Lysistrata emerges and looks expectantly up and down the street.*]

LYSISTRATA   Now if someone had invited the women to a revel for Bacchos, or to Pan's shrine, or to Genetyllis's at Kolias, they'd be jamming the streets with their tambourines.[3] But now there's not a single woman here. [*The far door opens.*] Except for my own neighbor there. Good morning, Kalonike.

KALONIKE   You too, Lysistrata. What's bothering you? Don't frown, child. Knitted brows are no good for your looks.

LYSISTRATA   But my heart's on fire, Kalonike, and I'm terribly annoyed about us women. You know, according to the men we're capable of all sorts of mischief—

KALONIKE   And that we are, by Zeus!

LYSISTRATA   But when they're told to meet here to discuss something that really matters, they're sleeping in and don't show up!

KALONIKE   Honey, they'll be along. For wives to get out of the house is a lot of trouble, you know: we've got to look after the husband or wake up a slave or put the baby to bed, or give it a bath or feed it a snack.

LYSISTRATA   Sure, but there's other business they ought to take more seriously than that stuff.

KALONIKE   Well, Lysistrata dear, what exactly *is* this business you're calling us women together for? What's the deal? Is it a big one?

LYSISTRATA   Big!

KALONIKE   Not hard as well?

LYSISTRATA   It's big *and* hard, by Zeus.

KALONIKE   Then how come we're not all here?

LYSISTRATA   That's not what I meant! If it were, we'd all have shown up fast enough. No, it's something I've been thinking hard *about*, kicking it around, night after sleepless night.

KALONIKE   All those kicks must have made it really smart.

LYSISTRATA   Smart enough that the salvation of all Greece lies in the women's hands!

KALONIKE   In the *women's* hands? That's hardly reassuring!

LYSISTRATA   It's true: our country's future depends on *us*: whether the Peloponnesians[4] become extinct—

KALONIKE   Well, that would be just fine with me, by Zeus!

LYSISTRATA   And all the Boiotians get annihilated—

KALONIKE   Not *all* of them, though: please spare the eels![5]

LYSISTRATA   I won't say anything like that about the Athenians, but you know what I *could* say. But if the women gather together here—the

---

3. The references are to fertility cults with erotic overtones in which women could participate. Bacchos (or Bacchus, another name for Dionysus) was especially associated with wine. His worshippers often used flutes and drums with cymbals attached, like the modern tambourine.   4. Inhabitants of the peninsula that forms the southern part of the Greek mainland. Led by Sparta, they, along with the Boiotians (Boeotians) north of Attica, were Athens' main enemies in the Peloponnesian War.   5. Eels from Lake Kopais in Boiotia, a much-prized delicacy, were now under embargo because Boiotia was enemy territory.

Boiotian women, the Peloponnesian women and ourselves—together we'll be able to rescue Greece!

KALONIKE But what can mere *women* do that's intelligent or noble? We sit around the house looking pretty, wearing saffron dresses and make-up and Kimberic gowns and canoe-sized slippers.[6]

LYSISTRATA Exactly! That's exactly what I think will rescue Greece: our fancy little dresses, our perfumes and our slippers, our rouge and our see-through underwear!

KALONIKE How do you mean? I'm lost.

LYSISTRATA They'll guarantee that not a single one of the men who are still alive will raise his spear against another—

KALONIKE Then, by the Two Goddesses,[7] I'd better get my party dress dyed saffron!

LYSISTRATA nor hoist his shield—

KALONIKE I'll wear a Kimberic gown!

LYSISTRATA nor even pull a knife!

KALONIKE I've got to buy some slippers!

LYSISTRATA So shouldn't the women have gotten here by now?

KALONIKE By *now?* My god, they should have taken wing and flown here ages ago!

LYSISTRATA My friend, you'll see that they're typically Athenian: everything they do, they do too late. There isn't even a single woman here from the Paralia, nor from Salamis.[8]

KALONIKE Oh, them: I just *know* they've been up since dawn, straddling their mounts.

LYSISTRATA And the women I reckoned would be here first, and counted on, the women from Acharnai,[9] they're not here either.

KALONIKE Well, Theogenes' wife,[1] for one, was set to make a fast get-away. [*Groups of women begin to enter from both sides.*] But look, here come some of your women now!

LYSISTRATA And here come some others, over there!

KALONIKE Phew! Where are *they* from?

LYSISTRATA From Dungstown.

KALONIKE It seems they've got some sticking to their shoes.

MYRRHINE I hope we're not too late, Lysistrata. What do you say? Why don't you say something?

LYSISTRATA Myrrhine, I've got no medal for anyone who shows up late for important business.

MYRRHINE Look, I couldn't find my girdle; it was dark. But now we're here, so tell us what's so important.

LYSISTRATA No, let's wait a little while, until the women from Boiotia and the Peloponnesos come.

MYRRHINE That's a much better plan. And look, there's Lampito coming now!

---

6. Evidently, expensive imports. Among the stereotypes of women was their extravagance.   7. Demeter and her daughter Kore (Persephone), fertility goddesses worshipped especially at Eleusis in Athenian territory.   8. An island just off the Attic coast. *The Paralia:* a district along the southern shore of Attica. 9. A district of Attica.   1. Presumably the Athenians knew who she was and got the joke, which is obscure to us.

[*Enter* LAMPITO, *accompanied by a group of other Spartan women, a Theban woman* (ISMENIA) *and a Korinthian woman.*]

LYSISTRATA Greetings, my very dear Spartan Lampito! My darling, how dazzling is your beauty! What rosy cheeks, what firmness of physique! You could choke a bull![2]

LAMPITO Is true, I think, by Twain Gods.[3] Much exercise, much leaping to harden buttocks.[4]

KALONIKE And what a beautiful pair of boobs you've got!

LAMPITO Hey, you feel me up like sacrificial ox!

LYSISTRATA And this other young lady here, where's *she* from?

LAMPITO By Twain Gods, she come as representative of Boiotia.

MYRRHINE She's certainly *like* Boiotia, by Zeus, with all her lush bottom-land.

KALONIKE Yes indeed, her bush has been most elegantly pruned.[5]

LYSISTRATA And who's this other girl?

LAMPITO Lady of substance, by Twain Gods, from Korinth.[6]

KALONIKE She's substantial all right, both frontside and backside.

LAMPITO Who convenes this assembly of women here?

LYSISTRATA I'm the one.

LAMPITO Then please to tell what you want of us.

KALONIKE That's right, dear lady, speak up. What's this important business of yours?

LYSISTRATA I'm ready to tell you. But before I tell you, I want to ask you a small question; it won't take long.

KALONIKE Ask away.

LYSISTRATA Don't you all pine for your children's fathers when they're off at war? I'm sure that every one of you has a husband who's away.

KALONIKE My husband's been away five months, my dear, at the Thracian front; he's guarding Eukrates.[7]

MYRRHINE And *mine's* been at Pylos[8] *seven* whole months.

LAMPITO And *mine,* soon as he come home from regiment, is strapping on the shield and flying off.

KALONIKE Even *lovers* have disappeared without a trace, and ever since the Milesians revolted from us, I haven't even seen a six-inch dildo, which might have been a consolation, however small.[9]

LYSISTRATA Well, if I could devise a plan to end the war, would you be ready to join me?

KALONIKE By the Two Goddesses, I would, even if I had to pawn this dress and on the very same day—drink up the proceeds!

MYRRHINE And *I* think I would even cut myself in two like a flounder and donate half to the cause!

---

2. Spartan women took part in athletics and were in other ways less restricted than women in other Greek cities.   3. The Dioskouroi, Kastor and Pollux, quintessential Spartan gods.   4. Aristophanes caricatures the Spartan dialect of Greek, a variety of Doric, which could sound strange to the ears of the Athenians, who spoke Attic-Ionic. Speakers of both dialects could understand each other, however.   5. Depilation of the pubic hair was expected of well-groomed women.   6. A city in the northern Peloponnesus, a bitter enemy of Athens.   7. We expect a place-name and get the name of an Athenian, perhaps a general. *The Thracian front:* in northeastern Greece, the scene of considerable fighting during the war.   8. A district located in the southern Peloponnesus and strategically important against Sparta. Pylos had been occupied by the Athenians since 425 B.C.E.   9. Leather dildos were evidently a manufacturing specialty of Miletos, a Greek city on the coast of Asia Minor that had recently revolted from the Athenian alliance and gone over to Sparta.

LAMPITO And I would climb up to summit of Taÿgeton,[1] if I'm able to see where peace may be from there.

LYSISTRATA Here goes then; no need to beat around the bush. Ladies, if we're going to force the men to make peace, we're going to have to give up—

KALONIKE Give up what? Tell us.

LYSISTRATA You'll do it, then?

KALONIKE We'll do it, even if it means our death!

LYSISTRATA All right. We're going to have to give up—cock. Why are you turning away from me? Where are you going? Why are you all pursing your lips and shaking your heads? What means thine altered color and tearful droppings?[2] Will you do it or not? What are you waiting for?

KALONIKE Count me out; let the war drag on.

MYRRHINE Me too, by Zeus; let the war drag on.

LYSISTRATA This from you, Ms. Flounder? Weren't you saying just a moment ago that you'd cut yourself in half?

KALONIKE Anything else you want, anything at all! I'm even ready to walk through fire; *that* rather than give up cock. There's nothing like it, Lysistrata dear.

LYSISTRATA And what about you?

WOMAN I'm ready to walk through fire too.

LYSISTRATA Oh what a low and horny race are we! No wonder men write tragedies about us: we're nothing but Poseidon and a bucket.[3] Dear Spartan, if you alone would side with me we might still salvage the plan; give me your vote!

LAMPITO By Twain Gods, is difficult for females to sleep alone without the hard-on. But anyway, I assent; is need for peace.

LYSISTRATA You're an absolute dear, and the only real woman here!

KALONIKE Well, what if we *did* abstain from, uh, what you say, which heaven forbid: would peace be likelier to come on account of *that*?

LYSISTRATA Absolutely, by the Two Goddesses. If we sat around at home all made up, and walked past them wearing only our see-through underwear and with our pubes plucked in a neat triangle, and our husbands got hard and hankered to ball us, but we didn't go near them and kept away, they'd sue for peace, and pretty quick, you can count on that!

LAMPITO Like Menelaos! Soon as he peek at Helen's bare melons, he throw his sword away, I think.[4]

KALONIKE But what if our husbands pay us no attention?

LYSISTRATA As Pherekrates said, skin the skinned dog.[5]

KALONIKE Facsimiles are nothing but poppy-cock. And what if they grab us and drag us into the bedroom by force?

LYSISTRATA Hold onto the door.

KALONIKE And what if they beat us up?

LYSISTRATA Submit, but disagreeably: men get no pleasure in sex when

---

1. The massive mountain range that towers over Sparta.   2. Lysistrata breaks into tragic language, very different from the less elevated, frequently obscene style of comedy. In Greek comedy characters often parody or quote tragedy.   3. The mythical heroine Tyro slept with Poseidon, god of the sea, and exposed the resulting twins in a tub by the river where she was seduced.   4. As Troy was being sacked, Menelaos was about to kill Helen in revenge for her adultery. She bared her breasts and, overcome by her beauty, he dropped his sword.   5. Pherekrates was another comic poet slightly earlier than Aristophanes. His advice amounts to "use a dildo."

they have to force you. And make them suffer in other ways as well.
Don't worry, they'll soon give in. No husband can have a happy life if his
wife doesn't want him to.

KALONIKE Well, if the two of you agree to this, then we agree as well.

LAMPITO And we shall bring *our* menfolk round to making everyway fair
and honest peace. But how do you keep Athenian rabble from acting like
lunatics?[6]

LYSISTRATA Don't worry, we'll handle the persuasion on *our* side.

LAMPITO Not so, as long as your battleships are afoot and your Goddess'
temple have bottomless fund of money.[7]

LYSISTRATA In fact, that's also been well provided for: we're going to
occupy the Akropolis this very day. The older women are assigned that
part: while we're working out our agreement down here, they'll occupy
the Akropolis, pretending to be up there for a sacrifice.

LAMPITO Sounds perfect, like rest of your proposals.

LYSISTRATA Then why not ratify them immediately by taking an oath, Lampito, so that the terms will be binding?

LAMPITO Reveal an oath, then, and we all swear to it.

LYSISTRATA Well said. Where's the Skythian[8] girl? [*A slave-girl comes out
of the stage-building with a shield.*] What are you gawking at? Put that
shield down in front of us—no, the other way—and someone give me
the severings.[9]

KALONIKE Lysistra, what kind of oath are you planning to make us swear?

LYSISTRATA What kind? The kind they say Aischylos once had people
swear: slaughtering an animal over a shield.[1]

KALONIKE Lysistrata, you don't take an oath about peace over a shield!

LYSISTRATA Then what kind of oath will it be?

KALONIKE What if we got a white stallion somewhere and cut a piece off
him?

LYSISTRATA What stallion? Get serious.

KALONIKE Well, how *are* we going to swear the oath?

LYSISTRATA By Zeus, if you'd like to know, I can tell you. We put a big
black wine-bowl hollow-up right here, we slaughter a magnum of Thasian
wine into it, and we swear not to pour any water into the bowl![2]

LAMPITO Oh da, I cannot find words to praise that oath!

LYSISTRATA Somebody go inside and fetch a bowl and a magnum. [*The
SLAVE-GIRL takes the shield inside and returns with a large wine-bowl and
a large cup.*]

MYRRHINE Dearest ladies, what a conglomeration of pottery!

KALONIKE [*Grabbing at the bowl.*] Just touching this could make a person
glad!

LYSISTRATA Put it down! And join me in laying hands upon this boar. [*All
the women put a hand on the magnum.*] Mistress Persuasion and Bowl

---

6. A jab at the Athenian democracy. Sparta had a very different constitution, but some Athenians took the
same view of democracy.   7. Athenian power was based on its navy and on the money that flowed from
the annual tribute of the "allies." The tribute was stored in Athena's temple, the Parthenon, on the Acropolis.
8. From Scythia, a region near the Black Sea in Asia Minor and a source of Athenian slaves.   9. Oaths
were sworn—always by men—standing on parts of the animal victims and touching its blood.   1. In
Seven against Thebes (467 B.C.E.).   2. Greek men heavily diluted their wine with water; drinking wine
neat (as does the Cyclops in *Odyssey* 9), was a sign of intemperance and barbarity. Women (according to
men) had no self-restraint, a lack displayed in their alleged fondness for wine as well as sex.

of Fellowship, graciously receive this sacrifice from the women. [*She opens the magnum and pours wine into the bowl.*]

KALONIKE   The blood's a good color and spurts out nicely.

LAMPITO   It smell good too, by Kastor!

MYRRHINE   Ladies, let me be the first to take the oath!

KALONIKE   Hold on, by Aphrodite! Not unless you draw the first lot!

LYSISTRATA   *All* of you lay your hands upon the bowl; you too Lampito. Now one of you, on behalf of you all, must repeat after me the terms of the oath, and the rest of you will then swear to abide by them. No man of any kind, lover or husband—

KALONIKE   No man of any kind, lover or husband—

LYSISTRATA   shall approach me with a hard-on. I can't hear you!

KALONIKE   shall approach me with a hard-on. Oh god, my knees are buckling, Lysistrata!

LYSISTRATA   At home in celibacy shall I pass my life—

KALONIKE   At home in celibacy shall I pass my life—

LYSISTRATA   wearing a party-dress and makeup—

KALONIKE   wearing a party-dress and makeup—

LYSISTRATA   so that my husband will get as hot as a volcano for me—

KALONIKE   so that my husband will get as hot as a volcano for me—

LYSISTRATA   but never willingly shall I surrender to my husband.

KALONIKE   but never willingly shall I surrender to my husband.

LYSISTRATA   If he should use force to force me against my will—

KALONIKE   If he should use force to force me against my will—

LYSISTRATA   I will submit coldly and not move my hips.

KALONIKE   I will submit coldly and not move my hips.

LYSISTRATA   I will not raise my oriental slippers toward the ceiling.

KALONIKE   I will not raise my oriental slippers toward the ceiling.

LYSISTRATA   I won't crouch down like the lioness on a cheesegrate.[3]

KALONIKE   I won't crouch down like the lioness on a cheesegrate.

LYSISTRATA   If I live up to these vows, may I drink from this bowl.

KALONIKE   If I live up to these vows, may I drink from this bowl.

LYSISTRATA   But if I break them, may the bowl be full of water.

KALONIKE   But if I break them, may the bowl be full of water.

LYSISTRATA   So swear you one and all?

ALL   So swear we all!

LYSISTRATA   All right, then, I'll consecrate the bowl. [*She takes a long drink.*]

KALONIKE   Only your share, my friend; let's make sure we're all on friendly terms right from the start.

[*After they drink, a women's joyful cry is heard offstage.*]

LAMPITO   What's that hurrah?

LYSISTRATA   It's just what I was telling you before: the women have occupied the Akropolis and the Goddess' temple. Now, Lampito: you take off and arrange things in Sparta, but leave these women here with us as hostages. [*Exit* LAMPITO.] Meanwhile, we'll go inside with the other women on the Akropolis and bolt the gates behind us.

---

3. I.e., in order to be penetrated from behind. The handles of metal utensils were often in the form of animals.

KALONIKE   But don't you think the men will launch a concerted attack on us, and very soon?

LYSISTRATA   I'm not worried about *them*. They can't come against us with enough threats or fire to get these gates open, except on the terms we've agreed on.

KALONIKE   No they can't, by Aphrodite![4] Otherwise we women wouldn't deserve to be called rascals you can't win a fight with!

[*All exit into the central door of the scene-building, which now represents the Akropolis.*]

PARODOS[5]

[*A semichorus composed of twelve old men, poorly dressed, slowly makes its way along one of the wings into the orchestra. Each carries a pair of logs, an unlit torch and a bucket of live coals.*]

MEN'S LEADER   Onward, Drakes,[6] lead the way, even if your shoulder *is* sore; you've got to keep toting that load of green olivewood, no matter how heavy it is.

MEN (*strophe*)

If you live long enough you'll get many surprises, yes sir!
Strymodoros: who in the world ever thought we'd hear
that women, the very creatures we've kept in our homes,
an obvious nuisance, now control the Sacred Image[7]
and occupy *my* Akropolis, and not only that,
they've locked the citadel gates with bolts and bars!

MEN'S LEADER   Let's hurry to the Akropolis, Philourgos, full speed ahead, so we can lay these logs in a circle all around them, around all the women who have instigated or abetted this business! We'll erect a single pyre and condemn them all with a single vote, then throw them on top with our own hands, starting with Lykon's wife![8]

MEN (*antistrophe*)

By Demeter, while I still live they'll never laugh at me!
Not even Kleomenes,[9] the first to occupy this place,
left here intact. No, for all he breathed the Spartan spirit,
he left without his weapons—surrendered to *me*!
with only a little bitty jacket on his back, starving,
filthy, unshaven and unwashed for six whole years.

MEN'S LEADER   That's the way I laid siege to *that* fellow—savagely! We kept watch on these gates in ranks seventeen deep. So: am I to stand by *now* and do nothing to put down the effrontery of these *women*, enemies of all the gods and of Euripides?[1] If so, take down my trophy that stands at Marathon![2]

---

4. Goddess of love.   **5.** The entrance song of the chorus. Because the women have seized the Acropolis, the old men make a comically pathetic attempt to "liberate" it.   **6.** In comedy, in contrast to tragedy, individual chorus members were often given personal names.   **7.** The ancient olive-wood statue of Athena Polias ("Goddess of the City").   **8.** Notorious for loose morals.   **9.** Leader of the Spartans who in 508 B.C.E. tried to intervene in Athens on behalf of the aristocratic resistance to the democratic reforms of Cleisthenes. They seized the Acropolis, were besieged there by the Athenians, and withdrew from the city after two days.   **1.** Aristophanes always presents the tragedian Euripides, improbably, as a misogynist and hence as hated by women in return.   **2.** Town on the north coast of Attica where in 490 B.C.E. a small Athenian army repelled a large Persian expedition. Victorious armies erected a trophy (from the Greek word for "turn") on the battlefield to mark the spot where the enemy turned and retreated.

MEN (strophe)
> I'm almost at the end of my trek;
> all that remains is the steep stretch
> up to the Akropolis; can't wait to get there!
> How in the world are we going to haul
> these loads up there without a donkey?
> This pair of logs is utterly crushing my shoulder!
> But I've got to soldier on,
> and keep my fire alight.
> It mustn't go out on me before I've reached my goal.
>   [*They blow into their buckets of coals.*]
> Ouch, ugh! The smoke!

(antistrophe)
> How terribly, Lord Herakles, this smoke
> jumped from the bucket and attacked me!
> It bit both my eyes like a rabid bitch!
> And as for this fire, it's Lemnian[3]
> in every possible way; otherwise
> it wouldn't have buried its teeth in my eyeballs that way!
> Hurry forth to the citadel,
> run to the Goddess' rescue!
> If this isn't the time to help her, Laches, when will that time be?
>   [*They blow on their buckets of coals again.*]
> Ouch, ugh! The smoke!

MEN'S LEADER   Praise the gods, this fire's awake and plenty lively too. Let's place our logs right here, then dip our torches into the buckets, and when they're lighted we'll charge the gates like rams. If the women don't unbolt the gates when we invite their surrender, we'll set the portals afire and smoke them into submission. Very well, let's put the logs down. Phew, that smoke! Damn! Would any of the generals at Samos[4] care to help us with this wood? [*He laboriously wrestles his pair of logs to the ground.*] They've finally stopped crushing my back! Now it's *your* job, bucket, to rouse your coals to flame and thus supply me, first of all, with a lighted torch! Lady Victory,[5] be our ally, help us win a trophy over the women on the Akropolis and their present audacity!

> [*As the men crouch down to light their torches the second semichorus enters on the run. It is composed of twelve old women, nicely dressed and carrying pitchers of water on their heads.*[6]]

WOMEN'S LEADER   I think I can see sparks and smoke, fellow women, as if a fire were ablaze. We must hurry all the faster!

WOMEN (strophe)
> Fly, fly, Nikodike,
> before Kalyke and Kritylla[7] are incinerated,
> blown from all directions

---

3. From the volcanic island of Lemnos, which was sacred to Hephaestus, the blacksmith god. The adjective may also allude to the myth of the women of Lemnos, who killed their husbands.   4. An island in the eastern Aegean; it was the major Athenian naval base at this time.   5. Victory was personified as a goddess, but there is probably a specific reference to Athena Nike ("Bringer of Victory"), whose small, elegant temple stands on a parapet on the right as one climbs to the entrance to the Acropolis.   6. Fetching each day's water from the neighborhood spring was a normal household chore for women, but these women are bringing water to put out the men's fire.   7. Names of women chorus members.

by nasty winds and old men who mean death!
I'm filled with dread: am I too late to help?
I've just come from the well with my pitcher;
it was hard to fill by the light of dawn,
in the throng and crash and clatter of pots,
fighting the elbows of housemaids and branded slaves.
I hoisted it onto my head with zeal, and carry the water here
to assist the women, my fellow citizens faced with burning.

(*antistrophe*)

I've heard that some frantic old men
are on the loose with three talents[8] of logs,
like furnace-men at the public bathhouse.
They're coming to the Akropolis, screaming
the direst threats, that they mean to use their fire
"to turn these abominable women into charcoal."
Goddess, may I never see these women in flames;
instead let them rescue Greece and her citizens from war and madness!
O golden-crested Guardian of the citadel, that is why
they occupy your shrine. I invite thee to be our ally, Tritogeneia,[9]
defending it with water, should any man set it afire.

WOMEN'S LEADER   Hold on! Hey! What's this? Men! Awful, nasty men! No
gentlemen, no god-fearing men would ever be caught doing this!

MEN'S LEADER   This here's a complication we didn't count on facing: this
swarm of women outside the gates is here to help the others!

WOMEN'S LEADER   Fear and trembling, eh? Don't tell me we seem a lot to
handle: you haven't even seen the tiniest fraction of our forces yet!

MEN'S LEADER   Phaidrias, are we going to let these women go on jabbering
like this? Why hasn't somebody busted a log over their heads?

WOMEN'S LEADER   Let's ground our pitchers then; if anyone attacks us they
won't get in our way.

MEN'S LEADER   By Zeus, if someone had socked them in the mouth a couple of times, like Boupalos,[1] they wouldn't still be talking!

WOMEN'S LEADER   OK, here's my mouth; someone take a sock at it; I'll
stand here and take it. But then I'm the bitch who gets to grab you by
the balls!

MEN'S LEADER   If you don't shut up, I'll knock you right out of your old
hide!

WOMEN'S LEADER   Come over here and just touch Stratyllis with the tip of
your finger.

MEN'S LEADER   What if I give you the one-two punch? Got anything scary
to counter with?

WOMEN'S LEADER   I'll rip out your lungs and your guts with my fangs.

MEN'S LEADER   There isn't a wiser poet than Euripides: no beast exists so
shameless as women![2]

WOMEN'S LEADER   Let's pick up our pitchers of water, Rhodippe.

MEN'S LEADER   Why did you bring water here, you witch?

---

8. More than 170 pounds (a *talent* is a unit of weight).   9. An epithet of Athena.   1. Said to have
been driven to suicide by the scurrilous abuse of the poet Hipponax (6th century B.C.E.).   2. A sentence
in the tragic style, if not an actual quotation from a lost play of Euripides.

WOMEN'S LEADER   And why have *you* got fire, you tomb? To burn yourself up?

MEN'S LEADER   *I'm* here to build a pyre and burn up your friends.

WOMEN'S LEADER   And *I've* come to put it out with this.

MEN'S LEADER   *You're* going to put out *my* fire?

WOMEN'S LEADER   That's what you soon will see.

MEN'S LEADER   I think I might barbecue you with this torch of mine.

WOMEN'S LEADER   Got any soap with you? I'll give you a bath.

MEN'S LEADER   *You* give *me* a bath, you crone?

WOMEN'S LEADER   A bath fit for a bridegroom!

MEN'S LEADER   What insolence!

WOMEN'S LEADER   I'm a free woman!

MEN'S LEADER   I'll put a stop to your bellowing.

WOMEN'S LEADER   You're not on a jury now, you know.[3]

MEN'S LEADER   Torch her hair! [*The men advance.*]

WOMEN'S LEADER   Acheloos,[4] do your thing! [*The women douse them.*]

MEN'S LEADER   Oh! Damn!

WOMEN'S LEADER   It wasn't too hot, was it?

MEN'S LEADER   Hot? Stop it! What do you think you're doing?

WOMEN'S LEADER   I'm watering you, so you'll bloom.

MEN'S LEADER   But I'm already dried out from shivering!

WOMEN'S LEADER   You've got fire there; why not sit by it and get warm?

EPISODE

[*Enter the* MAGISTRATE, *an irascible old man, accompanied by two slaves carrying crowbars and four Skythian policemen.*[5]]

MAGISTRATE   So the women's depravity bursts into flame again: beating drums, chanting "Sabazios!", worshiping Adonis on the rooftops.[6] I heard it all once before while sitting in Assembly. Demostratos[7] (bad luck to him!) was moving that we send an armada to Sicily, while his wife was dancing and yelling "Poor young Adonis! Then Demostratos moved that we sign up some Zakynthian infantry, but his wife up on the roof was getting drunk and going "Beat your breast for Adonis!" But he just went on making his motions, that godforsaken, disgusting Baron Bluster! From women, I say, you get this kind of riotous extravagance!

MEN'S LEADER [*Pointing to the* CHORUS OF WOMEN.]   Save your breath till you hear about *their* atrocities! They've committed every kind, even doused us with those pitchers. Now we get to shake water out of our clothes as if we'd peed in them!

MAGISTRATE   By the salty sea-god it serves us right! When we ourselves are accomplices in our wives' misbehavior and teach them profligacy, these are the sort of schemes they bring to flower! Aren't *we* the ones who go to the shops and say stuff like, "goldsmith, about that necklace you made

---

3. Payment for jury service, instituted by Pericles, provided the aged and the poor something of a living.
4. One of the biggest rivers in Greece.   5. Slaves from Scythia made up the Athenian police force. *Magistrate:* one of a board of ten prominent citizens chosen in the wake of the Sicilian disaster to restrain possible legislative excesses by the Assembly.   6. The Asiatic cult of the vegetation god Adonis (Tammuz) was celebrated by women, who lamented the god's death each year on the roofs of their houses. In male eyes, the cult, as both Oriental and female, threatened the Greek ideal of self-restraint. *Sabazios:* a god whose cult, recently imported into Athens, involved wine drinking and appealed especially to women and slaves.   7. One of the supporters of the expedition to Sicily in 415 B.C.E., which was to prove disastrous.

me: my wife was having a ball the other night, and now the prong's slipped out of its hole. Me, I've got to cruise over to Salamis. So if you've got time, by all means visit her in the evening and fit a prong in her hole." Another husband says this to a teenage shoemaker with a very grown-up cock, "Shoemaker, my wife's pinky-toe hurts. It seems the top-strap is cramping the bottom, where she's tender. So why don't you drop in on her some lunchtime and loosen it up so there's more play down there?" That's the sort of thing that's led to *this*, when I, a Magistrate, have lined up timber for oars and now come to get the necessary funds, and find myself standing at the gate, locked out by women! But I'm not going to stand around. [*To the two slaves.*] Bring the crowbars; I'll put a stop to their arrogance. What are *you* gaping at, you sorry fool? And where are *you* staring? I said crowbar, not winebar! Come on, put those crowbars under the gates and start jimmying on that side; I'll help out on this side.

LYSISTRATA [*Emerging from the gates.*]   Don't jimmy the gates; I'm coming out on my very own. Why do you need crowbars? It's not crowbars you need; it's rather brains and sense.

MAGISTRATE   Really! You witch! Where's a policeman? Grab her and tie both hands behind her back! [*One of the policemen advances on* LYSISTRATA.]

LYSISTRATA   If he so much as touches me with his fingertip, by Artemis he'll go home crying, public servant or not! [*The policeman retreats.*]

MAGISTRATE   What, are you scared? [*To a second policeman.*] You there, help him out; grab her around the waist and tie her up, on the double!

[*A large old woman emerges from the gates.*]

FIRST OLD WOMAN   If you so much as lay a hand on her, by Pandrosos[8] I'll beat the shit out of you! [*Both policemen retreat.*]

MAGISTRATE   Beat the shit out of me! Where's another policeman? [*A third policeman steps forward.*] Tie *her* up first, the one with the dirty mouth!

[*A second old woman emerges from the gates.*]

SECOND OLD WOMAN   If you raise your fingertip to her, by our Lady of Light[9] you'll be begging for an eye-cup! [*The third archer retreats.*]

MAGISTRATE   What's going on? Where's a policeman? [*The fourth policeman steps forward.*] Arrest her. I'll foil *one* of these sallies of yours!

[*A third old woman emerges from the gates.*]

THIRD OLD WOMAN   If you come near her, by Eastern Artemis[1] I'll rip out your hair till it screams! [*The fourth policeman retreats.*]

MAGISTRATE   What a terrible setback! I'm out of policemen. But men must never, ever be worsted by women! Skythians, let's charge them *en masse*; form up ranks!

[*The four policemen prepare to charge.*]

LYSISTRATA   By the Two Goddesses, you'll soon discover that we also have four squadrons of fully armed combat-women, waiting inside!

MAGISTRATE   Skythians, twist their arms behind their backs!

[*The policemen advance.*]

LYSISTRATA [*Calling into the Akropolis like a military commander.*]   Women of the reserve, come out double-time! Forward, you spawn of the mar-

8. Daughter of Kekrops, the legendary king of Attica, who was worshipped with her sister Aglauros on the Acropolis.   9. Hekate, a goddess associated with the moon and childbirth.   1. Artemis, the huntress goddess worshipped in Tauris (the Crimean Peninsula) and also in Attica.

ketplace,[2] you soup and vegetable mongers! Forward, you landladies, you hawkers of garlic and bread! [*Four squadrons of tough old market-women rush out of the Akropolis and, together with the women already onstage, attack the four policemen.*] Tackle them! Hit them! Smash them! Call them names, the nastier the better! [*The policemen run away howling.*] That's enough! Withdraw! Don't strip the bodies!

[*The women of the reserve go back into the Akropolis.*]

MAGISTRATE Terrible! What a calamity for my men!

LYSISTRATA Well, what did you expect? Did you think you were going up against a bunch of slave-girls? Or did you think women lack gall?

MAGISTRATE They've got it aplenty, by Apollo, provided there's a wineshop nearby.

MEN'S LEADER You've little to show for all your talk, Magistrate of this country! What's the point of fighting a battle of words with these beasts? Don't you comprehend the kind of bath they've given us just now—when we were still in our clothes, and without soap to boot?

WOMEN'S LEADER Well, sir, you shouldn't lift your hand against your neighbors just anytime you feel like it. If you do, you're going to end up with a black eye. I'd rather be sitting at home like a virtuous maiden, making no trouble for anyone here, stirring not a single blade of grass. But if anyone annoys me and rifles my nest, they'll find a wasp inside!

ONSTAGE DEBATE

MEN (*strophe*)

Zeus, how in the world are we going to deal with these monsters?
They've gone beyond what I can bear! Now it's time for a trial:
together let's find out
what they thought they were doing
when they occupied Kranaos'[3] citadel
and the great crag of the Akropolis,
a restricted, holy place.

MEN'S LEADER Question her and don't give in; cross-examine what she says. It's scandalous to let this sort of behavior go unchallenged.

MAGISTRATE Here's the first thing I'd like to know, by Zeus: what do you mean by barricading our Akropolis?

LYSISTRATA To keep the money safe and to keep *you* from using it to finance the war.

MAGISTRATE So we're at war on account of the money?

LYSISTRATA Yes, and the money's why everything else got messed up too. Peisandros and the others aiming to hold office were always fomenting some kind of commotion so that they'd be able to steal it.[4] So let them keep fomenting to their hearts' content: they'll be withdrawing no more money from *this* place.

MAGISTRATE But what do you plan to do?

LYSISTRATA Don't you see? We'll manage it for you!

MAGISTRATE *You'll* manage the money?

---

2. Poor citizen women and slave women sold food in booths in the *agora*, or marketplace. 3. Another mythical king of Athens. 4. A few months after this play was performed, Peisandros and an oligarchic faction overthrew the democratic constitution, with widespread assassinations and confiscations. By the following year (410 B.C.E.), the democracy was restored.

LYSISTRATA   What's so strange in that? Don't we manage the household finances for you already?

MAGISTRATE   That's different!

LYSISTRATA   How so?

MAGISTRATE   These are *war* funds!

LYSISTRATA   But there shouldn't even *be* a war.

MAGISTRATE   How else are we to protect ourselves?

LYSISTRATA   We'll protect you.

MAGISTRATE   *You?*

LYSISTRATA   Yes, us.

MAGISTRATE   What brass!

LYSISTRATA   You'll be protected whether you like it or not!

MAGISTRATE   You're going too far!

LYSISTRATA   Angry, are you? We've got to do it anyway.

MAGISTRATE   By Demeter, you've got no right!

LYSISTRATA   You must be saved, dear fellow.

MAGISTRATE   Even if I don't ask to be?

LYSISTRATA   All the more so!

MAGISTRATE   And where do *you* get off taking an interest in war and peace?

LYSISTRATA   We'll tell you.

MAGISTRATE   Well, make it snappy, unless you want to get hurt.

LYSISTRATA   Listen then, and try to control your fists.

MAGISTRATE   I can't; I'm so angry I can't keep my hands to myself.

FIRST OLD WOMAN   Then *you're* the one'll get hurt!

MAGISTRATE   Croak those curses at yourself, old bag! [*To* LYSISTRATA.] Start talking.

LYSISTRATA   Gladly. All along, being proper women, we used to suffer in silence no matter what you men did, because you wouldn't let us make a sound. But you weren't exactly all we could ask for. No, we knew only too well what you were up to, and too many times we'd hear in our homes about a bad decision you'd made on some great issue of state. Then, masking the pain in our hearts, we'd put on a smile and ask you, "How did the Assembly go today? Any decision about a rider to the peace treaty?" And my husband would say, "What's that to you? Shut up!" And I'd shut up.

FIRST OLD WOMAN   *I* wouldn't have shut up!

MAGISTRATE   If you hadn't shut up you'd have got a beating!

LYSISTRATA   Well, that's why I *did* shut up. Later on we began to hear about even worse decisions you'd made, and then we would ask, "Husband, how come you're handling this so stupidly?" And right away he'd glare at me and tell me to get back to my sewing if I didn't want major damage to my head: "War shall be the business of menfolk,"[5] unquote.

MAGISTRATE   He was right on the mark, by Zeus.

LYSISTRATA   How could he be right, you sorry fool, when we were forbidden to offer advice even when your policy was *wrong*? But *then*—when we began to hear you in the streets openly crying, "There isn't a man left in the land," and someone else saying, "No, by Zeus, not a one"—after *that* we women decided to lose no more time and to band together to save Greece. What was the point of waiting any longer? So, if you're ready to

5. Hector's words to Andromache at *Iliad* 6.517.

take your turn at listening, we have some good advice, and if you shut up, as we used to, we can put you back on the righttrack.

MAGISTRATE   *You* put *us*—outrageous! I won't stand for it!

LYSISTRATA   Shut up!

MAGISTRATE   *Me* shut up for *you*? A damned woman, with a veil on your face too?[6] I'd rather die!

LYSISTRATA   If the veil's an obstacle, here, take mine, it's yours, put it on *your* face [*She removes her veil and puts it on the* MAGISTRATE'*s head.*], and *then* shut up!

FIRST OLD WOMAN   And take this sewing-basket too.

LYSISTRATA   Now hitch up your clothes and start sewing; chew some beans while you work. War shall be the business of womenfolk!

WOMEN'S LEADER   Come away from your pitchers, women: it's our turn to pitch in with a little help for our friends!

WOMEN (*antistrophe*)
Oh yes! I'll dance with unflagging energy;
the effort won't weary my knees.
I'm ready to face anything
with women courageous as these:
they've got character, charm and guts,
they've got intelligence and heart
that's both patriotic and smart!

WOMEN'S LEADER   Now, most valiant of prickly mommies and spikey grannies, attack furiously and don't let up: you're still running with the wind!

LYSISTRATA   If Eros of the sweet soul and Cyprian[7] Aphrodite imbue our thighs and breasts with desire, and infect the men with sensuous rigidity and club-cock, then I believe all Greece will one day call us Disbanders of Battles.

MAGISTRATE   What's your plan?

LYSISTRATA   First of all, we can stop people going to the market fully armed and acting crazy.

FIRST OLD WOMAN   Paphian[8] Aphrodite be praised!

LYSISTRATA   At this very moment, all around the market, in the pottery shops and the grocery stalls, they're walking around in arms like Korybantes.[9]

MAGISTRATE   Zeus, a man's got to act like a man!

LYSISTRATA   But it's totally ridiculous when he takes a shield with a Gorgon-blazon[1] to buy sardines!

FIRST OLD WOMAN   Yes, by Zeus, I saw a long-haired fellow, a cavalry captain, on horseback, getting porridge from an old women and sticking it into his brass hat. Another one, a Thracian, was shaking his shield and spear like Tereus;[2] he scared the fig-lady out of her wits and gulped down all the ripe ones!

6. Respectable women wore veils in public.   7. Of Cyprus, an island that was an important center of Aphrodite's cult.   8. Of Paphos, a city of Cyprus where a famous temple of Aphrodite was located. 9. Nature spirits who engaged in ecstatic dancing.   1. An image of the snake-haired monster, Medusa; warriors' shields often carried such pictures.   2. A mythical Thracian king who raped his sister-in-law, Philomela, and cut out her tongue to silence her. In revenge, she and his wife, Prokne, cooked and served him his son for dinner. He tried to attack them but was turned into a hoopoe, Prokne became a nightingale, and Philomela became a swallow. There is an allusion to tragedy here: Sophocles dramatized the myth in his *Tereus*.

MAGISTRATE   So how will you women be able to put a stop to such a complicated international mess, and sort it all out?

LYSISTRATA   Very easily.

MAGISTRATE   How? Show me.

[LYSISTRATA *uses the contents of the basket which the* MAGISTRATE *was
given to illustrate her demonstration.*]

LYSISTRATA   It's rather like a ball of yarn when it gets tangled up. We hold
it this way, and carefully wind out the strands on our spindles, now this
way, now that way. That's how we'll wind up this war, if allowed, unsnarl-
ing it by sending embassies, now this way, now that way.

MAGISTRATE   You really think your way with wool and yarnballs and spindles can stop a terrible crisis? How brainless!

LYSISTRATA   I do think so, and if *you* had any brains you'd handle *all* the
polis' business the way we handle our wool!

MAGISTRATE   Well, how then? I'm all ears.

LYSISTRATA   Imagine the polis as fleece just shorn. First, put it in a bath
and wash out all the sheep-dung; spread it on a pallet and beat out the
riff-raff with a stick and pluck out the thorns; as for those who clump
and knot themselves together to snag government positions, card them
out and pluck off their heads. Next, card the wool into a basket of unity
and goodwill, mixing in everyone. The resident aliens and any other foreigner who's your friend, and anyone who owes money to the people's
treasury, mix them in there too. And by Zeus, don't forget the cities that
are colonies of this land: they're like flocks of your fleece, each one separated from the others. So take all these flocks and bring them together
here, joining them all and making one big bobbin. And from this weave
a fine new cloak for the people!

MAGISTRATE   Isn't it awful how these women go like this with their sticks
and like this with their bobbins, when they share none of the war's burdens!

LYSISTRATA   None? You monster! We bear more than our fair share, first
of all by giving birth to sons and sending them off to the army—

MAGISTRATE   Enough of that! Let's not open old wounds.

LYSISTRATA   Then, when we ought to be having fun and enjoying our bloom
of youth, we sleep alone because of the campaigns. And to say no more
about *our* case, it pains me to think of the maidens growing old in their
rooms.

MAGISTRATE   Men grow old too, don't they?

LYSISTRATA   That's quite a different story. When a man comes home he
can quickly find a girl to marry, even if he's a greybeard. But a woman's
prime is brief; if she doesn't seize it no one wants to marry her,[3] and she
sits at home looking for good omens.

MAGISTRATE   But any man who can still get a hard-on—

LYSISTRATA   Why don't you just drop dead? Here's a grave-site; buy a coffin:
I'll start kneading you a honeycake.[4] [*Taking off her garland.*] Use these
as a wreath.

FIRST OLD WOMAN [*Handing him ribbons.*]   You can have these from me.

---

3. Greek girls were marriageable at an early age, sometimes shortly after puberty. Men married later, often
in their thirties. Losses in the war, especially in Sicily, had probably greatly reduced the number of male
citizens.   4. The dead were provided with a honey cake to throw to Cerberus, the three-headed dog that
guarded the entrance to the underworld. Funeral arrangements were part of women's duties.

SECOND OLD WOMAN   And this garland from me.

LYSISTRATA   All set? Need anything else? Get on the boat, then. Charon[5]
is calling your name and you're holding him up!

MAGISTRATE   Isn't it shocking that I'm being treated like this? By Zeus. I'm
going straight to the other magistrates to display myself just as I am![6]

LYSISTRATA [As Magistrate exits with his slaves.]   I hope you won't complain
about the funeral we gave you. I tell you what: the day after tomorrow;
first thing in the morning, we'll perform the third-day offerings at your
grave! [The women exit into the Akropolis.]

CHORAL DEBATE

MEN'S LEADER   No free man should be asleep now! Let's strip for action,
men, and meet this emergency! [The men remove their jackets.]

MEN (strophe a)
  I think I smell much bigger trouble in this,
  a definite whiff of Hippias'[7] tyranny!
  I'm terrified that certain men from Sparta
  have gathered at the house of Kleisthenes[8]
  and scheme to stir up our godforsaken women
  to seize the Treasury and my jury-pay,
  my very livelihood.

MEN'S LEADER   It's shocking, you know, that they're lecturing the citizens
now, and running their mouths—mere women!—about brazen shields.
And to top it all off they're trying to make peace between us and the men
of Sparta, who are no more trustworthy than a starving wolf. Actually,
this plot they weave against us, gentlemen, aims at tyranny! Well, they'll
never tyrannize over me: from now on I'll be on my guard, I'll "carry my
sword in a myrtle-branch" and go to market fully armed right up beside
Aristogeiton.[9] I'll stand beside him like this [Assuming the posture of Aristogeiton's statue.]: that way I'll be ready to smack this godforsaken old
hag right in the jaw! [He advances on the WOMEN'S LEADER with fist raised.]

WOMEN'S LEADER   Just try it, and your own mommy won't recognize you
when you get home! Come on, fellow hags, let's start by putting our
jackets on the ground. [The women remove their jackets.]

WOMEN (antistrophe a)
  Citizens of Athens, we want to start
  by offering the polis some good advice,
  and rightly, for she raised me in splendid luxury.
  As soon as I turned seven I was an Arrephoros;
  then I was a Grinder; when I was ten I shed
  my saffron robe for the Foundress at the Brauronia.
  And once, when I was a beautiful girl, I carried the Basket,
  wearing a necklace of dried figs.[1]

5. The ferryman who transported the dead over the river Styx.   6. That is, dressed as both a woman and
a corpse.   7. The last Athenian tyrant, expelled in 510 B.C.E.   8. Not the great reformer who set up
the democracy but a contemporary of Aristophanes, frequently lampooned by him as a homosexual. Pederasty may have been fashionable in Athens, at least among the upper classes, but a man who allowed
himself to be penetrated was viewed as effeminate.   9. One of the two assassins of Hippias's brother
Hipparchus (killed 514 B.C.E.). This murder was considered to have paved the way for Hippias's expulsion
and the liberation of Athens from tyranny. According to a popular drinking song, the tyrannicides hid their
swords in myrtle branches when they approached their victim. Their statues stood in the Agora.   1. These
lines describe the religious duties of an aristocratic Athenian girl as participant in various festivals.

WOMEN'S LEADER   Thus I *owe* it to the polis to offer some good advice. And even if I *was* born a woman, don't hold it against me if I manage to suggest something better than what we've got now. I have a stake in our community: my contribution is *men*. You miserable geezers have *no* stake, since you've squandered your paternal inheritance, won in the Persian Wars, and now pay no taxes in return. On the contrary, we're all headed for bankruptcy on account of you! Have you anything to grunt in rebuttal? Any more trouble from you and I'll clobber you with this rawhide boot right in the jaw! [*She raises her foot at the* MEN'S LEADER.]

MEN (*strophe b*)

> This behavior of theirs amounts to extreme hubris,
> and I do believe it's getting aggravated.
> No man with any balls can let it pass.

MEN'S LEADER   Let's doff our shirts, 'cause a man's gotta smell like a man from the word go and shouldn't be all wrapped up like souvlaki. [*The men remove their shirts.*]

MEN

> Come on, Whitefeet!
> We went against Leipsydrion[2]
> when we still were something;
> now we've got to rejuvenate, grow wings
> all over, shake off these old skins of ours!

MEN'S LEADER   If any man among us gives these women the tiniest thing to grab on to, there's no limit to what their nimble hands will do. Why, they'll even be building frigates and launching naval attacks, cruising against us like Artemisia.[3] And if they turn to horsemanship, you can scratch our cavalry; there's nothing like a woman when it comes to mounting and riding; even riding hard she won't slip off. Just look at the Amazons in Mikon's painting,[4] riding chargers in battle against men. Our duty is clear: grab each woman's neck and lock it in the wooden stocks! [*He moves toward the* WOMEN'S LEADER.]

WOMEN (*antistrophe b*)

> By the Two Goddesses, if you fire me up
> I'll come at you like a wild sow and clip you bare,
> and this very day you'll go bleating to your friends for help!

WOMEN'S LEADER   Quickly, women, let's also take off our tunics; a woman's gotta smell like a woman, mad enough to bite! [*The women remove their shirts.*]

WOMEN

> All right now, someone attack me!
> He'll eat no more garlic
> and chew no more beans.
> If you so much as curse at me, I boil over with such rage,
> I'll be the beetle-midwife to your eagle's eggs.[5]

WOMEN'S LEADER   You men don't worry me a bit, not while my Lampito's around and my Ismenia, the noble Theban girl. You'll have no power to

2. A fort in the hills north of the Attic plain used as a base by rebels in their first attempt to overthrow Hippias in 513 B.C.E.   3. Queen of Halicarnassus in Asia Minor; she was a prominent ally of Xerxes at Salamis.   4. The painter Mikon had lately decorated several public buildings with frescoes. The battles of the Greeks and Amazons (fierce women warriors from just south of the Black Sea in Asia Minor) were favorite subjects of sculptors and painters.   5. In a fable by Aesop, a beetle breaks an eagle's eggs in revenge for a wrong done by the eagle. Here, "eggs" are testicles.

do anything about us, not even if you pass seven decrees: that's how much everyone hates you, you good-for-nothing, and especially our neighbors. Why, just yesterday I threw a party for the girls in honor of Hekate, and I invited my friend from next door, a fine girl who's very special to me: an eel from Boiotia. But they said she couldn't come because of *your* decrees. And you'll *never* stop passing these decrees until someone grabs you by the leg and throws you away and breaks your neck!
[*She makes a grab for the* MEN'S LEADER's *leg.*]

EPISODE

[LYSISTRATA *comes out of the Akropolis and begins to pace.*]

WOMEN'S LEADER[6]
    O mistress of this venture and strategem,
    why com'st thou from thy halls so dour of mien?
LYSISTRATA
    The deeds of ignoble women and the female heart
    do make me pace dispirited to and fro.
WOMEN'S LEADER
    What say'st thou? What say'st thou?
LYSISTRATA   'Tis true, too true!
WOMEN'S LEADER
    What dire thing? Pray tell it to thy friends.
LYSISTRATA
    'Twere shame to say and grief to leave unsaid.
WOMEN'S LEADER
    Hide not from me the damage we have taken.
LYSISTRATA
    The story in briefest compass: we need to fuck!
WOMEN'S LEADER
    Ah, Zeus!
LYSISTRATA
    Why rend the air for Zeus? You see our plight.
The truth is, I can't keep the wives away from their husbands any longer; they're running off in all directions. The first one I caught was over there by Pan's Grotto, digging at her hole, and another was trying to escape by clambering down a pulley-cable. And yesterday another one mounted a sparrow and was about to fly off to Orsilochos'[7] house when I pulled her off by her hair. They're coming up with every kind of excuse to go home. [*A wife comes out of the Akropolis, looks around, and begins to run off-stage.*] Hey you! What's your hurry?
FIRST WIFE   I want to go home. I've got some Milesian wool in the house, and the moths are chomping it all up.
LYSISTRATA   Moths! Get back inside.
FIRST WIFE   By the Two Goddesses, I'll be right back; just let me spread it on the bed!
LYSISTRATA   You won't be spreading anything, nor be going anywhere.
FIRST WIFE   So I'm supposed to let my wool go to waste?

6. The exchange between Lysistrata and the Women's Leader is more tragic parody.   7. Presumably a notorious adulterer.

LYSISTRATA   If that's what it takes. [*As the first wife walks back toward* LYS-ISTRATA *a second runs out of the Akropolis.*]

SECOND WIFE   Oh my god, my god, the flax! I forgot to shuck it when I left the house!

LYSISTRATA   Here's another one off to shuck her flax. March right back here.

SECOND WIFE   By our Lady of Light, I'll be back in a flash; just let me do a little shucking.

LYSISTRATA   No! No shucking! If *you* start doing it, some other wife will want to do the same. [*While the second wife walks back toward Lysistrata a third runs out of the Akropolis, holding her bulging belly.*]

THIRD WIFE   O Lady of Childbirth, hold back the baby till I can get to a more profane spot![8]

LYSISTRATA   What are you raving about?

THIRD WIFE   I'm about to deliver a child!

LYSISTRATA   But you weren't pregnant yesterday.

THIRD WIFE   But today I am. Please, Lysistrata, send me home to the mid-wife, and right away!

LYSISTRATA   What's the story? [*She feels the wife's belly.*] What's this? It's hard.

THIRD WIFE   It's a boy.

LYSISTRATA [*Knocking on it.*].   By Aphrodite, it's obvious you've got some-thing metallic and hollow in there. Let's have a look. [*She lifts up the wife's dress, exposing a large bronze helmet.*] Ridiculous girl! You're big with the sacred helmet,[9] not with child!

THIRD WIFE   But I *am* with child, by Zeus!

LYSISTRATA   Then what were you doing with this?

THIRD WIFE   Well, if I began to deliver here in the citadel, I could get into the helmet and have my baby there, like a pigeon.

LYSISTRATA   What kind of story is that? Excuses! It's obvious what's going on. You'll have to stay here til your—helmet has its naming-day.

THIRD WIFE   But I can't even *sleep* on the Akropolis, ever since I saw the snake that guards the temple.[1]

FOURTH WIFE   And what about poor me—listening to the owls[2] go *woo woo* all night is killing me!

LYSISTRATA   You nutty girls, enough of your horror stories! I guess you do miss your husbands; but do you think they don't miss *you*? They're spend-ing some very rough nights, I assure you. Just be patient, good ladies, and put up with this, just a little bit longer. There's an oracle predicting victory for us, *if* we stick together. Here's the oracle right here. [*She produces a scroll.*]

THIRD WIFE   Tell us what it says.

LYSISTRATA
      Be quiet, then.
      Yea, when the swallows hole up in a single home,
      fleeing the hoopoes and leaving the penis alone,

---

8. As sacred ground, the Acropolis would be polluted by either childbirth or death.   9. From the statue of Athena Promachos ("Fighter in Behalf of the City") that stood on the Acropolis.   1. No one had ever seen the sacred snake that lived in the Erechtheum, another temple on the Acropolis.   2. Athena's sacred birds.

then are their problems solved, what's high is low:
so says high-thundering Zeus—
THIRD WIFE   You mean *we'll* be lying on top?
LYSISTRATA   But:
    if the swallows begin to argue and fly away
    down from the citadel holy, all will say,
    no bird more disgustingly horny lives today!
THIRD WIFE   A pretty explicit oracle. Ye gods!
LYSISTRATA   So let's hear no more talk of caving in. Let's go inside. Dear
    comrades, it would be a real shame if we betray the oracle. [*All enter the
    Akropolis.*]

CHORAL SONGS

MEN (*strophe*)
    I want to tell you all a tale
    that once I heard when but a lad.
    In olden times there lived a young man,
    his name was Melanion.
    He fled from marriage until
    he got to the wilderness.
    And he lived in the mountains
    and he had a dog,
    and he wove traps and hunted rabbits,
    but never went home again
    because of his hatred.
    That's how much *he* loathed women.
    And, being wise, *we* loathe them just
    as much as Melanion did.[3]
MEN'S LEADER   How about a kiss, old bag?
WOMEN'S LEADER   Try it, and you've eaten your last onion!
MEN'S LEADER   How about I haul off and kick you? [*He kicks up his leg.*]
WOMEN'S LEADER [*Laughing.*]   That's quite a bush you've got down there!
MEN'S LEADER
    Well, Myronides too was rough down there,
    and hairy-assed to all his enemies;
    so too was Phormion.[4]
WOMEN (*antistrophe*)
    I also want to tell you all a tale,
    a reply to your Melanion.
    There once was a drifter named Timon,[5]
    who fenced himself off with impregnable thorns,
    as implacable as a Fury.
    So this Timon too
    left home because of his hatred
    <and lived in the mountains,>

---

3. In the well-known myth involving Melanion, it was Atalanta who avoided marriage, swearing to marry
only that man who bested her in a footrace she always won, while the losing suitors were put to death.
Melanion threw a golden apple in front of her; when she stopped to pick it up, she lost the race to him.
4. Like Myronides, a famous Athenian general.   5. A famous misanthrope, and the subject of Shakespeare's play *Timon of Athens*. There is no evidence that he hated women any less than he hated men.

constantly cursing and railing
against the wickedness of men.
That's how much *he* loathed *you*,
wicked men, ever and always.
But he was a dear friend to women.

WOMEN'S LEADER How would you like a punch in the mouth?

MEN'S LEADER No way! You're really scaring me!

WOMEN'S LEADER Then how about a good swift kick?

MEN'S LEADER If you do you'll be flashing your twat!

WOMEN'S LEADER
Even so you'll never see
any hair down there on me:
I may be getting antiquated
but I keep myself well depilated.

[*The* WOMEN'S CHORUS *picks up their and the men's discarded clothing and both semichoruses withdraw from the center of the orchestra to sit along its edges; during the ensuing episode the women put their clothing back on.*]

EPISODE

[LYSISTRATA *appears on the roof of the stage-building, which represents the Akropolis ramparts, and walks to and fro, looking carefully in all directions; suddenly she stops and peers into the distance.*]

LYSISTRATA All right! Yes! Ladies, come here, quick!

[MYRRHINE *and several other wives join* LYSISTRATA.]

WIFE What is it? What's all the shouting?

LYSISTRATA A man! I see a man coming this way, stricken, in the grip of Aphrodite's mysterious powers. Lady Aphrodite, mistress of Cyprus and Kythera[6] and Paphos, make thy journey straight and upright!

WIFE Where is he, whoever he is?

LYSISTRATA He's by Chloe's shrine.

WIFE By Zeus, I see him now! But who is he?

LYSISTRATA Take a good look. Anyone recognize him?

MYRRHINE Oh God, I do. He's my own husband Kinesias!

LYSISTRATA All right, it's your job to roast him, to torture him, to bamboozle him, to love him and not to love him, and to give him anything he wants—except what you swore over the bowl not to.

MYRRHINE Don't you worry, I'll do it!

LYSISTRATA Great! I'll stick around here and help you bamboozle him and roast him. Now everyone get out of sight!

[*All the wives go back inside except* LYSISTRATA. *Enter* KINESIAS, *wearing a huge erect phallus and accompanied by a male slave holding a baby. He is in obvious pain.*]

KINESIAS [*To himself.*] Oh, oh, evil fate! I've got terrible spasms and cramps. It's like I'm being broken on the rack!

LYSISTRATA [*Leaning down from the ramparts.*] Who's that who's standing up within our defense perimeter?

---

6. An island off the southern tip of the Peloponnesus; in myth, a birthplace of Aphrodite.

KINESIAS Me.

LYSISTRATA A man?

KINESIAS [*Brandishing his phallus.*] Of course a man!

LYSISTRATA In that case please depart.

KINESIAS And who are *you* to throw me out?

LYSISTRATA The daytime guard.

KINESIAS Then in the gods' name call Myrrhine out here to me.

LYSISTRATA Listen to him, "call Myrrhine"! And who might *you* be?

KINESIAS Her husband, Kinesias, from Paionidai.[7]

LYSISTRATA Well, hello, dear chum! Among us *your* name is hardly unknown or without celebrity. Your wife always has you on her lips; she'll be eating an egg or an apple and she'll say, "This one's for Kinesias."

KINESIAS Oh gods!

LYSISTRATA Yes, by Aphrodite. And whenever the conversation turns to men, your wife speaks up forthwith and says, "Compared to Kinesias, everything else is trash!"

KINESIAS Come on now, call her out!

LYSISTRATA Well? Got anything for me?

KINESIAS [*Indicating his phallus.*] Indeed I do, if you want it. [LYSISTRATA *looks away.*] What about this? [*He tosses her a purse.*] It's all I've got, and you're welcome to it.

LYSISTRATA OK then, I'll go in and call her for you. [*She leaves the ramparts.*]

KINESIAS Make it quick, now! [*Alone.*] I've had no joy or pleasure in my life since the day Myrrhine left the house. I go into the house and feel agony: everything looks empty to me; I get no pleasure from the food I eat. Because I'm horny!

MYRRHINE [*Still out of sight, speaking to Lysistrata.*] I love that man, I love him! But he doesn't *want* my love. Please don't make me go out to him!

KINESIAS Myrrhinikins, dearest, why are you doing this? Get down here!

MYRRHINE [*Appearing at the ramparts.*] By Zeus I'm not going down there!

KINESIAS You won't come down even when I ask you, Myrrhine?

MYRRHINE You're asking me, but you don't want me at all.

KINESIAS Me not want you? Why, I'm desolate!

MYRRHINE I'm leaving.

KINESIAS No, wait! At least listen to the baby! [*He grabs the baby from the slave and holds it up towards* MYRRHINE.] Come on you, yell for mommy!

BABY Mommy! Mommy! Mommy!

KINESIAS [*To* MYRRHINE.] Hey, what's wrong with you? Don't you feel sorry for the baby, unwashed and unsuckled for six days now?

MYRRHINE *Him* I feel sorry for. Too bad his *father* doesn't care about him!

KINESIAS Get down here, you screwy woman, and see to your child!

MYRRHINE How momentous is motherhood! I've got no choice but to go down there. [*She leaves the ramparts.* KINESIAS *returns the baby to the slave.*]

KINESIAS <Absence really does make the heart grow fonder!>[8] She seems

---

7. A village or deme in Attica. Athenian male citizens were identified by name and deme. *Paionidae* suggests the verb *paiō* "beat," and thus another slang term for sexual intercourse ("bang"). On Kinesias's name, see above, p. 722 n. 2.   8. A line is missing from the manuscripts here. The translator has supplied what must have been its substance.

much younger than I remember, and she has a sexier look in her eyes. She acted prickly and very stuck-up too, but that just makes me want her even more!

[MYRRHINE *enters from the Akropolis gates and goes over to the baby, ignoring* KINESIAS.]

MYRRHINE Poor sweetie pie, with such a lousy father let me give you a kiss, mommy's little dearest!

KINESIAS [*To* MYRRHINE's *back.*] What do you think you're doing, you naughty girl, listening to those other women and giving me a hard time and hurting yourself as well? [*He puts a hand on her shoulder.*]

MYRRHINE [*Wheeling around.*] Don't you lay your hands on me!

KINESIAS You know you've let our house, your things and mine, become an utter mess?

MYRRHINE It doesn't bother me.

KINESIAS It doesn't bother you that the hens are pulling your woollens apart?

MYRRHINE Not a bit.

KINESIAS And what a long time it's been since you've celebrated Aphrodite's holy mysteries. Won't you come home?

MYRRHINE Not me, by Zeus; I'm going nowhere until you men agree to a settlement and stop the war.

KINESIAS Well, if that's what's decided, then that's what we'll do.

MYRRHINE Well, if that's what's decided, I'll be going home. But for the time being I've sworn to stay here.

KINESIAS But at least lie down here with me; it's been so long.

MYRRHINE No way. But I'm not saying I don't love you.

KINESIAS Love me? So why won't you lie down, Myrrhine?

MYRRHINE Right here in front of the baby? You must be joking!

KINESIAS Zeus no! Boy, take him home. [*Exit slave.*] There you are, the kid's out of our way. Now, why don't you just lie down?

MYRRHINE Lie down *where*, you silly man?

KINESIAS [*Looking around.*] Where? Pan's Grotto will do fine.

MYRRHINE But I need to be pure before I can go back up to the Akropolis.[9]

KINESIAS Very easily done: just wash off in the Klepsydra.[1]

MYRRHINE You're telling me, dear, that I should go back on the oath I swore?

KINESIAS Don't worry about any oath; let me take the consequences.

MYRRHINE All right then, I'll get us a bed.

KINESIAS No, don't; the ground's OK for us.

MYRRHINE Apollo no! I wouldn't dream of letting you lie on the ground, no matter what kind of man you are. [MYRRHINE *goes into one of the flanking doors, which represents Pan's Grotto.*]

KINESIAS She really loves me, that's quite obvious!

MYRRHINE [*Returning with a cot.*] There you are! Lie right down while I undress. [KINESIAS *lies on the cot.*] But wait, I forgot, what is it, yes, a mattress! Got to get one.

KINESIAS A mattress? Not for me, thanks.

---

9. No one who had had sexual intercourse could enter a sanctuary without bathing first.   1. A spring on the northwestern slope of the Acropolis, not far from the entrance gate where this scene is set.

MYRRHINE   By Artemis, it's shabby on cords.

KINESIAS   Well, give me a kiss.

MYRRHINE   [*Kissing him.*]   There. [*She returns to the Grotto.*]

KINESIAS   Oh lordy! Get the mattress quick!

MYRRHINE   [*Returning with a mattress.*]   There we are! Lie back down and I'll get my clothes off. But wait, what is it, a pillow, you haven't got a pillow!

KINESIAS   I don't need a pillow!

MYRRHINE   I do. [*She returns to the Grotto.*]

KINESIAS   Is this cock of mine supposed to be Herakles[2] waiting for his dinner?

MYRRHINE   [*Returning with a pillow.*]   Lift up now, upsy daisy. There, is that everything?

KINESIAS   Everything *I* need. Come here, my little treasure!

MYRRHINE   Just getting my breastband off. But remember: don't break your promise about a peace-settlement.

KINESIAS   May lightning strike me, by Zeus!

MYRRHINE   You don't have a blanket.

KINESIAS   It's not a blanket I want—I want to fuck!

MYRRHINE   That's just what you're going to get. Back in a flash. [*She returns to the Grotto.*]

KINESIAS   That woman drives me nuts with all her bedding!

MYRRHINE   [*Returning with a blanket.*]   Get up.

KINESIAS   [*Pointing to his phallus.*]   I've already got it up! [MYRRHINE *carefully arranges the blanket while* KINESIAS *fidgets.*]

MYRRHINE   Want some scent?

KINESIAS   Apollo no, none for me.

MYRRHINE   But *I* will, by Aphrodite, whether you like it or not.

KINESIAS   [*As* MYRRHINE *returns to the Grotto.*]   Then let the scent flow! Lord Zeus!

MYRRHINE   [*Returning with a round bottle of perfume.*]   Hold out your hand. Take some and rub it in.

KINESIAS   I don't like this scent, by Apollo; it takes a long time warming up and it doesn't smell like conjugal pleasures.

MYRRHINE   Oh silly me, I brought the Rhodian brand!

KINESIAS   No, wait, I like it! Let it go, you screwy woman!

MYRRHINE   What are you talking about? [*She returns to the Grotto.*]

KINESIAS   Goddamn the man who first decocted scent!

MYRRHINE   [*Returning with a long, cylindrical bottle.*]   Here, try this tube.

KINESIAS   [*Point to his phallus.*]   Got one already! Now lie down, you slut, and don't bring me anything more.

MYRRHINE   By Artemis I will. Just getting my shoes off. But remember, darling, you're going to vote for peace. [*At this,* KINESIAS *averts his eyes from* MYRRHINE *and fiddles with the blanket;* MYRRHINE *dashes off into the Akropolis.*]

KINESIAS   I'll give it serious consideration. [*He looks up again, only to find* MYRRHINE *gone.*] The woman's destroyed me, annihilated me! Not only that: she's pumped me up and dropped me flat!

---

2. The great mythological hero, often portrayed in comedy as a glutton.

[*During the ensuing duet both semichoruses return to the center of the orchestra; the women carry the shirts that the men had removed earlier.*][3]

Now what shall I do? Whom shall I screw?
I'm cheated of the sexiest girl I knew!
How will I raise and rear this orphaned cock?
Is Fox Dog[4] out there anywhere?
I need to rent a practical nurse!

MEN'S LEADER
Yea frightful agony, thou wretch,
dost rack the soul of one so sore bediddled.
Sure I do feel for thee, alack!
What kidney could bear it,
what soul, what balls,
what loins, what crotch,
thus stretched on the rack
and deprived of a morning fuck?

KINESIAS
Ah Zeus! The cramps attack anew!

MEN'S LEADER
And *this* is what she's done to you,
the detestable, revolting shrew!

WOMEN'S LEADER
No, she's totally sweet and dear!

MEN'S LEADER
Sweet, you say! She's wicked, wicked!

KINESIAS
You're right: wicked is what she is!
O Zeus, Zeus, raise up a great tornado,
with lightning bolts and all,
to sweep her up like a heap of grain
and twirl her into the sky,
and then let go and let her fall
back down to earth again,
and let her point of impact be
this dick of mine right here!

EPISODE

[*Enter a Spartan* HERALD, *both arms hidden beneath a long travelling cloak and pushing it out in front.*]

HERALD [*To* KINESIAS.]   Where be the Senate of Athens or the Prytanies?[5]
Have some news to tell them.

KINESIAS   And what might you be? Are you human? Or a Konisalos?[6]

HERALD   Am Herald, youngun, by the Twain, come from Sparta about settlement.

KINESIAS   And that's why you've come hiding a spear in your clothes?

HERALD   Not I, by Zeus, no spear!

---

3. What follows parodies tragic laments shared by hero and chorus.   4. Nickname of Philostratos, a famous pimp.   5. Subgroup of the council, chosen by lot, that oversaw the daily affairs of state.   6. A spirit endowed with an exaggerated erect phallus and associated with a Spartan dance.

KINESIAS Why twist away from me? And why hold your coat out in front of you? You've got a swollen groin from the long ride, maybe?

HERALD By Kastor, this guy crazy! [*He accidently reveals his erect phallus.*]

KINESIAS Hey, that's a hard-on, you rascal!

HERALD No, by Zeus, is not! Don't be silly!

KINESIAS Then what do you call *that?*

HERALD Is Spartan walking-stick.

KINESIAS [*Pointing to his own phallus.*] Then *this* is a Spartan walking-stick too. Listen, I know what's up; you can level with me. How are things going in Sparta?

HERALD All Sparta rise, also allies. All have hard-on. Need Pellana.[7]

KINESIAS What caused this calamity to hit you? Was it Pan?[8]

HERALD Oh no. Was Lampito started it, yes, and then other women in Sparta, they all start together like in footrace, keep men away from their hair-pies.

KINESIAS So how are you faring?

HERALD Hard! Walk around town bent over, like men carrying oil-lamp in wind. The women won't permit even to touch the pussy till all of us unanimously agree to make peace-treaty with rest of Greeks.

KINESIAS So this business is a global conspiracy by all the women! Now I get it! OK, get back to Sparta as quick as you can and arrange to send ambassadors here with full powers to negotiate a treaty. And I'll arrange for *our* Council to choose their own ambassadors; this cock of mine will be Exhibit A.

HERALD I fly away. You offer capital advice. [*He exits by the way he entered;* KINESIAS *exits in the opposite direction.*]

MEN'S LEADER
    A woman's harder to conquer than any beast,
    than fire, and no panther is quite so ferocious.

WOMEN'S LEADER
    You understand that, but then you still resist us?
    It's possible, you rascal, to have our lasting friendship.

MEN'S LEADER
    I'll never cease to loathe women!

WOMEN'S LEADER
    Well, whenever you like. But meanwhile I'll not stand
    for you to be undressed like that. Just look how ridiculous you are!
    I'm coming over to put your shirt back on.
        [*She walks over and replaces his shirt, and the other women each follow
        suit for one of the men.*]

MEN'S LEADER
    By god, that's no mean thing you've done for us.
    And now I'm sorry I got mad and took it off.

WOMEN'S LEADER
    And now you look like a man again, not so ridiculous.
    And if you weren't so hostile I'd have removed
    that bug in your eye, that's still in there, I see.

MEN'S LEADER So *that's* what's been driving me nuts! Here, take my ring;

7. The point of this reference is unknown.   8. The god of wild places, associated with disorder.

please dig it out of my eye, then show it to me;
by god, it's been biting my eye for quite some time.

WOMEN'S LEADER

All right, I will, though you're a grumpy man.
Great gods, what a humongous gnat you've got in there!
There, take a look. Isn't it positively Trikorysian?[9]

MEN'S LEADER

By god, you've helped me; that thing's been digging wells,
and now it's out my eyes are streaming tears.

WOMEN'S LEADER

Then I'll wipe them away, though you're a genuine rascal,
and kiss you.

MEN'S LEADER

          Don't kiss me!

WOMEN'S LEADER

                    I'll kiss you whether you like it or not!

[*She does so, and the other women follow suit as before.*]

MEN'S LEADER

The worst of luck to you! You're born sweet-talkers.
The ancient adage gets it in a nutshell:
"Can't live *with* the pests or without 'em either."
But now I'll make peace, and promise nevermore
to mistreat you or to take mistreatment *from* you.
Let's get together, then, and start our song.

[*The semichoruses become one and for the remainder of the play perform as a single chorus.*]

CHORUS (*strophe*)

We don't intend to say anything
the least bit slanderous about
any citizen, you gentlemen out there,
but quite the opposite: to say and do
only what's nice, because the troubles
you've got already are more than enough.

So let every man and woman tell us
if they need to have a little cash,
say two or three minas,[1] we've got it at home
and we've got some purses for it too.
And if peace should ever break out,
everyone that we lent money to
can forget to repay—if they got anything!

(*antistrophe*)

We're getting set to entertain
some visitors from Karystos[2] today;
they're fine and handsome gentlemen.
There'll be a special soup, and that piglet

---

9. Of Trikorythos, an Attic deme near a marsh.   1. A large sum of money.   2. A city in Euboea, the large island off the northern coast of Attica, and an ally of Athens.

of mine, I've sacrificed it on the grill,
and it's turning out to be fine and tender meat
So come on over to my house today:
get up early and take a bath,
and bathe the kids, and walk right in.
You needn't ask anyone's permission,
just go straight on inside like it was yours,
because the door will be locked!

EPISODE

[*The Spartan Ambassadors enter, their clothes concealing conspicuous bulges. They are accompanied by slaves.*]

CHORUS-LEADER   Hey! Here come ambassadors from Sparta, dragging long beards and wearing something around their waists that looks like a pigpen. [*To the Spartans.*] Gentlemen of Sparta: first, our greetings! Then tell us how you all are doing?

SPARTAN AMBASSADOR   No use to waste a lot of time describing. Is best to *show* how we're doing. [*The Spartans open their cloaks to reveal their erect phalli.*]

CHORUS-LEADER   Gosh! Your problem's grown very hard, and it seems to be even more inflamed than before.

SPARTAN AMBASSADOR   Unspeakable! What can one say? We wish for someone to come, make peace for us on any terms he like.

[ATHENIAN AMBASSADORS *enter from the opposite direction, with cloaks bulging.*]

CHORUS-LEADER   Look, I see a party of native sons approaching, like men wrestling, holding their clothes away from their bellies like that! Looks like a bad case of prickly heat.

FIRST ATHENIAN AMBASSADOR [*To the* CHORUS-LEADER.]   Who can tell us where Lysistrata is? The men are here, and we're . . . as you see. [*They reveal their own erect phalli.*]

CHORUS-LEADER   *Their* syndrome seems to be the same as *theirs*. These spasms: do they seize you in the wee hours?

FIRST ATHENIAN AMBASSADOR   Yes, and what's worse, we're worn totally raw by being in this condition! If someone doesn't get us a treaty pretty soon, there's no way we won't be fucking Kleisthenes![3]

CHORUS-LEADER   If you've got any sense, you'll cover up there: you don't want one of the Herm-Dockers to see you like this.[4]

FIRST ATHENIAN AMBASSADOR   By god, that's good advice. [*The Athenians rearrange their cloaks to cover their phalli.*]

SPARTAN AMBASSADOR   By the Twain Gods, yes indeed. Come, put cloaks back on! [*The Spartans follow suit.*]

FIRST ATHENIAN AMBASSADOR   Greetings, Spartans! We've had an awful time.

SPARTAN AMBASSADOR   Dear colleague, we've had a *fearful* time, if those men saw us fiddling with ourselves.

3. See above, p. 738 n. 8.   4. Just before the great expedition left for Sicily, rioters broke the erect phalluses off many of the statues of the god Hermes that stood at the doors of most Athenian houses.

FIRST ATHENIAN AMBASSADOR Come on, then, Spartans, let's talk details. The reason for your visit?

SPARTAN AMBASSADOR Are ambassadors, for settlement.

FIRST ATHENIAN AMBASSADOR That's very good; us too. So why not invite Lysistrata to our meeting, since she's the only one who can settle our differences?

SPARTAN AMBASSADOR Sure, by the Twain Gods, Lysistrata, and Lysistratos too if ye like!

[LYSISTRATA emerges from the Akropolis gate.]

FIRST ATHENIAN AMBASSADOR It looks as if we don't have to invite her: she must have heard us, for here she comes herself.

CHORUS-LEADER Hail, manliest of all women! Now is your time: be forceful and flexible, high-class and vulgar, haughty and sweet, a woman for all seasons; because the head men of Greece, caught by your charms, have gathered together with all their mutual complaints and are turning them over to you for settlement.

LYSISTRATA Well, it's an easy thing to do if you get them when they're hot for it and not testing each other for weaknesses. I'll soon know how ready they are. Where's Reconciliation? [A naked girl comes out of the Akropolis.] Take hold of the Spartans first and bring them here; don't handle them with a rough or mean hand, or crudely, the way our husbands used to handle us, but use a wife's touch, like home sweet home. [The SPARTAN AMBASSADOR refuses to give his hand.] If he won't give you his hand, lead him by his weenie. [The SPARTAN AMBASSADOR complies, and she leads him and his colleagues to LYSISTRATA, where they stand to her left.] Now go and fetch those Athenians too; take hold of whatever they give you and bring them here. [RECONCILIATION escorts the Athenians to LYSISTRATA's right.] Spartans, move in closer to me, and you Athenians too; I want you to listen to what I have to say. I am a woman, but still I've got a mind: I'm pretty intelligent in my own right, and because I've listened many a time to the conversations of my father and the other men I'm pretty well educated too. Now that you're a captive audience I'm ready to give you the tongue-lashing you deserve—both of you.

Don't both of you sprinkle altars from the same cup like kinsmen, at the Olympic Games, at Thermopylai, at Delphi,[5] and so many other places I could mention if I had to make a long list? Yet with plenty of enemies available with their barbarian armies, it's *Greek* men and *Greek* cities you're determined to destroy! That's the first point I wanted to make.

FIRST ATHENIAN AMBASSADOR [Gazing at RECONCILIATION.] My cock is bursting out of its skin and killing me!

LYSISTRATA Next I'm going to turn to *you*, Spartans. Don't you remember the time when Perikleidas the Spartan came here on bended knee and sat at Athenian altars, white-faced in his scarlet uniform, begging for a military contingent? That time when Messenia was up in arms against you and the god was shaking you with an earthquake? And Kimon came

5. Site of an important oracle of Apollo and of Panhellenic games. At the games held every four years at Olympia, a truce was observed. At Thermopylae in central Greece, a mostly Spartan army held off the invading Persians for a time but was finally destroyed (480 B.C.E.).

with four thousand infantrymen and rescued all Lakedaimon? And after that sort of treatment from the Athenians, you're now out to ravage their country, who've treated you so well?[6]

FIRST ATHENIAN AMBASSADOR   By Zeus they *are* guilty, Lysistrata!

SPARTAN AMBASSADOR   We're guilty—[*Looking at* RECONCILIATION.] but what an unspeakably fine ass!

LYSISTRATA   Do you Athenians think I'm going to let *you* off? Don't you remember the time when you were dressed in slaves' rags and the Spartans came in force and wiped out many Thessalian fighters, many friends and allies of Hippias? That day when they were the only ones helping you to drive him out? How they liberated you, and replaced your slaves' rags with a warm cloak, as suits a free people?[7]

SPARTAN AMBASSADOR   [*Still gazing at* RECONCILIATION.]   I never saw such a classy woman!

FIRST ATHENIAN AMBASSADOR   *I've* never seen a lovelier cunt!

LYSISTRATA   So after so many good deeds done, why are you at war? Why not stop this terrible behavior? Why not make peace? Come on, what's in the way?

[*During the following negotiations* RECONCILIATION's *body serves as a map of Greece.*]

SPARTAN AMBASSADOR   We are ready, if they ready to return to us this abutment.

LYSISTRATA   Which one, sir?

SPARTAN AMBASSADOR   Back Door[8] here, that we for long time count on having, and grope for.

FIRST ATHENIAN AMBASSADOR   By Poseidon, that you *won't* get!

LYSISTRATA   Give it to them, good sir.

FIRST ATHENIAN AMBASSADOR   Then who will *we* be able to harrass?

LYSISTRATA   Just ask for some other place in return for that one.

FIRST ATHENIAN AMBASSADOR   Well, let's see now. First of all give us Echinous here and the Malian Gulf behind it and both Legs.

SPARTAN AMBASSADOR   By Twain Gods, we will not give *everything*, dear fellow!

LYSISTRATA   Let it go: don't be squabbling about legs.

FIRST ATHENIAN AMBASSADOR   Now I'm ready to strip down and do some ploughing!

SPARTAN AMBASSADOR   Me first, by Twain Gods: before one ploughs one spreads manure!

LYSISTRATA   You may do that when you've ratified the settlement. If, after due deliberation, you do decide to settle, go back and confer with your allies.

6. After a disastrous earthquake the Spartans were in great danger as a result of a rebellion of their serfs, the Messenian helots. The Athenians sent a large military force under Kimon to help them (464 B.C.E.). Lysistrata conveniently neglects to mention that the Spartans sent the army home—an affront that led to Kimon's exile and aggravated anti-Spartan feelings in Athens.   7. Hippias the tyrant had allowed exiled democrats to return to Attica, but they had to stay outside the city and wear sheepskins so that they could readily be identified. With the help of Spartan soldiers, the exiles and the people of Attica finally defeated the Thessalian troops of Hippias (510 B.C.E.). Lysistrata again omits the sequel, the attempt several years later by the Spartan king Kleomenes to overthrow the democracy that succeeded the tyranny (see above, p. 729 n. 9).   8. Pylos. Spartan men's supposed predilection for anal intercourse with either women or other men was a stock Athenian joke. The next lines also refer simultaneously to territories in dispute in the war and to salient portions of Reconciliation's anatomy.

FIRST ATHENIAN AMBASSADOR *Allies*, dear lady? We're too hard up for that! Won't our allies, all of them, come to the same decision *we* have, namely, to fuck?

SPARTAN AMBASSADOR *Ours* will, by Twain Gods!

FIRST ATHENIAN AMBASSADOR And so will the Karystians, by Zeus!

LYSISTRATA You make a strong case. For the time being see to it you remain pure, so that we women can host you on the Akropolis with what we brought in our boxes. There you may exchange pledges of mutual trust, and after that each of you may reclaim his wife and go home.

FIRST ATHENIAN AMBASSADOR What are we waiting for?

SPARTAN AMBASSADOR [*To* LYSISTRATA.] Lead on wherever you wish.

FIRST ATHENIAN AMBASSADOR By Zeus yes, as quick as you can.

    [LYSISTRATA *escorts* RECONCILIATION *inside, followed by the* SPARTAN *and* ATHENIAN AMBASSADORS; *the Spartans' slaves sit down outside the door, which is attended by a doorkeeper.*]

CHORUS (*strophe*)
    Intricate tapestries,
    nice clothes and fine gowns
    and gold jewellery: all that I own
    is yours for the asking
    for your sons and for your daughter too,
    when she's picked to march with the basket.[9]
    I declare my home open to everyone
    to take anything you want.
    Nothing is sealed up so tight
    that you won't be able to break the seals
    and take away what you find inside.
    But you won't see anything
    unless your eyes are sharper than mine.

(*antistrophe*)
    If anyone's out of bread
    but has slaves and lots of little kids to feed,
    you can get flour from my house:
    puny grains, but a pound of them
    grow up to be a loaf
    that looks very hearty.
    Any of you poor people are welcome
    to come to my house with sacks and bags
    to carry the flour away; my houseboy will load them up.
    A warning though: don't knock at my door—
    beware of the watchdog there!

EPISODE

FIRST ATHENIAN AMBASSADOR [*Still inside, knocking at the door and yelling to the doorkeeper.*] Open the door, you! [*He bursts through the door, sending the doorkeeper tumbling down the steps. He wears a garland and carries a torch, as from a drinking-party.*] You should have got out of the

---

9. Girls carried baskets in processions at many religious festivals.

way. [*Other Athenians emerge, similarly equipped. To the slaves.*] You
there, why are you sitting around? Want me to singe you with this torch?
What a stale routine! I refuse to do it. [*Encouragement from the spectators.*] Well, if it's absolutely necessary we'll go the extra mile, to do you
all a favor. [*He begins to chase the slaves with his torch.*]

SECOND ATHENIAN AMBASSADOR [*Jointing the* FIRST.] And we'll help you go
that extra mile! [*To the slaves.*] Get lost! You'll cry for your hair if you
don't!

FIRST ATHENIAN AMBASSADOR Yes, get lost, so the Spartans can come out
after their banquet without being bothered. [*The slaves are chased off.*]

SECOND ATHENIAN AMBASSADOR I've never been at a better party! The Spartans were really great guys, and we made wonderful company ourselves
over the drinks.

FIRST ATHENIAN AMBASSADOR Stands to reason: when we're sober we're not
ourselves. If the Athenians will take my advice, from now on we'll do all
our ambassadorial business drunk. As it is, whenever we go to Sparta
sober, we start right in looking for ways to stir up trouble. When they
say something we don't hear it, and when they don't say something we're
convinced that they did say it, and we each return with completely different reports. But this time everything turned out fine. When somebody
sang the Telamon Song when he should have been singing the Kleitagora
Song,[1] everybody would applaud and even swear up and down what a
fine choice it was. [*Some of the slaves approach the door again.*] Hey,
those slaves are back! Get lost, you whip-fodder! [*They chase the slaves
away.*]

SECOND ATHENIAN AMBASSADOR Yes, by Zeus, here they come out of the
door. [*The* SPARTAN AMBASSADORS *file out; their leader carries bagpipes.*]

SPARTAN AMBASSADOR [*To the stage-piper or to a piper who accompanies the
Spartans.*] Take pipes, my good man, and I dance two-step and sing
nice song for Athenians and ourselves.

FIRST ATHENIAN AMBASSADOR God yes, take the pipes: I love to watch you
people dance!

SPARTAN AMBASSADOR

Memory, speed to this lad
your own Muse, who knows
about us and the Athenians,
about that day at Artemision
when *they* spread sail like gods
against the armada
and whipped the Medes,
while Leonidas led *us*,[2]
like wild boars we were, yes,
gnashing our tusks, our jaws running
streams of foam, and our legs too.
The enemy, the Persians,
outnumbered the sand on the shore.

---

1. Evidently songs about war and peace, respectively.   2. While the Spartans under their king Leonidas
were holding the pass against the invading Persians at Thermopylae in 480 B.C.E., an indecisive naval battle
took place off Cape Artemision nearby.

Goddess of the Wilds, Virgin Beast-Killer,[3]
come this way, this way to the treaty,
and keep us together for a long long while.
Now let friendship in abundance
attend our agreement always,
and may we ever abandon
foxy strategems.
Come this way, this way,
Virgin Huntress!

[*A mute* LYSISTRATA *comes out of the Akropolis, followed by the Athenian and Spartan wives.*]

FIRST ATHENIAN AMBASSADOR   Well! Now that everything else has been
wrapped up so nicely, it's time for you Spartans to reclaim these wives
of yours; and you Athenians, these here. Let's have husband stand by
wife and wife by husband; then to celebrate our great good fortune let's
have a dance for the gods. And let's be sure never again to make the
same mistakes! [*The couples descend into the orchestra to dance to the*
AMBASSADOR's *song; around them dance the members of the* CHORUS, *who
are also paired in couples.*]

Bring on the dance, include the Graces,
and invite Artemis,
and her twin brother, the benign Healer,[4]
and the Nysian[5] whose eyes flash
bacchic among his maenads,
and Zeus alight with flame
and the thriving Lady his consort;[6]
and invite the divine powers
we would have as witnesses
to remember always
this humane peace,
which the goddess Kypris[7] has fashioned

CHORUS

Alalai, yay Paian!
Shake a leg, iai!
Dance to victory, iai!
Evoi evoi, evai evai!

FIRST ATHENIAN AMBASSADOR   Now, my dear Spartan, *you* give us some
music: a new song to match the last one!

SPARTAN AMBASSADOR

Come back again from fair Taygetos,
Spartan Muse, and distinguish this occasion
with a hymn to the God of Amyklai[8]
and Athena of the Brazen House[9]
and Tyndareos' fine sons,[1]
who gallop beside the Eurotas.[2]
Ho there, hop!

3. Artemis. 4. Apollo. 5. Dionysus. 6. Hera. 7. Aphrodite. 8. Apollo. 9. Athena had a
bronze-plated temple in Sparta.   1. Kastor and Pollux.   2. The river that runs by Sparta.

Hey there, jump!
Let's sing a hymn to Sparta,
home of dance divine
and stomping feet,
where by the Eurotas' banks
young girls frisk like fillies,
raising dust-clouds underfoot
and tossing their tresses
like maenads[3] waving their wands and playing,
led by Leda's daughter,[4]
their chorus-leader pure and pretty.

[To the CHORUS.] Come on now, hold your hair in your hand, get your feet hopping like a deer and start making some noise to spur the dance! And sing for the goddess who's won a total victory, Athena of the Brazen House!

[All exit dancing, the CHORUS singing a traditional hymn to Athena.]

---

3. Female devotees of Dionysus.   4. Helen, who was worshipped as a goddess in Sparta.

PLATO
429–347 B.C.E.

Socrates began a revolution in Western thought and laid the foundations for philosophy as we know it, but he wrote nothing. We know what we do about him mainly from the writings of his pupil Plato, a philosophical and literary genius of the first rank. It is very difficult to distinguish between what Socrates actually said and what Plato put into his mouth, but there is general agreement that the *Apology* is the clearest picture we have of the historical Socrates. In 399 B.C.E., Socrates was put on trial for impiety and "corrupting the youth" of Athens. The *Apology*—the Greek word means "defense speech" and unlike the English word carries no admission of wrongdoing—is Plato's version of the speech Socrates gave at his trial. In it, Socrates does what he so often challenged others to do: he gives an account of himself and of the questioning, thought, and conversation to which he devoted his life. More than a simple rebuttal of the charges, the speech is an eloquent statement of the value of the life of philosophy (literally, "love of wisdom"), and of why the most important thing we can do with our lives is the care of the soul.

Only five years before Socrates' trial, the Peloponnesian War ended in Athens' defeat. The victorious Spartans abolished the democracy and installed a repressive dictatorial regime dominated by thirty Athenians of oligarchic sympathies. "The Thirty," as they came to be known, were overthrown eight months later and a democratic constitution was reinstituted. Some members of the Thirty, as well as other prominent Athenians who had or were suspected of antidemocratic leanings, were associates of Socrates. His trial may well have been part of the reaction against the Thirty, especially since one of his main accusers, Anytus, was a leader of the restored democracy.

If there was a political motive in the background, the reason for his trial given by

Socrates in the *Apology* is also surely right: he unsettled and angered a lot of people. He would approach them with deceptively simple questions to which they thought they knew the answers. "What is piety?" "What is rhetoric, and is it an art?" "Can goodness be taught, or is it something we are just born with?" Through a process of question and answer that is still known as the Socratic method, he would get them to admit that they were wrong, that their certainties did not stand up to scrutiny, and that they did not know what they thought they knew. To have one's ignorance exposed and one's assumptions about the world shaken can provide a profoundly educational shock. It can also be infuriating. Many people probably found it easier to silence Socrates than to rethink their values and ideas.

The *Apology* shows why Socrates had to die and why that death was unjust. It is a defiant speech; Socrates rides roughshod over legal forms and seems to neglect no opportunity of outraging his listeners. But this defiance is not stupidity (as he hints himself, he could, if he had wished, have made a speech to please the court), nor is it a deliberate courting of martyrdom. It is the only course possible for him in the circumstances if he is not to betray his life's work, for Socrates knows as well as his accusers that what the Athenians really want is to silence him without having to take his life. What Socrates is making clear is that there is no such easy way out; he will have no part of any compromise that would restrict his freedom of speech or undermine his moral position. The speech is a sample of what the Athenians will have to put up with if they allow him to live; he will continue to be the gadfly that stings the sluggish horse. He will go on persuading them not to be concerned for their persons or their property but first and chiefly to care about the improvement of the soul. He has spent his life denying the validity of worldly standards, and he will not accept them now. To do so would be, as he says, to allow his enemies to harm him.

He was declared guilty and condemned to death. Though influential friends offered means of escape (and there is reason to think the Athenians would have been glad to see him go), Socrates refused to disobey the laws; in any case he had already, in his court speech, rejected the possibility of living in some foreign city.

The sentence was duly carried out. And in Plato's account of the execution in the *Phaedo*, we can see the calmness and kindness of a man who has led a useful life and who is secure in his faith that, contrary to appearances, "no evil can happen to a good man, either in life or after death."

The form of the *Apology* is dramatic: Plato re-creates the personality of his beloved teacher by presenting him as speaking directly to the reader. In most of the many books that he wrote in the course of a long life, Plato continued to feature Socrates as the principal speaker in philosophical dialogues that explored the ethical and political problems of the age. These dialogues (the *Republic* the most famous) were preserved in their entirety and have exerted an enormous influence on Western thought ever since. Plato also founded a philosophical school, the Academy, in 385 B.C.E., and it remained active as a center of philosophical training and research until it was suppressed by the Roman emperor Justinian in 529 C.E. Plato came from an aristocratic Athenian family and as a young man thought of a political career; the execution of Socrates by the courts of democratic Athens disgusted him with politics and prompted his famous remark that there was no hope for the cities until the rulers became philosophers or the philosophers, rulers. His own attempts to influence real rulers—the tyrant Dionysius of Syracuse in Sicily and, later, his son—ended in failure, however.

PRONOUNCING GLOSSARY

The following list uses common English syllables and stress accents to provide rough equivalents of selected words whose pronunciation may be unfamiliar to the general reader.

Adeimantus: *a-day-mant'-us*

Aeacus: *ee'-ak-us / ai'-ak-us*

Aeantodorus: *ee-ant-o-dor'-us / ai-ant-o-dor'-tus*

Aeschines: *es'-kin-eez / ais'-kin-eez*

Amphipolis: *am-fip'-o-lis*

Anytus: *an'-i-tus*

Arginusae: *ar-gin-oo'-sai*

Asclepius: *as-klee'-pee-us*

Cebes: *see'-beez / kee'-beez*

Ceos: *ke'-os*

Cephisus: *ke'-fi-sus*

Chaerephon: *kai'-re-fon*

Crito: *crai'-toh*

Critobulus: *cri-to'-boo-luhs*

Demodocus: *de-mod'-o-kus*

Echecrates: *ek-ek'-rat-eez*

Epigenes: *e-pig'-en-eez*

Evenus: *ee-vee'-nus / e-way'-nus*

Gorgias: *gor'-jee-as / gor'-gi-as*

Leontium: *lay-on'-tee-um*

Lysanias: *lai-san'-ee-as*

Meletus: *mee-lee'-tus*

Minos: *mai'-nos / mi'-nos*

Musaeus: *myoo-zee'-us / moo-sai'-us*

Nicostratus: *ni-kos'-tra-tus*

Palamedes: *pal-am-ee'-deez*

Phaedo: *fee'-doh*

Potidaea: *pot-i-dee'-ah / pot-i-dai'-ah*

Prodicus: *proh'-di-kus*

Prytanes: *pri'-tan-eez*

Prytaneum: *pri-tan-ee'-um / pri-tan-ay'-um*

Rhadamanthus: *rad-am-anth'-us*

Simmias: *sim'-ee-as*

Theages: *thee-ah'-jeez / thee-ah'-geez*

Theosdotides: *thee-os-dot'-id-eez*

Triptolemus: *trip-to'-le-muhs*

The Apology of Socrates[1]

I don't know, men of Athens, how you were affected by my accusers. As for me, I was almost carried away by them, they spoke so persuasively. And yet almost nothing they said is true. Among their many falsehoods, however, one especially amazed me: that you must be careful not to be deceived by me, since I'm a dangerously clever speaker. That they aren't ashamed at being immediately refuted by the facts, once it becomes apparent that I'm not a clever speaker at all, that seems to me most shameless of them. Unless, of course, the one they call "clever" is the one who tells the truth. If that's what they mean, I'd agree that I'm an orator—although not one of their sort. No, indeed. Rather, just as I claimed, they have said little or nothing true, whereas from me you'll hear the whole truth. But not, by Zeus, men of Athens, expressed in elegant language like theirs, arranged in fine words and phrases. Instead, what you hear will be spoken extemporaneously in whatever

1. Translated by C. D. Reeve.

words come to mind, and let none of you expect me to do otherwise—for I put my trust in the justice of what I say. After all, it wouldn't be appropriate at my age, gentlemen, to come before you speaking in polished, artificial language like a young man.

Indeed, men of Athens, this I positively entreat of you: if you hear me making my defense using the same sort of language that I'm accustomed to use both in the marketplace next to the bankers' tables—where many of you have heard me—and also in other places, please don't be surprised or create an uproar on that account. For the fact is that this is the first time I've appeared before a law court, although I'm seventy years old. So the language of this place is totally foreign to me. Now, if I were really a foreigner, you'd certainly forgive me if I spoke in the accents and manner in which I'd been raised. So now too, I'm asking you, justly it seems to me, to overlook my manner of speaking (maybe it will be less good, maybe it will be better), but consider and apply your mind to this alone, whether I say what's just or not. For that's the virtue or excellence of a juror, just as the orator's lies in telling the truth.

The first thing justice demands, then, men of Athens, is that I defend myself from the first false accusations made against me and from my first accusers, and then from the later accusations and the later accusers.[2] You see, many people have been accusing me in front of you for very many years now—and nothing they say is true. And I fear them more than Anytus[3] and the rest, though the latter are dangerous as well. But the earlier ones, gentlemen, are more dangerous. They got hold of most of you from childhood and persuaded you with their accusations against me—accusations no more true than the current ones. They say there's a man called Socrates, a "wise" man, a thinker about things in the heavens, an investigator of all things below the earth, and someone who makes the weaker argument the stronger.[4] Those who've spread this rumor, men of Athens, are my dangerous accusers, since the people who hear them believe that those who investigate such things do not acknowledge the gods either. Moreover, those accusers are numerous and have been accusing me for a long time now. Besides, they also spoke to you at that age when you would most readily believe them, when some of you were children or young boys. Thus they simply won their case by default, as there was no defense. But what's most unreasonable in all this is that I can't discover even their names and tell them to you—unless one of them happens to be a comic playwright.[5] In any case, the ones who used malicious slander

---

2. Socrates had been the object of much criticism and satire for many years before the trial. The earlier accusations are thus the accumulated prejudices that lie behind the formal charge now brought against him. 3. Socrates' principal accuser in the present trial. He was a leader of the restored democracy that followed the overthrow in 403 B.C.E. of the Thirty, whose government had been installed by Sparta in the wake of Athens' defeat in the Peloponnesian War. 4. The first charge, speculation about the physical nature of the heavens and the earth, would excite the suspicions of religiously minded traditionalists. The second, making the weaker argument seem stronger, associated Socrates with the Sophists, professional teachers of rhetoric and other subjects; they were thought by many (including Plato) to value persuasion above, and even at the expense of, the truth. 5. Aristophanes (450?–385? B.C.E.), whose comedy Clouds (423 B.C.E.) is a broad satire on Socrates and his associates as (allegedly) exemplars of the Sophistic movement. The play is a good example of the prejudice Socrates is talking about (though it is an open question how seriously Aristophanes intended his barbs against Socrates), for it represents him as propounding fantastic theories about matter and religion and teaching students how to avoid paying debts.

to persuade you—as well as those who persuaded others after having been persuaded themselves—all of these are impossible to deal with. One cannot bring any of them here to court or cross-examine them. One must literally fight with shadows to defend oneself and cross-examine with no one to respond.

So you too, then, should allow, as I claimed, that there are two groups of accusers: those who accused me just now and the older ones I've been discussing. Moreover, you should consider it proper for me to defend myself against the latter first, since you've heard them accusing me earlier, and at much greater length, than these recent ones here.

All right. I must defend myself, then, men of Athens, and try to take away in this brief time[6] prejudices you acquired such a long time ago. Certainly, that's the outcome I'd wish for—if it's in any way better for you and for me— and I'd like to succeed in my defense. But I think it's a difficult task, and I am not at all unaware of its nature. Let it turn out, though, in whatever way pleases the god. I have to obey the law and defend myself.

Let's examine, then, from the beginning, what the charge is from which the slander against me arose—the very one on which Meletus[7] relied when he wrote the present indictment of me. Well, then, what exactly did the slanderers say to slander me? Just as if they were real accusers their affidavit must be read. It's something like this:

> Socrates commits injustice and is a busybody, in that he investigates the things beneath the earth and in the heavens, makes the weaker argument the stronger, and teaches these things to others.

Indeed, you saw these charges expressed yourselves in Aristophanes' comedy. There, some fellow named Socrates swings around claiming he's walking on air and talking a lot of other nonsense on subjects that I know neither a lot nor a little but nothing at all about.[8] Not that I mean to disparage this knowledge, if anyone's wise in such subjects—I don't want to have to defend myself against more of Meletus' lawsuits!—but I, men of Athens, take no part in them. I call on the majority of you as witnesses to this, and I appeal to you to make it perfectly plain to one another—those of you who've heard me conversing (as many of you have). Tell one another, then, whether any of you has ever heard me discussing such subjects, either briefly or at length, and from this you'll realize that the other things commonly said about me are of the same baseless character.

In any case, none of them is true. And if you've heard from anyone that I undertake to educate people and charge fees, that's not true either. Although, it also seems to me to be a fine thing if anyone's able to educate people in the way Gorgias of Leontini does, and Prodicus of Ceos, and Hippias of Elis.[9] For each of them, gentlemen, can enter any city and persuade the young— who may associate with any of their own fellow citizens they want to free of

---

6. Speeches for prosecution and defense in Athenian law courts had time limits.   7. Another of Socrates' accusers.   8. In Aristophanes' *Clouds*, Socrates first appears suspended in a basket. When asked what he is doing, he replies, "I walk in air and contemplate the sun." He explains that only by suspending his intelligence can he investigate celestial matters.   9. Three of the most famous Sophists. Unlike Socrates, whose poverty Plato emphasizes, the Sophists charged high fees for their teachings and amassed large fortunes.

charge—to abandon those associations, and associate with them instead, pay them a fee, and be grateful to them besides.

Since we're on that topic, I heard that there's another wise gentleman here at present, from Paros. For I happened to run into a man who has spent more money on sophists than everyone else put together—Callias,[1] the son of Hipponicus. So I questioned him, since he has two sons himself.

"Callias," I said, "if your two sons had been born colts or calves, we could engage and pay a knowledgeable supervisor—one of those expert horse breeders or farmers—who could turn them into fine and good examples of their proper virtue or excellence. But now, seeing that they're human beings, whom do you have in mind to engage as a supervisor? Who is it that has the knowledge of *this* virtue, the virtue of human beings and of citizens? I assume you've investigated the matter, because you have two sons. Is there such a person," I asked, "or not?"

"Certainly," he replied.

"Who is he?" I said.

"His name's Evenus, Socrates," he replied, "from Paros. He charges five minas."[2]

I thought Evenus blessedly happy if he truly did possess that expertise and taught it for so modest a fee. I, at any rate, would pride myself and give myself airs if I had knowledge of those things. But in fact, men of Athens, I don't know them.

Now perhaps one of you will interject: "But Socrates, what, then, is *your* occupation? What has given rise to these slanders against you? Surely if you weren't in fact occupied with something out of the ordinary, if you weren't doing something different from most people, all this rumor and talk wouldn't have arisen. Tell us, then, what it is, so that we don't judge you hastily." These are fair questions, I think, for the speaker to ask, and I'll try to show you just what it is that has brought me this slanderous reputation. Listen, then. Perhaps, some of you will think I'm joking. But you may be sure that I'll be telling you the whole truth.

You see, men of Athens, I've acquired this reputation because of nothing other than a sort of wisdom. What sort of wisdom, you ask, is that? The very sort, perhaps, that is *human* wisdom. For it may just be that I really do have that sort of wisdom, whereas the people I mentioned just now may, perhaps, be wise because they possess *superhuman* wisdom. I don't know what else to call it, since I myself certainly don't possess that knowledge, and whoever says I do is lying and speaking in order to slander me.

Please don't create an uproar, men of Athens, even if you think I'm somehow making grand claims. You see, I'm not the author of the story I'm about to tell, though I'll refer you to a reliable source. In fact, as a witness to the existence of my wisdom—if indeed it is a sort of wisdom—and to its nature, I'll present the god at Delphi[3] to you.

---

1. Member of one of the richest families in Athens and prominent patron of the Sophists.   2. A substantial sum: there were 100 drachmas in a mina, and a day's wages for labor in Athens were a drachma or two. (Protagoras, one of the greatest Sophists, charged 100 minas for a course of instruction.)
3. Apollo. Delphi was the site of his main oracle, on the southern slopes of Mount Parnassus.

You remember Chaerephon,[4] no doubt. He was a friend of mine from youth and also a friend of your party, who shared your recent exile and restoration. You remember, then, what sort of man Chaerephon was, how intense he was in whatever he set out to do. Well, on one occasion in particular he went to Delphi and dared to ask the oracle—as I said, please don't create an uproar, gentlemen—he asked, exactly as I'm telling you, whether anyone was wiser than myself. The Pythia[5] drew forth the response that no one is wiser. His brother here will testify to you about it, since Chaerephon himself is dead.

Please consider my purpose in telling you this, since I'm about to explain to you where the slander against me has come from. You see, when I heard these things, I thought to myself as follows: "What can the god be saying? What does his riddle mean? For I'm only too aware that I've no claim to being wise in anything either great or small. What can he mean, then, by saying that I'm wisest? Surely he can't be lying: that isn't lawful[6] for him."

For a long time I was perplexed about what he meant. Then, very reluctantly, I proceeded to examine it in the following sort of way. I approached one of the people thought to be wise, assuming that in his company, if anywhere, I could refute the pronouncement and say to the oracle, "Here's someone wiser than I, yet you said I was wisest."

Then I examined this person—there's no need for me to mention him by name; he was one of our politicians. And when I examined him and talked with him, men of Athens, my experience was something like this: I thought this man seemed wise to many people, and especially to himself, but wasn't. Then I tried to show him that he thought himself wise, but wasn't. As a result, he came to dislike me, and so did many of the people present. For my part, I thought to myself as I left, "I'm wiser than that person. For it's likely that neither of us knows anything fine and good, but he thinks he knows something he doesn't know, whereas I, since I don't in fact know, don't think that I do either. At any rate, it seems that I'm wiser than he in just this one small way: that what I don't know, I don't think I know." Next, I approached another man, one of those thought to be wiser than the first, and it seemed to me that the same thing occurred, and so I came to be disliked by that man too, as well as by many others.

After that, then, I kept approaching one person after another. I realized, with distress and alarm, that I was arousing hostility. Nevertheless, I thought I must attach the greatest importance to what pertained to the god. So, in seeking what the oracle meant, I had to go to all those with any reputation for knowledge. And, by the dog,[7] men of Athens—for I'm obliged to tell the truth before you—I really did experience something like this: in my investigation in response to the god, I found that, where wisdom is concerned, those who had the best reputations were practically the most deficient, whereas men who were thought to be their inferiors were much better off. Accordingly, I must present all my wanderings to you as

---

4. One of Socrates' closest associates (he appears in Aristophanes' *Clouds*). He was an enthusiastic enough partisan of the democratic regime that he had to go into exile, along with many other democrats, in 404 B.C.E. when the Thirty carried on an oligarchic reign of terror (Socrates refers to this exile in the next sentence).   5. The priestess in Apollo's temple at Delphi who uttered the god's prophecies.   6. That is, according to the order of the world and the gods' nature. One way Apollo avoided lying was to give notoriously obscure or ambiguous oracles.   7. A euphemistic oath (compare "by George").

if they were labors of some sort that I undertook in order to prove the oracle utterly irrefutable.

You see, after the politicians, I approached the poets—tragic, dithyrambic,[8] and the rest—thinking that in their company I'd catch myself in the very act of being more ignorant than they. So I examined the poems with which they seemed to me to have taken the most trouble and questioned them about what they meant, in order that I might also learn something from them at the same time.

Well, I'm embarrassed to tell you the truth, gentlemen, but nevertheless it must be told. In a word, almost all the people present could have discussed these poems better than their authors themselves. And so, in the case of the poets as well, I soon realized it wasn't wisdom that enabled them to compose their poems, but some sort of natural inspiration, of just the sort you find in seers and soothsayers.[9] For these people, too, say many fine things, but know nothing of what they speak about. The poets also seemed to me to be in this sort of situation. At the same time, I realized that, because of their poetry, they thought themselves to be the wisest of people about the other things as well when they weren't. So I left their company, too, thinking that I had gotten the better of them in the very same way as of the politicians.

Finally, I approached the craftsmen. You see, I was conscious of knowing practically nothing myself, but I knew I'd discover that they, at least, would know many fine things. And I wasn't wrong about this. On the contrary, they did know things that I didn't know, and in that respect they were wiser than I. But, men of Athens, the good craftsmen also seemed to me to have the very same flaw as the poets: because he performed his own craft well, each of them also thought himself to be wisest about the other things, the most important ones; and this error of theirs seemed to overshadow their wisdom. So I asked myself on behalf of the oracle whether I'd prefer to be as I am, not in any way wise with their wisdom nor ignorant with their ignorance, or to have both qualities as they did. And the answer I gave to myself, and to the oracle, was that it profited me more to be just the way I was.

From this examination, men of Athens, much hostility has arisen against me of a sort that is harshest and most onerous. This has resulted in many slanders, including that reputation I mentioned of being "wise." You see, the people present on each occasion think that I'm wise about the subjects on which I examine others. But in fact, gentlemen, it's pretty certainly the god who is really wise, and by his oracle he meant that human wisdom is worth little or nothing. And it seems that when he refers to the Socrates here before you and uses my name, he makes me an example, as if he were to say, "That one among you is wisest, mortals, who, like Socrates, has recognized that he's truly worthless where wisdom's concerned."

So even now I continue to investigate these things and to examine, in response to the god, any person, citizen, or foreigner I believe to be wise. Whenever he seems not to be so to me, I come to the assistance of the god and show him that he's not wise. Because of this occupation, I've had no leisure worth talking about for either the city's affairs or my own domestic

---

8. The dithyramb was a short performance by a chorus at a public festival, produced, like tragedy, at state expense.   9. For a fuller exposition of this famous theory of poetic inspiration, see Plato's *Ion*.

ones; rather, I live in extreme poverty because of my service to the god.

In addition to these factors, the young people who follow me around of their own accord, those who have the most leisure, the sons of the very rich, enjoy listening to people being cross-examined. They often imitate me themselves and in turn attempt to cross-examine others. Next, I imagine they find an abundance of people who think they possess some knowledge, but in fact know little or nothing. The result is that those they question are angry not at themselves, but at me, and say that Socrates is a thoroughly pestilential fellow who corrupts the young. Then, when they're asked what he's doing or teaching, they've nothing to say, as they don't know. Yet, so as not to appear at a loss, they utter the stock phrases used against all who philosophize: "things in the sky and beneath the earth," and "not acknowledging the gods," and "making the weaker argument the stronger." For they wouldn't be willing to tell the truth, I imagine: that it has become manifest they pretend to know, but know nothing. So, seeing that these people are, I imagine, ambitious, vehement, and numerous, and have been speaking earnestly and persuasively about me, they've long been filling your ears with vehement slanders. On the basis of these slanders, Meletus has brought his charges against me, and Anytus and Lycon along with him: Meletus is aggrieved on behalf of the poets, Anytus on behalf of the artisans and politicians, and Lycon on behalf of the orators. So, as I began by saying, I'd be amazed if I could rid your minds of this slander in the brief time available, when there's so much of it in them.

There, men of Athens, is the truth for you. I've spoken it without concealing or glossing over anything, whether great or small. And yet I pretty much know that I make enemies by doing these very thing. And that's further evidence that I'm right—that this is the prejudice against me and these its causes. Whether you investigate these matters now or later, you'll find it to be so.

Enough, then, for my defense before you against the charges brought by my first accusers. Next, I'll try to defend myself against Meletus—who is, he claims, both good and patriotic—and against my later accusers. Once again, then, just as if they were really a different set of accusers, their affidavit must be examined in turn. It goes something like this:

> Socrates is guilty of corrupting the young, and of not acknowledging the gods the city acknowledges, but new daimonic activities[1] instead.

Such, then, is the charge. Let us examine each point in this charge.

Meletus says, then, that I commit injustice by corrupting the young. But I, men of Athens, reply that it's Meletus who is guilty of playing around with serious matters, of lightly bringing people to trial, and of professing to be seriously concerned about things he has never cared about at all—and I'll try to prove this.

---

1. The precise meaning of the charge is not clear. The Greek words may mean "new divinities," with a reference to Socrates' famous inner voice, which on occasion warned him against action on which he had decided and which he describes later in the speech. Or the words may mean "practicing strange rites." In any case, because the phrase implies religious belief of some sort, it can later be used against Meletus when he loses his head and accuses Socrates of atheism.

Step forward, Meletus, and answer me.[2] You regard it as most important, do you not, that our young people be as good as possible?

I certainly do.

Come, then, and tell these jurors who improves them. Clearly you know, since you care. For having discovered, as you assert, the one who corrupts them—namely, myself—you bring him before these jurors and accuse him. Come, then, speak up, tell the jurors who it is that improves them. Do you see, Meletus, that you remain silent and have nothing to say? Yet don't you think that's shameful and sufficient evidence of exactly what I say, that you care nothing at all? Speak up, my good man. Who improves them?

The laws.

But that's not what I'm asking, my most excellent fellow, but rather which *person*, who knows the laws themselves in the first place, does this?

These gentlemen, Socrates, the jurors.

What are you saying, Meletus? Are they able to educate and improve the young?

Most certainly.

All of them, or some but not others?

All of them.

That's good news, by Hera, and a great abundance of benefactors[3] that you speak of! What, then, about the audience present here? Do they improve the young or not?

Yes, they do so too.

And what about the members of the Council?[4]

Yes, the councilors too.

But, if that's so, Meletus, surely those in the Assembly, the assemblymen, won't corrupt the young, will they? Won't they all improve them too?

Yes, they will too.

But then it seems that all the Athenians except for me make young people fine and good, whereas I alone corrupt them. Is that what you're saying?

Most emphatically, that's what I'm saying.

I find myself, if you're right, in a most unfortunate situation. Now answer me this. Do you think that the same holds of horses? Do people in general improve them, whereas one particular person corrupts them or makes them worse? Or isn't it wholly the opposite: one particular person—or the very few who are horse trainers—is able to improve them, whereas the majority of people, if they have to do with horses and make use of them, make them worse? Isn't that true, Meletus, both of horses and of all other animals? Of course it is, whether you and Anytus say so or not. Indeed, our young people are surely in a very happy situation if only one person corrupts them, whereas all the rest benefit them.

Well then, Meletus, it has been adequately established that you've never given any thought to young people—you've plainly revealed your indifference—and that you care nothing about the issues on which you bring me to trial.

2. In Athens there was no office similar to that of our district attorney. Because the accuser also acted as prosecutor, Socrates can examine him as though he were a witness.   3. Probably about 500, all male citizens selected by lot. There was no judge in the Athenian law court. *Hera:* wife and sister of Zeus, the ruler of the gods.   4. The executive council of the Assembly, comprising 500 members chosen by lot. The Assembly was the sovereign body under the Athenian constitution; it consisted, at least in theory, of all male Athenian citizens.

Next, Meletus, tell us, in the name of Zeus, whether it's better to live among good citizens or bad ones. Answer me, sir. Surely, I'm not asking you anything difficult. Don't bad people do something bad to [whoever's][5] closest to them at the given moment, whereas good people do something good?

Certainly.

Now is there anyone who wishes to be harmed rather than benefited by those around him? Keep answering, my good fellow. For the law requires you to answer. Is there anyone who wishes to be harmed?

Of course not.

Well, then, when you summon me here for corrupting the young and making them worse, do you mean that I do so intentionally or unintentionally?

Intentionally, I say.

What's that, Meletus? Are you so much wiser at your age than I at mine, that you know bad people do something bad to [whoever's] closest to them at the given moment, and good people something good? Am I, by contrast, so very ignorant that I don't know even this: that if I do something bad to an associate, I risk getting back something bad from him in return? And is the result, as you claim, that I do so very bad a thing intentionally?

I'm not convinced by you of that, Meletus, and neither, I think, is anyone else. No, either I'm not corrupting the young or, if I am corrupting them, it's *un*intentionally, so that in either case what you say is false. But if I'm corrupting them unintentionally, the law doesn't require that I be brought to court for such mistakes—that is, unintentional ones—but that I be taken aside for private instruction and admonishment. For it's clear that if I'm instructed, I'll stop doing what I do unintentionally. You, however, avoided associating with me and were unwilling to instruct me. Instead, you bring me here, where the law requires you to bring those in need of punishment, not instruction.

Well, men of Athens, what I said before is absolutely clear by this point, namely, that Meletus has never cared about these matters to any extent, great or small. Nevertheless, please tell us now, Meletus, how is it you say I corrupt the young? Or is it absolutely clear, from the indictment you wrote, that it's by teaching them not to acknowledge the gods the city acknowledges, but new daimonic activities instead? Isn't that what you say I corrupt them by teaching?

I most emphatically do say that.

Then, in the name of those very gods we're now discussing, Meletus, speak yet more clearly, both for my sake and for that of these gentlemen. You see, I'm unable to tell what you mean. Is it that I teach people to acknowledge that some gods exist—so that I, then, acknowledge their existence myself and am not an out-and-out atheist and am not guilty of that—yet not, of course, the very ones acknowledged by the city, but different ones? Is that what you're charging me with, that they're different ones? Or are you saying that I myself don't acknowledge any gods at all, and that that's what I teach to others?

That's what I mean, that you don't acknowledge any gods at all.

You're a strange fellow, Meletus! Why [do] you say that? Do I not even acknowledge that the sun and the moon are gods, then, as other men do?

5. Bracketed words correct the translation, here and below.

No, by Zeus, gentlemen of the jury, he doesn't, since he says that the sun's a stone and the moon earth.

My dear Meletus, do you think it's Anaxagoras[6] you're accusing? Are you that contemptuous of the jury? Do you think they're so illiterate that they don't know that the books of Anaxagoras of Clazomenae are full of such arguments? And, in particular, do young people learn these views from me, views they can occasionally acquire in the Orchestra[7] for a drachma at most and that they'd ridicule Socrates for pretending were his own—especially as they're so strange? In the name of Zeus, is that really how I seem to you? Do I acknowledge the existence of no god at all?

No indeed, by Zeus, none at all.

You aren't at all convincing, Meletus, not even, it seems to me, to yourself. You see, men of Athens, this fellow seems very arrogant and intemperate to me and to have written this indictment simply out of some sort of arrogance, intemperance, and youthful rashness. Indeed, he seems to have composed a sort of riddle in order to test me: "Will the so-called wise Socrates recognize that I'm playing around and contradicting myself? Or will I fool him along with the other listeners?" You see, he seems to me to be contradicting himself in his indictment, as if he were to say, "Socrates is guilty of not acknowledging gods, but of acknowledging gods." And that's just childish playing around, isn't it?

Please examine with me, gentlemen, why it seems to me that this is what he's saying. And you, Meletus, answer us. But you, gentlemen, please remember what I asked of you at the beginning: don't create an uproar if I make my arguments in my accustomed manner.

Is there anyone, Meletus, who acknowledges that human activities exist but doesn't acknowledge human beings? Make him answer, gentlemen, and don't let him make one protest after another. Is there anyone who doesn't acknowledge horses but does acknowledge equine activities? Or who doesn't acknowledge that musicians exist but does acknowledge musical activities? There's no one, best of men—if you don't want to answer, I must answer for you and for the others here. But at least answer my next question. Is there anyone who acknowledges the existence of daimonic activities but doesn't acknowledge daimons?

No, there isn't.

How good of you to answer, if reluctantly and when compelled to by these gentlemen. Well then, you say that I acknowledge daimonic activities, whether new or familiar, and teach about them. But then, on your account, I do at any rate acknowledge daimonic activities, and to this you've sworn in your indictment against me. However, if I acknowledge daimonic activities, surely it's absolutely necessary that I acknowledge daimons. Isn't that so? Yes, it is—I assume you agree, since you don't answer. But don't we believe that daimons are either gods or, at any rate, children of gods?[8] Yes or no?

---

6. Philosopher (ca. 500–428 B.C.E.), born in Asia Minor, and an intimate friend of Pericles who was forced to leave Athens to escape an indictment for impiety. He is famous for his doctrine that matter was set in motion and ordered by Intelligence, which, however, did not create it. In Plato's *Phaedo*, Socrates says that he was attracted to this doctrine in his youth but criticizes Anaxagoras's views.   7. Evidently part of the *agora*, or marketplace. This passage is usually taken as one of the earliest references to a book trade in ancient Greece.   8. *Daimones* in Greek could range from lesser divinities outside the pantheon of Olympian gods to heroic mortals divinized after death to the general "divinity" when one felt the agency of some unidentified god behind an event. All these senses seem to underlie Socrates' words.

Of course.

Then, if indeed I do believe in daimons, as you're saying, and if daimons are gods of some sort, that's precisely what I meant when I said that you're presenting us with a riddle and playing around: you're saying that I don't believe in gods and, on the contrary, that I do believe in gods, since in fact I do at least believe in daimons. But if, on the other hand, daimons are children of gods, some sort of bastard offspring of a nymph, or of whomever else tradition says each one is the child, what man could possibly believe that children of gods exist, but not gods? That would be just as unreasonable as believing in the children of horses and asses—namely, mules—while not believing in the existence of horses and asses.

Well then, Meletus, you must have written these things to test us or because you were at a loss about what genuine injustice to charge me with. There's no conceivable way you could persuade any man with even the slightest intelligence that the same person believes in both daimonic activities and gods, and, on the contrary, that this same person believes neither in daimons, nor in gods, nor in heroes.

In fact, then, men of Athens, it doesn't seem to me to require a long defense to show that I'm not guilty of the charges in Meletus' indictment, but what I've said is sufficient. But what I was also saying earlier, that much hostility has arisen against me and among many people—you may be sure that's true. And *it's* what will convict me, if I am convicted: not Meletus or Anytus, but the slander and malice of many people. It has certainly convicted many other good men as well, and I imagine it will do so again. There's no danger it will stop with me.

But perhaps someone may say, "Aren't you ashamed, Socrates, to have engaged in the sort of occupation that has now put you at risk of death?" I, however, would be right to reply to him, "You're not thinking straight, sir, if you think that a man who's any use at all should give any opposing weight to the risk of living or dying, instead of looking to this alone whenever he does anything: whether his actions are just or unjust, the deeds of a good or bad man. You see, on your account, all those demigods who died on the plain of Troy were inferior people, especially the son of Thetis,[9] who was so contemptuous of danger when the alternative was something shameful. When he was eager to kill Hector,[1] his mother, since she was a goddess, spoke to him, I think, in some such words as these: 'My child, if you avenge the death of your friend Patroclus and slay Hector, you will die yourself immediately,' so the poem goes, 'as your death is fated to follow next after Hector's.' But though he heard that, he was contemptuous of death and danger, for he was far more afraid of living as a bad man and of failing to avenge his friends: 'Let me die immediately, then,' it continues, 'once I've given the wrongdoer his just deserts, so that I do not remain here by the curved ships, a laughingstock and a burden upon the earth.' Do you really suppose he gave a thought to death or danger?"

You see, men of Athens, this is the truth of the matter: Wherever someone has stationed himself because he thinks it best, or wherever he's been sta-

---

9. Achilles. Thetis was a sea nymph. See *Iliad* 18.100 ff.   1. The greatest of the Trojan warriors and eldest son of the king of Troy.

tioned by his commander, there, it seems to me, he should remain, steadfast in danger, taking no account at all of death or of anything else, in comparison to what's shameful. I'd therefore have been acting scandalously, men of Athens, if, when I'd been stationed in Potidea, Amphipolis, or Delium[2] by the leaders you had elected to lead me, I had, like many another, remained where they'd stationed me and run the risk of death. But if, when the god stationed me here, as I became thoroughly convinced he did, to live practicing philosophy, examining myself and others, I had—for fear of death or anything else—abandoned my station.

That would have been scandalous, and someone might have rightly and justly brought me to court for not acknowledging that gods exist, by disobeying the oracle, fearing death, and thinking I was wise when I wasn't. You see, fearing death, gentlemen, is nothing other than thinking one is wise when one isn't, since it's thinking one knows what one doesn't know. I mean, no one knows whether death may not be the greatest of all goods for people, but they fear it as if they knew for certain that it's the worst thing of all. Yet surely this is the most blameworthy ignorance of thinking one knows what one doesn't know. But I, gentlemen, may perhaps differ from most people by just this much in this matter too. And if I really were to claim to be wiser than anyone in any way, it would be in this: that as I don't have adequate knowledge about things in Hades, so too I don't think that I have knowledge. To act unjustly, on the other hand, to disobey someone better than oneself, whether god or man, that I do know to be bad and shameful. In any case, I'll never fear or avoid things that may for all I know be good more than things I know are bad.

Suppose, then, you're prepared to let me go now and to disobey Anytus, who said I shouldn't have been brought to court at all but that since I had been brought to court, you had no alternative but to put me to death[3] because, as he stated before you, if I were acquitted, soon your sons would all be entirely corrupted by following Socrates' teachings. Suppose, confronted with that claim, you were to say to me, "Socrates, we will not obey Anytus this time. Instead, we are prepared to let you go. But on the following condition: that you spend no more time on this investigation and don't practice philosophy, and if you're caught doing so, you'll die." Well, as I just said, if you were to let me go on these terms, I'd reply to you, "I've the utmost respect and affection for you, men of Athens, but I'll obey the god rather than you, and as long as I draw breath and am able, I won't give up practicing philosophy, exhorting you and also showing the way to any of you I ever happen to meet, saying just the sorts of things I'm accustomed to say:

> My excellent man, you're an Athenian, you belong to the greatest city, renowned for its wisdom and strength; are you not ashamed that you

---

2. Three battles of the Peloponnesian War in which Socrates had fought as an infantryman—at Potidaea (in northern Greece), in 432 B.C.E.; at Amphipolis (in northern Greece), of uncertain date; and at Delium (in central Greece), in 424 B.C.E. For a fuller account of Socrates' conduct at Potidaea and Delium, see Plato's *Symposium*. 3. The translator (in a note) suggests that Anytus assumed that Socrates would go into exile to avoid trial. Another way to understand the passage (which is perhaps more consistent with the Greek) is that Anytus argued against acquittal and implied that death was the only possible penalty upon conviction (a good rhetorical tactic).

take care to acquire as much wealth as possible—and reputation and honor—but that about wisdom and truth, about how your soul may be in the best possible condition, you take neither care nor thought?

Then, if one of you disagrees and says that he *does* care, I won't let him go away immediately, but I'll question, examine, and test him. And if he doesn't seem to me to possess virtue, though he claims he does, I'll reproach him, saying that he treats the most important things as having the least value, and inferior ones as having more. This I will do for anyone I meet, young or old, alien or fellow citizen—but especially for you, my fellow citizens, since you're closer kin to me. This, you may be sure, is what the god orders me to do. And I believe that no greater good for you has ever come about in the city than my service to the god. You see, I do nothing else except go around trying to persuade you, both young and old alike, not to care about your bodies or your money as intensely as about how your soul may be in the best possible condition. I say,

> It's not from wealth that virtue comes, but from virtue comes money, and all the other things that are good for human beings, both in private and in public life.

Now if by saying this, I'm corrupting the young, *this* is what you'd have to think to be harmful. But if anyone claims I say something other than this, he's talking nonsense."

"It's in that light," I want to say, "men of Athens, that you should obey Anytus or not, and let me go or not—knowing that I wouldn't act in any other way, not even if I were to die many times over."

Don't create an uproar, men of Athens. Instead, please abide by my request not to create an uproar at what I say, but to listen. For I think it will profit you to listen. You see, I'm certainly going to say some further things to you at which you may perhaps exclaim—but by no means do so.

You may be sure that if you put me to death—a man of the sort I said I was just now—you won't harm me more than you harm yourselves. Certainly, Meletus or Anytus couldn't harm me in any way: that's not possible. For I don't think it's lawful[4] for a better man to be harmed by a worse. He may, of course, kill me, or perhaps banish or disenfranchise me. And these *he* believes to be very bad things, and others no doubt agree. But I don't believe this. Rather, I believe that doing what he's doing now—attempting to kill a man unjustly—is far worse.

So, men of Athens, I'm far from pleading in my own defense now, as might be supposed. Instead, I'm pleading in yours, so that you don't commit a great wrong against the god's gift to you by condemning me. If you put me to death, you won't easily find another like me. For, even if it seems ridiculous to say so, I've literally been attached to the city, as if to a large thoroughbred horse that was somewhat sluggish because of its size and needed to be awakened by some sort of gadfly. It's as just such a gadfly, it seems to me, that the god has attached me to the city—one that awakens, cajoles, and reproaches each and every one of you and never stops alighting everywhere

---

4. That is, consistent with the moral order of the world, not "legal" in the narrower sense of "consistent with the city's law code."

on you the whole day. You won't easily find another like that, gentlemen. So if you obey me, you'll spare my life. But perhaps you'll be resentful, like people awakened from a doze, and slap at me. If you obey Anytus, you might easily kill me. Then you might spend the rest of your lives asleep, unless the god, in his compassion for you, were to send you someone else.

That I am indeed the sort of person to be given as a gift to the city by the god, you may recognize from this: it doesn't seem a merely human matter—does it?—for me to have neglected all my own affairs and to have put up with this neglect of my domestic life for so many years now, but always to have minded your business, by visiting each of you in private, like a father or elder brother, to persuade you to care about virtue. Of course, if I were getting anything out of it or if I were being paid for giving this advice, my conduct would be intelligible. But, as it is, you can plainly see for yourselves that my accusers, who so shamelessly accused me of everything else, couldn't bring themselves to be so utterly shameless as to call a witness to say that I ever once accepted or asked for payment. In fact, it's *I* who can call what I think is a sufficient witness that I'm telling the truth—my poverty.

But perhaps it may seem strange that I, of all people, give this advice by going around and minding other people's business in private, yet do not venture to go before your Assembly and give advice to the city in public. The reason for that, however, is one you've heard me give many times and in many places: A divine and daimonic thing comes to me—the very thing Meletus made mocking allusion to in the indictment he wrote. It's something that began happening to me in childhood: a sort of voice comes, which, whenever it does come, always holds me back from what I'm about to do but never urges me forward. *It* is what opposes my engaging in politics—and to me, at least, its opposition seems entirely right. For you may be sure, men of Athens, that if I'd tried to engage in politics I'd have perished long ago and have benefited neither you nor myself.

Please don't resent me if I tell you the truth. The fact is that no man will be spared by you or by any other multitude of people if he genuinely opposes a lot of unjust and unlawful actions and tries to prevent them from happening in the city. On the contrary, anyone who really fights for what's just, if indeed he's going to survive for even a short time, must act privately not publicly.

I'll present substantial evidence of that—not words, but what you value, deeds. Listen, then, to what happened to me, so you may see that fear of death wouldn't lead me to submit to a single person contrary to what's just, not even if I were to perish at once for not submitting. The things I'll tell you are of a vulgar sort commonly heard in the law courts, but they're true nonetheless.

You see, men of Athens, I never held any other public office in the city, but I've served on the Council.[5] And it happened that my own tribe, Antiochis, was presiding when you wanted to try the ten generals—the ones

---

5. Fifty members were chosen from each of the ten tribes into which the population was divided (all named after mythical heroes—in Socrates' case, Antiochis) to serve a year on the Council. Each tribal delegation acted as a standing committee of the whole body for a part of the year. The members of this standing committee were called Prytaneis. As a member of the Council, Socrates was not "engaging in politics" but simply fulfilling his duty as a citizen when called on.

who failed to rescue the survivors of the naval battle—as a group.[6] That was unlawful, as you all came to recognize at a later time. On that occasion, I was the only presiding member opposed to your doing something illegal, and I voted against you. And though the orators were ready to lay information against me and have me summarily arrested, and you were shouting and urging them on, I thought that I should face danger on the side of law and justice, rather than go along with you for fear of imprisonment or death when your proposals were unjust.

This happened when the city was still under democratic rule. But later, when the oligarchy[7] had come to power, it happened once more. The Thirty summoned me and four others to the Tholus and ordered us to arrest Leon of Salamis[8] and bring him from Salamis to die. They gave many such orders to many other people too, of course, since they wanted to implicate as many as possible in their crimes. On *that* occasion, however, I showed once again not by words but by deeds that I couldn't care less about death—if that isn't putting it too bluntly—but that all I care about is not doing anything unjust or impious. You see, that government, powerful though it was, didn't frighten me into unjust action: when we came out of the Tholus, the other four went to Salamis and arrested Leon, whereas I left and went home. I might have died for that if the government hadn't fallen shortly afterward.

There are many witnesses who will testify before you about these events.

Do you imagine, then, that I'd have survived all these years if I'd been regularly active in public affairs, and had come to the aid of justice like a good man, and regarded that as most important, as one should? Far from it, men of Athens, and neither would any other man. But throughout my entire life, in any public activities I may have engaged in, it was evident I was the sort of person—and in private life I was the same—who never agreed to anything with anyone contrary to justice, whether with others or with those whom my slanderers say are my students. In fact, I've never been anyone's teacher at any time. But if anyone, whether young or old, wanted to listen to me while I was talking and performing my own task, I never begrudged that to him. Neither do I engage in conversation only when I receive a fee and not when I don't. Rather, I offer myself for questioning to rich and poor alike, or, if someone prefers, he may listen to me and answer my questions. And if any one of these turned out well, or did not do so, I can't justly be held responsible, since I never at any time promised any of them that they'd learn anything from me or that I'd teach them. And if anyone says that he learned something from me or heard something in private that all the others didn't also hear, you may be sure he isn't telling the truth.

Why, then, you may ask, do some people enjoy spending so much time with me? You've heard the answer, men of Athens. I told you the whole truth:

6. In 406 B.C.E. the Athenians won a naval victory over Sparta at Arginusae off the coast of Asia Minor. Because the Athenian commanders failed to pick up the bodies of a large number of Athenians whose ships had been destroyed, all ten were put on trial not in a court of law but before the Assembly. They were condemned to death, and the six who had returned to Athens were executed, among them a son of Pericles. The procedure adopted—especially trying the generals as a group—may have been illegal, as Socrates claims; it was, at any rate, contrary to usual practice and unfair.   7. The Thirty, who came to power in 404 B.C.E. with Spartan backing and ruled for eight months. They included some men who had been associated with Socrates and influenced by him (especially Critias, a relative of Plato). Socrates is careful to give an instance of his opposition to the oligarchy to balance that of his opposition to an action by the democracy.   8. An island off the Piraeus (Athens' harbor), Athenian territory. Leon is otherwise unknown; the Thirty arrested a number of affluent citizens, whose property they confiscated. The Tholus: a circular building in the Agora in which the Prytaneis held their meetings and ate their meals.

it's because they enjoy listening to people being examined who think they're wise but aren't. For it's not unpleasant. In my case, however, it's something, you may take it from me, I've been ordered to do by the god, both in oracles and dreams, and in every other way that divine providence ever ordered any man to do anything at all.

All these things, men of Athens, are both true and easily tested. I mean, if I really do corrupt the young or have corrupted them in the past, surely if any of them had recognized when they became older that I'd given them bad advice at some point in their youth, they'd now have come forward themselves to accuse me and seek redress. Or else, if they weren't willing to come themselves, some of their family members—fathers, brothers, or other relatives—if indeed their kinsmen had suffered any harm from me—would remember it now and seek redress.

In any case, I see many of these people present here: first of all, there's Crito, my contemporary and fellow demesman,[9] the father of Critobulus here; then there's Lysanius of Sphettus, father of Aeschines here; next, there's Epigenes' father, Antiphon of Cephisia here. Then there are others whose brothers have spent time in this way: Nicostratus, son of Theozotides, Brother of Theodotus—by the way, Theodotus is dead, so that Nicostratus is at any rate not being held back by him; and Paralius here, son of Demodocus, whose brother was Theages; and there's Adeimantus, the son of Ariston, whose brother is Plato here,[1] and Aeantodorus, whose brother here is Apollodorus. And there are many others I could mention, some of whom Meletus most certainly ought to have called as witnesses in the course of his own speech. If he forgot to do so, let him call them now—I yield time to him. Let him tell us if he has any such witness. No, it's entirely the opposite, gentlemen. You'll find that they're all prepared to come to my aid, their corruptor, the one who, Meletus and Anytus claim, is doing harm to their families. Of course, the corrupted ones themselves might indeed have reason to come to my aid. But the *un*corrupted ones, their relatives, who are older men now, what reason could they possibly have to support me, other than the right and just one: that they know perfectly well that Meletus is lying, whereas I am telling the truth?

Well then, gentlemen, those, and perhaps other similar things, are pretty much all I have to say in my defense. But perhaps one of you might be resentful when he recalls his own behavior. Perhaps when he was contesting even a lesser charge than this charge, he positively entreated the jurors with copious tears, bringing forward his children and many other relatives and friends as well, in order to arouse as much pity as possible. And then he finds that I'll do none of these things, not even when I'm facing what might be considered the ultimate danger. Perhaps someone with these thoughts might feel more willful where I'm concerned and, made angry by these very same thoughts, cast his vote in anger.[2] Well, if there's someone like that among you—of course, I don't expect there to be, but *if* there is—I think it appro-

9. Resident of the same deme, a precinct of Attica (Athens's territory) and the local unit of government. Crito was a friend of Socrates who later tried to persuade him to escape from prison. 1. Plato is subtly claiming eyewitness authority for the version of Socrates' speech he gives in the *Apology*. 2. The accepted ending of the speech for the defense was an unrestrained appeal to the pity of the jury. Socrates' refusal to make it is another shock to the prejudices of the audience.

priate for me to answer him as follows: "I do indeed have relatives, my excellent man. As Homer puts it, I too 'wasn't born from oak or from rock'[3] but from human parents. And so I do have relatives, sons too, men of Athens, three of them, one already a young man while two are still children. Nonetheless, I won't bring any of them forward here and then entreat you to vote for my acquittal."

Why, you may ask, will I do none of these things? Not because I'm willful, men of Athens or want to dishonor you—whether I'm boldly facing death or not is a separate story. The point has to do with reputation—yours and mine and that of the entire city: it doesn't seem noble to me to do these things, especially at my age and with my reputation—for whether truly or falsely, it's firmly believed in any case that Socrates is superior to the majority of people in some way. Therefore, if those of *you* who are believed to be superior—either in wisdom or courage or any other virtue whatever—behave like that, it would be shameful.

I've often seen people of this sort when they're on trial: they're thought to be someone, yet they do astonishing things—as if they imagined they'd suffer something terrible if they died and would be immortal if only you didn't kill them. People like that seem to me to bring such shame to the city that any foreigner might well suppose that those among the Athenians who are superior in virtue—the ones they select from among themselves for political office and other positions of honor—are no better than women. I say this, men of Athens, because none of us who are in any way whatever thought to be someone should behave like that, nor, if we attempt to do so, should you allow it. On the contrary, you should make it clear you're far more likely to convict someone who makes the city despicable by staging these pathetic scenes than someone who minds his behavior.

Reputation aside, gentlemen, it doesn't seem just to me to entreat the jury—nor to be acquitted by entreating it—but rather to inform it and persuade it. After all, a juror doesn't sit in order to grant justice as a favor, but to decide where justice lies. And he has sworn on oath not that he'll favor whomever he pleases, but that he'll judge according to law. We shouldn't accustom you to breaking your oath, then, nor should you become accustomed to doing so—neither of us would be doing something holy if we did. Hence don't expect me, men of Athens, to act toward you in ways I consider to be neither noble, nor just, nor pious—most especially, by Zeus, when I'm being prosecuted for *impiety* by Meletus here. You see, if I tried to persuade and to force you by entreaties, after you've sworn an oath, I clearly would be teaching you not to believe in the existence of gods, and my defense would literally convict me of not acknowledging gods. But that's far from being the case: I do acknowledge them, men of Athens, as none of my accusers does. I turn it over to you and to the god to judge me in whatever way will be best for me and for yourselves.[4]

---

3. Penelope says to her husband, Odysseus (who is disguised as a beggar), "Tell me who you are. Where do you come from? You've hardly sprung from a rock or oak like some old man of legend" (*Odyssey* 19.183–84). 4. This is the end of the defense speech proper. It appears from what Socrates says later that the jury was split, 280–220, in reaching a verdict of guilty. The jury must now choose between the penalty proposed by the prosecution and one offered by the defense. Socrates must propose the lightest sentence he thinks he can get away with, but one heavy enough to satisfy the majority of the jury who voted to convict him. The prosecution probably expects him to propose exile from Athens, but Socrates surprises them.

There are many reasons, men of Athens, why I'm not resentful at this outcome—that you voted to convict me—and this outcome wasn't unexpected by me. I'm much more surprised at the number of votes cast on each side: I didn't think that the decision would be by so few votes but by a great many. Yet now, it seems, that if a mere thirty votes had been cast differently, I'd have been acquitted. Or rather, it seems to me that where Meletus is concerned I've been acquitted even as things stand. And not merely acquitted. On the contrary, one thing at least is clear to everyone: if Anytus had not come forward with Lycon to accuse me, Meletus would have been fined a thousand drachmas, since he wouldn't have received a fifth of the votes.[5]

But be that as it may, the man demands the death penalty for me. Well then, what counterpenalty should I now propose to you, men of Athens? Or is it clear that it's whatever I deserve? What then should it be? What do I deserve to suffer or pay just because I didn't mind my own business throughout my life? Because I didn't care about the things most people care about—making money, managing an estate, or being a general, a popular leader, or holding some other political office, or joining the cabals and factions that come to exist in a city—but thought myself too honest, in truth, to engage in these things and survive? Because I didn't engage in things, if engaging in them was going to benefit neither you nor myself, but instead went to each of you privately and tried to perform what I claim is the greatest benefaction? That was what I did. I tried to persuade each of you to care first not about any of his possessions, but about himself and how he'll become best and wisest; and not primarily about the city's possessions, but about the city itself; and to care about all other things in the same way.

What, then, do I deserve to suffer for being such a man? Something good, men of Athens, if I'm indeed to propose a penalty that I truly deserve. Yes, and the sort of good thing, too, that would be appropriate for me. What, then, is appropriate for a poor man who is a public benefactor and needs to have the leisure to exhort you? Nothing could be more appropriate, men of Athens, than for such a man to be given free meals in the Prytaneum[6]—much more so for him, at any rate, than for anyone of you who has won a victory at Olympia, whether with a single horse or with a pair or a team of four. You see, he makes you think you're happy, whereas I make you actually happy. Besides, he doesn't need to be sustained in that way, but I do need it. So if, as justice demands, I must propose a penalty I deserve, that's the penalty I propose: free meals in the Prytaneum.

Now perhaps when I say this, you may think I'm speaking in a quite willful manner—just as when I talked about appeals to pity and supplications. That's not so, men of Athens, rather it's something like this: I'm convinced that I never intentionally do injustice to any man—but I can't get you to share my conviction, because we've talked together a short time. I say this, because if you had a law, as other men in fact do, not to try a capital charge in a single

5. Socrates jokingly divides the votes against him into three parts, one for each of his three accusers, and suggests that Meletus's votes fall below the minimum needed to justify the trial. To discourage frivolous lawsuits, in such cases the accuser was fined.   6. A building near the Agora that housed the city's communal hearth; there the Prytaneis, as representatives of the city, entertained distinguished visitors, winners in the athletic contests at Olympia, and those who had done exceptional service to Athens (or in some cases their descendants). To be given free meals in the Prytaneum for life was an enormous honor.

day, but over several,[7] I think you'd be convinced. But as things stand, it isn't easy to clear myself of huge slanders in a short time.

Since *I'm* convinced that I've done injustice to no one, however, I'm certainly not likely to do myself injustice, to announce that I deserve something bad and to propose a penalty of that sort for myself. Why should I do that? In order not to suffer what Meletus proposes as a penalty for me when I say that I don't know whether it's a good or a bad thing? As an alternative to that, am I then to choose one of the things I know very well to be bad and propose it? Imprisonment, for example? And why should I live in prison, enslaved to the regularly appointed officers, the Eleven?[8] All right, a fine with imprisonment until I pay? But in my case the effect would be precisely the one I just now described, since I haven't the means to pay.

Well then, should I propose exile? Perhaps that's what *you'd* propose for me. But I'd certainly have to have an excessive love of life, men of Athens, to be so irrational as to do that. I see that you, my fellow citizens, were unable to tolerate my discourses and discussions but came to find them so burdensome and odious that you're now seeking to get rid of them. Is it likely, then, that I'll infer that others will find them easy to bear? Far from it, men of Athens. It would be a fine life for me, indeed, a man of my age,[9] to go into exile and spend his life exchanging one city for another, because he's always being expelled. You see, I well know that wherever I go, the young will come to hear me speaking, just as they do here. And if I drive them away, they will themselves persuade their elders to expel me; whereas if I don't drive them away, their fathers and relatives will expel me because of these same young people.

Now perhaps someone may say, "But by keeping quiet and minding your own business, Socrates, wouldn't it be possible for you to live in exile for us?" This is the very hardest point on which to convince some of you. You see, if I say that to do *that* would be to disobey the god, and that this is why I can't mind my own business you won't believe me, since you'll suppose I'm being ironical. But again, if I say it's the greatest good for a man to discuss virtue every day, and the other things you've heard me discussing and examining myself and others about, on the grounds that the unexamined life isn't worth living for a human being, you'll believe me even less when I say that. But in fact, things are just as I claim them to be, men of Athens, though it isn't easy to convince you of them. At the same time, I'm not accustomed to thinking that I deserve anything bad. If I had the means, I'd have proposed a fine of as much as I could afford to pay, since that would have done me no harm at all. But as things stand, I don't have them—unless you want me to propose as much as I'm in fact able to pay. Perhaps I could pay you about a mina of silver.[1] So I propose a fine of that amount.

One moment, men of Athens. Plato here, and Crito, Critobulus, and Apollodorus as well, are urging me to propose thirty minas and saying that they themselves will guarantee it. I propose a fine of that amount, therefore, and these men will be sufficient guarantors to you of the silver.[2]

---

7. There was such a law in Sparta. 8. A committee that had charge of prisons and public executions. 9. Seventy years old. 1. No small sum. In Aristotle's time (4th century B.C.E.), one mina was recognized as a fair ransom for a prisoner of war. 2. The jury decides for death. In the following section, Socrates makes a final statement to the court.

For the sake of a little time, men of Athens, you're going to earn from those who wish to denigrate our city both the reputation and the blame for having killed Socrates—that wise man. For those who wish to reproach you will, of course, claim that I'm wise, even if I'm not. In any case, if you'd waited a short time, this would have happened of its own accord. You, of course, see my age, you see that I'm already far along in life and close to death. I'm saying this not to all of you, but to those who voted for the death penalty. And to those same people I also say this: Perhaps you imagine, gentlemen, that I was convicted for lack of the sort of arguments I could have used to convince you, if I'd thought I should do or say anything to escape the penalty. Far from it. I *have* been convicted for a lack—not of arguments, however, but of boldfaced shamelessness and for being unwilling to say the sorts of things to you you'd have been most pleased to hear, with me weeping and wailing, and doing and saying many other things I claim are unworthy of me, but that are the very sorts of things you're used to hearing from everyone else. No, I didn't think then that I should do anything servile because of the danger I faced, and so I don't regret now that I defended myself as I did. I'd far rather die after such a defense than live like that.

You see, whether in a trial or in a war, neither I nor anyone else should contrive to escape death at all costs. In battle, too, it often becomes clear that one might escape death by throwing down one's weapons and turning to supplicate one's pursuers. And in each sort of danger there are many other ways one can contrive to escape death, if one is shameless enough to do or say anything. The difficult thing, gentlemen, isn't escaping death; escaping villainy is much more difficult, since it runs faster than death. And now I, slow and old as I am, have been overtaken by the slower runner while my accusers, clever and sharp-witted as they are, have been overtaken by the faster one—vice. And now I take my leave, convicted by you of a capital crime, whereas they stand forever convicted by the truth of wickedness and injustice. And just as I accept my penalty, so must they. Perhaps, things *had* to turn out this way, and I suppose it's good they have.

Next, I want to make a prophecy to those who convicted me. Indeed, I'm now at the point at which men prophesy most—when they're about to die. I say to you men who condemned me to death that as soon as I'm dead vengeance will come upon you, and it will be much harsher, by Zeus, than the vengeance you take in killing me. You did this now in the belief that you'll escape giving an account of your lives. But I say that quite the opposite will happen to you. There will be more people to test you, whom I now restrain, though you didn't notice my doing so. And they'll be all the harsher on you, since they're younger, and you'll resent it all the more. You see, if you imagine that by killing people you'll prevent anyone from reproaching you for not living in the right way, you're not thinking straight. In fact, to escape is neither possible nor noble. On the contrary, what's best and easiest isn't to put down other people, but to prepare oneself to be the best one can. With that prophecy to those of you who voted to convict me, I take my leave.

However, I'd gladly discuss this result with those who voted for my acquittal while the officers of the court are busy and I'm not yet on my way to the place where I must die. Please stay with me, gentlemen, just for that short time. After all, there's nothing to prevent us from having a talk with one another while it's still in our power. To you whom I regard as friends I'm willing to show the meaning of what has just now happened to me. You see, gentlemen of the jury—for in calling *you* "jurors" I no doubt use the term correctly—an amazing thing has happened to me. In previous times, the usual prophecies of my daimonic sign were always very frequent, opposing me even on trivial matters, if I was about do something that wasn't right. Now, however, something has happened to me, as you can see for yourselves, that one might think to be, and that's generally regarded as being, the worst of all bad things. Yet the god's sign didn't oppose me when I left home this morning, or when I came up here to the law court, or anywhere in my speech when I was about to say something, even though in other discussions it has often stopped me in the middle of what I was saying. Now, however, where this affair is concerned, it has opposed me in nothing I either said or did.

What, then, do I suppose is the explanation for that? I'll tell you. You see, it's likely that what has happened to me is a good thing and that those of you who suppose death to be bad make an incorrect supposition. I've strong evidence of this, since there's no way my usual sign would have failed to oppose me, if I weren't about to achieve something good.

But let's bear in mind that the following is also a strong reason to hope that death may be something good. Being dead is one of two things: either the dead are nothing, as it were, and have no awareness whatsoever of anything at all; or else, as we're told, it's some sort of change, a migration of the soul from here to another place. Now, if there's in fact no awareness, but it's like sleep—the kind in which the sleeper has no dream whatsoever— then death would be an amazing advantage. For I imagine that if someone had to pick a night in which he slept so soundly that he didn't even dream and had to compare all the other nights and days of his life with that one, and then, having considered the matter, had to say how many days or nights of his life he had spent better or more pleasantly than that night—I imagine that not just some private individual, but even the great king,[3] would find them easy to count compared to the other days and nights. Well, if death's like that, *I* say it's an advantage, since, in that case, the whole of time would seem no longer than a single night.

On the other hand, if death's a sort of journey from here to another place, and if what we're told is true, and all who've died are indeed there, what could be a greater good than that, gentlemen of the jury? If on arriving in Hades and leaving behind the people who claim to be jurors here, one's going to find those who are truly jurors or judges, the very ones who are said to sit in judgment there too—Minos, Rhadamanthys, Aeacus, Triptolemus,[4] and all the other demigods who were just in their own lifetimes—would the journey be a wretched one?

Or again, what would any one of you not give to talk to Orpheus and Museus, Hesiod[5] and Homer? I'd be willing to die many times over, if that were true. You see, for myself, at any rate, spending time there would be

---

3. The king of Persia, proverbial among the Greeks for wealth and power.   4. The mythical inventor of agriculture, identified as a judge of the dead only in this passage. The other three in Socrates' list were conventionally thought to be judges of the dead because of their just and upright lives. For Minos (legendary king of Crete), see *Odyssey* 11.650–55.   5. Greek poet (ca. 700 B.C.E.) who wrote the *Theogony* (a poem on the birth of the gods) and the *Works and Days* (a didactic poem containing precepts on farming and justice). Orpheus and Musaeus were legendary poets and religious teachers.

amazing: when I met Palamedes or Ajax,[6] the son of Telamon, or anyone else of old who died because of an unjust verdict, I could compare my own experience with theirs—as I suppose it wouldn't be unpleasing to do. And in particular, the most important thing: I could spend time examining and searching people there, just as I do here, to find out who among them is wise, and who thinks he is, but isn't.

What wouldn't one give, gentlemen of the jury, to be able to examine the leader of the great expedition against Troy,[7] or Odysseus, or Sisyphus,[8] or countless other men and women one could mention? To talk to them there, to associate with them and examine them, wouldn't that be inconceivable happiness? In any case, the people there certainly don't kill one for doing it. For if what we're told is true, the people there are both happier in all other respects than the people here and also deathless for the remainder of time.

But you too, gentlemen of the jury, should be of good hope in the face of death, and bear in mind this single truth: nothing bad can happen to a good man, whether in life or in death, nor are the gods unconcerned about his troubles. What has happened to me hasn't happened by chance; rather, it's clear to me that to die now and escape my troubles was a better thing for me. It was for this very reason that my sign never opposed me. And so, for my part, I'm not at all angry with those who voted to condemn me or with my accusers. And yet this wasn't what they had in mind when they were condemning and accusing me. No, they thought to harm me—and for that they deserve to be blamed.

This small favor, however, I ask of them. When my sons come of age, gentlemen, punish them by harassing them in the very same way that I harassed you, if they seem to you to take care of wealth or anything before virtue, if they think they're someone when they're no one. Reproach them, just as I reproached you: tell them that they don't care for the things they should and think they're someone when they're worth nothing. If you will do that, I'll have received my own just deserts from you, as will my sons.

But now it's time to leave, I to die and you to live. Which of us goes to the better thing, however, is unclear to everyone except the god.

---

6. Both were victims of unjust judgments. Palamedes, one of the Greek chieftains at Troy, was executed for treason on the false evidence of Odysseus early in the war. Ajax committed suicide after the armor of the dead Achilles was unfairly awarded to Odysseus as the bravest Greek warrior.   7. Agamemnon.
8. Famous for his unscrupulousness and cunning. Odysseus's guile is depicted favorably in the *Odyssey*, but other stories represented him as a duplicitous villain. Some made him the son of Sisyphus. Both men are presumably examples of those who think they are wise but are not.

ARISTOTLE
384–322 B.C.E.

One member of Plato's Academy, Aristotle, was to become as celebrated and influential as his teacher. He was not, like Plato, a native Athenian; he was born in northern Greece, at Stagira, close to the kingdom of Macedonia, which was eventually to become the dominant power in the Greek world. Aristotle entered the Academy at the age of seventeen but left it when Plato died (347 B.C.E.). He carried on his researches (he was especially interested in zoology) at various places on the Aegean; served as tutor to the young Alexander, son of Philip II of Macedon; and returned to Athens in 335, to found his own philosophical school, the Lyceum, where he established the world's first research library. At the Lyceum he and his pupils carried on research in zoology, botany, biology, physics, political science, ethics, logic, music, and mathematics. He left Athens when Alexander died in Babylon (323 B.C.E.) and the Athenians, for a while, were able to demonstrate their hatred of Macedon and everything connected with it; he died a year later.

The scope of his written work, philosophical and scientific, is immense. Even more than Plato, Aristotle has exerted a decisive influence on the Western philosophical and intellectual traditions. He is represented here by some excerpts from the *Poetics*, the first systematic work of literary criticism in the West, and one that has played a central role in shaping the theory and production of literature there.

From Poetics[1]

* * * Thus, Tragedy is an imitation of an action that is serious, complete, and possessing magnitude; in embellished language, each kind of which is used separately in the different parts; in the mode of action and not narrated; and effecting through pity and fear [what we call] the *catharsis*[2] of such emotions. By "embellished language" I mean language having rhythm and melody, and by "separately in different parts" I mean that some parts of a play are carried on solely in metrical speech while others again are sung.

The constituent parts of tragedy. Since the imitation is carried out in the dramatic mode by the personages themselves, it necessarily follows, first, that the arrangement of Spectacle will be a part of tragedy, and next, that Melody and Language will be parts, since these are the media in which they effect the imitation. By "language" I mean precisely the composition of the verses, by "melody" only that which is perfectly obvious. And since tragedy is the imitation of an action and is enacted by men in action, these persons must necessarily possess certain qualities of Character and Thought, since these are the basis for our ascribing qualities to the actions themselves— character and thought are two natural causes of actions—and it is in their actions that men universally meet with success or failure. The imitation of the action is the Plot. By plot I here mean the combination of the events; Character is that in virtue of which we say that the personages are of such and such a quality; and Thought is present in everything in their utterances that aims to prove a point or that expresses an opinion. Necessarily, therefore, there are in tragedy as a whole, considered as a special form, six constituent elements, viz. Plot, Character, Language, Thought, Spectacle,

1. Translated by James Hutton, who has added bracketed text for clarity. 2. This is probably the most disputed passage in the Western critical tradition. There are two main schools of interpretation, which differ in their understanding of the word *catharsis*. Some critics take it to mean "purification," implying a metaphor from the religious process of purification from guilt; the passions are "purified" by the tragic performance because the excitement of these passions by the performance weakens them and reduces them to just proportions in the individual. This theory was supported by the German critic G. E. Lessing. Others take the metaphor to be medical, reading the word as "purging" and interpreting the phrase to mean that the tragic performance excites the emotions only to allay them, thereby ridding the spectator of the disquieting emotions from which he or she suffers in everyday life. Tragedy thus has a therapeutic effect.

and Melody. Of these elements, two [Language and Melody] are the *media* in which they effect the imitation, one [Spectacle] is the *manner,* and three [Plot, Character, Thought] are the *objects* they imitate; and besides these there are no other parts. So then they employ these six forms, not just some of them so to speak; for every drama has spectacle, character, plot, language, melody, and thought in the same sense, but the most important of them is the organization of the events [the plot].

Plot and character. For tragedy is not an imitation of men but of actions and of life. It is in action that happiness and unhappiness are found, and the end[3] we aim at is a kind of activity, not a quality; in accordance with their characters men are of such and such a quality, in accordance with their actions they are fortunate or the reverse. Consequently, it is not for the purpose of presenting their characters that the agents engage in action, but rather it is for the sake of their actions that they take on the characters they have. Thus, what happens—that is, the plot—is the end for which a tragedy exists, and the end or purpose is the most important thing of all. What is more, without action there could not be a tragedy, but there could be without characterization. * * *

Now that the parts are established, let us next discuss what qualities the plot should have, since plot is the primary and most important part of tragedy. I have posited that tragedy is an imitation of an action that is a whole and complete in itself and of a certain magnitude—for a thing may be a whole, and yet have no magnitude to speak of. Now a thing is a whole if it has a beginning, a middle, and an end. A beginning is that which does not come necessarily after something else, but after which it is natural for another thing to exist or come to be. An end, on the contrary, is that which naturally comes after something else, either as its necessary sequel or as its usual [and hence probable] sequel, but itself has nothing after it. A middle is that which both comes after something else and has another thing following it. A well-constructed plot, therefore, will neither begin at some chance point nor end at some chance point, but will observe the principles here stated. * * *

Contrary to what some people think, a plot is not ipso facto a unity if it revolves about one man. Many things, indeed an endless number of things, happen to any one man some of which do not go together to form a unity, and similarly among the actions one man performs there are many that do not go together to produce a single unified action. Those poets seem all to have erred, therefore, who have composed a *Heracleid,* a *Theseid,* and other such poems, it being their idea evidently that since Heracles was one man, their plot was bound to be unified. * * *

From what has already been said, it will be evident that the poet's function is not to report things that have happened, but rather to tell of such things as might happen, things that are possibilities by virtue of being in themselves inevitable or probable. Thus the difference between the historian and the poet is not that the historian employs prose and the poet verse—the work of Herodotus[4] could be put into verse, and it would be no less a history with verses than without them; rather the difference is that the one tells of things

3. Purpose.   4. Historian of the Persian Wars (ca. 480–430/425? B.C.E.).

that have been and the other of such things as might be. Poetry, therefore, is a more philosophical and a higher thing than history, in that poetry tends rather to express the universal, history rather the particular fact. A universal is: The sort of thing that (in the circumstances) a certain kind of person will say or do either probably or necessarily, which in fact is the universal that poetry aims for (with the addition of names for the persons); a particular, on the other hand is: What Alcibiades[5] did or had done to him. * * *

Among plots and actions of the simple type, the episodic form is the worst. I call episodic a plot in which the episodes follow one another in no probable or inevitable sequence. Plots of this kind are constructed by bad poets on their own account, and by good poets on account of the actors; since they are composing entries for a competitive exhibition, they stretch the plot beyond what it can bear and are often compelled, therefore, to dislocate the natural order. * * *

Some plots are simple, others complex; indeed the actions of which the plots are imitation are at once so differentiated to begin with. Assuming the action to be continuous and unified, as already defined, I call that action simple in which the change of fortune takes place without a reversal or recognition, and that action complex in which the change of fortune involves a recognition or a reversal or both. These events [recognitions and reversals] ought to be so rooted in the very structure of the plot that they follow from the preceding events as their inevitable or probable outcome; for there is a vast difference between following from and merely following after. * * *

Reversal (Peripety) is, as aforesaid, a change from one state of affairs to its exact opposite, and this, too, as I say, should be in conformance with probability or necessity. For example, in *Oedipus,* the messenger[6] comes to cheer Oedipus by relieving him of fear with regard to his mother, but by revealing his true identity, does just the opposite of this. * * *

Recognition, as the word itself indicates, is a change from ignorance to knowledge, leading either to friendship or to hostility on the part of those persons who are marked for good fortune or bad. The best form of recognition is that which is accompanied by a reversal, as in the example from *Oedipus.* * * *

Next in order after the points I have just dealt with, it would seem necessary to specify what one should aim at and what avoid in the construction of plots, and what it is that will produce the effect proper to tragedy.

Now since in the finest kind of tragedy the structure should be complex and not simple, and since it should also be a representation of terrible and piteous events (that being the special mark of this type of imitation), in the first place, it is evident that good men ought not to be shown passing from prosperity to misfortune, for this does not inspire either pity or fear, but only revulsion; nor evil men rising from ill fortune to prosperity, for this is the most untragic plot of all—it lacks every requirement, in that it neither elicits human sympathy nor stirs pity or fear. And again, neither should an extremely wicked man be seen falling from prosperity into misfortune, for a plot so constructed might indeed call forth human sympathy, but would not

5. A brilliant but unscrupulous Athenian statesman (ca. 450–404 B.C.E.).   6. The Corinthian herdsman, in Sophocles' *Oedipus the King.*

excite pity or fear, since the first is felt for a person whose misfortune is undeserved and the second for someone like ourselves—pity for the man suffering undeservedly, fear for the man like ourselves—and hence neither pity nor fear would be aroused in this case. We are left with the man whose place is between these extremes. Such is the man who on the one hand is not pre-eminent in virtue and justice, and yet on the other hand does not fall into misfortune through vice or depravity, but falls because of some mistake;[7] one among the number of the highly renowned and prosperous, such as Oedipus and Thyestes[8] and other famous men from families like theirs.

It follows that the plot which achieves excellence will necessarily be single in outcome and not, as some contend, double, and will consist in a change of fortune, not from misfortune to prosperity, but the opposite from prosperity to misfortune, occasioned not by depravity, but by some great mistake on the part of one who is either such as I have described or better than this rather than worse. (What actually has taken place confirms this; for though at first the poets accepted whatever myths came to hand, today the finest tragedies are founded upon the stories of only a few houses, being concerned, for example, with Alcmeon, Oedipus, Orestes, Meleager, Thyestes, Telephus, and such others as have chanced to suffer terrible things or to do them.) So, then, tragedy having this construction is the finest kind of tragedy from an artistic point of view. And consequently, those persons fall into the same error who bring it as a charge against Euripides that this is what he does in his tragedies and that most of his plays have unhappy endings. For this is in fact the right procedure, as I have said; and the best proof is that on the stage and in the dramatic contests, plays of this kind seem the most tragic, provided they are successfully worked out, and Euripides, even if in everything else his management is faulty, seems at any rate the most tragic of the poets. * * *

In the characters and the plot construction alike, one must strive for that which is either necessary or probable, so that whatever a character of any kind says or does may be the sort of thing such a character will inevitably or probably say or do and the events of the plot may follow one after another either inevitably or with probability. (Obviously, then, the denouement of the plot should arise from the plot itself and not be brought about "from the machine,' as it is in *Medea* and in the embarkation scene in the *Iliad*.[9] The machine is to be used for matters lying outside the drama, either antecedents of the action which a human being cannot know, or things subsequent to the action that have to be prophesied and announced; for we accept it that the gods see everything. Within the events of the plot itself, however, there

---

7. The Greek word is *hamartia*. It has sometimes been translated as "flaw" (hence the expression "tragic flaw") and thought of as a moral defect, but comparison with Aristotle's use of the word in other contexts suggests strongly that he means by it "mistake" or "error" (of judgment).   8. Brother of Atreus and his rival over the kingship of Argos. Pretending to be reconciled, Atreus gave a feast at which he served Thyestes' own sons to their father. Thyestes' only surviving son, Aegisthus, later helped murder Atreus's son Agamemnon.   9. The reference is to an incident in the second book of the *Iliad:* an attempt of the Greek rank and file to return home and abandon the siege is arrested by the intervention of Athena. If it were a drama, she would appear literally on the *deus ex machina* ("god from the machine"), the machine that was employed in the theater to show the gods flying in space. It has come to mean any implausible way of solving complications of the plot. In Euripides' play, Medea escapes from Corinth "on the machine" in her magic chariot.

should be nothing unreasonable, or if there is, it should be kept outside the play proper, as is done in the *Oedipus* of Sophocles.) * * *

The chorus in tragedy. The chorus ought to be regarded as one of the actors, and as being part of the whole and integrated into performance, not in Euripides' way but in that of Sophocles. In the other poets, the choral songs have no more relevance to the plot than if they belonged to some other play. And so nowadays, following the practice introduced by Agathon,[1] the chorus merely sings interludes. But what difference is there between the singing of interludes and taking a speech or even an entire episode from one play and inserting it into another?

* * *

1. A younger contemporary of Euripides; most of his plays were produced in the 4th century B.C.E.

BELIEF SYSTEMS OF GREECE AND ROME

Belief systems are the ways, religious and otherwise, that societies and different groups within societies organize their understanding of the world and human life. At any given time, there may be several belief systems within a society that compete with each other for credibility or have no contact with each other; in the latter case, some people can subscribe to several at once, even when doing so involves holding contradictory beliefs simultaneously. Developments also occur over time; new systems of belief arise, replacing or absorbing some earlier ones, while others continue side by side with them.

To do full justice to the complexity of a culture's beliefs at any one time or over time is impossible, but it is both possible and useful to pick out certain dominant trends, especially when these form an essential background to literary texts (and often are articulated by them). So we can speak of Hesiod's systematization of divine genealogies and Olympian religion forming a background to the Greek Archaic worldview that Herodotus expresses, in which the gods are remote but see to it that human life is fragile and wrongdoing punished. Thucydides presupposes a very different outlook, one shaped to a great extent by the Sophists, in which much more confidence reposes in human capacities (for better or worse) and the traditional ethical framework is challenged (again, for better or worse) by a secular attitude that relies on human intelligence and the right of the stronger. In the fourth century B.C.E. philosophy develops, partly in continuation of and partly in reaction against this human-centered view. Such a sketch is valid—but we should also remember that throughout the sixth and fifth centuries B.C.E., alongside the Archaic religious worldview, "pre-Socratic" philosophers formed speculative theories about the nature of the world and its constituent parts that would be immensely important for Plato and Aristotle, especially when they disagreed with those theories. Conversely, religion and traditional piety flourished in the midst of the Sophistic revolution and the growth of philosophical systems. Though we often see the collision of these beliefs in Greek tragedy, the continued strength of religion is most evident in the building of temples and less formal shrines and in the huge number of dedications in all of them, acts of devotion by the faithful.

During the Hellenistic period (third to first centuries B.C.E.), there were important developments in religion, especially as a result of the Greeks' close contact with non-Greek peoples through imperial domination. Judaism flourished in Alexandria in Egypt as well as in Palestine and elsewhere. There was also at this time a great deal of important activity in philosophy (as well as in literature, the visual arts, and medicine). The Platonic (Academic) and the Aristotelian (Peripatetic) schools further developed their systems of thought and continued to do so long after. Neoplatonism would exert an important influence on Christianity, as would the writings of Aristotle much later (through their synthesis with Christian doctrine by Thomas Aquinas in the thirteenth century C.E.). Other important currents of thought also emerged in the Hellenistic period. Besides Cynicism and Skepticism, two in particular were very influential in Roman culture: Epicureanism and Stoicism. Their importance can be appreciated in (for example) the poetry of Lucretius and the prose writings of Seneca.

Finally, during the Roman period especially, certain cults foreign to Greece and Rome became important within Greco-Roman polytheism. To this amalgam, Christianity offered a strong, and ultimately victorious, alternative.

HESIOD
ca. 700 B.C.E.

Homer and Hesiod, wrote the historian Herodotus in the fifth century B.C.E., "were the ones who created a theogony for the Greeks and gave them their epithets, distinguished their domains and special skills, and described their appearance." We do not know whether Hesiod composed his poetry before or after Homer, but Herodotus considers his contribution to Greek culture to be on the same level as Homer's. Together, the two poets forged a Panhellenic religious system, one that could be shared by all Greeks and that eclipsed or subsumed local traditions. There are, however, differences between the two poets in religious feeling. Hesiod's gods are essentially serious, whereas Homer's gods are serious only sporadically.

The *Theogony,* or "Birth of the Gods," sets the Olympian religion familiar from Homer in the context of cosmic evolution. It describes the development of the world from the first elements through a series of divine genealogies that span three generations. Through these genealogies runs a narrative thread: the divine succession myth, the story of conflict within the ruling family of gods, and the overthrow of fathers by sons until Zeus establishes his rule securely by forestalling the birth of the son who is fated to overthrow him. The world order under Zeus is thus the culmination of the theogonic process. It offers stability under a ruler characterized by both physical might and intelligence, the positive qualities of whose reign are suggested by his marriages and daughters near the end of the poem. Zeus's triumph can also be seen as validating human institutions: rulership and hierarchies of power, the patriarchal family, and gender asymmetry.

From Theogony[1]

Chaos was born first and after her came Gaia[2]
the broad-breasted, the firm seat of all
the immortals who hold the peaks of snowy Olympos,[3]
and the misty Tartaros[4] in the depths of broad-pathed earth
and Eros,[5] the fairest of the deathless gods;   120
he unstrings the limbs and subdues both mind
and sensible thought in the breasts of all gods and all men.
Chaos gave birth to Erebos[6] and black Night;
then Erebos mated with Night and made her pregnant
and she in turn gave birth to Ether[7] and Day.   125
Gaia now first gave birth to starry Ouranos,[8]
her match in size, to encompass all of her,
and be the firm seat of all the blessed gods.
She gave birth to the tall mountains, enchanting haunts
of the divine nymphs who dwell in the woodlands;   130
and then she bore Pontos, the barren sea with its raging swell.
All these she bore without mating in sweet love. But then
she did couple with Ouranos to bear deep-eddying Okeanos,[9]
Koios and Kreios, Hyperion and Iapetos,
Theia and Rheia, Themis and Mnemosyne,   135
as well as gold-wreathed Phoibe and lovely Tethys.
Kronos, the sinuous-minded, was her last-born,
a most fearful child who hated his mighty father.
Then she bore the Kyklopes,[1] haughty in their might,
Brontes, Steropes, and Arges of the strong spirit,   140
who made and gave to Zeus the crushing thunder.
In all other respects they were like gods,
but they had one eye in the middle of their foreheads;
their name was Kyklopes because of this single
round eye that leered from their foreheads,   145
and inventive skill and strength and power were in their deeds.
Gaia and Ouranos had three other sons, so great
and mighty that their names are best left unspoken,
Kottos, Briareos, and Gyges, brazen sons all three.
From each one's shoulders a hundred invincible arms   150
sprang forth, and from each one's shoulders atop the sturdy trunk
there grew no fewer than fifty heads;
and there was matchless strength in their hulking frames.
All these awesome children born of Ouranos and Gaia
hated their own father from the day they were born,   155
for as soon as each one came from the womb,
Ouranos, with joy in his wicked work, hid it

---

1. Translated by Apostolos N. Athanassakis.   2. Earth. *Chaos*: a gap or chasm (from a word meaning "yawn" or "gape")—the space either beneath the earth's surface or between earth and sky.   3. A mountain range in northeastern Greece, believed to be the home of the gods.   4. The underworld.   5. Love. 6. The darkness characteristic of the underworld.   7. Region of brightness, the opposite of Erebos as Day is the opposite of Night.   8. The sky.   9. The river imagined to circle the earth (distinct from Pontos, the sea). The divinities named in the following lines compose the generation of Titans.   1. Unlike the sheepherding Cyclopes in book 9 of the *Odyssey*, these are craftsmen who forge the thunderbolt, the weapon Zeus uses against his enemies.

in Gaia's womb and did not let it return to the light.
Huge Gaia groaned within herself
and in her distress she devised a crafty and evil scheme. 160
With great haste she produced gray iron
and made a huge sickle and showed it to her children;
then, her heart filled with grief, she rallied them with these words:
"Yours is a reckless father; obey me, if you will,
that we may all punish your father's outrageous deed, 165
for he was first to plot shameful actions."
So she spoke, and fear gripped them all; not one of them
uttered a sound. Then great, sinuous-minded Kronos
without delay spoke to his prudent mother:
"Mother, this deed I promise you will be done, 170
since I loathe my dread-named father.
It was he who first plotted shameful actions."
So he spoke, and the heart of giant Earth was cheered.
She made him sit in ambush and placed in his hands
a sharp-toothed sickle and confided in him her entire scheme. 175
Ouranos came dragging with him the night, longing for Gaia's love,
and he embraced her and lay stretched out upon her.
Then his son reached out from his hiding place and seized him
with his left hand, while with his right he grasped
the huge, long, and sharp-toothed sickle and swiftly hacked off 180
his father's genitals and tossed them behind him—
and they were not flung from his hand in vain.
Gaia took in all the bloody drops that spattered off,
and as the seasons of the year turned round
she bore the potent Furies and the Giants, immense, 185
dazzling in their armor, holding long spears in their hands,
and then she bore the Ash Tree Nymphs of the boundless earth.
As soon as Kronos had lopped off the genitals with the sickle
he tossed them from the land into the stormy sea.
And as they were carried by the sea a long time, all around them 190
white foam rose from the god's flesh, and in this foam a maiden
was nurtured. First she came close to god-haunted Kythera
and from there she went on to reach sea-girt Cyprus.[2]
There this majestic and fair goddess came out, and soft grass
grew all around her soft feet. Both gods and men 195
call her Aphrodite, foam-born goddess, and fair-wreathed Kythereia;
Aphrodite because she grew out of *aphros*, foam that is,
and Kythereia because she touched land at Kythera.
She is called Kyprogenes, because she was born
in sea-girt Cyprus, and Philommedes,[3] fond of a man's genitals, 200
because to them she owed her birth. Fair Himeros[4] and Eros
became her companions when she was born and when she joined the
    gods.
And here is the power she has had from the start
and her share in the lives of men and deathless gods:
from her come young girls' whispers and smiles and deception 205

---

2. Kythera and Cyprus are both islands that were important centers of Aphrodite's cult.   3. A pun on *philommeidēs*, "laughter-loving," an epithet of Aphrodite in epic poetry.   4. Desire.

and honey-sweet love and its joyful pleasures.
But the great father Ouranos railed at his own children
and gave them the nickname Titans,[5] Overreachers,
because he said they had, with reckless power, overreached him
to do a monstrous thing that would be avenged some day.   210

* * *

Rhea succumbed to Kronos's love and bore him illustrious children,[6]
Hestia and Demeter and Hera, who walks in golden sandals,
imperious Hades, whose heart knows no mercy   455
in his subterranean dwelling, and the rumbling Earthshaker,[7]
and Zeus the counselor and father of gods and men,
Zeus under whose thunder the wide earth quivers.
But majestic Kronos kept on swallowing each child
as it moved from the holy womb toward the knees;   460
his purpose was to prevent any other child of the Sky Dwellers
from holding the kingly office among immortals.
He had learned from Gaia and starry Ouranos
that he, despite his power, was fated
to be subdued by his own son, a victim of his own schemes.   465
Therefore, he kept no blind watch, but ever wary
he gulped down his own children to Rhea's endless grief.
But as she was about to bear Zeus, father of gods
and men, she begged her own parents,
Gaia, that is, and starry Ouranos,   470
to contrive such a plan that the birth of her dear child
would go unnoticed and her father's Erinys would take revenge
for the children swallowed by majestic, sinuous-minded Kronos.
And they listened to their dear daughter and granted her wish
and let her know what fate had in store   475
for King Kronos and his bold-spirited son.
And so they sent her to Lyktos, in the rich land of Crete,
just as she was about to bear the last of her children,
great Zeus, whom huge Gaia would take into her care
on broad Crete, to nourish and foster with tender love.   480
She carried him swiftly in the darkness of night, and Lyktos was
the first place she reached; she took him in her arms
and hid him inside the god-haunted earth in a cave
lodged deep within a sheer cliff of densely wooded Mount Aigaion.
But to the great Lord Kronos, king of the older gods,   485
she handed a huge stone wrapped in swaddling clothes.
He took it in his hands and stuffed it into his belly—
the great fool! It never crossed his mind that the stone
was given in place of his son thus saved to become
carefree and invincible, destined to crush him by might of hand,   490
drive him out of his rule, and become king of the immortals.
The lord's strength and splendid limbs grew swiftly

---

5. A play on the verb *titainō*, "to stretch" or "strain." Ouranos pronounces a curse on his children, which will be fulfilled when Kronos is overthrown by his son Zeus. Note that the Furies (Erinyes) are born from the blood resulting from Ouranos's castration (line 185). Aeschylus's *Oresteia* will later trace a similar pattern of guilt and expiation descending through generations of a family.   6. The Olympian gods, the third divine generation.   7. Poseidon, god of the sea.

and, as the year followed its revolving course,
sinuous-minded Kronos was deceived by Gaia's
cunning suggestions to disgorge his own offspring—   495
overpowered also by the craft and brawn of his own son.
The stone last swallowed was first to come out,
and Zeus set it up on the broad-pathed earth,
at sacred Pytho,[8] under the rocky folds of Parnassos,
forever to be a marvel and a portent for mortal men.   500
He freed from their wretched bonds his father's brothers,
[Brontes and Steropes and Arges of the bold spirit,]
whom Ouranos, their father, had thrown into chains;
they did not forget the favors he had done them,
and they gave him the thunder and the smoky thunderbolt
and lightning, all of which had lain hidden in the earth.   505
Trusting in these, he ruled over mortals and immortals.
Iapetos took as his wife the fair-ankled Klymene,
daughter of Okeanos, and shared her bed,
and she bore him Atlas, a son of invincible spirit,
and Menoitios of the towering pride, and Prometheus,   510
whose mind was labyrinthine and swift, and foolish Epimetheus,[9]
who from the start brought harm to men who toil for bread;
he was first to accept the virgin woman fashioned by far-seeing Zeus,
who with flaming thunderbolt struck Menoitios
and cast him into murky Erebos   515
for his folly and reckless flaunting of manliness.
By harsh necessity, Atlas supports the broad sky
on his head and unwearying arms,
at the earth's limits, near the clear-voiced Hesperides,
for this is the doom decreed for him by Zeus the counselor.[1]   520
With shackles and inescapable fetters Zeus riveted Prometheus
on a pillar—Prometheus of the labyrinthine mind;
and he sent a long-winged eagle to swoop on him
and devour the god's liver; but what the long-winged bird ate
in the course of each day grew back and was restored to its full size. 525
But Herakles,[2] the mighty son of fair-ankled Alkmene,
slew the eagle, drove the evil scourge away
from the son of Iapetos and freed him from his sorry plight,
and did all this obeying the will of Olympian Zeus,
who rules on high, to make the glory of Herakles, child of Thebes,   530
greater than before over the earth that nurtures many.
Zeus so respected these things and honored his illustrious son
that he quelled the wrath he had nursed against Prometheus,
who had opposed the counsels of Kronos's mighty son.
When the gods and mortal men were settling their accounts[3]   535
at Mekone, Prometheus cheerfully took a great ox,
carved it up, and set it before Zeus to trick his mind.
He placed meat, entrails, and fat within a hide

8. Delphi, site of Apollo's famous oracle.   9. The Greeks interpreted Epimetheus's name as "After-thought" and his brother Prometheus's name as "Forethought."   1. Menoitios and Atlas may not have done anything in particular to incur punishment, but they are a physical threat to Zeus's supremacy. Prometheus threatens to rival him in cunning.   2. The son of Zeus, and the greatest of the Greek heroes.   3. Evidently they are separating, having lived together on terms of equality.

and covered them with the ox's tripe,
but with guile he arranged the white bones of the ox,   540
covered them with glistening fat, and laid them down as an offer.
Then indeed the father of gods and men said to him:
"Son of Iapetos, you outshine all other kings,
but, friend, you have divided with self-serving zeal."
These were the sarcastic words of Zeus, whose counsels never perish,   545
but Prometheus was a skillful crook and he smiled faintly,
all the while mindful of his cunning scheme,
and said: "Sublime Zeus, highest among the everlasting gods,
choose of the two portions whichever your heart desires."
He spoke with guileful intent, and Zeus, whose counsels never
     perish,   550
knew the guile and took note of it; so he pondered evils in his mind
for mortal men, evils he meant to bring on them.
With both hands he took up the white fat,
and spiteful anger rushed through his mind and heart
when he saw the white bones of the ox laid out in deceit.   555
From that time on the tribes of mortal men on earth
have burned the white bones for the gods on smoky altars.[4]
Then Zeus the cloud-gatherer angrily said:
"Son of Iapetos, no one matches your resourceful wits,
but, friend, your mind is clinging stubbornly to guile."   560
So Zeus, whose counsels never perish, spoke in anger
and thereafter never forgot that he had been beguiled
and never gave to ash trees the power of unwearying fire
for the good of men who live on this earth,
but the noble son of Iapetos deceived him again   565
and within a hollowed fennel stalk stole the far-flashing
unwearying fire. This stung the depths of Zeus's mind,
Zeus who roars on high, and filled his heart with anger,
when he saw among mortal men the far-seen flash of fire;
so straightaway because of the stolen fire he contrived an evil for
     men.   570
The famous lame smith[5] took clay and, through Zeus's counsels,
gave it the shape of a modest maiden.
Athena, the gray-eyed goddess, clothed her and decked her out
with a flashy garment and then with her hands
she hung over her head a fine draping veil, a marvel to behold;   575
Pallas Athena crowned her head with lovely wreaths
of fresh flowers that had just bloomed in the green meadows.
The famous lame smith placed on her head a crown of gold
fashioned by the skill of his own hands
to please the heart of Zeus the father.   580
It was a wondrous thing with many intricate designs
of all the dreaded beasts nurtured by land and sea.
Such grace he breathed into the many marvels therein
that they seemed endowed with life and voice.
Once he had finished—not something good but a mixture of good   585

4. An explanation of sacrifice, in which the victims' bones, wrapped in fat, are burned as an offering to the gods while mortals eat the meat. Sacrifice both expresses the distance between gods and mortals and is a way of communicating with the gods across that distance.   5. Hephaestus.

and bad—he took the maiden before gods and men,
and she delighted in the finery given her by gray-eyed Athena,
daughter of a mighty father. Immortal gods and mortal men
were amazed when they saw this tempting snare
from which men cannot escape. From her comes the fair sex;   590
yes, wicked womenfolk are her descendants.
They live among mortal men as a nagging burden
and are no good sharers of abject want, but only of wealth.
Men are like swarms of bees clinging to cave roofs
to feed drones that contribute only to malicious deeds;   595
the bees themselves all day long until sundown
are busy carrying and storing the white wax,
but the drones stay inside in their roofed hives
and cram their bellies full of what others harvest.
So, too, Zeus who roars on high made women   600
to be an evil for mortal men, helpmates in deeds of harshness.
And he bestowed another gift, evil in place of good:
whoever does not wish to marry, fleeing the malice of women,
reaches harsh old age with no one to care for him;
then even if he is well-provided,   605
he dies at the end only to have his livelihood shared
by distant kin. And even the man who does marry
and has a wife of sound and prudent mind
spends his life ever trying to balance
the bad and the good in her. But he who marries into a foul brood 610
lives plagued by unabating trouble in his heart
and in his mind, and there is no cure for his plight.
So there is no way to deceive or hide from the mind of Zeus,
for not even noble Prometheus, son of Iapetos,
escaped the heavy wrath of Zeus, but, despite his many skills,   615
succumbed to force and was bound in mighty chains.

*   *   *

But when the gods achieved their toilsome feat
and by brute force stripped the Titans of their claim to honor,
then, through Gaia's advice, they unflaggingly urged
Olympian Zeus, whose thunder is heard far and wide, to rule
over the gods, and he divided titles and power justly.   885
Zeus, king of the gods, took as his first wife Metis,[6]
a mate wiser than all gods and mortal men.
But when she was about to bear gray-eyed Athena,
then through the schemes of Gaia and starry Ouranos,
he deceived the mind of Metis with guile.   890
and coaxing words, and lodged her in his belly.
Such was their advice, so that of the immortals
none other than Zeus would hold kingly sway.
It was fated that Metis would bear keen-minded children,
first a gray-eyed daughter, Tritogeneia,[7]   895
who in strength and wisdom would be her father's match,

6. Personification of cunning intelligence. The series of Zeus's marriages (except the last two, to Leto and Hera), through his wives and the daughters they bear him, expresses qualities that will characterize his reign.　7. Athena.

and then a male child, high-mettled
and destined to rule over gods and men.
But Zeus lodged her in his belly before she did all this,
that she might advise him in matters good and bad.   900
His second wife was radiant Themis;[8] she bore the Seasons,
Lawfulness and Justice and blooming Peace,
who watch over the works of mortal men,
and also the Fates, to whom wise Zeus allotted high honors.
These are Klotho, Lachesis, and Atropos,   905
and they give mortals their share of good and evil.
Then Eurynome,[9] Ocean's fair daughter,
bore to Zeus the three Graces, all fair-cheeked,
Aglaia, Euphrosyne, and shapely Thalia;
their alluring eyes glance from under their brows,   910
and from their eyelids drips desire that unstrings the limbs.
After Zeus slept with Demeter who nurtures many,
she bore white-armed Persephone, whom Aidoneus[1]
snatched away from her mother with the consent of wise Zeus.
Then he fell in love with Mnemosyne[2] the lovely-haired,   915
who gave birth to the gold-filleted Muses,
lovers, all nine, of feasts and of enchanting song.
Leto lay in love with aegis-bearing Zeus
and gave birth to Apollon and arrow-shooting Artemis,
children comelier than all the other sky-dwellers.   920
Last of all, Zeus made Hera his buxom bride,
and she lay in love with the king of gods and men
and bore Hebe and Ares and Eileithyia.[3]
Then from his head he himself bore gray-eyed Athena,
wearliess leader of armies, dreaded and mighty goddess,   925
who stirs men to battle and is thrilled by the clash of arms.
Hera wrangled with her husband and because of anger,
untouched by him, she bore glorious Hephaistos
who surpasses all the other gods in craftsmanship.

*   *   *

8. Literally, What Is Right and Proper.   9. Wide-Ruling.   1. Another name for Hades, god of the underworld. Demeter: goddess of grain and fertility.   2. Memory.   3. Goddess of childbirth. Hebe: personification of Youth. Ares: god of war.

HERODOTUS
ca. 480–430/425? B.C.E.

Herodotus, the Greeks' first great writer of history, was born in Halicarnassus (the modern Turkish city of Bodrum) on the coast of Asia Minor. Exiled from his native city, he seems to have traveled widely in Greece, southern Italy, Asia Minor, and Egypt, gathering information about the past from physical evidence (buildings, monuments, and the like) and from local people's accounts of events. He probably spent time in Athens, and he took part in founding the Athenian colony of Thurii in south-ern Italy (444/3 B.C.E.), where he is said to have died. His monumental *Histories* (the Greek word *historia,* which Herodotus uses to describe his work, means literally "an inquiry") is a vast collection of stories and descriptions of non-Greek peoples and places; but its central theme is, as he tells us at the beginning, the cause of the war between the Persians and the Greeks. Accordingly, the work culminates in the inva-sion of Greece by the Persian king Xerxes and his massive army's defeat by a loose confederation of Greek cities in the naval battle of Salamis (480 B.C.E.) and the land battle of Plataea (479 B.C.E.).

Herodotus is our best source for Greek history of the Archaic period (seventh to early fifth centuries B.C.E.), and his work also eloquently conveys the religious outlook characteristic of that age. This attitude was informed not only by the conviction (expressed already by Hesiod) that the gods punish wrongdoing but also by a profound feeling for the fragility of human life—as, for example, when Solon tells Croesus, in the first selection printed below, that it is impossible to call a person happy until he or she has died without suffering misfortune. From this sense that life is inevitably a mixture of good and bad luck arose the notion that outstandingly prosperous people were especially vulnerable to ruin, that good fortune was therefore dangerous. For one thing, the gods were jealous; excessive prosperity raised people above the level proper to mortals and made them the gods' potential rivals. Presumption invited divine punishment. For another thing, the Greeks felt that great wealth and power fostered arrogance and made people more likely to do wrong. Such people's stories, they thought, exhibited a common pattern: a glut of wealth gave rise to pride, pride to blind folly, and folly to ruin.

The three men whose stories are touched on in the following selections all exem-plify these ideas. Croesus pays through his downfall for the crime of his ancestor Gyges, but although he does not seem a bad man, he is proud: he considers himself the happiest man alive because of his wealth. His lack of self-understanding, of any sense of his own vulnerability, is demonstrated by his incomprehension of Solon's wisdom and by his persistent misinterpretation of dreams and oracles. In deciding to attack Cyrus he disastrously overreaches, and he is ruined. His folly is emphasized by his act of crossing the river Halys at the edge of his own empire to launch his attack. Rivers function in Herodotus as natural boundaries for states and empires: attempts to gain territory beyond these boundaries risk growth beyond proper measure and so incur divine punishment. Polycrates, unlike Solon, heeds a warning about the dangers of prosperity and makes a good-faith effort to suffer a reverse; but he is dogged by his own good luck. Finally, Xerxes' defeat is also depicted as a story of excess, arrogance, folly, and ruin. Like Croesus, he crosses a riverlike boundary, and his yoking of Europe and Asia with his bridge expresses the vastness of his ambition. Even worse, when a storm destroys the bridge he punishes the Hellespont as he would a runaway slave. This action sums up the intellectual and moral blindness that dooms him to defeat.

From The Histories[1]

FROM BOOK 1

[Croesus and Solon]

So for these reasons—as well as to see the world—Solon[2] left home to visit Amasis in Egypt and especially Croesus in Sardis.[3] When he arrived, he was feasted in the palace by Croesus. Three or four days later, at Croesus' command, servants took Solon on a tour of the treasury and showed him how great and prosperous everything was. In due time, after Solon had observed and considered everything, Croesus asked, "Many stories have come to us, my Athenian guest, about your wisdom and your travels—how you have roamed around and seen so much of the world in your quest for knowledge. Well, this urge has come over me to ask you whether you have so far seen anybody you consider to be more fortunate than all other men."

He asked this expecting that the most fortunate of men would turn out to be himself. Solon did not use any delicate flattery, but told him the straight truth: "Tellus the Athenian, O King."

Croesus was amazed at what he said, and asked severely, "What makes you think that Tellus was so fortunate!"

Solon said, "In the first place, Tellus came from a thriving city and had honest, handsome sons. Also, he saw them all have children, all of whom survived. In the second place, he had a prosperous life, by our standards, and the end of that life was glorious. He came to the rescue during a battle between the Athenians and their neighbors in Eleusis[4] and died nobly after breaking the enemy's ranks. The Athenians honored him highly and buried him at the public expense right where he fell."

Solon had piqued Croesus with all that he had said about Tellus' good fortune, but Croesus, fully believing that he would at least come in second, asked who the next most fortunate might be.

Instead, Solon said, "Cleobis and Biton. They were Argives who made a good living and in addition to that had great physical strength. They were both prizewinning athletes, and this is the story most often told about them. The Argives were celebrating the feast of Hera, and it was absolutely necessary for their mother to be brought to the temple in her oxcart. But the oxen did not arrive from the field in time. Seeing that they were running out of time, the young men slipped in under the yoke themselves and dragged the wagon along with their mother riding in it. They arrived at the temple after covering over five and a half miles. Their action was seen by the entire congregation, and it was followed by the finest end a life can have. In it, god showed plainly through Cleobis and Biton that it is better for a man to die than to live.

"The Argive men gathered around congratulating the young men on their

1. Translated by Walter Blanco.   2. Athenian statesman and lawgiver; in 594 or 592 B.C.E. he reformed the laws of Athens. *These reasons*: Solon made the Athenians swear to abide by his laws for ten years and had gone abroad so that they could not force him to change them himself.   3. The capital city of Lydia, in Asia Minor. *Croesus*: king of Lydia in Asia Minor (ruled ca. 560–546 B.C.E.), proverbial for his wealth. His empire included the Anatolian plateau as far east as the Halys river. The story that Herodotus tells is so good that it hardly matters that the dates of Solon's reforms and Croesus's reign make the meeting of the two men impossible.   4. A city and plain on the western edge of Attica.

strength, while the women congratulated their mother. What sons she had! The mother was overjoyed both with the deed and with the praise. She stood before the statue of Hera and prayed that the goddess would give to her sons, Cleobis and Biton, who had honored her so highly, the very best thing that it was possible for a human being to have. After this prayer, while everyone was sacrificing and feasting, the young men lay down to sleep in that very same temple and never rose up again, transfixed in death. The Argives made the kind of statues of them that are made only for the very greatest men and dedicated them in Delphi."[5]

Solon, then, gave the second prize for happiness to these two, and Croesus angrily said, "So then, my Athenian guest, as far as you are concerned, our prosperity amounts to nothing, and you do not even consider us on a par with private citizens!"

Solon said, "When you ask me about human affairs, you ask someone who knows how jealous and provocative[6] god is. In the fullness of time, a man must see many things he doesn't want to see, and endure many things he doesn't want to endure. I'll set the limit of a person's life at seventy years. In those seventy years there are twenty-five thousand two hundred days, not counting any months thrown in.[7] But if you make every other year longer by a month so that the seasons come around to the right place, then besides the seventy years there are thirty-five months, or one thousand and fifty days. All in all, then, these seventy years add up to twenty-six thousand two hundred and fifty days, and from one day to the next absolutely nothing happens the same way twice. Thus, my dear Croesus, humans are the creatures of pure chance.

"Now, you seem to me to be very rich and to be the monarch of many people, but I couldn't say anything about this question you keep asking me until I find out that you have ended your life well, because the rich man isn't any better off than the man who has enough for his everyday needs unless his luck stays with him and he keeps on having the best of everything until he dies happily. Many people who are super rich are unlucky, you know, while many lucky people are just moderately well-off. Now, the very rich but unlucky man has only two advantages over the lucky man, while the lucky man has many advantages over the unlucky rich man. First, the rich man is better able to gratify his desires, and second, he is able to afford the trouble they bring. The lucky man, on the other hand, is better off than the unlucky rich man in these ways: while he is not as able to afford desire and trouble, his good luck keeps these things away from him. He suffers no bodily harm, he doesn't get sick, he experiences no misfortunes, he has good children, and he is handsome. If, in addition to all this, he dies happily, then he is the one you are looking for—the man who deserves to be called happy. Until he dies, though, you must hold off and not call him happy—just lucky.

"Of course, it is impossible for a mere mortal to combine all these things, just as no country is completely sufficient unto itself. It will have this, but it will lack that. The one that has the most—that one is the best. Thus, no one

---

5. Site of Apollo's oracle on the southern slopes of Mount Parnassus. These impressive statues were discovered and stand in the museum there; the bases are inscribed with the brothers' names.   6. The Greek word means literally "prone to stir up trouble." The gods' jealousy and penchant for troublemaking would be activated by great prosperity such as that of Croesus.   7. Most Greek cities used a lunar calendar with about 354 days, which was too short. At irregular intervals they would add an extra month to the year in order to bring the calendar back into phase with the cycle of seasons.

person is self-sufficient: he will have one thing, but he will be lacking in another. To me, whoever has the most of these things, and keeps on having them, and then happily ends his life, he is the one, Your Highness, who rightly carries the title you seek. You have to see how everything turns out, for god gives a glimpse of happiness to many people, and then tears them up by the very roots."

Solon did not at all please Croesus with what he said, and Croesus dismissed him without ceremony, thinking that someone who set aside the present good and urged you to look at how things turned out was a complete ignoramus.

After Solon left, though, Croesus got his great comeuppance[8] from god, I suppose because he thought that he was the happiest man in the world. As soon as he fell asleep that night, a dream came to him which showed him the truth about the disaster that would happen to his son. Croesus had two sons. One was a cripple—a deaf mute—and the other was by far the most outstanding young man of his generation. His name was Atys. Now, the dream showed Croesus that he would lose Atys through a wound from an iron spearhead. When he woke up, he gave this dreadful dream a great deal of thought. First, he chose a wife for his son. Also, Atys had been accustomed to command Lydian military forces, but Croesus no longer sent him anywhere on business of that kind. He took spears and javelins and all such weapons of war out of the men's living quarters and heaped them up in the women's bedrooms, lest one of them fall from a wall onto his son.

While Croesus was busy with the arrangements for his son's wedding, a man in the grip of a great misfortune came to Sardis, a man with blood on his hands. He was of Phrygian descent and belonged to the royal family. He came to Croesus' home and begged to be cleansed of his guilt according to the customs of the country; and Croesus purged his guilt away. The Lydian rite of purification is very similar to the Greek. After Croesus performed the customary ritual, he asked him who he was and where he came from, saying, "Who are you, stranger, and what part of Phrygia have you come from to be a supplicant at my hearth? What man or woman did you kill?"

He answered, "I am the son of Gordias, the son of Midas, Your Highness, and my name is Adrastus. I accidentally killed my own brother, and I am here because I was driven away and completely disinherited by my father."

Croesus replied: "You are descended from friends, and you have come among friends. Remain with us, where you shall want for nothing. You will gain all the more if you bear this misfortune as lightly as possible."

And so Adrastus lived with Croesus.

At the same time, a monster of a boar appeared on Mount Olympus,[9] in Mysias. He kept coming down from the mountain and destroying the fields and crops of the Mysians. The Mysians often went after him, but they could never do him any harm—he harmed them instead. Finally, some Mysian messengers went to Croesus and said, "A monster boar has appeared on our land, Your Majesty, and destroys our crops. We have tried our hardest to catch him, but we can't. We beg you to send your son with some dogs and some handpicked young men back with us so that we can drive this animal from our land."

---

8. In Greek, *nemesis*, "retribution" (on names, see p. 798, n. 1, below). 9. Location uncertain; perhaps west of Sardis, near the Aegean coast (not the famous Mount Olympus in Greece).

That is what they asked for, but Croesus remembered the message of the dream and said this to them: "Forget about my son—I couldn't send him with you. He is newly married, and that's what's on his mind now. I will, though, send the picked men and my whole pack of hunting dogs, and I'll order everyone who goes with you to do his utmost to rid your land of this beast."

That was his answer, and the Mysians were satisfied with it, but Croesus' son went up to him after hearing their request. Because Croesus was refusing to send him with them, the young man said, "The finest and noblest thing I once had was my reputation for hunting and fighting. But now you keep me away from both of them, though you don't see any cowardice or lack of enthusiasm in me. What kind of face am I supposed to wear when I go in and out of the marketplace? How do you suppose I look to my fellow citizens—to my bride! What kind of man will she think she's living with? Now, you must either let me go out after this animal or give me a good reason why what you have done is better for me."

Croesus said, "Son, I'm not doing this because I see any cowardice or other fault in you. A dream vision hovered over me in my sleep and said that you would have a short life because you would be killed by an iron spearpoint. It was because of this vision that I hurried up your marriage and will not send you out on this mission. I'm protecting you so that maybe I can steal you away from death while I live. You are my only son—I don't count that cripple as mine."

The young man answered, "I excuse you for protecting me after seeing such a vision. But you didn't understand it—the dream's meaning escaped you, and it's right that I should explain it to you. Now, you say that the dream told you that I would die because of an iron spearpoint. But what kind of hands does a boar have, and what kind of iron spearpoint are you so afraid of? If the dream had said that I would be killed by a tusk or by something else that belongs to this animal, then you would have to do what you are doing. But it was by a spear! So since this is not a battle against men, let me go."

Croesus answered, "Somehow, son, you've gotten the best of me with your interpretation of this dream, and since I've lost, I'll change my mind and let you go on the hunt."

After saying this, though, Croesus sent for Adrastus the Phrygian, and when he arrived, Croesus told him, "Adrastus, when you were struck down by your terrible misfortune—for which I do not blame you—I purged your guilt, welcomed you into my home, and took care of all your expenses. Now you owe me a favor in return for the favor I did for you. I want you to be my son's bodyguard while he goes out on this hunt in case any highwaymen show up and try to do you any harm on the road. Besides, you ought to go where you, too, can shine by your deeds. That is your birthright, and, anyway, you have the strength for it."

Adrastus answered, "Ordinarily I would not go on this mission. It's not fitting for me, after my terrible experience, to go among successful men my own age. I don't want to—and there are many reasons why I'd keep myself away from it. But now, since you insist, and since I must please you (for I do have an obligation to return your favors), I am ready to do this, and you can expect that your son, whom you order me to guard, will return none the worse for my protection."

After he gave Croesus this answer, the party set out, provided with picked men and dogs. When they arrived at Mount Olympus, they started hunting for the beast, and when they found it, they stood around it in a circle and hurled their spears at it. At that moment the stranger, the one who had been purged of his homicide, the man called Adrastus,[1] hurled his spear at the boar but missed it and hit the son of Croesus instead. Atys, struck with the point of the spear, fulfilled the prophecy of the dream.

Someone started running to Croesus to report the news. When he arrived in Sardis, this messenger told Croesus about the fight with the animal and the fate of his son. Croesus was utterly bewildered by his son's death and was especially outraged that the man who had killed him was the man he had purged of a homicide. He became so furious over the calamity that he bitterly invoked Zeus as "the Purifier," and called on him to witness what he had suffered from the stranger. Croesus also invoked the very same god under the epithets of "the God of Hospitality," and "the God of Friendship"— the God of Hospitality because he had unknowingly welcomed the stranger who was to be the killer of his son into his home and fed him, and the God of Friendship because he had sent that man as a protector and found him to be an enemy.

Later, the Lydians appeared bearing the corpse, with the killer following behind it. Then Adrastus stood in front of the body and with outstretched hands tried to surrender himself to Croesus, demanding to have his throat cut over the corpse. He talked about his first misfortune, and how on top of that he had destroyed the man who had cleansed him, and how he was not fit to live. Even though he was in his own private grief, Croesus pitied Adrastus when he heard these words and said, "I have all the justice I want from you, stranger, since you have pronounced a sentence of death on yourself. Besides, you are not the cause of my troubles; you just unwillingly brought them about. It was some god, who long ago foretold what the future would be."

Croesus gave his son a fitting burial. Then, after people had left, when all was quiet around the tomb, Adrastus, the son of Gordias, the son of Midas, he who was the killer of his own brother and, in a way, the killer of the man who had purged his guilt, believing himself to be the unluckiest man he had ever known, cut his own throat over the grave.

For two years, Croesus sat idle, in deep mourning over the loss of his son. Then, when the empire of Astyages, the son of Cyaxares, was destroyed by Cyrus,[2] the son of Cambyses, the growing strength of the Persians put an end to Croesus' grief, and he began to ponder whether he could seize that growing Persian power before it became too great. As soon as he had formed this intention, he tested the oracles in Greece and the one in Libya.

[Finding the Delphic oracle to be one of the two accurate oracles in the Greek world, Croesus sent staggeringly rich offerings to Delphi to win Apollo's favor. He then asked the oracle if he should attack Cyrus. The oracle replied that if he did so he would destroy a great empire. Delighted at the prospect of overthrowing the growing might

---

1. Adrastus's name sounds like the Greek word for "impossible to escape." The goddess Adrasteia ("Necessity") was closely identified with Nemesis, personification of retribution, the word Herodotus has used to characterize this story (see p. 796, n. 8, above). The name Atys would have suggested to a Greek atē, folly or the resulting ruin.   2. Founder of the Persian Empire (ruled 559–530 B.C.E.). Astyages: king of the Medes.

of Persia, Croesus attacked and indeed destroyed a great empire—his own. Crossing the Halys River, the boundary between Lydian and Persian territory, he fought a fierce but indecisive battle with Cyrus and then withdrew to Sardis. Cyrus invaded Lydia and captured Sardis and Croesus.]

The Persians, therefore, captured Sardis and took Croesus alive. He had ruled for fourteen years and had been under siege for fourteen days and had, in keeping with the oracle, destroyed his own mighty empire.

After capturing him, the Persians led him away to Cyrus, who piled up a huge heap of wood and mounted Croesus, bound in fetters, on top of it, along with fourteen Lydian boys beside him. Cyrus did this either because he had it in mind to make a burned offering of the firstfruits of his victory to one or another of the gods, or because he wanted to keep a vow—or maybe Cyrus mounted Croesus on the pyre because he had heard that Croesus was a religious man and he wanted to find out whether one of his gods would keep him from being burned alive.

That, anyway, is what Cyrus did, but they say that to Croesus, though standing in such terrible trouble on that pyre, there came the wisdom of Solon—spoken as if by the inspiration of a god—that no living man was ever truly happy. When this thought came into his head, he moaned and heaved a deep sigh, and after a moment of profound quiet called out the name Solon three times.

When Cyrus heard this, he commanded his interpreters to ask who Croesus was invoking. They approached him and asked. For a while, Croesus kept silent and would not answer the question, but they finally forced him to say, "A man I would give a great fortune to see talking with all the tyrants of the earth." Since his words made no sense to them, they again asked what he meant. They persisted and goaded until he told them how Solon, an Athenian, had visited him in the past, and how Solon had seen all of his prosperity and had belittled it in various ways. He told them everything had happened to him just as Solon had said, although it was as true for all of humanity as it was for him, and especially for those who thought that they themselves were happy. Croesus told them all this after the pyre was lit and the outer rims were burning. When Cyrus heard from his translators what Croesus had said, he changed his mind, realizing that he, a man, was about to burn another man alive—a man who had been no less prosperous than himself. In addition, fearing retribution and reflecting that nothing was sure in human affairs, he ordered that the fire be put out immediately and that Croesus and those who were with him be brought down. His men tried, but they could no longer control the fire.

The Lydians say that when Croesus realized that Cyrus had changed his mind—when he saw everyone trying unsuccessfully to put out the fire—he shouted an invocation to Apollo saying that if ever the god had been pleased with any of the gifts he had been given, he should stand beside him and protect him from the danger he was in. He appealed to the god with tears in his eyes, and then, suddenly, in a clear and windless sky, storm clouds gathered and burst and extinguished the fire with the most savage rain. After this, Cyrus knew that Croesus was a good man and that the gods loved him, so he took him down from the pyre and said, "Croesus, what man persuaded you to make war on my country and be my enemy instead of my friend?"

Croesus said, "I did it, Your Majesty, and it has worked out to your benefit and to my harm, but the cause of it all was the god of the Greeks, who incited me to make war. No one is so stupid that he would prefer war to peace, for in the one sons bury their fathers while in the other fathers bury their sons. But for some reason, this is what the god wanted to come to pass."

After Croesus said this, Cyrus untied him, gave him a seat near himself, and treated him with special respect—both he and everyone around him marveled at the sight of the man. But Croesus was silent, deep in thought. Eventually, though, he turned and saw the Persians plundering the Lydian city and said, "May I tell you what is on my mind right now, Your Majesty, or must I be quiet?"

Cyrus told him to say confidently whatever he liked, so Croesus asked, "What is that crowd over there so busy doing?"

"They are looting your city and carrying off your wealth," said Cyrus. But Croesus answered, "It's not my city or my wealth they're looting. None of it is mine any more. What they are looting and leading away belongs to *you.*"

Cyrus became anxious over what Croesus had said, so he dismissed everyone else and asked Croesus what he thought he should do under the circumstances.

"Since the gods have given me to you to be your slave," said Croesus, "I think that when I understand something more fully than you do it is right for me to tell you about it. Persians are unruly by nature, and they are also poor. Now, if you ignore these people who are looting and amassing great wealth, you can expect that it will occur to whichever one of them has the most wealth to rise up against you. Now then, if you are satisfied with what I say, this is what you should do. Station your bodyguards at every gate. Have them confiscate all the loot and tell the looters that they are required to give a tithe to Zeus. This way, you won't be resented for taking their wealth by force, and they will willingly hand it over, knowing that you are doing the right thing."

Cyrus was very pleased with what he heard, since it seemed to be good advice. He praised it highly and, after commanding his bodyguards to carry out Croesus' advice, said, "Though you are a king, Croesus, you are ready to give useful service and advice. Ask for whatever reward you like, and it will instantly be yours."

"Master," said Croesus, "you will make me most happy if you let me send these fetters to the god of the Greeks, the one I honored above all other gods, and to ask him whether it is his custom to deceive those who serve him well." Cyrus asked him what complaint he had against the god in making this request. Croesus went back to the beginning and told him about his intentions, about the oracles' answers, and especially his offerings, and about how, encouraged by the prophecy, he had made war on Persia. After relating all this, he ended up by again asking to be allowed to blame the god for the whole thing. Cyrus laughed and said, "You will get this from me, Croesus, and anything else you want whenever you want it."

When Croesus heard this, he sent some Lydians to Delphi with instructions to lay the fetters at the threshold of the temple and to ask whether the god was not ashamed to have egged Croesus on with prophecies to make war on Persia when that meant that the power of Croesus would be destroyed—

from which, they were to say as they showed the fetters, the god got firstfruits such as these. They should ask this, as well as whether it was customary for Greek gods to be so ungrateful.

It is said that the Lydians arrived and gave their messages and that the Pythian priestess told them this: "Even a god cannot avoid what has been foreordained. Croesus makes up for the crime of his ancestor five generations ago, that bodyguard of the Heraclids who truckled to a woman's guile, killed his master, and took a title that did not belong to him.[3] Loxian[4] Apollo would have liked the suffering of Sardis to happen in the time of Croesus' sons, and not in the time of Croesus, but he could not get around the Fates. Yet he granted as many favors as they allowed. He put off the fall of Sardis by three years—so let Croesus know that his capture came three years later than the appointed time. In addition to this, Loxias helped him when he was being burned alive. And, as far as the actual prophecy is concerned, Croesus complains about it unfairly, for Loxias prophesied to him that if he made war on Persia he would destroy a great empire. Now, if he was going to plan well, he ought to have sent someone to ask in response to this whether the god meant Cyrus' empire or his own. But he did not understand what was said and he did not ask any further questions, so he has no one to blame but himself. As to the last thing he consulted the oracle about, Loxias said what he said about the mule, and Croesus did not understand that, either.[5] Cyrus was really the mule because he was born to two people who were not of the same race, and his mother was superior to his father. She was a Mede and the daughter of Astyages, king of the Medes, while his father was a Persian— their subject—who lived with his own queen though he was beneath her in every way."

That was the answer the Pythian priestess gave to the Lydians, who brought it back to Sardis and repeated it to Croesus. He heard it, and acknowledged that the fault was his and not the god's.

FROM BOOK 3

[The Ring of Polycrates]

The power of Polycrates[6] grew in such a very short time that it made a noise throughout Ionia and the rest of Greece. Wherever he set out on a campaign, his good luck made everything go his way. He had a hundred penteconters[7] and one thousand archers. He carried off booty and captives from friend and foe alike, and said that you make your friends happier by giving back what you have taken than by never taking anything in the first place. He conquered numerous islands and many cities on the mainland. In a naval battle, he also defeated the Lesbians, who had gone out in full force to relieve the Mile-

---

3. In a story Herodotus has told earlier, Gyges, a bodyguard of the Lydian king Candaules (who traced his descent from the hero Heracles), was forced by the latter's wife to kill his master. He became king and founded a dynasty that ended with Croesus. 4. *Loxias* was a cult name of Apollo. 5. After inquiring about attacking Cyrus, Croesus asked the oracle if his own power would last long and was told that he should flee when a mule became king of the Medes. The offspring of a male donkey and a mare, a mule signifies mixed parentage; but Croesus interpreted the reply literally. 6. Tyrant of the Aegean island of Samos just off the coast of Asia Minor who seized power ca. 535 B.C.E. and was one of the most formidable figures in the sixth-century Greek world. Key to his conquests was his powerful navy. 7. Fifty-oared warships.

sians[8] and who, in chains, later dug the whole trench around the Samian wall.

Amasis[9] couldn't help noticing that Polycrates was having such huge success, and it made him a little anxious. When Polycrates' success became even greater still, Amasis wrote this letter on a piece of papyrus and sent it to Samos: "This is what Amasis has to say to Polycrates. It is usually pleasing to find out that a dear friend and ally is prospering, but your immense good luck does not please me, because I know that god is a jealous god. Now, I prefer that I and those I care about succeed in some things and fail in others, thus passing our lives with changing fortunes rather than with complete success. I have never heard tell of any totally lucky man who didn't finally end up in utter misery. Now, listen to me, and do the following about all this good luck: give some thought to what you regard as your most valuable possession—the one that it would give your heart the most pain to lose—and then throw it where no man can ever get to it again. If the good luck doesn't fall into a rhythm with the bad after you do this, then just keep following my prescription and you'll be cured."

After reading this letter and realizing that Amasis had given him good advice, Polycrates tried to figure out which of his heirlooms it would most vex his heart to lose, and after thinking it over, he realized that it was a signet ring he used to wear, an emerald set in gold, and the work of a Samian—Theodorus, son of Telecles. After he decided that this was what he was going to throw away, here is what he did: he manned a fifty-oared ship, boarded it, and ordered that it make for the open sea. When it was far from the island, he took off the ring and, with all of the sailors looking on, threw it into the sea. After doing this, he sailed back and became very despondent when he reached home.

Five or six days after these events, the following took place: a fisherman caught a beautiful huge fish, one he thought worthy of being given to Polycrates. So he brought it to the palace gates and said that he wanted to be admitted to Polycrates' presence. He succeeded in gaining admission, and as he presented Polycrates with the fish, he said, "Your Majesty, after I caught this fish, I didn't think it would be right to take it to the marketplace, even though I am a man who has to earn his own living. Instead, I thought it was worthy of you and your power, so I have brought it here and offer it to you."

Polycrates was delighted with the words of the fisherman and answered, "Thank you very much. You will be rewarded twice over both for your words and for your gift. You are even invited to dinner!"

Deeply honored, the fisherman went home while Polycrates' servants cut open the fish and found the signet ring in its guts. As soon as they saw the ring, they removed it, gleefully took it to Polycrates, and handed it over to him while they told him how it had been found. When he realized that this was the work of god, he wrote down on a papyrus how everything he had done had turned out and sent the letter off to Egypt.

---

8. Inhabitants of Miletus, an important Greek city in Asia Minor. *Lesbians:* inhabitants of the island of Lesbos, near the northern coast of Asia Minor.   9. Pharaoh of Egypt from 570 to 526 B.C.E. In response to the growth of Persian power, he made alliances with Croesus and several powerful Greek states, including Polycrates' Samos. The Persians conquered Egypt the year after his death.

After Amasis had read over Polycrates' letter, he understood that it was impossible for one man to save another from what had to be, and that Polycrates—so lucky in every way—was not destined to come to a happy end when he even found the things he threw away! Then Amasis sent a messenger to Samos and said that he was dissolving their alliance. He did this so that his spirit would not be pained over a friend when Polycrates was in the grip of a great and terrible circumstance.[1]

FROM BOOK 7

[Xerxes Punishes the Hellespont]

Next he prepared to march to Abydos.[2] There, Asia had just been yoked to Europe by a bridge across the Hellespont. Between Sestos and Madytus, in the Hellespontic Chersonese,[3] there is a rocky promontory stretching into the sea opposite Abydos. (Here, not much later, Athenian forces under general Xanthippus, son of Ariphron, captured Artayctes, the Persian satrap of Sestos, and nailed him alive to a plank for bringing women into the temple of Protesilaus[4] in Elaeus and having orgies with them.)

Starting from Abydos, the men responsible for this phase of operations brought their bridges of cable to the promontory—with the Phoenicians using cables of flax and the Egyptians cables of papyrus.[5] It is seven furlongs[6] across from Abydos. After the strait was bridged, though, a violent storm loosened the whole thing and broke it up.

When Xerxes heard this, he became furious and ordered that three hundred lashes be laid on the Hellespont with a whip and that a a pair of fetters be thrown into the water. I have even heard that he sent along men with branding irons to brand[7] the Hellespont! Be that as it may, he ordered the men to say these atrocious, barbarous[8] words while flogging the stream: "Your master imposes this punishment on you, O bitter water, because you did him wrong though you suffered no wrong from him. King Xerxes will cross over you whether you like it or not. No one sacrifices to you, and rightly so, you briny, muddy stream!" That, then, is the punishment Xerxes imposed on the water; as to the men in charge of bridging the Hellespont, he ordered that their heads be chopped off.[9]

---

1. In fact, Polycrates was lured to the mainland and killed by the local Persian governor (ca. 522 B.C.E.).
2. A city on the Asian shore of the Hellespont. *He*: Xerxes, king of Persia from 486 to 465 B.C.E.   3. A peninsula that forms the northern (European) shore of the Hellespont.   4. Supposedly the first Greek killed in the Trojan War, when the Greek ships arrived at Troy. *Satrap*: governor.   5. Both Phoenicians and Egyptians were at this time subject to Persia.   6. About 7/8 of a mile.   7. Like whipping and applying fetters, a customary Greek punishment of runaway or otherwise defiant slaves.   8. Because the Greeks considered rivers and riverlike bodies of water divine.   9. Xerxes had a new bridge built of ships lashed together and crossed into Europe with his army.

AESCHYLUS
524?–456 B.C.E.

Aeschylus fought at Salamis, and eight years later he produced his play *The Persians* (472 B.C.E.), which depicts the effect of the Greek victory on the Persians. The scene is set in the Persian capital city of Sousa. The chorus of Persian elders and Xerxes' mother are in suspense about how the king and his army are faring in Greece. A messenger arrives with a graphic description of the battle of Salamis and the news that Xerxes has fled Salamis and is on his way home. In fear for the future, the queen and elders conjure up the spirit of Dareius, Xerxes' father and predecessor as king. In the excerpt below, Dareius interprets the Persian defeat in the terms of Greek religion and predicts the further disaster that, in the following year (479 B.C.E.) at Plataea, befell the part of his army that Xerxes left behind.

For an introduction to Aeschylus, see pp. 502–6.

From The Persians[1]

* * *

DAREIUS   Ah! Swiftly the oracles have been fulfilled, and upon my son[2]
   Zeus has hurled their accomplishment.[3] I was sure   740
   That the gods would take their time in bringing these things about,
   But whenever a man is in a hurry, the god pitches in and abets him.
   Now I think evils have flooded over for all my family and people.
   My son—young, impetuous, blind—brought these things about.
   He thought to check the holy Hellespont in its flow,   745
   Bosporus,[4] the god's channel, with chains as though it were a slave,
   He sought a novel way to cross it, and he clamped iron-forged fetters
     on it
   To make an avenue for his vast army. He is mortal
   But—the fool—he thought he could command Poseidon[5]
   And all the gods. My son: a sickness of mind must have held him in its
     grip.   750
   All the wealth I toiled for now, I fear, lies free for anyone who comes
     along to take.

* * *

DAREIUS   Not even the army that has stayed in Greece now
   Will get home safely.
CHORUS   What do you mean? Won't the whole barbarian[6] army
   Cross Helle's strait[7] out of Europe?
DAREIUS   Just a few out of all who went, if we can trust   800
   The gods' oracles—and we can: consider what has just happened,

---

1. Translated by William Thalmann.   2. Xerxes, king of Persia from 486 to 465 B.C.E.   3. Dareius seems to be in possession of a complete set of prophecies about the disaster that has just occurred at Salamis and the one to come at Plataea. They appear to be Aeschylus's invention.   4. Strictly speaking, the narrow strait connecting the Propontis (into which the Hellespont leads from the Aegean) to the Black Sea, but here used of the whole passage between the Black Sea and the Aegean.   5. God of the sea.   6. That is, not speaking Greek. The word reflects a Greek point of view.   7. The Hellespont was named for Helle, who was being carried with her brother Phrixus on the back of a golden ram when she fell off in this strait and was drowned. Arriving in Colchis at the east end of the Black Sea, Phrixus sacrificed the ram and dedicated its fleece to Ares. This was later the object of the quest by Jason and the Argonauts.

And prophecies are not fulfilled by halves.
If so, he is leaving a choice part of his army behind, deluded by empty
  hopes.
They are waiting where the Asopus[8] waters the plain with its streams, 805
Making rich the soil of the Boeotians' land,
Where catastrophe lies in store for them to suffer,
In payment for their arrogance and thoughts that neglected the gods.
For when they invaded Greece no reverence held them
From plundering the gods' images and firing the temples.   810
The altars are gone, and the shrines of the gods uprooted from their
  foundations.
So their suffering matches the evils they did, and more is to come.
The foundation of evils is not yet laid, but is still being built,[9]   815
So thick the gore of bloody slaughter the Dorian[1] spear shall spill on
  Plataean earth.
Down to the third generation the heaps of corpses will give silent,
  visible warning
That mortals must not raise their thoughts too high.   820
For arrogance bursting into flower yields a crop of ruin,
And from it we reap a harvest of woe.
As witnesses to such heavy punishments for these acts
Remember Athens and Greece.
Let no one, desiring more in scorn for the good luck he has,   825
Pour his wealth and happiness away.
Zeus is there to chastise thoughts too high; his accounting falls heavy
  on us.

8. River in Boeotia, the district in which the city of Plataea lies. 9. The meaning of this line is obscure, and the last word uncertain. The point seems to be that many more evils are to come. Either the evils are seen as a building on which construction has barely started, or the bottom of evils has not yet been reached. 1. Greek, but perhaps with special reference to the Spartans, who were Doric and who played the leading role in the battle at Plataea.

THUCYDIDES
ca. 460–ca. 400 B.C.E.

In 424 B.C.E., during the Peloponnesian War, Thucydides was in command of Athenian troops on the northern Aegean island of Thasos when the Spartan general Brasidas attacked the strategically important Athenian colony of Amphipolis on the mainland nearby. Despite his best efforts, he was unable to prevent Brasidas from capturing the city. For this failure, the Athenians exiled him, and he sat out the rest of the war—for twenty years. The result of his forced leisure was his magnificent, though not quite complete, history of the Peloponnesian War. From his relatively detached position, he was able, as he tells us, to observe events on both sides and to think about their significance. Through his narrative, and through the many speeches by actors in that narrative that he re-creates for the reader, he offers a complex meditation on why individuals and states behave as they do.

One theme that runs through the work is how the pressure of war and its increasing ferocity helped open up for debate and redefinition a number of beliefs and values that had previously been widely shared and taken for granted because they formed part of the framework of traditional religion (as seen, for example, in Hesiod and Herodotus). The following selections develop this theme. In his graphic account of the plague in Athens, Thucydides describes how horror and fear drove people to abandon religious beliefs and standards of behavior in society. He uses the bloodshed of the civil war on the island of Corcyra as an occasion to tell how, as the war progressed, values and the words used to designate them were redefined throughout much of the Greek world to suit individual and party ambitions. In the Melian dialogue, he shows the Athenians refusing even to discuss such notions as justice and arguing instead that it is the interests of the stronger that determine human events. In sacking the main city on Melos, they act with perfect (and perfectly ruthless) consistency.

Thucydides' own aims in writing his history reflect a similar reliance on human intelligence and analysis. For example, he gives his reason for describing the plague: "I will say what it was like and how, should the disease ever strike again, someone who gives an examination may have some prior knowledge of it and not fail to recognize it." His method is analogous to that of contemporary medical writers. Close observation—Thucydides had the plague but survived—and methodical description of a disease's symptoms and progress will help those in the future understand and treat it when it occurs. In the introduction to the history, Thucydides describes his work as "a possession for all time": "those . . . who want to see things clearly as they were and, given human nature, as they will one day be again, more or less, may find this book a useful basis for judgment." As a doctor notices symptoms to diagnose and predict the course of a disease, so the student of history can understand events in the present by knowing what happened in the past. Patterns of action, in Thucydides' view, tend to repeat themselves with some degree of predictability because of an underlying "human nature." His is a human-centered understanding of the world, one in accord with prevailing intellectual trends in the Athens of the late fifth century B.C.E. These trends had been shaped by the Sophists, one of the greatest of whom, Protagoras, had said that human beings are "the measure of all things."

From The Peloponnesian War[1]

FROM BOOK 2

[The Plague in Athens]

47. These funeral rites[2] were celebrated that winter, after which the first year of the war came to an end. As soon as the summer began, the Peloponnesians and their allies—with two-thirds of their total force, as in the first year—invaded Attica under the command of Archidamus, son of Zeuxidamus and king of Sparta. They took up their positions and proceeded to scorch the earth. They had not been in Attica for very many days before the plague broke out in Athens for the first time. They say that it had already struck far and wide, including at Lemnos[3] and elsewhere, although there is no mention that it was a disease of such magnitude or that it caused such loss of life anywhere else. Physicians were the first to treat the disease, but they did so in ignorance of its nature and were no match for it. They died in large numbers, in direct proportion as they treated it. No other human skill did any good, either, and as to supplications in temples, consultations of oracles, and such like, these too were all to no avail. In the end, people gave up on all these things, defeated by the illness.

1. Translated by Walter Blanco.   2. The public funeral for those killed fighting in the war (the occasion of Pericles' famous funeral oration). The year is now 430 B.C.E.   3. An island in the northern Aegean and at this time part of the Athenian alliance.

48. They say that the disease first began south of Egypt, in Ethiopia, and then descended into Egypt, Libya, and most of the King of Persia's domains. It attacked Athens suddenly, getting its grip, at first, on the people of the Piraeus,[4] who said that the Peloponnesians had poisoned their cisterns—for there were not yet any wells in the Piraeus. It later advanced up into the city of Athens proper, and the deaths became much more numerous as a result. Let others, physician and layman alike, say what they know about the probable origin of the disease and about what they think enabled it to spread so far and to bring about so many violent changes. I will say what it was like and how, should the disease ever strike again, someone who gives an examination may have some prior knowledge of it and not fail to recognize it. I give this description having been sick myself and having myself seen others who suffered from the disease.

49. Everyone agrees that it was an unusually disease-free year with respect to other illnesses, and if anyone did have a prior condition, it always developed into this one. Other, healthy people were suddenly and for no discernible reason gripped first by severe feverish sensations in the head and by redness and inflammation of the eyes. Inside the head, the throat and tongue were swollen with blood, and breathing was irregular and foul-smelling. These symptoms were followed by sneezing and hoarseness, after which the affliction descended into the chest, accompanied by severe coughing. When the disease took hold in the stomach, there ensued heaving and the vomiting of every bilious substance ever given a name by physicians, and all this with terrible distress. In most people, there ensued a dry retching that gave way to severe convulsions, in some cases right after the retching abated and in others much later. The skin was not particularly hot to the touch, nor was it pale; it was a reddish blue and was broken out in small pimples and sores. Their innards, however, burned so much that they could not endure having the thinnest garments or linens thrown on them, nor anything but to be completely naked, and what they wanted most was to throw themselves into cold water. And indeed many of those who were unattended ran off to wells and cisterns and actually did so, in the grip of an unquenchable thirst. Their condition remained the same, however, no matter how much or how little they drank. In addition, they were beset by continual insomnia and restlessness. The body did not waste away during the time that the disease was at its height; on the contrary, it unexpectedly withstood the ordeal, with most people dying on the sixth or the eighth day as a result of the internal fever, even though they still retained some strength. If they escaped death then, though, the disease descended into the bowels, where it produced severe ulcerations followed by a liquid diarrhea, which so weakened them that most later died from it. Thus the disease ran its course through the whole body after beginning at the top and firmly planting its illness first in the head, and if anyone survived the most serious stages, it still left its mark by spreading to the body's extremities, attacking the genitals, fingers, and toes. Many of those who survived lost these, and some also lost their eyes.

50. As soon as they recovered, some were afflicted with a total amnesia and failed to recognize either their friends or themselves. You see, the shapes the plague took were greater than the mind could frame. Not only did it attack each person with symptoms more powerful than the human consti-

---

4. The port city of Athens.

tution could endure, but in this respect in particular it showed that it was a different kind of thing from any ordinary disease: many bodies were left unburied, but the birds and four-footed animals that feed on human corpses either did not approach the bodies or died if they did eat them. The proof of this is that there was a notable absence of carrion-eating birds: they were nowhere to be seen, not around the corpses or anywhere else. Dogs, however, who live among people, provided a better chance to see what happened to animals that ate the dead.

51. On the whole, then, this was the course of the disease, though I have omitted many peculiarities that may have occurred from case to case. During this time, none of the usual illnesses troubled people, and if it did, it developed into this one.

Some died in neglect, others while being fully cared for. There was not a single remedy to speak of that could be applied to bring relief, because what helped some, harmed others. No body type, whether weak or strong, stood out for its ability to withstand it; the disease carried off all alike regardless of the regimen they followed. The most awful thing of all was the despair of those who realized that they were sick, because their attitudes immediately became hopeless. They stopped resisting and were much more inclined to give themselves up for lost. Furthermore, when people attended to each other, they became infected and died like cattle. This is what did the greatest damage. Either people stayed away from one another out of fear and perished alone (and many households were left empty for want of any one to care for the sick) or they consorted with each other and died, especially those who made some claim to merit. These people were too embarrassed not to expose themselves by visiting their friends, since in the end even relatives were exhausted by the constant laments for the dying and were defeated by all the woe. Those who had escaped the disease, however, had the most pity on those who were suffering and dying, because they knew what the pain was like and because they were now full of confidence. You see, the disease did not attack the same person twice, at least not so as to kill him. So these people were congratulated by the others, and in the jubilance of the moment held the vain belief that they would never die from any other disease in the future either.

52. The basic calamity of the disease itself was aggravated by the crowding of people from the country into the city[5]—especially the newcomers. It was summer, they lived in stifling huts because they had no homes of their own, and the death rate was completely out of control. The dead had fallen on top of one another in their death-throes, after rolling around half-dead in the streets and near every spring in their desperate desire for water. The temples, in which they had pitched tents, were full of corpses because they died even there. Not knowing what was to become of them and completely overwhelmed by the illness, people lost respect for the sacred and the secular alike. All the burial customs they used to observe were thrown into confusion and they buried their dead as best they could. Many resorted to sacrilegious burial methods for want of appropriate ones, because of the many who had already died in their families. For example, they got a head start on people who had built funeral pyres by lighting them and piling on their own dead first, or they would throw the corpse they were carrying onto one that was already burning and go away.

---

5. To take refuge from the Spartans.

53. In addition to this, the plague initiated a more general lawlessness in the city. People dared to indulge more openly in their secret pleasures when they saw the swift change from well-being to sudden death, and from not having anything to immediately inheriting the property of the dead. As a result, they decided to go for instant gratifications that tended to sensuality because they regarded themselves and their property as equally short-lived. No one was willing to persevere in received ideas about "the good" because they were uncertain whether they would die before achieving it. Whatever was pleasurable, and whatever contributed to pleasure, wherever it came from, that was now the good and the useful. Fear of the gods? The laws of man? No one held back, concluding that as to the gods, it made no difference whether you worshipped or not since they saw that all alike were dying; and as to breaking the law, no one expected to live long enough to go to court and pay his penalty. The far more terrible verdict that had already been delivered against them was hanging over their heads—so it was only natural to enjoy life a little before it came down.

FROM BOOK 3

[Moral Breakdown Caused by War]

82. That was the kind of brutality the civil war[6] led to, though it seemed even worse, because it was the first in this war. Later virtually all of Greece was in a frenzy, with dissension everywhere, with the leaders of the people[7] trying to bring in the Athenians, and the oligarchs the Spartans. In peacetime, there would have been neither pretext nor inclination for inviting their intervention; but in war, where alliances are at one and the same time a way to hurt your enemies and gain something for yourself, inducements came easily to those who wanted radical change. Events struck these strife-torn cities (as they always do and always will for so long as human nature remains the same) hard and fast with more or less violence, quickly changing shape as change keeps pace with happenstance. In times of peace and prosperity, both cities and individuals can have lofty ideals because they have not fallen before the force of overwhelming necessity. War, however, which robs us of our daily needs, is a harsh teacher and absorbs most people's passions in the here and now.

But to resume. Once civil war had broken out in the cities, latecomers to the phenomenon learned about what had already happened elsewhere and went even further in rethinking accepted ideas about taking power, which became ever more cunning, and about taking revenge, which became ever more cruel. People even changed the accepted meanings of words as they saw fit. "Foolish boldness" came to be considered a "courageous devotion to the cause"; "watchful waiting" became "an excuse for cowardice." "Prudence" was a "mask for unmanliness," and "a jack of all trades" was "a master of none." Being "beside yourself with rage" was posited as "part of the human condition," and "thinking things over" to "be on the safe side" was "a glib excuse for a cop-out." The lover of violence was "semper fi,"[8] and the man

---

6. On the island of Corcyra, in the Ionian Sea west of the Greek mainland. In the civil war, members of the democratic faction (backed by Athens) ruthlessly murdered many of their opponents in the oligarchic party (427 B.C.E.).   7. I.e., of the democratic faction.   8. Short for *semper fidelis* (always faithful) the motto of the U.S. Marine Corps, which is equivalent to the Greek phrase Thucydides uses.

who challenged him a "subversive." If you plotted against someone and got away with it, you were "smart," and you were even more "brilliant" if you saw plots coming. But if you planned ahead so as to have no fear of plots and counterplots, you were a "traitor to the party" and "panicked by the opposition." In other words, you were praised for beating someone to it in doing harm and for egging on those who meant no harm at all.

Even relatives were rejected in favor of fellow party members, who were less likely to need a good reason to take risks. These parties did not operate in the service of legitimate interests according to established custom, but outside the rules for selfish gain, and mutual trust was not enforced by the invocation of the gods, but by complicity in crime. A fair proposal from the opposition was accepted by the party in power with safeguards for implementation and not in a spirit of well-bred liberality. People were willing to get hurt provided they were able to get even. If they ever took oaths of reconciliation, they did so in an emergency on the spur of the moment, and their promises derived no binding strength from anywhere else; but then, given the opportunity, the first side that was able to mobilize itself and to see an opening took greater pleasure in clandestine than in open revenge because of the trust of the other side, and figured not only that they would more safely win by deceit, but that they would gain kudos for having been smart. Your average ignoramus would prefer to be called a smart criminal than an honest man, and besides, "honest" makes him cringe while "smart" makes him proud.

The cause of all this was power pursued for the sake of greed and personal ambition, which led in turn to the entrenchment of a zealous partisanship. The leadership in the cities on both sides advanced high-sounding phrases like "The equality of free men before the law," or "A prudent aristocracy," but while serving the public interest in their speeches, they created a spoils system. Struggling with one another for supremacy in every way they could, they kept committing the most horrible crimes and escalated to ever greater revenges, never to promote justice and the best interests of the city, but— constantly setting the limit at whatever most pleased each side at any given moment—they were always prepared to sate their partisanship either by rigging votes or by seizing power with their bare hands. Thus neither side observed the rules of piety: they were more respected for the high words with which they got away with performing their base actions. As for the citizens who tried to be neutral, they were killed by both sides, either because they did not join in the fighting, or out of envy because they were managing to survive.

83. Thus the civil wars led to every sort of depravity imaginable in Greece, and openness, which is the better part of liberality, disappeared in utter ridicule. Ideological strife produced distrust everywhere, and nothing—no binding word or awe-inspiring oath—could end it, because when any one side had the upper hand, they were incapable of trusting others and made sure to provide against attack, convinced that they could not hope for security.

Lesser intellects fared best, on the whole, because their apprehensions about their own shortcomings and their opponents' intelligence, ability to manipulate ideas, and win debates, led them to get a head start in hatching plots, which they then moved boldly to execute. The more intelligent, disdainfully thinking that they would know about such things in time, and that they did not have to take by force what it was possible to achieve by policy, were often caught off guard and slaughtered.

FROM BOOK 5

[The Melian Dialogue]

84. The following summer, Alcibiades[9] sailed to Argos with twenty ships, seized three hundred Argives still suspected of having Spartan sympathies, and then imprisoned them on nearby islands under Athenian control. The Athenians also sent a fleet against the island of Melos.[1] Thirty of the ships were their own, six were from Chios, and two were from Lesbos.[2] Their own troops numbered twelve hundred hoplites,[3] three hundred archers, and twenty mounted archers. There were also about fifteen hundred hoplites from their allies on the islands. The Melians are colonists from Sparta and would not submit to Athenian control like the other islanders. At first, they were neutral and lived peaceably, but they became openly hostile after Athens once tried to compel their obedience by ravaging their land. The generals Cleomedes, son of Lycomedes, and Tisias, son of Tisimachus, bivouacked on Melian territory with their troops, but before doing any injury to the land, they sent ambassadors to hold talks with the Melians. The Melian leadership, however, did not bring these men before the popular assembly. Instead, they asked them to discuss their mission with the council and the privileged voters.[4] The Athenian ambassadors spoke as follows.

85. "We know that what you are thinking in bringing us before a few voters, and not before the popular assembly, is that now the people won't be deceived after listening to a single long, seductive, and unrefuted speech from us. Well, those of you who are sitting here can make things even safer for yourselves. When we say something that seems wrong, interrupt immediately, and answer, not in a set speech, but one point at a time.—But say first whether this proposal is to your liking."

86. The Melian councillors said, "There can be no objection to the reasonableness of quiet, instructive talks among ourselves. But this military force, which is here, now, and not off in the future, looks different from instruction. We see that you have come as judges in a debate, and the likely prize will be war if we win the debate with arguments based on right and refuse to capitulate, or servitude if we concede to you."

ATHENIANS

87. Excuse us, but if you're having this meeting to make guesses about the future or to do anything but look at your situation and see how to save your city, we'll leave. But if that's the topic, we'll keep talking.

MELIANS

88. It's natural and understandable that in a situation like this, people would want to express their thoughts at length. But so be it. This meeting is

---

9. A brilliant but erratic Athenian leader (450–404 B.C.E.), who would soon play an equivocal part in the war. The year is 416 B.C.E.   1. An island in the southwest part of the Cyclades.   2. Chios and Lesbos are islands in the eastern Aegean near the coast of Asia Minor; they were part of the Athenian alliance.   3. Heavily armed infantry.   4. Melos is an oligarchy: only a portion of the population, presumably selected on the basis of a property qualification, are fully franchised citizens, and the council is composed of members of the leading families.

about saving our city, and the format of the discussion will be as you have said.

ATHENIANS

89. Very well.

We Athenians are not going to use false pretenses and go on at length about how we have a right to rule because we destroyed the Persian empire,[5] or about how we are seeking retribution because you did us wrong. You would not believe us anyway. And please do not suppose that you will persuade *us* when you say that you did not campaign with the Spartans although you were their colonists, or that you never did us wrong. No, each of us must exercise what power he really thinks he can, and we know and you know that in the human realm, justice is enforced only among those who can be equally constrained by it, and that those who have power use it, while the weak make compromises.

MELIANS

90. Since you have ruled out a discussion of justice and forced us to speak of expediency, it would be inexpedient, at least as we see it, for you to eradicate common decency. There has always been a fair and right way to treat people who are in danger, if only to give them some benefit for making persuasive arguments by holding off from the full exercise of power. This applies to you above all, since you would set an example for others of how to take the greatest vengeance if you fall.

ATHENIANS

91. We're not worried about the end of our empire, if it ever does end. People who rule over others, like the Spartans, are not so bad to their defeated enemies. Anyway, we're not fighting the Spartans just now. What is really horrendous is when subjects are able to attack and defeat their masters.—But you let us worry about all that. We are here to talk about benefiting our empire and saving your city, and we will tell you how we are going to do that, because we want to take control here without any trouble and we want you to be spared for both our sakes.

MELIANS

92. And just how would it be as much to our advantage to be enslaved, as for you to rule over us?

ATHENIANS

93. You would benefit by surrendering before you experience the worst of consequences, and we would benefit by not having you dead.

MELIANS

94. So you would not accept our living in peace, being friends instead of enemies, and allies of neither side?

ATHENIANS

95. Your hatred doesn't hurt us as much as your friendship. That would show us as weak to our other subjects, whereas your hatred would be a proof of our power.

MELIANS

96. Would your subjects consider you reasonable if you lumped together colonists who had no connection to you, colonists from Athens, and rebellious colonists who had been subdued?

5. A reference to the battle of Salamis (480 B.C.E.) in which the Athenians played the decisive role.

ATHENIANS

97. They think there's justice all around. They also think the independent islands are strong, and that we are afraid to attack them. So aside from adding to our empire, your subjugation will also enhance our safety, especially since you are islanders and we are a naval power. Besides, you're weaker than the others—unless, that is, you show that you too can be independent.

MELIANS

98. Don't you think there's safety in our neutrality? You turned us away from a discussion of justice and persuaded us to attend to what was in your interest. Now it's up to us to tell you about what is to our advantage and to try to persuade you that it is also to yours. How will you avoid making enemies of states that are now neutral, but that look at what you do here and decide that you will go after them one day? How will you achieve anything but to make your present enemies seem more attractive, and to force those who had no intention of opposing you into unwilling hostility?

ATHENIANS

99. We do not think the threat to us is so much from mainlanders who, in their freedom from fear, will be continually putting off their preparations against us, as from independent islanders, like you, and from those who are already chafing under the restraints of rule. These are the ones who are most likely to commit themselves to ill-considered action and create foreseeable dangers for themselves and for us.

MELIANS

100. Well then, in the face of this desperate effort you and your slaves are making, you to keep your empire and they to get rid of it, wouldn't we, who are still free, be the lowest of cowards if we didn't try everything before submitting to slavery?

ATHENIANS

101. No, not if you think about it prudently. This isn't a contest about manly virtue between equals, or about bringing disgrace on yourself. You are deliberating about your very existence, about standing up against a power far greater than yours.

MELIANS

102. But we know that there are times when the odds in warfare don't depend on the numbers. If we give up, our situation becomes hopeless right away, but if we fight, we can still hope to stand tall.

ATHENIANS

103. In times of danger, hope is a comfort that can hurt you, but it won't destroy you if you back it up with plenty of other resources. People who gamble everything on it (hope is extravagant by nature, you see) know it for what it really is only after they have lost everything. Then, of course, when you can recognize it and take precautions, it's left you flat. You don't want to experience that. You Melians are weak, and you only have one chance. So don't be like all those people who could have saved themselves by their own efforts, but who abandoned their realistic hopes and turned in their hour of need to invisible powers—to prophecies and oracles and all the other nonsense that conspires with hope to ruin you.

MELIANS

104. As you well know, we too think it will be hard to fight both your power and the fortunes of war, especially with uneven odds. Still, we believe that

our fortune comes from god, and that we will not be defeated because we take our stand as righteous men against men who are in the wrong. And what we lack in power will be made up for by the Spartan League. They will have to help us, if only because of our kinship with them[6] and the disgrace they would feel if they didn't. So it's not totally irrational for us to feel hopeful.

ATHENIANS

105. Well, when it comes to divine good will, we don't think we'll be left out. We're not claiming anything or doing anything outside man's thinking about the gods or about the way the gods themselves behave. Given what we believe about the gods and know about men, we think that both are always forced by the law of nature to dominate everyone they can. We didn't lay down this law, it was there—and we weren't the first to make use of it. We took it as it was and acted on it, and we will bequeath it as a living thing to future generations, knowing full well that if you or anyone else had the same power as we, you would do the same thing. So we probably don't have to fear any disadvantage when it comes to the gods. And as to this opinion of yours about the Spartans, that you can trust them to help you because of their fear of disgrace—well, our blessings on your innocence, but we don't envy your foolishness. The Spartans do the right thing among themselves, according to their local customs. One could say a great deal about their treatment of others, but to put it briefly, they are more conspicuous than anyone else we know in thinking that pleasure is good and expediency is just. Their mindset really bears no relation to your irrational belief that there is any safety for you now.

MELIANS

106. But it's exactly because of this expediency that we trust them. They won't want to betray the Melians, their colonists, and prove themselves helpful to their enemies and unreliable to their well-wishers in Greece.

ATHENIANS

107. But don't you see that expediency is safe, and that doing the right and honorable thing is dangerous? On the whole, the Spartans are the last people to take big risks.

MELIANS

108. We think they'll take on dangers for us that they wouldn't for others and regard those dangers as less risky, because we are close to the Peloponnese from an operational point of view. Also, they can trust our loyalty because we are kin and we think alike.

ATHENIANS

109. Men who ask others to come to fight on their side don't offer security in good will but in real fighting power. The Spartans take this kind of thing more into consideration than others, because they have so little faith in their own resources that they even attack their neighbors with plenty of allies. So it's not likely that they'll try to make their way over to an island when we control the sea.

MELIANS

110. Then maybe they'll send their allies. The sea of Crete[7] is large, and it is harder for those who control the sea to catch a ship than it is for the

<hr>

6. Like the Spartans, the Melians were Doric Greeks.   7. The part of the Aegean Sea north of Crete and south of the Cycladic islands.

ship to get through to safety without being noticed. And if that doesn't work, they might turn against your territory or attack the rest of your allies, the ones Brasidas[8] didn't get to. And then the fight would shift from a place where you have no interest to your own land and that of your allies.

ATHENIANS

111. It's been tried and might even be tried for you—though surely you are aware that we Athenians have never abandoned a siege out of fear of anyone.

But it occurs to us that after saying you were going to talk about saving yourselves, you haven't in any of this lengthy discussion mentioned anything that most people would rely on for their salvation. Your strongest arguments are in the future and depend on hope. What you've actually got is too meager to give you a chance of surviving the forces lined up against you now. You've shown a very irrational attitude—unless, of course, you intend to reach some more prudent conclusion than this after you send us away and begin your deliberations. For surely you don't mean to commit yourselves to that "honor" which has been so destructive to men in clear and present dangers involving "dishonor." Many men who could still see where it was leading them have been drawn on by the allure of this so-called "honor," this word with its seductive power, and fallen with open eyes into irremediable catastrophe, vanquished in their struggle with a fine word, only to achieve a kind of dishonorable honor because they weren't just unlucky, they were fools. You can avoid this, if you think things over carefully, and decide that there is nothing so disgraceful in being defeated by the greatest city in the world, which invites you to become its ally on fair terms—paying us tribute, to be sure, but keeping your land for yourselves. You have been given the choice between war and security. Don't be stubborn and make the wrong choice. The people who are most likely to succeed stand up to their equals, have the right attitude towards their superiors, and are fair to those beneath them.

We will leave now. Think it over, and always remember that you are making a decision about your country. You only have one, and its existence depends on this one chance to make a decision, right or wrong.

112. Then the Athenians withdrew from the discussion. The Melians, left to themselves, came to the conclusion that had been implied by their responses in the talks. They answered the Athenians as follows: "Men of Athens, our decision is no different from what it was at first. We will not in this brief moment strip the city we have lived in for seven hundred years of its freedom. We will try to save it, trusting in the divine good fortune that has preserved us so far and in the help we expect from the Spartans and from others. We invite you to be our friends, to let us remain neutral, and to leave our territory after making a treaty agreeable to us both."

113. That was the Melian response. The talks were already breaking up when the Athenians said, "Well, judging from this decision, you seem to us to be the only men who can make out the future more clearly than what you can see, and who gaze upon the invisible with your mind's eye as if it were an accomplished fact. You have cast yourselves on luck, hope, and the Spartans, and the more you trust in them, the harder will be your fall."

---

8. Spartan general who had captured cities allied with Athens in northern Greece before his death in battle in 422 B.C.E.

114. Then the Athenian envoys returned to the camp. Since the Melians would not submit, the Athenian generals immediately took offensive action and, after dividing their men according to the cities they came from, began to build a wall around Melos. Later the Athenians left a garrison of their own and allied men to guard the land and sea routes and then withdrew with most of their army. The men who were left behind remained there and carried on the siege.

* * *

116. * * * By now,[9] the Melians were completely cut off, and there were traitors within the city itself. So, on their own initiative, they agreed to terms whereby the Athenians could do with them as they liked. The Athenians thereupon killed all the males of fighting age they could capture and sold the women and children into slavery. The Athenians then occupied the place themselves and later sent out five hundred colonists.

9. The following winter (416/5 B.C.E.).

PLATO
429–347 B.C.E.

Plato probably wrote his monumental *Republic*, a dialogue on the nature of justice, partly in response to the kind of political attitudes we see in Thucydides; the first book of the *Republic* contains a conversation between Socrates and the Sophist Thrasymachus, who argues that justice is the interest of the stronger in terms that recall the Athenians' position in the Melian dialogue. A different conception of justice presupposes a different understanding of the world and of reality. In the excerpt printed here, Socrates provides no less than such an understanding, as part of his argument about the nature of justice and the form that the right kind of city would take.

After Thrasymachus drops out of the dialogue at the end of book 1, Socrates continues the discussion with Glaucon and Adeimantus, who initially defend Thrasymachus's position. Gradually, with their agreement at each stage, Socrates builds a picture of the well-ordered city. He distinguishes three classes of citizen, male and female: the guardians, who rule; the army, allied with the guardians; and the subjects. The city's structure is only a large-scale version of the structure of the individual soul: a rational part, a passionate part, and an irrational part. In the well-ordered soul, the passionate element is allied with reason to keep irrational desires and impulses under control, just as the army supports the guardians in the well-ordered city. Justice, in the city and in the soul, consists of each individual fulfilling his or her proper function. The classes in the city are determined by the natural capacities of soul; thus the guardians are those with the largest capacity for reason. They are, in a word, philosophers. And so Socrates says that the proper city can come into being only if philosophers become kings or kings philosophers. Discussion of the nature of the philosopher leads to the question of what the philosopher ought to know, and this, says Socrates, is the good. At this point, he uses three figures to explain the good, in the passage reprinted below: the sun, the line, and the cave.

The sun is not itself the good; it is an image for the form of the good. What all three of these images assume, in fact, is a doctrine central to Plato's thought—the theory of forms (or ideas). Corresponding to each thing in our world is a form, which represents that thing's essence, or what it truly is. There might be, for instance, a form of the bed: bedness-in-itself, what it is to be a bed. Of this single form there are multiple copies in this world; each of these individual beds realizes in an only incomplete and imperfect way the essence of the bed, the form. Forms are intangible; as objects of knowledge they are not in but rather transcend the sensible world, although they provide the pattern for that world. For Plato it is especially important that there are forms not only of tangible objects but also of the best human qualities: a form of justice, of courage, of temperance, and so on. Superior to the other forms but lending them and our world its quality is the form of the good, and it is this above all that the philosopher strives to know.

Many consequences follow from this theory; two are especially relevant here. First, because the forms are what is genuinely real (being in its consummate sense) and because they are not of our world but transcendent, the things in our world are not truly real and are objects of belief, not knowledge. Second, because knowledge of the forms is the object of the rational part of the soul and thus the highest fulfillment of what we truly are, Plato is led not only to a downgrading of sense perception but also to a radical divorce between soul and body. The body is the locus of appetite, which threatens to distract the soul from the proper object of its efforts. The soul's union with the body impedes it. In the *Phaedo*, a dialogue set on Socrates' last day of life and concerned with the immortality of the soul, Socrates speaks of death as the soul's liberation from the body's prison and says that the philosopher's life is preparation "for dying and being dead." He means that freed of the body, the soul can enjoy direct apprehension of the forms, of what truly is.

The trajectory of thought from Socrates' statement in the *Apology* that the unexamined life is not worth living to the more abstract theory of forms, and all that it entails, is lengthy. But we can see that there is also continuity, that the vision of a transcendent reality and the possibility of the soul's ascent to it through philosophy deepens the sense of what the examined life might be.

From The Republic[1]

FROM BOOKS 6–7

[The Sun, the Divided Line, and the Cave]

Book 6. * * * 'Look at it this way. For hearing to hear, and sound to be heard, do they need some other class of thing as well? Without this third thing, will hearing fail to hear, and sound fail to be heard?'

'No, they don't need any other class of thing,' he[2] said.

'I suspect that many other faculties—I won't say all of them—have no need for any further thing of this sort. Can you think of any?'

'No, I can't.'

'How about the faculty of sight, and the thing which is seen? Has it ever struck you that those do need something of this sort?'

'How do you mean?'

'If there is sight in the eyes, and its possessor is trying to make use of it, you surely realise that even in the presence of colour sight will see nothing, and the colours will remain unseen, unless one further thing joins them, a third sort of thing which exists for precisely this purpose.'

1. Translated by Tom Griffith. 2. Glaucon.

'What thing do you mean?'

'The thing you call light.'

'True,' he said.

'In that case, because it involves a third thing of this important character, the link between the faculty of sight and the ability to be seen is something more valuable than the links between the other faculties and their objects. Unless of course light has no value.'

'Well, it certainly *does* have a value.'

'Which of the heavenly gods, then, do you take to be the agent responsible for this? Whose is the light which best enables our faculty of sight to see, and the things which are seen to be seen?'

'The one you or anyone else would take to be responsible,' he said. 'The one you're asking about is obviously the sun.'[3]

'Now, do you agree with me about the natural relationship of sight to this god?'

'What are you saying about it?'

'Sight is not the sun—neither sight itself, nor the place in which it occurs, and which we call the eye.'

'No. It isn't.'

'But of all the organs of perception, I would say, the eye is the most sun-*like*.'

'Much the most.'

'So the power which it has—the ability to see—it receives from the sun, as a kind of grant from an overflowing treasury?'

'Exactly.'

'So too, the sun is not sight, but it is the cause of sight and it can be seen *by* sight?'

'That is so,' he said.

'This is what you must take me to mean by the child of the good, which the good produces as its own analogue. In the world of thought the good stands in just the same relation to thinking and the things which can be thought as the sun, in the world of sight, stands to seeing and the things which can be seen.'

'What do you mean?' he said. 'Please explain that a bit further.'

'You know that when the eyes stop being directed at objects whose colours are in daylight, and turn to those whose colours are lit by the lights of the night, they are dimmed, and become virtually blind, as if there were no clear sight in them.'

'They certainly do.'

'Whereas when they are directed at things whose colours have the light of the sun shining on them, they see distinctly. The same eyes now manifestly do have sight in them.'

'Of course.'

'You can look at the soul in the same way. When it focuses where truth and that which is[4] shine forth, then it understands and knows what it sees, and does appear to possess intelligence. But when it focuses on what is mingled with darkness, on what comes into being and is destroyed, then it

---

3. The sun was traditionally considered a god.   4. That is, reality, the forms, as opposed to the objects of the sensible world, which are constantly coming into being and passing away.

resorts to opinion and is dimmed, as its opinions swing first one way and then another. Now, by contrast, it resembles something with no understanding.'

'None at all.'

'You can say that this thing which gives the things which are known their truth, and from which the knower draws his ability to know, is the form or character of the good. Because it is the cause of knowledge and truth, think of it by all means as something known. But you will be right to regard it as different from, and still more beautiful than, knowledge and truth, beautiful though both of these are. Just as in our example it is correct to think of light and vision as sun-*like*, but incorrect to think that they *are* the sun, in the same way here it is correct to think of knowledge and truth as good-*like*, but incorrect to think that either of them *is* the good. The good is something to be prized even more highly.'

'It's an incredible beauty you are talking about,' he said, 'if it is the cause of knowledge and truth, but itself surpasses them in beauty. And you of all people, presumably, are not going to say that it is pleasure.'

'Be silent,' I said. 'Don't even mention the word. No, take a closer look at our comparison.'

'How do you want me to look at it?'

'The sun gives to what is seen, I think you would say, not only its ability to be seen, but also birth, growth and sustenance—though it is not itself birth or generation.'

'Of course it isn't.'

'For the things which are known, say not only that their being known comes from the good, but also that they get their existence and their being from it as well—though the good is not being, but something far surpassing being in rank and power.'

'Ye gods,' Glaucon exclaimed, making us all laugh. 'What a miraculous transcendence.'

'Don't blame me,' I said. 'You were the one who compelled me to tell you what I thought about the subject.'

'I was. And whatever you do, don't stop now. If nothing else, at least go through your comparison with the sun, to make sure you haven't left anything out.'

'I've left all sorts of things out,' I said.

'Well, don't. Don't omit even the smallest detail.'

'I'm sure I shall omit something. Quite a lot, probably. All the same, as far as is possible on an occasion like this, I won't leave anything out on purpose.'

'No, don't, he said.

'Very well. You must be aware, as we said, that there are these two things. One of them is ruler of the category and realm of what can be understood. The other is ruler of what can be seen—of the heavenly scene, I could say, only I don't want you to think I'm playing with words. Anyway, be that as it may, you accept that there are these two forms of things, the seen and the understood?'

'Yes, I do.'

'Imagine taking a line which has been divided into two unequal sections, and dividing each section—the one representing the category of the seen and the one representing the category of the understood—again in the same proportion. The clearness or obscurity of the sections of the line, relative to one another, you will find to be as follows. In the category of the seen the first section is images, by which I mean in the first place shadows, and in the second place reflections in water, or any dense, smooth, shiny surface. Everything of that sort, if you see what I mean.'

'Yes, I do.'

'The second section you must regard as what the first section is an image *of*—the animals we see every day, the entire plant world, and the whole class of human artefacts.'

'Very well. I so regard it.'

'Now, looking at our division in terms of truth and its opposite, would you be prepared to say that the relation between the likeness and the thing it is a likeness *of* is equivalent to the relation between the object of opinion and the object of knowledge?'

'Yes, I would,' he said. 'Most emphatically.'

'Ask yourself next how the section which represents the understood should be divided.'

'How should it be?'

'Like this. In the first part the soul treats as images the things which in the other section of the line were originals. It is compelled to work from assumptions, proceeding to an end-point, rather than back to an origin or first principle. In the second part, by contrast, it goes from an assumption to an origin or first principle which is free from assumptions. It does not use the images which the first part uses, but makes its way in the investigation using forms alone, through themselves alone.'[5]

'I don't entirely follow what you just said.'

'Let's try again. You'll find it easier when you've heard what I have to say by way of introduction. You're aware, I imagine, that when people are doing things like geometry and arithmetic, there are some things they take for granted in their respective disciplines. Odd and even, figures and the three types of angle. That sort of thing. Taking these as known, they make them into assumptions. They see no need to justify them either to themselves or to anyone else. They regard them as plain to anyone. Starting from these, they then go through the rest of their argument, and finally reach, by agreed steps, that which they set out to investigate.'

'Yes, I am aware of that,' he said.

'And you will also be aware that they summon up the assistance of visible forms, and refer their discussion to them, although they're not thinking about these, but about the things these are images of. So their reasoning has in view the square itself, and the diagonal itself, not the diagonal they have

5. Socrates goes on to clarify what he says in this crucial but difficult paragraph by using the methods of geometry as an example. A triangle, or the drawing of a triangle, exists as an object in the world (the second division of the line) and can have an image—a reflection in a mirror, for example (the first division). For geometers, a triangle is also an image; they are not interested in the object itself but in using it to understand the properties of triangles as a class. They are operating with the methods and obtaining the knowledge of the third division of the line, but because they have to make assumptions and work from hypotheses— about the nature of angles, for instance—this is not the highest kind of knowledge. That highest knowledge, which is located on the fourth division of the line, would be intellection of what the essence of triangularity is without reliance on hypotheses—direct understanding of what a triangle is as a first principle, from which one could then proceed to explain everything that follows from it. Or, to use Socrates' own image, the sun is an object in the physical world (section 2 of the line) that has reflections in water or a mirror (section 1). Socrates has used it as an image to talk about the good (section 3), but such understanding via image is distinct from, and inferior to, direct knowledge of the good (section 4).

drawn. And the same with other examples. The models they construct, or figures they draw, which have their own shadows, and images in water—these they treat in their turn as images, in their attempt to see the corresponding things themselves which can be seen only through thinking.'

'True.'

'That is why I described this category as grasped by the understanding, but as requiring for its investigation that the soul make use of assumptions. The soul cannot make any progress towards a first principle, since it is unable to escape from these assumptions and move in an upwards direction. Instead it treats as images the things which were treated as originals, and copied, by what was in the section below them, and which are thought of as clear by comparison with those images, and valued for their clarity.'

'I see,' he said. 'You mean the realm of geometry and its related disciplines.'

'Finally, by the other section of the line representing the objects of understanding you must take me to mean what reason itself grasps by its power to conduct a rational discussion,[6] when it uses assumptions not as first principles, but as true "bases"—points to take off from, entry-points—until it gets to what is free from assumptions, and arrives at the origin or first principle of everything. This it seizes hold of, then turns round and follows the things which follow from this first principle, and so makes its way down to an end-point. It makes no use at all of any object of the senses, but only of pure forms—working through them and towards them. And it ends in forms.'

'I sort of see,' he said, 'though not as well as I'd like. I think what you're talking about is an enormous task, but I do at least understand that you want to take that which is, and is understood, and distinguish that part of it which is studied by the knowledge which comes from rational discussion as something clearer than the part which is studied by what are called the sciences. These use assumptions as first principles, and although those who study them are compelled to use thinking rather than their senses to do so, still, because their investigation does not make its way upwards to a first principle, but proceeds from assumptions, you do not regard them as having an intelligent understanding of their subjects, although with a first principle they *could* be understood. I also think that when people are doing subjects like geometry, you call their state of mind thinking rather than understanding, because you regard thinking as a halfway house between opinion and understanding.'

'You've grasped my meaning well enough,' I said. 'And please understand that there are four conditions arising in the soul, corresponding to the four sections of the line. Understanding corresponds to the highest section, thinking to the second, belief to the third, and conjecture to the last. Classify them accordingly, believing that the degree of clarity they possess is proportional to the truth possessed by their objects.'

'I understand. I agree. And I classify them in the way you suggest.'

Book 7. 'If we're thinking about the effect of education—or the lack of it—on our nature, there's another comparison we can make. Picture human beings living in some sort of underground cave dwelling, with an entrance which is long, as wide as the cave, and open to the light. Here they live, from

6. That is, dialectic, the step-by-step process of question and answer that is Socrates' characteristic method and that is the form taken by many Platonic dialogues (including the *Republic*).

earliest childhood, with their legs and necks in chains, so that they have to stay where they are, looking only ahead of them, prevented by the chains from turning their heads. They have light from a distant fire, which is burning behind them and above them. Between the fire and the prisoners, at a higher level than them, is a path along which you must picture a low wall that has been built, like the screen which hides people when they are giving a puppet show, and above which they make the puppets appear.'

'Yes, I can picture all that,' he said.

'Picture also, along the length of the wall, people carrying all sorts of implements which project above it, and statues of people, and animals made of stone and wood and all kinds of materials. As you'd expect, some of the people carrying the objects are speaking, while others are silent.'

'A strange picture. And strange prisoners.'

'No more strange than us,' I said. 'Do you think, for a start, that prisoners of that sort have ever seen anything more of themselves and of one another than the shadows cast by the fire on the wall of the cave in front of them?'

'How could they, if they had been prevented from moving their heads all their lives?'

'What about the objects which are being carried? Wouldn't they see only shadows of these also?'

'Yes, of course.'

'So if they were able to talk to one another, don't you think they'd believe that the things they were giving names to were the things they could see passing?'

'Yes, they'd be bound to.'

'What if the prison had an echo from the wall in front of them? Every time one of the people passing by spoke, do you suppose they'd believe the source of the sound to be anything other than the passing shadow?'

'No, that's exactly what they would think.'

'All in all, then, what people in this situation would take for truth would be nothing more than the shadows of the manufactured objects.'

'Necessarily.'

'Suppose nature brought this state of affairs to an end,' I said. 'Think what their release from their chains and the cure for their ignorance would be like. When one of them was untied, and compelled suddenly to stand up, turn his head, start walking, and look towards the light, he'd find all these things painful. Because of the glare he'd be unable to see the things whose shadows he used to see before. What do you suppose he'd say if he was told that what he used to see before was of no importance, whereas now his eyesight was better, since he was closer to what is, and looking at things which more truly are? Suppose further that each of the passing objects was pointed out to him, and that he was asked what it was, and compelled to answer. Don't you think he'd be confused? Wouldn't he believe the things he saw before to be more true than what was being pointed out to him now?'

'Yes, he would. Much more true.'

'If he was forced to look at the light itself, wouldn't it hurt his eyes? Wouldn't he turn away, and run back to the things he *could* see? Wouldn't he think those things really were clearer than what was being pointed out?'

'Yes,' he said.

'And if he was dragged out of there by force, up the steep and difficult path, with no pause until he had been dragged right out into the sunlight, wouldn't he find this dragging painful? Wouldn't he resent it? And when he came into the light, with his eyes filled with the glare, would he be able to see a single one of the things people call real?'

'No, he wouldn't. Not at first.'

'He'd need to acclimatise himself, I imagine, if he were going to see things up there. To start with, he'd find shadows the easiest things to look at. After that, reflections—of people and other things—in water. The things themselves would come later, and from those he would move on to the heavenly bodies and the heavens themselves. He'd find it easier to look at the light of the stars and the moon by night than look at the sun, and the light of the sun, by day.'

'Of course.'

'The last thing he'd be able to look at, presumably, would be the sun. Not its image, in water or some location that is not its own, but the sun itself. He'd be able to look at it by itself, in its own place, and see it as it really was.'

'Yes,' he said, 'unquestionably.'

'At that point he would work out that it was the sun which caused the seasons and the years, which governed everything in the visible realm, and which was in one way or another responsible for everything they used to see.'

'That would obviously be the next stage.'

'Now, suppose he were reminded of the place where he lived originally, of what passed for wisdom there, and of his former fellow-prisoners. Don't you think he would congratulate himself on the change? Wouldn't he feel sorry for them?'

'Indeed he would.'

'Back in the cave they might have had rewards and praise and prizes for the person who was quickest at identifying the passing shapes, who had the best memory for the ones which came earlier or later or simultaneously, and who as a result was best at predicting what was going to come next. Do you think he would feel any desire for these prizes? Would he envy those who were respected and powerful there? Or would he feel as Achilles does in Homer? Would he much prefer "to labour as a common serf, serving a man with nothing to his name,"[7] putting up with anything to avoid holding those opinions and living that life?'

'Yes,' he said. 'If you ask me, he'd be prepared to put up with anything to avoid that way of life.'

'There's another question I'd like to ask you,' I said. 'Suppose someone like that came back down into the cave and took up his old seat. Wouldn't he find, coming straight in from the sunlight, that his eyes were swamped by the darkness?'

'I'm sure he would.'

'And suppose he had to go back to distinguishing the shadows, in competition with those who had never stopped being prisoners. Before his eyes had grown accustomed to the dark, while he still couldn't see properly—and this period of acclimatisation would be anything but short—wouldn't he be

---

7. *Odyssey* 11.556–57. Achilles tells Odysseus that he would rather be the lowliest man imaginable, but alive, than king of the dead.

a laughing-stock? Wouldn't it be said of him that he had come back from his journey to the upper world with his eyesight destroyed, and that it wasn't worth even trying to go up there? As for anyone who tried to set them free, and take them up there, if they could somehow get their hands on him and kill him, wouldn't they do just that?'

'They certainly would,' he said.

'That is the picture, then, my dear Glaucon. And it fits what we were talking about earlier in its entirety. The region revealed to us by sight is the prison dwelling, and the light of the fire inside the dwelling is the power of the sun. If you identify the upward path and the view of things above with the ascent of the soul to the realm of understanding, then you will have caught my drift—my surmise—which is what you wanted to hear. Whether it is really true, perhaps only god knows. My own view, for what it's worth, is that in the realm of what can be known the thing seen last, and seen with great difficulty, is the form or character of the good. But when it is seen, the conclusion must be that it turns out to be the cause of all that is right and good for everything. In the realm of sight it produces light and light's sovereign, the sun, while in the realm of thought it is itself sovereign, producing truth and reason unassisted. I further believe that anyone who is going to act wisely either in private life or in public life must have had a sight of this.'

'Well, I for one agree with you,' he said. 'As far as I can follow, at any rate.'

'Can you agree with me, then, on one further point? It's no wonder if those who have been to the upper world refuse to take an interest in everyday affairs, if their souls are constantly eager to spend their time in that upper region. It's what you'd expect, presumably, if things really are like the picture we have just drawn.'

'Yes, it is what you'd expect.'

'And here's another question. Do you think it's at all surprising if a person who turns to everyday life after the contemplation of the divine cuts a sorry figure, and makes a complete fool of himself—if before he can see properly, or can get acclimatised to the darkness around him, he is compelled to compete, in the lawcourts or anywhere else, over the shadows of justice or the statues which cast those shadows, or to argue about the way they are understood by those who have never seen justice itself?'

'No, it's not in the least surprising,' he said.

'Anyone with any sense,' I said, 'would remember that people's eyesight can be impaired in two quite different ways, and for two quite different reasons. There's the change from light to darkness, and the change from darkness to light. He might then take it that the same is true of the soul, so that when he saw a soul in difficulties, unable to see, he would not laugh mindlessly, but would ask whether it had come from some brighter life and could not cope with the unfamiliar darkness, or whether it had come from greater ignorance into what was brighter, and was now dazzled by the glare. One he would congratulate on what it had seen, and on its way of life. The other he would pity. Or if he chose to laugh at it, his laughter would be less absurd than laughter directed at the soul which had come from the light above.'

'Yes. What you say is entirely reasonable.'

*   *   *

ARISTOTLE
384–322 B.C.E.

Plato laid the foundations for Western philosophy. Aristotle, his student for some twenty years, accepted some of the fundamental concepts of Plato's system (such as the forms) but made far-reaching changes and branched out in directions of his own. Later in his life, he founded his own philosophical school in a neighborhood just outside Athens known as the Lyceum. Eventually called the Peripatetic school, from the *peripatos* or colonnaded walkway on the outside of its building, it offered a philosophical system different from that of Plato's Academy (which took its name from the neighborhood outside Athens' walls where it was located).

Aristotle's inquiring mind ranged over nearly every area of nature and human culture; he investigated and wrote about physics (broadly conceived), biology, zoology, astronomy and meteorology, logic, metaphysics, ethics, the nature of the soul, rhetoric, poetry, politics, and much more. Nothing, it seems, escaped his curiosity. His method was empirical: he made systematic and exhaustive observations of particulars and drew general inferences from them. To take an example from one of the selections below: if the fact that plants take in nourishment, animals do this *and* move and have sense perception, and humans do all those things *and* think, means that there are different parts of the soul that impart these capacities, can the soul then be divided? No, because if you cut certain insects (or plants) into segments, these will continue to live and will generate limbs. From this observation he concludes that there is a complete soul in each segment, and soul is therefore indivisible.

Given his view of the limited reality of the world around us, Plato would no doubt have considered all these activities a waste of time. It was precisely here that Aristotle differed most fundamentally with his teacher. For him, the world we know through sense perception and thought *was* reality, or part of it, and therefore was the proper object of rational thought. There may be things transcending our world—divinity, for instance—but they were not more real. The forms were not outside and above observable phenomena; they were part of every plant, animal, and human being, giving them life and making them what they are. By themselves, forms are potentiality; they are active only when united with matter.

The selections from the immense body of Aristotle's writings that are printed here are meant to give an idea of his thought system on reality and being. One basic issue is causation: how do things come to be the way they are? In the excerpt from the *Physics*, Aristotle discusses the different meanings we can ascribe to the word *cause*, and the distinct ways in which results are produced. How cause and effect actually occur depends on the nature of "substance" (the Greek word, *ousia*, actually means "being," "that which is"). The *Metaphysics* (the title, which means simply "after the *Physics*," refers to the treatise's position in ancient editions of Aristotle) distinguishes three kinds of substance: matter, form, and the composite produced by their union. In the same essay, motion—a basic aspect of being (for one thing, it accounts for change)—also interests Aristotle. This topic leads him to consider those things that do not themselves move but that produce motion in other things: not only the unmoved mover of the world but also objects of thought that set the mind in motion through desire. And so Aristotle comes to consider what the highest type of thinking is. Mind is closely related to the nature of the soul, and in *On the Soul* Aristotle considers its structure and the interrelation of its parts, often rejecting as inadequate Plato's tripartite model. For Aristotle, the soul is more complex, and its activities are essential to life: not just desires, passion, and reason, as in Plato, but nutrition and sense perception as well as imagination, appetite, and thought. He will have none of Plato's soul/body antithesis. In the terms of his notion of substance, soul is the form that, joined to matter, produces the composite being (plant, animal, or human). It is at once the formal, efficient, and final cause; matter is the material cause (in the terms of the *Physics*). In the selection below from the *Nichomachean Ethics* (addressed to his son Nichomachus), we sample another side of Aristotle's thought. But his argument there that the highest happiness consists of the contemplative life is thoroughly consistent with the ideas developed in the *Metaphysics* and in *On the Soul* and should be seen in that context.

Though Aristotle's style is condensed and difficult (the texts we have often read like lecture notes, and perhaps they are), to follow the challenging paths of his reasoning is to observe an extraordinarily acute and rigorous mind at work. The result is intellectual excitement of the highest order.

For details of Aristotle's life, see pp. 779–80.

From Physics[1]

FROM BOOK 2

3 Now that we have established these distinctions, we must proceed to consider causes, their character and number. Knowledge is the object of our inquiry, and men do not think they know a thing till they have grasped the 'why' of it (which is to grasp its primary cause). So clearly we too must do this as regards both coming to be and passing away and every kind of physical change, in order that, knowing their principles, we may try to refer to these principles each of our problems.

In one sense, then, (1) that out of which a thing comes to be and which persists, is called 'cause',[2] e.g. the bronze of the statue, the silver of the bowl, and the genera of which the bronze and the silver are species.

In another sense (2) the form or the archetype,[3] i.e. the statement of the essence and its genera, are called 'causes' (e.g. of the octave the relation of 2 : 1, and generally number), and the parts in the definition.

Again (3) the primary source of the change or coming to rest;[4] e.g. the man who gave advice is a cause, the father is cause of the child, and generally what makes of what is made[5] and what causes change of what is changed.

Again (4) in the sense of end or 'that for the sake of which' a thing is done,[6] e.g. health is the cause of walking about. ('Why is he walking about?' we say. 'To be healthy', and, having said that, we think we have assigned the cause.) The same is true also of all the intermediate steps which are brought about through the action of something else as means towards the end, e.g. reduction of flesh, purging, drugs, or surgical instruments are means towards health.[7] All these things are 'for the sake of' the end, though they differ from one another in that some are activities, others instruments.

This then perhaps exhausts the number of ways in which the term 'cause' is used.

As the word has several senses, it follows that there are several causes of the same thing[8] (not merely in virtue of a concomitant attribute), e.g. both the art of the sculptor and the bronze are causes of the statue. These are causes of the statue *qua* statue, not in virtue of anything else that it may

---

1. Translated by R. P. Hardie and R. K. Gaye.   2. The material cause.   3. The formal cause—what kind of thing an object or being is.   4. The efficient cause (*efficient* derives from the Latin word for "make" or "bring about").   5. That is, what makes is the cause of what is made.   6. The final cause. 7. That is, health is their cause.   8. Causes of the thing itself in its essential character.

be—only not in the same way, the one being the material cause, the other the cause whence the motion comes. Some things cause each other reciprocally, e.g. hard work causes fitness and *vice versa*, but again not in the same way, but the one as end, the other as the origin of change. Further the same thing is the cause of contrary results. For that which by its presence brings about one result is sometimes blamed for bringing about the contrary by its absence. Thus we ascribe the wreck of a ship to the absence of the pilot whose presence was the cause of its safety.

From Metaphysics[1]

FROM BOOK 12

7   Since (1) this is a possible account of the matter, and (2) if it were not true, the world would have proceeded out of night and 'all things together' and out of non-being, these difficulties may be taken as solved.[2] There is, then, something which is always moved with an unceasing motion, which is motion in a circle; and this is plain not in theory only but in fact. Therefore the first heaven[3] must be eternal. There is therefore also something which moves it. And since that which is moved and moves is intermediate, there is something which moves without being moved, being eternal, substance, and actuality. And the object of desire and the object of thought move in this way; they move without being moved. The primary objects of desire and of thought are the same. For the apparent good is the object of appetite, and the real good is the primary object of rational wish. But desire is consequent on opinion rather than opinion on desire; for the thinking is the starting-point. And thought is moved by the object of thought, and one of the two columns of opposites is in itself the object of thought; and in this, substance is first, and in substance, that which is simple and exists actually. (The one and the simple are not the same; for 'one' means a measure, but 'simple' means that the thing itself has a certain nature.) But the beautiful, also, and that which is in itself desirable are in the same column; and the first in any class is always best, or analogous to the best.

That a final cause may exist among unchangeable entities is shown by the distinction of its meanings. For the final cause is (*a*) some being for whose good an action is done, and (*b*) something at which the action aims; and of these the latter exists among unchangeable entities though the former does not. The final cause, then, produces motion as being loved, but all other things move by being moved.

Now if something is moved it is capable of being otherwise than as it is. Therefore if its actuality is the primary form of spatial motion, then in so far as it is subject to change, in *this* respect it is capable of being otherwise—in place, even if not in substance. But since there is something which moves while itself unmoved, existing actually, this can in no way be otherwise than

---

1. Translated by W. D. Ross.   2. Aristotle has argued that actuality must precede potentiality; otherwise there is no necessity for anything to come into being. Therefore, he has rejected the derivation of the world from such potentialities as night or "all things together"—the theories of "theologians" and Anaxagoras (a 5th-century-B.C.E. pre-Socratic philosopher), respectively.   3. I.e., the outer sphere of the universe, that in which the fixed stars are set [Translator's note].

as it is. For motion in space is the first of the kinds of change, and motion in a circle the first kind of spatial motion; and this the first mover *produces.* The first mover, then, exists of necessity; and in so far as it exists by necessity, its mode of being is good, and it is in this sense a first principle. For the necessary has all these senses—that which is necessary perforce because it is contrary to the natural impulse, that without which the good is impossible, and that which cannot be otherwise but can exist only in a single way.

On such a principle, then, depend the heavens and the world of nature. And it is a life such as the best which we enjoy, and enjoy for but a short time (for it is ever in this state, which we cannot be), since its actuality is also pleasure. (And for this reason are waking, perception, and thinking most pleasant, and hopes and memories are so on account of these.) And thinking in itself deals with that which is best in itself, and that which is thinking in the fullest sense with that which is best in the fullest sense. And thought thinks on itself because it shares the nature of the object of thought; for it becomes an object of thought in coming into contact with and thinking its objects, so that thought and object of thought are the same. For that which is *capable* of receiving the object of thought, i.e. the essence, is thought. But it is *active* when it *possesses* this object. Therefore the possession rather than the receptivity is the divine element which thought seems to contain, and the act of contemplation is what is most pleasant and best. If, then, God is always in that good state in which we sometimes are, this compels our wonder; and if in a better this compels it yet more. And God *is* in a better state. And life also belongs to God; for the actuality of thought is life, and God is that actuality; and God's self-dependent actuality is life most good and eternal. We say therefore that God is a living being, eternal, most good, so that life and duration continuous and eternal belong to God; for this *is* God. * * *

It is clear then from what has been said that there is a substance which is eternal and unmovable and separate from sensible things. It has been shown also that this substance cannot have any magnitude, but is without parts and indivisible (for it produces movement through infinite time, but nothing finite has infinite power; and, while every magnitude is either infinite or finite, it cannot, for the above reason, have finite magnitude, and it cannot have infinite magnitude because there is no infinite magnitude at all). But it has also been shown that it is impassive and unalterable; for all the other changes are posterior to [4] change of place.

From On the Soul[1]

FROM BOOK 1

5 * * * From what has been said it is now clear that knowing as an attribute of soul cannot be explained by soul's being composed of the elements, and that it is neither sound nor true to speak of soul as moved. But since (*a*) knowing, perceiving, opining, and further (*b*) desiring, wishing, and generally all other modes of appetition, belong to soul, and (*c*) the local movements

4. I.e., depend on.   1. Translated by J. A. Smith.

of animals, and (*d*) growth, maturity, and decay are produced by the soul, we must ask whether each of these is an attribute of the soul as a whole, i.e. whether it is with the whole soul we think, perceive, move ourselves, act or are acted upon, or whether each of them requires a different part of the soul? So too with regard to life. Does it depend on one of the parts of soul? Or is it dependent on more than one? Or on all? Or has it some quite other cause?

Some[2] hold that the soul is divisible, and that one part thinks, another desires. If, then, its nature admits of its being divided, what can it be that holds the parts together? Surely not the body; on the contrary it seems rather to be the soul that holds the body together; at any rate when the soul departs the body disintegrates and decays. If, then, there is something else which makes the soul one, this unifying agency would have the best right to the name of soul, and we shall have to repeat for it the question: Is *it* one or multipartite? If it is one, why not at once admit that 'the soul' is one? If it has parts, once more the question must be put: What holds *its* parts together, and so *ad infinitum*?

The question might also be raised about the parts of the soul: What is the separate rôle of each in relation to the body? For, if the whole soul holds together the whole body, we should expect each part of the soul to hold together a part of the body. But this seems an impossibility; it is difficult even to imagine what sort of bodily part mind will hold together,[3] or how it will do this.

It is a fact of observation that plants and certain insects go on living when divided into segments; this means that each of the segments has a soul in it identical in species, though not numerically identical in the different segments, for both of the segments for a time possess the power of sensation and local movement. That this does not last is not surprising, for they no longer possess the organs necessary for self-maintenance. But, all the same, in each of the bodily parts there are present all the parts of soul, and the souls so present are homogeneous with one another and with the whole; this means that the several parts of the soul are indisseverable from one another, although the whole soul is divisible.[4] It seems also that the principle[5] found in plants is also a kind of soul; for this is the only principle which is common to both animals and plants; and this exists in isolation from the principle of sensation, though there is nothing which has the latter without the former.

FROM BOOK 2

1   Let the foregoing suffice as our account of the views concerning the soul which have been handed on by our predecessors; let us now dismiss them and make as it were a completely fresh start, endeavouring to give a precise answer to the question, What is soul? i.e. to formulate the most general possible definition of it.

We are in the habit of recognizing, as one determinate kind of what is, substance, and that in several senses, (*a*) in the sense of matter or that which in itself is not 'a this', and (*b*) in the sense of form or essence, which is that

---

2. Including Plato.   **3.** The Greeks did not locate thought or cognition in the brain.   **4.** That is, if, when plants and some insects are divided, each segment lives and possesses a complete soul, then soul must be divisible, though not into constituent parts but into two or more complete souls.   **5.** I.e., the principle of life and nutrition.

precisely in virtue of which a thing is called 'a this', and thirdly (c) in the sense of that which is compounded of both (a) and (b). Now matter is potentiality, form actuality; of the latter there are two grades related to one another as e.g. knowledge to the exercise of knowledge.

Among substances are by general consent reckoned bodies and especially natural bodies; for they are the principles of all other bodies. Of natural bodies some have life in them, others not; by life we mean self-nutrition and growth (with its correlative decay). It follows that every natural body which has life in it is a substance in the sense of a composite.

But since it is also a *body* of such and such a kind, viz. having life, the *body* cannot be soul; the body is the subject or matter, not what is attributed to it. Hence the soul must be a substance in the sense of the form of a natural body having life potentially within it. But substance is actuality, and thus soul is the actuality of a body as above characterized. Now the word actuality has two senses corresponding respectively to the possession of knowledge and the actual exercise of knowledge. It is obvious that the soul is actuality in the first sense, viz. that of knowledge as possessed, for both sleeping and waking presuppose the existence of soul, and of these waking corresponds to actual knowing, sleeping to knowledge possessed but not employed, and, in the history of the individual, knowledge comes before its employment or exercise.

That is why the soul is the first grade of actuality of a natural body having life potentially in it. The body so described is a body which is organized. The parts of plants in spite of their extreme simplicity are 'organs'; e.g. the leaf serves to shelter the pericarp, the pericarp to shelter the fruit, while the roots of plants are analogous to the mouth of animals, both serving for the absorption of food. If, then, we have to give a general formula applicable to all kinds of soul, we must describe it as the first grade of actuality of a natural organized body. That is why we can wholly dismiss as unnecessary the question whether the soul and the body are one: it is as meaningless as to ask whether the wax and the shape given to it by the stamp are one, or generally the matter of a thing and that of which it is the matter. Unity has many senses (as many as 'is' has), but the most proper and fundamental sense of both is the relation of an actuality to that of which it is the actuality.

We have now given an answer to the question, What is soul?—an answer which applies to it in its full extent. It is substance in the sense which corresponds to the definitive formula of a thing's essence. That means that it is 'the essential whatness' of a body of the character just assigned. Suppose that what is literally an 'organ', like an axe,[6] were a *natural* body, its 'essential whatness', would have been its essence, and so its soul; if this disappeared from it, it would have ceased to be an axe, except in name. As it is, it is just an axe; it wants the character which is required to make its whatness or formulable essence a soul; for that, it would have had to be a *natural* body of a particular kind, viz. one having *in itself* the power of setting itself in movement and arresting itself. Next, apply this doctrine in the case of the 'parts' of the living body. Suppose that the eye were an animal—sight would have been its soul, for sight is the substance or essence of the eye which

---

6. I.e., something made, and so artificial. The Greek word *organon* literally means "instrument."

corresponds to the formula,[7] the eye being merely the matter of seeing; when seeing is removed the eye is no longer an eye, except in name—it is no more a real eye than the eye of a statue or of a painted figure. We must now extend our consideration from the 'parts' to the whole living body; for what the departmental sense is to the bodily part which is its organ, that the whole faculty of sense is to the whole sensitive body as such.

* * *

2 * * * We resume our inquiry from a fresh starting-point by calling attention to the fact that what has soul in it differs from what has not in that the former displays life. Now this word has more than one sense, and provided any one alone of these is found in a thing we say that thing is living. Living, that is, may mean thinking or perception or local movement and rest, or movement in the sense of nutrition, decay and growth. Hence we think of plants also as living, for they are observed to possess in themselves an originative power through which they increase or decrease in all spatial directions; they grow up *and* down, and everything that grows increases its bulk alike in both directions or indeed in all, and continues to live so long as it can absorb nutriment.

This power of self-nutrition can be isolated from the other powers mentioned, but not they from it—in mortal beings at least. The fact is obvious in plants; for it is the only psychic[8] power they possess.

This is the originative power the possession of which leads us to speak of things as *living* at all, but it is the possession of sensation that leads us for the first time to speak of living things as animals; for even those beings which possess no power of local movement but do possess the power of sensation we call animals and not merely living things.

The primary form of sense is touch, which belongs to all animals. Just as the power of self-nutrition can be isolated from touch and sensation generally, so touch can be isolated from all other forms of sense. (By the power of self-nutrition we mean that departmental power of the soul which is common to plants and animals: all animals whatsoever are observed to have the sense of touch.) What the explanation of these two facts is, we must discuss later. At present we must confine ourselves to saying that soul is the source of these phenomena and is characterized by them, viz. by the powers of self-nutrition, sensation, thinking, and motivity.

* * *

Since the expression 'that whereby we live and perceive' has two meanings, just like the expression 'that whereby we know'—that may mean either (a) knowledge or (b) the soul, for we can speak of knowing by or with either, and similarly that whereby we are in health may be either (a) health or (b) the body or some part of the body; and since of the two terms thus contrasted knowledge or health is the name of a form, essence, or ratio, or if we so express it an actuality of a recipient matter—knowledge of what is capable of knowing, health of what is capable of being made healthy (for the operation of that which is capable of originating change terminates and has its seat in what is changed or altered); further, since it is the soul by or with

---

7. I.e., of what it is to be an eye.   8. I.e., having to do with the soul.

which primarily we live, perceive, and think:—it follows that the soul must be a ratio or formulable essence, not a matter or subject. For, as we said, the word substance has three meanings—form, matter, and the complex of both—and of these three what is called matter is potentiality, what is called form actuality. Since then the complex here is the living thing, the body cannot be the actuality of the soul; it is the soul which is the actuality of a certain kind of body. Hence the rightness of the view that the soul cannot be without a body, while it cannot *be* a body; it is not a body but something relative to a body. That is why it is *in* a body, and a body of a definite kind. It was a mistake, therefore, to do as former thinkers did, merely to fit it into a body without adding a definite specification of the kind or character of that body. Reflection confirms the observed fact; the actuality of any given thing can only be realized in what is already potentially that thing, i.e. in a matter of its own appropriate to it. From all this it follows that soul is an actuality or formulable essence of something that possesses a potentiality of being besouled.

3   Of the psychic powers above enumerated some kinds of living things, as we have said, possess all, some less than all, others one only. Those we have mentioned are the nutritive, the appetitive, the sensory, the locomotive, and the power of thinking. Plants have none but the first, the nutritive, while another order of living things has this *plus* the sensory. If any order of living things has the sensory, it must also have the appetitive; for appetite is the genus of which desire, passion, and wish are the species; now all animals have one sense at least, viz. touch, and whatever has a sense has the capacity for pleasure and pain and therefore has pleasant and painful objects present to it, and wherever these are present, there is desire, for desire is just appetition of what is pleasant. Further, all animals have the sense for food (for touch is the sense for food); the food of all living things consists of what is dry, moist, hot, cold, and these are the qualities apprehended by touch; all other sensible qualities are apprehended by touch only indirectly. Sounds, colours, and odours contribute nothing to nutriment; flavours fall within the field of tangible qualities. Hunger and thirst are forms of desire, hunger a desire for what is dry and hot, thirst a desire for what is cold and moist; flavour is a sort of seasoning added to both. We must later clear up these points, but at present it may be enough to say that all animals that possess the sense of touch have also appetition. The case of imagination is obscure; we must examine it later. Certain kinds of animals possess in addition the power of locomotion, and still another order of animate beings, i.e. man and possibly another order like man or superior to him, the power of thinking, i.e. mind.

*   *   *

4   * * * The soul is the cause or source of the living body. The terms cause and source have many senses. But the soul is the cause of its body alike in all three senses which we explicitly recognize. It is (*a*) the source or origin of movement, it is (*b*) the end, it is (*c*) the essence of the whole living body.[9]
   That it is the last, is clear; for in everything the essence is identical with

9. That is, according to the definitions set forth in the *Physics*, the soul is the (a) efficient, (b) final, and (c) formal cause of the living body. The natural body is the material cause.

the ground of its being, and here, in the case of living things, their being is to live, and of their being and their living the soul in them is the cause or source. Further, the actuality of whatever is potential is identical with its formulable essence.

It is manifest that the soul is also the final cause of its body. For Nature, like mind, always does whatever it does for the sake of something, which something is its end. To that something corresponds in the case of animals the soul and in this it follows the order of nature; all natural bodies are organs of the soul. This is true of those that enter into the constitution of plants as well as of those which enter into that of animals. This shows that that for the sake of which they are is soul. We must here recall the two senses of 'that for the sake of which', viz. (a) the end to achieve which, and (b) the being in whose interest, anything is or is done.

We must maintain, further, that the soul is also the cause of the living body as the original source of local movement. The power of locomotion is not found, however, in all living things. But change of quality and change of quantity are also due to the soul. Sensation is held to be a qualitative alteration, and nothing except what has soul in it is capable of sensation. The same holds of the quantitative changes which constitute growth and decay; nothing grows or decays naturally except what feeds itself, and nothing feeds itself except what has a share of soul in it.

* * *

FROM BOOK 3

9 The soul of animals is characterized by two faculties, (a) the faculty of discrimination which is the work of thought and sense, and (b) the faculty of originating local movement. Sense and mind we have now sufficiently examined. Let us next consider what it is in the soul which originates movement. Is it a single part of the soul separate either spatially or in definition? Or is it the soul as a whole? If it is a part, is that part different from those usually distinguished or already mentioned by us, or is it one of them? The problem at once presents itself, in what sense we are to speak of parts of the soul, or how many we should distinguish. For in a sense there is an infinity of parts: it is not enough to distinguish, with some thinkers,[1] the calculative, the passionate, and the desiderative, or with others the rational and the irrational; for if we take the dividing lines followed by these thinkers we shall find parts far more distinctly separated from one another than these, namely those we have just mentioned: (1) the nutritive, which belongs both to plants and to all animals, and (2) the sensitive, which cannot easily be classed as either irrational or rational; further (3) the imaginative, which is, in its being, different from all, while it is very hard to say with which of the others it is the same or not the same, supposing we determine to posit *separate* parts in the soul; and lastly (4) the appetitive, which would seem to be distinct both in definition and in power from all hitherto enumerated.[2]

1. Specifically, Plato, who sets forth this tripartite model of the soul in the *Republic*.   2. Aristotle omits from this list the rational or calculative part of the soul, although it slips into the discussion in the next paragraph. He is concerned here to show the inadequacy of the Platonic model (and by implication of the simpler division of the soul into rational and irrational parts) by arguing that the parts of the soul he has distinguished cannot be mapped onto that model. Because the rational part is shared by his and Plato's models, it is not pertinent in this context.

It is absurd to break up the last-mentioned faculty: as these thinkers do, for wish is found in the calculative part[3] and desire and passion in the irrational, and if the soul is tripartite appetite will be found in all three parts.

* * *

From Nicomachean Ethics[1]

FROM BOOK 10

7   If happiness is activity in accordance with virtue, it is reasonable that it should be in accordance with the highest virtue; and this will be that of the best thing in us. Whether it be reason or something else that is this element which is thought to be our natural ruler and guide and to take thought of things noble and divine, whether it be itself also divine or only the most divine element in us, the activity of this in accordance with its proper virtue will be perfect happiness. That this activity is contemplative we have already said.

Now this would seem to be in agreement both with what we said before and with the truth. For, firstly, this activity is the best (since not only is reason the best thing in us, but the objects of reason are the best of knowable objects); and, secondly, it is the most continuous, since we can contemplate truth more continuously than we can *do* anything. And we think happiness has pleasure mingled with it, but the activity of philosophic wisdom is admittedly the pleasantest of virtuous activities; at all events the pursuit of it is thought to offer pleasures marvellous for their purity and their enduringness, and it is to be expected that those who know will pass their time more pleasantly than those who inquire. And the self-sufficiency that is spoken of must belong most to the contemplative activity. For while a philosopher, as well as a just man or one possessing any other virtue, needs the necessaries of life, when they are sufficiently equipped with things of that sort the just man needs people towards whom and with whom he shall act justly, and the temperate man, the brave man, and each of the others is in the same case, but the philosopher, even when by himself, can contemplate truth, and the better the wiser he is; he can perhaps do so better if he has fellow-workers, but still he is the most self-sufficient. And this activity alone would seem to be loved for its own sake; for nothing arises from it apart from the contemplating, while from practical activities we gain more or less apart from the action. And happiness is thought to depend on leisure; for we are busy that we may have leisure, and make war that we may live in peace. Now the activity of the practical virtues is exhibited in political or military affairs, but the actions concerned with these seem to be unleisurely. Warlike actions are completely so (for no one chooses to be at war, or provokes war, for the sake of being at war; any one would seem absolutely murderous if he were to make enemies of his friends in order to bring about battle and slaughter);

---

3. Aristotle argues in the *Metaphysics* that "the real good is the primary object of rational wish."
1. Translated by W. D. Ross.

but the action of the statesman is also unleisurely, and—apart from the political action itself—aims at despotic power and honours, or at all events happiness, for him and his fellow citizens—a happiness different from political action, and evidently sought as being different. So if among virtuous actions political and military actions are distinguished by nobility and greatness, and these are unleisurely and aim at an end and are not desirable for their own sake, but the activity of reason, which is contemplative, seems both to be superior in serious worth and to aim at no end beyond itself, and to have its pleasure proper to itself (and this augments the activity), and the self-sufficiency, leisureliness, unweariedness (so far as this is possible for man), and all the other attributes ascribed to the supremely happy man are evidently those connected with this activity, it follows that this will be the complete happiness of man, if it be allowed a complete term of life (for none of the attributes of happiness is *in*complete).

But such a life would be too high for man; for it is not in so far as he is man that he will live so, but in so far as something divine is present in him; and by so much as this is superior to our composite nature is its activity superior to that which is the exercise of the other kind of virtue. If reason is divine, then, in comparison with man, the life according to it is divine in comparison with human life. But we must not follow those who advise us, being men, to think of human things, and, being mortal, of mortal things, but must, so far as we can, make ourselves immortal, and strain every nerve to live in accordance with the best thing in us; for even if it be small in bulk, much more does it in power and worth surpass everything. This would seem, too, to be each man himself, since it is the authoritative and better part of him. It would be strange, then, if he were to choose not the life of his self but that of something else. And what we said before will apply now; that which is proper to each thing is by nature best and most pleasant for each thing; for man, therefore, the life according to reason is best and pleasantest, since reason more than anything else *is* man. This life therefore is also the happiest.

8   But in a secondary degree the life in accordance with the other kind of virtue is happy; for the activities in accordance with this befit our human estate. Just and brave acts, and other virtuous acts, we do in relation to each other, observing our respective duties with regard to contracts and services and all manner of actions and with regard to passions; and all of these seem to be typically human. Some of them seem even to arise from the body, and virtue of character to be in many ways bound up with the passions. Practical wisdom, too, is linked to virtue of character, and this to practical wisdom, since the principles of practical wisdom are in accordance with the moral virtues and rightness in morals is in accordance with practical wisdom. Being connected with the passions also, the moral virtues must belong to our composite nature; and the virtues of our composite nature are human; so, therefore, are the life and the happiness which correspond to these. The excellence of the reason is a thing apart; we must be content to say this much about it, for to describe it precisely is a task greater than our purpose requires. It would seem, however, also to need external equipment but little, or less than moral virtue does. Grant that both need the necessaries, and do so equally, even if the statesman's work is the more concerned with the body and things of that sort; for there will be little difference there; but in what

they need for the exercise of their activities there will be much difference. The liberal man will need money for the doing of his liberal deeds, and the just man too will need it for the returning of services (for wishes are hard to discern, and even people who are not just pretend to wish to act justly); and the brave man will need power if he is to accomplish any of the acts that correspond to his virtue, and the temperate man will need opportunity; for how else is either he or any of the others to be recognized? It is debated, too, whether the will or the deed is more essential to virtue, which is assumed to involve both; it is surely clear that its perfection involves both; but for deeds many things are needed, and more, the greater and nobler the deeds are. But the man who is contemplating the truth needs no such thing, at least with a view to the exercise of his activity; indeed they are, one may say, even hindrances, at all events to his contemplation; but in so far as he is a man and lives with a number of people, he chooses to do virtuous acts; he will therefore need such aids to living a human life.

But that perfect happiness is a contemplative activity will appear from the following consideration as well. We assume the gods to be above all other beings blessed and happy; but what sort of actions must we assign to them? Acts of justice? Will not the gods seem absurd if they make contracts and return deposits, and so on? Acts of a brave man, then, confronting dangers and running risks because it is noble to do so? Or liberal acts? To whom will they give? It will be strange if they are really to have money or anything of the kind. And what would their temperate acts be? Is not such praise taste-less, since they have no bad appetites? If we were to run through them all, the circumstances of action would be found trivial and unworthy of gods. Still, every one supposes that they *live* and therefore that they are active; we cannot suppose them to sleep like Endymion.[2] Now if you take away from a living being action, and still more production, what is left but contemplation? Therefore the activity of God, which surpasses all others in blessedness, must be contemplative; and of human activities, therefore, that which is most akin to this must be most of the nature of happiness.

2. A mortal who was loved by Selene, the moon. Either at his request or as punishment for something he did, Zeus put him into a perpetual sleep.

LUCRETIUS
ca. 94–ca. 54 B.C.E.

We know virtually nothing about the life of Titus Lucretius Carus, except that he wrote one of the finest literary masterpieces of the late Roman republic: *De rerum natura*, "On the Nature of Things," or "On Reality." This didactic poem in six books is composed in dactylic hexameter, the meter of epic and particularly of Hesiod's didactic *Works and Days*. In it, Lucretius cast in poetic form the doctrines of Epicurus (341–270 B.C.E.), who founded in Athens the philosophical school that bears his name. Epicurus's philosophical concern was practical: how to achieve a happy life. He incorporated into his philosophical system the atomic theory of the fifth century B.C.E. natural philosopher Democritus.

Today the word *epicurean* is likely to conjure up visions of happy gluttons stuffing themselves with food and drink, but that vision is misleading. Epicurus did indeed consider pleasure the chief good in life, but it was pleasure arising from calm—what he called *ataraxia,* or "absence of disturbance." *Ataraxia* is the Epicurean goal, and excessive indulgence in sensual pleasures would upset that goal. So would competition for fame, power, and wealth, and the practical result of this philosophy is therefore quietism: indifference to the rewards and hazards of worldly ambition, a sufficiency of material resources rather than wealth, and a life of retirement in the company of a few like-minded friends.

In complete contrast to systems, such as Plato's, that postulated a transcendent reality, Epicureanism emphasized the importance of happiness in *this* life because there was no other. Democritus's atomic theory was useful because it provided a material basis for this view. Democritus claimed that the universe was composed of infinite space and an infinite number of tiny particles, which he called *atoms* (the name means "indivisible things"). Atoms were perpetually in motion, and they naturally tended to move in what, from our point of view, would be downward. There was an eccentricity or "swerve" in their paths, however, which caused them to collide. Some atoms would therefore move in the opposite direction, and the swerve also made it possible for them to combine and form larger wholes. Any given object or animate being is composed of atoms and void, which bounds the atoms and is bounded by them. Our world and everything in it is the result of the random convergence of atoms; and just as everything we see around us passes away by dissolving back into the constituent atoms, so our world will someday dissolve. Because space is infinite, there can be, and doubtless are, other worlds very different from this one. The atomic theory can (it was claimed) explain everything in our experience, not just the physical world but also phenomena like sense perception. A sweet taste, for example, is the result of particularly smooth atoms in food and liquids, a bitter taste the result of rough atoms. Hearing is caused by atoms bombarding our ears, and differences in sounds are produced by differences in the atoms' size, shape, and texture. Imagination and dreams can be referred to similar physical causes.

Epicureanism is thus a thoroughgoing materialist philosophy. One important consequence of its reliance on the atomic theory is that it views knowledge as based on sense perception; time and again, for example, as Lucretius explains and argues for the theory, he appeals to the evidence of the senses. Another consequence is that in contrast to Aristotle's teleology (in which everything tends toward a predetermined end), it presents our world and everything in it as unplanned, random, and unguided by any supernatural powers. The gods exist, but they pay no attention to human affairs. After all, they enjoy the best kind of life, which by definition entails complete *ataraxia.* Taking any interest—say, a concern to punish wrongdoing—would disturb this blissful state. If systems of value and belief cannot be referred to a higher power, the emphasis must lie on finding happiness in this life; Epicureanism is thus derived from a materialist foundation.

In *De rerum natura,* Lucretius systematically sets forth and defends the atomic theory and the ethical consequences that Epicurus drew from it. His goal, however, is a direct and practical one: to help the reader achieve Epicurean *ataraxia,* not only by informing him or her of the true nature of reality but especially by revealing as illusory all those things in life that trouble or frighten us, such as the striving for wealth or fame. Above all, it is a mistake to fear death. When we die, we merely dissolve into the atoms that compose us, and no awareness survives this dissolution. We do not need to fear suffering after death, as myths would have us do; there is no afterlife. Just like the body, the soul is composed of atoms (particularly fine and smooth ones), and they simply disperse at death. It is this concern to liberate us from what he considers superstition that gives Lucretius's poem its distinctive combination of rigorous thought and moral earnestness.

From On the Nature of Things[1]

FROM BOOK 1

[*Introduction to the Poem*]

Mother of Romans,[2] delight of gods and men,
Sweet Venus, who under the wheeling signs of heaven
Rouse the ship-shouldering sea and the fruitful earth
And make them teem—for through you all that breathe
Are begotten, and rise to see the light of the sun;   5
From you, goddess, the winds flee, from you and your coming
Flee the storms of heaven; for you the artful earth
Sends up sweet flowers, for you the ocean laughs
And the calm skies shimmer in a bath of light.
And now, when the gates are wide for spring and its splendor   10
And the west wind, fostering life, blows strong and free,
Pricked in their hearts by your power, the birds of the air
Give the first sign, goddess, of you and your entering;
Then through the fertile fields the love-wild beasts
Frolic, and swim the rapids (so seized with your charm   15
They eagerly follow wherever you may lead);
Yes, across seas and mountains and hungering rivers
And the leaf-springing homes of the birds and the greening fields,
Into all hearts you strike your lure of love
That by desire they propagate their kinds.   20
And since it is you alone who govern the birth
And growth of things, since nothing without you
Can be glad or lovely or rise to the shores of light,
I ask you to befriend me as I try
To pen these verses *On the Nature of Things*   25
For my friend Memmius,[3] whom you, goddess, have ever
Caused to excel, accomplished in all things.
All the more, goddess, grant them lasting grace!
In the meantime let the savage works of war
Rest easy, slumbering over land and sea.   30
For you alone can bless us mortal men
With quiet peace; Mars,[4] potent of arms, holds sway
In battle but surrenders at your bosom,
Vanquished by the eternal wound of love.
There, his chiseled neck thrown back, he gapes at you,   35
Goddess, and feeds his greedy eyes with love;
He reclines; his spirit lingers upon your lips.
Melting about him, goddess, as he rests
On your holy body, pour from your lips sweet nothings,
Seeking, renowned one, quiet peace for Rome.   40
For I cannot work with a clear mind while my country
Suffers, nor can the illustrious scion of

---

1. Translated by Anthony M. Esolen.   2. Venus, goddess of love and procreation, was the mother of Aeneas, mythical founder of Rome.   3. Roman aristocrat and literary patron active in politics in the 50s and 60s B.C.E. His conduct was not always creditable; in 52 he went into exile after being convicted of bribery in the consular elections of 54, in which he was a candidate.   4. God of war.

The Memmian house neglect the common good.
For by necessity the gods above
Enjoy eternity in highest peace,   45
Withdrawn and far removed from our affairs.
Free of all sorrow, free of peril, the gods
Thrive in their own works and need nothing from us,
Not won with virtuous deeds nor touched by rage.
Then withdraw[5] from cares and apply your cunning mind   50
To hear the truth of reasoned theory,
That the verses I give you, arranged with diligent love,
You will not scorn before you understand.
I open for you by discussing the ultimate law
Of the gods and sky; I reveal the atoms, whence   55
Nature creates and feeds and grows all things
And into which she resolves them when they are spent;
"Matter," "engendering bodies," "the seeds of things"
Are other terms for atoms which I use
In setting forth their laws; and "first beginnings"—   60
For from these elements all the world is formed.
When before our eyes man's life lay groveling, prostrate,
Crushed to the dust under the burden of Religion[6]
(Which thrust its head from heaven, its horrible face
Glowering over mankind born to die),   65
One man, a Greek,[7] was the first mortal who dared
Oppose his eyes, the first to stand firm in defiance.
Not the fables of gods, nor lightning,[8] nor the menacing
Rumble of heaven could daunt him, but all the more
They whetted his keen mind with longing to be   70
First to smash open the tight-barred gates of Nature.
His vigor of mind prevailed, and he strode far
Beyond the fiery battlements of the world,
Raiding the fields of the unmeasured All.[9]
Our victor returns with knowledge of what can arise,   75
What cannot, what law grants each thing its own
Deep-driven boundary stone and finite scope.
Religion now lies trampled beneath our feet,
And we are made gods by the victory.
You hear these things, and I fear you'll think yourself   80
On the road to evil, learning the fundamentals
Of blasphemy. Not so! Too often Religion
Herself gives birth to evil and blasphemous deeds.
At Aulis,[1] for instance: the pride of the Greek people,
The chosen peers, defiled Diana's altar   85
With the shameful blood of the virgin Iphigenia.
As soon as they tressed her hair with the ritual fillet,

5. Addressed to Memmius.   6. Lucretius means by this word not belief in the gods (he obviously believes that they exist) but "religious dread, superstition" (meanings that the Latin *religio* can encompass), and in particular the fear of death and punishment in an afterlife.   7. Epicurus.   8. In myth, Jupiter sometimes used the thunderbolt to kill presumptuous sinners. Epicurus, it is implied, shared their presumption, but to good effect.   9. A literal translation of the Greek term used by the Epicureans for the space (which Lucretius will argue is infinite) within which our bounded world is set.   1. Harbor where the Greek expedition against Troy sacrificed Agamemnon's daughter Iphigeneia to placate Artemis (Diana) and obtain favorable winds for their voyage. The episode is memorably recounted in the first choral ode of Aeschylus's *Agamemnon*, to which, along with Euripides' *Iphigeneia at Aulis*, this passage alludes.

The tassels spilling neatly upon each cheek,
And she sensed her grieving father beside the altar
With the acolytes nearby, hiding the knife, 90
And countrymen weeping to look upon her—mute
With fear, she fell to her knees, she groped for the earth.
Poor girl, what good did it do her then, that she
Was the first to give the king the name of "father"?
Up to the altar the men escorted her, trembling; 95
Not so that when her solemn rites were finished
She might be cheered in the ringing wedding-hymn,
But filthily, at the marrying age, unblemished
Victim, she fell by her father's slaughter-stroke
To shove his fleet off on a *bon voyage!* 100
Such wickedness Religion can incite!

[Atoms and the Void Are Infinite]

But since I have taught that the atoms, impermeable,
Fly never-vanquished through eternity, 950
Now is the time to unroll the question of whether
Their number is finite; so too with the void we've found—
The site or space in which all things occur—
Let's now observe whether emptiness too is bounded
Or whether it stretches vast and deep and endless. 955
Well, whatever road you take through the universe
You'll find no end; for it must then have some limit.
Now it's clear that nothing can be limited
Without something beyond for boundary, some
Point beyond which our sense can't follow it. 960
But you must admit that nothing exists beyond
This All; therefore it has no limit, no end.
Nor does it matter in what place you stand:
Take any point you like—you leave the whole
Unbounded in all regions equally. 965
Suppose, though, that this all-encompassing space
Were bounded; then if someone should race to the shore,
To the utter edge of the world, and fling a spear,
Would you say that the spear should spin from his strong arm
And fly far in the direction it was sent, 970
Or that something could prevent it and block its flight?
Confess: one or the other you must say.
Either one cuts off your retreat: you must
Concede, the world's extent is free and endless.
For if something or other should block the spear, prevent 975
Its flight to the target, something at the end
Or even beyond, that means we hadn't begun
From the true edge.[2] I'll follow you then; wherever
You place the shores, I ask, "What of the spear?
Where does it fly?" No end can be established; 980

2. Lucretius's argument is that no matter how far you proceed either the spear will be blocked and you can't find the true edge or, if it is not blocked, there is space beyond the boundary. Either case, he implies, thus suggests that the universe is infinite.

Immensity prolongs the flight forever.
Besides, if all the space of this whole world
Were finite, like a harbor huddled between
Specific shores, by now its plenty of matter
Would have sunk to the basin—nothing could happen beneath   985
Heaven's roof, if sky and sunlight could even exist,
For matter, all heaped up and clogged, would lie,
Settled in heaviness, age upon endless age.
But as it is, no quiet is granted the atoms,
The first-beginnings; there is no bottom to   990
The world, where they might flow and take their rest.
In tireless motion all things everywhere
Exist, and are propped and supplied from below by a wealth
Of matter speeding out of endless space.
Look around you. All things limit something else: 995
Hills divide air, air hedges one hill from another,
Land limits sea, sea limits all land, but nothing
Exists beyond this All to close it in.
Space—where things are—is so deep, that bright lightning
In all its speed cannot strike through to the end   1000
Even if granted perpetuity,
Or make the remaining journey any the shorter;
So plentifully does space extend around
All things—this way or that, space has no end.
In fact, Nature herself constrains the world   1005
From granting itself a limit. She forces the atoms
To be bounded by void, and to bound the void in turn;
By alternating these she gives the world
Endlessness. If they did not bound each other
One of them in pure form would stretch forever . . .[3]   1010
Neither sea nor earth nor the brilliant fields of the sky,
Nor mortal man nor the gods' most holy bodies
Could hold together for the tiniest moment.
Wrenched apart and set free from their alliance,
The atoms would drift along through the great void—   1015
And who knows, perhaps they could never have clung together
To create a thing, too scattered to combine.
For surely the atoms did not hold council, assigning
Order to each, flexing their keen minds with
Questions of place and motion and who goes where.   1020
But shuffled and jumbled in many ways, in the course
Of endless time they are buffeted, driven along,
Chancing upon all motions, combinations.
At last they fall into such an arrangement
As would create this universe, preserve it   1025
Through the Great Years,[4] so many and long, as soon
As its atoms should toss together in suitable motions—
Then at once the rivers brim, and spill their riches
To refresh the sea, and the earth, sun-cherished, warm,
Brings forth new brood; meek cattle brought to mate   1030

3. A line seems to be missing here.   4. Recurrent astral cycles, each lasting thousands of years.

Bloom, and the wheeling sky-flames come to life.
These things could never chance to be, without
An infinite supply of matter whence
They could repair their losses in due season.
For as an animal deprived of food   1035
Loses his matter, trickles away, so at once
All things dissolve when matter is somehow turned
Out of their path and fails to shore them up.[5]
As for the atoms beyond what's joined together,
The ones still free—they can't preserve the world.   1040
They can hammer away for a while and win some time
Till other atoms arrive to supply the whole.
But sometimes they'll be forced to ricochet,
And so lend ample space and time for the atoms
To fly and free themselves from their assemblies.   1045
So a multitude of atoms must come forth—
Even to keep those outside blows fresh-stocked
We will need countless atoms everywhere.

*   *   *

FROM BOOK 2

[Introduction: Freedom from Fear]

How sweet, to watch from the shore the wind-whipped ocean
Toss someone else's ship in a mighty struggle;
Not that the man's distress is cause for mirth—
Your freedom from those troubles is what's sweet;
And sweet, to see great lines of soldiers marshaled   5
In the plains of war, when you are free from peril;
But nothing is sweeter than to dwell in the calm
Temples of truth, the strongholds of the wise.
You can, from there, look down upon others wandering
Randomly, straying, seeking the path of life,   10
Warring with all their talent, wrestling for rank,
Night and day straining with the utmost toil
To fight their way to the heights of wealth and power.
O heart of man, how pitiful and blind!
In what benightedness with all its perils   15
Our time, so short, is squandered! And not to see
That our nature yelps after this alone: that the body
Be free of pain, the mind enjoy the sense
Of pleasure, far removed from care or fear!
And so we see what little our bodies need,   20
Only such things as soothe the pain away.
This little too will spread the table and make
Many delights more welcome—though Nature doesn't
Demand that golden statues of young men
Grasping the fiery torches in their hands   25

5. Part of Lucretius's theory is that all things created by combinations of atoms are constantly losing atoms.
These are replenished from the stream of atoms that is constantly bombarding the world, since atoms are
infinite in number and ceaselessly in motion.

Light up your midnight palace bacchanals,[6]
Or your halls blaze with silver or gleam with gold,
Or the lute resound from gilded tile and timber—
Rather, when friends in the soft grass lie at ease,
In the shade of a tall tree by the riverside,   30
Their bodies refreshed and gladdened, at no great cost,
Most pleasantly when the weather smiles and the season
Sprinkles the grassy meadow with new flowers.
But the flush of fever will not subside the sooner
For your floral quilts, your tossing and turning in purple,   35
Than if you slept in homely coverlets.
Since luxury, then, is useless for our bodies,
Nor can rank or rule do us the slightest good,
It stands to reason they cannot aid the mind—
Unless, perhaps, as you watch your troops in the drill field   40
Seething and swarming and spurring their shadow-battles,
Shored up with vast reserves and cavalry,
Each side adorned with equal arms and courage,
Or you see your fleet churn up the far-flung sea,
At the sight of these religion panics, flies   45
Quaking with fright from your soul; the fear of death
Will leave your heart then, light and free of care.[7]
But this is silly pomp and circumstance.
In fact, the fears of men, their dogged cares
Never fly the clashing of steel or the fierce spears,   50
But among kings and potentates yet strut
With bold contempt—won't bow to the flash of gold
Or the bright splendor of a purple robe.
Why doubt, the power belongs instead to reason,
Seeing that all life struggles in such darkness?   55
For as little boys tremble and fear whatever's lurking
In the blind dark, so we in the light of day
Tremble at what is no more terrible than
What little boys dream in the dark and fear will come.
And so this darkness and terror of the mind   60
Shall not by the sun's rays, by the bright lances of daylight
Be scattered, but by Nature and her law.

*　*　*

FROM BOOK 3

[Introduction: Praise of Epicurus]

Out of such darkness you[8] who were first to raise
So brilliant a light to show us the best of life,
I follow you, glory of Greece, and in the deep
Print of your traces I now fix my steps,
Not eager to strive with you, but longing in love   5
To imitate your work. For how can the swallow

6. An allusion to the golden statues that light Alcinous's hall in *Odyssey* 7.116–18.   7. The suggestion
that these spectacles banish, rather than arouse, religious dread is, of course, sarcastic.   8. Epicurus.

Contend with the song of the swan, or the spindly kid-goat
Gallop around the track with powerful horses?
You, father, are the founder of truth, you confirm us
With a father's lessons, and from your pages, sir,　　　　10
As bees sip all in the brambles decked with flowers,
So we partake of all your golden words,
Golden, and worthy of eternal life.
For once your teachings, sprung from a godlike mind,
Begin to trumpet the nature of things, the soul's　　　　15
Terrors flee, and the battlements of the world
Sunder; I see vast space and all its works.
The quiet dwellings of the gods appear,
Which winds can never lash nor storms defile
Nor the fall of biting snow and its hard sleet　　　　20
Mar with their gray; one still and cloudless sky
Is canopy, and laughs in a bath of light.[9]
Nature supplies their every need besides,
And nothing nibbles at their peace of mind.
But the halls of the dead—nowhere do *they* appear,　　　　25
Nor does the earth obstruct our looking down
On what occurs in space beneath our feet.[1]
When I think of these things, I am seized by a godlike pleasure
And I shudder with awe; for by your power, Nature's
Veil is stripped free, and all made manifest.　　　　30

[The Mortality of the Soul]

To begin, then. Since I've shown that the soul, so thin,　　　　425
So light, is made of the tiniest atoms, much
Smaller than those which make up the clear water
Or clouds or smoke (for in mobility
It far excels and moves at the slightest touch,
Why not? When it's moved by the *shadows* of cloud and smoke,　　　　430
The sort we see as we lie asleep and dream
Of the breath high over the altar, the drifting smoke—
Such things, no doubt, bring images to our minds),
And now too since you mark that when a jar
Is smashed the water spills away and scatters,　　　　435
And since clouds and smoke will scatter to the winds,
Trust that the soul spills too and perishes
The sooner and melts the quicker into its atoms
Once it's been drawn away from the human body.
In fact if the body—the soul's jar—is smashed　　　　440
Or so attenuated by loss of blood
It can no longer hold the soul inside,
What air do you think will hold the soul, when air
Is slighter than the body and less confining?
What's more, we see the body and mind are born　　　　445
Together, and grow old and weak together.
For as babies toddle about with bodies soft

---

9. Compare the description of Olympus in *Odyssey* 6.44–52.　　1. I.e., because Epicurus has revealed it—
as the ceaseless activity of atoms, *not* "the halls of the dead."

And tender, so their minds are wobbly too;
But when the trunk grows ripe with the strength of adulthood
The mind is better endowed, the reason stronger; 450
And last, when the might of Age has crushed the body
And the limbs have fallen, strengthless, beaten down,
Then the native talent hobbles, the tongue wanders,
Thoughts lapse—all powers fail at the same time.
It follows then that soul and spirit too 455
Dissolve like smoke into that sea of air,
For soul is born with the body and grows with it
And, as I've shown, cracks under the weight of age.
Here we should note that as the body itself
Is racked with violent sickness and sharp pain, 460
So the soul's seized with trouble and fear and sorrow.
It follows that the soul will share in Death.
For when the body is ill the soul will often
Wander; he loses his train of thought, he speaks
Astray, while drowsiness sinks him into a deep 465
And lasting coma—the head nods, the lids fall.
Where he is, he can hear no voices, recognize
No faces of those who surround him and call him back
To life, dewing their cheeks and lips with tears.
Admit, therefore, the soul dissolves—you must, 470
When the touch of sickness penetrates so far.
And pain and disease are both Death's artisans,
As we've learned so well from watching many die.
Yes, why is it then, when wine has stung a man
To the quick, his blood aglow with the heat it lends him, 475
The limbs, as a consequence, grow heavy; tripped, tangled,
Legs stagger, the thick speech lags, the thoughts are soused,
Eyes swim, and roaring and sobbing and brawls break out?
And all the rest of this sort of thing that follows,
Why is it? If not that the thrust and throttle of wine 480
Makes a habit of whipping the soul—and this, in the body!
But whatever can be throttled or trip-and-tangled,
Shows us that if a little rougher force
Finds a way in, it will die, its future lost.

[Death Is Not to Be Feared]

Death, then, is nothing to us, no concern,
Once we grant that the soul will also die.
Just as we felt no pain in ages past
When the Carthaginians swarmed to the attack[2]
And under the sky's high shores the whole world shook, 830
Struck by the shocks of war and alarm and riot,
All mankind over land and ocean in
The balance, whether to fall to the rule of either—
So too, when we no longer are, when our 835
Union of body and soul is put asunder,

2. In the Second Punic War (218–201 B.C.E.), the Carthaginians under Hannibal invaded Italy and almost defeated Rome. The argument is that just as we felt nothing about the most mighty events before we were born we will be indifferent to what happens to us after death.

Hardly shall anything then, when we are not,
Happen to us at all and stir the senses,
Not if earth were embroiled with the sea and the sea with heaven!
And even if the soul, ripped from the body,   840
Retained the power to feel, that still would be
Nothing to us, whose beings have been fashioned
By one fit marriage of one body and soul.
And if the Ages should collect our matter
After we die and return our present forms,   845
Lending us once again the light of life,
Even that won't mean anything to us,
Once our continuation has been snapped.
Who we once were can't touch us now at all;
Nor are we gripped with care for who we'll be.   850
When you reflect on the unmeasured span
Of ages past, how many and various were
The motions of matter, you may rest assured
That the seeds at times were placed in the same order
As these seeds which compose us now; a fact   855
That the mind can't retain in memory.
There's been a halt—hiatus—in our lives,
And all the motions of sense have gone astray.
Thus if your future is misery and sickness
You've got to exist in that same future time   860
For the ill to catch you. But since death clears the deck,
Forbidding that would-be sufferer to exist,
Nothing at all have we to fear from death;
He who cannot exist cannot feel pain,
Or care if he's never born again, once death   865
That does not die has seized his dying life.

* * *

But the things that are said to exist in the depths of Hell   975
Are all, to no surprise, part of our lives.
No fairy-tale Tantalus,[3] frozen in empty fear,
Pathetically shudders under a teetering stone;
Rather here, in life, an empty fear of the gods
Looms, and it's chance that brings the fall we dread.   980
No birds delve into a Tityus[4] flat in Hell
Or prick for a morsel left in that huge liver
Throughout time everlasting—really now!
Let him stretch out, if you like, immense in bulk,
His splayed limbs spanning not nine acres merely   985
But the whole globe; nevertheless, he'd not
Be able to suffer everlasting pain
Or offer the food of his body forever and ever.
Our Tityus is here—a man laid flat by love,

---

3. Tantalus, Tityus, and Sisyphus are the three proverbial sinners Odysseus sees being punished in *Odysseus* 11.660–89, to which Lucretius is alluding here. Many crimes were attributed to Tantalus, among them that he cooked and served to the gods his son Pelops, that he stole nectar and ambrosia from the gods, and that he told the gods' secrets. In the version followed by Lucretius, he was punished in the underworld with a rock always about to fall on his head.   4. A giant who tried to rape Leto, mother of Apollo and Artemis (Roman Diana). His punishment in the underworld was to lie flat on the ground while two vultures plucked and ate his liver for eternity.

Whom the birds peck apart—that's gnawing worry   990
Or other cares that tear us with desire.
In life we've Sisyphus[5] too, before our eyes,
Drunk with campaigning for the rods[6] of power,
And always the people send him home to sulk.
To canvass for power—unattainable, useless—   995
And ever to sweat and suffer hardship for it,
That's to push and push up a mountain a heavily-leaning
Boulder—which tumbles right back down from the summit
Anyhow, bouncing and bounding down to the plain.
Then to feed forever your ingrate heart, to take   1000
Your fill of the good things, stuffed but still not full
(As the returning seasons in their rounds
Bring us fresh life and harvest and delight,
The fruits of life that never seem to fill us)
That's the old tale, I think, of the ripe young virgins[7]   1005
Gathering water in a leaky pot
That couldn't be filled no matter what they did.
And Cerberus and the Furies,[8] see, and the darkness,
Tartarus[9] belching blasts from his horrible maw,
Really, they can't exist and never have!   1010
But in life infamous fear of punishment for
Infamous crimes is how we pay for evil.
Prison, and being flung from the frightful Rock,[1]
Flogging and chopping, racking, tarring, torching,
Take these away—still the man who knows his sin   1015
Anticipates, and whips himself hot with terror,
And never sees where misery can have
Its terminus, and punishments their limit;
He fears they may grow heavier still in death.
This life of fools, then, *this* is the true Hell.   1020

*   *   *

FROM BOOK 5

[The Origin of Religion]

How the idea of gods spread to all nations,
Stocking their cities with altars and making men tremble
To undertake the solemn rites, which flourish   1160
With all our luxury and magnificence
(Even now sowing in us the seeds of horror,
Urging us on to rear across the world
New shrines to the gods to crowd on festival days),
Is not hard to explain in a few words.   1165
In those days mortal men saw while awake

5. A trickster who tried to outwit death and become immortal. He was condemned perpetually to roll a
huge rock up a steep hill. As soon as he neared the top, the rock would roll back downhill and he would
have to start all over again.   6. Consuls and praetors (high Roman magistrates) had attendants who
carried bundles of rods and axes as symbols of their power.   7. Forced to marry their equally numerous
cousins, forty-nine of the fifty daughters of Danaus killed their husbands on their wedding night on their
father's order. Their punishment in the underworld was as Lucretius describes it.   8. Avenging spirits
who punish crimes, especially against blood relatives. Cerberus: the three-headed dog that guarded the
entrance to the underworld.   9. The underworld.   1. The Tarpeian Rock on the Capitol in Rome.
From it were thrown criminals condemned to death for murder or treason.

The excellent countenances of the gods,
Or rather in dreams they gasped at their vast size.
Men lent sensation to these giant forms
For they moved their limbs, it seemed, and spoke proud words   1170
As arrogant as their beauty and great strength.
Eternal life they gave them, for their faces
And their physiques persisted ever-present,
And they thought that beings endowed with such great power
Could never be put to rout by any force.   1175
They thought the gods preeminently blest,
For the fear of death could hardly trouble them;
Also because in dreams they saw them do
Miraculous things, and many, without an effort.
Then too they saw the systems of the sky   1180
Turn in sure order, and the changing seasons,
But could not understand why this occurred.
Their refuge, then: assign to the gods all things,
Have them steer all things with a single nod.
In the heavens they placed the holy haunts of the gods   1185
For through the heavens wheeled the night and the moon,
The moon and the day, the night and night's stark signs,
And night-roaming torches of heaven and gliding flames,
Clouds, sun, storms, snow, high winds and hail and lightning
And the sudden growl and great and menacing rumble.   1190
Unhappy human race—to grant such feats
To gods, and then to add vindictiveness!
What wailing did they bring forth for themselves,
What wounds for us, what tears for our descendants!
It's no piety to be seen at every altar,   1195
To cover your head and turn to the stone idol,
Or to flatten yourself on the ground and lift your palms
To the shrines, or to spray altars with the blood
Of cattle—so much!—or to string vow on vow.
To observe all things with a mind at peace   1200
Is piety.

* * *

SENECA
after 4 B.C.E.–65 C.E.

Born in Spain to parents of Italian descent, Lucius Annaeus Seneca went to Rome
as a student at an early age. By 39 C.E., he had held office and had gained a reputation
as an orator. In that year, he was exiled to the island of Corsica on charges of adultery
with the sister of the emperor Gaius (Caligula). He was recalled from exile in 49 with
the help of Agrippina, wife of the emperor Claudius, who made him tutor in rhetoric
to her son Nero. When Nero became emperor in 54, Seneca was one of his closest

advisors. Working with Burrus, the commander of the Praetorian Guard, he managed to curb Nero's worst tendencies and to ensure fairly good government for a time. In 59, Nero had Agrippina murdered and began to fall under the influence of less trustworthy people. Burrus's death in 62 ended Seneca's power, and by 64 he was in virtual retirement, devoting himself to philosophy. Nero, who by that time had given ample evidence of his own viciousness, forced Seneca to commit suicide in the wake of the Pisonian conspiracy in 65; Seneca was probably not involved in this attempt at regime change, although his nephew, the poet Lucan, probably was. His writings consist of moral essays (including *On Anger*), moral epistles, political essays, and nine tragedies. Most of these works are informed by Stoicism, which was one of the two most influential philosophical systems in Roman culture (the other was Epicureanism).

STOICISM

One of the most famous buildings in Athens, facing on the Agora, was the Painted Stoa, so called from the wall paintings it contained (a *stoa* was an oblong rectangular building with three sides solidly walled and its long front an open colonnade). Here, in the late fourth century B.C.E., Zeno of Citium taught his system of physics, logic, and ethics that became known as Stoicism, the "philosophy of the stoa." After Zeno's death his ideas were developed in various directions until the third century B.C.E., when Chrysippus, the successor of Zeno's successor as head of the Stoic school in Athens, restated and systematized them. Stoicism came to Rome in the second century B.C.E. through such figures as Panaetius of Rhodes, who lived there for a time in the 140s and who stressed to his Roman audience the implications of Stoicism for practical ethics. That is also the emphasis of Seneca's moral essays and epistles. But as Seneca was well aware, the ethical position was part of a much more comprehensive system whose parts, the Stoics maintained, were perfectly interdependent and seamlessly coherent.

Like Epicureanism, the ethical part of Stoicism aimed at achieving happiness and claimed a material basis in nature, but it defined these ideas very differently and reached conclusions that were often diametrically opposed to those of the other school. The world, the Stoics believed, was a single, unified being with both body and mind, and of all living creatures in the world humans were most akin to this being because they alone also possessed reason. Human beings thus should aim at developing their faculty of reason and at living in accordance with the rational order of the world, or nature. This was virtue, and the achievement of genuine happiness. One who lived in this way could not be harmed by what other people did or by misfortune, because compared to the exercise of reason all else was indifferent. Not that these other things were neutral in value; some, such as health, sufficient material wealth, and so on, were "preferable," and others—disease, financial ruin, and the like—were "to be avoided." But the only true calamity was to betray the dictates of reason, and those who did so lived an unhappy life even if they enjoyed material prosperity. True virtue made one impervious to what others might consider calamity. The Stoics emphasized personal responsibility and the importance of individual decisions. At the same time, they believed that everything that happened in the world was fated, but that fate was a rational plan. Thus falling ill or encountering another misfortune did not occur through random chance but instead advanced fate's intelligible plan for the world. Because reason was what humans had in common and what bound them together, they should strive to benefit each other and serve the larger community.

Stated baldly like this, these propositions sound like wishful thinking. But they grew out of a tightly and powerfully argued philosophical system. And they addressed in a new way—essentially by showing their unimportance—what could, under other systems of belief, be agonizing questions (as a glance at Greek tragedy will show): How can we explain instances of apparently undeserved suffering, when people, because of no discernible guilt of their own, become victims of others' actions or of impersonal forces? What can human life mean under such circumstances? What positive values can there be? Given its effectiveness at putting such questions into perspective, we can easily see how Stoicism might have been attractive to a Roman like Seneca, who lived at the center of one of the most capricious political regimes in Roman history.

From On Anger[1]

FROM BOOK 1

[*The Horrors of Anger*]

1 (1) You have demanded, Novatus,[2] that I write on how anger can be alleviated. I think that you were right to have a particular dread of this the most hideous and frenzied of all the emotions. The others have something quiet and placid in them, whereas anger is all excitement and impulse. Raving with a desire that is utterly inhuman for instruments of pain and reparations in blood, careless of itself so long as it harms the other, it rushes onto the very spear-points, greedy for vengeance that draws down the avenger with it.

(2) Some of the wise, accordingly, have described anger as 'brief insanity'—it is just as uncontrolled. Oblivious of decency, heedless of personal bonds, obstinate and intent on anything once started, closed to reasoning or advice, agitated on pretexts without foundation, incapable of discerning fairness or truth, it most resembles those ruins which crash in pieces over what they have crushed. (3) You can see that men possessed by anger are insane, if you look at their expression. The sure signs of raving madness are a bold and threatening look, a gloomy countenance, a grim visage, a rapid pace, restless hands, change of colour, heavy and frequent sighing. The marks of anger are the same: (4) eyes ablaze and glittering, a deep flush over all the face as blood boils up from the vitals, quivering lips, teeth pressed together, bristling hair standing on end, breath drawn in and hissing, the crackle of writhing limbs, groans and bellowing, speech broken off with the words barely uttered, hands struck together too often, feet stamping the ground, the whole body in violent motion 'menacing mighty wrath in mien',[3] the hideous horrifying face of swollen self-degradation—you would hardly know whether to call the vice hateful or ugly.

(5) Other passions can be concealed and nourished in secret. Anger parades itself; it shows on the face; the greater it is, the more obviously it seethes out. You can see how any animal, the moment it rears itself to do harm, shows some preliminary sign; the entire body forsakes its normal state of repose as it whets its savagery. (6) Boars foam at the mouth, grinding and sharpening their teeth; bulls toss their horns about, stamping and scattering the sand; lions growl; serpents swell at the neck when roused; rabid dogs are a grim spectacle—no animal has a nature so horrendous, so pernicious that it does not reveal, at the onset of anger, a fresh access of ferocity. (7) I know

---

1. Translated by John M. Cooper and J. F. Procopé. The material on Stoicism and the annotations to Seneca are indebted to their introduction and notes. 2. Seneca's older brother. 3. Evidently a line of poetry, quoted from an unknown source.

that other emotions, too, can scarce be concealed. Lust, fear and over-confidence have their indications, and can be told in advance. None, in fact, of the more violent disturbances makes its entry without causing some change to the face. What, then, is the difference? The other affections make themselves seen. Anger sticks right out. * * *

[Is Anger Natural?]

5 (1) We have asked what anger is, whether it occurs in any animal other than man, how it differs from irascibility, how many species of it there are. We must now ask whether anger accords with nature and whether it is useful and, in part, worth retaining.

(2) Is anger in accordance with nature? The answer will be clear, if we turn our eyes upon man. What is milder than man, when he is in his right mind? But what is crueller than anger? What is more loving of others than man is? What more adverse than anger? Man was begotten for mutual assistance, anger for mutual destruction. The one would flock together with his fellows, the other would break away. The one seeks to help, the other to harm; the one would succour even those unknown to him, the other would fly at even those who are dearest. Man will go so far as to sacrifice himself for the good of another; anger will plunge into danger, if it can draw the other down. (3) What greater ignorance of nature could there be than to credit its finest, most flawless work with this savage, ruinous fault? Anger, as I said, is greedy for punishment. That such a desire should reside in that most peaceful of dwellings, the breast of man, is utterly out of accord with his nature. Human life rests upon kindnesses and concord; bound together, not by terror but by love reciprocated, it becomes a bond of mutual assistance.

[Can Anger Be Useful, or Controlled?]

7 (1) Can it really be that anger, although it is not natural, should be adopted because it has often proved useful? 'It rouses and spurs on the mind. Without it, courage can achieve nothing magnificent in war—without the flame of anger beneath, to goad men on to meet danger with boldness.' Some, accordingly, think it best to moderate anger, not to remove it. They would confine it to a wholesome limit by drawing off any excess, while retaining what is essential for unenfeebled action, for unsapped force and vigour of spirit. (2) <Well>, in the first place, it is easier to exclude the forces of ruin than to govern them, to deny them admission than to moderate them afterwards. For once they have established possession, they prove to be more powerful than their governor, refusing to be cut back or reduced. (3) Moreover, reason itself, entrusted with the reins, is only powerful so long as it remains isolated from the affections. Mixed and contaminated with them, it cannot contain what it could previously have dislodged. Once the intellect has been stirred up and shaken out, it becomes the servant of the force which impels it. (4) Some things at the start are in our power; thereafter they sweep us on with a force of their own and allow no turning back. Bodies in free fall have no control over themselves. They cannot delay or resist the downward course. Any deliberation and second thoughts are cut short by the peremptory force of gravity. They cannot help completing a trajectory which they need not have begun. In the same way, the mind, if it throws itself into anger, love and other affections, is not allowed to restrain the impulse. It is bound to be swept along and driven to the bottom by its own weight and by the natural downward tendency of any failing.

8 (1) It is best to beat back at once the first irritations, to resist the very germs of anger and take care not to succumb. Once it has begun to carry us off course, the return to safety is difficult. Reason amounts to nothing, once the affection has been installed and we have voluntarily given it some legal standing. From then on, it will do what it wants, not what you allow it. (2) The enemy, I say, must be stopped at the very frontier; when he has invaded and rushed on the city gates, there is no 'limit' which his captives can make him accept. It is not the case that the mind stands apart, spying out its affections from without, to prevent their going too far—the mind itself turns into affection.[4] It cannot, accordingly, reinstate that useful and wholesome force[5] which it has betrayed and weakened. (3) As I said, it is not the case that they dwell apart, in isolation from one another. Reason and affection are the mind's transformations for better or for worse. How then can reason, under the oppressive domination of its failings, rise again, if it has already given way to anger? How can it free itself from the chaos, if the admixture of baser ingredients has prevailed? (4) 'But some people', it may be said, 'control their anger.' So as to do nothing that anger dictates—or some of it? If nothing, there is clearly no need, when it comes to doing things, of the anger which you recommend as somehow more forceful than reason. (5) Now my next question: is anger stronger than reason—or weaker? If stronger, how can reason put a limit on it? It is only the feebler, normally, who submit. If anger is weaker, reason can do without it. It is sufficient by itself for getting things done and has no need for a weaker ally. (6) 'But some people stay true to themselves and control themselves in their anger.' When? As their anger evaporates and departs of its own accord, not at its boiling-point—it is too strong then. (7) 'Well, is it not sometimes true that, even in anger, people release the objects of their hatred unharmed and untouched? Do they not refrain from harming them?' They do. But when? When affection has driven back affection, when fear or lust has obtained its demand. Quiet has ensued, thanks not to reason, but to an evil, untrustworthy armistice between the affections.

[The Use of Anger in War and in Peacetime]

9 (1) Again, there is nothing useful in anger. It does not whet the mind for deeds of war. Virtue needs no vice to assist it; it suffices for itself. Whenever impetus is necessary, it does not break out in anger; it rises to action aroused and relaxed to the extent that it thinks necessary, in just the same way that the range of a missile shot from a catapult is under the control of the operator. (2) 'Anger', says Aristotle, 'is needful; no fight can be won without it, without its filling the mind and kindling enthusiasm there; it must be treated

---

4. In contrast to Plato, the Stoics did not locate the emotions in a part of the psyche separate from reason but thought of it as something the mind becomes. This sentence makes the point clear, although Seneca's metaphor of an invading army obscures it.   5. I.e., reason.

however, not as a commander but as one of the rank and file.'[6] That is false. If it listens to reason and follows where led, it is no longer anger, the hallmark of which is wilful disobedience. But if it rebels against orders to stay still and follows its own ferocious fancy, it is as useless a subordinate in the soul as a soldier who ignores the signal for retreat. (3) So if it accepts a limit, it needs some other name, having ceased to be anger, which I understand to be something unbridled and ungoverned. If it does not, it is ruinous and not to be counted as an assistant. Either it is not anger at all, or it is useless. (4) Anyone who exacts punishment not through greed for the punishment itself, but because he should, does not count as angry. A good soldier is one who knows how to obey orders and carry out decisions. The affections are no less evil as subordinates than they are as commanders.

10   (1) So reason will never enlist the aid of reckless unbridled impulses over which it has no authority, which it can only contain by confronting them with matching and similar impulses—anger with fear, indolence with anger, fear with greed. (2) May virtue be spared the horror of reason's seeking refuge in vices! Trustworthy peace is impossible, turmoil and vacillation inevitable, for the mind that would find safety in its own evils. Incapable of bravery without anger, of industry without greed, of quietude without fear, it is doomed to live under a tyranny, once it has entered the service of an affection. Are you not ashamed to demote the virtues to dependency on vices? (3) Moreover, reason will cease to have any power at all, if it is powerless without affection. It will start to match and resemble it. For how will they differ? After all, affection without reason will be as unwise as reason without affection is unavailing. Each matches the other, where neither can exist without the other. But who would have the gall to make affection the equal of reason?

(4) 'Emotion does have some use,' it may be said, 'if it is moderate.' No. Only if its nature is to be useful. But if it will not submit to the command of reason, the sole consequence of moderation is that the less the affection the less its harm. Moderate affection means simply moderate evil.

[Anger and Greatness of Mind]

20   (1) Nor should you think even this, that anger contributes something to greatness of mind.[7] It is not a matter of greatness, but of morbid enlargement. Disease in bodies which bulge with a mass of tainted fluid is not 'growth' but pestilential excess. (2) All whose thoughts have been raised by derangement to superhuman heights, credit themselves with a spirit of lofty sublimity. But there is nothing solid beneath. Ruin awaits what has risen without foundation. Anger has no footing, no firm, lasting base on which to rise. Windy and void, it is as remote from greatness of mind as rash confidence is from courage, as cheek is from assurance or cruelty from sternness. (3) There is a great difference, I tell you, between a lofty and an arrogant mind. Bad temper achieves nothing imposing or handsome. On the contrary, I think it the mark of a morbid unhappy mind, aware of its own weakness,

6. This sentence is not found in any of Aristotle's surviving works.   7. If one thinks of heroes in the poetic tradition such as Achilles or of certain figures in Greek tragedy, anger might seem inseparable from greatness of mind. But for Stoicism, greatness of mind was imperviousness to external accidents and events.

to be constantly aching, like sore sick bodies which groan at the slightest touch. Anger is thus a particularly feminine and childish failing. 'But men, too, get it.' Yes. For men, too, can have feminine and childish characters.

(4) 'Tell me, then. Might not some utterances poured out in anger seem to be outpourings of a great mind?' You mean outpourings of ignorance about true greatness, like that dire, detestable saying: 'let them hate, provided that they fear.'[8] A sentence, as you can see, from the time of Sulla![9] I am not sure which wish was worse—to be hated or to be feared. 'Let them hate.' It occurred to him that he would be the object of curses, intrigues and crushing attack. So what did he add? He hit on a worthy remedy for hatred, confound him! 'Let them hate.' Then what? ' . . . provided that they obey?' No. ' . . . provided that they approve?' No. What, then? ' . . . provided that they fear!' On that condition, I would not wish even to be loved. (5) Is that the utterance of a great spirit, do you think? If you do, you are wrong. That is not greatness but frightfulness. You have no need to trust the words of the angry: their noise is great and threatening, the mind within terror-struck. (6) Nor need you think it true when Livy,[1] a masterly writer, says: 'a man of great rather than good character'. The two cannot be separated. Either it will be good as well, or it will not be great to start with. For 'greatness of mind', as I understand it, is something unshaken, solid within, firm and even from top to bottom—an impossibility in bad characters. (7) They can be terrifying, tumultuous, destructive; but they cannot be great. For the stay and strength of greatness is goodness. (8) Their speech, of course, their exertion and outward appointments may all make for belief in their greatness; they may say something which you might think was the utterance of a great mind, as did Gaius Caesar:[2] angry with heaven for drowning the noise of his clowns, whom he was keener to imitate than to watch, and for frightening his revels with thunderbolts (not, unfortunately, on target), he summoned Jove to combat—and mortal combat at that—with the line from Homer:

'Or let me lift thee, chief, or lift thou me.[3]

What madness! He thought that he could receive no harm from Jove himself or that he might even inflict harm on Jove. That utterance of his, I think, added quite some force to the motivation of the conspirators. Having to put up with a man who would not put up with Jove was the last straw.

21 (1) So there is nothing about anger, not even in the apparent extravagance of its disdain for gods and men, that is great or noble. If anyone does think that anger makes a great mind manifest, he might think the same about self-indulgence—with its wish to be borne on ivory, dressed in purple, roofed with gold, to transfer whole plots of land, enclose whole stretches of sea, turn rivers into cascades and woodland into hanging gardens. (2) Avarice, too, might betoken a great mind—watching, as it does, over stacks of gold and silver, cultivating estates on a par with provinces, delegating to single

---

8. A line from the tragedy *Atreus* by Lucius Accius (170–ca. 86 B.C.E.).   9. Aristocratic politician and general (138–79 B.C.E.). Made dictator after capturing Rome, Sulla had his enemies murdered in 82–81 B.C.E. through a device known as *proscription*, the publication of names of Roman citizens who were declared outlaws and could be hunted down and killed. He voluntarily relinquished power in 79. 1. Roman historian (59 B.C.E.–17 C.E.).   2. Third Roman emperor, better known as Caligula (12–41 C.E.). Notable for his cruelty and caprice, he was assassinated in the fourth year of his reign.   3. *Iliad* 23.724 (spoken by Ajax to Odysseus, his opponent in a wrestling match during the funeral games for Patroclus).

bailiffs lands with boundaries wider than those that used to be allotted to consuls. (3) So, too, might lust—it swims across the straits, castrates whole flocks of boys and braves the husband's sword in contempt of death. So, too, ambition—not content with yearly honours, it would, if possible, fill the consul list with one man's name alone, distributing his memorials all over the world. (4) But all these, no matter what lengths they go to or how wide they spread, are narrow, wretched, mean. Virtue alone is exalted and lofty. Nor is anything great which is not at the same time calm.

FROM BOOK 3

[Greatness of Mind Is Free from Disturbance]

6   (1) There is no surer proof of greatness than to be unprovoked by anything that can possibly happen. The higher and better ordered part of the world, the part near the stars, is neither compressed into cloud nor thrust into storm nor turned in the whirlwind, free as it is of all turbulence; the lower parts get the lightning. In the same way, a lofty mind, ever at rest in its calm anchorage, stifling anything which might induce anger, maintains its modesty, its claim to respect, its orderliness—none of which you will find in the angry. (2) Where a person is prey to pain and fury, his sense of shame is the first thing to be cast off. In making a violent, impulsive rush at someone, he throws away whatever there was to respect in him. His idea of what to do and the order in which to do it can hardly stay unshaken in his excited state. Can he hold his tongue, or control any part of his body? Has he any command of himself, once he is launched?

* * *

APULEIUS
ca. 125–after 170 C.E.

Throughout the centuries when philosophical systems were developing, the Olympian religion, as we know it from Homer, Hesiod, Virgil, and (with a heavy dose of parody at times) Ovid, continued to be observed in belief and ritual in Greece and Rome. The Greeks from at least the fourth century B.C.E., however, and the Romans to an even greater extent, were receptive to cults from outside their cultural sphere, especially Asia Minor. In the fifth century B.C.E., for example, the Athenians associated Cybele, the "Great Mother" from Anatolia, with Demeter, and her cult was imported into Rome in the late fourth century. The Iranian cult of Mithras was influential throughout the Roman Empire. A third very important cult found frequently in Greece and Italy in the imperial period was that of the Egyptian Isis. We have a good description of what her cult, and similar cults, might mean to a worshipper in the closing episodes of Apuleius's brilliant novel *The Golden Ass* (or *Metamorphoses*).

On a trip to Thessaly in northern Greece, Lucius, the hero of the novel, contrives, through a sexual liaison with a servant girl, to watch the practice of magic. The upshot is his transformation into an ass, although he keeps his human mind. Experiencing life as a beast of burden at first hand, he undergoes many adventures with a variety of people, most of them unsavory. Much of the novel is thus a risqué (and very enjoyable) picaresque romance; but in the eleventh and final book the tone changes. On the beach at the port of Cenchreae near Corinth, Lucius sees Isis in a vision; the following day, he encounters her cult procession and gains the means to transform himself back into human form. Finally, he is initiated into the goddess's mysteries. These climactic events retrospectively change the novel into a fable of conversion from entrapment in the lowest parts of human nature—sensuality, curiosity, magic—to a higher and more directed form of life that realizes the best human potential. Much of this significance derives from the nature of Isis and of her cult.

The Egyptian goddess was a sustainer of life. When her husband-brother Osiris was killed and dismembered by Seth (the incarnation of disorder), she searched for the pieces of Osiris's body, reconstituted it, and brought him back to life. She was thus associated with the promise of life after death, and also with the annual rising of the Nile that enriched the Egyptian soil. In the Hellenistic period, she was prominently associated with Sarapis—the hybrid of Osiris and the sacred Apis bull whose cult was introduced by the Ptolemies, the Greek dynasty that ruled Egypt in the wake of Alexander's conquests. It was especially at this time that the cult of Isis spread to Italy and Greece.

In Greco-Roman belief, Isis retained her nurturing function and was associated with the creative aspects of nature. As we see in her speech when she appears to Lucius in a vision, she was identified with a range of Greek and Roman goddesses (and also with Cybele). This process is sometimes called *syncretism* (a union), but more is involved than the matching of divinities from distinct religious traditions. At least as Apuleius presents her, Isis is a power who pervades what traditionally had been separate spheres of influence, possessed by different gods. She thus helps unify the worship of the life-giving forces in the world, which otherwise was dispersed among various cults.

In Lucius's encounter with Isis, two themes are especially prominent. First, she brings salvation to those in trouble—sailors at sea, for example, or a man trapped in his bestial nature. Second, she is identified with Fortuna, goddess of luck (as was actually the case), and indeed controls it. She gives coherence and direction—for the good—to what would otherwise be random chance. Thus Lucius's story can be seen from the perspective of its ending to have been directed toward his conversion to Isis: he had to wander and suffer in order to be saved from his afflictions. In a religious tradition that had often wondered whether luck, the things that happen to occur in our lives, was the result of chance or of providential guidance by a higher power, the belief that a nurturing goddess shaped fortune, or at least the fortune of her worshippers, must have been reassuring.

The Greco-Roman cult of Isis also gives us an example of a mystery religion. Although the cults of Mithras and Cybele were of this type, there was nothing "foreign" about mysteries; the Eleusinian Mysteries had been established in Greece since at least the sixth century B.C.E., if not before. The word *mystery* means simply "that in which one is initiated," and such cults involved rites of initiation and certain practices and beliefs that were shared only among initiates (hence the term's connotation of secrecy). The ceremony of initiation evidently involved a vivid religious experience (as Lucius says, "I drew near to the confines of death and trod the threshold of Proserpina, and before returning I journeyed through all the elements . . . I stood in the presence of the gods below and the gods above, and worshipped them from close at hand"), and initiates might be promised certain rewards in the afterlife. But it was possible to worship Isis without being an initiate. What mystery cults seem to have offered their initiates was a way of organizing the bewildering variety of experience in the terms of systematic belief and a set of goals (including life after death). Lucius's account of his experience vividly conveys the relief from anxiety and the joy that initiation could offer, the sense that a new life was beginning.

Apuleius was born in Madaurus in North Africa, which was a Roman province. He was educated in Carthage and then in Athens. After a rather spectacular interlude in Oea (the modern Tripoli), in which he was brought to trial for attracting the affections of a wealthy widow through witchcraft—his defense speech survives—he settled in Carthage, where he became a famous rhetorician. His writings included speeches and philosophy, as well as works on a wide range of scientific and other topics, in addition to his novel, the only complete specimen of this genre that survives in Latin (the fragmentary *Satyricon* of Petronius is of the same type).

From The Golden Ass[1]

FROM BOOK 11

1   A sudden fear aroused me at about the first watch of the night.[2] At that moment I beheld the full moon rising from the sea-waves, and gleaming with special brightness. In my enjoyment of the hushed isolation of the shadowy night, I became aware that the supreme goddess[3] wielded her power with exceeding majesty, that human affairs were controlled wholly by her providence, that the world of cattle and wild beasts and even things inanimate were lent vigour by the divine impulse of her light and power; that the bodies of earth, sea, and sky now increased at her waxing, and now diminished in deference to her waning. It seemed that Fate had now had her fill of my grievous misfortunes, and was offering hope of deliverance, however delayed. So I decided to address a prayer to the venerable image of the goddess appearing before my eyes. I hastily shook off my torpid drowsiness, and sprang up, exultant and eager. I was keen to purify myself at once, so I bathed myself in the sea-waters, plunging my head seven times beneath the waves, for Pythagoras[4] of godlike fame proclaimed that number to be especially efficacious in sacred rites. Then with tears in my eyes I addressed this prayer to the supremely powerful goddess:

2   'Queen of heaven, at one time you appear in the guise of Ceres, bountiful and primeval bearer of crops. In your delight at recovering your daughter, you dispensed with the ancient, barbaric diet of acorns and schooled us in civilized fare; now you dwell in the fields of Eleusis.[5] At another time you are heavenly Venus; in giving birth to Love when the world was first begun, you united the opposing sexes and multiplied the human race by producing ever abundant offspring; now you are venerated at the wave-lapped shrine of Paphos.[6] At another time you are Phoebus' sister; by applying soothing remedies you relieve the pain of childbirth, and have brought teeming numbers to birth; now you are worshipped in the famed shrines of Ephesus.[7] At

1. Translated by P. G. Walsh.   2. Having narrowly escaped being part of a humiliating public spectacle in the theater at Corinth, Lucius, still in the shape of an ass, has made his way to a beach near Cenchreae, the port of Corinth on the Saronic Gulf, and has fallen asleep. *First watch*: approximately 6–9 P.M. The Romans divided the night into four equal "watches," which varied in length according to the time of year.   3. Isis, who was variously identified with the moon and with the goddesses Lucius names in his prayer: Ceres, Venus, Diana ("Phoebus' sister"), and Proserpina.   4. A major Greek religious and scientific figure of the second half of the 6th century B.C.E. He taught the doctrine of the transmigration of souls and is credited with important discoveries in mathematics (such as the Pythagorean theorem) and music. His followers considered the number seven perfect and sacred.   5. Town near Athens and site of the mysteries of Demeter (Ceres). *Your daughter*: Persephone (Proserpina).   6. Important center of Venus's (Aphrodite's) cult on the island of Cyprus.   7. City in Asia Minor that had a famous temple to Artemis (Diana). One of Artemis's functions was as goddess of childbirth.

another time you are Proserpina, whose howls at night inspire dread,[8] and whose triple form restrains the emergence of ghosts as you keep the entrance to earth above firmly barred. You wander through diverse groves, and are appeased by varying rites. With this feminine light of yours you brighten every city and nourish the luxuriant seeds with your moist fire, bestowing your light intermittently according to the wandering paths of the sun. But by whatever name or rite or image it is right to invoke you, come to my aid at this time of extreme privation, lend stability to my disintegrating fortunes, grant respite and peace to the harsh afflictions which I have endured. Let this be the full measure of my toils and hazards; rid me of this grisly, four-footed form. Restore me to the sight of my kin; make me again the Lucius that I was. But if I have offended some deity who continues to oppress me with implacable savagery, at least allow me to die, since I cannot continue to live.'

3 These were the prayers which I poured out, supporting them with cries of lamentation. But then sleep enveloped and overpowered my wasting spirit as I lay on that couch of sand. But scarcely had I closed my eyes when suddenly from the midst of the sea a divine figure arose, revealing features worthy of veneration even by the gods. Then gradually the gleaming form seemed to stand before me in full figure as she shook off the sea-water. I shall try to acquaint you too with the detail of her wondrous appearance, if only the poverty of human speech grants me powers of description, or the deity herself endows me with a rich feast of eloquent utterance.[9]

To begin with, she had a full head of hair which hung down, gradually curling as it spread loosely and flowed gently over her divine neck. Her lofty head was encircled by a garland interwoven with diverse blossoms, at the centre of which above her brow was a flat disk resembling a mirror, or rather the orb of the moon, which emitted a glittering light. The crown was held in place by coils of rearing snakes on right and left, and it was adorned above with waving ears of corn. She wore a multicoloured dress woven from fine linen, one part of which shone radiantly white, a second glowed yellow with saffron blossom, and a third blazed rosy red. But what riveted my eyes above all else was her jet-black cloak, which gleamed with a dark sheen as it enveloped her. It ran beneath her right arm across to her left shoulder, its fringe partially descending in the form of a knot. The garment hung down in layers of successive folds, its lower edge gracefully undulating with tasselled fringes.

4 Stars glittered here and there along its woven border and on its flat surface, and in their midst a full moon exhaled fiery flames. Wherever the hem of that magnificent cloak billowed out, a garland composed of every flower and every fruit was inseparably attached to it. The goddess's appurtenances were extremely diverse. In her right hand she carried a bronze rattle;[1] it consisted of a narrow metal strip curved like a belt, through the middle of which were passed a few rods; when she shook the rattle vigorously three times with her arm, the rods gave out a shrill sound. From her left hand dangled a boat-shaped vessel, on the handle of which was the figure of a

---

8. As queen of the underworld, Proserpina was sometimes identified with Hecate, triple-bodied goddess of crossroads and patroness of magic and witchcraft.   9. The details of the description that follows all have parallels in Greco-Roman statues of Isis. Her attributes emphasize her various functions, especially natural fertility, the earth (snakes), and the sea (the boat).   1. The sistrum, carried by Isis's priests and a distinctive accessory in her cult.

serpent in relief, rearing high its head and swelling its broad neck. Her feet, divinely white, were shod in sandals fashioned from the leaves of the palm of victory. Such, then, was the appearance of the mighty goddess. She breathed forth the fertile fragrance of Arabia[2] as she deigned to address me in words divine:

5 'Here I am, Lucius, roused by your prayers. I am the mother of the world of nature, mistress of all the elements, first-born in this realm of time. I am the loftiest of deities, queen of departed spirits, foremost of heavenly dwellers, the single embodiment of all gods and goddesses. I order with my nod the luminous heights of heaven, the healthy sea-breezes, the sad silences of the infernal dwellers. The whole world worships this single godhead under a variety of shapes and liturgies and titles. In one land the Phrygians, firstborn of men, hail me as the Pessinuntian mother of the gods;[3] elsewhere the native dwellers of Attica call me Cecropian Minerva;[4] in other climes the wave-tossed Cypriots name me Paphian Venus; the Cretan archers, Dictynna[5] Diana; the trilingual Sicilians, Ortygian[6] Proserpina; the Eleusinians, the ancient goddess Ceres; some call me Juno, others Bellona,[7] others Hecate, and others still Rhamnusia.[8] But the peoples on whom the rising sun-god shines with his first rays—eastern and western Ethiopians, and the Egyptians who flourish with their time-honoured learning—worship me with the liturgy that is my own, and call me by my true name, which is queen Isis.

'I am here out of pity for your misfortunes; I am here to lend you kindly support. End now your weeping, abandon your lamentation, set aside your grief, for through my providence your day of salvation is now dawning. So pay careful attention to my commands. The day to be born of this night has been dedicated to me in religious observance from time immemorial. Now that the storms of winter are stilled, and the tempestuous waves of the ocean are calmed, the sea is now safe for shipping, and my priests entrust to it a newly built vessel dedicated as the first fruits of our journeys by sea.[9] You are to await this rite with an untroubled and reverent mind.

6 'As the procession forms up, a priest at my prompting will be carrying a garland of roses tied to the rattle in his right hand. So without hesitation part the crowd and join the procession, relying on my kindly care. Then, when you have drawn near, make as if you intend to kiss the priest's hand, and gently detach the roses;[1] at once then shrug off the skin of this most hateful of animals, which has long been abominable in my sight. Do not be fearful and regard any of these commands of mine as difficult, for at this moment as I stand before you I am also appearing to my priest as he sleeps, and am instructing him what to do following this. At my command the close-packed crowds will give way before you. In the midst of the joyous ritual and the jolly sights, no one will recoil from your ugly shape, nor put a malicious complexion on your sudden metamorphosis, and lay spiteful charges against you.

'What you must carefully remember and keep ever locked deep in your

2. A source of spices.   3. Cybele, mother-goddess worshipped in Anatolia in Asia Minor, where there was an important center of her cult at Pessinus.   4. Athena. *Cecropian:* from Cecrops, legendary king of Athens.   5. Cretan mother-goddess identified already in Greek times with Artemis (Diana).   6. Sicilian (Ortygia was an island in the harbor of Syracuse in Sicily). The Sicilians were "trilingual" because the island contained Carthaginian, Greek, and Roman settlements.   7. Roman goddess of war. *Juno:* Hera, wife and sister of Zeus (Jupiter or Jove), ruler of the gods.   8. Themis, the personification of what is right and proper, who had a temple at Rhamnous in Attica.   9. One of Isis's epithets was *pelagia,* "of the sea." Her connection to the sea had several aspects; among them was her protection of ships and sailors.
1. Lucius could regain his human shape only by eating roses.

heart is that the remaining course of your life until the moment of your last breath is pledged to me, for it is only right that all your future days should be devoted to the one whose kindness has restored you to the company of men. Your future life will be blessed, and under my protection will bring you fame; and when you have lived out your life's span and you journey to the realm of the dead, even there in the hemisphere beneath the earth you will constantly adore me, for I shall be gracious to you. You will dwell in the Elysian fields, while I, whom you now behold, shine brightly in the darkness of Acheron and reign in the inner Stygian[2] depths. But if you deserve to win my divine approval by diligent service, you will come to know that I alone can prolong your life even here on earth beyond the years appointed by your destiny.'

[A procession of Isis's priests and worshippers arrives to celebrate the rite of the launching of the ship sacred to her. As Isis foretold, Lucius eats the roses one of the priests is carrying and regains his human form. The priest now addresses him.]

15 'Lucius, the troubles which you have endured have been many and diverse. You have been driven before the heavy storms and the heaviest gales of Fortune, but you have finally reached the harbour of peace and the altar of mercy. Your high birth, and what is more, your rank and your accomplished learning have been of no avail to you whatever. In the green years of youth, you tumbled on the slippery slope into slavish pleasures, and gained the ill-omened reward of your unhappy curiosity. Yet somehow Fortune in her blind course, while torturing you with the most severe dangers, has in her random persecution guided you to this state of religious blessedness. So she can now head off and muster her most savage rage in search of some other victim for her cruelty, for hostile chance has no influence over those whose lives our majestic goddess has adopted into her service. Have brigands, or wild beasts, or slavery, or those winding, wholly crippling journeys to and fro, or the daily fear of death been of any avail to Fortune's malice? You have now been taken under the protection of Fortune with eyes,[3] who with the brilliance of her light lends lustre even to the other gods. Show now a happier face in keeping with your white garment, and join the procession of the saviour goddess with triumphal step. Let unbelievers see you, and as they see you let them recognize the error of their ways; for behold, Lucius is delivered from his earlier privations, and as he rejoices in the providence of the great Isis, he triumphs over his Fortune. But to ensure your greater safety under closer protection, enrol in this sacred army to which you were invited to swear allegiance not long ago. Consecrate yourself from this moment to the obedience of our religion, and of your own accord submit to the yoke of service. Once you have begun to serve the goddess, you will then better appreciate the reward of your freedom.'

[The sacred ship is piled with offerings and launched, and the procession returns to Isis's temple to complete the rite. Lucius is reunited with friends and family but devotes himself to the goddess, taking up residence in her temple precinct. In fulfill-

---

2. Of the Styx, a river of the underworld (as is Acheron). *Elysian Fields:* the region of the underworld where the souls of the virtuous enjoyed a blissful existence. See Virgil, *Aeneid* 6.853–972.   3. Isis was identified with the Roman goddess Fortuna, luck or chance, and was thought to control the fortunes of her initiates.

ment of a dream, two slaves and a horse he had lost when he was transformed into an ass are restored to him.]

21 This event made me perform my diligent service of worship more conscientiously, for these present blessings offered a pledge of hope for the future. Every day my longing to be admitted to the mysteries grew more and more, and I repeatedly greeted the chief priest with the most ardent requests that he should at last initiate me into the secret rites of the sanctified night. But he was in general a sober character, well known for his adhesion to a strict religious routine, and he treated me in the same way as parents often restrain their children's untimely desires. In a gentle and kind way he postponed my pressing request, whilst at the same time calming my agitation with the comforting expectation of a rosier future. He explained that the day on which a person could be initiated was indicated by the will of the goddess, that the priest who was to perform the sacred ritual was chosen by the foresight of that same goddess, and in addition the expenses necessary for the ceremonies were indicated in the same instruction. His advice was that I, like the others, should observe all these rules with reverent patience. It was my duty to take stringent precautions against both overenthusiasm and obstinacy, avoiding both faults so as not to hang back when summoned, nor to push forward unbidden. Not one individual in his community was so depraved in mind, or so enamoured of death as to undertake that ministry in a rash and sacrilegious spirit, without having received the call individually from his mistress; for that would incur a guilt that spelt death. Both the gates of hell and the guarantee of salvation lay in the control of the goddess. The act of initiation itself was performed as a rite of voluntary death and of salvation attained by prayer; indeed, it was the will of the goddess to select persons when their span of life was complete and they were poised on the very threshold of their final days. Such people could be safely entrusted with the profound mysteries of the sect. By her providence they were in some sense reborn, for she set them back on the course of renewed health. So I too was to submit to heaven's command, even though I had for long been named and designated for that blessed ministry by the notable and manifest favour of the great deity. Like the other worshippers, I should meanwhile abstain from profane and unlawful foods, to allow myself worthier access to the hidden secrets of that most hallowed religion.

[Isis now commands that Lucius be initiated into her mysteries.]

23 At once I energetically made the necessary preparations regardless of expense. Some I purchased personally, and others through my friends. The priest now told me that the required moment had come, so he led me to the baths close by in company with a group of initiates. First I was ushered into the normal bath. Then the priest first asked for the gods' blessing, and cleansed me by sprinkling water all over me until I was wholly purified. I was then escorted back to the temple. Two-thirds of the day had now elapsed; the priest set me before the very feet of the goddess, and gave me certain secret instructions too sacred to divulge. Then he commanded me openly, for all to witness, to discipline my pleasures in eating for the ensuing ten days, taking no animal flesh and drinking no wine.

I duly observed these commands with respectful self-discipline. The day now came which was appointed for my promise to the gods, and as the sun bent its course and ushered in the evening, suddenly crowds of initiates gathered from every side, and in accord with ancient custom they each paid me honour with a variety of gifts. Then all the noninitiates were removed to a distance. I was shrouded in a new linen garment, and the priest took my hand and led me into the heart of the sanctuary.

Perhaps the reader's interest is roused, and you are keen to enquire about the ensuing words and actions. I would tell you if it were permitted to reveal them; you would be told if you were allowed to hear. But both your ears and my tongue would incur equal guilt; my tongue for its impious garrulity, and your ears for their rash curiosity. I will not keep you long on tenterhooks, since your anxiety is perhaps motivated by religious longing. So listen, and be sure to believe that what you hear is true. I drew near to the confines of death and trod the threshold of Proserpina, and before returning I journeyed through all the elements. At dead of night I saw the sun gleaming with bright brilliance. I stood in the presence of the gods below and the gods above, and worshipped them from close at hand. Notice, then, that I have referred to things which you are not permitted to know, though you have heard about them. So I shall recount only what can be communicated without sacrilege to the understanding of non-initiates.

24 Morning came, and the rites were completed. I emerged sacramentally clothed in twelve garments. Though the clothing is quite germane to the ritual, there is no bar to my mentioning it, because at the time there were numerous persons present to see it. I took my stand as bidden on a wooden dais set before the statue of the goddess at the very heart of the sacred shrine. The linen garment that I wore made me conspicuous, for it was elaborately embroidered; the expensive cloak hung down my back from the shoulders to the heels, and from whatever angle you studied it, I was adorned all round with multicoloured animals. On one side were Indian snakes, and on the other Arctic gryphons[4] begotten by a world beyond this in the shape of winged birds. This garment the initiates call 'Olympian'. In my right hand I wielded a torch well alight; a garland of glinting palm-leaves projecting like the sun's rays encircled my head. When I was thus adorned to represent the sun and set there like a statue, the curtains were suddenly drawn back, and the people wandered in to gaze on me. Subsequently I celebrated a most happy birthday into the sacred mysteries; there was a pleasant banquet and a gathering of witty guests. There was also a third day of celebration with a similar programme of ceremonies, including a sacred breakfast and the official conclusion to the initiation.

For a few days I lingered on there, for I enjoyed the indescribable pleasure of gazing on the divine statue. I had pledged myself to Isis for the kindness which I could not repay. Finally, however, at the behest of the goddess I wound up my thanks, admittedly not expressed fully, but humbly and as far as my poor abilities allowed, and I prepared my long-delayed journey home. Even then the bonds of my most ardent yearning were hard to break. So finally I crouched before the image of the goddess, and for long rubbed her feet with my cheeks. With rising tears and frequent sobs I addressed her, choking on and swallowing my words.

4. Or griffins, mythical creatures that had the body of a lion and the beak and wings of an eagle.

25 'O holy, perennial saviour of the human race, you are ever generous in your care for mortals, and you bestow a mother's sweet affection upon wretched people in misfortune. No day, no period of sleep, no trivial moment hastens by which is not endowed with your kind deeds. You do not refrain from protecting mortals on sea and land, or from extending your saving hand to disperse the storms of life. With that hand you even wind back the threads of the Fates, however irretrievably twisted. You appease the storms raised by Fortune, and restrain the harmful courses of the stars. The gods above cultivate you, the spirits below court you. You rotate the world, lend the sun its light, govern the universe, crush Tartarus[5] beneath your heel. The stars are accountable to you, the seasons return at your behest, the deities rejoice before you, the elements serve you. At your nod breezes blow, clouds nurture the earth, seeds sprout, and buds swell. The birds coursing through the sky, the beasts wandering on the mountains, the snakes lurking in the undergrowth, the monsters that swim in the deep all tremble at your majesty. But my talent is too puny to sing your praises, and my patrimony is too meagre to offer you sacrificial victims; I have neither the richness of speech, nor a thousand mouths and as many tongues, nor an endless and uninhibited flow of words to express my feelings about your majesty. Therefore I shall be sure to perform the one thing that a pious but poor person can do: I shall preserve your divine countenance and your most holy godhead in the recess of my heart, and there I shall for ever guard it and gaze on it with the eyes of the mind.'

* * *

5. The underworld—i.e., death.

PLAUTUS
254?–184? B.C.E.

The comedies of Plautus are the earliest Roman literature that survives, and they make an exuberant beginning. With their drawing of human character types, their extravagant puns and wordplay, their ingenious plot twists, and their impeccable timing of jokes and pacing of action, they are gems of dramatic art, and their broad farce and physical humor have delighted audiences of all periods. Plautus helped shape the later European comic tradition, bequeathing to it not only plot elements and typical characters (the braggart, the grouch, the clever servant) but also whole plays. Shakespeare and Molière based comedies on Plautus's plays, and twentieth-century playwrights such as Friedrich Dürrenmatt and Jean Giraudoux continued to borrow from him. The Broadway hit and 1966 film *A Funny Thing Happened on the Way to the Forum* is a re-creation of Plautus's comedy that draws mainly on the play printed here, the *Pseudolus*.

Titus Maccius Plautus was born in the town of Sarsina in Umbria (northeastern Italy). Information about his life, as for many classical authors, is sparse. The traditional date of his birth is probably accurate to within a year or two. The date of his death is a mere guess, based on his apparent survival to a ripe old age. A much later writer says that Plautus made money in theatrical production as a young man, lost it in bad trading investments, and was reduced to working in a mill, where he wrote three of his plays; but these details are probably fictitious. He certainly wrote and produced his plays in Rome, and their theatrical brilliance suggests practical experience as an actor before he began to write—a supposition strengthened if his name means what it seems to ("Titus the Flatfoot Clown"?). The 20 comedies that survive complete (out of perhaps 130) probably date from the last decades of his life, from around 210 to 184 B.C.E.

ROMAN COMEDY

The kind of comedy that Plautus wrote represents the convergence of several traditions, including the burlesques on myth that were performed in the Greek areas of southern Italy and Sicily or native Italian farces improvised around stock situations and typical characters from daily life. The most important influence, however, was Greek New Comedy. The Old Comedy of Aristophanes—for example, *Lysistrata* (see p. 722)—which centered on extravagant fantasy, uninhibited obscenity, and pungent political and personal commentary, was a product of Athenian democracy. But the conquests of Alexander (356–323 B.C.E.), which ushered in the Hellenistic period, wrought huge changes in political conditions and in outlook. The New Comedy of this period, known to us mainly through substantial fragments and one complete play of the Greek poet Menander (344?–292? B.C.E.), reflects these altered conditions. Gone are fantasy, politics, and the chorus as an integral part of the drama. Instead, New Comedy portrays daily life centered on the family, with stereotyped situations and a repertoire of characters so typical that a conventional mask evolved for the actor playing each role: the audience could identify the character on sight (the slave, the young lovers, the old man, and so on). Much of the art of New Comedy was to combine and recombine stock characters and plot elements into new mixtures—a process that was infinitely extendable and, it seems, endlessly enjoyable to its audiences. Roman comic writers not only used these conventions; they also based each of their plays on a Greek comedy (or sometimes conflated two Greek models). They did more than translate or imitate, however. They rearranged freely, omitting some scenes and adding new ones, emphasizing certain themes at the expense of others, expanding and contracting various characters' roles. Plautus also recast as songs some scenes or passages that were spoken in the Greek plays, producing the metrically brilliant *cantica,* or lyric sections, that are a distinctive feature of his style.

Like his Greek models, Plautus presents typical characters responding in fairly predictable ways to stereotyped situations. An astonishing range of characters populates his plays: affluent citizens, respectable matrons, impecunious sons, parasites (professional meal-cadgers), slaves of both sexes, mercenary soldiers, prostitutes, pimps, cooks, quack doctors, and so on. These are caricatures of people who could be found filling well-defined social roles in any Hellenistic Greek city or in Rome itself. Many of these character types were to enjoy a long life on the European stage. Plautus's clever slaves, for example, are the ancestors of the irrepressible servant Dorine in Molière's *Tartuffe* (vol. 2, p. 12) and of the clever valets in Beaumarchais's eighteenth-century plays *The Marriage of Figaro* and *The Barber of Seville*. From such earlier examples as these to modern television sitcoms, stereotyped characters and situations have been used to reflect contemporary social concerns, just as they are in Greek New Comedy and Roman comedy.

One of the pleasures of comedy is that the sympathetic characters manage to overcome various obstacles to get what they want and achieve a happy ending. A common plot of this type in the ancient comedies revolves around a love intrigue. A young man of good family, dependent on his father for money and under his authority, is in love with a girl, but there is an impediment—social, economic, or both—to their union. The girl is apparently lowborn and a foreigner, and so the boy's father opposes the match (or would if he knew about it); someone else is in love with her and has the money to procure her; she is in the power of someone else (usually disreputable and greedy)—any or all of these conditions may obtain. The young man, usually despairing and ineffectual, is aided by a clever slave, who improvises a stratagem, often involving impersonation, to get the girl for his master. The blocking characters—those who stand in the way of the young couple's desires and often represent the repressive aspects of society—are punished or absorbed into the festivities that mark the wish-fulfilling end of the play, in which the girl often is discovered to be wellborn and a citizen, mislaid in infancy, and therefore marriageable. Thus erotic desire and the demands of society, whose conflict underlies many a tragic situation, are harmonized in the end, and youth succeeds in pressing its claims against old age. On the way to this happy conclusion, the play explores such issues as intergenerational relations (particularly those between fathers and sons), the social roles defined by gender and class, money and economic relations, marriage and the structure of the family, the distinction between slavery and freedom, and the question of who does and does not belong in the community.

Such issues must have been important for the ancient city-state at any time, but a form of drama that explored them and harmoniously reconciled them was especially pertinent to Rome in the opening decades of the second century B.C.E. The power and economic prosperity brought about by the defeat of Carthage and a number of subsequent military successes caused rapid social and cultural changes that were beginning to strain the traditional fabric of Roman society. The comedy of Plautus puts us in Rome at the historical moment of transition from city-state to world empire, just when the social and economic tensions it reflects were becoming urgent.

Rome had clear class divisions and a strict, traditional code of public and private morality, which was now challenged by the temptations of prosperity. Within the family, hierarchical authority was, if anything, more rigid still. The father controlled the property and had the power of life and death over his children as well as his slaves. Married women of any social standing were expected to behave beyond hint of reproach, especially where marital fidelity was concerned. And yet the Romans seem to have enjoyed the spectacle, offered in one comedy after another, of upstanding citizens tricked and made ridiculous, of lowlife pimps and soldiers wielding economic power over the supposedly respectable, of sons successfully eluding paternal author-ity, and of slaves much smarter than their owners. (Only the matronly ideal seems to have been off-limits to comedy, although the stage wife, more often than not, is a tiresome shrew.) Plautus, in fact, seems to have invented, or at least greatly expanded, the role of the clever slave, just at a time when slaves, captured in the Romans' many wars, were becoming more than ever a fact of Roman life. This systematic inversion of conventional social relations may have been permitted because comedy was per-formed at festivals, whose number had been growing in the late third century B.C.E. and continued to expand. The Romans had a well-developed sense of the distinction between business and leisure, and they were very good at enjoying themselves. The festival was a holiday from the business of daily life, and the normal rules could, while it lasted, be relaxed and even mocked. Comedy was part of this festive atmosphere; and if anyone thought that it allowed un-Roman behavior to go too far, it was always possible to reply that the characters and the plots were, after all, Greek. Although a bit of satire was possible and even expected, however, these plays did not mount any serious challenge to the social order. The festival, by providing a *temporary* relaxation of hierarchies and rules, ultimately strengthened them: when the festival was over, people went back to business as usual. In the same way, comedy did not seriously challenge the customary order of things but if anything affirmed it, for the plays usually end with an accommodation between social requirements and individual desire rather than the complete triumph of misrule.

Performances at these festivals were relatively informal, and because the plays had to compete with other events, such as gladiatorial shows, ropedancing, and boxing matches, they had to grab and keep the audience's attention. Temporary wooden scenery and seating were evidently erected for each festival and dismantled at its end (no permanent stone theater existed in Rome until the middle of the first century B.C.E.). The background scenery generally represented the facades of two, sometimes three, houses, each with a front door perhaps set within a roofed and columned porch. The setting was usually, though not always, in a town. The raised stage represented a street in front of the houses, and it was here, in the open, that the play's action occurred. Characters frequently engaged in asides to the audience, or could deliver soliloquies without seeing or being heard by others on stage. Conversely, one character or group of characters could spy on others from hiding. The side entrance on the audience's right (stage left) was imagined to lead to the forum; that on the left (stage right), to the harbor or outside the city. Seating was available to at least some of the audience. A portion of it was reserved for senators, and rank may have determined who got the rest as well, with the poor and slaves standing at the back. Social hierarchy therefore operated inside as well as outside the theater. It is fairly certain, in any case, that people from all levels of society could attend the plays, women and children as well as men, slaves as well as their masters. The actors were probably all men and wore masks. Many, if not all, may have been slaves themselves.

THE PSEUDOLUS

The *Pseudolus*, produced in 191 B.C.E., is a glorious example of Roman comedy. In adjacent houses represented by the background scenery, Simo and the pimp Ballio—types emblematic of social propriety and sleaze—live side by side. Their proximity illustrates the penetration of respectability by sordidness, and the hold Ballio has on his social superiors through their lust, their need for money, and his own shameless-ness provides some pointed commentary on social pretensions. What unites these two worlds in the play's action is a typical amatory intrigue. Simo's penniless son Calidorus is in love with Phoenicium, a girl in Ballio's establishment, who has been all but sold to a soldier. Calidorus plays the helpless lover to the hilt but gets Phoenicium through the machinations of his slave, the title character. Pseudolus—the name means "liar"—is Roman comedy's greatest portrait of the clever slave. His deceit and his zest for carrying it out provide the driving force of the play. Not only does he improvise a plot out of thin air, thinking at lightning speed to take advantage of every opportunity (and everyone else's stupidity), but he also tells his opponents Simo and Ballio exactly what he intends to do—and then, having maximized the challenge, he proceeds to demolish their defenses. Calidorus may get his girl, but the triumph belongs to Pseudolus.

One unusual feature of the love intrigue is that the girl, Phoenicium, appears only twice, both times briefly, and never speaks. In addition, there is never any suggestion that Calidorus will marry her, and she does not rise in status. The only female character (except for other prostitutes working for Ballio), she is the object of transactions among men, and her role reflects a view of women as a means to male ends common in patriarchal societies such as Rome's. This treatment of her also means that love itself is relatively unimportant as a theme of the play, outside of Calidorus's sentimental posturing, and the emphasis shifts to Pseudolus's plot and the obstacles he must overcome. As a blocking character, the father, Simo, is not very formidable, although he keeps his son on a short leash where money is concerned. He represents paternal severity, and his more tolerant contemporary and neighbor Callipho is there to serve as a foil to him and remind him that he had his share of fun in his youth. He does embody the obstacle to desire that the family structure poses, but he pales beside Ballio. In the pimp, and in the soldier who can afford to buy Phoenicium, we see economic power at its repressive worst. It is typical of comedy's life-affirming triumph of desire over economics that Pseudolus turns this weapon against Ballio, leveraging five minas (Greek coins) into twenty and making imaginary sums circulate as bets in a dizzying process. Fittingly, it is ultimately Pseudolus himself who gets twenty minas, which materialize in the money Simo has to pay him as a result of their wager.

In the end, the slave emerges paramount and rewarded, the young lovers are united, and the father must give way with what grace he can muster. But these inversions are not the play's last word. The *Pseudolus* ends, as so many comedies do, with a feast emblematic of the continuity of life and its energies, represented on stage by the drunken Pseudolus himself. In the play's last lines, Simo is invited to join the celebration and is included in the general merrymaking: his claims too are acknowledged. Only Ballio and the challenge to social order that he represents are rejected.

The *Pseudolus* represents a further important aspect of Plautus's art. It is one of the best examples among his plays of theatrical self-consciousness, or *metatheater*. Especially through Pseudolus's words, we are often reminded that we are watching a play in which the characters are filling roles—an effect of which modern playwrights such as Pirandello, Brecht, and Beckett are especially fond. Not only is the dramatic illusion broken in small ways ("I don't want to repeat myself: that's how plays become too long"), but the improvisation of Pseudolus's plot and the charade he stages with Simia's help to trick Ballio are compared to the way a poet creates plot and action out of nothing but fantasy. This emphasis on fiction making provides another link with the festival atmosphere surrounding the play and points explicitly to its removal from daily life. Through this device as well as in other ways, Plautine comedy offers a detached perspective from which Roman society could laugh at itself.

PRONOUNCING GLOSSARY

The following list uses common English syllables and stress accents to provide rough equivalents of selected words whose pronunciation may be unfamiliar to the general reader.

Ballio: *bahl'-ee-oh*

Calidorus: *kahl-i-doh'-rus*

Callipho: *kahl'-i-foh*

Charinus: *kahr-ee'-nus*

Plautus: *plaw'-tus*

Pseudolus: *soo'-doh-lus*

Pseudolus[1]

CHARACTERS

PSEUDOLUS, *a cunning slave*
CALIDORUS, *his master's teenaged son*
BALLIO, *a slave dealer and pimp*
SIMO, *Calidorus' father, a stern old man*
CALLIPHO, *Simo's friend, a tolerant old man*
HARPAX, *an officer's slave*
CHARINUS, *a young man, Calidorus' friend*
SIMIA, *a cunning slave*

YOUNG SLAVE, *an unnamed slave of Ballio's*
COOK, *anonymous, but not reticent*
COURTESANS, *Ballio's female slaves; silent roles*
  Delectium
  Obscenium
  Gymnasium
  Phoenicium
ATTENDANT SLAVES, *minor or silent roles*

---

1. Translated by Peter L. Smith, who uses a five-beat line for the spoken passages of the original, two four-beat lines for each of Plautus's lines in chanted passages, and lyric stanzas for the parts that were sung.

Prologue[2]

You'd better rise and stretch your legs,
    Walk up and down the aisle;
Here comes a Plautine comedy,
    It's bound to last a while.

Act I

[*The stage depicts three adjacent houses on a street in Athens. In the center is Simo's residence, flanked by the houses of his wealthy neighbor Callipho (stage right) and the disreputable pimp Ballio (stage left). As the play opens, the slave* PSEUDOLUS *and his young master,* CALIDORUS, *emerge from Simo's front door.*

PSEUDOLUS *wears the bizarre stock costume of the cunning slave—his physical appearance will be graphically described later in the play.* CALIDORUS *is a typical lovesick adolescent—a handsome, well-dressed, well-mannered, and appealing youth. Though he is not unintelligent, he is predictably unresourceful and naive. He is now preoccupied with the scrutiny of folding wooden letter-tablets, a standard form of ancient correspondence.*]

ACT I, SCENE 1

PSEUDOLUS   Master, if only I could read your mind
And learn the torture that's tormenting you,
I'd gladly spare two men a lot of bother:
I wouldn't need to ask, or you to answer.
Now, since that's impossible, necessity   5
Compels me to question you. Answer me this:
Why have you been acting half-alive
These last few days, toting letter-tablets
Everywhere and drenching them with tears,
Taking no one into your confidence?   10
[*Heroically.*] Give voice, that I may know what I know not.
CALIDORUS   Oh, Pseudolus, I'm suffering!
PSEUDOLUS   Jupiter forbid!
CALIDORUS   It's out of Jupiter's control;
Venus rules the region of my pain.
PSEUDOLUS   Am I allowed some knowledge? In the past,   15
You've made me privy-partner of your plans.
CALIDORUS   My attitude's unchanged.
PSEUDOLUS   Then state your problem.
I can offer cash, concern, or kind advice.
CALIDORUS [*Handing him the tablets.*]   Take this message; learn for
    yourself
Why I am quite consumptified with gloom and worry.   20
PSEUDOLUS   As you wish.
[*Examining tablets.*]   But oh! what's this?
CALIDORUS   What is it?

---

2. This short prologue (two lines of Latin) may be a later addition replacing a longer prologue by Plautus that explained the situation and plot to the audience.

PSEUDOLUS I think these letters must be sexy characters:
They're climbing all over each other.
CALIDORUS   Very funny.
PSEUDOLUS Holy Pol, unless the Sibyl[3] reads this first,
No one else could ever decipher it.   25
CALIDORUS Why are you so rude to charming letters,
Charming tablets, traced with a charming hand?
PSEUDOLUS Excuse me, sir; do chickens now have hands?
These are hen-tracts.
CALIDORUS   Oh, you make me sick.
Read it or hand it back.
PSEUDOLUS   All right, I'll read.   30
Take heart.
CALIDORUS   My heart is lost.
PSEUDOLUS   Well, find it again!
CALIDORUS No, I'll keep quiet; find it yourself in the wax.
That's where my heart resides—my breast is vacant now.
PSEUDOLUS [*Suddenly.*] I see your girl friend, Calidorus.
CALIDORUS [*Startled.*]   Where is she?
Where?
PSEUDOLUS [*Pointing to her name.*] Here, stretched out upon the
    boards,
relaxed in wax.[4]   35
CALIDORUS [*Furious.*] May the gods all smother you—
PSEUDOLUS   —with happiness.
CALIDORUS [*Tragically.*] My life's been brief, like a blade of summer
    grass:
Sudden was my birth, and suddenly I'm gone.
PSEUDOLUS Shut up, I'm trying to read.
CALIDORUS   Why not begin?
PSEUDOLUS [*Reading.*] "Phoenicium to her darling Calidorus: 40
With wax and string[5] and these appealing characters
I wish you love and health; your healing love I beg.
My eyes are moist, my heart and soul are faltering."
CALIDORUS I'm sunk, Pseudolus! I can't find the healing love
To send her back.
PSEUDOLUS   What healing love?
CALIDORUS   The silver kind.   45
PSEUDOLUS [*Waving the tablets.*] You're willing to repay her wooden love
With silver? Keep your wits about you, please!
CALIDORUS Read on, and soon the letter will explain
How urgently that silver must be found.
PSEUDOLUS "My pimp has sold me to a foreigner   50
(A Macedonian military man)
For twenty silver minas,[6] dearest love.
Before that soldier left, he paid out fifteen
In advance. Now there's a balance of only five.

---

3. Prophetess of Apollo. *Holy Pol*: a mild oath by Pollux (one of the Dioscuri, twin sons of Zeus).
4. Wood tablets were coated with wax, on which letters were incised with a stylus.   5. To tie together
the wooden tablets when they were folded face to face.   6. Athenian coins.

Therefore the soldier left a token here,   55
A portrait wax impression from his ring,[7]
And so, when someone brings a token like it,
I'm to be sent with him at once. A day is set
For the transaction: next Dionysia."
CALIDORUS   And that's tomorrow! I'm on the brink of doom,   60
Unless you've help to offer.
PSEUDOLUS   Let me finish.
CALIDORUS   Yes! I feel as though I'm talking with her.
Read—you give me bittersweet delight.
PSEUDOLUS [*Reading again, with increasing fervor.*] "Now our loves, our
     lives, our passionate embraces,
Laughter, fun, sweet talk, and sexy face-to-faces,   65
Slender little hips and thighs a-jiggle,
Tender little lips and tongues a-wiggle,
Juicy jousts of bouncy-boob and titty-tickle—
All our hopes of orgiastic consummation
Face dismemberment, disaster, desolation,   70
If we fail to find some mutual salvation.
Everything I know I've tried to tell you clearly:
Now I'll put you to the test. One question, merely:
Are you in love or just pretending?
                                    Yours sincerely."
CALIDORUS   An awful letter, Pseudolus.
PSEUDOLUS   Absolutely awful!   75
CALIDORUS   Why aren't you crying?
PSEUDOLUS   I've got stony eyes; I can't
Implore them to spit out a single tear.
CALIDORUS   How's that?
PSEUDOLUS   Hereditary dry-eye-itis.
CALIDORUS   Won't you help me just a little?
PSEUDOLUS   What should I do?
CALIDORUS   *Oh, dear!*
PSEUDOLUS   "Oh, dear"? Great Herc,[8] no need to scrimp   80
In that department; go ahead.
CALIDORUS   I'm so depressed, I can't find any cash to borrow—
PSEUDOLUS   *Oh, dear!*
CALIDORUS   There's not a penny in the house—
PSEUDOLUS   *Oh, dear!*
CALIDORUS   He's going to carry off my girl tomorrow—
PSEUDOLUS   *Oh, dear!*
CALIDORUS   Do you really think that helps?
PSEUDOLUS   I give what I've got: 85
I have an inexhaustible supply of groans.
CALIDORUS   It's all over for me today. But can you lend me
A single drachma[9] I'd pay back tomorrow?
PSEUDOLUS   Hardly—not if my life were on the line.

---

7. His seal ring, the impression of which in wax had the same function in antiquity as our signatures do
today.   8. Oath by Hercules, the great Greek hero (Heracles).   9. Another Athenian coin.

What will you do with a drachma?

CALIDORUS   Buy a rope.   90

PSEUDOLUS   What for?

CALIDORUS   To help me learn to swing. [*Tragically.*] I plan,
Ere shadows fall, to fall among the shades.

PSEUDOLUS   Then who'll pay back the drachma that I gave you?
Is that why you want to hang yourself, you sneak,
To dun me out of the drachma I've donated?   95

CALIDORUS   There's just no way that I can go on living
If she is grabbed from me and granted to another.
          [*Bursts into tears*].

PSEUDOLUS   Why cry, you cuckoo? You'll survive.

CALIDORUS   I've got to cry:
I haven't any money of my own,
No hope on earth of scraping up a scrap.   100

PSEUDOLUS   If I caught the drift of the lady's billet-doux,[1]
Your eyes have got to shower silver tears,
Or this pretentious crying act will help
As much as catching raindrops in a sieve.
Don't fear, my lovesick dear, I won't desert you.   105
Somewhere, somehow, some way (maybe) today
I'll find you silvery succor and salvation.
Where, oh where will it come from? I don't know,
But I know it will: I've got a twitching brow.

CALIDORUS   I only hope your deeds can match your words!   110

PSEUDOLUS   Holy Herc! If once I bang my holy gong,[2]
You know the holy rumpus I can raise!

CALIDORUS   You're now the repository of all my hopes.

PSEUDOLUS   Is it enough if I get this girl for you today
As your very own, or if I give you twenty minas?   115

CALIDORUS   It's enough—if it happens.

PSEUDOLUS   Demand your twenty minas,
So you'll know I'll carry out my promise to you.
Make it all quite legal: I'm itching to take the oath.

CALIDORUS [*Formally.*]   Sir, this day will you give me twenty minas?

PSEUDOLUS   Sir, I will. And now don't be a nuisance.   120
Listen to this, if you still have any doubts:
If all else fails, I'll pinch it from your papa.

CALIDORUS   God save you, I love you! But look: if possible,
For goodness' sake, put the pinch on Mother, too.

PSEUDOLUS   Dispel these worries from your fevered nose.   125

CALIDORUS   My fevered brain, do you mean?

PSEUDOLUS   I hate clichés.
[*Hailing the audience.*] Now hear ye, hear ye! Lend an ear, ye!
These are my solemn words of public warning
For the throng assembled here this morning,
All the citizens by tribe enrolled,   130
All my acquaintances and friends of old:

1. Love letter.   2. Literally, "set the sacred implements in motion," as if beginning a religious ritual.

If you should meet me, be on guard today,
And don't believe a single word I say.
CALIDORUS [*Startled by a noise from Ballio's house.*]   Shh!
                                                    Sweet
    Hercules, keep quiet!
PSEUDOLUS   Why, what's up?
CALIDORUS   The pimp's front door just gave a squeaking noise.   135
PSEUDOLUS   I'd rather twist his legs³ to make *him* squeak.
CALIDORUS   He's coming out in person: Lord of Lies!

ACT I, SCENE 2

[*As* PSEUDOLUS *and* CALIDORUS *make themselves inconspicuous,* BALLIO *emerges from his house, wielding a whip; the villainous slave dealer is berating a number of cowering male* SLAVES, *who are his household servants and personal attendants.*]

BALLIO   Get out! Come on, get out, you slugs!
        As merchandise you're rotten;
    You never do no good nohow:
        There's naught you've not forgotten!
    Unless I whip you up this way,   5
        You aren't the least bit useful;
    You're more like donkeys than like men,
        With ribs all striped and bruiseful.

    [*To audience.*] Flog 'em, you'll be the one to cry;
    These whipper-slappers always try,   10
    If given the chance, to have their fun:
    Grab, swipe, snitch, snatch, eat, drink, and run!
    That's just their nature; that's their way.
    And so, believe me when I say
    You'd rather wolves control your flock   15
    Than have these thugs patrol your block.

    It isn't always true, you know,
        That seeing is believing;
    Though their appearances aren't bad,
        Their actions are deceiving.   20

    [*Turning back to the* SLAVES.] Now unless you obey my command, all
        you guys,
    If you don't wipe the sleepiness out of your eyes,
        I'll embroider your hips
        With such colorful strips
            You'll resemble bright linen embroidered for feasts,   25
    Alexandrian coverlets covered with beasts.

---

3. Criminals were often punished by having their shins broken.

I issued orders yesterday,
Your provinces were all assigned;
But you're such crooked characters,
So careless, so devoid of mind,   30
You can't remember any job
Without a swift kick from behind.
    Perhaps you hope to get so tough
    That my whip won't be hard enough.

[*To audience.*] Just look at that! No concentration.   35
[*Cracking his whip at the* SLAVES.] Pay attention, look this way!
Make sure you point your ears at me,
You whip-lashed human specimens!
Your backsides can't get any harder
Than this rawhide whip of mine.   40
[*Flicking his whip at various victims.*] How now? That hurt? There!
    That's what's done
If any slave shows disrespect.

Now form a line in front of me
And pay attention to my words.
[*Pointing to a* SLAVE.] You with the jug: go fetch some water;   45
Fill the kettle for the cook.
[*To another.*] You with the axe: you'll oversee
The Province of Woodsplittia.

SLAVE   This axe is dull.

BALLIO   What if it is?
You're not so very sharp yourself.   50
Do I enjoy your service less
Because you're blunted with my blows?
[*To another.*] Your task is cleaning up the house.
You know the job. Hurry up! Go in!
[*To another.*] Be thou the Keeper of the Couch.   55
[*To another.*] You get to wash the silver plate.
Make sure these jobs are done when I
Return from town; I want to find
That everything's been swept and sprinkled,
Cleaned and leveled, washed and shined.   60
Today's my birthday, don't you see?
You all must celebrate with me.

Throw ham and pork-rind in the pot,
Get sweetbreads, sow-tits boiling hot!
I want to throw a banquet which   65
Will make the powerful think I'm rich.
Go in and quickly work away;
When cook comes, we want no delay.
     [*Except for one personal* ATTENDANT, *Ballio's male* SLAVES *now enter the
     house.*]

I'm off to market, where I wish
To buy the market out of fish.   70
Lead on, my boy, and guard your back:
Let no one grab my money sack.

Just wait! It nearly slipped my mind
There's something else I've got to do.
You women! Listen to me please: 75
My next announcement is for you.
        [*Ballio's contingent of lovely ladies* (COURTESANS) *files out of his house
            in response to his call.*]
All you who live the languid life
Of dissipation and decay,
Famed mistresses of mighty men,
I'll learn your preference today: 80
Choose gluttony or liberty;
Siestas or self-interest.
Which girls I free and which I sell
I'll find out by a simple test.
Make sure I'm loaded down with loot   85
From lover-boys that you delight.
Bring in a full year's keep today
Or work the street tomorrow night.

Today's my birthday, as you know.
Bring on the lads who find you fun,   90
Who call you "sweetheart," "dearest darling,"
"Smoochie-pooch" or "honey-bun."
    Make sure they march up by platoon,
    Each bearing a beautiful birthday boon.

Why do I give you clothing, jewelry,   95
    Everything you need,
When you repay me with obnoxious
    Drunkenness and greed?
    You soak and guzzle, getting high,
    While I sit soberly and cry.   100

    So now I'm going to call your names,
        Proceeding one by one;
    Don't try to tell me, by and by,
        If any job's undone,
    That tasks have not been all assigned.   105
        Attention, everyone!

I'll start with you, Delectium,
The darling of the grain suppliers.
All your lovers own vast stores
Of golden wheat piled mountain high.   110
Get grain delivered to us, please,

For me and all my household staff—
Enough to see us through the year.
Bring me such wheaty affluence
The citizens will change my name   115
From Ballio, the pauper pimp,
To Jason, prince of opulence.
        [*Exit* DELECTIUM.]
CALIDORUS [*To* PSEUDOLUS.]   You hear this jailbird chattering?
    He's quite a loudmouth, don't you think?
PSEUDOLUS   Dear Pollux, yes! A foulmouth, too.   120
    Be quiet, though, and listen on!
BALLIO   Obscenium, your patrons are
    The butchers, rivals of the pimps:
    They make their living, just like us,
    By selling poor and tainted meat.   125
    Unless I get three meat-racks jammed
    With juicy carcasses today,
    Tomorrow I'll copy what was done
    To Dirce by the sons of Jove:[4]
    They bound her to a raging bull;   130
    I'll stretch you on an empty meat-rack.
        [*Exit* OBSCENIUM.]
PSEUDOLUS [*To* CALIDORUS.]   This person makes me blazing mad!
    To think the manly youth of Athens
    Let him go on living here!
    Where do they hide, those lusty lads   135
    Who get their loving from a pimp?
    Why don't they meet and all combine
    To rid our public of these pests?
    But hey, no way!
    I've been too simple, too naive.   140
    Where would they get the nerve to hurt
    The men their love enslaves them to?
    Their passion keeps them all from doing
    Things their pimps would not approve.
CALIDORUS   Be quiet!
PSEUDOLUS   Why?
CALIDORUS   You bother me   145
    When you drown out this fellow's words.
PSEUDOLUS   Then I'll shut up.
CALIDORUS   I wish you would,
    Instead of saying that you will.
BALLIO   It's your turn now, Gymnasium,
    All of whose lover-boys possess   150
    Untold reserves of olive oil.
    If oil's not dumped in leather sacks
    And carried here to me forthwith,
    I'll have *you* dumped in a leather sack

---

4. Amphion and Zethus. In revenge for their stepmother Dirce's harsh treatment of their mother, Antiope, they bound Dirce to the horns of a bull.

And carried to the whorehouse shed.   155
There you'll be issued with a couch
Where you will get no sleep, but where,
To the point of sheer exhaustion. . . . Do you
Get the drift of my remarks?
[See here, you snake! When you've so many   160
Boyfriends oozing olive oil,
Do any of your fellow slaves
Have hair a wee bit glossier?
Do I enjoy a salad that's
A smidgen tastier? I know,   165
You don't care very much for oil;
You like to drench yourself in wine.
I'll check your faults in one fell swoop
If my commands aren't all obeyed.]⁵
          [Exit GYMNASIUM.]
But you, who are always on the point   170
Of paying cash for liberty,
So skilled in promising, less skilled
In having promises fulfilled:
Phoenicium, it's you I mean,
You plaything of the upper class!   175
Unless your boyfriends' grand estates
Provide me all your keep today,
Tomorrow, dear Phoenicium,
I'll tan your hide Phoenician red
And pack you off to the whorehouse shed.   180
          [Exit PHOENICIUM.]

ACT I, SCENE 3

CALIDORUS   Pseudolus, don't you hear what he's saying?
PSEUDOLUS   Sir, my attention's undivided.
CALIDORUS   Help me: what should I send this man
    To stop my girl from going on sale?
PSEUDOLUS   Don't worry! Keep your mind unclouded;   5
    I'll look after you and me.
    This fellow and I've been friends for years;
    We've traded favors back and forth.
    I'll send him a great big birthday gift:
    A bulging bundle of misery.   10
CALIDORUS   What's the use?
PSEUDOLUS   Can't you change the subject?
CALIDORUS   But—
PSEUDOLUS   Tut!
CALIDORUS   I'm tortured!
PSEUDOLUS   Toughen up!
CALIDORUS   I can't.
PSEUDOLUS   Well, force yourself!

5. The bracketed passage is thought to be a later addition to the original text.

CALIDORUS How can I?

PSEUDOLUS Try to control your emotions, man!
Concentrate on constructive thoughts; 15
When things go wrong, don't pander to passion.

CALIDORUS That's all nonsense; there's no pleasure
In love unless you can play the fool.

PSEUDOLUS Must you?

CALIDORUS Pseudolus, let me be silly. Please!

PSEUDOLUS I'll let you, if you let me leave. 20

CALIDORUS Wait! Wait! I'll be just the way you want me.

PSEUDOLUS Now you're sounding sensible.

BALLIO It's late; time's wasting. Move, slave, move!

[BALLIO *and his* SLAVE *start to move offstage.*]

CALIDORUS Hey, he's leaving. Why not call him?

PSEUDOLUS [*Restraining* CALIDORUS.] Slow down! Easy does it.

CALIDORUS He
mustn't leave. 25

BALLIO Dammit, move, you lazy slave!

PSEUDOLUS [*Aloud to* BALLIO.] Birthday boy! Hey, birthday boy!
I'm calling you. Hey, birthday boy!
Come on back, take a look at us.
Though you're such a busy person, 30
We'll detain you. Wait! See,
People want to talk to you!

BALLIO What's this? Who'd hold up
A very busy man like me?

PSEUDOLUS A friend and helpmate from your past. 35

BALLIO The past is dead; I live right now.

PSEUDOLUS You blasted boor!

BALLIO You blasted bother!

CALIDORUS Seize the fellow; chase him!

BALLIO [*To his* SLAVE.] Move on, boy.

PSEUDOLUS Let's go round and block his way.

BALLIO Jupiter damn you, whoever you are! 40

PSEUDOLUS I wish you—

BALLIO —the same to you both!
Come on, forward march, my boy.

PSEUDOLUS May we not have a word with you?

BALLIO No, you may not when I'm not in the mood.

PSEUDOLUS Not even something advantageous? 45

BALLIO Will you or won't you let me leave?

PSEUDOLUS No, wait!

BALLIO Let go.

CALIDORUS Ballio, listen! Are you deaf?

BALLIO Yes, to empty words and wallets.

CALIDORUS I always gave you cash in the past.

BALLIO Cash in the past is not what I'm after. 50

CALIDORUS I'll give when I get it.

BALLIO You'll have when you've got it.

CALIDORUS Oh, how foolishly I've wasted

All my presents and payments to you!
BALLIO Now that your account's defunct   55
   You want to pay me off in words.
   Stupid boy! Your books are closed.
PSEUDOLUS Just realize who this boy is!
BALLIO I've known for ages who he *was*;
   He should discover who he *is*.   60
   [*To his* SLAVE.] Let's get walking.
PSEUDOLUS   Ballio, could you
   Grant us just a single glance?
   There may be filthy lucre.
BALLIO   *Lucre!*
   That's a word that's worth a glance.
   If I were involved in sacrifice   65
   To mighty Jupiter on high,
   Holding sacred vessels in my hands,
   And there and then I saw a chance
   Of finding filthy lucre—well,
   I'd ditch the whole divine affair.   70
   All else aside, lucre's one
   Religious force I can't resist.
PSEUDOLUS [*To* CALIDORUS.]   The gods we honor and revere
   This fellow holds in total scorn.
BALLIO [*Aside.*] I'll speak to him. [*To* PSEUDOLUS.] My kindest
   greetings,   75
   Most egregious slave in Athens!
PSEUDOLUS This lad and I would like the gods
   To shower blessings on your head;
   But, if you get your just deserts,
   The gods are bound to cut you dead.   80
BALLIO [*Ignoring* PSEUDOLUS.]   What's the trouble, Calidorus?
CALIDORUS Love and cruel lack of cash.
BALLIO "What a pity!" I might say—
   If pity kept my stomach full.
PSEUDOLUS O.K. We know the type you are: 85
   No need at all to advertise.
   But do you know what we want?
BALLIO Oh, Pollux! Pretty well: trouble for me!
PSEUDOLUS That, too; but there is something else.
   Come on, pay attention.
BALLIO   I'm listening.   90
   Since you see I'm very busy,
   Keep your story cut and dried.
PSEUDOLUS My man's ashamed, because he promised
   On the appointed day to give you
   Twenty minas for his girl,   95
   And hasn't arranged delivery.
BALLIO If you've got to bear some burden,
   Shame's far easier than disgust.
   He hasn't delivered: he's feeling down;
   I haven't collected: I'm fed up!   100

PSEUDOLUS He'll come across, he'll raise the money;
    Just you wait a few more days.
    You see, he's terribly afraid
    You'll sell his girl friend out of spite.
BALLIO If he wanted, he had a chance   105
    To pay me the money long ago.
CALIDORUS What if I didn't have the cash?
BALLIO If you were in love, you'd have floated a loan.
    You could have gone to a financier;
    You could have carried a carrying charge;   110
    You could have defrauded dear old Dad.
PSEUDOLUS This boy defraud his dad? Outrageous!
    No danger you would ever suggest
    A moral act!
BALLIO   That would be un-pimp-ly.
CALIDORUS How could I defraud my father,   115
    When he's such a sly old man?
    And even if I had the chance,
    Filial love forbids!
BALLIO   I see.
    Then hug that filial love of yours
    At night instead of Phoenicium.   120
    But since you apparently prefer
    To put filial love before romance,
    Is every man alive your father?
    Is there no one you could ask
    To lend you money?
CALIDORUS   Lend? Oh, no: 125
    The word itself is dead and buried.
PSEUDOLUS Holy Herc, no lending these days!
    Bloated bankers leave the table
    Gorged on debts that they've recalled,
    And let their creditors go starving;[6]   130
    All the world is far too cagey
    Ever to credit another man.
CALIDORUS I'm most unhappy. I can't find
    A solitary silver piece;
    And so, unhappily I die   135
    Of love and lack of currency.
BALLIO Corner the market in olive oil!
    Speculate and sell for cash.
    By Herc, I'm sure that you could put
    At least two hundred in your pocket.   140
CALIDORUS Fat chance! The wretched law declares
    I'm underage.[7] Everyone's scared
    To give me credit.
BALLIO   That's my kind
    Of law: I'm scared to give you credit.

---

6. A year before the play was produced, bankers (who did their business at tables in the forum) were punished for cheating their own creditors. 7. I.e., under twenty-five and so legally prohibited from borrowing or engaging in business.

PSEUDOLUS   Credit! Hey, aren't you satisfied   145
  To know how useful he's been to you?
BALLIO   There's no such thing as a useful lover
  Unless he gives perpetually.
  Let him give, give; and when there's
  Nothing left, then let him cease to love.   150
CALIDORUS   Have you no pity?
BALLIO   Look: you're coming
  Empty-handed. Words don't clink.
  Yet I sincerely hope you'll live
  And thrive.
PSEUDOLUS   You speak as if he's dying.
BALLIO   Dead, as far as I'm concerned—   155
  If he keeps on talking the way he has.
  A lover's given up the ghost
  When he starts pleading with a pimp.
  Learn to sing a loud lament
  That has a silvery, tinkling tune;   160
  Toward your present woeful dirge
  About your lack of cash, I feel
  A stepmother's sympathy.
PSEUDOLUS   What?
  Were you once married to his father?
BALLIO   God forbid!
PSEUDOLUS   Do as we ask you, Ballio.   165
  Give *me* credit, if you're afraid
  To trust this boy. Within three days
  By land or sea (or somewhere else)
  I'll scrape this money up for you.
BALLIO   Give *you* credit?
PSEUDOLUS   Why not?
BALLIO   Well,   170
  To give you credit would be much
  Like tying up a hungry dog
  With twisted strips of mutton tripe.
CALIDORUS   How, when I'm so deserving, can you
  Show this kind of gratitude?   175
BALLIO   Well, what do you want?
CALIDORUS   I want you to wait,
  Six days only, more or less,
  And don't sell her or destroy me,
  The man who loves her.
BALLIO   Oh, cheer up!
  I'm prepared to wait six months.   180
CALIDORUS   Hurray! You dear, delightful man!
BALLIO   Hang on—do you want me to increase
  Your happiness a hundredfold?
CALIDORUS   How so?
BALLIO   By telling you, right now
  Phoenicium is not for sale.   185

CALIDORUS   She isn't?

BALLIO   That's a fact, by Herc!

CALIDORUS [*Ecstatically.*]   Pseudolus, go, get holy victims,
   Beasts and butchers; I would pay
   This Jove a sacrifice divine.
   I now regard our friend right here   190
   As a mightier Jove than Jupiter.

BALLIO   No victims, please. I much prefer
   To be appeased with chunks of lamb.

CALIDORUS   Hurry! Move! Go get the lambs!
   Do you hear what Jupiter has said?   195

PSEUDOLUS   I'll soon be back; but first I've got
   To run outside the city gate.

CALIDORUS   Why there?

PSEUDOLUS   I'll find two human butchers,[8]
   Armed with deadly warning bells;
   And while I'm there, I'll bring two flocks   200
   Of weeping-willow flogging whips:
   Today there'll be a sweet supply
   Of offerings for this Jupiter.

BALLIO   Go hang yourself!

PSEUDOLUS   No, hanging's what
   They do to a pimp-ly Jupiter.   205

BALLIO   You wouldn't stand to gain a thing
   If I should die.

PSEUDOLUS   Why not?

BALLIO   Well, look:
   If I were dead, in all of Athens
   There'd be no one worse than you.

CALIDORUS   Holy Herc, you've got to tell me—   210
   Answer seriously, please:
   You haven't got my girl for sale,
   My lovely, dear Phoenicium?

BALLIO   She's not for sale; by Pollux, no.
   You see, I sold her long ago.   215

CALIDORUS   You sold her? How?

BALLIO   Right off the stall:
   Neck and gizzard, guts and all.[9]

CALIDORUS   You sold my girl?

BALLIO   Precisely so;
   For twenty minas.

CALIDORUS   Twenty?

BALLIO   Yes.
   Or four times five, if you prefer.   220
   I sold her to a soldier boy,
   A captain out of Macedon.
   He paid me fifteen in advance.

CALIDORUS   What am I hearing?

---

8. Public executioners.   9. Like cattle, who were sold either gutted or with their entrails.

BALLIO   That your girl's   225
Converted into currency.

CALIDORUS   How could you?

BALLIO   Well, I felt like it;
And she was mine.

CALIDORUS   Ho! Pseudolus:
Run, fetch a sword!

PSEUDOLUS   Why do I need
A sword?

CALIDORUS   To kill this man—and me!

PSEUDOLUS   Why not just destroy yourself?   230
This fellow soon will starve to death.

CALIDORUS [To BALLIO.]   What do you say, you ultimate
Extreme of human perjury?
Did you swear that you would never
Sell her to anyone but me?   235

BALLIO   I did, and I admit it.

CALIDORUS   Well, then.
Hadn't you pledged, and formally, too?

BALLIO   Yes, but I fudged; I normally do.

CALIDORUS   Perjury! You criminal!

BALLIO   I put some money in my pocket.   240
If that's criminal, don't knock it.
You've got virtue and family fame—
But not a penny to your name.

CALIDORUS   Pseudolus, stand on the other side
And pile the curses on him.

PSEUDOLUS   Fine.   245
I wouldn't be more keen to run
To the praetor for my liberty.[1]

CALIDORUS   Bring on the insults!

PSEUDOLUS   Here we go;
My tongue will tear you limb from limb.
Shameless!

BALLIO   All right.

PSEUDOLUS   *Criminal!*   250

BALLIO   That's true enough.

PSEUDOLUS   *You whipping-boy!*

BALLIO   Why not?

PSEUDOLUS   *Grave-robber!*

BALLIO   Certainly.

PSEUDOLUS   *Filthy jailbird!*

BALLIO   Excellent!

PSEUDOLUS   *Treacherous swindler!*

BALLIO   That's my style.

PSEUDOLUS   *Foul assassin!*

BALLIO   Yes. Continue.   255

---

1. One of the procedures for legally setting a slave free involved the master and slave appearing before a magistrate such as a praetor, whose functions included administration of the law.

CALIDORUS	*Sacrilegious!*
BALLIO	I admit it.
CALIDORUS	*Perjurer!*
BALLIO	An old refrain.
CALIDORUS	*Lawbreaker!*
BALLIO	Most emphatically.
PSEUDOLUS	*Youth-corrupter!*
BALLIO	Ouch! That stings.
CALIDORUS	*Thief!*
BALLIO	Touché!
PSEUDOLUS	*Deserter!*
BALLIO	Bravo!
CALIDORUS	*Public fraud!*
BALLIO	Too obvious.
PSEUDOLUS	*Crooked cheater!*
CALIDORUS	*Dirty pimp!*
PSEUDOLUS	*You crud!*
BALLIO	Your voices are divine.
CALIDORUS	*You beat your father and your mother!*

BALLIO   And what's more, I killed them both 265
  Rather than provide them food;[2]
  Was that an awful thing to do?

PSEUDOLUS   We're pouring all our juicy words
  In a bottomless pot—a waste of time.

BALLIO   Is there nothing else you'd like to say? 270

CALIDORUS   Are you incapable of shame?

BALLIO   Or you—a lover who's been found
  As empty as a rotten nut?
  [*Reconsidering.*] And yet, although you've shouted many
  Nasty noises at my head, 275
  If that captain doesn't bring
  The other five he owes me still
  By today, the final deadline
  Formally agreed for payment—
  Well, if he can't deliver, then 280
  I think I can act in character.

CALIDORUS   How's that?

BALLIO   If *you* bring me the money,
  Then I'll break my word with *him:*
  I'm that kind of character. I'd gladly
  Chat with you, but it's not worthwhile. 285
  If you're broke, it's a hopeless effort
  Pleading with me to pity you.
  Here's my final word on the subject:
  Focus on the job at hand.

CALIDORUS   You're leaving?

---

2. Mistreatment of parents was particularly horrifying to the Romans, with their deeply traditional notions of paternal authority.

BALLIO   I've got many worries   290
  On my mind.
      [BALLIO *and his* SLAVE *leave for the marketplace, stage left.*]
PSEUDOLUS   You'll soon have more!
  [*To audience.*] I own that fellow now, unless
  All gods and men abandon me.
  I'll bone and fillet him, the way
  A cook prepares a slippery eel.   295
  Now, Calidorus, give me your
  Attention.
CALIDORUS   What is your command?
PSEUDOLUS   I want this town[3] placed under siege;
  I've got to capture it today.
  To do that, I'll require a man   300
  Who's wily, clever, cunning, crafty,
  Able to execute commands,
  Not fall asleep when he's on watch.
CALIDORUS   What do you intend to do?
PSEUDOLUS   When the time is ripe, I'll let you know.   305
  I don't want to repeat myself:
  That's how plays become too long.
CALIDORUS   Very good and very fair.
PSEUDOLUS   Hurry! Bring him right away.
CALIDORUS   Of all our friends, there are so few   310
  A man can really depend upon.
PSEUDOLUS   I know that. You've a double job:
  Prepare a prime selection drawn from
  All our friends; then pick out one
  That we can really count on.   315
CALIDORUS   I'll have him here at once.
PSEUDOLUS   Get moving,
  Won't you? Talking means delay.

ACT I, SCENE 4

[*As* CALIDORUS *leaves (stage right) to find an accomplice,* PSEUDOLUS *moves downstage to address the audience.*]

PSEUDOLUS   He's gone; you're on your own now, Pseudolus.
  Now what'll you do? You've loaded master's son
  With precious promises; can you get the goods?
  If you haven't a particle of a proper plan
  You can't begin to weave a cunning cloth   5
  Or execute a definite design.
  But look at the poet: when he starts to write,
  He seeks what doesn't exist, and then he finds it;
  He makes invented fiction look like truth.

---

3. Ballio. From here on, Pseudolus repeatedly refers to his plot against the pimp as if it were the siege of a city.

All right, I'll be a poet! Twenty coins,   10
Which don't exist on the face of earth, I'll find.
Ages ago I said I'd give him the money,
Hoping to lay a snare for our old man;
But somehow "Dad" got wind of what I wanted.

    [SIMO *and* CALLIPHO *appear from the forum, stage left.*]
I must control my voice and hold my tongue;   15
Look! Here's my master Simo coming this way,
Strolling with his neighbor Callipho.
Out of this old tomb today I'll dig up
Twenty coins to give to master's son.
I'll step aside and hear their conversation.   20

ACT I, SCENE 5

[*Enter the two old men and neighbors,* SIMO *and* CALLIPHO. SIMO, *who is Calidorus' father and Pseudolus' master, is severe in temperament;* CALLIPHO *is more tolerant and urbane.*]

SIMO   If all the spendthrifts and the lovesick boys
   In Athens met to elect a president,
   I'm sure that no one would defeat my son.
   He's the only topic of the town—
   How he wants to free his girl by scrounging   5
   Money to save her. People tell me this;
   In fact, I sniffed the truth a while back
   But pretended not to know.
PSEUDOLUS [*Aside.*]   His son must stink.
   The plot is killed; the whole affair is jammed.
   I meant to take this route to silver city;
   Now I find the road's completely blocked.   10
   He's on to us: no spoils for the despoilers!
CALLIPHO   People who blab or listen to slanderous gossip,
   If I were in charge of things, would all be hanged:
   Blabbers by the tongue, listeners by the ears.
   These stories that they tell you—that your son   15
   Is so in love he'd swindle you of silver—
   Chances are that these reports are lies.
   But even if they're absolutely true,
   In the light of present morals, what did he do
   Remarkable? What's new if a young man   20
   Loves or frees a mistress?
PSEUDOLUS[*Aside.*]   Charming fellow!
SIMO   As an old man I object.
CALLIPHO   But that's no use.
   You shouldn't have done these things when you were young.
   A father must be pure if he insists
   That his son be purer than he's been himself.   25
   When you were young, the damage that you caused

Was enough to share with every man alive!
"A chip off the old block": what's the big surprise?
PSEUDOLUS [*Aside.*] O Zeus, how few obliging men there are.   30
Hey! That's the kind of father a son should have.
SIMO   Who's talking here? It's my slave Pseudolus.
He's the corrupter of my son, the crook!
He's the leader, he's the teacher, he's the one
That I want crucified.
CALLIPHO   Now that's just silly,   35
Flying off the handle. How much better
To go up and ask him diplomatically
Whether those reports are true or false.
When times are tough, good heart is half the battle.
SIMO   I'll take your advice.
PSEUDOLUS [*Aside.*]   Here they come, Pseudolus.   40
Prepare your speech to take the old man on.
[*Aloud.*] Good health to master first, that's only fair;
What health is left can be his neighbor's share.
SIMO   Good day. What are you doing?
PSEUDOLUS   Standing here like this.
SIMO   See his attitude, Callipho? King of the roost!   45
CALLIPHO   I think he displays a fine self-confidence.
PSEUDOLUS   A slave who's free of crime and free of cunning
Should stand tall in his master's company.
CALLIPHO   We want to question you about some news
That's reached us, sort of drifting through a cloud.   50
SIMO   His words will now convince you that you've taken on
Not Pseudolus, but Socrates.
PSEUDOLUS   All right. I realize you've always put me down;
I know you've got no confidence in me.
You'd like me worthless; still, I'll be first-class.   55
SIMO   Keep your ear space vacant, Pseudolus;
Admit my words as tenants for a while.
PSEUDOLUS   Speak your mind, though I'm furious at you.
SIMO   A slave, furious at me, your master?
PSEUDOLUS   Does that
Seem so strange?
SIMO   Great Herc! According to you,   60
I've got to guard against your rage. You plan
To batter me the way I batter you.
[*To* CALLIPHO.] What do you think?
CALLIPHO   I feel his anger's justified,
When you place no confidence in him.
SIMO   All right,
Let him rage! I'll stop him doing any damage.   65
[*To* PSEUDOLUS.] Well? What about my question?
PSEUDOLUS   Go head and ask.
Treat my knowledge as your Delphic oracle.
SIMO   Pay attention, then, and remember your promise.
What do you say? Do you know my son's in love
With a music-girl?

PSEUDOLUS [*In oracular tones.*]   Yea, yea, forsooth.

SIMO   And he wants her
    freed?   70

PSEUDOLUS   In truth, forsooth.

SIMO   And twenty silver minas,
    Through skulduggery and dirty tricks,
    You're planning to snatch from me?

PSEUDOLUS   I? Snatch from you?

SIMO   Yes. To give my son, to free his girl.
    Confess it! Speak: in truth, forsooth?

PSEUDOLUS   In truth, forsooth.   75

SIMO   He admits it! Didn't I tell you, Callipho?

CALLIPHO   I remember.

SIMO   The moment you knew this, why was it
    Concealed from me? Why didn't I hear?

PSEUDOLUS   I'll tell you.
    I didn't want to breed a wicked custom
    By denouncing master A to master B.   80

SIMO   This fellow's fit for service in the mill!

CALLIPHO   But Simo, has he sinned?

SIMO   You bet he has!

PSEUDOLUS   Please stop. I keep my own books, Callipho;
    My sins belong to me. Just listen; I'll
    Explain why I shut you out of the love affair.   85
    I knew I'd land in the gristmill,[4] if I spoke.

SIMO   Didn't you know the mill would be your lot
    If you kept mum?

PSEUDOLUS   I knew.

SIMO   Why wasn't I told?

PSEUDOLUS   One fate was instant; one was more remote.
    Silence gained me a day or two of grace.   90

SIMO   What'll you do now? There's no hope of pinching
    Money out of me; I'm wide awake.
    I'll pass a law: *"Don't lend to Pseudolus!"*

PSEUDOLUS   Ye gods! I'll never beg from another man
    While you're alive. You'll give the cash yourself.   95
    I'll wheedle it from you.

SIMO   From me?

PSEUDOLUS   Precisely.

SIMO   Holy Herc, knock out my eye, if I give.

PSEUDOLUS   You'll give.
    Watch out; you've got fair warning.

CALLIPHO   One thing's sure:
    If you succeed, you'll stage a stunning coup!

PSEUDOLUS   I will.

SIMO   And if you don't?

PSEUDOLUS   Then flog me with canes.   100
    But what if I pull it off?

---

4. Hard labor often threatened to slaves in comedy. The huge stones that ground the wheat were turned
by animals or slaves.

SIMO   So help me Jove,
  You'll live your life unpunished.
PSEUDOLUS   Don't forget!
SIMO   You think I can't take care, when I'm forewarned?
PSEUDOLUS   You're warned: take care! You're told: take care! *Take care!*
  Those hands will bestow the cash on me today.   105
CALLIPHO   He's a living masterpiece if he keeps his word.
PSEUDOLUS   Haul me off into slavery if I fail.
SIMO   Very generous! You're mine already.
PSEUDOLUS   Do you want to hear a more amazing story?
CALLIPHO   Gladly! I love to listen to you talk.   110
PSEUDOLUS [*To* SIMO.]   Before I tackle you, I'll first engage
  Another foe in a memorable match.
SIMO   What other foe?
PSEUDOLUS   This pimp, your neighbor here.
  Through trickery and dirty double-dealing,
  I'll deprive our precious pandering pimp   115
  Of the music-girl your son adores.
SIMO   You will?
PSEUDOLUS   The two campaigns will be finished by this evening.
SIMO   If you carry out these tasks, as you declare,
  You'll be mightier than King Agathocles.[5]
  But if you fail, won't I be justified   120
  In sending you to the mill?
PSEUDOLUS   Not just for a day,
  But for all eternity! If I succeed,
  Will you give me the cash to pay the pimp,
  Of your own free will?
CALLIPHO [*To* SIMO.]   That's reasonable and fair;
  Say yes.
SIMO   But something's just occurred to me.   125
  What if there's collusion, Callipho,
  Or they've arranged some underhanded deal
  To dupe me of my wealth?
PSEUDOLUS   Not even I
  Would have the nerve to stoop so low! Look here:
  If there's collusion, Simo, or if we   130
  Have ever wheeled and dealed in such a way,
  Then use your whip like a writing instrument
  And scratch red letters all across my back.
SIMO   Your comedy can start now, any time.
PSEUDOLUS   Help me out today, please, Callipho;   135
  Don't get involved in any other scheme.
CALLIPHO   I had set up a visit to the country.
PSEUDOLUS   Un-set it then; upset your settled plans.
CALLIPHO   All right, I'll choose to stay on your account;
  I yearn to watch you in action, Pseudolus.   140
  And if I see him holding back the cash

---

5. Rose from humble origins to become tyrant and then king of Syracuse in Sicily, 316–289 B.C.E.

He promised, I'll come through with it myself.
SIMO   I won't renege.
PSEUDOLUS   By Pollux, if you do,
  You'll be dunned to death with a devastating din.
  Come on now, move along inside, you two,
  And give my tricks some room: it's their turn now.   145
CALLIPHO   All right; you'll get your way,
PSEUDOLUS   Remember, don't
  Leave home today.
CALLIPHO   I promise you my help.
    [CALLIPHO *enters his house.*]
SIMO   Well, I'm off to the forum. I'll be back here.
PSEUDOLUS   Make it soon!
    [*Exit* SIMO, *stage left.* PSEUDOLUS *moves downstage again to address the*
    audience.]
  I suspect that you're suspicious of me now.   150
  You think I'm making these grand promises
  To entertain you, till our play is done.
  You don't expect me to do what I said I would.
  Well, I won't back down. One fact I know for sure:
  I don't quite know just how I'll pull it off . . .   155
  And yet I'll manage! Somehow every actor ought
  To bring some novel innovation to the stage.
  If he can't, he should give way to one who can.

  I think I'll step inside here for a while
  To drill my regiment of roguery.
    I'll hurry back; expect a brief delay.   160
    Here's music[6] that will charm the time away.
    [*Exit into house.*]

Act II

[*A very short time has elapsed.* PSEUDOLUS *emerges from Simo's house, in obvious*
good spirits.]

ACT II, SCENE 1

PSEUDOLUS   Great Jupiter! How sweet to find
  That everything is working out!
  I've chased anxiety and doubt
  From this grand scheme I have in mind.
  It's stupid to entrust a plan
  To a weak or wishy-washy man;   5
  For all endeavors must depend
  On how much effort you expend.

  Inside my brain I've so prepared
  My tricky troops, my sneaky squad   10

---

6. An interlude of instrumental music often marked major divisions in the action of Roman comedy.

Of flimflam, fakery, and fraud,
That, after war has been declared,
My ancestral fortitude, combined
With hard work and a nasty mind,
Will snare my enemies with ease,   15
And falsely force them to their knees.

This adversary that I share
With all you lusty men out there,
This Ballio I'll bash and break:
Just pay attention, for my sake.   20

Today I will besiege this town,
Draw up my legions, tear it down;
And when I've stormed and scaled that wall
(My men won't find it hard at all),
I'll lead my army straightaway   25
To a second town, all old and gray.
This will provide my friends and me
With loads of booty, duty-free.
My destiny, the world will know,
Is striking panic in the foe.   30
It's in my blood: I feel the need
To carry out some doughty deed—
A hero's act, enshrined in fame,
That will perpetuate my name.

But who's this fellow striding up?   35
    He's quite unknown to me;
And why's he coming with that sword?
    I'll step aside and see.

ACT II, SCENE 2

[From the harbor (stage right) there appears a figure dressed in the conventional traveler's outfit of cloak, broad-brimmed hat, and conspicuous sword. It is HARPAX, *the somewhat dim-witted messenger slave of the Macedonian captain.]*

HARPAX   Here we are, the neighborhood
    My master carefully described.
    Everything seems to correspond
    With my instructions from the captain:
    Seventh block beyond the gate,   5
    The home of Ballio the pimp,
    The fellow I'm supposed to give
    This token and this moneybag.
    But I could use some guidance now.
    Which one's the pimp's establishment?   10

PSEUDOLUS [*Aside.*]   Quiet! Shh! I've got this man,
   If heaven and earth approve my plan.
   But I'll require a new invention:
   Here's a sudden, new dimension.
   Let's proceed with all dispatch;   15
   Scrap the old scheme, start from scratch!
   I'll pulverize and quite destroy
   This regimental errand-boy.
HARPAX   I'll knock on the door and see if I
   Can rouse up anyone inside.   20
   [*He knocks loudly on Ballio's door.*]
PSEUDOLUS [*Rushing up to* HARPAX].   Knock it off, whoever you are;
   Please save your knocks and spare these doors.
   I'm here to plead on their behalf
   As guardian patron of the portals.
HARPAX   Are you Ballio?
PSEUDOLUS   Not quite,   25
   But I'm Assistant Ballio.
HARPAX   What's that supposed to mean?
PSEUDOLUS   It means
   I'm Exchequer, In-checker, Prince of the Pantry.
HARPAX   Sort of majordomo?
PSEUDOLUS   Higher up
   In rank: I'm General Factotum.   30
HARPAX   What's your status, slave or free?
PSEUDOLUS   Right at the moment, I'm a slave.
HARPAX   You look the part. You don't appear
   A candidate for liberty.
PSEUDOLUS   Shouldn't you check the looking glass   35
   When you've got insults to unload?
HARPAX [*Aside.*]   This fellow's just a troublemaker.
PSEUDOLUS [*Aside.*]   Gods be gracious, here's an anvil
   For my craft! I'll hammer out
   A brazen masterpiece today.   40
HARPAX [*Aside.*]   Why's he talking to himself?
PSEUDOLUS   Look here, you youngster!
HARPAX   What do you want?
PSEUDOLUS   Do you or don't you represent
   That Macedonian officer
   Who bought a beauty from our stock,   45
   Who paid my master, Mister Pimp,
   A cash advance of fifteen minas,
   Five still owing?
HARPAX   I'm your man.
   But how in the world do you know me?
   Where have you seen or talked to me?   50
   I've never made a trip to Athens
   In the past, and till today,
   I'd never laid an eye on you.
PSEUDOLUS   It's just because you look the part.

When he left town, we all agreed   55
The balance would fall due today,
But no cold comfort has arrived.

HARPAX   Well, here it is.

PSEUDOLUS   You've brought it?

HARPAX   Yes.

PSEUDOLUS   Then why so slow to hand it over?

HARPAX   Give it to you?

PSEUDOLUS   Yes, Herc, to me!   60
I'm Ballio's financial wizard:
Bursar, purser, debt-disperser.

HARPAX   Holy Herc, if you controlled
The treasure of almighty Jove,
I'd never trust you with a single   65
Silver sliver!

PSEUDOLUS [Reaching for the bag.]   Quick as a wink
We'll see your debt discharged.

HARPAX [Protecting the bag.]   I'd rather keep these funds tied up.

PSEUDOLUS   Damn you! It's very obvious   70
You're smearing my integrity—
As though I'd never handled trust
Accounts a thousand times as large.

HARPAX   Well, maybe others have more faith;
You don't inspire my confidence.   75

PSEUDOLUS   Are you suggesting I might want
To con the silver out of you?

HARPAX   No. You're the source of that suggestion;
My suspicions are my own.
But what's your name?   80

PSEUDOLUS [Aside.]   This pimp has a slave called Syrus.
I'll pretend that's me [Aloud.] I'm Syrus.

HARPAX   Syrus?

PSEUDOLUS   Yessir, that's my name.

HARPAX   We're wasting time. If your master's home,
Why don't you call him to the door,   85
So I can get my business finished
Here, whatever your name may be.

PSEUDOLUS   If he were home, I'd summon him.
But trusting me with all the cash
Would be a more conclusive act   90
Than paying him.

HARPAX   Conclusive? Sure!
I'd close the deal and kiss it sweet
Goodbye! Of course, I realize
You're hot and bothered when you see
The money slipping through your claws.   95
I won't negotiate with anyone
But Ballio in person.

PSEUDOLUS   He's occupied and busy now:
He's got a case before the judge.

HARPAX   Good luck to him! I'll just return   100
   Another time, when he's at home.
   But take this letter from me, please,
   And give it to him. Inside he'll find
   The token our masters both agreed
   To use in dealing with the girl.   105
PSEUDOLUS   I understand. Your captain wanted
   Her released to anyone
   Who brought the cash, together with
   His portrait image, stamped in wax.
   He left a specimen with us.   110
HARPAX   You know about the whole affair.
PSEUDOLUS   Why shouldn't I?
HARPAX   Then give him the token.
PSEUDOLUS   O.K. But what's your name?
HARPAX   Harpax.[7]
PSEUDOLUS   Harp off, Harpax! You're not welcome.
   You won't get inside our house   115
   To play your snatching harpy acts.
HARPAX   I snatch great foes right off the battlefield:
   That's how I got my name.
PSEUDOLUS   I'm more inclined to think
   You snatch great pots right off the pantry shelf.   120
HARPAX   Not true! But Syrus, do you know
   What I would like?
PSEUDOLUS   I'll know if you tell me.
HARPAX   I've got a room beyond the gate,
   The third tavern on the right;
   My hostess is a tubby, chubby,   125
   Gimpy grandma, name of Chrysis.
PSEUDOLUS   What do you want from me?
HARPAX   Please reach me there, when your master comes.
PSEUDOLUS   As you would have it, certainly.
HARPAX   I'm now so weary from my travels,   130
   I must rest and freshen up.
PSEUDOLUS   A wise and admirable plan.
   But please make sure you don't go missing
   When I need to summon you.
HARPAX   No fear. I'll have a delicious meal,   135
   And then an after-dinner nap.
PSEUDOLUS   I quite approve.
HARPAX   And is that all?
PSEUDOLUS   Go off to slumberland.
HARPAX   I'm going.
   [Exit HARPAX, stage right.]
PSEUDOLUS   Just you listen, Harpy-boy:
   Bundle up in lots of blankets;   140
   Sweating makes a person sweet.

7. A name related to a Greek verb meaning "seize" or "plunder."

ACT II, SCENE 3

PSEUDOLUS [*Moving downstage to confide in the audience.*]   Immortal
    gods! I think this fellow
Saved my skin by coming here.
He's paid the ticket for my trip
From Way-off-course to Journey's-end.
Father Nick-of-Time himself   5
Couldn't have made a timelier entrance
Than this timeliest of letters
That has landed in my lap.

Here I've found my horn of plenty—
Plenty of everything I need: 10
A horn of hoax and hocus-pocus,
Sleight of hand, bamboozlement;
Plenty of cash, and a horny girl
To hug my master's horny son.

How I'm going to swagger now,   15
When I've got cause for confidence!
Already I'd laid out a plan
Of action, scheming how to snatch
The little lady from the pimp;
It all took shape inside my mind,   20
Well ordered, beautifully arranged.

But this will often be the case:
The plans of a hundred clever men
Can be overturned by a single goddess—
Luck. And isn't it the truth?   25
Depending on how a person uses Luck
He may succeed, and everyone of course
Will then pronounce him sensible and wise.
If a scheme should turn out well, then all the world
Declares him shrewd; but if disaster strikes,   30
We look upon him as an utter fool.

Well, we're the fools; we just can't see our folly!
All of us pursue our greedy goals,
Grasping at gain, as if we possibly
Could judge what serves our real interest.   35
We sacrifice the real world
By chasing unreality.
The outcome is predictable:
We groan and moan our lives away,
While death creeps closer all the while.   40

Enough profound philosophy!
My lectures always last too long.

Immortal gods! My little fib
Was worth its weight in platinum—
That sudden, spur-of-the-moment claim   45
That I belonged to Ballio.
Now I'll use this letter here
To dupe three victims: master, pimp,
And military messenger.

What's this? Oh bliss! I think another   50
Wish I made is coming true.
Look: Calidorus is approaching,
Leading someone by the hand.

ACT II, SCENE 4

[As PSEUDOLUS *steps aside to watch and listen,* CALIDORUS *returns (stage right) with* CHARINUS, *a bright and appealing youth of about his own age.*]

CALIDORUS   Sweet and bitter, I've revealed
    The truth in its entirety.
    You know my passion and my pain;
    You know my abject poverty.
CHARINUS   I remember everything;   5
    Just let me know what I should do.
CALIDORUS   Pseudolus commanded me
    To find a strong and sympathetic
    Friend, and then to bring him here.
CHARINUS   You've followed orders to the letter: 10
    Here's a friend and sympathy.
    But that man Pseudolus of yours
    Is new to me.
CALIDORUS   A living masterpiece!
    He's my inventive genius.
    He told me he could carry out   15
    The project I discussed with you.
PSEUDOLUS [*Aside.*]   I'll try the grand, heroic style.
CALIDORUS   Is that a voice?
PSEUDOLUS   Oh yea, rejoice!
    Dire despot, unto thee I bow;
    Pseudolus' sovereign lord art thou.
    A threefold pleasure, thrice prepared,   20
    Three victims cunningly ensnared
    Thou shalt possess: a triple treat;
    A triform triumph of deceit.
    Judge not this letter by its size:
    It holds a vast and precious prize.   25
CALIDORUS   That's him.
CHARINUS   A bold, bombastic beggar!
PSEUDOLUS   Forward march, extend your arm,
    And greet the answer to your prayer.

CALIDORUS   Pray, how should I greet you, Pseudolus?   30
  As Wishful Hope or Wish Fulfilled?
PSEUDOLUS   As both, I'd say.
CALIDORUS   As both, good day!
  But what's the news?
PSEUDOLUS   Dispel your fear!
CALIDORUS [*Identifying* CHARINUS *for* PSEUDOLUS.]   I packed this man
    out.
PSEUDOLUS   Come again?
CALIDORUS   I picked him out, I meant to say.   35
PSEUDOLUS   Who is he?
CALIDORUS   Charinus.
PSEUDOLUS   Gracious me!
  A graceful name! My gratitude.[8]
CHARINUS   Look, if I can be of service,
  Say the word.
PSEUDOLUS   Thanks just the same.
  Bless you, Charinus, I don't want   40
  The two of us to bother you.
CHARINUS   Could you two be a bother? Nothing
  Bothers me.
PSEUDOLUS   Then wait a while.
CALIDORUS   What's that you've got?
PSEUDOLUS   A letter
  I waylaid just now; a token, too.   45
CALIDORUS   A token? What do you mean, a token?
PSEUDOLUS   One the captain sent this way.
  His flunky was delivering it,
  Along with five bright silver coins;
  He'd come to fetch your ladylove,   50
  But I threw dust into his eyes.
CALIDORUS   How?
PSEUDOLUS   This audience has paid
  To see us act our comedy.
  They know precisely how it happened;
  You'll get caught up later on.   55
CALIDORUS   What's our next move?
PSEUDOLUS   Today your girl
  Will be free to take you in her arms.
CALIDORUS   Me?
PSEUDOLUS   Yes you, yourself, in person,
  If yours truly lives so long;
  And if you can find a man to help me—   60
  Quickly!
CHARINUS   What should he be like?
PSEUDOLUS   Immoral, clever, cunning, one
  Who quickly gets the hang of things

---

8. A pun: *Charinus* suggests the Greek word *charis*, "thanks" or "favor."

And then relies on native wit
To see what action he should take.
Someone unknown in these parts.   65

CHARINUS   If he's a slave, could that create
A problem?

PSEUDOLUS   Not at all; I much
Prefer the slave to the freeborn.[9]

CHARINUS   Well, I think I can provide your man: 70
Quick-witted, rotten to the core.
My father sent him from Carystus;[1]
So far, he hasn't ventured from
Our house, and never until yesterday
Had he set foot in Athens.   75

PSEUDOLUS   Wonderful! But I'll still need
To float a loan—five silver minas,
Which I'll pay back today; you see,
His father [*Pointing to* CALIDORUS.] owes a debt to me.

CHARINUS   I'll lend you the money; look no farther.   80

PSEUDOLUS   What a dear, obliging man!
I'll also need a cloak, a dagger,
And a broad-brimmed hat.

CHARINUS   Can do.

PSEUDOLUS   Immortal gods! This fellow's not
Charinus, he's sweet Charity!   85
Tell me about your father's slave:
Has he any sense about him?

CHARINUS   Armpit scents: he stinks to heaven.

PSEUDOLUS   Phew! We'll get him longer sleeves.
Can he be sanguine, sharp, and keen?   90

CHARINUS   His blood is two parts vinegar.

PSEUDOLUS   But what if he has to tap his veins
For sweeter fluids?

CHARINUS   Sweeter? He'll drip
Spiced liqueur and raisin brandy,
Muscatel and honey-mead;   95
In fact, he had a notion once
To start a walking winery.

PSEUDOLUS   Touché, Charinus! You're a treat;
You fleece me at my favorite game.
But how shall I address your flunky?   100

CHARINUS   Simia, alias Mister Monkey.[2]

PSEUDOLUS   When it's windy, can he whirl?

CHARINUS   He'd teach a twister how to twirl.

PSEUDOLUS   Is he cautious?

CHARINUS   Maybe not:
He's often cautioned, never caught.   105

PSEUDOLUS   What if they nail him fast and firm?

9. A slave could be unscrupulous in ways thought beneath a free man.   1. A city on Euboea, the long
island stretching along the north coast of the Athenian territory.   2. The name suggests the Greek *simos*,
"snub-nosed."

CHARINUS   He's just an eel: away he'll squirm.
PSEUDOLUS   And is he sharp at dirty tricks?
CHARINUS   Sharp enough for politics.
PSEUDOLUS   The man's an ideal choice, to judge   110
  From your account.
CHARINUS   If you only knew!
  He'll glance at you, and straightaway
  He'll tell you what you want him for.
  But what's your proposal?
PSEUDOLUS   I'll explain.
  When I have got him all dressed up,   115
  I want this fellow to become
  A counterfeit of the captain's slave;
  He'll take the token to the pimp,
  Along with the sack of silver coins,
  Then whisk the woman off to safety.   120

  Help! I've given the plot³ away!

  Any instructions that remain
  I'll tell the fellow face to face.
CALIDORUS   Then what are we doing standing here?
PSEUDOLUS   Get the man and all the trappings,   125
  Bring him right away to meet me
  At the countinghouse of Aeschinus.
  Be quick about it!
CALIDORUS   We'll be there
  Ahead of you.
        [*Exeunt* CALIDORUS AND CHARINUS, *stage left.*]
PSEUDOLUS   More haste, less speed!
  [*Addressing the audience.*] All my plans that earlier   130
  Were clouded and obscure have now
  Become transparent, and my vision's
  Crystal clear. The road's wide open:
  All my legions now are marshaled,
  Standards proudly raised on high.   135
  The birds are soaring overhead;
  The auspices all point my way.
  My heart's abrim with confidence
  That I can rout the enemy.
  Off to the forum, where I'll load   140
  My orders on this Simia:

  He mustn't trip, his leadership
  Is crucial in my grand design;
  I'll sound the call, we'll storm the wall,
  And then Fort Pimp will all be mine.   145
        [*Exit stage left.*]

3. I.e., of the play: a metatheatrical comment directed to the audience.

Act III

[*From* BALLIO's *doorway there emerges a* YOUNG SLAVE, *a wretched and timid boy in his early teens.*]

ACT III, SCENE 1

SLAVE   When the gods assign a boy the job of slaving
   For a pimp, and then they grant him ugliness,
   That boy has been assigned, if you ask me,
   A lousy load, a low-down dirty deal.
   Just look at me slaving here, where I'm obliged   5
   To shore up every shape and size of misery;
   And I can't find a single lover-boy
   To give me even a smidgen of tenderness.

   Today's the birthday of our boss the pimp;
   He's threatened the household, high and low alike: 10
   Whoever fails to give him a gift today
   Will die tomorrow in cruel agony.
   Hey! I don't know what I'm supposed to do;
   I lack the wherewithal all do it with.
   If I don't find a present for our pimp,   15
   I'm bound to get the long end of the stick.
   That's awful for a little kid like me!

   Gosh! I'm so scared of catching holy heck
   That if some fellow lays a load on me,
   Though people say that really makes you groan,   20
   I guess I'll somehow learn to clench my teeth.

   I'd better learn to clench my lips. Just look!
   My master's coming home; he's brought a cook.

ACT III, SCENE 2

[*As the* (YOUNG) SLAVE *tries to become invisible, enter (stage left)* BALLIO *and a* COOK, *accompanied by apprentice cooks and other* ATTENDANT (SLAVES).]

BALLIO   "Cook's Marketplace"—that's such a stupid name:
   Not cooks but crooks go on the market there.
   Upon my oath, I couldn't hope to find
   A worse type than this cook I've got in tow—
   A loud-mouthed, swaggering, useless nincompoop.   5

   The King of Hell refused to let him in:
   He's needed here to cater to the dead,
   Since he alone can satisfy their taste.
COOK   If you hold that opinion of me,
   Why did you hire me?

BALLIO   Scarcity: no choice!   10
    If you're a cook, why were you sitting there,
    Left out in the market all alone?
COOK   I'll tell you:
    Human greed's the cause of my decline,
    Not lack of talent.
BALLIO   How so?
COOK   Let me explain: 15
    As soon as people come to hire a cook,
    Nobody wants the best and highest priced;
    They'd rather hire the cheapest one around.
    That's why I sat alone in the marketplace.
    No drachma-per-diem dope am I; no one
    Gets me off my butt for less than double that.   20

    My dinner menu's not like other cooks',
    Who spice up mounds of mouldy meadow grass,
    Converting guests to cattle (greens galore!),
    Then lace that fodder with more foliage.
    They toss in coriander, fennel, garlic,   25
    Parsley, sorrel, cabbage, spinach, beet,
    Dissolve a pound of asafetida,
    Then grind in murderous mustard, guaranteed
    To make you howl before you touch the stuff.
    When these boys cook, their seasonings do not   30
    Consist of spices, but of vampire bats,
    To gnaw the living entrails from their guests.
    So that's why people here live such short lives,
    Their bellies bloated with this kind of fodder,
    Scary to mention, let alone to munch on.   35
    Humans choose the greens that cows refuse.
BALLIO   And you? Do you use heavenly seasoning
    That can extend the span of human life,
    Since you attack those spices?
COOK   Shout it aloud!
    People can aspire to live two hundred years   40
    By sticking to the spicy diets I've designed.
    When I've put scorchilender in the pan,
    Or torridopsis or inflammagon,
    The dish becomes red hot upon the spot.
    Those are my seasonings for Neptune's creatures;[4]   45
    Earth-born beasts I spice with yummiander,
    Smackalyptus, or delectamom.
BALLIO   May Jupiter and all the gods destroy you
    With your spices and your pack of lies!
COOK   Please let me speak.
BALLIO   Speak on, and go to hell!   50

---

4. Fish. *Neptune*: god of the sea.

COOK When the pans are boiling, I remove their lids:
    The savor flies to heaven on soaring feet.
BALLIO A savor with sore feet?
COOK   A careless slip.
BALLIO How so?
COOK   I meant to say, "on soaring wings."
    Jupiter dines daily on that scent.   55
BALLIO On your day off, what's Jupiter to eat?
COOK He goes to bed on an empty stomach.
BALLIO   Damn you!
    Is it for this I'm shelling out hard cash?
COOK Though I admit I'm an expensive cook,
    I promise that my hiring price is matched   60
    By service rendered.
BALLIO   Larceny, no doubt.[5]
COOK Do you expect to find a single cook
    Who's not equipped with grasping eagle talons?
BALLIO Do you expect to cook a single meal
    Without those grasping talons tightly tied?   65
    [Catching sight of the lurking (YOUNG) SLAVE.] Hey, boy, look lively!
      Here's a job for you!
    Get all my valuables locked away.
    Don't let this fellow's face out of your sight:
    If he looks sideways, you look sideways, too.
    If he steps forward, match him step for step.   70
    If he sticks out his hand, you do the same.
    If he should grab what's his, just let him grab it;
    But if he grabs what's mine, then hold him fast.
    He starts: you start. He stops: you stop likewise.
    He squats upon the ground: just squat away!   75
    And each apprentice cook gets a private guard.
COOK Come on, cheer up!
BALLIO   Will you explain how I
    Can be cheerful when I'm going home with you?
COOK Because today I'll dip you in my broth
    The way Medea cooked old Pelias.   80
    Her poisons and her magic drugs, they tell us,
    Made the old man a little lad again;[6]
    I'll do the same for you.
BALLIO   So you're also a poisoner?
COOK Heavens, no! I'm a man-preserver.
BALLIO   Ha!
    How much to teach me that single recipe?   85
COOK Which one?
BALLIO   Preserving you from fleecing me.
COOK Base price, if you trust me; otherwise, no deal.

---

5. Cooks in comedy are proverbial thieves. 6. In fact, Medea persuaded Pelias's daughters to chop him
up by promising that he would emerge from the cooking pot a young man, but when they did so nothing
happened.

But is it your friends or enemies you're going
To feast today?

BALLIO   Why, they're my friends, of course.

COOK   Why don't you call your enemies instead?   90
Today I'll give your guests a banquet so bespiced,
So sprinkled with sweet seasoning,
The instant someone samples my delights
He'll want to nibble off his fingertips.

BALLIO   By Herc, before you serve a single guest,   95
Be sure that you and your henchmen have a taste,
To make you nibble off your pilfering paws.

COOK   Perhaps you don't believe what I'm telling you.

BALLIO   Don't be a nuisance! Too much nagging! Shush!
Look: here's my house. Go in and cook your meal.   100
Hurry!

SLAVE:[7]   Why not sit down and call your guests?
The dinner's already a mess.

     [*The* COOK *and his retinue go into Ballio's house, leaving* BALLIO *alone
     on stage.*]

BALLIO   Just look at the sprig!
That rascal is the cook's assistant tongue.
Really, I don't know where to watch out first,
With thieves inside my house and a thug next door.   105
You see, my neighbor here (Calidorus' dad),
As he left for the forum, warned me specially
To be on guard against Pseudolus, his slave,
And not to trust him; for he's on the prowl today,
Hoping somehow to swindle the girl from me.   110
The old man said he'd promised solemnly
That he would filch away Phoenicium.

So now I'll go inside and tell my household staff
On no account to trust this Pseudolus riffraff.

     [*Goes into his house.*]

Act IV

[PSEUDOLUS *enters from the forum (stage left), singing exultantly to his newly
found assistant, the slave* SIMIA. SIMIA, *who does not appear immediately, is disguised as the messenger-slave Harpax, with cloak, broad hat, and conspicuous
sword; in guile and virtuosity, he can rival Pseudolus.*]

ACT IV, SCENE 1

PSEUDOLUS   If ever immortal benevolent gods
Get involved in our human condition,
They must want Calidorus and me to be saved,
And the pimp to go down to perdition.

---

7. Either Ballio's slave boy or the cook's assistant.

What a godsent support they've provided in you: 5
  You're a fellow so cunning and clever!
[*Looking back, and failing to see* SIMIA.] Where's he gone? If I've
  started to talk to myself,
  I'm becoming more loony than ever.

    By Herc, I'm tricked, it's plain to see:
    I failed to check a cheat like me.   10

Holy Pollux, I'm ruined if he's taken off,
  My design won't unfold as expected.
Look at that! There's my whipping-post strutting along,
  With his arrogant manner perfected.
[*To* SIMIA.] Hello, there, I was hunting all over for you;   15
  I was frightened that you had defected.
SIMIA   I confess I'm a frightfully flighty type.
PSEUDOLUS   Where were you dawdling?
SIMIA   Wherever I pleased.
PSEUDOLUS   I know that already.
SIMIA   Then why do you ask?
PSEUDOLUS   I want to school you in this scheme.   20
SIMIA   You need the school; don't scholar me.
PSEUDOLUS   You're treating me with cool contempt.
SIMIA   Don't you deserve contempt from me,
  A legendary legionary?
PSEUDOLUS   Concentrate on the job at hand.   25
SIMIA   Do you see my attention wandering?
PSEUDOLUS   Then walk along more quickly.
SIMIA   No, I like to take my time.
PSEUDOLUS   Here's our chance: while he's asleep,
  I want you to get the jump on him.   30
SIMIA   Why such a rush? Relax! No fear!
  If only Jupiter would place
  That soldier's emissary here
  To meet my challenge, face to face:
  There's no way he could ever be   35
  A Harpax half as good as me.
  Cheer up! I'll fix your fine affair,
  Untangling it with tender care.
  My tricks and lies will so dismay
  This foreign army type, he'll say   40
  He isn't who he seems to be;
  He'll calmly claim that I am he.
PSEUDOLUS   How come?
SIMIA   How dumb a question! I'm going to die!
PSEUDOLUS [*Aside.*]   A really charming sort of guy!   45
SIMIA   I'll outclass even you in lying,
  Master snitch, without half trying.
PSEUDOLUS   Jupiter watch over you
  For my sake!

SIMIA   And for my sake, too.
    Does this outfit suit me, would you say?   50
PSEUDOLUS   It's quite magnificent!
SIMIA   O.K.
PSEUDOLUS   I pray the kindly gods may grant you
    Everything for which you yearn;
    If I prayed them to grant what you were worth,
    You'd get less than nothing in return.   55
    [Aside.] He's so downright sly and sneaky;
    I've never seen a man more cheeky.
SIMIA   What's that I heard?
PSEUDOLUS   Hey, mum's the word.
    But what rewards you'll get from me
    If you manage this business properly!   60
SIMIA   Won't you shut up?
    Reminding the mindful is mindless and mad:
    The rememberer's memory may become bad.
    I've absorbed all the facts and I've learned them by heart;
    I've religiously practiced my fraudulent part.   65
PSEUDOLUS   An upright man!
SIMIA [Aside.]   Not he nor I.
PSEUDOLUS   Don't falter now!
SIMIA   Won't you shut up?
PSEUDOLUS   So help me heaven—
SIMIA   But heaven won't;
    You're spouting undiluted lies.
PSEUDOLUS   For your treachery, Simia, you have earned   70
    My love, my fear, my high esteem.
SIMIA   I've learned to hand out guff like that;
    You can't pat me upon the head.
PSEUDOLUS   What a lovely reception you'll get from me
    When you've done this job today!
SIMIA   Ha, ha!   75
PSEUDOLUS   With lovely food and wine and perfume,
    Succulent morsels and drinks galore.
    A lovely girl will be there as well,
    To lavish kisses upon you.
SIMIA   You're a lovely host.
PSEUDOLUS   I'll cause you to say   80
    Much more, if you pull off this job.
SIMIA   If I don't, may the crucifixioner
    Give me a cross reception!
    Now get a move on! Show me the mouth
    Of the pimp's establishment. Which door?   85
PSEUDOLUS   Third along here.
SIMIA   Shh! That mouth just
    Yawned.
PSEUDOLUS   The house has a bellyache,
    I'd say.
SIMIA   Why?
PSEUDOLUS   Because, so help me

Pollux, it's vomiting the pimp!

[PSEUDOLUS *and* SIMIA *make themselves inconspicuous, as* BALLIO
emerges from his house in an odd, furtive manner.]

SIMIA   Is that the man?

PSEUDOLUS   That's him.

SIMIA   What measly   90
Merchandise! Just take a look:
Forward motion's not for him;
He skitters sideways like a crab.

ACT IV, SCENE 2

BALLIO   I'll admit this cook's less foul
A character than I supposed;
So far he's pilfered nothing but
A ladle and a little mug.

PSEUDOLUS [*To* SIMIA, *sotto voce.*]   5
Here you go now, this is the perfect
Moment.

SIMIA   I agree with you.

PSEUDOLUS   Step out into the street. Be tricky!
I'll be waiting in ambush here.

SIMIA [*in a loud "soliloquy," moving toward* BALLIO.]   I've been counting
carefully:
Sixth lane from the city gate.   10
Here we are; this must be the alley
Where he told me to turn aside.
But how many houses down the alley,
That I really couldn't say.

BALLIO [*Aside.*]   Who's this fellow in the cloak?   15
Where's he come from? Who does he want?
He's got a sort of foreign look, and
I don't recognize his face.

SIMIA   Here's a man who's sure to know
The matter I'm unsure about.   20

BALLIO [*Aside.*]   He's heading straight for me. I wonder
Where in the world the fellow's from.

SIMIA   Hey there! You with the wild goatee,
I've got a question; answer me.

BALLIO   Well, well! You've no "good day" to share?   25

SIMIA   No, I have no good days to spare.

BALLIO   You'll get from me as good as you give.

PSEUDOLUS [*Aside.*]   A fine beginning: superlative!

SIMIA   Tell me, then, do you know any
Person living on this lane?   30

BALLIO   I know myself.

SIMIA   Few human beings
Reach the condition you describe.
Down in the forum I doubt you'd find
One man in ten who knows himself.

PSEUDOLUS [*Aside.*]   I'm safe; he's turned philosopher.   35
SIMIA   I'm looking for a nasty fellow—
   Scofflaw, low-life, perjurer,
   Degenerate.
BALLIO [*Aside.*]   It's me he wants.
   Those are my nicknames, sure enough.
   I hope he gets my surname right.   40
   [*Aloud.*] What is this fellow's name?
SIMIA   Pimp Ballio.
BALLIO   Do I know myself?
   I am the object of your search,
   Young man.
SIMIA   You're Ballio?
BALLIO   Me, yours truly.
SIMIA   The way you're dressed,   45
   You look like a second-story man.
BALLIO   If you spotted me on some dark street,
   I think you'd treat me with respect.
SIMIA   My master asked me to express
   His warmest compliments to you.   50
   Take this letter from me now;
   He told me to deliver it.
BALLIO   Just who issued the command?
PSEUD. [*Aside.*]   We're sunk! My man is all mucked up.
   Names weren't mentioned; what a mess!   55
BALLIO   Who do you say sent me this letter?
SIMIA   Look at his picture on the seal;
   Then, sir, *you* tell *me* his name,
   Proving to me that you are really
   Ballio.
BALLIO   Give me the letter.   60
SIMIA [*Handing it over.*]   Here: identify the seal.
BALLIO [*Aside, as he studies the seal.*]   Ah! Polymachaeroplagides:[8]
   Pure and simple recognition.
   [*To* SIMIA.] Hey! Polymachaeroplagides
   Is his name.
SIMIA   Now I know how right   65
   I was in giving you the letter,
   Seeing how you spoke the name
   Of Polymachaeroplagides.
BALLIO   What's he doing?
SIMIA   Playing the role
   Of brave heroic warrior.   70
   But hurry up and scrutinize
   This letter, please—I'm very rushed—
   Take the cash immediately
   And give the woman her release.
   I must be in Sicyon today   75

_____
8. "Son of Many Sword Wounds."

Or else tomorrow I die.
Master's very domineering.
BALLIO   Don't tell me; I know him too.
SIMIA   Come on, read the letter through, then.
BALLIO   Well, I will, if you'll shut up.   80
  [*Reads.*] "Captain Polymachaeroplagides
  Dispatches to the pimp named Ballio
  This letter sealed with a portrait mutually
  Agreed upon."
SIMIA   The token's in the letter.
BALLIO   I see; I'm satisfied. But does he never   85
  Start a letter with a friendly wish?
SIMIA   No; that would violate army protocol.
  By action he confers good health on friends
  And likewise deals destruction to his foes.
  But keep on reading, let experience teach you   90
  What this letter says.
BALLIO   Just listen, then:
  "Harpax, my aide, is on his way to you—"
  You're Harpax?
SIMIA   I'm your man, [*Aside.*] and harp I can.
BALLIO   "—Bearing this letter. He'll convey the cash;
  I want the woman sent with him at once.   95
  It's right to wish the righteous 'Best of health':
  I'd do so, if I thought you qualified."
SIMIA   What next?
BALLIO   Pay up and take away the girl.
SIMIA   What are we waiting for?
BALLIO   Follow inside, then.
SIMIA   Here I come.

                        ACT IV, SCENE 3

[As BALLIO *and* SIMIA *disappear into Ballio's house,* PSEUDOLUS *comes downstage
to address the audience yet again.*]

PSEUDOLUS   I swear to Pollux I've never seen a man
  More devious or deceitful than this Simia.
  I'm frightened of the fellow. I'm really scared
  I'll face the gory treatment Ballio got:
  My man may turn his lucky horns on me,   5
  If any chance of mischief should arise.
  Heavens! I hope not, for I wish him well.
  Now I'm feeling triply terrified.
  First, I'm nervous that my pal here could
  Desert me and defect to the enemy;   10
  Next, master might arrive back anytime,
  To snatch the loot and catch the looters, too;
  Finally, Harpax the First could reappear
  Before this Harpax gets the girl away.

Oh Herc, I'm doomed! They've been inside too long.   15
My heart is waiting with its suitcase packed;
It plans to fly away to distant realms,
Unless he brings the girl out right away.

[*Seeing Ballio's door open.*] I've won! I've overthrown my overseers!

ACT IV, SCENE 4

[SIMIA *reappears from Ballio's house, leading the girl* PHOENICIUM.]

SIMIA   Don't cry, you don't understand, Phoenicium.
You'll get the picture soon, at dinner time.
You're not being led to the fellow with the fangs,
That Macedonian who provokes your tears;
I'm taking you to your dearest sweet desire: 5
In a twinkling you'll be in Calidorus' arms.
PSEUDOLUS   Why did you loiter so long inside the house?
My heart's been battered, bruised, and beaten flat.
SIMIA   You jailbird, how can you find the luxury
Of grilling me when the enemy's everywhere?   10
I'd say, "Forward march, in double time!"
PSEUDOLUS   By Pollux, good advice from such a no-good thug!
Advance! Let's crown our win with a triumphant jug!
            [*They leave with* PHOENICIUM, *stage right.*]

ACT IV, SCENE 5

[BALLIO *comes out of his house, obviously pleased at the success of his transaction.*]

BALLIO   Ha, ha! At last my mind's been set at rest:
That fellow's gone; he's led the girl away.
Let Pseudolus come now, the dirty crook,
And try to snatch the girl by trickery!
By Herc, I'm positive I'd rather swear   5
An oath, commit a thousand perjuries,
Than let that swindler get the laugh on me.
Now when we meet, he'll be my laughingstock.
He's bound for the gristmill soon—that was the deal.

I'd love to meet old Simo, I confess;   10
How happily he'd share my happiness!

ACT IV, SCENE 6

[SIMO *enters from the forum, stage left.*]

SIMO   I'll see if my Ulysses has achieved
The sack of Ballio's sacred citadel.[9]

9. Troy could not be captured as long as it possessed the Palladium, a statue of Athena. Ulysses (Odysseus) stole it and guaranteed the Greek victory.

BALLIO   Give me your lucky hand, you lucky fellow,
   Simo.
SIMO   What's up?
BALLIO   Now—
SIMO   What now?
BALLIO   No problem!
SIMO   Why?
   Did my man come here?
BALLIO   No.
SIMO   Then what's so good?   5
BALLIO   Your twenty mina coins are safe and sound—
   The bet you made today with Pseudolus.
SIMO   I'd like to think so.
BALLIO   I'll pay up myself,
   If your slave gets possession of that girl
   Or else conveys her to your son, as pledged.   10
   Oh, Herc! Please bet me! I'm itching to give my word,
   To reassure you that your money's safe.
   You can even keep the woman as a gift.
SIMO   I see no risk in closing out the deal
   On those conditions. [Formally.] Twenty minas do you   15
   Swear to give?
BALLIO   I do.
SIMO   That's not so bad!
   But have you ever met Pseudolus?
BALLIO   Sure, with your son.
SIMO   What did he say to you? What words did he use?
BALLIO   Theater rubbish, standard pimp abuse
   From the comic stage, well known to every child: 20
   He called me a dirty double-crossing crook.
SIMO   He didn't tell a lie.
BALLIO   So I wasn't angry.
   How can it matter if you bad-mouth a man
   Who doesn't care and doesn't contradict?
SIMO   All right, I'd like to hear why he's no problem.   25
BALLIO   Because he'll never nab the girl from me:
   He can't! Remember I told you she was sold,
   Some time back, to a captain from Macedon?
SIMO   I do.
BALLIO   Well, sir, his slave brought me the cash,
   With a sign in sealing wax—
SIMO   Go on.   30
BALLIO   —As prearranged by the officer and me.
   He took away the girl a while ago.
SIMO   Is that the honest truth?
BALLIO   The what? From me?
SIMO   Watch out it's not some fabricated scheme.
BALLIO   The seal and the letter make me positive.   35
   He took her and left for Sicyon just now.
SIMO   Great Herc! Great work! I can hardly wait to appoint

Pseudolus Mayor of Millstone Colony.[1]
[*Looking offstage, left.*] But who's this in the cloak?

BALLIO   I've no idea.

Let's watch to see where he goes and what he does.   40

ACT IV, SCENE 7

[*The real* HARPAX *enters (stage right) singing a self-congratulatory solo.* BALLIO *and* SIMO *are not quite close enough to understand his words; at first,* BALLIO *will take him to be a young client, ripe for the plucking.*]

HARPAX   I find corrupt those slaves who flout
    Or disregard their master's rules.
Some can't perform a task without
    A blunt reminder: stupid fools!
No sooner out of master's sight   5
        They think they're free,
        At liberty
        To wench and brawl
        And squander all
They have; but they're still slaves, all right!   10
The only talent they possess
Is getting by on craftiness.
I've had no contact with that mob:
I've kept my distance, done my job.
In master's absence, I assume   15
My master's standing in the room.
I'm frightened when he's nowhere near;
When he's around I feel no fear.

And now for this assignment here!

I remained in the tavern for Syrus' call—   20
    He had taken the letter and told me to wait;
I expected some word when the pimp arrived home,
    But the man hasn't come and it's now getting late.
So I'm here to discover just what's going on;
    Did he take me, perhaps, for a bit of a ride?   25
Now my sensible move is to knock on the door
    And to summon somebody who may be inside.
        [*Waving the purse, as he moves toward Ballio's door.*]
        I want the pimp to take this fee
        And send the girl away with me.

BALLIO [*Whispering to* SIMO.]   Hey there!

SIMO   What is it?

BALLIO   The man is mine.   30

SIMO   How so?

---

1. The gristmill, here ironically called a colony (which would be settled only by free citizens).

BALLIO   Because this catch looks fine.
   He's got the dough, he wants a doll;
   I'm going to crunch him, bones and all.
SIMO   Will you devour him on the spot?
BALLIO   Yes, while he's fresh and piping hot.   35
   For while he's in a giving mood,
   Not to eat him would be rude.
      Upstanding fellows make me poor,
         And sinners make me fat;
      The public likes the hero type,   40
         But I prefer the rat.
SIMO [*Aside.*]   The gods will give you living hell
   For wickedness like that!
HARPAX [*Aside.*]   I'm wasting time; I'll give these doors a swat,
   To see if Ballio's at home or not.   45
BALLIO [*To* SIMO.]   It's Venus who confers these joys,
      Who sends me all these good-time boys,
   These damn-the-cost, let's-go-for-brokers,
      Self-indulgent, carefree jokers.
   Lads who eat and drink and screw,   50
      In temperament they're not like you:
   A pleasure-hater so repressed
      You spoil all pleasure for the rest.
HARPAX [*Shouting at the door.*]   Hey, anybody home?
BALLIO [*Aside.*]   I think
   He's heading straight toward my house.   55
   I'll get a load of loot from him;
   I recognize my lucky charm.
HARPAX [*Knocking loudly.*]   Will no one open?
BALLIO   You in the cloak!
   What debt are you collecting here?
HARPAX   I'm after Ballio the pimp,   60
   The master of this residence.
BALLIO   Whoever you may be, young fellow,
   Spare the effort of that search.
HARPAX   Why so?
BALLIO   Because he's here before you,
   Face to face and large as life.   65
HARPAX [*Pointing to* SIMO.]   You're him?
SIMO [*Outraged.*]   Watch out, you dressed-up lout,
   Beware my crooked walking stick
   And point your filthy finger this way:
   [*Indicating* BALLIO.] Here's the pimp.   70
BALLIO [*Indicating* SIMO.]   And here's the gent.
   But gentle sir, you've often heard
   The howls of raging creditors,
   When you've been penniless except
   For what this pimp's provided you.   75
HARPAX   Why don't you talk to me?

BALLIO   O.K.,
   I'm talking. What do you want?
HARPAX   For you to take some money.
BALLIO   Give!
   My hand is constantly outstretched.
HARPAX   Here, then. Take these silver minas—   80
   Five, all counted and correct.
   My master, Polymachaeroplagides,
   Said I should bring them here to you,
   The sum he owed, and you should send
   Phoenicium away with me.   85
BALLIO   Your master?
HARPAX   That's correct.
BALLIO   The soldier?
HARPAX   Yes, that's right.
BALLIO   From Macedon?
HARPAX   Exactly so.
BALLIO   Sent you to me?
   Polymachaeroplagides?
HARPAX   You speak the truth.
BALLIO   Instructing you   90
   To give me this cash?
HARPAX   If you're in fact
   Pimp Ballio.
BALLIO   And told you then
   To take the woman away from me?
HARPAX   Yes.
BALLIO   Did he say Phoenicium?
HARPAX   Your memory is excellent!
BALLIO   Wait here!   95
   I'll soon be back.
HARPAX   Well, hurry up;
   Be quick! I'm in a rush. You see
   How late in the day it is.
BALLIO   I do;
   But still I want this man's advice.
   Just wait right here, I'll soon   100
   Be back to see you.
   [Taking SIMO aside.] What now, Simo?
   What'll we do? He's caught in the act,
   This man who brought the moneybag.
SIMO   How so?
BALLIO   Don't you understand?   105
SIMO   My ignorance is absolute.
BALLIO   Your Pseudolus has hired this man
   To play the role of messenger
   From Macedon.
SIMO   Have you received
   His moneybag?

BALLIO   Is seeing believing?   110

SIMO   Say! In dealing with those spoils,
   Remember to give half to me:
   Friends should share and share alike.

BALLIO   Good grief! The whole amount is yours.

HARPAX [*Impatiently.*]   How soon will you attend to me?

BALLIO [*Aloud.*]   Hang on!   115
   [*Sotto voce.*] What do you suggest now, Simo?

SIMO   Let's have a little fun and games
   With this fictitious courier;
   We'll keep it up until he comes
   To realize the joke's on him.   120

BALLIO [*To* SIMO.]   Just follow me.
   [*To* HARPAX.]   Well, well! So you're
   His slave, you say?

HARPAX   Most certainly.

BALLIO   What was your purchase price?

HARPAX   His valor
   Won me on the battlefield.
   I was commanding officer   125
   In the place where I was born, back home.

SIMO   Did he ransack the city jail,
   The place where you were born, back home?

HARPAX   If you speak insulting words to me,
   You'll get them back.

BALLIO   How long a time   130
   Did it take to come from Sicyon?

HARPAX   I arrived the second day, at noon.[2]

BALLIO   Holy Herc! You made good time!

SIMO   The man's as speedy as can be:
   When you look at his calves, you know he's fit—   135
   To wear great thumping ankle-chains.

BALLIO   Tell me, were you accustomed to sleep
   In a cradle as a little boy?

SIMO   Of course he was.

BALLIO   And had you the habit
   Of doing (tut, tut!) . . . you know what I mean?   140

SIMO   Tut, tut! Of course he had.

HARPAX   Are you both
   Quite sane?

BALLIO   A probing question now:
   At night, when the captain took the watch
   And you stood guard along with him,
   Did his sword-blade always fit   145
   Inside your scabbard perfectly?

---

2. Noon of the day after he set out (the ancients counted inclusively). Sicyon, a city in the northern Peloponnesus, is about 50 miles southwest of Athens as the crow flies, and longer by road through the rugged mountains of the Isthmus of Corinth—an impressive distance to cover in a day and a half.

HARPAX Go hang yourself!
BALLIO   You'll get your chance
  At hanging soon enough today.
HARPAX Either bring me out the girl
  Or else return the money.
BALLIO   Wait!   150
HARPAX Why wait?
BALLIO   Tell us about this cloak:
  How much was the rental fee?
HARPAX   The which?
SIMO What does it cost to hire a sword?
HARPAX [*Aside.*] These men need their heads examined!
BALLIO Don't leave—
HARPAX   Let go!
BALLIO   That hat: what price   155
  Will it fetch its owner for the day?
HARPAX What "owner"? Are you raving mad?
  I own these clothes; I bought them as
  My private things.
BALLIO   You've got your only
  Private things between your legs.   160
HARPAX [*Aside.*] These gents are smeared with oil; they need
  A good old-fashioned rubbing down.
BALLIO Answer this question, in the name
  Of Herc (I'm very serious!):
  What are your wages? At what pittance   165
  Were you hired by Pseudolus?
HARPAX Who is that Pseudolus?
BALLIO   Your coach,
  Who trained you in this stratagem,
  So you could use more stratagems
  To snatch the girl away from me.   170
HARPAX What Pseudolus? What stratagems
  Do you keep going on about?
  I haven't the faintest notion who
  He is.
BALLIO Come on, away with you!
  Today there'll be no profit here   175
  For swindlers. Just tell Pseudolus
  Another fellow snatched the spoils,
  The first Harpax who came along.
HARPAX Honest to Pol, I'm really Harpax.
BALLIO Honest to Pol, you want to be.   180
  This is a swindle, pure and simple.
HARPAX I've handed you the moneybag;
  When I first came some time ago,
  I gave the token to your slave,
  Right here before your door—the letter   185
  Signed with the portrait of my master.

BALLIO   You gave a letter to my slave?
  Which slave?
HARPAX   Syrus was his name.
BALLIO [*To* SIMO.]   This swindle's based on more than nonsense:
  It's been thought out wickedly. 190
  That scoundrel of a Pseudolus!
  How cleverly he's planned it all!
  He gave him the exact amount
  Of money that the captain owed,
  And dressed the fellow up like this 195
  So he could take away the girl.
  [*Aloud.*] The real Harpax personally
  Brought that letter to me here.
HARPAX   My name is Harpax, and I am
  The Macedonian captain's slave. 200
  I've not been guilty of a single
  Wicked or deceitful deed,
  And I've no knowledge or awareness
  Of your precious Pseudolus.
SIMO   Barring a miracle, old pimp, 205
  You've forfeited the girl for good.
BALLIO   Ye gods, I'm getting really scared,
  The more I listen to his words.
  Ye gods, that Syrus fellow, too,
  Has left my heart frigidified— 210
  The one who took the token in.
  It's a wonder if he's not Pseudolus.
  [*To* HARPAX.] Hey, you, what did he look like, then,
  The man you gave the token to?
HARPAX   Bright red hair, protruding belly, 215
  Rather swarthy, chubby calves,
  With large head, ruddy face, sharp eyes,
  And utterly enormous feet.
BALLIO   You killed me when you reached those feet!
  It was Pseudolus himself. 220
  I'm done for! Now I'm dying, Simo.
HARPAX   I won't let you die, by Herc,
  Unless the money's paid me back—
  All twenty minas.
SIMO   In addition,
  Twenty minas more for me. 225
BALLIO [*To* SIMO.]   So will you take away the prize
  That I put forward as a joke?
SIMO   From wicked men it's right to take
  All loot and lucre that they make.
BALLIO   At least hand over Pseudolus. 230
SIMO   Hand over Pseudolus to you?
  What harm's he done? Did I not tell you
  A hundred times to watch for him?

BALLIO   He ruined me.
SIMO   He sentenced me
   To pay a twenty-mina fine.   235
BALLIO   What shall I do now?
HARPAX   Give me
   The money, then go hang yourself.
BALLIO   Damn you! Follow me this way, please,
   To the forum; I'll pay up.
HARPAX   I follow.
SIMO   What about me?
BALLIO   All foreigners get paid   240
   Today; but citizens, tomorrow.
   Pseudolus convened a court
   That put me on trial for life or death,
   When he dispatched that other man
   To steal the girl from me today.   245
   [To HARPAX.] Follow me. [To audience.] But don't you wait
   For me to take this road back home.
   The way life's gone, I've now decided
   Alley travel's best for me.
HARPAX   If you only walked at the rate you talked,   250
   We'd have reached the forum long ago.
      [Exit stage left.]
BALLIO   My happy birthday soon will be
   My gloomy death-day. Woe is me!
      [Exit.]

ACT IV, SCENE 8

SIMO   I've hit him up just fine, the way
   My slave has hit his enemy.
   Now I intend to lie in wait
   For Pseudolus—not the way it's done
   In other plays, where people lurk   5
   With whips and prods; I'll go inside
   To find the twenty minas that
   I promised if he did the job.
   I'll pay him of my own free will.
   The creature is so very clever,   10
   Very cunning, very sly.
   Pseudolus has quite surpassed
   The Trojan horse, Ulysses too.

   I'll get the money all prepared;
      Then Pseudolus will be ensnared.   15
      [Exit into his own house.]

Act V

[*Enter* PSEUDOLUS, *stage right, in wild disarray; he is wearing a garland and has obviously been drinking nonstop since he was last seen.*]

ACT V, SCENE 1

PSEUDOLUS What's up, feet? My word, feet!
    You're acting absurd, feet.
  Do you really suppose I'll be offered a hand
  When I wobble because you're unable to stand?
      If I stumble and fall,   5
      My tumble is all
       Your fault!
  Well, moving at last? Hey, foot, I feel
  You need your backside kicked, you heel.
  That's the trouble with wine: it always knows   10
  Like a sneaky wrestler, to tackle the toes.

  So help me Pollux, I do declare
  I've gone on a simply spectacular tear!

  Such an elegant spread, good taste sublime,
  A marvellous host and a marvellous time.   15
  No need for a rambling rhetorical style:
  Parties like this make life worthwhile!
  All forms of pleasure, all manner of love;
  The next best thing to heaven above.

  Two lovers locked in love's embrace,   20
    With lips engaged and tongues entwined;
  Two partners snuggling breast to breast,
    A couple with coupling on their mind.

  A snow-white hand, a toast, a sip,
  Sweet cup of love and fellowship.   25

  No hateful or obnoxious guest,
    No idiotic bore;
  Just perfumes, unguents, pretty ribbons,
    Floral wreaths galore,
  Provided in profusion there—   30
    Don't ask me any more.

      That's the way
      We spent the day,
  Young master and I, getting happy and tight,
      After I   35
      Accomplished my
  Objective by putting the foe to flight.

There I left them wining and dining,
    Reclining and fondling their ladies of leisure;
My sweetheart was acting the life of the party,   40
    Indulging herself with the utmost of pleasure.

I rose to leave; "Come, dance!" they cried.
    I gave a sort of jiggle,
This way; with expert skill I tried
    The Asiatic[3] wiggle.   45
All bundled in my frilly cloak,
    I did these steps (a silly joke);
They clapped, they shouted out "Encore!"
"Come back, we want a little more!"
I had my doubts, but just the same   50
Continued with my foolish game:
Parading for my girl, like this,
So she would offer me a kiss,
I pirouetted—and I fell!
That was my frolic's sad farewell;   55
For while I struggled, *oops!* Watch out!
I shit my cloak (or just about).
Sweet Pollux, how they roared at me
For such a loss of dignity!

I'm given a jug: I take a quaff.   60
I change my cloak, get that one off;
I head for home, and home I'll stay
Till this hangover goes away.

So long, young boss! Old boss must learn
    The bargain's satisfied.   65
[*Knocking on his own door.*] Hey, open up, somebody, hey!
    Tell Simo I'm outside.

ACT V, SCENE 2

SIMO [*Cautiously opening his door.*]   Some wretch at the door is calling
    me.
    What's this? How come? What do I see?
PSEUDOLUS   Your Pseudolus, garlanded and stewed.
SIMO [*Aside.*]   That's frank, at least. Some attitude!
    Is he scared on my account? No, sir!   5
    I wonder, should I growl or purr?
    [*Pointing to a purse that he is carrying.*] This moneybag rules out brute
        force;
    I hope to save it still, of course.
PSEUDOLUS [*Approaching* SIMO.]   Good man, meet bad man: how do you
    do.

---

3. Literally, "Ionic"—a reference to Greeks who lived on the Aegean Islands and on the coast of Asia
Minor. Ionic dancing was known for its lasciviousness.

SIMO   God bless you, Pseudolus! [*Recoiling.*] Phew!   10
   Get lost!
PSEUDOLUS   Hey, why am I rejected?
SIMO   What the hell had you expected,
   Drunk and belching in my face?
PSEUDOLUS   Just hold me gently, please, in case
   I crash. How can you fail to see   15
   That I am smashed quite smashingly?
SIMO   What gall is this, to come here tight,
   A wreath on your head, in broad daylight?
PSEUDOLUS   It gives me pleasure. [*Belches again.*]
SIMO   Pleasure, sure!
   You're pleased to belch in my face once more.   20
PSEUDOLUS   Belching's beautiful. Don't be a pain!
SIMO   I think, you rascal, you've the power
   To guzzle Massic wine and drain
   Four harvests in a single hour.
PSEUDOLUS   "In winter," add.[4]   25
SIMO   All right, not bad!
   From where exactly should I say
   You steered your loaded barge this way?
PSEUDOLUS   From a bash with your son.
   Oh, Simo, what fun   30
   To cheat Ballio!
   My mission's accomplished
   According to plan.
SIMO   You're a terrible man!
PSEUDOLUS   The girl's doing this. [*A lewd gesture.*]   35
   She's in bed with your boy
   And she's actually free.
SIMO   I know the whole story;
   No need to tell me.
PSEUDOLUS   Then where is my money   40
   And why the delay?
SIMO   You've got right on your side.
   I admit; I'll pay.
      [SIMO *hands the purse to* PSEUDOLUS.]
PSEUDOLUS   You said I'd never get it, yet it's mine.
   [*Pointing to his own shoulder.*] Just load this fellow up and fall in
     line.   45
SIMO [*To audience.*]   Load him up?
PSEUDOLUS   That's what I said.
SIMO [*To audience.*]   May I beat him up instead?
   Will he pinch my purse and laugh at me, the swine?
PSEUDOLUS   Woe to the vanquished!
SIMO   All right, turn your shoulder.   50

---

4. Because the Romans divided the daylight period into twelve hours, regardless of season, winter hours were of shorter duration [Translator's note].

[*Humiliated,* SIMO *places the purse over* PSEUDOLUS' *shoulder, and falls
    to his knees to beg for mercy.*]

PSEUDOLUS   Ah!

SIMO   I never thought I would become
  A suppliant at your feet. Oh dear! Oh dear!

PSEUDOLUS   Oh, stop it!

SIMO   I hurt!

PSEUDOLUS   If you didn't hurt, I would.

SIMO   Will you take this purse from master, Pseudolus, friend?

PSEUDOLUS   With all the feeling in my heart and soul!   55

SIMO   Please give me a tiny refund; you agree?

PSEUDOLUS   A greedy fellow: you can call me that,
  For you won't get a penny richer from this purse.
  You'd feel no pity for my wretched back,
  If I had not achieved my goal today.   60

SIMO   Someday, sure as I live, I'll get even with you!

PSEUDOLUS   Why do you threaten me? My skin is tough.

SIMO   Then go ahead. [*Starting to leave.*]

PSEUDOLUS   All right, come back.

SIMO   What for?

PSEUDOLUS   Come back, that's all; no trick involved.

SIMO   I'm here.

PSEUDOLUS   Come, join me for a drink together.

SIMO   Me?   65

PSEUDOLUS   Just do as I tell you. If you come, I'll give you
  Half or even more of your money back.

SIMO   I'll come; conduct me where you will.

PSEUDOLUS   Well, then. This business hasn't made you cross
  At me or my young master, has it, boss?   70

SIMO   Of course not!

PSEUDOLUS   Step this way; I'll follow you.

SIMO   Perhaps you should invite the audience, too.

PSEUDOLUS   Those cheapskates never have invited me;
  Why offer them our hospitality?
      [*To audience.*]
      But if you say   75
      You liked our play,
  And cheer our company before you go,
  Then I'll invite you—to tomorrow's show.
      [*Exeunt omnes.*]

CATULLUS

84?–54? B.C.E.

Gaius Valerius Catullus, born in the northern Italian city of Verona, lived out his short life in the last violent century of the Roman republic, but his poetry gives little hint that it was produced amid political upheaval. The 116 poems by him that have come down to us present a rich variety: imitations of Greek poets, long poems on Greek mythological themes, scurrilous personal attacks on contemporary politicians and private individuals, lighthearted verses designed to amuse his friends, and a magnificent marriage hymn. He also wrote a series of poems about his love affair with a Roman woman he calls Lesbia but who may have been Clodia, the enchanting but complex sister of one of Rome's most violent aristocrats turned political gangster. These poems, from which our selection is taken, present all the phases of the liaison, from the unalloyed happiness of the first encounters through doubt and hesitation to despair and virulent accusation, ending in heartbroken resignation to the bitter fact of Lesbia's betrayal.

Their tone ranges from the heights of joy at passionate love requited through the torments of simultaneous love and hate to the depths of morbid self-pity. Their direct and simple language seems to give readers immediate access to the experience of desire and betrayal and the feelings it arouses. In one sense, this impression is surely correct. But the poems are exceedingly complex. The passion is joined with considerable learning, and it is one of the remarkable characteristics of Catullus's poetry that strong emotion and sophistication are not at odds with each other but complementary. Poem 51, for example, powerfully describes the physical symptoms of love in the speaker; it is a translation into Latin of one of Sappho's most passionate Greek lyrics. Or consider poem 2, on Lesbia's pet sparrow: scholars have long suspected, probably correctly, an obscene double meaning in this pet.

There are further complexities. Many of the poems are addressed to someone—Lesbia, Catullus himself, or some third party—and the reader is a privileged audience to this communication. Who the addressee is and the relation between that person and the poet subtly shape the reader's view of the situation described in each poem. In poem 83, for example, when Lesbia seems to abuse "Catullus" in the presence of her husband, the speaker interprets this as a sign of love to which the husband is obtusely oblivious. Perhaps. Or is this a wishful interpretation? Who really is the dupe? Does the reader ever get access to Lesbia's feelings? Catullus's poetry is not simply a spontaneous outpouring of emotion but a carefully meditated portrayal of a love affair in which the poet's persona as well as his mistress is a character; and that gives depth and range to its passion.

PRONOUNCING GLOSSARY

The following list uses common English syllables and stress accents to provide rough equivalents of selected words whose pronunciation may be unfamiliar to the general reader.

Aurelius: *ow-ree'-lee-us*
Catullus: *kah-tul'-lus*

Hyrcani: *heer-kah'-nee*
Sagae: *sah'-gai*

5[1]

Lesbia, let us live only for loving,
and let us value at a single penny
all the loose flap of senile busybodies!
Suns when they set are capable of rising,
but at the setting of our own brief light   5
night is one sleep from which we never waken.
Give me a thousand kisses, then a hundred,
another thousand next, another hundred,
a thousand without pause & then a hundred,
until when we have run up our thousands   10
we will cry bankrupt, hiding our assets
from ourselves & any who would harm us,
knowing the volume of our trade in kisses.

2

Sparrow, you darling pet of my beloved,
which she caresses, presses to her body
or teases with the tip of one sly finger
until you peck at it in tiny outrage!
—for there are times when my desired, shining   5
lady is moved to turn to you for comfort,
to find (as I imagine) ease for ardor,
solace, a little respite from her sorrow—
if I could only play with you as she does,
and be relieved of my tormenting passion!   10

51[2]

To me that man seems like a god in heaven,
seems—may I say it?—greater than all gods are,
who sits by you & without interruption
        watches you, listens

to your light laughter, which casts such confusion   5
onto my senses, Lesbia, that when I
gaze at you merely, all of my well-chosen
        words are forgotten[3]

as my tongue thickens & a subtle fire
runs through my body while my ears are deafened   10

---

1. All selections translated by Charles Martin.   2. A translation into Latin of Sappho's Greek poem "He seems to me equal to gods" (see above, p. 498), that reproduces Sappho's metrical scheme (imitated in the English translation).   3. "All . . . forgotten" is a guess at the sense of a line missing in the original.

by their own ringing & at once my eyes are
   covered in darkness!

Leisure, Catullus. More than just a nuisance,
   leisure: you riot, overmuch enthusing.
Fabulous cities & their sometime kings have   15
   died of such leisure.[4]

86

Many find Quintia stunning. I find her attractive:
   tall, "regal," fair in complexion—these points are granted.
But stunning? No, I deny it: the woman is scarcely venerious,
   there's no spice at all in all the length of her body!
Now Lesbia is stunning, for Lesbia's beauty is total: 5
   and by that sum all other women are diminished.

87

No other woman can truthfully say she was cherished
   as much as Lesbia was when I was her lover.
Never, in any such bond, was fidelity greater
   than mine, in my love for you, ever discovered.

109

Darling, we'll both have equal shares in the sweet love you offer,
   and it will endure forever—you assure me.
O heaven, see to it that she can truly keep this promise,
   that it came from her heart & was sincerely given,
so that we may spend the rest of our days in this lifelong   5
   union, this undying compact of holy friendship.

83

Lesbia hurls abuse at me in front of her husband:
   that fatuous person finds it highly amusing!
Nothing gets through to you, jackass—for silence would signal
   that she'd been cured of me, but her barking & bitching
show that not only [have][5] I not been forgotten,   5
   —but that this burns her: and so she rants & rages.

4. The final stanza may not belong to this poem; if it does, it is Catullus's addition to the original by
Sappho.   5. Editorial substitution for the translator's *haven't.*

70

My woman says there is no one whom she'd rather marry
　　than me, not even Jupiter,[6] if he came courting.
That's what she says—but what a woman says to a passionate lover
　　ought to be scribbled on wind, on running water.

72

You used to say that you wished to know only Catullus,
　　Lesbia, and wouldn't take even Jove before me!
I didn't regard you just as my mistress then: I cherished you
　　as a father does his sons or his daughters' husbands.
Now that I know you, I burn for you even more fiercely,　　　　　　5
　　though I regard you as almost utterly worthless.
How can that be, you ask? It's because such cruelty forces
　　lust to assume the shrunken place of affection.

85

I hate & love. And if you should ask how I can do both,
　　I couldn't say; but I feel it, and it shivers me.

75

To such a state have I been brought by your mischief, my Lesbia,
　　and so completely ruined by my devotion,
that I couldn't think kindly of you if you did the best only,
　　nor cease to love, even if you should do—everything.

8

Wretched Catullus! You have to stop this nonsense,
　　admit that what you see has ended is over!
Once there were days which shone for you with rare brightness,
　　when you would follow wherever your lady led you,
the one we once loved as we will love no other;　　　　　　　　5
　　there was no end in those days to our pleasures,
when what you wished for was what she also wanted.
　　Yes, there were days which shone for you with rare brightness.

---

6. Jupiter (or Jove) was the supreme god of the Roman pantheon, corresponding to the Greek Zeus.

Now she no longer wishes; you mustn't want it,
you've got to stop chasing her now—cut your losses, 10
harden your heart & hold out firmly against her.
Goodbye now, lady. Catullus' heart is hardened,
he will not look to you nor call against your wishes—
how you'll regret it when nobody comes calling!
So much for you, bitch—your life is all behind you! 15
Now who will come to see you, thinking you lovely?
Whom will you love now, and whom will you belong to?
Whom will you kiss? And whose lips will you nibble?
But *you*, Catullus! *You* must hold out now, firmly!

58

Lesbia, Caelius[7]—yes, our darling,
yes, *Lesbia*, the Lesbia Catullus
once loved uniquely, more than any other!
—now on streetcorners & in wretched alleys
she shucks the offspring of greathearted Remus.[8] 5

11[9]

Aurelius & Furius, true comrades,
whether Catullus penetrates to where in
outermost India booms the eastern ocean's
    wonderful thunder;

whether he stops with Arabs or Hyrcani, 5
Parthian bowmen or nomadic Sagae;[1]
or goes to Egypt, which the Nile so richly
    dyes, overflowing;

even if he should scale the lofty Alps, or
summon to mind the mightiness of Caesar 10
viewing the Gallic Rhine, the dreadful Britons[2]
    at the world's far end—

you're both prepared to share in my adventures,
and any others which the gods may send me.
Back to my girl then, carry her this bitter 15
    message, these spare words:

---

7. Perhaps the Marcus Caelius Rufus who was one of Clodia's lovers and whom the statesman and orator Cicero defended when she sued him for trying to poison her.   8. Brother of Romulus, founder of Rome; symbol of Rome's greatness.   9. Like poem 51, also in Sapphic meter.   1. These are all peoples on the fringes of the Roman Empire (and so in Roman eyes exotic and menacing).   2. Julius Caesar (100–44 B.C.E.) began the conquest of Gaul in 58 and in 55 made an expedition to Britain.

May she have joy & profit from her cocksmen,
go down embracing hundreds all together,
never with love, but without interruption
    wringing their balls dry;   20

nor look to my affection as she used to,
for she has left it broken, like a flower
at the edge of a field after the plowshare
    brushes it, passing.

76

If any pleasure can come to a man through recalling
    decent behavior in his relations with others,
not breaking his word, and never, in any agreement,
    deceiving men by abusing vows sworn to heaven,
then countless joys will await you in old age, Catullus,   5
    as a reward for this unrequited passion!
For all of those things which a man could possibly say or
    do have all been said & done by you already,
and none of them counted for anything, thanks to her vileness!
    Then why endure your self-torment any longer?   10
Why not abandon this wretched affair altogether,
    spare yourself pain the gods don't intend you to suffer!
It's hard to break off with someone you've loved such a long time:
    it's hard, but you have to do it, somehow or other.
Your only chance is to get out from under this sickness,   15
    no matter whether or not you think you're able.
O gods, if pity is yours, or if ever to any
    who lay near death you offered the gift of your mercy,
look on my suffering: if my life seems to you decent,
    then tear from within me this devouring cancer,   20
this heavy dullness wasting the joints of my body,
    completely driving every joy from my spirit!
Now I no longer ask that she love me as I love her,
    or—even less likely—that she give up the others:
all that I ask for is health, an end to this foul sickness!   25
    O gods, grant me this in exchange for my worship.

VIRGIL
70–19 B.C.E.

Born in northern Italy, Publius Virgilius Maro became a leading member of the brilliant circle of literary artists that formed in Rome around the emperor Augustus. When he died in 19 B.C.E., just twelve years into Augustus's new regime, he left, not quite completed, an epic poem on the origins of Rome in the destruction of Troy: the journey of the Trojan Aeneas from Asia Minor to Italy, and his struggle to establish a home in his new land. This poem, the *Aeneid,* was meant to be a national epic for Augustan Rome, and it would become a profoundly influential text in the Western cultural and literary tradition.

We know little about Virgil, but the dates of his life tell us that he lived through the civil war that pitted Julius Caesar against the Roman Senate, and through the turbulent times that saw the collapse of the Roman republic and the emergence, under Augustus, of one-man rule over Italy and Rome's far-flung empire. As the new regime was getting established, at this moment of transition with enormous consequences not just for Rome but also for subsequent European history, Virgil looked back to distant origins to take stock of Rome's historical mission. Although not all readers today would endorse what sound like imperialist values, it is important to understand that when Virgil writes of Rome's civilizing and peace-bringing mission, he had years of political violence fresh in his memory. And so did his readers.

In using the past to assess the present, Virgil looked not only to the Aeneas legend but also to Greek literature, and especially to Homer. The story he tells combines the themes of the *Odyssey* (the wanderer in search of home) and the *Iliad* (the hero in battle). The first half of the poem (books 1–6) is modeled on the *Odyssey,* the second half (books 7–12) on the *Iliad.* Virgil borrows Homeric turns of phrase, similes, sentiments, and whole incidents; his Aeneas, like Achilles, sacrifices prisoners to the shade of a friend and, like Odysseus, descends alive to the world of the dead. But unlike Achilles, Aeneas does not satisfy the great passion of his life; nor does he, like Odysseus, find a home and peace. He sacrifices the personal objectives of both of Homer's heroes for a greater objective. His mission, imposed on him by the gods, is to found a city, from which, in the fullness of time, will spring the Roman state.

Homer presents us in the *Iliad* with the tragic pattern of the individual will, Achilles' wrath. But Aeneas is more than an individual. He is the prototype of the ideal Roman ruler; his qualities are the devotion to duty and the seriousness of purpose that were to give the Mediterranean world two centuries of ordered government after Augustus. Aeneas's mission begins in disorder in the burning city of Troy, but he leaves the carnage, carrying his father on his shoulders and leading his little son by the hand. This famous picture emphasizes the fact that unlike Achilles, he is securely set in a continuity of generations, the immortality of the family group, just as his mission to found a city, a home for the gods of Troy whose statues he carries with him, places him in a political and religious continuity. Achilles has no future. When he mentions his father and son, neither of whom he will see again, he emphasizes for us the loneliness of his short career. Odysseus has a father, wife, and son, and his heroic efforts are directed toward reestablishing himself in his proper context, that home in which he will be no longer a man in a world of magic and terror but a man in an organized and continuous community. But he fights for himself. Aeneas, on the other hand, suffers and fights not for himself but for the future. His own life is unhappy, and his death miserable. Yet he can console himself with the glory of his sons to come, the pageant of Roman achievement that he is shown by his father in the world below and that he carries on his shield. Aeneas's future is Virgil's present: the consolidation of the Roman peace under Augustus is the reward of Aeneas's unhappy life of effort and suffering.

Summarized like this, the *Aeneid* sounds like propaganda, which, in one sense of the word, it is. What saves it from the besetting fault of even the best propaganda—the partial concealment of the truth—is the fact that Virgil maintains an independence of the power that he is celebrating and sees his hero in the round. He knows that the Roman ideal of devotion to duty has another side, the suppression of many aspects of the personality, and that the man who wins and uses power must sacrifice much of himself, must live a life that, compared with that of Achilles or Odysseus, is constricted. In Virgil's poem Aeneas betrays the great passion of his life, his love for Dido, queen of Carthage. He does so reluctantly, but nevertheless he leaves her, and the full realization of what he has lost comes to him only when he meets her ghost in the world below. He weeps (as he did not at Carthage) and he pleads, in stronger terms than he did then, the overriding power that forced him to depart: "I left your land against my will, my queen." She leaves him without a word, her silence as impervious to pleas and tears as his was once at Carthage, and she goes back to join her first love, her husband, Sychaeus. Aeneas has sacrificed his love to something greater, but this does not insulate him from unhappiness. The limitations on the dedicated individual are emphasized by the contrasting figure of Dido, who follows her own impulse always, even in death. By her death, Virgil tells us expressly, she forestalls fate, breaking loose from the pattern in which Aeneas remains to the bitter end.

The Dido episode is an emphatic statement of the sacrifice that the Roman ideal of duty demands. Do we then admire Aeneas for his self-denial in service of a larger good to humanity? Or do we condemn him for cruelty to Dido and to himself? These questions are important because they have consequences for how we see Rome: is Rome worth such expenditure of lives? One can find justification in the text for both views. This is not an isolated example: the whole of Virgil's wondrously complex poem is open to different readings. An interpretation that sees it as straightforwardly celebrating Augustan Rome as the culmination of a historical process leading to peace and prosperity has to take account of apparently discordant elements. Why is Aeneas so different from the Homeric hero: introspective, uncertain, ambivalent (or so he often seems)? Why is he, the vehicle of the future, so given to nostalgia for a lost past? Why does Virgil emphasize that in going to a new home in Italy Aeneas is actually returning to the original home of the Trojan race? Or that Augustus is to restore the vanished Golden Age? What does progress mean if going forward actually means going back? Why does the poem end not with emphasis on Aeneas's triumph but with the death of his enemy Turnus, and why is killing the last action that this hero of civilization takes in the poem? These questions could be multiplied, but on the other hand the praise of Augustus, Rome, and Rome's imperial mission cannot be dismissed. In fact, the Augustan period was a time of unprecedented peace and stability. Was Virgil, then, paying tribute to what he saw as Rome's real achievements but balancing them against the costs?

VIRGIL IN LATIN

Conticuere omnes intentique ora tenebant;
inde toro pater Aeneas sic orsus ab alto:
    Infandum, regina, iubes renovare dolorem,
Troianas ut opes et lamentabile regnum
eruerint Danai, quaeque ipse miserrima uidi   5
et quorum pars magna fui. quis talia fando
Myrmidonum Dolopomue aut duri miles Ulixi
temperet a lacrimis? et iam nox umida caelo
praecipitat suadentque cadentia sidera somnos.
sed si tantus amor casus cognoscere nostros   10
et breviter Troiae supremum audire laborem,
quamquam animus meminisse horret luctuque refugit,
incipiam.

This is the beginning of book 2 of the *Aeneid*; Aeneas, at the banquet in Carthage, tells the story of the fall of Troy. The long lines do not employ rhyme but they have a regular rhythmic pattern based not on stress, as in English verse, but on length of syllable—that is, the time taken to pronounce it. Some vowels are naturally long, and others naturally short, but a short vowel may be made long by position (if it is followed by two consonants, it takes just as much time to pronounce as if it were naturally long). The line consists of six feet, each either a dactyl ($-\smile\smile$) or a spondee ($--$). In the first four feet various combinations are employed, but the last two feet, except in cases where a special effect is sought, are always dactyl plus spondee.

This hexameter (six-foot) line is capable of great variety, contained always in the formal pattern. Unfortunately, attempts to reproduce its disciplined variety in English stressed verse (Longfellow's "This is the forest primeval," for example) have not proved successful, and the translator has used a modern adaptation of the basic English line, the iambic pentameter of Shakespeare and Milton.

The subtle variation of the rhythm is not the only problem faced by translators; they must also try to compensate for the loss of effects that depend on the flexibility of Latin word order. In English, syntactical relationship is determined by that order: "man bites dog" means the opposite of "dog bites man." In Latin, because the terminations of the nouns show who does what to whom, "man bites dog" is *vir mordet canem,* and "dog bites man" *canis mordet virum.* Consequently, the words can be arranged in any order with no change of meaning. *Virum canis mordet, canis virum mordet,* and any other combination of these three elements all mean the same thing: "dog bites man." But the word order is not without its force; it can indicate emphasis. Normal order—subject, object, verb (for the Latin verb tends toward the end of the sentence)—would be *canis virum mordet.* But putting *virum,* the object, first—*virum canis mordet*—would draw attention to that word: "it was a *man* the dog bit."

This is a simple example; much more complicated effects are available to a poet in extended sentences. Line 3 of the passage quoted above, for example, uses the flexibility of word order not only for emphasis but also for exploring the possibilities of ambiguity and surprise offered by a highly inflected language. *Infandum* (unspeakable, something that cannot be said) is the first word, and we do not know from its termination whether it is subject or object or whether it is to be understood as a noun ("an unspeakable thing") or an adjective for which a noun will be supplied later. *Regina* (queen) could, according to its termination, be the subject of the sentence, but the context, Aeneas's reply to the queen's request for his story, suggests strongly that it is a form of address: "Unspeakable, oh Queen." The subject comes with the next word, the verb *iubes;* its termination shows that this is the second person, the "you" form—"you command." She has commanded something unspeakable. Is the reader being prepared for a refusal on the part of Aeneas to tell his story? *Renovare* defines the queen's order—"to renew"—and *dolorem* tells us what he is to renew— "sorrow." And the termination of this word suggests that the first word of the line, *infandum,* is in fact an adjective defining *dolorem.* The line, when one reaches this last word, re-forms itself into an unexpected pattern: "Unspeakable, oh Queen, is the sorrow you command me to renew." The line is enclosed between the two most important words in Aeneas's statement, *infandum* and *dolorem;* its last word imposes on us a slight change in our understanding of its first and so redirects attention to that solemn opening word of Aeneas's evocation of the fall of Troy, three long syllables heavy with grief for the lost splendor of a city that is now ash and rubble.

PRONOUNCING GLOSSARY

The following list uses common English syllables and stress accents to provide rough equivalents of selected words whose pronunciation may be unfamiliar to the general reader.

Aeneas: *i-nee'-uhs*

Aeneid: *i-nee'-id*

Aeolus: *ee'-o-lus / ai'-o-lus*

Anchises: *an-kai'-seez*

Andromachë: *an-dro'-ma-kee*

Aurora: *aw-roh'-rah / ow-roh'-rah*

Automedon: *aw-to'-me-don / ow-to'-me-don*

Charon: *kah'-ron*

Chimaera: *kai-meer'-uh / ki-mai'-ruh*

Cocytus: *ko-sai'-tus / ko'-ki-tus*

Creusa: *kree-oo'-sa / kray-oo'-sa*

Cyllene: *si-lee'-nee / ki-lay'-nay*

Cythera: *si'-ther-a / ki'-ther-a*

Cytherea: *si-the-ree'-uh / ki-ther-ay'-uh*

Danaans: *da'-nay-unz / dan'-a-ans*

Deiphobus: *day-i'-fo-bus*

Dido: *dai'-doh*

Dionysus: *dai-oh-nai'-sus*   Phrygian: *fri'-jun*

Eumenides: *yoo-me'-ni-deez*   Pirithoüs: *pi-ri'-thoh-us*

Hecate: *he'-kat-ee*   Scaean: *see'-an / skai'-an*

Iulus: *yoo'-lus / ee-yoo'-lus*   Teucer: *tyoo'-ser / tyoo'-ker*

Lethe: *lee'-thee*   Thymoetes: *thee-moy'-teez*

Musaeus: *moo-see'-us / moo-say'-us*   Tisiphone: *ti-si'-fo-nee*

Parcae: *par'-kai*   Xanthus: *zan'-thus / ksan'-thus*

Peneleus: *pee-ne'-lyoos*

From The Aeneid[1]

BOOK I

[A Fateful Haven]

I sing of warfare and a man at war.[2]
From the sea-coast of Troy in early days
He came to Italy by destiny,
To our Lavinian[3] western shore,
A fugitive, this captain, buffeted   5
Cruelly on land as on the sea
By blows from powers of the air—behind them
Baleful Juno[4] in her sleepless rage.
And cruel losses were his lot in war,
Till he could found a city and bring home   10
His gods to Latium,[5] land of the Latin race,
The Alban[6] lords, and the high walls of Rome.
Tell me the causes now, O Muse, how galled
In her divine pride, and how sore at heart
From her old wound, the queen of gods compelled him—   15
A man apart, devoted to his mission—
To undergo so many perilous days
And enter on so many trials. Can anger
Black as this prey on the minds of heaven?
Tyrian[7] settlers in that ancient time   20
Held Carthage,[8] on the far shore of the sea,
Set against Italy and Tiber's[9] mouth,
A rich new town, warlike and trained for war.
And Juno, we are told, cared more for Carthage
Than for any walled city of the earth,   25

---

1. Translated by Robert Fitzgerald.   2. Aeneas, a Trojan champion in the war at Troy, son of Venus (or Aphrodite), the goddess of love, and Anchises, a member of the Trojan royal house.   3. Named after the city of Lavinium near Rome. After the fall of Troy, Aeneas went in search of a new home, eventually settling here.   4. Wife and sister of the ruler of the gods (Hera in Greek). As in the *Iliad*, she is a bitter enemy of the Trojans.   5. The coastal plain on which Rome is situated.   6. The city of Alba Longa was founded by Aeneas's son, Ascanius. Romulus and Remus, the builders of Rome, were also from there.   7. From Tyre, on the coast of modern Lebanon, the principal city of the Phoenicians, a seafaring and trading people.   8. City on the coast of North Africa, opposite Sicily. Originally a Tyrian colony, it became a rich commercial center, controlling traffic in the western Mediterranean.   9. The river that flows through Rome.

More than for Samos,[1] even. There her armor
And chariot were kept, and, fate permitting,
Carthage would be the ruler of the world.
So she intended, and so nursed that power.
But she had heard long since   30
That generations born of Trojan blood
Would one day overthrow her Tyrian walls,
And from that blood a race would come in time
With ample kingdoms, arrogant in war,
For Libya's ruin: so the Parcae[2] spun.   35
In fear of this, and holding in memory
The old war she had carried on at Troy
For Argos'[3] sake (the origins of that anger,
That suffering, still rankled: deep within her,
Hidden away, the judgment Paris[4] gave,   40
Snubbing her loveliness; the race she hated;
The honors given ravished Ganymede[5]),
Saturnian Juno,[6] burning for it all,
Buffeted on the waste of sea those Trojans
Left by the Greeks and pitiless Achilles,   45
Keeping them far from Latium. For years
They wandered as their destiny drove them on
From one sea to the next: so hard and huge
A task it was to found the Roman people.

They were all under sail in open water   50
With Sicily just out of sight astern,
Lighthearted as they plowed the whitecapped sea
With stems of cutting bronze. But never free
Of her eternal inward wound, the goddess
Said to herself: 55
                 "Give up what I began?
Am I defeated? Am I impotent
To keep the king of Teucrians[7] from Italy?
The Fates forbid me; am I to suppose?
Could Pallas then consume the Argive fleet   60
With fire, and drown the crews,
Because of one man's one mad act—the crime
Of Ajax, son of Oïleus?[8] She—yes, she!—
Hurled out of cloudland lancing fire of Jove,
Scattered the ships, roughed up the sea with gales,   65
Then caught the man, bolt-struck, exhaling flames,

---

1. A large Greek island off the coast of Asia Minor, famous for its cult of Hera (Juno).   2. The Fates, who were imagined as female divinities who spun human destinies. *Libya's ruin*: Rome fought and won three wars against Carthage, finally destroying the city in 146 B.C.E. *Libya* is used as an inclusive name for the North African coast.   3. Home city of the Achaean (Greek) kings Agamemnon and Menelaus. Juno was on their side when they went to Troy to retrieve Helen, Menelaus's wife.   4. Son of King Priam of Troy. He was asked to judge which goddess—Venus, Juno, or Minerva (Athena)—was most beautiful. All three offered bribes, but Venus's promise of Helen's love prevailed, and Paris awarded her the prize.   5. A Trojan boy of extreme beauty who was taken up into heaven by Jupiter (Zeus), ruler of the gods.   6. Her father was Saturn, a Titan.   7. Trojans (so called from Teucer, one of the legendary kings of Troy).   8. One of the Greek heroes at Troy, a lesser warrior than Ajax son of Telamon. While the Greeks were sacking Troy, Priam's daughter Cassandra took refuge in the temple of Athena (Pallas). Ajax pulled her away from the goddess's statue and raped her. In revenge for this affront to her dignity, Athena set the Greek fleet on fire and overwhelmed it with a storm on its way home.

In a whirlwind and impaled him on a rock.
But I who walk as queen of all the gods,
Sister and wife of Jove, I must contend
For years against one people! Who adores   70
The power of Juno after this, or lays
An offering with prayer upon her altar?"

Smouldering, putting these questions to herself,
The goddess made her way to stormcloud country,
Aeolia, the weather-breeding isle.   75
Here in a vast cavern King Aeolus⁹
Rules the contending winds and moaning gales
As warden of their prison. Round the walls
They chafe and bluster underground. The din
Makes a great mountain murmur overhead.   80
High on a citadel enthroned,
Scepter in hand, he mollifies their fury,
Else they might flay the sea and sweep away
Land masses and deep sky through empty air.
In fear of this, Jupiter hid them away   85
In caverns of black night. He set above them
Granite of high mountains—and a king
Empowered at command to rein them in
Or let them go. To this king Juno now
Made her petition: 90
                    "Aeolus, the father
Of gods and men decreed and fixed your power
To calm the waves or make them rise in wind.
The race I hate is crossing the Tuscan sea,¹
Transporting Ilium² with her household gods—   95
Beaten as they are—to Italy.
                    Put new fury
Into your winds, and make the long ships founder!
Drive them off course! Throw bodies in the sea!
I have fourteen exquisite nymphs, of whom   100
The loveliest by far, Deïopëa,
Shall be your own. I'll join you two in marriage,
So she will spend all future years with you,
As you so well deserve,
And make you father of her lovely children."   105

Said Aeolus:
                "To settle on what you wish
Is all you need to do, your majesty.
I must perform it. You have given me
What realm I have. By your good offices   110
I rule with Jove's consent, and I recline
Among the gods at feasts, for you appoint me

---

9. Mythical ruler of the wind (see *Odyssey* 10).   1. The sea west of central Italy. The Trojans have almost
reached the future site of Rome.   2. Troy.

Lord of wind and cloud."
             Spearhaft reversed,
He gave the hollow mountainside a stroke,   115
And, where a portal opened, winds in ranks,
As though drawn up for battle, hurtled through,
To blow across the earth in hurricane.
Over the sea, tossed up from the sea-floor,
Eastwind and Southwind, then the wild Southwest   120
With squall on squall came scudding down,
Rolling high combers shoreward.
                Now one heard
The cries of men and screech of ropes in rigging
Suddenly, as the stormcloud whipped away   125
Clear sky and daylight from the Teucrians' eyes,
And gloom of night leaned on the open sea.
It thundered from all quarters, as it lightened
Flash on flash through heaven. Every sign
Portended a quick death for mariners.   130
Aeneas on the instant felt his knees
Go numb and slack, and stretched both hands to heaven,
Groaning out:
        "Triply lucky, all you men
To whom death came before your fathers' eyes   135
Below the wall at Troy! Bravest Danaan,
Diomedes, why could I not go down
When you had wounded me,[3] and lose my life
On Ilium's battlefield. Our Hector[4] lies there,
Torn by Achilles' weapon; there Sarpedon,[5]   140
Our giant fighter, lies; and there the river
Simoïs washes down so many shields
And helmets, with strong bodies taken under!"

As he flung out these words, a howling gust
From due north took the sail aback and lifted   145
Wavetops to heaven; oars were snapped in two;
The prow sheered round and left them broadside on
To breaking seas; over her flank and deck
A mountain of grey water crashed in tons.
Men hung on crests; to some a yawning trough   150
Uncovered bottom, boiling waves and sand.
The Southwind caught three ships and whirled them down
On reefs, hidden midsea, called by Italians
"The Altars"—razorbacks just under water.
The Eastwind drove three others from deep water   155
Into great shoals and banks, embedding them
And ringing them with sand, a desperate sight.
Before Aeneas' eyes a toppling billow
Struck the Lycians' ship, Orontes' ship,

---

3. In book 5 of the *Iliad*, Diomedes, one of the foremost warriors among the Greeks (Danaans), wounds Aeneas, who is rescued by his mother Aphrodite (Venus).   4. Oldest son of King Priam and Troy's chief defender, killed by Achilles, greatest warrior among the Greeks.   5. A Trojan ally killed by Achilles' comrade Patroclus.

Across the stern, pitching the steersman down   160
And overboard. Three times the eddying sea
Carried the ship around in the same place
Until the rapid whirlpool gulped it down.
A few men swimming surfaced in the welter.
So did shields, planks, precious things of Troy.   165
Ilioneus' good ship, brave Achates' ship,
The ship that carried Abas, and the one
Aletes sailed in, hale in his great age,
Were all undone by the wild gale: their seams
Parted and let the enemy pour in.   170
During all this, Neptune[6] became aware
Of hurly-burly and tempest overhead,
Bringing commotion to the still sea-depth
And rousing him. He lifted his calm brow
Above the surface, viewing the great sea,   175
And saw Aeneas' squadron far and wide
Dispersed over the water, saw the Trojans
Overwhelmed, the ruining clouds of heaven,
And saw his angry sister's[7] hand in all.
He called to him Eastwind and South and said: 180

"Are you so sure your line is privileged?
How could you dare to throw heaven and earth
Into confusion, by no will of mine,
And make such trouble? You will get from me—
But first to calm the rough sea; after this,   185
You'll pay a stricter penalty for your sins.
Off with you! Give this message to your king:
Power over the sea and the cruel trident
Were never his by destiny, but mine.
He owns the monstrous rocks, your home, Eastwind.   190
Let Aeolus ruffle in that hall alone
And lord it over winds shut in their prison."

Before the words were out, he quieted
The surging water, drove the clouds away,
And brought the sunlight back. Cymothoë   195
And Triton,[8] side by side, worked to dislodge
The grounded ships; then Neptune with his trident
Heaved them away, opened the miles of shoals,
Tempered the sea, and in his car departed
Gliding over the wave-tops on light wheels.   200

When rioting breaks out in a great city,
And the rampaging rabble goes so far
That stones fly, and incendiary brands—
For anger can supply that kind of weapon—
If it so happens they look round and see   205
Some dedicated public man, a veteran

---

6. God of the sea (Poseidon in Greek).   7. Juno.   8. A lesser sea god; Cymothoë is a sea nymph.

Whose record gives him weight, they quiet down,
Willing to stop and listen.
Then he prevails in speech over their fury
By his authority, and placates them.   210
Just so, the whole uproar of the great sea
Fell silent, as the Father of it all,
Scanning horizons under the open sky,
Swung his team around and gave free rein
In flight to his eager chariot.   215
                            Tired out,
Aeneas' people made for the nearest land,
Turning their prows toward Libya.[9] There's a spot
Where at the mouth of a long bay an island
Makes a harbor, forming a breakwater   220
Where every swell divides as it comes in
And runs far into curving recesses.
There are high cliffs on this side and on that,
And twin peaks towering heavenward impend
On reaches of still water. Over these,   225
Against a forest backdrop shimmering,
A dark and shaggy grove casts a deep shade,
While in the cliffside opposite, below
The overhanging peaks, there is a cave
With fresh water and seats in the living rock,   230
The home of nymphs. Here never an anchor chain,
Never an anchor's biting fluke need hold
A tired ship.
                        Aeneas put in here,
With only seven ships from his full number,   235
And longing for the firm earth underfoot
The Trojans disembarked, to take possession
Of the desired sand-beach. Down they lay,
To rest their brinesoaked bodies on the shore.
Achates[1] promptly struck a spark from flint   240
And caught it in dry leaves; he added tinder
Round about and waved it for a flame-burst.
Then they brought out the grain of Ceres,[2] tainted
By sea water, and Ceres' implements,
And, weary of their troubles, made all ready   245
To dry and grind with millstones what they had.

Meanwhile, Aeneas climbed one of the peaks
For a long seaward view, hoping to sight
Gale-worn Antheus and the Phrygian biremes,
Capys, or high poops bearing Caïcus'[3] arms.   250
He found no ship in sight, but on the shore
Three wandering stags. Behind them whole herds followed,
Grazing in a long line down the valleys.

---

9. The Trojans have been blown off course from the coast of Italy to North Africa.   1. Aeneas's most trusted companion.   2. Goddess of grain (Demeter in Greek).   3. All Trojans in charge of other ships that have disappeared. *Phrygian:* Trojan (after the district in Asia Minor in which Troy was located). *Biremes* were ships with two banks of oars.

Planting his feet, he took in hand the bow
And arrows carried by his aide, Achates, 255
Then, aiming for the leaders with heads high
And branching antlers, brought them first to earth.
Next he routed the whole herd,
Driving them with his shafts through leafy places,
Shooting and shooting till he won the hunt 260
By laying seven carcasses on the ground,
A number equal to his ships. Then back
To port he went, and parcelled out the game
To his ships' companies. There he divided
The wine courtly Acestes⁴ had poured out 265
And given them on the Sicilian shore—
Full jugs of it—when they were about to sail.
By this and by a simple speech Aeneas
Comforted his people:
                          "Friends and companions, 270
Have we not known hard hours before this?
My men, who have endured still greater dangers,
God will grant us an end to these as well.
You sailed by Scylla's rage, her booming crags,
You saw the Cyclops'⁵ boulders. Now call back 275
Your courage, and have done with fear and sorrow.
Some day, perhaps, remembering even this
Will be a pleasure. Through diversities
Of luck, and through so many challenges,
We hold our course for Latium, where the Fates 280
Hold out a settlement and rest for us.
Troy's kingdom there shall rise again. Be patient:
Save yourselves for more auspicious days."

So ran the speech. Burdened and sick at heart,
He feigned hope in his look, and inwardly 285
Contained his anguish. Now the Trojan crews
Made ready for their windfall and their feast.
They skinned the deer, bared ribs and viscera,
Then one lot sliced the flesh and skewered it
On spits, all quivering, while others filled 290
Bronze cooking pots and tended the beach fires.
All got their strength back from the meal, reclining
On the wild grass, gorging on venison
And mellowed wine. When hunger had been banished,
And tables put away, they talked at length 295
In hope and fear about their missing friends:
Could one believe they might be still alive,
Or had they suffered their last hour,
Never again to hear a voice that called them?
Aeneas, more than any, secretly 300

---

4. A king in Sicily who had given the Trojans shelter and whom the Trojans had just left when the storm hit.   5. Like Odysseus, Aeneas and his people encountered these monsters (whom tradition, by Roman times, had located in Sicily), as Aeneas will narrate in book 3.

Mourned for them all—for that fierce man, Orontes,
Then for Amycus, then for the bitter fate
Of Lycus, for brave Gyas, brave Cloanthus.

It was the day's end when from highest air
Jupiter looked down on the broad sea   305
Flecked with wings of sails, and the land masses,
Coasts, and nations of the earth. He stood
On heaven's height and turned his gaze toward Libya,
And, as he took the troubles there to heart,
Venus appealed to him, all pale and wan,   310
With tears in her shining eyes:
                              "My lord who rule
The lives of men and gods now and forever,
And bring them all to heel with your bright bolt,
What in the world could my Aeneas do,   315
What could the Trojans do, so to offend you
That after suffering all those deaths they find
The whole world closed to them, because of Italy?
Surely from these the Romans are to come
In the course of years, renewing Teucer's line,   320
To rule the sea and all the lands about it,
According to your promise. What new thought
Has turned you from them, Father? I consoled myself
For Troy's fall, that grim ruin, weighing out
One fate against another in the scales,   325
But now, when they have borne so many blows,
The same misfortune follows them. Great king,
What finish to their troubles will you give?
After Antenor[6] slipped through the Achaeans
He could explore Illyrian coves and reach   330
In safety the Liburnians' inland kingdoms
And source of the Timavus.[7] Through nine openings
With a great rumble in the mountain wall
It bursts from the ground there and floods the fields
In a rushing sea. And yet he chose that place   335
For Padua and new homes for Teucrians,
Gave them a name, set up the arms of Troy,
And now rests in his peace. As for ourselves,
Your own children, whom you make heirs of heaven,
Our ships being lost (this is unspeakable!),   340
We are forsaken through one enemy's rage
And kept remote from Italy. Is this
The palm for loyalty? This our power restored?"

He smiled at her, the father of gods and men,
With that serenity that calms the weather,   345
And lightly kissed his daughter. Then he said:

6. A leading Trojan who also escaped the city's destruction and came to Italy, settling near what is now
Venice on the Adriatic Sea.   7. Illyricum was a district, the Liburnians a people, and the Timavus a river
on the coast of the northern Adriatic.

"No need to be afraid, Cytherea.
Your children's destiny has not been changed.
As promised, you shall see Lavinium's walls
And take up, then, amid the stars of heaven   350
Great-souled Aeneas. No new thought has turned me.
No, he, your son—now let me speak of him,
In view of your consuming care, at length,
Unfolding secret fated things to come—
In Italy he will fight a massive war,   355
Beat down fierce armies, then for the people there
Establish city walls and a way of life.
When the Rutulians[8] are subdued he'll pass
Three summers of command in Latium,
Three years of winter quarters. But the boy,   360
Ascanius,[9] to whom the name of Iulus
Now is added—Ilus while Ilium stood—
Will hold the power for all of thirty years,
Great rings of wheeling months. He will transfer
His capital from Lavinium and make   365
A fortress, Alba Longa. Three full centuries
That kingdom will be ruled by Hector's race,
Until the queen and priestess, Ilia,
Pregnant by Mars, will bear twin sons to him.
Afterward, happy in the tawny pelt   370
His nurse, the she-wolf, wears, young Romulus[1]
Will take the leadership, build walls of Mars,
And call by his own name his people Romans.
For these I set no limits, world or time,
But make the gift of empire without end.   375
Juno, indeed, whose bitterness now fills
With fear and torment sea and earth and sky,
Will mend her ways, and favor them as I do,
Lords of the world, the toga-bearing Romans.
Such is our pleasure. As the years fall away,   380
An age comes when Assaracus'[2] royal house
Will bring to servitude Thessalian Phthia,
Renowned Mycenae, too; and subjugate
Defeated Argos.[3] From that comely line
The Trojan Caesar[4] comes, to circumscribe   385
Empire with Ocean, fame with heaven's stars.
Julius his name, from Iulus handed down:
All tranquil shall you take him heavenward
In time, laden with plunder of the East,

---

8. Inhabitants of Latium.   9. Aeneas's son.   1. Founder of Rome along with his twin brother, Remus
(whom he killed—a point Virgil leaves out here). As babies the twins were set out to die but survived when
a she-wolf suckled them.   2. One of the sons of Tros, an early king of Troy. Aeneas's father Anchises
was his grandson, and Priam, the last king of Troy, was descended from one of Assaracus's brothers.
3. I.e., conquer Greece (annexed as a Roman province in the 2nd century B.C.E.). Argos was the home of
the Greek warrior Diomedes, Agamemnon was from Mycenae and Achilles was from Phthia.   4. Julius
Caesar, founder of Rome's imperial power. His nephew and adopted son, Octavian, became the emperor
Augustus. The Julian family claimed descent from Iulus and through him from Aeneas. It is possible that
the reference is to Augustus himself ("plunder of the East" in line 389 would then allude to his victory over
Antony and Cleopatra in 31 B.C.E. in the naval battle at Actium which left him the undisputed master of
the Roman Empire).

And he with you shall be invoked in prayer. 390
Wars at an end, harsh centuries then will soften,
Ancient Fides and Vesta, Quirinus[5]
With Brother Remus, will be lawgivers,
And grim with iron frames, the Gates of War[6]
Will then be shut: inside, unholy Furor,[7] 395
Squatting on cruel weapons, hands enchained
Behind him by a hundred links of bronze,
Will grind his teeth and howl with bloodied mouth."

That said, he sent the son of Maia[8] down
From his high place to make the land of Carthage, 400
The new-built town, receptive to the Trojans,
Not to allow Queen Dido, all unknowing
As to the fated future, to exclude them.
Through the vast air with stroking wings he flew
And came down quickly on the Libyan coast, 405
Performing Jove's command, so that at once
Phoenicians put aside belligerence
As the god willed. Especially the queen
Took on a peaceful mood, an open mind
Toward Teucrians. 410

        But the dedicated[9] man,
Aeneas, thoughtful through the restless night,
Made up his mind, as kindly daylight came,
To go out and explore the strange new places,
To learn what coast the wind had brought him to 415
And who were living there, men or wild creatures—
For wilderness was all he saw—and bring
Report back to his company. The ships
He hid beneath a hollowed rocky cliff
And groves that made a vault, trees all around 420
And deep shade quivering. He took his way
With only one man at his side, Achates,
Hefting two hunting spears with broad steel points.
Then suddenly, in front of him,
His mother[1] crossed his path in mid-forest, 425
Wearing a girl's shape and a girl's gear—
A Spartan girl, or like that one of Thrace,
Harpalyce, who tires horses out,
Outrunning the swift Hebrus.[2] She had hung
About her shoulders the light, handy bow 430

5. Another name for Romulus. *Fides and Vesta*: two personifications worshipped as goddesses—Vesta, of the hearth and therefore of the family; Fides, of honesty, loyalty, and good faith (virtues highly prized in Roman culture).   6. These gates, in the temple of Janus, were kept open in wartime and closed in times of peace. They were closed in 25 B.C.E., early in Augustus's regime—for the first time since 235 B.C.E.   7. Personification of irrational fury and violence, especially of war (including the civil wars that plagued Rome before Augustus came to power).   8. Mercury (Hermes), messenger of the gods.   9. This word translates the Latin *pius*, a common epithet of Aeneas in the poem. *Pietas* (the related noun) is loyalty to family and country, and dedication to duty in general; it is the most important value in the *Aeneid*. "Unholy Furor" in line 395 is, in Latin, *Furor impius*—just the opposite of *pius*.   1. The goddess Venus.   2. A river in Thrace, the district north of the Aegean Sea. *Harpalyce* was a Thracian girl who lived in the wilds and devoted herself to hunting (in Greek tradition, a mark of resistance to marriage).

A huntress carries, and had given her hair
To the disheveling wind; her knees were bare,
Her flowing gown knotted and kirtled up.

She spoke first:
          "Ho, young fellows, have you seen—   435
Can you say where—one of my sisters here,
In a spotted lynx-hide, belted with a quiver,
Scouting the wood, or shouting on the track
Behind a foam-flecked boar?"
                   To Venus then   440
The son of Venus answered:
                  "No, I've heard
Or seen none of your sisters—only, how
Shall I address you, girl? Your look's not mortal,
Neither has your accent a mortal ring.   445
O Goddess, beyond doubt! Apollo's sister?[3]
One of the family of nymphs? Be kind,
Whoever you may be, relieve our trouble,
Tell us under what heaven we've come at last,
On what shore of the world are we cast up,   450
Wanderers that we are, strange to this country,
Driven here by wind and heavy sea.
By my right hand many an offering
Will be cut down for you before your altars."

Venus replied: 455
        "Be sure I am not fit
For any such devotion. Tyrian girls
Are given to wearing quivers and hunting boots
Of crimson, laced on the leg up to the knee.
This is the Punic[4] kingdom that you see,   460
The folk are Tyrian, the town Agenor's.[5]
But neighboring lands belong to Libya,
A nation hard to fight against in war.
The ruler here is Dido, of Tyre city,
In flight here from her brother—a long tale   465
Of wrong endured, mysterious and long.
But let me tell the main events in order.
Her husband was Sychaeus, of all Phoenicians
Richest in land, and greatly loved by her,
Ill-fated woman. Her father had given her,   470
A virgin still, in marriage, her first rite.
Her brother, though, held power in Tyre—Pygmalion,
A monster of wickedness beyond all others.
Between the two men furious hate arose,
And sacrilegiously before the altars,   475
Driven by a blind lust for gold, Pygmalion
Took Sychaeus by surprise and killed him
With a dagger blow in secret, undeterred

---

3. Diana (Artemis), virgin goddess of the hunt.   4. Carthaginian.   5. A mythical Phoenician king.

By any thought of Dido's love. He hid
What he had done for a long time, cozening her,   480
Deluding the sick woman with false hope.
But the true form of her unburied husband
Came in a dream: lifting his pallid face
Before her strangely, he made visible
The cruel altars and his body pierced,   485
Uncovering all the dark crime of the house.

He urged her then to make haste and take flight,
Leaving her fatherland, and to assist the journey
Revealed a buried treasure of old time,
Unknown to any, a weight of gold and silver.   490
Impelled by this, Dido laid her plans
To get away and to equip her company.
All who hated the tyrant, all in fear
As bitter as her own, now came together,
And ships in port, already fitted out,   495
They commandeered, to fill with gold: the riches
Pygmalion had itched for went to sea,
And captaining the venture was a woman.
They sailed to this place where today you'll see
Stone walls going higher and the citadel   500
Of Carthage, the new town. They bought the land,
Called Drumskin from the bargain made, a tract
They could enclose with one bull's hide.[6]

> But now,
What of yourselves? From what coast do you come?   505
Where are you bound?"

> Then to the questioner
He answered sighing, bringing out the words
From deep within him:

> "Goddess, if I should tell   510
Our story from the start, if you had leisure
To hear our annals of adversity,
Before I finished, the fair evening star
Would come to close Olympus and the day.
From old Troy—if the name of Troy has fallen   515
Perhaps upon your ears—we sailed the seas,
And yesterday were driven by a storm,
Of its own whim, upon this Libyan coast.
I am Aeneas, duty-bound, and known
Above high air of heaven by my fame,   520
Carrying with me in my ships our gods
Of hearth and home, saved from the enemy.
I look for Italy to be my fatherland,
And my descent is from all-highest Jove.
With twenty ships I mounted the Phrygian sea,   525
As my immortal mother showed the way.

6. They cut the hide into a very thin and very long strip.

I followed the given fates. Now barely seven
Ships are left, battered by wind and sea,
And I myself, unknown and unprovisioned,
Cross the Libyan wilderness, an exile   530
Driven from Europe and from Asia—"

But Venus chose to hear no more complaints
And broke in, midway through his bitterness:

"Whoever you are, I doubt Heaven is unfriendly
To you, as you still breathe life-giving air   535
On your approach to the Tyrian town. Go on:
Betake yourself this way to the queen's gate.
Your friends are back. This is my news for you:
Your ships were saved and brought to shore again
By winds shifting north, or else my parents   540
Taught me augury to no purpose. Look:
See the twelve swans in line rejoicing there!
Jove's eagle, like a bolt out of the blue,
Had flurried them in open heaven, but now
They seem to be alighting one by one   545
Or looking down on those already grounded.
As they disport themselves, with flapping wings,
After their chanting flight about the sky,
Just so your ships and your ships' companies
Are either in port or entering under sail.   550
Go on then, where the path leads, go ahead!"

On this she turned away. Rose-pink and fair
Her nape shone, her ambrosial hair exhaled
Divine perfume, her gown rippled full length,
And by her stride she showed herself a goddess.   555
Knowing her for his mother, he called out
To the figure fleeting away:
                          "You! cruel, too!
Why tease your son so often with disguises?
Why may we not join hands and speak and hear   560
The simple truth?"
                  So he called after her,
And went on toward the town. But Venus muffled
The two wayfarers in grey mist, a cloak
Of dense cloud poured around them, so that no one   565
Had the power to see or to accost them,
Make them halt, or ask them what they came for.
Away to Paphos[7] through high air she went
In joy to see her home again, her shrine
And hundred altars where Sabaean[8] incense   570
Fumed and garlands freshened the air.
                                    Meanwhile
The two men pressed on where the pathway led,
Soon climbing a long ridge that gave a view

---

7. On the island of Cyprus, center of an important cult of Aphrodite (Venus).   8. Arabian.

Down over the city and facing towers. 575
Aeneas found, where lately huts had been,
Marvelous buildings, gateways, cobbled ways,
And din of wagons. There the Tyrians
Were hard at work: laying courses for walls,
Rolling up stones to build the citadel, 580
While others picked out building sites and plowed
A boundary furrow. Laws were being enacted,
Magistrates and a sacred senate chosen.
Here men were dredging harbors, there they laid
The deep foundation of a theatre, 585
And quarried massive pillars to enhance
The future stage—as bees in early summer
In sunlight in the flowering fields
Hum at their work, and bring along the young
Full-grown to beehood; as they cram their combs 590
With honey, brimming all the cells with nectar,
Or take newcomers' plunder, or like troops
Alerted, drive away the lazy drones,
And labor thrives and sweet thyme scents the honey.
Aeneas said: "How fortunate these are 595
Whose city walls are rising here and now!"

He looked up at the roofs, for he had entered,
Swathed in cloud—strange to relate—among them,
Mingling with men, yet visible to none.
In mid-town stood a grove that cast sweet shade 600
Where the Phoenicians, shaken by wind and sea,
Had first dug up that symbol Juno showed them,
A proud warhorse's head: this meant for Carthage
Prowess in war and ease of life through ages.
Here being built by the Sidonian[9] queen 605
Was a great temple planned in Juno's honor,
Rich in offerings and the godhead there.
Steps led up to a sill of bronze, with brazen
Lintel, and bronze doors on groaning pins.
Here in this grove new things that met his eyes 610
Calmed Aeneas' fear for the first time.
Here for the first time he took heart to hope
For safety, and to trust his destiny more
Even in affliction. It was while he walked
From one to another wall of the great temple 615
And waited for the queen, staring amazed
At Carthaginian promise, at the handiwork
Of artificers and the toil they spent upon it:
He found before his eyes the Trojan battles
In the old war, now known throughout the world— 620
The great Atridae, Priam, and Achilles,
Fierce in his rage at both sides.[1] Here Aeneas

9. From Sidon, like Tyre a city in Phoenicia.   1. I.e., not just at the Trojans but at Agamemnon (with whom Achilles quarreled; see *Iliad* 1). *Atridae:* sons of Atreus, Agamemnon and Menelaus. *Priam:* king of Troy.

Halted, and tears came.
                                   "What spot on earth,"
He said, "what region of the earth, Achatës,   625
Is not full of the story of our sorrow?
Look, here is Priam. Even so far away
Great valor has due honor; they weep here
For how the world goes, and our life that passes
Touches their hearts. Throw off your fear. This fame   630
Insures some kind of refuge."
                                   He broke off
To feast his eyes and mind on a mere image,
Sighing often, cheeks grown wet with tears,
To see again how, fighting around Troy,   635
The Greeks broke here, and ran before the Trojans,
And there the Phrygians² ran, as plumed Achilles
Harried them in his warcar. Nearby, then,
He recognized the snowy canvas tents
Of Rhesus,³ and more tears came: these, betrayed   640
In first sleep, Diomedes devastated,
Swording many, till he reeked with blood,
Then turned the mettlesome horses toward the beachhead
Before they tasted Trojan grass or drank
At Xanthus ford.   645
                    And on another panel
Troilus,⁴ without his armor, luckless boy,
No match for his antagonist, Achilles,
Appeared pulled onward by his team: he clung
To his warcar, though fallen backward, hanging   650
On to the reins still, head dragged on the ground,
His javelin scribbling S's in the dust.
Meanwhile to hostile Pallas's⁵ shrine
The Trojan women walked with hair unbound,
Bearing the robe of offering, in sorrow,   655
Entreating her, beating their breasts. But she,
Her face averted, would not raise her eyes.
And there was Hector, dragged around Troy walls
Three times, and there for gold Achilles sold him,
Bloodless and lifeless. Now indeed Aeneas   660
Heaved a mighty sigh from deep within him,
Seeing the spoils, the chariot, and the corpse
Of his great friend, and Priam, all unarmed,
Stretching his hands out.⁶
                              He himself he saw   665
In combat with the first of the Achaeans,
And saw the ranks of Dawn, black Memnon's⁷ arms;

---

2. Trojans.   3. King of Thrace, who came to the aid of Troy just before the end of the war. In a night
raid on his camp, Odysseus and Diomedes killed him and many of his followers as they slept and drove his
horses back to the Greek camp. An oracle had proclaimed that if Rhesus's horses ate Trojan grass and
drank the water of the river Xanthus, Troy would not fall.   4. A young son of Priam.   5. Athena (see
Iliad 6.299–327).   6. The references are to Achilles' mistreatment of Hector's corpse in Iliad 22 and
Priam's ransoming of his son's body from Achilles in Iliad 24.   7. King of the Ethiopians, who fought on
the Trojan side. His mother was the dawn goddess Eos (in Latin, Aurora).

Then, leading the battalion of Amazons
With half-moon shields, he saw Penthesilea[8]
Fiery amid her host, buckling a golden   670
Girdle beneath her bare and arrogant breast,
A girl who dared fight men, a warrior queen.
Now, while these wonders were being surveyed
By Aeneas of Dardania,[9] while he stood
Enthralled, devouring all in one long gaze,   675
The queen paced toward the temple in her beauty,
Dido, with a throng of men behind.

As on Eurotas bank or Cynthus[1] ridge
Diana trains her dancers, and behind her
On every hand the mountain nymphs appear,   680
A myriad converging; with her quiver
Slung on her shoulders, in her stride she seems
The tallest, taller by a head than any,
And joy pervades Latona's[2] quiet heart:
So Dido seemed, in such delight she moved   685
Amid her people, cheering on the toil
Of a kingdom in the making. At the door
Of the goddess' shrine, under the temple dome,
All hedged about with guards on her high throne,
She took her seat. Then she began to give them   690
Judgments and rulings, to apportion work
With fairness, or assign some tasks by lot,
When suddenly Aeneas saw approaching,
Accompanied by a crowd, Antheus and Sergestus
And brave Cloanthus,[3] with a few companions,   695
Whom the black hurricane had driven far
Over the sea and brought to other coasts.
He was astounded, and Achates too
Felt thrilled by joy and fear: both of them longed
To take their friends' hands, but uncertainty   700
Hampered them. So, in their cloudy mantle,
They hid their eagerness, waiting to learn
What luck these men had had, where on the coast
They left their ships, and why they came. It seemed
Spokesmen for all the ships were now arriving,   705
Entering the hall, calling for leave to speak.
When all were in, and full permission given
To make their plea before the queen, their eldest,
Ilioneus, with composure said:
                         "Your majesty,   710
Granted by great Jupiter freedom to found
Your new town here and govern fighting tribes
With justice—we poor Trojans, worn by winds
On every sea, entreat you: keep away

---

8. Queen of the Amazons (a tribe of women warriors who lived in Asia Minor and also fought for Troy). Like Memnon, she was killed by Achilles.   9. The kingdom of Troy.   1. A mountain on the island of Delos, birthplace of Diana. *Eurotas*: a river near Sparta, where she was worshipped.   2. Diana's mother (Leto in Greek).   3. Ship captains of Aeneas's fleet, from whom he has been separated in the storm.

Calamity of fire from our ships! 715
Let a godfearing people live, and look
More closely at our troubles. Not to ravage
Libyan hearths or turn with plunder seaward
Have we come; that force and that audacity
Are not for beaten men. 720
                    There is a country
Called by the Greeks Hesperia, very old,
Potent in warfare and in wealth of earth;
Oenotrians farmed it; younger settlers now,
The tale goes, call it by their chief's name, Italy. 725
We laid our course for this.
But stormy Orion[4] and a high sea rising
Deflected us on shoals and drove us far,
With winds against us, into whelming waters,
Unchanneled reefs. We kept afloat, we few, 730
To reach your coast. What race of men is this?
What primitive state could sanction this behavior?
Even on beaches we are denied a landing,
Harried by outcry and attack, forbidden
To set foot on the outskirts of your country. 735
If you care nothing for humanity
And merely mortal arms, respect the gods
Who are mindful of good actions and of evil!

We had a king, Aeneas—none more just,
More zealous, greater in warfare and in arms. 740
If fate preserves him, if he does not yet
Lie spent amid the insensible shades but still
Takes nourishment of air, we need fear nothing;
Neither need you repent of being first
In courtesy, to outdo us. Sicily too 745
Has towns and plowlands and a famous king
Of Trojan blood, Acestes. May we be
Permitted here to beach our damaged ships,
Hew timbers in your forest, cut new oars,
And either sail again for Latium, happily, 750
If we recover shipmates and our king,
Or else, if that security is lost,
If Libyan waters hold you, Lord Aeneas,
Best of Trojans, hope of Iulus gone,
We may at least cross over to Sicily 755
From which we came, to homesteads ready there,
And take Acestes for our king."
                    Ilioneus
Finished, and all the sons of Dardanus
Murmured assent. Dido with eyes downcast 760
Replied in a brief speech:
                    "Cast off your fear,

4. The giant hunter turned constellation; his appearance marked the approach of winter (and thus stormy weather).

You Teucrians, put anxiety aside.
Severe conditions and the kingdom's youth
Constrain me to these measures, to protect 765
Our long frontiers with guards.
                              Who has not heard
Of the people of Aeneas, of Troy city,
Her valors and her heroes, and the fires
Of the great war? We are not so oblivious, 770
We Phoenicians. The sun yokes his team
Within our range at Carthage. Whether you choose
Hesperia Magna and the land of Saturn
Or Eryx[5] in the west and King Acestes,
I shall dispatch you safely with an escort, 775
Provisioned from my stores. Or would you care
To join us in this realm on equal terms?
The city I build is yours; haul up your ships;
Trojan and Tyrian will be all one to me.
If only he were here, your king himself, 780
Caught by the same easterly, Aeneas!
Indeed, let me send out trustworthy men
Along the coast, with orders to comb it all
From one end of Libya to the other,
In case the sea cast the man up and now 785
He wanders lost, in town or wilderness."

Elated at Dido's words, both staunch Achates
And father Aeneas had by this time longed
To break out of the cloud. Achates spoke
With urgency: 790
          "My lord, born to the goddess,
What do you feel, what is your judgment now?
You see all safe, our ships and friends recovered.
One is lost; we saw that one go down
Ourselves, amid the waves. Everything else 795
Bears out your mother's own account of it."

He barely finished when the cloud around them
Parted suddenly and thinned away
Into transparent air. Princely Aeneas
Stood and shone in the bright light, head and shoulders 800
Noble as a god's. For she who bore him
Breathed upon him beauty of hair and bloom
Of youth and kindled brilliance in his eyes,
As an artist's hand gives style to ivory,
Or sets pure silver, or white stone of Paros,[6] 805
In framing yellow gold. Then to the queen
He spoke as suddenly as, to them all,

5. A city at the west end of Sicily. Saturn (the Greek Cronus) was the father of Jupiter and was driven out by him from the kingship over the gods. Legend said that he took refuge in Italy (Hesperia), where the Golden Age that characterized his reign survived; this is an important theme of the second half of the *Aeneid*. 6. A Cycladic island; its marble was famous for its whiteness.

He had just appeared:
                          "Before your eyes I stand,
Aeneas the Trojan, that same one you look for,   810
Saved from the sea off Libya.
                          You alone,
Moved by the untold ordeals of old Troy,
Seeing us few whom the Greeks left alive,
Worn out by faring ill on land and sea,   815
Needy of everything—you'd give these few
A home and city, allied with yourselves.
Fit thanks for this are not within our power,
Not to be had from Trojans anywhere
Dispersed in the great world.   820
                          May the gods—
And surely there are powers that care for goodness,
Surely somewhere justice counts—may they
And your own consciousness of acting well
Reward you as they should. What age so happy   825
Brought you to birth? How splendid were your parents
To have conceived a being like yourself!
So long as brooks flow seaward, and the shadows
Play over mountain slopes, and highest heaven
Feeds the stars, your name and your distinction   830
Go with me, whatever lands may call me."

With this he gave his right hand to his friend
Ilioneus, greeting Serestus with his left,
Then took the hands of those brave men, Cloanthus,
Gyas, and the rest.   835
                  Sidonian Dido
Stood in astonishment, first at the sight
Of such a captain, then at his misfortune,
Presently saying:
                  "Born of an immortal   840
Mother though you are, what adverse destiny
Dogs you through these many kinds of danger?
What rough power brings you from sea to land
In savage places? Are you truly he,
Aeneas, whom kind Venus bore   845
To the Dardanian, the young Anchisës,
Near to the stream of Phrygian Simoïs?
I remember the Greek, Teucer,[7] came to Sidon,
Exiled, and in search of a new kingdom.
Belus, my father, helped him. In those days   850
Belus campaigned with fire and sword on Cyprus
And won that island's wealth. Since then, the fall
Of Troy, your name, and the Pelasgian[8] kings
Have been familiar to me. Teucer, your enemy,
Spoke often with admiration of the Teucrians   855

---

7. A warrior who fought at Troy (brother of the greater Ajax) and was later exiled from his home. He founded a city on the island of Cyprus.   8. Greek.

And traced his own descent from Teucrian stock.
Come, then, soldiers, be our guests. My life
Was one of hardship and forced wandering
Like your own, till in this land at length
Fortune would have me rest. Through pain I've learned   860
To comfort suffering men."
                              She led Aeneas
Into the royal house, but not before
Declaring a festal day in the gods' temples.
As for the ships' companies, she sent   865
Twenty bulls to the shore, a hundred swine,
Huge ones, with bristling backs, and fatted lambs,
A hundred of them, and their mother ewes—
All gifts for happy feasting on that day.

Now the queen's household made her great hall glow   870
As they prepared a banquet in the kitchens.
Embroidered table cloths, proud crimson-dyed,
Were spread, and set with massive silver plate,
Or gold, engraved with brave deeds of her fathers,
A sequence carried down through many captains   875
In a long line from the founding of the race.
Meanwhile paternal love would not allow
Aeneas' mind to rest. He sent Achates
On a quick mission to the ships, to tell
Ascanius and bring him to the city—   880
Fond father, as always thoughtful of his son—
And told Achates to fetch gifts as well,
Relics of Ilium: a robe stiff with figures
Worked in gold, and a veil woven round
With yellow acanthus flowers—both adornments   885
Worn by Argive Helen when she sailed
For Pergamum[9] and her forbidden marriage,
Marvelous keepsakes of her mother, Leda.
Along with these, a scepter Ilione,
Eldest of Priam's daughters, once had used,   890
A collar hung with pearls, and a coronet
Doubled in gems and gold,
                              Given these orders,
Achatës lost no time seeking the ships.

    Our Lady of Cythera,[1] however, pondered   895
New interventions, a new strategy:
That her young godling son, Desire,[2] should take
The face and figure of Ascanius,
Then come and use his gifts to make the queen
Infatuated, inflaming her with lust   900
To the marrow of her bones. Venus no doubt
Lacked faith in the ambiguous royal house

9. Troy.   1. Venus. Cythera, an island south of the Greek Peloponnesus, had an important cult to her.
2. Amor or Cupid (Greek Eros), god of sexual desire.

And Tyrians' double dealing; then, the spite
Of Juno vexed her. Her anxieties
Recurred as night came on. So she addressed him,   905
Amor, god of caressing wings:
                              "My son,
My strength, my greatest power, my one and only,
Making light of our High Father's bolt,
His giant-killer! I must turn to you   910
And beg the force of your divinity.
You know how Brother Aeneas has been tossed
From one coast to another on the high seas
By bitter Juno's hatred; you know this
And in my grieving for him grieve as well.   915
Now the Phoenician woman, Dido, has him,
Making him linger with her blandishments,
And what may come of this Junonian welcome
Worries me seriously. Juno will act
At such a crisis of affairs. Accordingly,   920
What I propose is to ensnare the queen
By guile beforehand, pin her down in passion,
So she cannot be changed by any power
But will be kept on my side by profound
Love of Aeneas. Take heed of our thought   925
How you may do this. The boy prince, my greatest
Care in the world, must go now to the city,
Summoned by his father, taking gifts
Saved from the great sea and the fires of Troy.
I'll drug him in his sleep, then hide him well   930
High up in Cythera, or on Cyprus, over
Idalium³ in my shrine. There is no way
For him to learn this trick or interfere.
You counterfeit his figure for one night,
No more, and make the boy's known face your mask,   935
So that when Dido takes you on her lap
Amid the banquetting and wine, in joy,
When she embraces you and kisses you,
You'll breathe invisible fire into her
And dupe her with your sorcery."   940
                        Amor
Agreed with his fond mother's plan of action,
Put off his wings and gaily walked as Iulus.
Venus in turn sent through Ascanius' body
Rills of slumber, caught him to her breast,   945
And bore him to Idalia's aerial groves
Where beds of marjoram
Embraced him in soft bloom and breathing shade.
Soon then the godling, doing as she wished,
Happily following where Achatës led,   950
Carried the royal gifts to the Tyrians.
He found the queen amid magnificence
Of tapestries, where she had placed herself

---

3. Another town in Cyprus that had a temple of Venus.

In the very center, on a golden couch.
Then Father Aeneas and the Trojan company   955
Came in to take their ease on crimson cloth.
Houseboys filled their finger bowls and brought them
Bread in baskets, napkins nubbled smooth.
In the great kitchen there were fifty maids
To set the dishes out in a long line   960
And tend the fires that shone for the hearth gods.
A hundred others, and as many boys
Of the same age, loaded the boards with meat
And placed the wine cups. Tyrians as well
Came crowding through the radiant doors, all bidden   965
To take their ease on figured cushioning.
There they admired Aeneas' gifts, admired
Iulus with his godling's face aglow
And simulated speech; then the great robe,
The veil that yellow acanthus flowers edged.   970
And more than anyone, the Phoenician queen,
Luckless, already given over to ruin,
Marveled and could not have enough: she burned
With pleasure in the boy and in the gifts.
After hugging Aeneas round the neck   975
And clinging to him, answering the love
Of the deluded father, he sought the queen;
And she with all her eyes and heart embraced him,
Fondling him at times upon her breast,
Oblivious of how great a god sat there   980
To her undoing. Mindful of his mother,
He had begun to make Sychaeus fade
From Dido's memory bit by bit, and tried
To waken with new love, a living love,
Her long settled mind and dormant heart.   985

After the first pause in the feast, and after
Trenchers were taken off, they put out wine bowls,
Grand and garlanded. A festive din
Now rose and echoed through the palace halls.
Lighted lamps hung from the coffered ceiling   990
Rich with gold leaf, and torches with high flames
Prevailed over the night. And now the queen
Called for a vessel heavy with gems and gold
That Belus and his line had always used.
She filled it, dipping wine, and her long hall   995
Fell silent.
          "Jupiter," she prayed,
"You make the laws for host and guest, they say.
Grant that this day be one of joy for Tyrians
And men of Troy; grant that it be remembered   1000
By our descendants. Now be with us, Bacchus,[4]
Giver of happiness, and kindly Juno,

4. God of wine (Dionysus).

And all you Tyrians attend
In friendliness this meeting that unites us."

At this she tilted a libation out   1005
And put the vessel lightly to her lips,
Then, with a jest, gave it to Bitias,
Who nearly immersed himself in brimming gold
As he drank down the foaming wine. The bowl
Passed then to other lords. And Lord Iopas,   1010
With flowing hair, whom giant Atlas⁵ taught,
Made the room echo to his golden lyre.
He sang the straying moon and toiling sun,
The origin of mankind and the beasts,
Of rain and fire; the rainy Hyades,   1015
Arcturus, the Great Bear and Little Bear;⁶
The reason winter suns are in such haste
To dip in Ocean, or what holds the nights
Endless in winter. Tyrians at this
Redoubled their applause; the Trojans followed.   1020
And Dido, fated queen, drew out the night
With talk of various matters, while she drank
Long draughts of love. Often she asked of Priam,
Often of Hector; now of the armor Memnon,
The son of Dawn, had worn; now of the team   1025
Diomedes drove; now of the huge Achilles.

"Come, rather," then she said, "dear guest, and tell us
From the beginning the Greek stratagems,
The ruin of your town and your sea-faring,
As now the seventh summer brings you here   1030
From wandering all the lands and all the seas."

BOOK II

[How They Took the City]

The room fell silent, and all eyes were on him,
As Father Aeneas from his high couch began:

"Sorrow too deep to tell, your majesty,
You order me to feel and tell once more.
How the Danaans leveled in the dust   5
The splendor of our mourned-forever kingdom—
Heartbreaking things I saw with my own eyes
And was myself a part of. Who could tell them,
Even a Myrmidon or Dolopian
Or ruffian of Ulysses,⁷ without tears?   10
Now, too, the night is well along, with dewfall
Out of heaven, and setting stars weigh down

---

5. A Titan condemned for his defiance of Jupiter to hold up the sky forever. He would probably be an appropriate teacher of the physical arrangement of the world.   6. The constellations Ursa Major and Ursa Minor. *Hyades:* the constellation that rises at the time of spring rains. *Arcturus:* the brightest star in Ursa Major.   7. Odysseus. Myrmidons and Dolopians were Achilles' soldiers.

Our heads toward sleep. But if so great desire
Moves you to hear the tale of our disasters,
Briefly recalled, the final throes of Troy,   15
However I may shudder at the memory
And shrink again in grief, let me begin.

Knowing their strength broken in warfare, turned
Back by the fates, and years—so many years—
Already slipped away, the Danaan captains   20
By the divine handicraft of Pallas built
A horse of timber, tall as a hill,
And sheathed its ribs with planking of cut pine.
This they gave out to be an offering
For a safe return by sea, and the word went round.   25
But on the sly they shut inside a company
Chosen from their picked soldiery by lot,
Crowding the vaulted caverns in the dark—
The horse's belly—with men fully armed.

Offshore there's a long island, Tenedos,   30
Famous and rich while Priam's kingdom lasted,
A treacherous anchorage now, and nothing more.
They crossed to this and hid their ships behind it
On the bare shore beyond. We thought they'd gone,
Sailing home to Mycenae before the wind,   35
So Teucer's town is freed of her long anguish,
Gates thrown wide! And out we go in joy
To see the Dorian⁸ campsites, all deserted,
The beach they left behind. Here the Dolopians
Pitched their tents, here cruel Achilles lodged,   40
There lay the ships, and there, formed up in ranks,
They came inland to fight us. Of our men
One group stood marveling, gaping up to see
The dire gift of the cold unbedded goddess,⁹
The sheer mass of the horse.   45
                              Thymoetes shouts
It should be hauled inside the walls and moored
High on the citadel—whether by treason
Or just because Troy's fate went that way now.
Capys opposed him; so did the wiser heads: 50
'Into the sea with it,' they said, 'or burn it,
Build up a bonfire under it,
This trick of the Greeks, a gift no one can trust,
Or cut it open, search the hollow belly!'

Contrary notions pulled the crowd apart.
Next thing we knew, in front of everyone,   55
Laocoön with a great company
Came furiously running from the Height,¹
And still far off cried out: 'O my poor people,

8. Greek.   9. Athena.   1. The citadel, the acropolis.

Men of Troy, what madness has come over you?   60
Can you believe the enemy truly gone?
A gift from the Danaans, and no ruse?
Is that Ulysses' way, as you have known him?
Achaeans must be hiding in this timber,
Or it was built to butt against our walls,   65
Peer over them into our houses, pelt
The city from the sky. Some crookedness
Is in this thing. Have no faith in the horse!
Whatever it is, even when Greeks bring gifts
I fear them, gifts and all.'   70
                  He broke off then
And rifled his big spear with all his might
Against the horse's flank, the curve of belly.
It stuck there trembling, and the rounded hull
Reverberated groaning at the blow.   75
If the gods' will had not been sinister,
If our own minds had not been crazed,
He would have made us foul that Argive den
With bloody steel, and Troy would stand today—
O citadel of Priam, towering still!   80

But now look: hillmen, shepherds of Dardania,
Raising a shout, dragged in before the king
An unknown fellow with hands tied behind—
This all as he himself had planned,
Volunteering, letting them come across him,   85
So he could open Troy to the Achaeans.
Sure of himself this man was, braced for it
Either way, to work his trick or die.
From every quarter Trojans run to see him,
Ring the prisoner round, and make a game   90
Of jeering at him. Be instructed now
In Greek deceptive arts: one barefaced deed
Can tell you of them all.
As the man stood there, shaken and defenceless,
Looking around at ranks of Phrygians,   95
'Oh god,' he said, 'what land on earth, what seas
Can take me in? What's left me in the end,
Outcast that I am from the Danaans,
Now the Dardanians will have my blood?'

The whimpering speech brought us up short; we felt   100
A twinge for him. Let him speak up, we said,
Tell us where he was born, what news he brought,
What he could hope for as a prisoner.
Taking his time, slow to discard his fright,
He said:
        'I'll tell you the whole truth, my lord,   105
No matter what may come of it. Argive
I am by birth, and will not say I'm not.
That first of all: Fortune has made a derelict

Of Sinon, but the bitch
Won't make an empty liar of him, too.   110
Report of Palamedes[2] may have reached you,
Scion of Belus' line, a famous man
Who gave commands against the war. For this,
On a trumped-up charge, on perjured testimony,
The Greeks put him to death—but now they mourn him,   115
Now he has lost the light. Being kin to him,
In my first years I joined him as companion,
Sent by my poor old father on this campaign,
And while he held high rank and influence
In royal councils, we did well, with honor.   120
Then by the guile and envy of Ulysses—
Nothing unheard of there!—he left this world,
And I lived on, but under a cloud, in sorrow,
Raging for my blameless friend's downfall.
Demented, too, I could not hold my peace   125
But said if I had luck, if I won through
Again to Argos, I'd avenge him there.
And I roused hatred with my talk; I fell
Afoul now of that man. From that time on,
Day in, day out, Ulysses   130
Found new ways to bait and terrify me,
Putting out shady rumors among the troops,
Looking for weapons he could use against me.
He could not rest till Calchas[3] served his turn—
But why go on? The tale's unwelcome, useless,   135
If Achaeans are all one,
And it's enough I'm called Achaean, then
Exact the punishment, long overdue;
The Ithacan[4] desires it; the Atridae
Would pay well for it.'   140
                 Burning with curiosity,
We questioned him, called on him to explain—
Unable to conceive such a performance,
The art of the Pelasgian. He went on,
Atremble, as though he feared us: 145
                 'Many times
The Danaans wished to organize retreat,
To leave Troy and the long war, tired out.
If only they had done it! Heavy weather
At sea closed down on them, or a fresh gale   150
From the Southwest would keep them from embarking,
Most of all after this figure here,
This horse they put together with maple beams,
Reached its full height. Then wind and thunderstorms
Rumbled in heaven. So in our quandary   155

---

2. A Greek warrior who advised Agamemnon to abandon the war against Troy; his downfall was engineered by Ulysses, who planted in his tent forged proofs of dealings with the enemy.   3. The prophet of the Greek army.   4. Ulysses.

We sent Eurypylus to Phoebus'[5] oracle,
And he brought back this grim reply:

'Blood and a virgin slain[6]
You gave to appease the winds, for your first voyage
Troyward, O Danaans. Blood again   160
And Argive blood, one life, wins your return.'

When this got round among the soldiers, gloom
Came over them, and a cold chill that ran
To the very marrow. Who had death in store?
Whom did Apollo call for? Now the man   165
Of Ithaca haled Calchas out among us
In tumult, calling on the seer to tell
The true will of the gods. Ah, there were many
Able to divine the crookedness
And cruelty afoot for me, but they   170
Looked on in silence. For ten days the seer
Kept still, kept under cover, would not speak
Of anyone, or name a man for death,
Till driven to it at last by Ulysses' cries—
By prearrangement—he broke silence, barely   175
Enough to designate me for the altar.[7]
Every last man agreed. The torments each
Had feared for himself, now shifted to another,
All could endure. And the infamous day came,
The ritual, the salted meal, the fillets[8] . . .   180
I broke free, I confess it, broke my chains,
Hid myself all night in a muddy marsh,
Concealed by reeds, waiting for them to sail
If they were going to.
                          Now no hope is left me   185
Of seeing my home country ever again,
My sweet children, my father, missed for years.
Perhaps the army will demand they pay
For my escape, my crime here, and their death,
Poor things, will be my punishment. Ah, sir,   190
I beg you by the gods above, the powers
In whom truth lives, and by what faith remains
Uncontaminated to men, take pity
On pain so great and so unmerited!'

For tears we gave him life, and pity, too.   195
Priam himself ordered the gyves removed
And the tight chain between. In kindness then
He said to him:
                  'Whoever you may be,
The Greeks are gone; forget them from now on;   200
You shall be ours. And answer me these questions:

---

5. Apollo. Eurypylus was a minor Greek chieftain.   6. Iphigenia, Agamemnon's daughter.   7. I.e., for
sacrifice.   8. Tufts of wool attached to the victim.

Who put this huge thing up, this horse?
Who designed it? What do they want with it?
Is it religious or a means of war?'

These were his questions. Then the captive, trained   205
In trickery, in the stagecraft of Achaea,
Lifted his hands unfettered to the stars.
'Eternal fires of heaven,' he began,
'Powers inviolable, I swear by thee,
As by the altars and blaspheming swords   210
I got away from, and the gods' white bands[9]
I wore as one chosen for sacrifice,
This is justice, I am justified
In dropping all allegiance to the Greeks—
As I had cause to hate them; I may bring   215
Into the open what they would keep dark.
No laws of my own country bind me now.
Only be sure you keep your promises
And keep faith, Troy, as you are kept from harm
If what I say proves true, if what I give   220
Is great and valuable.
            The whole hope
Of the Danaans, and their confidence
In the war they started, rested all along
In help from Pallas. Then the night came   225
When Diomedes and that criminal,
Ulysses, dared to raid her holy shrine.
They killed the guards on the high citadel
And ripped away the statue, the Palladium,[1]
Desecrating with bloody hands the virginal   230
Chaplets of the goddess. After that,
Danaan hopes waned and were undermined,
Ebbing away, their strength in battle broken,
The goddess now against them. This she made
Evident to them all with signs and portents.   235
Just as they set her statue up in camp,
The eyes, cast upward, glowed with crackling flames,
And salty sweat ran down the body. Then—
I say it in awe—three times, up from the ground,
The apparition of the goddess rose   240
In a lightning flash, with shield and spear atremble.
Calchas divined at once that the sea crossing
Must be attempted in retreat—that Pergamum
Cannot be torn apart by Argive swords
Unless at Argos first they beg new omens,   245
Carrying homeward the divine power
Brought overseas in ships. Now they are gone
Before the wind to the fatherland, Mycenae,
Gone to enlist new troops and gods. They'll cross

---

9. The fillets.　　1. The statue of Pallas Athena. An oracle stated that Troy could not be captured as long
as the Palladium remained in place in the shrine.

The water again and be here, unforeseen.   250
So Calchas read the portents. Warned by him,
They set this figure up in reparation
For the Palladium stolen, to appease
The offended power and expiate the crime.
Enormous, though, he made them build the thing   255
With timber braces, towering to the sky,
Too big for the gates, not to be hauled inside
And give the people back their ancient guardian.
If any hand here violates this gift
To great Minerva,[2] then extinction waits,   260
Not for one only—would god it were so—
But for the realm of Priam and all Phrygians.
If this proud offering, drawn by your hands,
Should mount into your city, then so far
As the walls of Pelops' town[3] the tide of Asia   265
Surges in war: that doom awaits our children.'

This fraud of Sinon, his accomplished lying,
Won us over; a tall tale and fake tears
Had captured us, whom neither Diomedes
Nor Larisaean[4] Achilles overpowered,   270
Nor ten long years, nor all their thousand ships.

And now another sign, more fearful still,
Broke on our blind miserable people,
Filling us all with dread. Laocoön,
Acting as Neptune's priest that day by lot,   275
Was on the point of putting to the knife
A massive bull before the appointed altar,
When ah—look there!
From Tenedos, on the calm sea, twin snakes—
I shiver to recall it—endlessly   280
Coiling, uncoiling, swam abreast for shore,
Their underbellies showing as their crests
Reared red as blood above the swell; behind
They glided with great undulating backs.
Now came the sound of thrashed seawater foaming;   285
Now they were on dry land, and we could see
Their burning eyes, fiery and suffused with blood,
Their tongues a-flicker out of hissing maws.
We scattered, pale with fright. But straight ahead
They slid until they reached Laocoön.   290
Each snake enveloped one of his two boys,
Twining about and feeding on the body.
Next they ensnared the man as he ran up
With weapons: coils like cables looped and bound him
Twice round the middle; twice about his throat   295
They whipped their back-scales, and their heads towered,

2. Athena.   3. Argos. Pelops was the grandfather of Agamemnon and Menelaus.   4. Of Larissa, a
town in Achilles' homeland of Thessaly.

While with both hands he fought to break the knots,
Drenched in slime, his head-bands black with venom,
Sending to heaven his appalling cries
Like a slashed bull escaping from an altar, 300
The fumbled axe shrugged off. The pair of snakes
Now flowed away and made for the highest shrines,
The citadel of pitiless Minerva,
Where coiling they took cover at her feet
Under the rondure of her shield. New terrors 305
Ran in the shaken crowd: the word went round
Laocoön had paid, and rightfully,
For profanation of the sacred hulk
With his offending spear hurled at its flank.
'The offering must be hauled to its true home,' 310
They clamored. 'Votive prayers to the goddess
Must be said there!'
            So we breached the walls
And laid the city open. Everyone
Pitched in to get the figure underpinned 315
With rollers, hempen lines around the neck.
Deadly, pregnant with enemies, the horse
Crawled upward to the breach. And boys and girls
Sang hymns around the towrope as for joy
They touched it. Rolling on, it cast a shadow 320
Over the city's heart. O Fatherland,
O Ilium, home of gods! Defensive wall
Renowned in war for Dardanus's people!
There on the very threshold of the breach
It jarred to a halt four times, four times the arms 325
In the belly thrown together made a sound—
Yet on we strove unmindful, deaf and blind,
To place the monster on our blessed height.
Then, even then, Cassandra's[5] lips unsealed
The doom to come: lips by a god's command 330
Never believed or heeded by the Trojans.
So pitiably we, for whom that day
Would be the last, made all our temples green
With leafy festal boughs throughout the city.

As heaven turned, Night from the Ocean stream 335
Came on, profound in gloom on earth and sky
And Myrmidons in hiding. In their homes
The Teucrians lay silent, wearied out,
And sleep enfolded them. The Argive fleet,
Drawn up in line abreast, left Tenedos 340
Through the aloof moon's friendly stillnesses
And made for the familiar shore. Flame signals
Shone from the command ship. Sinon, favored
By what the gods unjustly had decreed,

---

5. Daughter of King Priam. As punishment from Apollo, her prophecies were never believed (see Aeschylus, *Agamemnon* 1209 ff.).

Stole out to tap the pine walls and set free   345
The Danaans in the belly. Opened wide,
The horse emitted men; gladly they dropped
Out of the cavern, captains first, Thessandrus,
Sthenelus and the man of iron, Ulysses;
Hand over hand upon the rope, Acamas, Thoas,   350
Neoptolemus[6] and Prince Machaon,
Menelaus and then the master builder,
Epeos, who designed the horse decoy.
Into the darkened city, buried deep
In sleep and wine, they made their way,   355
Cut the few sentries down,
Let in their fellow soldiers at the gate,
And joined their combat companies as planned.
That time of night it was when the first sleep,
Gift of the gods, begins for all mankind,   360
Arriving gradually, delicious rest.
In sleep, in dream, Hector appeared to me,
Gaunt with sorrow, streaming tears, all torn—
As by the violent car on his death day—
And black with bloody dust,   365
His puffed-out feet cut by the rawhide thongs.
Ah god, the look of him! How changed
From that proud Hector who returned to Troy
Wearing Achilles' armor,[7] or that one
Who pitched the torches on Danaan ships;   370
His beard all filth, his hair matted with blood,
Showing the wounds, the many wounds, received
Outside his father's city walls. I seemed
Myself to weep and call upon the man
In grieving speech, brought from the depth of me: 375

'Light of Dardania, best hope of Troy,
What kept you from us for so long, and where?
From what far place, O Hector, have you come,
Long, long awaited? After so many deaths
Of friends and brothers, after a world of pain   380
For all our folk and all our town, at last,
Boneweary, we behold you! What has happened
To ravage your serene face? Why these wounds?'

He wasted no reply on my poor questions
But heaved a great sigh from his chest and said: 385
'Ai! Give up and go, child of the goddess,
Save yourself, out of these flames. The enemy
Holds the city walls, and from her height
Troy falls in ruin. Fatherland and Priam
Have their due; if by one hand our towers   390
Could be defended, by this hand, my own,

---

6. Son of Achilles.   7. Hector stripped it from the corpse of Patroclus, whom he had killed in battle.
Achilles avenged his friend Patroclus by killing Hector.

They would have been. Her holy things, her gods
Of hearth and household[8] Troy commends to you.
Accept them as companions of your days;
Go find for them the great walls that one day   395
You'll dedicate, when you have roamed the sea.'

As he said this, he brought out from the sanctuary
Chaplets and Vesta, Lady of the Hearth,
With her eternal fire.[9]
           While I dreamed,   400
The turmoil rose, with anguish, in the city.
More and more, although Anchises' house
Lay in seclusion, muffled among trees,
The din at the grim onset grew; and now
I shook off sleep, I climbed to the roof top   405
To cup my ears and listen. And the sound
Was like the sound a grassfire makes in grain,
Whipped by a Southwind, or a torrent foaming
Out of a mountainside to strew in ruin
Fields, happy crops, the yield of plowing teams,   410
Or woodlands borne off in the flood; in wonder
The shepherd listens on a rocky peak.
I knew then what our trust had won for us,
Knew the Danaan fraud: Deïphobus'[1]
Great house in flames, already caving in   415
Under the overpowering god of fire;
Ucalegon's already caught nearby;
The glare lighting the straits beyond Sigeum;[2]
The cries of men, the wild calls of the trumpets.

To arm was my first maddened impulse—not   420
That anyone had a fighting chance in arms;
Only I burned to gather up some force
For combat, and to man some high redoubt.
So fury drove me, and it came to me
That meeting death was beautiful in arms.   425
Then here, eluding the Achaean spears,
Came Panthus, Orthrys' son, priest of Apollo,
Carrying holy things, our conquered gods,
And pulling a small grandchild along: he ran
Despairing to my doorway.   430
               'Where's the crux,
Panthus,' I said. 'What strongpoint shall we hold?'

Before I could say more, he groaned and answered:
'The last day for Dardania has come,
The hour not to be fought off any longer.   435
Trojans we have been; Ilium has been;
The glory of the Teucrians is no more;

---

8. The Penates, kept in a shrine in Roman (not Trojan) homes.   9. The fire in Vesta's temple was never allowed to go out.   1. A son of Priam.   2. A promontory overlooking the strait that connects the Aegean with the Black Sea.

Black Jupiter has passed it on to Argos.
Greeks are the masters in our burning city.
Tall as a cliff, set in the heart of town,   440
Their horse pours out armed men. The conqueror,
Gloating Sinon, brews new conflagrations.
Troops hold the gates—as many thousand men
As ever came from great Mycenae; others
Block the lanes with crossed spears; glittering   445
In a combat line, swordblades are drawn for slaughter.
Even the first guards at the gates can barely
Offer battle, or blindly make a stand.'

Impelled by these words, by the powers of heaven,
Into the flames I go, into the fight,   450
Where the harsh Fury, and the din and shouting,
Skyward rising, calls. Crossing my path
In moonlight, five fell in with me, companions:
Ripheus, and Epytus, a great soldier,
Hypanis, Dymas, cleaving to my side   455
With young Coroebus, Mygdon's son. It happened
That in those very days this man had come
To Troy, aflame with passion for Cassandra,
Bringing to Priam and the Phrygians
A son-in-law's right hand. Unlucky one,   460
To have been deaf to what his bride foretold!
Now when I saw them grouped, on edge for battle,
I took it all in and said briefly,
                              'Soldiers,
Brave as you are to no end, if you crave   465
To face the last fight with me, and no doubt of it,
How matters stand for us each one can see.
The gods by whom this kingdom stood are gone,
Gone from the shrines and altars. You defend
A city lost in flames. Come, let us die,   470
We'll make a rush into the thick of it.
The conquered have one safety: hope for none.'

The desperate odds doubled their fighting spirit:
From that time on, like predatory wolves
In fog and darkness, when a savage hunger   475
Drives them blindly on, and cubs in lairs
Lie waiting with dry famished jaws—just so
Through arrow flights and enemies we ran
Toward our sure death, straight for the city's heart,
Cavernous black night over and around us.   480
Who can describe the havoc of that night
Or tell the deaths, or tally wounds with tears?
The ancient city falls, after dominion
Many long years. In windows, on the streets,
In homes, on solemn porches of the gods,   485
Dead bodies lie. And not alone the Trojans
Pay the price with their heart's blood; at times

Manhood returns to fire even the conquered
And Danaan conquerors fall. Grief everywhere,
Everywhere terror, and all shapes of death.   490

Androgeos was the first to cross our path
Leading a crowd of Greeks; he took for granted
That we were friends, and hailed us cheerfully:

'Men, get a move on! Are you made of lead
To be so late and slow? The rest are busy   495
Carrying plunder from the fires and towers.
Are you just landed from the ships?'
                                        His words
Were barely out, and no reply forthcoming
Credible to him, when he knew himself   500
Fallen among enemies. Thunderstruck,
He halted, foot and voice, and then recoiled
Like one who steps down on a lurking snake
In a briar patch and jerks back, terrified,
As the angry thing rears up, all puffed and blue.   505
So backward went Androgeos in panic.
We were all over them in a moment, cut
And thrust, and as they fought on unknown ground,
Startled, unnerved, we killed them everywhere.
So Fortune filled our sails at first. Coroebus,   510
Elated at our feat and his own courage,
Said:
      'Friends, come follow Fortune. She has shown
The way to safety, shown she's on our side.
We'll take their shields and put on their insignia! 515
Trickery, bravery: who asks, in war?
The enemy will arm us.'
                        He put on
The plumed helm of Androgeos, took the shield
With blazon and the Greek sword to his side.   520
Ripheus, Dymas—all were pleased to do it,
Making the still fresh trophies our equipment.
Then we went on, passing among the Greeks,
Protected by our own gods now no longer;
Many a combat, hand to hand, we fought   525
In the black night, and many a Greek we sent
To Orcus.[3] There were some who turned and ran
Back to the ships and shore; some shamefully
Clambered again into the horse, to hide
In the familiar paunch.   530
                        When gods are contrary
They stand by no one. Here before us came
Cassandra, Priam's virgin daughter, dragged
By her long hair out of Minerva's shrine,
Lifting her brilliant eyes in vain to heaven—   535

3. The abode of the dead.

Her eyes alone, as her white hands were bound.
Coroebus, infuriated, could not bear it,
But plunged into the midst to find his death.
We all went after him, our swords at play,
But here, here first, from the temple gable's height,   540
We met a hail of missiles from our friends,
Pitiful execution, by their error,
Who thought us Greek from our Greek plumes and shields.
Then with a groan of anger, seeing the virgin
Wrested from them, Danaans from all sides   545
Rallied and attacked us: fiery Ajax,[4]
Atreus' sons, Dolopians in a mass—
As, when a cyclone breaks, conflicting winds
Will come together, Westwind, Southwind, Eastwind
Riding high out of the Dawnland; forests   550
Bend and roar, and raging all in spume
Nereus[5] with his trident churns the deep.
Then some whom we had taken by surprise
Under cover of night throughout the city
And driven off, came back again: they knew   555
Our shields and arms for liars now, our speech
Alien to their own. They overwhelmed us.
Coroebus fell at the warrior goddess' altar,
Killed by Peneleus; and Ripheus fell,
A man uniquely just among the Trojans,   560
The soul of equity; but the gods would have it
Differently. Hypanis, Dymas died,
Shot down by friends; nor did your piety,
Panthus, nor Apollo's fillets shield you
As you went down.   565
                    Ashes of Ilium!
Flames that consumed my people! Here I swear
That in your downfall I did not avoid
One weapon, one exchange with the Danaans,
And if it had been fated, my own hand   570
Had earned my death. But we were torn away
From that place—Iphitus and Pelias too,
One slow with age, one wounded by Ulysses,
Called by a clamor at the hall of Priam.
Truly we found here a prodigious fight,   575
As though there were none elsewhere, not a death
In the whole city: Mars[6] gone berserk, Danaans
In a rush to scale the roof; the gate besieged
By a tortoise shell of overlapping shields.[7]
Ladders clung to the wall, and men strove upward   580
Before the very doorposts, on the rungs,
Left hand putting the shield up, and the right
Reaching for the cornice. The defenders

---

4. The lesser Ajax, son of Oileus.   5. An old sea god and father of the Nereids, the sea nymphs.
6. The war god (Ares in Greek).   7. When attacking a walled position, Roman soldiers protected themselves from overhead missiles by holding their shields above their heads; the resulting pattern looked like
the plates of a tortoiseshell.

Wrenched out upperworks and rooftiles: these
For missiles, as they saw the end, preparing   585
To fight back even on the edge of death.
And gilded beams, ancestral ornaments,
They rolled down on the heads below. In hall
Others with swords drawn held the entrance way,
Packed there, waiting. Now we plucked up heart   590
To help the royal house, to give our men
A respite, and to add our strength to theirs,
Though all were beaten. And we had for entrance
A rear door, secret, giving on a passage
Between the palace halls; in other days   595
Andromache, poor lady, often used it,
Going alone to see her husband's parents
Or taking Astyanax[8] to his grandfather.
I climbed high on the roof, where hopeless men
Were picking up and throwing futile missiles.   600
Here was a tower like a promontory
Rising toward the stars above the roof:
All Troy, the Danaan ships, the Achaean camp,
Were visible from this. Now close beside it
With crowbars, where the flooring made loose joints,   605
We pried it from its bed and pushed it over.
Down with a rending crash in sudden ruin
Wide over the Danaan lines it fell;
But fresh troops moved up, and the rain of stones
With every kind of missile never ceased.   610

Just at the outer doors of the vestibule
Sprang Pyrrhus,[9] all in bronze and glittering,
As a serpent, hidden swollen underground
By a cold winter, writhes into the light,
On vile grass fed, his old skin cast away,   615
Renewed and glossy, rolling slippery coils,
With lifted underbelly rearing sunward
And triple tongue a-flicker. Close beside him
Giant Periphas and Automedon,
His armor-bearer, once Achilles' driver,   620
Besieged the place with all the young of Scyros,[1]
Hurling their torches at the palace roof.
Pyrrhus shouldering forward with an axe
Broke down the stony threshold, forced apart
Hinges and brazen door-jambs, and chopped through   625
One panel of the door, splitting the oak,
To make a window, a great breach. And there
Before their eyes the inner halls lay open,
The courts of Priam and the ancient kings,
With men-at-arms ranked in the vestibule.   630
From the interior came sounds of weeping,

8. Son of Andromache and Hector.   9. Neoptolemus.   1. Island in the north Aegean where Neoptolemus grew up.

Pitiful commotion, wails of women
High-pitched, rising in the formal chambers
To ring against the silent golden stars;
And, through the palace, mothers wild with fright   635
Ran to and fro or clung to doors and kissed them.
Pyrrhus with his father's brawn stormed on,
No bolts or bars or men availed to stop him:
Under his battering the double doors
Were torn out of their sockets and fell inward.   640
Sheer force cleared the way: the Greeks broke through
Into the vestibule, cut down the guards,
And made the wide hall seethe with men-at-arms—
A tumult greater than when dykes are burst
And a foaming river, swirling out in flood,   645
Whelms every parapet and races on
Through fields and over all the lowland plains,
Bearing off pens and cattle. I myself
Saw Neoptolemus furious with blood
In the entrance way, and saw the two Atridae;   650
Hecuba² I saw, and her hundred daughters,
Priam before the altars, with his blood
Drenching the fires that he himself had blessed.
Those fifty bridal chambers, hope of a line
So flourishing; those doorways high and proud,   655
Adorned with takings of barbaric gold,
Were all brought low: fire had them, or the Greeks.

What was the fate of Priam, you may ask.
Seeing his city captive, seeing his own
Royal portals rent apart, his enemies   660
In the inner rooms, the old man uselessly
Put on his shoulders, shaking with old age,
Armor unused for years, belted a sword on,
And made for the massed enemy to die.
Under the open sky in a central court   665
Stood a big altar; near it, a laurel tree
Of great age, leaning over, in deep shade
Embowered the Penates. At this altar
Hecuba and her daughters, like white doves
Blown down in a black storm, clung together,   670
Enfolding holy images in their arms.
Now, seeing Priam in a young man's gear,
She called out:
                    'My poor husband, what mad thought
Drove you to buckle on these weapons?   675
Where are you trying to go? The time is past
For help like this, for this kind of defending,
Even if my own Hector could be here.
Come to me now: the altar will protect us,
Or else you'll die with us.'   680
                    She drew him close,

---

2. Wife of Priam and mother of Hector.

Heavy with years, and made a place for him
To rest on the consecrated stone.
                         Now see
Polites, one of Priam's sons, escaped   685
From Pyrrhus' butchery and on the run
Through enemies and spears, down colonnades,
Through empty courtyards, wounded. Close behind
Comes Pyrrhus burning for the death-stroke: has him,
Catches him now, and lunges with the spear.   690
The boy has reached his parents, and before them
Goes down, pouring out his life with blood.
Now Priam, in the very midst of death,
Would neither hold his peace nor spare his anger.

'For what you've done, for what you've dared,' he said,   695
'If there is care in heaven for atrocity,
May the gods render fitting thanks, reward you
As you deserve. You forced me to look on
At the destruction of my son: defiled
A father's eyes with death. That great Achilles   700
You claim to be the son of—and you lie—
Was not like you to Priam, his enemy;
To me who threw myself upon his mercy
He showed compunction, gave me back for burial
The bloodless corpse of Hector, and returned me   705
To my own realm.'
                    The old man threw his spear
With feeble impact; blocked by the ringing bronze,
It hung there harmless from the jutting boss.
Then Pyrrhus answered: 710
                        'You'll report the news
To Pelides,³ my father; don't forget
My sad behavior, the degeneracy
Of Neoptolemus. Now die.'
                           With this,   715
To the altar step itself he dragged him trembling,
Slipping in the pooled blood of his son,
And took him by the hair with his left hand.
The sword flashed in his right; up to the hilt
He thrust it in his body.   720
                          That was the end
Of Priam's age, the doom that took him off,
With Troy in flames before his eyes, his towers
Headlong fallen—he that in other days
Had ruled in pride so many lands and peoples,   725
The power of Asia.
                    On the distant shore
The vast trunk headless lies without a name.

For the first time that night, inhuman shuddering
Took me, head to foot. I stood unmanned,   730

---

3. Achilles, son of Peleus; he was killed by Paris before Troy fell.

And my dear father's image came to mind
As our king, just his age, mortally wounded,
Gasped his life away before my eyes.
Creusa[4] came to mind, too, left alone;
The house plundered; danger to little Iulus.   735
I looked around to take stock of my men,
But all had left me, utterly played out,
Giving their beaten bodies to the fire
Or plunging from the roof.
              It came to this,   740
That I stood there alone. And then I saw
Lurking beyond the doorsill of the Vesta,
In hiding, silent, in that place reserved,
The daughter of Tyndareus.[5] Glare of fires
Lighted my steps this way and that, my eyes   745
Glancing over the whole scene, everywhere.
That woman, terrified of the Trojans' hate
For the city overthrown, terrified too
Of Danaan vengeance, her abandoned husband's
Anger after years—Helen, that Fury   750
Both to her own homeland and Troy, had gone
To earth, a hated thing, before the altars.
Now fires blazed up in my own spirit—
A passion to avenge my fallen town
And punish Helen's whorishness.   755
                'Shall this one
Look untouched on Sparta and Mycenae
After her triumph, going like a queen,
And see her home and husband, kin and children,
With Trojan girls for escort, Phrygian slaves?   760
Must Priam perish by the sword for this?
Troy burn, for this? Dardania's littoral
Be soaked in blood, so many times, for this?
Not by my leave. I know
No glory comes of punishing a woman,   765
The feat can bring no honor. Still, I'll be
Approved for snuffing out a monstrous life,
For a just sentence carried out. My heart
Will teem with joy in this avenging fire,
And the ashes of my kin will be appeased.'   770

So ran my thoughts. I turned wildly upon her,
But at that moment, clear, before my eyes—
Never before so clear—in a pure light
Stepping before me, radiant through the night,
My loving mother came: immortal, tall,   775
And lovely as the lords of heaven know her.
Catching me by the hand, she held me back,
Then with her rose-red mouth reproved me:

                      'Son,

---

4. Aeneas's wife.   5. Helen.

Why let such suffering goad you on to fury 780
Past control? Where is your thoughtfulness
For me, for us? Will you not first revisit
The place you left your father, worn and old,
Or find out if your wife, Creusa, lives,
And the young boy, Ascanius—all these 785
Cut off by Greek troops foraging everywhere?
Had I not cared for them, fire would by now
Have taken them, their blood glutted the sword.
You must not hold the woman of Laconia,[6]
That hated face, the cause of this, nor Paris. 790
The harsh will of the gods it is, the gods,
That overthrows the splendor of this place
And brings Troy from her height into the dust.
Look over there: I'll tear away the cloud
That curtains you, and films your mortal sight, 795
The fog around you.—Have no fear of doing
Your mother's will, or balk at obeying her.—
Look: where you see high masonry thrown down,
Stone torn from stone, with billowing smoke and dust,
Neptune is shaking from their beds the walls 800
That his great trident pried up, undermining,
Toppling the whole city down. And look:
Juno in all her savagery holds
The Scaean Gates,[7] and raging in steel armor
Calls her allied army from the ships. 805
Up on the citadel—turn, look—Pallas Tritonia[8]
Couched in a stormcloud, lightening, with her Gorgon![9]
The Father himself empowers the Danaans,
Urges assaulting gods on the defenders.
Away, child; put an end to toiling so. 810
I shall be near, to see you safely home.'

She hid herself in the deep gloom of night,
And now the dire forms appeared to me
Of great immortals, enemies of Troy.
I knew the end then: Ilium was going down 815
In fire, the Troy of Neptune[1] going down,
As in high mountains when the countrymen
Have notched an ancient ash, then make their axes
Ring with might and main, chopping away
To fell the tree—ever on the point of falling, 820
Shaken through all its foliage, and the treetop
Nodding; bit by bit the strokes prevail
Until it gives a final groan at last
And crashes down in ruin from the height.

6. Helen. Laconia is Sparta, where her husband Menelaus is king.   7. One of the principal entrances
to Troy.   8. An epithet whose meaning is unclear.   9. The snake-haired monster at whose sight people
turned to stone; Athena had a Gorgon face on her shield.   1. Neptune was hostile to Troy, although he
had helped build the city.

Now I descended where the goddess guided,   825
Clear of the flames, and clear of enemies,
For both retired; so gained my father's door,
My ancient home. I looked for him at once,
My first wish being to help him to the mountains;
But with Troy gone he set his face against it,   830
Not to prolong his life, or suffer exile.

'The rest of you, all in your prime,' he said,
'Make your escape; you are still hale and strong.
If heaven's lords had wished me a longer span
They would have saved this home for me. I call it   835
More than enough that once before I saw
My city taken and wrecked,[2] and went on living.
Here is my death bed, here. Take leave of me.
Depart now. I'll find death with my sword arm.
The enemy will oblige; they'll come for spoils.   840
Burial can be dispensed with. All these years
I've lingered in my impotence, at odds
With heaven, since the Father of gods and men
Breathed high winds of thunderbolt upon me
And touched me with his fire.'[3]   845
                        He spoke on
In the same vein, inflexible. The rest of us,
Creusa and Ascanius and the servants,
Begged him in tears not to pull down with him
Our lives as well, adding his own dead weight   850
To the fates' pressure. But he would not budge,
He held to his resolve and to his chair.
I felt swept off again to fight, in misery
Longing for death. What choices now were open,
What chance had I?   855
                        'Did you suppose, my father,
That I could tear myself away and leave you?
Unthinkable; how could a father say it?
Now if it please the powers above that nothing
Stand of this great city; if your heart   860
Is set on adding your own death and ours
To that of Troy, the door's wide open for it:
Pyrrhus will be here, splashed with Priam's blood;
He kills the son before his father's eyes,
The father at the altars.   865
                        My dear mother,
Was it for this, through spears and fire, you brought me,
To see the enemy deep in my house,
To see my son, Ascanius, my father,
And near them both, Creusa,   870
Butchered in one another's blood? My gear,

---

2. By the hero Heracles, after Laömedon (then king of Troy) refused him promised payment.   3. Anchises was struck by a thunderbolt and crippled by Jupiter as punishment for being the lover of Venus.

Men, bring my gear. The last light calls the conquered.
Give me back to the Greeks. Let me take up
The combat once again. We shall not all
Die this day unavenged.'   875
                    I buckled on
Swordbelt and blade and slid my left forearm
Into the shield-strap, turning to go out,
But at the door Creusa hugged my knees,
Then held up little Iulus to his father.   880

'If you are going out to die, take us
To face the whole thing with you. If experience
Leads you to put some hope in weaponry
Such as you now take, guard your own house here.
When you have gone, to whom is Iulus left?   885
Your father? Wife?—one called that long ago.'

She went on, and her wailing filled the house,
But then a sudden portent came, a marvel:
Amid his parents' hands and their sad faces
A point on Iulus' head seemed to cast light,   890
A tongue of flame that touched but did not burn him,
Licking his fine hair, playing round his temples.
We, in panic, beat at the flaming hair
And put the sacred fire out with water;
Father Anchises lifted his eyes to heaven   895
And lifted up his hands, his voice, in joy:

'Omnipotent Jupiter, if prayers affect you,
Look down upon us, that is all I ask,
If by devotion to the gods we earn it,
Grant us a new sign, and confirm this portent!'   900
The old man barely finished when it thundered
A loud crack on the left. Out of the sky
Through depths of night a star fell trailing flame
And glided on, turning the night to day.
We watched it pass above the roof and go   905
To hide its glare, its trace, in Ida's⁴ wood;
But still, behind, the luminous furrow shone
And wide zones fumed with sulphur.
                                Now indeed
My father, overcome, addressed the gods,   910
And rose in worship of the blessed star.

'Now, now, no more delay. I'll follow you.
Where you conduct me, there I'll be.
                                Gods of my fathers,
Preserve this house, preserve my grandson. Yours   915
This portent was. Troy's life is in your power.

4. The mountain range near Troy.

I yield. I go as your companion, son.'
Then he was still. We heard the blazing town
Crackle more loudly, felt the scorching heat.

'Then come, dear father. Arms around my neck: 920
I'll take you on my shoulders, no great weight.
Whatever happens, both will face one danger,
Find one safety. Iulus will come with me,
My wife at a good interval behind.
Servants, give your attention to what I say.   925
At the gate inland there's a funeral mound
And an old shrine of Ceres the Bereft;[5]
Near it an ancient cypress, kept alive
For many years by our fathers' piety.
By various routes we'll come to that one place.   930
Father, carry our hearthgods, our Penates.
It would be wrong for me to handle them—
Just come from such hard fighting, bloody work—
Until I wash myself in running water.'
When I had said this, over my breadth of shoulder   935
And bent neck, I spread out a lion skin
For tawny cloak and stooped to take his weight.
Then little Iulus put his hand in mine
And came with shorter steps beside his father.
My wife fell in behind. Through shadowed places   940
On we went, and I, lately unmoved
By any spears thrown, any squads of Greeks,
Felt terror now at every eddy of wind,
Alarm at every sound, alert and worried
Alike for my companion and my burden.   945
I had got near the gate, and now I thought
We had made it all the way, when suddenly
A noise of running feet came near at hand,
And peering through the gloom ahead, my father
Cried out: 950
              'Run, boy; here they come; I see
Flame light on shields, bronze shining.'
                              I took fright,
And some unfriendly power, I know not what,
Stole all my addled wits—for as I turned   955
Aside from the known way, entering a maze
Of pathless places on the run—
                              Alas,
Creusa, taken from us by grim fate, did she
Linger, or stray, or sink in weariness?   960
There is no telling. Never would she be
Restored to us. Never did I look back
Or think to look for her, lost as she was,
Until we reached the funeral mound and shrine

---

5. So called because she mourns the loss of her daughter, Proserpina (Persephone in Greek), to the lord
of the underworld. Ceres' Greek name is Demeter.

Of venerable Ceres. Here at last   965
All came together, but she was not there;
She alone failed[6] her friends, her child, her husband.
Out of my mind, whom did I not accuse,
What man or god? What crueller loss had I
Beheld, that night the city fell? Ascanius,   970
My father, and the Teucrian Penates,
I left in my friends' charge, and hid them well
In a hollow valley.
                    I turned back alone
Into the city, cinching my bright harness.   975
Nothing for it but to run the risks
Again, go back again, comb all of Troy,
And put my life in danger as before:
First by the town wall, then the gate, all gloom,
Through which I had come out—and so on backward,   980
Tracing my own footsteps through the night;
And everywhere my heart misgave me: even
Stillness had its terror. Then to our house,
Thinking she might, just might, have wandered there.
Danaans had got in and filled the place,   985
And at that instant fire they had set,
Consuming it, went roofward in a blast;
Flames leaped and seethed in heat to the night sky.
I pressed on, to see Priam's hall and tower.
In the bare colonnades of Juno's shrine   990
Two chosen guards, Phoenix and hard Ulysses,
Kept watch over the plunder. Piled up here
Were treasures of old Troy from every quarter,
Torn out of burning temples: altar tables,
Robes, and golden bowls. Drawn up around them,   995
Boys and frightened mothers stood in line.
I even dared to call out in the night;
I filled the streets with calling; in my grief
Time after time I groaned and called Creusa,
Frantic, in endless quest from door to door.   1000
Then to my vision her sad wraith appeared—
Creusa's ghost, larger than life, before me.
Chilled to the marrow, I could feel the hair
On my head rise, the voice clot in my throat;
But she spoke out to ease me of my fear: 1005

'What's to be gained by giving way to grief
So madly, my sweet husband? Nothing here
Has come to pass except as heaven willed.
You may not take Creusa with you now;
It was not so ordained, nor does the lord   1010
Of high Olympus give you leave. For you
Long exile waits, and long sea miles to plough.

6. The original Latin does not imply fault and is better read "was not to be found" (literally, "was lacking to").

You shall make landfall on Hesperia
Where Lydian Tiber[7] flows, with gentle pace,
Between rich farmlands, and the years will bear   1015
Glad peace, a kingdom, and a queen for you.[8]
Dismiss these tears for your beloved Creusa.
I shall not see the proud homelands of Myrmidons
Or of Dolopians, or go to serve
Greek ladies, Dardan lady that I am   1020
And daughter-in-law of Venus the divine.
No: the great mother of the gods[9] detains me
Here on these shores. Farewell now; cherish still
Your son and mine.'
                  With this she left me weeping,   1025
Wishing that I could say so many things,
And faded on the tenuous air. Three times
I tried to put my arms around her neck,
Three times enfolded nothing, as the wraith
Slipped through my fingers, bodiless as wind,   1030
Or like a flitting dream.
              So in the end
As night waned I rejoined my company.
And there to my astonishment I found
New refugees in a great crowd: men and women   1035
Gathered for exile, young—pitiful people
Coming from every quarter, minds made up,
With their belongings, for whatever lands
I'd lead them to by sea.
                The morning star   1040
Now rose on Ida's ridges, bringing day.
Greeks had secured the city gates. No help
Or hope of help existed.
So I resigned myself, picked up my father,
And turned my face toward the mountain range.'   1045

[Aeneas goes on to tell the story of his wanderings in search of a new home. By the
end of the evening, Dido, who began to fall in love with him before the banquet
(through the intervention of Venus and Juno, who both promote the affair, each for
different reasons), now feels the full force of her passion for Aeneas.]

BOOK IV

[The Passion of the Queen]

The queen, for her part, all that evening ached
With longing that her heart's blood fed, a wound
Or inward fire eating her away.
The manhood of the man, his pride of birth,
Came home to her time and again; his looks,   5

---

7. The river was the center of many settlements of Etruscans, who were supposed to be immigrants from
Lydia, in Asia Minor.   8. Lavinia, daughter of the king of Latium, Latinus.   9. Cybele, an Asiatic
mother goddess worshipped (according to Virgil) at Troy.

His words remained with her to haunt her mind,
And desire for him gave her no rest.
                  When Dawn
Swept earth with Phoebus' torch and burned away
Night-gloom and damp, this queen, far gone and ill,   10
Confided to the sister of her heart:
"My sister Anna, quandaries and dreams
Have come to frighten me—such dreams!
                    Think what a stranger

Yesterday found lodging in our house: 15
How princely, how courageous, what a soldier.
I can believe him in the line of gods,
And this is no delusion. Tell-tale fear
Betrays inferior souls. What scenes of war
Fought to the bitter end he pictured for us!   20
What buffetings awaited him at sea!
Had I not set my face against remarriage
After my first love died and failed me, left me
Barren and bereaved—and sick to death
At the mere thought of torch and bridal bed—   25
I could perhaps give way in this one case
To frailty. I shall say it: since that time
Sychaeus, my poor husband, met his fate,
And blood my brother[1] shed stained our hearth gods,
This man alone has wrought upon me so   30
And moved my soul to yield. I recognize
The signs of the old flame, of old desire.
But O chaste life, before I break your laws,
I pray that Earth may open, gape for me
Down to its depth, or the omnipotent   35
With one stroke blast me to the shades, pale shades
Of Erebus[2] and the deep world of night!
That man who took me to himself in youth
Has taken all my love; may that man keep it,
Hold it forever with him in the tomb."   40

At this she wept and wet her breast with tears.
But Anna answered:
                "Dearer to your sister
Than daylight is, will you wear out your life,
Young as you are, in solitary mourning,   45
Never to know sweet children, or the crown
Of joy that Venus brings? Do you believe
This matters to the dust, to ghosts in tombs?
Granted no suitors up to now have moved you,
Neither in Libya nor before, in Tyre—   50
Iarbas[3] you rejected, and the others,
Chieftains bred by the land of Africa

---

1. Pygmalion, king of Tyre who killed Sychaeus, Dido's "first love" (line 23).   2. The lower depths of
Hades, the underworld.   3. The most prominent of Dido's African suitors.

Their triumphs have enriched—will you contend
Even against a welcome love? Have you
Considered in whose lands you settled here?   55
On one frontier the Gaetulans, their cities,
People invincible in war—with wild
Numidian horsemen, and the offshore banks,
The Syrtes; on the other, desert sands,
Bone-dry, where fierce Barcaean nomads range.[4]   60
Or need I speak of future wars brought on
From Tyre, and the menace of your brother?
Surely by dispensation of the gods
And backed by Juno's will, the ships from Ilium
Held their course this way on the wind.   65
                              Sister,
What a great city you'll see rising here,
And what a kingdom, from this royal match!
With Trojan soldiers as companions in arms
By what exploits will Punic glory grow!   70
Only ask the indulgence of the gods,
Win them with offerings, give your guests ease,
And contrive reasons for delay, while winter
Gales rage, drenched Orion storms at sea,
And their ships, damaged still, face iron skies.'   75

This counsel fanned the flame, already kindled,
Giving her hesitant sister hope, and set her
Free of scruple. Visiting the shrines
They begged for grace at every altar first,
Then put choice rams and ewes to ritual death   80
For Ceres Giver of Laws, Father Lyaeus,
Phoebus, and for Juno most of all
Who has the bonds of marriage in her keeping.[5]
Dido herself, splendidly beautiful,
Holding a shallow cup, tips out the wine   85
On a white shining heifer, between the horns,
Or gravely in the shadow of the gods
Approaches opulent altars. Through the day
She brings new gifts, and when the breasts are opened
Pores over organs, living still, for signs.[6]   90
Alas, what darkened minds have soothsayers!
What good are shrines and vows to maddened lovers?
The inward fire eats the soft marrow away,
And the internal wound bleeds on in silence.

4. Anna names African groups that lived near Carthage. The Gaetulans, a savage people, lived to the
southwest. The Numidians were the most powerful group. The Syrtes lived on the coast to the west. The
Barcaeans lived to the east.   5. Ceres, the goddess who guarantees the growth of crops; Lyaeus (Dionysus
or Bacchus), the wine god; and Phoebus (Apollo) are selected as deities especially connected with the
founding of cities. One of Apollo's titles is "founder," and Ceres and Lyaeus control the essential crops that
will enable the colonists to live. Dido prays to these gods at the moment when she is about to abandon her
responsibilities as founder of a city. A similar irony is present in her prayer to Juno, who oversees the
marriage bond, at the moment when she is about to break her long fidelity to the memory of Sychaeus.
6. An Etruscan and Roman practice was to inspect the entrails of the sacrificial victim and interpret
irregular or unusual features as signs of the future.

Unlucky Dido, burning, in her madness   95
Roamed through all the city, like a doe
Hit by an arrow shot from far away
By a shepherd hunting in the Cretan woods—
Hit by surprise, nor could the hunter see
His flying steel had fixed itself in her;   100
But though she runs for life through copse and glade
The fatal shaft clings to her side.
                          Now Dido
Took Aeneas with her among her buildings,
Showed her Sidonian wealth, her walls prepared,   105
And tried to speak, but in mid-speech grew still.
When the day waned she wanted to repeat
The banquet as before, to hear once more
In her wild need the throes of Ilium,
And once more hung on the narrator's words.   110
Afterward, when all the guests were gone,
And the dim moon in turn had quenched her light,
And setting stars weighed weariness to sleep,
Alone she mourned in the great empty hall
And pressed her body on the couch he left: 115
She heard him still, though absent—heard and saw him.
Or she would hold Ascanius in her lap,
Enthralled by him, the image of his father,
As though by this ruse to appease a love
Beyond all telling.   120
                 Towers, half-built, rose
No farther; men no longer trained in arms
Or toiled to make harbors and battlements
Impregnable. Projects were broken off,
Laid over, and the menacing huge walls   125
With cranes unmoving stood against the sky.

As soon as Jove's dear consort saw the lady
Prey to such illness, and her reputation
Standing no longer in the way of passion,
Saturn's daughter said to Venus: 130
                  "Wondrous!
Covered yourself with glory, have you not,
You and your boy, and won such prizes, too.
Divine power is something to remember
If by collusion of two gods one mortal   135
Woman is brought low.
                  I am not blind.
Your fear of our new walls has not escaped me,
Fear and mistrust of Carthage at her height.
But how far will it go? What do you hope for,   140
Being so contentious? Why do we not
Arrange eternal peace and formal marriage?
You have your heart's desire: Dido in love,
Dido consumed with passion to her core.
Why not, then, rule this people side by side   145

With equal authority? And let the queen
Wait on her Phrygian lord, let her consign
Into your hand her Tyrians as a dowry."

Now Venus knew this talk was all pretence,
All to divert the future power from Italy   150
To Libya; and she answered:
                        "Who would be
So mad, so foolish as to shun that prospect
Or prefer war with you? That is, provided
Fortune is on the side of your proposal.   155
The fates here are perplexing: would one city
Satisfy Jupiter's will for Tyrians
And Trojan exiles? Does he approve
A union and a mingling of these races?
You are his consort: you have every right   160
To sound him out. Go on, and I'll come, too."

But regal Juno pointedly replied:
"That task will rest with me. Just now, as to
The need of the moment and the way to meet it,
Listen, and I'll explain in a few words.   165
Aeneas and Dido in her misery
Plan hunting in the forest, when the Titan
Sun comes up with rays to light the world.
While beaters in excitement ring the glens
My gift will be a black raincloud, and hail,   170
A downpour, and I'll shake heaven with thunder.
The company will scatter, lost in gloom,
As Dido and the Trojan captain come
To one same cavern. I shall be on hand,
And if I can be certain you are willing,   175
There I shall marry them and call her his.
A wedding, this will be."
                        Then Cytherea,
Not disinclined, nodded to Juno's plea,
And smiled at the stratagem now given away.   180

Dawn came up meanwhile from the Ocean stream,
And in the early sunshine from the gates
Picked huntsmen issued: wide-meshed nets and snares,
Broad spearheads for big game, Massylian[7] horsemen
Trooping with hounds in packs keen on the scent.   185
But Dido lingered in her hall, as Punic
Nobles waited, and her mettlesome hunter
Stood nearby, cavorting in gold and scarlet,
Champing his foam-flecked bridle. At long last
The queen appeared with courtiers in a crowd,   190
A short Sidonian cloak edged in embroidery
Caught about her, at her back a quiver

---

7. African.

Sheathed in gold, her hair tied up in gold,
And a brooch of gold pinning her scarlet dress.
Phrygians came in her company as well,   195
And Iulus, joyous at the scene. Resplendent
Above the rest, Aeneas walked to meet her,
To join his retinue with hers. He seemed—
Think of the lord Apollo in the spring
When he leaves wintering in Lycia   200
By Xanthus torrent, for his mother's isle
Of Delos, to renew the festival;
Around his altars Cretans, Dryopes,
And painted Agathyrsans[8] raise a shout,
But the god walks the Cynthian ridge alone   205
And smooths his hair, binds it in fronded laurel,
Braids it in gold; and shafts ring on his shoulders.
So elated and swift, Aeneas walked
With sunlit grace upon him.
                                    Soon the hunters,   210
Riding in company to high pathless hills,
Saw mountain goats shoot down from a rocky peak
And scamper on the ridges; toward the plain
Deer left the slopes, herding in clouds of dust
In flight across the open lands. Alone,   215
The boy Ascanius, delightedly riding
His eager horse amid the lowland vales,
Outran both goats and deer. Could he only meet
Amid the harmless game some foaming boar,
Or a tawny lion down from the mountainside!   220

Meanwhile in heaven began a rolling thunder,
And soon the storm broke, pouring rain and hail.
Then Tyrians and Trojans in alarm—
With Venus' Dardan grandson[9]—ran for cover
Here and there in the wilderness, as freshets   225
Coursed from the high hills.
                             Now to the self-same cave
Came Dido and the captain of the Trojans.
Primal Earth herself and Nuptial Juno
Opened the ritual, torches of lightning blazed,   230
High Heaven became witness to the marriage,
And nymphs cried out wild hymns from a mountain top.
     That day was the first cause of death, and first
Of sorrow. Dido had no further qualms
As to impressions given and set abroad;   235
She thought no longer of a secret love
But called it marriage. Thus, under that name,
She hid her fault.
                    Now in no time at all
Through all the African cities Rumor goes—   240
Nimble as quicksilver among evils. Rumor

8. Pilgrims from various regions.   9. Ascanius.

Thrives on motion, stronger for the running,
Lowly at first through fear, then rearing high,
She treads the land and hides her head in cloud.
As people fable it, the Earth, her mother,   245
Furious against the gods, bore a late sister
To the giants Coeus and Enceladus,
Giving her speed on foot and on the wing:
Monstrous, deformed, titanic. Pinioned, with
An eye beneath for every body feather,   250
And, strange to say, as many tongues and buzzing
Mouths as eyes, as many pricked-up ears,
By night she flies between the earth and heaven
Shrieking through darkness, and she never turns
Her eye-lids down to sleep. By day she broods,   255
On the alert, on rooftops or on towers,
Bringing great cities fear, harping on lies
And slander evenhandedly with truth.
In those days Rumor took an evil joy
At filling countrysides with whispers, whispers,   260
Gossip of what was done, and never done:
How this Aeneas landed, Trojan born,
How Dido in her beauty graced his company,
Then how they reveled all the winter long
Unmindful of the realm, prisoners of lust.   265

These tales the scabrous goddess put about
On men's lips everywhere. Her twisting course
Took her to King Iarbas, whom she set
Ablaze with anger piled on top of anger.
Son of Jupiter Hammon by a nymph,   270
A ravished Garamantean,[1] this prince
Had built the god a hundred giant shrines,
A hundred altars, each with holy fires.
Alight by night and day, sentries on watch,
The ground enriched by victims' blood, the doors   275
Festooned with flowering wreaths. Before his altars
King Iarbas, crazed by the raw story,
Stood, they say, amid the Presences,
With supplicating hands, pouring out prayer:

"All powerful Jove, to whom the feasting Moors   280
At ease on colored couches tip their wine,
Do you see this? Are we then fools to fear you
Throwing down your bolts? Those dazzling fires
Of lightning, are they aimless in the clouds
And rumbling thunder meaningless? This woman   285
Who turned up in our country and laid down
A tiny city at a price, to whom
I gave a beach to plow—and on my terms—

---

1. African. Hammon or Ammon was a local god whom the Romans identified with Jupiter (and the Greeks with Zeus).

After refusing to marry me has taken
Aeneas to be master in her realm.   290
And now Sir Paris with his men, half-men,
His chin and perfumed hair tied up
In a Maeonian[2] bonnet, takes possession.
As for ourselves, here we are bringing gifts
Into these shrines—supposedly your shrines—   295
Hugging that empty fable."
                              Pleas like this
From the man clinging to his altars reached
The ears of the Almighty. Now he turned
His eyes upon the queen's town and the lovers   300
Careless of their good name; then spoke to Mercury,[3]
Assigning him a mission:
                          "Son, bestir yourself,
Call up the Zephyrs,[4] take to your wings and glide.
Approach the Dardan captain where he tarries   305
Rapt in Tyrian Carthage, losing sight
Of future towns the fates ordain. Correct him,
Carry my speech to him on the running winds:
No son like this did his enchanting mother
Promise to us, nor such did she deliver   310
Twice from peril at the hands of Greeks.
He was to be the ruler of Italy,
Potential empire, armorer of war;
To father men from Teucer's noble blood
And bring the whole world under law's dominion.   315
If glories to be won by deeds like these
Cannot arouse him, if he will not strive
For his own honor, does he begrudge his son,
Ascanius, the high strongholds of Rome?
What has he in mind? What hope, to make him stay   320
Amid a hostile race, and lose from view
Ausonian progeny, Lavinian lands?[5]
The man should sail: that is the whole point.
Let this be what you tell him, as from me."

He finished and fell silent. Mercury   325
Made ready to obey the great command
Of his great father, and he first tied on
The golden sandals, winged, that high in air
Transport him over seas or over land
Abreast of gale winds; then he took the wand   330
With which he summons pale souls out of Orcus
And ushers others to the undergloom,
Lulls men to slumber or awakens them,
And opens dead men's eyes. This wand in hand,
He can drive winds before him, swimming down   335
Along the stormcloud. Now aloft, he saw

2. Of Maeonia, or Lydia (i.e., Asiatic, and thus, according to a view originating with the Greeks, effeminate).   3. The messenger god.   4. The west winds.   5. The dowry of Aeneas's future wife, Lavinia.
Ausonian: Italian.

The craggy flanks and crown of patient Atlas,
Giant Atlas, balancing the sky
Upon his peak[6]—his pine-forested head
In vapor cowled, beaten by wind and rain.   340
Snow lay upon his shoulders, rills cascaded
Down his ancient chin and beard a-bristle,
Caked with ice. Here Mercury of Cyllene[7]
Hovered first on even wings, then down
He plummeted to sea-level and flew on   345
Like a low-flying gull that skims the shallows
And rocky coasts where fish ply close inshore.
So, like a gull between the earth and sky,
The progeny of Cyllene, on the wing
From his maternal grandsire, split the winds   350
To the sand bars of Libya.
                          Alighting tiptoe
On the first hutments, there he found Aeneas
Laying foundations for new towers and homes.
He noted well the swordhilt the man wore,   355
Adorned with yellow jasper; and the cloak
Aglow with Tyrian dye upon his shoulders—
Gifts of the wealthy queen, who had inwoven
Gold thread in the fabric. Mercury
Took him to task at once: 360
                    "Is it for you
To lay the stones for Carthage's high walls,
Tame husband that you are, and build their city?
Oblivious of your own world, your own kingdom!
From bright Olympus he that rules the gods   365
And turns the earth and heaven by his power—
He and no other sent me to you, told me
To bring this message on the running winds:
What have you in mind? What hope, wasting your days
In Libya? If future history's glories   370
Do not affect you, if you will not strive
For your own honor, think of Ascanius,
Think of the expectations of your heir,
Iulus, to whom the Italian realm, the land
Of Rome, are due."   375
                    And Mercury, as he spoke,
Departed from the visual field of mortals
To a great distance, ebbed in subtle air.
Amazed, and shocked to the bottom of his soul
By what his eyes had seen, Aeneas felt   380
His hackles rise, his voice choke in his throat.
As the sharp admonition and command
From heaven had shaken him awake, he now
Burned only to be gone, to leave that land
Of the sweet life behind. What can he do? How tell 385

---

6. The Atlas Mountains are in western North Africa; the reference here is also to the Titan Atlas.   7. A mountain in Arcadia and Mercury's birthplace.

The impassioned queen and hope to win her over?
What opening shall he choose? This way and that
He let his mind dart, testing alternatives,
Running through every one. And as he pondered
This seemed the better tactic: he called in   390
Mnestheus, Sergestus and stalwart Serestus,
Telling them:
         "Get the fleet ready for sea,
But quietly, and collect the men on shore.
Lay in ship stores and gear."   395
               As to the cause
For a change of plan, they were to keep it secret,
Seeing the excellent Dido had no notion,
No warning that such love could be cut short;
He would himself look for the right occasion,   400
The easiest time to speak, the way to do it.
The Trojans to a man gladly obeyed.

The queen, for her part, felt some plot afoot
Quite soon—for who deceives a woman in love?
She caught wind of a change, being in fear   405
Of what had seemed her safety. Evil Rumor,
Shameless as before, brought word to her
In her distracted state of ships being rigged
In trim for sailing. Furious, at her wits' end,
She traversed the whole city, all aflame   410
With rage, like a Bacchante[8] driven wild
By emblems shaken, when the mountain revels
Of the odd year possess her, when the cry
Of Bacchus rises and Cithaeron[9] calls
All through the shouting night. Thus it turned out   415
She was the first to speak and charge Aeneas:

"You even hoped to keep me in the dark
As to this outrage, did you, two-faced man,
And slip away in silence? Can our love
Not hold you, can the pledge we gave not hold you,   420
Can Dido not, now sure to die in pain?
Even in winter weather must you toil
With ships, and fret to launch against high winds
For the open sea? Oh, heartless!
                  Tell me now,   425
If you were not in search of alien lands
And new strange homes, if ancient Troy remained,
Would ships put out for Troy on these big seas?
Do you go to get away from me? I beg you,
By these tears, by your own right hand,[1] since I   430
Have left my wretched self nothing but that—
Yes, by the marriage that we entered on,

---

8. A female devotee of the god Bacchus, in an ecstatic trance at the festival held every other year in the
god's honor.   9. Mountain near Thebes, sacred to Bacchus.   1. The handclasp with which he pledged
his love and that Dido took as an earnest of marriage.

If ever I did well and you were grateful
Or found some sweetness in a gift from me,
Have pity now on a declining house!   435
Put this plan by, I beg you, if a prayer
Is not yet out of place.
Because of you, Libyans and nomad kings
Detest me, my own Tyrians are hostile;
Because of you, I lost my integrity   440
And that admired name by which alone
I made my way once toward the stars.
                                        To whom
Do you abandon me, a dying woman,
Guest that you are—the only name now left   445
From that of husband? Why do I live on?
Shall I, until my brother Pygmalion comes
To pull my walls down? Or the Gaetulan
Iarbas leads me captive? If at least
There were a child by you for me to care for,   450
A little one to play in my courtyard
And give me back Aeneas, in spite of all,
I should not feel so utterly defeated,
Utterly bereft."
                    She ended there.   455
The man by Jove's command held fast his eyes
And fought down the emotion in his heart.
At length he answered:
                          "As for myself, be sure
I never shall deny all you can say,   460
Your majesty, of what you meant to me.
Never will the memory of Elissa[2]
Stale for me, while I can still remember
My own life, and the spirit rules my body.
As to the event, a few words. Do not think   465
I meant to be deceitful and slip away.
I never held the torches of a bridegroom,
Never entered upon the pact of marriage.
If Fate permitted me to spend my days
By my own lights, and make the best of things   470
According to my wishes, first of all
I should look after Troy and the loved relics
Left me of my people. Priam's great hall
Should stand again; I should have restored the tower
Of Pergamum for Trojans in defeat.   475
But now it is the rich Italian land
Apollo tells me I must make for: Italy,
Named by his oracles. There is my love;
There is my country. If, as a Phoenician,
You are so given to the charms of Carthage,   480
Libyan city that it is, then tell me,
Why begrudge the Teucrian new lands

2. Dido.

For homesteads in Ausonia? Are we not
Entitled, too, to look for realms abroad?
Night never veils the earth in damp and darkness,   485
Fiery stars never ascend the east,
But in my dreams my father's troubled ghost[3]
Admonishes and frightens me. Then, too,
Each night thoughts come of young Ascanius,
My dear boy wronged, defrauded of his kingdom,   490
Hesperian lands of destiny. And now
The gods' interpreter, sent by Jove himself—
I swear it by your head and mine—has brought
Commands down through the racing winds! I say
With my own eyes in full daylight I saw him   495
Entering the building! With my very ears
I drank his message in! So please, no more
Of these appeals that set us both afire.
I sail for Italy not of my own free will."

During all this she had been watching him   500
With face averted, looking him up and down
In silence, and she burst out raging now:

"No goddess was your mother. Dardanus
Was not the founder of your family.
Liar and cheat! Some rough Caucasian cliff   505
Begot you on flint. Hyrcanian[4] tigresses
Tendered their teats to you. Why should I palter?
Why still hold back for more indignity?
Sigh, did he, while I wept? Or look at me?
Or yield a tear, or pity her who loved him?   510
What shall I say first, with so much to say?
The time is past when either supreme Juno
Or the Saturnian father[5] viewed these things
With justice. Faith can never be secure.
I took the man in, thrown up on this coast   515
In dire need, and in my madness then
Contrived a place for him in my domain,
Rescued his lost fleet, saved his shipmates' lives.
Oh, I am swept away burning by furies!
Now the prophet Apollo, now his oracles,   520
Now the gods' interpreter, if you please,
Sent down by Jove himself, brings through the air
His formidable commands! What fit employment
For heaven's high powers! What anxieties
To plague serene immortals![6] I shall not   525
Detain you or dispute your story. Go,
Go after Italy on the sailing winds,
Look for your kingdom, cross the deepsea swell!

3. Anchises had died in Sicily just before Aeneas, leaving for Italy, was blown by the storm winds to
Carthage.   4. Near the Caspian Sea. *Caucasian*: after the Caucasus Mountains, also near the Caspian
Sea. The adjective connoted outlandishness and cruelty.   5. Jupiter.   6. A reference to the Epicurean
idea that the gods are unaffected by human events.

If divine justice counts for anything,
I hope and pray that on some grinding reef   530
Midway at sea you'll drink your punishment
And call and call on Dido's name!
From far away I shall come after you
With my black fires, and when cold death has parted
Body from soul I shall be everywhere   535
A shade to haunt you! You will pay for this,
Unconscionable! I shall hear! The news will reach me
Even among the lowest of the dead!"

At this abruptly she broke off and ran
In sickness from his sight and the light of day,   540
Leaving him at a loss, alarmed, and mute
With all he meant to say. The maids in waiting
Caught her as she swooned and carried her
To bed in her marble chamber.
                       Duty-bound,   545
Aeneas, though he struggled with desire
To calm and comfort her in all her pain,
To speak to her and turn her mind from grief,
And though he sighed his heart out, shaken still
With love of her, yet took the course heaven gave him   550
And went back to the fleet. Then with a will
The Teucrians fell to work and launched ships
Along the whole shore: slick with tar each hull
Took to the water. Eager to get away,
The sailors brought oar-boughs out of the woods   555
With leaves still on, and oaken logs unhewn.
Now you could see them issuing from the town
To the water's edge in streams, as when, aware
Of winter, ants will pillage a mound of spelt
To store it in their granary; over fields   560
The black battalion moves, and through the grass
On a narrow trail they carry off the spoil;
Some put their shoulders to the enormous weight
Of a trundled grain, while some pull stragglers in
And castigate delay; their to-and-fro   565
Of labor makes the whole track come alive.
At that sight, what were your emotions, Dido?
Sighing how deeply, looking out and down
From your high tower on the seething shore
Where all the harbor filled before your eyes   570
With bustle and shouts! Unconscionable Love,
To what extremes will you not drive our hearts!
She now felt driven to weep again, again
To move him, if she could, by supplication,
Humbling her pride before her love—to leave   575
Nothing untried, not to die needlessly.

"Anna, you see the arc of waterfront
All in commotion: they come crowding in

From everywhere. Spread canvas calls for wind,
The happy crews have garlanded the sterns.   580
If I could brace myself for this great sorrow,
Sister, I can endure it, too. One favor,
Even so, you may perform for me.
Since that deserter chose you for his friend
And trusted you, even with private thoughts,   585
Since you alone know when he may be reached,
Go, intercede with our proud enemy.
Remind him that I took no oath at Aulis[7]
With Danaans to destroy the Trojan race;
I sent no ship to Pergamum. Never did I   590
Profane his father Anchises' dust and shade.
Why will he not allow my prayers to fall
On his unpitying ears? Where is he racing?
Let him bestow one last gift on his mistress:
This, to await fair winds and easier flight.   595
Now I no longer plead the bond he broke
Of our old marriage, nor do I ask that he
Should live without his dear love, Latium,
Or yield his kingdom. Time is all I beg,
Mere time, a respite and a breathing space   600
For madness to subside in, while my fortune
Teaches me how to take defeat and grieve.
Pity your sister. This is the end, this favor—
To be repaid with interest when I die."

She pleaded in such terms, and such, in tears,   605
Her sorrowing sister brought him, time and again.
But no tears moved him, no one's voice would he
Attend to tractably. The fates opposed it;
God's will blocked the man's once kindly ears.
And just as when the north winds from the Alps   610
This way and that contend among themselves
To tear away an oaktree hale with age,
The wind and tree cry, and the buffeted trunk
Showers high foliage to earth, but holds
On bedrock, for the roots go down as far   615
Into the underworld as cresting boughs
Go up in heaven's air: just so this captain,
Buffeted by a gale of pleas
This way and that way, dinned all the day long,
Felt their moving power in his great heart,   620
And yet his will stood fast; tears fell in vain.

On Dido in her desolation now
Terror grew at her fate. She prayed for death,
Being heartsick at the mere sight of heaven.
That she more surely would perform the act   625
And leave the daylight, now she saw before her

7. An allusion to Agamemnon's oath when he departed from Aulis for Troy.

A thing one shudders to recall: on altars
Fuming with incense where she placed her gifts,
The holy water blackened, the spilt wine
Turned into blood and mire. Of this she spoke   630
To no one, not to her sister even. Then, too,
Within the palace was a marble shrine
Devoted to her onetime lord, a place
She held in wondrous honor, all festooned
With snowy fleeces and green festive boughs.   635
From this she now thought voices could be heard
And words could be made out, her husband's words,
Calling her, when midnight hushed the earth;
And lonely on the rooftops the night owl
Seemed to lament, in melancholy notes,   640
Prolonged to a doleful cry. And then, besides,
The riddling words of seers in ancient days,
Foreboding sayings, made her thrill with fear.
In nightmare, fevered, she was hunted down
By pitiless Aeneas, and she seemed   645
Deserted always, uncompanioned always,
On a long journey, looking for her Tyrians
In desolate landscapes—

             as Pentheus[8] gone mad
Sees the oncoming Eumenides and sees   650
A double sun and double Thebes appear,
Or as when, hounded on the stage, Orestes[9]
Runs from a mother armed with burning brands,
With serpents hellish black,
And in the doorway squat the Avenging Ones.   655

So broken in mind by suffering, Dido caught
Her fatal madness and resolved to die.
She pondered time and means, then visiting
Her mournful sister, covered up her plan
With a calm look, a clear and hopeful brow.   660

"Sister, be glad for me! I've found a way
To bring him back or free me of desire.
Near to the Ocean boundary, near sundown,
The Aethiops' farthest territory lies,
Where giant Atlas turns the sphere of heaven   665
Studded with burning stars. From there
A priestess of Massylian stock has come;
She had been pointed out to me: custodian
Of that shrine named for daughters of the west,
Hesperides;[1] and it is she who fed   670

8. King of Thebes, who persecuted the worshippers of Bacchus and imprisoned the god himself. Pentheus was later mocked by the god, who inspired him with the Dionysiac spirit (and perhaps with wine) so that he saw double. In this state he was led off to his death on Cithaeron. These events are dramatized in Euripides' play The Bacchanals (Bacchae), which does not mention the Eumenides (Furies). Perhaps Virgil is using them simply as a symbol for madness. 9. Another reference to Greek tragedy: in Aeschylus's Choephoroe (The Libation Bearers), Orestes kills his mother, Clytaemnestra, and is pursued by the Furies. In other tragic contexts he is represented as pursued by the ghost of his mother. 1. Goddesses who lived in a garden that contained golden apples and was guarded by a dragon.

The dragon, guarding well the holy boughs
With honey dripping slow and drowsy poppy.
Chanting her spells she undertakes to free
What hearts she wills, but to inflict on others
Duress of sad desires; to arrest   675
The flow of rivers, make the stars move backward,
Call up the spirits of deep Night. You'll see
Earth shift and rumble underfoot and ash trees
Walk down mountainsides. Dearest, I swear
Before the gods and by your own sweet self,   680
It is against my will that I resort
For weaponry to magic powers. In secret
Build up a pyre in the inner court
Under the open sky, and place upon it
The arms that faithless man left in my chamber,   685
All his clothing, and the marriage bed
On which I came to grief—solace for me
To annihilate all vestige of the man,
Vile as he is: my priestess shows me this."

While she was speaking, cheek and brow grew pale.   690
But Anna could not think her sister cloaked
A suicide in these unheard-of rites;
She failed to see how great her madness was
And feared no consequence more grave
Than at Sychaeus' death. So, as commanded,   695
She made the preparations. For her part,
The queen, seeing the pyre in her inmost court
Erected huge with pitch-pine and sawn ilex,
Hung all the place under the sky with wreaths
And crowned it with funereal cypress boughs.   700
On the pyre's top she put a sword he left
With clothing, and an effigy on a couch,
Her mind fixed now ahead on what would come.
Around the pyre stood altars, and the priestess,
Hair unbound, called in a voice of thunder   705
Upon three hundred gods, on Erebus,
On Chaos, and on triple Hecate,[2]
Three-faced Diana. Then she sprinkled drops
Purportedly from the fountain of Avernus.[3]
Rare herbs were brought out, reaped at the new moon   710
By scythes of bronze, and juicy with a milk
Of dusky venom; then the rare love-charm
Or caul torn from the brow of a birthing foal
And snatched away before the mother found it.
Dido herself with consecrated grain   715
In her pure hands, as she went near the altars,
Freed one foot from sandal straps, let fall

2. Diana as goddess of sorcery and the moon. *Chaos:* the Greek personification of the void or disorder that, by Roman times, was thought to have preceded the creation of the universe.   3. A lake in southern Italy that was supposed to be the entrance to the lower world.

Her dress ungirdled, and, now sworn to death,
Called on the gods and stars that knew her fate.
She prayed then to whatever power may care   720
In comprehending justice for the grief
Of lovers bound unequally by love.

The night had come, and weary in every land
Men's bodies took the boon of peaceful sleep.
The woods and the wild seas had quieted   725
At that hour when the stars are in mid-course
And every field is still; cattle and birds
With vivid wings that haunt the limpid lakes
Or nest in thickets in the country places
All were asleep under the silent night.   730
Not, though, the agonized Phoenician queen:
She never slackened into sleep and never
Allowed the tranquil night to rest
Upon her eyelids or within her heart.
Her pain redoubled; love came on again,   735
Devouring her, and on her bed she tossed
In a great surge of anger.
                                  So awake,
She pressed these questions, musing to herself:

"Look now, what can I do? Turn once again   740
To the old suitors, only to be laughed at—
Begging a marriage with Numidians
Whom I disdained so often? Then what? Trail
The Ilian ships and follow like a slave
Commands of Trojans? Seeing them so agreeable,   745
In view of past assistance and relief,
So thoughtful their unshaken gratitude?
Suppose I wished it, who permits or takes
Aboard their proud ships one they so dislike?
Poor lost soul, do you not yet grasp or feel   750
The treachery of the line of Laömedon?⁴
What then? Am I to go alone, companion
Of the exultant sailors in their flight?
Or shall I set out in their wake, with Tyrians,
With all my crew close at my side, and send   755
The men I barely tore away from Tyre
To sea again, making them hoist their sails
To more sea-winds? No: die as you deserve,
Give pain quietus with a steel blade.
                                  Sister,   760
You are the one who gave way to my tears
In the beginning, burdened a mad queen
With sufferings, and thrust me on my enemy.
It was not given me to lead my life
Without new passion, innocently, the way   765

4. A king of Troy who twice broke his promise, once to Heracles and once to Apollo and Poseidon.

Wild creatures live, and not to touch these depths.
The vow I took to the ashes of Sychaeus
Was not kept."
     So she broke out afresh
In bitter mourning. On his high stern deck   770
Aeneas, now quite certain of departure,
Everything ready, took the boon of sleep.
In dream the figure of the god returned
With looks reproachful as before: he seemed
Again to warn him, being like Mercury   775
In every way, in voice, in golden hair,
And in the bloom of youth.
       "Son of the goddess,
Sleep away this crisis, can you still?
Do you not see the dangers growing round you,   780
Madman, from now on? Can you not hear
The offshore westwind blow? The woman hatches
Plots and drastic actions in her heart,
Resolved on death now, whipping herself on
To heights of anger. Will you not be gone   785
In flight, while flight is still within your power?
Soon you will see the offing boil with ships
And glare with torches; soon again
The waterfront will be alive with fires,
If Dawn comes while you linger in this country.   790
Ha! Come, break the spell! Woman's a thing
Forever fitful and forever changing."

At this he merged into the darkness. Then
As the abrupt phantom filled him with fear,
Aeneas broke from sleep and roused his crewmen: 795
"Up, turn out now! Oarsmen, take your thwarts!
Shake out sail! Look here, for the second time
A god from heaven's high air is goading me
To hasten our break away, to cut the cables.
Holy one, whatever god you are,   800
We go with you, we act on your command
Most happily! Be near, graciously help us,
Make the stars in heaven propitious ones!"

He pulled his sword aflash out of its sheath
And struck at the stern hawser. All the men   805
Were gripped by his excitement to be gone,
And hauled and hustled. Ships cast off their moorings,
And an array of hulls hid inshore water
As oarsmen churned up foam and swept to sea.

Soon early Dawn, quitting the saffron bed   810
Of old Tithonus,[5] cast new light on earth,

---

5. Human consort of Aurora, the dawn goddess. He is old because, although she made him immortal when she took him to her bed, she forgot to obtain for him the gift of eternal youth.

And as air grew transparent, from her tower
The queen caught sight of ships on the seaward reach
With sails full and the wind astern. She knew
The waterfront now empty, bare of oarsmen.   815
Beating her lovely breast three times, four times,
And tearing her golden hair,
                              "O Jupiter,"
She said, "will this man go, will he have mocked
My kingdom, stranger that he was and is?   820
Will they not snatch up arms and follow him
From every quarter of the town? and dockhands
Tear our ships from moorings? On! Be quick
With torches! Give out arms! Unship the oars!
What am I saying? Where am I? What madness   825
Takes me out of myself? Dido, poor soul,
Your evil doing has come home to you.
Then was the right time, when you offered him
A royal scepter. See the good faith and honor
Of one they say bears with him everywhere   830
The hearthgods of his country! One who bore
His father, spent with age, upon his shoulders!
Could I not then have torn him limb from limb
And flung the pieces on the sea? His company,
Even Ascanius could I not have minced   835
And served up to his father at a feast?
The luck of battle might have been in doubt—
So let it have been! Whom had I to fear,
Being sure to die? I could have carried torches
Into his camp, filled passage ways with flame,   840
Annihilated father and son and followers
And given my own life on top of all!
O Sun, scanning with flame all works of earth,
And thou, O Juno, witness and go-between
Of my long miseries; and Hecate,   845
Screeched for at night at crossroads in the cities;
And thou, avenging Furies, and all gods
On whom Elissa dying may call: take notice,
Overshadow this hell with your high power,
As I deserve, and hear my prayer!   850
If by necessity that impious wretch
Must find his haven and come safe to land,
If so Jove's destinies require, and this,
His end in view, must stand, yet all the same
When hard beset in war by a brave people,   855
Forced to go outside his boundaries
And torn from Iulus, let him beg assistance,
Let him see the unmerited deaths of those
Around and with him, and accepting peace
On unjust terms, let him not, even so,   860
Enjoy his kingdom or the life he longs for,
But fall in battle before his time and lie

Unburied on the sand![6] This I implore,
This is my last cry, as my last blood flows.
Then, O my Tyrians, besiege with hate   865
His progeny and all his race to come:
Make this your offering to my dust. No love,
No pact must be between our peoples; No,
But rise up from my bones, avenging spirit!
Harry with fire and sword the Dardan countrymen   870
Now, or hereafter, at whatever time
The strength will be afforded. Coast with coast
In conflict, I implore, and sea with sea,
And arms with arms: may they contend in war,
Themselves and all the children of their children!"[7]   875

Now she took thought of one way or another,
At the first chance, to end her hated life,
And briefly spoke to Barce, who had been
Sychaeus' nurse; her own an urn of ash
Long held in her ancient fatherland.   880
                              "Dear nurse,
Tell Sister Anna to come here, and have her
Quickly bedew herself with running water
Before she brings out victims for atonement.
Let her come that way. And you, too, put on   885
Pure wool around your brows. I have a mind
To carry out that rite to Stygian[8] Jove
That I have readied here, and put an end
To my distress, committing to the flames
The pyre of that miserable Dardan."   890

At this with an old woman's eagerness
Barce hurried away. And Dido's heart
Beat wildly at the enormous thing afoot.
She rolled her bloodshot eyes, her quivering cheeks
Were flecked with red as her sick pallor grew   895
Before her coming death. Into the court
She burst her way, then at her passion's height
She climbed the pyre and bared the Dardan sword—
A gift desired once, for no such need.
Her eyes now on the Trojan clothing there   900
And the familiar bed, she paused a little,
Weeping a little, mindful, then lay down
And spoke her last words:
                              "Remnants dear to me
While god and fate allowed it, take this breath   905

---

6. Dido's prophecy-wish does come true. Aeneas meets resistance in Italy, and at one point in the war he must leave Ascanius behind and beg aid from King Evander. One of the conditions of peace is that his people call themselves Latins (not Trojans). He is eventually drowned in an Italian river, never to see the glory of his descendants.   7. These prophecies also come true in the three Punic wars between the Romans and Carthaginians (all won by Rome).   8. The king of the underworld, Pluto (Hades in Greek); the Styx is one of the rivers of the underworld.

And give me respite from these agonies.
I lived my life out to the very end
And passed the stages Fortune had appointed.
Now my tall shade goes to the under world.
I built a famous town, saw my great walls,   910
Avenged my husband, made my hostile brother
Pay for his crime. Happy, alas, too happy,
If only the Dardanian keels had never
Beached on our coast." And here she kissed the bed.
"I die unavenged," she said, "but let me die.   915
This way, this way,[9] a blessed relief to go
Into the undergloom. Let the cold Trojan,
Far at sea, drink in this conflagration
And take with him the omen of my death!"

Amid these words her household people saw her   920
Crumpled over the steel blade, and the blade
Aflush with red blood, drenched her hands. A scream
Pierced the high chambers. Now through the shocked city
Rumor went rioting, as wails and sobs
With women's outcry echoed in the palace   925
And heaven's high air gave back the beating din,
As though all Carthage or old Tyre fell
To storming enemies, and, out of hand,
Flames billowed on the roofs of men and gods.
Her sister heard the trembling, faint with terror,   930
Lacerating her face, beating her breast,
Ran through the crowd to call the dying queen:

"It came to this, then, sister? You deceived me?
The pyre meant this, altars and fires meant this?
What shall I mourn first, being abandoned? Did you   935
Scorn your sister's company in death?
You should have called me out to the same fate!
The same blade's edge and hurt, at the same hour,
Should have taken us off. With my own hands
Had I to build this pyre, and had I to call   940
Upon our country's gods, that in the end
With you placed on it there, O heartless one,
I should be absent? You have put to death
Yourself and me, the people and the fathers
Bred in Sidon, and your own new city.   945
Give me fresh water, let me bathe her wound
And catch upon my lips any last breath
Hovering over hers."
               Now she had climbed
The topmost steps and took her dying sister   950
Into her arms to cherish, with a sob,
Using her dress to stanch the dark blood flow.
But Dido trying to lift her heavy eyes

9. In Latin *sic, sic*; the repetition represents two thrusts of the sword.

Fainted again. Her chest-wound whistled air.
Three times she struggled up on one elbow   955
And each time fell back on the bed. Her gaze
Went wavering as she looked for heaven's light
And groaned at finding it. Almighty Juno,
Filled with pity for this long ordeal
And difficult passage, now sent Iris[1] down   960
Out of Olympus to set free
The wrestling spirit from the body's hold.
For since she died, not at her fated span
Nor as she merited, but before her time
Enflamed and driven mad, Proserpina[2]   965
Had not yet plucked from her the golden hair,
Delivering her to Orcus of the Styx.
So humid Iris through bright heaven flew
On saffron-yellow wings, and in her train
A thousand hues shimmered before the sun.   970
At Dido's head she came to rest.
                        "This token
Sacred to Dis I bear away as bidden
And free you from your body."
                            Saying this,   975
She cut a lock of hair. Along with it
Her body's warmth fell into dissolution,
And out into the winds her life withdrew.

[After his hurried departure from Carthage, Aeneas goes to Sicily, to the kingdom of
his friend Acestes. There he organizes funeral games in honor of his father, Anchisës
(who had died in Sicily on their first visit there), and leaves behind those of his
following who are unwilling to go on to the uncertainty of a settlement in Italy. Once
on Italian soil, Aeneas, obeying instructions from his dead father, who had appeared
to him in a dream, consults the Sibyl, a prophetess of Apollo, who guides him down
to the world of the dead. There he is to see his father and the vision of his race, which
is to be his only reward, for he will die before his people are settled in their new
home.]

FROM BOOK VI

[Aeneas in the Underworld]

*   *   *

Gods who rule the ghosts; all silent shades;
And Chaos and infernal Fiery Stream,[3]
And regions of wide night without a sound,
May it be right to tell what I have heard,
May it be right, and fitting, by your will,   5
That I describe the deep world sunk in darkness

---

1. As in Homer, a divine messenger; sometimes identified with the rainbow.   2. Queen of the underworld. Before a human died she was thought to cut a lock of his or her hair as an offering to Dis, god of
the underworld. Dido (by suicide) dies unexpectedly; thus Juno sends Iris to cut the lock.   3. A translation
of *Phlegethon*, the name of one of the underworld rivers.

Under the earth.
                    Now dim to one another
In desolate night they[4] walked on through the gloom,
Through Dis's homes all void, and empty realms,   10
As one goes through a wood by a faint moon's
Treacherous light, when Jupiter veils the sky
And black night blots the colors of the world.
Before the entrance, in the jaws of Orcus,
Grief and avenging Cares have made their beds,   15
And pale Diseases and sad Age are there,
And Dread, and Hunger that sways men to crime,
And sordid Want—in shapes to affright the eyes—
And Death and Toil and Death's own brother, Sleep,
And the mind's evil joys; on the door sill   20
Death-bringing War, and iron cubicles
Of the Eumenides, and raving Discord,
Viperish hair bound up in gory bands.
In the courtyard a shadowy giant elm
Spreads ancient boughs, her ancient arms where dreams,   25
False dreams, the old tale goes, beneath each leaf
Cling and are numberless. There, too,
About the doorway forms of monsters crowd—
Centaurs, twiformed Scyllas, hundred-armed
Briareus, and the Lernaean hydra   30
Hissing horribly, and the Chimaera
Breathing dangerous flames, and Gorgons, Harpies,[5]
Huge Geryon, triple-bodied ghost.
Here, swept by sudden fear, drawing his sword,
Aeneas stood on guard with naked edge   35
Against them as they came. If his companion,
Knowing the truth, had not admonished him
How faint these lives were—empty images
Hovering bodiless—he had attacked
And cut his way through phantoms, empty air.   40

The path goes on from that place to the waves
Of Tartarus's Acheron. Thick with mud,
A whirlpool out of a vast abyss
Boils up and belches all the silt it carries
Into Cocytus.[6] Here the ferryman,   45
A figure of fright, keeper of waters and streams,
Is Charon, foul and terrible, his beard
Grown wild and hoar, his staring eyes all flame,
His sordid cloak hung from a shoulder knot.
Alone he poles his craft and trims the sails   50

---

4. Aeneas and the Sibyl.   5. All mythical creatures. Centaurs were half human and half horse. Scyllas
have many heads. Briareus had fifty heads. The Hydra had nine heads; but if one were cut off, two would
grow in its place. The Chimaera was one-third lion, one-third goat, and one-third snake. Here the Harpies
are spirits of the storm wind that carry souls to Hades.   6. A river of the underworld; the name suggests
"mourning" or "lamentation." Tartarus is in the lower depths of the underworld. Acheron is another river,
whose name suggests "woe."

And in his rusty hull ferries the dead,
Old now—but old age in the gods is green.[7]

Here a whole crowd came streaming to the banks,
Mothers and men, the forms with all life spent
Of heroes great in valor, boys and girls   55
Unmarried, and young sons laid on the pyre
Before their parents' eyes—as many souls
As leaves that yield their hold on boughs and fall
Through forests in the early frost of autumn,
Or as migrating birds from the open sea   60
That darken heaven when the cold season comes
And drives them overseas to sunlit lands.
There all stood begging to be first across
And reached out longing hands to the far shore.

But the grim boatman now took these aboard,   65
Now those, waving the rest back from the strand.
In wonder at this and touched by the commotion,
Aeneas said:
        "Tell me, Sister, what this means,
The crowd at the stream. Where are the souls bound?   70
How are they tested, so that these turn back,
While those take oars to cross the dead-black water?"

Briefly the ancient priestess answered him:

"Cocytus is the deep pool that you see,
The swamp of Styx beyond, infernal power   75
By which the gods take oath and fear to break it.
All in the nearby crowd you notice here
Are pauper souls, the souls of the unburied.
Charon's the boatman. Those the water bears
Are souls of buried men. He may not take them   80
Shore to dread shore on the hoarse currents there
Until their bones rest in the grave, or till
They flutter and roam this side a hundred years;
They may have passage then, and may return
To cross the deeps they long for."   85
                  Anchises' son
Had halted, pondering on so much, and stood
In pity for the souls' hard lot. Among them
He saw two sad ones of unhonored death,
Leucaspis and the Lycian fleet's commander,
Orontes,[8] who had sailed the windy sea   90
From Troy together, till the Southern gale
Had swamped and whirled them down, both ship and men.
Of a sudden he saw his helmsman, Palinurus,
Going by, who but a few nights before   95

---

7. I.e., age in gods does not affect their vitality or strength. Thus Charon, although old, is still able to ferry the souls of the dead over the river Styx.   8. Trojans lost at sea in the storm that took Aeneas to Carthage.

On course from Libya, as he watched the stars,
Had been pitched overboard astern. As soon
As he made sure of the disconsolate one
In all the gloom, Aeneas called:
                        "Which god   100
Took you away from us and put you under,
Palinurus? Tell me. In this one prophecy
Apollo, who had never played me false,
Falsely foretold you'd be unharmed at sea
And would arrive at the Ausonian coast.   105
Is the promise kept?"
                      But the shade said:
                                "Phoebus' caldron[9]
Told you no lie, my captain, and no god
Drowned me at sea. The helm that I hung on to,   110
Duty bound to keep our ship on course,
By some great shock chanced to be torn away,
And I went with it overboard. I swear
By the rough sea, I feared less for myself
Than for your ship: with rudder gone and steersman   115
Knocked overboard, it might well come to grief
In big seas running. Three nights, heavy weather
Out of the South on the vast water tossed me.
On the fourth dawn, I sighted Italy
Dimly ahead, as a wave-crest lifted me.   120
By turns I swam and rested, swam again
And got my footing on the beach, but savages
Attacked me as I clutched at a cliff-top,
Weighted down by my wet clothes. Poor fools,
They took me for a prize and ran me through.   125
Surf has me now, and sea winds, washing me
Close inshore.
                By heaven's happy light
And the sweet air, I beg you, by your father,
And by your hopes of Iulus' rising star,   130
Deliver me from this captivity,
Unconquered friend! Throw earth on me—you can—
Put in to Velia[1] port! Or if there be
Some way to do it, if your goddess mother
Shows a way—and I feel sure you pass   135
These streams and Stygian marsh by heaven's will—
Give this poor soul your hand, take me across,
Let me at least in death find quiet haven."
When he had made his plea, the Sibyl said:
"From what source comes this craving, Palinurus?   140
Would you though still unburied see the Styx
And the grim river of the Eumenides,
Or even the river bank, without a summons?
Abandon hope by prayer to make the gods

9. The three-legged shallow cauldron or tripod on which the Pythia, priestess of Apollo at Delphi, sat as
she delivered the god's prophecies.   1. South of the Bay of Naples, near Cape Palinuro (named after
Aeneas's pilot).

Change their decrees. Hold fast to what I say   145
To comfort your hard lot: neighboring folk
In cities up and down the coast will be
Induced by portents to appease your bones,
Building a tomb and making offerings there
On a cape forever named for Palinurus."   150

The Sibyl's words relieved him, and the pain
Was for a while dispelled from his sad heart,
Pleased at the place-name. So the two walked on
Down to the stream. Now from the Stygian water
The boatman, seeing them in the silent wood   155
And headed for the bank, cried out to them
A rough uncalled-for challenge:
                              "Who are you
In armor, visiting our rivers? Speak
From where you are, stop there, say why you come.   160
This is the region of the Shades, and Sleep,
And drowsy Night. It breaks eternal law
For the Stygian craft to carry living bodies.
Never did I rejoice, I tell you, letting
Alcides cross, or Theseus and Pirithoüs,[2]   165
Demigods by paternity though they were,
Invincible in power. One forced in chains
From the king's own seat the watchdog of the dead
And dragged him away trembling. The other two
Were bent on carrying our lady off   170
From Dis's chamber."
                         This the prophetess
And servant of Amphrysian Apollo[3]
Briefly answered:
                    "Here are no such plots,   175
So fret no more. These weapons threaten nothing.
Let the great watchdog at the door howl on
Forever terrifying the bloodless shades.
Let chaste Proserpina remain at home
In her uncle's house. The man of Troy, Aeneas,   180
Remarkable for loyalty, great in arms,
Goes through the deepest shades of Erebus
To see his father.
                    If the very image
Of so much goodness moves you not at all,   185
Here is a bough"[4]—at this she showed the bough
That had been hidden, held beneath her dress—
"You'll recognize it."
                       Then his heart, puffed up
With rage, subsided. They had no more words.   190

---

2. They came to kidnap Proserpina, failed, and were imprisoned. *Alcides:* Heracles. One of his labors was to bring Cerberus, the watchdog of Hades, up from the lower world, and he also rescued Theseus.   **3.** An elaborate learned allusion: Apollo had once served as herdsman to King Admetus on the banks of the river Amphrysus in Thessaly.   **4.** The golden bough that Aeneas had been ordered to take as tribute to Proserpina.

His eyes fixed on the ancient gift, the bough,
The destined gift, so long unseen, now seen,
He turned his dusky craft and made for shore.
There from the long thwarts where they sat he cleared
The other souls and made the gangway wide,   195
Letting the massive man step in the bilge.
The leaky coracle groaned at the weight
And took a flood of swampy water in.
At length, on the other side, he put ashore
The prophetess and hero in the mire,   200
A formless ooze amid the grey-green sedge.
Great Cerberus barking with his triple throat
Makes all that shoreline ring, as he lies huge
In a facing cave. Seeing his neck begin
To come alive with snakes, the prophetess   205
Tossed him a lump of honey and drugged meal
To make him drowse. Three ravenous gullets gaped
And he snapped up the sop. Then his great bulk
Subsided and lay down through all the cave.
Now seeing the watchdog deep in sleep, Aeneas   210
Took the opening: swiftly he turned away
From the river over which no soul returns.

Now voices crying loud were heard at once—
The souls of infants wailing. At the door
Of the sweet life they were to have no part in,   215
Torn from the breast, a black day took them off
And drowned them all in bitter death. Near these
Were souls falsely accused, condemned to die.
But not without a judge, or jurymen,
Had these souls got their places: Minos reigned   220
As the presiding judge, moving the urn,
And called a jury of the silent ones[5]
To learn of lives and accusations. Next
Were those sad souls, benighted, who contrived
Their own destruction, and as they hated daylight,   225
Cast their lives away. How they would wish
In the upper air now to endure the pain
Of poverty and toil! But iron law
Stands in the way, since the drear hateful swamp
Has pinned them down here, and the Styx that winds   230
Nine times around exerts imprisoning power.
Not far away, spreading on every side,
The Fields of Mourning came in view, so called
Since here are those whom pitiless love consumed
With cruel wasting, hidden on paths apart   235
By myrtle woodland growing overhead.
In death itself, pain will not let them be.
He saw here Phaedra, Procris, Eriphyle

---

5. The dead. Minos, once king of Crete, is now judge of the dead. The magistrate of a Roman court decided
the order in which cases were heard by drawing lots from an urn.

Sadly showing the wounds her hard son gave;
Evadne and Pasiphaë, at whose side   240
Laodamia walked, and Caeneus,[6]
A young man once, a woman now, and turned
Again by fate into the older form.
Among them, with her fatal wound still fresh,
Phoenician Dido wandered the deep wood.   245
The Trojan captain paused nearby and knew
Her dim form in the dark, as one who sees,
Early in the month, or thinks to have seen, the moon
Rising through cloud, all dim. He wept and spoke
Tenderly to her: 250
          "Dido, so forlorn,
The story then that came to me was true,
That you were out of life, had met your end
By your own hand. Was I, was I the cause?
I swear by heaven's stars, by the high gods,   255
By any certainty below the earth,
I left your land against my will, my queen.
The gods' commands drove me to do their will,
As now they drive me through this world of shades,
These mouldy waste lands and these depths of night.   260
And I could not believe that I would hurt you
So terribly by going. Wait a little.
Do not leave my sight.
Am I someone to flee from? The last word
Destiny lets me say to you is this."   265

Aeneas with such pleas tried to placate
The burning soul, savagely glaring back,
And tears came to his eyes. But she had turned
With gaze fixed on the ground as he spoke on,
Her face no more affected than if she were   270
Immobile granite or Marpesian[7] stone.
At length she flung away from him and fled,
His enemy still, into the shadowy grove
Where he whose bride she once had been, Sychaeus,
Joined in her sorrows and returned her love.   275
Aeneas still gazed after her in tears,
Shaken by her ill fate and pitying her.

With effort then he took the given way,
And they went on, reaching the farthest lands

6. Virgil's words in the original are ambiguous (perhaps to reflect the ambiguity of the sex of Caeneus).
The usual explanation of the passage is that Caenis (a woman) was changed by Neptune into a man
(Caeneus) but returned to her original sex after death. Because the name occurs here in a list of women,
this seems the most likely explanation. Phaedra was the wife of Theseus, king of Athens, who fell in love
with Hippolytus, her husband's son by another woman; the result was her death by suicide and Hippolytus's
death through his father's curse. Procris was killed by her husband in an accident that was brought about
by her own jealousy. Eriphyle betrayed her husband for gold and was killed by her own son. Evadne threw
herself on the pyre of her husband, who was killed by Jupiter for impiety. Pasiphaë was the wife of Minos;
she was made to fall in love with a bull, and their union produced the Minotaur. Laodamia begged to be
allowed to talk with her dead husband; the request was granted by the gods, and when his time came to
return she went with him to the underworld.   7. Marble from the island of Paros.

Where men famous in war gather apart.   280
Here Tydeus came to meet him, and then came
Parthenopaeus, glorious in arms,
Adrastus[8] then, a pallid shade. Here too
Were Dardans long bewept in the upper air,
Men who died in the great war. And he groaned   285
To pick these figures out, in a long file,
Glaucus, Medon, Thersilochus, besides
Antenor's three sons, then the priest of Ceres
Polyboetes, then Idaeus, holding
Still to his warcar, holding his old gear.   290
To right and left they crowd the path and stay
And will not have enough of seeing him,
But love to hold him back, to walk beside him,
And hear the story of why he came.
                                      Not so   295
Agamemnon's phalanx, chiefs of the Danaans:
Seeing the living man in bronze that glowed
Through the dark air, they shrank in fear. Some turned
And ran, as once, when routed, to the ships,
While others raised a battle shout, or tried to,   300
Mouths agape, mocked by the whispering cry.
Here next he saw Deïphobus, Priam's son,
Mutilated from head to foot, his face
And both hands cruelly torn, ears shorn away,
Nose to the noseholes lopped by a shameful stroke.   305
Barely knowing the shade who quailed before him
Covering up his tortured face, Aeneas
Spoke out to him in his known voice:
                                "Deïphobus,
Gallant officer in high Teucer's line,   310
Who chose this brutal punishment, who had
So much the upper hand of you? I heard
On that last night that you had fallen, spent
After a slaughter of Pelasgians—
Fallen on piled-up carnage. It was I   315
Who built on Rhoeteum Point an empty tomb
And sent a high call to your soul three times.
Your name, your armor, marks the place. I could not
Find you, friend, to put your bones in earth
In the old country as I came away."   320

And Priam's son replied:
                        "You left undone
Nothing, my friend, but gave all ritual due
Deïphobus, due a dead man's shade. My lot
And the Laconian woman's[9] ghastly doing   325
Sank me in this hell. These are the marks
She left me as her memorial. You know

---

8. Three of the seven Argive attackers of Thebes in the generation before the Trojan War. Tydeus was the
father of Diomedes.   9. Helen. Deïphobus had married her after the death of Paris.

How between one false gladness and another
We spent that last night—no need to remind you.
When the tall deadly horse came at one bound,   330
With troops crammed in its paunch, above our towers,
She made a show of choral dance and led
Our Phrygian women crying out on Bacchus
Here and there—but held a torch amid them,
Signalling to Danaans from the Height.   335
Worn by the long day, heavily asleep,
I lay in my unlucky bridal chamber,
And rest, profound and sweet, most like the rest
Of death, weighed on me as I lay. Meanwhile
She, my distinguished wife, moved all my arms   340
Out of the house—as she had slipped my sword,
My faithful sword, out from beneath my pillow—
Opened the door and called in Menelaus,
Hoping no doubt by this great gift to him,
Her lover, to blot old infamy out. Why hold back   345
From telling it? The two burst in the bedroom,
Joined by that ringleader of atrocity,
Ulysses, of the windking's[1] line. O gods,
If with pure lips I pray, requite the Greeks
With equal suffering! But you, now tell me   350
What in the world has brought you here alive:
Have you come from your sea wandering, and did heaven
Direct you? How could harrying fortune send you
To these sad sunless homes, disordered places?"

At this point in their talk Aurora,[2] borne   355
Through high air on her glowing rosy car
Had crossed the meridian: should they linger now
With stories they might spend the allotted time.
But at Aeneas' side the Sibyl spoke,
Warning him briefly: 360
                    "Night comes on, Aeneas,
We use up hours grieving. Here is the place
Where the road forks: on the right hand it goes
Past mighty Dis's walls, Elysium way,
Our way; but the leftward road will punish   365
Malefactors, taking them to Tartarus."
Deïphobus answered her:
                    "No need for anger,
Reverend lady. I'll depart and make
The tally in the darkness full again.   370
Go on, sir, glory of us all! Go on,
Enjoy a better destiny."
                    He spoke,
And even as he spoke he turned away.
Now of a sudden Aeneas looked and saw   375

---

1. Aeolus. His son was Sisyphus, one of the great tricksters of Greek legend, who was reputed to be Ulysses' actual father, rather than Laertes. 2. Dawn goddess.

To the left, under a cliff, wide buildings girt
By a triple wall round which a torrent rushed
With scorching flames and boulders tossed in thunder,
The abyss's Fiery River. A massive gate
With adamantine pillars faced the stream,   380
So strong no force of men or gods in war
May ever avail to crack and bring it down,
And high in air an iron tower stands
On which Tisiphone,[3] her bloody robe
Pulled up about her, has her seat and keeps   385
Unsleeping watch over the entrance way
By day and night. From the interior, groans
Are heard, and thud of lashes, clanking iron,
Dragging chains. Arrested in his tracks,
Appalled by what he heard, Aeneas stood.   390

"What are the forms of evil here? O Sister,
Tell me. And the punishments dealt out:
Why such a lamentation?"
                          Said the Sibyl:
"Light of the Teucrians, it is decreed   395
That no pure soul may cross the sill of evil.
When, however, Hecate appointed me
Caretaker of Avernus wood, she led me
Through heaven's punishments and taught me all.
This realm is under Cretan Rhadamanthus'[4]   400
Iron rule. He sentences. He listens
And makes the souls confess their crooked ways,
How they put off atonements in the world
With foolish satisfaction, thieves of time,
Until too late, until the hour of death.   405
At once the avenger girdled with her whip,
Tisiphone, leaps down to lash the guilty,
Vile writhing snakes held out on her left hand,
And calls her savage sisterhood. The awaited
Time has come, hell gates will shudder wide   410
On shrieking hinges. Can you see her now,
Her shape, as doorkeeper, upon the sill?
More bestial, just inside, the giant Hydra
Lurks with fifty black and yawning throats.
Then Tartarus itself goes plunging down   415
In darkness twice as deep as heaven is high
For eyes fixed on etherial Olympus.
Here is Earth's ancient race, the brood of Titans,[5]
Hurled by the lightning down to roll forever
In the abyss. Here, too, I saw those giant   420
Twins of Aloeus[6] who laid their hands
Upon great heaven to rend it and to topple

---

3. One of the Furies.   4. Brother of Minos, king of Crete, and like him a judge of the dead.   5. The
second generation of gods, offspring of Earth and Sky, overthrown by the Olympians under Jupiter (Zeus).
6. Otus and Ephialtes, who piled Mount Pelion on top of Mount Ossa in order to scale heaven and attack
Jupiter.

Jove from his high seat, and I saw, too,
Salmoneus paying dearly for the jape
Of mimicking Jove's fire, Olympus' thunder: 425
Shaking a bright torch from a four-horse car
He rode through Greece and his home town in Elis,
Glorying, claiming honor as a god—
Out of his mind, to feign with horses' hoofs
On bronze the blast and inimitable bolt.   430
The father almighty amid heavy cloud
Let fly his missile—no firebrand for him
Nor smoky pitchpine light—and spun the man
Headlong in a huge whirlwind.
                              One had sight   435
Of Tityos,[7] too, child of all-mothering Earth,
His body stretched out over nine whole acres
While an enormous vulture with hooked beak
Forages forever in his liver,
His vitals rife with agonies. The bird,   440
Lodged in the chest cavity, tears at his feast,
And tissues growing again get no relief.
As for the Lapiths, need I tell: Ixion,
Pirithoüs,[8] and the black crag overhead
So sure to fall it seems already falling.   445
Golden legs gleam on the feasters' couches,
Dishes in royal luxury prepared
Are laid before them—but the oldest Fury
Crouches near and springs out with her torch.
Her outcry, if they try to touch the meal.   450
Here come those who as long as life remained
Held brothers hateful, beat their parents, cheated
Poor men dependent on them; also those
Who hugged their newfound riches to themselves
And put nothing aside for relatives—   455
A great crowd, this—then men killed for adultery,
Men who took arms in war against the right,
Not scrupling to betray their lords. All these
Are hemmed in here, awaiting punishment.
Best not inquire what punishment, what form   460
Of suffering at their last end overwhelms them.
Some heave at a great boulder, or revolve,
Spreadeagled, hung on wheel-spokes. Theseus
Cleaves to his chair and cleaves to it forever.
Phlegyas[9] in his misery teaches all souls   465
His lesson, thundering out amid the gloom:
'Be warned and study justice, not to scorn
The immortal gods.' Here's one who sold his country,
Foisted a tyrant on her, set up laws

---

7. Punished for trying to rape Leto (Latona). Odysseus sees him in the land of the dead also (*Odyssey* 11.660–68).   8. Ixion tried to rape Juno, and Pirithoüs aided Theseus in his unsuccessful attempt to carry off Proserpina from the underworld. The punishment described here, however, was traditionally assigned to Tantalus, another of the great sinners.   9. A king in Boeotia who burned Apollo's temple at Delphi, enraged that the god had seduced his daughter.

Or nullified them for a price; another 470
Entered his daughter's room to take a bride
Forbidden him. All these dared monstrous wrong
And took what they dared try for. If I had
A hundred tongues, a hundred mouths, a voice
Of iron, I could not tell of all the shapes 475
Their crimes had taken, or their punishments."

All this he heard from her who for long years
Had served Apollo. Then she said:
                              "Come now,
Be on your way, and carry out your mission.
Let us go faster. I can see the walls 480
The Cyclops' forges built and, facing us,
The portico and gate¹ where they command us
To leave the gifts required."
                         On this the two 485
In haste strode on abreast down the dark paths
Over the space between, and neared the doors.
Aeneas gained the entrance, halted there,
Asperged his body with fresh water drops,
And on the sill before him fixed the bough. 490

Now that at last this ritual was performed,
His duty to the goddess done, they came
To places of delight, to green park land,
Where souls take ease amid the Blessed Groves.
Wider expanses of high air endow 495
Each vista with a wealth of light. Souls here
Possess their own familiar sun and stars.
Some train on grassy rings, others compete
In field games, others grapple on the sand.
Feet moving to a rhythmic beat, the dancers 500
Group in a choral pattern as they sing.
Orpheus,² the priest of Thrace, in his long robe
Accompanies, plucking his seven notes
Now with his fingers, now with his ivory quill.
Here is the ancient dynasty of Teucer, 505
Heroes high of heart, beautiful scions,
Born in greater days: Ilus, Assaracus,
And Dardanus,³ who founded Troy. Aeneas
Marvels to see their chariots and gear
Far off, all phantom: lances fixed in earth, 510
And teams unyoked, at graze on the wide plain.
All joy they took, alive, in cars and weapons,
As in the care and pasturing of horses,
Remained with them when they were laid in earth.
He saw, how vividly! along the grass 515
To right and left, others who feasted there

---

1. The entrance to Elysium, the paradise of the souls of the blessed. This gate can be passed only with the token of the golden bough.   2. The mythical singer who charmed all nature with his music.   3. Trojan ancestors.

And chorused out a hymn praising Apollo,
Within a fragrant laurel grove, where Po[4]
Sprang up and took his course to the world above,
The broad stream flowing on amid the forest.   520
This was the company of those who suffered
Wounds in battle for their country; those
Who in their lives were holy men and chaste
Or worthy of Phoebus in prophetic song;
Or those who bettered life, by finding out   525
New truths and skills; or those who to some folk
By benefactions made themselves remembered.
They all wore snowy chaplets on their brows.
To these souls, mingling on all sides, the Sibyl
Spoke now, and especially to Musaeus,[5]   530
The central figure, toward whose towering shoulders
All the crowd gazed:
                          "Tell us, happy souls,
And you, great seer, what region holds Anchises,
Where is his resting place? For him we came   535
By ferry across the rivers of Erebus."
And the great soul answered briefly:
                                      "None of us
Has one fixed home. We walk in shady groves
And bed on riverbanks and occupy   540
Green meadows fresh with streams. But if your hearts
Are set on it, first cross this ridge; and soon
I shall point out an easy path."
                                 So saying,
He walked ahead and showed them from the height   545
The sweep of shining plain. Then down they went
And left the hilltops.
                        Now Aeneas' father
Anchises, deep in the lush green of a valley,
Had given all his mind to a survey   550
Of souls, till then confined there, who were bound
For daylight in the upper world.[6] By chance
His own were those he scanned now, all his own
Descendants, with their futures and their fates,
Their characters and acts. But when he saw   555
Aeneas advancing toward him on the grass,
He stretched out both his hands in eagerness
As tears wetted his cheeks. He said in welcome:

"Have you at last come, has that loyalty
Your father counted on conquered the journey?   560
Am I to see your face, my son, and hear
Our voices in communion as before?
I thought so, surely; counting the months I thought
The time would come. My longing has not tricked me.

4. An Italian river.   5. A legendary singer, like Orpheus.   6. I.e., destined to be reincarnated, as
Anchises will explain.

I greet you now, how many lands behind you,   565
How many seas, what blows and dangers, son!
How much I feared the land of Libya
Might do you harm."
                          Aeneas said:
                                  "Your ghost,   570
Your sad ghost, father, often before my mind,
Impelled me to the threshold of this place.
My ships ride anchored in the Tuscan sea.
But let me have your hand, let me embrace you,
Do not draw back."   575
                          At this his tears brimmed over
And down his cheeks. And there he tried three times
To throw his arms around his father's neck,
Three times the shade untouched slipped through his hands,
Weightless as wind and fugitive as dream.   580
Aeneas now saw at the valley's end
A grove standing apart, with stems and boughs
Of woodland rustling, and the stream of Lethe[7]
Running past those peaceful glades. Around it
Souls of a thousand nations filled the air,   585
As bees in meadows at the height of summer
Hover and home on flowers and thickly swarm
On snow-white lilies, and the countryside
Is loud with humming. At the sudden vision
Shivering, at a loss, Aeneas asked   590
What river flowed there and what men were those
In such a throng along the riverside.
His father Anchises told him:
                          "Souls for whom
A second body is in store: their drink   595
Is water of Lethe, and it frees from care
In long forgetfulness. For all this time
I have so much desired to show you these
And tell you of them face to face—to take
The roster of my children's children here,   600
So you may feel with me more happiness
At finding Italy."
                          "Must we imagine,
Father, there are souls that go from here
Aloft to upper heaven, and once more   605
Return to bodies' dead weight? The poor souls,
How can they crave our daylight so?"
                                  "My son,
I'll tell you, not to leave you mystified,"
Anchises said, and took each point in order: 610

First, then, the sky and lands and sheets of water,
The bright moon's globe, the Titan sun and stars,
Are fed within by Spirit, and a Mind

---

7. Literally, "Forgetfulness" (Greek).

Infused through all the members of the world
Makes one great living body of the mass. 615
From Spirit come the races of man and beast,
The life of birds, odd creatures the deep sea
Contains beneath her sparkling surfaces,
And fiery energy from a heavenly source
Belongs to the generative seeds of these, 620
So far as they are not poisoned or clogged
By mortal bodies, their free essence dimmed
By earthiness and deathliness of flesh.
This makes them fear and crave, rejoice and grieve.
Imprisoned in the darkness of the body 625
They cannot clearly see heaven's air;[8] in fact
Even when life departs on the last day
Not all the scourges of the body pass
From the poor souls, not all distress of life.
Inevitably, many malformations, 630
Growing together in mysterious ways,
Become inveterate. Therefore they undergo
The discipline of punishments and pay
In penance for old sins: some hang full length
To the empty winds, for some the stain of wrong 635
Is washed by floods or burned away by fire.
We suffer each his own shade. We are sent
Through wide Elysium, where a few abide
In happy lands, till the long day, the round
Of Time fulfilled, has worn our stains away, 640
Leaving the soul's heaven-sent perception clear,
The fire from heaven pure.[9] These other souls,
When they have turned Time's wheel a thousand years,
The god calls in a crowd to Lethe stream,
That there unmemoried they may see again 645
The heavens and wish re-entry into bodies."
Anchises paused. He drew both son and Sibyl
Into the middle of the murmuring throng,
Then picked out a green mound from which to view
The souls as they came forward, one by one, 650
And to take note of faces.
                              "Come," he said,
"What glories follow Dardan generations
In after years, and from Italian blood
What famous children in your line will come, 655
Souls of the future, living in our name,
I shall tell clearly now, and in the telling
Teach you your destiny. That one you see,
The young man leaning on a spear unarmed,
Has his allotted place nearest the light. 660

8. The idea that the body is the tomb of the soul is found also in Plato. Like a number of other ideas in Anchises' speech (such as reincarnation), it was characteristic of Orphism, a set of beliefs that underlay various mystery rituals outside the state religions of Greece and Rome.   9. These souls, having successfully purged the impurities of the body, are now ready to return to the company of the gods. The other souls whom Anchises goes on to mention must undergo further rebirths before they are purified. They include the souls of the future Romans, whom Aeneas now surveys.

He will be first to take the upper air,
Silvius, a child with half Italian blood
And an Alban name, your last born, whom your wife,
Lavinia,[1] late in your great age will rear
In forests to be king and father of kings.   665
Through him our race will rule in Alba Longa.
Next him is Procas, pride of the Trojan line,
And Capys, too, then Numitor, then one
Whose name restores you: Silvius Aeneas,[2]
Both in arms and piety your peer,   670
If ever he shall come to reign in Alba.
What men they are! And see their rugged forms
With oakleaf crowns shadowing their brows. I tell you,
These are to found Nomentum, Gabii,
Fidenae town, Collatia's hilltop towers,   675
Pometii, Fort Inuus, Bola, Cora[3]—
Names to be heard for places nameless now.
Then Romulus, fathered by Mars, will come
To make himself his grandfather's companion,
Romulus, reared by his mother, Ilia,   680
In the blood-line of Assaracus. Do you see
The double plume of Mars fixed on his crest,
See how the father of the gods himself
Now marks him out with his own sign of honor?
Look now, my son: under his auspices   685
Illustrious Rome will bound her power with earth,
Her spirit with Olympus. She'll enclose
Her seven hills with one great city wall,
Fortunate in the men she breeds. Just so
Cybele Mother,[4] honored on Berecynthus,   690
Wearing her crown of towers, onward rides
By chariot through the towns of Phrygia,
In joy at having given birth to gods,
And cherishing a hundred grandsons, heaven
Dwellers with homes on high.   695
                       Turn your two eyes
This way and see this people, your own Romans.
Here is Caesar, and all the line of Iulus,
All who shall one day pass under the dome
Of the great sky: this is the man, this one,   700
Of whom so often you have heard the promise,
Caesar Augustus, son of the deified,[5]
Who shall bring once again an Age of Gold
To Latium, to the land where Saturn reigned
In early times. He will extend his power   705
Beyond the Garamants[6] and Indians,

---

1. The bride Aeneas will win by war in the second half of the poem.   2. Kings of Alba Longa, the city
(Rome's forerunner) founded in Italy by Ascanius. Silvius Aeneas was son of the Silvius mentioned in line
662 and grandson of Aeneas. Numitor was father of Ilia (or Rhea Silvia), the mother by Mars of Romulus
and Remus (see lines 678–84).   3. Towns near Rome.   4. The great mother goddess of Asia Minor,
whose cult was important in Rome from an early period. Mount Berecynthus, near Troy, was a center of
her Asian cult. One of her attributes was a crown that resembled a city wall with turrets.   5. Julius
Caesar, who after his assassination was recognized as a god.   6. A people of Africa.

Over far territories north and south
Of the zodiacal stars, the solar way,
Where Atlas, heaven-bearing, on his shoulder
Turns the night-sphere, studded with burning stars.   710
At that man's coming even now the realms
Of Caspia and Maeotia tremble, warned
By oracles, and the seven mouths of Nile
Go dark with fear. The truth is, even Alcides
Never traversed so much of earth—I grant   715
That he could shoot the hind with brazen hoofs
Or bring peace to the groves of Erymanthus,
Or leave Lerna affrighted by his bow.[7]
Neither did he who guides his triumphal car
With reins of vine-shoots twisted, Bacchus, driving   720
Down from Nysa's height his tiger team.
Do we lag still at carrying our valor
Into action? Can our fear prevent
Our settling in Ausonia?

                  Who is he   725
So set apart there, olive-crowned, who holds
The sacred vessels in his hands? I know
That snowy mane and beard: Numa,[8] the king,
Who will build early Rome on a base of laws,
A man sent from the small-town poverty   730
Of Cures to high sovereignty. After him
Comes Tullus, breaker of his country's peace,
Arousing men who have lost victorious ways,
Malingering men, to war. Near him is Ancus,
Given to boasting, even now too pleased   735
With veering popularity's heady air.
Do you care to see now, too, the Tarquin kings
And the proud soul of the avenger, Brutus,[9]
By whom the bundled *fasces* are regained?
Consular power will first be his, and his   740
The pitiless axes.[1] When his own two sons
Plot war against the city, he will call
For the death penalty in freedom's name—
Unhappy man, no matter how posterity
May see these matters. Love of the fatherland   745
Will sway him—and unmeasured lust for fame.
Now see the Decii and the Drusi there,
And stern Torquatus, with his axe, and see
Camillus[2] bringing the lost standards home.
That pair,[3] however, matched in brilliant armor,   750
Matched in their hearts' desire now, while night

---

7. Three of Hercules' labors: killing the Cerynaian stag, the Erymanthian boar, and the hydra of Lerna.
8. The second king of Rome. His successors are mentioned in the next ten lines.   9. Avenger of the rape
of Lucretia by Sextus, son of Tarquin the Proud; after Tarquin was expelled from Rome, the kingship was
abolished. This Brutus (claimed as ancestor by the assassin of Julius Caesar) was the first consul, chief
magistrate of the republic that succeeded the monarchy at Rome.   1. Rods (*fasces*) wrapped around an
ax were the symbol of the consul's power.   2. All heroic figures from Rome's past.   3. Julius Caesar
and his opponent in the Civil War, Pompey. The war was provoked in 49 B.C.E. when Caesar crossed the
Alps from Gaul and entered Italy with an army. Pompey had married Caesar's daughter, Julia.

Still holds them fast, once they attain life's light
What war, what grief, will they provoke between them—
Battle-lines and bloodshed—as the father
Marches from the Alpine ramparts, down   755
From Monaco's walled height, and the son-in-law,
Drawn up with armies of the East, awaits him.
Sons, refrain! You must not blind your hearts
To that enormity of civil war,
Turning against your country's very heart   760
Her own vigor of manhood. You above all
Who trace your line from the immortals, you
Be first to spare us. Child of my own blood,[4]
Throw away your sword!
                          Mummius[5] there,   765
When Corinth is brought low, will drive his car
As victor and as killer of Achaeans
To our high Capitol. Paulus will conquer
Argos and Agamemnon's old Mycenae,
Defeating Perseus,[6] the Aeacid,   770
Heir to the master of war, Achilles—thus
Avenging his own Trojan ancestors
And the defilement of Minerva's shrine.
Great Cato![7] Who would leave you unremarked,
Or, Cossus, you, or the family of Gracchi,   775
Or the twin Scipios, bright bolts of war,
The bane of Libya, or you, Fabricius,
In poverty yet powerful, or you,
Serranus, at the furrow, casting seed?
Where, though I weary, do you hurry me,   780
You Fabii? Fabius Maximus,
You are the only soul who shall restore
Our wounded state by waiting out the enemy.
Others will cast more tenderly in bronze
Their breathing figures, I can well believe,   785
And bring more lifelike portraits out of marble;
Argue more eloquently, use the pointer
To trace the paths of heaven accurately
And accurately foretell the rising stars.
Roman, remember by your strength to rule   790
Earth's peoples—for your arts are to be these:
To pacify, to impose the rule of law,
To spare the conquered, battle down the proud."
Anchises paused here as they gazed in awe,
Then added: 795
           "See there, how Marcellus[8] comes
With spoils of the commander that he killed:

---

4. Caesar's family, the Julii, traced their ancestry back through Ascanius (Iulus) to Aeneas and Anchises.
5. Roman general, one of the conquerors of Greece, who sacked the city of Corinth in 167 B.C.E.
6. Macedonian king defeated by the Roman general Aemilius Paulus in 168 B.C.E. He claimed descent from Achilles.   7. Statesman and orator (234–149 B.C.E.), known for his sternness and rigid morals (and so an embodiment of Romanness). He begins a list of illustrious figures out of Rome's past, almost all of them famous generals.   8. A Roman general famous for killing the leader of Gauls from northern Italy in 222 B.C.E. in single combat and for leading the Second Punic War against Hannibal.

How the man towers over everyone.
Cavalry leader, he'll sustain the realm
Of Rome in hours of tumult, bringing to heel   800
The Carthaginians and rebellious Gaul,
And for the third time in our history
He'll dedicate an enemy general's arms
To Father Romulus."
                          But here Aeneas   805
Broke in, seeing at Marcellus' side
A young man[9] beautifully formed and tall
In shining armor, but with clouded brow
And downcast eyes:
                          "And who is that one, Father 810
Walking beside the captain as he comes:
A son, or grandchild from the same great stock?
The others murmur, all astir. How strong
His presence is! But night like a black cloud
About his head whirls down in awful gloom."   815

His father Anchises answered, and the tears
Welled up as he began:
                          "Oh, do not ask
About this huge grief of your people, son.
Fate will give earth only a glimpse of him,
Not let the boy live on. Lords of the sky,   820
You thought the majesty of Rome too great
If it had kept these gifts. How many groans
Will be sent up from that great Field of Mars
To Mars' proud city, and what sad rites you'll see,   825
Tiber, as you flow past the new-built tomb.
Never will any boy of Ilian race
Exalt his Latin forefathers with promise
Equal to his; never will Romulus' land
Take pride like this in any of her sons.   830
Weep for his faithful heart, his old-world honor,
His sword arm never beaten down! No enemy
Could have come through a clash with him unhurt,
Whether this soldier went on foot or rode,
Digging his spurs into a lathered mount.   835
Child of our mourning, if only in some way
You could break through your bitter fate. For you
Will be Marcellus. Let me scatter lilies,
All I can hold, and scarlet flowers as well,
To heap these for my grandson's shade at least,   840
Frail gifts and ritual of no avail."

So raptly, everywhere, father and son
Wandered the airy plain and viewed it all.
After Anchises had conducted him

9. Another Marcellus, Augustus's nephew and presumptive heir, who died in 23 B.C.E. at the age of nineteen.

To every region and had fired his love   845
Of glory in the years to come, he spoke
Of wars that he must fight, of Laurentines,
And of Latinus' city, then of how
He might avoid or bear each toil to come.

There are two gates of Sleep, one said to be   850
Of horn, whereby the true shades pass with ease,
The other all white ivory agleam
Without a flaw, and yet false dreams are sent
Through this one by the ghosts to the upper world.
Anchises now, his last instructions given,   855
Took son and Sibyl there and let them go
By the Ivory Gate.
                Aeneas made his way
Straight to the ships to see his crews again,
Then sailed directly to Caieta's port.   860
Bow anchors out, the sterns rest on the beach.

[After returning from the underworld to the upper air, Aeneas begins his settlement
in Italy. He is offered the hand of the princess Lavinia by her father Latinus, but this
provokes a war against the Trojans, led by King Turnus of Laurentum. While Aeneas
is on an embassy to seek help from the Etruscans, his mother, Venus, comes to him
at night with the armor made for him by Vulcan (Hephaestus in Greek), her husband
and the guardian of fire. On the shield is carved a representation of the future glories
of Rome.]

FROM BOOK VIII

[The Shield of Aeneas]

*   *   *

          Venus the gleaming goddess,
Bearing her gifts, came down amid high clouds
And far away still, in a vale apart,
Sighted her son beside the ice-cold stream.
Then making her appearance as she willed   5
She said to him:
          "Here are the gifts I promised,
Forged to perfection by my husband's craft,
So that you need not hesitate to challenge
Arrogant Laurentines or savage Turnus,   10
However soon, in battle."
             As she spoke
Cytherea swept to her son's embrace
And placed the shining arms before his eyes
Under an oak tree. Now the man in joy   15
At a goddess' gifts, at being so greatly honored,
Could not be satisfied, but scanned each piece
In wonder and turned over in his hands
The helmet with its terrifying plumes

And gushing flames, the sword-blade edged with fate, 20
The cuirass of hard bronze, blood-red and huge—
Like a dark cloud burning with sunset light
That sends a glow for miles—the polished greaves[1]
Of gold and silver alloy, the great spear,
And finally the fabric of the shield 25
Beyond description.
               There the Lord of Fire,
Knowing the prophets, knowing the age to come,
Had wrought the future story of Italy,
The triumphs of the Romans: there one found 30
The generations of Ascanius' heirs,
The wars they fought, each one. Vulcan had made
The mother wolf, lying in Mars' green grotto;
Made the twin boys at play about her teats,[2]
Nursing the mother without fear, while she 35
Bent round her smooth neck fondling them in turn
And shaped their bodies with her tongue.
                     Nearby,
Rome had been added by the artisan,
And Sabine women roughly carried off 40
Out of the audience at the Circus games;
Then suddenly a new war coming on
To pit the sons of Romulus against
Old Tatius[3] and his austere town of Curës.
Later the same kings, warfare laid aside, 45
In arms before Jove's altar stood and held
Libation dishes as they made a pact
With offering of wine. Not far from this
Two four-horse war-cars, whipped on, back to back,
Had torn Mettus apart (still, man of Alba, 50
You should have kept your word) and Roman Tullus[4]
Dragged the liar's rags of flesh away
Through woods where brambles dripped a bloody dew.
There, too, Porsenna stood, ordering Rome
To take the exiled Tarquin back,[5] then bringing 55
The whole city under massive siege.
There for their liberty Aeneas' sons
Threw themselves forward on the enemy spears.
You might have seen Porsenna imaged there
To the life, a menacing man, a man in anger 60
At Roman daring: Cocles who downed the bridge,
Cloelia[6] who broke her bonds and swam the river.

1. Leg pieces.   2. The twins who were to build Rome, Romulus and Remus, sons of Mars the war god, were cast out into the woods and there suckled by a she-wolf.   3. A Sabine king. Because the new city of Rome consisted mostly of men, the Romans decided to steal women from the Sabines. The Romans invited them to an athletic festival, and at a given signal every Roman carried off a Sabine bride. The war that followed ended in the amalgamation of the Roman and Sabine peoples.   4. The king who punished Mettus for breaking an agreement made during the early wars of Rome. Mettus was torn apart by two chariots moving in opposite directions.   5. The Etruscan king Porsenna attempted to restore Tarquin, the last of the Roman kings, to the throne from which he had been expelled.   6. A Roman hostage held by Porsenna. Horatius Cocles, with two companions, defended the bridge across the Tiber to give the Romans time to destroy it.

On the shield's upper quarter Manlius,
guard of the Tarpeian Rock, stood fast
Before the temple and held the Capitol,[7]   65
Where Romulus' house[8] was newly thatched and rough.
Here fluttering through gilded porticos
At night, the silvery goose warned of the Gauls
Approaching: under cover of the darkness
Gauls amid the bushes had crept near   70
And now lay hold upon the citadel.
Golden locks they had and golden dress,
Glimmering with striped cloaks, their milky necks
Entwined with gold. They hefted Alpine spears,
Two each, and had long body shields for cover.   75
Vulcan had fashioned naked Luperci
And Salii[9] leaping there with woolen caps
And fallen-from-heaven shields, and put chaste ladies
Riding in cushioned carriages through Rome
With sacred images. At a distance then   80
He pictured the deep hell of Tartarus,
Dis's high gate, crime's punishments, and, yes,
You, Catiline,[1] on a precarious cliff
Hanging and trembling at the Furies' glare.
Then, far away from this, were virtuous souls   85
And Cato[2] giving laws to them. Mid-shield,
The pictured sea flowed surging, all of gold,
As whitecaps foamed on the blue waves, and dolphins
Shining in silver round and round the scene
Propelled themselves with flukes and cut through billows.   90
Vivid in the center were the bronze-beaked
Ships and the fight at sea off Actium.
Here you could see Leucata[3] all alive
With ships maneuvering, sea glowing gold,
Augustus Caesar leading into battle   95
Italians, with both senators and people,
Household gods and great gods: there he stood
High on the stern, and from his blessed brow
Twin flames gushed upward, while his crest revealed
His father's star. Apart from him, Agrippa,[4]   100
Favored by winds and gods, led ships in column,
A towering figure, wearing on his brows
The coronet adorned with warships' beaks,

---

7. In 392 B.C.E. Manlius was in charge of the citadel ("the Tarpeian Rock") at a time when the Gauls from the north held all the rest of the city. They made a night attack on the citadel, but Manlius, awakened by the cackling of the sacred geese, beat it off and saved Rome.   8. In Virgil's time there was still preserved at Rome a rustic building that was supposed to have been the dwelling place of Romulus.   9. The twelve priests of Mars, who danced in his honor carrying shields that had fallen from heaven. Luperci: priests of Lupercus, a Roman god corresponding to the Greek Pan.   1. Leader of a conspiracy to overthrow the republic; it was halted mainly through the efforts of Cicero, consul in 63 B.C.E. Catiline connotes the type of discord, represented by the civil war that almost destroyed the Roman state, to which Augustus later put an end.   2. The noblest of the republicans who had fought Julius Caesar; he stood for honesty and the seriousness that the Romans most admired. He committed suicide in 47 B.C.E. after Caesar's victory in Africa.   3. A promontory near Actium, on the west coast of Greece, which had a temple of Apollo on it. The naval battle fought here in 31 B.C.E. was the decisive engagement of the civil war. Augustus (then called Octavian), the master of the western half of the empire, defeated Antony, who held the eastern half and was supported by Cleopatra, queen of Egypt.   4. Augustus's admiral at Actium.

Highest distinction for command at sea.
Then came Antonius with barbaric wealth   105
And a diversity of arms, victorious
From races of the Dawnlands and Red Sea,
Leading the power of the East, of Egypt,
Even of distant Bactra[5] of the steppes
And in his wake the Egyptian consort came   110
So shamefully. The ships all kept together
Racing ahead, the water torn by oar-strokes,
Torn by the triple beaks, in spume and foam.
All made for the open sea. You might believe
The Cyclades[6] uprooted were afloat   115
Or mountains running against mountain heights
When seamen in those hulks pressed the attack
Upon the other turreted ships. They hurled
Broadsides of burning flax on flying steel,
And fresh blood reddened Neptune's fields. The queen   120
Amidst the battle called her flotilla on
With a sistrum's[7] beat, a frenzy out of Egypt,
Never turning her head as yet to see
Twin snakes of death behind, while monster forms
Of gods of every race, and the dog-god   125
Anubis[8] barking, held their weapons up
Against our Neptune, Venus, and Minerva.
Mars, engraved in steel, raged in the fight
As from high air the dire Furies came
With Discord, taking joy in a torn robe,   130
And on her heels, with bloody scourge, Bellona.[9]

Overlooking it all, Actian[1] Apollo
Began to pull his bow. Wild at this sight,
All Egypt, Indians, Arabians, all
Sabaeans[2] put about in flight, and she,   135
The queen, appeared crying for winds to shift
Just as she hauled up sail and slackened sheets.
The Lord of Fire had portrayed her there,
Amid the slaughter, pallid with death to come,
Then borne by waves and wind from the northwest,   140
While the great length of mourning Nile awaited her
With open bays, calling the conquered home
To his blue bosom and his hidden streams.
But Caesar then in triple triumph[3] rode
Within the walls of Rome, making immortal   145
Offerings to the gods of Italy—
Three hundred princely shrines throughout the city.
There were the streets, humming with festal joy
And games and cheers, an altar to every shrine,
To every one a mothers' choir, and bullocks   150

5. On the borders of India.   6. The islands of the southern Aegean Sea.   7. An Oriental rattle, used
in the worship of Isis.   8. The Egyptian death god, depicted with the head of a jackal.   9. A Roman
war goddess.   1. So called because of his temple at Actium; the temple (and its cult statue) overlooked
the sea battle.   2. Arabs from the Yemen.   3. For victories in Dalmatia and at Actium and Alexandria.

Knifed before the altars strewed the ground.
The man himself, enthroned before the snow-white
Threshold of sunny Phoebus, viewed the gifts
The nations of the earth made, and he fitted them
To the tall portals. Conquered races passed   155
In long procession, varied in languages
As in their dress and arms. Here Mulciber,[4]
Divine smith, had portrayed the Nomad tribes
And Afri with ungirdled flowing robes,
Here Leleges and Carians, and here   160
Gelonians[5] with quivers. Here Euphrates,
Milder in his floods now, there Morini,[6]
Northernmost of men; here bull-horned Rhine,
And there the still unconquered Scythian Dahae;
Here, vexed at being bridged, the rough Araxes.[7]   165
All these images on Vulcan's shield,
His mother's gift, were wonders to Aeneas.
Knowing nothing of the events themselves,
He felt joy in their pictures, taking up
Upon his shoulder all the destined acts   170
And fame of his descendants.

[In the course of the desperate battles that follow, the young Pallas, entrusted to
Aeneas's care by his father, is killed by the Italian champion Turnus, who takes and
wears the belt of Pallas as the spoil of victory. The fortunes of the war later change
in favor of the Trojans, and Aeneas kills the Etruscan king Mezentius, Turnus's ally.
Eventually, as the Italians prepare to accept the generous peace terms offered by
Aeneas, Turnus forestalls them by accepting Aeneas's challenge to single combat to
decide the issue. But this solution is frustrated by the intervention of Juno, who
foresees Aeneas's victory. She prompts Turnus's sister, the river nymph Juturna, to
intervene in an attempt to save Turnus's life. Juturna stirs up the Italians, who are
watching the champions prepare for the duel; the truce is broken, and in the subsequent fighting Aeneas is wounded by an arrow. Healed by Venus, he returns to the
fight, and the Italians are driven back. Turnus finally faces his adversary. His sword
breaks on the armor forged by Vulcan, and he runs from Aeneas. He is saved by
Juturna, who, assuming the shape of his charioteer, hands him a fresh sword. At this
point Jupiter intervenes to stop the vain attempts of Juno and Juturna to save Turnus.]

FROM BOOK XII

[The Death of Turnus]

* * *

Omnipotent Olympus' king meanwhile
Had words for Juno, as she watched the combat
Out of a golden cloud. He said:
                              "My consort,
What will the end be? What is left for you?   5
You yourself know, and say you know, Aeneas
Born for heaven, tutelary of this land,

---

4. Vulcan.   5. Peoples from Scythia (in the Balkans). The Leleges and Carians were from Asia Minor.
6. A Belgian tribe.   7. A turbulent river in Armenia. Augustus built a new bridge over it.

By fate to be translated to the stars.[8]
What do you plan? What are you hoping for,
Keeping your seat apart in the cold clouds? 10
Fitting, was it, that a mortal archer
Wound an immortal? That a blade let slip
Should be restored to Turnus, and new force
Accrue to a beaten man? Without your help
What could Juturna do? Come now, at last 15
Have done, and heed our pleading, and give way.
Let yourself no longer be consumed
Without relief by all that inward burning;
Let care and trouble not forever come to me
From your sweet lips. The finish is at hand. 20
You had the power to harry men of Troy
By land and sea, to light the fires of war
Beyond belief, to scar a family
With mourning before marriage.[9] I forbid
Your going further." 25
        So spoke Jupiter,
And with a downcast look Juno replied:

"Because I know that is your will indeed,
Great Jupiter, I left the earth below,
Though sore at heart, and left the side of Turnus. 30
Were it not so, you would not see me here
Suffering all that passes, here alone,
Resting on air. I should be armed in flames
At the very battle-line, dragging the Trojans
Into a deadly action. I persuaded 35
Juturna—I confess—to help her brother
In his hard lot, and I approved her daring
Greater difficulties to save his life,
But not that she should fight with bow and arrow.
This I swear by Styx' great fountainhead 40
Inexorable, which high gods hold in awe.
I yield now and for all my hatred leave
This battlefield. But one thing not retained
By fate I beg for Latium, for the future
Greatness of your kin: when presently 45
They crown peace with a happy wedding day—
So let it be—and merge their laws and treaties,
Never command the land's own Latin folk
To change their old name, to become new Trojans,
Known as Teucrians; never make them alter 50
Dialect or dress. Let Latium be.
Let there be Alban kings for generations,
And let Italian valor be the strength
Of Rome in after times. Once and for all
Troy fell, and with her name let her lie fallen." 55

8. Aeneas is destined for immortality, because after his death he will be worshipped as a local god.   9. A reference not only to the Italian losses but also to the suicide of Amata, wife of King Latinus, who hanged herself when the Trojans assaulted the city just before the duel between Aeneas and Turnus began.

The author of men and of the world replied
With a half-smile:
             "Sister of Jupiter[1]
Indeed you are, and Saturn's other child,
To feel such anger, stormy in your breast.   60
But come, no need; put down this fit of rage.
I grant your wish. I yield, I am won over
Willingly. Ausonian folk will keep
Their fathers' language and their way of life,
And, that being so, their name. The Teucrians   65
Will mingle and be submerged, incorporated.
Rituals and observances of theirs
I'll add, but make them Latin, one in speech.
The race to come, mixed with Ausonian blood,
Will outdo men and gods in its devotion,   70
You shall see—and no nation on earth
Will honor and worship you so faithfully."

To all this Juno nodded in assent
And, gladdened by his promise, changed her mind.
Then she withdrew from sky and cloud.   75
                            That done,
The Father set about a second plan—
To take Juturna from her warring brother.
Stories are told of twin fiends, called the Dirae,
Whom, with Hell's Megaera,[2] deep Night bore   80
In one birth. She entwined their heads with coils
Of snakes and gave them wings to race the wind.
Before Jove's throne, a step from the cruel king,
These twins attend him and give piercing fear
To ill mankind, when he who rules the gods   85
Deals out appalling death and pestilence,
Or war to terrify our wicked cities.
Jove now dispatched one of these, swift from heaven,
Bidding her be an omen to Juturna.
Down she flew, in a whirlwind borne to earth,   90
Just like an arrow driven through a cloud
From a taut string, an arrow armed with gall
Of deadly poison, shot by a Parthian[3]—
A Parthian or a Cretan[4]—for a wound
Immedicable; whizzing unforeseen   95
It goes through racing shadows: so the spawn
Of Night went diving downward to the earth.

On seeing Trojan troops drawn up in face
Of Turnus' army, she took on at once
The shape of that small bird[5] that perches late   100
At night on tombs or desolate roof-tops

---

1. Jupiter and Juno (like the Greek Zeus and Hera) are brother and sister as well as husband and wife.
2. A Fury. The Dirae are literally "Dreadful Ones."   3. Parthia was the most dangerous neighbor of the Roman Empire in the east.   4. Parthian mounted archers were famous, as were Cretan archers.
5. The owl.

And troubles darkness with a gruesome song.
Shrunk to that form, the fiend in Turnus' face
Went screeching, flitting, flitting to and fro
And beating with her wings against his shield.   105
Unstrung by numbness, faint and strange, he felt
His hackles rise, his voice choke in his throat.
As for Juturna, when she knew the wings,
The shriek to be the fiend's, she tore her hair,
Despairing, then she fell upon her cheeks   110
With nails, upon her breast with clenched hands.

"Turnus, how can your sister help you now?
What action is still open to me, soldierly
Though I have been? Can I by any skill
Hold daylight for you? Can I meet and turn   115
This deathliness away? Now I withdraw,
Now leave this war. Indecent birds, I fear you;
Spare me your terror. Whip-lash of your wings
I recognize, that ghastly sound, and guess
Great-hearted Jupiter's high cruel commands.   120
Returns for my virginity, are they?
He gave me life eternal[6]—to what end?
Why has mortality been taken from me?
Now beyond question I could put a term
To all my pain, and go with my poor brother   125
Into the darkness, his companion there.
Never to die? Will any brook of mine
Without you, brother, still be sweet to me?
If only earth's abyss were wide enough
To take me downward, goddess though I am,   130
To join the shades below!"
                              So she lamented,
Then with a long sigh, covering up her head
In her grey mantle, sank to the river's depth.

Aeneas moved against his enemy   135
And shook his heavy pine-tree spear. He called
From his hot heart:
                      "Rearmed now, why so slow?
Why, even now, fall back? The contest here
Is not a race, but fighting to the death   140
With spear and sword. Take on all shapes there are,
Summon up all your nerve and skill, choose any
Footing, fly among the stars, or hide
In caverned earth—"
                      The other shook his head,   145
Saying:
            "I do not fear your taunting fury,
Arrogant prince. It is the gods I fear
And Jove my enemy."

---

6. Jupiter had been the lover of Juturna and had rewarded her with immortality.

He said no more, 150
But looked around him. Then he saw a stone,
Enormous, ancient, set up there to prevent
Landowners' quarrels. Even a dozen picked men
Such as the earth produces in our day
Could barely lift and shoulder it. He swooped 155
And wrenched it free, in one hand, then rose up
To his heroic height, ran a few steps,
And tried to hurl the stone against his foe—
But as he bent and as he ran
And as he hefted and propelled the weight 160
He did not know himself. His knees gave way,
His blood ran cold and froze. The stone itself,
Tumbling through space, fell short and had no impact.

Just as in dreams when the night-swoon of sleep
Weighs on our eyes, it seems we try in vain 165
To keep on running, try with all our might,
But in the midst of effort faint and fail;
Our tongue is powerless, familiar strength
Will not hold up our body, not a sound
Or word will come: just so with Turnus now: 170
However bravely he made shift to fight
The immortal fiend blocked and frustrated him.
Flurrying images passed through his mind.
He gazed at the Rutulians,[7] and beyond them,
Gazed at the city, hesitant, in dread. 175
He trembled now before the poised spear-shaft
And saw no way to escape; he had no force
With which to close, or reach his foe, no chariot
And no sign of the charioteer, his sister.
At a dead loss he stood. Aeneas made 180
His deadly spear flash in the sun and aimed it,
Narrowing his eyes for a lucky hit.
Then, distant still, he put his body's might
Into the cast. Never a stone that soared
From a wall-battering catapult went humming 185
Loud as this, nor with so great a crack
Burst ever a bolt of lightning. It flew on
Like a black whirlwind bringing devastation,
Pierced with a crash the rim of sevenfold shield,
Cleared the cuirass' edge, and passed clean through 190
The middle of Turnus' thigh. Force of the blow
Brought the huge man to earth, his knees buckling,
And a groan swept the Rutulians as they rose,
A groan heard echoing on all sides from all
The mountain range, and echoed by the forests. 195
The man brought down, brought low, lifted his eyes
And held his right hand out to make his plea:

7. The Italian troops watching the combat between Turnus and Aeneas.

"Clearly I earned this, and I ask no quarter.
Make the most of your good fortune here.
If you can feel a father's grief—and you, too,   200
Had such a father in Anchises—then
Let me bespeak your mercy for old age
In Daunus,[8] and return me, or my body,
Stripped, if you will, of life, to my own kin.
You have defeated me. The Ausonians   205
Have seen me in defeat, spreading my hands.
Lavinia is your bride. But go no further
Out of hatred."
                Fierce under arms, Aeneas
Looked to and fro, and towered, and stayed his hand   210
Upon the sword-hilt. Moment by moment now
What Turnus said began to bring him round
From indecision. Then to his glance appeared
The accurst swordbelt surmounting Turnus' shoulder,
Shining with its familiar studs—the strap   215
Young Pallas wore when Turnus wounded him
And left him dead upon the field; now Turnus
Bore that enemy token on his shoulder—
Enemy still. For when the sight came home to, him,
Aeneas raged at the relic of his anguish   220
Worn by this man as trophy. Blazing up
And terrible in his anger, he called out:

"You in your plunder, torn from one of mine,
Shall I be robbed of you? This wound will come
From Pallas: Pallas makes this offering   225
And from your criminal blood exacts his due."

He sank his blade in fury in Turnus' chest.
Then all the body slackened in death's chill,
And with a groan for that indignity
His spirit fled into the gloom below.   230

8. Father of Turnus.

OVID

43 B.C.E.–17 C.E.

Born in the year after Julius Caesar's assassination, Publius Ovidius Naso did not
know the time of civil war, when no one's property, or life, was safe. He was twenty-
four when Virgil died, and he turned to different themes: the sophisticated and somewhat racy life of the urban elite in Rome, love in its manifold social and psychological
guises, Greco-Roman myth and local Italian legend. Like Catullus and Virgil, he was

profoundly influenced by the learned and polished works of the Greek Alexandrian period, but like his predecessors he translated their example into his personal idiom and used it for his own purposes. He was a versifier of genius. "Whatever I tried to say," he wrote, "came out in verse," and Alexander Pope adapted the line for his own case: "I lisped in numbers for the numbers came." Elegance, wit, and precision remained the hallmarks of Ovid's poetry throughout his long and productive career, and his way of telling stories was extraordinary for its subtlety and its depth of psychological understanding. His influence on the poets and artists of the Middle Ages, the Renaissance, and beyond was massive, second only, if at all, to Virgil's.

The early years of Ovid's manhood were marked by rapid literary and social success in the brilliant society of a capital intent on enjoying the peace and prosperity inaugurated by Augustus. The *Amores*, or "Love Affairs," unabashed chronicles of a Roman Don Juan, was his first publication. It was soon followed by the *Art of Love*, a handbook of seduction (originally circulated as books 1 and 2, for men; book 3, for women, was added by popular request). Not content with teaching his readers how to start a love affair, Ovid then advised them how to end it, in the *Remedies of Love*. At some point he wrote a poem on women's cosmetics; another, the *Fasti* (never finished), on the Roman calendar; and a collection of poetic letters, the *Heroides*, purporting to have been written by heroines of legend, such as Helen, to their lovers. In 8 C.E. Ovid was banished by imperial decree to the town of Tomi, in what is now Romania. It was on the fringe of the empire, and to a devotee of Roman high life it seemed a grim place indeed. He remained there until his death, sending back to Rome poetic epistles, collected as the *Sorrows* and the *Letters from Pontus*, that asked for pardon—to no effect. The reason for his banishment is not known. Involvement in some scandal concerning Augustus's daughter Julia is a possibility, but the ultimate cause was probably the love poetry, which ran afoul of Augustus's political and social program. Augustus was trying hard, by propaganda and legislation, to revive old Roman standards of morality and cannot have found Ovid's *Art of Love*, with its suggestion that Rome was a prime location for seduction, amusing. He correctly read the poem as political critique, a mode of resistance to the authoritarian imposition of moral reform. Ovid's greatest work, the *Metamorphoses*, suggests a similar critique. It was still unfinished at the time of his exile.

THE METAMORPHOSES

Virgil had written what Augustus wanted to be the "official" epic of the new order, which was to be seen as the fulfillment of a history that began with Aeneas's journey from Troy to Italy. The *Aeneid*, for all its innovations, was an epic in the traditional style: it focused on the deeds of a single hero, and it exemplified and transmitted its culture's dominant values. The *Metamorphoses* is recognizably epic; it is the only poem Ovid wrote in the epic meter, dactylic hexameter. But it can be seen as a critical response to Virgil, even an anti-*Aeneid*. Ovid produced a series of stories using the Alexandrian form of the *epyllion*, or "miniature epic," and he strung these together into a long narrative of fifteen books. The transitions between them, and the connections drawn by the narrator, are often transparently contrived—perhaps in mockery of the idea of narrative unity. There is no single hero, and one would have to seek hard for representative national values presented without irony. There is, however, a common element to these stories: all in one way or another involve changes of shape. And despite its leisurely and roundabout course, the narrative has a discernible direction—as Ovid says in his introduction, "from the world's beginning to the present day." Starting with the creation of the world, the transformation of matter into living bodies (the first great metamorphosis), Ovid regales his readers with tales of human beings changed into animals, flowers, and trees. He proceeds through Greek myth to stories of early Rome and so to his own time, including, as the final metamorphoses, the ascension of the murdered Julius Caesar to the heavens in the form of a star and the divine promise that Augustus too, far in the future, will become a god.

Fluidity, then, is a key concept of the *Metamorphoses*. It underlies both the narrative style and the vision of the world the poem projects. Virgil also told of a transformation, the new (Roman) order arising from the ruins of the old (Troy). But once the transformation was completed by the Augustan order, there was to be stability, permanence. Ovid tells of a world ceaselessly coming to be in a process that never ends. To Virgil's story of national origins he opposes creation itself, which sets the pattern of instability, the fleetingness of form, and constant transformation. Ambivalence and ambiguity there may be in the *Aeneid*—but within a single set of Roman values summed up in Aeneas himself. Ovid's epic without a hero presents shifting perspectives and offers the reader no single point of view or end point from which to judge his very complex narratives. Virgil responded to the chaos of civil war with a vision of political stability; Ovid responds in turn to the new order. To the forced imposition of political and moral unity he opposes fluidity itself.

The political implications do not exhaust the richness of the *Metamorphoses*, though they are never far to seek. Within the poem's large-scale framework, each story in turn engages and delights the reader with its verbal wit, the cunningly calculated emphasis on this or that telling detail, the shifts between pathos and ironic distance, and the brilliant psychological insights suggested by the narrative or the characters' words and actions. Ovid constantly plays with narrative technique. A story will be told partly from one character's perspective, and then, with a sudden shift, partly from another's. One story will be embedded in another, with a consequent imposition of one narrative voice on top of another, as when, in the excerpt from book 10 printed below, Venus tells Adonis the story of Atalanta. This story is set within the tale of the goddess's love for Adonis and of his death, which is one of a series of stories sung by Orpheus within the poem's main narrative. In such cases, both the immediate and the larger contexts give the same story different shades of meaning. And there are thematic connections between stories. Daphne and Syrinx are turned into plants (the laurel and the reed) that are henceforth attributes of the gods who tried to rape them: a form of appropriation that substitutes for sexual violence. Just as Jupiter turns Io, the girl *he* has raped, into a cow, so he tricks Europa, in order to possess her, by becoming a seductively handsome bull. Europa offers the god-bull flowers; the terrified Proserpina, victim of a far more direct and brutal rape, drops the flowers she has been collecting when the god of death carries her on his chariot beneath the Earth.

As these examples indicate, a common element of many stories in books 1 and 2 is the portrayal of important male gods as both destructive and ridiculous in their lust. "Slow down, I beg you," Apollo calls to the fleeing Daphne in fear that she will fall and disfigure herself, "restrain yourself in flight, / and I will follow at a lesser speed." Or, as the narrator comments on Jupiter-as-bull, "Majestic power and erotic love / do not get on together very well." As the examples also show, the poem contains a number of stories of rape. Ovid gives different perspectives on what is essentially the same situation in order to emphasize the variety of possible responses to it by different readers, and he leaves it to those readers to evaluate their own responses. That is, fluidity not only is a theme of the poem but also characterizes the multiple positions open to the reader. In addition, one of the possible implications of these stories of rape is, again, political, for rape is the ultimate imposition of control. When powerful gods, however ridiculous they may appear, force themselves on defenseless women, imposed authority is held up to questioning. After all, as Ovid points out gleefully in the *Art of Love*, a rape was at the heart of Rome's foundation legend: it was through the rape of the Sabine women that the male inhabitants of the new city acquired wives and were able to supply Rome with future citizens.

The stories selected here from later in the *Metamorphoses* bring out other aspects of gender and sexuality. From the story of Iphis and Ianthe we learn that the instability of gender is not a modern discovery; nor is the recognition that the roles it determines for women and men in society are more or less arbitrary. That episode, the last in book 9, ends with the triumph of heterosexual love. The tales from book 10 all have to do, in one way or another, with the psychopathology of love. The case of Pygmalion may seem an exception, but we should remember that it begins with his hatred of women for their loose morals, and that the story as a whole, whatever it may say about the power of art, can also be read as a fable of the male fabrication of woman—her person and her functions—according to his desires. In the same way, Atalanta's conquest by Hippomenes represents, in the Greek and Roman cultural code, the "taming" of the "wild" virgin into marriage; but the story ends as a tale of divine wrath against this couple, and it is told by Venus to a lover whom she is about to lose to death. These stories and others, including Myrrha's consummated love for her own father, are narrated by Orpheus, the archetypal poet, after his failure to bring Eurydice back from the underworld. Ovid tells us—and it seems to be his invention—that in reaction to his loss Orpheus had turned to pederasty, and that he was torn to pieces in his native Thrace by Maenads, female worshippers of Dionysus.

The Italian baroque sculptor Giovanni Bernini carved statue groups of Apollo and Daphne and of Hades and Proserpina—stunning translations of Ovid's poetry into marble. Among their many allusions to the *Metamorphoses*, Milton and Dante both used Ovid's version of the Proserpina story: the former in book 9 of *Paradise Lost* as an image of the entry of death into the world, the latter in the *Purgatorio* to emphasize redemption from death. It was surely not only the fact that the *Metamorphoses* draws into itself most of the major classical myths (and a number of lesser-known stories as well) that has made the poem a source of subjects for artists and poets ever since but also the memorable ways these stories are told and their rich potential for meaning. The poem has many themes, but it also tells about itself: the irresistible power of a well-told narrative to hold the attention and shape the imagination of those who read or listen to it.

PRONOUNCING GLOSSARY

The following list uses common English syllables and stress accents to provide rough equivalents of selected words whose pronunciation may be unfamiliar to the general reader.

Acheloüs: *a-kel-oh'-us*

Alpheus: *al'-fyoos*

Anapos: *a-nap'-os*

Arethusa: *a-reth-oos'-a*

Calliope: *kal-lai'-o-pee*

Cenchreis: *ken-kray'-is*

Ceres: *see'-reez / keé-res*

Cinyras: *sin-ai'-ras / kin-ee'-ras*

Cyane: *see-ah'-nee / kee-ah'-nay*

Daedalus: *dee'-dal-us / dai'-dal-us*

Epaphus: *e-paf'-us*

Erigone: *e-rig'-o-nee*

Europa: *yoo-roh'-pa*

Hippomenes: *hip-po'-men-eez*

Icarus: *i'-kar-us*

Inachus: *i'-na-kus*

Iphis: *i'-fis*

Isis: *ai'-sis*

Naiads: *nai'-adz*

Osiris: *oh-sai'-ris*

Pasiphaë: *pa-sif'-ay-ee*

Peneus: *pen'-yoos / pen-ay'-us*

Phoebus: *fee'-bus / foy-bus*

Proserpina: *pros-ehr'-pi-na*

Pygmalion: *pig-may'-lyon*

Satyr: *say'-ter*

Telethusa: *tel-e-thoo'-sa*

Typhoeus: *ti-foy'-oos*

Tenedos: *ten'-e-dos*

From Metamorphoses[1]

FROM BOOK I

[Proem]

My mind leads me to speak now of forms changed
into new bodies: O gods above, inspire
this undertaking (which you've changed as well)
and guide my poem in its epic sweep
from the world's beginning to the present day.   5

[The Creation]

Before the seas and lands had been created,
before the sky that covers everything,
Nature displayed a single aspect only
throughout the cosmos; Chaos was its name,
a shapeless, unwrought mass of inert bulk   10
and nothing more, with the discordant seeds
of disconnected elements all heaped
together in anarchic disarray.
  The sun as yet did not light up the earth,
nor did the crescent moon renew her horns,   15
nor was the earth suspended in midair,
balanced by her own weight, nor did the ocean
extend her arms to the margins of the land.
  Although the land and sea and air were present,
land was unstable, the sea unfit for swimming,   20
and air lacked light; shapes shifted constantly,
and all things were at odds with one another,
for in a single mass cold strove with warm,
wet was opposed to dry and soft to hard,
and weightlessness to matter having weight.   25
  Some god (or kinder nature) settled this
dispute by separating earth from heaven,
and then by separating sea from earth
and fluid aether[2] from the denser air;
and after these were separated out   30
and liberated from the primal heap,
he bound the disentangled elements
each in its place and all in harmony.
  The fiery and weightless aether leapt
to heaven's vault and claimed its citadel;   35
the next in lightness to be placed was air;
the denser earth drew down gross elements
and was compressed by its own gravity;
encircling water lastly found its place,

---

1. Translated by Charles Martin.   2. A region of refined air, fiery in nature, believed to be above the "denser air" that was closer to the earth and composed the breathable atmosphere.

encompassing the solid earth entire.[3]   40
   Now when that god (whichever one it was)
had given Chaos form, dividing it
in parts which he arranged, he molded earth
into the shape of an enormous globe,
so that it should be uniform throughout.   45
   And afterward he sent the waters streaming
in all directions, ordered waves to swell
under the sweeping winds, and sent the flood
to form new shores on the surrounded earth;
he added springs, great standing swamps and lakes,   50
as well as sloping rivers fixed between
their narrow banks, whose plunging waters (all
in varied places, each in its own channel)
are partly taken back into the earth
and in part flow until they reach the sea,   55
when they—received into the larger field
of a freer flood—beat against shores, not banks.
He ordered open plains to spread themselves,
valleys to sink, the stony peaks to rise,
and forests to put on their coats of green.   60
   And as the vault of heaven is divided
by two zones on the right and two on the left,
with a central zone, much hotter, in between,
so, by the care of this creator god,
the mass that was enclosed now by the sky   65
was zoned in the same way, with the same lines
inscribed upon the surface of the earth.
Heat makes the middle zone unlivable,
and the two outer zones are deep in snow;
between these two extremes, he placed two others   70
of temperate climate, blending cold and warmth.[4]
   Air was suspended over all of this,
proportionately heavier than aether,
as earth is heavier than water is.
He ordered mists and clouds into position,   75
and thunder, to make test of our resolve,[5]
and winds creating thunderbolts and lightning.
   Nor did that world-creating god permit
the winds to roam ungoverned through the air;
for even now, with each of them in charge   80
of his own kingdom, and their blasts controlled,
they scarcely can be kept from shattering
the world, such is the discord between brothers.
   Eurus[6] went eastward, to the lands of Dawn,
the kingdoms of Arabia and Persia,   85

3. From Homer on, the ancients conceived of Ocean as a stream that surrounded the earth. See the very end of the description of Achilles' shield in book 18 of Homer's *Iliad*, p. 173.   4. The sky, that is, is divided into five horizontal zones, and therefore so is the earth beneath it. On either side of the earth's uninhabitable torrid region, over which the sun passes, lies a temperate zone, and the northern one contains the inhabited, civilized lands on earth (ancient writers were vague about what the southern temperate zone contained). The two outermost zones, farthest from the sun, were too cold to live in.   5. Thunder was considered an omen.   6. The east wind. Zephyr, Boreas, and Auster were the west, north, and south winds, respectively.

and to the mountain peaks that lie below
the morning's rays; and Zephyr took his place
on the western shores warmed by the setting sun.
The frozen north and Scythia were seized
by bristling Boreas; the lands opposite,   90
continually drenched by fog and rain,
are where the south wind, known as Auster, dwells.
Above these winds, he set the weightless aether,
a liquid free of every earthly toxin.

No sooner had he separated all   95
within defining limits, when the stars,
which formerly had been concealed in darkness,
began to blaze up all throughout the heavens;
and so that every region of the world
should have its own distinctive forms of life,   100
the constellations and the shapes of gods
occupied the lower part of heaven;
the seas gave shelter to the shining fishes,
earth received beasts, and flighty air, the birds.

An animal more like the gods than these,   105
more intellectually capable
and able to control the other beasts,
had not as yet appeared: now man was born,
either because the framer of all things,
the fabricator of this better world,   110
created man out of his own divine
substance—or else because Prometheus[7]
took up a clod (so lately broken off
from lofty aether that it still contained
some elements in common with its kin),   115
and mixing it with water, molded it
into the shape of gods, who govern all.

And even though all other animals
lean forward and look down toward the ground,
he gave to man a face that is uplifted,   120
and ordered him to stand erect and look
directly up into the vaulted heavens
and turn his countenance to meet the stars;
the earth, that was so lately rude and formless,
was changed by taking on the shapes of men.   125

* * *

[Apollo and Daphne]

Daphne,[8] the daughter of the river god
Peneus, was the first love of Apollo;
this happened not by chance, but by the cruel
outrage of Cupid; Phoebus, in the triumph   630
of his great victory against the Python,[9]

---

7. A god best known for stealing fire from the gods and giving it to mortals. In some stories he also created humans out of clay.   8. Literally, "Laurel" (Greek).   9. The enormous snake that Apollo (Phoebus) had to kill in order to found his oracle at Delphi. *Cupid:* god of sexual desire.

observed him bending back his bow and said,
   "What are *you* doing with such manly arms,
lascivious boy? That bow befits *our* brawn,[1]   635
wherewith we deal out wounds to savage beasts
and other mortal foes, unerringly:
just now with our innumerable arrows
we managed to lay low the mighty Python,
whose pestilential belly covered acres!   640
Content yourself with kindling love affairs
with your wee torch—and don't claim *our* glory!"
    The son of Venus[2] answered him with this:
"Your arrow, Phoebus, may strike everything:
mine will strike you: as animals to gods,   645
your glory is so much the less than mine!"
    He spoke, and soaring upward through the air
on wings that thundered, in no time at all
had landed on Parnassus'[3] shaded height;
and from his quiver drew two arrows out   650
which operated at cross-purposes,
for one engendered flight, the other, love;
the latter has a polished tip of gold,
the former has a tip of dull, blunt lead;
with this one, Cupid struck Peneus' daughter,   655
while the other pierced Apollo to his marrow.
    One is in love now, and the other one
won't hear of it, for Daphne calls it joy
to roam within the forest's deep seclusion,
where she, in emulation of the chaste   660
goddess Phoebe,[4] devotes herself to hunting;
one ribbon only bound her straying tresses.
    Many men sought her, but she spurned her suitors,
loath to have anything to do with men,
and rambled through the wild and trackless groves   665
untroubled by a thought for love or marriage.
    Often her father said, "You owe it to me,
child, to provide me with a son-in-law
and grandchildren!"
               "Let me remain a virgin,
father most dear," she said, "as once before   670
Diana's father, Jove, gave her that gift."
    Although Peneus yielded to you, Daphne,
your beauty kept your wish from coming true,
your comeliness conflicting with your vow:
at first sight, Phoebus loves her and desires   675
to sleep with her; desire turns to hope,
and his own prophecy deceives the god.
    Now just as in a field the harvest stubble
is all burned off, or as hedges are set ablaze
when, if by chance, some careless traveler   680

---

1. The bow was one of Apollo's attributes.   2. Goddess of love (Aphrodite in Greek).   3. Mountain in central Greece, near Delphi.   4. Diana (Artemis in Greek), Apollo's sister, virgin goddess of the hunt.

should brush one with his torch or toss away
the still-smoldering brand at break of day—
just so the smitten god went up in flames
until his heart was utterly afire,
and hope sustained his unrequited passion.   685

   He gazes on her hair without adornment:
"What if it were done up a bit?" he asks,
and gazes on her eyes, as bright as stars,
and on that darling little mouth of hers,
though sight is not enough to satisfy;   690
he praises everything that he can see—
her fingers, hands, and arms, bare to her shoulders—
and what is hidden prizes even more.

   She flees more swiftly than the lightest breeze,
nor will she halt when he calls out to her: 695
"Daughter of Peneus, I pray, hold still,
hold still! I'm not a foe in grim pursuit!
Thus lamb flees wolf, thus dove from eagle flies
on trembling wings, thus deer from lioness,
thus any creature flees its enemy,   700
but I am stalking you because of love!

   "Wretch that I am: I'm fearful that you'll fall,
brambles will tear your flesh because of me!
The ground you're racing over's very rocky,
slow down, I beg you, restrain yourself in flight,   705
and I will follow at a lesser speed.

   "Just ask yourself who finds you so attractive!
I'm not a caveman, not some shepherd boy,
no shaggy guardian of flocks and herds—
you've no idea, rash girl, you've no idea   710
whom you are fleeing, that is why you flee!

   "Delphi, Claros, Tenedos are all mine,
I'm worshiped in the city of Patara![5]
Jove is my father, I alone reveal
what was, what is, and what will come to be!   715
The plucked strings answer my demand with song!

   "Although my aim is sure, another's arrow
proved even more so, and my careless heart
was badly wounded—the art of medicine
is my invention, by the way, the source   720
of my worldwide fame as a practitioner
of healing through the natural strength of herbs.

   "Alas, there is no herbal remedy
for the love that I must suffer, and the arts
that heal all others cannot heal their lord—"   725

   He had much more to say to her, but Daphne
pursued her fearful course and left him speechless,
though no less lovely fleeing him; indeed,
disheveled by the wind that bared her limbs
and pressed the blown robes to her straining body   730

---

5. All centers of Apollo's cult.

even as it whipped up her hair behind her,
the maiden was more beautiful in flight!
    But the young god had no further interest
in wasting his fine words on her; admonished
by his own passion, he accelerates,   735
and runs as swiftly as a Gallic hound[6]
chasing a rabbit through an open field;
the one seeks shelter and the other, prey—
he clings to her, is just about to spring,
with his long muzzle straining at her heels,   740
while she, not knowing whether she's been caught,
in one swift burst, eludes those snapping jaws,
no longer the anticipated feast;
so he in hope and she in terror race.
    But her pursuer, driven by his passion,   745
outspeeds the girl, giving her no pause,
one step behind her, breathing down her neck;
her strength is gone; she blanches at the thought
of the effort of her swift flight overcome,
but at the sight of Peneus, she cries,   750
"Help me, dear father! If your waters hold
divinity, transform me and destroy
that beauty by which I have too well pleased!"
    Her prayer was scarcely finished when she feels
a torpor take possession of her limbs—   755
her supple trunk is girdled with a thin
layer of fine bark over her smooth skin;
her hair turns into foliage, her arms
grow into branches, sluggish roots adhere
to feet that were so recently so swift,   760
her head becomes the summit of a tree;
all that remains of her is a warm glow.
    Loving her still, the god puts his right hand
against the trunk, and even now can feel
her heart as it beats under the new bark;   765
he hugs her limbs as if they were still human,
and then he puts his lips against the wood,
which, even now, is adverse to his kiss.
    "Although you cannot be my bride," he says,
"you will assuredly be my own tree,   770
O Laurel, and will always find yourself
girding my locks, my lyre, and my quiver too—
you will adorn great Roman generals
when every voice cries out in joyful triumph
along the route up to the Capitol;   775
you will protect the portals of Augustus,
guarding, on either side, his crown of oak;[7]
and as I am—perpetually youthful,
my flowing locks unknown to the barber's shears—

---

6. A hunting breed famous for speed.   7. The laurel tree, sacred to Apollo, was the symbol of victory
not only in athletic contests but also in war; victorious Roman generals honored with a triumphal procession
through the city to the Capitol wore a laurel wreath. The oak was sacred to Jupiter.

so you will be an evergreen forever   780
bearing your brilliant foliage with glory!"
    Phoebus concluded. Laurel shook her branches
and seemed to nod her summit in assent.

[Jove and Io]

There is a grove in Thessaly,[8] enclosed
on every side by high and wooded hills: 785
they call it Tempe. The river Peneus,
which rises deep within the Pindus range,
pours its turbulent waters through this gorge
and over a cataract that deafens all
its neighbors far and near, creating clouds   790
that drive a fine, cool mist along, until
it drips down through the summits of the trees.
    Here is the house, the seat, the inner chambers
of the great river; here Peneus holds court
in his rocky cavern and lays down the law   795
to water nymphs and tributary streams.
    First to assemble were the native rivers,
uncertain whether to congratulate,
or to commiserate with Daphne's father:
the Sperchios, whose banks are lined with poplars,   800
the ancient Apidanus and the mild
Aeas and Amprysus; others came later—
rivers who, by whatever course they take,
eventually bring their flowing streams,
weary of their meandering, to sea.   805
    Inachus[9] was the only river absent,
concealed in the recesses of his cave:
he added to his volume with the tears
he grimly wept for his lost daughter Io,
not knowing whether she still lived or not;   810
but since he couldn't find her anywhere,
assumed that she was nowhere to be found—
and in his heart, he feared a fate far worse.
    For Jupiter had seen the girl returning
from her father's banks and had accosted her: 815
"O maiden worthy of almighty Jove
and destined to delight some lucky fellow
(I know not whom) upon your wedding night,
come find some shade," he said, "in these deep woods—"
(showing her where the woods were very shady)   820
"while the sun blazes high above the earth!
    "But if you're worried about entering
the haunts of savage beasts all by yourself,
why, under the protection of a god
you will be safe within the deepest woods—   825
and no plebeian god, for I am he

8. A region of central Greece.   9. A river near Argos in the northeast Peloponnesus.

who bears the celestial scepter in his hand,
I am he who hurls the roaming thunderbolt—
don't run from me!"
     But run she did, through Lerna
and Lyrcea,[1] until the god concealed   830
the land entirely beneath a dense
dark mist and seized her and dishonored her.
 Juno,[2] however, happened to look down
on Argos, where she noticed something odd:
swift-flying clouds had turned day into night   835
long before nighttime. She realized
that neither falling mist nor rising fog
could be the cause of this phenomenon,
and looked about at once to find her husband,
as one too well aware of the connivings   840
of a mate so often taken in the act.
 When he could not be found above, she said,
"Either I'm mad—or I am being had."
She glided down to earth from heaven's summit
immediately and dispersed the clouds.   845
 Having intuited his wife's approach,
Jove had already metamorphosed Io
into a gleaming heifer—a beauty still,
even as a cow. Despite herself,
Juno gave this illusion her approval,   850
and feigning ignorance, asked him whose herd
this heifer had come out of, and where from;
Jove, lying to forestall all inquiries
as to her origin and pedigree,
replied that she was born out of the earth.   855
Then Juno asked him for her as a gift.
 What could he do? Here is his beloved:
to hand her over is unnatural,
but not to do so would arouse suspicion;
shame urged him onward while love held him back. 860
Love surely would have triumphed over shame,
except that to deny so slight a gift
to one who was his wife and sister both
would make it seem that this was no mere cow!
 Her rival given up to her at last,   865
Juno feared Jove had more such tricks in mind,
and couldn't feel entirely secure
until she'd placed this heifer in the care
of Argus, the watchman with a hundred eyes:
in strict rotation, his eyes slept in pairs,   870
while those that were not sleeping stayed on guard.
No matter where he stood, he looked at Io,
even when he had turned his back on her.
 He let her graze in daylight; when the sun

---

1. A mountain on the border between Argos and Arcadia to the west. *Lerna:* a marsh in the territory of Argos, near the coast. 2. Wife of Jupiter (Hera in Greek).

set far beneath the earth, he penned her in   875
and placed a collar on her indignant neck.
She fed on leaves from trees and bitter grasses,
and had no bed to sleep on, the poor thing,
but lay upon the ground, not always grassy,
and drank the muddy waters from the streams.   880
    Having no arms, she could not stretch them out
in supplication to her warden, Argus;
and when she tried to utter a complaint
she only mooed—a sound which terrified her,
fearful as she now was of her own voice.   885
    Io at last came to the riverbank
where she had often played; when she beheld
her own slack jaws and newly sprouted horns
in the clear water, she fled, terrified!
    Neither her naiad sisters[3] nor her father   890
knew who this heifer was who followed them
and let herself be petted and admired.
Inachus fed her grasses from his hand;
she licked it and pressed kisses on his palm,
unable to restrain her flowing tears.   895
    If words would just have come, she would have spoken,
telling them who she was, how this had happened,
and begging their assistance in her case;
but with her hoof, she drew lines in the dust,
and letters of the words she could not speak   900
told the sad story of her transformation.
    "Oh, wretched me," cried Io's father, clinging
to the lowing calf's horns and snowy neck.
"Oh, wretched me!" he groaned. "Are you the child
for whom I searched the earth in every part?   905
Lost, you were less a grief than you are, found!
    "You make no answer, unable to respond
to our speech in language of your own,
but from your breast come resonant deep sighs
and—all that you can manage now—you *moo!*   910
    "But I—all unaware of this—was busy
arranging marriage for you, in the hopes
of having a son-in-law and grandchildren.
Now I must pick your husband from my herd,
and now must find your offspring there as well!   915
    "Nor can I end this suffering by death;
it is a hurtful thing to be a god,
for the gates of death are firmly closed against me,
and our sorrows must go on forever."
    And while the father mourned his daughter's loss,   920
Argus of the hundred eyes removed her
to pastures farther off and placed himself
high on a mountain peak, a vantage point
from which he could keep watch in all directions.

---

3. River nymphs.

The ruler of the heavens cannot bear   925
the sufferings of Io any longer,
and calls his son, born of the Pleiades,[4]
and orders him to do away with Argus.

Without delay, he takes his winged sandals,
his magic, sleep-inducing wand, and cap;   930
and so equipped, the son of father Jove
glides down from heaven's summit to the earth,
where he removes and leaves behind his cap
and winged sandals, but retains the wand;
and sets out as a shepherd, wandering   935
far from the beaten path, driving before him
a flock of goats he rounds up as he goes,
while playing tunes upon his pipe of reeds.

The guardian of Juno is quite taken
by this new sound: "Whoever you might be,   940
why not come sit with me upon this rock,"
said Argus, "for that flock of yours will find
the grass is nowhere greener, and you see
that there is shade here suitable for shepherds."

The grandson of great Atlas takes his seat   945
and whiles away the hours, chattering
of this and that—and playing on his pipes,
he tries to overcome the watchfulness
of Argus, struggling to stay awake;
even though Slumber closes down some eyes,   950
others stay vigilant. Argus inquired
how the reed pipes, so recently invented,
had come to be, and Mercury responded:

"On the idyllic mountains of Arcadia,[5]
among the hamadryads[6] of Nonacris,   955
one was renowned, and Syrinx[7] was her name.
Often she fled—successfully—from Satyrs,[8]
and deities of every kind as well,
those of the shady wood and fruited plain.

"In her pursuits and in virginity   960
Diana was her model, and she wore
her robe hitched up and girt above the knees
just as her goddess did; and if her bow
had been made out of gold, instead of horn,
anyone seeing her might well have thought   965
she *was* the goddess—as, indeed, some did.

"Wearing his crown of sharp pine needles, Pan[9]
saw her returning once from Mount Lycaeus,[1]
and began to say. . . ."

There remained to tell

---

4. Mercury (Hermes in Greek) was the son of Maia, one of the Pleiades or daughters of Atlas. They were changed into stars when the hunter Orion was pursuing them along with their mother Pleione, whom he wanted to rape.   5. The rustic central region of the Peloponnesus. Nonacris was a town in its northern part.   6. Tree nymphs.   7. The name means "shepherd's pipe," a musical instrument made of reeds. 8. Woodland creatures—half man, bald, bearded, and highly sexed.   9. A god of the wild mountain pastures and woods, with goat's feet and horns. He was particularly associated with Arcadia.   1. A high mountain in Arcadia.

of how the maiden, having spurned his pleas,   970
fled through the trackless wilds until she came
to where the gently flowing Ladon stopped
her in her flight; how she begged the water nymphs
to change her shape, and how the god, assuming
that he had captured Syrinx, grasped instead   975
a handful of marsh reeds! And while he sighed,
the reeds in his hands, stirred by his own breath,
gave forth a similar, low-pitched complaint!
　　The god, much taken by the sweet new voice
of an unprecedented instrument,   980
said this to her: "At least we may converse
with one another—I can have that much."
　　That pipe of reeds, unequal in their lengths,
and joined together one-on-one with wax,
took the girl's name, and bears it to this day.   985
　　Now Mercury was ready to continue
until he saw that Argus had succumbed,
for all his eyes had been closed down by sleep.
He silences himself and waves his wand
above those languid orbs to fix the spell.   990
　　Without delay he grasps the nodding head
and where it joins the neck, he severs it
with his curved blade and flings it bleeding down
the steep rock face, staining it with gore.
O Argus, you are fallen, and the light   995
in all your lamps is utterly put out:
one hundred eyes, one darkness all the same!
　　But Saturn's daughter[2] rescued them and set
those eyes upon the feathers of her bird,[3]
filling his tail with constellated gems.   1000
　　Her rage demanded satisfaction, *now*:
the goddess set a horrifying Fury
before the eyes and the imagination
of her Grecian rival; and in her heart
she fixed a prod that goaded Io on,   1005
driving her in terror through the world
until at last, O Nile, you let her rest
from endless labor; having reached your banks,
she went down awkwardly upon her knees,
and with her neck bent backward, raised her face   1010
as only she could do it, to the stars;
and with her groans and tears and mournful mooing,
entreated Jove, it seemed, to put an end
to her great suffering.
　　　　　　　　　　Jove threw his arms   1015
around the neck of Juno in embrace,
imploring her to end this punishment:
"In future," he said, "put your fears aside:
never again will you have cause to worry—

2. Juno.　3. The peacock.

about *this* one." And swore upon the Styx.[4]
The goddess was now pacified, and Io   1020
at once began regaining her lost looks,
till she became what she had been before;
her body lost all of its bristling hair,
her horns shrank down, her eyes grew narrower,
her jaws contracted, arms and hands returned,   1025
and hooves divided themselves into nails;
nothing remained of her bovine nature,
unless it was the whiteness of her body.
She had some trouble getting her legs back,
and for a time feared speaking, lest she moo,   1030
and so quite timidly regained her speech.
She is a celebrated goddess now,
and worshiped by the linen-clad Egyptians.[5]
Her son, Epaphus, is believed to be
sprung from the potent seed of mighty Jove,   1035
and temples may be found in every city
wherein the boy is honored with his parent.

*   *   *

FROM BOOK II

[Jove and Europa]

When Mercury had punished her for these
impieties of thought and word,[6] he left
Athena's city, and on beating wings   1145
returned to heaven where his father Jove
took him aside and (without telling him
that his new passion was the reason) said:
"Dear son, who does my bidding faithfully,
do not delay, but with your usual   1150
swiftness fly down to earth and find the land
that looks up to your mother[7] on the left,
called Sidon[8] by the natives; there you will see
a herd of royal cattle some way off
upon a mountain; drive them down to shore."   1155
He spoke and it was done as he had ordered:
the cattle were immediately driven
down to a certain place along the shore
where the daughter of a great king used to play,
accompanied by maidens all of Tyre.[9]   1160
Majestic power and erotic love
do not get on together very well,
nor do they linger long in the same place:
the father and the ruler of all gods,

---

4. One of the rivers of the underworld; the gods swore solemn oaths by it.   5. Io was identified with Isis, at least by the Greeks and Romans.   6. Mercury has been in Athens, where he tried to have a love affair with Herse, daughter of King Cecrops; promised help and then betrayed by her sister Aglauros, he took his revenge on Aglauros by turning her into a statue.   7. Maia, Mercury's mother, had been transformed into a star among the Pleiades in the constellation Taurus.   8. One of the principal cities of Phoenicia (in modern Lebanon).   9. Another city of Phoenicia, but here used of Phoenicia itself.

who holds the lightning bolt in his right hand 1165
and shakes the world when he but nods his head,
now relinquishes authority and power,
assuming the appearance of a bull
to mingle with the other cattle, lowing
as gorgeously he strolls in the new grass. 1170
    He is as white as the untrampled snow
before the south wind turns it into slush.
The muscles stand out bulging on his neck,
and the dewlap[1] dangles on his ample chest;
his horns are crooked, but appear handmade, 1175
and flawless as a pair of matching gems.
His brow is quite unthreatening, his eye
excites no terror, and his countenance
is calm.
        The daughter of King Agenor[2]
admires him, astonished by the presence 1180
of peacefulness and beauty in the beast;
yet even though he seems a gentle creature,
at first she fears to get too close to him,
but soon approaching, reaches out her hand
and pushes flowers into his white mouth. 1185
    The lover, quite beside himself, rejoices,
and as a preview of delights to come,
kisses her fingers, getting so excited
that he can scarcely keep from doing it!
    Now he disports himself upon the grass, 1190
and lays his whiteness on the yellow sands;
and as she slowly overcomes her fear
he offers up his breast for her caresses
and lets her decorate his horns with flowers;
the princess dares to sit upon his back 1195
not knowing who it is that she has mounted,
and he begins to set out from dry land,
a few steps on false feet into the shallows,
then further out and further to the middle
of the great sea he carries off his booty; 1200
she trembles as she sees the shore receding
and holds the creature's horn in her right hand
and with the other clings to his broad back,
her garments streaming in the wind behind her.

FROM BOOK V

[Ceres and Proserpina]

As the Muse spoke,[3] Minerva could hear wings
beating on air, and cries of greeting came
from high in the trees. She peered into the foliage, 430

---

1. A fold of loose skin hanging from the neck.   2. Europa. Agenor was the Phoenician king.
3. Minerva (Athena in Greek) has come to Mount Helicon in central Greece, the home of the nine Muses (daughters of Zeus and Memory, they are patronesses of poetry and the other arts). One of the Muses has told her of an attempt recently made to trap and rape them by the wicked Pyreneus.

attempting to discover where those sounds,
the speech of human beings to be sure,
were emanating from: why, from some birds!
Bewailing their sad fate, a flock of nine
magpies (which mimic anyone they wish to)   435
had settled in the branches overhead.

    Minerva having shown astonishment,
the Muse gave her a little goddess-chat:
"This lot has only recently been added
to the throngs of birds. Why? They lost a contest!   440
Their father was Pierus, lord of Pella,[4]
their mother was Evippe of Paeonia;
nine times she called upon Lucina's[5] aid
and nine times she delivered. Swollen up
with foolish pride because they were so many,   445
that crowd of simpleminded sisters went
through all Haemonia and through Achaea[6] too,
arriving here to challenge us in song:

    " 'We'll show you girls just what real class is[7]
Give up tryin' to deceive the masses   450
Your rhymes are fake: accept our wager
Learn which of us is minor and which is major
There's nine of us here and there's nine of you
And you'll be nowhere long before we're through
Nothin's gonna save you 'cuz your songs are lame   455
And the way you sing 'em is really a shame
So stop with, "Well I *never*!" and "This *can't* be real!"
We're the newest New Thing and here is our deal
If we beat you, obsolete you, then you just get gone
From these classy haunts on Mount Helicon   460
We give you Macedonia—*if* we lose
An' that's an offer you just can't refuse
So take the wings off, sisters, get down and jam
And let the nymphs be the judges of our poetry slam!'

    "Shameful it was to strive against such creatures;   465
more shameful not to. Nymphs were picked as judges,
sworn into service on their river banks,
and took their seats on benches made of tufa.

    "And then—not even drawing lots!—the one
who claimed to be their champion commenced;   470
she sang of war between the gods and Giants,
giving the latter credit more than due
and deprecating all that the great gods did;
how Typhoeus,[8] from earth's lowest depths,
struck fear in every celestial heart,   475
so that they all turned tail and fled, until,
exhausted, they found refuge down in Egypt,

---

4. City of Macedonia, in northern Greece. The Paeonians were a tribe living north of Macedonia.
5. Goddess of childbirth. 6. Regions of central Greece (*Haemonia* is another name for Thessaly). The
sisters are traveling south toward Helicon. 7. Although there is no basis for it in the Latin text, the
translator uses dialect and rhyme in the speeches and song of Pierus's daughters to show how they challenge,
and partially deflate, the "high-culture" assumptions and language of the Muses. 8. Monstrous son of
Earth. Like the Earth-born Giants, he challenged Jupiter and the Olympian gods and was defeated.

where the Nile flows from seven distinct mouths;
she sang of how earthborn Typhoeus
pursued them even here and forced the gods   480
to hide themselves by taking fictive shapes:[9]
    " 'In Libya the Giants told the gods to scram.
The boss god they worship there has horns like a ram[1]
'Cuz Jupiter laid low as the leader of a flock
And Delius[2] his homey really got a shock   485
When the Giants left him with no place to go:
"Fuggedabout Apollo—make me a crow!"
And if you believe that Phoebus was a wuss
His sister Phoebe turned into a puss
Bacchus takes refuge in the skin of a goat   490
And Juno as a cow with a snow-white coat
Venus the queen of the downtown scene, yuh know what her wish is?
"Gimme a body just like a fish's"
Mercury takes on an ibis's shape
And that's how the mighty (**cheep cheep**) gods escape'   495
    "And then her song, accompanied on the lute,
came to an end, and it was our turn—
but possibly you haven't got the time
to listen to our song?"
                    "Oh, don't think that,"
Minerva said. "I want it word for word: 500
sing it for me just as you sang it then."
    The Muse replied: "We turned the contest over
to one of us, Calliope,[3] who rose,
and after binding up her hair in ivy
and lightly strumming a few plaintive chords,   505
she vigorously launched into her song:

    " 'Ceres[4] was first to break up the soil with a curved plowshare,
the first to give us the earth's fruits and to nourish us gently,
and the first to give laws: every gift comes from Ceres.
The goddess must now be my subject. Would that I *could* sing   510
a hymn that is worthy of her, for she surely deserves it.
    " 'Vigorous Sicily sprawled across the gigantic body
of one who had dared aspire to rule in the heavens;
the island's weight held Typhoeus firmly beneath it.
Often exerting himself, he strives yet again to rise up,   515
but there in the north, his right hand is held down by Pelorus,
his left hand by you, Pachynus; off in the west, Lilybaeum[5]
weighs on his legs, while Mount Etna[6] presses his head, as
under it, raging Typhoeus coughs ashes and vomits up fire.
Often he struggles, attempting to shake off the earth's weight   520
and roll its cities and mountains away from his body.
    " 'This causes tremors and panics the Lord of the Silent,[7]
who fears that the earth's crust will crack and break open,

9. An "explanation" of the Egyptian gods' animal forms.   1. Ammon, the chief Egyptian god, identified
by the Greeks and Romans with Zeus/Jupiter. He had an important oracular cult in the Libyan desert (west
of the Nile valley and part of Egypt under Roman rule).   2. Apollo, who was born on the island of Delos.
3. "Lovely Voice," the Muse of epic poetry.   4. Goddess of grain (Demeter).   5. Mountains on the
northeast, southeast, and western promontories of Sicily, respectively.   6. The large (and still active)
volcano near the center of the east coast of Sicily.   7. Pluto or Hades, king of the dead.

and daylight, let in, will frighten the trembling phantoms;
dreading disaster, the tyrant left his tenebrous kingdom;   525
borne in his chariot drawn by its team of black horses,
he crisscrossed Sicily, checking the island's foundation.
  " 'After his explorations had left him persuaded
that none of its parts were in imminent danger of falling,
his fears were forgotten, and Venus, there on Mount Eryx,[8]   530
observed him relaxing, and said, as she drew Cupid near her,
"My son, my sword, my strong right arm and source of my power,
take up that weapon by which all your victims are vanquished
and send your swift arrows into the breast of the deity
to whom the last part of the threefold realm[9] was allotted.   535
  " ' "You govern the gods and their ruler; you rule the defeated
gods of the ocean and govern the one who rules them, too;
why give up on the dead, when we can extend our empire
into their realm? A third part of the world is involved here!
And yet the celestial gods spurn our forbearance,   540
and the prestige of Love is diminished, even as mine is.
Do you not see how Athena and huntress Diana
have both taken leave of me?[1] The virgin daughter of Ceres
desires to do likewise—and will, if we let her!
But if you take pride in our alliance, advance it   545
by joining her to her uncle!"[2]
                    " 'Venus ceased speaking and Cupid
loosened his quiver, and, just as his mother had ordered,
selected, from thousands of missiles, the one that was sharpest
and surest and paid his bow the closest attention,
and using one knee to bend its horn back almost double,   550
he pierces the heart of Dis with his barb-tipped arrow.
  " 'Near Henna's[3] walls stands a deep pool of water, called Pergus:
not even the river Cayster,[4] flowing serenely,
hears more songs from its swans; this pool is completely surrounded
by a ring of tall trees, whose foliage, just like an awning,   555
keeps out the sun and preserves the water's refreshing coolness;
the moist ground is covered with flowers of Tyrian purple;
here it is springtime forever. And here Proserpina
was playfully picking its white lilies and violets,
and, while competing to gather up more than her playmates,   560
filling her basket and stuffing the rest in her bosom,
Dis saw her, was smitten, seized her and carried her off;
his love was that hasty. The terrified goddess cried out
for her mother, her playmates—but for her mother most often,
since she had torn the uppermost seam of her garment,   565
and the gathered flowers rained down from her negligent tunic;
because of her tender years and her childish simplicity,
even this loss could move her to maidenly sorrow.
  " 'Her abductor rushed off in his chariot, urging his horses,
calling each one by its name and flicking the somber,   570

8. Mountain in western Sicily with an important cult of Venus.   9. The underworld, ruled by Pluto. The
other parts of the "threefold realm" are the sea (ruled by Neptune) and the sky or Mount Olympus (Jupiter).
1. Both were perpetually virgin.   2. Pluto (also called Dis) was the brother of Jupiter, the father by Ceres
of Proserpina.   3. A city in central Sicily.   4. River in Lydia in Asia Minor, famous for its many swans.

rust-colored reins over their backs as they galloped
through the deep lakes and the sulphurous pools of Palike
that boil up through the ruptured earth, and where the Bacchiadae,
a race sprung from Corinth, that city between the two seas,
had raised their own walls between two unequal harbors.[5]   575

" 'There is a bay that is landlocked almost completely
between the two pools of Cyane and Pisaean Arethusa,
the residence of the most famous nymph in all Sicily,
Cyane, who gave her very own name to the fountain.
She showed herself now, emerged from her pool at waist level,   580
and recognizing the goddess, told Dis, "Go no further!
You cannot become the son-in-law of great Ceres
against her will: you should have asked and not taken!
If it is right for me to compare lesser with greater,
I accepted Anapis[6] when he desired to have me,   585
yielding to pleas and not—as in *this* case—to terror."
She spoke, and stretching her arms out in either direction,
kept him from passing. That son of Saturn could scarcely
hold back his anger; he urged on his frightening horses,
and then, with his strong right arm, he hurled his scepter   590
directly into the very base of the fountain;
the stricken earth opened a path to the underworld
and took in the chariot rushing down into its crater.

" 'Cyane, lamenting not just the goddess abducted,
but also the disrespect shown for *her* rights as a fountain,   595
tacitly nursed in her heart an inconsolable sorrow;
and she who had once been its presiding spirit,
reduced to tears, dissolved right into its substance.
You would have seen her members beginning to soften,
her bones and her fingertips starting to lose their old firmness;   600
her slenderest parts were the first to be turned into fluid:
her feet, her legs, her sea-dark tresses, her fingers
(for the parts with least flesh turn into liquid most quickly);
and after these, her shoulders and back and her bosom
and flanks completely vanished in trickling liquid;   605
and lastly the living blood in her veins is replaced by
springwater, and nothing remains that you could have seized on.

" 'Meanwhile, the terrified mother was pointlessly seeking
her daughter all over the earth and deep in the ocean.
Neither Aurora, appearing with dew-dampened tresses,   610
nor Hesperus[7] knew her to quit; igniting two torches
of pine from the fires of Etna, the care-ridden goddess
used them to illumine the wintery shadows of nighttime;
and when the dear day had once more dimmed out the bright stars,
she searched again for her daughter from sunrise to sunset.   615

" 'Worn out by her labors and suffering thirst, with no fountain
to wet her lips at, she happened upon a thatched hovel
and knocked at its humble door, from which there came forth

---

5. Syracuse, on the southeastern coast of Sicily, founded by Corinthian colonists in the eighth century
B.C.E. The Bacchiadae were a leading family who then ruled Corinth.   6. A river that empties into the
sea near Syracuse.   7. The evening star. *Aurora*: goddess of the dawn.

a crone who looked at the goddess, and, when asked for water,
gave her a sweet drink, sprinkled with toasted barley.   620
And, as she drank it, a boy with a sharp face and bold manner
stood right before her and mocked her and said she was greedy.
Angered by what he was saying, the goddess drenched him
with all she had not yet drunk of the barley mixture.
The boy's face thirstily drank up the spots as his arms were   625
turned into legs, and a tail was joined to his changed limbs;
so that he should now be harmless, the boy was diminished,
and he was transformed into a very small lizard.
Astonished, the old woman wept and reached out to touch him,
but the marvelous creature fled her, seeking a hideout.   630
He now has a name appropriate to his complexion,
Stellio, from the constellations spotting his body.

    " 'To speak of the lands and seas the goddess mistakenly searched
would take far too long; the earth exhausted her seeking;
she came back to Sicily; and, as she once more traversed it,   635
arrived at Cyane, who would have told her the story
had she not herself been changed; but, though willing in spirit,
her mouth, tongue, and vocal apparatus were absent;
nevertheless, she gave proof that was clear to the mother:
Persephone's girdle (which happened by chance to have fallen   640
into the fountain) now lay exposed on its surface.

    " 'Once recognizing it, the goddess knew that her daughter
had been taken, and tore her hair into utter disorder,
and repeatedly struck her breasts with the palms of both hands.
With her daughter's location a mystery still, she reproaches   645
the whole earth as ungrateful, unworthy her gift of grain crops,
and Sicily more than the others, where she has discovered
the proof of her loss; and so it was here that her fierce hand
shattered the earth-turning plows, here that the farmers and cattle
perished alike, and here that she bade the plowed fields   650
default on their trust by blighting the seeds in their keeping.
Sicilian fertility, which had been everywhere famous,
was given the lie when the crops died as they sprouted,
now ruined by too much heat, and now by too heavy a rainfall;
stars and winds harmed them, and the greedy birds devoured   655
the seed as it was sown; the harvest of wheat was defeated
by thorns and darnels and unappeasable grasses.

    " 'Then Arethusa[8] lifted her head from the Elean waters
and swept her dripping hair back away from her forehead,
saying, "O Mother of Grain—and mother, too, of that virgin   660
sought through the whole world—here end your incessant labors,
lest your great anger should injure the earth you once trusted,
and which, unwillingly pillaged, has done nothing ignoble;
nor do I plead for my nation, since I am a guest here:
my nation is Pisa, I am descended from Elis,   665
and live as a stranger in Sicily—this land that delights me
more than all others on earth; here Arethusa
dwells with her household gods. Spare it, merciful goddess,

---

8. A spring in Syracuse. Its waters are "Elean" because they were believed to originate in the district of
Pisa in Elis, a region of the western Peloponnesus in mainland Greece.

and when your cares and countenance both have been lightened,
there will come an opportune time to tell you the reason   670
why I was taken from home and borne off to Ortygia⁹
over a waste of waters. The earth gave me access,
showed me a path, and, swept on through underground caverns,
I raised my head here to an unfamiliar night sky.
But while gliding under the earth on a Stygian river,   675
I saw with my very own eyes your dear Proserpina;
grief and terror were still to be seen in her features,
yet she was nonetheless queen of that shadowy kingdom,
the all-powerful consort of the underworld's ruler."
    " 'The mother was petrified by the speech of the fountain,   680
and stood for a very long time as though she were senseless,
until her madness had been driven off by her outrage,
and then she set out in her chariot for the ethereal regions;
once there, with her face clouded over and hair all disheveled,
she planted herself before Jove and fiercely addressed him: 685
"Jupiter, I have come here as a suppliant, speaking
for my child—and yours: if you have no regard for her mother,
relent as her father—don't hold her unworthy, I beg you,
simply because *I* am the child's other parent!
The daughter I sought for so long is at last recovered,   690
if to recover means only to lose much more surely,
or if to recover means just to learn her location!
Her theft could be borne—if only he would return her!
Then let him do it, for surely *Jove's* daughter is worthy
of a mate who's no brigand, even if *my* daughter isn't."   695
    " 'Jupiter answered her, "She is indeed *our* daughter,
the pledge of our love and our common concern,
but if you will kindly agree to give things their right names,
this is not an injury requiring my retribution,
but an act of love by a son-in-law who won't shame you,   700
goddess, if you give approval; though much were lacking,
how much it is to be Jove's brother! But he lacks nothing,
and only yields to me that which the Fates have allotted.
Still, if you're so keen on parting them, your Proserpina
may come back to heaven—but only on one condition: 705
that she has not touched food, for so the Fates have required."

    " 'He spoke and Ceres was sure she would get back her daughter,
though the Fates were not, for the girl had already placated
her hunger while guilelessly roaming death's formal gardens,
where, from a low-hanging branch, she had plucked without thinking   710
a pomegranate, and peeling its pale bark off, devoured
seven of its seeds. No one saw her but Ascalaphus
(whom it is said that Orphne, a not undistinguished
nymph among those of Avernus, pregnant by Acheron,¹
gave birth to there in the underworld's dark-shadowed forest);   715
he saw, and by his disclosure, kept her from returning.

---

9. The island on which Syracuse was originally built and on which the Arethusan spring was located.
1. Acheron ("Woe") is one of the rivers, and Avernus a lake, in the underworld. The name *Orphne* means "darkness" in Greek.

" 'Raging, the Queen of the Underworld turned that informer
into a bird of ill omen: sprinkling the waters
of Phlegethon[2] into the face of Ascalaphus,
she gave him a beak and plumage and eyes quite enormous.   720
Lost to himself, he is clad now in yellow-brown pinions,
his head increases in size and his nails turn to talons,
but the feathers that spring from his motionless arms scarcely flutter;
a filthy bird he's become, the grim announcer of mourning,
a slothful portent of evil to mortals—the owl.   725

" 'That one, because of his tattling tongue, seems quite worthy
of punishment,—but you, daughters of Acheloüs,[3]
why do you have the plumage of birds and the faces of virgins?
Is it because while Proserpina gathered her flowers,
you, artful Sirens, were numbered among her companions?   730
No sooner had you scoured the whole earth in vain for her
than you desired the vast seas to feel your devotion,
and prayed to the gods, whom you found willing to help you,
that you might skim over the flood upon oars that were pinions,
then saw your limbs turn suddenly golden with plumage.   735
And so that your tunefulness, which the ear finds so pleasing,
should not be lost, nor your gifts of vocal expression,
your maidenly faces remain, along with your voices.

" 'But poised between his sorrowing sister and brother,
great Jove divided the year into two equal portions,   740
so now in two realms the shared goddess holds sway,
and as many months spent with her mother are spent with her husband.
She changed her mind then, and changed her expression to match it,
and now her fair face, which even Dis found depressing,
beams as the sun does, when, after having been hidden   745
before in dark clouds, at last it emerges in triumph.

" 'Her daughter safely restored to her, kindhearted Ceres
wishes to hear *your* story now, Arethusa—
what did you flee from and what changed you into a fountain?
The splashing waters are stilled: the goddess raises   750
her head from their depths and wrings dry her virid tresses,
then tells the old tale of the river Alpheus'[4] passion.
" ' "Once I was one of the nymphs who dwell in Achaea,"
she said, "and none had more zeal than I for traversing
the mountain pastures or setting out snares for small game.   755
But even though I did not seek to find fame as a beauty,
men called me that, my courage and strength notwithstanding;
nor was I pleased that my beauty was lauded so often,
and for my corporeal nature (which most other maidens
are wont to take pleasure in) I blushed like a rustic,   760
thinking it wrong to please men.
                                        " ' "Exhausted from hunting,
I was on my way back from the Stymphalian forest,[5]

---

2. Fiery river of the underworld.   3. The Sirens, familiar from book 12 of the *Odyssey* and often associated with death in post-Homeric literature and art. Acheloüs is a large river in northwest Greece.
4. River that flows past Olympia in Elis.   5. The woods surrounding Lake Stymphalus in Arcadia.

and the fierce heat of the day was doubled by my exertions.
By chance I came on a stream, gently and silently flowing,
clear to the bottom, where you could count every pebble,   765
water so still you would scarcely believe it was moving.
Silvery willows and poplars, which the stream nourished,
artlessly shaded its banks as they sloped to the water.
   " ' "At once I approach and wiggle my toes in its wetness,
then wade in up to my knees—not satisfied wholly,   770
I strip off my garments and hang them up on a willow,
and, naked, merge with the waters. I strike and stroke them,
gliding below and thrashing about on the surface,
then hear a strange murmur that seems to come from the bottom,
which sends me scampering onto the near bank in terror: 775
'Why the great rush?' Alpheus cries from his waters,
then hoarsely repeating, 'Why the great rush, Arethusa?'
Just as I am, I flee without clothing (my garments
were on the bank opposite); aroused, Alpheus pursues me,
my nakedness making me seem more ripe for the taking.   780
   " ' "Thus did I run, and thus did that fierce one press after,
as doves on trembling pinions flee from the kestrel,
as kestrels pursue the trembling doves and assault them.
To Orchomenus and past, to Psophis, Cyllene,
the folds of Maenalia, Erymanthus,[6] and Elis,   785
I continued to run, nor was he faster than I was;
but since Alpheus was so much stronger, I couldn't
outrun him for long, given his greater endurance.
   " ' "Nonetheless, I still managed to keep on running
across the wide fields, up wooded mountains,   790
on bare rocks, steep cliffs, in wastes wild and trackless;
with the sun at my back, I could see his shadow before me,
stretched out on the ground, unless my panic deceived me;
but surely I *did* hear those frightening footsteps behind me,
and felt his hot breath lifting the hair from my shoulders.   795
   " ' "Worn with exertion, I cried out, 'Help! Or I'm taken!
Aid your armoress, Diana—to whom you have often
entrusted your bow, along with your quiver of arrows!'
The goddess was moved by my plea and at once I was hidden
in a dense cloud of fine mist:[7] the river god, clueless,   800
circled around me, hidden in darkness, searching;
twice he unknowingly passed by the place where the goddess
had hidden me, and twice he called, 'Yo! Arethusa!'
How wretched was I? Why, even as the lamb is,
at hearing the howling of wolves around the sheepfold,   805
or as the rabbit in the briar patch who glimpses
the dog's fierce muzzle and feels too frightened to tremble.
   " ' "Alpheus remained there, for as he noticed no footprints
heading away from the cloud, he continued to watch it.
An icy sweat thoroughly drenched the limbs that he looked for,   810
and the dark drops poured from every part of my body;
wherever my foot had been, there was a puddle,
and my hair shed moisture. More swiftly than I can tell it,

---

6. Towns and mountains of Arcadia.   7. Conventional means in ancient epic of making someone invisible.

I turned into liquid—even so, he recognized me,
his darling there in the water, and promptly discarded   815
the human form he had assumed for the occasion,
reverting to river, so that our fluids might mingle.
Diana shattered the earth's crust; I sank down,
and was swept on through sightless caverns, off to Ortygia,
so pleasing to me because it's the goddess's birthplace;[8]   820
and here I first rose up into the air as a fountain."

 " 'Here Arethusa concluded. The fruitful goddess summoned
her team of dragons and yoked them onto her chariot;
and guiding their heads with the reins, she was transported
up through the middle air that lies between earth and heaven   825
until she arrived in Athens, and, giving her carriage
to Triptolemus,[9] ordered him to go off and scatter
grain on the earth—some on land that had never been broken,
and some on land that had been a long time fallow.
 " 'The young man was carried high up over Europe and Asia   830
until at last he came to the kingdom of Scythia.
Lyncus was king here; he brought him into his palace,
and asked him his name, his homeland, the cause of his journey,
and how he had come there.
      " ' "My well-known homeland," he
  answered,
"is Athens; I am Triptolemus; neither by ship upon water   835
nor foot upon land have I come here; the air itself parted
to make me a path on which I coursed through the heavens.
I bear you the gifts of Ceres, which, sown in your broad fields,
will yield a bountiful harvest of nourishing produce."
 " 'This the barbarian heard with great envy, and wishing   840
that he himself might be perceived as the donor,
took him in as a guest, and while the young man was sleeping,
approached with a sword, and as he attempted to stab him,
Ceres changed *Lyncus* to *lynx*, and ordered Triptolemus
to drive her sacred team through the air back to Athens.'   845

 "When our eldest sister had concluded
her superb performance, with one voice
the nymphs awarded victory to . . . the Muses!
 "And when the others, in defeat, reviled us,
I answered them: 'Since you display such nerve   850
in challenging the Muses, you deserve
chastisement—even more so since you've added
insult to outrage: our wise forbearance
is not without its limits, as you'll learn
when we get to the penalties, and vent   855
our righteous anger on your worthless selves.'
 "Then the Pierides[1] mock our threats,
and as they try to answer us by shouting
vulgarities and giving us the finger,

8. The Ortygia where Arethusa ended up was in Syracuse, but Delos, the Aegean island where Diana was born, was also called Ortygia. 9. Son of the king of Eleusis, the great cult center of Demeter (Ceres) near Athens. 1. I.e., the daughters of Pierus.

their fingers take on feathers and their arms   860
turn into pinions! Each one sees a beak
replace a sister's face, as a new bird
is added to the species of the forest;
and as they try to beat upon their breasts,
bewailing their new situation, they   865
all hang suspended, flapping in the air,
the forest's scandal—the P-Airides![2]
    "And even though they are all feathered now,
their speech remains as fluent as it was,
and they are famous for their noisiness   870
as well as for their love of argument."

FROM BOOK IX

[Iphis and Isis]

Rumor might very well have spread the news   960
of this unprecedented transformation[3]
throughout the hundred towns of Crete, if they
had not just had a wonder of their own
to talk about—the change that came to Iphis.
    For, once upon a time, there lived in Phaestus,   965
not far from the royal capital at Cnossus,
a freeborn plebeian named Ligdus, who
was otherwise unknown and undistinguished,
with no more property than fame or status,
and yet devout, and blameless in his life.   970
    His wife was pregnant. When her time had come,
he gave her his instructions with these words:
"There are two things I pray to heaven for
on your account: an easy birth and a son.
The other fate is much too burdensome,   975
for daughters need what Fortune has denied us:
a dowry.
        "Therefore—and may God prevent
this happening, but if, by chance, it does
and you should be delivered of a girl,
unwillingly I order this, and beg   980
pardon for my impiety—*But let it die!*"
    He spoke, and tears profusely bathed the cheeks
of the instructor and instructed both.
Telethusa continued to implore
her husband, praying him not to confine   985
their hopes so narrowly—to no avail,
for he would not be moved from his decision.
    Now scarcely able to endure the weight
of her womb's burden, as she lay in bed
at midnight, a dream-vision came to her: 990
the goddess Io[4] stood (or seemed to stand)

---

2. The translator's pun on the name Pierides.   3. The transformation of Byblis, who loved her brother
Caunus, into a fountain.   4. Identified with the Egyptian Isis, goddess of fertility, marriage, and maternity, whose cult was widespread in the Roman world. For Io, see pp. 1033–38.

before her troubled bed, accompanied
with solemn pomp by all her mysteries.
    She wore her crescent horns upon her brow
and a garland made of gleaming sheaves of wheat,   995
and a queenly diadem; behind her stood
the dog-faced god Anubis, and divine
Bubastis (who defends the lives of cats),
and Apis as a bull clothed in a hide
of varied colors, with Harpocrates,   1000
the god whose fingers, pressed against his lips,
command our silence; and one often sought
by his devoted worshipers—Osiris;[5]
and the asp, so rich in sleep-inducing drops.
She seemed to wake, and saw them all quite clearly.   1005
    These were the words the goddess spoke to her:
"O Telethusa, faithful devotee,
put off your heavy cares! Disobey your spouse,
and do not hesitate, when Lucina
has lightened the burden of your labor,   1010
to raise this child, whatever it will be,
I am that goddess who, when asked, delivers,
and you will have no reason to complain
that honors you have paid me were in vain."
After instructing her, the goddess left.   1015
    The Cretan woman rose up joyfully,
lifted her hands up to the stars, and prayed
that her dream-vision would be ratified.
    Then going into labor, she brought forth
a daughter—though her husband did not know it.   1020
The mother (with intention to deceive)
told them to feed the boy. Deception prospered,
since no one knew the truth except the nurse.
    The father thanked the gods and named the child
for its grandfather, Iphis; since this name   1025
was given men and women both, his mother
was pleased, for she could use it honestly.
So from her pious lie, deception grew.
She dressed it as a boy—its face was such
that whether boy or girl, it was a beauty.   1030
    Meanwhile, the years went by, thirteen of them:
your father, Iphis, has arranged for you
a marriage to the golden-haired Ianthe,
the daughter of a Cretan named Telestes,
the maid most praised in Phaestus[6] for her beauty.   1035
The two were similar in age and looks,
and had been taught together from the first.
    First love came unexpected to both hearts
and wounded them both equally—and yet
their expectations were quite different: 1040

---

5. Husband of Isis, killed by his brother Set and restored to life by Isis; he is thus a figure of rebirth.
6. A city in Crete.

Ianthe can look forward to a time
of wedding torches and of wedding vows,
and trusts that one whom she believes a man
will be *her* man. Iphis, however, loves
with hopeless desperation, which increases   1045
in strict proportion to its hopelessness,
and burns—a maiden—for another maid!

   And scarcely holding back her tears, she cries,
"Oh, what will be the end reserved for Iphis,
gripped by a strange and monstrous passion known   1050
to no one else? If the gods had wished to spare me,
they should have; if they wanted to destroy me,
they should have given me a natural affliction.

   "Cows do not burn for cows, nor mares for mares;
the ram will have his sheep, the stag his does,   1055
and birds will do the same when they assemble;
there are no animals whose females lust
for other females! I wish that I were dead!

   "That Crete might bring forth monsters of all kinds.
Queen Pasiphaë[7] was taken by a bull,   1060
yet even *that* was male-and-female passion!
My love is much less rational than hers,
to tell the truth. At least she had the hope
of satisfaction, taking in the bull
through guile, and in the image of a cow,   1065
thereby deceiving the adulterer!

   "If every form of ingenuity
were gathered here from all around the world,
if Daedalus[8] flew back on waxen wings,
what could he do? Could all his learnèd arts   1070
transform me from a girl into a boy?
Or could *you* change into a boy, Ianthe?

   "But really, Iphis, pull yourself together,
be firm, cast off this stultifying passion:
accept your birth—unless you would deceive   1075
yourself as well as others—look for love
where it is proper to, as a woman should!
Hope both creates and nourishes such love;
reality deprives you of all hope.

   "No watchman keeps you from her dear embrace,   1080
no husband's ever-vigilant concern,
no father's fierceness, nor does she herself
deny the gifts that you would have from her.
And yet you are denied all happiness,
nor could it have been otherwise if all   1085
the gods and men had labored in your cause.

   "But the gods have not denied me anything;
agreeably, they've given what they could;
my father wishes for me what *I* wish,

---

7. Wife of King Minos of Crete, and mother by a bull of the Minotaur.　　8. Fabled craftsman, who devised
the heifer disguise that enabled Pasiphaë to seduce the bull and, later, built the labyrinth for the Minotaur.
Forced to flee Crete, he made wings of feathers held together by wax for himself and his son Icarus.

she and her father both would have it be;   1090
but Nature, much more powerful than they are,
wishes it not—sole source of all my woe!

"But look—the sun has risen and the day
of our longed-for nuptials dawns at last!
Ianthe will be mine—and yet not mine: 1095
we die of thirst here at the fountainside.

"Why do you, Juno, guardian of brides,
and you, O Hymen, god of marriage, come
to these rites, which cannot be rites at all,
for no one takes the bride, and both are veiled?"   1100

She said no more. Nor did her chosen burn
less fiercely as she prayed you swiftly come,
O god of marriage.

                                        Fearing what you sought,
Telethusa postponed the marriage day
with one concocted pretext and another,   1105
a fictive illness or an evil omen.
But now she had no more excuses left,
and the wedding day was only one day off.

She tears the hair bands from her daughter's head
and from her own, and thus unbound, she prayed   1110
while desperately clinging to the altar:
"O holy Isis, who art pleased to dwell
and be worshiped at Paraetonium,
at Pharos, in the Mareotic fields,
and where the Nile splits into seven branches;   1115
deliver us, I pray you, from our fear!

"For I once saw thee and thy sacred emblems,
O goddess, and I recognized them all
and listened to the sound of brazen rattles[9]
and kept your orders in my memory.   1120

"And that my daughter still looks on the light,
and that I have not suffered punishment,
why, this is all your counsel and your gift;
now spare us both and offer us your aid."

Warm tears were in attendance on her words.   1125
The altar of the goddess seemed to move—
it *did* move, and the temple doors were shaken,
and the horns (her lunar emblem) glowed with light,
and the bronze rattles sounded.

                                    Not yet secure,
but nonetheless delighted by this omen,   1130
the mother left with Iphis following,
as was her wont, but now with longer strides,
darker complexion, and with greater force,
a keener countenance, and with her hair
shorter than usual and unadorned,   1135
and with more vigor than a woman has.

And you who were so recently a girl

---

9. Sistra, sacred rattles used in Isis's cult.

are now a boy! Bring gifts to the goddess!
Now boldly celebrate your faith in her!
They bring the goddess gifts and add to them   1140
a votive tablet with these lines inscribed:

> GIFTS IPHIS PROMISED WHEN SHE WAS A MAID
> TRANSFORMED INTO A BOY HE GLADLY PAID

The next day's sun revealed the great wide world
with Venus, Juno, and Hymen all together   1145
gathered beneath the smoking nuptial torches,
and Iphis in possession of Ianthe.

FROM BOOK X[1]

[Pygmalion]

"Pygmalion observed how these women[2] lived lives of sordid
indecency, and, dismayed by the numerous defects
of character Nature had given the feminine spirit,
stayed as a bachelor, having no female companion.   315
 "During that time he created an ivory statue,
a work of most marvelous art, and gave it a figure
better than any living woman could boast of,
and promptly conceived a passion for his own creation.
You would have thought it alive, so like a real maiden   320
that only its natural modesty kept it from moving:
art concealed artfulness. Pygmalion gazed in amazement,
burning with love for what was in likeness a body.
 "Often he stretched forth a hand to touch his creation,
attempting to settle the issue: *was* it a body,   325
or was it—this he would not yet concede—a mere statue?
He gives it kisses, and they are returned, he imagines;
now he addresses and now he caresses it, feeling
his fingers sink into its warm, pliant flesh, and
fears he will leave blue bruises all over its body;   330
he seeks to win its affections with words and with presents
pleasing to girls, such as seashells and pebbles, tame birds,
armloads of flowers in thousands of different colors,
lilies, bright painted balls, curious insects in amber;
he dresses it up and puts diamond rings on its fingers, 335
gives it a necklace, a lacy brassiere and pearl earrings,
and even though all such adornments truly become her,
she does not seem to be any less beautiful naked.
He lays her down on a bed with a bright purple cover
and calls her his bedmate and slips a few soft, downy pillows 340
under her head as though she were able to feel them.

---

1. This selection of stories is part of the song sung by Orpheus, the legendary singer, after he has failed
to redeem his wife, Eurydice, from the underworld. His theme, announced in the prologue of his song, is
"young boys whom the gods have desired, / and . . . girls seized by forbidden and blameworthy passions."
2. Orpheus has just told of the Propoetides of Cyprus, who, as punishment for having denied Venus's
divinity, became the first women to prostitute themselves.

"The holiday honoring Venus has come, and all Cyprus[3]
turns out to celebrate; heifers with gilded horns buckle
under the deathblow[4] and incense soars up in thick clouds;
having already brought his own gift to the altar,   345
Pygmalion stood by and offered this fainthearted prayer:
'If you in heaven are able to give us whatever
we ask for, then I would like as my wife—' and not daring
to say, '—my ivory maiden,' said, '—one like my statue!'
Since golden Venus was present there at her altar,   350
she knew what he wanted to ask for, and as a good omen,
three times the flames soared and leapt right up to the heavens.

    "Once home, he went straight to the replica of his sweetheart,
threw himself down on the couch and repeatedly kissed her;
she seemed to grow warm and so he repeated the action,   355
kissing her lips and exciting her breasts with both hands.
Aroused, the ivory softened and, losing its stiffness,
yielded, submitting to his caress as wax softens
when it is warmed by the sun, and handled by fingers,
takes on many forms, and by being used, becomes useful.   360
Amazed, he rejoices, then doubts, then fears he's mistaken,
while again and again he touches on what he has prayed for.
She is alive! And her veins leap under his fingers!

    "You can believe that Pygmalion offered the goddess
his thanks in a torrent of speech, once again kissing   365
those lips that were not untrue; that she felt his kisses,
and timidly blushing, she opened her eyes to the sunlight,
and at the same time, first looked on her lover and heaven!
The goddess attended the wedding since she had arranged it,
and before the ninth moon had come to its crescent, a daughter
was born to them—Paphos,[5] who gave her own name to the island.   370

    "She had a son named Cinyras, who would be regarded
as one of the blessèd, if he had only been childless.
I sing of dire events: depart from me, daughters,
depart from me, fathers; or, if you find my poems charming,   375
believe that I lie, believe these events never happened;
or, if you believe that they did, then believe they were punished.

    "If Nature allows us to witness such impious misdeeds,
then I give my solemn thanks that the Thracian people
and the land itself are far away from those regions[6]   380
where evil like that was begotten: let fabled Panchaea[7]
be rich in balsam and cinnamon, costum and frankincense,
the sweat that drips down from the trees; let it bear incense
and flowers of every description: it also bears myrrh, and
too great a price was paid for that new creation.   385

    "Cupid himself denies that his darts ever harmed you,
Myrrha, and swears that his torches likewise are guiltless;
one of the three sisters,[8] bearing a venomous hydra
and waving a Stygian firebrand, must have inspired your passion.

---

3. Island in the eastern Mediterranean sacred to Venus.   4. I.e., as they are sacrificed.   5. One of the cities of Cyprus, whose name is often used for the island as a whole.   6. A reminder that Orpheus is singing in Thrace (the region stretching along the north coast of the Aegean Sea).   7. An imaginary island near Arabia, rich in spices.   8. The Furies.

Hating a parent is wicked, but even more wicked   390
than hatred is this kind of love. Princes elected
from far and wide desire you, Myrrha; all Asia
sends its young men to compete for your hand in marriage:
choose from so many just one of these men for your husband,
so long as a certain one is not the one chosen.   395
   "She understood and struggled against her perversion,
asking herself, 'What have I begun? Where will it take me?
May heaven and piety and the sacred rights of fathers
restrain these unspeakable thoughts and repel my misfortune,
if this indeed *is* misfortune; yet piety chooses   400
not to condemn this love outright: without distinctions
animals copulate; it is no crime for the heifer
to bear the weight of her father upon her own back;
daughters are suitable wives in the kingdom of horses;
the billy goats enter the flocks that they themselves sire,   405
and birds are inseminated by those who conceive them:
blessed, the ones for whom such love is permitted!
   " 'Human morality gives us such stifling precepts,
and makes indecent what Nature freely allows us!
But people say there are nations where sons and their mothers,   410
where fathers and daughters, may marry each other, increasing
the bonds of piety by their redoubled affections.
Wretched am I, who hadn't the luck to be born there,
injured by nothing more than mischance of location!
   " 'Why do I obsess? Begone, forbidden desires;   415
of course he is worthy of love—but love for a father!
So, then, if I were not the daughter of great Cinyras,
I would be able to have intercourse with Cinyras:
though he is mine, he is not mine, and our nearness
ruins me: I would be better off as a stranger.   420
   " 'It would be good for me to go far away from my country,
as long as I could escape from my wicked desires,
for what holds me here is the passion that I have to see him,
to touch and speak to Cinyras and give him my kisses—
if nothing more is permitted. You impious maiden,   425
what more can you imagine will ever be granted?
Are you aware how you confuse all rights and relations?
Would you be your mother's rival? The whore of your father?
Would you be called your son's sister? Your brother's own mother?
Do you not shudder to think of the serpent-coiffed sisters[9]   430
thrusting their bloodthirsty torches into the faces
of the guilty wretches that those three appear to and torture?
   " 'But you, while your body is undefiled, keep your mind chaste,
and do not break Nature's law with incestuous pairing.
Think what you ask for: the very act is forbidden.   435
and he is devout and mindful of moral behavior—
ah, how I wish that he had a similar madness!'
   "She spoke and Cinyras, whom an abundance of worthy
suitors had left undecided, consulted his daughter,

---

9. Again, the Furies.

ran their names by her and asked whom she wished for a husband;   440
silent at first, she kept her eyes locked on her father,
seething until the hot tears spilled over her eyelids:
Cinyras, attributing this to the fears of a virgin,
bade her cease weeping, wiped off her cheeks, and kissed her;
Myrrha rejoiced overmuch at his gesture and answered   445
that she would marry a man 'just like you.' Misunderstanding
the words of his daughter, Cinyras approved them, replying,
'May you be this pious always.' Hearing that last word,
the virgin lowers her head, self-convicted of evil.

    "Midnight: now sleep dissolves all the cares of the body;   450
Cinyras' daughter, however, lies tossing, consumed by
the fires of passion, repeating her prayers in a frenzy;
now she despairs, now she'll attempt it; now she is shamefaced,
now eager: uncertain: *What should she do now?* She wavers,
just like a tree that the axe blade has girdled completely,   455
when only the last blow remains to be struck, and the woodsman
cannot predict the direction it's going to fall in,
she, after so many blows to her spirit, now totters,
now leaning in one, and now in the other, direction,
nor is she able to find any rest from her passion   460
save but in death. Death pleases her, and she gets up,
determined to hang herself from a beam with her girdle:
'Farewell, dear Cinyras: may you understand why I do this!'
she said, as she fitted the noose around her pale neck.

    "They say that, hearing her murmuring, her faithful old nurse   465
in the next chamber arose and entered her bedroom:
at sight of the grim preparations, she screams out, and striking
her breasts and tearing her garments, removes the noose from
around the girl's neck, and then, only then she collapses,
and weeping, embraces her, asking her why she would do it.   470

    "Myrrha remained silent, expressionless, with her eyes downcast,
sorrowing only because her attempt was detected.
But the woman persists, baring her flat breasts and white hair,
and by the milk given when she was a babe in the cradle
beseeches her to entrust her old nurse with the cause of her sorrow.   475
The girl turns away with a groan; the nurse is determined
to learn her secret, and promises not just to keep it:

    " 'Speak and allow me to aid you,' she says, 'for in my old age,
I am not utterly useless: if you are dying of passion,
my charms and herbs will restore you; if someone wishes you evil,   480
my rites will break whatever spell you are under;
is some god wrathful? A sacrifice placates his anger.
What else could it be? I can't think of anything—Fortune
favors your family, everything's going quite smoothly,
both of your parents are living, your mother, your father—'   485
Myrrha sighed deeply, hearing her father referred to,
but not even then did the nurse grasp the terrible evil
in the girl's heart, although she felt that her darling
suffered a passion of some kind for some kind of lover.

    "Nurse was unyielding and begged her to make known her secret.   490
whatever it was, pressing the tearful girl to her bosom;

and clasping her in an embrace that old age had enfeebled,
she said, 'You're in love—I am certain! I will be zealous
in aiding your cause, never you fear—and your father
will be none the wiser!'
               "Myrrha in frenzy leapt up   495
and threw herself onto the bed, pressing her face in the pillows:
'Leave me, I beg you,' she said. 'Avoid my wretched dishonor;
leave me or cease to ask me the cause of my sorrow:
what you attempt to uncover is sinful and wicked!'
    "The old woman shuddered: extending the hands that now trembled   500
with fear and old age, she fell at the feet of her darling,
a suppliant, coaxing her now, and now attempting to scare her;
threatening now to disclose her attempted self-murder,
but pledging to aid her if she confesses her passion.
    "She lifted her head with her eyes full of tears spilling over   505
onto the breast of her nurse and repeatedly tried to
speak out, but repeatedly stopped herself short of confession,
hiding her shame-colored face in the folds of her garments,
until she finally yielded, blurting her secret:
'O mother,' she cried, 'so fortunate you with your husband!'   510
and said no more but groaned.
                  "The nurse, who now understood it,
felt a chill run through her veins, and her bones shook with tremor,
and her white hair stood up in stiff bristles. She said whatever
she could to dissuade the girl from her horrible passion,
and even though Myrrha knew the truth of her warning,   515
she had decided to die if she could not possess him.
'Live, then,' the other replied, 'and possess your—' Not daring
to use the word 'father,' she left her sentence unfinished,
but called upon heaven to stand by her earlier promise.
    "Now it was time for the annual feast days of Ceres;   520
the pious, and married women clad in white vestments,
thronged to the celebration, offering garlands
of wheat as firstfruits of the season; now for nine nights
the intimate touch of their men is considered forbidden.
Among these matrons was Cenchreïs, wife of Cinyras,   525
for her attendance during these rites was required.
And so, while the queen's place in his bed was left vacant,
the overly diligent nurse came to Cinyras,
finding him drunk, and spoke to him of a maiden
whose passion for him was real (although her name wasn't)   530
and praising her beauty; when asked the age of this virgin,
she said, 'the same age as Myrrha.' Commanded to fetch her,
nurse hastened home, and entering, cried to her darling,
'Rejoice, my dear, we have won!' The unlucky maiden
could not feel joy in her heart, but only grim sorrow,   535
yet still she rejoiced, so distorted were her emotions.
    "Now it is midnight, when all of creation is silent;
high in the heavens, between the two Bears, Boötes[1]
had turned his wagon so that its shaft pointed downward;

---

1. The Ox-herder, a constellation that was thought to drive Ursa Major, the Great Bear.

Myrrha approaches her crime, which is fled by chaste Luna,[2]   540
while under black clouds the stars hide their scandalized faces;
Night lacks its usual fires; you, Icarus,[3] covered
your face and were followed at once by Erigone,
whose pious love of her father merited heaven.

    "Thrice Myrrha stumbles and stops each time at the omen,   545
and thrice the funereal owl sings her his poem of endings;
nevertheless she continues, her shame lessened by shadows.
She holds the left hand of her nurse, and gropes with the other
blindly in darkness: now at the bedchamber's threshold,
and now she opens the door: and now she is led within,   550
where her knees fail her; she falters, nearly collapsing,
her color, her blood, her spirit all flee together.

    "As she approaches the crime, her horror increases;
regretting her boldness, she wishes to turn back, unnoticed,
but even as she holds back, the old woman leads her   555
by the hand to the high bed, where she delivers her, saying,
'Take her, Cinyras—she's yours,' and unites the doomed couple.
The father accepts his own offspring in his indecent
bed and attempts to dispel the girl's apprehensions,
encouraging her not to be frightened of him, and   560
addressing her, as it happened, with a name befitting
her years: he called her 'daughter' while she called him 'father,'
so the right names were attached to their impious actions.

    "Filled with the seed of her father, she left his bedchamber,
having already conceived, in a crime against nature   565
which she repeated the following night and thereafter,
until Cinyras, impatient to see his new lover
after so many encounters, brought a light in,
and in the same moment discovered his crime and his daughter;
grief left him speechless; he tore out his sword from the scabbard;   570
Myrrha sped off, and, thanks to night's shadowy darkness,
escaped from her death. She wandered the wide-open spaces,
leaving Arabia, so rich in palms, and Panchaea,
and after nine months, she came at last to Sabaea,[4]
where she found rest from the weariness that she suffered,   575
for she could scarcely carry her womb's heavy burden.

    "Uncertain of what she should wish for, tired of living
but frightened of dying, she summed up her state in this prayer:
'O gods, if there should be any who hear my confession,
I do not turn away from the terrible sentence   580
that my misbehavior deserves; but lest I should outrage
the living by my survival, or the dead by my dying,
drive me from both of these kingdoms, transform me
wholly, so that both life and death are denied me.'

    "Some god *did* hear her confession, and heaven answered   585
her final prayer, for, even as she was still speaking,

---

2. The Moon, often associated with Diana, one of whose attributes was chastity.   3. More properly
Icarus, a mythic Athenian. He received Dionysus into the city, and the god rewarded him with wine, which
he shared with his countrymen. Feeling its effect, they thought they had been poisoned and killed him.
His daughter Erigone hanged herself in grief, and both were changed into stars.   4. Arabia Felix, the
southern tip of the Arabian Peninsula.

the earth rose up over her legs, and from her toes burst
roots that spread widely to hold the tall trunk in position;
her bones put forth wood, and even though they were still hollow,
they now ran with sap and not blood; her arms became branches,   590
and those were now twigs that used to be called her fingers,
while her skin turned to hard bark. The tree kept on growing,
over her swollen belly, wrapping it tightly,
and growing over her breast and up to her neck; she
could bear no further delay, and, as the wood rose,   595
plunged her face down into the bark and was swallowed.
    "Loss of her body has meant the loss of all feeling;
and yet she weeps, and the warm drops spill from her tree trunk;
those tears bring her honor: the distillate myrrh preserves and
will keep the name of its mistress down through the ages.   600
    "But under the bark, the infant conceived in such baseness
continued to grow and now sought a way out of Myrrha;
the pregnant trunk bulged in the middle and its weighty burden
pressed on the mother, who could not cry out in her sorrow
nor summon Lucina with charms to aid those in childbirth.   605
So, like a woman exerting herself to deliver,
the tree groaned and bent over double, wet from its weeping.
Gentle Lucina stood by the sorrowing branches,
laid her hands onto the bark and recited the charms that
aid in delivery; the bark split open; a fissure   610
ran down the trunk of the tree and its burden spilled out,
a bawling boychild, whom naiads placed in soft grasses
and bathed in the tears of its mother. Not even Envy
could have found fault with his beauty, for he resembled
one of the naked cherubs depicted by artists,   615
and would have been taken as one, if you had provided
him with a quiver or else removed one from those others.

[Venus and Adonis]

"Time swiftly glides by in secret, escaping our notice,
and nothing goes faster than years do: the son of his sister
by his grandfather, the one so recently hidden   620
within a tree, so recently born, a most beautiful infant,
now is an adolescent and now a young man
even more beautiful than he was as a baby,
pleasing now even to Venus and soon the avenger
of passionate fires that brought his mother to ruin.   625
    "For while her fond Cupid was giving a kiss to his mother,
he pricked her unwittingly, right in the breast, with an arrow
projecting out of his quiver; annoyed, the great goddess
swatted him off, but the wound had gone in more deeply
than it appeared to, and at the beginning deceived her.   630
    "Under the spell of this fellow's beauty, the goddess
no longer takes any interest now in Cythera,[5]
nor does she return to her haunts on the island of Paphon,

---

5. Island south of the Peloponnesus, and like Cyprus sacred to Venus.

or to fish-wealthy Cnidus or to ore-bearing Amathus;[6]
she avoids heaven as well, now—preferring Adonis,   635
and clings to him, his constant companion, ignoring
her former mode of unstrenuous self-indulgence,
when she shunned natural light for the parlors of beauty;
now she goes roaming with him through woods and up mountains
and over the scrubby rocks with her garments hitched up   640
and girded around her waist like a nymph of Diana,[7]
urging the hounds to pursue unendangering species,
hoppety hares or stags with wide-branching antlers,
or terrified does; but she avoids the fierce wild boars and
rapacious wolves and bears armed with sharp claws,   645
and shuns the lions, sated with slaughter of cattle.

  "And she warns you also to fear the wild beasts, Adonis,
if only her warning were heeded. 'Be bold with the timid,'
she said, 'but against the daring, daring is reckless.
Spare me, dear boy, the risk involved in your courage;   650
don't rile the beasts that Nature has armed with sharp weapons,
lest I should find the glory you gain much too costly!
For lions and bristling boars and other fierce creatures
look with indifferent eyes and minds upon beauty
and youth and other qualities Venus is moved by;   655
pitiless boars deal out thunderbolts with their curved tusks,
and none may withstand the frenzied assault of the lions,
whom I despise altogether.'

                                "And when he asked why,
she said, 'I will tell you this story which will amaze you,
with its retribution delivered for ancient wrongdoing.   660

  " 'But this unaccustomed labor has left me exhausted—
look, though—a poplar entices with opportune shade, and
offers a soft bed of turf we may rest on together,
as I would like to.' And so she lay down on the grasses
and on her Adonis, and using his breast as a pillow,   665
she told this story, mixing her words with sweet kisses:

  " 'Perhaps you'll have heard of a maiden able to vanquish
the swiftest of men in a footrace; this wasn't a fiction,
for she overcame all contestants; nor could you say whether
she deserved praise more for her speed or her beauty.   670
She asked some god about husbands. "A husband," he answered,
"is not for you, Atalanta: flee from a husband!
But you will not flee—and losing yourself, will live on!"

  " 'Frightened by his grim prediction, she went to the forest
and lived there unmarried, escaping the large and persistent   675
throng of her suitors by setting out cruel conditions;
"You cannot have me," she said, "unless you outrun me;
come race against me! A bride and a bed for the winner,
death to the losers. Those are the rules of the contest."

  " 'Cruel? Indeed—but such was this young maiden's beauty   680

---

6. All three were important centers of Venus's cult: Paphos and Amathus were cities on the island of
Cyprus, and Cnidus was a city in Asia Minor.   7. As a virgin and huntress, the antithesis of Venus.

that a foolhardy throng of admirers took up the wager.
As a spectator, Hippomenes sat in the grandstand,
asking why anyone ever would risk such a danger,
just for a bride, and disparaging their headstrong passion.
However, as soon as he caught a glimpse of her beauty, 685
like mine or like yours would be if you were a woman,'
said Venus, 'her face and her body, both bared for the contest,
he threw up both hands and cried out, "I beg your pardons,
who only a moment ago disparaged your efforts,
but truly I had no idea of the trophy you strive for!" 690
    " 'Praises ignited the fires of passion and made him
hope that no young man proved to be faster than she was
and fear that one would be. Jealous, he asked himself why he
was leaving the outcome of this competition unventured:
"God helps those who improve their condition by daring," 695
he said, addressing himself as the maiden flew by him.
Though she seemed no less swift than a Scythian arrow,
nevertheless, he more greatly admired her beauty,
and the grace of her running made her seem even more lovely;
the breezes blew back the wings attached to her ankles 700
while her loose hair streamed over her ivory shoulders
and her brightly edged knee straps fluttered lightly; a russet
glow fanned out evenly over her pale, girlish body,
as when a purple awning covers a white marble surface,
staining its artless candor with counterfeit shadow. 705
    " 'She crossed the finish line while he was taking it in, and
Atalanta, victorious, was given a crown and the glory;
the groaning losers were taken off: end of *their* story.
But the youth, undeterred by what had become of the vanquished,
stood on the track and fixed his gaze on the maiden: 710
"Why seek such an easy victory over these sluggards?
Contend with me," he said, "and if Fortune makes me the winner,
you will at least have been beaten by one not unworthy:
I am the son of Megareus, grandson of Neptune,
my great-grandfather; my valor is no less impressive 715
than is my descent; if you should happen to triumph,
you would be famous for having beaten Hippomenes."
    " 'And as he spoke, Atalanta's countenance softened:
she wondered whether she wished to win or to *be* won,
and asked herself which god, jealous of her suitor's beauty, 720
sought to destroy him by forcing him into this marriage:
"If *I* were judging, I wouldn't think I was worth it!
Nor am I moved by his beauty," she said, "though I could be,
but I *am* moved by his youth: his boyishness stirs me—
but what of his valor? His mind so utterly fearless? 725
What of his watery origins? His relation to Neptune?
What of the fact that he loves me and wishes to wed me,
and is willing to die if bitter Fortune denies him?
    " ' "Oh, flee from a bed that still reeks with the gore of past victims,
while you are able to, stranger; marrying *me* is 730
certain destruction! No one would wish to reject you,
and you may be chosen by a much wiser young lady!

" ' "But why should I care for you—after so many have perished?
Now *he* will learn! Let him die then, since the great slaughter
of suitors has taught him nothing! He must be weary of living!   735
So—must he die then, because he wishes to wed me,
and is willing to pay the ultimate price for his passion?
He shouldn't have to! And even though it won't be *my* fault,
my victory surely will turn the people against me!
        " ' "If only you would just give it up, or if only,   740
since you're obsessed with it, you were a little bit faster!
How very girlish is the boy's facial expression!
O poor Hippomenes! I wish you never had seen me!
You're worthy of life, and if only *my* life had been better,
or if the harsh Fates had not prevented my marriage,   745
you would have been the one I'd have chosen to marry!"
    " 'She spoke, and, moved by desire that struck without warning,
loved without knowing what she was doing or feeling.
Her father and people were clamoring down at the racecourse,
when Neptune's descendent Hippomenes anxiously begged me: 750
"Cytherian Venus, I pray you preside at my venture,
aiding the fires that you yourself have ignited."
A well-meaning breeze brought me this prayer, so appealing
that, I confess, it aroused me and stirred me to action,
though I had scant time enough to bring off his rescue.   755
    " 'There is a field upon Cyprus, known as Tamasus,
famed for its wealth; in olden days it was given
to me and provides an endowment now for my temples;
and there in this field is a tree; its leaves and its branches
glisten and shimmer, reflecting the gold they are made of;   760
now, as it happened, I'd just gotten back from a visit,
carrying three golden apples that I had selected:
and showing myself there to Hippomenes only,
approached him and showed him how to use them to advantage.
    " 'Both of them crouched for the start; when horns gave the signal,   765
they took off together, their feet barely brushing the surface;
you would have thought they were able to keep their toes dry
while skimming over the waves, and could touch on the ripened
heads of wheat in the field without bending them under.
    " 'Cries of support and encouragement cheered on the young man;   770
"Now is the time," they screamed, "go for it, go for it, hurry,
Hippomenes, give it everything that you've got now!
Don't hold back! Victory!" And I am uncertain whether
these words were more pleasing to him or to his Atalanta,
for often, when she could have very easily passed him,   775
she lingered beside, her gaze full of desperate longing,
until she reluctantly sped ahead of his features.
    " 'And now Hippomenes, dry-mouthed, was breathlessly gasping,
the finish line far in the distance; he threw out an apple,
and the sight of that radiant fruit astounded the maiden,   780
who turned from her course and retrieved the glittering missile;
Hippomenes passed her: the crowd roared its approval.
    " 'A burst of speed now and Atalanta makes up for lost time:
once more overtaking the lad, she puts him behind her!
A second apple: again she falls back, but recovers,

785

now she's beside him, now passing him, only the finish
remains: "Now, O goddess," he cries, "my inspiration, be with me!"
  " 'With all the strength of his youth he flings the last apple
to the far side of the field: *this* will really delay her!
The maiden looked doubtful about its retrieval: I forced her   790
to get it and add on its weight to the burden she carried:
time lost and weight gained were equal obstructions: the maiden
(lest my account should prove longer than even the race was)
took second place: the trophy bride left with the victor.
  " 'But really, Adonis, wasn't I worthy of being   795
thanked for my troubles? Offered a gift of sweet incense?
Heedless of all I had done, he offered me neither!
Immediate outrage was followed by keen indignation;
and firmly resolving not to be spurned in the future,
I guarded against it by making this pair an example.   800
  " 'Now they were passing a temple deep in the forest,
built long ago by Echion to honor Cybele,[8]
Mother of Gods, and now the length of their journey
urged them to rest here, where unbridled desire
possessed Hippomenes, moved by the strength of my godhead.   805
There was a dim and cave-like recess near the temple,
hewn out of pumice, a shrine to the ancient religion,
wherein a priest of these old rites had set a great many
carved wooden idols. Hippomenes entered that place, and
by his forbidden behavior defiled it;[9] in horror,   810
the sacred images turned away from the act, and Cybele
prepared to plunge the guilty pair in Stygian waters,
but that seemed too easy; so now their elegant pale necks
are cloaked in tawny manes; curved claws are their fingers;
arms are now forelegs, and all the weight of their bodies   815
shifts to their torsos; and now their tails sweep the arena;
fierce now, their faces; growls supplant verbal expression;
the forest now is their bedroom; a terror to others,
meekly these lions champ at the bit of the harness
on either side of the yoke of Cybele's chariot.   820
  " 'My darling, you must avoid these and all other wild beasts,
who will not turn tail, but show off their boldness in battle;
flee them or else your courage will prove our ruin!'

  "And after warning him, she went off on her journey,
carried aloft by her swans; but his courage resisted   825
her admonitions. It happened that as his dogs followed
a boar they were tracking, they roused it from where it was hidden,
and when it attempted to rush from the forest, Adonis
pierced it, but lightly, casting his spear from an angle;
with its long snout, it turned and knocked loose the weapon   830
stained with its own blood, then bore down upon our hero,
and, as he attempted to flee for his life in sheer terror,
it sank its tusks deep into the young fellow's privates,

---

8. A fertility goddess of Asia Minor known as the Great Mother. She was often pictured wearing a crown
that resembled a city wall with towers, and flanked by lions or riding in a cart drawn by them. 9. It was
considered sacrilege to have sexual intercourse in the precinct of a temple.

and stretched him out on the yellow sands, where he lay dying.
"Aloft in her light, swan-driven chariot, Venus   835
had not yet gotten to Cyprus; from a great distance
she recognized the dying groans of Adonis
and turned her birds back to him; when she saw from midair
his body lying there, lifeless, stained with its own blood,
she beat her breasts and tore at her hair and her garments,   840
and leapt from her chariot, raging, to argue with grim Fate:
   " 'It will not be altogether as you would have it,'
she said. 'My grief for Adonis will be remembered
forever, and every year will see, reenacted
in ritual form, his death and my lamentation;   845
and the blood of the hero will be transformed to a flower.
Or were *you* not once allowed to change a young woman[1]
to fragrant mint, Persephone? Do you begrudge me
the transformation of my beloved Adonis?'
   "And as she spoke, she sprinkled his blood with sweet nectar,   850
which made it swell up, like a transparent bubble
that rises from muck; and in no more than an hour
a flower sprang out of that soil, blood red in its color,
just like the flesh that lies underneath the tough rind
of the seed-hiding pomegranate. Brief is its season,   855
for the winds from which it takes its name, the anemone,
shake off those petals so lightly clinging and fated to perish."

1. Mentha, Hades' mistress, trampled by the jealous Proserpina and transformed into the mint (the meaning of her name).

PETRONIUS
died 66 C.E.

It is not certain that Titus Petronius (Arbiter) was the author of the *Satyricon*, but he is the best candidate. A friend of Nero's, he committed suicide at the imperial order after becoming involved in the Pisonian conspiracy against the emperor in 65 C.E. A brilliant account of Petronius's character and death is given by Tacitus in the *Annals* (book 16, chapters 18 and 19).

It is in the satiric masterpiece of this Roman aristocrat that the pragmatic, materialistic attitude Christianity was to supplant is most clearly displayed. It was probably written during the principate of Nero (54–68 C.E.), a period in which the material benefits and the spiritual weakness of the new order had already become apparent. The *Satyricon* itself has survived only in fragments; we know nothing certain about the scope of the work as a whole, but from the fragments it is clear that this book is the work of a satiric genius, perhaps the most original genius of Latin literature.

Dinner with Trimalchio, one of the longer fragments (printed here), shows us a tradesman's world. The narrator, a student of literature, and his cronies may have an aristocratic disdain for the businessmen at whose tables they eat, but they know that Trimalchio and his kind have inherited the Earth. Trimalchio began life as a foreign slave, but he is now a multimillionaire. The representative of culture, Agamemnon the teacher, drinks his wine and praises his fatuous remarks; he is content to be the court jester, the butt of Trimalchio's witticisms. Trimalchio knows no god but Mercury, the patron of business operations, but the gold bracelet, which represents a percentage of his income that he has dedicated to Mercury, he wears on his own arm rather than depositing it in a shrine of the god. He identifies himself with the god and worships himself, the living embodiment of the power of money. The conversation at his table is a sardonic revelation of the temper of a whole civilization. Written in brilliantly humorous and colloquial style, it exposes mercilessly a blindness to spiritual values of any kind, a distrust of the intellect, and a ferocious preoccupation with the art of cheating one's neighbor. The point is made more effective by the conscious evocation of the epic tradition throughout the work: the names alone of the teacher, Agamemnon, and his assistant in instruction, Menelaus; the wall paintings that show "the *Iliad*, and *Odyssey*, and the gladiatorial show given by Laenas"; Trimalchio's exhibition of monstrous ignorance of Homer (which nobody dares to correct); the Nestorian tone of Ganymedes, who regrets the old days when men were men (he is talking of the time when Safinius forced the bakers to lower the price of bread)—one touch after another reminds us that these figures are the final product of a tradition that began with Achilles and Odysseus.

The satire is witty, but it is nonetheless profound. Trimalchio and his friends all live for the moment, in material enjoyment, but they know that it cannot last. "Let us remember the living" is their watchword, but they cannot forget the dead. And as the banquet goes on, the thought of death, suppressed beneath the debased Epicureanism of Trimalchio and his associates, emerges slowly to the surface of their consciousness and comes to dominate it completely. The last arrival at the banquet is Habinnas the undertaker, and his coming coincides with the last stage of Trimalchio's drunkenness, the maudlin exhibition of his funeral clothes and the description of his tomb. "I want to die," says the Sibyl in the story Trimalchio tells early in the evening; at its end Trimalchio himself acts out his own funeral, complete with ointment, robes, wine, and trumpet players. The fact of death, the one fact that the practical materialism of Trimalchio and his circle can neither deny nor assimilate, asserts itself triumphantly as the supreme fact in the emptiness of Trimalchio's mind.

PRONOUNCING GLOSSARY

The following list uses common English syllables and stress accents to provide rough equivalents of selected words whose pronunciation may be unfamiliar to the general reader.

Encolpius: *en-kol'-pi-us*   Scintilla: *sin-til'-lah / skin-til'-ah*

Gaius: *gai'-us*   Trimalchio: *tri-mal'-ki-oh*

From The Satyricon[1]

[Dinner with Trimalchio]

[The narrator, Encolpius, is a penniless vagabond who is a student of rhetoric under a master named Agamemnon. His close associates are Ascyltus, a fellow student, and Giton, a handsome boy who has no particular occupation. After some disreputable and very tiring adventures they are invited, as pupils of Agamemnon, to a banquet. The scene of the story is an unidentified city in southern Italy, the time probably about 50 C.E.]

The next day but one finally arrived. But we were so knocked about that we wanted to run rather than rest. We were mournfully discussing how to avoid the approaching storm,[2] when one of Agamemnon's slaves broke in on our frantic debate.

"Here," said he, "don't you know who's your host today? It's Trimalchio—he's terribly elegant. . . . He has a clock in the dining-room and a trumpeter[3] all dressed up to tell him how much longer he's got to live."

This made us forget all our troubles. We dressed carefully and told Giton, who was very kindly acting as our servant, to attend us at the baths.[4]

We did not take our clothes off but began wandering around, or rather exchanging jokes while circulating among the little groups. Suddenly we saw a bald old man in a reddish shirt, playing ball with some long-haired boys. It was not so much the boys that made us watch, although they alone were worth the trouble, but the old gentleman himself. He was taking his exercise in slippers and throwing a green ball around. But he didn't pick it up if it touched the ground; instead there was a slave holding a bagful, and he supplied them to the players. We noticed other novelties. Two eunuchs stood around at different points: one of them carried a silver chamber pot, the other counted the balls, not those flying from hand to hand according to the rules, but those that fell to the ground. We were still admiring these elegant arrangements when Menelaus[5] hurried up to us.

"This is the man you'll be dining with," he said. "In fact, you are now watching the beginning of the dinner."

No sooner had Menelaus spoken than Trimalchio snapped his fingers. At the signal the eunuch brought up the chamber pot for him, while he went on playing. With the weight off his bladder, he demanded water for his hands, splashed a few drops on his fingers and wiped them on a boy's head.

It would take too long to pick out isolated incidents. Anyway, we entered the baths where we began sweating at once and we went immediately into the cold water. Trimalchio had been smothered in perfume and was already being rubbed down, not with linen towels, but with bath-robes of the finest wool. As this was going on, three masseurs sat drinking Falernian[6] in front of him. Through quarreling they spilled most of it and Trimalchio said they were drinking his health.[7] Wrapped in thick scarlet felt he was put into a

---

1. Translated by J. P. Sullivan.   2. A repetition of the unsavory incidents they have just experienced. 3. To sound off every hour on the hour. A clock was a rare and expensive item. The name Trimalchio suggests "triply blessed" or "triply powerful."   4. A public institution; they were magnificent buildings, containing not only baths of many types and temperatures but places for conversation and games, and even libraries.   5. Agamemnon's assistant in instruction.   6. A famous wine from Campania, south of Rome.   7. He claims they are pouring a libation.

litter. Four couriers with lots of medals went in front, as well as a go-cart in which his favourite boy was riding—a wizened, bleary-eyed youngster, uglier than his master. As he was carried off, a musician with a tiny set of pipes took his place by Trimalchio's head and whispered a tune in his ear the whole way.

We followed on, choking with amazement by now, and arrived at the door with Agamemnon at our side. On the doorpost a notice was fastened which read:

ANY SLAVE LEAVING THE HOUSE WITHOUT HIS MASTER'S PERMISSION WILL RECEIVE ONE HUNDRED LASHES

Just at the entrance stood the hall-porter, dressed in a green uniform with a belt of cherry red. He was shelling peas into a silver basin. Over the doorway hung—of all things—a golden cage from which a spotted magpie greeted visitors.

As I was gaping at all this, I almost fell over backwards and broke a leg. There on the left as one entered, not far from the porter's cubbyhole, was a huge dog with a chain round its neck. It was painted on the wall and over it, in big capitals, was written:

BEWARE OF THE DOG

My colleagues laughed at me, but when I got my breath back I went to examine the whole wall. There was a mural of a slave market, price tags and all. Then Trimalchio himself, holding a wand of Mercury and being led into Rome by Minerva.[8] After this a picture of how he learned accounting and, finally how he became a steward. The painstaking artist had drawn it all in great detail with descriptions underneath. Just where the colonnade ended Mercury hauled him up by the chin and rushed him to a high platform. . . .

I began asking the porter what were the pictures they had in the middle.

"The *Iliad,* and *Odyssey,* and the gladiatorial show given by Laenas," he told me.

Time did not allow us to look at many things there . . . by now we had reached the dining-room. . . .

Finally we took our places. Boys from Alexandria poured iced water over our hands. Others followed them and attended to our feet, removing any hangnails with great skill. But they were not quiet even during this troublesome operation: they sang away at their work. I wanted to find out if the whole staff were singers, so I asked for a drink. In a flash a boy was there, singing in a shrill voice while he attended to me—and anyone else who was asked to bring something did the same. It was more like a musical comedy than a respectable dinner party.

Some extremely elegant hors d'oeuvre were served at this point—by now everyone had taken his place with the exception of Trimalchio, for whom, strangely enough, the place at the top was reserved. The dishes for the first course included an ass of Corinthian bronze with two panniers, white olives on one side and black on the other. Over the ass were two pieces of plate,

---

8. Patron goddess of arts and skills (Athena in Greek). Mercury (Hermes in Greek), as a trickster, is the patron god of thieves and businessmen.

with Trimalchio's name and the weight of the silver inscribed on the rims. There were some small iron frames shaped like bridges supporting dormice sprinkled with honey and poppy seed. There were steaming hot sausages too, on a silver gridiron with damsons and pomegranate seeds underneath.

We were in the middle of these elegant dishes when Trimalchio himself was carried in to the sound of music and set down on a pile of tightly stuffed cushions. The sight of him drew an astonished laugh from the guests. His cropped head stuck out from a scarlet coat; his neck was well muffled up and he had put round it a napkin with a broad purple stripe and tassels dangling here and there. On the little finger of his left hand he wore a heavy gilt ring and a smaller one on the last joint of the next finger. This I thought was solid gold, but actually it was studded with little iron stars. And to show off even more of his jewellery, he had his right arm bare and set off by a gold armlet and an ivory circlet fastened with a gleaming metal plate.

After picking his teeth with a silver toothpick, he began: "My friends, I wasn't keen to come into the dining room yet. But if I stayed away any more, I would have kept you back, so I've deprived myself of all my little pleasures for you. However, you'll allow me to finish my game."

A boy was at his heels with a board of terebinth wood[9] with glass squares, and I noticed the very last word in luxury—instead of white and black pieces he had gold and silver coins. While he was swearing away like a trooper over his game and we were still on the hors d'oeuvre, a tray was brought in with a basket on it. There sat a wooden hen, its wings spread round it the way hens are when they are broody. Two slaves hurried up and as the orchestra played a tune they began searching through the straw and dug out peahens' eggs, which they distributed to the guests.

Trimalchio turned to look at this little scene and said: "My friends, I gave orders for that bird to sit on some peahens' eggs. I hope to goodness they are not starting to hatch. However, let's try them and see if they are still soft."

We took up our spoons (weighing at least half a pound each) and cracked the eggs, which were made of rich pastry. To tell the truth, I nearly threw away my share, as the chicken seemed already formed. But I heard a guest who was an old hand say: "There should be something good here." So I searched the shell with my fingers and found the plumpest little figpecker, all covered with yolk and seasoned with pepper.

At this point Trimalchio became tired of his game and demanded that all the previous dishes be brought to him. He gave permission in a loud voice for any of us to have another glass of mead if we wanted it. Suddenly there was a crash from the orchestra and a troop of waiters—still singing—snatched away the hors d'oeuvre. However in the confusion one of the side-dishes happened to fall and a slave picked it up from the floor. Trimalchio noticed this, had the boy's ears boxed and told him to throw it down again. A cleaner came in with a broom and began to sweep up the silver plate along with the rest of the rubbish. Two long-haired Ethiopians followed him, carrying small skin bottles like those they use for scattering sand in the circus, and they poured wine over our hands—no one ever offered us water.

---

9. A very hard wood that takes a high polish and is very expensive (like everything Trimalchio has).

Our host was complimented on these elegant arrangements. "You've got to fight fair," he replied. "That is why I gave orders for each guest to have his own table. At the same time these smelly slaves won't crowd so."

Carefully sealed wine bottles were immediately brought, their necks labelled:

FALERNIAN
CONSUL OPIMIUS[1]
ONE HUNDRED YEARS OLD

While we were examining the labels, Trimalchio clapped his hands and said with a sigh:

"Wine has a longer life than us poor folks. So let's wet our whistles. Wine is life. I'm giving you real Opimian. I didn't put out such good stuff yesterday, though the company was much better class."

Naturally we drank and missed no opportunity of admiring his elegant hospitality. In the middle of this a slave brought in a silver skeleton, put together in such a way that its joints and backbone could be pulled out and twisted in all directions. After he had flung it about on the table once or twice, its flexible joints falling into various postures, Trimalchio recited:

> "Man's life alas! is but a span,
> So let us live it while we can,
> We'll be like this when dead."

After our applause the next course was brought in. Actually it was not as grand as we expected, but it was so novel that everyone stared. It was a deep circular tray with the twelve signs of the Zodiac arranged round the edge. . . .

After this course Trimalchio got up and went to the toilet. Free of his domineering presence, we began to strike up a general conversation. Dama[2] started off by calling for bigger glasses.

"The day's nothin'," he said, "It's night 'fore y'can turn around. So the best thing's get out of bed and go straight to dinner. Lovely cold weather we've had too. M'bath hardly thawed me out. Still, a hot drink's as good as an overcoat. I've been throwin' it back neat, and I'm pretty tight—the wine's gone to m'head."

This started Seleucus off.

"Me now," he said, "I don't have a bath every day. It's like gettin' rubbed with fuller's earth,[3] havin' a bath. The water bites into you, and as the days go by, your heart turns to water. But when I've knocked back a hot glass of wine and honey, kiss-my-arse I say to the cold weather. Mind you, I couldn't have a bath—I was at a funeral today. Poor old Chrysanthus has just given up the ghost—nice man he was! It was only the other day he stopped me in the street. I still seem to hear his voice. Dear, dear! We're just so many walking bags of wind. We're worse than flies—at least flies have got some strength in them, but we're no more than empty bubbles.

"And what would he have been like if he hadn't been on a diet? For five days he didn't take a drop of water or a crumb of bread into his mouth. But he's gone to join the majority. The doctors finished him—well, hard luck, more like. After all, a doctor is just to put your mind at rest. Still, he got a good sendoff—he had a bier and all beautifully draped. His mourners—several of his slaves were left their freedom—did him proud, even though his widow was a bit mean with her tears. Suppose now he hadn't been so good to her! But women as a sex are real vultures. It's no good doing them a favour, you might as well throw it down a well. An old passion is just an ulcer."

He was being a bore and Phileros said loudly:

"Let's think of the living. He's got what he deserved. He lived an honest life and he died an honest death. What has he got to complain about? He started out in life with just a penny and he was ready to pick up less than that from a muck-heap, if he had to use his teeth. He went up in the world. He got bigger and bigger till he got where you see, like a honeycomb. I honestly think he left a solid hundred thousand and he had the lot in hard cash. But I'll be honest about it—seeing I'm a bit of a cynic—he had a foul mouth and too much lip. He wasn't a man, he was just murder.

"Now his brother was a fine man, a real friend to his friends, always ready with a helping hand or a decent meal.

"Chrysanthus had bad luck at first, but the first vintage set him on his feet. He fixed his own price when he sold the wine. And what properly kept his head above water was a legacy he came in for, when he pocketed more than was left to him. And the blockhead, when he had a quarrel with his brother, cut him out of his will in favour of some sod we've never heard of. You're leaving a lot behind when you leave your own flesh and blood. But he took advice from his slaves and they really fixed him. It's never right to believe all you're told, especially for a business man. But it's true he enjoyed himself while he lived. You got it, you keep it. He was certainly Fortune's favourite—lead turned to gold in his hand. Mind you, it's easy when everything runs smoothly.

"And how old do you think he was? Seventy or more! But he was hard as nails and carried his age well. His hair was black as a raven's wing. I knew the man for ages and ages and he was still an old lecher. I honestly don't think he left the dog alone. What's more, he liked little boys—he could turn his hand to anything. Well, I don't blame him—after all, he couldn't take anything else with him."

This was Phileros, then Ganymedes said:

"You're all talking about things that don't concern heaven or earth. Meanwhile, no one gives a damn the way we're hit by the corn[4] situation. Honest to God, I couldn't get hold of a mouthful of bread today. And look how there's still no rain. It's been absolute starvation for a whole year now. To hell with the food officers! They're in with the bakers—'You be nice to me and I'll be nice to you.' So the little man suffers, while those grinders of the poor never stop celebrating. Oh, if only we still had the sort of men I found here when I first arrived from Asia. Like lions they were. That was the life! Come one, come all! If white flour was inferior to the very finest, they'd thrash those bogeymen till they thought God Almighty was after them.

---

4. I.e., wheat.

"I remember Safinius—he used to live by the old arch then; I was a boy at the time. He wasn't a man, he was all pepper. He used to scorch the ground wherever he went. But he was dead straight—don't let him down and he wouldn't let you down. You'd be ready to play *morra*[5] with him in the dark. But on the city council, how he used to wade into some of them—no beating about the bush, straight from the shoulder! And when he was in court, his voice got louder and louder like a trumpet. He never sweated or spat—I think there was a touch of the old acid about him. And very affable he was when you met him, calling everyone by name just like one of us. Naturally at the time corn was dirt cheap. You could buy a penny loaf that two of you couldn't get through. Today—I've seen bigger bull's-eyes.

"Ah me! It's getting worse every day. This place is going down like a calf's tail. But why do we have a third-rate food officer who wouldn't lose a penny to save our lives? He sits at home laughing and rakes in more money a day than anyone else's whole fortune. I happen to know he's just made a thousand in gold. But if we had any balls at all, he wouldn't be feeling so pleased with himself. People today are lions at home and foxes outside.

"Take me, I've already sold the rags off my back for food and if this shortage continues, I'll be selling my bit of a house. What's going to happen to this place if neither god nor man will help us? As I hope to go home tonight, I'm sure all this is heaven's doing.

"Nobody believes in heaven, see, nobody fasts, nobody gives a damn for the Almighty. No, people only bow their heads to count their money. In the old days high-class ladies used to climb up the hill barefoot, their hair loose and their hearts pure, and ask God for rain. And he'd send it down in bucketfuls right away—it was then or never—and everyone went home like drowned rats. Since we've given up religion the gods nowadays keep their feet well wrapped up. The fields just lie . . ."

"Please, please," broke in Echion the rag merchant, "be a bit more cheerful. 'First it's one thing, then another,' as the yokel said when he lost his spotted pig. What we haven't got today, we'll have tomorrow. That's the way life goes. Believe me, you couldn't name a better country, if it had the people. As things are, I admit, it's having a hard time, but it isn't the only place. We mustn't be soft. The sky don't get no nearer wherever you are. If you were somewhere else, you'd be talking about the pigs walking round ready roasted back here.

"And another thing, we'll be having a holiday with a three-day show that's the best ever—and not just a hack troupe of gladiators but freedmen for the most part. My old friend Titus has a big heart and a hot head. Maybe this, maybe that, but something at all events. I'm a close friend of his and he does nothing by halves. He'll give us cold steel, no quarter and the slaughterhouse right in the middle where all the stands can see it. And he's got the wherewithal—he was left thirty million when his poor father died. Even if he spent four hundred thousand, his pocket won't feel it and he'll go down in history. He's got some big brutes already, and a woman who fights in a chariot and Glyco's steward, who was caught having fun with his mistress. You'll see quite a quarrel in the crowd between jealous husbands and roman-

---

5. A game (still played in southern Italy) that requires the players to match the number of fingers held out by the opponent.

tic lovers. But that half-pint Glyco threw his steward to the lions,[6] which is just giving himself away. How is it the servant's fault when he's forced into it? It's that old pisspot who really deserves to be tossed by a bull. But if you can't beat the ass you beat the saddle. But how did Glyco imagine the poisonous daughter of Hermogenes[7] would ever turn out well? The old man could cut the claws off a flying kite, and a snake don't hatch old rope. Glyco— well, Glyco's got his. He's branded for as long as he lives and only the grave will get rid of it. But everyone pays for their mistakes.

"But I can almost smell the dinner Mammaea is going to give us[8]—two denarii apiece for me and the family. If he really does it, he'll make off with all Norbanus's votes, I tell you he'll win at a canter. After all, what good has Norbanus done us? He put on some half-pint gladiators, so done in already that they'd have dropped if you blew at them. I've seen animal-killers[9] fight better. As for the horsemen killed, he got them off a lamp[1]—they ran round like cocks in a backyard. One was just a carthorse, the other couldn't stand up, and the reserve was just one corpse instead of another—he was practically hamstrung. One boy did have a bit of spirit—he was in Thracian armour,[2] and even he didn't show any initiative. In fact, they were all flogged afterwards, there were so many shouts of 'Give 'em what for!' from the crowd. Pure yellow, that's all. " 'Well, I've put on a show for you,' he says. 'And I'm clapping you,' says I. 'Reckon it up—I'm giving more than I got. So we're quits.'

"Hey, Agamemnon! I suppose you're saying 'What is that bore going on and on about?' It's because a good talker like you don't talk. You're a cut above us, and so you laugh at what us poor people say. We all know you're off your head with all that reading. But never mind! Some day I'll get you to come down to my place in the country and have a look at our little cottage. We'll find something to eat—a chicken, some eggs. It'll be nice, even though the unreliable weather this year has made off with everything. Anyway, we'll find enough to fill our bellies.

"And my kid is growing up to be a pupil of yours. He can divide by four already. If God spares him, you'll have him ready to do anything for you. In his spare time, he won't take his head out of his exercise book. He's clever and there's good stuff in him, even if he is crazy about birds. Only yesterday I killed his three goldfinches and told him a weasel ate them. But he's found some other silly hobbies, and he's having a fine time painting. Still, he's already well ahead with his Greek, and he's starting to take to his Latin, though his tutor is too pleased with himself and unreliable—he just comes and goes. He knows his stuff but doesn't want to work. There is another one as well, not so clever but he is conscientious—he teaches the boy more than he knows himself. In fact, he makes a habit of coming around on holidays, and whatever you give him, he's happy.

"Anyway, I've just bought the boy some law books, as I want him to pick up some legal training for home use. There's a living in that sort of thing. He's done enough dabbling in poetry and such like. If he objects, I've decided

6. Glyco was permitted by law to punish his slave by forcing him to fight wild beasts in the arena. 7. Presumably Glyco's father-in-law. 8. A public banquet given by Mammaea as part of his electoral campaign. His rival, Norbanus, has been giving gladiatorial shows. 9. Professional fighters of wild animals, considered inferior to gladiators. 1. I.e., they were as small as the horsemen depicted on a lamp. 2. Light armor, such as that worn by soldiers from Thrace, a savage country northeast of Greece.

he'll learn a trade—barber, auctioneer, or at least a barrister—something he can't lose till he dies. Well, yesterday I gave it to him straight: 'Believe me, my lad, any studying you do will be for your own good. You see Phileros the solicitor—if he hadn't studied, he'd be starving today. It's not so long since he was humping round loads on his back. Now he can even look Norbanus in the face. An education is an investment, and a proper profession never goes dead on you.'"

This was the sort of conversation flying round when Trimalchio came in, dabbed his forehead and washed his hands in perfume. There was a short pause, then he said:

"Excuse me, dear people, my inside has not been answering the call for several days now. The doctors are puzzled. But some pomegranate rind and resin in vinegar has done me good. But I hope now it will be back on its good behaviour. Otherwise my stomach rumbles like a bull. So if any of you wants to go out, there's no need for him to be embarrassed. None of us was born solid. I think there's nothing so tormenting as holding yourself in. This is the one thing even God Almighty can't object to. Yes, laugh, Fortunata,[3] but you generally keep me up all night with this sort of thing.

"Anyway, I don't object to people doing what suits them even in the middle of dinner—and the doctors forbid you to hold yourself in. Even if it's a longer business, everything is there just outside—water, bowls, and all the other little comforts. Believe me, if the wind goes to your brain it starts flooding your whole body too. I've known a lot of people die from this because they wouldn't be honest with themselves."

We thanked him for being so generous and considerate and promptly proceeded to bury our amusement in our glasses. Up to this point we'd not realized we were only in mid-stream, as you might say.

The orchestra played, the tables were cleared, and then three white pigs were brought into the dining-room, all decked out in muzzles and bells. The first, the master of ceremonies announced, was two years old, the second three, and the third six. I was under the impression that some acrobats were on their way in and the pigs were going to do some tricks, the way they do in street shows. But Trimalchio dispelled this impression by asking:

"Which of these would you like for the next course? Any clodhopper can do you a barnyard cock or a stew and trifles like that, but my cooks are used to boiling whole calves."

He immediately sent for the chef and without waiting for us to choose he told him to kill the oldest pig.

He then said to the man in a loud voice:

"Which division are you from?"

When he replied he was from number forty, Trimalchio asked:

"Were you bought or were you born here?"

"Neither," said the chef, "I was left to you in Pansa's will."

"Well, then," said Trimalchio, "see you serve it up carefully—otherwise I'll have you thrown into the messenger's division."

So the chef, duly reminded of his master's magnificence, went back to his kitchen, the next course leading the way.

Trimalchio looked around at us with a gentle smile: "If you don't like the

3. Trimalchio's wife.

wine, I'll have it changed. It is up to you to do it justice. I don't buy it, thank heaven. In fact, whatever wine really tickles your palate this evening, it comes from an estate of mine which as yet I haven't seen. It's said to join my estates at Tarracina and Tarentum. What I'd like to do now is add Sicily to my little bit of land, so that when I want to go to Africa, I could sail there without leaving my own property.

"But tell me, Agamemnon, what was your debate about today? Even though I don't go in for the law, still I've picked up enough education for home consumption. And don't you think I turn my nose up at studying, because I have two libraries, one Greek, one Latin. So tell us, just as a favour, what was the topic of your debate?"

Agamemnon was just beginning, "A poor man and a rich man were enemies . . ." when Trimalchio said: "What's a poor man?" "Oh, witty!" said Agamemnon, and then told us about some fictitious case or other. Like lightning Trimalchio said: "If this happened, it's not a fictitious case—if it didn't happen, then it's nothing at all."

We greeted this witticism and several more like it with the greatest enthusiasm.

"Tell me, my dear Agamemnon," continued Trimalchio, "do you remember the twelve labours of Hercules and the story of Ulysses—how the Cyclops tore out his thumb with a pair of pincers.[4] I used to read about them in Homer, when I was a boy. In fact, I actually saw the Sibyl at Cumae with my own eyes dangling in a bottle, and when the children asked her in Greek: 'What do you want, Sybil?' she used to answer: 'I want to die.' "

[Presents for the guests are distributed, with a slave announcing the nature of each gift and making in each case an atrocious pun on the name of the guest.]

We laughed for ages. There were hundreds of things like this but they've slipped my mind now.

Ascyltus, with his usual lack of restraint, found everything extremely funny, lifting up his hands and laughing till the tears came. Eventually one of Trimalchio's freedman[5] friends flared up at him—the one sitting above me, in fact.

"You with the sheep's eyes," he said, "what's so funny? Isn't our host elegant enough for you? You're better off, I suppose, and used to a bigger dinner. Holy guardian here preserve me! If I was sitting by him, I'd make him bleat! A fine pippin he is to be laughing at other people! Some fly-by-night from god knows where—not worth his own piss. In fact, if I pissed round him, he wouldn't know where to turn.

"By god, it takes a lot to make me boil, but if you're too soft, worms like this only come to the top. Look at him laughing! What's he got to laugh at? Did his father pay cash for him? You're a Roman knight,[6] are you? Well, my father was a king.

" 'Why are you only a freedman?' did you say? Because I went into service voluntarily. I wanted to be a Roman citizen, not a subject with taxes to pay. And today, I hope no one can laugh at the way I live. I'm a man among men,

---

4. Trimalchio refers to Ulysses' (Odysseus's) adventures in the cave of the Cyclops (*Odyssey* 9); despite what he goes on to say, he has obviously not read Homer.   5. A former slave who had bought his freedom.
6. A Roman class including all who had property above a certain amount.

and I walk with my head up. I don't owe anybody a penny—there's never been a court-order out for me. No one's said 'Pay up!' to me in the street.

"I've bought a bit of land and some tiny pieces of plate. I've twenty bellies to feed, as well as a dog. I bought my old woman's freedom so nobody could wipe his dirty hands on *her* hair. Four thousand I paid for myself. I was elected to the Augustan College[7] and it cost me nothing. I hope when I die I won't have to blush in my coffin.

"But you now, you're such a busybody you don't look behind you. You see a louse on somebody else, but not the fleas on your own back. You're the only one who finds us funny. Look at the professor now—he's an older man than you and we get along with him. But you're still wet from your mother's milk and not up to your ABC yet. Just a crackpot—you're like a piece of wash-leather in soak, softer but no better! You're grander than us—well, have two dinners and two suppers! I'd rather have my good name than any amount of money. When all's said and done, who's ever asked me for money twice? For forty years I slaved but nobody ever knew if I was a slave or a free man. I came to this colony when I was a lad with long hair—the town-hall hadn't been built then. But I worked hard to please my master—there was a real gentleman, with more in his little finger-nail than there is in your whole body. And I had people in the house who tried to trip me up one way or another, but still—thanks be to his guardian spirit!—I kept my head above water. That's real success: being born free is as easy as all get-out. Now what are you gawping at, like a goat in a vetch field?"

At this remark, Giton, who was waiting on me, could not suppress his laughter and let out a filthy guffaw, which did not pass unnoticed by Ascyltus's opponent. He turned his abuse on the boy.

"So!" he said, "you're amused too, are you, you curly-headed onion? A merry Saturnalia[8] to you! Is it December, I'd like to know? When did *you* pay your liberation tax?[9] Look, he doesn't know what to do, the gallow's bird, the crow's meat.

"God's curse on you, and your master too, for not keeping you under control! As sure as I get my bellyful, it's only because of Trimalchio that I don't take it out of you here and now. He's a freedman like myself. We're doing all right, but those good-for-nothings, well—. It's easy to see, like master, like man. I can hardly hold myself back, and I'm not naturally hot-headed— but once I start, I don't give a penny for my own mother.

"All right! I'll see you when we get outside, you rat, you excrescence. I'll knock your master in the dirt before I'm an inch taller or shorter. And I won't let you off either, by heaven, even if you scream down God Almighty. Your cheap curls and your no-good master won't be much use to you then—I'll see to that. I'll get my teeth into you, all right. Either I'm much mistaken about myself or you won't be laughing at us behind your golden beard. Athena's curse on you and the man who first made you such a forward brat.

"I didn't learn no geometry or criticism and such silly rubbish, but I can read the letters on a notice board and I can do my percentages in metal, weights, and money. In fact, if you like, we'll have a bet. Come on, here's

---

7. The state religion was the worship of Augustus, the emperor; the office of priest might be sold or conferred. 8. A December festival in honor of an ancient Italian deity at which the normal order of everyday life was reversed and the slaves and children made fun of their masters. 9. A freed slave had to pay 5 percent of his value to the treasury.

my cash. Now you'll see how your father wasted his money, even though you do know how to make a speech.

"Try this:

> Something we all have.
> Long I come, broad I come. What am I?

"I'll give you it: something we all have that runs and doesn't move from its place: something we all have that grows and gets smaller.[1]

"You're running round in circles, you've had enough, like the mouse in the pisspot. So either keep quiet or keep out of the way of your betters, they don't even know you're alive—unless you think I care about your box-wood rings that you swiped from your girl friend! Lord make me lucky! Let's go into town and borrow some money. You'll soon see they trust this iron one.

"Pah! a drownded fox makes a nice sight, I must say. As I hope to make my pile and die so famous that people swear by my dead body, I'll hound you to death. And he's a nice thing too—the one who taught you all these tricks—a muttonhead, not a master. We learned different. Our teacher used to say: 'Are your things in order? Go straight home. No looking around. And be polite to your elders.' Nowadays it's all an absolute muck-heap. They turn out nobody worth a penny. I'm like you see me and I thank God for the way I was learnt." . . .

In the middle of all this, a lictor[2] knocked at the double doors and a drunken guest entered wearing white, followed by a large crowd of people. I was terrified by this lordly apparition and thought it was the chief magistrate arriving. So I tried to rise and get my bare feet on the floor. Agamemnon laughed at this panic and said:

"Get hold of yourself, you silly fool. This is Habinnas—Augustan College and monumental mason."

Relieved by this information I resumed my position and watched Habinnas' entry with huge admiration. Being already drunk, he had his hands on his wife's shoulders; loaded with several garlands, oil pouring down his forehead and into his eyes, he settled himself into the place of honour and immediately demanded some wine and hot water. Trimalchio, delighted by these high spirits, demanded a larger cup for himself and asked how he had enjoyed it all.

"The only thing we missed," replied Habinnas, "was yourself—the apple of my eye was here. Still, it was damn good. Scissa was giving a ninth-day dinner[3] in honour of a poor slave of hers she'd freed on his death-bed. And I think she'll have a pretty penny to pay in liberation tax because they reckon he was worth fifty thousand. Still, it was pleasant enough, even if we did have to pour half our drinks over his wretched bones."

"Well," said Trimalchio, "what did you have for dinner?"

"I'll tell you if I can—I've such a good memory that I often forget my own name. For the first course we had a pig crowned with sausages and served with blood-puddings and very nicely done giblets, and of course beetroot and pure wholemeal bread—which I prefer to white myself: it's very strengthening and I don't regret it when I do my business. The next course was cold

---

1. There is no agreement about the correct answer to these riddles. Suggested answers are, to the first, the foot; the second, the eye; the third, hair. 2. A magistrate's attendant. 3. On the last day of the mourning period.

tart and a concoction of first-class Spanish wine poured over hot honey. I didn't eat anything at all of the actual tart, but I dived right into the honey. Scattered round were chickpeas, lupines, a choice of nuts and an apple apiece—though I took two. And look, I've got them tied up in a napkin, because if I don't take something in the way of a present to my youngster, I'll have a row on my hands.

"Oh, yes, my good lady reminds me. We had a hunk of bearmeat set before us, which Scintilla was foolish enough to try, and she practically spewed up her guts; but I ate more than a pound of it, as it tasted like real wild-boar. And I say if bears can eat us poor people, it's all the more reason why us poor people should eat bears.

"To finish up with, we had some cheese basted with new wine, snails all round, chitterlings, plates of liver, eggs in pastry hoods, turnips, mustard, and some filthy concoction—good riddance to that. There were pickled cumin seeds too, passed round in a bowl and some people were that bad-mannered they took three handfuls. You see, we sent the ham away.

"But tell me something, Gaius, now I ask—why isn't Fortunata at the table?"

"You know her," replied Trimalchio, "unless she's put the silver away and shared out the left-overs among the slaves, she won't put a drop of water to her mouth."

"All the same," retorted Habinnas, "unless she sits down, I'm shagging off."

And he was starting to get up, when at a given signal all the servants shouted "Fortunata" four or five times. So in she came with her skirt tucked up under a yellow sash to show her cerise petticoat underneath, as well as her twisted anklets and gold-embroidered slippers. Wiping her hands on a handkerchief which she carried round her neck, she took her place on the couch where Habbinas' wife was reclining. She kissed her. "Is it really you?" she said, clapping her hands together.

It soon got to the point where Fortunata took the bracelets from her great fat arms and showed them to the admiring Scintilla. In the end she even undid her anklets and her gold hair net, which she said was pure gold. Trimalchio noticed this and had it all brought to him and commented:

"A woman's chains, you see. This is the way us poor fools get robbed. She must have six and a half pounds on her. Still, I've got a bracelet myself, made up from one-tenth per cent to Mercury[4]—and it weighs not an ounce less than ten pounds."

Finally, for fear he looked like a liar, he even had some scales brought in and had them passed round to test the weight.

Scintilla was no better. From round her neck she took a little gold locket, which she called her "lucky box." From it she extracted two earrings and in her turn gave them to Fortunata to look at.

"A present from my good husband," she said, "and no one has a finer set."

"Hey!" said Habinnas, "you cleaned me out to buy you a glass bean. Honestly, if I had a daughter, I'd cut her little ears off. If there weren't any women, everything would be dirt cheap. As it is, we've got to drink cold water and piss it out hot."

Meanwhile, the women giggled tipsily between themselves and kissed each

---

4. Trimalchio sets aside a percentage of his profits to offer to his patron deity.

other drunkenly, one crying up her merits as a housewife, the other crying about her husband's demerits and boy friends. While they had their heads together like this, Habinnas rose stealthily and taking Fortunata's feet, flung them up over the couch.

"Oh, oh!" she shrieked, as her underskirt wandered up over her knees. So she settled herself in Scintilla's lap and hid her disgusting red face in her handkerchief.

Then came an interval, after which Trimalchio called for dessert. . . .

Fortunata was now wanting to dance, and Scintilla was doing more clapping than talking, when Trimalchio said:

"Philargyrus—even though you are such a terrible fan of the Greens[5]— you have my permission to join us. And tell your dear Menophila to sit down as well."

Need I say more? We were almost thrown out of our places, so completely did the household fill the dining-room. I even noticed that the chef was actually given a place above me, and he was reeking of pickles and sauce. And he wasn't satisfied with just having a place, but he had to start straight off on an imitation of the tragedian Ephesus, and then challenge his master to bet against the Greens winning at the next races.

Trimalchio became expansive after this argument.

"My dear people," he said, "slaves are human beings too. They drink the same milk as anybody else, even though luck's been agin 'em. Still, if nothing happens to me, they'll have their taste of freedom soon. In fact, I'm setting them all free in my will. I'm giving Philargyrus a farm, what's more, and the woman he lives with. As for Cario, I'm leaving him a block of flats, his five per cent manumission tax, and a bed with all the trimmings. I'm making Fortunata my heir, and I want all my friends to look after her.

"The reason I'm telling everyone all this is so my household will love me now as much as if I was dead."

Everyone began thanking his lordship for his kindness, when he became very serious and had a copy of his will brought in. Amid the sobs of his household he read out the whole thing from beginning to end.

Then looking at Habinnas, he said:

"What have you to say, my dear old friend? Are you building my monument the way I told you? I particularly want you to keep a place at the foot of my statue and put a picture of my pup there, as well as paintings of wreaths, scent-bottles, and all the contests of Petraites,[6] and thanks to you I'll be able to live on after I'm dead. And another thing! See that it's a hundred feet facing the road and two hundred back into the field. I want all the various sorts of fruit round my ashes and lots and lots of vines. After all, it's a big mistake to have nice houses just for when you're alive and not worry about the one we have to live in for much longer. And that's why I want this written up before anything else:

THIS MONUMENT DOES NOT GO TO THE HEIR

"But I'll make sure in my will that I don't get done down once I'm dead. I'll put one of my freedmen in charge of my tomb to look after it and not let people run up and shit on my monument. I'd like you to put some ships there

5. One of the teams in the chariot races.   6. A popular gladiator.

too, sailing under full canvas, and me sitting on a high platform in my robes of office, wearing five gold rings and pouring out a bagful of money for the people. You know I gave them all a dinner and two denarii apiece. Let's have in a banqueting hall as well, if you think it's a good idea, and show the whole town having a good time. Put up a statue of Fortunata on my right, holding a dove, and have her leading her little dog tied to her belt—and this dear little chap as well, and great big wine jars sealed up so the wine won't spill. And perhaps you could carve me a broken wine jar and boy crying over it. A clock in the middle, so that anybody who looks at the time, like it or not, has got to read my name. As for the inscription now, take a good look and see if this seems suitable enough:

> HERE SLEEPS
> GAIUS POMPEIUS TRIMALCHIO
> MAECENATIANUS
> ELECTED TO THE AUGUSTAN COLLEGE IN HIS ABSENCE
> HE COULD HAVE BEEN ON EVERY BOARD IN ROME
> BUT HE REFUSED
> GOD-FEARING BRAVE AND TRUE
> A SELF-MADE MAN
> HE LEFT AN ESTATE OF 30,000,000
> AND HE NEVER HEARD A PHILOSOPHER
> FAREWELL
> AND YOU FARE WELL, TRIMALCHIO."

[After a visit to the baths, where Encolpius and his friends make an unsuccessful attempt to escape, the dinner is resumed.]

After this dish Trimalchio looked at the servants and said:

"Why haven't you had dinner yet? Off you go and let some others come on duty."

Up came another squad and as the first set called out: "Good night, Gaius!" the new arrivals shouted: "Good evening, Gaius!"

This led to the first incident that damped the general high spirits. Not a bad-looking boy entered with the newcomers and Trimalchio jumped at him and began kissing him at some length. Fortunata, asserting her just and legal rights, began hurling insults at Trimalchio, calling him a low scum and a disgrace, who couldn't control his beastly desires. "You dirty dog!" she finally added.

Trimalchio took offence at this abuse and flung his glass into Fortunata's face. She screamed as though she'd lost an eye and put her trembling hands across her face. Scintilla was terrified too and hugged the quaking woman to her breast. An obliging slave pressed a little jug of cold water to her cheek, while Fortunata rested her head on it and began weeping. Trimalchio just said:

"Well, well, forgotten her chorus days, has she? She doesn't remember, but she was bought and sold, and I took her away from it all and made her as good as the next. Yet she puffs herself up like a frog and doesn't even spit for luck. Just a great hunk, not a woman. But those as are born over a shop don't dream of a house. May I never have a day's good luck again, if I don't teach that Cassandra in clogs some manners!

"There was I, not worth twopence, and I could have had ten million. And you know I'm not lying about it. Agatho, who ran a perfume shop for the lady next door, he took me on one side and said: 'You don't want to let your family die out, you know!' But me, trying to do the right thing and not wanting to look changeable, I cut my own throat.

"All right! I'll make you want to dig me up with your bare nails. Just so you'll know on the spot what you've done for yourself—Habinnas! I don't want you to put her statue on my tomb, so at least when I'm dead I won't have any more squabbles. And another thing! just to show I can get my own back—when I'm dead I don't want her to kiss me."

After this thunderbolt, Habinnas began asking him to calm down: "None of us are without faults," he said, "we're not gods, we're human!" Scintilla said the same, calling him Gaius, and she began asking him, in the name of his guardian spirit, to give in.

Trimalchio held back his tears no longer. "I ask you, Habinnas," he said, "as you hope to enjoy your bit of savings—if I did anything wrong, spit in my face. I kissed this very careful little fellow, not for his pretty face, but because he's careful with money—he says his ten times table, he reads a book at sight, he's got himself some Thracian kit out of his daily allowance, and he's bought himself an easy chair and two cups out of his own pocket. Doesn't he deserve to be the apple of my eye? But Fortunata won't have it.

"Is that the way you feel, high heels? I'll give you a piece of advice: don't let your good luck turn your head, you kite, and don't make me show my teeth, my little darling—otherwise you'll feel my temper. You know me: once I've decided on something, it's fixed with a twelve-inch nail.

"But to come back to earth—I want you to enjoy yourselves, my dear people. After all, I was once like you are, but being the right sort, I got where I am. It's the old headpiece that makes a man, the rest is all rubbish. 'Buy right—sell right!'—that's me! Different people will give you a different line. I'm just on top of the world, I'm that lucky.

"But you, you snoring thing, are you still moaning? I'll give you something to moan about in a minute.

"However, as I'd started to say, it was my shrewd way with money that got me to my present position. I came from Asia as big as this candlestick. In fact, every day I used to measure myself against it, and to get some whiskers round my beak quicker, I used to oil my lips from the lamp. Still, for fourteen years I was the old boy's fancy. And there's nothing wrong if the boss wants it. But I did all right by the old girl too. You know what I mean—I don't say anything because I'm not the boasting sort.

"Well, as heaven will have it, I became boss in the house, and the old boy, you see, couldn't think of anything but me. That's about it—he made me co-heir with the Emperor[7] and I got a senator's fortune. But nobody gets enough, never. I wanted to go into business. Not to make a long story of it, I built five ships, I loaded them with wine—it was absolute gold at the time—and I sent them to Rome. You'd have thought I ordered it—every single ship was wrecked. That's fact, not fable! In one single day Neptune[8] swallowed up thirty million. Do you think I gave up? This loss honestly wasn't more than

---

7. An honor that Trimalchio shared with many others, for it was customary (as a prudent measure, to avoid confiscation on some pretext or other) to include a bequest to the emperor in one's will.   8. God of the sea.

a flea-bite to me—it was as if nothing had happened. I built more boats, bigger and better and luckier, so nobody could say I wasn't a man of courage. You know, the greater the ship, the greater the confidence. I loaded them again—with wine, bacon, beans, perfumes and slaves. At this point Fortunata did the decent thing, because she sold off all her gold trinkets, all her clothes, and put ten thousand in gold pieces in my hand. This was the yeast my fortune needed to rise. What heaven wants, soon happens. In one voyage I carved out a round ten million. I immediately bought back all my old master's estates. I built a house, I invested in slaves, and I bought up the horse trade. Whatever I touched grew like a honeycomb. Once I had more than the whole country, then down tools! I retired from business and began advancing loans through freedmen.

"Actually I was tired of trading on my own account, but it was an astrologer who convinced me. He happened to come to our colony, a sort of Greek, Serapa by name, and he could have told heaven itself what to do. He even told me things I'd forgotten. He went through everything for me from A to Z. He knew me inside out—the only thing he didn't tell me was what I ate for dinner the day before. You'd have thought he'd never left my side.

"Wasn't there that thing, Habinnas?—I think you were there: 'You got your lady wife out of those *certain circumstances*. You are not lucky in your friends. Nobody thanks you enough for your trouble. You have large estates. You are nursing a viper in your bosom.'

"And he said—though I shouldn't tell you—I have thirty years, four months, two days to live. What's more, I shall soon receive a legacy. My horoscope tells me this. If I'm allowed to join my estates to Apulia,[9] I'll have lived enough.

"Meantime, under the protection of Mercury, I built this house. As you know, it was still a shack, now it's a shrine. It has four dining-rooms, twenty bedrooms, two marble colonnades, a row of boxrooms up above, a bedroom where I sleep myself, a nest for this viper, and a really good lodge for the porter. The guest apartment takes a hundred guests. In fact, when Scaurus[1] came here, he didn't want to stay anywhere else, even though he's got his father's guest house down by the sea. And there are a lot of other things I'll show you in a second.

"Believe me: have a penny, and you're worth a penny. You got something, you'll be thought something. Like your old friend—first a frog, now a king.

"Meantime, Stichus, bring out the shroud and the things I want to be buried in. Bring some cosmetic cream too, and a sample from that jar of wine I want my bones washed in."

Stichus did not delay over it, but brought his white shroud and his formal dress into the dining-room. . . . Trimalchio told us to examine them and see if they were made of good wool. Then he said with a smile:

"Now you, Stichus, see no mice or moths get at those—otherwise I'll burn you alive. I want to be buried in style, so the whole town will pray for my rest.'

He opened a bottle of nard on the spot, rubbed some on all of us and said:

---

9. The southeastern extremity of Italy.   1. Unidentified. The name is aristocratic, but it may be a reference to a well-known manufacturer of fish sauce from Pompeii.

"I hope this'll be as nice when I'm dead as when I'm alive.' The wine he had poured into a big decanter and he said:

"I want you to think you've been invited to my wake."

The thing was becoming absolutely sickening, when Trimalchio, showing the effects of his disgusting drunkenness, had a fresh entertainment brought into the dining-room, some cornet players. Propped up on a lot of cushions, he stretched out along the edge of the couch and said: "Pretend I'm dead and say something nice."

The cornet players struck up a dead march. One man in particular, the slave of his undertaker (who was the most respectable person present) blew so loudly that he roused the neighbourhood. As a result, the fire brigade, thinking Trimalchio's house was on fire, suddenly broke down the front door and began kicking up their own sort of din with their water and axes.

Seizing this perfect chance, we gave Agamemnon the slip and escaped as rapidly as if there really were a fire.

THE CHRISTIAN BIBLE: THE NEW TESTAMENT
ca. first century C.E.

The Christian Bible, as it evolved, incorporated many of the Hebrew sacred scriptures, now referred to collectively as the Old Testament (the word is a Latin translation of the Greek word for "covenant"), but added the canonical Christian scriptures—the Gospels, the Acts of the Apostles, the Epistles, and Revelation—as the New Testament. This bipartite structure of the Bible reflects the Christian understanding of how the events surrounding the birth and crucifixion of Jesus were related to Jewish history and belief: as a fulfillment of that history, and its completion. This view, based partly on an interpretation of a passage in the Hebrew prophet Jeremiah (31.31) foretelling a new covenant, was in accord with some of Jesus' own statements, such as "Do not think that I have come to destroy the law and the prophets. I have not come to destroy but to complete" (Matthew 5). It has various ramifications. The writers of the Gospels, especially Matthew, are at pains to point out correspondences between Jesus' life and death and the predictions of the Hebrew prophets. Doing so not only offered proof that Jesus was the Messiah and that he represented the fulfillment of earlier prophecies; it is also an example of how the Hebrew scriptures gave early Christians a way of interpreting his life. But the events of the New Testament were also seen as transcending those of the Old Testament. The Old Testament was to the New as body to spirit—an argument made in several epistles of Paul. Finally, it was a short step to viewing people and events of the Old Testament as prefiguring the New Testament, or as their types (this idea is called *typology*). Moses, for example, was a type of Jesus, the Flood a type of the coming of God's kingdom. Thus the Christian Bible, in its very structure, embodies a particular concept of history. In Jewish belief, history was open-ended, still in process; in contrast, the Christian notion of history looked backward and saw earlier events as ordered, and given meaning, by their end point and culmination.

When Jesus was born in the Roman province of Judea, there were four languages spoken in the area, a consequence of its complicated history. Classical Hebrew, the language of the sacred books of the Jews, was understood by educated people, especially the priestly caste, but the general population spoke Aramaic. This was a Semitic language close to classical Hebrew—the relationship has been compared with that between Portuguese and Spanish—but different enough to necessitate an Aramaic paraphrase of the sacred texts for use in the synagogue. Aramaic was the language in which Jesus preached to crowds and conversed with his disciples; the last words he spoke in agony on the cross were Aramaic: *Eli, eli, lama sabachthani?* (My God, my God, why have you forsaken me?).

But Judea, like all of the territory conquered by Alexander the Great, had come under Macedonian-Greek rule by the beginning of the second century B.C.E., and many Jews, especially those of the upper and educated classes, had learned Greek, which provided an entry to the new administrative, commercial, and cultural milieux of the Hellenistic empires. Finally, in the last half of the first century B.C.E. Judea became a Roman province, and Latin (the language of the Roman governor and the military establishment) became the language of government. Most cultured Romans, however, knew Greek, and Greek remained the lingua franca of the educated classes all over the huge territory now called the Middle East.

If the disciples of Jesus were to obey his command—"Go into all the world and preach the good news to all creation"—they would have to use Greek outside the Aramaic-speaking world. And it is in Greek that the four Gospels (the word is an Old English translation of the Greek for "good news") were written, probably some forty to sixty years after Jesus' death. They must have been based on the oral teaching of the original disciples, and the first three (selections from two of which are printed here) were clearly designed with an eye to different readerships. The Gospel according to Matthew, for example, has a Jewish public in mind; one of its main concerns is to convince its readers not only that Jesus was the legitimate heir to the throne of the royal house of David but also that Jesus was the king, the Messiah, announced by the Hebrew prophets. Mark, on the other hand, is clearly written with a Gentile audience in mind and pays particular attention to the needs of the Roman reader, translating Aramaic words and even explaining that the courtyard into which the Roman soldiers took Jesus after he was condemned was the place the Romans called the *praetorium*. And the Gospel according to Luke is obviously addressed to cultured Greek readers; it makes very few references to the Hebrew prophecies and is in fact dedicated to a Greek named Theophilos.

These three Gospels contain a central core of identical material that must come from an earlier source now lost (it is known as the Q document). The fourth Gospel, that of John, draws on different sources and also has greater theological density than the other three. The collection known to Christians as the New Testament was formed by combining the four Gospels with another book by Luke, the Acts of the Apostles, which is an account of Paul's missionary journeys to the cities of Greece and Asia Minor. Added to this were letters of Paul and others to the Christian communities in such cities as Corinth, Thessalonica, and Rome and the book called Revelation, a vision of the end of the world and the second coming of Jesus.

There were, of course, many other documents that gave accounts of the life and teaching of Jesus, but this particular collection contained those judged most reliable by the church authorities and was declared canonical some time in the third century. Latin translations of the Greek texts were made for the use of the churches of the Western Roman Empire, but there was no official version until in 382 Pope Damasus commissioned a scholar called Jerome to produce a correct translation. It soon became known as the Vulgate—the "common" or "popular" version. This was the text used and quoted by Augustine, and with some revisions over the centuries, the one that remained in use in the Christian churches of the West through the Middle Ages.

THE CHRISTIAN BIBLE: THE NEW TESTAMENT[1]

Luke 2

[The Birth and Youth of Jesus]

It happened in those days that a decree went forth from Augustus Caesar that all the world[2] should be enrolled in a census. This was the first census, when Quirinius was governor of Syria. And all went to be enrolled, each to his own city. And Joseph also went up from Galilee, from the city of Nazareth, to Judaea, to the city of David which is called Bethlehem, because he was of the house and family of David, to be enrolled with Mary his promised wife, who was pregnant. And it happened that while they were there her time was completed, and she bore a son, her first-born, and she wrapped him in swaddling clothes and laid him in a manger, because there was no room for them in the inn. And there were shepherds in that region, camping out at night and keeping guard over their flock. And an angel of the Lord stood before them, and the glory of the Lord shone about them, and they were afraid with a great fear. The angel said to them: Do not be afraid; behold, I tell you good news, great joy which shall be for all the people; because this day there has been born for you in the city of David a savior who is Christ[3] the Lord. And here is a sign for you; you will find a baby wrapped in swaddling clothes and lying in a manger. And suddenly with the angel there was a multitude of the heavenly host, praising God and saying: Glory to God in the highest and peace on earth among men of good will. And it happened that after the angels had gone off from them into the sky, the shepherds began saying to each other: Let us go to Bethlehem and see this thing which has happened, which the Lord made known to us; and they went, hastening, and found Mary and Joseph, and the baby lying in the manger; and when they had seen, they spread the news about what had been told them concerning this baby. And all who heard wondered at what had been told them by the shepherds; and Mary kept in mind all these sayings as she pondered them in her heart. And the shepherds returned, glorifying and praising God over all they had heard and seen, as it had been told them.

And when eight days were past, for his circumcision, his name was called Jesus, as it was named by the angel[4] before he was conceived in the womb.

And when the days for their purification according to the Law of Moses had been completed, they took him up to Jerusalem to set him before the Lord, as it has been written in the Law of the Lord: Every male child who opens the womb shall be called sacred to the Lord;[5] and to give sacrifice as it is stated in the Law of the Lord, a pair of turtle doves or two young pigeons. And behold, there was a man in Jerusalem whose name was Simeon, and this man was righteous and virtuous and looked forward to the consolation of Israel, and the Holy Spirit was upon him; and it had been prophesied to him by the Holy Spirit that he should not look upon his death until he had looked on the Lord's Anointed. And in the spirit he went into the temple; and as his parents brought in the child Jesus so that they could do for him

---

1. All selections translated by Richmond Lattimore.   2. The Roman Empire. *Augustus Caesar* (63 B.C.E.–14 C.E.): first Roman emperor.   3. Greek word for "anointed." The adjective is used of kings, priests, and the deliverer promised by the prophets.   4. In the Annunciation (Luke 1.31); *Jesus* is a form of the name *Joshua*, which means "he shall save."   5. The firstborn son is believed to belong to God (Exodus 13.2). The purification laws are given in Leviticus 12.

what was customary according to the law, Simeon himself took him in his arms and blessed God and said: Now, Lord, you release your slave, in peace, according to your word; because my eyes have looked on your salvation, what you made ready in the presence of all the peoples; a light for the revelation to the Gentiles,[6] and the glory of your people, Israel. And his father and his mother were in wonder at what was being said about him. And Simeon blessed them and said to Mary his mother: Behold, he is appointed for the fall and the rise[7] of many in Israel; and as a sign which is disputed; and through your soul also will pass the sword; so that the reasonings of many hearts may be revealed. And there was Anna, a prophetess, the daughter of Phanuel, of the tribe of Asher. And she was well advanced in years, having lived with her husband seven years from the time of her maidenhood, and now she was eighty-four years a widow. And she did not leave the temple, serving night and day with fastings and prayers. And at this same time she came near and gave thanks to God and spoke of the child to those who looked forward to the deliverance of Jerusalem.

And when they had done everything according to the Law of the Lord, they went back to Galilee, to their own city, Nazareth.

And the child grew in stature and strength as he was filled with wisdom, and the grace of God was upon him.

Now his parents used to journey every year to Jerusalem for the feast of the Passover. And when he was twelve years old, when they went up according to their custom for the festival and had completed their days there, on their return the boy Jesus stayed behind in Jerusalem, and his parents did not know it. And supposing that he was in their company they went a day's journey and then looked for him among their relatives and friends, and when they did not find him they turned back to Jerusalem in search of him. And it happened that after three days they found him in the temple sitting in the midst of the masters,[8] listening to them and asking them questions. And all who heard him were amazed at his intelligence and his answers. And they were astonished at seeing him, and his mother said to him: Child, why did you do this to us? See, your father and I have been looking for you, in distress. He said to them: But why were you looking for me? Did you not know that I must be in my father's house? And they did not understand what he had said to them. And he returned with them and came to Nazareth, and was in their charge. And his mother kept all his sayings in her heart. And Jesus advanced in wisdom and stature, and in the favor of God and men.

Matthew 5–7

[The Teaching of Jesus; The Sermon on the Mount]

And seeing the multitudes he went up onto the mountain, and when he was seated, his disciples came to him, and he opened his mouth and taught them, saying:

Blessed are the poor in spirit, because theirs is the Kingdom of Heaven.
Blessed are they who sorrow, because they shall be comforted.

---

6. Non-Jews. 7. The Greek word is the one always used of the resurrection of the dead. 8. Teachers, rabbis.

Blessed are the gentle, because they shall inherit the earth.

Blessed are they who are hungry and thirsty for righteousness, because they shall be fed.

Blessed are they who have pity, because they shall be pitied.

Blessed are the pure in heart, because they shall see God.

Blessed are the peacemakers, because they shall be called the sons of God.

Blessed are they who are persecuted for their righteousness, because theirs is the Kingdom of Heaven.

Blessed are you when they shall revile you and persecute you and speak every evil thing of you, lying, because of me. Rejoice and be glad, because your reward in heaven is great; for thus did they persecute the prophets before you.

You are the salt of the earth; but if the salt loses its power, with what shall it be salted?[1] It is good for nothing but to be thrown away and trampled by men. You are the light of the world. A city cannot be hidden when it is set on top of a hill. Nor do men light a lamp and set it under a basket, but they set it on a stand, and it gives its light to all in the house. So let your light shine before men, so that they may see your good works and glorify your father in heaven.

Do not think that I have come to destroy the law and the prophets. I have not come to destroy but to complete. Indeed, I say to you, until the sky and the earth are gone, not one iota[2] or one end of a letter must go from the law, until all is done. He who breaks one of the least of these commandments and teaches men accordingly shall be called the least in the Kingdom of Heaven; he who performs and teaches these commandments shall be called great in the Kingdom of Heaven. For I tell you, if your righteousness is not more abundant than that of the scribes and the Pharisees,[3] you may not enter the Kingdom of Heaven.

You have heard that it was said to the ancients: You shall not murder. He who murders shall be liable to judgment. I say to you that any man who is angry with his brother shall be liable to judgment; and he who says to his brother, fool, shall be liable before the council; and he who says to his brother, sinner, shall be liable to Gehenna.[4] If then you bring your gift to the altar, and there remember that your brother has some grievance against you, leave your gift before the altar, and go first and be reconciled with your brother, and then go and offer your gift. Be quick to be conciliatory with your adversary at law when you are in the street with him, for fear your adversary may turn you over to the judge, and the judge to the officer, and you be thrown into prison. Truly I tell you, you cannot come out of there until you pay the last penny.

You have heard that it has been said: You shall not commit adultery. I tell you that any man who looks at a woman so as to desire her has already committed adultery with her in his heart. If your right eye makes you go

1. That is, how can it regain its savor? 2. The smallest letter in the Greek alphabet, because it is the only letter made with a single stroke. 3. A sect that insisted on strict observance of the Mosaic law. *Scribes:* the official interpreters of the sacred scriptures. 4. Jesus compares the different degrees of punishment (administered by God) for the new sins listed here with the degrees of punishment recognized by Jewish law. The penalties that might be inflicted for murder were death by the sword (a sentence of a local court, "the judgment"), death by stoning (the sentence of a higher court, "the council"), and the burning of the criminal's body in the place where refuse was thrown, Gehenna, which is hence used as a name for hell.

amiss, take it out and cast it from you; it is better that one part of you should be lost instead of your whole body being cast into Gehenna. And if your right hand makes you go amiss, cut it off and cast it from you; it is better that one part of you should be lost instead of your whole body going to Gehenna. It has been said: If a man puts away his wife, let him give her a contract of divorce. I tell you that any man who puts away his wife, except for the reason of harlotry, is making her the victim of adultery; and any man who marries a wife who has been divorced is committing adultery. Again, you have heard that it has been said to the ancients: You shall not swear falsely, but you shall make good your oaths to the Lord. I tell you not to swear at all: not by heaven, because it is the throne of God; not by the earth, because it is the footstool for his feet; not by Jerusalem, because it is the city of the great king; not by your own head, because you cannot make one hair of it white or black. Let your speech be yes yes, no no; more than that comes from the evil one.

You have heard that it has been said: An eye for an eye and a tooth for a tooth. I tell you not to resist the wicked man, but if one strikes you on the right cheek, turn the other one to him also; and if a man wishes to go to law with you and take your tunic, give him your cloak also, and if one makes you his porter for a mile, go with him for two. Give to him who asks, and do not turn away one who wishes to borrow from you. You have heard that it has been said: You shall love your neighbor and hate your enemy. I tell you, love your enemies and pray for those who persecute you, so that you may be sons of your father who is in heaven, because he makes his sun rise on the evil and the good, and rains on the just and the unjust. For if you love those who love you, what reward do you have? Do not even the tax collectors do the same? And if you greet only your brothers, what do you do that is more than others do? Do not even the pagans do the same? Be perfect as your father in heaven is perfect.

Take care not to practice your righteousness publicly before men so as to be seen by them; if you do, you shall have no recompense from your father in heaven. Then when you do charity, do not have a trumpet blown before you, as the hypocrites do in the synagogues and the streets, so that men may think well of them. Truly I tell you, they have their due reward. But when you do charity, let your left hand not know what your right hand is doing, so that your charity may be in secret; and your father, who sees what is secret, will reward you. And when you pray, you must not be like the hypocrites, who love to stand up in the synagogues and the corners of the squares to pray, so that they may be seen by men. Truly I tell you, they have their due reward. But when you pray, go into your inner room and close the door and pray to your father, who is in secret; and your father, who sees what is secret, will reward you. When you pray, do not babble as the pagans do; for they think that by saying much they will be heard. Do not then be like them; for your father knows what you need before you ask him. Pray thus, then: Our father in heaven, may your name be hallowed, may your kingdom come, may your will be done, as in heaven, so upon earth. Give us today our sufficient bread, and forgive us our debts, as we also have forgiven our debtors. And do not bring us into temptation, but deliver us from evil. For if you forgive men their offenses, your heavenly father will forgive you; but if you do not forgive men, neither will your father forgive you your offenses. And when you fast, do not scowl like the hypocrites; for they make ugly faces so that men can see that they are fasting. Truly I tell you, they have their due reward. But when you fast, anoint your head and wash your face, so that you may not show as fasting to men, but to your father, in secret; and your father, who sees what is secret, will reward you.

Do not store up your treasures on earth, where the moth and rust destroy them, and where burglars dig through and steal them; but store up your treasures in heaven, where neither moth nor rust destroys them, and where burglars do not dig through[5] or steal; for where your treasure is, there also will be your heart. The lamp of the body is the eye. Thus if your eye is clear, your whole body is full of light; but if your eye is soiled, your whole body is dark. If the light in you is darkness, how dark it is. No man can serve two masters. For either he will hate the one and love the other, or he will cling to one and despise the other; you cannot serve God and mammon.[6] Therefore I tell you, do not take thought for your life, what you will eat, or for your body, what you will wear. Is not your life more than its food and your body more than its clothing? Consider the birds of the sky, that they do not sow or harvest or collect for their granaries, and your heavenly father feeds them. Are you not preferred above them? Which of you by taking thought can add one cubit to his growth? And why do you take thought about clothing? Study the lilies in the field, how they grow. They do not toil or spin; yet I tell you, not even Solomon in all his glory was clothed like one of these. But if God so clothes the grass of the field, which grows today and tomorrow is thrown in the oven, will he not much more clothe you, you men of little faith? Do not then worry and say: What shall we eat? Or: What shall we drink? Or: What shall we wear? For all this the Gentiles study. Your father in heaven knows that you need all these things. But seek out first his kingdom and his justice, and all these things shall be given to you. Do not then take thought of tomorrow; tomorrow will take care of itself. Sufficient to the day is its own evil.

Do not judge, so you may not be judged. You shall be judged by that judgment by which you judge, and your measure will be made by the measure by which you measure. Why do you look at the straw which is in the eye of your brother, and not see the log which is in your eye? Or how will you say to your brother: Let me take the straw out of your eye, and behold, the log is in your eye. You hypocrite, first take the log out of your eye, and then you will see to take the straw out of the eye of your brother. Do not give what is sacred to the dogs, and do not cast your pearls before swine, lest they trample them under their feet and turn and rend you. Ask, and it shall be given you; seek, and you shall find; knock, and the door will be opened for you. Everyone who asks receives, and he who seeks finds, and for him who knocks the door will be opened. Or what man is there among you, whose son shall ask him for bread, that will give him a stone? Or ask him for fish, that will give him a snake? If then you, who are corrupt, know how to give good gifts to your children, by how much more your father who is in heaven will give good

---

5. House walls were often made of mud brick, and burglars could dig through them.　6. Material wealth (from the Aramaic word for "riches").

things to those who ask him. Whatever you wish men to do to you, so do to them. For this is the law and the prophets.

Go in through the narrow gate; because wide and spacious is the road that leads to destruction, and there are many who go in through it; because narrow is the gate and cramped the road that leads to life, and few are they who find it. Beware of the false prophets, who come to you in sheep's clothing, but inside they are ravening wolves. From their fruits you will know them. Do men gather grapes from thorns or figs from thistles? Thus every good tree produces good fruits, but the rotten tree produces bad fruits. A good tree cannot bear bad fruits, and a rotten tree cannot bear good fruits. Every tree that does not produce good fruit is cut out and thrown in the fire. So from their fruits you will know them. Not everyone who says to me Lord Lord will come into the Kingdom of Heaven, but he who does the will of my father in heaven. Many will say to me on that day: Lord, Lord, did we not prophesy in your name, and in your name did we not cast out demons, and in your name did we not assume great powers? And then I shall admit to them: I never knew you. Go from me, for you do what is against the law.

Every man who hears what I say and does what I say shall be like the prudent man who built his house upon the rock. And the rain fell and the rivers came and the winds blew and dashed against that house, and it did not fall, for it was founded upon the rock. And every man who hears what I say and does not do what I say will be like the reckless man who built his house on the sand. And the rain fell and the rivers came and the winds blew and battered that house, and it fell, and that was a great fall.

And it happened that when Jesus had ended these words, the multitudes were astonished at his teaching, for he taught them as one who has authority, and not like their own scribes.

Luke 15

[The Teaching of Jesus; Parables]

All the tax collectors and the sinners kept coming around him, to listen to him. And the Pharisees and the scribes muttered, saying: This man receives sinners and eats with them. But he told them this parable, saying: Which man among you who has a hundred sheep and has lost one of them will not leave the ninety-nine in the wilds and go after the lost one until he finds it? And when he does find it, he sets it on his shoulders, rejoicing, and goes to his house and invites in his friends and his neighbors, saying to them: Rejoice with me, because I found my sheep which was lost. I tell you that thus there will be joy in heaven over one sinner who repents, rather than over ninety-nine righteous ones who have no need of repentance. Or what woman who has ten drachmas, if she loses one drachma, does not light the lamp and sweep the house and search diligently until she finds it? And finding it she invites in her friends and neighbors, saying: Rejoice with me, because I found the drachma I lost. Such, I tell you, is the joy among the angels of God over one sinner who repents.

And he said: There was a man who had two sons. And the younger of them said to his father: Father, give me my appropriate share of the property. And the father divided his substance between them. And not many days afterward the younger son gathered everything together and left the country for a distant land, and there he squandered his substance in riotous living. And after he had spent everything, there was a severe famine in that country, and he began to be in need. And he went and attached himself to one of the citizens of that country, who sent him out into the fields to feed the pigs. And he longed to be nourished on the nuts that the pigs ate, and no one would give to him. And he went and said to himself: How many hired servants of my father have plenty of bread while I am dying of hunger here. I will rise up and go to my father and say to him: Father, I have sinned against heaven and in your sight, I am no longer worthy to be called your son. Make me like one of your hired servants. And he rose up and went to his father. And when he was still a long way off, his father saw him and was moved and ran and fell on his neck and kissed him. The son said to him: Father, I have sinned against heaven and in your sight, I am no longer worthy to be called your son. But his father said to his slaves: Quick, bring the best clothing and put it on him, and have a ring for his hand and shoes for his feet, and bring the fatted calf, slaughter him, and let us eat and make merry because this man, my son, was a dead man and came to life. He was lost and he has been found. And they began to make merry. His older son was out on the estate, and as he came nearer to the house he heard music and dancing, and he called over one of the servants and asked what was going on. He told him: Your brother is here, and your father slaughtered the fatted calf, because he got him back in good health. He was angry and did not want to go in. But his father came out and entreated him. But he answered and said to his father: Look, all these years I have been your slave and never neglected an order of yours, but you never gave me a kid so that I could make merry with my friends. But when this son of yours comes back, the one who ate up your livelihood in the company of whores, you slaughtered the fatted calf for him. But he said to him: My child, you are always with me, and all that is mine is yours; but we had to make merry and rejoice, because your brother was a dead man and came to life. He was lost and has been found.

From Matthew 13

[*Why Jesus Teaches in Parables*]

On that day Jesus went out of the house and sat beside the sea; and a great multitude gathered before him, so that he went aboard a ship and sat there, and all the multitude stood on the shore. And he talked to them, speaking mostly in parables: Behold, a sower went out to sow. And as he sowed, some of the grain fell beside the way, and birds came and ate it. Some fell on stony ground where there was not much soil, and it shot up quickly because there was no depth of soil, but when the sun came up it was parched, and because it had no roots it dried away. Some fell among thorns, and the thorns grew up and stifled it. But some fell upon the good soil and bore fruit, some a hundredfold, some sixtyfold, some thirtyfold. He who has ears, let him hear. Then his disciples came to him and said: Why do you talk to them in parables? He answered them and said: Because it is given to you to understand the secrets of the Kingdom of Heaven, but to them it is not given. When a man has, he shall be given, and it will be more than he needs; but when he has not, even what he has shall be taken away from him. Therefore I talk to them in parables, because they have sight but do not see, and hearing but do not hear or understand. And for them is fulfilled the prophecy of Isaiah,[1] saying: With your hearing you shall hear and not understand, and you shall use your sight and look but not see. For the heart of this people is stiffened, and they hear with difficulty, and they have closed their eyes, so that they may never see with their eyes, or hear with their ears and with their hearts understand and turn back, so that I can heal them.

Blessed are your eyes because they see, and your ears because they hear. Truly I tell you that many prophets and good men have longed to see what you see, and not seen it, and to hear what you hear, and not heard it. Hear, then, the parable of the sower. To every man who hears the word of the Kingdom and does not understand it, the evil one comes and seizes what has been sown in his heart. This is the seed sown by the way. The seed sown on the stony ground is the man who hears the word and immediately accepts it with joy; but he has no root in himself, and he is a man of the moment, and when there comes affliction and persecution, because of the word, he does not stand fast. The seed sown among thorns is the man who hears the word, and concern for the world and the beguilement of riches stifle the word, and he bears no fruit. And the seed sown on the good soil is the man who hears the word and understands it, who bears fruit and makes it, one a hundredfold, one sixtyfold, and one thirtyfold.

He set before them another parable, saying: The Kingdom of Heaven is like a man who sowed good seed in his field. And while the people were asleep, his enemy came and sowed darnel in with the grain, and went away. When the plants grew and produced a crop, the darnel was seen. Then the slaves of the master came to him and said: Master, did you not sow good grain in your field? Where does the darnel[2] come from? He said to them: A man who is my enemy did it. His slaves said: Do you wish us to go out and gather it? But he said: No, for fear that when you gather the darnel you may pull up the grain with it. Let them both grow until harvest time, and in the time of harvest I shall say to the harvesters: First gather the darnel, and bind it in sheaves for burning, but store the grain in my granary.

He set before them another parable, saying: The Kingdom of Heaven is like a grain of mustard, which a man took and sowed in his field; which is the smallest of all seeds, but when it grows, it is the largest of the greens and grows into a tree, so that the birds of the air come and nest in its branches.

He told them another parable: The Kingdom of Heaven is like leaven, which a woman took and buried in three measures of dough, so that it all rose.

All this Jesus told the multitudes in parables, and he did not talk to them except in parables; so as to fulfill the word spoken by the prophet, saying: I will open my mouth in parables, and pour out what has been hidden since the creation.

* * *

1. See Isaiah 6.9–10. 2. A grassy kind of weed.

From Matthew 26

[*The Betrayal of Jesus*]

And at that time one of the twelve, he who was called Judas Iscariot, went to the high priests and said: What are you willing to give me if I betray him to you? And they paid him thirty pieces of silver. And from that time he looked for an opportunity to betray him.

On the first day of the feast of unleavened bread,[1] his disciples came to Jesus and said: Where do you wish us to make preparations for you to eat the feast of the Passover? He said: Go to the city, to the house of a certain man, and say to him: The teacher says: My time is near. I shall keep the Passover at your house, with my disciples. And his disciples did as Jesus instructed them, and made ready the Passover. When it was evening, he took his place at dinner with the twelve disciples. And as they were eating he said: Truly I tell you that one of you will betray me. They were bitterly hurt and began each one to say: Surely it is not I, Lord? He answered and said: The one who dips his hand in the dish with me, he is the one who will betray me. The son of man goes his way as it has been written for him to do, but woe to that man through whom the son of man is betrayed. It would have been well for that man if he had never been born. Judas, who had betrayed him, answered and said: Master, it is not I? Jesus said to him: It is you who said it. As they ate, Jesus took a loaf of bread, and blessed it, and broke it, and gave it to his disciples, and said: Take it; eat it; this is my body. And he took a cup and gave thanks and gave it to them, saying: Drink from it, all; for this is my blood, of the covenant,[2] which is shed for the sake of many, for the remission of sins. But I tell you, from now on I shall not drink of this produce of the vine, until that day when I drink it with you, new wine, in the kingdom of my father.

And they sang the hymn and went out to the Mount of Olives. Then Jesus said to them: All of you will be made to fail me in the course of this night. For it is written:[3] I will strike the shepherd, and the sheep of his flock will be scattered. But after my resurrection I will lead the way for you into Galilee. Peter spoke forth and said: Though all the others fail you, I will never fail you. Jesus said to him: Truly I tell you that on this night before the cock crows you will disown me three times. Peter said to him: Even if I must die with you, I will never disown you. And so spoke all the disciples.

Then Jesus went with them to a place called Gethsemane; and he said to his disciples: Sit down here, while I go over there and pray. He took with him Peter and the two sons of Zebedee;[4] and then he was in pain and distress. And he said to them: My soul is in anguish to the point of death. Stay here and keep watch with me. Then he went a little farther, and threw himself down on his face, and said in prayer: Father, if it is possible, let this cup pass me by; except only, let it be not as I wish, but as you wish. Then he went back to his disciples and found them asleep, and said to Peter: Are you not

1. Passover, held in remembrance of the delivery of the Jews from captivity in Egypt (Exodus 1–12).
2. The Greek word can mean either "agreement, arrangement" (covenant) or "will" (hence "the new testament" in the King James translation). Jesus compares himself to the lamb that was killed at the Passover as a sign of the covenant between God and the Jews. He thus places himself within the Jewish historical tradition even as he depicts the legacy of his sacrifice as the renewal and completion of that tradition.
3. In Zechariah 13.7.   4. James and John.

then strong enough to keep watch with me for a single hour? Be wakeful, and pray that you may not be brought to the test. The spirit is eager, but the flesh is weak. Again a second time he went off and prayed, saying: Father, if it is not possible for this cup to pass me by, but I must drink it, let your will be done. Then he came back and again found them sleeping, for their eyes were heavy; and leaving them he went back and prayed a third time, saying the same words as before. Then he came back to the disciples and said to them: So you are still asleep, and resting. Behold, the hour is near, and the son of man is betrayed into the hands of sinners. Rise up, let us go; see, my betrayer is near.

And while he was still speaking, behold, Judas came, one of the twelve, and with him a great crowd, with swords and clubs, from the high priests and the elders of the people. And he who betrayed him told them the signal, saying: The one I kiss will be the man. Seize him. And at once he came up to Jesus and said: Hail, master; and kissed him. Jesus said to him: My friend, why are you here? Then they came and laid hands on Jesus and bound him. And behold, one⁵ of those who were with Jesus put out his hand and drew his sword, and struck the slave of the high priest and took off his ear. Then Jesus said: Put away your sword where it belongs; for all who take up the sword shall die by the sword. Or do you not believe that I have the power to call upon my father, and he will at once send more than twelve legions⁶ of angels? But then, how to fulfill what has been written, that these things must be. At that time Jesus said to the multitude: You come out to arrest me with swords and clubs as if I were a highwayman? Day by day I sat in the temple, teaching, and you did not seize me.

But all this took place so that what was written by the prophets should be fulfilled.

At that time all his disciples left him and fled away.

But they who had seized Jesus brought him to the house of Caiaphas the high priest, where the scribes and elders were assembled. But Peter followed him at a distance as far as the courtyard of the high priest, and went inside and sat with the servingmen, to watch the event. And the high priests and the entire council were looking for some false evidence against Jesus, so that they might have him killed, and they could find none, though many false witnesses came forward. But later two came forward and spoke, saying: This man said this: I am able to tear down the temple of God and rebuild it within three days. Then the high priest stood up and said to him: Have you no answer? What is the testimony these bring against you? But Jesus remained silent. And the high priest said to him: I charge you by the living God that you tell us whether you are the Christ, the son of God. Jesus said to him: It is you who said it. But now I say to you, presently you shall see the son of man sitting on the right of the power and walking upon the clouds of the sky. Then the priest rent his clothing, saying: He has blasphemed. Why do we still need witnesses? Behold, you have heard the blasphemy. What is your decision? They answered and said: He has deserved death. Then they spat in his face and struck him with their fists and beat him, saying: Tell us, Christ, by prophecy, who hit you?

But Peter was sitting outside in the courtyard, and a serving girl came up

---

5. According to John 18.10, this was Peter.   6. A legion was a Roman military formation of six thousand soldiers.

to him and said: You also were with Jesus the Galilaean. But he denied it before them all, saying: I do not know what you mean. And as he went out to the gate another girl saw him and said to those who were there: This man was with Jesus the Nazarene. And again he denied it, with an oath, saying: I do not know the man. After a little those who were standing by came up to Peter and said: Truly you are one of them, for your way of speaking makes it clear. Then he began to swear with many oaths, saying: I do not know the man. And thereupon the cock crew. And Peter remembered the words of Jesus when he said: Before the cock crows you will disown me three times. And he went out and wept bitterly.

Matthew 27

[The Trial and Crucifixion of Jesus]

When morning came, all the high priests and elders of the people held a meeting against Jesus, to have him killed. And they bound him and took him away and gave him over to Pilate the governor.[1]

Then when Judas, who had betrayed him, saw that he had been condemned, he repented and proffered the thirty pieces of silver back to the high priests and the elders, saying: I did wrong to betray innocent blood. They said: What is that to us? You look to it. And he threw down the silver pieces in the temple and went away, and when he was alone he hanged himself. The high priests took up the silver pieces and said: We cannot put them in the treasury, since it is blood money. Then they took counsel together and with the money they bought the potter's field[2] to bury strangers in. Therefore that field has been called the Field of Blood, to this day. Then was fulfilled the word spoken by Jeremiah the prophet,[3] saying: I took the thirty pieces of silver, the price of him on whom a price was set, whom they priced from among the sons of Israel, and I gave the money for the field of the potter, as my Lord commanded me.

Now Jesus stood before the governor, and the governor questioned him, saying: Are you the King of the Jews? Jesus answered: It is you who say it. And while he was being accused by the high priests and the elders he made no answer. Then Pilate said to him: Do you not hear all their testimony against you? And he made no answer to a single word, so that the governor was greatly amazed.

For the festival, the governor was accustomed to release one prisoner for the multitude, whichever one they wished. And they had at that time a notorious man, who was called Barabbas.[4] Now as they were assembled Pilate said to them: Which one do you wish me to release for you, Barabbas, or Jesus, who is called Christ? For he knew that it was through malice that they had turned him over. Now as he was sitting on the platform, his wife sent him a message, saying: Let there be nothing between you and this just man,

---

1. Pilate's official title was procurator of the province of Judea. Roman policy was to allow the Jews as much independence as possible, especially in religious matters, but only the Roman authorities could impose a death sentence. 2. A field that had been dug for clay (used for making pottery), and thus was of little agricultural use. 3. Zechariah 11.12–13. 4. Under sentence of death for sedition and murder (Luke 23.19).

for I have suffered much today because of a dream about him. But the high priests and the elders persuaded the crowd to ask for Barabbas and destroy Jesus. Then the governor spoke forth and said to them: Which of the two shall I give you? They answered: Barabbas. Pilate said to them: What then shall I do with Jesus, who is called Christ? They all said: Let him be crucified.[5] But Pilate said: Why? What harm has he done? But they screamed all the more, saying: Let him be crucified. And Pilate, seeing that he was doing no good and that the disorder was growing, took water and washed his hands before the crowd, saying: I am innocent of the blood of this man. You see to it. And all the people answered and said: His blood is upon us and upon our children. Then Pilate gave them Barabbas, but he had Jesus flogged,[6] and gave him over to be crucified.

Then the soldiers of the governor took Jesus to the residence, and drew up all their battalion around him. And they stripped him and put a red mantle about him, and wove a wreath of thorns and put it on his head, and put a reed[7] in his right hand, and knelt before him and mocked him, saying: Hail, King of the Jews. And they spat upon him and took the reed and beat him on the head. And after they had mocked him, they took off the mantle and put his own clothes on him, and led him away to be crucified. And as they went out they found a man of Cyrene, named Simon. They impressed him[8] for carrying the cross.

Then they came to a place called Golgotha, which means the place of the skull, and gave him wine mixed with gall to drink. When he tasted it he would not drink it. Then they crucified him, and divided up his clothes, casting lots, and sat there and watched him. Over his head they put the label giving the charge against him, where it was written: This is Jesus, the King of the Jews. Then there were crucified with him two robbers, one on his right and one on his left. And those who passed by blasphemed against him, wagging their heads, and saying: You who tear down the temple and rebuild it in three days, save yourself, and come down from the cross, if you are the son of God. So too the high priests, mocking him along with the scribes and the elders, said: He saved others, he cannot save himself. He is King of Israel, let him come down from the cross and we will believe in him. He trusted in God, let him save him now, if he will; for he said: I am the son of God. And the robbers who were crucified with him spoke abusively to him in the same way.

But from the sixth hour there was darkness over all the earth until the ninth hour. But about the ninth hour Jesus cried out in a great voice, saying: *Elei elei lema sabachthanei?* Which is: My God, my God, why have you forsaken me?[9] But some of those who were standing there heard and said: This man calls to Elijah. And at once one of them ran and took a sponge, soaked it in vinegar and put it on the end of a reed, and gave it to him to drink. But the rest said: Let us see if Elijah comes to save him.

Then Jesus cried out again in a great voice, and gave up his life. And behold, the veil of the temple[1] was split in two from top to bottom, and the earth was shaken, and the rocks were split, and the tombs opened and many bodies of the holy sleepers rose up; and after his resurrection they came out

---

5. The regular Roman punishment for sedition. **6.** A routine part of the punishment. **7.** To represent the king's scepter. **8.** Pressed him into service. **9.** The opening verse of Psalm 22. Jesus spoke Aramaic, a language closely related to Hebrew. **1.** The curtain that screened off the holy of holies.

of their tombs and went into the holy city, and were seen by many. But the company commander and those with him who kept guard over Jesus, when they saw the earthquake and the things that happened, were greatly afraid, saying: In truth this was the son of God. And there were many women watching from a distance there, who had followed Jesus from Galilee, waiting on him. Among them were Mary the Magdalene, and Mary the mother of James and Joseph, and the mother of the sons of Zebedee.

When it was evening, there came a rich man of Arimathaea, Joseph by name, who also had been a disciple of Jesus. This man went to Pilate and asked for the body of Jesus. Then Pilate ordered that it be given up to him. And Joseph took the body and wrapped it in clean linen, and laid it in his new tomb, which he had cut in the rock, and rolled a great stone before the door of the tomb, and went away. But Mary the Magdalene and the other Mary were there, sitting before the tomb. On the next day, which is the day after the Day of Preparation, the high priests and the Pharisees gathered in the presence of Pilate, and said: Lord, we have remembered how that impostor said while he was still alive: After three days I shall rise up. Give orders, then, that the tomb be secured until after the third day, for fear his disciples may come and steal him away and say to the people: He rose from the dead. And that will be the ultimate deception, worse than the former one. Pilate said to them: You have a guard. Go and secure it as best you can. And they went and secured the tomb, sealing it with the help of the guard.

Matthew 28

[The Resurrection]

Late on the sabbath, as the light grew toward the first day after the sabbath, Mary the Magdalene and the other Mary came to visit the tomb. And behold, there was a great earthquake, for the angel of the Lord came down from heaven and approached the stone and rolled it away and was sitting on it. His look was like lightning, and his clothing white as snow. And those who were on guard were shaken with fear of him and became like dead men. But the angel spoke forth and said to the women: Do not you fear; for I know that you look for Jesus, who was crucified. He is not here. For he rose up, and he said. Come here, and look at the place where he lay. Then go quickly and tell his disciples that he has risen from the dead, and behold, he goes before you into Galilee. There you will see him. See; I have told you. And quickly leaving the tomb, in fear and great joy, they ran to tell the news to his disciples. And behold, Jesus met them, saying: I give you greeting. They came up to him and took his feet and worshipped him. Then Jesus said to them: Do not fear. Go and tell my brothers to go into Galilee, and there they will see me. And as they went on their way, behold, some of the guards went into the city and reported to the high priests all that had happened. And they met with the elders and took counsel together, and gave the soldiers a quantity of money, saying: Say that the disciples came in the night and stole him away while we were sleeping. And if this is heard in the house of the governor, we shall reason with him, and make it so that you have nothing to fear. And they took the money and did as they were instructed. And this is the story that has been spread about among the Jews, to this day.

Then the eleven disciples went on into Galilee, to the mountain where Jesus had given them instructions to go; and when they saw him, they worshipped him; but some doubted. And Jesus came up to them and talked with them, saying: All authority has been given to me, in heaven and on earth. Go out, therefore, and instruct all the nations, baptizing them in the name of the Father and the Son and the Holy Spirit, teaching them to observe all that I have taught you. And behold, I am with you, all the days until the end of the world.

LUCIAN
120?–190? C.E.

Satirist, rhetorician, parodist, creator of memorable fiction, Lucian brought his ironic sensibility to bear on the pretensions of people in his contemporary world and equally on the Greek traditions—historical, philosophic, religious, and literary—extending all the way back to Homer. Neither the gods on Olympus nor philosophers disputing the nature of reality were immune to his biting wit. Mixing together prose and poetry, dialogue and narrative, bits from all the established genres (that is, epic, tragedy, comedy, rhetoric, history, the philosophic dialogue), Lucian created new forms and renewed Greek literature in a late age even while he made affectionate fun of it. The eighty or so works that have survived under his name exerted a considerable influence in the Renaissance and after, both as vehicles for the transmission of Greek culture and as literary creations in their own right. The great Renaissance humanist Erasmus taught himself Greek by reading Lucian, and his *The Praise of Folly* (below, pp. 0000–0000) is a virtual re-creation of a Lucianic rhetorical satire. There is a direct line from Lucian's fictional travel tale *A True Story* to Thomas More's *Utopia*, Ariosto's *Orlando Furioso* (below, pp. 0000–0000), and Jonathan Swift's *Gulliver's Travels* (vol. 2, pp. 292–00). With its account of a trip to the Moon, *A True Story* also looks ahead to modern science fiction. In more recent times, however, Lucian has been relegated to the margins of literature or considered outside the canon. He has often been ignored as late and therefore decadent, too trivial to be included in the company of the giants of classical literature and thought, and beneath the established forms of "high" literature. These judgments are unfair. Modern solemnizers have just been fooled by the broadness of Lucian's grin into thinking that there is nothing behind it.

Lucian lived when the Roman Empire was at its height, but he wrote in Greek, not Latin. Although the empire unified a vast area politically, it remained culturally diverse. As the official language of government, Latin overrode local linguistic differences, especially in the western half of the empire, and in Italy itself a strong Latin literary tradition had developed. In the east, the situation was more complicated. From mainland Greece across the Aegean Sea to the coast and inland of Asia Minor, the great cities had a proud Greek heritage, which had been strengthened and spread through the Hellenistic culture inaugurated by the conquests of Alexander the Great (356–323 B.C.E.). Thus, in the eastern empire Greek was the language of the educated and political elite, and to write and speak in it was a mark of cultural prestige. It was here that important works—particularly rhetoric and prose narrative—were composed in Greek during the resurgence of Greek culture known as the Second Sophistic (late first to early third century C.E.; the name connects it to the Sophists of the fifth and fourth centuries B.C.E.). Lucian was one of the most remarkable writers in this movement.

What we can infer of Lucian's life (mainly from what he says in his fictions) illustrates the complexity of cultural identity in an Asia ruled by Rome. He was born in the Syrian city of Samosata, on the west bank of the Euphrates River. He probably grew up speaking not Greek but a Semitic language, Aramaic, most likely the dialect of it known as Syriac. For a man of his talents, however, the way to riches and high standing led through the Greek language and rhetoric. So Lucian indicates elaborately in a work titled *The Dream, or Lucian's Biography*. On the night after a disastrous first day of apprenticeship to his sculptor uncle, he says, two women appeared to him in a dream and disputed over him. Each urged him to become her disciple. Sculpture—mannish, with unkempt hair and calloused hands, covered with marble dust, and speaking with bad grammar—offered him strong muscles, artistic fame, and a settled life with no need to travel outside his native land. The more patrician Education promised him the full range of knowledge, the admiration of the rich and wellborn, clothing as fine as her own, instant recognition when he traveled abroad, and political influence at home through his eloquence. Lucian, of course, chose Education and the career as a professional rhetorician that she offered. But the dream captures nicely the class distinction between the two careers, and the social and political prestige that access to Greek culture entailed.

So Lucian the barbarian (in the Hellenic sense of one who did not know Greek) learned Greek and somehow absorbed the whole of its literature. He then set about fitting into the established structures supported by Roman rule, first putting his oratorical skills to practical use in the law courts and then becoming a professional rhetorician. Being a professional meant joining the circuit of traveling orators and giving public declamations, which consisted of a short prelude or rhetorical showpiece followed by a speech on a more weighty topic. Lucian's works include a number of such preludes, such as his speech in praise of a housefly and the *Dream*, evidently composed for a performance when Lucian visited his home town of Samosata as a local boy who had made good. The widespread interest in rhetoric and the public adulation it attracted are suggested in the *Dream* when Education promises Lucian, "If you give a speech, the common people will listen with their mouths agape, marveling and congratulating you on the power of your words and your father on his good fortune." Lucian's professional travels took him through the Ionian cities of Asia Minor, to mainland Greece, to Italy, and as far as Gaul, where he settled for some time in a (by his account) highly paid post as teacher of rhetoric. Around 160 C.E., however, at the age of forty, he shifted his career and probably went to live in Athens, which still, under Roman domination, enjoyed enormous prestige as the cradle of Greek culture. It is to this period that his great satirical and parodic works, including *A True Story*, belong. We last hear of him as holding an administrative position in the retinue of the Roman governor of Egypt—the kind of job given as patronage by influential officials. The post marks how far this provincial had moved, from the cultural margins into the center of imperial power, by means of Greek learning.

A TRUE STORY

Lucian's most famous and influential work, *A True Story* brilliantly parodies several kinds of narrative, such as earlier travel stories that purported to be true but retailed all kinds of fanciful descriptions and anecdotes. Another target is Herodotus, the "Father of History" (ca. 480–430/425? B.C.E.), who traveled around the eastern Mediterranean gathering information about the past and about contemporary geography. His descriptions of places at or beyond the fringes of the known world often include exotic giant or hybrid animals. Lucian condemns him for lying even while imitating such accounts as well as Herodotus's ethnographic descriptions of foreign peoples. Similarly, in the prologue of *A True Story* Lucian's narrator condemns Odysseus as a liar for the famous tales of his deep-sea adventures that he tells to the Phaeacians in books 9–12 of the *Odyssey*, which in that poem purport to be true. As we might expect, several incidents in *A True Story* allude to those tales. The narrator himself visits Calypso, bringing her a love note from Odysseus; the account of the islands of the Blest and the Damned recalls the visit to the dead in book 11 of the *Odyssey*; the island with streams of wine evokes the Lotus Eaters; and so on. And finally there must have been sea yarns and other travel tales circulating orally and in writing. The episode in the belly of the whale raises a strong suspicion that Lucian knew the biblical story of Jonah, perhaps in oral form.

Here and in many of Lucian's works, such parodies and recombinations of traditional forms challenge the authority of the Greek literary and cultural tradition, identified as it was with the values and outlook of the elite in the Greek east. They thus imply an alternative, more popular sensibility. At the same time, they also renew and reproduce the works of which they make fun; in this way, Lucian helped keep his Hellenized culture in touch with the past with which it proudly identified and to transmit that past to future ages. Another effect of the parody in *A True Story* is to raise the question of truth and fiction in narrative—even in those narratives that pretend to be true. Lucian's narrator-hero raises this issue right at the beginning when he claims that he will be engaging in "honest lying: The one and only truth you'll hear from me is that I *am* lying." This is, of course, a self-undermining statement: If he says that he is lying, can we be sure that he really is? Or is this statement too a lie? The title, *A True Story*, by itself raises these complicated ironies; and by presenting us with a thoroughly unreliable narrator, Lucian suggests that the fictions we enjoy, such as this work and all the works it parodies, escape our normal categories of truth and falsehood.

A True Story taps into the human impulse to wonder about what lies beyond the known world. Nowadays scientists are rapidly accumulating an enormous quantity of factual knowledge about what lies beyond Earth and beyond this solar system. This information will bring us into contact with what is truly other, what exists without any reference to human beings. But traditionally—and this is as true of Homer as it is of Lucian—works that imagine worlds beyond our own arrange them with reference to human institutions and experience. Such worlds may contrast with our own, by being either utopian or savage. Or they may reproduce human civilization both in its productive aspects and in its evil impulses, and thereby clarify our own culture for us. Or they may show alien beings engaged in activities similar to those of humans, but with implements adapted to the foreign setting. The Moonmen's helmets are made of beans, for example, and the plain on which they fight the Sunmen is woven from spiderwebs. In the royal palace on the moon is a well with a giant mirror suspended over it, through which life on Earth can be viewed in minutest detail. This arrangement is Lucian's image for what *A True Story* does: it presents our own world reflected in distant, imaginary ones.

PRONOUNCING GLOSSARY

The following list uses common English syllables and stress accents to provide rough equivalents of selected words whose pronunciation may be unfamiliar to the general reader.

Cinyras: *kin-ee'-ras*

Cnidus: *k-nee'-dus*

Ctesias: *ktay'-sias*

Ctesiochus: *ktay-see'-o-kus*

Diogenes: *dai-o'-jen-eez*

Empedocles: *em-ped'-o-kleez*

Endymion: *en-di'-mee-on*

Hippocrates: *hip-po'-cra-teez*

Nauplius: *now'-plee-us*

Palamedes: *pal-a-mee'-deez*

Phaëthon: *fa-ee'-thon*

Rhadamanthus: *ra-da-man'-thus*

Salmoneus: *sal-mon-ews'*

Scintharus: *skin'-tha-rus*

Zenodotus: *ze-no'-do-tus*

A True Story[1]

FROM PART I

No athlete or body-building enthusiast thinks only of exercising and being in condition. He thinks also of relaxing when the occasion calls for it and, as a matter of fact, he considers this the most important part of training. In my opinion the same holds for book enthusiasts: after poring over a lot of serious works, they ought give the mind a rest to get it into even better shape for the next workout. The most suitable way for them to spend the interval is with light, pleasant reading which, instead of merely entertaining, furnishes some intellectual fare as well—and this I think they'll agree is true of the present work.

It is a work that will appeal to them not only because of the exotic subject matter, the amusing plot, and the way I've told all sorts of lies with an absolutely straight face, but because I've included comic allusions to all our noted poets, historians, and philosophers of old who have written so many fabulous tall stories. I don't need to name names: you'll recognize them yourselves as you read along. Ctesias of Cnidus, the son of Ctesiochus, has written things about India and the Indians that he neither saw himself nor heard from anyone who had any respect for the truth. Iambulus[2] has written a lot of unbelievable stuff about the ocean; everyone knows he made it all up, yet, for all that, he has put together an amusing account. Lots of other writers have shown a preference for the same technique: under the guise of reporting their travels abroad they spin yarns of huge monsters, savage tribes, and strange ways of life. The arch-exponent of, and model for, this sort of tomfoolery is Homer's Odysseus telling the court of Alcinous about a bag with the winds in it, one-eyed giants, cannibals, savages, even many-headed monsters and magic drugs that change shipmates into swine—with one such story after another he had those simple-minded Phaeacians goggle-eyed.[3]

Now, I've read all the practitioners of this art and I've never been very hard on them for not telling the truth—not when I see how common this failing is even among those who profess to be writing philosophy. What I have wondered at, though, is the way they're convinced they can write pure fable and get away with it. Since I'm vain enough myself to want to leave something behind to posterity and since I have nothing true to record—I never had any experiences worth talking about—in order not to be the only writer without a stake in the right to make up tall tales, I, too, have turned to lying—but a much more honest lying than all the others. The one and only truth you'll hear from me is that I *am* lying; by frankly admitting that there isn't a word of truth in what I say, I feel I'm avoiding the possibility of attack from any quarter.

Well, then, I'm writing about things I neither saw nor heard of from another soul, things which don't exist and couldn't possibly exist. So all readers beware: don't believe any of it.

---

1. Translated by Lionel Casson.   2. Lucian here alludes to two of his predecessors in the kind of narrative he is writing. Ctesias (5th century B.C.E.) wrote the earliest known account of India, a romantic history of Persia, and a work on geography. Iambulus (probably 3rd century B.C.E.) wrote a fantastic description of a journey to the island of the sun (in the ocean) and of its inhabitants' idyllic existence.   3. In books 9–12 of the *Odyssey*.

Some time ago I set out on a voyage from the Straits of Gibraltar. A favorable breeze carried me into the Atlantic Ocean, and I was on my way. The basic reasons for the trip were my intellectual curiosity, my thirst for novelty, and the desire to find out what formed the farther border of the ocean and what peoples lived there. I had consequently put aboard a large stock of provisions and plenty of water and had taken on as crew fifty acquaintances who shared my interests; I had also laid in a good supply of weapons, induced—by the offer of a handsome salary—the best navigator available to go along, and had our vessel, a fast brig, made shipshape for a long and hard stay at sea.

* * *

[The first landfall is an island with rivers running with wine and vines in the shape of beautiful women.]

We then broke out the water jars, watered up—and also wined up from the river—and, after spending the night on the beach, sailed off at dawn before a moderate wind. Around noon, when the island had dropped out of sight, a typhoon suddenly hit us. It spun the ship around and lifted it about thirty miles high in the air. But, before it could let us drop back into the water, as we hung suspended in the sky, a wind filled our sails and carried us along. For seven days and nights we sailed the air. On the eighth we sighted a large land mass like an island in the sky. It was round and, illuminated by some immense light, shone brightly. We put in there, anchored, and disembarked, and, upon reconnoitering the countryside, found it was inhabited and under cultivation. During the day we could see no other land about but, when night came on, we saw a good many other islands the color of fire, some bigger than ours and some smaller. Below was another land mass with cities, rivers, seas, forests, and mountains; we guessed it was our own earth.

I decided to push farther inland. En route we ran into what is called locally the Buzzard Cavalry and were taken captive. Now the Buzzard Cavalry is made up of men who ride on buzzard back; they use birds the way we do horses. Their buzzards, you see, are enormous creatures, mostly three-headed; to give you an idea of their size I need only point out that any one of their wing feathers is longer and thicker than the mast on a big cargo vessel. This Buzzard Cavalry has orders to run patrol flights over the countryside and bring before the king any aliens they find. So we were arrested and brought before him. He looked us over and, guessing from the way we were dressed, said, "You are Greek, gentlemen?" We nodded. Then he said, "How did you get here with all that air to cross?" We told him our whole story and he, in turn, told us all about himself. His name was Endymion[4] and he, too, had come from earth: some time in the past he had been snatched up in his sleep, brought here, and made king of the place.

He explained to us that the land we were in was what appeared to people on earth as the moon. He told us, however, not to worry or be apprehensive, that we were in no danger, and that we would be given everything we needed. "Once I win this war I'm involved in against the people living on the sun," he added, "you can stay here with me and live happily ever after." We asked

4. Handsome mortal beloved by Selene, the moon.

him who his enemies were and how the disagreement had come about. "Phaëthon,"[5] he told us, "is king of the people living on the sun—the sun, you
see, is inhabited just like the moon—and he's been at war with us for a long
while. It all started this way. Some time ago I got the idea of collecting the
poorest among my subjects and sending them out to found a colony on the
Morning Star, which is completely bare and uninhabited. Phaëthon out of
spite called out his Ant Cavalry and intercepted the expedition before it had
gone halfway. We were beaten—we were no match for his forces at the
time—and turned back. Now I want to take the offensive again and establish
my colony. If you're willing, come, join our army. I'll supply each of your
men with one buzzard from the royal stables plus a complete outfit. We leave
tomorrow."

"If that's what you want, why, of course," I replied.

We stayed the night with him as his guests. At the crack of dawn his
lookouts reported that the enemy was approaching, and we rose and took
our positions. Endymion had 100,000 troops, not counting supply corps,
engineers, infantry, and contingents from foreign allies. Of the 100,000,
80,000 were Buzzard Cavalry and 20,000 Saladbird Cavalry. The saladbird
is an enormous bird covered all over with salad greens instead of feathers;
its wings look exactly like lettuce leaves. Alongside these were units of Pea-
shooters and Garlickeers. He also had some allied forces from the Big Dipper: 30,000 Fleaborne Bowmen and 50,000 Windrunners. The Fleaborne
Bowmen are mounted on huge fleas—hence the name—each as big as twelve
elephants. The Windrunners, though ground forces, are able to fly through
the air without wings. This is the way they do it: they wear shirts that go
down to their feet; by pulling these up through the belt and letting them
belly before the wind like sails, they're carried along the way a boat would
be. In battle they serve for the most part as mobile infantry. There was talk
that 70,000 Ostrich-Acorns and 50,000 Crane Cavalry were expected from
the stars over Cappadocia, but they never showed up so I didn't see them
and, consequently, haven't dared to describe what they're like—the fabulous
things I heard about them are unbelievable.

So much for the make-up of Endymion's army. The equipment was standard throughout: a helmet made from a bean (enormous, tough beans are
grown there), a breastplate of overlapping lupine husks (since the husks of
the local lupines are very hard, like horn, they are made into armor by being
stitched together), and a sword and shield of the Greek type.

At the appropriate moment Endymion drew up his forces for battle. The
Buzzard Cavalry together with the king and his elite guard (including us)
were on the right, the Saladbird Cavalry on the left, and, in the center, the
cavalry units from the foreign allies, each disposed as it chose. The infantry,
numbering about 60,000,000, he positioned as follows. He ordered the local
spiders—they are numerous and big, any one of them larger by far than the
average Aegean island—to span the air between the moon and the Morning
Star with a web; as soon as they finished he stationed the infantry on the
plain so formed, with General Nightly Goodday and two others in command.

On the enemy side the Ant Cavalry with Phaëthon in command formed

---

5. His father was the sun, or Apollo. The famous story of how he drove the sun's chariot too close to Earth
and plunged to his death is ignored here.

the left wing. This arm uses enormous winged beasts similar to our ants in every respect except size, for the largest can run upwards of two hundred feet in length. The mount as well as the rider fights, principally by using its feelers. Their number was reportedly 50,000. On the right wing were the Aerognats, bowmen astride huge gnats, also 50,000 in number, and, behind them, the Aerojumpers. These, although light-armed infantrymen, are especially dangerous because they have slings that fire elephantine radishes capable of inflicting in whomever they hit a gangrenous wound which spells instant death; rumor has it these missiles are tipped with mallow juice. On the Aerojumpers' flank were 10,000 Stalk-and-Mushroomeers, heavy-armed troops for hand-to-hand combat, so called because they use mushrooms for shields and asparagus stalks for spears. Nearby were 5000 Dog-Acorns, dog-faced men who fought mounted on winged acorns; they had been sent by the inhabitants of Sirius.[6] According to reports, Phaëthon had other allies who were late—the Cloud-Centaurs[7] and a detachment of slingers he had summoned from the Milky Way. The Cloud-Centaurs arrived after the battle had been decided. (How I wish they hadn't gotten there at all!) The slingers never showed up, and I've heard say that Phaëthon was so angry he subsequently laid their country waste with fire.

Such was the make-up of the force attacking us.[8] The standards were raised; donkeys—the substitute in these armies for trumpeters—brayed the charge on both sides; the lines clashed, and the battle was on. The sun's left immediately fled without waiting to engage our Buzzard Cavalry; we pursued, slaughtering as we galloped. Their right, however, overpowered our left, and the Aerognats gave chase all the way to where our infantry was drawn up. The infantry came to the rescue, and the Aerognats, well aware that their left had been defeated, gave way and ran. The retreat turned into a full-scale rout: our men killed or captured huge numbers. Streams of blood spilled over the clouds, drenching them and turning them the scarlet color they take on at sunset. Quite a lot dripped down on earth—which makes me wonder whether something similar hadn't occurred centuries ago and Homer simply jumped to the conclusion it was Zeus sending down a shower of blood to honor Sarpedon's death.[9]

As soon as we returned from the pursuit we erected two monuments, one on the cobwebs to commemorate the infantry battle, the other on the clouds for the air battle. Before we had finished, our lookouts reported the approach of the Cloud-Centaurs, the forces which were to have joined Phaëthon before the battle. Sure enough, they came into view, an absolutely incredible sight: each was a combination of man and winged horse, the human part as tall as the upper half of the Colossus of Rhodes[1] and the equine as big as a large cargo vessel. I won't put down their number; it was so great I'm afraid no one will believe it. Sagittarius, the archer from the Zodiac, was in command. When they realized their allies had been defeated, they sent word to Phaëthon to return to the attack and, lining up in battle formation, charged. The Moonmen who, because of the chase and subsequent search for plun-

6. The Dog Star.   7. Half human, half horse. When the legendary sinner Ixion tried to rape Hera, Zeus replaced her with an image made from a cloud. The Centaurs were born from this union.   8. This description of the battle lines of both sides parodies the battle narratives in Greek historians such as Thucydides.   9. *Iliad* 16.492–96.   1. Bronze statue of Helios, the sun god, over one hundred feet tall; one of the seven wonders of the ancient world.

der, had broken ranks and scattered all over, were routed to a man; the king himself was pursued to the walls of his capital, and most of his birds were killed. After tearing down our two monuments, the Cloud-Centaurs overran the entire plain woven by the spiders and, in the process, took me and two of my shipmates prisoner. When Phaëthon arrived on the scene, monuments were again erected—this time for his side.

The very same day we were carried off to the sun, our hands tied behind our backs with a strip of cobweb. The enemy decided against laying siege; instead, on the way back they set up a barricade in mid-air, a double wall of cloud, which cut the moon off completely from the sun's light. The moon consequently went into total eclipse and remained in the grip of perpetual night. Greatly upset, Endymion sent a message to the Sunmen imploring them to tear down the structure and not force his subjects to live their lives in pitch-darkness. He said he was ready to submit to taxation, furnish military aid when required, and enter into a nonaggression pact, and he volunteered to supply hostages to guarantee performance. Phaëthon and his people held two referendums: in the first they were as bitter as ever, but in the second they changed their minds and agreed to a treaty of peace worded thus:[2]

The Sunmen and their allies hereby agree to a treaty of peace with the Moonmen and their allies on the following terms:

The Sunmen shall tear down the barricade they erected, shall hereafter never make war on the moon, and shall return all prisoners at a ransom to be determined for each;

the Moonmen shall grant autonomy to all other stars and shall not bear arms against the sun;

each party shall render aid to the other in the event of aggression by a third party;

the king of the Moonmen shall pay to the king of the Sunmen an annual levy of 10,000 jars of dew and provide 10,000 hostages from his own subjects;

both parties shall co-operate in founding the colony on the Morning Star; interested nationals of any other country may take part;

this treaty shall be inscribed on a tablet of silver and gold to be erected in mid-air at the common frontier.

Sworn to by

Firestone
Heater
Burns
for the sun;
Nighting
Moony
Allbright
for the moon.[b]

Peace was made on these terms, and the moment it took effect the wall was torn down and the prisoners, including us, released. When we arrived back on the moon, our shipmates and Endymion himself came out a little way to meet us and welcomed us with tears in their eyes. Endymion asked

2. What follows is a parody of treaties quoted by Thucydides.

us to stay on and take part in founding the colony, promising to give me his own son in marriage (there are no women on the moon). I was not to be persuaded and requested instead to be sent back down to the ocean. When he realized my mind was made up he let us go after a week's entertainment as his guests.

* * *

[The narrator describes the peculiarities of the moon people and their culture, including the following.]

I am going to describe the kind of eyes they have, though I hesitate to do so since you're sure to think I'm lying. They have removable eyes: whenever they want they take them out and keep them safe until they need them; then they put them back and have sight again. Many who have lost their own borrow other people's, and some men, all well-to-do of course, own a good supply of spares. Everybody has ears of plane-tree leaves except the men hatched from acorns; theirs are of wood.

Another marvel I saw was in the royal palace. Here there is an enormous mirror suspended over a rather shallow well. If you stand in the well, you hear everything said on earth; if you look at the mirror, you see each city and nation as clearly as if you were standing over it. When I took a look, I saw my own homeland and my house and family; I can't say for sure whether they saw me.

Any person who doesn't believe that all this is so need only go there himself. He'll quickly discover I'm telling the truth.

* * *

[The narrator and his crew return with their ship to earth, where a whale swallows them. For twenty months they live on an island in the whale's belly, where they meet two other Greeks, Scintharus and his son, whom they defend from various monsters who also live in the whale. Finally they kill the whale and escape on their ship. After being trapped by ice and sailing through a sea of milk surrounding an island made of cheese, they meet men with huge feet made of cork who can run along the surface of the water.]

Soon a great many islands came into view. Nearby, to port, was the Cork our friends were hurrying to, a town built on a large dome-shaped piece of cork. Farther on, and more to starboard, five enormous islands towered upward; huge flames were spurting from their summits. Dead ahead, over fifty miles away, was a low, flat island. When we finally came within range, we were caressed by a marvelous offshore wind, sweetly scented like the breeze the historian Herodotus tells us carries the perfume of southern Araby. For it was like a blend of the fragrance of roses, narcissuses, hyacinths, lilies, and violets, plus myrrh, laurel, and wild-grape blooms. Soon we drew near, breathing in the aroma joyfully and looking forward to a respite from our long succession of hardships. We could see any number of harbors, all capacious and sheltered on every side, crystal-clear rivers flowing placidly toward the sea, meadows, woods, and a multitude of songbirds, some warbling on the shore and many in the trees. An atmosphere rare and pure pervaded the place. Sweet, gently blowing breezes stirred the trees, and the movement of the leaves produced a continuous melodic whistling like the sound from a shepherd's pipe in some deserted spot. And we could hear the mingled noises of a crowd, not a confused babel, but as at a banquet when some are playing music, some singing, and others beating time to the flute or lyre.

Entranced by it all, we headed for shore, moored, and disembarked, leaving Scintharus and two others in the boat. Advancing through a meadow filled with flowers, we ran into the local guards and sentries who bound us with rose garlands—the strongest fetters used there—and took us to their ruler. On the way we learned from them that the place was called the Isle of the Blest and that Rhadamanthus of Crete[3] ruled it. Sure enough, we were brought before him, and our hearing was put fourth on his docket. In the first case the defendant was Ajax the Greater: charged with having gone mad and committed suicide,[4] he was being tried to determine whether he should be allowed to associate with the Heroes. After a good deal of debate Rhadamanthus finally handed down his verdict: for the present Ajax was to take a dose of hellebore and be turned over to Dr. Hippocrates;[5] later, when he had regained his sanity, he could attend the daily Heroes' banquet. The second involved the eternal triangle: a wrangle between Theseus and Menelaus over which of them Helen should live with.[6] Rhadamanthus decided in favor of Menelaus because of all the trouble and danger he had gone through on behalf of his marriage, plus the fact that Theseus had a number of other wives, the Amazon girl and Minos' daughters.[7] The third was an argument between Alexander the Great and Hannibal of Carthage over precedence; judgment was in favor of Alexander, and a throne was set up for him alongside Cyrus the Elder of Persia.[8]

The fourth case was ours. We were brought before Rhadamanthus; he asked us how it was we had set foot on hallowed soil while still alive, and we gave him a complete account of our adventures. He then had us removed and deliberated for a long time with his associate justices—quite a few shared the bench with him, including Athens' Aristides the Just.[9] He closed the discussion, and they handed down their verdict: after death we were to stand trial for leaving home and meddling; for the present, however, we could remain a specified time on the island, attend the Heroes' banquet, and then leave. Our departure date was set at not more than seven months hence.

The next thing we knew, our fetters of flowers had fallen from us of their own accord and we were being led toward the city and the banquet of the blest. Now this city is all of gold and encircled by walls of emerald. There are seven gates, each made from a solid piece of cinnamonwood. The city rests on foundations of ivory, and the entire area within the walls is paved with ivory. All the gods have temples built of beryl; inside each is an altar

---

3. Traditionally, along with his brother Minos, one of the judges of the dead; he also appears in book 6 of Virgil's *Aeneid* (above, p. 1004, line 400) as judge of the wicked in Tartarus. But he was also ruler of extraordinary souls in Elysium, or the Isle of the Blest.   4. Because the Greeks awarded the dead Achilles' armor to Odysseus and not to him. See *Odyssey* 11.617–47.   5. Traditionally the founder of medicine (469–399 B.C.E.). *Hellebore*: an emetic used to cure madness.   6. Long before she married Menelaus, king of Sparta, Helen was carried off by the Athenian hero Theseus but was rescued by her brothers, Castor and Pollux.   7. Ariadne (whom he abandoned on the island of Naxos) and Phaedra. *The Amazon girl*: Hippolyta (or Antiope), who bore him Hippolytus.   8. Three great generals of antiquity: Alexander (356–323 B.C.E.) conquered as far east as India; Hannibal (247–183 B.C.E.), inflicted terrible defeats on the Romans, though he ultimately lost to them; and Cyrus (ruled 559–529 B.C.E.) founded the Persian Empire.   9. Athenian statesman (5th century B.C.E.), whose uprightness was proverbial.

made of a huge single block of amethyst, on which the hecatombs[1] are offered up. Around the city flows a river of the finest myrrh, almost two hundred feet wide and deep enough to swim in comfortably. The baths are large chambers of glass heated by cinnamonwood fires; instead of water the tubs are filled with warm dew. All clothing is made of finespun purple cobwebs.

The inhabitants are disembodied, i.e., they are without flesh or substance. They do have a discernible outline and form but no more than this. In spite of having no body, they stand and move, think and talk; in short, it's as if their naked souls were walking about clad in the semblance of their bodies. Without testing them by touch, you would never know you weren't looking at actual bodies; they're like shadows but shadows that stand erect and have color. They never grow old but remain the age they were when they arrived.

The island experiences neither night nor the full light of day. Something like the bright gray we see preceding the dawn, when the sun hasn't yet risen, illuminates the place at all times. There is only one season of the year, an eternal spring, and only one wind blows, the Zephyr.[2] The countryside is lush with every variety of flower and of fruit and shade tree. The vines bear twelve times a year and are harvested monthly. The pomegranate, apple, and other fruit trees bear, we were told, thirteen times a year since they bear twice during Minosmonth, as it's called in the local calendar. Instead of wheat the grain stalks are tipped with loaves of bread like mushrooms. Around the city are 365 springs of water, 365 of honey, and 500 of myrrh (smaller, however, than the others), plus seven rivers of milk and eight of wine.

The Heroes' banquet is held on the outskirts of town in what is called the Elysian Field, a lovely meadow in the center of a thick stand of trees of every kind which shade the diners. The couches are mounds of flowers. The winds wait on table and serve everything except wine. There's no need to serve this—the banqueting area is surrounded by large glass trees of the finest crystal whose fruit is wineglasses of all sizes and shapes; as each Hero takes his place at table, he harvests one or two, puts them by his setting, and they immediately fill themselves up. This takes care of the wine; for garlands the nightingales and other songbirds gather in their bills flowers from the nearby meadows and, hovering overhead and warbling sweetly, let them flutter down like snowflakes. And perfume is provided as follows: thick clouds suck up myrrh from the five hundred springs and the river, float over the banqueters, and, squeezed gently by the wind, send it down in a fine rain like the dew.

At table ample time is given over to music and singing. The songs are mostly from the epics of Homer (who is there in person, taking part in the festivities; his seat is just above Odysseus'). There's a boys' and a girls' chorus. The leaders, who also provide the musical accompaniment, are Locris' Eunomus, Lesbos' Arion, Anacreon, and Stesichorus (I actually saw him: since Helen had by this time forgiven him, he was one of the company).[3] When these choruses finish, a relief chorus of swans, swallows, and nightingales takes over and sings to a musical accompaniment supplied by the whole

---

1. Groups of one hundred animals for sacrifice.   2. The west wind, typically gentle and associated with fertility.   3. Eunomos and Arion were legendary singers; Anacreon and Stesichorus were lyric poets of the 6th century B.C.E. Stesichorus is said to have gone blind after writing a poem condemning Helen for her infidelity but to have regained his sight when he wrote another poem that absolved her of guilt.

forest under the leadership of the wind. What chiefly ensures a good time for all, however, is this: right beside the banquet area are two springs, one of laughter and the other of joy; inasmuch as all the guests begin the feast with a drink from each, they spend the rest of the time laughing and enjoying themselves.

I want to mention some of the celebrities I saw there. All the demigods were present, plus all the veterans of the Trojan War except Ajax the Lesser;[4] he, we were told, was the only one from either army undergoing punishment in the Land of the Damned. Of the non-Greeks, there were Cyrus the Elder and Younger, Scythia's Anacharsis, Thrace's Zamolxis, and Italy's Numa.[5] Also present were Sparta's Lycurgus, Athens' Phocion and Tellus, and all the Sages except Periander.[6] I saw Socrates chatting with Nestor and Palamedes[7] amid a circle of good-looking boys, among whom were Hyacinth, Narcissus, and Hylas.[8] I got the impression Hylas was the one he was in love with; at least it was mostly Hylas he was refuting. We heard that Rhadamanthus was annoyed with him and had threatened a number of times to throw him off the island if he kept on with his nonsense and refused to give up his Socratic irony and have fun. Plato wasn't there—the only one missing; they told us he was living in the republic he had invented, running it with the constitution and laws he had written.[9] Aristippus and Epicurus[1] were not only there but were the island's favorites—they were such nice, pleasant fellows and such good company at parties. I saw Aesop, who's assigned the role of buffoon at the banquets, and Diogenes,[2] so changed in his ways that he had married Lais the courtesan and gone in for drink; he was always getting up from the table to go into a dance or other alcoholic carryings-on. None of the Stoics was there: we were told that Chrysippus[3] had been denied permission to enter the island until he had had his fourth dose of hellebore, and all the others were still toiling up the straight and narrow path to virtue. We heard that the people of the Academy[4] wanted to come but were still holding off and arguing; the one point they couldn't come to any conclusion about was whether an island such as this existed. Besides, I imagine they were afraid to stand judgment before Rhadamanthus; after all, they were the ones who denied all standards of judgment. Rumor had it that a big group of them

---

4. Greek hero of the Trojan War who was shipwrecked and drowned on the voyage home for defying the gods.   5. Second king of Rome, thought to have established a framework of laws and religious cults in the city. The younger Cyrus was a Persian prince who died trying to depose his older brother from the throne at the end of the 5th century B.C.E.; the Greek writer Xenophon gives a favorable portrait of him. Anacharsis, a Scythian prince, was said to have traveled in Greece in the 6th century B.C.E. and was celebrated for his wisdom. Zamolxis was supposed to be either a Thracian god or a former slave of Pythagoras who successfully passed himself off as a god.   6. Tyrant of Corinth (ca. 625–585 B.C.E.), sometimes included among the Seven Sages—Greek thinkers and statesmen of the early 6th century B.C.E. whose sayings were widely quoted. Lycurgus was the legendary lawgiver of Sparta. Phocion (4th century B.C.E.), an Athenian general and statesman, was also a pupil of Plato. The Athenian Tellus was described by Solon as the embodiment of happiness, according to Herodotus (see p. 794).   7. Hero known for his cleverness, whose condemnation and death by the Greek army at Troy his rival Odysseus was said to have contrived. Nestor was the oldest and most experienced of the Greek leaders at Troy.   8. All beautiful youths who died young: *Hyacinth* was loved and accidentally killed by Apollo; *Narcissus*, beloved by Echo, fell in love with his own reflection to the nymph Echo's chagrin; and *Hylas*, the beloved of the great hero Heracles, was pulled into a pool and drowned by amorous nymphs.   9. The writings of Plato (429–347 B.C.E.) include the *Republic*, the *Statesman*, and the *Laws*.   1. Philosopher (341–270 B.C.E.) who based the happy life on pleasure, defined as an absence of disturbance. *Aristippus* (5th century B.C.E.): a friend of Socrates known for his luxurious style of living.   2. Leading Cynic philosopher (ca. 400–ca. 325 B.C.E.), known for the exceptional austerity of his life and for his acerbic attacks on all forms of social and civic convention. *Aesop* (early 6th century B.C.E.): legendary Greek teller of fables.   3. Philosopher (ca. 280–207 B.C.E.) who systematized Stoic thought.   4. A school established by Plato that lasted until the 6th century B.C.E. A rigorous skepticism became characteristic of its thought.

once did follow the people who were heading here but, being dawdlers and lacking the courage of conviction, fell behind and turned back at the halfway point.

These were the chief celebrities. Of them all the most respected was Achilles and, after him, Theseus.

Their attitude on sex and making love is as follows. They have intercourse with both males and females, and in public with everybody looking on; this doesn't strike them as anything to be the least bit ashamed of. Socrates is an exception. He swore up and down that his relations with young men were of the purest—and everybody there accused him of perjuring himself; as a matter of fact, he still insisted on it even after Hyacinth and Narcissus had a number of times confessed the truth. They all share women in common ungrudgingly;[5] on this point they're perfect Platonists. And young boys offer themselves without hesitation to whoever wants them.

I didn't let more than two or three days go by before I went to see Homer at a time when neither of us was busy and quizzed him at length. I made a point of asking him where his birthplace was, explaining that it was a matter people were still trying hard to settle at this late date. He told me he was aware that some thought it was Chios, others Smyrna, and most Colophon, but actually he was a Babylonian; his real name was Tigranes and he only changed it to Homer when he was later sent as a hostage (*homeros*) to Greece. Next I asked him about the verses marked by editors as spurious: had he written them? His answer was yes, every one; this made me realize what a lot of nonsense Professors Zenodotus and Aristarchus[6] had written. Since he had satisfied me on these points, I then asked why he had started the *Iliad* with the words "Sing of the wrath." For no particular reason, he replied; it had just come into his head that way. I also wanted to know whether he had written the *Odyssey* before the *Iliad* as is generally held, and the answer was no. And he's not blind, as is also generally believed; I knew that immediately—I didn't have to ask; I could see it with my own eyes. I quizzed him like this on a number of occasions later on as well, whenever I saw he had time to spare, and he answered all my questions readily—particularly after his success in the lawsuit. This was an action for criminal assault brought by Thersites[7] on the grounds that the poet had jeered at him in the *Iliad*; Homer retained Odysseus as attorney and won the case.

About this time Pythagoras[8] arrived; having gone through his seventh metamorphosis and seventh mortal existence, he was finally finished with the transmigrations of his soul. The whole right side of his body was of gold. He was judged qualified to join the company, although even when I left there was still uncertainty under what name, whether Pythagoras or Euphorbus. Then Empedocles[9] showed up, cooked through and through, his whole body roasted. In spite of all his begging he was denied admission.

Time passed, and the date came around for the athletic contests they call the Mortuaric Games. The board of commissioners consisted of Achilles,

5. A characteristic of the ideal state in Plato's *Republic*.   6. Heads of the great library at Alexandria in the 3rd and 2nd centuries B.C.E., whose work on Homer established texts of his poems that are the ancestors of our own. Both were concerned to identify interpolated lines and passages.   7. A common soldier, described as ugly and misshapen, who defies Agamemnon in book 2 of the *Iliad* and is beaten by Odysseus, to the Greek army's amusement.   8. Philosopher (6th century B.C.E.) who believed in reincarnation and claimed, it was said, that he had been the Trojan warrior Euphorbus.   9. Sicilian philosopher (ca. 492–ca. 432 B.C.E.) rumored to have committed suicide by throwing himself into the volcanic crater of Mount Etna.

serving his fifth consecutive term, and Theseus, serving his seventh. To go through the whole program would take too long, so I'll report on only the most important events. In wrestling Carus, one of Heracles' descendants, threw Odysseus to take the championship. In boxing Areus, the Egyptian whose grave is in Corinth, was paired with Epeus, and the match ended in a draw.[1] Combined boxing and wrestling wasn't on the program; they don't go in for it. I can't remember any longer who was the winner in track. In the poets' contest Hesiod[2] was awarded the victory, although Homer actually won by a wide margin. The prizes for all events were crowns made of plaited peacock feathers.

The games had scarcely ended when word came that the condemned in the Land of the Damned had broken their chains and overpowered the guards and were advancing on the island; the ringleaders were the Sicilian dictator Phalaris, the Egyptian despot Busiris, the Thracian despot Diomed, plus Sciron and Pityocamptes.[3] On receiving the news, Rhadamanthus mobilized the Heroes, and they formed up on the shore; the commanding officers were Theseus, Achilles, and Ajax, who had by now recovered his sanity. Battle was joined and the Heroes won, with most of the credit going to Achilles. Socrates also distinguished himself in action, much more than he had at Delium[4] during his lifetime. He was stationed on the right wing and, when four of the enemy charged him, he didn't retreat; he never once turned his back. For this he was afterward awarded a lovely, spacious estate in the suburbs where he would gather his disciples and hold dialogues with them; he named the place Post Mortem Academy. The defeated forces were rounded up and sent back in irons to serve even stiffer sentences. Homer wrote an epic about the fight and, when I left, gave me the manuscript to bring to the people on earth, but I subsequently lost it along with everything else. The first line went:

Sing to me this time, O Muse, of the war fought by ghosts of the Heroes.

After the battle they declared a holiday and, as is the custom whenever they win a war, cooked up beans for a great victory feast. Everyone took part except Pythagoras, who sat by himself and went hungry since he can't stand bean food.[5]

Six months had passed and we were in the middle of the seventh when an unexpected situation arose. For some time Scintharus' son Cinyras, a big, handsome boy, had been in love with Helen, and it wasn't hard to see that she was madly in love with him. In fact, time and again during the banqueting they would exchange signals or drink to each other or get up, just the two of them, and go wandering in the forest. The boy was so much in love that the moment came when he lost his head and made plans to abduct her—she was perfectly agreeable—and escape to one of the surrounding islands, either Cork or the Isle of Cheese. Well in advance they swore in the three most reckless men in my crew as accomplices. To his father Cinyras didn't men-

---

1. Areus was a philosopher at the court of Augustus and presumably a scrawny specimen. Epeus won the boxing crown at the funeral games for Patroclus (*Iliad* 23.664–99) [Translator's note]. 2. Poet (ca. 700 B.C.E.) whose works, especially the *Theogony* and the *Works and Days*, were often ranked with Homer's. According to an ancient story, Hesiod defeated Homer in a poetry contest by a decision of the judge that overrode the popular will. 3. Mythical rulers, all masters at particularly gruesome ways of killing people [Translator's note]. 4. Site of an Athenian defeat (424 B.C.E.) in the Peloponnesian War at which Socrates distinguished himself for courage. 5. Pythagoreans, though vegetarians, avoided beans.

tion a word; he knew the old man would have put a stop to the whole business. When the time seemed right they put their plan into action. After nightfall—I wasn't there; I was still at the banquet where I happened to have dozed off—giving everybody the slip, Cinyras smuggled Helen aboard our ship and quickly got under way. Toward midnight Menelaus woke up and, seeing his wife's bed empty, raised a hue and cry, routed out his brother,[6] and hurried to the chief authority, Rhadamanthus. When day dawned the lookouts reported they could see the ship well out to sea. So Rhadamanthus ordered fifty Heroes to take one of their men-of-war (galleys hewn from a single stalk of asphodel) and give chase. By rowing hard they caught up around noon, just as the runaways were about to enter the sea of milk near the Isle of Cheese; that's how close they had come to making their escape. The ship was taken in tow with a hawser of roses, and everybody returned. Helen was in tears and hid her face in shame. Cinyras and his accomplices were brought to Rhadamanthus who, before passing sentence, asked them whether there were any more in on the scheme; when they said no, he had them bound by the penis, flogged with mallow, and sent off to the Land of the Damned. The Assembly of Heroes then voted to expel us from the island before our time was up; we could stay the next day and no longer.

This filled me with dismay; I broke into tears at the thought of leaving such a good life and becoming a wanderer again. They consoled me with the assurance that I would be back before many years had passed, and even pointed out my future assembly seat and banquet couch, both in choice locations. I called on Rhadamanthus and begged him to tell me my future and show me my route. He vouchsafed that, after a good deal of wandering and danger, I would eventually return home, but he refused to add how long it would take. However, he did point to the surrounding islands—five were visible nearby and a sixth in the distance—and say, "These five, the ones you see spurting great flames, are where the damned are. That sixth is the City of Dreams. Beyond it is Calypso's island,[7] but you can't make it out from here. After sailing past all these you will come to the vast continent that lies across the sea from Europe. There you will have many adventures, pass through various lands, and live among hostile peoples before you finally reach your own continent."

This was all he would tell. But he plucked a mallow root[8] from the ground and, handing it to me, told me to pray to it when we were in mortal danger. And he warned me, when I did reach the land across the sea, not to poke fires with a sword, eat beans, or make love to boys over eighteen; if I kept these rules in mind, I could look forward to making my return to his island.

So I made the ship ready for sea and, when it was banquet time, had my final feast with the Heroes. The following day I went to see Homer and asked him to compose a two-line memorial for me. He did so, and I had it inscribed on a slab of beryl which I set up on the water front. The inscription read:

> Lucian, a man who is dear to the blessed immortals in heaven,
> Witnessed the things that are here, then returned to his dearly loved
> homeland.

---

6. Agamemnon.   **7.** Ogygia. Odysseus spent seven years there with the sea nymph Calypso before making his way to the Phaeacians and then home to Ithaca (see *Odyssey* 5).   **8.** An edible plant, proverbially food for paupers.

We stayed that day as well and the following morning, with all the Heroes on hand to see us off, sailed away. At the last minute, while Penelope[9] wasn't looking, Odysseus came up to me and handed me a letter to deliver to Calypso in Ogygia. Rhadamanthus had Nauplius the ferryman go along with us so that, in case we stopped off at the islands of the damned, we wouldn't be mistaken for the usual callers and arrested.

＊　＊　＊

[After leaving the Isle of the Blest, they pass the islands of the Damned and of Dreams, both of which the narrator describes.]

Three days later we put in at Ogygia and disembarked. The first thing I did was to open Odysseus' letter and read it. Here is what it said:

> Dear Calypso,
> Let me tell you what happened to me. Right after I finished the raft and sailed away from you, I was shipwrecked, and Leucothea barely managed to rescue me and bring me to Phaeacia. The Phaeacians escorted me home and there I found a mob of my wife's suitors living high, wide, and handsome at my expense. I killed them all, and Telegonus, the son I had by Circe,[1] later on killed me. Now I'm on the Isle of the Blest full of regrets at having given up my life with you and the immortality you offered me. If I ever get the chance, I'll run away and come to you.

This is how the letter read, except for a postscript about us, a request to furnish us hospitality. I went a short distance in from the beach and came upon the cave—it was just as Homer had described it—and the lady herself busy with her spinning. She took the letter, read it, and had a good long cry. But then she invited us to be her guests and, in the course of serving us a fine dinner, quizzed us about Penelope as well as Odysseus: What did she look like? Was she as discreet as Odysseus used to brag she was? We gave her the answers we imagined she wanted to hear.

＊　＊　＊

[After a series of adventures, including narrow escapes from the Bullheads and seductive women with donkeys' legs, they are shipwrecked on a continent that seems to be the one across the sea from Europe. Here the narrative ends, with the following conclusion.]

You now know our story up to the moment we reached this new continent: our adventures on the sea, during our trip around the islands, in the air, and, after that, inside the whale; then, after escaping from there, our further adventures among the Heroes, the dreams, and, finally, the Bullheads and Asslegs. What happened to us on the new continent I will tell in the subsequent volumes.[2]

---

9. Wife of Odysseus.　1. The enchantress with whom Odysseus had a year-long affair (*Odyssey* 10). A non-Homeric epic poem related his death by their son, Telegonus.　2. The biggest lie of all, as a disappointed ancient scribe noted in the margin of his copy [Translator's note].

AUGUSTINE
354–430 C.E.

Aurelius Augustine was born in 354 in Tagaste, in North Africa. He was baptized as a Christian in 387 and ordained bishop of Hippo, in North Africa, in 395. When he died there in 430, the city was besieged by Gothic invaders. Besides the *Confessions* (begun in 397) he wrote *The City of God* (finished in 426) and many polemical works against schismatics and heretics.

He was born into a world that no longer enjoyed the "Roman peace." Invading barbarians had pierced the empire's defenses and were increasing their pressure every year. The economic basis of the empire was cracking under the strain of the enormous taxation needed to support the army; the land was exhausted. The empire was Christian, but the church was split, beset by heresies and organized heretical sects. The empire was on the verge of ruin, and there was every prospect that the church would go down with it.

Augustine, one of the men responsible for the consolidation of the church in the West, especially for the systematization of its doctrine and policy, did not convert to Christianity until he had reached middle life. "Late have I loved Thee, O Beauty so ancient and so new," he says in his *Confessions*, written long after his conversion. The lateness of his conversion and his regret for his wasted youth were among the sources of the energy that drove him to assume the intellectual leadership of the Western church and to guarantee, by combating heresy on the one hand and laying new ideological foundations for Christianity on the other, the church's survival through the dark centuries to come. Augustine had been brought up in the literary and philosophical tradition of the classical world, and it is partly because of his assimilation of classical literature and method to Christian training and teaching that the literature of the ancient world survived at all when Roman power collapsed in a welter of bloodshed and destruction that lasted for generations.

In his *Confessions* he set down, for the benefit of others, the story of his early life and his conversion to Christianity. This is, as far as we know, the first authentic ancient autobiography, and that fact itself is a significant expression of the Christian spirit, which proclaims the value of the individual soul and the importance of its relation with God. Throughout the *Confessions* Augustine talks directly to God, in humility yet conscious that God is concerned for him personally. At the same time he comes to an understanding of his own feelings and development as a human being that marks his *Confessions* as one of the great literary documents of the Western world. His description of his childhood is the only detailed account of the childhood of a great man that antiquity has left us, and his accurate observation and keen perception are informed by the Hebrew and Christian idea of the sense of sin. "So small a boy and so great a sinner"—from the beginning of his narrative to the end Augustine sees individuals not as the Greeks at their most optimistic tended to see humanity, the center and potential masters of the universe, but as children, wandering in ignorance, capable of reclamation only through the divine mercy that waits eternally for them to turn to it.

In Augustine are combined the intellectual tradition of the ancient world and the religious feeling that was characteristic of the Middle Ages. The transition from the old world to the new can be seen in his pages; his analytical intellect pursues its odyssey through strange and scattered islands—the mysticism of the Manichees, the skepticism of the academic philosophers, the fatalism of the astrologers—until he finds his home in the church, to which he was to render such great service. His account of his conversion in the garden at Milan records the true moment of transition from the ancient to the medieval world. The innumerable defeats and victories, the burning towns and ravaged farms, the bloodshed, dates, and statistics of the end of an era are all illuminated and ordered by this moment in the history of the human spirit. Here is the point of change itself.

From Confessions[1]

[Childhood]

What have I to say to Thee, God, save that I know not where I came from, when I came into this life-in-death—or should I call it death-in-life? I do not know. I only know that the gifts Your mercy had provided sustained me from the first moment: not that I remember it but so I have heard from the parents of my flesh, the father from whom, and the mother in whom, You fashioned me in time.

Thus for my sustenance and my delight I had woman's milk: yet it was not my mother or my nurses who stored their breasts for me: it was Yourself, using them to give me the food of my infancy, according to Your ordinance and the riches set by You at every level of creation. It was by Your gift that I desired what You gave and no more, by Your gift that those who suckled me willed to give me what You had given them: for it was by the love implanted in them by You that they gave so willingly that milk which by Your gift flowed in the breasts. It was a good for them that I received good from them, though I received it not *from* them but only through them: since all good things are from You, O God, and *from God is all my health.*[2] But this I have learnt since: You have made it abundantly clear by all that I have seen You give, within me and about me. For at that time I knew how to suck, to lie quiet when I was content, to cry when I was in pain: and that was all I knew.

Later I added smiling to the things I could do, first in sleep, then awake. This again I have on the word of others, for naturally I do not remember; in any event, I believe it, for I have seen other infants do the same. And gradually I began to notice where I was, and the will grew in me to make my wants known to those who might satisfy them; but I could not, for my wants were within me and those others were outside: nor had they any faculty enabling them to enter into my mind. So I would fling my arms and legs about and utter sounds, making the few gestures in my power—these being as apt to express my wishes as I could make them: but they were not very apt. And when I did not get what I wanted, either because my wishes were not clear or the things not good for me, I was in a rage—with my parents as though I had a right to their submission, with free human beings as though they had been bound to serve me; and I took my revenge in screams. That infants are like this, I have learnt from watching other infants; and that I was like it myself I have learnt more clearly from these other infants, who did not know me, than from my nurses who did.

* * *

---

1. Translated by F. J. Sheed. 2. Throughout the *Confessions* Augustine quotes liberally from the Bible; the quotations are set off in italics. When a quotation bears on Augustine's situation, it is annotated.

From infancy I came to boyhood, or rather it came to me, taking the place of infancy. Yet infancy did not go: for where was it to go to? Simply it was no longer there. For now I was not an infant, without speech, but a boy, speaking. This I remember; and I have since discovered by observation how I learned to speak. I did not learn by elders teaching me words in any systematic way, as I was soon after taught to read and write. But of my own motion, using the mind which You, my God, gave me, I strove with cries and various sounds and much moving of my limbs to utter the feelings of my heart—all this in order to get my own way. Now I did not always manage to express the right meanings to the right people. So I began to reflect [I observed that][3] my elders would make some particular sound, and as they made it would point at or move towards some particular thing: and from this I came to realize that the thing was called by the sound they made when they wished to draw my attention to it. That they intended this was clear from the motions of their body, by a kind of natural language common to all races which consists in facial expressions, glances of the eye, gestures, and the tones by which the voice expresses the mind's state—for example whether things are to be sought, kept, thrown away, or avoided. So, as I heard the same words again and again properly used in different phrases, I came gradually to grasp what things they signified; and forcing my mouth to the same sounds, I began to use them to express my own wishes. Thus I learnt to convey what I meant to those about me; and so took another long step along the stormy way of human life in society, while I was still subject to the authority of my parents and at the beck and call of my elders.

O God, my God, what emptiness and mockeries did I now experience: for it was impressed upon me as right and proper in a boy to obey those who taught me, that I might get on in the world and excel in the handling of words[4] to gain honor among men and deceitful riches. I, poor wretch, could not see the use of the things I was sent to school to learn; but if I proved idle in learning, I was soundly beaten. For this procedure seemed wise to our ancestors: and many, passing the same way in days past, had built a sorrowful road by which we too must go, with multiplication of grief and toil upon the sons of Adam.

Yet, Lord, I observed men praying to You: and I learnt to do likewise, thinking of You (to the best of my understanding) as some great being who, though unseen, could hear and help me. As a boy I fell into the way of calling upon You, my Help and my Refuge; and in those prayers I broke the strings of my tongue—praying to You, small as I was but with no small energy, that I might not be beaten at school.[5] And when You did not hear me (*not as giving me over to folly*), my elders and even my parents, who certainly wished me no harm, treated my stripes as a huge joke, which they were very far from being to me. Surely, Lord, there is no one so steeled in mind or cleaving to You so close—or even so insensitive, for that might have the same effect— as to make light of the racks and hooks and other torture instruments[6] (from which in all lands men pray so fervently to be saved) while truly loving those

---

3. Words in brackets are the translator's.   4. The study of rhetoric, which was the passport to eminence in public life.   5. Augustine recognizes the necessity of this rigorous training; that he never forgot its harshness is clear from his remark in the *City of God* (21.14): "If a choice were given him between suffering death and living his early years over again, who would not shudder and choose death?"   6. The instruments of public execution.

who are in such bitter fear of them. Yet my parents seemed to be amused at the torments inflicted upon me as a boy by my masters, though I was no less afraid of my punishments or zealous in my prayers to You for deliverance. But in spite of my terrors I still did wrong, by writing or reading or studying less than my set tasks. It was not, Lord, that I lacked mind or memory, for You had given me as much of these as my age required; but the one thing I revelled in was play; and for this I was punished by men who after all were doing exactly the same things themselves. But the idling of men is called business; the idling of boys, though exactly like, is punished by those same men: and no one pities either boys or men. Perhaps an unbiased observer would hold that I was rightly punished as a boy for playing with a ball: because this hindered my progress in studies—studies which would give me the opportunity as a man to play at things more degraded. And what difference was there between me and the master who flogged me? For if on some trifling point he had the worst of the argument with some fellow-master, he was more torn with angry vanity than I when I was beaten in a game of ball.

* * *

But to continue with my boyhood, which was in less peril of sin than my adolescence. I disliked learning and hated to be forced to it. But I *was* forced to it, so that good was done to me though it was not my doing. Short of being driven to it, I certainly would not have learned. But no one does well against his will, even if the thing he does is a good thing to do. Nor did those who forced me do well: it was by You, O God, that well was done. Those others had no deeper vision of the use to which I might put all they forced me to learn, but to sate the insatiable desire of man for wealth that is but penury and glory that is but shame. But You, Lord, *by Whom the very hairs of our head are numbered,*[7] used for my good the error of those who urged me to study; but my own error, in that I had no will to learn, you used for my punishment—a punishment richly deserved by one so small a boy and so great a sinner. Thus, You brought good for me out of those who did ill, and justly punished me for the ill I did myself. So You have ordained and so it is: that every disorder of the soul is its own punishment.

To this day I do not quite see why I so hated the Greek tongue[8] that I was made to learn as a small boy. For I really liked Latin—not the rudiments that we got from our first teachers but the literature that we came to be taught later. For the rudiments—reading and writing and figuring—I found as hard and hateful as Greek. Yet this too could come only from sin and the vanity of life, because *I was flesh, and a wind that goes away and returns not.* For those first lessons were the surer. I acquired the power I still have to read what I find written and to write what I want to express; whereas in the studies that came later I was forced to memorize the wanderings of Aeneas[9]—whoever *he* was—while forgetting my own wanderings; and to weep for the death of Dido who killed herself for love,[1] while bearing dry-

7. Who knows and attends to the smallest detail of each life (compare Matthew 10.30). 8. Important not only for gaining knowledge of Greek literature but also because it was the official language of the Eastern Roman Empire. Augustine never really mastered Greek, though his remark elsewhere that he had acquired so little Greek that it amounted to practically none is overmodest. 9. Virgil's *Aeneid* 3. 1. *Aeneid* 4.

eyed my own pitiful state, in that among these studies I was becoming dead to You, O God, my life.

Nothing could be more pitiful than a pitiable creature who does not see to pity himself, and weeps for the death that Dido suffered through love of Aeneas and not for the death he suffers himself through not loving You, O God, Light of my heart, Bread of my soul, Power wedded to my mind and the depths of my thought. I did not love You and I went away from You in fornication:[2] and all around me in my fornication echoed applauding cries "Well done! Well done!" *For the friendship of this world is fornication against Thee:* and the world cries "Well done" so loudly that one is ashamed of unmanliness not to do it. And for this I did not grieve; but I grieved for Dido, slain as she sought by the sword an end to her woe, while I too followed after the lowest of Your creatures, forsaking You, earth going unto earth. And if I were kept from reading, I grieved at not reading the tales that caused me such grief. This sort of folly is held nobler and richer than the studies by which we learn to read and write!

But now let my God cry aloud in my soul, and let Your truth assure me that it is not so: the earlier study is the better. I would more willingly forget the wanderings of Aeneas and all such things than how to write and read. Over the entrance of these grammar schools hangs a curtain:[3] but this should be seen not as lending honor to the mysteries, but as a cloak to the errors taught within. Let not those masters—who have now lost their terrors for me—cry out against me, because I confess to You, my God, the desire of my soul, and find soul's rest in blaming my evil ways that I may love Your holy ways. Let not the buyers or sellers of book-learning cry out against me. If I ask them whether it is true, as the poet says, that Aeneas ever went to Carthage, the more ignorant will have to answer that they do not know, the more scholarly that he certainly did not. But if I ask with what letters the name Aeneas is spelt, all whose schooling has gone so far will answer correctly, according to the convention men have agreed upon for the use of letters. Or again, were I to ask which loss would be more damaging to human life—the loss from men's memory of reading and writing or the loss of these poetic imaginings—there can be no question what anyone would answer who had not lost his own memory. Therefore as a boy I did wrong in liking the empty studies more than the useful—or rather in loving the empty and hating the useful. For one and one make two, two and two make four, I found a loathsome refrain; but such empty unrealities as the Wooden Horse with its armed men, and Troy on fire, and Creusa's Ghost, were sheer delight.[4]

Give me leave, O my God, to speak of my mind, Your gift, and of the follies in which I wasted it. It chanced that a task was set me, a task which I did not like but had to do. There was the promise of glory if I won, the fear of ignominy, and a flogging as well, if I lost. It was to declaim the words uttered by Juno in her rage and grief when she could not keep the Trojan prince from coming to Italy.[5] I had learnt that Juno had never said these words, but

2. Here, metaphorically.   3. School was often held in a building open on one side and curtained off from the street.   4. *Aeneid* 2.   5. Augustine was assigned the task of delivering a prose paraphrase of Juno's angry speech in *Aeneid* 1 (pp. 931–32). In it she complains that her enemies, the Trojans under Aeneas, are on their way to their destined goal in Italy in spite of her resolution to prevent them. Rhetorical exercises such as this were common in the schools, because they served the double purpose of teaching both literature and rhetorical composition.

we were compelled to err in the footsteps of the poet who had invented them: and it was our duty to paraphrase in prose what he had said in verse. In this exercise that boy won most applause in whom the passions of grief and rage were expressed most powerfully and in the language most adequate to the majesty of the personage represented.

What could all this mean to me, O My true Life, My God? Why was there more applause for the performance I gave than for so many classmates of my own age? Was not the whole business so much smoke and wind? Surely some other matter could have been found to exercise mind and tongue. Thy praises, Lord, might have upheld the fresh young shoot of my heart, so that it might not have been whirled away by empty trifles, defiled, a prey to the spirits of the air. For there is more than one way of sacrificing to the fallen angels. * * *

FROM BOOK II

[The Pear Tree]

I propose now to set down my past wickedness and the carnal corruptions of my soul, not for love of them but that I may love Thee, O my God. I do it for love of Thy love, passing again in the bitterness of remembrance over my most evil ways that Thou mayest thereby grow ever lovelier to me, O Loveliness that dost not deceive, Loveliness happy and abiding: and I collect my self out of that broken state in which my very being was torn asunder because I was turned away from Thee, the One, and wasted myself upon the many.

Arrived now at adolescence I burned for all the satisfactions of hell, and I sank to the animal in a succession of dark lusts: *my beauty consumed away,* and I stank in Thine eyes, yet was pleasing in my own and anxious to please the eyes of men.

My one delight was to love and to be loved. But in this I did not keep the measure of mind to mind, which is the luminous line of friendship; but from the muddy concupiscence of the flesh and the hot imagination of puberty mists steamed up to becloud and darken my heart so that I could not distinguish the white light of love from the fog of lust. Both love and lust boiled within me, and swept my youthful immaturity over the precipice of evil desires to leave me half drowned in a whirlpool of abominable sins. Your wrath had grown mighty against me and I knew it not. I had grown deaf from the clanking of the chain of my mortality, the punishment for the pride of my soul: and I departed further from You, and You left me to myself: and I was tossed about and wasted and poured out and boiling over in my fornications: and You were silent, O my late-won Joy. You were silent, and I, arrogant and depressed, weary and restless, wandered further and further from You into more and more sins which could bear no fruit save sorrows.

* * *

Where then was I, and how far from the delights of Your house, in that sixteenth year of my life in this world, when the madness of lust—needing no licence from human shamelessness, receiving no licence from Your laws—took complete control of me, and I surrendered wholly to it? My family took no care to save me from this moral destruction by marriage: their only concern was that I should learn to make as fine and persuasive speeches as possible.

* * *

Your law, O Lord, punishes theft; and this law is so written in the hearts of men that not even the breaking of it blots it out: for no thief bears calmly being stolen from—not even if he is rich and the other steals through want. Yet I chose to steal, and not because want drove me to it—unless a want of justice and contempt for it and an excess for iniquity. For I stole things which I already had in plenty and of better quality. Nor had I any desire to enjoy the things I stole, but only the stealing of them and the sin. There was a pear tree near our vineyard, heavy with fruit, but fruit that was not particularly tempting either to look at or to taste. A group of young blackguards, and I among them, went out to knock down the pears and carry them off late one night, for it was our bad habit to carry on our games in the streets till very late. We carried off an immense load of pears, not to eat—for we barely tasted them before throwing them to the hogs. Our only pleasure in doing it was that it was forbidden. Such was my heart, O God, such was my heart: yet in the depth of the abyss You had pity on it. Let that heart now tell You what it sought when I was thus evil for no object, having no cause for wrongdoing save my wrongness. The malice of the act was base and I loved it— that is to say I loved my own undoing, I loved the evil in me—not the thing for which I did the evil, simply the evil: my soul was depraved, and hurled itself down from security in You into utter destruction, seeking no profit from wickedness but only to be wicked.

There is an appeal to the eye in beautiful things, in gold and silver and all such; the sense of touch has its own powerful pleasures; and the other senses find qualities in things suited to them. Worldly success has its glory, and the power to command and to overcome: and from this springs the thirst for revenge. But in our quest of all these things, we must not depart from You, Lord, or deviate from Your Law. This life we live here below has its own attractiveness, grounded in the measure of beauty it has and its harmony with the beauty of all lesser things. The bond of human friendship is admirable, holding many souls as one. Yet in the enjoyment of all such things we commit sin if through immoderate inclination to them—for though they are good, they are of the lowest order of good—things higher and better are forgotten, even You, O Lord our God, and Your Truth and Your Law. These lower things have their delights but not such as my God has, for He made them all: *and in Him doth the righteous delight, and He is the joy of the upright of heart.*

Now when we ask why this or that particular evil act was done, it is normal to assume that it could not have been done save through the desire of gaining or the fear of losing some one of these lower goods. For they have their own charm and their own beauty, though compared with the higher values of heaven they are poor and mean enough. Such a man has committed a murder. Why? He wanted the other man's wife or his property; or he had chosen robbery as a means of livelihood; or he feared to lose this or that through his victim's act; or he had been wronged and was aflame for vengeance. Would any man commit a murder for no cause, for the sheer delight of murdering? The thing would be incredible. There is of course the case of the man [Catiline] who was said[6] to be so stupidly and savagely cruel that he practised cruelty and evil even when he had nothing to gain by them. But even there a cause was stated—he did it, he said, lest through idleness his hand or his resolution should grow slack. And why did he want to prevent that? So that one day by the multiplication of his crimes the city should be his, and he would have gained honors and authority and riches, and would no longer be in fear of the law or in the difficulties that want of money and the awareness of his crimes had brought him. So that not even Catiline loved his crimes as crimes: he loved some other thing which was his reason for committing them.

What was it then that in my wretched folly I loved in you, O theft of mine, deed wrought in that dark night when I was sixteen? For you were not lovely: you were a theft. Or are you anything at all, that I should talk with you? The pears that we stole were beautiful for they were created by Thee, Thou most Beautiful of all, Creator of all, Thou good God, my Sovereign and true Good. The pears were beautiful but it was not pears that my empty soul desired. For I had any number of better pears of my own, and plucked those only that I might steal. For once I had gathered them I threw them away, tasting only my own sin and savouring that with delight; for if I took so much as a bite of any one of those pears, it was the sin that sweetened it. And now, Lord my God, I ask what was it that attracted me in that theft, for there was no beauty in it to attract. I do not mean merely that it lacked the beauty that there is in justice and prudence, or in the mind of man or his senses and vegetative life: or even so much as the beauty and glory of the stars in the heavens, or of earth and sea with their oncoming of new life to replace the generations that pass. It had not even that false show or shadow of beauty by which sin tempts us.

[For there *is* a certain show of beauty in sin.] Thus pride wears the mask of loftiness of spirit, although You alone, O God, are high over all. Ambition seeks honor and glory, although You alone are to be honored before all and glorious forever. By cruelty the great seek to be feared, yet who is to be feared but God alone: from His power what can be wrested away, or when or where or how or by whom? The caresses by which the lustful seduce are a seeking for love: but nothing is more caressing than Your charity, nor is anything more healthfully loved than Your supremely lovely, supremely luminous Truth. Curiosity may be regarded as a desire for knowledge, whereas You supremely know all things. Ignorance and sheer stupidity hide under the names of simplicity and innocence: yet no being has simplicity like to Yours: and none is more innocent than You, for it is their own deeds that harm the wicked. Sloth pretends that it wants quietude: but what sure rest is there save the Lord? Luxuriousness would be called abundance and completeness; but You are the fullness and inexhaustible abundance of incorruptible delight. Wastefulness is a parody of generosity: but You are the infinitely generous giver of all good. Avarice wants to possess overmuch: but You possess all. Enviousness claims that it strives to excel: but what can excel before You? Anger clamors for just vengeance: but whose vengeance is so just as Yours? Fear is the recoil from a new and sudden threat to something one holds dear, and a cautious regard for one's own safety: but nothing new or

---

6. By the Roman historian Sallust (*Catiline* 16). Cataline was a Roman politician whose conspiracy against the state was foiled by the consul Cicero in 63 B.C.E.

sudden can happen to You, nothing can threaten Your hold upon things loved, and where is safety secure save in You? Grief pines at the loss of things in which desire delighted: for it wills to be like to You from whom nothing can be taken away.

Thus the soul is guilty of fornication when she turns from You and seeks from any other source what she will nowhere find pure and without taint unless she returns to You. Thus even those who go from You and stand up against You are still perversely imitating You. But by the mere fact of their imitation, they declare that You are the creator of all that is, and that there is nowhere for them to go where You are not.

So once again what did I enjoy in that theft of mine? Of what excellence of my Lord was I making perverse and vicious imitation? Perhaps it was the thrill of acting against Your law—at least in appearance, since I had no power to do so in fact, the delight a prisoner might have in making some small gesture of liberty—getting a deceptive sense of omnipotence from doing something forbidden without immediate punishment. I was that slave, who fled from his Lord and pursued his Lord's shadow. O rottenness, O monstrousness of life and abyss of death! Could you find pleasure only in what was forbidden, and only because it was forbidden? * * *

FROM BOOK III

[*Student at Carthage*]

I came to Carthage[7] where a cauldron of illicit loves leapt and boiled about me. I was not yet in love, but I was in love with love, and from the very depth of my need hated myself for not more keenly feeling the need. I sought some object to love, since I was thus in love with loving; and I hated security and a life with no snares for my feet. For within I was hungry, all for the want of that spiritual food which is Thyself, my God; yet [though I was hungry for want of it] I did not hunger for it: I had no desire whatever for incorruptible food, not because I had it in abundance but the emptier I was, the more I hated the thought of it. Because of all this my soul was sick, and broke out in sores, whose itch I agonized to scratch with the rub of carnal things— carnal, yet if there were no soul in them, they would not be objects of love. My longing then was to love and to be loved, but most when I obtained the enjoyment of the body of the person who loved me.

Thus I polluted the stream of friendship with the filth of unclean desire and sullied its limpidity with the hell of lust. And vile and unclean as I was, so great was my vanity that I was bent upon passing for clean and courtly. And I did fall in love, simply from wanting to. O my God, my Mercy, with how much bitterness didst Thou in Thy goodness sprinkle the delights of that time! I was loved, and our love came to the bond of consummation: I wore my chains with bliss but with torment too, for I was scourged with the red hot rods of jealousy, with suspicions and fears and tempers and quarrels.

I developed a passion for stage plays, with the mirror they held up to my own miseries and the fuel they poured on my flame. How is it that a man wants to be made sad by the sight of tragic sufferings that he could not bear in his own person? Yet the spectator does want to feel sorrow, and it is

7. The capital city of the province, where Augustine went to study rhetoric.

actually his feeling of sorrow that he enjoys. Surely this is the most wretched lunacy? For the more a man feels such sufferings in himself, the more he is moved by the sight of them on the stage. Now when a man suffers himself, it is called misery; when he suffers in the suffering of another, it is called pity. But how can the unreal sufferings of the stage possibly move pity? The spectator is not moved to aid the sufferer but merely to be sorry for him; and the more the author of these fictions makes the audience grieve, the better they like him. If the tragic sorrows of the characters—whether historical or entirely fictitious—be so poorly represented that the spectator is not moved to tears, he leaves the theatre unsatisfied and full of complaints; if he *is* moved to tears, he stays to the end, fascinated and revelling in it.

* * *

Those of my occupations at that time which were held as reputable[8] were directed towards the study of the law, in which I meant to excel—and the less honest I was, the more famous I should be. The very limit of human blindness is to glory in being blind. By this time I was a leader in the School of Rhetoric and I enjoyed this high station and was arrogant and swollen with importance: though You know, O Lord, that I was far quieter in my behavior and had no share in the riotousness of the *eversores*—the Overturners[9]—for this blackguardly diabolical name they wore as the very badge of sophistication. Yet I was much in their company and much ashamed of the sense of shame that kept me from being like them. I was with them and I did for the most part enjoy their companionship, though I abominated the acts that were their specialty—as when they made a butt of some hapless newcomer, assailing him with really cruel mockery for no reason whatever, save the malicious pleasure they got from it. There was something very like the action of devils in their behavior. They were rightly called Overturners, since they had themselves been first overturned and perverted, tricked by those same devils who were secretly mocking them in the very acts by which they amused themselves in mocking and making fools of others.

With these men as companions of my immaturity, I was studying the books of eloquence; for in eloquence it was my ambition to shine, all from a damnable vaingloriousness and for the satisfaction of human vanity. Following the normal order of study I had come to a book of one Cicero, whose tongue[1] practically everyone admires, though not his heart. That particular book is called *Hortensius*[2] and contains an exhortation to philosophy. Quite definitely it changed the direction of my mind, altered my prayers to You, O Lord, and gave me a new purpose and ambition. Suddenly all the vanity I had hoped in I saw as worthless, and with an incredible intensity of desire I longed after immortal wisdom. I had begun that journey upwards by which I was to return to You. My father was now dead two years; I was eighteen and was receiving money from my mother for the continuance of my study of eloquence. But I used that book not for the sharpening of my tongue; what won me in it was what it said, not the excellence of its phrasing.

---

8. I.e., his rhetorical studies.   9. *Eversores* is the Latin word that means "overturners": a group of students who prided themselves on their wild actions and lack of discipline.   1. Style. Cicero (106–43 B.C.E.) is generally regarded as the greatest Roman orator; he wrote works of philosophy as well as rhetoric. 2. Only fragments of this dialogue remain. In it Cicero replies to an opponent of philosophy with an impassioned defense of the intellectual life.

* * *

So I resolved to make some study of the Sacred Scriptures and find what kind of books they were. But what I came upon was something not grasped by the proud, not revealed either to children, something utterly humble in the hearing but sublime in the doing, and shrouded deep in mystery. And I was not of the nature to enter into it or bend my neck to follow it. When I first read those Scriptures, I did not feel in the least what I have just said; they seemed to me unworthy to be compared with the majesty of Cicero. My conceit was repelled by their simplicity, and I had not the mind to penetrate into their depths. They were indeed of a nature to grow in Your little ones.[3] But I could not bear to be a little one; I was only swollen with pride, but to myself I seemed a very big man. * * *

FROM BOOK V

[Augustine Leaves Carthage for Rome]

It was by Your action upon me that I was moved to go to Rome and teach there what I had taught in Carthage. How I was persuaded to this, I shall not omit to confess to you, because therein Your most profound depths and Your mercy ever present towards us are to be meditated upon and uttered forth. My reason for going to Rome was not the greater earnings and higher dignity promised by the friends who urged me to go—though at that time, these considerations certainly influenced my mind: the principal and practically conclusive reason, was that I had heard that youths there pursued their studies more quietly and were kept within a stricter limit of discipline. For instance, they were not allowed to come rushing insolently and at will into the school of one who was not their own master, nor indeed to enter it at all unless he permitted.

At Carthage the licence of the students is gross and beyond all measure. They break in impudently and like a pack of madmen play havoc with the order which the master has established for the good of his pupils. They commit many outrages, extraordinarily stupid acts, deserving the punishment of the law if custom did not protect them. Their state is the more hopeless because what they do is supposed to be sanctioned, though by Your eternal law it could never be sanctioned; and they think they do these things unpunished, when the very blindness in which they do them is their punishment, so that they suffer things incomparably worse than they do. When I was a student I would not have such habits in myself, but when I became a teacher I had to endure them in others; and so I decided to go to a place where, as I had been told by all who knew, such things were not done. But You, O my Hope and my Portion in the land of the living, forced me to change countries for my soul's salvation: You pricked me with such goads at Carthage as drove me out of it, and You set before me certain attractions by which I might be drawn to Rome—in either case using men who loved this life of death, one set doing lunatic things, the other promising vain things: and to reform my ways You secretly used their perversity and my own. For those who had disturbed my peace were blind in the frenzy of their vicious-

---

3. Refers not only to the rhetorical simplicity of Jesus' teachings but also to his interest in teaching children; compare Matthew 19.14: "For of such is the kingdom of heaven."

ness, and those who urged me to go elsewhere savoured of earth. While I, detesting my real misery in the one place, hoped for an unreal happiness in the other.

Why I left the one country and went to the other, You Knew, O God, but You did not tell either me or my mother. She indeed was in dreadful grief at my going and followed me right to the seacoast. There she clung to me passionately, determined that I should either go back home with her or take her to Rome with me, but I deceived her with the pretence that I had a friend whom I did not want to leave until he had sailed off with a fair wind. Thus I lied to my mother, and such a mother; and so got away from her. But this also You have mercifully forgiven me, bringing me from the waters of that sea, filled as I was with execrable uncleanness, unto the water of Your grace; so that when I was washed clean, the floods that poured from my mother's eyes, the tears with which daily she watered the ground towards which she bent her face in prayer for me, should cease to flow. She would not return home without me, but I managed with some difficulty to persuade her to spend the night in a place near the ship where there was an oratory in memory of St. Cyprian. That night I stole away without her: she remained praying and weeping. And what was she praying for, O my God, with all those tears but that You should not allow me to sail! But You saw deeper and granted the essential of her prayer: You did not do what she was at that moment asking, that You might do the thing she was always asking. The wind blew and filled our sails and the shore dropped from our sight. And the next morning she was frantic with grief and filled Your ears with her moaning and complaints because You seemed to treat her tears so lightly, when in fact You were using my own desires to snatch me away for the healing of those desires, and were justly punishing her own too earthly affection for me with the scourge of grief. For she loved to have me with her, as is the way of mothers but far more than most mothers; and she did not realize what joys you would bring her from my going away. She did not realize it, and so she wept and lamented, and by the torments she suffered showed the heritage of Eve in her, seeking with sorrow what in sorrow she had brought forth. But when she had poured out all her accusation at my cruel deception, she turned once more to prayer to You for me. She went home and I to Rome. * * *

FROM BOOK VI

[Worldly Ambitions]

By this time my mother had come to me, following me over sea and land with the courage of piety and relying upon You in all perils. For they were in danger from a storm, and she reassured even the sailors—by whom travelers newly ventured upon the deep are ordinarily reassured—promising them safe arrival because thus You had promised her in a vision. She found me in a perilous state through my deep despair of ever discovering the truth. But even when I told her that if I was not yet a Catholic Christian, I was no longer a Manichean,[4] she was not greatly exultant as at some unlooked-for

4. Augustine had for nine years been a member of this religious sect, which followed the teaching of the Babylonian mystic Mani (216–277). The Manicheans believed that the world was a battleground for the forces of good and evil; redemption in a future life would come to the elect, who renounced worldly occupations and possessions and practiced a severe asceticism (including abstention from meat). Augustine's mother, Monica, was a Christian, and lamented her son's Manichean beliefs.

good news, because she had already received assurance upon that part of my misery; she bewailed me as one dead certainly, but certainly to be raised again by You, offering me in her mind as one stretched out dead, that You might say to the widow's son: *"Young man, I say to thee arise"*:[5] and he should sit up and begin to speak and You should give him to his mother.

* * *

Nor did I then groan in prayer for Your help. My mind was intent upon inquiry and unquiet for argumentation. I regarded Ambrose[6] as a lucky man by worldly standards to be held in honor by such important people: only his celibacy seemed to me a heavy burden. I had no means of guessing, and no experience of my own to learn from, what hope he bore within him, what struggles he might have against the temptations that went with his high place, what was his consolation in adversity, and on what joys of Your bread the hidden mouth of his heart fed. Nor did he know how I was inflamed nor the depth of my peril. I could not ask of him what I wished as I wished, for I was kept from any face to face conversation with him by the throng of men with their own troubles, whose infirmities he served. The very little time he was not with these he was refreshing either his body with necessary food or his mind with reading. When he read, his eyes traveled across the page and his heart sought into the sense, but voice and tongue were silent. No one was forbidden to approach him nor was it his custom to require that visitors should be announced: but when we came into him we often saw him reading and always to himself; and after we had sat long in silence, unwilling to interrupt a work on which he was so intent, we would depart again. We guessed that in the small time he could find for the refreshment of his mind, he would wish to be free from the distraction of other men's affairs and not called away from what he was doing. Perhaps he was on his guard lest [if he read aloud] someone listening should be troubled and want an explanation if the author he was reading expressed some idea over-obscurely, and it might be necessary to expound or discuss some of the more difficult questions. And if he had to spend time on this, he would get through less reading than he wished. Or it may be that his real reason for reading to himself was to pre-serve his voice, which did in fact readily grow tired. But whatever his reason for doing it, that man certainly had a good reason.

* * *

I was all hot for honors, money, marriage: and You made mock of my hotness. In my pursuit of these, I suffered most bitter disappointments, but in this You were good to me since I was thus prevented from taking delight in any-thing not Yourself. Look now into my heart, Lord, by whose will I remember all this and confess it to You. Let my soul cleave to You now that You have freed it from the tenacious hold of death. At that time my soul was in misery, and You pricked the soreness of its wound, that leaving all things it might turn to You, who are over all and without whom all would return to nothing, that it might turn to You and be healed. I was in utter misery and there was one day especially on which You acted to bring home to me the realization

5. Luke 7.14, recounting one of Christ's miracles. 6. The leading personality among the Christians of the West (339–397); not many years after this he defied the power of the emperor Theodosius and forced him to beg for God's pardon in the church at Milan for having put the inhabitants of Thessalonica to the sword.

of my misery. I was preparing an oration in praise of the Emperor[7] in which I was to utter any number of lies to win the applause of people who knew they were lies. My heart was much wrought upon by the shame of this and inflamed with the fever of the thoughts that consumed it. I was passing along a certain street in Milan when I noticed a beggar. He was jesting and laughing and I imagine more than a little drunk. I fell into gloom and spoke to the friends who were with me about the endless sorrows that our own insanity brings us: for here was I striving away, dragging the load of my unhappiness under the spurring of my desires, and making it worse by dragging it: and with all our striving, our one aim was to arrive at some sort of happiness without care: the beggar had reached the same goal before us, and we might quite well never reach it at all. The very thing that he had attained by means of a few pennies begged from passers-by—namely the pleasure of a temporary happiness—I was plotting for with so many a weary twist and turn.

Certainly his joy was no true joy; but the joy I sought in my ambition was emptier still. In any event he was cheerful and I worried, he had no cares and I nothing but cares. Now if anyone had asked me whether I would rather be cheerful or fearful, I would answer: "Cheerful"; but if he had gone on to ask whether I would rather be like that beggar or as I actually was, I would certainly have chosen my own state though so troubled and anxious. Now this was surely absurd. It could not be for any true reason. I ought not to have preferred my own state rather than his merely because I was the more learned, since I got no joy from my learning, but sought only to please men by it—not even to teach them, only to please them. Therefore did You break my bones with the rod of Your discipline.

* * *

Great effort was made to get me married. I proposed, the girl was promised me. My mother played a great part in the matter for she wanted to have me married and then cleansed with the saving waters of baptism,[8] rejoicing to see me grow every day more fitted for baptism and feeling that her prayers and Your promises were to be fulfilled in my faith. By my request and her own desire she begged You daily with the uttermost intensity of her heart to show her in a vision something of my future marriage, but You would never do it. She did indeed see certain vain fantasies, under the pressure of her mind's preoccupation with the matter; and she told them to me, not, however, with the confidence she always had when You had shown things to her, but as if she set small store by them; for she said that there was a certain unanalyzable savor, not to be expressed in words, by which she could distinguish between what You revealed and the dreams of her own spirit. Still she pushed on with the matter of my marriage, and the girl was asked for. She was still two years short of the age for marriage[9] but I liked her and agreed to wait.

There was a group of us friends who had much serious discussion together, concerning the cares and troubles of human life which we found so hard to endure. We had almost decided to seek a life of peace, away from the throng of men. This peace we hoped to attain by putting together whatever we could

---

7. Probably the young Valentinian (371–392), whose court was at Milan.   8. He could not be baptized while living in sin with his mistress, a liaison that resulted in the birth of a son, Adeodatus, who later accompanied Augustine to Italy.   9. The legal age was twelve years; Augustine was in his early thirties.

manage to get, and making one common household for all of us: so that in the clear trust of friendship, things should not belong to this or that individual, but one thing should be made of all our possessions, and belong wholly to each one of us, and everybody own everything. It seemed that there might be perhaps ten men in this fellowship. Among us there were some very rich men, especially Romanianus, our fellow townsman, who had been a close friend of mine from childhood and had been brought to the court in Milan by the press of some very urgent business. He was strongest of all for the idea and he had considerable influence in persuasion because his wealth was much greater than anyone else's. We agreed that two officers should be chosen every year to handle the details of our life together, leaving the rest undisturbed. But then we began to wonder whether our wives would agree, for some of us already had wives and I meant to have one. So the whole plan, which we had built up so neatly, fell to pieces in our hands and was simply dropped. We returned to our old sighing and groaning and treading of this world's broad and beaten ways:[1] for many thoughts were in our hearts, but *Thy counsel standeth forever.* And out of Thy counsel didst Thou deride ours and didst prepare Thine own things for us, meaning to *give us meat in due season and to open Thy hands and fill our souls with Thy blessing.*

Meanwhile my sins were multiplied. She with whom I had lived so long was torn from my side as a hindrance to my forthcoming marriage. My heart which had held her very dear was broken and wounded and shed blood. She went back to Africa, swearing that she would never know another man, and left with me the natural son I had had of her. But I in my unhappiness could not, for all my manhood, imitate her resolve. I was unable to bear the delay of two years which must pass before I was to get the girl I had asked for in marriage. In fact it was not really marriage that I wanted. I was simply a slave to lust. So I took another woman, not of course as a wife; and thus my soul's disease was nourished and kept alive as vigorously as ever, indeed worse than ever, that it might reach the realm of matrimony in the company of its ancient habit. Nor was the wound healed that had been made by the cutting off of my former mistress. For there was first burning and bitter grief; and after that it festered, and as the pain grew duller it only grew more hopeless. * * *

FROM BOOK VIII

[Conversion]

* * * Thus I was sick at heart and in torment, accusing myself with a new intensity of bitterness, twisting and turning in my chain in the hope that it might be utterly broken, for what held me was so small a thing! But it still held me. And You stood in the secret places of my soul, O Lord, in the harshness of Your mercy redoubling the scourges of fear and shame lest I should give way again and that small slight tie which remained should not be broken but should grow again to full strength and bind me closer even than before. For I kept saying within myself: "Let it be now, let it be now," and by the mere words I had begun to move toward the resolution. I almost made it, yet I did not quite make it. But I did not fall back into my original

---

1. Compare Matthew 7.13: "Broad is the way that leadeth to destruction," that is, to damnation.

state, but as it were stood near to get my breath. And I tried again and I was almost there, and now I could all but touch it and hold it: yet I was not quite there, I did not touch it or hold it. I still shrank from dying unto death and living unto life. The lower condition which had grown habitual was more powerful than the better condition which I had not tried. The nearer the point of time came in which I was to become different, the more it struck me with horror; but it did not force me utterly back nor turn me utterly away, but held me there between the two.

Those trifles of all trifles, and vanities of vanities, my one-time mistresses, held me back, plucking at my garment of flesh and murmuring softly: "Are you sending us away?" And "From this moment shall we not be with you, now or forever?" And "From this moment shall this or that not be allowed you, now or forever?" What were they suggesting to me in the phrase I have written "this or that," what were they suggesting to me, O my God? Do you in your mercy keep from the soul of Your servant the vileness and unclean- ness they were suggesting. And now I began to hear them not half so loud; they no longer stood against me face to face, but were softly muttering behind my back and, as I tried to depart, plucking stealthily at me to make me look behind. Yet even that was enough, so hesitating was I, to keep me from snatching myself free, from shaking them off and leaping upwards on the way I was called: for the strong force of habit said to me: "Do you think you can live without them?"

But by this time its voice was growing fainter. In the direction toward which I had turned my face and was quivering in fear of going, I could see the austere beauty of Continence, serene and indeed joyous but not evilly, honorably soliciting me to come to her and not linger, stretching forth loving hands to receive and embrace me, hands full of multitudes of good examples. With her I saw such hosts of young men and maidens, a multitude of youth and of every age, gray widows and women grown old in virginity, and in them all Continence herself, not barren but the fruitful mother of children, her joys, by You, Lord, her Spouse. And she smiled upon me and her smile gave courage as if she were saying: "Can you not do what these men have done, what these women have done? Or could men or women have done such in themselves, and not in the Lord their God? The Lord their God gave me to them. Why do you stand upon yourself and so not stand at all? Cast yourself upon Him and be not afraid; He will not draw away and let you fall. Cast yourself without fear, He will receive you and heal you."

Yet I was still ashamed, for I could still hear the murmuring of those vanities, and I still hung hesitant. And again it was as if she said: "Stop your ears against your unclean members, that they may be mortified. They tell you of delights, but not of such delights as the law of the Lord your God tells." This was the controversy raging in my heart, a controversy about myself against myself. And Alypius[2] stayed by my side and awaited in silence the issue of such agitation as he had never seen in me.

When my most searching scrutiny had drawn up all my vileness from the secret depths of my soul and heaped it in my heart's sight, a mighty storm arose in me, bringing a mighty rain of tears. That I might give way to my

2. A student of Augustine's at Carthage; he had joined the Manichees with Augustine, followed him to Rome and Milan, and now shared his desires and doubts. Alypius finally became a bishop in North Africa in 394.

tears and lamentations, I rose from Alypius: for it struck me that solitude was more suited to the business of weeping. I went far enough from him to prevent his presence from being an embarrassment to me. So I felt, and he realized it. I suppose I had said something and the sound of my voice was heavy with tears. I arose, but he remained where we had been sitting, still in utter amazement. I flung myself down somehow under a certain fig tree and no longer tried to check my tears, which poured forth from my eyes in a flood, *an acceptable sacrifice to Thee.* And much I said not in these words but to this effect: *"And Thou, O Lord, how long? How long, Lord; wilt Thou be angry forever? Remember not our former iniquities."*[3] For I felt that I was still bound by them. And I continued my miserable complaining: "How long, how long shall I go on saying tomorrow and again tomorrow? Why not now, why not have an end to my uncleanness this very hour?"

Such things I said, weeping in the most bitter sorrow of my heart. And suddenly I heard a voice from some nearby house, a boy's voice or a girl's voice, I do not know: but it was a sort of singsong, repeated again and again, "Take and read, take and read." I ceased weeping and immediately began to search my mind most carefully as to whether children were accustomed to chant these words in any kind of game, and I could not remember that I had ever heard any such thing. Damming back the flood of my tears I arose, interpreting the incident as quite certainly a divine command to open my book of Scripture and read the passage at which I should open. For it was part of what I had been told about Anthony,[4] that from the Gospel which he happened to be reading he had felt that he was being admonished as though what he read was spoken directly to himself: *Go, sell what thou hast and give to the poor and thou shalt have treasure in heaven; and come follow Me.*[5] By this experience he had been in that instant converted to You. So I was moved to return to the place where Alypius was sitting, for I had put down the Apostle's[6] book there when I arose. I snatched it up, opened it and in silence read the passage upon which my eyes first fell: *Not in rioting and drunkenness, not in chambering and impurities, not in contention and envy, but put ye on the Lord Jesus Christ and make not provision for the flesh in its concupiscences.* [Romans 13.13.] I had no wish to read further, and no need. For in that instant, with the very ending of the sentence, it was as though a light of utter confidence shone in all my heart, and all the darkness of uncertainty vanished away. Then leaving my finger in the place or marking it by some other sign, I closed the book and in complete calm told the whole thing to Alypius and he similarly told me what had been going on in himself, of which I knew nothing. He asked to see what I had read. I showed him, and he looked further than I had read. I had not known what followed. And this is what followed: *"Now him that is weak in faith, take unto you."* He applied this to himself and told me so. And he was confirmed by this message, and with no troubled wavering gave himself to God's goodwill and purpose—a purpose indeed most suited to his character, for in these matters he had been immeasurably better than I.

Then we went in to my mother and told her, to her great joy. We related how it had come about: she was filled with triumphant exultation, and

---

3. Compare Psalm 79.5–8; Augustine compares his spiritual despair with that of captive and subjected Israel.   **4.** The Egyptian saint (b. ca. 250) whose abstinence and self-control are still proverbial; he was one of the founders of the system of monastic life.   **5.** Luke 18.22.   **6.** Paul.

praised You who are mighty beyond what we ask or conceive: for she saw that You had given her more than with all her pitiful weeping she had ever asked. For You converted me to Yourself so that I no longer sought a wife nor any of this world's promises, but stood upon that same rule of faith in which You had shown me to her so many years before.[7] Thus You changed her mourning into joy, a joy far richer than she had thought to wish, a joy much dearer and purer than she had thought to find in grandchildren of my flesh.

FROM BOOK IX

[Death of His Mother]

* * * And I thought it would be good in Your sight if I did not dramatically snatch my tongue's service from the speech-market but quietly withdrew; but that in any event withdraw I must, so that youths—not students of Your law or Your peace but of lying follies and the conflicts of the law—should no longer buy at my mouth the tools of their madness. Fortunately it happened that there were only a few days left before the Vintage Vacation,[8] and I decided to endure them so that I might leave with due deliberation, seeing that I had been redeemed by You and was not going to put myself up for sale again. Our purpose therefore was known to You, but not to men other than our own friends. We had agreed among ourselves not to spread the news abroad at all, although, in our ascent from *the valley of tears and our singing of the song of degrees,* You had given us *sharp arrows* and *burning coals* against *cunning tongues* that might argue against us with pretended care for our interest, might destroy us saying that they loved us: as men consume food saying that they love it.

* * *

Furthermore that very summer, under the too heavy labor of teaching, my lungs had begun to give way and I breathed with difficulty,[9] the pain in my breast showed that they were affected and they no longer let me talk with any strength for too long at a time. At first this had disturbed me, because it made it practically a matter of necessity that I should lay down the burden of teaching, or at least give it up for the time if I was to be cured and grow well again. But when the full purpose of giving myself leisure to meditate on how You are the Lord arose in me and became a settled resolve—as you know, O my God—I actually found myself glad to have this perfectly truthful excuse to offer parents who might be offended and for their children's sake would never willingly have let me give up teaching. So I was full of joy, and I put up with the space of time that still had to run—I fancy it was about twenty days. But to bear the time took considerable fortitude. Desire for money, which formerly had helped me to bear the heavy labor of teaching, was quite gone; so that I should have [had nothing to help me bear it and so] found it altogether crushing if patience had not taken the place of cov-

---

7. At Carthage, when Augustine was still a Manichee, Monica had dreamed that she was standing on a wooden ruler weeping for her son and then saw that he was standing on the same ruler as herself.   8. This grape-harvesting and wine-making holiday lasted from the end of August to the middle of October.   9. Because he not only lectured but also read aloud, as is suggested by his comments on Ambrose's silent reading (book 6).

etousness. Some of Your servants, my brethren, may think that I sinned in this, since having enrolled with all my heart in Your service, I allowed myself to sit for so much as an hour in the chair of untruthfulness. It may be so. But, most merciful Lord, have You not pardoned and remitted this sin, along with others most horrible and deadly, in the holy water of baptism?

* * *

And now the day was come on which I was to be set free from the teaching of Rhetoric in fact, as I was already free in mind. And so it came about. You delivered my tongue as You had already delivered my heart, and I rejoiced and praised You, and so went off with my friends to the country-house.[1] The amount of writing I did there—the writing was now in your service but during this breathing-space still smacked of the school of pride—my books[2] exist to witness, with the record they give of discussions either with my friends there present or with Yourself when I was alone with You; and there are my letters to show what correspondence I had with Nebridius[3] while he was away.

* * *

When the Vintage Vacation was over I gave the people of Milan notice that they must find someone else to sell the art of words to their students, because I had chosen to serve You, and because owing to my difficulty in breathing and the pain in my lungs I could not continue my teaching. And in a letter I told Your bishop, the holy Ambrose, of my past errors and my present purpose, that he might advise me which of Your Scriptures I should especially read to prepare me and make me more fit to receive so great a grace. He told me to read Isaiah the prophet, I imagine because he more clearly foretells the gospel and the calling of the gentiles[4] than the other Old Testament writers; but I did not understand the first part of this book, and thinking that it would be all of the same kind, put it aside meaning to return to it when I should be more practised in the Lord's way of speech.

When the time had come to give in my name for baptism, we left the country and returned to Milan. Alypius had decided to be born again in You at the same time, for he was already endowed with the humility that Your sacraments require, and had brought his body so powerfully under control that he could tread the icy soil of Italy with bare feet, which required unusual fortitude. We also took with us the boy Adeodatus, carnally begotten by me in my sin. You had made him well. He was barely fifteen, yet he was more intelligent than many a grave and learned man. In this I am but acknowledging to You Your own gifts, O Lord my God, Creator of all and powerful to reshape our shapelessness: for I had no part in that boy but the sin. That he had been brought up by us in Your way was because You had inspired us, no other. I do but acknowledge to You Your own gifts. There is a book of mine called De Magistro:[5] it is a dialogue between him and me. You know,

---

1. At Cassiciacum, placed at his disposal by a friend. 2. While at Cassiciacum, Augustine wrote a book attacking the academic philosophers; a book on the happy life; and another titled De ordine, a treatise on divine providence. 3. Nebridius came from Carthage to Milan with Augustine, shared his spiritual pilgrimage through the pagan philosophies and Manichean doctrines to become a Christian, and returned to Africa, where he died. Augustine's letters to Nebridius are still extant. 4. The appeal of Christ's apostles to peoples outside the Hebrew nation: "I am sought of them that asked not for me; I am found of them that sought me not" (Isaiah 65.1). 5. The Teacher, written in Tagaste, Africa, two years after Augustine's baptism and shortly after his return from Italy; it concerns teaching and the thesis that only God is the cause for humankind's acquisition of learning and truth.

O God, that all the ideas which are put into the mouth of the other party to the dialogue were truly his, though he was but sixteen. I had experience of many other remarkable qualities in him. His great intelligence filled me with a kind of awe: and who but You could be the maker of things so wonderful? But You took him early from this earth, and I think of him utterly without anxiety, for there is nothing in his boyhood or youth or anywhere in him to cause me to fear. We took him along with us, the same age as ourselves in Your grace, to be brought up in Your discipline: and we were baptized, and all anxiety as to our past life fled away. The days were not long enough as I meditated, and found wonderful delight in meditating, upon the depth of Your design for the salvation of the human race. I wept at the beauty of Your hymns and canticles, and was powerfully moved at the sweet sound of Your Church's singing. Those sounds flowed into my ears, and the truth streamed into my heart: so that my feeling of devotion overflowed, and the tears ran from my eyes, and I was happy in them.

It was only a little while before that the church of Milan had begun to practice this kind of consolation and exultation, to the great joy of the brethen singing together with heart and voice. For it was only about a year, or not much more, since Justina, the mother of the boy emperor Valentinian, was persecuting Your servant Ambrose in the interests of her own heresy: for she had been seduced by the Arians.[6] The devoted people had stayed day and night in the church, ready to die with their bishop, Your servant. And my mother, Your handmaid, bearing a great part of the trouble and vigil, had lived in prayer. I also, though still not warmed by the fire of Your Spirit, was stirred to excitement by the disturbed and wrought-up state of the city. It was at this time that the practice was instituted of singing hymns and psalms after the manner of the Eastern churches,[7] to keep the people from being altogether worn out with anxiety and want of sleep. The custom has been retained from that day to this, and has been imitated by many, indeed in almost all congregations throughout the world.

At this time You revealed to Your bishop Ambrose in a vision the place where the bodies of the martyrs Protasius and Gervasius[8] lay hid, which You had for so many years kept incorrupt in the treasury of Your secret knowledge that You might bring them forth at the proper moment to check a woman's fury—the woman[9] being the ruler of the Empire! For when they were discovered and dug up and with due honor brought to Ambrose's basilica, not only were people cured who had been tormented by evil spirits—and the devils themselves forced to confess it—but also there was a man, a citizen well known to the city, who had been blind for many years: he asked what was the cause of the tumultuous joy of the people, and when he heard, he sprang up and asked his guide to lead him into the place. When he arrived there he asked to be allowed to touch with his handkerchief the place on which lay the saints, whose death is precious in Your sight. He did so, put

---

6. Members of a sect who followed the doctrine of Arius (250–336) that the Son had not existed from all eternity and was, therefore, inferior to the Father. At the Council of Nicaea (325) Arius and his followers were declared heretical, but the Arian heresy remained a serious problem for the church for many years. Justina demanded that Ambrose allow the Arians to hold public services inside the walls of Milan.   7. The Greek-speaking churches of the Eastern Roman Empire; they split off from the Catholic Church in the ninth century.   8. Two beheaded skeletons discovered by Ambrose at Milan were identified as the relics of these saints; nothing certain is known about them, but they were said to have been martyred in the second century.   9. Justina.

the handkerchief to his eyes, and immediately they were opened. The news spread abroad, Your praises glowed and shone, and if the mind of that angry woman was not brought to the sanity of belief, it was at least brought back from the madness of persecution. Thanks be to my God! From what and towards what have You led my memory, that it should confess to You these great things which I had altogether forgotten? Yet even then, *when the odor of Thy ointments was so sweet smelling,* I did *not run after Thee:* and for this I wept all the more now when I heard Your hymns and canticles, as one who had then sighed for You and now breathed in You, breathed so far as the air allows in this our house of grass.[1]

You, Lord, who make men of one mind to dwell in one house brought to our company a young man of our own town, Evodius. He had held office in the civil service, had been converted and baptized before us, had resigned from the state's service, and given himself to Yours. We kept together, meaning to live together in our devout purpose. We thought deeply as to the place in which we might serve You most usefully. As a result we started back for Africa. And when we had come as far as Ostia[2] on the Tiber, my mother died. I pass over many things, for I must make haste. Do You, O my God, accept my confessions and my gratitude for countless things of which I say nothing. But I will not omit anything my mind brings forth concerning her, Your servant, who brought me forth—brought me forth in the flesh to this temporal light, and in her heart to light eternal. Not of her gifts do I speak but of Your gifts in her. For she did not bring herself into the world or educate herself in the world: it was You who created her, nor did her father or mother know what kind of being was to come forth from them. It was the scepter of Your Christ, the discipline of your Only-Begotten, that brought her up in holy fear, in a Catholic family which was a worthy member of Your church. Yet it was not the devotion of her mother in her upbringing that she talked most of, but of a certain aged servant, who had indeed carried my mother's father on her back when he was a baby, as little ones are accustomed to be carried on the backs of older girls. Because of this, because also of her age and her admirable character, she was very much respected by her master and mistress in their Christian household. As a result she was given charge of her master's daughters. This charge she fulfilled most conscientiously, checking them sharply when necessary with holy severity and teaching them soberly and prudently. Thus, except at the times when they ate—and that most temperately—at their parents' table, she would not let them even drink water, no matter how tormenting their thirst. By this she prevented the forming of a bad habit, and she used to remark very sensibly: "Now you drink water because you are not allowed to have wine: but when you are married, and thus mistresses of food-stores and wine-cellars, you will despise water, but the habit of drinking will still remain." By this kind of teaching and the authority of her commands she moderated the greediness that goes with childhood and brought the little girls' thirst to such a control that they no longer wanted what they ought not to have.

Yet, as Your servant told me, her son, there did steal upon my mother an inclination to wine. For when, in the usual way, she was sent by her parents,

1. Compare Isaiah 40.6–8: "All flesh is grass. . . . The grass withereth, the flower fadeth: but the word of our God will stand forever." 2. On the southwest coast of Italy; it was the port of Rome and the point of departure for Africa.

as a well-behaved child, to draw wine from the barrel, she would dip the cup in, but before pouring the wine from the cup into the flagon, she would sip a little with the very tip of her lips, only a little because she did not yet like the taste sufficiently to take more. Indeed she did it not out of any craving for wine, but rather from the excess of childhood's high spirits, which tend to boil over in absurdities, and are usually kept in check by the authority of elders. And so, adding to that daily drop a little more from day to day—for he that despises small things, falls little by little—she fell into the habit, so that she would drink off greedily cups almost full of wine. Where then was that wise old woman with her forceful prohibitions? Could anything avail against the evil in us, unless Your healing, O Lord, watched over us? When our father and mother and nurses are absent, You are present, who created us, who call us, who can use those placed over us for some good unto the salvation of our souls. What did You do then, O my God? How did You cure her, and bring her to health? From another soul you drew a harsh and cutting sarcasm, as though bringing forth a surgeon's knife from Your secret store, and with one blow amputated that sore place. A maidservant with whom she was accustomed to go to the cellar, one day fell into a quarrel with her small mistress when no one else chanced to be about, and hurled at her the most biting insult possible, calling her a drunkard. My mother was pierced to the quick, saw her fault in its true wickedness, and instantly condemned it and gave it up. Just as the flattery of a friend can pervert, so the insult of an enemy can sometimes correct. Nor do You, O God, reward men according to what You do by means of them, but according to what they themselves intended. For the girl being in a temper wanted to enrage her young mistress, not to amend her, for she did it when no one else was there, either because the time and place happened to be thus when the quarrel arose, or because she was afraid that elders[3] would be angry because she had not told it sooner. But You, O Lord, Ruler of heavenly things and earthly, who turn to Your own purposes the very depths of rivers as they run and order the turbulence of the flow of time, did by the folly of one mind bring sanity to another; thus reminding us not to attribute it to our own power if another is amended by our word, even if we meant to amend him.

My mother, then, was modestly and soberly brought up, being rather made obedient to her parents by You than to You by her parents. When she reached the age for marriage, and was bestowed upon a husband, she served him as her lord. She used all her effort to win him to You, preaching You to him by her character, by which You made her beautiful to her husband, respected and loved by him and admirable in his sight. For she bore his acts of unfaithfulness quietly, and never had any jealous scene with her husband about them. She awaited Your mercy upon him, that he might grow chaste through faith in You. And as a matter of fact, though generous beyond measure, he had a very hot temper. But she knew that a woman must not resist a husband in anger, by deed or even by word. Only, when she saw him calm again and quiet, she would take the opportunity to give him an explanation of her actions, if it happened that he had been roused to anger unreasonably. The result was that whereas many matrons with much milder husbands carried the marks of blows to disfigure their faces, and would all get together to complain of the way their husbands behaved, my mother—talking lightly but

---

3. Leaders of the church.

meaning it seriously—advised them against their tongues: saying that from the day they heard the matrimonial contract read to them they should regard it as an instrument by which they became servants; and from that time they should be mindful of their condition and not set themselves up against their masters. And they often expressed amazement—for they knew how violent a husband she had to live with—that it had never been heard, and there was no mark to show, that Patricius[4] had beaten his wife or that there had been any family quarrel between them for so much as a single day. And when her friends asked her the reason, she taught them her rule, which was as I have just said. Those who followed it, found it good and thanked her; those who did not, went on being bullied and beaten.

Her mother-in-law began by being angry with her because of the whispers of malicious servants. But my mother won her completely by the respect she showed, and her unfailing patience and mildness. She ended by going to her son, telling him of the tales the servants had bandied about to the destruction of peace in the family between herself and her daughter-in-law, and asking him to punish them for it. So he, out of obedience to his mother and in the interests of order in the household and peace among his womenfolk, had the servants beaten whose names he had been given, as she had asked when giving them. To which she added the promise that anyone must expect a similar reward from her own hands who should think to please her by speaking ill of her daughter-in-law. And as no one had the courage to do so, they lived together with the most notable degree of kindness and harmony.

This great gift also, O my God, my Mercy, You gave to Your good servant, in whose womb You created me, that she showed herself, wherever possible, a peacemaker between people quarreling and minds at discord. For swelling and undigested discord often belches forth bitter words when in the venom of intimate conversation with a present friend hatred at its rawest is breathed out upon an absent enemy. But when my mother heard bitter things said by each of the other, she never said anything to either about the other save what would help to reconcile them. This might seem a small virtue, if I had not had the sorrow of seeing for myself so many people who—as if by some horrible widespreading infection of sin—not only tell angry people the things their enemies said in anger, but even add things that were never said at all. Whereas, on the contrary, ordinary humanity would seem to require not merely that we refrain from exciting or increasing wrath among men by evil speaking, but that we study to extinguish wrath by kind speaking. Such a one was she: and You were the master who taught her most secretly in the school of her heart.

The upshot was that toward the very end of his life she won her husband to You; and once he was a Christian she no longer had to complain of the things she had had to bear with before he was a Christian. Further, she was a servant of Your servants. Such of them as knew her praised and honored and loved You, O God, in her; for they felt Your presence in her heart, showing itself in the fruit of her holy conversation. She had been *the wife of one husband, had requited her parents, had governed her house* piously, *was well reported of for good works. She had brought up her children,*[5] being in labor of them as often as she saw them swerving away from You. Finally of

---

4. Augustine's father.   5. Augustine is paraphrasing Paul's description of the duties of a widow, given in 1 Timothy 5.

all of us Your servants, O Lord—since by Your gift You suffer us to speak—
who before her death were living together[6] after receiving the grace of baptism, she took as much care as if she had been the mother of us all, and
served us as if she had been the daughter of us all.

When the day was approaching on which she was to depart this life—a
day that You knew though we did not—it came about, as I believe by Your
secret arrangement, that she and I stood alone leaning in a window, which
looked inwards to the garden within the house where we were staying, at
Ostia on the Tiber; for there we were away from everybody, resting for the
sea voyage from the weariness of our long journey by land. There we talked
together, she and I alone, in deep joy; and *forgetting the things that were
behind and looking forward to those that were before*, we were discussing in
the presence of Truth, which You are, what the eternal life of the saints
could be like, *which eye has not seen nor ear heard, nor has it entered into the
heart of man*. But with the mouth of our heart we panted for the high waters
of Your fountain, the fountain of the life which is with You: that being sprinkled from that fountain according to our capacity, we might in some sense
meditate upon so great a matter.

And our conversation had brought us to this point, that any pleasure whatsoever of the bodily senses, in any brightness whatsoever of corporeal light,
seemed to us not worthy of comparison with the pleasure of that eternal
Light, not worthy even of mention. Rising as our love flamed upward towards
that Selfsame,[7] we passed in review the various levels of bodily things, up to
the heavens themselves, whence sun and moon and stars shine upon this
earth. And higher still we soared, thinking in our minds and speaking and
marveling at Your works: and so we came to our own souls, and went beyond
them to come at last to that region of richness unending, where You feed
Israel forever with the food of truth: and there life is that Wisdom by which
all things are made, both the things that have been and the things that are
yet to be. But this Wisdom itself is not made: it is as it has ever been, and
so it shall be forever: indeed "has ever been" and "shall be forever" have no
place in it, but it simply is, for it is eternal: whereas "to have been" and "to
be going to be" are not eternal. And while we were thus talking of His Wisdom and panting for it, with all the effort of our heart we did for one instant
attain to touch it; then sighing, and leaving the first fruits of our spirit bound
to it, we returned to the sound of our own tongue, in which a word has both
beginning and ending. For what is like to your Word, Our Lord, who abides
in Himself forever, yet grows not old and makes all things new!

So we said: If to any man the tumult of the flesh grew silent, silent the
images of earth and sea and air: and if the heavens grew silent, and the very
soul grew silent to herself and by not thinking of self mounted beyond self:
if all dreams and imagined visions grew silent, and every tongue and every
sign and whatsoever is transient—for indeed if any man could hear them,
he should hear them saying with one voice: We did not make ourselves, but
He made us who abides forever: but if, having uttered this and so set us to
listening to Him who made them, they all grew silent, and in their silence
He alone spoke to us, not by them but by Himself: so that we should hear

---

6. Augustine and his fellow converts.   7. Reality, the divine principle. This ecstasy of Augustine and
Monica is throughout described in philosophical terms, in which God is Wisdom.

His word, not by any tongue of flesh nor the voice of an angel nor the sound of thunder nor in the darkness of a parable,[8] but that we should hear Himself whom in all these things we love, should hear Himself and not them: just as we two had but now reached forth and in a flash of the mind attained to touch the eternal Wisdom which abides over all: and if this could continue, and all other visions so different be quite taken away, and this one should so ravish and absorb and wrap the beholder in inward joys that his life should eternally be such as that one moment of understanding for which we had been sighing—would not this be: *Enter Thou into the joy of Thy Lord?* But when shall it be? Shall it be when *we shall all rise again* and *shall not all be changed?*[9]

Such thoughts I uttered, though not in that order or in those actual words; but You know, O Lord, that on that day when we talked of these things the world with all its delights seemed cheap to us in comparison with what we talked of. And my mother said: "Son, for my own part I no longer find joy in anything in this world. What I am still to do here and why I am here I know not, now that I no longer hope for anything from this world. One thing there was, for which I desired to remain still a little longer in this life, that I should see you a Catholic Christian before I died. This God has granted me in superabundance, in that I now see you His servant to the contempt of all worldly happiness. What then am I doing here?"

What answer I made, I do not clearly remember; within five days or not much longer she fell into a fever. And in her sickness, she one day fainted away and for the moment lost consciousness. We ran to her but she quickly returned to consciousness, and seeing my brother and me standing by her she said as one wondering: "Where was I?" Then looking closely upon us as we stood wordless in our grief, she said: "Here you will bury your mother." I stayed silent and checked my weeping. But my brother said something to the effect that he would be happier if she were to die in her own land and not in a strange country. But as she heard this she looked at him anxiously, restraining him with her eye because he savored of earthly things, and then she looked at me and said: "See the way he talks." And then she said to us both: "Lay this body wherever it may be. Let no care of it disturb you: this only I ask of you that you should remember me at the altar of the Lord wherever you may be." And when she had uttered this wish in such words as she could manage, she fell silent as her sickness took hold of her more strongly.

But as I considered Your gifts, O unseen God, which You send into the hearts of Your faithful to the springing up of such wonderful fruits, I was glad and gave thanks to You, remembering what I had previously known of the care as to her burial which had always troubled her: for she had arranged to be buried by the body of her husband. Because they had lived together in such harmony, she had wished—so little is the human mind capable of rising to the divine—that it should be granted her, as an addition to her happiness and as something to be spoken of among men, that after her pilgrimage beyond the sea the earthly part of man and wife should lie together under

8. Compare Luke 8.10: "Unto you it is given to know the mysteries of the kingdom of God: but to others in parables; that seeing they might not see, and hearing they might not understand."   9. Compare 1 Corinthians 15.52: "the trumpet shall sound, and the dead shall be raised incorruptible, and we shall be changed," referring to the Last Judgment.

the same earth. Just when this vain desire had begun to vanish from her heart through the fullness of Your goodness, I did not know; but I was pleased and surprised that it had now so clearly vanished: though indeed in the conversation we had had together at the window, when she said: "What am I still doing here?" there had appeared no desire to die in her own land. Further I heard afterwards that in the time we were at Ostia, she had talked one day to some of my friends, as a mother talking to her children, of the contempt of this life and of the attraction of death. I was not there at the time. They marveled at such courage in a woman—but it was You who had given it to her—and asked if she was not afraid to leave her body so far from her own city. But she said: "Nothing is far from God, and I have no fear that He will not know at the end of the world from what place He is to raise me up." And so on the ninth day of her illness, in the fifty-sixth year of her life and the thirty-third of mine, that devout and holy soul was released from the body.

I closed her eyes; and an immeasurable sorrow flowed into my heart and would have overflowed in tears. But my eyes under the mind's strong constraint held back their flow and I stood dry-eyed. In that struggle it went very ill with me. As she breathed her last, the child Adeodatus broke out into lamentation and we all checked him and brought him to silence. But in this very fact the childish element in me, which was breaking out into tears, was checked and brought to silence by the manlier voice of my mind. For we felt that it was not fitting that her funeral should be solemnized with moaning and weeping and lamentation, for so it is normal to weep when death is seen as sheer misery or as complete extinction. But she had not died miserably, nor did she wholly die. Of the one thing we were sure by reason of her character, of the other by the reality of our faith.

What then was it that grieved my heart so deeply? Only the newness of the wound, in finding the custom I had so loved of living with her suddenly snapped short. It was a joy to me to have this one testimony from her: when her illness was close to its end, meeting with expressions of endearment such services as I rendered, she called me a dutiful loving son, and said in the great affection of her love that she had never heard from my mouth any harsh or reproachful word addressed to herself. But what possible comparison was there, O my God who made us, between the honor I showed her and the service she had rendered me?

Because I had now lost the great comfort of her, my soul was wounded and my very life torn asunder, for it had been one life made of hers and mine together. When the boy had been quieted and ceased weeping, Evodius took up the psalter and began to chant—with the whole house making the responses—the psalm *Mercy and judgment I will sing to Thee, O Lord.*[1] And when they heard what was being done, many of the brethren and religious women came to us; those whose office it was were making arrangement for the burial, while, in another part of the house where it could properly be done I discoursed, with friends who did not wish to leave me by myself, upon matters suitable for that time. Thus I used truth as a kind of fomentation[2] to bring relief to my torment, a torment known to You, but not known to those others: so that listening closely to me they thought that I lacked all

1. Compare Psalm 101.1.   2. Soothing dressing for a wound.

feeling of grief. But in Your ears, where none of them could hear, I accused the emotion in me as weakness; and I held in the flood of my grief. It was for the moment a little diminished, but returned with fresh violence, not with any pouring of tears or change of countenance: but I knew what I was crushing down in my heart. I was very much ashamed that these human emotions could have such power over me—though it belongs to the due order and the lot of our earthly condition that they should come to us—and I felt a new grief at my grief and so was afflicted with a twofold sorrow.

When the body was taken to burial, I went and returned without tears. During the prayers which we poured forth to you when the sacrifice of our redemption[3] was offered for her—while the body, as the custom there is, lay by the grave before it was actually buried—during those prayers I did not weep. Yet all that day I was heavy with grief within and in the trouble of my mind I begged of You in my own fashion to heal my pain; but You would not—I imagine because You meant to impress upon my memory by this proof how strongly the bond of habit holds the mind even when it no longer feeds upon deception. The idea came to me to go and bathe, for I had heard that the bath—which the Greeks call βαλανεῖον[4]—is so called because it drives anxiety from the mind. And this also I acknowledge to Your mercy, O Father of orphans, that I bathed and was the same man after as before. The bitterness of grief had not sweated out of my heart. Then I fell asleep, and woke again to find my grief not a little relieved. And as I was in bed and no one about, I said over those true verses that Your servant Ambrose wrote of You:

> Deus creator omnium
> polique rector vestiens
> diem decoro lumine,
> noctem sopora gratia,
>
> artus solutos ut quies
> reddat laboris usui
> mentesque fessas allevet
> luctusque solvat anxios.[5]

And then little by little I began to recover my former feeling about Your handmaid, remembering how loving and devout was her conversation with You, how pleasant and considerate her conversation with me, of which I was thus suddenly deprived. And I found solace in weeping in Your sight both about her and for her, about myself and for myself. I no longer tried to check my tears, but let them flow as they would, making them a pillow for my heart: and it rested upon them, for it was Your ears that heard my weeping, and not the ears of a man, who would have misunderstood my tears and despised them. But now, O Lord, I confess it to You in writing, let him read it who will and interpret it as he will: and if he sees it as sin that for so small a portion of an hour I wept for my mother, now dead and departed from my sight, who had wept so many years for me that I should live ever in Your sight—let him not scorn me but rather, if he is a man of great charity, let

---

3. Perhaps a communion service.　4. Augustine evidently derives *balaneion* ("bath") from the words *ballō* ("cast away") and *ania* ("sorrow").　5. God, the creator of all things / and ruler of the heavens / you who clothe the day with the glory of light, / and the night with the gift of sleep, / so that rest may relax the limbs / and restore them for the day's work / relieve the fatigue of the mind / and dispel anxiety and grief (Latin).

him weep for my sins to You, the Father of all the brethren of Your Christ.

Now that my heart is healed of that wound, in which there was perhaps too much of earthly affection, I pour forth to You, O our God, tears of a very different sort for Your handmaid—tears that flow from a spirit shaken by the thought of the perils there are for every soul that dies in Adam.[6] For though she had been made alive in Christ, and while still in the body had so lived that Your name was glorified in her faith and her character, yet I dare not say that from the moment of her regeneration in baptism no word issued from her mouth contrary to Your Command. Your Son, who is Truth, has said: *Whosoever shall say to his brother, Thou fool, shall be in danger of hell fire;*[7] and it would go ill with the most praiseworthy life lived by men, if You were to examine it with Your mercy laid aside! But because You do not enquire too fiercely into our sins, we have hope and confidence of a place with You. Yet if a man reckons up before You the merits he truly has, what is he reckoning except Your own gifts? If only men would know themselves to be but men, so that he that glories would glory in the Lord!

Thus, my Glory and my Life, God of my heart, leaving aside for this time her good deeds, for which I give thanks to Thee in joy, I now pray to Thee for my mother's sins. Grant my prayer through the true Medicine of our wounds,[8] who hung upon the cross and who now sitting at Thy right hand makes intercession for us. I know that she dealt mercifully, and from her heart forgave those who trespassed against her: do Thou also forgive such trespasses as she may have been guilty of in all the years since her baptism, forgive them, Lord, forgive them, I beseech Thee: enter not into judgment with her. Let Thy mercy be exalted above Thy justice for Thy words are true and Thou hast promised that the merciful shall obtain mercy. That they should be merciful is Thy gift who *hast mercy on whom Thou wilt, and wilt have compassion on whom Thou wilt.*

And I believe that Thou hast already done what I am now asking; but be not offended, Lord, at the things my mouth would utter. For on that day when her death was so close, she was not concerned that her body should be sumptuously wrapped or embalmed with spices, nor with any thought of choosing a monument or even for burial in her own country. Of such things she gave us no command, but only desired to be remembered at Thy altar, which she had served without ever missing so much as a day, on which she knew that the holy Victim was offered; *by whom the handwriting is blotted out of the decree that was contrary to us,*[9] by which offering too the enemy was overcome who, reckoning our sins and seeking what may be laid to our charge, found nothing in Him, in whom we are conquerors. Who shall restore to Him his innocent blood? Who shall give Him back the price by which He purchased us and so take us from Him? To this sacrament of our redemption Thy handmaid had bound her soul by the bond of faith. Let none wrest her from Thy protection; let neither the lion nor the dragon[1] bar her way by force or craft. For she will not answer that she owes nothing, lest she should be contradicted and confuted by that cunning accuser: but she will

---

6. That is, with the curse of Adam not nullified through baptism in Jesus Christ and conformity with his teachings.   7. From Matthew 5.22, Jesus' Sermon on the Mount. He is preaching a more severe moral code than the traditional one that whoever kills shall be liable to judgment.   8. Jesus.   9. An allusion to Christ's redemption of humanity from the curse of Adam through the Crucifixion.   1. Compare Psalm 91.13: "Thou shalt tread upon the lion and the adder: the young lion and the dragon shalt thou trample under feet, which invokes God's protection of the godly."

answer that her debts have been remitted by Him, to whom no one can hand back the price which He paid for us, though He owed it not.

So let her rest in peace, together with her husband, for she had no other before nor after him, but served him, in patience bringing forth fruit for Thee, and winning him likewise for Thee. And inspire, O my Lord my God, inspire Thy servants my brethren, Thy sons my masters, whom I serve with heart and voice and pen, that as many of them as read this may remember at Thy altar Thy servant Monica, with Patricius, her husband, by whose bodies Thou didst bring me into this life, though how I know not.[2] May they with loving mind remember these who were my parents in this transitory light, my brethren who serve Thee as our Father in our Catholic mother, and those who are to be fellow citizens with me in the eternal Jerusalem,[3] which Thy people sigh for in their pilgrimage from birth until they come there: so that what my mother at her end asked of me may be fulfilled more richly in the prayers of so many gained for her by my Confessions than by my prayers alone.

* * *

---

2. Augustine does not understand the seemingly miraculous process by which the fetus grows in the womb.
3. I.e., heaven.

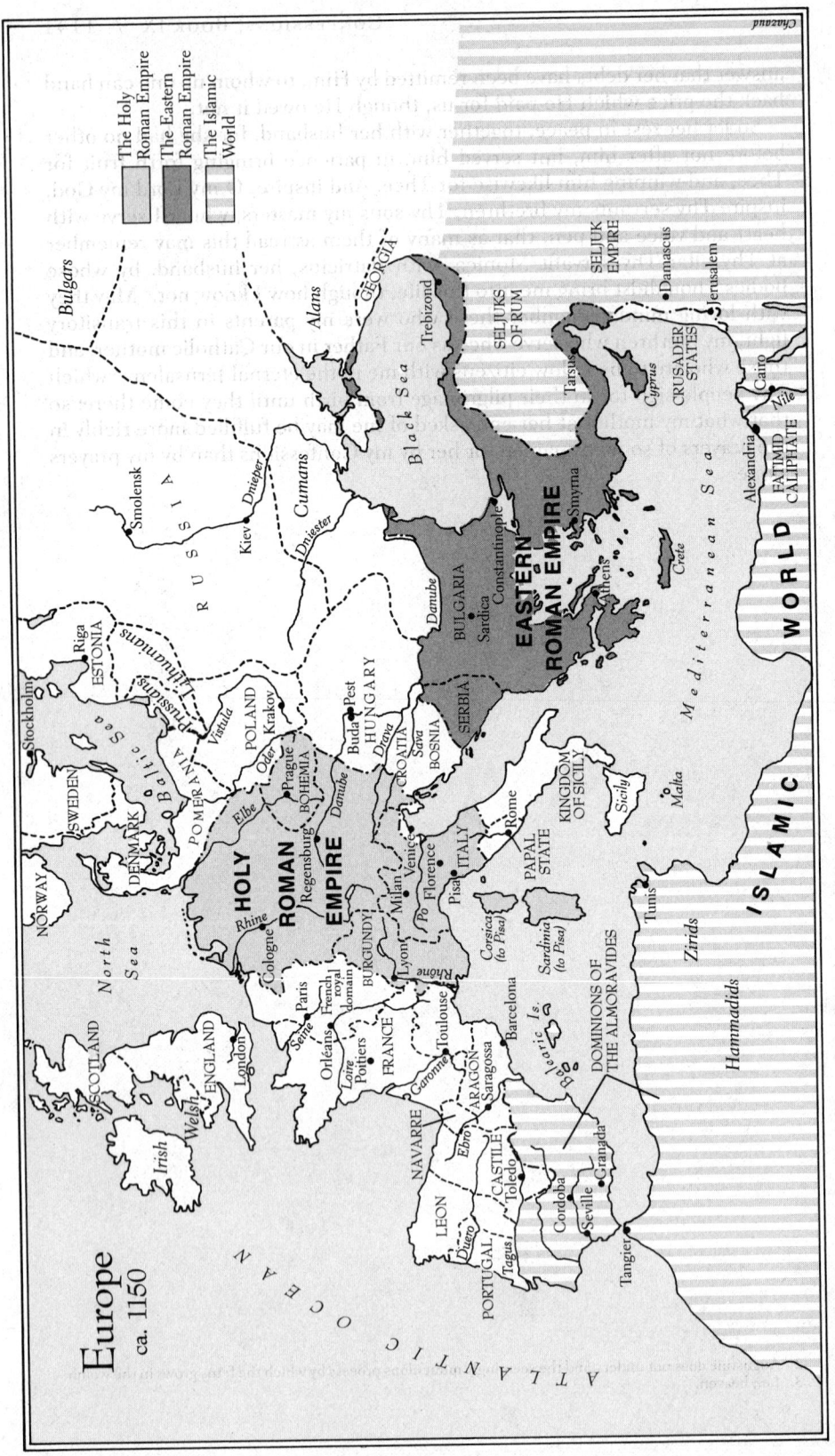

Europe
ca. 1150

The Holy Roman Empire
The Eastern Roman Empire
The Islamic World

Chazaud

ATLANTIC OCEAN

North Sea

SCOTLAND

Irish

Welsh

ENGLAND

London

NORWAY

SWEDEN

Stockholm

DENMARK

Baltic Sea

ESTONIA

Riga

Lithuanians

Prussians

POMERANIA

Oder

Vistula

RUSSIA

Smolensk

Dnieper

Kiev

Cumans

Dniester

Alans

GEORGIA

Bulgars

Trebizond

Black Sea

SELJUK EMPIRE

SELJUKS OF RUM

Tarsus

Damascus

Jerusalem

CRUSADER STATES

Cyprus

Cairo

Alexandria

Nile

FATIMID CALIPHATE

ISLAMIC WORLD

Mediterranean Sea

Crete

Athens

Smyrna

Constantinople

EASTERN ROMAN EMPIRE

Sardica

BULGARIA

SERBIA

BOSNIA

CROATIA

Sava

Drava

Danube

HUNGARY

Buda

Pest

POLAND

Krakov

Prague

BOHEMIA

Elbe

Regensburg

HOLY ROMAN EMPIRE

Rhine

Cologne

Paris

French royal domain

Seine

Orléans

Loire

Poitiers

FRANCE

Toulouse

Garonne

BURGUNDY

Lyons

Rhône

Po

Milan

Venice

Florence

Pisa

ITALY

Rome

PAPAL STATE

KINGDOM OF SICILY

Sicily

Malta

Tunis

Zirids

Hammadids

Corsica (to Pisa)

Sardinia (to Pisa)

Balearic Is.

DOMINIONS OF THE ALMORAVIDES

Barcelona

ARAGON

Saragossa

Ebro

NAVARRE

LEON

CASTILE

Toledo

Tagus

Duero

PORTUGAL

Seville

Cordoba

Granada

Tangier

The Middle Ages

The Middle Ages—approximately the thousand years from 500 to 1500—saw the classical civilization of Greece and Rome transformed by contact with three very different cultures. One was the Germanic culture of the tribes who invaded and, by the fifth century, had effectively conquered the western half of the Roman empire. The second was the Christianity that began in Palestine and then quickly spread throughout the empire until almost all of Western Europe was thoroughly Christianized by the eleventh century (as early as 325 the emperor Constantine had established Christianity as the official religion of the empire). The third influence—less pronounced but still important—was Islam, which arose in the Arabian peninsula in the seventh century and quickly spread throughout North Africa and into the Iberian peninsula, where it remained a powerful force until the fifteenth century. Because it was a combination of these vastly different cultural forces, medieval Europe displayed a wide range of values, ideas, and social forms. But for all this variety there emerged at the end of the process a recognizable culture. In the year 500 "the West" could hardly be defined either politically or culturally, but by 1500 the map of Europe looked very much as it does today. Many of the values we think of as characteristically Western—individualism, consensual government, a recognition of religious difference, even the idea of Europe itself—were emergent realities. Another central event within Western culture during this period was the emergence of vernacular literatures. The great national literatures of Europe took form during the Middle Ages, and here we find both individual literary masterpieces and traditions of writing that have continued to define Western literature.

Because it is the period during which the cultural identities of the European nations took shape, the Middle Ages has always generated both fascination and controversy. Take, for example, its distinctly odd name: the *middle* of what? The answer is that the period was named by the people who came immediately after it, who called their own age the Renaissance because they saw it as the time in which the cultural achievements of antiquity were being reborn. For them the immediately preceding period was a time of middleness, a space of cultural emptiness that separated them from the classical past they so admired: hence, the Middle Ages (or, in Latin, *medium aevum,* from which we get our term *medieval*). That this narrow view of cultural history is still in force today is shown by the way in which "medieval" continues to be used to mean antiquated, or quaint, or barbaric. It is also evident in the widespread notion that the Middle Ages was unusually homogeneous, a time in which all men and women thought and felt more or less the same things and behaved in much the same way. Yet in fact this period contains not one but many different kinds of people with many different cultures.

These cultures were oral and literate; Germanic and Latin; Arabic, Jewish, and Christian; secular and religious; tolerant and repressive; colloquial and learned; rural and urban; skeptical and pious; popular and aristocratic. For every example of one kind of cultural product we can find an example of another, and most significant literary works incorporated elements and values drawn from different and often conflicting traditions. *The Song of Roland,* for instance, composed in the eleventh century, promotes with unabashed enthusiasm the superiority of Christianity to Islam. Yet already in the ninth century, Islamic scholars had translated much of Greek science and philosophy into Arabic, preserving and enriching this tradition at the very time it was in decline in Western Europe. And beginning in the twelfth century, Muslim centers of learning in Spain, Sicily, and southern Italy made it possible for European scholars to regain access to these Greek originals and to study their Arabic commentators. Similarly complex is the way *The Song of Roland* struggles with internal contradictions of its own. The poem exalts a great warrior according to Germanic traditions of military heroism, but also affirms the necessity of subordinating individual accomplishment to the needs of a unified Christian community. Another example of the clash of competing interests can be found in the work of Geoffrey Chaucer, the founding poet of English literature. For the first two-thirds of his career he was a court poet who catered almost exclusively to the narrow tastes of an aristocratic readership, and yet in *The Canterbury Tales* he recorded the discontents and desires of men and women from almost every social class. These complexities and contradictions are everywhere in medieval writing, and if they frustrate modern attempts to define the period in simple terms they also make reading its literature a process of continuing surprise.

The most familiar description of the Middle Ages is as "an age of faith," by which is meant the notion that medieval people shared a uniform commitment to Catholic Christianity. The Roman empire had provided political unity, law, and order, but beyond that it had pretty much left moral and spiritual issues to be handled by the individual, either singly or in communities. As the Middle Ages developed, however, the Church gradually extended its spiritual and institutional authority across most of Europe. By 1200, with the exception of beleaguered Jewish communities, the area of the Iberian peninsula under Muslim control, and frontier lands in the Slavic east, Europe had become identical with Christendom. But this acknowledgment of the primacy of Christian doctrine and its rituals (such as baptism, communion, and confession) meant neither that religious values were universally recognized as primary nor that one single form of Christianity was placidly accepted by all medieval people. On the contrary, as the literature of the period makes clear, many people took the central doctrines of Christianity so much for granted that their daily lives seem largely untroubled by the moral and spiritual demands of religion. In the *Lais* of Marie de France, for example, and the vernacular love lyrics, men and women lead their romantic lives without giving much if any thought to Christian standards of behavior. In a more satiric vein, the French fabliaux and the tales from Boccaccio's *Decameron* provide an often acerbic and always witty puncturing of the pretensions of individual churchmen. The lecherous priest and the greedy friar are stock characters of medieval satire, as are the wayward nun and the gluttonous monk. Another pressure point at which Christian doctrine is tested is the Germanic epic *Beowulf*, a poem written by a believer who nonetheless deeply admires the pagan past that he knows must be left behind. Even in *The Divine Comedy*, the work that seems most securely located within the Christian worldview, Dante is poignantly aware of the gulf that separates him from the classical past, represented in the *Inferno* and *Purgatorio* by the man he calls "my author and my father," the pagan poet Virgil. The Middle Ages *is* an age of faith, but one that is also alert to the complexities and dilemmas that any faith poses to its adherents.

Another familiar description of the Middle Ages is as "an age of chivalry." Medieval literature for the most part expresses the values of the most powerful members of society, the aristocracy. These people achieved their domination through military might, both by imposing their will upon their neighbors and, more benevolently, by providing them with protection from invaders like the Vikings from the north, the Magyars and Mongols from the east, and the various Islamic peoples from the south. At times they became themselves the invaders, most notably in the various crusading expeditions that began in the eleventh century against Islam in the Iberian peninsula and the Middle East and, later, against the Slavs in what is now Eastern Europe. Not surprisingly, throughout its medieval history, from the time of *Beowulf* (eighth to the tenth centuries) to that of Malory's Arthurian tales (late fifteenth century), the

European nobility—and the writers they supported—celebrated military values. These included unwavering valor in the face of danger, loyalty to one's leader and companions, and an intense concern for personal honor. They also came to include a more or less explicit code of chivalry that stressed gentility of demeanor, generosity of both spirit and material goods, concern for the well-being of the powerless, and—above all—a capacity for experiencing a romantic love that was at once selfless and passionate. Whether or not medieval men actually lived up to these chivalric ideals is impossible to say, but that many believed in them—and believed that they achieved them—is undeniable. Yet many other members of medieval society, especially non-nobles like churchmen, urban dwellers, and peasants, were more likely than not to think that chivalry was just a fancy name for the heavy-handed imposition of force upon those least able to resist. More important for the writing of the time is the fact that chivalric values are never entirely consistent with each other. When does personal bravery give way to the needs of the group?—this is a question at the heart of both *Beowulf* and *The Song of Roland*. Can one be both a full-hearted lover and a loyal warrior? And can the same people perform both the deeds of war and those of civilization?—this is a question central to Western literature since the time of Homer and still challenging to us today.

The busy millennium we call, in the absence of a more precise term, the Middle Ages is thus dominated by certain leading concerns—the demands of religious faith and the appropriate use of physical force—that remain current. What continues to make its literature compelling to us is the skill with which individual writers dealt with these themes through the creation of unforgettable literary characters. For all its accomplishments in the arts of governing and the skills of commerce, in philosophy and theology, and in art and architecture, the most vivid legacy of the Middle Ages is the roster of characters it has contributed to world literature. Roland and Charlemagne, Robin Hood, Sir Gawain and Beowulf, the pilgrims of *The Canterbury Tales* and the lost souls of the *Inferno*: whether searching for the road to salvation or killing monsters, whether battling pagan enemies or hoodwinking unwary dupes, the protagonists of medieval literature continue to intrigue readers and inspire writers. In the last analysis the central concern of medieval literature is the individual human being working out his or her individual destiny.

THE MIDDLE AGES

TEXTS	CONTEXTS
	529 Foundation of Monte Cassino, the first Benedictine monastery
610–32 *The Koran*	
8th–10th centuries *Beowulf* • Latin lyrics, saints' lives, and histories	**8th–10th centuries** Invasions of Western Europe by Arabs, Norsemen, and Magyars
	800 Charlemagne crowned Holy Roman Emperor
	899 Alfred the Great, king of Wessex in England, dies
11th century Hispano-Arabic and Provençal lyrics • *The Song of Roland*	**11th century** Consolidation of feudal social structure
	1066 Norman invasion of England
	1099 Knights of the First Crusade capture Jerusalem
12th century Marie de France, *Lais* • Chrétien de Troyes, *Story of the Grail*	**12th century** Establishment of the universities of Paris, Oxford, and Bologna • Recovery of Aristotelian philosophy • Period of religious reform
	1187 Arabs recover Jerusalem permanently
13th century Fabliaux • *Romance of the Rose* • *Thorstein the Staff-Struck*	**13th century** Age of the great cathedrals and of scholastic philosophy
	1226 Francis of Assisi, founder of the first order of friars, dies
	1274 Thomas Aquinas, leading scholastic philosopher, dies
1301–21 Dante, *The Divine Comedy*	
	1337 War begins between France and England (The Hundred Years' War), ending only in 1453
	1348–50 Bubonic plague sweeps through Europe, killing over a third of the population
1353 Boccaccio, *The Decameron*	
1380? *Sir Gawain and the Green Knight*	
	1384 John Wyclif, promoter of religious views that prepare for the Reformation, dies
1386–1400 Chaucer, *The Canterbury Tales*	
14th century *The Thousand and One Nights*	**14th century** Peasant risings in England, France, Flanders, and Italy

Boldface titles indicate works in the anthology.

THE MIDDLE AGES

TEXTS	CONTEXTS
	15th century Growing centralization of state power throughout Europe
	1453 Fall of Constantinople to the Muslim Turks
	1455 Gutenberg prints the Bible, the first printed book
ca. 1470 Villon, *The Testament*	
	1492 Christopher Columbus's first voyage to the Western Hemisphere
1495? *Everyman*	

THE KORAN
610–632

For Muslims the Koran is something greater than prophetic revelation. It is an earthly duplicate of a divine Koran that exists in paradise engraved in figures of gold on tablets of marble. Like God, it was not created but exists for all eternity—a complete and sufficient guide to our conduct on earth. It is God's final revelation to humanity and was sent by Him to complete and correct all prior revelations. In its divinity it is greater than any prophet or any prophecy. It stands to Muslims as Christ does to Christians. To the glory of Muhammad's community, God chose to make this, His final revelation, in Arabic and through an Arab prophet. Because the Koran is, literally, God's word and is, like Him, miraculous and eternal, it cannot be translated. Interpretive renderings into other languages have been made and used for teaching purposes since the earliest period of Islam, but Muslims do not accept them as the Koran in the sense that Christians accept the Bible in English, or any of the other languages into which it has been translated, as still the Bible.

The Koran's revelations were received by Muhammad, known to Muslims as the Prophet of God, during the last two decades of his life—from roughly 610, when the angel Gabriel first appeared to him, to his death on June 8, 632. During his lifetime these revelations were recorded by various of his followers, but they were only gathered together into a comprehensive volume after his death. The title given this collection is the Koran (al-qur'ân), or the Recitation, and, as its title suggests, the Koran is a work to be heard and recited, an oral work with a music and rhythm of its own that does not appear to best advantage on the printed page. The text itself is far more dialogic than narrative. God speaks with Muhammad, or instructs him to give his community a particular message, or to "Recite!" Muhammad and other earlier prophets carry on frustrated dialogues with their doubting communities on the one hand and, on the other, with a demanding God. Only rarely does narrative replace the intermingling of voices in dialogue.

The revelations came to Muhammad in verses (âya) of varying length and number. These were gathered into larger divisions (Suras) that were organized roughly by subject. These gatherings often appear arbitrary, and there are abrupt transitions from subject in the longer Suras. Only the shortest are thematically unified and only Sura 12, Yusuf, tells a complete narrative. The Suras were then arranged by length, with the longer Suras preceding the shorter. Each Sura was given a name taken from some striking image or theme that appears in it. They are also identified as having been received in either Mecca or Medina, the two communities in which Muhammad lived. It is an article of faith with Muslims that the Koran we now have is a complete and accurate record of God's revelations to Muhammad and an exact copy of the divine Koran that exists in the seventh heaven.

Although the Koran was revealed over a relatively brief period, its style varies enormously. The earliest and shortest Suras sound like charms or incantations, evoking the wonder and glory of God:

> In the Name of God, the Compassionate, the Merciful
> Say: "I seek refuge in the Lord of men, the King of men, the God of men, from the mischief of the slinking prompter who whispers in the hearts of men; from jinn and men" (Men [entire] 114.1–6).

The later and longer ones are filled with legal prescriptions:

> Do not give the feeble-minded the property with which God has entrusted you for their support; but maintain and clothe them with its proceeds, and give them good advice (Women 4.6).

And many, perhaps most, of the Suras have the quality of sermons delivered in a highly charged and poetic language, often enriched by parables and brief narratives that exhort us to remember God and live pious lives. The earlier and longer Suras, like sermons, are mixtures of various styles—exhortation, evocation, legal prescription, and sage counsel.

The style of the individual Suras reflects in general terms the moments in Muhammad's life when they were revealed. In the early Meccan period of his mission, his concerns were those of an embattled prophet exhorting his community to believe in God and fear Him and defending himself against the hostility and skepticism of those who doubted both him and his God. The Suras from this period are filled with fierce and eloquent exhortations promising paradise to those who believe in God and eternal damnation to those who deny Him. These Suras are also marked by calls for social justice, expressed principally in concern for the plight of widows and orphans. It was in Mecca, too, that the accounts of earlier prophets from Noah (Nuh) to Jesus (Isâ)—who, like Muhammad, had to defend themselves against a hostile and unbelieving community—were revealed to him.

Eventually, Muhammad's success in creating a community of believers made him so unwelcome in his home that the Meccans forced him and his followers to emigrate to the nearby oasis of Medina. There he established his community among the tribes already settled around the oasis. While Muhammad continued to be the Prophet of Islam, the legal and political demands of his community now occupied most of his attention. He also had to cope with the growing number of believers who flocked to him and, eventually, to manage a war with the Meccans. The Suras revealed in Medina reflect these concerns in setting forth an extensive and detailed legal code that addresses the demands of the day-to-day life of the community as well as its spiritual needs.

These stylistic differences point out an obvious distinction between the Koran and the Bible. The essence of the Koran is admonition and guidance. No narrative thread runs through it, nor is it embedded in the history of a single people. The Koran's coherence is a product of the themes that are reiterated throughout its many Suras. For all the importance it gives to one language, Arabic, its message is a more general one. The many allusions to Moses (Musa), for example, stress that God may choose even an ordinary, flawed man to be His prophet and say nothing of Moses' role as the leader of his people. The meaning of the Koran, as it often asserts, is for all humanity.

The Exordium, the opening Sura of the Koran, has an exceptional resonance in the life of Muslims. They recite it at the beginning of every formal address and inscribe it at the head of every written document from works of scholarship to the stones that mark a grave. It begins every prayer.

Joseph (Sura 12) is, of course, not a prophet in Judaism or Christianity, but he is in Islam. He is also the only one whose tale is told continuously, and the only one to be mentioned exclusively in a single Sura. The Koranic version of this story includes most of the key events of Genesis 36–38 but excludes virtually everything that links Joseph to the Hebrews. In Genesis, Joseph is a divinely guided young man who is first tested severely and then becomes the leader of his people, guiding them to prosperity in Egypt. In the Koran he is a divinely guided young man but not the leader of any nation. Although God tests Joseph, it is to prove that only those who follow divine guidance prosper. In the most famous scene, the temptation by his master's wife, he is not more righteous than she, but God gives him a sign that he should not succumb. Islam does not believe in original sin, and is more accepting of human error than Genesis. Joseph's innocence in this encounter is also explicitly established in Sura 12, while in Genesis only we and God see that Joseph is blameless. His master's wife, identified as Zuleikha in the commentaries, is also treated in a more tolerant fashion than Potiphar's wife. In a remarkable scene she shows the women of the city that they, too, would have been seduced by Joseph's angelic beauty. In the Koran, in short, the story of Joseph has nothing of the epic dimensions it has in Genesis but focuses instead on the more general theme of the importance of trusting in divine guidance.

PRONOUNCING GLOSSARY

The following list uses common English syllables and stress accents to provide rough equivalents of selected words whose pronunciation may be unfamiliar to the general reader.

al-qur'ân: *al-ko-ran'*

âya: *eye'-yuh*

bahirah: *buh-hee'-ruh*

Idris: *ee-drees'*

Isâ: *ee'-suh*

Ka'ba: *ka'-buh*

Nuh: *nooh*

Potiphar: *poh'-tee-far*

saibah: *saw'-ee-buh*

Suwâ: *soo-wah'*

wasilah: *wuh-see'-luh*

Ya'uq: *yah-ook'*

Yaghuth: *yah-gooth'*

Yusuf: *you'-suff*

Zuleikha: *zoo-lay'-kuh*

FROM THE KORAN[1]

1. The Exordium

IN THE NAME OF GOD THE COMPASSIONATE THE MERCIFUL

> Praise be to God, Lord of the Universe,
> The Compassionate, the Merciful,[2]
> Sovereign of the Day of Judgement!
> You alone we worship, and to You alone
> we turn for help.
> Guide us to the straight path,
> The path of those whom You have favoured,
> Not of those who have incurred Your wrath,
> Nor of those who have gone astray.

From 4. Women

In the Name of God, the Compassionate, the Merciful

You people! Have fear of your Lord, who created you from a single soul. From that soul He created its spouse and through them He bestrewed the earth with countless men and women.

Fear God, in whose name you plead with one another, and honour the mothers who bore you. God is ever watching you.

Give orphans[3] the property which belongs to them. Do not exchange their

---

1. Translated by N. J. Dawood.   2. According to Islamic law, this phrase, spoken or written, must precede all written work.   3. Orphan girls.

valuables for worthless things or cheat them of their possessions; for this would surely be a grievous sin. If you fear that you cannot treat orphans with fairness, then you may marry other women who seem good to you: two, three, or four of them. But if you fear that you cannot maintain equality among them, marry one only or any slave-girls you may own. This will make it easier for you to avoid injustice.

Give women their dowry as a free gift; but if they choose to make over to you a part of it, you may regard it as lawfully yours.

Do not give the feeble-minded the property with which God has entrusted you for their support; but maintain and clothe them with its proceeds, and speak kind words to them.

Put orphans to the test until they reach a marriageable age. If you find them capable of sound judgement, hand over to them their property, and do not deprive them of it by squandering it before they come of age.

Let not the rich guardian touch the property of his orphan ward; and let him who is poor use no more than a fair portion of it for his own advantage.

When you hand over to them their property, call in some witnesses; sufficient is God's accounting of your actions.

Men shall have a share in what their parents and kinsmen leave; and women shall have a share in what their parents and kinsmen leave: whether it be little or much, they shall be legally entitled to a share.

If relatives, orphans, or needy men are present at the division of an inheritance, give them, too, a share of it, and speak kind words to them.

Let those who are solicitous about the welfare of their young children after their own death take care not to wrong orphans. Let them fear God and speak for justice.

Those that devour the property of orphans unjustly, swallow fire into their bellies; they shall burn in a mighty conflagration.

God has thus enjoined you concerning your children:

A male shall inherit twice as much as a female. If there be more than two girls, they shall have two-thirds of the inheritance; but if there be one only, she shall inherit the half. Parents shall inherit a sixth each, if the deceased have a child; but if he leave no child and his parents be his heirs, his mother shall have a third. If he have brothers, his mother shall have a sixth after payment of any legacy he may have bequeathed or any debt he may have owed.

You may wonder whether your parents or your children are more beneficial to you. But this is the law of God; surely God is all-knowing and wise.

You shall inherit the half of your wives' estate if they die childless. If they leave children, a quarter of their estate shall be yours after payment of any legacy they may have bequeathed or any debt they may have owed.

Your wives shall inherit one quarter of your estate if you die childless. If you leave children, they shall inherit one-eighth, after payment of any legacy you may have bequeathed or any debt you may have owed.

If a man or a woman leave neither children nor parents and have a brother or a sister, they shall each inherit one-sixth. If there be more, they shall equally share the third of the estate, after payment of any legacy he may have bequeathed or any debt he may have owed, without prejudice to the rights of the heirs. That is a commandment from God. God is all-knowing, and gracious.

Such are the bounds set by God. He that obeys God and His apostle shall dwell for ever in gardens watered by running streams. That is the supreme triumph. But he that defies God and His apostle and transgresses His bounds, shall be cast into a Fire wherein he will abide for ever. Shameful punishment awaits him.

If any of your women commit a lewd act, call in four witnesses from among yourselves against them; if they testify to their guilt confine them to their houses till death overtakes them or till God finds another way for them.

If two men among you commit a lewd act, punish them both. If they repent and mend their ways, let them be. God is forgiving and merciful.

God forgives those who commit evil in ignorance and then quickly turn to Him in penitence. God will pardon them. God is all-knowing and wise. But He will not forgive those who do evil and, when death comes to them, say: 'Now we repent!' Nor those who die unbelievers: for them We have prepared a woeful scourge.

Believers, it is unlawful for you to inherit the women of your deceased kinsmen against their will, or to bar them from re-marrying, in order that you may force them to give up a part of what you have given them, unless they be guilty of a proven lewd act. Treat them with kindness; for even if you dislike them, it may well be that you dislike a thing which God has meant for your own abundant good.

If you wish to replace one wife with another, do not take from her the dowry you have given her even if it be a talent of gold. That would be improper and grossly unjust; for how can you take it back when you have lain with each other and entered into a firm contract?

You shall not marry the women whom your fathers married: all previous such marriages excepted. That was an evil practice, indecent and abominable.

Forbidden to you are your mothers, your daughters, your sisters, your paternal and maternal aunts, the daughters of your brothers and sisters, your foster-mothers, your foster-sisters, the mothers of your wives, your step-daughters who are in your charge, born of the wives with whom you have lain (it is no offence for you to marry your step-daughters if you have not consummated your marriage with their mothers), and the wives of your own begotten sons.[4] You are also forbidden to take in marriage two sisters at one and the same time: all previous such marriages excepted. Surely God is forgiving and merciful. Also married women except those whom you own as slaves. Such is the decree of God. All women other than these are lawful for you, provided you court them with your wealth in modest conduct, not in fornication. Give them their dowry for the enjoyment you have had of them as a duty; but it shall be no offence for you to make any other agreement among yourselves after you have fulfilled your duty. Surely God is all-knowing and wise.

If any one of you cannot afford to marry a free believing woman, let him marry a slave-girl who is a believer (God best knows your faith: you are born one of another). Marry them with the permission of their masters and give them their dowry in all justice, provided they are honourable and chaste and have not entertained other men. If after marriage they commit adultery, they shall suffer half the penalty inflicted upon free adulteresses. Such is the law

4. Cf. Leviticus 18.

for those of you who fear to commit sin: but if you abstain, it will be better for you. God is forgiving and merciful.

God desires to make this known to you and to guide you along the paths of those who have gone before you, and to turn to you with mercy. God is all-knowing and wise.

God wishes to forgive you, but those who follow their own appetites wish to see you stray grievously into error. God wishes to lighten your burdens, for man was created weak.

Believers, do not consume your wealth among yourselves in vanity, but rather trade with it by mutual consent.

Do not kill yourselves.[5] God is merciful to you, but he that does that through wickedness and injustice shall be burned in fire. That is easy enough for God.

If you avoid the enormities you are forbidden, We shall pardon your misdeeds and usher you in with all honour. Do not covet the favours by which God has exalted some among you above others. Men shall be rewarded according to their deeds, and women shall be rewarded according to their deeds. Rather implore God to bestow on you His gifts. Surely God has knowledge of all things.

To every parent and kinsman We have appointed heirs who will inherit from them. As for those with whom you have entered into agreements, let them, too, have their share. Surely God bears witness to all things.

Men have authority over women because God has made the one superior to the other, and because they spend their wealth to maintain them. Good women are obedient. They guard their unseen parts because God has guarded them. As for those from whom you fear disobedience, admonish them and forsake them in beds apart, and beat them. Then if they obey you, take no further action against them. Surely God is high, supreme.

If you fear a breach between a man and his wife, appoint an arbiter from his people and another from hers. If they wish to be reconciled, God will bring them together again. Surely God is all-knowing and wise.

Serve God and associate none with Him. Show kindness to parents and kindred, to orphans and to the destitute, to near and distant neighbours, to those that keep company with you, to the traveller in need, and to the slaves you own. God does not love arrogant and boastful men, who are themselves tight-fisted and enjoin others to be tight-fisted; who conceal the riches which God of His bounty has bestowed upon them (We have prepared a shameful punishment for the unbelievers).

* * *

5. The Table

In the Name of God, the Compassionate, the Merciful

Believers, be true to your obligations. It is lawful for you to eat the flesh of all beasts other than that which is hereby announced to you. Game is

---

5. This is generally taken to mean: "Do not kill one another."

forbidden while you are on pilgrimage. God decrees what He will.

Believers, do not violate the rites of God, or the sacred month, or the offerings or their ornaments, or those that repair to the Sacred House seeking God's grace and pleasure. Once your pilgrimage is ended, you shall be free to go hunting.

Do not allow your hatred for those who would debar you from the Holy Mosque to lead you into sin. Help one another in what is good and pious, not in what is wicked and sinful. Have fear of God; God is stern in retribution.

You are forbidden carrion, blood, and the flesh of swine; also any flesh dedicated to any other than God. You are forbidden the flesh of strangled animals and of those beaten or gored to death; of those killed by a fall or mangled by beasts of prey (unless you make it clean by giving the death-stroke yourselves); also of animals sacrificed to idols.

You are forbidden to settle disputes by consulting the Arrows.[6] That is a pernicious practice.

The unbelievers have this day abandoned all hope of vanquishing your religion. Have no fear of them: fear Me.

This day I have perfected your religion for you and completed My favour to you. I have chosen Islām to be your faith.

He that is constrained by hunger to eat of what is forbidden, not intending to commit sin, will find God forgiving and merciful.

They ask you what is lawful for them. Say:"All wholesome things are lawful for you, as well as that which you have taught the birds and beasts of prey to catch, training them as God has taught you. Eat of what they catch for you, pronouncing upon it the name of God. And have fear of God: swift is God's reckoning."

All wholesome things have this day been made lawful for you. The food of those to whom the Book was given[7] is lawful for you, and yours for them.

Lawful for you are the believing women and the free women from among those who were given the Book before you, provided that you give them their dowries and live in honour with them, neither committing fornication nor taking them as mistresses.

He that denies the Faith shall gain nothing from his labours. In the world to come he will surely be among the losers.

Believers, when you rise to pray wash your faces and your hands as far as the elbow, and wipe your heads and your feet to the ankle. If you are unclean, cleanse yourselves. But if you are sick or on a journey, or if, when you have just relieved yourselves or had intercourse with women, you can find no water, take some clean sand and rub your faces and your hands with it. God does not wish to burden you; He seeks only to purify you and to perfect His favour to you, so that you may give thanks.

Remember God's favour to you, and the covenant with which He bound you when you said: "We hear and obey." Have fear of God. God knows the innermost thoughts of men.

Believers, fulfil your duties to God and bear true witness. Do not allow your hatred for other men to turn you away from justice. Deal justly; that will bring you closer to true piety. Have fear of God; God is cognizant of all your actions.

---

6. A form of casting lots.   7. The Jews.

God has promised those that have faith and do good works forgiveness and a rich reward. As for those who disbelieve and deny Our revelations, they are the heirs of Hell.

Believers, remember the favour which God bestowed upon you when He restrained the hands of those who sought to harm you. Have fear of God. In God let the faithful put their trust.

God made a covenant with the Israelites and raised among them twelve chieftains. God said: "I shall be with you. If you attend to your prayers and render the alms levy; if you believe in My apostles and assist them and give God a generous loan, I shall forgive you your sins and admit you to gardens watered by running streams. But he that hereafter denies Me shall stray from the right path."

But because they broke their covenant We laid on them Our curse and hardened their hearts. They have tampered with words out of their context and forgotten much of what they were enjoined. You will ever find them deceitful, except for a few of them. But pardon them and bear with them. God loves those who do good.

With those who said they were Christians We made a covenant also, but they too have forgotten much of what they were exhorted to do. Therefore We stirred among them enmity and hatred, which shall endure till the Day of Resurrection, when God will declare to them all that they have done.

People of the Book![8] Our apostle has come to reveal to you much of what you have hidden of the Scriptures, and to forgive you much. A light has come to you from God and a glorious Book, with which God will guide to the paths of peace those that seek to please Him; He will lead them by His will from darkness to the light; He will guide them to a straight path.

Unbelievers are those who declare: "God is the Messiah, the son of Mary." Say: "Who could prevent God, if He so willed, from destroying the Messiah, the son of Mary, his mother, and all the people of the earth? God has sovereignty over the heavens and the earth and all that lies between them. He creates what He will; and God has power over all things."

The Jews and the Christians say: "We are the children of God and His loved ones." Say: "Why then does He punish you for your sins? Surely you are mortals of His own creation. He forgives whom He will and punishes whom He pleases. God has sovereignty over the heavens and the earth and all that lies between them. All shall return to Him."

People of the Book! Our apostle has come to you with revelations after an interval which saw no apostles, lest you say: "No one has come to give us good news or to warn us." Now someone has come to give you good news and to warn you. God has power over all things.

Bear in mind the words of Moses to his people. He said: "Remember, my people, the favour which God has bestowed upon you. He has raised up prophets among you, made you kings, and given you that which He has given to no other nation. Enter, my people, the holy land which God has assigned for you. Do not turn back, and thus lose all."

"Moses," they replied, "a race of giants dwells in this land. We will not set foot in it till they are gone. As soon as they are gone we will enter."

Thereupon two God-fearing men whom God had favoured said: "Go in to them through the gates, and when you have entered you shall surely be

8. Here, Jews and Christians.

victorious. In God put your trust, if you are true believers."

But they replied: "Moses we will never go in as long as *they* are in it. Go, you and your Lord, and fight. Here we will stay."

"Lord," cried Moses, "I have none but myself and my brother. Keep us apart from these wicked people."

He replied: "They shall be forbidden this land for forty years, during which time they shall wander homeless on the earth. Do not grieve for these wicked people."

Recount to them in all truth the story of Adam's two sons: how they each made an offering, and how the offering of the one was accepted while that of the other was not. One said: "I will surely kill you." The other replied: "God accepts offerings only from the righteous. If you stretch your hand to kill me, I shall not stretch mine to slay you; for I fear God, Lord of the Universe. I would rather you should add your sin against me to your other sins and thus become an inmate of the Fire. Such is the recompense of the unjust."

His soul prompted him to slay his brother; he slew him, and thus became one of the lost. Then God sent down a raven, which clawed the earth to show him how to bury the naked corpse of his brother. "Alas!" he cried. "Have I not strength enough to do as this raven has done and so bury my brother's naked corpse?" And he repented.

That was why We laid it down for the Israelites that whoever killed a human being, except as punishment for murder or other villainy in the land, shall be regarded as having killed all mankind; and that whoever saved a human life shall be regarded as having saved all mankind.

Our apostles brought them veritable proofs: yet many among them, even after that, did prodigious evil in the land.

Those that make war against God and His apostle and spread disorder in the land shall be slain or crucified or have their hands and feet cut off on alternate sides, or be banished from the land. They shall be held up to shame in this world, and in the world to come grievous punishment awaits them: except those that repent before you reduce them. For you must know that God is forgiving and merciful.

Believers, have fear of God and seek the right path to Him. Fight valiantly for His cause, so that you may triumph.

As for the unbelievers, if they offered all that the earth contains and as much besides to redeem themselves from the torment of the Day of Resurrection, it shall not be accepted from them. Woeful punishment awaits them.

They will strive to get out of the Fire, but get out of it they shall not. Lasting punishment awaits them.

As for the man or woman who is guilty of theft, cut off their hands to punish them for their crimes. That is the punishment enjoined by God. God is mighty and wise. But whoever repents after committing evil, and mends his ways, shall be pardoned by God. God is forgiving and merciful.

Did you not know that God has sovereignty over the heavens and the earth? He punishes whom He will and forgives whom He pleases. God has power over all things.

Apostle, do not grieve for those who plunge headlong into unbelief; those who say with their mouths: "We believe," but have no faith in their hearts, and those Jews who listen to lies and listen to others who have not come to you. They tamper with words out of their context and say: "If such-a-such [a precept] be given you, accept it; if it be not given you, beware!"

You cannot help a man if God intends to try him. Those whose hearts God does not intend to purify shall be held up to shame in this world, and in the world to come grievous punishment awaits them.

They listen to falsehoods and practice what is unlawful. If they come to you, give them your judgement or avoid them. If you avoid them, they can in no way harm you; but if you do act as their judge, judge them with fairness. God loves those that deal justly.

But how will they come to you for judgement when they already have the Torah which enshrines God's own judgement? Soon after, they will turn their backs: they are no true believers.

We have revealed the Torah, in which there is guidance and light. By it the prophets who submitted to God judged the Jews, and so did the rabbis and the divines, according to God's Book which had been committed to their keeping and to which they themselves were witnesses.

Have no fear of man; fear Me, and do not sell My revelations for a paltry sum. Unbelievers are those who do not judge according to God's revelations.

Therein We decreed for them a life for a life, an eye for an eye, a nose for a nose, an ear for an ear, a tooth for a tooth, and a wound for a wound. But if a man charitably forbears from retaliation, his remission shall atone for him. Transgressors are those that do not judge according to God's revelations.

After them We sent forth Jesus son of Mary, confirming the Torah already revealed, and gave him the Gospel, in which there is guidance and light, corroborating what was revealed before it in the Torah: a guide and an admonition to the righteous. Therefore let those who follow the Gospel judge according to what God has revealed therein. Evil-doers are those that do not judge according to God's revelations.

And to you We have revealed the Book with the truth. It confirms the Scriptures which came before it and stands as a guardian over them. Therefore give judgement among men according to God's revelations and do not yield to their whims or swerve from the truth made known to you.

We have ordained a law and assigned a path for each of you. Had God pleased, He could have made of you one community: but it is His wish to prove you by that which He has bestowed upon you. Vie with each other in good works, for to God shall you all return and He will resolve your differences for you.

Pronounce judgement among them according to God's revelations and do not be led by their desires. Take heed lest they turn you away from a part of that which God has revealed to you. If they reject your judgement, know that it is God's wish to scourge them for their sins. A great many of mankind are evil-doers.

Is it pagan laws that they wish to be judged by? Who is a better judge than God for men whose faith is firm?

Believers, take neither the Jews nor the Christians for your friends. They are friends with one another. Whoever of you seeks their friendship shall become one of their number. God does not guide the wrong-doers.

You see the faint-hearted hastening to woo them. They say: "We fear lest a change of fortune should befall us." But it may well be that when God grants you victory or makes known His will, they will regret their secret plans. Then will the faithful say: "Are these the men who solemnly swore by God that they would stand by you?" Their works will come to nothing and they will lose all.

Believers, if any among you renounce the Faith, God will replace them by others who love Him and are loved by Him, who are humble towards the faithful and stern towards the unbelievers, zealous for God's cause and fearless of man's censure. Such is the grace of God: He bestows it on whom He will. God is munificent and all-knowing.

Your only protectors are God, His apostle, and the faithful: those who attend to their prayers, render the alms levy, and kneel down in worship. Those who seek the protection of God, His apostle, and the faithful must know that God's followers are sure to triumph.

Believers, do not seek the friendship of the infidels and those who were given the Book before you, who have made of your religion a jest and a diversion. Have fear of God, if you are true believers.

When you call them to pray, they treat their prayers as a jest and a diversion. This is because they are devoid of understanding.

Say: "People of the Book, is it not that you hate us only because we believe in God and in what has been revealed to us and what was formerly revealed, and because most of you are evil-doers?"

Say: "Shall I tell you who will receive a worse reward from God? Those whom God has cursed and with whom He has been angry, transforming them into apes and swine, and those who serve the devil. Worse is the plight of these, and they have strayed farther from the right path."

When they came to you they said: "We are believers." Indeed, infidels they came and infidels they departed. God knew best what they concealed.

You see many among them vie with one another in sin and wickedness and practise what is unlawful. Evil is what they do.

Why do their rabbis and divines not forbid them to blaspheme or to practise what is unlawful? Evil indeed are their doings.

The Jews say: "God's hand is chained." May their own hands be chained! May they be cursed for what they say! By no means. His hands are both outstretched: He bestows as He will.

That which is revealed to you from your Lord will surely increase the wickedness and unbelief of many among them. We have stirred among them enmity and hatred, which will endure till the Day of Resurrection. Whenever they kindle the fire of war, God puts it out. They spread evil in the land, but God does not love the evil-doers.

If the People of the Book accept the true faith and keep from evil, We will pardon them their sins and admit them to the gardens of delight. If they observe the Torah and the Gospel and what has been revealed to them from their Lord, they shall enjoy abundance from above and from beneath.

There are some among them who are righteous men; but there are many among them who do nothing but evil.

Apostle, proclaim what has been revealed to you from your Lord; if you do not, you will surely fail to convey His message. God will protect you from all men. God does not guide the unbelievers.

Say: "People of the Book, you will attain nothing until you observe the Torah and the Gospel and that which has been revealed to you from your Lord."

That which has been revealed to you from your Lord will surely increase the wickedness and unbelief of many among them. But do not grieve for the unbelievers.

Believers, Jews, Sabaeans and Christians—whoever believes in God and the Last Day and does what is right—shall have nothing to fear or to regret.

We made a covenant with the Israelites and sent forth apostles among them. But whenever an apostle came to them with a message that did not suit their inclinations, some they accused of lying and others they put to death. They thought no punishment would follow: they were blind and deaf. Then God turned to them in mercy, but many again were blind and deaf. God is ever watching their actions.

Unbelievers are those that say: "God is the Messiah, the son of Mary." For the Messiah himself said: "Children of Israel, serve God, my Lord and your Lord." He that worships other deities besides God, God will deny him Paradise, and the Fire shall be his home. None shall help the evil-doers.

Unbelievers are those that say: "God is one of three." There is but one God. If they do not desist from so saying, those of them that disbelieve shall be sternly punished.

Will they not turn to God in penitence and seek forgiveness of Him? God is forgiving and merciful.

The Messiah, the son of Mary, was no more than an apostle: other apostles passed away before him. His mother was a saintly woman. They both ate earthly food.

See how We make plain to them Our revelations. See how they ignore the truth.

Say: "Will you serve instead of God that which can neither harm nor help you? God is He who hears all and knows all."

Say: "People of the Book! Do not transgress the bounds of truth in your religion. Do not yield to the desires of those who have erred before; who have led many astray and have themselves strayed from the even path."

Those of the Israelites who disbelieved were cursed by David and Jesus son of Mary, because they rebelled and committed evil. Nor did they censure themselves for any wrong they did. Evil were their deeds.

You see many among them making friends with unbelievers. Evil is that to which their souls prompt them. They have incurred the wrath of God and shall endure eternal torment. Had they believed in God and the Prophet and that which has been revealed to him, they would not have befriended them. But many of them are evil-doers.

You will find that the most implacable of men in their enmity to the faithful are the Jews and the pagans, and that the nearest in affection to them are those who say: "We are Christians." That is because there are priests and monks among them; and because they are free from pride.

When they listen to that which was revealed to the Apostle, you see their eyes fill with tears as they recognize its truth. They say: 'Lord, we believe. Count us among the witnesses. Why should we not believe in God and in the truth that has come down to us? Why should we not hope our Lord will admit us among the righteous?' And for their words God has rewarded them with gardens watered by running streams, where they shall dwell for ever. Such is the recompense of the righteous. But those that disbelieve and deny Our revelations shall become the inmates of Hell.

Believers, do not forbid the wholesome things which God made lawful for you. Do not transgress; God does not love the transgressors. Eat of the lawful and wholesome things which God has given you. Have fear of God, in whom you do believe.

God will not punish you for that which is inadvertent in your oaths. But He will take you to task over the oaths which you solemnly swear. The penalty for a broken oath is the feeding of ten needy men with such food as you normally offer to your own people; or the clothing of ten needy men; or the freeing of a slave. He that cannot afford any of these must fast three days. In this way you shall expiate your broken oaths. Therefore be true to that which you have sworn. Thus God makes plain to you His revelations, so that you may give thanks.

Believers, wine and games of chance, idols and divining arrows, are abominations devised by Satan. Avoid them, so that you may prosper. Satan seeks to stir up enmity and hatred among you by means of wine and gambling, and to keep you from the remembrance of God and from your prayers. Will you not abstain from them?

Obey God, and obey the Apostle. Beware; if you pay no heed, know that Our apostle's duty is but to give clear warning.

In regard to any food they may have eaten, no blame shall be attached to those that have embraced the Faith and done good works so long as they fear God and believe in Him and do good works; so long as they fear God and believe in Him; so long as they fear God and do good works. God loves the charitable.

Believers, God will put you to the proof by means of the game which you can catch with your hands or with your spears, so that God may know those who fear Him in their hearts. He that transgresses hereafter, woeful punishment awaits him.

Believers, kill no game while on pilgrimage. He that kills game by design, shall present, as an offering to the Ka'bah, an animal equivalent to the one he killed, to be determined by two just men among you; or he shall, in expiation, either feed the destitute or fast, so that he may taste the evil consequences of his deed. God has forgiven what is past; but if anyone relapses into wrongdoing God will avenge Himself on him: God is mighty and capable of revenge.

Lawful for you is what you catch from the sea and the sustenance it provides; a wholesome food, for yourselves and for the seafarers. But you are forbidden the game of the land while you are on pilgrimage. Have fear of God, before whom you shall all be assembled.

God has made the Ka'bah, the Sacred House, the sacred month, and the sacrificial offerings with their ornaments, eternal values for mankind; so that you may know God has knowledge of all that the heavens and the earth contain; that God has knowledge of all things.

Know that God is stern in retribution, and that God is forgiving and merciful.

The Apostle's duty is but to give warning. God knows all that you reveal and all that you conceal.

Say: "Evil and good are not equal, even though the abundance of evil may tempt you. Have fear of God, you men of understanding, so that you may triumph."

Believers, do not ask questions about things which, if made known to you, would only pain you; but if you ask them when the Koran is being revealed, they shall be made plain to you. God will pardon you for this; God is forgiving and gracious. Other men inquired about them before you, only to disbelieve them thereafter.

God demands neither a *bahīrah*, nor a *sā'ibah*, nor a *waṣīlah*, nor a *ḥāmi*.[9] The unbelievers invent falsehoods about God. Most of them are lacking in judgement.

When they are told: "Come to that which God has revealed, and to the Apostle," they reply: "Sufficient for us is the faith we inherited from our fathers," even though their fathers knew nothing and were not rightly guided.

Believers, you are accountable for none but yourselves; he that strays cannot harm you if you are on the right path. To God shall you all return, and He will declare to you what you have done.

Believers, when death approaches you, let two just men from among you act as witnesses when you make your testament; or two men from another tribe if the calamity of death overtakes you while you are travelling the land. Detain them after prayers, and if you doubt their honesty, let them swear by God: "We will not sell our testimony for any price even to a kinsman. We will not hide the testimony of God; for we should then be evil-doers." If both prove dishonest, replace them by another pair from among those immediately concerned, and let them both swear by God, saying: "Our testimony is truer than theirs. We have told no lies, for we should then be wrongdoers." Thus will they be more likely to bear true witness or to fear that the oaths of others may contradict theirs. Have fear of God and be obedient. God does not guide the evil-doers.

One day God will gather all the apostles and ask them: "How were you received?" They will reply: "We have no knowledge. You alone know what is hidden." God will say: "Jesus son of Mary, remember the favour I bestowed on you and on your mother: how I strengthened you with the Holy Spirit, so that you preached to men in your cradle and in the prime of manhood; how I instructed you in the Book and in wisdom, in the Torah and in the Gospel; how by My leave you fashioned from clay the likeness of a bird and breathed into it so that, by My leave, it became a living bird; how, by My leave, you healed the blind man and the leper, and by My leave restored the dead to life; how I protected you from the Israelites when you had come to them with clear signs: when those of them who disbelieved declared: 'This is but plain sorcery'; how, when I enjoined the disciples to believe in Me and in My apostle, they replied: 'We believe; bear witness that we submit.'"

"Jesus son of Mary," said the disciples, "can your Lord send down to us from heaven a table spread with food?"

He replied: "Have fear of God, if you are true believers."

"We wish to eat of it," they said, "so that we may reassure our hearts and know that what you said to us is true, and that we may be witnesses of it."

"Lord," said Jesus son of Mary, "send down to us from heaven a table spread with food, that it may mark a feast for the first of us and and for the last of us: a sign from You. Give us our sustenance; You are the best provider."

---

9. Names given by pagan Arabs to sacred animals offered at the Ka'bah.

God replied: "I am sending one to you. But whoever of you disbelievers hereafter shall be punished as no man will ever be punished."

Then God will say: "Jesus son of Mary, did you ever say to mankind: "Worship me and my mother as gods besides God?"

"Glory be to You," he will answer, "I could never have claimed what I have no right to. If I had ever said so, You would have surely known it. You know what is in my mind, but I know not what is in Yours. You alone know what is hidden. I told them only what You bade me. I said: "Serve God, my Lord and your Lord." I watched over them while living in their midst, and ever since You took me to Yourself, You have been watching them. You are the witness of all things. If You punish them, they surely are Your servants; and if You forgive them, surely You are mighty and wise."

God will say: "This is the day when their truthfulness will benefit the truthful. They shall for ever dwell in gardens watered by running streams. God is pleased with them, and they are pleased with Him. That is the supreme triumph."

God has sovereignty over the heavens and the earth and all that they contain. He has power over all things.

10. Jonah

In the Name of God, the Compassionate, the Merciful

Alif lām rā'.[1] These are the verses of the Wise Book: Does it seem strange to mankind that We revealed Our will to a mortal from among themselves, saying: "Give warning to mankind, and proclaim good tidings to the faithful: their endeavours shall be rewarded by their Lord?"

The unbelievers say: "This man[2] is a skilled enchanter." Yet your Lord is God, who in six days created the heavens and the earth and then ascended the throne, ordaining all things. None has power to intercede for you, except him who has received His sanction. Such is God, your Lord: therefore serve Him. Will you not take heed?

To Him shall you all return: God's promise shall be fulfilled. He brings the Creation into being and will then restore it, so that He may justly recompense those who have believed in Him and done good works. As for the unbelievers, scalding water shall they drink, and for their unbelief woeful punishment awaits them.

It was He that gave the sun his brightness and the moon her light, ordaining her phases that you may learn to compute the seasons and the years. God created them only to manifest the Truth. He makes plain His revelations to men of knowledge.

In the alternation of night and day, and in all that God has created in the heavens and the earth, there are signs for righteous men.

Those who entertain no hope of meeting Us, being pleased and contented with the life of this world, and those who pay no heed to Our revelations, shall have the Fire as their home in requital for their deeds.

---

1. A number of Suras begin with several letters of the Arabic alphabet, the meaning of which is unclear.
2. Muhammad.

As for those that believe and do good works, God will guide them through their faith. Rivers will run at their feet in the Gardens of Delight. Their prayer will be: "Glory be to You, Lord!" and their greeting: "Peace!" "Praise be to God, Lord of the Universe" will be the burthen of their plea.

Had God hastened the punishment of men as they would hasten their reward, their fate would have been sealed. Therefore We leave those who entertain no hope of meeting Us to their wrongdoing, ever straying from the right path.

When misfortune befalls man, he prays to Us lying on his side, sitting, or standing on his feet. But as soon as We relieve his affliction he pursues his former ways, as though he never prayed for Our help. Thus do their foul deeds seem fair to the transgressors.

We destroyed generations before your time on account of the wrongs they did; their apostles came to them with veritable signs, but they would not believe. Thus shall We reward the guilty. Then We made you their successors in the land, so that We might observe how you would conduct yourselves.

When Our clear revelations are recited to them, those who entertain no hope of meeting Us say to you: "Give us a different Koran, or change it."

Say:[3] "It is not for me to change it, of my own accord. I follow only what is revealed to me, for I fear, if I disobey my Lord, the punishment of a fateful day."

Say: "Had God pleased, I would never have recited it to you, nor would He have made you aware of it. A whole lifetime I dwelt among you before its coming. Will you not understand?"

Who is more wicked than the man who invents a falsehood about God or denies His revelations? Truly, the evil-doers shall not triumph.

They worship idols that can neither harm nor help them, and say: "These will intercede for us with God."

Say: "Do you presume to tell God of what He knows to exist neither in the heavens nor on earth?" Glory be to Him! Exalted be He above the gods they serve besides Him!

There was a time when mankind were but one community. Then they disagreed among themselves: and but for a Word from your Lord, long since decreed, their differences would have been firmly resolved.

And they ask: "Why has no sign been sent down to him by his Lord?"

Say: "God alone has knowledge of what is hidden. Wait if you will: I too am waiting."

No sooner do We show mercy to a people after some misfortune has afflicted them than they begin to scheme against Our revelations. Say: "More swift is God's scheming. Our angels are recording your intrigues."

It is He who guides them by land and sea. They embark: and as the ships set sail, rejoicing in a favourable wind, a raging tempest overtakes them. Billows surge upon them from every side and they fear they are encompassed by death. They pray to God with all fervour, saying: "Deliver us from this peril and we will be truly thankful."

Yet when He does deliver them, they perpetrate corruption in the land and act unjustly.

You people! It is your own souls that you are corrupting. Take your enjoy-

---

3. God's instruction to Muhammad.

ment in this life: to Us shall you then return, and We will declare to you all
that you have done.

This present life is like the rich garment with which the earth adorns itself
when watered by the rain We send down from the sky. Crops, sustaining
man and beast, grow luxuriantly: but, as the earth's tenants begin to think
themselves its masters, down comes Our scourge upon it, by night or by day,
laying it waste, as though it did not blossom but yesterday. Thus do We make
plain Our revelations to thoughtful men.

God invites you to the Home of Peace. He guides whom He will to a
straight path.

Those that do good works shall have a good reward, and more besides.
Neither blackness nor misery shall overcast their faces. They are the heirs
of Paradise, wherein they shall abide for ever.

As for those that have done evil, evil shall be rewarded with evil. Misery
will oppress them (they shall have none to protect them from God), as though
patches of the night's own darkness veiled their faces. They are the heirs of
the Fire, wherein they shall abide for ever.

On the day We assemble them all together, We shall say to the idolaters:
"Keep to your places, you and your idols!" We will separate them one from
another, and then their idols will say to them: "It was not us that you worshipped. Sufficient is God as our witness, and your witness. Nor were we
aware of your worship."

Thereupon each soul will know what it has done. They shall be sent back
to God, their true Lord, and the idols they invented will forsake them.

Say: "Who provides for you from heaven and earth? Who has endowed
you with hearing and sight? Who brings forth the living from the dead, and
the dead from the living? Who ordains all things?"

They will reply: "God."

Say: "Will you not take heed, then? Such is God, your true Lord. That
which is not true must needs be false. How then can you turn away?"

Thus is the Word of your Lord made good about the evil-doers. They will
not believe.

Say: "Can any of your idols bring the Creation into being and then restore
it? Say: God brings the Creation into being and will then restore it. How is
it that you are so misled?"

Say: "Can any of your idols give guidance to the truth?" Say: "God gives
guidance to the truth. Who is more worthy to be followed: He that can give
guidance to the truth, or he that cannot and is himself in need of guidance?
What has come over you that you so judge?"

Most of them follow nothing but mere conjecture. But conjecture is in no
way a substitute for truth. God is cognizant of all their actions.

This Koran could not have been devised by any but God. It confirms what
was revealed before it and fully explains the Scriptures. It is beyond doubt
from the Lord of the Universe.

If they say: "He invented it himself," say: "Bring me one chapter like it.
Call on whom you may besides God to help you, if what you say be true!"

Indeed, they disbelieve what they cannot grasp, for they have not yet seen
its prophecy fulfilled. Likewise did those before them disbelieve. But see
what was the end of the wrongdoers.

Some believe in it, while others do not. But your Lord best knows the evil-
doers.

If they disbelieve you, say: "My deeds are mine and your deeds are yours. You are not accountable for my actions, nor am I accountable for what you do."

Some of them listen to you. But can you make the deaf hear you, incapable as they are of understanding?

Some of them look upon you. But can you show the way to the blind, bereft as they are of sight?

Indeed, in no way does God wrong mankind, but men wrong themselves.

The day will come when He will gather them all together, as though they had sojourned in this world but for an hour. They will acquaint themselves with each other. Losers shall be those who denied they would ever meet God and did not follow the right path.

Whether We let you glimpse in some measure the scourge We threaten them with, or call you back to Us before We smite them, to Us they shall return. God will then be witness to all their actions.

An apostle is sent to each community. When their apostle comes, justice is done among them; they are not wronged.

They ask: "When will this promise be fulfilled, if what you say be true?"

Say: "I have no control over any harm or benefit to myself, except by the will of God. A space of time is fixed for each community; when their time is come, not for one hour shall they delay: nor can they go before it."

Say: "Do but consider. Should His scourge fall upon you in the night or by the light of day, what punishment would the guilty hasten? Will you believe in it when it does overtake you, although it was your wish to hurry it on?"

Then will the wrongdoers be told: "Feel the everlasting torment! Shall you not be rewarded according only to your deeds?"

They ask you if it is true. Say: "Yes, by the Lord, it is certainly true! And you shall not escape."

To redeem himself then, each sinner would gladly give all that the earth contains if he possessed it. When they behold the scourge, they will repent in secret. But judgement shall be fairly passed upon them; they shall not be wronged.

Surely to God belongs all that the heavens and the earth contain. Surely the promise of God is true, though most of them may not know it. It is He who ordains life and death, and to Him shall you be recalled.

You people! An admonition has come to you from your Lord, a cure for the mind, a guide and a blessing to true believers.

Say: "In the grace and mercy of God let them rejoice, for these are better than the worldly riches they amass."

Say: "Do but consider the provision God has sent down for you. Some of it you pronounced unlawful and some, lawful." Say: "Was it God who gave you His leave, or do you invent falsehoods about God?"

What will they think, those who invent falsehoods about God, on the Day of Resurrection? God is bountiful to men: yet most of them do not give thanks.

You shall engage in no affair, you shall recite no verse from the Koran, you shall commit no act, but We will witness it. Not an atom's weight in earth or heaven escapes your Lord, nor is there any object smaller or greater, but is recorded in a glorious book.

Surely the servants of God have nothing to fear or to regret. Those that have faith and keep from evil shall rejoice both in this world and in the world to come: the words of God shall never change. That is the supreme triumph.

Let not their words grieve you. All glory belongs to God. He alone hears all and knows all.

Surely to God belong all who dwell in the heavens and on earth. Those that serve other gods besides God follow nothing but idle fancies and preach nothing but falsehoods.

He it is who has ordained the night for you to rest in and given the day its light for you to see with. Surely in this there are signs for prudent men.

They say: "God has begotten a son." God forbid! Self-sufficient is He. His is all that the heavens and the earth contain. Surely for this you have no sanction. Would you say of God what you know not?

Say: "Those that invent falsehoods about God shall not prosper. They may take their ease in this life, but to Us they shall then return, and for their unbelief We will make them taste the grievous torment."

Recount to them the tale of Noah. He said to his people: "If it offends you, my people, that I should dwell in your midst and preach to you God's revelations (for in God I have put my trust), muster all your idols and decide on your course of action. Do not intrigue in secret. Execute your judgement and give me no respite. If you turn away from me, remember I demand of you no recompense. Only God will reward me. I am commanded to be one of those who shall submit to Him."

But they disbelieved him. Therefore We saved Noah and those who were with him in the ark, so that they survived, and drowned the others who denied Our revelations. Consider the fate of those who were forewarned.

After him We sent apostles to their descendants. They showed them veritable signs, but they persisted in their unbelief. Thus do We seal up the hearts of the transgressors.

Then We sent forth Moses and Aaron with Our signs to Pharaoh and his nobles. But they responded with scorn, for they were wicked men. When the truth had come to them from Us, they declared: "Surely this is but plain sorcery."

Moses replied: "Is this what you say of the Truth when it has come to you? Is this sorcery? Sorcerers shall never prosper."

They said: "Have you come to turn us away from the faith of our fathers, so that you two may lord it over the land? We will never believe in the pair of you."

Then Pharaoh said: "Bring every learned sorcerer to my presence."

And when the sorcerers attended, Moses said to them: "Cast down what you wish to cast." And when they had thrown, he said: "The sorcery that you have wrought, God will surely bring to nothing. God does not bless the work of those who do evil. By His words God vindicates the truth, much as the guilty may dislike it."

Few of his[4] people believed in Moses, for they feared the persecution of Pharaoh and his nobles. Surely Pharaoh was a tyrant in the land, a man of rampant wickedness.

Moses said: "If you believe in God, my people, and have submitted to Him, in Him alone then put your trust."

---

4. Pharaoh's.

They replied: "In God we have put our trust. Lord, do not let us suffer at the hands of wicked men. Deliver us, through Your mercy, from the unbelievers."

We revealed Our will to Moses and his brother, saying: "Build houses in Egypt for your people and make your homes places of worship. Conduct prayers and give good tidings to the faithful."

"Lord," said Moses, "You have bestowed on Pharaoh and his nobles splendour and riches in this life, so that they may stray from Your path. Lord, destroy their riches and harden their hearts, so that they shall persist in unbelief until they face the woeful scourge."

He replied: "Your prayer shall be answered. Follow the straight path and do not walk in the footsteps of ignorant men."

We led the Israelites across the sea, and Pharaoh and his legions pursued them with wickedness and spite. But as he was drowning, Pharaoh cried: "Now I believe no god exists except the God in whom the Israelites believe. To Him I give up myself."

"Only now! But before this you were a rebel and a wrongdoer. We shall today save your body, so that you may become a sign for all posterity: a great many of mankind do not heed Our signs."

We settled the Israelites in a secure land and provided them with wholesome things. Nor did they disagree among themselves until knowledge was given them. Your Lord will on the Day of Resurrection judge their differences.

If you doubt what We have revealed to you, ask those who have read the Scriptures before you. The truth has come to you from your Lord: therefore do not doubt it. Nor shall you deny the revelations of God, for then you will surely be among the lost.

Those for whom the word of your Lord shall be fulfilled will not have faith, even if they be given every sign, until they face the woeful scourge. Were it otherwise, every community, had it believed, would have profited from its faith. But it was so only with Jonah's people. When they believed, We spared them the penalty of disgrace in this nether life and suffered them to take their ease a while. Had your Lord pleased, all the people of the earth would have believed in Him, one and all. Would you then force people to have faith?

None can have faith except by God's leave. He will visit His scourge upon the senseless.

Say: "Behold what the heavens and the earth contain!" But neither signs nor warnings will avail the unbelievers.

What can they wait for but the fate of those who have gone before them? Say: "Wait if you will; I too am waiting."

We shall save Our apostles and the true believers. It is but just that We should save the faithful.

Say: "You people! Doubt my religion if you will, but never will I worship those that you worship besides God. I worship God, who will reclaim you all: for I am thus commanded to be a believer: 'Dedicate yourself to the Faith in all uprightness and serve none besides God. You shall not pray to idols which can neither help nor harm you, for if you do, you will become a wrongdoer. If God afflicts you with a misfortune, none can remove it but He; and if He bestows on you a favour, none can withhold His bounty. He is bountiful to whom He will. He is the Forgiving One, the Merciful.' "

Say: "You people! The truth has come to you from your Lord. He that follows the right path follows it for his own good, and he that strays from the right path does so at his own peril. I am not your keeper."

Observe what is revealed to you, and have patience till God make known His judgement. He is the best of judges.

12. Joseph

In the Name of God, the Compassionate, the Merciful

Alif lām rā'. These are the verses of the Glorious Book. We have revealed the Koran in the Arabic tongue so that you may grow in understanding.

In revealing this Koran We will recount to you the best of narratives, though before it you were heedless.

Joseph said to his father: "Father, I dreamt of eleven stars and the sun and the moon; I saw them prostrate themselves before me."[5]

"My son," he replied, "say nothing of this dream to your brothers, lest they plot evil against you: Satan is the sworn enemy of man. Even thus shall you be chosen by your Lord. He will teach you to interpret visions, and will perfect His favour to you and to the house of Jacob, as He perfected it to your forefathers Abraham and Isaac before you. Your Lord is all-knowing and wise."

Surely in Joseph and his brothers there are signs for doubting men.

They said to each other: "Surely Joseph and his brother[6] are dearer to our father than ourselves, though we are many. Truly, our father is much mistaken. Let us slay Joseph, or cast him away in some far-off land, so that we may have no rivals in our father's love, and after that be honourable men."

One of the brothers said: "Do not slay Joseph; but, if you must, rather cast him into a dark pit. Some caravan will take him up."

They said to their father: "Why do you not trust us with Joseph? Surely we wish him well. Send him with us tomorrow, that he may play and enjoy himself. We will take good care of him."

He replied: "It would much grieve me to let him go with you; for I fear lest the wolf should eat him when you are off your guard."

They said: "If the wolf could eat him despite our number, then we should surely be lost!"

And when they took him with them, they resolved to cast him into a dark pit. We revealed to him Our will, saying: "You shall tell them of all this when they will not know you."

At nightfall they returned weeping to their father. They said: "We went off to compete together, and left Joseph with our packs. The wolf devoured him. But you will not believe us, though we speak the truth." And they showed him their brother's shirt, stained with false blood.

"No!" he cried. "Your souls have tempted you to evil. Sweet patience! God alone can help me bear the loss you speak of."

And a caravan passed by, who sent their water-bearer to the pit. And when he had let down his pail, he cried: "Rejoice! A boy!"

---

5. Cf. Genesis 37.9.   6. His full brother, Benjamin.

They concealed him as part of their merchandise. But God knew what they did. They sold him for a trifling price, for a few pieces of silver. They cared nothing for him.

The Egyptian who bought him said to his wife:[7] "Be kind to him. He may prove useful to us, or we may adopt him as our son."

Thus We established Joseph in the land, and taught him to interpret dreams. God has power over all things, though most men may not know it. And when he reached maturity We bestowed on him wisdom and knowledge. Thus do We reward the righteous.

His master's wife attempted to seduce him. She bolted the doors and said: "Come!"

"God forbid!" he replied. "My lord has treated me with kindness. Wrongdoers shall never prosper."

She made for him, and he himself would have succumbed to her had he not seen a sign from his Lord. Thus did We shield him from evil-doing and lechery, for he was one of Our faithful servants.

They both rushed to the door. She tore his shirt from behind. And at the door they met her husband.

She cried: "Shall not the man who wished to violate your wife be thrown into prison or sternly punished?"

Joseph said: "It was she who attempted to seduce me."

"If his shirt is torn from the front," said one of her people, "she is speaking the truth and he is lying. If it is torn from behind, then he is speaking the truth, and she is lying."

And when her husband saw that Joseph's shirt was rent from behind, he said to her: "This is but one of your tricks. Your cunning is great indeed! Joseph, say no more about this. Woman, ask pardon for your sin. You have assuredly done wrong."

In the city, women were saying: "The Prince's wife has sought to seduce her servant. She has conceived a passion for him. We can see that she had clearly gone astray."

When she heard of their intrigues, she invited them to a banquet prepared at her house. To each she gave a knife, and ordered Joseph to present himself before them. When they saw him, they were amazed at him and cut their hands, exclaiming: "God preserve us! This is no mortal, but a gracious angel."

"This is he," she said, "on whose account you blamed me. I attempted to seduce him, but he was unyielding. If he declines to do my bidding, he shall be thrown into prison and shall be held in scorn."

"Lord," said Joseph, "sooner would I go to prison than give in to their advances. Shield me from their cunning, or I shall yield to them and lapse into folly."

His Lord answered his prayer and warded off their wiles from him. He hears all and knows all.

Yet, for all the evidence they had seen, they thought it right to jail him for a time.

Two young men entered the prison with him. One said: "I dreamt that I was pressing grapes." And the other: "I dreamt I was carrying a loaf upon my head, and the birds came and ate of it. Tell us the meaning of these dreams, for we can see you are a man of virtue."

7. Traditionally given the name Zuleikha.

Joseph replied: "Whatever food you are provided with, I can divine for you its meaning, even before it reaches you. This knowledge my Lord has given me, for I have left the faith of those that disbelieve in God and deny the life to come. I follow the faith of my forefathers, Abraham, Isaac and Jacob. We will serve no idols besides God. Such is the grace which God has bestowed on us and on all mankind. Yet most men do not give thanks.

"Fellow prisoners! Are sundry gods better than God, the One who conquers all? Those you serve besides Him are nothing but names which you and your fathers have devised and for which God has revealed no sanction. Judgement rests only with God. He has commanded you to worship none but Him. That is the true faith; yet most men do not know it.

"Fellow prisoners, one of you will serve his lord with wine. The other will be crucified, and the birds will peck at his head. That is the answer to your question."

And Joseph said to the prisoner who he knew would survive. "Remember me in the presence of your lord."

But Satan made him forget to mention Joseph to his lord, so that he stayed in prison for several years.

The king said: "I saw seven fatted cows which seven lean ones devoured; also seven green ears of corn and seven others dry. Tell me the meaning of this vision, my nobles, if you can interpret visions."

They replied: "They are but a medley of dreams; nor are we skilled in the interpretation of dreams."

Thereupon the man who had been freed remembered after all that time. He said: "I shall tell you what it means. Give me leave to go."

"Joseph," he said, "man of truth, tell us of the seven fatted cows which seven lean ones devoured; also of the seven green ears of corn and the other seven which were dry: so that I may go back to my masters and inform them."

He replied: "You shall sow for seven consecutive years. Leave in the ear the corn you reap, except a little which you may eat. There shall follow seven hungry years which will consume all but a little of what you scored. Then will come a year of abundant rain, in which the people will press the grape."

The king said: "Bring this man before me."

But when the envoy came to him, Joseph said: "Go back to your master and ask him about the women who cut their hands. My master knows their cunning."

The king questioned the women, saying: "What made you attempt to seduce Joseph?"

"God forbid!" they replied. "We know no evil of him."

"Now the truth must come to light," said the Prince's wife. "It was I who attempted to seduce him. He has told the truth."

"From this," said Joseph, "my lord will know that I did not betray him in his absence, and that God does not guide the mischief of the treacherous. Not that I claim to be free from sin: man's soul is prone to evil, except his to whom my Lord has shown mercy. My Lord is forgiving and merciful."

The king said: "Bring him before me. I will choose him for my own."

And when he had spoken with him, the king said: "You shall henceforth dwell with us, honoured and trusted."

Joseph said: "Give me charge of the granaries of the land. I shall husband them wisely."

Thus did We establish Joseph in the land, and he dwelt there as he pleased. We bestow Our mercy on whom We will, and shall never deny the righteous their reward. Surely better is the recompense of the life to come for those who believe in God and keep from evil.

Joseph's brothers arrived and presented themselves before him. He recognized them, but they knew him not. And when he had given them their provisions, he said: "Bring me your other brother from your father. Do you not see that I give just measure and am the best of hosts? If you refuse to bring him, you shall have no measure, nor shall you come near me again."

They replied: "We will endeavour to fetch him from his father. This we will surely do."

He said to his servants: "Put their silver[8] into their packs, so that they may discover it when they return to their people. Perchance they will come back."

When they returned to their father, they said: "Father, corn is henceforth denied us. Send our brother with us and we shall have our measure. We will take good care of him."

He replied: "Am I to trust you with him as I once trusted you with his brother? But God is the best of guardians: and of all those that show mercy He is the most merciful."

When they opened their packs, they discovered that their silver had been returned to them. "Father," they said, "what more can we desire? Here is our silver returned to us. We will buy provisions for our people, and take good care of our brother. We should receive an extra camel-load; a camel-load should be easy enough."

He replied: "I will not send him with you until you promise in God's name to bring him back to me, unless the worst befall you."

And when they had given him their pledge, he said: "God is the witness of what we say. My sons, do not enter from one gate; enter from different gates. In no way can I shield you from the might of God; judgement is His alone. In Him I have put my trust. In Him let the faithful put their trust."

And when they entered as their father bade them, he could in no way shield them from the might of God. It was but a wish in Jacob's soul which he had thus fulfilled. He was possessed of knowledge which We had given him. But most men have no knowledge.

When they went in to Joseph, he embraced his brother, and said: "I am your brother. Do not grieve at what they did."

And when he had given them their provisions, he hid a drinking-cup in his brother's pack.

Then a crier called out after them: "Travellers, you are surely thieves!"

They turned back, and asked: "What have you lost?"

"We miss the king's drinking-cup," they replied. "He that brings it shall have a camel-load of corn. I pledge my word for it."

"In God's name," they cried, "you know we did not come to do evil in the land. We are no thieves."

The Egyptians said: "What punishment shall be his who stole it, if you prove to be lying?"

They replied: "He in whose pack the cup is found shall render himself

---

8. Literally, "their merchandise."

your bondsman: that shall be his punishment. Thus do we punish the wrong-doers."

Joseph searched their bags before his brother's, and then took out the cup from his brother's bag.

Thus We directed Joseph. By the king's law he had no right to seize his brother: but God willed otherwise. We exalt whom We will to a lofty station: and above those that have knowledge there is One who is all-knowing.

They said: "If he has stolen—know then that a brother of his stole before him."[9]

But Joseph kept his secret and revealed nothing to them. He said: "Your deed was worse. God best knows the things you speak of."

They said: "Noble prince, this boy has an aged father. Take one of us, instead of him. We can see you are a generous man."

He replied: "God forbid that we should take any but the man with whom our property was found: for then we should surely be unjust."

When they despaired of him, they went aside to confer in private. The eldest said: "Do you not know that your father took from you a pledge in God's name, and that long ago you did your worst with Joseph? I will not stir from the land until my father gives me leave or God makes known to me His judgement: He is the best of judges. Return to your father and say to him: 'Father, your son has stolen. We testify only to what we know. We could not guard against the unforeseen. Inquire at the city where we lodged, and from the caravan with which we travelled. We surely speak the truth.'"

"No!" cried their father. "Your souls have tempted you to evil. But I will have sweet patience. God may bring them all to me. He alone is all-knowing and wise." And he turned away from them, crying: "Alas for Joseph!" His eyes went white with grief, and he was oppressed with silent sorrow.

His sons exclaimed: "In God's name, will you not cease to think of Joseph until you ruin your health and die?"

He replied: "I complain to God of my sorrow and sadness. God has made known to me things that you know not. Go, my sons, and seek news of Joseph and his brother. Do not despair of God's spirit; none but unbelievers despair of God's spirit."

And when they went in to him, they said: "Noble prince, we and our people are scourged with famine. We have brought but little money. Give us our full measure, and be charitable to us: God surely rewards the charitable."

"Do you know," he replied, "what you did to Joseph and his brother? You are surely unaware."

They cried: "Can you indeed be Joseph?"

"I am Joseph," he answered, "and this is my brother. God has been gracious to us. Those that keep from evil and endure with fortitude, God will not deny them their reward."

"By the Lord," they said, "God has exalted you above us all. We have indeed done wrong."

He replied: "None shall reproach you this day. May God forgive you: of all those that show mercy He is the most merciful. Take this shirt of mine

9. Commentators say that Joseph had stolen an idol of his maternal grandfather's and broken it, so that he might not worship it.

and throw it over my father's face: he will recover his sight. Then return to me with all your people."

When the caravan departed their father said: "I feel the breath of Joseph, though you will not believe me."

"In God's name," said those who heard him, "it is but your old illusion."

And when the bearer of good news arrived, he threw Joseph's shirt over the old man's face, and he regained his sight. He said: "Did I not tell you, God has made known to me what you know not?"

His sons said: "Father, implore forgiveness for our sins. We have indeed done wrong."

He replied: "I shall implore my Lord to forgive you. He is forgiving and merciful."

And when they went in to Joseph, he embraced his parents and said: "Welcome to Egypt, safe, if God wills!"

He helped his parents to a couch, and they all fell on their knees and prostrated themselves before him.

"This," said Joseph to his father, "is the meaning of my old vision: my Lord has fulfilled it. He has been gracious to me. He has released me from prison, and brought you out of the desert after Satan had stirred up strife between me and my brothers. My Lord is gracious to whom He will. He alone is all-knowing and wise.

"Lord, You have given me authority and taught me to interpret dreams. Creator of the heavens and the earth, my Guardian in this world and in the world to come! Allow me to die in submission, and admit me among the righteous."

That which We have now revealed to you[1] is a tale of the unknown. You were not present when Joseph's brothers conceived their plans and schemed against him. Yet strive as you may, most men will not believe.

You shall demand of them no recompense for this. It is but an admonition to all mankind.

Many are the marvels of the heavens and the earth; yet they pass them by and pay no heed to them. The greater part of them believe in God only if they can worship other gods besides Him.

Are they confident that God's scourge will not fall upon them, or that the Hour of Doom will not overtake them unawares, without warning?

Say: "This is my path. With sure knowledge I call on you to have faith in God, I and all my followers. Glory be to God! I am no idolater."

Nor were the apostles whom We sent before you other than mortals inspired by Our will and chosen from among their people.

Have they not travelled the land and seen what was the end of those who disbelieved before them? Surely better is the life to come for those that keep from evil. Can you not understand?

And when at length the apostles despaired and thought they were denied, Our help came down to them, delivering whom We pleased. The evil-doers could not be saved from Our scourge. Their annals point a moral to men of understanding.

This[2] is no invented tale, but a confirmation of previous scriptures, an explanation of all things, a guide and a blessing to true believers.

1. Muhammad.　2. The Koran.

BEOWULF

ca. ninth century

Beowulf, composed perhaps (but not certainly) about 850 in the Anglo-Saxon language then current in England, is both a heroic poem of dark magnificence and the most vivid account left to us of the social world and life experiences of the Germanic and Scandinavian peoples who overran the Roman empire. The poem is a fairy-tale story of how the hero, Beowulf, conquers three monsters: first a man-eating, troll-like creature named Grendel, then Grendel's vengeance-seeking mother, and finally—when Beowulf has become an old man—a fire-breathing dragon. From these unlikely events the poet has fashioned a poem that describes not merely the details of the warrior life of the Germanic tribes but its meaning to the people who lived it. Although himself a Christian, the poet provides us with a unique insight into a pagan world that had passed away by the time he was writing, but one whose legends and values he knows well. Like the Homeric poems and *The Song of Roland,* the historical period of the action of *Beowulf* is many centuries prior to the poem's date of composition: the one event in the poem that can be dated—the death of Beowulf's lord, Hygelac, in a raid on the Franks—occurred around 520. The protagonists of the poem are not the English who were its audience but two of their forebears, the Germanic tribes of the South Danes, who lived in Denmark, and their neighbors to the east, the Geats, who lived in southern Sweden. In addition to these two groups the poem alludes to the history of other northern European peoples, especially the Swedes, the Frisians, and the Franks, and it mentions as well more obscure tribal groupings like the Heatho-Bards, the Wulfings, and the Waegmundings. In reading the poem, we enter into a pre-Christian Germanic world that is both mysterious and fascinating. And that world is also, as Beowulf himself comes to understand, doomed.

The most important fact about Germanic tribal society is its violence. Each of the various tribes is in competition with the others for land and plunder, and even within tribes there are constant struggles for power. The central bond that holds society together is the loyalty between a lord and his warriors, or thanes. The lord is a "ring-giver," which means that he distributes to his thanes objects of value that include bracelets and necklaces ("rings"), armor and weapons, and even land and political authority. In return the thane is expected to provide unswerving loyalty on the battlefield and good counsel during times of peace. More important, this bond of loyalty establishes the community within which individuals find meaning.

In the Germanic world the worst condition into which a man can fall is to be an outlaw or wanderer, someone who has no home. This is the situation of the monster Grendel, described in the poem as a "grim demon / haunting the marches, marauding round the heath / and the desolate fens" (102–104). The Christian poet interprets Grendel and his mother as deriving from the race of Cain, who was condemned by God to wander the earth after his murder of Abel. The poem begins with Grendel's attack upon the great hall Heorot, built as a place to celebrate community solidarity and the goodness of the gods by Hrothgar, the old Danish king. What motivates Grendel's attack is his sense of exclusion: in this world, to be an independent individual is to be isolated and rejected. Appropriately, Grendel's slayer, Beowulf, is himself something of an individual, who, by this act, achieves inclusion within his own social world. Almost two-thirds of the way through the poem we learn that Beowulf "had been poorly regarded / for a long time" by his people, the Geats: "They firmly believed that he lacked force, / that the prince was a weakling" (2183–88). But the victory over Grendel and his mother, and the gifts he receives from the Danes and gives in turn to his own lord, Hygelac, change all that. Hygelac gives him a sword that had belonged to his own father, Hrethel, and grants him land and lordship: "a hall and a throne." After the deaths of Hygelac and his son Heardred, the Geats then turn to Beowulf to become their king, and he rules for fifty years until his fatal battle with a dragon.

Given that martial prowess is the primary means by which a man earns the respect of his fellows—Beowulf is recognized as worthy not because he is thoughtful or self-controlled (although he is both) but because he is fierce in battle—we should not be surprised that the poet presents a tribal world constantly engulfed in violence. The monster-killing that constitutes the main action of the poem is located within a dense context of tribal feuding. These feuds are mentioned so allusively and indirectly that we can assume the poet's English audience was fully informed about the early history of their Germanic ancestors. But the modern reader does not know this history, and it will be helpful to outline it here. (The genealogical table will help to keep the characters straight.)

The poem tells us of five primary feuds. The most important, which we learn about only toward the end of the poem (2379–96, 2472–89, 2922–98), is between the Geats and the Swedes, and takes place in two phases. The first phase begins when the Swedes, under their king Ongentheow, defeat the Geats in a battle at Hreosnahill (or Sorrow Hill) in which great slaughter is committed by Ongentheow's sons, Ohthere and Onela. This slaughter is then avenged by the killing of Ongentheow by the Geat Eofer in the battle of Ravenswood, in which the Geatish king Haethcyn also dies. The second phase of the Swedish-Geatish feud is initiated by a civil war within the Swedish royal family. After the death of his elder brother Ohthere, Onela seizes the throne and drives out the rightful heirs, Ohthere's sons Eanmund and Eadgils. They find refuge with the Geats, then being led by Hygelac's son Heardred. Onela attacks the Geats, killing both Heardred and one of the brothers, Eanmund. (The warrior who actually kills Eanmund is named Weohstan and is the father of Wiglaf, who at the end of the poem is the only one of Beowulf's thanes to stand by him in the attack on the dragon. How Wiglaf—who like Beowulf is referred to as a Waegmunding—came to be accepted among the Geats is never explained.) Heardred's death leaves Beowulf king of the Geats, and he later supports Eadgils, who kills Onela and regains the Swedish throne. Yet despite this apparent alliance, after the death of Beowulf we are told that "this vicious feud" (3000) between the Swedes and Geats will now lead to renewed Swedish attacks on the leaderless Geats (possibly because Wiglaf, the apparent heir to the Geatish throne, is the son of the slayer of Eanmund, Eadgils's brother).

The second feud mentioned in the poem is that between the Heatho-Bards and the Danes. While Beowulf is visiting Hrothgar in order to deal with the monsters, there are several cryptic references to a deadly fire that awaits the great hall Heorot. When Beowulf returns from his adventure and describes the trip to Hygelac, he explains that Hrothgar's daughter Freawaru is promised to Ingeld, the son of the murdered Heatho-Bard king Froda. Yet Beowulf predicts, in a sinister description of the way that enmity will be stirred up when a Heatho-Bard warrior sees a Dane wearing Froda's armor, that the peace will not hold: "But generally the spear / is prompt to retaliate when a prince is killed, / no matter how admirable the bride may be" (2029–31).

The third feud, predicted but not described, is within the Danish royal house. The old king Hrothgar has two young sons, Hrethric and Hrothmund, and his queen, Wealhtheow, asks Beowulf to protect them from their uncle Hrothulf after the death of Hrothgar—protection Beowulf will be unable to provide.

As to the fourth feud, Hrothgar tells Beowulf that Beowulf's father, Ecgtheow, started a feud with the Wulfings by killing a man called Heatholaf, and that the Geats exiled him in order to protect themselves from retaliation. Hrothgar, however, not only provided Ecgtheow with asylum but also settled the feud by paying compensation to the Wulfings for Heatholaf, a compensation known among the Germanic tribes as *wergild*, or "man-money."

The fifth feud is that between the Geats and three tribes to the south of them, the

Frisians, the Hetware, and the Franks. This feud started when the Geatish king Hyge-lac raided the other tribes' territory—as mentioned, there is an independent record of this raid, which took place about 520—and was killed in the process. As he prepares to fight the dragon, Beowulf tells us that he avenged Hygelac's death: "I killed / Dayraven the Frank in front of the two armies" (2501–502). After Beowulf's death the Geats are told that they face harsh battle at the hands of the Franks.

In addition to these feuds, which occur within the historical world of the poem, one other is mentioned in detail in a song sung by a *scop*, or bard, during the cele-brations after the death of Grendel. This is known as the fight at Finnsburg. A Dane named Hnaef and his entourage of warriors, while visiting the Jute Finn at the fortress of Finnsburg, are attacked by the Jutes despite the fact that Finn is married to Hnaef's sister Hildeburh (doubtless as part of an effort to patch up a previous feud). Hnaef is killed, along with the son of Finn and Hildeburh. Neither party is powerful enough to finish off the other, and they agree to a truce: they will winter together in Finns-burg, and the Danes will sail home in the spring. Not surprisingly, the coming of spring also awakens "longing . . . for vengeance" (1138–40), and the Danes slaughter Finn and the other Jutes in their hall, returning home with plunder and with the bereft Hildeburh, whose son and husband are now dead.

The poet makes clear that the awful cost of their violence is not lost on these people. The description of the future that awaits the leaderless Geats now that Beowulf is dead—delivered to the waiting people by a messenger sent from the battle with the dragon—is only one of several chilling passages that acknowledge the effect of tribal warfare:

> . . . Many a spear,
> dawn-cold to the touch will be taken down
> and waved on high; the swept harp
> won't waken warriors, but the raven winging
> darkly over the doomed will have news,
> tidings for the eagle of how he hoked and ate,
> how the wolf and he made short work of the dead. (3021–27)

Nor will things go better for the women of the tribe:

> . . . often, repeatedly, in the path of exile
> they shall walk bereft, bowed under woe,
> now that [Beowulf's] laugh is silenced. (3018–20)

Yet the poem also argues that it is only by violence that civilization can be maintained. The attacks by both Grendel and his mother are themselves a feud, in the first instance against God (hence the monsters' descent from the race of Cain), more immediately against the peaceful society that Hrothgar has established in Heorot. As Wealhtheow says of Heorot,

> "Here each comrade is true to the other,
> loyal to lord, loving in spirit.
> The thanes have one purpose, the people are ready:
> having drunk and pledged, the ranks do as I bid." (1228–31)

Grendel wants to destroy this social harmony, and his mother is an avenging spirit who seeks retaliation for the death of her offspring. Similarly, the dragon is roused to rage by the need to avenge the theft of a drinking cup from the hoard he guards: "he worked himself up / by imagining battle" (2298–99). Thus the monsters can be understood, at least in part, as embodiments of the feuding principle that is inevitably destroying Germanic society. Yet in killing them Beowulf is involved in a paradox: violence can be controlled only by violence, a circle from which no one in the poem is able to escape.

Violence is thus part and parcel of this civilization. After Grendel's mother has killed one of Hrothgar's men, Beowulf advises the Danish king, in a succinct sentence that could stand as a motto for the poem, "It is always better / to avenge dear ones than to indulge in mourning" (1384–85). The miserable condition of the man who cannot avenge the death of a kinsman is vividly described in the story Beowulf tells about Hygelac's father, Hrethel. Hrethel had three sons, Herebeald, Haethcyn, and Hygelac. In an accident, Haethcyn killed Herebeald; because it was an accident, and because the perpetrator was his own son, Hrethel could not compensate himself for his loss with either *wergild* or vengeance. As Beowulf arms himself for the battle with the dragon he tells this grim story, and he draws a parallel between Hrethel's unassuageable grief and the sorrow of the father who sees his son die on the gallows as an outlaw. The grieving father looks at his son's empty dwelling-place, the silent winehall, and he goes then to his bed, chanting grief-songs: "everything seems too large, / the steadings and the fields" (2461–62). This sense of emptiness is an effect of more than simply the technical problem of how to find satisfaction for certain kinds of injury. By having Beowulf tell this story as he prepares for what he knows will be his final battle, the poet shows us that the hero understands at some level the futility of the entire world of Germanic heroism that he himself so fully represents. Trolls and dragons can be killed, but how does one eradicate the violence that serves to constitute society itself? The monsters are, finally, instances of a social sickness that infects the culture as a whole: they may be killed, but the violence they represent will continue unabated. Perhaps Beowulf's greatest act of heroism is found not in the physical courage he displays in his battles against human and superhuman foes but in his spiritual capacity to persevere despite knowing that his efforts are futile.

The poem survives in only a single manuscript written about 1000, but it was composed earlier, probably over a period of many years. Like the Homeric poems and *The Song of Roland, Beowulf* emerged from an oral tradition of composition (for a discussion of oral composition, see above, pp. 100–1). It was put into its final form by a Christian, but one who is both careful to preserve the distinction between his Christian present and the pagan past and unusually tolerant of the culture of his forebears. For one thing, he avoids putting Christian sentiments in the mouths of pre-Christian characters. The terms with which the characters refer to the deity— God, the Lord, Heavenly Powers, Almighty God, Lord of Ages, Heavenly Shepherd, King of Heaven, and so forth—are, in their original Anglo-Saxon forms, the same terms as appear in explicitly non-Christian writings. We should also remember that the habit of capitalizing sacred names is a modern convention: in the manuscript they are, like all proper names, lowercase. For example, when the Geats arrive in Denmark they are described in the translation as having "thanked God" (227) that the trip was successful. But the Anglo-Saxon could just as accurately be translated "thanked a god," which has a very different implication. Another example is the way in which the translator has Hrothgar say that Beowulf was sent to the Danes by "Holy God . . . in His goodness" (381–82); again, one could just as accurately, and more consistently, translate this as "by a divine god of his kindness." Hrothgar's speech of advice to Beowulf is certainly consistent with Christianity, but it contains nothing out of character with the values of the Germanic, pagan world in which Hrothgar and Beowulf live. Perhaps most important, the poet refrains from criticizing his pagan characters for their paganism. While he makes it clear that the Danes are wrong to offer sacrifices to their heathen gods in an effort to fend off Grendel's attacks, he is more sorrowful than judgmental or moralistic (175–88). They commit this error because they do not yet know of the true, Christian God whom the poet himself worships, just as they cannot know that the monsters are of the race of Cain. They do indeed live in a world ruled over by the Christian God: as the poet says, "Past and present, God's will prevails" (1057). But while the audience knows this truth, their pagan forebears cannot. Moreover, the poet shows remarkable restraint in not criticizing pagan practices— such as cremation—that were strictly forbidden by Christian doctrine. Indeed, in its respect for the past the poem participates in its own central theme. Feuding, after all, is caused by an inability to make peace with the past, an unwillingness to put aside what has happened and move into a new future. *Beowulf* confronts this dilemma by asking, How can one celebrate one's own cultural past while admitting that it must be left behind?

The translation is by Seamus Heaney, the Nobel Prize–winning poet from Northern Ireland. Heaney has included in his translation some Northern Irish words, encouraging us to think about the relation of the violence depicted in the poem to the violence of our own time. The original Anglo-Saxon poem is written in an alliterative verse in which each line has four stresses, three of which usually alliterate, and with a strong break or caesura in the middle of the line. For instance, the fourth and fifth lines of the poem read in the original (*sc* is pronounced as *sh* in Anglo-Saxon):

> Oft Scyld Scefing   sceathena threatum
> monegum maegthum   meodsetla ofteah.

These lines can be translated word for word: "Often Scyld Scefing from troops of the enemies, / from many races, mead-benches deprived." Heaney's translation reads: "There was Shield Sheafson, scourge of many tribes / a wrecker of mead-benches, rampaging among foes." While he does not here keep to the Anglo-Saxon pattern of alliteration, he nonetheless provides us with lines that include strong alliteration and a caesura—and one that retains the sense of the original and captures the energy both of the verse and of the world it depicts.

PRONOUNCING GLOSSARY

The following list uses common English syllables and stress accents to provide rough equivalents of selected words whose pronunciation may be unfamiliar to the general reader.

Aeschere: *ash'-hair-uh*

Eadgils: *ay-ahd'-gils*

Eanmund: *ay-ahn'-mund*

Ecglaf: *etch'-lahf*

Ecgtheow: *etch'-thee-ow*

Eofor: *ay-oh'-for*

Freawaru: *fray-ah'-wah-roo*

Geats: *yay'-ats*

Haethcyn: *hath'-kin*

Heardred: *hay-ahr'-dred*

Heatho-Bards: *hay-ath'-oh–bards*

Heatholaf: *hay-ath'-oh-lahf*

Heorogar: *hay-ah'-roh-gahr*

Heorot: *hay'-oh-rot*

Herebeald: *her'-uh-bay-ald*

Hildeburh: *hil'-de-burhk*

Hnaef: *hnaf*

Hondscio: *hond'-shee-oh*

Hreosnahill: *hray-ohs'-nah-hill*

Hrethel: *hray'-thuhl*

Hrethric: *hreth'-rich*

Hrothgar: *hroth'-gahr*

Hrothmund: *hroth'-mund*

Hrothulf: *hroth'-ulf*

Hygd: *higd*

Hygelac: *hig'-uh-lahk*

Ohthere: *ohkt'-her-uh*

Onela: *oh-nay'-lah*

Ongentheow: *ohn-gen'-thay-ow*

Waegmundings: *wahg'-mund-ings*

Wealhtheow: *way-ahl'-thay-ow*

Weohstan: *way'oh-stahn*

Wiglaf: *wig'-lahf*

TRIBES AND GENEALOGIES

1. *The Danes (Bright-, Half-, Ring-, Spear-, North-, East-, South-, West-Danes; Shield-ings, Honor-, Victor-, War-Shieldings: Ing's friends).*

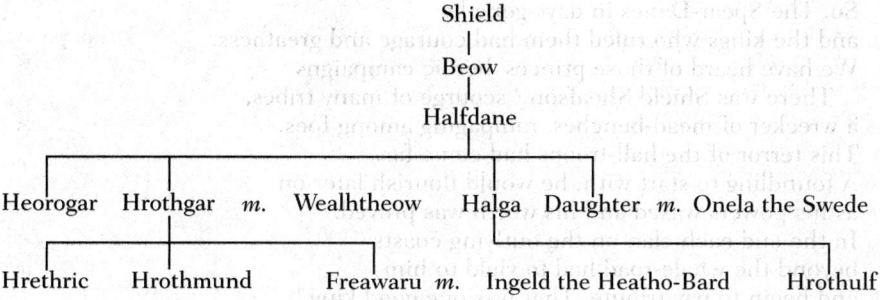

2. *The Geats (Sea-, War-, Weather-Geats).*

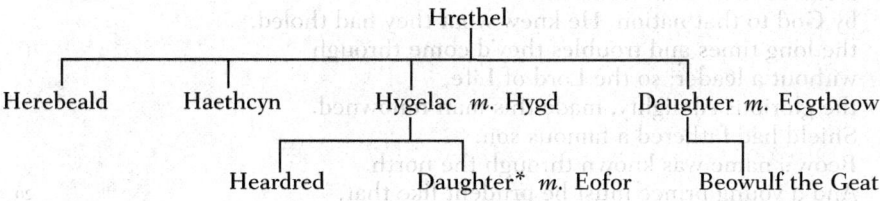

3. *The Swedes*

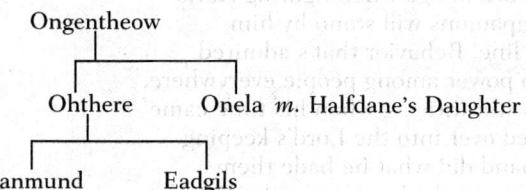

4. *Miscellaneous.*

A. Half-Danes (also called Shieldings) involved in the fight at Finnsburg may represent a different tribe from the Danes described above. Their king Hoc had a son, Hnaef, who succeeded him, and a daughter Hildeburh, who married Finn, king of the Jutes.

B. The Jutes, or Frisians, are represented as enemies of the Danes in the fight at Finnsburg and as allies of the Franks at the time Hygelac the Geat made the attack in which he lost his life and from which Beowulf swam home. Also allied with the Franks at this time were the Hetware.

C. The Heatho-Bards (i.e., "Battle-Bards") are represented as inveterate enemies of the Danes. Their king Froda had been killed in an attack on the Danes, and Hrothgar's attempt to make peace with them by marrying his daughter Freawaru to Froda's son Ingeld failed when the latter attacked Heorot. The attack was repulsed, although Heorot was burned.

---

* The daughter of Hygelac who was given to Eofor may have been born to him by a former wife, older than Hygd.

Beowulf[1]

[PROLOGUE: THE RISE OF THE DANISH NATION]

So. The Spear-Danes in days gone by
and the kings who ruled them had courage and greatness.
We have heard of those princes' heroic campaigns.
    There was Shield Sheafson,[2] scourge of many tribes,
a wrecker of mead-benches, rampaging among foes.   5
This terror of the hall-troops had come far.
A foundling to start with, he would flourish later on
as his powers waxed and his worth was proved.
In the end each clan on the outlying coasts
beyond the whale-road had to yield to him   10
and begin to pay tribute. That was one good king.
    Afterward a boy-child was born to Shield,
a cub in the yard, a comfort sent
by God to that nation. He knew what they had tholed,[3]
the long times and troubles they'd come through   15
without a leader; so the Lord of Life,
the glorious Almighty, made this man renowned.
Shield had fathered a famous son:
Beow's name was known through the north.
And a young prince must be prudent like that,   20
giving freely while his father lives
so that afterward in age when fighting starts
steadfast companions will stand by him
and hold the line. Behavior that's admired
is the path to power among people everywhere.   25
    Shield was still thriving when his time came
and he crossed over into the Lord's keeping.
His warrior band did what he bade them
when he laid down the law among the Danes:
they shouldered him out to the sea's flood,   30
the chief they revered who had long ruled them.
A ring-whorled prow rode in the harbor,
ice-clad, outbound, a craft for a prince.
They stretched their beloved lord in his boat,
laid out by the mast, amidships,   35
the great ring-giver. Far-fetched treasures
were piled upon him, and precious gear.
I never heard before of a ship so well furbished
with battle-tackle, bladed weapons
and coats of mail. The massed treasure   40
was loaded on top of him: it would travel far
on out into the ocean's sway.
They decked his body no less bountifully
with offerings than those first ones did

---

1. Translated by Seamus Heaney.   2. Translates Scyld Scefing, which probably means "son of Sheaf."
Scyld's origins are mysterious.   3. An Anglo-Saxon word that means "suffered, endured" and that survives
in the translator's native land of Northern Ireland. In using this word, he also maintains an alliterative
pattern similar to the original ("that . . . they . . . tholed").

who cast him away when he was a child   45
and launched him alone out over the waves.[4]
And they set a gold standard up
high above his head and let him drift
to wind and tide, bewailing him
and mourning their loss. No man can tell,   50
no wise man in hall or weathered veteran
knows for certain who salvaged that load.

    Then it fell to Beow to keep the forts.
He was well regarded and ruled the Danes
for a long time after his father took leave   55
of his life on earth. And then his heir,
the great Halfdane, held sway
for as long as he lived, their elder and warlord.
He was four times a father, this fighter prince:
one by one they entered the world,   60
Heorogar, Hrothgar, the good Halga,
and a daughter,[5] I have heard, who was Onela's queen,
a balm in bed to the battle-scarred Swede.

    The fortunes of war favored Hrothgar.
Friends and kinsmen flocked to his ranks,   65
young followers, a force that grew
to be a mighty army. So his mind turned
to hall-building: he handed down orders
for men to work on a great mead-hall
meant to be a wonder of the world forever;   70
it would be his throne-room and there he would dispense
his God-given goods to young and old—
but not the common land or people's lives.[6]
Far and wide through the world, I have heard,
orders for work to adorn that wallstead   75
were sent to many peoples. And soon it stood there
finished and ready, in full view,
the hall of halls. Heorot[7] was the name
he had settled on it, whose utterance was law.
Nor did he renege, but doled out rings   80
and torques[8] at the table. The hall towered,
its gables wide and high and awaiting
a barbarous burning.[9] That doom abided,
but in time it would come: the killer instinct
unleashed among in-laws, the blood-lust rampant.   85

[HEOROT IS ATTACKED]

    Then a powerful demon, a prowler through the dark,
nursed a hard grievance. It harrowed him

---

4. Since Shield arrived with nothing, this sentence is a litotes or understatement, a characteristic of the laconic style of old Germanic poetry.   5. The text is faulty here, so that the name of Halfdane's daughter has been lost. *Halfdane*: according to another source, Halfdane's mother was Swedish; hence his name. 6. Apparently, slaves, along with pastureland used by all, were not in the king's power to give away. 7. I.e., "hart," a symbol of royalty.   8. Golden bands worn around the neck.   9. The destruction by fire of Heorot occurred at a later time than that of the poem's action, when the Heatho-Bard Ingeld attacked his father-in-law, Hrothgar. For a more detailed account of this feud and of Hrothgar's hope that it could be settled by the marriage of his daughter to Ingeld, see lines 2020–69.

to hear the din of the loud banquet
every day in the hall, the harp being struck
and the clear song of a skilled poet   90
telling with mastery of man's beginnings,
how the Almighty had made the earth
a gleaming plain girdled with waters;
in His splendor He set the sun and the moon
to be earth's lamplight, lanterns for men,   95
and filled the broad lap of the world
with branches and leaves; and quickened life
in every other thing that moved.

   So times were pleasant for the people there
until finally one, a fiend out of hell,   100
began to work his evil in the world.
Grendel was the name of this grim demon
haunting the marches, marauding round the heath
and the desolate fens; he had dwelt for a time
in misery among the banished monsters,   105
Cain's clan, whom the Creator had outlawed
and condemned as outcasts.[1] For the killing of Abel
the Eternal Lord had exacted a price:
Cain got no good from committing that murder
because the Almighty made him anathema   110
and out of the curse of his exile there sprang
ogres and elves and evil phantoms
and the giants too who strove with God
time and again until He gave them their reward.[2]

   So, after nightfall, Grendel set out   115
for the lofty house, to see how the Ring-Danes
were settling into it after their drink,
and there he came upon them, a company of the best
asleep from their feasting, insensible to pain
and human sorrow. Suddenly then   120
the God-cursed brute was creating havoc:
greedy and grim, he grabbed thirty men
from their resting places and rushed to his lair,
flushed up and inflamed from the raid,
blundering back with the butchered corpses.   125

   Then as dawn brightened and the day broke,
Grendel's powers of destruction were plain:
their wassail was over, they wept to heaven
and mourned under morning. Their mighty prince,
the storied leader, sat stricken and helpless,   130
humiliated by the loss of his guard,
bewildered and stunned, staring aghast
at the demon's trail, in deep distress.
He was numb with grief, but got no respite
for one night later merciless Grendel   135
struck again with more gruesome murders.

---

1. Genesis 4.9–12.   2. The poet is thinking here of Genesis 6.2–8, where the Latin Bible in use at the time refers to giants mating with women who were understood to be the descendents of Cain, and thus creating the wicked race that God destroyed with the flood.

Malignant by nature, he never showed remorse.
It was easy then to meet with a man
shifting himself to a safer distance
to bed in the bothies,[3] for who could be blind   140
to the evidence of his eyes, the obviousness
of the hall-watcher's hate? Whoever escaped
kept a weather-eye open and moved away.
    So Grendel ruled in defiance of right,
one against all, until the greatest house   145
in the world stood empty, a deserted wallstead.
For twelve winters, seasons of woe,
the lord of the Shieldings[4] suffered under
his load of sorrow; and so, before long,
the news was known over the whole world.   150
Sad lays were sung about the beset king,
the vicious raids and ravages of Grendel,
his long and unrelenting feud,
nothing but war; how he would never
parley or make peace with any Dane   155
nor stop his death-dealing nor pay the death-price.[5]
No counselor could ever expect
fair reparation from those rabid hands.
All were endangered; young and old
were hunted down by that dark death-shadow   160
who lurked and swooped in the long nights
on the misty moors; nobody knows
where these reavers from hell roam on their errands.
    So Grendel waged his lonely war,
inflicting constant cruelties on the people,   165
atrocious hurt. He took over Heorot,
haunted the glittering hall after dark,
but the throne itself, the treasure-seat,
he was kept from approaching; he was the Lord's outcast.
    These were hard times, heartbreaking   170
for the prince of the Shieldings; powerful counselors,
the highest in the land, would lend advice,
plotting how best the bold defenders
might resist and beat off sudden attacks.
Sometimes at pagan shrines they vowed   175
offerings to idols, swore oaths
that the killer of souls might come to their aid
and save the people.[6] That was their way,
their heathenish hope; deep in their hearts
they remembered hell. The Almighty Judge   180
of good deeds and bad, the Lord God,
Head of the Heavens and High King of the World,
was unknown to them. Oh, cursed is he

---

3. Outlying buildings; the word is current in Northern Ireland.   4. I.e., Hrothgar; as descendents of
Shield, the Danes are called Shieldings.   5. According to Germanic law, a slayer could achieve peace
with his victim's kinsmen only by paying them *wergild* ("man-price") as compensation for the slain man.
6. The poet interprets the heathen gods to whom the Danes make offerings as different incarnations of
Satan. Naturally, the pagan Danes do not think of their gods in these biblical terms, but as the poet makes
clear in the following lines, they have no other recourse.

who in time of trouble has to thrust his soul
in the fire's embrace, forfeiting help;   185
he has nowhere to turn. But blessed is he
who after death can approach the Lord
and find friendship in the Father's embrace.

[THE HERO COMES TO HEOROT]

So that troubled time continued, woe
that never stopped, steady affliction   190
for Halfdane's son, too hard an ordeal.
There was panic after dark, people endured
raids in the night, riven by the terror.
When he heard about Grendel, Hygelac's thane
was on home ground, over in Geatland.   195
There was no one else like him alive.
In his day, he was the mightiest man on earth,
highborn and powerful. He ordered a boat
that would ply the waves. He announced his plan:
to sail the swan's road[7] and seek out that king,   200
the famous prince who needed defenders.
Nobody tried to keep him from going,
no elder denied him, dear as he was to them.
Instead, they inspected omens and spurred
his ambition to go, whilst he moved about   205
like the leader he was, enlisting men,
the best he could find; with fourteen others
the warrior boarded the boat as captain,
a canny pilot along coast and currents.
Time went by, the boat was on water,   210
in close under the cliffs.
Men climbed eagerly up the gangplank,
sand churned in surf, warriors loaded
a cargo of weapons, shining war-gear
in the vessel's hold, then heaved out,   215
away with a will in their wood-wreathed ship.
Over the waves, with the wind behind her
and foam at her neck, she flew like a bird
until her curved prow had covered the distance,
and on the following day, at the due hour,   220
those seafarers sighted land,
sunlit cliffs, sheer crags
and looming headlands, the landfall they sought.
It was the end of their voyage and the Geats vaulted
over the side, out on to the sand,   225
and moored their ship. There was a clash of mail
and a thresh of gear. They thanked God
for that easy crossing on a calm sea.
When the watchman on the wall, the Shieldings' lookout

---

7. I.e., the sea. This is an example of a "kenning," a metaphoric phrase that is used to describe a common
object. These kennings are very common throughout Anglo-Saxon poetry. See, for another instance, line
258, where the poet describes a man's capacity for speech as his "word-hoard."

whose job it was to guard the sea-cliffs,   230
saw shields glittering on the gangplank
and battle-equipment being unloaded
he had to find out who and what
the arrivals were. So he rode to the shore,
this horseman of Hrothgar's, and challenged them   235
in formal terms, flourishing his spear:
"What kind of men are you who arrive
rigged out for combat in your coats of mail,
sailing here over the sea-lanes
in your steep-hulled boat? I have been stationed   240
as lookout on this coast for a long time.
My job is to watch the waves for raiders,
any danger to the Danish shore.
Never before has a force under arms
disembarked so openly—not bothering to ask   245
if the sentries allowed them safe passage
or the clan had consented. Nor have I seen
a mightier man-at-arms on this earth
than the one standing here: unless I am mistaken,
he is truly noble. This is no mere   250
hanger-on in a hero's armor.
So now, before you fare inland
as interlopers, I have to be informed
about who you are and where you hail from.
Outsiders from across the water,   255
I say it again: the sooner you tell
where you come from and why, the better."
     The leader of the troop unlocked his word-hoard;
the distinguished one delivered this answer:
"We belong by birth to the Geat people   260
and owe allegiance to Lord Hygelac.
In his day, my father was a famous man,
a noble warrior-lord named Ecgtheow.
He outlasted many a long winter
and went on his way. All over the world   265
men wise in counsel continue to remember him.
We come in good faith to find your lord
and nation's shield, the son of Halfdane.
Give us the right advice and direction.
We have arrived here on a great errand   270
to the lord of the Danes, and I believe therefore
there should be nothing hidden or withheld between us.
So tell us if what we have heard is true
about this threat, whatever it is,
this danger abroad in the dark nights,   275
this corpse-maker mongering death
in the Shieldings' country. I come to proffer
my wholehearted help and counsel.
I can show the wise Hrothgar a way
to defeat his enemy and find respite—   280
if any respite is to reach him, ever.

I can calm the turmoil and terror in his mind.
Otherwise, he must endure woes
and live with grief for as long as his hall
stands at the horizon on its high ground." 285

Undaunted, sitting astride his horse,
the coast-guard answered: "Anyone with gumption
and a sharp mind will take the measure
of two things: what's said and what's done.
I believe what you have told me, that you are a troop 290
loyal to our king. So come ahead
with your arms and your gear, and I will guide you.
What's more, I'll order my own comrades
on their word of honor to watch your boat
down there on the strand—keep her safe 295
in her fresh tar, until the time comes
for her curved prow to preen on the waves
and bear this hero back to Geatland.
May one so valiant and venturesome
come unharmed through the clash of battle." 300

So they went on their way. The ship rode the water,
broad-beamed, bound by its hawser
and anchored fast. Boar-shapes[8] flashed
above their cheek-guards, the brightly forged
work of goldsmiths, watching over 305
those stern-faced men. They marched in step,
hurrying on till the timbered hall
rose before them, radiant with gold.
Nobody on earth knew of another
building like it. Majesty lodged there, 310
its light shone over many lands.
So their gallant escort guided them
to that dazzling stronghold and indicated
the shortest way to it; then the noble warrior
wheeled on his horse and spoke these words: 315
"It is time for me to go. May the Almighty
Father keep you and in His kindness
watch over your exploits. I'm away to the sea,
back on alert against enemy raiders."

It was a paved track, a path that kept them 320
in marching order. Their mail-shirts glinted,
hard and hand-linked; the high-gloss iron
of their armor rang. So they duly arrived
in their grim war-graith[9] and gear at the hall,
and, weary from the sea, stacked wide shields 325
of the toughest hardwood against the wall,
then collapsed on the benches; battle-dress
and weapons clashed. They collected their spears
in a seafarers' stook,[1] a stand of grayish
tapering ash. And the troops themselves 330

---

8. Images of boars—a cult animal among the Germanic tribes and sacred to the god Freyr—were fixed atop helmets in the belief that they would provide protection from enemy blows.   9. *Graith* is an archaic word for equipment or armor.   1. *Stook* is an archaic word for a pile or mass.

were as good as their weapons.
                          Then a proud warrior
questioned the men concerning their origins:
"Where do you come from, carrying these
decorated shields and shirts of mail,
these cheek-hinged helmets and javelins?   335
I am Hrothgar's herald and officer.
I have never seen so impressive or large
an assembly of strangers. Stoutness of heart,
bravery not banishment, must have brought you to Hrothgar."
    The man whose name was known for courage,   340
the Geat leader, resolute in his helmet,
answered in return: "We are retainers
from Hygelac's band. Beowulf is my name.
If your lord and master, the most renowned
son of Halfdane, will hear me out   345
and graciously allow me to greet him in person,
I am ready and willing to report my errand."
    Wulfgar replied, a Wendel[2] chief
renowned as a warrior, well known for his wisdom
and the temper of his mind: "I will take this message,   350
in accordance with your wish, to our noble king,
our dear lord, friend of the Danes,
the giver of rings. I will go and ask him
about your coming here, then hurry back
with whatever reply it pleases him to give."   355
    With that he turned to where Hrothgar sat,
an old man among retainers;
the valiant follower stood foursquare
in front of his king: he knew the courtesies.
Wulfgar addressed his dear lord: 360
"People from Geatland have put ashore.
They have sailed far over the wide sea.
They call the chief in charge of their band
by the name of Beowulf. They beg, my lord,
an audience with you, exchange of words   365
and formal greeting. Most gracious Hrothgar,
do not refuse them, but grant them a reply.
From their arms and appointment, they appear well born
and worthy of respect, especially the one
who has led them this far: he is formidable indeed."   370
    Hrothgar, protector of Shieldings, replied:
"I used to know him when he was a young boy.
His father before him was called Ecgtheow.
Hrethel the Geat[3] gave Ecgtheow
his daughter in marriage. This man is their son,   375
here to follow up an old friendship.
A crew of seamen who sailed for me once

---

2. The *Wendels* or Vandals are another Germanic nation; it is not unusual for a person to be a member of
a nation different from the one in which he resides. Hence Beowulf himself is both a Geat and a Waegmunding.   3. The leader of the Geats prior to his son Hygelac, who is the current leader. Note that
Ecgtheow's marriage to Hrethel's daughter makes Beowulf part of the royal line.

with a gift-cargo across to Geatland
returned with marvelous tales about him:
a thane,[4] they declared, with the strength of thirty   380
in the grip of each hand. Now Holy God
has, in His goodness, guided him here
to the West-Danes, to defend us from Grendel.
This is my hope; and for his heroism
I will recompense him with a rich treasure.   385
Go immediately, bid him and the Geats
he has in attendance to assemble and enter.
Say, moreover, when you speak to them,
they are welcome to Denmark."
                      At the door of the hall,
Wulfgar duly delivered the message: 390
"My lord, the conquering king of the Danes,
bids me announce that he knows your ancestry;
also that he welcomes you here to Heorot
and salutes your arrival from across the sea.
You are free now to move forward   395
to meet Hrothgar in helmets and armor,
but shields must stay here and spears be stacked
until the outcome of the audience is clear."
    The hero arose, surrounded closely
by his powerful thanes. A party remained   400
under orders to keep watch on the arms;
the rest proceeded, led by their prince
under Heorot's roof. And standing on the hearth
in webbed links that the smith had woven,
the fine-forged mesh of his gleaming mail-shirt,   405
resolute in his helmet, Beowulf spoke:
"Greetings to Hrothgar. I am Hygelac's kinsman,
one of his hall-troop. When I was younger,
I had great triumphs. Then news of Grendel,
hard to ignore, reached me at home: 410
sailors brought stories of the plight you suffer
in this legendary hall, how it lies deserted,
empty and useless once the evening light
hides itself under heaven's dome.
So every elder and experienced councilman   415
among my people supported my resolve
to come here to you, King Hrothgar,
because all knew of my awesome strength.
They had seen me boltered[5] in the blood of enemies
when I battled and bound five beasts,   420
raided a troll-nest and in the night-sea
slaughtered sea-brutes. I have suffered extremes
and avenged the Geats (their enemies brought it
upon themselves; I devastated them).
Now I mean to be a match for Grendel,   425

---

4. I.e., a warrior in the service of a lord like Hrethel or Hrothgar himself.   5. Clotted, sticky—a Northern Irish term.

settle the outcome in single combat.
And so, my request, O king of Bright-Danes,
dear prince of the Shieldings, friend of the people
and their ring of defense, my one request
is that you won't refuse me, who have come this far, 430
the privilege of purifying Heorot,
with my own men to help me, and nobody else.
I have heard moreover that the monster scorns
in his reckless way to use weapons;
therefore, to heighten Hygelac's fame 435
and gladden his heart, I hereby renounce
sword and the shelter of the broad shield,
the heavy war-board: hand-to-hand
is how it will be, a life-and-death
fight with the fiend. Whichever one death fells 440
must deem it a just judgment by God.
If Grendel wins, it will be a gruesome day;
he will glut himself on the Geats in the war-hall,
swoop without fear on that flower of manhood
as on others before. Then my face won't be there 445
to be covered in death: he will carry me away
as he goes to ground, gorged and bloodied;
he will run gloating with my raw corpse
and feed on it alone, in a cruel frenzy
fouling his moor-nest. No need then 450
to lament for long or lay out my body:
if the battle takes me, send back
this breast-webbing that Weland[6] fashioned
and Hrethel gave me, to Lord Hygelac.
Fate goes ever as fate must." 455
　　Hrothgar, the helmet of Shieldings, spoke:
"Beowulf, my friend, you have traveled here
to favor us with help and to fight for us.
There was a feud one time, begun by your father.
With his own hands he had killed Heatholaf 460
who was a Wulfing;[7] so war was looming
and his people, in fear of it, forced him to leave.
He came away then over rolling waves
to the South-Danes here, the sons of honor.
I was then in the first flush of kingship, 465
establishing my sway over the rich strongholds
of this heroic land. Heorogar,
my older brother and the better man,
also a son of Halfdane's, had died.
Finally I healed the feud by paying: 470
I shipped a treasure-trove to the Wulfings,
and Ecgtheow acknowledged me with oaths of allegiance.
　　"It bothers me to have to burden anyone
with all the grief that Grendel has caused
and the havoc he has wreaked upon us in Heorot, 475

6. The blacksmith of the Norse gods.　　7. The *Wulfings* are another Germanic nation.

our humiliations. My household-guard
are on the wane, fate sweeps them away
into Grendel's clutches—but God can easily
halt these raids and harrowing attacks!
  "Time and again, when the goblets passed   480
and seasoned fighters got flushed with beer
they would pledge themselves to protect Heorot
and wait for Grendel with their whetted swords.
But when dawn broke and day crept in
over each empty, blood-spattered bench,   485
the floor of the mead-hall where they had feasted
would be slick with slaughter. And so they died,
faithful retainers, and my following dwindled.
Now take your place at the table, relish
the triumph of heroes to your heart's content."   490

[FEAST AT HEOROT]

  Then a bench was cleared in that banquet hall
so the Geats could have room to be together
and the party sat, proud in their bearing,
strong and stalwart. An attendant stood by
with a decorated pitcher, pouring bright   495
helpings of mead. And the minstrel sang,
filling Heorot with his head-clearing voice,
gladdening that great rally of Geats and Danes.
  From where he crouched at the king's feet,
Unferth, a son of Ecglaf's, spoke   500
contrary words.[8] Beowulf's coming,
his sea-braving, made him sick with envy:
he could not brook or abide the fact
that anyone else alive under heaven
might enjoy greater regard than he did: 505
"Are you the Beowulf who took on Breca
in a swimming match[9] on the open sea,
risking the water just to prove that you could win?
It was sheer vanity made you venture out
on the main deep. And no matter who tried,   510
friend or foe, to deflect the pair of you,
neither would back down: the sea-test obsessed you.
You waded in, embracing water,
taking its measure, mastering currents,
riding on the swell. The ocean swayed,   515
winter went wild in the waves, but you vied
for seven nights; and then he outswam you,
came ashore the stronger contender.
He was cast up safe and sound one morning

---

8. Unferth is Hrothgar's *thyle*, a kind of licensed spokesman who here engages Beowulf in a traditional "flytting" or verbal combat; see the note to line 1457. Ecglaf appears in the poem only as the father of Unferth.   9. The original Anglo-Saxon describing this contest can be interpreted in such a way that Breca and Beowulf are competing not in swimming but in rowing, which is more plausible.

among the Heatho-Reams,[1] then made his way   520
to where he belonged in Bronding[2] country,
home again, sure of his ground
in strongroom and bawn.[3] So Breca made good
his boast upon you and was proved right.
No matter, therefore, how you may have fared   525
in every bout and battle until now,
this time you'll be worsted; no one has ever
outlasted an entire night against Grendel."
   Beowulf, Ecgtheow's son, replied:
"Well, friend Unferth, you have had your say   530
about Breca and me. But it was mostly beer
that was doing the talking. The truth is this:
when the going was heavy in those high waves,
I was the strongest swimmer of all.
We'd been children together and we grew up   535
daring ourselves to outdo each other,
boasting and urging each other to risk
our lives on the sea. And so it turned out.
Each of us swam holding a sword,
a naked, hard-proofed blade for protection   540
against the whale-beasts. But Breca could never
move out farther or faster from me
than I could manage to move from him.
Shoulder to shoulder, we struggled on
for five nights, until the long flow   545
and pitch of the waves, the perishing cold,
night falling and winds from the north
drove us apart. The deep boiled up
and its wallowing sent the sea-brutes wild.
My armor helped me to hold out;   550
my hard-ringed chain-mail, hand-forged and linked,
a fine, close-fitting filigree of gold,
kept me safe when some ocean creature
pulled me to the bottom. Pinioned fast
and swathed in its grip, I was granted one   555
final chance: my sword plunged
and the ordeal was over. Through my own hands,
the fury of battle had finished off the sea-beast.
   "Time and again, foul things attacked me,
lurking and stalking, but I lashed out,   560
gave as good as I got with my sword.
My flesh was not for feasting on,
there would be no monsters gnawing and gloating
over their banquet at the bottom of the sea.
Instead, in the morning, mangled and sleeping   565
the sleep of the sword, they slopped and floated

---

1. The *Heatho-Reams* are a people of southern Norway.   2. The *Brondings* are the nation to which Breca belonged, but nothing is known of their territory.   3. Fortified outwork of a court or castle. The word was used by English planters in Ulster to describe fortified dwellings they erected on lands confiscated from the Irish [Translator's note].

like the ocean's leavings. From now on
sailors would be safe, the deep-sea raids
were over for good. Light came from the east,
bright guarantee of God, and the waves   570
went quiet; I could see headlands
and buffeted cliffs. Often, for undaunted courage,
fate spares the man it has not already marked.
However it occurred, my sword had killed
nine sea-monsters. Such night dangers   575
and hard ordeals I have never heard of
nor of a man more desolate in surging waves.
But worn out as I was, I survived,
came through with my life. The ocean lifted
and laid me ashore, I landed safe   580
on the coast of Finland.

          Now I cannot recall
any fight you entered, Unferth,
that bears comparison. I don't boast when I say
that neither you nor Breca were ever much
celebrated for swordsmanship   585
or for facing danger on the field of battle.
You killed your own kith and kin,
so for all your cleverness and quick tongue,
you will suffer damnation in the depths of hell.[4]
The fact is, Unferth, if you were truly   590
as keen or courageous as you claim to be
Grendel would never have got away with
such unchecked atrocity, attacks on your king,
havoc in Heorot and horrors everywhere.
But he knows he need never be in dread   595
of your blade making a mizzle[5] of his blood
or of vengeance arriving ever from this quarter—
from the Victory-Shieldings, the shoulderers of the spear.
He knows he can trample down you Danes
to his heart's content, humiliate and murder   600
without fear of reprisal. But he will find me different.
I will show him how Geats shape to kill
in the heat of battle. Then whoever wants to
may go bravely to mead,[6] when the morning light,
scarfed in sun-dazzle, shines forth from the south   605
and brings another daybreak to the world."

    Then the gray-haired treasure-giver was glad;
far-famed in battle, the prince of Bright-Danes
and keeper of his people counted on Beowulf,
on the warrior's steadfastness and his word.   610
So the laughter started, the din got louder
and the crowd was happy. Wealhtheow came in,
Hrothgar's queen, observing the courtesies.
Adorned in her gold, she graciously saluted

---

4. The manuscript is damaged here, and the word "hell" may well be "hall": "You will suffer condemnation in the hall" is an acceptable translation of the line. 5. I.e., drizzle. 6. *Mead* is an alcoholic drink made by fermenting honey and adding water.

the men in the hall, then handed the cup   615
first to Hrothgar, their homeland's guardian,
urging him to drink deep and enjoy it
because he was dear to them. And he drank it down
like the warlord he was, with festive cheer.
So the Helming woman went on her rounds,   620
queenly and dignified, decked out in rings,
offering the goblet to all ranks,
treating the household and the assembled troop,
until it was Beowulf's turn to take it from her hand.
With measured words she welcomed the Geat   625
and thanked God for granting her wish
that a deliverer she could believe in would arrive
to ease their afflictions. He accepted the cup,
a daunting man, dangerous in action
and eager for it always. He addressed Wealhtheow;   630
Beowulf, son of Ecgtheow, said:
"I had a fixed purpose when I put to sea.
As I sat in the boat with my band of men,
I meant to perform to the uttermost
what your people wanted or perish in the attempt,   635
in the fiend's clutches. And I shall fulfill that purpose,
prove myself with a proud deed
or meet my death here in the mead-hall."
This formal boast by Beowulf the Geat
pleased the lady well and she went to sit   640
by Hrothgar, regal and arrayed with gold.
     Then it was like old times in the echoing hall,
proud talk and the people happy,
loud and excited; until soon enough
Halfdane's heir had to be away   645
to his night's rest. He realized
that the demon was going to descend on the hall,
that he had plotted all day, from dawn-light
until darkness gathered again over the world
and stealthy night-shapes came stealing forth   650
under the cloud-murk. The company stood
as the two leaders took leave of each other:
Hrothgar wished Beowulf health and good luck,
named him hall-warden and announced as follows:
"Never, since my hand could hold a shield   655
have I entrusted or given control
of the Danes' hall to anyone but you.
Ward and guard it, for it is the greatest of houses.
Be on your mettle now, keep in mind your fame,
beware of the enemy. There's nothing you wish for   660
that won't be yours if you win through alive."

[THE FIGHT WITH GRENDEL]

     Hrothgar departed then with his house-guard.
The lord of the Shieldings, their shelter in war,

left the mead-hall to lie with Wealhtheow,
his queen and bedmate. The King of Glory   665
(as people learned) had posted a lookout
who was a match for Grendel, a guard against monsters,
special protection to the Danish prince.
And the Geat placed complete trust
in his strength of limb and the Lord's favor.   670
    He began to remove his iron breast-mail,
took off the helmet and handed his attendant
the patterned sword, a smith's masterpiece,
ordering him to keep the equipment guarded.
And before he bedded down, Beowulf,   675
that prince of goodness, proudly asserted:
"When it comes to fighting, I count myself
as dangerous any day as Grendel.
So it won't be a cutting edge I'll wield
to mow him down, easily as I might.   680
He has no idea of the arts of war,
of shield or sword-play, although he does possess
a wild strength. No weapons, therefore,
for either this night: unarmed he shall face me
if face me he dares. And may the Divine Lord   685
in His wisdom grant the glory of victory
to whichever side He sees fit."
    Then down the brave man lay with his bolster
under his head and his whole company
of sea-rovers at rest beside him.   690
None of them expected he would ever see
his homeland again or get back
to his native place and the people who reared him.
They knew too well the way it was before,
how often the Danes had fallen prey   695
to death in the mead-hall. But the Lord was weaving
a victory on His war-loom for the Weather-Geats.
Through the strength of one they all prevailed;
they would crush their enemy and come through
in triumph and gladness. The truth is clear: 700
Almighty God rules over mankind
and always has.
              Then out of the night
came the shadow-stalker, stealthy and swift.
The hall-guards were slack, asleep at their posts,
all except one; it was widely understood   705
that as long as God disallowed it,
the fiend could not bear them to his shadow-bourne.
One man, however, was in fighting mood,
awake and on edge, spoiling for action.
    In off the moors, down through the mist-bands   710
God-cursed Grendel came greedily loping.
The bane of the race of men roamed forth,
hunting for a prey in the high hall.
Under the cloud-murk he moved toward it

until it shone above him, a sheer keep 715
of fortified gold. Nor was that the first time
he had scouted the grounds of Hrothgar's dwelling—
although never in his life, before or since,
did he find harder fortune or hall-defenders.
Spurned and joyless, he journeyed on ahead 720
and arrived at the bawn. The iron-braced door
turned on its hinge when his hands touched it.
Then his rage boiled over, he ripped open
the mouth of the building, maddening for blood,
pacing the length of the patterned floor 725
with his loathsome tread, while a baleful light,
flame more than light, flared from his eyes.
He saw many men in the mansion, sleeping,
a ranked company of kinsmen and warriors
quartered together. And his glee was demonic, 730
picturing the mayhem: before morning
he would rip life from limb and devour them,
feed on their flesh; but his fate that night
was due to change, his days of ravening
had come to an end.
          Mighty and canny, 735
Hygelac's kinsman was keenly watching
for the first move the monster would make.
Nor did the creature keep him waiting
but struck suddenly and started in;
he grabbed and mauled a man on his bench, 740
bit into his bone-lappings,[7] bolted down his blood
and gorged on him in lumps, leaving the body
utterly lifeless, eaten up
hand and foot. Venturing closer,
his talon was raised to attack Beowulf 745
where he lay on the bed, he was bearing in
with open claw when the alert hero's
comeback and armlock forestalled him utterly.
The captain of evil discovered himself
in a handgrip harder than anything 750
he had ever encountered in any man
on the face of the earth. Every bone in his body
quailed and recoiled, but he could not escape.
He was desperate to flee to his den and hide
with the devil's litter, for in all his days 755
he had never been clamped or cornered like this.
Then Hygelac's trusty retainer recalled
his bedtime speech, sprang to his feet
and got a firm hold. Fingers were bursting,
the monster back-tracking, the man overpowering. 760
The dread of the land was desperate to escape,
to take a roundabout road and flee
to his lair in the fens. The latching power

7. I.e., joints.

in his fingers weakened; it was the worst trip
the terror-monger had taken to Heorot. 765
And now the timbers trembled and sang,
a hall-session[8] that harrowed every Dane
inside the stockade: stumbling in fury,
the two contenders crashed through the building.
The hall clattered and hammered, but somehow 770
survived the onslaught and kept standing:
it was handsomely structured, a sturdy frame
braced with the best of blacksmith's work
inside and out. The story goes
that as the pair struggled, mead-benches were smashed 775
and sprung off the floor, gold fittings and all.
Before then, no Shielding elder would believe
there was any power or person upon earth
capable of wrecking their horn-rigged hall
unless the burning embrace of a fire 780
engulf it in flame. Then an extraordinary
wail arose, and bewildering fear
came over the Danes. Everyone felt it
who heard that cry as it echoed off the wall,
a God-cursed scream and strain of catastrophe, 785
the howl of the loser, the lament of the hell-serf
keening his wound. He was overwhelmed,
manacled tight by the man who of all men
was foremost and strongest in the days of this life.
    But the earl-troop's leader was not inclined 790
to allow his caller to depart alive:
he did not consider that life of much account
to anyone anywhere. Time and again,
Beowulf's warriors worked to defend
their lord's life, laying about them 795
as best they could, with their ancestral blades.
Stalwart in action, they kept striking out
on every side, seeking to cut
straight to the soul. When they joined the struggle
there was something they could not have known at the time, 800
that no blade on earth, no blacksmith's art
could ever damage their demon opponent.
He had conjured the harm from the cutting edge
of every weapon.[9] But his going away
out of this world and the days of his life 805
would be agony to him, and his alien spirit
would travel far into fiends' keeping.
    Then he who had harrowed the hearts of men
with pain and affliction in former times
and had given offense also to God 810
found that his bodily powers failed him.

---

8. In Hiberno-English the word "session" (*seissiún* in Irish) can mean a gathering where musicians and singers perform for their own enjoyment [Translator's note]. In other words, the poet is making a laconic joke, since the main function of the hall is celebration and singing.   9. Grendel is magically protected from weapons.

Hygelac's kinsman kept him helplessly
locked in a handgrip. As long as either lived,
he was hateful to the other. The monster's whole
body was in pain; a tremendous wound   815
appeared on his shoulder. Sinews split
and the bone-lappings burst. Beowulf was granted
the glory of winning; Grendel was driven
under the fen-banks, fatally hurt,
to his desolate lair. His days were numbered,   820
the end of his life was coming over him,
he knew it for certain; and one bloody clash
had fulfilled the dearest wishes of the Danes.
The man who had lately landed among them,
proud and sure, had purged the hall,   825
kept it from harm; he was happy with his nightwork
and the courage he had shown. The Geat captain
had boldly fulfilled his boast to the Danes:
he had healed and relieved a huge distress,
unremitting humiliations,   830
the hard fate they'd been forced to undergo,
no small affliction. Clear proof of this
could be seen in the hand the hero displayed
high up near the roof: the whole of Grendel's
shoulder and arm, his awesome grasp.   835

[CELEBRATION AT HEOROT]

Then morning came and many a warrior
gathered, as I've heard, around the gift-hall,
clan-chiefs flocking from far and near
down wide-ranging roads, wondering greatly
at the monster's footprints. His fatal departure   840
was regretted by no one who witnessed his trail,
the ignominious marks of his flight
where he'd skulked away, exhausted in spirit
and beaten in battle, bloodying the path,
hauling his doom to the demons' mere.[1]   845
The bloodshot water wallowed and surged,
there were loathsome upthrows and overturnings
of waves and gore and wound-slurry.
With his death upon him, he had dived deep
into his marsh-den, drowned out his life   850
and his heathen soul: hell claimed him there.
Then away they rode, the old retainers
with many a young man following after,
a troop on horseback, in high spirits
on their bay steeds. Beowulf's doings   855
were praised over and over again.
Nowhere, they said, north or south
between the two seas or under the tall sky

---

1. A lake or pool.

on the broad earth was there anyone better
to raise a shield or to rule a kingdom.   860
Yet there was no laying of blame on their lord,
the noble Hrothgar; he was a good king.

    At times the war-band broke into a gallop,
letting their chestnut horses race
wherever they found the going good   865
on those well-known tracks. Meanwhile, a thane
of the king's household, a carrier of tales,
a traditional singer deeply schooled
in the lore of the past, linked a new theme
to a strict meter.[2] The man started   870
to recite with skill, rehearsing Beowulf's
triumphs and feats in well-fashioned lines,
entwining his words.
                        He told what he'd heard
repeated in songs about Sigemund's exploits,[3]
all of those many feats and marvels,   875
the struggles and wanderings of Waels's son,
things unknown to anyone
except to Fitela, feuds and foul doings
confided by uncle to nephew when he felt
the urge to speak of them: always they had been   880
partners in the fight, friends in need.
They killed giants, their conquering swords
had brought them down.
                        After his death
Sigemund's glory   grew and grew
because of his courage   when he killed the dragon,   885
the guardian of the hoard.   Under gray stone
he had dared to enter   all by himself
to face the worst   without Fitela.
But it came to pass   that his sword plunged
right through   those radiant scales   890
and drove into the wall.   The dragon died of it.
His daring had given him   total possession
of the treasure-hoard,   his to dispose of
however he liked.   He loaded a boat:
Waels's son   weighted her hold   895
with dazzling spoils.   The hot dragon melted.
    Sigemund's name   was known everywhere.
He was utterly valiant   and venturesome,
a fence round his fighters   and flourished therefore
after King Heremod's   prowess declined   900
and his campaigns slowed down.   The king was betrayed,
ambushed in Jutland,   overpowered
and done away with.   The waves of his grief

---

2. The singer or *scop* composes extemporaneously in alliterative verse.   3. According to Norse legend,
Sigemund, the son of Waels (or Volsung, as he is known in Norse), slept with his sister Sigurth, who bore
a son named Fitela; Fitela was thus also Sigemund's nephew, as he is described here. The singer here
contrasts Sigemund's bravery in killing a dragon with the defeat of the Danish king Heremod, who could
not protect his people. For more on Heremod as a bad king, see lines 1709–22.

had beaten him down,   made him a burden,
a source of anxiety   to his own nobles:
that expedition   was often condemned
in those earlier times   by experienced men,
men who relied   on his lordship for redress,
who presumed that the part   of a prince was to thrive
on his father's throne   and defend the nation,
the Shielding land   where they lived and belonged,
its holdings and strongholds.   Such was Beowulf
in the affection of his friends   and of everyone alive.
But evil entered   into Heremod.

    Meanwhile, the Danes kept racing their mounts
down sandy lanes. The light of day
broke and kept brightening. Bands of retainers
galloped in excitement to the gabled hall
to see the marvel; and the king himself,
guardian of the ring-hoard, goodness in person,
walked in majesty from the women's quarters
with a numerous train, attended by his queen
and her crowd of maidens, across to the mead-hall.
    When Hrothgar arrived at the hall, he spoke,
standing on the steps, under the steep eaves,
gazing toward the roofwork and Grendel's talon:
"First and foremost, let the Almighty Father
be thanked for this sight. I suffered a long
harrowing by Grendel. But the Heavenly Shepherd
can work His wonders always and everywhere.
Not long since, it seemed I would never
be granted the slightest solace or relief
from any of my burdens: the best of houses
glittered and reeked and ran with blood.
This one worry outweighed all others—
a constant distress to counselors entrusted
with defending the people's forts from assault
by monsters and demons. But now a man,
with the Lord's assistance, has accomplished something
none of us could manage before now
for all our efforts. Whoever she was
who brought forth this flower of manhood,
if she is still alive, that woman can say
that in her labor the Lord of Ages
bestowed a grace on her. So now, Beowulf,
I adopt you in my heart as a dear son.
Nourish and maintain this new connection,
you noblest of men; there'll be nothing you'll want for,
no worldly goods that won't be yours.
I have often honored smaller achievements,
recognized warriors not nearly as worthy,
lavished rewards on the less deserving.
But you have made yourself immortal
by your glorious action. May the God of Ages
continue to keep and requite you well."

905
910
915
920
925
930
935
940
945
950
955

Beowulf, son of Ecgtheow, spoke:
"We have gone through with a glorious endeavor
and been much favored in this fight we dared
against the unknown. Nevertheless,
if you could have seen the monster himself   960
where he lay beaten, I would have been better pleased.
My plan was to pounce, pin him down
in a tight grip and grapple him to death—
have him panting for life, powerless and clasped
in my bare hands, his body in thrall.   965
But I couldn't stop him from slipping my hold.
The Lord allowed it, my lock on him
wasn't strong enough; he struggled fiercely
and broke and ran. Yet he bought his freedom
at a high price, for he left his hand   970
and arm and shoulder to show he had been here,
a cold comfort for having come among us.
And now he won't be long for this world.
He has done his worst but the wound will end him.
He is hasped and hooped and hirpling[4] with pain,   975
limping and looped in it. Like a man outlawed
for wickedness, he must await
the mighty judgment of God in majesty."
    There was less tampering and big talk then
from Unferth the boaster, less of his blather   980
as the hall-thanes eyed the awful proof
of the hero's prowess, the splayed hand
up under the eaves. Every nail,
claw-scale and spur, every spike
and welt on the hand of that heathen brute   985
was like barbed steel. Everybody said
there was no honed iron hard enough
to pierce him through, no time-proofed blade
that could cut his brutal, blood-caked claw.
    Then the order was given for all hands   990
to help to refurbish Heorot immediately:
men and women thronging the wine-hall,
getting it ready. Gold thread shone
in the wall-hangings, woven scenes
that attracted and held the eye's attention.   995
But iron-braced as the inside of it had been,
that bright room lay in ruins now.
The very doors had been dragged from their hinges.
Only the roof remained unscathed
by the time the guilt-fouled fiend turned tail   1000
in despair of his life. But death is not easily
escaped from by anyone:
all of us with souls, earth-dwellers
and children of men, must make our way
to a destination already ordained   1005

---

4. I.e., limping.

where the body, after the banqueting,
sleeps on its deathbed.   Then the due time arrived
for Halfdane's son to proceed to the hall.
The king himself would sit down to feast.
No group ever gathered in greater numbers   1010
or better order around their ring-giver.
The benches filled with famous men
who fell to with relish; round upon round
of mead was passed; those powerful kinsmen,
Hrothgar and Hrothulf, were in high spirits   1015
in the raftered hall. Inside Heorot
there was nothing but friendship. The Shielding nation
was not yet familiar with feud and betrayal.[5]
    Then Halfdane's son presented Beowulf
with a gold standard as a victory gift,   1020
an embroidered banner; also breast-mail
and a helmet; and a sword carried high,
that was both precious object and token of honor.
So Beowulf drank his drink, at ease;
it was hardly a shame to be showered with such gifts   1025
in front of the hall-troops. There haven't been many
moments, I am sure, when men exchanged
four such treasures at so friendly a sitting.
An embossed ridge, a band lapped with wire
arched over the helmet: head-protection   1030
to keep the keen-ground cutting edge
from damaging it when danger threatened
and the man was battling behind his shield.
Next the king ordered eight horses
with gold bridles to be brought through the yard   1035
into the hall. The harness of one
included a saddle of sumptuous design,
the battle-seat where the son of Halfdane
rode when he wished to join the sword-play:
wherever the killing and carnage were the worst,   1040
he would be to the fore, fighting hard.
Then the Danish prince, descendant of Ing,[6]
handed over both the arms and the horses,
urging Beowulf to use them well.
And so their leader, the lord and guard   1045
of coffer and strongroom, with customary grace
bestowed upon Beowulf both sets of gifts.
A fair witness can see how well each one behaved.
    The chieftain went on to reward the others:
each man on the bench who had sailed with Beowulf   1050
and risked the voyage received a bounty,
some treasured possession. And compensation,
a price in gold, was settled for the Geat

---

5. The poet here refers to the later history of the Danes, when after Hrothgar's death his nephew Hrothulf drove his son Hrethric from the throne. For Wealhtheow's fear that this betrayal will indeed come to pass, see lines 1168–90. 6. Ing is a Germanic deity and the protector of the Danes.

Grendel had cruelly killed earlier—
as he would have killed more, had not mindful God
and one man's daring prevented that doom.
Past and present, God's will prevails.
Hence, understanding is always best
and a prudent mind. Whoever remains
for long here in this earthly life
will enjoy and endure more than enough.

   They sang then and played to please the hero,
words and music for their warrior prince,
harp tunes and tales of adventure:
there were high times on the hall benches,
and the king's poet performed his part
with the saga of Finn and his sons, unfolding
the tale of the fierce attack in Friesland
where Hnaef, king of the Danes, met death.[7]

Hildeburh
> had little cause

to credit the Jutes:
> son and brother,

she lost them both
> on the battlefield.

She, bereft
> and blameless, they

foredoomed, cut down
> and spear-gored. She,

the woman in shock,
> waylaid by grief,

Hoc's daughter—
> how could she not

lament her fate
> when morning came

and the light broke
> on her murdered dears?

And so farewell
> delight on earth,

war carried away
> Finn's troop of thanes

all but a few.
> How then could Finn

hold the line
> or fight on

to the end with Hengest,
> how save

the rump of his force

---

7. This song recounts the fight at Finnsburg, described in the headnote, between the Dane Hengest and the Jute (or Frisian) Finn. The poet begins with the bereft Hildeburh, daughter of the Danish king Hoc and wife of the Jute Finn, whose unnamed son and brother Hnaef have already been killed in the first battle with Finn. He then tells how Hengest, the new leader of the Danes, is offered a truce by the weakened Finn, how together they cremate their dead, and then how Hengest and the remaining Danes spend the winter with Finn and the Jutes. But with the coming of spring, the feud breaks out again and Finn and the Jutes are slaughtered by Hengest with the help of two other Danes, Guthlaf and Oslaf.

from that enemy chief?
So a truce was offered
                        as follows: first   1085
separate quarters
                        to be cleared for the Danes,
hall and throne
                        to be shared with the Frisians.
Then, second:
                        every day
at the dole-out of gifts
                        Finn, son of Focwald,
should honor the Danes,
                        bestow with an even   1090
hand to Hengest
                        and Hengest's men
the wrought-gold rings,
                        bounty to match
the measure he gave
                        his own Frisians—
to keep morale
                        in the beer-hall high.
Both sides then
                        sealed their agreement.   1095
With oaths to Hengest
                        Finn swore
openly, solemnly,
                        that the battle survivors
would be guaranteed
                        honor and status.
No infringement
                        by word or deed,
no provocation
                        would be permitted.   1100
Their own ring-giver
                        after all
was dead and gone,
                        they were leaderless,
in forced allegiance
                        to his murderer.
So if any Frisian
                        stirred up bad blood
with insinuations
                        or taunts about this,   1105
the blade of the sword
                        would arbitrate it.
A funeral pyre
                        was then prepared,
effulgent gold
                        brought out from the hoard.
The pride and prince
                        of the Shieldings lay
awaiting the flame.

Everywhere   1110
there were blood-plastered
                         coats of mail.
The pyre was heaped
                 with boar-shaped helmets
forged in gold,
                with the gashed corpses
of wellborn Danes—
                 many had fallen.
Then Hildeburh
                 ordered her own   1115
son's body
                 be burnt with Hnaef's
the flesh on his bones
                 to sputter and blaze
beside his uncle's.
                 The woman wailed
and sang keens,
                 the warrior went up.[8]
Carcass flame
                 swirled and fumed,   1120
they stood round the burial
                      mound and howled
as heads melted,
                 crusted gashes
spattered and ran
                 bloody matter.
The glutton element
                 flamed and consumed
the dead of both sides.
                      Their great days were gone.   1125
Warriors scattered
                 to homes and forts
all over Friesland,
                 fewer now, feeling
loss of friends.
                 Hengest stayed,
lived out that whole
                 resentful, blood-sullen
winter with Finn,
                 homesick and helpless.   1130
No ring-whorled prow
                      could up then
and away on the sea.
                 Wind and water
raged with storms,
                 wave and shingle
were shackled in ice
                 until another year
appeared in the yard

---

8. *Keens* is an Irish word for funeral laments; the warrior (Hildeburh's son) either goes up on the pyre or up in smoke.

           as it does to this day,   1135
the seasons constant,
           the wonder of light
coming over us.
           Then winter was gone,
earth's lap grew lovely,
           longing woke
in the cooped-up exile
           for a voyage home—
but more for vengeance,
           some way of bringing   1140
things to a head:
           his sword arm hankered
to greet the Jutes.
           So he did not balk
once Hunlafing[9]
           placed on his lap
Dazzle-the-Duel,
           the best sword of all,
whose edges Jutes
           knew only too well.   1145
Thus blood was spilled,
           the gallant Finn
slain in his home
           after Guthlaf and Oslaf[1]
back from their voyage
           made old accusation:
the brutal ambush,
           the fate they had suffered,
all blamed on Finn.
           The wildness in them   1150
had to brim over.
           The hall ran red
with blood of enemies.
           Finn was cut down,
the queen brought away
           and everything
the Shieldings could find
           inside Finn's walls—
the Frisian king's
           gold collars and gemstones—   1155
swept off to the ship.
           Over sea-lanes then
back to Daneland
           the warrior troop
bore that lady home.

         The poem was over,
the poet had performed, a pleasant murmur
started on the benches, stewards did the rounds   1160

---

9. A Danish follower of Hengest.   1. Danes who seem to have gone home in order to bring reinforcements to Hengest. But it is possible that these two have been with Hengest all along and that "their voyage" is an unrelated journey.

with wine in splendid jugs, and Wealhtheow came to sit
in her gold crown between two good men,
uncle and nephew, each one of whom
still trusted the other;[2] and the forthright Unferth,
admired by all for his mind and courage   1165
although under a cloud for killing his brothers,
reclined near the king.
               The queen spoke:
"Enjoy this drink, my most generous lord;
raise up your goblet, entertain the Geats
duly and gently, discourse with them,   1170
be open-handed, happy and fond.
Relish their company, but recollect as well
all of the boons that have been bestowed on you.
The bright court of Heorot has been cleansed
and now the word is that you want to adopt   1175
this warrior as a son. So, while you may,
bask in your fortune, and then bequeath
kingdom and nation to your kith and kin,
before your decease. I am certain of Hrothulf.
He is noble and will use the young ones well.   1180
He will not let you down. Should you die before him,
he will treat our children truly and fairly.
He will honor, I am sure, our two sons,
repay them in kind, when he recollects
all the good things we gave him once,   1185
the favor and respect he found in his childhood."
She turned then to the bench where her boys sat,
Hrethric and Hrothmund, with other nobles' sons,
all the youth together; and that good man,
Beowulf the Geat, sat between the brothers.   1190
   The cup was carried to him, kind words
spoken in welcome and a wealth of wrought gold
graciously bestowed: two arm bangles,
a mail-shirt and rings, and the most resplendent
torque of gold I ever heard tell of   1195
anywhere on earth or under heaven.
There was no hoard like it since Hama snatched
the Brosings' neck-chain and bore it away
with its gems and settings to his shining fort,
away from Eormenric's wiles and hatred,   1200
and thereby ensured his eternal reward.[3]
Hygelac the Geat, grandson of Swerting,
wore this neck-ring on his last raid;[4]
at bay under his banner, he defended the booty,
treasure he had won. Fate swept him away   1205
because of his proud need to provoke

---

2. See note 5 to lines 1017–18.   3. The legend alluded to here seems to be that Hama stole the golden
necklace of the Brosings from Eormenric (a historical figure, the king of the Ostrogoths, who died ca. 375),
and then gave it to the goddess Freya.   4. The poet here refers to the death of Hygelac while raiding the
Frisian territory of the Franks. This raid and Hygelac's death are recorded by the historian Gregory of Tours
(d. 594) as having taken place about 520.

a feud with the Frisians. He fell beneath his shield,
in the same gem-crusted, kingly gear
he had worn when he crossed the frothing wave-vat.
So the dead king fell into Frankish hands.
They took his breast-mail, also his neck-torque,   1210
and punier warriors plundered the slain
when the carnage ended; Geat corpses
covered the field.

               Applause filled the hall.
Then Wealhtheow pronounced in the presence of the company: 1215
"Take delight in this torque, dear Beowulf,
wear it for luck and wear also this mail
from our people's armory: may you prosper in them!
Be acclaimed for strength, for kindly guidance
to these two boys, and your bounty will be sure.   1220
You have won renown: you are known to all men
far and near, now and forever.
Your sway is wide as the wind's home,
as the sea around cliffs. And so, my prince,
I wish you a lifetime's luck and blessings   1225
to enjoy this treasure. Treat my sons
with tender care, be strong and kind.
Here each comrade is true to the other,
loyal to lord, loving in spirit.
The thanes have one purpose, the people are ready: 1230
having drunk and pledged, the ranks do as I bid."

   She moved then to her place. Men were drinking wine
at that rare feast; how could they know fate,
the grim shape of things to come,
the threat looming over many thanes   1235
as night approached and King Hrothgar prepared
to retire to his quarters? Retainers in great numbers
were posted on guard as so often in the past.
Benches were pushed back, bedding gear and bolsters
spread across the floor, and one man   1240
lay down to his rest, already marked for death.
At their heads they placed their polished timber
battle-shields; and on the bench above them,
each man's kit was kept to hand:
a towering war-helmet, webbed mail-shirt   1245
and great-shafted spear. It was their habit
always and everywhere to be ready for action,
at home or in the camp, in whatever case
and at whatever time the need arose
to rally round their lord. They were a right people.   1250

[ANOTHER ATTACK]

   They went to sleep. And one paid dearly
for his night's ease, as had happened to them often,
ever since Grendel occupied the gold-hall,
committing evil until the end came,

death after his crimes. Then it became clear,   1255
obvious to everyone once the fight was over,
that an avenger lurked and was still alive,
grimly biding time. Grendel's mother,
monstrous hell-bride, brooded on her wrongs.
She had been forced down into fearful waters,   1260
the cold depths, after Cain had killed
his father's son, felled his own
brother with a sword. Branded an outlaw,
marked by having murdered, he moved into the wilds,
shunned company and joy. And from Cain there sprang   1265
misbegotten spirits, among them Grendel,
the banished and accursed, due to come to grips
with that watcher in Heorot waiting to do battle.
The monster wrenched and wrestled with him,
but Beowulf was mindful of his mighty strength,   1270
the wondrous gifts God had showered on him:
he relied for help on the Lord of All,
on His care and favor. So he overcame the foe,
brought down the hell-brute. Broken and bowed,
outcast from all sweetness, the enemy of mankind   1275
made for his death-den. But now his mother
had sallied forth on a savage journey,
grief-racked and ravenous, desperate for revenge.
    She came to Heorot. There, inside the hall,
Danes lay asleep, earls who would soon endure   1280
a great reversal, once Grendel's mother
attacked and entered. Her onslaught was less
only by as much as an amazon warrior's
strength is less than an armed man's
when the hefted sword, its hammered edge   1285
and gleaming blade slathered in blood,
razes the sturdy boar-ridge off a helmet.
Then in the hall, hard-honed swords
were grabbed from the bench, many a broad shield
lifted and braced; there was little thought of helmets   1290
or woven mail when they woke in terror.
    The hell-dam was in panic, desperate to get out,
in mortal terror the moment she was found.
She had pounced and taken one of the retainers
in a tight hold, then headed for the fen.   1295
To Hrothgar, this man was the most beloved
of the friends he trusted between the two seas.
She had done away with a great warrior,
ambushed him at rest.
                        Beowulf was elsewhere.
Earlier, after the award of the treasure,   1300
the Geat had been given another lodging.
    There was uproar in Heorot. She had snatched their trophy,
Grendel's bloodied hand. It was a fresh blow
to the afflicted bawn. The bargain was hard,
both parties having to pay   1305

with the lives of friends. And the old lord,
the gray-haired warrior, was heartsore and weary
when he heard the news: his highest-placed adviser,
his dearest companion, was dead and gone.

    Beowulf was quickly brought to the chamber: 1310
the winner of fights, the arch-warrior,
came first-footing in with his fellow troops
to where the king in his wisdom waited,
still wondering whether Almighty God
would ever turn the tide of his misfortunes.   1315
So Beowulf entered with his band in attendance
and the wooden floorboards banged and rang
as he advanced, hurrying to address
the prince of the Ingwins,[5] asking if he'd rested
since the urgent summons had come as a surprise.   1320

    Then Hrothgar, the Shieldings' helmet, spoke:
"Rest? What is rest? Sorrow has returned.
Alas for the Danes! Aeschere is dead.
He was Yrmenlaf's elder brother
and a soul-mate to me, a true mentor,   1325
my right-hand man when the ranks clashed
and our boar-crests had to take a battering
in the line of action. Aeschere was everything
the world admires in a wise man and a friend.
Then this roaming killer came in a fury   1330
and slaughtered him in Heorot. Where she is hiding,
glutting on the corpse and glorying in her escape,
I cannot tell; she has taken up the feud
because of last night, when you killed Grendel,
wrestled and racked him in ruinous combat   1335
since for too long he had terrorized us
with his depredations. He died in battle,
paid with his life; and now this powerful
other one arrives, this force for evil
driven to avenge her kinsman's death.   1340
Or so it seems to thanes in their grief,
in the anguish every thane endures
at the loss of a ring-giver, now that the hand
that bestowed so richly has been stilled in death.

    "I have heard it said by my people in hall,   1345
counselors who live in the upland country,
that they have seen two such creatures
prowling the moors, huge marauders
from some other world. One of these things,
as far as anyone ever can discern,   1350
looks like a woman; the other, warped
in the shape of a man, moves beyond the pale
bigger than any man, an unnatural birth
called Grendel by the country people
in former days. They are fatherless creatures,   1355

---

5. The *Ingwins* are the friends of the god Ing—i.e., the Danes. See n. 6 to line 1042, above.

and their whole ancestry is hidden in a past
of demons and ghosts.[6] They dwell apart
among wolves on the hills, on windswept crags
and treacherous keshes, where cold streams
pour down the mountain and disappear   1360
under mist and moorland.
               A few miles from here
a frost-stiffened wood waits and keeps watch
above a mere; the overhanging bank
is a maze of tree-roots mirrored in its surface.
At night there, something uncanny happens: 1365
the water burns. And the mere bottom
has never been sounded by the sons of men.
On its bank, the heather-stepper halts:
the hart in flight from pursuing hounds
will turn to face them with firm-set horns   1370
and die in the wood rather than dive
beneath its surface. That is no good place.
When wind blows up and stormy weather
makes clouds scud and the skies weep,
out of its depths a dirty surge   1375
is pitched toward the heavens. Now help depends
again on you and on you alone.
The gap of danger where the demon waits
is still unknown to you. Seek it if you dare.
I will compensate you for settling the feud   1380
as I did the last time with lavish wealth,
coffers of coiled gold, if you come back."

[BEOWULF FIGHTS GRENDEL'S MOTHER]

Beowulf, son of Ecgtheow, spoke:
"Wise sir, do not grieve. It is always better
to avenge dear ones than to indulge in mourning.   1385
For every one of us, living in this world
means waiting for our end. Let whoever can
win glory before death. When a warrior is gone,
that will be his best and only bulwark.
So arise, my lord, and let us immediately   1390
set forth on the trail of this troll-dam.
I guarantee you: she will not get away,
not to dens under ground nor upland groves
nor the ocean floor. She'll have nowhere to flee to.
Endure your troubles today. Bear up   1395
and be the man I expect you to be."
   With that the old lord sprang to his feet
and praised God for Beowulf's pledge.
Then a bit and halter were brought for his horse
with the plaited mane. The wise king mounted   1400
the royal saddle and rode out in style

6. Note that Hrothgar doesn't know of the biblical genealogy of Grendel and his mother that the poet has given us in lines 102–14.

with a force of shield-bearers. The forest paths
were marked all over with the monster's tracks,
her trail on the ground wherever she had gone
across the dark moors, dragging away   1405
the body of that thane, Hrothgar's best
counselor and overseer of the country.
So the noble prince proceeded undismayed
up fells and screes, along narrow footpaths
and ways where they were forced into single file,   1410
ledges on cliffs above lairs of water-monsters.
He went in front with a few men,
good judges of the lie of the land,
and suddenly discovered the dismal wood,
mountain trees growing out at an angle   1415
above gray stones: the bloodshot water
surged underneath. It was a sore blow
to all of the Danes, friends of the Shieldings,
a hurt to each and every one
of that noble company when they came upon   1420
Aeschere's head at the foot of the cliff.
    Everybody gazed as the hot gore
kept wallowing up and an urgent war-horn
repeated its notes: the whole party
sat down to watch. The water was infested   1425
with all kinds of reptiles. There were writhing sea-dragons
and monsters slouching on slopes by the cliff,
serpents and wild things such as those that often
surface at dawn to roam the sail-road
and doom the voyage. Down they plunged,   1430
lashing in anger at the loud call
of the battle-bugle. An arrow from the bow
of the Geat chief got one of them
as he surged to the surface: the seasoned shaft
stuck deep in his flank and his freedom in the water   1435
got less and less. It was his last swim.
He was swiftly overwhelmed in the shallows,
prodded by barbed boar-spears,
cornered, beaten, pulled up on the bank,
a strange lake-birth, a loathsome catch   1440
men gazed at in awe.
                    Beowulf got ready,
donned his war-gear, indifferent to death;
his mighty, hand-forged, fine-webbed mail
would soon meet with the menace underwater.
It would keep the bone-cage of his body safe: 1445
no enemy's clasp could crush him in it,
no vicious armlock choke his life out.
To guard his head he had a glittering helmet
that was due to be muddied on the mere bottom
and blurred in the upswirl. It was of beaten gold,   1450
princely headgear hooped and hasped
by a weapon-smith who had worked wonders

in days gone by and adorned it with boar-shapes;
since then it had resisted every sword.
And another item lent by Unferth   1455
at that moment of need was of no small importance:
the brehon⁷ handed him a hilted weapon,
a rare and ancient sword named Hrunting.
The iron blade with its ill-boding patterns
had been tempered in blood. It had never failed   1460
the hand of anyone who hefted it in battle,
anyone who had fought and faced the worst
in the gap of danger. This was not the first time
it had been called to perform heroic feats.

When he lent that blade to the better swordsman,   1465
Unferth, the strong-built son of Ecglaf,
could hardly have remembered the ranting speech
he had made in his cups. He was not man enough
to face the turmoil of a fight under water
and the risk to his life. So there he lost   1470
fame and repute. It was different for the other
rigged out in his gear, ready to do battle.

Beowulf, son of Ecgtheow, spoke:
"Wisest of kings, now that I have come
to the point of action, I ask you to recall   1475
what we said earlier: that you, son of Halfdane
and gold-friend to retainers, that you, if I should fall
and suffer death while serving your cause,
would act like a father to me afterward.
If this combat kills me, take care   1480
of my young company, my comrades in arms.
And be sure also, my beloved Hrothgar,
to send Hygelac the treasures I received.
Let the lord of the Geats gaze on that gold,
let Hrethel's son take note of it and see   1485
that I found a ring-giver of rare magnificence
and enjoyed the good of his generosity.
And Unferth is to have what I inherited:
to that far-famed man I bequeath my own
sharp-honed, wave-sheened wonder-blade.   1490
With Hrunting I shall gain glory or die."

After these words, the prince of the Weather-Geats
was impatient to be away and plunged suddenly:
without more ado, he dived into the heaving
depths of the lake. It was the best part of a day   1495
before he could see the solid bottom.

Quickly the one who haunted those waters,
who had scavenged and gone her gluttonous rounds
for a hundred seasons, sensed a human
observing her outlandish lair from above.   1500
So she lunged and clutched and managed to catch him

---

7. One of an ancient class of lawyers in Ireland [Translator's note]. The word is used to translate the Anglo-Saxon *thyle*.

in her brutal grip; but his body, for all that,
remained unscathed: the mesh of the chain-mail
saved him on the outside. Her savage talons
failed to rip the web of his war-shirt. 1505
Then once she touched bottom, that wolfish swimmer
carried the ring-mailed prince to her court
so that for all his courage he could never use
the weapons he carried; and a bewildering horde
came at him from the depths, droves of sea-beasts 1510
who attacked with tusks and tore at his chain-mail
in a ghastly onslaught. The gallant man
could see he had entered some hellish turn-hole
and yet the water there did not work against him
because the hall-roofing held off 1515
the force of the current; then he saw firelight,
a gleam and flare-up, a glimmer of brightness.
    The hero observed that swamp-thing from hell,
the tarn-hag[8] in all her terrible strength,
then heaved his war-sword and swung his arm: 1520
the decorated blade came down ringing
and singing on her head. But he soon found
his battle-torch extinguished; the shining blade
refused to bite. It spared her and failed
the man in his need. It had gone through many 1525
a hand-to-hand fight, had hewed the armor
and helmets of the doomed, but here at last
the fabulous powers of that heirloom failed.
    Hygelac's kinsman kept thinking about
his name and fame: he never lost heart. 1530
Then, in a fury, he flung his sword away.
The keen, inlaid, worm-loop-patterned steel
was hurled to the ground: he would have to rely
on the might of his arm. So must a man do
who intends to gain enduring glory 1535
in a combat. Life doesn't cost him a thought.
Then the prince of War-Geats, warming to this fight
with Grendel's mother, gripped her shoulder
and laid about him in a battle frenzy:
he pitched his killer opponent to the floor 1540
but she rose quickly and retaliated,
grappled him tightly in her grim embrace.
The sure-footed fighter felt daunted,
the strongest of warriors stumbled and fell.
So she pounced upon him and pulled out 1545
a broad, whetted knife: now she would avenge
her only child. But the mesh of chain-mail
on Beowulf's shoulder shielded his life,
turned the edge and tip of the blade.
The son of Ecgtheow would have surely perished 1550
and the Geats lost their warrior under the wide earth

8. A *tarn* is a small lake.

had the strong links and locks of his war-gear
not helped to save him: holy God
decided the victory. It was easy for the Lord,
the Ruler of Heaven, to redress the balance   1555
once Beowulf got back up on his feet.

    Then he saw a blade that boded well,
a sword in her armory, an ancient heirloom
from the days of the giants, an ideal weapon,
one that any warrior would envy,   1560
but so huge and heavy of itself
only Beowulf could wield it in a battle.
So the Shieldings' hero hard-pressed and enraged,
took a firm hold of the hilt and swung
the blade in an arc, a resolute blow   1565
that bit deep into her neck-bone
and severed it entirely, toppling the doomed
house of her flesh; she fell to the floor.
The sword dripped blood, the swordsman was elated.

    A light appeared and the place brightened   1570
the way the sky does when heaven's candle
is shining clearly. He inspected the vault:
with sword held high, its hilt raised
to guard and threaten, Hygelac's thane
scouted by the wall in Grendel's wake.   1575
Now the weapon was to prove its worth.
The warrior determined to take revenge
for every gross act Grendel had committed—
and not only for that one occasion
when he'd come to slaughter the sleeping troops,   1580
fifteen of Hrothgar's house-guards
surprised on their benches and ruthlessly devoured,
and as many again carried away,
a brutal plunder. Beowulf in his fury
now settled that score: he saw the monster   1585
in his resting place, war-weary and wrecked,
a lifeless corpse, a casualty
of the battle in Heorot. The body gaped
at the stroke dealt to it after death:
Beowulf cut the corpse's head off.   1590

    Immediately the counselors keeping a lookout
with Hrothgar, watching the lake water,
saw a heave-up and surge of waves
and blood in the backwash. They bowed gray heads,
spoke in their sage, experienced way   1595
about the good warrior, how they never again
expected to see that prince returning
in triumph to their king. It was clear to many
that the wolf of the deep had destroyed him forever.

    The ninth hour of the day arrived.   1600
The brave Shieldings abandoned the cliff-top
and the king went home; but sick at heart,
staring at the mere, the strangers held on.

They wished, without hope, to behold their lord,
Beowulf himself.

     Meanwhile, the sword   1605
began to wilt into gory icicles
to slather and thaw. It was a wonderful thing,
the way it all melted as ice melts
when the Father eases the fetters off the frost
and unravels the water-ropes, He who wields power 1610
over time and tide: He is the true Lord.
  The Geat captain saw treasure in abundance
but carried no spoils from those quarters
except for the head and the inlaid hilt
embossed with jewels; its blade had melted   1615
and the scrollwork on it burned, so scalding was the blood
of the poisonous fiend who had perished there.
Then away he swam, the one who had survived
the fall of his enemies, flailing to the surface.
The wide water, the waves and pools,   1620
were no longer infested once the wandering fiend
let go of her life and this unreliable world.
  The seafarers' leader made for land,
resolutely swimming, delighted with his prize,
the mighty load he was lugging to the surface.   1625
His thanes advanced in a troop to meet him,
thanking God and taking great delight
in seeing their prince back safe and sound.
Quickly the hero's helmet and mail-shirt
were loosed and unlaced. The lake settled,   1630
clouds darkened above the bloodshot depths.
  With high hearts they headed away
along footpaths and trails through the fields,
roads that they knew, each of them wrestling
with the head they were carrying from the lakeside cliff, 1635
men kingly in their courage and capable
of difficult work. It was a task for four
to hoist Grendel's head on a spear
and bear it under strain to the bright hall.
But soon enough they neared the place,   1640
fourteen Geats in fine fettle,
striding across the outlying ground
in a delighted throng around their leader.
  In he came then, the thanes' commander,
the arch-warrior, to address Hrothgar: 1645
his courage was proven, his glory was secure.
Grendel's head was hauled by the hair,
dragged across the floor where the people were drinking,
a horror for both queen and company to behold.
They stared in awe. It was an astonishing sight. 1650

[ANOTHER CELEBRATION AT HEOROT]

Beowulf, son of Ecgtheow, spoke:
"So, son of Halfdane, prince of the Shieldings,

we are glad to bring this booty from the lake.
It is a token of triumph and we tender it to you.
I barely survived the battle under water.   1655
It was hard-fought, a desperate affair
that could have gone badly; if God had not helped me,
the outcome would have been quick and fatal.
Although Hrunting is hard-edged,
I could never bring it to bear in battle.   1660
But the Lord of Men allowed me to behold—
for He often helps the unbefriended—
an ancient sword shining on the wall,
a weapon made for giants, there for the wielding.
Then my moment came in the combat and I struck   1665
the dwellers in that den. Next thing the damascened[9]
sword blade melted; it bloated and it burned
in their rushing blood. I have wrested the hilt
from the enemies' hand, avenged the evil
done to the Danes; it is what was due.   1670
And this I pledge, O prince of the Shieldings:
you can sleep secure with your company of troops
in Heorot Hall. Never need you fear
for a single thane of your sept[1] or nation,
young warriors or old, that laying waste of life   1675
that you and your people endured of yore."
       Then the gold hilt was handed over
to the old lord, a relic from long ago
for the venerable ruler. That rare smithwork
was passed on to the prince of the Danes   1680
when those devils perished; once death removed
that murdering, guilt-steeped, God-cursed fiend,
eliminating his unholy life
and his mother's as well, it was willed to that king
who of all the lavish gift-lords of the north   1685
was the best regarded between the two seas.
       Hrothgar spoke; he examined the hilt,
that relic of old times. It was engraved all over
and showed how war first came into the world
and the flood destroyed the tribe of giants.   1690
They suffered a terrible severance from the Lord;
the Almighty made the waters rise,
drowned them in the deluge for retribution.
In pure gold inlay on the sword-guards
there were rune-markings correctly incised,   1695
stating and recording for whom the sword
had been first made and ornamented
with its scrollworked hilt. Then everyone hushed
as the son of Halfdane spoke this wisdom:
"A protector of his people, pledged to uphold   1700
truth and justice and to respect tradition,

9. Ornamented with inlaid designs.   1. An Irish term meaning a clan or division of a tribe.

is entitled to affirm that this man
was born to distinction. Beowulf, my friend,
your fame has gone far and wide,
you are known everywhere. In all things you are even-tempered,   1705
prudent and resolute. So I stand firm by the promise of friendship
we exchanged before. Forever you will be
your people's mainstay and your own warriors'
helping hand.

               Heremod was different,
the way he behaved to Ecgwela's sons.[2]
His rise in the world brought little joy   1710
to the Danish people, only death and destruction.
He vented his rage on men he caroused with,
killed his own comrades, a pariah king
who cut himself off from his own kind,   1715
even though Almighty God had made him
eminent and powerful and marked him from the start
for a happy life. But a change happened,
he grew bloodthirsty, gave no more rings
to honor the Danes. He suffered in the end   1720
for having plagued his people for so long:
his life lost happiness.

                  So learn from this
and understand true values. I who tell you
have wintered into wisdom.

                  It is a great wonder
how Almighty God in His magnificence   1725
favors our race with rank and scope
and the gift of wisdom; His sway is wide.
Sometimes He allows the mind of a man
of distinguished birth to follow its bent,
grants him fulfillment and felicity on earth   1730
and forts to command in his own country.
He permits him to lord it in many lands
until the man in his unthinkingness
forgets that it will ever end for him.
He indulges his desires; illness and old age   1735
mean nothing to him; his mind is untroubled
by envy or malice or the thought of enemies
with their hate-honed swords. The whole world
conforms to his will, he is kept from the worst
until an element of overweening   1740
enters him and takes hold
while the soul's guard, its sentry, drowses,
grown too distracted. A killer stalks him,
an archer who draws a deadly bow.
And then the man is hit in the heart,   1745
the arrow flies beneath his defenses,
the devious promptings of the demon start.

---

2. *Ecgwela's sons* are the Danes. He was evidently a former king of the Danes.

His old possessions seem paltry to him now.
He covets and resents; dishonors custom
and bestows no gold; and because of good things   1750
that the Heavenly Powers gave him in the past
he ignores the shape of things to come.
Then finally the end arrives
when the body he was lent collapses and falls
prey to its death; ancestral possessions   1755
and the goods he hoarded are inherited by another
who lets them go with a liberal hand.
    "O flower of warriors, beware of that trap.
Choose, dear Beowulf, the better part,
eternal rewards. Do not give way to pride.   1760
For a brief while your strength is in bloom
but it fades quickly; and soon there will follow
illness or the sword to lay you low,
or a sudden fire or surge of water
or jabbing blade or javelin from the air   1765
or repellent age. Your piercing eye
will dim and darken; and death will arrive,
dear warrior, to sweep you away.
    "Just so I ruled the Ring-Danes' country
for fifty years, defended them in wartime   1770
with spear and sword against constant assaults
by many tribes: I came to believe
my enemies had faded from the face of the earth.
Still, what happened was a hard reversal
from bliss to grief. Grendel struck   1775
after lying in wait. He laid waste to the land
and from that moment my mind was in dread
of his depredations. So I praise God
in His heavenly glory that I lived to behold
this head dripping blood and that after such harrowing   1780
I can look upon it in triumph at last.
Take your place, then, with pride and pleasure,
and move to the feast. Tomorrow morning
our treasure will be shared and showered upon you."
    The Geat was elated and gladly obeyed   1785
the old man's bidding; he sat on the bench.
And soon all was restored, the same as before.
Happiness came back, the hall was thronged,
and a banquet set forth; black night fell
and covered them in darkness.
                        Then the company rose   1790
for the old campaigner: the gray-haired prince
was ready for bed. And a need for rest
came over the brave shield-bearing Geat.
He was a weary seafarer, far from home,
so immediately a house-guard guided him out,   1795
one whose office entailed looking after
whatever a thane on the road in those days
might need or require. It was noble courtesy.

[BEOWULF RETURNS HOME]

That great heart rested. The hall towered,
gold-shingled and gabled, and the guest slept in it   1800
until the black raven with raucous glee
announced heaven's joy, and a hurry of brightness
overran the shadows. Warriors rose quickly,
impatient to be off: their own country
was beckoning the nobles; and the bold voyager   1805
longed to be aboard his distant boat.
Then that stalwart fighter ordered Hrunting
to be brought to Unferth, and bade Unferth
take the sword and thanked him for lending it.
He said he had found it a friend in battle   1810
and a powerful help; he put no blame
on the blade's cutting edge. He was a considerate man.
    And there the warriors stood in their war-gear,
eager to go, while their honored lord
approached the platform where the other sat.   1815
The undaunted hero addressed Hrothgar.
Beowulf, son of Ecgtheow, spoke:
"Now we who crossed the wide sea
have to inform you that we feel a desire
to return to Hygelac. Here we have been welcomed   1820
and thoroughly entertained. You have treated us well.
If there is any favor on earth I can perform
beyond deeds of arms I have done already,
anything that would merit your affections more,
I shall act, my lord, with alacrity.   1825
If ever I hear from across the ocean
that people on your borders are threatening battle
as attackers have done from time to time,
I shall land with a thousand thanes at my back
to help your cause. Hygelac may be young   1830
to rule a nation, but this much I know
about the king of the Geats: he will come to my aid
and want to support me by word and action
in your hour of need, when honor dictates
that I raise a hedge of spears around you.   1835
Then if Hrethric should think about traveling
as a king's son to the court of the Geats,
he will find many friends. Foreign places
yield more to one who is himself worth meeting."
    Hrothgar spoke and answered him: 1840
"The Lord in his wisdom sent you those words
and they came from the heart. I have never heard
so young a man make truer observations.
You are strong in body and mature in mind,
impressive in speech. If it should come to pass   1845
that Hrethel's descendant dies beneath a spear,
if deadly battle or the sword blade or disease
fells the prince who guards your people

and you are still alive, then I firmly believe
the seafaring Geats won't find a man   1850
worthier of acclaim as their king and defender
than you, if only you would undertake
the lordship of your homeland. My liking for you
deepens with time, dear Beowulf.
What you have done is to draw two peoples,   1855
the Geat nation and us neighboring Danes,
into shared peace and a pact of friendship
in spite of hatreds we have harbored in the past.
For as long as I rule this far-flung land
treasures will change hands and each side will treat   1860
the other with gifts; across the gannet's bath,
over the broad sea, whorled prows will bring
presents and tokens. I know your people
are beyond reproach in every respect,
steadfast in the old way with friend or foe."   1865
    Then the earls' defender furnished the hero
with twelve treasures and told him to set out,
sail with those gifts safely home
to the people he loved, but to return promptly.
And so the good and gray-haired Dane,   1870
that highborn king, kissed Beowulf
and embraced his neck, then broke down
in sudden tears. Two forebodings
disturbed him in his wisdom, but one was stronger:[3]
nevermore would they meet each other   1875
face to face. And such was his affection
that he could not help being overcome:
his fondness for the man was so deep-founded,
it warmed his heart and wound the heartstrings
tight in his breast.
                      The embrace ended   1880
and Beowulf, glorious in his gold regalia,
stepped the green earth. Straining at anchor
and ready for boarding, his boat awaited him.
So they went on their journey, and Hrothgar's generosity
was praised repeatedly. He was a peerless king   1885
until old age sapped his strength and did him
mortal harm, as it has done so many.
    Down to the waves then, dressed in the web
of their chain-mail and war-shirts the young men marched
in high spirits. The coast-guard spied them,   1890
thanes setting forth, the same as before.
His salute this time from the top of the cliff
was far from unmannerly; he galloped to meet them
and as they took ship in their shining gear,
he said how welcome they would be in Geatland.   1895
Then the broad hull was beached on the sand

3. We are not told what the other foreboding is, but it is probably the old man's awareness of the imminence
of his own death.

to be cargoed with treasure, horses and war-gear.
The curved prow motioned; the mast stood high
above Hrothgar's riches in the loaded hold.
    The guard who had watched the boat was given   1900
a sword with gold fittings, and in future days
that present would make him a respected man
at his place on the mead-bench.
                     Then the keel plunged
and shook in the sea; and they sailed from Denmark.
    Right away the mast was rigged with its sea-shawl;   1905
sail-ropes were tightened, timbers drummed
and stiff winds kept the wave-crosser
skimming ahead; as she heaved forward,
her foamy neck was fleet and buoyant,
a lapped prow loping over currents,   1910
until finally the Geats caught sight of coastline
and familiar cliffs. The keel reared up,
wind lifted it home, it hit on the land.
    The harbor guard came hurrying out
to the rolling water: he had watched the offing   1915
long and hard, on the lookout for those friends.
With the anchor cables, he moored their craft
right where it had beached, in case a backwash
might catch the hull and carry it away.
Then he ordered the prince's treasure-trove   1920
to be carried ashore. It was a short step
from there to where Hrethel's son and heir,
Hygelac the gold-giver, makes his home
on a secure cliff, in the company of retainers.
    The building was magnificent, the king majestic, 1925
ensconced in his hall; and although Hygd, his queen,
was young, a few short years at court,
her mind was thoughtful and her manners sure.
Haereth's daughter[4] behaved generously
and stinted nothing when she distributed   1930
bounty to the Geats.
              Great Queen Modthryth
perpetrated terrible wrongs.[5]
If any retainer ever made bold
to look her in the face, if an eye not her lord's[6]
stared at her directly during daylight,   1935
the outcome was sealed: he was kept bound,
in hand-tightened shackles, racked, tortured
until doom was pronounced—death by the sword,
slash of blade, blood-gush, and death-qualms
in an evil display. Even a queen   1940
outstanding in beauty must not overstep like that.
A queen should weave peace, not punish the innocent
with loss of life for imagined insults.

4. I.e., Hygd.   5. A Danish queen whose wickedness is being used as a foil to Hygd.   6. Probably her
father, although the Anglo-Saxon word can also refer to a husband.

But Hemming's kinsman put a halt to her ways
and drinkers round the table had another tale: 1945
she was less of a bane to people's lives,
less cruel-minded, after she was married
to the brave Offa,[7] a bride arrayed
in her gold finery, given away
by a caring father, ferried to her young prince   1950
over dim seas. In days to come
she would grace the throne and grow famous
for her good deeds and conduct of life,
her high devotion to the hero king
who was the best king, it has been said,   1955
between the two seas or anywhere else
on the face of the earth. Offa was honored
far and wide for his generous ways,
his fighting spirit and his farseeing
defense of his homeland; from him there sprang Eomer,   1960
Garmund's grandson, kinsman of Hemming,[8]
his warriors' mainstay and master of the field.

　　Heroic Beowulf and his band of men
crossed the wide strand, striding along
the sandy foreshore; the sun shone,   1965
the world's candle warmed them from the south
as they hastened to where, as they had heard,
the young king, Ongentheow's killer[9]
and his people's protector, was dispensing rings
inside his bawn. Beowulf's return   1970
was reported to Hygelac as soon as possible,
news that the captain was now in the enclosure,
his battle-brother back from the fray
alive and well, walking to the hall.
Room was quickly made, on the king's orders,   1975
and the troops filed across the cleared floor.

　　After Hygelac had offered greetings
to his loyal thane in a lofty speech,
he and his kinsman, that hale survivor,
sat face to face. Haereth's daughter[1]   1980
moved about with the mead-jug in her hand,
taking care of the company, filling the cups
that warriors held out. Then Hygelac began
to put courteous questions to his old comrade
in the high hall. He hankered to know   1985
every tale the Sea-Geats had to tell:
"How did you fare on your foreign voyage,
dear Beowulf, when you abruptly decided
to sail away across the salt water
and fight at Heorot? Did you help Hrothgar   1990

---

7. *Offa* was a legendary king of the Angles, one of the Germanic peoples who invaded England and established a kingdom named Mercia in the north of the country prior to the composition of *Beowulf*. Hemming
is evidently a forebear of the Angles.　　8. *Garmund* is Offa's father, *Eomer* his son.　　9. *Ongentheow's
killer* is Hygelac, king of the Geats; he led the attack against the Swedes, although a Geat named Eofor
actually killed Ongentheow. This is the first reference to the feud between the Geats and the Swedes (or
Shylfings) detailed in the headnote (see below, lines 2379–96, 2468–89, 2922–98).　　1. I.e., Hygd.

much in the end? Could you ease the prince
of his well-known troubles? Your undertaking
cast my spirits down, I dreaded the outcome
of your expedition and pleaded with you
long and hard to leave the killer be,   1995
let the South-Danes settle their own
blood-feud with Grendel. So God be thanked
I am granted this sight of you, safe and sound."
    Beowulf, son of Ecgtheow, spoke:
"What happened, Lord Hygelac, is hardly a secret   2000
any more among men in this world—
myself and Grendel coming to grips
on the very spot where he visited destruction
on the Victory-Shieldings and violated
life and limb, losses I avenged   2005
so no earthly offspring of Grendel's
need ever boast of that bout before dawn,
no matter how long the last of his evil
family survives.
            When I first landed
I hastened to the ring-hall and saluted Hrothgar.   2010
Once he discovered why I had come,
the son of Halfdane sent me immediately
to sit with his own sons on the bench.
It was a happy gathering. In my whole life
I have never seen mead enjoyed more   2015
in any hall on earth. Sometimes the queen
herself appeared, peace-pledge between nations,[2]
to hearten the young ones and hand out
a torque to a warrior, then take her place.
Sometimes Hrothgar's daughter distributed   2020
ale to older ranks, in order on the benches:
I heard the company call her Freawaru
as she made her rounds, presenting men
with the gem-studded bowl, young bride-to-be
to the gracious Ingeld,[3] in her gold-trimmed attire.   2025
The friend of the Shieldings favors her betrothal:
the guardian of the kingdom sees good in it
and hopes this woman will heal old wounds
and grievous feuds.
            But generally the spear
is prompt to retaliate when a prince is killed,   2030
no matter how admirable the bride may be.
    "Think how the Heatho-Bards are bound to feel,
their lord, Ingeld, and his loyal thanes,
when he walks in with that woman to the feast:
Danes are at the table, being entertained,   2035

---

2. Wealhtheow, Hrothgar's queen, is called a "peace-pledge between nations" because kings attempted to
end feuds by marrying their daughters to the sons of the kings of enemy nations. But as we have already
seen in the case of the marriage of the Dane Hildeburh to the Jute Finn, and as we shall shortly learn
again, such a strategy seems rarely to have worked. **3.** *Ingeld* is the king of the Heatho-Bards, whose
father, Froda, was killed by the Danes.

honored guests in glittering regalia,
burnished ring-mail that was their hosts' birthright,
looted when the Heatho-Bards could no longer wield
their weapons in the shield-clash, when they went down
with their beloved comrades and forfeited their lives.　　2040
Then an old spearman will speak while they are drinking,
having glimpsed some heirloom that brings alive
memories of the massacre; his mood will darken
and heart-stricken, in the stress of his emotion,
he will begin to test a young man's temper　　2045
and stir up trouble, starting like this:
'Now, my friend, don't you recognize
your father's sword, his favorite weapon,
the one he wore when he went out in his war-mask
to face the Danes on that final day?　　2050
After Withergeld[4] died and his men were doomed,
the Shieldings quickly claimed the field;
and now here's a son of one or other
of those same killers coming through our hall
overbearing us, mouthing boasts,　　2055
and rigged in armor that by right is yours.'
And so he keeps on, recalling and accusing,
working things up with bitter words
until one of the lady's retainers lies
spattered in blood, split open　　2060
on his father's account.[5] The killer knows
the lie of the land and escapes with his life.
Then on both sides the oath-bound lords
will break the peace, a passionate hate
will build up in Ingeld, and love for his bride　　2065
will falter in him as the feud rankles.
I therefore suspect the good faith of the Heatho-Bards,
the truth of their friendship and the trustworthiness
of their alliance with the Danes.

　　　　　　　　　　But now, my lord,
I shall carry on with my account of Grendel,　　2070
the whole story of everything that happened
in the hand-to-hand fight.

　　　　　　　　　After heaven's gem
had gone mildly to earth, that maddened spirit,
the terror of those twilights, came to attack us
where we stood guard, still safe inside the hall.　　2075
There deadly violence came down on Hondscio[6]
and he fell as fate ordained, the first to perish,
rigged out for the combat. A comrade from our ranks
had come to grief in Grendel's maw:
he ate up the entire body.　　2080
There was blood on his teeth, he was bloated and dangerous,
all roused up, yet still unready

---

4. A Heatho-Bard warrior.　5. A Danish attendant to Freawaru, whose father killed a Heatho-Bard in the original battle; this action is envisioned as taking place at Ingeld's court after the marriage.　6. A Geat who was accompanying Beowulf; his name means "glove."

to leave the hall empty-handed;
renowned for his might, he matched himself against me,
wildly reaching. He had this roomy pouch,[7]   2085
a strange accoutrement, intricately strung
and hung at the ready, a rare patchwork
of devilishly fitted dragon-skins.
I had done him no wrong, yet the raging demon
wanted to cram me and many another   2090
into this bag—but it was not to be
once I got to my feet in a blind fury.
It would take too long to tell how I repaid
the terror of the land for every life he took
and so won credit for you, my king,   2095
and for all your people. And although he got away
to enjoy life's sweetness for a while longer,
his right hand stayed behind him in Heorot,
evidence of his miserable overthrow
as he dived into murk on the mere bottom.   2100
    "I got lavish rewards from the lord of the Danes
for my part in the battle, beaten gold
and much else, once morning came
and we took our places at the banquet table.
There was singing and excitement: an old reciter,   2105
a carrier of stories, recalled the early days.
At times some hero made the timbered harp
tremble with sweetness, or related true
and tragic happenings; at times the king
gave the proper turn to some fantastic tale,   2110
or a battle-scarred veteran, bowed with age,
would begin to remember the martial deeds
of his youth and prime and be overcome
as the past welled up in his wintry heart.
    "We were happy there the whole day long   2115
and enjoyed our time until another night
descended upon us. Then suddenly
the vehement mother avenged her son
and wreaked destruction. Death had robbed her,
Geats had slain Grendel, so his ghastly dam   2120
struck back and with bare-faced defiance
laid a man low. Thus life departed
from the sage Aeschere, an elder wise in counsel.
But afterward, on the morning following,
the Danes could not burn the dead body   2125
nor lay the remains of the man they loved
on his funeral pyre. She had fled with the corpse
and taken refuge beneath torrents on the mountain.
It was a hard blow for Hrothgar to bear,
harder than any he had undergone before.   2130
And so the heartsore king beseeched me
in your royal name to take my chances

---

7. The Anglo-Saxon word translated as "pouch" literally means "glove."

underwater, to win glory
and prove my worth. He promised me rewards.
Hence, as is well known, I went to my encounter   2135
with the terror-monger at the bottom of the tarn.
For a while it was hand-to-hand between us,
then blood went curling along the currents
and I beheaded Grendel's mother in the hall
with a mighty sword. I barely managed   2140
to escape with my life; my time had not yet come.
But Halfdane's heir, the shelter of those earls,
again endowed me with gifts in abundance.
    "Thus the king acted with due custom.
I was paid and recompensed completely,   2145
given full measure and the freedom to choose
from Hrothgar's treasures by Hrothgar himself.
These, King Hygelac, I am happy to present
to you as gifts. It is still upon your grace
that all favor depends. I have few kinsmen   2150
who are close, my king, except for your kind self."
Then he ordered the boar-framed standard to be brought,
the battle-topping helmet, the mail-shirt gray as hoar-frost,
and the precious war-sword; and proceeded with his speech:
"When Hrothgar presented this war-gear to me   2155
he instructed me, my lord, to give you some account
of why it signifies his special favor.
He said it had belonged to his older brother,
King Heorogar, who had long kept it,
but that Heorogar had never bequeathed it   2160
to his son Heoroward, that worthy scion,
loyal as he was.
                    Enjoy it well."
    I heard four horses were handed over next.
Beowulf bestowed four bay steeds
to go with the armor, swift gallopers,   2165
all alike. So ought a kinsman act,
instead of plotting and planning in secret
to bring people to grief, or conspiring to arrange
the death of comrades. The warrior king
was uncle to Beowulf and honored by his nephew: 2170
each was concerned for the other's good.
    I heard he presented Hygd with a gorget,
the priceless torque that the prince's daughter,
Wealhtheow, had given him; and three horses,
supple creatures brilliantly saddled.   2175
The bright necklace would be luminous on Hygd's breast.
    Thus Beowulf bore himself with valor;
he was formidable in battle yet behaved with honor
and took no advantage; never cut down
a comrade who was drunk, kept his temper   2180
and, warrior that he was, watched and controlled
his God-sent strength and his outstanding
natural powers. He had been poorly regarded

for a long time, was taken by the Geats
for less than he was worth: and their lord too   2185
had never much esteemed him in the mead-hall.
They firmly believed that he lacked force,
that the prince was a weakling; but presently
every affront to his deserving was reversed.

    The battle-famed king, bulwark of his earls,   2190
ordered a gold-chased heirloom of Hrethel's[8]
to be brought in; it was the best example
of a gem-studded sword in the Geat treasury.
This he laid on Beowulf's lap
and then rewarded him with land as well,   2195
seven thousand hides;[9] and a hall and a throne.
Both owned land by birth in that country,
ancestral grounds; but the greater right
and sway were inherited by the higher born.

[THE DRAGON WAKES]

A lot was to happen in later days   2200
in the fury of battle. Hygelac fell
and the shelter of Heardred's shield proved useless
against the fierce aggression of the Shylfings:[1]
ruthless swordsmen, seasoned campaigners,
they came against him and his conquering nation,   2205
and with cruel force cut him down
so that afterwards
            the wide kingdom
reverted to Beowulf. He ruled it well
for fifty winters, grew old and wise
as warden of the land
            until one began   2210
to dominate the dark, a dragon on the prowl
from the steep vaults of a stone-roofed barrow[2]
where he guarded a hoard; there was a hidden passage,
unknown to men, but someone managed[3]
to enter by it and interfere   2215
with the heathen trove. He had handled and removed
a gem-studded goblet; it gained him nothing,
though with a thief's wiles he had outwitted
the sleeping dragon. That drove him into rage,
as the people of that country would soon discover.   2220
    The intruder who broached the dragon's treasure
and moved him to wrath had never meant to.
It was desperation on the part of a slave
fleeing the heavy hand of some master,
guilt-ridden and on the run,   2225

---

8. Hygelac's father and, through his daughter, Beowulf's grandfather.   9. A *hide* varied in size, but was considered to be sufficient land to support a peasant and his family.   1. Hygelac died in the raid against the Franks (see n. 4 to lines 1202–203); Heardred died in the long feud against the Swedes or Shylfings described in the headnote.   2. A *barrow* is a burial mound.   3. In the single manuscript of *Beowulf*, the page containing lines 2215–31 is badly damaged, and the translation is therefore conjectural. The ellipses of lines 2227–30 indicate lines that cannot be reconstructed at all.

going to ground. But he soon began
to shake with terror; . . . . . . in shock
the wretch . . . .
. . . . panicked and ran
away with the precious   2230
metalwork. There were many other
heirlooms heaped inside the earth-house,
because long ago, with deliberate care,
somebody now forgotten
had buried the riches of a highborn race   2235
in this ancient cache. Death had come
and taken them all in times gone by
and the only one left to tell their tale,
the last of their line, could look forward to nothing
but the same fate for himself: he foresaw that his joy   2240
in the treasure would be brief.
                    A newly constructed
barrow stood waiting, on a wide headland
close to the waves, its entryway secured.
Into it the keeper of the hoard had carried
all the goods and golden ware   2245
worth preserving. His words were few:
"Now, earth, hold what earls once held
and heroes can no more; it was mined from you first
by honorable men. My own people
have been ruined in war; one by one   2250
they went down to death, looked their last
on sweet life in the hall. I am left with nobody
to bear a sword or to burnish plated goblets,
put a sheen on the cup. The companies have departed.
The hard helmet, hasped with gold,   2255
will be stripped of its hoops; and the helmet-shiner
who should polish the metal of the war-mask sleeps;
the coat of mail that came through all fights,
through shield-collapse and cut of sword,
decays with the warrior. Nor may webbed mail   2260
range far and wide on the warlord's back
beside his mustered troops. No trembling harp,
no tuned timber, no tumbling hawk
swerving through the hall, no swift horse
pawing the courtyard. Pillage and slaughter   2265
have emptied the earth of entire peoples."
And so he mourned as he moved about the world,
deserted and alone, lamenting his unhappiness
day and night, until death's flood
brimmed up in his heart.
                    Then an old harrower of the dark   2270
happened to find the hoard open,
the burning one who hunts out barrows,
the slick-skinned dragon, threatening the night sky
with streamers of fire. People on the farms
are in dread of him. He is driven to hunt out   2275

hoards under ground, to guard heathen gold
through age-long vigils, though to little avail.
For three centuries, this scourge of the people
had stood guard on that stoutly protected
underground treasury, until the intruder   2280
unleashed its fury; he hurried to his lord
with the gold-plated cup and made his plea
to be reinstated. Then the vault was rifled,
the ring-hoard robbed, and the wretched man
had his request granted. His master gazed   2285
on that find from the past for the first time.
　　When the dragon awoke, trouble flared again.
He rippled down the rock, writhing with anger
when he saw the footprints of the prowler who had stolen
too close to his dreaming head.   2290
So may a man not marked by fate
easily escape exile and woe
by the grace of God.
　　　　　　　　　The hoard-guardian
scorched the ground as he scoured and hunted
for the trespasser who had troubled his sleep.   2295
Hot and savage, he kept circling and circling
the outside of the mound. No man appeared
in that desert waste, but he worked himself up
by imagining battle; then back in he'd go
in search of the cup, only to discover   2300
signs that someone had stumbled upon
the golden treasures. So the guardian of the mound,
the hoard-watcher, waited for the gloaming
with fierce impatience; his pent-up fury
at the loss of the vessel made him long to hit back   2305
and lash out in flames. Then, to his delight,
the day waned and he could wait no longer
behind the wall, but hurtled forth
in a fiery blaze. The first to suffer
were the people on the land, but before long   2310
it was their treasure-giver who would come to grief.
　　The dragon began to belch out flames
and burn bright homesteads; there was a hot glow
that scared everyone, for the vile sky-winger
would leave nothing alive in his wake.   2315
Everywhere the havoc he wrought was in evidence.
Far and near, the Geat nation
bore the brunt of his brutal assaults
and virulent hate. Then back to the hoard
he would dart before daybreak, to hide in his den.   2320
He had swinged[4] the land, swathed it in flame,
in fire and burning, and now he felt secure
in the vaults of his barrow; but his trust was unavailing.
　　Then Beowulf was given bad news,

---

4. I.e., singed, scorched.

the hard truth: his own home,   2325
the best of buildings, had been burned to a cinder,
the throne-room of the Geats. It threw the hero
into deep anguish and darkened his mood:
the wise man thought he must have thwarted
ancient ordinance of the eternal Lord,   2330
broken His commandment. His mind was in turmoil,
unaccustomed anxiety and gloom
confused his brain; the fire-dragon
had razed the coastal region and reduced
forts and earthworks to dust and ashes,   2335
so the war-king planned and plotted his revenge.
The warriors' protector, prince of the hall-troop,
ordered a marvelous all-iron shield
from his smithy works. He well knew
that linden boards would let him down   2340
and timber burn. After many trials,
he was destined to face the end of his days,
in this mortal world, as was the dragon,
for all his long leasehold on the treasure.

   Yet the prince of the rings was too proud   2345
to line up with a large army
against the sky-plague. He had scant regard
for the dragon as a threat, no dread at all
of its courage or strength, for he had kept going
often in the past, through perils and ordeals   2350
of every sort, after he had purged
Hrothgar's hall, triumphed in Heorot
and beaten Grendel. He outgrappled the monster
and his evil kin.
           One of his cruelest
hand-to-hand encounters had happened   2355
when Hygelac, king of the Geats, was killed
in Friesland: the people's friend and lord,
Hrethel's son, slaked a sword blade's
thirst for blood. But Beowulf's prodigious
gifts as a swimmer guaranteed his safety: 2360
he arrived at the shore, shouldering thirty
battle-dresses, the booty he had won.
There was little for the Hetware[5] to be happy about
as they shielded their faces and fighting on the ground
began in earnest. With Beowulf against them,   2365
few could hope to return home.

   Across the wide sea, desolate and alone,
the son of Ecgtheow swam back to his people.
There Hygd offered him throne and authority
as lord of the ring-hoard: with Hygelac dead,   2370
she had no belief in her son's ability
to defend their homeland against foreign invaders.
Yet there was no way the weakened nation

---

5. The *Hetware* are a Frankish tribe.

could get Beowulf to give in and agree
to be elevated over Heardred as his lord   2375
or to undertake the office of kingship.
But he did provide support for the prince,
honored and minded him until he matured
as the ruler of Geatland.
                Then over sea-roads
exiles arrived, sons of Ohthere.[6]   2380
They had rebelled against the best of all
the sea-kings in Sweden, the one who held sway
in the Shylfing nation, their renowned prince,
lord of the mead-hall. That marked the end
for Hygelac's son: his hospitality   2385
was mortally rewarded with wounds from a sword.
Heardred lay slaughtered and Onela returned
to the land of Sweden, leaving Beowulf
to ascend the throne, to sit in majesty
and rule over the Geats. He was a good king.   2390
    In days to come, he contrived to avenge
the fall of his prince; he befriended Eadgils
when Eadgils was friendless, aiding his cause
with weapons and warriors over the wide sea,
sending him men. The feud was settled   2395
on a comfortless campaign when he killed Onela.
    And so the son of Ecgtheow had survived
every extreme, excelling himself
in daring and in danger, until the day arrived
when he had to come face to face with the dragon.   2400
The lord of the Geats took eleven comrades
and went in a rage to reconnoiter.
By then he had discovered the cause of the affliction
being visited on the people. The precious cup
had come to him from the hand of the finder,   2405
the one who had started all this strife
and was now added as a thirteenth to their number.
They press-ganged and compelled this poor creature
to be their guide. Against his will
he led them to the earth-vault he alone knew,   2410
an underground barrow near the sea-billows
and heaving waves, heaped inside
with exquisite metalwork. The one who stood guard
was dangerous and watchful, warden of the trove
buried under earth: no easy bargain   2415
would be made in that place by any man.
    The veteran king sat down on the cliff-top.
He wished good luck to the Geats who had shared
his hearth and his gold. He was sad at heart,
unsettled yet ready, sensing his death.   2420

---

6. *Ohthere* was king of the Swedes or Shylfings, but after his death his sons, Eanmund and Eadgils, were driven out by their uncle Onela. They were taken in by Heardred, Hygelac's son, who was then king of the Geats, who was then in turn attacked and killed (along with Eanmund) by Onela. At this point Beowulf became king of the Geats and supported Eadgils in his successful attack on Onela.

His fate hovered near, unknowable but certain:
it would soon claim his coffered soul,
part life from limb. Before long
the prince's spirit would spin free from his body.

    Beowulf, son of Ecgtheow, spoke: 2425
"Many a skirmish I survived when I was young
and many times of war: I remember them well.
At seven, I was fostered out by my father,
left in the charge of my people's lord.
King Hrethel kept me and took care of me,   2430
was openhanded, behaved like a kinsman.
While I was his ward, he treated me no worse
as a wean[7] about the place than one of his own boys,
Herebeald and Haethcyn, or my own Hygelac.
For the eldest, Herebeald, an unexpected   2435
deathbed was laid out, through a brother's doing,
when Haethcyn bent his horn-tipped bow
and loosed the arrow that destroyed his life.
He shot wide and buried a shaft
in the flesh and blood of his own brother.   2440
That offense was beyond redress, a wrongfooting
of the heart's affections; for who could avenge
the prince's life or pay his death-price?
It was like the misery felt by an old man
who has lived to see his son's body   2445
swing on the gallows. He begins to keen
and weep for his boy, watching the raven
gloat where he hangs: he can be of no help.
The wisdom of age is worthless to him.
Morning after morning, he wakes to remember   2450
that his child is gone; he has no interest
in living on until another heir
is born in the hall, now that his first-born
has entered death's dominion forever.
He gazes sorrowfully at his son's dwelling,   2455
the banquet hall bereft of all delight,
the windswept hearthstone; the horsemen are sleeping,
the warriors under ground; what was is no more.
No tunes from the harp, no cheer raised in the yard.
Alone with his longing, he lies down on his bed   2460
and sings a lament; everything seems too large,
the steadings and the fields.
                    Such was the feeling
of loss endured by the lord of the Geats
after Herebeald's death. He was helplessly placed
to set to rights the wrong committed,   2465
could not punish the killer in accordance with the law
of the blood-feud, although he felt no love for him.
Heartsore, wearied, he turned away
from life's joys, chose God's light

---

7. A young child [Translator's note]; a Northern Irish word.

and departed, leaving buildings and lands   2470
to his sons, as a man of substance will.
   "Then over the wide sea Swedes and Geats
battled and feuded and fought without quarter.
Hostilities broke out when Hrethel died.
Ongentheow's sons[8] were unrelenting,   2475
refusing to make peace, campaigning violently
from coast to coast, constantly setting up
terrible ambushes around Hreosnahill.[9]
My own kith and kin avenged
these evil events, as everybody knows,   2480
but the price was high: one of them paid
with his life. Haethcyn, lord of the Geats,
met his fate there and fell in the battle.
Then, as I have heard, Hygelac's sword
was raised in the morning against Ongentheow,   2485
his brother's killer. When Eofor cleft
the old Swede's helmet, halved it open,
he fell, death-pale: his feud-calloused hand
could not stave off the fatal stroke.
   "The treasures that Hygelac lavished on me   2490
I paid for when I fought, as fortune allowed me,
with my glittering sword. He gave me land
and the security land brings, so he had no call
to go looking for some lesser champion,
some mercenary from among the Gifthas[1]   2495
or the Spear-Danes or the men of Sweden.
I marched ahead of him, always there
at the front of the line; and I shall fight like that
for as long as I live, as long as this sword
shall last, which has stood me in good stead   2500
late and soon, ever since I killed
Dayraven the Frank in front of the two armies.
He brought back no looted breastplate
to the Frisian king but fell in battle,
their standard-bearer, highborn and brave.   2505
No sword blade sent him to his death:
my bare hands stilled his heartbeats
and wrecked the bone-house. Now blade and hand,
sword and sword-stroke, will assay the hoard."

[BEOWULF ATTACKS THE DRAGON]

   Beowulf spoke, made a formal boast   2510
for the last time: "I risked my life
often when I was young. Now I am old,
but as king of the people I shall pursue this fight

---

8. *Ongentheow's sons* are Ohthere and Onela, who attacked the Geats and killed Haethcyn; Haethcyn was then avenged by his brother Hygelac, whose attack on the Swedes resulted in the death of Ongentheow at the hands of the Geat Eofor (described below in lines 2922–98). These events took place before those of lines 2379–96, which describe the Geats' role in the struggle between Onela and Ohthere's two sons after Ongentheow's death.   9. The place of the battle can be translated as Sorrow Hill.   1. A tribe related to the Goths.

for the glory of winning, if the evil one will only
abandon his earth-fort and face me in the open."   2515
    Then he addressed each dear companion
one final time, those fighters in their helmets,
resolute and highborn: "I would rather not
use a weapon if I knew another way
to grapple with the dragon and make good my boast   2520
as I did against Grendel in days gone by.
But I shall be meeting molten venom
in the fire he breathes, so I go forth
in mail-shirt and shield. I won't shift a foot
when I meet the cave-guard: what occurs on the wall   2525
between the two of us will turn out as fate,
overseer of men, decides. I am resolved.
I scorn further words against this sky-borne foe.
    "Men-at-arms, remain here on the barrow,
safe in your armor, to see which one of us   2530
is better in the end at bearing wounds
in a deadly fray. This fight is not yours,
nor is it up to any man except me
to measure his strength against the monster
or to prove his worth. I shall win the gold   2535
by my courage, or else mortal combat,
doom of battle, will bear your lord away."
    Then he drew himself up beside his shield.
The fabled warrior in his war-shirt and helmet
trusted in his own strength entirely   2540
and went under the crag. No coward path.
    Hard by the rock-face that hale veteran,
a good man who had gone repeatedly
into combat and danger and come through,
saw a stone arch and a gushing stream   2545
that burst from the barrow, blazing and wafting
a deadly heat. It would be hard to survive
unscathed near the hoard, to hold firm
against the dragon in those flaming depths.
Then he gave a shout. The lord of the Geats   2550
unburdened his breast and broke out
in a storm of anger. Under gray stone
his voice challenged and resounded clearly.
Hate was ignited. The hoard-guard recognized
a human voice, the time was over   2555
for peace and parleying. Pouring forth
in a hot battle-fume, the breath of the monster
burst from the rock. There was a rumble under ground.
Down there in the barrow, Beowulf the warrior
lifted his shield: the outlandish thing   2560
writhed and convulsed and viciously
turned on the king, whose keen-edged sword,
an heirloom inherited by ancient right,
was already in his hand. Roused to a fury,
each antagonist struck terror in the other.   2565

Unyielding, the lord of his people loomed
by his tall shield, sure of his ground,
while the serpent looped and unleashed itself.
Swaddled in flames, it came gliding and flexing
and racing toward its fate. Yet his shield defended   2570
the renowned leader's life and limb
for a shorter time than he meant it to:
that final day was the first time
when Beowulf fought and fate denied him
glory in battle. So the king of the Geats   2575
raised his hand and struck hard
at the enameled scales, but scarcely cut through:
the blade flashed and slashed yet the blow
was far less powerful than the hard-pressed king
had need of at that moment. The mound-keeper   2580
went into a spasm and spouted deadly flames:
when he felt the stroke, battle-fire
billowed and spewed. Beowulf was foiled
of a glorious victory. The glittering sword,
infallible before that day,   2585
failed when he unsheathed it, as it never should have.
For the son of Ecgtheow, it was no easy thing
to have to give ground like that and go
unwillingly to inhabit another home
in a place beyond; so every man must yield   2590
the leasehold of his days.

               Before long
the fierce contenders clashed again.
The hoard-guard took heart, inhaled and swelled up
and got a new wind; he who had once ruled
was furled in fire and had to face the worst.   2595
No help or backing was to be had then
from his highborn comrades; that hand-picked troop
broke ranks and ran for their lives
to the safety of the wood. But within one heart
sorrow welled up: in a man of worth   2600
the claims of kinship cannot be denied.
   His name was Wiglaf, a son of Weohstan's,
a well-regarded Shylfing warrior
related to Aelfhere.[2] When he saw his lord
tormented by the heat of his scalding helmet,   2605
he remembered the bountiful gifts bestowed on him,
how well he lived among the Waegmundings,
the freehold he inherited from his father[3] before him.
He could not hold back: one hand brandished
the yellow-timbered shield, the other drew his sword—   2610
an ancient blade that was said to have belonged

2. *Wiglaf* is, like Beowulf, a member of the clan of the Waegmundings (see lines 2813–14), although both
consider themselves Geats as well. See note 2 to line 347. Nothing is known of Aelfhere.   3. Wiglaf's
father is Weohstan, who, as we learn shortly, was the man who killed Eanmund, Ohthere's son, when he
had taken refuge among the Geats (2379–84). How Wiglaf then became a Geat is not clear, although it
may have been when Beowulf helped Eanmund's brother Eadgils avenge himself on Onela, who had
usurped the throne of the Swedes; Eadgils then became king.

to Eanmund, the son of Ohthere, the one
Weohstan had slain when he was an exile without friends.
He carried the arms to the victim's kinfolk,
the burnished helmet, the webbed chain-mail   2615
and that relic of the giants. But Onela returned
the weapons to him, rewarded Weohstan
with Eanmund's war-gear. He ignored the blood-feud,
the fact that Eanmund was his brother's son.[4]
Weohstan kept that war-gear for a lifetime,   2620
the sword and the mail-shirt, until it was the son's turn
to follow his father and perform his part.
Then, in old age, at the end of his days
among the Weather-Geats, he bequeathed to Wiglaf
innumerable weapons.
                          And now the youth   2625
was to enter the line of battle with his lord,
his first time to be tested as a fighter.
His spirit did not break and the ancestral blade
would keep its edge, as the dragon discovered
as soon as they came together in the combat.   2630
    Sad at heart, addressing his companions,
Wiglaf spoke wise and fluent words:
"I remember that time when mead was flowing,
how we pledged loyalty to our lord in the hall,
promised our ring-giver we would be worth our price,   2635
make good the gift of the war-gear,
those swords and helmets, as and when
his need required it. He picked us out
from the army deliberately, honored us and judged us
fit for this action, made me these lavish gifts—   2640
and all because he considered us the best
of his arms-bearing thanes. And now, although
he wanted this challenge to be one he'd face
by himself alone—the shepherd of our land,
a man unequaled in the quest for glory   2645
and a name for daring—now the day has come
when this lord we serve needs sound men
to give him their support. Let us go to him,
help our leader through the hot flame
and dread of the fire. As God is my witness,   2650
I would rather my body were robed in the same
burning blaze as my gold-giver's body
than go back home bearing arms.
That is unthinkable, unless we have first
slain the foe and defended the life   2655
of the prince of the Weather-Geats. I well know
the things he has done for us deserve better.
Should he alone be left exposed
to fall in battle? We must bond together,

4. That is, Onela ignored the fact that Weohstan had killed his nephew Eanmund since he in fact wanted
Eanmund dead.

shield and helmet, mail-shirt and sword."   2660
Then he waded the dangerous reek and went
under arms to his lord, saying only:
"Go on, dear Beowulf, do everything
you said you would when you were still young
and vowed you would never let your name and fame   2665
be dimmed while you lived. Your deeds are famous,
so stay resolute, my lord, defend your life now
with the whole of your strength. I shall stand by you."
   After those words, a wildness rose
in the dragon again and drove it to attack,   2670
heaving up fire, hunting for enemies,
the humans it loathed. Flames lapped the shield,
charred it to the boss, and the body armor
on the young warrior was useless to him.
But Wiglaf did well under the wide rim   2675
Beowulf shared with him once his own had shattered
in sparks and ashes.
                          Inspired again
by the thought of glory, the war-king threw
his whole strength behind a sword stroke
and connected with the skull. And Naegling snapped.   2680
Beowulf's ancient iron-gray sword
let him down in the fight. It was never his fortune
to be helped in combat by the cutting edge
of weapons made of iron. When he wielded a sword,
no matter how blooded and hard-edged the blade,   2685
his hand was too strong, the stroke he dealt
(I have heard) would ruin it. He could reap no advantage.
   Then the bane of that people, the fire-breathing dragon,
was mad to attack for a third time.
When a chance came, he caught the hero   2690
in a rush of flame and clamped sharp fangs
into his neck. Beowulf's body
ran wet with his life-blood: it came welling out.
   Next thing, they say, the noble son of Weohstan
saw the king in danger at his side   2695
and displayed his inborn bravery and strength.
He left the head alone,[5] but his fighting hand
was burned when he came to his kinsman's aid.
He lunged at the enemy lower down
so that his decorated sword sank into its belly   2700
and the flames grew weaker.
                               Once again the king
gathered his strength and drew a stabbing knife
he carried on his belt, sharpened for battle.
He stuck it deep in the dragon's flank.
Beowulf dealt it a deadly wound.   2705
They had killed the enemy, courage quelled his life;
that pair of kinsmen, partners in nobility,

5. I.e., the dragon's flame-breathing head.

had destroyed the foe. So every man should act,
be at hand when needed; but now, for the king,
this would be the last of his many labors   2710
and triumphs in the world.
                          Then the wound
dealt by the ground-burner earlier began
to scald and swell; Beowulf discovered
deadly poison suppurating inside him,
surges of nausea, and so, in his wisdom,   2715
the prince realized his state and struggled
toward a seat on the rampart. He steadied his gaze
on those gigantic stones, saw how the earthwork
was braced with arches built over columns.
And now that thane unequaled for goodness   2720
with his own hands washed his lord's wounds,
swabbed the weary prince with water,
bathed him clean, unbuckled his helmet.
    Beowulf spoke: in spite of his wounds,
mortal wounds, he still spoke   2725
for he well knew his days in the world
had been lived out to the end—his allotted time
was drawing to a close, death was very near.
    "Now is the time when I would have wanted
to bestow this armor on my own son,   2730
had it been my fortune to have fathered an heir
and live on in his flesh. For fifty years
I ruled this nation. No king
of any neighboring clan would dare
face me with troops, none had the power   2735
to intimidate me. I took what came,
cared for and stood by things in my keeping,
never fomented quarrels, never
swore to a lie. All this consoles me,
doomed as I am and sickening for death;   2740
because of my right ways, the Ruler of mankind
need never blame me when the breath leaves my body
for murder of kinsmen. Go now quickly,
dearest Wiglaf, under the gray stone
where the dragon is laid out, lost to his treasure;   2745
hurry to feast your eyes on the hoard.
Away you go: I want to examine
that ancient gold, gaze my fill
on those garnered jewels; my going will be easier
for having seen the treasure, a less troubled letting-go   2750
of the life and lordship I have long maintained."
    And so, I have heard, the son of Weohstan
quickly obeyed the command of his languishing
war-weary lord; he went in his chain-mail
under the rock-piled roof of the barrow,   2755
exulting in his triumph, and saw beyond the seat
a treasure-trove of astonishing richness,
wall-hangings that were a wonder to behold,

glittering gold spread across the ground,
the old dawn-scorching serpent's den   2760
packed with goblets and vessels from the past,
tarnished and corroding. Rusty helmets
all eaten away. Armbands everywhere,
artfully wrought. How easily treasure
buried in the ground, gold hidden   2765
however skillfully, can escape from any man!
   And he saw too a standard, entirely of gold,
hanging high over the hoard,
a masterpiece of filigree; it glowed with light
so he could make out the ground at his feet   2770
and inspect the valuables. Of the dragon there was no
remaining sign: the sword had dispatched him.
Then, the story goes, a certain man[6]
plundered the hoard in that immemorial howe,[7]
filled his arms with flagons and plates,   2775
anything he wanted; and took the standard also,
most brilliant of banners.
                 Already the blade
of the old king's sharp killing-sword
had done its worst: the one who had for long
minded the hoard, hovering over gold,   2780
unleashing fire, surging forth
midnight after midnight, had been mown down.
   Wiglaf went quickly, keen to get back,
excited by the treasure. Anxiety weighed
on his brave heart—he was hoping he would find   2785
the leader of the Geats alive where he had left him
helpless, earlier, on the open ground.
   So he came to the place, carrying the treasure
and found his lord bleeding profusely,
his life at an end; again he began   2790
to swab his body. The beginnings of an utterance
broke out from the king's breast-cage.
The old lord gazed sadly at the gold.
   "To the everlasting Lord of all,
to the King of Glory, I give thanks   2795
that I behold this treasure here in front of me,
that I have been allowed to leave my people
so well endowed on the day I die.
Now that I have bartered my last breath
to own this fortune, it is up to you   2800
to look after their needs. I can hold out no longer.
Order my troop to construct a barrow
on a headland on the coast, after my pyre has cooled.
It will loom on the horizon at Hronesness[8]
and be a reminder among my people—   2805
so that in coming times crews under sail
will call it Beowulf's Barrow, as they steer

6. I.e., Wiglaf.   7. *Howe* is an Irish word for dwelling.   8. The name means "Whaleness."

ships across the wide and shrouded waters."
    Then the king in his great-heartedness unclasped
the collar of gold from his neck and gave it   2810
to the young thane, telling him to use
it and the war-shirt and gilded helmet well.
"You are the last of us, the only one left
of the Waegmundings. Fate swept us away,
sent my whole brave highborn clan   2815
to their final doom. Now I must follow them."
    That was the warrior's last word.
He had no more to confide. The furious heat
of the pyre would assail him. His soul fled from his breast
to its destined place among the steadfast ones.   2820

[BEOWULF'S FUNERAL]

    It was hard then on the young hero,
having to watch the one he held so dear
there on the ground, going through
his death agony. The dragon from underearth,
his nightmarish destroyer, lay destroyed as well,   2825
utterly without life. No longer would his snakefolds
ply themselves to safeguard hidden gold.
Hard-edged blades, hammered out
and keenly filed, had finished him
so that the sky-roamer lay there rigid,   2830
brought low beside the treasure-lodge.
    Never again would he glitter and glide
and show himself off in midnight air,
exulting in his riches: he fell to earth
through the battle-strength in Beowulf's arm.   2835
There were few, indeed, as far as I have heard,
big and brave as they may have been,
few who would have held out if they had had to face
the outpourings of that poison-breather
or gone foraging on the ring-hall floor   2840
and found the deep barrow-dweller
on guard and awake.
                The treasure had been won,
bought and paid for by Beowulf's death.
Both had reached the end of the road
through the life they had been lent.
                  Before long   2845
the battle-dodgers abandoned the wood,
the ones who had let down their lord earlier,
the tail-turners, ten of them together.
When he needed them most, they had made off.
Now they were ashamed and came behind shields,   2850
in their battle-outfits, to where the old man lay.
They watched Wiglaf, sitting worn out,
a comrade shoulder to shoulder with his lord,
trying in vain to bring him round with water.

Much as he wanted to, there was no way   2855
he could preserve his lord's life on earth
or alter in the least the Almighty's will.
What God judged right would rule what happened
to every man, as it does to this day.
   Then a stern rebuke was bound to come   2860
from the young warrior to the ones who had been cowards.
Wiglaf, son of Weohstan, spoke
disdainfully and in disappointment:
"Anyone ready to admit the truth
will surely realize that the lord of men   2865
who showered you with gifts and gave you the armor
you are standing in—when he would distribute
helmets and mail-shirts to men on the mead-benches,
a prince treating his thanes in hall
to the best he could find, far or near—   2870
was throwing weapons uselessly away.
It would be a sad waste when the war broke out.
Beowulf had little cause to brag
about his armed guard; yet God who ordains
who wins or loses allowed him to strike   2875
with his own blade when bravery was needed.
There was little I could do to protect his life
in the heat of the fray, but I found new strength
welling up when I went to help him.
Then my sword connected and the deadly assaults   2880
of our foe grew weaker, the fire coursed
less strongly from his head. But when the worst happened
too few rallied around the prince.
   "So it is good-bye now to all you know and love
on your home ground, the open-handedness,   2885
the giving of war-swords. Every one of you
with freeholds of land, our whole nation,
will be dispossessed, once princes from beyond
get tidings of how you turned and fled
and disgraced yourselves. A warrior will sooner   2890
die than live a life of shame."
   Then he ordered the outcome of the fight to be reported
to those camped on the ridge, that crowd of retainers
who had sat all morning, sad at heart,
shield-bearers wondering about   2895
the man they loved: would this day be his last
or would he return? He told the truth
and did not balk, the rider who bore
news to the cliff-top. He addressed them all:
"Now the people's pride and love,   2900
the lord of the Geats, is laid on his deathbed,
brought down by the dragon's attack.
Beside him lies the bane of his life,
dead from knife-wounds. There was no way
Beowulf could manage to get the better   2905
of the monster with his sword. Wiglaf sits

at Beowulf's side, the son of Weohstan,
the living warrior watching by the dead,
keeping weary vigil, holding a wake
for the loved and the loathed.
                Now war is looming   2910
over our nation, soon it will be known
to Franks and Frisians, far and wide,
that the king is gone. Hostility has been great
among the Franks since Hygelac sailed forth
at the head of a war-fleet into Friesland: 2915
there the Hetware harried and attacked
and overwhelmed him with great odds.
The leader in his war-gear was laid low,
fell among followers: that lord did not favor
his company with spoils. The Merovingian king   2920
has been an enemy to us ever since.
    "Nor do I expect peace or pact-keeping
of any sort from the Swedes. Remember:
at Ravenswood, Ongentheow
slaughtered Haethcyn, Hrethel's son,   2925
when the Geat people in their arrogance
first attacked the fierce Shylfings.
The return blow was quickly struck
by Ohthere's father.[9] Old and terrible,
he felled the sea-king and saved his own   2930
aged wife, the mother of Onela
and of Ohthere, bereft of her gold rings.
Then he kept hard on the heels of the foe
and drove them, leaderless, lucky to get away
in a desperate rout into Ravenswood.   2935
His army surrounded the weary remnant
where they nursed their wounds; all through the night
he howled threats at those huddled survivors,
promised to axe their bodies open
when dawn broke, dangle them from gallows   2940
to feed the birds. But at first light
when their spirits were lowest, relief arrived.
They heard the sound of Hygelac's horn,
his trumpet calling as he came to find them,
the hero in pursuit, at hand with troops.   2945
    "The bloody swathe that Swedes and Geats
cut through each other was everywhere.
No one could miss their murderous feuding.
Then the old man made his move,
pulled back, barred his people in: 2950
Ongentheow withdrew to higher ground.
Hygelac's pride and prowess as a fighter
were known to the earl; he had no confidence
that he could hold out against that horde of seamen,
defend his wife and the ones he loved   2955

9. Ongentheow.

from the shock of the attack. He retreated for shelter
behind the earthwall. Then Hygelac swooped
on the Swedes at bay, his banners swarmed
into their refuge, his Geat forces
drove forward to destroy the camp. 2960
There in his gray hairs, Ongentheow
was cornered, ringed around with swords.
And it came to pass that the king's fate
was in Eofor's hands,[1] and in his alone.
Wulf, son of Wonred, went for him in anger, 2965
split him open so that blood came spurting
from under his hair. The old hero
still did not flinch, but parried fast,
hit back with a harder stroke:
the king turned and took him on. 2970
Then Wonred's son, the brave Wulf,
could land no blow against the aged lord.
Ongentheow divided his helmet
so that he buckled and bowed his bloodied head
and dropped to the ground. But his doom held off. 2975
Though he was cut deep, he recovered again.
   "With his brother down, the undaunted Eofor,
Hygelac's thane, hefted his sword
and smashed murderously at the massive helmet
past the lifted shield. And the king collapsed, 2980
the shepherd of people was sheared of life.
Many then hurried to help Wulf,
bandaged and lifted him, now that they were left
masters of the blood-soaked battle-ground.
One warrior stripped the other, 2985
looted Ongentheow's iron mail-coat,
his hard sword-hilt, his helmet too,
and carried the graith[2] to King Hygelac,
he accepted the prize, promised fairly
that reward would come, and kept his word. 2990
For their bravery in action, when they arrived home,
Eofor and Wulf were overloaded
by Hrethel's son, Hygelac the Geat,
with gifts of land and linked rings
that were worth a fortune. They had won glory, 2995
so there was no gainsaying his generosity.
And he gave Eofor his only daughter
to bide at home with him, an honor and a bond.
   "So this bad blood between us and the Swedes,
this vicious feud, I am convinced, 3000
is bound to revive; they will cross our borders
and attack in force when they find out
that Beowulf is dead. In days gone by
when our warriors fell and we were undefended,
he kept our coffers and our kingdom safe. 3005

---

1. The killing of Ongentheow by Eofor has been previously described in lines 2486–89.   2. Armor.

He worked for the people, but as well as that
he behaved like a hero.
                      We must hurry now
to take a last look at the king
and launch him, lord and lavisher of rings,
on the funeral road. His royal pyre   3010
will melt no small amount of gold:
heaped there in a hoard, it was bought at heavy cost,
and that pile of rings he paid for at the end
with his own life will go up with the flame,
be furled in fire: treasure no follower   3015
will wear in his memory, nor lovely woman
link and attach as a torque around her neck—
but often, repeatedly, in the path of exile
they shall walk bereft, bowed under woe,
now that their leader's laugh is silenced,   3020
high spirits quenched. Many a spear
dawn-cold to the touch will be taken down
and waved on high; the swept harp
won't waken warriors, but the raven winging
darkly over the doomed will have news,   3025
tidings for the eagle of how he hoked[3] and ate,
how the wolf and he made short work of the dead."
    Such was the drift of the dire report
that gallant man delivered. He got little wrong
in what he told and predicted.
                     The whole troop   3030
rose in tears, then took their way
to the uncanny scene under Earnaness.[4]
There, on the sand, where his soul had left him,
they found him at rest, their ring-giver
from days gone by. The great man   3035
had breathed his last. Beowulf the king
had indeed met with a marvelous death.
    But what they saw first was far stranger:
the serpent on the ground, gruesome and vile,
lying facing him. The fire-dragon   3040
was scaresomely burned, scorched all colors.
From head to tail, his entire length
was fifty feet. He had shimmered forth
on the night air once, then winged back
down to his den; but death owned him now,   3045
he would never enter his earth-gallery again.
Beside him stood pitchers and piled-up dishes,
silent flagons, precious swords
eaten through with rust, ranged as they had been
while they waited their thousand winters under ground.   3050
That huge cache, gold inherited
from an ancient race, was under a spell—

---

3. *Hoked*: rooted about, a Northern Irish word [adapted from Translator's note].   4. The place where
Beowulf fought the dragon; it means "Eagleness."

which meant no one was ever permitted
to enter the ring-hall unless God Himself,
mankind's Keeper, True King of Triumphs,   3055
allowed some person pleasing to Him—
and in His eyes worthy—to open the hoard.
    What came about brought to nothing
the hopes of the one who had wrongly hidden
riches under the rock-face. First the dragon slew   3060
that man among men, who in turn made fierce amends
and settled the feud. Famous for his deeds
a warrior may be, but it remains a mystery
where his life will end, when he may no longer
dwell in the mead-hall among his own.   3065
So it was with Beowulf, when he faced the cruelty
and cunning of the mound-guard. He himself was ignorant
of how his departure from the world would happen.
The highborn chiefs who had buried the treasure
declared it until doomsday so accursed   3070
that whoever robbed it would be guilty of wrong
and grimly punished for their transgression,
hasped in hell-bonds in heathen shrines.
Yet Beowulf's gaze at the gold treasure
when he first saw it had not been selfish.   3075
    Wiglaf, son of Weohstan, spoke:
"Often when one man follows his own will
many are hurt. This happened to us.
Nothing we advised could ever convince
the prince we loved, our land's guardian,   3080
not to vex the custodian of the gold,
let him lie where he was long accustomed,
lurk there under earth until the end of the world.
He held to his high destiny. The hoard is laid bare,
but at a grave cost; it was too cruel a fate   3085
that forced the king to that encounter.
I have been inside and seen everything
amassed in the vault. I managed to enter
although no great welcome awaited me
under the earthwall. I quickly gathered up   3090
a huge pile of the priceless treasures
handpicked from the hoard and carried them here
where the king could see them. He was still himself,
alive, aware, and in spite of his weakness
he had many requests. He wanted me to greet you   3095
and order the building of a barrow that would crown
the site of his pyre, serve as his memorial,
in a commanding position, since of all men
to have lived and thrived and lorded it on earth
his worth and due as a warrior were the greatest.   3100
Now let us again go quickly
and feast our eyes on that amazing fortune
heaped under the wall. I will show the way
and take you close to those coffers packed with rings

and bars of gold. Let a bier be made   3105
and got ready quickly when we come out
and then let us bring the body of our lord,
the man we loved, to where he will lodge
for a long time in the care of the Almighty."
    Then Weohstan's son, stalwart to the end,   3110
had orders given to owners of dwellings,
many people of importance in the land,
to fetch wood from far and wide
for the good man's pyre:
                            "Now shall flame consume
our leader in battle, the blaze darken   3115
round him who stood his ground in the steel-hail,
when the arrow-storm shot from bowstrings
pelted the shield-wall. The shaft hit home.
Feather-fledged, it finned the barb in flight."
    Next the wise son of Weohstan   3120
called from among the king's thanes
a group of seven: he selected the best
and entered with them, the eighth of their number,
under the God-cursed roof; one raised
a lighted torch and led the way.   3125
No lots were cast for who should loot the hoard
for it was obvious to them that every bit of it
lay unprotected within the vault,
there for the taking. It was no trouble
to hurry to work and haul out   3130
the priceless store. They pitched the dragon
over the cliff-top, let tide's flow
and backwash take the treasure-minder.
Then coiled gold was loaded on a cart
in great abundance, and the gray-haired leader,   3135
the prince on his bier, borne to Hronesness.
    The Geat people built a pyre for Beowulf,
stacked and decked it until it stood foursquare,
hung with helmets, heavy war-shields
and shining armor, just as he had ordered.   3140
Then his warriors laid him in the middle of it,
mourning a lord far-famed and beloved.
On a height they kindled the hugest of all
funeral fires; fumes of woodsmoke
billowed darkly up, the blaze roared   3145
and drowned out their weeping, wind died down
and flames wrought havoc in the hot bone-house,
burning it to the core. They were disconsolate
and wailed aloud for their lord's decease.
A Geat woman too sang out in grief;   3150
with hair bound up, she unburdened herself
of her worst fears, a wild litany
of nightmare and lament: her nation invaded,
enemies on the rampage, bodies in piles,
slavery and abasement. Heaven swallowed the smoke.   3155

Then the Geat people began to construct
a mound on a headland, high and imposing,
a marker that sailors could see from far away,
and in ten days they had done the work.
It was their hero's memorial; what remained from the fire   3160
they housed inside it, behind a wall
as worthy of him as their workmanship could make it.
And they buried torques in the barrow, and jewels
and a trove of such things as trespassing men
had once dared to drag from the hoard.   3165
They let the ground keep that ancestral treasure,
gold under gravel, gone to earth,
as useless to men now as it ever was.
Then twelve warriors rode around the tomb,
chieftains' sons, champions in battle,   3170
all of them distraught, chanting in dirges,
mourning his loss as a man and a king.
They extolled his heroic nature and exploits
and gave thanks for his greatness; which was the proper thing,
for a man should praise a prince whom he holds dear   3175
and cherish his memory when that moment comes
when he has to be convoyed from his bodily home.
So the Geat people, his hearth-companions,
sorrowed for the lord who had been laid low.
They said that of all the kings upon earth   3180
he was the man most gracious and fair-minded,
kindest to his people and keenest to win fame.

THE SONG OF ROLAND
ca. 1100

The Song of Roland is the foundation of the French literary tradition. One of the earliest poems written in French, it describes the process by which France left behind its Germanic past as a loose confederation of powerful families and accepted its future as a Christian nation united by loyalties to king and country. This story is told as a clash of powerful personalities who are together engaged in a holy war against the Muslims in Spain. The central protagonist is the great warrior Roland, who embodies in a pure form the spirit of feudal loyalty to one's overlord. The emperor Charlemagne is the object of this loyalty, but his commitments are split: he owes to Roland a reciprocal loyalty, but he is also the head of the Holy Roman Empire, the institutional heir to classical Rome that is endowed with the mission not merely to defend but to expand Christendom. Opposed to Roland is his stepfather Ganelon, a member of Charlemagne's Frankish nobility who believes he can pursue a feud with Roland without compromising his loyalty to the king. And surrounding these three main characters are men who provide further perspectives on the central issue of what kind of loyalty is valid. Oliver, Roland's closest companion in arms, criticizes Roland's narrow conception of his duty; Turpin, a warrior archbishop, provides justifications for Roland's actions that may be merely rationalizations; Pinabel, one of Ganelon's kinsmen, comes to his defense when he is charged with treason for his part in Roland's death; and Tierri, a warrior, challenges Pinabel not merely to defend Roland or even Charlemagne but to promote national and supranational loyalties that transcend Ganelon's tribal conception.

Many modern readers have been tempted to read the poem as a kind of medieval *Iliad*, with the heroic yet arrogantly intransigent Roland as a French Achilles. Yet in the manuscript the poem is untitled, Roland dies less than two-thirds of the way through, and the beginning and ending of the poem focus on "Charles the King, our Emperor, the Great." The poem could with equal justice be entitled—as indeed it was in some of its medieval versions—*The Song of Charlemagne*. In fact, the relation of Roland's story to Charles's—the relation, that is, of the heroic acts of one man to the historically transcendent mission of establishing a universal Christian empire— is the poem's overriding theme. Roland embodies the unswerving and reciprocal allegiance that bound together lord and vassal into a stable unit, a relationship that made possible the establishment of the feudal system that, from the tenth through twelfth centuries, came to dominate Europe. From his first appearance in the poem, at the council scene in which the Franks debate whether to accept the offer of the Saracen leader Marsilion to submit to Charles if the Franks will leave Spain, Roland both promotes and himself displays this fidelity. He argues against accepting the offer for three reasons, all of them having to do with loyalty. First, Marsilion has already been proven untrustworthy in fulfilling his sworn oath; second, Basan and Basile, the ambassadors whom Marsilion killed during the previous negotiations, must be avenged (they were, Roland reminds Charles, "*your* men"); and third, Charles must also be true to his commitment to conquer Spain ("Fight the war you came to fight!"), an obligation he owes to God, who has sanctioned this Holy War. Again, the poem's climactic scene, in which the members of the rear guard are ambushed and Roland refuses to blow his horn to call back the army to help them, has often been read as expressing Roland's intemperate and unjustified reliance upon his own prowess. Yet another interpretation, centered on loyalty, is also possible. As the leader of the rear guard, Roland has sworn to protect the army: to call it back now, in the face of overwhelming enemy forces, would be to place it in danger and to betray his commitment. Indeed, when he accepted this dangerous assignment—dangerous because everyone, including Roland, suspected that Ganelon had conspired with the Saracens to set a trap—he promised Charles not victory over any Saracen attack but rather that he would not lose any part of his baggage train "that has not first been bought and paid for with swords." In other words, Roland swore an oath to fight to the utmost to protect the army, and this he must now do. At this point in the poem he explicitly describes the values that guide his life:

> We know our duty: to stand here for our King.
> A man must bear some hardships for his lord,
> stand everything, the great heat, the great cold,
> lose the hide and hair on him for his good lord.
> Now let each man make sure to strike hard here:
> let them not sing a bad song about us!

Certainly Roland is concerned with personal honor, but this depends above all not on valor but on loyalty: he fights not for himself but "for his good lord." Surprisingly, however, when it is clear that the Saracens have been defeated at the cost of the whole of the rear guard, Roland does blow the horn. Is this an admission that he was wrong before, as his companion Oliver implies? Perhaps; yet Turpin says that Roland should blow the horn to summon Charles so that he may, as is required of a good lord, avenge the deaths of the men who died for him. Moreover, it is this final act of feudal loyalty, and not the wounds inflicted by the Saracens, that kills Roland: the force of the horn blast bursts his temples. As the battle nears its end the poet describes

Roland as "a brave man keeping faith," and the religious imagery with which his passing is surrounded makes it clear that, whatever the modern reader may think, the poet wants his audience to approve of Roland's choices. Yet we also cannot forget that Roland has said that his companions died "for me," which could mean simply that they performed their feudal duty to him but could also mean that they died "because of me."

If loyalty is the theme of the poem, it is analyzed rather than simply celebrated. The poem provides three other perspectives from which to make an assessment. One is provided by Oliver. In a famous line, we are told that "Roland is good [*proz*], and Oliver is wise [*sages*]." It is not easy to know exactly what the poet means by these terms. Is Roland primarily a fighter, a man of prowess, while Oliver is a strategist, a man of thought? While the poem is unwilling to criticize Roland's decisions about the horn, it also presents Oliver as capable of a larger, more pragmatic view than his companion. As Oliver urges him to look at the surrounding pagan hordes, Roland gazes instead at his sword, Durendal; as Oliver argues for Charles's need for the twelve peers and the warriors of the rear guard, Roland focuses only on the immediate challenge posed by the Saracen ambush. Roland's intensity and narrow commitment may be necessary for the functioning of the feudal system, but the poet also wants us to know that it is bought at a fearful price, that there are other ways of understanding one's duty.

The same could be said of Ganelon. He is no petty traitor: as the poet says of him at his trial, he would have been "a great man, had he been loyal." His behavior as an ambassador at Marsilion's camp is both shrewd and courageous. In order to accomplish Roland's downfall he must first provoke the now peacefully inclined Marsilion to wrath and then turn his anger against Roland. To this end he takes a calculated risk for the sake of a calculated—but far from guaranteed—result. Insulting Marsilion deliberately, in the name of the emperor, he makes himself the first target of the Saracen king's fury and certainly endangers his own life. Luckily for him, the king's hand is stayed, and the Saracens applaud Ganelon's magnificent courage. We are never told, however, why this otherwise admirable man so loathes Roland that he betrays both his companions and his lord—and himself—in order to bring about his death. Ganelon is Roland's stepfather, and the poet may have known of the legend that made Roland the offspring of an incestuous relationship between Charlemagne and his sister and thus (as with Arthur and Mordred) both his nephew and his son. But nothing is made of these family relationships, and we are probably on firmer ground to think that Ganelon simply cannot bear Roland's utter self-confidence in his own virtue and prowess. The story—perhaps true, perhaps not—that he tells the Saracen Blancandrin of Roland's plundering expedition, and of his haughty offer to Charles of a bright red apple as a sign that he can deliver to him "the crowns of all earth's kings," is a more reliable indicator of Ganelon's hatred than of Roland's character. At his trial Ganelon claims that his betrayal of the rear guard was justified by his formal defiance of Roland: this was a private matter, a feud, and no business of Charles's. But we get no sense that this argument carries much weight with either the Franks or the poet. The reluctance of Charles's council to punish Ganelon comes not from sympathy with his self-justification but from fear of his champion Pinabel. The danger Ganelon presents, then, is that he will return the Franks to a world of private vengeance where might makes right and where the larger interests of the community can be sacrificed to the impulses of its individual members. If Oliver sees the largest view, Ganelon sees the narrowest.

The final perspective we are offered is Charles's. He is in some ways the most complex character in the poem. On the one hand, he is the great Christian emperor, the agent of God in bringing about the unification of the world under the cross. As Roland lies dying, he recites a list of the lands he has brought under Charles's rule—a list that includes not just France but most of Europe, exceeding the boundaries of even the huge empire ruled over by the historical Charlemagne (742–814). This idea of a single Christendom under a divinely authorized emperor was one of the persistent dreams of medieval Christians. It was part of the justification for the crusades, and we will meet it again in Dante's *Divine Comedy*. It also contributed to the incapacity of most medieval Christians to recognize cultural differences as anything other than either threatening or contemptible, an affront to the cultural unity that God desired. In this poem Islamic religion and culture are presented in a degrading travesty: the Saracens are shown as idolaters and worshipers of Muhammad and Apollo, when in fact Islam rejects religious images, regards Muhammad as a prophet, not a god, and is monotheistic. (This ill-informed picture was produced, ironically, at the very time that Christian scholars were beginning to benefit from contact with their far more sophisticated Arab contemporaries, who had direct access to Greek texts, especially those of Aristotle, that were lost to the Latin West.) In any case, the fullest expression of Charles's role as God's agent in spreading Christian rule comes in the battle against Marsilion's overlord Baligant. Omitted in this selection, this battle is presented as an apocalyptic confrontation between good and evil, and Charles's victory is capped by the conversion of Marsilion's queen Bramimonde and her renaming as Juliana.

Yet Charles is also a human being, in some ways the most human in the poem. He is the only character whose inner life is made visible to us, partly in his dreams, partly in the single, sad line he speaks when informed by the angel Gabriel that further campaigns await him: " 'God!' said the King, 'the pains, the labors of my life!' " Charles embodies the weariness that made the Franks vulnerable to Marsilion's and Ganelon's deceptions at the outset, and that led them to want to avoid confronting Ganelon and Pinabel at the end. This is a weariness that is utterly foreign to Roland, a fatigue he seems not even to notice much less sympathize with. That the poet allows it so much room in his poem, while acknowledging that it must not be allowed to prevail, is testimony to the breadth of his own sympathies.

The Song of Roland derives ultimately from a historical event. In the year 778 the thirty-six-year-old Charles, then king of the Franks (he did not become the emperor Charlemagne until 800), entered Spain at the request of an Arabic ruler in revolt against his overlord. But Charles's self-interested intervention in this Muslim civil war went awry, and by the end of July he had decided to return to France. On August 15, as the army made its way through the narrow valleys of the Pyrenees, the rear guard protecting its retreat was annihilated in an ambush set by the native Basques. Among those killed was one Hruodlandus, governor of the marches (or borders) of Brittany. About 350 years later, between 1125 and 1150, someone wrote out the manuscript that contains the poem that we now call *The Song of Roland*. This manuscript was written in the French spoken at the time in England, a dialect known as Anglo-Norman, but the poem itself was composed in continental French around the year 1100. This date fits well with two contemporary conditions. One is the struggle then under way between the French king Philip I and the powerful barons who were technically subordinate to him but controlled much of what now constitutes France—a struggle that finds a parallel in the poem in the confrontation between Charles and Ganelon. The other is the growing interest in crusading. Throughout the eleventh century French knights fought against the Arab rulers of Spain, and in 1095 Pope Urban urged the nobility of Europe, and especially of France, to direct their martial energies away from their internal wrangling and toward the Holy Land, at the time governed by Muslim "infidels" (although governed in fact in a spirit of religious tolerance). The result was the First Crusade, which succeeded in capturing Jerusalem in 1099, in massacring most of the non-Christian population, and in establishing the French-controlled Kingdom of Jerusalem. *The Song of Roland* is steeped in this crusading spirit: as Roland says, and as the poem continually insists, "Pagans are wrong and Christians are right!"

Although there have been a number of theories, no one really knows how—or why—the story of the ill-fated Hruodlandus survived. It was a traditional story by at least the eleventh century: one later medieval chronicler even tells us that a minstrel called Taillefer sang about Roland to the Norman army of William the Conqueror before the battle of Hastings in 1066. The poem shows unmistakable signs of having emerged from a period of oral composition. As in the Homeric poems and *Beowulf,* many of its phrases are metrical formulas originally combined by an oral poet into complete lines and then larger passages as he re-created the poem anew at each performance (for a fuller account of oral composition, see above, pp. 100–1). As testimony to its oral prehistory, the vocabulary of the whole of *The Song of Roland* comprises only some eighteen hundred words. In its written form the poem is comprised of 291 stanzas, or *laisses* (from the Latin *lectio,* or "reading"); the number of lines in each *laisse* varies widely, but it averages about fourteen. Each line contains ten or eleven syllables, with a strong caesura, or break, in the middle; the lines are then linked by assonance, which means that their final stressed vowels are identical (the final words of lines 1240–42, for example, are *vil, guarit,* and *murir,* the *i* being pronounced the same in each case). Even when written, the poem was almost certainly presented orally by a minstrel, or *jongleur* (like Taillefer), who would accompany himself with a simple stringed instrument. Like *Beowulf,* the poem would be chanted rather than sung, producing an effect of cadenced, ritualistic ceremony. This effect was doubtless enhanced by the so-called *laisses similaires,* groups of *laisses* that repeat, with variations, an especially significant scene or act (see, for example, lines 1049–92). These groups of *laisses* endow such moments with a powerful sense of solemnity and consequence.

PRONOUNCING GLOSSARY

The following list uses common English syllables to provide rough equivalents of selected words whose pronunciation may be unfamiliar to the general reader.

Aquitaine: *ah-kee-ten*
Blancandrin: *blanh-cahn-drinh*
Durendal: *dur-ahn-dahl*
Gerer: *zhehr-air*
Gerin: *zhehr-anh'*
Halteclere: *ahl-te-clehr'*
Haltille: *ahl-tee*
Malduit: *mahl-dwee*

Marsilion: *mahr-see-lyonh'*
Munjoie: *munh-zhwah*
Ogier: *oh-zhyay*
Rencesvals: *ren-ses-vahls*
Roland: *roh-lanh*
Rousillon: *roo-see-yonh*
Veillantif: *ve-yanh-teef*

From The Song of Roland[1]

1

Charles the King, our Emperor, the Great,
has been in Spain for seven full years,
has conquered the high land down to the sea.
There is no castle that stands against him now,
no wall, no citadel left to break down—
except Saragossa, high on a mountain.[2]
King Marsilion holds it, who does not love God,

5

---

1. Translated by Frederick Goldin. Many of Goldin's notes have been adapted for use here. 2. Saragossa, in northeastern Spain, is not actually on a mountaintop. The poet's geography is not always accurate.

who serves Mahumet and prays to Apollin.[3]
He cannot save himself: his ruin will find him there. AOI.[4]

2

King Marsilion was in Saragossa.   10
He has gone forth into a grove, beneath its shade,
and he lies down on a block of blue marble,
twenty thousand men, and more, all around him.
He calls aloud to his dukes and his counts:
"Listen, my lords, to the troubles we have.   15
The Emperor Charles of the sweet land of France
has come into this country to destroy us.
I have no army able to give him battle,
I do not have the force to break his force.
Now act like my wise men: give me counsel,   20
save me, save me from death, save me from shame!"
No pagan there has one word to say to him
except Blancandrin, of the castle of Valfunde.

3

One of the wisest pagans was Blancandrin,
brave and loyal, a great mounted warrior,   25
a useful man, the man to aid his lord;
said to the King: "Do not give way to panic.
Do this: send Charles, that wild, terrible man,
tokens of loyal service and great friendship:
you will give him bears and lions and dogs,   30
seven hundred camels, a thousand molted hawks,
four hundred mules weighed down with gold and silver,
and fifty carts, to cart it all away:
he'll have good wages for his men who fight for pay.
Say he's made war long enough in this land: 35
let him go home, to France, to Aix, at last—
come Michaelmas[5] you will follow him there,
say you will take their faith, become a Christian,
and be his man with honor, with all you have.
If he wants hostages, why, you'll send them,   40
ten, or twenty, to give him security.
Let us send him the sons our wives have borne.
I'll send my son with all the others named to die.
It is better that they should lose their heads[6]
than that we, Lord, should lose our dignity   45
and our honors—and be turned into beggars!" AOI.

---

3. The Greek god Apollo; but the poet is mistaken, for these people worship only one god, Allah. *Mahumet*: Muhammad, founder of the Islamic religion. 4. These three mysterious letters appear at certain moments throughout the text, 180 times in all. No one has ever adequately explained them, though every reader feels their effect. 5. The feast of St. Michael, September 29. *Aix*: Aix-la-Chapelle, or Aachen, was the capital of Charlemagne's empire. 6. The speaker expects that the hostages will be killed by the French when the deception becomes clear. Sometime before, hostages sent by the French had been similarly slain (see lines 207–209).

4

Said Blancandrin: "By this right hand of mine
and by this beard that flutters on my chest,
you will soon see the French army disband,
the Franks will go to their own land, to France.
When each of them is in his dearest home,   50
King Charles will be in Aix, in his chapel.
At Michaelmas he will hold a great feast—
that day will come, and then our time runs out,
he'll hear no news, he'll get no word from us.   55
This King is wild, the heart in him is cruel:
he'll take the heads of the hostages we gave.
It is better, Lord, that they lose their heads
than that we lose our bright, our beautiful Spain—
and nothing more for us but misery and pain!"   60
The pagans say: "It may be as he says."

5

King Marsilion brought his counsel to end,
then he summoned Clarin of Balaguét,
Estramarin and Eudropin, his peer,
And Priamun, Guarlan, that bearded one,   65
and Machiner and his uncle Maheu,
and Joüner, Malbien from over-sea,
and Blancandrin, to tell what was proposed.
From the worst of criminals he called these ten.
"Barons, my lords, you're to go to Charlemagne;   70
he's at the siege of Cordres,[7] the citadel.
Olive branches are to be in your hands—
that signifies peace and humility.
If you've the skill to get me an agreement,
I will give you a mass of gold and silver   75
and lands and fiefs, as much as you could want."
Say the pagans: "We'll benefit from this!" AOI.

6

Marsilion brought his council to an end,
said to his men: "Lords, you will go on now,
and remember: olive branches in your hands;   80
and in my name tell Charlemagne the King
for his god's sake to have pity on me—
he will not see a month from this day pass
before I come with a thousand faithful;
say I will take that Christian religion   85
and be his man in love and loyalty.
If he wants hostages, why, he'll have them."
Said Blancandrin: "Now you will get good terms." AOI.

7. Córdoba, in southern Spain, at that time part of the Muslim empire.

7

King Marsilion had ten white mules led out,
sent to him once by the King of Suatilie,[8]   90
with golden bits and saddles wrought with silver.
The men are mounted, the men who brought the message,
and in their hands they carry olive branches.
They came to Charles, who has France in his keeping.
He cannot prevent it: they will fool him. AOI.   95

8

The Emperor is secure and jubilant:
he has taken Cordres, broken the walls,
knocked down the towers with his catapults.
And what tremendous spoils his knights have won—
gold and silver, precious arms, equipment.   100
In the city not one pagan remained
who is not killed or turned into a Christian.
The Emperor is in an ample grove,
Roland and Oliver are with him there,
Samson the Duke and Ansëis the fierce,   105
Geoffrey d'Anjou, the King's own standard-bearer;
and Gerin and Gerer, these two together always,
and the others, the simple knights, in force:
fifteen thousand from the sweet land of France.
The warriors sit on bright brocaded silk;   110
they are playing at tables to pass the time,
the old and the wisest men sitting at chess,
the young light-footed men fencing with swords.
Beneath a pine, beside a wild sweet-briar,
there was a throne, every inch of pure gold.   115
There sits the King, who rules over sweet France.
His beard is white, his hair flowering white.
That lordly body! the proud fierce look of him!—
If someone should come here asking for him,
     there'd be no need to point out the King of France.
The messengers dismounted, and on their feet   120
they greeted him in all love and good faith.

9

Blancandrin spoke, he was the first to speak,
said to the King: "Greetings, and God save you,
that glorious God whom we all must adore.
Here is the word of the great king Marsilion: 125
he has looked into this law of salvation,
wants to give you a great part of his wealth,
bears and lions and hunting dogs on chains,
seven hundred camels, a thousand molted hawks,
four hundred mules packed tight with gold and silver,   130

---

8. A subordinate king, owing allegiance to Marsilion.

and fifty carts, to cart it all away;
and there will be so many fine gold bezants,[9]
you'll have good wages for the men in your pay.
You have stayed long—long enough!—in this land,
it is time to go home, to France, to Aix.   135
My master swears he will follow you there."
The Emperor holds out his hands toward God,
bows down his head, begins to meditate. AOI.

10

The Emperor held his head bowed down;
never was he too hasty with his words: 140
his custom is to speak in his good time.
When his head rises, how fierce the look of him;
he said to them: "You have spoken quite well.
King Marsilion is my great enemy.
Now all these words that you have spoken here—   145
how far can I trust them? How can I be sure?"
The Saracen: "He wants to give you hostages.
How many will you want? ten? fifteen? twenty?
I'll put my son with the others named to die.[1]
You will get some, I think, still better born.   150
When you are at home in your high royal palace,
at the great feast of Saint Michael-in-Peril,[2]
the lord who nurtures me will follow you,
and in those baths[3]—the baths God made for you—
my lord will come and want to be made Christian."   155
King Charles replies: "He may yet save his soul." AOI.

11

Late in the day it was fair, the sun was bright.
Charles has them put the ten mules into stables.
The King commands a tent pitched in the broad grove,
and there he has the ten messengers lodged;   160
twelve serving men took splendid care of them.
There they remained that night till the bright day.
The Emperor rose early in the morning,
the King of France, and heard the mass and matins.
And then the King went forth beneath a pine,   165
calls for his barons to complete his council:
he will proceed only with the men of France. AOI.

12

The Emperor goes forth beneath a pine,
calls for his barons to complete his council:

9. Gold coins; the name is derived from Byzantium.   1. I.e., if the promise is broken. *Saracen:* the usual
term for the enemy.   2. The epithet *in peril of the sea* was applied to the famous sanctuary Mont-St.-
Michel off the Normandy coast because it could be reached on foot only at low tide, and pilgrims were
endangered by the incoming tide. Eventually, the phrase was applied to the saint himself.   3. Famous
healing springs at Aix-la-Chapelle.

Ogier the Duke, and Archbishop Turpin,   170
Richard the Old, and his nephew Henri;
from Gascony, the brave Count Acelin,
Thibaut of Reims, and his cousin Milun;
and Gerer and Gerin, they were both there,
and there was Count Roland, he came with them,   175
and Oliver, the valiant and well-born;
a thousand Franks of France, and more, were there.
Ganelon came, who committed the treason.
Now here begins the council that went wrong.[4] AOI.

13

"Barons, my lords," said Charles the Emperor,   180
"King Marsilion has sent me messengers,
wants to give me a great mass of his wealth,
bears and lions and hunting dogs on chains,
seven hundred camels, a thousand molting hawks,
four hundred mules packed with gold of Araby,   185
and with all that, more than fifty great carts;
but also asks that I go back to France:
he'll follow me to Aix, my residence,
and take our faith, the one redeeming faith,
become a Christian, hold his march[5] lands from me.   190
But what lies in his heart? I do not know."
And the French say: "We must be on our guard!" AOI.

14

The Emperor has told them what was proposed.
Roland the Count will never assent to that,
gets to his feet, comes forth to speak against it;   195
says to the King: "Trust Marsilion—and suffer!
We came to Spain seven long years ago,
I won Noples for you, I won Commibles,
I took Valterne and all the land of Pine,
and Balaguer and Tudela and Seville.   200
And then this king, Marsilion, played the traitor:
he sent you men, fifteen of his pagans—
and sure enough, each held an olive branch;
and they recited just these same words to you.
You took counsel with all your men of France;   205
they counseled you to a bit of madness:
you sent two Counts across to the Pagans,
one was Basan, the other was Basile.
On the hills below Haltille, he took their heads.
They were your men. Fight the war you came to fight!   210
Lead the army you summoned on to Saragossa!

4. The poet anticipates that the plan adopted at the council will prove to be a mistake and that Ganelon
will commit treason.   5. A frontier province or territory.

Lay siege to it all the rest of your life!
Avenge the men that this criminal murdered!" AOI.

15

The Emperor held his head bowed down with this,
and stroked his beard, and smoothed his mustache down,   215
and speaks no word, good or bad, to his nephew.
The French keep still, all except Ganelon:
he gets to his feet and, come before King Charles,
how fierce he is as he begins his speech;
said to the King: "Believe a fool—me or   220
another—and suffer! Protect your interest!
When Marsilion the King sends you his word
that he will join his hands[6] and be your man,
and hold all Spain as a gift from your hands
and then receive the faith that we uphold—   225
whoever urges that we refuse this peace,
that man does not care, Lord, what death we die.
That wild man's counsel must not win the day here—
let us leave fools, let us hold with wise men!" AOI.

16

And after that there came Naimon the Duke—   230
no greater vassal in that court than Naimon—
said to the King: "You've heard it clearly now,
Count Ganelon has given you your answer:
let it be heeded, there is wisdom in it.
King Marsilion is beaten in this war,   235
you have taken every one of his castles,
broken his walls with your catapults,
burnt his cities and defeated his men.
Now when he sends to ask you to have mercy,
it would be a sin to do still more to him.   240
Since he'll give you hostages as guarantee,
this great war must not go on, it is not right."
And the French say: "The Duke has spoken well." AOI.

17

"Barons, my lords, whom shall we send down there,
to Saragossa, to King Marsilion?"   245
Naimon replies, "I'll go, if you grant it!
At once, my lord! give me the glove and the staff."[7]
The King replies: "You're a man of great wisdom:
now by my beard, now by this mustache of mine,
you will not go so far from me this year; or ever.   250
Go take your seat when no one calls on you."

---

6. Part of the gesture of homage; the lord enclosed the joined hands of his vassal with his own.   7. Symbols of his commission from the emperor Charles.

18

"Barons, my lords, whom can we send down there,
to this Saracen who holds Saragossa?"
Roland replies: "I can go there! No trouble!"
"No, no, not you!" said Oliver the Count,   255
"that heart in you is wild, spoils for a fight,
how I would worry—you'd fight with them, I know.
Now I myself could go, if the King wishes."
The King replies: "Be still, the two of you!
Not you, not he—neither will set foot there.   260
Now by this beard, as sure as you see white,
let no man here name one of the Twelve Peers!"
The French keep still, see how he silenced them.

19

Turpin of Reims has come forth from the ranks,
said to the King: "Let your Franks have a rest.   265
You have been in this land for seven years,
the many pains, the struggles they've endured!
I'm the one, Lord, give me the glove and the staff,
and I'll go down to this Saracen of Spain
and then I'll see what kind of man we have."   270
The Emperor replies to him in anger:
"Now you go back and sit on that white silk
and say no more unless I command it!" AOI.

20

"My noble knights," said the Emperor Charles,
"choose me one man: a baron from my march,[8]   275
to bring my message to King Marsilion."
And Roland said: "Ganelon, my stepfather."
The French respond: "Why, that's the very man!
pass this man by and you won't send a wiser."
And hearing this Count Ganelon began to choke,   280
pulls from his neck the great furs of marten
and stands there now, in his silken tunic,
eyes full of lights, the look on him of fury,
he has the body, the great chest of a lord;
stood there so fair, all his peers gazed on him;   285
said to Roland: "Madman, what makes you rave?
Every man knows I am your stepfather,
yet you named me to go to Marsilion.
Now if God grants that I come back from there,
you will have trouble: I'll start a feud with you,   290
it will go on till the end of your life."
Roland replies: "What wild words—all that blustering!

---

8. Charlemagne wants them to choose a baron from an outlying region and not one of the Twelve Peers, the circle of his dearest men.

Every man knows that threats don't worry me.
But we need a wise man to bring the message:
if the King wills, I'll gladly go in your place."   295

21

Ganelon answers: "You will not go for me. AOI.
You're not my man, and I am not your lord.
Charles commands me to perform this service:
I'll go to Marsilion in Saragossa.
And I tell you, I'll play a few wild tricks   300
before I cool the anger in me now."
When he heard that, Roland began to laugh. AOI.

22

Ganelon sees: *Roland laughing at him!*
and feels such pain he almost bursts with rage,
needs little more to go out of his mind;   305
says to the Count: "I have no love for you,
you *made* this choice fall on me, and that was wrong.
Just Emperor, here I am, before you.
I have one will: to fulfill your command."

23

"I know now I must go to Saragossa. AOI.   310
Any man who goes there cannot return.
And there is this: I am your sister's husband,
have a son by her, the finest boy there can be,
Baldewin," says he, "who will be a good man.
To him I leave my honors, fiefs, and lands.   315
Protect my son: these eyes will never see him."
Charles answers him: "That tender heart of yours!
You have to go, I have commanded it."

24

And the King said: "Ganelon, come forward, AOI.
come and receive the staff and the glove.   320
You have heard it: the Franks have chosen you."
Said Ganelon: "Lord, it's Roland who did this.
In all my days I'll have no love for him,
or Oliver, because he's his companion,
or the Twelve Peers, because they love him so.   325
I defy them, here in your presence, Lord."
And the King said: "What hate there is in you!
You will go there, for I command you to."
"I can go there, but I'll have no protector. AOI.
Basile had none, nor did Basan his brother."   330

25

The Emperor offers him his right glove.
But Ganelon would have liked not to be there.
When he had to take it, it fell to the ground.
"God!" say the French, "What's that going to mean?
What disaster will this message bring us!"   335
Said Ganelon: "Lords, you'll be hearing news."

26

Said Ganelon: "Lord, give me leave to go,
since go I must, there's no reason to linger."
And the King said: "In Jesus' name and mine,"
absolved him and blessed him with his right hand.   340
Then he gave him the letter and the staff.

27

Count Ganelon goes away to his camp.
He chooses, with great care, his battle-gear,
picks the most precious arms that he can find.
The spurs he fastened on were golden spurs;   345
he girds his sword, Murgleis, upon his side;
he has mounted Tachebrun, his battle horse,
his uncle, Guinemer, held the stirrup.
And there you would have seen brave men in tears,
his men, who say: "Baron, what bad luck for you!   350
All your long years in the court of the King,
always proclaimed a great and noble vassal!
Whoever it was doomed you to go down there—
Charlemagne himself will not protect that man.
Roland the Count should not have thought of this—   355
and you the living issue of a mighty line!"
And then they say: "Lord, take us there with you!"
Ganelon answers: "May the Lord God forbid!
It is better that I alone should die
      than so many good men and noble knights.
You will be going back, Lords, to sweet France: 360
go to my wife and greet her in my name,
and Pinabel, my dear friend and peer,
and Baldewin, my son, whom you all know:
give him your aid, and hold him as your lord."
And he starts down the road; he is on his way. AOI.   365

28

Ganelon rides to a tall olive tree,
there he has joined the pagan messengers.
And here is Blancandrin, who slows down for him:
and what great art they speak to one another.

Said Blancandrin: "An amazing man, Charles! 370
conquered Apulia, conquered all of Calabria,
crossed the salt sea on his way into England,
won its tribute,[9] got Peter's pence[1] for Rome:
what does he want from us here in our march?"
Ganelon answers: "That is the heart in him. 375
There'll never be a man the like of him." AOI.

29

Said Blancandrin: "The Franks are a great people.
Now what great harm all those dukes and counts do
to their own lord when they give him such counsel:
they torment him, they'll destroy him, and others." 380
Ganelon answers: "Well, now, I know no such man
except Roland, who'll suffer for it yet.
One day the Emperor was sitting in the shade:
his nephew came, still wearing his hauberk,
he had gone plundering near Carcassonne; 385
and in his hand he held a bright red apple:
'Dear Lord, here, take,' said Roland to his uncle;
'I offer you the crowns of all earth's kings.'
Yes, Lord, that pride of his will destroy him,
for every day he goes riding at death. 390
And *should* someone kill him, we would have peace." AOI.

30

Said Blancandrin: "A wild man, this Roland!
wants to make every nation beg for his mercy
and claims a right to every land on earth!
But what men support him, if that is his aim?" 395
Ganelon answers: "Why, Lord, the men of France.
They love him so, they will never fail him.
He gives them gifts, masses of gold and silver,
mules, battle horses, brocaded silks, supplies.
And it is all as the Emperor desires: 400
he'll win the lands from here to the Orient." AOI.

31

Ganelon and Blancandrin rode on until
each pledged his faith to the other and swore
they'd find a way to have Count Roland killed.
They rode along the paths and ways until, 405
in Saragossa, they dismount beneath a yew.
There was a throne in the shade of a pine,
covered with silk from Alexandria.

---

9. Although begun perhaps as early as the eighth century, the tribute was not the result of any effort of
Charlemagne, who did not in fact visit England. **1.** A tribute of one penny per house "for the use of
Saint Peter," i.e., for the pope in Rome.

There sat the king who held the land of Spain,
and around him twenty thousand Saracens.   410
There is no man who speaks or breathes a word,
poised for the news that all would like to hear.
Now here they are: Ganelon and Blancandrin.

32

Blancandrin came before Marsilion,
his hand around the fist of Ganelon,   415
said to the King: "May Mahumet save you,
and Apollin, whose sacred laws we keep!
We delivered your message to Charlemagne:
when we finished, he raised up both his hands
and praised his god. He made no other answer.   420
Here he sends you one of his noble barons,
a man of France, and very powerful.
You'll learn from him whether or not you'll have peace."
"Let him speak, we shall hear him," Marsilion answers. AOI.

33

But Ganelon had it all well thought out.   425
With what great art he commences his speech,
a man who knows his way about these things;
said to the King: "May the Lord God save you,
that glorious God, whom we must all adore.
Here is the word of Charlemagne the King: 430
you are to take the holy Christian faith;
he will give you one half of Spain in fief.
If you refuse, if you reject this peace,
you will be taken by force, put into chains,
and then led forth to the King's seat at Aix;   435
you will be tried; you will be put to death:
you will die there, in shame, vilely, degraded."
King Marsilion, hearing this, was much shaken.
In his hand was a spear, with golden feathers.
He would have struck, had they not held him back. AOI.   440

34

Marsilion the King—his color changed!
He shook his spear, waved the shaft to and fro.
When he saw that, Ganelon laid hand to sword,
he drew it out two fingers from its sheath;
and spoke to it: "How beautiful and bright!   445
How long did I bear you in the King's court
before I died! The Emperor will not say
I died alone in that foreign country:
they'll buy you first, with the best men they have!"
The pagans say: "Let us break up this quarrel!"   450

35

The pagan chiefs pleaded with Marsilion
till he sat down once again on his throne.
The Caliph² spoke: "You did us harm just now,
served us badly, trying to strike this Frenchman.
You should have listened, you should have heard him out."   455
Said Ganelon: "Lord, I must endure it.
I shall not fail, for all the gold God made,
for all the wealth there may be in this land,
to tell him, as long as I have breath, all
that Charlemagne—that great and mighty King!—   460
has sent through me to his mortal enemy."
He is buckled in a great cloak of sable,
covered with silk from Alexandria:
he throws it down. Blancandrin picks it up.
But his great sword he will never throw down!   465
In his right fist he grasps its golden pommel.
Say the pagans: "That's a great man! A noble!" AOI.

36

Now Ganelon drew closer to the King
and said to him: "You are wrong to get angry,
for Charles, who rules all France, sends you this word: 470
you are to take the Christian people's faith;
he will give you one half of Spain in fief,
the other half goes to his nephew: Roland—
quite a partner you will be getting there!
If you refuse, if you reject this peace,   475
he will come and lay siege to Saragossa;
you will be taken by force, put into chains,
and brought straight on to Aix, the capital.
No saddle horse, no war horse for you then,
no he-mule, no she-mule for you to ride: 480
you will be thrown on some miserable dray;
you will be tried, and you will lose your head.
Our Emperor sends you this letter."
He put the letter in the pagan's right fist.

37

Marsilion turned white; he was enraged;   485
he breaks the seal, he's knocked away the wax,
runs through the letter, sees what is written there:
"Charles sends me word, this king who rules in France:
I'm to think of his anger and his grief—
he means Basan and his brother Basile,   490
I took their heads in the hills below Haltille;
if I want to redeem the life of my body,

---

2. A high official of King Marsilion.

I must send him my uncle: the Algalife.[3]
And otherwise he'll have no love for me."
Then his son came and spoke to Marsilion,   495
said to the King: "Ganelon has spoken madness.
He crossed the line, he has no right to live.
Give him to me, I will do justice on him."
When he heard that, Ganelon brandished his sword;
he runs to the pine, set his back against the trunk.   500

38

King Marsilion went forth into the orchard,
he takes with him the greatest of his men;
Blancandrin came, that gray-haired counselor,
and Jurfaleu, Marsilion's son and heir,
the Algalife, uncle and faithful friend.   505
Said Blancandrin: "Lord, call the Frenchman back.
He swore to me to keep faith with our cause."
And the King said: "Go, bring him back here, then."
He took Ganelon's right hand by the fingers,
leads him into the orchard before the King.   510
And there they plotted that criminal treason. AOI.

39

Said Marsilion: "My dear Lord Ganelon,
that was foolish, what I just did to you,
I showed my anger, even tried to strike you.
Here's a pledge of good faith, these sable furs,   515
the gold alone worth over five hundred pounds:
I'll make it all up before tomorrow night."
Ganelon answers: "I will not refuse it.
May it please God to reward you for it." AOI.

40

Said Marsilion: "I tell you, Ganelon,   520
I have a great desire to love you dearly.
I want to hear you speak of Charlemagne.
He is so old, he's used up all his time—
from what I hear, he is past two hundred!
He has pushed his old body through so many lands,   525
taken so many blows on his buckled shield,
made beggars of so many mighty kings:
when will he lose the heart for making war?"
Ganelon answers: "Charles is not one to lose heart.
No man sees him, no man learns to know him   530
who does not say: the Emperor is great.
I do not know how to praise him so highly
that his great merit would not surpass my praise.

3. The Caliph.

Who could recount his glory and his valor?
God put the light in him of such lordliness,   535
he would choose death before he failed his barons."

41

Said the pagan: "I have reason to marvel
at Charlemagne, a man so old and gray—
he's two hundred years old, I hear, and more;
he has tortured his body through so many lands,   540
and borne so many blows from lance and spear,
made beggars of so many mighty kings:
when will he lose the heart for making war?"
"Never," said Ganelon, "while his nephew lives,
he's a fighter, there's no vassal like him   545
     under the vault of heaven. And he has friends.
There's Oliver, a good man, his companion.
And the Twelve Peers, whom Charles holds very dear,
form the vanguard, with twenty thousand knights.
Charles is secure, he fears no man on earth." AOI.

42

Said the pagan: "Truly, how I must marvel   550
at Charlemagne, who is so gray and white—
over two hundred years, from what I hear;
gone through so many lands a conqueror,
and borne so many blows from strong sharp spears,
killed and conquered so many mighty kings: 555
when will he lose the heart for making war?"
"Never," said Ganelon, "while one man lives: Roland!
no man like him from here to the Orient!
There's his companion, Oliver, a brave man.
And the Twelve Peers, whom Charles holds very dear,
form the vanguard, with twenty thousand Franks.   560
Charles is secure, he fears no man alive." AOI.

43

"Dear Lord Ganelon," said Marsilion the King,
"I have my army, you won't find one more handsome:
I can muster four hundred thousand knights!   565
With this host, now, can I fight Charles and the French?"
Ganelon answers: "No, no, don't try that now,
you'd take a loss: thousands of your pagans!
Forget such foolishness, listen to wisdom:
send the Emperor so many gifts   570
there'll be no Frenchman there who does not marvel.
For twenty hostages—those you'll be sending—
he will go home: home again to sweet France!
And he will leave his rear-guard behind him.

There will be Roland, I do believe, his nephew,   575
and Oliver, brave man, born to the court.
These Counts are dead, if anyone trusts me.
Then Charles will see that great pride of his go down,
he'll have no heart to make war on you again." AOI.

44

"Dear Lord Ganelon," said Marsilion the King,   580
"What must I do to kill Roland the Count?"
Ganelon answers: "Now I can tell you that.
The King will be at Cize,[4] in the great passes,
he will have placed his rear-guard at his back:
there'll be his nephew, Count Roland, that great man,   585
and Oliver, in whom he puts such faith,
and twenty thousand Franks in their company.
Now send one hundred thousand of your pagans
against the French—let them give the first battle.
The French army will be hit hard and shaken.   590
I must tell you: your men will be martyred.
Give them a second battle, then, like the first.
One will get him, Roland will not escape.
Then you'll have done a deed, a noble deed,
and no more war for the rest of your life!" AOI.   595

45

"If someone can bring about the death of Roland,
then Charles would lose the right arm of his body,
that marvelous army would disappear—
never again could Charles gather such forces.
Then peace at last for the Land of Fathers!"[5]   600
When Marsilion heard that, he kissed his neck.
Then he begins to open up his treasures. AOI.

46

Marsilion said, "Why talk. . . .
No plan has any worth which one. . . .[6]
Now swear to me that you will betray Roland."   605
Ganelon answers: "Let it be as you wish."
On the relics in his great sword Murgleis
he swore treason and became a criminal. AOI.

47

There stood a throne made all of ivory.
Marsilion commands them bring forth a book: 610

---

4. The pass through the Pyrenees.   5. *Tere Major*, in the original; it can mean either "the great land"
or "the land of fathers, ancestors." It always refers to France.   6. Parts of lines 603–4 are unintelligible
in the manuscript.

it was the law of Mahum and Tervagant.[7]
This is the vow sworn by the Saracen of Spain:
if he shall find Roland in the rear-guard,
he shall fight him, all his men shall fight him,
and once he finds Roland, Roland will die. 615
Says Ganelon: "May it be as you will." AOI.

48

And now there came a pagan, Valdabrun,
he was the man who raised Marsilion.
And, all bright smiles, he said to Ganelon:
"You take my sword, there's no man has one better: 620
a thousand coins, and more, are in the hilt.
It is a gift, dear lord, made in friendship,
only help us to Roland, that great baron,
let us find him standing in the rear-guard."
"It shall be done," replies Count Ganelon. 625
And then they kissed, on the face, on the chin.

49

And there came then a pagan, Climborin,
and, all bright smiles, he said to Ganelon:
"You take my helmet, I never saw one better,
only help us to Roland, lord of the march, 630
show us the way to put Roland to shame."
"It shall be done," replied Count Ganelon.
And then they kissed, on the face, on the mouth. AOI.

50

And then there came the Queen, Bramimunde;
said to the Count: "Lord, I love you well,
for my lord and all his men esteem you so. 635
I wish to send your wife two necklaces,
they are all gold, jacinths, and amethysts,
they are worth more than all the wealth of Rome.
Your Emperor has never seen their like."
He has taken them, thrusts them into his boot. AOI. 640

51

The King calls for Malduit, his treasurer:
"The gifts for Charles—is everything prepared?"
And he replies: "Yes, Lord, and well prepared:
seven hundred camels, packed with gold and silver, 645
and twenty hostages, the noblest under heaven." AOI.

---

7. A fictitious deity whom the poet mistakenly says the Saracens worshiped.

52

Marsilion took Ganelon by the shoulder
and said to him: "You're a brave man, a wise man.
Now by that faith you think will save your soul,
take care you do not turn your heart from us.   650
I will give you a great mass of my wealth,
ten mules weighed down with fine Arabian gold;
and come each year, I'll do the same again.
Now you take these, the keys to this vast city:
present King Charles with all of its great treasure;   655
then get me Roland picked for the rear-guard.
Let me find him in some defile or pass,
I will fight him, a battle to the death."
Ganelon answers: "It's high time that I go."
Now he is mounted, and he is on his way. AOI.   660

53

The Emperor moves homeward, he's drawing near.
Now he has reached the city of Valterne:
Roland had stormed it, destroyed it, and it stood
from that day forth a hundred years laid waste.
Charles is waiting for news of Ganelon   665
and the tribute from Spain, from that great land.
In the morning, at dawn, with the first light,
Count Ganelon came to the Christian camp. AOI.

54

The Emperor rose early in the morning,
the King of France, and has heard mass and matins.   670
On the green grass he stood before his tent.
Roland was there, and Oliver, brave man,
Naimon the Duke, and many other knights.
Ganelon came, the traitor, the foresworn.
With what great cunning he commences his speech;   675
said to the King: "May the Lord God save you!
Here I bring you the keys to Saragossa.
And I bring you great treasure from that city,
and twenty hostages, have them well guarded.
And good King Marsilion sends you this word: 680
Do not blame him concerning the Algalife:
I saw it all myself, with my own eyes:
     four hundred thousand men, and all in arms,
their hauberks on, some with their helms laced on,
swords on their belts, the hilts enameled gold,
who went with him to the edge of the sea.   685
They are in flight: it is the Christian faith—
they do not want it, they will not keep its law.
They had not sailed four full leagues out to sea

when a high wind, a tempest swept them up.
They were all drowned; you will never see them;   690
if he were still alive, I'd have brought him.
As for the pagan King, Lord, believe this:
before you see one month from this day pass,
he'll follow you to the Kingdom of France
and take the faith—he will take your faith, Lord,   695
and join his hands and become your vassal.
He will hold Spain as a fief from your hand."
Then the King said: "May God be thanked for this.
You have done well, you will be well rewarded."
Throughout the host they sound a thousand trumpets.   700
The French break camp, strap their gear on their pack-horses.
They take the road to the sweet land of France. AOI.

55

King Charlemagne laid waste the land of Spain,
stormed its castles, ravaged its citadels.
The King declares his war is at an end.   705
The Emperor rides toward the land of sweet France.
Roland the Count affixed the gonfanon,[8]
raised it toward heaven on the height of a hill;
the men of France make camp across that country.
Pagans are riding up through these great valleys,   710
their hauberks on, their tunics of double mail,
their helms laced on, their swords fixed on their belts,
shields on their necks, lances trimmed with their banners.
In a forest high in the hills they gathered:
four hundred thousand men waiting for dawn.   715
God, the pity of it! the French do not know! AOI.

56

The day goes by; now the darkness of night.
Charlemagne sleeps, the mighty Emperor.
He dreamt he was at Cize, in the great passes,
and in his fists held his great ashen lance.   720
Count Ganelon tore it away from him
and brandished it, shook it with such fury
the splinters of the shaft fly up toward heaven.
Charlemagne sleeps, his dream does not wake him.

57

And after that he dreamed another vision: 725
he was in France, in his chapel at Aix,
a cruel wild boar was biting his right arm;
saw coming at him—from the Ardennes—a leopard,
it attacked him, fell wildly on his body.

8. Pennant.

And a swift hound running down from the hall   730
came galloping, bounding over to Charles,
tore the right ear off that first beast, the boar,
turns, in fury, to fight against the leopard.
And the French say: It is a mighty battle,
but cannot tell which one of them will win.   735
Charlemagne sleeps, his dream does not wake him. AOI.

58

The day goes by, and the bright dawn arises.
Throughout that host. . . .⁹
The Emperor rides forth with such fierce pride.
"Barons, my lords," said the Emperor Charles,   740
"look at those passes, at those narrow defiles—
pick me a man to command the rear-guard."
Ganelon answers: "Roland, here, my stepson.
You have no baron as great and brave as Roland."
When he hears that, the King stares at him in fury;   745
and said to him: "You are the living devil,
a mad dog—the murderous rage in you!
And who will precede me, in the vanguard?"
Ganelon answers, "Why, Ogier of Denmark,
you have no baron who could lead it so well."   750

59

Roland the Count, when he heard himself named,
knew what to say, and spoke as a knight must speak:
"Lord Stepfather, I have to cherish you!
You have had the rear-guard assigned to me.
Charles will not lose, this great King who rules France,   755
I swear it now, one palfrey, one war horse—
        while I'm alive and know what's happening—
one he-mule, one she-mule that he might ride,
Charles will not lose one sumpter, not one pack horse
that has not first been bought and paid for with swords."
Ganelon answers: "You speak the truth, I know." AOI.   760

60

When Roland hears he will lead the rear-guard,
he spoke in great fury to his stepfather:
"Hah! you nobody, you base-born little fellow,
and did you think the glove would fall from my hands
as the staff fell¹ from yours before King Charles?" AOI.   765

---

9. The rest of the line is unintelligible in the manuscript.   1. Ganelon had let fall a glove, not a staff (line 333). For this and other less objective reasons, some editors have questioned the authenticity of this *laisse.*

61

"Just Emperor," said Roland, that great man,
"give me the bow that you hold in your hand.
And no man here, I think, will say in reproach
I let it drop, as Ganelon let the staff drop[2]
from his right hand, when he should have taken it."   770
The Emperor bowed down his head with this,
he pulled his beard, he twisted his mustache,
cannot hold back, tears fill his eyes, he weeps.

62

And after that there came Naimon the Duke,
no greater vassal in the court than Naimon,   775
said to the King: "You've heard it clearly now:
it is Count Roland. How furious he is.
He is the one to whom the rear-guard falls,
no baron here can ever change that now.
Give him the bow that you have stretched and bent,   780
and then find him good men to stand with him."
The King gives him the bow; Roland has it now.

63

The Emperor calls forth Roland the Count:
"My lord, my dear nephew, of course you know
I will give you half my men, they are yours.
Let them serve you, it is your salvation."   785
"None of that!" said the Count. "May God strike me
if I discredit the history of my line.
I'll keep twenty thousand Franks—they are good men.
Go your way through the passes, you will be safe.   790
You must not fear any man while I live."

64

Roland the Count mounted his battle horse. AOI.
Oliver came to him, his companion.
And Gerin came, and the brave Count Gerer,
and Aton came, and there came Berenger,   795
and Astor came, and Anseïs, fierce and proud,
and the old man Gerard of Roussillon,
and Gaifier, that great and mighty duke.
Said the Archbishop: "I'm going, by my head!"
"And I with you," said Gautier the Count,
"I am Count Roland's man and must not fail him."   800
And together they choose twenty thousand men. AOI.

2. In this *laisse* a reviser tried to make the text more consistent by adding the reference to the staff.

65

Roland the Count summons Gautier de l'Hum:
"Now take a thousand Franks from our land, France,
and occupy those passes and the heights there.   805
The Emperor must not lose a single man." AOI.
Gautier replies: "Lord, I'll fight well for you."
And with a thousand French of France, their land,
Gautier rides out to the hills and defiles;
will not come down, for all the bad news, again,   810
till seven hundred swords have been drawn out.
King Almaris of the Kingdom of Belferne
gave them battle that day, and it was bitter.

66

High are the hills, the valleys tenebrous,
the cliffs are dark, the defiles mysterious.   815
That day, and with much pain, the French passed through.
For fifteen leagues around one heard their clamor.
When they reach Tere Majur, the Land of Fathers,
they beheld Gascony, their lord's domain.
Then they remembered: their fiefs, their realms, their honors,   820
remembered their young girls, their gentle wives:
not one who does not weep for what he feels.
Beyond these others King Charles is in bad straits:
his nephew left in the defiles of Spain!
feels the pity of it; tears break through. AOI.   825

67

And the Twelve Peers are left behind in Spain,
and twenty thousand Franks are left with them.
They have no fear, they have no dread of death.
The Emperor is going home to France.
Beneath his cloak, his face shows all he feels.   830
Naimon the Duke is riding beside him;
and he said to the King: "What is this grief?"
And Charles replies: "Whoever asks me, wrongs me.
I feel such pain, I cannot keep from wailing.
France will be destroyed by Ganelon.   835
Last night I saw a vision brought by angels:
the one who named my nephew for the rear-guard
shattered the lance between my fists to pieces.
I have left him in a march among strangers.
If I lose him, God! I won't find his like." AOI.   840

68

King Charles the Great cannot keep from weeping.
A hundred thousand Franks feel pity for him;

and for Roland, an amazing fear.
Ganelon the criminal has betrayed him;
got gifts for it from the pagan king,   845
gold and silver, cloths of silk, gold brocade,
mules and horses and camels and lions.
Marsilion sends for the barons of Spain,
counts and viscounts and dukes and almaçurs,
and the emirs,[3] and the sons of great lords: 850
four hundred thousand assembled in three days.
In Saragossa he has them beat the drums,
they raise Mahumet upon the highest tower:
no pagan now who does not worship him
and adore him. Then they ride, racing each other,   855
search through the land, the valleys, the mountains;
and then they saw the banners of the French.
The rear-guard of the Twelve Companions
will not fail now, they'll give the pagans battle.

69

Marsilion's nephew has come forward   860
riding a mule that he goads with a stick;
said—a warrior's laugh on him—to his uncle:
"Dear Lord and King, how long I have served you,
and all the troubles, the pains I have endured,
so many battles fought and won on the field   865
Give me a fief, the first blow at Roland.
I will kill him, here's the spear I'll do it with.
If Mahumet will only stand by me,
I will set free every strip of land in Spain,
from the passes of Aspre to Durestant.   870
Charles will be weary, his Franks will give it up:
and no more war for the rest of your life!"
King Marsilion gave him his glove, as sign. AOI.

70

The King's nephew holds the glove in his fist,
speaks these proud words to Marsilion his uncle: 875
"You've given me, dear Lord, King, a great gift!
Choose me twelve men, twelve of your noble barons,
and I will fight against the Twelve Companions."
And Falsaron was the first to respond—
he was the brother of King Marsilion: 880
"Dear Lord, Nephew, it's you and I together!
We'll fight, that's sure! We'll battle the rear-guard
of Charlemagne's grand army! We are the ones!
We have been chosen. We'll kill them all! It is fated." AOI.

3. All lords of high rank.

71

And now again: there comes King Corsablis,   885
a Berber, a bad man, a man of cunning;
and now he spoke as a brave vassal speaks:
for all God's gold he would not be a coward.
Now rushing up: Malprimis de Brigal,
faster on his two feet than any horse;   890
and cries great-voiced before Marsilion:
"I'm on my way to Rencesvals to fight!
Let me find Roland, I won't stop till I kill him!"

[Lines 894–993 continue the roll call of volunteers.]

79

They arm themselves in Saracen hauberks,
all but a few are lined with triple mail;   995
they lace on their good helms of Saragossa,
gird on their swords, the steel forged in Vienne;
they have rich shields, spears of Valencia,
and gonfanons of white and blue and red.
They leave the mules and riding horses now,   1000
mount their war horses and ride in close array.
The day was fair, the sun was shining bright,
all their armor was aflame with the light;
a thousand trumpets blow: that was to make it finer.
That made a great noise, and the men of France heard.   1005
Said Oliver: "Companion, I believe
we may yet have a battle with the pagans."
Roland replies: "Now may God grant us that.
We know our duty: to stand here for our King.
A man must bear some hardships for his lord,   1010
stand everything, the great heat, the great cold,
lose the hide and hair on him for his good lord.
Now let each man make sure to strike hard here:
let them not sing a bad song about us!
Pagans are wrong and Christians are right!   1015
They'll make no bad example of me this day!" AOI.

80

Oliver climbs to the top of a hill,
looks to his right, across a grassy vale,
sees the pagan army on its way there;
and called down to Roland, his companion:
"That way, toward Spain: the uproar I see coming!   1020
All their hauberks, all blazing, helmets like flames!
It will be a bitter thing for our French.
Ganelon knew, that criminal, that traitor,
when he marked us out before the Emperor."   1025

"Be still, Oliver," Roland the Count replies.
"He is my stepfather—my stepfather.
 I won't have you speak one word against him."

81

Oliver has gone up upon a hill,
sees clearly now: the kingdom of Spain,
and the Saracens assembled in such numbers:
helmets blazing, bedecked with gems in gold,   1030
those shields of theirs, those hauberks sewn with brass,
and all their spears, the gonfanons affixed;
cannot begin to count their battle corps,
there are too many, he cannot take their number.   1035
And he is deeply troubled by what he sees.
He made his way quickly down from the hill,
came to the French, told them all he had seen.

82

Said Oliver: "I saw the Saracens,
no man on earth ever saw more of them—   1040
one hundred thousand, with their shields, up in front,
helmets laced on, hauberks blazing on them,
the shafts straight up, the iron heads like flames—
you'll get a battle, nothing like it before.
My lords, my French, may God give you the strength.   1045
Hold your ground now! Let them not defeat us!"
And the French say: "God hate the man who runs!
We may die here, but no man will fail you." AOI.

83

Said Oliver: "The pagan force is great;
from what I see, our French here are too few.
Roland, my companion, sound your horn then,   1050
Charles will hear it, the army will come back."
Roland replies: "I'd be a fool to do it.
I would lose my good name all through sweet France.
I will strike now, I'll strike with Durendal,
the blade will be bloody to the gold from striking!   1055
These pagan traitors came to these passes doomed!
I promise you, they are marked men, they'll die." AOI.

84

"Roland, Companion, now sound the olifant,[4]
Charles will hear it, he will bring the army,   1060

---

4. A form of *elephant*, which means "ivory" or "a horn made of ivory." It is used specifically, almost as a proper name, to denote Roland's horn, made of an elephant's tusk and adorned with gold and jewels about the rim.

the King will come with all his barons to help us."
Roland replies: "May it never please God
that my kin should be shamed because of me,
or that sweet France should fall into disgrace.
Never! Never! I'll strike with Durendal,   1065
I'll strike with this good sword strapped to my side,
you'll see this blade running its whole length with blood.
These pagan traitors have gathered here to die.
I promise you, they are all bound for death." AOI.

85

"Roland, Companion, sound your olifant now,   1070
Charles will hear it, marching through those passes.
I promise you, the Franks will come at once."
Roland replies: "May it never please God
that any man alive should come to say
that pagans—pagans!—once made me sound this horn: 1075
no kin of mine will ever bear that shame.
Once I enter this great battle coming
and strike my thousand seven hundred blows,
you'll see the bloody steel of Durendal.
These French are good—they will strike like brave men.   1080
Nothing can save the men of Spain from death."

86

Said Oliver: "I see no blame in it—
I watched the Saracens coming from Spain,
the valleys and mountains covered with them,
every hillside and every plain all covered,   1085
hosts and hosts everywhere of those strange men—
and here we have a little company."
Roland replies: "That whets my appetite.
May it not please God and his angels and saints
to let France lose its glory because of me—   1090
let me not end in shame, let me die first.
The Emperor loves us when we fight well."

87

Roland is good, and Oliver is wise,
both these vassals men of amazing courage:
once they are armed and mounted on their horses,   1095
they will not run, though they die for it, from battle.
Good men, these Counts, and their words full of spirit.
Traitor pagans are riding up in fury.
Said Oliver: "Roland, look—the first ones,
on top of us—and Charles is far away.   1100
You did not think it right to sound your olifant:
if the King were here, we'd come out without losses.

Now look up there, toward the passes of Aspre—
you can see the rear-guard: it will suffer.
No man in that detail will be in another."
Roland replies: "Don't speak such foolishness— 1105
shame on the heart gone coward in the chest.
We'll hold our ground, we'll stand firm—we're the ones!
We'll fight with spears, we'll fight them hand to hand!" AOI.

88

When Roland sees that there will be a battle, 1110
it makes him fiercer than a lion or leopard;
shouts to the French, calls out to Oliver:
"Lord, companion: friend, do not say such things.
The Emperor, who left us these good French,
had set apart these twenty thousand men: 1115
he knew there was no coward in their ranks.
A man must meet great troubles for his lord,
stand up to the great heat and the great cold,
give up some flesh and blood—it is his duty.
Strike with the lance, I'll strike with Durendal— 1120
it was the King who gave me this good sword!
If I die here, the man who gets it can say:
it was a noble's, a vassal's, a good man's sword."

89

And now there comes the Archbishop Turpin.
He spurs his horse, goes up into a mountain, 1125
summons the French; and he preached them a sermon:
"Barons, my lords, Charles left us in this place.
We know our duty: to die like good men for our King.
Fight to defend the holy Christian faith.
Now you will have a battle, you know it now, 1130
you see the Saracens with your own eyes.
Confess your sins, pray to the Lord for mercy.
I will absolve you all, to save your souls.
If you die here, you will stand up holy martyrs,
you will have seats in highest Paradise." 1135
The French dismount, cast themselves on the ground;
the Archbishop blesses them in God's name.
He commands them to do one penance: strike.

90

The French arise, stand on their feet again;
they are absolved, released from all their sins: 1140
the Archbishop has blessed them in God's name.
Now they are mounted on their swift battle horses,
bearing their arms like faithful warriors;
and every man stands ready for the battle.

Roland the Count calls out to Oliver: 1145
"Lord, Companion, you knew it, you were right,
Ganelon watched for his chance to betray us,
got gold for it, got goods for it, and money.
The Emperor will have to avenge us now.
King Marsilion made a bargain for our lives, 1150
but still must pay, and that must be with swords." AOI.

91

Roland went forth into the Spanish passes
on Veillantif, his good swift-running horse.
He bears his arms—how they become this man!—
grips his lance now, hefting it, working it, 1155
now swings the iron point up toward the sky,
the gonfanon all white laced on above—
the golden streamers beat down upon his hands:
a noble's body, the face aglow and smiling.
Close behind him his good companion follows; 1160
the men of France hail him: their protector!
He looks wildly toward the Saracens,
and humbly and gently to the men of France;
and spoke a word to them, in all courtesy:
"Barons, my lords, easy now, keep at a walk. 1165
These pagans are searching for martyrdom.
We'll get good spoils before this day is over,
no king of France ever got such treasure!"
And with these words, the hosts are at each other. AOI.

92

Said Oliver: "I will waste no more words. 1170
You did not think it right to sound your olifant,
there'll be no Charles coming to your aid now.
He knows nothing, brave man, he's done no wrong;
those men down there—they have no blame in this.
Well, then, ride now, and ride with all your might! 1175
Lords, you brave men, stand your ground, hold the field!
Make up your minds, I beg you in God's name,
to strike some blows, take them and give them back!
Here we must not forget Charlemagne's war cry."
And with that word the men of France cried out. 1180
A man who heard that shout: Munjoie! Munjoie!⁵
would always remember what manhood is.
Then they ride, God! Look at their pride and spirit!
and they spur hard, to ride with all their speed,
come on to strike—what else would these men do? 1185
The Saracens kept coming, never fearing them.
Franks and pagans, here they are, at each other.

---

5. For the poet's derivation of this war cry, see *laisse* 183, below.

93

Marsilion's nephew is named Aëlroth.
He rides in front, at the head of the army,
comes on shouting insults against our French:
"French criminals, today you fight our men.   1190
One man should have saved you: he betrayed you.
A fool, your King, to leave you in these passes.
This is the day sweet France will lose its name,
and Charlemagne the right arm of his body."   1195
When he hears that—God!—Roland is outraged!
He spurs his horse, gives Veillantif its head.
The Count comes on to strike with all his might,
smashes his shield, breaks his hauberk apart,
and drives: rips through his chest, shatters the bones,   1200
knocks the whole backbone out of his back,
casts out the soul of Aëlroth with his lance;
which he thrusts deep, makes the whole body shake,
throws him down dead, lance straight out,[6] from his horse;
he has broken his neck; broken it in two.   1205
There is something, he says, he must tell him:
"Clown! Nobody! Now you know Charles is no fool,
he never was the man to love treason.
It took his valor to leave us in these passes!
France will not lose its name, sweet France! today.   1210
Brave men of France, strike hard! The first blow is ours!
We're in the right, and these swine in the wrong!" AOI.

94

A duke is there whose name is Falsaron,
he was the brother of King Marsilion,
held the wild land of Dathan and Abiram;[7]   1215
under heaven, no criminal more vile;
a tremendous forehead between his eyes—
a good half-foot long, if you had measured it.
His pain is bitter to see his nephew dead;
rides out alone, baits the foe with his body,   1220
and riding shouts the war cry of the pagans,
full of hate and insults against the French:
"This is the day sweet France will lose its honor!"
Oliver hears, and it fills him with fury,
digs with his golden spurs into his horse,   1225
comes on to strike the blow a baron strikes,
smashes his shield, breaks his hauberk apart,
thrusts into him the long streamers of his gonfalon,
knocks him down, dead, lance straight out, from the saddle;

---

6. The lance is held, not thrown, and used to knock the enemy from his horse. To throw one's weapons is savage and ignoble. See *laisses* 154 and 160 and the outlandish names of the things the pagans throw at Roland, Gautier, and Turpin.   7. See Numbers 16.1–35.

looks to the ground and sees the swine stretched out,   1230
and spoke these words—proud words, terrible words:
"You nobody, what are your threats to me!
Men of France, strike! Strike and we will beat them!"
Munjoie! he shouts—the war cry of King Charles. AOI.

95

A king is there whose name is Corsablis,   1235
a Berber, come from that far country.
He spoke these words to all his Saracens:
"Now here's one battle we'll have no trouble with,
look at that little troop of Frenchmen there,
a few odd men—they're not worth noticing!   1240
King Charles won't save a single one of them.
Their day has come, they must all die today."
And Archbishop Turpin heard every word:
no man on earth he wants so much to hate!
digs with spurs of fine gold into his horse,   1245
comes on to strike with all his awful might;
smashed through his shield, burst the rings of his hauberk,
sent his great lance into the body's center,
drove it in deep, he made the dead man shake,
knocked him down, dead, lance straight out, on the road;   1250
looks to the ground and sees the swine stretched out;
there is something, he says, he must tell him:
"You pagan! You nobody! You told lies there:
King Charles my lord is our safeguard forever!
Our men of France have no heart for running.   1255
As for your companions—we'll nail them to the ground;
and then you must all die the second death.[8]
At them, you French! No man forget what he is!
Thanks be to God, now the first blow is ours";
and shouts Munjoie! Munjoie! to hold the field.   1260

[Lines 1261–1319 narrate a series of single combats, many of them quite similar.]

104

The battle is fearful and wonderful   1320
and everywhere. Roland never spares himself,
strikes with his lance as long as the wood lasts:
the fifteenth blow he struck, it broke, was lost.
Then he draws Durendal, his good sword, bare,
and spurs his horse, comes on to strike Chernuble,   1325
smashes his helmet, carbuncles shed their light,
cuts through the coif, through the hair on his head,
cut through his eyes, through his face, through that look,
the bright, shining hauberk with its fine rings,
down through the trunk to the fork of his legs,   1330

---

8. The death of the soul, eternal damnation (see Revelation 20.14 and 21.8).

through the saddle, adorned with beaten gold,
into the horse; and the sword came to rest:
cut through the spine, never felt for the joint;
knocks him down, dead, on the rich grass of the meadow;
then said to him: "You were doomed when you started,   1335
Clown! Nobody! Let Mahum help you now.
No pagan swine will win this field today."

105

Roland the Count comes riding through the field,
holds Durendal, that sword! it carves its way!
and brings terrible slaughter down on the pagans.   1340
To have seen him cast one man dead on another,
the bright red blood pouring out on the ground,
his hauberk, his two arms, running with blood,
his good horse—neck and shoulders running with blood!
And Oliver does not linger, he strikes!   1345
and the Twelve Peers, no man could reproach them;
and the brave French, they fight with lance and sword.
The pagans die, some simply faint away!
Said the Archbishop: "Bless our band of brave men!"
Munjoie! he shouts—the war cry of King Charles. AOI.   1350

106

Oliver rides into that battle-storm,
his lance is broken, he holds only the stump;
comes on to strike a pagan, Malsarun;
and he smashes his shield, all flowers and gold,
sends his two eyes flying out of his head,   1355
and his brains come pouring down to his feet;
casts him down, dead, with seven hundred others.
Now he has killed Turgis and Esturguz,
and the shaft bursts, shivers down to his fists.
Count Roland said: "Companion, what are you doing?   1360
Why bother with a stick in such a battle?
Iron and steel will do much better work!
Where is your sword, your Halteclere—that name!
Where is that crystal hilt, that golden guard?"
"Haven't had any time to draw it out,   1365
been so busy fighting," said Oliver. AOI.

107

Lord Oliver has drawn out his good sword—
that sword his companion had longed to see—
and showed him how a good man uses it:
strikes a pagan, Justin of Val Ferrée,   1370
and comes down through his head, cuts through the center,
through his body, his hauberk sewn with brass,

the good saddle beset with gems in gold,
into the horse, the backbone cut in two;
knocks him down, dead, before him on the meadow.   1375
Count Roland said: "Now I know it's you, Brother.
The Emperor loves us for blows like that."
Munjoie! that cry! goes up on every side. AOI.

108

Gerin the Count sits on his bay Sorél
and Gerer his companion on Passe-Cerf;   1380
and they ride, spurring hard, let loose their reins,
come on to strike a pagan, Timozel,
one on his shield, the other on his hauberk.
They broke their two lances in his body;
turn him over, dead, in a fallow field.   1385
I do not know and have never heard tell
which of these two was swifter, though both were swift.
Esperveris: he was the son of Borel
and now struck dead by Engeler of Bordeaux.
Turpin the Archbishop killed Siglorel,   1390
the enchanter, who had been in Hell before:
Jupiter brought him there, with that strange magic.
Then Turpin said: "That swine owed us his life!
Roland replies: "And now the scoundrel's dead.
Oliver, Brother, those were blows! I approve!"   1395

109

In the meantime, the fighting grew bitter.
Franks and pagans, the fearful blows they strike—
those who attack, those who defend themselves;
so many lances broken, running with blood,
the gonfanons in shreds, the ensigns torn,   1400
so many good French fallen, their young lives lost:
they will not see their mothers or wives again,
or the men of France who wait for them at the passes. AOI.
Charlemagne waits and weeps and wails for them.
What does that matter? They'll get no help from him.   1405
Ganelon served him ill that day he sold,
in Saragossa, the barons of his house.
He lost his life and limbs for what he did:
was doomed to hang in the great trial at Aix,
and thirty of his kin were doomed with him,   1410
who never expected to die that death. AOI.

110

The battle is fearful and full of grief.
Oliver and Roland strike like good men,
the Archbishop, more than a thousand blows,

and the Twelve Peers do not hang back, they strike! 1415
the French fight side by side, all as one man.
The pagans die by hundreds, by thousands:
whoever does not flee finds no refuge from death,
like it or not, there he ends all his days.
And there the men of France lose their greatest arms; 1420
they will not see their fathers, their kin again,
or Charlemagne, who looks for them in the passes.
Tremendous torment now comes forth in France,
a mighty whirlwind, tempests of wind and thunder,
rains and hailstones, great and immeasurable, 1425
bolts of lightning hurtling and hurtling down:
it is, in truth, a trembling of the earth.
From Saint Michael-in-Peril to the Saints,
from Besançon to the port of Wissant,
there is no house whose veil of walls does not crumble. 1430
A great darkness at noon falls on the land,
there is no light but when the heavens crack.
No man sees this who is not terrified,
and many say: "The Last Day! Judgment Day!
The end! The end of the world is upon us!" 1435
They do not know, they do not speak the truth:
it is the worldwide grief for the death of Roland.

111

The French have fought with all their hearts and strength,
pagans are dead by the thousands, in droves:
of one hundred thousand, not two are saved. 1440
Said the Archbishop: "Our men! What valiant fighters!
No king under heaven could have better.
It is written in the Gesta Francorum:[9]
our Emperor's vassals were all good men."
They walk over the field to seek their dead, 1445
they weep, tears fill their eyes, in grief and pity
for their kindred, with love, with all their hearts.
Marsilion the King, with all his men
    in that great host, rises up before them. AOI.

112

King Marsilion comes along a valley
with all his men, the great host he assembled: 1450
twenty divisions, formed and numbered by the King,
helmets ablaze with gems beset in gold,
and those bright shields, those hauberks sewn with brass.
Seven thousand clarions sound the pursuit,
and the great noise resounds across that country. 1455
Said Roland then: "Oliver, Companion, Brother,
that traitor Ganelon has sworn our deaths:

9. The Deeds of the French (Latin), title of an account of these events that has not survived.

it is treason, it cannot stay hidden,
the Emperor will take his terrible revenge.
We have this battle now, it will be bitter, 1460
no man has ever seen the like of it.
I will fight here with Durendal, this sword,
and you, my companion, with Halteclere—
we've fought with them before, in many lands!
how many battles have we won with these two! 1465
Let no one sing a bad song of our swords." AOI.

113

When the French see the pagans so numerous,
the fields swarming with them on every side,
they call the names of Oliver, and Roland,
and the Twelve Peers: protect them, be their warranter. 1470
The Archbishop told them how he saw things:
"Barons, my lords, do not think shameful thoughts,
do not, I beg you all in God's name, run.
Let no brave man sing shameful songs of us:
let us all die here fighting: that is far better. 1475
We are promised: we shall soon find our deaths,
after today we won't be living here.
But here's one thing, and I am your witness:
Holy Paradise lies open to you,
you will take seats among the Innocents."[1] 1480
And with these words the Franks are filled with joy,
there is no man who does not shout Munjoie! AOI.

114

A Saracen was there of Saragossa,
half that city was in this pagan's keeping,
this Climborin, who fled before no man, 1485
who took the word of Ganelon the Count,
kissed in friendship the mouth that spoke that word,
gave him a gift: his helmet and its carbuncle.
Now he will shame, says he, the Land of Fathers,
he will tear off the crown of the Emperor; 1490
sits on the horse that he calls Barbamusche,
swifter than the sparrowhawk, than the swallow;
digs in his spurs, gives that war horse its head,
comes on to strike Engeler of Gascony,
whose shield and fine hauberk cannot save him; 1495
gets the head of his spear into his body,
drives it in deep, gets all the iron through,
throws him back, dead, lance straight out, on the field.
And then he cries: "It's good to kill these swine!
At them, Pagans! At them and break their ranks!" 1500
"God!" say the French, "the loss of that good man!" AOI.

1. The infants slain by King Herod (see Matthew 2.16).

115

Roland the Count calls out to Oliver:
"Lord, Companion, there is Engeler dead,
we never had a braver man on horse."
The Count replies: "God let me avenge him";   1505
and digs with golden spurs into his horse,
grips—the steel running with blood—Halteclere,
comes on to strike with all his mighty power:
the blow comes flashing down; the pagan falls.
Devils take away the soul of Climborin.   1510
And then he killed Alphaïen the duke,
cut off the head of Escababi,
struck from their horses seven great Arrabites:
they'll be no use for fighting any more!
And Roland said: "My companion is enraged!   1515
Why, he compares with me! he earns his praise!
Fighting like that makes us dearer to Charles";
lifts up his voice and shouts: "Strike! you are warriors!" AOI.

[Lines 1519–1627 narrate another series of single combats.]

125

Marsilion sees his people's martyrdom.
He commands them: sound his horns and trumpets;
and he rides now with the great host he has gathered.   1630
At their head rides the Saracen Abisme:
no worse criminal rides in that company,
stained with the marks of his crimes and great treasons,
lacking the faith in God, Saint Mary's son.
And he is black, as black as melted pitch,   1635
a man who loves murder and treason more
than all the gold of rich Galicia,
no living man ever saw him play or laugh;
a great fighter, a wild man, mad with pride,
and therefore dear to that criminal king;   1640
holds high his dragon,[2] where all his people gather.
The Archbishop will never love that man,
no sooner saw than wanted to strike him;
considered quietly, said to himself:
"That Saracen—a heretic, I'll wager.   1645
Now let me die if I do not kill him—
I never loved cowards or cowards' ways." AOI.

126

Turpin the Archbishop begins the battle.
He rides the horse that he took from Grossaille,
who was a king this priest once killed in Denmark.   1650

---

2. Banner.

Now this war horse is quick and spirited,
his hooves high-arched, the quick legs long and flat,
short in the thigh, wide in the rump, long in the flanks,
and the backbone so high, a battle horse!
and that white tail, the yellow mane on him,   1655
the little ears on him, the tawny head!
No beast on earth could ever run with him.
The Archbishop—that valiant man!—spurs hard,
he will attack Abisme, he will not falter,
strikes on his shield, a miraculous blow: 1660
a shield of stones, of amethysts, topazes,
esterminals,[3] carbuncles all on fire—
a gift from a devil, in Val Metas,
sent on to him by the Amiral Galafre.
There Turpin strikes, he does not treat it gently—   1665
after that blow, I'd not give one cent for it;
cut through his body, from one side to the other,
and casts him down dead in a barren place.
And the French say: "A fighter, that Archbishop!
Look at him there, saving souls with that crozier!"   1670

127

Roland the Count calls out to Oliver:
"Lord, Companion, now you have to agree
the Archbishop is a good man on horse,
there's none better on earth or under heaven,
he knows his way with a lance and a spear."   1675
The Count replies: "Right! Let us help him then."
And with these words the Franks began anew,
the blows strike hard, and the fighting is bitter;
there is a painful loss of Christian men.
To have seen them, Roland and Oliver,   1680
these fighting men, striking down with their swords,
the Archbishop with them, striking with his lance!
One can recount the number these three killed:
it is written—in charters, in documents;
the Geste tells it: it was more than four thousand.   1685
Through four assaults all went well with our men;
then comes the fifth, and that one crushes them.
They are all killed, all these warriors of France,
all but sixty, whom the Lord God has spared:
they will die too, but first sell themselves dear. AOI.   1690

128

Count Roland sees the great loss of his men,
calls on his companion, on Oliver:
"Lord, Companion, in God's name, what would you do?
All these good men you see stretched on the ground.

---

3. Precious ornaments.

We can mourn for sweet France, fair land of France!   1695
a desert now, stripped of such great vassals.
Oh King, and friend, if only you were here!
Oliver, Brother, how shall we manage it?
What shall we do to get word to the King?"
Said Oliver: "I don't see any way.   1700
I would rather die now than hear us shamed." AOI.

129

And Roland said: "I'll sound the olifant,
Charles will hear it, drawing through the passes,
I promise you, the Franks will return at once."
Said Oliver: "That would be a great disgrace,   1705
a dishonor and reproach to all your kin,
the shame of it would last them all their lives.
When I urged it, you would not hear of it;
you will not do it now with my consent.
It is not acting bravely to sound it now—   1710
look at your arms, they are covered with blood."
The Count replies: "I've fought here like a lord."⁴ AOI.

130

And Roland says: "We are in a rough battle.
I'll sound the olifant, Charles will hear it."
Said Oliver: "No good vassal would do it.   1715
When I urged it, friend, you did not think it right.
If Charles were here, we'd come out with no losses.
Those men down there—no blame can fall on them."
Oliver said: "Now by this beard of mine,
If I can see my noble sister, Aude,   1720
once more, you will never lie in her arms!"⁵AOI.

131

And Roland said: "Why are you angry at me?"
Oliver answers: "Companion, it is your doing.
I will tell you what makes a vassal good:
    it is judgment, it is never madness;
restraint is worth more than the raw nerve of a fool.   1725
Frenchmen are dead because of your wildness.
And what service will Charles ever have from us?
If you had trusted me, my lord would be here,
we would have fought this battle through to the end,
Marsilion would be dead, or our prisoner.   1730
Roland, your prowess—had we never seen it!
    And now, dear friend, we've seen the last of it.

---

4. Some have found lines 1710–12 difficult. Oliver means, "We have fought this far—look at the enemy's blood on your arms: It is too late, it would be a disgrace to summon help when there is no longer any chance of being saved." But Roland thinks that that is the one time when it is not a disgrace.   5. Aude had been betrothed to Roland.

No more aid from us now for Charlemagne,
a man without equal till Judgment Day,
you will die here, and your death will shame France.
We kept faith, you and I, we were companions;
    and everything we were will end today.   1735
We part before evening, and it will be hard." AOI.

132

Turpin the Archbishop hears their bitter words,
digs hard into his horse with golden spurs
and rides to them; begins to set them right:
"You, Lord Roland, and you, Lord Oliver,   1740
I beg you in God's name do not quarrel.
To sound the horn could not help us now, true,
but still it is far better that you do it:
let the King come, he can avenge us then—
these men of Spain must not go home exulting!   1745
Our French will come, they'll get down on their feet,
and find us here—we'll be dead, cut to pieces.
They will lift us into coffins on the backs of mules,
and weep for us, in rage and pain and grief,
and bury us in the courts of churches;   1750
and we will not be eaten by wolves or pigs or dogs."
Roland replies, "Lord, you have spoken well." AOI.

133

Roland has put the olifant to his mouth,
he sets it well, sounds it with all his strength.
The hills are high, and that voice ranges far,   1755
they heard it echo thirty great leagues away.
King Charles heard it, and all his faithful men.
And the King says: "Our men are in a battle."
And Ganelon disputed him and said:
"Had someone else said that, I'd call him liar!" AOI.   1760

134

And now the mighty effort of Roland the Count:
he sounds his olifant; his pain is great,
and from his mouth the bright blood comes leaping out,
and the temple bursts in his forehead.
That horn, in Roland's hands, has a mighty voice: 1765
King Charles hears it drawing through the passes.
Naimon heard it, the Franks listen to it.
And the King said: "I hear Count Roland's horn;
he'd never sound it unless he had a battle."
Says Ganelon: "Now no more talk of battles!   1770
You are old now, your hair is white as snow,
the things you say make you sound like a child.

You know Roland and that wild pride of his—
what a wonder God has suffered it so long!
Remember? he took Noples without your command: 1775
the Saracens rode out, to break the siege;
they fought with him, the great vassal Roland.
Afterwards he used the streams to wash the blood
from the meadows: so that nothing would show.
He blasts his horn all day to catch a rabbit,   1780
he's strutting now before his peers and bragging—
who under heaven would dare meet him on the field?
So now: ride on! Why do you keep on stopping?
The Land of Fathers lies far ahead of us." AOI.

135

The blood leaping from Count Roland's mouth,   1785
the temple broken with effort in his forehead,
he sounds his horn in great travail and pain.
King Charles heard it, and his French listen hard.
And the King said: "That horn has a long breath!"
Naimon answers: "It is a baron's breath.   1790
There is a battle there, I know there is.
He betrayed him! and now asks you to fail him!
Put on your armor! Lord, shout your battle cry,
and save the noble barons of your house!
You hear Roland's call. He is in trouble."   1795

136

The Emperor commanded the horns to sound,
the French dismount, and they put on their armor:
their hauberks, their helmets, their gold-dressed swords,
their handsome shields; and take up their great lances,
the gonfalons of white and red and blue.   1800
The barons of that host mount their war horses
and spur them hard the whole length of the pass;
and every man of them says to the other:
"If only we find Roland before he's killed,
we'll stand with him, and then we'll do some fighting!"   1805
What does it matter what they say? They are too late.

137

It is the end of day, and full of light,
arms and armor are ablaze in the sun,
and fire flashes from hauberks and helmets,
and from those shields, painted fair with flowers,   1810
and from those lances, those gold-dressed gonfanons.
The Emperor rides on in rage and sorrow,
the men of France indignant and full of grief.
There is no man of them who does not weep,

they are in fear for the life of Roland.   1815
The King commands: seize Ganelon the Count!
and gave him over to the cooks of his house;
summons the master cook, their chief, Besgun:
"Guard him for me like the traitor he is:
he has betrayed the barons of my house."   1820
Besgun takes him, sets his kitchen comrades,
a hundred men, the best, the worst, on him;
and they tear out his beard and his mustache,
each one strikes him four good blows with his fist;
and they lay into him with cudgels and sticks,   1825
put an iron collar around his neck
and chain him up, as they would chain a bear;
dumped him, in dishonor, on a packhorse,
and guard him well till they give him back to Charles.

138

High are the hills, and tenebrous, and vast, AOI.   1830
the valleys deep, the raging waters swift;
to the rear, to the front, the trumpets sound:
they answer the lone voice of the olifant.
The Emperor rides on, rides on in fury,
the men of France in grief and indignation.   1835
There is no man who does not weep and wail,
and they pray God: protect the life of Roland
till they come, one great host, into the field
and fight at Roland's side like true men all.
What does it matter what they pray? It does no good.   1840
They are too late, they cannot come in time. AOI.

139

King Charles the Great rides on, a man in wrath,
his great white beard spread out upon his hauberk.[6]
All the barons of France ride spurring hard,
there is no man who does not wail, furious   1845
not to be with Roland, the captain count,
who stands and fights the Saracens of Spain,
so set upon, I cannot think his soul abides.
God! those sixty men who stand with him, what men!
No king, no captain ever stood with better. AOI.   1850

140

Roland looks up on the mountains and slopes,
sees the French dead, so many good men fallen,
and weeps for them, as a great warrior weeps:
"Barons, my lords, may God give you his grace,
may he grant Paradise to all your souls,   1855

---

6. A gesture of defiance toward the enemy.

make them lie down among the holy flowers.
I never saw better vassals than you.
All the years you've served me, and all the times,
the mighty lands you conquered for Charles our King!
The Emperor raised you for this terrible hour! 1860
Land of France, how sweet you are, native land,
laid waste this day, ravaged, made a desert.
Barons of France, I see you die for me,
and I, your lord—I cannot protect you.
May *God* come to your aid, that God who never failed. 1865
Oliver, brother, now I will not fail *you*.
I will die here—of grief, if no man kills me.
Lord, Companion, let us return and fight."

141

Roland returned to his place on the field,
strikes—a brave man keeping faith—with Durendal, 1870
struck through Faldrun de Pui, cut him to pieces,
and twenty-four of the men they valued most;
no man will ever want his vengeance more!
As when the deer turns tail before the dogs,
so the pagans flee before Roland the Count. 1875
Said the Archbishop: "You! Roland! What a fighter!
Now that's what every knight must have in him
who carries arms and rides on a fine horse:
he must be strong, a savage, when he's in battle;
for otherwise, what's he worth? Not four cents! 1880
Let that four-cent man be a monk in some minster,
and he can pray all day long for our sins."
Roland replies: "Attack, do not spare them!"
And with that word the Franks began again.
There was a heavy loss of Christian men. 1885

142

When a man knows there'll be no prisoners,
what will that man not do to defend himself!
And so the Franks fight with the fury of lions.
Now Marsilion, the image of a baron,
mounted on that war horse he calls Gaignun, 1890
digs in his spurs, comes on to strike Bevon,
who was the lord of Beaune and of Dijon;
smashes his shield, rips apart his hauberk,
knocks him down, dead, no need to wound him more.
And then he killed Yvorie and Yvon, 1895
and more: he killed Gerard of Rousillon.
Roland the Count is not far away now,
said to the pagan: "The Lord God's curse on you!
You kill my companions, how you wrong me!
You'll feel the pain of it before we part, 1900
you will learn my sword's name by heart today";

comes on to strike—the image of a baron.
He has cut off Marsilion's right fist;
now takes the head of Jurfaleu the blond—
the head of Jurfaleu! Marsilion's son.   1905
The pagans cry: "Help, Mahumet! Help us!
Vengeance, our gods, on Charles! the man who set
these criminals on us in our own land,
they will not quit the field, they'll stand and die!"
And one said to the other: "Let *us* run then."   1910
And with that word, some hundred thousand flee.
Now try to call them back: they won't return. AOI.

143

What does it matter? If Marsilion has fled,
his uncle has remained: the Algalife,[7]
who holds Carthage, Alfrere, and Garmalie,   1915
and Ethiopia: a land accursed;
holds its immense black race under his power,
the huge noses, the enormous ears on them;
and they number more than fifty thousand.
These are the men who come riding in fury,   1920
and now they shout that pagan battle cry.
And Roland said: "Here comes our martyrdom;
I see it now: we have not long to live.
But let the world call any man a traitor
     who does not make them pay before he dies!
My lords, attack! Use those bright shining swords!   1925
Fight a good fight for your deaths and your lives,
let no shame touch sweet France because of us!
When Charles my lord comes to this battlefield
and sees how well we punished these Saracens,
finds fifteen of their dead for one of ours,   1930
I'll tell you what he will do: he will bless us." AOI.

144

When Roland sees that unbelieving race,
those hordes and hordes blacker than blackest ink—
no shred of white on them except their teeth—
then said the Count: "I see it clearly now,   1935
we die today: it is there before us.
Men of France, strike! I will start it once more."
Said Oliver: "God curse the slowest man."
And with that word, the French strike into battle.

145

The Saracens, when they saw these few French,   1940
looked at each other, took courage, and presumed,

---

7. The Caliph, Marsilion's uncle, whom Ganelon lied about to Charlemagne (see lines 680–91).

telling themselves: "The Emperor is wrong!"
The Algalife rides a great sorrel horse,
digs into it with his spurs of fine gold,
strikes Oliver, from behind, in the back,   1945
shattered the white hauberk upon his flesh,
drove his spear through the middle of his chest;
and speaks to him: "Now you feel you've been struck!
Your great Charles doomed you when he left you in this pass.
That man wronged us, he must not boast of it.   1950
I've avenged all our dead in you alone!"

146

Oliver feels: he has been struck to death;
grips Halteclere, that steel blade shining, strikes
on the gold-dressed pointed helm of the Algalife,
sends jewels and flowers crackling down to the earth,   1955
into the head, into the little teeth;
draws up his flashing sword, casts him down, dead,
and then he says: "Pagan, a curse on you!
If only I could say Charles has lost nothing—
but no woman, no lady you ever knew   1960
will hear you boast, in the land you came from,
that you could take one thing worth a cent from me,
or do me harm, or do any man harm";
then cries out to Roland to come to his aid. AOI.

147

Oliver feels he is wounded to death,   1965
will never have his fill of vengeance, strikes,
as a baron strikes, where they are thickest,
cuts through their lances, cuts through those buckled shields,
through feet, through fists, through saddles, and through flanks.
Had you seen him, cutting the pagans limb   1970
from limb, casting one corpse down on another,
you would remember a brave man keeping faith.
Never would he forget Charles' battle-cry,
Munjoie! he shouts, that mighty voice ringing;
calls to Roland, to his friend and his peer: 1975
"Lord, Companion, come stand beside me now.
We must part from each other in pain today." AOI.

148

Roland looks hard into Oliver's face,
it is ashen, all its color is gone,
the bright red blood streams down upon his body,   1980
Oliver's blood spattering on the earth.
"God!" said the Count, "I don't know what to do,
Lord, Companion, your fight is finished now.

There'll never be a man the like of you.
Sweet land of France, today you will be stripped   1985
of good vassals, laid low, a fallen land!
The Emperor will suffer the great loss";
faints with that word, mounted upon his horse. AOI.

149

Here is Roland, lords, fainted on his horse,
and Oliver the Count, wounded to death: 1990
he has lost so much blood, his eyes are darkened—
he cannot see, near or far, well enough
to recognize a friend or enemy:
struck when he came upon his companion,
strikes on his helm, adorned with gems in gold,   1995
cuts down straight through, from the point to the nasal,[8]
but never harmed him, he never touched his head.
Under this blow, Count Roland looked at him;
and gently, softly now, he asks of him:
"Lord, Companion, do you mean to do this?   2000
It is Roland, who always loved you greatly.
You never declared that we were enemies."
Said Oliver: "Now I hear it is you—
I don't see you, may the Lord God see you.
Was it you that I struck? Forgive me then."   2005
Roland replies: "I am not harmed, not harmed,
I forgive you, Friend, here and before God."
And with that word, each bowed to the other.
And this is the love, lords, in which they parted.

150

Oliver feels: death pressing hard on him;   2010
his two eyes turn, roll up into his head,
all hearing is lost now, all sight is gone;
gets down on foot, stretches out on the ground,
cries out now and again: *mea culpa!*[9]
his two hands joined, raised aloft toward heaven,   2015
he prays to God: grant him His Paradise;
and blesses Charles, and the sweet land of France,
his companion, Roland, above all men.
The heart fails him, his helmet falls away,
the great body settles upon the earth.   2020
The Count is dead, he stands with us no longer.
Roland, brave man, weeps for him, mourns for him,
you will not hear a man of greater sorrow.

151

Roland the Count, when he sees his friend dead,
lying stretched out, his face against the earth,   2025

---

8. The nosepiece protruding down from the cone-shaped helmet.   9. My guilt (Latin); a formula used
in the confession of one's sins.

softly, gently, begins to speak the regret:[1]
"Lord, Companion, you were brave and died for it.
We have stood side by side through days and years,
you never caused me harm, I never wronged you;
when you are dead, to be alive pains me."   2030
And with that word the lord of marches faints
upon his horse, which he calls Veillantif.
He is held firm by his spurs of fine gold,
whichever way he leans, he cannot fall.

152

Before Roland could recover his senses   2035
and come out of his faint, and be aware,
a great disaster had come forth before him:
the French are dead, he has lost every man
except the Archbishop, and Gautier de l'Hum,
who has come back, down from that high mountain: 2040
he has fought well, he fought those men of Spain.
His men are dead, the pagans finished them;
flees now down to these valleys, he has no choice,
and calls on Count Roland to come to his aid:
"My noble Count, my brave lord, where are you?   2045
I never feared whenever you were there.
It is Walter: I conquered Maëlgut,
my uncle is Droün, old and gray: your Walter
and always dear to you for the way I fought;
and I have fought this time: my lance is shattered,   2050
my good shield pierced, my hauberk's meshes broken;
and I am wounded, a lance struck through my body.
I will die soon, but I sold myself dear."
And with that word, Count Roland has heard him,
he spurs his horse, rides spurring to his man. AOI.   2055

153

Roland in pain, maddened with grief and rage:
rushes where they are thickest and strikes again,
strikes twenty men of Spain, strikes twenty dead,
and Walter six, and the Archbishop five.
The pagans say: "Look at those criminals!   2060
Now take care, Lords, they don't get out alive,
only a traitor will not attack them now!
Only a coward will let them save their skins!"
And then they raise their hue and cry once more,
rush in on them, once more, from every side. AOI.   2065

154

Count Roland was always a noble warrior,
Gautier de l'Hum is a fine mounted man,

---

1. What follows is a formal and customary lament for the dead.

the Archbishop, a good man tried and proved:
not one of them will ever leave the others;
strike, where they are thickest, at the pagans.   2070
A thousand Saracens get down on foot,
and forty thousand more are on their mounts:
and I tell you, not one will dare come close,
they throw, and from afar, lances and spears,
wigars and darts, mizraks, javelins, pikes.   2075
With the first blows they killed Gautier de l'Hum
and struck Turpin of Reims, pierced through his shield,
broke the helmet on him, wounded his head;
ripped his hauberk, shattered its rings of mail,
and pierced him with four spears in his body,   2080
the war horse killed under him; and now there comes
great pain and rage when the Archbishop falls. AOI.

155

Turpin of Reims, when he feels he is unhorsed,
struck to the earth with four spears in his body,
quickly, brave man, leaps to his feet again;   2085
his eyes find Roland now, he runs to him
and says one word: "See! I'm not finished yet!
What good vassal ever gives up alive!";
and draws Almace, his sword, that shining steel!
and strikes, where they are thickest, a thousand blows, and more. 2090
Later, Charles said: Turpin had spared no one;
he found four hundred men prostrate around him,
some of them wounded, some pierced from front to back,
some with their heads hacked off. So says the Geste,
and so says one who was there, on that field,   2095
the baron Saint Gilles,[2] for whom God performs miracles,
who made the charter setting forth these great things
      in the Church of Laon. Now any man
who does not know this much understands nothing.

156

Roland the Count fights well and with great skill,
but he is hot, his body soaked with sweat;   2100
has a great wound in his head, and much pain,
his temple broken because he blew the horn.
But he must know whether King Charles will come;
draws out the olifant, sounds it, so feebly.
The Emperor drew to a halt, listened.   2105
"Seigneurs," he said, "it goes badly for us—
My nephew Roland falls from our ranks today.
I hear it in the horn's voice: he hasn't long.
Let every man who wants to be with Roland

2. St. Gilles of Provence. These lines explain how the story of Rencesvals could be told after all who had
fought there died.

ride fast! Sound trumpets! Every trumpet in this host!"   2110
Sixty thousand, on these words, sound, so high
the mountains sound, and the valleys resound.
The pagans hear: it is no joke to them;
cry to each other: "We're getting Charles on us!"

157

The pagans say: "The Emperor is coming, AOI.   2115
listen to their trumpets—it is the French!
If Charles comes back, it's all over for us,
if Roland lives, this war begins again
and we have lost our land, we have lost Spain."
Some four hundred, helmets laced on, assemble,   2120
some of the best, as they think, on that field.
They storm Roland, in one fierce, bitter attack.
And now Count Roland has some work on his hands. AOI.

158

Roland the Count, when he sees them coming,
how strong and fierce and alert he becomes!   2125
He will not yield to them, not while he lives.
He rides the horse they call Veillantif, spurs,
digs into it with his spurs of fine gold,
and rushes at them all where they are thickest,
the Archbishop—that Turpin!—at his side.   2130
Said one man to the other: "Go at it, friend.
The horns we heard were the horns of the French,
King Charles is coming back with all his strength."[3]

159

Roland the Count never loved a coward,
a blusterer, an evil-natured man,   2135
a man on horse who was not a good vassal.
And now he called to Archbishop Turpin:
"You are on foot, Lord, and here I am mounted,
and so, here I take my stand: for love of you.
We'll take whatever comes, the good and bad,   2140
together, Lord: no one can make me leave you.
They will learn our swords' names today in battle,
the name of Almace, the name of Durendal!"
Said the Archbishop: "Let us strike or be shamed!
Charles is returning, and he brings our revenge."   2145

160

Say the pagans: "We were all born unlucky!
The evil day that dawned for us today!

---

3. The lines could be spoken either by Roland and the archbishop or by the pagans.

We have lost our lords and peers, and now comes Charles—
that Charlemagne!—with his great host. Those trumpets!
that shrill sound on us—the trumpets of the French!   2150
And the loud roar of that Munjoie! This Roland
is a wild man, he is too great a fighter—
What man of flesh and blood can ever hope
to bring him down? Let us cast at him, and leave him there."
And so they did: arrows, wigars, darts,   2155
lances and spears, javelots dressed with feathers;
struck Roland's shield, pierced it, broke it to pieces,
ripped his hauberk, shattered its rings of mail,
but never touched his body, never his flesh.
They wounded Veillantif in thirty places,   2160
struck him dead, from afar, under the Count.
The pagans flee, they leave the field to him.
Roland the Count stood alone, on his feet. AOI.

161

The pagans flee, in bitterness and rage,
strain every nerve running headlong toward Spain,   2165
and Count Roland has no way to chase them,
he has lost Veillantif, his battle horse;
he has no choice, left alone there on foot.
He went to the aid of Archbishop Turpin,
unlaced the gold-dressed helmet, raised it from his head,   2170
lifted away his bright, light coat of mail,
cut his under tunic into some lengths,
stilled his great wounds with thrusting on the strips;
then held him in his arms, against his chest,
and laid him down, gently, on the green grass;   2175
and softly now Roland entreated him:
"My noble lord, I beg you, give me leave:
our companions, whom we have loved so dearly,
are all dead now, we must not abandon them.
I want to look for them, know them once more,   2180
and set them in ranks, side by side, before you."
Said the Archbishop: "Go then, go and come back.
The field is ours, thanks be to God, yours and mine."

162

So Roland leaves him, walks the field all alone,
seeks in the valleys, and seeks in the mountains.   2185
He found Gerin, and Gerer his companion,
and then he found Berenger and Otun,
Anseïs and Sansun, and on that field
he found Gerard the old of Roussillon;
and carried them, brave man, all, one by one,   2190
came back to the Archbishop with these French dead,
and set them down in ranks before his knees.
The Archbishop cannot keep from weeping,
raises his hand and makes his benediction;

and said: "Lords, Lords, it was your terrible hour.   2195
May the Glorious God set all your souls
among the holy flowers of Paradise!
Here is my death, Lords, pressing on me,
I shall not see our mighty Emperor."

163

And Roland leaves, seeks in the field again;   2200
he has found Oliver, his companion,
held him tight in his arms against his chest;
came back to the Archbishop, laid Oliver
down on a shield among the other dead.
The Archbishop absolved him, signed him with the Cross.   2205
And pity now and rage and grief increase;
and Roland says: "Oliver, dear companion,
you were the son of the great duke Renier,
who held the march of the vale of Runers.
Lord, for shattering lances, for breaking shields,   2210
for making men great with presumption weak with fright,
for giving life and counsel to good men,
for striking fear in that unbelieving race,
no warrior on earth surpasses you."

164

Roland the Count, when he sees his peers dead,   2215
and Oliver, whom he had good cause to love,
felt such grief and pity, he begins to weep;
and his face lost its color with what he felt:
a pain so great he cannot keep on standing,
he has no choice, falls fainting to the ground.   2220
Said the Archbishop: "Baron, what grief for you."

165

The Archbishop, when he saw Roland faint,
felt such pain then as he had never felt;
stretched out his hand and grasped the olifant.
At Rencesvals there is a running stream: 2225
he will go there and fetch some water for Roland;
and turns that way, with small steps, staggering;
he is too weak, he cannot go ahead,
he has no strength: all the blood he has lost.
In less time than a man takes to cross a little field   2230
that great heart fails, he falls forward, falls down;
and Turpin's death comes crushing down on him.

166

Roland the Count recovers from his faint,
gets to his feet, but stands with pain and grief;

looks down the valley, looks up the mountain, sees: 2235
on the green grass, beyond his companions,
that great and noble man down on the ground,
the Archbishop, whom God sent in His name;
who confesses his sins, lifts up his eyes,
holds up his hands joined together to heaven,   2240
and prays to God: grant him that Paradise.
Turpin is dead, King Charles' good warrior.
In great battles, in beautiful sermons
he was ever a champion against the pagans.
Now God grant Turpin's soul His holy blessing. AOI.   2245

167

Roland the Count sees the Archbishop down,
sees the bowels fallen out of his body,
and the brain boiling down from his forehead.
Turpin has crossed his hands upon his chest
beneath the collarbone, those fine white hands.   2250
Roland speaks the lament, after the custom
followed in his land: aloud, with all his heart:
"My noble lord, you great and well-born warrior,
I commend you today to the God of Glory,
whom none will ever serve with a sweeter will.   2255
Since the Apostles no prophet the like of you[4]
arose to keep the faith and draw men to it.
May your soul know no suffering or want,
and behold the gate open to Paradise."

168

Now Roland feels that death is very near.   2260
His brain comes spilling out through his two ears;
prays to God for his peers: let them be called;
and for himself, to the angel Gabriel;
took the olifant: there must be no reproach!
took Durendal his sword in his other hand,   2265
and farther than a crossbow's farthest shot
he walks toward Spain, into a fallow land,
and climbs a hill: there beneath two fine trees
stand four great blocks of stone, all are of marble;
and he fell back, to earth, on the green grass,   2270
has fainted there, for death is very near.

169

High are the hills, and high, high are the trees;
there stand four blocks of stone, gleaming of marble.
Count Roland falls fainting on the green grass,

---

4. Cf. Deuteronomy 34.10, on the death of Moses: "And there arose not a prophet since in Israel like unto Moses, whom the Lord knew face to face."

and is watched, all this time, by a Saracen: 2275
who has feigned death and lies now with the others,
has smeared blood on his face and on his body;
and quickly now gets to his feet and runs—
a handsome man, strong, brave, and so crazed with pride
that he does something mad and dies for it: 2280
laid hands on Roland, and on the arms of Roland,
and cried: "Conquered! Charles's nephew conquered!
I'll carry this sword home to Arabia!"
As he draws it, the Count begins to come round.

170

Now Roland feels: *someone taking his sword!*   2285
opened his eyes, and had one word for him:
"I don't know you, you aren't one of ours";
grasps that olifant that he will never lose,
strikes on the helm beset with gems in gold,
shatters the steel, and the head, and the bones,   2290
sent his two eyes flying out of his head,
dumped him over stretched out at his feet dead;
and said: "You nobody! how could you dare
lay hands on me—rightly or wrongly: how?
Who'll hear of this and not call you a fool?   2295
Ah! the bell-mouth of the olifant is smashed,
the crystal and the gold fallen away."

171

Now Roland the Count feels: his sight is gone;
gets on his feet, draws on his final strength,
the color on his face lost now for good.   2300
Before him stands a rock; and on that dark rock
in rage and bitterness he strikes ten blows:
the steel blade grates, it will not break, it stands unmarked.
"Ah!" said the Count, "Blessed Mary, your help!
Ah Durendal, good sword, your unlucky day,   2305
for I am lost and cannot keep you in my care.
The battles I have won, fighting with you,
the mighty lands that holding you I conquered,
that Charles rules now, our King, whose beard is white!
Now you fall to another: it must not be
        a man who'd run before another man!   2310
For a long while a good vassal held you:
there'll never be the like in France's holy land."

172

Roland strikes down on that rock of Cerritania:
the steel blade grates, will not break, stands unmarked.
Now when he sees he can never break that sword,   2315

Roland speaks the lament, in his own presence:
"Ah Durendal, how beautiful and bright!
so full of light, all on fire in the sun!
King Charles was in the vales of Moriane
when God sent his angel and commanded him, 2320
from heaven, to give you to a captain count.
That great and noble King girded it on me.
And with this sword I won Anjou and Brittany,
I won Poitou, I won Le Maine for Charles,
and Normandy, that land where men are free, 2325
I won Provence and Aquitaine with this,
and Lombardy, and every field of Romagna,
I won Bavaria, and all of Flanders,
all of Poland, and Bulgaria, for Charles,
Constantinople, which pledged him loyalty, 2330
and Saxony, where he does as he wills;
and with this sword I won Scotland and Ireland,
and England, his chamber, his own domain—
the lands, the nations I conquered with this sword,
for Charles, who rules them now, whose beard is white! 2335
Now, for this sword, I am pained with grief and rage:
Let it not fall to pagans! Let me die first!
Our Father God, save France from that dishonor."

173

Roland the Count strikes down on a dark rock,
and the rock breaks, breaks more than I can tell, 2340
and the blade grates, but Durendal will not break,
the sword leaped up, rebounded toward the sky.
The Count, when he sees that sword will not be broken,
softly, in his own presence, speaks the lament:
"Ah Durendal, beautiful, and most sacred, 2345
the holy relics in this golden pommel!
Saint Peter's tooth and blood of Saint Basile,
a lock of hair of my lord Saint Denis,
and a fragment of blessed Mary's robe:
your power must not fall to the pagans, 2350
you must be served by Christian warriors.
May no coward ever come to hold you!
It was with you I conquered those great lands
that Charles has in his keeping, whose beard is white,
the Emperor's lands, that make him rich and strong." 2355

174

Now Roland feels: death coming over him,
death descending from his temples to his heart.
He came running underneath a pine tree
and there stretched out, face down, on the green grass,
lays beneath him his sword and the olifant. 2360
He turned his head toward the Saracen hosts,

and this is why: with all his heart he wants
King Charles the Great and all his men to say,
he died, that noble Count, a conqueror;
makes confession, beats his breast often, so feebly,   2365
offers his glove, for all his sins, to God. AOI.

175

Now Roland feels that his time has run out;
he lies on a steep hill, his face toward Spain;
and with one of his hands he beat his breast:
"Almighty God, *mea culpa* in thy sight,[5]   2370
forgive my sins, both the great and the small,
sins I committed from the hour I was born
until this day, in which I lie struck down."
And then he held his right glove out to God.
Angels descend from heaven and stand by him. AOI.   2375

176

Count Roland lay stretched out beneath a pine;
he turned his face toward the land of Spain,
began to remember many things now:
how many lands, brave man, he had conquered;
and he remembered: sweet France, the men of his line,   2380
remembered Charles, his lord, who fostered him:
cannot keep, remembering, from weeping, sighing;
but would not be unmindful of himself:
he confesses his sins, prays God for mercy:
"Loyal Father, you who never failed us,   2385
who resurrected Saint Lazarus from the dead,
and saved your servant Daniel from the lions:[6]
now save the soul of me from every peril
for the sins I committed while I still lived."
Then he held out his right glove to his Lord: 2390
Saint Gabriel took the glove from his hand.
He held his head bowed down upon his arm,
he is gone, his two hands joined, to his end.
Then God sent him his angel Cherubin[7]
and Saint Michael, angel of the sea's Peril;   2395
and with these two there came Saint Gabriel:
they bear Count Roland's soul to Paradise.

177

Roland is dead, God has his soul in heaven.
The Emperor rides into Rencesvals;
there is no passage there, there is no track,   2400

---

5. See Psalm 51.4: "Against thee, thee only, have I sinned, and done this evil in thy sight."   **6.** See Daniel 6.12–23. For the raising of Lazarus, see John 11.1–44.   **7.** The poet seems to have regarded this as the name of a single angel.

no empty ground, not an elle, not one foot,
that does not bear French dead or pagan dead.
King Charles cries out: "Dear Nephew, where are you?
Where is the Archbishop? Count Oliver?
Where is Gerin, his companion Gerer? 2405
Where is Otun, where is Count Berenger,
Yves and Yvoire, men I have loved so dearly?
What has become of Engeler the Gascon,
Sansun the Duke, and Anseïs, that fighter?
Where is Gerard the Old of Roussillon, 2410
and the Twelve Peers, whom I left in these passes?"
And so forth—what's the difference? No one answered.
"God!" said the King, "how much I must regret
I was not here when the battle began";
pulls his great beard, a man in grief and rage. 2415
His brave knights weep, their eyes are filled with tears,
twenty thousand fall fainting to the ground;
Duke Naimon feels the great pity of it.

178

There is no knight or baron on that field
who does not weep in bitterness and grief; 2420
for they all weep: for their sons, brothers, nephew,
weep for their friends, for their sworn men and lords;
the mass of them fall fainting to the ground.
Here Naimon proved a brave and useful man:
he was the first to urge the Emperor: 2425
"Look ahead there, two leagues in front of us,
you can see the dust rising on those wide roads:
the pagan host—and how many they are!
After them now! Ride! Avenge this outrage!"
"Oh! God!" said Charles, "look how far they have gotten! 2430
Lord, let me have my right, let me have honor,
they tore from me the flower of sweet France."
The King commands Gebuïn and Othon,
Thibaut of Reims and Count Milun his cousin:
"Now guard this field, the valleys, the mountains, 2435
let the dead lie, all of them, as they are,
let no lion, let no beast come near them,
let no servant, let no groom come near them,
I command you, let no man come near these dead
until God wills we come back to this field." 2440
And they reply, gently, and in great love:
"Just Emperor, dear Lord, we shall do that."
They keep with them a thousand of their knights. AOI.

179

The Emperor has his high-pitched trumpets sound,
and then he rides, brave man, with his great host. 2445

They made the men of Spain show them their heels,
and they keep after them, all as one man.
When the King sees the twilight faltering,
he gets down in a meadow on the green grass,
lies on the ground, prays to the Lord his God   2450
to make the sun stand still for him in heaven,
hold back the night, let the day linger on.
Now comes the angel[8] always sent to speak with Charles;
and the angel at once commanded him:
"Charles, ride: God knows. The light will not fail you.   2455
God knows that you have lost the flower of France.
You can take vengeance now on that criminal race."
The Emperor, on that word, mounts his horse. AOI.

180

God made great miracles for Charlemagne,
for on that day in heaven the sun stood still.   2460
The pagans flee, the Franks keep at their heels,
catch up with them in the Vale Tenebrous,
chase them on spurring hard to Saragossa,
and always killing them, striking with fury;
cut off their paths, the widest roads away: 2465
the waters of the Ebro lie before them,
very deep, an amazing sight, and swift;
and there is no boat, no barge, no dromond, no galley.
They call on Tervagant, one of their gods.
Then they jump in, but no god is with them: 2470
those in full armor, the ones who weigh the most,
sank down, and they were many, to the bottom;
the others float downstream: the luckiest ones,
who fare best in those waters, have drunk so much,
they all drown there, struggling, it is amazing.   2475
The French cry out: "Curse the day you saw Roland!" AOI.

181

When Charlemagne sees all the pagans dead,
many struck down, the great mass of them drowned—
the immense spoils his knights win from that battle!—
the mighty King at once gets down on foot,   2480
lies on the ground, and gives thanks to the Lord.
When he stands up again, the sun has set.
Said the Emperor: "It is time to make camp.
It is late now to return to Rencesvals;
our horses are worn out, they have no strength—   2485
take off their saddles, the bridles on their heads,
let them cool down and rest in these meadows."
The Franks reply: "Yes, as you well say, Lord." AOI.

8. Gabriel. Cf. *laisses* 185, 291, and others.

182

The Emperor commands them to make camp.
The French dismount into that wilderness;   2490
they have removed the saddles from their horses,
and the bridles, dressed in gold, from their heads,
free them to the meadows and the good grass;
and that is all the care they can give them.
Those who are weary sleep on the naked earth;   2495
and all sleep, they set no watch that night.

183

The Emperor lay down in a meadow,
puts his great spear, brave man, beside his head;
he does not wish, on this night, to disarm:
he has put on his bright, brass-sewn hauberk,   2500
laced on his helm, adorned with gems in gold,
and girded on Joiuse, there never was its like:
each day it shines with thirty different lights.
There are great things that we can say about the lance
with which Our Lord was wounded on the Cross: 2505
thanks be to God, Charles has its iron point,
he had it mounted in that sword's golden pommel.
For this honor, and for this mighty grace,
the name Joiuse was given to that sword.
Brave men of France must never forget this: 2510
from this sword's name they get their cry Munjoie!
This is why no nation can withstand them.

184

The night is clear, the moon is shining bright,
Charles lies down in grief and pain for Roland,
and for Oliver, it weighs down on him hard,   2515
for the Twelve Peers, for all the men of France
whom he left dead, covered with blood, at Rencesvals;
and cannot keep from weeping, wailing aloud,
and prays to God: lead their souls to safety.
His weariness is great, for his pain is great;   2520
he has fallen asleep, he cannot go on.
Through all the meadows now the Franks are sleeping.
There is no horse that has the strength to stand:
if one wants grass, he grazes lying down.
He has learned much who knows much suffering.   2525

185

Charlemagne sleeps, a man worn out with pain.
God sent Saint Gabriel to him that night
with this command: watch over the Emperor.

All through the night the angel stands at his head;
and in a vision he brought the King dread tidings   2530
of a great battle soon to come against him:
revealed to him its grave signification:
Charles raised his eyes and looked up to the sky,
he sees the thunder, the winds, the blasts of ice,
the hurricanes, the dreadful tempests,   2535
the fires and flames made ready in the sky.
And suddenly all things fall on his men.
Their lances burn, the wood of ash and apple,
and their shields burn down to their golden bosses,
the shafts of their sharp spears burst into pieces,   2540
then the grating of hauberks, helmets of steel.
He sees his warriors in great distress—
leopards and bears furious to devour them,
serpents, vipers, dragons, demons of hell,
swarms of griffins, thirty thousand and more,   2545
and all come swooping down upon the French;
and the French cry: "Charlemagne, come help us!"
The King is filled with rage and pain and pity,
wants to go there, but something blocks his way:
out of a wood a great lion coming at him,   2550
it is tremendous, wild, and great with pride:
seeks the King's very body, attacks the King!
and they lock arms, King and lion, to fight,
and still he cannot tell who strikes, who falls.
The Emperor sleeps, his dream does not wake him.   2555

186

And after this he was shown another vision:
he was in France, at Aix, on a stone step,
and two chains in his hands holding a bear;
from the Ardennes he saw thirty bears coming,
and each of them was speaking like a man;   2560
they said to him: "Lord, give him back to us,
you must not keep him longer, it is not right;
he is our kin, we must deliver him."
From his palace a greyhound now, running,
leaps on the greatest bear among them all,   2565
on the green grass beyond his companions,
there the King sees an amazing struggle
but cannot tell who conquers, who goes down.
These are the things God's angel showed this baron.
Charles sleeps until the morning and the bright day.   2570

[Lines 2571–3675 describe the death of Marsilion and Charlemagne's defeat of the
army of Baligant, the emir of Cairo and Marsilion's overlord.]

267

Night passes on, and the bright day appears.
Charles fortified the towers of Saragossa,

left a thousand knights there, fighting men all;
they guard the city in the Emperor's name.
Now the King mounts his horse, all his men mount,   3680
and Bramimunde, whom he leads prisoner,
though he has but one will: to do her good.
They turn toward home, in joy, in jubilation,
and pass in force, a mighty host, through Nerbone;
and Charles came to Bordeaux, that . . . city, sets[9]   3685
on the altar of the baron saint Sevrin
the olifant, filled with gold and pagan coins—
pilgrims passing can see it there today;
crosses the Gironde in great ships that lie there;
he has escorted as far as Blaye his nephew   3690
and Oliver, his noble companion,
and the Archbishop, who was so wise and brave;
and bids these lords be laid in white stone coffins:
at Saint-Romain the brave men lie there still;
the Franks leave them to the Lord and His Names.[1]   3695
And Charles rides over the valleys and the mountains,
would take no rest all the long way to Aix,
and rode until he dismounts at the steps.
When he is in his sovereign high palace,
he summons all his judges, sends messengers: 3700
Saxons, Bavarians, Frisians, men of Lorraine,
the Alemans, the men of Burgundy,
the Poitevins, the Normans, the Bretons,
the wisest men among the men of France.
And now begins the trial of Ganelon.   3705

268

The Emperor is home again from Spain,
and comes to Aix, best residence of France,
ascends to the palace; entered the hall.
And now comes Aude, fair maid, before the King;
and said to him: "Where is Roland the captain,   3710
who swore to me to take me for his wife?"
And Charlemagne feels the weight and grief of this,
tears fill his eyes, he weeps, pulls his white beard:
"Sweet friend, dear sister, you ask for a dead man.
I will give you a good man in his place,   3715
it is Louis, I cannot name a better—
he is my son, he will possess my marches."
And Aude replies: "How strange these words sound to me.
May it never please God or his angels or saints
that I should go on living after Roland";   3720
loses color, falls at Charlemagne's feet,

---

9. The line is incomplete in the manuscript.   1. A reference to prayers containing some of the many
names (Adonai, Emmanuel, Yehovah, and so on) by which God is called in sacred writings. These prayers
were considered effective in times of danger.

already dead, God take pity on her soul.
Brave men of France weep and lament for Aude.

269

Aude the fair maid is gone now to her end;
the King believes that she has only fainted;   3725
and he is moved, the Emperor weeps for Aude,
takes her two hands; now he has raised her up,
her head sinks down, fallen upon her shoulders;
when Charlemagne sees she is dead in his arms,
he has four countesses sent for at once,   3730
and Aude is borne to a minster of nuns;
all through the night till dawn they wake beside her,
then nobly buried her by an altar.
The King gave Aude great honors, the church great gifts. AOI.

270

The Emperor has come home again to Aix.   3735
In iron chains, the traitor Ganelon
stands before the palace, within the city.
He has been bound, and by serfs, to a stake;
they tie his hands with deerhide straps and thongs,
and beat him hard, with butcher's hooks, with clubs—   3740
for what better reward has this man earned?
There he stands, in pain and rage, awaiting his trial.

271

It is written in the ancient Geste
that Charles summons his vassals from many lands;
they are gathered in the chapel at Aix,   3745
a high day this, a very solemn feast,
the feast, some say, of the baron saint Sylvester.[2]
Now here begin the trial and the pleadings
of Ganelon, who committed treason.
The Emperor has had this man brought forth. AOI.   3750

272

"Barons, my lords," said Charlemagne the King,
"judge what is right concerning Ganelon.
He was with me, came in my army to Spain,
and took from me twenty thousand of my French,
and my nephew, whom you'll not see again,   3755
and Oliver, brave man, born to the court,
and the Twelve Peers—betrayed them all for money."

2. The feast of Saint Sylvester: December 31.

Said Ganelon: "Let me be called a traitor
    if I hide what I did. It was Roland
who cheated me of gold and goods; and so I wanted
to make him suffer and die; and found the way.   3760
But treason, no—I'll grant no treason there!"
The Franks reply: "We shall take counsel now."

273

And there Ganelon stood, before the King,
breathing power—that lordly color on his face:
the image of a great man, had he been loyal.   3765
He sees his judges, he sees the men of France,
and his kinsmen, the thirty with him there;
then he cried out, with that great ringing voice:
"Barons, hear me, hear me for the love of God!
I was in that army with the Emperor   3770
and served him well, in love and loyalty.
Then his nephew Roland began to hate me,
and he doomed me to die an outrageous death:
I was sent as messenger to King Marsilion.
I used my wits, and I came back alive.   3775
Now I had challenged Roland, that great fighter,
and Oliver, and all of their companions:
King Charles heard it, and all his noble barons.
I took *revenge*, but there's no treason there."
The Franks reply: "We shall go into council."   3780

274

When Ganelon sees that his great trial commences,
he got his thirty kinsmen all around him.
There is one man the others listen to:
it is Pinabel of the castle of Sorence,
a man who counsels well and judges well,   3785
a valiant fighter—no man can win his arms. AOI.
Said Ganelon: "In you, friend . . . [3]
free me from death and from this accusation!"
Said Pinabel: "You will soon be out of this.
Let one Frenchman dare sentence you to hang: 3790
once the Emperor sets us down man to man,
I will give him the lie with this steel sword."
And Ganelon, the Count, falls at his feet.

275

Bavarians, Saxons have gone into council,
Poitevins and Normans and men of France,   3795
the Alemans, the Germans from the North,
men of Auvergne, the courtliest of all.

---

3. The line is incomplete in the manuscript.

They keep their voices low, because of Pinabel;
said to each other: "Best to let it stop here—
let's leave this trial and then entreat the King   3800
to let Count Ganelon go free this time
and serve henceforth in love and loyalty.
Roland is dead: you won't see him again,
he will not come for gold or goods again:
only a fool would fight over this now."   3805
All go along, no one there disagrees
except one man, Lord Gefrei's brother: Tierri. AOI.

276

The barons now come back to Charlemagne,
say to the King: "Lord, this we beg of you:
let Ganelon go free, renounce your claim,   3810
then let him serve you in love and loyalty:
let this man live, for his family is great.
Roland is dead: we'll not see a hair of him,
    though we die for it, not a shred of his garment,
or get him back for gold or goods again."
And the King said: "You are all my traitors." AOI.   3815

277

When Charles perceives all have abandoned him,
he bowed his head with that and hid his face,
and in such pain calls himself wretched man.
But now we see: a warrior before him,
Tierri, brother of Gefrei, a duke of Anjou—   3820
the meager body on him, such a slight man!
his hair all black, and his face rather dark;
hardly a giant, but at least not too small;
said to the Emperor, as one born to the court:
"Dear Lord and King, do not lament before us.   3825
You know I have served you well: I have the right,
my forebears' right! to give this judgment here:
Whatever wrong Count Roland may have done
to Ganelon, he was in your service,
    and serving you should have protected him,
Ganelon is a traitor: he betrayed Roland.   3830
It's you he wronged when he perjured himself,
and broke faith. Therefore, I sentence him
to die, to hang . . . his body cast . . . [4]
like a traitor, a man who committed treason.
If his kinsman wants to give me the lie,   3835
here is my sword, girded on: and with this sword
I am ready to make my judgment good."
The Franks reply: "Now you have spoken well."

4. The line is incomplete in manuscript.

278

Now Pinabel has come before the King:
a huge man of swift grace, a valiant man—   3840
time has run out for the poor wretch he strikes!—
said to the King: "Lord, is this not your court?
Give orders then, tell them to stop this noise.
Here I see Tierri, who has given his judgment:
I declare it is false; I shall fight with him";   3845
places his deerhide glove in Charles's fist.
Said the Emperor: "I must have good surety."
Thirty kinsmen go hostage for his loyalty.
Then the King said: "I shall release him then";
and has them guarded until justice is done. AOI.   3850

279

When Tierri sees the battle will take place
he gave to Charles his own right glove as gage.
The Emperor sets him free, for hostages;
then has four benches set round that battle ground:
there they will sit: the two men pledged to fight.   3855
The others judge they have been duly summoned,
Oger of Denmark had settled every question.
And then they call for their horses and arms.

280

Now since both men have been brought forth for battle, AOI.
they make confession and are absolved and blessed;   3860
they hear their mass, receive the Sacrament,
lay down great offerings in these minsters.
Now the two men have come back before Charles.
They have fastened their spurs upon their feet,
and they put on white hauberks, strong and light,   3865
and laced their bright helmets glowing upon their heads,
gird on their swords, the hilts of purest gold;
hang their great quartered shields upon their necks,
take hold of their sharp spears in their right fists;
now they are mounted upon their swift war horses.   3870
And then a hundred thousand warriors wept,
moved for love of Roland to pity Tierri.
The Lord well knows how this battle will end.

281

Down below Aix there is a broad meadow;
there the battle is joined between these barons.   3875
They are brave men, great warriors keeping faith,
and their horses are swift and spirited.
They spur them hard, reins loosened all the way,
come on to strike, the great strength that is theirs!
their two shields burst in that attack to pieces,

3880

their hauberks tear, their saddle girths rip open,
the bosses turn, the saddles fall to earth.
A hundred thousand men, who watch them, weep.

282

Now the two warriors are on the ground, AOI.
now on their feet, and with what speed! again—   3885
the grace and lightness, the strength of Pinabel!—
fall on each other, they have no horses now,
strike with their swords, the hilts of purest gold,
and strike again on these helmets of steel
tremendous blows—blows that cut through helms of steel!   3890
The knights of France are wild with grief and worry.
"Oh, God," said Charles, "make the right between
        them clear!"

283

Said Pinabel: "Tierri, now give it up!
I'll be your man, in love and loyalty,
I'll give you all I own, take what you please,   3895
only make peace with the King for Ganelon."
Tierri replies: "I cannot hear of that,
call me traitor if I consent to that!
May God do right between us two today." AOI.

284

Now Tierri spoke: "Pinabel, you are good,   3900
the great body on you formed like a lord's;
your peers know you: all that a vassal should be;
let this battle go then, let it end here,
I will make peace for you with Charlemagne.
But justice will be done on Ganelon,
        such justice will be done on his body,   3905
no day will pass that men do not speak of it."
Said Pinabel: "May the Lord God forbid!
I will stand up for all my kin, I'll fight,
no man alive will make me quit my kin
        and cry defeat and beg for his mercy,
I'd sooner die than be reproached for that."   3910
And they begin to beat down with their swords
on these helmets beset with gems in gold,
and the bright fires fly from that fight toward heaven;
and no chance now that these two can be parted:
it cannot end without one of them dead. AOI.   3915

285

Pinabel of Sorence, that valiant man,
strikes Tierri now on that helm of Provence:
the fire shoots out and sets the grass aflame;

and shows Tierri the point of that steel sword:
he brought it down. Pinabel brought it down   3920
on his forehead, and down across his face,
the whole right cheek is bloody from that blow,
his hauberk runs with blood down to his waist.
God protects him, he is not struck down dead. AOI.

286

And Tierri sees: he is struck on the face—   3925
the bright blood falling on the grass in the meadow;
strikes Pinabel on his helm of bright steel,
and shattered it, split it to the nosepiece,
struck his brain out spattering from his head;
and raised his sword; he has cast him down, dead.   3930
That was the blow, and the battle is won.
The Franks cry out: "God has made a miracle!
Now Ganelon must hang, it is right now,
and all his kin who stood for him in court." AOI.

287

Now when Tierri had won his great battle,   3935
there came to him the Emperor Charlemagne,
and forty of his barons along with him,
Naimon the Duke, and Oger of Denmark,
William of Blaye, and Gefrei of Anjou.
The King has taken Tierri into his arms,   3940
he wipes his face with his great furs of marten,
throws them aside; they clasp new furs round him.
Very gently, they disarm the warrior,
then they mount him on a mule of Araby,
and he comes home in joy among brave men.   3945
They come to Aix, it is there they dismount.
It is the time now for the executions.

288

Now Charlemagne summons his counts and dukes:
"What is your counsel regarding those I have held?
They came to court to stand for Ganelon,   3950
bound themselves hostages for Pinabel."
The Franks reply: "Not one of them must live."
The King commands his officer, Basbrun:
"Go, hang them all on the accursed tree,
and by this beard, by the white hairs in this beard,   3955
if one escapes, you are lost, a dead man."
Basbrun replies: "What should I do but hang them?";
leads them, by force, with a hundred sergeants.
They are thirty men, and thirty men are hanged.
A traitor brings death, on himself and on others. AOI.   3960

289

Bavarians and Alemans returned,
and Poitevins, and Bretons, and Normans,
and all agreed, the Franks before the others,
Ganelon must die, and in amazing pain.
Four war horses are led out and brought forward;   3965
then they attach his two feet, his two hands.
These battle horses are swift and spirited,
four sergeants come and drive them on ahead
toward a river in the midst of a field.
Ganelon is brought to terrible perdition,   3970
all his mighty sinews are pulled to pieces,
and the limbs of his body burst apart;
on the green grass flows that bright and famous blood.
Ganelon died a traitor's and recreant's death.
Now when one man betrays another,
      it is not right that he should live to boast of it.   3975

290

When the Emperor had taken his revenge,
he called to him his bishops of France,
Bavaria, Germany: "In my household
there is a noble captive, and she has heard,
for so long now, such sermons and examples,   3980
she longs for faith in God, the Christian faith.
Baptize this Queen, that God may have her soul."
And they reply: "Let her be baptized now
by godmothers, ladies of noble birth."
At the baths of Aix there is a great crowd gathered,   3985
there they baptized the noble Queen of Spain,
and they found her the name Juliana;
she is Christian, by knowledge of the Truth.

291

When the Emperor had brought his justice to pass
and peace comes now to that great wrath of his,   3990
he put the Christian faith in Bramimunde;
the day passes, the soft night has gathered,
the King lay down in his vaulted chamber.
Saint Gabriel! come in God's name to say:
"Charles, gather the great hosts of your Empire!   3995
Go to the land of Bire, with all your force,
you must relieve King Vivien at Imphe,
the citadel, pagans have besieged it:
Christians are calling you, they cry your name!"
The Emperor would have wished not to go.   4000
"God!" said the King, "the pains, the labors of my life!";
weeps from his eyes, pulls his white beard.

Here ends the song   that Turold composes, paraphrases, amplifies,[5] 4003
                              that Turold completes, relates,
Here ends the tale   that Turold declaims, recounts, narrates,
                              that Turold copies, transcribes,
Here ends the geste   for Turold grows weak, grows weary, declines,
Here ends the written history,
Here ends the source   that Turold turns into poetry.

5. The last line of the poem reads *Ci falt la geste que Turoldus declinet.* The meaning of the words *geste* and *declinet* and the syntax of *que* have never been finally settled, and no line in the poem contains so many possible meanings as the last one. Some of the interpretations that have been proposed are given here, and every one is plausible.

MARIE DE FRANCE
twelfth century

The first woman writer in French (at least so far as we know), Marie de France created her work at a crucial time in the history of literature. In the twelfth century most of the major forms and themes that have shaped Western literature emerged in the vernacular languages of Europe. Primary among them were the works we now call romances, novelistic narratives that dealt with adventure and—above all—love. The most familiar of these narratives are the stories of King Arthur and his knights, tales as popular in the Middle Ages as today. The Arthurian legends were part of a vast mythology developed by the Celts of Western Europe, peoples who were driven from their lands by the Germanic invaders of the fourth and fifth centuries and took refuge on the Atlantic fringe of the continent in what are now Ireland, Wales, and Brittany. Yet if they were conquered as a people, the Celts triumphed through their stories. Much of medieval literature reveals the influence of Celtic mythology.

Less popular than the long Arthurian narratives but more finely crafted as works of art were the short narratives of love, adventure, and the supernatural, also of Celtic origin, known as *lais* or, in English, lays. As a form of literature, the lay first appears in a collection composed about 1165 by a woman who identifies herself only as "Marie." In another work she tells us that she is "from France," and ever since the Renaissance she has been given the designation "Marie de France." From the evidence of her writing, we know that she was a noblewoman, that she could read French, English, and Latin, and that she was familiar with a royal household, probably that of Henry II, king of England (reigned 1154–89). She may well have been a nun or even an abbess, since many noble daughters were placed in the elegant aristocratic convents of Europe. All of her work, including the twelve lays that survive, is written in octosyllabic verse in Anglo-Norman, a French dialect spoken by the nobility of postconquest England. The sources for her lays, she tells us, were stories that she heard, and while she provides us with several Breton terms—like the word *laüstic* for nightingale—we cannot know if she heard these stories in English, French, or Breton.

The two lays presented here deal with a topic that is central to the collection as a whole. These are stories in which love serves as an alternative—in one case successfully, in the other not—to an uncaring or unjust society. In both stories Marie combines an acute awareness of contemporary social conditions with sympathy for individuals who seek personal fulfillment. In the lay that bears his name, Lanval is a young foreigner who has come to the Arthurian court to seek his fortune. He is the son of a king, but his "inheritance"—by which Marie means his ancestral domain—

is far away. The implication is that Lanval, like many noble young men in twelfth-century France and England, was a younger son excluded from inheriting the family land under the recently established system of primogeniture, by which only the eldest son inherited. Thus when at the beginning of the story Arthur hands out lands and wives to his knights but neglects the deserving Lanval, he is dooming Lanval to a life of continued obscurity and lonely service. Rescue comes to him in the form of the fairy lover, who is not merely beautiful and loving but—as Marie is careful to stress—rich. Now that Lanval can comport himself with the confidence and generosity that befits a nobleman, he becomes attractive to the queen (presumably Guinevere, although she is not named). And in rejecting her advances he asserts not simply the superior beauty of his lady but the superiority of her handmaiden, making it clear that he is attached to a court that surpasses in its grandeur that of Arthur himself. This is why Arthur so quickly supports his queen in her false accusation, and why Lanval is accused not just of a social gaffe but of felony and treason. For as Arthur's barons say, Lanval ought to honor his lord at all times, while he is acting (rightly, as it turns out) as if he is obligated to a different sovereign entirely. Yet the power of Marie's story derives from the fact that, despite this emphasis on social and material benefits, Lanval is primarily distressed because he has lost not the fairy queen's financial support but her love. And when the two pairs of damsels appear, he remains true to her by refusing to claim either of them as proof that his rash words to the queen were true. Perhaps because he passes this test his lover herself then appears and takes him away with her to Avalon, a world in which the petty jealousies of the Arthurian court can be forgotten. Here love seems to conquer all, but its triumph is possible only in the fantasy world of fiction.

Laüstic, on the other hand, is a story of unfulfilled love. In this case the social reality to which the story is addressed is the aristocratic custom of arranged marriages. In *Lanval* Arthur gives away wives, yet there is no indication that the women involved have any say in their marital fate. Yet at the same time as the European nobility was treating marriage as a financial and political matter, the Church was teaching that marriage was above all a matter of free consent, that what made two people husband and wife was their agreement to enter into marriage with each other. Marie's lays are filled with unhappy wives—unhappy not only because they were forced into marriages against their will but because they know they deserve better (indeed, perhaps we should understand Guinevere's misbehavior in *Lanval* as caused by such knowledge). The young wife in *Laüstic* can only dream of escape as she gazes out her confining room at her would-be lover. The nightingale that she invokes to quiet her jealous husband becomes a symbol of this yearning to escape, and when her husband brutally kills it and throws its bleeding corpse at her, we can understand that the stain it leaves on the breast of her tunic is the outward sign of a broken heart. Yet this is not the end, for the golden casket in which her lover entombs the nightingale serves to celebrate a love that may not have found earthly fulfillment but has achieved another, higher permanence. In its exquisite concision, *Laüstic* is itself a literary version of that golden casket, a verbal equivalent to the jeweled reliquaries in which medieval people encased the bodies of their saints.

Lanval[1]

Just as it happened, I shall relate to you the story of another lay, which tells of a very noble young man whose name in Breton is Lanval.

Arthur, the worthy and courtly king, was at Carlisle[2] on account of the Scots and the Picts who were ravaging the country, penetrating into the land of Logres[3] and frequently laying it waste.

The king was there during the summer, at Pentecost,[4] and he gave many rich gifts to counts and barons and to those of the Round Table: there was no such company in the whole world. He apportioned wives and lands to all, save to one who had served him: this was Lanval, whom he did not remember, and for whom no one put in a good word. Because of his valor, generosity, beauty and prowess, many were envious of him. There were those who pretended to hold him in esteem, but who would not have uttered a single regret if misfortune had befallen him. He was the son of a king of noble birth, but far from his inheritance, and although he belonged to Arthur's household he had spent all his wealth, for the king gave him nothing and Lanval asked for nothing. Now he was in a plight, very sad and forlorn. Lords, do not be surprised: a stranger bereft of advice can be very downcast in another land when he does not know where to seek help.

This knight whose tale I am telling you had served the king well. One day he mounted his horse and went to take his ease. He left the town and came alone to a meadow, dismounting by a stream; but there his horse trembled violently, so he loosened its saddlegirth and left it, allowing it to enter the meadow to roll over on its back. He folded his cloak, which he placed beneath his head, very disconsolate because of his troubles, and nothing could please him. Lying thus, he looked downriver and saw two damsels coming, more beautiful than any he had ever seen: they were richly dressed in closely fitting tunics of dark purple and their faces were very beautiful. The older one carried dishes of gold, well and finely made—I will not fail to tell you the truth—and the other carried a towel. They went straight to where the knight lay and Lanval, who was very well-mannered, stood up to meet them. They first greeted him and then delivered their message: "Sir Lanval, my damsel, who is very worthy, wise and fair, has sent us for you. Come with us, for we will conduct you safely. Look, her tent is near." The knight went with them, disregarding his horse which was grazing before him in the meadow. They led him to the tent, which was so beautiful and well-appointed that neither Queen Semiramis at the height of her wealth, power and knowledge, nor the Emperor Octavian,[5] could have afforded even the right-hand side of it. There was a golden eagle placed on the top, the value of which I cannot tell, nor of the ropes or the poles which supported the walls of the tent. There is no king under the sun who could afford it, however much he might give. Inside this tent was the maiden who surpassed in beauty the lily and the new rose when it appears in summer. She lay on a very beautiful bed—the coverlets cost as much as a castle—clad only in her shift. Her body was well formed and handsome, and in order to protect herself from the heat of the sun, she

---

1. Translated by Glyn S. Burgess and Keith Busby. 2. City near the Scottish border. 3. The Arthurian name for England. 4. A feast day celebrated on the seventh Sunday after Easter. 5. Roman emperor Caesar Augustus (63 B.C.E.–14 C.E.); *Semiramis*: a legendary queen of Assyria.

had cast about her a costly mantle of white ermine covered with Alexandrian purple. Her side, though, was uncovered, as well as her face, neck and breast; she was whiter than the hawthorn blossom.

The maiden called the knight, who came forward and sat before the bed. "Lanval," she said, "fair friend, for you I came from my country. I have come far in search of you and if you are worthy and courtly, no emperor, count or king will have felt as much joy or happiness as you, for I love you above all else." He looked at her and saw that she was beautiful. Love's spark pricked him so that his heart was set alight, and he replied to her in seemly manner: "Fair lady, if it were to please you to grant me the joy of wanting to love me, you could ask nothing that I would not do as best I could, be it foolish or wise. I shall do as you bid and abandon all others for you. I never want to leave you and this is what I most desire." When the girl heard these words from the man who loved her so, she granted him her love and her body. Now Lanval was on the right path! She gave him a boon, that henceforth he could wish for nothing which he would not have, and however generously he gave or spent, she would still find enough for him. Lanval was very well lodged, for the more he spent, the more gold and silver he would have. "Beloved," she said, "I admonish, order, and beg you not to reveal this secret to anyone! I shall tell you the long and the short of it: you would lose me forever if this love were to become known. You would never be able to see me or possess me." He replied that he would do what she commanded. He lay down beside her on the bed: now Lanval was well lodged. That afternoon he remained with her until evening and would have done so longer had he been able and had his love allowed him, "Beloved," she said, "arise! You can stay no longer. Go from here and I shall remain, but I shall tell you one thing: whenever you wish to speak with me, you will not be able to think of a place where a man may enjoy his love without reproach or wickedness, that I shall not be there with you to do your bidding. No man save you will see me or hear my voice." When he heard this, Lanval was well pleased and, kissing her, he arose. The damsels who had led him to the tent dressed him in rich garments, and in his new clothes there was no more handsome young man on earth. He was neither foolish nor ill-mannered. The damsels gave him water to wash his hands and a towel to dry them and then brought him food. He took his supper, which was not to be disdained, with his beloved. He was very courteously served and dined joyfully. There was one dish in abundance that pleased the knight particularly, for he often kissed his beloved and embraced her closely.

When they had risen from table, his horse was brought to him, well saddled. Lanval was richly served there. He took his leave, mounted, and went towards the city, often looking behind him, for he was greatly disturbed, thinking of his adventure and uneasy in his heart. He was at a loss to know what to think, for he could not believe it was true. When he came to his lodgings, he found his men finely dressed. That night he offered lavish hospitality but no one knew how this came to be. There was no knight in the town in sore need of shelter whom he did not summon and serve richly and well. Lanval gave costly gifts, Lanval freed prisoners, Lanval clothed the jongleurs,[6] Lanval performed many honorable acts. There was no one,

---

6. Minstrels.

stranger or friend, to whom he would not have given gifts. He experienced great joy and pleasure, for day or night he could see his beloved often and she was entirely at his command.

In the same year, I believe, after St John's day,[7] as many as thirty knights had gone to relax in a garden beneath the tower where the queen was staying. Gawain was with them and his cousin, the fair Ywain. Gawain, the noble and the worthy, who endeared himself to all, said: "In God's name, lords, we treat our companion Lanval ill, for he is so generous and courtly, and his father is a rich king, yet we have not brought him with us." So they returned, went to his lodgings and persuaded him to come with them.

The queen, in the company of three ladies, was reclining by a window cut out of the stone when she caught sight of the king's household and recognized Lanval. She called one of her ladies to summon her most elegant and beautiful damsels to relax with her in the garden where the others were. She took more than thirty with her, and they went down the steps where the knights, glad of their coming, came to meet them. They took the girls by the hand and the conversation was not uncourtly. Lanval withdrew to one side, far from the others, for he was impatient to hold his beloved, to kiss, embrace and touch her. He cared little for other people's joy when he could not have his own pleasure. When the queen saw the knight alone, she approached him straightaway. Sitting down beside him, she spoke to him and opened her heart. "Lanval, I have honored, cherished and loved you much. You may have all my love: just tell me what you desire! I grant you my love and you should be glad to have me." "Lady," he said, "leave me be! I have no desire to love you, for I have long served the king and do not want to betray my faith. Neither you nor your love will ever lead me to wrong my lord!" The queen became angry and distressed, and spoke unwisely: "Lanval," she said, "I well believe that you do not like this kind of pleasure. I have been told often enough that you have no desire for women. You have well-trained young men and enjoy yourself with them. Base coward, wicked recreant, my lord is extremely unfortunate to have suffered you near him. I think he may have lost his salvation because of it!"

When he heard her, he was distressed, but not slow to reply. He said something in spite that he was often to regret. "Lady, I am not skilled in the profession you mention, but I love and am loved by a lady who should be prized above all others I know. And I will tell you one thing: you can be sure that one of her servants, even the very poorest girl, is worth more than you, my lady the Queen, in body, face and beauty, wisdom and goodness." Thereupon the queen left and went in tears to her chamber, very distressed and angry that he had humiliated her in this way. She took to her bed ill and said that she would never again get up, unless the king saw that justice was done her in respect of her complaint.

The king had returned from the woods after an extremely happy day. He entered the queen's apartments and when she saw him, she complained aloud, fell at his feet, cried for mercy and said that Lanval had shamed her. He had requested her love and because she had refused him, had insulted and deeply humiliated her. He had boasted of a beloved who was so well-bred, noble, and proud that her chambermaid, the poorest servant she had,

7. June 24.

was worthier than the queen. The king grew very angry and swore an oath that, if Lanval could not defend himself in court, he would have him burned or hanged. The king left the room, summoned three of his barons and sent them for Lanval, who was suffering great pain. He had returned to his lodgings, well aware of having lost his beloved by revealing their love. Alone in his chamber, distraught and anguished, he called his beloved repeatedly, but to no avail. He lamented and sighed, fainting from time to time; a hundred times he cried to her to have mercy, to come and speak with her beloved. He cursed his heart and his mouth and it was a wonder he did not kill himself. His cries and moans were not loud enough nor his agitation and torment such that she would have mercy on him, or even permit him to see her. Alas, what will he do?

The king's men arrived and told Lanval to go to court without delay: the king had summoned him through them, for the queen had accused him. Lanval went sorrowfully and would have been happy for them to kill him. He came before the king, sad, subdued and silent, betraying his great sorrow. The king said to him angrily: "Vassal, you have wronged me greatly! You were extremely ill-advised to shame and vilify me, and to slander the queen. You boasted out of folly, for your beloved must be very noble for her handmaiden to be more beautiful and more worthy than the queen."

Lanval denied point by point having offended and shamed his lord, and maintained that he had not sought the queen's love, but he acknowledged the truth of his words about the love of which he had boasted. He now regretted this, for as a result he had lost her. He told them he would do whatever the court decreed in this matter, but the king was very angry and sent for all his men to tell him exactly what he should do, so that his action would not be unfavorably interpreted. Whether they liked it or not, they obeyed his command and assembled to make a judgment, deciding that a day should be fixed for the trial, but that Lanval should provide his lord with pledges that he would await his judgment and return later to his presence. Then the court would be larger, for at that moment only the king's household itself was present. The barons returned to the king and explained their reasoning. The king asked for pledges, but Lanval was alone and forlorn, having no relation or friend there. Then Gawain approached and offered to stand bail, and all his companions did likewise. The king said to them: "I entrust him to you on surety of all that you hold from me, lands and fiefs, each man separately." When this had been pledged, there was no more to be done, and Lanval returned to his lodging with the knights escorting him. They chastised him and urged him strongly not to be so sorrowful, and cursed such foolish love. They went to see him every day, as they wished to know whether he was drinking and eating properly, being very much afraid that he might harm himself.

On the appointed day the barons assembled. The king and queen were there and the guarantors brought Lanval to court. They were all very sad on his account and I think there were a hundred who would have done all in their power to have him released without a trial because he had been wrongly accused. The king demanded the verdict according to the charge and the rebuttal, and now everything lay in the hands of the barons. They considered their judgment, very troubled and concerned on account of this noble man from abroad, who was in such a plight in their midst. Some of them wanted to harm him in conformity with their lord's will. Thus spoke the count of Cornwall: "There shall be no default on our part. Like it or not, right must prevail. The king accused his vassal, whom I heard you call Lanval, of a felony and charged him with a crime, about a love he boasted of which angered my lady. Only the king is accusing him, so by the faith I owe you, there ought, to tell the truth, to be no case to answer, were it not that one should honor one's lord in all things. An oath will bind Lanval and the king will put the matter in our hands. If he can provide proof and his beloved comes forward, and if what he said to incur the queen's displeasure is true, then he will be pardoned, since he did not say it to spite her. And if he cannot furnish proof, then we must inform him that he will lose the king's service and that the king must banish him." They sent word to the knight and informed him that he should send for his beloved to defend and protect him. He told them that this was not possible and that he would receive no help from her. The messengers returned to the judges, expecting no help to be forthcoming for Lanval. The king pressed them hard because the queen was waiting for them.

When they were about to give their verdict, they saw two maidens approaching on two fine ambling palfreys. They were extremely comely and dressed only in purple taffeta, next to their bare skin; the knights were pleased to see them. Gawain and three other knights went to Lanval, told him about this, and pointed the two maidens out to him. Gawain was very glad and strongly urged Lanval to tell him if this was his beloved, but he told them that he did not know who they were, whence they came or where they were going. The maidens continued to approach, still on horseback, and then dismounted before the dais where King Arthur was seated. They were of great beauty and spoke in courtly fashion: "King, make your chambers available and hang them with silken curtains so that my lady may stay here, for she wishes to lodge with you." This he granted them willingly and summoned two knights who led them to the upper chambers. For the moment they said no more.

The king asked his barons for the judgment and the responses, and said that they had greatly angered him by the long delay. "Lord," they said, "we are deliberating, but because of the ladies we saw, we have not reached a verdict. Let us continue with the trial." So they assembled in some anxiety, and there was a good deal of commotion and contention.

While they were in this troubled state, they saw two finely accoutred maidens coming along the street, dressed in garments of Phrygian[8] silk and riding on Spanish mules. The vassals were glad of this and they said to each other that Lanval, the worthy and brave, was now saved. Ywain went up to him with his companions, and said: "Lord, rejoice! For the love of God, speak to us! Two damsels are approaching, very comely and beautiful. It is surely your beloved." Lanval quickly replied that he did not recognize them, nor did he know or love them. When they had arrived, they dismounted before the king and many praised them highly for their bodies, faces, and complexions. They were both more worthy than the queen had ever been. The older of the two, who was courtly and wise, delivered her message fittingly: "King, place your chambers at our disposal for the purpose of lodging my lady. She is coming

---

8. Phrygia is in modern Turkey, but here designates more generally the East.

here to speak with you." He ordered them to be taken to the others who had arrived earlier. They paid no heed to their mules, and, as soon as they had left the king, he summoned all his barons so that they might deliver their verdict. This had taken up too much of the day and the queen, who had been waiting for them for such a long time, was getting angry.

Just as they were about to give their verdict, a maiden on horseback entered the town. There was none more beautiful in the whole world. She was riding a white palfrey which carried her well and gently; its neck and head were well-formed and there was no finer animal on earth. The palfrey was richly equipped, for no count or king on earth could have paid for it, save by selling or pledging his lands. The lady was dressed in a white tunic and shift, laced left and right so as to reveal her sides. Her body was comely, her lips low, her neck whiter than snow on a branch; her eyes were bright and her face white, her mouth fair and her nose well-placed; her eyebrows were brown and her brow fair, and her hair curly and rather blond. A golden thread does not shine as brightly as the rays reflected in the light from her hair. Her cloak was of dark silk and she had wrapped its skirts about her. She held a sparrowhawk on her wrist and behind her there followed a dog. There was no one in the town, humble or powerful, old or young, who did not watch her arrival, and no one jested about her beauty. She approached slowly and the judges who saw her thought it was a great wonder. No one who had looked at her could have failed to be inspired with real joy. Those who loved the knight went and told him about the maiden who was coming and who, please God, would deliver him. "Lord and friend, here comes a lady whose hair is neither tawny nor brown. She is the most beautiful of all women in the world." Lanval heard this and raised his head, for he knew her well, and sighed. His blood rushed to his face and he was quick to speak: "In faith," he said, "it is my beloved! If she shows me no mercy, I hardly care if anyone should kill me, for my cure is in seeing her." The lady entered the palace, where no one so beautiful had ever before been seen. She dismounted before the king, and in the sight of all, let her cloak fall so that they could see her better. The king, who was well-mannered, rose to meet her, and all the others honored her and offered themselves as her servants. When they had looked at her and praised her beauty greatly, she spoke thus, for she had no wish to remain: "King, I have loved one of your vassals, Lanval, whom you see there. Because of what he said, he was accused in your court, and I do not wish him to come to any harm. You should know that the queen was wrong, as he never sought her love. As regards the boast he made, if he can be acquitted by me, let your barons release him!" The king granted that it should be as the judges recommended, in accordance with justice. There was not one who did not consider that Lanval had successfully defended himself, and so he was freed by their decision. The maiden, who had many servants, then left, for the king could not retain her. Outside the hall there was a large block of dark marble on to which heavily armed men climbed when they left the king's court. Lanval mounted it and when the maiden came through the door, he leapt in a single bound on to the palfrey behind her. He went with her to Avalon,[9] so the Bretons tell us, to a very beautiful island. Thither the

___

9. The Celtic isle of the blessed.

young man was borne and no one has heard any more about him, nor can I relate any more.

Laüstic[1]

I shall relate an adventure to you from which the Bretons composed a lay. *Laüstic* is its name, I believe, and that is what the Bretons call it in their land. In French the title is *Rossignol,* and Nightingale is the correct English word.

In the region of St Malo[2] was a famous town and two knights dwelt there, each with a fortified house. Because of the fine qualities of the two men the town acquired a good reputation. One of the knights had taken a wise, courtly and elegant wife who conducted herself, as custom dictated, with admirable propriety. The other knight was a young man who was well known amongst his peers for his prowess and great valor. He performed honorable deeds gladly and attended many tournaments, spending freely and giving generously whatever he had. He loved his neighbor's wife and so persistently did he request her love, so frequent were his entreaties and so many qualities did he possess that she loved him above all things, both for the good she had heard about him and because he lived close by. They loved each other prudently and well, concealing their love carefully to ensure that they were not seen, disturbed or suspected. This they could do because their dwellings were adjoining. Their houses, halls and keeps were close by each other and there was no barrier or division, apart from a high wall of dark-hued stone. When she stood at her bedroom window, the lady could talk to her beloved in the other house and he to her, and they could toss gifts to each other. There was scarcely anything to displease them and they were both very content except for the fact that they could not meet and take their pleasure with each other, for the lady was closely guarded when her husband was in the region. But they were so resourceful that day or night they managed to speak to each other and no one could prevent their coming to the window and seeing each other there. For a long time they loved each other, until one summer when the copses and meadows were green and the gardens in full bloom. On the flower-tops the birds sang joyfully and sweetly. If love is on anyone's mind, no wonder he turns his attention towards it. I shall tell you the truth about the knight. Both he and the lady made the greatest possible effort with their words and with their eyes. At night, when the moon was shining and her husband was asleep, she often rose from beside him and put on her mantle. Knowing her beloved would be doing the same, she would go and stand at the window and stay awake most of the night. They took delight in seeing each other, since they were denied anything more. But so frequently did she stand there and so frequently leave her bed that her husband became angry and asked her repeatedly why she got up and where she went. "Lord," replied the lady, "anyone who does not hear the song of the nightingale knows none of the joys of this world. This is why I come and stand here. So sweet is the song I hear by night that it brings me great pleasure. I take such delight in

---

1. Translated by Glyn S. Burgess and Keith Busby.   2. A town in Brittany.

it and desire it so much that I can get no sleep at all." When the lord heard what she said, he gave a spiteful, angry laugh and devised a plan to ensnare the nightingale. Every single servant in his household constructed some trap, net or snare and then arranged them throughout the garden. There was no hazel tree or chestnut tree on which they did not place a snare or bird-lime, until they had captured and retained it. When they had taken the nightingale, it was handed over, still alive, to the lord, who was overjoyed to hold it in his hands. He entered the lady's chamber. "Lady," he said, "where are you? Come forward and speak to us. With bird-lime I have trapped the nightingale which has kept you awake so much. Now you can sleep in peace, for it will never awaken you again." When the lady heard him she was grief-stricken and distressed. She asked her husband for the bird, but he killed it out of spite, breaking its neck wickedly with his two hands. He threw the body at the lady, so that the front of her tunic was bespattered with blood, just on her breast. Thereupon he left the chamber. The lady took the tiny corpse, wept profusely and cursed those who had betrayed the nightingale by constructing the traps and snares, for they had taken so much joy from her. "Alas," she said, "misfortune is upon me. Never again can I get up at night or go to stand at the window where I used to see my beloved. I know one thing for certain. He will think I am faint-hearted, so I must take action. I shall send him the nightingale and let him know what has happened." She wrapped the little bird in a piece of samite, embroidered in gold and covered in designs. She called one of her servants, entrusted him with her message and sent him to her beloved. He went to the knight, greeted him on behalf of his lady, related the whole message to him and presented him with the nightingale. When the messenger had finished speaking, the knight, who had listened attentively, was distressed by what had happened. But he was not uncourtly or tardy. He had a small vessel prepared, not of iron or steel, but of pure gold with fine stones, very precious and valuable. On it he carefully placed a lid and put the nightingale in it. Then he had the casket sealed and carried it with him at all times.

This adventure was related and could not long be concealed. The Bretons composed a lay about it which is called *Laüstic*.

CHRÉTIEN DE TROYES

ca. 1185

Although there is evidence that Arthur was regarded as a heroic figure in Britain as early as the seventh century, it was not until Geoffrey of Monmouth composed his pseudohistorical work *The History of the Kings of Britain* in the 1130s that the Arthurian stories began to achieve the immense popularity that has continued to the present day. Geoffrey's "history" claimed that Britain had been founded by a Trojan refugee named Brutus (in imitation of the founding of Rome by Aeneas in Virgil's *Aeneid*), and he presented Arthur as the greatest of all British kings, whose court was preeminent for its elegance and chivalry. While Geoffrey's work gained immediate popularity, the first Arthurian romances, with their now familiar cast of characters, their fanciful and seemingly random adventures, and their interest in the ethics of the chivalric life, did not appear until the work of Chrétien de Troyes, whose five Arthurian romances were composed between about 1170 and 1190. As his name suggests, Chrétien was a native of Troyes, a prosperous city in the county of Champagne in northwest France. His first romance, *Erec and Enide*, usually dated in the early 1170s, was almost certainly written in the context of the court of Henry II of England (ruled 1155–89); his second, third, and fourth romances, *Cligés*, *Lancelot*, and *Yvain*, were written in the context of the court of the count of Champagne, Henry the Liberal and his wife Marie de Champagne, who ruled the county after her husband's death in 1181 until the majority of her son in 1187. These courts were among the leading literary centers of Europe, so it is not surprising that Chrétien should have worked in these milieux. His final romance, *The Story of the Grail*, was dedicated to Count Philip of Flanders, who died while on crusade in the Holy Land in 1191. The romance is unfinished, but we do not know if this is because Chrétien died, because the story had reached an impasse from which he could not rescue it, or because he felt that its incompleteness was important to its overall meaning. In any case, the fascination created by Chrétien's account of the Grail—which appears in his romance for the very first time in Western literature—led to many continuations and rewritings of the story, a process that continues to the present. Indeed, so successful were these subsequent stories that *The Story of the Grail*, along with Chrétien's other romances, virtually disappeared from view as early as the fourteenth century, replaced by the ever more elaborate narratives they had inspired. Yet they remain not simply inspirations for others but great works in themselves, and none more so than the Grail romance.

If Arthur was in fact a historical figure, little of substance is known about him. The ultimate sources for the Arthurian stories were Celtic legends, legends that may once have emerged from historical events but that became vehicles for transmitting myths central to Celtic religious and social traditions. These legends were kept alive through storytellers and oral poets, traditional performers who were still active in the twelfth century. Chrétien seems to have known their stories primarily through the Celtic inhabitants of Brittany: there were substantial contacts between Bretons and French throughout the period. Chrétien's achievement was not simply to present these stories in French—the most influential literary language throughout the European Middle Ages—but to transform them into skillfully shaped and intriguing narratives. Moreover, Chrétien's romances dealt with issues that were of primary concern to the aristocracy of his time. What constitutes a truly ethical chivalric code? What is the relation of the warrior ethos of the knight to the domestic and more psychologically complex issue of love? And how is the knight to accommodate his quest for honor and renown to the spiritual demands of Christianity? It is this last question that is at the center of *The Story of the Grail*.

The exact source for Chrétien's romance is not known. He twice mentions a "book" from which he took the story, but this is almost certainly a conventional gesture toward authenticity rather than reference to a real source. For Chrétien the Grail was simply a large, flat dish that did not itself have any specific value (the French word comes from the medieval Latin term *gradale*, which means a platter or serving dish). The importance of the Grail was what it carried, which we come to learn in the course of the romance is a single communion wafer or Host, the only sustenance required by the Grail King. Later romancers identified the Grail with the chalice used by Christ at the Last Supper. At the Grail castle Perceval also sees a miraculous bleeding lance, which later romancers identified with the lance that pierced Christ's side while he was on the cross. But these are later developments, and are almost certainly irrelevant to Chrétien's story. He seems to have learned of a magic dish that provides endless sustenance and a bleeding lance from Celtic mythology. For him the story is above all about the education of a young man, Perceval, and the dilemma he faces in trying to reconcile knightly prowess with Christian spirituality. The story begins as a typical account of the transformation of a young man from a naive rustic into an accomplished knight, endowed with honor and a wife who brings with her land to provide him with the wealth necessary to maintain his station. Perceval's initial ventures into the chivalric world are comically inept, but when he arrives at Arthur's court he is the object of prophecies that mark him as elected to fulfill a great destiny. After having won a suit of armor by killing its unworthy owner, he arrives at the manor of Gornemant de Gohort, who instructs the young man in the use of his weapons and in chivalric etiquette and then knights his accomplished pupil. Perceval proceeds to rescue the beautiful Blanchflor from her wicked oppressor, and having been granted her love he seems to have achieved all that a young man could want. His only unfinished business is to return home to reassure his mother of his success. But on the way back he encounters the Fisher King and his magical castle, and it is there that he witnesses the mysterious Grail procession. The Grail and bleeding lance are carried into another room past the silent Perceval, who has been instructed by Gornemant not to ask questions lest he be thought a simpleton. The next morning he finds the castle deserted, and once on his way he encounters a damsel who tells him that in not asking about the Grail and the lance he has committed a grievous error, one caused by the sin he committed in causing the death of his sorrowing mother when he initially left home. As his journey continues he confronts further evidence of his culpability. Only after five years of fruitless questing does he meet a hermit who explains to him the crucial tenets of Christianity and leads him to a life of penance by which he can atone for the sins he has—albeit unwittingly—committed. At this point Perceval disappears from the romance, not to reappear again. While the hermit assures him that he can have both chivalric renown and salvation, nothing in the romance indicates how these values are in fact to be reconciled.

Perceval's failure to ask the crucial questions at the Grail castle seems to have two causes, one immediate, the other more distant. The immediate cause is that he follows Gornemant's instruction not to ask questions. In following this advice even when it seems inappropriate, Perceval is continuing a habit of excessive literalism that has been typical of him throughout the narrative. Chrétien's point seems to be that in accepting his adventures as not requiring thought or introspection, Perceval has made himself vulnerable to error. The larger lesson is that the questing knight must always be alert to the *significance* of his experience and not simply regard it as an opportunity for personal achievement. Chrétien's world is evidently ordered by a providential force that offers people the opportunity for spiritual growth rather than simply social achievement. The mysterious and apparently random series of events that occur are occasions for self-knowledge if only the knight will seek to understand them—a challenge of interpretation that confronts the reader as well. This theme is part of an interest in introspection that develops throughout the twelfth century, a growing realization that importance resides less in outward action than in inward understanding. This development will reach its medieval fulfillment in Dante's *Divine Comedy*, in *Sir Gawain and the Green Knight*, and in Chaucer's *Canterbury Tales*.

The other cause of Perceval's failure is the sin of abandoning his mother. Yet just as Perceval's naïveté is the condition for his early success, so too he is here involved in a kind of paradox. If he had not left his mother he would never have become a knight, never have arrived at the Grail Castle at all, and therefore never have been in a position even to ask the crucial questions—questions he cannot ask precisely because he has done those things that put him in the position to ask them. This double bind is at the center of the story. Chrétien is exploring the unhappy fact that humans are fallible creatures who always seem to discover their fallibility too late. As the story proceeds, we learn that Perceval is enmeshed in a web of familial relationships of which he at first knows very little. The Fisher King whom he has not healed is his maternal uncle, who is wounded in exactly the same way as was his father. So he has, then, failed to cure his very own family, both his mother's kin and, at least symbolically, his father's as well. And he has failed because he has unknowingly committed a sin against both those kin groups: he has abandoned and in effect killed his mother (despite the fact that his mother not only prepared him for his departure, but wished him joy); and he has followed the path taken by his father and two brothers, for whom knighthood resulted only in suffering and death. The ultimate irony is that the only way in which he can atone for these inevitable misdeeds is to lead a life of penance rather than chivalry, a life that will take him even further away from the very family that he wishes so deeply to heal.

Chrétien is thus exploring two related issues, issues that are as relevant to life today as they were in the twelfth century. One concerns the complex web of guilt and responsibility that seems to be a result of growing up within a family; the other is the personal issue of one's own spiritual life. To become a mature adult each individual needs to break away from the family, a process that however necessary often feels like a transgression or even a betrayal. And once this process of growth has been accomplished, how is the guilt that accompanies it to be dealt with? Writing within a Christian context, Chrétien answers this last question by turning to the religious values of his day as they are expressed by the hermit at the end of the story. Sin is defined as a violation of family bonds (the killing of his mother by leaving home, the failure to heal his uncle by not asking the crucial questions at the Grail castle). Yet sin is unavoidable. Once it has been committed, the need for *personal* salvation preempts the possibility of correcting the wrongs committed against the family and even society at large. The selections of *The Story of the Grail* printed here comprise all of Perceval's adventures, but omit about half of the full romance. The omitted parts concern the adventures of Gawain, which parallel those of Perceval but which lack any sense of religious significance. Moreover, Gawain's adventures become ever more trivial, so that as Perceval moves further away from the chivalric life, Gawain's adventures reveal that life to be superficial and even demeaning. In sum, Chrétien is the first great celebrant of the world of Arthurian chivalry who nonetheless ends his career by calling into question chivalry's pursuit of worldly honor. This irony—that chivalric achievement is challenged at the very moment of its greatest success—will haunt both Arthurian literature and the literature of the warrior class of the Western world throughout medieval history. It is an irony that continues to the present day.

From The Story of the Grail[1]

He who sows little reaps little, and let him who wishes to reap scatter his seed on ground that will yield him a hundredfold, for on poor earth good seed dries up and dies.[2] Chrétien sows the romance which he is beginning in so good a place that he cannot fail to gain great profit, for he does it for the worthiest man in the empire of Rome; that is, the Count Philip of Flanders,[3] who is of greater worth than Alexander was. Though Alexander is said to be a model,[4] I will prove that he did not equal the Count, for he gathered in himself all the sins and vices from which the Count is pure and free.

The Count does not listen to coarse buffoonery or insolent boasts, and grieves if he hears slander spoken of anyone. The Count loves justice, loyalty, and Holy Church, and hates all uncourtly behavior. His generosity is greater than anyone knows, for he gives without hypocrisy and without guile, accord-

1. Translated from the French by R. S. Loomis.   2. The opening phrase about sowing is from 2 Corinthians 9.6; this phrase then leads into a discussion of the parable of the sower (Matthew 13.3–23; Mark 4.3–20; Luke 8.5–15). Chrétien quotes Luke 8.8.   3. Philip of Flanders became Chrétien's patron after 1181; he died in 1191.   4. Alexander the Great was renowned in the Middle Ages above all for his generosity, but Chrétien here contrasts this pagan hero to the Christian Philip. This unusual contrast, and the biblical allusions, indicates the importance of Christian values to the poem.

ing to the gospel, which says: "Let not thy left hand know what they right hand doeth."[5] Only they know his largess who receive it, and God, who sees all secrets and knows the inmost feelings of the heart and the bowels. Why does the Gospel say: "Hide thy good deeds from they left hand"? The left hand, according to the story, means vainglory, which comes from false hypocrisy. What does the right hand mean? Charity, which does not boast of its good works but rather covers them up so that no one knows of them save Him who is called both God and charity. According to the text, God is charity, and whoever lives in charity—St. Paul says it and I have read it— abides in God and God in him.[6]

Understand truly, therefore, that the gifts which the good Count Philip makes are gifts of charity; for no one persuades him but his generous, noble heart, which counsels him to do good. Is he not worth more than Alexander, who cared nothing for charity or any other virtue? Yes, without the slightest doubt. Therefore, Chrétien will not have toiled in vain when by the command of the Count he strives to put into rhyme the best tale which may be told in a royal court. That is the story of the Grail, of which the Count gave him the book.[7] You will now hear how he acquits himself.

It was in the season when trees bloom, bushes put forth leaves, meadows turn green, birds sweetly sing in their language at dawn, and all things are aflame with joy, that the son of the widow lady of the lonely Wild Forest[8] arose and easily saddled his hunter, took three javelins, and thus left his mother's manor, thinking that he would go to see his mother's harrowers, who were harrowing her oats with twelve oxen and six harrows.[9] So he entered the forest, and at once his heart rejoiced at the sweet season and at hearing the warbling of the birds. All these things pleased him, and, filled with the sweetness of the calm weather, he took the bridle from his hunter and let him graze the fresh, greening grass. And the lad, who knew well how to cast the javelins that he carried, walked about casting them, now behind, now before, now low, now high, until he heard coming through the wood five knights, armed at all points. Their arms made a great crashing as they came, for the branches of the oaks and hornbeams[1] struck them, the lances knocked against the shields, and all the coats of mail clinked. The wood of the shields and the steel of the mail cried out. The noble youth heard but did not see those who were approaching at a rapid pace; he wondered and said: "By my soul, the lady my mother told me the truth when she said that devils are the most terrible thing in the world and taught me that one ought to cross oneself against them. But I scorn her teaching and will not cross myself; rather I will strike the strongest with one of the javelins I am carrying, so that none of the others, I think, will dare to come near me."

Thus the youth talked to himself before he caught sight of them. But when he saw them clearly as they appeared out of the wood and observed the jingling coats of mail and the bright, gleaming helmets and the lances and

---

5. Matthew 6.3.   6. The actual reference is not to one of Paul's Epistles but to 1 John 4.16.   7. This reference to a source is almost certainly apocryphal; in giving credit to Philip for the story, Chrétien is implying that Philip is the source of the virtues that the romance will explore.   8. *Wild Forest* signifies both a specific place and the fact that Perceval lives in an uncultured environment.   9. *Harrows* are heavy wooden frames set with teeth that are dragged over plowed land to break up or spread soil after it has been sown but before the seeds have begun to germinate. By beginning the story in this way Chrétien draws a connection with the prologue, implying that the story will in some sense parallel the parable of the sower.   1. Common European trees with very hard wood (hence their name).

the shields, such as he had never seen before, and when he descried the green and the vermilion catching the light of the sun, and the gold, blue, and silver, he was so delighted that he exclaimed: "Ah, Lord God, have mercy! These are angels that I see. Alas, now I was very wrong when I said that they were devils! My mother, who told me that angels were the most beautiful things there are, except God, who is more beautiful than everything else, was telling no lie. Here I see God himself, I think, for one of them is so fair to look at that the others, God keep me! have not a tenth of his beauty. My mother herself said that one must believe in God and adore, bow the knee, and honor Him. I will adore this one and all the others too."

At once he threw himself on the ground, reciting the creed and the prayers which his mother had taught him. The master of the knights saw him and said: "Stay back! For this youth has fallen to the ground for fear at sight of us. If we all went together toward him, it seems to me he would be so frightened he would die and he could not reply to anything I asked him."

They stopped, and the leader went quickly to the youth, greeted and reassured him, saying: "Young sir, do not be afraid."

"I am not afraid," said the youth, "by the Savior in whom I believe. Are you God?"

"No, by my faith."

"Who are you then?"

"I am a knight."

"I have never known a knight," said the youth, "nor have I seen one, nor ever heard talk of one. But you are more beautiful than God. If only I could be like you, so shining and shaped just so!"

At this word the knight drew near him and asked: "Have you seen in this glade five knights and three maidens?"

The youth had his mind set on asking about other matters. He put out his hand and took hold of the knight's lance, and said: "Fair dear sir, you who call yourself a knight, what is this that you hold?"

"Now you have given me very useful instructions, it seems!" said the knight. "I expected to get some information from you, my good friend, and now you want to learn something from me. But I will tell you; it is my lance."

"Tell me, does one cast it as I do my javelins?"

"Not at all, young sir, you are very foolish. One uses it to strike a blow."

"Then one of my three javelins that you see here is better, for, whenever I want to, I kill birds and animals with them as far away as a crossbow will shoot an arrow."

"Young sir, I have nothing to do with that. But answer my question about the knights. Tell me if you know where they are, and have you seen the maidens?"

The youth took hold of the edge of the shield and said: "What is this and what is it for?"

"Young sir, this is a trick to make me talk of things other than those which I asked about. So God help me, I expected you to give me news rather than to give instructions to you! Now you expect me to teach you! I will tell you, then, how this is managed, for you please me. This thing I carry is called a shield."

"Is called a shield?"

"Certainly, and I must never despise it, for it is so trustworthy that if anyone throws or shoots at me, it wards off all the blows. That is the service it renders me."

Then the knights who had remained behind rode up to their lord and said at once: "Sir, what does this Welsh lad tell you?"

The lord said: "He knows nothing of manners, so God help me, for he never answers properly any question I ask, but instead he asks the name of anything he sees and what it is good for."

"Sir, be assured that the Welsh are all by nature more stupid than beasts at pasture, and this one too is like a beast.[2] It is a foolish man who stops to deal with him unless he wishes to trifle away his time."

"So God keep me, I do not know, but before I go farther, I will tell him whatever he wishes, and I will not depart otherwise." Then he asked again: "Young sir, do not be annoyed, but tell me if you have met or seen the five knights and the maidens."

The youth grasped and pulled the skirt of the coat of mail and said: "Tell me, good sir, what is this you are wearing?"

"Young sir, do you not know?"

"I do not."

"Young sir, it is my hauberk,[3] and is heavy as iron."

"Is it of iron?"

"You see that it is."

"I know nothing about it, but, so God save me, it is very beautiful. What do you do with it and what use is it?"

"Young sir, that is easy to say. If now you wished to throw javelins or shoot arrows at me, you could do me no harm."

"Sir knight, God keep the hinds and the harts from wearing such hauberks, for then I could not kill any or chase them."

The knight repeated: "Young sir, so God help you, can you give me news of the knights and the maidens?"

The boy, who had little sense, said: "Were you born like this?"

"Not at all, young sir, no one can be born like this."

"Who, then, dressed you this way?"

"Young sir, I will tell you."

"Tell me then."

"Willingly. It is not yet five whole days since King Arthur knighted me and gave me all this armor. But now answer me; what has become of the knights who passed this way, escorting the three maidens? Were they riding slowly or were they in flight?"

The youth said: "Sir, now look at that very high wood which surrounds that mountain: there is the pass of Snowdon."[4]

"And what of that, fair brother?"

"There are my mother's laborers who harrow and plow her fields, and if those people passed that way they would see them and tell you."

The knights agreed to go with him if he would lead them to the men who were harrowing the field of oats. The youth mounted his hunter and went

2. The knight is expressing a common attitude of the French and Anglo-Norman aristocracy toward the Celts who lived in what were considered the wilds of Brittany and Wales. He also thinks that Perceval is a peasant and, therefore, according to a widespread aristocratic prejudice, is only barely human.   3. The basic element of 12th-century armor, long-sleeved shirts of chain mail extending to the knees.   4. Snowdon is a mountain in northwest Wales.

where the laborers were harrowing. When they spied their lord, they trembled for fear. Do you know why? Because of the knights whom they saw accompanying him in arms, for they knew well that if the knights told him of their way of life he would wish to be one also, and his mother would go out of her mind. She had taken precautions to prevent him from ever seeing a knight or learning anything of knighthood.

The youth said to the ox-drivers: "Have you seen five knights and three maidens come this way?"

"They have been following the pass all this day," said the ox-drivers.

The youth said to the knight who had been conversing with him: "Sir, the knights and the maidens have taken this road. But now tell me more of the king who makes knights and where is he most often found."

"Young sir, I will tell you; the King is now at Carlisle.[5] Five days have not passed since he was there, for I was there and saw him. If you do not find him there, there will be someone surely to direct you; he will not yet have gone so far that you will not hear news of him there."

At once the knight departed at a great gallop, so that he should not be too late to overtake the others. The youth was not slow to return to his manor, where his mother grieved in her heart for his delay. But she rejoiced the moment she saw him and could not hide her delight, and like a doting mother ran to him and called him "fair son, fair son" more than a hundred times. "Fair son, my heart has been torn by your absence. I have almost died of anxiety. Where have you been so long today?"

"Where, lady? I will tell you without any lies that I have seen something that made me very happy. Have you not often told me that the angels of our Lord God are so beautiful that Nature never made any creature so beautiful and that nothing in the world is more beautiful?"

"Fair son, I say it again; I said it truly and I repeat it."

"Hush, Mother! Did I not see just now the most beautiful things there are, passing through the wild forest? They are more beautiful, I think, than God and his angels."

The mother took him in her arms and said: "Fair son, I entrust you to God, for I am in terror for you. I believe you have seen those angels of whom everyone complains and who kill all they meet."

"I have not, Mother; truly I have not. They say they are called knights."

The mother swooned at the word when she heard him mention knights, and when she recovered she spoke like a woman in anger: "Alas, wretch that I am! Fair sweet son, I thought I would protect you so well from chivalry that you would never hear or see anything of it. You would have become a knight, fair son, if it had pleased God that your father and your friends had the care of you. There was no knight so honored and so feared, fair son, as your father was in all the Isles of the Sea.[6] You can boast indeed that neither his lineage nor mine is a disgrace to you, for I am descended from the best knights of this country. In the Isles of the Sea there was no family better than mine in my time. But the best have fallen on evil days. One can see in many places that misfortunes overtake those who uphold honor and prowess. Wickedness, shame, and sloth prosper, for they cannot fall, but the good are

---

5. A city on the border between England and Scotland.   6. This term probably refers to Britain.

doomed to ruin. If you do not know it, your father was wounded through the thighs so that he was maimed in body.[7] The great lands and great treasures which he had won by his valor, all were lost and he fell into great poverty. After the death of King Uther Pendragon, the father of King Arthur, the noblemen were wrongfully impoverished, disinherited, and banished. Their lands were devastated and the poorer folk rendered destitute. Whoever could flee, fled. Your father had this manor here in this wild forest. He could not flee but had himself brought here hastily in a litter, for he knew no other refuge. You were a little suckling, scarce more than two years old. You had two very fair brothers. When they were big enough, they went by their father's counsel to royal courts to receive arms and horses. The elder went to the King of Escavalon and served him till he was dubbed knight. The younger took service with King Ban of Gomeret.[8] On one and the same day both the youths were made knights, and on that day they started to return home, wishing to bring joy to me and their father, who never saw them alive, for they were both vanquished in combat and slain in combat. For this I suffer great anguish and grief. A strange thing happened to the elder: crows and rooks pecked out his eyes; thus people found them dead.[9] Their father died of sorrow for his sons, and I have led a bitter life since his death. You were all the comfort and all the good I had, for all others were gone. God had left me nothing else to gladden my heart."

The youth hardly listened to what his mother told him, but said: "Give me something to eat. I do not know what you are talking about, but I want to go to the king who makes knights, and I will go, whomever it may displease!"

His mother detained and kept him as long as she could, and fitted him out with a large canvas shirt and breeches made in the fashion of Wales, where they make breeches and hose of one piece, I think; he had also a coat and hood of buckskin which fastened about him. Thus his mother equipped him. He stayed only three days; her caresses availed no longer to keep him.

Then his mother felt a strange grief; weeping, she kissed and embraced him, and said: "I feel a deep sorrow now that I see you depart, fair son. You will go to the court of the King and ask him to give you arms. There will be no refusal; I know he will give them to you. But when you try to use those arms, what will happen? How will you know how to do what you have never done before and never seen others doing? I fear you will do badly; you will be wholly unskilled, and it does not seem strange to me that one does not know what one has not learned. Rather is it strange when one fails to learn what one has often heard and seen. Fair son, I wish to teach you a lesson which you will do well to hear, and if it pleases you to remember it, great profit can come to you. You will soon become a knight, my son, if it please God, and I approve it. If, near or far, you find a lady who needs help, or a maiden in distress, do not withhold your aid if they ask for it; for in this all

---

7. This description of the father's wound is a euphemism for castration. The collapse of economic power and the retreat to the Wild Forest connects Chrétien's story to the age-old belief that the fertility of the land is dependent upon the sexual potency of the ruler. It was this anthropological aspect that attracted T. S. Eliot to the Grail myth in *The Waste Land*, for instance.　8. As is often the case with Chrétien, these two kings have no special relevance to the story; they are part of a larger world of political intrigue—such as the collapse of the kingdom after the death of Uther Pendragon—that we are made aware of without ever being given enough information fully to understand them.　9. Again, a mysterious detail that is never explained. Many of these details may have had a specific significance in the original Celtic legend, but Chrétien seems to include them in order to give his story an aura of mystery rather than to make any clear point.

honor lies. He who does not yield honor to ladies, loses his own honor. Serve ladies and maidens, and you will receive honor everywhere. If you ask a favor of any, avoid offending her and do nothing to displease her. He who wins a kiss from a maiden receives much; if she permits you to kiss her, I forbid you to take more if, for my sake, you are willing to forego it. If she has a ring on her finger or a purse at her girdle, and if for love or for entreaty she gives it to you, it will be right and proper for you to wear her ring; I give you leave to take the ring or the purse.[1] Fair son, I would tell you another thing: never on the road or at an inn keep company long with someone before inquiring his name. Learn his name, for by the name one knows the man. Fair son, speak with noble men and go with them; a noble man never gives bad counsel to those who frequent his company. Above everything I beseech you to enter church and minster and pray Our Lord to give you honor in this world and grant you so to act that you may come to a good end."

"Mother, what is church?"

"A place where service is rendered to Him who made heaven and earth and placed men and animals on it."

"And what is minster?"

"The same, my son; a beautiful and holy house, with relics and treasures, where one sacrifices the body of Jesus Christ, the holy prophet,[2] whom the Jews treated so shamefully. He was betrayed and wrongly condemned and suffered the agony of death for men and women; for their souls, when they left their bodies, went to hell, and it was He who delivered them. He was bound to a pillar, scourged, and crucified, wearing a crown of thorns. I charge you to go to the minsters to hear Masses and matins and to worship that Lord."

"Then I will gladly go to churches and minsters from this time on," said the youth; "I give you my promise."

Without further delay he took his leave, and his mother wept. His saddle was ready, and he himself was equipped after the Welsh fashion with brogues of rawhide. Wherever he went he was wont to carry three javelins, and he had intended to take them, but his mother made him leave two behind so that he would not seem too Welsh, and she would gladly have made him leave all three if it had been possible. He carried a willow switch in his right hand to whip his horse. Weeping, his mother kissed him whom she loved so dearly at his departure, and prayed God to keep him.

"Fair son," she said, "God give you wherever you go greater joy than remains with me!"

After the youth had ridden a stone's throw, he looked back and saw his mother fallen at the end of the bridge; she lay in a swoon as if she had dropped dead. But he applied his switch to the croup of his hunter, which went off without stumbling and carried him at high speed through the great dark forest. He rode from morning till evening, and lay in the forest that night till the bright day dawned.

The youth rose early, to the song of birds, mounted, and rode steadily till he saw a tent pitched in a fair meadow beside a spring. The tent was won-

---

1. If a purse were given to a knight, it would be as a love token, similar to a ring, not because it contained money.   2. By referring to Jesus as a prophet rather than the Son of God, Perceval's mother may be revealing her own inadequate religious understanding or inadvertently misleading her son.

derfully beautiful; a part was scarlet, the other green, striped with gold embroidery. On top was a gilded eagle, on which the sun struck clear and red, so that the whole meadow was brightened by the brilliance of the tent. Around the tent, which was the most beautiful in the world, were arranged leafy bowers and Welsh lodges. The youth rode toward the tent, and before entering, said: "O God, it is Thy house I see. I should do wrong if I did not go and worship Thee. Surely my mother was telling the truth when she said that a minster was the most beautiful thing there is, and told me that if ever I found one I should go and worship the Creator in whom I believe. I will go pray Him to give me something to eat, for I need it badly."

Then he came to the tent, found it open, and saw, within, a bed covered with a silk brocade. On the bed there lay alone a damsel sleeping. Her maidens were far away, for they had gone to pick fresh flowers with intent to strew them over the floor of the pavilion, according to custom. As the youth entered, his horse stumbled so heavily that the damsel heard it and awoke trembling. The youth spoke in his innocence: "Maiden, I greet you as my mother told me to do. My mother taught me to greet maidens wherever I met them."

The maiden quaked for fear of the youth, whom she took for an idiot, and she blamed her own folly for being discovered by him thus alone. She cried: "Young sir, go away! Flee, that my lover may not see you!"

"By my head," said the youth, "I will kiss you first, no matter whom it annoys, for my mother taught me to."

"I will not kiss you, indeed," said the maiden, "if I can help it. Flee, so that my lover will not find you, for if he does, you are as good as dead."

The youth had strong arms and embraced her clumsily, knowing no better, and stretched her out under him, and though she defended herself and struggled to escape as best she could, her effort was vain. For the youth kissed her willy-nilly twenty times without stopping, as the tale tells, until he saw on her finger a ring with a very bright emerald.

"My mother told me besides," said he, "to take the ring on your finger, but not to do anything more. Here, give me the ring; I want it."

"Indeed," said the maiden, "you will not have my ring, of that be assured, unless you snatch it from my finger by force."

The youth seized her hand, stretched out her finger by force, took the ring, slipped it on his own finger, and said: "I wish you well. I will go away now quite happy. Your kisses are much better than any handmaid's in my mother's household, for your mouth is not bitter."

She wept and said to the youth: "Do not take away my ring, for I shall be in a sad state, and you will lose your life, sooner or later, I promise you."

The youth paid no attention to what he heard, but was dying of hunger because of his fast. He spied a leather bottle full of wine and beside it a silver goblet and on a bundle of rushes a new white towel. He lifted it and found underneath three good venison pasties, new made. This was a repast for which he felt no repugnance. Consumed with hunger, he broke one of the pasties before him and ate it with avidity, filled the silver cup with wine which was by no means bad, took big and frequent drafts, and said: "Maiden, I cannot finish these pasties today. Come and eat; they are good. One apiece will be enough for us, and there will be a whole one left."

All this while she wept, though he prayed and urged her. She answered not a word but wept piteously and loud and wrung her hands. He ate as much as he wished and drank till he had had enough. Then he covered up the remainder and promptly took his leave and commended her to God, though little it pleased her. "God save you," said he, "fair friend! For God's sake, do not be sorry for the ring I am taking, because I will repay you for it before I die. Now, with your leave, I am going."

She wept and refused to commend him to God, for on his account she was bound to endure such disgrace and trouble as no wretched woman ever had, and so long as he lived she would receive no help from him; let him understand that he had betrayed her.

Thus she remained in tears. Before long her lover returned from hunting in the wood. Seeing the hoof tracks of the youth who had gone his way, he was troubled, and when he found his mistress weeping, he said: "Damsel, I perceive by these signs that a knight has been here."

"No, my lord, on my faith. But there has been a Welsh lad, a rude, clownish fool, who drank all he pleased of your wine and ate one of your pasties."

"Why do you weep for that, my fair one? If he had drunk and eaten everything, I would have been willing."

"There was more, my lord," said she. "There was a struggle for my ring. He took it from me and carried it away. I would rather die than have him bear it away."

At that the man was disturbed and troubled in his heart. "By my faith," said he, "that was an insult! But since he has taken it, let him keep it. But I suspect that there was more; if there was, do not hide it."

"My lord," said she, "he kissed me."

"Kissed you?"

"Indeed, I tell you the truth, but it was against my will."

"Say rather that you took pleasure in it and refused him nothing!" said he, in a torment of jealousy. "Do you think that I do not know you? Surely, I know you too well and am not so blind or so squint-eyed that I do not see your falsity. You have started on a wicked path; you have taken a painful road. Your horse shall not have his feed of oats nor shall he be let blood until I am avenged. If he casts a shoe, he shall not be shod again. If he dies, you shall follow me on foot. The clothes which you are wearing shall not be changed, but you shall follow me on foot and naked until I have his head. No other punishment will I choose." He then sat down and began to eat.

Meanwhile, the youth rode on until he saw a charcoal-burner approaching, driving an ass before him. "Carl, you there, driving the ass, show me the shortest way to Carlisle. They tell me that there King Arthur, whom I want to see, makes knights."

"Young sir, in that direction there is a castle standing by the sea. If you go there, good friend, you will find King Arthur in the castle, both happy and sad."

"Now tell me what I want to know, how the King can be both happy and sad."

"I will tell you very quickly. King Arthur with all his army has fought with King Rion, and the King of the Isles[3] was beaten, and it is that which makes

---

3. King Rion is the King of the Isles.

King Arthur glad. He is angry with his companions who have gone back to their castles where they find it pleasanter to live, and he does not know what has happened to them. That makes the King sad."

The youth did not care a penny for the information, except that he took the road which the charcoal-burner had shown. He saw a splendid, strong castle well situated above the sea, and presently descried issuing from the gate an armed knight bearing a golden cup in his hand. With his left hand he held his lance, bridle, and shield, and the golden cup in his right. His arms, all scarlet, became him well. The youth, seeing the fresh, handsome arms, was pleased and said to himself: "By my faith, I will ask the King for these. If he gives them to me, I shall be well satisfied, and a curse on him who would want any others!"

At once, feeling impatient to reach the court, he rode rapidly toward the castle until he met the knight, who stopped him for a moment and asked: "Young sir, where are you going, tell me?"

"I am going to court to ask the King for these arms of yours."

"Young sir, it is right for you to do so. Go quickly and return. Tell the evil King if he will not hold his land as my vassal, let him yield it, or let him send someone out to defend it against me, for I declare that it is mine. Let him believe you by this token that just now I seized in his presence the cup I am carrying, with all the wine he was drinking."

The knight might better have found someone else to take the message, for the youth did not listen to a word, but hastened to the court where the King and the knights were seated at their repast. He rode into the hall, which was on the ground level, paved and as long as wide. King Arthur sat at the head of the table, sunk in thought; all the rest talked and amused themselves, save him who remained pensive and mute. The youth advanced, but he did not know whom to greet, for he did not recognize the King. Yonet, holding a knife in his hand, came to meet him. The newcomer said: "Young sir, you there, with the knife in your hand, show me who is the King."

Yonet was very courteous and replied: "Friend, behold him there."

The youth rode at once toward the King and greeted him as best as he knew how. The King remained brooding and uttered no word. Again the youth spoke; still the King brooded and uttered no sound.

"By my faith," said the youth then, "this King never made a knight! When I cannot drag a word out of him, how could he make a knight?"

Preparing to depart, the youth turned the head of his hunter, but, like an idiot, he had brought him so close to the King that actually the horse knocked the cap off his head onto the table. The King raised his head, turned toward the youth, and, dismissing his cares, said: "Good brother, welcome! Pray do not take it ill that I met your greeting with silence. Anger kept me from replying. My worst enemy, who hates and terrifies me most, has even here laid claim to my land, and is so mad as to threaten to take it, whether I will or no. He is called the Red Knight of the Forest of Quinqueroi.[4] The Queen had come to sit with me in order to see and comfort these wounded knights.[5]

---

4. *Quinqueroi* is a Celtic and specifically Breton name (cf. the Breton city of Quimper in contemporary France).   5. Presumably the knights still at the Arthurian court are those recovering from their wounds from the battle against King Rion. Why the Red Knight is an enemy of Arthur, or on what basis he lays claim to the Arthurian lands, is unknown; the important point is that Perceval will serve, unintentionally, as Arthur's savior.

That knight would not have roused my anger, whatever he said, but he snatched the cup before me and raised it so wildly that all the wine with which it was filled poured over the Queen. That was a vile and churlish deed! Therefore the Queen, burning with sorrow and anger, has gone to her chamber, where she will die. So help me God, I do not believe she can escape alive."

The youth did not care an onion for what the King said; nor did his grief nor the Queen's humiliation make any impression. "Make me a knight, sir King," said he, "because I am eager to be gone."

The eyes in the countenance of the young barbarian were bright and smiling. Though no one who saw him thought him other than mad, all found him handsome and noble.[6] "Friend," said the King, "dismount and give your hunter to this squire, who will care for it and perform your pleasure. I vow to God that your request shall be granted, to my honor and to your profit."

The youth answered: "The knights I met in the glade did not dismount, and you want me to dismount? But knight me quickly and then I will go."

"Ah," said the King, "dear good friend, I will do it gladly, to your profit and my honor."

"By the faith I owe my Maker, good sir King," said the youth, "I will never be a knight unless I am a red knight. Give me the arms of the man I met outside the gate who was carrying away your golden cup."

The seneschal,[7] who was wounded, was angry at what he heard and said: "Friend, you are right. Go at once and take away his arms, for they are yours. You were no fool when you came here to get them."

"Kay," said the King, "in God's name, I beg you. You are too ready to mock and do not care who is the butt. It is unbecoming a gentleman. If the youth is simple-minded, he is still, I think, well born. If he has been thus trained by a boorish master, he may yet prove brave and wise. It is churlish to make a jest of others and to promise without giving. A gentleman should not promise anything that he cannot or will not bestow, for he earns the ill will of him who, but for that promise, would be his friend and who, after the promise is made, expects it to be kept. You should learn that it is better to refuse outright than to rouse vain expectations. To tell the truth, he mocks and deceives himself who promises and does not fulfill, for he loses the heart of his friend."

Thus the King rebuked Kay. As the youth departed, he noticed a fair maiden and greeted her. She returned his greeting and said, laughing: "Young sir, if you live long enough, I believe in my heart that in all the world there will not be, nor will there be acknowledged, a better knight than you. This is my faith and firm belief."

Now this maiden had not laughed for more than six years, and she spoke so loudly that all heard her. Kay, touched to the quick by these words, leaped up, and with the palm of his hand dealt her tender face such a stout blow that he stretched her on the ground. After striking the maiden, he was about to return to his seat when he came upon a fool, standing by the fireplace, and kicked him into the flames in anger because the fool had often declared: "This maiden will never laugh till she sees him who will win the lordship of

6. Most medieval literature assumes that nobility will ultimately reveal itself, even when disguised in rustic manners, but that nobody born a peasant could ever become a knight. In reality class boundaries were more permeable than this assumption claims.   7. An official at a medieval court responsible for overseeing domestic arrangements as well as administering justice.

knighthood." The dwarf screamed, the maiden wept, but the youth did not pause and, without asking counsel of anyone, rode after the Red Knight.

Yonet, who knew all the shortest passages and was eager to bring news to the court, ran alone through a garden beside the hall and descended through a postern[8] till he came to the road just where the Red Knight was waiting for a knightly adventure. The Welsh youth now approached at high speed to seize his arms. The knight, while waiting, had set down the golden cup on a block of brown stone. As soon as the youth came within hearing, he cried: "Lay down your weapons! Carry them no longer, for King Arthur sends you this order!"

The knight inquired: "Young sir, does no one dare to come here to uphold the King's cause? If so, do not hide it from me."

"What the devil! Are you jesting with me, sir knight, that you have not yet stripped off my arms? Take them off at once, I command you."

"Young sir, I ask you whether anyone is coming on the King's behalf to fight with me."

"Sir knight, take off the arms at once, or I will take them off myself, for I will not let you keep them longer. Understand me, I will strike you if you make me talk any more about it."

Then the knight was furious, raised his lance with both hands, and gave the youth a blow across the shoulders with the butt, so that he made him crouch over the neck of his horse. The youth, enraged in his turn when he felt himself bruised by the stroke, aimed as well as he could at the knight's eye and let fly a javelin. It struck him through the eye and brain, so that he saw and heard no more, and the blood and brains oozed out at the nape of his neck. With the agony his heart stopped, and he fell full length to the earth. The youth alighted, laid the lance aside, took the shield from his neck, but could not remove the helm from his head, for he did not know how to grasp it. He sought to ungird the sword, but he did not know how, and he could not draw it from the sheath, but grasped the sheath and pulled and pulled

Yonet began to laugh when he saw the youth so occupied. "What is it, friend?" he said; "what are you doing?"

"I do not know. I thought your King had given me these arms, but I will have to cut up the dead man for chops before I can get any of them, for they stick so to the body that the inside and the outside seem to be of one piece; they hold together so fast."

"Do not vex yourself," said Yonet, "for I will separate them if you wish."

"Do so then at once," said the youth, "and give them to me without delay."

Yonet promptly stripped the body, even down to the toes, removing coat and hose of mail, helmet, and every other piece of armor. But the youth would not take off his own garments, nor, in spite of anything Yonet said, would he put on the comfortable padded silk tunic which the knight had worn under his coat of mail; nor would he remove the brogues from his own feet, but said: "What the devil! are you mocking me? Change my good clothes that my mother made for me the other day for the clothes of this knight? Do you wish me to put off my thick shirt of hemp for this soft thin one, and my jacket that keeps out the water for this that will not stop a drop? Shame on

8. A back or side entrance.

his neck who would exchange his good clothes for another's bad ones!"

It is a hard task to teach a fool. The lad would take nothing but the arms and would heed no request. Yonet laced the mail hose on his legs, attached the spurs to his brogues, then put on the coat of mail so that none ever looked better, fitted the helm over the padded skullcap[9] becomingly, and showed how to gird on the sword so that it swung loosely. Then he placed the lad's foot in the stirrup[1] and made him mount the war horse. The youth had never seen a stirrup before and was not used to spurs but only to whip or willow switch. Yonet brought the shield and lance and handed them over to him. Before Yonet departed, the youth said: "Friend, take my hunter and lead him away, for he is a very good one. I give him to you because I have no more need of him. And take the cup to the King and greet him for me. And tell the maiden whom Kay struck on the cheek that if I can, before I die, I hope to cook him such a dish that she will be well avenged."

Yonet replied that he would return the cup to the King and carry the message faithfully. So the two parted. Yonet entered through the door the hall where the barons were gathered, bringing the cup back to the King, and said: "Sire, rejoice now, for your knight who was here returns your cup to you."

"Of what knight do you speak?" said the King, who was still in a rage of anger.

"In God's name, sire," said Yonet, "I speak of the youth who but now departed."

"Do you speak," said the King, "of the Welsh youth who asked me for the red colored arms of the knight who has many times done all he could to humiliate me?"

"Sire, indeed it is he."

"How did he recover my cup? Did the knight love him or prize him so much that he yielded it of his free will?"

"Nay; rather, the youth made him pay dearly, for he killed the knight."

"How was that, good friend?"

"Sire, I know only that the knight struck the youth a painful blow with his lance, and the youth struck him back with a javelin through the eyehole so that the blood and the brains flowed out behind, and hurled him dead to the earth."

Then the King said to the seneschal: "Ah, Kay, what harm you have done me today! By your evil tongue, so ready with idle chatter, you have driven away a knight who this day has done me great service."

"Sire," said Yonet to the King, "by my head, he sent a message by me to the Queen's handmaid, whom Kay struck in hatred and scorn, that he would avenge her if he lives and if the chance offers."

The fool, who was sitting beside the fire, heard these words, leapt to his feet, came before the King, and skipped and danced for glee, saying: "Lord King, so God save me, your adventures now begin, and often you will find them perilous and hard. I pledge you that Kay will surely regret his feet and his hands and his stupid, churlish tongue. Before forty days have passed, the young knight will have avenged the kick Kay gave me, and the buffet he gave the maiden will be well paid back, for his right arm will be broken between

---

9. A close-fitting cap worn under a helmet.   1. A *stirrup* (one of a pair) was necessary for a knight to brace himself while using a lance.

the elbow and the shoulder, and he will carry it slung from his shoulder for half a year; he can escape it no more than death."

At this speech Kay was so enraged that he almost burst with malice and anger and could hardly keep from killing the fool before the whole court. But he did not attack him because it would displease the King. The King exclaimed: "Ah, ah, Kay, how you have offended me today! If anyone had taught and trained the youth a little about the arms so that he would know how to defend himself, and likewise about his shield and lance, he without doubt would have been a good knight. But the youth knows little of arms or anything else, for he could not even draw a sword if there were need. There he is sitting on his horse; he will meet a knight who will not hesitate to maim him for the sake of his horse. He will speedily be left dead or crippled. He is so simple-minded and brutish that he will soon have played his last stake."

Thus the King mourned for the youth and looked downcast, but there was nothing to be gained by that, and he fell silent. Meanwhile, the youth without a pause went spurring through the forest till he came to a plain bordering a river which was wider than a crossbow shot, for all the water of the countryside flowed through its bed. He crossed a meadow toward the great rushing river but he did not descend into it, for he saw that it was very deep and black and swifter than the Loire.[2] So he followed the bank. Opposite, there was a tall cliff whose base was washed by the stream, and on the side which sloped toward the sea there stood a noble, strong castle. Where the river entered the bay the youth turned to the left and saw the towers of the castle, which seemed to him to grow out of the castle. In the middle stood a huge and mighty keep. Toward the bay, where the river fought with the tide, stood a strong barbican,[3] and the waves beat against its foot. At the four corners of the walls, built of hard stone, there were four low turrets, strong and fair. The castle was finely situated and well furnished within. In front of a round outwork a bridge of sandstone and limestone was built across the river, strong, high, with battlemented parapets, and in the middle a tower. At the near end was a drawbridge, fitted for its purpose, to serve as a passageway by day and as a closed gate by night. The youth proceeded to the bridge.

On it a lord, clad in an ermine robe, was pacing for his pleasure, and he waited the approach of the newcomer. He was holding for dignity's sake a short staff, and near him were two squires without mantles. The newcomer remembered well his mother's lesson, for he bowed to the lord and said: "Sir, my mother taught me that."

"God bless you, fair brother!" said the lord, who perceived that the stranger was uncouth and silly of speech, and he added: "Fair brother, whence have you come?"

"Whence? From King Arthur's court."

"What did you do there?"

"The King made me a knight, good luck to him!"

"A knight? God save me, but I did not think that at this time his mind was on such things. I thought rather that he was concerned with other matters than making knights.[4] Now tell me, gentle brother, who gave you these arms?"

"The King gave them to me."

2. A major river in the north of France.   3. A small blockhouse that protected the main gate of a castle.
4. Another hint that the Arthurian world is in some sort of crisis.

"Gave them? How?"

The youth related what you have already heard; to retell it would be tedious and futile, for no story gains by repetition. The lord then asked what he did with his horse.

"I make him run up hill and down dale, just as I used to make the hunter I had in my mother's house."

"Tell me also, fair friend, what you can do with your arms."

"I know well how to put them on and take them off, just as the squire did who put them on me and took them off the knight whom I had killed. And they are so light to wear that they do not tire me at all."

"By God's soul," said the lord, "that I am glad to hear. Now tell me, if it does not annoy you, what errand brought you here."

"Sir, my mother taught me to go to men of rank to get their advice and to trust it, because good comes to those who believe them."

The lord replied: "Fair brother, blessed be your mother, for she gave you sound counsel. But have you more to say?"

"Yes."

"What?"

"Only this and no more, that you give me lodging tonight."

"Gladly," said the lord; "but grant me a favor which will bring you much good."

"What is it?"

"That you take your mother's advice and mine."

"By my faith, I grant it."

"Then dismount."

The youth dismounted, and one of the two squires who had come up took his horse and the other removed his arms, so that he stood in his rude costume, with the brogues and in the ill-made and ill-fitting coat of buckskin which his mother had given him. The lord then had the sharp steel spurs which the youth had brought attached to his own feet, mounted the horse, hung the shield by the strap around his neck, grasped the lance, and said: "Friend, now take a lesson in arms and watch how to hold a lance, and how to spur and check a horse."

Then he displayed the pennon and showed how to hold the shield, a little forward so that it touched the horse's neck. He laid the lance in rest,[5] and pricked the horse, worth a hundred marks, which no other surpassed for ardor, speed, and strength. The lord was skilled in the management of shield, horse, and lance, since he had been trained in it from boyhood. All that he did delighted the youth, and when he had finished his expert tilting before the youth, who had watched it closely, he returned with his lance upright, and inquired: "Friend, would you too like to know how to manage lance and shield and how to spur and control a horse?"

The youth answered at once that he did not care to live another day or to own wealth or lands before he had learned how to do the same. The lord said: "Dear good friend, what one does not know one can learn if he will take the pains. Every profession demands effort, heart, and practice; every knowledge comes by these three. But since you have never done these things nor seen others do them, you cannot be shamed or blamed if you do not know how."

---

5. Placed his lance in its support preparatory to a charge.

Then the lord caused the youth to mount, and he began to carry lance and shield as adroitly as if he had passed all his days in tourneys and wars and had journeyed throughout the world seeking battle and adventure. For it came to him by nature, and when Nature teaches and the heart attends, nothing can be too hard. With the aid of these two, the youth performed so well that it greatly pleased the lord, and he said in his heart that if his pupil had devoted all his life to arms, he would have become a master. When the youth had carried out the exercise, he returned to the lord with his lance erect as he had seen it held, and said: "Sir, did I do well? Do you think that I will learn it if I take pains? My eyes have never seen anything that I am so eager to master. I long to know as much about it as you do."

"Friend," said the lord, "if you set your heart on it, you will learn without any difficulty."

Three times the lord mounted and three times showed all he knew of the handling of arms till he thought it was enough, and three times he made the youth mount. After the last he said: "Friend, if you met a knight and he struck you, what would you do?"

"I would strike him back."

"And if your lance broke?"

"Then there would be nothing to do but to attack him with my fists."

"Friend, never do that."

"What should I do?"

"You must use your sword and fence with him."

Then the lord planted the lance in the ground, for he wished to teach him how to defend himself with the sword or to attack with it, as circumstances required. He grasped the sword and said: "In this way you should defend yourself if anyone assails you."

"As for that, so God save me, no one knows more than I, because I have often practiced on cushions and shields at my mother's house until I was tired out."

"Then let us go inside," said the lord, "for there is no other lodging, and, whoever may object, you will enjoy no mean hospitality tonight."

Then, as the two went in, side by side, the youth said to his host: "Sir, my mother taught me that I should never be long in the company of anyone without knowing his name; so, as my mother taught me, I would ask your name."

"Fair sweet friend," said the lord, "my name is Gornemant of Gohort."

They entered hand in hand, and as they mounted the steps a squire of his own accord came running with a short mantle which he cast over the youth that he might not, after the heat of exercise, take a bad cold. The buildings of the lord were rich and large, his servants pleasant to look upon, and an excellent meal was prepared. So the knights washed and sat down to eat. The lord seated the youth beside him and caused him to eat from the same dish. I will not say how many courses they had or what they were, but they had plenty to eat and drink; I do not need to tell more of the repast.

When they had risen from table, the courteous lord besought the youth who had sat beside him to stay a month; indeed, he would gladly keep him a whole year if he wished, and he would meanwhile teach him such things as would help him in case of need. The youth replied: "Sir, I do not know whether I am near the manor where my mother lives, but I pray God to guide me so that I may see her again, for I saw her fall in a swoon at the end of the bridge before her gate, and I do not know whether she is alive or dead. But I do know that she fainted for sorrow at my leaving her, and so until I know how she is I cannot stay here long. I must leave tomorrow early."

The lord perceived that prayers would be of no avail, and held his peace. Without more debate they retired to rest, for the beds were already made. Early on the morrow the lord arose and went where he found the youth lying in bed, and brought him as a present a shirt and breeches of fine linen, hose dyed red, and a tunic of indigo silk woven in India. He told him to put them on, saying: "Friend, if you trust me, dress yourself in the clothes you see here."

The youth answered: "Fair sir, surely you could give me better advice, for the clothes that my mother made me, are they not better than these, and yet you wish me to put these on?"

"Young sir," said the lord, "by my head, they are worse. You promised me, good friend, when I brought you here that you would obey all my orders."

"I will do so," said the youth; "I will not oppose you."

Without a pause he donned the new clothes and left those of his mother. The lord, bending over, fastened on his heel the right spur, such was the custom for him who made a knight. Many squires were present, and each, as opportunity offered, helped in the arming. The lord took the sword, girded it on the youth, kissed him, and said that with the sword he had given him the highest order that God had made and decreed—namely, the stainless order of knighthood. He continued: "Remember this, fair brother, I pray you: if it happens that in combat with a knight you gain the upper hand and he is unable to defend himself longer, have mercy on him and do not kill him wittingly. Beware also of talking too much and of gossiping. No one can talk too much without saying something rude. The wise man declares: 'He who talks too much commits sin.' Therefore, fair brother, I forbid you to talk overmuch. Moreover, I beg you, if you find man or woman, whether damsel or lady, in distress, advise them so far as you can and if you have the power to help. One more thing I would have you learn, and do not despise it, for it is not to be scorned. Go to the minster and pray to Him who made all things, to have mercy on your soul and to keep you a good Christian in this earthly life."

The youth said to the lord: "Good sir, may you be blessed by all the Apostles of Rome! That is what I once heard my mother say."

"Now, fair brother," said the lord, "hereafter do not keep saying that your mother taught you this or that. Till now I do not blame you at all, but, begging your pardon, I ask that henceforth you correct yourself, for if you persist, you will be taken for a fool. So I pray you, avoid it."

"What shall I say then, good sir?"

"You may say that the vavasor[6] who buckled on your spur taught you so."

The youth promised that he would never as long as he lived utter a word of any other master, for he saw clearly that the lord's teaching was good. His host then made the sign of the cross over him and, with hand uplifted, said: "Fair sir, God preserve you! Adieu, and may He guide you, for the delay is irksome to you."

6. The vassal of an important noble rather than of the king; the term means literally the vassal of a vassal.

The new knight departed from his host, and he was impatient to go to his mother and find her alive and well. He plunged into the wild forests, where he was more at home than on the level lands, and he rode till he saw a strong, well-placed castle, but outside the walls there was nothing but sea and water and ravaged fields. Hastening toward it, he arrived at the gate, but before he could enter he had to cross a bridge so feeble that he doubted whether it would hold up under him. But he mounted it and passed over without any harm or humiliation. When he arrived at the gate, he found it locked. He did not knock softly or call in a low voice, but struck so hard that presently there appeared at a window of the hall a thin and pale maiden. She asked: "Who is it calls there?"

The youth looked up at the maiden and said: "Fair friend, I am a knight and I ask you to let me in and give me lodging for the night."

"Sir," said she, "you will have it, though you may not be pleased with our entertainment; nevertheless, we will do the best we can."

Then the damsel withdrew, and he who was waiting at the gate feared that he might be kept too long and resumed his knocking. Soon, four servants, bearing great axes on their shoulders and girded with swords, came and opened the door saying: "Sir, enter."

In better days the servants would have been handsome fellows, but through lack of food and sleep they were wonderfully changed, and if the fields outside were ravaged and stripped, it was no better within. Wherever the new knight passed, he found the streets empty and the old houses tumbled down, and there was neither man nor woman about. There were two abbeys in the town, one of terrified nuns, the other of helpless monks, and the buildings were not in a good state, and the walls were cracked and the towers roofles and the gates open both night and day. No mill was grinding or oven baking in the whole town; there was no bread or cake or even a penny's worth of anything for sale. The knight found the castle so desolate that there was no bread, pastry, wine, cider, or ale.

The four servants led him to a slate-roofed hall, there caused him to alight, and removed his arms. Promptly a squire descended the steps of the hall bearing a gray mantle and fastened it round his neck, while another stabled his horse in a stall where there was no grain or hay and only a little straw; there was no more in the house. The other squires made him ascend the stairs before them, and in the stately hall two lords and a maiden advanced to meet him. The hair of the lords was grizzled but not white, and they would have been at the peak of their ardor and strength if they had not suffered hardship.

The maiden approached, more gracious and glowing with life than sparrow hawk or parrot. Her mantle and her gown were of a dark silk, starred with gold and trimmed with fine ermine, and the collar of the mantle was of black and gray sable, neither too long nor too wide. And if ever I have described the beauty with which God endowed the body and the visage of a woman, I will try again without varying from the truth by a word. Her tresses flowed free and the beholder would mistake them, if it were possible, for fine gold, they were so lustrous. Her forehead was high, white, and smooth, as if it had been carved of marble or ivory or fine wood; her eyebrows dark and wide apart; her eyes smiling, bright, and large; her nose straight and regular; the red glowed on her white skin more charmingly than vermilion on silver. To steal away the minds and hearts of men, God made of her a wonder, and never before or since has He made her equal.

When the knight saw her, he greeted her, and she and the two attendant knights responded. The damsel took his hand courteously and said: "Fair sir, our lodging tonight will not be such as a man of rank deserves. If I tell you at once of our condition, you may think perhaps that I speak out of hostility, to induce you to leave. But may it please you to remain and to accept our hospitality, such as it is, and may God grant you a better tomorrow."

Then she led him by the hand into a fair, wide, and long chamber with a vaulted ceiling, and there they seated themselves on a couch, spread with a coverlet of samite.[7] Knights entered in groups of four, five, and six, and sat down but said not a word, looking at the guest who sat silent beside their lady. And he refrained from speaking because he remembered the charge which Gornemant had laid upon him. Then all the knights began to whisper among themselves. "By God," said each, "I wonder if this knight is dumb; it would be a great pity, for never was so handsome a knight born of woman. How well he looks beside my lady, and she beside him, if only they were not both so silent. They are both so beautiful that never knight and maiden looked better together. It seems as if God had made each for the other in order that he might join them."

They all continued to talk together, while the damsel waited for her guest to address her. Perceiving at last that he would not speak unless spoken to, she said courteously: "Sir, whence did you come today?"

"Damsel," said he, "I lay last night at the castle of a nobleman, where I had good lodging. There were five towers, exceeding strong, one big and four little ones. I cannot tell you all about it and I do not know what the castle is called, but I know well the name of the nobleman, Gornemant of Gohort."

"Ah, fair friend," said the maiden, "well have you spoken and courteously. May God the King reward you for calling your host a nobleman. You have never uttered a truer word, for he is a noble man, by St. Richier;[8] that I can vouch for. Know, then, that I am his niece, but it is long since I have set eyes on him. Surely, since you left your home, you have not met a nobler man, to my thinking. As a noble and gracious host, powerful and prosperous, he must have given you cheerful and joyous entertainment. But here there are only six loaves, which a holy prior, my uncle, has sent me for supper tonight, with a bottle of boiled wine. There is no other provender except a buck which one of my servants shot with an arrow this morning."

She ordered the tables to be set up, and when this was done, all sat down to supper. They did not linger long at the meal but ate ravenously. Afterwards those remained who had kept watch the night before and who were now due to sleep, while fifty servants and squires whose duty it was to keep watch that night over the castle went out. The rest busied themselves in making their guest comfortable, and those who attended to the bedding spread fair sheets and a costly coverlet and laid a pillow at the head. The youth enjoyed that night in his bed all the comfort and pleasure imaginable except the delight of a maiden's or a lady's company, if it had pleased or been permitted him; but of that he knew and thought nothing, and free from care he went promptly to sleep.

7. A heavy silk fabric. 8. St. Richier or Riquier was a 7th-century French monk.

But his hostess, who was shut in her chamber, did not rest. While he slept peacefully, she, who had no defense in the struggle which went on within her, brooded, turning and tossing, till at last she donned a short mantle of scarlet silk over her shift, and set out on a bold enterprise. It was no trifling matter; rather she planned to go to her guest and tell him something of her plight. Leaving her bed, she issued from her chamber, perspiring and trembling in every limb with terror. She came to the bed where the knight was sleeping, wept and sighed deeply, and knelt so that the tears wetted his face; she did not dare to be bolder. At last he woke, startled and wondering how his face was so wet, and found her on her knees beside the bed and her arms around his neck. He had the courtesy to embrace her in turn, and drew her toward him, saying: "Fair lady, what do you wish? What has brought you here?"

"Ah, gentle knight, have mercy! I implore you for God's sake and for His Son's not to take me for a vile thing because I have come to you thus, and though I am nearly nude, I have no light, wicked, or coarse design. In the whole world there is no living creature so wretched and poor that I am not more so. I have nothing to cheer me; every day is a grief. I shall never see another night nor another day than tomorrow, but I will kill myself with my own hand. Of three hundred and ten knights who garrisoned this castle, only fifty are left. Forty-eight have been led away and either killed or imprisoned by an evil knight, Anguingueron, seneschal of Clamadeu of the Isles.[9] I grieve as much for those who are in prison as for the dead, for I know that they will die too, for they can never escape. So many brave men have been killed for my sake that I have a right to mourn. For a whole winter and a summer Anguingueron has laid close siege to us, and while his forces increase, ours dwindle, and our provisions are spent, so that there is not enough to feed a bee. Tomorrow, unless God wills otherwise, this castle must surrender, for it can no longer be defended, and I with it. But surely, before Anguingueron takes me alive, I will kill myself, and he will have only my corpse. Then little shall I care, though Clamadeu, who hopes to possess me, gain his end, for he will have the body without life and soul. I keep in my casket a knife of fine steel, which I intend to plunge into my body. I have said enough. I will now go back and leave you to your rest."

Here then was an opportunity for the knight to win fame if he had the courage, for the maiden had come and shed tears over his face for no other purpose than to inspire him to do battle, if he dared, in defense of her land and herself. He spoke: "Dear friend, be of good cheer tonight. Take comfort, stop crying, come close to me, and wipe the tears from your eyes. God, if He pleases, will better by you tomorrow than what you have told me. Come and lie in this bed beside me, for it is wide enough for us both. Do not leave me now."

She replied: "If it pleases you, I will do so."

Then, holding her in his arms, he kissed her and drew her softly under the coverlet, and she did not resist his kisses and I do not think that they dis-

---

9. The arithmetic is faulty, unless we are to think that the 212 knights who are missing were not victims of Anguingueron's most recent attack but were killed earlier during the long siege; later Anguingueron will say that he has killed or captured "all [the lady's] knights this past year." In any case, numbers in many medieval texts are often only approximate. Neither Anguingueron nor Clamadeu of the Isles appear in any earlier texts.

pleased him. Thus they lay that night beside each other, mouth to mouth, until dawn approached. That night gave him so much delight that they slept together mouth to mouth, in close embrace.[1] When day came the maiden returned to her chamber and dressed herself without the aid of her women, who were not yet awake. The guards who had watched through the night, as soon as they saw daylight, woke those who were sleeping and made them rise from their beds without delay. The maiden herself went back to her knight and said courteously: "Sir, God give you good day! I do not expect that you will make a long stay or find anything to do here; it would be of no use, and I will not take it ill if you go, for it would not be polite of me. We have done nothing for your ease and comfort. But I pray God to arrange better lodging for you and more bread, wine, salt, and every provision, than you have found here."

He answered: "Fair maiden, I will not look today for any other lodging, but if I can I will restore peace to all your land. If I find your enemy yonder outside, I shall not be happy if he stays longer, for he has no right to torment you. But if I defeat and kill him, I will ask you to be my love as a reward. I will take no other pay."

She courteously replied: "Sir, it is a poor and contemptible thing you now request of me, but if I refuse, you will think me proud, and therefore I will not deny you. Nevertheless, do not say that I become your love on condition that you go forth to die for my sake; that would be outrageous. Be assured that you have not the strength or the age to hold your own in battle against a knight so big and hardy as he who waits outside yonder."

"You will see today," said he, "for I will go and fight with him. I will not stop for anyone's advice."

Thus she warned him against a plan which she wished him to execute. Often, when one sees a man eager to carry out a wish, one hides one's real desire in order to make him more ardent. So she behaved shrewdly, rebuking Perceval for doing what she had put it in his heart to do. He called for his arms, and when they were brought, and the gate was opened, attendants armed him and had him mount a caparisoned steed, in the open square. Everyone showed signs of grief and said: "Sir, God give you aid this day, and bring to an evil end Anguingueron, the seneschal, who has destroyed this country."

Thus both men and women wept as they accompanied him to the gate, and when they saw him sally from the castle, they said with one voice: "May the true cross, on which God allowed His Son to suffer, protect you this day from mortal peril and from prison and bring you back safe to the place where you may have peace and joy!"

Thus they all prayed. Meanwhile the besiegers saw him coming and pointed him out to Anguingueron, who was sitting before his tent, confident that the castle would be surrendered before nightfall or that someone would come out to meet him in bodily combat. He had already had his mail hose laced, and his men were exulting at the thought that the castle and the land were as good as conquered. When Anguingueron saw the knight, he hastily completed his arming, rode swiftly toward him on a strong, heavily built

---

1. Chrétien seems to want us to think that Perceval does not violate his mother's command to do nothing more than kiss a lady.

charger, and called: "Young sir, who has sent you? Tell me your purpose. Have you come to seek peace or battle?"

"But you, tell me first what you are doing in this land," said the youth. "Why have you killed the knights and ravaged all the country?"

Arrogant was the reply: "I demanded that this day the castle be vacated and the keep[2] surrendered; it has been defended too long. And my master must have the maiden."

"A curse on this answer and on him who makes it!" said the youth. "It is you, rather, who must give up all claims against her."

"You are plying me with lies, by St. Peter," said Anguingueron. "Many a man pays the penalty who never committed the fault."

The youth grew restive, laid his lance in rest, and each spurred against his opponent as fast as his horse could carry him. Furiously and with mighty blows they reduced what remained of their lances to splinters. Anguingueron fell from his saddle, painfully wounded in the arm and side. The youth, not knowing how to deal with him on horseback, sprang to the ground, drew his sword, and laid on again. I cannot describe all the strokes, but they were heavy and the fight lasted long, until Anguingueron fell. The youth still attacked him fiercely till he begged for mercy, but the youth declared that he would grant none. Then he remembered that Gornemant had taught him never wittingly to slay a knight after he had vanquished him, and the seneschal cried: "Fair friend, do not be so cruel as to refuse me mercy. I acknowledge that you have the best of me and are a very great knight, but no one who knew us both and had not seen it would ever believe that you alone had killed me in battle with your arms. But I will bear witness that you have fairly overcome me in battle, in the sight of my people before my tent, and my word will be accepted and your glory will be known; no knight ever had greater. Think, too, if you have a lord who has shown you favor and whom you have not yet repaid; send me to him and I will go and report how you have defeated me and give myself up as a prisoner to do with what he pleases."

"A curse on him who would expect more! Do you know where you must go? To that castle yonder, and say to the beautiful maiden who is my ladylove that never in all your life will you do her harm and that you put yourself wholly at her mercy."

Anguingueron replied: "Then kill me, for so she would have me killed, and she desires nothing so much as my ruin and death. I was at the death of her father, and this year I have slain or imprisoned all her knights. To send me to her would place me in a dungeon cell, and nothing could be worse. If you have no other friend, man or woman, send me to someone who bears me no grudge. This lady, if she had me in her power, would not fail to take my life."

Then the youth commanded the seneschal to go to the castle of a nobleman and told him the name, and described the architecture as well as any mason in the world. He praised the river, the bridge, the little towers, the keep, and the outworks so well that the seneschal recognized that he was to be sent as captive to the place where he was hated most. "Good sir," he said, "if you send me there, I shall be no safer. God help me, but you are bent on putting me on a fatal journey into fatal hands. In this war I slew one of that

2. The central tower of a castle.

lord's brothers, and you slay me too, good friend, if you force me to go to him. It will be my death."[3]

"Then," said the youth, "you shall go as a captive to King Arthur. Greet him, and ask him for my sake to show you the maiden whom Kay the seneschal struck when she laughed on seeing me. Give yourself up to her and tell her, if you please, that I pray God not to let me die before I have avenged her."

Anguingueron replied that he would gladly do this service, and then the victor returned to the castle. His prisoner departed, caused his banner to be borne away, and lifted the siege, so that no one of the host, be his hair dark or light, remained. The men of the castle sallied forth to meet the returning hero, but they were disgusted that he had not taken the head of the vanquished knight and given it to them. With great joy they caused him to dismount at a horseblock and disarmed him, saying: "Sir, since you have not brought Anguingueron back, why did you not bring his head?"

The knight answered: "Sirs, by my faith, that would not have been right. Because he killed your relatives, he would have had no warrant for his safety, and you would have killed him in spite of me. There would be little left of my honor if, after getting the best of him, I had not granted his plea for mercy. Do you know what I granted? He will go, if he keeps his promise, as a prisoner to King Arthur."

Just then the damsel arrived and made great joy of him and led him to her chamber to rest and take his ease. Nor was she coy with her kisses and embraces, but they amused themselves thus and in gracious talk, instead of in drinking and eating.

Meanwhile Clamadeu was indulging in foolish anticipations as he traveled toward the castle, thinking at last to take it without resistance. A squire met him on the road, lamenting loudly, and gave him the news of his seneschal, Anguingueron. "In God's name, lord," said the squire, tearing his hair in distress, "the worst has happened."

Clamadeu replied: "What is that?"

"Lord," said the squire, "on my faith, your seneschal has been overcome by arms and has gone to give himself up to King Arthur."

"Who, tell me, squire, has done this and how could it happen? Whence could the knight have come who could make so noble and valiant a man surrender?"

The squire answered: "My dear lord, I do not know who the knight was; I know only that I saw him come out of Belrepeire, wearing red arms."

"What do you advise, squire?" said his master, who was nearly out of his mind with rage.

"What, sire? It is best to turn back, for if you proceed you will gain nothing."

At this word there came forward a grizzled knight, who was the counselor of Clamadeu, and said: "Squire, you do not speak wisely. It is best to follow more sensible advice than yours. If he takes yours, he will act like a fool. My counsel is to go on." Then he added: "Sire, would you like to know how to capture the knight and the castle? I will tell you how, and it will be easy. Within the walls of Belrepeire there is neither drink nor food, and the knights are weak, while we are strong and hale, and, suffering neither thirst nor

---

3. These revelations are designed to show the level of violence and unresolved antagonism at work in the chivalric world into which the naïve Perceval has just entered.

hunger, we can put up a stout fight. If the defenders dare to make a sally and engage in battle outside, let us send twenty knights to offer battle before the gate. The knight who is dallying with Blancheflor, his sweet mistress, will be eager to undertakes feats of arms beyond his powers and will be captured or slain. The other knights will be so feeble that they can give him little aid, and our twenty will retreat before them until we burst upon them through this valley and surround them."

"By my faith, I commend the plan that you propose," said Clamadeu. "We have here picked men, five hundred fully armed knights and a thousand well-equipped foot, and it will be like capturing a troop of dead men."

Clamadeu sent accordingly twenty knights toward the gate, with their various gonfalons and banners unfurled to the wind. When those within the castle saw them, they opened the gate wide, for the youth willed it so. He himself rode out at their head to encounter the foe, and attacked them all boldly and fiercely. Those he met did not take him for an apprentice in arms. That day his lance head was felt in many a gut. One he pierced in the chest, one in the nipple, of one he broke the arm, of one the collarbone. Him he killed, him he maimed, him he unhorsed, him he captured. He turned over the captives and the horses to those who were charged with the duty of taking them.

Now the troops who had ascended the valley came in sight of the battle, and they were five hundred knights by count, besides a thousand foot. The defenders were staying close to the open gate, and when the new arrivals saw their own comrades maimed and dead, they made a wild and disorderly rush toward the gate. The defenders, however, held their ranks at the gate and bravely met the onslaught, but they were few and weak. The attackers were now reinforced by the foot soldiers who had followed them, so that the defense was obliged to withdraw into the castle. Archers posted over the gate shot into the dense mass which was struggling ardently to make an entry. At last a small body forced its way in. But the defenders dropped a portcullis[4] which killed and crushed all those whom it struck in its fall. Clamadeu never saw anything that made him sadder, for many of his men were slain at the portcullis and he himself was shut out. There was nothing to do but take a rest, for another hasty assault would only be wasted effort.

His counselor advised him: "Sire, it is no wonder if a wise and worthy man sometimes fails. As God wills, good and evil fortune come to every man. You have lost the battle, that is plain; but there is no saint who does not have a feast day. You have been struck by a storm; your men are crippled, and the defenders have won the day. But, rest assured, their turn will come to lose. Pluck out both my eyes if they hold out two more days. The castle and the keep will be yours, and they will all place themselves at your mercy. If you stay only today and tomorrow, the castle will be in your hands, and the maiden who has refused you so long will implore you in God's name to take her."

Then those who had brought tents and pavilions pitched them, and the others camped as best they could. The men of the castle disarmed the knights they had captured, but did not put them in dungeons or in irons, but only made them pledge on their honor as knights not to attempt an escape and

---

4. A heavy grating that is dropped from above to block a gateway.

never to do them injury again. So it was arranged within the castle.

Now that very day a high wind drove a barge, heavily laden with wheat and other provisions, across the sea and, as God willed, brought it safely before the castle.[5] When the besieged saw it, they sent to inquire who the new arrivals were and what they wanted, and descending to the barge they asked what sort of people they were, whence they came, and whither they were bound. The answer was: "We are merchants, bringing food for sale, bread, wine, salt bacon, and, if there is need, oxen and swine for slaughtering."

The men of the castle exclaimed: "Blessed be God, who lent strength to the wind and brought you here under full sail! Welcome! Come ashore, for your whole cargo is already sold at as high a price as you wish, and take your payment at once, for you will have plenty to do, counting and carrying away the gold and silver ingots that we will give you for the wheat, and you may, if necessary, require a cart to load the meat and wine."

So those who bought and those who sold made a good bargain. They saw to the unloading of the ship and had everything carried up for the relief of the castle. When those within spied the bearers of the food approaching, you can imagine their delight, and with all speed they hastened to prepare a meal. Clamadeu, who was idling away the time outside, might now have long to wait, for the besieged were provided with oxen, swine, and salt meat in plenty, and wheat enough to last till harvest. The cooks were not sluggish; the kitchen boys lighted the fires for the roasts. Carefree, the youth may now disport himself with his love; she embraces him, he kisses her, and thus each gives joy to the other. The hall was no longer quiet, but was full of noise and gaiety. Everyone was merry over the repast, which they had craved so long, and the cooks worked fast and made those sit down to eat who had the greatest need. When they had finished, they rose to give place to others.

Clamadeu and his men, however, who had heard news of the good fortune which had come to the besieged, were dismayed, and there were those who said it was best to depart, because the castle could not be starved out and the siege had been undertaken for nothing. But Clamadeu, mad with rage, sent a message to the castle without asking counsel of anyone, informing the red knight that until noon the next day he could be found on the plain ready to meet him in single combat, if he dared come out. When the maiden heard this challenge delivered to her lover, she was torn with grief, but he returned answer that, since Clamadeu had demanded battle, he should have it. This only aggravated the maiden's sorrow, but it was of no avail. All the others, men and women, besought the youth not to go out to fight with one who had never yet met his match in battle.

"Sir," said the youth, "you would do well to be still, for I will not be stopped for anything or for any man in the world."

Thus they had their answer, and dared speak no more, but retired to bed and slept till the sun rose on the morrow. They grieved that their prayers had not succeeded in persuading their lord to heed their advice. The same night his love pleaded with him not to go out to battle but to rest in peace, for the besieged no longer cared a whit for Clamadeu and his men. It was

5. The miraculous arrival of this ship is the latest in a series of events that reveal Perceval's course as being providentially directed.

all in vain; and that was strange, for her blandishments were very sweet to him, and with every word she kissed him so tenderly that she placed the key of love into the lock of his heart. Nevertheless, she could not dissuade him from his purpose. He called for his arms, they were quickly brought, and as he donned them, both men and women lamented. He commended them all to the King of Kings, then mounted a steed from Norway which had been led up, and rode away, leaving them in their grief.

When Clamadeu saw his adversary approaching, he felt a foolish confidence that he would soon make him void his saddle. The heath was fair, level, and empty except for the two combatants, for Clamadeu had sent back all his people. Each laid his lance in rest and spurred against the other without shouting a defiance. Each had a thick but manageable lance of ash wood, with a sharp head; the horses were swift; their masters were strong and hated each other with a mortal hatred. They struck each other so that the shields and the lances were broken, and they were both thrown to the earth. But they quickly sprang up and renewed the combat on foot with their swords, and long the issue hung in the balance. If I wished I could describe it fully, but I will not, since one word is as good as twenty. At last Clamadeu was forced to beg mercy, and promised everything, except that, like his seneschal, he would not be imprisoned at Belrepeire, nor would he go for all the empire of Rome to the nobleman who possessed the castle so grandly placed, but he would consent gladly to become the prisoner of King Arthur, and would deliver the message to the maiden whom Kay had brutally struck—namely, that the youth would avenge her in time if God gave him the power, in spite of anyone's displeasure. The youth made him promise also that the next day before dawn all the prisoners in his towers would be allowed to return freely, and that if ever in his life an army laid siege to Belrepeire he would disperse them if he could, and that never would he or his men do injury to its mistress.

So Clamadeu departed to his own land, and when he arrived, he commanded that all the prisoners be freed, and so by his orders they departed, unhindered, with all their equipment. Clamadeu himself took the road alone. It was the custom of that country, as we find it written, that a vanquished knight was allowed to proceed to the place of his captivity with such arms as he was wearing, neither less nor more. So equipped, Clamadeu followed the road Anguingueron had taken to Dinasdaron,[6] where the King was said to hold court.

But there was great rejoicing at Belrepeire when those who had long suffered vile imprisonment returned. The hall and the quarters of the knights resounded with mirth. The bells in the chapels and minsters rang out gaily, and there was no monk or nun who did not render thanks to the Lord. Men and women danced through the streets and market places. Throughout the castle and town there was exultation that the war was over.

Anguingueron meantime had completed his journey, and Clamadeu, following, put up three nights in the same lodgings, as he knew by his traces, and arrived at Dinasdaron in Wales, where King Arthur was holding high feast in his halls. They saw Clamadeu approaching, fully armed, as was his right. Anguingueron had already the evening before delivered his message,

---

6. A castle in Wales.

and had been asked to remain as one of the King's household and council. When he saw his lord stained with blood, he recognized him and exclaimed: "Sirs, sirs, behold a wonder! The youth with the red arms, believe me, has sent here that knight whom you see. He must have conquered him, I am certain, because he is covered with blood. I recognize his shield and the man himself, for he is my lord and I am his man. His name is Clamadeu of the Isles, and I believed that there was no better knight in the empire of Rome. But many a mighty man comes to grief."

So Anguingueron spoke as Clamadeu approached, and then each ran to meet the other. It was the feast of Pentecost,[7] and the Queen was sitting at Arthur's side at the head of the dais, and there were counts, dukes, kings, queens, countesses in plenty, and they had come from hearing all the masses at the minster. Kay walked through the hall, without mantle, in his right hand a small staff, a cap of goodly stuff on his head, his blond hair twined in a single tress. There was no handsomer knight in the world, but his evil speech detracted from his good looks and his prowess. His tunic was of rich colored silk. About his waist was a girdle finely wrought, with a buckle and ornaments of gold, as the story testifies. Everyone got out of his way as he came through the hall, they so dreaded his raillery and his malicious tongue. For it is a sensible man who fears public slander, whether in jest or earnest. So no one spoke to Kay, and he walked up to where the King was sitting and said: "Sire, if you please, you may eat at once."

"Kay," the King replied, "leave me in peace, for by the eyes in my head, I will not begin eating at a high feast such as this until some new tidings are brought to my court."

As they talked, Clamadeu entered, in arms, as was proper, to give himself up as a prisoner; and he said: "God save and bless the best king living, the most generous and courteous, as all those bear witness who have heard of his great deeds! Now harken, good lord, to the message that I would deliver. Though it pains me, I will nevertheless confess that I was sent here by a knight who conquered me, and must surrender to you, for I cannot do otherwise. If asked what his name is, I must admit my ignorance, but will report that his arms are red and that he says you gave them to him."

"Friend," said the King, "so may God keep you, tell me truly whether he is well and vigorous?"

"Yes, you may be quite sure, dear good lord," said Clamadeu; "he is the most valiant knight whom I have known. Furthermore, he told me that I should speak to the maiden who laughed when she saw him and whom Kay struck shamefully on the cheek, and tell her that he will avenge her, if God grants him the power."

The fool, hearing this speech, leapt for joy and cried: "Lord King, so may God bless me, she shall be well repaid for the buffet; and do not take it for a jest, for Kay will have his arm broken and his collarbone put out."

Hearing these words, Kay took them for utter nonsense, and if he let them pass, it was not because of cowardice but from respect for the royal presence. The King shook his head, saying: "Ah, Kay, I am sorely distressed that the youth is not here among us. It was you and your foolish tongue that drove him away, to my sorrow."

---

7. *Pentecost* is the Christian feast day celebrating the descent of the Holy Spirit upon the Apostles, as described in Acts 2. In Arthurian tales it is often the day on which the court is visited by a stranger bearing news of adventures abroad in the land.

At these words Giflet rose and Sir Ivain,[8] who shed refinement on all those about him, and the King told them to lead Clamadeu to the chambers where the Queen's damsels were making merry. The knight bowed and was led to the chambers, where the maiden was pointed out to him. There he gave her the tidings she was eager to hear. Though she had recovered from the blow on her cheek, she had not forgotten the shame of it. It is very wrong to forget shame or injury. Pain passes, but shame lasts in a strong and steadfast man; while in an evil man it cools and dies. Clamadeu had now performed his errand, and the King retained him the rest of his life in his household.

Now he who had contested with Clamadeu the maiden Blancheflor and her land took his ease and delight with his fair love, and the land would have been entirely his if his mind had not turned elsewhere. He thought again of his mother, whom he had seen falling in a swoon, and he yearned to see her more than anything else. He did not dare to take leave of his love, for she forbade it and sent all her folk to beseech him to stay. But their prayers availed only to win a promise that if he found his mother alive, he would bring her back with him and would then take over the land, and if she were dead, he would return likewise. Thus he set out on the promise of return, but he left his gracious lady angry and sorrowful, and her people also. As he rode out of the town, there was such a procession as on Ascension Day[9] or on a Sunday. All the monks had gone out, clad in silken copes, and all the veiled nuns, and both monks and nuns pleaded: "Sir, you who have delivered us from exile and restored us to our houses, it is no wonder if we mourn when you leave us so soon. Our grief is such that it could not be greater."

He replied: "Weep no longer; it is not fitting. I will come back, if God keeps me. Tears are worth nothing. Do you not believe that it would be good for me to see my mother, who used to live in that wood which is called the Wild Forest? I will come back, whether she lives or not, for my mind is set. If she is alive, I will make her a veiled nun in your church; if dead, I will arrange a service for her soul every year that God may place her in Abraham's bosom among the pious souls. Reverend monks and you, fair ladies, this ought not to cause you sorrow, because I will make great provision for her soul if God brings me back."

Then the monks, nuns, and all the others went their ways, and Perceval set forth, lance in rest, armed at all points as he had come there. All day he journeyed without meeting earthly creature or Christian man or woman to direct him. He did not cease to beseech the Lord, the sovereign Father, if it were His will, to grant that he might find his mother in life and health. He was still praying when he came at the bottom of a hill to a river. Gazing upon the deep and rapid water, he did not dare to descend into it but said: "Ah, Almighty God, if I could cross this stream, I believe I would find my mother, if she is still alive."

So he rode along the bank till he came to a cliff washed by the stream, so that he could not pass. Then he caught sight of a boat floating downstream and two men in it. He waited, expecting them to come up to him. But they stopped in the middle of the river and dropped anchor. The man in the bow had a line and was baiting his hook with a fish somewhat larger than a

---

8. *Giflet* and *Ivain* are two of Arthur's knights.   9. *Ascension Day* is the feast day celebrating Christ's ascension into heaven forty days after the resurrection.

minnow. The knight, not knowing where to find passage, greeted them and asked: "Sirs, tell me if there is a ford or a bridge on this river?"

The fisherman answered: "No, brother, on my faith there is not for twenty leagues up or down a boat larger than this, which would not carry five men, and one cannot cross on horseback, for there is no ferry, bridge, or ford."

"Then tell me, in God's name, where I may find shelter."

The fisherman replied: "Indeed you will have need of that and more. I will myself give you lodging tonight. Ride up by the cleft in this rock, and when you have reached the top, you will see before you in a valley a house where I dwell, near the river and near the wood."

Without further pause the knight ascended, and at the top of the hill he gazed long ahead without seeing anything but sky and earth. He exclaimed: "What has brought me here? Stupidity and trickery. God bring shame on him today who sent me here! Truly he put me on the right path when he said that at the top I would spy a house! Fisherman, you foully deceived me if you spoke out of malice!"

At that instant he spied before him in a valley the top of a tower. One might seek as far as Beirut without finding one as noble or as well situated.[1] It was square, built of dark stone, and flanked by two lesser towers. The hall stood in front of the tower, and before the hall an arcade. As the youth descended he confessed that the fisherman had given him good directions, and praised him and no longer called him a treacherous liar, since now he had found harborage. So he proceeded to the gate, before which there was a drawbridge lowered. As he crossed, four squires came to meet him; two removed his arms; a third led his horse away to give him fodder and oats; the fourth clad the youth in a scarlet mantle, fresh and new. Then they led him to the arcade, and be assured that none as splendid could be found as far as Limoges. There he waited till the lord of the castle sent two squires to fetch him, and he accompanied them to the square hall, which was as long as it was wide. In the middle he saw, sitting on a couch, a handsome nobleman with grizzled locks, on his head a sable cap, black as a mulberry, with a crimson lappet below and a robe of the same. He was reclining on his elbow, and in front of him a great fire of dry branches blazed between four columns. Four hundred men could seat themselves comfortably around it. The four strong columns which supported the hood of the fireplace were of massive bronze.

The squires brought the youth before his host and stood on either side of him. When the lord saw him approach, he promptly greeted him, saying: "Friend, do not take it amiss if I do not rise to meet you, but I cannot do so easily."

"In God's name, sire, do not speak of it, for, as God may give me joy and health, it does not offend me."

The nobleman raised himself with difficulty, as much as he could, and said: "Friend, draw nearer; do not be abashed but sit here at my side, for so I bid you."

As the youth sat beside him, the nobleman inquired: "Friend, from what place did you come today?"

"Sire, this morning I left the castle called Belrepeire."

---

1. The suddenness with which the castle appears marks it as having a special significance; some scholars see Perceval as here entering into a version of the Celtic otherworld. A similar effect occurs when Gawain arrives at his destination in *Sir Gawain and the Green Knight*.

"So help me God," exclaimed the nobleman, "you have had a long day's ride. You must have departed before the watchman blew his horn at dawn." "No," the youth answered, "prime[2] had already been rung, I assure you."

As they talked, a squire came in at the door, a sword suspended from his neck. He handed it to the rich host, who drew it halfway from the sheath and observed where it was forged, for it was written on the blade. He saw too that it was of such fine steel that it could not break save only in one peril which no one knew but him who had forged and tempered it. The squire who had brought it announced: "Sire, the fair-haired maiden, your beautiful niece, sends you this gift. You have never seen one lighter for its length and breadth. You may present it to whom you please, but my lady would be glad if you would bestow it where it would be well employed. He who forged it made only three, and he will die before he can make another."

At once the lord, taking the sword by the hangings, which were worth a great treasure, gave it to the newcomer. The pommel was of the best gold of Arabia or Greece, and the sheath was covered with Venetian gold embroidery. This richly mounted sword the lord gave to the youth, saying: "Good sir, this was destined for you, and I desire you to have it. Gird it on and then draw it."

The youth thanked him and fastened the girdle so that it was not too tight. Then he drew out the naked blade from the sheath and after holding it a little put it back. Rest assured that it became him well hanging at his side, and better still when gripped in his fist; and it surely seemed that it would do him knightly service in time of need. Looking about, he noted standing behind him around the brightly burning fire some squires, and he entrusted the sword to the keeping of the one who had charge of his arms. Then he returned to his seat beside the lord, who showed him great honor. The light of the candles was the brightest that one could find in any mansion.

While they were talking of this and that, a squire entered from a chamber, grasping by the middle a white lance, and passed between the fire and those seated on the couch. All present beheld the white lance and the white point, from which a drop of red blood ran down to the squire's hand. The youth who had arrived that night watched this marvel, but he refrained from asking what this meant, for he was mindful of the lesson which Gornemant gave him, warning him against too much speech, and he feared that if he asked, it would be considered rude. So he held his peace.

Then two other squires came in, right handsome, bearing in their hands candelabra of fine gold and niello work, and in each candelabrum were at least ten candles. A damsel came in with these squires, holding between her two hands a grail. She was beautiful, gracious, splendidly garbed, and as she entered with the grail in her hands, there was such a brilliant light that the candles lost their brightness, just as the stars do when the moon or the sun rises. After her came a damsel holding a carving platter of silver. The grail which preceded her was of refined gold; and it was set with precious stones of many kinds, the richest and the costliest that exist in the sea or in the earth. Without question those set in the grail surpassed all other jewels. Like the lance, these damsels passed before the couch and entered another chamber.

The youth watched them pass, but he did not dare to ask concerning the

2. About 9 A.M.

grail and whom one served with it, for he kept in his heart the words of the wise nobleman. I fear that harm will come of this, because I have heard say that one can be too silent as well as be too loquacious. But, for better or for worse, the youth put no question.

The lord then ordered the water to be brought and the cloths to be spread, and this was done by those whose duty and custom it was. The lord and his guest washed their hands with moderately warm water. Two squires brought a wide table top of ivory, which, according to the story, was all of a piece, and they held it a moment before the lord and the youth, till two other squires came bringing trestles. The wood of which they were made possessed two virtues which made them last forever. Of what were they made? Of ebony. What is the property of that wood? It cannot rot and it cannot burn; these two dangers it does not heed. The table top was placed on the trestles, and the cloth was laid. What should I say of the cloth? No legate, cardinal, or even pope ever ate on one so white.

The first course was a haunch of venison, peppered and cooked in grease. There was no lack of clear wine or grape juice to drink from a cup of gold. Before them a squire carved the peppered venison which he had set on a silver carving platter, and then he placed the slices on large pieces of bread in front of them.

Meanwhile the grail passed again before them, and still the youth did not ask concerning the grail, whom one served with it. He restrained himself because the nobleman had so gently charged him not to speak too much, and he had treasured this in his heart and remembered it. But he was silent longer than was proper, for as each course was served, he saw the grail pass before him in plain view, and did not learn whom one served with it though he would have liked much to know. Instead he said to himself that he would really ask one of the squires of the court before he departed, but would wait till the morning when he took leave of the lord and his attendants. So he postponed the matter and put his mind on eating and drinking; in no stingy fashion were the delicious viands and wines brought to the table. The food was excellent; indeed, all the courses that king or count or emperor are wont to have were served to that noble and the youth that night.

After the repast the two passed the evening in talk, while the squires made up the beds for the night and prepared the rarest fruits: dates, figs, nutmegs, cloves, pomegranates, electuaries,[3] gingerbread of Alexandria, aromatic jelly, and so forth. Afterwards they had many droughts of piment without honey or pepper, mulberry wine, and clear syrup. At all this the youth wondered, for he had never experienced the like. At last the nobleman said: "Friend, it is time to go to bed, and do not take it ill that I depart to my chamber to sleep. And when you please, you may lie here. Because of my infirmity I must be carried."

Four nimble and strong servants came out of a chamber, took hold by the four corners the coverlet of the couch on which the nobleman was lying, and carried him away. Other squires remained with the youth to serve him as was needed. When he wished, they removed his hose and other clothing and put him to bed in white linen sheets.

He slept till break of day, but the household had already risen. When he

---

3. A medicinal concoction, consisting of herbs mixed in a syrup or honey.

looked about, he saw no one, and was obliged to get up alone; though he was annoyed, he rose since he must, drew on hose without help, and took his arms, which he found at the head of the dais, where they had been brought. When he had armed himself well, he walked past the doors of chambers which he had seen open the night before. But all in vain, for he found them closed. He shouted and knocked. No one opened; there was no response. When he had called long enough, he went to the door of the hall, found it open, descended the steps, and found his horse saddled and his lance and shield leaning against the wall. He then mounted and searched about the courtyard, but saw neither servant nor squire. He rode to the gate and found the drawbridge lowered, for it had been so left that nothing should prevent him from passing it freely at any hour. Then he thought, since the bridge was down, that the squires must have gone into the forest to examine the nets and traps. So, having no reason to wait longer, he said to himself that he would follow after them and learn, if possible, from one of them why the lance bled and whither the grail was carried. He passed out through the gate, but before he had crossed the drawbridge, he felt that the feet of his horse were rising, and the animal made a great leap, and if he had not done so, both he and his rider would have come to grief. The youth turned his head to see what had happened and perceived that someone had raised the drawbridge. He called out, but no one answered.

"Speak," said he, "you who have raised the bridge! Speak to me! Where are you, for I do not see you? Show yourself, and I would ask you a question."

Thus he wasted his words, for no one would reply. So he rode toward the forest and entered on a path where there were fresh hoofprints of horses. "This is the way," said he to himself, "which the men I am seeking have taken."

Then he galloped through the forest as long as the tracks lasted, until he spied by chance a maiden under an oak tree, crying and lamenting in her distress. "Alas, wretch that I am, in an evil hour was I born! Cursed be that hour and that in which I was begotten! Never before has anything happened to enrage me so. Would that God had not pleased to make me hold my dead lover in my arms! He would have done better to let me die and let my lover live. O Death, why did you take his soul rather than mine? When I see him whom I loved best dead, what is life worth? Without him I care nothing for my life and my body. Death, cast out my soul that it may, if his soul deigns to accept it, be its handmaid and companion."

Thus she was mourning over the headless body of a knight which she clasped. The youth did not stop when he saw her, but approached and greeted her. She returned his greeting with head lowered, but did not cease her lament. The youth asked: "Who killed this knight who lies in your lap?"

"Good sir," the maiden replied, "a knight killed him this very morning. But one thing I see which amazes me. For people say that one may ride twenty-five leagues in the direction from which you came without finding an honest and clean lodging place, and yet your horse's flanks are smooth and his hide is curried. Whoever it was who washed and combed him, fed him on oats and bedded him with hay, the beast could not have a fuller belly and a neater hide. And you yourself look as if you had enjoyed a night of comfortable repose."

"By my faith, fair lady," said he, "I had indeed as much comfort last night as was possible, and if it appears so, there is good reason. If anyone gave a loud shout here where we are, it would be heard clearly where I lay last night. You cannot know this country well, for without doubt I have had the best lodging I ever enjoyed."

"Ah, sir, did you lie then at the dwelling of the rich Fisher King?"

"Maiden, by the Savior, I do not know if he is fisherman or king, but he is very rich and courteous. I can say no more than that late last evening I met two men floating slowly in a boat. One was rowing, the other was fishing with a hook, and he directed me to his house and there gave me lodging."

The maiden said: "Good sir, he is a king, I assure you, but he was wounded and maimed in a battle so that he cannot move himself, for a javelin wounded him through the two thighs.[4] He is still in such pain that he cannot mount a horse, but when he wishes to divert himself, he has himself placed in a boat and goes fishing with a hook; therefore he is called the Fisher King. He can endure no other pastime, neither hunting nor hawking, but he has his fowlers, archers, and huntsmen to pursue game in his forests. Therefore he enjoys this place; in all the world no better dwelling could be found for his purposes, and he has built a mansion befitting a rich king."

"Damsel," said he, "by my faith, what you say is true, for last evening I was filled with wonder as soon as I came before him. I stood at a little distance, but he told me to come and sit beside him, and bade me not think that he did not rise out of pride, for he had not the strength."

"Surely he did you a great honor when he seated you beside him. Tell me, when you were sitting there, did you see the lance of which the point bleeds, though there is no flesh or vein there?"

"Did I see it? Yes, by my faith."

"Did you ask why it bled?"

"I said nothing about it."

"So help me God, learn, then, that you have done ill. Did you see the grail?"

"Yes, indeed."

"And who held it?"

"A maiden."

"And whence did she come?"

"From a chamber."

"Whither did she go?"

"Into another chamber."

"Did no one precede the grail?"

"Yes."

"Who?"

"Only two squires."

"What did they hold in their hands?"

"Candelabra full of candles."

"Who came after the grail?"

"Another maiden."

"What did she hold?"

"A little carving dish of silver."

---

4. This is the same wound as suffered by Perceval's father. Some scholars have even suggested that Perceval's father and the Fisher King are the same person. It is striking if enigmatic that the Fisher King was wounded not by a lance or arrow bolt but by a javelin, the weapon Perceval used to kill the Red Knight.

"Did you not ask anyone where they were going?"

"No question came from my mouth."

"So help me God, that was worse. What is your name, friend?"

Then he who did not know his name divined it and said that his name was Perceval of Wales.[5] He did not know whether he told the truth or not, but it was the truth though he did not know it. When the damsel heard it, she rose and faced him, saying angrily: "Your name is changed, good friend."

"What is it?"

"Perceval the wretched! Ah, unfortunate Perceval, how unlucky it was that you did not ask all those things! For you would have cured the maimed King, so that he would have recovered the use of his limbs and would have ruled his lands and great good would have come of it! But now you must know that much misery will come upon you and others. This has happened to you, understand, because of your sin against your mother; she has died of grief for you. I know you better than you know me, for you do not know who I am. I was reared with you in the house of your mother long ago. I am your first cousin and you are mine. I grieve no less because you have had the misfortune not to learn what is done with the grail and to whom it is carried than because of the death of your mother or because of this knight whom I loved dearly, seeing he called me his dear mistress and loved me as a brave and loyal knight."

"Ah, cousin," said Perceval, "if what you say is true, tell me how you know it."

"I know it," the damsel answered, "as truly as one who saw her laid in the earth."

"Now may God of his goodness have mercy on her soul!" cried Perceval. "It is a sorrowful tale you have told. Now that she is laid in earth, what is there left for me to seek? For I was journeying only to see her. I must now take another road. If you are willing to accompany me, I should be pleased. He who lies dead here can no longer serve you, I warrant. The dead to the dead, the living to the living.[6] Let us go together, for it seems very foolish for you to watch here alone over this body. Let us pursue the slayer, and I promise and swear that, if I overtake him, either he will force me to surrender, or I will force him."

She, unable to suppress the great woe in her heart, said: "Good friend, I cannot go with you or leave my lover until I have buried him. If you listen to me, follow this paved road, since it is by this way that the evil, insolent knight who killed my sweet lover departed. So help me God, I have not said this because I wish you to pursue him, though I wish him as much harm as if he had slain me. But where did you get the sword which hangs at your left side and which has never drawn blood and has never been unsheathed in the hour of need? I know well where it was forged and by whom. Do not trust it, for it will betray you in battle and fly in pieces."

"Fair cousin, one of the nieces of my good host sent it to him last evening, and he gave it to me, and I was well pleased. But you terrify me if what you have said is true. Tell me now, if you know: if the sword should break, will it ever be repaired?"

"Yes, but with much hardship. If one could find the way to the lake which

---

5. This moment of Perceval's self-identification marks a crucial turn in his development toward maturity.
6. See Luke 9.60.

is near the Firth of Forth, he could have it hammered, tempered, and made whole again. If chance should take you there, go to a smith called Trebuchet, because he made it and will reforge it; it can be done by no other man."[7]

"Surely," said Perceval, "if it breaks, I shall be in grievous peril."

Then he went his way, and she remained, unwilling to part from him whose death wrung her heart. Perceval followed the tracks until he came up with a lean and weary palfrey, which was walking ahead of him and by its wretched appearance seemed to have fallen into bad hands. It was travel-worn and starved like a hired horse which has been ridden hard all day and poorly cared for at night. It was so gaunt that it trembled as if with a distemper.[8] The neck was shrunk, and the ears drooped. Its bones were covered only with hide, so that mastiffs and hounds would have expected to make a meal of it. There was a saddle on its back and a bridle on its head such as befitted such a beast.

The rider was a maiden. No one ever saw a more wretched, though she would have been beautiful if her fate had been happier. She was in such evil case that not a palm's breadth of her dress was whole and her nipples showed through the rents. Here and there it was fastened together with knots and rude stitches. Her skin seemed to be scratched, as if with a lancet,[9] and it was tanned with heat and cracked with hail and frost. Her hair was loose, she wore no mantle, and on her face were the ugly traces of tears which ceaselessly flowed down to her breast and over her dress to her knees. Well might the heart feel anguish when the body suffered such pain.

As soon as Perceval perceived her, he rode up swiftly. She drew her robe about her to cover her skin, but as soon as she closed one hole, she opened a hundred others. Perceval approached her in her discolored and pitiful state and heard her bitterly complaining of her sorrow and pain: "O God, may it please Thee to end my life! I have suffered too long and too grievously, and I have not deserved it! O God, since Thou knowest well that I am innocent, send, if it please Thee, someone to free me from this misery, or do Thou deliver me from him who makes me live in such shame. I find no mercy in him. I cannot escape from him alive, nor will he kill me. I do not understand why he desires my company in this manner unless he enjoys my disgrace and woe. Even if he were certain that I deserved this usage, even if I am not dear to him, he ought to have pity on me since I have already paid so heavily. But it is sure that he does not love me when he puts this humiliation on me and shows no concern."

Then Perceval said: "Fair lady, God save you!"

When the damsel heard him, she bowed and said in a low voice: "Sir, for your greeting may you have all that your heart desires, and yet I have no cause to say this."

Perceval changed color for shame and replied: "In God's name, fair friend, what do you mean? Surely I do not know that I have ever seen you before or done you any wrong."

"You have indeed," said she. "You have made me so wretched that no one should greet me, and I sweat with fear when anyone stops me or looks at me."

7. *Trebuchet* is mentioned only here.   8. An equine disease.   9. A small knife.

"Truly," said Perceval, "I was not aware that I had injured you. I did not come here to do you shame or harm, but was following my road. Since I caught sight of you so poorly and scantily clad, I cannot be happy until I learn what chance has brought you to this sorrowful state."

"Ah, sir," said she, "have pity! Say no more but flee and leave me in peace. You do wrong to tarry. Be wise and flee!"

"I must know," said he, "for what danger or what threat I should flee when no one is pursuing me."

"Sir," said she, "be not offended, but flee while you can, before the Proud Knight of the Glade, who seeks nothing but strife and battle, finds us together. If he discovers you, he will kill you at once. He is so furious when anyone stops me that no one can depart with his head who is caught with me. It is but a short while since he killed a man. First, however, he tells each one why he holds me so vile and treats me so cruelly."

While they were talking, the Proud Knight came out of the wood and, raising a cloud of sand and dust, rode up like thunder, shouting: "In an evil hour did you halt to converse with the maiden! I would have you know that your end has come because you made her pause for a single step. But I will not kill you before I have told you for what misdeed I have put her to such shame. Listen and you will hear the story. One day I had gone hunting and had left this damsel, whom I loved more than all else, in my tent, when by chance a Welsh youth came there. I do not know what happened except that he kissed her by force and she has confessed it. If she lied, what harm was it? If he kissed her against her will, did he not afterward have all his desire? No one would believe that he would kiss her without doing more, for one deed leads on to another. One who kisses a woman and does no more when they are alone together is a faintheart. A woman who grants her mouth easily gives the rest; that indeed is what she intends. Beyond a doubt, as everyone knows, though a woman may defend herself, she has no wish to be victor in this struggle. Even when she takes a man by the throat and scratches, bites, and half kills him, she wishes to be overcome, however much she defends herself and delays. She is reluctant to surrender, for she prefers to be forced, and then she shows no gratitude. Therefore I believe that the youth lay with her. Besides he seized a ring that she wore on her finger and carried it away, and sorely it vexes me. And before that he drank some strong wine and ate one of three pasties I had ordered kept for me. But now my mistress is doing a noble penance, as you see. Whoever indulges in folly, let him pay for it so that he may beware of repeating it. When I returned and learned the truth, imagine my anger. I swore—and I was right—that her palfrey should have no oats nor be bled nor be shod again, and that she herself should wear no other tunic or mantle than the one she was then wearing, until I should have the best of him who had forced her, killed him and cut off his head."

When Perceval had heard this, he replied: "Friend, I assure you that she has done her penance. I am the youth who kissed her against her will and to her distress; I took her ring from her finger, but that was all. And if I ate one and a half of the three pasties and drank my fill of wine, I swear it was merely my stupidity."

"By my head," said the Proud Knight, "it is a wonderful thing to hear your confession! If it is true, you have richly deserved death."

"Still, my death is not as near as you think," said Perceval.

Without another word they gave their horses the spur and met with such fury that they splintered their lances and were hurled from their saddles, but they sprang up at once, drew their swords and exchanged great blows. The combat was stern, but it would be wasted time to say more than that they fought till the Proud Knight of the Glade surrendered and begged for mercy. Perceval, who never forgot the nobleman who had charged him not to kill any knight who begged for mercy, said: "Knight, I will have mercy on you only when you pardon your lady. She has never deserved, I swear, the harsh treatment you have given her."

The knight, who really loved the maiden more than the apple of his eye, said: "Good sir, by your counsel I will make amends to her. You cannot command anything that I am not ready to do. My heart is somber with grief for the suffering I have caused her."

"Go then," said Perceval, "to the nearest manor you own hereabouts, so that she may bathe and rest till she is well again. Then make ready and take her, suitably garbed, to King Arthur, greet him for me, and place yourself at his mercy, equipped as you are here. If he asks who sent you, you will say: he whom he made a red knight at the advice of my lord Kay, the seneschal. And the suffering and the wrong you have done to your damsel, that you must rehearse before all the court so that all may hear it, including the Queen and her fair maidens. Of these I prize one above all. Kay struck her on the cheek and stunned her, merely because she laughed with pleasure at seeing me. Seek her out, I command you, and give her this message, that I will not be moved by any plea to join King Arthur's court till I have so avenged her that she will rejoice."

The Proud Knight replied that he would go and say everything that Perceval had enjoined, and that he would not delay except such time as was needed for his damsel to rest and make ready. He invited Perceval also to stay with him till his wounds healed. But Perceval said: "Go your way and may you have good adventure. But I have other plans and will seek shelter elsewhere."

Without further words they parted. That evening the Proud Knight arranged that his mistress should be bathed and richly robed, and thereafter saw that she was so well cared for that her beauty returned. Then they both took the direct road to Caerleon,[1] where King Arthur was holding court, but it was a small assemblage, for there were only three thousand valiant knights. Before them all the knight came, bringing his damsel, that he might surrender to King Arthur, and addressed him thus: "Sire, I am your prisoner to do with what you will. It is right and reasonable since that is the command of the youth who asked and obtained red arms from you."

As soon as the King heard this, he understood its meaning and said: "Disarm yourself, good sir. Joy and good adventure be his who has sent you as a gift to me, and you yourself are right welcome. For his sake you will be cherished and honored in my household."

"Sire," said the knight, "before I disarm, I have one thing more to say. I would ask that the Queen and her maidens come to hear the news that I have brought, for it will not be disclosed till she comes who was struck on the cheek because of a single laugh; that was her only offense."

1. A town in Wales.

He ceased, and the King, hearing what was required, sent for the Queen, and she came with all her maidens, two by two and hand in hand. When the Queen was seated beside her lord King Arthur, the Proud Knight of the Glade spoke: "Lady, a knight whom I honor highly and who overcame me in combat sends you greeting. I have no more to say of him save that he sends you this maiden, my mistress."

"Friend," said the Queen, "he has my great thanks."

Then the knight related all the cruelty, shame, and suffering he had long inflicted on her, and the reason for his behavior—all without concealment. Then the damsel whom Kay the seneschal had struck was pointed out to him, and he said: "He who sent me here, maiden, asked me to give you his greeting, and not to stir a foot hence till I had told you this: he will never, so may God help him, enter King Arthur's court till he has avenged you for the buffet you received on his account."

When the fool heard this, he leapt to his feet and cried: "Lord Kay, may God bless me, you will surely pay for that injury, and that right soon."

After the fool, the King spoke: "Ah, Kay, that was not courtesy when you mocked the youth. By your jest you robbed me of him so that I never expect to see him again."

Then the King caused the knight, his prisoner, to sit before him, freed him, and bade him disarm. Sir Gawain, who was sitting at the King's right, asked: "In God's name, sire, who can it be who, alone, vanquished by his arms as good a knight as this? In all the isles of the sea I have not heard of a knight, nor have I seen or known one, who could compare with him in arms and chivalry."

"Good nephew," said the King, "I do not know who he is though I have seen him; but when I saw him, I failed to ask. He demanded that I make him a knight on the instant, and, seeing him handsome and comely, I said: 'Brother, I will do so, but dismount till someone brings you gilded arms.' He refused to take them or to alight till he had red arms. He added other strange things, saying that he would accept no arms but those of the knight who had carried off my golden cup. Kay, who was and is and always will be ill-mannered and who never says a good word, spoke to him: 'Brother, the King gives you the arms; go take them at once.' The youth, who did not understand the jest, thought that Kay was telling the truth, followed the Red Knight, and killed him with the cast of a javelin. I do not know how the fight began, but only that the Red Knight of the Forest of Quinqueroi struck him, I know not why, with his lance, in contemptuous fashion. The youth then hit him in the eye with his javelin, killed him, and took his arms. Since then he has done me such good service that, by my lord St. David, to whom men pray in Wales,[2] I will never lie two nights in the same chamber or hall till I see him, if he is alive, whether on sea or land, but I will start presently to seek him."

When the King had sworn this oath, all understood that the time had come to depart. One could have seen men packing bedclothes, coverlets, and pillows, filling chests, trussing pack horses, loading a large train of carts, stowing tents and pavilions. A clever and well-lettered cleric could not describe in a whole day all the baggage and provisions that were promptly got ready.

---

2. St. David, reputed to have lived in the 6th century, is the patron saint of Wales.

Thus the King departed from Caerleon as if he led an army, and his barons followed, while the Queen, with equal pomp and majesty, took her whole retinue and left not a maiden behind. That night they camped in a meadow near a forest. Before morning there was a heavy fall of snow.

That same morning Perceval had risen early, according to custom, to seek adventure, and came to the meadow, covered with frost and snow, where the royal host had camped. But before he came to the tents, he saw and heard a flock of wild geese, which had been blinded by the snow and were flying with a clamor before a pursuing falcon. When one of them became separated from the flock, the falcon pounced on her and struck her to the ground, but since it was too early, left her without feeding. Perceval galloped toward the spot. The goose had been wounded in the neck and had shed three drops of blood[3] which spread on the white snow like a natural color, but she was not injured so badly that she could not leave the earth, and before Perceval arrived, had flown away. When he saw the snow where the goose had lain beaten down and the blood drops around it, he leaned on his lance to gaze at the spectacle. The blood melting into the snow reminded him of the fresh hues of his lady's face, and he mused till he forgot himself. For so did the red of her cheeks stand out against the white as the three drops of blood stood out against the white snow. The sight pleased him so much that he seemed to behold the fresh color of his fair lady.

Perceval mused upon the drops of blood while the morning passed, until the squires, issuing from the tents, saw him in a reverie and thought that he was asleep. Returning, they encountered before the royal tent, where the King was still sleeping, Sagremor, who was called the Hothead because of his hot temper.

"Tell me," he cried, "and conceal nothing! Why are you in such haste?"

"Sir," they answered, "outside this camp we have seen a knight sleeping on his steed."

"Is he armed?"

"In faith, yes."

"I will go to speak with him," said he, "and bring him to the court."

At once Sagremor ran to the King's tent and waked him, saying: "Sire, on the heath yonder there is a knight sleeping."

The King bade him go and fetch the knight if he consented to come. Without delay Sagremor ordered his horse to be led out and his arms brought. His command was obeyed and, being promptly and fully armed, he rode out from the camp and approached the knight, saying: "Sir, you must come to the court."

Perceval did not move and seemed not to hear. Sagremor spoke again, and, when the other did not stir, he grew angry and shouted: "By St. Peter the apostle, you will come willy-nilly. I am sorry that I asked you, for I wasted my breath."

Then he unfurled the pennon wrapped round his lance, took his position, and then gave spurs to his horse, warning his adversary to beware, for he would strike him if he did not defend himself. Perceval looked and saw Sagremor charging at full speed. Emerging from his reverie, he spurred against him. At the encounter Sagremor's lance shattered, but Perceval's did not

---

3. To a religious sensibility, the three drops of blood would have recalled the Trinity.

break or bend but struck his opponent with such force that he was hurled to the ground. The steed fled, head up, toward the tents, where those who were just rising saw it with great dismay. Kay, who could never refrain from mockery, said in jest to the King: "Good sir, see how Sagremor is returning. He is leading the knight by the bridle and bringing him against his will."

"Kay," said the King, "you do not well to make a mock of brave men. Go now and let us see whether you will fare better than he."

"Sire," said Kay, "I am very glad that you wish me to go. I will bring him back by force, whether he will or no, and make him tell his name."

Then he had himself armed, mounted, and rode toward him who was so absorbed in contemplating the three drops that he was oblivious to everything else. From a distance Kay shouted: "Knight, knight, come to the King! By my faith, you shall come, or you will pay dearly."

Hearing the threat, Perceval turned the head of his horse and pricked him with his steel spurs into a gallop. Both adversaries were eager to do their best and drove at each other in earnest. Kay splintered his lance in the shock, as if it had been a piece of bark. And Perceval was not slack but hit Kay above the boss of his shield[4] and hurled him onto a rock, so that his collarbone was dislocated and his right arm was broken between the elbow and the armpit like a dry stick, just as the fool had foreseen and often described it. The lackwit's prophecy proved true. Kay fainted with the pain, and his horse trotted rapidly away toward the tents. The Britons saw it returning without the seneschal; squires rode to meet it, and ladies and knights bestirred themselves. When they found the seneschal in a swoon, they felt sure that he was dead and set up a loud lamentation, both men and women. Perceval returned to gaze on the three drops, leaning on his lance.

But the King was deeply concerned over the seneschal's injury and sorrowed until he was informed that he need not be distressed, because Kay would recover, provided that he had a leech to restore the collarbone to its place and to set the broken arm. So the King, who had a tender feeling for Kay, sent a wise leech and three maidens trained in his school, who restored the collarbone and bandaged the arm so that the broken bone would knit together. Then they brought him to the King's tent, comforted him, and told him that he need not be anxious, for he would be cured. Sir Gawain addressed the King: "Sire, so help me God, it is not right, as you know and have always said, for one knight to disturb another's thoughts for any cause, and this your two knights have done. I do not know that they were wrong, but that they came to grief is certain. Perhaps the knight was brooding over some loss or was cast down because his lady had been stolen from him. Now, if it is your pleasure, I will go to observe him, and if I find that he has stopped brooding, I will request him to come to you here."

At these words Kay broke out in anger: "Ah, Sir Gawain, you expect to lead the knight here by the hand, even if he is reluctant. That will be a gallant deed, if he permits you and yields the upper hand to you. Many a prisoner you have won in this way. When a knight is weary and has had his fill of fighting, that is a fit time for a gallant knight to ask permission to go forth and subdue him! A thousand curses on my neck, Gawain, if you are not so wise that one can take lessons from you! You know how to make your fine,

---

4. A *boss* is a projecting knob in the center of the shield.

polished words pay! You would speak proud and insulting words to him? A curse on him who believed or believes that. Indeed you could carry out that errand in a silken gown, without drawing sword or breaking lance. You may well pride yourself that if your tongue is able to say: 'Sir, God save you and give you joy and health!' he will do your will. I do not speak for your instruction, for you know quite well how to smooth him down as one strokes a cat. Then people will say: 'Now Sir Gawain is waging a fierce battle!' "

"Ah, Sir Kay!," said Gawain, "you could surely speak more kindly. Do you think to get your revenge by pouring out your fury on me? In faith, good friend, I will bring him back, and without a broken arm or a dislocated collarbone, for I do not like such wages."

"Go now, nephew," said the King; "you have spoken with courtesy. Bring the knight if you can, but take all your arms, for you must not go defenseless."

Gawain, who was renowned for all the virtues, had himself armed speedily, mounted a strong and spirited horse, and came straight to the knight, who was still leaning on his lance and enjoying his reverie. But the sun had now melted away two of the drops of blood in the snow, and the third was disappearing, and so the knight was not so deep in thought as he had been. Sir Gawain approached him quietly, at an amble, without any hostile show, and said: "Sir, I would have greeted you if I had known your heart as I do my own; but I may say this, that I am a messenger of the King, who sends and begs you through me to come and speak with him."

"Two men have already been here," said Perceval, "who drove away my joy and the happy thoughts which absorbed me, and who treated me as if I were a captive. Anyone who tried to make me leave this place was not seeking my welfare. Before me were three drops of fresh blood which brightened the snow, and, looking at them, I seemed to see the fresh color in the face of my lovely mistress, so that I would never seek to leave."

"Truly," said Sir Gawain, "that was no boorish fancy, but right courteous and sweet. He who took your mind from it was a fool and overbold. But now I would gladly know what you intend to do. If it would not displease you, I will readily bring you to the King."

"Tell me first, dear good friend," said Perceval, "is Kay the seneschal there?"

"In faith, he is; and you may know that it was he who jousted with you but now, and the joust cost him a broken right arm and a dislocated collarbone."

"Then," said Perceval, "I have well avenged the maiden for the blow he gave her."

When Sir Gawain heard that, he gave a start in his amazement, and said: "Sir, God save me, it is you for whom the King is searching. What is your name?"

"Perceval, sir; and what is yours?"

"Sir, believe me truly that I received in baptism the name of Gawain."

"Gawain?"

"Indeed, good sir."

Perceval, filled with joy, said: "Sir, I have heard speak of you in many places, and I would greatly desire your acquaintance, if it would not displease you."

"Be assured," said Sir Gawain, "that it would not please me less than you, but rather more."

Perceval replied: "In faith, I will gladly go wherever you will, for it is right, and I shall regard myself more highly now that I am your friend."

They met and embraced; then they began to unlace helms, coifs, ventails,[5] drew down the mail from their heads, and departed, making great joy. Squires who had witnessed their delight from an outpost ran to the King, exclaiming: "Sire, sire, in faith, Sir Gawain is bringing the knight, and they are rejoicing together."

There was no one who heard the news but left his tent and went to meet them. Kay said to his lord, the King: "Now the honor belongs to Sir Gawain, your nephew. The fight must have been right stiff and dangerous, if I do not lie, because he is returning as whole and sound as he went out, as if he had never received a blow nor given one. He uttered no word of defiance. So it is right that he should have the glory and that men should say that he has accomplished what we others could not, in spite of all the strength and effort we put into it."

So Kay said his say according to his wont, whether right or wrong. Sir Gawain did not wish to bring his companion to court all armed, but had him disarmed in his tent, and a chamberlain drew a robe out of his chest and presented it to Perceval to wear. When he had donned a tunic and a fine, becoming mantle, the two proceeded hand in hand to the King, who was sitting before his tent. "Sire, sire," said Sir Gawain, "I bring you the knight whom you have wished to see this fortnight past. It is he of whom you have spoken much, it is he whom you set out to find. I present him to you, for here he is."

"Good nephew, many thanks!" said the King, rising to his feet in honor of the newcomer. "Good sir, you are right welcome! Pray tell me what I should call you."

"In faith, good lord King," said Perceval, "I will not hide my name. It is Perceval of Wales."

"Ah, Perceval, sweet good friend, now that you have come to my court, you shall not leave it by my will. I have been much troubled since I first saw you, not knowing the amends which God had destined for you. It was foreseen clearly by the maiden and the fool whom Kay the seneschal smote, so that all my court was aware of it. You have indeed fulfilled their prophecy in every point, so that no one can doubt it, for I have heard the truth about your exploits."

As he spoke, the Queen arrived, having heard tidings of the newcomer. When Perceval saw her and learned who she was, and recognized the damsel who followed her as her who laughed for joy at sight of him, he went to meet them, saying: "God give joy and honor to one who, by the testimony of all the eyes who see or have seen her, is the most beautiful and the best lady alive."

The Queen replied: "You are most welcome, as a knight whose high and noble prowess has been well proved."

---

5. Detachable flaps of mail, laced by leather thongs to the mail hoods or coifs to protect the knights' lower faces.

Then Perceval greeted the maiden who had laughed, and embraced her, saying: "Fair one, if there is ever need, I would gladly be the knight whose aid will never fail you." And for this the maiden thanked him.

Great was the joy which the King, the Queen, and the barons made over Perceval of Wales. They returned that evening with him to Caerleon, and the rejoicing lasted that night and through the morrow. On the third day they saw a damsel come riding on a tawny mule, with a scourge in her right hand. Her hair hung in two black twisted braids, and if the book describes her truly, never was there a creature so loathly save in hell. Her neck and hands were blacker than any iron ever seen, yet these were less ugly than the rest of her. Her eyes were two holes, as small as those of a rat; her nose was like that of a monkey or a cat; her lips were like those of an ass or an ox; her teeth resembled in color the yolk of an egg; she had a beard like a goat. In the middle of her chest rose a hump; her backbone was crooked; her hips and shoulders were well shaped for dancing! Her back was hunched, and her legs were twisted like two willow wands. Her figure was perfect for leading a dance!

Into the King's presence the damsel urged her mule; never had such a creature come to a royal court. She gave a general greeting to the King and all the barons, but, seated on her tawny mule, she addressed Perceval alone, in these words: "Ah, Perceval, Fortune is bald behind, but has a forelock in front.[6] A curse on him who greets or wishes you well, for you did not seize Fortune when you met her. You entered the dwelling of the Fisher King; you saw the lance which bleeds. Was it so painful to open your mouth that you could not ask why the drop of blood sprang from the white point of the lance? When you saw the grail, you did not inquire who was the rich man whom one served with it. Most unfortunate is he who when the weather is fairer than usual waits for even fairer to come. It was you, unfortunate man, who saw that the time and the place were right for speech, and yet remained mute. You had ample opportunity, but in an evil hour you kept silence. If you had asked, the rich King, who is now sore troubled, would have been wholly cured of his wound and would have held his land in peace—land which he will never hold again. Do you know what will happen if the King does not hold his land and is not healed of his wound? Ladies will lose their husbands, lands will be laid waste, maidens, helpless, will remain orphans, and many knights will die. All these calamities will befall because of you!"

Then, turning to the King, she said: "Oh King, I depart, and may it not offend you, for this night I must take my lodging far from here. I do not know if you have heard speak of Castle Orgulous; it is there that I am bound to go tonight. In that castle are five hundred and sixty-six knights of fame, and be assured that none but has a ladylove with him, noble, courteous, and fair. I tell you this because no one goes there without finding joust or battle; he who would perform feats of chivalry will not fail of his purpose if he seeks there. But if any would have the supreme glory of the world, I know the place, the very spot, where he may best win it, if he dares. On the hill which stands below Montesclaire a damsel is besieged. Great would be the honor

6. The metaphor derives from the idea that as Fortune rises on her wheel you can grab her by the hair in front, but since she is bald behind she cannot be seized as she descends. The idea, then, is that with foresight you can take advantage of Fortune, but hindsight is useless.

he would win who would raise the siege and deliver the maiden. All praise would be his, and if God grants him that good fortune, he will be able to gird on without fear the Sword with the Strange Hangings."

After saying all it pleased her to say, the damsel ceased and departed without another word. Sir Gawain then leapt up and vowed that he would go to Montescleire and do all in his power to rescue the lady. Giflet, son of Do, in turn announced that, if God aided him, he would make his way to Castle Orgulous. Kahedin spoke: "And I will ascend Mount Dolorous, and will not pause till I arrive."

But Perceval spoke otherwise, and vowed that henceforth he would not lie two nights in the same lodging, nor avoid any strange passage of which he might hear, nor fail to engage in combat with any knight who claimed to be superior to every other or even two other knights, until he could learn whom one served with the grail, and until he had found the lance that bleeds, and had heard the true reason why it bled. He would not give up the quest for any suffering. Thus as many as fifty arose and swore, one to another, that they would not fail to purse any adventure or seek any marvel of which they heard, even though it were in the most perilous land. [Here Chrétien inserted adventures of Gawain.]

Perceval, as the story tells, had so lost his memory that he had forgotten God. Five times April and May had passed, five whole years indeed, since he had entered a minster or worshipped God or His cross. But for all that he did not cease to pursue chivalry, and sought out strange and stern adventures and proved his mettle and undertook no exploit from which he did not emerge triumphant. Within the five years he sent sixty knights of fame to Arthur's court as prisoners. Throughout this time he did not think of God.

Toward the end he was journeying, all armed as was his wont, through a wilderness, when he came upon three knights and ten ladies walking shoeless, in woolen gowns, their heads deep in their hoods. The ladies, who for the salvation of their souls were doing penance on foot for their sins, were astonished to see Perceval coming all armed, holding lance and shield. One of the three knights stopped Perceval and said: "Dear good sir, do you not believe in Jesus Christ, who wrote the new law and gave it to Christians? It is surely not right but rather a great sin to bear arms on the day that Jesus Christ died."

Perceval, who gave no heed to day or hour, answered: "What day is this then?"

"What day, sir? Do you not know? It is the holy Friday, the day when every man should adore the cross and weep for his sins, for today He who was sold for thirty pence was hung upon the cross. He who was clean of all sin saw the sins in which the whole world was bound and befouled and became a man for our sins. In truth He was both God and man, for the Virgin bore a Son, conceived by the Holy Ghost. In Him God received flesh and blood, so that His deity was concealed in human flesh. This is a certainty, and whoever does not believe it will never see His face. He was born of the Virgin Lady and took the form and the soul of man, together with the holy Deity. On this day He was crucified and delivered His friends from hell. Right holy was that death which saved the living and restored the dead to life. The wicked Jews, whom one should kill like dogs, in their hatred wrought their own harm and our good when they raised Him on the cross. Themselves they destroyed, and us they saved. All who believe in Him ought to spend this day in penitence. Today no man who believes in God should bear arms on field or road."

"Whence do you now come?" asked Perceval.

"Sir, we come from a good man, a holy hermit, who dwells in this forest, and, so great is his sanctity, he lives by the glory of heaven alone."

"In God's name, sirs, what were you doing there? What did you ask for or desire?"

"What, sir?" said one of the ladies. "We asked counsel for our sins and made confession—the highest work which a Christian can do who would draw near to God."

Hearing them, Perceval was moved to tears, and determined to go speak with the holy man. "I would go to the hermit," he said, "if I but knew the path or the road."

"Sir," was the answer, "whoever would go there should follow this path by which we have come, through this thick, scrubby wood, and let him watch for the twigs which we knotted with our hands as we came. We left such signs in order that no one seeking the holy hermit would lose his way."

Then they commended each other to God, without further inquiry. Perceval started on the path, sighing from the bottom of his heart because he felt that he had sinned against God and was deeply repentant. So, weeping, he traversed the wood and came to the hermitage. There he dismounted, removed his arms, and tethered his horse to a hornbeam. Entering a little chapel, he found the hermit, a priest, and another ministrant about to begin the highest and the sweetest service that can be celebrated in a church. As soon as Perceval entered the chapel he fell on his knees, and the good man called to him, seeing that he was humble and that the water flowed from his eyes to his chin. Perceval, who greatly dreaded that he had offended God, grasped the foot of the hermit, bent before him, and with joined hands begged for counsel of which he had great need. The good man bade him make his confession, for unless he were confessed and repentant, he could have no remission.

"Sir," said Perceval, "for five years I have not known where I was. I did not love God nor believe in Him, and I have done nothing but evil."

"Ah, good friend," said the worthy man, "tell me why you have done so, and pray God to have mercy on the soul of His sinner."

"Sir, I was once at the house of the Fisher King, and saw the lance of which the point truly bleeds, but concerning that drop of blood which I saw hanging from the white steel, I did not ask, and ever since I have fared ill. Nor do I know whom one serves with the grail which I saw, and since then I have endured such sorrow that I would willingly have died. I forgot God, and have not implored His mercy and have done nothing, to my knowledge, to obtain pardon."

"Ah, good friend," said the worthy man, "tell me your name."

The other replied: "Perceval, sir."

At this word the worthy man, who recognized the name, sighed and said: "Brother, a sin of which you know nothing has wrought this harm. It was the sorrow you caused your mother when you left her, for she fell swooning to the earth at the end of the bridge before her gate, and died of that grief. Because of the sin you then committed it came to pass that you failed to ask concerning the lance and the grail. Thus many evils have befallen you, and know that you would not have endured so long if she had not commended you to God. But her prayer had such power, that God for her sake has preserved you from death and from prison. Sin cut off your tongue when you saw before you the bleeding point which never has been staunched, and did not ask the reason. And great was your folly when you did not learn whom one served with the grail. It was my brother, and his sister and mine was your mother. And believe me that the rich Fisher is the son of the King who causes himself to be served with the grail. But do not think that he takes from it a pike, a lamprey, or a salmon. The holy man sustains and refreshes his life with a single Mass wafer. So sacred a thing is the grail, and he himself is so spiritual, that he needs no more for his sustenance than the Mass wafer which comes in the grail. Fifteen years he has been thus without issuing from the chamber where you saw the grail enter. Now will I enjoin penance on you for your sin."

"Good Uncle," said Perceval, "with all my heart will I perform it. Since my mother was your sister, rightly should you call me nephew, and rightly I should call you uncle and love you the better."

"It is true, good nephew. But now listen: if your soul is seized with pity, you are indeed repentant, and for atonement go to the minster every day before any other place, and it will be for your good. Do not neglect it for any cause, but if you are in any place where there is minster, chapel, or parish church, go there when the bell rings, or earlier if you are already risen. Never will you regret it, but rather will your soul be benefited. If the Mass is begun, it will be all the better, and stay until the priest has finished his prayers and chants. If you choose to do so, you can still advance in worth and enjoy both honor and paradise. Believe in God, love God, worship God. Honor good men and good women. Rise in the presence of a priest; it is a service which costs little and God in truth loves it because it comes from humility. If a maiden asks your help, or a widow or an orphan girl, give it, and yours will be the gain. Such service is the highest. Aid them, and on no account weaken in welldoing. This is what I would have you do to atone for your sins and to recover all the graces which once were yours. Tell me now if you assent."

"Yes," said Perceval, "right gladly."

"Now I pray you that you stay two whole days with me and as a penance take only such food as mine."

Perceval agreed, and the hermit taught him an orison and repeated it till he knew it by heart. In this prayer were many names of our Lord, and they were so great that mouth of man ought not to utter them save in the fear of death.[7] So after teaching the prayer, he forbade Perceval to say it except in great peril, and Perceval said: "Sir, I will not." So he remained and heard the service with great delight. After the service he adored the cross, wept for his sins, and repented of them heartily. Thus he meditated, and for supper that night he ate what the holy hermit pleased to give him, herbs such as chervil, lettuce, and cress, bread of barley and oats, and clear water of the spring, while his horse had straw and a basin full of barley, and was properly groomed and stabled.

---

7. In Jewish tradition the many names used to designate the deity are sacred, and this sense of awe was adopted by Christians and applied to Jesus, for whom many names and titles are given in the New Testament.

Thus Perceval learned how God was crucified and died on a Friday, and on Easter Day he received the communion. Of him the tale tells no more at this point.

[The rest of the poem is occupied with the adventures of Gawain and ends without returning to Perceval.]

THORSTEIN THE STAFF-STRUCK
thirteenth century

Medieval Iceland produced not only a unique and highly interesting body of poetry but also some of the finest prose narratives in European literature. Some of these, like the *Saga of the Volsungs,* deal with figures of early Germanic tradition. But some thirty or forty, called sagas of Icelanders, are about men and women who lived in Iceland (and often in Norway in their youth) from the late ninth to the early eleventh centuries. Written mostly in the thirteenth century, they may remind us a bit of the historical novels of a later time. But in the historical novel, usually the major characters are fictional, products of the author's invention, while those well known to history serve as framework or background. In the Icelandic saga the converse is true: the principal figures were actual people attested by documents and other evidence, as were also most of the events and acts attributed to them. Oral tradition bridged the interval between the tenth century and the thirteenth. Thus the author of an extant saga was free to shape characterization, motivation, mood, and tone as he saw fit. It is now believed that the milieu of thirteenth-century Iceland may have influenced features of some of these narratives. A few may have been entirely fictional, except for the use of the names of actual persons. The sagas are nearly always anonymous. Some of the most notable are of novel length, like the *Saga of the Laxdalers* or the Grettir saga, or the *Saga of Burnt Njal,* greatest of all.

The story of Thorstein the Staff-Struck is very short; in fact, it was not called a saga but a *thattr,* literally, a "thread." Nevertheless, it shows the characteristic features of a family saga. Although the action is "strong," to use a modern term—people kill and are killed—violence is not included for its own sake; instead, it interests the narrator chiefly as an expression of personality and character. The incidents of the story are conducted in such a way as to distinguish sharply nearly all of the participants; these are all members of one or the other of two families or households who live in northeast Iceland. The "fierce," now aged, but still irascible Thorarin is contrasted with his husky and confident but even-tempered son, Thorstein; only when the insolent Thord willfully insults him does Thorstein take action. In prosecuting Thorstein for manslaughter, Bjarni, Thord's employer and also the district chieftain, fulfills a more or less automatic obligation. However, when Thorstein ignores the sentence of exile, Bjarni (whose responsibility it was to attack Thorstein) takes no action. We learn that he is unwilling to deprive the infirm, nearly blind Thorarin of his son's support. Nevertheless, when Bjarni overhears the malicious gossip of Thorhall and Thorvald, he sends them out with instructions to kill Thorstein. We are not told what he expected would happen, but when he learns that Thorstein has slain the two brothers, once again he does nothing; when his wife Rannveig goads him, he remarks that "Thorstein has never killed anyone without a good reason." All the same, when she tells him of the taunts in circulation about him, he decides that he cannot avoid a confrontation with Thorstein.

Although the circumstances are different, Bjarni's motive in his (reluctant) challenge of Thorstein is the same as the latter's when he (at last) challenges Thord. Each man considers the respect of the community essential to his self-respect; hence they act as the code requires, regardless of their personal inclination or of the intrinsic merits of the case. The thirteenth-century Christian author faithfully presents this pre-Christian pattern; the ethical dilemma, unacknowledged by the protagonists, is implicit in the narration. Hence in the final encounter Bjarni and Thorstein carry out the *form* of conduct that tradition makes obligatory, while the *manner* in which they do so ensures a morally satisfactory result.

Readers will enjoy this succinct narrative best if they ask themselves such questions—among others—as: What purposes are served by the dialogue? What is Thorarin's motive for each of his acts? How does the author make use of the two female characters?

PRONOUNCING GLOSSARY

The following list uses common English syllables to provide rough equivalents of selected words whose pronunciation may be unfamiliar to the general reader.

Bjorni: *b-yorn'-ee*   Thorstein: *thor'-stain*

Thorstein the Staff-Struck[1]

There was a man called Thorarin who lived at Sunnudale; he was old and nearly blind. He had been a fierce viking in his younger years, and even in his old age he was very hard to deal with. He had an only son, Thorstein, who was a tall man, powerful but even-tempered; he worked so hard on his father's farm that three other men could hardly have done any better. Thorarin had little money, but a good many weapons. He and his son owned some breeding horses and that was their main source of income, for the young colts they sold never failed in spirit or strength.

Bjarni of Hof[2] had a servant called Thord who looked after his riding horses and was considered very good at the job. Thord was an arrogant man and would never let anyone forget the fact that he was in the service of a chieftain. But this didn't make him a better man and added nothing to his popularity. Bjarni also had two brothers working for him who were called Thorhall and Thorvald, both great scandalmongers about any gossip they heard in the district.

Thorstein and Thord arranged a horse-fight for their young stallions.[3] During the fight, Thord's horse started giving way, and when Thord realized he was losing, he struck Thorstein's horse a hard blow on the jaw. Thorstein saw this and hit back with an even heavier blow at Thord's horse, forcing it to back away. This got the spectators shouting with excitement. Then Thord aimed a blow at Thornstein with his horse-goad, hitting him so hard on the eye-brow that the skin broke and the lid fell hanging down over the eye. Thorstein tore a piece off his shirt and bandaged his head. He said nothing about what had happened, apart from asking people to keep this from his

1. Translated, with footnotes, by Hermann Pálsson.   2. Bjarni of Hof was the local chieftain, and the wealthiest and most powerful farmer in the district.   3. Horse-fights used to be a favorite sport in Iceland. Two stallions were pitted against one another, and behind each of them there was a man equipped with a goad to prod them on. At these horse-fights tempers would often run high.

father. That should have been the end of the incident, but Thorvald and Thorhall kept jeering at Thorstein and gave him the nickname Staff-Struck.

One morning that winter just before Christmas, when the women at Sunnudale were getting up for their work, Thorstein went out to feed the cattle. He soon came back and lay down on a bench. His father, old Thorarin, came into the room and asked who was lying there. Thorstein told him.

"Why are you up so early, son?" said Thorarin.

Thorstein answered, "It seems to me there aren't many men about to share the work with me."

"Have you got a head-ache, son?" said Thorarin.

"Not that I've noticed," said Thorstein.

"What can you tell me about the horse-fight last summer, son?" said Thorarin. "Weren't you beaten senseless like a dog?"

"It's no credit to me if you call it a deliberate blow, not an accident," said Thorstein.

Thorarin said, "I'd never have thought I could have a coward for a son."

"Father," said Thorstein, "Don't say anything now that you'll live to regret later."

"I'm not going to say as much as I've a mind to," said Thorarin.

Thorstein got to his feet, seized his weapons and set off. He came to the stable where Thord was grooming Bjarni's horses, and when he saw Thord he said, "I'd like to know, friend Thord, whether it was accidental when you hit me in the horse-fight last summer, or deliberate. If it was deliberate, you'll be willing to pay me compensation."

"If only you were double-tongued," said Thord, "then you could easily speak with two voices and call the blow accidental with one and deliberate with the other. That's all the compensation you're getting from me."

"In that case don't expect me to make this claim a second time," said Thorstein.

With that he rushed at Thord and dealt him his death-blow. Then he went up to the house at Hof where he saw a woman standing outside the door. "Tell Bjarni that a bull has gored Thord, his horse-boy," he said to her, "and also that Thord will be waiting for him at the stable."

"Go back home, man," she said. "I'll tell Bjarni in my own good time."

Thorstein went back home, and the woman carried on with her work.

After Bjarni had got up that morning and was sitting at table, he asked where Thord could be, and was told he had gone to see to the horses.

"I'd have thought he'd be back by now, unless something has happened to him," said Bjarni.

The woman Thorstein had spoken to broke in. "It's true what we women are often told, we're not very clever. Thorstein the Staff-Struck came here this morning and he said Thord had been gored by a bull and couldn't look after himself. I didn't want to wake you, and then I forgot all about it."

Bjarni left the table, went over to the stable and found Thord lying there, dead. Bjarni had him buried, then brought a court action against Thorstein and had him sentenced to outlawry for manslaughter. But Thorstein stayed on at Sunnudale and worked for his father, and Bjarni did nothing more about it.

One day in the autumn when the men of Hof were busy singeing sheep's heads,[4] Bjarni lay down on top of the kitchen wall to listen to their talk. Now the brothers Thorhall and Thorvald started gossiping; "It never occurred to us when we came to live here with Killer-Bjarni[5] that we'd be singeing lambs' heads while his outlaw Thorstein is singeing the heads of wethers. It would have been better for Bjarni to have been more lenient with his kinsmen at Bodvarsdale and not to let his outlaw at Sunnudale act just like his own equal. But 'A wounded coward lies low,' and it's not likely that he'll ever wipe away this stain on his honor."

One of the men said, "Those words were better left unsaid, the trolls must have twisted your tongue. I think Bjarni simply isn't prepared to take the only breadwinner at Sunnudale away from Thorstein's blind father and other dependents there. I'll be more than surprised if you singe many more lambs' heads here, or tattle on much longer about the fight at Bodvarsdale."

Then they went inside to have their meal, and after that to bed. Bjarni gave no sign that he had heard anything of what had been said. But early next morning he roused Thorhall and Thorvald and told them to ride over to Sunnudale and bring him Thorstein's severed head before mid-morning. "I think you're more likely than anyone else to wipe away that stain from my honor, since I haven't the courage to do it for myself," he said.

The brothers realized they had said too much, but they set off and went over to Sunnudale. Thorstein was standing in the doorway, sharpening a short sword. He asked them where they were going, and they told him they were looking for some horses. Thorstein said they didn't have very far to go. "The horses are down by the fence."

"We're not sure we'll be able to find them unless you tell us more precisely," they said.

Thorstein came outside, and as they were walking together across the meadow, Thorvald raised his axe and rushed at him. But Thorstein pushed him back so hard that he fell, then ran him through with the short sword. Thorhall tried to attack Thorstein and went the same way as his brother. Thorstein tied them to their saddles, fixed the reins to the horses' manes, and drove them off.

The horses went back to Hof. Some of the servants there were out of doors and went inside to tell Bjarni that Thorvald and Thorhall had come back and their journey hadn't been wasted. Bjarni went outside and saw what had happened. He said nothing and had the two men buried. Then everything was quiet till after Christmas.

One evening after Bjarni and his wife Rannveig had gone to bed, she said to him, "What do you think everyone in the district is talking about these days?"

"I couldn't say," said Bjarni. "In my opinion most people talk a lot of rubbish."

"This is what people are mainly talking about now," she continued: "They're wondering how far Thorstein the Staff-Struck can go before you bother to take revenge. He's killed three of your servants, and your supporters

---

4. In Iceland, as in some other sheep-raising countries, sheep's heads were (and still are) considered a great delicacy. The heads are singed over a fire to remove all traces of wool before they are cleaned and cooked.   5. The name Killer-Bjarni is an allusion to the fact that Bjarni fought and killed some of his own kinsmen in the battle of Bodvarsdale which is mentioned in the following sentence.

are beginning to doubt whether you can protect them, seeing that you've failed to avenge this. You often take action when you shouldn't and hold back when you should."

"It's the same old story," said Bjarni, "no one seems willing to learn from another man's lesson. Thorstein has never killed anyone without a good reason—but still, I'll think about your suggestion."

With that they dropped the subject and slept through the night. In the morning Rannveig woke up as Bjarni was taking down his sword and shield. She asked him where he was going.

"The time has come for me to settle that matter of honor between Thorstein of Sunnudale and myself," he said.

"How many men are you taking with you?" she asked.

"I'm not taking a whole army to attack Thorstein," he said. "I'm going alone."

"You mustn't do that," she said, "risking your life against the weapons of that killer."

"You're a typical woman," said Bjarni, "arguing against the very thing you were urging just a few hours ago! There's a limit to my patience, I can only stand so much taunting from you and others. And once my mind's made up, there's no point in trying to hold me back."

Bjarni went over to Sunnudale. He saw Thorstein standing in the doorway, and they exchanged some words.

"You'll fight me in single combat," said Bjarni, "on that hillock over there in the home-meadow."

"I'm in no way good enough to fight you," said Thorstein. "I give you my promise to leave the country with the first ship that sails abroad. I know a generous man like you will provide my father with labor to run the farm if I go away."

"You can't talk yourself out of this now," said Bjarni.

"You'll surely let me go and see my father first," said Thorstein.

"Certainly," said Bjarni.

Thorstein went inside and told his father that Bjarni had come and challenged him to a duel.

The old man said, "Anybody who offends a more powerful man in his own district can hardly expect to wear out many more new shirts. In my opinion your offences are so serious, I can't find any excuse for you. So you'd better take your weapons and defend yourself the best you can. In my younger days I'd never have given way before someone like Bjarni, great fighting-man though he may be. I'd much rather lose you than have a coward for a son."

Thorstein went outside and walked with Bjarni up the hillock. They started fighting with determination and destroyed each other's shield. When they had been fighting for a long time, Bjarni said to Thorstein, "I'm getting very thirsty now, I'm not so used to hard work as you are."

"Go down to the stream then and drink," said Thorstein.

Bjarni did so, and laid the sword down beside him. Thorstein picked it up, examined it and said, "You can't have been using this sword at Bodvarsdale."

Bjarni said nothing, and they went back to the hillock. After they'd been fighting for a time, it became obvious to Bjarni that Thorstein was a highly skilled fighter, and the outcome seemed less certain than he'd expected.

"Everything seems to go wrong for me today," he said. "Now my shoe-thong's loose."

"Tie it up then," said Thorstein.

When Bjarni bent down to tie it, Thorstein went into the house and brought back two shields and a sword. He joined Bjarni on the hillock and said, "Here's a sword and shield my father sends you. The sword shouldn't get so easily blunted as the one you've been using. And I don't want to stand here any longer with no shield to protect me against your blows. I'd very much like us to stop this game now, for I'm afraid your good luck will prove stronger than my bad luck. Every man wants to save his life, and I would too, if I could."

"There's no point in your trying to talk yourself out of this," said Bjarni. "The fight must go on."

"I wouldn't like to be the first to strike," said Thorstein.

Then Bjarni struck at Thorstein, destroying his shield, and Thorstein hacked down Bjarni's shield in return.

"That was a blow," said Bjarni.

Thorstein replied, "Yours wasn't any lighter."

Bjarni said, "Your sword seems to be biting much better now than it was earlier."

"I want to save myself from the foulest of luck if I possibly can," said Thorstein. "It scares me to have to fight you, so I want you yourself to settle the matter between us."

It was Bjarni's turn to strike. Both men had lost their shields. Bjarni said, "It would be a great mistake in one stroke both to throw away good fortune and do wrong. In my opinion I'd be fully paid for my three servants if you took their place and served me faithfully."

Thorstein said, "I've had plenty of opportunity today to take advantage of you, if my bad luck had been stronger than your good luck. I'll never deceive you."

"Now I can see what a remarkable man you must be," said Bjarni. "You'll allow me to go inside to see your father and tell him about this in my own words?"

"You can go if you want as far as I'm concerned," said Thorstein, "but be on your guard."

Bjarni went up to the bed-closet where Old Thorarin was lying. Thorarin asked who was there, and Bjarni told him.

"What's your news, friend Bjarni?" said Thorarin.

"The killing of Thorstein, your son," said Bjarni.

"Did he put up any defence at all?" asked Thorarin.

"I don't think there's ever been a better fighter than your son, Thorarin," said Bjarni.

"It's no wonder your opponents at Bodvarsdale found you so hard to deal with," said Thorarin, "seeing that you've overcome my son."

Bjarni said, "I want to invite you to come over to Hof and take the seat of honor there for the rest of your life. I'll be just like a son to you."

"I'm in the same position now as any other pauper," said Thorarin. "Only a fool accepts a promise gladly, and promises of chieftains like yourself aren't usually honored for more than a month after the event, while you're trying to console us. After that we're treated as ordinary paupers, though our grief doesn't grow any the less for that. Still, anyone who shakes hands on a bargain with a man of your character should be satisfied, in spite of other men's lessons. So I'd like to shake hands with you, and you'd better come into the bed-closet to me. Come closer now, for I'm an old man and trembling on my feet because of ill-health and old age. And I must admit, the loss of my son has upset me a bit."

Bjarni went into the bed-closet and shook Thorarin by the hand. Then he realized the old man was groping for a short sword with the idea of thrusting it at him. Bjarni pulled back his hand and said, "You merciless old rascal! I can promise you now you'll get what you deserve. Your son Thorstein is alive and well, and he'll come with me over to Hof, but you'll be given slaves to run the farm for you, and never suffer any want for the rest of your life."

Thorstein went with Bjarni over to Hof, and stayed in his service for the rest of his life. He was considered a man of great courage and integrity. Bjarni kept his standing and became better-liked and more self-controlled the older he grew. He was a very trustworthy man. In the last years of his life he became a devout Christian and went to Rome on pilgrimage. He died on that journey, and is buried at a town called Sutri,[6] just north of Rome.[7]

✻ ✻ ✻

6. The town Sutri is mentioned elsewhere in early Icelandic records.   7. The story concludes with a long account of Bjarni's descendants, extending into the thirteenth century.

MEDIEVAL LYRICS: A SELECTION

While in classical Greece the term *lyric* referred to poems sung to the accompaniment of the lyre, the short poems of Rome, such as those by Catullus, were composed to be read silently. The medieval period saw a return to the tradition of poetry as performance. Most medieval lyrics, including many written in Latin, were verses sung to an accompanying tune. One major reason for this return to performance was the influence of the vernacular traditions of song brought into prominence by the various cultures that reshaped Europe after the fall of Rome. All the peoples that together created the Middle Ages—the multifarious nations of the Roman Empire (from the Persians in the east to the Celts in the west), the tribes (Germanic, Scandinavian, Slavic, and Eurasian) that divided the fallen Roman empire, and the inhabitants (both Arabic and non-Arabic) of the Islamic world—had traditions of song that stretched back into time immemorial. By their very nature most of these songs were ephemeral. Arabic and Anglo-Saxon songs do survive from as early as the seventh and eighth centuries, and early Latin lyrics show the influence of vernacular forms. But we lack all but a very few of the vernacular songs composed prior to about the year 1100. The reason is not just that it is less likely for a vernacular text to be preserved in an expensive manuscript than one in Latin, but that virtually all medieval lyrics were performed in public rather than read in private. Those that were written down and survived thus are only a small fraction of the lyrics that actually circulated throughout the Middle Ages.

The medieval lyrics selected here represent the most important linguistic communities and demonstrate both the range of topics treated by medieval lyricists and their extraordinary skill. While the poems are printed in chronological order, regardless of their original language of composition, readers will notice that certain topics recur with some frequency. Unsurprisingly, the most common is love. Most important here are the lyrics written beginning around 1100 in Provençal, a literary language derived from the various dialects spoken in the southern half of France and the bordering regions of Italy and Spain. Here we find expressed, if not for the first time in Western literature, then in terms that became decisive, our modern form of romantic love. Often called *courtly love*, a term coined by French scholars in the nineteenth century, it was in the Middle Ages known as *fin'amors* (Provençal), *fine amour* (French), or *minne* (German). Its central elements are that love is an overwhelming emotion that promises ecstatic bliss but also causes painful yearning; that the beloved is an embodiment of all virtue and yet often remains cool and distant, even unaware of the lover's sufferings; and that love is an ennobling emotion, in the sense both that it can be fully experienced only by gentlemen and ladies and that it causes them to behave in exalted and selfless ways. Various aspects of this emotional complex are certainly present in earlier writing. In the *Phaedrus* and the *Symposium*, for instance, Plato (429–347 B.C.E.) described erotic love between men as providing a means for philosophical and moral improvement, and the Roman poet Ovid (43 B.C.E.–C.E. 17) described passionate, unrequited love between men and women in terms that medieval poets knew and imitated. So too, as early as the Umayyad period (C.E. 650–750) Arabic poets described a love—known as 'Udhrite love—that was ardent, chaste, and incapacitating to the point of death. Indeed, it is likely that the Provençal poets were influenced by singers and composers from the Iberian peninsula who continued to celebrate this kind of love. One of these Arabic lyrics is *The Singing Lute*, written by a poet of whom we know only his name, Ibn Arfa' Ra'suh. (In the manuscripts medieval lyrics are untitled, so that all titles are supplied by the editor or translator.) The poem was composed in Spain—or al-Andalus, as it was known to its Arab rulers—in the mid-eleventh century to celebrate the poet's patron, known as al-Ma'mūn or Yahya ibn Dhī n-Nūn, the ruler of Toledo. Written according to a strict scheme of meter and rhyme, and deploying the delicate natural imagery characteristic of medieval Arabic poetry, it compares the disdain of the beautiful lady to the haughtiness of the great warrior, a comparison that implies that because he is "the terrorizer of armies" al-Maʾmūn is able to sustain a sophisticated culture that supports both poetry and love. Other love poems from al-Andalus included here are the beautiful *Summer*, written in Hebrew by Judah Halevi, perhaps the most distinguished of the many Jewish scholars and poets who flourished under Arab rule, and the compact *In Battle*, by the Arabic poet Abu-l-Hasan ibn Al-Qabturnuh, a poem that combines love and war in a surprisingly effective way.

Quite apart from its originality or sources, the influence of the Provençal celebration of *fin'amors* was enormous. Like the poets of al-Andalus, those of Provence drew connections among the virtuosity and elegance of their lyrics, the exalted delicacy of the emotion they celebrated, and the aristocratic courts in which they lived and composed. In this way the love lyric became not merely a private statement but an expression of a way of life that was elegantly mannered and knowingly sophisticated. As the French term *courtoisie*, or "courtliness," suggests, the love lyric described values that derived from noble society: intensity of feeling matched elevation of social standing. In this way the poetry combined private and public concerns, and the relation of lover to beloved is often phrased in the same terms as the feudal relation of a lord to his vassal (the beloved was, in Provençal poetry, referred to as *midons*, "my lord"). It is hardly surprising, then, that many of the poems that survive are written by noble authors. The ability to compose both lyrics and music was one that every well-bred aristocrat wanted to possess. Certainly there were professional composers and performers, but they often served as mouthpieces or instructors to their noble patrons. The oldest datable Provençal lyrics are by William IX, duke of Aquitaine (ca. 1071–1127). He is represented here by his *Spring Song*, which includes in a few stanzas a remarkable range of amorous feelings, from a rather conventional statement about love in general through an anxious lover's doubt to a rousing celebration of mutual pleasure and a scornful rejection of mere braggarts. Another noble author is Beatrice, countess of Dia—one of a significant number of women troubadours—whose witty *A Lover's Prize* begins with resentment at her lover's betrayal and ends with a boldly explicit insistence on her own rights as a lover. On the other hand, the "Love Song" by Jaufré Rudel, who was probably not an aristocrat, begins by celebrating love, but the possibility of disappointment leads him to turn away from eroticism to religion: according to tradition, Jaufré died on crusade. In *The Art of Love*, Arnaut Daniel, one of the most technically proficient of the troubadours, draws a connection between the control required for poetic virtuosity and the overwhelming ardor caused by love, a paradox that he triumphantly accepts in the poem's final lines.

Beginning in Provence around the year 1100, then, the love lyric spread throughout Europe to Sicily, Italy, France, Germany, and England. In each of these environments it took on slightly different characteristics. In Sicily and Italy there was a strong interest both in verbal and metrical virtuosity and in the way in which intense love could lead to religious truth. The great Italian poets of the late thirteenth century created what Dante called the *dolce stil nuovo*, or "sweet new manner" (see below, p. 1590). By this Dante meant that poetic virtuosity was not opposed to but rather expressed the intensity and authenticity of the lover's feelings; and above all, that the lady opened her admirer to a love that was genuinely religious. As he said in his lyric autobiography, the *Vita nuova* or *New Life*, the lady "seems to be a creature come from Heaven to earth, to manifest a miracle." Dante and the other *stilnovisti*, as they are called, were thus the direct precursors of Petrarch. The earliest of the four Italian poems selected here is by Guido Guinizzelli, a Bolognese poet much admired by Dante. This famous poem, *Love and Nobility*, argues that true nobility is a function not of ancestry but of virtue, and that virtue is in turn a function of a love that is more philosophical and religious than emotional. The next poem, *An Encounter*, is by Guido Cavalcanti, a friend of Dante and the true founder of the *dolce stil nuovo*. Avoiding philosophical speculations about love, his poem celebrates instead a dream-like moment of amorous fulfillment. The sonnet that follows, *Love and Poetry*, is addressed by Dante to Guido Cavalcanti and another poet of their circle, Lapo Gianni. Here Dante invokes a company of poets "enchanted" by Merlin and devoted to a love that is simultaneously earthly and heavenly, a charmingly lighthearted treatment of a theme that in other places he expresses with greater seriousness. An example is the next sonnet, in which Dante provides his own version of Guinizzelli's equation of nobility, virtue, and love.

The two German love poems show how both the Provençal interest in the psychology of love and the Italian concern with its philosophical meaning were taken up by the poets of the north. *The Wound of Love*, by Heinrich von Morungen, one of the earliest of the *minnesingers*, combines the troubadour theme of unrequited love with an awareness that hostility often accompanies desire, a complexity of feeling intensified by the reduction of both lover and lady to two pairs of lips. Walther von der Vogelweide, generally regarded as the finest of the *minnesingers*, is represented here by *Dancing Girl*, which hides great depths beneath its apparently simple surface: vacillating between dreaming and waking, the poem ends with the poet searching for an ideal that is again more than simply amorous. Another poem that begins as a love poem but then develops into an enigmatic account of a natural creature that is more than natural is *The Fox*, by Dafydd ap Gwilym, the best-known representative of the rich poetic traditions of medieval Wales.

The two French love poems included here also show how the motifs of the Provençal lyric continued to provide poets with fresh inspiration until the very end of the Middle Ages. *Aubade* is an anonymous dawn song, a traditional poem in which lovers—in this case, the woman only—lament the coming of day because it will mean their parting. Charles d'Orléans, the author of the *Balade*, was captured at the battle of Agincourt in 1415 and spent twenty-five years as a prisoner in England. This delicate lyric, written in a traditional form, neatly combines the old feudal metaphors of the lady as lord and the lover as vassal with commercial imagery that derives from a new and very different world.

While medieval lyricists were preoccupied by love in its many manifestations, they also used the short poem to express and explore religious feelings. Many of these poems are in Latin, the language of the Church, and they are often written to serve as part of a religious service. The poems by Notker Balbulus, a monk in the great monastery at St. Gall in present-day Switzerland, and by Hildegard of Bingen, a German nun who became famous as a religious visionary, scientist, poet, musician, and reformer of Church abuses, are the words to a musical work known as a sequence, a chant sung during the Mass. Notker's *Hymn to Holy Women*, written to be sung on the feast days of holy women, is based on the traditional idea that Mary was the New Testament counterpart to Eve: where Eve had brought human beings into the grasp of Satan by her disobedience, it was through Mary that Christ came to free them. The other central idea of the poem is the harrowing of hell, when Christ, after his death on the cross, descended into hell and released the souls of the just held captive by the Devil, represented in the poem by the Ethiop and the dragon. Here the cross is symbolized both by the ladder that stretches up to heaven and by the hook that pierces the dragon's jaw, an image derived from the Book of Job. Hildegard's sequence, *A Hymn to St. Maximinus*, celebrates an early Christian saint. Using images derived from the Bible, and especially the Song of Songs, Hildegard describes a vision in which Maximinus is seen both as a priest celebrating the Mass and as a saint welcomed into heaven. He is both an embodiment of divine virtue and the means by which others can ascend to it. Other Latin poems drew upon the themes of secular poetry and turned them to religious purposes. *Song of Summer* is an anonymous work found in an anthology of poems that were originally composed in Germany, France, and Italy and were copied together into a manuscript in eleventh-century England. By means of a catalog of birds and their songs it celebrates the fecundity, variety, and beauty of nature, invoking in its final stanza the Virgin Mary, who as the Mother of God is simultaneously the source of this goodness, a perfect instance of it, and—paradoxically—an alternative to it (hence she is represented by the bee rather than by a bird).

By no means were all religious poems in Latin, however, and vernacular poets were adept at expressing powerful religious feelings and complex thoughts. Two English examples are *Calvary*, which encapsulates the meaning of the Crucifixion in only four lines, and the late poem *Lament of the Virgin*, which describes the sufferings of the Virgin in a voice that reaches out to all men and women. Another example of the way secular and religious languages are brought together is *Strawberry Picking*, by the mysterious poet known as Alexander the Wild (i.e., the Vagabond), a poem that oscillates delicately between secular and religious meanings, between an observant realism and a suggestive symbolism. Finally, the woman writer Hadewijch of Antwerp (or Brabant), who composed in Flemish, is represented by *The Cult of Love*, a poem that begins within the conventions of troubadour verse but transforms them into a personal experience that is both intense and enigmatic: is it an earthly lover of whom she speaks, or—as we would expect of a religious writer like Hadewijch—Christ?

The subjects treated by medieval lyrics were by no means confined to love and religion. Then as now, one of the most common lyric themes was loss, and medieval poems are often elegiac. The first poem in our selection was written by a German monk named Walahfrid Strabo in 829, when he was about twenty: in order to further his education, he had been sent from Reichenau, a monastery on an island in Lake Constance where he had grown up, to Fulda, a monastery several hundred miles away. In the poem Walahfrid connects his own loneliness to the idea that all Christians are exiles from their true homeland, heaven, a heaven of which the island monastery is an earthly image; he defines himself as the child not of earthly parents—who no doubt committed him to the monastery at an early age—but as the son of his first teacher who was his spiritual father, of the monastery that is his spiritual mother, and finally of God Himself; and in the course of the poem he comes to understand that the "wisdom" he has come to Fulda to find can also be found in "the teaching of life" that his exile has forced upon him. Some ten years later Walahfrid did in fact return to Reichenau as its abbot. Another elegy, written almost six hundred years later, in the early 1400s, is *Alone in Martyrdom,* by Christine de Pizan, a remarkable writer who composed a wide range of works, including treatises on moral, political, and feminist issues. Here she laments the early death of her husband in a graceful lyric whose elegance enhances its depth of feeling. A similar elegy, but one in which loss finds compensation in the thought of God's mercy, is *A Letter from the Grave,* by the Hebrew poet Meir Halevi Abulafia, written for his sister in 1212. Conversely, a poem that functions as an elegy for an entire civilization is the Anglo-Saxon *The Ruin.* Composed probably in the ninth or tenth century, it describes the wonder with which someone from the Germanic world—in which most building was done with timber—gazes on the mighty architectural achievements of the Romans (who preceded the Anglo-Saxons as rulers of England) while implicitly acknowledging the transience of all human accomplishment. Finally, *The Sacrifice of Isaac,* by Rabbi Ephraim ben Jacob of Bonn, combines elegy with prayer. Ephraim was a Hebrew scholar who witnessed and chronicled the massacres endured by the Jews of the Rhineland in 1146 during the Second Crusade, as they had endured similarly pitiless massacres in 1096 at the time of the First Crusade. His powerful poem memorializes these dreadful events—in which rather than abandon their religion Jews chose suicide or murder, often killing their own children—by locating them in the context of the biblical story of the sacrifice of Isaac. Ephraim here adopts an ancient Jewish tradition that interpreted the biblical story to mean that Isaac was actually killed by his father, Abraham, but resurrected, transported to Eden, and then returned to his father. Yet Ephraim's poem refuses to embrace any easy consolation, and it remains an unflinching affirmation of faith in the face of injustice and terrible suffering.

Last but not least, medieval poets often wrote poems simply about themselves—or, more accurately, about selves they pretended (or wanted) to be. A salient example is *The Archpoet's Confession.* The Archpoet is the name given to an anonymous writer who made popular the idea of the vagabond-poet, and while his vivid picture of the riotous life of the wandering scholar has been very influential, it now seems to have been composed as much of theatrical extravagance as hard fact. Similarly theatrical are two other "autobiographical" poems. *In Praise of War,* by Bertran de Born, a minor noble and notorious troublemaker, celebrates with unrestrained enthusiasm the war-making that was so central a part of the life of the twelfth-century knight and brought misery to so many ordinary people (Bertran appears in Dante's *Inferno* among the sowers of discord [p. 1555]). And a selection from François Villon's *Testament* also moves us away from the aristocratic world of much medieval lyric to the harsher realities of economic and emotional necessity endured by the population at large. Villon, a man who knew both poverty and imprisonment, provides us with the dramatic monologue of an old woman who—like Chaucer's Wife of Bath—expresses the familiar medieval concern about mutability with a powerful sense of its personal meaning. These apparently personal poems are best read as dramatic monologues, virtually as theatrical performances. But that doesn't mean that they don't express, as do all of these lyrics, human feelings that were as real to medieval people as they are to us. Perhaps more immediate in its appeal, albeit deriving from the other end of the social scale, is *The Scorpions* by Alfonso X, a thirteenth-century king of Castile and Léon, who created at his court an environment in which Christian, Jewish, and Muslim scholars and poets worked in harmony. In this poem Alfonso wistfully yearns to escape from the demands of kingship, and perhaps especially from the armed rebellions that characterized his reign, into the life of the merchant, which he romanticizes in an act of wistful imaginative freedom.

PRONOUNCING GLOSSARY

The following list uses common English syllables and stress accents to provide rough equivalents of selected words whose pronunciation may be unfamiliar to the general reader.

Abu-1-Hasan ibn Al-Qabturnuh: *a-boo-1-ha'san ibun al-kwab-turn-uh*

al-Mamun: *al-ma-moon'*

Annwn: *an'-wun*

Arnaut Daniel: *ahr-nowt'dan-yel'*

Dafydd ap Gwilem: *daff'-id ap gwil'-em*

François Villon: *frahn-swah' vee-yonh'*

Guido Guinizzelli: *gwee'-do gween'-itz-e-lli*

Hadewijch: *had'-e-witch*

Ibn Arfa' Ra'suh: *i'bun ar'-fah rah'-suh*

Jaufré Rudel: *joh-fray roo-del'*

Meir Halevi Abulafia: *mey-er hal-ay-vee a-bool-a-fia'*

Reichenau: *raik'-en-ow*

Sulayma: *sul-ay'-ma*

Walther von der Vogelweide: *val'ter von der vo'-gel-vai'-duh*

Yahya ibn Dhi n-Nun: *ya'hya ibun thee' en-noon'*

Ya'rub: *yah'-roob*

WALAHFRID STRABO
808/9–849

Elegy on Reichenau[1]

Sister Muse, lament for my pain,
speak of my sad parting,
alas, from the land of my fathers, ceaselessly
harassed as I was by shameful penury.

Wretched, I seek heart-felt wisdom,   5
and so I leave my homeland,
stricken by many kinds of hardship, I lament,
loathed and in exile.

No kindly teacher consoles me,
nor does any good master hearten me;   10
the only thing that keeps my miserable body alive
is the food I eat.

Bitter cold assails my naked flesh,
there is no warmth in my hands,
goose-pimples stand out on my feet   15
and my face flinches before the harsh winter.

Indoors I suffer the icy cold,
the sight of my frozen bed gives no pleasure,

---

1. Translated from the Latin by Peter Godman. Reichenau is a monastery on an island in Lake Constance, which is located on what is now the Swiss-German border.

warm neither when I get up nor where I sleep,
I snatch what rest I can.   20

If only wisdom which I esteem
could take hold in my mind
even the smallest part of it, the warmth of my wits
would make me safer.

Alas, father,[2] if only you were there—   25
you whom I have followed to the ends of the earth—
I believe that no harm would have come
to the poor little heart of your pupil.

Look, tears burst forth as I recall
how good was the peace I long ago enjoyed,   30
when happy Reichenau gave me
a modest roof over my head.

May you always be my holy and dear, dear
mother, consecrated by your throngs of saints,
through praise-giving, the promotion of good deeds, and worship,   35
happy island.

Now too let us call that island holy
because there the mother of God is richly worshipped,
so that we joyously cry out as we should,
happy island!   40

Although you are surrounded by deep waters,
nonetheless your foundations are firm in love,
and you spread its holy teachings among all men,
happy island.

Always wishing to see you,   45
I remember you day and night,
recalling all the kindness you bring me,
happy island.

Grow now and flourish, develop and prosper
so that, following the Lord's will,   50
with your children you may be called
happy Reichenau!

Let almighty Christ grant in His mercy
that I may return and rejoice on your site,
saying: "Hail, glorious mother,   55
forever!"

Christ, king of kings, lord of the mighty,
you who are called wisdom of the Father,

2. An older monk named Grimald.

deign to refresh my heart
with the teaching of life.   60

Grant, redeemer, I pray, a span of years,
so that, on returning to the bosom of my fatherland[3]
for which I have longed, I may sing
to Christ in songs of praise.

We sing in thanks to the highest father,   65
joined to His son in all-embracing love
and to the Spirit ruling with equal power
forever and ever. Amen.

3. Could refer either to Reichenau or to heaven.

NOTKER BALBULUS
ca. 840–912

A Hymn to Holy Women[1]

1. A ladder stretching up to heaven,
      circled by torments—

2. At whose foot an attentive
      dragon
   stands on guard, forever
      awake,

3. So that no one can climb even
      to the first rung and not be
      torn—

4. The ascent of the ladder barred
      by an Ethiop,[2] brandishing
   a drawn sword, threatening
      death,

5. While over the topmost rung
      leans a young man, radiant,
   a golden bough in his hand—

6. This is the ladder the love of
      Christ
   made so free for women
   that, treading down the
      dragon
   and striding past the Ethiop's
      sword,

7. By way of torments of every kind
      they can reach heaven's
         summit
   and take the golden laurel
   from the hand of the strength-
         giving king.

8. What good did it do you,
      impious serpent,
   once to have deceived a
      woman,

9. Since a virgin brought forth
         God incarnate,
   only-begotten of the Father:

1. Translated from the Latin by Peter Dronke.   2. I.e., the Devil.

10. He who took your spoils away
    and pierces your jaw with a hook[3]

11. To make of it an open gate
    for Eve's race, whom you long to
    hold.

12. So now you can see girls
    defeating you, envious one,

13. And married women now
    bearing sons who please
    God.

14. Now you groan at the loyalty
    of widows to their dead
    husbands,

15. You who once seduced a girl
    to disloyalty towards her
    creator.

16. Now you can see women made
    captains
    in the war that is waged against
    you,

17. Women who spur on their sons
    bravely to conquer all your
    tortures.

18. Even courtesans, your vessels,
    are purified by God,

19. Transmuted into a burnished
    temple for him alone.

20. For these graces let us now
    glorify him together,
    both the sinners and those who
    are just,

21. Him who strengthens those who
    stand
    and gives his right hand to
    the fallen,
    that at least after crimes we may
    rise.

3. See Job 40.20.

ANONYMOUS
ca. ninth or tenth century

The Ruin[1]

Marvelous is this wall-stone—but the fates broke,
smashed this city; this work of giants is decaying.
The roofs are fallen, the towers are in ruins,
the frosty gate is despoiled, frost is on the masonry,
damaged buildings are torn, collapsed,   5
undermined by age. The grasp of the earth holds
the master builder, he's dead and gone
into the hard grasp of the ground, until a hundred generations
of people shall have passed away. Often this wall,
red-stained and gray with lichen, one reign after another,   10
has withstood storms; high and wide, now it has fallen.

1. Translated from the Anglo-Saxon by Lee Patterson. The poem survives in fragmentary form.

The wall-stone still survives, broken down by the weather . . .
. . . .
. . . he put together a shrewd,
keen plan with rings, the clever man who bound
these wall braces together with wire, wonderfully!   20
Bright were the city halls, many the bath-houses,
high the crowd of gables, loud the noise of warriors,
many the mead-halls[2] full of people's joy—
until fate the powerful overturned all that.
Slaughtered men died everywhere, days of pestilence came,   25
death took away all the brave men.
Their sanctuaries became waste places,
their city decayed. The craftsmen died,
the warriors fell to the earth. So these halls decay,
and this red-curved roof of the vault splits off from   30
its tiles. The ruin fell to the ground,
broken into heaps, where once many a man,
happy of heart and bright with gold, adorned with splendor,
proud and flushed with wine, shone in his armor,
gazed on his treasure, on his silver, on jewels,   35
on wealth, on possessions, on valuable stone,
on this bright city and its broad kingdom.
Stone halls stood here, the streams gave off heat
in a great surge; the wall enclosed everything
in its bright bosom, there where the baths were.   40
hot to the core. That was elegant!
They let the hot streams gush . . .
over the gray stone . . .
. . . .
. . . there the baths were . . .   46
. . . .
. . . That is a kingly thing,
a house . . . . a city . . . .

2. *Mead* is an alcoholic drink made from honey.

ANONYMOUS

ca. eleventh century

Song of Summer[1]

The woodlands clothe the slender shoots
of boughs, laden with fruits;
from high perches wood pigeons sing
songs to one and all.

1. Translated from the Latin by Jan Ziolkowski.

Here the turtledove moans, here the thrush resounds,   5
here the age-old song of blackbirds rings out,
and the sparrow, not silent, with its chatter
    takes possession of the heights beneath the elms.
Here the nightingale sings, delighting in leafy boughs,
pours out a long warbling through the breeze,   10
solemnly, and with tremulous voice the kite
    causes the sky to echo.
The eagle as it soars starward sings, upon the breezes
the lark sings and produces sounds in melodies.
From above it swoops, with a different melody
    as it touches ground.   15
The swift swallow ever makes its call,
the quail sings, the jackdaw resounds:
thus birds everywhere celebrate for everyone
    the song of summer.   20
None among the birds is like the bee,
who represents the ideal of chastity,
if not she who bore Christ in her womb
    inviolate.

IBN ARFA' RA'SUH
eleventh century

The Singing Lute[1]

The lute trills the most wondrous melodies
And the watercourses cut through the flower beds of the gardens.
The birds sing on the branches of the *bān*,[2]
And joy enlivens the lions of the battlefield.
Every one of us is an Emir[3] and a sultan because of the wine.   5
The lute-strings speak with eloquent charm
While the birds respond to them from the myrtle branches.
Come, give me wine to drink for the garden exudes fragrance;
The Pleiads[4] have set and it is sweet to take the morning drink
Offered to me by a lovely gazelle   10
Who is like a tender branch enveloped in a cloak of eglantine,
Whose sides are covered in embroidered silks, who almost breaks
    because he is so tender.
Hold fast to the love and drink to the health
    of the Possessor of Dual Glory,[5]

---

1. Translated from the Arabic by James T. Monroe. Bracketed words are the translator's interpolation.
2. The bonduc, or horse-radish tree, which has fragrant white flowers.   3. A ruler.   4. A constellation.
5. The poet's patron, who is here presented as ruling over both the Islamic east (Persia, Arabia, and Egypt) and west (Spain).

Who supports the lands of the East and the West,
And who gives succor to believers, a descendant of Yaʾrub,[6]   15
The lofty king, who humbles sultans,
Who leads cavalcades, and is the lion of the battlefields.
He is a king whose heart is braver than the lion's,
Just as his finger is more generous than the rain clouds.
Should Time ever appear frowning or with a severe face   20
He meets it smiling like the flowers in the gardens.
His deeds are stars [shining out over] this world and religion.
The beloved refuses to return the greeting
While the heart is aflame from the excess of love.
Thus the sorrowing one sings the song of one confused by love: 25
"You go by, yet you give no greeting as though you were al-Maʾmūn,[7]
The terrorizer of armies, Yahya ibn Dhī n-Nūn."[8]

6. The mythical ancestor of the patron's tribe.   7. One of the patron's names.   8. Another of the patron's names.

WILLIAM IX, DUKE OF AQUITAINE
1071–1127

Spring Song[1]

In the sweetness of new spring
the woods grow leafy, little birds,
each in their own language, sing,
rehearse new stanzas with new words,
and it is good that man should find   5
the joy that most enchants his mind.

I see no messenger or note
from her, my first source of delight;
my heart can neither sleep nor laugh,
I dare not make a further move,   10
till I know what the end will be—
is she what I would have her be?

Our love together goes the way
of the branch on the hawthorn-tree,
trembling in the night, a prey   15
to the hoar-frost and the showers,
till next morning, when the sun
enfolds the green leaves and the boughs.

1. Translated from the Provençal by Peter Dronke.

One morning I remember still
we put an end to skirmishing,   20
and she gave me so great a gift:
her loving body, and her ring.
May God keep me alive until
my hands again move in her mantle!

For I shun that strange talk which might pull   25
my Helpmeet and myself apart;
I know that words have their own life,
and swift discourses spread about—
let others vaunt love as they will,
we have love's food, we have the knife!   30

JUDAH HALEVI
ca. 1075–1141

Summer[1]

The earth, like a girl, sipped the rains
Of winter past, and those the ministering cloud distilled
Or perhaps, like a secluded bride in winter,
Whose soul longs for the coming of love's time
She waited, and sought the season ripe for love   5
Till summer came, and calmed her anxious heart
Wearing golden tunics and white embroidered flax.
Like a girl who delights in her finery and raiment,
Every day she renews the grace of her embroiderers
And provides all her neighbors with new garments.   10
Every day she changes the colors of her fields
Now with strings of pearls, now with emeralds or rubies,
Offering her meadows now white or green or gold
Or blushing like the sweetheart kissing her beloved.
Her trellises display such gorgeous flowers   15
It seems as if she stole the stars from heaven.
Here is paradise, whose sheltered buds are clustered
Among the vines, kindled with blushes that incite to love.
The grapes are cold as snow in the hand of him who plucks them.
But in his entrails, they burn as hot as fire.   20
From the whirling cask, the wine, like sun, is rising.
And we shall bring our onyx[2] cups to pour it.
In the love of wine we shall stroll beneath the bowers
Around the garden, and smile with tears of rain,
Bright with shining drops spilled by the clouds   25
That scatter round like strings of pearls.

1. Translated from the Hebrew by William M. Davis.   2. A semiprecious stone.

She finds joy in the song of the swallow, and in the song of the vintagers,
And in cooing pigeons tamed by love.
She twitters in the branches, as the maiden sings
Behind her zither, swaying as she dances.   30
My soul is attentive to the breeze of dawn,
For it fondles the breath of my beloved.
A wanton breeze it is, that steals the scent of myrtles
To waft it off to lovers apart.
The heads of the myrtle rise and nod in turn   35
While the tremulous fronds of the palm tree
Seem to applaud the singing of the birds.

ABU-L-HASAN IBN AL-QABTURNUH
twelfth century

In Battle[1]

I remembered Sulayma[2] when the passion
        of battle was as fierce
as the passion of my body when we parted.

I thought I saw, among the lances, the tall
        perfection of her body,
and when they bent toward me I embraced them.   5

1. Translated from the Arabic by Lysander Kemp.   2. The name of the beloved.

HILDEGARD OF BINGEN
1098–1179

A Hymn to St. Maximinus[1]

1A

The dove peered in
through the latticed window,
where before her gaze
raining, a balm rained down
from the brightness of Maximinus.[2]   5

1. Translated from the Latin by Peter Dronke.   2. A 4th-century saint, patron of the nuns at the Benedictine Abbey at Trier for whom Hildegard probably wrote this sequence.

1B

The sun's heat blazed
and streamed into the darkness
from which blossomed the gem
—in the building of the temple—
of the purest generous heart.   10

2A

He, the sublime tower
made of Lebanon's tree,[3]
made of cypress,
is decked with jacinth and sardonyx,[4]
city that no architect's skill can match.   15

2B

He, the swift hart
ran up to the fountain
of purest water
bubbling from the mightiest stone
whose moisture made the sweet perfumes flow.   20

3A

You perfumers
who live in the gentlest greenness
of the king's gardens,
you who mount into the heights
when you have consummated   25
the only sacrifice among the rams,

3B

Lucent[5] among you
is this architect, wall of the temple,
he who longed
for an eagle's wings as he kissed   30
his foster-mother, Wisdom,
in Ekklesia's[6] glorious fecundity!

4A

Maximinus, you are mountain and valley,
and in both you appear, a pinnacle,
where the mountain-goat walked, and the elephant,   35
and Wisdom played in her delight.

---

3. The cypress.   4. Precious stones.   5. I.e., glowing.   6. The Church.

4B

You are both brave and gentle;
in the rites and in the sparkling of the altar
you mount as a smoke of fragrant spices
to the column of praise   40

5

Where you plead the cause of your people
who aspire to the mirror of light
for which there is praise on high.

THE ARCHPOET
d. 1165?

His Confession[1]

Seething over inwardly
    With fierce indignation,
In my bitterness of soul,
    Hear my declaration.
I am of one element,   5
    Levity my matter,
Like enough a withered leaf
    For the winds to scatter.

Since it is the property
    Of the sapient   10
To sit firm upon a rock,
    It is evident
That I am a fool, since I
    Am a flowing river,
Never under the same sky,   15
    Transient for ever.

Hither, thither, masterless
    Ship upon the sea,
Wandering through the ways of air,
    Go the birds like me.   20
Bound am I by ne'er a bond,
    Prisoner to no key,
Questing go I for my kind,
    Find depravity.

---

1. Translated from the Latin by Helen Waddell.

Never yet could I endure 25
 Soberness and sadness,
Jests I love and sweeter than
 Honey find I gladness.
Whatsoever Venus bids
 Is a joy excelling, 30
Never in an evil heart
 Did she make her dwelling.

Down the broad way do I go,
 Young and unregretting,
Wrap me in my vices up, 35
 Virtue all forgetting,
Greedier for all delight
 Than heaven to enter in:
Since the soul in me is dead,
 Better save the skin. 40

Pardon, pray you, good my lord,
 Master of discretion,
But this death I die is sweet,
 Most delicious poison.
Wounded to the quick am I 45
 By a young girl's beauty:
She's beyond my touching? Well,
 Can't the mind do duty?

Hard beyond all hardness, this
 Mastering of Nature: 50
Who shall say his heart is clean,
 Near so fair a creature?
Young are we, so hard a law,
 How should we obey it?
And our bodies, they are young, 55
 Shall they have no say in't?

Sit you down amid the fire,
 Will the fire not burn you?
To Pavia² come, will you
 Just as chaste return you? 60
Pavia, where Beauty draws
 Youth with finger-tips,
Youth entangled in her eyes,
 Ravished with her lips.

Let you bring Hippolytus,³ 65
 In Pavia dine him,
Never more Hippolytus
 Will the morning find him.

---

2. Italian city then known for its wild life.   3. Legendary figure of ancient Greece, noted for his vehement
opposition to the pleasures of the flesh.

In Pavia not a road
    But leads to venery,
Nor among its crowding towers
    One to chastity.   70

Yet a second charge they bring:
    I'm for ever gaming.
Yea, the dice hath many a time   75
    Stripped me to my shaming.
What an if the body's cold,
    If the mind is burning,
On the anvil hammering,
    Rhymes and verses turning?   80

Look again upon your list.
    Is the tavern on it?
Yea, and never have I scorned,
    Never shall I scorn it,
Till the holy angels come,   85
    And my eyes discern them,
Singing for the dying soul,
    Requiem aeternam.[4]

For on this my heart is set:
    When the hour is nigh me,   90
Let me in the tavern die,
    With a tankard by me,
While the angels looking down
    Joyously sing o'er me,
Deus sit propitius   95
    Huic potatori.[5]

'Tis the fire that's in the cup
    Kindles the soul's torches,
'Tis the heart that drenched in wine
    Flies to heaven's porches.   100
Sweeter tastes the wine to me
    In a tavern tankard
Than the watered stuff my Lord
    Bishop hath decanted.

Let them fast and water drink,   105
    All the poets' chorus,
Fly the market and the crowd
    Racketing uproarious:
Sit in quiet spots and think,
    Shun the tavern's portal,
Write, and never having lived,   110
    Die to be immortal.

---

4. Eternal rest (Latin), the opening words of the Catholic Mass for the dead.   5. May God be gracious to this drinker (Latin).

Never hath the spirit of
   Poetry descended,
Till with food and drink my lean   115
   Belly was distended,
But when Bacchus lords it in
   My cerebral story,
Comes Apollo with a rush,
   Fills me with his glory.   120

Unto every man his gift.
   Mine was not for fasting.
Never could I find a rhyme
   With my stomach wasting.
As the wine is, so the verse: 125
   'Tis a better chorus
When the landlord hath a good
   Vintage set before us.

Good my lord, the case is heard,
   I myself betray me,
And affirm myself to be   130
   All my fellows say me.
See, they in thy presence are:
   Let whoe'er hath known
His own heart and found it clean,   135
   Cast at me the stone.

JAUFRÉ RUDEL
twelfth century

Love Song[1]

When the nightingale in the leaves
Gives, seeks, and takes love,
And happily begins his song,
And gazes often at his mate,
And the streams are clear and the meadows fair,   5
Because of the new pleasure which prevails,
A great joy settles in my heart.

I am eager for a love affair—
For I know no more worthy enjoyment—
Which I pray for and desire, and it would be good   10
If she made me a gift of love;
For she has a full body, delicate and fair,

---

1. Translated from the Provençal by George Wolf and Roy Rosenstein.

With nothing that could be unbecoming,
And her good, pleasurable love.

I am preoccupied with this love   15
Awake and then asleep in dreams,
For there I have amazing joy,
Because I enjoy her and am joyously happy;
But her beauty is worth nothing to me,
Because no friend will inform me   20
How I might obtain this pleasure.

I am so anxious about this love
That when I go running towards her
It seems to me I'm turning
Backwards and that she's fleeing;   25
And my horse runs so slowly . . .
I do not think I shall ever get there,
Unless love makes her hold back.

Love, I leave you cheerfully,
For I seek what is best for me;   30
And I am so fortunate in this
That I am still rejoicing,
Thanks to my Good Protector
Who wants, calls, and approves me,
And has made me very hopeful.   35

And whoever stays here enjoying himself,
And does not follow God to Bethlehem,
I do not know how he will ever be worthy,
Or how he will ever reach salvation;
For I know and indeed believe   40
That whoever teaches of Jesus
Holds a good school.

RABBI EPHRAIM BEN JACOB
1132–1200

The Sacrifice of Isaac[1]

Let me recall my Fathers' (names)
   Today before Thee, examiner and knower (of hearts).
Oh grant the Fathers' merits to the sons,
   The father an old man, and the child, of his old age.[2]

1. Translated from the Hebrew by Judah Goldin; the parenthetical phrases are expansions of the original by the translator. For the biblical story of Abraham's obedience to God's command that he sacrifice his son Isaac, see Genesis 22.1–19.　2. Genesis 44.20; the last line of each stanza is a citation from the Bible.

You told your favorite[3] to offer up his only one,[4]   5
    On one of the mountains to enact the priest:
"Offer Me as sacrifice the soul of him you love,
    Get it for Me, for it pleases Me well."[5]

You called upon him to withstand the trial,
    As calls a king upon a seasoned warrior: 10
By this you shall be tested and prove victorious.
    The Lord trieth the righteous.[6]

The wild ass took pride in his bleeding and brayed:
    Drops of my blood I gave at the age of thirteen![7]
The beloved whispered: Oh that God would take me,   15
    Yea, let Him take all.[8]

Alert, (the father) ran to carry out a *mitsvah*,[9]
    And yearned to saddle his own ass himself,
(Bound to God) by a knot of love, that outweighed dignity.
    Behold, O Lord, Thou knowest it altogether.[1]   20

Then came the Satan, standing close by them,
    Murmuring, "Might one exchange a word with thee?"
Cried the perfect one, "I will walk in mine integrity,"
    For so the King has appointed.[2]

On the third day they arrived at Scopus,[3]   25
    Then to their Maker they looked:
The pillar of cloud shone in its splendor
    On the top of the mount, like devouring fire.[4]

The alert one piled on his son
    Faggots for the sacrifice, for the burnt offering.   30
Then the son opened his mouth to ask,
    Behold fire and wood, but where is the lamb for a burnt offering?[5]

In his reply, the saint spoke the rightful thing:
    The Lord will make it known who shall be His.
My son, the Master will look to His lamb   35
    And who is holy, He will draw to Him.[6]

The Pure One showed him the altar of the ancients.
    A male without blemish you shall offer of your own free will.
Whispered the soft-spoken dove:[7] Bind me as sacrifice
    With cords to the horns of the altar.[8]   40

---

3. Abraham.   4. Isaac.   5. Judges 14.3.   6. Psalms 11.5.   7. *The wild ass* refers to Ishmael, Isaac's half-brother; he was circumcised at thirteen (Genesis 17.25), and according to Jewish tradition he taunted Isaac that he was the more pious because he felt the pain of circumcision, while Isaac was circumcised when only eight days old.   8. 2 Samuel 19.30.   9. Sacrifice.   1. Psalms 139.4.   2. Esther 1.8.   3. A mountain near Jerusalem.   4. Exodus 24.17.   5. Genesis 22.7.   6. Numbers 16.5.   7. Isaac.   8. Psalms 118.28.

Bind for me my hands and my feet
    Lest I be found wanting and profane the sacrifice.
I am afraid of panic; I am concerned to honor you,
    My will is to honor you greatly.[9]

When the one whose life was bound up in the lad's   45
    Heard this, he bound him hand and foot like the perpetual offering.
In their right order he prepared fire and wood,
    And offered upon them the burnt offering.[1]

Then did the father and the son embrace,
    Mercy and Truth met and kissed each other.   50
Oh, my father, fill your mouth with praise,
    For He doth bless the sacrifice.[2]

I long to open my mouth to recite the Grace:
    Forever blessed be the Lord. Amen.
Gather my ashes, bring them to the city,   55
    Unto the tent, to Sarah.[3]

He made haste, he pinned him down with his knees,
    He made his two arms strong.
With steady hands he slaughtered him according to the rite,
    Full right was the slaughter.[4]   60

Down upon him fell the resurrecting dew, and he revived.
    (The father) seized him (then) to slaughter him once more.
Scripture, bear witness! Well-grounded is the fact:
    And the Lord called Abraham, even a second time from heaven.[5]

The ministering angels cried out, terrified: 65
    Even animal victims, were they ever slaughtered twice?
Instantly they made their outcry heard on high,
    Lo, Ariels cried out above the earth.[6]

We beg of Thee, have pity upon him!
    In his father's house, we were given hospitality.
He was swept by the flood of celestial tears   70
    Into Eden, the garden of God.[7]

The pure one thought: The child is free of guilt,
    Now I, whither shall I go?
Then he heard: Your son was found an acceptable sacrifice,   75
    By Myself have I sworn it, saith the Lord.[8]

In a nearby thicket did the Lord prepare
    A ram, meant for this *mitsvah*[9] even from Creation.
The proxy caught its leg in the skirts of his coat,
    And behold, he stood by his burnt offering.[1]   80

9. Numbers 24.11.   **1.** Exodus 40.29.   **2.** Psalms 89.53.   **3.** Genesis 18.6. Sarah is Isaac's mother.
4. Genesis 43.16.   **5.** Genesis 22.15.   **6.** Isaiah 33.7.   **7.** Ezekiel 28.13.   **8.** Genesis 22.16.
9. Sacrifice.   **1.** Numbers 23.17.

So he offered the ram, as he desired to do,
  Rather than his son, as a burnt offering.
Rejoicing, he beheld the ransom of his only one
  Which God delivered into his hand.[2]

This place he called Adonai-Yireh,[3]   85
  The place where light and the law are manifest.
He swore to bless it as the Temple site,
  For there the Lord commanded the blessing.[4]

Thus prayed the binder and the bound,
  That when their descendants commit a wrong   90
This act be recalled to save them from disaster,
  From all their transgressions and sins.[5]

O Righteous One, do us this grace!
  You promised our fathers mercy to Abraham.[6]
Let then their merit stand as our witness,   95
  And pardon our iniquity and our sin, and take us for Thine inheritance.[7]

Recall to our credit the many Akedahs,[8]
  The saints, men and women, slain for Thy sake.
Remember the righteous martyrs of Judah,
  Those that were bound of Jacob.[9]   100

Be Thou the shepherd of the surviving flock
  Scattered and dispersed among the nations.
Break the yoke and snap the bands
  Of the bound flock that yearns toward Thee[1]

O GOD! O KING . . .   105

2. Exodus 21.13. Isaac returns to his father from Eden.   3. Provision of the Lord.   4. Psalms 133.3.
5. Leviticus 16.16.   6. Abraham figures here as both an individual and Israel as a whole.   7. Exodus
34.9.   8. Sacrifices.   9. Genesis 30.42.   1. Genesis 30.41.

BEATRICE, COUNTESS OF DIA
ca. 1150–1200

A Lover's Prize[1]

I have been in great distress
for a knight for whom I longed;
I want all future times to know
how I loved him to excess
  Now I see I am betrayed—   5

1. Translated from the Provençal by Peter Dronke.

he claims I did not give him love—
such was the mistake I made,
   naked in bed, and dressed.

How I'd long to hold him pressed
naked in my arms one night—
if I could be his pillow once,   10
would he not know the height of bliss?
   Floris was all to Blanchefleur,[2]
yet not so much as I am his:
I am giving my heart, my love,   15
   my mind, my life, my eyes.

Fair, gentle lover, gracious knight,
if once I held you as my prize
and lay with you a single night
and gave you a love-laden kiss—   20
   my greatest longing is for you
to lie there in my husband's place,
but only if you promise this:
   to do all I'd want to do.

2. Lovers in a well-known romance.

BERTRAN DE BORN
ca. 1140–ca. 1215

In Praise of War[1]

I love the joyful time of Easter,
that makes the leaves and flowers come forth,
and it pleases me to hear the mirth
of the birds, who make their song
resound through the woods,   5
and it pleases me to see upon the meadows
tents and pavilions planted,
and I feel a great joy
when I see ranged along the field
knights and horses armed for war.   10

And it pleases me when the skirmishers
make the people and their baggage run away,
and it pleases me when I see behind them coming
a great mass of armed men together,
and I have pleasure in my heart   15

1. Translated from the Provençal by Frederick Goldin.

when I see strong castles besieged,
the broken ramparts caving in,
and I see the host on the water's edge,
closed in all around by ditches,
with palisades, strong stakes close together   20

And I am as well pleased by a lord
when he is first in the attack,
armed, upon his horse, unafraid,
so he makes his men take heart
by his own brave lordliness.   25
And when the armies mix in battle,
each man should be poised
to follow him, smiling,
for no man is worth a thing
till he has given and gotten blow on blow.   30

Maces and swords and painted helms,
the useless shields cut through,
we shall see as the fighting starts,
and many vassals together striking,
and wandering wildly,   35
the unreined horses of the wounded and dead.
And once entered into battle
let every man proud of his birth
think only of breaking arms and heads,
for a man is worth more dead than alive and beaten.   40

I tell you there is not so much savor
in eating or drinking or sleeping,
as when I hear them scream, "There they are! Let's get them!"
on both sides, and I hear riderless
horses in the shadows, neighing,   45
and I hear them scream, "Help! Help!"
and I see them fall among the ditches,
little men and great men on the grass,
and I see fixed in the flanks of the corpses
stumps of lances with silken streamers.   50

Barons, pawn your castles,
and your villages, and your cities
before you stop making war on one another.

Papiols,[2] gladly go
fast to my Lord Yes-and-No[3]   55
and tell him he has lived in peace too long.

---

2. Bertran's *joglar*, or minstrel, who will sing the lyric.   3. A mocking reference to Bertran's lord at the time, Richard the Lion-Hearted, whom he accuses of indecisiveness.

HEINRICH VON MORUNGEN
ca. 1150–1222

The Wound of Love[1]

She has wounded me
  in my innermost soul,
within the mortal core,
when I told her
  that I was raving and anguished   5
in desire for her glorious lips.
Once I bade my own lips
  to commend me to her service,
  and to steal me
a tender kiss of hers,   10
  that I might for ever be well.

How I begin to hate
  her rose-red lips,
which I never yet forgot!
It troubles me still,   15
  that they once refused me
with such vehemence.
Thus I have grown so weak
  that I would far rather—alive—
  burn in the abyss   20
of hell than serve her still,
  not knowing to what end.

1. Translated from the German by Peter Dronke.

ARNAUT DANIEL
twelfth century

The Art of Love[1]

To this sweet and pretty air
I set words that I plane and finish;
and every word will fit well,
once I have passed the file there,
for at once Love polishes and aureates   5
my song, which proceeds from her,
ruler and guardian of merit.

1. Translated from the Provençal by Frederick Goldin.

Each day I am a better man and purer,
for I serve the noblest lady in the world,
and I worship her, I tell you this in the open.   10
I belong to her from my foot to the top of my head;
and let the cold wind blow,
love raining in my heart
keeps me warm when it winters most.

I hear a thousand masses and pay to have them said,   15
I burn lights of wax and oil,
so may God give me good luck with her,
for no defense against her does me any good.
When I look at her golden hair,
her soft young spirited body,   20
if someone gave me Luserna,[2] I'd still love her more.

I love her and seek her out with a heart so full,
I think I am stealing her out of my own hands by too much wanting,
if a man can lose a thing by loving it well.
For the heart of her submerges   25
mine and does not abate.
So usurious is her demand,
she gets craftsman and workshop together.

I do not want the empire of Rome,
do not make me pope of it   30
so that I could not turn back to her
for whom the heart in me burns and breaks apart.
If she does not cure me of this torment
with a kiss before new year's,
she murders me and sends herself to hell.   35

But this torment I endure
could not make me turn away from loving well,
though it holds me fast in loneliness,
for in this desert I cast my words in rhyme.
I labor in loving more than a man who works the earth,   40
for the Lord of Moncli did not love
N'Audierna an egg's worth more.[3]

I am Arnaut, who hoards the wind,
and chases the hare on an ox,
and swims against the tide.   45

---

2. A city, probably in Spain.   3. Both the Lord of Moncli and his love, N'Audierna, have not been identified.

WALTHER VON DER VOGELWEIDE
ca. 1170–ca. 1230

Dancing Girl[1]

"Lady, accept this garland"—
these were the words I spoke to a pretty girl:
"then you will grace the dance
with the lovely flowers crowning you.
If I had priceless stones,   5
they would be for your hair—
indeed you must believe me,
by my faith, I mean it truly!"

She took my offering
as a gently nurtured child would take it.   10
Her cheeks became as red
as the rose that stands beside the lilies.
Her shining eyes were lowered then in shame,
yet she curtsied graciously.
That was my reward—   15
if any more becomes mine, I'll hold it secret.

"You are so fair,
that I want to give you my chaplet now,
the very best I have.
I know of many flowers, white and red,   20
so far away, on the heath over there,
where they spring up beautiful,
and where the birds are singing—
let us pluck them together there."

I thought that never yet   25
had I known such bliss as I knew then.
From the tree the flowers
rained on us endlessly as we lay in the grass.
Yes, I was filled with laughter in sheer joy.
Just then, when I was so gloriously   30
rich in my dreaming,
then day broke, and I was forced to wake.

She has stirred me so
that this summer, with every girl I meet,
I must gaze deep in her eyes: 35
perhaps one will be mine: then all my cares are gone.
What if she were dancing here?
Ladies, be so kind,
set your hats back a little.
Oh, if only, under a garland, I could see that face!   40

1. Translated from the German by Peter Dronke.

MEIR HALEVI ABULAFIA
ca. 1170–1244

A Letter from the Grave[1]

He wrote this when his sister—may God delight in her—died on the Sabbath of 10 November 1212; he wrote to his father, in the name of his sister, to inform him and to bring him comfort.

O clouds, bear these greetings to my father from my grave, in words not spoken but written. Tell him, with the dumb lips of my disaster, what has become of my lips and my voice. But take care that my distress should not overwhelm him, that my great sorrow should not oppress him. What good would it do to oppress him with my sorrow? Would his pain spare me mine? Would it be right to tear open his heart because of me? No, I would be wronging my father, whose loving wings were my bed, whose compassionate shoulders were my chariot. Once I shone like a sun in his house, but now I have set in the abyss.

Turn away from me! How much longer will you call to me? Know that the hand of God has touched me. Death, like a ravening lion, tore me out of the room of my beloved. No longer can I cast my fortunes on the dear friend of my youth; now I must commit my fortunes to the grave. They buried me, covering my face with the very dust which only yesterday I trampled underfoot. But I shall draw all men after me; both my loved ones and my rivals will join me. God summons all mortals to the house of the dead. Sinner and prophet perish alike. When He restores all souls to their bodies, then shall I come into your presence again.

Though He has made your heart—my heart's guardian—share my grief, though He has made a sea of tears flow over you and almost flooded you with weeping, He will now fill my grave with His dew of sparkling light, He will say to your welling tears: "Subside and dry!"

1. Translated from the Hebrew by T. Carmi.

HADEWIJCH OF BRABANT
thirteenth century

The Cult of Love[1]

The birds have long been silent
that were blithe here before:

1. Translated from the Flemish by Peter Dronke.

their blitheness has departed,
they have lost their summer now;
they would swiftly sing again
if that summer came again,   5
which they have chosen above all
and for which they were born:
one hears it in their voices then.

I'll say no more of birds' laments: 10
their joy, their pain, is quickly gone;
I have more grievous cause to moan:
Love, to whom we should aspire,
weighs us down with her noble cares,
so we chase after false delights   15
and Love cannot enfold us then.
Ah, what has baseness done to us!
Who shall erase that faithlessness?

The mighty ones, whose hand is strong,
it is on them I still rely,   20
who work at all times in Love's bond,
heedless of pain, grief, tragedy;
they want to ride through all the land
that lovers loving by love have found,
so perfect is their noble heart;   25
they know what Love can teach by love,
how Love exalts lovers by love.

Why then should anyone refuse,
since by loving Love can be won?
Why not ride, longing, through the storm,   30
trusting in the power of Love,
aspiring to the cult of Love?
Love's peerlessness will then be seen—
there, in the brightness of Love's dawn,
where for Love's sake is shunned no pain   35
and no pain caused by Love weighs down.

Often I call for help as a lost one,
but then, when you come close, my dear one,
with new solace you bear me up
and with high spirit I ride on,   40
sport with my dear so joyously
as if north and south and east
and west all lands belonged to me!
Then suddenly I am dashed down.—
Oh, what use to tell my pain?   45

ALFONSO X
1221–1284

The Scorpions[1]

I cannot find such great delight
in the song
of birds, or in their twittering,
in love or in ambition
or in arms—for I fear   5
that these indeed
are fraught with danger—
as in a good galleon
that can take me speedily
from this demonic landscape   10
where the scorpions dwell;
for within my heart
I have felt their sting!

And by the holy God I swear
I would wear   15
neither cloak nor beard,
nor would I involve myself in love
or arms, for injury
and lamentation
come from these at every season—   20
no, I'd pilot a merchant-ship
and sail across the ocean,
selling vinegar and flour,
and I would fly from the poison
of the scorpion, for I know   25
no other medicine against it.

I can take no pleasure here
in tilting,
nor, God save the mark,
in mock-tournaments;   30
as for going armed by night
or patrolling,
I do it without any joy—
for I find more enchantment in the sea
than in being a knight: 35
long ago I was a mariner,
and henceforth I long to guard
myself against the scorpion, and return
to what I was in the beginning.

1. Translated from the Spanish by Peter Dronke.

I must try to explain to you: 40
the demon
will never be able to trick me
now into speaking the language
of arms, for this is not my role—
(useless   45
for me to reason thus,
I have not even arms to try)—
rather, I long to go alone
and in a merchant's guise
to find some land   50
where they cannot strike at me:
the black scorpion, and the mottled.

GUIDO GUINIZZELLI
thirteenth century

Love and Nobility[1]

Love always repairs to the noble heart
  Like a bird winging back into its grove:
Nor was love made before the noble heart,
  Nor did nature, before the heart, make love.
For they were there as long as was the Sun,   5
  Whose splendor's ever bright;
Never did love before that shining come.
Love nestles deep inside nobility
  Exactly the way
One sees the heart within the fiery blaze.   10

Fire of love in noble heart is caught
  Like power gleaming inside a precious stone.
The value does not come down from the stars
  Until the Sun has blenched the stone all pure.
Only after the might of the Sun   15
  Has drawn out all that's vile
Does the star bestow its noble power.
Just so a heart transformed by nature pure,
  Noble and elect,
A woman starlike with her love injects.   20

Love for this reason stays in noble heart
  Like a waving flame atop a burning brand,
Shining, its own delight, subtle and bright;
  It is so proud, it knows no other way.

1. Translated from the Italian by James J. Wilhelm.

Yet a nature which is still debased   25
    Greets love as water greets the fire,
With the cold hissing against the heat.
Love in noble heart will find a haven
    Like the shine
Of a diamond glinting in ore within the mine.   30

Sun beats against the mud the livelong day;
    Mud it remains; Sun does not lose its ray;
The haughty one says: "I am noble by my tribe."
    He is the mud; Sun is the noble power.
Man must never believe   35
    That nobility exists outside the heart
In the grandness of his ancestry,
For without virtue, heart has no noble worth;
    It's a ray through a wave;
The heavens retain the sparkle and splendor they gave.   40

Shines among the powers of heaven
    God the creator, more than Sun in our eye;
Each angel knows the Maker beyond its sphere,
    And turning its circle, obeys God's noble power.
And thus it follows at once: 45
    The blesséd tasks of the Master transpire.
In the same way, in all truth, the beautiful lady
Should behave, for in her eyes reflects the desire
    Of a noble man
Who will turn his every thought to her command.   50

Lady, God will ask me: "Why did you presume?"
    When my soul stands before his mighty throne.
"You passed the heavens, came all the way to me,
    And cheapened me in the light of profane love.
To me is due all the praise   55
    And to the Queen of the Royal Realm[2]
Who makes all fraudulence cease."
I'll tell him then: "She had an angel look—
    A heavenly face.
What harm occurred if my love in her was placed?"   60

_____

2. The Virgin Mary.

GUIDO CAVALCANTI
ca. 1255–1300

An Encounter[1]

Once within a little grove a shepherdess I spied;
More than any star of sky beauteous did she prove.

Ringlets she had, blonde and curly locks,
Eyes filled with love, a face of rosy hue,
And with her staff she led her gentle flocks,   5
Barefoot, with their feet bathed by the dew.
She sang, indeed, as if she were enamored;
She had the glamour of every pleasing art.

I greeted her, and asked her then at once
If she had any company that day;   10
She answered sweetly: "For the nonce,
Alone throughout this grove I make my way."
And added: "Listen, but when the gentle bird is heard,
A friend should have my heart."

And when she told me of this state of mind,   15
Suddenly I heard birdsongs in the wood.
I said to myself: "This surely would be the time
To take from this shepherdess what joy I could."
Grace I requested—just to kiss her face—
And then embrace if she should feel like me.   20

She took my hand, seized with love's old power,
And said she'd give me her heart too;
She led me then into a fresh green bower,
And there I saw flowers of every hue.
And I was filled so full of sweetened joy   25
Love's godlike boy[2] there too I seemed to see.

1. Translated from the Italian by James J. Wilhelm.   2. Cupid.

DANTE ALIGHIERI
1265–1321

Love and Poetry[1]

Guido, I wish that you and Lapo[2] and I,
Spirited on the wings of a magic spell,
Could drift in a ship where every rising swell
Would sweep us at our will across the skies;
Then tempest never, or any weather dire   5
Could ever make our blissful living cease;
No, but abiding in a steady, blesséd peace
Together we'd share the increase of desire.

And Lady Vanna and Lady Lagia[3] then
And she[4] who looms above the thirty best[5]   10
Would join us at the good enchanter's[6] behest;
And there we'd talk of Love without an end
To make those ladies happy in the sky—
With Lapo enchanted too, and you and I.

Sonnet[1]

Love and the gentle heart are one thing,
even as the sage[2] affirms in his poem,
and so one can be without the other
as much as rational soul without reason.
Nature creates them when she is amorous: 5
Love as lord and the heart as his mansion,
in which, sleeping, he rests
sometimes a brief and sometimes a long season.
Beauty appears in a wise lady, then,
which so pleases the eyes that in the heart   10
is born a desire for that which pleases;
and so long it lasts sometimes therein
that it wakens the spirit of Love.
And the same to a lady does a worthy man.

---

1. Translated from the Italian by James J. Wilhelm.   2. Guido Cavalcanti and Lapo Gianni were poets in Dante's literary circle.   3. Giovanna and Lagia were Guido and Lapo's ladies.   4. Beatrice, Dante's beloved.   5. Dante wrote a poem naming the most beautiful ladies of Florence.   6. Merlin.
1. Translated from the Italian by Dino Cervigni and Edward Vasta.   2. Guido Guinizzelli; see above, p. 1411.

ANONYMOUS
thirteenth century

Calvary

Now goeth sonne[1] under wood,
Me rueth, Mary, thy fair rood;[2]
Now goeth sonne under tree,
Me rueth, Mary, thy son and thee.

1. Both "sun" and "son."   2. Both "face" and "cross."

ALEXANDER THE WILD
thirteenth century

Strawberry Picking[1]

Long ago, when we were children,
in the time that spanned the years
when we ran across the meadows,
over from those, now back to these,
there, where we at times   5
found violets,
you now see cattle leap for flies.

I remember how we sat
deep in flowers, and decided
which girl was the prettiest.   10
Our young looks were radiant then
with the new garland
for the dance.
And so the time goes by.

Look, there we ran to find strawberries,   15
ran to the beech from the fir-tree,
over sticks and stones,
as long as the sun shone.
Then a forester called out
through the branches   20
"Come along, children, go home!"

All our hands were stained,
picking strawberries yesterday;
to us it was nothing but play.

1. Translated from the German by Peter Dronke.

Then, again and again, we heard 25
our shepherd calling
and moaning:
"Children, the forest is full of snakes!"

One child walked in the tall grass,
started, and cried aloud: 30
"Children, right here there was a snake!
He has bitten our pony—
it will never heal;
it must always
remain poisoned and unwell." 35

"Come along then, out of the forest!
If you do not now make haste
it will happen as I say:
if you are not sure to be gone
from the forest while there is day, 40
you will lose your way
and your joy will become a moan."

Do you know that five young women
loitered in the meadow-lands
till the king locked up his hall? 45
Great were their moans and their distress—
for the bailiffs tore
their clothes away,
so that they stood naked, without a dress.[2]

2. Probably an allusion to the parable of the five foolish virgins in the New Testament of the Bible: see
Matthew 25.1–13.

DAFYDD AP GWILYM
ca. 1310–1370

The Fox[1]

Yesterday was I, sure of purpose,
Under the trees (alas that the girl doesn't see it)
Standing under Ovid's[2] stems
And waiting for a pretty girl beneath the trees;
She made me weep on her way. 5
I saw when I looked there
(An ape's shape where I did not love)

1. Translated from the Welsh by Richard Morgan Loomis.   2. Roman love poet (43 B.C.E.–17 C.E.).

A red fox (he doesn't love our hounds' place)
Sitting like a tame animal,
On his haunches near his den.   10

    I drew between my hands
A bow of yew there, it was brave,
About, like an armed man,
On the brow of the hill, a stirring of high spirits,
Weapon for coursing along a district,   15
To hit him with a long, stout bolt.
I drew for a try a shaft
Clear past the jaw.
My grief, my bow went
In three pieces, luckless disaster.   20

    I got mad (I did not dread him,
Unhappy bear) at the fox.
He's a lad who'd love a hen,
A silly bird, and bird flesh;
He doesn't follow the cry of horns,   25
Rough his voice and his carol.
Ruddy is he in front of a talus[3] slope,
Like an ape among green trees.
At both ends of a field there turns up
A dog-shape looking for a goose.   30
Crows' beacon near the brink of a hill,
Acre-strider, color of an ember,
Likeness of a lure for crows and magpies at a fair,
Portent looking like a dragon.
Lord of excitement, chewer of a fat hen,   35
Of acclaimed fleece, glowing flesh.
An awl of hollowed-out fine earth,
Fire-dish at the edge of a shuttered window.
Copper bow of light feet,
Tongs like a beak of blood.   40

    Not easy for me to follow him,
And his dwelling toward Annwn.[4]
Red roamer, he was found to be too fierce,
He'd run ahead of a course of hounds.
Sharp his rushing, gorse-strider,   45
Leopard with a dart in his rump.

---

3. A pile of rock fragments.   4. The otherworld of Welsh myth.

ANONYMOUS
fourteenth century

Aubade[1]

Deep in an orchard, under hawthorn leaves,
the lady holds her lover in her arms,
until the watcher cries, he sees the dawn.
Dear God, the daybreak! oh how soon it comes!

"If only God let night stay without end,   5
and my beloved never left my side,
and never again the guard saw day or dawn—
dear God, the daybreak! oh how soon it comes!"

"Let us kiss, sweet beloved, you and I,
down in the meadows where the birds now sing—   10
defy my jealous husband and do all!
Dear God, the daybreak! oh how soon it comes!

"Let us create new love-sports, sweet beloved,
down in the meadows where the birds now sing—
until the watcher plays his pipe again.   15
Dear God, the daybreak! oh how soon it comes!

"In the sweet wind that came to me from there
I drank a ray of my beloved's breath,
my fair and joyous, gracious lover's breath—
dear God, the daybreak! oh how soon it comes!"   20

The lady is delightful, lovable,
admired by many for her beauty's sake,
and holds her heart most loyally in love.
Dear God, the daybreak! oh how soon it comes!

1. Translated from the French by Peter Dronke.

CHRISTINE DE PIZAN
ca. 1364–ca. 1431

Alone in Martyrdom[1]

Alone in martyrdom I have been left
In the desert of this world, that's full of sadness,
By my sweet love, who held my heart

1. Translated from the French by Muriel Kittel.

In sorrowless joy and in perfect gladness;
But he is dead, and such deep griefs oppress   5
Me, my weary heart such sorrows gnaw,
I shall bewail his death for evermore.

What can I ever do but weep and sigh for
My departed love, what wonder is this?
For when my heart profoundly ponders how   10
I lived secure and without bitterness,
Since childhood and early youthfulness
With him—at me such sufferings gnaw
I shall bewail his death for evermore.

As the turtledove without her mate does turn   15
To dry things only, nor cares more for greenness;
As the ewe that the wolf seeks to kill
Is terrified, by her shepherd left defenseless;
So am I left in great distress
By my dear love whose loss to me is sore;   20
I shall bewail his death for evermore.

ANONYMOUS
fifteenth century

Lament of the Virgin

Of all women that ever were born,
That bear children, abide and see,
How my son lies me before,
Upon my knee, taken from the tree.
Your children ye dance upon your knee.   5
With laughing, kissing and merry cheer;
Behold my child, behold now me,
For now lies dead my dear son dear.

O woman, woman, well is thee,
Thy child's cap thee dotes upon;   10
Thou picks his hair, beholds his ble,[1]
Thou wost not well when thou hast done.
But ever, alas, I make my moan
To see my son's head as it is here;
I pick out thorns by one and one,   15
For now lies dead my dear son dear.

O woman, a chaplet chosen thou has
Thy child to wear, it does thee great liking;

---

1. Complexion.

Thou pins it on with great solace, 20
And I sit with my son sore weeping.
His chaplet is thorns' sore pricking,
His mouth I kiss with a careful[2] cheer;
I sit weeping and thou singing,
For now lies dead my dear son dear.

O woman, look to me again, 25
That plays and kisses your children's pappis.[3]
To see my son I have great pain,
In his breast so great a gap is.
And on his body so many swappis.[4]
With bloody lips I kiss him here, 30
Alas! full hard methink me happis,[5]
For now lies dead my dear son dear.

O woman, thou takes thy child by the hand
And says, "My son, give me a strake!"[6]
My son's hands are sorely bleeding; 35
To look on him me list not lake.[7]
His hands he suffered for thy sake
Thus to be bored with nail and spear;
When thou make mirth great sorrow I make,
For now lies dead my dear son dear. 40

Behold, women, when that ye play
And have your children on knees dansand;[8]
You feel their feet, so feat[9] are they,
And to your sight well likand,[1]
But the most[2] finger of any hand, 45
Through my son's feet I may put here,
And pull it out sorely bledand,[3]
For now lies dead my dear son dear.

Therefore, women, by town and street,
Your children's hands when ye behold 50
Their breasts, their body, and their feet,
Then good it were on my son think you wolde,[4]
How care has made my heart full cold
To see my son, with nail and spear,
With scourge and thorns many-fold, 55
Wounded and dead, my dear son dear.

Thou hast thy son full whole and sound,
And mine is dead upon my knee;
Thy child is loose and mine is bound,
Thy child is alive and mine dead is he. 60
Why was this ought[5] but for thee?
For my child trespassed never here.

---

2. Woeful.   3. Breasts.   4. Wounds.   5. I suffer.   6. Stroke—i.e., caress.   7. Is no pleasure to me.   8. Dancing.   9. Pretty.   1. Liking.   2. Largest.   3. Bleeding.   4. Would.   5. At all.

Me thinks ye be holden to weep with me,
For now lies dead my dear son dear.

Weep with me, both man and wife,   65
My child is yours and loves you well.
If your child had lost his life
You would weep at every mele.[6]
But for my son weep ye never a del.[7]
If you love yours, mine has no peer;   70
He sends yours both hap and hele[8]
And for you died my dear son dear.

Now all women that have your wit,[9]
And see my child on my knees dead,
Weep not for yours but weep for it,   75
And ye shall have full muchel mede.[1]
He would again for your love bleed
Rather than that ye damnéd were.
I pray you all to him take heed,
For now lies dead my dear son dear.   80

Farewell, woman, I may no more
For dread of death rehearse his pain.
Ye may laugh when ye list[2] and I weep sore,
That may ye see and ye look to me again.
To love my son and ye be fain,[3]   85
I will love yours with heart entere,[4]
And he shall bring your children and you, certain,
To bliss where is my dear son dear.

6. Occasion.   7. Not at all.   8. Both fortune and health.   9. I.e., wits.   1. A great reward.
2. Please.   3. If you be willing.   4. Entire.

CHARLES D'ORLÉANS
ca. 1394–1465

Balade[1]

If you wish to sell your kisses,
I will gladly buy some,
And in return you will have my heart as deposit.
To use them as inheritance,
By the dozens, hundreds, or thousands.   5
Don't sell them to me at as high a price
As you would to a total stranger
For you are receiving me as your liegeman.

1. Translated from the French by Sarah Spence.

If you wish to sell your kisses,
I will gladly buy some.   10
And in return you will have my heart as deposit.
My complete wish and desire
Are yours in spite of all suspicion;
Allow, as a faithful and wise woman,
That for my reward and share
I may be among the first served,   15
If you wish to sell your kisses.

FRANÇOIS VILLON
1431–ca. 1470

From The Testament[1]

*   *   *

Now I think I hear the laments
Of the once-beautiful Helmet-seller[2]
Wishing she were a girl again   455
And saying something like this
"Ah, cruel, arrogant old age
Why have you beaten me down so soon?
What holds me back from striking myself
From killing myself with a blow?   460

"You have taken from me the high hand
That I had by right of beauty
Over clerics, merchants, men of the Church
For then there wasn't a man born
Who wouldn't have given me all he owned   465
Repent though he might later on
If I'd just have let him have
What now tramps won't take for free.

"To many a man I refused it
Which wasn't exactly good sense   470
For the love of a smooth operator
Whom I gave free play with it
And what if I did fool around
I swear I loved him truly
But he just gave me a hard time   475
And loved me for my money.

1. Translated from the French by Galway Kinnell.   2. A woman who sells armor.

"He could wipe the floor with me
Or kick me I loved him still
And even if he's broken my back
He could just ask for a kiss   480
And I'd forget my misery
The rascal rotten right through
Would take me in his arms (a lot I got for it)
What's left? The shame and sin.

"Dead he's been these thirty years   485
And here I am old and grizzled
When I think also of the happy times
What I was, what I've become
When I look at myself naked
And see how I've changed so much   490
Poor, dried-up, lean and bony
I nearly go off my head.

"What's become of the smooth forehead
The yellow hair, the arching eyebrows
The wide-set eyes, the fair gaze   495
That took in all the cleverest men
The straight nose neither large nor small
The little flattened ears
The dimpled chin, the bright rounded cheeks
And the lips beautiful and red?   500

"The delicate little shoulders
The long arms and slender hands
The small breasts, the full buttocks
High, broad, perfectly built
For holding the jousts of love   505
The wide loins and the sweet quim
Set over thick firm thighs
In its own little garden?

"The forehead lined, the hair gray
The eyebrows all fallen out, the eyes clouded   510
Which threw those bright glances
That felled many a poor devil
The nose hooked far from beauty
The ears hairy and lopping down
The cheeks washed out, dead and pasty   515
The chin furrowed, the lips just skin.

"This is what human beauty comes to
The arms short, the hands shriveled
The shoulders all hunched up
The breasts? Shrunk in again   520
The buttocks gone the way of the tits
The quim? aagh! As for the thighs

They aren't thighs now but sticks
Speckled all over like sausages.

"This is how we lament the good old days   525
Among ourselves, poor silly crones
Dumped down on our hunkers
In little heaps like so many skeins
Around a tiny hempstalk fire
That's soon lit and soon gone out   530
And once we were so adorable
So it goes for men and women.

"Now look here pretty Glover
Who used to study under me
And you too Blanche the Shoe-fitter   535
It's time you got it straight
Take what you can right and left
Don't spare a man I beg you
For there's no run on old crones
No more than cried-down money.   540

"And you sweet Sausage-filler
Such a born dancer
And Guillemette the Tapester[3]
Don't fall out with your man
Soon you'll have to close up shop   545
When you've gotten old and flabby
And good for no one but an old priest
No more than cried-down money.

"Jeanneton the Bonnet-maker
Don't let that one lover tie you down   550
And Catherine the Purse-seller
Stop putting men out to pasture
She who's lost her looks can ask them
To come back, she can flash her smile
But ugly old age can't buy love   555
No more than cried-down money.

"Girls, stop a moment
And let it sink in why I weep and cry
I can't get back in circulation
No more than cried-down money."   560

*   *   *

---

3. Properly a maker or seller of rugs; her shop may have been headquarters for a prostitute.

MEDIEVAL TALES: A SELECTION

Among the most popular forms of literature in the Middle Ages were brief narratives, some little more than anecdotes or jokes, some as ambitious as short stories. Indeed, as a glance at the table of contents of this anthology will show, some of the greatest medieval masterpieces—the *Lais* of Marie de France, Boccaccio's *Decameron*, Chaucer's *Canterbury Tales*, the *Arabian Nights*, and even Dante's *Divine Comedy*—are collections of stories. Yet these works derive from a vast network of largely anonymous stories that have their own kind of genius. If they are less carefully crafted works of art than their more illustrious literary progeny, they nonetheless display an uninhibited energy, a willingness to explore nonconformist attitudes, and a satiric vigor that the more official works tend to moderate. And these tales often seem to aim at no higher effect than to provide pleasure: wit and high spirits are, despite their moralizing claims to the contrary, the qualities these tales prize above all others.

While medieval audiences probably didn't much care what type of story they were listening to, many medieval writers did have a sense of the various genres available to them, even though the boundaries between them were often blurred. The most capacious of these generic types was the *exemplum*, by which is meant a story that provides an example of a general principle. From the time of the Gospels, Christian teachers had relied upon exemplary stories to drive home moral points. By the early twelfth century, collections of these *exempla* began to appear, and in the thirteenth century, when public preaching had become a central aspect of religious life, these collections grew and became more carefully organized. A preacher looking for a story to illustrate a specific theme could now find in a handbook a number of stories located under various spiritual or moral categories. (A good instance of using an *exemplum* to enliven a sermon is found in Chaucer's *Pardoner's Tale*.) *Exempla* were also widely used in various kinds of didactic treatises, some secular and concerned with transmitting philosophical, political, or general moral truths, some religious and concerned with helping Christians understand both the elements of their faith and the nature of sin. Not surprisingly, some of the more severe moralists rejected *exempla* entirely, arguing that stories simply distracted the audience from the lesson being taught. Yet this moralizing severity had an unexpected literary benefit, for in the hands of skillful storytellers the relation of the story to the moral became itself a source of interest; and some storytellers actually challenged their listeners to find any moral at all while simultaneously making their stories irresistibly interesting.

In this small selection from the literally hundreds of medieval tales that survive we have included three *exempla*. The first two are from the earliest collection in Latin, made by Petrus Alfonsi in the first decades of the twelfth century. Petrus was born in 1062 as Moshe Sephardi, a member of the Jewish community in Huesca, Spain, a town at the time controlled by the Arabs. In 1096 the town was captured by the Christians, and on St. Peter's Day, June 29, 1106, Moshe himself converted to Christianity, taking his name from his patron saint Peter and from his godfather, King Alfonso I of Aragon. Well educated in both Hebrew and Arabic science, Petrus served as a physician first for Alfonso and then for Henry I of England. It was probably in England that he wrote the *Dialogue of Peter and Moses* justifying his conversion, as well as important astronomical works that for the first time made the sophisticated science then flourishing in Arabic Spain available to the Latin West. There is evidence that around 1125 Peter returned to Spain and took up residence in Toledo, where he continued his role as a transmitter of Arabic and Hebrew knowledge to the Latin West. The selection here is drawn from his work called the *Disciplina clericalis*. The title means literally *Rule for Clerics* but is more informatively translated as *The Scholar's Guide*: the book is meant to provide wisdom to those who can read Latin. In compiling his book Petrus drew upon Hebrew wisdom literature, Arabic proverbs, and tales drawn from the rich folklore of India, Byzantium, Persia, Israel, and Arabia.

The *Disciplina* seems first to have been written in either Arabic or Hebrew and then translated into Latin prose, either by Petrus alone or with a collaborator. Its subsequent influence was enormous. Not only was it translated into most of the European languages, but its stories found their way, for the most part indirectly, into preachers' handbooks and vernacular collections like the *Decameron* and *The Canterbury Tales*. The two tales included here are based upon one of the most popular medieval narrative themes, the outwitting of the powerful by an apparently weaker opponent. In the first case we see peasant cunning vanquishing the arrogance of two city-dwellers; in the second it is Nehudi the apprentice who outsmarts his master. In both cases we are given morals that are acceptable but hardly exhaust the meanings of the narratives. For one thing, the tales are placed in the context of a conversation between a wise man and his son, and so we are encouraged to ask how they comment on that relationship. For another, the interest in the stories derives not simply from their moral significance but from an unexpected twist. While we think we know how the stories are going to turn out, each one ends with a verbal cleverness we had not anticipated. In a sense, the stories outwit the reader: we expect to be instructed but are instead charmed, an effect that forces us to examine our own scale of values.

Our second selection consists of four fabliaux. The fabliau (the term derives from the Northern French word for "little fable") is a short tale in rhyming couplets that must meet one criterion above all: humor. The earliest fabliaux date from the end of the twelfth century: *The Wild Dream* is ascribed in its final lines to Jean Bodel, author of a number of other works, who died in 1210. Of the 160 or so surviving fabliaux, almost all come from the north of France; there are a few English examples, but most—like Chaucer's *Miller's Tale*—have French sources. We know the names of only a few of the authors. Most of the authors seem to have been professional minstrels, and no doubt many of the fabliaux circulated orally before being written down. Although many fabliaux end with a lesson, few actually claim to offer much moral improvement: as one poet says, fabliaux "are a great comfort to the frivolous and idle." The values the fabliaux promote are frankly hedonistic. They celebrate the pleasures of food and wine, comfortable lodgings, and—above all—sex. Many are unapologetically obscene, although it is difficult to know if medieval men and women had the same standards of verbal propriety as many modern readers. Fabliaux also celebrate specifically literary pleasures. They are written in a jaunty verse form (nicely imitated in this translation), they delight in witty rhymes and clever puns, and they often display playfully overelaborate plotting. Because of the nonaristocratic social status of most of their protagonists, and their raucous behavior, it used to be thought that the fabliaux were lower-class works. But we now know that they circulated in aristocratic circles as well, and the picture they present of the lower classes contains a strong element of the stereotype. Among the misdemeanors that the fabliaux most delight in punishing are social affectation and priestly misbehavior. But these affronts can offend members of every social class.

The Wild Dream and *The Ring That Controlled Erections* are two tales that display one of the most prominent characteristics of the fabliau, its capacity to give free rein to sexual fantasy. Yet in both cases the fantasy is located within a controlling context. In *The Wild Dream* that context is provided by the carefully detailed account of the genial domestic world of the husband and wife. The husband's good-humored acceptance of his wife's teasing, along with the wife's equally good-humored acceptance of her husband's physical limits, show how fantasy can actually serve to improve the workings of real life—a lesson that applies to the fabliau itself. *The Three Hunchbacks* is a much less cheerful story, in part because it expresses with shocking directness the medieval contempt for the deformed, in part because of the story's casual violence and complacent amoralism. Whether the price we have to pay for the story's wit is too high is a question readers will have to answer for themselves—bearing in mind, however, that this may well be the question that the fabliau means to pose. *The Butcher of Abbeville* is a good example of a number of central fabliau values: wit, as shown in the cleverness both of the protagonist and of the fabliau plot itself; realism, as in the careful rendering of the dialogue among the priest's household; hedonism, as in the butcher's loving description of the fine meal the purloined sheep will provide and his appreciation of the sexual pleasures he solicits from the household; and above all the pleasure of storytelling itself, as the narrative lovingly unfolds its deliciously inevitable denouement. It is, finally, this unabashed celebration of pleasure for its own sake that is the fabliau's greatest contribution to medieval culture.

With the final selection we return to the *exemplum,* in this case a tale found in a work called *Handling Sin,* written in the first two decades of the fourteenth century by Robert Mannyng, an English cleric. Composed in rough English couplets, the work is freely adapted from a French book called the *Manual of Sins.* As both the French and English titles imply, these works are meant to provide readers (or listeners, since Robert seems to have expected his work to have been read aloud) with information about sin. In the twelfth century, the Church had decreed that every Christian was to go to confession at least once a year: these works—and many others like them— were designed to teach the laity how to "handle sin" by teaching them what acts were sinful and the remedies, especially confession, that could be marshaled against them. In the course of his exposition of various transgressions Robert includes a large num- ber of illustrative *exempla.* The story of the dancers of Colbeck was widely known throughout Europe: Robert is correct when he says that it appears in many foreign chronicles. His source for the story is not in fact the French *Manual of Sins,* where a simpler, less interesting version appears. Instead Robert turned to a Latin saint's life written in the late eleventh century by a monk named Goscelin, a typical example of the complicated route by which these tales circulated throughout Europe. Within its context in *Handling Sin* Robert presents the story as illustrating the sin of sacrilege; he also wants his listeners to be respectful of priests. Yet he seems himself to realize that the story can hardly be contained by such a simple frame. He adds at the end that it is also about cursing, and readers will quickly see that other themes are involved. But what is most striking about the story is the contrast between its simple— even simplistic—form and its deeply mysterious content. Both dancers and priest are together caught up in an action they cannot themselves fully understand but that nonetheless reveals a complex and enigmatic purposiveness. God, we are led to believe, is the true author of this story, but exactly what is He telling us? The story's refusal to reveal its ultimate meaning leaves readers free to meditate on their own understanding of divine justice.

PETRUS ALFONSI
1062–ca. 1110

From The Scholar's Guide[1]

The Two City Dwellers and the Country Man

Once there were two city men and a country man who were going to Mecca on a pilgrimage. They ate together until they came near Mecca, where their provisions gave out, and they had nothing left but a little flour with which they could make one small loaf.

1. Translated from the Latin by J. R. Jones and J. E. Keller.

The city men, seeing this, said to each other, "We have little bread and our companion eats much; we should think how we can get his share of the bread and eat it by ourselves."

They all three agreed to the following plan: that they would make the loaf and bake it; and while it was cooking, they would go to sleep, and whoever had the most extraordinary dream should have the bread for himself. The city dwellers said this as a trick because they thought the country man was stupid enough to believe such ruses. They made the loaf, put it on the fire, and then lay down to sleep.

The country man, aware of the trick, took the half-baked loaf from the fire while his companions were sleeping, ate it, and lay down again.

One of the city dwellers, as if frightened by a dream, awoke and called to his companion. The second city dweller said, "What is the matter?"

And the first said, "I had a wonderful dream: it seemed that two angels opened the gates of heaven, took me up, and led me before God."

His companion said to him, "This dream is wonderful, but I dreamt that with two angels leading me and opening the earth, I was taken to hell."

The peasant heard all this and still pretended to be asleep; but the deceitful city men, who had already been deceived, called the country man to wake up. And he, slyly, as if he were frightened, answered, "Who is calling me?"

They said, "We, your companions."

And he said, "Have you returned already?"

And they said, "Where did we go, that we should return?"

And the rustic said, "I dreamed that two angels took one of you and opened the gates of heaven and took him before God; then two other angels took the other and opened the earth and took him to hell. When I saw these things, I thought that neither of you would ever return, and I got up and ate the bread."

The father: "So it happened, my son, that those who wanted to deceive their companion were tricked by their own ruse."

Then the son said, "It happened to them just as it says in the proverb: He who wanted all, lost all. These men resemble the dog, whose nature inclines him to take the food of the other dog. If they had imitated the camel, they would have imitated a more gentle nature. For the nature of the camel is such that when many are given feed at the same time, none of them eats until all eat at the same time. And if one is so sick that he is unable to eat, the others will not eat until it is led away. These two city men, when they decided to behave as animals, should have copied the nature of the gentlest animal. They deserved to lose their food.

"But I wish that they had been whipped, as the king's tailor was beaten through the cleverness of his pupil Nedui; I heard about it from my teacher some time ago."

The father: "Tell me, my boy, what you have heard. What happened to the pupil? Such a story should be very amusing!"

The son:

The King's Tailor's Apprentice

My teacher told me that a king had a tailor who cut different clothes for him suitable for different seasons, and the tailor had apprentices who sewed skillfully whatever the master tailor cut. Among the apprentices was one called Nedui, who was better than all his companions in the art of sewing.

Since a holiday was approaching, the king called his tailor and ordered him to prepare for him and his family expensive clothing for the occasion; and so that it could be done more quickly and without delay, he placed a eunuch, one of his chamberlains, as supervisor (for that was his task) over the men who sewed, and asked him to watch them closely and give them whatever was necessary.

One day the king's servants gave the tailor and his assistants hot bread and honey, with the other food, and those who were there began to eat.

The eunuch said to those eating, "Why do you eat when Nedui is not here and not wait for him?"

The master tailor said, "Because he would not eat honey even if he were here."

And they ate it all. Then Nedui came and said, "Why did you eat without me and not keep my share for me?"

The eunuch said to him, "Your master said that even if you were here you would not eat honey." Nedui said nothing, but he was thinking how he could get even with his master. He devised a plan, and later, the master being absent, in secrecy, he said to the eunuch:

"Sir, my master sometimes has spells of madness and loses his mind, and he beats and kills those who are near him without distinction."

The eunuch said to him, "If I knew when he was about to have a seizure, I would tie him up and whip him so that he would do nothing rash."

And Nedui said, "When you see him looking all around and feeling the floor with his hands and getting up from his seat and picking up the chair on which he is seated, then you will know that he is mad, and if you do not protect yourself and your servants, he will beat you on the head with a club."

"God bless you," said the eunuch, "I shall at once take precautions for myself and my servants."

The next day Nedui hid his master's shears, and when the master looked for his shears and did not find them, he began to feel around the floor with his hands and to look here and there and get up off his seat and to move the chair on which he was seated.

Seeing this, the eunuch immediately called his servants and ordered them to tie the tailor and beat him fiercely so that he could not beat the others.

The tailor screamed, "What harm have I done, that you torment me with this beating?"

But they, beating him more fiercely, said nothing; and when they were tired of beating him and he of being beaten they let him loose, half dead. When he came to after a long time, he asked the eunuch what crime he had committed, and the eunuch said to him:

"Nedui, your apprentice, told me that sometimes you went mad and that you did not stop until you were tied and beaten; therefore I had you tied and beaten."

The tailor, when he heard this, called Nedui and said to him, "Friend, when have you ever seen me crazy?"

The apprentice: "When have you ever seen me refuse to eat honey?"

The eunuch and the others, hearing this, laughed and judged that each one deserved the punishment he suffered.

To this the father answered: "The tailor deserved his punishment because if he had kept the precept of Moses, to love his brother as himself, this would not have happened to him."

FOUR FABLIAUX[1]

thirteenth century

The Butcher of Abbeville[2]

My lords, here's something marvelous—
you've never heard the like of this
which I am now about to tell,
so set your minds to listen well,
for words, when no one lends an ear,   5
in the end simply disappear.
   In Abbeville a butcher dwelt.
In high esteem the man was held:
he wasn't base or slanderous,
but wise, well-bred and virtuous;   10
he plied his trade with honesty
and often in adversity
helped out his neighbors who were needy;
he wasn't covetous or greedy.
   One All Saints' Day, as was his wont,   15
the butcher went to Oisemont[3]
to purchase livestock at the fair,
but all his time was wasted there:
he found the animals too pricy,
the pigs looked dangerous and feisty,   20
a wretched and degraded breed;
nothing was there that met his need,
his whole trip was to no avail,
he'd keep his cash—forget the sale!
His meager marketing now done,   25
he quickly turned his steps toward home
with cape and sword, since day was ending
and twilight soon would be descending.
Listen, and you'll hear how he fared.
Night overtook him unprepared   30
when halfway home, there in Bailleul.[4]
The day was gone, the night was full;
it was so dark, he thought he'd stay
and go no further on his way,
because he feared the many robbers   35

---

1. Translated from the French by Ned Dubin.   2. A town in northeastern France.   3. A nearby town.
4. A village between Oisement and Abbeville.

the countryside around there harbors
might steal the money he had brought.
Before the entrance to a courtyard he caught sight of a poor woman.
He asked of her, calling her to him,   40
"Say, do you know some place nearby
where for a price a man can buy
the basic comforts for his body?
I'd not intrude on anybody."
The worthy woman in reply   45
said, "Sir, by all the world's saints, my
employer here, good Master Miles,
says there's no wine around for miles,
except Father Gautier, our priest,
has two casks at the very least,   50
brought all the way from Nogentel.[5]
There's always wine there, I hear tell.
See if he'll put you up tonight."
The butcher said, "I'll go there right
away, good woman. God defend you."   55
"Sir, to His keeping I commend you."
    Before his doorstep he found seated
the deacon, who was most conceited.
The butcher greeted him and said,
"Father, as God may send you aid,   60
I ask your hospitality
in honor and in charity."
"Go seek your shelter with the Lord!
By Saint Hubert, I'll not accord
a layman lodgings for the night!   65
You'll find some other place, all right,
where you can stay somewhere in town—
just go on searching up and down
till someone offers you a bed.
I promise you, I'll not be led   70
to let you spend the night inside
this house of mine—it's occupied;
nor should a priest in any case
open his home to someone base."
"Base, father? Are you telling me   75
that you despise the laity?"
"Indeed I do, and I am right.
You've shown me disrespect and spite.
Now get off of my property!"
"What spite? It would be charity   80
for you to let me stay here, father,
for I'm not like to find another.
I spend my money willingly:
if you've something to sell to me,
I'll buy it of you, never fret,   85

5. A town some 150 miles away, known for its fine wine.

and be in your eternal debt.
I'd never dream, sir, to impose."
"You'd do as well to knock, Lord knows,
against a stone wall with your head,
by Saint Peter!" the deacon said.   90
"I won't give you a place to rest."
"The devil come and be your guest,"
the butcher said, "dishonest priest!
You are a scoundrel and a beast!"
He went away—why waste his breath?—   95
but he was smouldering with wrath.
    What happened to him? Be it known
that just as he was leaving town,
before an old abandoned shelter
with rafters fallen helter-skelter   100
he met up with a flock of ewes.
Now you will hear a piece of news!
He gave the herding-man a call,
who'd had many a cow and bull
under his care back in his youth: 105
"God give you joy, shepherd. In truth,
whose beasts are these?" "Our priest's, in faith."
"God! can this really be the case?"
Hear what the butcher did next: he
purloined a sheep so cleverly   110
the shepherd didn't see the theft;
he was so tricky and so deft
it all escaped the shepherd's eyes.
The butcher quickly takes his prize
and hoists it up onto his back   115
and takes a detour to go back,
arriving at the deacon's manse
who's so puffed up with arrogance
as he's about to close the door,
and, saddled with a sheep, once more   120
he said, "May God, who rules mankind,
be good to you, father, and kind."
The deacon bid the man the same
and promptly asked from where he came.
"From Abbeville. Today I went   125
to market down in Oisemont.
This sheep is all I found to buy,
but it looks meaty in the thigh.
Will you not let me be your guest
tonight, for I'm in need of rest?   130
I'm not a stingy man, nor cheap.
Tonight we'll cook and eat the sheep
if you would like to, 'cause I've found
it quite a load to tote around.
It's big, and it has so much meat   135
we all will have enough to eat."
The priest approves—he has intense

desire to dine at his expense.
(He loves a funeral, which brings
him in more than four christenings.) 140
"Why certainly, sir, with a will!
If there were three of you here, still
I'd house you all and you would lack
for nothing. I'm not one to slack
on honor and consideration! 145
You seem to be a man of station,
and I would like to know your name."
"Father, by God, know that I came
to be called David by baptism
when I received the oil and chrism.[6] 150
May God not smile on in the least
the man who raised so large a beast!—
I'm tired from bearing such a load.
Your hearth means rest after the road."
    They went inside then. At that late 155
hour a fire sparkled in the grate.
He put the sheep down on the ground
and turned his head and looked around
requesting someone bring an axe,
which came as soon as he had asked. 160
He killed the beast and skinned it; after
he hung the skin up from a rafter
nearby for all of them to see.
"Father," he said, "what quality!
See for yourself, for love of God, 165
what first-class meat marbled with lard—
it's even better than I thought!
I must admit that having brought
it so far hurt my neck a bit.
Now do with it as you see fit. 170
Make a roast of the shoulder quarter
and a pot full of boiling water
for stock for all the house to share
around. I think that it is fair
to say that this meat is the most 175
fine I've seen. Put it up to roast!
How tender and juicy it looks—
it will be done before the cooks
have even finished with the sauce!
I won't give orders. You're the boss, 180
good host—you've but to say the word,
so have them quickly lay the board:
it's ready! Let's wash up a bit
and have some candles brought and lit."
    Here's something now that's just for your 185
ears: the priest had a paramour
for whom he felt such jealousy

---

6. *Chrism* is oil mixed with cream, used for anointing a baptized infant.

whenever he had company
he sent her to stay in her room,
but on this night he called her to him   190
to table to join their repast
in honor of his special guest.
When they had eaten royally,
the lady made especially
for their guest's comfort a fine bed   195
with white, fresh laundered sheets and spread.
The deacon called his serving-maid:
"I order you, sister," he said,
"that Master David here, our guest,
be waited on as he likes best.   200
Let nothing at all disagree
with him—he's been good company."
The deacon went off to his room
(his lady friend, too, I assume);
the butcher remained by the fire.   205
He'd everything to his desire:
good lodgings, also bonhomie.
He called the maid: "Come here to me—
a word with you, wench. Come on over,
grant me the favors of a lover,   210
and you will get a princely gift."
"How dare you? Hush!" she answered, miffed:
"Lord! men are such ill-mannered beasts!
Hands off! and let me be in peace!
What do I know of such a sin?"   215
"In faith, I'm sure that you'll give in
when you have heard my proposition."
"Come, out with it, and I will listen."
"If you will sleep with me tonight
and give me pleasure and delight,   220
I swear to God, I'll let you keep
in payment the skin of my sheep."
"Don't even think it! Stop your noise!
I see you don't go in for boys,
by God, to ask that thing of me!   225
Your mind is full of lechery,
you're such a crazy fool, I swear!
I'd do it, but I just don't dare:
tomorrow you would tell Madame."
"I'll keep it secret like a clam,   230
God bless my soul! I'd never use you,
then turn around, dear, and accuse you."
So she agreed to do his whim
and promptly gave herself to him.
    She lay with him until day broke.   235
She lit the fire when she awoke,
then did her chores and milked the cow.
The deacon, too, has woken now.
He leaves for church, where at the altar

This terra-cotta fragment dating from the fifteenth century B.C.E. represents a portion of the Babylonian epic of *Gilgamesh*. Many such tablets have been discovered in modern-day Turkey, Syria, Israel (where this particular fragment was discovered), and—not surprisingly—Iraq, where the epic originated. The cuneiform (wedge-shaped) markings on the surface of this tablet were made by pressing the edge of a reed stylus into the soft clay in different combinations and at different angles. The clay tablet was then baked in order to harden the surface and preserve the markings.

Cuneiform writing first appeared as simple pictograms that were used by the ancient Sumerians for business and administrative records. These pictograms were later transformed into an ideographic (and, even later, a syllabic) writing system by the Babylonians, Assyrians, and Persians, and employed to record a wide variety of literary texts in several languages, and in stone as well as clay tablets.

The so-called Mask of Agamemnon was discovered by the German archaeologist Heinrich Schliemann (1822–1890) in one of the royal shaft graves at Mycenae in the northern Peloponnesus of Greece. The site of a great palace complex excavated by Schliemann after his excavation at Hissarlik (Troy) in Turkey, Mycenae was, according to Homer, the stronghold of Agamemnon. Schliemann believed that the grave from which this funeral mask was taken contained the remains (and the buried treasure) of Agamemnon, Cassandra, and his companions, killed at a banquet on their return from Troy by Clytemnestra and her lover, Aegisthus. The mask is now believed to be the likeness of an Achaean king from the sixteenth century B.C.E.—much earlier than the assumed era of the Trojan War.

A common feature of male aristocratic social life in fifth-century Athens was the symposium—a gathering of upper-class men that centered on drinking and conversation, often supplemented by music, games, and sexual activity. Many aspects of the symposia were informal, but there was a ritualized set of expectations about what would occur at these gatherings, and the objects involved in preparing and serving the wine give some evidence of the cultural seriousness of the occasion. Each of the vases pictured here may have played some role in a symposium: an amphora [1] was a large vessel used to store olive oil, honey, or wine; a krater [2] was the vessel in which the wine would be mixed with water (the Greeks drank their wine diluted); and a kylix [3] was a broad, flat cup from which the wine would be drunk (this picture is a detail of the bottom inside of the kylix).

These common objects are also masterpieces of classical Greek art—exceptionally beautiful examples of "black figure" and "red figure" vase painting. The first [1] (by Exekias, the most celebrated black-figure painter whose work is known to us) features a

[1]

scene of Achilles (left) and Ajax (right) taking a break from battle to play a game. The other two (by artists known only through their work) feature, respectively, [2] Orestes at Delphi (by the Eumenides Painter) being purified of the murder of his mother, Clytemnestra, by the blood of a young pig (held above his head in the painting), and [3] Oedipus pondering the Sphinx's riddle (by the Oedipus Painter). Painted pottery was created by Greeks in various countries, and elite Greek men everywhere attended symposia. These scenes would be familiar to any Athenian, literate or not, and would reassure the participants in the symposia that their gathering had a foundation in, and a connection to, their culture's heroic past.

[2]

[3]

The theater of the sanctuary of Asklepios in Epidaurus, Greece, is the finest surviving example of ancient Greek theatrical architecture. Built in two stages from the fourth through the second centuries B.C.E., the theater was partially restored in the 1950s and 1960s to accommodate theatrical performances. Despite its size (it can seat nearly twelve thousand spectators), the theater's acoustics are exceptional: performers' voices are audible from the furthest reaches of the cavea (the seating area), even when the performers are speaking in a whisper.

Behind the round orchestra (stage area) are remnants of a number of structures that were not restored in the twentieth century, including the skene, a small building that served as a backdrop to the play's action. Scenery would have included movable screens for backdrops, a wheeled wooden platform to provide "interior" scenes, and a crane to bring in the gods from heaven.

This fresco portrait of a Roman husband and wife was removed from the atrium of a house in Pompeii—a city that was completely buried (and remarkably well preserved) by ash from an eruption of Mt. Vesuvius in 79 c.e. Excavations of Pompeii have been ongoing since the eighteenth century, and the archaeological project continues to yield intriguing glimpses into the everyday lives of first-century Romans.

This double portrait of a Pompeiian couple is an excellent example of the realistic strand in Roman art. In sharp contrast to the idealized aesthetics of classical Greek art, these sensitive likenesses depict a particular man and woman (probably the attorney Terentius Neo and his wife), together with conventionalized attributes of their daily life: a scroll (perhaps a marriage contract) for the husband, and wax tablets and a stylus for the wife (possibly household notes). The individualized features of the two sitters, from the man's slight beard and wrinkled brow to the woman's finely detailed coiffure, are evidence of a desire to pass on a realistic representation of their appearance and symbols of their social roles.

Although the Roman Empire suffered severe decline during much of the third century C.E. (a fifty-year civil war ravaged the economy, and the lack of stable political succession left the frontiers of the empire open to attack), two figures—Diocletian and Constantine ("the Great")—rescued the empire from chaos and reorganized it in ways that allowed it to survive in a different form for several centuries more. Constantine emerged as ruler of a reunited empire in 324, after a nearly twenty-year struggle for power that followed Diocletian's abdication in 305. In 330, the new emperor built a capital city for the empire in Byzantium and renamed it Constantinople ("city of Constantine").

Constantine is remembered partly for his favorable treatment of the newly emerging Christian religion. In 313, when he was sharing power with a rival, he issued the Edict of Milan, essentially ending official persecution of Christians. By the time of the Council of Nicea, convened in 325 to resolve a doctrinal dispute, Christianity was the official religion of the empire. Constantine was himself baptized into the faith on his deathbed in 337.

The massive marble fragments pictured above were part of a thirty-foot-tall seated statue that once dominated the main interior of Constantine's huge administrative building, the Basilica Nova in Rome (since destroyed). The gigantic head alone stands eight and a half feet tall and weighs approximately

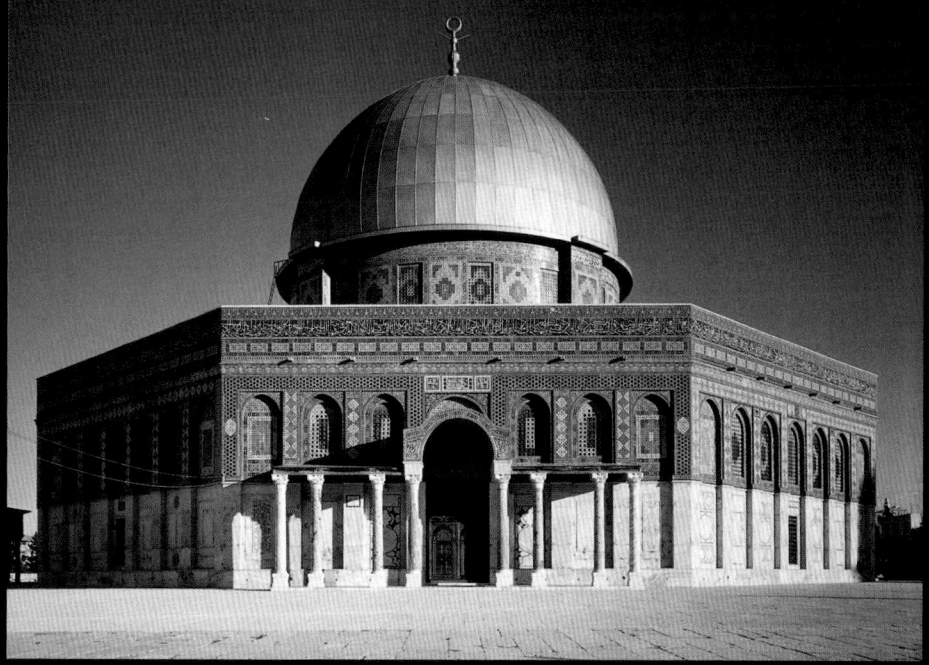

After Muhammad's death in 632, the tribes of Arabia, only recently united and inspired by the faith of Islam, conquered the Persian and Byzantine empires to the east and west of them, radically altering the history of the world in the process. Within a century the Islamic Empire stretched from southern Spain to northern India and from the Caucasus to the Indian Ocean.

The Mosque of Umar in Jerusalem, more commonly known as the Dome of the Rock, is the first great architectural monument to the remarkable early triumph of Islam. Originally constructed by the Umayyad dynasty of caliphs between 687 and 692, this octagonal mosque was built atop the rock that Muslims believe was the site of Muhammad's ascension (mi'raj) to heaven and his return to earth. The mosque's significance as a marker of Islamic imperial success is underscored by the fact that the site is revered by Jews as the traditional site of Adam's burial and Abraham's near-sacrifice of Isaac, as well as the former site of the Temple of Solomon, which the Romans demolished in 70 C.E. The overall structure of the Dome of the Rock bears little resemblance to the distinctly Islamic architecture that would follow over the centuries, but the use of calligraphy and the abstract geometric designs in tile mosaics (all of which were added during subsequent restorations) are typical features of Islamic architectural decoration and help distinguish it from its Greek, Roman, and Byzantine predecessors.

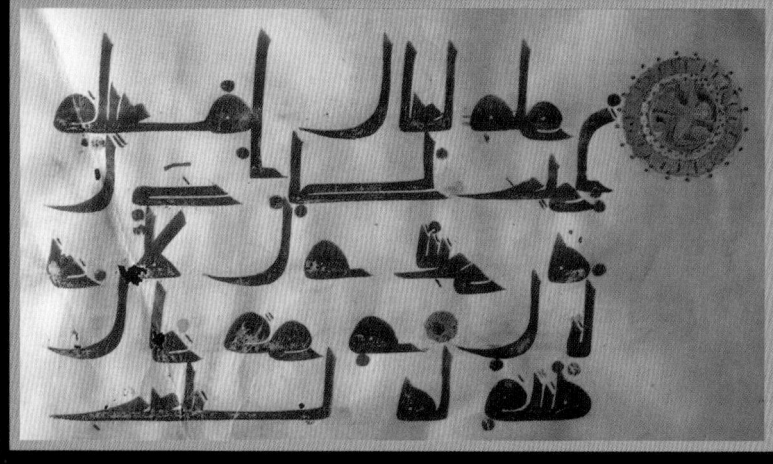

[1]

Islam established Arabic as the dominant language of religion, trade, and learning throughout the vast Islamic Empire. Obviously, the most important Arabic text is the Koran—the worldly replica of divine wisdom that Muslims believe exists in paradise, engraved in gold (in Arabic) on marble tablets. The page from the Koran above [1] is rendered in kufic script, a style that originated in Hirah in Iraq before the time of Muhammad and was widely used in the first centuries of the Islamic era. It contributed its name to the city of Kufa, where it was first adopted as the official script.

Arabic also became the language of all branches of scientific knowledge and the vehicle through which many Greek texts were preserved. The page below [2] is taken from an early Arabic translation of the major pharmacological treatise of the late-classical world: Dioscorides' *De Materia Medica*, a five-volume encyclopedia of approximately six hundred plants and one thousand medications that we know in part only through its Arabic translations. Dioscorides' work stimulated the study of medicine and medicinal plants within Islam. Between 900 and 1250 Islamic scientists made many significant contributions to medicine. *The Canon of Medicine* by Avicenna (in Arabic, Ibn Sina, 980–1037), for instance, was translated into Latin in the thirteenth century and remained a standard medical text in European universities until the late 1600s.

[2]

[1]

In 1939, a burial mound in Suffolk, England, was excavated to reveal a treasure-laden oak ship nearly one hundred feet long. The Sutton Hoo treasure is believed to be a burial tribute to the East Anglian king Raedwald (who died in 625 C.E.). Raedwald was apparently baptized into the Christian faith during his adulthood (an interesting though debatable clue to his conversion is the presence of two spoons among the burial treasures that are inscribed respectively with "Saulus" and "Paulus"—the names of Saint Paul before and after his own conversion), but the mere fact that this burial mound exists means that he partially or completely abandoned the faith by the time of his death.

The parallels between the burial mound at Sutton Hoo and the Anglo-Saxon burial traditions recounted in *Beowulf* (for instance, the burial of Shield at sea [lines 26–52] and the creation of a burial mound in tribute to the slain Beowulf [lines 3156–3183]) have been noted by scholars ever since the discovery of the treasure. The two objects pictured here—an iron helmet with decorative bronze panels [1] and the gold, glass, and enamel cloisonné purse cover [2]—are intended to mark the buried king's military prowess, statesmanship, wealth, and status.

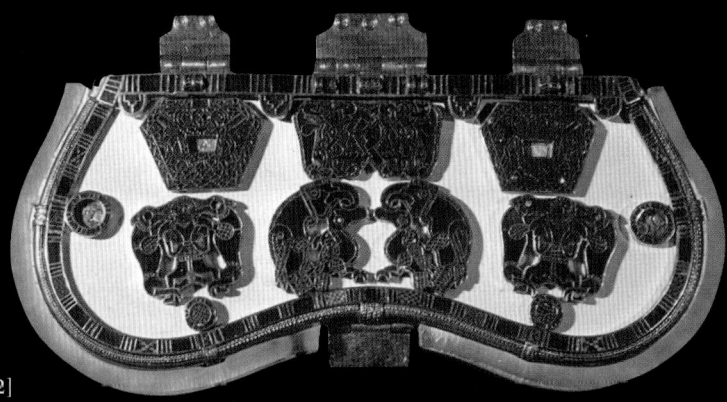

[2]

The European Middle Ages saw the development of a technology (and cultural object) that today we take for granted: the ████ book. For most of the period, the mode of book production was slow and painstaking since each copy of any one text had to be rendered by hand by a scribe (the mechanical process of printing wouldn't arise until 1455 with Gutenberg's Bible), and most books were religious in nature, produced to accompany the devotions of the wealthy and the powerful. Inspired by religious feeling and the luxurious tastes of the ultimate recipients of the books, monastic scribes devoted considerable energy and talent to surrounding the religious texts with didactic and sumptuous illustrations.

By the late thirteenth century, illuminated manuscripts of secular texts were quite common. In addition to classical texts, homegrown literary treasures written in vernacular languages, such as Dante's *Inferno* [1] and Chaucer's *Canterbury Tales* [2], received lush treatment. The illustration above from a fourteenth-century manuscript of *Inferno* shows Dante (on the far left) and Virgil talking with two plague-stricken "Falsifiers"—Griffolino and Cappochio—in the eighth circle of hell (canto XXIX, lines 73–139). The second image is a detail of the opening page of the Wife of Bath's tale from the Ellesmere manuscript of the *Canterbury Tales*. The Ellesmere manuscript, produced very soon after Chaucer's death (ca. 1410), is lavishly illuminated throughout, offering not only individual illustrations of the various pilgrims (all of them, like the Wife of Bath here, on horseback), but also the first known portrait of Chaucer himself.

[1]

[2]

Like his near-contemporary Desiderius Erasmus (author of *The Praise of Folly*), Hieronymus Bosch used parody to reveal human foibles and to critique medieval practices and beliefs that were giving way to a new sense of human potential, later called "the Renaissance."

In this painting, *The Cure of Folly* (also *Cutting the Stone*) (1475–80), Bosch shows an unlucky man (apparently suffering from mental illness) undergoing a trephining procedure to remove "the stone of madness" from his skull. What emerges instead is a small flower—a twin to another flower already lying on the table, perhaps the result of an earlier excision. The scene is generally taken as a satire on medieval medical practice: the quack doctor has an inverted funnel on his head, the hapless patient has tucked his shoes neatly under the chair, and the nun with a book on her head (possibly Saint Sophia, representing wisdom) stares into the distance, ignoring the whole operation. The painting is both amusing and enigmatic, a collection of puzzling images and allusions, and a comic suggestion that the surgery itself is a mistake. The ornamental Gothic calligraphy framing the scene spells out, in letters of gold, a suggestion that the patient has already had one valuable asset removed: "Master, cut out the stone. My name is Gelded Badger."

Although the literary monuments of the European Renaissance sprung from all corners of Western Europe, the major achievements of the visual arts were more concentrated. In particular, the period that art historians have called the High Renaissance and that is associated with the northern cities of Italy (Florence, Milan, and Rome) is credited primarily to four artists (Leonardo da Vinci, Michelangelo, Raphael, and Titian) and is generally limited to the thirty years between 1495 and 1525.

Raphael, while less innovative than Leonardo and less brilliantly tempestuous than Michelangelo, created a visual style that synthesized the best qualities from the work of both of his elders, work that is recognizable to us today as distinctly representative of Renaissance art. The painting above—*Madonna of the Meadow* (1505)—perfectly illustrates the way that Renaissance artists were able to endow religious subjects with down-to-earth realism (here, a mother watching children at play) and also convey an appreciation for sensuous beauty. The domestic scene—and especially Mary, strikingly beautiful and flowingly posed—might just as easily distract believers from devotional thoughts as inspire them.

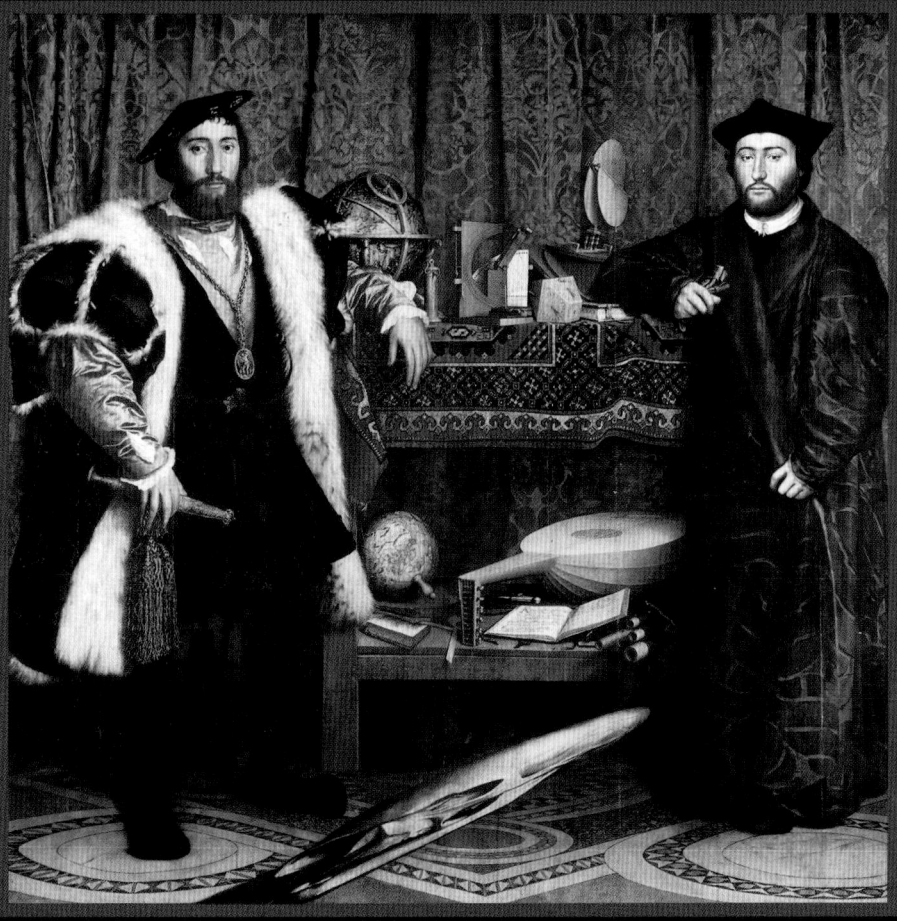

A central assumption underlying Renaissance thought was a strongly affirmed awareness of the intellectual and physical "virtues" of the human being and the worthiness of human accomplishments: in brief, the concept of humanism. Rejecting the medieval emphasis on religious topics and perspectives, Renaissance artists, thinkers, and writers asserted throughout their work that there are certain earthly actions highly worth doing, and that by choosing and accomplishing these actions, humanity proves its special dignity. Looming behind this profound delight in earthly achievements, however, was also a nagging doubt about their ultimate purpose and a constant awareness of human mortality. The resulting attitude, which has been called "Renaissance melancholy," underlay much of Renaissance art and literature.

The Ambassadors (1533) by the Flemish artist Hans Holbein the Younger is a double portrait of the French ambassadors to England during the reign of Henry VIII. Their expression and posture convey an easy confidence in their status and character while their clothing and the objects around them suggest their worldliness as well as their interest in science, religion, art, and music. Lurking at their feet, however, is a strange object that, when viewed at an angle from the lower left, reveals itself to be a human skull.

The French "discovered" Italy in the mid-fifteenth century, both through travel
and through military invasions. Under Francis I (who ruled from 1515 to 1547),
France laid claim to territories in northern Spain, the Netherlands, and Italy, gaining a secure toehold in Milan. In an attempt to glorify himself and his country,
Francis invited some of the most accomplished Italian artists and architects to his
court, including Leonardo da Vinci, Andrea del Sarto, and Rosso Fiorentino, who
became an official court painter in 1530.

The Chateau de Chambord, pictured above, is the largest of the chateaux built
in France's Loire valley and is a treasure of northern Renaissance architecture.
Although the architect is unknown, apocryphal tales connecting Leonardo to its
early design (especially to the design of its spectacular double spiral staircase)
underscore the chateau's debt to Italian architectural ideas, at least in its three
lower levels. The cylindrical towers above the third level are distinctly French.
Work began on Chambord in 1519 but was halted from 1525 through 1526
because of Francis's capture by the Spanish at the battle of Pavia and the subsequent (financially ruinous) ransom that was negotiated by his sister, Marguerite de
Navarre. Although Francis loved the building, he didn't live to see it completed;
the finishing touches weren't made until 150 years later, during Louis XIV's reign.
Despite its magnificence, the chateau was difficult to heat and maintain, and the
king visited it chiefly during summer. Molière presented performances of his plays
at Chambord for Louis XIV.

Born in Crete and trained in Venice, El Greco ("the Greek") is associated with the spirit and character of sixteenth-century Spain, his home from 1577 until his death in 1614. He was especially attuned to the fervent religiosity of his adopted countrymen, producing emotionally vivid pictures for Catholic patrons and the Church itself.

El Greco was a contemporary of Miguel de Cervantes, whose novel, *Don Quixote,* takes a parodic stab at both the image of the Spanish nobleman and the long literary tradition of the chivalric romance. The portrait above, in contrast, is an earnest attempt to capture the appearance and character of a real, not imagined, sixteenth-century Spanish nobleman on the occasion of his knighthood. Pictured here is Don Juan de Silva, Notary Mayor of Toledo, in the late 1570s, in a pose and manner that clearly signals his piety, relative austerity, and moral seriousness.

Astronomicum Cæsareum:

Historicus, diuina gerens, sophiǽq́ perit°,
    Hic sua cognoscet, si bona nosse volet.
Namq́ vetustatis miratot tempora rebus
    Distribuet, verè dum canet historias.
Ipse sacri præses no̅ res æquare diebus

Discet, & hinc serie festa locare sua,
    Ipseq́ naturæ rimator mira cometæ
    Percipiet, nulli dicta vel acta prius,
Sed caueant animis adsint liuore perustis,
    Hæc etenim labes cernere vera neg̅t̅

Published in the same year (1540) in which Copernicus announced his theory that the Earth revolves around the Sun, this book (*Astronomicum Caesareum*, "The Emperor's Astronomy") colorfully illuminated the principles of the longstanding Ptolemaic worldview, a philosophy of the cosmos that placed Earth (and by extension, human beings) at the center of the known universe. Copernicus's ideas would eventually replace those articulated in the *Astronomicum*, but his heliocentric (sun-centered) worldview was met initially by tremendous opposition because it directly contradicted both religious and humanist beliefs of the time.

he and his cleric sing the psalter,   240
and lets his concubine sleep late.
David the butcher doesn't wait
now that it's morning and time presses,
but quickly grabs his shoes and dresses;
to the room where his hostess lies   245
he now goes to say his goodbyes,
draws back the latch, opens the door.
To see her guest standing before
her bed when she opens her eyes,
the lovely lady shows surprise   250
and can't imagine to what ends
he's come there and what he intends.
"Let me express my gratitude,
lady," he says. "Nobody could
have shown more hospitality   255
and gracious generosity."
Having said this, he draws up closer
and lays his head down on the bolster,
pulls back the sheet and catches sight
of her breasts, beautiful and white.   260
"My God!" he says, "now here's a wonder!
Sweet blessed Virgin! Yes, by thunder,
this deacon really has it good
to lie with such a lady nude!
So help me Saint Honorius,[7]   265
a king would be content with less!
If it were given to me to
lie here at night in bed with you,
I'd be contented and made whole!"
"David, it's wrong, upon my soul,   270
for you to say the things you say!
Now leave me! Get your hands away!
My man won't be in church that long;
he'd think we'd done him grievous wrong
if he came in the room and saw.   275
He wouldn't love me anymore,
thanks to you. It would cost me dear."
He does his best to calm her fear:
"Lady," he tells her, "I will not,
for love of God, move from this spot   280
for any man alive. The same
holds for the deacon: if he came
and uttered so much as a word,
however prideful and absurd,
in protest like some uncouth villain,   285
I wouldn't hesitate to kill him.
But if you'll satisfy my wish,
sweet lady, I will make you rich:
that first-rate sheepskin will be yours."

---

7. Bishop of Amiens, a nearby city, in the 6th century.

"But what will people say?—because   290
I think that you're so indiscreet
you'll brag about it in the street."
"Will you not trust me when I've promised
that while I live I will be honest?
No one will know, woman or man,   295
by the saints in the Vatican."
He goes on urging and insists
until no longer she resists
and lets the butcher at his pleasure
enjoy her favors in full measure.   300
    After, he left,—why hang around?—
went to the church, and there he found
the priest, who had begun the readings
and never halted the proceedings.
Right at the *Jube Domine*[8]   305
the butcher came to him to say,
"Let me express my gratitude
for housing me; nobody could
have done so more hospitably,
but I would ask you to agree   310
to do something for me and buy
the skin of that fine sheep which I
brought you, for it would ease my road.
The wool must be a three-pound load
and first-rate. I'll sell it to you,   315
though it's worth three, for only two
shillings, and be grateful to boot."
"Most welcome guest, for you I'll do 't
gladly, if it's expedient.
Your company is excellent;   320
come back and visit frequently."
He sells him his own skin, then he
bids him farewell, and off he goes.
    The deacon's lady friend arose,
who was so lovely and flirtatious;   325
her bluish-gray eyes were vivacious;
she chose to wear a bright green gown
with deep and large pleats hanging down
and tucked in tightly at the waist
(such vanity suited her taste);   330
she was, in short, coquette and fair.
She went and sat down in a chair,
whereon without delay the maid
approached the skin and would have laid
her hands on it, had not her mistress   335
forbid her, saying, "Now what business
do you have with that sheepskin there?"
"Lady, I think that's my affair.

---

8. The beginning of a Latin phrase—"Father, do you wish to bless me?"—that the clerk directs to the priest before reading the lesson.

I mean to hang it up outside
in the bright sunshine till it's dried."   340
"Oh no, you won't! You do your chores
and leave it hanging here indoors.
It's not disturbing anyone."
"But mistress, all my chores are done.
I got up earlier than you."   345
"I bet!" "Well, anyway, it's true,
while you slept late, so hold your peace."
"Be off! and don't dare touch that fleece!
Don't you so much as lay a hand
or fiddle with it—understand?"   350
"In God's name, lady, and why not?
I'll fiddle with it a whole lot.
I may, since it belongs to me."
"You say the skin's your property?"
"Indeed I do." "Oh, is that so?   355
You put that sheepskin down and go
hang yourself! Drown in a latrine!
I'm livid! Who has ever seen
a servant try to be so bossy?
You two-faced, stinking, brazen hussy!   360
Get out! Don't dare darken my door!"
"What do you carry on so for,
and why insult me for what's mine?
So what if you'd swear on divine
relics?—it's mine beyond a doubt."   365
"Get out before I throw you out!
Your service here is terminated!
You're shameless and you're self-inflated!
The priest himself may contradict it,
but all the same you are evicted,   370
you fill me with such strong dislike!"
"I'm going,—may the black plague strike
who works for you a single day!—
but till the master comes I'll stay.
I mean to let him know completely,   375
in every detail, how you treat me."
"How *I* treat *you*? What cheek! You blasted
immoral bitch! You trull! You bastard!"
"Me? bastard? If you say so, that's
because the deacon sired your brats,   380
no doubt, in a more legal fashion?"
"Put down my sheepskin, by God's passion,
or you'll come to a sorry pass!
You'll wish that you were in Arras,[9]
or even in Cologne, by God!"   385
And then the woman struck her hard
using her distaff. The maid shouted,
"That skin will cost you, never doubt it!

9. A town about forty miles away.

My Saint Marie's pure reputation,
you hit me without provocation! 390
Although it kill me, you shall pay!"
She burst in tears and wailed away.
    Amid the ruckus and the fight
the priest returned and said, "All right,
who struck you? What's this argument?" 395
"My mistress, but I'm innocent!"
"She had some cause, and you know why,
so let me hear it, and don't lie."
"Indeed, sir, it was for the hide
that's hanging there by the fireside. 400
Remember, master, how you said
last evening when you went to bed
that I should do my level best
to entertain David, our guest?
I did as you commanded; he 405
in gratitude presented me
the sheepskin, and, by all that's holy,
I swear to you I earned it fully."
The deacon heard her and deduced
from what she said, she'd been seduced 410
and their guest had given his word
to make the sheepskin her reward.
It raised the hackles on his back,
but still he kept his true thoughts back
and said, "Now, lady, by our Savior, 415
I don't approve of your behavior.
You flaunt me and make a disturbance
and beat up on my household servants."
"What? Just because she wants our fleece?
I'm sure if you knew but a piece 420
of the shame she heaped on my head,
you'd pay her back for what she said.
The things she said about your children!
What kind of man are you, who're willing
to permit me to be the butt 425
of insults for this foul-mouthed slut?
Whatever else you may decide,
I will not let her have my hide.
I say the sheepskin isn't hers."
"Whose is it then?" "Why, mine, of course." 430
"It's yours?" "Why, yes." "Why should that be?"
"We showed him hospitality,
we gave him covers, sheets, a roof—
I'd think that was sufficient proof,
yet here I stand interrogated!" 435
"Dear lady, say, is what you've stated
true, by your promised honesty
when you first came to live with me?
Are you the owner of the pelt?"
"Saint Peter, yes! You heard me tell 't!" 440

Just then the serving-maid broke in:
"It was to me he gave the skin!
She's handing you a pack of lies!"
"Whore! what foul stars were in the skies
when you were born? He had his way   445
with you! Clear out of here today!
For shame! to boast of it aloud!"
The priest said, "By the sacred shroud
of Compiègne,¹ control yourself!
"I hate her more than death itself!   450
When she speaks there is no believing
her, and I've caught the baggage thieving!"
"What did I ever take from you?"
"My oats, my wheat, my barley, too,
my peas, my lard, my fresh-baked loaves!   455
How can you treat her with kid gloves
and let her so get on our nerves,
sir. Let her have what she deserves!
For God's sake, get rid of this menace!"
"Lady," he answered, "by Saint Dennis,²   460
listen to me. I want to know
to which of you the skin should go.
Now tell me who made you this gift."
"Our guest did, right before he left."
"How so?—for, by Saint Martin's maw,   465
this morning he got up before
the sun had risen in the sky!"
"How blasphemous! I can't think why
you need to swear with such élan.
When it was time to go the man   470
took fitting leave and was well-bred."
"He saw you getting out of bed?"
"No way!" "Then when?" "I was reposing
and scarcely noticed in my dozing
when he came up to me. I fail   475
to see the need for such detail."
"With what words did he bid farewell?"
"You're out to trap me, I can tell!
He said: 'Lady, farewell. God bless!'
That's all he did or said—no less,   480
no more,—and so he took his leave.
He asked for nothing, I believe,
to cause you any harm or shame,
and now you're seeking to place blame!
You never did believe in me,   485
and yet there's nothing there to see
except great virtue, God be praised!,
still you accuse me as if crazed
and anger me in such a fashion

---

1. A town about eighty miles away, which claimed to possess the shroud in which Jesus had been wrapped after his death.   2. The patron saint of France.

my flesh turns colors out of passion."   490
"Aha!" he cries, "deceitful shrew!
I went too far in coddling you!
I'll have you thrashed! I'll see you dead!
I know you fucked with him in bed!
You could have cried out—tell me why   495
you had to break our sacred tie?
I cast you out! Get out of here!
On the church altar I will swear
no more to lie beside you naked
in bed. You are repudiated!"   500
    The priest sat, overcome with choler,
sorrow, despondency and dolor.
On seeing him so irritated,
the lady heartily regretted
she'd been so headstrong and perverse   505
and, fearing he might yet do worse,
went to her room. Right then in sallied
the shepherd, who, it seems, had tallied
all of his sheep, and the count proved
that one of them had been removed.   510
He'd no idea what had become
of his sheep, and came at a run
to the priest's house, scratching his crotch.
The priest sat, taken down a notch,
angry and fuming, at his bible.   515
"The devil take you! What's the trouble,
you no good bum? What brings you here?
What's with this frown from ear to ear,
son of a bitch? You hick! You creep!
You should be out watching your sheep!   520
I ought to give you a good shaking."
"But one of your sheep has been taken,
master, the best of all the herd!
I can't think how or what occurred."
"So, now you've gone and lost a sheep—   525
that shows what kind of watch you keep!
You should be hanged or thrown in prison!"
The shepherd answered, "Master, listen!
Late in the evening yesterday
I met a stranger on the way   530
back into town, whom I had never
seen in the fields or road, wherever,
who eyed my flock most carefully
and made a point of asking me
who owned such admirable beasts,   535
and I said, 'Sir, they are our priest's.'
He, I imagine, was the thief."
"David, by my Christian belief!
Our guest last night!" exclaimed the priest.
"I've been outsmarted! I've been fleeced!   540
He's fucked all of the women in

my house and sold me my own skin!
He's wiped my nose on my own sleeve!
I must be a born fool to live
so long and still be caught off guard.   545
You're always learning, if you're smart.
With my own crust he bakes me pies!
The sheepskin, would you recognize
it?" "Master, what? If I've a chance
to look, I'll know it at a glance.   550
For seven years I've had that flock."
He takes the hide and has a look;
the ears and head identified
the sheep that had supplied the hide.
"Aha! Master," exclaimed the bilious   555
shepherd, "by God, why that's Cornelius,
my most favorite animal
and much the gentlest of them all!
By Saint Vincent,[3] whose faith I keep,
you couldn't find a fatter sheep,   560
and I know well of what I'm speaking."
"You come here, lady," said the deacon,
"and state your case, I order you;
and you, our servant, come here too
and speak, for I'll not be denied.   565
What claim do you have on the hide?"
"I swear that as I love you, sire,
it's mine alone, whole and entire."
"And you, fair lady, what's your claim?"
"Sir, God forgive me, all the same,   570
it should be mine, and for good cause."
"It will be neither hers nor yours.
I paid good money for the fleece
and mean to keep the entire piece.
He asked I buy it at the altar   575
when I was reading from my psalter,
so, by God's true apostle Peter,
it won't be yours, no, nor hers either
unless a magistrate decides!"
   To you, my lords, who all are wise,   580
I, Eustace d'Amiens[4] submit
their case that you may settle it,
and ask you with due courtesy
to render judgment loyally.
Each one of you will speak his piece: 585
which of the three should have the fleece—
the deacon or his deaconess
or their maid (bless her sauciness).

3. A third-century deacon, reputedly tortured to death for his faith.   4. Nothing is known of Eustace except that he came from Amiens, a city near Abbeville.

The Three Hunchbacks

My lords, if you have time to spare,
though but a moment, you may hear
a little fabliau I wrote
in rhyme, based on an anecdote,
and not one word of it's a lie.   5
    In a walled town in days gone by
(but I've forgotten the town's name—
let's say Douay;[1] it's all the same)
there dwelt a worthy citizen
of decent means, the best of men,   10
who among his good friends could count
the foremost tradespeople around,
and, though he did not have great wealth,
who was respected for himself
and his good sense by all the city.   15
He had a daughter. She was pretty;
so pretty, she was a delight.
If I were to describe her right,
I doubt that Nature ever made
a creature fairer than this maid,   20
but I do not intend to dwell
on how she looked or try to tell
her beauty, because I'm afraid
you'd just discredit what I said,
so better leave the matter be   25
than understate reality.
    In that same town, not far from them,
a hunchback lived, a ruffian,
whose head was his outstanding feature.
Nature, I think, who made this creature,   30
struggled immensely when she formed
him—nothing else was so deformed
and hideous beyond compare:
he'd a large head and shaggy hair,
a short neck and, as huge as boulders,   35
set too high up, enormous shoulders.
The man who'd foolishly detail
his ugliness is bound to fail.
His vicious way of life accorded
with how he looked, because he hoarded   40
all of his life to pile up gain.
To tell you truly and speak plain,
this hunchback was richer than Croesus[2]—
unless report of him deceives us,
none in town had more wealth than he.   45
What can I say? From A to Z,
that's how the hunchback's life was led.

---

1. A town located in northeastern France.   2. A mythological king of immense wealth.

Because of all the wealth he had,
his friends arranged to wed the lout
to the fair maid I told about,   50
but from the moment they were wed
he couldn't get out of his head
the beauty which she was endowed
with, and his jealousy allowed
him not a second of respite.   55
He always kept his doors shut tight
and let nobody in his home
who hadn't come there for a loan
or else had money to repay.
   Thus he sat keeping watch all day,   60
till once on Christmas there came three
strolling players, humpbacked as he,
where he was standing by the door
and said that they'd like nothing more
than to observe the holiday   65
with him—since he's humpbacked as they
and in the town there's no one else
as much like them as he himself,
they'd not do better anywheres.
He led the three of them upstairs   70
(for his house had a second floor),
where a repast was ready for
them all, and they sat down to dine.
Their meal was copious and fine,
to tell the truth, for this time he   75
was neither tight nor niggardly,
but offered his guests to partake in
a capon roast and peas with bacon,
and, when at length dinner was done,
distributed to every one   80
of the three hunchback minstrels plenty
of Paris pennies (I think, twenty).
Last of all, he forbade the men
that they ever appear again
inside his house or in his yard—   85
if caught there, then things would go hard:
they'd have a bath to make them shiver
in the cold water of the river.
(His house was set on the canal,
and it was wide, and deep as well).   90
The hunchbacks listened to their host
and left his house directly, most
willingly, in a festive mood,
because that day had been a good
one for them, of that they'd no doubt;   95
and then their host also went out
to the bridge and took up his station.
   His wife, who'd heard the celebration
and how the hunchbacks sang and played,

sent for them to come back and bade   100
them sing for her delight,
and had the household doors shut tight.
Now, while the hunchbacks sang their air
and entertained the lady there,
her husband, who had not been gone   105
too long, came back home thereupon.
He called in a commanding voice
from the door; when she heard the noise,
she recognized him in a wink.
For all the world she couldn't think   110
of any place where she could hide
the hunchbacks she had asked inside.
There was a bed beside the hearth
they used to carry back and forth
with three drawers built inside of it.   115
What can I say? Here's what she did:
she put one hunchback in each drawer
and let her husband in the door,
who went and sat by her since he
took pleasure in her company,   120
but not for too long did he stay
before he rose and went away,
climbed back downstairs and left the house.
It didn't incommode his spouse
her husband didn't hang about;   125
she wished to get the hunchbacks out,
the three she'd hidden in the drawers.
She had an awful shock, because,
when she had opened up the bed
and looked inside, she found them dead.   130
    When she saw all three had expired,
she ran to the door and required
a passing porter she waylaid
in God's name to come to her aid.
The young man, when he heard her call,   135
came running, didn't wait at all.
"My friend," she said, "I have a question.
Say, can I count on your discretion
and promise not to inculpate
me in the matter I'll relate?   140
I'll see to it it's worth your while,
for when you've done my errand I'll
reward you thirty pounds in cash."
The porter heard and in a flash
agreed to get her business done—he   145
wasn't a man to turn down money,
and so the job was to his taste.
He followed her upstairs in haste.
She opened one drawer in the bed;
"No need to be afraid," she said.   150

"Just dump this corpse in the canal
and I will say you've served me well."
She gave him a sack; in a minute
he'd packed away the hunchback in it,
and then he lifted up the sack,   155
went downstairs with it on his back,
ran straight down to the river's edge
and up onto the highest bridge
and tossed the hunchback in the drink.
Before you'd have had time to blink   160
he set off back home on the double.
The lady, with no end of trouble,
had taken out one hunchback more.
Lifting him up was quite a chore,
and, out of breath from her endeavor,   165
she drew aside from the cadaver.
The porter came back much elated:
"It's time that I were compensated,
lady. I got rid of your dwarf."
"What kind of joke would you pull off,   170
mister?" she said. "You dunce! you bounder!
The hunchback's back; he's still around here.
I don't think that you ever threw
him in. You brought him back with you.
If you don't trust me, look and see!"   175
"How in the name of Hell could he
have ever come back here, by thunder?
It baffles me, I'm filled with wonder.
Why, he was dead! I'd be surprised
if he were not the Antichrist!   180
I swear that it won't help him any!"
He grabbed the second hunchback, then he
shoved him into the sack and lifted
it on his shoulders, then he shifted
the weight for comfort and set out,   185
whereon the woman turned about,
opened the third drawer and drew forth
the hunchback, laid him by the hearth
and waited at the door. The porter
emptied the sack into the water,   190
letting the hunchback fall head first,
and told him, "May you be accursed
if you come back to me! Now go!"
and hurried back. He wasn't slow
to ask the lady for his fee,   195
which she accorded readily
and told him he would be well paid.
Then back to the fireplace she led
him, as if she were not aware
the third hunchback was lying there.   200
"What's this?" she said. "As God may strike

me dead, who's ever heard the like
of this? See where our hunchback's lying!"
The long-suffering porter, spying
him by the fire, was not amused   205
and cried, "Christ! Will my day be used
up lugging this damned dwarf around?
God's carcass! Was there ever found
a more persistent minstrel? Never!
I go and toss him in the river   210
only to find that he's come back!"
He stuffs the third one in the sack
and heaves it up onto his shoulders.
With anger and dismay he smolders,
irately turns and goes to trundle   215
back down the stairs toting his bundle,
and flings the final hunchback down
in the canal that flows through town.
"Good riddance, and the devil take you!
I've lugged you all day. I can't shake you,   220
but if again I catch you headed
back home, I tell you, you'll regret it!
You have bewitched me, I believe,
but, by God, by Whose grace I breathe,
if you come following behind,   225
with the first sword or stick I find
I'll strike your neck in such a manner
to leave you with a red bandanna!"
This said, he went straight back and strode
on up the steps of her abode.   230
    Now, well before he reached the top,
he glanced behind, came to a stop
to see her husband on his way
home again. In no mood for play,
he signed the cross thrice in succession   235
and prayed for divine intercession,
exclaiming, stricken to the quick,
"In God's name, is the creature sick
with rabies to tag after me
and dog me through eternity?   240
Now by the wheel that broke Saint Martin,[3]
he takes me for a hick, that's certain—
I just keep toting; when I'm done,
it's his idea of having fun
to come back for another ride!"   245
He grabbed a club which hung beside
the door with both fists, then he ran
back to the flight of stairs again.
The husband was close to the top.
"How, Mr. Hunchback? Go back! Stop!   250

---

3. The meaning of this reference is unknown.

How stubborn can a person be?
I promise you, by Saint Marie,
you'll rue having come back once more!
What kind of stooge d'you take me for?"
Without a pause he raised the club   255
and brought it down with such a thud
on the hunchback's enormous head
that on the stairs he struck him dead
with his brains spattered left and right,
then bagged him, tied the sack up tight   260
with a cord, then went at a run
the same way he had often gone
and pitched his burden in the river,
hunchback and sack, the two together,
for he was scared that for the fourth   265
time he'd be followed by the dwarf.
"Bad luck to you!" he said. "Now sink!
This time I can be sure, I think,
you won't return to give me grief
until the forests are in leaf!"   270
    He went right back to see the lady
and asked her if he might be paid—he
had done her errand to perfection.
The woman offered no objection,
but gave the young man his reward   275
of thirty pounds, not one cent short,
freely and generously paid,
the best bargain she'd ever made,
she said, delighted with her day,
because he'd got out of the way   280
her husband, who was so disfigured.
For the rest of her days, she figured,
she'd never suffer pain or strife
now her spouse is out of her life.
    Durant[4] says, rounding off his tale,   285
that everything on earth's for sale—
there's not a girl that can't be bought,
nor any treasure that God wrought,
however valuable and good,
that, if the truth be understood,   290
cannot be had for the right price.
The hunchback used wealth to entice
his marriage with a lady fair.
Shame on the man whose only care
is massing money for his purse!   295
And on who coined it first, a curse!

4. Nothing is known of Durant.

The Wild Dream

I'll tell as briefly as I can
about a woman and a man
and what befell them, if I may.
I heard about it in Douay.
I do not know his or her name,   5
but I can affirm all the same
what fine, upstanding folk they were
and that she loved him and he her.
    The good man had to leave one day
and go on business far away,   10
and thus for three full months he stayed
in foreign parts engaged in trade,
and he was so successful there
that he returned walking on air
to Douay on a Thursday evening.   15
Don't think that his wife felt like grieving
to have her husband back again;
the fuss she made over him then
gave proof of her wifely devotion
and of the strength of her emotion.   20
When she had hugged, kissed and embraced
him, so he could relax, she placed
a low-slung, comfortable chair
near her and then went to prepare
their meal. All in good time they ate   25
seated on cushions by the gate,
where a fire crackled warm and bright,
without smoke, but with lots of light.
They'd fish and meat, good, hearty fare,
and wine from Soissons and Auxerre,[1]   30
white linen, and fresh, healthful meat.
It pleased his wife to watch him eat;
she saw that he got all the fine,
choice morsels, and, with each bite, wine.
Eager to please her man, the lady   35
was more than willing, more than ready
to satisfy his every whim,
expecting in return from him
the welcome for which she was aching,
but it turned out she was mistaken   40
in plying him with all that drink,
for wine made his libido shrink,
and afterwards, when the man got in
their bed, that pleasure was forgotten.
Not by his wife—it filled her head   45
when she climbed next to him in bed,
nor would he have needed to ask,

---

1. Two cities in northern France.

for she was ready for the task.
He had no thought for his poor spouse,
who would have liked them to carouse   50
and stay awake a while still.
Don't think the lady just sits still
while her husband sleeps like a stone:
"Ha!" she protests, "he sure has shown
himself a stinking, oafish creep!   55
He should be up, but he's asleep!
My happy hopes have turned to pain.
Three months have passed since we have lain
together, and yet, sure enough,
the devil makes the man doze off.   60
Well, he can take him, if he will!"
She lies there quietly and still;
what's on her mind remains unspoken—
she doesn't wake him up or poke him,
though in her mind she's sorely vexed,   65
lest he should think she's oversexed.
This reason makes her disregard her
thoughts of love-making and ardor
which she has entertained tonight.
She turns in, feeling wrath and spite.   70
    She dreamt a dream while she was lying
there fast asleep—don't think I'm lying!—
that she'd gone to a yearly fair,
the likes of which you have to hear,
for every stall and shop display   75
there, every house and place to stay,
every exchange and table was
not selling bolts of cloth or furs
or linen, wool or silks of price,
it seemed to her, or dyes, or spice,   80
or goods, or pharmaceuticals—
just penises and testicles
in wild profusion, for the sellers
had filled their houses, rooms and cellars
with the commodity, and porters   85
came toting them across the borders
upon their backs, while down the road
they rolled in by the wagonload.
Despite the massive inventory,
the merchants had no need to worry   90
of not exhausting their supplies.
The thirty-shilling merchandise
was awesome, good ones cost a pound,
and for the poor folk could be found
some smaller ones, which still could sate   95
a girl for ten or nine or eight.
They sold in gross and in detail.
The best and biggest ones for sale
were closely watched and very dear.

The wife went looking everywhere 100
and put much effort in her quest
till at one stall she came to rest
on seeing one so long and wide, it
just had to be hers, she decided.
The shaft was large and well-endowed 105
with a big head, cocky and proud,
and, if you want to hear the whole
truth, you could toss into the hole
with ease a round, ripe cherry, and it
would go on falling till it landed 110
down in the scrotum, which was made
like the shovel-end of a spade.
No man has ever seen its like.
The wife decided she would strike
a bargain, and she asked how much. 115
"If you were my own sister, such
as this would cost two marks of silver.
This penis is no scrawny sliver,
but of the finest Loheringian[2]
stock, both testicles and engine, 120
a worthy wand for a magician.
You would do well to take possession
of it. Do come give it a feel."
"Friend, why should we drag out the deal?
I'll buy it from you, if you're willing 125
to part with it for fifty shillings.
You won't get so much for it anywhere, and I'll throw in a penny
for God, that it may bring me bliss."
"A giveaway, that's what it is, 130
but I'm won over, and so suit yourself, and I hope in the future
you'll try it out and praise the vendor.
I think from now on you'll remember
me when you pray or sing a psalm." 135
The woman lifted up her palm
to give him high five, well-disposed
on account of the deal she'd closed . . . .
. . . and hits her husband in the jaw
with so much force, she feels her sore 140
hand turn bright red, tingle and burn,
and one can easily discern
the finger marks from chin to ear,
and he wakes up in startled fear
and sits bolt upright upon waking, 145
and his wife also wakens, shaking,
who'd sooner sleep on till tomorrow,
since now her joy has turned to sorrow.
She has no way to go on keeping

2. From Lorraine, a province in northern France, where men were reputed to be sexually well endowed.

the joy she bought herself while sleeping, 150
so she'd prefer to stay asleep.
"Wife," the man says, "pray do not keep
from me the dream that made you go
just now and strike me such a blow.
Were you asleep then or awake?" 155
"Don't say such things, for goodness sake,"
she tells him, "sir. Hit you? Who, me?"
"In affection and harmony,
by the strength of your marriage vow,
what were you thinking of just now? 160
Don't keep it back for any cause."
I'll have you know, without a pause
the woman launched into her tale,
like it or not, and didn't fail
to lay all of the details bare 165
of her dream of the penis fair,
how some were good and some were bad,
and she bought the largest they had,
by far more impressive than any,
for fifty shillings and a penny. 170
"Sir," she explains, "here's what occurred.
To close the deal, I gave my word
and went to shake hands with good grace,
hitting you squarely in the face,
but only did it in my sleep. 175
For God's sake, dearest husband, keep
your temper, for as I admit
my error and sincere regret,
I beg your pardon for the blow."
"In faith, sweet wife," he says, "you know 180
I pardon you, and so should God!"
He embraces and hugs her hard
and kisses her sweet mouth as well,
and his penis begins to swell,
for she charms him and turns him on. 185
He lays his penis in her palm
as soon as he feels that it's ready,
and asks, "By your love for me, lady,
as God may keep you free from sin,
at that fair, what would it bring in, 190
the one you're holding on to now?"
"As I hope to survive, I vow
that someone selling a full coffer
of them would find no one who'd offer
a speck of money for the lot. 195
Why, even those the paupers bought
were such that one of them with ease
would equal at least two of these
the way it is now. Look here, sire!
There it would never find a buyer 200
who'd ask to see the thing up close."

"So what?" he says. "That's how it goes.
Take this one—the others don't matter!—
until you think you can do better."
(And so she did, if I am right).   205
    Together they thus passed the night,
but I think his judgment unsound,
for the next day he spread it round
till a rhymer of fabliaux,
Jean Bodel,[3] also came to know   210
of it, and for its merits he
put it in his anthology
neither embellished nor extended,
which means the lady's dream has ended.

The Ring That Controlled Erections

Haiseau[1] has yet another thing
to tell. A man once owned a ring
which, when worn, by a magic spell
at once would make his manhood swell.
It happened one day that he rode   5
across a field where a stream flowed.
He got off his horse when he saw it,
strode to the bank and crouched before it
and washed his hands, also his face
and ring, which he took from its case.   10
At length he got up and rode on,
but left the ring there on the lawn.
    A bishop soon came riding by.
As soon as the stream caught his eye,
he dismounted and found the ring,   15
and, enthralled by its glittering,
he picked it up and put it on.
His virile member thereupon
began to stiffen in due course.
The bishop, now back on his horse,   20
was disconcerted to detect
his member had grown quite erect
and this growth didn't seem to end it,
for it grew ever more distended
and so enlarged, it burst the stitches   25
at the seams of the bishop's britches.
Ashamed, the bishop shows his servants
what hard luck mortifies and burdens
him, but they've no way of construing
this mischief is all the ring's doing.   30
    It grew till it dragged on the ground.

---

3. The author of this and other fabliaux.   1. Either the author or the minstrel.

He sent his messengers around
to find someone who could advise
him how to bring it back to size.
The man who'd lost the ring got word   35
of what strange marvel had occurred,
and to the bishop straightaway
he went and asked how much he'd pay
him if he could effect a cure.
He said, unable to endure   40
such agony, "Just name your fee."
"Then I will ask you to agree
to give me those two rings you wear
and one hundred pounds as my share."
Without the rings on, his incessant   45
erection became detumescent.
Before the bishop paid his hundred-
pound fee, he was disencumbered,
and wasn't it a fair exchange
when each was glad to have the change?   50

ROBERT MANNYNG

early fourteenth century

The Cursed Dancers of Colbeck[1]

Carols,[2] wrestling, or summer games—whoever practices such disgraceful behavior in church or churchyard should be afraid of sacrilege. Interludes[3] or singing, beating the tabor[4] or piping—all these things are forbidden while the priest is conducting mass. These things are hateful to the good priest, and he'll be angry about them much sooner than will an ignorant man who doesn't understand Holy Writ, especially if people sing carols and read out rhymes[5] during feast days. In any holy place where the priest says his beads or is praying or performing any other devotion—it's all sacrilege, these and many other things.

But in order to persuade you not to dance in church I shall tell you about a remarkable event, most of which is the gospel truth. * * * It was upon a Christmas Eve that twelve fools made a carol—madly, as a kind of challenge—in a town called Colbeck.[6] The church in that town is dedicated to the martyr St. Magnus, and to his sister, St. Bukcester. The names of all of the carollers are written down, and you shall know them. Their leader, who made the music, was called Gerlew. The other twelve were as follows: Theodoric, Meinhold, Bovoline, Gerard, Edbert, Wenseline, Aceline, Folkward,

---

1. Translated from the Middle English by Lee Patterson.   2. Circle dances usually accompanied with singing.   3. Short plays or mimed performances.   4. A small drum.   5. I.e., tell rhyming tales, or sing ballads.   6. Kölbigk, in Saxony, an area in eastern Germany just north of the present-day Czech border.

Hildebrand, Aelward, Benne, and Odricus. There were also two maidens in their band, Mersewine and Wisbessine.[7] All of these people came because of the daughter of the town priest. The priest was called Robert, I believe, and his son was called Ayone. His daughter, whom these men wanted, was named Ave.

Together they agreed that both Wisbessine and Mersewine should go to entice Ave out. These women went and persuaded her to come and carol with them around the church. Benne organized the carol and Gerlew composed the song they should sing, as it says in the Latin:

> By the leafy wood rode Bovoline,
> With him he led the fair Mersewine.
> Why are we waiting? Why don't we go?[8]

This is the carol that Gerlew wrote, the song they sung in the church yard—they weren't afraid of being foolish—until matins[9] was finished and the priest robed himself to begin the Mass. Nevertheless they didn't leave off, but continued dancing as they had begun: despite the Mass, they didn't stop. The priest, who stood at the altar and heard their noise and their uproar, came down from the altar and went out to the church porch. "For God's sake," he said, "I prohibit you from continuing. But come in a seemly fashion to hear God's service, behave as Christians, and for reverence of Christ stop this carolling. With all your heart worship him who was born this night of the Virgin." For all his asking they wouldn't stop, but continued dancing as they pleased.

Distressed by this, the priest prayed to the God of his faith that on behalf of St. Magnus, in whose honor the church was built, He would arrange it so that they would suffer such vengeance that they would continue in this way for a full year until they might depart. (In the Latin that I read he said not a year but forever.) He cursed them there all together as they carolled for fun. As soon as the priest had spoken, every hand was fast locked into the others so that no man might part them asunder for a twelvemonth. The priest went in then and commanded his son Ayone that he should go quickly after Ave, and bring her out of that carol. But all too late was that word said, for vengeance had been laid on all of them. Ayone expected to succeed, and he quickly went to the carol. He grabbed his sister by the arm but the arm separated from the body. All the people there wondered, but you will hear of a greater miracle: since he had the arm in his hand, the body went forth carolling, and neither body nor arm bled but was as dry, as was the shoulder, as if a branch were torn from a tree trunk.

Ayone went to his father and brought him a sad present. "Look, father," he said, "you have here the arm of your daughter, that was my own sister Ave whom I thought I might save. Your vengeance is now made manifest on your own flesh. Savagely and hastily you cursed: you asked for vengeance and you have your wish." You don't need to ask if there was grief for the priest and for many others. The priest that cursed because of that dance saw the harsh effect fall on his own.

---

7. A total of fifteen people are named, but presumably only the twelve men are actual dancers, Gerlew supplying the music and the two women being companions of dubious character.   8. Robert cites these lines in Latin and then translates them into Middle English.   9. The regular morning church service that did not usually include the Mass.

He took his daughter's bereft arm and buried it the next morning. But the next day he found Ave's arm lying upon the grave. He buried it again, and again it appeared upon the grave. He buried it a third time, and again it was cast out of the pit. The priest wouldn't bury it again—he feared some vengeance. Instead he bore it into the church, for fear of more harm, and set it up so as to be visible to everyone.

These people who were carolling, all that year, hand in hand, never left that place nor might anyone lead them away. Where the cursing first began they continued to race about. Unlike many bodies, they felt no weariness, nor did they eat food or taste drink, nor sleep even a single wink. They knew nothing of either day nor night, when it was come, when it was gone. Frost nor snow, hail nor rain, of cold and heat they felt no pain. Their nails did not grow, their clothes did not get dirty, their complexions did not change. Thunder nor lightning gave them no fear: God's mercy warded it off them. But they sang the song that wrought their woe: "Why are we waiting? Why don't we go?"

What person alive would not journey to see this thing? Emperor Henry[1] came from Rome to see this harsh punishment. When he saw them he wept bitterly for the suffering he saw there. He arranged for carpenters to make a covering over them to protect them from storms, but whatever they made was in vain. Whatever they set up one day was down the next. Once, twice, thrice they built, and all their work was for nothing. No covering might protect the dancers from the cold until the time of mercy that Christ willed.

The time of grace arrived through His might and at the end of the twelve-month, on Christmas Eve. The same hour that the priest bound them was the same hour when they came apart; the same hour that he cursed them was the same hour they separated. And in the twinkling of an eye they flew into the church, and on the pavement they all fell down as if they were dead or in a faint. For three days each lay still without stirring flesh or bone, and at the end of three days God granted that they should return to life. They stood up and spoke openly to the parish priest, sir Robert. "You are both an example and a cause of our long confusion; you are the maker of our travail that has been a marvel to so many. And you shall soon end your own travail, for to your eternal home you shall soon go." At that time they all rose except Ave: she lay dead beside them. Her father and brother had great sorrow; all the others felt wonder and fear. They feared, I believe, not that her soul was dead but of the pain that brought bodily death.[2]

The first man who died after the daughter was her father, the priest. For Ave's arm, that none might lay in a grave, the Emperor made a vessel to put it in and hang in the church, so that all men might see it and know and think on this event when they saw it. These people that had gone carolling all the year hand in hand, even though they were now apart everyone still spoke of this miracle. That same skipping that they first did—they continued that dance through lands and nations. But as they might not first be unbound, so might they now never again come together into one place. Four went to the court of Rome, and always skipping they went about. With many leaps they came there, but they never came together again. Their clothes didn't

---

1. Henry II, Holy Roman Emperor from 1002 to 1024.   2. By the death of the soul the author means eternal damnation.

rot nor their nails grow; their hair didn't lengthen nor their complexions change. Nor did they ever have relief, so far as we have heard, at any shrine, except at that of the virgin saint Edith: there Theodoric was cured on Lady's Day in Lent as he slept beside her tomb. There he had his medicine from St. Edith, the holy virgin.[3]

Bruning, bishop of St. Toule, wrote this marvelous tale. Afterward his name was better known: men called him Pope Leo.[4] They know this story at the court of Rome, and it is written in chronicles in many places beyond the sea—more so than in this country.

Therefore people say and truly it is believed, "The nearer the church, the further from God." So people regard this tale: some hold it an idle story, while in other places it is held dearly and people take it for a great marvel. It is a tale of clear illustration, an example of and a warning against cursing. I told you this tale to make you afraid to carol in a church or churchyard, especially against the priest's will. Stop when he bids you to be still: jangling[5] is a form of sacrilege.

3. A tenth-century nun whose shrine was located at Wilton in England.   4. Goscelin, Robert's source, credits the story to Bruno, bishop of Toul (b. 1002), who presided as Pope Leo IX from 1048 until his death in 1054.   5. Chattering, babbling.

DANTE ALIGHIERI
1265–1321

Called by its author a comedy, and named by later ages—in recognition of both its subject matter and its achievement—*The Divine Comedy*, Dante's poem is one of the indisputably great works of world literature. It combines into a coherent whole a wide range of disparate literary elements. It is organized with the precision and harmony of the great philosophical systems and the vast Gothic cathedrals of its time; and yet it attends with extraordinary care to the tiniest detail. It celebrates with unqualified enthusiasm and at times even dogmatism the central doctrines of medieval Christianity; and yet it remains persistently alert to the sympathies of the human heart. It is epic in its scope and its central themes; and yet it sings with an exquisite lyricism. It is a poem that declares everywhere its commitment to the culture of medieval Christendom; and yet it celebrates the achievements of the classical world and extends its admiration even to Islamic philosophy. It is one of the most deeply serious works in world literature, concerned with nothing less than the relation of the Creator to His creatures and the ultimate destiny of the human soul; and yet it has room for not just grim irony but scenes of generous good humor and even vulgar horseplay. It does not shy away from episodes that the German writer Goethe accurately called "repulsive and often disgusting"; and yet it also includes moments of sublime beauty that have been rarely matched and never surpassed. Perhaps above all, it showed that a great work of literary art, equal to the great works of antiquity, can be created in the vernacular, providing the declaration of independence that made possible the various national traditions of post-medieval literature. In this sense *The Divine Comedy* is the foundational text for the European literary imagination.

Dante was born in Florence in the spring of 1265. In his early years he wrote some ninety lyrics, thirty-one of which he collected and provided with a narrative commentary in a work he called the *Vita nuova* or *New Life* (completed between 1292

Dante's Hell

	cantos
Dark Wood	1–2
Ante-Inferno Neutrals	3
CIRCLE I Virtuous Pagans	4
CIRCLE II Lustful	5
CIRCLE III Gluttons	6
CIRCLE IV Prodigal and Miserly	7
CIRCLE V Wrathful	8
CIRCLE VI Arch-Heretics	9–10

Acheron

Minos

Cerberus

Plutus

Styx

City of Dis

Minotaur

INCONTINENT (wolf)

CIRCLE VII
Violent—

—against neighbors	12
—against self	13
—against God	14–16

VIOLENT (lion)

Phlegethon

Wood of Suicides

Burning Plain

Great Barrier

Geryon — 17

CIRCLE VIII

i. Panderers and Seducers	18
ii. flatterers	
iii. Simonists	19
iv. Soothsayers	20
v. Grafters	21–22
vi. Hypocrites	23
vii. Thieves	24–25
viii. Deceivers	26–27
ix. Sowers of Discord	28
x. Falsifiers	29–30

FRAUDULENT (leopard)

Antaeus

CIRCLE IX
Treacherous—

—to kindred: Caina	32
—to country: Antenora	33
—to guests: Tolomea	
—to benefactors: Judecca	34

Satan

and 1295). This work recounted his love for a young woman he named Beatrice ("blessed" in Italian), who died in 1290. More than a love story, it described how Beatrice led him from a merely human love to something transcendental, almost divine. Dante realized that this transformation also required a new form of poetry, and it is from the *New Life* that *The Divine Comedy* was to spring as both a fulfillment and an alternative.

Meanwhile, however, political conflicts had decisively altered Dante's life. The Florentine political class, like that of much of northern Italy, was divided into two factions. The Guelphs, generally members of the urban elite and artisans, supported Florentine independence and resisted the claims of the Holy Roman Empire to sovereignty over the city or indeed any part of Italy, often by soliciting the support of the military power of the papacy. The Ghibellines, on the other hand, were drawn from the ancient feudal aristocracy and saw the empire as a means of furthering their own interests. After a series of bitter struggles, the Florentine Guelphs—of which Dante was a member—were triumphant. Around 1300, however, the Guelphs themselves broke into two parties, the Blacks and the Whites, and civil strife was renewed. The Whites, with Dante as a member, became associated with the Ghibellines in their resistance to the power of the pope. In 1301, while Dante was on a diplomatic mission for the city, the Blacks staged a coup with the help of Pope Boniface VII and his ally, the Frenchman Charles of Anjou. The next year Dante was condemned to exile, and he never returned to Florence. This experience of exile is central to *The Divine Comedy*, which on the most literal level recounts the journey of a lost traveler back to his ultimate homeland, Heaven. Also central is Dante's outrage at the internecine strife that tore northern Italy apart throughout his lifetime. Soon he came to believe that only the Holy Roman Emperor could bring order out of chaos, and he condemned the interference of the Church, and especially the pope, in political affairs, just as he condemned the Ghibellines' misuse of the empire's prestige for their own, self-seeking purposes. Dante's politics in *The Divine Comedy* are also religious and prophetic: he is concerned with restoring the conditions in which Christ first came—when Caesar Augustus presided over the "Roman peace" or *pax Romana*—so that He can come again and usher in the Final Judgment. Thus for Dante the Roman Empire is divinely ordained: it first provided the earthly unity and order appropriate to the birth of Christ, and only when it is restored will His second coming be possible.

As a sign of the availability of the divine, this unity and order are everywhere present in Dante's poem. The three parts or canticles—the *Inferno, Purgatorio,* and *Paradiso*—are of equal length. Each of the latter two has thirty-three cantos; the first, the *Inferno,* has thirty-four, but the first canto is a prologue to the whole. This threefold pattern serves to embody the Trinity within the very structure of the poem, as does the verse form. Dante created a verse known as *terza rima,* which rhymes in the Italian original according to the scheme *aba bcb cdc* and so on. The lines thus form groups of three (known in Italian as *terzine,* or tercets) interlocked by a repeated rhyme word—a verbal equivalent to the three-in-one of the Trinity. Moreover, since each line contains eleven syllables, the total number of syllables in each tercet is thirty-three, the same as the number of cantos in each canticle (again, if we take *Inferno* 1 as a prologue). Each canticle even ends with the same word, *stelle* (stars), objects that are for Dante the visible signs of God's providential oversight. Nine, the square of three, figures centrally in the interior structure of each canticle. In Hell, the lost souls are arranged in three main groups and occupy nine circles; Purgatory is divided into an Ante-Purgatory, seven terraces, and the Earthly Paradise, for a total of nine locations; and Heaven consists of nine embedded spheres beyond which lies the infinite Empyrean of the Trinity.

In addition to these structures, the poem is organized according to an ethical pattern. For Dante, as for medieval philosophy generally, the natural inclination of every human being is love, a movement toward something outside the self. The natural and proper object of love is God, either directly or as mediated through the created world.

Sin occurs when love is immoderately directed to the wrong object, when the creature (including the self) is loved not *for* but *instead of* the Creator. In Hell, perverse love is represented in three forms, as incontinence, violence, and fraudulence. In Purgatory, it is also represented in three forms, as misdirected (pride, envy, and wrath), as defective (sloth), and as excessive (avarice, gluttony, and lust). In Paradise, the blessed are distinguished by the extent to which they enjoy the vision of God, and are again divided into three categories: those whose vision is limited by incomplete love, those who have fulfilled the four cardinal virtues (wisdom, fortitude, justice, and temperance), and finally those—like the angels—whose love comes nearest to perfection. Finally, Dante's geography is equally symmetrical. The globe is divided into a northern and southern hemisphere, but only the northern is inhabited. Its central point is Jerusalem, while to the east lies the Ganges and to the west the straits of Gibraltar. Hell is a huge funnel extending into the center of the Earth that was created when Lucifer fell from Heaven. The earth displaced by his fall rose into the southern hemisphere—which had previously been covered entirely with water—and formed Mount Purgatory. This mountain, organized into its three parts as described above, has at its top the Earthly Paradise, or Eden, the original home of the human race. After descending into Hell, climbing up through the Earth, and then mounting to the Earthly Paradise, Dante is transported through the nine spheres described by medieval astronomy—those of the moon, Mercury, Venus, the sun, Mars, Jupiter, Saturn, the fixed stars, and the *primum mobile*, or outermost sphere, which moves the others—until he reaches the Empyrean, which exists beyond time and space. This final vision is presented in our selection from the *Paradiso*.

There is, finally, one other organizing principle that governs the form of the poem as a whole. When Dante is told that he is to journey through Hell, Purgatory, and Paradise, he protests that he is not worthy by comparing himself to two previous otherworldly travelers: "I am not Aeneas, I am not Paul" (*Inferno* 2.32). Aeneas visits the underworld in book 6 of Virgil's *Aeneid,* and Virgil plays a large role as both a literary influence and a character in Dante's poem. The reference to Paul is to a passage in 2 Corinthians 12.2: "I knew a man in Christ above fourteen years ago (whether in the body, I cannot tell; whether out of the body, I cannot tell; God knoweth;) such a one caught up to the third heaven." Medieval readers understood Paul to be talking about himself, but their problem was to understand what he meant by the third heaven, since there is presumably only one kingdom of God. The solution was provided by Augustine in one of his commentaries on Genesis, in which he argued that the three Pauline "heavens" were really metaphors for three ways in which human beings can know. These three are, in ascending order of clarity, "corporeal vision," or knowledge by means of the senses; "spiritual" or "imaginative vision," or knowledge through images that have corporeal shape without corporeal substance, as in dreams; and finally "intellectual vision," which is the direct knowledge of God and other realities, such as love, that have neither corporeal shape nor corporeal substance. God can be known in all three ways, which Augustine illustrated by passages from the Bible. He is known corporeally by Moses and the burning bush (Exodus 3–4); spiritually or imaginatively in the symbolic images of the Book of Revelation; and intellectually by Paul's vision, which he himself describes in 1 Corinthians 13.12: "For now we see through a glass, darkly but then face to face: now I know in part; but then shall I know even as also I am known."

The important point for us is that the three canticles of *The Divine Comedy* are each constructed according to one of these modes of vision. The *Purgatorio*, for example, is a place of images that have corporeal shape but not corporeal substance. In *Purgatorio* 2 we have a vivid illustration of this in a scene that appears in both Homer's and Virgil's underworlds: Dante tries three times to embrace his old friend Casella and three times he fails. With the form of a human being but not the substance, Casella is not merely *seen* by the imagination; he *exists* as an image rather than a thing. He is dematerialized, which shows that he is on his way up to Paradise. For in the *Paradiso* we find that its inhabitants are neither bodies nor images but simply lights. Furthermore, Dante himself, as he ascends the paradisal ladder, becomes "enlightened" or "illuminated." But because he is still in this life rather than a pure spirit this happens to him not literally but metaphorically, as he is instructed by various people in the nature of ultimate truth. This is the reason why the *Paradiso* is so didactic, with characters talking little about themselves and instead explaining what are to us often abstruse points of theological or scholastic teaching. In the *Paradiso* Dante is "enlightened" or "illuminated" by this teaching. So what do we find in the *Inferno*? Not only are the inhabitants of Hell known corporeally but they *are* corporeal, and indeed become all the more so as Dante descends deeper into the pit. At the beginning of the journey, while Dante is in the upper levels, the characters flit about like the shades we expect them to be (as in canto 5), but very soon they become more and more substantial, so that—for example—Virgil and Dante can actually touch them, as in canto 8, where Virgil hurls Filippo Argenti back into the mud. Appropriately, the most corporeal place in Hell is the bottom circle, which is the most materialistic place in the universe. Dante calls it "the center / of the universe, where all weights must converge" (*Inferno* 32.73–74), because it is furthest from the pure spirituality and immateriality of Paradise (the Empyrean). At the bottom of Hell we find the heaviest thing in the universe, Satan: although originally Lucifer, the Angel of Light, he is now the being with the least amount of spirit, a speechless creature from whose mouths—he has three heads, an infernal parody of the Trinity, to prove that God is present even here in the pit of Hell—flows a bloody drool, what Dante calls in Italian *bava,* a word that refers to infantile slaver.

If the least sinful people are spun round with wind, then, the worst are frozen into ice and utterly immobile. This is Dante's way of showing us that the perfect order of the universe includes the moral law that one's punishment is not merely appropriate to the crime but *is* the crime: these are the sinners who most fully denied the spirit, and so their spirit, which was created eternal by God, has come as close to pure matter as is possible. This moral law is called by one of the sinners a "counter-penalty," or *contrapasso.* It is clear from discussions by philosophers known to Dante—such as Thomas Aquinas—that the Latin term *contrapassum* meant "retribution" according to the law of retribution as defined in the Old Testament: an eye for an eye, a tooth for a tooth (see Exodus 21.23–24). But this is not really the principle that governs the distribution of punishment in Hell: this is what the sinners think, but they are oversimplifying. On the contrary, the moral economy of Hell is explained in a single sentence by another of the sinners (Capaneus): "What I once was, alive, I still am, dead" (*Inferno* 14.51). The punishment of sin is the sin itself, as Augustine taught in the *Confessions:* "So You [God] have ordained and so it is: that every disorder of the soul is its own punishment." In the *Inferno* every sinner commits his sin forever, for all of eternity, and that is his punishment.

Before exploring in more detail the workings of divine justice in the *Inferno,* we need to understand the role of Virgil, and of the *Aeneid,* in the poem. When Dante protests in *Inferno* 2 that he is neither Aeneas nor Paul, he is indicating that his poem will bring together, in a combination that will find its ultimate fulfillment in Milton's *Paradise Lost,* both the classical and the Christian traditions. This is a bold and largely unprecedented ambition in Western literature. In the *Confessions* Augustine struggles with and finally rejects the *Aeneid:* he describes how as a student he was seduced by the beauty of Virgil's poetry into weeping for the death of Dido while ignoring the spiritual death of his own soul. For Augustine the poem's poetic power was irresistible, but its meaning was worse than useless to the Christian; as another of the Church Fathers put it, the *Aeneid* was "a beautiful vase filled with vipers." For Virgil's poem celebrated the founding of an earthly empire and, worse, one that Jupiter prophesied would continue "without end." In the *City of God,* written in part to defend Christians from the charge that it was their rejection of Rome's traditional deities that had caused the sack of Rome by the Goths in 410, Augustine poured scorn on these words, "without end." For him there was only one city, the Heavenly Jerusalem, which was not a physical place at all but a condition of the soul—a vision of peace—available both in this life and in the life to come to those who have faith. The "eternal city" was not Rome but the City of God, populated by citizens faithful not to the emperor or the Roman deities but to the gospel of Jesus Christ.

But for Dante, as we have seen, Rome had a different meaning. For him, the establishment of the empire by Augustus, and the extension of Roman peace over the Western world, were the necessary preconditions for the birth of Christ. It was not just one city among many but the source of an imperial order that was divinely sanctioned. For Dante, since Virgil was the prophet and celebrant of this empire, he was—although he could not know it—inspired in writing the *Aeneid* not by Jupiter but by the Christian God. This notion of Virgilian inspiration was furthered by a Christian interpretation of one of Virgil's early poems, the Fourth Eclogue. The poem begins:

> Now comes the last age [prophesied] by the song of the Cumaean sybil; the great order of the ages is born anew; now the Virgin returns, now the reign of Saturn comes again; now a new child is sent down from heaven above.

It's easy enough to see how a devout reader could see in these words a prophecy of the birth of Christ, although Virgil was probably thinking of a son born to some prominent Roman, perhaps even to Augustus. Dante believed that the second coming of Christ, and the fulfillment of history, was dependent upon the reestablishment of the imperial authority whose initial establishment Virgil had described in the *Aeneid*. This is why it is Virgil who in *Inferno* 1 provides an obscure prophecy of a savior who will bring peace to the war-torn cities of Italy. In sum, for Dante, Rome and its empire played a crucial role in history.

So part of the reason Virgil is chosen as the guide is that he is a poet who was divinely inspired to make known the meaning of history, a role that Dante assumes for himself as well—hence the political prophecies scattered throughout the poem. But Virgil is also chosen because he taught Dante what in *Inferno* 1 Dante calls "the noble style." What he means by this is that reading Virgil allowed him to move beyond the lyric love poetry that had characterized the early part of his career. This poetry was, as Dante's discussion in *Purgatorio* 24 and 26 makes clear, a necessary precondition to the writing of the *Comedy*. But it was Virgil who showed him that poetry might aspire to a vision of experience that dealt with the ultimate issues of life and death, and with a vision of the meaning of history. It was Virgil, in other words, who persuaded him that poetry could be a vehicle for moral and philosophical truth, and a means of self-fulfillment, as his final ratification of Dante's spiritual growth in *Purgatorio* 30 shows.

Yet despite the fact that Virgil is Dante's "master and author," there are important differences between them. Indeed, a central theme in both the *Inferno* and the *Purgatorio* is the fluctuation in the relationship between Dante and Virgil. Dante is usually submissive before Virgil, but there are moments when Virgil appears baffled and even inept. One of these occurs in canto 9 of the *Inferno*, when the devils in the City of Dis refuse Virgil entrance and he has to call upon a divine messenger sent from Heaven. In that canto the Furies threaten to bring Medusa in order to turn Dante to stone; Virgil makes Dante turn around and then covers up his eyes with both Dante's and his own hands. As soon as Virgil does this, Dante speaks—in the present tense—to the reader:

> O all of you whose intellects are sound,
> look now and see the meaning that is hidden
> beneath the veil that covers my strange verses. (9.61–63)

While Virgil the non-Christian covers up, Christian readers must *uncover*: they must interpret this action and this scene as a whole in order to understand the nature of the spiritual—not literal—threat posed by the Furies and Medusa. The answer has to do with the meaning of *petrification*, which in Christian terms means turning the heart to stone, being hard-hearted or *impenitent*; and the greatest source of impenitence is *despair*, which is the belief that you have committed sins so grave that they cannot be forgiven. The Furies are, for the Middle Ages, symbols of this despair, and despair is the condition of everyone in Hell, including Virgil: they have abandoned all hope of being saved. That is why in this very canto Dante mentions "that first circle / whose pain is all in having hope cut off" (9.17–18) and Virgil mentions "the pit of Judas," (9.27) Judas representing the New Testament type of despair. As a pagan, Virgil can *experience* this condition but cannot *understand* it: the despair or absence of hope at work here is Virgil's—he doesn't think they will get into the city of Dis—not Dante's; and the heavenly messenger who arrives is "filled with scorn" (9.88) not only because of the useless resistance of the inhabitants of Dis but also because of Virgil's incapacity. To appreciate something of the subtlety of Dante's poetry, we should notice that this messenger opens the gate with a touch of his wand, or *verghetta*. In the Middle Ages the power of Virgil's poetry was such that there developed a tradition that he was a magician, perhaps even a soothsayer: we meet this tradition in canto 20, where Dante will have Virgil revise his own poem so as to distance himself from this accusation. But one of the effects of this connection between Virgil and magic was that the spelling of his name was revised from Vergil— in Latin his name is *Vergilius Maro*—to Virgil by assimilation with the Latin word for a magician's wand, which is *virga*. In other words, Virgil wields a *virga*. But here Virgil's powers fail him, and it is an angel of God—the God whom Virgil did not know—who wields the *verghetta*.

There are many examples of the way in which Dante marks the difference between Virgil's pre-Christian understanding and his own confident Christianity. The reader might want to compare, for instance, the description in *Aeneid* 6 of the souls awaiting their trip across the river Acheron with its rewriting in *Inferno* 3, or any of the other passages—indicated in the notes—where Dante draws directly upon the *Aeneid*. In addition to this indication of cultural and (for Dante) spiritual difference, Dante's relation to Virgil is not just literary but deeply emotional. Virgil may be a figure of authority, but he is also one of pathos, and nowhere more so than in the *Purgatorio*. There, in cantos 21 and 22, he meets his disciple Statius, the author of an epic poem that was, as Statius says, inspired by the *Aeneid*. More important is that Dante, quite unhistorically, presents Statius as having converted to Christianity by reading the lines from Virgil's Fourth Eclogue cited above. Statius says to Virgil,

> You were the lonely traveler in the dark
> who holds his lamp behind him, shedding light
> not for himself but to make others wise. (*Purgatorio* 22.67–69)

Dante is here, even more anachronistically, having Statius apply to Virgil a description that in one of his treatises Augustine applied to the Jews: "O Jews, you carried in your hands the lamp of the law in order to show the way to others while you remained in the darkness." The point is twofold: Virgil is a classical version of Moses, who saw the promised land but could not himself enter; and Virgil is to Statius (and to Dante) as Moses is to Christ: he is the prefiguration, and they are the fulfillment. This sense of Virgil's exclusion from the ultimate reward of the righteous life is expressed with great poignancy in *Purgatorio* 30, where Virgil disappears from the poem to be replaced by Beatrice.

A further distinction between Dante and Virgil is generic: in *Inferno* 20, Virgil refers to his poem as "my high tragedy"; in the next canto, Dante calls his poem "my Comedy." What are the differences between tragedy and comedy? In the Middle Ages, there are essentially four. First, *narrative structure*: a tragedy begins in happiness and ends in misery, while a comedy works in reverse, so that Dante begins in Hell and ends in Paradise. Second, *style*: tragedy is exalted in style, while comedy can indulge in a range of styles, and we see this in the *Inferno*, for example, where canto 21 provides a wonderful scene of a group of naughty devils who tease Virgil by pretending to be Roman soldiers but then, as they set off on their march, signal their departure with an obscene gesture. Third, *character*: a tragedy deals with important historical figures, while a comedy deals with all sorts of people, the common as well as the highborn—and certainly this is true of Dante's poem. And fourth, *subject matter*: tragedy deals with events of grand historical importance while comedy deals with people's private or inward lives.

We can understand this last, most important difference in the way Dante manipulates the word "pity" (*pietà* in the Italian). This is the Italian version of the key Virgilian term *pietas*: for Virgil piety means essentially a dutiful or obedient compliance to a larger responsibility—one that in fact entails the abandonment of one's own personal or inner self. But for Dante *pietà* means pity or compassion. In Virgil *pietas* is always good; but in Dante pity is not. In *Inferno* 2, for instance, Virgil explains that Beatrice feels compassion or *pietà* for Dante, but that the sufferings of those in Hell, including Virgil himself, do not touch her. It would have been wrong for her to feel pity for Virgil: everyone in Hell is there as an effect not just of God's justice but of his love as well, as the inscription over the gate in canto 3 tells us. As Virgil says to Dante in a line where the translator makes clear the distinction between the two words, "In this place piety lives when pity is dead" (20. 28). In a larger sense, one of the central concerns of the poem is precisely what the protagonist feels and the shifts of his personality—the turmoil within his inner self—throughout the course of the journey he undertakes. This is clearly not true, for example, of Aeneas, who is denied any but the most obvious emotions—and often not many of them. Indeed, Aeneas's piety is fully accomplished precisely when he has sacrificed his personality in the interest of founding Rome, whereas *The Divine Comedy* is concerned throughout with the spiritual development of its protagonist.

The Divine Comedy is concerned as well with the spiritual development of its readers. As Augustine's *Confessions* make clear, for the medieval Christian reading was itself a spiritual action with serious moral consequences. One of the greatest impediments to Augustine's conversion was his inability to understand how the Hebrew Bible—with what he thought was its unsophisticated language and outlandish narratives—could compete with either the wisdom available in Greek philosophy or the beautiful style of Latin poetry, or how it could be reconciled to Christian doctrine. But he learned, with the help of Bishop Ambrose of Milan, to read the Bible not literally but, as he calls it, spiritually. He means by this what we would call allegorical reading. For example, throughout the Middle Ages the Song of Songs in the Hebrew Bible was read not as a love poem but as an allegory about the love of God for the individual soul, or of Christ for the Church, or of the Holy Spirit for the Virgin Mary. Moses, Isaac, Noah, and the other patriarchs were seen not just as leaders of Israel but as prefigurations of Christ. And so on: virtually every passage in the Hebrew Bible was interpreted so as to render it consistent with both the New Testament and Christian doctrine as defined by the Church. In 2 Corinthians 3.6 Paul says that "the letter killeth, but the spirit giveth life." To read the Bible only literally, simply as a series of historical narratives, is not merely to miss its deeper significance but to place oneself in spiritual danger, to risk one's very soul. As Augustine argues, to read literally is to read carnally or corporeally, with the eye of the flesh; but to interpret is to read spiritually, with the eye of the heart.

We have already seen how at a crucial moment in the *Inferno* (canto 9) Virgil seeks to cover Dante's eyes while Dante himself urges the reader to uncover the meaning of the events being portrayed. Throughout the *Comedy*, and especially in the *Inferno*, the most corporeal of the three canticles, both Dante the pilgrim and the reader are tempted to read carnally or corporeally, to be distracted from the need for interpretation by the visually powerful scenes presented to them. An example is the account in canto 5 of Paolo and Francesca, who are located in the third circle, where the lustful are punished. These young lovers are here because they committed adultery, and the winds that blow them about are an infernal version of the gusts of desire that drove them in life. But if we stop here we will make the same mistake as does the pilgrim Dante, who feels for them exactly the wrong sort of pity. For Francesca's punishment is not to whirl about endlessly, locked in the arms of her beloved: after all, is that really a punishment? No, her punishment is to repeat throughout eternity the act of seduction that brought about her damnation; and Paolo's punishment is to watch her as she works her wiles. It is no accident that in the conversation with Dante and Virgil Paolo says not a word but only sobs; indeed, Francesca refers to him only once, with the contemptuous demonstrative pronoun *questi*, "this one who never shall leave my side." And whom does Francesca seduce? After listening to her tell her carefully crafted tale of love—one that incorporates within it lines from the kind of lyric poetry that Dante himself had written as a youth—Dante falls to the ground with pity. Indeed, his description is painfully apt: he "fell to Hell's floor as a body, dead, falls"—an act all too appropriate for a man in Hell. Nor does Francesca's power stop at Dante, for it has worked its magic on generations of readers. The challenge of this scene is to remember its deep significance—that this woman is in Hell, that she is currently repeating the very sin that put her there—while she does everything in her power to make you forget.

The interpretive drama acted out in this scene is repeated throughout the *Inferno*. The poem is peopled with brilliantly realized personalities who engage in rhetorical subtleties that simultaneously conceal and yet reveal their moral corruption. Farinata and Cavalcanti, Pier delle Vigne, Brunetto Latini, Vanni Fucci, Ulysses, Guido da Montefeltro, Bertran de Born, Geri del Bello, Ugolino—these and more provide a human drama that is unsurpassed in Western literature. Yet we are simultaneously never allowed to forget that they are all damned by a divine justice that is, for Dante, infallible. We are simultaneously intrigued and wary, powerfully drawn toward these men and women whose personalities have here, in eternity, achieved their full and at times glorious potential and yet also on the alert for the full meaning of their words. Of all the accomplishments of this great poem, perhaps its most enduring achievement is its capacity to provide the reader with a virtually limitless sense of the deep meaningfulness that literature can provide. For Dante this meaningfulness derived from God, but whatever its source, we can still agree with those readers who thought the poem divine.

PRONOUNCING GLOSSARY

The following list uses common English syllables to provide rough equivalents of selected words whose pronunciation may be unfamiliar to the general reader.

Abbagliato: *ah-bahl-lee-ah'-toh*	Gianni Schicchi: *jyahn'-ee skee'-kee*
Aghinolfo: *ah-gee-nol'-foh*	Hypsipyle: *hip-sip'-il-ay*
Alichino: *a-lee-kee'-noh*	Maghinardo: *mah-ghee-nard'-oh*
Bacchiglione: *bahk-eel-lee-oh'-nay*	Malebolge: *mahl-uh-bowl'-jay*
Barbariccia: *bar-bar-eetch'-yah*	Malebranche: *mahl-uh-branck'-eh*
Caccia: *cah'-chyah*	Paolo: *powl'-oh*
Capocchio: *ka-pawk'-yoh*	Peschiera: *pes-kee-ehr'-ah*
Ciacco: *chyah'-koh*	Puccio: *poo'-chyoh*
Draghignazzo: *drah-gee-nyah'-zoh*	Rinier: *ree-nyay'*
Focaccia: *foh-cah'-chyah*	Romagna: *row-mah'-nyah*
Gianfigliazzi: *jyahn'-feel-yah-tzee*	Ruggieri: *roo-jyehr'-ee*

Tagliacozzo: *tah-lyah-cot'-soh*   Uguiccione: *oo-gwee-chyoh'-nay*
Tegghiaio: *teh-gyai'-oh*   Verrucchio: *vehr-oo'-kyoh*

From The Divine Comedy[1]

Inferno

CANTO I

Halfway through his life, Dante the Pilgrim wakes to find himself lost in a dark wood. Terrified at being alone in so dismal a valley, he wanders until he comes to a hill bathed in sunlight, and his fear begins to leave him. But when he starts to climb the hill his path is blocked by three fierce beasts: first a Leopard, then a Lion, and finally a She-Wolf. They fill him with fear and drive him back down to the sunless wood. At that moment the figure of a man appears before him; it is the shade of Virgil, and the Pilgrim begs for help. Virgil tells him that he cannot overcome the beasts which obstruct his path; they must remain until a "Greyhound" comes who will drive them back to Hell. Rather by another path will the Pilgrim reach the sunlight, and Virgil promises to guide him on that path through Hell and Purgatory, after which another spirit, more fit than Virgil, will lead him to Paradise. The Pilgrim begs Virgil to lead on, and the Guide starts ahead. The Pilgrim follows.

Midway along the journey of our life[2]
  I woke to find myself in a dark wood,
  for I had wandered off from the straight path.[3]
How hard it is to tell what it was like,
  this wood of wilderness, savage and stubborn
  (the thought of it brings back all my old fears),
a bitter place! Death could scarce be bitterer.
  But if I would show the good that came of it
  I must talk about things other than the good.
How I entered there I cannot truly say,
  I had become so sleepy[4] at the moment
  when I first strayed, leaving the path of truth;[5]
but when I found myself at the foot of a hill,
  at the edge of the wood's beginning, down in the valley,
  where I first felt my heart plunged deep in fear,
I raised my head and saw the hilltop shawled
  in morning rays of light sent from the planet
  that leads men straight ahead on every road.[6]
And then only did terror start subsiding,

        3

        6

        9

        12

        15

        18

1. Translated by Mark Musa. The notes are by Lee Patterson.   2. Born in 1265, Dante was thirty-five in 1300, the fictional date of the poem. The biblical span of human life is seventy (see Psalms 90.10 and Isaiah 38.10).   3. See Proverbs 2.13–14 and 4.18–19, and also 2 Peter 2.15.   4. See Romans 13.11–12.   5. See Psalms 23.3.   6. The sun, which in the astronomical system of Dante's time was a planet thought to revolve around the Earth.

in my heart's lake,[7] which rose to heights of fear
   that night I spent in deepest desperation.   21
Just as a swimmer, still with panting breath,
   now safe upon the shore, out of the deep,
   might turn for one last look at the dangerous waters,   24
so I, although my mind was turned to flee,
   turned round to gaze once more upon the pass
   that never let a living soul escape.[8]   27
I rested my tired body there awhile
   and then began to climb the barren slope
   (I dragged my stronger foot and limped along).[9]   30
Beyond the point the slope begins to rise
   sprang up a leopard, trim and very swift!
   It was covered by a pelt of many spots.   33
And, everywhere I looked, the beast was there
   blocking my way, so time and time again
   I was about to turn and go back down.   36
The hour was early in the morning then,
   the sun was climbing up with those same stars
   that had accompanied it on the world's first day,   39
the day Divine Love set their beauty turning;[1]
   so the hour and sweet season of creation
   encouraged me to think I could get past   42
that gaudy beast, wild in its spotted pelt,
   but then good hope gave way and fear returned
   when the figure of a lion loomed up before me,   45
and he was coming straight toward me, it seemed,
   with head raised high, and furious with hunger—
   the air around him seemed to fear his presence.   48
And now a she-wolf came, that in her leanness
   seemed racked with every kind of greediness
   (how many people she has brought to grief!).   51
This last beast brought my spirit down so low
   with fear that seized me at the sight of her,
   I lost all hope of going up the hill.[2]   54
As a man who, rejoicing in his gains,
   suddenly seeing his gain turn into loss,
   will grieve as he compares his then and now,   57
so she made me do, that relentless beast;
   coming toward me, slowly, step by step,
   she forced me back to where the sun is mute.   60
While I was rushing down to that low place,

7. This phrase refers to the inner chamber of the heart, a cavity that in the physiology of Dante's time was the location of fear. Not coincidentally, Dante's last stop in the *Inferno* ends at the lake of Cocytus (see 31.123). **8.** This simile of Dante as the survivor of a passage through the sea invokes the story of the escape of the Israelites from Egypt through the Red Sea, a central metaphor throughout the *Comedy* (see *Purgatorio* 24.46): see Exodus 14. There is also probably an allusion to the opening of the *Aeneid*, where Aeneas and his men survive a storm. **9.** The pilgrim is limping because he suffers from the injury of original sin. **1.** In the Middle Ages it was thought that the world was created in spring, when the sun is in the constellation Aries. **2.** The meaning of the leopard, lion, and she-wolf is open to a number of interpretations, the most plausible being that they represent the three major forms of sin found in Hell, respectively fraud, violence, and incontinence or immoderation (see 11.78 ff.). The structure of Hell indicates that the last is the least serious morally, but its role in this canto shows that it is the most difficult to overcome psychologically. Dante probably took the identities of these three beasts from a passage in Jeremiah 5.6.

my eyes made out a figure coming toward me
  of one grown faint, perhaps from too much silence.[3]
And when I saw him standing in this wasteland,   63
  "Have pity on my soul," I cried to him,
  "whichever you are, shade or living man!"
"No longer living man, though once I was,"   66
  he said, "and my parents were from Lombardy,
  both of them were Mantuans by birth.[4]
I was born, though somewhat late, *sub Julio*,[5]   69
  and lived in Rome when good Augustus reigned,
  when still the false and lying gods were worshipped.   72
I was a poet and sang of that just man,
  son of Anchises, who sailed off from Troy
  after the burning of proud Ilium.[6]   75
But why retreat to so much misery?
  Why not climb up this blissful mountain here,
  the beginning and the source of all man's joy?"   78
"Are you then Virgil, are you then that fount
  from which pours forth so rich a stream of words?"
  I said to him, bowing my head modestly.   81
"O light and honor of the other poets,
  may my long years of study, and that deep love
  that made me search your verses, help me now!   84
You are my teacher, the first of all my authors,
  and you alone the one from whom I took
  the noble style that was to bring me honor.   87
You see the beast that forced me to retreat;
  save me from her, I beg you, famous sage,
  she makes me tremble, the blood throbs in my veins."   90
"But you must journey down another road,"
  he answered, when he saw me lost in tears,
  "if ever you hope to leave this wilderness;
this beast, the one you cry about in fear,   93
  allows no soul to succeed along her path,
  she blocks his way and puts an end to him.   96
She is by nature so perverse and vicious,
  her craving belly is never satisfied,
  still hungering for food the more she eats.   99
She mates with many creatures, and will go on
  mating with more until the greyhound comes
  and tracks her down to make her die in anguish.[7]   102
He will not feed on either land or money:
  his wisdom, love, and virtue shall sustain him;
  he will be born between Feltro and Feltro.[8]   105
He comes to save that fallen Italy

---

3. The Roman poet Virgil's voice has not been heard since he died in 19 B.C.E.   **4.** Lombardy is the most
northern area of Italy; Mantua is located to the east of Milan.   **5.** Virgil (70–19 B.C.E.) was born *sub
Julio*, during the reign of Julius Caesar (assassinated in 44 B.C.E.), who was regarded by Dante as the founder
of the Roman Empire.   **6.** Aeneas, the hero of Virgil's *Aeneid*.   **7.** Dante's prediction of a modern
political redeemer is so enigmatic that there can be no certainty of his identity. Most commentators think
it is Cangrande (i.e., the great dog) della Scala of Verona, Dante's benefactor after his exile from Florence.
8. Feltre and Montefeltro are towns that roughly mark the limits of Cangrande's domains. But other
interpretations are possible.

for which the maid Camilla gave her life
    and Turnus, Nisus, Euryalus died of wounds.[9]   108
And he will hunt for her through every city
    until he drives her back to Hell once more,
    whence Envy first unleashed her on mankind.   111
And so, I think it best you follow me
    for your own good, and I shall be your guide
    and lead you out through an eternal place   114
where you will hear desperate cries, and see
    tormented shades, some old as Hell itself,
    and know what second death is, from their screams.[1]   117
And later you will see those who rejoice
    while they are burning, for they have hope of coming,
    whenever it may be, to join the blessèd[2]—   120
to whom, if you too wish to make the climb,
    a spirit, worthier than I, must take you;[3]
    I shall go back, leaving you in her care,   123
because that Emperor dwelling on high
    will not let me lead any to His city,
    since I in life rebelled against His law.[4]   126
Everywhere He reigns, and there He rules;
    there is His city, there is His high throne.
    Oh, happy the one He makes His citizen!"   129
And I to him: "Poet, I beg of you,
    in the name of God, that God you never knew,
    save me from this evil place and worse,   132
lead me there to the place you spoke about
    that I may see the gate Saint Peter guards
    and those whose anguish you have told me of."   135
Then he moved on, and I moved close behind him.

CANTO II

*But the pilgrim begins to waver; he expresses to Virgil his misgivings about his ability
to undertake the journey proposed by Virgil. His predecessors have been Aeneas and
Saint Paul, and he feels unworthy to take his place in their company. But Virgil rebukes
his cowardice, and relates the chain of events that led him to come to Dante. The Virgin
Mary took pity on the Pilgrim in his despair and instructed Saint Lucia to aid him. The
Saint turned to Beatrice because of Dante's great love for her, and Beatrice in turn went
down to Hell, into Limbo, and asked Virgil to guide her friend until that time when
she herself would become his guide. The Pilgrim takes heart at Virgil's explanation and
agrees to follow him.*

The day was fading and the darkening air
    was releasing all the creatures on our earth
    from their daily tasks, and I, one man alone,   3
was making ready to endure the battle
    of the journey, and of the pity it involved,
    which my memory, unerring, shall now retrace.   6

9. Characters in the *Aeneid* who die during Aeneas's conquest of Italy.   1. The second death is damnation; see Revelation 21.8.   2. The souls in Purgatory; the blessèd are the saved in Paradise.   3. Beatrice.   4. Virgil "rebelled" against God because he was not a Christian.

O Muses! O high genius! Help me now!
  O memory that wrote down what I saw,
  here your true excellence shall be revealed!   9
Then I began: "O poet come to guide me,
  tell me if you think my worth sufficient
  before you trust me to this arduous road.   12
You wrote about young Sylvius's father,[5]
  who went beyond, with flesh corruptible,
  with all his senses, to the immortal realm;   15
but if the Adversary of all evil
  was kind to him, considering who he was,
  and the consequence that was to come from him,   18
this cannot seem, to thoughtful men, unfitting,
  for in the highest heaven he was chosen
  father of glorious Rome and of her empire,   21
and both the city and her lands, in truth,
  were established as the place of holiness
  where the successors of great Peter sit.[6]   24
And from this journey you celebrate in verse,
  Aeneas learned those things that were to bring
  victory for him, and for Rome, the Papal seat;   27
then later the Chosen Vessel, Paul, ascended
  to ring back confirmation of that faith
  which is the first step on salvation's road.[7]   30
But why am I to go? Who allows me to?
  I am not Aeneas, I am not Paul,
  neither I nor any man would think me worthy;   33
and so, if I should undertake the journey,
  I fear it might turn out an act of folly—
  you are wise, you see more than my words express."   36
As one who unwills what he willed, will change
  his purpose with some new second thought,
  completely quitting what he first had started,   39
so I did, standing there on that dark slope,
  thinking, ending the beginning of that venture
  I was so quick to take up at the start.   42
"If I have truly understood your words,"
  that shade of magnanimity replied,
  "your soul is burdened with that cowardice   45
which often weighs so heavily on man,
  it turns him from a noble enterprise
  like a frightened beast that shies at its own shadow.   48
To free you from this fear, let me explain
  the reason I came here, the words I heard
  that first time I felt pity for your soul: 51
I was among those dead who are suspended,[8]
  when a lady summoned me. She was so blessed
  and beautiful, I implored her to command me.[9]   54
With eyes of light more bright than any star,

---

5. Aeneas, who visited the underworld in *Aeneid* 6.   6. The apostle Peter is considered by the Catholic Church to be the first pope.   7. St. Paul; see 2 Corinthians 12.2–4.   8. In Limbo, where the souls experience "neither joy nor sorrow" (4.84).   9. As we soon learn, the lady is Beatrice.

in low, soft tones she started to address me
in her own language, with an angel's voice: 57
'O noble soul, courteous Mantuan,
whose fame the world continues to preserve
and will preserve as long as world there is, 60
my friend, who is no friend of Fortune's, strays
on a desert slope; so many obstacles
have crossed his path, his fright has turned him back 63
I fear he may have gone so far astray,
from what report has come to me in Heaven,
that I may have started to his aid too late. 66
Now go, and with your elegance of speech,
with whatever may be needed for his freedom,
give him your help, and thereby bring me solace. 69
I am Beatrice, who urges you to go;
I come from the place I am longing to return to;[1]
love moved me, as it moves me now to speak. 72
When I return to stand before my Lord,
often I shall sing your praises to Him.'
And then she spoke no more. And I began, 75
'O Lady of Grace, through whom alone mankind
may go beyond all worldy things contained
within the sphere that makes the smallest round,[2] 78
your plea fills me with happy eagerness—
to have obeyed already would still seem late!
You needed only to express your wish. 81
But tell me how you dared to make this journey
all the way down to this point of spacelessness,
away from your spacious home that calls you back.' 84
'Because your question searches for deep meaning,
I shall explain in simple words,' she said,
'just why I have no fear of coming here. 87
A man must stand in fear of just those things
that truly have the power to do us harm,
of nothing else, for nothing else is fearsome. 90
God gave me such a nature through His Grace,
the torments you must bear cannot affect me,
nor are the fires of Hell a threat to me. 93
A gracious lady[3] sits in Heaven grieving
for what happened to the one I send you to,
and her compassion breaks Heaven's stern decree. 96
She called Lucia[4] and making her request,
she said, "Your faithful one is now in need
of you, and to you I now commend his soul." 99
Lucia, the enemy of cruelty,
hastened to make her way to where I was,
sitting by the side of ancient Rachel,[5] 102
and said to me: "Beatrice, God's true praise,

1. Paradise.   2. The sphere of the moon.   3. The Virgin Mary.   4. St. Lucy, a 3rd-century martyr
and the patron saint of those afflicted with poor or damaged sight.   5. Rachel signifies the contemplative
life: see Genesis 29.16–17.

will you not help the one whose love was such
  it made him leave the vulgar crowd for you?
Do you not hear the pity of his weeping,   105
  do you not see what death it is that threatens him
  along that river the sea shall never conquer?"[6]   108
There never was a wordly person living
  more anxious to promote his selfish gains
  than I was at the sound of words like these—   111
to leave my holy seat and come down here
  and place my trust in you, in your noble speech
  that honors you and all those who have heard it!' 114
When she had finished reasoning, she turned
  her shining eyes away, and there were tears
  How eager then I was to come to you!   117
And I have come to you just as she wished,
  and I have freed you from the beast that stood
  blocking the quick way up the mount of bliss.   120
So what is wrong? Why, why do you delay?
  Why are you such a coward in your heart,
  why aren't you bold and free of all your fear,   123
when three such gracious ladies, who are blessed,
  watch out for you up there in Heaven's court,
  and my words, too, bring promise of such good?" 126
As little flowers from the frosty night
  are closed and limp, and when the sun shines down
  on them, they rise to open on their stem,   129
my wilted strength began to bloom within me,
  and such warm courage flowed into my heart
  that I spoke like a man set free of fear.   132
"O she, compassionate, who moved to help me!
  And you, all kindness, in obeying quick
  those words of truth she brought with her for you— 135
you and the words you spoke have moved my heart
  with such desire to continue onward
  that now I have returned to my first purpose. 138
Let us start, for both our wills, joined now, are one.
  You are my guide, you are my lord and teacher."
  These were my words to him and, when he moved, 141
I entered on that deep and rugged road.

CANTO III

As the two poets enter the vestibule that leads to Hell itself, Dante sees the inscription above the gate, and he hears the screams of anguish from the damned souls. Rejected by God and not accepted by the powers of Hell, the first group of souls are "nowhere," because of their cowardly refusal to make a choice in life. Their punishment is to follow a banner at a furious pace forever, and to be tormented by flies and hornets. The Pilgrim recognizes several of these shades but mentions none by name. Next they come to the River Acheron, where they are greeted by the infernal boatman, Charon. Among those doomed souls who are to be ferried across the river, Charon sees the living man and

6. These are the metaphoric waters of 1.22–24.

challenges him, but Virgil lets it be known that his companion must pass. Then across the landscape rushes a howling wind, which blasts the Pilgrim out of his senses, and he falls to the ground.

I AM THE WAY INTO THE DOLEFUL CITY,
   I AM THE WAY INTO ETERNAL GRIEF,
   I AM THE WAY TO A FORSAKEN RACE.   3
JUSTICE IT WAS THAT MOVED MY GREAT CREATOR;
   DIVINE OMNIPOTENCE CREATED ME,
   AND HIGHEST WISDOM JOINED WITH PRIMAL LOVE.[7]   6
BEFORE ME NOTHING BUT ETERNAL THINGS
   WERE MADE, AND I SHALL LAST ETERNALLY.
   ABANDON EVERY HOPE, ALL YOU WHO ENTER.   9
I saw these words spelled out in somber colors
   inscribed along the ledge above a gate;
   "Master," I said, "these words I see are cruel."   12
He answered me, speaking with experience:
   "Now here you must leave all distrust behind;
   let all your cowardice die on this spot.   15
We are at the place where earlier I said
   you could expect to see the suffering race
   of souls who lost the good of intellect."[8]   18
Placing his hand on mine, smiling at me
   in such a way that I was reassured,
   he led me in, into those mysteries.   21
Here sighs and cries and shrieks of lamentation
   echoed throughout the starless air of Hell;
   at first these sounds resounding made me weep: 24
tongues confused, a language strained in anguish
   with cadences of anger, shrill outcries
   and raucous groans that joined with sounds of hands, 27
raising a whirling storm that turns itself
   forever through that air of endless black,
   like grains of sand swirling when a whirlwind blows. 30
And I, in the midst of all this circling horror,
   began, "Teacher, what are these sounds I hear?
   What souls are these so overwhelmed by grief?"   33
And he to me: "This wretched state of being
   is the fate of those sad souls who lived a life
   but lived it with no blame and with no praise.   36
They are mixed with that repulsive choir of angels
   neither faithful nor unfaithful to their God,
   who undecided stood but for themselves.[9]   39
Heaven, to keep its beauty, cast them out,
   but even Hell itself would not receive them,
   to fear the damned might glory over them."   42
And I. "Master, what torments do they suffer
   that force them to lament so bitterly?"

---

7. God as Father, Son, and Holy Ghost.   8. *The good of intellect:* i.e., God.   9. The "neutral angels," not mentioned in the Bible but discussed by theologians throughout the Middle Ages, were those who declined to choose either side when Satan rebelled against God.

He answered: "I will tell you in few words: 45
these wretches have no hope of truly dying,
    and this blind life they lead is so abject
    it makes them envy every other fate.
The world will not record their having been there; 48
    Heaven's mercy and its justice turn from them.
    Let's not discuss them; look and pass them by." 51
And so I looked and saw a kind of banner
    rushing ahead, whirling with aimless speed
    as though it would not ever take a stand; 54
behind it an interminable train
    of souls pressed on, so many that I wondered
    how death could have undone so great a number. 57
When I had recognized a few of them,
    I saw the shade of the one who must have been
    the coward who had made the great refusal.[1] 60
At once I understood, and I was sure
    this was that sect of evil souls who were
    hateful to God and to His enemies. 63
These wretches, who had never truly lived,
    went naked, and were stung and stung again
    by the hornets and the wasps that circled them 66
and made their faces run with blood in streaks;
    their blood, mixed with their tears, dripped to their feet,
    and disgusting maggots collected in the pus. 69
And when I looked beyond this crowd I saw
    a throng upon the shore of a wide river,
    which made me ask, "Master, I would like to know: 72
who are these people, and what law is this
    that makes those souls so eager for the crossing—
    as I can see, even in this dim light?" 75
And he: "All this will be made plain to you
    as soon as we shall come to stop awhile
    upon the sorrowful shore of Acheron."[2] 78
And I, with eyes cast down in shame, for fear
    that I perhaps had spoken out of turn,
    said nothing more until we reached the river. 81
And suddenly, coming toward us in a boat,
    a man of years[3] whose ancient hair was white
    shouted at us, "Woe to you, perverted souls! 84
Give up all hope of ever seeing Heaven:
    I come to lead you to the other shore,
    into eternal darkness, ice, and fire. 87
And you, the living soul, you over there,
    get away from all these people who are dead."
    But when he saw I did not move aside, 90
he said, "Another way, by other ports,
    not here, shall you pass to reach the other shore;

1. This is Pope Celestine V, who was elected in July 1294 but resigned five months later.   **2.** The first of the four rivers of Hell.   **3.** Charon; see *Aeneid* 6.

a lighter skiff than this must carry you."[4]   93
And my guide, "Charon, this is no time for anger!
  It is so willed, there where the power is
  for what is willed; that's all you need to know."   96
These words brought silence to the woolly cheeks
  of the ancient steersman of the livid marsh,
  whose eyes were set in glowing wheels of fire.   99
But all those souls there, naked, in despair,
  changed color and their teeth began to chatter
  at the sound of his announcement of their doom.   102
They were cursing God, cursing their own parents,
  the human race, the time, the place, the seed
  of their beginning, and their day of birth.   105
Then all together, weeping bitterly,
  they packed themselves along the wicked shore
  that waits for every man who fears not God.   108
The devil, Charon, with eyes of glowing coals,
  summons them all together with a signal,
  and with an oar he strikes the laggard sinner.   111
As in autumn when the leaves begin to fall,
  one after the other (until the branch
  is witness to the spoils spread on the ground),   114
so did the evil seed of Adam's Fall
  drop from that shore to the boat, one at a time,
  at the signal, like the falcon to its lure.[5]   117
Away they go across the darkened waters,
  and before they reach the other side to land,
  a new throng starts collecting on this side.   120
"My son," the gentle master said to me,
  "all those who perish in the wrath of God
  assemble here from all parts of the earth;   123
they want to cross the river, they are eager;
  it is Divine Justice that spurs them on,
  turning the fear they have into desire.   126
A good soul never comes to make this crossing,
  so, if Charon grumbles at the sight of you,
  you see now what his words are really saying."   129
He finished speaking, and the grim terrain
  shook violently; and the fright it gave me
  even now in recollection makes me sweat.   132
Out of the tear-drenched land a wind arose
  which blasted forth into a reddish light,
  knocking my senses out of me completely,   135
and I fell as one falls tired into sleep.[6]

---

4. Charon knows that after death Dante will be taken not to Hell but to Purgatory in a "swift and light" vessel piloted by an angel; the arrival of the souls in Purgatory is described in *Purgatorio* 2.22–48. This is the first of several places in the *Commedia* where Dante predicts his own salvation.   5. These similes are drawn from *Aeneid* 6.56–60 (all line references are to the edition in this anthology).   6. Dante is describing an earthquake, which medieval science understood as the escape of vapors from within the earth; it is while he is unconscious that he crosses Acheron into Hell proper.

CANTO IV

Waking from his swoon, the Pilgrim is led by Virgil to the First Circle of Hell, known as Limbo, where the sad shades of the virtuous non-Christians dwell. The souls here, including Virgil, suffer no physical torment, but they must live, in desire, without hope of seeing God. Virgil tells about Christ's descent into Hell and His salvation of several Old Testament figures. The poets see a light glowing in the darkness, and as they proceed toward it, they are met by the four greatest (other than Virgil) pagan poets: Homer, Horace, Ovid, and Lucan, who take the Pilgrim into their group. As they come closer to the light, the Pilgrim perceives a splendid castle, where the greatest non-Christian thinkers dwell together with other famous historical figures. Once within the castle, the Pilgrim sees, among others, Electra, Aeneas, Caesar, Saladin, Aristotle, Plato, Orpheus, Cicero, Avicenna, and Averroës. But soon they must leave; and the poets move from the radiance of the castle toward the fearful encompassing darkness.

A heavy clap of thunder ! I awoke
   from the deep sleep that drugged my mind—startled,
   the way one is when shaken out of sleep.   3
I turned my rested eyes from side to side,
   already on my feet and, staring hard,
   I tried my best to find out where I was,   6
and this is what I saw: I found myself
   upon the brink of grief's abysmal valley
   that collects the thunderings of endless cries.   9
So dark and deep and nebulous it was,
   try as I might to force my sight below,
   I could not see the shape of anything.   12
"Let us descend into the sightless world,"
   began the poet (his face was deathly pale):
   "I will go first, and you will follow me."   15
And I, aware of his changed color, said:
   "But how can I go on if you are frightened?
   You are my constant strength when I lose heart."   18
And he to me: "The anguish of the souls
   that are down here paints my face with pity—
   which you have wrongly taken to be fear.   21
Let us go, the long road urges us."
   He entered then, leading the way for me
   down to the first circle of the abyss.   24
Down there, to judge only by what I heard,
   there were no wails but just the sounds of sighs
   rising and trembling through the timeless air,   27
the sounds of sighs of untormented grief
   burdening these groups, diverse and teeming,
   made up of men and women and of infants.   30
Then the good master said, "You do not ask
   what sort of souls are these you see around you.
   Now you should know before we go on farther,   33
they have not sinned. But their great worth alone
   was not enough, for they did not know Baptism,
   which is the gateway to the faith you follow,   36
and if they came before the birth of Christ,

they did not worship God the way one should;
  I myself am a member of this group. 39
For this defect, and for no other guilt,
  we here are lost. In this alone we suffer:
  cut off from hope, we live on in desire." 42
The words I heard weighed heavy on my heart;
  to think that souls as virtuous as these
  were suspended in that limbo, and forever! 45
"Tell me, my teacher, tell me, O my master,"
  I began (wishing to have confirmed by him
  the teachings of unerring Christian doctrine), 48
"did any ever leave here, through his merit
  or with another's help, and go to bliss?"
And he, who understood my hidden question,[7] 51
answered: "I was a novice in this place
  when I saw a mighty lord descend to us
  who wore the sign of victory as his crown. 54
He took from us the shade of our first parent,[8]
  of Abel, his good son, of Noah, too,
  and of obedient Moses, who made the laws; 57
Abram, the Patriarch, David the King,
  Israel with his father and his children,
  with Rachel, whom he worked so hard to win; 60
and many more he chose for blessedness;
  and you should know, before these souls were taken,
  no human soul had ever reached salvation." 63
We did not stop our journey while he spoke,
  but continued on our way along the woods—
  I say the woods, for souls were thick as trees. 66
We had not gone too far from where I woke
  when I made out a fire up ahead,
  a hemisphere of light that lit the dark. 69
We were still at some distance from that place,
  but close enough for me vaguely to see
  that honorable souls possessed that spot. 72
"O glory of the sciences and arts,
  who are these souls enjoying special honor,
  dwelling apart from all the others here?" 75
And he to me: "The honored name they bear
  that still resounds above in your own world
  wins Heaven's favor for them in this place."[9] 78
And as he spoke I heard a voice announce:
  "Now let us honor our illustrious poet,
  his shade that left is now returned to us." 81
And when the voice was silent and all was quiet
  I saw four mighty shades approaching us,
  their faces showing neither joy nor sorrow. 84
Then my good master started to explain:

---

7. Dante's question is about the Harrowing of Hell, when according to Christian doctrine, Christ descended into Hell after the crucifixion and rescued the souls of the righteous of Israel; see also 12.44.   8. Adam.
9. The "honored name" is "poet."

"Observe the one who comes with sword in hand,
　leading the three as if he were their master.   87
It is the shade of Homer, sovereign poet,
　and coming second, Horace, the satirist;
　Ovid is the third, and last comes Lucan.[1]   90
Since they all share one name with me, the name
　you heard resounding in that single voice,
　they honor me and do well doing so."   93
So I saw gathered there the noble school
　of the master singer of sublimest verse,
　who soars above all others like the eagle.   96
And after they had talked awhile together,
　they turned and with a gesture welcomed me,
　and at that sign I saw my master smile.   99
Greater honor still they deigned to grant me:
　they welcomed me as one of their own group,
　so that I numbered sixth among such minds.   102
We walked together toward the shining light,
　discussing things that here are best kept silent,
　as there they were most fitting for discussion.   105
We reached the boundaries of a splendid castle
　that seven times was circled by high walls
　defended by a sweetly flowing stream.[2]   108
We walked right over it as on hard ground;
　through seven gates I passed with those wise spirits,
　and then we reached a meadow fresh in bloom.[3]   111
There people were whose eyes were calm and grave,
　whose bearing told of great authority;
　seldom they spoke and always quietly.   114
Then moving to one side we reached a place
　spread out and luminous, higher than before,
　allowing us to view all who were there.   117
And right before us on the lustrous green
　the mighty shades were pointed out to me
　(my heart felt glory when I looked at them).   120
There was Electra standing with a group,
　among whom I saw Hector and Aeneas,
　and Caesar, falcon-eyed and fully armed.[4]   123
I saw Camilla and Penthesilea;
　across the way I saw the Latian King,
　with Lavinia, his daughter, by his side.[5]   126
I saw the Brutus who drove out the Tarquin;
　Lucretia, Julia, Marcia, and Cornelia;
　off, by himself, I noticed Saladin,[6]   129

1. Horace, Ovid, and Lucan are famous Roman poets.   2. Commentators have suggested that this is a Castle of Fame, its seven walls symbolizing the seven liberal arts, a system of knowledge developed in the classical period.   3. A locale reminiscent of the classical Elysian fields as described in *Aeneid* 6.468–73.   4. Julius Caesar (d. 44 B.C.E.). *Electra:* the mother of Dardanus, the founder of Troy. *Hector:* the leading warrior of the Trojans in the *Iliad. Aeneas:* the hero of the *Aeneid.*   5. Heiress to King Latinus who ruled the area of Italy where Rome was later located and who married Aeneas. *Camilla:* a female warrior in the *Aeneid,* where she is compared to *Penthesilea,* who fought for the Trojans against the Greeks.   6. Admired for his chivalry in fighting against the crusaders, he was sultan of Egypt and Syria and died in 1193. *Brutus:* not the Brutus who killed Julius Caesar, but an earlier Roman who drove out the tyrant Tarquin. All four of the women mentioned were virtuous Roman matrons.

and when I raised my eyes a little higher
  I saw the master sage of those who know,[7]
  sitting with his philosophic family.   132
All gaze at him, all pay their homage to him;
  and there I saw both Socrates and Plato,
  each closer to his side than any other;   135
Democritus, who said the world was chance,
  Diogenes, Thales, Anaxagoras,
  Empedocles, Zeno, and Heraclitus;   138
I saw the one who classified our herbs:
  Dioscorides I mean. And I saw Orpheus,
  Tully, Linus, Seneca the moralist,[8]   141
Euclid the geometer, and Ptolemy,
  Hippocrates, Galen, Avicenna,
  and Averroës, who made the Commentary.[9]   144
I cannot tell about them all in full;
  my theme is long and urges me ahead,
  often I must omit things I have seen.   147
The company of six becomes just two;
  my wise guide leads me by another way
  out of the quiet into tempestuous air.   150
I come into a place where no light is.

CANTO V

From Limbo Virgil leads his ward down to the threshold of the Second Circle of Hell, where for the first time he will see the damned in Hell being punished for their sins. There, barring their way, is the hideous figure of Minòs, the bestial judge of Dante's underworld; but after strong words from Virgil, the poets are allowed to pass into the dark space of this circle, where can be heard the wailing voices of the Lustful, whose punishment consists in being forever whirled about in a dark, stormy wind. After seeing a thousand or more famous lovers—including Semiramis, Dido, Helen, Achilles, and Paris—the Pilgrim asks to speak to two figures he sees together. They are Francesca da Rimini and her lover, Paolo, and the scene in which they appear is probably the most famous episode of the Inferno. At the end of the scene, the Pilgrim, who has been overcome by pity for the lovers, faints to the ground.

This way I went, descending from the first
  into the second round, that holds less space
  but much more pain—stinging the soul to wailing.   3
There stands Minòs grotesquely, and he snarls,
  examining the guilty at the entrance;
  he judges and dispatches, tail in coils.[1]   6
By this I mean that when the evil soul

---

7. Aristotle (384–322 B.C.E.), Greek philosopher. The men mentioned in lines 132–38 are Greek philosophers of the 7th through the 4th centuries B.C.E.   8. Roman philosopher and dramatist, killed by Nero in 65 C.E. *Dioscorides:* Greek physician (1st century C.E.) *Orpheus:* mythical Greek poet. *Tully:* Cicero (d. 43 B.C.E.), Roman orator.   9. Avicenna (d. 1037) and Averroës (d. 1198) were Islamic philosophers who wrote commentaries on Aristotle's works that were highly influential in Christian Europe. *Euclid:* Greek mathematician (4th century B.C.E.). *Ptolemy:* Greek astronomer and geographer (1st century C.E.) credited with devising the cosmological system that was accepted until the time of Copernicus in the 16th century (hence the term *Ptolomaic universe*). *Hippocrates and Galen:* Greek physicians (4th and 2nd centuries B.C.E., respectively).   1. In *Aeneid* 6.207–11 Minos is described as judge of the underworld.

appears before him, it confesses all,
  and he, who is the expert judge of sins,
knows to what place in Hell the soul belongs;   9
  the times he wraps his tail around himself
  tell just how far the sinner must go down.   12
The damned keep crowding up in front of him:
  they pass along to judgment one by one;
  they speak, they hear, and then are hurled below.   15
"O you who come to the place where pain is host,"
  Minòs spoke out when he caught sight of me,
  putting aside the duties of his office,   18
"be careful how you enter and whom you trust
  it's easy to get in, but don't be fooled!"
  And my guide said to him: "Why keep on shouting?   21
Do not attempt to stop his fated journey;
  it is so willed there where the power is
  for what is willed,[2] that's all you need to know."   24
And now the notes of anguish start to play
  upon my ears; and now I find myself
  where sounds on sounds of weeping pound at me.   27
I came to a place where no light shone at all,
  bellowing like the sea racked by a tempest,
  when warring winds attack it from both sides.   30
The infernal storm, eternal in its rage,
  sweeps and drives the spirits with its blast:
  it whirls them, lashing them with punishment.   33
When they are swept back past their place of judgment,
  then come the shrieks, laments, and anguished cries;
  there they blaspheme God's almighty power.   36
I learned that to this place of punishment
  all those who sin in lust have been condemned,
  those who make reason slave to appetite;   39
and as the wings of starlings in the winter
  bear them along in wide-spread, crowded flocks,
  so does that wind propel the evil spirits: 42
now here, then there, and up and down, it drives them
  with never any hope to comfort them—
  hope not of rest but even of suffering less.   45
And just like cranes in flight, chanting their lays,
  stretching an endless line in their formation,
  I saw approaching, crying their laments,   48
spirits carried along by the battling winds,
  And so I asked, "Teacher, tell me, what souls
  are these punished in the sweep of the black wind?"   51
"The first of those whose story you should know,"
  my master wasted no time answering,
  "was empress over lands of many tongues;   54
her vicious tastes had so corrupted her
  she licensed every form of lust with laws
  to cleanse the stain of scandal she had spread;   57

---

2. It is willed in Heaven by God, who has the power to accomplish whatever He wills.

she is Semiramis,[3] who, legend says,
    was Ninus' wife as well as his successor;
    she governed all the land the Sultan rules.   60
The next is she who killed herself for love
    and broke faith with the ashes of Sichaeus;[4]
    and there is Cleopatra, who loved men's lusting.   63
See Helen there, the root of evil woe
    lasting long years, and see the great Achilles,
    who lost his life to love, in final combat;[5]   66
see Paris, Tristan[6]—then, more than a thousand
    he pointed out to me, and named them all,
    those shades whom love cut off from life on earth.   69
After I heard my teacher call the names
    of all these knights and ladies of ancient times,
    pity confused my senses, and I was dazed.   72
I began: "Poet, I would like, with all my heart,
    to speak to those two there who move together
    and seem to be so light upon the winds."[7]   75
And he: "You'll see when they are closer to us;
    if you entreat them by that love of theirs
    that carries them along, they'll come to you."   78
When the winds bent their course in our direction
    I raised my voice to them, "O wearied souls,
    come speak with us if it be not forbidden."   81
As doves, called by desire to return
    to their sweet nest, with wings raised high and poised,
    float downward through the air, guided by will,   84
so these two left the flock where Dido is
    and came toward us through the malignant air,
    such was the tender power of my call.   87
"O living creature, gracious and so kind,
    who makes your way here through this dingy air
    to visit us who stained the world with blood,   90
if we could claim as friend the King of Kings,
    we would beseech him that he grant you peace,
    you who show pity for our atrocious plight.   93
Whatever pleases you to hear or speak
    we will hear and we will speak about with you
    as long as the wind, here where we are, is silent.   96
The place where I was born lies on the shore
    where the river Po with its attendant streams
    descends to seek its final resting place.[8]   99
Love, quick to kindle in the gentle heart,
    seized this one for the beauty of my body,
    torn from me, (How it happened still offends me!)   102

---

3. Renowned for licentiousness, a mythical queen of Assyria and wife of Ninus, the legendary founder of Ninevah. Because both the capital of Assyria and Old Cairo were known as Babylon, her land is here confused with that ruled by the sultan of Egypt.   4. Dido, whose suicide for love of Aeneas is described in *Aeneid* 4.542–942, was the widow of Sichaeus. Cleopatra killed herself after the death of her lover, Marc Antony, in 30 B.C.E.   5. The medieval version of the Troy story described Achilles as enamored of a Trojan princess, Polyxena, and killed in an ambush set by Paris when he went to meet her. Helen's seduction by Paris (see line 67) was the cause of the Trojan War.   6. The lover of Iseult, wife of his lord King Mark.   7. Francesca da Rimini and her brother-in-law Paolo Malatesta.   8. The *Po* is a river in northern Italy that empties into the Adriatic sea at Ravenna.

Love, that excuses no one loved from loving,
  seized me so strongly with delight in him
  that, as you see, he never leaves my side. 105
Love led us straight to sudden death together.[9]
  Caïna awaits the one who quenched our lives."[1]
  These were the words that came from them to us. 108
When those offended souls had told their story,
  I bowed my head and kept it bowed until
  the poet said, "What are you thinking of?" 111
When finally I spoke, I sighed, "Alas,
  all those sweet thoughts, and oh, how much desiring
  brought these two down into this agony." 114
And then I turned to them and tried to speak;
  I said, "Francesca, the torment that you suffer
  brings painful tears of pity to my eyes. 117
But tell me, in that time of your sweet sighing
  how, and by what signs, did love allow you
  to recognize your dubious desires?" 120
And she to me: "There is no greater pain
  than to remember, in our present grief,
  past happiness (as well your teacher knows)! 123
But if your great desire is to learn
  the very root of such a love as ours,
  I shall tell you, but in words of flowing tears. 126
One day we read, to pass the time away,
  of Lancelot,[2] of how he fell in love;
  we were alone, innocent of suspicion. 129
Time and again our eyes were brought together
  by the book we read; our faces flushed and paled.
  To the moment of one line alone we yielded: 132
it was when we read about those longed-for lips
  now being kissed by such a famous lover,
  that this one (who shall never leave my side) 135
then kissed my mouth, and trembled as he did.
  Our Galehot[3] was that book and he who wrote it.
  That day we read no further."[4] And all the while 138
the one of the two spirits spoke these words,
  the other wept, in such a way that pity
  blurred my senses; I swooned as though to die, 141
and fell to Hell's floor as a body, dead, falls.

CANTO VI

*On recovering consciousness the Pilgrim finds himself with Virgil in the Third Circle,
where the Gluttons are punished. These shades are mired in filthy muck and are eternally battered by cold and dirty hail, rain, and snow. Soon the travelers come upon*

9. These seven lines (100–6) should be compared to the love sonnets by Guido Guinizzelli and Dante
included in *Medieval Lyrics: A Selection* (pp. 1411 and 1414).   **1.** *Caïna* is the circle of Cain (described
in canto 32), where those who killed their kin are punished; the lovers were killed by Gianciotto Malatesta,
Francesca's husband and Paolo's brother.   **2.** In Arthurian legend, the lover of Arthur's wife, Guinevere.
3. The knight who, in the French romance being read by the lovers, acted as a go-between for Lancelot
and Guinevere.   **4.** Compare this line to Augustine's account of his conversion by reading a passage in
Paul's Epistle to the Romans: see pp. 1127 ff. above.

Cerberus, the three-headed, doglike beast who guards the Gluttons, but Virgil pacifies him with fistfuls of slime and the two poets pass on. One of the shades recognizes Dante the Pilgrim and hails him. It is Ciacco, a Florentine who, before they leave, makes a prophecy concerning the political future of Florence. As the poets move away, the Pilgrim questions Virgil about the Last Judgment and other matters until the two arrive at the next circle.

Regaining now my senses, which had fainted
   at the sight of these two who were kinsmen lovers,
   a piteous sight confusing me to tears,   3
new suffering and new sinners suffering
   appeared to me, no matter where I moved
   or turned my eyes, no matter where I gazed.   6
I am in the third circle, in the round of rain
   eternal, cursed, cold, and falling heavy,
   unchanging beat, unchanging quality.   9
Thick hail and dirty water mixed with snow
   come down in torrents through the murky air,
   and the earth is stinking from this soaking rain.   12
Cerberus,[5] a ruthless and fantastic beast,
   with all three throats howls out his doglike sounds
   above the drowning sinners of this place.   15
His eyes are red, his beard is slobbered black,
   his belly swollen, and he has claws for hands;
   he rips the spirits, flays and mangles them.   18
Under the rain they howl like dogs, lying
   now on one side with the other as a screen,
   now on the other turning, these wretched sinners.   21
When the slimy Cerberus caught sight of us,
   he opened up his mouths and showed his fangs;
   his body was one mass of twitching muscles.   24
My master stooped and, spreading wide his fingers,
   he grabbed up heaping fistfuls of the mud
   and flung it down into those greedy gullets.   27
As a howling cur, hungering to get fed,
   quiets down with the first mouthful of his food,
   busy with eating, wrestling with that alone,   30
so it was with all three filthy heads
   of the demon Cerberus, used to barking thunder
   on these dead souls, who wished that they were deaf.   33
We walked across this marsh of shades beaten
   down by the heavy rain, our feet pressing
   on their emptiness that looked like human form.   36
Each sinner there was stretched out on the ground
   except for one[6] who quickly sat up straight,
   the moment that he saw us pass him by.   39
"O you there being led through this inferno,"
   he said, "try to remember who I am,
   for you had life before I gave up mine."[7]   42
I said: "The pain you suffer here perhaps

---

5. For this creature as one of the guardians of Hell, see *Aeneid* 6.190–97.   **6.** A Florentine named Ciacco, known only through his appearance here.   **7.** "You were born before I died."

disfigures you beyond all recognition:
   I can't remember seeing you before.   45
But tell me who you are, assigned to grieve
   in this sad place, afflicted by such torture
   that—worse there well may be, but none more foul."   48
"Your own city," he said, "so filled with envy
   its cup already overflows the brim,
   once held me in the brighter life above.   51
You citizens gave me the name of Ciacco;
   and for my sin of gluttony I am damned,
   as you can see, to rain that beats me weak.   54
And my sad sunken soul is not alone,
   for all these sinners here share in my pain
   and in my sin." And that was his last word.   57
"Ciacco," I said to him, "your grievous state
   weighs down on me, it makes me want to weep;
   but tell me what will happen, if you know,   60
to the citizens of that divided state?
   And are there any honest men among them?
   And tell me, why is it so plagued with strife?"   63
And he replied:[8] "After much contention
   they will come to bloodshed; the rustic party
   will drive the other out by brutal means.   66
Then it will come to pass, this side will fall
   within three suns, and the other rise to power
   with the help of one now listing toward both sides.   69
For a long time they will keep their heads raised high,
   holding the others down with crushing weight,
   no matter how these weep or squirm for shame.   72
Two just men there are,[9] but no one listens,
   for pride, envy, avarice are the three sparks
   that kindle in men's hearts and set them burning."   75
With this his mournful words came to an end.
   But I spoke back: "There's more I want to know;
   I beg you to provide me with more facts: 78
Farinata and Tegghiaio, who were so worthy,
   Jacopo Rusticucci, Arrigo, Mosca,
   and all the rest so bent on doing good,[1]   81
where are they? Tell me what's become of them;
   one great desire tortures me: to know
   whether they taste Heaven's sweetness or Hell's gall." 84
"They lie below with blacker souls," he said,
   "by different sins pushed down to different depths;
   if you keep going you may see them all.   87
But when you are once more in the sweet world
   I beg you to remind our friends of me.
   I speak no more; no more I answer you."   90

8. The enigmatic "prophecy" that follows refers first to the triumph of the Whites, or "the rustic party" (to which Dante was allied), in 1300 and then their defeat by the Blacks, aided by Pope Boniface ("one now listing toward both sides"), in 1302, at which time Dante was exiled.   9. The identity of these two is unknown.   1. Dante asks about famous Florentines; he will find Farinata in canto 10, Tegghiaio and Rusticucci in canto 16, and Mosca in canto 28. Arrigo does not appear.

He twisted his straight gaze into a squint
   and stared awhile at me, then bent his head,
      falling to join his other sightless peers   93
My guide then said to me: "He'll wake no more
   until the day the angel's trumpet blows,
      when the unfriendly Judge shall come down here;   96
each soul shall find again his wretched tomb,
   assume his flesh and take his human shape,
      and hear his fate resound eternally."[2]   99
And so we made our way through the filthy mess
   of muddy shades and slush, moving slowly,
      talking a little about the afterlife.   102
I said, "Master, will these torments be increased,
   or lessened, on the final Judgment Day,
      or will the pain be just the same as now?"   105
And he: "Remember your philosophy:
   the closer a thing comes to its perfection,
      more keen will be its pleasure or its pain.   108
Although this cursèd race of punished souls
   shall never know the joy of true perfection,
      more perfect will their pain be then than now."[3] 111
We circled round that curving road while talking
   of more than I shall mention at this time,
      and came to where the ledge begins descending; 114
there we found Plutus, mankind's arch-enemy.[4]

CANTO VII

At the boundary of the Fourth Circle the two travelers confront clucking Plutus, the god of wealth, who collapses into emptiness at a word from Virgil. Descending farther, the Pilgrim sees two groups of angry, shouting souls who clash huge rolling weights against each other with their chests. They are the Prodigal and the Miserly. Their earthly concern with material goods prompts the Pilgrim to question Virgil about Fortune and her distribution of the worldly goods of men. After Virgil's explanation, they descend to the banks of the swamplike river Styx, which serves as the Fifth Circle. Mired in the bog are the Wrathful, who constantly tear and mangle each other. Beneath the slime of the Styx, Virgil explains, are the Slothful; the bubbles on the muddy surface indicate their presence beneath. The poets walk around the swampy area and soon come to the foot of a high tower.

"Pape Satàn, pape Satàn aleppe!"[5]
   the voice of Plutus clucked these words at us,
      and that kind sage, to whom all things were known,   3
said reassuringly: "Do not let fear
   defeat you, for whatever be his power,
      he cannot stop our journey down this rock."   6
Then he turned toward that swollen face of rage,
   crying, "Be quiet, cursèd wolf of Hell:

---

2. Virgil refers to the Last Judgment, when the dead will regain their bodies.   3. They will be more perfect because body and soul will be reunited (a principle derived from Aristotelian science), which will only increase their pain.   4. Dante combines Pluto, the classical god of the underworld, with Plutus, the classical god of wealth.   5. Virgil apparently understands this mysterious outburst regarding Satan, but commentators have remained baffled.

feed on the burning bile that rots your guts. 9
This journey to the depths does have a reason,
   for it is willed on high, where Michael wrought
   a just revenge for the bold assault on God."[6] 12
As sails swollen by wind, when the ship's mast breaks,
   collapse, deflated, tangled in a heap,
   just so the savage beast fell to the ground. 15
And then we started down a fourth abyss,
   making our way along the dismal slope
   where all the evil of the world is dumped. 18
Ah, God's avenging justice! Who could heap up
   suffering and pain as strange as I saw here?
   How can we let our guilt bring us to this? 21
As every wave Charybdis[7] whirls to sea
   comes crashing against its counter-current wave,
   so these folks here must dance their roundelay. 24
More shades were here than anywhere above,
   and from both sides, to the sound of their own screams,
   straining their chests, they rolled enormous weights. 27
And when they met and clashed against each other
   they turned to push the other way, one side
   screaming, "Why hoard?," the other side, "Why waste?" 30
And so they moved back round the gloomy circle,
   returning on both sides to opposite poles
   to scream their shameful tune another time; 33
again they came to clash and turn and roll
   forever in their semicircle joust.
   And I, my heart pierced through by such a sight, 36
spoke out, "My Master, please explain to me
   who are these people here? Were they all priests,
   these tonsured[8] souls I see there to our left?" 39
He said, "In their first life all you see here
   had such myopic minds they could not judge
   with moderation when it came to spending; 42
their barking voices make this clear enough,
   when they arrive at the two points on the circle
   where opposing guilts divide them into two. 45
The ones who have the bald spot on their heads
   were priests and popes and cardinals, in whom
   avarice is most likely to prevail." 48
And I: "Master, in such a group as this
   I should be able to recognize a few
   who dirtied themselves by such crimes as these." 51
And he replied, "Yours is an empty hope:
   their undistinguished life that made them foul
   now makes it harder to distinguish them. 54
Eternally the two will come to blows;
   then from the tomb they will be resurrected:
   these with tight fists, those without any hair. 57

6. A reference to the battle in heaven between the Archangel Michael and Satan in the form of a dragon: see *Revelation* 12.7–9.   7. A famous whirlpool in the Straits of Messina, between Sicily and Italy, described in *Aeneid* 3.   8. The tonsure—a shaving of part of the head—was a mark of clerical status.

It was squandering and hoarding that have robbed them
   of the lovely world, and got them in this brawl:
   I will not waste choice words describing it!   60
You see, my son, the short-lived mockery
   of all the wealth that is in Fortune's keep,
   over which the human race is bickering;   63
for all the gold that is or ever was
   beneath the moon won't buy a moment's rest
   for even one among these weary souls."   66
"Master, now tell me what this Fortune is
   you touched upon before. What is she like
   who holds all worldly wealth within her fists?"   69
And he to me, "O foolish race of man,
   how overwhelming is your ignorance!
   Now listen while I tell you what she means:[9]   72
that One, whose wisdom knows infinity,
   made all the heavens and gave each one a guide,
   and each sphere shining shines on all the others,   75
so light is spread with equal distribution:
   for worldly splendors He decreed the same
   and ordained a guide and general ministress   78
who would at her discretion shift the world's
   vain wealth from nation to nation, house to house,
   with no chance of interference from mankind;   81
so while one nation rules, another falls,
   according to whatever she decrees
   (her sentence hidden like a snake in grass).   84
Your knowledge has no influence on her;
   for she foresees, she judges, and she rules
   her kingdom as the other gods do theirs.   87
Her changing changes never take a rest;
   necessity keeps her in constant motion,
   as men come and go to take their turn with her.   90
And this is she so crucified and cursed;
   even those in luck, who should be praising her,
   instead revile her and condemn her acts.   93
But she is blest and in her bliss hears nothing;
   with all God's joyful first-created creatures
   she turns her sphere and, blest, turns it with joy. 96
Now let's move down to greater wretchedness;
   the stars that rose when I set out for you
   are going down—we cannot stay too long."[1]   99
We crossed the circle to its other bank,
   passing a spring that boils and overflows
   into a ditch the spring itself cut out.   102
The water was a deeper dark than perse,
   and we, with its gray waves for company,

---

9. Virgil now explains that each area of life is presided over by a *guide*, a kind of angel, under the ultimate authority of God. The classical goddess Fortune—the "ministress" of line 78—who was thought to distribute the world's goods capriciously is here described as acting according to God's supervision.   **1.** The stars that were rising at the start of the journey (1.37–40) are now setting: Good Friday has passed, and the time is now the early hours of Holy Saturday.

made our way down along a rough, strange path.   105
This dingy little stream, when it has reached
  the bottom of the gray malignant slopes,
  becomes a swamp that has the name of Styx.[2]   108
And I, intent on looking as we passed,
  saw muddy people moving in that marsh,
  all naked, with their faces scarred by rage.   111
They fought each other, not with hands alone,
  but struck with head and chest and feet as well,
  with teeth they tore each other limb from limb.   114
And the good teacher said: "My son, now see
  the souls of those that anger overcame;
  and I ask you to believe me when I say,   117
beneath the slimy top are sighing souls
  who make these waters bubble at the surface;
  your eyes will tell you this—just look around.   120
Bogged in this slime they say, 'Sluggish we were
  in the sweet air made happy by the sun,
  and the smoke of sloth was smoldering in our hearts;   123
now we lie sluggish here in this black muck!'
  This is the hymn they gurgle in their throats
  but cannot sing in words that truly sound."   126
Then making a wide arc, we walked around
  the pond between the dry bank and the slime,
  our eyes still fixed on those who gobbled mud.   129
We came, in time, to the foot of a high tower.[3]

CANTO VIII

But before they had reached the foot of the tower, the Pilgrim had noticed two signal
flames at the tower's top, and another flame answering from a distance; soon he realizes
that the flames are signals to and from Phlegyas, the boatman of the Styx, who suddenly
appears in a small boat speeding across the river. Wrathful and irritated though he is,
the steersman must grant the poets passage, but during the crossing an angry shade rises
from the slime to question the Pilgrim. After a brief exchange of words, scornful on the
part of the Pilgrim, who has recognized this sinner, the spirit grabs hold of the boat.
Virgil pushes him away, praising his ward for his just scorn, while a group of the wrathful
attack the wretched soul, whose name is Filippo Argenti. At the far shore the poets
debark and find themselves before the gates of the infernal City of Dis, where howling
figures threaten them from the walls. Virgil speaks with them privately, but they slam
the gate shut in his face. His ward is terrified, and Virgil too is shaken, but he insists
that help from Heaven is already on the way.

I must explain, however, that before
  we finally reached the foot of that high tower,
  our eyes had been attracted to its summit   3
by two small flames we saw flare up just there;
  and, so far off the eye could hardly see,
  another burning torch flashed back a sign.   6

2. The second river of Hell. 3. This watchtower guards the entrance to lower Hell or the city of Dis—
another name for Pluto, the classical god of the underworld, that is throughout the *Inferno* applied to Satan
(see 11.65 and 34.20).

I turned to that vast sea of human knowledge:
    "What signal is this? And the other flame,
    what does it answer? And who's doing this?"   9
And he replied: "You should already see
    across the filthy waves what has been summoned,
    unless the marsh's vapors hide it from you."   12
A bowstring never shot an arrow off
    that cut the thin air any faster than
    a little boat I saw that very second   15
skimming along the water in our direction,
    with a solitary steersman, who was shouting,
    "Aha, I've got you now, you wretched soul!"   18
"Phlegyas, Phlegyas,[4] this time you shout in vain,"
    my lord responded, "you will have us with you
    no longer than it takes to cross the muck."   21
As one who learns of some incredible trick
    just played on him flares up resentfully—
    so, Phlegyas there was seething in his anger.   24
My leader calmly stepped into the skiff
    and when he was inside, he had me enter,
    and only then it seemed to carry weight.   27
Soon as my guide and I were in the boat
    the ancient prow began to plough the water,
    more deeply, now, than any time before.[5]   30
And as we sailed the course of this dead channel,
    before me there rose up a slimy shape
    that said: "Who are you, who come before your time?"   33
And I spoke back, "Though I come, I do not stay;
    but who are you, in all your ugliness?"
    "You see that I am one who weeps," he answered.   36
And then I said to him: "May you weep and wail,
    stuck here in this place forever, you damned soul,
    for, filthy as you are, I recognize you."   39
With that he stretched both hands out toward the boat
    but, on his guard, my teacher pushed him back:
    "Away, get down there with the other curs!"   42
And then he put his arms around my neck
    and kissed my face and said, "Indignant soul,
    blessèd is she in whose womb you were conceived.[6]   45
In the world this man was filled with arrogance,
    and nothing good about him decks his memory;
    for this, his shade is filled with fury here.   48
Many in life esteem themselves great men
    who then will wallow here like pigs in mud,
    leaving behind them their repulsive fame."   51
"Master, it certainly would make me happy
    to see him dunked deep in this slop just once
    before we leave this lake—it truly would."   54
And he to me, "Before the other shore

---

4. A mythological figure condemned to Hell for setting fire to the temple of Apollo in revenge for the god's seduction of his daughter; Dante found him in *Aeneid* 6.444–47.   **5.** Because of the weight of the living Dante.   **6.** See Luke 11.27, where these words are applied to Jesus.

comes into sight, you will be satisfied:
  a wish like that is worthy of fulfillment."   57
Soon afterward, I saw the wretch so mangled
  by a gang of muddy souls that, to this day,
  I thank my Lord and praise Him for that sight: 60
"Get Filippo Argenti!"[7] they all cried.
  And at those shouts the Florentine, gone mad,
  turned on himself and bit his body fiercely.   63
We left him there, I'll say no more about him.
  A wailing noise began to pound my ears
  and made me strain my eyes to see ahead.   66
"And now, my son," the gentle teacher said,
  "coming closer is the city we call Dis,
  with its great walls and its fierce citizens."   69
And I, "Master, already I can see
  the clear glow of its mosques above the valley,
  burning bright red, as though just forged, and left   72
to smolder." And he to me: "Eternal fire
  burns within, giving off the reddish glow
  you see diffused throughout this lower Hell."   75
And then at last we entered those deep moats
  the circled all of this unhappy city
  whose walls, it seemed to me, were made of iron.   78
For quite a while we sailed around, until
  we reached a place and heard our boatsman shout
  with all his might, "Get out! Here is the entrance."   81
I saw more than a thousand fiendish angels[8]
  perching above the gates enraged, screaming:
  "Who is the one approaching? Who, without death,   84
dares walk into the kingdom of the dead?"
  And my wise teacher made some kind of signal
  announcing he would speak to them in secret.   87
They managed to suppress their great resentment
  enough to say: "You come, but he must go
  who thought to walk so boldly through this realm.   90
Let him retrace his foolish way alone,
  just let him try. And you who led him here
  through this dark land, you'll stay right where you are."   93
And now, my reader, consider how I felt
  when those foreboding words came to my ears!
  I thought I'd never see our world again!   96
"O my dear guide, who more than seven times
  restored my confidence, and rescued me
  from the many dangers that blocked my going on,   99
don't leave me, please," I cried in my distress,
  "and if the journey onward is denied us
  let's turn our footsteps back together quickly."   102
Then that lord who had brought me all this way
  said, "Do not fear, the journey we are making

---

7. A Florentine contemporary of Dante.   8. The rebel angels, cast out of Heaven; see Luke 10.18 and
Revelation 12.9.

none can prevent: such power did decree it. 105
Wait here for me and feed your weary spirit
   with comfort and good hope; you can be sure
   I will not leave you in this underworld." 108
With this he walks away. He leaves me here,
   that gentle father, and I stay, doubting,
   and battling with my thoughts of "yes"—but "no." 111
I could not hear what he proposed to them,
   but they did not remain with him for long;
   I saw them race each other back for home. 114
Our adversaries slammed the heavy gates
   in my lord's face, and he stood there outside,
   then turned toward me and walked back very slowly 117
with eyes downcast, all self-assurance now
   erased from his forehead—sighing, "Who are these
   to forbid my entrance to the halls of grief!" 120
He spoke to me: "You need not be disturbed
   by my vexation, for I shall win the contest,
   no matter how they plot to keep us out! 123
This insolence of theirs is nothing new;
   they used it once at a less secret gate,[9]
   which is, and will forever be, unlocked; 126
you saw the deadly words inscribed above it;
   and now, already past it, and descending,
   across the circles, down the slope, alone, 129
comes one by whom the city will be opened."

CANTO IX

The help from Heaven has not yet arrived; the Pilgrim is afraid and Virgil is obviously worried. He reassures his ward by telling him that, soon after his own death, he was forced by the Sorceress Erichtho to resume mortal shape and go to the very bottom of Hell in order to bring up the soul of a traitor; thus Virgil knows the way well. But no sooner is the Pilgrim comforted than the Three Furies appear before him, on top of the tower, shrieking and tearing their breasts with their nails. They call for Medusa, whose horrible face has the power of turning anyone who looks on her to stone. Virgil turns his ward around and covers his eyes. After an "address to the reader" calling attention to the coming allegory, a strident blast splits the air, and the poets perceive an Angel coming through the murky darkness to open the gates of the City for them. Then the angel returns on the path whence he had come, and the two travelers enter the gate. Within are great open burning sarcophagi, from which groans of torment issue. Virgil explains that these are Arch-Heretics and their lesser counterparts.

The color of the coward on my face,
   when I realized my guide was turning back,
   made him quickly change the color of his own. 3
He stood alert, like one who strains to hear;
   his eyes could not see far enough ahead
   to cut the heavy fog of that black air. 6
"But surely we were meant to win this fight,"

9. A reference to Christ's descent into Hell after the crucifixion for the "harrowing": see above, Canto 4.52.

he said, "or else . . . but no, such help was promised!
   Oh, how much time it's taking him to come!"   9
I saw too well how quickly he amended
   his opening words with what he added on!
   They were different from the ones he first pronounced;   12
but nonetheless his words made me afraid,
   perhaps because the phrase he left unfinished
   I finished with worse meaning than he meant.   15
"Has anyone before ever descended
   to this sad hollow's depths from that first circle
   whose pain is all in having hope cut off?"[1]   18
I put this question to him. He replied,
   "It is not usual for one of us
   to make the journey I am making now.   21
But it happens I was down here once before,
   conjured by that heartless witch, Erichtho[2]
   (who could recall the spirit to its body).   24
Soon after I had left my flesh in death
   she sent me through these walls, and down as far
   as the pit of Judas to bring a spirit out;   27
and that place is the lowest and the darkest
   and the farthest from the sphere that circles all;[3]
   I know the road, and well, you can be sure.   30
This swamp that breathes with a prodigious stink
   lies in a circle round the doleful city
   that now we cannot enter without strife."   33
And he said other things, but I forget them,
   for suddenly my eyes were drawn above,
   up to the fiery top of that high tower   36
where in no time at all and all at once
   sprang up three hellish Furies[4] stained with blood,
   their bodies and their gestures those of females;   39
their waists were bound in cords of wild green hydras,
   horned snakes and little serpents grew as hair,
   and twined themselves around the savage temples.   42
And he who had occasion to know well
   the handmaids of the queen of timeless woe[5]
   cried out to me "Look there! The fierce Erinyes!   45
That is Megaera, the one there to the left,
   and that one raving on the right, Alecto,
   Tisiphone, in the middle." He said no more.   48
With flailing palms the three would beat their breasts,
   then tear them with their nails, shrieking so loud,
   I drew close to the poet, confused with fear.   51
"Medusa,[6] come, we'll turn him into stone,"

1. "Has anyone from Limbo ever descended into lower Hell before?"   2. A legendary sorceress. The story of Virgil's prior descent into Hell is apparently Dante's own invention, although in the Middle Ages Virgil had the reputation of being a magician.   3. Judecca, the last subdivision of the last circle of Hell, where Judas is punished.   4. Three mythological monsters who represent the spirit of vengeance, known in Greek as the Erinyes (see below, line 45, and lines 46–48 for their individual names); they figure prominently in the *Aeneid* and other Latin poetry.   5. In classical mythology the queen of Hell is Hecate, or Proserpina, the wife of Pluto.   6. A mythological figure known as a Gorgon (line 56), so frightful in appearance that she turned those who gazed on her into stone.

they shouted all together glaring down,
    "how wrong we were to let off Theseus[7] lightly!"   54
"Now turn your back and cover up your eyes,
    for if the Gorgon comes and you should see her,
    there would be no returning to the world!"   57
These were my master's words. He turned me round
    and did not trust my hands to hide my eyes
    but placed his own on mine and kept them covered.   60
O all of you whose intellects are sound,
    look now and see the meaning that is hidden
    beneath the veil that covers my strange verses:[8]   63
and then, above the filthy swell, approaching,
    a blast of sound, shot through with fear, exploded,
    making both shores of Hell begin to tremble;   66
it sounded like one of those violent winds,
    born from the clash of counter-temperatures,
    that tear through forests; raging on unchecked,   69
it splits and rips and carries off the branches
    and proudly whips the dust up in its path
    and makes the beasts and shepherds flee its course!   72
He freed my eyes and said, "Now turn around
    and set your sight along the ancient scum,
    there where the marsh's mist is hovering thickest."   75
As frogs before their enemy, the snake,
    all scatter through the pond and then dive down
    until each one is squatting on the bottom,   78
so I saw more than a thousand fear-shocked souls
    in flight, clearing the path of one who came
    walking the Styx, his feet dry on the water.[9]   81
From time to time with his left hand he fanned
    his face to push the putrid air away,
    and this was all that seemed to weary him.   84
I was certain now that he was sent from Heaven.
    I turned to my guide, but he made me a sign
    to keep my silence and bow low to this one.   87
Ah, the scorn that filled his holy presence!
    He reached the gate and touched it with a wand;
    it opened without resistance from inside.   90
"O Heaven's outcasts, despicable souls,"
    he started, standing on the dreadful threshold,
    "what insolence is this that breeds in you?   93
Why do you stubbornly resist that will
    whose end can never be denied and which,
    more than one time, increased your suffering?   96
What do you gain by locking horns with fate?
    If you remember well, your Cerberus
    still bears his chin and throat peeled clean for that!"[1]   99

---

7. *Theseus*, a legendary Athenian hero, descended into the underworld in order to try to rescue Proserpina, whom Pluto had abducted, and was rescued by Hercules.   8. Dante here reminds us of the need to interpret his poetry, although the lesson of this particular episode is far from self-evident.   9. This is an angel, although described in a way reminiscent of Mercury, the classical messenger of the gods.   1. According to classical mythology, Hercules dragged Cerberus into the daylight.

He turned then and retraced the squalid path,
    without one word to us, and on his face
    the look of one concerned and spurred by things   102
that were not those he found surrounding him.
    And then we started moving toward the city
    in the safety of the holy words pronounced.   105
We entered there, and with no opposition.
    And I, so anxious to investigate
    the state of souls locked up in such a fortress,   108
once in the place, allowed my eyes to wander,
    and saw, in all directions spreading out,
    a countryside of pain and ugly anguish.   111
As at Arles where the Rhône turns to stagnant waters
    or as at Pola near Quarnero's Gulf
    that closes Italy and bathes her confines,   114
the sepulchers make all the land uneven,
    so they did here, strewn in all directions,
    except the graves here served a crueler purpose:[2] 117
for scattered everywhere among the tombs
    were flames that kept them glowing far more hot
    than any iron an artisan might use.   120
Each tomb had its lid loose, pushed to one side,
    and from within came forth such fierce laments
    that I was sure inside were tortured souls.   123
I asked, "Master, what kind of shades are these
    lying down here, buried in the graves of stone,
    speaking their presence in such dolorous sighs?"   126
And he replied: "There lie arch-heretics
    of every sect, with all of their disciples;
    more than you think are packed within these tombs.   129
Like heretics lie buried with their like
    and the graves burn more, or less, accordingly."
    Then turning to the right, we moved ahead   132
between the torments there and those high walls.

CANTO X

They come to the tombs containing the Epicurean heretics, and as they are walking by them, a shade suddenly rises to full height in one tomb, having recognized the Pilgrim's Tuscan dialect. It is the proud Farinata, who, in life, opposed Dante's party; while he and the Pilgrim are conversing, another figure suddenly rises out of the same tomb. It is the shade of Cavalcante de Cavalcanti, who interrupts the conversation with questions about his son Guido. Misinterpreting the Pilgrim's confused silence as evidence of his son's death, Cavalcante falls back into his sepulcher and Farinata resumes the conversation exactly where it had been broken off. He defends his political actions in regard to Florence and prophesies that Dante, like himself, will soon know the pain of exile. But the Pilgrim is also interested to know how it is that the damned can see the future but not the present. When his curiosity is satisfied, he asks Farinata to tell Cavalcante that his son is still alive, and that his silence was caused only by his confusion about the shade's inability to know the present.

---

2. *Arles,* located on the Rhone River in southern France, and *Pola,* located on the bay of Quarnero in what is now Yugoslavia, were sites of Roman cemeteries.

Now onward down a narrow path, between
    the city's ramparts and the suffering,
    my master walks, I following close behind.   3
"O lofty power who through these impious gyres[3]
    lead me around as you see fit," I said,
    "I want to know, I want to understand: 6
the people buried there in sepulchers,
    can they be seen? I mean, since all the lids
    are off the tombs and no one stands on guard."   9
And he: "They will forever be locked up,
    when they return here from Jehoshaphat
    with the bodies that they left up in the world.[4]   12
The private cemetery on this side
    serves Epicurus[5] and his followers,
    who make the soul die when the body dies.   15
As for the question you just put to me,
    it will be answered soon, while we are here;
    and the wish you are keeping from me will be granted."[6]   18
And I: "O my good guide, I do not hide
    my heart; I'm trying not to talk too much,
    as you have told me more than once to do."   21
"O Tuscan walking through our flaming city,
    alive, and speaking with such elegance,
    be kind enough to stop here for a while.   24
Your mode of speech identifies you clearly
    as one whose birthplace is that noble city
    with which in my time, perhaps, I was too harsh."   27
One of the vaults resounded suddenly
    with these clear words, and I, intimidated,
    drew up a little closer to my guide,   30
who said, "What are you doing? Turn around
    and look at Farinata,[7] who has risen,
    you will see him from the waist up standing straight."   33
I already had my eyes fixed on his face,
    and there he stood out tall, with his chest and brow
    proclaiming his disdain for all this Hell.   36
My guide, with a gentle push, encouraged me
    to move among the sepulchers toward him:
    "Be sure you choose your words with care," he said.   39
And when I reached the margin of his tomb
    he looked at me, and half-contemptuously
    he asked, "And *who* would *your* ancestors be?"   42
And I who wanted only to oblige him
    held nothing back but told him everything
    At this he lifted up his brows a little,   45
then said, "Bitter enemies of mine they were
    and of my ancestors and of my party;

---

3. *Gyres*: circular turns. 4. According to the Bible, the Last Judgment when the dead will again receive their bodies will take place in the Valley of Jehoshaphat: see Joel 3.2 and 3.12, and Matthew 25.31–32. 5. Greek philosopher (d. 270 B.C.E.) who rejected the idea of the immortality of the soul. 6. Presumably Dante's desire to see the Florentines who inhabit this circle. 7. Farinata degli Uberti (d. 1264), a leader of the Ghibelline faction in Florence.

I had to scatter them not once but twice."[8]   48
"They were expelled, but only to return
    from everywhere," I said, "not once but twice—
    an art your men, however, never mastered!"[9]   51
Just then along that same tomb's open ledge
    a shade appeared, but just down to his chin,
    beside this other; I think he got up kneeling.[1]   54
He looked around as though he hoped to see
    if someone else, perhaps, had come with me
    and, when his expectation was deceived,   57
he started weeping: "If it be great genius
    that carries you along through this blind jail,
    where is my son? Why is he not with you?"   60
"I do not come alone," I said to him,
    "that one waiting over there guides me through here,
    the one, perhaps, your Guido held in scorn."[2]   63
(The place of pain assigned him, and what he asked,
    already had revealed his name to me
    and made my pointed answer possible.)   66
Instantly, he sprang to his full height and cried,
    "What did you say? He *held*? Is he not living?
    The day's sweet light no longer strikes his eyes?"[3]   69
And when he heard the silence of my delay
    responding to his question, he collapsed
    into his tomb, not to be seen again.   72
That other stately shade, at whose request
    I had first stopped to talk, showed no concern
    nor moved his head nor turned to see what happened;   75
he merely picked up where we had left off:
    "If that art they did not master," he went on,
    "that gives me greater pain than does this bed.   78
But the face of the queen who reigns down here[4] will glow
    not more than fifty times before you learn
    how hard it is to master such an art;[5]   81
and as I hope that you may once more know
    the sweet world, tell me, why should your party be
    so harsh to my clan in every law they make?"   84
I answered: "The massacre and butchery
    that stained the waters of the Arbia red[6]
    now cause such laws to issue from our councils."   87
He sighed, shaking his head. "It was not I
    alone took part," he said, "not certainly

8. Dante's family were Guelphs, who were driven out of Florence twice, in 1248 and 1260.   9. The Ghibellines were exiled in 1280, never to return.   1. This is Cavalcante de Cavalcanti, father of Dante's friend and fellow poet Guido; a Guelph, Guido married the daughter of Farinata in an unsuccessful attempt to heal the feud. In June 1300—after the fictional date of this conversation—Guido was exiled to a part of Italy where he caught the malaria from which he died in August. Dante was at that time a member of the governing body that made the decision to exile Guido.   2. The passage is ambiguous in the original Italian: as translated here, the "one" refers to Virgil; but the Italian word can also be translated to refer to Beatrice, so that these two lines would then read: "that one waiting over there guides me through here, / *to her* whom your Guido perhaps held in scorn."   3. In line 61 Dante used a verbal form known in Italian as the remote past, which leads Cavalcante to believe, wrongly, that now, in April 1300, Guido is dead—although, ironically, in about four months he will indeed die, as Dante knew when he was writing this canto.   4. Proserpina, who is also the goddess of the moon.   5. Farinata here predicts Dante's own exile.   6. A stream near the hill of Montaperti, where the Ghibellines defeated the Guelphs in 1260.

would I have joined the rest without good cause.   90
But I alone stood up when all of them
    were ready to have Florence razed. It was *I*
    who openly stood up in her defense."   93
"And now, as I would have your seed find peace,"
    I said, "I beg you to resolve a problem
    that has kept my reason tangled in a knot: 96
if I have heard correctly, all of you
    can see ahead to what the future holds
    but your knowledge of the present is not clear."   99
"Down here we see like those with faulty vision
    who only see," he said, "what's at a distance;
    this much the sovereign lord grants us here.   102
When events are close to us, or when they happen,
    our mind is blank, and were it not for others
    we would know nothing of your living state.   105
Thus you can understand how all our knowledge
    will be completely dead at that time when
    the door to future things is closed forever."[7]   108
Then I, moved by regret for what I'd done[8]
    said, "Now, will you please tell the fallen one
    his son is still on earth among the living;   111
and if, when he asked, silence was my answer,
    tell him: while he was speaking, all my thoughts
    were struggling with that point you solved for me."   114
My teacher had begun to call me back,
    so I quickly asked that spirit to reveal
    the names of those who shared the tomb with him.   117
He said, "More than a thousand lie with me,
    the Second Frederick[9] is here and the Cardinal[1]
    is with us. And the rest I shall not mention."   120
His figure disappeared. I made my way
    to the ancient poet, reflecting on those words
    those words which were prophetic enemies.[2]   123
He moved, and as we went along he said,
    "What troubles you? Why are you so distraught?"
    And I told him all the thoughts that filled my mind.   126
"Be sure your mind retains," the sage commanded,
    "those words you heard pronounced against yourself,
    and listen carefully now." He raised a finger: 129
"When at last you stand in the glow of her sweet ray,[3]
    the one whose splendid eyes see everything,
    from her you'll learn your life's itinerary."   132
Then to the left he turned. Leaving the walls,
    he headed toward the center by a path
    that strikes into a vale, whose stench arose,   135
disgusting us as high up as we were.

---

7. The damned can see the future but not the present; after the Last Judgment, when human time is abolished, they will know nothing.   8. See note 3 to line 69 above.   9. Frederick II, Holy Roman emperor from 1215 until his death in 1250; he reputedly denied that there was life after death.   1. Ottaviano degli Ubaldini (d. 1273), who is reputed to have said, "If I have a soul, I have lost it for the Ghibellines."   2. That is, Farinata's prediction of his exile.   3. Beatrice's.

CANTO XI

Continuing their way within the Sixth Circle, where the heretics are punished, the poets are assailed by a stench rising from the abyss ahead of them which is so strong that they must stop in order to accustom themselves to the odor. They pause beside a tomb whose inscription declares that within is Pope Anastasius. When the Pilgrim expresses his desire to pass the time of waiting profitably, Virgil proceeds to instruct him about the plan of punishments in Hell. Then, seeing that dawn is only two hours away, he urges the Pilgrim on.

We reached the curving brink of a steep bank
   constructed of enormous broken rocks;
   below us was a crueler den of pain.   3
And the disgusting overflow of stench
   the deep abyss was vomiting forced us
   back from the edge. Crouched underneath the lid   6
of some great tomb, I saw it was inscribed:
   "Within lies Anastasius, the pope
   Photinus lured away from the straight path."[4]   9
"Our descent will have to be delayed somewhat
   so that our sense of smell may grow accustomed
   to these vile fumes; then we will not mind them,"   12
my master said. And I: "You will have to find
   some way to keep our time from being wasted."
   "That is precisely what I had in mind,"   15
he said, and then began the lesson:[5] "My son,
   within these boulders' bounds are three more circles,
   concentrically arranged like those above,   18
all tightly packed with souls; and so that, later,
   the sight of them alone will be enough,
   I'll tell you how and why they are imprisoned.   21
All malice has injustice as its end,
   an end achieved by violence or by fraud;
   while both are sins that earn the hate of Heaven,   24
since fraud belongs exclusively to man,
   God hates it more and, therefore, far below,
   the fraudulent are placed and suffer most.   27
In the first of the circles below are all the violent;
   since violence can be used against three persons,
   into three concentric rounds it is divided: 30
violence can be done to God, to self,
   or to one's neighbor—to him or to his goods,
   as my reasoned explanation will make clear.   33
By violent means a man can kill his neighbor
   or wound him grievously; his goods may suffer
   violence by arson, theft, and devastation;   36
so, homicides and those who strike with malice,

4. Pope Anastasius (d. 498) was thought, wrongly, to have accepted a heresy promoted by the 5th-century theologian Photinus that Christ was not divine but only human.   5. Virgil now describes the three remaining circles of Hell, the seventh, eighth, and ninth. The seventh is for the violent and is divided into three parts; the eighth and ninth are for the fraudulent, the eighth for those who deceive generally, the ninth for those who betray those who love them. For the scheme of Hell as a whole, see the diagram on p. 1458.

those who destroy and plunder, are all punished
  in the first round, but all in different groups.   39
Man can raise violent hands against himself
  and his own goods; so in the second round,
  paying the debt that never can be paid,   42
are suicides, self-robbers of your world,
  or those who gamble all their wealth away
  and weep up there when they should have rejoiced.   45
One can use violence against the deity
  by heartfelt disbelief and cursing Him,
  or by despising Nature and God's bounty;   48
therefore, the smallest round stamps with its seal
  both Sodom and Cahors[6] and all those souls
  who hate God in their hearts and curse His name.   51
Fraud, that gnaws the conscience of its servants,
  can be used on one who puts his trust in you
  or else on one who has no trust invested.   54
This latter sort seems only to destroy
  the bond of love that Nature gives to man;
  so in the second circle there are nests   57
of hypocrites, flatterers, dabblers in sorcery,
  falsifiers, thieves, and simonists,[7]
  panders, seducers, grafters, and like filth.   60
The former kind of fraud both disregards
  the love Nature enjoys and that extra bond
  between men which creates a special trust;   63
thus, it is in the smallest of the circles,
  at the earth's center, around the throne of Dis,[8]
  that traitors suffer their eternal pain."   66
And I, "Master, your reasoning runs smooth,
  and your explanation certainly makes clear
  the nature of this pit and of its inmates,   69
but what about those in the slimy swamp,
  those driven by the wind, those beat by rain,
  and those who come to blows with harsh refrains?   72
Why are they, too, not punished here inside
  the city of flame, if they have earned God's wrath?
  If they have not, why are they suffering?"   75
And he to me, "Why do you let your thoughts
  stray from the path they are accustomed to?
  Or have I missed the point you have in mind?   78
Have you forgotten how your *Ethics*[9] reads,
  those terms it explicates in such detail:
  the three conditions that the heavens hate,   81
incontinence, malice, and bestiality?
  Do you not remember how incontinence

---

6. In the Middle Ages the names of Sodom (see Genesis 18.20–19.26) and Cahors, a city in southern France, became synonymous with sodomites and userers respectively. Usury, forbidden by the medieval church, is charging interest on loans; the logic of this prohibition—based on the argument that usury, like sodomy, is unnatural—is explained in lines 97–111 below.   7. Simony is the sin of selling a spiritual good, such as a church office or a sacrament like confession, for material gain. It is named after Simon Magus, a magician who sought to buy from the Apostles the power of baptism in Acts 8.9–24.   8. *Dis* is Satan, who is found at the bottom of Hell (see canto 34).   9. Aristotle's *Nicomachean Ethics*.

offends God least, and merits the least blame? 84
If you will reconsider well this doctrine
    and then recall to mind who those souls were
    suffering pain above, outside the walls, 87
you will clearly see why they are separated
    from these malicious ones, and why God's vengeance
    beats down upon their souls less heavily." 90
"O sun that shines to clear a misty vision,
    such joy is mine when you resolve my doubts
    that doubting pleases me no less than knowing! 93
Go back a little bit once more," I said
    "to where you say that usury offends
    God's goodness, and untie that knot for me." 96
"Philosophy," he said, "and more than once,
    points out to one who reads with understanding
    how Nature takes her course from the Divine 99
Intellect, from its artistic workmanship,[1]
    and if you have your *Physics*[2] well in mind
    you will find, not many pages from the start, 102
how your art too, as best it can, imitates
    Nature, the way an apprentice does his master;
    so your art may be said to be God's grandchild. 105
From Art and Nature man was meant to take
    his daily bread to live—if you recall
    the book of Genesis near the beginning,[3] 108
but the usurer, adopting other means,
    scorns Nature in herself and in her pupil,
    Art—he invests his hope in something else[4] 111
Now follow me, we should be getting on;
    the Fish are shimmering over the horizon,
    the Wain is now exactly over Caurus,[5] 114
and the passage down the bank is farther on."

CANTO XII

They descend the steep slope into the Seventh Circle by means of a great landslide, which was caused when Christ descended into Hell. At the edge of the abyss is the Minotaur, who presides over the circle of the Violent and whose own bestial rage sends him into such a paroxysm of violence that the two travelers are able to run past him without his interference. At the base of the precipice, they see a river of boiling blood, which contains those who have inflicted violence upon others. But before they can reach the river they are intercepted by three fierce Centaurs, whose task it is to keep those who are in the river at their proper depth by shooting arrows at them if they attempt to rise. Virgil explains to one of the centaurs (Chiron) that this journey of the Pilgrim and himself is ordained by God; and he requests him to assign someone to guide the two of them to the ford in the river and carry the Pilgrim across it to the other bank. Chiron gives the task to Nessus, one of the centaurs, who, as he leads them to the river's ford, points out many of the sinners there in the boiling blood.

1. The laws of nature are determined by God.   2. Aristotle's *Physics*, which argues that human art should follow natural laws.   3. In Genesis 3.17–19, God decrees that because of the Fall people must toil, supporting themselves by the sweat of their brows.   4. The usurer makes money not from labor but from money itself, which is an unnatural and therefore illicit art.   5. The position of stars shows that it is now about 4 A.M. on Holy Saturday.

Not only was that place, where we had come
   to descend, craggy, but there was something there
   that made the scene appalling to the eye.   3
Like the ruins this side of Trent left by the landslide
   (an earthquake or erosion must have caused it)
   that hit the Adige on its left bank,[6]   6
when, from the mountain's top where the slide began
   to the plain below, the shattered rocks slipped down,
   shaping a path for a difficult descent—   9
so was the slope of our ravine's formation.
   And at the edge, along the shattered chasm,
   there lay stretched out the infamy of Crete:[7]   12
the son conceived in the pretended cow.
   When he saw us he bit into his flesh,
   gone crazy with the fever of his rage.   15
My wise guide cried to him: "Perhaps you think
   you see the Duke of Athens come again,
   who came once in the world to bring your death?[8]   18
Begone, you beast, for this one is not led
   down here by means of clues your sister[9] gave him;
   he comes here only to observe your torments."   21
The way a bull breaks loose the very moment
   he knows he has been dealt the mortal blow,
   and cannot run but jumps and twists and turns,   24
just so I saw the Minotaur perform,
   and my guide, alert, cried out: "Run to the pass!
   While he still writhes with rage, get started down."   27
And so we made our way down through the ruins
   of rocks, which often I felt shift and tilt
   beneath my feet from weight they were not used to.   30
I was deep in thought when he began: "Are you,
   perhaps, thinking about these ruins protected
   by the furious beast I quenched in its own rage?   33
Now let me tell you that the other time
   I came down to the lower part of Hell,
   this rock had not then fallen into ruins;   36
but certainly, if I remember well,
   it was just before the coming of that One
   who took from Hell's first circle the great spoil,   39
that this abyss of stench, from top to bottom
   began to shake,[1] so I thought the universe
   felt love—whereby, some have maintained, the world   42
has more than once renewed itself in chaos.[2]

---

6. A famous landslide on a mountain on the Adige River near Trent, a city in northern Italy.   7. The Minotaur, half man and half bull, was conceived when Pasiphaë, the wife of King Minos of Crete, had a wooden cow built within which she placed herself so as to have intercourse with a bull. The story of the Minotaur is told by Ovid, *Metamorphoses* 8.   8. Virgil is referring to Theseus, who killed the Minotaur in the labyrinth in which it was imprisoned.   9. Ariadne, daughter of Minos and Pasiphaë, who taught Theseus how to escape from the labyrinth within which the Minotaur was imprisoned.   1. Because of the earthquake that accompanied Christ's death, which occurred just before his descent to Hell and the "harrowing," Christ's rescue from the First Circle of the virtuous Israelites (see above, canto 4.52–63). 2. A reference to a theory of the Greek philosopher Empedocles that the universe is held together by alternating forces of love and hate, and that if either one predominates the result is chaos. This classical theory is not consistent with the Christian belief that the universe is created and organized by God's love.

That was the moment when this ancient rock
  was split this way—here, and in other places.   45
But now look down the valley. Coming closer
  you will see the river of blood that boils the souls
  of those who through their violence injured others."   48
(Oh, blind cupidity[3] and insane wrath,
  spurring us on through our short life on earth
  to steep us then forever in such misery!)   51
I saw a river—wide, curved like a bow—
  that stretched embracing all the flatland there,
  just as my guide had told me to expect.   54
Between the river and the steep came centaurs,[4]
  galloping in single file, equipped with arrows,
  off hunting as they used to in the world;   57
then, seeing us descend, they all stopped short
  and three of them departed from the ranks
  with bows and arrows ready from their quivers.   60
One of them cried from his distant post: "You there,
  on your way down here, what torture are you seeking?
  Speak where you stand, if not, I draw my bow."   63
And then my master shouted back: "Our answer
  we will give to Chiron[5] when we're at his side;
  as for you, I see you are as rash as ever!"   66
He nudged me, saying: "That one there is Nessus,[6]
  who died from loving lovely Dejanira,
  and made of himself, of his blood, his own revenge. 69
The middle one, who contemplates his chest,
  is great Chiron, who reared and taught Achilles;
  the last is Pholus,[7] known for his drunken wrath. 72
They gallop by the thousands round the ditch,
  shooting at any daring soul emerging
  above the bloody level of his guilt."   75
When we came closer to those agile beasts,
  Chiron drew an arrow, and with its notch
  he parted his beard to both sides of his jaws,   78
and when he had uncovered his great mouth
  he spoke to his companions: "Have you noticed,
  how the one behind moves everything he touches? 81
This is not what a dead man's feet would do!"
  And my good guide, now standing by the torso
  at the point the beast's two natures joined,[8] replied: 84
"He is indeed alive, and so alone
  that I must show him through this dismal valley;
  he travels by necessity, not pleasure.   87
A spirit[9] came, from singing Alleluia,
  to give me this extraordinary mission;

---

3. Desire for wealth.   4. Mythological creatures that are half man and half horse.   5. A centaur renowned for wisdom who educated many legendary Greek heroes, including Achilles.   6. Nessus fell in love with Dejanira, wife of Hercules, who killed him; while dying, Nessus poisoned with his own blood a robe that killed Hercules when he put it on.   7. Another centaur, killed by Hercules, whose rage is typical of the race.   8. When standing, Virgil reaches to the centaur's chest where his human and animal natures join.   9. Beatrice.

he is no rogue nor I a criminal spirit.[1]   90
Now, in the name of that power by which I move
    my steps along so difficult a road,
    give us one of your troop to be our guide: 93
to lead us to the ford and, once we are there,
    to carry this one over on his back,
    for he is not a spirit who can fly."   96
Chiron looked over his right breast and said
    to Nessus, "You go, guide them as they ask,
    and if another troop protests, disperse them!"   99
So with this trusted escort we moved on
    along the boiling crimson river's bank,[2]
    where piercing shrieks rose from the boiling souls.   102
There I saw people sunken to their eyelids,
    and the huge centaur explained, "These are the tyrants
    who dealt in bloodshed and plundered wealth.   105
Their tears are paying for their heartless crimes:
    here stand Alexander and fierce Dionysius,
    who weighed down Sicily with years of pain;[3]   108
and there, that forehead smeared with coal-black hair,
    is Azzolino;[4] the other one, the blond,
    Opizzo d'Esti, who, and this is true,   111
was killed by his own stepson in your world."[5]
    With that I looked to Virgil, but he said
    "Let him instruct you now, don't look to me."   114
A little farther on, the centaur stopped
    above some people peering from the blood
    that came up to their throats. He pointed out   117
a shade off to one side, alone, and said:
    "There stands the one who, in God's keep, murdered
    the heart still dripping blood above the Thames."[6]   120
Then I saw other souls stuck in the river
    who had their heads and chests above the blood,
    and I knew the names of many who were there.   123
The river's blood began decreasing slowly
    until it cooked the feet and nothing more,
    and here we found the ford where we could cross.   126
"Just as you see the boiling river here
    on this side getting shallow gradually,"
    the centaur said, "I would also have you know   129
that on the other side the riverbed
    sinks deeper more and more until it reaches
    the deepest meeting place where tyrants moan: 132
it is there that Heaven's justice strikes its blow
    against Attila,[7] known as the scourge of earth,

---

1. Virgil is answering the question of lines 61–62, which assumes that they are condemned spirits.   2. A river of blood, which we later learn is named Phlegethon (see 14.116).   3. Alexander the Great (d. 323 B.C.E.) and Dionysius of Syracuse in Sicily (d. 367 B.C.E.).   4. Azzolino III (d. 1259), a brutal ruler in northern Italy.   5. Opizzo II d'Este (d. 1293), another cruel northern Italian tyrant, reputedly murdered by his son; he is called "stepson" either because of the unnaturalness of the crime or because Opizzo suspected his wife of adultery.   6. Guy de Montfort (d. 1298), who killed his cousin Prince Henry of Cornwall during a church service ("in God's keep") in the Italian city of Viterbo. Nessus's image of the blood dripping from the victim's heart indicates his focus on the fact that the murder is still unavenged.   7. Attila the Hun (d. 453).

against Pyrrhus and Sextus,[8] and forever   135
extracts the tears the scalding blood produces,
    from Rinier da Corneto and Rinier Pazzo,[9]
    whose battlefields were highways where they robbed."   138
Then he turned round and crossed the ford again.

CANTO XIII

*No sooner are the poets across the Phlegethon than they encounter a dense forest, from
which come wails and moans, and which is presided over by the hideous harpies—half-
woman, half-beast, bird-like creatures. Virgil tells his ward to break off a branch of one
of the trees; when he does, the tree weeps blood and speaks. In life he was Pier Delle
Vigne, chief counselor of Frederick II of Sicily; but he fell out of favor, was accused
unjustly of treachery, and was imprisoned, whereupon he killed himself. The Pilgrim is
overwhelmed by pity. The sinner also explains how the souls of the suicides come to this
punishment and what will happen to them after the Last Judgment. Suddenly they are
interrupted by the wild sounds of the hunt, and two naked figures, Lano of Siena and
Giacomo da Sant' Andrea, dash across the landscape, shouting at each other, until one
of them hides himself in a thorny bush; immediately a pack of fierce, black dogs rush
in, pounce on the hidden sinner, and rip his body, carrying away mouthfuls of flesh.
The bush, which has been torn in the process, begins to lament. The two learn that the
cries are those of a Florentine who had hanged himself in his own home.*

Not yet had Nessus reached the other side
    when we were on our way into a forest
    that was not marked by any path at all.   3
No green leaves, but rather black in color,
    no smooth branches, but twisted and entangled,
    no fruit, but thorns of poison bloomed instead.   6
No thick, rough, scrubby home like this exists—
    not even between Cecina and Corneto[1]
    for those wild beasts that hate the run of farmlands.   9
Here the repulsive Harpies[2] twine their nests,
    who drove the Trojans from the Strophades
    with filthy forecasts of their close disaster.   12
Wide-winged they are, with human necks and faces,
    their feet are clawed, their bellies fat and feathered;
    perched in the trees they shriek their strange laments.   15
"Before we go on farther," my guide began,
    "remember, you are in the second round
    and shall be till we reach the dreadful sand,[3]   18
now look around you carefully and see
    with your own eyes what I will not describe,
    for if I did, you wouldn't believe my words."   21
Around me wails of grief were echoing,
    and I saw no one there to make those sounds;
    bewildered by all this, I had to stop.   24

8. Sextus, the son of the Roman consul Pompey, became a pirate (1st century B.C.E.); Pyrrhus, Achilles'
son, killed the aged Priam at the fall of Troy, as described in *Aeneid* 2.595–704.   9. Both Riniers were
bandits of Dante's day; they are now weeping from pain, whereas in life they never wept for their sins.
1. Two towns that mark the limits of the Maremma, a desolate area in Tuscany.   2. Birds with the faces
of women and clawed hands; in *Aeneid* 3 they drive the wandering Trojans from their refuge in the Stro-
phades Islands and predict their future suffering.   3. The *dreadful sand* is in the third ring or "round" of
the seventh circle, described in the next canto.

I think perhaps he thought I might be thinking
   that all the voices coming from those stumps
   belonged to people hiding there from us, 27
and so my teacher said, "If you break off
   a little branch of any of these plants,
   what you are thinking now will break off too."[4] 30
Then slowly raising up my hand a bit
   I snapped the tiny branch of a great thornbush,
   and its trunk cried: "Why are you tearing me?"[5] 33
And when its blood turned dark around the wound,
   it started saying more: "Why do you rip me?
   Have you no sense of pity whatsoever? 36
Men were we once, now we are changed to scrub;
   but even if we had been souls of serpents,
   your hand should have shown more pity than it did." 39
Like a green log burning at one end only,
   sputtering at the other, oozing sap,
   and hissing with the air it forces out, 42
so from that splintered trunk a mixture poured
   of words and blood. I let the branch I held
   fall from my hand and stood there stiff with fear. 45
"O wounded soul," my sage replied to him,
   "if he had only let himself believe
   what he had read in verses I once wrote,[6] 48
he never would have raised his hand against you,
   but the truth itself was so incredible,
   I urged him on to do the thing that grieves me. 51
But tell him who you were; he can make amends,
   and will, by making bloom again your fame
   in the world above, where his return is sure." 54
And the trunk: "So appealing are your lovely words,
   I must reply. Be not displeased if I
   am lured into a little conversation.[7] 57
I am that one who held both of the keys
   that fitted Frederick's heart; I turned them both,
   locking and unlocking, with such finesse 60
that I let few into his confidence.
   I was so faithful to my glorious office,
   I lost not only sleep but life itself. 63
That courtesan who constantly surveyed
   Caesar's household with her adulterous eyes,
   mankind's undoing, the special vice of courts,[8] 66
inflamed the hearts of everyone against me,

---

4. Your thoughts that the moans come from people concealed among the trees will cease or "break off."
5. This episode derives from *Aeneid* 3, where Aeneas and his Trojan companions, stopping in their search
for a new home, discover Polydorus transformed into a bush. Sent out by Priam during the war to solicit
aid from the Thracians, Polydorus had been murdered by his hosts, and the javelins with which his body
had been pierced had grown into the bush from which Aeneas breaks off a branch that bleeds. See also
Ovid, *Metamorphoses* 2.   6. Had Dante been able to believe the story of Polydorus recounted in the
Aeneid.   7. This is the soul of Pier della Vigna (ca. 1190–1249), who had risen to become minister to
the Emperor Frederick II (on whom see note 9 on 10.119); Frederick is referred to here as "Caesar" and
"Augustus" because he sought to imitate the imperial court of Rome. Pier's name means Peter of the Vine,
probably because his father had been a simple worker in a vineyard.   8. Pier means Envy, on whom he
blames his fall from favor.

and these, inflamed, inflamed in turn Augustus,
  and my happy honors turned to sad laments.   69
My mind, moved by scornful satisfaction,
  believing death would free me from all scorn,
  made me unjust to me, who was all just.[9]   72
By these strange roots of my own tree I swear
  to you that never once did I break faith
  with my lord, who was so worthy of all honor.   75
If one of you should go back to the world,
  restore the memory of me, who here
  remain cut down by the blow that Envy gave."   78
My poet paused awhile, then said to me,
  "Since he is silent now, don't lose your chance,
  ask him, if there is more you wish to know."   81
"Why don't you keep on questioning," I said,
  "and ask him, for my part, what I would ask,
  for I cannot, such pity chokes my heart."   84
He began again: "That this man may fulfill
  generously what your words cry out for,
  imprisoned soul, may it please you to continue   87
by telling us just how a soul gets bound
  into these knots, and tell us, if you know,
  whether any soul might someday leave his branches."   90
At that the trunk breathed heavily, and then
  the breath changed to a voice that spoke these words:
  "Your question will be answered very briefly.   93
The moment that the violent soul departs
  the body it has torn itself away from,
  Minòs sends it down to the seventh hole;   96
it drops to the wood, not in a place allotted,
  but anywhere that fortune tosses it.
There, like a grain of spelt,[1] it germinates,   99
soon springs into a sapling, then a wild tree;
  at last the Harpies, feasting on its leaves,
  create its pain, and for the pain an outlet.   102
Like the rest, we shall return to claim our bodies,[2]
  but never again to wear them—wrong it is
  for a man to have again what he once cast off.   105
We shall drag them here and, all along the mournful
  forest, our bodies shall hang forever more,
  each one on a thorn of its own alien shade."   108
We were standing still attentive to the trunk,
  thinking perhaps it might have more to say,
  when we were startled by a rushing sound,   111
such as the hunter hears from where he stands:
  first the boar, then all the chase approaching,
  the crash of hunting dogs and branches smashing,   114
then, to the left of us appeared two shapes[3]
  naked and gashed, fleeing with such rough speed

9. I unjustly committed suicide even though I was innocent of the accusations brought against me.
1. Wheat. 2. At the Last Judgment. 3. Lano of Siena and Giacomo da Sant' Andrea of Padua, two Italians of a generation earlier than Dante's; both were reputed to be spendthrifts.

they tore away with them the bushes' branches.   117
The one ahead: "Come on, come quickly, Death!"
    The other, who could not keep up the pace,
    screamed, "Lano, your legs were not so nimble   120
when you jousted in the tournament of Toppo!"[4]
    And then, from lack of breath perhaps, he slipped
    into a bush and wrapped himself in thorns.   123
Behind these two the wood was overrun
    by packs of black bitches ravenous and ready,
    like hunting dogs just broken from their chains;   126
they sank their fangs in that poor wretch who hid,
    they ripped him open piece by piece, and then
    ran off with mouthfuls of his wretched limbs.   129
Quickly my escort took me by the hand
    and led me over to the bush that wept
    its vain laments from every bleeding sore.[5]   132
"O Giacomo da Sant' Andrea," it said,
    "what good was it for you to hide in me?
    What fault have I if you led an evil life?"   135
My master, standing over it, inquired:
    "Who were you once that now through many wounds
    breathes a grieving sermon with your blood?"   138
He answered us: "O souls who have just come
    in time to see this unjust mutilation
    that has separated me from all my leaves,   141
gather them round the foot of this sad bush.
    I was from the city that took the Baptist
    in exchange for her first patron,[6] who, for this,   144
swears by his art she will have endless sorrow;
    and were it not that on the Arno's[7] bridge
    some vestige of his image still remains,   147
those citizens who built anew the city
    on the ashes that Attila left behind
    would have accomplished such a task in vain;[8]   150
I turned my home into my hanging place."

CANTO XIV

They come to the edge of the Wood of the Suicides, where they see before them a stretch of burning sand upon which flames rain enternally and through which a stream of boiling blood is carried in a raised channel formed of rock. There, many groups of tortured souls are on the burning sand; Virgil explains that those lying supine on the ground are the Blasphemers, those crouching are the Usurers, and those wandering aimlessly, never stopping, are the Sodomites. Representative of the blasphemers is Capaneus, who died cursing his god. The Pilgrim questions his guide about the source of the river of boiling blood; Virgil's reply contains the most elaborate symbol in the Inferno, that of the Old Man of Crete, whose tears are the source of all the rivers in Hell.

4. Lano was killed at a battle on the river Toppo in 1287.   5. Nothing is known about this suicide, who hanged himself from his own house.   6. Florence; when the Florentines converted to Christianity, John the Baptist replaced Mars as patron of the city, and therefore Mars will forever persecute the city with civil war.   7. The river that runs through Florence.   8. According to legend, Attila the Hun destroyed Florence when he invaded Italy in the 5th century.

The love we both shared for our native city
   moved me to gather up the scattered leaves
   and give them back to the voice that now had faded.   3
We reached the confines of the woods that separate
   the second from the third round.[9] There I saw
   God's justice in its dreadful operation.   6
Now to picture clearly these unheard-of things:
   we arrived to face an open stretch of flatland
   whose soil refused the roots of any plant;   9
the grieving forest made a wreath around it,
   as the sad river of blood enclosed the woods.
   We stopped right here, right at the border line.   12
This wasteland was a dry expanse of sand,
   thick, burning sand, no different from the kind
   that Cato's[1] feet packed down in other times.   15
O just revenge of God! how awesomely
   you should be feared by everyone who reads
   these truths that were revealed to my own eyes!   18
Many separate herds of naked souls I saw,
   all weeping desperately; it seemed each group
   had been assigned a different penalty: 21
some souls were stretched out flat upon their backs,
   others were crouching there all tightly hunched,
   some wandered, never stopping, round and round.   24
Far more there were of those who roamed the sand
   and fewer were the souls stretched out to suffer,
   but their tongues were looser, for the pain was greater.   27
And over all that sandland, a fall of slowly
   raining broad flakes of fire showered steadily
   (a mountain snowstorm on a windless day),   30
like those that Alexander saw descending
   on his troops while crossing India's torrid lands:
   flames falling, floating solid to the ground,   33
and he with all his men began to tread
   the sand so that the burning flames might be
   extinguished one by one before they joined.[2]   36
Here too a never-ending blaze descended,
   kindling the sand like tinder under flint-sparks,
   and in this way the torment there was doubled.   39
Without a moment's rest the rhythmic dance
   of wretched hands went on, this side, that side,
   brushing away the freshly fallen flames.   42
And I: "My master, you who overcome
   all opposition (except for those tough demons
   who came to meet us at the gate of Dis),   45
who is that mighty one that seems unbothered

---

9. The third ring of the seventh circle is surrounded by the second ring of the woods through which Dante has just passed and the first ring of the river of blood described in canto 12.   1. Roman general (1st century B.C.E.) who campaigned in Libya.   2. Dante is here following an account by the philosopher Albertus Magnus (d. 1280) of a legendary adventure that befell Alexander the Great in his conquest of India.

by burning, stretched sullen and disdainful there,
looking as if the rainfall could not tame him?"[3]
And that very one, who was quick to notice me
inquiring of my guide about him, answered:
"What I was once, alive, I still am, dead!
Let Jupiter wear out his smith,[4] from whom
he seized in anger that sharp thunderbolt
he hurled, to strike me down, my final day;
let him wear out those others, one by one,
who work the soot-black forge of Mongibello[5]
(as he shouts, 'Help me, good Vulcan, I need your help,'
the way he cried that time at Phlegra's battle),[6]
and with all his force let him hurl his bolts at me,
no joy of satisfaction would I give him!"
My guide spoke back at him with cutting force,
(I never heard his voice so strong before):
"O Capaneus, since your blustering pride
will not be stilled, you are made to suffer more:
no torment other than your rage itself
could punish your gnawing pride more perfectly."
And then he turned a calmer face to me,
saying, "That was a king, one of the seven
besieging Thebes; he scorned, and would seem still
to go on scorning God and treat him lightly,
but, as I said to him, he decks his chest
with ornaments of lavish words that prick him.
Now follow me and also pay attention
not to put your feet upon the burning sand,
but to keep them well within the wooded line."
Without exchanging words we reached a place
where a narrow stream came gushing from the woods
(its reddish water still runs fear through me!);
like the one that issues from the Bulicame,[7]
whose waters are shared by prostitutes downstream,
it wore its way across the desert sand.
This river's bed and banks were made of stone,
so were the tops on both its sides; and then
I understood this was our way across.
"Among the other marvels I have shown you,
from the time we made our entrance through the gate
whose threshold welcomes every evil soul,
your eyes have not discovered anything
as remarkable as this stream you see here
extinguishing the flames above its path."
These were my master's words, and I at once
implored him to provide me with the food
for which he had given me the appetite.

48
51
54
57
60
63
69
72
75
78
81
84
87
90
93

---

3. Capaneus, one of the seven legendary kings who besieged Thebes as described in the *Thebaid* by Statius (d. 95 C.E.). He was struck with a thunderbolt when he boasted that not even Jupiter could stop him. 4. Vulcan. 5. The Sicilian name for Mt. Etna, thought to be Vulcan's furnace. *Those others* are the Cyclopes, Vulcan's helpers. 6. Jove defeated the rebellious Titans at the battle of Phlegra (see 31.43). 7. A hot sulphurous spring that supplied water to brothels in an area of northern Italy.

"In the middle of the sea there lies a wasteland,"
   he immediately began, "that is known as Crete,
   under whose king the world knew innocence.[8]   96
There is a mountain there that was called Ida;
   then happy in its verdure and its streams,
   now deserted like an old, discarded thing;   99
Rhea chose it once as a safe cradle
   for her son, and, to conceal his presence better,
   she had her servants scream loud when he cried.[9]   102
In the mountain's core an ancient man stands tall;
   he has his shoulders turned toward Damietta[1]
   and faces Rome as though it were his mirror.   105
His head is fashioned of the finest gold;
   pure silver are his arms and hands and chest;
   from there to where his legs spread, he is brass;   108
the rest of him is all of chosen iron,
   except his right foot which is terra cotta;
   he puts more weight on this foot than the other.[2]   111
Every part of him, except the gold, is broken
   by a fissure dripping tears down to his feet,
   where they collect to erode the cavern's rock;   114
from stone to stone they drain down here, becoming
   rivers: the Acheron, Styx, and Phlegethon,
   then overflow down through this tight canal   117
until they fall to where all falling ends:
   they form Cocytus.[3] What that pool is like
   I need not tell you. You will see, yourself."   120
And I to him: "If this small stream beside us
   has its source, as you have told me, in our world,
   why have we seen it only on this ledge?"   123
And he to me: "You know this place is round,
   and though your journey has been long, circling
   toward the bottom, turning only to the left,   126
you still have not completed a full circle;
   so you should never look surprised, as now,
   if you see something you have not seen before."   129
And I again: "Where, Master, shall we find
   Lethe and Phlegethon? You omit the first
   and say the other forms from the rain of tears."   132
"I am very happy when you question me,"
   he said, "but that the blood-red water boiled
   should answer certainly one of your questions.[4]   135
And Lethe you shall see, but beyond this valley,
   at a place where souls collect to wash themselves
   when penitence has freed them of their guilt.[5]   138

---

8. Saturn, mythical king of Crete during the golden age.   9. Jupiter was hidden by his mother, Rhea, from his father, Saturn, who tried to devour all his children to thwart a prophecy that he would be dethroned by one of them. So that Saturn would not hear the infant's cries, Rhea had her servants cry out and beat their shields with their swords.   1. A city in Egypt. The Old Man has been interpreted as an emblem of the decline of human history.   2. The four metals and the clay represent the degeneration of history; Dante took them from Daniel 2.31–35.   3. The frozen lake at the bottom of Hell: see 32.22–30 and 34.52.   4. See note to 12.101.   5. Lethe is crossed when Dante passes into the Earthly Paradise on the top of Mount Purgatory.

Now it is time to leave this edge of woods,"
   he added. "Be sure you follow close behind me:
   the margins are our road, they do not burn,   141
and all the flames above them are extinguished."

CANTO XV

They move out across the plain of burning sand, walking along the ditchlike edge of the conduit through which the Phlegethon flows, and after they have come some distance from the wood they see a group of souls running toward them. One, Brunetto Latini, a famous Florentine intellectual and Dante's former teacher, recognizes the Pilgrim and leaves his band to walk and talk with him. Brunetto learns the reason for the Pilgrim's journey and offers him a prophecy of the troubles lying in wait for him—an echo of Ciacco's words in Canto VI. Brunetto names some of the others being punished with him (Priscian, Francesco D'Accorso, Andrea de' Mozzi); but soon, in the distance, he sees a cloud of smoke approaching, which presages a new group, and because he must not associate with them, like a foot-racer Brunetto speeds away to catch up with his own band.

Now one of those stone margins bears us on
   and the river's vapors hover like a shade,
   sheltering the banks and the water from the flames.   3
As the Flemings, living with the constant threat
   of flood tides rushing in between Wissant
   and Bruges,[6] build their dikes to force the sea back;   6
as the Paduans build theirs on the shores of Brenta[7]
   to protect their town and homes before warm weather
   turns Chiarentana's snow to rushing water—   9
so were these walls we walked upon constructed,
   though the engineer, whoever he may have been,
   did not make them as high or thick as those.   12
We had left the wood behind (so far behind,
   by now, that if I had stopped to turn around,
   I am sure it could no longer have been seen)   15
when we saw a troop of souls come hurrying
   toward us beside the bank, and each of them
   looked us up and down, as some men look   18
at other men, at night, when the moon is new.
   They strained their eyebrows, squinting hard at us,
   as an old tailor might at his needle's eye.   21
Eyed in such a way by this strange crew,
   I was recognized by one of them, who grabbed
   my garment's hem and shouted: "How marvelous!"   24
And I, when he reached out his arm toward me,
   straining my eyes, saw through his face's crust,
   through his burned features that could not prevent   27
my memory from bringing back his name;
   and bending my face down to meet with his,

---

6. Cities that, for Dante, mark the two ends of the dike that protects Flanders from the sea.   **7.** A river that flows through Padua, fed by the melting snows in the mountains of the province of Chiarentana (modern Carinthia in Austria).

I said: "Is this really you, here, Ser Brunetto?"[8]   30
And he: "O my son, may it not displease you
  if Brunetto Latini lets his troop file on
  while he walks at your side for a little while."   33
And I: "With all my heart I beg you to,
  and if you wish me to sit here with you,
  I will, if my companion does not mind."   36
"My son," he said, "a member of this herd
  who stops one moment lies one hundred years
  unable to brush off the wounding flames,   39
so, move on; I shall follow at your hem
  and then rejoin my family that moves
  along, lamenting their eternal pain."   42
I did not dare step off the margin-path
  to walk at his own level but, with head
  bent low in reverence, I moved along.   45
He began: "What fortune or what destiny
  leads you down here before your final hour?
  And who is this one showing you the way?"   48
"Up there above in the bright living life
  before I reached the end of all my years,
  I lost myself in a valley," I replied;   51
"just yesterday at dawn I turned from it.
  This spirit here appeared as I turned back,
  and by this road he guides me home again."   54
He said to me: "Follow your constellation
  and you cannot fail to reach your port of glory,
  not if I saw clearly in the happy life;   57
and if I had not died just when I did,
  I would have cheered you on in all your work,
  seeing how favorable Heaven was to you.   60
But that ungrateful and malignant race
  which descended from the Fiesole[9] of old,
  and still have rock and mountain in their blood,   63
will become, for your good deeds, your enemy—
  and right they are: among the bitter berries
  there's no fit place for the sweet fig to bloom.[1]   66
They have always had the fame of being blind,
  an envious race, proud and avaricious;
  you must not let their ways contaminate you,   69
Your destiny reserves such honors for you:
  both parties shall be hungry to devour you,
  but the grass will not be growing where the goat is.[2]   72
Let the wild beasts of Fiesole make fodder
  of each other, and let them leave the plant untouched

---

8. Brunetto Latini (ca. 1220–1294), active in Florentine politics and the author of—among other works—
two books: a prose encyclopedia in French called the *Tresor*, which emphasizes the qualities needed for
civic duty, and a shorter allegorical poem in Italian called the *Tesoretto*, which combines autobiography
with philosophy.   9. A hill town north of Florence whose rustic inhabitants were supposed to have joined
with noble Romans in the founding of Florence, creating an unstable mixture.   1. The *bitter berries* are
the Florentines descended from Fiesole; the *sweet fig* is Brunetto's term for the aristocratic Dante.   2. Either both parties will ask you to join them or both parties will want to devour you—but keep yourself apart.

(so rare it is that one grows in their dung-heap)   75
in which there lives again the holy seed
    of those remaining Romans who survived there
    when this new nest of malice was constructed."   78
"Oh, if all I wished for had been granted,"
    I answered him, "you certainly would not,
    not yet, be banished from our life on earth;   81
my mind is etched (and now my heart is pierced)
    with your kind image, loving and paternal,
    when, living in the world, hour after hour   84
you taught me how man makes himself eternal.[3]
    And while I live my tongue shall always speak
    of my debt to you, and of my gratitude.   87
I will write down what you tell me of my future
    and save it, with another text, to show
    a lady who can interpret, if I can reach her.[4]   90
This much, at least, let me make clear to you:
    if my conscience continues not to blame me,
    I am ready for whatever Fortune wants.   93
This prophecy is not new to my ears,
    and so let Fortune turn her wheel, spinning it
    as she pleases, and the peasant turn his spade."[5]   96
My master, hearing this, looked to the right,
    then, turning round and facing me, he said:
    "He listens well who notes well what he hears."   99
But I did not answer him; I went on talking,
    walking with Ser Brunetto, asking him
    who of his company were most distinguished.   102
And he: "It might be good to know who some are,
    about the rest I feel I should be silent,
    for the time would be too short, there are so many.   105
In brief, let me tell you, all here were clerics
    and respected men of letters of great fame,
    all befouled in the world by one same sin:[6]   108
Priscian is traveling with that wretched crowd
    and Franceso d'Accorso too,[7] and also there,
    if you could have stomached such repugnancy,   111
you might have seen the one the Servant of Servants
    transferred to the Bacchiglione from the Arno
    where his sinfully erected nerves were buried.[8]   114
I would say more, but my walk and conversation
    with you cannot go on, for over there
    I see a new smoke rising from the sand: 117
people approach with whom I must not mingle.
    Remember my Trésor, where I live on,
    this is the only thing I ask of you."   120

3. In the *Tresor* Brunetto says that earthly glory gives man a second life through an enduring reputation.
4. Beatrice.   5. The traditional image of Fortune and her wheel is here compared to the rustic image of
the peasant turning the soil with his hoe.   6. Sodomy, condemned in the Middle Ages as unnatural.
7. *Priscian* was a Greek grammarian (6th century C.E.), *Francesco d'Accorso* a Florentine law professor (d.
1293).   8. Andrea de' Mozzi, bishop of Florence (1287–95), transferred by Pope Boniface (designated
here by an official title for the pope, *the Servant of* [Christ's] *Servants*) from Florence to Vicenza; the Arno
runs through Florence, the Bacchiglione through Vicenza.

Then he turned back, and he seemed like one of those
   who run Verona's race across its fields
   to win the green cloth prize;[9] and he was like   123
the winner of the group, not the last one in.

CANTO XVI

*Continuing through the third round of the Circle of Violence, the Pilgrim hears the
distant roar of a waterfall, which grows louder as he and his guide proceed. Suddenly
three shades, having recognized him as a Florentine, break from their company and
converse with him, all the while circling like a turning wheel. Their spokesman, Jacopo
Rusticucci, identifies himself and his companions (Guido Guerra and Tegghiaio Aldo-
brandini) as well-known and honored citizens of Florence, and begs for news of their
native city. The three ask to be remembered in the world and then rush off. By this time
the sound of the waterfall is so deafening that it almost drowns out speech, and when
the poets reach the edge of the precipice, Virgil takes a cord which had been bound
around his pupil's waist and tosses it into the abyss. It is a signal, and in response a
monstrous form looms up from below, swimming through the air. On this note of suspense, the canto ends.*

Already we were where I could hear the rumbling
   of the water plunging down to the next circle,
   something like the sound of beehives humming,   3
when three shades with one impulse broke away,
   running, from a group of spirits passing us
   beneath the rain of bitter suffering.   6
They were coming toward us shouting with one voice:
   "O you there, stop! From the clothes you wear, you seem
   to be a man from our perverted city."[1]   9
Ah, the wounds I saw covering their limbs,
   some old, some freshly branded by the flames!
   Even now, when I think back to them, I grieve.   12
Their shouts caught the attention of my guide,
   and then he turned to face me, saying, "Wait,
   for these are shades that merit your respect.   15
And were it not the nature of this place
   to rain with piercing flames, I would suggest
   you run toward *them*, for it would be more fitting."[2]   18
When we stopped, they resumed their normal pace
   and when they reached us, then they started circling;
   the three together formed a turning wheel,   21
just like professional wrestlers stripped and oiled,
   eyeing one another for the first, best grip
   before the actual blows and thrusts begin.[3]   24
And circling in this way each kept his face
   pointed up at me, so that their necks and feet
   moved constantly in opposite directions.   27
"And if the misery along these sterile sands,"
   one of them said, "and our charred and peeling flesh

9. A footrace run at Verona on the first Sunday in Lent, the prize being a piece of green cloth. For the
race to be run by the Christian, see I Corinthians 9.24–25.   1. Florence.   2. To hurry was considered
undignified.   3. The three naked Florentines form a circle and are compared to oiled wrestlers (a sport
practiced in Dante's time).

make us, and what we ask, repulsive to you,   30
let our great wordly fame persuade your heart
    to tell us who you are, how you can walk
    safely with living feet through Hell itself.   33
This one in front, whose footsteps I am treading,
    even though he runs his round naked and skinned,
    was of noble station, more than you may think: 36
he was the grandson of the good Gualdrada;
    his name was Guido Guerra,⁴ and in his life
    he accomplished much with counsel and with sword.   39
This other one, who pounds the sand behind me,
    is Tegghiaio Aldobrandi,⁵ whose wise voice
    the world would have done well to listen to.   42
And I, who share this post of pain with them,
    was Jacopo Rusticucci⁶ and for sure
    my reluctant wife first drove me to my sin."   45
If I could have been sheltered from the fire,
    I would have thrown myself below with them,
    and I think my guide would have allowed me to;   48
but, as I knew I would be burned and seared,
    my fear won over my first good intention
    that made me want to put my arms around them.   51
And then I spoke: "Repulsion, no, but grief
    for your condition spread throughout my heart
    (and years will pass before it fades away),   54
as soon as my lord here began to speak
    in terms that led me to believe a group
    of such men as yourselves might be approaching.   57
I am from your city, and your honored names
    and your accomplishments I have always heard
    rehearsed, and have rehearsed, myself, with fondness.   60
I leave the bitter gall, and journey toward
    those sweet fruits promised me by my true guide,⁷
    but first I must go down to the very center."   63
"So may your soul remain to guide your body
    for years to come," that same one spoke again,
    "and your fame's light shine after you are gone,   66
tell us if courtesy and valor dwell
    within our city as they used to do,
    or have they both been banished from the place?   69
Guglielmo Borsiere,⁸ who joined our painful ranks
    of late, and travels there with our companions,
    has given us reports that make us grieve."⁹   72
"A new breed of people with their sudden wealth
    have stimulated pride and unrestraint
    in you, O Florence, made to weep so soon."   75
These words I shouted with my head strained high,
    and the three below took this to be my answer

---

4. A leading participant in the civil strife in Florence (d. 1272).   5. An ally of Guido (see 6.79).   6. An
ally of Tegghiaio who blames his wife for his sodomy (see 6.80).   7. Leave Hell and head for Paradise.
8. An elegant member of Florentine society.   9. An account of the recent dissension within the city, to
which Dante himself was soon to fall victim.

and looked, as if on truth, at one another. 78
"If you always answer questions with such ease,"
    they all spoke up at once, "O happy you,
    to have this gift of ready, open speech; 81
therefore, if you survive these unlit regions
    and return to gaze upon the lovely stars,
    when it pleases you to say 'I was down there,' 84
do not fail to speak of us to living men."
    They broke their man-made wheel and ran away,
    their nimble legs were more like wings in flight. 87
"Amen" could not have been pronounced as quick
    as they were off, and vanished from our sight;
    and then my teacher thought it time to leave. 90
I followed him, and we had not gone far
    before the sound of water was so close
    that if we spoke we hardly heard each other. 93
As that river on the Apennines' left slope,[1]
    first springing from its source at Monte Veso,
    then flowing eastward holding its own course 96
(called Acquacheta at its start above
    before descending to its lower bed
    where, at Forli, it has another name), 99
reverberates there near San Benedetto
    dell'Alpe (plunging in a single bound),
    where at least a thousand vassals could be housed, 102
so down a single rocky precipice
    we found the tainted waters falling, roaring
    sound loud enough to deafen us in seconds. 105
I wore a cord that fastened round my waist,[2]
    with which I once had thought I might be able
    to catch the leopard with the gaudy skin.[3] 108
As soon as I removed it from my body
    just as my guide commanded me to do,
    I gave it to him looped into a coil. 111
Then taking it and turning to the right,
    he flung it quite a distance past the bank
    and down into the deepness of the pit. 114
"Now surely something strange is going to happen,"
    I thought to myself, "to answer the strange signal
    whose course my master follows with his eyes." 117
How cautious a man must be in company
    with one who can not only see his actions
    but read his mind and understand his thoughts![4] 120
He spoke: "Soon will rise up what I expect;
    and what you are trying to imagine now
    soon must reveal itself before your eyes." 123
It is always better to hold one's tongue than speak

1. Dante compares the roar of Phlegethon to the Montone River in northern Italy, whose course he traces in the next nine lines. 2. While commentators disagree, it seems likely that this cord is a reference both to Job 41.1, where God says He can draw Leviathan up with a hook and bind his tongue with a cord, and to Francis of Assisi, who wore a cord as a sign of humility and obedience. As a layman, Dante may have had a connection with the Franciscan friars, a common circumstance at the time. 3. The leopard of canto 1, representing fraud. 4. Dante now realizes that Virgil can read his thoughts.

a truth that seems a bold-faced lie when uttered,
　since to tell this truth could be embarrassing;　　　　126
but I shall not keep quiet; and by the verses
　of my *Comedy*—so may they be received
　with lasting favor, Reader—I swear to you　　　　129
I saw a figure coming, it was swimming
　through the thick and murky air, up to the top
　(a thing to startle even stalwart hearts),　　　　132
like one returning who has swum below
　to free the anchor that has caught its hooks
　on a reef or something else the sea conceals,　　　　135
spreading out his arms, and doubling up his legs.

CANTO XVII

The beast that had been seen approaching at the end of the last canto is the horrible monster Geryon; his face is appealing like that of an honest man, but his body ends in a scorpionlike stinger. He perches on the edge of the abyss and Virgil advises his ward, who has noticed new groups of sinners squatting on the fiery sand, to learn who they are, while he makes arrangements with Geryon for the descent. The sinners are the Usurers, unrecognizable except by the crests on the moneybags hanging about their necks, which identify them as members of the Gianfigliazzi, Ubriachi, and Scrovegni families. The Pilgrim listens to one of them briefly but soon returns to find his master sitting on Geryon's back. After he conquers his fear and mounts, too, the monster begins the slow, spiraling descent into the Eighth Circle.

"And now, behold the beast with pointed tail
　that passes mountains, annulling walls and weapons,
　behold the one that makes the whole world stink!"[5]　　3
These were the words I heard my master say
　as he signaled for the beast to come ashore,
　up close to where the rocky levee ends.　　　　6
And that repulsive spectacle of fraud
　floated close, maneuvering head and chest
　on to the shore, but his tail he let hang free.　　　　9
His face was the face of any honest man,
　it shone with such a look of benediction;
　and all the rest of him was serpentine;　　　　12
his two clawed paws were hairy to the armpits,
　his back and all his belly and both flanks
　were painted arabesques and curlicues:　　　　15
the Turks and Tartars never made a fabric
　with richer colors intricately woven,
　nor were such complex webs spun by Arachne.[6]　　18
As sometimes fishing boats are seen ashore,
　part fixed in sand, and part still in the water;
　and as the beaver,[7] living in the land　　　　21
of drunken Germans,[8] squats to catch his prey,

---

5. Geryon, the embodiment of fraud. For this figure Dante drew upon classical literature, where he had not three natures—human, reptilian, and bestial—combined into one, as here, but three bodies and three heads.　6. A woman in classical literature famous for weaving, turned into a spider: see Ovid, *Metamorphoses* 6.　7. Which was thought to catch fish by putting its tail into the water.　8. A tradition going back to the Romans accused the Germans of drunkenness.

just so that beast, the worst of beasts, hung waiting
   on the bank that bounds the stretch of sand in stone.   24
In the void beyond he exercised his tail,
   twitching and twisting-up the venomed fork
   that armed its tip just like a scorpion's stinger.   27
My leader said: "Now we must turn aside
   a little from our path, in the direction
   of that malignant beast that lies in wait."   30
Then we stepped off our path down to the right
   and moved ten paces straight across the brink
   to keep the sand and flames at a safe distance.   33
And when we stood by Geryon's side, I noticed,
   a little farther on, some people crouched
   in the sand quite close to the edge of emptiness.   36
Just then my master spoke: "So you may have
   a knowledge of this round that is complete,"
   he said, "go and see their torment for yourself.   39
But let your conversation there be brief;
   while you are gone I shall speak to this one
   and ask him for the loan of his strong back."   42
So I continued walking, all alone,
   along the seventh circle's outer edge
   to where the group of sufferers were sitting.   45
The pain was bursting from their eyes; their hands
   went scurrying up and down to give protection
   here from the flames, there from the burning sands.   48
They were, in fact, like a dog in summertime
   busy, now with his paw, now with his snout,
   tormented by the fleas and flies that bite him.   51
I carefully examined several faces
   among this group caught in the raining flames
   and did not know a soul, but I observed   54
that around each sinner's neck a pouch was hung,
   each of a different color, with a coat of arms,
   and fixed on these they seemed to feast their eyes.⁹   57
And while I looked about among the crowd,
   I saw something in blue on a yellow purse
   that had the face and bearing of a lion;   60
and while my eyes continued their inspection
   I saw another purse as red as blood
   exhibiting a goose more white than butter.   63
And one who had a blue sow, pregnant-looking,
   stamped on the whiteness of his moneybag
   asked me: "What are you doing in this pit?   66
Get out of here! And since you're still alive,
   I'll tell you that my neighbor Vitaliano
   will come to take his seat on my left side.¹   69
Among these Florentines I sit, one Paduan:

---

9. These are usurers, men who lent money for interest, which was forbidden by the Church in the Middle Ages (although often practiced). Each has a coat of arms on his purse by which he can be identified; all are Italians.   1. The speaker is from Padua and here maliciously identifies another Paduan who will soon be joining him.

time after time they fill my ears with blasts
  of shouting: 'Send us down the sovereign knight[2]   72
who will come bearing three goats on his pouch.'"
  As final comment he stuck out his tongue—
    as far out as an ox licking its nose.   75
And I, afraid my staying there much longer
  might anger the one who warned me to be brief,
    turned my back on these frustrated sinners.   78
I found my guide already sitting high
  upon the back of that fierce animal;
    he said: "And now, take courage and be strong.   81
From now on we descend by stairs like these.
  Get on up front. I want to ride behind,
    to be between you and the dangerous tail."[3]   84
A man who feels the shivers of a fever
  coming on, his nails already dead of color,
    will tremble at the mere sight of cool shade;   87
I was that man when I had heard his words.
  But then I felt those stabs of shame that make
    a servant brave before his valorous master.   90
As I squirmed around on those enormous shoulders,
  I wanted to cry out, "Hold on to me,"
    but I had no voice to second my desire.   93
Then he who once before had helped me out
  when I was threatened put his arms around me
    as soon as I was settled, and held me tight;   96
and then he cried: "Now Geryon, start moving,
  descend with gentle motion, circling wide:
    remember you are carrying living weight."   99
Just as a boat slips back away from shore,
  back slowly, more and more, he left that pier;
    and when he felt himself all clear in space,   102
to where his breast had been he swung his tail
  and stretched it undulating like an eel,
    as with his paws he gathered in the air.   105
I doubt if Phaëthon[4] feared more—that time
  he dropped the sun-reins of his father's chariot
    and burned the streak of sky we see today—   108
or if poor Icarus[5] did—feeling his sides
  unfeathering as the wax began to melt,
    his father shouting: "Wrong, your course is wrong"—   111
than I had when I felt myself in air
  and saw on every side nothing but air;
    only the beast I sat upon was there.   114
He moves along slowly, and swimming slowly,
  descends a spiral path—but I know this
    only from a breeze ahead and one below;   117
I hear now on my right the whirlpool roar

---

2. A prominent Florentine banker.   3. Virgil protects Dante from Geryon's scorpion's tail.   4. Son of Apollo, *Phaëthon* tried to drive the chariot of the sun, but when it got out of control it scorched both Earth and the heavens, creating the Milky Way (Ovid, *Metamorphoses* 2).   5. Flying with wings made of wax and feathers, *Icarus* went too near the sun and fell (Ovid, *Metamorphoses* 8).

with hideous sound beneath us on the ground;
   at this I stretch my neck to look below,   120
but leaning out soon made me more afraid,
   for I heard moaning there and saw the flames;
   trembling, I cowered back, tightening my legs,   123
and I saw then what I had not before:
   the spiral path of our descent to torment
   closing in on us, it seemed, from every side.   126
As the falcon on the wing for many hours,
   having found no prey, and having seen no signal
(so that his falconer sighs: "Oh, he falls already"),   129
descends, worn out, circling a hundred times
   (instead of swooping down), settling at some distance
   from his master, perched in anger and disdain,[6]   132
so Geryon brought us down to the bottom
   at the foot of the jagged cliff, almost against it,
   and once he got our bodies off his back,   135
he shot off like a shaft shot from a bowstring.

CANTO XVIII

The Pilgrim describes the view he had of the Eighth Circle of Hell while descending through the air on Geryon's back. It consists of ten stone ravines called Malebolge *(Evil Pockets), and across each* bolgia *is an arching bridge. When the poets find themselves on the edge of the first ravine they see two lines of naked sinners, walking in opposite directions. In one are the Pimps or Panderers, and among them the Pilgrim recognizes Venedico Caccianemico; in the other are the Seducers, among whom Virgil points out Jason. As the two move toward the next* bolgia, *they are assailed by a terrible stench; for here the Flatterers are immersed in excrement. Among them are Alessio Interminei and Thaïs the whore.*

There is a place in Hell called Malebolge,
   cut out of stone the color of iron ore,
   just like the circling cliff that walls it in.   3
Right at the center of this evil plain
   there yawns a very wide, deep well, whose structure
   I will talk of when the place itself is reached.[7]   6
That belt of land remaining, then, runs round
   between the well and cliff, and all this space
   is divided into ten descending valleys,   9
just like a ground-plan for successive moats
   that in concentric circles bind their center
   and serve to protect the ramparts of the castle.   12
This was the surface image they presented;
   and as bridges from a castle's portal stretch
   from moat to moat to reach the farthest bank,   15
so, from the great cliff's base, just spokes of rock,
   crossing from bank to bank, intersecting ditches
   until the pit's hub cuts them off from meeting.   18
This is the place in which we found ourselves,

---

6. Unless it sights prey or is called back with a lure by its master, a trained falcon will continue flying until exhaustion compels it to descend.   7. The last, or ninth, circle of Hell, described in cantos 21–34.

once shaken from the back of Geryon.
   The poet turned to the left, I walked behind him.   21
There, on our right, I saw new suffering souls,
   new means of torture, and new torturers,
   crammed into the depths of the first ditch.   24
Two files of naked souls walked on the bottom,
   the ones on our side faced us as they passed,
   the others moved as we did but more quickly.   27
The Romans, too, in the year of the Jubilee[8]
   took measures to accommodate the throngs
   that had to come and go across their bridge: 30
they fixed it so on one side all were looking
   at the castle, and were walking to St. Peter's;
   on the other, they were moving toward the mount.   33
On both sides, up along the deadly rock,
   I saw horned devils with enormous whips
   lashing the backs of shades with cruel delight.   36
Ah, how they made them skip and lift their heels
   at the very first crack of the whip! Not one of them
   dared pause to take a second or a third!   39
As I walked on my eyes met with the glance
   of one down there; I murmured to myself:
   "I know this face from somewhere, I am sure."[9]   42
And so I stopped to study him more closely;
   my leader also stopped, and was so kind
   as to allow me to retrace my steps;   45
and that whipped soul thought he would hide from me
   by lowering his face—which did no good.
   I said, "O you, there, with your head bent low,   48
if the features of your shade do not deceive me,
   you are Venedico Caccianemico, I'm sure.
   How did you get yourself in such a pickle?"   51
"I'm not so keen on answering," he said,
   "but I feel I must; your plain talk is compelling,
   it makes me think of old times in the world.   54
I was the one who coaxed Ghisolabella
   to serve the lusty wishes of the Marquis,
   no matter how the sordid tale is told;   57
I'm not the only Bolognese who weeps here—
   hardly! This place is packed with us; in fact,
   there are more of us here than there are living tongues,   60
between Savena and Reno, saying 'Sipa';[1]
   I call on your own memory as witness:
   remember we have avaricious hearts."   63
Just at that point a devil let him have
   the feel of his tailed whip and cried: "Move on,
   you pimp, you can't cash in on women here!"   66

8. The year 1300 was a Jubilee Year, and Dante here describes the crowd control on the bridge that ran between the Castle of St. Angelo and St. Peter's.   9. This is Venedico Caccianemico, a man from Bologna who was reputed to have turned his sister Ghisolabella over to the Marquis of Este.   1. *Sipa* is a word for "yes" in the dialect spoken in the territory between the rivers Savena and Reno, which comprise the boundaries of Bologna.

I turned and hurried to rejoin my guide;
  we walked a few more steps and then we reached
  the rocky bridge that juts out from the bank.   69
We had no difficulty climbing up,
  and turning right, along the jagged ridge,
  we left those shades to their eternal circlings.   72
When we were where the ditch yawned wide below
  the ridge, to make a passage for the scourged,
  my guide said: "Stop and stand where you can see   75
these other misbegotten souls, whose faces
  you could not see before, for they were moving
  in the same direction we were, over there."   78
So from the ancient bridge we viewed the train
  that hurried toward us along the other tract—
  kept moving, like the first, by stinging whips.   81
And the good master, without my asking him,
  said, "Look at that imposing one approaching,
  who does not shed a single tear of pain: 84
what majesty he still maintains down there!
  He is Jason,[2] who by courage and sharp wits,
  fleeced the Colchians of their golden ram.   87
He later journeyed through the isle of Lemnos,
  whose bold and heartless females, earlier,
  had slaughtered every male upon the island;   90
there with his words of love, and loving looks,
  he succeeded in deceiving young Hypsipyle,
  who had in turn deceived the other women.   93
He left her there, with child, and all alone:
  such sin condemns him to such punishment,
  and Medea, too, gets her revenge on him.   96
With him go all deceivers of this type,
  and let this be enough to know concerning
  the first valley and the souls locked in its jaws."   99
We were already where the narrow ridge
  begins to cross the second bank, to make it
  an abutment for another ditch's arch.   102
Now we could hear the shades in the next pouch
  whimpering, making snorting grunting sounds
  and sounds of blows, slapping with open palms.   105
From a steaming stench below, the banks were coated
  with a slimy mold that stuck to them like glue,
  disgusting to behold and worse to smell.   108
The bottom was so hollowed out of sight,
  we saw it only when we climbed the arch
  and looked down from the bridge's highest point: 111
there we were, and from where I stood I saw
  souls in the ditch plunged into excrement
  that might well have been flushed from our latrines;   114

2. *Jason* led the Argonauts on the voyage to the island of Colchis, where they stole the golden fleece. He seduced and abandoned Hypsipyle, who had hidden her father when the other women of Lemnos were killing all the males. He also abandoned Medea, the daughter of the king of Colchis. For his story, see Ovid, *Metamorphoses* 7.

my eyes were searching hard along the bottom,
   and I saw somebody's head so smirched with shit,
   you could not tell if he were priest or layman.   117
He shouted up: "Why do you feast your eyes
   on me more than these other dirty beasts?"
   And I replied: "Because, remembering well,   120
I've seen you with your hair dry once or twice.
   You are Alessio Interminei from Lucca,[3]
   that's why I stare at you more than the rest."   123
He beat his slimy forehead as he answered:
   "I am stuck down here by all those flatteries
   that rolled unceasing off my tongue up there."   126
He finished speaking, and my guide began:
   "Lean out a little more, look hard down there
   so you can get a good look at the face   129
of that repulsive and disheveled tramp
   scratching herself with shitty fingernails,
   spreading her legs while squatting up and down: 132
it is Thaïs the whore,[4] who gave this answer
   to her lover when he asked: 'Am I very worthy
   of your thanks?': 'Very? Nay, incredibly so!'   135
I think our eyes have had their fill of this."

CANTO XIX

*From the bridge above the Third Bolgia can be seen a rocky landscape below filled with
holes, from each of which protrude a sinner's legs and feet; flames dance across their
soles. When the Pilgrim expresses curiosity about a particular pair of twitching legs,
Virgil carries him down into the bolgia so that the Pilgrim himself may question the
sinner. The legs belong to Pope Nicholas III, who astounds the Pilgrim by mistaking
him for Boniface VIII, the next pope, who, as soon as he dies, will fall to the same hole,
thereby pushing Nicholas farther down. He predicts that soon after Boniface, Pope
Clement V will come, stuffing both himself and Boniface still deeper. To Nicholas's
rather rhetoric-filled speech the Pilgrim responds with equally high language, inveighing
against the Simonists, the evil churchmen who are punished here. Virgil is much pleased
with his pupil and, lifting him in an affectionate embrace, he carries him to the top of
the arch above the next bolgia.*

O Simon Magus![5] O scum that followed him!
   Those things of God that rightly should be wed
   to holiness, you, rapacious creatures,   3
for the price of gold and silver, prostitute.
   Now, in your honor, I must sound my trumpet
   for here in the third pouch is where you dwell.   6
We had already climbed to see this tomb,
   and were standing high above it on the bridge,
   exactly at the mid-point of the ditch.   9
O Highest Wisdom, how you demonstrate
   your art in Heaven, on earth, and here in Hell!

---

3. A prominent citizen of Lucca, in northern Italy.   4. A character in a play by the Roman writer Terence
(186 or 185–159? B.C.E.).   5. Because in the Bible *Simon Magus* tried to buy spiritual power from the
apostles (Acts 8.9–24), the selling of any spiritual good for material gain was known in the Middle Ages as
simony. The most common form of simony was the selling of Church offices.

How justly does your power make awards!⁶   12
I saw along the sides and on the bottom
   the livid-colored rock all full of holes;
   all were the same in size, and each was round.   15
To me they seemed no wider and no deeper
   than those inside my lovely San Giovanni,⁷
   in which the priest would stand or baptize from;   18
and one of these, not many years ago,
   I smashed for someone who was drowning in it:
   let this be mankind's picture of the truth!   21
From the mouth of every hole were sticking out
   a single sinner's feet, and then the legs
   up to the calf—the rest was stuffed inside.   24
The soles of every sinner's feet were flaming;
   their naked legs were twitching frenziedly—
   they would have broken any chain or rope.   27
Just as a flame will only move along
   an object's oily outer peel, so here
   the fire slid from heel to toe and back.   30
"Who is that one, Master, that angry wretch,
   who is writhing more than any of his comrades,"
   I asked, "the one licked by a redder flame?"⁸   33
And he to me, "If you want to be carried down
   along that lower bank to where he is,
   you can ask him who he is and why he's here."   36
And I, "My pleasure is what pleases you:
   you are my lord, you know that from your will
   I would not swerve. You even know my thoughts."   39
When we reached the fourth bank, we began to turn
   and, keeping to the left, made our way down
   to the bottom of the holed and narrow ditch.   42
The good guide did not drop me from his side
   until he brought me to the broken rock
   of that one who was fretting with his shanks.   45
"Whatever you are, holding your upside down,
   O wretched soul, stuck like a stake in ground,
   make a sound or something," I said, "if you can."   48
I stood there like a priest who is confessing
   some vile assassin who, fixed in his ditch,
   has called him back again to put off dying.⁹   51
He cried: "Is that *you*, here, already, upright?
   Is that you here already upright, Boniface?
   By many years the book has lied to me!   54
Are you fed up so soon with all that wealth
   for which you did not fear to take by guile

---

6. Dante is here applauding the artfulness of divine justice because the simoniacs, who cared most for their purses, are here stuffed into fiery purses hewn into the rock; see line 72 below.   7. The baptistery in Florence where Dante was baptized. The subsequent personal reference has never been satisfactorily explained.   8. Pope Nicholas III (pope 1277–80). He mistakenly believes that one of his successors, Boniface VIII, has come to be squeezed into the hole (line 53). Like all damned souls, Nicholas has foreknowledge, and because Boniface did not die until 1303 Nicholas is surprised at what he thinks is his appearance in 1300.   9. Hired murderers were occasionally executed by being placed head-down in a ditch and then buried alive.

the Lovely Lady,[1] then tear her asunder?"   57
I stood there like a person just made fun of,
    dumbfounded by a question for an answer,
    not knowing how to answer the reply.   60
Then Virgil said: "Quick, hurry up and tell him:
    'I'm not the one, I'm not the one you think!'"
    And I answered just the way he told me to.   63
The spirit heard, and twisted both his feet,
    then, sighing with a grieving, tearful voice,
    he said: "Well then, what do you want of me?   66
If it concerns you so to learn my name
    that for this reason you came down the bank,
    know that I once was dressed in the great mantle.   69
But actually I was the she-bear's son,[2]
    so greedy to advance my cubs, that wealth
    I pocketed in life, and here, myself.   72
Beneath my head are pushed down all the others
    who came, sinning in simony, before me,
    squeezed tightly in the fissures of the rock.   75
I, in my turn, shall join the rest below
    as soon as *he* comes, the one I thought you were
    when, all too quick, I put my question to you.   78
But already my feet have baked a longer time
    (and I have been stuck upside-down like this)
    than he will stay here planted with feet aflame: 81
soon after him shall come one from the West,[3]
    a lawless shepherd, one whose fouler deeds
    make him a fitting cover for us both.   84
He shall be another Jason,[4] like the one
    in Maccabees: just as his king was pliant,
    so France's king shall soften to this priest."   87
I do not know, perhaps I was too bold here,
    but I answered him in tune with his own words:
    "Well, tell me now: what was the sum of money   90
that holy Peter had to pay our Lord
    before He gave the keys into his keeping?
    Certainly He asked no more than 'Follow me.'[5]   93
Nor did Peter or the rest extort gold coins
    or silver from Matthias when he was picked
    to fill the place the evil one had lost.[6]   96
So stay stuck there, for you are rightly punished,
    and guard with care the money wrongly gained
    that made you stand courageous against Charles.[7]   99
And were it not for the reverence I have
    for those highest of all keys that you once held
    in the happy life—if this did not restrain me,   102

1. The church.   2. The arms of Nicholas's family (the Orsini) included a *she-bear*.   3. Clement V, who became pope in 1305 after agreeing with the French king to remove the papacy to Avignon in France. He is *from the West* because he was born in western France.   4. Jason became high priest of the Jews by bribing the king: see 2 Maccabees 4.7–9.   5. See Matthew 16.18–19: the keys are the church's power to bind (condemn) and to loose (absolve). For *follow me*, see Matthew 4.18–19.   6. *Matthias* was chosen by lot to fill the place of Judas (Acts 1.23–26).   7. Nicholas was supposed to be involved in a plot against Charles of Anjou (1226–1285), ruler of Naples and Sicily.

I would use even harsher words than these,
  for your avarice brings grief upon the world,
  crushing the good, exalting the depraved. 105
You shepherds it was the Evangelist[8] had in mind
  when the vision came to him of her who sits
  upon the waters playing whore with kings: 108
that one who with the seven heads was born
  and from her ten horns managed to draw strength
  so long as virtue was her bridegroom's joy. 111
You have built yourselves a God of gold and silver!
  How do you differ from the idolator,
  except he worships one, you worship hundreds? 114
O Constantine,[9] what evil did you sire,
  not by your conversion, but by the dower
  that the first wealthy Father got from you!" 117
And while I sang these very notes to him,
  his big flat feet kicked fiercely out of anger,
  —or perhaps it was his conscience gnawing him. 120
I think my master liked what I was saying,
  for all the while he smiled and was intent
  on hearing the ring of truly spoken words. 123
Then he took hold of me with both his arms,
  and when he had me firm against his breast,
  he climbed back up the path he had come down. 126
He did not tire of the weight clasped tight to him,
  but brought me to the top of the bridge's arch,
  the one that joins the fourth bank to the fifth. 129
And here he gently set his burden down—
  gently, for the ridge, so steep and rugged,
  would have been hard even for goats to cross. 132
From there another valley opened to me.

CANTO XX

In the Fourth Bolgia *they see a group of shades weeping as they walk slowly along the valley; they are the Soothsayers and their heads are twisted completely around so that their hair flows down their fronts and their tears flow down to their buttocks. Virgil points out many of them, including Amphiaraus, Tiresias, Aruns, and Manto. It was Manto who first inhabited the site of Virgil's home city of Mantua, and the poet gives a long description of the city's founding, after which he names more of the condemned soothsayers: Eurypylus, Michael Scot, Guido Bonatti, and Asdente.*

Now I must turn strange torments into verse
  to form the matter of the twentieth canto
  of the first chant, the one about the damned. 3
Already I was where I could look down

---

8. John, author of Revelation, who in the Middle Ages was identified with the author of the Gospel according to John: for this passage, which was originally interpreted as referring to pagan Rome but which Dante applies to the corrupt Church, see Revelation 17.1–18. The *seven heads* are the seven Sacraments; the *ten horns*, the Ten Commandments; the *bridegroom*, God.   9. Roman Emperor (d. 337) who was the supposed author of a document—known as the Donation of Constantine—in which he granted temporal power and the right to acquire wealth to Pope Sylvester I, the *first wealthy Father* of this passage. The document was proved to be a forgery in the 15th century.

into the depths of the ditch: I saw its floor
 was wet with anguished tears shed by the sinners,   6
and I saw people in the valley's circle,
 silent, weeping, walking at a litany pace
 the way processions push along in our world.[1]   9
And when my gaze moved down below their faces,
 I saw all were incredibly distorted,
 the chin was not above the chest, the neck   12
was twisted—their faces looked down on their backs;
 they had to move ahead by moving backward,
 for they never saw what was ahead of them.   15
Perhaps there was a case of someone once
 in a palsy fit becoming so distorted,
 but none that I know of! I doubt there could be!   18
So may God grant you, Reader, benefit
 from reading of my poem, just ask yourself
 how I could keep my eyes dry when, close by,   21
I saw the image of our human form
 so twisted—the tears their eyes were shedding
 streamed down to wet their buttocks at the cleft.   24
Indeed I did weep, as I leaned my body
 against a jut of rugged rock. My guide:
 "So you are still like all the other fools?   27
In this place piety lives when pity is dead,
 for who could be more wicked than that man
 who tries to bend divine will to his own![2]   30
Lift your head up, lift it, see him for whom
 the earth split wide before the Thebans's eyes,
 while they all shouted, 'Where are you rushing off to,   33
Amphiaraus?[3] Why do you quit the war?'
 He kept on rushing downward through the gap
 until Minòs, who gets them all, got him.   36
You see how he has made his back his chest:
 because he wished to see too far ahead,
 he sees behind and walks a backward track.   39
Behold Tiresias,[4] who changed his looks:
 from a man he turned himself into a woman,
 transforming all his body, part for part;   42
then later on he had to take the wand
 and strike once more those two snakes making love
 before he could get back his virile parts.   45
Backing up to this one's chest comes Aruns,[5]
 who, in the hills of Luni, worked by peasants
 of Carrara dwelling in the valley's plain,   48
lived in white marble cut into a cave,
 and from this site, where nothing blocked his view,

---

1. A *litany* is a form of public prayer, often recited during stately *processions* in the church. 2. This is a rebuke to Dante, who errs by showing sympathy for the damned. 3. A priest swallowed up by the Earth in a battle against the Thebans as described in Statius's *Thebaid* (see note 3 to 14.48). For Minos, see 5.4. 4. A soothsayer of Thebes, he struck two coupling serpents with his rod and was transformed into a woman. Seven years later he repeated the action and was changed back into a man. See Ovid, *Metamorphoses* 3. 5. An Etruscan soothsayer from the city of Luni, in the area of Carrera where marble is quarried, is described by the Roman poet Lucan (d. 65 c.E.) in his *Pharsalia*.

he could observe the sea and stars with ease.   51
And that one, with her hair loose, flowing back
  to cover both her breasts you cannot see,
  and with her hairy parts in front behind her,   54
was Manto,[6] who had searched through many lands
  before she came to dwell where I was born;
  now let me tell you something of her story.   57
When her father had departed from the living,
  and Bacchus' sacred city[7] fell enslaved,
  she wandered through the world for many years.   60
High in fair Italy there spreads a lake,
  beneath the mountains bounding Germany
  beyond the Tyrol, known as Lake Benaco;[8]   63
by a thousand streams and more, I think, the Alps
  are bathed from Garda to the Val Camonica[9]
  with the waters flowing down into that lake;   66
at its center is a place where all three bishops
  of Trent and Brescia and Verona could,
  if they would ever visit there, say Mass;   69
Peschiera[1] sits, a handsome well-built fortress,
  to ward off Brescians and the Bergamese,
  along the lowest point of that lake's shore,   72
where all the water that Benaco's basin
  cannot hold must overflow to make a stream
  that winds its way through countrysides of green;   75
but when the water starts to flow, its name
  is not Benaco, but Mencio, all the way
  to Governol,[2] where it falls into the Po;   78
but before its course is run it strikes a lowland,
  on which it spreads and turns into a marsh
  that can become unbearable in summer.   81
Passing this place one day the savage virgin
  saw land that lay in the center of the mire,
  untilled and empty of inhabitants.   84
There, to escape all human intercourse,
  she stopped to practice magic with her servants;
  there she lived, and there she left her corpse.   87
Later on, the men who lived around there gathered
  on that very spot, for it was well protected
  by the bog that girded it on every side.   90
They built a city over her dead bones,
  and for her, the first to choose that place, they named it
  Mantua,[3] without recourse to sorcery.   93
Once, there were far more people living there,
  before the foolish Casalodi listened
  to the fraudulent advice of Pinamonte.[4]   96

6. Another Theban soothsayer described by Roman poets.   7. Thebes.   8. The present-day Lake Garda in northern Italy, located in terms of an island where the boundaries of the three dioceses of Trent, Brescia, and Verona meet.   9. *Garda* is a town by the lake and *Val Camonica* a valley below it.   1. *Peschiera* is a town on the south shore of the lake; the *Brescians* and the *Bergamese* are inhabitants of two towns to the northwest of Peschiera.   2. A town some thirty miles south of Peschiera. Presumably Virgil provides this detailed geography to illustrate that he is a native of this region.   3. Virgil's native city. 4. A reference to the internal intrigues of the rulers of Mantua in the 13th century.

And so, I warn you, should you ever hear
    my city's origin told otherwise,
    let no false tales adulterate the truth."⁵   99
And I replied: "Master, your explanations
    are truth for me, winning my faith entirely;
    any others would be just like burned-out coals.   102
But speak to me of these shades passing by,
    if you see anyone that is worth noting;
    for now my mind is set on only that."   105
He said: "That one, whose beard flows from his cheeks
    and settles on his back and makes it dark,
    was (when the war stripped Greece of all its males, 108
so that the few there were still rocked in cradles)
    an augur who, with Calchas,⁶ called the moment
    to cut the first ship's cable free at Aulis: 111
he is Eurypylus. I sang his story
    this way, somewhere in my high tragedy:
    you should know where—you know it, every line.   114
That other one, whose thighs are scarcely fleshed,
    was Michael Scot,⁷ who most assuredly
    knew every trick of magic fraudulence.   117
See there Guido Bonatti; see Asdente,⁸
    who wishes now he had been more devoted
    to making shoes—too late now for repentance. 120
And see those wretched hags⁹ who traded in
    needle, spindle, shuttle, for fortune-telling,
    and cast their spells with image-dolls and potions. 123
Now come along. Cain¹ with his thorn-bush straddles
    the confines of both hemispheres already
    and dips into the waves below Seville;   126
and the moon last night already was at full;
    and you should well remember that at times
    when you were lost in the dark wood she helped you." 129
And we were moving all the time he spoke.

CANTO XXI

When the two reach the summit of the arch over the Fifth Bolgia, they see in the ditch below the bubbling of boiling pitch. Virgil's sudden warning of danger frightens the Pilgrim even before he sees a black devil rushing toward them, with a sinner slung over his shoulder. From the bridge the devil flings the sinner into the pitch, where he is poked at and tormented by the family of Malebranche devils. Virgil, advising his ward to hide behind a rock, crosses the bridge to face the devils alone. They threaten him with their

by *the men who lived around there* (see line 88, above). It is not clear why Dante has Virgil contradict his own poem unless he is trying to clear Virgil of any taint of himself being a magician (see note 2 to 9.23).   6. *Calchas* and *Eurypylus* were prophets (or augurs) involved in the Trojan War; here Virgil says that they determined when the Greeks were to set out for the war from the island of Aulis, although *Aeneid* 2 gives a different account.   7. A famous scientist, philosopher, and astrologer from Scotland, Scot spent many years at the court of Frederick II (10.119) in Palermo and died in 1235.   8. A shoemaker famous as a soothsayer in 13th-century Italy. *Guido Bonatti*: an astrologer at the court of Guido da Montefeltro (see canto 32).   9. Common soothsayers and potion makers.   1. Popular belief held that God placed Cain in the moon after the murder of Abel; *Cain with his thorn-bush* means the moon with its spots, which is now setting at the western edge of the Northern Hemisphere. Overhead, in Jerusalem, it is the dawn of Holy Saturday.

pitchforks, but when he announces to their leader, Malacoda, that Heaven has willed that he lead another through Hell, the devil's arrogance collapses. Virgil calls the Pilgrim back to him. Scarmiglione, who tries to take a poke at him, is rebuked by his leader, who tells the travelers that the sixth arch is broken here but farther on they will find another bridge to cross. He chooses a squad of his devils to escort them there: Alichino, Calcabrina, Cagnazzo, Barbariccia, Libicocco, Draghignazzo, Ciriatto, Graffiacane, Farfarello, and Rubicante. The Pilgrim's suspicion about their unsavory escorts is brushed aside by his guide, and the squad starts off, giving an obscene salute to their captain, who returns their salute with a fart.

From this bridge to the next we walked and talked
  of things my Comedy does not care to tell;
  and when we reached the summit of the arch,

we stopped to see the next fosse² of Malebolge   3
  and to hear more lamentation voiced in vain:
  I saw that it was very strangely dark!

In the vast and busy shipyard of the Venetians³   6
  there boils all winter long a tough, thick pitch
  that is used to caulk the ribs of unsound ships.

Since winter will not let them sail, they toil: 9
  some build new ships, others repair the old ones,
  plugging the planks come loose from many sailings;

some hammer at the bow, some at the stern,   12
  one carves the oars while others twine the ropes,
  one mends the jib, one patches up the mainsail;

here, too, but heated by God's art, not fire,   15
  a sticky tar was boiling in the ditch
  that smeared the banks with viscous residue.

I saw it there, but I saw nothing in it,   18
  except the rising of the boiling bubbles
  breathing in air to burst and sink again.

I stood intently gazing there below,   21
  my guide, shouting to me: "Watch out, watch out!"
  took hold of me and drew me to his side.

I turned my head like one who can't resist   24
  looking to see what makes him run away
  (his body's strength draining with sudden fear),

but, looking back, does not delay his flight;   27
  and I saw coming right behind our backs,
  rushing along the ridge, a devil, black!

His face, his look, how frightening it was!   30
  With outstretched wings he skimmed along the rock,
  and every single move he made was cruel;

on one of his high-hunched and pointed shoulders   33
  he had a sinner slung by both his thighs,
  held tightly clawed at the tendons of his heels.

He shouted from our bridge: "Hey, Malebranche,⁴   36
  here's one of Santa Zita's elders for you!
  You stick him under—I'll go back for more;

       39

2. Ditch or pouch.   **3.** The huge shipyard at Venice was called the Arsenal.   **4.** *Malebranche* (Evil-claws) is the generic name for the devils in this ditch, and each has a proper name as well (lines 76, 105, 118–26). The elders of *Saint Zita* in Lucca (a town near Florence) were ten citizens who ran the government.

I've got that city stocked with the likes of him,
　　they're all a bunch of grafters, save Bonturo![5]
　　You can change a 'no' to 'yes' for cash in Lucca."　　　　42
He flung him in, then from the flinty cliff
　　sprang off. No hound unleashed to chase a thief
　　could have taken off with greater speed than he.　　　　45
That sinner plunged, then floated up stretched out,
　　and the devils underneath the bridge all shouted:
　　"You shouldn't imitate the Holy Face!　　　　48
The swimming's different here from in the Serchio![6]
　　We have our grappling-hooks along with us—
　　don't show yourself above the pitch, or else!"　　　　51
With a hundred prongs or more they pricked him, shrieking:
　　"You've got to do your squirming under cover,
　　try learning how to cheat beneath the surface."　　　　54
They were like cooks who make their scullery boys
　　poke down into the caldron with their forks
　　to keep the meat from floating to the top.　　　　57
My master said: "We'd best not let them know
　　that you are here with me; crouch down behind
　　some jutting rock so that they cannot see you;　　　　60
whatever insults they may hurl at me,
　　you must not fear, I know how things are run here;
　　I have been caught in as bad a fix before."[7]　　　　63
He crossed the bridge and walked on past the end;
　　as soon as he set foot on the sixth bank
　　he forced himself to look as bold as possible.　　　　66
With all the sound and fury that breaks loose
　　when dogs rush out at some poor begging tramp,
　　making him stop and beg from where he stands,　　　　69
the ones who hid beneath the bridge sprang out
　　and blocked him with a flourish of their pitchforks,
　　but he shouted: "All of you behave yourselves!　　　　72
Before you start to jab me with your forks,
　　let one of you step forth to hear me out,
　　and then decide if you still care to grapple."　　　　75
They all cried out: "Let Malacoda[8] go!"
　　One stepped forward—the others stood their ground—
　　and moving, said, "What good will this do him?"　　　　78
"Do you think, Malacoda," said my master,
　　"that you would see me here, come all this way,
　　against all opposition, and still safe,　　　　81
without propitious fate and God's permission?
　　Now let us pass, for it is willed in Heaven
　　that I lead another by this savage path."　　　　84
With this the devil's arrogance collapsed,
　　his pitchfork, too, dropped right down to his feet,
　　as he announced to all: "Don't touch this man!"　　　　87

---

5. A current official in Lucca, Bonturo Dati was in fact known as the most corrupt of all; the devil is being ironic.　　6. The *Serchio* is a river near Lucca. The *Holy Face* of Lucca was a venerated icon.　　7. Virgil may be referring to his difficulties with the devils in 8.82–130, when he and Dante tried to enter the city of Dis.　　8. Evil-tail.

"You, hiding over there," my guide called me,
  "behind the bridge's rocks, curled up and quiet,
  come back to me, you may return in safety."   90
At his words I rose and then I ran to him
  and all the devils made a movement forward;
  I feared they would not really keep their pact.   93
(I remember seeing soldiers under truce,
  as they left the castle of Caprona, frightened
  to be passing in the midst of such an enemy.)[9]   96
I drew up close to him, as close as possible,
  and did not take my eyes from all those faces
  that certainly had nothing good about them.   99
Their prongs were aimed at me, and one was saying:
  "Now do I let him have it in the rump?"
  They answered all for one: "Sure, stick him good!"   102
But the devil who had spoken with my guide
  was quick to spin around and scream an order:
  "At ease there, take it easy, Scarmiglione!"   105
Then he said to us: "You cannot travel straight
  across this string of bridges, for the sixth arch
  lies broken at the bottom of its ditch;[1]   108
if you have made your mind up to proceed,
  you must continue on along this ridge;
  not far, you'll find a bridge that crosses it.[2]   111
Five hours more and it will be one thousand,
  two hundred sixty-six years and a day
  since the bridge-way here fell crumbling to the ground.[3]   114
I plan to send a squad of mine that way
  to see that no one airs himself down there;
  go along with them, they will not misbehave.   117
Front and center, Alichino, Calcabrina,"
  he shouted his commands, "you too, Cagnazzo;
  Barbariccia, you be captain of the squad.   120
Take Libicocco with you and Draghignazzo,
  toothy Ciriatto and Graffiacane,
  Farfarello and our crazy Rubicante.[4]   123
Now tour the ditch, inspect the boiling tar;
  these two shall have safe passage to the bridge
  connecting den to den without a break."   126
"O master, I don't like the looks of this,"
  I said, "let's go, just you and me, no escort,
  you know the way. I want no part of them!   129
If you're observant, as you usually are,
  why is it you don't see them grind their teeth
  and wink at one another?—we're in danger!"   132

---

9. A battle outside Florence in 1289, in which Dante may have taken part.   1. The bridge across the
fifth ditch was smashed, as Malacoda explains, by the earthquake that occurred at the time of the Crucifixion.   2. As the travelers discover, this is a lie.   3. According to medieval tradition, Christ's death on
the cross occurred on Good Friday at noon, in his thirty-third year, which would be 34 C.E.; the time at
which Dante and Vigil are in this fifth ditch of Malebolge is 7 A.M. of Holy Saturday, 1300, which is 1266
years plus one day, less five hours later.   4. These names—like Scarmiglione in line 105—imply raffish
irreverence in general, although some do have specific if ignoble meanings: Cagnazzo = "Big Dog," Barbariccia = "Curly Beard," Graffiacane = "Dog-Scratcher."

And he to me: "I will not have you frightened;
   let them do all the grinding that they want,
   they do it for the boiling souls, not us."   135
Before they turned left-face along the bank
   each one gave their good captain a salute
   with farting tongue pressed tightly to his teeth,   138
and he blew back with his bugle of an ass-hole.

CANTO XXII

The note of grotesque comedy in the bolgia *of the* Malebranche *continues, with a comparison between Malacoda's salute to his soldiers and different kinds of military signals the Pilgrim has witnessed in his lifetime. He sees many Grafters squatting in the pitch, but as soon as the* Malebranche *draw near, they dive below the surface. One unidentified Navarrese, however, fails to escape and is hoisted up on Graffiacane's hooks; Rubicante and the other Malebranche start to tear into him, but Virgil, at his ward's request, manages to question him between torments. The sinner briefly tells his story, and then relates that he has left below in the pitch an Italian, Fra Gomita, a particularly adept grafter, who spends his time talking to Michel Zanche.*

The Navarrese sinner promises to lure some of his colleagues to the surface for the devils' amusement, if the tormentors will hide themselves for a moment. Cagnazzo is skeptical but Alichino agrees, and no sooner do the Malebranche *turn away than the crafty grafter dives below the pitch. Alichino flies after him, but too late; now Calcabrina rushes after Alichino and both struggle above the boiling pitch, and then fall in. Barbariccia directs the rescue operation as the two poets steal away.*

I have seen troops of horsemen breaking camp,
   opening the attack, or passing in review,
   I have even seen them fleeing for their lives;   3
I have seen scouts ride, exploring your terrain,
   O Aretines,[5] and I have seen raiding-parties
   and the clash of tournaments, the run of jousts—   6
to the tune of trumpets, to the ring of clanging bells,
   to the roll of drums, to the flash of flares on ramparts,
   to the accompaniment of every known device;   9
but I never saw cavalry or infantry
   or ships that sail by landmarks or by stars
   signaled to set off by such strange bugling!   12
So, on our way we went with those ten fiends.
   What savage company! But—in church, with saints—
   with rowdy good-for-nothings, in the tavern![6]   15
My attention now was fixed upon the pitch
   to see the operations of this *bolgia,*
   and how the cooking souls got on down there.   18
Much like the dolphins that are said to surface
   with their backs arched to warn all men at sea
   to rig their ships for stormy seas ahead,[7]   21
so now and then a sinner's back would surface
   in order to alleviate his pain,
   then dive to hide as quick as lightning strikes.   24

---

5. The people of Arezzo, a city south of Florence.   6. A popular proverb.   7. A common medieval belief.

Like squatting frogs along the ditch's edge,
  with just their muzzles sticking out of water,
    their legs and all the rest concealed below,   27
these sinners squatted all around their pond;
  but as soon as Barbariccia would approach
    they quickly ducked beneath the boiling pitch.   30
I saw (my heart still shudders at the thought)
  one lingering behind[8]—as it sometimes happens
    one frog remains while all the rest dive down—
and Graffiacan, standing in front of him,   33
  hooked and twirled him by his pitchy hair
    and hoisted him. He looked just like an otter!   36
By then I knew the names of all the fiends:
  I had listened carefully when they were chosen,
    each of them stepping forth to match his name.   39
"Hey, Rubicante, dig your claws down deep
  into his back and peel the skin off him,"
    this fiendish chorus egged him on with screams.   42
I said: "Master, will you, if you can, find out
  the name of that poor wretch who has just fallen
    into the cruel hands of his adversaries?"   45
My guide walked right up to the sinner's side
  and asked where he was from, and he replied:
    "I was born and bred in the kingdom of Navarre;   48
my mother gave me to a lord to serve,
  for she had me by some dishonest spendthrift
    who ran through all he owned and killed himself.   51
Then I became a servant in the household
  of good King Thibault. There I learned my graft,
    and now I pay my bill by boiling here."   54
Ciriatto, who had two tusks sticking out
  on both sides of his mouth, just like a boar's,
    let him feel how just one tusk could rip him open.   57
The mouse had fallen prey to evil cats,
  but Barbariccia locked him with his arms,
    shouting: "Get back while I've got hold of him!"   60
Then toward my guide he turned his face and said:
  "If you want more from him, keep questioning
    before he's torn to pieces by the others."   63
My guide went on: "Then tell me, do you know
  of some Italian stuck among these sinners
    beneath the pitch?" And he, "A second ago   66
I was with one who lived around those parts.
  Oh, I wish I were undercover with him now!
    I wouldn't have these hooks or claws to fear."   69
Libicocco cried: "We've waited long enough,"
  then with his fork he hooked the sinner's arm
    and, tearing at it, he pulled out a piece.   72
Draghignazzo, too, was anxious for some fun;

---

8. The identity of this sinner is not known, but he was employed in the household of Thibaut II of Champagne, a man renowned for his honesty who was also king of Navarre, the area of Spain that is now Basque country.

he tried the wretch's leg, but their captain quickly
   spun around and gave them all a dirty look.   75
As soon as they calmed down a bit, my master
   began again to interrogate the wretch,
   who still was contemplating his new wound: 78
"Who was it, you were saying, that unluckily
   you left behind you when you came ashore?"
   "Gomita," he said, "the friar from Gallura,[9]   81
receptacle for every kind of fraud:
   when his lord's enemies were in his hands,
   the treatment they received delighted them: 84
he took their cash, and as he says, hushed up
   the case and let them off; none of his acts
   was petty grafting, all were of sovereign order.   87
He spends his time with don Michele Zanche
   of Logodoro, talking on and on
   about Sardinia—their tongues no worse for wear!   90
Oh, but look how that one grins and grinds his teeth;
   I could tell you so much more, but I am afraid
   he is going to grate my scabby hide for me."   93
But their master-sergeant turned to Farfarello,
   whose wild eyes warned he was about to strike,
   shouting, "Get away, you filthy bird of prey."   96
"If you would like to see Tuscans or Lombards,"
   the frightened shade took up where he left off,
   "and have a talk with them, I'll bring some here;   99
but the Malebranche must back up a bit,
   or else those shades won't risk a surfacing;
   I, by myself, will bring you up a catch   102
of seven, without moving from this spot,
   just by whistling—that's our signal to the rest
   when one peers out and sees the coast is clear."   105
Cagnazzo raised his snout at such a story,
   then shook his head and said: "Listen to the trick
   he's cooked up to get off the hook by jumping!"   108
And he, full of the tricks his trade had taught him,
   said: "Tricky, I surely am, especially
   when it comes to getting friends into worse trouble."   111
But Alichin could not resist the challenge,
   and in spite of what the others thought, cried out:
   "If you jump, I won't come galloping for you,   114
I've got my wings to beat you to the pitch.
   We'll clear this ledge and wait behind that slope.
   Let's see if one of you can outmatch us!"   117
Now listen, Reader, here's a game that's strange:
   they all turned toward the slope, and first to turn
   was the fiend who from the start opposed the game.   120
The Navarrese had perfect sense of timing:
   feet planted on the ground, in a flash he jumped,

---

9. A friar who was chancellor of the Gallura district on the island of Sardinia. He was hanged by his master, a lord of Pisa, when it was discovered that he had sold prisoners their freedom.   1. Little is known of this sinner, except that he too was a Sardinian.

the devil's plan was foiled, and he was free.   123
The squad was stung with shame but most of all
  the one who brought this blunder to perfection;[2]
  he swooped down, howling, "Now I've got you caught!"   126
Little good it did, for wings could not outstrip
  the flight of terror: down the sinner dived
  and up the fiend was forced to strain his chest   129
like a falcon swooping down on a wild duck:
  the duck dives quickly out of sight, the falcon
  must fly back up dejected and defeated.   132
In the meantime, Calcabrina, furious,
  also took off, hoping the shade would make it,
  so he could pick a fight with his companion.   135
And when he saw the grafter hit the pitch,
  he turned his claws to grapple with his brother,
  and they tangled in mid-air above the ditch;   138
but the other was a full-fledged hawk as well
  and used his claws on him, and both of them
  went plunging straight into the boiling pond.   141
The heat was quick to make them separate,
  but there seemed no way of getting out of there;
  their wings were clogged and could not lift them up.   144
Barbariccia, no less peeved than all his men,
  sent four fiends flying to the other shore
  with their equipment at top speed; instantly,   147
some here, some there, they took the posts assigned them.
  They stretched their hooks to reach the pitch-dipped pair,
  who were by now deep-fried within their crusts.   150
And there we left them, all messed up that way.

CANTO XXIII

*The antics of Ciampolo, the Navarrese, and the Malebranche bring to the Pilgrim's
mind the fable of the frog, the mouse, and the hawk—and that in turn reminds him of
the immediate danger he and Virgil are in from the angry Malebranche. Virgil senses
the danger too, and grabbing his ward as a mother would her child, he dashes to the
edge of the bank and slides down the rocky slope into the Sixth Bolgia—not a moment
too soon, for at the top of the slope they see the angry Malebranche. When the Pilgrim
looks around him he sees weeping shades slowly marching in single file, each one covered
from head to foot with a golden cloak lined with lead, which weights them down. These
are the Hypocrites. Two in this group identify themselves as Catalano de' Malavolti and
Loderingo degli Andalò, two Jovial Friars. The Pilgrim is about to address them when
he sees the shade of Caiaphas (the evil counselor who advised Pontius Pilate to crucify
Christ), crucified and transfixed by three stakes to the ground. Virgil discovers from the
two friars that in order to leave this bolgia they must climb up a rockslide; he also learns
that this is the only bolgia over which the bridge is broken. Virgil is angry with himself
for having believed Malacoda's lie about the bridge over the Sixth Bolgia (canto XXI,
iii).*

In silence, all alone, without an escort,
  we moved along, one behind the other,

2. Alichin.

like minor friars[3] bent upon a journey.   3
I was thinking over one of Aesop's fables[4]
    that this recent skirmish had brought back to mind,
    where he tells the story of the frog and mouse;   6
for "yon" and "there" could not be more alike
    than the fable and the fact, if one compares
    the start and finish of both incidents.   9
As from one thought another often rises,
    so this thought gave quick birth to still another,
    and then the fear I first had felt was doubled.   12
I was thinking: "Since these fiends, on our account,
    were tricked and mortified by mockery,
    they certainly will be more than resentful;   15
with rage now added to their evil instincts,
    they will hunt us down with all the savagery
    of dogs about to pounce upon the hare."   18
I felt my body's skin begin to tighten—
    I was so frightened!—and I kept looking back:
    "O master," I said, "if you do not hide   21
both of us, and very quick, I am afraid
    of the Malebranche—right now they're on our trail—
    I feel they're there, I think I hear them now."   24
And he replied: "Even if I were a mirror
    I could not reflect your outward image faster
    than your inner thoughts transmit themselves to me.   27
In fact, just now they joined themselves with mine,
    and since they were alike in birth and form,
    I decided to unite them toward one goal: 30
if the right-hand bank should slope in such a way
    as to allow us to descend to the next *bolgia*,
    we could escape that chase we have imagined."   33
He had hardly finished telling me his plan
    when I saw them coming with their wings wide open
    not too far off, and now they meant to get us!   36
My guide instinctively caught hold of me,
    like a mother waking to some warning sound,
    who sees the rising flames are getting close   39
and grabs her son and runs—she does not wait
    the short time it would take to put on something;
    she cares not for herself, only for him.   42
And over the edge, then down the stony bank
    he slid, on his back, along the sloping rock
    that walls the higher side of the next *bolgia*.   45
Water that turns a mill wheel never ran
    the narrow sluice at greater speed, not even
    at the point before it hits the paddle-blades,[5]   48
than down that sloping border my guide slid,

---

3. Franciscan friars, who were known as "minor" or "lesser" friars because Francis of Assisi, the founder of the order, insisted upon humility.   4. The fable that Dante seems to be referring to tells how a frog offers to ferry a mouse across a river, then halfway over tries to drown him, only to be seized by a kite (a hawklike bird) while the mouse escapes.   5. A mill built on the land while the water of the river turns its wheel.

bearing me with him, clasping me to his chest
as though I were his child, not his companion.   51
His feet had hardly touched rock bottom, when
there they were, the ten of them, above us
on the height; but now there was no need to fear: 54
High Providence that willed for them to be
the ministers in charge of the fifth ditch
also willed them powerless to leave their realm.   57
And now, down there, we found a painted people,
slow-motioned; step by step, they walked their round
in tears, and seeming wasted by fatigue.   60
All were wearing cloaks with hoods pulled low
covering the eyes (the style was much the same
as those the Benedictines wear at Cluny),[6]   63
dazzling, gilded cloaks outside, but inside
they were lined with lead, so heavy that the capes
King Frederick used, compared to these, were straw.[7]   66
O cloak of everlasting weariness!
We turned again, as usual, to the left
and moved with them, those souls lost in their mourning;   69
but with their weight that tired-out race of shades
paced on so slowly that we found ourselves
in new company with every step we took;   72
and so I asked my guide: "Please look around
and see, as we keep walking, if you find
someone whose name or deeds are known to me."   75
And one who overheard me speaking Tuscan
cried out somewhere behind us: "Not so fast,
you there, rushing ahead through this heavy air,   78
perhaps from me you can obtain an answer."
At this my guide turned toward me saying, "Stop,
and wait for him, then match your pace with his."   81
I paused and saw two shades with straining faces
revealing their mind's haste to join my side,
but the weight they bore and the crowded road delayed them.   84
When they arrived, they looked at me sideways
and for some time, without exchanging words;
then they turned to one another and were saying: 87
"He seems alive, the way his throat is moving,
and if both are dead, what privilege allows them
to walk uncovered by the heavy cloak?"   90
Then they spoke to me: "O Tuscan who has come
to visit the college of the sullen hypocrites,
do not disdain to tell us who you are."   93
I answered them: "I was born and I grew up
in the great city on the lovely Arno's shore,
and I have the body I have always had.   96
But who are you, distilling tears of grief,

6. One of the largest monasteries in Europe, located in Burgundy in France; the *Benedictines* are monks who follow the Rule of St. Benedict (d. 587), one of the founders of monasticism. 7. Frederick II (see note to 10.119) was reported to have punished traitors by encasing them in lead and throwing them into heated cauldrons.

so many I see running down your cheeks?
And what kind of pain is this that it can glitter?" 99
One of them answered: "The orange-gilded cloaks
are thick with lead so heavy that it makes us,
who are the scales it hangs on, creak as we walk. 102
Jovial Friars we were, both from Bologna.
My name was Catalano, his, Loderingo,
and both of us were chosen by your city, 105
that usually would choose one man alone,
to keep the peace. Evidence of what we were
may still be seen around Gardingo's parts."[8] 108
I began: "O Friars, all your wretchedness . . . ."
but said no more; I couldn't, for I saw
one crucified with three stakes on the ground.[9] 111
And when he saw me all his body writhed,
and through his beard he heaved out sighs of pain;
then Friar Catalano, who watched the scene, 114
remarked: "That impaled figure you see there
advised the Pharisees it was expedient
to sacrifice one man for all the people. 117
Naked he lies stretched out across the road,
as you can see, and he must feel the load
of every weight that steps on him to cross. 120
His father-in-law[1] and the other council members,
who were the seed of evil for all Jews,
are racked the same way all along this ditch." 123
And I saw Virgil staring down amazed
at this body stretching out in crucifixion,
so vilely punished in the eternal exile. 126
Then he looked up and asked one of the friars:
"Could you please tell us, if your rule permits:
is there a passage-way on the right, somewhere, 129
by which the two of us may leave this place
without summoning one of those black angels
to come down here and raise us from this pit?" 132
He answered: "Closer than you might expect,
a ridge jutting out from the base of the great circle
extends, and bridges every hideous ditch 135
except this one, whose arch is totally smashed
and crosses nowhere; but you can climb up
its massive ruins that slope against this bank." 138
My guide stood there awhile, his head bent low,
then said: "He told a lie about this business,
that one who hooks the sinners over there."[2] 141
And the friar: "Once, in Bologna, I heard discussed
the devil's many vices; one of them is

---

8. *Gardingo*: a district in Florence, was destroyed by a civil war incited by their meddling in Florentine affairs. *Jovial Friars*: a military and religious order in Bologna called the Knights of the Blessed Virgin Mary, or popularly the Jovial Friars because of the laxity of its rules. The members were meant to fight only in order to protect the weak and enforce peace. *Catalano* and *Loderingo* were two citizens of Bologna who were involved in founding the Jovial Friars in 1261.   9. This is Caiaphas, the high priest under Pontius Pilate who advised that Christ be crucified (John 11.45–52).   1. Annas; see John 18.13.   2. See 21.111.

that he tells lies and is father of all lies."[3]   144
In haste, taking great strides, my guide walked off,
  his face revealing traces of his anger.
  I turned and left the heavy-weighted souls   147
to make my way behind those cherished footprints.

CANTO XXIV

After an elaborate simile describing Virgil's anger and the return of his composure, the two begin the difficult, steep ascent up the rocks of the fallen bridge. The Pilgrim can barely make it to the top even with Virgil's help, and after the climb he sits down to catch his breath; but his guide urges him on, and they make their way back to the bridge over the Seventh Bolgia. From the bridge confused sounds can be heard rising from the darkness below. Virgil agrees to take his pupil down to the edge of the eighth encircling bank, and once they are there, the scene reveals a terrible confusion of serpents, and Thieves madly running.

Suddenly a snake darts out and strikes a sinner's neck, whereupon he flares up, turning into a heap of crumbling ashes; then the ashes gather together into the shape of a man. The metamorphosed sinner reveals himself to be Vanni Fucci, a Pistoiese condemned for stealing the treasure of the sacristy of the church of San Zeno at Pistoia. He makes a prophecy about the coming strife in Florence.

In the season of the newborn year, when the sun
  renews its rays beneath Aquarius[4]
  and nights begin to last as long as days,   3
at the time the hoarfrost paints upon the ground
  the outward semblance of his snow-white sister[5]
  (but the color from his brush soon fades away),   6
the peasant wakes, gets up, goes out and sees
  the fields all white. No fodder for his sheep!
  He smites his thighs in anger and goes back   9
into his shack and, pacing up and down,
  complains, poor wretch, not knowing what to do;
  once more he goes outdoors, and hope fills him   12
again when he sees the world has changed its face
  in so little time, and he picks up his crook
  and out to pasture drives his sheep to graze—   15
just so I felt myself lose heart to see
  my master's face wearing a troubled look,
  and as quickly came the salve to heal my sore: 18
for when we reached the shattered heap of bridge,
  my leader turned to me with that sweet look
  of warmth I first saw at the mountain's foot.   21
He opened up his arms (but not before
  he had carefully studied how the ruins lay
  and found some sort of plan) to pick me up.   24
Like one who works and thinks things out ahead,
  always ready for the next move he will make,
  so, while he raised me up toward one great rock,   27
he had already singled out another,
  saying, "Now get a grip on that rock there,

3. For this description of the devil, see John 8.44. 4. January 21–February 21. 5. I.e., snow.

but test it first to see it holds your weight."   30
It was no road for one who wore a cloak!
  Even though I had his help and he weighed nothing,
  we could hardly lift ourselves from crag to crag.   33
And had it not been that the bank we climbed
  was lower than the one we had slid down[6]—
  I cannot speak for him—but I for one   36
surely would have quit. But since the Evil Pits
  slope toward the yawning well that is the lowest,
  each valley is laid out in such a way   39
that one bank rises higher than the next.
  We somehow finally reached the point above
  where the last of all that rock was shaken loose.   42
My lungs were so pumped out of breath by the time
  I reached the top, I could not go on farther,
  and instantly I sat down where I was.   45
"Come on, shake off the covers of this sloth,"
  the master said, "for sitting softly cushioned,
  or tucked in bed, is no way to win fame;   48
and without it man must waste his life away,
  leaving such traces of what he was on earth
  as smoke in wind and foam upon the water.   51
Stand up! Dominate this weariness of yours
  with the strength of soul that wins in every battle
  if it does not sink beneath the body's weight.   54
Much steeper stairs than these we'll have to climb;[7]
  we have not seen enough of sinners yet!
  If you understand me, act, learn from my words."   57
At this I stood up straight and made it seem
  I had more breath than I began to breathe,
  and said: "Move on, for I am strong and ready."   60
We climbed and made our way along the bridge,
  which was jagged, tight and difficult to cross,
  and steep—far more than any we had climbed.   63
Not to seem faint, I spoke while I was climbing;
  then came a voice from the depths of the next chasm,
  a voice unable to articulate.   66
I don't know what it said, even though I stood
  at the very top of the arch that crosses there;
  to me it seemed whoever spoke, spoke running.   69
I was bending over, but no living eyes
  could penetrate the bottom of that darkness;
  therefore I said: "Master, why not go down   72
this bridge onto the next encircling bank,[8]
  for I hear sounds I cannot understand,
  and I look down but cannot see a thing."   75
"No other answer," he replied, "I give you
  than doing what you ask, for a fit request
  is answered best in silence and in deed."   78

6. Because the whole of the eighth circle is tilted downward, the downside wall of each ditch is lower than that on the upside.   7. Both the climb from the pit of Hell back to Earth and the climb up Mount Purgatory.   8. Of the seventh ditch.

From the bridge's height we came down to the point
  where it ends and joins the edge of the eighth bank,
    and then the *bolgia* opened up to me:[9]
down there I saw a terrible confusion
  of serpents, all of such a monstrous kind
    the thought of them still makes my blood run cold.[1] 84
Let all the sands of Libya boast no longer,
  for though she breeds chelydri and jaculi,
    phareans, cenchres, and head-tailed amphisbenes, 87
she never bred so great a plague of venom,
  not even if combined with Ethiopia
    or all the sands that lie by the Red Sea. 90
Within this cruel and bitterest abundance
  people ran terrified and naked, hopeless
    of finding hiding-holes or heliotrope.[2] 93
Their hands were tied behind their backs with serpents,
  which pushed their tails and heads around the loins
    and coiled themselves in knots around the front. 96
And then—at a sinner running by our bank
  a snake shot out and, striking, hit his mark:
    right where the neck attaches to the shoulder. 99
No *o* or *i* was ever quicker put
  by pen to paper than he flared up and burned,
    and turned into a heap of crumbled ash; 102
and then, these ashes scattered on the ground
  began to come together on their own
    and quickly take the form they had before: 105
precisely so, philosophers declare,
  the phoenix dies to be reborn again
    as she approaches her five-hundredth year;[3] 108
alive, she does not feed on herbs or grain,
  but on teardrops of frankincense and balm,
    and wraps herself to die in nard and myrrh. 111
As a man in a fit will fall, not knowing why
  (perhaps some hidden demon pulls him down,
    or some oppilation chokes his vital spirits), 114
then, struggling to his feet, will look around,
  confused and overwhelmed by the great anguish
    he has suffered, moaning as he stares about— 117
so did this sinner when he finally rose.
  Oh, how harsh the power of the Lord can be,
    raining in its vengeance blows like these! 120
My guide asked him to tell us who he was,
  and he replied: "It's not too long ago
    I rained from Tuscany to this fierce gullet. 123
I loved the bestial life more than the human,

9. They cross the bridge over the seventh ditch and then climb down the wall between the seventh and eighth ditches.   1. The following list of exotic serpents derives from a description by the Roman poet Lucan (39–65 C.E.) of the plagues of Libya.   2. A fictitious stone that was supposed to make the bearer invisible.   3. The *phoenix* is a mythical bird that is supposed to burn to death in its own nest every five hundred years, after which either itself or its son is reborn from the ashes; for these details, including its diet of exotic herbs and its funeral preparations (lines 110–11), see Ovid, *Metamorphoses* 15. In medieval mythography the phoenix was often taken as a symbol of Christ.

like the bastard that I was; I'm Vanni Fucci,
    the beast! Pistoia was my fitting den."[4]   126
I told my guide: "Tell him not to run away;
    ask him what sin has driven him down here,
    for I knew him as a man of bloody rage."   129
The sinner heard and did not try to feign;
    directing straight at me his mind and face,
    he reddened with a look of ugly shame,   132
and said: "That you have caught me by surprise
    here in this wretched *bolgia*, makes me grieve
    more than the day I lost my other life.   135
Now I am forced to answer what you ask:
    I am stuck so far down here because of theft:
    I stole the treasure of the sacristy—   138
a crime falsely attributed to another.
    I don't want you to rejoice at having seen me,
    if ever you escape from these dark pits,   141
so open your ears and hear my prophecy:[5]
    Pistoia first shall be stripped of all its Blacks,
    and Florence then shall change its men and laws;   144
from Valdimagra Mars shall thrust a bolt
    of lightning wrapped in thick, foreboding clouds,
    then bolt and clouds will battle bitterly   147
in a violent storm above Piceno's fields,
    where rapidly the bolt will burst the cloud,
    and no White will escape without his wounds.   150
And I have told you this so you will suffer!"

CANTO XXV

The wrathful Vanni Fucci directs an obscene gesture to God, whereupon he is attacked by several snakes, which coil about him, tying him so tight that he cannot move a muscle. As soon as he flees, the centaur Cacus gallops by with a fire-breathing dragon on his back, and following close behind are three shades, concerned because they cannot find Cianfa—who soon appears as a snake and attacks Agnèl; the two merge into one hideous monster, which then steals off. Next, Guercio, in the form of a snake, strikes Buoso, and the two exchange shapes. Only Puccio Sciancato is left unchanged.

When he had finished saying this, the thief
    shaped his fists into figs[6] and raised them high
    and cried: "Here, God, I've shaped them just for you!"   3
From then on all those snakes became my friends,
    for one of them at once coiled round his neck
    as if to say, "That's all you're going to say,"   6
while another twisted round his arms in front;
    it tied itself into so tight a knot,

4. The illegitimate son of a noble father of *Pistoia*, a town just north of Florence; known as "the beast" because of the extravagance of his misbehavior. He reputedly robbed a church in Pistoia, a crime for which a similarly named man was wrongly hanged.   5. Vanni Fucci now prophesies, in the enigmatic terms appropriate to the genre, that the party of the Blacks (of which he was a member) will first be expelled from Pistoia by the Whites, but that then the Whites of Florence (Dante's party) will be defeated. The prophecy refers to events that occurred in either 1302 or 1306.   6. An obscene gesture made by thrusting a protruding thumb between the first and second fingers of a closed fist.

between the two he could not move a muscle.   9
Pistoia, ah, Pistoia! why not resolve
    to burn yourself to ashes, ending all,
    since you have done more evil than your founders?[7]   12
Throughout the circles of this dark inferno
    I saw no shade so haughty toward his God,
    not even he who fell from Thebes' high walls.[8]   15
Without another word he fled, and then
    I saw a raging centaur gallop up
    roaring: "Where is he, where is that untamed beast?"   18
I think that all Maremma[9] does not have
    as many snakes as he had on his back,
    right up to where his human form begins.   21
Upon his shoulders, just behind the nape,
    a dragon with its wings spread wide was crouching
    and spitting fire at whoever came its way.   24
My master said to me: "That one is Cacus,[1]
    who more than once in the grotto far beneath
    Mount Aventine spilled blood to fill a lake.   27
He does not go the same road as his brothers
    because of the cunning way he committed theft
    when he stole his neighbor's famous cattle-herd;   30
and then his evil deeds came to an end
    beneath the club of Hercules, who struck
    a hundred blows, and he, perhaps, felt ten."   33
While he was speaking Cacus galloped off;
    at the same time three shades appeared below us;
    my guide and I would not have seen them there   36
if they had not cried out: "Who are you two?"
    At this we cut our conversation short
    to give our full attention to these three.   39
I didn't know who they were, but then it happened,
    as often it will happen just by chance,
    that one of them was forced to name another: 42
"Where did Cianfa[2] go off to?" he asked. And then,
    to keep my guide from saying anything,
    I put my finger tight against my lips.   45
Now if, my reader, you should hesitate
    to believe what I shall say, there's little wonder,
    for I, the witness, scarcely can believe it.   48
While I was watching them, all of a sudden
    a serpent—and it had six feet—shot up
    and hooked one of these wretches with all six.   51
With the middle feet it hugged the sinner's stomach
    and, with the front ones, grabbed him by the arms,
    and bit him first through one cheek, then the other;   54
the serpent spread its hind feet round both thighs,
    then stuck its tail between the sinner's legs,

7. The most important founder of Pistoia was Catiline, who was a traitor against the Roman republic in the 1st century B.C.E.   8. Capaneus (see 14.46–75).   9. A region infested with snakes; see 13.8.
1. A monster who lived in a cave on Mount Aventine in Rome and was killed by Hercules, from whom he stole cattle; see *Aeneid* 8.   2. A noble Florentine, reputedly a thief.

and up against his back the tail slid stiff. 57
No ivy ever grew to any tree
   so tight entwined, as the way that hideous beast
   had woven in and out its limbs with his; 60
and then both started melting like hot wax
   and, fusing, they began to mix their colors
   (so neither one seemed what he was before), 63
just as a brownish tint, ahead of flame,
   creeps up a burning page that is not black
   completely, even though the white is dying. 66
The other two who watched began to shout:
   "O Agnèl![3] If you could see how you are changing!
   You're not yourself, and you're not both of you!" 69
The two heads had already fused to one
   and features from each flowed and blended into
   one face where two were lost in one another; 72
two arms of each were four blurred strips of flesh;
   and thighs with legs, then stomach and the chest
   sprouted limbs that human eyes have never seen. 75
Each former likeness now was blotted out:
   both, and neither one it seemed—this picture
   of deformity. And then it sneaked off slowly. 78
Just as a lizard darting from hedge to hedge,
   under the stinging lash of the dog-days' heat,
   zips across the road, like a flash of lightning, 81
so, rushing toward the two remaining thieves,
   aiming at their guts, a little serpent,
   fiery with rage and black as pepper-corn, 84
shot up and sank its teeth in one of them,
   right where the embryo receives its food,
   then back it fell and lay stretched out before him. 87
The wounded thief stared speechless at the beast,
   and standing motionless began to yawn
   as though he needed sleep, or had a fever. 90
The snake and he were staring at each other;
   one from his wound, the other from its mouth
   fumed violently, and smoke with smoke was mingling. 93
Let Lucan from this moment on be silent,
   who tells of poor Nasidius and Sabellus,[4]
   and wait to hear what I still have in store; 96
and Ovid, too, with his Cadmus and Arethusa—[5]
   though he metamorphosed one into a snake,
   the other to a fountain, I feel no envy, 99
for never did he interchange two beings
   face to face so that both forms were ready
   to exchange their substance, each one for the other's, 102
an interchange of perfect symmetry:
   the serpent split its tail into a fork,

---

3. Another noble Florentine thief.   4. Two soldiers bitten by serpents in Lucan's *Pharsalia*.   5. See *Metamorphoses* 4.

and the wounded sinner drew his feet together; 105
the legs, with both the thighs, closed in to join
   and in a short time fused, so that the juncture
   didn't show signs of ever having been there, 108
the while the cloven tail assumed the features
   that the other one was losing, and its skin
   was growing soft, the other's getting scaly; 111
I saw his arms retreating to the armpits,
   and the reptile's two front feet, that had been short,
   began to stretch the length the man's had shortened; 114
the beast's hind feet then twisted round each other
   and turned into the member man conceals,
   while from the wretch's member grew two legs. 117
The smoke from each was swirling round the other,
   exchanging colors, bringing out the hair
   where there was none, and stripping off the other's. 120
The one rose up, the other sank, but neither
   dissolved the bond between their evil stares,
   fixed eye to eye, exchanging face for face; 123
the standing creature's face began receding
   toward the temples; from the excess stuff pulled back,
   the ears were growing out of flattened cheeks, 126
while from the excess flesh that did not flee
   the front, a nose was fashioned for the face,
   and lips puffed out to just the normal size. 129
The prostrate creature strains his face out long
   and makes his ears withdraw into his head,
   the way a snail pulls in its horns. The tongue, 132
that once had been one piece and capable
   of forming words, divides into a fork,
   while the other's fork heals up. The smoke subsides. 135
The soul that had been changed into a beast
   went hissing off along the valley's floor,
   the other close behind him, spitting words. 138
Then he turned his new-formed back on him and said
   to the shade left standing there: "Let Buoso run
   the valley on all fours, the way I did."[6] 141
Thus I saw the cargo of the seventh hold
   exchange and interchange; and let the strangeness
   of it all excuse me, if my pen has failed. 144
And though this spectacle confused my eyes
   and stunned my mind, the two thieves could not flee
   so secretly I did not recognize 147
that one was certainly Puccio Sciancato[7]
   (and he alone, of that company of three
   that first appeared, did not change to something else), 150
the other, he who made you mourn, Gaville.[8]

---

6. The identity of this *Buoso* is uncertain.   7. This third thief is also a noble Florentine.   8. The *little serpent* of line 83 above is now identified as Francesco de Cavalcanti, a Florentine nobleman who lived in *Gaville*, a town south of Florence. When he was murdered by his townsmen, his kinsmen took brutal revenge.

CANTO XXVI

From the ridge high above the Eighth Bolgia can be perceived a myriad of flames
flickering far below, and Virgil explains that within each flame is the suffering soul of
a Deceiver. One flame, divided at the top, catches the Pilgrim's eye and he is told that
within it are jointly punished Ulysses and Diomed. Virgil questions the pair for the
benefit of the Pilgrim. Ulysses responds with the famous narrative of his last voyage,
during which he passed the Pillars of Hercules and sailed the forbidden sea until he
saw a mountain shape, from which came suddenly a whirlwind that spun his ship
around three times and sank it.

Be joyful, Florence, since you are so great
    that your outstretched wings beat over land and sea,
    and your name is spread throughout the realm of Hell!   3
I was ashamed to find among the thieves
    five of your most eminent citizens,[9]
    a fact which does you very little honor   6
But if early morning dreams have any truth,
    you will have the fate, in not too long a time,
    that Prato and the others crave for you.[1]   9
And were this the day, it would not be too soon!
    Would it had come to pass, since pass it must!
    The longer the delay, the more my grief.   12
We started climbing up the stairs of boulders
    that had brought us to the place from where we watched;
    my guide went first and pulled me up behind him.   15
We went along our solitary way
    among the rocks, among the ridge's crags,
    where the foot could not advance without the hand.   18
I know that I grieved then, and now again
    I grieve when I remember what I saw,
    and more than ever I restrain my talent   21
lest it run a course that virtue has not set;
    for if a lucky star or something better
    has given me this good, I must not misuse it.   24
As many fireflies (in the season when
    the one who lights the world hides his face least,
    in the hour when the flies yield to mosquitoes)   27
as the peasant on the hillside at his ease
    sees, flickering in the valley down below,
    where perhaps he gathers grapes or tills the soil—   30
with just so many flames all the eighth *bolgia*
    shone brilliantly, as I became aware
    when at last I stood where the depths were visible.   33
As he[2] who was avenged by bears beheld
    Elijah's chariot at its departure,
    when the rearing horses took to flight toward Heaven,   36
and though he tried to follow with his eyes,

---

9. Cianfa (25.43), Agnello (25.68), Francesco (25.82, 149), Buoso (25.140), and Puccio (25.148) are all
Florentines.   1. A town just north of Florence, on the way to Pistoia. The reason for this threat is unclear.
2. Elisha, an Old Testament prophet, was mocked by children, who were then attacked by bears. He saw
the ascent to heaven of the prophet Elijah in his chariot and continued Elijah's mission: 2 Kings 2.1–25.

he could not see more than the flame alone
  like a small cloud once it had risen high— 39
so each flame moves itself along the throat
  of the abyss, none showing what it steals
  but each one stealing nonetheless a sinner. 42
I was on the bridge, leaning far over—so far
  that if I had not grabbed some jut of rock
  I could easily have fallen to the bottom. 45
And my guide, who saw me so absorbed, explained:
  "There are souls concealed within these moving fires,
  each one swathed in his burning punishment." 48
"O master," I replied, "from what you say
  I know now I was right; I had guessed already
  it might be so, and I was about to ask you: 51
Who's in that flame with its tip split in two,
  like that one which once sprang up from the pyre
  where Eteocles was placed beside his brother?"[3] 54
He said: "Within, Ulysses and Diomed[4]
  are suffering in anger with each other,
  just vengeance makes them march together now. 57
And they lament inside one flame the ambush
  of the horse become the gateway that allowed
  the Romans' noble seed[5] to issue forth. 60
Therein they mourn the trick that caused the grief
  of Deïdamia,[6] who still weeps for Achilles;
  and there they pay for the Palladium." 63
"If it is possible for them to speak
  from within those flames," I said, "master, I pray
  and repray you—let my prayer be like a thousand— 66
that you do not forbid me to remain
  until the two-horned flame comes close to us;
  you see how I bend toward it with desire!" 69
"Your prayer indeed is worthy of highest praise,"
  he said to me, "and therefore I shall grant it;
  but see to it your tongue refrains from speaking. 72
Leave it to me to speak, for I know well
  what you would ask; perhaps, since they were Greeks,
  they might not pay attention to your words."[7] 75
So when the flame had reached us, and my guide
  decided that the time and place were right,
  he addressed them and I listened to him speaking: 78
"O you who are two souls within one fire,
  if I have deserved from you when I was living,
  if I have deserved from you much praise or little, 81
when in the world I wrote my lofty verses,

3. *Eteocles* and his brother, Polynices, were the sons of Oedipus; cursed by their father for their imprisonment of him, they engaged in a civil war over Thebes, killed each other, and were cremated on the same
pyre, the flame of which divided into two as a sign of their enmity.   4. Two of the Greek leaders in the
Trojan War. They devised the trick of the Trojan horse and stole the Palladium, a statue of Pallas Athena
that protected the city. Their villainy is described by Aeneas in *Aeneid* 2.   5. The Trojan survivors, who
founded Rome.   6. Achilles' lover, who tried to prevent him from going to the Trojan War but was
thwarted by Ulysses.   7. Virgil may assume that Greeks would disdain anyone who, like Dante, did not
know Greek (and was therefore a "barbarian"); or that because he derives from the classical world he is the
more appropriate interlocutor.

do not move on; let one of you tell where
    he lost himself through his own fault, and died."   84
The greater of the ancient flame's two horns
    began to sway and quiver, murmuring
    just like a flame that strains against the wind;   87
then, while its tip was moving back and forth,
    as if it were the tongue itself that spoke,
    the flame took on a voice and said: "When I   90
set sail from Circe,[8] who, more than a year,
    had kept me occupied close to Gaëta
    (before Aeneas called it by that name),[9]   93
not sweetness of a son, not reverence
    for an aging father, not the debt of love
    I owed Penelope[1] to make her happy,   96
could quench deep in myself the burning wish
    to know the world and have experience
    of all man's vices, of all human worth.   99
So I set out on the deep and open sea
    with just one ship and with that group of men,
    not many, who had not deserted me.   102
I saw as far as Spain, far as Morocco,
    both shores; I had left behind Sardinia,
    and the other islands which that sea encloses.   105
I and my mates were old and tired men.
    Then finally we reached the narrow neck
    where Hercules put up his signal-pillars   108
to warn men not to go beyond that point.[2]
    On my right I saw Seville, and passed beyond;
    on my left, Ceüta had already sunk behind me.   111
'Brothers,' I said, 'who through a hundred thousand
    perils have made your way to reach the West,
    during this so brief vigil of our senses   114
that is still reserved for us, do not deny
    yourself experience of what there is beyond,
    behind the sun, in the world they call unpeopled.[3]   117
Consider what you came from: you are Greeks!
    You were not born to live like mindless brutes
    but to follow paths of excellence and knowledge.'   120
With this brief exhortation I made my crew
    so anxious for the way that lay ahead,
    that then I hardly could have held them back;   123
and with our stern turned toward the morning light,
    we made our oars our wings for that mad flight,
    gaining distance, always sailing to the left.   126
The night already had surveyed the stars

8. Dante places Circe's home near *Gaëta*, on the coast of Italy north of Naples; she was a sorceress who transformed men into beasts.   9. Aeneas named it after his nurse Caieta, who died there: *Aeneid* 7. 1. Ulysses' faithful wife.   2. The straits of Gibraltar, with Seville on the European side and Ceüta on the African. According to myth, Hercules separated a single mountain into two to mark the point beyond which human beings should not venture.   3. According to the geography of Dante's day, the southern hemisphere was made up entirely of water, with the only land being Mount Purgatory. To go *behind the sun* means to follow a westward course.

the other pole contains; it saw ours so low
    it did not show above the ocean floor.[4]   129
Five times we saw the splendor of the moon
    grow full and five times wane away again
    since we had entered through the narrow pass—   132
when there appeared a mountain shape, darkened
    by distance, that arose to endless heights.
    I had never seen another mountain like it.[5]   135
Our celebrations soon turned into grief:
    from the new land there rose a whirling wind
    that beat against the forepart of the ship   138
and whirled us round three times in churning waters;
    the fourth blast raised the stern up high, and sent
    the bow down deep, as pleased Another's will.   141
And then the sea was closed again, above us."

CANTO XXVII

*As soon as Ulysses has finished his narrative, another flame—its soul within having
recognized Virgil's Lombard accent—comes forward asking the travelers to pause and
answer questions about the state of affairs in the region of Italy from which he came.
The Pilgrim responds by outlining the strife in Romagna and ends by asking the flame
who he is. The flame, although he insists he does not want his story to be known among
the living, answers because he is supposedly convinced that the Pilgrim will never return
to earth. He is another famous deceiver, Guido da Montefeltro, a soldier who became
a friar in his old age; but he was untrue to his vows when, at the urging of Pope Boniface
VIII, he counseled the use of fraud in the pope's campaign against the Colonna family.
He was damned to Hell because he failed to repent his sins, trusting instead in the pope's
fraudulent absolution.*

By now the flame was standing straight and still,
    it said no more and had already turned
    from us, with sanction of the gentle poet,   3
when another, coming right behind it,
    attracted our attention to its tip,
    where a roaring of confusing sounds had started.   6
As the Sicilian bull—that bellowed first
    with cries of that one (and it served him right)
    who with his file had fashioned such a beast[6]—   9
would bellow with the victim's voice inside,
    so that, although the bull was only brass,
    the effigy itself seemed pierced with pain: 12
so, lacking any outlet to escape
    from the burning soul that was inside the flame,
    the suffering words became the fire's language.   15
But after they had made their journey upward
    to reach the tip, giving it that same quiver
    the sinner's tongue inside had given them,   18

4. They had crossed the equator and could see only the stars of the Southern Hemisphere.   5. This is
Mount Purgatory.   6. According to classical legend, Phalaris, the tyrant of Agrigentum in Sicily, had an
artisan build a brazen bull in which he roasted his victims alive, their shrieks emerging as the sounds of a
bull's bellowing. His first victim was the artisan himself, Perillus.

we heard the words:[7] "O you to whom I point
   my voice, who spoke just now in Lombard,[8] saying:
   'you may move on, I won't ask more of you.'   21
although I have been slow in coming to you,
   be willing, please, to pause and speak with me.
   You see how willing I am—and I burn!   24
If you have just now fallen to this world
   of blindness, from that sweet Italian land
   where I took on the burden of my guilt,
tell me, are the Romagnols[9] at war or peace?   27
   For I come from the hills between Urbino
   and the mountain chain that lets the Tiber loose."   30
I was still bending forward listening
   when my master touched my side and said to me:
   "*You* speak to him; *this* one is Italian."   33
And I, who was prepared to answer him,
   began without delaying my response:
   "O soul who stands concealed from me down there,   36
your Romagna is not now and never was
   without war in her tyrants' hearts, although
   there was no open warfare when I came here.   39
Ravenna's[1] situation has not changed:
   the eagle of Polenta broods up there,
   covering all of Cervia with its pinions;   42
the land[2] that stood the test of long endurance
   and left the French piled in a bloody heap
   is once again beneath the verdant claws.   45
Verrucchio's Old Mastiff and its New One,[3]
   who both were bad custodians of Montagna,
   still sink their fangs into their people's flesh;   48
the cities by Lamone and Santerno[4]
   are governed by the Lion of the White Lair,
   who changes parties every change of season.   51
As for the town[5] whose side the Savio bathes:
   just as it lies between the hills and plains,
   it lives between freedom and tyranny.   54
And now I beg you tell us who you are—
   grant me my wish as yours was granted you—
   so that your fame may hold its own on earth."   57
And when the fire, in its own way, had roared
   awhile, the flame's sharp tip began to sway
   to and fro, then released a blow of words: 60

7. The speaker is Guido da Montefeltro (d. 1298), a nobleman deeply involved in the constant warfare of thirteenth-century Italy but who became a friar two years before his death (see line 67).   8. The dialect of northern Italy. Dante believed that since Virgil came from Mantua, his spoken language would be not Latin but this dialect.   9. The people of Romagna, an area northeast of Florence and bordering the Adriatic Sea; the city of Urbino marks its southern limit, the Apennine mountains its northern. The subsequent passage describes the political conditions in the cities of Romagna.   1. The major city of Romagna, ruled at the time by the Polenta family, who also controlled the small city of Cervia.   2. Forlì, which defeated French invaders but then fell under the control of the tyrannical Ordelaffi family, which had green paws on its coat of arms.   3. Malatesta de Verrucchio and his son Malatestino were tyrants of Rimini who killed their enemy *Montagna*.   4. The cities of Faenza and Imola, on the Lamone and Santerno Rivers respectively, governed by an unreliable ruler who had a lion on a white ground on his coat of arms.   5. Cesena, located on the Savio River, was a free municipality although its politics were dominated by a single family.

"If I thought that I were speaking to a soul
   who someday might return to see the world,
   most certainly this flame would cease to flicker;   63
but since no one, if I have heard the truth,
   ever returns alive from this deep pit,
   with no fear of dishonor I answer you: 66
I was a man of arms and then a friar,
   believing with the cord to make amends;
   and surely my belief would have come true   69
were it not for that High Priest[6] (his soul be damned!)
   who put me back among my early sins;
   I want to tell you why and how it happened.   72
While I still had the form of the bones and flesh
   my mother gave me, all my actions were
   not those of a lion, but those of a fox;   75
the wiles and covert paths, I knew them all,
   and so employed my art that rumor of me
   spread to the farthest limits of the earth.   78
When I saw that the time of life had come
   for me, as it must come for every man,
   to lower the sails and gather in the lines,   81
things I once found pleasure in then grieved me;
   repentant and confessed, I took the vows
   a monk takes. And, oh, to think it could have worked!   84
And then the Prince of the New Pharisees
   chose to wage war upon the Lateran
   instead of fighting Saracens or Jews,[7]   87
for all his enemies were Christian souls
   (none among the ones who conquered Acri,[8]
   none a trader in the Sultan's kingdom).   90
His lofty papal seat, his sacred vows
   were no concern to him, nor was the cord
   I wore (that once made those it girded leaner).[9]   93
As Constantine once had Silvestro brought
   from Mount Soracte to cure his leprosy,[1]
   so this one sought me out as his physician   96
to cure his burning fever caused by pride.
   He asked me to advise him. I was silent,
   for his words were drunken. Then he spoke again: 99
'Fear not, I tell you: the sin you will commit,
   it is forgiven. Now you will teach me how
   I can level Palestrina[2] to the ground.   102
Mine is the power, as you cannot deny,
   to lock and unlock Heaven. Two keys I have,
   those keys my predecessor did not cherish."[3]   105

---

6. Pope Boniface VIII.   7. Boniface was struggling to retain the papacy against the challenge of another Roman family, the Colonnas.   8. City in the Holy Land, captured by the crusaders and then recaptured by the Saracens.   9. Guido refers to the rough cord worn as a belt by Franciscan friars, a symbol of both obedience and poverty (hence it would make the wearer *leaner*); for another reference to this cord, see 16.106.   1. According to legend, the Emperor Constantine (d. 337) was cured of his leprosy by Pope Sylvester, who was hiding on Mount Soracte, some twenty miles north of Rome; see 19.115.   2. The fortress of the Colonnas.   3. The keys are those of damnation and absolution, given by Christ to Peter; see 19.92. Boniface's *predecessor* was Celestine V, who resigned after five months; see 3.59–60.

And when his weighty arguments had forced me
   to the point that silence seemed the poorer choice,
   I said: 'Father, since you grant me absolution   108
for the sin I find I must fall into now:
   ample promise with a scant fulfillment
   will bring you triumph on your lofty throne.'   111
Saint Francis[4] came to get me when I died,
   but one of the black Cherubim cried out:
   'Don't touch him, don't cheat me of what is mine!   114
He must come down to join my other servants
   for the false counsel he gave. From then to now
   I have been ready at his hair, because   117
one cannot be absolved unless repentant,
   nor can one both repent and will a thing
   at once—the one is canceled by the other!'[5]   120
O wretched me! How I shook when he took me,
   saying: 'Perhaps you never stopped to think
   that I might be somewhat of a logician!'[6]   123
He took me down to Minòs,[7] who eight times
   twisted his tail around his hardened back,
   then in his rage he bit it, and announced: 126
'He goes with those the thievish fire burns.'
   And here you see me now, lost, wrapped this way,
   moving, as I do, with my resentment."   129
When he had brought his story to a close,
   the flame, in grievous pain, departed from us
   gnarling and flickering its pointed horn.   132
My guide and I moved farther on; we climbed
   the ridge until we stood on the next arch
   that spans the fosse where penalties are paid   135
by those who, sowing discord, earned Hell's wages.

CANTO XXVIII

In the Ninth Bolgia the Pilgrim is overwhelmed by the sight of mutilated, bloody shades, many of whom are ripped open, with entrails spilling out. They are the Sowers of Scandal and Schism, and among them are Mahomet, Ali, Pier da Medicina, Gaius Scribonius Curio, Mosca de' Lamberti, and Bertran de Born. All bemoan their painful lot, and Mahomet and Pier da Medicina relay warnings through the Pilgrim to certain living Italians who are soon to meet terrible ends. Bertran de Born, who comes carrying his head in his hand like a lantern, is a particularly arresting example of a Dantean con-trapasso.

Who could, even in the simplest kind of prose
   describe in full the scene of blood and wounds
   that I saw now—no matter how he tried!   3
Certainly any tongue would have to fail:
   man's memory and man's vocabulary

---

4. Francis of Assisi (1181/82–1226), founder of the order of friars joined by Guido.   **5.** Guido wanted forgiveness for his sin of guile at the same time as he was committing it; in willing the sin he showed that he was not truly repentant, the precondition for forgiveness.   **6.** The devil is referring to the logical law of noncontradiction.   **7.** For Minos, see 5.4.

are not enough to comprehend such pain. 6
If one could bring together all the wounded
    who once upon the fateful soil of Puglia
    grieved for their life's blood spilled by the Romans,⁸ 9
and spilled again in the long years of the war
    that ended in great spoils of golden rings
    (as Livy's history tells, that does not err),⁹ 12
and pile them with the ones who felt the blows
    when they stood up against great Robert Guiscard,¹
    and with those others whose bones are still in heaps 15
at Ceprano² (there where every Puglian
    turned traitor), and add those from Tagliacozzo,³
    where old Alardo conquered, weaponless— 18
if all these maimed with limbs lopped off or pierced
    were brought together, the scene would be nothing
    to compare with the foul ninth bolgia's bloody sight. 21
No wine cask with its stave or cant-bar sprung
    was ever split the way I saw someone
    ripped open from his chin to where we fart. 24
Between his legs his guts spilled out, with the heart
    and other vital parts, and the dirty sack
    that turns to shit whatever the mouth gulps down. 27
While I stood staring into his misery,
    he looked at me and with both hands he opened
    his chest and said: "See how I tear myself! 30
See how Mahomet⁴ is deformed and torn!
    In front of me, and weeping, Ali walks,
    his face cleft from his chin up to the crown. 33
The souls that you see passing in this ditch
    were all sowers of scandal and schism in life,
    and so in death you see them torn asunder. 36
A devil stands back there who trims us all
    in this cruel way, and each one of this mob
    receives anew the blade of the devil's sword 39
each time we make one round of this sad road,
    because the wounds have all healed up again
    by the time each one presents himself once more. 42
But who are you there, gawking from the bridge
    and trying to put off, perhaps, fulfillment
    of the sentence passed on you when you confessed?" 45
"Death does not have him yet, he is not here
    to suffer for his guilt," my master answered;
    "but that he may have full experience, 48

8. *Puglia* is in southern Italy, and Dante refers here to those killed when the Trojans conquered it in the *Aeneid* 7–12. 9. *Livy* is a Roman historian (d. 17 C.E.) and the *war* he chronicled is the Second Punic War (218–201 B.C.E.) between Rome and Carthage under Hannibal. After the Battle of Cannae (216) the victorious Carthaginians displayed rings taken from fallen Romans. 1. A Norman conquerer (1015–1085) who fought the Greeks and Saracens for control of Sicily and southern Italy in the 11th century. 2. A town that the barons of Puglia were pledged to defend for Manfred, the natural son of Frederick II (10.119), but whom they betrayed; he was then killed at the battle of Benevento in 1266. 3. A town where in 1268 Manfred's nephew Conradin was defeated by the strategy rather than the brute force of Alardo de Valery. 4. Founder of Islam (570–632), regarded by some medieval Christians as a renegade Christian and a creator of religious disunity. Ali was his nephew and son-in-law, and his disputed claim to the rulership (or caliphate) divided Islam into Suni and Shia sects.

I, who am dead, must lead him through this Hell
   from round to round, down to the very bottom,
   and this is as true as my presence speaking here."   51
More than a hundred in that ditch stopped short
   to look at me when they had heard his words,
   forgetting in their stupor what they suffered.   54
"And you, who will behold the sun, perhaps
   quite soon, tell Fra Dolcino⁵ that unless
   he wants to follow me here quick, he'd better   57
stock up on food, or else the binding snows
   will give the Novarese their victory,
   a conquest not won easily otherwise."   60
With the heel of one foot raised to take a step,
   Mahomet said these words to me, and then
   stretched out and down his foot and moved away.   63
Another, with his throat slit, and his nose
   cut off as far as where the eyebrows start
   (and he only had a single ear to show),   66
who had stopped like all the rest to stare in wonder,
   stepped out from the group and opened up his throat,
   which ran with red from all sides of his wound,   69
and spoke: "O you whom guilt does not condemn,
   whom I have seen in Italy up there,
   unless I am deceived by similarity,   72
recall to mind Pier da Medicina,⁶
   should you return to see the gentle plain
   declining from Vercelli to Marcabò,   75
and inform the two best citizens of Fano⁷—
   tell Messer Guido and tell Angiolello—
   that, if our foresight here is no deception,   78
from their ship they shall be hurled bound in a sack
   to drown in the water near Cattolica,
   the victims of a tyrant's treachery;   81
between the isles of Cyprus and Mallorca
   so great a crime Neptune never witnessed
   among the deeds of pirates or the Argives.⁸   84
That traitor, who sees only with one eye
   and rules the land that someone with me here
   wishes he'd never fed his eyes upon,⁹   87
will have them come to join him in a parley,
   then see to it they do not waste their breath
   on vows or prayers to escape Focara's wind."   90
And I to him: "If you want me to bring back
   to those on earth your message—who is the one
   sated with the bitter sight? Show him to me."   93

---

5. In 1300 *Fra Dolcino* was head of a reformist order known as the Apostolic Brothers that was condemned as heretical by the pope. He and his followers escaped to the hills near the town of Novara, but starvation forced them out and many were executed.   6. The town of *Medicina* lies in the Po Valley between Vercelli and Marcabò. Nothing certain is known of Pier de Medicina.   7. A town on the Adriatic coast of Italy; its two leaders—named in the next line—were drowned in 1312 by the one-eyed tyrant Malatestino of Rimini (27.46) near the promontory of Focara (see line 90) after he had invited them to the town of La Cattolica for a parley.   8. *Cyprus and Majorca* are islands at the western and eastern ends of the Mediterranean. *Neptune* is the classical god of the sea and *Argives* is another name for Greeks.   9. This *someone* is Caius Curio, whose story is told in lines 94–102.

At once he grabbed the jaws of a companion[1]
  standing near by, and squeezed his mouth half open,
  announcing, "Here he is, and he is mute.   96
This man, in exile, drowned all Caesar's doubts
  and helped him cast the die, when he insisted:
  'A man prepared, who hesitates, is lost.' "   99
How helpless and bewildered he appeared,
  his tongue hacked off as far down as the throat,
  this Curio, once so bold and quick to speak!   102
And one[2] who had both arms but had no hands,
  raising the gory stumps in the filthy air
  so that the blood dripped down and smeared his face,   105
cried: "You, no doubt, also remember Mosca,
  who said, alas, 'What's done is over with,'
  and sowed the seed of discord for the Tuscans."   108
"And of death for all your clan," I quickly said,
  and he, this fresh wound added to his wound,
  turned and went off like one gone mad from pain.   111
But I remained to watch the multitude,
  and saw a thing that I would be afraid
  to tell about without more evidence,   114
were I not reassured by my own conscience—
  that good companion enheartening a man
  beneath the breastplate of its purity.   117
I saw it, I'm sure, and I seem to see it still:
  a body with no head that moved along,
  moving no differently from all the rest;   120
he held his severed head up by its hair,
  swinging it in one hand just like a lantern,
  and as it looked at us it said: "Alas!"   123
Of his own self he made himself a light
  and they were two in one and one in two.
  How could this be? He who ordained it knows.   126
And when he had arrived below our bridge,
  he raised the arm that held the head up high
  to let it speak to us at closer range.   129
It spoke:[3] "Now see the monstrous punishment,
  you there still breathing, looking at the dead,
  see if you find suffering to equal mine!   132
And that you may report on me up there,
  know that I am Bertran de Born, the one
  who evilly encouraged the young king.   135
Father and son I set against each other:
  Achitophel with his wicked instigations
  did not do more with Absalom and David.   138

---

1. Caius Curio, a Roman of the 1st century B.C.E., was bribed by Julius Caesar to betray his friends; he urged Caesar to cross the Rubicon and invade the Roman republic, starting a civil war.   2. A Florentine noble, who in 1215 started the civil strife that tore the city apart by advising a father to avenge the slight to his daughter by killing the man who had broken his engagement to her. Mosca's own family was a victim of the strife some sixty years later.   3. This is Bertran de Born, a Provençal nobleman and poet, who reputedly advised the son of Henry II of England to rebel against his father. For Achitophel's similar scheming between David and his son Absalom, see 2 Samuel 15–17. A poem by Bertran is included in *Medieval Lyrics: A Selection* (pp. 1403–4).

Because I cut the bonds of those so joined,
    I bear my head cut off from its life-source,
      which is back there, alas, within its trunk.   141
In me you see the perfect *contrapasso*!"[4]

CANTO XXIX

*When the Pilgrim is rebuked by his mentor for his inappropriate interest in these
wretched shades, he replies that he was looking for someone. Virgil tells the Pilgrim that
he saw the person he was looking for, Geri del Bello, pointing a finger at him. They
discuss Geri until they reach the edge of the next* bolgia, *where all types of Falsifiers are
punished. There miserable, shrieking shades are afflicted with diseases of various kinds
and are arranged in various positions. Sitting back to back, madly scratching their
leprous sores, are the shades of Griffolino da Arezzo and one Capocchio, who talk to
the Pilgrim, the latter shade making wisecracks about the Sienese.*

The crowds, the countless, different mutilations,
    had stunned my eyes and left them so confused
      they wanted to keep looking and to weep,   3
but Virgil said: "What are you staring at?
    Why do your eyes insist on drowning there
      below, among those wretched, broken shades?   6
You did not act this way in other *bolge*.
    If you hope to count them one by one, remember
      the valley winds some twenty-two miles around;[5]   9
and already the moon is underneath our feet;
    the time remaining to us now is short[6]—
      and there is more to see than you see here."   12
"If you had taken time to find out what
    I was looking for," I started telling him,
      "perhaps you would have let me stay there longer."   15
My guide was moving on, with me behind him,
    answering as I did while we went on,
      and adding: "Somewhere down along this ditch   18
that I was staring at a while ago,
    I think there is a spirit of my family
      mourning the guilt that's paid so dear down there."   21
And then my master said: "From this time on
    you should not waste another thought on him;
      think on ahead, and let him stay behind,   24
for I saw him standing underneath the bridge
    pointing at you, and threatening with his gesture,
      and I heard his name called out: Geri del Bello.[7]   27
That was the moment you were so absorbed
    with him who was the lord of Altaforte[8]
      that you did not look his way before he left."   30
"Alas, my guide," I answered him, "his death

---

4. For *contrapasso*, see the headnote to Dante, p. 1460.   5. The reason for this exact measurement is
not known. At 30.86 we are told that the circumference of the ninth circle is eleven miles, showing that
Hell is shaped like a funnel.   6. This means that the sun (which they cannot see) is over their heads,
and the time is about 2 P.M. The journey to the center of Hell lasts twenty-four hours, so only four hours
are left.   7. First cousin to Dante's father; his death at the hands of a member of another Florentine
family initiated a feud between the two families that lasted some fifty years.   8. Bertran de Born (see
28.134).

by violence, which has not yet been avenged
   by anyone who shares in his disgrace, 33
made him resentful, and I suppose for this
   he went away without a word to me,
   and because he did I feel great piety." 36
We spoke of this until we reached the start
   of the bridge across the next *bolgia*, from which
   the bottom, with more light, might have been seen. 39
Having come to stand above the final cloister
   of Malebolge, we saw it spreading out,
   revealing to our eyes its congregation. 42
Weird shrieks of lamentation pierced through me
   like arrow-shafts whose tips are barbed with pity,
   so that my hands were covering my ears. 45
Imagine all the sick in the hospitals
   of Maremma, Valdichiana, and Sardinia
   between the months of July and September,[9] 48
crammed all together rotting in one ditch—
   such was the misery here; and such a stench
   was pouring out as comes from flesh decaying. 51
Still keeping to our left, we made our way
   down the long bridge onto the final bank,
   and now my sight was clear enough to find 54
the bottom where the High Lord's ministress,
   Justice infallible, metes out her punishment
   to falsifiers she registers on earth. 57
I doubt if all those dying in Aegina[1]
   when the air was blowing sick with pestilence
   and the animals, down to the smallest worm, 60
all perished (later on this ancient race,
   according to what the poets tell as true,
   was born again from families of ants) 63
offered a scene of greater agony
   than was the sight spread out in that dark valley
   of heaped-up spirits languishing in clumps. 66
Some sprawled out on others' bellies, some
   on others' backs, and some, on hands and knees,
   dragged themselves along that squalid alley. 69
Slowly, in silence, slowly we moved along,
   looking, listening to the words of all those sick,
   who had no strength to raise their bodies up. 72
I saw two sitting, leaning against each other
   like pans propped back to back against a fire,[2]
   and they were blotched from head to foot with scabs. 75
I never saw a curry-comb[3] applied
   by a stable-boy who is harried by his master,
   or simply wants to finish and go to bed, 78

9. The region of *Maremma*, the river valley of *Val di Chiana*, and the island of *Sardinia* were all plagued
by malaria. 1. A mythical island that was infected by Juno with a pestilence that killed all its inhabitants
and was then repopulated when Jupiter turned ants into men: see Ovid, *Metamorphoses* 7. 2. The image
is of pans leaned against one another before a kitchen fireplace. 3. A *curry-comb* is a bristled brush used
to groom horses.

the way those two applied their nails and dug
   and dug into their flesh, crazy to ease
   the itching that can never find relief.   81
They worked their nails down, scraping off the scabs
   the way one works a knife to scale a bream[4]
   or some other fish with larger, tougher scales.   84
"O you there scraping off your scabs of mail
   and even making pincers of your fingers,"
   my guide began to speak to one of them,   87
"so may your fingernails eternally
   suffice their task, tell us: among the many
   packed in this place is anyone Italian?"   90
"Both of us whom you see disfigured here,"
   one answered through his tears, "we are Italians.
   But you, who ask about us, who are you?"   93
"I am one accompanying this living man
   descending bank from bank," my leader said,
   "and I intend to show him all of Hell."   96
With that each lost the other back's support
   and each one, shaky, turned to look at me,
   as others did who overheard these words.   99
My gentle master came up close to me
   and said: "Now ask them what you want to know,"
   and since he wanted me to speak, I started: 102
"So may the memory of you not fade
   from the minds of men up there in the first world,
   but rather live on under many suns,   105
tell me your names and where it was you lived;
   do not let your dreadful, loathsome punishment
   discourage you from speaking openly."   108
"I'm from Arezzo," one of them replied,
   "and Albert of Siena had me burned,
   but I'm not here for what I died for there;[5]   111
it's true I told him, jokingly, of course:
   'I know the trick of flying through the air,'
   and he, eager to learn and not too bright,   114
asked me to demonstrate my art; and only
   just because I didn't make him Daedalus,
   he had me burned by one whose child he was.   117
But here, to the last *bolgia* of the ten,
   for the alchemy[6] I practiced in the world
   I was condemned by Minòs, who cannot err."   120
I said to my poet: "Have you ever known
   people as silly as the Sienese?
   Even the French cannot compare with them!"   123
With that the other leper[7] who was listening

---

4. A *bream* is a large fish like a carp.   5. Griffolino of Arezzo cheated Albero of Siena by promising to teach him the art of Daedalus—flying. The bishop of Siena, father of the illegitimate Albero, had Griffolino burned as a heretic.   6. A practice that sought to turn base metals like lead into gold.   7. The speaker is Capocchio, a Florentine burned in 1293 for alchemy, which he here admits was mere counterfeiting. The people he lists were rich young noblemen of Siena who joined a "Spendthrifts' Club"—the *fashionable club* of line 130—and sought to outdo each other in profligacy. For another member of this club, Lano of Siena, see 13.115.

feigned exception to my quip: "Excluding,
   of course, Stricca, who lived so frugally,   126
and Niccolo, the first to introduce
   the luxury of the clove for condiment
   into that choice garden where the seed took root,   129
and surely not that fashionable club
   where Caccia squandered all his woods and vineyards
   and Abbagliato flaunted his great wit!   132
That you may know who this is backing you
   against the Sienese, look sharply at me
   so that my face will give you its own answer,   135
and you will recognize Capocchio's shade,
   betrayer of metals with his alchemy;
   you'll surely recall—if you're the one I think—   138
how fine an ape of nature[8] I once was."

CANTO XXX

Capocchio's remarks are interrupted by two mad, naked shades who dash up, and one of them sinks his teeth into Capocchio's neck and drags him off; he is Gianni Schicchi and the other is Myrrha of Cyprus. When they have gone, the Pilgrim sees the ill-proportioned and immobile shade of Master Adamo, a counterfeiter, who explains how members of the Guidi family had persuaded him to practice his evil art in Romena. He points out the fever-stricken shades of two infamous liars, Potiphar's Wife and Sinon the Greek, whereupon the latter engages Master Adamo in a verbal battle. Virgil rebukes the Pilgrim for his absorption in such futile wrangling, but his immediate shame wins Virgil's immediate forgiveness.

In ancient times when Juno was enraged
   against the Thebans because of Semele[9]
   (she showed her wrath on more than one occasion),   3
she made King Athamas go raving mad:
   so mad that one day when he saw his wife
   coming with his two sons in either arm,   6
he cried: "Let's spread the nets, so I can catch
   the lioness with her lion cubs at the pass!"
Then he spread out his insane hands, like talons,   9
and, seizing one of his two sons, Learchus,
   he whirled him round and smashed him on a rock.
   She drowned herself with the other in her arms.   12
And when the wheel of Fortune brought down low
   the immeasurable haughtiness of Trojans,[1]
   destroying in their downfall king and kingdom,   15
Hecuba sad, in misery, a slave
   (after she saw Polyxena lie slain,
   after this grieving mother found her son   18

8. By *ape of nature* Capocchio means that he merely imitated change in his alchemical displays rather than actually accomplishing it.   9. Daughter of the king of Thebes, *Semele* was loved by Jupiter and therefore incited the wrath of Juno, who drove her brother-in-law Athamas insane. While mad, Athamas thought his wife, Ino, and his two sons, Learchus and Melicertes, were a lioness and two cubs; he killed Learchus, and Ino drowned herself and Melicertes. See Ovid, *Metamorphoses* 4.   1. Parallel to the fate of Thebes is that of Troy, which is here represented by the madness into which Queen Hecuba fell when she saw her daughter Polyxena sacrificed on Achilles' tomb and the unburied body of her betrayed son Polydorus. See Ovid, *Metamorphoses* 13.

Polydorus left unburied on the shore),
  now gone quite mad, went barking like a dog—
  it was the weight of grief that snapped her mind.   21
But never in Thebes or Troy were madmen seen
  driven to acts of such ferocity
  against their victims, animal or human,   24
as two shades I saw, white with rage and naked,
  running, snapping crazily at things in sight,
  like pigs, directionless, broken from their pen.   27
One, landing on Capocchio, sank his teeth
  into his neck, and started dragging him
  along, scraping his belly on the rocky ground.   30
The Aretine[2] spoke, shaking where he sat:
  "You see that batty shade? He's Gianni Schicchi![3]
  He's rabid and he treats us all that way."   33
"Oh," I answered, "so may that other shade
  never sink its teeth in you—if you don't mind,
  please tell me who it is before it's gone."   36
And he to me: "That is the ancient shade
  of Myrrha,[4] the depraved one, who became,
  against love's laws, too much her father's friend.   39
She went to him, and there she sinned in love,
  pretending that her body was another's—
  just as the other there fleeing in the distance,   42
contrived to make his own the 'queen of studs,'
  pretending that he was Buoso Donati,
  making his will and giving it due form."   45
Now that the rabid pair had come and gone
  (from whom I never took my eyes away),
  I turned to watch the other evil shades.   48
And there I saw a soul shaped like a lute,
  if only he'd been cut off from his legs
  below the belly, where they divide in two.   51
The bloating dropsy,[5] disproportioning
  the body's parts with unconverted humors,
  so that the face, matched with the paunch, was puny,   54
forced him to keep his parched lips wide apart,
  as a man who suffers thirst from raging fever
  has one lip curling up, the other sagging.   57
"O you who bear no punishment at all
  (I can't think why) within this world of sorrow,"
  he said to us, "pause here and look upon   60
the misery of one Master Adamo:[6]
  in life I had all that I could desire,
  and now, alas, I crave a drop of water.   63

---

2. Griffolino (see 29.111).   3. A Florentine who impersonated Buoso Donati (line 44), who had just died, and dictated a new will that gave him Buoso's best beast (*the 'queen of studs'* of line 43).   4. *Myrrha* impersonated another woman in order to sleep with her father: see Ovid, *Metamorphoses* 10.   5. A disease in which fluid (*humors* of line 53) gathers in the cells and the affected part becomes grotesquely swollen. 6. A counterfeiter, burned in 1281, who made coins stamped with the image of John the Baptist, the patron saint of Florence, that contained twenty-one rather than twenty-four carets of gold (see line 90); he worked for a noble family of Romena (individual members are mentioned in line 77), a town in the Florentine district of Casentino.

The little streams that flow from the green hills
   of Casentino, descending to the Arno,
   keeping their banks so cool and soft with moisture,   66
forever flow before me, haunting me;
   and the image of them leaves me far more parched
   than the sickness that has dried my shriveled face.   69
Relentless Justice, tantalizing me,
   exploits the countryside that knew my sin,
   to draw from me ever new sighs of pain: 72
I still can see Romena, where I learned
   to falsify the coin stamped with the Baptist,
   for which I paid with my burned body there;   75
but if I could see down here the wretched souls
   of Guido or Alexander or their brother,
   I would not exchange the sight for Branda's fountain.[7]   78
One is here already, if those maniacs
   running around this place have told the truth,
   but what good is it, with my useless legs?   81
If only I were lighter, just enough
   to move one inch in every hundred years,
   I would have started on my way by now   84
to find him somewhere in this gruesome lot,
   although this ditch winds round eleven miles
   and is at least a half a mile across.   87
It's their fault I am here with this choice family:
   they encouraged me to turn out florins
   whose gold contained three carats' worth of alloy."   90
And I to him: "Who are those two poor souls
   lying to the right, close to your body's boundary,
   steaming like wet hands in wintertime?"   93
"When I poured into this ditch, I found them here,"
   he answered, "and they haven't budged since then,
   and I doubt they'll move through all eternity.   96
One is the false accuser of young Joseph;
   the other is false Sinon, the Greek in Troy:[8]
   it's their burning fever makes them smell so bad."   99
And one of them, perhaps somewhat offended
   at the kind of introduction he received,
   with his fist struck out at the distended belly,   102
which responded like a drum reverberating;
   and Master Adam struck him in the face
   with an arm as strong as the fist he had received,   105
and he said to him: "Although I am not free
   to move around, with swollen legs like these,
   I have a ready arm for such occasions."   108
"*But* it was *not* as free and ready, was it,"
   the other answered, "when you went to the stake?
   Of course, when you were coining, it was readier!"   111
And he with the dropsy: "*Now* you tell the truth,

7. A fountain near Romena.   8. The *false accuser* is Potiphar's wife, who falsely accused Joseph of trying
to lie with her (Genesis 39.6–20); *Sinon* is the Greek priest who persuaded the Trojans to accept the
wooden horse (*Aeneid* 2).

but you were not as full of truth that time
   when you were asked to tell the truth at Troy!" 114
"My words were false—so were the coins you made,"
   said Sinon, "and *I* am here for one false act
   but *you* for more than any fiend in hell!" 117
"The horse, recall the horse, you falsifier,"
   the bloated paunch was quick to answer back,
   "may it burn your guts that all the world remembers!" 120
"May your guts burn with thirst that cracks your tongue,"
   the Greek said, "may they burn with rotting humors
   that swell your hedge of a paunch to block your eyes!" 123
And then the money-man: "So there you go,
   your evil mouth pours out its filth as usual;
   for if *I* thirst, and humors swell me up, 126
you burn more, and your head is fit to split,
   and it wouldn't take much coaxing to convince you
   to lap the mirror of Narcissus dry!"[9] 129
I was listening, all absorbed in this debate,
   when the master said to me: "Keep right on looking,
   a little more, and I shall lose my patience." 132
I heard the note of anger in his voice
   and turned to him; I was so full of shame
   that it still haunts my memory today. 135
Like one asleep who dreams himself in trouble
   and in his dream he wishes he were dreaming,
   longing for that which is, as if it were not, 138
just so I found myself: unable to speak,
   longing to beg for pardon and already
   begging for pardon, not knowing that I did. 141
"Less shame than yours would wash away a fault
   greater than yours has been," my master said,
   "and so forget about it, do not be sad. 144
If ever again you should meet up with men
   engaging in this kind of futile wrangling,
   remember I am always at your side; 147
to have a taste for talk like this is vulgar!"

CANTO XXXI

Through the murky air they move, up across the bank that separates the Malebolge *from the pit of Hell, the Ninth (and last) Circle of the* Inferno. *From a distance is heard the blast of a mighty horn, which turns out to have been that of the giant Nimrod. He and other giants, including Ephialtes, are fixed eternally in the pit of Hell; all are chained except Antaeus, who, at Virgil's request, lifts the two poets in his monstrous hand and deposits them below him, on the lake of ice known as Cocytus.*

The very tongue that first spoke—stinging me,
   making the blood rush up to both my cheeks—
   then gave the remedy to ease the pain, 3
just as, so I have heard, Achilles' lance,

---

9. Narcissus saw his reflection in a pool of water, referred to here as a *mirror* (Ovid, *Metamorphoses* 3).

belonging to his father, was the source
of pain, and then of balm, to him it struck.[1]   6
Turning our backs on that trench of misery
gaining the bank again that walls it in,
we cut across, walking in dead silence.   9
Here it was less than night and less than day,
so that my eyes could not see far ahead;
but then I heard the blast of some high horn   12
which would have made a thunder-clap sound dim;
it drew my eyes directly to one place,
as they retraced the sound's path to its source.   15
After the tragic rout when Charlemagne[2]
lost all his faithful, holy paladins,
the sound of Roland's horn was not as ominous.   18
Keeping my eyes still turned that way, I soon
made out what seemed to be high, clustered towers.
"Master," I said, "what city lies ahead?"   21
"Because you try to penetrate the shadows,"
he said to me, "from much too far away,
you confuse the truth with your imagination.   24
You will see clearly when you reach that place
how much the eyes may be deceived by distance,
and so, just push ahead a little more."   27
Then lovingly he took me by the hand
and said: "But now, before we go on farther,
to prepare you for the truth that could seem strange,   30
I'll tell you these aren't towers, they are giants;
they're standing in the well around the bank—
all of them hidden from their navels down."   33
As, when the fog begins to thin and clear,
the sight can slowly make out more and more
what is hidden in the mist that clogs the air,   36
so, as I pierced the thick and murky air,
approaching slowly, closer to the well,
confusion cleared and my fear took on more shape.   39
For just as Montereggion[3] is crowned with towers
soaring high above its curving ramparts,
so, on the bank that runs around the well,   42
towering with only half their bodies out,
stood the terrible giants,[4] forever threatened
by Jupiter in the heavens when he thunders.   45
And now I could make out one of the faces,
the shoulders, the chest and a good part of the belly
and, down along the sides, the two great arms.[5]   48
Nature, when she cast away the mold

1. Achilles' father, Peleus, gave him a lance that would heal any wound it inflicted.   2. In *The Song of Roland*. Roland blows his horn to alert Charlemagne to the fact that the rear guard Roland commands has been slaughtered. *Paladins* are the twelve peers or great warriors of Charlemagne's court.   3. A castle surrounded by towers, built to protect Siena from attack by Florence.   4. These *giants* are the mythological Titans, monsters born of the Earth who assaulted Olympus and were defeated and imprisoned by Jupiter.   5. This is Nimrod, described in Genesis as "the first on earth to be a mighty man" (10.8) and understood by medieval commentators to be a giant. He ruled over Babylon, where the tower of Babel was built (11.1–9).

for shaping beasts like these, without a doubt
   did well, depriving Mars of more such agents.
And if she never did repent of whales   51
   and elephants, we must consider her,
   on sober thought, all the more just and wary: 54
for when the faculty of intellect
   is joined with brute force and with evil will,
   no man can win against such an alliance.   57
His face, it seemed to me, was about as long
   and just as wide as St. Peter's cone in Rome,[6]
   and all his body's bones were in proportion,   60
so that the bank which served to cover him
   from his waist down showed so much height above
   that three tall Frisians[7] on each other's shoulders   63
could never boast of stretching to his hair,
   for downward from the place men clasp their cloaks
   I saw a generous thirty hand-spans of him.[8]   66
"Raphel may amech zabi almi!"[9]
   He played these sputtering notes with prideful lips
   for which no sweeter psalm was suitable.   69
My guide called up to him: "Blathering idiot,
   stick to your horn[1] and take it out on that
   when you feel a fit of anger coming on;   72
search round your neck and you will find the strap
   it's tied to, you poor muddle-headed soul,
   and there's the horn so pretty on your chest."   75
And then he turned to me: "His words accuse him.
   He is Nimrod, through whose infamous device
   the world no longer speaks a common language.   78
But let's leave him alone and not waste breath,
   for he can no more understand our words
   than anyone can understand his language."   81
We had to walk still farther than before,
   continuing to the left, a full bow's-shot,
   to find another giant,[2] huger and more fierce.   84
What engineer it took to bind this brute
   I cannot say, but there he was, one arm
   pinned to his back, the other locked in front,   87
with a giant chain winding around him tight,
   which, starting from his neck, made five great coils—
   and that was counting only to his waist.   90
"This beast of pride decided he would try
   to pit his strength against almighty Jove,"
   my leader said, "and he has won this prize.   93
He's Ephialtes, who made his great attempt
   when the giants arose to fill the Gods with panic;

---

6. This bronze pine cone, over twelve feet high, stood outside St. Peter's Cathedral in Dante's time; today it can be seen in the papal gardens in the Vatican.   7. Inhabitants of the northernmost province of what is now the Netherlands, considered the tallest men of the time.   8. About fifteen feet.   9. Appropriately for the builder of Babel, he speaks an incomprehensible language.   1. Nimrod has a *horn* because in the Bible he is described as a hunter (Genesis 10.9).   2. This is Ephialtes, a Titan who with his twin brother Otus tried to attack Olympus by piling Mount Ossa on Mount Pelion; see Virgil, *Aeneid* 6.

the arms he lifted then, he moves no more." 96
And I to him: "If it were possible,
   I would really like to have the chance to see
   the fantastic figure of Briareus."[3] 99
His answer was: "Not far from here you'll see
   Antaeus,[4] who can speak and is not chained;
   he will set us down in the very pit of sin. 102
The one you want to see is farther off;
   he too is bound and looks just like this one,
   except for his expression, which is fiercer." 105
No earthquake of the most outrageous force
   ever shook a tower with such violence
   as, suddenly, Ephialtes shook himself. 108
I never feared to die as much as then,
   and my fear might have been enough to kill me,
   if I had not already seen those chains. 111
We left him and continued moving on
   and came to where Antaeus stood, extending
   from the well a good five ells up to his head.[5] 114
"O you who in the celebrated valley[6]
   (that saw Scipio become the heir of glory,
   when Hannibal with all his men retreated) 117
once captured a thousand lions as your quarry
   (and with whose aid, had you chosen to take part
   in the great war with your brothers, the sons of earth 120
would, as many still think, have been the victors),
   do not disdain this modest wish: take us,
   and put us down where ice locks in Cocytus.[7] 123
Don't make us go to Tityus or Typhon;[8]
   this man can give you what all long for here,
   and so bend down, and do not scowl at us. 126
He still can spread your legend in the world,
   for he yet lives, and long life lies before him,
   unless Grace summons him before his time." 129
Thus spoke my master, and the giant in haste
   stretched out the hands whose formidable grip
   great Hercules once felt, and took my guide. 132
And Virgil, when he felt the grasping hands,
   called out: "Now come and I'll take hold of you."
   Clasped together, we made a single burden. 135
As the Garisenda[9] looks from underneath
   its leaning side, at the moment when a cloud
   comes drifting over against the tower's slant, 138
just so the bending giant Antaeus seemed
   as I looked up, expecting him to topple.
   I wished then I had gone another way. 141
But he, most carefully, handed us down

---

3. Another Titan.   4. A Titan born too late to participate in the rebellion against Jupiter and therefore not chained; he was known for eating lions (line 118) and was defeated by Hercules in a wrestling match (line 132).   5. About fifteen feet.   6. The *valley* of the Bagradas River in Tunisia, where the Roman Scipio defeated the Carthaginian Hannibal in 202 B.C.E.   7. The frozen lake of *Cocytus* is in the ninth and last circle of Hell.   8. Two more Titans.   9. A leaning tower of Bologna; when a cloud passes over it, moving opposite to the tower's slant, it appears to be falling away from the sky.

to the pit that swallows Lucifer with Judas.[1]
And then, the leaning giant immediately   144
drew himself up as tall as a ship's mast.

CANTO XXXII

*They descend farther down into the darkness of the immense plain of ice in which shades
of Traitors are frozen. In the outer region of the ice-lake, Caïna, are those who betrayed
their kin in murder; among them, locked in a frozen embrace, are Napoleone and
Alessandro of Mangona, and others are Mordred, Focaccia, Sassol Mascheroni, and
Camicion de'Pazzi. Then the two travelers enter the area of ice called Antenora, and
suddenly the Pilgrim kicks one of the faces sticking out of the ice. He tries to force the
sinner to reveal his name by pulling out his hair, and when another shade identifies
him as Bocca Degli Abati, the Pilgrim's fury mounts still higher. Bocca, himself furious,
names several other sinners in Antenora, including Buoso da Duera, Tesauro dei Beccheria, Gianni de' Soldanier, Ganelon, and Tibbald. Going farther on, the Pilgrim sees
two heads frozen in one hole, the mouth of one gnawing at the brain of the other.*

If I had words grating and crude enough
    that really could describe this horrid hole
    supporting the converging weight of Hell,   3
I could squeeze out the juice of my memories
    to the last drop. But I don't have these words,
    and so I am reluctant to begin.   6
To talk about the bottom of the universe
    the way it truly is, is no child's play,
    no task for tongues that gurgle baby-talk.   9
But may those heavenly ladies[2] aid my verse
    who aided Amphion to wall-in Thebes,
    that my words may tell exactly what I saw.   12
O misbegotten rabble of all rabble,
    who crowd this realm, hard even to describe,
    it were better you had lived as sheep or goats!   15
When we reached a point of darkness in the well
    below the giant's feet, farther down the slope,
    and I was gazing still at the high wall,   18
I heard somebody say: "Watch where you step!
    Be careful that you do not kick the heads
    of this brotherhood of miserable souls."   21
At that I turned around and saw before me
    a lake of ice stretching beneath my feet,
    more like a sheet of glass than frozen water.[3]   24
In the depths of Austria's wintertime, the Danube
    never in all its course showed ice so thick,
    nor did the Don beneath its frigid sky,   27
as this crust here; for if Mount Tambernic[4]
    or Pietrapana would crash down upon it,
    not even at its edges would a crack creak.   30
The way the frogs (in the season when the harvest

1. Two of the inhabitants of Cocytus.   2. The Muses who helped the legendary musician Amphion raise
the walls of Thebes with the music of his lyre.   3. The water for this lake derives from the crack in the
Old Man of Crete (14.103).   4. Probably Mount Tambura, close to Mount Pietrapana in the Italian Alps.

will often haunt the dreams of the peasant girl)
   sit croaking with their muzzles out of water,   33
so these frigid, livid shades were stuck in ice
   up to where a person's shame appears;
   their teeth clicked notes like storks' beaks snapping shut.[5]   36
And each one kept his face bowed toward the ice:
   the mouth bore testimony to the cold,
   the eyes, to sadness welling in the heart.   39
I gazed around awhile and then looked down,
   and by my feet I saw two figures clasped
   so tight that one's hair could have been the other's.   42
"Tell me, you two, pressing your chests together,"
   I asked them, "who are you?"[6] Both stretched their necks
   and when they had their faces raised toward me,   45
their eyes, which had before been only glazed,
   dripped tears down to their lips, and the cold froze
   the tears between them, locking the pair more tightly.   48
Wood to wood with iron was never clamped
   so firm! And the two of them like billy-goats
   were butting at each other, mad with anger.   51
Another one with both ears frozen off,
   and head still bowed over his icy mirror,
   cried out: "What makes you look at us so hard?   54
If you're interested to know who these two are:
   the valley where Bisenzio's waters[7] flow
   belonged to them and to their father, Albert;   57
the same womb bore them both, and if you scour
   all of Caïna,[8] you will not turn up one
   who's more deserving of this frozen aspic—   60
not him who had his breast and shadow pierced
   with one thrust of the lance from Arthur's hand;[9]
   not Focaccia, not even this one here,   63
whose head gets in my way and blocks my view,
   known in the world as Sassol Mascheroni,[1]
   and if you're Tuscan you must know who he was.   66
To save me from your asking for more news:
   I was Camicion de' Pazzi,[2] and I await
   Carlin,[3] whose guilt will make my own seem less."   69
Farther on I saw a thousand doglike faces,
   purple from the cold. That's why I shudder,
   and always will, when I see a frozen pond.   72
While we were getting closer to the center

5. A harsh, clacking sound. *Where a person's shame appears* is the face because of blushing.   6. These are the two sons of Count Alberto degli Alberti of Florence; when he died (ca. 1280), they killed each other over politics and their inheritance.   7. *Bisenzio* is a river north of Florence.   8. Named after Cain: this first of the four subdivisions of Cocytus is where those who betrayed their kin are imprisoned.   9. *Not him . . . hand:* This is Mordred, Arthur's nephew and son; when Arthur pierced him with a sword, he created a wound so large that the sun shone through, thus creating a hole in Mordred's shadow. *Focaccia* in the next line is a nobleman of Pistoia who killed his cousin.   1. A Florentine nobleman who murdered a relative.   2. A Florentine who killed his kinsman.   3. A Florentine who betrayed a castle belonging to his party. When he dies he will therefore be sent to the next subdivision, Antenora, for those who committed treachery against their country, city, or party—a harsher punishment, which Camicion says *will make my own [guilt] seem less.*

of the universe,[4] where all weights must converge,
   and I was shivering in the eternal chill— 75
by fate or chance or willfully perhaps,
   I do not know—but stepping among the heads,
   my foot kicked hard against one of those faces. 78
Weeping, he screamed: "Why are you kicking me?[5]
   You have not come to take revenge on me
   for Montaperti, have you? Why bother me?" 81
And I: "My master, please wait here for me,
   let me clear up a doubt concerning this one,
   then I shall be as rapid as you wish." 84
My leader stopped, and to that wretch, who still
   had not let up in his barrage of curses,
   I said: "Who are you, insulting other people?" 87
"And you, who are *you* who march through Antenora[6]
   kicking other people in their faces?
   No living man could kick as hard!" he answered. 90
"I am a living man," was my reply,
   "and it might serve you well, if you seek fame,
   for me to put your name down in my notes." 93
And he said: "That's the last thing I would want!
   That's not the way to flatter in these lowlands!
   Stop pestering me like this—get out of here!" 96
At that I grabbed him by his hair in back[7]
   and said: "You'd better tell me who you are
   or else I'll not leave one hair on your head." 99
And he to me: "Go on and strip me bald
   and pound and stamp my head a thousand times,
   you'll never hear my name or see my face." 102
I had my fingers twisted in his hair
   and already I'd pulled out more than one fistful,
   while he yelped like a cur with eyes shut tight, 105
when someone else[8] yelled: "What's the matter, Bocca?
   It's bad enough to hear your shivering teeth;
   now you bark! What the devil's wrong with you?" 108
"There's no need now for you to speak," I said,
   "you vicious traitor! Now I know your name
   and I'll bring back the shameful truth about you." 111
"Go away!" he answered. "Tell them what you want;
   but if you do get out of here, be sure
   you also tell about that blabbermouth, 114
who's paying here what the French silver cost him:
   'I saw,' you can tell the world, 'the one from Duera
   stuck in with all the sinners keeping cool,' 117
And if you should be asked: 'Who else was there?'
   Right by your side is the one from Beccheria[9]

4. The *center of the universe* is where gravity is most strong and to which all material things are drawn.
5. Bocca degli Abati (his name is betrayed by one of the fellow damned in line 106); Bocca betrayed his
party at the battle of Montaperti in 1260.   6. Dante and Virgil have moved into the second subdivision
of Caïna, which is named after Antenor, a Trojan who betrayed the city to the Greeks; it is the location of
those who betrayed their country.   7. The hair at the nape of the neck.   8. This is Buoso da Duera,
who betrayed Manfred, the ruler of Naples, to his enemy Charles of Anjou in 1265.   9. Tesauro de'
Beccheria, a churchman executed for treason in Florence in 1258.

whose head was chopped off by the Florentines.   120
As for Gianni Soldanier,[1] I think you'll find him
   farther along with Ganelon and Tibbald,
   who opened up Faenza while it slept."   123
Soon after leaving him I saw two souls
   frozen together in a single hole,
   so that one head used the other for a cap.   126
As a man with hungry teeth tears into bread,
   the soul with capping head had sunk his teeth
   into the other's neck, just beneath the skull.   129
Tydeus[2] in his fury did not gnaw
   the head of Menalippus with more relish
   than this one chewed that head of meat and bones.   132
"O you who show with every bestial bite
   your hatred for the head you are devouring,"
   I said, "tell me your reason, and I promise,   135
if you are justified in your revenge,
   once I know who you are and this one's sin,
   I'll repay your confidence in the world above   138
unless my tongue dry up before I die."

CANTO XXXIII

Count Ugolino is the shade gnawing at the brain of his one-time associate Archbishop Ruggieri, and Ugolino interrupts his gruesome meal long enough to tell the story of his imprisonment and cruel death, which his innocent offspring shared with him. Moving farther into the area of Cocytus known as Tolomea, where those who betrayed their guests and associates are condemned, the Pilgrim sees sinners with their faces raised high above the ice, whose tears freeze and lock their eyes. One of the shades agrees to identify himself on condition that the ice be removed from his eyes. The Pilgrim agrees, and learns that this sinner is Friar Alberigo and that his soul is dead and damned even though his body is still alive on earth, inhabited by a devil. Alberigo also names a fellow sinner with him in the ice, Branca d'Oria, whose body is still functioning up on earth. But the Pilgrim does not honor his promise to break the ice from Alberigo's eyes.

Lifting his mouth from his horrendous meal,
   this sinner[3] first wiped off his messy lips
   in the hair remaining on the chewed-up skull,   3
then spoke: "You want me to renew a grief
   so desperate that just the thought of it,
   much less the telling, grips my heart with pain;   6
but if my words can be the seed to bear
   the fruit of infamy for this betrayer,
   who feeds my hunger, then I shall speak—in tears.   9
I do not know your name, nor do I know
   how you have come down here, but Florentine
   you surely seem to be, to hear you speak.   12

---

1. *Gianni Soldanier* was a Florentine nobleman who switched political parties; *Ganelon* (line 122) is the betrayer of Roland in *The Song of Roland; Tibbald* (line 122) was the citizen of Faenza (a town east of Florence) who betrayed it to its enemies.   2. In the war against Thebes, *Tydeus* was mortally wounded by Menalippus, whom he killed and whose skull he gnawed in fury while dying.   3. Ugolino, a governor of Pisa who was betrayed by his enemy Archbishop Ruggieri in 1288. His own crime is obliquely explained by his narrative.

First you should know I was Count Ugolino
   and my neighbor here, Ruggieri the Archbishop;
   now I'll tell you why I'm so unneighborly.   15
That I, trusting in him, was put in prison
   through his evil machinations, where I died,
   this much I surely do not have to tell you.   18
What you could not have known, however, is
   the inhuman circumstances of my death.
   Now listen, then decide if he has wronged me!   21
Through a narrow slit of window high in that mew[4]
   (which is called the tower of hunger, after me,
   and I'll not be the last to know that place)   24
I had watched moon after moon after moon go by,
   when finally I dreamed the evil dream
   which ripped away the veil that hid my future.   27
I dreamed of this one here as lord and huntsman,
   pursuing the wolf and the wolf cubs up the mountain[5]
   (which blocks the sight of Lucca from the Pisans)   30
with skinny bitches, well trained and obedient;
   he had out front as leaders of the pack
   Gualandi with Sismondi and Lanfranchi.[6]   33
A short run, and the father with his sons
   seemed to grow tired, and then I thought I saw
   long fangs sunk deep into their sides, ripped open.   36
When I awoke before the light of dawn,
   I heard my children sobbing in their sleep
   (you see they, too, were there), asking for bread.   39
If the thought of what my heart was telling me
   does not fill you with grief, how cruel you are!
   If you are not weeping now—do you ever weep?   42
And then they awoke. It was around the time
   they usually brought our food to us. But now
   each one of us was full of dread from dreaming;   45
then from below I heard them driving nails
   into the dreadful tower's door; with that,
   I stared in silence at my flesh and blood.   48
I did not weep, I turned to stone inside;
   they wept, and my little Anselmuccio spoke:
   'What is it, father? Why do you look that way?'   51
For them I held my tears back, saying nothing,
   all of that day, and then all of that night,
   until another sun shone on the world.   54
A meager ray of sunlight found its way
   to the misery of our cell, and I could see
   myself reflected four times in their faces;   57
I bit my hands in anguish. And my children,

---

4. A cage for birds; the prison in Pisa where Ugolino and his relatives were confined became known as the Torre de Fame or Tower of Hunger.   5. Mount San Giuliano lies between Pisa and Lucca. *The Wolf and the wolf cubs*: Ugolino and his four sons, each of whom are named in subsequent lines (50, 68, 89). In fact, Ugolino was imprisoned with two sons (who were grown men) and two adolescent grandsons. 6. Pisan families of the political party opposed to that of Ugolino.

who thought that hunger made me bite my hands,
were quick to draw up closer to me, saying: 60
'O father, you would make us suffer less,
if you would feed on us: you were the one
who gave us this sad flesh; you take it from us!'[7]   63
I calmed myself to make them less unhappy.
That day we sat in silence, and the next day.
O pitiless earth! You should have swallowed us!   66
The fourth day came, and it was on that day
my Gaddo fell prostrate before my feet,
crying: 'Why don't you help me? Why, my father?'[8]   69
There he died. Just as you see me here,
I saw the other three fall one by one,
as the fifth day and the sixth day passed. And I,   72
by then gone blind, groped over their dead bodies.
Though they were dead, two days I called their names.
Then hunger proved more powerful than grief."   75
He spoke these words; then, glaring down in rage,
attacked again the wretched skull with his teeth
sharp as a dog's, and as fit for grinding bones.   78
O Pisa, blot of shame upon the people
of that fair land where the sound of "sì" is heard![9]
Since your neighbors hesitate to punish you,   81
let Capraia and Gorgona[1] move and join,
damming up the River Arno at its mouth,
and let every Pisan perish in its flood!   84
For if Count Ugolino was accused
of turning traitor, trading-in your castles,[2]
you had no right to make his children suffer.   87
Their newborn years (O newborn Thebes!)[3] made them
all innocents: Brigata, Uguiccione,
and the other two soft names my canto sings.   90
We moved ahead to where the frozen water
wraps in harsh wrinkles another sinful race,
with faces not turned down but looking up.[4]   93
Here, the weeping puts an end to weeping,
and the grief that finds no outlet from the eyes
turns inward to intensify the anguish: 96
for the tears they first wept knotted in a cluster
and like a visor made for them in crystal,
filled all the hollow part around their eyes.   99
Although the bitter coldness of the dark
had driven all sensation from my face,
as though it were not tender skin but callous,   102
I thought I felt the air begin to blow,

7. See Job 1.21.   8. See Matthew 27.46.   9. I.e., Italy, where *si* means "yes."   1. Islands belonging
to Pisa that lie close to the mouth of the Arno, which flows through Pisa.   2. In 1285 Ugolino conveyed
three Pisan castles to Lucca and Florence.   3. In classical mythology, *Thebes* was notorious for its internecine violence, such as the story of Oedipus, his father, Laius, and his sons, Eteocles and Polynices (see
26.54).   4. Virgil and Dante pass into the third subdivision of Cocytus, called Tolomea (line 124) after
Ptolemy, governor of Jericho, who killed his father-in-law, Simon, and two of his sons while they were
dining with him (1 Maccabees 16.11–17). In Tolomea those who have betrayed their guests are punished.

and I: "What causes such a wind, my master?
  I thought no heat could reach into these depths."[5]   105
And he to me: "Before long you will be
  where your own eyes can answer for themselves,
  when they will see what keeps this wind in motion."   108
And one of the wretches with the frozen crust
  screamed out at us: "O wicked souls, so wicked
  that you have been assigned the ultimate post,   111
break off these hard veils covering my eyes
  and give relief from the pain that swells my heart—
  at least until the new tears freeze again."   114
I answered him: "If this is what you want,
  tell me your name; and if I do not help you,
  may I be forced to drop beneath this ice!"   117
He answered then: "I am Friar Alberigo,[6]
  I am he who offered fruit from the evil orchard:
  here dates are served me for the figs I gave."   120
"Oh, then!" I said. "Are you already dead?"
  And he to me: "Just how my body is
  in the world above, I have no way of knowing.   123
This zone of Tolomea is very special,
  for it often happens that a soul falls here
  before the time that Atropos[7] should send it.   126
And that you may more willingly scrape off
  my cluster of glass tears, let me tell you:
  whenever a soul betrays the way I did,   129
a demon takes possession of the body,
  controlling its maneuvers from then on,
  for all the years it has to live up there,   132
while the soul falls straight into this cistern here;
  and the shade in winter quarters just behind me
  may well have left his body up on earth.   135
But you should know, if you've just come from there:
  he is Ser Branca D'Oria;[8] and many years
  have passed since he first joined us here, icebound."   138
"I think you're telling me a lie," I said,
  "for Branca D'Oria is not dead at all;
  he eats and drinks, he sleeps and wears out clothes."   141
"The ditch the Malebranche watch above,"
  he said, "the ditch of clinging, boiling pitch,
  had not yet caught the soul of Michel Zanche,   144
when Branca left a devil in his body
  to take his place, and so did his close kinsman,
  his accomplice in this act of treachery.   147
But now, at last, give me the hand you promised.
  Open my eyes." I did not open them.

5. Since the sun's heat was thought to cause wind, Dante wonders why he feels wind in this cold place. The answer will be given in 34.46–52.   6. A member of the Jovial Friars (see 23.103), he killed two of his relatives during a banquet at his house, signaling the assassins with an order to bring the fruit. In saying that he is now being served dates instead of figs, he is ironically complimenting God for His generosity, since a date would be more valuable than a fig.   7. One of the mythological figures known as the Fates; she is the one who cuts the thread of life.   8. A nobleman of Genoa (a *Genovese* in line 151), who with a *close kinsman* (line 146) killed his father-in-law, *Michel Zanche* (line 144) at a banquet in 1275 or 1290.

To be mean to him was a generous reward. 150
O all you Genovese, you men estranged
   from every good, at home with every vice,
   why can't the world be wiped clean of your race? 153
For in company with Romagna's rankest soul[9]
   I found one of your men, whose deeds were such
   that his soul bathes already in Cocytus 156
but his body seems alive and walks among you.

CANTO XXXIV

*Far across the frozen ice can be seen the gigantic figure of Lucifer, who appears from
this distance like a windmill seen through fog; and as the two travelers walk on toward
that terrifying sight, they see the shades of sinners totally buried in the frozen water. At
the center of the earth Lucifer stands frozen from the chest downward, and his horrible
ugliness (he has three faces) is made more fearful by the fact that in each of his three
mouths he chews on one of the three worst sinners of all mankind, the worst of those
who betrayed their benefactors: Judas Iscariot, Brutus, and Cassius. Virgil, with the
Pilgrim on his back, begins the descent down the shaggy body of Lucifer. They climb
down through a crack in the ice, and when they reach the Evil One's thighs, Virgil turns
and begins to struggle upward (because they have passed the center of the earth), still
holding on to the hairy body of Lucifer, until they reach a cavern, where they stop for
a short rest. Then a winding path brings them eventually to the earth's surface, where
they see the stars.*

"*Vexilla regis prodeunt Inferni,*"[1]
   my master said, "closer to us, so now
   look ahead and see if you can make him out." 3
A far-off windmill turning its huge sails
   when a thick fog begins to settle in,
   or when the light of day begins to fade, 6
that is what I thought I saw appearing.
   And the gusts of wind it stirred made me shrink back
   behind my guide, my only means of cover. 9
Down here,[2] I stood on souls fixed under ice
   (I tremble as I put this into verse);
   to me they looked like straws worked into glass. 12
Some lying flat, some perpendicular,
   either with their heads up or their feet,
   and some bent head to foot, shaped like a bow. 15
When we had moved far enough along the way
   that my master thought the time had come to show me
   the creature who was once so beautiful,[3] 18
he stepped aside, and stopping me, announced:
   "This is he, this is Dis;[4] this is the place
   that calls for all the courage you have in you." 21
How chilled and nerveless, Reader, I felt then;

9. That is, Friar Alberigo (line 118); *Romagna* is the part of Italy from which he and Branca come.
1. The first three words—"the banners of the king advance"—are the opening lines of a sixth-century Latin
hymn traditionally sung during Holy Week to celebrate Christ's Passion. Dante has added the last word,
Inferni—"the banners of the king of Hell advance"—in order to apply the words to Satan.   2. This is the
last and lowest subdivision of Caïna, known as Judecca after Judas; the sinners here are those who betrayed
their benefactors.   3. Lucifer, the "light-bearer," was the most beautiful of angels before he rebelled and
was renamed Satan.   4. A classical name for Pluto, here applied to Satan (see also 11.65 and 12.39).

do not ask me—I cannot write about it—
　　there are no words to tell you how I felt.
I did not die—I was not living either!　　　　　　24
　　Try to imagine, if you can imagine,
　　me there, deprived of life and death at once.　　27
The king of the vast kingdom of all grief
　　stuck out with half his chest above the ice;
　　my height is closer to the height of giants　　　30
than theirs is to the length of his great arms;
　　consider now how large all of him was:
　　this body in proportion to his arms.　　　　　33
If once he was as fair as now he's foul
　　and dared to raise his brows against his Maker,
　　it is fitting that all grief should spring from him.　　36
Oh, how amazed I was when I looked up
　　and saw a head—one head wearing three faces![5]
　　One was in front (and that was a bright red),　　39
the other two attached themselves to this one
　　just above the middle of each shoulder,
　　and at the crown all three were joined in one:　　42
The right face was a blend of white and yellow,
　　the left the color of those people's skin
　　who live along the river Nile's descent.[6]　　　45
Beneath each face two mighty wings stretched out,
　　the size you might expect of this huge bird
　　(I never saw a ship with larger sails):　　　　48
not feathered wings but rather like the ones
　　a bat would have. He flapped them constantly,
　　keeping three winds continuously in motion　　51
to lock Cocytus eternally in ice.
　　He wept from his six eyes, and down three chins
　　were dripping tears all mixed with bloody slaver.　　54
In each of his three mouths he crunched a sinner,
　　with teeth like those that rake the hemp and flax,
　　keeping three sinners constantly in pain;　　　57
the one in front—the biting he endured
　　was nothing like the clawing that he took:
　　sometimes his back was raked clean of its skin.　　60
"That soul up there who suffers most of all,"
　　my guide explained, "is Judas Iscariot:
　　the one with head inside and legs out kicking.　　63
As for the other two whose heads stick out,
　　the one who hangs from that black face is Brutus[7]—
　　see how he squirms in silent desperation;　　　66
the other one is Cassius,[8] he still looks sturdy.
　　But soon it will be night. Now is the time

---

5. Satan's three faces (and much else) make him an infernal parody of the Trinity.　6. I.e., Ethiopians.
The significance of these three colors is not certain; it has been suggested that they represent hatred,
impotence, and ignorance as the opposites of the Divine attributes of love, omnipotence, and wisdom (see
3.5–6).　7. The murderer of Julius Caesar in 44 B.C.E. and thus for Dante a betrayer of the empire.
8. The other murderer of Caesar.

to leave this place, for we have seen it all."   69
I held on to his neck, as he told me to,
    while he watched and waited for the time and place,
    and when the wings were stretched out just enough,   72
he grabbed on to the shaggy sides of Satan;
    then downward, tuft by tuft, he made his way
    between the tangled hair and frozen crust.   75
When we had reached the point exactly where
    the thigh begins, right at the haunch's curve,
    my guide, with strain and force of every muscle,   78
turned his head toward the shaggy shanks of Dis
    and grabbed the hair as if about to climb—
    I thought that we were heading back to Hell.[9]   81
"Hold tight, there is no other way," he said,
    panting, exhausted, "only by these stairs
    can we leave behind the evil we have seen."   84
When he had got me through the rocky crevice,
    he raised me to its edge and set me down,
    then carefully he climbed and joined me there.   87
I raised my eyes, expecting I would see
    the half of Lucifer I saw before.
    Instead I saw his two legs stretching upward.   90
If at that sight I found myself confused,
    so will those simple-minded folk who still
    don't see what point it was I must have passed.   93
"Get up," my master said, "get to your feet,
    the way is long, the road a rough climb up,
    already the sun approaches middle tierce!"[1]   96
It was no palace promenade we came to,
    but rather like some dungeon Nature built:
    it was paved with broken stone and poorly lit.   99
"Before we start to struggle out of here,
    O master," I said when I was on my feet,
    "I wish you would explain some things to me.   102
Where is the ice? And how can he be lodged
    upside-down? And how, in so little time,
    could the sun go all the way from night to day?"   105
"You think you're still on the center's other side,"
    he said, "where I first grabbed the hairy worm
    of rottenness that pierces the earth's core;   108
and you *were* there as long as I moved downward
    but, when I turned myself, you passed the point
    to which all weight from every part is drawn.[2]   111

9. Virgil's reversal marks the point at which the two travelers pass from the northern to the southern hemisphere. They began by climbing down Satan's body, but now reverse directions and climb up from the Earth's center (hence when they have passed through the center Dante sees Satan's legs sticking up (line 90). Note that the travelers pass through the glassy ice, a passage that probably echoes 1 Corinthians 13.12: "We see now through a glass in a dark manner; but then face to face."   1. About 7:30 A.M. on Holy Saturday. Dante has added twelve hours to his scheme so that the travelers will emerge from the Earth and arrive at the shore of Mount Purgatory just before sunrise on the next day, Easter Sunday.   2. The center of the earth, which is for Dante the center of the universe, and therefore the place where gravity is the strongest. Being furthest from Heaven, it is also the place which is most material and least spiritual.

Now you are standing beneath the hemisphere[3]
   which is opposite the side covered by land,
   where at the central point was sacrificed 114
the Man whose birth and life were free of sin.
   You have both feet upon a little sphere
   whose other side Judecca occupies; 117
when it is morning here, there it is evening.[4]
   And he whose hairs were stairs for our descent
   has not changed his position since his fall. 120
When he fell from the heavens on this side,[5]
   all of the land that once was spread out here,
   alarmed by his plunge, took cover beneath the sea 123
and moved to our hemisphere; with equal fear
   the mountain-land, piled up on this side, fled
   and made this cavern here when it rushed upward. 126
Below somewhere there is a space, as far
   from Beelzebub[6] as the limit of his tomb,
   known not by sight but only by the sound 129
of a little stream[7] that makes its way down here
   through the hollow of a rock that it has worn,
   gently winding in gradual descent." 132
My guide and I entered that hidden road
   to make our way back up to the bright world.
   We never thought of resting while we climbed. 135
We climbed, he first and I behind, until,
   through a small round opening ahead of us
   I saw the lovely things the heavens hold, 138
and we came out to see once more the stars.[8]

From Purgatorio

CANTO I

*Having left the Inferno behind, Dante announces his intention to sing of the second
kingdom, Purgatory, and calls upon the Muses, in particular Calliope, to accompany
his song. As the dawn approaches, he feels a sense of renewal, and, looking up into the*

3. I.e., under the Southern Hemisphere, exactly opposite Jerusalem where Christ (*the Man whose birth
and life were free of sin*) was crucified. Jerusalem is the center of the Northern Hemisphere (see Ezekiel
5.5) and is located directly over the cavity of Hell.   4. The *little sphere* upon which they stand is the
other side of Judecca, which is a hollow. The sun is now over the Southern Hemisphere, and therefore it
is night in the Northern, where Hell is located.   5. The land that was in the Southern Hemisphere before
Satan fell fled to the Northern to avoid him; hence the Southern Hemisphere is composed of water. The
exception is that when Satan plunged into the center of the world, the earth close to his body in the Northern
Hemisphere moved *with equal fear* (line 124) to the Southern Hemisphere and became *mountain-land*
(line 125), which is Mount Purgatory. *This cavern* (line 126) refers to Hell; Mount Purgatory is thus
comprised of the land displaced by Satan in his fall. This elaborate explanation for medieval geography is
Dante's own poetic scheme.   6. Satan.   7. This stream must flow down from Purgatory, perhaps from
Lethe. It finds its source in *a space* (line 127) on Mount Purgatory; thus it is *as far from Beelzebub as the
limit of his tomb*—that is, it is located on the surface of the Southern Hemisphere, which since Satan is at
the center of the earth is the same distance from him as Hell (his *tomb*) is deep. When Dante has Virgil
say that it is *below* (line 127) he must be writing from the perspective of the Northern Hemisphere, since
Mount Purgatory is at this moment above the travelers.   8. Each of the three parts of the *Divine Comedy*
end with the word *stars* as an affirmation of God's benevolent order.

heavens, he sees four stars. Turning his gaze earthward again, he discovers standing near him a dignified old man: Cato of Utica. Cato thinks Dante and Virgil are refugees from Hell, and he questions them as to how they managed to escape. Virgil explains that Dante is still a living man, and that, at the command of a lady from Heaven, he, Virgil, has been sent to guide this man on a journey for the purpose of his salvation. Already this journey has taken them through Hell, and now it is their intention to see the souls of Purgatory. Cato assents to their passage. He then instructs Virgil to bind a reed around the Pilgrim's waist and to be sure to cleanse him of every trace of stain from the infernal regions. The two poets descend to the shore, where they proceed to carry out Cato's instructions. The purgation is marked by a miracle: when Virgil pulls a reed from the ground, another springs up immediately to take its place.

For better waters, now, the little bark
   of my poetic powers hoists its sails,
   and leaves behind that cruelest of the seas.[9]   3
And I shall sing about that second realm
   where man's soul goes to purify itself
   and become worthy to ascend to Heaven.   6
Here let death's poetry arise to life,
   O Muses sacrosanct whose liege I am!
   And let Calliope[1] rise up and play   9
her sweet accompaniment in the same strain
   that pierced the wretched magpies with the truth
   of unforgivable presumptuousness.[2]   12
The tender tint of orient sapphire,
   suffusing the still reaches of the sky,
   as far as the horizon deeply clear,[3]   15
renewed my eyes' delight, now that I found
   myself free of the deathly atmosphere
   that had weighed heavy on my eyes and heart.   18
The lovely planet kindling love in man[4]
   made all the eastern sky smile with her light,
   veiling the Fish[5] that shimmered in her train.   21
Then to my right I turned to contemplate
   the other pole and there saw those four stars
   the first man saw, and no man after him.[6]   24
The heavens seemed to revel in their flames.
   O widowed Northern Hemisphere, deprived
   forever of the vision of their light![7]   27
And when I looked away from those four stars,
   turning a little toward the other pole,
   where no sign of the Wain[8] was visible,   30

---

9. The metaphor of the poem as a ship (*bark*) is traditional; the *better waters* refer to Purgatory, while *that cruelest of the seas* is Hell.   **1.** The Muse of epic poetry.   **2.** The nine daughters of Pierus—the Pierides—challenged the Muses to a singing contest and, having lost, were turned into magpies: see Ovid, *Metamorphoses* 5.   **3.** The time is just before sunrise on Easter Sunday, 1300.   **4.** Venus, the morning star, although in fact on this date Venus would have been visible only after sunrise.   **5.** The constellation Pisces, in which Venus would have been located if it had risen before the sun on this date.   **6.** Prior to their expulsion from Eden, which is located on the summit of Mount Purgatory, Adam and Eve saw four stars above the South Pole. These stars symbolize the four cardinal virtues: prudence, temperance, justice, and fortitude.   **7.** Dante is lamenting the corruption of his present time compared to the perfection of life before the Fall.   **8.** The constellation Ursa Major, which never disappears from northern skies but is not visible to an observer in the Southern Hemisphere. *The other pole:* the North Pole.

I saw near me an ancient man,[9] alone,
  whose face commanded all the reverence
  that any son could offer to his sire.   33
Long-flowing was his beard and streaked with white,
  as was his hair, which in two tresses fell
  to rest upon his chest on either side.   36
The rays of light from those four sacred stars
  struck with such radiance upon his face,
  it was as if the sun were shining there.   39
"Who are you two who challenged the blind stream[1]
  and have escaped from the eternal prison?"
  he said, moving his venerable locks.   42
"Who guided you? What served you as a lamp
  to light your way out of the heavy night
  that keeps the pit of Hell forever black?   45
Are all the laws of God's Abyss destroyed?
  Have new decisions now been made in Heaven
  so that, though damned, you come up to my cliff?"   48
My leader quickly seized me by the arm;
  his words, his touch, the way he looked at me,
  compelled my knees and brow to reverence.   51
Then he addressed him: "Not on my behalf
  have I come here; a lady sent from Heaven[2]
  asked me to guide this man along his way.   54
But since it is your will that we reveal
  the circumstances of our presence here,
  how can my will deny yours what it asks?   57
This man has not yet seen his final hour,
  although so close to it his folly brought him
  that little time was left to change his ways.   60
So I was sent to help him, as I said;
  there was no other way to save his soul
  than by my guiding him along this road.   63
Already I have shown him all the Damned;
  I want to show him now the souls of those
  who purge themselves of guilt in your domain.   66
How we came here would take too long to tell;
  from Heaven comes the power that has served
  to lead him here to see and hear you now.   69
May it please you to welcome him—he goes
  in search of freedom, and how dear that is,
  the man who gives up life for it well knows.   72
You know, you found death sweet in Utica
  for freedom's sake; there you put off that robe
  which will be radiant on the Great Day.[3]   75
We have not broken Heaven's timeless laws.
  This man still lives; Minòs does not bind me;[4]

---

9. Cato (95–46 B.C.E.), a Roman known for his uncompromising morality and love of liberty; rather than submit to what he saw as Julius Caesar's tyranny, he committed suicide in Utica, a city in North Africa. Dante is here influenced by Virgil's treatment of Cato in the underworld, where he is presented not as a suicide but as the lawgiver to the righteous (*Aeneid* 6).   1. Lethe (see *Inferno* 34.130–32).   2. Beatrice.   3. *That robe* is the body, which will be glorified in its resurrection on Judgment Day.   4. See *Inferno* 5.4.

I come from that same Round where the chaste eyes   78
of your dear Marcia[5] still plead with your soul,
 O blessed heart, to hold her as your own;
 for love of her, then, bend your will to ours,   81
allow us to go through your seven realms,
 and I shall tell her how you have been kind—
 if you will let me speak your name below."   84
"Marcia was so enchanting to my eyes,"
 he answered then, "that while I was alive,
 there was no wish of hers I would not grant.   87
She dwells beyond the evil river now,
 and can no longer move me by that law
 decreed upon the day I issued forth.[6]   90
But if a heavenly lady, as you say,
 moves and directs you, why your flattery?
 Ask in her name, there is no need for more.   93
Go with this man, see that you gird his waist
 with a smooth reed;[7] take care to bathe his face
 till every trace of filth has disappeared,   96
for it would not be fitting that he go
 with vision clouded by the mists of Hell,
 to face the first of Heaven's ministers.   99
Around this little island at its base,
 down there, just where the waves break on the shore,
 you will find rushes growing in soft sand.   102
No other plant producing leaves or stalk
 that hardens could survive in such a place—
 only the reeds that yield to buffeting.   105
When you are ready to begin to scale
 the mountainside, do not come back this way;
 the rising sun will show you where to climb."   108
With that he vanished. From my knees I rose,
 and silent, drawing closer to my guide,
 I looked into his eyes. He said to me: 111
"Follow my footsteps; now we must turn back,
 for over there the plain begins to slope,
 descending gently to the shore below."   114
The dawn was gaining ground, putting to flight
 the last hour of the night; I recognized,
 far off, the rippling waters of the sea.   117
We made our way along that lonely plain
 like men who seek the right path they have lost,
 counting each step a loss till it is found.   120
When we had reached a place where the cool shade
 allowed the dew to linger on the slope,
 resisting a while longer the sun's rays,   123
my master placed both of his widespread hands

---

5. Cato's wife, now in Limbo (see *Inferno* 4.128); according to a story told by the Roman poet Lucan (C.E. 39–65), Cato ceded Marcia to his friend Hortensius, but on Hortensius's death Marcia's entreaty to Cato that he remarry her was granted. **6.** Cato was freed during the Harrowing of Hell (see *Inferno* 4.52) and is now unmoved by the sufferings of those left behind. *The evil river*: Acheron. **7.** The *reed* is a symbol of humility.

gently upon the tender grass, and I,
  who understood what his intention was,
offered my tear-stained face to him, and he   126
  made my face clean, restoring its true color,
  once buried underneath the dirt of Hell.   129
At last we touched upon the lonely shore
  that never yet has seen its waters sailed
  by one who then returned to tell the tale.   132
There, as another willed, he girded me.
  Oh, miracle! When he pulled out the reed,
  immediately a second humble plant   135
sprang up from where the first one had been picked.

CANTO II

*As the sun rises, Dante and Virgil are still standing at the water's edge and wondering
which road to take in order to ascend the mountain of Purgatory, when the Pilgrim sees
a reddish glow moving across the water. The light approaches at an incredible speed,
and eventually they are able to discern the wings of an angel. The angel is the miraculous
pilot of a ship containing souls of the Redeemed, who are singing the psalm* In exitu
Israël de Aegypto. *At a sign from the angel boatsman, these souls disembark, only to
roam about on the shore. Apparently, they are strangers, and, mistaking Virgil and Dante
for familiars of the place, they ask them which road leads up the mountainside. Virgil
answers that they, too, are pilgrims, only recently arrived. At this point some of the souls
realize that the Pilgrim is still alive, and they stare at him in fascination. Recognizing
a face that he knows in this crowd of souls, Dante tries three times in vain to embrace
the shade of his old friend Casella, a musician; then he asks Casella for a song and, as
he sings, all the souls are held spellbound. Suddenly the Just Old Man, Cato, appears
to disperse the rapt crowd, sternly rebuking them for their negligence and exhorting
them to run to the mountain to begin their ascent.*

The sun was touching the horizon now,[8]
  the highest point of whose meridian arc
  was just above Jerusalem; and Night,   3
revolving always opposite to him,
  rose from the Ganges with the Scales that fall
  out of her hand when she outweighs the day.   6
Thus, where we were, Aurora's lovely face
  with a vermilion flush on her white cheeks
  was aging in a glow of golden light.   9
We were still standing at the water's edge,
  wondering about the road ahead, like men
  whose thoughts go forward while their bodies stay,   12
when, suddenly, I saw, low in the west
  (like the red glow of Mars that burns at dawn
  through the thick haze that hovers on the sea),   15
a light—I hope to see it come again!—
  moving across the waters at a speed
  faster than any earthly flight could be.   18

8. The opening nine lines designate the time by reference to *Jerusalem* (where the sun is setting), *the
Ganges* (where it is midnight, and where the constellation Libra—*the Scales*—is in the sky), and Mount
Purgatory (where the dawn—*Aurora*—is gradually reddening).

I turned in wonder to my guide, and then,
  when I looked back at it again, the light
  was larger and more brilliant than before, 21
and there appeared, on both sides of this light,
  a whiteness indefinable, and then,
  another whiteness grew beneath the shape. 24
My guide was silent all the while, but when
  the first two whitenesses turned into wings,
  and he saw who the steersman was, he cried: 27
"Fall to your knees, fall to your knees! Behold
  the angel of the Lord! And fold your hands.
  Expect to see more ministers like him. 30
See how he scorns to use man's instruments;
  he needs no oars, no sails, only his wings
  to navigate between such distant shores. 33
See how he has them pointing up to Heaven:
  he fans the air with these immortal plumes
  that do not moult as mortal feathers do." 36
Closer and closer to our shore he came,
  brighter and brighter shone the bird of God,
  until I could no longer bear the light, 39
and bowed my head. He steered straight to the shore,
  his boat so swift and light upon the wave,
  it left no sign of truly sailing there; 42
and the celestial pilot stood astern
  with blessedness inscribed upon his face.
  More than a hundred souls were in his ship: 45
In exitu Israël de Aegypto,[9]
  they all were singing with a single voice,
  chanting it verse by verse until the end. 48
The angel signed them with the holy cross,
  and they rushed from the ship onto the shore;
  he disappeared, swiftly, as he had come. 51
The souls left there seemed strangers to this place:
  they roamed about, while looking all around,
  endeavoring to understand new things. 54
The sun, which with its shafts of light had chased
  the Goat out of the heavens' highest field,[1]
  was shooting rays of day throughout the sky, 57
when those new souls looked up to where we were,
  and called to us: "If you should know the road
  that leads up to the mountainside, show us." 60
And Virgil answered them: "You seem to think
  that we are souls familiar with this place,
  but we, like all of you, are pilgrims here; 63
we just arrived, not much ahead of you,
  but by a road which was so rough and hard—

9. "When Israel went out of Egypt" (Latin). This is the first verse of Psalm 113 (114 in Protestant Bibles), which is a song of thanksgiving for the liberation of the Israelites from Egypt. Christians understood this liberation as prefiguring the salvation of sinners through Christ. That the day is Easter Sunday gives the psalm special relevance. 1. The constellation Capricorn can now not be seen because of the growing light.

to climb this mountain now will be like play." 66
Those souls who noticed that my body breathed,
   and realized that I was still alive,
   in their amazement turned a deathly pale. 69
Just as a crowd, greedy for news, surrounds
   the messenger who bears the olive branch,
   and none too shy to elbow-in his way, 72
so all the happy souls of these Redeemed
   stared at my face, forgetting, as it were,
   the way to go to make their beauty whole. 75
One of these souls pushed forward, arms outstretched,
   and he appeared so eager to embrace me
   that his affection moved me to show mine. 78
O empty shades, whose human forms seem real!
   Three times I clasped my hands around his form,
   as many times they came back to my breast.[2] 81
I must have been the picture of surprise,
   for he was smiling as he drew away,
   and I plunged forward still in search of him. 84
Then, gently, he suggested I not try,
   and by his voice I knew who this shade was;
   I begged him stay and speak to me awhile. 87
"As once I loved you in my mortal flesh,
   without it now I love you still," he said.
   "Of course I'll stay. But tell me why you're here." 90
"I make this journey now, O my Casella,
   hoping one day to come back here again,"[3]
   I said. "But how did you lose so much time?" 93
He answered: "I cannot complain if he
   who, as he pleases, picks his passengers,
   often refused to take me in his boat, 96
for that Just Will is always guiding his.[4]
   But for the last three months, indulgently,
   he has been taking all who wish to cross;[5] 99
so, when I went to seek the shore again,
   where Tiber's waters turn to salty sea,[6]
   benignly, he accepted me aboard. 102
Now, back again he flies to Tiber's mouth,
   which is the meeting place of all the dead,
   except for those who sink to Acheron's shore."[7] 105
"If no new law prevents remembering
   or practicing those love songs that once brought
   peace to my restless longings in the world," 108
I said, "pray sing, and give a little rest
   to my poor soul which, burdened by my flesh,

---

2. In his visit to the underworld in book 6 of the *Aeneid*, Aeneas also tries three times to embrace his father Anchisës.   3. He journeys now so that after death he may return to Purgatory. *Casella*, a Florentine musician, was said to have set some of Dante's lyrics to music. The question that follows assumes that Casella died well before the present moment.   4. The angel who chooses the souls to cross in his boat is directed by God.   5. Pope Boniface proclaimed 1300—the year of the poem's action—a Jubilee or Holy Year, when those making pilgrimage to Rome were granted release from punishments for their sins (see *Inferno* 18, 28). Dante follows popular belief in assuming that this grant applies to the souls awaiting transport to Purgatory as well as to the living.   6. At Ostia, where the Tiber enters the sea.   7. Hell.

has climbed this far and is exhausted now."   111
Amor che ne la mente mi ragiona.[8]
    began the words of his sweet melody—
    their sweetness still is sounding in my soul.   114
My master and myself and all those souls
    that came with him were deeply lost in joy,
    as if that sound were all that did exist.   117
And while we stood enraptured by the sound
    of those sweet notes—a sudden cry: "What's this,
    you lazy souls?" It was the Just Old Man.[9]   120
"What negligence to stand around like this!
    Run to the mountain, shed that slough which still
    does not let God be manifest to you!"   123
Just as a flock of pigeons in a field
    peacefully feeding on the grain and tares,
    no longer strutting proud of how they look,   126
immediately abandon all their food,
    flying away, seized by a greater need—
    if something should occur that startles them—   129
so did that new-formed flock of souls give up
    their feast of song, and seek the mountainside,
    rushing to find a place they hoped was there.   132
And we were just as quick to take to flight.

*   *   *

CANTO XXI

As the Pilgrim and Virgil walk along the Terrace of the Avaricious, a shade appears and speaks to them. Virgil explains that the Pilgrim is still alive, and he relates the nature and purpose of their journey, finally asking the shade why the mountain has just trembled. The shade explains that the mountain of Purgatory is not subject to the vicissitudes of Nature such as rain, wind, and lightning, but that when a soul feels that the time of its purification has come to an end and it is ready to ascend to Heaven, then the mountain shakes and voices shout praises to God. The shade speaking is the one who has just experienced this release after more than five hundred years of purgation. He identifies himself as Statius, the author of the Thebaid *and the unfinished* Achilleid. *Statius claims that he has derived his poetic inspiration from the* Aeneid, *and he expresses his ardent wish to have lived when Virgil was alive, and to have met the great poet. At these words the Pilgrim smiles knowingly, and with his guide's permission, reveals to Statius that he is standing in the presence of his mentor. Forgetting himself, Statius bends down to embrace Virgil's knees, but is gently reminded by that prince of poets that they are only empty shades.*

The natural thirst which nothing satisfies
    except that water begged for long ago
    by the poor woman of Samaria
tormented me,[1] and haste was urging me   3
    along the crowded path, and I was still

8. "Love that speaks to me in my mind" is the first line of a lyric that Dante included in his prose philosophical work, the *Convivio*, which he left incomplete.   9. Cato.   1. The thirst for knowledge can be quenched only by divine revelation. In the previous canto Dante has heard a cry of exultation and felt Mount Purgatory shake; it is the meaning of these events that he wishes to know. For the woman of Samaria, see John 4.5–15.

grieving at the just pain those souls must pay,   6
when suddenly—just as we read in Luke
  that Christ, new-risen from the tomb, appeared
  to the two men on the Emmaus road[2]—   9
a shade appeared! He had come from behind
  while we were trying not to step on shades,[3]
  quite unaware of him until he spoke: 12
"May God, my brothers, give you peace." At that,
  we quickly turned around, and Virgil then
  responded to his words appropriately,   15
and said: "May God's True Court which sentenced me
  to eternal banishment, lead you in peace
  into the Congregation of the Blest."   18
"What's that?" he said as we kept forging on.
  "If you are souls whom God will not receive,
  who let you climb His stairway this far up?"   21
And then my teacher said: "If you observe
  those marks the angel has traced on his brow,
  you'll see that he must dwell among the Just.[4]   24
But she who labors spinning day and night,
  had not spun out for him the flax which Clotho
  packs on her distaff for each one of us;[5]   27
therefore, his soul, sister to yours and mine,
  in coming up, could not come by itself,
  because it does not see as our eyes do.   30
And so I was brought up from Hell's wide throat
  to serve him as a guide, and guide I shall
  as far as my own knowledge will permit.   33
But can you tell me why the mountain shook
  so hard just now, and why all of the souls
  down to its marshy base, cried out as one?"   36
My leader's question pierced the needle's eye
  of my desire, and with the eager hope
  that this aroused, I felt my thirst relieved.   39
The shade said: "Sacred laws that rule this mount
  will not let anything take place that is
  uncustomary or irregular.   42
This place is not subject to any change:
  what Heaven takes from itself into itself,
  and nothing else, can serve as cause up here;[6]   45
therefore no rain, no hail, no snow can fall,
  nor dew nor hoarfrost form at any point
  beyond the three-step stairway down below.[7]   48
There are no clouds, misty or dense, no sign
  of lightning or of Thaumas' daughter,[8] she

---

2. Luke 24.13–17.   3. The avaricious are punished by being bound prone to the Earth since they worshiped earthly things in life.   4. Before Dante entered Purgatory proper, an angel traced seven Ps upon his forehead, one for each deadly sin (*peccatum* in Latin): see *Purgatorio* 9.112–14. The marks disappear one by one as he climbs the mountain and passes through each of the seven terraces appointed for the purgation of a sin.   5. According to classical mythology, the three Fates determine the span of a person's life: Clotho holds the spool, Lachesis spins the thread, and Atropos cuts it at the predestined time. 6. Purgatory is free from any earthly influence, and therefore any change must be caused by motion from above.   7. To reach the gate of Purgatory proper one must climb three steps, which represent the three stages of penance: contrition of heart, confession of mouth, and satisfaction by deeds.   8. Iris, goddess of the rainbow.

who often moves from place to place below; 51
nor can dry vapors rise beyond the height
  of those three steps of which I just now spoke,
  whereon Saint Peter's vicar[9] rests his feet. 54
Quakes may occur below, slight or severe,
  but tremors caused by winds hid in the earth
  (I know not why) have never reached this high. 57
Up here the mountain trembles when some soul
  feels itself pure enough to stand erect
  or start at once to climb—then, comes the shout. 60
The will to rise, alone, proves purity:
  once freed, it takes possession of the soul
  and wills the soul to change its company. 63
It willed to climb before, but the desire
  High Justice set against it, inspired it
  to wish to suffer—as once it wished to sin. 66
And I, who for five hundred years and more,
  have lain here in my pain, felt only now
  will free to raise me to a higher sill. 69
That's why you felt the quake and why you heard
  the pious dwellers on the mount praise God.
  May He soon call them up to be with Him." 72
This was his explanation. And my joy
  was inexpressible: the more the thirst,
  the more enjoyable becomes the drink. 75
And my wise leader: "Now I see what net
  holds you bound here, and how the mesh is torn,
  why the mount shakes, why you rejoice as one. 78
Now, if it please you, I would like to know
  who you once were, and learn from your own words
  why you have lain so many centuries here."[1] 81
"During the rule of the good Titus, who,
  assisted by the King of Kings, avenged
  the wounds that poured forth blood which Judas sold,[2] 84
I bore the title that endures the most
  and which is honored most," that soul replied;
  "renown I had, not yet the Christian faith.[3] 87
The spirit of my verses was so sweet
  that from Toulouse,[4] Rome called me to herself,
  and judged me worthy of the myrtle crown. 90
My name is Statius, still well known on earth.
  I sang of Thebes, then of Achilles' might,
  but found that second weight too great to bear. 93
The spark that kindled my poetic ardor
  came from the sacred flame that set on fire
  more than a thousand poets: I mean the *Aeneid*. 96
That was the mother of my poetry,

9. The angel who guards the entrance to Purgatory and who marked Dante's forehead.   1. The spirit reveals himself to be Statius (d. 96 C.E.), a Roman poet who composed an epic on the story of Thebes called the *Thebaid* and an unfinished epic on Achilles, the *Achilleid*.   2. The destruction of Jerusalem in 70 C.E. by the Roman Emperor Titus in response to a rebellion was understood by Christians to be a divine punishment for the crucifixion of Christ.   3. He was a poet but not yet a Christian.   4. A city in southern France; Statius actually came from Naples, but Dante is following a medieval tradition.

the nurse that gave it suck. Without that poem,
   my verses would have not been worth a thing.   99
And if only I could have been alive
   when Virgil lived, I would consent to spend
   an extra year of exile on the mount."   102
At these words Virgil turned to me. His look
   told me in silence: "Silence!" But the power
   of a man's will is often powerless: 105
laughter and tears follow so close upon
   the passions that provoke them that the more
   sincere the man, the less they obey his will.   108
I smiled and unsmiled quicker than a blink,
   but he stopped speaking; staring straight at me,
   into the eyes, where secrets are betrayed: 111
"So may your toiling win you grace," he said,
   "tell me the reason for your smile just now—
   that smile that quickly came and quickly went."   114
Here I am caught between opposing sides:
   the one tells me be quiet, the other bids
   me to speak up. And so, I sigh. My guide   117
perfectly understood: "Don't be afraid
   to speak," he said: "speak to him, answer now
   the question he has asked so earnestly."   120
"You seem to find my smiling very strange,"
   I said to him, "O ancient spirit, but
   I have to tell you something stranger still: 123
This shade here who directs my eyes to Heaven
   is the poet Virgil, who bequeathed to you
   the power to sing the deeds of men and gods.   126
In truth, the only reason for my smile,
   is that you chose to mention Virgil here:
   your very words are guilty of my smile."   129
Already he was bending to embrace
   my teacher's feet, but Virgil: "Brother, no!
   You are a shade; it is a shade you see."   132
And Statius, rising: "Now you understand
   how much my love for you burns deep in me,
   when I forget about our emptiness   135
and deal with shadows as with solid things."

FROM CANTO XXII

*Leaving the Fifth Terrace, the Pilgrim and Virgil, now accompanied by Statius, are
directed to the next ledge by an angel who removes another P from the Pilgrim's forehead
and pronounces those blessed who thirst for righteousness. Virgil tells Statius that he
has felt a great deal of good will toward him ever since Juvenal had come down to Limbo
with the report of Statius's love and admiration for Virgil. But he is puzzled as to how
such a magnanimous spirit could find room in its heart for avarice. Statius explains that
his sin was not Avarice, but Prodigality, and that whenever two sins are the immediate
opposite of one another, they are purged together on the same terrace of the mountain
of Purgatory. Virgil then asks Statius how he came to be a Christian, and Statius replies
that it was Virgil's Fourth Eclogue that eventually led him to give ear to the Christian
preachers. Once converted, however, he kept his faith a secret, and for this lack of zeal
was consigned to spend four hundred years on the Terrace of the Slothful.*

By now we had already left behind
　　the angel who directs to the Sixth Round
　　and from my brow erased another scar,[5]　　　　3
saying that all who looked for righteousness
　　are blest—omitting the *esuriunt*,
　　and predicating only *sitiunt*.[6]　　　　　　6
And I, lighter than I had felt before
　　at any other stairs,[7] moved easily
　　upward, behind those swiftly climbing shades.　9
Now, Virgil was already speaking: "Love,
　　kindled by virtue, always kindles love,
　　if the first flame is clearly visible;[8]　　　12
thus, ever since the day that Juvenal[9]
　　came down to Hell's Limbo to be with us,
　　and told me of the love you felt for me,　　15
I have felt more good will toward you, more than
　　was felt toward any person not yet seen;
　　and so, these stairs will seem much shorter now.　18
But tell me—speak to me as to a friend,
　　and as a friend, forgive me if I seem
　　too bold in slackening decorum's reins—　　21
how could your heart find room for avarice,
　　with that abundant store of sound, good sense
　　which you acquired with such diligence?"　　24
These words of Virgil brought to Statius' lips
　　a briefly lingering smile; then he replied:
　　"All you have said reveals your love for me.　27
Appearances will often, it is true,
　　give rise to false assumptions, when the truth
　　to be revealed is hidden from our eyes.　　30
Your question makes it clear to me that you
　　believe my sin on earth was Avarice—
　　perhaps because you found me where you did.　33
In truth, I had no part of Avarice;
　　in fact, too little! The sin I purged below,
　　thousands of months, was Prodigality.[1]　　36
And if I had not come to change my ways
　　while meditating on those lines you wrote,
　　where you, enraged by human nature, cry:　39
'To what extremes, O cursèd lust for gold
　　will you not drive man's appetite?'[2] I would
　　be rolling weights now in the dismal jousts.[3]　42
But when I understood how hands could spread
　　their wings too wide in spending, then that sin,

5. The *scar* is a *P* for avarice, the sin cleansed on the previous terrace.　　6. The angel quotes the beginning of the Fourth Beatitude from the Sermon on the Mount, "Blessed are they which do hunger and thirst after righteousness: for they shall be filled" (Matthew 5.6). He mentions only "thirst" (*sitiunt* in Latin), omitting hunger, which will appear at the end of the journey through the sixth terrace, where gluttony is purged. 7. Dante grows lighter as he is gradually relieved of the sins, symbolized by the *P*s on his forehead, that weigh him down.　　8. Virtuous love, such as Statius displayed at the end of canto 21, will elicit a similar response.　　9. A Roman poet, contemporary with Statius but who outlived him (dying about 140 C.E.), located with Virgil in Limbo, as described in *Inferno* 4.　　1. Prodigality is a vice opposite to Avarice but its counterpart: both involve an excess in the use of money; in *Inferno* 7 the avaricious and the prodigal are punished together.　　2. Statius is quoting from *Aeneid* 3.　　3. Be punished in the fourth circle of Hell, described in *Inferno* 7.

and all my others, I repented of. 45
How many shall rise bald the Final Day
    through ignorance of this vice, forbidding them
    repentance during life or on death's bed?[4] 48
And know that when the vice of any sin
    is the rebuttal of its opposite,
    the two of them wither together here. 51
So, though to purge myself I spent my time
    among those souls who weep for Avarice,
    my sin was just the opposite of theirs."
"Now, when you sang about the bitter strife 54
    of the twin sources of Jocasta's grief,"[5]
    the bard of the *Bucolics*[6] said to him, 57
"from what you wrote in Clio's[7] company,
    it does not seem that you were faithful then
    to that faith without which virtue is vain.[8] 60
If this be so, tell me—what heavenly sun
    or earthly beam lit up your course so that
    you could set sail behind the Fisherman."[9] 63
Statius said: "It was you directed me
    to drink Parnassus' waters[1]—it was you
    whose radiance revealed the way to God. 66
You were the lonely traveller in the dark
    who holds his lamp behind him, shedding light
    not for himself but to make others wise; 69
for you once wrote: 'The world is born again;
    Justice returns, and the first age of man,
    and a new progeny descends from heaven.'[2] 72
Through you I was a poet, through you, a Christian.
    And now, to show you better what I mean,
    I shall fill in my outline with more color. 75
By then, the world was laboring in the birth
    of the true faith, sown by the messengers
    of the Eternal Kingdom;[3] and your words, 78
which I just quoted now, so harmonized
    with what the new preachers were saying then,
    that I would often go to hear them speak. 81
These men became so holy in my eyes
    that when Domitian[4] persecuted them,
    I wept, as they wept in their suffering, 84
and, for as long as I remained alive,
    I helped them, and their righteous way of life

---

4. The close-cropped heads of the prodigal are described in *Inferno* 7.57.   5. Statius's *Thebaid* deals with the history of Thebes: *Jocasta's* husband, Laius, was unwittingly killed by their son, Oedipus, who then—again in ignorance—married Laius's widow, Oedipus's own mother. Their sons, Polynices and Eteocles, imprisoned their father in a dungeon and then fought over the throne of Thebes in a war in which they killed each other. It is this fratricidal war, in which Jocasta lost both her sons at once, to which Virgil refers.   6. Virgil's *Bucolics* contain his *Georgics* and *Eclogues*, which is quoted in line 70.   7. The Muse of history, whom Statius invokes in the *Thebaid*.   8. I.e., Christianity.   9. I.e., followed Peter, a fisherman who became a fisher of men (see Mark 1.17).   1. Dante follows a tradition that takes *Parnassus*, a mountain in Greece, as the home of the Muses.   2. A slightly altered citation from Virgil's *Fourth Eclogue*. A pastoral poem written about 40 B.C.E., it celebrated the birth of the son of an important Roman politician but was taken by medieval Christians as a prophecy of the birth of Christ.   3. The apostles. 4. Roman emperor, C.E. 81–91, thought by early Christian historians to have persecuted Christians although there is little evidence for this.

taught me to scorn all other faiths but theirs.
Before I brought the Greeks to Theban streams
   with my poetic art,[5] I was baptized,
   but was a secret Christian out of fear,
pretending to be pagan many years;
   and for this lack of zeal, I had to run
   four hundred years on the Fourth Circle.[6] Now,
please tell me, you who did remove the veil
   that once concealed from me the good I praise,
   tell me, while there is still some time to climb,
where is our ancient Terence, do you know?
   And Plautus, and Caecilius and Varius?[7]
   Have they been damned? If so, where are they lodged?"
"They all, along with Persius and me
   and others," said my guide, "are with that Greek
   the Muses suckled more than all the rest,
in the First Round of Hell's unlighted jail.
   We often talk about the mountain slope
   where our nine nurses[8] dwell eternally.
Euripides walks with us; Antiphon,
   Simonides, and Agathon are there,
   and other Greeks who wear the laurel crown.[9]
With us are many of your people too:
   Antigone, Deïphyle, Argia,
   Ismene, sad as she has ever been,
and she who showed Langia to the Greeks,
   and Thetis, and the daughter of Tiresias,
   Deïdamia with her sisters, too."[1]
The poets now were free of walls and stairs,
   both of them standing silent on the ledge,
   eager again to gaze at everything.
Already the four handmaids of the day[2]
   were left behind, and at the chariot-pole,
   the fifth was tilting up the blazing tip,
when my guide said: "I think we ought to move
   with our right shoulders to the outer edge,
   the way we always have gone round this mount."[3]
So, habit was our guide there, and we went
   our way with much less hesitation now,
   since worthy Statius gave us his assent.
They walked ahead and I, behind, alone,
   was paying close attention to their words,
   which taught me things about the art of verse.[4]

87

90

93

96

99

102

105

108

111

114

117

120

123

126

129

*   *   *

5. The *Thebaid* describes how six Greek rulers joined with Polynices to invade Thebes and topple Eteocles from the throne.   6. Where Sloth, which is the cause of the failure to perform religious duties, is purged. 7. These men and *Persius* (line 100) are Roman poets now in Limbo with Homer (lines 101–102). 8. The Muses walk on Mount Parnassus.   9. Greek dramatists and poets.   1. Characters from Statius's *Thebaid* and *Achilleid*, which Dante considered historical epics.   2. The hours, the fifth of which is guiding the chariot of the sun: it is between 10 and 11 A.M.   3. Mount Purgatory is climbed by turning to the right; the travelers descended into Hell by turning to the left.   4. The canto continues with a new episode, not relevant to the literary issues that have so far occupied it.

FROM CANTO XXIV

The pilgrim and Virgil are now on the sixth terrace, where Gluttony is punished. Among other sinners, they meet Bonagiunta Orbicciana, a Florentine poet who was acquainted with Dante. This selection from this canto begins with Bonagiunta citing one of Dante's most famous sonnets.

"But, tell me, do I not see standing here
  him who brought forth the new poems that begin:
  'Ladies who have intelligence of Love.'"[5]   51
I said to him, "I am one who, when Love
  inspires me, takes careful note and then,
  gives form to what he dictates in my heart."   54
"My brother, now I see," he said, "the knot
  that held Guittone and the Notary
  and me back from the sweet new style[6] I hear!   57
Now, I see very clearly how your wings
  fly straight behind the dictates of that Love—
  this, certainly, could not be said of ours;   60
and no one who examines the two styles
  can clarify the difference more than I."
  Then, pleased with what he said, he said no more.   63

*   *   *

FROM CANTO XXVI

Dante and Virgil are now on the seventh terrace, where Lechery is punished. Here they meet another of Dante's literary contemporaries and continue the discussion of literary issues.

As for my name, I can fulfill your wish:
  I am Guido Guinizelli[7]—here so soon,
  for I repented long before I died."   93
As King Lycurgus raged with grief, two sons
  discovered their lost mother and rejoiced[8]—
  I felt the same (though more restrained) to hear   96
that spirit name himself—father of me
  and father of my betters, all who wrote
  a sweet and graceful poetry of love.   99
I heard no more, I did not speak, I walked
  deep in my thoughts, my eyes fixed on his shade;
  the flames kept me from coming close to him.   102
At last my eyes were satisfied. And then
  I spoke, convincing him of my deep wish
  to serve him in whatever way I could.[9]   105
He answered me: "What I just heard you say
  has made a deep impression on my mind,

5. The first line of the first lyric in Dante's *New Life*, which tells the story in poetry and prose of his transformation by his love for Beatrice.   6. The *dolce stil novo* that Dante saw as characterizing his own poetry and that was first defined for him by Guido Guinizelli, whom he will meet in canto 26; see above, p. 1382. The *Notary* (Giacomo da Lentini) and Guittone d'Arezzo, like Bonagiunta, were Italian poets of the generation before Dante's.   7. Bolognese poet (d. ca. 1276), considered the greatest Italian poet prior to Dante. A poem by him is included in *Medieval Lyrics: A Selection* (pp. 1411–12).   8. In an episode in Statius's *Thebaid*, a woman condemned to death by the warrior Lycurgus is saved at the last moment by the arrival of her twin sons.   9. Dante here swears an oath to Guinizelli to which the reader is not given access.

which even Lethe[1] cannot wash away.   108
But if what you have told me is the truth,
  now tell me what it is that makes you show
  in words and looks this love you have for me?"   111
And I to him: "Those graceful poems of yours,
  which, for as long as our tongue serves for verse,
  will render precious even the ink you used."   114
"My brother, I can show you now," he said
  (he pointed to a spirit up ahead)[2]
  "a better craftsman of his mother tongue.   117
Poets of love, writers of tales in prose—
  better than all of them he was! They're fools
  who think him of Limoges a greater poet![3]   120
They judge by reputation, not by truth,
  their minds made up before they know the rules
  of reason and the principles of art.   123
Guittone[4] was judged this way in the past;
  many praised him and him alone—though, now,
  most men have been won over to the truth.   126
But now, if that high privilege be yours
  of climbing to the cloister, there where Christ
  is Abbot of the holy college, then,   129
please say a *Paternoster*[5] for me there—
  at least the part appropriate for us,
  who are by now delivered from all evil."   132
Then, to make room for someone else, perhaps,
  he disappeared into the depths of fire
  the way fish seeking deeper waters fade.   135
I moved up toward the shade just pointed out,
  and told him my desire had prepared
  a gracious place of welcome for his name.   138
He readily and graciously replied:[6]
  "Tan m'abellis vostre cortes deman,
  Qu'ieu no me puesc no voill a vos cobrire.   141
Ieu sui Arnaut, que plor e vau cantan;
  consiros vei la passada folor,
  e vei jausen lo joi qu'esper, denan.   144
Ara vos prec, per aquella valor
  que vos guida al som de l'escalina,
  sovenha vos a temps de ma dolor!"   147
Then in the purifying flames he hid.

FROM CANTO XXVII

The sun is near setting when the poets leave the souls of the Lustful and encounter the angel of Chastity, singing the beatitude "Blessed are the Pure of Heart." The angel tells them that they can go no farther without passing through the flames, but, numbed with

---

1. The river of forgetfulness that the fully purged souls will pass through in order to renounce their earthly lives.   2. Guinizzelli is indicating Arnaut Daniel (d. ca. 1210), a Provençal poet. A poem by him is included in *Medieval Lyrics: A Selection* (pp. 1405–6)   3. The reference is to Giraut de Borneil (d. ca. 1220), another Provençal poet.   4. See *Purgatorio* 24.56.   5. The Lord's Prayer.   6. Arnaut speaks not in Italian but in Provençal. His speech can be translated: "Your elegant request so pleases me, / I could not possibly conceal my name. / I am Arnaut, singing now through my tears, / regretfully recalling my past follies / and joyfully anticipating joy. / I beg you, in the name of the great power / guiding you to the summit of the stairs, / remember in good times my suffering here."

fear, the Pilgrim hesitates for a long time. Finally Virgil prevails upon him and they make the crossing through the excruciating heat. As they emerge on the other side, they hear the invitation "Come O ye blessed of my Father," and an angel exhorts them to climb as long as there is still daylight. But soon the sun sets and the poets are overcome by sleep. Toward morning the Pilgrim dreams of Leah and Rachel, who represent the active and contemplative lives, respectively. When he awakes, he is refreshed and eager and races up the remaining steps. In the last few lines, included here, Virgil describes the moral development achieved by the Pilgrim—such that he no longer needs his guidance. These are the last words that Virgil will speak in the poem.

* * *

And now, before the splendor of the dawn
   (more welcomed by the homebound pilgrim now,
    the closer he awakes to home each day),   111
night's shadows disappeared on every side;
   my sleep fled with them: I rose to my feet,
    for my great teachers were already up.   114
"That precious fruit which all men eagerly
   go searching for on many different boughs
    will give, today, peace to your hungry soul."[7]   117
These were the words that Virgil spoke to me,
   and never was a more auspicious gift
    received, or given, with more joyfulness.   120
Growing desire, desire to be up there,
   was rising in me: with every step I took
    I felt my wings were growing for the flight.   123
Once the stairs, swiftly climbed, were all behind
   and we were standing on the topmost step,
    Virgil addressed me, fixing his eyes on mine: 126
"You now have seen, my son, the temporal
   and the eternal fire,[8] you've reached the place
    where my discernment now has reached its end. 129
I led you here with skill and intellect;
   from here on, let your pleasure be your guide:
    the narrow ways, the steep, are far below.   132
Behold the sun shining upon your brow,
   behold the tender grass, the flowers, the trees,
    which, here, the earth produces of itself.   135
Until those lovely eyes rejoicing come,
   which, tearful, once urged me to come to you,[9]
    you may sit here, or wander, as you please.   138
Expect no longer words or signs from me.
   Now is your will upright, wholesome and free,
    and not to heed its pleasure would be wrong: 141
I crown and miter you lord of yourself!"

FROM CANTO XXX

Dante has arrived at the Earthly Paradise on the top of Mount Purgatory. There Beatrice appears. The Pilgrim turns to Virgil to confess his overpowering emotions, only to find

7. On this day Dante will enter the Earthly Paradise and find Beatrice, who will conduct him through Paradise.   8. Purgatory and Hell.   9. See *Inferno* 2.55–74.

that Virgil has disappeared! Beatrice speaks sternly to Dante, calling him by name and reprimanding him for having wasted his God-given talents, wandering from the path that leads to Truth. So hopeless, in fact, was his case, to such depths did he sink, that the journey to see the souls of the Damned in Hell was the only way left of setting him back on the road to salvation.

* * *

Sometimes, as day approaches, I have seen
   all of the eastern sky a glow of rose,
     the rest of heaven beautifully clear,
the sun's face rising in a misty veil   24
   of tempering vapors that allow the eye
     to look straight at it for a longer time:
even so, within a nebula of flowers   27
   that flowed upward from angels' hands and then
     poured down, covering all the chariot,[1]
appeared a lady—over her white veil   30
   an olive crown and, under her green cloak,
     her gown, the color of eternal flame.[2]
And instantly—though many years had passed   33
   since last I stood trembling before her eyes,
     captured by adoration, stunned by awe—[3]
my soul, that could not see her perfectly,   36
   still felt, succumbing to her mystery
     and power, the strength of its enduring love.
No sooner were my eyes struck by the force   39
   of the high, piercing virtue I had known
     before I quit my boyhood years,[4] than I
turned to the left—with all the confidence   42
   that makes a child run to its mother's arms,
     when he is frightened or needs comforting—
to say to Virgil: "Not one drop of blood   45
   is left inside my veins that does not throb:
     I recognize signs of the ancient flame."[5]
But Virgil was not there. We found ourselves   48
   without Virgil, sweet father, Virgil to whom
     for my salvation I gave up my soul.[6]
All the delights around me, which were lost   51
   by our first mother,[7] could not keep my cheeks,
     once washed with dew, from being stained with tears.
"Dante,[8] though Virgil leaves you, do not weep,   54
   not yet, that is, for you shall have to weep
     from yet another wound.[9] Do not weep yet."
Just as an admiral, from bow or stern,   57
   watches his men at work on other ships,
     encouraging their earnest labors—so,   60

---

1. Beatrice appears in a chariot accompanied by messengers of eternal life.   **2.** The colors are symbolic: white signifies hope; green, faith; and red, charity.   **3.** Beatrice died in 1290, so it has been ten years since Dante saw her.   **4.** Dante was nine when he fell in love with Beatrice.   **5.** A quotation from Virgil's *Aeneid* 4; it is Dido's response upon first seeing Aeneas.   **6.** This tercet echoes Virgil's *Georgics* 4.525–27, in which Orpheus looks back and laments the loss of Eurydice.   **7.** Eve, who caused the loss of the Eden in which Dante is now located.   **8.** This is the only time Dante's name appears in the *Commedia.*   **9.** The sharp words Beatrice will now speak.

rising above the chariot's left rail
   (when I turned round, hearing my name called out,
   which of necessity I here record),   63
I saw the lady who had first appeared
   beneath the angelic festival of flowers
   gazing upon me from beyond the stream.   66
Although the veil that flowed down from her head,
   fixed by the crown made of Minerva's leaves,[1]
   still kept me from a perfect view of her,   69
I sensed the regal sternness of her face,
   as she continued in the tone of one
   who saves the sharpest words until the end: 72
"Yes, look at me! Yes, I am Beatrice!
   So, you at last have deigned to climb the mount?
   You learned at last that here lies human bliss?"   75
I lowered my head and looked down at the stream,
   but, filled with shame at my reflection there,
   I quickly fixed my eyes upon the grass.   78
I was the guilty child facing his mother,
   abject before her harshness: harsh, indeed,
   is unripe pity not yet merciful.[2]   81

*   *   *

From Paradiso

CANTO XXXIII

Dante has been led by Beatrice and other guides to the highest point of the universe, the Empyrean. The final canto of the poem begins with a prayer by Bernard of Clairvaux (1091–1153), abbot of the monastery of Clairvaux in France and one of the great spiritual leaders and mystical writers of the Middle Ages. Bernard is present here both as a mystic and because of the role his writings played in developing the cult of the Virgin Mary. St. Bernard lovingly praises the Virgin Mary and then recounts the Pilgrim's journey through Hell, Purgatory, and the celestial spheres, entreating the Virgin to clear away the obstacles from the Pilgrim's eyes so that he may behold God's glory. Bernard then signals the Pilgrim to look upward, but he has already done so, spurred on by his clearer sight. He sees the multiform world bound in a single unity with love. Then, as he gazes into the Divine Light, he sees three rings of three different colors all of which share and are bound by one and the same circumference. The first ring of color reflects the second; both reflect the third: the miracle of the Trinity. Again the poet's words begin to fail him. He fixes his eyes on the second ring of reflected light and perceives God in the image of man, but he is unable to grasp how the forms coincide. Then with a sudden flash the Pilgrim's mind is illuminated by the Truth and he feels, now that the ultimate vision has been granted him, his desire and will turning in harmony with Divine Love, "the Love that moves the sun and the other stars."

"Oh Virgin Mother, daughter of your son,
   most humble, most exalted of all creatures

---

1. These are olive leaves, sacred to Minerva, the Roman goddess of wisdom.   2. Beatrice's *pity* is *unripe* because it is not yet time for her to show it to Dante, the erring child.

chosen of God in His eternal plan,   3
you are the one who ennobled human nature
  to the extent that He did not disdain,
  Who was its Maker, to make Himself man.   6
Within your womb rekindled was the love
  that gave the warmth that did allow this flower[3]
  to come to bloom within this timeless peace.   9
For all up here you are the noonday torch
  of charity, and down on earth, for men,
  the living spring of their eternal hope.   12
Lady, you are so great, so powerful,
  that who seeks grace without recourse to you
  would have his wish fly upward without wings.   15
Not only does your loving kindness rush
  to those who ask for it, but often times
  it flows spontaneously before the plea.   18
In you is tenderness, in you is pity,
  in you munificence—in you unites
  all that is good in God's created beings.   21
This is a man who from the deepest pit
  of all the universe up to this height
  has witnessed, one by one, the lives of souls,   24
who begs you that you grant him through your grace
  the power to raise his vision higher still
  to penetrate the final blessedness.   27
And I who never burned for my own vision
  more than I burn for his, with all my prayers
  I pray you—and I pray they are enough—   30
that you through your own prayers dispel the mist
  of his mortality, that he may have
  the Sum of Joy revealed before his eyes.   33
I pray you also, Queen who can achieve
  your every wish, keep his affections sound
  once he has had the vision and returns.   36
Protect him from the stirrings of the flesh:
  you see, with Beatrice, all the Blest,
  hands clasped in prayer, are praying for my prayer."   39
Those eyes so loved and reverenced by God,
  now fixed on him who prayed, made clear to us
  how precious true devotion is to her;   42
then she looked into the Eternal Light,
  into whose being, we must believe, no eyes
  of other creatures pierce with such insight.   45
And I who was approaching now the end
  of all man's yearning, strained with all the force
  in me to raise my burning longing high.   48
Bernard then gestured to me with a smile
  that I look up, but I already was
  instinctively what he would have me be: 51
for now my vision as it grew more clear

3. In *Paradiso* 30 Dante saw the blessed souls arranged in a vast rose, to which Bernard now refers.

was penetrating more and more the Ray
  of that exalted Light of Truth Itself. 54
And from then on my vision rose to heights
  higher than words, which fail before such sight,
  and memory fails, too, at such extremes. 57
As he who sees things in a dream and wakes
  to feel the passion of the dream still there
  although no part of it remains in mind, 60
just such am I: my vision fades and all
  but ceases, yet the sweetness born of it
  I still can feel distilling in my heart: 63
so imprints on the snow fade in the sun,
  and thus the Sibyl's oracle of leaves
  was swept away and lost into the wind.[4] 66
O Light Supreme, so far beyond the reach
  of mortal understanding, to my mind
  relend now some small part of Your own Self, 69
and give to my tongue eloquence enough
  to capture just one spark of all Your glory
  that I may leave for future generations; 72
for, by returning briefly to my mind
  and sounding, even faintly, in my verse,
  more of Your might will be revealed to men. 75
If I had turned my eyes away, I think,
  from the sharp brilliance of the living Ray
  which they endured, I would have lost my senses. 78
And this, as I recall, gave me more strength
  to keep on gazing till I could unite
  my vision with the Infinite Worth I saw. 81
O grace abounding and allowing me to dare
  to fix my gaze on the Eternal Light,
  so deep my vision was consumed in It! 84
I saw how it contains within its depths
  all things bound in a single book by love
  of which creation is the scattered leaves: 87
how substance, accident, and their relation[5]
  were fused in such a way that what I now
  describe is but a glimmer of that Light. 90
I know I saw the universal form,
  the fusion of all things, for I can feel,
  while speaking now, my heart leap up in joy. 93
One instant brings me more forgetfulness
  than five and twenty centuries brought the quest
  that stunned Neptune when he saw Argo's keel.[6] 96
And so my mind was totally entranced
  in gazing deeply, motionless, intent;
  the more it saw the more it burned to see. 99

4. In *Aeneid* 3 Virgil describes how the Sibyl of Cumae writes down the future on leaves that the wind then scatters. 5. In the philosophical tradition followed by Dante, a *substance* is that which subsists in and of itself, an *accident* exists only as a quality or an attribute of a substance, and their *relation* is the way substances and accidents are bound together. 6. The voyage of Jason and the Argonauts after the golden fleece was thought to have occurred about 1300 B.C.E.; see *Inferno* 18.86–87.

And one is so transformed within that Light
   that it would be impossible to think
   of ever turning one's eyes from that sight,   102
because the good which is the goal of will
   is all collected there, and outside it
   all is defective that is perfect there.   105
Now, even in the things I do recall
   my words have no more strength than does a babe
   wetting its tongue, still at its mother's breast.   108
Not that within the Living Light there was
   more than a sole aspect of the Divine
   which always is what It has always been,   111
yet as I learned to see more, and the power
   of vision grew in me, that single aspect
   as I changed, seemed to me to change Itself.   114
Within Its depthless clarity of substance
   I saw the Great Light shine into three circles
   in three clear colors bound in one same space;[7]   117
the first seemed to reflect the next like rainbow
   on rainbow, and the third was like a flame
   equally breathed forth by the other two.   120
How my weak words fall short of my conception,
   which is itself so far from what I saw
   that "weak" is much too weak a word to use!   123
O Light Eternal fixed in Self alone,
   known only to Yourself, and knowing Self,
   You love and glow, knowing and being known!   126
That circling which, as I conceived it, shone
   in You as Your own first reflected light
   when I had looked deep into It a while,   129
seemed in Itself and in Its own Self-color
   to be depicted with man's very image.[8]
   My eyes were totally absorbed in It.   132
As the geometer who tries so hard
   to square the circle, but cannot discover,
   think as he may, the principle involved,[9]   135
so did I strive with this new mystery:
   I yearned to know how could our image fit
   into that circle, how could it conform;   138
but my own wings could not take me so high—
   then a great flash of understanding struck
   my mind, and suddenly its wish was granted.   141
At this point power failed high fantasy[1]
   but, like a wheel in perfect balance turning,
   I felt my will and my desire impelled   144
by the Love that moves the sun and the other stars.[2]

7. Signifying the Trinity.   8. Dante seems to see a human image in the center of the Godhead.   9. The problem of constructing a square equal in area to a circle is a proverbially insoluble mathematical problem. 1. By *fantasy* Dante means the capacity of the mind to form images; it is *high* because it is capable of representing in visible form invisible truths.   2. As in the *Inferno* and the *Purgatorio*, the last word of the *Paradiso* is *stars*, returning us to the perspective of the human gazing up at that which is beyond the human.

GIOVANNI BOCCACCIO
1313–1375

The *Decameron* by Giovanni Boccaccio has a reputation as a ribald classic, and certainly many of its stories—including some selected here—deal with sexual misadventures. But it also gathers into its hundred stories the diversity and energy that made fourteenth-century Italy one of the great cultural resources of medieval Europe. With his predecessor Dante and his slightly older contemporary Petrarch, Boccaccio established Italy and specifically Florence as a center of literary production that influenced European writing for centuries.

Boccaccio was born in Tuscany, probably in Florence, to a merchant and banker who did not marry the child's mother until some five years later. At fourteen he was taken to Naples, where his father made him spend six years studying arithmetic and then, when it became clear that Boccaccio would not make a successful merchant, another six years preparing for a career as a lawyer. But this enterprise also failed, for Boccaccio was drawn to the sophisticated circle of writers and scholars that the ruler of southern Italy, Robert of Anjou, had assembled into a court that was the most advanced cultural center of its time. Although known to modern readers almost exclusively through the *Decameron*, Boccaccio wrote primarily either courtly tales of love in Italian verse or learned treatises on subjects such as history, classical mythology, and geography in Latin prose. Along with Petrarch, Boccaccio was one of the many medieval writers who worked to revive the literary heritage of the classical world. In a poem called the *Teseida* he produced the first vernacular version of a classical epic, initiating a tradition that was to culminate in Milton's *Paradise Lost,* and he sponsored the first translation of Homer from Greek (in this case into Latin). The humanism that was to come to fruition in the Renaissance finds one of its most important medieval inspirations in the work of Boccaccio.

The *Decameron* represents another aspect of Boccaccio's literary personality. Locating the collection, written between 1350 and 1353, in a specific historical context, Boccaccio first describes the devastating effects of the bubonic plague (or Black Death) of 1348–50 on Florence. Indeed, while the plague killed at least one-third of the European population (as well as millions elsewhere in the world), in Florence the death rate was as high as 70 percent. Despite the vividness of Boccaccio's description, his account is not in fact based on experience. On the contrary, he borrowed historians' descriptions of earlier plagues. He emphasizes the destruction of both the social fabric of the city and the moral restraints on individual behavior, in effect the disappearance of civilization itself: "all respect for the laws of God and man had virtually broken down and been extinguished in our city." Partly in response to this collapse, but also partly as an effect of it, Boccaccio imagines an alternative society. He describes how seven young ladies of good family are joined by three young men and retreat from the ravaged city to a beautiful country estate. Here they restore themselves with pleasure, but a pleasure that is carefully regulated: as their leader, Pampinea, says, they will enjoy themselves in the country "without in any way overstepping the bounds of what is reasonable." Among their recreations is a tale-telling game: for ten days each member of the group tells a story, creating the hundred stories that comprise the *Decameron*.

But if Boccaccio presents these tales as an alternative to the social and moral collapse of plague-stricken Florence, he also insists that pleasure is itself healthful. In this he sets his work in opposition to that of one of his own literary heroes, Dante. Much of Boccaccio's work is heavily influenced by Dante, and near the end of his life he both wrote a treatise celebrating Dante and delivered a set of lectures commenting in detail on the first twenty-eight cantos of the *Inferno*. Yet the *Decameron* is an implicitly anti-Dantean work. Its division into one hundred tales echoes Dante's division of his *Comedy* into one hundred cantos, and Boccaccio gives his work an alternative title—"Prince Galahalt"—that refers to a crucial moment in the *Inferno*. In canto 5 of the *Inferno* Francesca explains to Dante that she and her brother-in-law Paolo fell in love while reading the story of Lancelot and Guinevere. She blames the book for their fall, calling it a Galahalt: she is referring to the knight in the Arthurian court who served as a go-between for the lovers. Dante is implying here that reading, and especially reading for pleasure, can be morally dangerous. Yet Boccaccio insists by his subtitle, by the Prologue that defines his book as a consolation and distraction for lovesick ladies, and by the very occasion for the story-telling, that literature can provide a pleasure that is not merely legitimate but restorative.

Many different kinds of pleasure are both described in and made available by the *Decameron*. While the members of the company are flirtatious but always decorous, many of the stories told, especially by the men, celebrate sexual pleasure with a frank good humor. The sixth story of the ninth day is a good example. The story is a version of a tale that also survives as a French fabliau, which may have been the form in which Boccaccio first heard it. Despite all the shenanigans and illicit sexuality, the story insists that no harm has been done, and the duped father and husband are treated with genial warmth. The story is typical as well in its celebration of values associated with the vigorous merchant class from which Boccaccio derived and that was largely dominant in Italy. The story describes a world of bewildering fluctuation. One of the literary pleasures it provides its readers is the plotting out of movements from bed to bed that occur during the night. To do so is to see that the baby's cradle is both the narrative device that makes the amorous events of the night possible and a metaphor for the circulation of sexual favors, much as commodities circulate throughout the mercantile world. Indeed, to succeed in the world of this story, as in commerce, requires a quick wit, a flexible sense of propriety, and an alertness to one's own self-interest without a vengeful desire to harm others that might make permanent enemies. On the whole, the *Decameron* celebrates just this pragmatic and relativistic value system, refusing to endow any single set of values with ultimate authority. If one story teaches one lesson, then the next will teach a contradictory one, and readers are allowed to decide for themselves where true value is to be found.

In this relativism Boccaccio's *Decameron* is very different from Dante's *Divine Comedy*. Dante is an absolutist: he insists throughout his great work that there *is* a single truth, and the many details of the poem are controlled by Christian doctrine. But without being in any sense unmindful of the claims of religion—Boccaccio was certainly a fully devout Christian—the *Decameron* describes a much more multifarious, much less easily judged world than does *The Divine Comedy*. The first story tells of a thoroughgoing rogue, Ser Cepperello, who provides an outrageously false deathbed confession to a credulous and self-seeking friar. But while Cepperello seems to damn himself by his impenitent mockery of the salvation offered by the Church, we are aware that he is acting out of charitable motives in trying to protect his Florentine friends. So it becomes difficult to know if the townspeople are entirely wrong in thinking he is a saint. And we are also aware that the good deed performed is itself an act of tale-telling, and a tale that is both an outrageous lie and a pleasure to read. On the other side, the story of Nastagio and the hunt of love (the eighth story of the fifth day) presents a scene straight out of the *Inferno*: a scornful lady is eternally hunted down and eviscerated by her suicidal lover. Are we to think that here divine justice is being done? The context in which the scene is placed might give us pause. Used by Nastagio to persuade his lady to accept him as a lover, this scene reveals both the obsessions of the courtly lover—as does the ninth story of the fourth day, in which the noble lady commits suicide in order to remain magnificently true to her lover—but also its cruelty and violence. Finally, these complexities are brought together in the story of Griselda (the tenth story of the tenth day), which proved to be one of the most popular stories of the later Middle Ages (both Petrarch and Chaucer produced versions). Is Griselda a saint of patience who is finally rewarded for her virtue? Or is she an unreasonably passive creature who solicits her own victimization?

Is Walter a monster, a tyrant both politically and domestically, and the story a psychological study of despotism? Or is he an agent of God who makes possible the revelation of Griselda's superhuman virtue, or perhaps even God himself? In this fascinating puzzle of a story, Boccaccio poses questions without providing any obvious answer, showing us that perhaps the deepest pleasure that literature can offer is the pleasure of interpretation.

PRONOUNCING GLOSSARY

The following list uses common English syllables to provide rough equivalents of selected words whose pronunciation may be unfamiliar to the general reader.

Cepperello Dietaiuti: *chep-er-el-lo dee-ay-tie-yu'-tee*

Giannùcole: *gee-an-ooh'-co-lay*

Gualtieri: *gwal-tee-ay'-ree*

Guido degli Anastagi: *gwee'-do day'-lee an-as-ta'-jee*

Guillaume de Cabestanh: *gee-ohm' de cab-es-stan'*

Guillaume de Roussillon: *gee-ohm' de roo-see-yonh*

Musciatto: *mus-chee-at'-to*

Nastagio degli Onesti: *nas-taj'-io day'-lee on-es'-tee*

Paolo Traversari: *pow'-lo tra-ver-sa'-ree*

Pinuccio: *pin-ooch'-ee-o*

The Decameron[1]

Here begins the book called Decameron,[2] *otherwise known as Prince Galahalt, wherein are contained a hundred stories told in ten days by seven ladies and three young men.*

[THE PROLOGUE]

To take pity on people in distress is a human quality which every man and woman should possess, but it is especially requisite in those who have once needed comfort, and found it in others. I number myself as one of these, because if ever anyone required or appreciated comfort, or indeed derived pleasure therefrom, I was that person. For from my earliest youth until the present day, I have been inflamed beyond measure with a most lofty and noble love, far loftier and nobler than might perhaps be thought proper, were I to describe it, in a person of my humble condition.[3] And although people of good judgment, to whose notice it had come, praised me for it and rated me much higher in their esteem, nevertheless it was exceedingly difficult for me to endure. The reason, I hasten to add, was not the cruelty of my lady-love, but the immoderate passion engendered within my mind by a craving that was ill-restrained. This, since it would allow me no proper respite, often caused me an inordinate amount of distress. But in my anguish I have on occasion derived much relief from the agreeable conversation and the admirable expressions of sympathy offered by friends, without which I am firmly convinced that I should have perished. However, the One who is infinite decreed by immutable law that all earthly things should come to an end. And

---

1. Translated by G. H. McWilliam.   2. The title is a pseudo-Greek word meaning "Ten Days"; it also ironically refers to a medieval devotional text called the Hexaemeron (Six Days) about the six days of creation described in Genesis.   3. This claim to love a noble lady is conventional in medieval literature.

it pleased Him that this love of mine, whose warmth exceeded all others, and which had stood firm and unyielding against all the pressures of good intention, helpful advice, and the risk of danger and open scandal, should in the course of time diminish of its own accord. So that now, all that is left of it in my mind is the delectable feeling which Love habitually reserves for those who refrain from venturing too far upon its deepest waters. And thus what was once a source of pain has now become, having shed all discomfort, an abiding sensation of pleasure.

But though the pain has ceased, I still preserve a clear recollection of the kindnesses I received in the past from people who, prompted by feelings of goodwill towards me, showed a concern for my sufferings. This memory will never, I think, fade for as long as I live. And since it is my conviction that gratitude, of all the virtues, is most highly to be commended and its opposite condemned. I have resolved, in order not to appear ungrateful, to employ what modest talents I possess in making restitution for what I have received. Thus, now that I can claim to have achieved my freedom, I intend to offer some solace, if not to those who assisted me (since their good sense or good fortune will perhaps render such a gift superfluous), at least to those who stand in need of it. And even though my support, or if you prefer, my encouragement, may seem very slight (as indeed it is) to the people concerned, I feel none the less that it should for preference be directed where it seems to be most needed, because that is the quarter in which it will be more effective and, at the same time, more readily welcomed.

And who will deny that such encouragement, however small, should much rather be offered to the charming ladies than to the men? For the ladies, out of fear or shame, conceal the flames of passion within their fragile breasts, and a hidden love is far more potent than one which is worn on the sleeve, as everyone knows who has had experience of these matters. Moreover they are forced to follow the whims, fancies and dictates of their fathers, mothers, brothers and husbands, so that they spend most of their time cooped up within the narrow confines of their rooms, where they sit in apparent idleness, wishing one thing and at the same time wishing its opposite, and reflecting on various matters, which cannot possibly always be pleasant to contemplate. And if, in the course of their meditations, their minds should be invaded by melancholy arising out of the flames of longing, it will inevitably take root there and make them suffer greatly, unless it be dislodged by new interests. Besides which, their powers of endurance are considerably weaker than those that men possess.

When men are in love, they are not affected in this way, as we can see quite plainly. They, whenever they are weighed down by melancholy or ponderous thoughts, have many ways of relieving or expelling them. For if they wish, they can always walk abroad, see and hear many things, go fowling, hunting, fishing, riding and gambling, or attend to their business affairs. Each of these pursuits has the power of engaging men's minds, either wholly or in part, and diverting them from their gloomy meditations, at least for a certain period: after which, some form of consolation will ensue, or the affliction will grow less intense.

So in order that I may to some extent repair the omissions of Fortune, which (as we may see in the case of the more delicate sex) was always more sparing of support wherever natural strength was more deficient, I intend to provide succor and diversion for the ladies, but only for those who are in love, since the others can make do with their needles, their reels and their spindles. I shall narrate a hundred stories or fables or parables or histories or whatever you choose to call them, recited in ten days by a worthy band of seven ladies and three young men, who assembled together during the plague which recently took such heavy toll of life. And I shall also include some songs, which these seven ladies sang for their mutual amusement.

In these tales will be found a variety of love adventures, bitter as well as pleasing, and other exciting incidents, which took place in both ancient and modern times. In reading them, the aforesaid ladies will be able to derive, not only pleasure from the entertaining matters therein set forth, but also some useful advice. For they will learn to recognize what should be avoided and likewise what should be pursued, and these things can only lead, in my opinion, to the removal of their affliction. If this should happen (and may God grant that it should), let them give thanks to Love, which, in freeing me from its bonds, has granted me the power of making provision for their pleasures.

FIRST DAY

Here begins the First Day of the Decameron, *wherein first of all the author explains the circumstances in which certain persons, who presently make their appearance, were induced to meet for the purpose of conversing together, after which, under the rule of* Pampinea, *each of them speaks on the subject they find most congenial.*

Whenever, fairest ladies, I pause to consider how compassionate you all are by nature, I invariably become aware that the present work will seem to you to possess an irksome and ponderous opening. For it carries at its head the painful memory of the deadly havoc wrought by the recent plague, which brought so much heartache and misery to those who witnessed, or had experience of it. But I do not want you to be deterred, for this reason, from reading any further, on the assumption that you are to be subjected, as you read, to an endless torrent of tears and sobbing. You will be affected no differently by this grim beginning than walkers confronted by a steep and rugged hill, beyond which there lies a beautiful and delectable plain. The degree of pleasure they derive from the latter will correspond directly to the difficulty of the climb and the descent. And just as the end of mirth is heaviness, so sorrows are dispersed by the advent of joy.

This brief unpleasantness (I call it brief, inasmuch as it is contained within few words) is quickly followed by the sweetness and the pleasure which I have already promised you, and which, unless you were told in advance, you would not perhaps be expecting to find after such a beginning as this. Believe me, if I could decently have taken you whither I desire by some other route, rather than along a path so difficult as this, I would gladly have done so. But since it is impossible without this memoir to show the origin of the events you will read about later, I really have no alternative but to address myself to its composition.

I say, then, that the sum of thirteen hundred and forty-eight years had elapsed since the fruitful Incarnation of the Son of God, when the noble city of Florence, which for its great beauty excels all others in Italy, was visited by the deadly pestilence. Some say that it descended upon the human race through the influence of the heavenly bodies, others that it was a punishment signifying God's righteous anger at our iniquitous way of life. But whatever its cause, it had originated some years earlier in the East, where it had claimed countless lives before it unhappily spread westward, growing in strength as it swept relentlessly on from one place to the next.[4]

In the face of its onrush, all the wisdom and ingenuity of man were unavailing. Large quantities of refuse were cleared out of the city by officials specially appointed for the purpose, all sick persons were forbidden entry, and numerous instructions were issued for safeguarding the people's health, but all to no avail. Nor were the countless petitions humbly directed to God by the pious, whether by means of formal processions or in all other ways, any less ineffectual. For in the early spring of the year we have mentioned, the plague began, in a terrifying and extraordinary manner, to make its disastrous effects apparent. It did not take the form it had assumed in the East, where if anyone bled from the nose it was an obvious portent of certain death. On the contrary, its earliest symptom, in men and women alike, was the appearance of certain swellings in the groin or the armpit, some of which were egg-shaped whilst others were roughly the size of the common apple. Sometimes the swellings were large, sometimes not so large, and they were referred to by the populace as *gavòccioli*.[5] From the two areas already mentioned, this deadly *gavòcciolo* would begin to spread, and within a short time it would appear at random all over the body. Later on, the symptoms of the disease changed, and many people began to find dark blotches and bruises on their arms, thighs, and other parts of the body, sometimes large and few in number, at other times tiny and closely spaced. These, to anyone unfortunate enough to contract them, were just as infallible a sign that he would die as the *gavòcciolo* had been earlier, and as indeed it still was.

Against these maladies, it seemed that all the advice of physicians and all the power of medicine were profitless and unavailing. Perhaps the nature of the illness was such that it allowed no remedy or perhaps those people who were treating the illness (whose numbers had increased enormously because the ranks of the qualified were invaded by people, both men and women, who had never received any training in medicine), being ignorant of its causes, were not prescribing the appropriate cure. At all events, few of those who caught it ever recovered, and in most cases death occurred within three days from the appearance of the symptoms we have described, some people dying more rapidly than others, the majority without any fever or other complications.

But what made this pestilence even more severe was that whenever those suffering from it mixed with people who were still unaffected, it would rush upon these with the speed of a fire racing through dry or oily substances that happened to come within its reach. Nor was this the full extent of its evil, for not only did it infect healthy persons who conversed or had any dealings with the sick, making them ill or visiting an equally horrible death upon them, but it also seemed to transfer the sickness to anyone touching the clothes or other objects which had been handled or used by its victims.

---

4. The bubonic plague originated on the steppes of central Asia and was carried to Europe by fleas that infested rats on the ships of European traders.   **5.** The medical name for these swellings is *buboes* (from Greek), whence the name bubonic plague.

It is a remarkable story that I have to relate. And were it not for the fact that I am one of many people who saw it with their own eyes, I would scarcely dare to believe it, let alone commit it to paper, even though I had heard it from a person whose word I could trust. The plague I have been describing was of so contagious a nature that very often it visibly did more than simply pass from one person to another. In other words, whenever an animal other than a human being touched anything belonging to a person who had been stricken or exterminated by the disease, it not only caught the sickness, but died from it almost at once. To all of this, as I have just said, my own eyes bore witness on more than one occasion. One day, for instance, the rags of a pauper who had died from the disease were thrown into the street, where they attracted the attention of two pigs. In their wonted fashion, the pigs first of all gave the rags a thorough mauling with their snouts, after which they took them between their teeth and shook them against their cheeks. And within a short time they began to writhe as though they had been poisoned, then they both dropped dead to the ground, spread-eagled upon the rags that had brought about their undoing.

These things, and many others of a similar or even worse nature, caused various fears and fantasies to take root in the minds of those who were still alive and well. And almost without exception, they took a single and very inhuman precaution, namely to avoid or run away from the sick and their belongings, by which means they all thought that their own health would be preserved.

Some people were of the opinion that a sober and abstemious mode of living considerably reduced the risk of infection. They therefore formed themselves into groups and lived in isolation from everyone else. Having withdrawn to a comfortable abode where there were no sick persons, they locked themselves in and settled down to a peaceable existence, consuming modest quantities of delicate foods and precious wines and avoiding all excesses. They refrained from speaking to outsiders, refused to receive news of the dead or the sick, and entertained themselves with music and whatever other amusements they were able to devise.

Others took the opposite view, and maintained that an infallible way of warding off this appalling evil was to drink heavily, enjoy life to the full, go round singing and merrymaking, gratify all of one's cravings whenever the opportunity offered, and shrug the whole thing off as one enormous joke. Moreover, they practised what they preached to the best of their ability, for they would visit one tavern after another, drinking all day and night to immoderate excess; or alternatively (and this was their more frequent custom), they would do their drinking in various private houses, but only in the ones where the conversation was restricted to subjects that were pleasant or entertaining. Such places were easy to find, for people behaved as though their days were numbered, and treated their belongings and their own persons with equal abandon. Hence most houses had become common property, and any passing stranger could make himself at home as naturally as though he were the rightful owner. But for all their riotous manner of living, these people always took good care to avoid any contact with the sick.

In the face of so much affliction and misery, all respect for the laws of God and man had virtually broken down and been extinguished in our city. For like everybody else, those ministers and executors of the laws who were not either dead or ill were left with so few subordinates that they were unable to discharge any of their duties. Hence everyone was free to behave as he pleased.

There were many other people who steered a middle course between the two already mentioned, neither restricting their diet to the same degree as the first group, nor indulging so freely as the second in drinking and other forms of wantonness, but simply doing no more than satisfy their appetite. Instead of incarcerating themselves, these people moved about freely, holding in their hands a posy of flowers, or fragrant herbs, or one of a wide range of spices, which they applied at frequent intervals to their nostrils, thinking it an excellent idea to fortify the brain with smells of that particular sort; for the stench of dead bodies, sickness, and medicines seemed to fill and pollute the whole of the atmosphere.

Some people, pursuing what was possibly the safer alternative, callously maintained that there was no better or more efficacious remedy against a plague than to run away from it. Swayed by this argument, and sparing no thought for anyone but themselves, large numbers of men and women abandoned their city, their homes, their relatives, their estates and their belongings, and headed for the countryside, either in Florentine territory or, better still, abroad. It was as though they imagined that the wrath of God would not unleash this plague against men for their iniquities irrespective of where they happened to be, but would only be aroused against those who found themselves within the city walls; or possibly they assumed that the whole of the population would be exterminated and that the city's last hour had come.

Of the people who held these various opinions, not all of them died. Nor, however, did they all survive. On the contrary, many of each different persuasion fell ill here, there, and everywhere, and having themselves, when they were fit and well, set an example to those who were as yet unaffected, they languished away with virtually no one to nurse them. It was not merely a question of one citizen avoiding another, and of people almost invariably neglecting their neighbors and rarely or never visiting their relatives, addressing them only from a distance; this scourge had implanted so great a terror in the hearts of men and women that brothers abandoned brothers, uncles their nephews, sisters their brothers, and in many cases wives deserted their husbands. But even worse, and almost incredible, was the fact that fathers and mothers refused to nurse and assist their own children, as though they did not belong to them.

Hence the countless numbers of people who fell ill, both male and female, were entirely dependent upon either the charity of friends (who were few and far between) or the greed of servants, who remained in short supply despite the attraction of high wages out of all proportion to the services they performed. Furthermore, these latter were men and women of coarse intellect and the majority were unused to such duties, and they did little more than hand things to the invalid when asked to do so and watch over him when he was dying. And in performing this kind of service, they frequently lost their lives as well as their earnings.

As a result of this wholesale desertion of the sick by neighbors, relatives and friends, and in view of the scarcity of servants, there grew up a practice almost never previously heard of, whereby when a woman fell ill, no matter how gracious or beautiful or gently bred she might be, she raised no objection to being attended by a male servant, whether he was young or not. Nor did she have any scruples about showing him every part of her body as freely as she would have displayed it to a woman, provided that the nature of her infirmity required her to do so; and this explains why those women who recovered were possibly less chaste in the period that followed.

Moreover a great many people died who would perhaps have survived had they received some assistance. And hence, what with the lack of appropriate means for tending the sick, and the virulence of the plague, the number of deaths reported in the city whether by day or by night was so enormous that it astonished all who heard tell of it, to say nothing of the people who actually witnessed the carnage. And it was perhaps inevitable that among the citizens who survived there arose certain customs that were quite contrary to established tradition.

It had once been customary, as it is again nowadays, for the women relatives and neighbors of a dead man to assemble in his house in order to mourn in the company of the women who had been closest to him; moreover his kinsfolk would forgather in front of his house along with his neighbors and various other citizens, and there would be a contingent of priests, whose numbers varied according to the quality of the deceased; his body would be taken thence to the church in which he had wanted to be buried, being borne on the shoulders of his peers amidst the funeral pomp of candles and dirges. But as the ferocity of the plague began to mount, this practice all but disappeared entirely and was replaced by different customs. For not only did people die without having many women about them, but a great number departed this life without anyone at all to witness their going. Few indeed were those to whom the lamentations and bitter tears of their relatives were accorded; on the contrary, more often than not bereavement was the signal for laughter and witticisms and general jollification—the art of which the women, having for the most part suppressed their feminine concern for the salvation of the souls of the dead, had learned to perfection. Moreover it was rare for the bodies of the dead to be accompanied by more than ten or twelve neighbors to the church, nor were they borne on the shoulders of worthy and honest citizens, but by a kind of gravedigging fraternity, newly come into being and drawn from the lower orders of society. These people assumed the title of sexton, and demanded a fat fee for their services, which consisted in taking up the coffin and hauling it swiftly away, not to the church specified by the dead man in his will, but usually to the nearest at hand. They would be preceded by a group of four or six clerics, who between them carried one or two candles at most, and sometimes none at all. Nor did the priests go to the trouble of pronouncing solemn and lengthy funeral rites, but, with the aid of these so-called sextons, they hastily lowered the body into the nearest empty grave they could find.

As for the common people and a large proportion of the bourgeoisie, they presented a much more pathetic spectacle, for the majority of them were constrained, either by their poverty or the hope of survival, to remain in their houses. Being confined to their own parts of the city, they fell ill daily in their thousands, and since they had no one to assist them or attend to their needs, they inevitably perished almost without exception. Many dropped dead in the open streets, both by day and by night, whilst a great many others, though dying in their own houses, drew their neighbors' attention to the fact more by the smell of their rotting corpses than by any other means. And what with these, and the others who were dying all over the city, bodies were here, there and everywhere.

Whenever people died, their neighbors nearly always followed a single, set routine, prompted as much by their fear of being contaminated by the decaying corpse as by any charitable feelings they may have entertained towards the deceased. Either on their own, or with the assistance of bearers whenever these were to be had, they extracted the bodies of the dead from their houses and left them lying outside their front doors, where anyone going about the streets, especially in the early morning, could have observed countless numbers of them. Funeral biers would then be sent for, upon which the dead were taken away, though there were some who, for lack of biers, were carried off on plain boards. It was by no means rare for more than one of these biers to be seen with two or three bodies upon it at a time; on the contrary, many were seen to contain a husband and wife, two or three brothers and sisters, a father and son, or some other pair of close relatives. And times without number it happened that two priests would be on their way to bury someone, holding a cross before them, only to find that bearers carrying three or four additional biers would fall in behind them; so that whereas the priests had thought they had only one burial to attend to, they in fact had six or seven, and sometimes more. Even in these circumstances, however, there were no tears or candles or mourners to honor the dead; in fact, no more respect was accorded to dead people than would nowadays be shown towards dead goats. For it was quite apparent that the one thing which, in normal times, no wise man had ever learned to accept with patient resignation (even though it struck so seldom and unobtrusively), had now been brought home to the feeble-minded as well, but the scale of the calamity caused them to regard it with indifference.

Such was the multitude of corpses (of which further consignments were arriving every day and almost by the hour at each of the churches), that there was not sufficient consecrated ground for them to be buried in, especially if each was to have its own plot in accordance with long-established custom. So when all the graves were full, huge trenches were excavated in the churchyards, into which new arrivals were placed in their hundreds, stowed tier upon tier like ships' cargo, each layer of corpses being covered over with a thin layer of soil till the trench was filled to the top.

But rather than describe in elaborate detail the calamities we experienced in the city at that time, I must mention that, whilst an ill wind was blowing through Florence itself, the surrounding region was no less badly affected. In the fortified towns, conditions were similar to those in the city itself on a minor scale; but in the scattered hamlets and the countryside proper, the poor unfortunate peasants and their families had no physicians or servants whatever to assist them, and collapsed by the wayside, in their fields, and in their cottages at all hours of the day and night, dying more like animals than human beings. Like the townspeople, they too grew apathetic in their ways, disregarded their affairs, and neglected their possessions. Moreover they all behaved as though each day was to be their last, and far from making provision for the future by tilling their lands, tending their flocks, and adding to their previous labors, they tried in every way they could think of to squander the assets already in their possession. Thus it came about that oxen, asses, sheep, goats, pigs, chickens, and even dogs (for all their deep fidelity to man) were driven away and allowed to roam freely through the fields, where the crops lay abandoned and had not even been reaped, let alone gathered in. And after a whole day's feasting, many of these animals, as though possessing the power of reason, would return glutted in the evening to their own quarters, without any shepherd to guide them.

But let us leave the countryside and return to the city. What more remains to be said, except that the cruelty of heaven (and possibly, in some measure, also that of man) was so immense and so devastating that between March and July of the year in question, what with the fury of the pestilence and the fact that so many of the sick were inadequately cared for or abandoned in their hour of need because the healthy were too terrified to approach them, it is reliably thought that over a hundred thousand human lives were extinguished within the walls of the city of Florence? Yet before this lethal catastrophe fell upon the city, it is doubtful whether anyone would have guessed it contained so many inhabitants.

Ah, how great a number of splendid palaces, fine houses, and noble dwellings, once filled with retainers, with lords and with ladies, were bereft of all who had lived there, down to the tiniest child! How numerous were the famous families, the vast estates, the notable fortunes, that were seen to be left without a rightful successor! How many gallant gentlemen, fair ladies, and sprightly youths, who would have been judged hale and hearty by Galen, Hippocrates, and Aesculapius[6] (to say nothing of others), having breakfasted in the morning with their kinsfolk, acquaintances, and friends, supped that same evening with their ancestors in the next world!

The more I reflect upon all this misery, the deeper my sense of personal sorrow; hence I shall refrain from describing those aspects which can suitably be omitted, and proceed to inform you that these were the conditions prevailing in our city, which was by now almost emptied of its inhabitants, when one Tuesday morning (or so I was told by a person whose word can be trusted) seven young ladies were to be found in the venerable church of Santa Maria Novella,[7] which was otherwise almost deserted. They had been attending divine service, and were dressed in mournful attire appropriate to the times. Each was a friend, a neighbor, or a relative of the other six, none was older than twenty-seven or younger than eighteen, and all were intelligent, gently bred, fair to look upon, graceful in bearing, and charmingly unaffected. I could tell you their actual names, but refrain from doing so for a good reason, namely that I would not want any of them to feel embarrassed, at any time in the future, on account of the ensuing stories, all of which they either listened to or narrated themselves. For nowadays, laws relating to pleasure are somewhat restrictive, whereas at that time, for the reasons indicated above, they were exceptionally lax, not only for ladies of their own age but also for much older women. Besides, I have no wish to supply envious tongues, ever ready to censure a laudable way of life, with a chance to besmirch the good name of these worthy ladies with their lewd and filthy

6. The mythical *Aesculapius* is the classical god of medicine; *Hippocrates* (d. ca. 377 B.C.E.) is regarded as the founder of medicine; *Galen* (d. 199 C.E.), also a Greek, was a famous medical authority. 7. An important church in Florence, perhaps chosen as the origin of the frame-story because its name *novella* can mean both *new* (which is why it was attached to this church) and *story*. The present church has a façade added in the 15th century.

gossip. And therefore, so that we may perceive distinctly what each of them had to say, I propose to refer to them by names which are either wholly or partially appropriate to the qualities of each. The first of them, who was also the eldest, we shall call Pampinea, the second Fiammetta, Filomena the third, and the fourth Emilia, then we shall name the fifth Lauretta, and the sixth Neifile, whilst to the last, not without reason, we shall give the name of Elissa.[8]

Without prior agreement but simply by chance, these seven ladies found themselves sitting, more or less in a circle, in one part of the church, reciting their paternosters. Eventually, they left off and heaved a great many sighs, after which they began to talk among themselves on various different aspects of the times through which they were passing. But after a little while, they all fell silent except for Pampinea, who said:

"Dear ladies, you will often have heard it affirmed, as I have, that no man does injury to another in exercising his lawful rights. Every person born into this world has a natural right to sustain, preserve, and defend his own life to the best of his ability—a right so freely acknowledged that men have sometimes killed others in self-defence, and no blame whatever has attached to their actions. Now, if this is permitted by the laws, upon whose prompt application all mortal creatures depend for their well-being, how can it possibly be wrong, seeing that it harms no one, for us or anyone else to do all in our power to preserve our lives? If I pause to consider what we have been doing this morning, and what we have done on several mornings in the past, if I reflect on the nature and subject of our conversation, I realize, just as you also must realize, that each of us is apprehensive on her own account. This does not surprise me in the least, but what does greatly surprise me (seeing that each of us has the natural feelings of a woman) is that we do nothing to requite ourselves against the thing of which we are all so justly afraid.

"Here we linger for no other purpose, or so it seems to me, than to count the number of corpses being taken to burial, or to hear whether the friars of the church, very few of whom are left, chant their offices at the appropriate hours, or to exhibit the quality and quantity of our sorrows, by means of the clothes we are wearing, to all those whom we meet in this place. And if we go outside, we shall see the dead and the sick being carried hither and thither, or we shall see people, once condemned to exile by the courts for their misdeeds, careering wildly about the streets in open defiance of the law, well knowing that those appointed to enforce it are either dead or dying; or else we shall find ourselves at the mercy of the scum of our city who, having scented our blood, call themselves sextons and go prancing and bustling all over the place, singing bawdy songs that add insult to our injuries. Moreover, all we ever hear is 'So-and-so's dead' and 'So-and-so's dying'; and if there were anyone left to mourn, the whole place would be filled with sounds of weeping and wailing.

"And if we return to our homes, what happens? I know not whether your own experience is similar to mine, but my house was once full of servants, and now that there is no one left apart from my maid and myself, I am filled

8. The first four names derive from earlier works by Boccaccio himself; the last three refer, respectively, to the poetry of Petrarch, Dante, and Virgil, the three poets whom Boccaccio most admired.

with foreboding and feel as if every hair of my head is standing on end. Wherever I go in the house, wherever I pause to rest, I seem to be haunted by the shades of the departed, whose faces no longer appear as I remember them but with strange and horribly twisted expressions that frighten me out of my senses.

"Accordingly, whether I am here in church or out in the streets or sitting at home, I always feel ill at ease, the more so because it seems to me that no one possessing private means and a place to retreat to is left here apart from ourselves. But even if such people are still to be found, they draw no distinction, as I have frequently heard and seen for myself, between what is honest and what is dishonest; and provided only that they are prompted by their appetites, they will do whatever affords them the greatest pleasure, whether by day or by night, alone or in company. It is not only of lay people that I speak, but also of those enclosed in monasteries, who, having convinced themselves that such behavior is suitable for them and is only unbecoming in others, have broken the rules of obedience and given themselves over to carnal pleasures, thereby thinking to escape, and have turned lascivious and dissolute.

"If this be so (and we plainly perceive that it is), what are we doing here? What are we waiting for? What are we dreaming about? Why do we lag so far behind all the rest of the citizens in providing for our safety? Do we rate ourselves lower than all other women? Or do we suppose that our own lives, unlike those of others, are bound to our bodies by such strong chains that we may ignore all those things which have the power to harm them? In that case we are deluded and mistaken. We have only to recall the names and the condition of the young men and women who have fallen victim to this cruel pestilence, in order to realize clearly the foolishness of such notions.

"And so, lest by pretending to be above such things or by becoming complacent we should succumb to that which we might possibly avoid if we so desired, I would think it an excellent idea (though I do not know whether you would agree with me) for us all to get away from this city, just as many others have done before us, and as indeed they are doing still. We could go and stay together on one of our various country estates, shunning at all costs the lewd practices of our fellow citizens and feasting and merrymaking as best we may without in any way overstepping the bounds of what is reasonable.

"There we shall hear the birds singing, we shall see fresh green hills and plains, fields of corn undulating like the sea, and trees of at least a thousand different species; and we shall have a clearer view of the heavens, which, troubled though they are, do not however deny us their eternal beauties, so much more fair to look upon than the desolate walls of our city. Moreover the country air is much more refreshing, the necessities of life in such a time as this are more abundant, and there are fewer obstacles to contend with. For although the farmworkers are dying there in the same way as the townspeople here in Florence, the spectacle is less harrowing inasmuch as the houses and people are more widely scattered. Besides, unless I am mistaken we shall not be abandoning anyone by going away from here; on the contrary, we may fairly claim that we are the ones who have been abandoned, for our kinsfolk are either dead or fled, and have left us to fend for ourselves in the midst of all this affliction, as though disowning us completely.

"Hence no one can reproach us for taking the course I have advocated, whereas if we do nothing we shall inevitably be confronted with distress and mourning, and possibly forfeit our lives into the bargain. Let us therefore do as I suggest, taking our maidservants with us and seeing to the dispatch of all the things we shall need. We can move from place to place, spending one day here and another there, pursuing whatever pleasures and entertainments the present times will afford. In this way of life we shall continue until such time as we discover (provided we are spared from early death) the end decreed by Heaven for these terrible events. You must remember, after all, that it is no more unseemly for us to go away and thus preserve our own honor than it is for most other women to remain here and forfeit theirs."

Having listened to Pampinea's suggestion, the other ladies not only applauded it but were so eager to carry it into effect that they had already begun to work out the details amongst themselves, as though they wanted to rise from their pews and set off without further ado. But Filomena, being more prudent than the others, said:

"Pampinea's arguments, ladies, are most convincing, but we should not follow her advice as hastily as you appear to wish. You must remember that we are all women, and every one of us is sufficiently adult to acknowledge that women, when left to themselves, are not the most rational of creatures, and that without the supervision of some man or other their capacity for getting things done is somewhat restricted. We are fickle, quarrelsome, suspicious, cowardly, and easily frightened; and hence I greatly fear that if we have none but ourselves to guide us, our little band will break up much more swiftly, and with far less credit to ourselves, than would otherwise be the case. We would be well advised to resolve this problem before we depart."

Then Elissa said:

"It is certainly true that man is the head of woman,[9] and that without a man to guide us it rarely happens that any enterprise of ours is brought to a worthy conclusion. But where are we to find these men? As we all know, most of our own menfolk are dead, and those few that are still alive are fleeing in scattered little groups from that which we too are intent upon avoiding. Yet we cannot very well go away with total strangers, for if self-preservation is our aim, we must so arrange our affairs that wherever we go for our pleasure and repose, no trouble or scandal should come of it."

Whilst the talk of the ladies was proceeding along these lines there came into the church three young men, in whom neither the horrors of the times nor the loss of friends or relatives nor concern for their own safety had dampened the flames of love, much less extinguished them completely. I have called them young, but none in fact was less than twenty-five years of age, and the first was called Panfilo, the second Filostrato, and the last Dioneo.[1] Each of them was most agreeable and gently bred, and by way of sweetest solace amid all this turmoil they were seeking to catch a glimpse of their lady-loves, all three of whom, as it happened, were among the seven we have mentioned, whilst some of the remaining four were closely related to one or other of the three. No sooner did they espy they young ladies than they too were espied, whereupon Pampinea smiled and said:

9. Here Elissa (whose name is also one given by Virgil to Dido in book 4 of the *Aeneid*) is quoting St. Paul (Ephesians 5.23). It is difficult to decide if Boccaccio is being ironic.   1. The first two names derive from Boccaccio's earlier work; the name Dioneo is associated with Aphrodite, the classical goddess of love.

"See how Fortune favors us right from the beginning, in setting before us three young men of courage and intelligence, who will readily act as our guides and servants if we are not too proud to accept them for such duties."

Then Neifile, whose face had turned all scarlet with confusion since she was the object of one of the youth's affections, said:

"For goodness' sake do take care, Pampinea, of what you are saying! To my certain knowledge, nothing but good can be said of any one of them, and I consider them more than competent to fulfil the office of which we were speaking. I also think they would be good, honest company, not only for us, but for ladies much finer and fairer than ourselves. But since it is perfectly obvious that they are in love with certain of the ladies here present, I am apprehensive lest, by taking them with us, through no fault either of theirs or of our own, we should bring disgrace and censure on ourselves."

"That is quite beside the point," said Filomena. "If I live honestly, and my conscience is clear, then people may say whatever they like. God and Truth will take up arms in my defence. Now, if only they were prepared to accompany us, we should truly be able to claim as Pampinea has said, that Fortune favors our enterprise."

Filomena's words reassured the other ladies, who not only withdrew their objections but unanimously agreed to call the young men over, explain their intentions, and inquire whether they would be willing to join their expedition. And so, without any further discussion, Pampinea, who was a blood relation to one of the young men, got up and walked towards them. They were standing there gazing at the young ladies, and Pampinea, having offered them a cheerful greeting, told them what they were planning to do, and asked them on behalf of all her companions whether they would be prepared to join them in a spirit of chaste and brotherly affection.

The young men thought at first that she was making mock of them, but when they realized she was speaking in earnest, they gladly agreed to place themselves at the young ladies' disposal. So that there should be no delay in putting the plan into effect, they made provision there and then for the various matters that would have to be attended to before their departure. Meticulous care was taken to see that all necessary preparations were put in hand, supplies were sent on in advance to the place at which they intended to stay, and as dawn was breaking on the morning of the next day, which was a Wednesday, the ladies and the three young men, accompanied by one or two of the maids and all three manservants, set out from the city. And scarcely had they travelled two miles from Florence before they reached the place at which they had agreed to stay.

The spot in question was some distance away from any road, on a small hill that was agreeable to behold for its abundance of shrubs and trees, all bedecked in green leaves. Perched on its summit was a palace, built round a fine, spacious courtyard, and containing loggias, halls, and sleeping apartments, which were not only excellently proportioned but richly embellished with paintings depicting scenes of gaiety. Delectable gardens and meadows lay all around, and there were wells of cool, refreshing water. The cellars were stocked with precious wines, more suited to the palates of connoisseurs than to sedate and respectable ladies. And on their arrival the company discovered, to their no small pleasure, that the place had been cleaned from top to bottom, the beds in the rooms were made up, the whole house was adorned with seasonable flowers of every description, and the floors had been carpeted with rushes.

Soon after reaching the palace, they all sat down, and Dioneo, a youth of matchless charm and readiness of wit, said:

"It is not our foresight, ladies, but rather your own good sense, that has led us to this spot. I know not what you intend to do with your troubles; my own I left inside the city gates when I departed thence a short while ago in your company. Hence you may either prepare to join with me in as much laughter, song and merriment as your sense of decorum will allow, or else you may give me leave to go back for my troubles and live in the afflicted city."

Pampinea, as though she too had driven away all her troubles, answered him in the same carefree vein.

"There is much sense in what you say, Dioneo," she replied. "A merry life should be our aim, since it was for no other reason that we were prompted to run away from the sorrows of the city. However, nothing will last for very long unless it possesses a definite form. And since it was I who led the discussions from which this fair company has come into being, I have given some thought to the continuance of our happiness, and consider it necessary for us to choose a leader, drawn from our own ranks, whom we would honor and obey as our superior, and whose sole concern will be that of devising the means whereby we may pass our time agreeably. But so that none of us will complain that he or she has had no opportunity to experience the burden of responsibility and the pleasure of command associated with sovereign power, I propose that the burden and the honor should be assigned to each of us in turn for a single day. It will be for all of us to decide who is to be our first ruler, after which it will be up to each ruler, when the hour of vespers[2] approaches, to elect his or her successor from among the ladies and gentlemen present. The person chosen to govern will be at liberty to make whatever arrangements he likes for the period covered by his rule, and to prescribe the place and the manner in which we are to live."

Pampinea's proposal was greatly to everyone's liking, and they unanimously elected her as their queen for the first day, whereupon Filomena quickly ran over to a laurel bush, for she had frequently heard it said that laurel leaves were especially worthy of veneration and that they conferred great honor upon those people of merit who were crowned with them.[3] Having plucked a few of its shoots, she fashioned them into a splendid and venerable garland, which she set upon Pampinea's brow, and which thenceforth became the outward symbol of sovereign power and authority to all the members of the company, for as long as they remained together.

Upon her election as their queen, Pampinea summoned the servants of the three young men to appear before her together with their own maidservants, who were four in number. And having called upon everyone to be silent, she said:

"So that I may begin by setting you all a good example, through which, proceeding from good to better, our company will be enabled to live an ordered and agreeable existence for as long as we choose to remain together,

2. *Vespers* is the hour at which evening prayer would be said, usually at sunset.   3. Crowning with laurel leaves was a form of accolade common in the classical world; here there may also be an allusion to the Laura who was celebrated by Petrarch in his lyric poetry.

I first of all appoint Dioneo's manservant, Parmeno,[4] as my steward, and to him I commit the management and care of our household, together with all that appertains to the service of the hall. I desire that Panfilo's servant, Sirisco, should act as our buyer and treasurer, and carry out the instructions of Parmeno. As well as attending to the needs of Filostrato, Tindaro will look after the other two gentlemen in their rooms whenever their own manservants are prevented by their offices from performing such duties. My own maidservant, Misia, will be employed full-time in the kitchen along with Filomena's maidservant, Licisca, and they will prepare with diligence whatever dishes are prescribed by Parmeno. Chimera and Stratilia, the servants of Lauretta and Fiammetta, are required to act as chambermaids to all the ladies, as well as seeing that the places we frequent are neatly and tidily maintained. And unless they wish to incur our royal displeasure, we desire and command that each and every one of the servants should take good care, no matter what they should hear or observe in their comings and goings, to bring us no tidings of the world outside these walls unless they are tidings of happiness."

Her orders thus summarily given, and commended by all her companions, she rose gaily to her feet, and said:

"There are gardens here, and meadows, and other places of great charm and beauty, through which we may now wander in search of our amusement, each of us being free to do whatever he pleases. But on the stroke of tierce,[5] let us all return to this spot, so that we may breakfast together in the shade."

The merry company having thus been dismissed by their newly elected queen, the young men and their fair companions sauntered slowly through a garden, conversing on pleasant topics, weaving fair garlands for each other from the leaves of various trees, and singing songs of love.

After spending as much time there as the queen had allotted them, they returned to the house to find that Parmeno had made a zealous beginning to his duties, for as they entered the hall on the ground floor, they saw the tables ready laid, with pure white tablecloths and with goblets shining bright as silver, whilst the whole room was decorated with broom blossom. At the queen's behest, they rinsed their hands in water, then seated themselves in the places to which Parmeno had assigned them.

Dishes, daintily prepared, were brought in, excellent wines were at hand, and without a sound the three manservants promptly began to wait upon them. Everyone was delighted that these things had been so charmingly and efficiently arranged, and during the meal there was pleasant talk and merry laughter from all sides. Afterwards, the tables were cleared, and the queen sent for musical instruments so that one or two of their number, well versed in music, could play and sing, whilst the rest, ladies and gentlemen alike, could dance a *carole*.[6] At the queen's request, Dioneo took a lute and Fiammetta a viol, and they struck up a melodious tune, whereupon the queen, having sent the servants off to eat, formed a ring with the other ladies and the two young men, and sedately began to dance. And when the dance was over, they sang a number of gay and charming little songs.

---

4. The names of the servants are taken from comic characters in classical drama.   5. Like vespers, *tierce* is also an hour at which prayer was said, in this case about 9 A.M.   6. A round dance.

In this fashion they continued until the queen decided that the time had come for them to retire to rest, whereupon she dismissed the whole company. The young men went away to their rooms which were separated from those of the ladies, and found that, like the hall, they too were full of flowers, and that their beds were neatly made. The ladies made a similar discovery in theirs, and having undressed, they lay down to rest.

The queen rose shortly after nones,[7] and caused the other ladies to be roused, as also the young men, declaring it was harmful to sleep too much during the day. They therefore betook themselves to a meadow, where the grass, being protected from the heat of the sun, grew thick and green, and where, perceiving that a gentle breeze was stirring, the queen suggested that they should all sit on the green grass in a circle. And when they were seated, she addressed them as follows:

"As you can see, the sun is high in the sky, it is very hot, and all is silent except for the cicadas in the olive-trees. For the moment, it would surely be foolish of us to venture abroad, this being such a cool and pleasant spot in which to linger. Besides, as you will observe, there are chessboards and other games here, and so we are free to amuse ourselves in whatever way we please. But if you were to follow my advice, this hotter part of the day would be spent, not in playing games (which inevitably bring anxiety to one of the players, without offering very much pleasure either to his opponent or to the spectators), but in telling stories—an activity that may afford some amusement both to the narrator and to the company at large. By the time each one of you has narrated a little tale of his own or her own, the sun will be setting, the heat will have abated, and we shall be able to go and amuse ourselves wherever you choose. Let us, then, if the idea appeals to you, carry this proposal of mine into effect. But I am willing to follow your own wishes in this matter, and if you disagree with my suggestion, let us all go and occupy our time in whatever way we please until the hour of vespers."

The whole company, ladies and gentlemen alike, were in favor of telling stories.

"Then if it is agreeable to you," said the queen, "I desire that on this first day each of us should be free to speak upon whatever topic he prefers."

And turning to Panfilo, who was seated on her right, she graciously asked him to introduce the proceedings with one of his stories. No sooner did he receive this invitation than Panfilo began as follows, with everyone listening intently:

[THE FIRST STORY OF THE FIRST DAY]

Ser Cepperello deceives a holy friar with a false confession, then he dies; and although in life he was a most wicked man, in death he is reputed to be a Saint, and is called Saint Ciappelletto.

It is proper, dearest ladies, that everything made by man should begin with the sacred and admirable name of Him that was maker of all things. And therefore, since I am the first and must make a beginning to our story-telling,

7. About 3 p.m.

I propose to begin by telling you of one of His marvellous works, so that, when we have heard it out, our hopes will rest in Him as in something immutable, and we shall forever praise His name. It is obvious that since all temporal things are transient and mortal, so they are filled and surrounded by troubles, trials and tribulations, and fraught with infinite dangers which we, who live with them and are part of them, could without a shadow of a doubt neither endure, nor defend ourselves against, if God's special grace did not lend us strength and discernment. Nor should we suppose that His grace descends upon and within us through any merit of our own, for it is set in motion by His own loving-kindness, and is obtained by the pleas of people who like ourselves were mortal, and who, by firmly doing His pleasure whilst they were in this life, have now joined Him in eternal blessedness. To these, as to advocates made aware, through experience, of our frailty (perhaps because we have not the courage to submit our pleas personally in the presence of so great a judge) we present whatever we think is relevant to our cause. And our regard for Him, who is so compassionate and generous towards us, is all the greater when, the human eye being quite unable to penetrate the secrets of divine intelligence, common opinion deceives us and perhaps we appoint as our advocate in His majestic presence one who has been cast by Him into eternal exile. Yet He from whom nothing is hidden, paying more attention to the purity of the supplicant's motives than to his ignorance or to the banishment of the intercessor, answers those who pray to Him exactly as if the advocate were blessed in His sight. All of which can clearly be seen in the tale I propose to relate; and I say clearly because it is concerned, not with the judgment of God, but with that of men.

It is said, then, that Musciatto Franzesi,[8] having become a fine gentleman after acquiring enormous wealth and fame as a merchant in France, was obliged to come to Tuscany with the brother of the French king, the Lord Charles Lackland,[9] who had been urged and encouraged to come by Pope Boniface. But finding that his affairs, as is usually the case with merchants, were entangled here, there, and everywhere, and being unable quickly or easily to unravel them, he decided to place them in the hands of a number of different people. All this he succeeded in arranging, except that he was left with the problem of finding someone capable of recovering certain loans which he had made to various people in Burgundy.[1] The reason for his dilemma was that he had been told the Burgundians were a quarrelsome, thoroughly bad and unprincipled set of people; and he was quite unable to think of anyone he could trust, who was at the same time sufficiently villainous to match the villainy of the Burgundians. After devoting much thought to this problem, he suddenly recalled a man known as Ser Cepperello, of Prato,[2] who had been a frequent visitor to his house in Paris. This man was short in stature and used to dress very neatly, and the French, who did not know the meaning of the word Cepperello, thinking that it signified *chapel*, which in their language means "garland," and because as we have said he was a little man, used to call him, not Ciappello, but Ciappelletto:

8. Like many other characters in the *Decameron*, those appearing in this first story are based on actual people. Musciatto was a Florentine financier who made a huge fortune in France by dubious means; Cepperello Dietaiuti was one of his associates. 9. Brother of King Philip of France, who invaded Italy in 1301. 1. A region of northeastern France. 2. A city just to the north of Florence.

and everywhere in that part of the world, where few people knew him as Ser Cepperello, he was known as Ciappelletto.[3]

This Ciappelletto was a man of the following sort: a notary by profession, he would have taken it as a slight upon his honor if one of his legal deeds (and he drew up very few of them) were discovered to be other than false. In fact, he would have drawn up free of charge as many false documents as were requested of him, and done it more willingly than one who was highly paid for his services. He would take great delight in giving false testimony, whether asked for it or not. In those days, great reliance was placed in France upon sworn declarations, and since he had no scruples about swearing falsely, he used to win, by these nefarious means, every case in which he was required to swear upon his faith to tell the truth. He would take particular pleasure, and a great amount of trouble, in stirring up enmity, discord and bad blood between friends, relatives and anybody else; and the more calamities that ensued, the greater would be his rapture. If he were invited to witness a murder or any other criminal act, he would never refuse, but willingly go along; and he often found himself cheerfully assaulting or killing people with his own hands. He was a mighty blasphemer of God and His Saints, losing his temper on the tiniest pretext, as if he were the most hot-blooded man alive. He never went to church, and he would use foul language to pour scorn on all of her sacraments, declaring them repugnant. On the other hand, he would make a point of visiting taverns and other places of ill repute, and supplying them with his custom. Of women he was as fond as dogs are fond of a good stout stick; in their opposite, he took greater pleasure than the most depraved man on earth. He would rob and pilfer as conscientiously as if he were a saintly man making an offering. He was such a prize glutton and heavy drinker, that he would occasionally suffer for his over-indulgence in a manner that was most unseemly. He was a gambler and a card-sharper of the first order. But why do I lavish so many words upon him? He was perhaps the worst man ever born. Yet for all his villainy, he had long been protected by the power and influence of Messer Musciatto, on whose account he was many a time treated with respect, both by private individuals, whom he frequently abused, and by the courts of law, which he was forever abusing.

So that when Musciatto, who was well acquainted with his way of living, called this Ser Ciappelletto to mind, he judged him to be the very man that the perverseness of the Burgundians required. He therefore sent for him and addressed him as follows:

"Ser Ciappelletto, as you know, I am about to go away from here altogether, but I have some business to settle, among others with the Burgundians. These people are full of tricks, and I know of no one better fitted than yourself to recover what they owe me. And so, since you are not otherwise engaged at present, if you will attend to this matter I propose to obtain favors for you at court, and allow you a reasonable portion of the money you recover."

Ser Ciappelletto, who was out of a job at the time and ill-supplied with worldly goods, seeing that the man who had long been his prop and stay was

3. This nickname assumes that Ciappello's name derives from the Italian word *ceppo* ("log" or "tree-stump"), and the suffix-*etto* is a diminutive. Hence the name means "little stump," which may have an obscene connotation.

about to depart, made up his mind without delay and said (for he really had no alternative) that he would do it willingly. So that when they had agreed on terms, Ser Ciappelletto received powers of attorney from Musciatto and letters of introduction from the King, and after Musciatto's departure he went to Burgundy, where scarcely anybody knew him. And there, in a gentle and amiable fashion that ran contrary to his nature, as though he were holding his anger in reserve as a last resort, he issued his first demands and began to do what he had gone there to do. Before long, however, while lodging in the house of two Florentine brothers who ran a money-lending business there and did him great honor out of their respect for Musciatto, he happened to fall ill; whereupon the two brothers promptly summoned doctors and servants to attend him, and provided him with everything he needed to recover his health. But all their assistance was unavailing, because the good man, who was already advanced in years and had lived a disordered existence, was reported by his doctors to be going each day from bad to worse, like one who was suffering from a fatal illness. The two brothers were filled with alarm, and one day, alongside the room in which Ser Ciappelletto was lying, they began talking together.

"What are we to do about the fellow?" said one to the other. "We've landed ourselves in a fine mess on his account, because to turn him away from our house in his present condition would arouse a lot of adverse comment and show us to be seriously lacking in common sense. What would people say if they suddenly saw us evicting a dying man after giving him hospitality in the first place, and taking so much trouble to have him nursed and waited upon, when he couldn't possibly have done anything to offend us? On the other hand, he has led such a wicked life that he will never be willing to make his confession or receive the sacraments of the Church; and if he dies unconfessed, no church will want to accept his body and he'll be flung into the moat like a dog. But even if he makes his confession, his sins are so many and so appalling that the same thing will happen, because there will be neither friar nor priest who is either willing or able to give him absolution; in which case, since he will not have been absolved, he will be flung into the moat just the same. And when the townspeople see what has happened, they'll create a commotion, not only because of our profession which they consider iniquitous and never cease to condemn, but also because they long to get their hands on our money, and they will go about shouting: 'Away with these Lombard dogs[4] that the Church refuses to accept'; and they'll come running to our lodgings and perhaps, not content with stealing our goods, they'll take away our lives into the bargain. So we shall be in a pretty fix either way, if this fellow dies."

Ser Ciappelletto, who as we have said was lying near the place where they were talking, heard everything they were saying about him, for he was sharp of hearing, as invalids invariably are. So he called them in to him, and said:

"I don't want you to worry in the slightest on my account, nor to fear that I will cause you to suffer any harm. I heard what you were saying about me and I agree entirely that what you predict will actually come to pass, if matters take the course you anticipate; but they will do nothing of the kind. I have done our good Lord so many injuries whilst I lived, that to do Him

---

4. Outside Italy, Italian bankers were known as Lombards, even if they came from a different province.

another now that I am dying will be neither here nor there. So go and bring me the holiest and ablest friar you can find, if there is such a one, and leave everything to me, for I shall set your affairs and my own neatly in order, so that all will be well and you'll have nothing to complain of."

Whilst deriving little comfort from all this, the two brothers nevertheless went off to a friary and asked for a wise and holy man to come and hear the confession of a Lombard who was lying ill in their house. They were given an ancient friar of good and holy ways who was an expert in the Scriptures and a most venerable man, towards whom all the townspeople were greatly and specially devoted, and they conducted him to their house.

On reaching the room where Ser Ciappelletto was lying, he sat down at his bedside, and first he began to comfort him with kindly words, then he asked him how long it was since he had last been to confession. Whereupon Ser Ciappelletto, who had never been to confession in his life, replied:

"Father, it has always been my custom to go to confession at least once every week, except that there are many weeks in which I go more often. But to tell the truth, since I fell ill, nearly a week ago, my illness has caused me so much discomfort that I haven't been to confession at all."

"My son," said the friar, "you have done well, and you should persevere in this habit of yours. Since you go so often to confession, I can see that there will be little for me to hear or to ask."

"Master friar," said Ser Ciappelletto, "do not speak thus, for however frequently or regularly I confess, it is always my wish that I should make a general confession of all the sins I can remember committing from the day I was born till the day of my confession. I therefore beg you, good father, to question me about everything, just as closely as if I had never been confessed. Do not spare me because I happen to be ill, for I would much rather mortify this flesh of mine than that, by treating it with lenience, I should do anything that could lead to the perdition of my soul, which my Savior redeemed with His precious blood."

These words were greatly pleasing to the holy friar, and seemed to him proof of a well-disposed mind. Having warmly commended Ser Ciappelletto for this practice of his, he began by asking him whether he had ever committed the sin of lust with any woman. To which, heaving a sigh, Ser Ciappelletto replied:

"Father, I am loath to tell you the truth on this matter, in case I should sin by way of vainglory."

To which the holy friar replied:

"Speak out freely, for no man ever sinned by telling the truth, either in confession or otherwise."

"Since you assure me that this is so," said Ser Ciappelletto, "I will tell you. I am a virgin as pure as on the day I came forth from my mother's womb."

"Oh, may God give you His blessing!" said the friar. "How nobly you have lived! And your restraint is all the more deserving of praise in that, had you wished, you would have had greater liberty to do the opposite than those who, like ourselves, are expressly forbidden by rule."

Next he asked him whether he had displeased God by committing the sin of gluttony; to which, fetching a deep sigh, Ser Ciappelletto replied that he had, and on many occasions. For although, apart from the periods of fasting normally observed in the course of the year by the devout, he was accustomed

to fasting on bread and water for at least three days every week, he had drunk
the water as pleasurably and avidly (especially when he had been fatigued
from praying or going on a pilgrimage) as any great bibber of wine; he had
often experienced a craving for those dainty little wild herb salads that
women eat when they go away to the country; and sometimes the thought
of food had been more attractive to him than he considered proper in one
who, like himself, was fasting out of piety. Whereupon the friar said:

"My son, these sins are natural and they are very trivial, and therefore I
would not have you burden your conscience with them more than necessary.
No matter how holy a man may be, he will be attracted by the thought of
food after a long spell of fasting, and by the thought of drink when he is
fatigued."

"Oh!" said Ser Ciappelletto. "Do not tell me this to console me, father. As
you are aware, I know that things done in the service of God must all be
done honestly and without any grudge; and if anyone should do otherwise,
he is committing a sin."

The friar, delighted, said to him:

"I am contented to see you taking such a view, and it pleases me greatly
that you should have such a good and pure conscience in this matter. But
tell me, have you ever been guilty of avarice, by desiring to have more than
was proper, or keeping what you should not have kept?"

To which Ser Ciappelletto replied:

"Father, I would not wish you to judge me ill because I am in the house
of these money-lenders. I have nothing to do with their business; indeed I
had come here with the express intention of warning and reproaching them,
and dissuading them from this abominable form of money-making; and I
think I would have succeeded, if God had not stricken me in this manner.
However, I would have you know that my father left me a wealthy man, and
when he was dead, I gave the greater part of his fortune to charity. Since
then, in order to support myself and enable me to assist the Christian poor,
I have done a small amount of trading, in the course of which I have desired
to gain, and I have always shared what I have gained with the poor, allocating
one half to my own needs and giving the other half to them. And in this I
have had so much help from my Creator that I have continually gone from
strength to strength in the management of my affairs."

"You have done well," said the friar, "but tell me, how often have you lost
your temper?"

"Oh!" said Ser Ciappelletto, "I can assure you I have done that very often.
But who is there who could restrain himself, when the whole day long he
sees men doing disgusting things, and failing to observe God's commandments, or to fear His terrible wrath? There have been many times in the
space of a single day when I would rather have been dead than alive, looking
about me and seeing young people frittering away their time, telling lies,
going drinking in taverns, failing to go to church, and following the ways of
the world rather than those of God."

"My son," said the friar, "this kind of anger is justified, and for my part I
could not require you to do penance for it. But has it ever happened that
your anger has led you to commit murder or to pour abuse on anyone or do
them any other form of injury?"

To which Ser Ciappelletto replied:

"Oh, sir, however could you, that appear to be a man of God, say such a thing? If I had thought for a single moment of doing any of the things you mention, do you suppose I imagine that God would have treated me so generously? Those things are the business of cut-throats and evildoers, and whenever I have chanced upon one of their number, I have always sent him packing, and offered up a prayer for his conversion!"

"May God give you His blessing," said the friar, "but now, tell me, my son: have you ever borne false witness against any man, or spoken ill of people, or taken what belonged to others without seeking their permission?"

"Never, sir, except on one occasion," replied Ser Ciappelletto, "when I spoke ill of someone. For I once had a neighbor who, without the slightest cause, was forever beating his wife, so that on this one occasion I spoke ill of him to his wife's kinsfolk, for I felt extremely sorry for that unfortunate woman. Whenever the fellow had had too much to drink, God alone could tell you how he battered her."

Then the friar said:

"Let me see now, you tell me you were a merchant. Did you ever deceive anyone, as merchants do?"

"Faith, sir, I did," said Ser Ciappelletto. "But all I know about him is that he was a man who brought me some money that he owed me for a length of cloth I had sold him. I put the money away in a box without counting it, and a whole month passed before I discovered there were four pennies more than there should have been. I kept them for a year with the intention of giving them back, but I never saw him again, so I gave them away to a beggar."

"That was a trivial matter," said the friar, "and you did well to dispose of the money as you did."

The holy friar questioned him on many other matters, but always he answered in similar vein, and hence the friar was ready to proceed without further ado to give him absolution. But Ser Ciappelletto said:

"Sir, I still have one or two sins I have not yet told you about."

The friar asked him what they were, and he said:

"I recall that I once failed to show a proper respect for the Holy Sabbath, by making one of my servants sweep the house after nones[5] on a Saturday."

"Oh!" said the friar. "This, my son, is a trifling matter."

"No, father," said Ser Ciappelletto, "you must not call it trifling, for the Sabbath has to be greatly honored, seeing that this was the day on which our Lord rose from the dead."

Then the friar said:

"Have you done anything else?"

"Yes, sir," replied Ser Ciappelletto, "for I once, without thinking what I was doing, spat in the house of God."

The friar began to smile, and said:

"My son, this is not a thing to worry about. We members of religious orders spit there continually."

"That is very wicked of you," said Ser Ciappelletto, "for nothing should be kept more clean than the holy temple in which sacrifice is offered up to God."

In brief, he told the friar many things of this sort, and finally he began to

---

5. A church service held about 3 P.M.

sigh, and then to wail loudly, as he was well able to do whenever he pleased.

"My son," said the holy friar. "What is the matter?"

"Oh alas, sir," replied Ser Ciappelletto, "I have one sin left to which I have never confessed, so great is my shame in having to reveal it; and whenever I remember it, I cry as you see me doing now, and feel quite certain that God will never have mercy on me for this terrible sin."

"Come now, my son," said the holy friar, "what are you saying? If all the sins that were ever committed by the whole of mankind, together with those that men will yet commit till the end of the world, were concentrated in one single man, and he was as truly repentant and contrite as I see you to be, God is so benign and merciful that He would freely remit them on their being confessed to Him; and therefore you may safely reveal it."

Then Ser Ciappelletto said, still weeping loudly:

"Alas, father, my sin is too great, and I can scarcely believe that God will ever forgive me for it, unless you intercede with your prayers."

To which the friar replied:

"You may safely reveal it, for I promise that I will pray to God on your behalf."

Ser Ciappelletto went on weeping, without saying anything, and the friar kept encouraging him to speak. But after Ser Ciappelletto, by weeping in this manner, had kept the friar for a very long time on tenterhooks, he heaved a great sigh, and said:

"Father, since you promise that you will pray to God for me, I will tell you. You are to know then that once, when I was a little boy, I cursed my mother." And having said this, he began to weep loudly all over again.

"There now, my son," said the friar, "does this seem so great a sin to you? Why, people curse God the whole day long, and yet He willingly forgives those who repent for having cursed Him. Why then should you suppose He will not forgive you for this? Take heart and do not weep, for even if you had been one of those who set Him on the cross, I can see that you have so much contrition that He would certainly forgive you."

"Oh alas, father," said Ser Ciappelletto, "what are you saying? My dear, sweet mother, who carried me day and night for nine months in her body, and held me more than a hundred times in her arms! It was too wicked of me to curse her, and the sin is too great; and if you do not pray to God for me, it will never be forgiven me."

Perceiving that Ser Ciappelletto had nothing more to say, the friar absolved him and gave him his blessing. He took him for a very saintly man indeed, being fully convinced that what Ser Ciappelletto had said was true; but then, who is there who would not have been convinced, on hearing a dying man talk in this fashion? Finally, when all this was done, he said to him:

"Ser Ciappelletto, with God's help you will soon be well again. But in case it were to happen that God should summon your blessed and well-disposed soul to His presence, are you willing for your body to be buried in our convent?"

To which Ser Ciappelletto replied:

"Yes, father. In fact, I would not wish to be elsewhere, since you have promised that you will pray to God for me. Besides, I have always been especially devoted to your Order. So when you return to your convent, I beg you to see that I am sent that true body of Christ which you consecrate every morning on the altar. For although I am unworthy of it, I intend with your permission to take it, and afterwards to receive the holy Extreme Unction,[6] so that, having lived as a sinner, I shall at least die as a Christian."

The holy man said that he was greatly pleased, that the words were well spoken, and that he would see it was brought to him at once; and so it was.

The two brothers, who strongly suspected that Ser Ciappelletto was going to deceive them, had posted themselves behind a wooden partition which separated the room where Ser Ciappelletto was lying from another, and as they stood there listening they could easily follow what Ser Ciappelletto was saying to the friar. When they heard the things he confessed to having done, they were so amused that every so often they nearly exploded with mirth, and they said to each other:

"What manner of man is this, whom neither old age nor illness, nor fear of the death which he sees so close at hand, nor even the fear of God, before whose judgment he knows he must shortly appear, have managed to turn from his evil ways, or persuade to die any differently from the way he has lived?"

Seeing, however, that he had said all the right things to be received for burial in a church, they cared nothing for the rest.

Shortly thereafter Ser Ciappelletto made his communion, and, failing rapidly, he received Extreme Unction. Soon after vespers[7] on the very day that he had made his fine confession, he died. Whereupon the two brothers made all necessary arrangements, using his own money to see that he had an honorable funeral, and sending news of his death to the friars and asking them to come that evening to observe the customary vigil, and the following morning to take away the body.

On hearing that he had passed away, the holy friar who had received his confession arranged with the prior for the chapterhouse bell to be rung, and to the assembled friars he showed that Ser Ciappelletto had been a saintly man, as his confession had amply proved. He expressed the hope that through him the Lord God would work many miracles, and persuaded them that his body should be received with the utmost reverence and loving care. Credulous to a man, the prior and the other friars agreed to do so, and that evening they went to the place where Ser Ciappelletto's body lay, and celebrated a great and solemn vigil over it; and in the morning, dressed in albs and copes,[8] carrying books in their hands and bearing crosses before them, singing as they went, they all came for the body, which they then carried back to their church with tremendous pomp and ceremony, followed by nearly all the people of the town, men and women alike. And when it had been set down in the church, the holy friar who had confessed him climbed into the pulpit and began to preach marvelous things about Ser Ciappelletto's life, his fasts, his virginity, his simplicity and innocence and saintliness, relating among other things what he had tearfully confessed to him as his greatest sin, and describing how he had barely been able to convince him that God would forgive him, at which point he turned to reprimand his audience, saying:

---

6. The sacrament in which a dying person is anointed by a priest.   7. A church service held at eventide.
8. *Albs* and *copes* are religious vestments worn by priests while performing a religious ritual.

"And yet you miserable sinners have only to catch your feet in a wisp of
straw for you to curse God and the Virgin and all the Saints in heaven."

Apart from this, he said much else about his loyalty and his purity of heart.
And in brief, with a torrent of words that the people of the town believed
implicitly, he fixed Ser Ciappelletto so firmly in the minds and affections of
all those present that when the service was over, everyone thronged round
the body to kiss his feet and his hands, all the clothes were torn from his
back, and those who succeeded in grabbing so much as a tiny fragment felt
they were in Paradise itself. He had to be kept lying there all day, so that
everyone could come and gaze upon him, and on that same night he was
buried with honor in a marble tomb in one of the chapels. From the next
day forth, people began to go there to light candles and pray to him, and
later they began to make votive offerings and to decorate the chapel with
figures made of wax, in fulfilment of promises they had given.

The fame of his saintliness, and of the veneration in which he was held,
grew to such proportions that there was hardly anyone who did not pray for
his assistance in time of trouble, and they called him, and call him still, Saint
Ciappelletto. Moreover it is claimed that through him God has wrought many
miracles, and that He continues to work them on behalf of whoever commends himself devoutly to this particular Saint.

It was thus, then, that Ser Cepperello of Prato lived and died, becoming
a Saint in the way you have heard. Nor would I wish to deny that perhaps
God has blessed and admitted him to His presence. For albeit he led a
wicked, sinful life, it is possible that at the eleventh hour he was so sincerely
repentant that God had mercy upon him and received him into His kingdom.
But since this is hidden from us, I speak only with regard to the outward
appearance, and I say that the fellow should rather be in Hell, in the hands
of the devil, than in Paradise. And if this is the case, we may recognize how
very great is God's loving-kindness towards us, in that it takes account, not
of our error, but of the purity of our faith, and grants our prayers even when
we appoint as our emissary one who is His enemy, thinking him to be His
friend, as though we were appealing to one who was truly holy as our intercessor for His favor. And therefore, so that we, the members of this joyful
company, may be guided safely and securely by His grace through these
present adversities, let us praise the name of Him with whom we began our
storytelling, let us hold Him in reverence, and let us commend ourselves to
Him in the hour of our need, in the certain knowledge that we shall be heard.

And there the narrator fell silent.

[THE NINTH STORY OF THE FOURTH DAY][9]

*Guillaume de Roussillon causes his wife to eat the heart of her lover, Guillaume de
Cabestanh,[1] whom he has secretly murdered. When she finds out, she kills herself by
leaping from a lofty casement to the ground below, and is subsequently buried with the
man she loved.*

You must know, then, that according to the Provençals, there once lived
in Provence two noble knights, each of whom owned several castles and had

9. This story is told by Dioneo, one of the young men.   1. The story is based on a poetic account of the
love affair between an early 13th-century Provençal poet of this name and the wife of his lord, Raimon de
Castel-Roussillon.

a number of dependants. The name of the first was Guillaume de Roussillon, whilst the other was called Guillaume de Cabestanh. Since both men excelled in feats of daring, they were bosom friends and made a point of accompanying one another to jousts and tournaments and other armed contests, each bearing the same device.[2]

Although the castles in which they lived were some ten miles apart, Guillaume de Cabestanh chanced to fall hopelessly in love with the charming and very beautiful wife of Guillaume de Roussillon, and, notwithstanding the bonds of friendship and brotherhood that united the two men, he managed in various subtle ways to bring his love to the lady's notice. The lady, knowing him to be a most gallant knight, was deeply flattered, and began to regard him with so much affection that there was nothing she loved or desired more deeply. All that remained for him to do was to approach her directly, which he very soon did, and from then on they met at frequent intervals for the purpose of making passionate love to one another.

One day, however, they were incautious enough to be espied by the lady's husband, who was so incensed by the spectacle that his great love for Cabestanh was transformed into mortal hatred. He firmly resolved to do away with him, but concealed his intentions far more successfully than the lovers had been able to conceal their love.

His mind being thus made up, Roussillon happened to hear of a great tournament that was to be held in France. He promptly sent word of it to Cabestanh and asked him whether he would care to call upon him, so that they could talk it over together and decide whether or not to go and how they were to get there. Cabestanh was delighted to hear of it, and sent back word to say that he would come and sup with him next day without fail.

On receiving Cabestanh's message, Roussillon judged this to be his opportunity for killing him. Next day, he armed himself, took horse with a few of his men, and lay in ambush about a mile away from his castle, in a wood through which Cabestanh was bound to pass. After a long wait, he saw him approaching, unarmed, and followed by two of his men, who were likewise unarmed, for he never suspected for a moment that he was running into danger. Roussillon waited until Cabestanh was at close range, then he rushed out at him with murder and destruction in his heart, brandishing a lance above his head and shouting: "Traitor, you are dead!" And before the words were out of his mouth he had driven the lance through Cabestanh's breast.

Cabestanh was powerless to defend himself, or even to utter a word, and on being run through by the lance he fell to the ground. A moment later he was dead, and his men, without stopping to see who had perpetrated the deed, turned the heads of their horses and galloped away as fast as they could in the direction of their master's castle.

Dismounting from his horse, Roussillon cut open Cabestanh's chest with a knife, tore out the heart with his own hands, and, wrapping it up in a banderole,[3] told one of his men to take it away. Having given strict orders that no one was to breathe a word about what had happened, he then remounted and rode back to his castle, by which time it was already dark.

The lady had heard that Cabestanh was to be there that evening for supper and was eagerly waiting for him to arrive. When she saw her husband arriving without him she was greatly surprised, and said to him:

2. Coat of arms.   3. A long narrow flag or streamer.

"And how is it, my lord, that Cabestanh has not come?"

To which her husband replied:

"Madam, I have received word from him that he cannot be here until tomorrow."

Roussillon left her standing there, feeling somewhat perturbed, and when he had dismounted, he summoned the cook and said to him:

"You are to take this boar's heart and see to it that you prepare the finest and most succulent dish you can devise. When I am seated at table, send it in to me in a silver tureen."

The cook took the heart away, minced it, and added a goodly quantity of fine spices, employing all his skill and loving care and turning it into a dish that was too exquisite for words.

When it was time for dinner, Roussillon sat down at the table with his lady. Food was brought in, but he was unable to do more than nibble at it because his mind was dwelling upon the terrible deed he had committed. Then the cook sent in his special dish, which Roussillon told them to set before his lady, saying that he had no appetite that evening.

He remarked on how delicious it looked, and the lady, whose appetite was excellent, began to eat it, finding it so tasty a dish that she ate every scrap of it.

On observing that his lady had finished it down to the last morsel, the knight said:

"What did you think of that, madam?"

"In good faith, my lord," replied the lady, "I liked it very much."

"So help me God," exclaimed the knight, "I do believe you did. But I am not surprised to find that you liked it dead, because when it was alive you liked it better than anything else in the whole world."

On hearing this, the lady was silent for a while; then she said:

"How say you? What is this that you have caused me to eat?"

"That which you have eaten," replied the knight, "was in fact the heart of Guillaume de Cabestanh, with whom you, faithless woman that you are, were so infatuated. And you may rest assured that it was truly his, because I tore it from his breast myself, with these very hands, a little before I returned home."

You can all imagine the anguish suffered by the lady on hearing such tidings of Cabestanh, whom she loved more dearly than anything else in the world. But after a while, she said:

"This can only have been the work of an evil and treacherous knight, for if, of my own free will, I abused you by making him the master of my love, it was not he but I that should have paid the penalty for it. But God forbid that any other food should pass my lips now that I have partaken of such excellent fare as the heart of so gallant and courteous a knight as Guillaume de Cabestanh."

And rising to her feet, she retreated a few steps to an open window, through which without a second thought she allowed herself to fall.

The window was situated high above the ground, so that the lady was not only killed by her fall but almost completely disfigured.

The spectacle of his wife's fall threw Roussillon into a panic and made him repent the wickedness of his deed. And fearing the wrath of the local people and of the Count of Provence, he had his horses saddled and rode away.

By next morning the circumstances of the affair had become common knowledge throughout the whole of the district, and people were sent out from the castles of the lady's family and of Guillaume de Cabestanh to gather up the two bodies, which were later placed in a single tomb in the chapel of the lady's own castle amid widespread grief and mourning. And the tombstone bore an inscription, in verse, to indicate who was buried there and the manner and the cause of their deaths.

[THE EIGHTH STORY OF THE FIFTH DAY][4]

In his love for a young lady of the Traversari family, Nastagio degli Onesti squanders his wealth without being loved in return. He is entreated by his friends to leave the city, and goes away to Classe, where he sees a girl being hunted down and killed by a horseman, and devoured by a brace of hounds. He then invites his kinsfolk and the lady he loves to a banquet, where this same girl is torn to pieces before the eyes of his beloved, who, fearing a similar fate, accepts Nastagio as her husband.

In Ravenna,[5] a city of great antiquity in Romagna, there once used to live a great many nobles and men of property, among them a young man called Nastagio degli Onesti, who had inherited an incredibly large fortune on the deaths of his father and one of his uncles. Being as yet unmarried, he fell in love, as is the way with young men, with a daughter of Messer Paolo Traversari, a girl of far more noble lineage than his own, whose love he hoped to win by dint of his accomplishments. But though these were very considerable, and splendid, and laudable, far from promoting his cause they appeared to damage it, inasmuch as the girl he loved was persistently cruel, harsh and unfriendly toward him. And on account possibly of her singular beauty, or perhaps because of her exalted rank, she became so haughty and contemptuous of him that she positively loathed him and everything he stood for.

All of this was so difficult for Nastagio to bear that he was frequently seized, after much weeping and gnashing of teeth, with the longing to kill himself out of sheer despair. But, having stayed his hand, he would then decide that he must give her up altogether, or learn if possible to hate her as she hated him. All such resolutions were unavailing, however, for the more his hopes dwindled, the greater his love seemed to grow.

As the young man persisted in wooing the girl and spending money like water, certain of his friends and relatives began to feel that he was in danger of exhausting both himself and his inheritance. They therefore implored and advised him to leave Ravenna and go to live for a while in some other place, with the object of curtailing both his wooing and his spending. Nastagio rejected this advice as often as it was offered, but they eventually pressed him so hard that he could not refuse them any longer, and agreed to do as they suggested. Having mustered an enormous baggage-train, as though he were intending to go to France or Spain or some other remote part of the world, he mounted his horse, rode forth from Ravenna with several of his friends, and repaired to a place which is known as Classe, some three miles distant from the city. Having sent for a number of tents and pavilions, he told his companions that this was where he intended to stay, and that they could all go back to Ravenna. So Nastagio pitched his camp in this place, and began to live in as fine and lordly a fashion as any man ever born, from

4. The teller is Filomena, one of the young ladies.   5. On the west coast of Italy.

time to time inviting various groups of friends to dine or breakfast with him, as had always been his custom.

Now, it so happened that one Friday morning toward the beginning of May, the weather being very fine, Nastagio fell to thinking about his cruel mistress. Having ordered his servants to leave him to his own devices so that he could meditate at greater leisure, he sauntered off, lost in thought, and his steps led him straight into the pinewoods. The fifth hour of the day was already spent, and he had advanced at least half a mile into the woods, oblivious of food and everything else, when suddenly he seemed to hear a woman giving vent to dreadful wailing and ear-splitting screams. His pleasant reverie being thus interrupted, he raised his head to investigate the cause, and discovered to his surprise that he was in the pinewoods. Furthermore, on looking straight ahead he caught sight of a naked woman, young and very beautiful, who was running through a dense thicket of shrubs and briars towards the very spot where he was standing. The woman's hair was dishevelled, her flesh was all torn by the briars and brambles, and she was sobbing and screaming for mercy. Nor was this all, for a pair of big, fierce mastiffs were running at the girl's heels, one on either side, and every so often they caught up with her and savaged her. Finally, bringing up the rear he saw a swarthy-looking knight, his face contorted with anger, who was riding a jet-black steed and brandishing a rapier, and who, in terms no less abusive than terrifying, was threatening to kill her.[6]

This spectacle struck both terror and amazement into Nastagio's breast, to say nothing of compassion for the hapless woman, a sentiment that in its turn engendered the desire to rescue her from such agony and save her life, if this were possible. But on finding that he was unarmed, he hastily took up a branch of a tree to serve as a cudgel, and prepared to ward off the dogs and do battle with the knight. When the latter saw what he was doing, he shouted to him from a distance:

"Keep out of this, Nastagio! Leave me and the dogs to give this wicked sinner her deserts!"

He had no sooner spoken than the dogs seized the girl firmly by the haunches and brought her to a halt. When the knight reached the spot he dismounted from his horse, and Nastagio went up to him saying:

"I do not know who you are, or how you come to know my name; but I can tell you that it is a gross outrage for an armed knight to try and kill a naked woman, and to set dogs upon her as though she were a savage beast. I shall do all in my power to defend her, of that you may be sure."

Whereupon the knight said:

"I was a fellow citizen of yours, Nastagio, my name was Guido degli Anastagi, and you were still a little child when I fell in love with this woman. I loved her far more deeply than you love that Traversari girl of yours, but her pride and cruelty led me to such a pass that, one day, I killed myself in sheer despair with this rapier that you see in my hand, and thus I am condemned to eternal punishment. My death pleased her beyond measure, but shortly thereafter she too died, and because she had sinned by her cruelty and by gloating over my sufferings, and was quite unrepentant, being convinced that she was more of a saint than a sinner, she too was condemned to the pains

6. Cf. the account of the punishment of the spendthrifts in Dante's *Inferno*, canto 13.

of Hell. No sooner was she cast into Hell than we were both given a special punishment, which consisted in her case of fleeing before me, and in my own of pursuing her as though she were my mortal enemy rather than the woman with whom I was once so deeply in love. Every time I catch up with her, I kill her with this same rapier by which I took my own life; then I slit her back open, and (as you will now observe for yourself) I tear from her body that hard, cold heart to which neither love nor pity could ever gain access, and together with the rest of her entrails I cast it to these dogs to feed upon.

"Within a short space of time, as ordained by the power and justice of God, she springs to her feet as though she had not been dead at all, and her agonizing flight begins all over again, with the dogs and myself in pursuit. Every Friday at this hour I overtake her in this part of the woods, and slaughter her in the manner you are about to observe; but you must not imagine that we are idle for the rest of the week, because on the remaining days I hunt her down in other places where she was cruel to me in thought and deed. As you can see for yourself, I am no longer her lover but her enemy, and in this guise I am obliged to pursue her for the same number of years as the months of her cruelty towards me. Stand aside, therefore, and let me carry out the judgment of God. Do not try to oppose what you cannot prevent."

On hearing these words, Nastagio was shaken to the core, there was scarcely a single hair on his head that was not standing on end, and he stepped back to fix his gaze on the unfortunate girl, waiting in fear and trembling to see what the knight would do to her. This latter, having finished speaking, pounced like a mad dog, rapier in hand, upon the girl, who was kneeling before him, held by the two mastiffs, and screaming for mercy at the top of her voice. Applying all his strength, the knight plunged his rapier into the middle of her breast and out again at the other side, whereupon the girl fell on her face, still sobbing and screaming, whilst the knight, having laid hold of a dagger, slashed open her back, extracted her heart and everything else around it, and hurled it to the two mastiffs, who devoured it greedily on the instant. But before very long the girl rose suddenly to her feet as though none of these things had happened, and sped off in the direction of the sea, being pursued by the dogs, who kept tearing away at her flesh as she ran. Remounting his horse, and seizing his rapier, the knight too began to give chase, and within a short space of time they were so far away that Nastagio could no longer see them.

For some time after bearing witness to these events, Nastagio stood rooted to the spot out of fear and compassion, but after a while it occurred to him that since this scene was enacted every Friday, it ought to prove very useful to him. So he marked the place and returned to his servants; and when the time seemed ripe, he sent for his friends and kinsfolk, and said to them:

"For some little time you have been urging me to desist from wooing this hostile mistress of mine and place a curb on my extravagance, and I am willing to do so on condition that you obtain for me a single favor, which is this: that on Friday next you arrange for Messer Paolo Traversari and his wife and daughter and all their womenfolk, together with any other lady you care to invite, to join me in this place for breakfast. My reason for wanting this will become apparent to you on the day itself."

They thought this a very trifling commission for them to undertake, and promised him they would do it. On their return to Ravenna, they invited all the people he had specified. And although they had a hard job, when the time came, in persuading Nastagio's beloved to go, she nevertheless went there along with the others.

Nastagio saw to it that a magnificent banquet was prepared, and had the tables placed beneath the pine-trees in such a way as to surround the place where he had witnessed the massacre of the cruel lady. Moreover, in seating the ladies and gentlemen at table, he so arranged matters that the girl he loved sat directly facing the spot where the scene would be enacted.

The last course had already been served, when they all began to hear the agonized yells of the fugitive girl. Everyone was greatly astonished and wanted to know what it was, but nobody was able to say. So they all stood up to see if they could find out what was going on, and caught sight of the wailing girl, together with the knight and the dogs. And shortly thereafter they came into the very midst of the company.

Everyone began shouting and bawling at the dogs and the knight, and several people rushed forward to the girl's assistance; but the knight, by repeating to them the story he had related to Nastagio, not only caused them to retreat but filled them all with terror and amazement. And when he dealt with the girl in the same way as before, all the ladies present (many of whom, being related either to the suffering girl or to the knight, still remembered his great love and the manner of his death) wept as plaintively as though what they had witnessed had been done to themselves.

When the spectacle was at an end, and the knight and the lady had gone, they all began to talk about what they had seen. But none was stricken with so much terror as the cruel maiden loved by Nastagio, for she had heard and seen everything distinctly and realized that these matters had more to do with herself than with any of the other guests, in view of the harshness she had always displayed towards Nastagio; consequently, she already had the sensation of fleeing before her enraged suitor, with the mastiffs tearing away at her haunches.

So great was the fear engendered within her by this episode, that in order to avoid a similar fate she converted her enmity into love; and, seizing the earliest opportunity (which came to her that very evening), she privily sent a trusted maidservant to Nastagio, requesting him to be good enough to call upon her, as she was ready to do anything he desired. Nastagio was overjoyed, and told her so in his reply, but added that if she had no objection he preferred to combine his pleasure with the preservation of her good name, by making her his lawful wedded wife.

Knowing that she alone was to blame for the fact that she and Nastagio were not already married, the girl readily sent him her consent. And so, acting as her own intermediary, she announced to her father and mother, to their enormous satisfaction, that she would be pleased to become Nastagio's wife. On the following Sunday Nastagio married her, and after celebrating their nuptials they settled down to a long and happy life together.

Their marriage was by no means the only good effect to be produced by this horrible apparition, for from that day forth the ladies of Ravenna in general were so frightened by it that they became much more tractable to men's pleasures than they had ever been in the past.

Two young men lodge overnight at a cottage, where one of them goes and sleeps with their host's daughter, whilst his wife inadvertently sleeps with the other. The one who was with the daughter clambers into bed beside her father, mistaking him for his companion, and tells him all about it. A great furor then ensues, and the wife, realizing her mistake, gets into her daughter's bed, whence with a timely explanation she restores the peace.

Not long ago, there lived in the valley of the Mugnone[8] a worthy man who earned an honest penny by supplying food and drink to wayfarers; and although he was poor, and his house was tiny, he would from time to time, in cases of urgent need, offer them a night's lodging, but only if they happened to be people he knew.

Now, this man had a most attractive wife, who had borne him two children, the first being a charming and beautiful girl of about fifteen or sixteen, as yet unmarried, whilst the second was an infant, not yet twelve months old, who was still being nursed at his mother's breast.

The daughter had caught the eye of a lively and handsome young Florentine gentleman who used to spend much of his time in the countryside, and he fell passionately in love with her. Nor was it long before the girl, being highly flattered to have won the affection of so noble a youth, which she strove hard to retain by displaying the greatest affability towards him, fell in love with him. And neither of the pair would have hesitated to consummate their love, but for the fact that Pinuccio (for such was the young man's name) was not prepared to expose the girl or himself to censure.

At length however, his ardor growing daily more intense, Pinuccio was seized with a longing to consort with her, come what may, and it occurred to him that he must find some excuse for lodging with her father overnight, since, being conversant with the layout of the premises, he had good reason to think that he and the girl could be together without anyone ever being any the wiser. And no sooner did this idea enter his head than he promptly took steps to carry it into effect.

Late one afternoon, he and a trusted companion of his called Adriano, who knew of his love for the girl, hired a couple of pack-horses, and having laden them with a pair of saddlebags, filled probably with straw, they set forth from Florence; and after riding round in a wide circle they came to the valley of the Mugnone, some time after nightfall. They then wheeled their horses round to make it look as though they were returning from Romagna, rode up to the cottage of our worthy friend, and knocked at the door. And since the man was well acquainted with both Pinuccio and his companion, he immediately came down to let them in.

"You'll have to put us up for the night," said Pinuccio. "We had intended to reach Florence before dark, but as you can see, we've made such slow progress that this is as far as we've come, and it's too late to enter the city at this hour."

"My dear Pinuccio," replied the host, "as you know, I can't exactly offer you a princely sort of lodging. But no matter: since night has fallen and you've nowhere else to go, I shall be glad to put you up as best I can."

So the two young men dismounted, and having seen that their nags were comfortably stabled, they went into the house, where, since they had brought plenty to eat with them, they made a hearty supper along with their host. Now, their host had only one bedroom, which was very tiny, and into this he had crammed three small beds, leaving so little space that it was almost impossible to move between them. Two of the beds stood alongside one of the bedroom walls, whilst the third was against the wall on the opposite side of the room; and having seen that the least uncomfortable of the three was made ready for his guests, the host invited them to sleep in that for the night. Shortly afterward, when they appeared to be asleep, though in reality they were wide awake, he settled his daughter in one of the other two beds, whilst he and his wife got into the third; and beside the bed in which she was sleeping, his wife had placed the cradle containing her infant son.

Having made a mental note of all these arrangements, Pinuccio waited until he was sure that everyone was asleep, then quietly left his bed, stole across to the bed in which his lady-love was sleeping, and lay down beside her. Although she was somewhat alarmed, the girl received him joyously in her arms, and they then proceeded to take their fill of that sweet pleasure for which they yearned above all else.

Whilst Pinuccio and the girl were thus employed, a cat, somewhere in the house, happened to knock something over, causing the man's wife to wake up with a start. Being anxious to discover what it was, she got up and groped her way naked in the dark towards that part of the house from which the noise had come.

Meanwhile Adriano also happened to get up, not for the same reason, but in order to obey the call of nature, and as he was groping his way towards the door with this purpose in view, he came in contact with the cradle deposited there by the woman. Being unable to pass without moving it out of his way, he picked it up and set it down beside his own bed; and after doing what he had to do, he returned to his bed and forgot all about it.

Having discovered the cause of the noise and assured herself that nothing important had fallen, the woman swore at the cat, and, without bothering to light a lamp and explore the matter further, returned to the bedroom. Picking her way carefully through the darkness, she went straight to the bed where her husband was lying; but on finding no trace of the cradle, she said to herself: "How stupid I am! What a fine thing to do! Heavens above, I was just about to step into the bed where my guests are sleeping." So she walked a little further up the room, found the cradle, and got into bed beside Adriano, thinking him to be her husband.

On perceiving this, Adriano, who was still awake, gave her a most cordial reception; and without a murmur he tacked hard to windward over and over again, much to her delight and satisfaction.

This, then, was how matters stood when Pinuccio, who had gratified his longings to the full and was afraid of falling asleep in the young lady's arms, abandoned her so as to go back and sleep in his own bed. But on reaching the bed to find the cradle lying there, he moved on, thinking he had mistaken his host's bed for his own, and ended up by getting into bed with the host, who was awakened by his coming. And being under the impression that the man who lay beside him was Adriano, Pinuccio said:

"I swear to you that there was never anything so delicious as Niccolosa. By the body of God, no man ever had so much pleasure with any woman as I have been having with her. Since the time I left you, I assure you I've been to the bower of bliss half a dozen times at the very least."

The host was not exactly pleased to hear Pinuccio's tidings, and having first of all asked himself what the devil the fellow was doing in his bed, he allowed his anger to get the better of his prudence, and exclaimed:

"What villainy is this, Pinuccio? I can't think why you should have played me so scurvy a trick, but by all that's holy, I shall pay you back for it."

Now, Pinuccio was not the wisest of young men, and on perceiving his error, instead of doing all he could to remedy matters, he said:

"Pay me back? How? What could you do to me?"

Whereupon the host's wife, thinking she was with her husband, said to Adriano:

"Heavens! Just listen to the way those guests of ours are arguing with one another!"

Adriano laughed, and said:

"Let them get on with it, and to hell with them. They had far too much to drink last night."

The woman had already thought she could detect the angry tones of her husband, and on hearing Adriano's voice, she realized at once whose bed she was sharing. So being a person of some intelligence, she promptly got up without a word, seized her baby's cradle, and having picked her way across the room, which was in total darkness, she set the cradle down beside the bed in which her daughter was sleeping and scrambled in beside her. Then, pretending to have been aroused by the noise her husband was making, she called out to him and demanded to know what he was quarrelling with Pinuccio about. Whereupon her husband replied:

"Don't you hear what he says he has done to Niccolosa this night?"

"He's telling a pack of lies," said the woman. "He hasn't been anywhere near Niccolosa, for I've been lying beside her myself the whole time and I haven't managed to sleep a wink. You're a fool to take any notice of him. You men drink so much in the evening that you spend the night dreaming and wandering all over the place in your sleep, and imagine you've performed all sorts of miracles: it's a thousand pities you don't trip over and break your necks! What's Pinuccio doing there anyway? Why isn't he in his own bed?"

At which point, seeing how adroitly the woman was concealing both her own and her daughter's dishonor, Adriano came to her support by saying:

"How many times do I have to tell you, Pinuccio, not to wander about in the middle of the night? You'll land yourself in serious trouble one of these days, with this habit of walking in your sleep, and claiming to have actually done the fantastic things you dream about. Come back to bed, curse you!"

When he heard Adriano confirm what his wife had been saying, the host began to think that Pinuccio really had been dreaming after all; and seizing him by the shoulder, he shook him and yelled at him, saying:

"Wake up, Pinuccio! Go back to your own bed!"

Having taken all of this in, Pinuccio now began to thresh about as though he were dreaming again, causing his host to split his sides with laughter. But in the end, after a thorough shaking, he pretended to wake up; and calling to Adriano, he said:

"Why have you woken me up? Is it morning already?"

"Yes," said Adriano. "Come back here."

Pinuccio kept up the pretence, showing every sign of being extremely drowsy, but in the end he left his host's side and staggered back to bed with Adriano. When they got up next morning, their host began to laugh and make fun of Pinuccio and his dreams. And so, amid a constant stream of merry banter, the two young men saddled and loaded their horses, and after drinking the health of their host, they remounted and rode back to Florence, feeling no less delighted with the manner than with the outcome of the night's activities.

From then on, Pinuccio discovered other ways of consorting with Niccolosa, who meanwhile assured her mother that he had certainly been dreaming. And thus the woman, who retained a vivid memory of Adriano's embraces, was left with the firm conviction that she alone had been awake on the night in question.

[THE TENTH STORY OF THE TENTH DAY][9]

The Marquis of Saluzzo, obliged by the entreaties of his subjects to take a wife, follows his personal whims and marries the daughter of a peasant. She bears him two children, and he gives her the impression that he has put them to death. Later on, pretending that she has incurred his displeasure and that he has remarried, he arranges for his own daughter to return home and passes her off as his bride, having meanwhile turned his wife out of doors in no more than the shift she is wearing. But on finding that she endures it all with patience, he cherishes her all the more deeply, brings her back to his house, shows her their children, who have now grown up, and honors her as the Marchioness, causing others to honor her likewise.

A very long time ago, there succeeded to the marquisate of Saluzzo[1] a young man called Gualtieri, who, having neither wife nor children, spent the whole of his time hunting and hawking, and never even thought about marrying or raising a family, which says a great deal for his intelligence. His followers, however, disapproved of this, and repeatedly begged him to marry so that he should not be left without an heir nor they without a lord. Moreover, they offered to find him a wife whose parentage would be such as to strengthen their expectations and who would make him exceedingly happy.

So Gualtieri answered them as follows:

"My friends, you are pressing me to do something that I had always set my mind firmly against, seeing how difficult it is to find a person who will easily adapt to one's own way of living, how many thousands there are who will do precisely the opposite, and what a miserable life is in store for the man who stumbles upon a woman ill-suited to his own temperament. Moreover it is foolish of you to believe that you can judge the character of daughters from the ways of their fathers and mothers, hence claiming to provide me with a wife who will please me. For I cannot see how you are to know the fathers, or to discover the secrets of the mothers; and even if this were possible, daughters are very often different from either of their parents. Since, however, you are so determined to bind me in chains of this sort, I

9. The teller is Dioneo, the young man who tells the last story of each day.   1. A town at the foot of the Alps about thirty miles south of Turin.

am ready to do as you ask; but so that I have only myself to blame if it should turn out badly, I must insist on marrying a wife of my own choosing. And I hereby declare that no matter who she may be, if you fail to honor her as your lady you will learn to your great cost how serious a matter it is for you to have urged me to marry against my will."

To this the gentlemen replied that if only he would bring himself to take a wife, they would be satisfied.

Now, for some little time, Gualtieri had been casting an appreciative eye on the manners of a poor girl from a neighboring village, and thinking her very beautiful, he considered that a life with her would have much to commend it. So without looking further afield, he resolved to marry the girl; and having summoned her father, who was very poor indeed, he arranged with him that he should take her as his wife.

This done, Gualtieri brought together all his friends from the various parts of his domain, and said to them:

"My friends, since you still persist in wanting me to take a wife, I am prepared to do it, not because I have any desire to marry, but rather in order to gratify your wishes. You will recall the promise you gave me, that no matter whom I should choose, you would rest content and honor her as your lady. The time has now come when I want you to keep that promise, and for me to honor the promise I gave to you. I have found a girl after my own heart, in this very district, and a few days hence I intend to marry her and convey her to my house. See to it, therefore, that the wedding-feast lacks nothing in splendor, and consider how you may honorably receive her, so that all of us may call ourselves contented—I with you for keeping your promise, and you with me for keeping mine."

As of one voice, the good folk joyously gave him their blessing, and said that whoever she happened to be, they would accept her as their lady and honor her as such in all respects. Then they all prepared to celebrate the wedding in a suitably grand and sumptuous manner, and Gualtieri did the same. A rich and splendid nuptial feast was arranged, to which he invited many of his friends, his kinsfolk, great nobles and other people of the locality; moreover he caused a quantity of fine, rich robes to be tailored to fit a girl whose figure appeared to match that of the young woman he intended to marry; and lastly he laid in a number of rings and ornamental belts, along with a precious and beautiful crown, and everything else that a bride could possibly need.

Early on the morning of the day he had fixed for the nuptials, Gualtieri, his preparations now complete, mounted his horse together with all the people who had come to do him honor, and said:

"Gentlemen, it is time for us to go and fetch the bride."

He then set forth with the whole of the company in train, and eventually they came to the village and made their way to the house of the girl's father, where they met her as she was returning with water from the fountain, making great haste so that she could go with other women to see Gualtieri's bride arriving. As soon as Gualtieri caught sight of her, he called to her by her name, which was Griselda, and asked her where her father was, to which she blushingly replied:

"My lord, he is at home."

So Gualtieri dismounted, and having ordered everyone to wait for him outside, he went alone into the humble dwelling, where he found the girl's father, whose name was Giannùcole, and said to him:

"I have come to marry Griselda, but first I want to ask her certain questions in your presence." He then asked her whether, if he were to marry her, she would always try to please him and never be upset by anything he said or did, whether she would obey him, and many other questions of this sort, to all of which she answered that she would.

Whereupon Gualtieri, having taken her by the hand, led her out of the house, and in the presence of his whole company and of all the other people there he caused her to be stripped naked. Then he called for the clothes and shoes which he had had specially made, and quickly got her to put them on, after which he caused a crown to be placed upon the dishevelled hair of her head. And just as everyone was wondering what this might signify, he said:

"Gentlemen, this is the woman I intend to marry, provided she will have me as her husband." Then, turning to Griselda, who was so embarrassed that she hardly knew where to look, he said: "Griselda, will you have me as your wedded husband?"

To which she replied:

"I will, my lord."

"And I will have you as my wedded wife," said Gualtieri, and he married her then and there before all the people present. He then helped her mount a palfrey, and led her back, honorably attended, to his house, where the nuptials were as splendid and as sumptuous, and the rejoicing as unrestrained, as if he had married the King of France's daughter.

Along with her new clothes, the young bride appeared to take on a new lease of life, and she seemed a different woman entirely. She was endowed, as we have said, with a fine figure and beautiful features, and lovely as she already was, she now acquired so confident, graceful and decorous a manner that she could have been taken for the daughter, not of the shepherd Giannùcole, but of some great nobleman, and consequently everyone who had known her before her marriage was filled with astonishment. But apart from this, she was so obedient to her husband, and so compliant to his wishes, that he thought himself the happiest and most contented man on earth. At the same time she was so gracious and benign towards her husband's subjects, that each and every one of them was glad to honor her, and accorded her his unselfish devotion, praying for her happiness, prosperity, and greater glory. And whereas they had been wont to say that Gualtieri had shown some lack of discretion in taking this woman as his wife, they now regarded him as the wisest and most discerning man on earth. For no one apart from Gualtieri could ever have perceived the noble qualities that lay concealed beneath her ragged and rustic attire.

In short, she comported herself in such a manner that she quickly earned widespread acclaim for her virtuous deeds and excellent character not only in her husband's domain but also in the world at large; and those who had formerly censured Gualtieri for choosing to marry her were now compelled to reverse their opinion.

Not long after she had gone to live with Gualtieri she conceived a child, and in the fullness of time, to her husband's enormous joy, she bore him a daughter. But shortly thereafter Gualtieri was seized with the strange desire to test Griselda's patience, by subjecting her to constant provocation and making her life unbearable.

At first he lashed her with his tongue, feigning to be angry and claiming that his subjects were thoroughly disgruntled with her on account of her lowly condition, especially now that they saw her bearing children; and he said they were greatly distressed about this infant daughter of theirs, of whom they did nothing but grumble.

The lady betrayed no sign of bitterness on hearing these words, and without changing her expression she said to him:

"My lord, deal with me as you think best[2] for your own good name and peace of mind, for I shall rest content whatever you decide, knowing myself to be their inferior and that I was unworthy of the honor which you so generously bestowed upon me."

This reply was much to Gualtieri's liking, for it showed him that she had not been puffed with pride by any honor that he or others had paid her.

A little while later, having told his wife in general terms that his subjects could not abide the daughter she had borne him, he gave certain instructions to one of his attendants, whom he sent to Griselda. The man looked very sorrowful, and said:

"My lady, if I do not wish to die, I must do as my lord commands me. He has ordered me to take this daughter of yours, and to . . ." And his voice trailed off into silence.

On hearing these words and perceiving the man's expression, Griselda, recalling what she had been told, concluded that he had been instructed to murder her child. So she quickly picked it up from its cradle, kissed it, gave it her blessing, and albeit she felt that her heart was about to break, placed the child in the arms of the servant without any trace of emotion, saying:

"There: do exactly as your lord, who is my lord too, has instructed you. But do not leave her to be devoured by the beasts and the birds, unless that is what he has ordered you to do."

The servant took away the little girl and reported Griselda's words to Gualtieri, who, marvelling at her constancy, sent him with the child to a kinswoman of his in Bologna,[3] requesting her to rear and educate her carefully, but without ever making it known whose daughter she was.

Then it came about that his wife once more became pregnant, and in due course she gave birth to a son, which pleased Gualtieri enormously. But not being content with the mischief he had done already, he abused her more viciously than ever, and one day he glowered at her angrily and said:

"Woman, from the day you produced this infant son, the people have made my life a complete misery, so bitterly do they resent the thought of a grandson of Giannùcole succeeding me as their lord. So unless I want to be deposed, I'm afraid I shall be forced to do as I did before, and eventually to leave you and marry someone else."

His wife listened patiently, and all she replied was:

"My lord, look to your own comfort, see that you fulfil your wishes, and spare no thought for me, since nothing brings me pleasure unless it pleases you also."

Before many days had elapsed, Gualtieri sent for his son in the same way that he had sent for his daughter, and having likewise pretended to have had the child put to death, he sent him, like the little girl, to Bologna. To all of

2. See Luke 1.38, where the Virgin Mary replies to the Angel Gabriel, "Be it unto me according to thy word." 3. A city in northern Italy, not far from Florence.

this his wife reacted no differently, either in her speech or in her looks, than she had on the previous occasion, much to the astonishment of Gualtieri, who told himself that no other woman could have remained so impassive. But for the fact that he had observed her doting upon the children for as long as he allowed her to do so, he would have assumed that she was glad to be rid of them, whereas he knew that she was too judicious to behave in any other way.

His subjects, thinking he had caused the children to be murdered, roundly condemned him and judged him a cruel tyrant, whilst his wife became the object of their deepest compassion. But to the women who offered her their sympathy in the loss of her children, all she ever said was that the decision of their father was good enough for her.

Many years after the birth of his daughter, Gualtieri decided that the time had come to put Griselda's patience to the final test. So he told a number of his men that in no circumstances could he put up with Griselda as his wife any longer, having now come to realize that his marriage was an aberration of his youth. He would therefore do everything in his power to obtain a dispensation from the Pope, enabling him to divorce Griselda and marry someone else. For this he was chided severely by many worthy men, but his only reply was that it had to be done.

On learning of her husband's intentions, from which it appeared she would have to return to her father's house, in order perhaps to look after the sheep as she had in the past, meanwhile seeing the man she adored being cherished by some other woman, Griselda was secretly filled with despair. But she prepared herself to endure this final blow as stoically as she had borne Fortune's earlier assaults.

Shortly thereafter, Gualtieri arranged for some counterfeit letters of his to arrive from Rome, and led his subjects to believe that in these, the Pope had granted him permission to abandon Griselda and remarry.

He accordingly sent for Griselda, and before a large number of people he said to her:

"Woman, I have had a dispensation from the Pope, allowing me to leave you and take another wife. Since my ancestors were great noblemen and rulers of these lands, whereas yours have always been peasants, I intend that you shall no longer be my wife, but return to Giannùcole's house with the dowry you brought me, after which I shall bring another lady here. I have already chosen her and she is far better suited to a man of my condition."

On hearing these words, the lady, with an effort beyond the power of any normal woman's nature, suppressed her tears and replied:

"My lord, I have always known that my lowly condition was totally at odds with your nobility, and that it is to God and to yourself that I owe whatever standing I possess. Nor have I ever regarded this as a gift that I might keep and cherish as my own, but rather as something I have borrowed; and now that you want me to return it, I must give it back to you with good grace. Here is the ring with which you married me: take it. As to your ordering me to take away the dowry that I brought, you will require no accountant, nor will I need a purse or a pack-horse, for this to be done. For it has not escaped my memory that you took me naked as on the day I was born.[4] If you think

---

4. See Job 1.21: "Naked came I out of my mother's womb, and naked shall I return thither: the Lord gave, and the Lord hath taken away."

it proper that the body in which I have borne your children should be seen by all the people, I shall go away naked. But in return for my virginity, which I brought to you and cannot retrieve, I trust you will at least allow me, in addition to my dowry, to take one shift away with me."

Gualtieri wanted above all else to burst into tears, but maintaining a stern expression he said:

"Very well, you may take a shift."

All the people present implored Gualtieri to let her have a dress, so that she who had been his wife for thirteen years and more would not have to suffer the indignity of leaving his house in a shift, like a pauper; but their pleas were unavailing. And so Griselda, wearing a shift, barefoot, and with nothing to cover her head, having bidden them farewell, set forth from Gualtieri's house and returned to her father amid the weeping and the wailing of all who set eyes upon her.

Giannùcole, who had never thought it possible that Gualtieri would keep his daughter as his wife, and was daily expecting this to happen, had preserved the clothes she discarded on the morning Gualtieri had married her. So he brought them to her, and Griselda, having put them on, applied herself as before to the menial chores in her father's house, bravely enduring the cruel assault of hostile Fortune.

No sooner did Gualtieri drive Griselda away, than he gave his subjects to understand that he was betrothed to a daughter of one of the Counts of Panago.[5] And having ordered that grandiose preparations were to be made for the nuptials, he sent for Griselda and said to her:

"I am about to fetch home this new bride of mine, and from the moment she sets foot inside the house, I intend to accord her an honorable welcome. As you know, I have no women here who can set the rooms in order for me, or attend to many of the things that a festive occasion of this sort requires. No one knows better than you how to handle these household affairs, so I want you to make all the necessary arrangements. Invite all the ladies you need, and receive them as though you were mistress of the house. And when the nuptials are over, you can go back home to your father."

Since Griselda was unable to lay aside her love for Gualtieri as readily as she had dispensed with her good fortune, his words pierced her heart like so many knives. But she replied:

"My lord, I am ready to do as you ask."[6]

And so, in her coarse, thick, woollen garments, Griselda returned to the house she had quitted shortly before in her shift, and started to sweep and tidy the various chambers. On her instructions, the beds were draped with hangings, the benches in the halls were suitably adorned, the kitchen was made ready; and she set her hand, as though she were a petty serving wench, to every conceivable household task, never stopping to draw breath until she had everything prepared and arranged as befitted the occasion.

Having done all this, she caused invitations to be sent, in Gualtieri's name, to all the ladies living in those parts, and began to await the event. And when at last the nuptial day arrived, heedless of her beggarly attire, she bade a cheerful welcome to each of the lady guests, displaying all the warmth and courtesy of a lady of the manor.

Gualtieri's children having meanwhile been carefully reared by his kins-

5. An area near Bologna.   6. See again Luke 1.38: "Behold the handmaid of the Lord."

woman in Bologna, who had married into the family of the Courts of Panago, the girl was now twelve years old, the loveliest creature ever seen, whilst the boy had reached the age of six. Gualtieri had sent word to his kinswoman's husband, asking him to do him the kindness of bringing this daughter of his to Saluzzo along with her little brother, to see that she was nobly and honorably escorted, and to tell everyone he met that he was taking her to marry Gualtieri, without revealing who she really was to a living soul.

In accordance with the Marquis's request, the gentleman set forth with the girl and her brother and a noble company, and a few days later, shortly before the hour of breakfast, he arrived at Saluzzo, where he found that all the folk thereabouts, and numerous others from neighboring parts, were waiting for Gualtieri's latest bride.

After being welcomed by the ladies, she made her way to the hall where the tables were set, and Griselda, just as we have described her, went cordially up to meet her, saying:

"My lady, you are welcome."

The ladies, who in vain had implored Gualtieri to see that Griselda remained in another room, or to lend her one of the dresses that had once been hers, so that she would not cut such a sorry figure in front of his guests, took their seats at table and addressed themselves to the meal. All eyes were fixed upon the girl, and everyone said that Gualtieri had made a good exchange. But Griselda praised her as warmly as anyone present, speaking no less admiringly of her little brother.

Gualtieri felt that he had now seen all he wished to see of the patience of his lady, for he perceived that no event, however singular, produced the slightest change in her demeanor, and he was certain that this was not because of her obtuseness, as he knew her to be very intelligent. He therefore considered that the time had come for him to free her from the rancor that he judged her to be hiding beneath her tranquil outward expression. And having summoned her to his table, before all the people present he smiled at her and said:

"What do you think of our new bride?"

"My lord," replied Griselda, "I think very well of her. And if, as I believe, her wisdom matches her beauty, I have no doubt whatever that your life with her will bring you greater happiness than any gentleman on earth has ever known. But with all my heart I beg you not to inflict those same wounds upon her that you imposed upon her predecessor, for I doubt whether she could withstand them, not only because she is younger, but also because she has had a refined upbringing, whereas the other had to face continual hardship from her infancy."

On observing that Griselda was firmly convinced that the young lady was to be his wife, and that even so she allowed no hint of resentment to escape her lips, Gualtieri got her to sit down beside him, and said:

"Griselda, the time has come for you to reap the reward of your unfailing patience, and for those who considered me a cruel and bestial tyrant, to know that whatever I have done was done of set purpose, for I wished to show you how to be a wife, to teach these people how to choose and keep a wife, and to guarantee my own peace and quiet for as long as we were living beneath the same roof. When I came to take a wife, I was greatly afraid that this peace would be denied me, and in order to prove otherwise I tormented and provoked you in the ways you have seen. But as I have never known you to oppose my wishes, I now intend, being persuaded that you can offer me all the happiness I desired, to restore to you in a single instant that which I took from you little by little, and delectably assuage the pains I have inflicted upon you. Receive with gladsome heart, then, this girl whom you believe to be my bride, and also her brother. These are our children, whom you and many others have long supposed that I caused to be cruelly murdered; and I am your husband, who loves you above all else, for I think I can boast that there is no other man on earth whose contentment in his wife exceeds my own."

Having spoken these words, he embraced and kissed Griselda, who by now was weeping with joy; then they both got up from table and made their way to the place where their daughter sat listening in utter amazement to these tidings. And after they had fondly embraced the girl and her brother, the mystery was unravelled to her, as well as to many of the others who were present.

The ladies rose from table in transports of joy, and escorted Griselda to a chamber, where, with greater assurance of her future happiness, they divested her of her tattered garments and clothed her anew in one of her stately robes. And as their lady and their mistress, a rôle which even in her rags had seemed to be hers, they led her back to the hall, where she and Gualtieri rejoiced with the children in a manner marvelous to behold.

Everyone being delighted with the turn that events had taken, the feasting and the merrymaking were redoubled, and continued unabated for the next few days. Gualtieri was acknowledged to be very wise, though the trials to which he had subjected his lady were regarded as harsh and intolerable, whilst Griselda was accounted the wisest of all.

The Count of Panago returned a few days later to Bologna, and Gualtieri, having removed Giannùcole from his drudgery, set him up in a style befitting his father-in-law, so that he lived in great comfort and honor for the rest of his days. As for Gualtieri himself, having married off his daughter to a gentleman of renown, he lived long and contentedly with Griselda, never failing to honor her to the best of his ability.

What more needs to be said, except that celestial spirits may sometimes descend even into the houses of the poor, whilst there are those in royal palaces who would be better employed as swineherds than as rulers of men? Who else but Griselda could have endured so cheerfully the cruel and unheard of trials that Gualtieri imposed upon her without shedding a tear? For perhaps it would have served him right if he had chanced upon a wife, who, being driven from the house in her shift, had found some other man to shake her skin-coat for her, earning herself a fine new dress in the process.

SIR GAWAIN AND THE GREEN KNIGHT
1380?

Although concerned with King Arthur and his knights, *Sir Gawain and the Green Knight* is far from a typical Arthurian romance. It focuses on a single knight, it displays a remarkable economy and elegance of narrative form, and it deals not with deeds of martial prowess but with an inner moral testing. In addition, it is written not only in verse, unlike the vast majority of late medieval romances, but in a verse of such subtlety and beauty that the work stands out as a masterpiece of literary craftsmanship. *Gawain* was composed sometime between 1370 and 1390 in the northwest midlands in England, in an area near the present city of Birmingham, and its anonymous author used alliteration for his primary poetic form. Each line has four stresses, at least two and usually three of which fall on words that begin with the same sound: "King Arthur was counted most courteous of all." The only exception to this pattern is the five-line verse that ends each stanza, known as a *bob and wheel*. The translation reproduces this pattern with great skill and fidelity, one result of which is the occasional use of unusual words or ordinary words in slightly unaccustomed senses: some of these have been glossed, while the meanings of others may be surmised from the context or, if necessary, found in a dictionary. This minor difficulty also replicates the experience of reading the original, which is written not only in a provincial dialect but with a deliberately artful vocabulary. The poem is, as the poet says, "linked in measures meetly / By letters tried and true," and much of its success derives from its verbal virtuosity.

In using this alliterative line the poet was harking back to the tradition of Anglo-Saxon verse, as represented in this anthology by *Beowulf* and by the lyric poem *The Ruin*. We do not know how this tradition survived from the middle of the twelfth century, when it disappeared from view under the influence of continental forms imported by the conquering Normans, until the second half of the fourteenth, when it burst forth in an impressive number of excellent poems. But the *Gawain*-poet seems to have been aware that he was using a native tradition, for one of the themes of his work is the contrast between Bertilak, who for all his sophistication is powerfully linked to a vividly described natural world, and Gawain, the representative of an elegant court that may be a bit too civilized. The poem is constructed from two originally separate narrative motifs, "The Beheading Game" and "The Exchange of Winnings." In both cases Gawain must meet a standard of behavior that is both courtly and more than courtly. He must show himself to be honorable both in submitting to the blow of an ax that must surely prove fatal and in exchanging with his host what each man has won that day. This second test then has an added challenge: each morning the host goes out hunting, while his wife offers *herself* to her husband's guest. Much of the comedy of the poem derives from the way in which Gawain refuses this attractive offer while avoiding any hint of discourtesy. But in both of the main tests the hero's resolve is weakened by the most natural of impulses: self-preservation. When he finally does accept from the lady what she says is a magic belt that will preserve his life, he violates his agreement with his host by not offering this gift in exchange for the pelt he receives. When his deception is discovered, Gawain is deeply humiliated and berates both himself and the lady, who has, he thinks, finally seduced him into disloyalty. But Bertilak is far less disturbed: he recognizes that Gawain is, after all, only a human being, not a paragon of perfect virtue. One way the poet stresses this theme is in the contrast between the pentangle that Gawain carries on his shield—a symbol of perfect fidelity—and the green baldric that he comes to wear as a sign of his fallibility. When upon his return to the court Arthur and his household adopt the green baldric as a sign of honor, Gawain is suddenly placed in the unusual—and difficult—position of knowing more about human nature, both his own and others, than does his sovereign. And oddly enough, not even the reader can be certain that Gawain's acceptance of the baldrick, which he sees as his failure, did not in fact save his life.

One of the most striking aspects of the poem is the symmetry it establishes between Bertilak's three days of hunting and the three wooing scenes between Gawain and his host's wife. The precise significance of this symmetry has never been satisfactorily explained, but every reader recognizes its instinctive fittingness. As Bertilak rushes through the wintry landscape in pursuit of his prey, Gawain uses his verbal dexterity to evade the lady's none too subtle advances. Gawain may be warmly tucked up in bed, but we can well imagine that he would prefer to be testing his mettle in a more active, less social way. But his fate is to be denied the opportunity to act, and perhaps the most subtle aspect of the poet's genius is his ability to get us to admire a hero who must learn to succeed by doing nothing.

PRONOUNCING GLOSSARY

The following list uses common English syllables and stress accents to provide rough equivalents of selected words whose pronunciation may be unfamiliar to the general reader.

Bertilak: *behr-tee-lak'*   Sauvage: *soh-vazh'*

Sir Gawain and the Green Knight[1]

PART I

Since the siege and the assault was ceased at Troy,
The walls breached and burnt down to brands and ashes,
The knight that had knotted the nets of deceit
Was impeached for his perfidy,[2] proven most true,
It was high-born Aeneas and his haughty race   5
That since prevailed over provinces, and proudly reigned
Over well-nigh all the wealth of the West Isles.[3]
Great Romulus[4] to Rome repairs in haste;
With boast and with bravery builds he that city
And names it with his own name, that it now bears.   10
Ticius to Tuscany,[5] and towers raises,
Langobard[6] in Lombardy lays out homes,
And far over the French Sea, Felix Brutus[7]
On many broad hills and high Britain he sets,[8]
                most fair.   15
        Where war and wrack and wonder
        By shifts have sojourned there,
        And bliss by turns with blunder
        In that land's lot had share.

And since this Britain was built by this baron great,   20
Bold boys bred there, in broils delighting,

---

1. Translated by Marie Borroff. Many of the notes are by E. Talbot Donaldson.   2. The treacherous knight is either Aeneas himself or Antenor, both of whom were, according to medieval tradition, traitors to their city, Troy; but Aeneas was actually tried ("impeached") by the Greeks for his refusal to hand over to them his sister Polyxena.   3. Perhaps western Europe.   4. The legendary founder of Rome is here given Trojan ancestry, like Aeneas.   5. A region north of Rome; modern Florence is located in it. *Ticius:* not otherwise known.   6. The reputed founder of Lombardy, a region in the north centered on modern Milan.   7. Great-grandson of Aeneas and legendary founder of Britain; not elsewhere given the name *Felix* (Latin "happy"). *French Sea:* the North Sea, including the English Channel.   8. Establishes.

That did in their day many a deed most dire.
More marvels have happened in this merry land
Than in any other I know, since that olden time,
But of those that here built, of British kings,　　　　　25
King Arthur was counted most courteous of all,
Wherefore an adventure I aim to unfold,
That a marvel of might some men think it,
And one unmatched among Arthur's wonders.
If you will listen to my lay but a little while,　　　　30
As I heard it in hall, I shall hasten to tell
　　　　　　　anew,
　　　　As it was fashioned featly
　　　　In tale of derring-do,
　　　　And linked in measures meetly[9]　　　　35
　　　　By letters tried and true.

This king lay at Camelot[1] at Christmastide;
Many good knights and gay his guests were there,
Arrayed of the Round Table rightful brothers,[2]
With feasting and fellowship and carefree mirth.　　　40
There true men contended in tournaments many,
Joined there in jousting these gentle knights,
Then came to the court for carol-dancing,
For the feast was in force full fifteen days,
With all the meat and the mirth that men could devise,　45
Such gaiety and glee, glorious to hear,
Brave din by day, dancing by night.
High were their hearts in halls and chambers,
These lords and these ladies, for life was sweet.
In peerless pleasures passed they their days,　　　50
The most noble knights known under Christ,
And the loveliest ladies that lived on earth ever,
And he the comeliest king, that that court holds,
For all this fair folk in their first age
　　　　　　　were still.　　　　55
　　　　Happiest of mortal kind,
　　　　King noblest famed of will;
　　　　You would now go far to find
　　　　So hardy a host on hill.

While the New Year was new, but yesternight come,　60
This fair folk at feast two-fold was served,
When the king and his company were come in together,
The chanting in chapel achieved and ended.
Clerics and all the court acclaimed the glad season,
Cried Noel anew, good news to men;　　　　65
Then gallants gather gaily, hand-gifts to make,
Called them out clearly, claimed them by hand,

9. Suitably.　1. Capital of Arthur's kingdom, presumably located in southwest England or southern Wales.　2. According to legend, the Round Table was made by Merlin, the wise magician who had helped Arthur become king after a dispute broke out among Arthur's knights about precedence: it seated one hundred knights. The table described in the poem is not round.

Bickered long and busily about those gifts.
Ladies laughed aloud, though losers they were,
And he that won was not angered, as well you will know.[3]   70
All this mirth they made until meat was served;
When they had washed them worthily, they went to their seats,
The best seated above, as best it beseemed,
Guenevere the goodly queen gay in the midst
On a dais well-decked and duly arrayed   75
With costly silk curtains, a canopy over,
Of Toulouse and Turkestan tapestries rich,
All broidered and bordered with the best gems
Ever brought into Britain, with bright pennies
                to pay.   80
        Fair queen, without a flaw,
        She glanced with eyes of grey.
        A seemlier[4] that once he saw,
        In truth, no man could say.

But Arthur would not eat till all were served;   85
So light was his lordly heart, and a little boyish;
His life he liked lively—the less he cared
To be lying for long, or long to sit,
So busy his young blood, his brain so wild.
And also a point of pride pricked him in heart,   90
For he nobly had willed, he would never eat
On so high a holiday, till he had heard first
Of some fair feat or fray, some far-borne tale,
Of some marvel of might, that he might trust,
By champions of chivalry achieved in arms,   95
Or some suppliant came seeking some single knight
To join with him in jousting, in jeopardy each
To lay life for life, and leave it to fortune
To afford him on field fair hap[5] or other.
Such is the king's custom, when his court he holds   100
At each far-famed feast amid his fair host
               so dear.
        The stout king stands in state
        Till a wonder shall appear;
        He leads, with heart elate,   105
        High mirth in the New Year.

So he stands there in state, the stout young king,
Talking before the high table[6] of trifles fair.
There Gawain the good knight by Guenevere sits,
With Agravain à la dure main[7] on his other side,   110
Both knights of renown, and nephews of the king.
Bishop Baldwin above begins the table,
And Yvain, son of Urien, ate with him there.
These few with the fair queen were fittingly served;

3. The dispensing of New Year's gifts seems to have involved kissing.   4. More suitable and pleasing (queen).   5. Good luck.   6. The high table is on a dais; the side tables (line 115) are on the main floor and run along the walls at a right angle to the high table.   7. Of the hard hand.

At the side-tables sat many stalwart knights.   115
Then the first course comes, with clamor of trumpets
That were bravely bedecked with bannerets bright,
With noise of new drums and the noble pipes.
Wild were the warbles that wakened that day
In strains that stirred many strong men's hearts.   120
There dainties were dealt out, dishes rare,
Choice fare to choose, on chargers so many
That scarce was there space to set before the people
The service of silver, with sundry meats,
               on cloth.   125
          Each fair guest freely there
          Partakes, and nothing loth;[8]
          Twelve dishes before each pair;
          Good beer and bright wine both.

Of the service itself I need say no more,   130
For well you will know no tittle was wanting.
Another noise and a new was well-nigh at hand,
That the lord might have leave his life to nourish;
For scarce were the sweet strains still in the hall,
And the first course come to that company fair,   135
There hurtles in at the hall-door an unknown rider,
One the greatest on ground in growth of his frame:
From broad neck to buttocks so bulky and thick,
And his loins and his legs so long and so great,
Half a giant on earth I hold him to be,   140
But believe him no less than the largest of men,
And that the seemliest in his stature to see, as he rides,
For in back and in breast though his body was grim,
His waist in its width was worthily small,
And formed with every feature in fair accord   145
               was he.
          Great wonder grew in hall
          At his hue most strange to see,
          For man and gear and all
          Were green as green could be.   150

And in guise all of green, the gear and the man:
A coat cut close, that clung to his sides,
And a mantle to match, made with a lining
Of furs cut and fitted—the fabric was noble,
Embellished all with ermine, and his hood beside,   155
That was loosed from his locks, and laid on his shoulders.
With trim hose and tight, the same tint of green,
His great calves were girt, and gold spurs under
He bore on silk bands that embellished his heels,
And footgear well-fashioned, for riding most fit.   160
And all his vesture verily was verdant green;
Both the bosses[9] on his belt and other bright gems

---

8. Not unwillingly.   9. Ornamental knobs.

That were richly ranged on his raiment noble
About himself and his saddle, set upon silk,
That to tell half the trifles would tax my wits,   165
The butterflies and birds embroidered thereon
In green of the gayest, with many a gold thread.
The pendants of the breast-band, the princely crupper,[1]
And the bars of the bit were brightly enameled;
The stout stirrups were green, that steadied his feet,   170
And the bows of the saddle and the side-panels both,
That gleamed all and glinted with green gems about.
The steed he bestrides of that same green
                so bright.
        A green horse great and thick;   175
        A headstrong steed of might;
        In broidered bridle quick,
        Mount matched man aright.

Gay was this goodly man in guise all of green,
And the hair of his head to his horse suited;   180
Fair flowing tresses enfold his shoulders;
A beard big as a bush on his breast hangs,
That with his heavy hair, that from his head falls,
Was evened all about above both his elbows,
That half his arms thereunder were hid in the fashion   185
Of a king's cap-à-dos,[2] that covers his throat.
The mane of that mighty horse much to it like,
Well curled and becombed, and cunningly knotted
With filaments of fine gold amid the fair green,
Here a strand of the hair, here one of gold;   190
His tail and his foretop twin in their hue,
And bound both with a band of a bright green
That was decked adown the dock[3] with dazzling stones
And tied tight at the top with a triple knot
Where many bells well burnished rang bright and clear.   195
Such a mount in his might, nor man on him riding,
None had seen, I dare swear, with sight in that hall
                so grand.
        As lightning quick and light
        He looked to all at hand;   200
        It seemed that no man might
        His deadly dints withstand.

Yet had he no helm, nor hauberk[4] neither,
Nor plate, nor appurtenance appending to arms,
Nor shaft pointed sharp, nor shield for defense,   205
But in his one hand he had a holly bob
That is goodliest in green when groves are bare,
And an ax in his other, a huge and immense,
A wicked piece of work in words to expound:

---

1. *Breast-band . . . crupper:* parts of the horse's harness.   **2.** Or *capados*, interpreted by the translator as a garment covering its wearer "from head to back."   **3.** The solid part of the tail.   **4.** Tunic of chain mail.

The head on its haft was an ell[5] long;   210
The spike of green steel, resplendent with gold;
The blade burnished bright, with a broad edge,
As well shaped to shear as a sharp razor;
Stout was the stave in the strong man's gripe,
That was wound all with iron to the weapon's end,   215
With engravings in green of goodliest work.
A lace lightly about, that led to a knot,
Was looped in by lengths along the fair haft,
And tassels thereto attached in a row,
With buttons of bright green, brave to behold.   220
This horseman hurtles in, and the hall enters;
Riding to the high dais, recked he no danger;
Not a greeting he gave as the guests he o'erlooked,
Nor wasted his words, but "Where is," he said,
"The captain of this crowd? Keenly I wish   225
To see that sire with sight, and to himself say

           my say."
        He swaggered all about
        To scan the host so gay;
        He halted, as if in doubt   230
        Who in that hall held sway.

There were stares on all sides as the stranger spoke,
For much did they marvel what it might mean
That a horseman and a horse should have such a hue,
Grow green as the grass, and greener, it seemed,   235
Than green fused on gold more glorious by far.
All the onlookers eyed him, and edged nearer,
And awaited in wonder what he would do,
For many sights had they seen, but such a one never,
So that phantom and faerie the folk there deemed it,   240
Therefore chary of answer was many a champion bold,
And stunned at his strong words stone-still they sat
In a swooning silence in the stately hall.
As all were slipped into sleep, so slackened their speech
           apace   245
        Not all, I think, for dread,
        But some of courteous grace
        Let him who was their head
        Be spokesman in that place.

Then Arthur before the high dais that entrance beholds,   250
And hailed him, as behooved, for he had no fear,
And said "Fellow, in faith you have found fair welcome;
The head of this hostelry Arthur am I;
Leap lightly down, and linger, I pray,
And the tale of your intent you shall tell us after."   255
"Nay, so help me," said the other, "He that on high sits,
To tarry here any time, 'twas not mine errand;

5. Three or four feet long.

But as the praise of you, prince, is puffed up so high,
And your court and your company are counted the best,
Stoutest under steel-gear on steeds to ride,   260
Worthiest of their works the wide world over,
And peerless to prove in passages of arms,
And courtesy here is carried to its height,
And so at this season I have sought you out.
You may be certain by the branch that I bear in hand   265
That I pass here in peace, and would part friends,
For had I come to this court on combat bent,
I have a hauberk at home, and a helm beside,
A shield and a sharp spear, shining bright,
And other weapons to wield, I ween[6] well, to boot,   270
But as I willed no war, I wore no metal.
But if you be so bold as all men believe,
You will graciously grant the game that I ask
           by right."
        Arthur answer gave   275
        And said, "Sir courteous knight,
        If contest here you crave,
        You shall not fail to fight."

"Nay, to fight, in good faith, is far from my thought;
There are about on these benches but beardless children,   280
Were I here in full arms on a haughty steed,
For measured against mine, their might is puny.
And so I call in this court for a Christmas game,
For 'tis Yule and New Year, and many young bloods about;
if any in this house such hardihood claims,   285
Be so bold in his blood, his brain so wild,
As stoutly to strike one stroke for another,
I shall give him as my gift this gisarme[7] noble,
This ax, that is heavy enough, to handle as he likes,
And I shall bide[8] the first blow, as bare as I sit.   290
If there be one so wilful my words to assay,
Let him leap hither lightly, lay hold of this weapon;
I quitclaim it forever, keep it[9] as his own,
And I shall stand him a stroke, steady on this floor,
So you grant me the guerdon[1] to give him another,   295
           sans[2] blame.
        In a twelvemonth and a day
        He shall have of me the same;
        Now be it seen straightway
        Who dares take up the game."   300

If he astonished them at first, stiller were then
All that household in hall, the high and the low;
The stranger on his green steed stirred in the saddle,
And roisterously his red eyes he rolled all about,
Bent his bristling brows, that were bright green,   305

---

6. Believe.   7. Weapon.   8. Endure.   9. I.e., let him keep it.   1. Reward.   2. Without.

Wagged his beard as he watched who would arise.
When the court kept its counsel he coughed aloud,
And cleared his throat coolly, the clearer to speak:
"What, is this Arthur's house," said that horseman then,
"Whose fame is so fair in far realms and wide?   310
Where is now your arrogance and your awesome deeds,
Your valor and your victories and your vaunting words?
Now are the revel and renown of the Round Table
Overwhelmed with a word of one man's speech,
For all cower and quake, and no cut felt!"   315
With this he laughs so loud that the lord grieved;
The blood for sheer shame shot to his face,
                            and pride.
            With rage his face flushed red,
            And so did all beside.   320
            Then the king as bold man bred
            Toward the stranger took a stride.

And said "Sir, now we see you will say but folly,
Which whoso has sought, it suits that he find.
No guest here is aghast of your great words.   325
Give to me your gisarme, in God's own name,
And the boon you have begged shall straight be granted."
He leaps to him lightly, lays hold of his weapon;
The green fellow on foot fiercely alights.
Now has Arthur his ax, and the haft grips,   330
And sternly stirs it about, on striking bent.
The stranger before him stood there erect,
Higher than any in the house by a head and more;
With stern look as he stood, he stroked his beard,
And with undaunted countenance drew down his coat,   335
No more moved nor dismayed for his mighty dints
Than any bold man on bench had brought him a drink
                            of wine.
            Gawain by Guenevere
            Toward the king doth now incline: 340
            "I beseech, before all here,
            That this melee may be mine."

"Would you grant me the grace," said Gawain to the king,
"To be gone from this bench and stand by you there,
If I without discourtesy might quit this board,   345
And if my liege lady³ misliked it not,
I would come to your counsel before your court noble.
For I find it not fit, as in faith it is known,
When such a boon is begged before all these knights,
Though you be tempted thereto, to take it on yourself   350
While so bold men about upon benches sit,
That no host under heaven is hardier of will,
Nor better brothers-in-arms where battle is joined;

---

3. Lady entitled to the knight's feudal service.

I am the weakest, well I know, and of wit feeblest;
And the loss of my life would be least of any;   355
That I have you for uncle is my only praise;
My body, but for your blood, is barren of worth;
And for that this folly befits not a king,
And 'tis I that have asked it, it ought to be mine,
And if my claim be not comely let all this court judge,   360
                    in sight."
            The court assays the claim,
            And in counsel all unite
            To give Gawain the game
            And release the king outright.   365

Then the king called the knight to come to his side,
And he rose up readily, and reached him with speed,
Bows low to his lord, lays hold of the weapon,
And he releases it lightly, and lifts up his hand,
And gives him God's blessing, and graciously prays   370
That his heart and his hand may be hardy both.
"Keep, cousin," said the king, "what you cut with this day,
And if you rule it aright, then readily, I know,
You shall stand the stroke it will strike after."
Gawain goes to the guest with gisarme in hand,   375
And boldly he bides there, abashed not a whit.
Then hails he Sir Gawain, the horseman in green:
"Recount we our contract, ere you come further.
First I ask and adjure you, how you are called
That you tell me true, so that trust it I may."   380
"In good faith," said the good knight, "Gawain am I
Whose buffet befalls you, whate'er betide after,
And at this time twelvemonth take from you another
With what weapon you will, and with no man else
                    alive."   385
            The other nods assent:
            "Sir Gawain, as I may thrive,
            I am wondrous well content
            That you this dint shall drive."

"Sir Gawain," said the Green Knight, "By God, I rejoice   390
That your fist shall fetch this favor I seek,
And you have readily rehearsed, and in right terms,
Each clause of my covenant with the king your lord,
Save that you shall assure me, sir, upon oath,
That you shall seek me yourself, wheresoever you deem   395
My lodgings may lie, and look for such wages
As you have offered me here before all this host."
"What is the way there?" said Gawain, "Where do you dwell?
I heard never of your house, by Him that made me,
Nor I know you not, knight, your name nor your court.   400
But tell me truly thereof, and teach me your name,
And I shall fare forth to find you, so far as I may,
And this I say in good certain, and swear upon oath."

"That is enough in New Year, you need say no more,"
Said the knight in the green to Gawain the noble,   405
"If I tell you true, when I have taken your knock,
And if you handily have hit, you shall hear straightway
Of my house and my home and my own name;
Then follow in my footsteps by faithful accord.
And if I spend no speech, you shall speed the better: 410
You can feast with your friends, nor further trace
                  my tracks.
          Now hold your grim tool steady
          And show us how it hacks."
          "Gladly, sir; all ready,"   415
          Says Gawain; he strokes the ax.

The Green Knight upon ground girds him with care:
Bows a bit with his head, and bares his flesh:
His long lovely locks he laid over his crown,
Let the naked nape for the need be shown.   420
Gawain grips to his ax and gathers it aloft—
The left foot on the floor before him he set—
Brought it down deftly upon the bare neck,
That the shock of the sharp blow shivered the bones
And cut the flesh cleanly and clove it in twain,   425
That the blade of bright steel bit into the ground.
The head was hewn off and fell to the floor;
Many found it at their feet, as forth it rolled;
The blood gushed from the body, bright on the green,
Yet fell not the fellow, nor faltered a whit,   430
But stoutly he starts forth upon stiff shanks,
And as all stood staring he stretched forth his hand,
Laid hold of his head and heaved it aloft,
Then goes to the green steed, grasps the bridle,
Steps into the stirrup, bestrides his mount,   435
And his head by the hair in his hand holds,
And as steady he sits in the stately saddle
As he had met with no mishap, nor missing were
                  his head.
          His bulk about he haled,[4]   440
          That fearsome body that bled;
          There were many in the court that quailed
          Before all his say was said.

For the head in his hand he holds right up;
Toward the first on the dais directs he the face,   445
And it lifted up its lids, and looked with wide eyes,
And said as much with its mouth as now you may hear:
"Sir Gawain, forget not to go as agreed,
And cease not to seek till me, sir, you find,
As you promised in the presence of these proud knights.   450
To the Green Chapel come, I charge you, to take

---

4. Hauled.

Such a dint as you have dealt—you have well deserved
That your neck should have a knock on New Year's morn.
The Knight of the Green Chapel I am well-known to many,
Wherefore you cannot fail to find me at last;   455
Therefore come, or be counted a recreant[5] knight."
With a roisterous rush he flings round the reins,
Hurtles out at the hall-door, his head in his hand,
That the flint-fire flew from the flashing hooves.
Which way he went, not one of them knew   460
Nor whence he was come in the wide world
     so fair.
   The king and Gawain gay
   Make game of the Green Knight there,
   Yet all who saw it say   465
   'Twas a wonder past compare.

Though high-born Arthur at heart had wonder,
He let no sign be seen, but said aloud
To the comely queen, with courteous speech,
"Dear dame, on this day dismay you no whit;   470
Such crafts are becoming at Christmastide,
Laughing at interludes, light songs and mirth,
Amid dancing of damsels with doughty knights.
Nevertheless of my meat now let me partake,
For I have met with a marvel, I may not deny."   475
He glanced at Sir Gawain, and gaily he said,
"Now, sir, hang up your ax, that has hewn enough,"
And over the high dais it was hung on the wall
That men in amazement might on it look,
And tell in true terms the tale of the wonder.   480
Then they turned toward the table, these two together,
The good king and Gawain, and made great feast,
With all dainties double, dishes rare,
With all manner of meat and minstrelsy both,
Such happiness wholly had they that day   485
     in hold.
   Now take care, Sir Gawain,
   That your courage wax not cold
   When you must turn again
   To your enterprise foretold.   490

PART II

This adventure had Arthur of handsels[6] first
When young was the year, for he yearned to hear tales;
Though they wanted for words when they went to sup,
Now are fierce deeds to follow, their fists stuffed full.
Gawain was glad to begin those games in hall,   495
But if the end be harsher, hold it no wonder,
For though men are merry in mind after much drink,

---

5. Cowardly. 6. Gifts to mark the New Year.

A year passes apace, and proves ever new:
First things and final conform but seldom.
And so this Yule to the young year yielded place,   500
And each season ensued at its set time;
After Christmas there came the cold cheer of Lent,
When with fish and plainer fare our flesh we reprove;
But then the world's weather with winter contends:
The keen cold lessens, the low clouds lift;   505
Fresh falls the rain in fostering showers
On the face of the fields; flowers appear.
The ground and the groves wear gowns of green;
Birds build their nests, and blithely sing
That solace of all sorrow with summer comes   510
> ere long.
>> And blossoms day by day
>> Bloom rich and rife in throng;
>> Then every grove so gay
>> Of the greenwood rings with song.   515

And then the season of summer with the soft winds,
When Zephyr sighs low over seeds and shoots;
Glad is the green plant growing abroad,
When the dew at dawn drops from the leaves,
To get a gracious glance from the golden sun.   520
But harvest with harsher winds follows hard after,
Warns him to ripen well ere winter comes;
Drives forth the dust in the droughty season,
From the face of the fields to fly high in air.
Wroth winds in the welkin[7] wrestle with the sun,   525
The leaves launch from the linden and light on the ground,
And the grass turns to gray, that once grew green.
Then all ripens and rots that rose up at first,
And so the year moves on in yesterdays many,
And winter once more, by the world's law,   530
> draws nigh.
>> At Michaelmas[8] the moon
>> Hangs wintry pale in sky;
>> Sir Gawain girds him soon
>> For travails yet to try.   535

Till All-Hallows' Day[9] with Arthur he dwells,
And he held a high feast to honor that knight
With great revels and rich, of the Round Table.
Then ladies lovely and lords debonair
With sorrow for Sir Gawain were sore at heart;   540
Yet they covered their care with countenance glad:
Many a mournful man made mirth for his sake.
So after supper soberly he speaks to his uncle
Of the hard hour at hand, and openly says,
"Now, liege lord of my life, my leave I take;   545

7. The heavens.   8. September 29.   9. November 1.

The terms of this task too well you know—
To count the cost over concerns me nothing.
But I am bound forth betimes[1] to bear a stroke
From the grim man in green, as God may direct."
Then the first and foremost came forth in throng: 550
Yvain and Eric and others of note,
Sir Dodinal le Sauvage, the Duke of Clarence,
Lionel and Lancelot and Lucan the good,
Sir Bors and Sir Bedivere, big men both,
And many manly knights more, with Mador de la Porte.   555
All this courtly company comes to the king
To counsel their comrade, with care in their hearts;
There was much secret sorrow suffered that day
That one so good as Gawain must go in such wise
To bear a bitter blow, and his bright sword   560
              lay by.
        He said, "Why should I tarry?"
        And smiled with tranquil eye;
        "In destinies sad or merry,
        True men can but try."   565

He dwelt there all that day, and dressed in the morning;
Asked early for his arms, and all were brought.
First a carpet of rare cost was cast on the floor
Where much goodly gear gleamed golden bright;
He takes his place promptly and picks up the steel,   570
Attired in a tight coat of Turkestan silk
And a kingly cap-à-dos, closed at the throat,
That was lavishly lined with a lustrous fur.
Then they set the steel shoes on his sturdy feet
And clad his calves about with comely greaves,   575
And plate well-polished protected his knees,
Affixed with fastenings of the finest gold.
Fair cuisses enclosed, that were cunningly wrought,
His thick-thewed thighs, with thongs bound fast,
And massy chain-mail of many a steel ring   580
He bore on his body, above the best cloth,
With brace burnished bright upon both his arms,
Good couters[2] and gay, and gloves of plate,
And all the goodly gear to grace him well
              that tide.
        His surcoat[3] blazoned bold;   585
        Sharp spurs to prick with pride;
        And a brave silk band to hold
        The broadsword at his side.

When he had on his arms, his harness was rich,   590
The least latchet or loop laden with gold;
So armored as he was, he heard a mass,

---

1. Soon.   2. Armor for the elbows.   3. Cloth tunic worn over the armor.

Honored God humbly at the high altar.
Then he comes to the king and his comrades-in-arms,
Takes his leave at last of lords and ladies,   595
And they clasped and kissed him, commending him to Christ.
By then Gringolet⁴ was girt with a great saddle
That was gaily agleam with fine gilt fringe,
New-furbished for the need with nail-heads bright;
The bridle and the bars bedecked all with gold;   600
The breast-plate, the saddlebow, the side-panels both,
The caparison and the crupper accorded in hue,
And all ranged on the red the resplendent studs
That glittered and glowed like the glorious sun.
His helm now he holds up and hastily kisses,   605
Well-closed with iron clinches, and cushioned within;
It was high on his head, with a hasp behind,
And a covering of cloth to encase the visor,
All bound and embroidered with the best gems
On broad bands of silk, and bordered with birds,   610
Parrots and popinjays preening their wings,
Lovebirds and love-knots as lavishly wrought
As many women had worked seven winters thereon,
                            entire.
                    The diadem costlier yet   615
                    That crowned that comely sire,
                    With diamonds richly set,
                    That flashed as if on fire.

Then they showed forth the shield, that shone all red,
With the pentangle⁵ portrayed in purest gold.   620
About his broad neck by the baldric⁶ he casts it,
That was meet for the man, and matched him well.
And why the pentangle is proper to that peerless prince
I intend now to tell, though detain me it must.
It is a sign by Solomon sagely devised   625
To be a token of truth, by its title of old,
For it is a figure formed of five points,
And each line is linked and locked with the next
For ever and ever, and hence it is called
In all England, as I hear, the endless knot.   630
And well may he wear it on his worthy arms,
For ever faithful five-fold in five-fold fashion
Was Gawain in good works, as gold unalloyed,
Devoid of all villainy, with virtues adorned
                            in sight.   635
                    On shield and coat in view
                    He bore that emblem bright,
                    As to his word most true
                    And in speech most courteous knight.

---

4. Gawain's horse.   5. A five-pointed star, formed by five lines drawn without lifting the pen, supposed
to have mystical significance; as Solomon's sign (line 625), it was enclosed in a circle.   6. Belt worn
diagonally across the chest.

And first, he was faultless in his five senses, 640
Nor found ever to fail in his five fingers,
And all his fealty was fixed upon the five wounds
That Christ got on the cross, as the creed tells;
And wherever this man in melee took part,
His one thought was of this, past all things else, 645
That all his force was founded on the five joys⁷
That the high Queen of heaven had in her child.
And therefore, as I find, he fittingly had
On the inner part of his shield her image portrayed,
That when his look on it lighted, he never lost heart. 650
The fifth of the five fives followed by this knight
Were beneficence boundless and brotherly love
And pure mind and manners, that none might impeach,
And compassion most precious—these peerless five
Were forged and made fast in him, foremost of men. 655
Now all these five fives were confirmed in this knight,
And each linked in other, that end there was none,
And fixed to five points, whose force never failed,
Nor assembled all on a side, nor asunder either,
Nor anywhere at an end, but whole and entire 660
However the pattern proceeded or played out its course.
And so on his shining shield shaped was the knot
Royally in red gold against red gules,⁸
That is the peerless pentangle, prized of old
     in lore. 665
    Now armed is Gawain gay,
    And bears his lance before,
    And soberly said good day,
    He thought forevermore.

He struck his steed with the spurs and sped on his way 670
So fast that the flint-fire flashed from the stones.
When they saw him set forth they were sore aggrieved,
And all sighed softly, and said to each other,
Fearing for their fellow, "Ill fortune it is
That you, man, must be marred, that most are worthy! 675
His equal on this earth can hardly be found;
To have dealt more discreetly had done less harm,
And have dubbed him a duke, with all due honor.
A great leader of lords he was like to become,
And better so to have been than battered to bits, 680
Beheaded by an elf-man,⁹ for empty pride!
Who would credit that a king could be counseled so,
And caught in a cavil in a Christmas game?"
Many were the warm tears they wept from their eyes
When goodly Sir Gawain was gone from the court 685

---

7. These were the annunciation to Mary that she was to bear the Son of God, Christ's Nativity, Resurrection, and Ascension into heaven, and the "Assumption" or bodily taking up of Mary into heaven to join Him. 8. Background (*gules* is the heraldic name for red). 9. Supernatural being, in this case obviously not small.

> that day.
> No longer he abode,
> But speedily went his way
> Over many a wandering road,
> As I heard my author say.   690

Now he rides in his array through the realm of Logres,[1]
Sir Gawain, God knows, though it gave him small joy!
All alone must he lodge through many a long night
Where the food that he fancied was far from his plate;
He had no mate but his mount, over mountain and plain,   695
Nor man to say his mind to but almighty God,
Till he had wandered well-nigh into North Wales.
All the islands of Anglesey he holds on his left,
And follows, as he fares, the fords by the coast,
Comes over at Holy Head, and enters next   700
The Wilderness of Wirral[2]—few were within
That had great good will toward God or man.
And earnestly he asked of each mortal he met
If he had ever heard aught of a knight all green,
Or of a Green Chapel, on ground thereabouts,   705
And all said the same, and solemnly swore
They saw no such knight all solely green
> in hue.
> Over country wild and strange
> The knight sets off anew;   710
> Often his course must change
> Ere the Chapel comes in view.

Many a cliff must he climb in country wild;
Far off from all his friends, forlorn must he ride;
At each strand or stream where the stalwart passed   715
'Twere a marvel if he met not some monstrous foe,
And that so fierce and forbidding that fight he must.
So many were the wonders he wandered among
That to tell but the tenth part would tax my wits.
Now with serpents he wars, now with savage wolves,   720
Now with wild men of the woods, that watched from the rocks,
Both with bulls and with bears, and with boars besides,
And giants that came gibbering from the jagged steeps.
Had he not borne himself bravely, and been on God's side,
He had met with many mishaps and mortal harms.   725
And if the wars were unwelcome, the winter was worse,
When the cold clear rains rushed from the clouds
And froze before they could fall to the frosty earth.
Near slain by the sleet he sleeps in his irons
More nights than enough, among naked rocks,   730
Where clattering from the crest the cold stream ran
And hung in hard icicles high overhead.

---

1. Another name for Arthur's kingdom.   2. *North Wales . . . Wirral:* Gawain went from Camelot north to the northern coast of Wales, opposite the islands of Anglesey; there he turned east across the river Dee to the forest of Wirral, near what is now Liverpool.

Thus in peril and pain and predicaments dire
He rides across country till Christmas Eve,
              our knight.   735
              And at that holy tide
              He prays with all his might
              That Mary may be his guide
              Till a dwelling comes in sight.

By a mountain next morning he makes his way   740
Into a forest fastness, fearsome and wild;
High hills on either hand, with hoar woods below,
Oaks old and huge by the hundred together.
The hazel and the hawthorn were all intertwined
With rough raveled moss, that raggedly hung,   745
With many birds unblithe upon bare twigs
That peeped most piteously for pain of the cold.
The good knight on Gringolet glides thereunder
Through many a marsh and mire, a man all alone;
He feared for his default, should he fail to see   750
The service of that Sire that on that same night
Was born of a bright maid, to bring us His peace.
And therefore sighing he said, "I beseech of Thee, Lord,
And Mary, thou mildest mother so dear,
Some harborage where haply I might hear mass   755
And Thy matins tomorrow—meekly I ask it,
And thereto proffer and pray my pater and ave[3]
                        and creed."
              He said his prayer with sighs,
              Lamenting his misdeed;
              He crosses himself, and cries   760
              On Christ in his great need.

No sooner had Sir Gawain signed himself[4] thrice
Than he was ware, in the wood, of a wondrous dwelling,
Within a moat, on a mound, bright amid boughs   765
Of many a tree great of girth that grew by the water—
A castle as comely as a knight could own,
On grounds fair and green, in a goodly park
With a palisade of palings planted about
For two miles and more, round many a fair tree.   770
The stout knight stared at that stronghold great
As it shimmered and shone amid shining leaves,
Then with helmet in hand he offers his thanks
To Jesus and Saint Julian,[5] that are gentle both,
That in courteous accord had inclined to his prayer;   775
"Now fair harbor," said he, "I humbly beseech!"
Then he pricks his proud steed with the plated spurs,
And by chance he has chosen the chief path
That brought the bold knight to the bridge's end

3. Two prayers, the Pater Noster ("Our Father," the Lord's Prayer) and Ave Maria ("Hail Mary").
4. Made the Sign of the Cross over his own chest.   5. Patron saint of hospitality.

in haste. 780

The bridge hung high in air;
The gates were bolted fast;
The walls well-framed to bear
The fury of the blast.

The man on his mount remained on the bank 785
Of the deep double moat that defended the place.
The wall went in the water wondrous deep,
And a long way aloft it loomed overhead.
It was built of stone blocks to the battlements' height,
With corbels under cornices[6] in comeliest style; 790
Watch-towers trusty protected the gate,
With many a lean loophole, to look from within:
A better-made barbican the knight beheld never.
And behind it there hoved a great hall and fair:
Turrets rising in tiers, with tines[7] at their tops, 795
Spires set beside them, splendidly long,
With finials well-fashioned, as filigree fine.
Chalk-white chimneys over chambers high
Gleamed in gay array upon gables and roofs;
The pinnacles in panoply, pointing in air, 800
So vied there for his view that verily it seemed
A castle cut of paper for a king's feast.
The good knight on Gringolet thought it great luck
If he could but contrive to come there within
To keep the Christmas feast in that castle fair 805
and bright.
There answered to his call
A porter most polite;
From his station on the wall
He greets the errant knight.</div> 810

"Good sir," said Gawain, "Wouldst go to inquire
If your lord would allow me to lodge here a space?"
"Peter!"[8] said the porter, "For my part, I think
So noble a knight will not want for a welcome!"
Then he bustles off briskly, and comes back straight, 815
And many servants beside, to receive him the better.
They let down the drawbridge and duly went forth
And kneeled down on their knees on the naked earth
To welcome this warrior as best they were able.
They proffered him passage—the portals stood wide— 820
And he beckoned them to rise, and rode over the bridge.
Men steadied his saddle as he stepped to the ground,
And there stabled his steed many stalwart folk.
Now come the knights and the noble squires
To bring him with bliss into the bright hall. 825
When his high helm was off, there hied forth a throng
Of attendants to take it, and see to its care;

6. Ornamental projections supporting the top courses of stone.   7. Sharp points. *Hoved*: arose.
8. I.e., "By Saint Peter!"

They bore away his brand[9] and his blazoned shield;
Then graciously he greeted those gallants each one,
And many a noble drew near, to do the knight honor.   830
All in his armor into hall he was led,
Where fire on a fair hearth fiercely blazed.
And soon the lord himself descends from his chamber
To meet with good manners the man on his floor.
He said, "To this house you are heartily welcome: 835
What is here is wholly yours, to have in your power
                and sway."
        "Many thanks," said Sir Gawain;
        "May Christ your pains repay!"
        The two embrace amain   840
        As men well met that day.

Gawain gazed on the host that greeted him there,
And a lusty fellow he looked, the lord of that place:
A man of massive mold, and of middle age;
Broad, bright was his beard, of a beaver's hue,   845
Strong, steady his stance, upon stalwart shanks,
His face fierce as fire, fair-spoken withal,
And well-suited he seemed in Sir Gawain's sight
To be a master of men in a mighty keep.
They pass into a parlor, where promptly the host   850
Has a servant assigned him to see to his needs,
And there came upon his call many courteous folk
That brought him to a bower where bedding was noble,
With heavy silk hangings hemmed all in gold,
Coverlets and counterpanes curiously wrought,   855
A canopy over the couch, clad all with fur,
Curtains running on cords, caught to gold rings,
Woven rugs on the walls of eastern work,
And the floor, under foot, well-furnished with the same.
With light talk and laughter they loosed from him then   860
His war-dress of weight and his worthy clothes.
Robes richly wrought they brought him right soon,
To change there in chamber and choose what he would.
When he had found one he fancied, and flung it about,
Well-fashioned for his frame, with flowing skirts,   865
His face fair and fresh as the flowers of spring,
All the good folk agreed, that gazed on him then,
His limbs arrayed royally in radiant hues,
That so comely a mortal never Christ made
            as he.   870
        Whatever his place of birth,
        It seemed he well might be
        Without a peer on earth
        In martial rivalry.

A couch before the fire, where fresh coals burned,   875
They spread for Sir Gawain splendidly now

9. Sword.

With quilts quaintly stitched, and cushions beside,
And then a costly cloak they cast on his shoulders
Of bright silk, embroidered on borders and hems,
With furs of the finest well-furnished within, 880
And bound about with ermine, both mantle and hood;
And he sat at that fireside in sumptuous estate
And warmed himself well, and soon he waxed merry.
Then attendants set a table upon trestles broad,
And lustrous white linen they laid thereupon, 885
A saltcellar of silver, spoons of the same.
He washed himself well and went to his place,
Men set his fare before him in fashion most fit.
There were soups of all sorts, seasoned with skill,
Double-sized servings, and sundry fish, 890
Some baked, some breaded, some broiled on the coals,
Some simmered, some in stews, steaming with spice,
And with sauces to sup that suited his taste.
He confesses it a feast with free words and fair;
They requite him as kindly with courteous jests, 895
                              well-sped.
            "Tonight you fast and pray;
            Tomorrow we'll see you fed."
            The knight grows wondrous gay
            As the wine goes to his head. 900

Then at times and by turns, as at table he sat,
They questioned him quietly, with queries discreet,
And he courteously confessed that he comes from the court,
And owns him of the brotherhood of high-famed Arthur,
The right royal ruler of the Round Table, 905
And the guest by their fireside is Gawain himself,
Who has happened on their house at that holy feast.
When the name of the knight was made known to the lord,
Then loudly he laughed, so elated he was,
And the men in that household made haste with joy 910
To appear in his presence promptly that day,
That of courage ever-constant, and customs pure,
Is pattern and paragon, and praised without end:
Of all knights on earth most honored is he.
Each said solemnly aside to his brother, 915
"Now displays of deportment shall dazzle our eyes
And the polished pearls of impeccable speech;
The high art of eloquence is ours to pursue
Since the father of fine manners is found in our midst.
Great is God's grace, and goodly indeed, 920
That a guest such as Gawain he guides to us here
When men sit and sing of their Savior's birth
                              in view.
            With command of manners pure
            He shall each heart imbue; 925
            Who shares his converse, sure,
            Shall learn love's language true."

When the knight had done dining and duly arose,
The dark was drawing on; the day nigh ended.
Chaplains in chapels and churches about   930
Rang the bells aright, reminding all men
Of the holy evensong of the high feast.
The lord attends alone; his fair lady sits
In a comely closet, secluded from sight.
Gawain in gay attire goes thither soon;   935
The lord catches his coat, and calls him by name,
And has him sit beside him, and says in good faith
No guest on God's earth would he gladlier greet.
For that Gawain thanked him; the two then embraced
And sat together soberly the service through.   940
Then the lady, that longed to look on the knight,
Came forth from her closet with her comely maids.
The fair hues of her flesh, her face and her hair
And her body and her bearing were beyond praise,
And excelled the queen herself, as Sir Gawain thought.   945
He goes forth to greet her with gracious intent;
Another lady led her by the left hand
That was older than she—an ancient, it seemed,
And held in high honor by all men about.
But unlike to look upon, those ladies were,   950
For if the one was fresh, the other was faded:
Bedecked in bright red was the body of one;
Flesh hung in folds on the face of the other;
On one a high headdress, hung all with pearls;
Her bright throat and bosom fair to behold,   955
Fresh as the first snow fallen upon hills;
A wimple[1] the other one wore round her throat;
Her swart chin well swaddled, swathed all in white;
Her forehead enfolded in flounces of silk
That framed a fair fillet,[2] of fashion ornate,   960
And nothing bare beneath save the black brows,
The two eyes and the nose, the naked lips,
And they unsightly to see, and sorrily bleared.
A beldame, by God, she may well be deemed,
                         of pride!   965
              She was short and thick of waist,
              Her buttocks round and wide;
              More toothsome, to his taste,
              Was the beauty by her side.

When Gawain had gazed on that gay lady,   970
With leave of her lord, he politely approached;
To the elder in homage he humbly bows;
The lovelier he salutes with a light embrace.
He claims a comely kiss, and courteously he speaks;
They welcome him warmly, and straightway he asks   975

---

1. A garment covering the neck and sides of the head.   2. Ornamental ribbon or headband.

To be received as their servant, if they so desire.
They take him between them; with talking they bring him
Beside a bright fire; bade then that spices
Be freely fetched forth, to refresh them the better,
And the good wine therewith, to warm their hearts.   980
The lord leaps about in light-hearted mood;
Contrives entertainments and timely sports;
Takes his hood from his head and hangs it on a spear,
And offers him openly the honor thereof
Who should promote the most mirth at that Christmas feast;   985
"And I shall try for it, trust me—contend with the best,
Ere I go without my headgear by grace of my friends!"
Thus with light talk and laughter the lord makes merry
To gladden the guest he had greeted in hall
      that day.   990
   At the last he called for light
   The company to convey;
   Gawain says goodnight
   And retires to bed straightway.

On the morn when each man is mindful in heart   995
That God's son was sent down to suffer our death,
No household but is blithe for His blessed sake;
So was it there on that day, with many delights.
Both at larger meals and less they were lavishly served
By doughty lads on dais, with delicate fare;   1000
The old ancient lady, highest she sits;
The lord at her left hand leaned, as I hear;
Sir Gawain in the center, beside the gay lady,
Where the food was brought first to that festive board,
And thence throughout the hall, as they held most fit,   1005
To each man was offered in order of rank.
There was meat, there was mirth, there was much joy,
That to tell all the tale would tax my wits,
Though I pained me, perchance, to paint it with care;
But yet I know that our knight and the noble lady   1010
Were accorded so closely in company there,
With the seemly solace of their secret words,
With speeches well-sped, spotless and pure,
That each prince's pastime their pleasures far
      outshone.   1015
   Sweet pipes beguile their cares,
   And the trumpet of martial tone;
   Each tends his affairs
   And those two tend their own.

That day and all the next, their disport was noble,   1020
And the third day, I think, pleased them no less;
The joys of St. John's Day[3] were justly praised,

---

3. December 27.

And were the last of their like for those lords and ladies;
Then guests were to go in the gray morning,
Wherefore they whiled the night away with wine and with mirth,   1025
Moved to the measures of many a blithe carol;
At last, when it was late, took leave of each other,
Each one of those worthies, to wend his way.
Gawain bids goodbye to his goodly host
Who brings him to his chamber, the chimney beside,   1030
And detains him in talk, and tenders his thanks
And holds it an honor to him and his people
That he has harbored in his house at that holy time
And embellished his abode with his inborn grace.
"As long as I may live, my luck is the better   1035
That Gawain was my guest at God's own feast!"
"Noble sir," said the knight, "I cannot but think
All the honor is your own—may heaven requite it!
And your man to command I account myself here
As I am bound and beholden, and shall be, come   1040
                what may."
        The lord with all his might
        Entreats his guest to stay;
        Brief answer makes the knight:
        Next morning he must away.   1045

Then the lord of that land politely inquired
What dire affair had forced him, at that festive time,
So far from the king's court to fare forth alone
Ere the holidays wholly had ended in hall.
"In good faith," said Gawain, "you have guessed the truth: 1050
On a high errand and urgent I hastened away,
For I am summoned by myself to seek for a place—
I would I knew whither, or where it might be!
Far rather would I find it before the New Year
Than own the land of Logres, so help me our Lord!   1055
Wherefore, sir, in friendship this favor I ask,
That you say in sober earnest, if something you know
Of the Green Chapel, on ground far or near,
Or the lone knight that lives there, of like hue of green.
A certain day was set by assent of us both   1060
To meet at that landmark, if I might last,
And from now to the New Year is nothing too long,
And I would greet the Green Knight there, would God but allow,
More gladly, by God's Son, than gain the world's wealth!
And I must set forth to search, as soon as I may;   1065
To be about the business I have but three days
And would as soon sink down dead as desist from my errand."
Then smiling said the lord, "Your search, sir, is done,
For we shall see you to that site by the set time.
Let Gawain grieve no more over the Green Chapel;   1070
You shall be in your own bed, in blissful ease,
All the forenoon, and fare forth the first of the year,
And make the goal by midmorn, to mind your affairs,

no fear!

Tarry till the fourth day 1075
And ride on the first of the year.
We shall set you on your way;
It is not two miles from here."

Then Gawain was glad, and gleefully he laughed:
"Now I thank you for this, past all things else! 1080
Now my goal is here at hand! With a glad heart I shall
Both tarry, and undertake any task you devise."
Then the host seized his arm and seated him there;
Let the ladies be brought, to delight them the better,
And in fellowship fair by the fireside they sit; 1085
So gay waxed the good host, so giddy his words,
All waited in wonder what next he would say.
Then he stares on the stout knight, and sternly he speaks:
"You have bound yourself boldly my bidding to do—
Will you stand by that boast, and obey me this once?" 1090
"I shall do so indeed," said the doughty knight;
"While I lie in your lodging, your laws will I follow."
"As you have had," said the host, "many hardships abroad
And little sleep of late, you are lacking, I judge,
Both in nourishment needful and nightly rest; 1095
You shall lie abed late in your lofty chamber
Tomorrow until mass, and meet then to dine
When you will, with my wife, who will sit by your side
And talk with you at table, the better to cheer

our guest. 1100
A-hunting I will go
While you lie late and rest."
The knight, inclining low,
Assents to each behest.

"And Gawain," said the good host, "agree now to this: 1105
Whatever I win in the woods I will give you at eve,
And all you have earned you must offer to me;
Swear now, sweet friend, to swap as I say,
Whether hands, in the end, be empty or better."
"By God," said Sir Gawain, "I grant it forthwith! 1110
If you find the game good, I shall gladly take part."
"Let the bright wine be brought, and our bargain is done,"
Said the lord of that land—the two laughed together.
Then they drank and they dallied and doffed all constraint,
These lords and these ladies, as late as they chose, 1115
And then with gaiety and gallantries and graceful adieux
They talked in low tones, and tarried at parting.
With compliments comely they kiss at the last;
There were brisk lads about with blazing torches
To see them safe to bed, for soft repose 1120

long due.
Their covenants, yet awhile,

They repeat, and pledge anew;
That lord could well beguile
Men's hearts, with mirth in view.   1125

PART III

Long before daylight they left their beds;
Guests that wished to go gave word to their grooms,
And they set about briskly to bind on saddles,
Tend to their tackle, tie up trunks.
The proud lords appear, appareled to ride,   1130
Leap lightly astride, lay hold of their bridles,
Each one on his way to his worthy house.
The liege lord of the land was not the last
Arrayed there to ride, with retainers many;
He had a bite to eat when he had heard mass;   1135
With horn to the hills he hastens amain.
By the dawn of that day over the dim earth,
Master and men were mounted and ready.
Then they harnessed in couples the keen-scented hounds,
Cast wide the kennel-door and called them forth,   1140
Blew upon their bugles bold blasts three;
The dogs began to bay with a deafening din,
And they quieted them quickly and called them to heel,
A hundred brave huntsmen, as I have heard tell,
                    together.   1145
        Men at stations meet;
        From the hounds they slip the tether;
        The echoing horns repeat,
        Clear in the merry weather.

At the clamor of the quest, the quarry trembled;   1150
Deer dashed through the dale, dazed with dread;
Hastened to the high ground, only to be
Turned back by the beaters, who boldly shouted.
They harmed not the harts, with their high heads,
Let the bucks go by, with their broad antlers,   1155
For it was counted a crime, in the close[4] season,
If a man of that demesne should molest the male deer.
The hinds were headed up, with "Hey!" and "Ware!"
The does with great din were driven to the valleys.
Then you were ware, as they went, of the whistling of arrows;   1160
At each bend under boughs the bright shafts flew
That tore the tawny hide with their tapered heads.
Ah! They bray and they bleed, on banks they die,
And ever the pack pell-mell comes panting behind;
Hunters with shrill horns hot on their heels—   1165
Like the cracking of cliffs their cries resounded.
What game got away from the gallant archers

4. Or closed.

Was promptly picked off at the posts below
When they were harried on the heights and herded to the streams:
The watchers were so wary at the waiting-stations,   1170
And the greyhounds so huge, that eagerly snatched,
And finished them off as fast as folk could see
               with sight.
         The lord, now here, now there,
         Spurs forth in sheer delight.   1175
         And drives, with pleasures rare,
         The day to the dark night.

So the lord in the linden-wood leads the hunt
And Gawain the good knight in gay bed lies,
Lingered late alone, till daylight gleamed,   1180
Under coverlet costly, curtained about.
And as he slips into slumber, slyly there comes
A little din at his door, and the latch lifted,
And he holds up his heavy head out of the clothes;
A corner of the curtain he caught back a little   1185
And waited there warily, to see what befell.
Lo! it was the lady, loveliest to behold,
That drew the door behind her deftly and still
And was bound for his bed—abashed was the knight,
And laid his head low again in likeness of sleep;   1190
And she stepped stealthily, and stole to his bed,
Cast aside the curtain and came within,
And set herself softly on the bedside there,
And lingered at her leisure, to look on his waking.
The fair knight lay feigning for a long while,   1195
Conning in his conscience what his case might
Mean or amount to—a marvel he thought it.
But yet he said within himself, "More seemly it were
To try her intent by talking a little."
So he started and stretched, as startled from sleep,   1200
Lifts wide his lids in likeness of wonder,
And signs himself swiftly, as safer to be,
               with art.
         Sweetly does she speak
         And kindling glances dart,   1205
         Blent white and red on cheek
         And laughing lips apart.

"Good morning, Sir Gawain," said that gay lady,
"A slack sleeper you are, to let one slip in!
Now you are taken in a trice—a truce we must make,   1210
Or I shall bind you in your bed, of that be assured."
Thus laughing lightly that lady jested.
"Good morning, good lady," said Gawain the blithe,
"Be it with me as you will; I am well content!
For I surrender myself, and sue for your grace,   1215
And that is best, I believe, and behooves me now."
Thus jested in answer that gentle knight.

"But if, lovely lady, you misliked it not,
And were pleased to permit your prisoner to rise,
I should quit this couch and accoutre me better,
And be clad in more comfort for converse here."   1220
"Nay, not so, sweet sir," said the smiling lady;
"You shall not rise from your bed; I direct you better:
I shall hem and hold you on either hand,
And keep company awhile with my captive knight.
For as certain as I sit here, Sir Gawain you are,   1225
Whom all the world worships, whereso you ride;
Your honor, your courtesy are highest acclaimed
By lords and by ladies, by all living men;
And lo! we are alone here, and left to ourselves: 1230
My lord and his liegemen are long departed,
The household asleep, my handmaids too,
The door drawn, and held by a well-driven bolt,
And since I have in this house him whom all love,
I shall while the time away with mirthful speech   1235
                at will.
          My body is here at hand,
          Your each wish to fulfill;
          Your servant to command
          I am, and shall be still."   1240

"In good faith," said Gawain, "my gain is the greater,
Though I am not he of whom you have heard;
To arrive at such reverence as you recount here
I am one all unworthy, and well do I know it.
By heaven, I would hold me the happiest of men   1245
If by word or by work I once might aspire
To the prize of your praise—'twere a pure joy!"
"In good faith, Sir Gawain," said that gay lady,
"The well-proven prowess that pleases all others,
Did I scant or scout[5] it, 'twere scarce becoming.   1250
But there are ladies, believe me, that had liefer far[6]
Have thee here in their hold, as I have today,
To pass an hour in pastime with pleasant words,
Assuage all their sorrows and solace their hearts,
Than much of the goodly gems and gold they possess.   1255
But laud be to the Lord of the lofty skies,
For here in my hands all hearts' desire
                doth lie."
          Great welcome got he there
          From the lady who sat him by;   1260
          With fitting speech and fair
          The good knight makes reply.

"Madame," said the merry man, "Mary reward you!
For in good faith, I find your beneficence noble.

5. Mock.   6. Would much rather.

And the fame of fair deeds runs far and wide, 1265
But the praise you report pertains not to me,
But comes of your courtesy and kindness of heart."
"By the high Queen of heaven" (said she) "I count it not so,
For were I worth all the women in this world alive,
And all wealth and all worship were in my hands, 1270
And I should hunt high and low, a husband to take,
For the nurture I have noted in thee, knight, here,
The comeliness and courtesies and courtly mirth—
And so I had ever heard, and now hold it true—
No other on this earth should have me for wife." 1275
"You are bound to a better man," the bold knight said,
"Yet I prize the praise you have proffered me here,
And soberly your servant, my sovereign I hold you,
And acknowledge me your knight, in the name of Christ."
So they talked of this and that until 'twas nigh noon, 1280
And ever the lady languishing in likeness of love.
With feat[7] words and fair he framed his defence,
For were she never so winsome, the warrior had
The less will to woo, for the wound that his bane
            must be. 1285
        He must bear the blinding blow,
        For such is fate's decree;
        The lady asks leave to go;
        He grants it full and free.

Then she gaily said goodbye, and glanced at him, laughing, 1290
And as she stood, she astonished him with a stern speech:
"Now may the Giver of all good words these glad hours repay!
But our guest is not Gawain—forgot is that thought."
"How so?" said the other, and asks in some haste,
For he feared he had been at fault in the forms of his speech. 1295
But she held up her hand, and made answer thus:
"So good a knight as Gawain is given out to be,
And the model of fair demeanor and manners pure,
Had he lain so long at a lady's side,
Would have claimed a kiss, by his courtesy, 1300
Through some touch or trick of phrase at some tale's end."
Said Gawain, "Good lady, I grant it at once!
I shall kiss at your command, as becomes a knight,
And more, lest you mislike, so let be, I pray."
With that she turns toward him, takes him in her arms, 1305
Leans down her lovely head, and lo! he is kissed.
They commend each other to Christ with comely words,
He sees her forth safely, in silence they part,
And then he lies no later in his lofty bed,
But calls to his chamberlain, chooses his clothes, 1310
Goes in those garments gladly to mass,
Then takes his way to table, where attendants wait,
And made merry all day, till the moon rose

7. Fitting.

in view
Was never knight beset   1315
'Twixt worthier ladies two:
The crone and the coquette;
Fair pastimes they pursue.

And the lord of the land rides late and long,
Hunting the barren hind[8] over the broad heath.   1320
He had slain such a sum, when the sun sank low,
Of does and other deer, as would dizzy one's wits.
Then they trooped in together in triumph at last,
And the count of the quarry quickly they take.
The lords lent a hand with their liegemen many,   1325
Picked out the plumpest and put them together
And duly dressed the deer, as the deed requires.
Some were assigned the assay of the fat:
Two fingers'-width fully they found on the leanest.
Then they slit the slot[9] open and searched out the paunch,   1330
Trimmed it with trencher-knives and tied it up tight.
They flayed the fair hide from the legs and trunk,
Then broke open the belly and laid bare the bowels,
Deftly detaching and drawing them forth.
And next at the neck they neatly parted   1335
The weasand[1] from the windpipe, and cast away the guts.
At the shoulders with sharp blades they showed their skill,
Boning them from beneath, lest the sides be marred;
They breached the broad breast and broke it in twain,
And again at the gullet they begin with their knives,   1340
Cleave down the carcass clear to the breach;
Two tender morsels they take from the throat,
Then round the inner ribs they rid off a layer
And carve out the kidney-fat, close to the spine,
Hewing down to the haunch, that all hung together,   1345
And held it up whole, and hacked it free,
And this they named the numbles,[2] that knew such terms
of art.
They divide the crotch in two,
And straightway then they start   1350
To cut the backbone through
And cleave the trunk apart.

With hard strokes they hewed off the head and the neck,
Then swiftly from the sides they severed the chine,
And the corbie's bone[3] they cast on a branch.   1355
Then they pierced the plump sides, impaled either one
With the hock of the hind foot, and hung it aloft,
To each person his portion most proper and fit.
On a hide of a hind the hounds they fed
With the liver and the lights,[4] the leathery paunches,   1360

---

8. Female deer that are not pregnant.   9. The hollow above the breastbone.   1. Esophagus.
2. Other internal organs.   3. A bit of gristle for a raven (*corbie*).   4. Lungs.

And bread soaked in blood well blended therewith.
High horns and shrill set hounds a-baying,
Then merrily with their meat they make their way home,
Blowing on their bugles many a brave blast.
Ere dark had descended, that doughty band   1365
Was come within the walls where Gawain waits
                                        at leisure.
                        Bliss and hearth-fire bright
                        Await the master's pleasure;
                        When the two men met that night,   1370
                        Joy surpassed all measure.

Then the host in the hall his household assembles,
With the dames of high degree and their damsels fair.
In the presence of the people, a party he sends
To convey him his venison in view of the knight.   1375
And in high good-humor he hails him then,
Counts over the kill, the cuts on the tallies,[5]
Holds high the hewn ribs, heavy with fat.
"What think you, sir, of this? Have I thriven well?
Have I won with my woodcraft a worthy prize?"   1380
"In good earnest," said Gawain, "this game is the finest
I have seen in seven years in the season of winter."
"And I give it to you, Gawain," said the goodly host,
"For according to our covenant, you claim it as your own."
"That is so," said Sir Gawain, "the same say I: 1385
What I worthily have won within these fair walls,
Herewith I as willingly award it to you."
He embraces his broad neck with both his arms,
And confers on him a kiss in the comeliest style.
"Have here my profit, it proved no better;   1390
Ungrudging do I grant it, were it greater far."
"Such a gift," said the good host, "I gladly accept—
Yet it might be all the better, would you but say
Where you won this same award, by your wits alone."
"That was no part of the pact; press me no further,   1395
For you have had what behooves; all other claims
                                        forbear."
                        With jest and compliment
                        They conversed, and cast off care;
                        To the table soon they went;   1400
                        Fresh dainties wait them there.

And then by the chimney-side they chat at their ease;
The best wine was brought them, and bounteously served;
And after in their jesting they jointly accord
To do on the second day the deeds of the first: 1405
That the two men should trade, betide as it may,
What each had taken in, at eve when they met.
They seal the pact solemnly in sight of the court;
Their cups were filled afresh to confirm the jest;

5. Notched sticks were used to count the animals taken in the hunt.

Then at last they took their leave, for late was the hour,   1410
Each to his own bed hastening away.
Before the barnyard cock had crowed but thrice
The lord had leapt from his rest, his liegemen as well.
Both of mass and their meal they made short work:
By the dim light of dawn they were deep in the woods   1415
               away.
        With huntsmen and with horns
        Over plains they pass that day;
        They release, amid the thorns,
        Swift hounds that run and bay.   1420

Soon some were on a scent by the side of a marsh;
When the hounds opened cry, the head of the hunt
Rallied them with rough words, raised a great noise.
The hounds that had heard it came hurrying straight
And followed along with their fellows, forty together.   1425
Then such a clamor and cry of coursing hounds
Arose, that the rocks resounded again.
Hunters exhorted them with horn and with voice;
Then all in a body bore off together
Between a mere[6] in the marsh and a menacing crag,   1430
To a rise where the rock stood rugged and steep,
And boulders lay about, that blocked their approach.
Then the company in consort closed on their prey:
They surrounded the rise and the rocks both,
For well they were aware that it waited within,   1435
The beast that the bloodhounds boldly proclaimed.
Then they beat on the bushes and bade him appear,
And he made a murderous rush in the midst of them all;
The best of all boars broke from his cover,
That had ranged long unrivaled, a renegade old,   1440
For of tough-brawned boars he was biggest far,
Most grim when he grunted—then grieved were many,
For three at the first thrust he threw to the earth,
And dashed away at once without more damage.
With "Hi!" "Hi!" and "Hey!" "Hey!" the others followed,   1445
Had horns at their lips, blew high and clear.
Merry was the music of men and of hounds
That were bound after this boar, his bloodthirsty heart
               to quell.
        Often he stands at bay,   1450
        Then scatters the pack pell-mell;
        He hurts the hounds, and they
        Most dolefully yowl and yell.

Men then with mighty bows moved in to shoot,
Aimed at him with their arrows and often hit,   1455
But the points had no power to pierce through his hide,
And the barbs were brushed aside by his bristly brow;
Though the shank of the shaft shivered in pieces,

6. Pool.

The head hopped away, wheresoever it struck.
But when their stubborn strokes had stung him at last,   1460
Then, foaming in his frenzy, fiercely he charges,
Hies at them headlong that hindered his flight,
And many feared for their lives, and fell back a little.
But the lord on a lively horse leads the chase;
As a high-mettled huntsman his horn he blows;   1465
He sounds the assembly and sweeps through the brush,
Pursuing this wild swine till the sunlight slanted.
All day with this deed they drive forth the time
While our lone knight so lovesome lies in his bed,
Sir Gawain safe at home, in silken bower   1470
               so gay.
        The lady, with guile in heart,
        Came early where he lay;
        She was at him with all her art
        To turn his mind her way.   1475

She comes to the curtain and coyly peeps in;
Gawain thought it good to greet her at once,
And she richly repays him with her ready words,
Settles softly at his side, and suddenly she laughs,
And with a gracious glance, she begins on him thus: 1480
"Sir, if you be Gawain, it seems a great wonder—
A man so well-meaning, and mannerly disposed,
And cannot act in company as courtesy bids,
And if one takes the trouble to teach him, 'tis all in vain.
That lesson learned lately is lightly forgot,   1485
Though I painted it as plain as my poor wit allowed."
"What lesson, dear lady?" he asked all alarmed;
"I have been much to blame, if your story be true."
"Yet my counsel was of kissing," came her answer then,
"Where favor has been found, freely to claim   1490
As accords with the conduct of courteous knights."
"My dear," said the doughty man, "dismiss that thought;
Such freedom, I fear, might offend you much;
It were rude to request if the right were denied."
"But none can deny you," said the noble dame,   1495
"You are stout enough to constrain with strength, if you choose,
Were any so ungracious as to grudge you aught."
"By heaven," said he, "you have answered well,
But threats never throve among those of my land,
Nor any gift not freely given, good though it be.   1500
I am yours to command, to kiss when you please;
You may lay on as you like, and leave off at will."
              With this,
        The lady lightly bends
        And graciously gives him a kiss;   1505
        The two converse as friends
        Of true love's trials and bliss.

"I should like, by your leave," said the lovely lady,
"If it did not annoy you, to know for what cause

So brisk and so bold a young blood as you,   1510
And acclaimed for all courtesies becoming a knight—
And name what knight you will, they are noblest esteemed
For loyal faith in love, in life as in story;
For to tell the tribulations of these true hearts,
Why, 'tis the very title and text of their deeds,   1515
How bold knights for beauty have braved many a foe,
Suffered heavy sorrows out of secret love,
And then valorously avenged them on villainous churls
And made happy ever after the hearts of their ladies.
And you are the noblest knight known in your time;   1520
No household under heaven but has heard of your fame,
And here by your side I have sat for two days
Yet never has a fair phrase fallen from your lips
Of the language of love, not one little word!
And you, that with sweet vows sway women's hearts,   1525
Should show your winsome ways, and woo a young thing,
And teach by some tokens the craft of true love.
How! are you artless, whom all men praise?
Or do you deem me so dull, or deaf to such words?
       Fie! Fie!   1530
    In hope of pastimes new
    I have come where none can spy;
    Instruct me a little, do,
    While my husband is not nearby."

"God love you, gracious lady!" said Gawain then;   1535
"It is a pleasure surpassing, and a peerless joy,
That one so worthy as you would willingly come
And take the time and trouble to talk with your knight
And content you with his company—it comforts my heart.
But to take to myself the task of telling of love,   1540
And touch upon its texts, and treat of its themes
To one that, I know well, wields more power
In that art, by a half, than a hundred such
As I am where I live, or am like to become,
It were folly, fair dame, in the first degree!   1545
In all that I am able, my aim is to please,
As in honor behooves me, and am evermore
Your servant heart and soul, so save me our Lord!"
Thus she tested his temper and tried many a time,
Whatever her true intent, to entice him to sin,   1550
But so fair was his defense that no fault appeared,
Nor evil on either hand, but only bliss
       they knew.
    They linger and laugh awhile;
    She kisses the knight so true,   1555
    Takes leave in comeliest style
    And departs without more ado.

Then he rose from his rest and made ready for mass,
And then a meal was set and served, in sumptuous style;
He dallied at home all day with the dear ladies,   1560

But the lord lingered late at his lusty sport;
Pursued his sorry swine, that swerved as he fled,
And bit asunder the backs of the best of his hounds
When they brought him to bay, till the bowmen appeared
And soon forced him forth, though he fought for dear life, 1565
So sharp were the shafts they shot at him there.
But yet the boldest drew back from his battering head,
Till at last he was so tired he could travel no more,
But in as much haste as he might, he makes his retreat
To a rise on rocky ground, by a rushing stream. 1570
With the bank at his back he scrapes the bare earth,
The froth foams at his jaws, frightful to see.
He whets his white tusks—then weary were all
Those hunters so hardy that hoved[7] round about
Of aiming from afar, but ever they mistrust 1575
                    his mood.
          He had hurt so many by then
          That none had hardihood
          To be torn by his tusks again,
          That was brainsick, and out for blood. 1580

Till the lord came at last on his lofty steed,
Beheld him there at bay before all his folk;
Lightly he leaps down, leaves his courser,
Bares his bright sword, and boldly advances;
Straight into the stream he strides towards his foe. 1585
The wild thing was wary of weapon and man;
His hackles rose high; so hotly he snorts
That many watched with alarm, lest the worst befall.
The boar makes for the man with a mighty bound
So that he and his hunter came headlong together 1590
Where the water ran wildest—the worse for the beast,
For the man, when they first met, marked him with care,
Sights well the slot, slips in the blade,
Shoves it home to the hilt, and the heart shattered,
And he falls in his fury and floats down the water, 1595
                  ill-sped.
          Hounds hasten by the score
          To maul him, hide and head;
          Men drag him in to shore
          And dogs pronounce him dead. 1600

With many a brave blast they boast of their prize,
All hallooed in high glee, that had their wind;
The hounds bayed their best, as the bold men bade
That were charged with chief rank in that chase of renown.
Then one wise in woodcraft, and worthily skilled, 1605
Began to dress the boar in becoming style:
He severs the savage head and sets it aloft,
Then rends the body roughly right down the spine;

7. Hovered.

Takes the bowels from the belly, broils them on coals,
Blends them well with bread to bestow on the hounds.   1610
Then he breaks out the brawn in fair broad flitches,
And the innards to be eaten in order he takes.
The two sides, attached to each other all whole,
He suspended from a spar that was springy and tough;
And so with this swine they set out for home;   1615
The boar's head was borne before the same man
That had stabbed him in the stream with his strong arm,
                    right through.
            He thought it long indeed
            Till he had the knight in view;   1620
            At his call, he comes with speed
            To claim his payment due.

The lord laughed aloud, with many a light word,
When he greeted Sir Gawain—with good cheer he speaks.
They fetch the fair dames and the folk of the house;   1625
He brings forth the brawn, and begins the tale
Of the great length and girth, the grim rage as well,
Of the battle of the boar they beset in the wood.
The other men meetly commended his deeds
And praised well the prize of his princely sport,   1630
For the brawn of that boar, the bold knight said,
And the sides of that swine surpassed all others.
Then they handled the huge head; he owns it a wonder,
And eyes it with abhorrence, to heighten his praise.
"Now, Gawain," said the good man, "this game becomes yours   1635
By those fair terms we fixed, as you know full well."
"That is true," returned the knight, "and trust me, fair friend,
All my gains, as agreed, I shall give you forthwith."
He clasps him and kisses him in courteous style,
Then serves him with the same fare a second time.   1640
"Now we are even," said he, "at this evening feast,
And clear is every claim incurred here to date,
                    and debt."
            "By Saint Giles!" the host replies,
            "You're the best I ever met!   1645
            If your profits are all this size,
            We'll see you wealthy yet!"

Then attendants set tables on trestles about,
And laid them with linen; light shone forth,
Wakened along the walls in waxen torches.   1650
The service was set and the supper brought;
Royal were the revels that rose then in hall
At that feast by the fire, with many fair sports:
Amid the meal and after, melody sweet,
Carol-dances comely and Christmas songs,   1655
With all the mannerly mirth my tongue may describe.
And ever our gallant knight beside the gay lady;
So uncommonly kind and complaisant was she,

With sweet stolen glances, that stirred his stout heart,
That he was at his wits' end, and wondrous vexed;   1660
But he could not in conscience her courtship repay,
Yet took pains to please her, though the plan might
                 go wrong.
           When they to heart's delight
           Had reveled there in throng,   1665
           To his chamber he calls the knight,
           And thither they go along.

And there they dallied and drank, and deemed it good sport
To enact their play anew on New Year's Eve,
But Gawain asked again to go on the morrow,   1670
For the time until his tryst was not two days.
The host hindered that, and urged him to stay,
And said, "On my honor, my oath here I take
That you shall get to the Green Chapel to begin your chores
By dawn on New Year's Day, if you so desire.   1675
Wherefore lie at your leisure in your lofty bed,
And I shall hunt hereabouts, and hold to our terms,
And we shall trade winnings when once more we meet,
For I have tested you twice, and true have I found you;
Now think this tomorrow: the third pays for all;   1680
Be we merry while we may, and mindful of joy,
For heaviness of heart can be had for the asking."
This is gravely agreed on and Gawain will stay.
They drink a last draught and with torches depart
                 to rest.   1685
           To bed Sir Gawain went;
           His sleep was of the best;
           The lord, on his craft intent,
           Was early up and dressed.

After mass, with his men, a morsel he takes;   1690
Clear and crisp the morning; he calls for his mount;
The folk that were to follow him afield that day
Were high astride their horses before the hall gates.
Wondrous fair were the fields, for the frost was light;
The sun rises red amid radiant clouds,   1695
Sails into the sky, and sends forth his beams.
They let loose the hounds by a leafy wood;
The rocks all around re-echo to their horns;
Soon some have set off in pursuit of the fox,
Cast about with craft for a clearer scent;   1700
A young dog yaps, and is yelled at in turn;
His fellows fall to sniffing, and follow his lead,
Running in a rabble on the right track,
And he scampers all before; they discover him soon,
And when they see him with sight they pursue him the faster,   1705
Railing at him rudely with a wrathful din.
Often he reverses over rough terrain,
Or loops back to listen in the lee of a hedge;

At last, by a little ditch, he leaps over the brush,
Comes into a clearing at a cautious pace, 1710
Then he thought through his wiles to have thrown off the hounds
Till he was ware, as he went, of a waiting-station
Where three athwart his path threatened him at once,
     all gray.
    Quick as a flash he wheels 1715
    And darts off in dismay;
    With hard luck at his heels
    He is off to the wood away.

Then it was heaven on earth to hark to the hounds
When they had come on their quarry, coursing together! 1720
Such harsh cries and howls they hurled at his head
As all the cliffs with a crash had come down at once.
Here he was hailed, when huntsmen met him;
Yonder they yelled at him, yapping and snarling;
There they cried "Thief!" and threatened his life, 1725
And ever the harriers at his heels, that he had no rest.
Often he was menaced when he made for the open,
And often rushed in again, for Reynard was wily;
And so he leads them a merry chase, the lord and his men,
In this manner on the mountains, till midday or near, 1730
While our hero lies at home in wholesome sleep
Within the comely curtains on the cold morning.
But the lady, as love would allow her no rest,
And pursuing ever the purpose that pricked her heart,
Was awake with the dawn, and went to his chamber 1735
In a fair flowing mantle that fell to the earth,
All edged and embellished with ermines fine;
No hood on her head, but heavy with gems
Were her fillet and the fret[8] that confined her tresses;
Her face and her fair throat freely displayed; 1740
Her bosom all but bare, and her back as well.
She comes in at the chamber-door, and closes it with care,
Throws wide a window—then waits no longer,
But hails him thus airily with her artful words,
     with cheer: 1745
    "Ah, man, how can you sleep?
    The morning is so clear!"
    Though dreams have drowned him deep,
    He cannot choose but hear.

Deep in his dreams he darkly mutters 1750
As a man may that mourns, with many grim thoughts
Of that day when destiny shall deal him his doom
When he greets his grim host at the Green Chapel
And must bow to his buffet, bating all strife.
But when he sees her at his side he summons his wits, 1755
Breaks from the black dreams, and blithely answers.

8. Ornamental net.

That lovely lady comes laughing sweet,
Sinks down at his side, and salutes him with a kiss.
He accords her fair welcome in courtliest style;
He sees her so glorious, so gaily attired, 1760
So faultless her features, so fair and so bright,
His heart swelled swiftly with surging joys.
They melt into mirth with many a fond smile,
And there was bliss beyond telling between those two,
    at height.   1765
   Good were their words of greeting;
   Each joyed in other's sight;
   Great peril attends that meeting
   Should Mary forget her knight.

For that high-born beauty so hemmed him about, 1770
Made so plain her meaning, the man must needs
Either take her tendered love or distastefully refuse.
His courtesy concerned him, lest crass he appear,
But more his soul's mischief, should he commit sin
And belie his loyal oath to the lord of that house. 1775
"God forbid!" said the bold knight, "That shall not befall!"
With a little fond laughter he lightly let pass
All the words of special weight that were sped his way;
"I find you much at fault," the fair one said,
"Who can be cold toward a creature so close by your side, 1780
Of all women in this world most wounded in heart,
Unless you have a sweetheart, one you hold dearer,
And allegiance to that lady so loyally knit
That you will never love another, as now I believe.
And, sir, if it be so, then say it, I beg you; 1785
By all your heart holds dear, hide it no longer
    with guile."
   "Lady, by Saint John,"
   He answers with a smile,
   "Lover have I none,   1790
   Nor will have, yet awhile."

"Those words," said the woman, "are the worst of all,
But I have had my answer, and hard do I find it!
Kiss me now kindly; I can but go hence
To lament my life long like a maid lovelorn." 1795
She inclines her head quickly and kisses the knight,
Then straightens with a sigh, and says as she stands,
"Now, dear, ere I depart, do me this pleasure:
Give me some little gift, your glove or the like,
That I may think on you, man, and mourn the less." 1800
"Now by heaven," said he, "I wish I had here
My most precious possession, to put it in your hands,
For your deeds, beyond doubt, have often deserved
A repayment far passing my power to bestow.
But a love-token, lady, were of little avail; 1805
It is not to your honor to have at this time

A glove as a guerdon from Gawain's hand,
And I am here on an errand in unknown realms
And have no bearers with baggage with becoming gifts,
Which distresses me, madame, for your dear sake.   1810
A man must keep within his compass: account it neither grief
                                            nor slight."
                    "Nay, noblest knight alive,"
                    Said that beauty of body white,
                    "Though you be loath to give,   1815
                    Yet you shall take, by right."

She reached out a rich ring, wrought all of gold,
With a splendid stone displayed on the band
That flashed before his eyes like a fiery sun;
It was worth a king's wealth, you may well believe.   1820
But he waved it away with these ready words:
"Before God, good lady, I forego all gifts;
None have I to offer, nor any will I take."
And she urged it on him eagerly, and ever he refused,
And vowed in very earnest, prevail she would not.   1825
And she sad to find it so, and said to him then,
"If my ring is refused for its rich cost—
You would not be my debtor for so dear a thing—
I shall give you my girdle;[9] you gain less thereby."
She released a knot lightly, and loosened a belt   1830
That was caught about her kirtle, the bright cloak beneath,
Of a gay green silk, with gold overwrought,
And the borders all bound with embroidery fine,
And this she presses upon him, and pleads with a smile,
Unworthy though it were, that it would not be scorned.   1835
But the man still maintains that he means to accept
Neither gold nor any gift, till by God's grace
The fate that lay before him was fully achieved.
"And be not offended, fair lady, I beg,
And give over your offer, for ever I must   1840
                    decline.
                    I am grateful for favor shown
                    Past all deserts of mine,
                    And ever shall be your own
                    True servant, rain or shine."   1845

"Now does my present displease you," she promptly inquired,
"Because it seems in your sight so simple a thing?
And belike, as it is little, it is less to praise,
But if the virtue that invests it were verily known,
It would be held, I hope, in higher esteem.   1850
For the man that possesses this piece of silk,
If he bore it on his body, belted about,
There is no hand under heaven that could hew him down,
For he could not be killed by any craft on earth."

9. Belt.

Then the man began to muse, and mainly he thought   1855
It was a pearl for his plight, the peril to come
When he gains the Green Chapel to get his reward:
Could he escape unscathed, the scheme were noble!
Then he bore with her words and withstood them no more,
And she repeated her petition and pleaded anew,   1860
And he granted it, and gladly she gave him the belt,
And besought him for her sake to conceal it well,
Lest the noble lord should know—and the knight agrees
That not a soul save themselves shall see it thenceforth
                         with sight.   1865
          He thanked her with fervent heart,
          As often as ever he might;
          Three times, before they part,
          She has kissed the stalwart knight.

Then the lady took her leave, and left him there,   1870
For more mirth with that man she might not have.
When she was gone, Sir Gawain got from his bed,
Arose and arrayed him in his rich attire;
Tucked away the token the temptress had left,
Laid it reliably where he looked for it after.   1875
And then with good cheer to the chapel he goes,
Approached a priest in private, and prayed to be taught
To lead a better life and lift up his mind,
Lest he be among the lost when he must leave this world.
And shamefaced at shrift[1] he showed his misdeeds   1880
From the largest to the least, and asked the Lord's mercy,
And called on his confessor to cleanse his soul,
And he absolved him of his sins as safe and as clean
As if the dread Day of Judgment should dawn on the morrow.
And then he made merry amid the fine ladies   1885
With deft-footed dances and dalliance light,
As never until now, while the afternoon wore
                       away.
          He delighted all around him,
          And all agreed, that day,   1890
          They never before had found him
          So gracious and so gay.

Now peaceful be his pasture, and love play him fair!
The host is on horseback, hunting afield;
He has finished off this fox that he followed so long: 1895
As he leapt a low hedge to look for the villain
Where he heard all the hounds in hot pursuit,
Reynard comes racing out of a rough thicket,
And all the rabble in a rush, right at his heels.
The man beholds the beast, and bides his time,   1900
And bares his bright sword, and brings it down hard,
And he blenches from the blade, and backward he starts;

---

1. Confession.

A hound hurries up and hinders that move,
And before the horse's feet they fell on him at once
And ripped the rascal's throat with a wrathful din.   1905
The lord soon alighted and lifted him free,
Swiftly snatched him up from the snapping jaws,
Holds him over his head, halloos with a will,
And the dogs bayed the dirge, that had done him to death.
Hunters hastened thither with horns at their lips,   1910
Sounding the assembly till they saw him at last.
When that comely company was come in together,
All that bore bugles blew them at once,
And the others all hallooed, that had no horns.
It was the merriest medley that ever a man heard,   1915
The racket that they raised for Sir Reynard's soul
                          that died.
          Their hounds they praised and fed,
          Fondling their heads with pride,
          And they took Reynard the Red   1920
          And stripped away his hide.

And then they headed homeward, for evening had come,
Blowing many a blast on their bugles bright.
The lord at long last alights at his house,
Finds fire on the hearth where the fair knight waits,   1925
Sir Gawain the good, that was glad in heart.
With the ladies, that loved him, he lingered at ease;
He wore a rich robe of blue, that reached to the earth
And a surcoat lined softly with sumptuous furs;
A hood of the same hue hung on his shoulders;   1930
With bands of bright ermine embellished were both.
He comes to meet the man amid all the folk,
And greets him good-humoredly, and gaily he says,
"I shall follow forthwith the form of our pledge
That we framed to good effect amid fresh-filled cups."   1935
He clasps him accordingly and kisses him thrice,
As amiably and as earnestly as ever he could.
"By heaven," said the host, "you have had some luck
Since you took up this trade, if the terms were good."
"Never trouble about the terms," he returned at once,   1940
"Since all that I owe here is openly paid."
"Marry!" said the other man, "mine is much less,
For I have hunted all day, and nought have I got
But this foul fox pelt, the fiend take the goods!
Which but poorly repays those precious things   1945
That you have cordially conferred, those kisses three
                          so good."
          "Enough!" said Sir Gawain;
          "I thank you, by the rood!"[2]
          And how the fox was slain   1950
          He told him, as they stood.

2. Cross.

With minstrelsy and mirth, with all manner of meats,
They made as much merriment as any men might
(Amid laughing of ladies and light-hearted girls,
So gay grew Sir Gawain and the goodly host)   1955
Unless they had been besotted, or brainless fools.
The knight joined in jesting with that joyous folk,
Until at last it was late; ere long they must part,
And be off to their beds, as behooved them each one.
Then politely his leave of the lord of the house   1960
Our noble knight takes, and renews his thanks:
"The courtesies countless accorded me here,
Your kindness at this Christmas, may heaven's King repay!
Henceforth, if you will have me, I hold you my liege,
And so, as I have said, I must set forth tomorrow,   1965
If I may take some trusty man to teach, as you promised,
The way to the Green Chapel, that as God allows
I shall see my fate fulfilled on the first of the year."
"In good faith," said the good man, "with a good will
Every promise on my part shall be fully performed."   1970
He assigns him a servant to set him on the path,
To see him safe and sound over the snowy hills,
To follow the fastest way through forest green
                              and grove.
                    Gawain thanks him again,   1975
                    So kind his favors prove,
                    of the ladies then
                    He takes his leave, with love.

Courteously he kissed them, with care in his heart,
And often wished them well, with warmest thanks,   1980
Which they for their part were prompt to repay.
They commend him to Christ with disconsolate sighs;
And then in that hall with the household he parts—
Each man that he met, he remembered to thank
or his deeds of devotion and diligent pains,   1985
And the trouble he had taken to tend to his needs;
And each one as woeful, that watched him depart,
As he had lived with him loyally all his life long.
By lads bearing lights he was led to his chamber
And blithely brought to his bed, to be at his rest.   1990
How soundly he slept, I presume not to say,
For there were matters of moment his thoughts might well
                              pursue.
                    Let him lie and wait;
                    He has little more to do,   1995
                    Then listen, while I relate
                    How they kept their rendezvous.

PART IV

Now the New Year draws near, and the night passes,
The day dispels the dark, by the Lord's decree;
But wild weather awoke in the world without: 2000

The clouds in the cold sky cast down their snow
With great gusts from the north, grievous to bear.
Sleet showered aslant upon shivering beasts;
The wind warbled wild as it whipped from aloft,
And drove the drifts deep in the dales below.   2005
Long and well he listens, that lies in his bed;
Though he lifts not his eyelids, little he sleeps;
Each crow of the cock he counts without fail.
Readily from his rest he rose before dawn,
For a lamp had been left him, that lighted his chamber.   2010
He called to his chamberlain, who quickly appeared,
And bade him get him his gear, and gird his good steed,
And he sets about briskly to bring in his arms,
And makes ready his master in manner most fit.
First he clad him in his clothes, to keep out the cold,   2015
And then his other harness, made handsome anew,
His plate-armor of proof, polished with pains,
The rings of his rich mail rid of their rust,
And all was fresh as at first, and for this he gave thanks
                              indeed.   2020
            With pride he wears each piece,
            New-furbished for his need:
            No gayer from here to Greece;
            He bids them bring his steed.

In his richest raiment he robed himself then: 2025
His crested coat-armor, close-stitched with craft,
With stones of strange virtue on silk velvet set;
All bound with embroidery on borders and seams
And lined warmly and well with furs of the best.
Yet he left not his love-gift, the lady's girdle;   2030
Gawain, for his own good, forgot not that:
When the bright sword was belted and bound on his haunches,
Then twice with that token he twined him about.
Sweetly did he swathe him in that swatch of silk,
That girdle of green so goodly to see,   2035
That against the gay red showed gorgeous bright.
Yet he wore not for its wealth that wondrous girdle,
Nor pride in its pendants, though polished they were,
Though glittering gold gleamed at the tips,
But to keep himself safe when consent he must   2040
To endure a deadly dint, and all defense
                              denied.
            And now the bold knight came
            Into the courtyard wide;
            That folk of worthy fame   2045
            He thanks on every side.

Then was Gringolet girt, that was great and huge,
And had sojourned safe and sound, and savored his fare;
He pawed the earth in his pride, that princely steed.
The good knight draws near him and notes well his look,   2050
And says sagely to himself, and soberly swears,

"Here is a household in hall that upholds the right!
The man that maintains it, may happiness be his!
Likewise the dear lady, may love betide her!
If thus they in charity cherish a guest   2055
That are honored here on earth, may they have His reward
That reigns high in heaven—and also you all;
And were I to live in this land but a little while,
I should willingly reward you, and well, if I might."
Then he steps into the stirrup and bestrides his mount;   2060
His shield is shown forth; on his shoulder he casts it;
Strikes the side of his steed with his steel spurs,
And he starts across the stones, nor stands any longer
　　　　　　　　to prance.
　　　　　　　On horseback was the swain   2065
　　　　　　　That bore his spear and lance;
　　　　　　　"May Christ this house maintain
　　　　　　　And guard it from mischance!"

The bridge was brought down, and the broad gates
Unbarred and carried back upon both sides;   2070
He commended him[3] to Christ, and crossed over the planks;
Praised the noble porter, who prayed on his knees
That God save Sir Gawain, and bade him good day,
And went on his way alone with the man
That was to lead him ere long to that luckless place   2075
Where the dolorous dint must be dealt him at last.
Under bare boughs they ride, where steep banks rise,
Over high cliffs they climb, where cold snow clings;
The heavens held aloof, but heavy thereunder
Mist mantled the moors, moved on the slopes.   2080
Each hill had a hat, a huge cape of cloud;
Brooks bubbled and broke over broken rocks,
Flashing in freshets that waterfalls fed.
Roundabout was the road that ran through the wood
Till the sun at that season was soon to rise,   2085
　　　　　　　　that day.
　　　　　　　They were on a hilltop high;
　　　　　　　The white snow round them lay;
　　　　　　　The man that rode nearby
　　　　　　　Now bade his master stay.   2090

"For I have seen you here safe at the set time,
And now you are not far from that notable place
That you have sought for so long with such special pains.
But this I say for certain, since I know you, sir knight,
And have your good at heart, and hold you dear—   2095
Would you heed well my words, it were worth your while—
You are rushing into risks that you reck not of:
There is a villain in yon valley, the veriest on earth,
For he is rugged and rude, and ready with fists,

---

3. I.e., himself.

And most immense in his mold of mortals alive,   2100
And his body bigger than the best four
That are in Arthur's house, Hector[4] or any.
He gets his grim way at the Green Chapel;
None passes by that place so proud in his arms
That he does not dash him down with his deadly blows,   2105
For he is heartless wholly, and heedless of right,
For be it chaplain or churl that by the Chapel rides,
Monk or mass-priest or any man else,
He would as soon strike him dead as stand on two feet.
Wherefore I say, just as certain as you sit there astride,   2110
You cannot but be killed, if his counsel holds,
For he would trounce you in a trice, had you twenty lives
> for sale.
>> He has lived long in this land
>> And dealt out deadly bale;   2115
>> Against his heavy hand
>> Your power cannot prevail.

"And so, good Sir Gawain, let the grim man be;
Go off by some other road, in God's own name!
Leave by some other land, for the love of Christ,   2120
And I shall get me home again, and give you my word
That I shall swear by God's self and the saints above,
By heaven and by my halidom[5] and other oaths more,
To conceal this day's deed, nor say to a soul
That ever you fled for fear from any that I knew."   2125
"Many thanks!" said the other man—and demurring he speaks—
"Fair fortune befall you for your friendly words!
And conceal this day's deed I doubt not you would,
But though you never told the tale, if I turned back now,
Forsook this place for fear, and fled, as you say,   2130
I were a caitiff[6] coward; I could not be excused.
But I must to the Chapel to chance my luck
And say to that same man such words as I please,
Befall what may befall through Fortune's will
> or whim.   2135
>> Though he be a quarrelsome knave
>> With a cudgel great and grim,
>> The Lord is strong to save:
>> His servants trust in Him."

"Marry," said the man, "since you tell me so much,   2140
And I see you are set to seek your own harm,
If you crave a quick death, let me keep you no longer!
Put your helm on your head, your hand on your lance,
And ride the narrow road down yon rocky slope
Till it brings you to the bottom of the broad valley.   2145
Then look a little ahead, on your left hand,

---

4. Either the Trojan hero or one of Arthur's knights.   5. Holiness or, more likely, patron saints.

And you will soon see before you that self-same Chapel,
And the man of great might that is master there.
Now goodbye in God's name, Gawain the noble!
For all the world's wealth I would not stay here, 2150
Or go with you in this wood one footstep further!"
He tarried no more to talk, but turned his bridle,
Hit his horse with his heels as hard as he might,
Leaves the knight alone, and off like the wind
                goes leaping. 2155
         "By God," said Gawain then,
         "I shall not give way to weeping;
         God's will be done, amen!
         I commend me to His keeping."

He puts his heels to his horse, and picks up the path; 2160
Goes in beside a grove where the ground is steep,
Rides down the rough slope right to the valley;
And then he looked a little about him—the landscape was wild,
And not a soul to be seen, nor sign of a dwelling,
But high banks on either hand hemmed it about, 2165
With many a ragged rock and rough-hewn crag;
The skies seemed scored by the scowling peaks.
Then he halted his horse, and hoved there a space,
And sought on every side for a sight of the Chapel,
But no such place appeared, which puzzled him sore, 2170
Yet he saw some way off what seemed like a mound,
A hillock high and broad, hard by the water,
Where the stream fell in foam down the face of the steep
And bubbled as if it boiled on its bed below.
The knight urges his horse, and heads for the knoll; 2175
Leaps lightly to earth; loops well the rein
Of his steed to a stout branch, and stations him there.
He strides straight to the mound, and strolls all about,
Much wondering what it was, but no whit the wiser;
It had a hole at one end, and on either side, 2180
And was covered with coarse grass in clumps all without,
And hollow all within, like some old cave,
Or a crevice of an old crag—he could not discern
                aright.
         "Can this be the Chapel Green? 2185
         Alack!" said the man, "Here might
         The devil himself be seen
         Saying matins[7] at black midnight!"

"Now by heaven," said he, "it is bleak hereabouts;
This prayer-house is hideous, half-covered with grass! 2190
Well may the grim man mantled in green
Hold here his orisons, in hell's own style!
Now I feel it is the Fiend, in my five wits,
That has tempted me to this tryst, to take my life;

_____
7. Morning prayers.

This is a Chapel of mischance, may the mischief take it!   2195
As accursed a country church as I came upon ever!"
With his helm on his head, his lance in his hand,
He stalks toward the steep wall of that strange house.
Then he heard, on the hill, behind a hard rock,
Beyond the brook, from the bank, a most barbarous din: 2200
Lord! it clattered in the cliff fit to cleave it in two,
As one upon a grindstone ground a great scythe!
Lord! it whirred like a mill-wheel whirling about!
Lord! it echoed loud and long, lamentable to hear!
Then "By heaven," said the bold knight, "That business up there   2205
Is arranged for my arrival, or else I am much
                    misled.
          Let God work! Ah me!
          All hope of help has fled!
          Forfeit my life may be   2210
          But noise I do not dread."

Then he listened no longer, but loudly he called,
"Who has power in this place, high parley to hold?
For none greets Sir Gawain, or gives him good day;
If any would a word with him, let him walk forth   2215
And speak now or never, to speed his affairs."
"Abide," said one on the bank above over his head,
"And what I promised you once shall straightway be given."
Yet he stayed not his grindstone, nor stinted its noise,
But worked awhile at his whetting before he would rest,   2220
And then he comes around a crag, from a cave in the rocks,
Hurtling out of hiding with a hateful weapon,
A Danish ax devised for that day's deed,
With a broad blade and bright, bent in a curve,
Filed to a fine edge—four feet it measured   2225
By the length of the lace that was looped round the haft.
And in form as at first, the fellow all green,
His lordly face and his legs, his locks and his beard,
Save that firm upon two feet forward he strides,
Sets a hand on the ax-head, the haft to the earth;   2230
When he came to the cold stream, and cared not to wade,
He vaults over on his ax, and advances amain
On a broad bank of snow, overbearing and brisk
                  of mood.
          Little did the knight incline   2235
          When face to face they stood;
          Said the other man, "Friend mine,
          It seems your word holds good!"

"God love you, Sir Gawain!" said the Green Knight then,
"And well met this morning, man, at my place!   2240
And you have followed me faithfully and found me betimes,[8]
And on the business between us we both are agreed:

8. In good time.

Twelve months ago today you took what was yours,
And you at this New Year must yield me the same.
And we have met in these mountains, remote from all eyes: 2245
There is none here to halt us or hinder our sport;
Unhasp your high helm, and have here your wages;
Make no more demur than I did myself
When you hacked off my head with one hard blow."
"No, by God," said Sir Gawain, "that granted me life,   2250
I shall grudge not the guerdon, grim though it prove;
Bestow but one stroke, and I shall stand still,
And you may lay on as you like till the last of my part
           be paid."
         He proffered, with good grace,   2255
         His bare neck to the blade,
         And feigned a cheerful face:
         He scorned to seem afraid.

Then the grim man in green gathers his strength,
Heaves high the heavy ax to hit him the blow.   2260
With all the force in his frame he fetches it aloft,
With a grimace as grim as he would grind him to bits;
Had the blow he bestowed been as big as he threatened,
A good knight and gallant had gone to his grave.
But Gawain at the great ax glanced up aside   2265
As down it descended with death-dealing force,
And his shoulders shrank a little from the sharp iron.
Abruptly the brawny man breaks off the stroke,
And then reproved with proud words that prince among knights.
"You are not Gawain the glorious," the green man said,   2270
"That never fell back on field in the face of the foe,
And now you flee for fear, and have felt no harm:
Such news of that knight I never heard yet!
I moved not a muscle when you made to strike,
Nor caviled at the cut in King Arthur's house;   2275
My head fell to my feet, yet steadfast I stood,
And you, all unharmed, are wholly dismayed—
Wherefore the better man I, by all odds,
           must be."
         Said Gawain, "Strike once more;   2280
         I shall neither flinch nor flee;
         But if my head falls to the floor
         There is no mending me!

"But go on, man, in God's name, and get to the point!
Deliver me my destiny, and do it out of hand,   2285
For I shall stand to the stroke and stir not an inch
Till your ax has hit home—on my honor I swear it!"
"Have at thee then!" said the other, and heaves it aloft,
And glares down as grimly as he had gone mad.
He made a mighty feint, but marred not his hide;   2290
Withdrew the ax adroitly before it did damage.
Gawain gave no ground, nor glanced up aside,

But stood still as a stone, or else a stout stump
That is held in hard earth by a hundred roots.
Then merrily does he mock him, the man all in green: 2295
"So now you have your nerve again, I needs must strike;
Uphold the high knighthood that Arthur bestowed,
And keep your neck-bone clear, if this cut allows!"
Then was Gawain gripped with rage, and grimly he said,
"Why, thrash away, tyrant, I tire of your threats; 2300
You make such a scene, you must frighten yourself."
Said the green fellow, "In faith, so fiercely you speak
That I shall finish this affair, nor further grace
                    allow."
            He stands prepared to strike 2305
            And scowls with both lip and brow;
            No marvel if the man mislike
            Who can hope no rescue now.

He gathered up the grim ax and guided it well:
Let the barb at the blade's end brush the bare throat; 2310
He hammered down hard, yet harmed him no whit
Save a scratch on one side, that severed the skin;
The end of the hooked edge entered the flesh,
And a little blood lightly leapt to the earth.
And when the man beheld his own blood bright on the snow, 2315
He sprang a spear's length with feet spread wide,
Seized his high helm, and set it on his head,
Shoved before his shoulders the shield at his back,
Bares his trusty blade, and boldly he speaks—
Not since he was a babe born of his mother 2320
Was he once in this world one-half so blithe—
"Have done with your hacking—harry me no more!
I have borne, as behooved, one blow in this place;
If you make another move I shall meet it midway
And promptly, I promise you, pay back each blow 2325
                    with brand.
            One stroke acquits me here;
            So did our covenant stand
            In Arthur's court last year—
            Wherefore, sir, hold your hand!" 2330

He lowers the long ax and leans on it there,
Sets his arms on the head, the haft on the earth,
And beholds the bold knight that bides there afoot,
How he faces him fearless, fierce in full arms,
And plies him with proud words—it pleases him well. 2335
Then once again gaily to Gawain he calls,
And in a loud voice and lusty, delivers these words:
"Bold fellow, on this field your anger forbear!
No man has made demands here in manner uncouth,
Nor done, save as duly determined at court. 2340
I owed you a hit and you have it; be happy therewith!
The rest of my rights here I freely resign.

Had I been a bit busier, a buffet, perhaps,
I could have dealt more directly, and done you some harm.
First I flourished with a feint, in frolicsome mood,   2345
And left your hide unhurt—and here I did well
By the fair terms we fixed on the first night;
And fully and faithfully you followed accord:
Gave over all your gains as a good man should.
A second feint, sir, I assigned for the morning   2350
You kissed my comely wife—each kiss you restored.
For both of these there behooved but two feigned blows
                    by right.
          True men pay what they owe;
          No danger then in sight.   2355
          You failed at the third throw,
          So take my tap, sir knight.

"For that is my belt about you, that same braided girdle,
My wife it was that wore it; I know well the tale,
And the count of your kisses and your conduct too,   2360
And the wooing of my wife—it was all my scheme!
She made trial of a man most faultless by far
Of all that ever walked over the wide earth;
As pearls to white peas, more precious and prized,
So is Gawain, in good faith, to other gay knights.   2365
Yet you lacked, sir, a little in loyalty there,
But the cause was not cunning, nor courtship either,
But that you loved your own life; the less, then, to blame."
The other stout knight in a study stood a long while,
So gripped with grim rage that his great heart shook.   2370
All the blood of his body burned in his face
As he shrank back in shame from the man's sharp speech.
The first words that fell from the fair knight's lips:
"Accursed be a cowardly and covetous heart!
In you is villainy and vice, and virtue laid low!"   2375
Then he grasps the green girdle and lets go the knot,
Hands it over in haste, and hotly he says:
"Behold there my falsehood, ill hap betide it!
Your cut taught me cowardice, care for my life,
And coveting came after, contrary both   2380
To largesse and loyalty belonging to knights.
Now am I faulty and false, that fearful was ever
Of disloyalty and lies, bad luck to them both!
                    and greed.
          I confess, knight, in this place,   2385
          Most dire is my misdeed;
          Let me gain back your good grace,
          And thereafter I shall take heed."

Then the other laughed aloud, and lightly he said,
"Such harm as I have had, I hold it quite healed.   2390
You are so fully confessed, your failings made known,
And bear the plain penance of the point of my blade,

I hold you polished as a pearl, as pure and as bright
As you had lived free of fault since first you were born.
And I give you, sir, this girdle that is gold-hemmed   2395
And green as my garments, that, Gawain, you may
Be mindful of this meeting when you mingle in throng
With nobles of renown—and known by this token
How it chanced at the Green Chapel, to chivalrous knights.
And you shall in this New Year come yet again   2400
And we shall finish out our feast in my fair hall,
                              with cheer."
                    He urged the knight to stay,
                    And said, "With my wife so dear
                    We shall see you friends this day,   2405
                    Whose enmity touched you near."

"Indeed," said the doughty knight, and doffed his high helm,
And held it in his hands as he offered his thanks,
"I have lingered long enough—may good luck be yours,
And He reward you well that all worship bestows!   2410
And commend me to that comely one, your courteous wife,
Both herself and that other, my honoured ladies,
That have trapped their true knight in their trammels so quaint.
But if a dullard should dote, deem it no wonder,
And through the wiles of a woman be wooed into sorrow,   2415
For so was Adam by one, when the world began,
And Solomon by many more, and Samson the mighty—
Delilah was his doom, and David thereafter
Was beguiled by Bathsheba, and bore much distress;
Now these were vexed by their devices—'twere a very joy   2420
Could one but learn to love, and believe them not.
For these were proud princes, most prosperous of old,
Past all lovers lucky, that languished under heaven,
                              bemused.
                    And one and all fell prey   2425
                    To women that they had used;
                    If I be led astray,
                    Methinks I may be excused.

"But your girdle, God love you! I gladly shall take
And be pleased to possess, not for the pure gold,   2430
Nor the bright belt itself, nor the beauteous pendants,
Nor for wealth, nor worldly state, nor workmanship fine,
But a sign of excess it shall seem oftentimes
When I ride in renown, and remember with shame
The faults and the frailty of the flesh perverse,   2435
How its tenderness entices the foul taint of sin;
And so when praise and high prowess have pleased my heart,
A look at this love-lace will lower my pride.
But one thing would I learn, if you were not loath,
Since you are lord of yonder land where I have long sojourned   2440
With honor in your house—may you have His reward
That upholds all the heavens, highest on throne!

How runs your right name?—and let the rest go."
"That shall I give you gladly," said the Green Knight then;
"Bercilak de Hautdesert this barony I hold,   2445
Through the might of Morgan le Fay,⁹ that lodges at my house,
By subtleties of science and sorcerers' arts,
The mistress of Merlin, she has caught many a man,
For sweet love in secret she shared sometime
With that wizard, that knows well each one of your knights   2450
                    and you.
              Morgan the Goddess, she,
              So styled by title true;
              None holds so high degree
              That her arts cannot subdue.   2455

"She guided me in this guise to your glorious hall,
To assay, if such it were, the surfeit of pride
That is rumored of the retinue of the Round Table.
She put this shape upon me to puzzle your wits,
To afflict the fair queen, and frighten her to death   2460
With awe of that elvish man that eerily spoke
With his head in his hand before the high table.
She was with my wife at home, that old withered lady,
Your own aunt is she,¹ Arthur's half-sister,
The Duchess's daughter of Tintagel, that dear King Uther   2465
Got Arthur on after, that honored is now.
And therefore, good friend, come feast with your aunt;
Make merry in my house; my men hold you dear,
And I wish you as well, sir, with all my heart,
As any mortal man, for your matchless faith."   2470
But the knight said him nay, that he might by no means.
They clasped then and kissed, and commended each other
To the Prince of Paradise, and parted with one
                    assent.
              Gawain sets out anew;   2475
              Toward the court his course is bent;
              And the knight all green in hue,
              Wheresoever he wished, he went.

Wild ways in the world our worthy knight rides
On Gringolet, that by grace had been granted his life.   2480
He harbored often in houses, and often abroad,
And with many valiant adventures verily he met
That I shall not take time to tell in this story.
The hurt was whole that he had had in his neck,
And the bright green belt on his body he bore,   2485
Oblique, like a baldric, bound at his side,
Below his left shoulder, laced in a knot,
In betokening of the blame he had borne for his fault;
And so to court in due course he comes safe and sound.

9. Arthur's half-sister, an enchantress (*Faye:* fairy) who sometimes abetted him, sometimes made trouble
for him.   1. Morgan was the daughter of Igraine, duchess of Tintagel, and her husband, the duke. Igraine
conceived Arthur when his father, Uther, lay with her through one of Merlin's trickeries.

Bliss abounded in hall when the high-born heard 2490
That good Gawain was come; glad tidings they thought it.
The king kisses the knight, and the queen as well,
And many a comrade came to clasp him in arms,
And eagerly they asked, and awesomely he told,
Confessed all his cares and discomfitures many, 2495
How it chanced at the Chapel, what cheer made the knight,
The love of the lady, the green lace at last.
The nick on his neck he naked displayed
That he got in his disgrace at the Green Knight's hands,
       alone. 2500
   With rage in heart he speaks,
   And grieves with many a groan;
   The blood burns in his cheeks
   For shame at what must be shown.

"Behold, sir," said he, and handles the belt, 2505
"This is the blazon of the blemish that I bear on my neck;
This is the sign of sore loss that I have suffered there
For the cowardice and coveting that I came to there;
This is the badge of false faith that I was found in there,
And I must bear it on my body till I breathe my last. 2510
For one may keep a deed dark, but undo it no whit,
For where a fault is made fast, it is fixed evermore."
The king comforts the knight, and the court all together
Agree with gay laughter and gracious intent
That the lords and the ladies belonging to the Table, 2515
Each brother of that band, a baldric should have,
A belt borne oblique, of a bright green,
To be worn with one accord for that worthy's sake.
So that was taken as a token by the Table Round,
And he honored that had it, evermore after, 2520
As the best book of knighthood bids it be known.
In the old days of Arthur this happening befell;
The books of Brutus' deeds bear witness thereto
Since Brutus, the bold knight, embarked for this land
After the siege ceased at Troy and the city fared 2525
      amiss.
   Many such, ere we were born,
   Have befallen here, ere this.
   May He that was crowned with thorn
   Bring all men to His bliss! Amen. 2530

HONY SOYT QUI MAL PENCE

GEOFFREY CHAUCER
1340?–1400

Chaucer is not only one of the earliest poets in the English literary tradition but also one of the greatest. Apart from the poetic virtuosity, psychological subtlety, and humane good humor of his writing, he is worthy of his place here because he is the poet who endowed English literature with a status equal to that of the other European vernaculars—who in effect showed that it could become a world literature. Ironically, the earliest important body of vernacular writing in the medieval period was that of Anglo-Saxon England (represented in this anthology by *Beowulf* and by the lyric poem "The Ruin"). With the Norman conquest of England in 1066 this rich tradition was soon extinguished, and cultural leadership was assumed by literature written in the languages of France—French, Provençal (the dialect of southern France), and Anglo-Norman (the dialect of Normandy and England)—and, to a lesser extent, Italy. Having undergone the break in cultural continuity caused by the Norman conquest, and hindered by the internal struggle for cultural dominance between French and English, English speakers did not develop their own national literature in their own language until the last third of the fourteenth century. This was when *Sir Gawain and the Green Knight* was written, and when other significant writers emerged, especially William Langland, the author of a brilliantly difficult long poem called *Piers Plowman*, and John Gower, who wrote in French and Latin but also composed a major English poem, the *Confessio amantis* (or *Lover's Confession*). Both Langland and Gower lived and worked in London, which was also Chaucer's home. But unlike these contemporaries, Chaucer was very much aware of the European literary traditions not just as collections of texts but as *traditions*, as ongoing cultural projects. This awareness gave to his poetry an artistic subtlety and cultural sophistication that has ensured his position in world literature. But just as important, it also allowed Chaucer to conceive of—and to accomplish—the establishment of an English literary tradition. For it was to his poetry that later English poets, including Shakespeare, Spenser, and Milton, turned to find the foundations of an English literary tradition upon which they could then build.

Chaucer was the son of a wealthy London merchant, and like many children in his position he was sent at an early age to serve as a page in a noble household, in his case that of the countess of Ulster, who was married to one of the sons of King Edward III. Although from a bourgeois background, Chaucer would there have been educated in the values of the aristocratic culture of the time, including its literary tastes, which were for the most part formed on French models. In 1359–60 Chaucer participated in one of the king's military expeditions against the French, was captured, and as was usual at the time, was ransomed by the king. By 1367 Chaucer was a squire in the king's household. This meant not that he resided with the king (although he may have), but that he was called upon to perform a number of services, primarily traveling abroad on the king's business. Chaucer undertook diplomatic journeys to Spain, to France, and—first in 1372–73, then again in 1378—to Italy. These last trips are particularly important because they suggest that Chaucer knew Italian (which he could have learned in London from dealings with the many Italian merchants and bankers who lived there). His poetry—virtually alone among his contemporaries—shows the strong influence of Dante, Petrarch, and Boccaccio, and it is in part their example that provided him with the model for a national literature. In 1374 Chaucer became the Controller of the Customs in London, and he leased a house there (he had already been married for some eight years). He kept this job until 1386, when—probably under political pressure—he resigned. By this time the king was the young Richard II, who had ascended the throne in 1377 at the age of ten. Richard was throughout his reign involved in dangerous struggles for power with the leading members of the aristocracy, and in 1386 he seemed on the verge of being deposed. Chaucer was probably a member of the king's party, and his resignation reflects the decline of Richard's power. By 1389 Richard had regained command, and Chaucer was given other posts and gifts, but ten years later Richard was first deposed and then murdered by Henry Bolingbroke, who became Henry IV. This made little financial difference to Chaucer, who had long maintained a relationship with Henry's father, John of Gaunt, and with Henry himself: his annuity was quickly renewed.

As even this brief account suggests, Chaucer lived in turbulent times. In addition to the struggles for power among the royal family, England was throughout this time at war with France and with the Scots, wars that went progressively badly. It was also during this time—in 1381—that England experienced the shock of the Peasants' Revolt, a violent rebellion that accomplished little substantively but made disturbingly clear the intense animosity that existed between the classes. Finally, this was a period of religious turmoil, when John Wyclif and his supporters were challenging the Church in terms of both its doctrine and its immense economic power—a challenge that would finally culminate in the Protestant Reformation of the sixteenth century. Oddly enough, most of these events find only the barest mention in Chaucer's poetry. Unlike Dante, he seems not to have held strong political convictions, and his religious commitments seem both generally orthodox and lacking in any special intensity. Finally, although Chaucer was generously rewarded by the great men of his day, there is no clear evidence that these rewards were given to him because he wrote poetry. He seems to have followed a career path much like that of other men of his background, and we do not know to what extent, if any, his extraordinary talent was appreciated in his own day. Indeed, two of the characteristics that make Chaucer such an appealing writer are a tolerant inquisitiveness toward all sorts of people and opinions and a self-effacing if sometimes disingenuous modesty. While he lacks Dante's learning, for example, and his intensity, he is a far more agreeable poet: one can hardly imagine Dante appreciating either the Miller's hilarious bawdy or the witty self-promotions of the Wife of Bath.

Chaucer's career as a poet can be usefully divided into three stages. The first stage comprises the poetry he wrote primarily under the influence of the fashionable French court poetry of the time. When Chaucer was a young man the literary language of the king's household was probably French, yet Chaucer seems to have written only in English. The earliest poem we can date with any certainty is an elegy, in English, for Blanche, duchess of Lancaster and the wife of John of Gaunt, who died in 1368. But while written in English, much of this poem is derived from the work of contemporary French court poets: Chaucer here gratifies the tastes of an elegant society hypersensitive to French fashions. This interest continues in all the poetry Chaucer wrote prior to *The Canterbury Tales*, even when his work begins to show the powerful influence of the Italian poets. This second phase begins as early as the late 1370s, when in a poem called the *House of Fame* Chaucer struggles to locate himself in relation to Dante, whose work he seems to have found both intimidating and pretentious. In the 1380s he wrote *Troilus and Criseyde*, a very beautiful narrative love poem based on a poem by Boccaccio, which explores the psychological depths and the ethical questions that are now treated by the novel. The third part of Chaucer's career is called the English period and comprises *The Canterbury Tales*, a work begun about 1386 and left incomplete. The twenty-four tales that Chaucer completed in fact draw on a wide variety of sources, almost all of them Continental: Chaucer was never very interested in what native tradition of English writing there was. But *The Canterbury Tales* is still a very English work. It begins with a *General Prologue* that describes a group of about thirty pilgrims who meet by chance at an inn in a suburb of London prior to the trip to the shrine of St. Thomas à Becket at Canterbury cathedral. These pilgrims are drawn from almost every rank of fourteenth-century English society, with a decided emphasis on the middle strata, and the reader is left in no doubt that one of the purposes of the work as a whole is to provide a kind of portrait of the nation as a whole. Here Chaucer moves beyond the aristocratic circles to which all of his previous work had been addressed and writes for a larger, national audience. Whether he found such an audience in his own lifetime is very doubtful, but certainly his ambition has been amply rewarded by posterity.

The Canterbury Tales, like the Decameron and The Thousand and One Nights, is a collection of tales located within a frame. At the urging of their host, Harry Bailly, the pilgrims who have gathered at the Tabard Inn agree to tell two tales each, one while going to and one while returning from Canterbury. It seems doubtful that Chaucer himself meant to compose 120 tales, and there are clear indications that the tale-telling game is meant to end before the pilgrims reach Canterbury. Whether Chaucer decided that the twenty-four tales he did include were sufficient is not known, but he certainly did not complete all the links between the tales, and as a result the order in which many of the tales should be read is unclear. Yet this is not a serious impediment to understanding the individual tales, which together provide a brilliant anthology of virtually every medieval kind of writing. Chaucer offers us fabliaux, a mini-epic, romances, saints' lives, exempla, a lay, an animal fable, anecdotes, and even two prose treatises dealing with political and spiritual behavior. If he wants to show us almost every kind of person to be found in late medieval England, he also wants to survey almost the full range of medieval writing. Even the General Prologue, which describes with an air of casual spontaneity the pilgrims who gather at the Tabard Inn, is a recognizable kind of medieval writing. Medieval social theory held that society was divided into three estates, or classes: the nobility, who ruled; the clergy, who prayed; and the laborers, who worked. Much social criticism of the time was offered in the form of a critical commentary on the members of each of these estates. These works are known as estates satires, and the General Prologue fits the pattern. Chaucer begins with portraits of the knightly estate (the Knight, the Squire, and their servant, the Yeoman), then moves to the clergy (the Prioress, Monk, and Friar), and then to the largest group of all, the estate of those who work for a living. And if he doesn't keep strictly to this scheme—the Clerk, the Parson, the Summoner, and the Pardoner are all technically members of the clergy—he nonetheless includes two "ideal" portraits of each estate: the Knight and the Squire, the Clerk and the Parson, and the Yeoman and the Plowman. Yet, as is usual with Chaucer, he adopts a conventional form only in order to revise it in a new direction. The estates satire is a social form: its focus is on the ills of society and how they can be cured. But Chaucer's focus in the General Prologue is primarily on individuals and their psychological makeup. We are much less interested in the degree to which the Prioress fulfills her spiritual duties than we are in the needs she seeks to fulfill with her elegant dress, her love of pets, and her refined but avid dining. We know that the Friar violates his vows, but our attention is drawn to the sort of person he is. Striking in this regard is the fact that not until the final portraits does Chaucer pay much attention to the social effects of his characters' misbehavior: until we come to the out-and-out rogues (the Manciple, Miller, Reeve, Summoner and Pardoner—a group in which the narrator places himself!), there is remarkably little sense of anyone being seriously victimized by the pilgrims' foibles. This is not to say that Chaucer is uninterested in morality, but that the moralist's responsibility to judge seems often to conflict with the artist's desire to understand and to appreciate. This conflict corresponds to one within the General Prologue itself, between the duty of pilgrimage and the pleasure of tale-telling. In reading this vivid gallery of portraits, then, we do well to try to balance moral judgment with psychological analysis, and to seek to understand the many motivations and needs of these characters and the differing attitudes that the enthusiastic narrator—who is not to be identified with the historical Chaucer—takes toward them.

When the tale-telling game begins, the Knight—the highest representative of the aristocratic estate—is asked to tell the first story. He responds with a medievalized version of a classical epic: it deals with the fervent love of two knights for a fair maiden, and the inconclusive efforts of a wise ruler to bring order out of the chaos their passion creates. The Host then begins to call upon the highest representative of the clergy, the Monk, but is rudely interrupted by one of the lowest ranking members of the third estate, the Miller. The Miller says he will "pay off" the Knight, which means that he will both reward him and retaliate against him. But the social tensions of the time that for a moment burst into the tale-telling game are immediately displaced into *The Miller's Tale,* which is itself about reward and retaliation. Like the Knight, the Miller tells of two young men (Nicholas and Absalom) who desire a beautiful woman (Alison), and of an older man (John) who tries unsuccessfully to control events. But rather than the Knight's high seriousness the Miller presents ribald comedy; and rather than the courtly love the Knight celebrates the Miller presents sexual desire in much less exalted terms. *The Miller's Tale* is a fabliau—indeed, it is two fabliaux brought brilliantly together. One deals with the triangle of Nicholas, Alison, and John and ends with Nicholas's triumph and John's humiliation; the other is the triangle of Nicholas, Absalom and Alison and ends with both men humiliated and Alison cheerfully unscathed. Both these plots are brought together with a single word—"Water!"—that creates an almost metaphysical sense of harmonious resolution. Two stories have unfolded in apparently random ways, and yet suddenly we see that they are in fact one beautifully complex story. One is tempted to say that each story "pays off"—rewards and retaliates against—the other. But does the harmony of the plot extend to the theme as well? Is there moral as well as narrative order? To answer this question the reader must realize that what is being punished is not transgression against social or religious conventions but a presumptuous desire to overcontrol. All three men want to control Alison, but she not only has a mind of her own but also knows when a joke has gone far enough. It is this combination of frank self-gratification with prudent self-restraint that the Miller seems to admire, and that the three men lack.

The Wife of Bath is also called Alison, and it is not unreasonable to see her as Chaucer's idea of how the Miller's beautiful young woman might deal with growing old. But instead of being primarily an object that men desire, this Alison is endowed with a vivid personality and a complex inner life that she herself tells us all about. In her *Prologue* she sets her female experience against the misogynist stereotypes of women, as lawless, sexually voracious, and manipulative creatures, promoted by certain traditions of medieval religious thought. Yet the reader is forced to ask if the Wife's frank celebration of her own sexuality, and her account of the torment she has inflicted on her three old husbands, does not actually confirm those stereotypes. An answer is suggested by the Wife's claim that in her *Prologue* she is only playing: indeed, at one point she speaks as if she were showing her almost exclusively male audience how she would conduct a kind of school for wives. She seems, in other words, to be putting on a performance, pretending to reveal to her fascinated audience the secrets that women share among themselves and so letting men witness the intimate life of a woman. Yet as the *Prologue* proceeds we feel that her playful dramatics give way to a more serious, more authentic self-revelation. We learn that not only have her husbands suffered in marriage but that she has too, that she is unavoidably (if cheerfully) aware of the advancing years. Moreover, what she seems most to value is neither money nor the sex she so aggressively celebrates but the companionship and love she comes finally to share with Jankin. In the same way her *Tale* gradually reveals itself to be more than simply a nostalgic wish fulfillment for the return of youth and beauty. When the criminal knight tries to learn what women most desire he is offered a series of misogynist answers, but when forced to marry he discovers, through the moral lecture his old wife delivers, that she possesses a wisdom he himself lacks. This is why he leaves the final decision about what form she will assume up to her, and in granting her mastery he is rewarded not merely with youth and beauty but with a marriage of mutual affection. It is through this experience, then, rather than by relying on the authority of time-honored opinions, that the knight comes to learn about the true nature of women.

The Pardoner provides a performance that is very similar to that of the Wife, but his subject is not marriage but religion. His function is to raise money for a charitable institution—in this case, a hospital—by selling papal indulgences. These were documents by which the Church remitted some of the punishment that awaited sinners in purgatory by virtue of their charitable gifts. On no account, despite what this Pardoner says, did indulgences remit the guilt of sin: only Christ could do that. In his *Prologue* the Pardoner admits that he is a thorough rogue—indeed, he trumpets his viciousness, and his impenitent lack of concern for his own spiritual future, so loudly and so brazenly that we may think he protests too much. Even in the *Prologue* we get hints that the Pardoner harbors somewhere in his tortured soul the thought that he is, despite himself, doing God's work. And in fact the story he tells is one of the most brilliantly effective religious stories in all medieval literature. Generically it is an exemplum, one of those tales with which preachers would enliven their sermons. It demonstrates with an almost mathematical efficiency that the wages of sin are death, and it also provides us with a startling insight into the Pardoner himself. For he too is seeking the spiritual death of damnation, and in the figure of the eerie old man he expresses with painful vividness the common medieval understanding of damnation as a condition of perpetual dying, a dying that never finds death. Just as the Wife of Bath is more than a stereotype, so too the Pardoner is more than an impenitent sinner. On the contrary, Chaucer allows us to see the deep suffering endured by a man who mocks religious truths while simultaneously yearning for them.

CHAUCER IN MIDDLE ENGLISH

Chaucer is presented here in a Modern English version by Theodore Morrison, which is remarkably clear, accurate, and easy to read. But, to get some idea of Chaucer's original language, we may profitably compare the first eighteen lines of the *General Prologue* in the two forms. It will be possible to point out only a few of the changes that have occurred in pronunciation, in grammatical forms, and sometimes in the use and meaning of words.

> Whan that Aprille with his shoures sote
> The droghte of Marche hath perced to the rote,
> And bathed every veyne in swich licour,
> Of which vertu engendred is the flour;
> When Zephirus eek with his swete breeth   5
> Inspired hath in every holt and heeth
> The tendre croppes, and the yonge sonne
> Hath in the Ram his halfe cours y-ronne,
> And smale fowles maken melodye,
> That slepen al the night with open yë,   10
> So priketh hem nature in hir corages:
> Than longen folk to goon on pilgrimages
> And palmers for to seken straunge strandes
> To ferne halwes, couthe in sondry landes;
> And specially, from every shires ende   15
> Of Engeland, to Caunterbury they wende,
> The holy blisful martir for to seke,
> That hem hath holpen, whan that they were seke.

In Middle English of the late fourteenth century, the letters representing the stressed vowels were pronounced about as they are in Spanish or Italian in our time. Thus the *A* of *Aprille* sounded like *a* in our *father*; the first *e* in *swete* (line 5) was like the *a* in modern English *late*; and the second *i* in *Inspired* (line 6) was like *i* in our *machine.* In verbs, the third person singular ended in *-th,* not *-s,* as in *hath* (line 2); and the plural ending, either *-en* or *-e,* formed a separate syllable, as in *maken* (line 9), *slepen* (line 10), and *wende* (line 16). Among the pronouns and pronominal adjectives, Chaucer's language did not have our *its, their,* or *them.* Instead, the corresponding forms were, respectively, *his* (line 1), *hir(e)* (line 11), and *hem* (line 18). Changes in the meaning or use of words may compel a substitution. Thus Chaucer's *couthe* (line 14) has become obsolete and hence is translated as *renowned* instead; so also *corages* (line 11) becomes *hearts,* and *ferne halwes* (line 14) becomes *foreign shrines.* Recordings of Chaucer's poetry read in its original language can be found at <*http://icg.fas.harvard.edu/chaucer/*> and <*http://academics.vmi.edu/english/audio/audio_index.html*>.

The Canterbury Tales[1]

General Prologue

As soon as April pierces to the root
The drought of March, and bathes each bud and shoot
Through every vein of sap with gentle showers
From whose engendering liquor spring the flowers;
When zephyrs[2] have breathed softly all about   5
Inspiring every wood and field to sprout,
And in the zodiac the youthful sun
His journey halfway through the Ram[3] has run;
When little birds are busy with their song
Who sleep with open eyes the whole night long   10
Life stirs their hearts and tingles in them so,
Then off as pilgrims people long to go,
And palmers[4] to set out for distant strands
And foreign shrines renowned in many lands.
And specially in England people ride   15
To Canterbury from every countryside
To visit there the blessed martyred saint[5]
Who gave them strength when they were sick and faint.
    In Southwark at the Tabard[6] one spring day
It happened, as I stopped there on my way,   20
Myself a pilgrim with a heart devout
Ready for Canterbury to set out,
At night came all of twenty-nine assorted
Travelers, and to that same inn resorted,
Who by a turn of fortune chanced to fall   25
In fellowship together, and they were all
Pilgrims who had it in their minds to ride
Toward Canterbury. The stable doors were wide,
The rooms were large, and we enjoyed the best,
And shortly, when the sun had gone to rest,   30
I had so talked with each that presently

1. Translated by Theodore Morrison.   2. The west wind.   3. A sign of the zodiac (Aries); the sun is in the Ram from March 12 to April 11.   4. Pilgrims, who, originally, brought back palm leaves from the Holy Land.   5. St. Thomas à Becket, slain in Canterbury cathedral in 1170.   6. An inn at Southwark, across the river Thames from London.

I was a member of their company
And promised to rise early the next day
To start, as I shall show, upon our way.
    But none the less, while I have time and space,   35
Before this tale has gone a further pace,
I should in reason tell you the condition
Of each of them, his rank and his position,
And also what array they all were in;
And so then, with a knight I will begin.   40
    A Knight was with us, and an excellent man,
Who from the earliest moment he began
To follow his career loved chivalry,
Truth, openhandedness, and courtesy.
He was a stout man in his lord's campaigns   45
And in that cause had gripped his horse's reins
In Christian lands and pagan through the earth,
None farther, and always honored for his worth.
He was on hand at Alexandria's[7] fall.
He had often sat in precedence to all   50
The nations at the banquet board in Prussia.[8]
He had fought in Lithuania and in Russia,
No Christian knight more often; he had been
In Moorish Africa at Benmarin,
At the siege of Algeciras in Granada,   55
And sailed in many a glorious armada
In the Mediterranean, and fought as well
At Ayas and Attalia when they fell
In Armenia and on Asia Minor's coast.
Of fifteen deadly battles he could boast,   60
And in Algeria, at Tremessen,
Fought for the faith and killed three separate men
In single combat. He had done good work
Joining against another pagan Turk
With the king of Palathia.[9] And he was wise,   65
Despite his prowess, honored in men's eyes,
Meek as a girl and gentle in his ways.
He had never spoken ignobly all his days
To any man by even a rude inflection.
He was a knight in all things to perfection.   70
He rode a good horse, but his gear was plain,
For he had lately served on a campaign.
His tunic was still spattered by the rust
Left by his coat of mail, for he had just
Returned and set out on his pilgrimage.   75
    His son was with him, a young Squire, in age
Some twenty years as near as I could guess.
His hair curled as if taken from a press.
He was a lover and would become a knight.
In stature he was of a moderate height   80

7. In Egypt, captured in 1365 by King Peter of Cyprus.   8. A reference to crusades against the still-pagan Slavs.   9. An independent emirate on the southwest coast of Turkey.

But powerful and wonderfully quick.
He had been in Flanders, riding in the thick
Of forays in Artois and Picardy,[1]
And bore up well for one so young as he,
Still hoping by his exploits in such places   85
To stand the better in his lady's graces.
He wore embroidered flowers, red and white,
And blazed like a spring meadow to the sight.
He sang or played his flute the livelong day.
He was as lusty as the month of May.   90
His coat was short, its sleeves were long and wide.
He sat his horse well, and knew how to ride,
And how to make a song and use his lance,
And he could write and draw well, too, and dance.
So hot his love that when the moon rose pale   95
He got no more sleep than a nightingale.
He was modest, and helped whomever he was able,
And carved as his father's squire at the table.
   But one more servant had the Knight beside,
Choosing thus simply for the time to ride: 100
A Yeoman, in a coat and hood of green.
His peacock-feathered arrows, bright and keen,
He carried under his belt in tidy fashion.
For well-kept gear he had a yeoman's passion,
No draggled feather might his arrows show,   105
And in his hand he held a mighty bow.
He kept his hair close-cropped, his face was brown.
He knew the lore of woodcraft up and down.
His arm was guarded from the bowstring's whip
By a bracer, gaily trimmed. He had at hip   110
A sword and buckler, and at his other side
A dagger whose fine mounting was his pride,
Sharp-pointed as a spear. His horn he bore
In a sling of green, and on his chest he wore
A silver image of St. Christopher,   115
His patron, since he was a forester.
   There was also a Nun, a Prioress,
Whose smile was gentle and full of guilelessness.
"By St. Loy!"[2] was the worst oath she would say.
She sang mass well, in a becoming way,   120
Intoning through her nose the words divine,
And she was known as Madame Eglantine.
She spoke good French, as taught at Stratford-Bow[3]
For the Parisian French she did not know.
She was schooled to eat so primly and so well   125
That from her lips no morsel ever fell.
She wet her fingers lightly in the dish
Of sauce, for courtesy was her first wish.
With every bite she did her skillful best

1. Provinces in the north of France and in Flanders.   2. Perhaps St. Eligius, apparently a popular saint
at this time.   3. In Middlesex, near London, where there was a nunnery.

To see that no drop fell upon her breast.   130
She always wiped her upper lip so clean
That in her cup was never to be seen
A hint of grease when she had drunk her share.
She reached out for her meat with comely air.
She was a great delight, and always tried   135
To imitate court ways, and had her pride,
Both amiable and gracious in her dealings.
As for her charity and tender feelings,
She melted at whatever was piteous.
She would weep if she but came upon a mouse   140
Caught in a trap, if it were dead or bleeding.
Some little dogs that she took pleasure feeding
On roasted meat or milk or good wheat bread
She had, but how she wept to find one dead
Or yelping from a blow that made it smart,   145
And all was sympathy and loving heart.
Neat was her wimple in its every plait,
Her nose well formed, her eyes as gray as slate.
Her mouth was very small and soft and red.
She had so wide a brow I think her head   150
Was nearly a span broad, for certainly
She was not undergrown, as all could see.
She wore her cloak with dignity and charm,
And had her rosary about her arm,
The small beads coral and the larger green,   155
And from them hung a brooch of golden sheen,
On it a large A and a crown above;[4]
Beneath, "All things are subject unto love."
      A Priest accompanied her toward Canterbury,
And an attendant Nun, her secretary.   160
      There was a Monk, and nowhere was his peer,
A hunter, and a roving overseer.[5]
He was a manly man, and fully able
To be an abbot. He kept a hunting stable,
And when he rode the neighborhood could hear   165
His bridle jingling in the wind as clear
And loud as if it were a chapel bell.
Wherever he was master of a cell
The principles of good St. Benedict,[6]
For being a little old and somewhat strict,   170
Were honored in the breach, as past their prime.
He lived by the fashion of a newer time.
He would have swapped that text for a plucked hen
Which says that hunters are not holy men,
Or a monk outside his discipline and rule   175
Is too much like a fish outside his pool;
That is to say, a monk outside his cloister.
But such a text he deemed not worth an oyster.

---

4. The A stands for Amor, Latin for "love"; in the original the motto is Amor vincit omnia, "Love conquers all."   5. He is responsible for the monastery's outlying properties.   6. Monastic rules authored by St. Benedict in the 6th century.

I told him his opinion made me glad.
Why should he study always and go mad, 180
Mewed in his cell with only a book for neighbor?
Or why, as Augustine[7] commanded, labor
And sweat his hands? How shall the world be served?
To Augustine be all such toil reserved!
And so he hunted, as was only right. 185
He had greyhounds as swift as birds in flight.
His taste was all for tracking down the hare,
And what his sport might cost he did not care.
His sleeves I noticed, where they met his hand,
Trimmed with gray fur, the finest in the land. 190
His hood was fastened with a curious pin
Made of wrought gold and clasped beneath his chin,
A love knot at the tip. His head might pass,
Bald as it was, for a lump of shining glass,
And his face was glistening as if anointed. 195
Fat as a lord he was, and well appointed.
His eyes were large, and rolled inside his head
As if they gleamed from a furnace of hot lead.
His boots were supple, his horse superbly kept.
He was a prelate to dream of while you slept. 200
He was not pale nor peaked like a ghost.
He relished a plump swan as his favorite roast.
He rode a palfrey brown as a ripe berry.
    A Friar was with us, a gay dog and a merry,
Who begged his district with a jolly air. 205
No friar in all four orders[8] could compare
With him for gallantry; his tongue was wooing.
Many a girl was married by his doing,
And at his own cost it was often done.
He was a pillar, and a noble one, 210
To his whole order. In his neighborhood
Rich franklins[9] knew him well, who served good food,
And worthy women welcomed him to town;
For the license that his order handed down,
He said himself, conferred on him possession 215
Of more than a curate's[1] power of confession.
Sweetly the list of frailties he heard,
Assigning penance with a pleasant word.
He was an easy man for absolution
Where he looked forward to a contribution, 220
For if to a poor order a man has given
It signifies that he has been well shriven,[2]
And if a sinner let his purse be dented
The Friar would stake his oath he had repented.
For many men become so hard of heart 225
They cannot weep, though conscience makes them smart.
Instead of tears and prayers, then, let the sinner

7. St. Augustine (354–430 c.e.) argued that monks should perform manual labor. 8. Most friars belonged to one of four groups, or orders. 9. Landowners or country squires, not belonging to the nobility. 1. A parish priest. 2. Confessed.

Supply the poor friars with the price of dinner.
For pretty women he had more than shrift.[3]
His cape was stuffed with many a little gift,   230
As knives and pins and suchlike. He could sing
A merry note, and pluck a tender string,
And had no rival at all in balladry.
His neck was whiter than a fleur-de-lis,[4]
And yet he could have knocked a strong man down.   235
He knew the taverns well in every town.
The barmaids and innkeepers pleased his mind
Better than beggars and lepers and their kind.
In his position it was unbecoming
Among the wretched lepers to go slumming.   240
It mocks all decency, it sews no stitch
To deal with such riffraff, but with the rich,
With sellers of victuals, that's another thing.
Wherever he saw some hope of profiting,
None so polite, so humble. He was good,   245
The champion beggar of his brotherhood.
Should a woman have no shoes against the snow,
So pleasant was his *"In principio"*[5]
He would have her widow's mite before he went.
He took in far more than he paid in rent   250
For his right of begging within certain bounds.[6]
None of his brethren trespassed on his grounds!
He loved as freely as a half-grown whelp.
On arbitration-days[7] he gave great help,
For his cloak was never shiny nor threadbare   255
Like a poor cloistered scholar's. He had an air
As if he were a doctor or a pope.
It took stout wool to make his semicope[8]
That plumped out like a bell for portliness.
He lisped a little in his rakishness   260
To make his English sweeter on his tongue,
And twanging his harp to end some song he'd sung
His eyes would twinkle in his head as bright
As the stars twinkle on a frosty night.
Hubert this gallant Friar was by name.   265
    Among the rest a Merchant also came.
He wore a forked beard and a beaver hat
From Flanders. High up in the saddle he sat,
In figured cloth,[9] his boots clasped handsomely,
Delivering his opinions pompously,   270
Always on how his gains might be increased.
At all costs he desired the sea policed[1]
From Middleburg in Holland to Orwell.[2]
He knew the exchange rates, and the time to sell
French currency, and there was never yet   275

---

3. Confession.   4. Lily.   5. In the beginning (Latin); the opening phrase of a famous passage in the New Testament of the Bible (John 1.1–16).   6. The territory in which he could beg, for which he paid a fee.   7. Days appointed for settling disputes.   8. A short cape.   9. Cloth of mixed color.   1. For protection from piracy.   2. An English port near Harwich.

A man who could have told he was in debt
So grave he seemed and hid so well his feelings
With all his shrewd engagements and close dealings.
You'd find no better man at any turn;
But what his name was I could never learn.   280
   There was an Oxford Student too, it chanced,
Already in his logic well advanced.
He rode a mount as skinny as a rake,
And he was hardly fat. For learning's sake
He let himself look hollow and sober enough.   285
He wore an outer coat of threadbare stuff,
For he had no benefice[3] for his enjoyment
And was too unworldly for some lay employment.
He much preferred to have beside his bed
His twenty volumes bound in black or red   290
All packed with Aristotle from end to middle
Than a sumptuous wardrobe or a merry fiddle.
For though he knew what learning had to offer
There was little coin to jingle in his coffer.
Whatever he got by touching up a friend   295
On books and learning he would promptly spend
And busily pray for the soul of anybody
Who furnished him the wherewithal for study.
His scholarship was what he truly heeded.
He never spoke a word more than was needed,   300
And that was said with dignity and force,
And quick and brief. He was of grave discourse
Giving new weight to virtue by his speech,
And gladly would he learn and gladly teach.
   There was a Lawyer, cunning and discreet,   305
Who had often been to St. Paul's porch[4] to meet
His clients. He was a Sergeant of the Law,[5]
A man deserving to be held in awe,
Or so he seemed, his manner was so wise.
He had often served as Justice of Assize[6]   310
By the king's appointment, with a broad commission,
For his knowledge and his eminent position.
He had many a handsome gift by way of fee.
There was no buyer of land as shrewd as he.
All ownership to him became fee simple.[7]   315
His titles were never faulty by a pimple.
None was so busy as he with case and cause,
And yet he seemed much busier than he was.
In all cases and decisions he was schooled
That were of record since King William[8] ruled.   320
No one could pick a loophole or a flaw
In any lease or contract he might draw.
Each statute on the books he knew by rote.

---

3. A paid position in the Church.   4. A meeting place for lawyers and their clients in the porch of St. Paul's Cathedral, London.   5. Sergeants of the Law were the most prestigious and powerful lawyers of the time.   6. A judge in the circuit court.   7. Owned outright without legal impediments.   8. The Conqueror (ruled 1066–1087).

He traveled in a plain, silk-belted coat.
   A Franklin traveled in his company. 325
Whiter could never daisy petal be
Than was his beard. His ruddy face gave sign
He liked his morning sop of toast in wine.
He lived in comfort, as he would assure us,
For he was a true son of Epicurus[9] 330
Who held the opinion that the only measure
Of perfect happiness was simply pleasure.
Such hospitality did he provide,
He was St. Julian[1] to his countryside.
His bread and ale were always up to scratch. 335
He had a cellar none on earth could match.
There was no lack of pasties in his house,
Both fish and flesh, and that so plenteous
That where he lived it snowed of meat and drink.
With every dish of which a man can think, 340
After the various seasons of the year,
He changed his diet for his better cheer.
He had coops of partridges as fat as cream,
He had a fishpond stocked with pike and bream.
Woe to his cook for an unready pot 345
Or a sauce that wasn't seasoned and spiced hot!
A table in his hall stood on display
Prepared and covered through the livelong day.
He presided at court sessions for his bounty
And sat in Parliament often for his county. 350
A well-wrought dagger and a purse of silk
Hung at his belt, as white as morning milk.
He had been a sheriff and county auditor.
On earth was no such rich proprietor!
   There were five Guildsmen, in the livery 355
Of one august and great fraternity,[2]
A Weaver, a Dyer, and a Carpenter,
A Tapestry-maker and a Haberdasher.
Their gear was furbished new and clean as glass.
The mountings of their knives were not of brass 360
But silver. Their pouches were well made and neat,
And each of them, it seemed, deserved a seat
On the platform at the Guildhall,[3] for each one
Was likely timber to make an alderman.
They had goods enough, and money to be spent, 365
Also their wives would willingly consent
And would have been at fault if they had not.
For to be "Madamed" is a pleasant lot,
And to march in first at feasts for being well married,
And royally to have their mantles carried. 370
   For the pilgrimage these Guildsmen brought their own

---

9. Greek philosopher whose teaching (presented here in a somewhat debased form) is believed to make pleasure the goal of life.   1. Patron saint of hospitality.   2. Members of a parish fraternity, an organization centered on the parish church that served both religious and social purposes.   3. London's city hall.

Cook to boil their chicken and marrow bone
With seasoning powder and capers and sharp spice.
In judging London ale his taste was nice.
He well knew how to roast and broil and fry, 375
To mix a stew, and bake a good meat pie,
Or capon creamed with almond, rice, and egg.
Pity he had an ulcer on his leg!
    A Skipper was with us, his home far in the west.
He came from the port of Dartmouth,[4] as I guessed. 380
He sat his carthorse pretty much at sea
In a coarse smock that joggled on his knee.
From his neck a dagger on a string hung down
Under his arm. His face was burnished brown
By the summer sun. He was a true good fellow. 385
Many a time he had tapped a wine cask mellow
Sailing from Bordeaux[5] while the owner slept.
Too nice a point of honor he never kept.
In a sea fight, if he got the upper hand,
Drowned prisoners floated home to every land. 390
But in navigation, whether reckoning tides,
Currents, or what might threaten him besides,
Harborage, pilotage, or the moon's demeanor,
None was his like from Hull to Cartagena.[6]
He knew each harbor and the anchorage there 395
From Gotland to the Cape of Finisterre[7]
And every creek in Brittany and Spain,
And he had called his ship the *Madeleine*.
    With us came also an astute Physician.
There was none like him for a disquisition 400
On the art of medicine or surgery,
For he was grounded in astrology.
He kept his patient long in observation,
Choosing the proper hour for application
Of charms and images by intuition 405
Of magic, and the planets' best position.
For he was one who understood the laws
That rule the humors, and could tell the cause
That brought on every human malady,
Whether of hot or cold, or moist or dry. 410
He was a perfect medico, for sure.
The cause once known, he would prescribe the cure
For he had his druggists ready at a motion
To provide the sick man with some pill or potion—
A game of mutual aid, with each one winning. 415
Their partnership was hardly just beginning!
He was well versed in his authorities,
Old Aesculapius, Dioscorides,
Rufus, and old Hippocrates, and Galen,
Haly, and Rhazes, and Serapion, 420

---

4. On the southwest coast.   5. On the southwest coast of France.   6. A Spanish port. *Hull:* an English port.   7. On the Spanish coast. *Gotland:* a Swedish island.

Averroës, Bernard, Johannes Damascenus,
Avicenna, Gilbert, Gaddesden, Constantinus.[8]
He urged a moderate fare on principle,
But rich in nourishment, digestible;
Of nothing in excess would he admit.   425
He gave but little heed to Holy Writ.
His clothes were lined with taffeta; their hue
Was all of blood red and of Persian blue,
Yet he was far from careless of expense.
He saved his fees from times of pestilence,   430
For gold is a cordial,[9] as physicians hold,
And so he had a special love for gold.

   A worthy woman there was from near the city
Of Bath,[1] but somewhat deaf, and more's the pity.
For weaving she possessed so great a bent   435
She outdid the people of Ypres and of Ghent.[2]
No other woman dreamed of such a thing
As to precede her at the offering,
Or if any did, she fell in such a wrath
She dried up all the charity in Bath.   440
She wore fine kerchiefs of old-fashioned air,
And on a Sunday morning, I could swear,
She had ten pounds of linen on her head.
Her stockings were of finest scarlet-red,
Laced tightly, and her shoes were soft and new.   445
Bold was her face, and fair, and red in hue.
She had been an excellent woman all her life
Five men in turn had taken her to wife,
Omitting other youthful company—
But let that pass for now! Over the sea   450
She had traveled freely; many a distant stream
She crossed, and visited Jerusalem
Three times. She had been at Rome and at Boulogne,
At the shrine of Compostella, and at Cologne.[3]
She had wandered by the way through many a scene.   455
Her teeth were set with little gaps between.[4]
Easily on her ambling horse she sat.
She was well wimpled, and she wore a hat
As wide in circuit as a shield or targe.[5]
A skirt swathed up her hips, and they were large.   460
Upon her feet she wore sharp-roweled spurs.
She was a good fellow; a ready tongue was hers.
All remedies of love she knew by name,[6]
For she had all the tricks of that old game.

   There was a good man of the priests' vocation,   465
A poor town Parson of true consecration,
But he was rich in holy thought and work.

---

8. Eminent medical authorities from ancient Greece, ancient and medieval Arabic civilization, and England in the 13th and 14th centuries. 9. *Gold* was thought to be a stimulant. 1. A town in southwest England. 2. Towns in Flanders famous for their cloth. 3. Sites of shrines much visited by pilgrims. 4. I.e., gap-toothed; in a woman considered a sign of sexual prowess. 5. A small shield. 6. Chaucer has Ovid's *Love Cures* (*Remedia Amoris*) in mind.

Learned he was, in the truest sense a clerk
Who meant Christ's gospel faithfully to preach
And truly his parishioners to teach.
He was a kind man, full of industry,   470
Many times tested by adversity
And always patient. If tithes[7] were in arrears,
He was loth to threaten any man with fears
Of excommunication; past a doubt   475
He would rather spread his offering about
To his poor flock, or spend his property.
To him a little meant sufficiency.
Wide was his parish, with houses far asunder,
But he would not be kept by rain or thunder,   480
If any had suffered a sickness or a blow,
From visiting the farthest, high or low
Plodding his way on foot, his staff in hand.
He was a model his flock could understand,
For first he did and afterward he taught.   485
That precept from the Gospel he had caught,
And he added as a metaphor thereto,
"If the gold rusts, what will the iron do?"
For if a priest is foul, in whom we trust,
No wonder a layman shows a little rust.   490
A priest should take to heart the shameful scene
Of shepherds filthy while the sheep are clean.
By his own purity a priest should give
The example to his sheep, how they should live.
He did not rent his benefice for hire,[8]   495
Leaving his flock to flounder in the mire,
And run to London, happiest of goals,
To sing paid masses in St. Paul's for souls,[9]
Or as chaplain from some rich guild take his keep,
But dwelt at home and guarded well his sheep   500
So that no wolf should make his flock miscarry.
He was a shepherd, and not a mercenary.
And though himself a man of strict vocation
He was not harsh to weak souls in temptation,
Not overbearing nor haughty in his speech,   505
But wise and kind in all he tried to teach.
By good example and just words to turn
Sinners to heaven was his whole concern.
But should a man in truth prove obstinate,
Whoever he was, of rich or mean estate,   510
The Parson would give him a snub to meet the case.
I doubt there was a priest in any place
His better. He did not stand on dignity
Nor affect in conscience too much nicety,
But Christ's and his disciples' words he sought   515
To teach, and first he followed what he taught.

---

7. Payments due to the priest, usually a tenth of annual income.   8. Rent out his appointment to a substitute.   9. Many wealthy people endowed positions for priests, who would sing Masses for the souls of their patrons after their deaths.

There was a Plowman with him on the road,
His brother, who had forked up many a load
Of good manure. A hearty worker he,
Living in peace and perfect charity.[1]   520
Whether his fortune made him smart or smile,
He loved God with his whole heart all the while
And his neighbor as himself. He would undertake,
For every luckless poor man, for the sake
Of Christ to thresh and ditch and dig by the hour   525
And with no wage, if it was in his power.
His tithes on goods and earnings he paid fair.
He wore a coarse, rough coat and rode a mare.
      There also were a Manciple, a Miller,
A Reeve, a Summoner, and a Pardoner,[2]   530
And I—this makes our company complete.
      As tough a yokel as you care to meet
The Miller was. His big-beefed arms and thighs
Took many a ram put up as wrestling prize.
He was a thick, squat-shouldered lump of sins.   535
No door but he could heave it off its pins
Or break it running at it with his head.
His beard was broader than a shovel, and red
As a fat sow or fox. A wart stood clear
Atop his nose, and red as a pig's ear   540
A tuft of bristles on it. Black and wide
His nostrils were. He carried at his side
A sword and buckler.[3] His mouth would open out
Like a great furnace, and he would sing and shout
His ballads and jokes of harlotries and crimes.   545
He could steal corn and charge for it three times,
And yet was honest enough, as millers come,
For a miller, as they say, has a golden thumb.[4]
In white coat and blue hood this lusty clown,
Blowing his bagpipes, brought us out of town.   550
      The Manciple was of a lawyers' college,[5]
And other buyers might have used his knowledge
How to be shrewd provisioners, for whether
He bought on cash or credit, altogether
He managed that the end should be the same: 555
He came out more than even with the game.
Now isn't it an instance of God's grace
How a man of little knowledge can keep pace
In wit with a whole school of learned men?
He had masters to the number of three times ten   560
Who knew each twist of equity and tort;[6]
A dozen in that very Inn of Court
Were worthy to be steward of the estate

---

1. Ache.   2. A seller of indulgences that purported to release sinful souls from purgatory early. *Manciple:* an officer in charge of supplies. *Reeve:* farm overseer. *Summoner:* he summoned people to appear before the church court (presided over by the archdeacon) and in general acted as a kind of bailiff.   3. Shield.
4. A reference to the proverb "an honest miller has a golden thumb," i.e., there are no honest millers.
5. The Manciple manages the affairs of an Inn of Court (see line 562), an institution where young men training to be lawyers lived and worked.   6. Different kinds of legal cases.

To any of England's lords, however great,
And keep him to his income well confined 565
And free from debt, unless he lost his mind,
Or let him scrimp, if he were mean in bounty;
They could have given help to a whole county
In any sort of case that might befall;
And yet this Manciple could cheat them all! 570
    The Reeve was a slender, fiery-tempered man.
He shaved as closely as a razor can.
His hair was cropped about his ears, and shorn
Above his forehead as a priest's is worn.[7]
His legs were very long and very lean. 575
No calf on his lank spindles could be seen.
But he knew how to keep a barn or bin,
He could play the game with auditors and win.
He knew well how to judge by drought and rain
The harvest of his seed and of his grain. 580
His master's cattle, swine, and poultry flock,
Horses and sheep and dairy, all his stock,
Were altogether in this Reeve's control.
And by agreement, he had given the sole
Accounting since his lord reached twenty years. 585
No man could ever catch him in arrears.
There wasn't a bailiff, shepherd, or farmer working
But the Reeve knew all his tricks of cheating and shirking.
He would not let him draw an easy breath.
They feared him as they feared the very death. 590
He lived in a good house on an open space,
Well shaded by green trees, a pleasant place.
He was shrewder in acquisition than his lord.
With private riches he was amply stored.
He had learned a good trade young by work and will. 595
He was a carpenter of first-rate skill.
On a fine mount, a stallion, dappled gray.
Whose name was Scot, he rode along the way.
He wore a long blue coat hitched up and tied
As if it were a friar's, and at his side 600
A sword with rusty blade was hanging down.
He came from Norfolk, from nearby the town
That men call Bawdswell.[8] As we rode the while,
The Reeve kept always hindmost in our file.
    A Summoner in our company had his place. 605
Red as the fiery cherubim[9] his face.
He was pocked and pimpled, and his eyes were narrow.
He was lecherous and hot as a cock sparrow.
His brows were scabby and black, and thin his beard.
His was a face that little children feared. 610
Brimstone or litharge bought in any quarter,
Quicksilver, ceruse, borax, oil of tartar,

---

7. His head was shaved in the form of the tonsure that indicated clerical status.   8. A town in northern Norfolk, a county northwest of London.   9. An order of angels that Chaucer seems to have thought (wrongly) were represented with red faces.

No salve nor ointment that will cleanse or bite
Could cure him of his blotches, livid white,
Or the nobs and nubbins sitting on his cheeks.[1]   615
He loved his garlic, his onions, and his leeks.
He loved to drink the strong wine down blood-red.
Then would he bellow as if he had lost his head.
And when he had drunk enough to parch his drouth,
Nothing but Latin issued from his mouth.   620
He had smattered up a few terms, two or three,
That he had gathered out of some decree—
No wonder; he heard law Latin all the day,
And everyone knows a parrot or a jay
Can cry out "Wat" or "Poll" as well as the pope;   625
But give him a strange term, he began to grope.
His little store of learning was paid out,
So "Questio quod juris"[2] he would shout.
He was a goodhearted bastard and a kind one.
If there were better, it was hard to find one.   630
He would let a good fellow, for a quart of wine,
The whole year round enjoy his concubine
Scot-free from summons, hearing, fine, or bail,
And on the sly he too could flush a quail.
If he liked a scoundrel, no matter for church law.   635
He would teach him that he need not stand in awe
If the archdeacon threatened with his curse—
That is, unless his soul was in his purse,
For in his purse he would be punished well.
"The purse," he said, "is the archdeacon's hell."[3]   640
Of course I know he lied in what he said.
There is nothing a guilty man should so much dread
As the curse that damns his soul, when, without fail,
The church can save him, or send him off to jail.
He had the young men and girls in his control   645
Throughout the diocese; he knew the soul
Of youth, and heard their every last design.
A garland big enough to be the sign
Above an alehouse balanced on his head,
And he made a shield of a great round loaf of bread.   650
     There was a Pardoner of Rouncivalle
With him, of the blessed Mary's hospital,[4]
But now come straight from Rome (or so said he).
Loudly he sang, "Come hither, love, to me,"
While the Summoner's counterbass trolled out profound—   655
No trumpet blew with half so vast a sound.
This Pardoner had hair as yellow as wax,
But it hung as smoothly as a hank of flax.
His locks trailed down in bunches from his head,

---

1. The Summoner seems to suffer from a form of leprosy; these remedies were recommended by medieval physicians for his condition.   2. The question is, what (part) of the law [applies] (Latin).   3. I.e., the archdeacon would punish sinners with a fine rather than send them to hell by excommunicating them, a view with which the narrator disagrees in the following lines.   4. The hospital of St. Mary of Rouncivalle was located at Charing Cross, now part of London. The money the Pardoner collects is supposed to go to the hospital.

And he let the ends about his shoulders spread, 660
But in thin clusters, lying one by one.
Of hood, for rakishness, he would have none,
For in his wallet he kept it safely stowed.
He traveled, as he thought, in the latest mode,
Disheveled. Save for his cap, his head was bare, 665
And in his eyes he glittered like a hare.
A Veronica⁵ was stitched upon his cap
His wallet lay before him in his lap
Brimful of pardons from the very seat
In Rome. He had a voice like a goat's bleat. 670
He was beardless and would never have a beard.
His cheek was always smooth as if just sheared.
I think he was a gelding or a mare;
But in this trade, from Berwick down to Ware,⁶
No pardoner could beat him in the race, 675
For in his wallet he had a pillow case
Which he represented as Our Lady's veil;
He said he had a piece of the very sail
St. Peter, when he fished in Galilee
Before Christ caught him, used upon the sea. 680
He had a latten⁷ cross embossed with stones
And in a glass he carried some pig's bones,
And with these holy relics, when he found
Some village parson grubbing his poor ground,
He would get more money in a single day 685
Than in two months would come the parson's way.
Thus with his flattery and his trumped-up stock
He made dupes of the parson and his flock.
But though his conscience was a little plastic
He was in church a noble ecclesiastic. 690
Well could he read the Scripture or saint's story,
But best of all he sang the offertory,
For he understood that when this song was sung,
Then he must preach, and sharpen up his tongue
To rake in cash, as well he knew the art, 695
  And so he sang out gaily, with full heart.
  Now I have set down briefly, as it was,
Our rank, our dress, our number, and the cause
That made our sundry fellowship begin
In Southwark, at this hospitable inn 700
Known as the Tabard, not far from the Bell.
But what we did that night I ought to tell,
And after that our journey, stage by stage,
And the whole story of our pilgrimage.
But first, in justice, do not look askance 705
I plead, nor lay it to my ignorance
If in this matter I should use plain speech

5. A reproduction of the handkerchief bearing the miraculous impression of Christ's face, said to have been impressed on the handkerchief that St. Veronica gave Him to wipe His face with on the way to His Crucifixion. 6. Berwick was at the northern end of the Great North Road that traversed England; Ware, at the southern. 7. An alloy of copper and tin made to resemble brass.

And tell you just the words and style of each,
Reporting all their language faithfully.
For it must be known to you as well as me   710
That whoever tells a story after a man
Must follow him as closely as he can.
If he takes the tale in charge, he must be true
To every word, unless he would find new
Or else invent a thing or falsify.   715
Better some breadth of language than a lie!
He may not spare the truth to save his brother.
He might as well use one word as another.
In Holy Writ Christ spoke in a broad sense
And surely his word is without offense.   720
Plato, if his pages you can read,
Says let the word be cousin to the deed.[8]
So I petition your indulgence for it
If I have cut the cloth just as men wore it,
Here in this tale, and shown its very weave.   725
My wits are none too sharp, you must believe.
  Our Host gave each of us a cheerful greeting
And promptly of our supper had us eating.
The victuals that he served us were his best.
The wine was potent, and we drank with zest.   730
Our Host cut such a figure, all in all,
He might have been a marshal in a hall.
He was a big man, and his eyes bulged wide.
No sturdier citizen lived in all Cheapside,[9]
Lacking no trace of manhood, bold in speech,   735
Prudent, and well versed in what life can teach,
And with all this he was a jovial man.
And so when supper ended he began
To jolly us, when all our debts were clear.
"Welcome," he said. "I have not seen this year   740
So merry a company in this tavern as now,
And I would give you pleasure if I knew how.
And just this very minute a plan has crossed
My mind that might amuse you at no cost.
  "You go to Canterbury—may the Lord   745
Speed you, and may the martyred saint reward
Your journey! And to while the time away
You mean to talk and pass the time of day,
For you would be as cheerful all alone
As riding on your journey dumb as stone.   750
Therefore, if you'll abide by what I say,
Tomorrow, when you ride off on your way,
Now, by my father's soul, and he is dead,
If you don't enjoy yourselves, cut off my head!
Hold up your hands, if you accept my speech."   755
  Our counsel did not take us long to reach.

---

8. The Platonic text to which Chaucer refers is the *Timaeus*, but he knew it indirectly through references
in Latin works.   9. A London district.

We bade him give his orders at his will.
"Well, sirs," he said, "then do not take it ill,
But hear me in good part, and for your sport.
Each one of you, to make our journey short,   760
Shall tell two stories, as we ride, I mean,
Toward Canterbury; and coming home again
Shall tell two other tales he may have heard
Of happenings that some time have occurred.
And the one of you whose stories please us most,   765
Here in this tavern, sitting by this post
Shall sup at our expense while we make merry
When we come riding home from Canterbury.
And to cheer you still the more, I too will ride
With you at my own cost, and be your guide.   770
And if anyone my judgment shall gainsay
He must pay for all we spend along the way.
If you agree, no need to stand and reason.
Tell me, and I'll be stirring in good season."
    This thing was granted, and we swore our pledge   775
To take his judgment on our pilgrimage,
His verdict on our tales, and his advice.
He was to plan a supper at a price
Agreed upon; and so we all assented
To his command, and we were well contented.   780
The wine was fetched; we drank, and went to rest.
    Next morning, when the dawn was in the east,
Up spring our Host, who acted as our cock,
And gathered us together in a flock,
And off we rode, till presently our pace   785
Had brought us to St. Thomas' watering place.[1]
And there our Host began to check his horse.
"Good sirs," he said, "you know your promise, of course.
Shall I remind you what it was about?
If evensong and matins don't fall out,[2]   790
We'll soon find who shall tell us the first tale.
But as I hope to drink my wine and ale,
Whoever won't accept what I decide
Pays everything we spend along the ride.
Draw lots, before we're farther from the Inn.   795
Whoever draws the shortest shall begin.
Sir Knight," said he, "my master, choose your straw.
Come here, my lady Prioress, and draw,
And you, Sir Scholar, don't look thoughtful, man!
Pitch in now, everyone!" So all began   800
To draw the lots, and as the luck would fall
The draw went to the Knight, which pleased us all.
And when this excellent man saw how it stood,
Ready to keep his promise, he said, "Good!
Since it appears that I must start the game,   805

1. A stream about a mile from London on the road to Canterbury.   2. Evening and morning church services; the Host is asking if what was said in the evening is still acceptable in the morning.

Why then, the draw is welcome, in God's name.
Now let's ride on, and listen, what I say."
And with that word we rode forth on our way,
And he, with his courteous manner and good cheer,
Began to tell his tale, as you shall hear.   810

The Miller's Prologue and Tale

THE PROLOGUE

When the Knight had finished,[3] no one, young or old,
In the whole company, but said he had told
A noble story, one that ought to be
Preserved and kept alive in memory,
Especially the gentlefolk, each one.   5
Our good Host laughed, and swore, "The game's begun,
The ball is rolling! This is going well.
Let's see who has another tale to tell.
Come, match the Knight's tale if you can, Sir Monk!"
    The Miller, who by this time was so drunk   10
He looked quite bloodless, and who hardly sat
His horse, he was never one to doff his hat
Or stand on courtesy for any man.
Like Pilate in the Church plays[4] he began
To bellow. "Arms and blood and bones," he swore,   15
"I know a yarn that will even up the score,
A noble one, I'll pay off the Knight's tale!"
    Our Host could see that he was drunk on ale.
"Robin," he said, "hold on a minute, brother.
Some better man shall come first with another.   20
Let's do this right. You tell yours by and by."
    "God's soul," the Miller told him, "that won't I!
Either I'll speak, or go on my own way."
    "The devil with you! Say what you have to say,"
Answered our Host. "You are a fool. Your head   25
Is overpowered."
                   "Now," the Miller said,
"Everyone listen! But first I will propound
That I am drunk, I know it by my sound.
If I can't get my words out, put the blame
On Southwark ale, I ask you, in God's name!   30
For I'll tell a golden legend and a life[5]
Both of a carpenter and of his wife,
How a student put horns on the fellow's head."
    "Shut up and stop your racket," the Reeve said.
"Forget your ignorant drunken bawdiness.   35
It is a sin and a great foolishness
To injure any man by defamation
And to give women such a reputation.
Tell us of other things; you'll find no lack."

---

3. *The Knight's Tale* is the first told, immediately following the *General Prologue.*   4. Mystery plays
represented Pilate as a braggart and loudmouth.   5. A saint's life.

Promptly this drunken Miller answered back:⁣ 40
"Oswald, my brother, true as babes are suckled,
The man who has no wife, he is no cuckold.
I don't say for this reason that you are.
There are plenty of faithful wives, both near and far,
Always a thousand good for every bad, 45
And you know this yourself, unless you're mad.
I see you are angry with my tale, but why?
You have a wife; no less, by God, do I.
But I wouldn't, for the oxen in my plow,
Shoulder more than I need by thinking how 50
I may myself, for aught I know, be one.
I'll certainly believe that I am none.
A husband mustn't be curious, for his life,
About God's secrets or about his wife.
If she gives him plenty and he's in the clover, 55
No need to worry about what's left over."
    The Miller, to make the best of it I can,
Refused to hold his tongue for any man,
But told his tale like any low-born clown.
I am sorry that I have to set it down, 60
And all you people, for God's love, I pray,
Whose taste is higher, do not think I say
A word with evil purpose; I must rehearse
Their stories one and all, both better and worse,
Or play false with my matter, that is clear. 65
Whoever, therefore, may not wish to hear,
Turn over the page and choose another tale;
For small and great, he'll find enough, no fail,
Of things from history, touching courtliness,
And virtue too, and also holiness. 70
If you choose wrong, don't lay it on my head.
You know the Miller couldn't be called well bred.
So with the Reeve, and many more as well,
And both of them had bawdy tales to tell.
Reflect a little, and don't hold me to blame. 75
There's no sense making earnest out of game.

THE TALE

There used to be a rich old oaf who made
His home at Oxford, a carpenter by trade,
And took in boarders. With him used to dwell
A student who had done his studies well,
But he was poor; for all that he had learned, 5
It was toward astrology his fancy turned.
He knew a number of figures and constructions
By which he could supply men with deductions
If they should ask him at a given hour
Whether to look for sunshine or for shower, 10
Or want to know whatever might befall,
Events of all sorts, I can't count them all.

He was known as handy Nicholas,[6] this student.
Well versed in love, he knew how to be prudent,
Going about unnoticed, sly, and sure.   15
In looks no girl was ever more demure.
Lodged at this carpenter's, he lived alone;
He had a room there that he made his own,
Festooned with herbs, and he was sweet himself
As licorice or ginger. On a shelf   20
Above his bed's head, neatly stowed apart,
He kept the trappings that went with his art,
His astrolabe,[7] his books—among the rest,
Thick ones and thin ones, lay his *Almagest*[8]—
And the counters for his abacus as well.   25
Over his cupboard a red curtain fell
And up above a pretty zither lay
On which at night so sweetly would he play
That with the music the whole room would ring.
"Angelus to the Virgin"[9] he would sing   30
And then the song that's known as "The King's Note."[1]
Blessings were called down on his merry throat!
So this sweet scholar passed his time, his end
Being to eat and live upon his friend.[2]
    This carpenter had newly wed a wife   35
And loved her better than he loved his life.
He was jealous, for she was eighteen in age;
He tried to keep her close as in a cage,
For she was wild and young, and old was he
And guessed that he might smack of cuckoldry.   40
His ignorant wits had never chanced to strike
On Cato's[3] word, that man should wed his like;
Men ought to wed where their conditions point,
For youth and age are often out of joint.
But now, since he had fallen in the snare,   45
He must, like other men, endure his care.
    Fair this young woman was, her body trim
As any mink, so graceful and so slim.
She wore a striped belt that was all of silk;
A piece-work apron, white as morning milk,   50
About her loins and down her lap she wore.
White was her smock, her collar both before
And on the back embroidered all about
In coal-black silk, inside as well as out.
And like her collar, her white-laundered bonnet   55
Had ribbons of the same embroidery on it.
Wide was her silken fillet, worn up high,
And for a fact she had a willing eye.
She plucked each brow into a little bow,

6. Chaucer's word is hendë, implying both *ready to hand* and *ingratiating* [Translator's note].   7. An astronomical instrument for telling time.   8. A 2nd-century treatise by Ptolemy, an astronomy textbook.   9. A song about the Annunciation, when the angel Gabriel tells Mary she is to bear Jesus.   1. Unidentified.   2. I.e., the friend who provided him with money for his education.   3. Dionysius Cato, the supposed author of a book of maxims employed in elementary education.

And each one was as black as any sloe.[4] 60
She was a prettier sight to see by far
Than the blossoms of the early pear tree are,
And softer than the wool of an old wether.
Down from her belt there hung a purse of leather
With silken tassels and with studs of brass. 65
No man so wise, wherever people pass,
Who could imagine in this world at all
A wench like her, the pretty little doll!
Far brighter was the dazzle of her hue
Than a coin struck in the Tower,[5] fresh and new. 70
As for her song, it twittered from her head
Sharp as a swallow perching on a shed.
And she could skip and sport as a young ram
Or calf will gambol, following his dam.
Her mouth was sweet as honey-ale or mead 75
Or apples in the hay, stored up for need.
She was as skittish as an untrained colt,
Slim as a mast and straighter than a bolt.
On her simple collar she wore a big brooch-pin
Wide as a shield's boss underneath her chin. 80
High up along her legs she laced her shoes.
She was a pigsney,[6] she was a primrose
For any lord to tumble in his bed
Or a good yeoman honestly to wed.
    Now sir, and again sir, this is how it was: 85
A day came round when handy Nicholas,
While her husband was at Oseney,[7] well away,
Began to fool with this young wife, and play.
These students always have a wily head.
He caught her in between the legs, and said, 90
"Sweetheart, unless I have my will with you
I'll die for stifled love, by all that's true,"
And held her by the haunches, hard. "I vow
I'll die unless you love me here and now,
Sure as my soul," he said, "is God's to save." 95
She shied just as a colt does in the trave,[8]
And turned her head hard from him, this young wife,
And said, "I will not kiss you, on my life.
Why, stop it now," she said, "stop, Nicholas,
Or I will cry out 'Help, help,' and 'Alas!' 100
Be good enough to take your hands away."
    "Mercy," this Nicholas began to pray,
And spoke so well and poured it on so fast
She promised she would be his love at last,
And swore by Thomas à Becket, saint of Kent, 105
That she would serve him when she could invent
Or spy out some good opportunity.
"My husband is so full of jealousy

4. The sloeberry. 5. Minted in the Tower of London. 6. *Pig's eye*, probably the name of a wild flower.
7. A town near Oxford. 8. A wooden frame confining a horse being shod.

You must be watchful and take care," she said,
"Or well I know I'll be as good as dead.   110
You must go secretly about this business."
      "Don't give a thought to that," said Nicholas.
"A student has been wasting time at school
If he can't make a carpenter a fool."
And so they were agreed, these two, and swore   115
To watch their chance, as I have said before.
When Nicholas had spanked her haunches neatly
And done all I have spoken of, he sweetly
Gave her a kiss, and then he took his zither
And loudly played, and sang his music with her.   120
      Now in her Christian duty, one saint's day,
To the parish church this good wife made her way,
And as she went her forehead cast a glow
As bright as noon, for she had washed it so
It glistened when she finished with her work.   125
      Serving this church there was a parish clerk
Whose name was Absolom, a ruddy man
With goose-gray eyes and curls like a great fan
That shone like gold on his neatly parted head.
His tunic was light blue and his nose red,   130
And he had patterns that had been cut through
Like the windows of St. Paul's in either shoe.[9]
He wore above his tunic, fresh and gay,
A surplice white as a blossom on a spray.
A merry devil, as true as God can save,   135
He knew how to let blood, trim hair, and shave,
Or write a deed of land in proper phrase,
And he could dance in twenty different ways
In the Oxford fashion, and sometimes he would sing
A loud falsetto to his fiddle string   140
Or his guitar. No tavern anywhere
But he had furnished entertainment there.
Yet his speech was delicate, and for his part
He was a little squeamish toward a fart.
      This Absolom, so jolly and so gay,   145
With a censer[1] went about on the saint's day
Censing the parish women one and all.
Many the doting look that he let fall,
And specially on this carpenter's young wife.
To look at her, he thought, was a good life,   150
She was so trim, so sweetly lecherous.
I dare say that if she had been a mouse
And he a cat, he would have made short work
Of catching her. This jolly parish clerk
Had such a heartful of love-hankerings   155
He would not take the women's offerings;
No, no, he said, it would not be polite.

---

9. The patterns cut in his shoes resembled the windows in St. Paul's Cathedral in London.   1. A receptacle for incense with which to bless (or "cense") the wives of the parish as they made their offerings in church.

The moon, when darkness fell, shone full and bright
And Absolom was ready for love's sake
With his guitar to be up and awake,   160
And toward the carpenter's, brisk and amorous,
He made his way until he reached the house
A little after the cocks began to crow.
Under a casement he sang sweet and low,
"Dear lady, by your will, be kind to me,"   165
And strummed on his guitar in harmony.
This lovelorn singing woke the carpenter
Who said to his wife, "What, Alison, don't you hear
Absolom singing under our bedroom wall?"
    "Yes, God knows, John," she answered, "I hear it all."   170
    What would you like? In this way things went on
Till jolly Absolom was woebegone
For wooing her, awake all night and day.
He combed his curls and made himself look gay.
He swore to be her slave and used all means   175
To court her with his gifts and go-betweens.
He sang and quavered like a nightingale.
He sent her sweet spiced wine and seasoned ale,
Cakes that were piping hot, mead sweet with honey,
And since she was town-bred, he proffered money.   180
For some are won by wealth, and some no less
By blows, and others yet by gentleness.
    Sometimes, to keep his talents in her gaze,
He acted Herod[2] in the mystery plays
High on the stage. But what can help his case?   185
For she so loves this handy Nicholas
That Absolom is living in a bubble.
He has nothing but a laugh for all his trouble.
She leaves his earnestness for scorn to cool
And makes this Absolom her proper fool.   190
For this is a true proverb, and no lie;
"It always happens that the nigh and sly
Will let the absent suffer." So 'tis said,
And Absolom may rage or lose his head
But just because he was farther from her sight   195
This nearby Nicholas got in his light.
    Now hold your chin up, handy Nicholas,
For Absolom may wail and sing "Alas!"
One Saturday when the carpenter had gone
To Oseney, Nicholas and Alison   200
Agreed that he should use his wit and guile
This simple jealous husband to beguile.
And if it happened that the game went right
She would sleep in his arms the livelong night,
For this was his desire and hers as well.   205
At once, with no more words, this Nicholas fell
To working out his plan. He would not tarry,

---

2. A role traditionally played as a bully in the mystery plays.

But quietly to his room began to carry
Both food and drink to last him out a day,
Or more than one, and told her what to say   210
If her husband asked her about Nicholas.
She must say she had no notion where he was;
She hadn't laid eyes on him all day long;
He must be sick, or something must be wrong;
No matter how her maid had called and cried   215
He wouldn't answer, whatever might betide.

   This was the plan, and Nicholas kept away,
Shut in his room, for that whole Saturday.
He ate and slept or did as he thought best
Till Sunday, when the sun was going to rest,   220
This carpenter began to wonder greatly
Where Nicholas was and what might ail him lately,
"Now, by St. Thomas, I begin to dread
All isn't right with Nicholas," he said.
"He hasn't, God forbid, died suddenly!   225
The world is ticklish these days, certainly.
Today I saw a corpse to church go past,
A man that I saw working Monday last!
Go up," he told his chore-boy, "call and shout,
Knock with a stone, find what it's all about   230
And let me know."
              The boy went up and pounded
And yelled as if his wits had been confounded.
"What, how, what's doing, Master Nicholas?
How can you sleep all day?" But all his fuss
Was wasted, for he could not hear a word.   235
He noticed at the bottom of a board
A hole the cat used when she wished to creep
Into the room, and through it looked in deep
And finally of Nicholas caught sight.
This Nicholas sat gaping there upright   240
As though his wits were addled by the moon
When it was new. The boy went down, and soon
Had told his master how he had seen the man.

   The carpenter, when he heard this news, began
To cross himself. "Help us, St. Frideswide![3]   245
Little can we foresee what may betide!
The man's astronomy has turned his wit,
Or else he's in some agonizing fit.
I always knew that it would turn out so.
What God has hidden is not for men to know.   250
Aye, blessed is the ignorant man indeed,
Blessed is he that only knows his creed!
So fared another scholar of the sky,
For walking in the meadows once to spy
Upon the stars and what they might foretell,   255

---

3. An 8th-century English saint noted for her ability to cast out devils. She was the patron saint of Oxford.

Down in a clay-pit suddenly he fell!
He overlooked that! By St. Thomas, though,
I'm sorry for handy Nicholas. I'll go
And scold him roundly for his studying
If so I may, by Jesus, heaven's king!   260
Give me a staff, I'll pry up from the floor
While you, Robin, are heaving at the door.
He'll quit his books, I think."
                                    He took his stand
Outside the room. The boy had a strong hand
And by the hasp he heaved it off at once.   265
The door fell flat. With gaping countenance
This Nicholas sat studying the air
As still as stone. He was in black despair,
The carpenter believed, and hard about
The shoulders caught and shook him, and cried out   270
Rudely, "What, how! What is it? Look down at us!
Wake up, think of Christ's passion, Nicholas!
I'll sign you with the cross to keep away
These elves and things!" And he began to say,
Facing the quarters of the house, each side,   275
And on the threshold of the door outside,
The night-spell:[4] "Jesu and St. Benedict
From every wicked thing this house protect . . ."
    Choosing his time, this handy Nicholas
Produced a dreadful sigh, and said, "Alas,   280
This world, must it be all destroyed straightway?"
    "What," asked the carpenter, "what's that you say?
Do as we do, we working men, and think
Of God."
              Nicholas answered, "Get me a drink,
And afterwards I'll tell you privately   285
Of something that concerns us, you and me.
I'll tell you only, you among all men."
    This carpenter went down and came again
With a draught of mighty ale, a generous quart.
As soon as each of them had drunk his part   290
Nicholas shut the door and made it fast
And sat down by the carpenter at last
And spoke to him. "My host," he said, "John dear,
You must swear by all that you hold sacred here
That not to any man will you betray   295
My confidence. What I'm about to say
Is Christ's own secret. If you tell a soul
You are undone, and this will be the toll:
If you betray me, you shall go stark mad."
    "Now Christ forbid it, by His holy blood,"   300
Answered this simple man. "I don't go blabbing.
If I say it myself, I have no taste for gabbing.
Speak up just as you like, I'll never tell,

---

4. A magic charm said at night to protect a house from evil spirits.

Not wife nor child, by Him that harrowed hell."[5]
"Now, John," said Nicholas, "this is no lie.   305
I have discovered through astrology,
And studying the moon that shines so bright
That Monday next, a quarter through the night,
A rain will fall, and such a mad, wild spate
That Noah's flood was never half so great.   310
This world," he said, "in less time than an hour
Shall drown entirely in that hideous shower.
Yes, every man shall drown and lose his life."
    "Alas," the carpenter answered, "for my wife!
Alas, my Alison! And shall she drown?"   315
For grief at this he nearly tumbled down,
And said, "But is there nothing to be done?"
    "Why, happily there is, for anyone
Who will take advice," this handy Nicholas said.
"You mustn't expect to follow your own head.   320
For what said Solomon, whose words were true?
'Proceed by counsel, and you'll never rue.'
If you will act on good advice, no fail,
I'll promise, and without a mast or sail,
To see that she's preserved, and you and I.   325
Haven't you heard how Noah was kept dry
When, warned by Christ beforehand, he discovered
That the whole earth with water should be covered?"
    "Yes," said the carpenter, "long, long ago."
    "And then again," said Nicholas, "don't you know   330
The grief they all had trying to embark
Till Noah could get his wife into the Ark?[6]
That was a time when Noah, I dare say,
Would gladly have given his best black wethers away
If she could have had a ship herself alone.   335
And therefore do you know what must be done?
This demands haste, and with a hasty thing
People can't stop for talk and tarrying.
    "Start out and get into the house right off
For each of us a tub or kneading-trough,   340
Above all making sure that they are large,
In which we'll float away as in a barge.
And put in food enough to last a day.
Beyond won't matter; the flood will fall away
Early next morning. Take care not to spill   345
A word to your boy Robin, nor to Jill
Your maid. I cannot save her, don't ask why.
I will not tell God's secrets, no, not I.
Let it be enough, unless your wits are mad,
To have as good a grace as Noah had.   350
I'll save your wife for certain, never doubt it.
Now go along, and make good time about it.

---

5. I.e., Christ, who descended into hell and led away Adam, Eve, the Patriarchs, John the Baptist, and others, redeeming and releasing them.   6. A stock comedy scene in the mystery plays.

"But when you have, for her and you and me,
Brought to the house these kneading-tubs, all three,
Then you must hang them under the roof, up high,   355
To keep our plans from any watchful eye.
When you have done exactly as I've said,
And put in snug our victuals and our bread,
Also an ax to cut the ropes apart
So when the rain comes we can make our start,   360
And when you've broken a hole high in the gable
Facing the garden plot, above the stable,
To give us a free passage out, each one,
Then, soon as the great fall of rain is done,
You'll swim as merrily, I undertake,   365
As the white duck paddles along behind her drake.
Then I shall call, 'How, Alison! How, John!
Be cheerful, for the flood will soon be gone.'
And 'Master Nicholas, what ho!' you'll say.
'Good morning, I see you clearly, for it's day.'   370
Then we shall lord it for the rest of life
Over the world, like Noah and his wife.
    "But one thing I must warn you of downright.
Use every care that on that selfsame night
When we have taken ship and climbed aboard,   375
No one of us must speak a single word,
Nor call, nor cry, but pray with all his heart.
It is God's will. You must hang far apart,
You and your wife, for there must be no sin
Between you, no more in a look than in   380
The very deed. Go now, the plans are drawn.
Go, set to work, and may God spur you on!
Tomorrow night when all men are asleep
Into our kneading-troughs we three shall creep
And sit there waiting, and abide God's grace.   385
Go along now, this isn't the time or place
For me to talk at length or sermonize.
The proverb says, 'Don't waste words on the wise.'
You are so wise there is no need to teach you.
Go, save our lives—that's all that I beseech you!"   390
    This simple carpenter went on his way.
Many a time he said, "Alack the day,"
And to his wife he laid the secret bare.
She knew it better than he; she was aware
What this quaint bargain was designed to buy.   395
She carried on as if about to die,
And said, "Alas, go get this business done.
Help us escape, or we are dead, each one.
I am your true, your faithful wedded wife.
Go, my dear husband, save us, limb and life!"   400
    Great things, in all truth, can the emotions be!
A man can perish through credulity
So deep the print imagination makes.
This simple carpenter, he quails and quakes.

He really sees, according to his notion,   405
Noah's flood come wallowing like an ocean
To drown his Alison, his pet, his dear.
He weeps and wails, and gone is his good cheer,
And wretchedly he sighs. But he goes off
And gets himself a tub, a kneading-trough,   410
Another tub, and has them on the sly
Sent home, and there in secret hangs them high
Beneath the roof. He made three ladders, these
With his own hands, and stowed in bread and cheese
And a jug of good ale, plenty for a day.   415
Before all this was done, he sent away
His chore-boy Robin and his wench likewise
To London on some trumped-up enterprise,
And so on Monday, when it drew toward night,
He shut the door without a candlelight   420
And saw that all was just as it should be,
And shortly they went clambering up, all three.
They sat there still, and let a moment pass.
    "Now then, 'Our Father,' mum!" said Nicholas,
And "Mum!" said John, and "Mum!" said Alison,   425
And piously this carpenter went on
Saying his prayers. He sat there still and straining,
Trying to make out whether he heard it raining.
    The dead of sleep, for very weariness,
Fell on this carpenter, as I should guess,   430
At about curfew time, or little more.
His head was twisted, and that made him snore.
His spirit groaned in its uneasiness.
Down from his ladder slipped this Nicholas,
And Alison too, downward she softly sped   435
And without further word they went to bed
Where the carpenter himself slept other nights.
There were the revels, there were the delights!
And so this Alison and Nicholas lay
Busy about their solace and their play   440
Until the bell for lauds[7] began to ring
And in the chancel friars began to sing.
    Now on this Monday, woebegone and glum
For love, this parish clerk, this Absolom
Was with some friends at Oseney, and while there   445
Inquired after John the carpenter.
A member of the cloister drew him away
Out of the church, and told him, "I can't say.
I haven't seen him working hereabout
Since Saturday. The abbot sent him out   450
For timber, I suppose. He'll often go
And stay at the granary a day or so.
Or else he's at his own house, possibly.
I can't for certain say where he may be."

---

7. The second of the seven church services celebrated each day; it took place before sunrise.

Absolom at once felt jolly and light,   455
And thought, "Time now to be awake all night,
For certainly I haven't seen him making
A stir about his door since day was breaking.
Don't call me a man if when I hear the cock
Begin to crow I don't slip up and knock   460
On the low window by his bedroom wall.
To Alison at last I'll pour out all
My love-pangs, for at this point I can't miss,
Whatever happens, at the least a kiss.
Some comfort, by my word, will come my way.   465
I've felt my mouth itch the whole livelong day,
And that's a sign of kissing at the least.
I dreamed all night that I was at a feast.
So now I'll go and sleep an hour or two,
And then I'll wake and play the whole night through."   470
    When the first cockcrow through the dark had come
Up rose this jolly lover Absolom
And dressed up smartly. He was not remiss
About the least point. He chewed licorice
And cardamom to smell sweet, even before   475
He combed his hair. Beneath his tongue he bore
A sprig of Paris[8] like a truelove knot.
He strolled off to the carpenter's house, and got
Beneath the window. It came so near the ground
It reached his chest. Softly, with half a sound,   480
He coughed, "My honeycomb, sweet Alison,
What are you doing, my sweet cinnamon?
Awake, my sweetheart and my pretty bird,
Awake, and give me from your lips a word!
Little enough you care for all my woe,   485
How for your love I sweat wherever I go!
No wonder I sweat and faint and cannot eat
More than a girl; as a lamb does for the teat
I pine. Yes, truly, I so long for love
I mourn as if I were a turtledove."   490
    Said she, "You jack-fool, get away from here!
So help me God, I won't sing 'Kiss me, dear!'
I love another more than you. Get on,
For Christ's sake, Absolom, or I'll throw a stone.
The devil with you! Go and let me sleep."   495
    "Ah, that true love should ever have to reap
So evil a fortune," Absolom said. "A kiss,
At least, if it can be no more than this,
Give me, for love of Jesus and of me."
    "And will you go away for that?" said she.   500
    "Yes, truly, sweetheart," answered Absolom.
    "Get ready then," she said, "for here I come,"
And softly said to Nicholas, "Keep still,
And in a minute you can laugh your fill."

---

8. A cloverlike plant.

This Absolom got down upon his knee   505
And said, "I am a lord of pure degree,
For after this, I hope, comes more to savor.
Sweetheart, your grace, and pretty bird, your favor!"
   She undid the window quickly. "That will do,"
She said. "Be quick about it, and get through,   510
For fear the neighbors will look out and spy."
   Absolom wiped his mouth to make it dry.
The night was pitch dark, coal-black all about.
Her rear end through the window she thrust out.
He got no better or worse, did Absolom,   515
Than to kiss her with his mouth on the bare bum
Before he had caught on, a smacking kiss.
   He jumped back, thinking something was amiss.
A woman had no beard, he was well aware,
But what he felt was rough and had long hair.   520
   "Alas," he cried, "what have you made me do?"
   "Te-hee!" she said, and banged the window to.
Absolom backed away a sorry pace.
   "You've bearded him!"[9] said handy Nicholas.
"God's body, this is going fair and fit!"   525
   This luckless Absolom heard every bit,
And gnawed his mouth, so angry he became.
He said to himself, "I'll square you, all the same."
   But who now scrubs and rubs, who chafes his lips
With dust, with sand, with straw, with cloth and chips   530
If not this Absolom? "The devil," says he,
"Welcome my soul if I wouldn't rather be
Revenged than have the whole town in a sack!
Alas," he cries, "if only I'd held back!"   535
His hot love had become all cold and ashen.
He didn't have a curse to spare for passion
From the moment when he kissed her on the ass.
That was the cure to make his sickness pass!
He cried as a child does after being whipped;
He railed at love. Then quietly he slipped   540
Across the street to a smith who was forging out
Parts that the farmers needed round about.
He was busy sharpening colter[1] and plowshare
When Absolom knocked as though without a care.
   "Undo the door, Jervice, and let me come."   545
   "What? Who are you?"
                "It is I, Absolom."
   "Absolom, is it! By Christ's precious tree,
Why are you up so early? Lord bless me,
What's ailing you? Some gay girl has the power
To bring you out, God knows, at such an hour!   550
Yes, by St. Neot,[2] you know well what I mean!"
   Absolom thought his jokes not worth a bean.

---

9. "To beard" in Middle English means to trick, but Nicholas is also punning on the literal meaning of the word.   1. A turf cutter on a plow.   2. A 9th-century English saint.

Without a word he let them all go by.
He had another kind of fish to fry
Than Jervice guessed. "Lend me this colter here   555
That's hot in the chimney, friend," he said. "Don't fear,
I'll bring it back right off when I am through.
I need it for a job I have to do."
    "Of course," said Jervice. "Why, if it were gold
Or coins in a sack, uncounted and untold,   560
As I'm a rightful smith, I wouldn't refuse it.
But, Christ's foot! how on earth do you mean to use it?"
    "Let that," said Absolom, "be as it may.
I'll let you know tomorrow or next day,"
And took the colter where the steel was cold   565
And slipped out with it safely in his hold
And softly over to the carpenter's wall.
He coughed and then he rapped the window, all
As he had done before.
                            "Who's knocking there?"
Said Alison. "It is a thief, I swear."   570
    "No, no," said he. "God knows, my sugarplum,
My bird, my darling, it's your Absolom.
I've brought a golden ring my mother gave me,
Fine and well cut, as I hope that God will save me.
It's yours, if you will let me have a kiss."   575
    Nicholas had got up to take a piss
And thought he would improve the whole affair.
This clerk, before he got away from there,
Should give *his* ass a smack; and hastily
He opened the window, and thrust out quietly,   580
Buttocks and haunches, all the way, his bum.
Up spoke this clerk, this jolly Absolom:
"Speak, for I don't know where you are, sweetheart."
    Nicholas promptly let fly with a fart
As loud as if a clap of thunder broke,   585
So great he was nearly blinded by the stroke,
And ready with his hot iron to make a pass,
Absolom caught him fairly on the ass.
    Off flew the skin, a good handbreadth of fat
Lay bare, the iron so scorched him where he sat.   590
As for the pain, he thought that he would die,
And like a madman he began to cry.
"Help! Water! Water! Help, for God's own heart!"
    At this the carpenter came to with a start.
He heard a man cry "Water!" as if mad.   595
"It's coming now," was the first thought he had.
"It's Noah's flood, alas, God be our hope!"
He sat up with his ax and chopped the rope
And down at once the whole contraption fell.
He didn't take time out to buy or sell   600
Till he hit the floor and lay there in a swoon.
    Then up jumped Nicholas and Alison
And in the street began to cry, "Help, ho!"

The neighbors all came running, high and low,
And poured into the house to see the sight. 605
The man still lay there, passed out cold and white,
For in his tumble he had broken an arm.
But he himself brought on his greatest harm,
For when he spoke he was at once outdone
By handy Nicholas and Alison 610
Who told them one and all that he was mad.
So great a fear of Noah's flood he had,
By some delusion, that in his vanity
He had bought himself these kneading-troughs, all three.
And hung them from the roof there, up above, 615
And he had pleaded with them, for God's love,
To sit there in the loft for company.
   The neighbors laughed at such a fantasy,
And round the loft began to pry and poke
And turned his whole disaster to a joke. 620
He found it was no use to say a word.
Whatever reason he offered, no one heard.
With oaths and curses people swore him down
Until he passed for mad in the whole town.
Wit, clerk, and student all stood by each other. 625
They said, "It's clear the man is crazy, brother."
Everyone had his laugh about this feud.
So Alison, the carpenter's wife, got screwed
For all the jealous watching he could try,
And Absolom, he kissed her nether eye, 630
And Nicholas got his bottom roasted well.
God save this troop! That's all I have to tell.

The Wife of Bath's Prologue and Tale

THE PROLOGUE

"Experience, though all authority
Was lacking in the world, confers on me
The right to speak of marriage, and unfold
Its woes. For, lords, since I was twelve years old[3]
—Thanks to eternal God in heaven alive— 5
I've married at church door no less than five
Husbands, provided that I can have been
So often wed,[4] and all were worthy men.
But I was told, indeed, and not long since,
That Christ went to a wedding only once 10
At Cana, in the land of Galilee.[5]
By this example he instructed me
To wed once only—that's what I have heard!
Again, consider now what a sharp word,
Beside a well, Jesus, both God and man, 15

---

3. According to Church law, twelve was the earliest age at which a girl could be married; the Wife is probably bragging rather than telling the literal truth.   4. Assuming so many marriages are legitimate.
5. John 2.1–2.

Spoke in reproving the Samaritan:
'Five husbands thou hast had'—this certainly
He said to her—'and the man that now hath thee
Is not thy husband.'[6] True, he spoke this way,
But what he meant is more than I can say   20
Except that I would ask why the fifth man
Was not a husband to the Samaritan?
To just how many could she be a wife?
I've never heard this number all my life
Determined up to now. For round and round   25
Scholars may gloze,[7] interpret, and expound,
But plainly, this I know without a lie,
God told us to increase and multiply.[8]
That noble text I can well understand.
My husband—this too I have well in hand—   30
Should leave both father and mother and cleave to me.[9]
Number God never mentioned, bigamy,
No, nor even octogamy; why do men
Talk of it as a sin and scandal, then?
    "Think of that monarch, wise King Solomon.   35
It strikes me that *he* had more wives than one![1]
To be refreshed, God willing, would please me
If I got it half as many times as he!
He had a gift, and one of God's own giving,
For all his wives! There isn't a man now living   40
Who has the like. By all that I make out
On the first night this king had many a bout
With each, he was so thoroughly alive.
Blessed be God that I have married five,
And always, for the money in his chest   45
And for his nether purse, I picked the best.
In divers schools ripe scholarship is made,
And various practice in all kinds of trade
Makes perfect workmen, as the world can see.
Five husbands have had turns at schooling me.   50
Welcome the sixth, whenever I am faced
With yet another. I don't mean to be chaste
At all costs. When a spouse of mine is gone,
Some other Christian man shall take me on,
For then, says the Apostle, I'll be free   55
To wed, in God's name, where it pleases me.[2]
To marry is no sin, as we can learn
From him; better to marry than to burn,[3]
He says. Why should I care what obloquy
Men heap on Lamech and his bigamy?   60
Abraham was, by all that I can tell,
A holy man; so Jacob[4] was as well,

6. John 4.6–19.   7. Gloss, or interpret.   8. Genesis 1.28.   9. Matthew 19.5–6.   1. 1 Kings 11.3
describes Solomon as having seven hundred wives and three hundred concubines.   2. The Apostle is
Paul, and the reference is to 1 Corinthians 7.39; throughout her *Prologue* the Wife returns to this chapter,
sometimes using (or misusing) Paul to support her views, sometimes arguing against him.   3. 1 Cor. 7.9.
4. See Genesis 29.15–30. For Lamech, see Genesis 4.19–23. For Abraham, Genesis 16.1–6.

And each of them took more than two as brides,
And many another holy man besides.
Where, may I ask, in any period,   65
In plain words can you show Almighty God
Forbade us marriage? Point it out to me!
Or where did he command virginity?
The Apostle, when he speaks of maidenhood,
Lays down no law.[5] This I have understood   70
As well as you, milords, for it is plain.
Men may advise a woman to abstain
From marriage, but mere counsels aren't commands.
He left it to our judgment, where it stands.
Had God enjoined us all to maidenhood   75
Then marriage would have been condemned for good.
But truth is, if no seed were ever sown,
In what soil could virginity be grown?
Paul did not dare command a thing at best
On which his Master left us no behest.   80
    "But now the prize goes to virginity.
Seize it whoever can, and let us see
What manner of man shall run best in the race!
But not all men receive this form of grace
Except where God bestows it by his will.   85
The Apostle was a maid, I know; but still,
Although he wished all men were such as he,
It was only *counsel* toward virginity.[6]
To be a wife he gave me his permission,
And so it is no blot on my condition   90
Nor slander of bigamy upon my state
If when my husband dies I take a mate.
A man does virtuously, St. Paul has said,
To touch no woman[7]—meaning in his bed.
For fire and fat are dangerous friends at best.   95
You know what this example should suggest.
Here is the nub: he held virginity
Superior to wedded frailty,
And frailty I call it unless man
And woman both are chaste for their whole span.   100
    "I am not jealous if maidenhood outweighs
My marriages; I grant it all the praise.
It pleases, them, these virgins, flesh and soul
To be immaculate. I won't extol
My own condition. In a lord's household   105
You know that every vessel can't be gold.
Some are of wood, and serve their master still.
God calls us variously to do his will.
Each has his proper gift, of all who live,
Some this, some that, as it pleases God to give.   110
    "Virginity is a high and perfect course,
And continence is holy. But the source

5. 1 Cor. 7.25.   6. 1 Cor. 7.8.   7. 1 Cor. 7.1.

Of all perfection, Jesus, never bade
Each one of us to go sell all he had
And give it to the poor; he did not say   115
That all should follow him in this one way.
He spoke to those who would live perfectly,[8]
And by your leave, lords, that is not for me!
The flower of my best years I find it suits
To spend on the acts of marriage and its fruits.   120
    "Tell me this also: why at our creation
Were organs given us for generation,
And for what profit were we creatures made?
Believe me, not for nothing! Ply his trade
Of twisting texts who will, and let him urge   125
That they were only given us to purge
Our urine; say without them we should fail
To tell a female rightly from a male
And that's their only object—say you so?
It won't work, as experience will show.   130
Without offense to scholars, I say this,
That they were made for both these purposes,
That we may both be cleansed, I mean, and eased
Through intercourse, where God is not displeased.
Why else in books is this opinion met,   135
That every man should pay his wife his debt?[9]
Tell me with what a man should hope to pay
Unless he put his instrument in play?
They were supplied us, then, for our purgation,
But they were also meant for generation.   140
    "But none the less I do not mean to say
That all those who are furnished in this way
Are bound to go and practice intercourse.
The world would then grant chastity no force.
Christ was a maid, yet he was formed a man,   145
And many a saint, too, since the world began,
And yet they lived in perfect chastity.
I am not spiteful toward virginity.
Let virgins be white bread of pure wheat-seed.
Barley we wives are called, and yet I read   150
In Mark, and tell the tale in truth he can,
That Christ with barley bread cheered many a man.[1]
In the state that God assigned to each of us
I'll persevere. I'm not fastidious.
In wifehood I will use my instrument   155
As freely by my Maker it was lent.
If I hold back with it, God give me sorrow!
My husband shall enjoy it night and morrow
Whenever it pleases him to pay his debt.
A husband, though—I've not been thwarted yet—   160
Shall always be my debtor and my slave.
From tribulation he shall never save

8. Matthew 9.16–22.   9. 1 Cor. 7.3.   1. The reference is actually found not in Mark but in John 6.9.

His flesh, not for as long as I'm his wife![2]
I have the power, during all my life,
Over his very body, and not he. 165
For so the Apostle has instructed me,
Who bade men love their wives for better or worse.
It pleases me from end to end, that verse!"[3]

    The Pardoner, before she could go on,
Jumped up and cried, "By God and by St. John, 170
Upon this topic you preach nobly, Dame!
I was about to wed, but now, for shame,
Why should my body pay a price so dear?
I'd rather not be married all this year!"

    "Hold on," she said. "I haven't yet begun. 175
You'll drink a keg of this before I'm done,
I promise you, and it won't taste like ale!
And after I have told you my whole tale
Of marriage, with its fund of tribulation—
And I'm the expert of my generation, 180
For I myself, I mean, have been the whip—
You can decide then if you want a sip
Out of the barrel that I mean to broach.
Before you come too close in your approach,
Think twice. I have examples, more than ten! 185
'The man who won't be warned by other men,
To other men a warning he shall be.'
These are the words we find in Ptolemy.
Go read them right there in his *Almagest*."[4]

    "Now, Madame, if you're willing, I suggest," 190
Answered the Pardoner, "as you began,
Continue with your tale, and spare no man.
Teach us young men your practice as our guide."

    "Gladly, if it will please you," she replied.
"But first I ask you, if I speak my mind, 195
That all this company may be well inclined,
And will not take offense at what I say.
I only mean it, after all, in play.

    "Now, sirs, I will get onward with my tale.
If ever I hope to drink good wine or ale, 200
I'm speaking truth: the husbands I have had,
Three of them have been good, and two were bad.
The three were kindly men, and rich, and old.
But they were hardly able to uphold
The statute which had made them fast to me. 205
You know well what I mean by this, I see!
So help me God, I can't help laughing yet
Thinking of how at night I made them sweat,
And I thought nothing of it, on my word!
Their land and wealth they had by then conferred 210
On me, and so I safely could neglect

---

2. 1 Cor. 7.28; this verse, with its reference to the "tribulation of the flesh," is central to the Wife's *Prologue*.
3. 1 Cor. 7.4.   4. The *Almagest* is a second-century treatise on astronomy; this proverb appears in a preface that was later added to the work.

Tending their love or showing them respect.
So well they loved me that by God above
I hardly set a value on their love.
A woman who is wise is never done   215
Busily winning love when she has none,
But since I had them wholly in my hand
And they had given me their wealth and land,
Why task myself to spoil them or to please
Unless for my own profit and my ease?   220
I set them working so that many a night
They sang a dirge, so grievous was their plight!
They never got the bacon, well I know,
Offered as prize to couples at Dunmow
Who live a year in peace, without repentance![5]   225
So well I ruled them, by my law and sentence,
They gladly brought me fine things from the fair,
Happy whenever I spoke with a mild air,
For God knows I could chide outrageously.
     "Now judge if I could do it properly!   230
You wives who understand and who are wise,
This is the way to throw dust in their eyes.
There isn't on the earth so bold a man
He can swear false or lie as a woman can.
I do not urge this course in every case,   235
Just when a prudent wife is caught off base;
Then she should swear the parrot's mad who tattled
Her indiscretions, and when she's once embattled
Should call her maid as witness, by collusion.
But listen, how I threw them in confusion: 240
     " 'Sir dotard, this is how you live?' I'd say.
'How can my neighbor's wife be dressed so gay?
She carries off the honors everywhere.
I sit at home. I've nothing fit to wear.
What were you doing at my neighbor's house?   245
Is she so handsome? Are you so amorous?
What do you whisper to our maid? God bless me,
Give up your jokes, old lecher. They depress me.
When I've a harmless friend myself, you balk
And scold me like a devil if I walk   250
For innocent amusement to his house.
You drink and come home reeling like a souse
And sit down on your bench, worse luck, and preach.
Taking a wife who's poor—this is the speech
That you regale me with—costs grievously,   255
And if she's rich and of good family,
It is a constant torment, you decide,
To suffer her ill humor and her pride.
And if she's fair, you scoundrel, you destroy her
By saying that every lecher will enjoy her;   260
For she can't long keep chastity intact

5. At Dunmow, in Essex, a side of bacon was given to the couple who had lived a year without quarreling.

Who is from every side at once attacked.
    " 'Some want us for our wealth, so you declare,
Some for our figure, some think we are fair,
Some want a woman who can dance or sing,   265
Some want kindness, and some philandering,
Some look for hands and arms well turned and small.
Thus, by your tale, the devil may take us all!
Men cannot keep a castle or redoubt
Longer, you tell me, than it can hold out.   270
Or if a woman's plain, you say that she
Is one who covets each man she may see,
For at him like a spaniel she will fly
Until she finds some man that she can buy.
Down to the lake goes never a goose so gray   275
But it will have a mate, I've heard you say.
It's hard to fasten—this too I've been told—
A thing that no man willingly will hold.
Wise men, you tell me as you go to bed,
And those who hope for heaven should never wed.   280
I hope wild lightning and a thunderstroke
Will break your wizened neck! You say that smoke
And falling timbers and a railing wife
Drive a man from his house. Lord bless my life!
What ails an old man, so to make him chide?   285
We cover our vices till the knot is tied,
We wives, you say, and then we trot them out.
Here's a fit proverb for a doddering lout!
An ox or ass, you say, a hound or horse,
These we examine as a matter of course.   290
Basins and also bowls, before we buy them,
Spoons, spools, and such utensils, first we try them,
And so with pots and clothes, beyond denial;
But of their wives men never make a trial
Until they are married. After that, you say,   295
Old fool, we put our vices on display.
    " 'I'm in a pique if you forget your duty
And aren't forever praising me for beauty
Or aren't at all hours doting on my face
And calling me "fair dame" in every place,   300
Or fail to give a feast on my birthday
To keep my spirits fresh and make me gay,
Or if all proper courtesies aren't paid
My nurse, and equally my chambermaid,
My father's kin with all his family ties—   305
You say so, you old barrelful of lies!
    " 'Yet just because he has a head of hair
Like shining gold, and squires me everywhere,
You have a false suspicion in your heart
Of Jenkin, our apprentice. For my part   310
I wouldn't have him if you died tomorrow!
But tell me this, or go and live in sorrow:
That chest of yours, why do you hide the keys

Away from me? It's my wealth, if you please,
As much as yours. Will you make a fool of me,   315
The mistress of our house? You shall not be
Lord of my body and my wealth at once!
No, by St. James himself, you must renounce
One or the other, if it drives you mad!
What do you gain by spying? You'd be glad   320
To lock me up, I think, inside your chest.
"Enjoy yourself, and go where you think best,"
You ought to say; "I won't hear tales of malice.
I know you for a faithful wife, Dame Alice."
A woman loves no man who keeps close charge   325
Of where she goes. We want to be at large.
Blessed above all other men was he,
The wise astrologer, Don Ptolemy,
Who has this proverb in his *Almagest*:
"Of all wise men his wisdom is the best   330
Who does not care who has the world in hand."[6]
Now by this proverb you should understand,
Since you have plenty, it isn't yours to care
Or fret how richly other people fare,
For by your leave, old dotard, you for one   335
Can have all you can take when day is done.
The man's a niggard to the point of scandal
Who will not lend his lamp to light a candle;
His lamp won't lose although the candle gain.
If you've enough, you ought not to complain.   340
   " 'You say, too, if we make ourselves look smart,
Put on expensive clothes and dress the part,
We lay our virtue open to disgrace.
And then you try to reinforce your case
By saying these words in the Apostle's name: 345
"In chaste apparel, with modesty and shame,
So shall you women clothe yourselves," said he,
"And not in rich coiffure or jewelry,
Pearls or the like, or gold, or costly wear."[7]
Now both your text and rubric,[8] I declare,   350
I will not follow as I would a gnat!
   " 'You told me once that I was like a cat,
For singe her skin and she will stay at home,
But if her skin is smooth, the cat will roam.
No dawn but finds her on the neighbors calling   355
To show her skin, and go off caterwauling.
If I am looking smart, you mean to say,
I'm off to put my finery on display.
   " 'What do you gain, old fool, by setting spies?
Though you beg Argus[9] with his hundred eyes   360
To be my bodyguard, for all his skill
He'll keep me only by my own free will.

---

6. See note to line 189 above.   7. 1 Timothy 2.9.   8. The rubric was a heading to the text written in red (*ruber* in Latin).   9. Argus was a hundred-eyed creature sent by Juno to watch over Io, whom Jove loved and had turned into a heifer; see Ovid, *Metamorphoses* 1.

I know enough to blind him, as I live!
" 'There are three things, you also say, that give
Vexation to this world both south and north.   365
You add that no one can endure the fourth.
Of these catastrophes a hateful wife—
You precious wretch, may Christ cut short your life!—
Is always reckoned, as you say, for one.
Is this your whole stock of comparison,   370
And why from all your parables of contempt
Can luckless helpmates never be exempt?
You also liken woman's love to hell,
To barren land where water will not dwell.
I've heard you call it an unruly fire;   375
The more it burns, the hotter its desire
To burn up everything that burned will be.
You say that just as worms destroy a tree
A wife destroys her spouse, as they have found
Who get themselves in holy wedlock bound.'   380
    "By these devices, lords, as you perceive,
I got my three old husbands to believe
That in their cups they said things of this sort,
And all of it was false; but for support
Jenkin bore witness, and my niece did too.   385
These innocents, Lord, what I put them through!
God's precious pains! And they had no recourse,
For I could bite and whinny like a horse.
Though in the wrong, I kept them well annoyed,
Or oftentimes I would have been destroyed!   390
First to the mill is first to grind his grain.
I was always the first one to complain,
And so our peace was made; they gladly bid
For terms to settle things they never did!
    "For wenching I would scold them out of hand   395
When they were hardly well enough to stand.
But this would tickle a man; it would restore him
To think I had so great a fondness for him!
I'd vow when darkness came and out I stepped,
It was to see the girls with whom he slept.   400
Under this pretext I had plenty of mirth!
Such wit as this is given us at our birth.
Lies, tears, and needlework the Lord will give
In kindness to us women while we live.
And thus in one point I can take just pride: 405
I showed myself in the end the stronger side.
By sleight or strength I kept them in restraint,
And chiefly by continual complaint.
In bed they met their grief in fullest measure.
There I would scold; I would not do their pleasure.   410
Bed was a place where I would not abide
Feeling my husband's arm across my side
Till he agreed to square accounts and pay,
And after that I'd let him have his way.

To every man, therefore, I tell this tale: 1415
Win where you're able, all is up for sale.
No falcon by an empty hand is lured.
For victory their cravings I endured
And even feigned a show of appetite.
And yet in old meat I have no delight;   1420
It made me always rail at them and chide them,
For though the pope himself sat down beside them
I would not give them peace at their own board.
No, on my honor, I paid them word for word.
Almighty God so help me, if right now   1425
I had to make my last will, I can vow
For every word they said to me, we're quits.
For I so handled the contest by my wits
That they gave up, and took it for the best,
Or otherwise we should have had no rest.   1430
Like a mad lion let my husband glare,
He finally got the worst of the affair.
    "Then I would say, 'My dear, you ought to keep
In mind how gentle Wilkin looks, our sheep.
Come here, my husband, let me kiss your cheek!   1435
You should be patient, too; you should be meek.
Of Job and of his patience when you prate
Your conscience ought to show a cleaner slate.
He should be patient who so well can preach.
If not, then it will fall on me to teach   1440
The beauty of a peaceful wedded life.
For one of us must give in, man or wife,
And since men are more reasonable creatures
Than women are, it follows that *your* features
Ought to exhibit patience. Why do you groan?   1445
You want my body yours, and yours alone?
Why, take it all! Welcome to every bit!
But curse you, Peter,[1] unless you cherish it!
Were I inclined to peddle my *belle chose*,[2]
I could walk out dressed freshly as a rose.   1450
But I will keep it for your own sweet tooth.
It's your fault if we fight. By God, that's truth!'
    "This was the way I talked when I had need.
But now to my fourth husband I'll proceed.
    "This fourth I married was a roisterer.   1455
He had a mistress, and my passions were,
Although I say it, strong; and altogether
Stubborn and young I was, and pert in feather.
If anyone took up his harp to play,
How I could dance! I sang as merry a lay   1460
As any nightingale when of sweet wine
I'd drunk my draft. Metellius,[3] the foul swine,
Who beat his spouse until he took her life

1. This is not the husband's name but an oath by St. Peter.   2. Pretty thing (French).   3. A virtuous Roman husband who reputedly killed his wife for drinking wine.

For drinking wine, if I had been his wife,
He'd never have frightened me away from drinking!   465
But after a drink, Venus gets in my thinking,
For just as true as cold engenders hail
A thirsty mouth goes with a thirsty tail.
Drinking destroys a woman's last defense
As lechers well know by experience.   470
   "But, Lord Christ, when it all comes back to me,
Remembering my youth and jollity,
It tickles me to the roots. It does me good
Down to this very day that while I could
I took my world, my time, and had my fling.   475
But age, alas, that poisons everything
Has robbed me of my beauty and my pith.
Well, let it go! Good-by! The devil with
What cannot last! There's only this to tell:
The flour is gone, I've only chaff to sell.   480
Yet I'll contrive to keep a merry cheek!
But now of my fourth husband I will speak.
   "My heart was, I can tell you, full of spite
That in another he should find delight.
I paid him for this debt; I made it good.   485
I furnished him a cross of the same wood,
By God and by St. Joce[4]—in no foul fashion,
Not with my flesh; but I put on such passion
And rendered him so jealous, I'll engage
I made him fry in his own grease for rage!   490
On earth, God knows, I was his purgatory;
I only hope his soul is now in glory.
God knows it was a sad song that he sung
When the shoe pinched him; sorely was he wrung!
Only he knew, and God, the devious system,   495
By which outrageously I used to twist him.
He died when I came home from Jerusalem.
He's buried near the chancel,[5] under the beam
That holds the cross. His tomb is less ornate
Than that where King Darius lies in state   500
And which the paintings of Appelles graced
With subtle work.[6] It would have been a waste
To bury him lavishly. Farewell! God save
His soul and give him rest! He's in his grave.
   "And now of my fifth husband let me tell.   505
God never let his soul go down to hell
Though he of all five was my scourge and flail!
I feel it on my ribs, right down the scale,
And ever shall until my dying day.
And yet he was so full of life and gay   510

---

4. A 7th-century Breton saint, whose relics were at an abbey near the Tabard Inn. 5. The part of the church used by the officiating clergy; often a cross was placed on a beam that divided it from the nave, where the congregation sat. 6. Darius, king of the Persians, reputedly had a tomb decorated by the famous Jewish craftsman Appelles; Chaucer derived this fictional information from a 12th-century Latin poem.

In bed, and could so melt me and cajole me
When on my back he had a mind to roll me,
What matter if on every bone he'd beaten me!
He'd have my love, so quickly he could sweeten me.
I loved him best, in fact; for as you see, 515
His love was a more arduous prize for me.
We women, if I'm not to tell a lie,
Are quaint in this regard. Put in our eye
A thing we cannot easily obtain,
All day we'll cry about it and complain. 520
Forbid a thing, we want it bitterly,
But urge it on us, then we turn and flee.
We're chary of what we hope that men will buy.
A throng at market makes the prices high;
Men set no value on cheap merchandise, 525
A truth all women know if they are wise.
    "My fifth, may God forgive his every sin,
I took for love, not money. He had been
An Oxford student once, but in our town
Was boarding with my good friend, Alison. 530
She knew each secret that I had to give
More than our parish priest did, as I live!
I told her my full mind, I shared it all.
For if my husband pissed against a wall
Or did a thing that might have cost his life, 535
To her, and to another neighbor's wife,
And to my niece, a girl whom I loved well,
His every thought I wouldn't blush to tell.
And often enough I told them, be it said.
God knows I made his face turn hot and red 540
For secrets he confided to his shame.
He knew he only had himself to blame.
    "And so it happened once that during Lent,
As I did often, to Alison's I went,
For I have loved my life long to be gay 545
And to walk out in April or in May
To hear the talk and seek a favorite haunt.
Jenkin the student, Alice, my confidante,
And I myself into the country went.
My husband was in London all that Lent. 550
I had the greater liberty to see
And to be seen by jolly company.
How could I tell beforehand in what place
Luck might be waiting with a stroke of grace?
And so I went to every merrymaking. 555
No pilgrimage was past my undertaking.
I was at festivals, and marriages,
Processions, preachings, and at miracle plays,
And in my scarlet clothes I made a sight.
Upon that costume neither moth nor mite 560
Nor any worm with ravening hunger fell.
And how so? It was kept in use too well.

"Now for what happened. In the fields we walked,
The three of us, and gallantly we talked,
The student and I, until I told him he,   565
If I became a widow, should marry me.
For I can say, and not with empty pride,
I've never failed for marriage to provide
Or other things as well. Let mice be meek;
A mouse's heart I hold not worth a leek.   570
He has one hole to scurry to, just one,
And if that fails him, he is quite undone.
    "I let this student think he had bewitched me.
(My mother with this piece of guile enriched me!)
All night I dreamed of him—this too I said;   575
He was about to kill me flat in bed;
My very bed in fact was full of blood;
But still I hoped it would result in good,
For blood betokens gold, as I have heard.
It was a fiction, dream and every word,   580
But I was following my mother's lore
In all this matter, as in many more.
    "Sirs—let me see; what did I mean to say?
Aha! By God, I have it! When he lay,
My fourth, of whom I've spoken, on his bier,   585
I wept of course; I showed but little cheer,
As wives must do, since custom has its place,
And with my kerchief covered up my face.
But since I had provided for a mate,
I did not cry for long, I'll freely state.   590
And so to church my husband on the morrow
Was borne away by neighbors in their sorrow.
Jenkin, the student, was among the crowd,
And when I saw him walk, so help me God,
Behind the bier, I thought he had a pair   595
Of legs and feet so cleanly turned and fair
I put my heart completely in his hold.
He was in fact some twenty winters old
And I was forty, to confess the truth;
But all my life I've still had a colt's tooth.   600
My teeth were spaced apart; that was the seal
St. Venus printed, and became me well.
So help me God, I was a lusty one,
Pretty and young and rich, and full of fun.
And truly, as my husbands have all said,   605
I was the best thing there could be in bed.
For I belong to Venus in my feelings,
Yet have the heart of Mars in all my dealings.
From Venus come my lust and appetite,
From Mars I get my courage and my might,   610
Born under Taurus, while Mars stood therein.
Alas, alas, that ever love was sin!
I yielded to my every inclination
Through the predominance of my constellation;

This made me so I never could withhold   615
My chamber of Venus, if the truth be told,
From a good fellow; yet upon my face
Mars left his mark, and in another place.
Never, so may Christ grant me intercession,
Have I yet loved a fellow with discretion,   620
But always I have followed appetite,
Let him be long or short or dark or light.
I never cared, as long as he liked me,
What his rank was or how poor he might be.
   "What should I say, but when the month ran out,   625
This jolly student, always much about,
This Jenkin married me in solemn state.
To him I gave land, titles, the whole slate
Of goods that had been given me before;
But my repentance afterward was sore!   630
He wouldn't endure the pleasures I held dear.
By God, he gave me a lick once on the ear,
When from a book of his I tore a leaf,
So hard that from the blow my ear grew deaf.
Stubborn I was as a lioness with young,   635
And by the truth I had a rattling tongue,
And I would visit, as I'd done before,
No matter what forbidding oath he swore.
Against this habit he would sit and preach me
Sermons enough, and he would try to teach me   640
Old Roman stories,[7] how for his whole life
The man Sulpicius Gallus left his wife
Only because he saw her look one day
Bareheaded down the street from his doorway.
   "Another Roman he told me of by name   645
Who, since his wife was at a summer's game
Without his knowledge, thereupon forsook
The woman. In his Bible he would look
And find that proverb of the Ecclesiast[8]
Where he enjoins and makes the stricture fast   650
That men forbid their wives to rove about.
Then he would quote me this, you needn't doubt:
'Build a foundation over sands or shallows,
Or gallop a blind horse across the fallows,
Let a wife traipse to shrines that some saint hallows,   655
And you are fit to swing upon the gallows.'
Talk as he would, I didn't care two haws
About his proverbs or his stale old saws.
Set right by him I never meant to be.
I hate the man who tells my faults to me,   660
And more of us than I do, by your pleasure.
This made him mad with me beyond all measure.
Under his yoke in no case would I go.

7. This and much of the following information is derived from a collection of Latin misogynist and anti-matrimonial literature popular in the Middle Ages; see note to line 667 below.   8. Ecclesiasticus 25.31.

"No, by St. Thomas, I will let you know
Why from that book of his I tore a leaf,   665
For which I got the blow that made me deaf.
    "He had a book,⁹ *Valerius*, he called it,
And *Theophrastus*, and he always hauled it
From where it lay to read both day and night
And laughed hard at it, such was his delight.   670
There was another scholar, too, at Rome,
A cardinal, whose name was St. Jerome;
He wrote a book against Jovinian.
The book included too Tertullian,
Chrysippus, Trotula, Abbess Héloïse   675
Who lived near Paris; it contained all these,
Bound in a single volume, and many a one
Besides; the Parables of Solomon
And Ovid's *Art of Love*. On such vacation
As he could snatch from worldly occupation   680
He dredged this book for tales of wicked wives.
He knew more stories of their wretched lives
Than those told of good women in the Bible.
No scholar ever lived who did not libel
Women, believe me; to speak well of wives   685
Is quite beyond them, unless it be in lives
Of holy saints; no woman else will do.
Who was it painted the lion, tell me who?¹
By God, if women had only written stories
Like wits and scholars in their oratories,   690
They would have pinned on men more wickedness
Than the whole breed of Adam can redress.
Venus's children clash with Mercury's;²
The two work evermore by contraries.
Knowledge and wisdom are of Mercury's giving,   695
Venus loves revelry and riotous living,
And with these clashing dispositions gifted
Each of them sinks when the other is uplifted.
Thus Mercury falls, God knows, in desolation
In Pisces, which is Venus' exaltation.   700
And Venus falls when Mercury is raised.
Thus by a scholar no woman can be praised.
The scholar, when he's old and cannot do
The work of Venus more than his old shoe,
Then sits he down, and in his dotage fond   705
Writes that no woman keeps her marriage bond!
    "But now for the story that I undertook—
To tell how I was beaten for a book.

9. Jenkin's book contains treatises called *Valerius* (written in the 12th century) and *Theophrastus* (2nd century), Jerome's *Letter Against Jovinian* (4th century), and works by Tertullian (d. ca. 230), Crisippus (a writer mentioned in Jerome's *Letter*), Trotula (an 11th-century woman physician who wrote gynecological works), and Heloise (the lover of Abelard, who argued in her letters that a philosopher should never marry). The *Parables of Solomon* is a reference to the biblical book of Proverbs, ascribed to Solomon in the Middle Ages, while Ovid's *Art of Love* is a guidebook for seducers.   1. A reference to Aesop's fable in which a lion objects to a picture of a lion eating a man, arguing that if the lion had painted the picture it would have been quite different.   2. Mercury is the planet that rules over scholars, its "children."

"Jenkin, one night, who never seemed to tire
Of reading in his book, sat by the fire   710
And first he read of Eve, whose wickedness
Delivered all mankind to wretchedness
For which in his own person Christ was slain
Who with his heart's blood bought us all again.
'By this,' he said, 'expressly you may find   715
That woman was the loss of all mankind.'

"He read me next how Samson lost his hair.
Sleeping, his mistress clipped it off for fair;
Through this betrayal he lost both his eyes.
He read me then—and I'm not telling lies—   720
How Deianeira, wife of Hercules,
Caused him to set himself on fire.[3] With these
He did not overlook the sad to-do
Of Socrates with *his* wives—he had two.[4]
Xantippe emptied the pisspot on his head.   725
This good man sat as patient as if dead.
He wiped his scalp; he did not dare complain
Except to say 'With thunder must come rain.'

"Pasiphaë,[5] who was the queen of Crete,
For wickedness he thought her story sweet.   730
Ugh! That's enough, it was a grisly thing,
About her lust and filthy hankering!
And Clytemnestra[6] in her lechery
Who took her husband's life feloniously,
He grew devout in reading of her treason.   735
And then he told me also for what reason
Unhappy Amphiaraus[7] lost his life.
My husband had the story of *his* wife,
Eriphyle, who for a clasp of gold
Went to his Grecian enemies and told   740
The secret of her husband's hiding place,
For which at Thebes he met an evil grace.
Livia and Lucilia,[8] he went through
Their tale as well; they killed their husbands, too.
One killed for love, the other killed for hate.   745
At evening Livia, when the hour was late,
Poisoned her husband, for she was his foe.
Lucilia doted on her husband so
That in her lust, hoping to make him think
Ever of her, she gave him a love-drink   750
Of such a sort he died before the morrow.
And so at all turns husbands come to sorrow!

"He told me then how one Latumius,[9]
Complaining to a friend named Arrius,

3. Driven by jealousy, Hercules's wife, Deianeira, prepared for him a poisoned shirt that burned him to
death.   4. This apocryphal story is derived from Jerome's *Letter*.   5. Pasiphaë made love with a bull
and gave birth to the Minotaur.   6. She murdered her husband, Agamemnon, on his return from Troy.
7. The prophet Amphiaraus attempted to avoid joining a military expedition against Thebes that he knew
to be doomed, but was betrayed by his wife.   8. Roman wives; Livia poisoned her husband at the insti-
gation of her lover, while Lucilia poisoned hers with a love potion.   9. This unpleasant story appears in
a collection of popular tales.

Told him that in his garden grew a tree   755
On which his wives had hanged themselves, all three,
Merely for spite against their partnership.
'Brother,' said Arrius, 'let me have a slip
From this miraculous tree, for, begging pardon,
I want to go and plant it in my garden.'   760
    "Then about wives in recent times he read,
How some had murdered husbands lying abed
And all night long had let a paramour
Enjoy them with the corpse flat on the floor;
Or driven a nail into a husband's brain   765
While he was sleeping, and thus he had been slain;
And some had given them poison in their drink.
He told more harm than anyone can think,
And seasoned his wretched stories with proverbs
Outnumbering all the blades of grass and herbs   770
On earth. 'Better a dragon for a mate,
Better,' he said, 'on a lion's whims to wait
Than on a wife whose way it is to chide.
Better,' he said, 'high in the loft to bide
Than with a railing wife down in the house.   775
They always, they are so contrarious,
Hate what their husbands like,' so he would say.
'A woman,' he said, 'throws all her shame away
When she takes off her smock.' And on he'd go:
'A pretty woman, unless she's chaste also,   780
Is like a gold ring stuck in a sow's nose.'
Who could imagine, who would half suppose
The gall my heart drank, raging at each drop?
    "And when I saw that he would never stop
Reading all night from his accursed book,   785
Suddenly, in the midst of it, I took
Three leaves and tore them out in a great pique,
And with my fist I caught him on the cheek
So hard he tumbled backward in the fire.
And up he jumped, he was as mad for ire   790
As a mad lion, and caught me on the head
With such a blow I fell down as if dead.
And seeing me on the floor, how still I lay,
He was aghast, and would have fled away,
Till I came to at length, and gave a cry.   795
'You'd kill me for my lands? Before I die,
False thief,' I said, 'I'll give you a last kiss!'
    "He came to me and knelt down close at this,
And said, 'So help me God, dear Alison,
I'll never strike you. For this thing I've done   800
You are to blame. Forgive me, I implore.'
So then I hit him on the cheek once more
And said, 'Thus far I am avenged, you thief.
I cannot speak. Now I shall die for grief.'
But finally, with much care and ado,   805
We reconciled our differences, we two.

He let me have the bridle in my hand
For management of both our house and land.
To curb his tongue he also undertook,
And on the spot I made him burn his book. 810
And when I had secured in full degree
By right of triumph the whole sovereignty,
And he had said, 'My dear, my own true wife,
Do as you will as long as you have life;
Preserve your honor and keep my estate.'[1] 815
From that day on we'd settled our debate.
I was as kind, God help me, day and dark,
As any wife from India to Denmark,
And also true, and so he was to me.
I pray the Lord who sits in majesty 820
To bless his soul for Christ's own mercy dear.
And now I'll tell my tale, if you will hear."
"Dame," laughed the Friar, "as I hope for bliss,
It was a long preamble to a tale, all this!"
"God's arms!" the Summoner said, "it is a sin, 825
Good people, how friars are always butting in!
A fly and a friar will fall in every dish
And every question, whatever people wish.
What do you know, with your talk about 'preambling'?
Amble or trot or keep still or go scrambling, 830
You interrupt our pleasure."
               "You think so,
Sir Summoner?" said the Friar. "Before I go,
I'll give the people here a chance or two
For laughs at summoners, I promise you."
"Curse on your face," the Summoner said, "curse me, 835
If I don't tell some stories, two or three,
On friars, before I get to Sittingborne,[2]
With which I'll twist your heart and make it mourn,
For you have lost your temper, I can see."
"Be quiet," cried our Host, "immediately," 840
And ordered, "Let the woman tell her tale.
You act like people who've got drunk on ale.
Do, Madame, tell us. That is the best measure."
"All ready, sir," she answered, "at your pleasure,
With license from this worthy Friar here." 845
"Madame, tell on," he said. "You have my ear."

THE TALE

In the old days when King Arthur ruled the nation,
Whom Welshmen speak of with such veneration,
This realm we live in was a fairy land.
The fairy queen danced with her jolly band
On the green meadows where they held dominion. 5
This was, as I have read, the old opinion;

---

1. Status.   2. A town about two-thirds of the way to Canterbury.

I speak of many hundred years ago.
But no one sees an elf now, as you know,
For in our time the charity and prayers
And all the begging of these holy friars   10
Who swarm through every nook and every stream
Thicker than motes of dust in a sunbeam,
Blessing our chambers, kitchens, halls, and bowers,
Our cities, towns, and castles, our high towers,
Our villages, our stables, barns, and dairies,   15
They keep us all from seeing any fairies,
For where you might have come upon an elf
There now you find the holy friar himself
Working his district on industrious legs
And saying his devotions while he begs.   20
Women are safe now under every tree.
No incubus[3] is there unless it's he,
And all they have to fear from him is shame.
    It chanced that Arthur had a knight who came
Lustily riding home one day from hawking,   25
And in his path he saw a maiden walking
Before him, stark alone, right in his course.
This young knight took her maidenhead by force,
A crime at which the outcry was so keen
It would have cost his neck, but that the queen,   30
With other ladies, begged the king so long
That Arthur spared his life, for right or wrong,
And gave him to the queen, at her own will,
According to her choice, to save or kill.
    She thanked the king, and later told this knight, 35
Choosing her time, "You are still in such a plight
Your very life has no security.
I grant your life, if you can answer me
This question: what is the thing that most of all
Women desire? Think, or your neck will fall   40
Under the ax! If you cannot let me know
Immediately, I give you leave to go
A twelvemonth and a day, no more, in quest
Of such an answer as will meet the test.
But you must pledge your honor to return   45
And yield your body, whatever you may learn."
    The knight sighed; he was rueful beyond measure.
But what! He could not follow his own pleasure.
He chose at last upon his way to ride
And with such answer as God might provide   50
To come back when the year was at the close.
And so he takes his leave, and off he goes.
    He seeks out every house and every place
Where he has any hope, by luck or grace,
Of learning what thing women covet most.   55
But he could never light on any coast

---

3. A wicked spirit that fornicates with women.

Where on this point two people would agree,
For some said wealth and some said jollity,
Some said position, some said sport in bed
And often to be widowed, often wed.   60
Some said that to a woman's heart what mattered
Above all else was to be pleased and flattered.
That shaft, to tell the truth, was a close hit.
Men win us best by flattery, I admit,
And by attention. Some say our greatest ease   65
Is to be free and do just as we please,
And not to have our faults thrown in our eyes,
But always to be praised for being wise.
And true enough, there's not one of us all
Who will not kick if you rub us on a gall.   70
Whatever vices we may have within,
We won't be taxed with any fault or sin.
    Some say that women are delighted well
If it is thought that they will never tell
A secret they are trusted with, or scandal.   75
But that tale isn't worth an old rake handle!
We women, for a fact, can never hold
A secret. Will you hear a story told?
Then witness Midas![4] For it can be read
In Ovid that he had upon his head   80
Two ass's ears that he kept out of sight
Beneath his long hair with such skill and sleight
That no one else besides his wife could guess.
He loved her well, and trusted her no less.
He begged her not to make his blemish known,   85
But keep her knowledge to herself alone.
She swore that never, though to save her skin,
Would she be guilty of so mean a sin,
And yet it seemed to her she nearly died
Keeping a secret locked so long inside.   90
It swelled about her heart so hard and deep
She was afraid some word was bound to leap
Out of her mouth, and since there was no man
She dared to tell, down to a swamp she ran—
Her heart, until she got there, all agog—   95
And like a bittern[5] booming in the bog
She put her mouth close to the watery ground:
"Water, do not betray me with your sound!
I speak to you, and you alone," she said.
"Two ass's ears grow on my husband's head!   100
And now my heart is whole, now it is out.
I'd burst if I held it longer, past all doubt."
Safely, you see, awhile you may confide
In us, but it will out; we cannot hide
A secret. Look in Ovid if you care   105

---

4. The story of Midas and his ass's ears (given to him because he preferred Pan's songs to those of Apollo) is found in Ovid, *Metamorphoses* 11.174–93. In Ovid the secret is known not to Midas's wife but to his barber.   5. A kind of heron.

To learn what followed; the whole tale is there.
    This knight, when he perceived he could not find
What women covet most, was low in mind;
But the day came when homeward he must ride,
And as he crossed a wooded countryside   110
Some four and twenty ladies there by chance
He saw, all circling in a woodland dance,
And toward this dance he eagerly drew near
In hope of any counsel he might hear.
But the truth was, he had not reached the place   115
When dance and all, they vanished into space.
No living soul remained there to be seen
Save an old woman sitting on the green,
As ugly a witch as fancy could devise.
As he approached her she began to rise   120
And said, "Sir knight, here runs no thoroughfare.
What are you seeking with such anxious air?
Tell me! The better may your fortune be.
We old folk know a lot of things," said she.
    "Good mother," said the knight, "my life's to pay,   125
That's all too certain, if I cannot say
What women covet most. If you could tell
That secret to me, I'd requite you well."
    "Give me your hand," she answered. "Swear me true
That whatsoever I next ask of you,   130
You'll do it if it lies within your might
And I'll enlighten you before the night."
    "Granted, upon my honor," he replied.
    "Then I dare boast, and with no empty pride,
Your life is safe," she told him. "Let me die   135
If she, the queen, won't say the same as I.
Let's learn if the haughtiest of all who wear
A net or coverchief upon their hair
Will be so forward as to answer 'no'
To what I'll teach you. No more; let us go."   140
With that she whispered something in his ear,
And told him to be glad and have no fear.
    When they had reached the court, the knight declared
That he had kept his day, and was prepared
To give his answer, standing for his life.   145
Many the wise widow, many the wife,
Many the maid who rallied to the scene,
And at the head as justice sat the queen.
Then silence was enjoined; the knight was told
In open court to say what women hold   150
Precious above all else. He did not stand
Dumb like a beast, but spoke up at command
And plainly offered them his answering word
In manly voice, so that the whole court heard.
    "My liege and lady, most of all," said he,   155
"Women desire to have the sovereignty
And sit in rule and government above

Their husbands, and to have their way in love.
This is what most you want. Spare me or kill
As you may like; I stand here by your will."   160
   No widow, wife, or maid gave any token
Of contradicting what the knight had spoken.
He should not die; he should be spared instead;
He well deserved his life, the whole court said.
   The old woman whom the knight met on the grass   165
Sprang up at this. "My sovereign lady queen,
Before your court has risen, do me right!
I taught, myself, this answer to the knight,
For which he pledged his honor in my hand,
Solemnly, that the first thing I demand,   170
He'd do it, if it lay within his might.
Before the court I ask you, then, sir knight,
To take me," said the woman, "as your wife,
For well you know that I have saved your life.
Deny me, on your honor, if you can."   175
   "Alas," replied this miserable man,
"That was my promise, it must be confessed.
For the love of God, though, choose a new request!
Take all my wealth, and let my body be."
   "If that's your tune, then curse both you and me,"   180
She said. "Though I am ugly, old, and poor,
I'll have, for all the metal and the ore
That under earth is hidden or lies above,
Nothing, except to be your wife and love."
   "My love? No, my damnation, if you can!   185
Alas," he said, "that any of my clan
Should be so miserably misallied!"
   All to no good; force overruled his pride,
And in the end he is constrained to wed,
And marries his old wife and goes to bed.   190
   Now some will charge me with an oversight
In failing to describe the day's delight,
The merriment, the food, the dress at least.
But I reply, there was no joy nor feast;
Nothing but sorrow and sharp misery.   195
He married her in private, secretly,
And all day after, such was his distress,
Hid like an owl from his wife's ugliness.
   Great was the woe this knight had in his head
When in due time they both were brought to bed.   200
He shuddered, tossed, and turned, and all the while
His old wife lay and waited with a smile.
"Is every knight so backward with a spouse?
Is it," she said, "a law in Arthur's house?
I am your love, your own, your wedded wife.   205
I am the woman who has saved your life.
I've never done you anything but right.
Why do you treat me this way the first night?
You must be mad, the way that you behave!

Tell me my fault, and as God's love can save,   210
I will amend it, truly, if I can."
   "Amend it?" answered this unhappy man.
"It never can be amended, truth to tell.
You are so loathsome and so old as well,
And your low birth besides is such a cross   215
It is no wonder that I turn and toss.
God take my woeful spirit from my breast!"
   "Is this," she said, "the cause of your unrest?"
"No wonder!" said the knight. "It truly is."
   "Now sir," she said, "I could amend all this   220
Within three days, if it should please me to,
And if you deal with me as you should do.
   "But since you speak of that nobility
That comes from ancient wealth and pedigree,
As if that constituted gentlemen,   225
I hold such arrogance not worth a hen!
The man whose virtue is pre-eminent,
In public and alone, always intent
On doing every generous act he can,
Take him—he is the greatest gentleman!   230
Christ wills that we should claim nobility
From him, not from old wealth or family.
Our elders left us all that they were worth
And through their wealth and blood we claim high birth,
But never, since it was beyond their giving,   235
Could they bequeath to us their virtuous living;
Although it first conferred on them the name
Of gentlemen, they could not leave that claim!
   "Dante the Florentine on this was wise:
'Frail is the branch on which man's virtues rise'—   240
Thus runs his rhyme—'God's goodness wills that we
Should claim from him alone nobility.'[6]
Thus from our elders we can only claim
Such temporal things as men may hurt and maim.
   "It's plain enough that true nobility   245
Is not bequeathed along with property,
For many a lord's son does a deed of shame
And yet, God knows, enjoys his noble name.
But he, though scion of a noble house
And elders who were wise and virtuous,   250
Who will not follow his elders, who are dead,
But leads, himself, a shameful life instead,
He is not noble, be he duke or earl.
It is the churlish deed that makes the churl.
And therefore, my dear husband, I conclude   255
That though my ancestors were rough and rude,
Yet may Almighty God confer on me
The grace to live, as I hope, virtuously.
Call me of noble blood when I begin

---

6. Chaucer's sources are Dante's *Convivio* and *Purgatorio* 7.121–23.

To live in virtue and to cast out sin.   260
   "As for my poverty, at which you grieve,
Almighty God in whom we all believe
In willful poverty chose to lead his life,
And surely every man and maid and wife
Can understand that Jesus, heaven's king,   265
Would never choose a low or vicious thing.
A poor and cheerful life is nobly led;
So Seneca[7] and others have well said.
The man so poor he doesn't have a stitch
Who thinks himself repaid, I count as rich.   270
He that is covetous, he is the poor man,
Pining to have the things he never can.
It is of cheerful mind, true poverty.
Juvenal[8] says about it happily:
'The poor man as he goes along his way   275
And passes thieves is free to sing and play.'
Poverty is a good we loathe, a great
Reliever of our busy worldly state,
A great amender also of our minds
As he that patiently will bear it finds.   280
And poverty, for all it seems distressed,
Is a possession no one will contest.
Poverty, too, by bringing a man low,
Helps him the better God and self to know.
Poverty is a glass where we can see   285
Which are our true friends, as it seems to me.
So, sir, I do not wrong you on this score;
Reproach me with my poverty no more.
   "Now, sir, you tax me with my age; but, sir,
You gentlemen of breeding all aver   290
That men should not despise old age, but rather
Grant an old man respect, and call him 'father.'
   "If I am old and ugly, as you have said,
You have less fear of being cuckolded,
For ugliness and age, as all agree,   295
Are notable guardians of chastity.
But since I know in what you take delight,
I'll gratify your worldly appetite.
   "Choose now, which of two courses you will try:
To have me old and ugly till I die   300
But evermore your true and humble wife,
Never displeasing you in all my life,
Or will you have me rather young and fair
And take your chances on who may repair
Either to your house on account of me   305
Or to some other place, it well may be.
Now make your choice, whichever you prefer."
   The knight took thought, and sighed, and said to her
At last, "My love and lady, my dear wife,

---

7. A Roman philosopher.   8. A Roman poet.

In your wise government I put my life.   310
Choose for yourself which course will best agree
With pleasure and honor, both for you and me.
I do not care, choose either of the two;
I am content, whatever pleases you."

"Then have I won from you the sovereignty,   315
Since I may choose and rule at will?" said she.
    He answered, "That is best, I think, dear wife."
    "Kiss me," she said. "Now we are done with strife,
For on my word, I will be both to you,
That is to say, fair, yes, and faithful too.   320
May I die mad unless I am as true
As ever wife was since the world was new.
Unless I am as lovely to be seen
By morning as an empress or a queen
Or any lady between east and west,   325
Do with my life or death as you think best.
Lift up the curtain, see what you may see."
    And when the knight saw what had come to be
And knew her as she was, so young, so fair,
His joy was such that it was past compare.   330
He took her in his arms and gave her kisses
A thousand times on end; he bathed in blisses.
And she obeyed him also in full measure
In everything that tended to his pleasure.
    And so they lived in full joy to the end.   335
And now to all us women may Christ send
Submissive husbands, full of youth in bed,
And grace to outlive all the men we wed.
And I pray Jesus to cut short the lives
Of those who won't be governed by their wives;   340
And old, ill-tempered niggards who hate expense,
God promptly bring them down with pestilence!

The Pardoner's Prologue and Tale

Now my fine friend," he⁹ said, "you Pardoner,
Be quick, tell us a tale of mirth or fun."
    "St. Ninian!"¹ he said, "it shall be done,
But at this tavern here, before my tale,
I'll just go in and have some bread and ale."   5
    The proper pilgrims in our company
Cried quickly, "Let him speak no ribaldry!
Tell us a moral tale, one to make clear
Some lesson to us, and we'll gladly hear."
    "Just as you wish," he said. "I'll try to think   10
Of something edifying while I drink."

9. The Host; the Physician has just finished his tale.   1. A Scottish saint.

THE PROLOGUE

"In churches," said the Pardoner, "when I preach,
I use, milords, a lofty style of speech
And ring it out as roundly as a bell,
Knowing by rote all that I have to tell.
My text is ever the same, and ever was: 5
Radix malorum est cupiditas.[2]
    "First I inform them whence I come; that done,
I then display my papal bulls,[3] each one.
I show my license[4] first, my body's warrant,
Sealed by the bishop, for it would be abhorrent   10
If any man made bold, though priest or clerk,
To interrupt me in Christ's holy work.
And after that I give myself full scope.
Bulls in the name of cardinal and pope,
Of bishops and of patriarchs I show.   15
I say in Latin some few words or so
To spice my sermon; it flavors my appeal
And stirs my listeners to greater zeal.
Then I display my cases made of glass
Crammed to the top with rags and bones. They pass   20
For relics with all the people in the place.
I have a shoulder bone in a metal case,
Part of a sheep owned by a holy Jew.
'Good men,' I say, 'heed what I'm telling you:
Just let this bone be dipped in any well   25
And if cow, calf, or sheep, or ox should swell
From eating a worm, or by a worm be stung,
Take water from this well and wash its tongue
And it is healed at once. And furthermore
Of scab and ulcers and of every sore   30
Shall every sheep be cured, and that straightway,
That drinks from the same well. Heed what I say:
If the good man who owns the beasts will go,
Fasting, each week, and drink before cockcrow
Out of this well, his cattle shall be brought   35
To multiply—that holy Jew so taught
Our elders—and his property increase.
    " 'Moreover, sirs, this bone cures jealousies.
Though into a jealous madness a man fell,
Let him cook his soup in water from this well,   40
He'll never, though for truth he knew her sin,
Suspect his wife again, though she took in
A priest, or even two of them or three.
    " 'Now here's a mitten that you all can see.
Whoever puts his hand in it shall gain,   45
When he sows his land, increasing crops of grain,
Be it wheat or oats, provided that he bring

---

2. Avarice is the root of all evil (Latin).   3. Letters of indulgence, with the pope's seal (Latin *bulla*), which promise the purchaser release from some of the pains of purgatory.   4. A license from the bishop was required of all those who would preach in his diocese.

His penny or so to make his offering.
  " 'There is one word of warning I must say,
Good men and women. If any here today   50
Has done a sin so horrible to name
He daren't be shriven[5] of it for the shame,
Or if any woman, young or old, is here
Who has cuckolded her husband, be it clear
They may not make an offering in that case   55
To these my relics; they have no power nor grace.
But any who is free of such dire blame,
Let him come up and offer in God's name
And I'll absolve him through the authority
That by the pope's bull has been granted me.'   60
  "By such hornswoggling I've won, year by year,
A hundred marks[6] since being a pardoner.
I stand in my pulpit like a true divine,
And when the people sit I preach my line
To ignorant souls, as you have heard before,   65
And tell skullduggeries by the hundred more.
Then I take care to stretch my neck well out
And over the people I nod and peer about
Just like a dove perching on a shed.
My hands fly and my tongue wags in my head   70
So busily that to watch me is a joy.
Avarice is the theme that I employ
In all my sermons, to make the people free
In giving pennies—especially to me.
My mind is fixed on what I stand to win   75
And not at all upon correcting sin.
I do not care, when they are in the grave,
If souls go berry-picking that I could save.
Truth is that evil purposes determine,
And many a time, the origin of a sermon: 80
Some to please people and by flattery
To gain advancement through hypocrisy,
Some for vainglory, some again for hate.
For when I daren't fight otherwise, I wait
And give him a tongue-lashing when I preach.   85
No man escapes or gets beyond the reach
Of my defaming tongue, supposing he
Has done a wrong to my brethren or to me.
For though I do not tell his proper name,
People will recognize him all the same.   90
By sign and circumstance I let them learn.
Thus I serve those who have done us an ill turn.
Thus I spit out my venom under hue
Of sanctity, and seem devout and true!
  "But to put my purpose briefly, I confess   95
I preach for nothing but for covetousness.
That's why my text is still and ever was

Radix malorum est cupiditas.
For by this text I can denounce, indeed,
The very vice I practice, which is greed.   100
But though that sin is lodged in my own heart,
I am able to make other people part
From avarice, and sorely to repent,
Though that is not my principal intent.
    "Then I bring in examples, many a one,   105
And tell them many a tale of days long done.
Plain folk love tales that come down from of old.
Such things their minds can well report and hold.
Do you think that while I have the power to preach
And take in silver and gold for what I teach   110
I shall ever live in willful poverty?
No, no, that never was my thought, certainly.
I mean to preach and beg in sundry lands.
I won't do any labor with my hands,
Nor live by making baskets.[7] I don't intend   115
To beg for nothing; that is not my end.
I won't ape the apostles; I must eat,
I must have money, wool, and cheese, and wheat,
Though I took it from the meanest wretch's tillage
Or from the poorest widow in a village,   120
Yes, though her children starved for want. In fine,
I mean to drink the liquor of the vine
And have a jolly wench in every town.
But, in conclusion, lords, I will get down
To business: you would have me tell a tale.   125
Now that I've had a drink of corny ale,
By God, I hope the thing I'm going to tell
Is one that you'll have reason to like well.
For though myself a very sinful man,
I can tell a moral tale, indeed I can,   130
One that I use to bring the profits in
While preaching. Now be still, and I'll begin."

THE TALE

There was a company of young folk living
One time in Flanders, who were bent on giving
Their lives to follies and extravagances,
Brothels and taverns, where they held their dances
With lutes, harps, and guitars, diced at all hours,   5
And also ate and drank beyond their powers,
Through which they paid the devil sacrifice
In the devil's temple with their drink and dice,
Their abominable excess and dissipation.
They swore oaths that were worthy of damnation;   10
It was grisly to be listening when they swore.
The blessed body of our Lord they tore[8]—

7. A medieval tradition asserted that the apostle Paul was a basket maker.   8. They swore by the various parts of Christ's body (see line 171 for examples).

The Jews, it seemed to them, had failed to rend
His body enough—and each laughed at his friend
And fellow in sin. To encourage their pursuits   15
Came comely dancing girls, peddlers of fruits,
Singers with harps, bawds and confectioners
Who are the very devil's officers
To kindle and blow the fire of lechery
That is the follower of gluttony.   20
     Witness the Bible, if licentiousness
Does not reside in wine and drunkenness!
Recall how drunken Lot, unnaturally,
With his two daughters lay unwittingly,
So drunk he had no notion what he did.[9]   25
     Herod, the stories tell us, God forbid,
When full of liquor at his banquet board
Right at his very table gave the word
To kill the Baptist, John, though guiltless he.[1]
     Seneca says a good word, certainly.   30
He says there is no difference he can find
Between a man who has gone out of his mind
And one who carries drinking to excess,
Only that madness outlasts drunkenness.[2]
O gluttony, first cause of mankind's fall,[3]   35
Of our damnation the cursed original
Until Christ bought us with his blood again!
How dearly paid for by the race of men
Was this detestable iniquity!
This whole world was destroyed through gluttony.   40
     Adam our father and his wife also
From paradise to labor and to woe
Were driven for that selfsame vice, indeed.
As long as Adam fasted—so I read—
He was in heaven; but as soon as he   45
Devoured the fruit of that forbidden tree
Then he was driven out in sorrow and pain.
Of gluttony well ought we to complain!
Could a man know how many maladies
Follow indulgences and gluttonies   50
He would keep his diet under stricter measure
And sit at table with more temperate pleasure.
The throat is short and tender is the mouth,
And hence men toil east, west, and north, and south,
In earth, and air, and water—alas to think—   55
Fetching a glutton dainty meat and drink.
     This is a theme, O Paul, that you well treat:
"Meat unto belly, and belly unto meat,
God shall destroy them both," as Paul has said.[4]
When a man drinks the white wine and the red—   60
This is a foul word, by my soul, to say,

9. Genesis 19.33–35.   1. Matthew 14.1–11; Mark 6.14–28.   2. Seneca's *Epistles* 83.   3. Since the
Fall was caused by eating the forbidden fruit.   4. 1 Corinthians 6.13.

And fouler is the deed in every way—
He makes his throat his privy through excess.
   The Apostle says, weeping for piteousness,
"There are many of whom I told you—at a loss   65
I say it, weeping—enemies of Christ's cross,
Whose belly is their god; their end is death."[5]
O cursed belly! Sack of stinking breath
In which corruption lodges, dung abounds!
At either end of you come forth foul sounds.   70
Great cost it is to fill you, and great pain!
These cooks, how they must grind and pound and strain
And transform substance into accident[6]
To please your cravings, though exorbitant!
From the hard bones they knock the marrow out.   75
They'll find a use for everything, past doubt,
That down the gullet sweet and soft will glide.
The spiceries of leaf and root provide
Sauces that are concocted for delight,
To give a man a second appetite.   80
But truly, he whom gluttonies entice
Is dead, while he continues in that vice.
   O drunken man, disfigured is your face,
Sour is your breath, foul are you to embrace!
You seem to mutter through your drunken nose   85
The sound of "Samson, Samson," yet God knows
That Samson never indulged himself in wine.[7]
Your tongue is lost, you fall like a stuck swine,
And all the self-respect that you possess
Is gone, for of man's judgment, drunkenness   90
Is the very sepulcher and annihilation.
A man whom drink has under domination
Can never keep a secret in his head.
Now steer away from both the white and red,
And most of all from that white wine keep wide   95
That comes from Lepe.[8] They sell it in Cheapside
And Fish Street.[9] It's a Spanish wine, and sly
To creep in other wines that grow nearby,
And such a vapor it has that with three drinks
It takes a man to Spain; although he thinks   100
He is home in Cheapside, he is far away
At Lepe. Then "Samson, Samson" will he say!
   By God himself, who is omnipotent,
All the great exploits in the Old Testament
Were done in abstinence, I say, and prayer.   105
Look in the Bible, you may learn it there.
   Attila,[1] conqueror of many a place,
Died in his sleep in shame and in disgrace
Bleeding out of his nose in drunkenness.
A captain ought to live in temperateness!   110

---

5. Philippians 3.18–19.   6. A distinction was made in philosophy between *substance*, the real nature of a thing, and *accident*, its merely sensory qualities, such as flavor.   7. Judges 13.4.   8. A town in Spain noted for strong wines.   9. London streets.   1. Leader of the Hun invasion of Europe, 5th century.

And more than this, I say, remember well
The injunction that was laid on Lemuel[2]—
Not Samuel, but Lemuel, I say!
Read in the Bible; in the plainest way
Wine is forbidden to judges and to kings.   115
This will suffice; no more upon these things.
    Now that I've shown what gluttony will do,
Now I will warn you against gambling, too;
Gambling, the very mother of low scheming,
Of lying and forswearing and blaspheming   120
Against Christ's name, of murder and waste as well
Alike of goods and time; and, truth to tell,
With honor and renown it cannot suit
To be held a common gambler by repute.
The higher a gambler stands in power and place,   125
The more his name is lowered in disgrace.
If a prince gambles, whatever his kingdom be,
In his whole government and policy
He is, in all the general estimation,
Considered so much less in reputation.   130
    Stilbon,[3] who was a wise ambassador,
From Lacedaemon once to Corinth bore
A mission of alliance. When he came
It happened that he found there at a game
Of hazard all the great ones of the land,   135
And so, as quickly as it could be planned,
He stole back, saying, "I will not lose my name
Nor have my reputation put to shame
Allying you with gamblers. You may send
Other wise emissaries to gain your end,   140
For by my honor, rather than ally
My countrymen to gamblers, I will die.
For you that are so gloriously renowned
Shall never with this gambling race be bound
By will of mine or treaty I prepare."   145
Thus did this wise philosopher declare.
    Remember also how the Parthians' lord
Sent King Demetrius, as the books record,
A pair of golden dice, by this proclaiming
His scorn, because that king was known for gaming,   150
And the king of Parthia therefore held his crown
Devoid of glory, value, or renown.
Lords can discover other means of play
More suitable to while the time away.
    Now about oaths I'll say a word or two,   155
Great oaths and false oaths, as the old books do.
Great swearing is a thing abominable,
And false oaths yet more reprehensible.
Almighty God forbade swearing at all,

---

2. Proverbs 31.4–7.   3. Chaucer adapted this and the next story—both fictitious—from a 12th-century work.

Matthew be witness;[4] but specially I call   160
The holy Jeremiah on this head.
"Swear thine oaths truly, do not lie," he said.
"Swear under judgment, and in righteousness."[5]
But idle swearing is a great wickedness.
Consult and see, and he that understands   165
In the first table of the Lord's commands
Will find the second of his commandments this:
"Take not the Lord's name idly or amiss."[6]
If a man's oaths and curses are extreme,
Vengeance shall find his house, both roof and beam.   170
"By the precious heart of God," and "By his nails"—
"My chance is seven,[7] by Christ's blood at Hailes,[8]
Yours five and three." "Cheat me, and if you do,
By God's arms, with this knife I'll run you through!"—
Such fruit comes from the bones,[9] that pair of bitches: 175
Oaths broken, treachery, murder. For the riches
Of Christ's love, give up curses, without fail,
Both great and small!—Now, sirs, I'll tell my tale.
    These three young roisterers of whom I tell
Long before prime had rung from any bell   180
Were seated in a tavern at their drinking,
And as they sat, they heard a bell go clinking
Before a corpse being carried to his grave.
One of these roisterers, when he heard it, gave
An order to his boy: "Go out and try   185
To learn whose corpse is being carried by.
Get me his name, and get it right. Take heed."
    "Sir," said the boy, "there isn't any need.
I learned before you came here, by two hours.
He was, it happens, an old friend of yours,   190
And all at once, there on his bench upright
As he was sitting drunk, he was killed last night.
A sly thief, Death men call him, who deprives
All the people in this country of their lives,
Came with his spear and smiting his heart in two   195
Went on his business with no more ado.
A thousand have been slaughtered by his hand
During this plague. And, sir, before you stand
Within his presence, it should be necessary,
It seems to me, to know your adversary.   200
Be evermore prepared to meet this foe.
My mother taught me thus; that's all I know."
    "Now by St. Mary," said the innkeeper,
"This child speaks truth. Man, woman, laborer,
Servant, and child the thief has slain this year   205
In a big village a mile or more from here.
I think it is his place of habitation.
It would be wise to make some preparation

---

4. Matthew 5.34.   **5.** Jeremiah 4.2.   **6.** Exodus 20.7.   **7.** I.e., "My number is seven."   **8.** An abbey in Gloucestershire, where some of Christ's blood was believed to be preserved.   **9.** Dice.

Before he brought a man into disgrace."
    "God's arms!" this roisterer said. "So that's the case!   210
Is it so dangerous with this thief to meet?
I'll look for him by every path and street,
I vow it, by God's holy bones! Hear me,
Fellows of mine, we are all one, we three.
Let each of us hold up his hand to the other   215
And each of us become his fellow's brother.
We'll slay this Death, who slaughters and betrays.
He shall be slain whose hand so many slays,
By the dignity of God, before tonight!"
    The three together set about to plight   220
Their oaths to live and die each for the other
Just as though each had been to each born brother,
And in their drunken frenzy up they get
And toward the village off at once they set
Which the innkeeper had spoken of before,   225
And many were the grisly oaths they swore.
They rent Christ's precious body limb from limb—
Death shall be dead, if they lay hands on him!
    When they had hardly gone the first half mile,
Just as they were about to cross a stile,   230
An old man, poor and humble, met them there.
The old man greeted them with a meek air
And said, "God bless you, lords, and be your guide."
    "What's this?" the proudest of the three replied.
"Old beggar, I hope you meet with evil grace!   235
Why are you all wrapped up except your face?
What are you doing alive so many a year?"
    The old man at these words began to peer
Into this gambler's face. "Because I can,
Though I should walk to India, find no man,"   240
He said, "in any village or any town,
Who for my age is willing to lay down
His youth. So I must keep my old age still
For as long a time as it may be God's will.
Nor will Death take my life from me, alas!   245
Thus like a restless prisoner I pass
And on the ground, which is my mother's gate,
I walk and with my staff both early and late
I knock and say, 'Dear mother, let me in!
See how I vanish, flesh, and blood, and skin!   250
Alas, when shall my bones be laid to rest?
I would exchange with you my clothing chest,
Mother, that in my chamber long has been
For an old haircloth rag to wrap me in.'
And yet she still refuses me that grace.   255
All white, therefore, and withered is my face.
    "But, sirs, you do yourselves no courtesy
To speak to an old man so churlishly
Unless he had wronged you either in word or deed.
As you yourselves in Holy Writ may read,   260

'Before an aged man whose head is hoar
Men ought to rise.'[1] I counsel you, therefore,
No harm nor wrong here to an old man do,
No more than you would have men do to you
In your old age, if you so long abide.   265
And God be with you, whether you walk or ride!
I must go yonder where I have to go."
  "No, you old beggar, by St. John, not so,"
Said another of these gamblers. "As for me,
By God, you won't get off so easily!   270
You spoke just now of that false traitor, Death,
Who in this land robs all our friends of breath.
Tell where he is, since you must be his spy,
Or you will suffer for it, so say I
By God and by the holy sacrament.   275
You are in league with him, false thief, and bent
On killing us young folk, that's clear to my mind."
  "If you are so impatient, sirs, to find
Death," he replied, "turn up this crooked way,
For in that grove I left him, truth to say,   280
Beneath a tree, and there he will abide.
No boast of yours will make him run and hide.
Do you see that oak tree? Just there you will find
This Death, and God, who bought again mankind,
Save and amend you!" So said this old man;   285
And promptly each of these three gamblers ran
Until he reached the tree, and there they found
Florins of fine gold, minted bright and round,
Nearly eight bushels of them, as they thought.
And after Death no longer then they sought.   290
Each of them was so ravished at the sight,
So fair the florins glittered and so bright,
That down they sat beside the precious hoard.
The worst of them, he uttered the first word.
  "Brothers," he told them, "listen to what I say.   295
My head is sharp, for all I joke and play.
Fortune has given us this pile of treasure
To set us up in lives of ease and pleasure.
Lightly it comes, lightly we'll make it go.
God's precious dignity! Who was to know   300
We'd ever tumble on such luck today?
If we could only carry this gold away,
Home to my house, or either one of yours—
For well you know that all this gold is ours—
We'd touch the summit of felicity.   305
But still, by daylight that can hardly be.
People would call us thieves, too bold for stealth,
And they would have us hanged for our own wealth.
It must be done by night, that's our best plan,
As prudently and slyly as we can.   310

1. Leviticus 19.32.

Hence my proposal is that we should all
Draw lots, and let's see where the lot will fall,
And the one of us who draws the shortest stick
Shall run back to the town, and make it quick,
And bring us bread and wine here on the sly,   315
And two of us will keep a watchful eye
Over this gold; and if he doesn't stay
Too long in town, we'll carry this gold away
By night, wherever we all agree it's best."
   One of them held the cut out in his fist   320
And had them draw to see where it would fall,
And the cut fell on the youngest of them all.
At once he set off on his way to town,
And the very moment after he was gone
The one who urged this plan said to the other: 325
"You know that by sworn oath you are my brother.
I'll tell you something you can profit by.
Our friend has gone, that's clear to any eye,
And here is gold, abundant as can be,
That we propose to share alike, we three.   330
But if I worked it out, as I could do,
So that it could be shared between us two,
Wouldn't that be a favor, a friendly one?"
   The other answered, "How that can be done,
I don't quite see. He knows we have the gold.   335
What shall we do, or what shall he be told?"
   "Will you keep the secret tucked inside your head?
And in a few words," the first scoundrel said,
"I'll tell you how to bring this end about."
   "Granted," the other told him. "Never doubt,   340
I won't betray you, that you can believe."
   "Now," said the first, "we are two, as you perceive,
And two of us must have more strength than one.
When he sits down, get up as if in fun
And wrestle with him. While you play this game   345
I'll run him through the ribs. You do the same
With your dagger there, and then this gold shall be
Divided, dear friend, between you and me.
Then all that we desire we can fulfill,
And both of us can roll the dice at will."   350
Thus in agreement these two scoundrels fell
To slay the third, as you have heard me tell.
   The youngest, who had started off to town,
Within his heart kept rolling up and down
The beauty of those florins, new and bright.   355
"O Lord," he thought, "were there some way I might
Have all this treasure to myself alone,
There isn't a man who dwells beneath God's throne
Could live a life as merry as mine should be!"
And so at last the fiend, our enemy,   360
Put in his head that he could gain his ends
If he bought poison to kill off his friends.

Finding his life in such a sinful state,
The devil was allowed to seal his fate.
For it was altogether his intent   365
To kill his friends, and never to repent.
So off he set, no longer would he tarry,
Into the town, to an apothecary,
And begged for poison; he wanted it because
He meant to kill his rats; besides, there was   370
A polecat living in his hedge, he said,
Who killed his capons; and when he went to bed
He wanted to take vengeance, if he might,
On vermin that devoured him by night.
   The apothecary answered, "You shall have   375
A drug that as I hope the Lord will save
My soul, no living thing in all creation,
Eating or drinking of this preparation
A dose no bigger than a grain of wheat,
But promptly with his death-stroke he shall meet.   380
Die, that he will, and in a briefer while
Than you can walk the distance of a mile,
This poison is so strong and virulent."
   Taking the poison, off the scoundrel went,
Holding it in a box, and next he ran   385
To the neighboring street, and borrowed from a man
Three generous flagons. He emptied out his drug
In two of them, and kept the other jug
For his own drink; he let no poison lurk
In that! And so all night he meant to work   390
Carrying off the gold. Such was his plan,
And when he had filled them, this accursed man
Retraced his path, still following his design,
Back to his friends with his three jugs of wine.
   But why dilate upon it any more?   395
For just as they had planned his death before,
Just so they killed him, and with no delay.
When it was finished, one spoke up to say:
"Now let's sit down and drink, and we can bury
His body later on. First we'll be merry,"   400
And as he said the words, he took the jug
That, as it happened, held the poisonous drug,
And drank, and gave his friend a drink as well,
And promptly they both died. But truth to tell,
In all that Avicenna[2] ever wrote   405
He never described in chapter, rule, or note
More marvelous signs of poisoning, I suppose,
Than appeared in these two wretches at the close.
Thus they both perished for their homicide,
And thus the traitorous poisoner also died.   410
   O sin accursed above all cursedness,
O treacherous murder, O foul wickedness,

2. An Arab physician.

O gambling, lustfulness, and gluttony,
Traducer of Christ's name by blasphemy
And monstrous oaths, through habit and through pride! 415
Alas, mankind! Ah, how may it betide
That you to your Creator, he that wrought you
And even with his precious heart's blood bought you,
So falsely and ungratefully can live?
  And now, good men, your sins may God forgive 420
And keep you specially from avarice!
My holy pardon will avail in this,
For it can heal each one of you that brings
His pennies, silver brooches, spoons, or rings.
Come, bow your head under this holy bull! 425
You wives, come offer up your cloth or wool!
I write your names here in my roll, just so.
Into the bliss of heaven you shall go!
I will absolve you here by my high power,[3]
You that will offer, as clean as in the hour 430
When you were born.—Sirs, thus I preach. And now
Christ Jesus, our souls' healer, show you how
Within his pardon evermore to rest,
For that, I will not lie to you, is best.
  But in my tale, sirs, I forgot one thing. 435
The relics and the pardons that I bring
Here in my pouch, no man in the whole land
Has finer, given me by the pope's own hand.
If any of you devoutly wants to offer
And have my absolution, come and proffer 440
Whatever you have to give. Kneel down right here,
Humbly, and take my pardon, full and clear,
Or have a new, fresh pardon if you like
At the end of every mile of road we strike,
As long as you keep offering ever newly 445
Good coins, not counterfeit, but minted truly.
Indeed it is an honor I confer
On each of you, an authentic pardoner
Going along to absolve you as you ride.
For in the country mishaps may betide— 450
One or another of you in due course
May break his neck by falling from his horse.
Think what security it gives you all
That in this company I chanced to fall
Who can absolve you each, both low and high, 455
When the soul, alas, shall from the body fly!
By my advice, our Host here shall begin,
For he's the man enveloped most by sin.
Come, offer first, Sir Host, and once that's done,
Then you shall kiss the relics, every one, 460
Yes, for a penny! Come, undo your purse!

---

3. The Pardoner is overstating the effect of his indulgences, which can promise relief only from punishment of sin, not from its guilt. According to medieval doctrine, full absolution can be provided only by Christ.

"No, no," said he. "Then I should have Christ's curse!
I'll do nothing of the sort, for love or riches!
You'd make me kiss a piece of your old britches
And for a saintly relic make it pass   465
Although it had the tincture of your ass.
By the cross St. Helen[4] found in the Holy Land,
I wish I had your balls here in my hand
For relics! Cut 'em off, and I'll be bound
If I don't help you carry them around.   470
I'll have the things enshrined in a hog's turd!"
   The Pardoner did not answer; not a word,
He was so angry, could he find to say.
   "Now," said our Host, "I will not try to play
With you, nor any other angry man."   475
   Immediately the worthy Knight began,
When he saw that all the people laughed, "No more,
This has gone far enough. Now as before,
Sir Pardoner, be gay, look cheerfully,
And you, Sir Host, who are so dear to me,   480
Come, kiss the Pardoner, I beg of you,
And Pardoner, draw near, and let us do
As we've been doing, let us laugh and play."
And so they kissed, and rode along their way.

4. Mother of Constantine the Great; believed to have found the True Cross.

THE THOUSAND AND ONE NIGHTS
fourteenth century

The Thousand and One Nights is rich in paradoxes. An anonymous work, it is nevertheless more widely known in the Arab world than any other work of Arabic literature.
It is almost as well known in Europe, and so far is the only work of Arabic letters to
become a permanent part of European and, indeed, of world literature. Despite this
great popularity, and despite its shaping influence on modern literature, traditional
Arabic literary scholars have never recognized it as a work of serious literature, and
it is still occasionally banned as immoral by Arab governments.

   The history of *The Thousand and One Nights* is vague, and its shape as hard to pin
down as a cloud's. The starting point of the work in Arabic was probably a collection
of tales in Middle Persian called the "thousand stories" that had been translated or
adapted from Sanskrit in the time of the Sassanids (226–652), the last pre-Islamic
Iranian dynasty. During the ninth and tenth centuries a great deal of Persian literature, both popular and courtly, was translated into Arabic, particularly at the caliphal
court in Baghdad. The tales that became the core of the *Nights* were probably among
them. The Perso-Indian origins of the prologue and other tales are suggested by the
Persian personal names—Shahrayar, Shahzaman, Shahrazad—and place names—
Indochina, Samarkand—of the prologue. Stories set in the Baghdad of the late eighth
century—those that mention the caliph Haroun al-Rashid and his vizier Ja'far the

Barmakid, for instance—indicate that the original translator, or later copyists, felt free to add local tales to the originals. From Baghdad, manuscripts of this original translation circulated widely to other parts of the Islamic world, especially Syria and Egypt. The tales were also transmitted orally and adapted and translated into other languages of the region. Indeed, the initial translation into Arabic may have been an oral one—the work of a Persian storyteller who came to the great metropolis of Baghdad and adapted his wares to the language of his audience. What we know for certain is that written and oral transmissions of the tales have intermingled down to the present day. Oral versions were written down and written tales were memorized and added to oral repertories.

We can discern two quite distinct branches in the written transmission of the *Nights*. The earliest surviving manuscript, which dates from fourteenth-century Syria, belongs to the more conservative branch. Later manuscripts derived from it adhere closely to it in substance, form, and style. Others, known collectively as the Egyptian branch, depart widely from it, deleting some of the original stories and adding others from Indian, Persian, Turkish, and Egyptian sources. The story of Sindbad is one of the earliest such additions, and that of Aladdin and the magic lamp one of the latest. At times it seems that the copyists were determined to expand the number of tales to fit the fanciful "one thousand and one" of the title. The first European translator of the *Nights*, the French scholar and traveler Jean Antoine Galland (1646–1715), followed the example of the copyists in the Egyptian branch, translating whatever stories he could find. The great success of his work encouraged other European translators, notably Sir Richard Burton (1821–1890), to do likewise. Some of the tales that Galland and Burton translated from oral sources were retranslated from French or English back into Arabic for new Arabic printings of the *Nights*, and the original character of the *Nights* was distorted almost beyond recognition. The first scholarly edition of *The Thousand and One Nights*, the first, that is, to be based on the fourteenth-century Syrian manuscript, was completed only in 1984, and the selection printed here was translated from it.

From the very beginning classical Arabic literature was unable to find a place for the *Nights*. It was a work neither of history nor of useful knowledge and moral instruction. It was not composed in an elegant, poetic style but in ordinary prose that was very close to common speech. It was filled with magical and fantastic stories that were clearly untrue. While such extravagant and improbable fabrications might be tolerated in poetry, they were unacceptable in a work of prose, since prose was expected to be more serious and substantial than poetry. The qualities that exclude the *Nights* from the canon of classical Arabic are, of course, the very ones that ensure its wide popular acceptance. It is a brilliantly entertaining work, and its stories vary from lighthearted and frivolous to touchingly romantic or terrifying and painful. The themes set forth in the prologue—lust, madness, violence, justice, retribution, and heroism—are weighty ones, and they are grounded in the stuff of everyday life. But they are told with great artistry and made magical by luxurious settings, fantastic adventures, magical turns of fortune, and the timely intervention of demons and sorcerers.

THE PROLOGUE: THE STORY OF THE MERCHANT AND THE DEMON

In the *Prologue*, Shahrayar is a monarch driven mad by the infidelity of his wife. To ensure that another such humiliation will not occur, he has decided to marry a new young woman each night and murder her the next morning—before she has a chance to betray him. Three years pass in this way and Shahrayar has drastically depleted the number of marriageable young women in the kingdom. His chief vizier has been unable to think of a way to dissuade his monarch from this mad, self-destructive policy, but the vizier's elder daughter, Shahrazad, a young woman of exceptional learning and courage, has a plan. She will voluntarily marry Shahrayar and then use her skill as a storyteller to manipulate him into deferring her death endlessly. Her father tries, unsuccessfully, to dissuade her by telling her tales that are both irrelevant and unpersuasive, but she launches her scheme with the help of her sister, Dinarzad. Each night Shahrazad tells Shahrayar stories to while away the long hours, stopping each sunrise just before some crisis and counting on Shahrayar's eagerness to hear the end of the story to dissuade him from having her executed. In this way, she is able to hold his murderous impulses in check until the passage of time and the healing effect of the tales can do their work, and Shahrayar at last pardons her and abandons his policy.

To Western readers, the *Nights* most resembles such other famous collections of tales as Chaucer's *Canterbury Tales*, Boccaccio's *Decameron*, and Marguerite de Navarre's *Heptameron*. Like these, its tales are set within the frame of another, larger tale. The prologue of the *Nights* does not surround or frame the tales it includes, however. There are examples of such framed collections within the *Nights*, starting with the first set that Shahrazad recites, but the *Prologue* is a frame tale with a difference. It has a single narrator, not many; and as a consequence there is none of the interplay between narrators, or between narrators and the tales they tell, that marks these other collections. That is, while there are many narrators, and tales within tales, all the stories are ultimately recounted by Shahrazad. Moreover, her motive throughout is the single and compelling one of preventing the destruction of herself and the other young women of her community. The formulaic exchange among Shahrazad, Shahrayar, and Dinarzad that is repeated each dawn and evening reminds us that Shahrazad is not telling tales simply to while away the time.

The image of Shahrazad deftly employing her skills as a narrator to buy her life a day at a time has captured the fancy of all who have read the *Nights*, but there may be more to her tales than an endlessly deferred conclusion. That is, her tales can also be read as a means of healing the wound inflicted on Shahrayar by his wife's infidelity, and of teaching him that not all women wish him ill. That she may have cure in mind as much as delay is suggested by the neat fit between the first set of tales she tells and her own plight. In the first story, for example, a demon sets a precedent for allowing Shahrazad to purchase her life with her tales by allowing three old men to pay the merchant's blood price with theirs. This story also suggests that the demon is too harsh in threatening to kill the merchant for a crime that is at worst accidental. How much more innocent of any wrongdoing are the young women of Shahrayar's realm? In each of the tales a benign but powerful woman undoes the harm caused by an ill-intentioned one. The wicked characters are punished according to their crimes, and never by death. All this suggests that Shahrazad is not simply distracting Shahrayar with her tales, she is educating him or, better, attempting to cure him of his madness. Her choice of a cure may suggest that these tales were shaped by female narrators as well as male or at least by narrators who had an understanding and appreciation of women. A more characteristically male solution to the problem that Shahrayar poses might have been to depose or destroy him.

THE FISHERMAN AND THE DEMON

Shahrazad's second series of tales falls into two parts. In the first, the fisherman and the jinn are, as the title promises, the principals. In the second, the demon vanishes from the stage entirely, and the fisherman moves into a supporting role. The focus of the first set of stories is a battle of wits between fisherman and demon. The injustice of the demon's plan to kill the blameless fisherman provides both the recurrent theme of the tales that the fisherman and the demon tell and the principal link between these stories and those of the three old men. Yet the links between them seem more tenuous, and the story of the deceitful wife actually celebrates fraud as a means of escaping just retribution. The *Tale of the Enchanted King*, however, which makes up the whole of the second narrative, draws us once more back into the world of Shahrayar and Shahrazad. The cruel sorceress queen, her deformed lover, and the innocent king immediately suggest the story that sets the *Nights* in motion. The one important change in this narrative structure is the substitution of a good man for a good woman as the agent whereby justice is done and the king and his kingdom are returned to health.

PRONOUNCING GLOSSARY

The following list uses common English syllables and stress accents to provide rough equivalents of selected words whose pronunciation may be unfamiliar to the general reader.

Dinarzad: *dee-nar-zahd'*

Haroun al-Rashid: *ha-roon'ar—ra-sheed'*

Ja'far the Barmakid: *juh-far' the bar'-muh-kid*

Sa'd al-Din Mas'ud: *sad' ad—deen mass-ood'*

Shahrazad: *shah-ruh-zahd'*

Shahrayar: *shah-ruh-yahr'*

Shahzaman: *shah-zuh-mahn'*

From The Thousand and One Nights[1]

Prologue

[*The Story of King Shahrayar and Shahrazad, His Vizier's[2] Daughter*]

It is related—but God knows and sees best what lies hidden in the old accounts of bygone peoples and times—that long ago, during the time of the Sasanid dynasty,[3] in the peninsulas of India and Indochina, there lived two kings who were brothers. The older brother was named Shahrayar, the younger Shahzaman. The older, Shahrayar, was a towering knight and a daring champion, invincible, energetic, and implacable. His power reached the remotest corners of the land and its people, so that the country was loyal to him, and his subjects obeyed him. Shahrayar himself lived and ruled in India and Indochina, while to his brother he gave the land of Samarkand[4] to rule as king.

Ten years went by, when one day Shahrayar felt a longing for his brother the king, summoned his vizier (who had two daughters, one called Shahrazad, the other Dinarzad) and bade him go to his brother. Having made preparations, the vizier journeyed day and night until he reached Samarkand. When Shahzaman heard of the vizier's arrival, he went out with his retainers to meet him. He dismounted, embraced him, and asked him for news from his older brother, Shahrayar. The vizier replied that he was well, and that he had sent him to request his brother to visit him. Shahzaman complied with his brother's request and proceeded to make preparations for the journey. In the meantime, he had the vizier camp on the outskirts of the city, and took care of his needs. He sent him what he required of food and fodder, slaugh-

---

1. All selections translated by Husain Haddawy except for *The Third Old Man's Tale*, translated by Jerome W. Clinton.   2. One who bears burdens (literal trans.); the highest state official or administrator under a caliph or shah.   3. The last pre-Islamic dynasty (226–652).   4. A city and province in central Asia, now in Uzbekistan.

tered many sheep in his honor, and provided him with money and supplies, as well as many horses and camels.

For ten full days he prepared himself for the journey; then he appointed a chamberlain in his place, and left the city to spend the night in his tent, near the vizier. At midnight he returned to his palace in the city, to bid his wife good-bye. But when he entered the palace, he found his wife lying in the arms of one of the kitchen boys. When he saw them, the world turned dark before his eyes and, shaking his head, he said to himself, "I am still here, and this is what she has done when I was barely outside the city. How will it be and what will happen behind my back when I go to visit my brother in India? No. Women are not to be trusted." He got exceedingly angry, adding, "By God, I am king and sovereign in Samarkand, yet my wife has betrayed me and has inflicted this on me." As his anger boiled, he drew his sword and struck both his wife and the cook. Then he dragged them by the heels and threw them from the top of the palace to the trench below. He then left the city and going to the vizier ordered that they depart that very hour. The drum was struck, and they set out on their journey, while Shahzaman's heart was on fire because of what his wife had done to him and how she had betrayed him with some cook, some kitchen boy. They journeyed hurriedly, day and night, through deserts and wilds, until they reached the land of King Shahrayar, who had gone out to receive them.

When Shahrayar met them, he embraced his brother, showed him favors, and treated him generously. He offered him quarters in a palace adjoining his own, for King Shahrayar had built two beautiful towering palaces in his garden, one for the guests, the other for the women and members of his household. He gave the guest house to his brother, Shahzaman, after the attendants had gone to scrub it, dry it, furnish it, and open its windows, which overlooked the garden. Thereafter, Shahzaman would spend the whole day at his brother's, return at night to sleep at the palace, then go back to his brother the next morning. But whenever he found himself alone and thought of his ordeal with his wife, he would sigh deeply, then stifle his grief, and say, "Alas, that this great misfortune should have happened to one in my position!" Then he would fret with anxiety, his spirit would sag, and he would say, "None has seen what I have seen." In his depression, he ate less and less, grew pale, and his health deteriorated. He neglected everything, wasted away, and looked ill.

When King Shahrayar looked at his brother and saw how day after day he lost weight and grew thin, pale, ashen, and sickly, he thought that this was because of his expatriation and homesickness for his country and his family, and he said to himself, "My brother is not happy here. I should prepare a goodly gift for him and send him home." For a month he gathered gifts for his brother; then he invited him to see him and said, "Brother, I would like you to know that I intend to go hunting and pursue the roaming deer, for ten days. Then I shall return to prepare you for your journey home. Would you like to go hunting with me?" Shahzaman replied, "Brother, I feel distracted and depressed. Leave me here and go with God's blessing and help." When Shahrayar heard his brother, he thought that his dejection was because of his homesickness for his country. Not wishing to coerce him, he left him behind, and set out with his retainers and men. When they entered the wilderness, he deployed his men in a circle to begin trapping and hunting.

After his brother's departure, Shahzaman stayed in the palace and, from the window overlooking the garden, watched the birds and trees as he thought of his wife and what she had done to him, and sighed in sorrow. While he agonized over his misfortune, gazing at the heavens and turning a distracted eye on the garden, the private gate of his brother's palace opened, and there emerged, strutting like a dark-eyed deer, the lady, his brother's wife, with twenty slave-girls, ten white and ten black. While Shahzaman looked at them, without being seen, they continued to walk until they stopped below his window, without looking in his direction, thinking that he had gone to the hunt with his brother. Then they sat down, took off their clothes, and suddenly there were ten slave-girls and ten black slaves dressed in the same clothes as the girls. Then the ten black slaves mounted the ten girls, while the lady called, "Mas'ud, Mas'ud!" and a black slave jumped from the tree to the ground, rushed to her, and, raising her legs, went between her thighs and made love to her. Mas'ud topped the lady, while the ten slaves topped the ten girls, and they carried on till noon. When they were done with their business, they got up and washed themselves. Then the ten slaves put on the same clothes again, mingled with the girls, and once more there appeared to be twenty slave-girls. Mas'ud himself jumped over the garden wall and disappeared, while the slave-girls and the lady sauntered to the private gate, went in and, locking the gate behind them, went their way.

All of this happened under King Shahzaman's eyes. When he saw this spectacle of the wife and the women of his brother the great king—how ten slaves put on women's clothes and slept with his brother's paramours and concubines and what Mas'ud did with his brother's wife, in his very palace—and pondered over this calamity and great misfortune, his care and sorrow left him and he said to himself, "This is our common lot. Even though my brother is king and master of the whole world, he cannot protect what is his, his wife and his concubines, and suffers misfortune in his very home. What happened to me is little by comparison. I used to think that I was the only one who has suffered, but from what I have seen, everyone suffers. By God, my misfortune is lighter than that of my brother." He kept marveling and blaming life, whose trials none can escape, and he began to find consolation in his own affliction and forget his grief. When supper came, he ate and drank with relish and zest and, feeling better, kept eating and drinking, enjoying himself and feeling happy. He thought to himself, "I am no longer alone in my misery; I am well."

For ten days, he continued to enjoy his food and drink, and when his brother, King Shahrayar, came back from the hunt, he met him happily, treated him attentively, and greeted him cheerfully. His brother, King Shahrayar, who had missed him, said, "By God, brother, I missed you on this trip and wished you were with me." Shahzaman thanked him and sat down to carouse with him, and when night fell, and food was brought before them, the two ate and drank, and again Shahzaman ate and drank with zest. As time went by, he continued to eat and drink with appetite, and became lighthearted and carefree. His face regained color and became ruddy, and his body gained weight, as his blood circulated and he regained his energy; he was himself again, or even better. King Shahrayar noticed his brother's condition, how he used to be and how he had improved, but kept it to himself until he took him aside one day and said, "My brother Shahzaman, I would like you to do something for me, to satisfy a wish, to answer a question truthfully." Shahzaman asked, "What is it, brother?" He replied, "When you first came to stay with me, I noticed that you kept losing weight, day after day, until your looks changed, your health deteriorated, and your energy sagged. As you continued like this, I thought that what ailed you was your homesickness for your family and your country, but even though I kept noticing that you were wasting away and looking ill, I refrained from questioning you and hid my feelings from you. Then I went hunting, and when I came back, I found that you had recovered and had regained your health. Now I want you to tell me everything and to explain the cause of your deterioration and the cause of your subsequent recovery, without hiding anything from me." When Shahzaman heard what King Shahrayar said, he bowed his head, then said, "As for the cause of my recovery, that I cannot tell you, and I wish that you would excuse me from telling you." The king was greatly astonished at his brother's reply and, burning with curiosity, said, "You must tell me. For now, at least, explain the first cause."

Then Shahzaman related to his brother what happened to him with his own wife, on the night of his departure, from beginning to end, and concluded, "Thus all the while I was with you, great King, whenever I thought of the event and the misfortune that had befallen me, I felt troubled, careworn, and unhappy, and my health deteriorated. This then is the cause." Then he grew silent. When King Shahrayar heard his brother's explanation, he shook his head, greatly amazed at the deceit of women, and prayed to God to protect him from their wickedness, saying, "Brother, you were fortunate in killing your wife and her lover, who gave you good reason to feel troubled, careworn, and ill. In my opinion, what happened to you has never happened to anyone else. By God, had I been in your place, I would have killed at least a hundred or even a thousand women. I would have been furious; I would have gone mad. Now praise be to God who has delivered you from sorrow and distress. But tell me what has caused you to forget your sorrow and regain your health?" Shahzaman replied, "King, I wish that for God's sake you would excuse me from telling you." Shahrayar said, "You must." Shahzaman replied, "I fear that you will feel even more troubled and careworn than I." Shahrayar asked, "How could that be, brother? I insist on hearing your explanation."

Shahzaman then told him about what he had seen from the palace window and the calamity in his very home—how ten slaves, dressed like women, were sleeping with his women and concubines, day and night. He told him everything from beginning to end (but there is no point in repeating that). Then he concluded, "When I saw your own misfortune, I felt better—and said to myself, 'My brother is king of the world, yet such a misfortune has happened to him, and in his very home.' As a result I forgot my care and sorrow, relaxed, and began to eat and drink. This is the cause of my cheer and good spirits."

When King Shahrayar heard what his brother said and found out what had happened to him, he was furious and his blood boiled. He said, "Brother, I can't believe what you say unless I see it with my own eyes." When Shahzaman saw that his brother was in a rage, he said to him, "If you do not believe me, unless you see your misfortune with your own eyes, announce that you plan to go hunting. Then you and I shall set out with your troops, and when we get outside the city, we shall leave our tents and camp with the men behind, enter the city secretly, and go together to your palace. Then the next morning you can see with your own eyes."

King Shahrayar realized that his brother had a good plan and ordered his army to prepare for the trip. He spent the night with his brother, and when God's morning broke, the two rode out of the city with their army, preceded by the camp attendants, who had gone to drive the poles and pitch the tents where the king and his army were to camp. At nightfall King Shahrayar summoned his chief chamberlain and bade him take his place. He entrusted him with the army and ordered that for three days no one was to enter the city. Then he and his brother disguised themselves and entered the city in the dark. They went directly to the palace where Shahzaman resided and slept there till the morning. When they awoke, they sat at the palace window, watching the garden and chatting, until the light broke, the day dawned, and the sun rose. As they watched, the private gate opened, and there emerged as usual the wife of King Shahrayar, walking among twenty slave-girls. They made their way under the trees until they stood below the palace window where the two kings sat. Then they took off their women's clothes, and suddenly there were ten slaves, who mounted the ten girls and made love to them. As for the lady, she called, "Mas'ud, Mas'ud," and a black slave jumped from the tree to the ground, came to her, and said, "What do you want, you slut? Here is Sa'ad al-Din Mas'ud." She laughed and fell on her back, while the slave mounted her and like the others did his business with her. Then the black slaves got up, washed themselves, and, putting on the same clothes, mingled with the girls. Then they walked away, entered the palace, and locked the gate behind them. As for Mas'ud, he jumped over the fence to the road and went on his way.

When King Shahrayar saw the spectacle of his wife and the slave-girls, he went out of his mind, and when he and his brother came down from upstairs, he said, "No one is safe in this world. Such doings are going on in my kingdom, and in my very palace. Perish the world and perish life! This is a great calamity, indeed." Then he turned to his brother and asked, "Would you like to follow me in what I shall do?" Shahzaman answered, "Yes. I will." Shahrayar said, "Let us leave our royal state and roam the world for the love of the Supreme Lord. If we should find one whose misfortune is greater than ours, we shall return. Otherwise, we shall continue to journey through the land, without need for the trappings of royalty." Shahzaman replied, "This is an excellent idea. I shall follow you."

Then they left by the private gate, took a side road, and departed, journeying till nightfall. They slept over their sorrows, and in the morning resumed their day journey until they came to a meadow by the seashore. While they sat in the meadow amid the thick plants and trees, discussing their misfortunes and the recent events, they suddenly heard a shout and a great cry coming from the middle of the sea. They trembled with fear, thinking that the sky had fallen on the earth. Then the sea parted, and there emerged a black pillar that, as it swayed forward, got taller and taller, until it touched the clouds. Shahrayar and Shahzaman were petrified; then they ran in terror and, climbing a very tall tree, sat hiding in its foliage. When they looked again, they saw that the black pillar was cleaving the sea, wading in the water toward the green meadow, until it touched the shore. When they looked again, they saw that it was a black demon, carrying on his head a large glass chest with four steel locks. He came out, walked into the meadow, and where should he stop but under the very tree where the two kings were hiding. The demon sat down and placed the glass chest on the ground. He took out four keys and, opening the locks of the chest, pulled out a full-grown woman. She had a beautiful figure, and a face like the full moon, and a lovely smile. He took her out, laid her under the tree, and looked at her, saying, "Mistress of all noble women, you whom I carried away on your wedding night, I would like to sleep a little." Then he placed his head on the young woman's lap, stretched his legs to the sea, sank into sleep, and began to snore.

Meanwhile, the woman looked up at the tree and, turning her head by chance, saw King Shahrayar and King Shahzaman. She lifted the demon's head from her lap and placed it on the ground. Then she came and stood under the tree and motioned to them with her hand, as if to say, "Come down slowly to me." When they realized that she had seen them, they were frightened, and they begged her and implored her, in the name of the Creator of the heavens, to excuse them from climbing down. She replied, "You must come down to me." They motioned to her, saying, "This sleeping demon is the enemy of mankind. For God's sake, leave us alone." She replied, "You must come down, and if you don't, I shall wake the demon and have him kill you." She kept gesturing and pressing, until they climbed down very slowly and stood before her. Then she lay on her back, raised her legs, and said, "Make love to me and satisfy my need, or else I shall wake the demon, and he will kill you." They replied, "For God's sake, mistress, don't do this to us, for at this moment we feel nothing but dismay and fear of this demon. Please, excuse us." She replied, "You must," and insisted, swearing, "By God who created the heavens, if you don't do it, I shall wake my husband the demon and ask him to kill you and throw you into the sea." As she persisted, they could no longer resist and they made love to her, first the older brother, then the younger. When they were done and withdrew from her, she said to them, "Give me your rings," and, pulling out from the folds of her dress a small purse, opened it, and shook out ninety-eight rings of different fashions and colors. Then she asked them, "Do you know what these rings are?" They answered, "No." She said, "All the owners of these rings slept with me, for whenever one of them made love to me, I took a ring from him. Since you two have slept with me, give me your rings, so that I may add them to the rest, and make a full hundred. A hundred men have known me under the very horns of this filthy, monstrous cuckold, who has imprisoned me in this chest, locked it with four locks, and kept me in the middle of this raging, roaring sea. He has guarded me and tried to keep me pure and chaste, not realizing that nothing can prevent or alter what is predestined and that when a woman desires something, no one can stop her." When Shahrayar and Shahzaman heard what the young woman said, they were greatly amazed, danced with joy, and said, "O God, O God! There is no power and no strength, save in God the Almighty, the Magnificent. Great is women's cunning." Then each of them took off his ring and handed it to her. She took them and put them with the rest in the purse. Then sitting again by the demon, she lifted his head, placed it back on her lap, and motioned to them, "Go on your way, or else I shall wake him."

They turned their backs and took to the road. Then Shahrayar turned to his brother and said, "My brother Shahzaman, look at this sorry plight. By God, it is worse than ours. This is no less than a demon who has carried a young woman away on her wedding night, imprisoned her in a glass chest, locked her up with four locks, and kept her in the middle of the sea, thinking that he could guard her from what God had foreordained, and you saw how she has managed to sleep with ninety-eight men, and added the two of us to make a hundred. Brother, let us go back to our kingdoms and our cities, never to marry a woman again. As for myself, I shall show you what I will do."

Then the two brothers headed home and journeyed till nightfall. On the morning of the third day, they reached their camp and men, entered their tent, and sat on their thrones. The chamberlains, deputies, princes, and viziers came to attend King Shahrayar, while he gave orders and bestowed robes of honor, as well as other gifts. Then at his command everyone returned to the city, and he went to his own palace and ordered his chief vizier, the father of the two girls Shahrazad and Dinarzad, who will be mentioned below, and said to him, "Take that wife of mine and put her to death." Then Shahrayar went to her himself, bound her, and handed her over to the vizier, who took her out and put her to death. Then King Shahrayar grabbed his sword, brandished it, and, entering the palace chambers, killed every one of his slave-girls and replaced them with others. He then swore to marry for one night only and kill the woman the next morning, in order to save himself from the wickedness and cunning of women, saying, "There is not a single chaste woman anywhere on the entire face of the earth." Shortly thereafter he provided his brother Shahzaman with supplies for his journey and sent him back to his own country with gifts, rarities, and money. The brother bade him good-bye and set out for home.

Shahrayar sat on his throne and ordered his vizier, the father of the two girls, to find him a wife from among the princes' daughters. The vizier found him one, and he slept with her and was done with her, and the next morning he ordered the vizier to put her to death. That very night he took one of his army officers' daughters, slept with her, and the next morning ordered the vizier to put her to death. The vizier, who could not disobey him, put her to death. The third night he took one of the merchants' daughters, slept with her till the morning, then ordered his vizier to put her to death, and the vizier did so. It became King Shahrayar's custom to take every night the daughter of a merchant or a commoner, spend the night with her, then have her put to death the next morning. He continued to do this until all the girls perished, their mothers mourned, and there arose a clamor among the fathers and mothers, who called the plague upon his head, complained to the Creator of the heavens, and called for help on Him who hears and answers prayers.

Now, as mentioned earlier, the vizier, who put the girls to death, had an older daughter called Shahrazad and a younger one called Dinarzad. The older daughter, Shahrazad, had read the books of literature, philosophy, and medicine. She knew poetry by heart, had studied historical reports, and was acquainted with the sayings of men and the maxims of sages and kings. She was intelligent, knowledgeable, wise, and refined. She had read and learned. One day she said to her father, "Father, I will tell you what is in my mind." He asked, "What is it?" She answered, "I would like you to marry me to King Shahrayar, so that I may either succeed in saving the people or perish and die like the rest." When the vizier heard what his daughter Shahrazad said, he got angry and said to her, "Foolish one, don't you know that King Shahrayar has sworn to spend but one night with a girl and have her put to death the next morning? If I give you to him, he will sleep with you for one night and will ask me to put you to death the next morning, and I shall have to do it, since I cannot disobey him." She said, "Father, you must give me to him, even if he kills me." He asked, "What has possessed you that you wish to imperil yourself?" She replied, "Father, you must give me to him. This is absolute and final." Her father the vizier became furious and said to her, "Daughter, 'He who misbehaves, ends up in trouble,' and 'He who considers not the end, the world is not his friend.' As the popular saying goes, 'I would be sitting pretty, but for my curiosity.' I am afraid that what happened to the donkey and the ox with the merchant will happen to you." She asked, "Father, what happened to the donkey, the ox, and the merchant?" He said:

[The Tale of the Ox and the Donkey]

There was a prosperous and wealthy merchant who lived in the countryside and labored on a farm. He owned many camels and herds of cattle and employed many men, and he had a wife and many grown-up as well as little children. This merchant was taught the language of the beasts, on condition that if he revealed his secret to anyone, he would die; therefore, even though he knew the language of every kind of animal, he did not let anyone know, for fear of death. One day, as he sat, with his wife beside him and his children playing before him, he glanced at an ox and a donkey he kept at the farmhouse, tied to adjacent troughs, and heard the ox say to the donkey, "Watchful one, I hope that you are enjoying the comfort and the service you are getting. Your ground is swept and watered, and they serve you, feed you sifted barley, and offer you clear, cool water to drink. I, on the contrary, am taken out to plow in the middle of the night. They clamp on my neck something they call yoke and plow, push me all day under the whip to plow the field, and drive me beyond my endurance until my sides are lacerated, and my neck is flayed. They work me from nighttime to nighttime, take me back in the dark, offer me beans soiled with mud and hay mixed with chaff, and let me spend the night lying in urine and dung. Meanwhile you rest on well-swept, watered, and smoothed ground, with a clean trough full of hay. You stand in comfort, save for the rare occasion when our master the merchant rides you to do a brief errand and returns. You are comfortable, while I am weary; you sleep, while I keep awake."

When the ox finished, the donkey turned to him and said, "Greenhorn, they were right in calling you ox, for you ox harbor no deceit, malice, or meanness. Being sincere, you exert and exhaust yourself to comfort others. Have you not heard the saying 'Out of bad luck, they hastened on the road'? You go into the field from early morning to endure your torture at the plow to the point of exhaustion. When the plowman takes you back and ties you to the trough, you go on butting and beating with your horns, kicking with your hoofs, and bellowing for the beans, until they toss them to you; then you begin to eat. Next time, when they bring them to you, don't eat or even touch them, but smell them, then draw back and lie down on the hay and straw. If you do this, life will be better and kinder to you, and you will find relief."

As the ox listened, he was sure that the donkey had given him good advice.

He thanked him, commended him to God, and invoked His blessing on him, and said, "May you stay safe from harm, watchful one." All of this conversation took place, daughter, while the merchant listened and understood. On the following day, the plowman came to the merchant's house and, taking the ox, placed the yoke upon his neck and worked him at the plow, but the ox lagged behind. The plowman hit him, but following the donkey's advice, the ox, dissembling, fell on his belly, and the plowman hit him again. Thus the ox kept getting up and falling until nightfall, when the plowman took him home and tied him to the trough. But this time the ox did not bellow or kick the ground with his hoofs. Instead, he withdrew, away from the trough. Astonished, the plowman brought him his beans and fodder, but the ox only smelled the fodder and pulled back and lay down at a distance with the hay and straw, complaining till the morning. When the plowman arrived, he found the trough as he had left it, full of beans and fodder, and saw the ox lying on his back, hardly breathing, his belly puffed, and his legs raised in the air. The plowman felt sorry for him and said to himself, "By God, he did seem weak and unable to work." Then he went to the merchant and said, "Master, last night, the ox refused to eat or touch his fodder."

The merchant, who knew what was going on, said to the plowman, "Go to the wily donkey, put him to the plow, and work him hard until he finishes the ox's task." The plowman left, took the donkey, and placed the yoke upon his neck. Then he took him out to the field and drove him with blows until he finished the ox's work, all the while driving him with blows and beating him until his sides were lacerated and his neck was flayed. At nightfall he took him home, barely able to drag his legs under his tired body and his drooping ears. Meanwhile the ox spent his day resting. He ate all his food, drank his water, and lay quietly, chewing his cud in comfort. All day long he kept praising the donkey's advice and invoking God's blessing on him. When the donkey came back at night, the ox stood up to greet him saying, "Good evening, watchful one! You have done me a favor beyond description, for I have been sitting in comfort. God bless you for my sake." Seething with anger, the donkey did not reply, but said to himself, "All this happened to me because of my miscalculation. 'I would be sitting pretty, but for my curiosity.' If I don't find a way to return this ox to his former situation, I will perish." Then he went to his trough and lay down, while the ox continued to chew his cud and invoke God's blessing on him.

"You, my daughter, will likewise perish because of your miscalculation. Desist, sit quietly, and don't expose yourself to peril. I advise you out of compassion for you." She replied, "Father, I must go to the king, and you must give me to him." He said, "Don't do it." She insisted, "I must." He replied, "If you don't desist, I will do to you what the merchant did to his wife." She asked, "Father, what did the merchant do to his wife?" He said:

[The Tale of the Merchant and His Wife]

After what had happened to the donkey and the ox, the merchant and his wife went out in the moonlight to the stable, and he heard the donkey ask the ox in his own language, "Listen, ox, what are you going to do tomorrow morning, and what will you do when the plowman brings you your fodder?"

The ox replied, "What shall I do but follow your advice and stick to it? If he brings me my fodder, I will pretend to be ill, lie down, and puff my belly." The donkey shook his head, and said, "Don't do it. Do you know what I heard our master the merchant say to the plowman?" The ox asked, "What?" The donkey replied, "He said that if the ox failed to get up and eat his fodder, he would call the butcher to slaughter him and skin him and would distribute the meat for alms and use the skin for a mat. I am afraid for you, but good advice is a matter of faith; therefore, if he brings you your fodder, eat it and look alert lest they cut your throat and skin you." The ox farted and bellowed.

The merchant got up and laughed loudly at the conversation between the donkey and the ox, and his wife asked him, "What are you laughing at? Are you making fun of me?" He said, "No." She said, "Tell me what made you laugh." He replied, "I cannot tell you. I am afraid to disclose the secret conversation of the animals." She asked, "And what prevents you from telling me?" He answered, "The fear of death." His wife said, "By God, you are lying. This is nothing but an excuse. I swear by God, the Lord of heaven, that if you don't tell me and explain the cause of your laughter, I will leave you. You must tell me." Then she went back to the house crying, and she continued to cry till the morning. The merchant said, "Damn it! Tell me why you are crying. Ask for God's forgiveness, and stop questioning and leave me in peace." She said, "I insist and will not desist." Amazed at her, he replied, "You insist! If I tell you what the donkey said to the ox, which made me laugh, I shall die." She said, "Yes, I insist, even if you have to die." He replied, "Then call your family," and she called their two daughters, her parents and relatives, and some neighbors. The merchant told them that he was about to die, and everyone, young and old, his children, the farmhands, and the servants began to cry until the house became a place of mourning. Then he summoned legal witnesses, wrote a will, leaving his wife and children their due portions, freed his slave-girls, and bid his family good-bye, while everybody, even the witnesses, wept. Then the wife's parents approached her and said, "Desist, for if your husband had not known for certain that he would die if he revealed his secret, he wouldn't have gone through all this." She replied, "I will not change my mind," and everybody cried and prepared to mourn his death.

Well, my daughter Shahrazad, it happened that the farmer kept fifty hens and a rooster at home, and while he felt sad to depart this world and leave his children and relatives behind, pondering and about to reveal and utter his secret, he overheard a dog of his say something in dog language to the rooster, who, beating and clapping his wings, had jumped on a hen and, finishing with her, jumped down and jumped on another. The merchant heard and understood what the dog said in his own language to the rooster, "Shameless, no-good rooster. Aren't you ashamed to do such a thing on a day like this?" The rooster asked, "What is special about this day?" The dog replied, "Don't you know that our master and friend is in mourning today? His wife is demanding that he disclose his secret, and when he discloses it, he will surely die. He is in this predicament, about to interpret to her the language of the animals, and all of us are mourning for him, while you clap your wings and get off one hen and jump on another. Aren't you ashamed?" The merchant heard the rooster reply, "You fool, you lunatic! Our master and friend claims to be wise, but he is foolish, for he has only one wife, yet he does not know how to manage her." The dog asked, "What should he do with her?"

The rooster replied, "He should take an oak branch, push her into a room, lock the door, and fall on her with the stick, beating her mercilessly until he breaks her arms and legs and she cries out, 'I no longer want you to tell me or explain anything.' He should go on beating her until he cures her for life, and she will never oppose him in anything. If he does this, he will live, and live in peace, and there will be no more grief, but he does not know how to manage." Well, my daughter Shahrazad, when the merchant heard the conversation between the dog and the rooster, he jumped up and, taking an oak branch, pushed his wife into a room, got in with her, and locked the door. Then he began to beat her mercilessly on her chest and shoulders and kept beating her until she cried for mercy, screaming, "No, no, I don't want to know anything. Leave me alone, leave me alone. I don't want to know anything," until he got tired of hitting her and opened the door. The wife emerged penitent, the husband learned good management, and everybody was happy, and the mourning turned into a celebration.

"If you don't relent, I shall do to you what the merchant did to his wife." She said, "Such tales don't deter me from my request. If you wish, I can tell you many such tales. In the end, if you don't take me to King Shahrayar, I shall go to him by myself behind your back and tell him that you have refused to give me to one like him and that you have begrudged your master one like me." The vizier asked, "Must you really do this?" She replied, "Yes, I must."

Tired and exhausted, the vizier went to King Shahrayar and, kissing the ground before him, told him about his daughter, adding that he would give her to him that very night. The king was astonished and said to him, "Vizier, how is it that you have found it possible to give me your daughter, knowing that I will, by God, the Creator of heaven, ask you to put her to death the next morning and that if you refuse, I will have you put to death too?" He replied, "My King and Lord, I have told her everything and explained all this to her, but she refuses and insists on being with you tonight." The king was delighted and said, "Go to her, prepare her, and bring her to me early in the evening."

The vizier went down, repeated the king's message to his daughter, and said, "May God not deprive me of you." She was very happy and, after preparing herself and packing what she needed, went to her younger sister, Dinarzad, and said, "Sister, listen well to what I am telling you. When I go to the king, I will send for you, and when you come and see that the king has finished with me, say, 'Sister, if you are not sleepy, tell us a story.' Then I will begin to tell a story, and it will cause the king to stop his practice, save myself, and deliver the people." Dinarzad replied, "Very well."

At nightfall the vizier took Shahrazad and went with her to the great King Shahrayar. But when Shahrayar took her to bed and began to fondle her, she wept, and when he asked her, "Why are you crying?" she replied, "I have a sister, and I wish to bid her good-bye before daybreak." Then the king sent for the sister, who came and went to sleep under the bed. When the night wore on, she woke up and waited until the king had satisfied himself with her sister Shahrazad and they were by now all fully awake. Then Dinarzad cleared her throat and said, "Sister, if you are not sleepy, tell us one of your lovely little tales to while away the night, before I bid you good-bye at daybreak, for I don't know what will happen to you tomorrow." Shahrazad turned to King Shahrayar and said, "May I have your permission to tell a story?" He replied, "Yes," and Shahrazad was very happy and said, "Listen":

[The Story of the Merchant and the Demon]

THE FIRST NIGHT

It is said, O wise and happy King, that once there was a prosperous merchant who had abundant wealth and investments and commitments in every country. He had many women and children and kept many servants and slaves. One day, having resolved to visit another country, he took provisions, filling his saddlebag with loaves of bread and with dates, mounted his horse, and set out on his journey. For many days and nights, he journeyed under God's care until he reached his destination. When he finished his business, he turned back to his home and family. He journeyed for three days, and on the fourth day, chancing to come to an orchard, went in to avoid the heat and shade himself from the sun of the open country. He came to a spring under a walnut tree and, tying his horse, sat by the spring, pulled out from the saddlebag some loaves of bread and a handful of dates, and began to eat, throwing the date pits right and left until he had had enough. Then he got up, performed his ablutions, and performed his prayers.

But hardly had he finished when he saw an old demon, with sword in hand, standing with his feet on the ground and his head in the clouds. The demon approached until he stood before him and screamed, saying, "Get up, so that I may kill you with this sword, just as you have killed my son." When the merchant saw and heard the demon, he was terrified and awestricken. He asked, "Master, for what crime do you wish to kill me?" The demon replied, "I wish to kill you because you have killed my son." The merchant asked, "Who has killed your son?" The demon replied, "You have killed my son." The merchant said, "By God, I did not kill your son. When and how could that have been?" The demon said, "Didn't you sit down, take out some dates from your saddlebag, and eat, throwing the pits right and left?" The merchant replied, "Yes, I did." The demon said, "You killed my son, for as you were throwing the stones right and left, my son happened to be walking by and was struck and killed by one of them, and I must now kill you." The merchant said, "O my lord, please don't kill me." The demon replied, "I must kill you as you killed him—blood for blood." The merchant said, "To God we belong and to God we turn. There is no power or strength, save in God the Almighty, the Magnificent. If I killed him, I did it by mistake. Please forgive me." The demon replied, "By God, I must kill you, as you killed my son." Then he seized him, and throwing him to the ground, raised the sword to strike him. The merchant began to weep and mourn his family and his wife and children. Again, the demon raised his sword to strike, while the merchant cried until he was drenched with tears, saying, "There is no power or strength, save in God the Almighty, the Magnificent." Then he began to recite the following verses:

Life has two days: one peace, one wariness,
And has two sides: worry and happiness.
Ask him who taunts us with adversity,
"Does fate, save those worthy of note, oppress?

> Don't you see that the blowing, raging storms 5
> Only the tallest of the trees beset,
> And of earth's many green and barren lots,
> Only the ones with fruits with stones are hit,
> And of the countless stars in heaven's vault
> None is eclipsed except the moon and sun? 10
> You thought well of the days, when they were good,
> Oblivious to the ills destined for one.
> You were deluded by the peaceful nights,
> Yet in the peace of night does sorrow stun."

When the merchant finished and stopped weeping, the demon said, "By God, I must kill you, as you killed my son, even if you weep blood." The merchant asked, "Must you?" The demon replied, "I must," and raised his sword to strike.

But morning overtook Shahrazad, and she lapsed into silence, leaving King Shahrayar burning with curiosity to hear the rest of the story. Then Dinarzad said to her sister Shahrazad, "What a strange and lovely story!" Shahrazad replied, "What is this compared with what I shall tell you tomorrow night if the king spares me and lets me live? It will be even better and more entertaining." The king thought to himself, "I will spare her until I hear the rest of the story; then I will have her put to death the next day." When morning broke, the day dawned, and the sun rose; the king left to attend to the affairs of the kingdom, and the vizier, Shahrazad's father, was amazed and delighted. King Shahrayar governed all day and returned home at night to his quarters and got into bed with Shahrazad. Then Dinarzad said to her sister Shahrazad, "Please, sister, if you are not sleepy, tell us one of your lovely little tales to while away the night." The king added, "Let it be the conclusion of the story of the demon and the merchant, for I would like to hear it." Shahrazad replied, "With the greatest pleasure, dear, happy King":

THE SECOND NIGHT

It is related, O wise and happy King, that when the demon raised his sword, the merchant asked the demon again, "Must you kill me?" and the demon replied, "Yes." Then the merchant said, "Please give me time to say good-bye to my family and my wife and children, divide my property among them, and appoint guardians. Then I shall come back, so that you may kill me." The demon replied, "I am afraid that if I release you and grant you time, you will go and do what you wish, but will not come back." The merchant said, "I swear to keep my pledge to come back, as the God of Heaven and earth is my witness." The demon asked, "How much time do you need?" The merchant replied, "One year, so that I may see enough of my children, bid my wife good-bye, discharge my obligations to people, and come back on New Year's Day." The demon asked, "Do you swear to God that if I let you go, you will come back on New Year's Day?" The merchant replied, "Yes, I swear to God."

After the merchant swore, the demon released him, and he mounted his horse sadly and went on his way. He journeyed until he reached his home and came to his wife and children. When he saw them, he wept bitterly, and when his family saw his sorrow and grief, they began to reproach him for his behavior, and his wife said, "Husband, what is the matter with you? Why do you mourn, when we are happy, celebrating your return?" He replied, "Why not mourn when I have only one year to live?" Then he told her of his encounter with the demon and informed her that he had sworn to return on New Year's Day, so that the demon might kill him.

When they heard what he said, everyone began to cry. His wife struck her face in lamentation and cut her hair, his daughters wailed, and his little children cried. It was a day of mourning, as all the children gathered around their father to weep and exchange good-byes. The next day he wrote his will, dividing his property, discharged his obligations to people, left bequests and gifts, distributed alms, and engaged reciters to read portions of the Quran in his house. Then he summoned legal witnesses and in their presence freed his slaves and slave-girls, divided among his elder children their shares of the property, appointed guardians for his little ones, and gave his wife her share, according to her marriage contract. He spent the rest of the time with his family, and when the year came to an end, save for the time needed for the journey, he performed his ablutions, performed his prayers, and, carrying his burial shroud, began to bid his family good-bye. His sons hung around his neck, his daughters wept, and his wife wailed. Their mourning scared him, and he began to weep, as he embraced and kissed his children good-bye. He said to them, "Children, this is God's will and decree, for man was created to die." Then he turned away and, mounting his horse, journeyed day and night until he reached the orchard on New Year's Day.

He sat at the place where he had eaten the dates, waiting for the demon, with a heavy heart and tearful eyes. As he waited, an old man, leading a deer on a leash, approached and greeted him, and he returned the greeting. The old man inquired, "Friend, why do you sit here in this place of demons and devils? For in this haunted orchard none come to good." The merchant replied by telling him what had happened to him and the demon, from beginning to end. The old man was amazed at the merchant's fidelity and said, "Yours is a magnificent pledge," adding, "By God, I shall not leave until I see what will happen to you with the demon." Then he sat down beside him and chatted with him. As they talked . . .

But morning overtook Shahrazad, and she lapsed into silence. As the day dawned, and it was light, her sister Dinarzad said, "What a strange and wonderful story!" Shahrazad replied, "Tomorrow night I shall tell something even stranger and more wonderful than this."

THE THIRD NIGHT

When it was night and Shahrazad was in bed with the king, Dinarzad said to her sister Shahrazad, "Please, if you are not sleepy, tell us one of your lovely little tales to while away the night." The king added, "Let it be the conclusion of the merchant's story." Shahrazad replied, "As you wish":

I heard, O happy King, that as the merchant and the man with the deer sat talking, another old man approached, with two black hounds, and when he reached them, he greeted them, and they returned his greeting. Then he asked them about themselves, and the man with the deer told him the story of the merchant and the demon, how the merchant had sworn to return on New Year's Day, and how the demon was waiting to kill him. He added that when he himself heard the story, he swore never to leave until he saw what would happen between the merchant and the demon. When the man with the two dogs heard the story, he was amazed, and he too swore never to leave them until he saw what would happen between them. Then he questioned the merchant, and the merchant repeated to him what had happened to him with the demon.

While they were engaged in conversation, a third old man approached and greeted them, and they returned his greeting. He asked, "Why do I see the two of you sitting here, with this merchant between you, looking abject, sad, and dejected?" They told him the merchant's story and explained that they were sitting and waiting to see what would happen to him with the demon. When he heard the story, he sat down with them, saying, "By God, I too like you will not leave, until I see what happens to this man with the demon." As they sat, conversing with one another, they suddenly saw the dust rising from the open country, and when it cleared, they saw the demon approaching, with a drawn steel sword in his hand. He stood before them without greeting them, yanked the merchant with his left hand, and, holding him fast before him, said, "Get ready to die." The merchant and the three old men began to weep and wail.

But dawn broke and morning overtook Shahrazad, and she lapsed into silence. Then Dinarzad said, "Sister, what a lovely story!" Shahrazad replied, "What is this compared with what I shall tell you tomorrow night? It will be even better; it will be more wonderful, delightful, entertaining, and delectable if the king spares me and lets me live." The king was all curiosity to hear the rest of the story and said to himself, "By God, I will not have her put to death until I hear the rest of the story and find out what happened to the merchant with the demon. Then I will have her put to death the next morning, as I did with the others." Then he went out to attend to the affairs of his kingdom, and when he saw Shahrazad's father, he treated him kindly and showed him favors, and the vizier was amazed. When night came, the king went home, and when he was in bed with Shahrazad, Dinarzad said, "Sister, if you are not sleepy, tell us one of your lovely little tales to while away the night." Shahrazad replied, "With the greatest pleasure":

THE FOURTH NIGHT

It is related, O happy King, that the first old man with the deer approached the demon and, kissing his hands and feet, said, "Fiend and King of the demon kings, if I tell you what happened to me and that deer, and you find it strange and amazing, indeed stranger and more amazing than what happened to you and the merchant, will you grant me a third of your claim on him for his crime and guilt?" The demon replied, "I will." The old man said:

[The First Old Man's Tale]

Demon, this deer is my cousin, my flesh and blood. I married her when I was very young, and she a girl of twelve, who reached womanhood only afterward. For thirty years we lived together, but I was not blessed with children, for she bore neither boy nor girl. Yet I continued to be kind to her, to care for her, and to treat her generously. Then I took a mistress, and she bore me a son, who grew up to look like a slice of the moon.[5] Meanwhile, my wife grew jealous of my mistress and my son. One day, when he was ten, I had to go on a journey. I entrusted my wife, this one here, with my mistress and son, bade her take good care of them, and was gone for a whole year. In my absence my wife, this cousin of mine, learned soothsaying and magic and cast a spell on my son and turned him into a young bull. Then she summoned my shepherd, gave my son to him, and said, "Tend this bull with the rest of the cattle." The shepherd took him and tended him for a while. Then she cast a spell on the mother, turning her into a cow, and gave her also to the shepherd.

When I came back, after all this was done, and inquired about my mistress and my son, she answered, "Your mistress died, and your son ran away two months ago, and I have had no news from him ever since." When I heard her, I grieved for my mistress, and with an anguished heart I mourned for my son for nearly a year. When the Great Feast of the Immolation[6] drew near, I summoned the shepherd and ordered him to bring me a fat cow for the sacrifice. The cow he brought me was in reality my enchanted mistress. When I bound her and pressed against her to cut her throat, she wept and cried, as if saying, "My son, my son," and her tears coursed down her cheeks. Astonished and seized with pity, I turned away and asked the shepherd to bring me a different cow. But my wife shouted, "Go on. Butcher her, for he has none better or fatter. Let us enjoy her meat at feast time." I approached the cow to cut her throat, and again she cried, as if saying, "My son, my son." Then I turned away from her and said to the shepherd, "Butcher her for me." The shepherd butchered her, and when he skinned her, he found neither meat nor fat but only skin and bone. I regretted having her butchered and said to the shepherd, "Take her all for yourself, or give her as alms to whomever you wish, and find me a fat young bull from among the flock." The shepherd took her away and disappeared, and I never knew what he did with her.

Then he brought me my son, my heartblood, in the guise of a fat young bull. Then my son saw me, he shook his head loose from the rope, ran toward me, and, throwing himself at my feet, kept rubbing his head against me. I was astonished and touched with sympathy, pity, and mercy, for the blood hearkened to the blood and the divine bond, and my heart throbbed within me when I saw the tears coursing over the cheeks of my son the young bull, as he dug the earth with his hoofs. I turned away and said to the shepherd, "Let him go with the rest of the flock, and be kind to him, for I have decided to spare him. Bring me another one instead of him." My wife, this very deer, shouted, "You shall sacrifice none but this bull." I got angry and replied, "I listened to you and butchered the cow uselessly. I will not listen to you and kill this bull, for I have decided to spare him." But she pressed me, saying, "You must butcher this bull," and I bound him and took the knife . . .

But dawn broke, and morning overtook Shahrazad, and she lapsed into silence, leaving the king all curiosity for the rest of the story. Then her sister Dinarzad said, "What an entertaining story!" Shahrazad replied, "Tomorrow night I shall tell you something even stranger, more wonderful, and more entertaining if the king spares me and lets me live."

THE FIFTH NIGHT

The following night, Dinarzad said to her sister Shahrazad, "Please, sister, if you are not sleepy, tell us one of your little tales." Shahrazad replied, "With the greatest pleasure":

I heard, dear King, that the old man with the deer said to the demon and to his companions:

I took the knife and as I turned to slaughter my son, he wept, bellowed, rolled at my feet, and motioned toward me with his tongue. I suspected something, began to waver with trepidation and pity, and finally released him, saying to my wife, "I have decided to spare him, and I commit him to your care." Then I tried to appease and please my wife, this very deer, by slaughtering another bull, promising her to slaughter this one next season. We slept that night, and when God's dawn broke, the shepherd came to me without letting my wife know, and said, "Give me credit for bringing you good news." I replied, "Tell me, and the credit is yours." He said, "Master, I have a daughter who is fond of soothsaying and magic and who is adept at the art of oaths and spells. Yesterday I took home with me the bull you had spared, to let him graze with the cattle, and when my daughter saw him, she laughed and cried at the same time. When I asked her why she laughed and cried, she answered that she laughed because the bull was in reality the son of our master the cattle owner, put under a spell by his step-mother, and that she cried because his father had slaughtered the son's mother. I could hardly wait till daybreak to bring you the good news about your son."

Demon, when I heard that, I uttered a cry and fainted, and when I came to myself, I accompanied the shepherd to his home, went to my son, and threw myself at him, kissing him and crying. He turned his head toward me, his tears coursing over his cheeks, and dangled his tongue, as if to say, "Look at my plight." Then I turned to the shepherd's daughter and asked, "Can you release him from the spell? If you do, I will give you all my cattle and all my possessions." She smiled and replied, "Master, I have no desire for your wealth, cattle, or possessions. I will deliver him, but on two conditions: first, that you let me marry him; second, that you let me cast a spell on her who had cast a spell on him, in order to control her and guard against her evil power." I replied, "Do whatever you wish and more. My possessions are for you and my son. As for my wife, who has done this to my son and made me slaughter his mother, her life is forfeit to you." She said, "No, but I will let her taste what she has inflicted on others." Then the shepherd's daughter filled a bowl of water, uttered an incantation and an oath, and said to my son, "Bull, if you have been created in this image by the All-Conquering, Almighty Lord, stay as you are, but if you have been treacherously put under a spell, change back to your human form, by the will of God, Creator of the wide world." Then she sprinkled him with the water, and he shook himself and changed from a bull back to his human form.

As I rushed to him, I fainted, and when I came to myself, he told me what my wife, this very deer, had done to him and to his mother. I said to him, "Son, God has sent us someone who will pay her back for what you and your mother and I have suffered at her hands." Then, O demon, I gave my son in marriage to the shepherd's daughter, who turned my wife into this very deer, saying to me, "To me this is a pretty form, for she will be with us day and night, and it is better to turn her into a pretty deer than to suffer her sinister looks." Thus she stayed with us, while the days and nights followed one another, and the months and years went by. Then one day the shepherd's daughter died, and my son went to the country of this very man with whom you have had your encounter. Some time later I took my wife, this very deer, with me, set out to find out what had happened to my son, and chanced to stop here. This is my story, my strange and amazing story.

The demon assented, saying, "I grant you one-third of this man's life."

Then, O King Shahrayar, the second old man with the two black dogs approached the demon and said, "I too shall tell you what happened to me and to these two dogs, and if I tell it to you and you find it stranger and more amazing than this man's story will you grant me one-third of this man's life?" The demon replied, "I will." Then the old man began to tell his story, saying . . .

But dawn broke, and morning overtook Shahrazad, and she lapsed into silence. Then Dinarzad said, "This is an amazing story," and Shahrazad replied, "What is this compared with what I shall tell you tomorrow night if the king spares me and lets me live!" The king said to himself, "By God, I will not have her put to death until I find out what happened to the man with the two black dogs. Then I will have her put to death, God the Almighty willing."

THE SIXTH NIGHT

When the following night arrived and Shahrazad was in bed with King Shahrayar, her sister Dinarzad said, "Sister, if you are not sleepy, tell us a little tale. Finish the one you started." Shahrazad replied, "With the greatest pleasure":

I heard, O happy King, that the second old man with the two dogs said:

[*The Second Old Man's Tale*]

Demon, as for my story, these are the details. These two dogs are my brothers. When our father died, he left behind three sons, and left us three thousand dinars,[7] with which each of us opened a shop and became a shopkeeper. Soon my older brother, one of these very dogs, went and sold the contents of his shop for a thousand dinars, bought trading goods, and, having prepared himself for his trading trip, left us. A full year went by, when one day, as I sat in my shop, a beggar stopped by to beg. When I refused him, he tearfully asked, "Don't you recognize me?" and when I looked at him closely, I recognized my brother. I embraced him and took him into the shop, and when I asked him about his plight, he replied, "The money is gone, and the situation is bad." Then I took him to the public bath, clothed him in one

---

7. Gold coins; the basic Muslim money units [Translator's note].

of my robes, and took him home with me. Then I examined my books and checked my balance, and found out that I had made a thousand dinars and that my net worth was two thousand dinars. I divided the amount between my brother and myself, and said to him, "Think as if you have never been away." He gladly took the money and opened another shop.

Soon afterward my second brother, this other dog, went and sold his merchandise and collected his money, intending to go on a trading trip. We tried to dissuade him, but he did not listen. Instead, he bought merchandise and trading goods, joined a group of travelers, and was gone for a full year. Then he came back, just like his older brother. I said to him, "Brother, didn't I advise you not to go?" He replied tearfully, "Brother, it was foreordained. Now I am poor and penniless, without even a shirt on my back." Demon, I took him to the public bath, clothed him in one of my new robes, and took him back to the shop. After we had something to eat, I said to him, "Brother, I shall do my business accounts, calculate my net worth for the year, and after subtracting the capital, whatever the profit happens to be, I shall divide it equally between you and myself. When I examined my books and subtracted the capital, I found out that my profit was two thousand dinars, and I thanked God and felt very happy. Then I divided the money, giving him a thousand dinars and keeping a thousand for myself. With that money he opened another shop, and the three of us stayed together for a while. Then my two brothers asked me to go on a trading journey with them, but I refused, saying, "What did you gain from your ventures that I can gain?"

They dropped the matter, and for six years we worked in our stores, buying and selling. Yet every year they asked me to go on a trading journey with them, but I refused, until I finally gave in. I said, "Brothers, I am ready to go with you. How much money do you have?" I found out that they had eaten and drunk and squandered everything they had, but I said nothing to them and did not reproach them. Then I took inventory, gathered all I had together, and sold everything. I was pleased to discover that the sale netted six thousand dinars. Then I divided the money into two parts, and said to my brothers, "The sum of three thousand dinars is for you and myself to use on our trading journey. The other three thousand I shall bury in the ground, in case what happened to you happens to me, so that when we return, we will find three thousand dinars to reopen our shops." They replied, "This is an excellent idea." Then, demon, I divided my money and buried three thousand dinars. Of the remaining three I gave each of my brothers a thousand and kept a thousand for myself. After I closed my shop, we bought merchandise and trading goods, rented a large seafaring boat, and after loading it with our goods and provisions, sailed day and night, for a month.

But morning overtook Shahrazad, and she lapsed into silence. Then her sister Dinarzad said, "Sister, what a lovely story!" Shahrazad replied, "Tomorrow night I shall tell you something even lovelier, stranger, and more wonderful if I live, the Almighty God willing."

THE SEVENTH NIGHT

The following night Dinarzad said to her sister Shahrazad, "For God's sake, sister, if you are not sleepy, tell us a little tale." The king added, "Let it be the completion of the story of the merchant and the demon." Shahrazad replied, "With the greatest pleasure":

I heard, O happy King, that the second old man said to the demon:

For a month my brothers, these very dogs, and I sailed the salty sea, until we came to a port city. We entered the city and sold our goods, earning ten dinars for every dinar. Then we bought other goods, and when we got to the seashore to embark, I met a girl who was dressed in tatters. She kissed my hands and said, "O my lord, be charitable and do me a favor, and I believe that I shall be able to reward you for it." I replied, "I am willing to do you a favor regardless of any reward." She said, "O my lord, marry me, clothe me, and take me home with you on this boat, as your wife, for I wish to give myself to you. I, in turn, will reward you for your kindness and charity, the Almighty God willing. Don't be misled by my poverty and present condition." When I heard her words, I felt pity for her, and guided by what God the Most High had intended for me, I consented. I clothed her with an expensive dress and married her. Then I took her to the boat, spread the bed for her, and consummated our marriage. We sailed many days and nights, and I, feeling love for her, stayed with her day and night, neglecting my brothers. In the meantime they, these very dogs, grew jealous of me, envied me for my increasing merchandise and wealth, and coveted all our possessions. At last they decided to betray me and, tempted by the Devil, plotted to kill me. One night they waited until I was asleep beside my wife; then they carried the two of us and threw us into the sea.

When we awoke, my wife turned into a she-demon and carried me out of the sea to an island. When it was morning, she said, "Husband, I have rewarded you by saving you from drowning, for I am one of the demons who believe in God.[8] When I saw you by the seashore, I felt love for you and came to you in the guise in which you saw me, and when I expressed my love for you, you accepted me. Now I must kill your brothers." When I heard what she said, I was amazed and I thanked her and said, "As for destroying my brothers, this I do not wish, for I will not behave like them." Then I related to her what had happened to me and them, from beginning to end. When she heard my story, she got very angry at them, and said, "I shall fly to them now, drown their boat, and let them all perish." I entreated her, saying, "For God's sake, don't. The proverb advises 'Be kind to those who hurt you.' No matter what, they are my brothers after all." In this manner, I entreated her and pacified her. Afterward, she took me and flew away with me until she brought me home and put me down on the roof of my house. I climbed down, threw the doors open, and dug up the money I had buried. Then I went out and, greeting the people in the market, reopened my shop. When I came home in the evening, I found these two dogs tied up, and when they saw me, they came to me, wept, and rubbed themselves against me. I started, when I suddenly heard my wife say, "O my lord, these are your brothers." I asked, "Who has done this to them?" She replied, "I sent to my sister and asked her to do it. They will stay in this condition for ten years, after which they may be delivered." Then she told me where to find her and

8. According to the Koran God created both humans and demons (jinns), some of whom accepted Islam.

departed. The ten years have passed, and I was with my brothers on my way to her to have the spell lifted, when I met this man, together with this old man with the deer. When I asked him about himself, he told me about his encounter with you, and I resolved not to leave until I found out what would happen between you and him. This is my story. Isn't it amazing?

The demon replied, "By God, it is strange and amazing. I grant you one-third of my claim on him for his crime."

Then the third old man said, "Demon, don't disappoint me. If I told you a story that is stranger and more amazing than the first two would you grant me one-third of your claim on him for his crime?" The demon replied, "I will." Then the old man said, "Demon, listen":

But morning overtook Shahrazad, and she lapsed into silence. Then her sister said, "What an amazing story!" Shahrazad replied, "The rest is even more amazing." The king said to himself, "I will not have her put to death until I hear what happened to the old man and the demon; then I will have her put to death, as is my custom with the others."

THE EIGHTH NIGHT

The following night Dinarzad said to her sister Shahrazad, "For God's sake, sister, if you are not sleepy, tell us one of your lovely little tales to while away the night." Shahrazad replied, "With the greatest pleasure":

[The Third Old Man's Tale][9]

The demon said, "This is a wonderful story, and I grant you a third of my claim on the merchant's life."

The third sheikh approached and said to the demon, "I will tell you a story more wonderful than these two if you will grant me a third of your claim on his life, O demon!"

To which the demon agreed.

So the sheikh began:

O sultan and chief of the demons, this mule was my wife. I had gone off on a journey and was absent from her for a whole year. At last I came to the end of my journey and returned home late one night. When I entered the house I saw a black slave lying in bed with her. They were chatting and dallying and laughing and kissing and quarreling together. When she saw me my wife leaped out of bed, ran to the water jug, recited a spell over it, then splashed me with some of the water and said, "Leave this form for the form of a dog."

Immediately I became a dog and she chased me out of the house. I ran out of the gate and didn't stop running until I reached a butcher's shop. I entered it and fell to eating the bones lying about. When the owner of the shop saw me, he grabbed me and carried me into his house. When his daughter saw me, she hid her face and said, "Why are you bringing this strange man in with you?"

9. Because the earliest manuscript does not include a story for the third sheikh, later narrators supplied one. This brief anecdote comes from a manuscript found in the library of the Royal Academy in Madrid.

"What man?" her father asked.

"This dog is a man whose wife has put a spell on him," she said, "but I can set him free again." She took a jug of water, recited a spell over it, then splashed a little water from it on me, and said, "Leave this shape for your original one."

And I became myself again. I kissed her hand and said, "I want to cast a spell on my wife as she did on me. Please give me a little of that water."

"Gladly," she said, "if you find her asleep, sprinkle a few drops on her and she will become whatever you wish."

Well, I did find her asleep, and I sprinkled some water on her and said, "Leave this shape for the shape of a she mule." She at once became the very mule you see here, oh sultan and chief of the demons."

The demon then turned to him and asked, "Is this really true?"

"Yes," he answered, nodding his head vigorously, "it's all true."

When the sheikh had finished his story, the demon shook with laughter and granted him a third of his claim on the merchant's blood.

Then the demon released the merchant and departed. The merchant turned to the three old men and thanked them, and they congratulated him on his deliverance and bade him good-bye. Then they separated, and each of them went on his way. The merchant himself went back home to his family, his wife, and his children, and he lived with them until the day he died. But this story is not as strange or as amazing as the story of the fisherman.

Dinarzad asked, "Please, sister, what is the story of the fisherman?" Shahrazad said: . . .

[The Story of the Fisherman and the Demon]

It is related that there was a very old fisherman who had a wife and three daughters and who was so poor that they did not have even enough food for the day. It was this fisherman's custom to cast his net four times a day. One day, while the moon was still up, he went out with his net at the call for the early morning prayer. He reached the outskirts of the city and came to the seashore. Then he set down his basket, rolled up his shirt, and waded to his waist in the water. He cast his net and waited for it to sink; then he gathered the rope and started to pull. As he pulled little by little, he felt that the net was getting heavier until he was unable to pull any further. He climbed ashore, drove a stake into the ground, and tied the end of the rope to the stake. Then he took off his clothes, dove into the water, and went around the net, shaking it and tugging at it until he managed to pull it ashore. Feeling extremely happy, he put on his clothes and went back to the net. But when he opened it, he found inside a dead donkey, which had torn it apart. The fisherman felt sad and depressed and said to himself, "There is no power and no strength save in God, the Almighty, the Magnificent," adding, "Indeed, this is a strange catch!" Then he began to recite the following verses:

> O you who brave the danger in the dark,
> Reduce your toil, for gain is not in work.
> Look at the fisherman who labors at his trade,

As the stars in the night their orbits make,
And deeply wades into the raging sea,   5
Steadily gazing at the swelling net,
Till he returns, pleased with his nightly catch,
A fish whose mouth the hook of death has cut,
And sells it to a man who sleeps the night,
Safe from the cold and blessed with every wish.   10
Praised be the Lord who blesses and withholds:
This casts the net, but that one eats the fish.

*But morning overtook Shahrazad, and she lapsed into silence. Then her sister
Dinarzad said, "Sister, what a lovely story!" Shahrazad replied, "Tomorrow
night I shall tell you the rest, which is stranger and more wonderful, if the king
spares me and lets me live!"*

THE NINTH NIGHT

*The following night Dinarzad said to her sister Shahrazad, "Sister, if you are
not sleepy, finish the fisherman's story." Shahrazad replied, "With the greatest
pleasure":*

I heard, O happy King, that when the fisherman finished reciting his
verses, he pushed the donkey out of the net and sat down to mend it. When
he was done, he wrung it out and spread it to dry. Then he waded into the
water and, invoking the Almighty God, cast the net and waited for it to sink.
Then he pulled the rope little by little, but this time the net was even more
firmly snagged. Thinking that it was heavy with fish, he was extremely happy.
He took off his clothes and, diving into the water, freed the net and struggled
with it until he reached the shore, but inside the net he found a large jar full
of nothing but mud and sand. When he saw this, he felt sad and, with tears
in his eyes, said to himself, "This is a strange day! God's we are and to God
we turn," and he began to recite the following verses:

O my tormenting fate, forbear,
Or if you can't, at least be fair.
I went to seek my daily bread,
But they said to me it was dead.
And neither luck nor industry   5
Brought back my daily bread to me.
The Pleiads[1] many fools attain,
While sages sit in dark disdain.

Then the fisherman threw the jar away, washed his net, and, wringing it
out, spread it to dry. Then he begged the Almighty God for forgiveness and
went back to the water. For the third time, he cast the net and waited for it
to sink. But when he pulled it up, he found nothing inside but broken pots
and bottles, stones, bones, refuse, and the like. He wept at this great injustice
and ill luck and began to recite the following verses:

---

1. Cluster of stars in the constellation of Taurus.

Your livelihood is not in your own hands;
Neither by writing nor by the pen you thrive.
Your luck and your wages are by lot;
Some lands are waste, and some are fertile lands.
The wheel of fortune lowers the man of worth,   5
Raising the base man who deserves to fall.
Come then, O death, and end this worthless life,
Where the ducks soar, while the falcons are bound to earth.
No wonder that you see the good man poor,
While the vicious exalts in his estate.   10
Our wages are alloted; 'tis our fate
To search like birds for gleanings everywhere.
One bird searches the earth from east to west,
Another gets the tidbits while at rest.

Then the fisherman raised his eyes to the heavens and, seeing that the sun
had risen and that it was morning and full daylight, said, "O Lord, you know
that I cast my net four times only. I have already cast it three times, and
there is only one more try left. Lord, let the sea serve me, even as you let it
serve Moses."[2] Having mended the net, he cast it into the sea, and waited
for it to sink. When he pulled, he found that it was so heavy that he was
unable to haul it. He shook it and found that it was caught at the bottom.
Saying "There is no power or strength save in God, the Almighty, the Magnificent," he took off his clothes and dove for the net. He worked at it until
he managed to free it, and as he hauled it to the shore, he felt that there was
something heavy inside. He struggled with the net, until he opened it and
found a large long-necked brass jar, with a lead stopper bearing the mark of
a seal ring.[3] When the fisherman saw the jar, he was happy and said to
himself, "I will sell it in the copper market, for it must be worth at least two
measures of wheat." He tried to move the jar, but it was so full and so heavy
that he was unable to budge it. Looking at the lead stopper, he said to himself, "I will open the jar, shake out the contents, then roll it before me until
I reach the copper market." Then he took out a knife from his belt and began
to scrape and struggle with the lead stopper until he pried it loose. He held
the stopper in his mouth, tilted the jar to the ground, and shook it, trying to
pour out its contents, but when nothing came out, he was extremely surprised.

After a while, there began to emerge from the jar a great column of smoke,
which rose and spread over the face of the earth, increasing so much that it
covered the sea and rising so high that it reached the clouds and hid the
daylight. For a long time, the smoke kept rising from the jar; then it gathered
and took shape, and suddenly it shook and there stood a demon, with his
feet on the ground and his head in the clouds. He had a head like a tomb,
fangs like pincers, a mouth like a cave, teeth like stones, nostrils like trumpets, ears like shields, a throat like an alley, and eyes like lanterns. In short,
all one can say is that he was a hideous monster. When the fisherman saw
him, he shook with terror, his jaws locked together, and his mouth went dry.

2. Moses is a prophet in Islam, as well.   3. A ring that houses a precious or semiprecious stone (usually
agate) engraved with the name of a person and used to imprint a signature, or in other instances engraved
with talismanic words and used as a charm.

The demon cried, "O Solomon,[4] prophet of God, forgive me, forgive me. Never again will I disobey you or defy your command."

But morning overtook Shahrazad, and she lapsed into silence. Then Dinarzad said, "Sister, what a strange and amazing story!" Shahrazad replied, "Tomorrow night I shall tell you something stranger and more amazing if I stay alive."

THE TENTH NIGHT

The following night, when Shahrazad was in bed with King Shahrayar, her sister Dinarzad said, "Please, sister, finish the story of the fisherman." Shahrazad replied, "With the greatest pleasure":

I heard, O happy King, that when the fisherman heard what the demon said, he asked, "Demon, what are you saying? It has been more than one thousand and eight hundred years since the prophet Solomon died, and we are now ages later. What is your story, and why were you in this jar?" When the demon heard the fisherman, he said, "Be glad!" The fisherman cried, "O happy day!" The demon added, "Be glad that you will soon be put to death." The fisherman said, "You deserve to be put to shame for such tidings. Why do you wish to kill me, I who have released you and delivered you from the bottom of the sea and brought you back to this world?" The demon replied, "Make a wish!" The fisherman was happy and asked, "What shall I wish of you?" The demon replied, "Tell me how you wish to die, and what manner of death you wish me to choose." The fisherman asked, "What is my crime? Is this my reward from you for having delivered you?" The demon replied, "Fisherman, listen to my story." The fisherman said, "Make it short, for I am at my rope's end."

The demon said, "You should know that I am one of the renegade, rebellious demons. I, together with the giant Sakhr, rebelled against the prophet Solomon, the son of David, who sent against me Asif ibn-Barkhiya, who took me by force and bade me be led in defeat and humiliation before the prophet Solomon. When the prophet Solomon saw me, he invoked God to protect him from me and my looks and asked me to submit to him, but I refused. So he called for this brass jar, confined me inside, and sealed it with a lead seal on which he imprinted God's Almighty name. Then he commanded his demons to carry me and throw me into the middle of the sea. I stayed there for two hundred years, saying to myself, 'Whoever sets me free during these two hundred years, I will make him rich.' But the two hundred years went by and were followed by another two hundred, and no one set me free. Then I vowed to myself, 'Whoever sets me free, I will open for him all the treasures of the earth,' but four hundred years went by, and no one set me free. When I entered the next hundred years, I vowed to myself, 'Whoever delivers me, during these hundred years, I will make him king, make myself his servant, and fulfill every day three of his wishes,' but that hundred years too, plus all the intervening years, went by, and no one set me free. Then I raged and raved and growled and snorted and said to myself, 'Whoever delivers me from

---

4. Solomon (Suleiman) is mentioned as a prophet in the Koran.

now on, I will either put him to the worst of deaths or let him choose for himself the manner of death.' Soon you came by and set me free. Tell me how you wish to die."

When the fisherman heard what the demon said, he replied, "To God we belong and to Him we return. After all these years, with my bad luck, I had to set you free now. Forgive me, and God will grant you forgiveness. Destroy me, and God will inflict on you one who will destroy you." The demon replied, "It must be. Tell me how you wish to die." When the fisherman was certain that he was going to die, he mourned and wept, saying, "O my children, may God not deprive us of each other." Again he turned to the demon and said, "For God's sake, release me as a reward for releasing you and delivering you from this jar." The demon replied, "Your death is your reward for releasing me and letting me escape." The fisherman said, "I did you a good turn, and you are about to repay me with a bad one. How true is the sentiment of the following lines:

> Our kindness they repaid with ugly deeds,
> Upon my life, the deeds of men depraved.
> He who the undeserving aids will meet
> The fate of him who the hyena saved."

The demon said, "Be brief, for as I have said, I must kill you." Then the fisherman thought to himself, "He is only a demon, while I am a human being, whom God has endowed with reason and thereby made superior to him. He may use his demonic wiles on me, but I will use my reason to deal with him." Then he asked the demon, "Must you kill me?" When the demon replied, "I must," the fisherman said, "By the Almighty name that was engraved on the ring of Solomon the son of David, will you answer me truthfully if I ask you about something?" The demon was upset and said with a shudder, "Ask, and be brief!"

But morning overtook Shahrazad, and she lapsed into silence. Then Dinarzad said, "Sister, what an amazing and lovely story!" Shahrazad replied, "What is this compared with what I shall tell you tomorrow night if the king spares me and lets me live! It will be even more amazing."

THE ELEVENTH NIGHT

The following night Dinarzad said to her sister Shahrazad, "Sister, if you are not sleepy, finish the story of the fisherman and the demon." Shahrazad replied, "With the greatest pleasure":

I heard, O King, that the fisherman said, "By the Almighty name, tell me whether you really were inside this jar." The demon replied, "By the Almighty name, I was imprisoned in this jar." The fisherman said, "You are lying, for this jar is not large enough, not even for your hands and feet. How can it be large enough for your whole body?" The demon replied, "By God, I was inside. Don't you believe that I was inside it?" The fisherman said, "No, I don't." Whereupon the demon shook himself and turned into smoke, which rose, stretched over the sea, spread over the land, then gathered, and, little by little, began to enter the jar. When the smoke disappeared completely, the demon shouted from within, "Fisherman, here I am in the jar. Do you believe me now?"

The fisherman at once took out the sealed lead stopper and hurriedly clamped it on the mouth of the jar. Then he cried out, "Demon, now tell me how you wish to die. For I will throw you into this sea, build a house right here, and sit here and stop any fisherman who comes to fish and warn him that there is a demon here, who will kill whoever pulls him out and who will let him choose how he wishes to die." When the demon heard what the fisherman said and found himself imprisoned, he tried to get out but could not, for he was prevented by the seal of Solomon the son of David. Realizing that the fisherman had tricked him, the demon said, "Fisherman, don't do this to me. I was only joking with you." The fisherman replied, "You are lying, you the dirtiest and meanest of demons," and began to roll the jar toward the sea. The demon shouted, "Don't, don't!" But the fisherman replied, "Yes, yes." Then in a soft and submissive voice the demon asked, "Fisherman, what do you intend to do?" The fisherman replied, "I intend to throw you into the sea. The first time you stayed there for eight hundred years. This time I will let you stay until Doomsday. Haven't I said to you, 'Spare me, and God will spare you. Destroy me, and God will destroy you'? But you refused, and persisted in your resolve to do me in and kill me. Now it is my turn to do you in." The demon said, "Fisherman, if you open the jar, I will reward you and make you rich." The fisherman replied, "You are lying, you are lying. Your situation and mine is like that of King Yunan and the sage Duban." The demon asked, "What is their story?" The fisherman said:

[The Tale of King Yunan and the Sage Duban]

Demon, there was once a king called Yunan, who reigned in one of the cities of Persia, in the province of Zuman.[5] This king was afflicted with leprosy, which had defied the physicians and the sages, who, for all the medicines they gave him to drink and all the ointments they applied, were unable to cure him. One day there came to the city of King Yunan a sage called Duban. This sage had read all sorts of books, Greek, Persian, Turkish, Arabic, Byzantine, Syriac, and Hebrew, had studied the sciences, and had learned their groundwork, as well as their principles and basic benefits. Thus he was versed in all the sciences, from philosophy to the lore of plants and herbs, the harmful as well as the beneficial. A few days after he arrived in the city of King Yunan, the sage heard about the king and his leprosy and the fact that the physicians and the sages were unable to cure him. On the following day, when God's morning dawned and His sun rose, the sage Duban put on his best clothes, went to King Yunan and, introducing himself, said, "Your Majesty, I have heard of that which has afflicted your body and heard that many physicians have treated you without finding a way to cure you. Your Majesty, I can treat you without giving you any medicine to drink or ointment to apply." When the king heard this, he said, "If you succeed, I will bestow on you riches that would be enough for you and your grandchildren. I will bestow favors on you, and I will make you my companion and friend." The king bestowed robes of honor on the sage, treated him kindly, and then asked him, "Can you really cure me from my leprosy without any medicine to drink

5. Modern Armenia.

or ointment to apply?" The sage replied, "Yes, I will cure you externally." The king was astonished, and he began to feel respect as well as great affection for the sage. He said, "Now, sage, do what you have promised." The sage replied, "I hear and obey. I will do it tomorrow morning, the Almighty God willing." Then the sage went to the city, rented a house, and there he distilled and extracted medicines and drugs. Then with his great knowledge and skill, he fashioned a mallet with a curved end, hollowed the mallet, as well as the handle, and filled the handle with his medicines and drugs. He likewise made a ball. When he had perfected and prepared everything, he went on the following day to King Yunan and kissed the ground before him.

But morning overtook Shahrazad, and she lapsed into silence. Then her sister Dinarzad said, "What a lovely story!" Shahrazad replied, "You have heard nothing yet. Tomorrow night I shall tell you something stranger and more amazing if the king spares me and lets me live!"

THE TWELFTH NIGHT

The following night Dinarzad said to her sister Shahrazad, "Please, sister, finish the rest of the story of the fisherman and the demon." Shahrazad replied, "With the greatest pleasure":

I heard, O King, that the fisherman said to the demon:

The sage Duban came to King Yunan and asked him to ride to the playground to play with the ball and mallet. The king rode out, attended by his chamberlains, princes, viziers, and lords and eminent men of the realm. When the king was seated, the sage Duban entered, offered him the mallet, and said, "O happy King, take this mallet, hold it in your hand, and as you race on the playground, hold the grip tightly in your fist, and hit the ball. Race until you perspire, and the medicine will ooze from the grip into your perspiring hand, spread to your wrist, and circulate through your entire body. After you perspire and the medicine spreads in your body, return to your royal palace, take a bath, and go to sleep. You will wake up cured, and that is all there is to it." King Yunan took the mallet from the sage Duban and mounted his horse. The attendants threw the ball before the king, who, holding the grip tightly in his fist, followed it and struggled excitedly to catch up with it and hit it. He kept galloping after the ball and hitting it until his palm and the rest of his body began to perspire, and the medicine began to ooze from the handle and flow through his entire body. When the sage Duban was certain that the medicine had oozed and spread through the king's body, he advised him to return to his palace and go immediately to the bath. The king went to the bath and washed himself thoroughly. Then he put on his clothes, left the bath, and returned to his palace.

As for the sage Duban, he spent the night at home, and early in the morning, he went to the palace and asked for permission to see the king. When he was allowed in, he entered and kissed the ground before the king; then, pointing toward him with his hand, he began to recite the following verses:

> The virtues you fostered are great;
> For who but you could sire them?
> Yours is the face whose radiant light

> Effaces the night dark and grim.
> Forever beams your radiant face;   5
> That of the world is still in gloom.
> You rained on us with ample grace,
> As the clouds rain on thirsty hills,
> Expending your munificence,
> Attaining your magnificence.   10

When the sage Duban finished reciting these verses, the king stood up and embraced him. Then he seated the sage beside him, and with attentiveness and smiles, engaged him in conversation. Then the king bestowed on the sage robes of honor, gave him gifts and endowments, and granted his wishes. For when the king had looked at himself the morning after the bath, he found that his body was clear of leprosy, as clear and pure as silver. He therefore felt exceedingly happy and in a very generous mood. Thus when he went in the morning to the reception hall and sat on his throne, attended by the mamluks[6] and chamberlains, in the company of the viziers and the lords of the realm, and the sage Duban presented himself, as we have mentioned, the king stood up, embraced him, and seated him beside him. He treated him attentively and drank and ate with him.

But morning overtook Shahrazad, and she lapsed into silence. Then her sister Dinarzad said, "Sister, what a lovely story!" Shahrazad replied, "The rest of the story is stranger and more amazing. If the king spares me and I am alive tomorrow night, I shall tell you something even more entertaining."

THE THIRTEENTH NIGHT

The following night Dinarzad said to her sister Shahrazad, "Sister, if you are not sleepy, tell us one of your lovely little tales to while away the night." Shahrazad replied, "With the greatest pleasure":

I heard, O happy King who is praiseworthy by the Grace of God, that King Yunan bestowed favors on the sage, gave him robes of honor, and granted his wishes. At the end of the day he gave the sage a thousand dinars and sent him home. The king, who was amazed at the skill of the sage Duban, said to himself, "This man has treated me externally, without giving me any draught to drink or ointment to apply. His is indeed a great wisdom for which he deserves to be honored and rewarded. He shall become my companion, confidant, and close friend." Then the king spent the night, happy at his recovery from his illness, at his good health, and at the soundness of his body. When morning came and it was light, the king went to the royal reception hall and sat on the throne, attended by his chief officers, while the princes, viziers, and lords of the realm sat to his right and left. Then the king called for the sage, and when the sage entered and kissed the ground before him, the king stood up to salute him, seated him beside him, and invited him to eat with him. The king treated him intimately, showed him favors, and bestowed on him robes of honor and many other gifts. Then he spent the whole day conversing with him, and at the end of the day he ordered that he

---

6. Literally "slaves," but here members of a military force who were originally of Caucasian slaves.

be given a thousand dinars. The sage went home and spent the night with his wife, feeling happy and thankful to God the Arbiter.

In the morning, the king went to the royal reception hall, and the princes and viziers came to stand in attendance. It happened that King Yunan had a vizier who was sinister, greedy, envious, and fretful, and when he saw that the sage had found favor with the king, who bestowed on him much money and many robes of honor, he feared that the king would dismiss him and appoint the sage in his place; therefore, he envied the sage and harbored ill will against him, for "nobody is free from envy." The envious vizier approached the king and, kissing the ground before him, said, "O excellent King and glorious Lord, it was by your kindness and with your blessing that I rose to prominence; therefore, if I fail to advise you on a grave matter, I am not my father's son. If the great King and noble Lord commands, I shall disclose the matter to him." The king was upset and asked, "Damn you, what advice have you got?" The vizier replied, "Your Majesty, 'He who considers not the end, fortune is not his friend.' I have seen your Majesty make a mistake, for you have bestowed favors on your enemy who has come to destroy your power and steal your wealth. Indeed, you have pampered him and shown him many favors, but I fear that he will do you harm." The king asked, "Whom do you accuse, whom do you have in mind, and at whom do you point the finger?" The vizier replied, "If you are asleep, wake up, for I point the finger at the sage Duban, who has come from Byzantium." The king replied, "Damn you, is he my enemy? To me he is the most faithful, the dearest, and the most favored of people, for this sage has treated me simply by making me hold something in my hand and has cured me from the disease that had defied the physicians and the sages and rendered them helpless. In all the world, east and west, near and far, there is no one like him, yet you accuse him of such a thing. From this day onward, I will give him every month a thousand dinars, in addition to his rations and regular salary. Even if I were to share my wealth and my kingdom with him, it would be less than he deserves. I think that you have said what you said because you envy him. This is very much like the situation in the story told by the vizier of King Sinbad[7] when the king wanted to kill his own son.

But morning overtook Shahrazad, and she lapsed into silence. Then her sister Dinarzad said, "Sister, what a lovely story!" Shahrazad replied, "What is this compared with what I shall tell you tomorrow night! It will be stranger and more amazing."

THE FOURTEENTH NIGHT

The following night, when the king got into bed and Shahrazad got in with him, her sister Dinarzad said, "Please, sister, if you are not sleepy, tell us one of your lovely little tales to while away the night." Shahrazad replied, "Very well":

I heard, O happy King, that King Yunan's vizier asked, "King of the age, I beg your pardon, but what did King Sindbad's vizier tell the king when he

---

7. Not to be confused with Sinbad the Sailor.

wished to kill his own son?" King Yunan said to the vizier, "When King Sindbad, provoked by an envious man, wanted to kill his own son, his vizier said to him, 'Don't do what you will regret afterward.' "

[The Tale of the Husband and the Parrot]

I have heard it told that there was once a very jealous man who had a wife so splendidly beautiful that she was perfection itself. The wife always refused to let her husband travel and leave her behind, until one day when he found it absolutely necessary to go on a journey. He went to the bird market, bought a parrot, and brought it home. The parrot was intelligent, knowledgeable, smart, and retentive. Then he went away on his journey, and when he finished his business and came back, he brought the parrot and inquired about his wife during his absence. The parrot gave him a day-by-day account of what his wife had done with her lover and how the two carried on in his absence. When the husband heard the account, he felt very angry, went to his wife, and gave her a sound beating. Thinking that one of her maids had informed her husband about what she did with her lover in her husband's absence, the wife interrogated her maids one by one, and they all swore that they had heard the parrot inform the husband.

When the wife heard that it was the parrot who had informed the husband, she ordered one of her maids to take the grinding stone and grind under the cage, ordered a second maid to sprinkle water over the cage, and ordered a third to carry a steel mirror and walk back and forth all night long. That night her husband stayed out, and when he came home in the morning, he brought the parrot, spoke with it, and asked about what had transpired in his absence that night. The parrot replied, "Master, forgive me, for last night, all night long, I was unable to hear or see very well because of the intense darkness, the rain, and the thunder and lightning." Seeing that it was summertime, during the month of July, the husband replied, "Woe unto you, this is no season for rain." The parrot said, "Yes, by God, all night long, I saw what I told you." The husband, concluding that the parrot had lied about his wife and had accused her falsely, got angry, and he grabbed the parrot and, taking it out of the cage, smote it on the ground and killed it. But after the parrot's death, the husband heard from his neighbors that the parrot had told the truth about his wife, and he was full of regret that he had been tricked by his wife to kill the parrot.

King Yunan concluded, "Vizier, the same will happen to me."

But morning overtook Shahrazad, and she lapsed into silence. Then her sister Dinarzad said, "What a strange and lovely story!" Shahrazad replied, "What is this compared with what I shall tell you tomorrow night! If the king spares me and lets me live, I shall tell you something more amazing." The king thought to himself, "By God, this is indeed an amazing story."

THE FIFTEENTH NIGHT

The following night Dinarzad said to her sister Shahrazad, "Please, sister, if you are not sleepy, tell us one of your lovely little tales, for they entertain and help everyone to forget his cares and banish sorrow from the heart." Shahrazad replied, "With the greatest pleasure." King Shahrayar added, "Let it be the remainder of the story of King Yunan, his vizier, and the sage Duban, and of the fisherman, the demon, and the jar." Shahrazad replied, "With the greatest pleasure":

I heard, O happy King, that King Yunan said to his envious vizier, "After the husband killed the parrot and heard from his neighbors that the parrot had told him the truth, he was filled with remorse. You too, my vizier, being envious of this wise man, would like me to kill him and regret it afterward, as did the husband after he killed the parrot." When the vizier heard what King Yunan said, he replied, "O great king, what harm has this sage done to me? Why, he has not harmed me in any way. I am telling you all this out of love and fear for you. If you don't discover my veracity, let me perish like the vizier who deceived the son of the king." King Yunan asked his vizier, "How so?" The vizier replied:

[The Tale of the King's Son and the She-Ghoul]

It is said, O happy King, that there was once a king who had a son who was fond of hunting and trapping. The prince had with him a vizier appointed by his father the king to follow him wherever he went. One day the prince went with his men into the wilderness, and when he chanced to see a wild beast, the vizier urged him to go after it. The prince pursued the beast and continued to press in pursuit until he lost its track and found himself alone in the wilderness, not knowing which way to turn or where to go, when he came upon a girl, standing on the road, in tears. When the young prince asked her, "Where do you come from?" she replied, "I am the daughter of an Indian king. I was riding in the wilderness when I dozed off and in my sleep fell off my horse and found myself alone and helpless." When the young prince heard what she said, he felt sorry for her, and he placed her behind him on his horse and rode on. As they passed by some ruins, she said, "O my lord, I wish to relieve myself here." He let her down and she went into the ruins. Then he went in after her, ignorant of what she was, and discovered that she was a she-ghoul, who was saying to her children, "I brought you a good, fat boy." They replied, "Mother, bring him to us, so that we may feed on his innards." When the young prince heard what they said, he shook with terror, and fearing for his life, ran outside. The she-ghoul followed him and asked, "Why are you afraid?" and he told her about his situation and his predicament, concluding, "I have been unfairly treated." She replied, "If you have been unfairly treated, ask the Almighty God for help, and He will protect you from harm." The young prince raised his eyes to Heaven . . .

But morning overtook Shahrazad, and she lapsed into silence. Then her sister Dinarzad said, "What a strange and lovely story!" Shahrazad replied, "What is this compared with what I shall tell you tomorrow night! It will be even stranger and more amazing."

THE SIXTEENTH NIGHT

The following night Dinarzad said, "Please, sister, if you are not sleepy, tell us one of your lovely little tales." Shahrazad replied, "I shall with pleasure":

I heard, O King, that the vizier said to King Yunan:

When the young prince said to the she-ghoul, "I have been unfairly treated," she replied, "Ask God for help, and He will protect you from harm." The young prince raised his eyes to Heaven and said, "O Lord, help me to prevail upon my enemy, for 'everything is within your power.'" When the she-ghoul heard his invocation, she gave up and departed, and he returned safely to his father and told him about the vizier and how it was he who had urged him to pursue the beast and drove him to his encounter with the she-ghoul. The king summoned the vizier and had him put to death.

The vizier added, "You too, your Majesty, if you trust, befriend, and bestow favors on this sage, he will plot to destroy you and cause your death. Your Majesty should realize that I know for certain that he is a foreign agent who has come to destroy you. Haven't you seen that he cured you externally, simply with something you held in your hand?" King Yunan, who was beginning to feel angry, replied, "You are right, vizier. The sage may well be what you say and may have come to destroy me. He who has cured me with something to hold can kill me with something to smell." Then the king asked the vizier, "My vizier and good counselor, how should I deal with him?" The vizier replied, "Send for him now and have him brought before you, and when he arrives, strike off his head. In this way, you will attain your aim and fulfill your wish." The king said, "This is good and sound advice." Then he sent for the sage Duban, who came immediately, still feeling happy at the favors, the money, and the robes the king had bestowed on him. When he entered, he pointed with his hand toward the king and began to recite the following verses:

> If I have been remiss in thanking you,
> For whom then have I made my verse and prose?
> You granted me your gifts before I asked,
> Without deferment and without excuse.
> How can I fail to praise your noble deeds,   5
> Inspired in private and in public by my muse?
> I thank you for your deeds and for your gifts,
> Which, though they bend my back, my care reduce.

The king asked, "Sage, do you know why I have had you brought before me?" The sage replied, "No, your Majesty." The king said, "I brought you here to have you killed and to destroy the breath of life within you." In astonishment Duban asked, "Why does your Majesty wish to have me put to death, and for what crime?" The king replied, "I have been told that you are a spy and that you have come to kill me. Today I will have you killed before you kill me. 'I will have you for lunch before you have me for dinner.'" Then the king called for the executioner and ordered him, saying, "Strike off the head of this sage and rid me of him! Strike!"

When the sage heard what the king said, he knew that because he had been favored by the king, someone had envied him, plotted against him, and lied to the king, in order to have him killed and get rid of him. The sage realized then that the king had little wisdom, judgment, or good sense, and he was filled with regret, when it was useless to regret. He said to himself,

"There is no power and no strength, save in God the Almighty, the Magnificent. I did a good deed but was rewarded with an evil one." In the meantime, the king was shouting at the executioner, "Strike off his head." The sage implored, "Spare me, your Majesty, and God will spare you; destroy me, and God will destroy you." He repeated the statement, just as I did, O demon, but you too refused, insisting on killing me. King Yunan said to the sage, "Sage, you must die, for you have cured me with a mere handle, and I fear that you can kill me with anything." The sage replied, "This is my reward from your Majesty. You reward good with evil." The king said, "Don't stall; you must die today without delay." When the sage Duban became convinced that he was going to die, he was filled with grief and sorrow, and his eyes overflowed with tears. He blamed himself for doing a favor for one who does not deserve it and for sowing seeds in a barren soil and recited the following verses:

> Maimuna was a foolish girl,
> Though from a sage descended,
> And many with pretense to skill
> Are e'en on dry land upended.

The executioner approached the sage, bandaged his eyes, bound his hands, and raised the sword, while the sage cried, expressed regret, and implored, "For God's sake, your Majesty, spare me, and God will spare you; destroy me, and God will destroy you." Then he tearfully began to recite the following verses:

> They who deceive enjoy success,
> While I with my true counsel fail
> And am rewarded with disgrace.
> If I live, I'll nothing unveil;
> If I die, then curse all the men,   5
> The men who counsel and prevail.

Then the sage added, "Is this my reward from your Majesty? It is like the reward of the crocodile." The king asked, "What is the story of the crocodile?" The sage replied, "I am in no condition to tell you a story. For God's sake, spare me, and God will spare you. Destroy me, and God will destroy you," and he wept bitterly.

Then several noblemen approached the king and said, "We beg your Majesty to forgive him for our sake, for in our view, he has done nothing to deserve this." The king replied, "You do not know the reason why I wish to have him killed. I tell you that if I spare him, I will surely perish, for I fear that he who has cured me externally from my affliction, which had defied the Greek sages, simply by having me hold a handle, can kill me with anything I touch. I must kill him, in order to protect myself from him." The sage Duban implored again, "For God's sake, your Majesty, spare me, and God will spare you. Destroy me, and God will destroy you." The king insisted, "I must kill you."

Demon, when the sage realized that he was surely going to die, he said, "I beg your Majesty to postpone my execution until I return home, leave instructions for my burial, discharge my obligations, distribute alms, and donate my scientific and medical books to one who deserves them. I have in particular a book entitled *The Secret of Secrets,* which I should like to give you for safekeeping in your library." The king asked, "What is the secret of this book?" The sage replied, "It contains countless secrets, but the chief one is that if your Majesty has my head struck off, opens the book on the sixth leaf, reads three lines from the left page, and speaks to me, my head will speak and answer whatever you ask."

The king was greatly amazed and said, "Is it possible that if I cut off your head and, as you say, open the book, read the third line, and speak to your head, it will speak to me? This is the wonder of wonders." Then the king allowed the sage to go and sent him home under guard. The sage settled his affairs and on the following day returned to the royal palace and found assembled there the princes, viziers, chamberlains, lords of the realm, and military officers, as well as the king's retinue, servants, and many of his citizens. The sage Duban entered, carrying an old book and a kohl[8] jar containing powder. He sat down, ordered a platter, and poured out the powder and smoothed it on the platter. Then he said to the king, "Take this book, your Majesty, and don't open it until after my execution. When my head is cut off, let it be placed on the platter and order that it be pressed on the powder. Then open the book and begin to ask my head a question, for it will then answer you. There is no power and no strength save in God, the Almighty, the Magnificent. For God's sake, spare me, and God will spare you; destroy me, and God will destroy you." The king replied, "I must kill you, especially to see how your head will speak to me." Then the king took the book and ordered the executioner to strike off the sage's head. The executioner drew his sword and, with one stroke, dropped the head in the middle of the platter, and when he pressed the head on the powder, the bleeding stopped. Then the sage Duban opened his eyes and said, "Now, your Majesty, open the book." When the king opened the book, he found the pages stuck. So he put his finger in his mouth, wetted it with his saliva, and opened the first page, and he kept opening the pages with difficulty until he turned seven leaves. But when he looked in the book, he found nothing written inside, and he exclaimed, "Sage, I see nothing written in this book." The sage replied, "Open more pages." The king opened some more pages but still found nothing, and while he was doing this, the drug spread through his body—for the book had been poisoned—and he began to heave, sway, and twitch.

But morning overtook Shahrazad, and she lapsed into silence. Then her sister Dinarzad said, "Sister, what an amazing and entertaining story!" Shahrazad replied, "What is this compared with what I shall tell you tomorrow night if the king spares me and lets me live!"

THE SEVENTEENTH NIGHT

The following night Dinarzad said to her sister Shahrazad, "Please, sister, if you are not sleepy, tell us one of your lovely little tales to while away the night." The king added, "Let it be the rest of the story of the sage and the king and of the fisherman and the demon." Shahrazad replied, "Very well, with the greatest pleasure":

8. Cosmetic, used by Eastern, especially Muslim, women to darken the eyelids.

I heard, O King, that when the sage Duban saw that the drug had spread through the king's body and that the king was heaving and swaying, he began to recite the following verses:

> For long they ruled us arbitrarily,
> But suddenly vanished their powerful rule.
> Had they been just, they would have happily
> Lived, but they oppressed, and punishing fate
> Afflicted them with ruin deservedly,   5
> And on the morrow the world taunted them,
> " 'Tis tit for tat; blame not just destiny."

As the sage's head finished reciting the verses, the king fell dead, and at that very moment the head too succumbed to death. Demon, consider this story.

But morning overtook Shahrazad, and she lapsed into silence. Then her sister Dinarzad said, "Sister, what an entertaining story!" Shahrazad replied, "What is this compared with what I shall tell you tomorrow night if I live!"

THE EIGHTEENTH NIGHT

The following night, Dinarzad said to her sister Shahrazad, "Please, sister, if you are not sleepy, tell us one of your lovely little tales to while away the night." The king added, "Let it be the rest of the story of the fisherman and the demon." Shahrazad replied, "With the greatest pleasure":

I heard, O King, that the fisherman said to the demon, "Had the king spared the sage, God would have spared him and he would have lived, but he refused and insisted on destroying the sage, and the Almighty God destroyed him. You too, demon, had you from the beginning agreed to spare me, I would have spared you, but you refused and insisted on killing me; therefore, I shall punish you by keeping you in this jar and throwing you into the bottom of the sea." The demon cried out, "Fisherman, don't do it. Spare me and save me and don't blame me for my action and my offense against you. If I did ill, you should do good. As the saying goes, 'Be kind to him who wrongs you.' Don't do what Imama did to 'Atika." The fisherman asked, "What did Imama do to 'Atika?" The demon replied, "This is no time and this narrow prison is no place to tell a story, but I shall tell it to you after you release me." The fisherman said, "I must throw you into the sea. There is no way I would let you out and set you free, for I kept imploring you and calling on you, but you refused and insisted on killing me, without any offense or injury that merits punishment, except that I had set you free. When you treated me in this way, I realized that you were unclean from birth, that you were ill-natured, and that you were one who rewards good with ill. After I throw you into the sea, I shall build me a hut here and live in it for your sake, so that if anyone pulls you out, I shall acquaint him with what I suffered at your hands and shall advise him to throw you back into the sea and let you perish or languish there to the end of time, you the dirtiest of demons." The demon replied, "Set me free this time, and I pledge never to bother you or harm you, but to make you rich." When he heard this, the fisherman made the demon pledge and covenant that if the fisherman released him and let him out, he would not harm him but would serve him and be good to him.

After the fisherman secured the demon's pledge, by making him swear by the Almighty Name, he opened the seal of the jar, and the smoke began to rise. When the smoke was completely out of the jar, it gathered and turned again into a full-fledged demon, who kicked the jar away and sent it flying to the middle of the sea. When the fisherman saw what the demon had done, sure that he was going to meet with disaster and death, he wet himself and said, "This is a bad omen." Then he summoned his courage and cried out, "Demon, you have sworn and given me your pledge. Don't betray me. Come back, lest the Almighty God punish you for your betrayal. Demon, I repeat to you what the sage Duban said to King Yunan, 'Spare me, and God will spare you; destroy me, and God will destroy you.'" When the demon heard what the fisherman said, he laughed, and when the fisherman cried out again, "Demon, spare me," he replied, "Fisherman, follow me," and the fisherman followed him, hardly believing in his escape, until they came to a mountain outside the city. They climbed over to the other side and came to a vast wilderness, in the middle of which stood a lake surrounded by four hills.

The demon halted by the lake and ordered the fisherman to cast his net and fish. The fisherman looked at the lake and marveled as he saw fish in many colors, white, red, blue, and yellow. He cast his net, and when he pulled, he found four fish inside, one red, one white, one blue, and one yellow. When he saw them, he was full of admiration and delight. The demon said to him, "Take them to the king of your city and offer them to him, and he will give you enough to make you rich. Please excuse me, for I know no other way to make you rich. But don't fish here more than once a day." Then, saying, "I shall miss you," the demon kicked the ground with his foot, and it opened and swallowed him. The fisherman, O King, returned to the city, still marveling at his encounter with the demon and at the colored fish. He entered the royal palace, and when he offered the fish to the king, the king looked at them . . .

But morning overtook Shahrazad, and she lapsed into silence. Then Dinarzad said, "Sister, what an amazing and entertaining story!" Shahrazad replied, "What is this compared with what I shall tell you tomorrow night if the king spares me and lets me live!"

THE NINETEENTH NIGHT

The following night Dinarzad said to her sister Shahrazad, "Sister, tell us the rest of the story and what happened to the fisherman." Shahrazad replied, "With the greatest pleasure":

I heard, O King, that when the fisherman presented the fish to the king, and the king looked at them and saw that they were colored, he took one of them in his hand and looked at it with great amazement. Then he said to his vizier, "Take them to the cook whom the emperor of Byzantium has given us as a present." The vizier took the fish and brought them to the girl and said to her, "Girl, as the saying goes, 'I save my tears for the time of trial.' The king has been presented these four fish, and he bids you fry them well." Then the vizier went back to report to the king, and the king ordered him to give the fisherman four hundred dirhams.[9] The vizier gave the money to the fisherman, who, receiving it, gathered it in the folds of his robe and went away, running, and as he ran, he stumbled and kept falling and getting up, thinking that he was in a dream. Then he stopped and bought some provisions for his family.

So far for the fisherman, O King. In the meantime the girl scaled the fish, cleaned them, and cut them into pieces. Then she placed the frying pan on the fire and poured in the sesame oil, and when it began to boil, she placed the fish in the frying pan. When the pieces were done on one side, she turned them over, but no sooner had she done this than the kitchen wall split open and there emerged a maiden with a beautiful figure, smooth cheeks, perfect features, and dark eyes. She wore a short-sleeved silk shirt in the Egyptian style, embroidered all around with lace and gold spangles. In her ears she wore dangling earrings; on her wrists she wore bracelets; and in her hand she held a bamboo wand. She thrust the wand into the frying pan and said in clear Arabic, "O fish, O fish, have you kept the pledge?" When the cook saw what had happened, she fainted. Then the maiden repeated what she had said, and the fish raised their heads from the frying pan and replied in clear Arabic, "Yes, yes. If you return, we shall return; if you keep your vow, we shall keep ours; and if you forsake us, we shall be even." At that moment the maiden overturned the frying pan and disappeared as she had come, and the kitchen wall closed behind her.

When the cook came to herself, she found the four fish charred, and she felt sorry for herself and afraid of the king, saying to herself, " 'He broke his lance on his very first raid.' " While she remonstrated with herself, the vizier suddenly stood before her, saying, "Give me the fish, for we have set the table before the king, and he is waiting for them." The girl wept and told the vizier what she had seen and witnessed and what had happened to the fish. The vizier was astonished and said, "This is very strange." Then he sent an officer after the fisherman, and he returned a while later with the fisherman. The vizier shouted at him, saying, "Bring us at once four more fish like the ones you brought us before, for we have had an accident with them." When he followed with threats, the fisherman went home and, taking his fishing gear, went outside the city, climbed the mountain, and descended to the wilderness on the other side. When he came to the lake, he cast his net, and when he pulled up, he found inside four fish, as he had done the first time. Then he brought them back to the vizier, who took them to the girl and said, "Fry them in front of me, so that I can see for myself." The girl prepared the fish at once, placed the frying pan over the fire, and threw them in. When the fish were done, the wall split open, and the maiden appeared in her elegant clothes, wearing necklaces and other jewelry and holding in her hand the bamboo wand. Again she thrust the wand into the frying pan and said in clear Arabic, "O fish, have you kept the pledge?" and again the fish raised their heads and replied, "Yes, yes. If you return, we shall return; if you keep your vow, we shall keep ours; and if you forsake us, we shall be even."

But morning overtook Shahrazad, and she lapsed into silence. Then Dinarzad said, "What an entertaining story!" Shahrazad replied, "What is this com-

9. Small silver coins.

pared with what I shall tell you tomorrow night if I live, the Almighty God willing!"

THE TWENTIETH NIGHT

The following night Dinarzad said to her sister Shahrazad, "Please, sister, if you are not sleepy, tell us one of your lovely little tales to while away the night." Shahrazad replied, "With the greatest pleasure":

I heard, O happy King, that after the fish spoke, the maiden overturned the frying pan with the wand and disappeared into the opening from which she had emerged, and the wall closed behind her. The vizier said to himself, "I can no longer hide this affair from the king," and he went to him and told him what had happened to the fish before his very eyes.

The king was exceedingly amazed and said, "I wish to see this with my own eyes." Then he sent for the fisherman, who came after a little while, and the king said to him, "I want you to bring me at once four more fish like the ones you brought before. Hurry!" Then he assigned three officers to guard the fisherman and sent him away. The fisherman disappeared for a while and returned with four fish, one red, one white, one blue, and one yellow. The king commanded, "Give him four hundred dirhams," and the fisherman, receiving the money, gathered it in the folds of his robe and went away. Then the king said to the vizier, "Fry the fish here in my presence." The vizier replied, "I hear and obey," and he called for a stove and a frying pan and sat to clean the fish. Then he lit the fire and, pouring the sesame oil, placed the fish in the frying pan.

When they were almost done, the palace wall split open, and the king and vizier began to tremble, and when they looked up, they saw a black slave who stood like a towering mountain or a giant descendant of the tribe of 'Ad.[1] He was as tall as a reed, as wide as a stone bench, and he held a green palm leaf in his hand. Then in clear but unpleasant language, he said, "O fish, O fish, have you kept the pledge?" and the fish raised their heads from the frying pan and said, "Yes, yes. If you return, we shall return; if you keep your vow, we shall keep ours; and if you forsake us, we shall be even." At that moment, the black slave overturned the frying pan, in the middle of the hall, and the fish turned into charcoal. Then the black slave departed as he had come, and the wall closed behind him. When the black slave disappeared, the king said, "I cannot sleep over this affair, for there is no doubt a mystery behind these fish." Then he bade the fisherman be brought before him again.

When the fisherman arrived, the king said to him, "Damn you, where do you catch these fish?" The fisherman replied, "My lord, I catch them in a lake that lies among four hills, on the other side of the mountain." The king turned to the vizier and asked, "Do you know this lake?" The vizier replied, "No, by God, your Majesty. For sixty years, I have hunted, traveled, and roamed far and wide, sometimes for a day or two, sometimes for a month or two, but I have never seen or known that such a lake existed on the other side of the mountain." Then the king turned to the fisherman and asked him, "How far is this lake from here?" The fisherman replied, "King of the age,

---

1. Tribe supposedly destroyed by God's wrath (Koran 41.15).

it is one hour from here." The king was astonished, and he ordered his soldiers to be ready. Then he rode out with his troops, behind the fisherman, who led the way under guard, muttering curses on the demon as he went.

They rode until they were outside the city. Then they climbed the mountain, and when they descended to the other side, they saw a vast wilderness that they had never seen in all their lives, as well as the four hills and the lake in whose clear water they saw the fish in four colors, red, white, blue, and yellow. The king stood marveling; then he turned to the vizier, princes, chamberlains, and deputies and asked, "Have any of you ever seen this lake before?" They replied, "Never." He asked, "And none of you knew where it was?" They kissed the ground before him and replied, "By God, your Majesty, till now we have never in our lives seen this lake or known about it, even though it is close to our city." The king said, "There is a mystery behind this. By God, I shall not return to the city until I find the answer to the mystery behind this lake and these fish in four colors." Then he ordered his men to halt and pitch the tents, and he dismounted and waited.

When it was dark, he summoned the vizier, who was an experienced and wise man of the world. The vizier came to the king, without being seen by the soldiers, and when he arrived, the king said, "I wish to reveal to you what I intend to do. At this very hour, I shall go all by myself to look for an answer to the mystery of this lake and these fish. Early tomorrow morning you shall sit at the entrance of my tent and tell the princes that the king is indisposed and that he has given you orders not to let anyone be admitted to his presence. You must not let anyone know about my departure and absence, and you must wait for me for three days." The vizier, unable to disobey him, abided by the order, saying, "I hear and obey."

Then the king packed, prepared himself, and girded himself with the royal sword. Then he climbed one of the four hills, and when he reached the top, he journeyed on for the rest of the night. In the morning, when the sun rose and steeped the mountaintop with light, the king looked and sighted a dark mass in the distance. When he saw it, he was glad, and he headed in its direction, saying to himself, "There may be someone there to give me information." He journeyed on, and when he arrived, he found a palace, built under a lucky star, with black stones and completely overlaid with iron plates. It had double doors, one open, one shut. Pleased, the king knocked gently at the door and waited patiently for a while without hearing any reply. He knocked again, this time more loudly than before, but again waited without hearing any reply or seeing anyone. He knocked for the third time and kept knocking repeatedly but once more waited without hearing any reply or seeing anyone. Then he said to himself, "There is no doubt that there is no one inside, or perhaps the palace is deserted." Summoning his courage, he entered and shouted from the hallway, "O inhabitants of the palace, I am a stranger and a hungry traveler. Have you any food? Our Lord will requite you and reward you for it." He shouted a second and a third time but heard no reply. Feeling bold and determined, he advanced from the hallway into the center of the palace and looked around, but saw no one.

But morning overtook Shahrazad, and she lapsed into silence. Then Dinarzad said, "Sister, what an amazing and entertaining story!" Shahrazad replied,

"What is this compared with what I shall tell you tomorrow night if I live, the Almighty God willing!"

THE TWENTY-FIRST NIGHT

The following night Dinarzad said to her sister Shahrazad, "For God's sake, sister, if you are not sleepy, tell us one of your lovely little tales to while away the night." Shahrazad replied, "With the greatest pleasure":

I heard, O King, that the king walked to the center of the palace and looked around, but saw no one. The palace was furnished with silk carpets and leather mats and hung with drapes. There were also settees, benches, and seats with cushions, as well as cupboards. In the middle there stood a spacious courtyard, surrounded by four adjoining recessed courts facing each other. In the center stood a fountain, on top of which crouched four lions in red gold, spouting water from their mouths in droplets that looked like gems and pearls, and about the fountain singing birds fluttered under a high net to prevent them from flying away. When the king saw all this, without seeing anyone, he was astonished and regretted that he found none to give him any information. He sat pensively by one of the recessed courts, when he heard sad moans and lamentations and the following plaintive verses:

> My soul is torn between peril and toil;
> O life, dispatch me with one mighty blow.
> Lover, neither a bankrupt nor a noble man
> Humbled by love's law do you pity show.
> Ev'n from the breeze I jealously used to guard you,   5
> But at the blow of fate the eyes blind go.
> When, as he pulls to shoot, the bowstring breaks
> What can the bowman facing his foes do?
> And when the foes begin to congregate
> How can he then escape his cruel fate?   10

When the king heard the lamentation and the verses, he rose and moved toward the source of the voice until he came to a doorway behind a curtain, and when he lifted the curtain, he saw at the upper end of the room a young man sitting on a chair that rose about twenty inches above the floor. He was a handsome young man, with a full figure, clear voice, radiant brow, bright face, downy beard, and ruddy cheeks, graced with a mole like a speck of amber, just as the poet describes it:

> Here is a slender youth whose hair and face
> All mortals envelope with light or gloom.
> Mark on his cheek the mark of charm and grace,
> A dark spot on a red anemone.

The king greeted the seated young man, pleased to see him. The young man wore a long-sleeved robe of Egyptian silk with gold embroidery, and on his head he wore an Egyptian conical head covering, but his face showed signs of grief and sorrow. When the king greeted him, the young man greeted him back courteously and said, "Pardon me, sir, for not rising, for you deserve even a greater honor." The king replied, "Young man, you are pardoned. I myself am your guest, having come to you on a serious mission. Pray tell me the story behind the lake and the colored fish, as well as this palace and the fact that you sit alone and mourn with no one to console you." When the young man heard this, his tears began to flow over his cheeks until they drenched his breast. Then he sang the following *Mawwaliya* verses:[2]

> Say to the man whom life with arrows shot,
> "How many men have felt the blows of fate!"
> If you did sleep, the eyes of God have not;
> Who can say time is fair and life in constant state?

Then he wept bitterly. The king was astonished and asked, "Young man, why do you cry?" The young man replied, "Sir, how can I refrain from crying in my present condition?" Then he lifted the skirt of his robe, and the king saw that while one half of the young man, from the navel to the head, was human flesh, the other half, from the navel to the feet, was black stone.

But morning overcame Shahrazad, and she lapsed into silence. Then King Shahrayar thought to himself, "This is an amazing story. I am willing to postpone her execution even for a month, before having her put to death." While the king was thinking to himself, Dinarzad said to her sister Shahrazad, "Sister, what an entertaining story!" Shahrazad replied, "What is this compared with what I shall tell you tomorrow night if I live, the Almighty God willing!"

THE TWENTY-SECOND NIGHT

The following night Shahrazad said:

I heard, O King, that when the king saw the young man in this condition, he felt very sad and sorry for him, and said with a sigh, "Young man, you have added one more worry to my worries. I came to look for an answer to the mystery of the fish, in order to save them, but ended up looking for an answer to your case, as well as the fish. There is no power and no strength save in God, the Almighty, the Magnificent. Hurry up, young man, and tell me your story." The young man replied, "Lend me your ears, your eyes, and your mind." The king replied, "My ears, my eyes, and my mind are ready." The young man said:

[The Tale of the Enchanted King]

My story, and the story of the fish, is a strange and amazing one, which, if it could be engraved with needles at the corner of the eye,[3] would be a lesson to those who would consider. My lord, my father was the king of this city, and his name was King Mahmud of the Black Islands. For these four hills were islands. He ruled for seventy years, and when he died, I succeeded him and married my cousin. She loved me very much, so much so that if I was away from her even for a single day, she would refuse to eat and drink until I returned to her. In this way, we lived together for five years until one

---

2. Poems in colloquial language, often sung to the accompaniment of a reed pipe.   **3.** I.e., if a master calligrapher could by a miracle of his art write the entire story at the corner of an eye, it would then be read as a double miracle, one for the extraordinary events, one for the extraordinary art.

day she went to the bath and I ordered the cook to grill meat and prepare a sumptuous supper for her. Then I entered this palace, lay down in this very spot where you are sitting now, and ordered two maids to sit down, one at my head and one at my feet, to fan me. But I felt uneasy and could not go to sleep. While I lay with my eyes closed, breathing heavily, I heard the girl at my head say to the one at my feet, "O Mas'uda, what a pity for our poor master with our damned mistress, and him so young!" The other one replied, "What can one say? May God damn all treacherous, adulterous women. Alas, it is not right that such a young man like our master lives with this bitch who spends every night out." Mas'uda added, "Is our master stupid? When he wakes up at night, doesn't he find that she is not by his side?" The other replied, "Alas, may God trip the bitch our mistress. Does she leave our master with his wits about him? No. She places a sleeping potion in the last drink he takes, offers him the cup, and when he drinks it, he sleeps like a dead man. Then she leaves him and stays out till dawn. When she returns, she burns incense under his nose, and when he inhales it, he wakes up. What a pity!"

My lord, when I heard the conversation between the two maids, I was extremely angry and I could hardly wait for the night to come. When my wife returned from the bath, we had the meal served but ate very little. Then we retired to my bed and I pretended to drink the contents of the cup, which I poured out, and went to sleep. No sooner had I fallen on my side than my wife said, "Go to sleep, and may you never rise again. By God, your sight disgusts me and your company bores me." Then she put on her clothes, perfumed herself with burning incense and, taking my sword, girded herself with it. Then she opened the door and walked out. My lord, I got up . . .

But morning overtook Shahrazad, and she lapsed into silence. Then Dinarzad said, "O my lady, what an amazing and entertaining story!" Shahrazad replied, "What is this compared with what I shall tell you tomorrow night!"

THE TWENTY-THIRD NIGHT

The following night Dinarzad said to her sister Shahrazad, "Please, sister, if you are not sleepy, tell us one of your lovely little tales." Shahrazad replied, "With the greatest pleasure":

It is related, O King, that the enchanted young man said to the king:

Then I followed her, as she left the palace and traversed my city until she stood at the city gate. There she uttered words I could not understand, and the locks fell off and the gate opened by itself. She went out, and I followed her until she slipped through the trash mounds and came to a hut built with palm leaves, leading to a domed structure built with sun-dried bricks. After she entered, I climbed to the top of the dome, and when I looked inside, I saw my wife standing before a decrepit black man sitting on reed shavings and dressed in tatters. She kissed the ground before him and he raised his head and said, "Damn you, why are you late? My black cousins were here. They played with the bat and ball, sang, and drank brewed liquor. They had a good time, each with his own girlfriend, except for myself, for I refused even to drink with them because you were absent."

My wife replied, "O my lord and lover, don't you know that I am married to my cousin, who finds me most loathsome and detests me more than anyone else? Were it not for your sake, I would not have let the sun rise before reducing his city to rubble, a dwelling place for the bears and the foxes, where the owl hoots and the crow crows, and would have hurled its stones beyond Mount Qaf."[4] He replied, "Damn you, you are lying. I swear in the name of black chivalry that as of tonight, if our cousins visit me and you fail to be present, I will never befriend you, lie down with you, or let my body touch yours. You cursed woman, you have been playing with me like a piece of marble, and I am subject to your whims, you cursed, rotten woman." My lord, when I heard their conversation, the world started to turn black before my eyes, and I lost my senses. Then I heard my wife crying and imploring, "O my lover and my heart's desire, if you remain angry at me, whom else have I got, and if you turn me out, who will take me in, O my lord, my lover, and light of my eye?" She kept crying and begging until he was appeased. Then, feeling happy, she took off her outer garments, and asked, "My lord, have you anything for your little girl to eat?" The black man replied, "Open the copper basin," and when she lifted the lid, she found some leftover fried rat bones. After she ate them, he said to her, "There is some brewed liquor left in that jug. You may drink it." She drank the liquor and washed her hands and lay beside the black man on the reed shavings. Then she undressed and slipped under his tatters. I climbed down from the top of the dome and, entering through the door, grabbed the sword that my wife had brought with her, and drew it, intending to kill both of them. I first struck the black man on the neck and thought that I had killed him.

But morning overtook Shahrazad, and she lapsed into silence. Then Dinarzad said, "Sister, what an entertaining story!" Shahrazad replied, "Tomorrow night I shall tell you something more entertaining if I live!"

THE TWENTY-FOURTH NIGHT

The following night Dinarzad said to her sister Shahrazad, "For God's sake, sister, if you are not sleepy, tell us one of your lovely little tales." Shahrazad replied, "With the greatest pleasure":

I heard, O King, that the enchanted young man said to the king:

My lord, I struck the black man on the neck, but failed to cut the two arteries. Instead I only cut into the skin and flesh of the throat and thought that I had killed him. He began to snort violently, and my wife pulled away from him. I retreated, put the sword back in its place, and went back to the city. I entered the palace and went to sleep in my bed till morning. When my wife arrived and I looked at her, I saw that she had cut her hair and put on a mourning dress. She said, "Husband, don't reproach me for what I am

---

4. Legendary mountain cited for its remoteness.

doing, for I have received news that my mother has died, that my father was killed in the holy war, and that my two brothers have also lost their lives, one in battle, the other bitten by a snake. I have every reason to weep and mourn." When I heard what she said, I did not reply, except to say, "I don't reproach you. Do as you wish."

She mourned for an entire year, weeping and wailing. When the year ended, she said to me, "I want you to let me build inside the palace a mausoleum for me to use as a special place of mourning and to call it the house of sorrows." I replied, "Go ahead." Then she gave the order, and a house of mourning was erected for her, with a domed mausoleum and a tomb inside. Then, my lord, she moved the wounded black man to the mausoleum and placed him in the tomb. But, although he was still alive, from the day I cut his throat, he never spoke a word or was able to do her any good, except to drink liquids. She visited him in the mausoleum every day, morning and evening, bringing with her beverages and broth, and she kept at it for an entire year, while I held my patience and left her to her own devices. One day, while she was unaware, I entered the mausoleum and found her crying and lamenting:

> When I see your distress,
> It pains me, as you see.
> And when I see you not,
> It pains me, as you see.
> O speak to me, my life,   5
> My master, talk to me.

Then she sang:

> The day I have you is the day I crave;
> The day you leave me is the day I die.
> Were I to live in fear of promised death,
> I'd rather be with you than my life save.

Then she recited the following verses:

> If I had every blessing in the world
> And all the kingdom of the Persian king,
> If I see not your person with my eyes,
> All this will not be worth an insect's wing.

When she stopped crying, I said to her, "Wife, you have mourned and wept enough and further tears are useless." She replied, "Husband, do not interfere with my mourning. If you interfere again, I will kill myself." I kept quiet and left her alone, while she mourned, wept, and lamented for another year. One day, after the third year, feeling the strain of this drawn-out, heavy burden, something happened to trigger my anger, and when I returned, I found my wife in the mausoleum, beside the tomb, saying, "My lord, I have not had any word from you. For three years I have had no reply." Then she recited the following verses:

> O tomb, O tomb, has he his beauties lost,
> Or have you lost yourself that radiant look?
> O tomb, neither a garden nor a star,
> The sun and moon at once how can you host?

These verses added anger to my anger, and I said to myself, "Oh, how much longer shall I endure?" Then I burst out with the following verses:

O tomb, O tomb, has he his blackness lost,
Or have you lost yourself that filthy look?
O tomb, neither a toilet nor a heap of dirt,
Charcoal and mud at once how can you host?

When my wife heard me, she sprang up and said, "Damn you, dirty dog. It was you who did this to me, wounded my beloved, and tormented me by depriving me of his youth, while he has been lying here for three years, neither alive nor dead." I said to her, "You, dirtiest of whores and filthiest of all venal women who ever desired and copulated with black slaves, yes it was I who did this to him." Then I grabbed my sword and drew it to strike her. But when she heard me and realized that I was determined to kill her, she laughed and said, "Get away, you dog. Alas, alas, what is done cannot be undone; nor will the dead come back to life, but God has delivered into my hand the one who did this to me and set my heart ablaze with the fire of revenge." Then she stood up, uttered words I could not understand, and cried, "With my magic and cunning, be half man, half stone." Sir, from that instant, I have been as you now see me, dejected and sad, helpless and sleepless, neither living with the living nor dead among the dead.

But morning overtook Shahrazad, and she lapsed into silence. Then Dinarzad said, "Sister, what an amazing and entertaining story!" Shahrazad replied, "Tomorrow night I shall tell you something more entertaining if the king spares me and lets me live!"

THE TWENTY-FIFTH NIGHT

The following night Dinarzad said to her sister Shahrazad, "Sister, if you are not sleepy, tell us one of your lovely little tales to while away the night." Shahrazad replied, "With the greatest pleasure":

It is related, O King, that the enchanted young man said to the king:

"After my wife turned me into this condition, she cast a spell on the city, with all its gardens, fields, and markets, the very place where your troops are camping now. My wife turned the inhabitants of my city, who belonged to four sects, Muslims, Magians,[5] Christians, and Jews, into fish, the Muslims white, the Magians red, the Christians blue, and the Jews yellow. Likewise, she turned the islands into four hills surrounding the lake. As if what she has done to me and the city is not enough, she strips me naked every day and gives me a hundred lashes with the whip until my back is lacerated and begins to bleed. Then she clothes my upper half with a hairshirt like a coarse rug and covers it with these luxurious garments." Then the young man burst into tears and recited the following verses:

---

5. Zoroastrian priests. Zoroastrianism is the religion of ancient Persia, based on the recognition of the dual principle of good and evil or light and darkness.

O Lord, I bear with patience your decree,
And so that I may please you, I endure,
That for their tyranny and unfair use
Our recompense your Paradise may be.
You never let the tyrant go, my Lord;   5
Pluck me out of the fire, Almighty God.

The king said to the young man, "Young man, you have lifted one anxiety but added another worry to my worries. But where is your wife, and where is the mausoleum with the wounded black man?" The young man replied, "O King, the black slave is lying in the tomb inside the mausoleum, which is in the adjoining room. My wife comes to visit him at dawn every day, and when she comes, she strips me naked and gives me a hundred lashes with the whip, while I cry and scream without being able to stand up and defend myself, since I am half stone, half flesh and blood. After she punishes me, she goes to the black slave to give him beverages and broth to drink. Tomorrow at dawn she will come as usual." The king replied, "By God, young man, I shall do something for you that will go down in history and commemorate my name." Then the king sat to converse with the young man until night fell and they went to sleep.

The king got up before dawn, took off his clothes, and, drawing his sword, entered the room with the domed mausoleum and found it lit with candles and lamps and scented with incense, perfume, saffron, and ointments. He went straight to the black man and killed him. Then he carried him out and threw him in a well inside the palace. When he came back, he put on the clothes of the black man, covered himself, and lay hiding at the bottom of the tomb, with the drawn sword hidden under his clothes.

A while later, the cursed witch arrived, and the first thing she did was to strip her husband naked, take a whip, and whip him again and again, while he cried, "Ah wife, have pity on me; help me; I have had enough punishment and pain; have pity on me." She replied, "You should have had pity on me and spared my lover."

But morning overtook Shahrazad, and she lapsed into silence. Then Dinarzad said, "Sister, what an amazing and entertaining story!" Shahrazad replied, "What is this compared with what I shall tell you tomorrow night if I live!" King Shahrayar, with a mixture of amazement, pain, and sorrow for the enchanted youth, said to himself, "By God, I shall postpone her execution for tonight and many more nights, even for two months, until I hear the rest of the story and find out what happened to the enchanted young man. Then I shall have her put to death, as I did the others." So he said to himself.

THE TWENTY-SIXTH NIGHT

The following night Dinarzad said to Shahrazad, "Sister, if you are not sleepy, tell us one of your lovely little tales to while away the night." Shahrazad replied, "With the greatest pleasure":

I heard, O King, that after the witch punished her husband by whipping him until his sides and shoulders were bleeding and she satisfied her thirst for revenge, she dressed him with the coarse hairshirt and covered it with the outer garments. Then she headed to the black man, with the usual cup of drink and the broth. She entered the mausoleum, reached the tomb, and began to cry, wail, and lament, saying, "Lover, denying me yourself is not your custom. Do not be stingy, for my foes gloat over our separation. Be generous with your love, for forsaking is not your custom. Visit me, for my life is in your visit. O my lord, speak to me; O my lord, entertain me." Then she sang the following verses of the *Mufrad*[6] variety:

> For how long is this cruel disdain,
> Have I not paid with enough tears?
> O lover, talk to me,
> O lover, speak to me,
> O lover, answer me.   5

The king lowered his voice, stammered, and, simulating the accent of black people, said, "Ah, ah, ah! There is no power and no strength save in God the Almighty, the Magnificent." When she heard him speak, she screamed with joy and fainted, and when she came to herself, she cried, "Is it true that you spoke to me?" The king replied, "Damn you, you don't deserve that anyone should speak to you or answer you." She asked, "What is the cause?" He replied, "All day long you punish your husband, while he screams for help. From sunset till dawn he cries, implores, and invokes God against you and me, with his deafening and enervating cries that deprive me of sleep. If it had not been for this, I would have recovered a long time ago, and this is why I have not spoken to you or answered you." She said, "My lord, if you allow me, I shall deliver him from his present condition." He replied, "Deliver him and rid us of his noise."

She went out of the mausoleum, took a bowl, and, filling it with water, uttered a spell over it, and the water began to boil and bubble as in a caldron over fire. Then she sprinkled the young man with the water and said, "By the power of my spell, if the Creator has created you in this form, or if he has turned you into this form out of anger at you, stay as you are, but if you have been transformed by my magic and cunning, turn back to your normal form, by the will of God, Creator of the world." The young man shook himself at once and stood up, erect and sound, and he rejoiced and thanked God for his deliverance. Then his wife said to him, "Get out of my sight and don't ever come back, for if you do and I see you here, I shall kill you." She yelled at him, and he went away.

Then she returned to the mausoleum and, descending to the tomb, called out, "My sweet lord, come out and let me see your handsome face." The king replied in a muffled voice, "You have rid me of the limb, but failed to rid us of the body." She asked, "My sweet lord, what do you mean by the body?" He replied, "Damn you, cursed woman, it is the inhabitants of this city and its four islands, for every night at midnight, the fish raise their heads from the lake to implore and invoke God against me, and this is why I do not recover. Go to them and deliver them at once; then come back to hold my hand and help me rise, for I am beginning to feel better already." When she

6. Literally "single," a verse form.

heard him, she rejoiced and replied joyfully, "Yes, my lord, yes, with God's help, my sweetheart." Then she rose, went to the lake, and took a little of its water.

But morning overtook Shahrazad, and she lapsed into silence. Then Dinarzad said, "What an amazing and entertaining story!" Shahrazad replied, "What is this compared with what I shall tell you tomorrow night if the king spares me and I live!"

THE TWENTY-SEVENTH NIGHT

The following night Dinarzad said to her sister Shahrazad, "If you are not sleepy, tell us one of your lovely little tales to while away the night." Shahrazad replied, "With the greatest pleasure":

It is related, O King, that the wife uttered some words over the lake, and the fish began to dance, and at that instant the spell was lifted, and the townspeople resumed their usual activities and returned to their buying and selling. Then she went back to the palace, entered the mausoleum, and said, "My lord, give me your gracious hand and rise." The king replied in a muffled voice, "Come closer to me." She moved closer, while he urged her, "Come closer still," and she moved until her body touched his. Then he pushed her back and with one stroke of the sword sliced her in half, and she fell in two to the ground.

Then the king went out and, finding the enchanted young man waiting for him, congratulated him on his deliverance, and the young man kissed his hand, thanked him, and invoked God's blessing on him. Then the king asked him, "Do you wish to stay here or come with me to my city?" The young man replied, "King of the age, and Lord of the world, do you know the distance between your city and mine?" The king replied, "It is a half-day journey." The young man said, "O King, you are dreaming, for between your city and mine it is a full year's journey. You reached us in half a day because the city was enchanted." The king asked, "Still, do you wish to stay here in your city or come with me?" The young man replied, "O King, I shall not part from you, even for one moment." The king was happy and said, "Thank God who has given you to me. You shall be a son to me, for I have never had one." They embraced, holding each other closely, and felt happy. Then they walked together back to the palace, and when they entered the palace, the enchanted young king announced to the eminent men of his kingdom and to his retinue that he was going on a journey.

He spent ten days in preparation, packing what he needed, together with the gifts that the princes and merchants of the city had given him for his journey. Then he set out with the king, with his heart on fire to be leaving his city for a whole year. He left, with fifty Mamluks and many guides and servants, bearing one hundred loads of gifts, rarities, and treasures, as well as money. They journeyed on, evening and morning, night and day, for a whole year until God granted them safe passage and they reached their destination. Then the king sent someone to inform the vizier of his safe return, and the vizier came out with all the troops and most of the townspeople to meet him. Having given him up for lost, they were exceedingly happy, and the city was decorated and its streets were spread with silk carpets. The vizier and the soldiers dismounted and, kissing the ground before the king, congratulated him on his safety and invoked God's blessing on him.

Then they entered the city, and the king sat on his throne and, meeting with the vizier, explained to him why he had been absent for an entire year. He told him the story of the young man and how he, the king, had dealt with the young man's wife and saved him and the city, and the vizier turned to the young man and congratulated him on his deliverance. Then the princes, viziers, chamberlains, and deputies took their places, and the king bestowed on them robes of honor, gifts, and other favors. Then he sent for the fisherman, who was the cause of saving the young man and the city, and when the fisherman stood before the king, the king bestowed on him robes of honor, and then asked him, "Do you have any children?" The fisherman replied that he had one boy and two girls. The king had them brought before him, and he himself married one of the girls, while he married the other to the enchanted young man. Moreover, the king took the fisherman's son into his service and made him one of his attendants. Then he conferred authority on the vizier, appointing him king of the city of the Black Islands, supplied him with provisions and fodder for the journey, and ordered the fifty Mamluks, who had come with them, as well as a host of other people, to go with him. He also sent with him many robes of honor and many fine gifts for all the princes and prominent men there. The vizier took his leave, kissed the king's hand, and departed. The king, the enchanted young man, and the fisherman lived peacefully thereafter, and the fisherman became one of the richest men of his time, with daughters married to kings.

But morning overtook Shahrazad, and she lapsed into silence. Then Dinarzad said, "What an amazing and entertaining story!" Shahrazad replied, "What is this compared with what I shall tell you tomorrow night if the king spares me and lets me live!"

EVERYMAN
1495?

Although drama never attained the status of a dominant literary form in the Middle Ages, in the later centuries of the period it was popular, fairly abundant, and varied in character. It began with the impersonation or dramatization of passages from the liturgy of the Resurrection and the Nativity of Christ. Produced at first in the Latin language and inside a church, it was later moved outside and Latin was replaced with the vernacular languages of several European peoples. By the fourteenth century, if not earlier, whole "cycles" of short plays were performed on certain feast days of the Church, especially Corpus Christi. A complete sequence began with the revolt of Satan and his followers against God and ended with the Last Judgment; inside these limits, some forty "one-act" pieces presented the important events in the divine plan for human history. These plays were produced in the towns, with each of the various craft and trade guilds responsible for one of the plays. The carpenters, for example, would perform the story of Noah, while the "pinners," or nail-makers, would perform the Crucifixion. Because of their scriptural content, modern scholars sometimes called these works *miracle plays,* but the more current term is *mystery plays,* referring not to their content but to the guilds that mounted them: in Middle English a craft or trade is known as a *mystery.*

About the time when the mystery plays had reached their fullest development, another kind of dramatic composition emerged, also religious in nature and purpose. As the mystery plays dramatize biblical events, so the *morality* plays dramatize the content of a typical homily or sermon. By common consent, *Everyman* is regarded as the best of this kind of drama. We do not know the author's name, but the play belongs to the late fifteenth century; it almost certainly derives from a Dutch piece on the same theme. Whereas mystery plays were produced in a long sequence, with amateur casts, morality plays may have been acted by professional or semiprofessional companies. Nothing is actually known about the original productions of *Everyman;* it is well suited, however, to outdoor performance. Its comparative length, along with the large role of the title character, favors the possibility of some degree of professionalism in the cast.

The modern reader may find it profitable to compare *Everyman* with such different kinds of drama as Greek tragedy or Samuel Beckett's *Endgame.* In its brevity, simplicity, and concentration on a single theme and situation, it recalls especially the shorter plays of the ancient Greeks. Its topic has much in common with that of Beckett's play—facing death and coming to terms with life—but the choices involved and the consequent ending (or "ending," in Beckett's work) are different.

As in most morality plays, the characters are personifications of more-abstract concepts. Everyman himself, of course, represents all humanity. But we should not assume in advance that "abstract" characters make a dull play. In the first place, dramatizing the characters gives them actuality; the actors must be flesh and blood. Then, in *Everyman,* the situations, the speech, and the behavior of the various characters are thoroughly realistic as well as representative of their generalized significance. For example, Fellowship does and says what a single boon companion would be likely to say and do under the same circumstances. Good Deeds is not a static figure: we see her first bound to the Earth (the floor of the stage) by Everyman's sins; when he scourges himself in penance, she rises joyfully to accompany him. The author's ingenuity is notable in the character Goods (Riches): Goods is offstage when Everyman calls him; the audience hears but does not see him at first as he explains that he lies there in corners, trussed and piled up, locked in chests, stuffed in bags! Surely he must have got a laugh when he did come on stage. And of course God, who instigates the action by sending Death to call Everyman to his account, is no abstraction. He was probably a voice offstage rather than an actor—but a very effective character nonetheless.

Together with the lean and rapidly moving plot, it is the rightness of its words that makes *Everyman* a success. God speaks with an unfailing simplicity and directness:

> Charyte they do all clene forgete.
> I hoped well that every man
> In my glory shulde make his mansyon;
> And thereto I had them all electe. . . .
> They be so combred with worldly ryches
> That nedes on them I must do iustyce. . . .

Nor is humor absent from the play. Cousin, asked by Everyman to go with him at the summons of Death, exclaims: "No, by Our Lady! I have the crampe in my to[e]"; and later, Beauty replies to the same effect: "I crosse out all this! Adewe, by Saynt Iohan! / I take my cap in my lappe, and am gone." There is irony in Fellowship's farewell verse: "For you I wyll remembre that partynge is mournynge." Best of all, perhaps, are the short speeches, scattered throughout the earlier parts of the play especially, which express Everyman's disappointment in his friends and consequent disillusion. One example must suffice. After a long colloquy with Goods, that character asks Everyman, "What! wenest thou that I am thyne?" Reversal, the necessary prelude to reorientation, is condensed in Everyman's brief reply: "I had weened [believed] so."

Everyman[1]

DRAMATIS PERSONAE

MESSENGER	KNOWLEDGE
GOD	CONFESSION
DEATH	BEAUTY
EVERYMAN	STRENGTH
FELLOWSHIP	DISCRETION
KINDRED	FIVE-WITS
COUSIN	ANGEL
GOODS	DOCTOR
GOOD DEEDS	

Here Beginneth a Treatise How the High Father of
Heaven Sendeth Death to Summon Every Creature
to Come and Give Account of Their Lives in This
World, and is in Manner of a Moral Play

[*Enter* MESSENGER.]

MESSENGER   I pray you all give your audience,
　And hear this matter with reverence,
　By figure[2] a moral play,
　The Summoning of Everyman called it is,
　That of our lives and ending shows　　　　　　　　　　5
　How transitory we be all day.[3]
　The matter is wonder precious,
　But the intent of it is more gracious
　And sweet to bear away.
　The story saith: Man, in the beginning　　　　　　　　10
　Look well, and take good heed to the ending,
　Be you never so gay.
　You think sin in the beginning full sweet,
　Which in the end causeth the soul to weep,
　When the body lieth in clay.　　　　　　　　　　　　15
　Here shall you see how fellowship and jollity,
　Both strength, pleasure, and beauty,
　Will fade from thee as flower in May.
　For ye shall hear how our Heaven-King
　Calleth Everyman to a general reckoning.　　　　　　　20
　Give audience and hear what he doth say.
　　　[*Exit* MESSENGER.—*Enter* GOD.]

1. Modernized text by E. Talbot Donaldson, whose notes have been adapted here.　2. In form.

GOD   I perceive, here in my majesty,
How that all creatures be to me unkind,[4]
Living without dread in worldly prosperity.
Of ghostly[5] sight the people be so blind,   25
Drowned in sin, they know me not for their God.
In worldly riches is all their mind:
They fear not of my righteousness the sharp rod;
My law that I showed when I for them died
They forget clean, and shedding of my blood red.   30
I hanged between two,[6] it cannot be denied:
To get them life I suffered to be dead.
I healed their feet, with thorns hurt was my head.
I could do no more than I did, truly—
And now I see the people do clean forsake me.   35
They use the seven deadly sins damnable,
As pride, coveitise,[7] wrath, and lechery
Now in the world be made commendable.
And thus they leave of angels the heavenly company.
Every man liveth so after his own pleasure,   40
And yet of their life they be nothing sure.
I see the more that I them forbear,
The worse they be from year to year:
All that liveth appaireth[8] fast.
Therefore I will, in all the haste,   45
Have a reckoning of every man's person.
For, and[9] I leave the people thus alone
In their life and wicked tempests,
Verily they will become much worse than beasts;
For now one would by envy another up eat.   50
Charity do they all clean forgeet.
I hoped well that every man
In my glory should make his mansion,
And thereto I had them all elect.[1]
But now I see, like traitors deject,[2]   55
They thank me not for the pleasure that I to them meant,
Nor yet for their being that I them have lent.
I proffered the people great multitude of mercy,
And few there be that asketh it heartily.
They be so cumbered with worldly riches   60
That needs on them I must do justice—
On every man living without fear.
Where art thou, Death, thou mighty messenger?
        [*Enter* DEATH.]
DEATH   Almighty God, I am here at your will,
Your commandment to fulfill.   65
GOD   Go thou to Everyman,
And show him, in my name,

---

4. Thoughtless.   5. Spiritual.   6. The two thieves between whom Christ was crucified.   7. Avarice.
8. Degenerates.   9. If.   1. Chosen.   2. Abased.

A pilgrimage he must on him take,
Which he in no wise may escape;
And that he bring with him a sure reckoning   70
Without delay or any tarrying.
DEATH   Lord, I will in the world go run over all,
And cruelly out-search both great and small.
          [*Exit* GOD.]
Everyman will I beset that liveth beastly
Out of God's laws, and dreadeth not folly.   75
He that loveth riches I will strike with my dart,
His sight to blind, and from heaven to depart[3]—
Except that Almsdeeds be his good friend—
In hell for to dwell, world without end.
Lo, yonder I see Everyman walking: 80
Full little he thinketh on my coming;
His mind is on fleshly lusts and his treasure,
And great pain it shall cause him to endure
Before the Lord, Heaven-King.
          [*Enter* EVERYMAN.]
Everyman, stand still! Whither art thou going   85
Thus gaily? Hast thou thy Maker forgeet?
EVERYMAN   Why askest thou?
Why wouldest thou weet?[4]
DEATH   Yea, sir, I will show you:
In great haste I am sent to thee   90
From God out of his majesty.
EVERYMAN   What! sent to me?
DEATH   Yea, certainly.
Though thou have forgot him here,
He thinketh on thee in the heavenly sphere,   95
As, ere we depart, thou shalt know.
EVERYMAN   What desireth God of me?
DEATH   That shall I show thee:
A reckoning he will needs have
Without any longer respite.   100
EVERYMAN   To give a reckoning longer leisure I crave.
This blind[5] matter troubleth my wit.
DEATH   On thee thou must take a long journay:
Therefore thy book of count with thee thou bring,
For turn again thou cannot by no way.   105
And look thou be sure of thy reckoning,
For before God thou shalt answer and shew
Thy many bad deeds and good but a few—
How thou hast spent thy life and in what wise,
Before the Chief Lord of Paradise.   110
Have ado that we were in that way,[6]
For weet thou well thou shalt make none attornay.[7]

3. Separate.   4. Know.   5. Unexpected.   6. Let's get started at once.   7. None to appear in your
stead.

EVERYMAN   Full unready I am such reckoning to give.
   I know thee not. What messenger art thou?
DEATH   I am Death that no man dreadeth,[8]   115
   For every man I 'rest, and no man spareth;
   For it is God's commandment
   That all to me should be obedient.
EVERYMAN   O Death, thou comest when I had thee least in mind.
   In thy power it lieth me to save: 120
   Yet of my good will I give thee, if thou will be kind,
   Yea, a thousand pound shalt thou have—
   And defer this matter till another day.
DEATH   Everyman, it may not be, by no way.
   I set nought by gold, silver, nor riches,   125
   Nor by pope, emperor, king, duke, nor princes,
   For, and I would receive gifts great,
   All the world I might get.
   But my custom is clean contrary:
   I give thee no respite. Come hence and not tarry!   130
EVERYMAN   Alas, shall I have no longer respite?
   I may say Death giveth no warning.
   To think on thee it maketh my heart sick,
   For all unready is my book of reckoning.
   But twelve year and I might have a biding,[9]   135
   My counting-book I would make so clear
   That my reckoning I should not need to fear.
   Wherefore, Death, I pray thee, for God's mercy,
   Spare me till I be provided of remedy.
DEATH   Thee availeth not to cry, weep, and pray;   140
   But haste thee lightly[1] that thou were gone that journay,
   And prove thy friends, if thou can.
   For weet thou well the tide abideth no man,
   And in the world each living creature
   For Adam's sin must die of nature.[2]   145
EVERYMAN   Death, if I should this pilgrimage take
   And my reckoning surely make,
   Show me, for saint[3] charity,
   Should I not come again shortly?
DEATH   No, Everyman. And thou be once there,   150
   Thou mayst never more come here,
   Trust me verily.
EVERYMAN   O gracious God in the high seat celestial,
   Have mercy on me in this most need!
   Shall I have no company from this vale terrestrial   155
   Of mine acquaintance that way me to lead?
DEATH   Yea, if any be so hardy
   That would go with thee and bear thee company.
   Hie thee that thou were gone to God's magnificence,

---

8. That fears nobody.   9. If I might have a delay for just twelve years.   1. Quickly.   2. Naturally.

Thy reckoning to give before his presence. 160
What, weenest[4] thou thy life is given thee,
And thy worldly goods also?
EVERYMAN   I had weened so, verily.
DEATH   Nay, nay, it was but lent thee.
For as soon as thou art go, 165
Another a while shall have it and then go therefro,
Even as thou hast done.
Everyman, thou art mad! Thou hast thy wits[5] five,
And here on earth will not amend thy life!
For suddenly I do come. 170
EVERYMAN   O wretched caitiff! Whither shall I flee
That I might 'scape this endless sorrow?
Now, gentle Death, spare me till tomorrow,
That I may amend me
With good advisement.[6] 175
DEATH   Nay, thereto I will not consent,
Nor no man will I respite,
But to the heart suddenly I shall smite,
Without any advisement.
And now out of thy sight I will me hie: 180
See thou make thee ready shortly,
For thou mayst say this is the day
That no man living may 'scape away.
        [*Exit* DEATH.]
EVERYMAN   Alas, I may well weep with sighs deep:
Now have I no manner of company 185
To help me in my journey and me to keep.
And also my writing[7] is full unready—
How shall I do now for to excuse me?
I would to God I had never be geet![8]
To my soul a full great profit it had be. 190
For now I fear pains huge and great.
The time passeth: Lord, help, that all wrought!
For though I mourn, it availeth nought.
The day passeth and is almost ago:
I wot[9] not well what for to do. 195
To whom were I best my complaint to make?
What and I to Fellowship thereof spake,
And showed him of this sudden chance?
For in him is all mine affiance,[1]
We have in the world so many a day 200
Be good friends in sport and play.
I see him yonder, certainly.
I trust that he will bear me company.
Therefore to him will I speak to ease my sorrow.
        [*Enter* FELLOWSHIP.]

4. Suppose. 5. Senses. 6. Preparation. 7. Ledger. 8. Beenbegotten. 9. Know.
1. Trust.

Well met, good Fellowship, and good morrow!   205
FELLOWSHIP   Everyman, good morrow, by this day!
   Sir, why lookest thou so piteously?
   If anything be amiss, I pray thee me say,
   That I may help to remedy.
EVERYMAN   Yea, good Fellowship, yea: 210
   I am in great jeopardy.
FELLOWSHIP   My true friend, show to me your mind.
   I will not forsake thee to my life's end
   In the way of good company.
EVERYMAN   That was well spoken, and lovingly!   215
FELLOWSHIP   Sir, I must needs know your heaviness.
   I have pity to see you in any distress.
   If any have you wronged, ye shall revenged be,
   Though I on the ground be slain for thee,
   Though that I know before that I should die.   220
EVERYMAN   Verily, Fellowship, gramercy.[2]
FELLOWSHIP   Tush! by thy thanks I set not a stree.[3]
   Show me your grief and say no more.
EVERYMAN   If I my heart should to you break,[4]
   And then you to turn your mind fro me,   225
   And would not me comfort when ye hear me speak,
   Then should I ten times sorrier be.
FELLOWSHIP   Sir, I say as I will do, indeed.
EVERYMAN   Then be you a good friend at need.
   I have found you true herebefore.   230
FELLOWSHIP   And so ye shall evermore.
   For, in faith, and thou go to hell,
   I will not forsake thee by the way.
EVERYMAN   Ye speak like a good friend. I believe you well.
   I shall deserve[5] it, and I may.   235
FELLOWSHIP   I speak of no deserving, by this day!
   For he that will say and nothing do
   Is not worthy with good company to go.
   Therefore show me the grief of your mind,
   As to your friend most loving and kind.   240
EVERYMAN   I shall show you how it is:
   Commanded I am to go a journey,
   A long way, hard and dangerous,
   And give a strait[6] count, without delay,
   Before the high judge Adonai.[7]   245
   Wherefore I pray you bear me company,
   As ye have promised, in this journey.
FELLOWSHIP   This is matter indeed! Promise is duty—
   But, and I should take such a voyage on me,
   I know it well, it should be to my pain.   250
   Also it maketh me afeard, certain.
   But let us take counsel here, as well as we can—

2. Many thanks.   3. Straw.   4. Disclose.   5. Repay.   6. Strict.   7. God.

For your words would fear a strong man.

EVERYMAN   Why, ye said if I had need,
Ye would me never forsake, quick ne dead,   255
Though it were to hell, truly.

FELLOWSHIP   So I said, certainly.
But such pleasures[8] be set aside, the sooth to say.
And also, if we took such a journay,
When should we again come?   260

EVERYMAN   Nay, never again, till the day of doom.

FELLOWSHIP   In faith, then will not I come there!
Who hath you these tidings brought?

EVERYMAN   Indeed, Death was with me here.

FELLOWSHIP   Now by God that all hath bought,[9]   265
If Death were the messenger,
For no man that is living today
I will not go that loath journay—
Not for the father that begat me!

EVERYMAN   Ye promised otherwise, pardie.[1]   270

FELLOWSHIP   I wot well I said so, truly.
And yet, if thou wilt eat and drink and make good cheer,
Or haunt to women the lusty company,
I would not forsake you while the day is clear,
Trust me verily!   275

EVERYMAN   Yea, thereto ye would be ready—
To go to mirth, solace,[2] and play:
Your mind to folly will sooner apply
Than to bear me company in my long journay.

FELLOWSHIP   Now in good faith, I will not that way.   280
But, and thou will murder or any man kill,
In that I will help thee with a good will.

EVERYMAN   O that is simple[3] advice, indeed!
Gentle fellow, help me in my necessity:
We have loved long, and now I need—   285
And now, gentle Fellowship, remember me!

FELLOWSHIP   Whether ye have loved me or no,
By Saint John, I will not with thee go!

EVERYMAN   Yet I pray thee take the labor and do so much for me,
To bring me forward,[4] for saint charity,   290
And comfort me till I come without the town.

FELLOWSHIP   Nay, and thou would give me a new gown,
I will not a foot with thee go.
But, and thou had tarried, I would not have left thee so.
And as now, God speed thee in thy journey!   295
For from thee I will depart as fast as I may.

EVERYMAN   Whither away, Fellowship? Will thou forsake me?

FELLOWSHIP   Yea, by my fay! To God I betake[5] thee.

EVERYMAN   Farewell, good Fellowship! For thee my heart is sore.

8. Jokes.   9. Redeemed.   1. By God.   2. Pleasure.   3. Foolish.   4. Escort me.   5. Commend.

Adieu forever—I shall see thee no more   300
FELLOWSHIP   In faith, Everyman, farewell now at the ending:
For you I will remember that parting is mourning.
        [*Exit* FELLOWSHIP.]
EVERYMAN   Alack, shall we thus depart[6] indeed—
Ah, Lady, help!—without any more comfort?
Lo, Fellowship forsaketh me in my most need!   305
For help in this world whither shall I resort?
Fellowship herebefore with me would merry make,
And now little sorrow for me doth he take.
It is said, "In prosperity men friends may find
Which in adversity be full unkind."   310
Now whither for succor shall I flee,
Sith[7] that Fellowship hath forsaken me?
To my kinsmen I will, truly,
Praying them to help me in my necessity.
I believe that they will do so,   315
For kind will creep where it may not go.[8]
I will go 'say[9]—for yonder I see them—
Where[1] be ye now my friends and kinsmen.
        [*Enter* KINDRED *and* COUSIN.]
KINDRED   Here be we now at your commandment:
Cousin, I pray you show us your intent   320
In any wise, and not spare.
COUSIN   Yea, Everyman, and to us declare
If ye be disposed to go anywhither.
For, weet you well, we will live and die togither.
KINDRED   In wealth and woe we will with you hold,   325
For over his kin a man may be bold.
EVERYMAN   Gramercy, my friends and kinsmen kind.
Now shall I show you the grief of my mind.
I was commanded by a messenger
That is a high king's chief officer: 330
He bade me go a pilgrimage, to my pain—
And I know well I shall never come again.
Also I must give a reckoning strait,
For I have a great enemy that hath me in wait,[2]
Which intendeth me to hinder.   335
KINDRED   What account is that which ye must render?
That would I know.
EVERYMAN   Of all my works I must show
How I have lived and my days spent;
Also of ill deeds that I have used   340
In my time sith life was me lent,
And of all virtues that I have refused.
Therefore I pray you go thither with me
To help me make mine account, for saint charity.

6. Part.   7. Since.   8. For kinship will creep where it cannot walk (or kinsmen will suffer hardship for one another).   9. Assay.   1. Whether.   2. Satan lies in ambush for me.

COUSIN   What, to go thither? Is that the matter?   345
   Nay, Everyman, I had liefer fast[3] bread and water
   All this five year and more!
EVERYMAN   Alas, that ever I was bore!
   For now shall I never be merry
   If that you forsake me.   350
KINDRED   Ah, sir, what? Ye be a merry man:
   Take good heart to you and make no moan.
   But one thing I warn you, by Saint Anne,
   As for me, ye shall go alone.
EVERYMAN   My Cousin, will you not with me go?   355
COUSIN   No, by Our Lady! I have the cramp in my toe:
   Trust not to me. For, so God me speed,
   I will deceive you in your most need.
KINDRED   It availeth you not us to 'tice.[4]
   Ye shall have my maid with all my heart: 360
   She loveth to go to feasts, there to be nice,[5]
   And to dance, and abroad to start.[6]
   I will give her leave to help you in that journey,
   If that you and she may agree.
EVERYMAN   Now show me the very effect of your mind: 365
   Will you go with me or abide behind?
KINDRED   Abide behind? Yea, that will I and I may!
   Therefore farewell till another day.
      [*Exit* KINDRED.]
EVERYMAN   How should I be merry or glad?
   For fair promises men to me make,   370
   But when I have most need they me forsake.
   I am deceived. That maketh me sad.
COUSIN   Cousin Everyman, farewell now,
   For verily I will not go with you;
   Also of mine own an unready reckoning   375
   I have to account—therefore I make tarrying.
   Now God keep thee, for now I go.
      [*Exit* COUSIN.]
EVERYMAN   Ah, Jesus, is all come hereto?
   Lo, fair words maketh fools fain:[7]
   They promise and nothing will do, certain.   380
   My kinsmen promised me faithfully
   For to abide with me steadfastly,
   And now fast away do they flee.
   Even so Fellowship promised me.
   What friend were best me of to provide?   385
   I lose my time here longer to abide.
   Yet in my mind a thing there is:
   All my life I have loved riches;
   If that my Goods[8] now help me might,
   He would make my heart full light.   390

---

3. Rather fast on.   4. Entice.   5. Wanton.   6. To go gadding about.   7. Glad.   8. Goods.

I will speak to him in this distress.
Where art thou, my Goods and riches?
GOODS [*Within.*]   Who calleth me? Everyman? What, hast thou haste?
I lie here in corners, trussed and piled so high,
And in chests I am locked so fast—   395
Also sacked in bags—thou mayst see with thine eye
I cannot stir, in packs low where I lie.
What would ye have? Lightly[9] me say.
EVERYMAN   Come hither, Goods, in all the haste thou may,
For of counsel I must desire thee.   400
          [*Enter* GOODS.]
GOODS   Sir, and ye in the world have sorrow or adversity,
That can I help you to remedy shortly.
EVERYMAN   It is another disease[1] that grieveth me:
In this world it is not, I tell thee so.
I am sent for another way to go,   405
To give a strait count general
Before the highest Jupiter of all.
And all my life I have had joy and pleasure in thee:
Therefore I pray thee go with me,
For peradventure, thou mayst before God Almighty   410
My reckoning help to clean and purify.
For it is said ever among[2]
That money maketh all right that is wrong.
GOODS   Nay, Everyman, I sing another song:
I follow no man in such voyages.   415
For, and I went with thee,
Thou shouldest fare much the worse for me;
For because on me thou did set thy mind,
Thy reckoning I have made blotted and blind,[3]
That thine account thou cannot make truly—   420
And that hast thou for the love of me.
EVERYMAN   That would grieve me full sore,
When I should come to that fearful answer.
Up, let us go thither together.
GOODS   Nay, not so, I am too brittle, I may not endure.   425
I will follow no man one foot, be ye sure.
EVERYMAN   Alas, I have thee loved and had great pleasure
All my life-days on good and treasure.
GOODS   That is to thy damnation, without leasing,[4]
For my love is contrary to the love everlasting.   430
But if thou had me loved moderately during,
As to the poor to give part of me,
Then shouldest thou not in this dolor be,
Nor in this great sorrow and care.
EVERYMAN   Lo, now was I deceived ere I was ware,   435
And all I may wite[5] misspending of time.

9. Quickly.   1. Distress.   2. Now and then.   3. Illegible.   4. Lie.   5. Blame on.

GOODS   What, weenest[6] thou that I am thine?
EVERYMAN   I had weened so.
GOODS   Nay, Everyman, I say no.
 As for a while I was lent thee;   440
 A season thou hast had me in prosperity.
 My condition is man's soul to kill;
 If I save one, a thousand I do spill.
 Weenest thou that I will follow thee?
 Nay, from this world, not verily.   445
EVERYMAN   I had weened otherwise.
GOODS   Therefore to thy soul Goods is a thief;
 For when thou art dead, this is my guise[7]—
 Another to deceive in the same wise
 As I have done thee, and all to his soul's repreef.[8] 450
EVERYMAN   O false Goods, cursed thou be,
 Thou traitor to God, that hast deceived me
 And caught me in thy snare!
GOODS   Marry, thou brought thyself in care,[9]
 Whereof I am glad: 455
 I must needs laugh, I cannot be sad.
EVERYMAN   Ah, Goods, thou hast had long my heartly[1] love;
 I gave thee that which should be the Lord's above.
 But wilt thou not go with me, indeed?
 I pray thee truth to say.   460
GOODS   No, so God me speed!
 Therefore farewell and have good day.
   [Exit GOODS.]
EVERYMAN   Oh, to whom shall I make my moan
 For to go with me in that heavy journay?
 First Fellowship said he would with me gone: 465
 His words were very pleasant and gay,
 But afterward he left me alone.
 Then spake I to my kinsmen, all in despair,
 And also they gave me words fair—
 They lacked no fair speaking,   470
 But all forsake me in the ending.
 Then went I to my Goods that I loved best,
 In hope to have comfort; but there had I least,
 For my Goods sharply did me tell
 That he bringeth many into hell.   475
 Then of myself I was ashamed,
 And so I am worthy to be blamed:
 Thus may I well myself hate.
 Of whom shall I now counsel take?
 I think that I shall never speed   480
 Till that I go to my Good Deed.
 But alas, she is so weak

6. Suppose. 7. Custom. 8. Shame. 9. Sorrow. 1. Sincere.

That she can neither go[2] nor speak.
Yet will I venture[3] on her now.
My Good Deeds, where be you?   485
GOOD DEEDS [*Speaking from the ground.*]   Here I lie, cold in the ground:
  Thy sins hath me sore bound
  That I cannot stear.[4]
EVERYMAN   O Good Deeds, I stand in fear:
  I must you pray of counsel,   490
  For help now should come right well.
GOOD DEEDS   Everyman, I have understanding
  That ye be summoned, account to make,
  Before Messiah of Jer'salem King.
  And you do by me, that journey with you will I take.   495
EVERYMAN   Therefore I come to you my moan to make.
  I pray you that ye will go with me.
GOOD DEEDS   I would full fain, but I cannot stand, verily.
EVERYMAN   Why, is there anything on you fall?
GOOD DEEDS   Yea, sir, I may thank you of all: 500
  If ye had perfectly cheered me,
  Your book of count full ready had be.
        [GOOD DEEDS *shows him the account book.*]
  Look, the books of your works and deeds eke,[5]
  As how they lie under the feet,
  To your soul's heaviness.   505
EVERYMAN   Our Lord Jesus help me!
  For one letter here I cannot see.
GOOD DEEDS   There is a blind reckoning in time of distress!
EVERYMAN   Good Deeds, I pray you help me in this need,
  Or else I am forever damned indeed.   510
  Therefore help me to make reckoning
  Before the Redeemer of all thing
  That King is and was and ever shall.
GOOD DEEDS   Everyman, I am sorry of your fall
  And fain would help you and I were able.   515
EVERYMAN   Good Deeds, your counsel I pray you give me.
GOOD DEEDS   That shall I do verily,
  Though that on my feet I may not go;
  I have a sister that shall with you also,
  Called Knowledge, which shall with you abide   520
  To help you to make that dreadful reckoning.
        [*Enter* KNOWLEDGE.]
KNOWLEDGE   Everyman, I will go with thee and be thy guide,
  In thy most need to go by thy side.
EVERYMAN   In good condition I am now in everything,
  And am whole content with this good thing,   525
  Thanked be God my Creator.
GOOD DEEDS   And when she hath brought you there
  Where thou shalt heal thee of thy smart,[6]

---

2. Walk.   3. Gamble.   4. Stir.   5. Also.   6. Pain.

Then go you with your reckoning and your Good Deeds together
  For to make you joyful at heart   530
  Before the blessed Trinity.
EVERYMAN My Good Deeds, gramercy!
  I am well content, certainly,
  With your words sweet.
KNOWLEDGE Now go we together lovingly   535
  To Confession, that cleansing river.
EVERYMAN For joy I weep—I would we were there!
  But I pray you give me cognition,
  Where dwelleth that holy man Confession?
KNOWLEDGE In the House of Salvation: 540
  We shall find him in that place
  That shall us comfort, by God's grace.
      [KNOWLEDGE *leads* EVERYMAN *to* CONFESSION.]
  Lo, this is Confession: kneel down and ask mercy,
  For he is in good conceit[7] with God Almighty.
EVERYMAN [*Kneeling.*] O glorious fountain that all uncleanness doth
    clarify,[8]   545
  Wash from me the spots of vice unclean,
  That on me no sin may be seen.
  I come with Knowledge for my redemption,
  Redempt with heart and full contrition,
  For I am commanded a pilgrimage to take   550
  And great accounts before God to make.
  Now I pray you, Shrift, mother of Salvation,
  Help my Good Deeds for my piteous exclamation.
CONFESSION I know your sorrow well, Everyman:
  Because with Knowledge ye come to me,   555
  I will you comfort as well as I can,
  And a precious jewel I will give thee,
  Called Penance, voider of adversity.
  Therewith shall your body chastised be—
  With abstinence and perseverance in God's service.   560
  Here shall you receive that scourge of me,
  Which is penance strong that ye must endure,
  To remember thy Savior was scourged for thee
  With sharp scourges, and suffered it patiently.
  So must thou ere thou 'scape that painful pilgrimage.   565
  Knowledge, keep him in this voyage,
  And by that time Good Deeds will be with thee.
  But in any wise be secure of mercy—
  For your time draweth fast—and ye will saved be.
  Ask God mercy and he will grant, truly.   570
  When with the scourge of penance man doth him bind,
  The oil of forgiveness then shall he find.
EVERYMAN Thanked be God for his gracious work,
  For now I will my penance begin.

---

7. Esteem. 8. Purify.

This hath rejoiced and lighted my heart, 575
Though the knots be painful and hard within.9
KNOWLEDGE   Everyman, look your penance that ye fulfill,
   What pain that ever it to you be;
   And Knowledge shall give you counsel at will
   How your account ye shall make clearly. 580
EVERYMAN   O eternal God, O heavenly figure,
   O way of righteousness, O goodly vision,
   Which descended down in a virgin pure
   Because he would every man redeem,
   Which Adam forfeited by his disobedience; 585
   O blessed Godhead, elect and high Divine,
   Forgive my grievous offense!
   Here I cry thee mercy in this presence:
   O ghostly Treasure, O Ransomer and Redeemer,
   Of all the world Hope and Conduiter,1 590
   Mirror of joy, Foundator of mercy,
   Which enlumineth heaven and earth thereby,
   Hear my clamorous complaint, though it late be;
   Receive my prayers, of thy benignity.
   Though I be a sinner most abominable, 595
   Yet let my name be written in Moses' table.2
   O Mary, pray to the Maker of all thing
   Me for to help at my ending,
   And save me from the power of my enemy,
   For Death assaileth me strongly. 600
   And Lady, that I may by mean of thy prayer
   Of your Son's glory to be partner—
   By the means of his passion I it crave.
   I beseech you help my soul to save.
   Knowledge, give me the scourge of penance: 605
   My flesh therewith shall give acquittance.3
   I will now begin, if God give me grace.
KNOWLEDGE   Everyman, God give you time and space!4
   Thus I bequeath you in the hands of our Savior:
   Now may you make your reckoning sure. 610
EVERYMAN   In the name of the Holy Trinity
   My body sore punished shall be:
   Take this, body, for the sin of the flesh!
   Also5 thou delightest to go gay and fresh,
   And in the way of damnation thou did me bring, 615
   Therefore suffer now strokes of punishing!
   Now of penance I will wade the water clear,
   To save me from purgatory, that sharp fire.
GOOD DEEDS   I thank God, now can I walk and go,
   And am delivered of my sickness and woe. 620
   Therefore with Everyman I will go, and not spare:

9. To my senses. The *knots* are on the scourge (whip) of penance.   1. Guide.   2. Tablet on which are recorded those who have been baptized and have done penance.   3. Satisfaction for sins.   4. Opportunity.   5. As.

His good works I will help him to declare.

KNOWLEDGE Now Everyman, be merry and glad:
 Your Good Deeds cometh now, ye may not be sad.
 Now is your Good Deeds whole and sound,   625
 Going upright upon the ground.

EVERYMAN My heart is light, and shall be evermore.
 Now will I smite faster than I did before.

GOOD DEEDS Everyman, pilgrim, my special friend,
 Blessed be thou without end!   630
 For thee is preparate the eternal glory.
 Ye have me made whole and sound
 Therefore I will bide by thee in every stound.[6]

EVERYMAN Welcome, my Good Deeds! Now I hear thy voice,
 I weep for very sweetness of love.   635

KNOWLEDGE Be no more sad, but ever rejoice:
 God seeth thy living in his throne above.
 Put on this garment to thy behove,[7]
 Which is wet with your tears—
 Or else before God you may it miss   640
 When ye to your journey's end come shall.

EVERYMAN Gentle Knowledge, what do ye it call?

KNOWLEDGE It is a garment of sorrow;
 From pain it will you borrow:[8]
 Contrition it is   645
 That getteth forgiveness;
 It pleaseth God passing[9] well.

GOOD DEEDS Everyman, will you wear it for your heal?[1]

EVERYMAN Now blessed be Jesu, Mary's son,
 For now have I on true contrition.   650
 And let us go now without tarrying.
 Good Deeds, have we clear our reckoning?

GOOD DEEDS Yea, indeed, I have it here.

EVERYMAN Then I trust we need not fear.
 Now friends, let us not part in twain.   655

KNOWLEDGE Nay, Everyman, that will we not, certain.

GOOD DEEDS Yet must thou lead with thee
 Three persons of great might.

EVERYMAN Who should they be?

GOOD DEEDS Discretion and Strength they hight,[2]   660
 And thy Beauty may not abide behind.

KNOWLEDGE Also ye must call to mind
 Your Five-Wits as for your counselors.

GOOD DEEDS You must have them ready at all hours.

EVERYMAN How shall I get them hither?   665

KNOWLEDGE You must call them all togither,
 And they will be here incontinent.[3]

EVERYMAN My friends, come hither and be present,

---

6. Trial. 7. Advantage. 8. Redeem. 9. Surpassingly. 1. Welfare. 2. Are called. 3. At once.

Discretion, Strength, my Five-Wits, and Beauty!
   [*They enter.*]
BEAUTY Here at your will we be all ready.   670
  What will ye that we should do?
GOOD DEEDS That ye would with Everyman go
  And help him in his pilgrimage.
  Advise you: will ye with him or not in that voyage?
STRENGTH We will bring him all thither,   675
  To his help and comfort, ye may believe me.
DISCRETION So will we go with him all togither.
EVERYMAN Almighty God, loved might thou be!
  I give thee laud that I have hither brought
  Strength, Discretion, Beauty, and Five-Wits—lack I nought—   680
  And my Good Deeds, with Knowledge clear,
  All be in my company at my will here:
  I desire no more to my business.
STRENGTH And I, Strength, will by you stand in distress,
  Though thou would in battle fight on the ground.   685
FIVE-WITS And though it were through the world round,
  We will not depart for sweet ne sour.
BEAUTY No more will I, until death's hour,
  Whatsoever thereof befall.
DISCRETION Everyman, advise you first of all: 690
  Go with a good advisement[4] and deliberation.
  We all give you virtuous monition[5]
  That all shall be well.
EVERYMAN My friends, hearken what I will tell;
  I pray God reward you in his heaven-sphere;   695
  Now hearken all that be here,
  For I will make my testament,
  Here before you all present:
  In alms half my good I will give with my hands twain,
  In the way of charity with good intent;   700
  And the other half, still[6] shall remain,
  I 'queath to be returned there it ought to be.
  This I do in despite of the fiend of hell,
  To go quit out of his perel,[7]
  Ever after and this day.   705
KNOWLEDGE Everyman, hearken what I say:
  Go to Priesthood, I you advise,
  And receive of him, in any wise,
  The holy sacrament and ointment[8] togither;
  Then shortly see ye turn again hither: 710
  We will all abide you here.
FIVE-WITS Yea, Everyman, hie you that ye ready were.
  There is no emperor, king, duke, ne baron,
  That of God hath commission

---

4. Preparation.   5. Confident prediction.   6. Which still.   7. To go free from danger from him.
8. Extreme unction.

As hath the least priest in the world being: 715
For of the blessed sacraments pure and bening[9]
He beareth the keys, and thereof hath the cure[1]
For man's redemption—it is ever sure—
Which God for our souls' medicine
Gave us out of his heart with great pine,[2]   720
Here in this transitory life for thee and me.
The blessed sacraments seven there be:
Baptism, confirmation, with priesthood[3] good,
And the sacrament of God's precious flesh and blood,
Marriage, the holy extreme unction, and penance: 725
These seven be good to have in remembrance,
Gracious sacraments of high divinity.

EVERYMAN   Fain would I receive that holy body,
And meekly to my ghostly[4] father I will go.

FIVE-WITS   Everyman, that is the best that ye can do: 730
God will you to salvation bring.
For priesthood exceedeth all other thing:
To us Holy Scripture they do teach,
And converteth man from sin, heaven to reach;
God hath to them more power given   735
Than to any angel that is in heaven.
With five words[5] he may consecrate
God's body in flesh and blood to make,
And handleth his Maker between his hands.
The priest bindeth and unbindeth all bands,[6]   740
Both in earth and in heaven.
Thou ministers[7] all the sacraments seven;
Though we kiss thy feet, thou were worthy;
Thou art surgeon that cureth sin deadly;
No remedy we find under God   745
But all only priesthood.[8]
Everyman, God gave priests that dignity
And setteth them in his stead among us to be.
Thus be they above angels in degree.
          [Exit EVERYMAN.]

KNOWLEDGE   If priests be good, it is so, surely.   750
But when Jesu hanged on the cross with great smart,[9]
There he gave out of his blessed heart
The same sacrament in great torment,
He sold them not to us, that Lord omnipotent:
Therefore Saint Peter the Apostle doth say   755
That Jesu's curse hath all they
Which God their Savior do buy or sell,[1]

---

9. Benign.   1. Care.   2. Torment.   3. Ordination.   4. Spiritual.   5. "For this is my body,"
spoken by the priest when he offers the wafer at Communion.   6. A reference to the power of the keys,
inherited by the priesthood from St. Peter, who received it from Christ with the promise that whatever St.
Peter bound or loosed on Earth would be bound or loosed in heaven (Matthew 16.19).   7. Administers.
8. Except from priesthood alone.   9. Pain.   1. To give or receive money for the sacraments is simony,
named after Simon, who wished to buy the gift of the Holy Ghost and was cursed by St. Peter.

Or they for any money do take or tell.[2]
Sinful priests giveth the sinners example bad:
Their children sitteth by other men's fires, I have heard;   760
And some haunteth women's company
With unclean life, as lusts of lechery.
These be with sin made blind.

FIVE-WITS   I trust to God no such may we find.
Therefore let us priesthood honor,   765
And follow their doctrine for our souls' succor.
We be their sheep and they shepherds be
By whom we all be kept in surety.
Peace, for yonder I see Everyman come,
Which hath made true satisfaction.   770

GOOD DEEDS   Methink it is he indeed.

[Re-enter EVERYMAN.]

EVERYMAN   Now Jesu be your alder speed![3]
I have received the sacrament for my redemption,
And then mine extreme unction.
Blessed be all they that counseled me to take it!   775
And now, friends, let us go without longer respite.
I thank God that ye have tarried so long.
Now set each of you on this rood[4] your hond
And shortly follow me:
I go before there[5] I would be. God be our guide!   780

STRENGTH   Everyman, we will not from you go
Till ye have done this voyage long.

DISCRETION   I, Discretion, will bide by you also.

KNOWLEDGE   And though this pilgrimage be never so strong,
I will never part you fro.   785

STRENGTH   Everyman, I will be as sure by thee
As ever I did by Judas Maccabee.[6]

EVERYMAN   Alas, I am so faint I may not stand—
My limbs under me doth fold!
Friends, let us not turn again to this land,   790
Not for all the world's gold.
For into this cave must I creep
And turn to earth, and there to sleep.

BEAUTY   What, into this grave, alas?

EVERYMAN   Yea, there shall ye consume, more and lass.[7]   795

BEAUTY   And what, should I smother here?

EVERYMAN   Yea, by my faith, and nevermore appear.
In this world live no more we shall,
But in heaven before the highest Lord of all.

BEAUTY   I cross out all this! Adieu, by Saint John—   800
I take my tape in my lap and am gone.[8]

---

2. Or who, for any sacrament, take or count out money.   3. The prosperer of you all.   4. Cross.
5. Where.   6. Judas Maccabaeus was an enormously powerful warrior in the defense of Israel against
the Syrians in late Old Testament times.   7. Decay, all of you.   8. I tuck my skirts in my belt and am
off.

EVERYMAN   What, Beauty, whither will ye?
BEAUTY   Peace, I am deaf—I look not behind me,
   Not and thou wouldest give me all the gold in thy chest.
    [*Exit* BEAUTY.]
EVERYMAN   Alas, whereto may I trust?   805
   Beauty goeth fast away fro me—
   She promised with me to live and die!
STRENGTH   Everyman, I will thee also forsake and deny.
   Thy game liketh me not at all.
EVERYMAN   Why then, ye will forsake me all?   810
   Sweet Strength, tarry a little space.
STRENGTH   Nay, sir, by the rood of grace,
   I will hie me from thee fast,
   Though thou weep till thy heart tobrast.[9]
EVERYMAN   Ye would ever bide by me, ye said.   815
STRENGTH   Yea, I have you far enough conveyed!
   Ye be old enough, I understand,
   Your pilgrimage to take on hand:
   I repent me that I hither came.
EVERYMAN   Strength, you to displease I am to blame,   820
   Yet promise is debt, this ye well wot.[1]
STRENGTH   In faith, I care not:
   Thou art but a fool to complain;
   You spend your speech and waste your brain.
   Go, thrust thee into the ground.   825
    [*Exit* STRENGTH.]
EVERYMAN   I had weened[2] surer I should you have found.
   He that trusteth in his Strength
   She him deceiveth at the length.
   Both Strength and Beauty forsaketh me—
   Yet they promised me fair and lovingly.   830
DISCRETION   Everyman, I will after Strength be gone:
   As for me, I will leave you alone.
EVERYMAN   Why Discretion, will ye forsake me?
DISCRETION   Yea, in faith, I will go from thee.
   For when Strength goeth before,   835
   I follow after evermore.
EVERYMAN   Yet I pray thee, for the love of the Trinity,
   Look in my grave once piteously.
DISCRETION   Nay, so nigh will I not come.
   Farewell everyone!   840
    [*Exit* DISCRETION.]
EVERYMAN   Of all thing faileth save God alone—
   Beauty, Strength, and Discretion.
   For when Death bloweth his blast
   They all run fro me full fast.
FIVE-WITS   Everyman, my leave now of thee I take.   845
   I will follow the other, for here I thee forsake.

9. Break.   1. Know.   2. Supposed.

EVERYMAN   Alas, then may I wail and weep,
  For I took you for my best friend.
FIVE-WITS   I will no longer thee keep.
  Now farewell, and there an end!   850
     [*Exit* FIVE-WITS.]
EVERYMAN   O Jesu, help, all hath forsaken me!
GOOD DEEDS   Nay, Everyman, I will bide with thee:
  I will not forsake thee indeed;
  Thou shalt find me a good friend at need.
EVERYMAN   Gramercy, Good Deeds! Now may I true friends see.   855
  They have forsaken me every one—
  I loved them better than my Good Deeds alone.
  Knowledge, will ye forsake me also?
KNOWLEDGE   Yea, Everyman, when ye to Death shall go,
  But not yet, for no manner of danger.   860
EVERYMAN   Gramercy, Knowledge, with all my heart!
KNOWLEDGE   Nay, yet will I not from hence depart
  Till I see where ye shall become.
EVERYMAN   Methink, alas, that I must be gone
  To make my reckoning and my debts pay,   865
  For I see my time is nigh spent away.
  Take example, all ye that this do hear or see,
  How they that I best loved do forsake me,
  Except my Good Deeds that bideth truly.
GOOD DEEDS   All earthly things is but vanity.   870
  Beauty, Strength, and Discretion do man forsake,
  Foolish friends and kinsmen that fair spake—
  All fleeth save Good Deeds, and that am I.
EVERYMAN   Have mercy on me, God most mighty,
  And stand by me, thou mother and maid, holy Mary!   875
GOOD DEEDS   Fear not: I will speak for thee.
EVERYMAN   Here I cry God mercy!
GOOD DEEDS   Short our end, and 'minish our pain.[3]
  Let us go, and never come again.
EVERYMAN   Into thy hands, Lord, my soul I commend: 880
  Receive it, Lord, that it be not lost.
  As thou me boughtest,[4] so me defend,
  And save me from the fiend's boast,
  That I may appear with that blessed host
  That shall be saved at the day of doom.   885
  In manus tuas, of mights most,
  Forever *commendo spiritum meum.*[5]
     [EVERYMAN *and* GOOD DEEDS *descend into the grave.*]
KNOWLEDGE   Now hath he suffered that we all shall endure,
  The Good Deeds shall make all sure.
  Now hath he made ending,   890
  Methinketh that I hear angels sing
  And make great joy and melody

---

3. Make our dying quick and diminish our pain.   4. Redeemed.   5. Into thy hands, O greatest of
powers, I commend my spirit forever (Latin).

Where Everyman's soul received shall be.
ANGEL [*Within.*]   Come, excellent elect spouse to Jesu![6]
 Here above thou shalt go   895
 Because of thy singular virtue.
 Now the soul is taken the body fro,
 Thy reckoning is crystal clear:
 Now shalt thou into the heavenly sphere—
 Unto the which all ye shall come   900
 That liveth well before the day of doom.
    [*Enter* DOCTOR.[7]]
DOCTOR   This memorial[8] men may have in mind:
 Ye hearers, take it of worth, old and young,
 And forsake Pride, for he deceiveth you in the end.
 And remember Beauty, Five-Wits, Strength, and Discretion,   905
 They all at the last do Everyman forsake,
 Save his Good Deeds there doth he take—
 But beware, for and they be small,
 Before God he hath no help at all—
 None excuse may be there for Everyman.   910
 Alas, how shall he do than?[9]
 For after death amends may no man make,
 For then mercy and pity doth him forsake.
 If his reckoning be not clear when he doth come,
 God will say, "*Ite, maledicti, in ignem eternum!*"[1]   915
 And he that hath his account whole and sound,
 High in heaven he shall be crowned,
 Unto which place God bring us all thither,
 That we may live body and soul togither.
 Thereto help, the Trinity!   920
 Amen, say ye, for saint charity.

6. The soul is often referred to as the bride of Jesus.   7. The learned theologian who explains the meaning of the play.   8. Reminder.   9. Then.   1. Depart, ye cursed, into everlasting fire (Latin).

MEDIEVAL WOMEN

One of the questions that most challenged medieval people was the nature and status of woman. From both classical antiquity and the Hebrew Bible the Middle Ages received accounts that defined woman as inferior to man. According to Aristotle, "the female is a defective male"; the Bible taught that because of Eve's transgression, woman "shalt be under the man's power" (Genesis 3.16); Aristotle taught that in the act of generation man is the active power, supplying the form, while the woman is passive, supplying mere matter; the Bible showed that man was made in the image of God, while woman was made from man. These authorities, and many others, led to the creation of a set of distinctions that left woman in the inferior position: man is reason, woman emotion; man is intellect, woman is body; man is culture, woman is nature; man is self-controlled, woman is disorderly. With the advent of Christianity, these distinctions were developed in ways that led to an attitude toward women that was deeply misogynistic. But there was another side to the argument. Both the *Odyssey* and the *Aeneid* contained, in the characters of Penelope and Dido, admirable and powerful women; if the Bible placed Eve under Adam's subjection, it also defined her as "a helpmate like to himself" (Ecclesiasticus 17.5), and if mankind had been lost through Eve, it had been redeemed through the Virgin Mary; the classical poets, as we see from the example of Catullus, were fully alive to the power of passionate love between man and woman; and while Eve was made from Adam, if she was not made from his head, she was also not made—as the great medieval philosopher Thomas Aquinas (1225–1274) argued—from his feet, for it was "not right for her to be subject to man's contempt as his slave," but from his rib, "to signify the social union of man and woman," a union that many medieval writers took to require equality and mutuality. In fact, despite a prevailing attitude that women were inferior to men, the modern ideas of "companionate marriage" and of "marital affection" were alive and well in the Middle Ages. And then, of course, there was the reality of the lives that men and women lived—lives that reveal a wide range of attitudes toward women and an equally wide range of opportunities for women of ambition and capacity. That these opportunities were far less than those available to men should not blind us to the evidence that many women were able to lead fulfilling and surprisingly independent lives. Indeed, historians now generally agree that the position of women in the Middle Ages was significantly better than in the Renaissance and succeeding centuries. It was not until the nineteenth century that the process began that has led to the idea of full equality that our own society is striving to achieve.

The writings included in this section cover a wide range of medieval attitudes and practices. We begin with the misogynistic writings of two of the Church fathers. Tertullian was born about 160 C.E., probably in Carthage in North Africa; he became a Christian in his thirties and died, after a long and contentious career, around 250 C.E. In this selection Tertullian promotes two of the most harmful ideas about women—that all women are guilty through Eve's transgression in the garden of Eden, and that women are dangerous because they cause men to sin. John Chrysostom (347–407 C.E.) lived in the East—he was born in Antioch, a great city in what is now Turkey—and wrote in Greek, but his works were widely translated and known in the West. In this selection he asserts the central tenet of misogyny—that woman is inferior to man in everything—but he also stresses one of the central themes of this kind of writing, that women are chronic and even dangerous talkers. Andreas Capellanus wrote in the late twelfth century, and in this brief selection from his satirical work *On Love* he expands on the dangers of a woman's tongue. To show that this idea had real-life consequences, two selections from the legal records of late medieval England are included. The first documents a case of slander in fifteenth-century Yorkshire, the other a regulation to govern women's talking in the town of Hereford. Interestingly, similar records concerning slander and the restraint of the tongue are far less frequently concerned with men, although it is hard to believe from modern experience that men were less given to either gossip or belittling comments about their acquaintances than women.

Another aspect of medieval misogyny was its attack on marriage. In part this derived from the growing interest in clerical celibacy, which did not become an official Church regulation until the late eleventh century and was never effectively enforced throughout the Middle Ages. But in part it derived from a classical opinion that since men were by definition more rational than women, they should devote themselves to philosophy, a commitment that marriage made impossible. In 393, Jerome—the translator of the Bible into Latin and one of the greatest of the Church fathers—wrote a treatise attacking the opinions of a man named Jovinian, who claimed that virgins, widows, and married women were all of equal merit. Jerome, himself celibate, wrote a strongly worded response, not only defending virginity but attacking, with considerable violence, marriage. In his response he included a little treatise called *On Marriage* by an author whom we know only as Theophrastus. Both Jerome's

Against Jovinian and Theophrastus's *On Marriage* led a long and colorful life throughout the Middle Ages: they are the among the primary texts that comprise, for example, the "book of wicked wives" that the Wife of Bath tears from her husband's hands as he tauntingly reads out insulting passages. A real life example of a philosopher whose life was transformed by marriage was Peter Abelard (d. 1142), a brilliant and controversial thinker whose ground-breaking work prepared the way for the great scholastics, like Thomas Aquinas, of the next century. While in his thirties and teaching in Paris, Abelard became enamored of a young woman named Heloise, and while he was supposed to be tutoring her they fell into a passionate love affair. Heloise became pregnant, and Abelard married her, but then sent her to stay at a nunnery outside Paris. Heloise's uncle apparently thought that Abelard had rejected Heloise, and in revenge he hired men to assault the philosopher; whether at the uncle's direction or not, Abelard was castrated. He then entered a monastery, although he continued to teach and write throughout his life, and Heloise became a nun and eventually the prioress of a nunnery called the Paraclete. Abelard wrote a self-accusing and self-pitying account of his fate in a work called *The History of My Calamities* in 1132. When Heloise read it, she wrote to him, and two letters by each of the former lovers have been preserved. The one included here is an extraordinary display of Heloise's intelligence and learning, but even more of her emotional honesty. For here she admits that her desire for Abelard has never diminished and she includes details that one hardly expects from a nun. But her letter is also written within the traditions of antimatrimonial and misogynistic literature, and it is not clear whether she is telling the truth about herself or instead adopting the stereotype of the lustful woman in order to make Abelard feel less guilty. Lest we should assume that marriage was looked down on by the medieval church, included here is a sermon for a wedding by a thirteenth-century friar named Guillaume de Mailly. Guillaume asserts that the primary purpose of marriage is procreation, but he also insists that a truly Christian marriage is one in which there is "intimate or deep-seated love of the heart," and he illustrates this by quoting one of Paul's Epistles, "Husbands, love your wives." Moreover, in his insistence that the couple have "the right intention" in marrying, he is following the Church's teaching that the only thing required for a true marriage is the mutual consent of the partners. Although the Church preferred couples to have a church wedding, it was never required; and neither the state nor—more important—parents could prevent a marriage to which the partners consented. In reality, of course, aristocratic parents often dictated, or tried to dictate, whom their children should marry. But for the vast majority of the population, including members of the wealthy merchant class, the choice of a marriage partner was their own.

Many medieval writers confronted the misogynistic tradition not only by defending women but by showing how unrealistic and illogical its attacks were. Two examples are presented here. One is from a late thirteenth-century English work called by modern scholars *The Southern Passion*. This is a metrical account of the events of Christ's life from Good Friday through Easter, but it also includes a vigorous defense of Mary Magdalene, one of the women who wept at the foot of the cross and to whom Christ first appeared after the resurrection on Easter. This defense also shows the way in which men blame women for their own erotic desires, and argues that it is absurd to blame women as a class for the faults of a few. A second defense is offered by Christine de Pizan, a remarkable woman who lived in Paris in the first part of the fifteenth century. Widowed at an early age, Christine supported herself by her writing, and many of her works are explicitly feminist. The selection here is from one of her earliest works, *Letter from the God of Love*. The premise of the work is that women complain to Cupid of men's slander, and the *Letter* is Cupid's response. In it Christine provides an especially shrewd analysis of the motivations for both clerical and courtly misogyny, and she reminds men that in slandering women they are slandering their own mothers and sisters. Surprisingly modern in their attitudes, both *The Southern Passion* and Christine's poem show that both men and women were quite capable of understanding not only the psychology that motivates prejudice but also the damage that it inflicts upon human relations.

The final and longest selection presented here is one of the most remarkable documents to survive from the Middle Ages. Throughout the fourteenth and fifteenth centuries the English monarchy sought to enforce a very dubious claim to the throne of France. It was this effort that resulted in the so-called Hundred Years' War, which lasted from 1337 until 1453, when the English were finally expelled from France for good. After his overwhelming victory at Agincourt in 1415, Henry V of England and Charles VI of France agreed that Henry would marry Charles's daughter Katherine and that their son would become King of England and France. In 1422 Henry died, leaving his six-month-old son Henry as the inheritor of this dual monarchy. Meanwhile, in 1419, the son of Charles VI, known as the dauphin, was implicated in the murder of the duke of Burgundy, who controlled much of what is now eastern and northern France. As a result, the Burgundians joined with the English against the French. The dauphin was driven from Paris and established himself in Bourges, where he reigned as Charles VII after his father's death, also in 1422. The country was divided between the English north of the Loire, the Burgundians in the east and far north, and the French from the Loire south, except for Aquitaine, which was controlled by the English. Throughout all of this territory armed bands of undisciplined soldiers brought misery to ordinary people, and reduced the country to helpless despair. In 1428 the English besieged the French-held city of Orleans, and threatened to break through into French territory. It was at this desperate moment that a savior appeared, Joan of Arc. A mere peasant girl about seventeen years old—she was known to her contemporaries as *Jeanne la Pucelle*, Maid Joan—she managed to travel from her village in northeastern France to Chinon, where Charles was then living, and to obtain an interview with the king. She convinced him of his legitimacy as the rightful ruler of France, and then, in May 1429, led a rescue party to Orleans and raised the siege. Then she led Charles to Rheims, a city in what was nominally English territory, where he was invested with the crown of France in a ceremony that established the young king's religious and political legitimacy. Joan now wished to return home but was persuaded to continue to fight; and in May 1430 she was taken prisoner by the Burgundians at Compiègne. The Burgundians sold her to the English, and beginning in February 1431, she was put on trial at Rouen as a heretic before judges who were French in nationality but loyal to the English. The transcript of her interrogation by the judges survives, and here—at times in her own words—we learn about the life and mission of this astonishing young woman who was to become an enduring symbol of French patriotism.

There are several themes that dominate Joan's testimony. One is her gradual admission that she is inspired not just by disembodied "voices" but by an angel—St. Michael—and two saints, Margaret and Catherine. The choice of these figures is not arbitrary. The Archangel Michael was, according to medieval belief, the standard bearer of the heavenly host that defeated Satan and his rebel angels and cast them out of Heaven. Moreover, the famous monastery of Mont St. Michel on the coast of Normandy retained its loyalty to the French monarchy although surrounded by English territory. According to legend, Margaret of Antioch was an early Christian saint who protected her virginity by assuming male clothing and entering a monastery; the little church in Joan's village of Domremy had within it a statue of St. Margaret. Catherine of Alexandria was also an early Christian virgin saint who, at the age of eighteen, protested the Roman emperor's plans to martyr Christians and when confronted with the arguments of fifty of his best philosophers succeeded in converting them to Christianity. For Joan, who was wearing male clothing as she set out on a mission to persuade the king of France that only she could rescue his kingdom from the enemy, these figures must have provided powerful examples. Moreover, in the later Middle Ages visionary women such as Joan became more and more common—a development that did not always please the men of the Church hierarchy. A second important theme is Joan's clothing. The inquisitors seem almost obsessed with it, and clearly it is crucial to Joan's own sense of her identity. She explains it as a demand made of her by God, but it also represents her own sense of herself as not merely a virgin but as somehow transcending traditional sex roles. Like the Archangel Michael (and all angels, according to medieval theologians), her clothing defines her as beyond and above sexual definition, a being who was at once a woman and a man and therefore more than either. For her judges, who had a highly traditional view of woman's place, this was obviously deeply disturbing, and it became one of the "errors" for which she was convicted. The third theme is Joan's extraordinary resilience and courage in the face of a barrage of questions from over twenty judges and their entourage of over a hundred assistants. Sometimes she would be questioned for four hours in the morning and then for another three in the afternoon, with her answers often being interrupted by questions shouted at her from all sides. Yet always she retains not just her composure but her utter confidence in her mission, in her voices, and in God. Over and over the inquisitors try to trap her with elaborate theological questions about, for example, the nature of angels. Yet Joan replies with the assurance of innocence. Why was she, of all people, sent to rescue France, she is asked. "It pleased God so to do," she answers, "by means of a simple maid to drive back the king's enemies." To this reply her enemies could respond only with the brutality of the stake.

TERTULLIAN
ca. 160–225

From The Appearance of Women[1]

If there were faith on earth equal to the reward for faith which is hoped for in heaven, none of you, my most beloved sisters, from when you became aware of the living God and came to understand your nature as women, would have wanted a very glamorous or ostentatious style of dress. Rather, you would go about in mourning clothes and even neglect your appearance, giving the impression of a mourning and repentant Eve so that, adopting all the clothing of the penitent, you might atone more fully for what derives from Eve, namely the disgrace of the first sin and the hatred which followed because of the fall of the human race. "In sorrows and care you will give birth, woman, and be dependent on your husband; and he is lord over you."[2] Do you not know that you are Eve? The judgment of God upon this sex lives on in this age; therefore, necessarily the guilt should live on also. You are the gateway of the devil; you are the one who unseals the curse of that tree, and you are the first one to turn your back on the divine law; you are the one who persuaded him whom the devil was not capable of corrupting; you easily destroyed the image of God, Adam. Because of what you deserve, that is, death, even the Son of God had to die. And do you still think of adorning yourself above and beyond your tunics of animal skin?[3]

You should know that in order to achieve perfect, that is, Christian, chas-

---

1. Translated from the Latin by C. W. Marx.　2. Genesis 3.16.　3. See Genesis 3.21.

tity you must not only not seek to be the object of desire, but also despise the very idea of being one. First, because the desire to please through appearance does not come from a sound conscience, since we know that appearance naturally excites sexual desire. Why therefore do you arouse this evil toward yourself? Why do you excite what you declare to be foreign to you? Second, because we ought not to open the way to temptations. These sometimes, by their urgency, perpetrate sin—and may God drive this away from His own—and indeed they stir up the spirit by offering opportunities to sin.

Why are we a danger to another? Why do we cause desire in another? If the Lord in elaborating the law does not make a distinction in penalty between the fact of sexual intercourse and desire,[4] I do not know whether He may leave unpunished a person who has brought someone else to damnation. For that man is lost as soon as he desires your beauty, and he has committed already in his mind what he desired and you have become his sword. Since we and others are concerned about the desire for beauty which is so dangerous, you should now realize not only that you must reject the preparation of false and contrived beauty, but also that you must remove the splendor of natural beauty by concealing and neglecting it as dangerous to the sight of the eyes. For, although we should not find fault with beauty as something good bestowed on the body by nature, as an additional gift of divine creation, and as good clothing for the soul, we must however be wary of it, because of the injury and violence which it brings to those who pursue it. For the lives of Christians are characterized less by gold than by iron, for the robes are being prepared for the martyrs, and the angels who will bear them up are being made ready. Go forth adorned with the ointments and ornaments of the prophets and the apostles, taking your radiance from simplicity, your rosy complexion from your chastity; paint your eyes with modesty and your mouth with silence; hang on your ears the word of God and fasten round your necks the collar of Christ. Bow your heads to your husbands and that will be ornament for you. Keep your hands busy with spinning and stay at home,[5] and you will be more pleasing than if you were adorned with gold. Dress yourselves in the silk of modesty, with the linen of holiness, and with the purple of chastity. Dressed up in this way, you will have God as your lover.

---

4. See Matthew 5.28. 5. Spinning or weaving was considered to be woman's appropriate work throughout the Middle Ages; see Exodus 35.25.

ST. JOHN CHRYSOSTOM[1]
347–407

From A Sermon

The blessed Paul requires great modesty and great decorum of women, and not only as regards their dress and appearance: he proceeds even to regulate their speech. And what does he say? "Let the woman learn in silence"; that is, let her not speak at all in the church; a rule he has also given in his Epistle to the Corinthians, where he says, "It is a shame for women to speak in the church" and the reason is that the law has made them subject to men. Furthermore, "if they will learn any thing, let them ask their husbands at home."[2] At that time, under such instruction, women did indeed keep silence; but now there tends to be a lot of noise among them, much racket and talking, and nowhere so much as in this place. They may all be seen here talking more than in the market, or at the baths. They are all busily conversing on unfruitful matters, as if they came here for relaxation. So there is general confusion and they do not seem to understand that unless they are quiet they cannot learn anything useful. For when our preaching has to compete with the chatter and no one attends to what is said, what good can it do them? The extent of the silence required of women is that they are not to speak even of spiritual matters, let alone worldly ones, in the church. This is good order and decorum; this will make her fairer than any dress. Clothed like this, she will be able to offer her prayers most pleasingly.

"But I suffer not a woman to teach." Having said that he wished them not to speak in the church, in order to eliminate every reason for conversation, he says, let them not teach, but have the status of learners. In this way they will show submission by their silence. For their sex is somewhat talkative by nature; on that account he restrains them on all sides. "For Adam," he says, "was first formed, then Eve. And Adam was not deceived, but the woman being deceived transgressed."

It may be asked, What has this to do with today's women? It shows that the male sex enjoyed the higher honor. Man was formed first; and elsewhere Paul shows man's superiority: "Neither was the man created for the woman, but the woman for the man."[3] Why does he say this? He wishes for the man to have the pre-eminence in every way; let man take precedence, he means, both for the reason already given[4] and because of what happened afterward. The woman taught the man once and made him guilty of disobedience, and ruined everything. Therefore, because she made bad use of her power over the man, or rather her equality with him, God made her subject to her husband.

---

1. Translated from the Latin by Henry Tweed and Alcuin Blamires. Chrysostom's text is 1 Timothy 2:11–15, where St. Paul writes: "Let the woman learn in silence, with all subjection. But I suffer not women to teach, nor to use authority over the man: but to be in silence. For Adam was first formed; then Eve. And Adam was not seduced; but the woman being seduced, was in the transgression. Yet she shall be saved through child-bearing; if she continue in faith, and love, and sanctification, with sobriety." **2.** For both these citations from Paul, see 1 Corinthians 14.34–35. **3.** 1 Corinthians 11.9. **4.** I.e., because man was created first.

"THEOPHRASTUS"

dates unknown

From On Marriage[1]

Theophrastus's book about marriage, in which he asks whether a wise man should marry, is said to be worth its weight in gold. And after specifying that, yes, occasionally a wise man might venture on marriage—if the woman is beautiful, virtuous, and from a good family, and he himself healthy and rich—he immediately concludes: but all these things rarely coexist in a marriage. Therefore a wise man should not marry.

For, first, marriage impedes the pursuit of philosophy, nor may any man serve both books and a wife. There are many things which are necessary for married women's practices: expensive clothes, gold, gems, shopping sprees, maids, all kinds of furniture, litters, a gilt two-wheeled chariot. Then, all night long, the nagging complaints: "That woman looks so much prettier when she goes out; this one is honored by everyone; when women get together, they despise me as a wretch. Why were you staring at the woman next door? What were you talking about with the maid? What did you bring home from the forum?" We cannot even have a friend or a companion. Only hatred suspects that its own love belongs to another. If there is a really learned teacher in another city, we can neither leave our wife behind nor travel there with that baggage.

It is hard to support a poor one, a torment to put up with a rich one. Add to that that there is no picking out a wife, but we have to take whatever comes along. If she has a temper, if she is foolish, malformed, proud, smelly, whatever vice it is, we learn of it only after the wedding. A horse, a donkey, a bull, a dog, and the most worthless slaves, even clothes and kettles, a wooden stool, a goblet, and an earthen pitcher are all tested first and then bought or not. Only a wife is not shown, lest she should displease before she is wed. Her face must always be noticed and her beauty praised, lest, if you look at another woman, she'll think that she displeases you. You have to call her "lady," celebrate her birthday, toast her health, and wish for her to outlive you. You have to show deference to her nurse and her maid, the servant from her father's house, and her foster-child, and her handsome attendant and her curly-haired "assistant," and her eunuch, gelded to prolong her pleasure and to make it safe;[2] behind these titles there is an adulterer hiding. Those whom she loves must be loved in return, whether they want to or not.

If you put her in charge of the whole household, you become one of the servants. If you keep some matters for your own judgment, she will think you don't trust her, and turn to hatred and bickering, and, if you do not change your mind immediately, she will get the poison ready. If you let into the house old women and goldsmiths and soothsayers and peddlers of gems and of silk clothing, it is a threat to her chastity; if you keep them out, she takes offense because you suspect her. But in truth what does even diligent watchfulness avail, since an immodest wife can not be guarded, and a modest one should not be? Necessity is a faithless watchkeeper over chastity; and only a woman who could have sinned, if she wanted to, can truly be called

---

1. Translated from the Latin by Ralph Hanna III and Traugott Lawler.   2. Men who are castrated in adulthood generally do not lose the desire or capacity for sexual intercourse, but they are of course sterile.

modest. A beautiful wife will be quickly surrounded by lovers, an ugly one will have difficulty restraining her desires. What many love is hard to keep; to have what no one else wants is irksome. Still it is less painful to have an ugly wife than to keep a beauty. Nothing is safe that the whole population is longing and sighing for. One man tempts by his shape, another by his brains, another by his jokes, yet another by his generosity. What is attacked from all sides will fall, one way or another.[3]

People take wives to manage their household, to care for them when they are sick, and to avoid loneliness. But a faithful servant will manage things much better, one obedient to his master's authority and complying with his way of running things, than a wife, who thinks herself the mistress in this alone, that she should do the opposite of her husband's will, that is, what she likes, not what she is told. As for waiting on us when we are sick, friends and household slaves we have bound to us by our kindness to them can do that better than a woman—who will weep and blame us, and sell us floods of tears in hope of the inheritance and, by making a great show of her own anxiety, drive her poor sick husband to despair. But if she gets sick, we have to be sick with her and never leave her bedside. Or if she is a good and kind wife, which is nonetheless a rare bird, when she gives birth, we groan with her; when she is in danger, we, too, are tortured with her. However, a wise man can never be alone.[4] He has with him all men who are and who have ever been good, and he turns his free mind wherever he likes. What his body cannot do, he embraces in his thought. And if he lacks men to speak to, he speaks with God. He will never be less alone than when he is alone.

3. The unpalatable choice between a faithful ugly wife and an untrustworthy beautiful one is presented to a man at the end of the *Wife of Bath's Tale*. The choice, in other words, itself derives from the misogynist tradition, which is perhaps one reason why the man is rewarded for leaving the decision up to a woman.
4. By *wise man* is meant a man committed to the philosophic life.

HELOISE
1101–1164

From Letter to Abelard[1]

Of all wretched women I am the most wretched, and amongst the unhappy I am unhappiest. The higher I was exalted when you preferred me to all other women, the greater my suffering over my own fall and yours, when I was flung down; for the higher the ascent, the heavier the fall. Has Fortune ever set any great or noble woman above me or made her my equal, only to be similarly cast down and crushed with grief? What glory she gave me in you, what ruin she brought upon me through you! Violent in either extreme, she showed no moderation in good or evil. To make me the saddest of all women she first made me blessed above all, so that when I thought how much I had lost, my consuming grief would match my crushing loss, and my sorrow for what was taken from me would be the greater for the fuller joy of possession

1. Translated from Latin by Betty Radice.

which had gone before; and so that the happiness of supreme ecstasy would end in the supreme bitterness of sorrow.

Moreover, to add to my indignation at the outrage you suffered, all the laws of equity in our case were reversed. For while we enjoyed the pleasures of an uneasy love and abandoned ourselves to fornication (if I may use an ugly but expressive word) we were spared God's severity. But when we amended our unlawful conduct by what was lawful, and atoned for the shame of fornication by an honorable marriage, then the Lord in his anger laid his hand heavily upon us, and would not permit a chaste union though he had long tolerated one which was unchaste. The punishment you suffered would have been proper vengeance for men caught in open adultery. But what others deserve for adultery came upon you through a marriage which you believed had made amends for all previous wrong doing; what adulterous women have brought upon their lovers, your own wife brought on you. Nor was this at the time when we abandoned ourselves to our former delights, but when we had already parted and were leading chaste lives, you presiding over the school in Paris and I at your command living with the nuns at Argenteuil.[2] Thus we were separated, to give you more time to devote yourself to your pupils, and me more freedom for prayer and meditation on the Scriptures, both of us leading a life which was holy as well as chaste. It was then that you alone paid the penalty in your body for a sin we had both committed. You alone were punished though we were both to blame, and you paid all, though you had deserved less, for you had made more than necessary reparation by humbling yourself on my account and had raised me and all my kind to your own level—so much less then, in the eyes of God and of your betrayers, should you have been thought deserving of such punishment.

What misery for me—born as I was to be the cause of such a crime! Is it the general lot of women to bring total ruin on great men? Hence the warning about women in Proverbs: "But now, my son, listen to me, attend to what I say: do not let your heart entice you into her ways, do not stray down her paths; she has wounded and laid low so many, and the strongest have all been her victims. Her house is the way to hell, and leads down to the halls of death."[3] And in Ecclesiastes: "I put all to the test . . . I find woman more bitter than death; she is a snare, her heart a net, her arms are chains. He who is pleasing to God eludes her, but the sinner is her captive."[4] It was the first woman in the beginning who lured man from Paradise, and she who had been created by the Lord as his helpmate became the instrument of his total downfall. And that mighty man of God, the Nazarite whose conception was announced by an angel,[5] Delilah alone overcame; betrayed to his enemies and robbed of his sight, he was driven by his suffering to destroy himself along with his enemies. Only the woman he had slept with could reduce to folly Solomon, wisest of all men; she drove him to such a pitch of madness that although he was the man whom the Lord had chosen to build the temple in preference to his father David, who was a righteous man, she plunged him into idolatry until the end of his life, so that he abandoned the worship of God which he had preached and taught in word and writing.[6] Job, holiest of men, fought his last and hardest battle against his wife, who urged him

2. A convent outside Paris. 3. Proverbs 7.24–27. 4. Ecclesiastes 7.26. 5. Samson in Judges 13.3. 6. 1 Kings 11.1–8.

to curse God.[7] The cunning arch-tempter well knew from repeated experience that men are most easily brought to ruin through their wives, and so he directed his usual malice against us too, and attacked you by means of marriage when he could not destroy you through fornication. Denied the power to do evil through evil, he effected evil through good.

At least I can thank God for this: the tempter did not prevail on me to do wrong of my own consent, like the women I have mentioned, though in the outcome he made me the instrument of his malice. But even if my conscience is clear through innocence, and no consent of mine makes me guilty of this crime, too many earlier sins were committed to allow me to be wholly free from guilt. I yielded long before to the pleasures of carnal desires, and merited then what I weep for now. The sequel is a fitting punishment for my former sins, and an evil beginning must be expected to come to a bad end. For this offence, above all, may I have strength to do proper penance, so that at least by long contrition I can make some amends for your pain from the wound inflicted on you; and what you suffered in the body for a time, I may suffer, as is right, throughout my life in contrition of mind, and thus make reparation to you at least, if not to God.

For if I truthfully admit to the weakness of my unhappy soul, I can find no penitence whereby to appease God, whom I always accuse of the greatest cruelty in regard to this outrage. By rebelling against his ordinance, I offend him more by my indignation than I placate him by making amends through penitence. How can it be called repentance for sins, however great the mortification of the flesh, if the mind still retains the will to sin and is on fire with its old desires? It is easy enough for anyone to confess his sins, to accuse himself, or even to mortify his body in outward show of penance, but it is very difficult to tear the heart away from hankering after its dearest pleasures. Quite rightly then, when the saintly Job said, "I will speak out against myself," that is, "I will loose my tongue and open my mouth in confession to accuse myself of my sins," he added at once "I will speak out in bitterness of soul."[8] St. Gregory comments on this: "There are some who confess their faults aloud but in doing so do not know how to groan over them—they speak cheerfully of what should be lamented. And so whoever hates his faults and confesses them must still confess them in bitterness of spirit, so that this bitterness may punish him for what his tongue, at his mind's bidding, accuses him."[9] But this bitterness of true repentance is very rare, as St. Ambrose observes, when he says: "I have more easily found men who have preserved their innocence than men who have known repentance."[1]

In my case, the pleasures of lovers which we shared have been too sweet—they can never displease me, and can scarcely be banished from my thoughts. Wherever I turn they are always there before my eyes, bringing with them awakened longings and fantasies which will not even let me sleep. Even during the celebration of the Mass, when our prayers should be purer, lewd visions of those pleasures take such a hold upon my unhappy soul that my thoughts are on their wantonness instead of on prayers. I should be groaning over the sins I have committed, but I can only sigh for what I have lost. Everything we did and also the times and places are stamped on my heart

---

7. Job 2.9–10.   8. Job 10.1.   9. Pope Gregory the Great (d. 604), wrote a famous commentary on Job called the *Moralia*, from which Heloise is quoting.   1. Heloise is here quoting a treatise on penance by Ambrose, bishop of Milan (d. 397).

along with your image, so that I live through it all again with you. Even in sleep I know no respite. Sometimes my thoughts are betrayed in a movement of my body, or they break out in an unguarded word. In my utter wretchedness, that cry from a suffering soul could well be mine: "Miserable creature that I am, who is there to rescue me out of the body doomed to this death?" Would that in truth I could go on: "The grace of God through Jesus Christ our Lord."[2] This grace, my dearest, came upon you unsought—a single wound of the body by freeing you from these torments has healed many wounds in your soul. Where God may seem to you an adversary he has in fact proved himself kind; like an honest doctor who does not shrink from giving pain if it will bring about a cure. But for me, youth and passion and experience of pleasures which were so delightful intensify the torments of the flesh and longings of desire, and the assault is the more overwhelming as the nature they attack is the weaker.

Men call me chaste; they do not know the hypocrite I am. They consider purity of the flesh a virtue, though virtue belongs not to the body but to the soul. I can win praise in the eyes of men but deserve none before God, who searches our hearts and loins and sees in our darkness.[3] I am judged religious at a time when there is little in religion which is not hypocrisy, when whoever does not offend the opinions of men receives the highest praise.[4] And yet perhaps there is some merit and it is somehow acceptable to God, if a person whatever his intention gives no offence to the Church in his outward behavior, does not blaspheme the name of the Lord in the hearing of unbelievers nor disgrace the Order of his profession amongst the worldly. And this too is a gift of God's grace and comes through his bounty—not only to do good but to abstain from evil—though the latter is vain if the former does not follow from it, as it is written: "Turn from evil and do good."[5] Both are vain if not done for love of God.

At every stage of my life up to now, as God knows, I have feared to offend you rather than God, and tried to please you more than him. It was your command, not love of God which made me take the veil. Look at the unhappy life I lead, pitiable beyond any other, if in this world I must endure so much in vain, with no hope of future reward. For a long time my pretense deceived you, as it did many, so that you mistook hypocrisy for piety; and therefore you commend yourself to my prayers and ask me for what I expect from you. I beg you, do not feel so sure of me that you cease to help me by your own prayers. Do not suppose me healthy and so withdraw the grace of your healing. Do not believe I want for nothing and delay helping me in my hour of need. Do not think me strong, lest I fall before you can sustain me. False praise has harmed many and taken from them the support they needed. The Lord cries out through Isaiah: "O my people! Those who call you happy lead you astray and confuse the path you should take."[6] And through Ezekiel he says: "Woe upon you women who hunt men's lives by sewing magic bands upon the wrists and putting veils over the heads of persons of every age."[7] On the other hand, through Solomon it is said that "the sayings of the

---

2. Heloise is quoting Paul's Epistle to the Romans 7.24.   3. Psalm 8.10.   4. Here Heloise is adopting Abelard's contempt for the current state of theological studies rather than attacking the Church as a whole. 5. Psalm 38.27.   6. Isaiah 3.12.   7. Ezekiel 13.18. Heloise seems to understand this verse as an attack on those who practice magic.

wise are sharp as goads, like nails driven home."[8] That is to say, nails which cannot touch wounds gently, but only pierce through them.

Cease praising me, I beg you, lest you acquire the base stigma of being a flatterer or the charge of telling lies, or the breath of my vanity blows away any merit you saw in me to praise. No one with medical knowledge diagnoses an internal ailment by examining only outward appearance. What is common to the damned and the elect can win no favor in the eyes of God: of such a kind are the outward actions which are performed more eagerly by hypocrites than by saints. "The heart of man is deceitful and inscrutable; who can fathom it?"[9] And: "A road may seem straightforward to a man, yet may end as the way to death."[1] It is rash for man to pass judgment on what is reserved for God's scrutiny, and so it is also written: "Do not praise a man in his lifetime."[2] By this is meant, do not praise a man while in doing so you can make him no longer praiseworthy.

To me your praise is the more dangerous because I welcome it. The more anxious I am to please you in everything, the more I am won over and delighted by it. I beg you, be fearful for me always, instead of feeling confidence in me, so that I may always find help in your solicitude. Now particularly you should fear, now when I no longer have in you an outlet for my incontinence. I do not want you to exhort me to virtue and summon me to the fight, saying "Power comes to its full strength in weakness" and "He cannot win a crown unless he has kept the rules."[3] I do not seek a crown of victory; it is sufficient for me to avoid danger, and this is safer than engaging in war. In whatever corner of heaven God shall place me, I shall be satisfied. No one will envy another there, and what each one has will suffice. Let the weight of authority reinforce what I say—let us hear St. Jerome: "I confess my weakness, I do not wish to fight in hope of victory, lest the day comes when I lose the battle. What need is there to forsake what is certain and pursue uncertainty?"[4]

8. Ecclesiastes 12.11; in the Middle Ages it was thought that Solomon was the author of this book. 9. Jeremiah 17.9. 1. Proverbs 14.12 and 16.25. 2. Ecclesiasticus 11.28; the interpretation Heloise then gives of this verse is (deliberately?) strained. 3. 2 Corinthians 12.9 and 2 Timothy 2.5. 4. Jerome, translator of the Bible into Latin, died in 420; Heloise is quoting his treatise, *Against Vigilantius.*

ANDREAS CAPELLANUS
twelfth century

From On Love[1]

As a general rule, every woman is also known to be envious, always eaten with jealousy at another's beauty and discontented with her material lot. Even if she hears her own daughter's beauty praised she can scarcely stop

1. Translated from the Latin by P. G. Walsh.

herself being gnawed by the fire of inner envy. She sees the considerable poverty and excessive indigence of neighboring women as abundant wealth and plentiful riches. So I think the old proverb sought to designate the female sex alone and without exception when it says

> The crops are lusher in a neighbor's field,
> Their neighbor's cattle heavier udders yield.[2]

It is almost inconceivable that one woman should praise the moral character or beauty of another. If she does happen to praise her in one thing, she will at once add a criticism of something else to cancel out the praise she uttered. So reasonably enough it follows that a woman is a slanderer, because slander is the outcome of nothing but envy and hate. Woman has never sought to dispense with these prescriptive rights, but tries to keep them wholly undiminished. It would be hard to find a woman whose tongue could ever be merciful or leave slander unsaid. Every woman believes that she is advancing her glory and her own good name if she seeks to detract in this way from the praises of other women; and this is a clear indication to all that there is little wisdom stirring within women, for everyone in the world is aware of the general and constant rule that slander only damages the good name and harms the reputation of the slanderer. But this does not make women stop their slander or assaults on the praises of good men, and so I think we should maintain stoutly that there is no woman with a whit of sound instruction. All that wise men hold is quite foreign to a woman; she gets her notions at random, dwells happily on her own upraises, and behaves contrary to wisdom in other ways which would be tedious for me to mention individually.

* * *

All women are also free with their tongues, for not one of them can restrain her tongue from reviling people, or from crying out all day long like a barking dog over the loss of a single egg, disturbing the whole neighborhood for a trifle. A woman gossiping with other women would never willingly give another a chance to speak; she always tries to dominate the conversation with her own opinions, and to go on talking longest. Her tongue or breath could never be exhausted by talking. We see, too, numerous women on many occasions who are so keen to talk that when they are alone they break into speech, and speak out aloud to themselves. Then too a woman recklessly contradicts everyone, and could never agree with anyone's opinion, but always strives to put her own view first on every topic. Besides this, no woman can keep a secret. The more she is bidden to keep something in confidence, the more eagerly she strains to tell it to everybody. No woman to this day has been found to keep any secret undivulged, no matter how important or even likely to cause someone's death. Any secret confided to a woman's trust seems to burn her up inside if she does not first expose the confidences so disastrously reposed in her. You could not prevent women acting like this by bidding them do the opposite because all women take the greatest pleasure in gossiping about something new. So be sure to keep your secret from every women.

---

2. This is a slightly modified quotation from a poem by Ovid called *Tristia*.

GUILLAUME DE MAILLY
thirteenth century

From A Sermon[1]

[The topic to be discussed] is sacramental [marriage], which is bodily marriage, and this is marriage in the literal sense with which the present Gospel deals. For we are taught in this Gospel how that marriage should be maintained, and how it should come about, by the fact that Jesus was invited. For the purpose of this kind of marriage should be that Jesus, that is, salvation, be there. But for salvation to be there, three things are necessary, namely, a right intention in contracting it, fidelity in maintaining it, and inseparability in living it.[2]

First, I say, the right intention in contracting marriage is required, in order that it should have the good of children, which happens when marriage is contracted with the intention of procreating children and educating them to give worship to God. Not so the usurers or avaricious, who contract marriage in order to accumulate wealth. These men contract marriage with money rather than with a bride. Therefore of such men it is said in Psalms: "They have slept their sleep." For the life of such men is only a kind of sleep or dream. Note the story about the man who dreams he is a king: when he wakes up, he is sorrowful, though he was happy when he was asleep. So it is with men of that sort: "all the men of riches have found nothing in their hands" [Psalms 75 (76); 6]. "For they brought nothing into this world: certainly they can carry nothing out," as is said at I Timothy 6.7. Such men do not contract marriage with the right intention, but this is demanded in order that Jesus be present at the marriage in this way. "Let her marry to whom she will, only in the Lord" [I Corinthians 7.39], that is, for the honor of the Lord. Note the story about the philosopher who, when his daughter had the choice between two men, one stupid and rich, the other poor and wise, said: "I prefer to give my daughter to a man in need of money than to money in need of a man." * * *

Second, fidelity in preserving the marriage once contracted, so that it should have the good of faith. This fidelity shows itself in four things. First, in an intimate or deep-seated love of the heart. "Husbands, love your wives" [Ephesians 5.25]. This is one thing which pleases God to the highest degree: "With three things my spirit is pleased, which are approved before God and men: the concord of brethren, the love of neighbors, and a man and wife that agree well [that is, in what is good] together" [Ecclesiasticus 25.1–2]. For they should not love one another in a disordered fashion, since, as the saint says, "The vehement lover of his wife is an adulterer,"[3] indeed, worse than an adulterer, because he turns that which was given to him as a remedy into a poison. For marriage was instituted to this end: that it should be a

---

1. Translated from the Latin by David d'Avray. The text on which this sermon is based, as is the case with almost all marriage sermons, is John 2.1: "There was a marriage at Cana in Galilee," a passage that describes Jesus' presence at a wedding and the miracle of turning water into wine, events that showed to medieval readers that Jesus approved of marriage.   2. Note that Guillaume does not mention either a church ritual, any authorization by the state, or any permission of the partners' parents. In the later Middle Ages the Church taught that a legitimate marriage could be contracted simply by the consent of the two partners, who could marry each other simply by saying, "I marry you."   3. The saint is Jerome, who says this in his treatise *Against Jovinian*, which defends virginity as a higher spiritual state than marriage.

remedy against incontinence. "If they do not contain themselves, let them marry. It is better to marry than to burn" [I Corinthians 7.9]. Second, this fidelity consists in service to each other with regard to temporal things; for as it is said in Ephesians 5.29, "No one ever hated his own flesh, but nourishes and cherishes it." "He who is with a wife thinks the things of this world and . . . she that is married thinks on the things of this world" [I Corinthians 7.33–34], namely, about providing for her household. Third, it consists in the paying of mutual honor: "Sara obeyed Abraham, calling him Lord; likewise husbands, giving honor to the female as to the weaker vessel" [I Peter 3.6–7]. Fourth, it consists in both members of the couple preserving the law of the marriage bed without any violation. "The woman has not power of her own body, but her husband" and vice versa. And therefore it is commanded that the husband render the debt to his wife, and vice versa [I Corinthians 7.3–4]. Concerning the last two things, that is, honor and the preservation of the marriage bed, it is said in the final chapter of Hebrews 13.4, "Marriage honorable in all," with respect to the first point, "and the bed undefiled" with respect to the second. But alas, today one can say of many the words of Wisdom 14.24: "nor do they now keep marriage undefiled." For as it is said in the same place, in many there is "inconstancy in marriage, the disorder of adultery and of immodesty." * * *

Third, inseparability in living is required, so that the good of the sacrament be present. And so, "To those who are joined together in marriage, not I, but the Lord, commands that the wife depart not from her husband; if she departs, however, that she remain unmarried," and "If any brother has a wife who is not a believer and she consents to dwell with him, let him not put her away," similarly with a husband [I Corinthians 7.10–12].

In such a marriage, therefore, in which these three things come together, Jesus is present.

THE SOUTHERN PASSION
late thirteenth century

From The Southern Passion[1]

[When] the sweet king Jesus appeared to any mortal person after His Resurrection on Easter Day He chose rather to show himself to a woman, Mary Magdalene, than to any other person, and in this He did a great honor to woman—indeed to all sinful people, in that she was such a sinner.[2] (We sinners need not lose hope, seeing that Jesus wants to come to us in such a way.) Here in this example any person of understanding can perceive that

---

1. Translated from Middle English by Alcuin Blamires.　　2. In the New Testament Mary Magdalene is mentioned among the women who accompanied Christ and ministered to Him (Luke 8.2–3), where it is also said that seven devils had been cast out of her (Mark 16.9). She is next named as standing at the foot of the cross (Mark 15.40; Matthew 27.56; John 19.25; Luke 23.49). She saw Christ laid in the tomb, and she was the first recorded witness of the Resurrection. In Catholic tradition she is identified as the "sinner" or prostitute of Luke 7.36–50, who anointed Christ's feet with oil and whose sins He forgave; and also as the sister of Martha and Lazarus (Luke 10.38–42 and John 11). She is considered a saint by the Catholic Church.

women are loyal enough when they commit themselves to virtue; for, although the disciples whom our Lord loved and his closest kin, Saints James and John, were full of grief, they left Him abandoned in His sepulcher without a friend, whereas Mary sought Him out. Yet even after Peter and St. John had gone to the sepulcher, they went off again and let things be. But she stayed there weeping, in much distress, unwilling to leave.

So I conclude that ultimately there is no love as loyal as that of a morally committed woman. How is it then that women are so criticized in verses and sayings and books, which claim that they are false, untrustworthy, fickle, and wicked, to many a man's cost? Tell me truthfully, where is any woman who goes asking *men* to lie with her—whereas all the time men ask *women* to do this, using their wealth to give silver or other presents in order to satisfy their lust? What foolishness! Where would you find a man so steadfast, if a nice, attractive, charming woman were to come and keep on begging him for sex, that he would not change his tune and do it in the end? If he didn't, he'd be reckoned a saint fit to lie in a shrine! So, how should we rate a *woman* (and this includes most women) who does not give in to any amount of importuning, as can be seen every day? *She* won't be thought a saint—it will pass without notice. What logic is there in this attitude? Who on earth can see sense in it? But if a woman is discovered to have gone astray just once, she will be blamed at least a thousand times more than a man; moreover, if a woman is given a bad reputation—however contrary to the facts—any man will be loath to marry her, as one sees all the time. Yet take a man who has slept with a hundred women and may be the vilest lecher on earth, and there is still no delay in a wife being found for him, whether he is knight, baron, or whatever, so long as he's rich. The girl can be absolutely virginal and innocent, her spouse as corrupt as you like. What logic can anyone see in this? It should properly be described as debauchery and wickedness and rampant promiscuity.

If it is as evil to do lechery as the Bible and the Lord Himself tell us, then who is the more blameworthy: the one who instigates it, or the one who doesn't so much do it as suffer what men do to her? You know very well that it is the male who does it, and whoever says otherwise is wrong and is lying through his teeth, unless he has no teeth—and would to God he hadn't. The nature of all other animals will teach us the real truth, that women's goodness and chastity exceed men's, so that it is unfair for them to be criticized. You can see clearly that among sheep, oxen, dogs, hens and geese, horses, all sorts of animals, the female keeps herself quietly to herself, unexcited, as if sex didn't exist, except when her season duly comes round. Indeed, some of them are sexually inactive for a whole year or even two unless put to lush pasture. What do you think of the males? Do they behave similarly?—No, not many of them, if they get the chance, because they are always ready for it, summer or winter, when they can find a mate; very few hang back. And if they pick up a mating scent from the far end of town, they'll soon be there, doing the act so sinfully that it doesn't bear thinking about.

Let louts learn a lesson from this, and stifle their malicious talk! When they are enjoying themselves on the pub bench, with a jug and a glass and a barman there to serve up, then their chatter and their fun is to pass judgment on some innocent girl—would to God they'd drown in a beer barrel for it! Why won't they reflect on other animals, as I have just said, and see that woman's nature is more chaste than their own? These loudmouths and liars sitting with their friends commit slander against women; I'll explain how. If a cleric or priest has stupidly committed theft or lechery, up jumps each lout with a bit of coarse slander: "Just look what these clerics get up to! So-and-so stole an ox and did such-and-such wrong, and so-and-so went to bed with that man's wife. These lousy clerics, they're all the same—they ought to be butchered down to the last one." So, if men come across one cleric who has done wrong, every lout will say it is characteristic of *all* clerics. How rational is this? Tell the truth: stop yourself lying about it! It is simply malicious intent and foul gossip to generalize about all men on the basis of the culpability of one man seen doing wrong.

Women fare just the same among malicious tongues. When the men hear (which is seldom) that one woman is going astray—no doubt at the importuning of some lecher, since few would do so otherwise—then plenty of louts will voice their smut: "Do you see that woman who seduced that reeve, who puts on such goody-goody airs and graces (so much for believing any woman) and acts as pious as a nun? Do you see what she's done, how she has behaved? It's clear what they are—not one's to be trusted—for they are all wicked and false, shame on the lot of them." So, for one lapse that a good-for-nothing brings a woman to, though it happens rarely or is even a lie, they'll criticize every woman including good ones and claim they all behave like that. But what reasoning is this, to criticize an innocent majority who seldom make a slip, for a single act? This is not right. Why can't blame be borne individually for individual guilt? Instead, one person's wrongdoing gets blamed on all. But for the love of Christ, those of you with some sense, do not blame the innocent without cause. For if, every time you see one man doing wrong, you're going to accuse all men likewise, it won't take long in any one day before you'll be saying that all men ought to be hung. If one man is a rogue, are all men too? No, there's no logic in that; you know what's true. Were a man hung or dismembered for theft, and they proposed to dish up the same treatment to you, you wouldn't consider it legal. You would look quite unamused, and take the liberty of bidding goodbye to all who pronounced that sort of judgment. Think of others as you would have them think of you. Should a woman importuned by a lecher do wrong, don't thrust forward your half-baked logic claiming falsely that all women behave so, and all deserve disgrace. Don't blame any woman unfairly for another's guilt. Let each bear guilt individually as is only right—and as you'd wish to be upheld in your own case if you were innocent.

When all is said, may God bring shame on all who blame a good woman without reason, for there is no greater mildness and goodness in any earthly creature, no greater kindness and loyalty than in a good woman. You see how Mary Magdalene alone sought our Lord, when the Apostles who were with Him all abandoned Him. Whose love was clearer in this case, hers or theirs? Don't tell a lie! Was there anyone more steadfast than holy Mary Magdalene?

WOMEN AND THE LAW[1]
fifteenth century

A Case in York, England, in 1422

Ralph Arncotes of the parish of Holy Trinity, King's Court,[2] chaplain, aged fifty years says that he knew Agnes, about whom this case is concerned, for the past twelve years and more and that during that time he never told or heard say other than that Agnes was a trustworthy woman of good reputation and of honest conversation. He says that on Sunday last of the present month, immediately after vespers[3] had been sung in the aforesaid parish church of Holy Trinity and at the time when the parishioners of the same church were returning to their homes in great number, this witness was present in person in the cemetery of the parish church. He heard Emma,[4] about whom this case is also concerned, publicly and in a loud voice call out and name the said Agnes as she was going from the vespers and the cemetery to her own home in Colliergate, York, which was right by the cemetery and the church, "old whore of monks and friars," in English "ald munkhore and ald frerehor," and "thief and attainted[5] thief," in English "ald rank[6] tayntyd thefe." The said Emma at that time and place in the presence, as the witness believes, of sixty men and women returning from the parish church and vespers, as stated before, and other men and women of other parishes and places present there in many various places repeated and publicly proclaimed these words with great spirit and great malice out of wickedness and hatred with the intention of publicly defaming Agnes, so that by the pronouncement of these words and Emma's malice all who heard and saw Emma knew and would clearly be able to know that Emma, although she appeared somewhat infirm in body, had a tongue flexible and vigorous for articulating her talkativeness, and a spirit full of malice and irascibility because Emma purposed and desired to hit the same Agnes with a club which she then had and held in her hand had she not gone back into her home more quickly. Because of the defamatory words, Agnes's character was besmirched and her standing, esteem, and reputation gravely and abusively defamed and injured. Because of these defamatory words to the knowledge and hearing of this witness, certain of Agnes's neighbors refused to have dealings with Agnes as they used to, and the husband of the same Agnes would have driven her from his society and his home were it not for the special request and entreaty of his neighbors.

An Ordinance from the Town of Hereford, 1486

Also, concerning scolds, it was agreed that through such women many ills in the city arose, *viz.* quarreling, beating, defamation, disturbing the peace of the night, discord frequently stirred between neighbors, as well as opposing the bailiffs, officers, and others and abusing them in their own person, and often raising hue and cry and breaking the peace of the lord king, and

1. Translated by P. J. P. Goldberg.   2. A district in the city of York.   3. The evening service.
4. *Emma* originally appeared as "Emmot" in the translation by Goldberg, "Excerpts from Laws and Customs," in *Women in England c. 1275–1525*, pp. 230, 234–35.   5. Convicted.   6. Corrupt.

to the disturbance of the city's tranquility. Consequently, whenever scolds shall be taken and convicted, they shall have their judgment of the cucking stool.[7] And they shall stand[8] there with bare feet and the hair of the head hanging loose for the whole time that they may be seen by all traveling on the road. And afterwards when judgment has been made they shall be taken to the lord king's jail and shall stay there until they make fine. And if they refuse to be punished by such a judgment, they shall be thrown out of the city.

7. A chair on which an offender—often a scold or a dishonest tradesman—was confined while on display either outside the door of his or her house or, as in this case, in a public place. People thus displayed were insulted and often pelted with refuse or manure.   8. I.e., stay.

CHRISTINE DE PIZAN
ca. 1365–ca. 1430

From Letter from the God of Love[1]

If they are not careful, ladies are often deceived, for they are trusting and only see the good side of things. Because of this, whether they want to or not, it often happens that they fall in love with deceivers, and are betrayed before they become aware of what is happening. And when they have been completely taken in by the disloyal lovers who have tricked them, listen to how these lovers behave toward them: it is not enough for them to have betrayed the ladies; they have companions in their wicked behavior. There is no deed or promise that they do not recount to one another, nor do they neglect to exaggerate their amorous successes: they brag that they live in the bedrooms of the ladies who love them; then they swear body and soul that this is the truth, and tell how they lay naked in their ladies' arms. They tell their drinking companions; and the noblemen gossip together in ducal or royal courts, or elsewhere; these are the kinds of lessons they teach. There are many who should be using their words to recount true and valuable stories, chivalric exploits; but instead, comfortably relaxing in front of a warm fire of an evening, they tease each other, and reproachfully say to one another: "I know how you work. Lady X is your lover, and you play the gay blade for the sake of her love; but many share in it; she receives you after having just dismissed your predecessor!" Thus envious men defame the fair lady, with no grounds, without knowing anything negative about her. And the one who is teased pretends to be hurt by this, but in fact he is very pleased with this treatment. And, he speaks many blameful words, although he makes apologies for this: in making his apologies he names and thus accuses the lady; he pretends to conceal and to hide that which he is delighted to tell and to reveal.

There are others who provoke teasing against themselves, in order to get their companions to chide them into recounting what they in fact want everyone to know. They laugh off the chiding by naming ladies' names, and thereby excuse themselves in a cowardly way. And there are others who have

1. Translated from the French by Kevin Brownlee and Renate Blumenfeld-Kosinski.

taken great trouble to succeed in love, but have failed. They are ashamed because they have been refused. They do not want others to think that they have wasted their time, and therefore they brag about things that have never occurred. If they have visited the lady's house for any reason whatsoever, they recount every detail of how the household functions in order to support their boasts. Many ugly things are said in this context; and he who does not want to express himself explicitly uses innuendo to make his point. Thus women are often very slanderously identified and blamed without justification; even certain very elevated ladies, both blondes and brunettes. God, what speakers! God, what encounters where the honor of ladies is stolen away!

And how does this kind of defamation profit those who should arm themselves in order to guard and to protect women's honor? For every man should be well disposed toward women, who are the mothers of all of them; nor are mothers bitter or fickle toward their offspring, but rather soothing, sweet, and friendly. They are responsive and helpful to the needs of their sons; they have done and continue to do so many good things for their sons: they consider any activity good which leads to the gentle nourishment of man's body. At his birth, during his lifetime, at his death, women are helpful and useful to him—understanding, sweet, and obliging. The man who slanders women is self-centered, rude, and full of ingratitude. Furthermore, I say that a man behaves unnaturally when he defames, or slanders, or reproaches woman, whether it is a question of one, or two, or of all women generally.[2]

In addition, the above-mentioned ladies complain of the many clerks who accuse them in prose and verse books, defaming their morals in varied words; and they give these books as school texts to their young, beginning students, by way of example and doctrine, to be retained into adulthood. Some tell in verse how Adam, David, Samson, and many other men were deceived by women both early and late: what living man will escape? Others say that women are very deceitful, crafty, false, and worthless. Still others say that they are highly untruthful, changeable, inconstant, and flighty. Yet others accuse them of many terrible vices, and cast much blame on them, while excusing them for nothing. Thus the clerks write their verses both morning and evening, now in French, now in Latin, basing themselves on who knows what books that repeat more lies than a drunkard.

Ovid said much evil of women (which I consider to be a misdeed) in a book he wrote which he called *Love's Remedies* in which he accused them of dishonorable, filthy, ugly, uncouth behavior.[3] I deny that they possess such vices, and I stand ready to do battle on this issue with anyone who wants to throw down the gauntlet—of course, I mean honorable women; I am not concerned with the worthless ones. Clerks are taught this book from their earliest youth, in their beginning grammar classes, and they teach it to others, so that none will undertake to love a woman. They are, however, foolish and waste their time in this endeavor; it is useless to try to prevent love in this way. For as long as the world lasts we will never allow—my lady Nature and myself—that women not be cherished and loved, in spite of all those who would like to condemn them. They will steal away and capture the hearts

---

2. Christine's point is that it is unnatural for a man to blame women since he is implicitly attacking his own mother.   3. This poem by the Roman poet Ovid (43 B.C.E.–ca. 17 C.E.) provides a misogynistic account of women as a way of protecting men from love. Christine later refers to Ovid's *Art of Love*, which gives cynical advice about how to seduce women; it was widely read throughout the Middle Ages. As Christine mentions later, Ovid was exiled by the emperor Caesar Augustus to a small town on the Black Sea for an unknown offense.

of many who most blame them. By our commandments, without fraud or extortion men will no longer be so instructed by subtle clerks, nor by their writings, despite the fact that many books treat the topic of women and condemn them as being worth little. And if anyone says that we should believe these books which were written by men of great renown and wisdom, who would not have deigned to lie, books which prove women's evil nature, I answer that those who wrote these things in their books were only interested in deceiving women. They could never possess enough women; every day they wanted new ones, without being loyal even to the most beautiful. How did David or King Solomon behave?[4] They angered God who punished their transgressions. Many others have been like this, including even Ovid, who desired so many of them, then tried to defame them. And all the clerks who have spoken so much about women were much more obsessed with them than were other people, not with one woman only, but with a thousand.

With regard to deception, I do not know how to imagine or to conceive how woman can deceive man. She does not go looking for him, or asking after him, or seeking for him at his home; nor does she think of him, or remember him, when he comes to deceive and to tempt. How does he tempt her? Truly in such a way that no trouble is too much for him, no burden too heavy. He enjoys nothing except using his heart, body, and wealth in order to deceive her. And this torment and pain continue for a long time, and are repeated many times, despite the fact that men very often fail in their quest, no matter how hard they try. Ovid speaks of these men in his treatise on *The Art of Love*: because of his great pity for them he compiled a book in which he wrote and openly taught them how to deceive women, and how to win their love through dissembling; and he called the book *The Art of Love*; but it does not teach the condition or the ways of loving well, but rather the contrary. For he who wants to act according to this book will never love, no matter how much he is loved. And for this reason the book is badly named, for it is the book of *The Art of Great Deceit and of False Appearance*, such is the name I give it.

Why then if women are weak and flighty, and easily manipulated, silly and lacking self-control, as some clerkly authors say, why do those who pursue them have any need of ruse? And why do women not give in at once, without requiring that strategies and tricks be used to catch them? For it is not necessary to go to war for a castle that is already captured. And even a poet as subtle as Ovid, who was later exiled, and Jean de Meun in the *Romance of the Rose*:[5] what great exertion! What an elaborate enterprise! And what great learning, both accessible and obscure, what adventures he described there! And how many people are entreated and begged, and how much effort and trickery is there in order to accomplish nothing more than the deception of a maid through fraud and cunning, for that is the ultimate goal! Does a weakly fortified place require such an assault? How can one try so hard for

4. For David and Bathsheba, see 2 Samuel 11.1–27; for Solomon and the queen of Sheba, and his many foreign wives who turned him to strange gods in his old age, see 1 Kings 11.1–10 and 2 Chronicles 9.1–12. In the Vulgate, these accounts are found at 2 Kings 11.1–27 (David) and 3 Kings 10.1–13 and 3 Kings 11.1–11 (Solomon).   5. The *Romance of the Rose* is a rambling narrative of some 26,000 lines composed in French by two authors, Guillaume de Lorris, who wrote the first 4,000 lines in about 1225, and Jean de Meun, who completed the poem about 1275. It is an elaborate allegory about seduction, with many sidetracks, and, in certain passages by Jean de Meun, it has a strongly misogynist tone, although it is far from clear that these passages represent the opinion of the author. It was one of the most widely read books in the Middle Ages, and Christine attacked it in another work, setting off a lively literary controversy among contemporary French writers.

so easy a prize? I do not understand or believe that such great effort is needed to capture a weakly fortified place, nor scheming, nor ingenuity, nor great subtlety. It is necessary to conclude that, since scheming, great ingenuity and great effort are required to deceive noble or low-born women, they are not so fickle as is said, nor is their behavior so changeable.

And if anyone says to me that books are full of such fickle women (a charge made by many, and one that I dislike), I answer that women did not write the books, nor did they put into them the things one reads there against women and their behavior. Thus do male authors write to their hearts' delight their descriptions of women; these authors show no mercy when they plead their own cases, happy to yield in nothing and to take for themselves the spoils of victory: for aggressive people quickly attack those who do not defend themselves. But if women had written books, I know for a fact that they would have been written differently, for women well know that they are wrongly condemned. The parts are not fairly distributed, for the strongest take the largest pieces, and the one who divides up the pieces takes the best for himself.[6] Furthermore, the wicked slanderers who despise women say that they are all false, always have been and always will be; that none have ever had any loyalty, and that he who loves any woman whatsoever finds that they are all like this when he tries them out. They are put in the wrong in every case; no matter who has acted badly, the blame is placed on women.

But this is a wicked lie; the contrary is true. For as far as love is concerned, many women have been, are, and will be loyal, in spite of their having been treated falsely, treacherously, deceitfully, and mendaciously. How did Medea act toward the false Jason?[7] She was very loyal, and through her subtle cleverness, she enabled him to win the Golden Fleece, for which he was more famous than a hundred thousand other men. Because of her, his renown was greater than anyone else's, and he promised her that he would be her sweet, loyal love, belonging only to her; but he broke his word, left her for someone else, and departed. How did Dido act toward Aeneas, when she was queen of Carthage, filled with great love and loyalty, and he was an exile from Troy, sailing wearily, dejectedly, and unhappily, having almost perished along with his men?[8] He was taken in when he was in great need by that beautiful woman whom he falsely deceived. For she received him and his followers with very great honor and did much good for him; and afterward he behaved very badly toward her. Despite the fact that he had pledged his faith and his love to her (truly, as a deception), he then left her never to return and placed his love elsewhere. As a result, she died of grief for love of him, in a very piteous way. Anyone who wanted to tell all the trials of Penelope, Ulysses's wife, would have much to say about her goodness which is irreproachable. She was very beautiful, sought after, and well beloved, noble, wise, courageous, and famed. Many other women, so many that they cannot be counted, have been, are, and will be in this category. But I will now be silent concerning them, for it would take a very long time to tell their stories.

6. Christine seems here to be referring to an animal fable that describes how the lion, the king of the beasts, divided up his prey among the other animals and ended up keeping the whole of it for himself on the principle that might makes right. 7. Jason's betrayal of Medea after her crucial help in his conquest of the Golden Fleece is a standard example of masculine faithlessness in the Middle Ages (see Ovid, *Metamorphoses* 7.1–158, 7.350–403 and Dante's *Inferno* 18.83–99, where Jason is punished for his betrayal of women in the First Bolgia of the Eighth Circle, among the Panderers and Seducers). 8. Aeneas's "betrayal" of Dido is described in book 4 of Virgil's *Aeneid*.

Was not the great city of Troy, which had been so gloriously strong, captured long ago through deceptions, false counsel, clever treachery, mendacious speeches, tricks, and broken promises; and burned to the ground? And are not kings and kingdoms betrayed every day by tricks and plots? Books and romances are full of stories of how effectively deceptive beautiful blandishments are; it is therefore not surprising that working hard at lying and conniving leads to victory over something as simple as an ignorant little woman. And if she is sneaky and cunning, is it not because she is under the control of a malicious, sharp-eyed man, who uses against her all the pain with which he is filled? In these ways are women defamed and wrongly blamed by many men; this is how, both in speech and in writing, whether true or not, women are depicted.

I do not, however, find this in any book or writing (in spite of what has been slanderously spoken or written) about the life of Jesus or about his death, effected through envy. Similarly, neither the deeds of the Apostles who underwent much hardship for the faith nor the Gospels show women in a bad light. On the contrary, much good is said there concerning women: they are shown as having a very high calling, great prudence, much sense and constancy, perfect love, great firmness of faith, great charity, strong willpower, strong hearts entirely fixed on serving God, and they gave clear evidence of this, for they never abandoned Him either alive or dead.[9] Sweet Jesus, when wounded, injured, and dead, was abandoned by all except women. The entirety of the faith remained in a single woman. Therefore anyone who defames women is extremely foolish, if only because of the reverence required by the Queen of Heaven, in memory of her goodness, which was so noble and worthy that She was elected to carry the son of God. God the Father conferred great honor on women by choosing a woman to be his wife and mother, God's temple joined to the Trinity. Women should thus be joyous and gay, for they have the same form as She; God never created anything else of comparable dignity or goodness, excepting only the person of Jesus.

Thus he who mocks women is very foolish, when a woman is seated on the highest throne, next to her son, at the right hand of the Father: this is a great honor for women's maternity. And we can find no instance where the good Jesus reproached women; rather, he loved them and valued them. God formed women in his worthy image and gave to her knowledge, awareness, and the gift of understanding, so that she might save herself. He gave her a very noble form and created her out of the most noble material, for He did not make her out of mud and earth, but only out of man's rib, man's body being the most noble of terrestrial creations. And the ancient true stories of the Bible, which cannot ever lie, tell us that in the Earthly Paradise woman was created first, not man.[1] And, concerning the deception because of which God sent us bitter consequences, for which lady Eve, our mother, is blamed,

9. Christine is referring here to the "Three Marys," Mary Magdalene, Mary of Bethany (the sister of Lazarus, who was raised from the dead by Jesus), and the Virgin Mary. They held vigil beside his tomb and it was to them that he first appeared when resurrected. Misogynist writers claimed that this was because Jesus knew that women could not keep quiet about anything and that therefore they would spread the good news.   1. Since Adam was created before Eden was established, it was assumed that Eve was the first to be created within Eden itself. Church Fathers and theologians differed in their interpretation of this: in the late 4th century Ambrose stated that given this advantage, one would expect woman to be superior to man, but she is not. On the other hand, the 12th-century theologian Peter Abelard saw "a certain dignity enhancing woman's creation, since she was made in paradise but man outside it."

I say in truth that she did not deceive Adam, but simply repeated to him the words that the Devil had said to her, believing them to be sincere and true. Thus it was not fraud or deception, for innocence, with no concealed malice, should not be called deception. Without intending to deceive others, one cannot deceive them, for this is not true deception. Of what great evils can women thus be accused? Do not women have Paradise as their reward? Of what crimes can one accuse them? And if some foolish men wish to amuse themselves with love (may they be cursed for this), they cannot succeed; let wise men refrain from this; he who, having planned deceit, is himself deceived has no one but himself to blame.

Let everyone judge my case, and equitably make a decision according to the truth. He shall find, if he judges correctly, that women's greatest faults cause very little damage: they do not kill people, or wound, or maim; nor do they undertake and pursue treachery; they do not burn out or disinherit people; they do not poison or steal gold or silver; they do not cheat people out of their wealth or their inheritances through false contracts; nor do they damage kingdoms, duchies, or empires. Disaster rarely follows, even from the worst women. In general, one woman's behavior does not establish a rule for all. And whoever wants to cite historical or biblical examples against me, of one woman, or two, or several who were condemned for wickedness would be citing exceptions. For I am speaking about the average woman, and there are very few who resort to wicked ways.

And if someone were to say to me that women's nature and characteristics do not incline them in this direction, or toward giving battle, or killing people, or making torches to set fires, or any such things; and for the reason that women do not and should not deserve any special fame, praise or credit for refraining from these activities, I reply (with all due respect) that indeed women are not inclined in this direction, or toward cruelty. For woman's nature is mild, very piteous, fearful and hesitant, humble, sweet, calm and very charitable, lovable, devout, modest in peace, fearful in war, unpretentious and pious, with an anger that is quickly appeased, unable to bear the sight of cruelty or suffering: these are in sum, the natural attributes of women. And those who through some accident do not possess them act against nature; for cruelty in women is a fault, and only women's gentleness deserves to be prized.

Since women are neither accustomed nor inclined to shed blood or to kill, they do not commit other ugly and horrible capital sins, indeed, great and enormous sins, of which they are thus free and innocent. Each human being is stained with some vice, but women cannot thereby be guilty of wicked actions in which they are not implicated. They will thus not be punished or held guilty for them, since they did not commit them. Thus I can say (without being accused of heresy) that God on high behaved with great courtliness toward women, when He created them without the predispositions which push people to commit great transgressions: for from desires result the deeds that blemish the souls of many people. It is therefore better not to have desires whose fulfillment often leads to death. Only a heretic would want to maintain that there is no merit in abstaining from sin because one feels no temptation. Such reasoning cannot be defended, for we see the contrary in the lives of the saints: St. Nicholas was incapable of sinning; he never sinned, nor was he ever tempted to do so; and many other saints did not have the desire to sin.[2] I am speaking of mortal sins, since they could commit venial sins; but all of the saints are rightly called the chosen ones, predestined and elected by God.

For all these reasons I conclude by wanting to prove that women's behavior is to be greatly approved and praised; and to recommend their nature which is not oriented toward the vices that spoil human nature and make people suffer. Through these just and true arguments, I conclude that all reasonable men must prize, cherish and love women; nor should they want to denigrate those through whom every man is born. Let them not return evil for the good they have received, for woman constitutes the single best and most natural object in the world for men's love. It is therefore quite despicable and very shameful to blame the thing that one should love most which brings the greatest joy to every man. There is no joy in a natural man's life without woman: she is his mother, his sister, his beloved; it is very rare that she is his enemy. It is right for her to be compatible with him, the thing that is most pleasing to him; any man who condemns women cannot win fame or praise, but only great condemnation. There is no blame so vile and harmful as being considered a slanderer, and most especially in defaming women as a group: this is a contemptible and wicked act of villainy. Let all noble hearts, therefore, keep away from it, for it leads to nothing good, but rather to great harm, shame, spite and all vile things.

2. St. Nicholas, an early saint about whom little is known, was renowned for his chastity. It was said that as an infant he refused to be suckled on Friday because it was a fast day. Because several of the legends about him featured children, he became their patron saint and presents were given to children on his feast day (December 6). Eventually this tradition developed into the familiar Santa Claus of today.

THE TRIAL OF JOAN OF ARC
1431

The Trial of Joan of Arc[1]

February 21, 1431

The bishop[2] caused Joan to come before him, charitably admonished her, and told her that she should tell the truth concerning the things which would be asked her, as much for the shortening of her trial as for the unburdening of her conscience, without subterfuge or craft; and that she should swear on the Holy Gospels to tell the truth concerning everything she should be asked. Joan answered: "I do not know on what you may wish to question me. Perhaps you may ask such things as I will not answer." Whereupon the bishop said to her: "You will swear to tell the truth about whatever you are asked concerning the Catholic Faith, and all else that you may know." To which Joan answered that concerning her father and mother, and concerning everything she had done since she took the road for France,[3] she would willingly

1. Translated from the French by W. S. Scott and edited by Lee Patterson.   2. This is Pierre de Cauchon, bishop of Beauvais and the presiding judge.   3. By *France*, Joan means those parts of the country that were loyal to Charles VII.

swear. But as for revelations sent her from God, never had she told or revealed them save to Charles, who she said was her king. And if they cut her head off, she would not reveal them; for she knew from her visions that she must keep them secret. But within eight days she would know if she ought to reveal them. After these words the bishop admonished her, and asked her to take the oath to tell the truth concerning the Faith. Joan knelt down, her two hands on the book, that is to say a missal,[4] and swore that she would tell the truth in all matters asked her concerning the Faith. But that, about the aforesaid revelations, she would not tell anyone.

Joan, being questioned as to her name and surname, answered that, in the place where she was born, she was called Jeannette, and in France, Jeanne; of a surname she knew nothing. Questioned as to the place of her birth, she answered that she was born in a village called Domremy de Greux.[5] Questioned as to the name of her father and mother, she answered that her father was named Jacques Tart[6] and her mother Ysabeau. Questioned as to where she had been baptized, she answered that it was in the church of Domremy. Questioned as to who were her godfathers and godmothers, she answered that they were a woman named Agnes and another called Joan; and a man called Jean Bavent was her godfather. She said also that she had heard her mother say that she had other godfathers and godmothers as well as these. Questioned as to how old she was, she answered that she was nineteen or thereabouts. She said also that her mother taught her the *Pater Noster, Ave Maria* and *Credo*,[7] and that no one else save her mother taught her her faith. Being required to repeat the *Pater Noster* and *Ave Maria*, she answered that she would say it willingly, provided that my lord bishop of Beauvais, who was present, would hear her confession. And then the bishop said: "I will give you one or two notable persons of this company to whom you will say your *Pater Noster* and *Ave Maria*." To which she answered: "I will not say them at all, if they do not hear me in confession."

February 22, 1431

[Joan was again asked to take an oath but again refused, saying she would not tell her judges everything. Bishop Cauchon then asked her if she would tell the truth, to which she replied, "You may well ask me such things that as to some I shall tell the truth, as to others, not." She said further: "If you are well informed about me, you would wish that I were out of your hands. I have done nothing save by revelation."] Questioned as to what age she was when she left her father's house, she said that she did not know the answer. Questioned as to whether she had learned any craft or trade, she said yes; and that her mother had taught her to sew; and that she did not believe there was any woman in Rouen who could teach her anything in this matter. She said also that she had left her father's house partly for fear of the Burgundians; and that she went to Neufchateau with a woman named La Rousse, where she stayed a fortnight.[8] In this house she did the household tasks,

---

4. A prayer book that contains the service for the Mass.   5. Domremy is located in the northeast part of France, on what was then the border between France and Burgundy.   6. It is probable that the person who transcribed Joan's testimony misheard her. Near Domremy is a village named Arc-en-Barrois, from which her father, who was not born in Domremy, derived his surname.   7. Two prayers—"Our Father" and "Hail Mary"—and the Creed (literally, "I believe").   8. A town near Domremy in the hands of the supporters of Charles VII; the d'Arc family escaped there when Domremy was attacked by the Burgundians in 1428. La Rousse (whose name means "The Redhead") was an inhabitant of Neufchateau who took Joan in. Afterward the d'Arc family returned to Domremy.

and did not go into the fields to keep the sheep or other animals.

Asked whether she made her confession every year, she said yes, to her own curé. And if he were prevented, she confessed to another priest, with her curé's leave.[9] And she also said that she had confessed two or three times to mendicant friars. And that she received the Body of Our Lord every year at Easter. And she said that from the age of thirteen, she received revelation from Our Lord by a voice which taught her how to behave. And the first time she was greatly afraid. And she said that the voice came that time at noon, on a summer's day, a fast day, when she was in her father's garden, and that the voice came on her right side, in the direction of the church. And she said that the voice was hardly ever without a light, which was always in the direction of the voice. She said further that after she had heard it three times, she knew that it was the voice of an angel. She said also that this voice had always taken good care of her. Questioned as to what teaching this voice gave her as to the salvation of her soul, she answered that it taught her how to behave. And it said to her that she ought to go often to church. And later it said to her that it was necessary that she should go into France. And it said to her two or three times a week that she must leave and go into France. And that her father knew nothing of her going. And with this, it said to her that she must hurry and go and raise the siege of Orleans; and that she should go to Robert de Baudricourt, captain of Vaucouleurs;[1] and that he would give her men to accompany her. To which she answered that she was only a poor woman, who knew nothing of riding or of making war. And after these words, she went to an uncle's house, where she stayed a week, after which her uncle brought her to Robert de Baudricourt, whom she recognized, although she had never seen him before. And she said that she recognized him by her voices, which had told her that it was he. [Joan then describes how de Baudricourt twice refused to help her but finally agreed; and that the duke of Lorraine asked to see her, apparently hoping that she would cure him of an illness that afflicted him.]

She said further that when she left Vaucouleurs, she took man's dress, and also a sword which de Baudricourt gave her, but no other armor. She said further that it was absolutely essential that she change her dress.[2] She said also that she went to her king without hindrance. Further, she said that she found her king at Chinon,[3] where she arrived about noon, and lodged at an inn, and after dinner went to the king who was in the castle. She said that she went right into the room where the king was, whom she recognized among many others by the advice of the voice.[4] She said that she told the king that she wished to make war on the English. She said also that before the king set her to work, he had several apparitions and glorious revelations. Questioned as to what revelations, she answered: "I shall not tell you yet; go

9. Annual confession, preferably to one's own priest, was required of all Christians.   1. Vaucouleurs is a small town near Neufchateau where the French had a castle and a garrison.   2. Joan's point is that she did not change her dress for frivolous reasons or of her own will, which would violate social convention, biblical injunction (see Deuteronomy 22.5), and Church law (according to which, "If a woman, *judging it useful according to her own decision*, puts on male clothing, she is anathematized because this is imitating male dress"). But if a woman is forced to wear male clothing to protect herself, especially when traveling, this is considered legitimate. Joan's answer here allows her interrogators to think that this is the reason, although later she will offer a different explanation.   3. Chinon is a castle south of the Loire and west of Bourges where Charles was living at that time.   4. According to later testimony, Charles was not seated on his throne at the head of the hall but standing among other members of his household as a way of testing Joan's inspiration.

to the king and he will tell you." She said further that the voice promised her that very soon after she arrived the king would receive her. She said also that those of her party[5] well knew that the voice came from God; and that they saw and knew the voice; and that she knows this well. She said that the king and several members of his Council heard and saw the voices who came to her.

She said also that she never asked anything of the voice save at the last the salvation of her soul. She said further that the voice told her that she should stay at St. Denis in France; and there she wished to remain.[6] But the lords were not willing to leave her there, because she was wounded; otherwise she would not have left. And she said that she was wounded in the moat of Paris, of which wound she was cured within five days. She said that she had made a great assault on Paris. Asked whether the day she made this assault were a feast day, she answered, after being questioned several times, that she believed it was a feast. Asked if she thought it a good thing to make an assault on a feast day, she replied, "Go on to the next question."

February 24, 1431

[Again the session opened with an argument between Joan and her judges over the oath that she would take, Joan insisting that "I am ready to swear and to say all that I know concerning my trial, but I will not say all that I know." She also said that she came from God, and ought not to be here; and said that they should remit her into the hands of God, from Whom she came. The questioning on this day immediately turned to the voice that instructed Joan and she told her judges that she had heard the voice three times, both the day before and on this day, when she was awakened by the voice.] Asked if she did not thank the voice, and kneel down, she answered that she thanked it, being seated on her bed. And she said that she joined her hands together, and begged and prayed that it might help and advise her in what she had to do. To which the voice told her to answer boldly. She said several times to the bishop, "You say that you are my judge; consider well what you do; for in truth I am sent from God, and you are putting yourself in great peril." Asked if this voice had ever varied in its advice, she answered that she had never found in it two contradictory words. Asked whether it were an angel coming direct from God, or if it were a saint, she answered that it came from God. And added, "I am not telling you all I know, for I am greatly afraid of saying something displeasing to it in my answers to you." And she said further, "In this questioning I beg you that I may be allowed a delay."

Asked if she believed that God would be displeased if she told the truth, she answered my lord of Beauvais that the voices had told her to say some things to the king and not to him. She also said that the voice told her that night things concerning the king's good, things that she wished the king to know immediately. Asked if she could make this heavenly voice obey her and carry a message to her king, she answered that she did not know whether it would be willing to obey her, unless it were the will of God, and that Our Lord agreed. And that, if it pleased God, it would be able to reveal it to the

---

5. That is, those who supported Charles, known as Armagnacs.   6. *St. Denis* was a monastery and nunnery located outside Paris supported by the French monarchy. Joan is referring here to a period of recuperation she spent at St. Denis in the fall of 1429 after she led an unsuccessful attack on Paris.

king; if so, "I would be very happy." Questioned as to why she cannot now speak with her king, as she used to do in his presence, she said that she did not know if it were God's will. She said further that if she were not in the grace of God she could do nothing. She said also that there is a saying among little children that people are often hanged for telling the truth. Asked if she knew whether she were in the grace of God, she answered, "If I am not, may God put me there; if I am, may He keep me there."[7] She said further that if she knew she were not in the grace of God, she would be the most miserable person in the world. She said also that if she were in mortal sin, the voice would not come to her. And she would that everyone might hear them as well as she did.

She said that she thought she was thirteen years of age when the voice came to her the first time. Asked whether in her childhood she used to go and play in the fields with the others, she said she did so sometimes. But she did not know at what age. Asked if the people of Domremy sided with the Burgundians or the Armagnacs, she answered that she only knew one Burgundian, whose head she would like to see chopped off, that is if it had pleased God. Asked whether at Maxey[8] they were Burgundians or Armagnacs, she said they were Burgundians.

Questioned as to whether her voice told her in her childhood to hate the Burgundians, she answered that ever since she learned that the voices were for the King of France, she did not love the Burgundians. She added that the Burgundians would have war, if they did not do as they ought; she knew this from the voice. Asked if the voice told her in her childhood that the English should come into France, she said they were already in France when the voice first spoke to her. Asked if she were ever with the other children when they played at fights between English and French, she said no, as far as she could remember. But she had often seen those of her village fighting against those of Maxey, and coming back wounded and bleeding. Asked if in her youth she had a great desire to defeat the Burgundians, she answered that she had a great desire that the king should have his kingdom. Asked if she had wanted to be a man when she knew she had to come into France, she said that she had answered elsewhere.[9]

Questioned concerning the tree, she answered that quite close to Domremy there was a tree which was called the Ladies' Tree; others called it the Fairies' Tree; and near there was a spring; and she had heard it said that persons suffering from fever drank of it; and she has seen them going to it to be cured. But she did not know whether they were cured or not. She said also that she had heard that the sick, when they could get up, went to the tree to walk about; and she said it was a large tree called a beech, from whence comes the *beau mai*[1] and it belonged to Messire Pierre de Bourlémont.[2] She said that she sometimes went there with the other girls in summer time, and made wreaths for Notre Dame de Domremy. She had heard several old folk say, not of her family, that the fairies frequented it; and she had heard her godmother Joan say that she had seen them there. Whether

---

7. Joan is here echoing a common prayer familiar to her from church services at Domremy.   8. A village near to Domremy under the control of the Burgundians.   9. Joan is referring here and in the next answer either to private interrogations prior to the public trial or to an earlier examination at Poitiers undertaken by Charles's clerical advisors.   1. A branch from a tree.   2. The family of de Bourlémont were lords of the village of Domremy. The château of Bourlémont still stands not far from the village.

this was true, she does not know. She said that she herself had never seen a fairy, as far as she knew, neither at the tree or anywhere else. She said further that she had seen garlands hung on the branches of the tree by the girls; and she herself had hung them there with the other girls.[3] Sometimes they took them away, and sometimes they left them. She also said that ever since she learned that she must come into France, she played very little, the least that she could. And she did not know whether, since she had reached years of discretion, she had danced near the tree. Sometimes she may have danced there with the children, but she more often sang than danced. She also said that there was a wood called the *Bois Chenu*[4] that she could see from her father's house, not more than a league away; but she was unaware and had never heard it said that the fairies frequented it. She said that she heard from her brother that it was said that she received her revelations at the tree and from the fairies. But she had not. She said further that when she came before the king, many people asked whether in her country there was not a wood called the *Bois Chenu*, for there was a prophecy that from the *Bois Chenu* should come a maiden who would perform marvelous acts; but she put no faith in it.

Questioned as to whether she wanted a woman's dress, she answered, "If you give me permission, give me one, and I will take it and go. Otherwise no. I am content with this one, since it is God's will that I wear it."[5]

February 27, 1431

[After the usual debate about taking the oath, Joan was questioned again about her voices, and after some resistance she provided the following testimony.] Questioned as to whether it were the voice of an angel, or of a saint, or directly from God, she answered that the voices were those of St. Catherine and of St. Margaret. "And their heads are crowned with beautiful crowns, most richly and preciously. And," she said, "for telling you this I have leave from Our Lord. If you doubt it, send to Poitiers where I have been previously examined."[6] Asked how she knew that it was these two saints, and if she could tell the one from the other, she answered that she was certain that it was these; and that she well knew the one from the other. She also said that it was seven years since they first began to guide her. She also said she knows them because they tell her their names. She said also that she received counsel from St. Michael. Questioned which came first, she said it was St. Michael. Asked if it were long ago, she answered, "I do not speak of St. Michael's voice, but of the great comfort he brought me." Asked which was the first voice that came to her when she was thirteen, she said it was St. Michael whom she saw before her eyes; and he was not alone, but was accompanied by angels from heaven. She said also that she would not have

3. Joan is here referring either to springtime rituals characteristic of medieval country life, and dating back to pre-Christian days, or to church services that were sometimes performed outdoors at springtime as a replacement for these rituals.   4. An oak forest; there was current at the time a prophecy that a maid would come from the *Bois Chenu* and deliver France. This prophecy ultimately derives from a 12th-century work known as the *Prophecies of Merlin*, although the people of Domremy would have known of it only orally.   5. Joan is apparently saying that she will wear a woman's dress if she is released, but if not to be released, she will continue to wear the men's clothing she had on when captured. This is the first time she suggests that her clothing is more than merely a necessity.   6. Joan is referring here to an examination conducted by clergy at Poitiers at the request of Charles in the spring of 1429; their conclusion was that the king might find Joan useful in relieving the siege of Orleans.

come into France had it not been for God's command. Asked if she saw St. Michael and the angels corporeally and in reality, she answered, "I saw them with my bodily eyes, as well as I am seeing you." And when they left her, she wept and greatly longed that they would have taken her with them.[7]

Asked if the voice ordered her to wear a man's dress, she answered that the dress is but a small matter; and that she had not taken it by the advice of any living man; and that she did not take this dress nor do anything at all save by the command of Our Lord and the angels. Questioned as to whether it seemed to her that this command to take male dress was a lawful one, she answered that everything she had done was at Our Lord's command, and if He had ordered Joan to take a different dress, she would have been at God's command. Asked whether she had been to St. Catherine de Fierbois, she answered yes.[8] And there she heard three masses in one day. She said further that she had a sword, which, when she was in Tours or in Chinon, she sent to be looked for at St. Catherine de Fierbois. This sword was in the ground, behind the altar of St. Catherine, and it was immediately found there, all rusted. Asked how she knew the sword was there, she said it was in the ground, all rusted, and upon it were five crosses. This she knew from her voices, saying that she never saw the man who was sent to look for the sword. She wrote to the clergy of the place asking that it might please them to let her have the sword, which they sent her. It was not deep in the ground behind the altar, so she thought, although in truth she was not certain whether it were in front of it or behind, but she believed that she wrote that it was behind the altar. She added that as soon as the sword was found, the clergy of the place rubbed it, and the rust fell off without any effort; and that it was an armorer of Tours who went to find the sword. And the clergy of St. Catherine and the citizens of Tours both gave her sheaths for it. They made two sheaths, one of crimson velvet and the other of cloth of gold. She herself had another made of very strong leather. She also stated that when she was taken prisoner she no longer had this sword; but that she had always worn it until her departure from St. Denis.[9] Asked whether she had ever said or caused to be said a blessing upon this sword, she said no, nor would she have known how to do so. She said also that she greatly prized this sword, since it was found in the church of St. Catherine, whom she much loved. Asked whether she had placed her sword upon any altar, she said no, as far as she knew, nor had she done so in order that it might have better fortune. Asked if she had her sword when she was taken prisoner, she said no, but that she had one which was taken from a Burgundian. She added that she had this sword at Lagny, and from Lagny to Compiégne she wore the Burgundian's sword, because it was a good sword for war, useful for giving hard clouts.[1]

Asked whether, when she was before the city of Orleans, she had a standard, and of what color it was, she replied that it had a field sown with fleurs-de-lis, and showed a world with an angel on either side, white in color, of linen; and she thought that the names JESUS MARIA were written on it;

7. This is the beginning of the inquisitors' attempts to show that Joan did not show a proper skepticism about the appearance of this spirit, since according to Church teaching evil spirits often appeared in the guise of angels or saints in order to tempt the unwary into evil actions.   8. This was a chapel dedicated to St. Catherine on the route from Vaucouleurs to Chinon.   9. There was a tradition that Charles Martel, king of the Franks, placed his sword in the chapel of St. Catherine de Fierbois in thanks for his victory over Moslem invaders at Tours in 732.   1. Joan is referring to her final campaign, in the spring of 1430.

and it had a silk fringe.[2] Asked if these names JESUS MARIA were written at the top or the bottom, or along the side, she answered that she thought they were along the side. Asked which she preferred, her sword or her standard, she replied that she was forty times fonder of her standard than she was of her sword. Asked who persuaded her to have this design on her standard, she said, "I have told you often enough that I have done nothing save by God's command." She said moreover that she herself bore her standard during an attack, in order to avoid killing anyone. And she added that she had never killed anyone at all.

March 1, 1431

[Joan is asked which of the three claimants to the papacy her voices told her to support, and she replies that they gave her no advice but that she believes "one ought to obey our lord the Pope at Rome." From this exchange, it is clear that Joan has no knowledge of or interest in church politics. The questioning then turns to the appearance of the angels and the language in which they speak.] She said that they spoke most excellently and beautifully; and that she understood them perfectly. She said that the voice was lovely, sweet and low in tone, and spoke in French. Asked if that voice, that is to say St. Margaret, spoke English, she answered, "Why should she speak English? She is not on the side of the English." Asked who gave her the ring which the Burgundians have, she answered, her father or mother; and she thought that JESUS MARIA was written on it. But she did not know who had had this written; she did not think there was any stone in it; and it was given to her at Domremy. She said also that her brother had given her a ring which we, the bishop, now have; and she requested us to give it to the church. She said further that she had never cured anyone with any rings. Asked whether St. Catherine and St. Margaret had spoken to her beneath the tree, she answered, "I do not know." Being repeatedly asked if the saints had spoken to her at the aforementioned spring, she replied yes; and she had heard them there. But what they then said to her she does not know. Being again asked if they had made any promises to her there or elsewhere, she replied that they did not make any promise to her, except by leave of Our Lord. Amongst other things, they told her that her king would be reestablished in his kingdom, whether his enemies wished it or no. She said that the saints promised to bring her to Paradise, as she had asked them. She said that those who wished to remove her from this world might well go themselves first. And she added, "One day I must be freed." She said also that she would be dead, were it not for the revelation which comforts her each day.

Asked what she has done with her mandrake,[3] she answered that she never had one; but that she had heard it said that there was one near her village, but that she had never seen it. She had heard it said that it was a dangerous and evil thing to him who keeps it, but she does not know its purpose. Asked where is the place where this thing of which she has heard is to be found, she replied that she had heard that it is the ground near the tree, but she

---

2. Joan was illiterate; at the interview at Poitiers she reportedly said that she knew "neither A nor B." Whenever she says she "wrote" something, she means that she had it written for her at her dictation.
3. A *mandrake* is a root plant of the potato family. Little images made of this root, which often looked like the lower limbs of a man, were reputed to be used in witchcraft.

does not know the spot. But she has heard it said that over the place grows a tree called a hazel. Asked what purpose this mandrake serves, she answered that she had heard it said that it attracts money, but she does not believe it, and on this matter her voices have never told her anything at all.

March 3, 1431

Over and over again did Maitre Jean Beaupêre, by order of my lord the Bishop of Beauvais, put questions to Joan, repeating to her that she had said that St. Michael had wings; and yet had not said anything of the bodies or limbs of St. Catherine and St. Margaret.[4] She answered, "I have told you what I know; and I will not answer you further." She said also that she had seen them so clearly that she was well assured that they were saints in heaven. Asked if she had seen more than their faces, she answered, "I have told you what I know. I would rather you cut my throat than tell you more." Asked if St. Michael and St. Gabriel had natural heads, she said, "Yes, so I saw them. And I believe that it was they, as certainly as I believe that God exists."[5] Asked whether she believes that God made them with heads as she saw them, she answered, "I saw them with my own eyes. I will not say anything else." Asked if she had seen or known by revelation that she would escape, she answered, "That does not concern your trial. Do you want me to speak against myself?"[6]

Asked whether, when she first came before her king, he asked her if it were by revelation that she changed her dress, she answered. "I have told you; although I do not remember if I was asked." She said also that it was written down at Poitiers. Questioned whether she was not required at Beaurevoir[7] to change her dress, she answered, "Yes, indeed. And I answered that I would not change it without Our Lord's leave." She said also that the duchess of Luxembourg asked my lord of Luxembourg not to hand her over to the English. She said also that the duchess of Luxembourg and the lady of Beaurevoir offered her a woman's dress, or cloth to make one, asking her to wear it. And she answered that she had not Our Lord's permission to do so, and it was not yet time. Asked whether she believed she would have done wrong or committed mortal sin in taking a woman's dress, she answered that she did better to obey and serve her sovereign Lord, that is God, than men. She also said that if she had to do so, she would sooner have done it at the request of these two ladies than of any other ladies in France, except the queen. Asked whether, when God revealed to her that she should change her dress, it was by the voice of St. Michael, St. Catherine, and St. Margaret, she said, "You will have nothing else from me at present."

Asked if she ever knew Brother Richard,[8] she answered, "I had never seen him until I came before Troyes."[9] Asked what greeting Brother Richard gave her, she answered that the people of Troyes sent him to her, as she thought, saying that they were doubtful as to whether she was sent by God. And when

---

4. These questions are designed to show that Joan's guides were not real angels, as the Church defined them, but evil spirits.   5. This is the first mention of the angel Gabriel, who makes only a few appearances in the testimony.   6. Joan here shows an unusual sophistication about the law, since important medieval legal authorities upheld the right of the accused to avoid self-incrimination.   7. *Beaurevoir* is the name of the castle of John, duke of Luxembourg, an ally of the Burgundians and whose troops captured Joan. In her answer Joan will refer to his wife and his step-daughter.   8. A preaching friar active in France at the time.   9. A town in eastern France, loyal to Charles.

he came near he made the sign of the Cross and sprinkled holy water, and she said to him, "Approach boldly. I shall not fly away."[1] Asked if she was aware that some of her party had had Mass celebrated and prayers said for her, she said she did not know. But if they had held a service it was not at her orders; and if they prayed for her, she is sure that they did no wrong. Asked whether those of her party firmly believed that she was sent by God, she answered, "I do not know whether they believe it, and refer to their opinions. But even if they do not believe it, still I am sent from God." Asked if she thinks that in believing she was sent from God they believed rightly, she answered, "If they believe that I am sent from God, they are not deceived." Asked if she were not well aware of the thoughts of those of her party, when they kissed her feet and hands and clothing, she replied, "Many people gladly came to see me." And that they kissed her clothing as little as she could help. But she said that the poor gladly came to her, because she did them no unkindness, but upheld and helped them as much as she could. Asked if good women did not touch their rings with the ring she was wearing, she answered, "Many women touched her hands and her rings." But she does not know their thoughts or intentions. Asked who were those other company who caught butterflies in her standard before Château-Thierry,[2] she replied that it was never done or said by their party; but that those of the other party invented it.[3] Asked what she did at Rheims with the gloves when her king was crowned, she answered that gifts of gloves were made to the knights and nobles who were there, and there was one who lost his gloves; but she did not say that she would find them.[4]

Asked whether, when traveling about the country, she received the sacrament of penance and of the altar frequently, when she was in the good towns,[5] she said, "Yes, from time to time." Asked if she had received the said sacraments wearing man's dress, she said yes; but does not remember having received it in armor. Asked what was the age of the child at Lagny that she went to see, she replied, "The baby was three days old." And it was brought to Lagny to Notre Dame. And she was told that the maidens of the town were before the statue of Our Lady; and that she might like to go and pray to God and Our Lady that it might live. And she went there and prayed to God with the others. And finally life appeared in it, and it yawned three times; then it was baptized and immediately after died, and was buried in consecrated ground. For three days, they said, no life had appeared in the child; and it was as black as her tunic. But when it yawned, the color began to come back. And she was with the maidens on her knees in front of Our Lady, offering prayers. Asked if it were not said by the town that she had brought this about, and that it was by her intercession, she replied, "I never inquired."

Asked if she knew Catherine de la Rochelle, or had seen her, she said yes, at Jargeau; and at Montfaucon-en-Berry.[6] Asked what she said to her, she answered that this Catherine said to her that a woman appeared, a white lady, dressed in cloth of gold, who told her to go through the good towns,

1. I.e., I am not a witch. 2. The idea behind this question is that witches used various kinds of insects to work their magic; *Château-Thierry* is a town in northern France. 3. The two parties to which Joan refers are the French and their opposition, the English and Burgundians. 4. Again, the question is designed to get Joan to admit that she could do things, such as find missing objects, by witchcraft. 5. That is, the towns loyal to Charles. 6. This incident with *Catherine de la Rochelle* took place in the winter of 1429–30, while Joan was engaged in an unsuccessful siege of a town named La Charité.

and that the king would give her heralds and trumpets to proclaim that whoever had gold, silver, or treasure should at once bring it forth; and that she would know those who did not and those who had hidden it; and would know where to find the treasure; and it would serve to pay Joan's men-at-arms. To which she had answered that Catherine should return to her husband, and look after her household and children. And, in order to be certain of the truth, she had spoken to St. Catherine and St. Margaret, who told her that this Catherine was mad and a liar. So she wrote to her king that she would tell him what ought to be done. And when she arrived, she informed him that Catherine was only a fool and a liar. However, Brother Richard wanted them to set her to work, which she would not permit, wherefore Brother Richard and Catherine were displeased with her. She said also to Catherine, who wished to go to the Duke of Burgundy to make peace, that it was her opinion that they would find no peace save at the lance's point. She also asked Catherine if this Lady appeared every night; and if so, she would sleep with her. And she did so, but kept awake till midnight, saw nothing, and then went to sleep. And when morning came, she asked if the Lady had appeared. And Catherine answered that she had come, but Joan was asleep, and she had not been able to wake her. So she asked her if the Lady would come the next night. And Catherine said yes. On this account Joan slept during the day in order that she might keep awake at night. And she shared Catherine's bed again the following night, and kept awake throughout the night. But she saw no one, although she often asked, "Will she come soon?" To which Catherine answered, "Yes, soon." Nevertheless, she knew through St. Catherine and St. Margaret that as for the affair of Catherine de la Rochelle, it was all nonsense.

March 12, 1431

Asked whether, when she promised Our Lord to keep her virginity, she had spoken to Him, she answered, "It ought to be sufficient to promise it to those who were sent by Him, that is to St. Catherine and St. Margaret." Asked who had persuaded her to cite a man at Toul in an action for marriage,[7] she said, "I did not cite him; it was he who cited me." And there she swore before the judge to tell the truth; and in fact she never had made any promise to him. She said also that the first time she heard her voice, she vowed her virginity as long as it should be pleasing to God. She was then of the age of thirteen years or thereabouts. She said further that her voices had assured her that she would win her case.

Asked if she had ever spoken of these visions either to her curé or to any other churchman, she said no; but only to Robert de Baudricourt and to her king. And she also said that she was never compelled by her voices to keep them secret; but she was greatly afraid of telling about them, for fear of the Burgundians preventing her making her journey; and especially was she afraid of her father, that he too might hinder her journey. Asked if she believed that she had done well in leaving without the permission of her father or mother, seeing that it is said that one should honor one's father and mother, she replied that in everything else she had been most obedient

---

7. This questioning refers to a charge against Joan that she had broken her promise to marry a man whose name remains unknown. Later in the trial it was suggested that the man in question refused to marry Joan on account of her evil life and association with prostitutes at Neufchateau.

to them, save for this departure; but that she later had written to them, and they had forgiven her. Asked if when she left her father and mother she believed that she had not committed a sin, she answered, "Since God so commanded, I had to obey." She added that since God so commanded, if she had had a hundred fathers and mothers, and if she had been a king's daughter, she would still have gone. Questioned whether she had asked her voices to tell her father and mother of her leaving, she answered that, as for her father and mother, the voices were well enough pleased that she should tell them, had it not been for the trouble that they would have caused if she did tell them. For herself, she would not tell them for anything. She added that her voices left it to her to tell her father and mother, or to keep silence.

Asked whether, when she saw St. Michael and the angels, she made any reverence to them, she said yes; after they left she had kissed the ground on which they stood, doing them reverence. Asked if they stayed long with her, she answered, "They often come to Christians who do not see them." She added that she had often seen them among Christian folk. Asked if her voices had ever called her Daughter of God, Daughter of the Church, Great-hearted Maid, she answered that, both before the raising of the siege of Orleans, and afterwards, every day when they spoke to her, they have often called her Joan the Pucelle, Daughter of God. Asked why, since she calls herself Daughter of God, she was unwilling to say the *Pater Noster*, she replied that she would willingly say it. And previously when she refused to say it, it was with the intention that my lord of Beauvais should hear her in confession.

Questioned concerning her father's dreams, she replied that when she was still with her father and mother, she was often told by her mother that her father had said that he dreamed his daughter Joan would go off with the soldiers; and that her mother and father took great care to keep her safely; that they were very strict with her; and that she was always obedient to them save in the incident at Toul, the action for breach of promise of marriage. She said further that she had heard her mother say that her father had said to her brothers, "If I thought that such a thing could happen as I have dreamed, I should want you to drown her; and if you did not, I would drown her myself." And that she greatly feared that they would lose their minds when she left to go to Vaucouleurs. Asked if his thoughts and dreams had come to her father after she had her visions, she replied, "Yes, more than two years after she first heard the voices."

March 13, 1431

[The session begins with questions about the sign that appeared to Charles when Joan met him at Chinon, and after resisting Joan finally provides an account of how an angel brought her before Charles, and that Charles himself saw the angel, who offered him a crown.] She said that when the angel came she accompanied him, and went with him up the stairs to the king's chamber, and the angel entered first. Then she herself said to the king, "Sire, here is your sign: take it." Asked where it was he appeared to her, she answered, "I often prayed that God should send the king a sign, and was in my lodging at the house of a good woman near the castle of Chinon, when he came. And then we went together to the king, and he was accompanied by a number of other angels whom no one could see." She said further that, had it not been for the love of her, and release her from the trouble caused by those who opposed her, she truly believed that a number of people would have seen the angel, who did not see him. Asked how the angel left her, she replied that he departed from her in a little chapel, and she was much disturbed at his leaving, and wept, and would gladly have gone with him; that is, that her soul would have gone. "He did not leave me frightened, but dismayed at his leaving." Asked if it were on account of her merits that God sent His angel, she answered that he came for a great purpose, and hoped that the king would believe in the sign, and that they would stop opposing her; and to give help to the good people of Orleans; and also on account of the merits of the king and the good duke of Orleans.[8] Asked why she, sooner than another, she answered, "It pleased God so to do, by means of a simple maid to drive back the king's enemies."

March 14, 1431

Asked when she said that my lord of Beauvais had put himself in danger in trying her, what was the danger into which my lord of Beauvais and the others had put themselves, she replied that this was and is what she said to my lord of Beauvais: "You say that you are my judge. I do not know whether you are. But I warn you not to judge me wrongfully for you would so put yourself in great danger. But I warn you, so that if Our Lord punish you for it, I shall have done my duty in so warning you." Asked whether, since her voices have told her that in the end she will come to the Kingdom of Heaven, she believes herself assured of salvation, and that she will not be damned in hell, she said that she firmly believes what her voices have told her, that she will be saved, as firmly as if she were already there. And when they told her that this answer had great weight, she answered that she, too, accounted it a great treasure. Questioned as to whether, after this revelation, she believes that she cannot commit mortal sin, she answered, "As to this I know nothing; but commit myself in all things to the Lord."

March 17, 1431

Asked to say whether she will submit to the decision of the Church, she answered, "I refer in this to Our Lord Who sent me, to Our Lady and to all the blessed saints in heaven." And it is her opinion that the Church and Our Lord are one; and that they ought not to make difficulties seeing that they are one. Then she was told that there is the Church Triumphant, where are God, the saints, and the souls that are saved; and there is the Church Militant, that is to say our Holy Father the Pope, God's Vicar upon earth, the cardinals, the prelates of the Church, and the clergy, and all good Catholic Christians; and this Church when assembled cannot err, and is governed by the Holy Spirit. Wherefore, being asked if she will not submit to the Church Militant, as it has been explained to her, she answered that it was from God, from the Virgin Mary, and from all the blessed saints in heaven, and from the Church Triumphant on high, and by their commands, that she came to the King of France. And to this Church she submits all her good deeds, and everything that she has done or is to do. And in answer to whether she would

---

8. Charles's brother, at the time imprisoned in England.

submit to the Church Militant, she said that she would not now make any other answer.

Asked what she says as to the woman's dress that they offered her in order that she might go and hear Mass, she said that as to the woman's dress, she would not take it yet, not till it pleased Our Lord. And if it must be that she is found guilty, then she begs the lords of the Church to grant her the grace of a woman's dress and a hood for her head; that she would rather die than go back on what Our Lord had commanded her to do; and firmly believes that Our Lord will not suffer her to be brought so low, that she might not receive help from God by a miracle. Asked why, since she has said that she wears man's dress by God's command, she asks a woman's dress to wear in her last hours, she answered, "It suffices that it be long."[9] Asked whether her saying that she would take a woman's dress if they would let her go was pleasing to God, she answered that if they let her go in a woman's dress, she would at once put on man's dress and do as Our Lord commanded her. She has said this before. And she would not for anything take the oath that she would not take up arms or wear male dress to do Our Lord's will. Asked what warrant and help she expected to have from Our Lord in taking man's dress, she said, both in the manner of this dress and in the other things she had done, she sought nothing but the salvation of her soul.

Asked if she did not believe before to-day that the fairies were evil spirits, she answered that she knew nothing about it. Asked if her godmother who saw the fairies is considered a wise woman,[1] she said that she is considered a sensible and upright woman; not a witch or a sorceress. Asked if she knew whether St. Catherine and St. Margaret hated the English, she said, "They love what Our Lord loves, and hate what God hates." Asked whether God hates the English, she said that as to the love or hate that God has for the English, or what He would do for their souls, she knows nothing; but she is well assured that they will be driven out of France, except those who die there; and that God will send the French victory over the English. Questioned as to whether God were for the English while their cause prospered in France, she answered that she did not know whether God hated the French; but she believes that He will allow them to be defeated for their sins, if in fact they are in a state of sin.

On March 27 Joan was read the list of 59 charges and replied to most of them by referring to her earlier testimony. She was accused, among other things, of having been taught "magic and sorcery" by her parents and god-mother (who was herself accused of being "a witch and a sorceress"), that she frequented the tree and the spring in the woods, "often at night [while] dancing and chanting spells," and of wearing male dress, "violating canon law, to the scandal of her sex and womanly modesty, and to the perversion of all decent behavior." To this last charge Joan referred to her earlier testimony, but then added: "And as for womanly duties," she said, "there were enough other women to do them."

On May 2 she was publically admonished by the bishop of Beauvais to

---

9. Joan is concerned that if she were to be stripped to her shirt, as was commonly done to a man about to be executed, her legs would be exposed; hence it is out of modesty that she asks for a woman's dress.
1. See above, the interrogation for February 24.

submit to the Church, but Joan refused, saying, "I wait upon God my Creator in all. I love Him with all my heart. I trust in my judge, that is the King of Heaven and earth. I believe in the Church on earth; but for my deeds and words, as I have previously said, I refer the whole matter to God, who caused me to do what I have done. I have a good Master, Our Lord, in Whom I trust for everything, and not in any other." It was decided by the judges that Joan should not be tortured, and on May 23 she was given a "charitable admonition" to abjure her previous testimony and submit to the Church by admitting that her revelations were from the devil and not God. Joan replied: "I will maintain what I have always said at my trial. And if I were to be condemned and saw the fire lit and the wood prepared and the executioner who was to burn me ready to cast me into the fire, still in the fire would I not say anything other than what I have said. And I will maintain what I have said until death."

The next day, as the sentence of death by fire was being read, it is reported that Joan retracted her previous testimony, submitted to the Church, and agreed to wear women's clothing. She was then sentenced to perpetual imprisonment. But four days later, on May 28, she was found in the prison wearing male clothing, and she maintained that "her voices had told her that she had done great wrong to God in confessing that what she had done was not well done," and that she had submitted only "for fear of the fire." Since she had been said to have earlier recanted, she was now a relapsed heretic. On the next day, May 29, Joan was handed over to the secular authorities for execution and on May 30, 1431, was burned to death in the market square of Rouen. Her final word was reported to have been "Jesu." In 1455–56, after the English had been finally expelled from France, a trial of rehabilitation was held and Joan was exonerated. After much controversy and resistance from conservative members of the Roman curia, Joan was declared a saint in 1920.

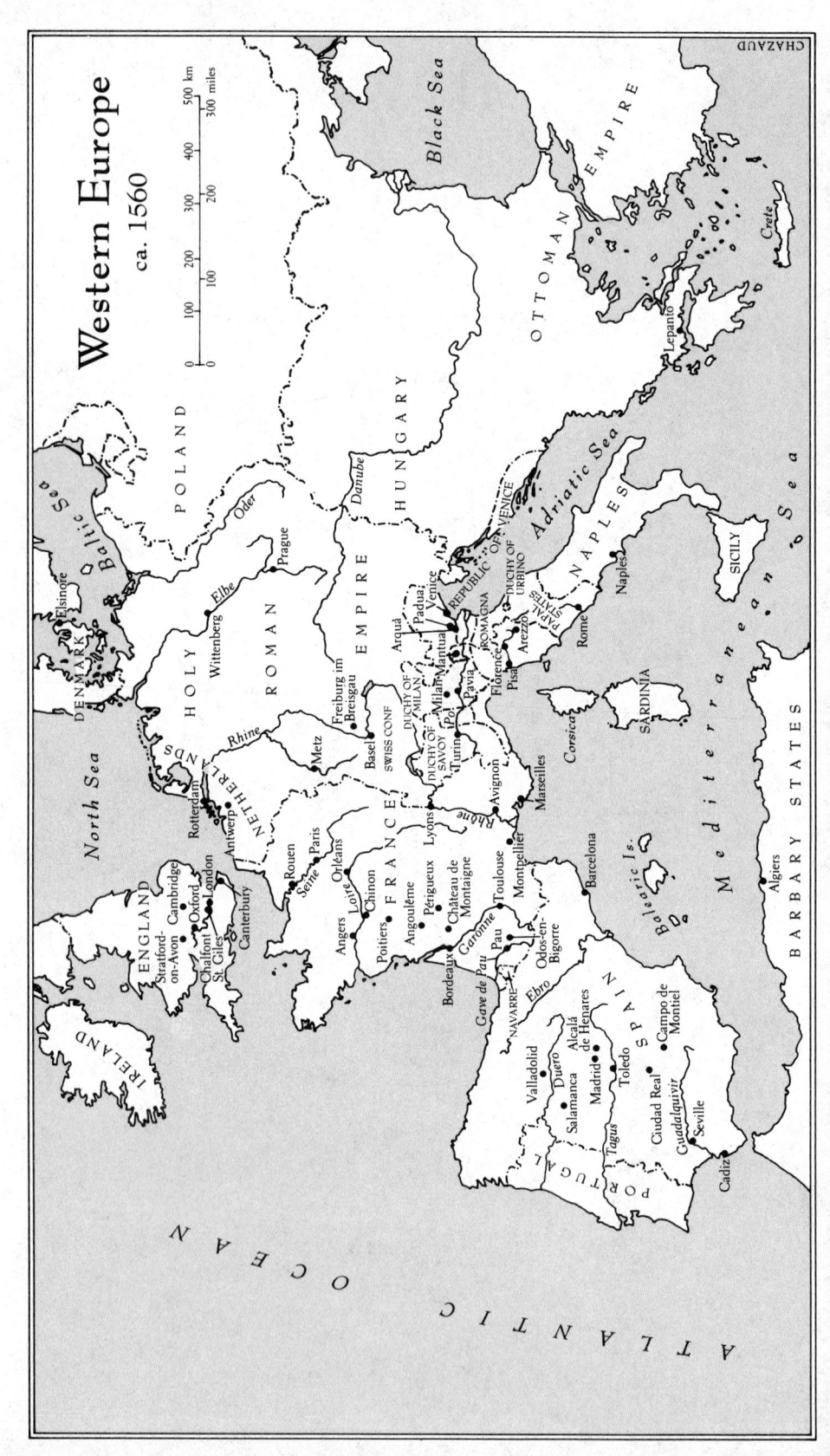

Western Europe
ca. 1560

0 100 200 300 400 500 km
0   100   200   300 miles

Black Sea

OTTOMAN EMPIRE

Crete

Lepanto

Baltic Sea

Elsinore

DENMARK

POLAND

Oder

Prague

Elbe

Wittenberg

HOLY ROMAN EMPIRE

Danube

HUNGARY

Adriatic Sea

NAPLES

Naples

SICILY

North Sea

Rotterdam

Antwerp

NETHERLANDS

Rhine

Metz

Basel

SWISS CONF

Freiburg im Breisgau

DUCHY OF MILAN

DUCHY OF SAVOY

Turin

Pavia

Milan

Mantua

Padua

Arquà

REPUBLIC OF VENICE

Venice

DUCHY OF URBINO

ROMAGNA

PAPAL STATES

Florence

Arezzo

Pisa

Rome

SARDINIA

Corsica

IRELAND

ENGLAND

Stratford-on-Avon

Oxford

Cambridge

London

Chalfont St. Giles

Canterbury

Rouen

Paris

Seine

Orléans

Angers

Loire

Chinon

FRANCE

Poitiers

Angoulême

Périgueux

Château de Montaigne

Lyons

Rhône

Avignon

Marseilles

Montpellier

Toulouse

Bordeaux

Garonne

Gave de Pau

Pau

Odos-en-Bigorre

NAVARRE

Ebro

Barcelona

Balearic Is.

Mediterranean Sea

Algiers

BARBARY STATES

SPAIN

Valladolid

Duero

Salamanca

Alcalá de Henares

Madrid

Tagus

Toledo

Ciudad Real

Campo de Montiel

Guadalquivir

Seville

Cadiz

PORTUGAL

ATLANTIC OCEAN

CHAZAUD

The Renaissance

"All the world's a stage, / And all the men and women merely players": Shakespeare's famous comparison of human beings to actors playing their various roles in the great theater of the world conjures up the exhilarating liberty and mobility we associate with the Renaissance and with the lively characters produced in the literature of the period. Since "merely" meant, in Shakespeare's day, "wholly" and "entirely," the line evokes a lively sense of the men and women of that world performing their roles with the gusto of actors. Their social roles as princes, clowns, thieves, or housewives appear, from one angle, exciting opportunities for the characters to explore. Yet such roles are also clearly confining: Renaissance men and women were born into societies that strictly regulated their actions and even their clothing—only actors had the right to vary their garb and dress above their station. Whether Renaissance subjects relished the pleasures of playing or resented the constraints of their social roles is a subject often taken up in the literature of the day.

When Renaissance writers explore the relationship of literary characters and their social roles, they partly follow in the tradition exemplified in the Middle Ages by Chaucer's *Canterbury Tales*. Yet the most memorable characters of Renaissance literature enjoy greater autonomy and more fully realized personalities than Chaucer's pilgrims. Rabelais's broad-minded giant, Gargantua; Cervantes's idealistic but mad Quixote; Shakespeare's brillant but tormented Hamlet; and Milton's "domestic" Adam and "adventurous" Eve are frequently presented in acts of thought, fantasy, planning, doubt, and internal debate. Deliberating with others and themselves about what to do seems at least as important to these characters as putting their plans into action.

One reason for this shift toward internal, mental, and psychological portraiture is that Renaissance authors, like the characters they invent, inhabited a world of such widespread revolutionary change that they could not passively receive the traditional wisdom of previous ages. When Nicolaus Copernicus (1473–1543) discovered that the Earth moves around the sun and when Galileo Galilei (1564–1642) turned his telescope up to the heavens, the Renaissance mind had to reconceive the nature of the universe and Creation. When Christopher Columbus (1451–1506) sailed to what he thought were the Indies, he proved that the Earth was not flat and introduced a New World to Europe, which began for the first time to think of itself as the Old World. Around the time that Columbus was sailing to America, humanist scholars in Italy began to use new scholarly methods that gave them fuller access to the cultural legacy of the ancient world of Greece and Rome and a new sense of their own place in history. On scientific, geographical, and scholarly fronts, the world of Renaissance Europe was undergoing revolutionary change.

The new discoveries' challenge to European and human centrality in the world and in Creation met with fervent, if varied, responses. In 1633 the Inquisition forced Galileo to repudiate the Copernican theory that the Earth rotates around the sun. In his dialogue *The City of the Sun* (1602) Galileo's friend and supporter Tommasso Campanella (1568–1639) optimistically asserted that the three great inventions of his day—the compass, the printing press, and the gun—were "signs of the union of the entire world." François Rabelais, less sanguine about the idea of world union enforced by the gun and artillery, placed his hopes for peace only on the printing press, an instrument for intellectual deliberation and the dissemination of ideas. In

The First Anniversary, John Donne (1572–1631), on the other hand, focused on the psychological threat of the new discoveries and theories to individuals unable to cope with so much uncertainty:

> The new philosophy calls all in doubt,
> The element of fire is quite put out;
> The sun is lost and the earth, and no man's wit
> Can well direct him where to look for it.
> And freely men confess that this world's spent,
> When in the planets and the firmament
> They seek so many new; they see that this
> Is crumbled out again to his atomies . . .

In Donne's poem, the new discoveries amount to a second creation, so radical is the new theory of the world's construction. For Renaissance intellectuals and for the literary characters they created, there was almost literally no firm ground to stand on as they moved through life in an increasingly complex and uncertain world. Although received wisdom appeared from one angle like an anchor in a sea of change, from another it seemed like a shackle to error: it is no wonder, then, that the reasoning and choices of the characters in Renaissance poetry and prose began to matter enormously.

As with other terms that have currency in cultural history (for instance, *Romanticism*), the usefulness of the term *Renaissance* depends on its keeping a certain degree of elasticity. The literal meaning of the word—"rebirth"—suggests that one impulse toward the great intellectual and artistic achievements of the period came from the example of ancient culture, or even better, from a certain vision that the artists and intellectuals of the Renaissance possessed of the world of antiquity, which they saw as "reborn" through their work. The restoration of ancient arts and learning was regarded as a glorious achievement to be set beside the thrilling discoveries of their own age. "For now," Rabelais writes through his Gargantua,

> all courses of study have been restored, and the acquisition of languages has become supremely honorable: Greek, without which it is shameful for any man to be called a scholar; Hebrew; Chaldean; and Latin. And in my time we have learned how to produce wonderfully elegant and accurate printed books, just as, on the other hand, we have also learned (by diabolic suggestion) how to make cannon and other such fearful weapons.

Machiavelli, whose love of antiquity is as typical a trait as his better-known political realism, suggests in the opening of his *Discourses on the First Ten Books of Livy* (1513–21) that rulers should be as keen on the imitation of ancient "virtues" as are artists, lawyers, and the scientists: "The civil laws are nothing but decisions given by the ancient jurisconsults. . . . And what is the science of medicine, but the experience of ancient physicians, which their successors have taken for their guide?"

Elasticity should likewise be maintained in regard to the chronological span of the Renaissance as a "movement" extending through varying periods of years and as including phases and traits of the epoch that is otherwise known as the Middle Ages (and vice versa). The peak of the Renaissance can be shown to have occurred at different times in different countries, the "movement" having had its inception in Italy, where its impact was at first most remarkable in the visual arts, while in England, for instance, it developed later and its main achievements were in literature, particularly the drama. The meaning of the term has also, in the course of time, widened considerably. Nowadays it conveys, to say the least, a general notion of artistic creativity, of extraordinary zest for life and knowledge, of sensory delight in opulence and magnificence, of spectacular individual achievement, thus extending far beyond the literal meaning of rebirth and the strict idea of a revival and imitation of antiquity.

Even in its stricter sense, however, the term continues to have its function. The degree to which European intellectuals of the period possessed and were possessed by the writings of the ancient world is difficult for modern readers to realize. For these writers references to classical mythology, philosophy, and literature are not ornaments or affectations. Along with references to the Scriptures they are part, and a major part, of their mental equipment and way of thinking. For example, Erasmus, in his *The Praise of Folly*, speaks in a cluster of classical allusions to introduce the lineage of his character, Folly: "Neither Chaos . . . nor Orcus, nor Saturn, nor Jape-tus, nor any other of these worn-out, moldy old gods was my father. Rather, it was Plutus [god of wealth], the one and only father of men and gods alike, Hesiod and Homer and even Jupiter himself to the contrary notwithstanding" (p. 1922). Similarly, Machiavelli writes to a friend: "I get up before daylight, prepare my birdlime, and go out with a bundle of cages on my back, so that I look like Geta when he came back from the harbor with the books of Amphitryo" (p. 1948, n. 3). The words have by no means the sound of erudite self-gratification that they might have today. These remarks may seem to show off erudite learning in an exaggerated manner. But in their historical context, they are part of the common linguistic currency of the Renais-sance intellectual.

When we are overcome by sudden emotion, our first exclamations are likely to be in the language most familiar to us—our dialect, if we happen to have one. Montaigne relates of himself that when once his father unexpectedly fell back in his arms in a swoon, the first words he uttered under the emotion of that experience were in Latin. Similarly Benvenuto Cellini, the Italian sculptor, goldsmith, and autobiographer, talk-ing to his patron and expressing admiration of a Greek statue, establishes with the ancient artist an immediate contact, a proud familiarity:

> I cried to the Duke: "My lord, this is a statue in Greek marble, and it is a miracle
> of beauty. . . . If your Excellency permits, I should like to restore it—head and
> arms and feet. . . . It is certainly not my business to patch up statues, that being
> the trade of botchers, who do it in all conscience villainously ill; yet the art
> displayed by this great master of antiquity cries out to me to help him."

The people who, starting at about the middle of the fourteenth century, gave new impulse to this emulation of the classics are often referred to as humanists. The word in that sense is related to what we call the humanities, and the humanities at that time were Latin and Greek. Every cultivated person wrote and spoke Latin, with the result that a Western community of intellectuals could exist, a spiritual "republic of letters" above individual nations. There was also a considerable amount of individual contact among humanists. In glancing at the biographies of the authors included in this section, the extensiveness of their travels may strike us as remarkable or even surprising, considering the hardships and slowness of traveling during those centu-ries.

The archetype of literature as a vocation is often said to be Petrarch—the first author in this section—who anticipated certain ideals of the high Renaissance: a lofty conception of the literary art, a taste for the good life, a basic pacifism, and a strong sense of the memories and glories of antiquity. In this last respect, what should be emphasized is the imaginative quality, the visionary impulse with which the writers of the period looked at those memories—the same vision and imagination with which they regarded such contemporary heroes as the great navigators and astronomers. The Renaissance view of the cultural monuments of antiquity was far from being that of the philologist and the antiquarian; indeed, familiarity was facilitated by the very lack of a scientific sense of history. We find the visionary and imaginative element not only in the creations of poets and dramatists (Shakespeare's Romans, to give an obvious example) but also in the works of political writers: as when Machiavelli describes himself entering, through his reading, the

> ancient courts of ancient men, where, being lovingly received, I feed on that food
> which alone is mine, and which I was born for; I am not ashamed to speak with
> them and to ask the reasons for their actions, and they courteously answer me.

> For . . . hours I feel no boredom and forget every worry; I do not fear poverty, and death does not terrify me. I give myself completely over to the ancients.

Imitation of antiquity acquires, in Machiavelli and many others, a special quality; whereas "academic" imitations transcribe, Machiavelli plunges into vital and reciprocal communication—even communion—with the ancients.

The vision of an ancient age of glorious intellectual achievement that is "now" brought to life again implies, of course, however roughly, the idea of an intervening "middle" time, by comparison ignorant and dark. The commonplace but vastly inaccurate notion that the "light" of the Renaissance broke through a long "night" of the Middle Ages was not devised by subsequent "enlightened" centuries; it was held by the humanist scholars of the Renaissance themselves. In his genealogy of giants from Grangousier to Gargantua to Pantagruel, Rabelais conveniently represents the generations of modern learning with their varying degrees of enlightenment. Thus Gargantua writes to his son:

> Though my late father of worthy memory, Grandgousier, devoted all his energy to those things of which I might take the fullest advantage, and from which I might acquire the most sensible knowledge, and though my own effort matched his—or even surpassed it—still, as you know very well, it was neither so fit nor so right a time for learning as exists today, nor was there an abundance of such teachers as you have had. It was still a murky, dark time, oppressed by the misery, unhappiness, and disasters of the Goths, who destroyed all worthwhile literature of every sort. But divine goodness has let me live to see light and dignity returned to humanistic studies, and to see such an improvement, indeed, that it would be hard for me to qualify for the very first class of little schoolboys—I who, in my prime, had the reputation (and not in error) of the most learned man of my day.

The combination of self-deprecation, aspiration, and arrogance aptly characterizes the period's sense of its own achievements and its standing in relation to antiquity and the Middle Ages.

Definitions of the Renaissance must also take account of the period's preoccupation with this life rather than with the life beyond. The contrast of an ideal medieval man or woman, whose mode of action is basically oriented toward the thought of the afterlife (and who therefore conceives of life on Earth as transient and preparatory) with an ideal Renaissance man or woman, possessing and cherishing earthly interests so concrete and self-sufficient that the very realization of the ephemeral quality of life is to him or her nothing but an added spur to its immediate enjoyment—this is a useful contrast even though it represents an enormous oversimplification of the facts.

The same emphasis on the immediate and tangible is reflected in the earthly, amoral, and aesthetic character of what we may call the Renaissance code of behavior. According to this "code," human action is judged not in terms of right and wrong, of good and evil (as it is judged when life is viewed as a moral "test," with reward or punishment in the afterlife), but in terms of its present concrete validity and effectiveness, of the delight it affords, of its memorability and its beauty. In that sense a good deal that is typical of the Renaissance, from architecture to poetry, from sculpture to rhetoric, may be related to a taste for the harmonious and the memorable, for the spectacular effect, for the successful striking of a pose. Individual human action, seeking as it were in itself its own reward, finds justification in its formal appropriateness; in its being a well-rounded achievement, perfect of its kind; in the zest and gusto with which it is, here and now, performed; and, finally, in its proving worthy of remaining as a testimony to the performer's power on Earth.

A convenient way to illustrate this emphasis is to consider certain words especially expressive of the interests of the period—"virtue," "fame," "glory." "Virtue," particularly in its Italian form, *virtù*, is to be understood in a wide sense. As we may see even now in some relics of its older meanings, the word (from the Latin *vir*, "man") connotes active power—the intrinsic force and ability of a person or thing (the "virtue" of a law or of a medicine)—and hence, also, technical skill (the capacity of the "virtuoso"). The Machiavellian prince's "virtues," therefore, are not necessarily goodness, temperance, clemency, and the like; they are whatever forces and skills may help him in the efficient management and preservation of his princely powers. The idealistic, intangible part of the prince's success is consigned to such concepts as "fame" and "glory," but even in this case the dimension within which human action is considered is still an earthly one. These concepts connote the hero's success and reputation with his contemporaries, or look forward to splendid recognition from posterity, on Earth.

In this sense (though completely pure examples of such an attitude are rare) the purpose of life is the unrestrained and self-sufficient practice of one's "virtue," the competent and delighted exercise of one's skill. At the same time, there is no reason to forget that such virtues and skills are God's gift. The worldview of even some of the most clearly earthbound Renaissance writers was hardly godless; Machiavelli, Rabelais, Cellini take for granted the presence of God in their own and in their heroes' lives:

> . . . we have before our eyes extraordinary and unexampled means prepared by God. The sea has been divided. A cloud has guided you on your way. The rock has given forth water. Manna has fallen. Everything has united to make you great. The rest is for you to do. God does not intend to do everything, lest he deprive us of our free will and the share of glory that belongs to us. (Machiavelli)

> And then Gargantua and Powerbrain would briefly recapitulate, according to the Pythagorean fashion, everything Gargantua had read and seen and understood, everything he had done and heard, all day long.
> They would both pray to God their Creator, worshiping, reaffirming their faith, glorifying Him for His immense goodness and thanking Him for all they had been given, and forever placing themselves in His hands.
> And then they would go to sleep. (Rabelais)

> I found that all the bronze my furnace contained had been exhausted in the head of this figure [of the statue of Perseus]. It was a miracle to observe that not one fragment remained in the orifice of the channel, and that nothing was wanting to the statue. In my great astonishment I seemed to see in this the hand of God arranging and controlling all. (Cellini)

Yet if we compare the attitudes of these authors with the view of the world and of the value of human action that emerges from the major literary work of the Middle Ages, *The Divine Comedy*, and with the manner in which human action is there seen within a grand extratemporal design, we see that the presence of God in the Renaissance writers cited above is conspicuously less dominating.

Renaissance intellectuals, artists, aristocrats, and princes did not lack in abiding religious faith or fervor. The most powerful lords of opulent Renaissance courts would unhesitatingly affirm John Calvin's starkly religious assessment of earthly life and gain:

> For if heaven is our country, what is earth but a place of exile! If the departure out of the world is an entrance into life, what is the world but a sepulchre? What is a continuance in it but an absorption in death? If deliverance from the body is an introduction into complete liberty, what is the body but a prison? Therefore, if the terrestrial life be compared with the celestial, it should undoubtedly be despised and accounted of no value.

These princes, however, sharply felt the conflict between the values of worldly goods and spiritual renunciation. The religious conviction in the transitory nature of earthly possessions, moreover, did not prevent princes and lords from seeking to expand their kingdoms. An anonymous Spanish writer was inspired to celebrate Spain's growing empire as "the greatest event since the making of the world, apart from the incarnation and death of him who created it," a phrase that today rings with more patriotism than piety. At the time it was written, however, Church and state seemed inextricably bound together. The Papacy was a political and military power as well as a spiritual one; Charles V of Spain united most of Europe under his rule and declared himself the Holy Roman Emperor; and Henry VIII of England broke with the Catholic Church and declared himself head of the Church of England. Even movements originally intended to reform the Catholic Church—such as the Reformist movements associated with Martin Luther (1483–1546), Ulrich Zwingli (1484–1531), and John Calvin (1509–1564)—were rapidly adopted by Renaissance princes bridling under papal authority. Given the political force of the Catholic Church and the Protestant Reformation, it is no wonder that the Renaissance often appears to be more preoccupied with earthly princes and empires than with the heavenly King.

In a similar vein, religious convictions in no way hamper the capacity for Renaissance princes and poets to appreciate sensuous beauty and pleasure. Just as the sensuous appraisal of a woman's beauties plays a large part in the Song of Songs from the Hebrew Bible, for example, so Ludovico Ariosto rhapsodically describes the temptress Alcina as

> so beautifully modelled, no painter, however much he applied himself, could have achieved anything more perfect. Her long blonde tresses were gathered in a knot: pure gold itself could have no finer lustre. Roses and white privet blooms lent their colours to suffuse her delicate cheeks. Her serene brow was like polished ivory, and in perfect proportion. / Beneath two of the thinnest black arches, two dark eyes—or rather, two bright suns; soft was their look, gentle their movement . . . down the midst of the face, the nose. . . . / Below this, the mouth, set between two dimples; it was imbued with native cinnabar. Here a beautiful soft pair of lips opened to disclose a double row of choicest pearls. . . . / Snow-white was her neck, milky her breast; the neck was round, the breast broad and full. A pair of apples, not yet ripe, fashioned in ivory, rose and fell like the sea-swell at times when a gentle breeze stirs the ocean. . . . You could easily judge that what lay hidden did not fall short of what was exposed to view.

Alcina is, evidently, at once a spiritual experience and "a paradise on earth" to conquer. The loving description of a woman's body often goes hand in glove with the idea of conquest and world-discovery: when John Donne, for example, finally succeeds in stripping his beloved of all her clothing, he bursts out, "O my America, my newfound land!"

If the mistresses of courtly writers inspired them to praise all the world had to offer, their princes also received the admiration of these writers for their generosity in supporting the arts. Castiglione in the first pages of the *Courtier* pays homage to the memory of the late lord of Montefeltro, in whose palace at Urbino the book's personages hold their lofty debate on the idea of a perfect gentleman (an earlier Montefeltro appears in Dante's Hell, another in Dante's Purgatory); but Castiglione praises him only for his achievements as a man of arms and a promoter of the arts. There is no thought of either the salvation or the damnation of his soul (though the general tone of the work would seem to imply his salvation); he is exalted instead for military victories, and even more warmly, for having built a splendid palace:

> He built on the rugged site of Urbino a palace thought by many the most beautiful to be found anywhere in all Italy and he furnished it so well with every suitable thing that it seemed not a palace but a city in the form of a palace; and furnished it not only with what is customary, such as silver vases, wall hangings of the richest cloth of gold, silk, and other like things, but for ornament he added countless ancient statues of marble and bronze, rare paintings, and musical

instruments of every sort; nor did he wish to have anything there that was not most rare and excellent. Then, at great expense, he collected many very excellent and rare books in Greek, Latin, and Hebrew, all of which he adorned with gold and silver, deeming these to be the supreme excellence of his great palace.

The almost legendary Duke Federico defines, through his life's history, the ideal prince as a heroic empire-builder, able to tame "rugged" terrain by force, amass luxurious wealth, and best of all, collect fine arts. The supreme testimony to his heroic virtue is his library of costly and sumptuous volumes, all collected to conserve the wisdom of antiquity and to promote the exchange of ideas at Urbino.

Thus the popular view that associates the idea of the Renaissance especially with the flourishing of the arts is correct. The leaders of the period saw in a work of art the clearest instance of beautiful, harmonious, and self-justified performance. To create such a work became the valuable occupation par excellence, the most satisfactory display of *virtù*. The Renaissance view of antiquity exemplifies this attitude. The artists and intellectuals of the period not only drew on antiquity for certain practices and forms but also found there a recognition of the place of the arts among outstanding modes of human action. In this way, the concepts of "fame" and "glory" became particularly associated with the art of poetry because the Renaissance drew from antiquity the idea of the poet as celebrator of high deeds, the "dispenser of glory."*

There is, then, an important part of the Renaissance mind that sees terrestrial life as positive fulfillment. This is especially clear where there is a close association between the practical and the intellectual, as in the exercise of political power, the act of scientific discovery, the creation of works of art. The Renaissance assumption is that there are things highly worth doing, within a strictly temporal pattern. By doing them, humanity proves its privileged position in Creation and therefore incidentally follows God's intent. The often cited phrase "the dignity of man" describes this positive, strongly affirmed awareness of the intellectual and physical "virtues" of the human being, and of the individual's place in Creation.

It is important, however, to see this fact about the Renaissance in the light of another phenomenon. Where there is a singularly high capacity for feeling the delight of earthly achievement, there is a possibility that its ultimate worth will also be questioned profoundly. What (the Renaissance mind usually seems to ask at some point) is the purpose of all this activity? What meaningful relation does it bear to any all-inclusive, cosmic pattern? The Renaissance coincided with, and perhaps to some extent occasioned, a loss of firm belief in the final unity and the final intelligibility of the universe, such belief as underlies, for example, *The Divine Comedy,* enabling Dante to say in Paradise:

> I saw within Its depth how It conceives
>   all things in a single volume bound by Love,
>   of which the universe is the scattered leaves;
> substance, accident, and their relation
>   so fused that all I say could do no more
>   than yield a glimpse of that bright revelation.

Once the notion of this grand unity of design has lost its authority, certainty about the final value of human actions is no longer to be found. For some minds, indeed, the sense of void becomes so strong as to paralyze all aspiration to power or thirst for knowledge or delight in beauty; the resulting attitude we may call Renaissance melancholy, whether it be openly shown (as by some characters in Elizabethan drama) or provide an undercurrent of sadness, or incite to ironical forms of compromise, to

---

*And, of course, a typical guarantee of memorability was having oneself portrayed—perhaps at various stages in life—by some of the magnificent and highly honored painters of the period.

some sort of wise adjustment (as in Erasmus or Montaigne.) Thus while on one, and perhaps the better-known, side of the picture human intellect in Renaissance literature enthusiastically expatiates over the realms of knowledge and unveils the mysteries of the universe, on the other it is beset by puzzling doubts and a profound mistrust of its own powers.

Doubts about the value of human action within the scheme of eternity did not, however, diminish the outpouring of ideas about the ideal ordering of this world. Renaissance poets and intellectuals turned to the printing press as the means to disseminate and test ideas about the ideal prince, courtier, councilor, and humble subject as well as the ideal court and society. Renaissance epics, such as Ludovico Ariosto's *Orlando Furioso*, use the resources of comedy and tragedy (among other genres) to explore what is gained and lost in achieving that crystallization of the civilizing process, the imperial court. Niccolò Machiavelli turns to print in order to propose his amoral ideas about the effective (rather than ideal) prince; Baldassare Castiglione uses the dialogue form to define and expand the role of the courtier who would serve and, it is hoped, counsel the powerful prince. Other writers shift the focus from the court to the entire commonwealth. Marguerite de Navarre examines the strategies of individuals from the lower classes whose only resource against the abuses of powerful lords and clergymen is their own ingenuity. Lope de Vega transforms the historical case of a peasant uprising against a highly abusive military commander into a play, *Fuente Ovejuna*, which possesses the artistic charm of comedy and the weight of political ethics. In all these works of imaginative scope and supreme artistic skill, Renaissance writers can be seen tirelessly examining the nature of their own world, the problem of power, and the vexed relations between the absolute authority of the prince and the rights and liberties of the people. Its zeal for defining the social contract partly explains why the Renaissance is often viewed as the "early modern" period; the "rebirth" and flourishing of antiquity also heralded ideas that we associate with the modern political world.

The joining of philosophical and imaginative thinking in literary expression is characteristic of the Renaissance, which cultivated the idea of "serious play." Throughout the literature of the period, we see the creative and restless mind of the Renaissance intellectual "freely ranging," as Sir Philip Sidney put it, "only in the zodiac of his own wit," creating fictional characters and worlds that might, if the poet is sufficiently persuasive, be put into practice and change the nature of the real world.

THE RENAISSANCE

TEXTS	CONTEXTS
1335 Petrarch's poems to Laura, including **Sonnets,** under way (published 1360)	
	1338–1453 Hundred Years' War
	1348–1350 The Black Death: Petrarch's Laura dies in the plague
1349–1353 Boccaccio's **Decameron** in progress	
1387–1399 Chaucer's **The Canterbury Tales** in progress; he dies in 1400	
	1428 Joan of Arc liberates Orléans from the British; she is burned at the stake for heresy in 1431
	1453 Constantinople falls to the Turks, increasing dissemination of Greek culture in Western Europe
	1473 Printing comes to Spain
	1474 William Caxton prints the first book in English
	1492 Columbus discovers America • Expulsion of the Jews from Spain • Spanish reconquest of Granada • Expedition of Charles VIII of France
1494 Sebastian Brandt's **Ship of Fools**	
	1502 The "Nuremberg Egg," first portable timepiece
	1503 Leonardo da Vinci paints the **Mona Lisa**
1511 Erasmus's **The Praise of Folly** published	
	1512 Michelangelo completes the Sistine Chapel ceiling
1516 Erasmus's edition of the New Testament of the Bible • First publication of Ariosto's **Orlando Furioso**	
	1517 Luther's Ninety-five Theses denounces abuses of the Roman Church
	1519 Charles I of Spain becomes Holy Roman Emperor, Charles V
1521 Second edition of **Orlando Furioso**	**1521** Luther is excommunicated
	1524 Francis I is captured in battle against the armies of Charles V

Boldface titles indicate works in the anthology.

THE RENAISSANCE

TEXTS	CONTEXTS
	1527 Rome sacked by the French • Castiglione, now bishop of Avila, is accused of treachery • Marguerite marries Henri d'Albret, king of Navarre
1528 Castiglione's *Book of the Courtier* published; he dies the following year	
1531 Erasmus publishes first complete edition of Aristotle's works	
1532 Rabelais's *Pantagruel* • Machiavelli's *The Prince* • Final publication of *Orlando Furioso*; Ariosto dies the following year	
	1533 Sorbonne accuses Marguerite's chaplain of heresy
1534 Rabelais's *Gargantua*	1534 Henry VIII breaks with Rome and becomes head of the Church of England
1536 John Calvin's *Institutes of the Christian Religion*	
1546 Rabelais's *Third Book*	
	1547 Francis I dies; Henry II accedes to the French throne
1549 Rabelais's *Fourth Book*	1549 England declares war on France
1551 First English translation of More's *Utopia*; More had been executed for high treason by Henry VIII in 1535	
	1555 Tobacco brought to Spain from America for the first time
1558 Marguerite de Navarre's *Heptameron* published	
	1559 Spain's most severe Index of banned books
	1563 Council of Trent concludes
	1571 Spain's battle of Lepanto against the Turks
1571? Montaigne's *Essays* in progress; books 1 and 2 published in 1580; complete publication in 1588	
1581 Tasso's *Jerusalem Delivered*	
	1586 El Greco paints the *Burial of Count Orgaz*
	1588 Spain's Invincible Armada defeated by England

THE RENAISSANCE

TEXTS	CONTEXTS
1590 Sir Philip Sidney's revised *Arcadia*	
1596 Edmund Spenser's *The Faerie Queene* 1–6 plus the "Mutabilitie Cantos"	
1597 Tasso's revised *Jerusalem Conquered*	
1597–1604 Cervantes's ***Don Quixote*** in progress; part 1 was published in 1605, part 2 in 1615	
	1598 Philip II of Spain dies; Philip III crowned • Literary quarrel between Lope de Vega and Luis de Gongora
1600 Shakespeare's *Hamlet* appears	
	1608 Dutch scientist Johann Lippershey invents the telescope
1611 King James version of the Bible published	
	1620 Colony founded by Pilgrims at Plymouth, Massachusetts
	1633 Galileo forced by the Inquisition to repudiate Copernican theory that Earth rotates around the sun
1641 René Descartes publishes his *Meditations on First Philosophy*	
	1643–1715 Reign of Louis XIV of France, "the Sun King"
	1645–1649 England's Charles I surrenders to antimonarchical forces of Oliver Cromwell and is executed; monarchy is abolished
1655? Milton's *Paradise Lost* in progress; published 1667	**1655** Velázquez paints *Las Meninas*
	1660 Charles II restores the English monarchy

FRANCIS PETRARCH
1304–1374

Although Petrarch, a contemporary of Dante and Boccaccio, lived and died in the Middle Ages, he did everything in his power to distinguish himself and his scholarship from the period he dismissed as the "Dark Ages." Frustrated with the corruption of scholarly Latin, Petrarch dedicated himself to the recovery of classical learning in a spirit commonly associated with a later period. If Petrarch can be called a precursor of the Renaissance, it is not for his scholarly output in Latin or his reforms to Latin prose style. The credit is instead due to an aspect of Petrarch's work that neither he nor his contemporaries regarded as a lasting contribution to letters: Petrarch's 366 lyric poems in the vernacular, mostly dedicated to his frustrated desire for an elusive woman named Laura. Petrarch's art, experience of love, and sense of his own fragmented, fluid, and metamorphic self set the standard for the lyric expression of subjective and erotic experience in the Renaissance. His efforts to scrutinize himself intently and at times unflatteringly and to capture his own elusive inner workings in verse inspired a poetic tradition that has influenced lyric sequences from Shakespeare's sonnets to Walt Whitman's *Leaves of Grass* and to modern pop lyrics.

Francesco Petrarca was born in Arezzo on July 20, 1304, three years after his father (along with Dante) was exiled from Florence. In 1314, Petrarch's father moved his family to Avignon, the new seat of the papacy (1309–77), where he became prosperous in the legal profession. Petrarch himself trained as a law student for ten years, but chose to pursue the study of classical culture and literature. He soon came to the attention of the powerful Colonna family, whose patronage launched his career as a diplomat-scholar and allowed him to travel widely and move in the intimate circles of European princes and scholars. He conducted diplomatic missions for popes and princes, but refused the offices of bishop and papal secretary, preferring instead to ground his growing prestige in his humanistic scholarship. He did not always manage to protect his scholarly independence from the manipulations of the powerful, such as the tyrannical Visconti family in Milan (as his usually admiring friend Boccaccio remarked). His politics are not easy to decipher: although he served as diplomat for the Visconti at one time, at another he supported the republican dream of the Roman tribune, Cola di Rienzo. Petrarch bequeathed to later humanists the hope that scholar-poets might one day be recognized as shaping forces of the nation-state; in practice, however, he established the humanist scholar's ambiguous position as councillor and exploited servant of powerful princes.

Petrarch expected that he would secure enduring fame through the *Africa*, his unfinished epic poem in Latin hexameters on the life of Scipio Africanus, who embodied the valiant and pious virtues that Petrarch admired in Roman heroism. Of greater importance were Petrarch's manuscript discoveries of Cicero's *Pro Archia* (For Archias), a Roman "defense of poetry," in 1333 and letters to Atticus in 1345. The discovery of Cicero's personal correspondence inspired Petrarch to compose his own familiar letters, learned, intellectually exploratory, often moving, and profoundly dialogical. Addressed to his many friends and even to the ancients themselves, these letters illustrate how essential the dialogue was to Petrarch as a literary form and as a way of thinking about the past. Imaginative conversation with the ancients, like imitation of their poetry, brought him into volatile contact with the past: his research into classical history and arts profoundly influenced his sense of himself and his own cultural moment. He had discovered how faulty the medieval transmission of classical culture was, with a paradoxical result: he was convinced that he was at the cusp of a classical revival and tragically aware that the classical world was irretrievably lost. By learning that the past was like a foreign world, Petrarch discovered a modern sense of alienation. He understood, too, that the dislocations of history affect cultural and individual identity. This awareness ties Petrarch's thought and work to the aspects of the Renaissance that most anticipate modernity. In 1370, Petrarch retired to the Euganean hills at Arquà near Padua, where he lived with his daughter, Francesca (his estranged son, Giovanni, died of the plague in 1361). When Petrarch died on the night of July 18, 1374, his head was resting on an open volume of his beloved Virgil.

Petrarch's most famous work, the *Rime Sparse* (Scattered rhymes) or *Rerum Fragmenta Vulgarium* (Fragments in the vernacular), is a collection of 366 songs and sonnets (based on the calendar year associated with the liturgy) of extraordinary technical virtuosity and variety. Written in Italian and woven into a highly introspective narrative, the lyric collection takes the poet himself as its object of study; the poems painstakingly record how his thoughts and identity are scattered and transformed by the experience of love for a beautiful, unattainable woman named Laura. Even some of his friends suspected that Laura was merely the theme and emblem of his lyric poetry and not a historical woman; she appears to have been both. On the flyleaf of his magnificent copy of Virgil, Petrarch inscribed a note on her life:

> Laura, illustrious through her own virtues, and long famed through my verses, first appeared to my eyes in my youth, in the year of our Lord 1327, on the sixth day of April, in the church of St. Clare in Avignon, at matins; and in the same city, also on the sixth day of April, at the same first hour, but in the year 1348, the light of her life was withdrawn from the light of day, while I, as it chanced, was in Verona, unaware of my fate.* * * Her chaste and lovely form was laid to rest at vesper time.* * * I am persuaded that her soul returned to the heaven from which it came, as Seneca says of Africanus. I have thought to write this, in bitter memory, yet with a certain bitter sweetness, here in this place that is often before my eyes, so that I may be admonished, by the sight of these words and by the consideration of the swift flight of time, that there is nothing in this life in which I should find pleasure; and that it is time, now that the strongest tie is broken, to flee from Babylon; and this, by the prevenient grace of God, should be easy for me, if I meditate deeply and manfully on the futile cares, the empty hopes, and the unforeseen events of my past years. (Translated by E. H. Wilkins)

Petrarch's note illuminates the powerful role that Laura plays in his personal struggles between spiritual aspirations and earthly attachments. His thoughts of Laura habitually turn his mind to the problem of his own will, torn between spiritual and sensual desires, always delaying worldly renunciation. Even when he expresses disgust with earthly rewards and pleasures, his habitual ambivalence makes a last-minute entrance in the conditional "if" upon which his renunciation depends: he will choose the right course of action, Petrarch writes, *if* he meditates "deeply and manfully" on the disappointments and failures of his past and denies memory's seductively bittersweet pleasures.

In the *Rime Sparse*, Laura's ambiguous position between divine guide and earthly temptress contrasts sharply with the role that Beatrice played in Dante's spiritual pilgrimage. Whereas Dante's love finally leads him to paradise, it is never clear to Petrarch whether he is pursuing heavenly or earthly delights and whether his amorous and philosophical wanderings will lead him to any destination or "port" (in the nautical image of sonnet 189) at all. When Dante looks into Beatrice's eyes on Mt. Purgatory, he sees a reflection of the heavens; when Petrarch gazes into Laura's eyes, he sees himself. Not even his use of the liturgical year (especially the anniversaries of Christ's death and resurrection) to structure his account of their relationship guarantees that a spiritual conversion will follow Petrarch's self-analysis or "confession" of his life. It might instead represent a trap, as it does in sonnet 211, written on the eleventh anniversary of his first glimpse of Laura: "One thousand three hundred twenty seven, exactly at the first hour of the sixth day of April, I entered the labyrinth, nor do I see where I may get out of it." The image of the labyrinth evokes Petrarch's tortuous experience of love and mental wandering: apparently fresh paths turn into dead ends and avenues already traced in frustration. An allusion to the maze that the mythical Greek artist Daedalus created to contain the Minotaur, Petrarch's labyrinth also suggests that a threat lies at the center of the ingeniously crafted lyric collection. The metaphor of the self-enclosed and secretive labyrinth hints that love of the very classical figures that prompt philosophical discoveries may bar the poet from the less sensually appealing knowledge of Christian truths. For this reason, Dante must finally move beyond the guidance of his beloved Virgil. Petrarch is less confident: in a contrary and skeptical mood at the end of one of his most philosophical poems (song 264), Petrarch asserts, "I see the better, but choose the worse."

In terms of literary and moral authorities, the "better" models that Petrarch employs in his poetry are Dante and St. Augustine, both of whom famously described their lives in narratives of conversion (Dante's *The New Life* and St. Augustine's *Confessions*). The "worse" model—the one Petrarch repeatedly chooses to represent his own wayward mind—is Ovid. Of particular importance is the *Metamorphoses,* the classical counterepic that artfully uses fragmentation, fluid change, and scattering as principles of narrative composition and as motifs describing the effects of power—divine, political, or erotic—on bodies and on minds. Petrarch refers to a variety of Ovidian figures in the *Rime Sparse,* including Narcissus and Echo, Actaeon and Diana, Medusa, and Pygmalion. His chief Ovidian model, however, is the story of Apollo, the god who "invents" the genre of lyric during his amorous chase of the nymph Daphne. While running, Apollo describes her various beauties—eyes, figure, and hair—and imaginatively embellishes what he sees. When Daphne eludes him through her transformation into the laurel, Apollo claims her as his tree, if not his lover, and declares that the laurel will be the sign of triumph in letters and warfare.

Like Ovid's Apollo, Petrarch uses language to possess as well as describe his lady. Her name interweaves key attributes of Petrarch's poetic imagination: *lauro* and *alloro* ("laurel"), *oro* ("gold," for her tresses and value), *l'aura* ("breeze" and "inspiration," which etymologically relates to "breath"), *laus* or *lauda* ("praise"). Such play on words suggests the selective, even obsessive character of Petrarch's poetic style. Like Apollo, Petrarch also "translates" his beloved's elusive body into the more tangible "figures" of rhetoric: her physical attributes reflect the style of his poetry and proclaim his triumphant glory. The Ovidian model poses the threat of the labyrinth, the trap of the artist's own making: the most significant and evocative words limit the poet to ranging within his well-defined obsessions. The Ovidian lover in Petrarch can expect no transcendence, only repeated and uncontrollable metamorphoses of the mind (e.g., despair, hope, ecstasy).

Petrarch's great legacy to Renaissance European literature is the *Rime Sparse*'s language of self-description. He absorbed the conventional use of hyperbole, antithesis, and oxymoron (rhetorical exaggeration and opposition) from troubadour songs, provençal lyric, and classical love elegy: *I freeze and burn, love is bitter and sweet, my sighs are tempests and my tears are floods, I am in ecstasy and agony, I am possessed by memories of her and I am in exile from myself.* Petrarch forged such rhetorical figures or tropes of love into a powerful language of introspection and self-fashioning that swept through European literature. Although it was often faddish and stylized, it had quite serious dimensions that helped articulate growing questions about the self: is it determined by God or flexible and in the shaping hands of men? Do culture, history, and force of will compose and transform it? The beloved does not fare as well: the eloquent expression of the male poet-lover's complex *interior* life depends, as Petrarchan successors noticed, on a correspondingly detailed description of the beloved's *exterior*. In *Paradise Lost,* for example, the angel Raphael chastises Adam for placing Eve's beauty above his own manly reason: "What admir'st thou," the angel chides, "what transports thee so, / An outside?" In the Petrarchan inventory of the beloved's adorable parts, from eyes to hair, cheeks, and hand, the poet converts her living body to ornaments, metal, and minerals, such as gold, topaz, and pearls. Although any one of her beauties is capable of scattering the poet's thoughts, the beloved herself has little independent coherence. Some of her parts, as critics have noticed, are greater than their sum.

PRONOUNCING GLOSSARY

The following list uses common English syllables and stress accents to provide rough equivalents of selected words whose pronunciation may be unfamiliar to the general reader.

Acheron: *ah'-ker-on*

Aigues Mortes: *ayg mort*

Bologna: *bo-lon'-yah*

Dionisio: *dee-oh-nee'-zyoh*

Malaucène: *ma-loh-sen'*

Ventoux: *von-too'*

Letter to Dionisio da Borgo San Sepolcro[1]

[The Ascent of Mount Ventoux]

To-day[2] I made the ascent of the highest mountain in the region, which is not improperly called Ventosum.[3] My only motive was the wish to see what so great an elevation had to offer. I have had the expedition in mind for many years; for as you know, I have lived in this region from infancy, having been cast here by that fate which determines the affairs of men. Consequently the mountain, which is visible from a great distance, was ever before my eyes, and I conceived the plan of some time doing what I have at last accomplished to-day. The idea took hold upon me with especial force when, in re-reading Livy's *History of Rome,* yesterday, I happened upon the place where Philip of Macedon, the same who waged war against the Romans, ascended Mount Haemus in Thessaly, from whose summit he was able, it is said, to see two seas, the Adriatic and the Euxine.[4] Whether this be true or false I have not been able to determine, for the mountain is too far away, and writers disagree. Pomponius Mela, the cosmographer—not to mention others who have spoken of this occurrence—admits its truth without hesitation;[5] Titus Livius, on the other hand, considers it false. I, assuredly, should not have left the question long in doubt, had that mountain been as easy to explore as this one. Let us leave this matter to one side, however, and return to my mountain here,—it seems to me that a young man in private life may well be excused for attempting what an aged king could undertake without arousing criticism.

When I came to look about for a companion I found, strangely enough, that hardly one among my friends seemed suitable, so rarely do we meet with just the right combination of personal tastes and characteristics, even among those who are dearest to us. This one was too apathetic, that one over-anxious; this one too slow, that one too hasty; one was too sad, another over-

---

1. Translated by James Harvey Robinson and Henry Winchester Rolfe. Letter 4.1 from *De Rebus Familiaribus.* Dionisio, or Dionigi, da Borgo San Sepolcro was an Augustinian monk whom Petrarch had probably met in Paris in 1333. A learned theologian, he taught at Paris and in 1339 was appointed bishop of Monopoli. He spent the last part of his life in Naples at the court of the learned king Robert d'Anjou and died there in 1342 (Petrarch wrote a verse epistle on his death).   2. April 26. From internal evidence the year should be 1336, ten years after Petrarch left Bologna, but the letter was probably revised and made into an "allegory" at a later date (see n. 8, p. 1898).   3. Windy. Mount Ventoux (six thousand feet) is near Malaucène, not far from Petrarch's home in Vaucluse.   4. Compare Livy's *Roman History* 40.21.2.   5. Pomponius Mela (1st century C.E.), Roman geographer of Spanish birth. The passage referred to his *Corographia* 2.17.

cheerful; one more simple, another more sagacious, than I desired. I feared this one's taciturnity and that one's loquacity. The heavy deliberation of some repelled me as much as the lean incapacity of others. I rejected those who were likely to irritate me by a cold want of interest, as well as those who might weary me by their excessive enthusiasm. Such defects, however grave, could be borne with at home, for charity suffereth all things, and friendship accepts any burden; but it is quite otherwise on a journey, where every weakness becomes much more serious. So, as I was bent upon pleasure and anxious that my enjoyment should be unalloyed, I looked about me with unusual care, balanced against one another the various characteristics of my friends, and without committing any breach of friendship I silently condemned every trait which might prove disagreeable on the way. And—would you believe it?—I finally turned homeward for aid, and proposed the ascent to my only brother, who is younger than I,[6] and with whom you are well acquainted. He was delighted and gratified beyond measure by the thought of holding the place of a friend as well as of a brother.

At the time fixed we left the house, and by evening reached Malaucène, which lies at the foot of the mountain, to the north. Having rested there a day, we finally made the ascent this morning, with no companions except two servants; and a most difficult task it was. The mountain is a very steep and almost inaccessible mass of stony soil. But, as the poet[7] has well said, "Remorseless toil conquers all." It was a long day, the air fine. We enjoyed the advantages of vigor of mind and strength and agility of body, and everything else essential to those engaged in such an undertaking, and so had no other difficulties to face than those of the region itself. We found an old shepherd in one of the mountain dales, who tried, at great length, to dissuade us from the ascent, saying that some fifty years before he had, in the same ardour of youth, reached the summit, but had gotten for his pains nothing except fatigue and regret, and clothes and body torn by the rocks and briars. No one, so far as he or his companions knew, had ever tried the ascent before or after him. But his counsels increased rather than diminished our desire to proceed, since youth is suspicious of warnings. So the old man, finding that his efforts were in vain, went a little way with us, and pointed out a rough path among the rocks, uttering many admonitions, which he continued to send after us even after we had left him behind. Surrendering to him all such garments or other possessions as might prove burdensome to us, we made ready for the ascent, and started off at a good pace. But, as usually happens, fatigue quickly followed upon our excessive exertion, and we soon came to a halt at the top of a certain cliff. Upon starting on again we went more slowly, and I especially advanced along the rocky way with a more deliberate step. While my brother chose a direct path straight up the ridge,[8] I weakly took an easier one which really descended. When I was called back, and the right road was shown me, I replied that I hoped to find a better way round on the other side, and that I did not mind going farther if the path were only less steep. This was just an excuse for my laziness; and when the others had already reached a considerable height I was still wandering in the valleys. I had failed to find an easier path, and had only increased the distance

---

6. Gherardo, who was about three years younger. 7. Virgil in *Georgics* 1.145–46. 8. In the allegorical reading of the letter, this could be an allusion to Gherardo achieving God and salvation more directly (he became a monk in 1342, retiring into the monastery of Montrieux).

and difficulty of the ascent. At last I became disgusted with the intricate way I had chosen, and resolved to ascend without more ado. When I reached my brother, who, while waiting for me, had had ample opportunity for rest, I was tired and irritated. We walked along together for a time, but hardly had we passed the first spur when I forgot about the circuitous route which I had just tried, and took a lower one again. Once more I followed an easy, round-about path through winding valleys, only to find myself soon in my old difficulty. I was simply trying to avoid the exertion of the ascent; but no human ingenuity can alter the nature of things, or cause anything to reach a height by going down. Suffice it to say that, much to my vexation and my brother's amusement, I made this same mistake three times or more during a few hours.

After being frequently misled in this way, I finally sat down in a valley and transferred my winged thoughts from things corporeal to the immaterial, addressing myself as follows:—"What thou hast repeatedly experienced to-day in the ascent of this mountain, happens to thee, as to many, in the journey toward the blessed life. But this is not so readily perceived by men, since the motions of the body are obvious and external while those of the soul are invisible and hidden. Yes, the life which we call blessed is to be sought for on a high eminence, and strait is the way that leads to it. Many, also, are the hills that lie between, and we must ascend, by a glorious stairway, from strength to strength. At the top is at once the end of our struggles and the goal for which we are bound. All wish to reach this goal, but, as Ovid says, 'To wish is little; we must long with the utmost eagerness to gain our end.'[9] Thou certainly dost ardently desire, as well as simply wish, unless thou deceivest thyself in this matter, as in so many others. What, then, doth hold thee back? Nothing, assuredly, except that thou wouldst take a path which seems, at first thought, more easy, leading through low and worldly pleasures. But nevertheless in the end, after long wanderings, thou must perforce either climb the steeper path, under the burden of tasks foolishly deferred, to its blessed culmination, or lie down in the valley of thy sins, and (I shudder to think of it!), if the shadow of death overtake thee, spend an eternal night amid constant torments." These thoughts stimulated both body and mind in a wonderful degree for facing the difficulties which yet remained. Oh, that I might traverse in spirit that other road for which I long day and night, even as to-day I overcame material obstacles by my bodily exertions! And I know not why it should not be far easier, since the swift immortal soul can reach its goal in the twinkling of an eye, without passing through space, while my progress to-day was necessarily slow, dependent as I was upon a failing body weighed down by heavy members.

One peak of the mountain, the highest of all, the country people call "Sonny," why, I do not know, unless by antiphrasis,[1] as I have sometimes suspected in other instances; for the peak in question would seem to be the father of all the surrounding ones. On its top is a little level place, and here we could at least rest our tired bodies.

Now, my father, since you have followed the thoughts that spurred me on in my ascent, listen to the rest of the story, and devote one hour, I pray you, to reviewing the experiences of my entire day. At first, owing to the unac-

---

9. *Ex Ponto* 3.1.35.   1. The rhetorical use of a word in a sense opposite to its actual meaning.

customed quality of the air and the effect of the great sweep of view spread out before me, I stood like one dazed. I beheld the clouds under our feet, and what I had read of Athos and Olympus seemed less incredible as I myself witnessed the same things from a mountain of less fame. I turned my eyes toward Italy, whither my heart most inclined. The Alps, rugged and snow-capped, seemed to rise close by, although they were really at a great distance; the very same Alps through which that fierce enemy of the Roman name once made his way, bursting the rocks, if we may believe the report, by the application of vinegar. I sighed, I must confess, for the skies of Italy, which I beheld rather with my mind than with my eyes. An inexpressible longing came over me to see once more my friend and my country. At the same time I reproached myself for this double weakness, springing, as it did, from a soul not yet steeled to manly resistance. And yet there were excuses for both of these cravings, and a number of distinguished writers might be summoned to support me.

Then a new idea took possession of me, and I shifted my thoughts to a consideration of time rather than place. "To-day it is ten years since, having completed thy youthful studies, thou didst leave Bologna. Eternal God! In the name of immutable wisdom, think what alterations in thy character this intervening period has beheld! I pass over a thousand instances. I am not yet in a safe harbor where I can calmly recall past storms. The time may come when I can review in due order all the experiences of the past, saying with St. Augustine, 'I desire to recall my foul actions and the carnal corruption of my soul, not because I love them, but that I may the more love thee, O my God.'[2] Much that is doubtful and evil still clings to me, but what I once loved, that I love no longer. And yet what am I saying? I still love it, but with shame, but with heaviness of heart. Now, at last, I have confessed the truth. So it is. I love, but love what I would not love, what I would that I might hate. Though loath to do so, though constrained, though sad and sorrowing, still I do love, and I feel in my miserable self the truth of the well known words, 'I will hate if I can; if not, I will love against my will.'[3] Three years have not yet passed since that perverse and wicked passion which had a firm grasp upon me and held undisputed sway in my heart began to discover a rebellious opponent, who was unwilling longer to yield obedience. These two adversaries have joined in close combat for the supremacy, and for a long time now a harassing and doubtful war has been waged in the field of my thoughts."

Thus I turned over the last ten years in my mind, and then, fixing my anxious gaze on the future, I asked myself, "If, perchance, thou shouldst prolong this uncertain life of thine for yet two lustres, and shouldst make an advance toward virtue proportionate to the distance to which thou hast departed from thine original infatuation during the past two years, since the new longing first encountered the old, couldst thou, on reaching thy fortieth year, face death, if not with complete assurance, at least with hopefulness, calmly dismissing from thy thoughts the residuum of life as it faded into old age?"

These and similar reflections occurred to me, my father. I rejoiced in my progress, mourned my weaknesses, and commiserated the universal insta-

2. *Confessions* 2.1.1.   3. Ovid's *Amores* 3.2.35.

bility of human conduct. I had well-nigh forgotten where I was and our object in coming; but at last I dismissed my anxieties, which were better suited to other surroundings, and resolved to look about me and see what we had come to see. The sinking sun and the lengthening shadows of the mountain were already warning us that the time was near at hand when we must go. As if suddenly wakened from sleep, I turned about and gazed toward the west. I was unable to discern the summits of the Pyrenees, which form the barrier between France and Spain; not because of any intervening obstacle that I know of but owing simply to the insufficiency of our mortal vision. But I could see with the utmost clearness, off to the right, the mountains of the region about Lyons, and to the left the bay of Marseilles and the waters that lash the shores of Aigues Mortes, altho' all these places were so distant that it would require a journey of several days to reach them. Under our very eyes flowed the Rhone.

While I was thus dividing my thoughts, now turning my attention to some terrestial object that lay before me, now raising my soul, as I had done my body, to higher planes, it occurred to me to look into my copy of St. Augustine's *Confessions*, a gift that I owe to your love, and that I always have about me, in memory of both the author and the giver. I opened the compact little volume, small indeed in size, but of infinite charm, with the intention of reading whatever came to hand, for I could happen upon nothing that would be otherwise than edifying and devout. Now it chanced that the tenth book presented itself. My brother, waiting to hear something of St. Augustine's from my lips, stood attentively by. I call him, and God too, to witness that where I first fixed my eyes it was written: "And men go about to wonder at the heights of the mountains, and the mighty waves of the sea, and the wide sweep of rivers, and the circuit of the ocean, and the revolution of the stars, but themselves they consider not."[4] I was abashed, and asking my brother (who was anxious to hear more), not to annoy me, I closed the book, angry with myself that I should still be admiring earthly things who might long ago have learned from even the pagan philosophers that nothing is wonderful but the soul, which, when great itself, finds nothing great outside itself. Then, in truth, I was satisfied that I had seen enough of the mountain; I turned my inward eye upon myself, and from that time not a syllable fell from my lips until we had reached the bottom again. Those words had given me occupation enough, for I could not believe that it was by a mere accident that I happened upon them. What I had there read I believed to be addressed to me and to no other, remembering that St. Augustine had once suspected the same thing in his own case, when, on opening the book of the Apostle, as he himself tells us,[5] the first words that he saw there were, "Not in rioting and drunkenness, not in chambering and wantonness, not in strife and envying. But put ye on the Lord Jesus Christ, and make not provision for the flesh, to fulfil the lusts thereof."[6]

The same thing happened earlier to St. Anthony, when he was listening to the Gospel where it is written, "If thou wilt be perfect, go and sell that thou hast, and give to the poor, and thou shalt have treasure in heaven: and come and follow me."[7] Believing this scripture to have been read for his especial benefit, as his biographer Athanasius[8] says, he guided himself by its

---

4. *Confessions* 10.8.15.   **5.** *Confessions* 8.12.29.   **6.** Romans 13.13–14.   **7.** Matthew 19.21.
8. A saint and doctor of the Church (ca. 295–373), in his *Vita Antonii* 2.

aid to the Kingdom of Heaven. And as Anthony on hearing these words waited for nothing more, and as Augustine upon reading the Apostle's admonition sought no farther, so I concluded my reading in the few words which I have given. I thought in silence of the lack of good counsel in us mortals, who neglect what is noblest in ourselves, scatter our energies in all directions, and waste ourselves in a vain show, because we look about us for what is to be found only within. I wondered at the natural nobility of our soul, save when it debases itself of its own free will, and deserts its original estate, turning what God has given it for its honor into dishonor. How many times, think you, did I turn back that day, to glance at the summit of the mountain, which seemed scarcely a cubit high compared with the range of human contemplation,—when it is not immersed in the foul mire of earth? With every downward step I asked myself this: If we are ready to endure a little nearer heaven, how can a soul struggling toward God, up the steeps of human pride and human destiny, fear any cross or prison or sting of fortune? How few, I thought, but are diverted from their path by the fear of difficulties or the love of ease! How happy the lot of those few, if any such there be! It is to them, assuredly, that the poet was thinking, when he wrote:

> Happy the man who is skilled to understand
> Nature's hid causes; who beneath his feet
> All terrors casts, and death's relentless doom,
> And the loud roar of greedy Acheron.[9]

How earnestly should we strive, not to stand on mountain-tops, but to trample beneath us those appetites which spring from earthy impulses.

With no consciousness of the difficulties of the way, amidst these preoccupations which I have so frankly revealed, we came, long after dark, but with the full moon lending us its friendly light, to the little inn which we had left that morning before dawn. The time during which the servants have been occupied in preparing our supper, I have spent in a secluded part of the house, hurriedly jotting down these experiences on the spur of the moment, lest, in case my task were postponed, my mood should change on leaving the place, and so my interest in writing flag.

You will see, my dearest father, that I wish nothing to be concealed from you, for I am careful to describe to you not only my life in general but even my individual reflections. And I beseech you, in turn, to pray that these vague and wandering thoughts of mine may some time become firmly fixed, and, after having been vainly tossed about from one interest to another, may direct themselves at last toward the single, true, certain, and everlasting good.

MALAUCÈNE, April 26.

---

9. Virgil's *Georgics* 2.490–92.

Sonnets

1[1]

O you who hear within these scattered verses[2]
the sound of sighs with which I fed my heart
in my first errant youthful days when I
in part was not the man I am today;

for all the ways in which I weep and speak   5
between vain hopes, between vain suffering,
in anyone who knows love through its trials,
in them, may I find pity and forgiveness.

But now I see how I've become the talk
so long a time of people all around   10
(it often makes me feel so full of shame),

and from my vanities there comes shame's fruit,
and my repentance, and the clear awareness
that worldly joy is just a fleeting dream.

3[3]

It was the day the sun's ray had turned pale
with pity for the suffering of his Maker[4]
when I was caught (and I put up no fight),
my lady, for your lovely eyes had bound me.

It seemed no time to be on guard against   5
Love's blows; therefore, I went my way
secure and fearless—so, all my misfortunes
began in midst of universal woe.[5]

Love found me all disarmed and saw the way
was clear to reach my heart down through the eyes,   10
which have become the halls and doors of tears.

It seems to me it did him little honor
to wound me with his arrow in my state[6]
and to you, armed, not show his bow at all.

---

1. Translated by Mark Musa.   2. The *scattered verses* refer to the sonnet collection's title, *Rime Sparse*.
3. Translated by Mark Musa.   4. The anniversary of Christ's crucifixion. Elsewhere (sonnet 211 and a
note in Petrarch's copy of Virgil) given as April 6, 1327.   5. The communal Christian grief that contrasts
with Petrarch's private woes.   6. State of grief over the crucifixion.

61[7]

Blest be the day, and blest the month and year,
Season and hour[8] and very moment blest,
The lovely land and place[9] where first possessed
By two pure eyes I found me prisoner;

And blest the first sweet pain, the first most dear,   5
Which burnt my heart when Love came in as guest;
And blest the bow, the shafts which shook my breast,
And even the wounds which Love delivered there.

Blest be the words and voices which filled grove
And glen with echoes of my lady's name;   10
The sighs, the tears, the fierce despair of love;

And blest the sonnet-sources of my fame;
And blest that thought of thoughts which is her own,
Of her, her only, of herself alone!

62[1]

Father in heaven, after each lost day,
Each night spent raving with that fierce desire
Which in my heart has kindled into fire
Seeing your acts adorned for my dismay;

Grant henceforth that I turn, within your light[2]   5
To another life and deeds more truly fair,
So having spread to no avail the snare
My bitter foe[3] might hold it in despite.

The eleventh year,[4] my Lord, has now come round
Since I was yoked beneath the heavy trace   10
That on the meekest weighs most cruelly.

Pity the abject plight where I am found;
Return my straying thoughts to a nobler place;
Show them this day you were on Calvary.

---

7. Translated by Joseph Auslander.   8. April 6, 1327; Spring; sunrise.   9. The Church of Saint Clare
at Avignon.   1. Translated by Bernard Bergonzi.   2. Of grace.   3. Satan.   4. I.e., 1338.

78[5]

When Simon[6] first received that high idea
which for my sake he used his drawing pen,
had he then given to his gracious work
a voice and intellect as well as form,

he would have freed my breast of many sighs   5
that make what others cherish vile to me,
for she appears so humble in her image
and her expression promises me peace.

And then when I begin to speak to her,
most kindly she appears to hear me speak—   10
if only she could answer what I say!

Pygmalion,[7] how happy you should be
with your creation, since a thousand times
you have received what I yearn for just once!

90[8]

She used to let her golden hair fly free
For the wind to toy and tangle and molest;
Her eyes were brighter than the radiant west.
(Seldom they shine so now.) I used to see

Pity look out of those deep eyes on me.   5
("It was false pity," you would now protest.)
I had love's tinder heaped within my breast;
What wonder that the flame burned furiously?

She did not walk in any mortal way,[9]
But with angelic progress; when she spoke,   10
Unearthly voices sang in unison.

She seemed divine among the dreary folk
Of earth. You say she is not so today?
Well, though the bow's unbent, the wound bleeds on.

---

5. Translated by Mark Musa.   **6.** Simone Martini (active 1315–44), a Sienese painter. His painting of
Laura is the occasion of the poem.   **7.** Sculptor, from Ovid's *Metamorphoses* 10.243–97, who fell in love
with his own ivory statue, which Venus brought to life. Whereas Ovid's Pygmalion enjoys a thousand
physical embraces, Petrarch yearns only for a reply to his words, or poem.   **8.** Translated by Morris
Bishop.   **9.** Like Venus in book 1 of Virgil's *Aeneid*, when the goddess of love appears to Aeneas in the
guise of a Spartan huntress. In the Renaissance, the image of Venus armed conjured up an ideal synthesis
of eroticism and chastity.

126[1]

Clear, fresh, sweet waters,[2] where she who alone seems lady
to me rested her lovely body,
    gentle branch where it pleased her (with sighing I remember)
to make a column for her lovely side,
    grass and flowers that her rich garment covered along with   5
her angelic breast, sacred bright air where Love opened my heart
with her lovely eyes: listen all together to my sorrowful dying
words.

    If it is indeed my destiny and Heaven exerts itself that Love
close these eyes while they are still weeping,   10
    let some grace bury my poor body among you and let my soul
return naked to this its own dwelling;
    death will be less harsh if I bear this hope to the fearful pass,
for my weary spirit could never in a more restful port or a more
tranquil grave flee my laboring flesh and my bones.   15

    There will come a time perhaps when to her accustomed
sojourn the lovely, gentle wild one will return
    and, seeking me, turn her desirous and happy eyes toward
where she saw me on that blessed day,
    and oh the pity! seeing me already dust amid the stones,   20
Love will inspire her to sigh so sweetly that she will win mercy
for me and force Heaven, drying her eyes with her lovely veil.

    From the lovely branches was descending (sweet in
memory) a rain of flowers over her bosom,
    and she was sitting humble in such a glory,[3] already covered   25
with the loving cloud;
    this flower was falling on her skirt, this one on her blond
braids, which were burnished gold and pearls to see that day;
this one was coming to rest on the ground, this one on the water,
this one, with a lovely wandering, turning about seemed to say: 30
"Here reigns Love."[4]

    How many times did I say to myself then, full of awe: "She was
surely born in Paradise!"
    Her divine bearing and her face and her words and her sweet
smile had so laden me with forgetfulness   35
    and so divided me from the true image, that I was sighing:
"How did I come here and when?" thinking I was in Heaven, not
there where I was. From then on this grass has pleased me so that
elsewhere I have no peace.

    If you had as many beauties as you have desire, you could   40
boldly leave the wood and go among people.[5]

---

1. Translated by Robert M. Durling.   2. Of the river Sorgue.   3. An image associated with the Virgin
Mary.   4. Amor (Cupid) or Christ. The floral and bejewelled images associate Laura's body with the bride
of the Song of Songs, whose erotic chastity is celebrated as an "enclosed garden," and "fountain sealed."
5. The last two lines are addressed to the poem.

189[6]

My ship full of forgetful cargo sails
through rough seas at the midnight of a winter
between Charybdis and the Scylla reef,
my master, no, my foe,[7] is at the helm;

at each oar sits a quick and insane thought   5
that seems to scorn the storm and what it brings;
the sail, by wet eternal winds of sighs,
of hopes and of desires blowing, breaks;

a rain of tears, a mist of my disdain
washes and frees those all too weary ropes   10
made up of wrong entwined with ignorance.

Hidden are those two trusty signs of mine;[8]
dead in the waves is reason as is skill,
and I despair of ever reaching port.

190[9]

A doe of purest white upon green grass
wearing two horns of gold appeared to me
between two streams beneath a laurel's shade
at sunrise in that season not yet ripe.

The sight of her was so sweetly austere   5
that I left all my work to follow her,
just like a miser who in search of treasure
with pleasure makes his effort bitterless.

"No one touch me,"[1] around her lovely neck
was written out in diamonds, and in topaz: 10
"It pleased my Caesar to create me free."

The sun by now had climbed the sky midway,
my eyes were tired but not full from looking
when I fell in the water and she vanished.

---

6. Translated by Mark Musa.   **7.** Love. *Charybdis* and *Scylla* are the twinned oceanic dangers through which Odysseus, in Homer's *Odyssey*, and Aeneas, in Virgil's *Aeneid*, must chart a middle course. Forgetfulness of oneself and of God is sinful in Augustinian terms. The ship, captained by Reason, is a traditional figure for the embodied soul.   **8.** Laura's eyes.   **9.** Translated by Mark Musa.   **1.** These are Christ's words to Mary Magdalene at the Resurrection.

333[2]

Go, grieving rimes of mine, to that hard stone
Whereunder lies my darling, lies my dear,
And cry to her to speak from heaven's sphere.
Her mortal part with grass is overgrown.

Tell her, I'm sick of living; that I'm blown   5
By winds of grief from the course I ought to steer,
That praise of her is all my purpose here
And all my business; that of her alone

Do I go telling, that how she lived and died
And lives again in immortality,   10
All men may know, and love my Laura's grace.

Oh, may she deign to stand at my bedside
When I come to die; and may she call to me
And draw me to her in the blessèd place!

2. Translated by Morris Bishop.

Lyric Poetry: After Petrarch

Petrarch created a poetic style that inspired countless imitations and adaptations in the Renaissance. His influence can still be felt today. Whether the love symptoms are found in Elizabethan sonnets or in modern-day pop lyrics (e.g., "The Tracks of My Tears" by Smokey Robinson and the Miracles or "Every Breath You Take" by Sting), the obsessive lover who adores from afar, who dies and is reborn a thousand times a day, who is mentally scattered and physically immobile, and who is never more alone than in a crowd, has been forged in the icy fire of Petrarchan love. Petrarch did not invent the idea of the divided and tormented lover, but his authoritative self-portrait defined an entire tradition in which love is described and understood.

The poems that follow—by William Shakespeare, Sir Philip Sidney, Edmund Spenser, and Sir Thomas Wyatt in English; Francesco Berni, Michelangelo Buonarotti, Veronica Franco, and Giambattista Marino in Italian; and Maurice Scève in French—owe debts, and pay tribute, to Petrarch. The uses that these poets find for Petrarchan poetry vary considerably: while many Renaissance poets imitated Petrarch faithfully or without innovation, the poets represented here adapt the Petrarchan tradition to distinctive and personal uses. Michelangelo and Scève, for example, cultivate and extend the spiritual intellectualism associated with Petrarch. In their poems, the familiar language of contradiction and opposition (such as antithesis, paradox, and oxymoron) represents the irreconcilable differences in the poets' experience of the world, real and ideal. For them, the rhetoric of contradiction lends itself to philosophical insight into the tensions in the human experience of the physical and spiritual worlds.

By contrast, Berni, Shakespeare, and Marino deny the spiritual side of Petrarchan poetry entirely. In their hands, the Petrarchan tradition seems to be the victim of its own success. Marino treats it as an opulent toy, subject to the whims of the witty poet. Berni and Shakespeare, on the other hand, parody the fetishistic quality of Petrarchan description, especially as it applies to the lover's apparently inexhaustible desire to compare his lady, in minute detail, to ornamental objects of gold, silver, pearl, or coral. The one female poet presented here, Veronica Franco, uses the Petrarchan lady's position as the object (not the subject) of love poetry as her point of entry: she takes arms against an unnamed man who has defamed her and derided her poetry and, simultaneously, battles against a cultural tradition that requires passivity and silence, not authorship, from her. These examples demonstrate the extent to which the prestigious tradition of Petrarchan lyric inspired and even goaded later poets to take up a pen and write.

There is no single story to be told about the Petrarchan lyric and certainly no evolutionary model of its uses. Centuries after Petrarch's death, poets could treat his lyric tradition either as a dead end, best suited for parody, or—as Wyatt, Sidney, and Spenser do below—as a supple language, endlessly adaptable to the task of exploring and understanding the loving heart in its many sufferings and contradictions.

MICHELANGELO BUONAROTTI
1475–1564

Sonnets

83[1]

I see in your beautiful face, my lord,
what can scarcely be related in this life:
my soul, although still clothed in its flesh,
has already risen often with it to God.
   And if the evil, cruel, and stupid rabble   5
point the finger at others for what they feel themselves,
my intense longing is no less welcome to me,
nor my love, my faith, and my virtuous desire.
   To people of good judgment, every beauty
seen here resembles, more than anything else does,   10
that merciful fountain[2] from which we all derive;
   nor have we another sample or other fruit
of heaven on earth; so he who loves you in faith
rises up to God and holds death sweet.

162[3]

Now on the right foot and now on the left,[4]
  shifting back and forth, I search for my salvation.
    Between virtue and vice,
  my bewildered heart distresses and wearies me;

1. Translated by James M. Saslow. One of Michelangelo's best-known sonnets, written for Tommaso de' Cavalieri, a young Roman nobleman.   2. God.   3. Translated by James M. Saslow. This poem was written for Vittoria Colonna.   4. Symbolically, virtue and vice. The poet evokes the dilemma of Hercules, forced to choose at a crossroads between the paths of virtue and vice.

I'm like one who can't see heaven,[5]
who gets lost on every path and misses his goal.
I offer my blank page
to your sacred ink,[6] so that
love's deceptions may vanish and mercy may write the truth;
that my soul, freed from itself,
may not subject to our errors
the little that's left me,[7] and I may live less blind.
I beg to know from you,
high and godly lady, whether humbled sin
holds a lower rank in heaven than sheer good.[8]

235[9]

A man within a woman,[1] or rather a god
speaks through her mouth, so that I,
by having listened to her,
have been made such that I'll never be my own again.[2]
I do believe, since I've been
taken from myself by her,
that, being outside myself, I'll take pity on myself;
her beautiful face spurs me
so far above vain desire
that I see death in every other beauty.
O lady who pass souls
through fire and water on to days of joy:[3]
Pray, make me never turn back to myself again.

236[4]

If the portion that's divine has well conceived
the face and gestures of someone, then through that
double power, and with a short-lived, lowly model,[5]
he can give life to stone, which is beyond craft's power.[6]
And it's no different with the roughest sketch:
before one's eager hand takes up the brush,[7]
he checks and reworks the most beautiful and clever
of his learned ideas, and lays out his subjects.
It's the same with me: at birth I was a model
of little worth, to be reborn through you,[8]
noble and worthy lady, as a noble and perfect thing.

5. One who has lost sight of spiritual comfort.   6. Michelangelo presents himself as dependent on
Colonna's inspirational poetry and letters for spiritual guidance.   7. I.e., the short time remaining to me
in this life.   8. As in the biblical parable of the lost lamb, Michelangelo hopes that heaven will look as
kindly on a penitent sinner as on someone whose life has been entirely free from sin.   9. Translated by
James M. Saslow.   1. This poem was written for Vittoria Colonna, whom Michelangelo described as a
"very great friend," using the masculine form *amico*, corresponding to his description of her here as "a man
within a woman."   2. I will no longer have control over myself or my emotions.   3. You lead souls to
a blessed life by causing the transforming pain of love (fire) and tears (water).   4. Translated by James
M. Saslow. Written for Vittoria Colonna, this poem is concerned with the Neoplatonic theory of art. Michelangelo praises the idea or conception of the artist, which is inspired by God, over the manual aspects of
art.   5. The artist's mind or intellect.   6. In the sense of a small-scale preliminary study in clay or wax
(hence fragile and cheap) for a permanent sculpture.   7. By using the skills of both the mind and the
hand, the end product will be raised above the level of mere craft to true art.   8. Through your work of
moral inspiration, which amounts to artistic revision of my original, lowly form.

If your grace builds up what I lack, and files down
my excess, what penitence should my fierce ardor
expect, if it[9] is to chastise and teach me?

9. The penitence exacted by the lady in the name of "correcting" Michelangelo's defective "model."

FRANCESCO BERNI
1497–1535

[Hair of Fine Silver, Shaggy and Twisted][1]

Hair of fine silver, shaggy and twisted
Tastelessly around a beautiful face of gold:
Wrinkled brow, gazing at which I pale,
Whereon Love and Death break their arrow points.
Shimmering eyes of pearl, beams turned away   5
By every object unequal to them;
Eyebrows of snow, and you, which move my heart,
Fingers and hands, delightfully thick and short.

Lips of milk, large azure mouth,
Teeth of ebony, rare and wandering,   10
Unheard of, ineffable harmony;
Manners haughty and ponderous; to you, divine
Servants of Love, I now make plain that such
Are the charms of my lady.

1. Translated by Luciano Rebay. Parodies or mock praise in the Petrarchan style, such as is found here,
were popular.

MAURICE SCÈVE
1500?–1564

From *Delie*

Dizain 378[2]

With shining gold and rose Aurora[3] white
Had scarcely finish'd crowning her fair head,
When my spirit, which had laps'd and perished quite
At the tangled source where diverse things are led,

2. Translated by Frank J. Warnke. A *dizain* is a verse of ten lines.   3. Goddess of the dawn.

Return'd to me across the curtain'd bed 5
To render me against my Death secure.
But you, who (you alone) have power sure
To put an end to my fatality,
Shall be to me the uncorrupted Myrrh[4]
Against the worms of my mortality. 10

4. Used to anoint corpses.

THOMAS WYATT
1503–1542

Whoso List to Hunt[5]

Whoso list to hunt, I know where is an hind,
But as for me, alas, I may no more;
The vain travail hath wearied me so sore,
I am of them that furthest come behind.
Yet may I by no means my wearied mind 5
Draw from the deer, but as she fleeth afore
Fainting I follow; I leave off therefore
Since in a net I seek to hold the wind.
Who list her hunt, I put him out of doubt,
As well as I, may spend his time in vain. 10
And graven with diamonds in letters plain
There is written her fair neck round about,
"*Noli me tangere* for Caesar's I am,
And wild for to hold, though I seem tame."[6]

My Galley Chargèd with Forgetfulness[7]

My galley chargèd with forgetfulness
Through sharp seas, in winter nights doth pass
'Tween rock and rock; and eke mine enemy,[8] alas,
That is my lord, steereth with cruelness,
And every oar a thought in readiness, 5
As though that death were light in such a case.
An endless wind doth tear the sail apace
Of forcèd sighs and trusty fearfulness.

5. This adaptation of Petrarch's sonnet 190 translates the earlier poem's spiritual themes into thoroughly secular ones. 6. Whereas Petrarch's "Caesar" was God, Wyatt's is King Henry VIII, who had married Anne Boleyn, beloved of Wyatt and the deer (or dear) of this poem. 7. Adaptation of Petrarch sonnet 189. 8. Through Satan.

A rain of tears, a cloud of dark disdain,
Hath done the wearied cords great hinderance;   10
Wreathèd with error and eke with ignorance.
The stars be hid that led me to this pain.
Drownèd is reason that should me consort,
And I remain despairing of the port.

They Flee from Me That Sometime Did Me Seek

They[9] flee from me that sometime did me seek
With naked foot, stalking in my chamber.
I have seen them gentle, tame, and meek,
That now are wild and do not remember
That sometime they put themselves in danger   5
To take bread at my hand; and now they range,
Busily seeking with a continual change.

Thanked be fortune it hath been otherwise
Twenty times better; but once in special,
In thin array after a pleasant guise,
When her loose gown from her shoulders did fall,   10
And she me caught in her arms long and small;[1]
And therewithal sweetly did me kiss
And softly said, "dear heart, how like you this?"

It was no dream: I lay broad waking.   15
But all is turned thorough my gentleness
Into a strange fashion of forsaking;
And I have leave to go of her goodness,
And she also, to use newfangleness.[2]
But since that I so kindly am served   20
I would fain know what she hath deserved.

9. Although "they" remain unidentified throughout the poem, Wyatt refers chiefly to the woman who loved
and left him.   1. Slender.   2. A new word in the period referring to innovations in style.

VERONICA FRANCO
1546–1591

Capitolo 13[3]

A CHALLENGE TO A LOVER WHO HAS OFFENDED HER

No more words! To deeds, to the battlefield, to arms!
For, resolved to die, I want to free myself
from such merciless mistreatment.

    Should I call this a challenge? I do not know,
since I am responding to a provocation;   5
but why should we duel over words?

    If you like, I will say that you've challenged me;
if not, I challenge you; I'll take any route,
and any opportunity suits me equally well.

    Yours be the choice of place or of arms,   10
and I will make whatever choice remains;
rather, let both be your decision.

    At once, I am sure, you will realize
how ungrateful and faithless you have been
and how wrongfully you have betrayed me.   15

    And unless my rage yields to overwhelming love,
with these very hands I will, in all boldness,
tear your living heart from your very breast.

    The deceiving tongue that lies to do me harm
I will tear out by its root, after it's been bitten   20
against the palate with repentant teeth;

    and if this brings no relief to my life,
abandoning all hope, I will rejoice
at having turned to bloodshed for my revenge.

    Then, with the same knife, my own breast,   25
satisfied and appeased by slaying you,
I may cut open, regretting my deed.

    Now, while I'm intent on pursuing revenge,
enter the arena, cruel, rebellious lover,
and present at once whatever arms you wish.   30

    Do you wish, for the field, the secret inn
that, hardhearted and deceptive, once watched
over so many of my now bitter delights?

    Here before me now stands the bed
where I took you in my arms, and which still   35
preserves the imprint of our bodies, breast to breast.

    In it I find now neither joy nor sleep,
but only weeping, by night and by day,
which transforms me into a river of tears.

    But this very place, which once was   40

---

3. Translated by Ann Rosalind Jones and Margaret F. Rosenthal, this poem is written in the *terza rima* that Dante used in *The Divine Comedy*. Franco had been maligned by an anonymous critic and, here, she goes on the counterattack, thinking her betrayer is a man (probably Marco Venier), with whom she has had sexual relations.

the cherished shelter of my joys,
where I now live alone, in torment and grief,
   choose this as a battleground, so that the news
of your betrayal will reach no other place
but die here with you, cruel, faithless man.   45
     Come here, and, full of most wicked desire,
braced stiff for your sinister task,
bring with daring hand a piercing blade.
     Whatever weapon you hand over to me,
I will gladly take, especially if it is sharp   50
and sturdy and also quick to wound.
     Let all armor be stripped from your naked breast,
so that, unshielded and exposed to blows,
it may reveal the valor it harbors within.
     Let no one else intervene in this match,   55
let it be limited to the two of us alone,
behind closed doors, with all seconds sent away.
     This is the custom of noble knights,
who, without clamor, strive to clear their names
when they consider their honor to be stained: 60
   either they reach an agreement on their own,
or, if they can find no road to peace,
they may sate their thirst for each other's blood.
     This is the style in which I like to fight,
and this manner fulfills and satisfies   65
my desire for bitter revenge.
     Although I hope, without any doubt, to spill
a river of your blood—indeed, I am certain
I can, without shedding a drop of my own—
   what if you were to offer me peace?   70
What if, all weapons laid aside, you took
the path opened to a love match in bed?
     Must I continue to battle against you,
since whoever refuses pardon when asked
wends his erring way reputed a coward?   75
     When you finally came to this point
with me, I'd not, perhaps, depart
from what is decent and proper to do.
     Perhaps I would even follow you to bed,
and, stretched out there in skirmishes with you,   80
I would yield to you in no way at all.
     To take revenge for your unfair attack,
I'd fall upon you, and in daring combat,
as you too caught fire defending yourself,
   I would die with you, felled by the same blow.   85
Oh, empty hopes, over which cruel fate
forces me to weep forever!
     But hold firm, my strong, undaunted heart,
and with that felon's final destruction,
avenge your thousand deaths with his one.   90
     Then end your agony with the same blade.

EDMUND SPENSER
1552–1599

From Amoretti

34[4]

Like as a ship that through the Ocean wide,
By conduct of some star doth make her way,
Whenas a storm hath dimmed her trusty guide,
Out of her course doth wander far astray.
So I whose star, that wont with her bright ray,   5
Me to direct, with clouds is overcast,
Do wander now in darkness and dismay,
Through hidden perils round about me plast.[5]
Yet hope I well, that when this storm is past
My *Helice* the lodestar[6] of my life   10
Will shine again, and look on me at last,
With lovely light to clear my cloudy grief.
Till then I wander carefull comfortless,
In secret sorrow and sad pensiveness.

37

What guile is this, that those her golden tresses
She doth attire under a net of gold;[7]
And with sly skill so cunningly them dresses,
That which is gold or hair may scarce be told?
Is it that men's frail eyes, which gaze too bold,   5
She may entangle in that golden snare;
And, being caught, may craftily enfold
Their weaker hearts,[8] which are not well aware?
Take heed, therefore, mine eyes, how ye do stare
Henceforth too rashly on that guileful net,   10
In which, if ever ye entrapped are,
Out of her bands ye by no means shall get.
Fondness it were for any, being free,
To cover fetters, though they golden be.

---

4. From the *Amoretti* (Little Loves), a sonnet sequence addressed primarily to Elizabeth Boyle, whom Spenser later married. It is based on Petrarch's sonnet 189.   **5.** Placed.   **6.** The pole star, in this case probably the constellation Ursa Major.   **7.** Focused, as many of Petrarch's poems are, on the lady's golden hair, which is imagined as a net or lure in hunting.   **8.** The familiar pun on harts (stags) and hearts sustains the hunting image.

SIR PHILIP SIDNEY
1554–1586

From Astrophil and Stella

1[9]

Loving in truth, and fain in verse my love to show,
That she, dear she, might take some pleasure of my pain,
Pleasure might cause her read, reading might make her know,
Knowledge might pity win, and pity grace obtain,[1]
I sought fit words to paint the blackest face of woe;   5
Studying inventions fine her wits to entertain,
Oft turning others' leaves, to see if thence would flow
Some fresh and fruitful showers upon my sunburned brain.
But words came halting forth, wanting invention's stay;[2]
Invention, Nature's child, fled step-dame Study's blows;   10
And others' feet[3] still seemed but strangers in my way.
Thus great with child to speak and helpless in my throes,
Biting my truant pen, beating myself for spite,
"Fool," said my Muse to me, "look in they heart, and write."

31

With how sad steps, O Moon, thou climb'st the skies!
How silently, and with how wan a face!
What, may it be that even in heav'nly place
That busy archer[4] his sharp arrows tries!
Sure, if that long-with love-acquainted eyes   5
Can judge of love, thou feel'st a lover's case,[5]
I read it in thy looks; thy languished grace
To me, that feel the like, thy state descries.[6]
Then, even of fellowship, O Moon, tell me,
Is constant love deemed there but want of wit?   10
Are beauties there as proud as here they be?
Do they above love to be loved, and yet
Those lovers scorn whom that love doth possess?
Do they call virtue there ungratefulness?

9. The first poem of *Astrophil and Stella*, the sonnet sequence addressed chiefly to Penelope Rich, here called "Stella" or star. Sidney's speaker is Astrophil or "Star-lover" (with an additional pun on Sidney's first name, Philip).   1. The logical sequence from the lover's pain to the lady's grace or acceptance is called, in rhetoric, a *gradatio* or "ladder."   2. Support.   3. Metrical feet.   4. Cupid.   5. Plight or emotional situation; legal case.   6. Shows.

WILLIAM SHAKESPEARE
1564–1616

130[7]

My mistress' eyes are nothing like the sun;
Coral is far more red than her lips' red;
If snow be white, why then her breasts are dun;
If hairs be wires, black wires grow on her head.
I have seen roses damask'd,[8] red and white,   5
But no such roses see I in her cheeks;
And in some perfumes is there more delight
Than in the breath that from my mistress reeks.
I love to hear her speak, yet well I know
That music hath a far more pleasing sound;   10
I grant I never saw a goddess go;
My mistress, when she walks, treads on the ground.
   And yet, by heaven, I think my love as rare
   As any she belied with false compare.

7. A famous parody of Petrarchan love.   8. In an image borrowed from textiles, the lady's *damask'd* cheeks are seen as richly patterned cloth.

GIAMBATTISTA MARINO
1569–1625

While His Lady Combs Her Hair[9]

Through waves of gold, the waves which were her hair,
A little ship of ivory sailed one day,
A hand of ivory steered it on its way
Through precious undulations here and there.

And while along the tremulous surge of beauty   5
She drove a straight and never-ending furrow,
From the rows of tumbled gold Love sought to borrow
Chains to reduce a rebel to his duty.

My shipwrecked heart veers down to death so fast
In this stormy, blond and gilded sea that I   10
Am caught forever in its waves at last.
In golden gulfs, at least, I come to my
Tempestuous end, on rocks of diamond press'd,
  —O rich disaster in which submerged I die.

9. Translated by Frank J. Warnke.

DESIDERIUS ERASMUS
1466?–1536

It is not too much to say that Desiderius Erasmus set the standard for scholarship and pedagogy in the Western tradition. He carefully cultivated the ideal of the scholar-teacher that holds sway even today: wise, experienced, and learned, yet personally modest, forbearing, and affectionate with his students and peers. He had good reason to fashion an image of himself as the Socrates of Christian humanism (a blend of classical learning and Christian philosophy). He hoped to influence the social signif-icance of intellectual labor, and to achieve his goal he needed to be known for more than his editions of important texts (such the New Testament and collected works of St. Jerome) and popular treatises on moral behavior (including his *Handbook of the Christian Soldier* and *Education of a Christian Prince*). To overturn the cult of received wisdom, Erasmus had to revolutionize the very idea of the scholar. His greatest work was, in a sense, himself: he created the model of the tireless, curious, and non-dogmatic intellectual in pursuit of enlightenment.

His most enduring literary creation, however, is *The Praise of Folly*, a mock assault on wisdom and celebration of the mind in the act of play. No literary work more charmingly or memorably illustrates the Renaissance concept of "serious play." Although elegant and comic in style, *The Praise of Folly* takes up themes that are philosophical and moral: it deals with the power (and arrogance) of the human intel-lect, the worth (and futility) of knowledge, and above all the folly (and wisdom) of human behavior.

Erasmus was born at Rotterdam, probably in 1466. As a youth, he studied first at Gouda and then at Deventer until the deaths of his parents, when he was urged by his guardians to enter into the monastic life. Erasmus, who had hoped for a university education, reluctantly entered the Augustinian canons at Steyn and was ordained in 1492. He gained the bishop's consent in 1495 to leave the monastery for Paris and the most famous of all universities. At the University of Paris, he became the tutor of William Blount, Lord Mountjoy, who arranged for Erasmus to visit England in 1499–1500. There he befriended Sir Thomas More and John Colet, both of whom profoundly influenced Erasmus's intellectual life. Colet, a passionate student of reli-gion, turned Erasmus's mind from exclusively literary and classical interests to the-ological scholarship. Colet inspired in Erasmus a new dedication to religious morals and scholarship: at a time when Greek was largely forgotten, Erasmus labored to teach himself Greek in order to study the New Testament in its original language.

Throughout his career, Erasmus committed himself to research and travels. He visited England again in 1505–1506 and met the archbishop of Canterbury (William Warham) and influential members of the court. As tutor to the son of Henry VII's Italian physician (Giovanni Battista Boerio), he visited Italy, the original home of humanist studies. He stayed at the universities of Turin (where he received a doctor-ate of theology), and Bologna; he also visited Padua, Florence, Rome, and Venice, where he befriended the great printer, Aldus Manutius. He returned to England in 1509, following the coronation of Henry VIII, from whom Erasmus had hopes of financial support for his scholarly work. During his five-year stay, he lectured in Greek and divinity at Cambridge University and worked to edit, translate, and annotate the Greek New Testament. England lost its charms for Erasmus in 1514, however, when the country was swept up in a militaristic fervor following English victories over France and Scotland. Erasmus traveled to Basel, where he took his publishing ven-tures to a new level: he not only worked but also lived in the publishing house of Johannes Froben, who produced Erasmus's editions of Jerome and the New Testa-ment in 1516. This period of his life brings us the now familiar image of Erasmus, surrounded by disciples and the bustle of the printing house, producing some of his most demanding and influential work. His crowning achievement was to become a councillor to the young Charles V, a post that prompted him to write his *Education of a Christian Prince.*

Despite his success, Erasmus found himself increasingly at odds with traditional Catholic scholars, who recognized that his editions of the New Testament and Jerome implicitly challenged the authority of the Church. His work also drew the favorable notice of Martin Luther, whose reformist zeal inspired both sympathy and anxiety in Erasmus. In October 1517, in the hope of generating debate about the system of papal indulgences, Luther nailed his *Ninety-five Theses* to the Castle Church door in Wittenburg. Erasmus at first hoped to negotiate a peaceful compromise between the Protestant reformers and the Catholic conservatives, but the differences between his temperament and intellectual qualities and Luther's were ultimately insuperable. Shaking all Europe, Luther rejected the highest ecclesiastical authority, a challenge he summed up in his famous declaration, "Here I stand." Erasmus, by contrast, chose to explore all dimensions of intellectual problems. An old anecdote has it that Luther, annoyed at Erasmus's refusal to side with or against the reformers, demanded, "Where do you stand?" to which Erasmus responded, "I stand *here.* And here. And here." Reluctantly, Erasmus finally took issue with Luther in print. Their exchange, which focused on the necessity of free will (Erasmus) and God's uncircumscribed majesty (Luther), was bitter and led to their decisive break. Despite Erasmus's efforts to affirm his faith and seek peaceful reform, many of his works, including *The Praise of Folly,* were enrolled in the notorious Index of books banned by the Church. In 1535 Erasmus received the devastating news of Sir Thomas More's execution, and on July 12, 1536, following an illness, he died in Freiburg.

While crossing the Alps on his third visit to England, Erasmus conceived *The Praise of Folly,* his celebrated investigation of the relationship between wisdom and folly. He drafted the work at the home of Sir Thomas More, who inspired its playful style and serious theme (More's name, Erasmus gleefully noted, means "fool," *mora*). The classical precedent on which he drew is the genre of mock praise, developed by Greek and Roman orators, on such unpleasant themes as tyrants, the fever, flies, and baldness. Erasmus, however, departs from his models in important ways. To begin with, he does not speak in his own voice but instead creates a dramatic character to serve as his authority: Folly herself, a witty and ingratiating entertainer. She immediately seizes the stage by commenting on her warm reception: "You all suddenly perked up," she tells us, "and greeted me with happy, congenial laughter—so much so that every last one of you here before me, wherever I look, seems to be high on the nectar of the Homeric gods." Once she has put herself on familiar terms with her audience, Folly begins her comic monologue on her favorite subject: herself. It may initially come as a surprise that she successfully proves that she is a blessing, not a curse, to human beings. Her audience welcomes her because—unlike a tyrant, fever, or baldness—folly brings joy, especially when the burdens of human existence seem most oppressive. Folly is not only a pleasure (a point on which Folly dwells at length) but is so essential to human nature that it cannot be eradicated even from the wisest person.

Folly's major argument, which she lays out in three parts, is that we owe our joys to illusions, without which life would be unbearable. To illustrate her point, she first singles out the Stoics, who pride themselves on their indifference to joy and pleasure, as her targets of satire. These philosophers, she argues, lead their lives as an extended renunciation of life itself. Folly is "not altogether fool," as one of Shakespeare's characters remarks of King Lear's Fool, when she emphasizes that the wisdom of the Stoics, who place their own passions under close surveillance and restraint, acts as a kind of prison rather than a force of intellectual liberation. True to her nature, however, Folly habitually mounts compelling arguments in favor of folly only to conclude them with classical quotations, lifted out of context, that undermine her own position. After demolishing the Stoics, she borrows an improbable line from Sophocles: "Not to think, that is the good life." The great paradox of Erasmus's text is that Folly is both the object and source of praise, and her oration both celebrates and exposes its speaker's foolishness.

In the next part of Folly's speech, Erasmus turns to the abuse of power by religious and political authorities. The responsibilities of political and ecclesiastical office are heavy, Folly maintains, and were it not for her influence, no one would undertake such joyless work. When she describes the vices of ecclesiastical and political administrators, she adopts a comically non-judgmental approach: "Popes, however diligent in harvesting money, delegate their excessively apostolic labors to the bishops, the bishops to the pastors, the pastors to their vicars, the vicars to the mendicant friars, and they too foist off their charge on those who shear the fleece of the flock." Erasmus's satire of corruption, although more heavy-handed than usual, is leavened with subtle touches: the images of harvest and sheep-shearing conjure up a lively sense of the victims (sheep-like manual laborers) and the predators, who have turned their pastoral care into a financial enterprise.

The most radical part of her speech elaborates the assertion of the Apostle Paul that evangelists, who neglect worldly interest and reputation, are "fools for Christ" (1 Corinthians 4.9–10). Folly regards this contingent of her following with wonder:

> they throw away their possessions, ignore injuries, allow themselves to be deceived, make no distinction between friend and foe, shudder at the thought of pleasure, find satisfaction in fasts, vigils, tears, and labors, shrink from life, desire death above all else—in short, they seem completely devoid of normal human responses, just as if their minds were living somewhere else, not in their bodies.

The possible responses of Erasmus's readers to Folly's account of ideal Christian behavior are legion. They might laugh at her ironic portrait of virtue and admire her dexterous ability to cite and twist authorities. They might instead worry that renunciation of the self seems possible only to Christians who reject the entire world (the good and bad alike) and its social responsibilities. They might experience revelation at the religious ecstasy she succinctly describes or, on the other hand, a loss of equilibrium as they sway between the evangelical authorities she cites and her own exuberant, destabilizing text. Nowhere does Erasmus more radically question the sources and authorities with which people justify their choices and actions.

Modern readers may wonder why Erasmus chose a literary frolic as a means to communicate ideas about religious and political reform. His original audience would have known that Erasmus's spirit of fun comes from the popular tradition that combined rough play and social rebellion. The tradition flourished around the figure of the Fool, dressed in cap and bells and carrying a bauble. Fools, who were figures of serious cultural play, presided over the popular carnivalesque festivities that took place during the liturgical year (e.g., May Day, Whitsuntide, Halloween, and Christmastide). During the festivals, common people and lower clergy were temporarily liberated from fixed social and ecclesiastical hierarchies: women and servants were "on top" and the people elected their own Lord of Misrule. In the Feast of Fools, the lower clergy elected a bishop or even a pope of Fools to lead a raucous parody of the ecclesiastical service. The French sociétés joyeux ("joyous societies") featured a mock sermon on the life of a "saint" (e.g., St. Onion), and joked about love, women, and marriage, as well as taverns and drink.

The figure of the Fool also shielded Erasmus from a backlash against his biting social criticisms. Court Fools enjoyed unique privileges: one of the most famous was Henry VIII's beloved Archie Armstrong, who not only joked, sang, and conversed with the king but also challenged him when he seemed unwilling to hear the concerns of the common people. Only the "all-licensed Fool," as Shakespeare calls him in *King Lear*, has the liberty to mock the king to his face when he appeared to abuse his power. It is to the Fool's license that Erasmus refers in a public letter to a critic of the *Folly*: "Even the most savage tyrants put up with their buffoons and court fools, who sometimes taunt their masters with open insults." The prudent response to mockery, he continues, is to laugh and admit or dissemble one's own faults. Through the idea of the licensed fool, Erasmus encourages his readers to question the oppressive or tyrannical exercise of authority.

From The Praise of Folly[1]

Folly Herself Speaks:

Whatever mortals commonly say about me—and I am not unaware of how bad Folly's reputation is, even among the biggest fools of all—still it is quite clear that I myself, the very person now standing here before you, I and I alone pour forth joy into the hearts of gods and men alike. Hence it is that as soon as I came out to speak to this numerous gathering, the faces of all of you immediately brightened up with a strange, new expression of joy. You all suddenly perked up and greeted me with happy, congenial laughter—so much so that every last one of you here before me, wherever I look, seems to be high on the nectar of the Homeric gods, and on the drug nepenthe[2] too, whereas before you all sat there downcast and tense, as if you had just come back from the cave of Trophonius.[3] But when the sun first reveals his fair golden face to the earth, or when a harsh winter yields to the balmy breezes of early spring, everything suddenly takes on a new appearance, a new color, and a certain youthful freshness: so too, when you caught sight of me, your faces were transformed. Thus, what these eloquent orators can hardly accomplish in a long and carefully thought out speech—namely, to clear the mind of troubles and sorrows—that very goal I achieved in a flash simply by making an appearance.

* * * But since there are not very many who know my lineage, I will try (with the help of the Muses) to explain it. Neither Chaos, however, nor Orcus, nor Saturn, nor Japetus, nor any other of these worn-out, moldy old gods was my father. Rather, it was Plutus, the one and only father of men and gods alike, Hesiod and Homer and even Jupiter[4] himself to the contrary notwithstanding. Plutus alone, as it is now and ever has been, has everything and everyone, sacred and secular alike, at his beck and call: he keeps the whole pot boiling. His decision governs war, peace, kingdoms, counsels, judgments, agreements, marriages, pacts, treaties, laws, arts, recreations, serious business—I'm running out of breath—in short, all the affairs, public or private, in which mortals engage. Without his help that whole crew of poetic divinities—I will go further, even the so-called "select" gods—would either not exist at all or would eke out a miserable existence as homebodies. Whoever is frowned on by him can never find enough help even from Pallas[5] herself. Conversely, whoever is smiled on by Plutus can afford to tell Jupiter himself to go to hell, thunderbolt and all. Such is the father I can boast. And this great god certainly did not give birth to me from his brain, as Jupiter did

---

1. Translated by Clarence Miller.   2. Legendary drug causing oblivion.   3. Seat of a particularly awesome oracle.   4. Sometimes called Jove (and Zeus in Greek), king of the gods. Plutus was the god of wealth and abundance. Hesiod (ca. 700 B.C.E.), Greek didactic poet, cited here because he was author of the *Theogony* (about the generation and genealogy of the gods).   5. Pallas Athena, daughter of Jove and goddess of wisdom.

to that sour stick-in-the-mud Pallas. Rather, he begot me on Neotes (Youth), the fairest, the most charming nymph of all. Moreover, he did not do it within the forbidding bonds of matrimony, like the progenitor of that limping black-smith,[6] but rather in a fashion not a little sweeter, "mingled together in passionate love," as my friend Homer says. But make no mistake, I was not begotten by Plutus[7] as Aristophanes represents him, his eyesight completely gone and one foot already in the grave, but rather when he was young, sound, and hot-blooded, inflamed not merely by youth but even more by nectar, which on that occasion he had drunk at the banquet of the gods, perhaps in larger, stronger drafts than usual.

But if anyone wants to know my birthplace—since nowadays people seem to think one of the most important points of nobility is the place where a person gives out his first wails—I was brought forth neither in wandering Delos, nor in the waves of the sea, nor in hollow-echoing caverns, but rather in the Isles of the Blest,[8] where everything grows without effort—they plough not, neither do they sow. In those isles there is no work, no old age, no disease. Nowhere in their fields do you see asphodel, mallows, sea onions, lupines, beans, or any such trash as that. Instead, both sight and smell are gratified by moly, panace, nepenthe, amaracus, ambrosia, lotus, roses, vio-lets, hyacinths, a veritable garden of Adonis. Born as I was among all these delights, I certainly did not begin my life by crying, but rather immediately smiled at my mother.

Far be it from me to envy the mighty son of Cronos the goat which gave him suck, since I was nursed at the breasts of two most elegant nymphs: Methe (Drunkenness), begotten by Bacchus, and Apaedia (Stupidity), the daughter of Pan. You can see them both here among my other attendants and handmaidens. If you want to know the names of the rest of them, you'll not get them from me in any language but Greek. This one—you see how she raises her eyebrows—is obviously Philautia (Selflove). The one you see here, with smiling eyes and clapping hands, is named Kolakia (Flattery). This one, dosing and half asleep, is Lethe (Forgetfulness). This one, leaning on her elbows with her hands clasped, is Misoponia (Laziness). This one, wreathed with roses and drenched with sweet-smelling lotions, is Hedone (Pleasure). This one, with the restless glance and the rolling eyes, is Anoia (Madness). This one, with the smooth complexion and the plump, well-rounded figure, is Tryphe (Luxury). You also see two gods among the girls: one is called Comos (Rowdiness), the other Negreton Hypnon (Sweet Sleep). This, then, is the loyal retinue which helps me to subject the whole world to my dominion, lording it over the greatest lords.

You have heard about my birth, upbringing, and companions. Now, lest my claim to divinity should seem unsubstantiated, listen carefully and I will show you how many benefits I bestow on gods and men alike and how widely my divine power extends. Consider, if that author (whoever he was) was not far from the mark when he wrote that the essence of divinity is to give aid to mortals, and if the persons who taught mortals how to produce wine or

6. Hephaestus (Vulcan), whose parents were Zeus and his wife, Hera (Juno). 7. Plutus was usually represented as a boy with a cornucopia. 8. The mythical and remote islands where, according to Greek tradition, some favorites of the gods dwelt in immortality and bliss. *Delos:* in Greek myth, once a floating island and birthplace of Apollo, god of sunlight, prophecy, music, and poetry. *Waves of the sea:* from which Venus (Aphrodite), goddess of love, emerged. *In hollow-echoing caverns:* a Homeric expression.

grain or some other commodity have been justly elevated to the senate of the gods, why should I not rightly be considered and called the very *alpha*[9] of all the gods, since I alone bestow all things on all men?

First, what can be sweeter or more precious than life itself? But to whom should you attribute the origin of life if not to me? For it is not the spear of stern-fathered Pallas or the aegis of cloud-gathering Zeus which begets and propagates the human race. No, Jupiter himself, father of the gods and king over men, whose mere nod shakes all Olympus, even he must put aside that three-forked lightning bolt of his; he must dispense with that fierce Titanic countenance (with which he can, at his pleasure, terrify all the gods); clearly, he must change his role like an actor and play a humble part whenever he wants to do what in fact he is forever doing—that is, make a baby. To be sure, the Stoics[1] rank themselves only a little lower than the gods. But give me a man who is a Stoic three or four times over, a Stoic to the nth degree, and he too, though he may not have to shave off his beard—the sign of wisdom (though goats also have one)—he certainly will have to swallow his pride; he will have to smooth out his frowns, put aside his iron clad principles, and indulge just a bit in childish and fantastic trifles. In short, I am the one that wise man must come to—I repeat, he must come to me—if he ever wants to be a father.

But let me take you into my confidence even more candidly, as is my fashion. I ask you, is it the head, or the face, or the chest, or the hand, or the ear—all considered respectable parts of the body—is it any of these which generates gods and men? No, I think not. Rather, the human race is propagated by the part which is so foolish and funny that it cannot even be mentioned without a snicker. That is the sacred fount from which all things draw life, not the Pythagorean tetrad.[2] Come now, would any man ever submit to the halter of matrimony if he followed the usual method of these wisemen and first considered the drawbacks of that state of life? Or what woman would ever yield to a man's advances if she either knew about or at least called to mind the perilous labor of childbirth, the trials and tribulations of raising children? So, if you owe your life to matrimony, and you owe matrimony to my handmaid Anoia, you can easily see how much you owe to me. Then again, what woman who has once had this experience would ever consent to go through it again if it were not for the divine influence of Lethe? Even Venus herself (in spite of what Lucretius[3] says) would never deny that her power is crippled and useless without the infusion of our divine influence. Thus, this game of ours, giddy and ridiculous as it is, is the source of supercilious philosophers (whose place has now been taken by so-called monks), and kings in their scarlet robes, and pious priests, and pope-holy pontiffs and, finally, even that assembly of poetic gods, so numerous that Olympus, large as it is, can hardly accommodate the crowd.

But it would be little enough for me to assert my role as the fountain and

---

9. First letter of the Greek alphabet, hence "beginning" or "origin." The author is Pliny.　1. Stoicism originated in the Stoa Poikile ("painted porch"), a building in the marketplace in Athens where the philosopher Zeno (4th century B.C.E.) lectured; later it was perhaps the principal philosophy of the Roman elite. It became known during the Renaissance, especially through Seneca. Here the Stoics are the butt of Folly's irony because of their supposedly godlike disregard of the passions.　2. The first four numbers (which then added together equal the ideal number, ten); according to Pythagoras (6th century B.C.E.), the tetrad signified the root of all being.　3. Poet (ca. 94–ca. 54 B.C.E.) who, in *On the Nature of Things*, invokes Venus because "all living things" are conceived through her.

nursery of life, if I did not also show that all the benefits of life depend completely on my good offices. After all, what is this life itself—can you even call it life if you take away pleasure? . . . Your applause has answered for you. I was certain that none of you is so wise, or rather foolish—no, I mean wise— as to be of that opinion. In fact, even these Stoics do not scorn pleasure, however diligently they pretend to—ripping it to shreds in their public pronouncements for the very good reason that when they have driven others away from it they can enjoy it all the better by themselves. But for god's sake, I wish they would tell me, is there any part of life that is not sad, cheerless, dull, insipid, and wearisome unless you season it with pleasure, that is, with the spice of folly? To this fact Sophocles, a poet beyond all praise, offered ample testimony when he paid us that most elegant compliment: "Never to think, that is the good life."[4]

* * *

* * * If someone should try to strip away the costumes and makeup from the actors performing a play on the stage and to display them to the spectators in their own natural appearance, wouldn't he ruin the whole play? Wouldn't all the spectators be right to throw rocks at such a madman and drive him out of the theater? Everything would suddenly look different: the actor just now playing a woman would be seen to be a man; the one who had just now been playing a young man would look old; the man who played the king only a moment ago would become a pauper; the actor who played god would be revealed as a wretched human being. But to destroy the illusions in this fashion would spoil the whole play. This deception, this disguise, is the very thing that holds the attention of the spectators. Now the whole life of mortal men, what is it but a sort of play, in which various persons make their entrances in various costumes, and each one plays his own part until the director gives him his cue to leave the stage? Often he also orders one and the same actor to come on in different costumes, so that the actor who just now played the king in royal scarlet now comes on in rags to play a miserable servant. True, all these images are unreal, but this play cannot be performed in any other way.

If at this point some wiseman, dropped down direct from heaven, should suddenly jump up and begin shouting that this figure whom everyone reverences as if he were the lord god is not even a man because he is controlled by his passions like an animal, that he is a servant of the lowest rank because he willingly serves so many filthy masters; or if he should turn to another man who is mourning the death of his parent and tell him to laugh instead because the dead man has at last really begun to live, whereas this life is really nothing but a sort of death; if he should see another man glorying in his noble lineage and call him a low-born bastard because he is so far removed from virtue, which is the only true source of nobility; and if he addressed everyone else in the same way, I ask you, what would he accomplish except to make everyone take him for a raving lunatic? Just as nothing is more foolish than misplaced wisdom, so too, nothing is more imprudent than perverse prudence. And surely it is perverse not to adapt yourself to the

---

4. Compare Sophocles' *Ajax*, lines 554–55: "life is sweetest before the feelings are awake—until one learns to know joy and pain."

prevailing circumstances, to refuse "to do as the Romans do," to ignore the party-goer's maxim "take a drink or take your leave," to insist that the play should not be a play. True prudence, on the other hand, recognizes human limitations and does not strive to leap beyond them; it is willing to run with the herd, to overlook faults tolerantly or to share them in a friendly spirit. But, they say, that is exactly what we mean by folly. I will hardly deny it— as long as they will reciprocate by admitting that this is exactly what it means to perform the play of life.

Another point—by all the gods in heaven! Should I say it or keep still? But why keep still, since it is "truer than truth itself." But perhaps in such a weighty matter it would be well to summon the Muses from Helicon[5]—the poets often enough invoke them for the merest trifles. Be present, then, you daughters of Jove, for a bit, while I show that no one can reach the heights of wisdom and the very "inner sanctum," as they themselves say, "of happiness" except with the guidance of Folly.

First of all, everyone admits that the emotions all belong to Folly. Thus, the usual distinction between a wiseman and a fool is that the fool is governed by emotion, the wiseman by reason. That is why the Stoics eliminate from their wiseman all emotional perturbations, as if they were diseases. But actually the emotions not only function as guides to those who are hastening to the haven of wisdom, but also, in the whole range of virtuous action, they operate like spurs or goads, as it were, encouraging the performance of good deeds. I know that died-in-the-wool Stoic, Seneca, strenuously denies this, removing all emotion whatsoever from his wiseman. But by doing this he is left with something that cannot even be called human; he fabricates some new sort of divinity that has never existed and never will. Frankly, he sets up a marble statue of a man, utterly unfeeling and quite impervious to all human emotion. They can enjoy their wiseman all they like and have him all to themselves, or (if they prefer) they can live with him in Plato's republic, or in the realm of Platonic ideas, or in "the gardens of Tantalus."[6] Who would not flee in horror from such a man, as he would from a monster or a ghost—a man who is completely deaf to all human sentiment, who is untouched by emotion, no more moved by love or pity than "a chunk of flint or a mountain crag," who never misses anything, who never makes a mistake, who sees through everything as if he had "x-ray vision," measures everything "with plumb line and T square," never forgives anything, who is uniquely self-satisfied, who thinks he alone is rich, he alone is healthy, regal, free, in brief, he thinks that he alone is all things (but he is also alone in thinking so), who cares nothing about friendship, who makes friends with no one, who would not hesitate to tell the gods themselves to go hang, who can find nothing in all human life that he does not condemn and ridicule as madness? Yet just such a creature as this is that perfect wiseman of theirs. I ask you, if an office were to be awarded by election, what state would choose such a man for civic office, what army would select him for their general? Indeed, what woman would consent to marry him or put up with him as a husband? What host would want him (or tolerate him) as a guest? What servant would ever enter his service or continue in it? Who would not prefer someone chosen

5. Mythical mountain, home of the Muses.   6. In Tantalus's garden in Hades, rich fruit is always just beyond his grasp. All the individuals here are characterized by the presence of abstraction and figments. *Realm of Platonic ideas*: the celestial ideal models of which real things are only imperfect realizations.

at random from the mob of out-and-out fools? Being a fool himself, he could either command fools or obey them, please his peers (who are clearly in the majority), be companionable with his wife, cheerful with his friends, a fine table companion, an easy-going messmate. In short, he considers nothing human foreign to him.[7] But for some time now I have been sick and tired of this wiseman. Therefore I shall proceed in my speech by returning to the remaining benefits.

Just think, if a person could look down from a watchtower, as Jupiter sometimes does according to the poets, and could see how many disasters human life is exposed to, how miserable and messy childbirth is, how toilsome it is to bring children up, how defenseless they are against injuries, how young men must make their way by the sweat of their brow, how burdensome old age is, how death comes cruel and ineluctable; and then too, if he could see during the course of life itself how man is besieged by a whole army of diseases, threatened by accidents, assailed by misfortunes, how everything everywhere is tinged with bitterness—to say nothing of the evils men inflict on each other, such as poverty, prison, disgrace, shame, torture, entrapment, betrayal, insults, quarrels, deception, but I might as well try "to number the sands of the seashore"—now, as for what crimes man committed to deserve all this or which god in his anger caused men to be born to all these miseries, those are things it is not proper for me to declare at the present time, but whoever gives these things serious consideration cannot but approve the example of the Milesian virgins,[8] however pitiable their case was. But in fact, who have been the most likely to commit suicide out of weariness with life? Isn't it those who have come closest to wisdom? Among these (to say nothing of such people as Diogenes, Xenocrates, Cato, Cassius, and Brutus) was Chiron,[9] who had an opportunity to be immortal but freely chose death instead. You can see, I imagine, what would happen if men everywhere were wise: we would need another batch of clay, another potter like Prometheus.[1] But I, partly through ignorance, partly through thoughtlessness, sometimes through forgetfulness of past misfortunes, sometimes through hope of good things to come, now and then mixing some honey with their pleasures, I rescue men from such terrible sufferings—so effectively that they are even unwilling to leave this life behind when the thread is all unwound and life leaves them behind. The less cause they have to remain in this life, the more they want to stay alive—so little are they touched by the tedium of life.

It is my doing that you see everywhere men as old as Nestor,[2] who no longer even look like men: driveling, doting, toothless, whitehaired, bald, or (in the words of Aristophanes) "filthy, crookbacked, wretched, shriveled, bald, toothless, and lame of their best limb";[3] but yet they are so in love with life and "have such young ideas" that one of them will dye his hair, another will hide his baldness with a toupee, another will wear false teeth (borrowed

---

7. From a proverbial phrase in Terence's *Self-Tormentor*, line 77: "I am a man: nothing human do I consider alien to me."   8. From the city of Miletus, in Asia Minor; according to an ancient tale, most of them, seemingly gone insane, hanged themselves.   9. The centaur (half man, half horse) who, incurably wounded and suffering great pain, asked Zeus for relief from his own immortality [Editor's note]. Of the philosophers *Diogenes* and *Xenocrates*, the first killed himself, but the second died by accident (Diogenes Laertius 6.77–78, 4.14–15). *Cato* of Utica, *Brutus*, and *Cassius* committed suicide after being defeated in battle [Translator's note].   1. He supposedly molded the human race out of clay.   2. The old, eloquent sage in the Homeric epic.   3. *Plutus*, lines 266–67.

perhaps from some hog), another will fall head over heels in love with some young girl and outdo any beardless youth in amorous idiocy. In fact, to see old codgers with one foot in the grave marry some sweet young thing—with no dowry at that, and of far more use to other men than to him—this sort of thing happens so often that people almost consider it praiseworthy.

But it is even more amusing to see these old women, so ancient they might as well be dead and so cadaverous they look as if they had returned from the grave, yet they are always mouthing the proverb "life is sweet." They are as hot as bitches in heat, or (as the Greeks say) they rut like goats. They pay a good price for the services of some handsome young Adonis. They never cease smearing their faces with makeup. They can't tear themselves away from the mirror. They pluck and thin their pubic bush. They show off their withered and flabby breasts. They whip up their languid lust with quavering whines and whimpers. They drink a lot. They mingle with the young girls on the dance floor. They write billets-doux. Everyone laughs at these things as utterly foolish (and indeed they are), but the old bags themselves are perfectly self-satisfied. They lead a life of the utmost pleasure. They swim in honey up to their ears. Through my blessing, they live in bliss. Now if anyone thinks such goings-on are absurd, I wish he would take the trouble to decide whether he thinks it better to live a life of perfect bliss by means of such folly or to look for a way to "end it all," as they say.

Now, the fact that such absurdities are generally considered disgraceful, that doesn't bother my fools at all: they are either unaware of their notoriety, or, if they are aware, they find it easy to ignore it. If a rock falls on your head, that is certainly bad for you. But shame, disgrace, reproaches, curses do harm only insofar as they are perceived. If they are not noticed, they are not harmful. "What harm if all the crowd should hiss and boo; you're safe as long as you can clap for you." But that is made possible only by Folly.

Even so, I can imagine the philosophers' objections: "But to be caught in the toils of such folly, to err, to be deceived, to be ignorant—such an existence is itself miserable." One thing is sure: such it is to be a man. But I don't see why they should call him miserable, since this is the way you are born, this is the way you are formed and fashioned, this is the common lot of everyone. But nothing is miserable merely because it follows its own nature, unless perhaps someone thinks man's lot is deplorable because he cannot fly like the birds, or run on all fours like other animals, and is not armed with horns like a bull. But by the same token, he should argue that even a fine, thoroughbred horse is unhappy because he has never learned grammar and doesn't eat pancakes, or that a bull is miserable because he cannot work out in the gym. Therefore, just as a horse who is ignorant of grammar is not miserable, so too, a man who is a fool is not unhappy, because these things are inherent in their natures.

But these word-jugglers are back at it again: "The knowledge of various branches of learning," they say, "was especially added to human nature so that with their help he could use his mental skill to compensate for what Nature left out." As if it were the least bit likely that Nature, who was so alert in providing for gnats (and even for tiny flowers and blades of grass), should have nodded only in equipping mankind, so that there should be a need for the different branches of learning—which were actually thought up by Theutus,[4] a spirit quite hostile to mankind, as instruments of man's utter ruination. So little do they contribute to man's happiness, that they defeat the very purpose for which they were supposedly invented—as that most wise king in Plato cleverly argues concerning the invention of writing.[5] Thus, the branches of learning crept in along with the other plagues of man's life, and from the very same source from which all shameful crimes arise, namely, the demons—who also derive their name from this fact, since "demon" comes from δαήμονες ("scientes," knowing ones). Now the simple people of the golden age, who were not armed with any formal learning, lived their lives completely under the guidance of natural impulses. What need was there for grammar when everyone spoke the same language and when speech served no other purpose than to let one person understand another? What use was there for dialectic, when there was no disagreement among conflicting opinions? What room was there for rhetoric when there were no litigious troublemakers? What demand was there for legal learning when there was no such thing as bad morals—for good laws undoubtedly sprang from bad conduct. Then too, they had more reverence than to pry into the secrets of Nature with irreligious curiosity—to measure the stars, their motions and effects, to seek the causes of mysterious phenomena—for they considered it unlawful for mortals to seek knowledge beyond the limits of their lot. As for what is beyond the range of the furthest stars, the madness of exploring such things never even entered their minds. But when the purity of the golden age had gradually declined, then evil spirits, as I said, first began to invent the learned disciplines, but only a few at first and even those taken up only by a few. Afterwards, the superstition of the Chaldeans and the idle frivolity of the Greeks added hundreds more, all of them nothing but forms of mental torture, so painful that the grammar of even one language is more than enough to make life a perpetual agony.

Still, even among these disciplines, the ones held in highest esteem are those which come closest to the ordinary understanding—that is, the folly—of mankind. Theologians starve, physicists freeze, astronomers are ridiculed, logicians are ignored. "One physician alone is worth whole hosts of other men."[6] And even among physicians, the more ignorant, bold, and thoughtless one of them is, the more he is valued by these high and mighty princes. Besides, medicine (certainly as it is now practiced by most doctors) is nothing but a subdivision of flattery, just like rhetoric. The next rank beneath the doctors belongs to pettifogging lawyers; in fact, I wonder if they don't hold the highest rank of all, since their profession—not to speak of it myself—is universally ridiculed as asinine by the philosophers. Still, all business transactions, from the smallest to the greatest, are absolutely controlled by these asses. They acquire large estates, while a theologian who has carefully read through whole bookcases of divinity nibbles on dried peas, waging continual warfare with bedbugs and lice.

Moreover, just as those disciplines which are most closely related to Folly contribute most to happiness, so too, those men who have nothing whatever to do with any branch of learning and follow Nature as their only guide are

---

4. In Plato's *Phaedrus*, an Egyptian god who brought the art of writing to King Thamus. 5. King Thamus argued that the invention of writing would produce only false wisdom and destroy the power of people's memory. 6. Homer, *Iliad* 11.514.

by far the happiest of all. For she is completely adequate in every way, unless perhaps someone wants to leap over the bounds of human destiny. Nature hates disguises, and whatever has not been spoiled by artifice always produces the happiest results. After all, don't you see that, among all the other kinds of living creatures, those which remain at the furthest remove from any formal learning and take Nature for their only teacher lead the happiest lives? What could be happier or more marvelous than the bees? And yet they do not even have all the bodily senses. What architect has ever produced buildings like theirs? What philosopher has ever established a comparable republic? The horse, on the other hand, because his senses resemble those of man and because he left his original abode to dwell with men, has also become a sharer in the sufferings of men. Thus, often enough a horse that is ashamed to be defeated in a race becomes broken-winded, and a horse that strives for victory in warfare is stabbed and bites the dust with his rider. To say nothing of the sharp-toothed curb bits, the points of the spurs, the imprisonment of the stable, the whips, cudgels, fetters, the rider—in short, that whole miserable panorama of servitude that he willingly accepted when (like brave men of honor) he was overcome by a burning desire for revenge on his enemy. How much more attractive is the life of flies and little birds, who live for the moment purely by natural instinct, as long as they can avoid the snares of men. But if they should be put into cages and learn to speak human sounds, it is quite remarkable how they decline from their native sleekness and elegance. So certain is it that the creations of Nature are in every way more joyous than the fabrications of artifice.

Accordingly, I could never bestow sufficient praise on that cock embodying Pythagoras,[7] who had been, in his single person, a philosopher, a man, a woman, a king, a private citizen, a fish, a horse, a frog, even a sponge (I think), but who decided that no creature was more miserable than man because all the others were content to remain within the limits of Nature, while man alone tried to go beyond the bounds of his lot. Moreover, among men he places natural-born fools far above great and learned men; and Gryllus[8] was not a little wiser than wily Odysseus, since he preferred to grunt in the pigsty instead of being exposed with Odysseus to so many unexpected calamities. With Gryllus and the cock, Homer himself, the father of foolish fables, seems to be in agreement, since he repeatedly calls all mortals "miserable and wretched" and frequently applies the epithet "unhappy" to Ulysses, his model of wisdom, but never to Paris or Ajax or Achilles. And why this distinction? Wasn't it because the clever and cunning Ulysses never did anything without consulting Pallas Athene and was too smart for his own good, departing as far as possible from the guidance of Nature?

Therefore, just as among mortals those men who seek wisdom are furthest from happiness—indeed, they are fools twice over because, forgetting the human condition to which they were born, they aspire to the life of the immortal gods and (like the giants)[9] wage war against Nature with the

---

7. In Lucian's *The Dream, or the Cock* (2nd century C.E.) the cock upholds the Pythagorean notion of transmigration of souls from one body to another by claiming that he is Pythagoras. 8. Character in a dialogue by Plutarch, changed into a pig by Circe. 9. Following the example of the giants, or Titans, of Greek mythology, who, inspired by their wronged mother, Gaea (Earth), fought the Olympian gods and were defeated.

engines of learning—so too, the least miserable among men are those who come closest to the level of intelligence (that is, the folly) of brute animals and never undertake anything beyond human nature. Come on, then, let us see if we can't show this, not with the fine-spun arguments of the Stoics, but with some plain, ordinary example. But by all the gods above! is anyone happier than the sort of men who are usually called fools, dolts, simpletons, nincompoops—actually very fine titles, as I see it? At first glance, what I am saying may perhaps seem foolish and absurd, but it is nevertheless true as can be.

First, they are spared all fear of death, a burden hardly to be taken lightly. They are not tortured by pangs of conscience. They are not frightened by silly tales about the underworld. They are not terrified by apparitions and ghosts. They are not tormented by the fear of impending evils, nor kept on tenterhooks by the hope of coming good. In brief, they are not harried by the thousands of cares to which this life is subject. They feel no shame, no fear, no ambition, no envy, no love. Finally, if they come close to the ignorance of brute animals, they do not even commit sins, according to theologians. Now at this point, most foolish wiseman, do me a favor: just consider how many ways your mind is tortured day and night—pile up all the troubles of your life into a single heap, and then you will finally understand how many evils I have spared my fools. On top of that, note that they not only rejoice continually themselves—playing, laughing, and singing little tunes—but also, wherever they turn, they provide everyone else with entertainment, jokes, fun and laughter, as if the gods in their goodness had granted them to men for the specific purpose of brightening up the gloominess of man's life. Hence, whereas various people react variously to other people, everyone agrees unanimously in claiming these fools as their own—they seek them out, maintain them, pamper them, coddle them, help them in time of need, freely allow them to do or say anything they like. So far is anyone from wishing to harm them that even savage beasts refrain from hurting them, out of a certain natural awareness of their innocence. As a matter of fact, they are sacred to the gods, especially to me, and therefore it is not without reason that everyone treats them with such respect.

In fact, even the mightiest monarchs are so delighted with them that without these fools some of them can neither eat breakfast, nor make their entry, nor even so much as survive for a single hour. And they value these simpletons far more than those sour wisemen, though it is true that they usually maintain some of them too, for the sake of appearances. The reason why they value them more is not far to seek, I think, and ought not to surprise anyone, since those wisemen normally offer princes nothing but melancholy—indeed, relying on their learning, they sometimes do not hesitate to make harsh truth grate upon their tender ears—whereas fools provide the very thing for which princes are always on the lookout: jokes, laughs, guffaws, fun. And don't forget another talent, by no means contemptible, that is peculiar to fools: they alone speak the plain, unvarnished truth. And what is more worthy of praise than truthfulness? True, Alcibiades' proverb in Plato attributes truthfulness to wine and children,[1] but actually the praise for that virtue

1. See Plato's *Symposium*.

is all mine and mine alone, as Euripides himself testifies in that famous saying about us which has come down from him: "a fool speaks like a fool."[2] Whatever a fool has in his heart, he reveals in his face and expresses in his speech. But wisemen have those two tongues, also mentioned by Euripides:[3] with one they speak the truth, with the other whatever they think convenient for the moment. They are the ones who turn black into white, who blow hot and cold in one breath, who profess to believe one thing in their speech but conceal quite another in their hearts. Princes, then, for all their great happiness, still seem to me most unhappy in one respect: there is no one from whom they can hear the truth, and they are forced to take flatterers for their friends.

But "a prince's ears tingle at the truth," someone will say, "and for that very reason they shun those wisemen: they are afraid that perhaps one of them might be so frank as to say what is true rather than pleasant." Quite right—kings do hate the truth. But my fools, on the other hand, have a marvelous faculty of giving pleasure not only when they speak the truth but even when they utter open reproaches, so that the very same statement which would have cost a wiseman his life causes unbelievable pleasure if spoken by a fool. For truthfulness has a certain inherent power of giving pleasure, if it contains nothing that gives offense. But the skill to manage this the gods have granted only to fools.

For almost the same reasons women, who naturally tend to be more inclined to pleasures and trifles, are extraordinarily fond of this kind of men. Accordingly, whatever they do with this sort of person (even though it is sometimes sufficiently serious), they explain away as mere entertainment and amusement—as indeed the fair sex is quite clever, especially in covering up their faux pas.

Therefore, to return to the happiness of simpletons, having lived their lives with great joy, with no fear or even awareness of death, they depart directly to the Elysian fields, where their antics continue to delight the leisurely souls of the blessed.

And now let us compare the lot of this fool with any wiseman whatsoever. Imagine, if you please, a model of wisdom to set over against the fool: a man who has wasted his whole childhood and youth in mastering the branches of learning and has lost the sweetest part of life in sleepless nights and endless painstaking labors, a man who even in the rest of his life has not tasted the tiniest crumb of pleasure, always frugal, poor, gloomy, surly, unfair and harsh to himself, severe and hateful to others, wasted away into a pale, thin, sickly, blear-eyed figure, old and gray long before his time, hastening to a premature grave—though what does it matter when such a person dies, since he never really lived at all? And there you have a fine picture of your wiseman.

But here the frogs of the Stoic ilk croak at me once again. "Nothing," they say, "is more miserable than madness. But extraordinary folly is either very close to madness or is actually identical with it. For what does it mean to be mad but to be of unsound mind?" But these cavilers are completely "on the wrong track." Come, let us demolish this syllogism also, with the help of the Muses. The argument is clever indeed, but just as Plato's Socrates taught

---

2. *The Bacchanals (Bacchae)*, line 369.   3. *Rhesus*, lines 394–95; *Andromache*, lines 451–52.

when he divided one Venus into two and split one Cupid into two,[4] so, these dialecticians should have distinguished one kind of madness from the other if they ever intended to pass for sane themselves. For every sort of madness is not necessarily disastrous, in and of itself. Otherwise Horace would not have said "Or am I beguiled by a lovely madness"[5] nor would Plato have placed the frenzy of poets, prophets, and lovers among the chief goods of life; nor would the prophetess have called the labor of Aeneas mad.[6]

For there are two kinds of madness: one which is sent up from the under-world by the avenging Furies whenever they dart forth their serpents and inspire in the breasts of mortals a burning desire for war, or unquenchable thirst for gold, or disgraceful and wicked lust, or parricide, incest, sacrilege, or some other such plague, or when they afflict the guilty thoughts of some criminal with the maddening firebrands of terror. There is another kind far different from the first, namely the kind which takes its origin from me and is most desirable. It occurs whenever a certain pleasant mental distraction relieves the heart from its anxieties and cares and at the same time soothes it with the balm of manifold pleasures. Indeed, in a letter to Atticus, Cicero wishes for this mental distraction as a great gift from the gods, because it would have deprived him of all awareness of the great evils around him. Nor was there anything wrong with the judgment of the Greek who was so mad that he sat alone in the theater for whole days on end, laughing, applauding, enjoying himself, because he thought that wonderful tragedies were being acted there, whereas nothing at all was being performed. But in the other duties of life he conducted himself very well: he was cheerful with his friends, agreeable with his wife; he could overlook the faults of his servants and not fly into a mad rage when he found a winejar had been secretly tapped. Through the efforts of his friends he took some medicine which cured him of his disease, but when he was completely himself again, he took issue with his friends in this fashion: "Damn it all!" he said, "you have killed me, my friends, not cured me, by thus wresting my enjoyment from me and forcibly depriving me of a most pleasant delusion."[7] And rightly enough. For they were the ones who were deluded, and they had more need of hellebore than he did, since they thought such a felicitous and gratifying madness was some kind of evil that needed to be expelled by means of potions.

But in fact I haven't yet decided whether just any error of the senses or the mind ought to be designated by the name madness. Certainly, if a man with poor eyesight thinks a mule is an ass, or if someone takes a piece of doggerel for a very skillful poetic composition, he does not immediately strike everyone as mad. But if a person is deceived not only in the perceptions of his senses but also in the judgments of his mind, and if his deception is continual and beyond the usual share, only then will he be thought to verge on madness—as, for instance, if a person who hears an ass braying thinks he is listening to a marvelous choir, or if some poor beggar, born into the very lowest level of society, believes he is Croesus,[8] king of Lydia. But this kind of madness, if it errs in the direction of pleasure (as it usually does), brings no small share of delight both to those who experience it and to those who observe it without being mad to the same degree themselves. For this

---

4. I.e., in distinguishing heavenly love from other types of love.   5. *Odes* 3.4.5–6.   6. *Aeneid* 6.135.
7. This passage is a paraphrase of Horace's *Epistles* 2.128–40.   8. Proverbially wealthy man.

species of madness is far more widespread than most people realize. But one madman mocks another, and they maintain between them a mutual interchange of merriment. And not infrequently you see the greater madman laugh louder at the less. Still, everyone is all the happier the more ways he is deluded, as far as Folly can judge, as long as he remains within the category of madness that belongs peculiarly to us—a category which is in fact so widespread that I hardly know whether anyone at all can be found from the whole sum of mortals who is always impeccably wise and who is not subject to some kind of madness. The real difference is only this: the man who sees a cucumber and thinks it is a woman is labeled mad because this happens very rarely. But if a man who shares his wife in common with many other men nevertheless swears that she is more faithful than Penelope and warmly congratulates himself in his ignorant bliss, no one calls him mad because they see that this sort of thing happens to husbands everywhere.

This class of madness also includes those who look down on everything except hunting wild animals and whose spirits are incredibly exhilarated whenever they hear the nerve-shattering blasts on the horns or the baying of the hounds. I imagine that even the dung of the dogs smells like cinnamon to them. And then what exquisite pleasure they feel when the quarry is to be butchered! Lowly peasants may butcher bulls and rams, but only a nobleman may cut up wild animals. Baring his head and kneeling down, he takes a special blade set aside for that purpose (for it would hardly do to use just any knife) and exercises the most devout precision, in cutting up just these parts, with just these movements, in just this order. Meanwhile, the surrounding crowd stands in silent wonder, as if they were seeing some new religious ceremony, although they have beheld the same spectacle a thousand times before. Then, whoever gets a chance to taste some of the beast is quite convinced that he has gained no small share of added nobility. Thus, though these men have accomplished nothing more by constantly chasing and eating wild animals than to lower themselves almost to the level of the animals they hunt, still in the meantime they think they are living like kings.

Very like them is the sort of men who burn with an insatiable desire to build, replacing round structures with square and square with round. Nor is there an end to it, nor any limit, until they are reduced to such utter poverty that nothing at all is left—neither place to live nor food to eat. What of it? In the meantime they have passed several years with the greatest pleasure.

The group that comes closest to these builders, I think, consists of those who strive to change one substance into another by means of novel, occult arts, and move heaven and earth to track down a certain fifth element or "quintessence."[9] This honied hope entices them so powerfully that they spare no effort or expense. They are wonderfully clever in thinking up some new way to deceive themselves. They cheat themselves with a pleasing sort of fraud, until they have spent everything and don't even have enough left to fire their furnaces.[1] But still they never stop dreaming sweet dreams, and they also do everything they can to encourage others to pursue the same happiness. Even when they have been completely deprived of all hope whatsoever, there is still one saying left—a great comfort indeed: "in great affairs

---

9. A substance (in addition to the four traditional elements—earth, water, air, and fire) of which the heavenly bodies were believed to be composed.   1. For alchemical experiments.

the intent alone's enough." And then they rail against the shortness of life, because it is inadequate for an enterprise of such great moment.

As to gamblers, I am in some doubt whether they should be admitted to our fellowship. But still it is a foolish and altogether absurd spectacle to see some of them so addicted to it that their hearts leap up and throb as soon as they hear the clatter of the dice. Finally, when the hope of winning has kept luring them onward until they suffer the shipwreck of all their resources, splitting the ship of their fortune against the dice-reef (hardly less fearful than the coast of Malea),[2] and when they have barely escaped from the sea with the shirts on their backs, they will cheat anyone rather than the winner of their money, lest anyone should think they are not men of honor. What shall we say when even old men who are already half-blind go on playing with the aid of eye-glasses? Or when they pay good money to hire a stand-in to roll the dice for them because their own finger-joints have been crippled by a well-earned attack of gout? A pleasant spectacle indeed, except that sometimes such gambling ends in violent quarrels and hence falls into the province of the Furies, not in mine.

But there can be no question at all that another group is entirely enlisted "under my banner": those who delight in hearing or telling miracles and monstrous lies. They can never get enough of such tales whenever strange horrors are told about apparitions, ghosts, specters, dead souls, and thousands of such marvels as these. And the further such tall tales are from the truth, the more easily they gain credence and the more delicately they tickle the ears of the listeners. Besides, they are not only wonderfully useful in relieving the boredom of the passing hours, but they also produce a fine profit, especially for priests and preachers.[3]

Closely related to such men are those who have adopted the very foolish (but nevertheless quite agreeable) belief that if they look at a painting or statue of that huge Polyphemus Christopher, they will not die on that day; or, if they address a statue of Barbara[4] with the prescribed words, they will return from battle unharmed; or, if they accost Erasmus on certain days, with certain wax tapers, and in certain little formulas of prayer, they will soon become rich. Moreover, in George they have discovered a new Hercules, just as they have found a new Hippolytus.[5] They all but worship George's horse, most religiously decked out in breastplates and bosses, and from time to time oblige him with some little gift. To swear by his bronze helmet is thought to be an oath fit for a king.

Now what shall I say about those who find great comfort in soothing self-delusions about fictitious pardons for their sins, measuring out the times in purgatory down to the droplets of a waterclock, parceling out centuries, years, months, days, hours, as if they were using mathematical tables? Or what about those who rely on certain little magical tokens and prayers thought up by some pious impostor for his own amusement or profit? They promise themselves anything and everything: wealth, honor, pleasure, an abundance of everything, perpetual health, a long life, flourishing old age,

---

2. In Greece, proverbially dangerous.   3. Cf. Chaucer's *The Pardoner's Tale* (p. 1756).   4. St. Barbara is supposed to protect her worshipers against fire and artillery. Polyphemus is the Cyclops (one-eyed giant) in Homer's *Odyssey*. St. Christopher is also represented with only one eye.   5. In Greco-Roman mythology, both fought against monsters.

and finally a seat next to Christ among the saints, though this last they don't want for quite a while yet—that is, when the pleasures of this life, to which they cling with all their might, have finally slipped through their fingers, then it will be soon enough to enter into the joys of the saints. Imagine here, if you please, some businessman or soldier or judge who thinks that if he throws into the collection basket one coin from all his plunder, the whole cesspool of his sinful life will be immediately wiped out. He thinks all his acts of perjury, lust, drunkenness, quarreling, murder, deception, dishonesty, betrayal are paid off like a mortgage, and paid off in such a way that he can start off once more on a whole new round of sinful pleasures.

Now who could be more foolish—rather, who could be happier—than those who assure themselves they will have the very ultimate felicity because they have recited daily those seven little verses from the holy psalms? A certain devil—certainly a merry one, but too loose-lipped to be very clever—is believed to have mentioned them to St. Bernard, but the poor devil was cheated by a clever trick.[6] Such absurdities are so foolish that even I am almost ashamed of them, but still they are approved not only by the common people but even by learned teachers of religion.

And then too, isn't it pretty much the same sort of nonsense when particular regions lay claim to a certain saint, when they parcel out particular functions to particular saints, and assign to particular saints certain modes of worship: one offers relief from a toothache, another helps women in labor, another restores stolen goods; one shines as a ray of hope in a shipwreck, another takes care of the flocks—and so on with the others, for it would take far too long to list all of them. Some saints have a variety of powers, especially the virgin mother of God, to whom the ordinary run of men attribute more almost than to her son.

But what do men end up asking from these saints except things that pertain to folly? Just think, among all the votive tablets that you see covering the walls and even the ceilings of some churches, have you ever seen anyone who escaped from folly or who became the least bit wiser? One saved his life by swimming. Another was stabbed by an enemy but recovered. Another, with no less luck than bravery, fled from the battle while the rest were fighting. Another who had been hung on the gallows fell down by the favor of some saint friendly to thieves, so that he could proceed in his career of disburdening those who are sadly overburdened by their riches. Another escaped by breaking out of jail. Another, much to the chagrin of his physician, recovered from a fever. For another, a poisonous potion, because it worked as a purge, was curative rather than fatal, though his wife (who lost her effort and expense) was not exactly overjoyed at the result. Another, whose wagon had overturned, drove his horses home uninjured. Another, buried by the collapse of a building, was not killed. Another, caught by a husband, managed to get away. No one gives thanks for escaping from folly. To lack all wisdom is so very agreeable that mortals will pray to be delivered from anything rather than from folly.

But why have I embarked on this vast sea of superstitions?

---

6. A devil had told St. Bernard that repeating seven particular verses of the Psalms would bring him the certainty of salvation. The *clever trick* was that of proposing to recite all the Psalms.

> Not if I had a hundred tongues, a hundred mouths,
> A voice of iron, could I survey all kinds
> Of fools, or run through all the forms of folly.[7]

So rife, so teeming with such delusions is the entire life of all Christians everywhere. And yet priests are not unwilling to allow and even foster such delusions because they are not unaware of how many emoluments accumulate from this source. In the midst of all this, if some odious wiseman should stand up and sing out the true state of affairs: "You will not die badly if you live well. You redeem your sins if to the coin you add a hatred of evil deeds, then tears, vigils, prayers, fasts, and if you change your whole way of life. This saint will help you if you imitate his life"—if that wiseman were to growl out such assertions and more like them, look how much happiness he would immediately take away from the minds of mortals, look at the confusion he would throw them into!

Of the same stripe are those who prescribe in great detail, while they are still alive, how they wish to be buried, giving exact numbers for the torches, the people in mourning garments, the singers, the official mourners that they want in the funeral procession, as if they could have any awareness of this spectacle or as if the dead would be ashamed unless their corpses were grandly planted in the ground—they seem for all the world like political candidates staging a campaign dinner complete with entertainers.

Even though I am in a hurry, I can hardly pass over in silence those who preen themselves on the empty title of nobility, even though they are no different from the lowliest shoemaker. One traces his ancestry back to Aeneas, another to Brut,[8] another to Arthur. Everywhere they display statues and pictures of their ancestors, they count up their great-grandfathers and great-great-grandfathers, they rehearse their ancient family names, while they themselves are not much better than dumb statues, almost inferior to the very symbols they display. And yet this pleasant Selflove enables them to lead an altogether happy life. Nor is there any lack of others, equally foolish, who revere this class of beasts as if they were gods.

But why should I be talking about one group or another, as if such Selflove did not render almost everyone everywhere most happy in a variety of marvelous ways? One man who is uglier than any monkey is quite confident that he is as handsome as Nereus. Another, as soon as he can draw three lines with a compass, immediately thinks he is another Euclid. Another, who sounds like an "ass playing a harp and who sings no better than the bird that gives the hen uxorious nips," still thinks he is another Hermogenes. But by far the most entertaining kind of madness is the sort which causes some people to boast of any talent among their servants as if it were their own. This was displayed by that twice-blessed rich man in Seneca[9] who always kept servants at hand when he intended to tell an anecdote so that they could prompt him with the names. He wouldn't have hesitated to engage in a fist fight (though he himself was so infirm he was just barely alive) because he relied on the many strapping servants he had at home.

As for professors of the arts, why bother to mention them?—since Selflove

7. A variation on a passage in the *Aeneid* (6.625–27) in which, however, Virgil is talking of "forms of crime," not folly.   8. The legendary founder of Britain.   9. *Epistles* 27.4–6.

is the special prerogative of all of them, so much so that you will sooner find one who will admit that his father's farm is second-rate than one who will accept second rank in intelligence. But this is especially true of actors, singers, orators, and poets: the more ignorant anyone of them is, the more arrogant his self-complacence, conceit, and braggadocio. And "birds of a feather", or like will to like—in fact, the less skillful anything is, the more admirers it obtains, according to the rule that the worst things usually please most people, because the majority of men, as we said, are subject to folly. Therefore, if a man acquires more pleasure for himself and more admiration from others according to the depth of his ignorance, why on earth should he choose real learning? First of all it costs a great deal, and then it will make him more disagreeable and timid, and finally it will please far fewer people.

Then again, I see that Nature has not only given every mortal his own brand of Selflove but has also grafted a sort of communal form of it to particular nations and even cities. Hence it is that the British lay claim above all to good looks, music, and fine food. The Scots pride themselves on their nobility and close blood-ties to the royal house, not to mention dialectical subtlety. The French claim for themselves refinement of manners. The Parisians arrogate to themselves theological learning, to the exclusion of almost everyone else.[1] The Italians lay claim to literature and eloquence, and on one point they all preen themselves most complacently: that, of all mortals, they alone are not barbarians. In this sort of happiness the Romans lead the way, and still dream sweet dreams about that ancient Rome of theirs. The Venetians are happy in their reputation for nobility. The Greeks, as the founders of the various branches of learning, emblazon themselves with the ancient renown of their famous heroes. The Turks and all that scum of the real barbarians claim for themselves the praise due to religion, ridiculing Christians, precisely because of their superstitions. But the Jews have it even better, still waiting faithfully for their Messiah and clinging to their Moses tooth and nail even to this day. Spaniards yield to no one in military glory. The Germans pride themselves on their tallness and their knowledge of magic. But, not to run through all of them one by one, you see (I think) how much pleasure Selflove everywhere supplies to individual mortals and to mankind as a whole, and in this function her sister Flattery is almost her equal.

For Selflove is nothing but the soothing praise which a person bestows on himself. If he bestows it on someone else, then it is Kolakia. Nowadays flattery is thought of as disreputable, but only by people who are more concerned about words than about things themselves. They judge that flattery is inconsistent with good faith. That the fact is quite otherwise, we can learn even by examples drawn from dumb animals. Is there any animal more fawning than a dog? But then again, is there any more faithful? Is any creature more obsequious than a squirrel? But is any more friendly to man? Unless perhaps you think fierce lions or cruel tigers or treacherous panthers contribute more to man's life! True, there is a certain kind of flattery which is altogether destructive, the kind employed by some unprincipled cynics to ruin their wretched victims. But this Flattery of mine proceeds from a kind disposition and a certain frankness which is much closer to a virtue than the opposite

1. The Sorbonne, the theological faculty in Paris, was the center of theological studies in Europe.

qualities, "sourness" and peevishness, "jangling" (as Horace[2] says) "and dour." This kind of flattery gives a lift to those whose spirits are low, consoles those who mourn, stimulates the apathetic, rouses the dull, cheers the sick, tames the fierce, unites lovers and keeps them united. It entices children to learn their lessons, it cheers up old people, it advises and teaches princes under the cover of an encomium, without giving offense. In short, it makes everyone more agreeable and indulgent to himself—and this is surely the chief ingredient of happiness. What is more courteous than for one person to scratch another's back? Not to mention that this flattery plays a large part in that eloquence everyone praises, a larger in medicine, and the largest of all in poetry—in sum, it is the honey and spice of all human intercourse.

But to be deceived, they say, is miserable. Quite the contrary—not to be deceived is most miserable of all. For nothing could be further from the truth than the notion that man's happiness resides in things as they actually are. It depends on opinions. For human affairs are so manifold and obscure that nothing can be clearly known, as is rightly taught by my friends the Academics,[3] the least arrogant of the philosophers. Or, if anything can be known, it often detracts from the pleasures of life. Finally, the human mind is so constituted that it is far more taken with appearances than reality. If anyone wants clear and obvious evidence of this fact, he should go to church during sermons: if the preacher is explaining his subject seriously, they all doze, yawn, and are sick of it. But if that screacher—I beg your pardon, I meant to say preacher—tells some old wives' tale, as they often do, the whole congregation sits up and listens with open mouths. Likewise, if any saint is more legendary or poetic—for example, think of George or Christopher or Barbara—you will see that such a saint is worshiped with far more devotion than Peter or Paul or Christ himself. But such things are out of place here.

And then, how much less it costs to gain such happiness! Sometimes it requires a great deal of effort to acquire the real article, even if it is something quite trivial, such as grammar. But to think you have acquired it—nothing could be easier, and yet such an opinion contributes as much or more to happiness. Consider, if someone eats a rotten pickled fish, the mere smell of which would be unbearable to another person, and yet the one who eats it thinks it tastes like ambrosia, what difference does it make to his happiness? Conversely, if some delicacy like sturgeon turns another man's stomach, it will hardly add anything to his happiness. If someone who has an extraordinarily ugly wife still thinks that she could compete with Venus herself, isn't it quite the same as if she were really beautiful? If someone values and admires a canvas daubed with red and yellow, quite convinced that it is by Apelles of Zeuxis, isn't he actually happier than the man who has paid a high price for the real work of those painters but who perhaps takes less pleasure in viewing them than the other man? I know a certain man named after me[4] who gave his bride some imitation gems, assuring her (and he is a clever jokester) that they were not only real and genuine but also that they were of unparalleled and inestimable value. I ask you, what difference did it make to the girl since she feasted her eyes and mind no less pleasantly on glass and kept them hidden among her things as if they were an extraordinary

2. *Epistles* 1.18.6.   3. Philosophers of Plato's school, the Academy, which later became a school of the skeptics.   4. Sir Thomas More (1478–1535), a close friend of Erasmus. The pun is with *moria* (Latin for "folly").

treasure? Meanwhile, the husband avoided expense and profited by his wife's mistake, nor was she any less grateful to him than if he had given her very costly gifts. Surely you don't believe that there is any difference between those who sit in Plato's cave[5] gazing in wonder at the images and likeness of various things—as long as they desire nothing more and are no less pleased—and that wiseman who left the cave and sees things as they really are? Now if Lucian's Mycillus[6] had been allowed to dream forever that rich, golden dream of his, he would have had no reason to wish for any other happiness.

Thus, there is either no difference, or if there is, the lot of fools is clearly preferable. First, because their happiness costs them so little—nothing more than a touch of persuasion. Then too, they enjoy it in common with most other men. And, of course, nothing is really enjoyable without someone to share it with. And who does not know how few wisemen there are—if, in fact, any at all can be found? True, out of so many centuries the Greeks count seven altogether,[7] but if you examine even those very carefully, may I drop dead on the spot if you can find so much as a semi-wiseman, or even a hemi-demi-semi-wiseman.

Now, among the many benefits for which Bacchus is praised, the chief one is held (and rightly so) to be that he clears the mind of its troubles—and that only for a short time, since as soon as you have slept off your little wine-drinking spree, all your anxieties come rushing back to your mind "post-haste," as they say. But how much more ample and lasting is the benefit I provide, a sort of continuous inebriation which fills the mind with joy, delight, and exquisite pleasure—and all with no effort from you. Nor do I ever refuse any mortal a share of my gifts, whereas other endowments of the gods are distributed some to one, some to another. It is not every vineyard that produces a noble, mellow wine, one that drives away care, one that enriches us with surging hope. Few have been endowed with delicate beauty, the gift of Venus; even fewer with eloquence, a benefit given by Mercury. Not so very many have received wealth through the good offices of Hercules. Homer's Jupiter has hardly granted everyone political supremacy. Very often Mars favors neither side. Many depart quite disappointed from the tripod of Apollo's oracle. The son of Saturn often hurls his lightning bolt. Phoebus sometimes throws down missiles armed with the plague. Neptune drowns more than he saves. I might also mention in passing such powers as Vejovis, Pluto, Ate, the Poenae,[8] the god of Fever and the like—not really gods, but tormentors. I, Folly, am the only one who embraces everyone equally with such ready and easy generosity. I do not care for vows, nor do I grow angry and demand expiatory gifts if some point of ceremony is overlooked. Nor do I go on a rampage if someone invites the other gods and leaves me sitting at home with no share of the fragrant steam rising from the sacrificial victims. For the other gods are so touchy about such things that it is more advantageous, and even safer, to leave them alone than to follow their cult—just as there are some men who are so hard to please and quick to take offense that it is better to have nothing at all to do with them than to cultivate their friendship.

---

5. In Plato's allegory in the *Republic* (book 7) he compares the soul in the body to a prisoner chained in a cave, his or her back against the light, able to see only the shadows of things outside. 6. A character in *The Dream, or the Cock* who dreams that he has taken the place of a rich man. 7. Philosophers in the 6th century B.C.E.; among them were Thales and Solon. 8. Poena was goddess of punishment. Vejovis was hostile to men. Pluto was god of the underworld. Ate was goddess of revenge and discord.

But no one sacrifices to Folly, they say, and no one has built a temple dedicated to her. Indeed, I myself, as I said, find this ingratitude somewhat surprising. Still, I am good-natured enough to take this also in good part, though I couldn't really want such things anyway. Why should I need a bit of incense or grain or a goat or a hog, when all mortals everywhere in the world worship me with the kind of homage that even the theologians rank highest of all? Unless perhaps I should envy Diana because human blood is sacrificed in her honor! I consider that I am being worshiped with the truest devotion when men everywhere do precisely what they now do: embrace me in their hearts, express me in their conduct, represent me in their lives. Clearly this sort of devotion to the saints, even among Christians, is not exactly common. What a huge flock of people light candles to the virgin mother of God—even at noon, when there is no need! But how few of them strive to imitate her chastity, her modesty, her love for the things of heaven! For, in the last analysis, that is true worship, the kind which is by far the most pleasing to the saints in heaven. Furthermore, why should I want a temple, since the whole world, unless I am badly mistaken, is a splendid temple dedicated to me? Nor will there ever be a lack of worshipers, as long as there is no lack of men. Moreover, I am not so foolish as to require stone statues decked out in gaudy colors. For sometimes these are a drawback to the worship of us gods—that is, when stupid numbskulls adore the figures instead of the divinities, and then we are left in the position of those who have been edged out of their jobs by substitutes. I consider that as many statues have been set up for me as there are men who display, sometimes even unwillingly, a living image of me. And so, there is no reason why I should envy the other gods because each is worshiped in his own corner of the world, and on set days too—as, for example, Phoebus is honored at Rhodes, Venus on Cyprus, Juno at Argos, Minerva at Athens, Jupiter on Olympus, Neptune at Terentum, Priapus[9] at Lampsacus—as long as the whole world in perfect unanimity never ceases to offer me far superior victims.

Now if anyone thinks my claims reveal more boldness than truth, come on, let's examine the actual lives of men for a bit, to make it clear just how much they owe me—throughout all society from top to bottom—and how highly they value me.

* * *

But why should I fret uselessly, trying to establish these things through so much testimony from various witnesses,[1] when Christ himself in the mystical psalms openly says to the Father, "You know my folly"?[2] Nor is it merely an accident that fools are so extremely pleasing to God. I think the reason is simply this: just as great rulers suspect and despise those who are too intelligent (as Caesar did Brutus and Cassius, whereas he had no fear of the drunken Anthony, and as Nero did Seneca, and Dionysius[3] did Plato) but are delighted with crude and simple minds, so too Christ always despises and condemns those savants who rely on their own wisdom. Paul testifies very clearly on this point when he says "What is foolish to the world, God has chosen,"[4] and when he says that God was pleased to save the world

9. A god of procreation, son of Dionysus and Aphrodite.   1. I.e., of the relationship between Folly and Christianity.   2. Psalm 69.5. The speaker is not Christ but the psalmist.   3. Dionysius the Younger (4th century B.C.E.), tyrant of Syracuse, in Sicily.   4. 1 Corinthians 1.27.

through folly because it could not be redeemed by wisdom.[5] Indeed, God himself makes the same point clear enough when he cries out through the mouth of the prophet, "I will destroy the wisdom of the wise and the prudence of the prudent I will reject,"[6] and again when he gives thanks that the mystery of salvation has been hidden from the wise and revealed to the simple, that is, to fools.[7] For the Greek for "simple" is νηπίοις, which he contrasted with σοφοῖς (wise). Relevant here, too, are his attacks everywhere in the gospel against the scribes and pharisees and doctors of the law, whereas he carefully protected the ignorant populace. For isn't "Woe to you, scribes and pharisees"[8] equivalent to "Woe to you, wisemen"? But he seems to have taken the greatest delight in simple people, women, and fishermen. In fact, even on the level of animal creatures, Christ is most pleased with those who are farthest removed from the slyness of the fox. Hence he preferred to ride on an ass, when if he wished he could have mounted on a lion's back with impunity. And the Holy Spirit came down in the shape of a dove, not an eagle or a hawk. Moreover, throughout Holy Scripture, harts, young mules, and lambs are frequently mentioned. Consider also that he calls his own followers, destined for immortal life, sheep. No other animal is more stupid, as is quite clear from the Aristotelian proverb "a mind like a sheep's," which (as he informs us) is derived from that animal's stupidity and is frequently leveled at blockheads and dolts as an insult. But, of such a flock as this, Christ professes to be the shepherd. Even more, he himself delighted in the title "lamb," as when John pointed him out with, "Behold, the lamb of God,"[9] which is also frequently mentioned in the Apocalypse.

Do not all these witnesses cry out with one voice that all mortals are fools, even the pious? And that even Christ, though he was the wisdom of the Father,[1] became somehow foolish in order to relieve the folly of mortals when he took on human nature and appeared in the form of a man? Just as he became sin in order to heal sins.[2] Nor did he choose any other way to heal them but through the folly of the cross, through ignorant and doltish apostles. For them, too, he carefully prescribed folly, warning them against wisdom, when he set before them the example of children, lilies, mustard seed, and sparrows[3]—stupid creatures lacking all intelligence, leading their lives according to the dictates of nature, artless and carefree—and also when he forbad them to be concerned about how they should speak before magistrates, and when he enjoined them not to examine dates and times, so as to keep them from relying on their own wisdom and make them depend on him heart and soul. To the same effect is the prohibition of God, the architect of the world, that they should not eat any fruit from the tree of knowledge, as if knowledge would poison their happiness. For that matter, Paul openly condemns knowledge as dangerous because it puffs men up.[4] St. Bernard, I imagine, was following Paul when he interpreted the mountain on which Lucifer established his throne as the mountain of knowledge.

Perhaps we ought not to omit the argument that folly is pleasing to the

---

5. 1 Corinthians 1.21: "It pleased God by the foolishness of preaching to save them that believe." **6.** 1 Corinthians 1.19. **7.** Matthew 11.25: "I thank thee, O Father, Lord of heaven and earth, because thou hast hid these things from the wise and prudent, and hast revealed them unto babes." **8.** Luke 11.44. **9.** John 1.29. **1.** 1 Corinthians 1.24: "But unto them which are called, both Jews and Greeks, Christ the power of God, and the wisdom of God." **2.** 2 Corinthians 5.21. **3.** Matthew 10.29. *Children:* Luke 18.17. *Lilies:* Matthew 6.28. *Mustard seed:* Luke 17.6. **4.** 1 Corinthians 8.1: "Knowledge puffeth up, but charity edifieth."

powers above because it alone can win pardon for mistakes, whereas a knowledgeable man is not forgiven. Hence, those who pray for forgiveness, even if they sinned knowingly, still employ folly as a pretext and defense. For this is the way Aaron prays to avert the punishment of his sister in The Book of Numbers, if I remember correctly: "I beg you, Lord, do not hold us responsible for this sin, which we have committed in our folly."[5] So too Saul begged David to forgive his offense, saying, "For it is clear that I acted in my folly."[6] Again, David himself coaxes the Lord in these words: "But I beg you, Lord, to take away the iniquity of your servant, because we have acted in our folly,"[7] as if he would not obtain pardon unless he pleaded folly and ignorance as excuses. But what is even more compelling, when Christ on the cross prayed for his enemies, "Father, forgive them," the only excuse he made for them was their ignorance: "for they do not know," he said, "what they are doing."[8] In the same way Paul, writing to Timothy: "For this reason I obtained mercy from God, because I acted ignorantly, as an unbeliever."[9] What does "I did it ignorantly" amount to but "I did it in my folly, not with malice?" What does "For this reason I obtained mercy" mean but that he would not have obtained it if he had not been recommended by the patronage of folly? Our case is also strengthened by that mystical psalmist, who did not occur to us in the proper place: "Do not remember the sins of my youth and my stupidities."[1] You hear the two excuses he makes: namely, youth, to whom I am a regular companion, and stupidities—and in the plural at that, so that we may understand the full force of his folly.

And now, to stop running through endless examples and to put it in a nutshell, it seems to me that the Christian religion taken all together has a certain affinity with some sort of folly and has little or nothing to do with wisdom. If you want some proof of this, notice first of all that children, old people, women, and retarded persons are more delighted than others with holy and religious matters and hence are always nearest to the altar, simply out of a natural inclination. Moreover, you see how those first founders of religion were remarkably devoted to simplicity and bitterly hostile to literature. Finally, no fools seem more senseless than those people who have been completely taken up, once and for all, with a burning devotion to Christian piety: they throw away their possessions, ignore injuries, allow themselves to be deceived, make no distinction between friend and foe, shudder at the thought of pleasure, find satisfaction in fasts, vigils, tears, and labors, shrink from life, desire death above all else—in short, they seem completely devoid of normal human responses, just as if their minds were living somewhere else, not in their bodies. Can such a condition be called anything but insanity? In this light, it is not at all surprising that the apostles seemed to be intoxicated with new wine and that Paul seemed mad to the judge Festus.[2]

* * *

* * * In absolutely every activity of life, the pious man flees from whatever is related to the body and is carried away in the pursuit of the eternal and

---

5. Numbers 12.11: "And Aaron said unto Moses, Alas, my lord, I beseech thee, lay not the sin upon us, wherein we have done foolishly, and wherein we have sinned." 6. 1 Samuel 26.21: "Behold, I have played the fool, and I have erred exceedingly." 7. 1 Chronicles 21.8. 8. Luke 23.34. 9. 1 Timothy 1.13: "But I obtained mercy, because I did it ignorantly in unbelief." 1. Psalm 25.7. 2. Acts 26.24: "Festus said with a loud voice, Paul, thou art beside thyself; much learning doth make thee mad."

invisible things of the spirit. Hence, since these two groups[3] are in such utter disagreement on all matters, the result is that each thinks the other is insane—though that word applies more properly to the pious than to ordinary men, if you want my opinion. This will be much clearer if, according to my promise, I devote a few words to showing that their supreme reward is no more than a certain insanity.

First, therefore, consider that Plato had some glimmer of this notion when he wrote that the madness of lovers is the height of happiness.[4] For a person who loves intensely no longer lives in himself but rather in that which he loves, and the farther he gets from himself and the closer to it, the happier he is. Moreover, when the mind is set on leaving the body and no longer has perfect control over the bodily organs, no doubt you would rightly call this condition madness. Otherwise what is the meaning of such common expressions as "he is out of his wits," "come to your senses," and "he is himself once more." Also, the more perfect the love, the greater and happier is the madness. What, then, is that future life in heaven for which pious minds long so eagerly? I'll tell you: the spirit, stronger at last and victorious, will absorb the body. And it will do so all the more easily, partly because it is in its own kingdom now, partly because even in its former life it had purged and refined the body in preparation for such a transformation. Then the spirit will be absorbed by that highest mind of all, whose power is infinitely greater, in such a way that the whole man will be outside himself, and will be happy for no other reason than that he is located outside himself, and will receive unspeakable joy from that Highest Good which gathers all things to Himself.

Now, although this happiness is not absolutely perfect until the mind, having received its former body, is endowed with immortality, nevertheless it happens that, because the life of the pious is nothing but a meditation and a certain shadow (as it were) of that other life, they sometimes experience a certain flavor or odor of that reward. And this, even though it is like the tiniest droplet by comparison with that fountain of eternal happiness, nevertheless far surpasses all pleasures of the body, even if all the delights of all mortals were gathered into one. So much beyond the body are the things of the spirit; things unseen, beyond what can be seen. This, indeed, is what the prophet promises: "Eye has not seen, nor ear heard, nor has the heart of man conceived what things God has prepared for those who love him."[5] And this is Folly's part, which shall not be taken from her by the transformation of life, but shall be perfected. Those who have the privilege of experiencing this (and it happens to very few) undergo something very like madness: they talk incoherently, not in a human fashion, making sounds without sense. Then the entire expression of their faces vacillates repeatedly: now happy, now sad; now crying, now laughing, now sighing—in short, they are completely beside themselves. Soon after, when they come to themselves, they say they do not know where they have been, whether in the body or out of it, whether waking or sleeping. They do not remember what they heard or saw or said or did except in a cloudy way, as if it were a dream. All they know is that they were never happier than while they were transported with such madness. Thus, they lament that they have come to their senses and want above all else to be forever mad with this kind of madness. And this is only a faint taste, as it were, of that future happiness.

---

3. The pious and the ordinary.   4. *Phaedrus*, line 245.   5. 1 Corinthians 2.9.

But I have long since forgotten myself and "have gone beyond the pale." If you think my speech has been too pert or wordy, keep in mind that you've been listening to Folly and to a woman. But also remember that Greek proverb "Often a foolish man says something to the point"—unless, perhaps, you think it doesn't apply to women.

I see that you are waiting for an epilogue, but you are crazy if you think I still have in mind what I have said, after pouring forth such a torrent of jumbled words. The old saying was "I hate a drinking-companion with a memory." Updated, it is "I hate a listener with a memory." Therefore, farewell, clap your hands, live well, drink your fill, most illustrious initiates of Folly.

NICCOLÒ MACHIAVELLI
1469–1527

The most famous and controversial political writer and theorist of his time—indeed, possibly of all time—Niccolò Machiavelli was born in Florence on May 3, 1469. Little is known of his schooling, but it is obvious from his works that he knew the Latin and Italian writers well. He entered public life in 1494 as a clerk and from 1498 to 1512 was secretary to the second chancery of the commune of Florence, whose magistrates were in charge of internal and war affairs. During the conflict between Florence and Pisa, he dealt with military problems firsthand. Thus he had a direct experience of war as well as of diplomacy; he was entrusted with many missions—among others, to King Louis XII of France in 1500 and in 1502 to Cesare Borgia, duke of Valentinois or "il duca Valentino," the favorite son of Pope Alexander VI. Machiavelli described the duke's ruthless methods in crushing a conspiracy during his conquest of the Romagna region in a terse booklet *Of the Method Followed by Duke Valentino in Killing Vitellozzo Vitelli*, which already shows direct insight into the type of the amoral and technically efficient "prince." In 1506 Machiavelli went on a mission to Pope Julius II, whose expedition into Romagna (an old name for north-central Italy) he followed closely. From this and other missions—to Emperor Maximilian (1508) and again to the king of France (1509)—Machiavelli drew his two books of observations or *Portraits* of the affairs of those territories, written in 1508 and 1510.

Preeminently a student of politics and an acute observer of historical events, Machiavelli endeavored to apply his experience of other states to the strengthening of his own, the Florentine republic, and busied himself in 1507 with the establishment of a Florentine militia, encountering great difficulties. When the republican regime came to an end, he lost his post and was exiled from the city proper, though forbidden to leave Florentine territory. The new regime of the Medici accused him unjustly of conspiracy, and he was released only after a period of imprisonment and torture. To the period of his exile (spent near San Casciano, a few miles from Florence, where he retired with his wife, Marietta Corsini, and his five children), we owe his major works: the *Discourses on the First Ten Books of Livy* (1513–21) and *The Prince*, written in 1513 with the hope of obtaining public office from the Medici. In 1520 Machiavelli was commissioned to write a history of Florence, which he presented in 1525 to Pope Clement VII (Giulio de' Medici). The following year, conscious of imminent dangers, he took part in the work to improve the military fortifications of Florence. The fate of the city at this point depended on the outcome of the larger struggle between

Francis I of France and the Holy Roman Emperor, Charles V. Pope Clement's siding with the king of France led to the disastrous "Sack of Rome" by Charles V in 1527, and the result for Florence was the collapse of Medici domination. Machiavelli's hopes, briefly raised by the reestablishment of the republic, came to naught, because he was now regarded as a Medici sympathizer. This last disappointment may have accelerated his end. He died on June 22, 1527, and was buried in the church of Santa Croce.

Though Machiavelli has a place in literary history for a short novel and two plays—one of which, La mandragola (The mandrake), first performed in the early 1520s, belongs in the upper rank of Italian comedies of intrigue—his world reputation is based on The Prince. This "handbook" on how to obtain and keep political power consists of twenty-six chapters. The first eleven deal with different types of dominions and the ways in which they are acquired and preserved—the early title of the whole book, in Latin, was De principatibus (Of princedoms)—and the twelfth to fourteenth chapters focus particularly on problems of military power. The book's astounding fame, however, is based on the final part (from chapter fifteen to the end), which deals primarily with the attributes and "virtues" of the prince himself. In other words, despite its reputation for cool, precise realism, the work presents a hypothetical type, the idealized portrait of a certain kind of person.

Manuals of this sort may be classified, in one sense, as pedagogical literature. Because of their merits of form and of vivid, if stylized, characterization they can be considered works of art, but their overt purpose is to codify a certain set of manners and rules of conduct; the authors, therefore, present themselves as especially wise, experts in the field, "minds" offering advice to the executive "arm." Machiavelli is a clear example of this approach. His fervor, the dramatic, oratorical way he confronts his reader, the wealth and pertinence of his illustrations are all essential qualities of his pedagogical persona: "Either you are already prince, or you are on the way to become one. In the first case liberality is dangerous; in the second it is very necessary to be thought liberal. Caesar was one of those. . . . Somebody may answer. . . . I answer." Relying on his direct knowledge of politics, he uses examples he can personally vouch for:

> Men are so simple and so subject to present needs that he who deceives in this way will always find those who will let themselves be deceived.
>   I do not wish to keep still about one of the recent instances. Alexander VI did nothing else than deceive men, and had no other intention. . . .

The implied tone of I know, I have seen such things myself adds a special immediacy to Machiavelli's prose. His view of the practical world may have been an especially startling one, but the sensation caused by his work would have been far less without the rhetorical power, the drama of argumentation, that makes The Prince a unique example of "the art of persuasion."

The view of humanity in Machiavelli is not at all cheerful. Indeed, the pessimistic notion that humanity is evil is not so much Machiavelli's conclusion about human nature as his premise; it is the point of departure of all subsequent reasoning on the course for a ruler to follow. The very fact of its being given as a premise, however, tends to qualify it; it is not a firm philosophical judgment but a stratagem, dictated by the facts as they are seen by a lucid observer of the here and now. The author is committed to his view of the human being not as a philosopher or as a religious man but as a practical politician. He indicates the rules of the game as his experience shows it must, under the circumstances, be played.

> A prudent ruler . . . cannot and should not observe faith when such observance is to his disadvantage and the causes that made him give his promise have vanished. If men were all good, this advice would not be good, but since men are wicked and do not keep their promises to you, you likewise do not have to keep yours to them.

A basic question in the study of Machiavelli, therefore, is "How much of a realist is he?" His picture of the perfectly efficient ruler has something of the quality of an abstraction; it shows, though much less clearly than Castiglione's portrayal of the courtier, the well-known Renaissance tendency toward "perfected" form. Machiavelli's abandonment of complex actualities in favor of an ideal vision is shown most clearly at the conclusion of the book, particularly in the last chapter. This is where he offers what amounts to the greatest of his illustrations as the prince's preceptor and counselor: the ideal ruler, now technically equipped by his pedagogue, is to undertake a mission—the liberation of Machiavelli's Italy. If we regard the last chapter of *The Prince* as a culmination of Machiavelli's discussion rather than as a dissonant addition to it, we are likely to feel at that point not only that Machiavelli's realistic method is ultimately directed toward an ideal task but also that his conception of that task, far from being based on immediate realities, is founded on cultural and poetic myths. Machiavelli's method here becomes imaginative rather than scientific. His exhortation to liberate Italy, and his final prophecy, belong to the tradition of poetic visions in which a present state of decay is lamented and a hope of future redemption is expressed (as in Dante's *Purgatorio*, canto 6). And a very significant part of this hope is presented not in terms of technical political considerations (choice of the opportune moment, evaluation of military power) but in terms of a poetic justice for which precedents are sought in religious and ancient history and in mythology:

> . . . if it was necessary to make clear the ability of Moses that the people of Israel should be enslaved in Egypt, and to reveal Cyrus's greatness of mind that the Persians should be oppressed by the Medes, and to demonstrate the excellence of Theseus that the Athenians should be scattered, so at the present time. . . . Everything is now fully disposed for the work . . . if only your House adopts the methods of those I have set forth as examples. Moreover, we have before our eyes extraordinary and unexampled means prepared by God. The sea has been divided. . . . Manna has fallen.

Machiavelli's Italy, as he observes in chapter 25, is now a country "without dykes and without any wall of defence." It has suffered from "deluges," and its present rule, a "barbarian" one, "stinks in every nostril." Something is rotten in it, in short, as in Hamlet's Denmark. And we become more and more detached even from the particular example, Italy, as we recognize in the situation a pattern frequently exemplified in tragedy: the desire for communal regeneration, for the cleansing of the city-state, the *polis*. Of this cleansing, Italy on the one side and the imaginary prince on the other may be taken as symbols. The envisaged redemption is identified with antiquity and Roman virtue, while the realism of the political observer is here drowned out by the cry of the humanist dreaming of ancient glories.

PRONOUNCING GLOSSARY

The following list uses common English syllables and stress accents to provide rough equivalents of selected words whose pronunciation may be unfamiliar to the general reader.

Borgia: *bor'-juh*	Pistoia: *pees-toh'-yah*
Chiron: *kai'-ron*	San Casciano: *san ka-shah'-noh*
de' Medici: *day may'-dee-chee*	Santa Croce: *san'-tuh croh'-chay*
Machiavelli: *ma-kee-ah-vel'-lee*	

Letter to Francesco Vettori[1]

["That Food Which Alone Is Mine"]

I am living on my farm, and since my last troubles[2] I have not been in Florence twenty days, putting them all together. Up to now I have been setting snares for thrushes with my own hands; I get up before daylight, prepare my birdlime, and go out with a bundle of cages on my back, so that I look like Geta when he came back from the harbor with the books of Amphitryo,[3] and catch at the least two thrushes and at the most six. So I did all of September; then this trifling diversion, despicable and strange as it is, to my regret failed. What my life is now I shall tell you.

In the morning I get up with the sun and go out into a grove that I am having cut; there I remain a couple of hours to look over the work of the past day and kill some time with the woodmen, who always have on hand some dispute either among themselves or among their neighbors. . . .

When I leave the grove, I go to a spring, and from there into my aviary. I have a book in my pocket, either Dante or Petrarch or one of the minor poets, as Tibullus,[4] Ovid, and the like. I read about their tender passions and their loves, remember mine, and take pleasure for a while in thinking about them. Then I go along the road to the inn, talk with those who pass by, ask the news of their villages, learn various things, and note the varied tastes and different fancies of men. It gets to be dinner time, and with my troop I eat what food my poor farm and my little property permit. After dinner, I return to the inn; there I usually find the host, a butcher, a miller, and two furnace-tenders. With these fellows I sink into vulgarity for the rest of the day, playing at cricca and tricche-trach;[5] from these games come a thousand quarrels and numberless offensive and insulting words; we often dispute over a penny, and all the same are heard shouting as far as San Casciano.[6] So, involved in these trifles, I keep my brain from getting mouldy, and express the perversity of Fate, for I am willing to have her drive me along this path, to see if she will be ashamed of it.

In the evening, I return to my house, and go into my study. At the door I take off the clothes I have worn all day, mud spotted and dirty, and put on regal and courtly garments. Thus appropriately clothed, I enter into the ancient courts of ancient men,[7] where, being lovingly received, I feed on that food which alone is mine, and which I was born for; I am not ashamed to speak with them and to ask the reasons for their actions, and they courteously answer me. For four hours I feel no boredom and forget every worry; I do not fear poverty, and death does not terrify me. I give myself completely over to the ancients. And because Dante says that there is no knowledge unless one retains what one has read,[8] I have written down the profit I have gained

---

1. Translated by Allan H. Gilbert. From a letter dated December 10, 1513, to Vettori, ambassador in Rome. 2. Machiavelli had been suspected of participation in a conspiracy led by two young friends of his and had been imprisoned and subjected to torture before his innocence was recognized. 3. Allusion to a popular tale in which Amphitryo, returning to Thebes after having studied at Athens, sends forward from the harbor his servant Geta to announce his arrival to his wife, Alemene, and loads him with his books. 4. Albius Tibullus (1st century B.C.E.), Roman elegiac poet. 5. Two popular games, the first played with cards, the second with dice thrown to regulate the movements of pawns on a chessboard. 6. Nearby village, in the region around Florence. 7. Machiavelli here refers figuratively to his study of ancient history. 8. *Paradiso* 5.41–42: "For knowledge none can vaunt / Who retains not, although he have understood."

from their conversation, and composed a little book *De principatibus*,[9] in which I go as deep as I can into reflections on this subject, debating what a principate is, what the species are, how they are gained, how they are kept, and why they are lost. If ever any of my trifles can please you, this one should not displease you; and to a prince, and especially a new prince, it ought to be welcome.

From The Prince[1]

New Princedoms Gained with Other Men's Forces and through Fortune

FROM CHAPTER 7

* * *

[*Cesare Borgia*][2]

* * * Cesare Borgia, called by the people Duke Valentino, gained his position through his father's Fortune and through her lost it, notwithstanding that he made use of every means and action possible to a prudent and vigorous man for putting down his roots in those states that another man's arms and Fortune bestowed on him. As I say above, he who does not lay his foundations beforehand can perhaps through great wisdom and energy lay them afterward, though he does so with trouble for the architect and danger to the building. So on examining all the steps taken by the Duke, we see that he himself laid mighty foundations for future power. To discuss these steps is not superfluous; indeed I for my part do not see what better precepts I can give a new prince than the example of Duke Valentino's actions. If his arrangements did not bring him success, the fault was not his, because his failure resulted from an unusual and utterly malicious stroke of Fortune.[3]

[*Pope Alexander VI Attempts to Make Cesare a Prince*]

Alexander VI,[4] in his attempt to give high position to the Duke his son, had before him many difficulties, present and future. First, he saw no way in which he could make him lord of any state that was not a state of the Church, yet if the Pope tried to take such a state from the Church, he knew that the Duke of Milan and the Venetians[5] would not allow it because both Faenza and Rimini were already under Venetian protection. He saw, besides, that the weapons of Italy, especially those of which he could make use, were in the hands of men who had reason to fear the Pope's greatness; therefore he could not rely on them, since they were all among the Orsini and the Colonnesi[6] and their allies. He therefore was under the necessity of disturb-

9. Of princedoms (Latin title of *The Prince*). All chapter headings are also in Latin in the original.
1. Translated by Allan H. Gilbert.   2. Son of Pope Alexander VI and duke of Valentinois and Romagna. His skillful and merciless subjugation of the local lords of Romagna occurred between 1499 and 1502.
3. Ill health.   4. Rodrigo Borgia (1431?–1503), pope (1492–1503), father of Cesare and Lucrezia Borgia.   5. The Venetian Republic opposed the expansion of the papal states. *Duke of Milan:* Ludovico Il Moro, the flamboyant duke of the Sforza family.   6. Powerful Roman families.

ing the situation and embroiling the states of Italy so that he could safely master part of them. This he found easy since, luckily for him, the Venetians, influenced by other reasons, had set out to get the French to come again into Italy. He not merely did not oppose their coming; he made it easier by dissolving the early marriage of King Louis.[7] The King then marched into Italy with the Venetians' aid and Alexander's consent; and he was no sooner in Milan than the Pope got soldiers from him for an attempt on Romagna; these the King granted for the sake of his own reputation.[8]

[Borgia Determines to Depend on Himself]

Having taken Romagna, then, and suppressed the Colonnesi, the Duke, in attempting to keep the province and to go further, was hindered by two things: one, his own forces, which he thought disloyal; the other, France's intention. That is, he feared that the Orsini forces which he had been using would fail him and not merely would hinder his gaining but would take from him what he had gained, and that the King would treat him in the same way. With the Orsini, he had experience of this when after the capture of Faenza he attacked Bologna, for he saw that they turned cold over that attack. And as to the King's purpose, the Duke learned it when, after taking the dukedom of Urbino, he invaded Tuscany—an expedition that the King made him abandon. As a result, he determined not to depend further on another man's armies and Fortune.

[The Duke Destroys His Disloyal Generals]

The Duke's first act to that end was to weaken the Orsini and Colonnesi parties in Rome by winning over to himself all their adherents who were men of rank, making them his own men of rank and giving them large subsidies; and he honored them, according to their stations, with military and civil offices, so that within a few months their hearts were emptied of all affection for the Roman parties, and it was wholly transferred to the Duke. After this, he waited for a good chance to wipe out the Orsini leaders, having scattered those of the Colonna family; such a chance came to him well and he used it better. When the Orsini found out, though late, that the Duke's and the Church's greatness was their ruin, they held a meeting at Magione, in Perugian territory. From that resulted the rebellion of Urbino, the insurrections in Romagna, and countless dangers for the Duke, all of which he overcame with the aid of the French. Thus having got back his reputation, but not trusting France or other outside forces, in order not to have to put them to a test, he turned to trickery. And he knew so well how to falsify his purpose that the Orsini themselves, by means of Lord Paulo,[9] were reconciled with him (as to Paulo the Duke did not omit any sort of gracious act to assure him, giving him money, clothing and horses) so completely that their folly took them to Sinigaglia into his hands. Having wiped out these leaders, then, and changed their partisans into his friends, the Duke had laid very good foundations for his power, holding all the Romagna along with the dukedom

---

7. Louis XII, king of France (d. 1515).   8. According to his agreement with Pope Alexander VI.
9. Member of the Orsini.

of Urbino, especially since he believed he had made the Romagna his friend and gained the support of all those people, through their getting a taste of well-being.

[Peace in Romagna; Remirro de Orco]

Because this matter is worthy of notice and of being copied by others, I shall not omit it. After the Duke had seized the Romagna and found it controlled by weak lords who had plundered their subjects rather than governed them, and had given them reason for disunion, not for union, so that the whole province was full of thefts, brawls, and every sort of excess, he judged that if he intended to make it peaceful and obedient to the ruler's arm, he must of necessity give it good government. Hence he put in charge there Messer Remirro de Orco, a man cruel and ready, to whom he gave the most complete authority. This man in a short time rendered the province peaceful and united, gaining enormous prestige. Then the Duke decided there was no further need for such boundless power, because he feared it would become a cause for hatred; so he set up a civil court in the midst of the province, with a distinguished presiding judge, where every city had its lawyer. And because he knew that past severities had made some men hate him, he determined to purge such men's minds and win them over entirely by showing that any cruelty which had gone on did not originate with himself but with the harsh nature of his agent. So getting an opportunity for it, one morning at Cesena he had Messer Remirro laid in two pieces in the public square with a block of wood and a bloody sword near him. The ferocity of this spectacle left those people at the same time gratified and awe-struck.

[Princely Virtues]

FROM CHAPTER 15

On the Things for Which Men, and Especially Princes, Are Praised or Censured

* * * Because I know that many have written on this topic, I fear that when I too write I shall be thought presumptuous, because, in discussing it, I break away completely from the principles laid down by my predecessors. But since it is my purpose to write something useful to an attentive reader, I think it more effective to go back to the practical truth of the subject than to depend on my fancies about it. And many have imagined republics and principalities that never have been seen or known to exist in reality. For there is such a difference between the way men live and the way they ought to live, that anybody who abandons what is for what ought to be will learn something that will ruin rather than preserve him, because anyone who determines to act in all circumstances the part of a good man must come to ruin among so many who are not good. Hence, if a prince wishes to maintain himself, he must learn how to be not good, and to use that ability or not as is required.

Leaving out of account, then, things about an imaginary prince, and considering things that are true, I say that all men, when they are spoken of, and especially princes, because they are set higher, are marked with some of the qualities that bring them either blame or praise. To wit, one man is thought liberal, another stingy (using a Tuscan word, because *avaricious* in our language is still applied to one who desires to get things through violence, but *stingy* we apply to him who refrains too much from using his own property); one is thought open-handed, another grasping; one cruel, the other compassionate; one is a breaker of faith, the other reliable; one is effeminate and cowardly, the other vigorous and spirited; one is philanthropic, the other egotistic; one is lascivious, the other chaste; one is straight-forward, the other crafty; one hard, the other easy to deal with; one is firm, the other unsettled; one is religious, the other unbelieving; and so on.

And I know that everybody will admit that it would be very praiseworthy for a prince to possess all of the above-mentioned qualities that are considered good. But since he is not able to have them or to observe them completely, because human conditions do not allow him to, it is necessary that he be prudent enough to understand how to avoid getting a bad name because he is given to those vices that will deprive him of his position. He should also, if he can, guard himself from those vices that will not take his place away from him, but if he cannot do it, he can with less anxiety let them go. Moreover, he should not be troubled if he gets a bad name because of vices without which it will be difficult for him to preserve his position. I say this because, if everything is considered, it will be seen that some things seem to be virtuous, but if they are put into practice will be ruinous to him; other things seem to be vices, yet if put into practice will bring the prince security and well-being.

FROM CHAPTER 16

On Liberality and Parsimony

Beginning, then, with the first of the above-mentioned qualities, I assert that it is good to be thought liberal.[1] Yet liberality, practiced in such a way that you get a reputation for it, is damaging to you, for the following reasons: If you use it wisely and as it ought to be used, it will not become known, and you will not escape being censured for the opposite vice. Hence, if you wish to have men call you liberal, it is necessary not to omit any sort of lavishness. A prince who does this will always be obliged to use up all his property in lavish actions; he will then, if he wishes to keep the name of liberal, be forced to lay heavy taxes on his people and exact money from them, and do everything he can to raise money. This will begin to make his subjects hate him, and as he grows poor he will be little esteemed by anybody. So it comes about that because of this liberality of his, with which he has damaged a large number and been of advantage to but a few, he is affected by every petty annoyance and is in peril from every slight danger. If he recognizes this and wishes to draw back, he quickly gets a bad name for stinginess.

Since, then, a prince cannot without harming himself practice this virtue of liberality to such an extent that it will be recognized, he will, if he is prudent, not care about being called stingy. As time goes on he will be

---

1. Generous, openhanded.

thought more and more liberal, for the people will see that because of his economy his income is enough for him, that he can defend himself from those who make war against him, and that he can enter upon undertakings without burdening his people. Such a prince is in the end liberal to all those from whom he takes nothing, and they are numerous; he is stingy to those to whom he does not give, and they are few. In our times we have seen big things done only by those who have been looked on as stingy; the others have utterly failed. Pope Julius II,[2] though he made use of a reputation for liberality to attain the papacy, did not then try to maintain it, because he wished to be able to make war. The present King of France[3] has carried on great wars without laying unusually heavy taxes on his people, merely because his long economy has made provision for heavy expenditures. The present King of Spain,[4] if he had continued liberal, would not have carried on or completed so many undertakings.

Therefore a prince ought to care little about getting called stingy, if as a result he does not have to rob his subjects, is able to defend himself, does not become poor and contemptible, and is not obliged to become grasping. For this vice of stinginess is one of those that enables him to rule. Somebody may say: Caesar, by means of his liberality became emperor, and many others have come to high positions because they have been liberal and have been thought so. I answer: Either you are already prince, or you are on the way to become one. In the first case liberality is dangerous; in the second it is very necessary to be thought liberal. Caesar was one of those who wished to attain dominion over Rome. But if, when he had attained it, he had lived for a long time and had not moderated his expenses, he would have destroyed his authority. Somebody may answer: Many who have been thought very liberal have been princes and done great things with their armies. I answer: The prince spends either his own property and that of his subjects or that of others. In the first case he ought to be frugal; in the second he ought to abstain from no sort of liberality. When he marches with his army and lives on plunder, loot, and ransom, a prince controls the property of others. To him liberality is essential, for without it his soldiers would not follow him. You can be a free giver of what does not belong to you or your subjects, as were Cyrus, Caesar, and Alexander, because to spend the money of others does not decrease your reputation but adds to it. It is only the spending of your own money that hurts you.

There is nothing that eats itself up as fast as does liberality, for when you practice it you lose the power to practice it, and become poor and contemptible, or else to escape poverty you become rapacious and therefore are hated. And of all the things against which a prince must guard himself, the first is being an object of contempt and hatred. Liberality leads you to both of these. Hence there is more wisdom in keeping a name for stinginess, which produces a bad reputation without hatred, than in striving for the name of liberal, only to be forced to get the name of rapacious, which brings forth both bad reputation and hatred.

---

2. Giuliano della Rovere (1443–1513), elected to the papacy in 1503 at the death of Pius III, who had been successor to Alexander VI (Rodrigo Borgia). Alexander VI is discussed in chap. 18. Julius II's character is discussed in chap. 25. 3. Louis XII (1462–1515). 4. Ferdinand II, "the Catholic" (1452–1516).

FROM CHAPTER 17

On Cruelty and Pity, and Whether It Is Better to Be Loved or to Be Feared, and Vice Versa

Coming then to the other qualities already mentioned, I say that every prince should wish to be thought compassionate and not cruel; still, he should be careful not to make a bad use of the pity he feels. Cesare Borgia[5] was considered cruel, yet this cruelty of his pacified the Romagna, united it, and changed its condition to that of peace and loyalty. If the matter is well considered, it will be seen that Cesare was much more compassionate than the people of Florence, for in order to escape the name of cruel they allowed Pistoia to be destroyed.[6] Hence a prince ought not to be troubled by the stigma of cruelty, acquired in keeping his subjects united and faithful. By giving a very few examples of cruelty he can be more truly compassionate than those who through too much compassion allow disturbances to continue, from which arise murders or acts of plunder. Lawless acts are injurious to a large group, but the executions ordered by the prince injure a single person. The new prince, above all other princes, cannot possibly avoid the name of cruel, because new states are full of perils. Dido in Vergil puts it thus: "Hard circumstances and the newness of my realm force me to do such things, and to keep watch and ward over all my lands."[7]

All the same, he should be slow in believing and acting, and should make no one afraid of him; his procedure should be so tempered with prudence and humanity that too much confidence does not make him incautious, and too much suspicion does not make him unbearable.

All this gives rise to a question for debate: Is it better to be loved than to be feared, or the reverse? I answer that a prince should wish for both. But because it is difficult to reconcile them, I hold that it is much more secure to be feared than to be loved, if one of them must be given up. The reason for my answer is that one must say of men generally that they are ungrateful, mutable, pretenders and dissemblers, prone to avoid danger, thirsty for gain. So long as you benefit them they are all yours; as I said above, they offer you their blood, their property, their lives, their children, when the need for such things is remote. But when need comes upon you, they turn around. So if a prince has relied wholly on their words, and is lacking in other preparations, he falls. For friendships that are gained with money, and not with greatness and nobility of spirit, are deserved but not possessed, and in the nick of time one cannot avail himself of them. Men hesitate less to injure a man who makes himself loved than to injure one who makes himself feared, for their love is held by a chain of obligation, which, because of men's wickedness, is broken on every occasion for the sake of selfish profit; but their fear is secured by a dread of punishment which never fails you.

Nevertheless the prince should make himself feared in such a way that, if he does not win love, he escapes hatred. This is possible, for to be feared and not to be hated can easily coexist. In fact it is always possible, if the ruler abstains from the property of his citizens and subjects, and from their women. And if, as sometimes happens, he finds that he must inflict the

---

5. See n. 2, p. 1949. 6. By internal dissensions, because the Florentines, Machiavelli contends, failed to treat the leaders of the dissenting parties with an iron hand. 7. *Aeneid* 1.563–64.

penalty of death, he should do it when he has proper justification and evident reason. But above all he must refrain from taking property, for men forget the death of a father more quickly than the loss of their patrimony. Further, causes for taking property are never lacking, and he who begins to live on plunder is always finding cause to seize what belongs to others. But on the contrary, reasons for taking life are rare and fail sooner.

But when a prince is with his army and has a great number of soldiers under his command, then above all he must pay no heed to being called cruel, because if he does not have that name he cannot keep his army united or ready for duty. It should be numbered among the wonderful feats of Hannibal that he led to war in foreign lands a large army, made up of countless types of men, yet never suffered from dissension, either among the soldiers or against the general, in either bad or good fortune. His success resulted from nothing else than his inhuman cruelty, which, when added to his numerous other strong qualities, made him respected and terrible in the sight of his soldiers. Yet without his cruelty his other qualities would not have been adequate. So it seems that those writers have not thought very deeply who on one side admire his accomplishment and on the other condemn the chief cause for it.

The truth that his other qualities alone would not have been adequate may be learned from Scipio,[8] a man of the most unusual powers not only in his own times but in all ages we know of. When he was in Spain his armies mutinied. This resulted from nothing other than his compassion, which had allowed his soldiers more license than befits military discipline. This fault was censured before the Senate by Fabius Maximus, and Scipio was called by him the corrupter of the Roman soldiery. The Locrians[9] were destroyed by a lieutenant of Scipio's, yet he did not avenge them or punish the disobedience of that lieutenant. This all came from his easy nature, which was so well understood that one who wished to excuse him in the Senate said there were many men who knew better how not to err than how to punish errors. This easy nature would in time have overthrown the fame and glory of Scipio if, in spite of this weakness, he had kept on in independent command. But since he was under the orders of the Senate, this bad quality was not merely concealed but was a glory to him.

Returning, then, to the debate on being loved and feared, I conclude that since men love as they please and fear as the prince pleases, a wise prince will evidently rely on what is in his own power and not on what is in the power of another. As I have said, he need only take pains to avoid hatred.

FROM CHAPTER 18

In What Way Faith Should Be Kept by Princes

Everybody knows how laudable it is in a prince to keep his faith and to be an honest man and not a trickster. Nevertheless, the experience of our times shows that the princes who have done great things are the ones who have taken little account of their promises and who have known how to addle the

8. Publius Cornelius Scipio Africanus the Elder (235–183 B.C.E.). The episode of the mutiny occurred in 206 B.C.E.   9. Citizens of Locri, in Sicily.

brains of men with craft. In the end they have conquered those who have put their reliance on good faith.

You must realize, then, that there are two ways to fight. In one kind the laws are used, in the other, force. The first is suitable to man, the second to animals. But because the first often falls short, one has to turn to the second. Hence a prince must know perfectly how to act like a beast and like a man. This truth was covertly taught to princes by ancient authors, who write that Achilles and many other ancient princes[1] were turned over for their up-bringing to Chiron the centaur, that he might keep them under his tuition. To have as teacher one who is half beast and half man means nothing else than that a prince needs to know how to use the qualities of both creatures. The one without the other will not last long.

Since, then, it is necessary for a prince to understand how to make good use of the conduct of the animals, he should select among them the fox and the lion, because the lion cannot protect himself from traps, and the fox cannot protect himself from the wolves. So the prince needs to be a fox that he may know how to deal with traps, and a lion that he may frighten the wolves. Those who act like the lion alone do not understand their business. A prudent ruler, therefore, cannot and should not observe faith when such observance is to his disadvantage and the causes that made him give his promise have vanished. If men were all good, this advice would not be good, but since men are wicked and do not keep their promises to you, you likewise do not have to keep yours to them. Lawful reasons to excuse his failure to keep them will never be lacking to a prince. It would be possible to give innumerable modern examples of this and to show many treaties and prom-ises that have been made null and void by the faithlessness of princes. And the prince who has best known how to act as a fox has come out best. But one who has this capacity must understand how to keep it covered, and be a skilful pretender and dissembler. Men are so simple and so subject to present needs that he who deceives in this way will always find those who will let themselves be deceived.

I do not wish to keep still about one of the recent instances. Alexander VI[2] did nothing else than deceive men, and had no other intention; yet he always found a subject to work on. There never was a man more effective in swearing that things were true, and the greater the oaths with which he made a promise, the less he observed it. Nonetheless his deceptions always suc-ceeded to his wish, because he thoroughly understood this aspect of the world.

It is not necessary, then, for a prince really to have all the virtues men-tioned above, but it is very necessary to seem to have them. I will even venture to say that they damage a prince who possesses them and always observes them, but if he seems to have them they are useful. I mean that he should seem compassionate, trustworthy, humane, honest, and religious, and actually be so; but yet he should have his mind so trained that, when it is necessary not to practice these virtues, he can change to the opposite, and do it skilfully. It is to be understood that a prince, especially a new prince, cannot observe all the things because of which men are considered good, because he is often obliged, if he wishes to maintain his government, to act contrary to faith, contrary to charity, contrary to humanity, contrary to reli-

1. E.g., Theseus, Jason, and Hercules.   2. Pope from 1492 to 1503; father of Cesare Borgia.

gion. It is therefore necessary that he have a mind capable of turning in whatever direction the winds of Fortune and the variations of affairs require, and, as I said above, that he should not depart from what is morally right, if he can observe it, but should know how to adopt what is bad, when he is obliged to.

A prince, then, should be very careful that there does not issue from his mouth anything that is not full of the above-mentioned five qualities. To those who see and hear him he should seem all compassion, all faith, all honesty, all humanity, all religion. There is nothing more necessary to make a show of possessing than this last quality. For men in general judge more by their eyes than by their hands; everybody is fitted to see, few to understand. Everybody sees what you appear to be; few make out what you really are. And these few do not dare to oppose the opinion of the many, who have the majesty of the state to confirm their view. In the actions of all men, and especially those of princes, where there is no court to which to appeal, people think of the outcome. A prince needs only to conquer and to maintain his position. The means he has used will always be judged honorable and will be praised by everybody, because the crowd is always caught by appearance and by the outcome of events, and the crowd is all there is in the world; there is no place for the few when the many have room enough. A certain prince[3] of the present day, whom it is not good to name, preaches nothing else than peace and faith, and is wholly opposed to both of them, and both of them, if he had observed them, would many times have taken from him either his reputation or his throne.

[*"Fortune Is a Woman"*]

FROM CHAPTER 25

The Power of Fortune in Human Affairs, and to What Extent She Should Be Relied On

It is not unknown to me that many have been and still are of the opinion that the affairs of this world are so under the direction of Fortune and of God that man's prudence cannot control them; in fact, that man has no resource against them. For this reason many think there is no use in sweating much over such matters, but that one might as well let Chance take control. This opinion has been the more accepted in our times, because of the great changes in the state of the world that have been and now are seen every day, beyond all human surmise. And I myself, when thinking on these things, have now and then in some measure inclined to their view. Nevertheless, because the freedom of the will should not be wholly annulled, I think it may be true that Fortune is arbiter of half of our actions, but that she still leaves the control of the other half, or about that, to us.

I liken her to one of those raging streams that, when they go mad, flood the plains, ruin the trees and the buildings, and take away the fields from one bank and put them down on the other. Everybody flees before them; everybody yields to their onrush without being able to resist anywhere. And though this is their nature, it does not cease to be true that, in calm weather,

---

3. Ferdinand II. In refraining from mentioning him, Machiavelli apparently had in mind the good relations existing between Spain and the house of Medici.

men can make some provisions against them with walls and dykes, so that, when the streams swell, their waters will go off through a canal, or their currents will not be so wild and do so much damage. The same is true of Fortune. She shows her power where there is no wise preparation for resisting her, and turns her fury where she knows that no walls and dykes have been made to hold her in. And if you consider Italy—the place where these variations occur and the cause that has set them in motion—you will see that she is a country without dykes and without any wall of defence. If, like Germany, Spain, and France, she had had a sufficient bulwark of military vigor, this flood would not have made the great changes it has, or would not have come at all.

And this, I think, is all I need to say on opposing oneself to Fortune, in general. But limiting myself more to particulars, I say that a prince may be seen prospering today and falling in ruin tomorrow, though it does not appear that he has changed in his nature or any of his qualities. I believe this comes, in the first place, from the causes that have been discussed at length in preceding chapters. That is, if a prince bases himself entirely on Fortune, he will fall when she varies. I also believe that a ruler will be successful who adapts his mode of procedure to the quality of the times, and likewise that he will be unsuccessful if the times are out of accord with his procedure. Because it may be seen that in things leading to the end each has before him, namely glory and riches, men proceed differently. One acts with caution, another rashly; one with violence, another with skill; one with patience, another with its opposite; yet with these different methods each one attains his end. Still further, two cautious men will be seen, of whom one comes to his goal, the other does not. Likewise you will see two who succeed with two different methods, one of them being cautious and the other rash. These results are caused by nothing else than the nature of the times, which is or is not in harmony with the procedure of men. It also accounts for what I have mentioned, namely, that two persons, working differently, chance to arrive at the same result; and that of two who work in the same way, one attains his end, but the other does not.

On the nature of the times also depends the variability of the best method. If a man conducts himself with caution and patience, times and affairs may come around in such a way that his procedure is good, and he goes on successfully. But if times and circumstances change, he is ruined, because he does not change his method of action. There is no man so prudent as to understand how to fit himself to this condition, either because he is unable to deviate from the course to which nature inclines him, or because, having always prospered by walking in one path, he cannot persuade himself to leave it. So the cautious man, when the time comes to go at a reckless pace, does not know how to do it. Hence he comes to ruin. Yet if he could change his nature with the times and with circumstances, his fortune would not be altered.

Pope Julius II proceeded rashly in all his actions, and found the times and circumstances so harmonious with his mode of procedure that he was always so lucky as to succeed. Consider the first enterprise he engaged in, that of Bologna, while messer Giovanni Bentivogli[4] was still alive. The Venetians

---

4. Of the ruling family Bentivogli. The pope undertook to dislodge him from Bologna in 1506. *Messer:* my lord.

were not pleased with it; the King of Spain felt the same way; the Pope was debating such an enterprise with the King of France. Nevertheless, in his courage and rashness Julius personally undertook that expedition. This movement made the King of Spain and the Venetians stand irresolute and motionless, the latter for fear, and the King because of his wish to recover the entire kingdom of Naples. On the other side, the King of France was dragged behind Julius, because the King, seeing that the Pope had moved and wishing to make him a friend in order to put down the Venetians, judged he could not refuse him soldiers without doing him open injury. Julius, then, with his rash movement, attained what no other pontiff, with the utmost human prudence, would have attained. If he had waited to leave Rome until the agreements were fixed and everything arranged, as any other pontiff would have done, he would never have succeeded, for the King of France would have had a thousand excuses, and the others would have raised a thousand fears. I wish to omit his other acts, which are all of the same sort, and all succeeded perfectly. The brevity of his life did not allow him to know anything different. Yet if times had come in which it was necessary to act with caution, they would have ruined him, for he would never have deviated from the methods to which nature inclined him.

I conclude, then, that since Fortune is variable and men are set in their ways, they are successful when they are in harmony with Fortune and unsuccessful when they disagree with her. Yet I am of the opinion that it is better to be rash than over-cautious, because Fortune is a woman and, if you wish to keep her down, you must beat her and pound her. It is evident that she allows herself to be overcome by men who treat her in that way rather than by those who proceed coldly. For that reason, like a woman, she is always the friend of young men, because they are less cautious, and more courageous, and command her with more boldness.

[The Roman Dream]

FROM CHAPTER 26

An Exhortation to Take Hold of Italy and Restore Her to Liberty from the Barbarians

Having considered all the things discussed above, I have been turning over in my own mind whether at present in Italy the time is ripe for a new prince to win prestige, and whether conditions there give a wise and vigorous ruler occasion to introduce methods that will do him honor, and bring good to the mass of the people of the land. It appears to me that so many things unite for the advantage of a new prince, that I do not know of any time that has ever been more suited for this. And, as I said, if it was necessary to make clear the ability of Moses that the people of Israel should be enslaved in Egypt, and to reveal Cyrus's greatness of mind that the Persians should be oppressed by the Medes, and to demonstrate the excellence of Theseus that the Athenians should be scattered, so at the present time, in order to make known the greatness of an Italian soul, Italy had to be brought down to her present position, to be more a slave than the Hebrews, more a servant than the Persians, more scattered than the Athenians; without head, without government; defeated, plundered, torn asunder, overrun; subject to every sort of disaster.

And though before this, certain persons[5] have showed signs from which it could be inferred that they were chosen by God for the redemption of Italy, nevertheless it has afterwards been seen that in the full current of action they have been cast off by Fortune. So Italy remains without life and awaits the man, whoever he may be, who is to heal her wounds, put an end to the plundering of Lombardy and the tribute laid on Tuscany and the kingdom of Naples, and cure her of those sores that have long been suppurating. She may be seen praying God to send some one to redeem her from these cruel and barbarous insults. She is evidently ready and willing to follow a banner, if only some one will raise it. Nor is there at present anyone to be seen in whom she can put more hope than in your illustrious House, because its fortune and vigor, and the favor of God and of the Church, which it now governs,[6] enable it to be the leader in such a redemption. This will not be very difficult, as you will see if you will bring to mind the actions and lives of those I have named above. And though these men were striking exceptions, yet they were men, and each of them had less opportunity than the present gives; their enterprises were not more just than this, nor easier, nor was God their friend more than he is yours. Here justice is complete. "A way is just to those to whom it is necessary, and arms are holy to him who has no hope save in arms."[7] Everything is now fully disposed for the work, and when that is true an undertaking cannot be difficult, if only your House adopts the methods of those I have set forth as examples. Moreover, we have before our eyes extraordinary and unexampled means prepared by God. The sea has been divided. A cloud has guided you on your way. The rock has given forth water. Manna has fallen.[8] Everything has united to make you great. The rest is for you to do. God does not intend to do everything, lest he deprive us of our free will and the share of glory that belongs to us.

It is no wonder if no one of the above-named Italians[9] has been able to do what we hope your illustrious House can. Nor is it strange if in the many revolutions and military enterprises of Italy, the martial vigor of the land always appears to be exhausted. This is because the old military customs were not good, and there has been nobody able to find new ones. Yet nothing brings so much honor to a man who rises to new power, as the new laws and new methods he discovers. These things, when they are well founded and have greatness in them, make him revered and worthy of admiration. And in Italy matter is not lacking on which to impress forms of every sort. There is great vigor in the limbs if only it is not lacking in the heads. You may see that in duels and combats between small numbers, the Italians have been much superior in force, skill, and intelligence. But when it is a matter of armies, Italians cannot be compared with foreigners. All this comes from the weakness of the heads, because those who know are not obeyed, and each man thinks he knows. Nor up to this time has there been a man able to raise himself so high, through both ability and fortune, that the others would yield to him. The result is that for the past twenty years, in all the wars that have been fought when there has been an army entirely Italian, it has always made

5. Possibly Cesare Borgia and Francesco Sforza, who were discussed earlier in the book.   6. Pope Leo X (1475–1521) was a Medici (Giovanni de' Medici). *House:* of Medici. *The Prince* was first meant for Giuliano de' Medici. After Giuliano's death it was dedicated to his nephew Lorenzo, later duke of Urbino.   7. Livy's *History* 9.1, para. 10.   8. Another allusion to Moses.   9. Perhaps another reference to Borgia and Sforza.

a bad showing. Proof of this was given first at the Taro, and then at Alessandria, Capua, Genoa, Vailà, Bologna, and Mestri.[1]

If your illustrious House, then, wishes to imitate those excellent men who redeemed their countries, it is necessary, before everything else, to furnish yourself with your own army, as the true foundation of every enterprise. You cannot have more faithful, nor truer, nor better soldiers. And though every individual of these may be good, they become better as a body when they see that they are commanded by their prince, and honored and trusted by him. It is necessary, therefore, that your House should be prepared with such forces, in order that it may be able to defend itself against the foreigners with Italian courage.

And though the Swiss and the Spanish infantry are properly estimated as terribly effective, yet both have defects. Hence a third type would be able not merely to oppose them but to feel sure of overcoming them. The fact is that the Spaniards are not able to resist cavalry, and the Swiss have reason to fear infantry, when they meet any as determined in battle as themselves. For this reason it has been seen and will be seen in experience that the Spaniards are unable to resist the French cavalry, and the Swiss are overthrown by Spanish infantry. And though of this last a clear instance has not been observed, yet an approach to it appeared in the battle of Ravenna,[2] when the Spanish infantry met the German battalions, who use the same methods as the Swiss. There the Spanish, through their ability and the assistance given by their shields, got within the points of the spears from below, and slew their enemies in security, while the Germans could find no means of resistance. If the cavalry had not charged the Spanish, they would have annihilated the Germans. It is possible, then, for one who realizes the defects of these two types, to equip infantry in a new manner, so that it can resist cavalry and not be afraid of foot-soldiers; but to gain this end they must have weapons of the right sorts, and adopt varied methods of combat. These are some of the things which, when they are put into service as novelties, give reputation and greatness to a new ruler.[3]

This opportunity, then, should not be allowed to pass, in order that after so long a time Italy may see her redeemer. I am unable to express with what love he would be received in all the provinces that have suffered from these foreign deluges; with what thirst for vengeance, what firm faith, what piety, what tears! What gates would be shut against him? what peoples would deny him obedience? what envy would oppose itself to him? what Italian would refuse to follow him? This barbarian rule stinks in every nostril. May your illustrious House, then, undertake this charge with the spirit and the hope with which all just enterprises are taken up, in order that, beneath its ensign, our native land may be ennobled, and, under its auspices, that saying of Petrarch may come true: "Manhood[4] will take arms against fury, and the combat will be short, because in Italian hearts the ancient valor is not yet dead."

1. Sites of battles occurring between the end of the century and 1513.　2. Between Spain and France in April 1512.　3. Machiavelli was subsequently the author of the treatise Art of War (1521).　4. An etymological translation of the original virtù (from the Latin vir, "man"). The quotation is from the canzone "My Italy."

LUDOVICO ARIOSTO
1474–1533

The *Orlando Furioso* (Orlando gone crazy), Ludovico Ariosto's seriocomic romance epic, is as witty and playful in tone as it is philosophically and politically serious. The most important achievement of Renaissance Italy's greatest poet, it is also a study in contrasts, at once brilliantly original and self-consciously derivative. Ariosto, like many Renaissance writers, made use of literary "imitation," the method of allusion and adaptation by which writers simultaneously composed original works and competed with their contemporaries and predecessors. While the best "imitations" can be read independently of the literary traditions they engage, their full dimensions emerge only in comparison with the literature they imitate, parody, and honor. Such a poem is *Orlando Furioso,* which blithely recycles classical, medieval, and contemporary texts yet is not hampered by its web of allusions. In his title, which recalls a popular romance epic, *Orlando in Love* (the *Orlando Innamorato* of Count Matteo Maria Boiardo), Ariosto announces his plan to outstrip other poets in the romance epic tradition: he will show how Orlando, under the influence of desire, crosses the line from love to lunacy. As the shift in title indicates, much of Ariosto's humor comes from placing heroes of the past in new and unexpected situations. Readers of this anthology have at their fingertips a wide range of Ariosto's favorite models for his witty, subtle, and often irreverent imitations: the works of Homer, Virgil, Ovid, St. Augustine, Dante, Boccaccio, and Petrarch as well as *The Song of Roland,* from which Ariosto's title hero ultimately derives. The *Orlando Furioso* is, in turn, itself a source of inspiration to such writers of the later Renaissance as Rabelais, Cervantes, Shakespeare, and Milton.

Ludovico Ariosto's life as a poet and diplomat was inextricably woven into the dramatic political career of the Este family of Ferrara. In 1472 Niccolò Ariosti was made a count by Ercole d'Este, duke of Ferrara, for the dubious service of trying to assassinate Ercole's nephew and rival. Niccolò married in 1473, and his firstborn son, Ludovico, was born in Reggio Emilia in 1474. In 1485 Niccolò moved his family to Ferrara, where he prospered in the service of Duke Ercole and pressed his reluctant son to study law. Ludovico preferred poetry and drama, and an apocryphal story told by his affectionate younger brother describes young Ludovico listening humbly while his father severely chastised him for laziness, only to light up joyfully when his father left the room and adapt the lecture to the needs of a comedy he was writing. When Ludovico gained court notice by performing in festivities given for the Sforza family in 1494, Niccolò released his son from legal studies and found him a tutor, the humanist Gregorio da Spoleto. In 1502 Ludovico wrote a poem for the marriage of Alfonso d'Este and Lucrezia Borgia (whom he unblushingly praised as a virgin), and in 1503 he entered the service of Ippolito d'Este, the warlike and profligate cardinal. His most memorable adventure under Ippolito was a diplomatic mission to Pope Julius II: although the pope at first listened tolerantly to Ariosto's speech, he lost patience when a second diplomat arrived with the same message, and threatened to hang one and throw the other (Ariosto) in the Tiber River.

Ariosto assumed financial responsibility for his family when his father died in 1500, and his financial distresses at times interfered with his work on the *Orlando Furioso.* Cardinal Ippolito could be demanding, stingy, and unprincipled (for example, he had his servants put out the eyes of his half brother because they had attracted the interest of Angela Borgia, whom the Cardinal himself passionately desired); but he understood Ariosto's importance as a poet well enough to finance the publication of the first edition of the *Orlando Furioso* in 1516. When Ariosto refused to join him on a mission to Hungary in 1517, however, he fired the poet on the spot, and Ariosto transferred his services to the more cultured Duke Alfonso in 1518. The financial strains that threatened Ariosto's family worsened when one of his cousins died intestate: Duke

Alfonso appropriated the inheritance and, despite litigation, refused to reconsider his action. Alfonso was himself strapped for cash in his constant negotiations with the Venetian Republic, King Francis I of France, and the Emperor Charles V to keep the pope from seizing Ferrara; his solution to Ariosto's financial woes was to make him governor of the bandit-infested Ganfagnana in 1522 (the year after the second edition of the *Orlando Furioso* appeared). In 1525, after begging for release from his onerous administrative duties, Ariosto returned to Ferrara, to Alessandra Benucci—the great love of life—and his beloved son, Virginio, and to his poetic labors. He died in 1533 after seeing the final edition of the *Orlando Furioso* through publication in 1532.

Variety and broad scope are the hallmarks of the *Orlando Furioso*. The mood of the poem moves up and down the scale of genres, from epic fury to romance dalliance to pastoral repose, from tragedy to comedy, from panegyric (song of praise) to satire, and from the sublime to the grotesque. Characters within the poem also explore heights and depths: in a parody of Dante's pilgrimage through hell and purgatory to paradise in *The Divine Comedy*, the comic knight Astolfo visits hell but, finding the stench unbearable, heads upward to the earthly paradise at the highest point of the world (in Nubia) and finally leaves the terrestrial sphere to visit the moon. Range also characterizes the *Orlando Furioso*'s geography, which stretches from France, Italy, Spain, Holland, England, Scotland, India, Tunisia, Libya, Syria, and Nubia to Byzantium and beyond. From these diverse countries come Christian and pagan knights who mingle and clash as they try to make names for themselves. The breadth of the *Orlando Furioso*'s survey of Europe, the Levant, and the New World is matched by the depth of its scrutiny of human psychology and of the interior lives of its characters. During the course of the poem, its Christians and pagans, men and women, nobles and servants find themselves in wild adventures and compromising situations, which cause them to experience every passion dreamed of in the philosophy of Ariosto's day.

Wrath and desire are the passions Ariosto explores in greatest depth, and no character experiences them more violently than Orlando. For the first twenty-three cantos of the poem, he pursues his obsessive love for the beautiful Chinese princess, Angelica; at the poem's exact center, he enters into a frenzy of epic proportions (if not beyond). Although love-madness is considered sacred by the Neoplatonic philosophers of Renaissance Italy, Orlando's "great folly" turns out to be debasing and profane. We might consider Orlando's love-madness in light of Ariosto's many images of horsemen governing and giving way to impetuous horses that stand for the passions. In the allegory of the soul presented in Plato's dialogue the *Phaedrus*, Socrates describes the soul as three-part and compares it to a charioteer managing two contrasting horses, which represent the divine and physical dimensions of desire. Whereas one of the horses is easily restrained, well-formed, and noble, the other is willful, misshapen, and lustful. If the charioteer attains the Platonic ideal and masters the stubborn wrath of the lustful horse, his love becomes holy. For Ariosto, however, passion brings less insight into spiritual matters than it brings ethical blindness and psychological confusion. When Orlando discovers that Angelica loves another man and that the pair have consummated their mutual passion, he experiences a "deep, bitter hate" and a "burning wrath" that leave him motionless on the grass for three days and nights without food or sleep, after which

his bitter agony grew and grew until it drove him out of his mind.
On the fourth day, worked into a great frenzy, he stripped off his armor and chain-mail. / The helmet landed here, the shield there, more pieces of armor further off, the breastplate further still: arms and armor all found their resting-place here and there about the wood. Then he tore off his clothes and exposed his hairy belly and all his chest and back.
Now began the great madness, so horrifying that none will ever know a worse instance. / He fell into a frenzy so violent that his every sense was darkened.

Abandoning his duty, his reason, and his very identity, Orlando is soon more bestial than human and, in fact, comes to behave exactly like the lustful and rebellious horse in Plato's allegory. When he comes across Angelica, he gallops after her in an attempt to rape her, kill her, or eat her (it is hard to say which), but he lands on her horse after Angelica has fallen off: "He followed the steed across the bare sand, constantly gaining on her; now he could touch her . . . he had her by the mane . . . now by the bridle . . . at last he held her. / He seized her as gleefully as another man would a maiden." Crazed Orlando rides the poor beast to death and drags it yet further; as Ariosto remarks, Angelica herself would have fared no better.

Orlando's story is not the sole, or even the most important, of Ariosto's tales; the poet weaves into a single tapestry an extraordinary range of story lines. In addition to Orlando's amorous search, his great madness, and the devastation they bring to his dearest friends, for example, Ariosto describes the trials of the woman Orlando pursues, following Angelica as she flees from a series of lecherous men (including some of Ariosto's redoubtable heroes) and discovers passion with Medor, the one man who demands nothing of her. Ariosto also presents the travails of the hero Rinaldo, an admirer of Angelica who eventually learns important lessons about marriage, trust, and jealousy. In further strands, the poet narrates the adventures of a woman warrior, Marfisa, who encounters a colony of man-hating women and a city governed by a woman-hating tyrant, and he traces the development of Rodomont, a proud and warlike follower of Islam, into the poem's antihero. As the description of even a few of the poem's story lines indicates, it is easy, while reading the *Orlando Furioso*, to become so engrossed in the pleasures of romance adventures that one periodically "forgets" to notice how artfully Ariosto controls the design of his larger narrative.

What is more, readers swept up in the romance often fail to care about the moral purpose that, according to ancient and contemporary defenses of poetry, justifies pleasure in reading. When readers grow entranced by Ariosto's narrative digressions from and suspensions of the moral, they resemble Ariosto's own wandering and desiring characters. To this extent, Ariosto's poem mirrors his enchanted castle in which "the ladies and knights who venture" into it chase after various objects of desire:

> they all imagine they are espying the object of their quest, be it a lady, a page, a friend, or comrade—human desire differing in its objectives. So they search the palace through and through to no avail; and yet so great is their hope and their desire to find what they are searching for that they are unable to tear themselves away.

Prisoners of their own desires and illusions, characters in the labyrinthine castle seem caught in an eternal moment of pursuit. Much as Ariosto's readers suspend the educative purpose of reading for the sensual pleasures of romance, the characters run in circles both literally and figuratively.

As the design of the *Orlando Furioso* gradually takes shape, a larger purpose dominates the story lines. The main story, which comes from epic rather than romance, concerns the founding of the Este dynasty at Ferrara, the family and court that Ariosto served. Ariosto's premiere lady knight, Bradamant, undertakes an epic quest to rescue and marry her beloved Ruggiero, the young pagan knight destined to become the father of the Este family. Ruggiero's adventures in love, arms, and religious conversion form the theme of the "education of the prince" that is central to many Renaissance epics. Throughout the *Orlando Furioso*, Ruggiero faces ethical dilemmas: should he choose the seductive witch, Alcina, or his betrothed, Bradamant? After he rescues the gorgeous, naked Angelica from the virgin-eating sea monster, should he seize her for himself? Should he return to his liege lord, the pagan king Agrican, or conclude his personal quest? The pattern of evaluating moral alternatives casts Ruggiero as a new Hercules, the legendary hero of the Greco-Roman world who faced the choice between Virtue and Vice when he came to a crossroads. Ruggiero has a more complicated problem: if he has the power to know the good, does he also have the strength to choose the good? For Renaissance interpreters of Hercules's story, the difficulty lay not in recognizing but in choosing the better course of action: "I see the better, but choose the worse," Petrarch remarked in a line that might stand as an epigraph for Ariosto's poem. For Ariosto, the scene of Hercules-at-the-crossroads brings up the central question of the will: are human beings masters or slaves of their passions? Are moral deliberations doomed, for the most part, to end in the justification of acts one knows to be wrong? Ruggiero's final choice radically tests his heroic character: at the end of the poem, he must choose between his loyalty to his liege lord, who made Ruggiero a knight, and his newly plighted troth to Charlemagne, Christianity, and Bradamant. Since loyalty to one side means a betrayal of the other, he has no irreproachable choice between virtue and vice. Ruggiero must choose between two distinct models of faith and their systems of self-esteem; not until the end of the poem, when Rodomont challenges him as a "betrayer of the faith," is he in a position to prove, in combat, that his choice was the most virtuous. The epic component of the poem, dedicated to the loftier and directly political goals of Ariosto's poem, ultimately defines heroic identity as forceful yet cautious—qualities Ariosto views as appropriate to the court at Ferrara in fifteenth-century Italy.

The wandering, digressive nature of Ariostan romance comes to an ending of high seriousness when Ruggiero converts to Christianity, emerges as the poem's true hero (in place of Orlando), and founds the Este dynasty. At the poem's conclusion, Ariosto draws all of its populous world back to the Christian camp for a final battle between Ruggiero and Rodomont, the pagan antihero. Bradamant undergoes a social "conversion" when she discards her armor and independence before marrying Ruggiero. The fantastically resilient knights who once battled headless giants and sea monsters begin to confront tragic loss and death. The poem's vast geographical range and cultural mix shrink into a moralized opposition between East and West, pagan and Christian. By its ending, the *Orlando Furioso* shifts from an exploratory to a prescriptive mood: after enthusiastically testing authority and raising doubts during the vast bulk of the poem, Ariosto finally establishes fixed values and beliefs. With the move into epic seriousness, the *Orlando Furioso* acknowledges a certain loss of imaginative freedom that accompanies the triumph of civilized order; simultaneously, it confers on the Este family a memorable role in the cultural achievement of Renaissance Italy.

Orlando Furioso[1]

CANTO 1

I sing of knights and ladies, of love and arms, of courtly chivalry,[2] of courageous deeds—all from the time when the Moors crossed the sea from Africa and wrought havoc in France. I shall tell of the anger, the fiery rage of young Agramant their king, whose boast it was that he would avenge himself on Charles, Emperor of Rome, for King Trojan's[3] death. / I shall tell of Orlando,[4] setting down what has never before been recounted in prose or rhyme: of Orlando, driven raving mad by love—and he a man who had been always esteemed for his great prudence—if she,[5] who has reduced me almost to a like condition, and even now is eroding my last fragments of sanity, leaves me yet with sufficient to complete what I have undertaken. / Seed of Ercole, adornment and splendor of our age, Hippolytus,[6] great of heart, may

1. Translated by Guido Waldman.   2. Ariosto expands the opening line of Virgil's *Aeneid*, "I sing of arms and the man" (which Robert Fitzgerald expansively translates, "I sing of warfare and a man at war").   3. Agramant's father, killed by Orlando in Provence. *Moors*: Arabs who invaded France during the reign of Charles Martel.   4. Nephew of Charlemagne and hero of *The Song of Roland* and Boiardo's *Orlando Innamorato*.   5. Ariosto's great love was Alessandra Benucci.   6. Ippolito d'Este, son of Duke Ercole, and Ariosto's patron.

it please you to accept this which your lowly servant would, and alone is able to, give you. My debt to you I can in part repay with words, with an outlay of ink; hold me not, though, a parsimonious giver, for all I have to give, I give you. / Among the most illustrious heroes to whose names I am about to pay honor you will hear mention of Ruggiero,[7] your forefather, the founder of your noble line. I shall tell you of his pre-eminent valor, his splendid actions, if you will pay heed to me and make room in your mind, busied with matters of moment, for these my verses. /

Orlando, who had long been in love with the beautiful Angelica,[8] and who had for her sake left countless immortal trophies in India, in Media, in Tartary, had now returned with her to the West, to where, at the foot of the lofty Pyrenees, King Charlemagne and the hosts of France and Germany were assembled in their tented camp to / force Kings Agramant and Marsilius[9] once more to lament their rash stupidity—the one for leading from Africa as many men as could bear lance and sword; the other for inciting Spain to visit destruction upon the lovely realm of France. So Orlando arrived at a good moment; but he was quick to regret his return, / for his lady was taken from him. Such is the waywardness of human judgment! The damsel, whom he had defended so constantly all the way from the Hesperides to the shores of Sunrise, was taken from him now, now that he was surrounded by friends, in his own land, with not a blow struck. It was the wise emperor, anxious to extinguish a serious fire, who took her from him. / A quarrel had arisen a few days earlier between Count Orlando and his cousin Rinaldo, for both of them were aflame with love for this ravishing beauty. Charles, who could not abide this conflict, which rendered them questionable allies, gave this damsel, the cause of the quarrel, into the keeping of Namo, Duke of Bavaria; / and promised her as a prize to whichever of the two slaughtered the greater number of Infidels[1] and wrought him the worthiest assistance in the vital conflict of that day. The outcome, however, was not in keeping with their prayers: the ranks of the baptized were put to flight, and among the many captives was the duke, whose tent was abandoned. /

Here the damsel was left who was to have been the victor's prize; she had mounted her horse before the crucial moment and, when that came, foreseeing that Fortune was that day to turn traitor to those of the Christian faith, she turned and fled. Entering a wood and following a narrow path she came upon a knight who was approaching on foot. / He wore a breastplate, and on his head a helmet; his sword hung by his side, and on his arm he bore his shield; and he came running through the forest more fleet of foot than the lightly-clad athlete sprinting for the red mantle at the village games. Never did a timid shepherd-girl start back more violently from a horrid snake than did Angelica, jerking on the reins the moment she saw the armed man approach on foot. / The man was none other than Rinaldo, son of Aymon, lord of Montauban, and a doughty paladin, whose charger,[2] Bayard, had only a little earlier made off without him—a strange turn of affairs. When his eyes lit on the woman, he recognized her angel's countenance, even from a distance, and the lovely face which held him in amorous thraldom. / The damsel turned her palfrey's head and galloped off through the forest at full tilt. She made no attempt to choose the best and surest path, or to avoid the

---

7. Progenitor of the Este dynasty.   8. Daughter of the khan of Cathay and great Petrarchan beauty, as her "angelic" face suggests (cf. Petrarch's sonnet 126 above).   9. King of Spain and ally of Agramant. 1. Chivalric romances refer to all non-Christians as "infidels," "Saracens," and "pagans."   2. Horse.

thickets and the underbrush: pale and trembling and quite unstrung, she left it to her horse to find his own way through. High and low, on and on through the deep, grim forest she coursed, until she came to a river. /

On the river-bank stood Ferrau,[3] clothed in sweat and grime: a great need to slake his thirst and to rest had withdrawn him early from the battle. But here he was now forced to tarry, for in his greedy haste to drink he had dropped his helmet into the river, and was still trying to recover it. / The damsel, screaming with terror, came galloping in headlong flight. Hearing her voice, the Saracen leapt up the bank and peered at her face. As soon as she was close he recognized her: many a day though it was since he had last had news of her, and pale and distraught though she now appeared, she could be none other than the fair Angelica. / As he was chivalrous, and no less hot-headed than the two cousins, he hastened boldly to her rescue, reckless of his lost helmet. Drawing his sword, he ran full of menace toward Rinaldo, who feared him but little: many a time had they set eyes on each other, and indeed tested each other's valor at arms. / Both of them were on foot as they flung themselves upon each other with naked sword; no armor plate, no chain-mail could have resisted the blows they delivered—enough to split an anvil. Now, while the two warriors were hewing each other, the damsel's horse had perforce to pick his way with care, for as hard as she could dig her heels she spurred him faster and faster through the woods and fields. / For a long time the two champions strove in vain each to gain the upper hand, but neither was less skilled than the other in the use of arms.

The lord of Montauban it was who first broke silence and addressed the Spanish knight, and spoke like one whose heart is all consumed with fire. / "You are thinking," said he to the pagan, "that you will be doing injury to me alone, and yet you will hurt yourself as well as me: if all this is because the brilliant rays of the new Sun have set your heart afire, what do you win by delaying me here? Even if you were to take my life or capture me, the beautiful lady will not be yours for all that—see, while we tarry here, she is slipping away. / You would do far better, if you still love her, to go and stand in her path, make her stop, detain her before she goes any further. Once we have her in our keeping, then let us make trial with our swords to see whose she should be. Otherwise, after a weary struggle, I can see that we shall both be the losers." /

The pagan was not displeased with the proposal, and so they deferred their battle; indeed, the truce so drew them together, excluding from their thoughts both hatred and anger, that as they departed from the refreshing stream, the pagan would not suffer good Aymon's son to go on foot, but pressed him to come up and mount behind him; then they galloped away after Angelica. / Great was the goodness of the knights of old! Here they were, rivals, of different faiths, and they still ached all over from the cruel and vicious blows they had dealt each other; still, off they went together in mutual trust, through the dark woods and crooked paths. Goaded by four spurs, the charger came to a fork where the road divided. / Here, not knowing which path the damsel had taken (for in both there were fresh tracks which were not to be distinguished from each other), they left the decision to Fate: Rinaldo took the one path, the Saracen the other.

Ferrau thrust further and further through the wood, and in the end found

3. Nephew of Marsilius.

himself at the place whence he had started. / Back he was by the river's side, at the point where his helmet had fallen in. With no further hope of finding the damsel, he went down to the water's edge to recover his helmet where it lay buried in the river; but it was sunk so deep in sand that he was to have much work to do ere he set hands on it. / He had fashioned a long pole out of the branch of a tree, shorn of its foliage, and with this he searched the river bed, prodding and poking every inch of it. While he was thus passing the time with ill-contained impatience, he noticed a knight of fierce countenance emerging chest-deep from the middle of the river. / He was fully armed except for his head, and in his right hand he bore a helmet: the very helmet for which Ferrau had so long been searching in vain. He addressed Ferrau with angry words and said: "O vile deceiver,[4] why take you so ill the loss of your helmet when you should long ago have surrendered it to me? / Remember, pagan, when you killed Angelica's brother (I am he): you promised me that after a few days you would throw the helmet into the river, after the other arms. If Fortune now carries my wishes into effect (which you were unwilling to do), be not dismayed. Or rather, be dismayed, if you must, but at your faithlessness. / But if you still crave for a fine helmet, find yourself another one, and acquire it with greater honor. Orlando the paladin has such a one, and Rinaldo too—perhaps his is even better; the one belonged once to Almont, the other to Mambrino.[5] Bear off one of those two with your valor, for this you would do well to leave to me, as earlier you promised." /

When the phantom surged up out of the water, the Saracen's hair stood on end and he paled, and his voice died in his throat. Then, hearing Argalia[6] tax him with his broken pledge (Argalia was he called, whom he had slain here), he blazed inwardly with fury, and blushed for shame. / Having no time to invent an excuse, and well knowing that the phantom spoke true, he made no answer, but kept his lips sealed; his spirit, though, was so pierced with shame that he swore on Lanfusa's[7] life to set his heart on no helmet other than the prize one that Orlando had wrested once from proud Almont's head in Aspromont. / This oath he observed more faithfully than that which he had earlier sworn. He set off, then, in such a bitter mood that many days later he still fretted and fumed. His only thought was to seek out the paladin, searching wherever he thought he might be. Rinaldo, following another route from Ferrau's, encountered different adventures. / He had not gone far before his fiery charger leapt into view. "Stop, Bayard, oh stop! I cannot endure to be without you." Deaf to his words, the steed would not approach, but drew away from him, faster and faster. Rinaldo followed, consumed with anger. But let us pursue Angelica in her flight. /

Through fearful dark woods she fled, through wild, desolate and deserted places. The stirring of a branch, of a green leaf of oak, elm or beech would make her swerve in fright; at each shadow she espied, whether by hill or dale, she imagined that Rinaldo was still close behind her. / Like a baby fawn or kid, who has watched through the leaves of the wood where he was born, and has seen the leopard's fangs close on his mother's throat, seen her flank and breast torn open; he flees through the thickets to escape the monster,

---

4. Argalia's insult in full, "deceiver of your faith, *marano*," refers to the converted Jews in Spain and to the Spanish Moslems, who, after the fall of Granada in 1492, also fell under the surveillance of the Inquisition.
5. A king killed by Rinaldo; his helmet originally belonged to Hector of Troy. *Almont:* brother of Trojan, killed by Orlando in Aspromont. 6. Angelica's brother, killed by Ferraù. 7. Ferraù's mother.

trembling with terror and alarm; and every time he brushes against a twig he sees himself already in the cruel beast's jaws. / That day and night, and half the next day onward she pressed, and knew not whither. At last she came to a pleasant grove whose trees gently rustled in a delicious breeze; two limpid brooks murmured close by so that the grass was ever fresh and tender; the quiet waters, breaking as they flowed softly over the little pebbles, sounded musically. / Here she felt safe, and a thousand miles from Rinaldo, and she decided to rest a little from her weary journey and the summer's heat. She stepped down amid the flowers and, unbridling her horse, let him wander away to graze by the crystal waters whose verges were fresh with new grass. / Close by she noticed a beautiful thicket of flowering hawthorn and red roses mirrored in the limpid rippling water and sheltered from the sun by tall shady oaks. It was hollowed in the middle and offered a refreshing bower amid the deepest shade: the branches and leaves were so disposed that no sun—nor indeed any lesser observer—could peep in. / Soft young grass made an inviting bed for whoever ventured here. The lovely damsel stepped into the bower, lay down, and fell asleep. Not for long, however, for she thought she heard the trample of approaching feet. Silently she arose, and espied an armored knight who had come to the water's edge. /

Whether he be friend or foe she could not tell; her doubting heart was assailed by hope and fear; as she waited to see how it would turn out, not so much as a sigh did she permit to escape her lips. The knight sat down on the bank of the stream and rested his cheek on his arm; so deeply did he lapse into thought that he might have been turned to unfeeling stone. / More than an hour, my Lord,[8] the sorrowing knight sat, his head bowed in thought. Then he began to lament, a mournful, weary sound, and yet so sweet that out of compassion the very rocks would have split, and a cruel tigress would have turned gentle.

He sighed and wept; tears streamed down his cheeks. His heart was a furnace. / He spoke: "You, thought, who set my heart afire and turn it to ice, and cause the pain which ever gnaws within me, what am I to do? For I have been late in coming, and another has been first to cull the fruit.[9] Little has fallen to me but words and looks while another has gathered the best of the crop. If I am to be denied both fruit and blossom, why does my heart keep aching for her? / A virgin is like a rose: while she remains on the thorn whence she sprang, alone and safe in a lovely garden, no flock, no shepherd approaches. The gentle breeze and the dewy dawn, water, and earth pay her homage; amorous youths and loving maidens like to deck their brows with her, and their breasts. / But no sooner is she plucked from her mother-stalk, severed from her green stem, than she loses all, all the favor, grace, and beauty wherewith heaven and men endowed her. The virgin who suffers one to cull her flower—of which she should be more jealous than of her own fair eyes, than of her life—loses the esteem she once enjoyed in the hearts of all her other wooers. / Let her be abhorred by those others, and loved only by him to whom she gave herself so abundantly. O cruel enemy, Fortune! The others triumph and I die of need. What then: am I to find her no longer pleasing? Am I to relinquish my own heart's life? Ah, let this day be my last, let me live no longer if I am no longer to love her." /

8. Ippolito d'Este.   9. Angelica's virginity.

Should anyone ask me who it is who was shedding such copious tears into the brook, well, he was the King of Circassia, the love-lorn Sacripant. Love, let me add, was the prime and only cause for his cruel sorrow: he was, indeed, one of the lovers of this damsel, who at once recognized him. / For love of her he had come out of the East to where the sun sets, for in India he had learned, to his great sorrow, that she had followed Orlando to the West; then in France he had learned how the emperor had set her apart, promising her as the prize to whichever of the two yielded greater assistance to the Golden Lilies.[1] He had been in the field of battle, had witnessed the rout of King Charlemagne. He had gone in search of fair Angelica, but so far he had been unable to find her. This, then, was the sad tale, this the plight which weighed so heavy on his love-lorn heart, provoking his grief to utterance in words which might have made even the sun pause for pity. /

While he was thus lamenting and shedding hot tears in copious streams, and uttering these words and many more which I think I need not relate, by a fortunate turn in his affairs, his words came to the ears of Angelica; and so in one hour he reached a point which otherwise he would never have reached, not in a thousand years. / The lovely woman paid the closest attention to the tears, the speech and behavior of this man who was so assiduous a lover, even though this was not the first time she had heard him. Hard, though, and cold as a stone pillar, she would not stoop to pity: it would seem she disdained all human kind, and believed that no man was worthy of her. / And yet, seeing herself all alone amid those woods, she conceived the idea of taking him as a guide—for when the water is up to your neck you must be truly stubborn not to cry for help. If she let this occasion slip she would never again find so trusty an escort: she had already long experience of the king's rare fidelity in love. / She had no mind, however, to alleviate the misery which rent her lover, or to heal the wounds he had suffered by affording him the pleasure which all lovers crave. No, she would spin a tale, devise a subterfuge to maintain him in hope for so long as she had need of him; afterwards, she would revert to her accustomed hardness. /

Forth she stepped from the blind concealment of the thicket, and made so radiant and unlooked-for an appearance, she might have been Diana, or Venus[2] issuing forth from a shady grove. Emerging, she said: "Peace be with you. God protect you and my good name: pray, do not entertain so false an opinion of me—it goes against all reason." / Never was such joy, such amazement to be seen in a mother's eyes when she lifted them to look on her son whom she had bewailed and lamented for dead as she heard the troops return without him: such, though, was the Saracen's joy, such his wonder on suddenly beholding her angel's face, her graceful movements, her overwhelming presence. / Brimful of gentle, loving thoughts he ran to his lady, his goddess, who threw her arms tightly about his neck—which she would perhaps not have done in her native Cathay. Now that she had his company, her thoughts turned to her father's kingdom, the cradle of her birth; hope suddenly revived in her of soon regaining her precious home. / She told him all that had befallen her since the day when she had sent him to the King of the Nabateans of Sericana to ask for help; and how Orlando had frequently saved her from death and outrage and all manner of evils; and how her virginal flower

---

1. Charlemagne's emblem.   2. Goddess of love. *Diana:* goddess of virginity and the hunt.

was still as intact as the day she had borne it from her mother's womb. / This may have been true, but scarcely plausible to anyone in his right mind; to him it seemed quite possible, however, lost as he was in a far deeper delusion. What a man sees, Love can make invisible—and what is invisible, that can Love make him see. This, then, was believed, for a poor wretch will readily believe whatever suits him. / "If the knight of Anglant[3] was so stupid as to neglect his opportunity, so much the worse for him: never again will Fortune offer him so rare a gift," remarked Sacripant to himself. "Far be it from me to imitate him, foregoing the offer of so great a good and then having only myself to blame. / I shall pluck the morning-fresh rose which I might lose were I to delay. Full well I know that there is nothing that a woman finds so delectable and pleasing, even when she pretends to resent it and will sometimes burst into tears. I shall not be put off by any repulse or show of anger, but shall carry into effect what I propose." /

Thus spoke he. But while he was preparing for his gentle assault, a terrible din from the wood close by resounded in his ears, so that he regretfully had to give up his enterprise, and put on his helmet—for it was his habit to go about fully armed. He approached his charger, bridled him, climbed into the saddle and grasped his lance. / Out of the wood a knight appeared. Stalwart and proud was his mien. His raiment was white as snow, and a white plume crested his helmet. King Sacripant could not endure this importunate fellow's arrival, just in time to interfere with the pleasure which lay in store, and the look he darted at him was fraught with menace. / When the other drew near he challenged him to battle, confident that he would sweep him from the saddle. But the other, who did not deem himself a jot inferior, and was ready to prove it, cut short his haughty threats, setting spurs to his steed and lowering his lance. Sacripant was off, too, like a hurricane, and they charged straight at each other. / No lions in the tall scrub, no bulls charging each other full tilt ever met with the impact of those two knights: each ran his lance through the other's shield. The clash reverberated all about, from the grassy valleys even to the summits of the barren hills. Lucky it was that the warriors wore good, sound breastplates, for these defended their chests. / Neither steed swerved from his course, indeed they butted each other head on, like rams. The pagan warrior's died almost instantly; alive, he had proved himself a champion. The other's fell also, but no sooner did he feel the prick of the spurs in his side than he rose to his feet. But the horse of the Saracen king lay inert, his full weight resting upon his master.[4]

The unknown champion, who had remained in the saddle and seen the other overthrown, horse and rider, decided he had had enough of this skirmish and felt no need to carry it further. So he pulled away and rode off at a fast gallop along the path which ran straight through the forest; and before the pagan had extricated himself, the other was little short of a mile away. / Just as a ploughman, dazed and stunned, gets up when the lightning has passed, from where the shattering thunderburst has thrown him down beside his dead oxen; he gets up and beholds the pine standing bereft of its leaves and of its dignity, the very pine he was accustomed to see in the distance. So it was with the pagan when he regained his feet. Angelica had been witness of this dire event. / He sighed and groaned, not because his arm or

---

3. Orlando.   4. Horses traditionally depict passions that must be reined in.

foot may have been broken or sprained, but simply for shame: never in his life, before or since, was his face so red. This was not only because of his fall, but all the more so in that his lady it was who had pulled the heavy weight off him. He would have remained dumb, I am convinced, were it not that she restored him to speech. / "Alas, good sir, take it not so hardly," she said, "for it was no fault of yours if you fell, but rather of the horse, who was less prepared for another fray than for rest and nourishment. Nor will this have added a jot to that warrior's glory, for he was quite clearly the loser: this is how I construe it, inasmuch as he was the first to leave the field." /

While she was thus consoling the Saracen, who should arrive at a gallop but a messenger, mounted on a palfrey; he carried his horn and his pouch at his side, and looked tired and dispirited. When he drew near to Sacripant he asked him whether he had seen a warrior come this way through the forest, with a white shield and crested with a white plume. / "As you see, he has overthrown me, and has only just departed," replied Sacripant. "Now tell me his name, so that I may know who it was who unseated me." "On that point," said the other, "I can satisfy you at once. You must know that the rare valor which swept you from the saddle was that of a gentle damsel. / She is brave, but, more than that, she is beautiful. Her name is famous and I shall keep it from you no longer: it is Bradamant[5] who has stripped you of all the honors you have won hitherto."

With these words he galloped off, leaving the Saracen far from pleased: he knew not what to do or say, and blushed crimson with shame. / After long and useless reflection on what had taken place, coming back always to his defeat by a woman—the more he thought about it, the more it hurt—he mounted the other horse without a word; and without a word he drew Angelica up behind him, and reserved her for happier entertainment in more tranquil surroundings. /

They had not gone two miles when a terrific noise filled the forest all about and seemed to send a shiver through it from end to end. Shortly after, a great war-horse came into view, richly caparisoned in cloth-of-gold; he came bounding over streams, over briars, and splintered trees and whatever else stood in his path. / "If the deep shade and the thickly meshed foliage do not impair my vision," said the damsel, "this charger forcing his boisterous passage through the choked wood is Bayard. Yes, this is certainly Bayard, I recognize him. Ah, how well he understands our need: one palfrey is quite unsuited to carry the two of us, and he is coming quickly to our assistance." / The Circassian dismounted and approached the horse, meaning to grasp his reins. But the charger pivoted round quick as a flash and presented his hindquarters; he did not reach the point, though, of unleashing a kick. A sad knight he would have been, had he been struck full on, for the horse had such power in his heels, he could have shattered a whole mountain of metal. / Then he meekly approached the damsel; he was almost human in his gesture of humility, like a dog dancing around his master who has just returned after a few days' absence. Bayard still remembered her, for she had tended him in Albracca in the days when she was so enamored of Rinaldo, who was so cruel to her then, so unresponsive to her love. / She took his reins in her left hand, and with the other hand she caressed his neck and chest.

---

5. Lady knight, Rinaldo's sister, and future mother of the Este dynasty, she is on her epic quest to find and marry her beloved Ruggiero.

The horse, who was of remarkable intelligence, submitted to her as meekly as a lamb. Sacripant meanwhile seized his opportunity: he mounted Bayard and spurred him and reined him in. Now that her own steed was lightened of his burden, the damsel moved from his hindquarters and resumed her place in the saddle. /

She happened then to look round, and her eyes fell upon a man of imposing stature advancing on foot, with much clanking of armor. She flared up with anger and vexation, for she recognized him as Rinaldo, Duke Aymon's son. He loved her, coveted her more than his life, but she loathed and avoided him, as a crane will flee from a falcon. Once upon a time it was he who hated her worse than death, while she loved him; now they had changed roles. / And the cause was to be found in two springs in the Ardennes,[6] not far apart, whose waters produce diverging effects: the one inclines the heart to love, whereas love loses place in the heart of whoever drinks from the other; what first is fire turns to ice. Rinaldo had tasted the one, and love held him in thrall: Angelica the other, and she hated and shunned him. / The effect of that liquid blended with secret venom, transforming love into loathing, was to cast a pall over the damsel's limpid eyes the moment she had set them upon Rinaldo. With tremulous voice and anxious face she begged and entreated Sacripant not to wait for the warrior to approach any nearer, but to turn with her and flee. /

"Am I," replied the Saracen, "am I held in so little esteem by you, that you reckon me of no use, of no avail to defend you against him? Have you already forgotten the battles at Albracca, and the night when I alone stood as your shield and refuge against Agrican and all his men?" / She made no answer, and knew not what to do, for Rinaldo was now too close at hand: he arrived threatening the Saracen from a distance once he saw and recognized the horse, and recognized the angel-face which had kindled a furnace in his heart. What passed between these two champions I mean to defer to the next canto.

Summary   Bradamant seeks Ruggiero, who has been captured and confined in an enchanted castle by his protector, the sorcerer Atlas. Pinabello, from the enemy house of Maganza, pushes Bradamant into an underground cavern that turns out to be the tomb of Merlin, wizard of the Arthurian legends. Merlin's spirit prophesies the coming Este dynasty, of which Bradamant and Ruggiero will be the progenitors, and the sorceress Melissa describes Bradamant's illustrious female descendants. Melissa also tells her how to destroy Atlas's spell and free Ruggiero. When Bradamant succeeds, the two lovers greet each other ecstatically, but they are swiftly separated when Ruggiero mounts Atlas's flying steed, the hippogryph (a cross between a horse and a gryphon), who takes to flight and carries Ruggiero away from the lamenting Bradamant.

FROM CANTOS 6 AND 7

[Ruggiero Visits the Isle of Alcina and Logistilla]

* * *

But now it is time to return to Ruggiero, still coursing through the sky on the wind-borne beast. / Courageous man that he was, Ruggiero's face

---

6. In Boiardo's poem, Angelica loved Rinaldo, who hated her, until she drank from a stream that caused hatred at the very moment that he drank from another whose waters induced love.

retained its normal hue; but I do believe that his heart within him was trembling like a leaf. He had left the European mainland far behind him, and had passed way out beyond the bounds which matchless Hercules had set for mariners.[7] / That great and wondrous bird, the hippogryph, bore him away so fast in winged flight that he far outpaced the eagle when it guides the falling thunderbolt. No creature sweeps through the air at a speed to equal his—I doubt whether thunder and lightning are more swift when they dart from the heavens. / The winged steed, after flying straight as an arrow for many a league, never once deflecting from his course, finally, as though sated with the air, began in lazy gyres to descend upon an island. After long hiding from her lover and taxing his constancy, the virgin Arethusa[8] came to just such an island by a dark, hollow passage beneath the sea. /

No lovelier, no happier land than this did he behold of any over which the steed had stretched his wings; were he to search the whole wide world, a more delightful land than this he would never find; here the great bird, after a broad circular sweep, descended with Ruggiero. Here were well-tilled plains and neat hills, limpid waters, shady banks, and soft meadows, / enticing thickets of cool laurel, of palms and loveliest myrtle, of cedar and orange-trees whose fruit and blossoms were disposed in sundry harmonious ways—these all afforded shade, with their thick spreading foliage, against the searing heat of the summer's day. And, safe amid their branches, flitted melodious nightingales. / Hares and rabbits were to be espied hopping among the deep-red roses and white lilies which a temperate breeze kept ever fresh; and deer, holding high their splendid heads, roamed about, stooping to crop the grass, quite unafraid that any might slay or capture them. Fawns and nimble goats skipped deftly—many was their number in these rustic parts. /

When the hippogryph was so close to the ground that to jump from his back would be less perilous, Ruggiero quickly slipped from the saddle and set foot on the green sward. He kept firm hold of the reins, though, lest the steed once more took wing, and tethered him to a green myrtle branch growing by the sea, by the water's edge, between a laurel and a pine. / And close by, where a spring bubbled up surrounded by cedars and fruitful palms, he set down his shield, drew off his helm and gauntlets, and turned his face now to the sea, now to the hills to capture the fresh vigorous breeze which, with a cheerful murmur, set the high tree-tops—the beeches and firs—a-rustling. / He dipped his parched lips in the fresh crystal pool and splashed himself to cool his veins, for he was overheated in his armor and little wonder if he found it burdensome, for not a solitary soul had presented himself for battle, and here he had travelled, all of three thousand miles at a stretch, armed to the teeth. /

While Ruggiero was here, his steed, which he had left in the cool shade of a dense thicket, shied away, frightened by I know not what he had descried in the tangled wood. He so tore apart the myrtle to which he was tethered that he became ensnared in the branches strewn underfoot; he tugged at the myrtle, bringing down a shower of leaves, but was unable to pull free. / If a log with but a soft core of pith is placed in the fire, it starts to whine, because the intense heat consumes the vaporous air inside it, and it sizzles noisily so long as the vapor forces a way out. Just so, the damaged myrtle moaned and

---

7. Columns established by Hercules, marking the limits of the Western world: the straits of Gibraltar.
8. Ovidian nymph transformed into a spring as she tried to elude the river god, Alpheus; her stream took an underground course to an island, where his waters joined hers.

hissed in vexation, and finally a sad, tearful voice / issued from an open pore, and framed words pronounced with utmost clarity: "If you are good and kind, as your fair looks suggest, loose this animal from my branches. Let my own ill-fortune be sufficient torment without the addition of more evil, more pain inflicted upon me from without." / At the first sound of this voice Ruggiero turned his face and jumped up; when he realized that it issued from the tree, he was no little astonished.[9]

He hastened to untie the hippogryph and, blushing for shame, "Whatever you are," he said, "whether human spirit or woodland goddess, pardon me. / If I deranged your fair branches and wrought damage to your living myrtle, it was through not knowing that a human spirit was hidden beneath your rough bark. But do not deny me an answer: tell me who you are, who live and speak, a rational being in a spiky, contorted body—so may heaven's hailstones ever spare you! / And if now or in the future I can do you some favor by way of amends, I promise you, by the fair woman[1] in whose keeping lies the best part of me, that I shall so perform in word and action that you shall have just cause to thank me." Thus spoke Ruggiero, and the myrtle quivered from head to foot. / Perspiration now beaded through the tree's bark, like a faggot green from the forest which feels the flame overwhelm it after vainly trying to resist the heat.

"Your courtesy so prevails upon me that I must tell you both who I was and who it is who has changed me into this myrtle by the soft sea-shore. / Astolfo was my name; I was a paladin, much feared in battle; Orlando and Rinaldo were my cousins, whose fame has broken all bounds. I was heir, after my father Otho, to the crown of England. Handsome I was, and graceful, so that I was beloved by not a few ladies—yet in the end I proved my own undoing. /

"I was returning from those distant isles washed on the East by the Indian Sea, where with Rinaldo and others I had been shut away in a darkened vault until Orlando there displayed his utmost strength. We were journeying Westward, then, along the dunes which endure the wrath of the North winds. / Hard, spiteful Fate traced our path which brought us out, one morning, onto a lovely beach on which stood a castle of the potent Alcina.[2] She had come forth from it, and we found her standing alone at the edge of the sea: she was pulling ashore all the fishes she wanted, though she had neither net nor hook. / Swift-moving dolphins hastened to her, and ponderous tunny, open-mouthed; the sperm whales and the sea-lions were disturbed out of their indolent sleep; mullet and jelly-fish, salmon and black-fish came in shoals, as fast as they could swim; sea-wolves and cachalots, grampus and orcs rose out of the sea with their monstrous backs. / We descried a whale, the largest one ever to be seen in the ocean: its vast shoulders protruded eleven cubits and more above the briny waves. All of us fell into the same deception—we took it for an island, it lay so still with never even a ripple, and its two extremities were at so great a distance apart. / Alcina drew the fishes out of the water with simple words and magic charms. She and the witch Morgana were born of the same mother, but whether she was delivered first or last, or whether both at once I cannot say.

"Well, Alcina looked at me, and she liked what she saw, as was clear from

9. Ariosto imitates Virgil's Polidorus (*Aeneid* 3) and Dante's suicide, Pier delle Vigne (*Inferno* 13, 40), both turned into plants that bleed when torn. 1. Bradamant. 2. A sorceress and temptress like Homer's Circe.

her face; so she devised a crafty ruse to take me away from my companions; and here she succeeded. / With a cheerful smile she came to meet us, and showed easy courtesy as she addressed us: 'Good sirs, if you would like to abide with me today, I shall show you every manner of fish among those I have caught: some with scales, some all pulpy, some fur-clad, and more abundant than the stars in the sky. / And should you wish to see a siren, who can still the waves with her sweet singing, go with me to this further beach where she always comes at this hour.' She pointed to the vast whale which, as I said, looked like a small island. I, who have always (to my regret) been too impetuous, stepped onto that fish. / Rinaldo, and Dudone likewise, signalled to me not to go, but to no avail. Smiling, Alcina left them to themselves and stepped on behind me. The whale, faithful to its office, swam off through the salt waves. I was not long in regretting my folly, but by then I was too far from the shore. / Rinaldo flung himself into the sea to help me, but he almost sank, for a raging wind blew up from the South, drawing a dark veil over sky and sea. I know not what became of him. Alcina meanwhile addressed herself to reassuring me.

"All that day and through the night she kept me in the midst of the sea on the monster's back, / until we came to this beautiful island. Alcina owns a great part of it, having stolen a share from Logistilla, a sister of hers who, as the only legitimate daughter, had been left the whole of it by their father. Alcina and Morgana, as she fully avowed to me, were both born of incest. / A wicked, pernicious pair they make, surfeited with every sort of ugly infamy; not so Logistilla[3]—she is one who has steeped her heart in all that is virtuous, and lives in chastity. The two have conspired against her, and have recruited more than one army to drive her from the island; time and again they have seized castles from her—over a hundred of them; / indeed, Logistilla would be left with not so much as a parcel of land were it not that the island is narrowed on one side by a creek, and on the other by a deserted mountain— similar to the mountain and the firth which separate England from Scotland. Not that this deters Alcina and Morgana from trying to wrest from her what little is left. / The pair of them, being vicious to the core, cannot endure her, because she is chaste and good.

"But I was telling you how it came about that I was turned into a tree: Alcina entertained me in luxury, all ablaze as she was with love for me—and I burned for her no less ardently, seeing how beautiful she was, and how indulgent. / In her delicate body I found all my delight; every treasure was concentrated here, so it seemed to me, which is normally shared out among human kind, some enjoying more, others less, and no one having a large share. Lost in contemplation of her looks, I quite forgot about France and all else—my every thought, my every good design ended in her, and never went beyond. / I was her beloved, too, as much as she was mine, or more. Alcina gave no further thought to anyone else: she had abandoned all her other lovers—for before me there had been a fair number. She made me her councillor, kept me at her side day and night, set all the others under my command. Me she believed, to me she referred everything; night and day she would never address another, only me. / Alas! Why must I keep touching my

3. Logistilla (from Greek *logos* "word" or "reason") represents virtue and reason, while Alcina, a figure of romance poetry, represents material pleasures with no transcendence.

wounds when I have no hope of a balm? Why must I recollect the good that was, now that I am suffering the most rigorous penitence? Whilst I counted myself happy, and whilst I believed I stood highest in Alcina's love, she took back from me the gift of her heart, and threw herself body and soul into a fresh infatuation.[4]

"I was late in discovering the fickleness of her nature, prone to falling in and out of love all at once. I had reigned in her affection for but two months when a new lover was assumed in my place. She drove me out disdainfully, and withdrew her favor from me. Later I learnt that she had meted similar treatment to a thousand lovers before me, and always without cause. / And, to prevent their spreading about the world the story of her wanton ways, she transforms them, every one, planting them here and there in the fertile soil, changing one into a fir-tree, another into an olive, another into a palm or cedar, or into the guise in which you see me on this verdant bank; yet others the proud enchantress changes into liquid springs, or into beasts, just as it suits her. /

"Now you, sir, have reached this enchanted island by an unusual way, and some lover shall, on your account, be turned into stone or water or something of the sort. A scepter shall be yours, from Alcina's hand, and you shall reign, and you shall be the happiest of mortal men: but make no mistake—your time will soon come to be changed into a beast or a fountain, into wood or rock. / I have gladly given you warning, not that I imagine it will be of any use to you; and yet it is better that you should not go unprepared but rather knowing something of her ways. Perhaps, as faces differ, so do wit and skill, and you will devise some way to forestall the worst—some way which a thousand before you have not discovered." /

Ruggiero had heard that Astolfo was cousin to his lady, Bradamant, and he was deeply afflicted on seeing the change the knight had undergone from his true self into a scrawny, sterile shrub. And for the love he bore his lady, he would gladly have been of service to him (if only he had known how); but all he could do was to offer him consolation. / This he did as best he could; then he asked him if there was a way to reach the territory of Logistilla, whether by hill or by dale, so as to avoid passing through that of Alcina. There was indeed, returned the myrtle, a way studded with sheer rocks, if he went on a little towards the right, and climbed the hill towards the craggy peak. / But he was not to reckon on making much headway along that path, for he would come upon a whole band of pugnacious roughs, who would provide no easy passage. Alcina deployed them there to act as a wall or dyke stopping whoever would seek to escape from her clutches. Ruggiero thanked the myrtle for everything, then left him, duly forewarned. /

He approached the hippogryph, untethered him, grasped his reins and walked him away instead of mounting him, as he had done before: he was not this time going to be carried off against his wishes. He pondered how best to reach Logistilla's realm in safety; he was firmly disposed to do whatever was necessary to avoid falling into Alcina's power. / He considered mounting his steed and spurring him on to a new flight through the air, but he feared this might prove a distinct mistake, seeing how little notice the beast took of the bridle. "I shall force my way through, if I go the right way

4. Like the medieval figure of Lady Fortune, she strikes down those at the height of happiness.

about it," he told himself, but all in vain—he had not gone two miles from the shore when Alcina's splendid city came into view. / Off in the distance stood a wall which curved away, embracing a vast stretch of land; it was so high, its top seemed to merge with the heavens, and it looked as if it were solid gold from summit to foot. (There are some who part company with me here and maintain that it is an effect of alchemy;[5] they may know better than I, but, again, they may be quite mistaken. To me it looks like gold, the way it gleams.) / When he was close to these walls whose splendour is unmatched by any others in the world, the doughty knight left the road, which ran broad and straight across the plain to the massive gates, and veered off to the right along the safer path leading up to the mountain heights.

Soon, however, his journey was disturbed and interrupted by the onslaught of the band of ruffians. / Never did you set eyes on a more fantastic throng, or see faces so monstrous and misshapen.[6] Some of them were human from the neck down, but with the head of a monkey or of a cat; some stumped about on cloven hoofs; some were quick, agile centaurs. Some were young and pert, others old and stupid. Some were naked, others clad in strange pelts. / One galloped on an unbridled horse, another plodded along on a donkey or an ox, and yet another mounted a centaur; many rode on the backs of ostriches, eagles, and cranes. Some set a horn to their lips, some their cup. They were male and female—some of them both at once. One carried a hook, the next a rope ladder, another a crowbar, yet another a stealthy file. / Their captain could be seen sitting astride a tortoise which shuffled stolidly along; he had a swollen paunch, the captain, and a fat face, and henchmen to support him on either side, as he was drunk and his head kept lolling forward. Some dabbed his forehead and chin while others flapped their garments to fan him. / A creature whose feet and belly were human, but whose neck, head, and ears were those of a dog, barked at Ruggiero to make him turn off towards the fair city which lay behind him. "Not I," retorted the knight, "so long as I have strength to wield this"—and he flourished his sword, aiming its sharp point at the creature's face. /

The monster attacked him with a spear, but Ruggiero let fly at him and ran him through the paunch so that his sword stuck out through his back a palm's width. He grasped his shield and leapt in all directions, but the enemy thronged round him, pricking him here, clawing at him there. He whirled his sword and laid about him savagely, / splitting one open down to the jaw, the next right down to the chest, for this breed of scoundrels goes unarmored (and besides, no helmet, shield, breastplate, or chain-mail can resist his sword). But he was so hemmed in on all sides that if he was to give himself room and hold this scum at bay, he would have needed more arms and hands than Briareus.[7] / Had he thought of bringing out the shield of Atlas[8]—the shield of the blinding light, which the magician had left suspended from the saddle—he would have overcome the ugly mob in a trice, and made them all fall down in a dazzle. It could be that he would not stoop to using it, preferring to rely on valor rather than on guile. / Be that as it may, he would sooner have died than fall a prisoner to so scurvy a crew.

Now who should sally forth from a gate in the walls (all gold and glitter,

5. Pseudoscience and philosophy concerned with turning base metals into gold. 6. Grotesque figures of vice. 7. A one-hundred-armed giant. 8. Uncovered, the shield belonging to Ruggiero's wizard mentor dazzles beholders and knocks them unconscious.

as I said), but two damsels. To judge by their bearing and apparel, they were clearly not of mean birth, brought up in poverty by shepherds, but reared amid the opulence of a royal palace. / They each rode on a unicorn whiter than the whitest ermine; both were of great beauty, and so exquisite in their dress and manners that a man would have needed the eyes of a god to look at their appearance and judge them for what they were. They could have passed for Beauty (had she a body) and Grace. / They both came to where Ruggiero was being hard pressed by the brutish throng. These all now melted away and the damsels held out their hand to the knight, who blushingly thanked them for their act of kindness. And, to do their pleasure, he was glad to go with them back to the golden gate. /

Above the gate, and jutting a little over it, the wall was ornamented, and there was not an inch but was encrusted in the rarest jewels from the Levant. Great columns made of solid diamond flanked the gate through the thickness of the walls. Whether they presented a true or false image to the eye, there was nothing like them for grace and felicity. / On the threshold and among the columns nymphs played and frolicked wantonly—their beauty might have been enhanced had they been more jealous of the respect which should have been their due as women. They were all dressed in green skirts and crowned with spring garlands. All smiles and charm, they welcomed Ruggiero into paradise. / The place could well be called by that name: I do believe it was the cradle of Love. Here it was all dancing and play-time, and the hours went by in one continuous festivity. Grey-headed Thought could not dwell here in a single heart, not even for a moment. There was no entrance here for Discomfort or Dearth, but Plenty was ever in attendance with her copious horn.[9] / This was the abode of youths and maidens, here where soft April, presenting a serene and merry face, seemed constantly to smile. By a spring, some there were who sang in sweet, melodious voice; in the shade of a tree or a cliff others played and danced and indulged in honest fun. Another had gone apart, and was communing with his true-love. / Round the tops of the pines and laurels, of the tall beeches and shaggy fir-trees the little cupids flitted and swooped merrily. Some of them were gloating contentedly over their victories; some were carefully aiming their heart-piercing arrows; others were spreading nets. Down by a stream one was honing darts, while another was sharpening his against a smooth stone. / Here Ruggiero was presented with a majestic bay charger; sturdy and robust he was, and his trappings were spangled with precious stones and embroidered with thread of gold. The winged horse, the same which used to do the old Moorish wizard's[1] bidding, was entrusted to a youth, who was to lead him after Ruggiero at a slower pace. /

The two lovesome maidens, the pretty pair who had protected Ruggiero from the band of knaves, the knaves who had forestalled him on the path he had taken off to the right, now addressed him: "Your valorous deeds, sir, of which we have heard tell, embolden us to avail ourselves of your assistance. / We shall soon be coming to a bog which divides this plain in two. The bridge across it is held by a savage woman called Erifilla,[2] who bullies and tricks and robs whoever would cross to the other side. She is built like a

---

9. Horn of plenty, the cornucopia.   1. Atlas, Ruggiero's boyhood protector.   2. Signifies avarice and betrayal (from Erifila, who betrayed her husband for jewels).

giant; her teeth are fangs and her bite venomous; her nails are pointed and she claws like a bear. / Not only does she keep molesting us on our path, which would be free of obstacle were it not for her, but also she often runs about the garden making a nuisance of herself in one way and another. Many of the murderous mob that attacked you outside the gate are spawn of hers— all of them are her followers, evil, like her, inhospitable and rapacious." / Answered Ruggiero: "For you I shall gladly fight not merely one battle but a hundred! Command my person as you will, to the limits of its resources—if I wear plastron and coat of mail, it is not to win myself land or silver, but simply to serve and prosper others, the more so when they are lovely ladies like yourselves." /

The ladies replied with thanks as befitted a knight of his sort, and they continued in conversation until they came in sight of the bog and the bridge. Here they saw the insolent woman, armed—her arms were made of gold and adorned with emeralds and sapphires. The story of how Ruggiero risked her onslaught I shall defer to the next canto.[3]

* * *

He who travels far afield beholds things which lie beyond the bounds of belief; and when he returns to tell of them, he is not believed, but is dismissed as a liar, for the ignorant throng will refuse to accept his word, but needs must see with their own eyes, touch with their own hands. This being so, I realize that my words will gain scant credence where they outstrip the experience of my hearers. / Still, whatever degree of reliance is placed on my word, I shall not trouble myself about the ignorant and mindless rabble: I know that you, my sharp, clear-headed listeners, will see the shining truth of my tale. To convince you, and you alone, is all that I wish to strive for, the only reward I seek.

I left off at the point where they came in sight of the bog and the bridge over it which was guarded by proud Erifilla. / Her armor was of the finest metal, encrusted with gems of various colors—red rubies, yellow topaz, green emeralds, and golden hyacinth. She was mounted, but not upon a horse: she had saddled a wolf, instead, with a saddle of unusual splendor, and this beast she was urging onto the bridge. / I doubt whether in Apulia there would be found one of his size—he bulked even larger than an ox. She had thrust no bit into his mouth to bring the foam to his lips—in fact I have no idea how she schooled him to her bidding. Her Pestilence wore a sand-colored cape over her armor; apart from its color, it was not unlike that which bishops and prelates wear at court. / On her shield and helmet she sported a bloated, poisonous toad. The damsels pointed her out to the knight: she had crossed to their side of the bridge to block his path, to joust with him and bring him to shame, as she was normally inclined to do. She shouted to Ruggiero to turn back, but he grasped a lance, and yelled defiance at her. / The massive Amazon did not hesitate: she straightway set spurs to her wolf, braced herself firmly in the saddle and charged, setting her lance in rest as she came; the ground shuddered. But, after the impact, she was left lying on the field— Ruggiero caught her under the helmet and tipped her from the saddle with such force, he carried her back some six lengths. / Now, drawing the sword

---

3. Three bullets (as below) mark the end of each canto.

he had buckled on, he was coming to sever her proud head from her shoulders, as well he could do, for Erifilla was lying prostrate amid the meadow-flowers. But the ladies called to him: "She is overthrown—that is enough: no need to wreak any starker vengeance upon her. Sheathe your sword, gentle knight; let us cross the bridge and continue on our way." /

Their path led through a wood; it was somewhat rough and hard-going, for it was narrow and stony, and climbed steeply. When they reached the top of the hill, though, they came out into broad, open fields, and here they set eyes on the most splendid and delightful palace to be seen in the whole wide world. / From the outer gates stepped forth beauteous Alcina, and came to meet Ruggiero; and, surrounded by a handsome and dignified retinue, she extended to him a regal welcome. The whole court now paid such honor and respect to the valiant knight, they could not have done more had God himself come down from Heaven. / What was remarkable about the splendid palace was not its opulence (unrivaled though it was) so much as its inhabitants—the most attractive, courteous people in the world.

For youth and comeliness there was little to judge between them all; only Alcina outstripped them every one in beauty, as the sun is more radiant than any star. / She was so beautifully modelled, no painter, however much he applied himself, could have achieved anything more perfect. Her long blonde tresses were gathered in a knot: pure gold itself could have no finer lustre. Roses and white privet blooms lent their colors to suffuse her delicate cheeks. Her serene brow was like polished ivory, and in perfect proportion. / Beneath two of the thinnest black arches, two dark eyes—or rather, two bright suns; soft was their look, gentle their movement. Love seemed to flit, frolicsome, about them; indeed, Love from this vantage point would let fly his full quiver and openly steal away all hearts. Down the midst of the face, the nose— Envy herself could find no way of bettering it. / Below this, the mouth, set between two dimples; it was imbued with native cinnabar.[4] Here a beautiful soft pair of lips opened to disclose a double row of choicest pearls. Here was the course of those winning words which could not but soften every heart, however rugged and uncouth. Here was formed the melodious laughter which made a paradise on earth. / Snow-white was her neck, milky her breast; the neck was round, the breast broad and full. A pair of apples, not yet ripe, fashioned in ivory, rose and fell like the sea-swell at times when a gentle breeze stirs the ocean. Argus[5] himself could not see them entire, but you could easily judge that what lay hidden did not fall short of what was exposed to view. / Her arms were justly proportioned, and her lily-white hands were often to be glimpsed: they were slender and tapering, and quite without a knot or swelling vein. A pair of small, neat, rounded feet completes the picture of this august person. Her looks were angelic, heaven-sent—no veil could have concealed them. / Everything about her was an enticement, whether she spoke or laughed or sang, whether she but moved a step.

Little wonder that Ruggiero was ensnared, finding her, as he did, so entrancing. Little did it profit him to have been warned by the myrtle of her evil, treacherous nature—it did not seem to him possible for deceit and perfidy to keep company with so charming a smile. / On the contrary, he

---

4. The language is from the biblical Song of Songs, the possibly allegorical love song between the bride and bridegroom. 5. A mythological creature with one hundred eyes.

preferred to believe that if she had changed Astolfo into a myrtle by the sandy shore, it was because he had treated her with stark ingratitude, and so deserved his fate and worse. Everything he had been told about her he dismissed as false, deeming rather that the wretch was moved by spite and envy and was a shameless liar. / Intensely though he loved fair Bradamant, she was here and now wrested from his heart, for by magic Alcina erased all trace of the pangs with which up till now his soul was smitten. She alone became the unique burden of his love, she alone was now engraved upon his heart. Good Ruggiero must be forgiven, then, for this show of inconstancy. /

Around the festive board zithers, harps, and lyres set the air vibrating with delightful sounds, with soft harmony and tuneful notes. There was song, too, song of love's joys and ecstasies, and recitals of pleasing fantasies framed in verse of happiest inspiration. / Which of the splendid and sumptuous banquets arranged by any of those who sat upon King Ninus's throne, which of the many celebrated feasts offered by Cleopatra to the victorious Roman, which of these can compare to the banquet that the loving sorceress prepared for the paladin? No such feast, I am sure, was ever set out on Olympus when Ganymede[6] ministered to imperial Jove. / When the food and the tables were cleared away, they all sat down in a circle to play a merry game which consisted in each whispering into his neighbor's ear to ask a secret—any secret. This gave the lovers ample occasion to disclose their passion without hindrance; the final outcome was an assignation for that very night. / This game was not continued for long—it was ended far sooner than was the normal custom.

The pages then led the way into the palace with torches, driving out the darkness with an abundance of light. Preceded and followed by elegant company, Ruggiero was escorted to his downy bed in a little bedroom: it was airy and pleasantly decorated, the first choice of all the rooms in the palace. / Once more he was pressed to partake of sweet delicacies and choice wines, after which the company bowed respectfully and withdrew to their own quarters. Ruggiero slipped between the perfumed sheets, which might well have been the handiwork of Arachne[7] herself; he strained his ears now to listen for the approach of lovely Alcina. / At the slightest movement he heard, he would raise his head, hoping it was she; often he heard sounds when in fact there was nothing to hear—and then he would realize his mistake and sigh. Now and then he would jump out of bed, open the door, and look outside, but there was nothing to be seen. Endlessly he cursed weary time for moving so sluggishly. / Often he would tell himself: "Now she has set out"—and he would start counting the steps which must separate Alcina's room from the one where he awaited her. These and other vain fancies occupied him in the interval before she came, and frequently he feared lest some obstacle be placed between his hand and the fruit. / Alcina all the while was steeping herself in precious perfumes; she put an end to these labors once all was at peace in the household and there was no need for further delay. Now she slipped out of her room and stole by a secret passage to where Ruggiero awaited her; in his heart all this time hope and fear had fought many a round. /

---

6. A beautiful Trojan boy snatched by Jupiter, in the shape of an eagle, to be his cup-bearer. *Victorious Roman:* Pompey the Great, Julius Caesar, or Marc Antony. *Ninus:* king of Assyria, husband and son of Semiramis; his successor was the profligate Sardanapalus.   7. Ovid's master weaver, who challenged Minerva to a weaving contest and was transformed into a spider.

When Astolfo's successor looked up to see those joyful-twinkling stars, he felt as though hot sulphur were coursing through his veins, which threatened to start out from his skin. Now he was engulfed up to his eyes in sheer sweetness, in loveliness. He jumped out of bed and gathered her into his arms, quite unable to wait for her to undress— / for all that she was wearing neither gown nor petticoat: she had come in a light mantle which she had thrown over a white nightgown of gossamer texture. The mantle she abandoned to Ruggiero as he embraced her; this left only the insubstantial gossamer-gown which, before and behind, concealed no more than would a pane of glass placed before a spray of roses or lilies. / Ivy never clung so tightly to the stem round which it was entwined as did the two lovers cling to each other, drawing from each other's lips pollen so fragrant that it will be found on no flower which grows in the scented Indian or Arabian sands. As for describing their pleasure, better to leave this to them—the more so as they frequently had a second tongue in their mouth. / Such matters were kept a secret, or, if no secret, at least they were not spoken of: a seal on the lips often merits praise, seldom blame.

The whole court, astute company that it was, offered Ruggiero its service and a cheerful welcome; everybody reverenced him, deferred to him, for such was the will of love-struck Alcina. / There was not a pleasure which was overlooked, for the love-pavilion afforded every one of them. Two and three times a day they would change their costume depending on the pastime they next intended. Banqueting often, festival ever was the order of the day, with tourneys and trials of strength, with masques, and dances and bathing. Beside a spring, on a shady hillside they would read what was written of love in olden times; / or else they would course through the wooded valleys and over the glad hills, chasing the timid hare; or with their cunning hounds they would flush the frantic, flapping partridge from her cover amid the stubble and the underbrush; they would snare the thrush amid the scented juniper, using a running noose or a soothing lure. Or else they would bait their hooks or cast their nets to disturb the fish out of their contented secrecy. /

Thus did Ruggiero bask in every sort of pleasure, while toil was the lot of Charles the Emperor and of Agramant the King: I should not wish to forget their story, nor to leave aside Bradamant, who for many days bitterly lamented the loss of her lover whom she had seen borne off along so strange a path, she knew not whither. / Before taking up the kings' story, I shall take up hers: for many a day she scoured the country in vain, searching the shady forests and sunny fields, searching farmsteads and cities, hills and plains; but she could glean nothing about her dearest love who was so far, far away. Often she visited the Saracen host, but not a trace could she pick up of her Ruggiero. / Each day she would question over a hundred souls, but not one of them could give her news of him. She would go from one encampment to the next, seeking for him in every tent and pavilion. This was not difficult, for she could go among the mounted troops and those on foot thanks to the ring which, against all human experience, made her vanish when she put it in her mouth. / She could not, nor would she, seek him among the dead: the mighty downfall of a man so great would have made itself heard from the Indus to the lands of the setting sun. She could not tell, she could not imagine where his path lay, on or above the earth, and yet pitifully she kept searching for him, with sighs and tears and every kind of sorrow for companions. /

Eventually she thought of returning to the cave which sheltered the prophet Merlin's bones;[8] she would scream so piercingly about his tomb that the cold marble would be moved to pity. And whether Ruggiero still lived, or whether Death—that ultimate necessity—had cut short his happy years, she would here discover. Then she would pursue whatever course was best proposed. /

Thus decided, she set off towards the forests neighboring Ponthieu, where, in wild and hilly country, was concealed the tomb from which Merlin spoke. Now the enchantress who had ever followed Bradamant in her thoughts, I mean the one who had instructed her about her posterity in the gorgeous cavern— / the good and wise enchantress, who had always taken care of her, knowing her destiny as mother of unconquerable men, indeed of demigods—sought daily to know what she was doing, what saying, and daily cast spells to favor her. Ruggiero's delivery from Atlas, his abduction, where now he was in India, all this was known to her. / She had seen him mounted on that unbridled horse which he could not control, sailing out into the distance along so perilous and strange a path. Full well she knew how he was passing his time now in amusements, in dancing and feasting, in soft, pampered indolence, forgetful of his Liege, of his beloved, of his own renown.[9] / And it might therefore have been the lot of so goodly a knight to pass the best years of his life in sustained idleness, only to lose his soul and body all at once. And that odor, which is all we leave behind once our frail carcass falls to dust, and saves us from the tomb and keeps us ever-living, that odor would be like a fragrant flower severed from its stem or plucked out from the grass. / But the kind sorceress, who took more care of him than he did of himself, thought how to bring him back to true virtue, despite himself, by a hard and rugged way—just like a skilled physician who treats a wound with iron and fire, and often with poison: even though at first he causes much pain, he ultimately does good, and receives thanks. /

She showed him no indulgence: a transcendent love made her so blind to all else that she had, like Atlas, set her heart upon restoring his life to him. Atlas, however, would have him enjoy long life bereft of honor and renown rather than forego one year of his carefree existence for all the praise the world could accord him. / He had sent Ruggiero to Alcina's island to make him, at her court, forget about arms. And, being a magician of consummate art, skilled in every kind of magic spell, he had bound that queen's[1] heart to his in so strong a bond that there was no question of her breaking free, though Ruggiero were to grow as old as Nestor.[2] /

But back to the enchantress who could see into the future: she set out and found the wandering Bradamant on her way to see her. Coming upon her friend the enchantress, Bradamant found new hope in place of the anguish which had hitherto been all her company. The prophetess disclosed the truth to her—that her Ruggiero had been carried off to Alcina. / The maiden was stunned to learn just how far away was her beloved—and worse, that without immediate and effective help, their very love for each other was imperiled. But the kind enchantress comforted her and was quick to apply a dressing to the throbbing wound: she gave her word that within a few days she would restore Ruggiero to her. /

8. Where she met the sorceress Melissa and heard Merlin's prophecy of the dynasty she and Ruggiero would found.   9. Agramant, Bradamant, and his reputation.   1. Alcina, who now resembles Virgil's Queen Dido.   2. I.e., ancient: Nestor saw three generations, according to Homer.

"As you possess the ring,"[3] she said, "which is proof against every magic spell, I have not the least doubt that if I take it with me to the place where Alcina is purloining your treasure, I shall foil her designs and bring back to you your only-beloved. I shall set out this evening with the gathering dusk, and as dawn breaks I shall be in India." / She went on to explain to her the manner in which she intended to use the ring so as to rescue her loved one from the soft, womanly realm and bring him back to France. Bradamant drew the ring from her finger; not only this would she have handed over, but also her heart, her very life, if this might have procured help for her Ruggiero. / She gave her the ring, and commended herself to the enchantress; even more did she commend Ruggiero to her, bidding her convey to him all her fondest love. Then, by a different path, she set out towards Provence.

The enchantress went her own way, and, to put her plan into effect, she that evening conjured up a palfrey; he was black all over, except for a red foot. / I believe he must have been some spirit she had summoned in that shape from hell. Barefoot and ungirded, she mounted him; her hair, now hideously withered, fell loose about her. She took the ring off her finger lest it would inhibit her own magic. Then she left in such haste that the following morning found her on Alcina's island. / Here she underwent a remarkable transformation: she put on almost a foot in height, grew her limbs stouter, and ended up so proportioned that she passed for Atlas, the wizard who had brought up Ruggiero so dotingly. She clothed her chin in a long beard and induced wrinkles on her brow and all over. / In face, speech, and person she took him off so perfectly that she seemed none other than the sorcerer himself.

Then she concealed herself, and remained alert for the moment when at last Ruggiero did not have the love-sick Alcina at his side—this was a stroke of fortune, for, go or stay, she could not stand being parted from him for even an hour. / She found him all on his own, as she wanted, enjoying the freshness and peace of the morning beside a delightful stream which flowed down a hillside towards a pleasant, limpid lake. The delicious softness of his dress suggested sloth and sensuality; Alcina had woven the garment with her own hands in silk and gold, a subtle work. / A glittering, richly jewelled necklace fastened round his neck and hung to his chest, while his two arms, hitherto so virile, were now each clasped by a lustrous bangle. Each ear was pierced by a fine gold ring from which a fat pearl hung, such as no Arabian or Indian ever boasted. / His curly locks were saturated in perfumes, the most precious and aromatic that exist. His every gesture was mincing, as though he were accustomed to waiting on ladies in Valencia. All about him was sickly, all but his name; the rest was but corruption and decay.[4] Thus was Ruggiero discovered, thus changed from his true self by sorcery. /

The enchantress, then, presented herself to Ruggiero in Atlas's likeness, with Atlas's grave, venerable face which had always commanded his respect; on his face he wore the look of angry menace which Ruggiero had feared from early childhood.

"Are these then the fruits," she exclaimed, "for which I have toiled so long? / Early I fed you on the marrow of bears and lions; I accustomed you as a child to strangle snakes in grottoes and wild ravines, to disarm the clawing

3. A magical ring originally belonging to Angelica; worn on the finger, it protects wearers from magical deceptions; placed in the mouth, it grants invisibility. 4. Ruggiero outdoes Aeneas in being decorated and smothered by Dido (in *Aeneid* 4). *Valencia:* Spanish city notorious in the 1500s for dissolute behavior.

panthers and tigers and draw the tusks off live boars—was all this schooling to no better purpose than to make you play Adonis, or Atys,[5] to Alcina? / Was this, then, the promise of your manhood, made to me when you were still but a child at the breast—this the promise of the stars I studied, and the sacral threads, the conjunctions, the dreams and auguries and omens which have been my all-too-assiduous study? It was in deeds of arms that you were to stand out, a matchless champion. / A goodly beginning, this, from which we can hope soon to see you become another Alexander, Scipio, or Caesar![6] Alas, who could ever have dreamed it possible that you of all people would become a bondsman to Alcina! To make this obvious to everyone, you wear about your neck and on your arms the chains with which she drags you to her bidding. /

"Though you care nothing for your own renown, and for the shining deeds for which Heaven has appointed you, why must you defraud your own posterity of all the good which I have a thousand times predicted to you? What of the womb in which—so Heaven has decreed—you're to conceive a glorious and god-like race, more radiant than the sun: why must you suffer it to remain eternally sealed? / The noblest spirits conceived in the Eternal Mind must at their appointed time take human form, springing from the stock rooted in you: prevent them not! Do not prevent the triumphant and victorious deeds whereby your children, and your children's children, shall heal Italy of her dread afflictions and dire injuries, and restore her to her pristine glory. / Many and many a gracious soul, brilliant, illustrious, eminent, peerless, and holy, is to be sprung as shoots from your fecund tree; even if all of these cannot weigh upon your decision, yet but one pair should be sufficient: Hippolytus and his brother,[7] the likes of whom have seldom been encountered in the world to this day, for sheer eminence of virtue. / I used to speak to you more often of these two than of all the others put together, for, among them all, they shall enjoy the lion's share of pre-eminent qualities; also, when I spoke of them, I saw you pay closer attention than when I spoke of other of your seed—I saw you rejoice that such illustrious heroes were to be descended from you. /

"This woman you have made your queen, what has she to distinguish her from a thousand other whores? This woman, she's the whole world's concubine: judge for yourself whether she can really satisfy! Now, that you may know who Alcina is, stripped of her artifices and deceits, put this ring on your finger and return to her, and you shall realize just how fair are her looks." /

Ruggiero stood shamefaced and silent, staring at the ground, not knowing what to say. The enchantress put the ring on his little finger, and brought him back to reality. Coming to himself, Ruggiero was so overwhelmed with shame that he wished himself a thousand feet below ground, so that no one could look him in the face. / After these words, the enchantress switched back into her own likeness, as she had no further need to borrow Atlas's, her effect once achieved. What I neglected to tell you earlier was her name: Melissa. She now gave Ruggiero a true account of herself and of her mission. / She had been sent, she explained, by one who loved him and ever longed

5. A youth who castrated himself for the mother goddess, Cybele. *Adonis:* boy loved by Venus.   6. Famed world-conquerors of Greece and Rome.   7. Alfonso d'Este, duke of Ferrara, and Ippolito d'Este, the cardinal and Ariosto's patron.

for him, by one who could not be without him; she had come to deliver him from the shackles which had been forced upon him by sorcery. And in order the better to gain his confidence, she had assumed Atlas's form. But now that she had restored him to his senses, she would set all the facts before him. /

"A most worthy lady who loves you, and who would be deserving of your love—and, unless you are forgetful, you must realize how much you owed your liberty to the service she rendered you—this lady sends you this ring, proof against all magic. Her very heart she would have sent, had her heart possessed the same virtues as this ring to procure your safety." / She went on to speak of the love which Bradamant bore him, and she commended her merits in terms which combined truth with warmth of feeling. Being a skilled messenger, she chose her words to the best advantage, and she implanted in Ruggiero an utter revulsion for Alcina, such as one would feel for any loathsome object. /

She made her an object of disgust to him, for all that he had loved her up till now; be not surprised, though—his love had been wrought out of enchantment, and, with the ring, the spell was broken. What else the ring showed up was that Alcina's beauty was in every detail an imposture: it was wholly fraudulent—nothing, from her soles up to her tresses, was natural to her. Her beauty evaporated, leaving nothing but dregs. / If a child sets aside a ripe fruit and then, forgetting where he put it, is brought to the very place many days later and happens upon his fruit, he is amazed to find it all rotten and putrid, and not at all as he had left it; and though he normally had a weakness for that sort of fruit, he throws this one away in loathing and revulsion— / so it was with Ruggiero: once Melissa had made him set eyes again upon Alcina, but this time wearing the ring that makes the wearer, while he has it on his finger, totally immune to magic, he was astonished to find that in place of the beauty he had just parted from, he was confronted with a woman so hideous that her equal for sheer ugliness and decrepitude could be found nowhere on earth. / She was whey-faced, wrinkled, and hollow-cheeked; her hair was white and sparse; she was not four feet high; the last tooth had dropped out of her jaw; she had lived longer than anyone on earth, longer than Hecuba or the Cumaean Sibyl.[8] But she made such use of arts unknown in our day that she could pass for young and fair. / Young and fair she made herself by artifice, and deceived many as she deceived Ruggiero. But now, with the ring, he could read the cards[9] aright and see the truth which for so many years had been kept hidden. Small wonder, then, if Ruggiero could no longer find in himself the slightest inclination to love Alcina, now that he was so equipped when he came upon her that her deceit could no longer serve her. /

But, as Melissa advised him, he betrayed no change in his face until he had resumed his armor, from head to foot, which for so many days he had neglected. And, so as to avert Alcina's suspicions, he pretended to try it on just to see how easily he could manage it—he pretended to see if he could still squeeze into it after so many days since he last wore it. / Then he buckled on his sword, which was called Balisard, and took up the miraculous shield,

8. Apollo gave her immortality but not eternal youth. *Hecuba:* queen of Troy and Priam's wife.   9. Italian *carte*, meaning maps and pages of a book.

which not merely dazzles the eyes but so clouds the spirit that, to all appearances, it takes leave of the body. He took up the shield, then, still sheathed in its silken drape, and slung it from his shoulder. / Next, he went to the stables and had a horse saddled and bridled—a black horse, black as pitch, chosen on Melissa's instructions, for she knew that he could run like the wind. Those who knew him called him Rabican—he was the very horse which was borne on whale-back to this place, together with the knight who is now the sport of the breeze by the edge of the sea. / He might have taken the hippogryph, who was tethered next to Rabican, but Melissa had told him, "Bear in mind that he is, as you know, too unruly." And she gave him to hope that the next day she would take out the hippogryph and help Ruggiero to learn little by little how to control him and make him go anywhere. / Leaving him alone, too, Ruggiero would not arouse suspicions about the secret escape he was contriving. He did as Melissa directed—she kept, unseen, by his ear the whole time.

Thus feigning, he slipped out of the ancient harlot's palace, all soft sensuality, and came to a gate which gave onto the road leading to Logistilla's domain. / He drove into the sentinels, sword in hand, and caught them unawares; some he left wounded, others slain, and then charged out across the bridge. Before Alcina had an inkling of what had befallen, Ruggiero was already well away. In the next canto I shall tell you what path he took, and how he came to the realm of Logistilla.

FROM CANTOS 8 AND 9

[Angelica Travels Alone, and Orlando Has a Dream]

Sorcerers and sorceresses, we may not know it but you thrive among us! Artfully you disguise your faces and ensnare the hearts of the opposite sex. You work your magic not by virtue of obedient sprites nor by conning the stars for signs: by trickery, lies, and dissimulation you bind the hearts of others with knots that cannot be untied. / Those of us who possessed Angelica's ring—I mean the ring of Reason—could descry each person's true face, undisguised by cunning artifice. A man who passes for handsome and kind may well, beneath his veneer, look like an ugly brute. Ruggiero, then, was most fortunate to have the ring which disclosed to him the truth. /

As I said, Ruggiero feigned his way out and came to the gates, armed and mounted on Rabican. He took the guards unawares and, as he drove into them, he did not leave his sword in its sheath. Some he left dead, others the worse for wear, before he rode out across the bridge and smashed his way through the palisade. He set out towards the woods, but after only a short way he came upon one of Alcina's minions. / On his wrist the man was carrying some bird of prey which he liked to take out with him daily into the fields or to a nearby pond where there was always plenty of game to be caught. At his side trotted his faithful hound, and he was riding a quite ordinary hack. Seeing how fast Ruggiero was approaching, he judged that he must be a fugitive. /

The fellow made towards him and in an arrogant tone enquired: "Why such haste?" Ruggiero did not see fit to reply, so the other, more certain than ever that he was a fugitive, decided he must be stopped. He extended his left hand and cried: "What will you say if I stop you in your tracks—you'll find no shelter from this bird of mine!" / The huntsman released his bird, which winged away so fast that Rabican could not outdistance it. Then he jumped off his horse and in a trice had unbridled him: the horse became like an arrow shot from a bow and arrived kicking and biting viciously. Right behind him came the huntsman, as though borne on a lick of flame, or on the very wind. / Now the hound did not wish to play the laggard, but was off after Rabican like a hunting-cat after a hare. Ruggiero would have deemed it cowardly not to stand his ground, so he turned to face the man approaching at such a dashing stride. For all weapons the fellow carried only a small stick—the kind used to teach a dog obedience—so Ruggiero did not deign to draw his sword. / The huntsman reached him and landed him a powerful blow, while the hound sunk his teeth into his left foot. The unbridled horse meanwhile kicked out repeatedly with his back legs, which thudded against Ruggiero's right side. The bird wheeled and circled, every so often ripping at him with its talons, and so terrifying the charger with its shrieks that he scarce answered to spur or rein. / Finally Ruggiero's sword flashed out: if he was to stop their molesting him, there was no other way. Cut and thrust, he threatened the beasts and their master in turn, but his assailants only pinned him down the more: together they had closed the whole width of the path to him. Ruggiero foresaw the shame and evil he must incur if they delayed him further. / He knew that if he tarried there longer, any moment would bring into view Alcina and her minions. Already the valleys were ringing to the sound of bells, trumpets, and drums. He could see that against an unarmed groom with a dog his sword was not the answer: he would obtain better and faster results if he disclosed the shield which Atlas had made. / He stripped off the scarlet cloth which had covered the shield these many days, and the dazzle achieved its well-proved effect the moment it caught the eye of the beholders. The huntsman was left senseless; horse and hound collapsed all of a heap, and the bird's pinions fell inert, powerless to sustain it in flight. Ruggiero was glad to leave them all a prey to sleep. /

Alcina, meanwhile, had been told how Ruggiero had stormed the gates and killed several of the guard. She could almost have died for grief; she rent her garments and flayed her cheeks, cursing herself for an idiot and a fool. She raised the alarm at once and summoned her henchmen to her, every one. / She split them into two groups, sending one along the path Ruggiero had taken, and assembling the other at the harbor to board ship and put out from shore: in the shadow of the spreading sails the whole sea grew dark. Alcina embarked with these; such was her desperation, such her devouring lust for Ruggiero that she left her city unguarded. /

She left no one to guard her palace, which gave Melissa the opportunity for which she had been waiting, to steal into this sinister stronghold and liberate the unfortunates detained there. Here was her opportunity to find everything in its proper place and lay her hands on it—figurines to burn, seals to remove, knots, magic squares, and whorls to disarrange. / Then, hastening through the countryside in search of the discarded lovers whom Alcina had turned—a great host of them—into wood or stone, into springs or wild beasts, she restored them all to their proper selves. Finding themselves now able to move freely, they all set off in the footsteps of good Ruggiero, and so made their escape to Logistilla's kingdom, whence they returned each to his own land—Greece, Persia, Scythia, India. / Melissa sent them each back to his own land, laden with a debt of gratitude which could never be repaid.

The first to be restored to human form was Astolfo, the duke of the English, thanks to the kinship he enjoyed with Ruggiero, and to this knight's intercession for him; beside commending Astolfo to her, he gave Melissa the ring, the better to be able to help him. / At Ruggiero's behest, then, the paladin was restored to his true self. But Melissa felt she had accomplished nothing until she had restored to him his weapons and his golden lance which has only to touch a person to tip him from the saddle. This lance was Argalia's, but then fell to Astolfo; it brought high honor to both of them in France. / Melissa found the golden lance, which Alcina had put away in her palace, and all the rest of the duke's arms which had been taken from him in that haunt of evil. She mounted the charger which had belonged to Atlas, the Moorish wizard, and had Astolfo climb on behind; then, taking flight for Logistilla's, they arrived there an hour before Ruggiero. /

Ruggiero, meanwhile, was making his way to Logistilla, the kindly enchantress. His path lay amid hard boulders and bramble thickets, from one hill's crest to the next; one path he followed and another, ever steep and solitary, wild and inhospitable. Strained and weary, he came out upon a beach hemmed in between the mountains and the sea; it was in the heat of mid-afternoon, and the place was exposed to the South, arid and bare, sterile and desolate. / The blazing sun beat down upon the hill nearby, which reflected back a heat so intense that it set the air simmering, and the sand: it would have taken less heat to liquefy glass. Every bird sat silent in the soft shade; alone the cricket amid the thick, leafy shrubs shrilled his monotonous refrain, which filled, which deafened, the hills and valleys, the sea and sky. / Tedious and oppressive was the heat, the thirst and weariness which were all Ruggiero had for company as he pursued his sand-strewn way along the sun-drenched desert shore.[1]

* * *

But ought I not, my Lord, to do as the good musician playing his subtle instrument? He will select different strings, fresh harmonies, as he seeks effects, now muted, now strident. And I, intent on unfolding Rinaldo's story, have just remembered sweet Angelica: I left her fleeing from him,[2] and falling in with a hermit. / I shall pursue her story a little. I told you how earnestly she enquired how she might reach the sea-coast, for she was so terrified of Rinaldo that she felt certain of dying if she did not cross the sea, imagining herself unsafe anywhere in Europe. But the hermit took his time, for he enjoyed her company. / Such rare beauty inflamed his heart and warmed the chill marrow in his bones. But, seeing that she took little notice of him, and indeed showed no disposition to bide with him, he mercilessly goaded and spurred his little mule, without being able to rouse him from his lethargic gait; the mule would walk only a few paces, and quite refused to trot—as for a full canter, that was out of the question. /

Now, as he was dropping a long way behind, and in a while would completely lose her traces, the hermit had recourse to his dark cave, and sum-

1. Typologically, a spiritual middle ground, based on the Israelites' passage through the desert from Egypt to the promised land and through idolatry to true worship.   2. In canto 1, Charlemagne then sent Rinaldo on a mission to Scotland.

moned forth a host of demons. He selected one of them and told him what it was he wanted; after which, he bade him enter into Angelica's palfrey which was bearing away the lady—and his heart. / A cunning hound, well used to hunting the fox or the hare in the mountains, will see the prey going by one path, and will himself choose another, as though disdaining to follow the scent; but where the fugitive's path comes out, that is where he will station himself, and he will seize his prey in his jaws and rend open its flanks. Thus did the hermit, taking another path to come up with the damsel, whichever way she went. / What he planned to do is obvious to me, and I shall tell you—later on.

Angelica, all unsuspecting, rode on, covering unequal daily stages. But in her horse the demon lay concealed, as sometimes a fire is concealed only to blaze forth in a while so mightily that there is no putting it out, and to escape from it is difficult. / The damsel followed the path which lay beside the broad sea which washes the land of the Gascons; she rode close to the water's edge, picking her way where the ground was firmest. But her steed was drawn into the water by the powerful demon, and began to swim; the fearful maiden knew not what to do—she just clung tightly to the saddle. / She tugged and tugged on the reins, but could not turn her steed, who was swimming straight out into the deep. She drew up her skirts so as to keep them dry, and pulled her feet clear of the water. Her tresses hung loose about her shoulders, while the lascivious breeze caressed her. The great winds fell silent: perhaps they, like the sea, were arrested by so rare a vision of beauty. / In vain she turned her soft eyes towards the shore, and bathed her face and breast with tears; she saw the land ever receding and growing smaller and smaller.[3] After swimming in a great arc, ever to the right, the beast carried her back to the shore, where it was all dark rocks and dreadful caverns.

Night was falling. / Finding herself alone in this desolate spot—the very look of the place was enough to inspire dread—at the hour when Phoebus[4] sinks into the ocean, leaving a pall of darkness in the air and over the land, Angelica stood motionless: anyone descrying her there would have been in some doubt whether she was a real, sentient woman, or simply a rock tinted to look like one. / She stood paralyzed in the shifting sand, her hair dishevelled, her hands clasped, her lips motionless; her langorous eyes were raised to heaven, as though accusing the Great Mover of having set all the Fates against her. She stood awhile as though in a trance, then tears came welling up and her tongue found utterance for her grief. /

"Fortune, what more have you to do," she said, "before you are sated and replete with hounding me? What have I still left to give you, except for this wretched life of mine? But you do not want it, for you have been so prompt to save it from the sea where it might have found an end to its sorrows. You must have wanted to see me tormented still more before I die. / But I cannot see how you can hurt me more than you have done already. You have had me banished from my royal home, whither I have no hope of returning. I have lost my good name,[5] which is worse: for though I have committed no fault, yet I give everyone the excuse to hold that, being a wanderer, I must be a loose woman. / Deprive a woman of her virtue, and what other blessing

---

3. The scene echoes Ovid's tale of Europa, abducted by Jupiter in the guise of a bull, in *Metamorphoses* 2.   4. The sun god.   5. Reputation; compare with Ruggiero's loss of all but his name on Alcina's island.

can she enjoy in this world? I suffer for being young, alas, and for being accounted, whether rightly or wrongly, beautiful. I cannot thank Heaven for this gift, as it is the source of all my sorrows. It was on this account that Argalia my brother died—little good did his enchanted weapons do him. / It was on this account that Agrican, King of Tartary, defeated my father Galafron, Great Khan of Cathay and the Indies, which led to my present sorry state, shifting my dwelling from day to day. Now that you have taken from me all my possessions, my honor and those dear to me, and done your worst to me, for what further misery are you preparing me? / If drowning me in the sea did not seem to you a cruel enough death, I'll not recoil if you send a wild beast to devour me and put an end to my torments, if only that will satisfy you. Send me any affliction, any at all and, as long as I die of it, I'll not be able to thank you enough." Thus spoke the maiden through her tears. The next moment the hermit appeared. /

The hermit, from the top of a high rock, had been observing Angelica who, all bewildered and forlorn, had been set ashore at the base of it. He had come six days before, borne hither by a demon who took an untrodden route. Now he approached her, with a show of piety as profound as that of Paul or Hilarion.[6] / When the damsel noticed him, she took comfort, for she did not know him; her terror gradually abated, though her face still remained pale and drawn. When he was close by she said, "Mercy, good father! I've come to a pitiful pass!" And, her voice choked with sobs, she explained to him what he already knew full well. / The hermit offered her good, devout words of comfort, and as he spoke, he boldly placed his hands now on her breast, now on her tear-stained cheeks. Then, gaining confidence, he tried to embrace her, but she angrily struck at his chest and pushed him away, her face suffused with a modest blush. / Out of his pocket the hermit now drew a phial of liquid and lightly sprayed a drop of it onto the maiden's eyes—eyes which sparkled with the most blazing brand in Cupid's armory. The liquid drops put her to sleep: she lay supine on the sand, now a prey to the lustful old lecher. / He hugged her and felt her at his pleasure: she was asleep and could offer no resistance. He planted kisses on her lovely breast and on her lips; there was no one to see him in that wild, deserted spot. But when he came to the impact, his charger stumbled, for his wasted body would not answer to his desire—his was too elderly, unsuitable a jade, and the harder he forced him the worse his success. / He tried one way, then another, but could not get his flop-eared nag to jump; vainly he shook his reins and spurred him on, but there was no making him raise his head. Eventually he fell asleep beside the damsel, who was now to suffer a worse assault: when Fortune takes it into her head to make play with a mortal, she does nothing by halves. /

But, before I tell you what happened, I must make a slight digression. In the northern seas, over towards the setting sun, out beyond Ireland, there lies an island; its name is Ebuda. It has only a few inhabitants, the survivors of the destruction wrought upon it by the horrid orc and the other sea-beasts brought thither by Proteus, the vengeful god.[7] /

An old legend, possibly true, relates that once upon a time a powerful king ruled the island; he had a daughter of such entrancing beauty that, when she walked on the briny beach, she could without effort leave Proteus burn-

---

6. First hermit of Palestine. *Paul:* the apostle to the Gentiles. 7. Shape-shifting sea god.

ing even in the middle of his watery realm. And Proteus, coming upon her alone one day, caught her in an embrace and left her pregnant. / Her father, who was of exceedingly harsh and severe disposition, regarded the matter as an intolerable injury, so much so that no excuse, no pity would stay him from ordering her beheaded—passionate anger ruled him. Nor would he defer the execution of his cruel command in view of her pregnant condition. And the little grandson who had committed no fault: he had him slain even before he was born. / Proteus, the sea-god who pastures the proud flocks of Neptune, ruler of the Ocean, heard the dreadful torment of his lady and broke all bounds in his seething wrath. At once he sent onshore his orcs and sealions and all his watery flock to ravage the sheep and cattle, yes, and the hamlets and farms and those who toiled there; / often, too, they surged up to the town walls and laid siege to them from all sides. The townsfolk had to stand armed guard day and night—a wearisome duty, and terrifying. Everyone had withdrawn from the open fields. Eventually, to find some remedy, they repaired to the oracle for a consultation, and this was its reply: / They must find a maiden as beautiful as the first and take her to the water's edge and offer her to the irate god to compensate for the one who was slain. If he was satisfied with her beauty he would keep her, and would harass them no further; but if he rejected her they must offer him another and yet another until he was content. / Thus among the comeliest of the fair sex a hard toll began to be exacted: each day one of them was offered to Proteus until one acceptable to him were found. The first met her death, and so did all who followed, for one and all were engulfed in the maw of a great orc who remained near the river's mouth after the rest of the terrible sea-herd was dispersed. /

Whether or not there is any truth in this story about Proteus, I really have no idea; at all events, a wicked, ancient law was there enforced against women, on the basis of such a story: the monstrous orc, who visits their shore every day, must be fed on their flesh. To be a woman is a hard enough lot at the best of times—but here particularly so. / Poor wretched damsels, borne by injurious Fate to so inclement a shore where the islanders keep watch upon the sea to make a wicked holocaust of alien women: for the more damsels from abroad who are sacrificed, the smaller the inroads they have to make among their own womenfolk. But as the wind does not always blow the prey in their direction, they go out scavenging along every other shore. / They scour every sea in their galleys and brigs and other vessels and from near and far they fetch in what they need to relieve their torment. Many women they carry off by force, a few they lure and entice, others they buy with gold; they keep gathering them in from all quarters and pack them into their prisons and keeps. /

As one of their galleys was passing close inshore, coasting along the deserted strand where poor Angelica lay asleep on the grass amid the underbrush, a number of sailors landed to refurbish their supplies of wood and fresh water. So they came upon this, the flower of feminine beauty and grace, lying clasped in the venerable father's arms. / Alas, too precious, too exalted a prey for men so base, so barbarous! Oh cruel Fortune, who would ever imagine that you could exercise such power over human affairs! You would feed a monster with the fairest of the fair, who stirred King Agrican to leave the Caucasian gates with half of Scythia in his train, and invade India, there to meet his death; / the fairest beauty, whom Sacripant preferred to his own honor and goodly kingdom; she who made Orlando, Duke of Anglant, besmirch his name and sully his lofty genius; she for whom, in massive disarray, the entire Orient stood to arms: now so abandoned is she, there is not one she can turn to for so much as a word of help. /

Oppressed by sleep, beautiful Angelica was shackled before she could rouse herself. With her they carried off the hermit in the ship already crowded with grieving humanity. The sail was hoisted to the masthead and drew the ship back to the grim island, where they shut the maiden in a dungeon until her turn arrived. / But her beauty produced such an effect upon those hardened folk that out of pity they postponed her sacrifice for many days, reserving her till the last possible moment. So long as there was another alien damsel to replace her, she was saved by her angelic countenance.

Finally, though, she was brought to the sea-monster, with the whole population following, weeping, in her train. / Who shall describe the sobs and shrieks and wails which mounted to the heavens? I am amazed that the shore did not gape open when she was exposed on the cold rock, to wait, chained and abandoned by all, for a stark, dreadful death. I shall not tell you more—it is too painful, and sorrow drives me to turn my rhymes in some other direction, / and find less harrowing verses until my weary spirit recovers: the baleful viper, the jealous tiger whipped up into a frenzy of rage, and whatever venomous species creep through the hot sands between the Atlantic and the Red Sea shore—they could none of them behold or contemplate without compassion the sight of Angelica tied to the bare rock. / Ah, if her Orlando had known—he had gone to Paris in search of her—or the two knights who were tricked by the wily old hermit who sent them his infernal messenger! They would have risked a thousand deaths to follow Angelica's traces and bring her aid. And yet, even had they known where to find her, what could they have done, seeing the distance that separated them from her? /

Paris meanwhile lay besieged by Agramant, King Trojan's famous son; and the day came when the city was reduced to such straits that it almost fell to the enemy. Were it not that God accepted the Christians' prayers and flooded the plain in a murky downpour, the Sacred Empire and the mighty name of France would that day have fallen to the African spears. / The Almighty Creator turned His eyes to the just lament of the old emperor, and dowsed the fires in a sudden rainstorm; probably no human ingenuity would have been able to master them. Wise is the man who always turns to God: for no one else can give him better assistance. The pious monarch well recognized this, owing his rescue to divine intervention. /

That night, Orlando imparted his fleeting thoughts to his restless bed. This way and that he drove them, and herded them all together, but could never pen them in. They were like the tremulous gleam which a limpid pool gives off under the rays of the sun or moon—high and low, to right and left it fans out, and leaps over the broad roof-tops.[8] / His lady returned to haunt his mind—not that she had ever been absent from it—and stoked up to a new incandescence the fire which during the day seemed to have waned. She had

---

8. Echoes Virgil's simile from *Aeneid* 8.22; Aeneas leaves camp to find allies, whereas Orlando abandons his sovereign and uncle for love.

come with him to the West from Cathay; and now, with Charles's defeat at Bordeaux, he had lost all trace of her. / Bitterly Orlando regretted this, and vainly brooded on his stupidity.

"What a coward's role I played, my love!" said he. "Alas, how sickened I am to think that I could have had you with me night and day, for of your own goodness you did not deny me this, but I let you be handed over to Namo's⁹ keeping, and knew not how to forestall such an affront! / Did not I have reason to make a stand? Aye, and supposing Charles had stood his ground? Well, supposing he had—who could have forced my hand? Who was going to take you away in the teeth of my opposition? Could I not have fought, sword in hand, or made them first tear my heart out of my breast? Neither Charles nor all his henchmen together were capable of wresting you from me by force. / He might at least have left her well guarded in Paris or some / other stronghold. If he gave her into Namo's keeping, it must surely have been with a view to losing her. Who could have guarded her better than I? Who would have guarded her with his own life, more jealously than his own heart, his very eyes? I should and could have done so, but I did not. / Where are you now, my love, my pretty nursling, where are you without me? Are you not like the ewe lamb lost in the wood as the daylight wanes—hither and yon she wanders, bleating, and hopes the shepherd will hear her; it is the wolf, though, that hears from afar, and the poor shepherd weeps for his lamb in vain. / Where are you, hope of my heart? Are you still a-wandering all by yourself? Or have the wicked wolves found you unprotected by your faithful Orlando? And your flower,¹ which could set me among the heavenly gods, the flower which I preserved for you intact, so as not to sadden your chaste heart, will they, alas, have plucked and despoiled it? / O, woe upon me, what would I but to die if they have plucked my pretty flower! Almighty God, afflict me with any sorrow, any, but not this! If this has truly come to pass, I must with my own hands take my life and damn my despairing soul."

Thus cried Orlando, tormented knight, amid sighs and bitter tears. / Now was the time when every living creature concedes rest to his careworn spirit—some lying in feather-beds, others on hard stones or on the grass, or in the branches of beech and myrtle-trees. But you, Orlando, you scarcely shut your eyelids, pricked as you are by sharp and jagged thoughts, which leave you no peace to enjoy even the briefest snatch of slumber. / Orlando dreamed of a green bank all scattered with fragrant flowers, and there he saw a vision of ivory-white blent with a flush of crimson painted by Love's own hand, and a pair of limpid stars whose light nourished his soul, caught in Love's toils—I mean he saw the lovely eyes and face which had plucked his heart from his breast. / He enjoyed a wonderful sense of happiness and well-being, as deep as a man can feel who is happy in love. But a sudden storm blew up, which ravaged the flowers and threw down the trees—a storm the like of which you will not see when Aquilo, Auster, and Levanter meet and contend. He dreamed that he wandered through a wilderness in vain search of shelter. / Meanwhile the hapless lover somehow or other loses his lady in the failing light, and searches here and there through the woods and moors calling her name. And while in vain he cries, "Woe is me! Who is it

9. Duke of Bavaria, Charlemagne's trusted friend and adviser.   1. Angelica's virginity; compare Orlando's speech with Sacripant's in canto 1.

who has changed my solace into poison?" he hears his lady tearfully calling to him for help. / He runs to where he thinks the cries come from, and searches desperately high and low; imagine his searing grief when he can no longer descry his love's sweet radiance. Now he hears a voice from a different quarter, which cries: "Look no more to have joy from her here below."[2]

At this dreadful cry he woke, to find himself bathed in tears. / Unmindful that the pictures must be false that fear or hope projects in the dreaming mind, Orlando was so wrought up about his lady, believing that some danger or disgrace must have overtaken her, that he leapt, fulminating, out of bed, clad himself in armor and chain-mail and all else he needed, then fetched Brigliador;[3] but he dispensed with the services of a squire. / And to go anywhere at will without compromising his reputation, he wore not his distinguished emblem of red and white quarterings, but chose a black one—perhaps it was consonant with his sense of mourning. This sable emblem he had wrested from one Amostant whom he had slain a few years earlier. / He stole off in the depth of the night, greeting nobody and leaving no word for the emperor, his uncle; he did not bid farewell even to Brandimart,[4] his boon companion whom he loved so well. But when the golden-haired Sun set forth from Tithonus's[5] splendid halls and routed the dark shades of night, the emperor realized that the paladin was gone. / Charles was profoundly displeased to discover that his nephew had made off in the night, when he was most bound to stay with him and lend his assistance. And, unable to restrain his anger, he broke out in imprecations against him and heaped abuse upon him, uttering threats if he did not return, and promising to make him sorry for such a dereliction. /

Now Brandimart, who loved Orlando as much as his own self, was quick to act, whether in the hope of persuading the paladin to return, or simply from anger at hearing him the butt of such abuse and raillery. He scarcely waited for dusk to gather than he set out in his turn, without a word to his Fiordiligi for fear she try to oppose his decision. / She was a damsel he deeply loved, and he was seldom apart from her: she was comely, graceful, and of gentle manners; nor was she lacking in shrewdness and wisdom. If he did not take leave of her, it was because he planned to return to her within the day; but events so fell out that he was delayed beyond the expected time. / After vainly waiting for him, and finding him still not returned after nearly a month, her desire for him was so sharpened that she set off without guides or any company. She traveled through many lands searching for him, as at the proper time her story shall reveal.

But I shall not for the present say more about these two: I am more concerned about Orlando, the lord of Anglant. / Once he had altered the glorious emblem of Almont, he went to the gate and whispered into the ear of the captain of the guard, "I am the count." Immediately the drawbridge was lowered for him, and he took the road leading directly to the enemy camp. What followed you shall discover in the next canto.

* * *

Cruel, treacherous Love! See what it can do to a heart, once conquered! It can make Orlando forget the sovereign fealty that he owes his lord. Once

2. Orlando's dream is intensely Petrarchan; cf. especially Petrarch's sonnet 126 above. 3. Orlando's horse. 4. Orlando's closest friend. 5. Ancient husband of the dawn, Aurora.

upon a time he was a man of sound judgment, awake to his duty, a true defender of Holy Church. But now? Thanks to feckless Love, he pays no heed to his uncle, none to his self-respect, still less to God. / I can forgive him, though, with all my heart. Indeed, I am delighted to have such a partner in crime: for my own efforts at self-improvement are something short of zealous, but when it comes to harmful pursuits, I run with the foremost.

Off he went, dressed all in black, with no concern for the many friends he was forsaking, and passed amid the tented camp of the Africans and Spaniards: / or rather, not tented, for the rain had driven them to shelter under trees and roofs. There they were, then, bedded down in groups of ten, twenty, four, seven, eight, some further off, others closer in. They were all sleeping, haggard and exhausted, some spread-eagled on the ground, others with their heads pillowed on their hands. All asleep—and the count was free to slaughter all he wanted, but not once did he set his hand to Durindana.[6] / For Orlando is great of heart, and would not stoop to striking men who sleep. Hither and thither he moved, intent on picking up the traces of his lady. And every time he came upon someone awake, with many a sigh he would give a description of her and of her apparel, and entreat the man out of kindness to tell him which way she went. / When the day dawned bright and clear he continued his search throughout the Moorish camp; this he could safely do, dressed as he was in Arab costume. He was also aided by the fact that French was not his only tongue: he spoke African with such fluency that he could have passed for a native of Tripoli. / Here he stopped, then, for three days, wholly intent on making a thorough search. After this he started to explore every town and village around; he not only visited those of the Ile-de-France, but also passed again through the Auvergne and Gascony, searching every last hamlet. From Provence to Brittany he searched, and from Picardy to the confines of Spain. /

It was the end of October and the onset of November, the season when the trees can be seen shedding their leafy raiment until they stand stripped and shivering in their nakedness, and the birds fly together in tight flocks. This was when Orlando began his amorous quest; all that winter he continued it, and still on into the following spring. / In the course of these wanderings from village to village he came one day to a river which separates the Normans from the Bretons and flows softly to the sea close by. It was swollen at present, and streaked with froth from the melting snows and the rains up in the mountains. And the current had demolished the bridge and swept it away so there was no crossing. / The paladin looked closely at each shore in turn to see how he was to reach the other side (inasmuch as he was neither bird nor fish). And what did he see but a boat coming toward him with a damsel sitting in the stern. She signed to him that she was coming, but stopped a little short of the bank. / She did not put into the shore, as though fearing lest the passenger come on board uninvited.

Orlando besought her to take him in her boat and land him on the other side, but "No knight crosses here," she replied, "who has not first given me his word that he will do battle at my request—the most just and honorable battle in the world. / If then, sir, you wish me to help you set foot on the other side, promise me that, before this next month is out, you will go to the King of Hibernia and join the fine host assembling there to destroy the island

6. Orlando's sword.

of Ebuda, the most sinister of any island set in the sea. / You must know that beyond Ireland there are many islands and one of them is Ebuda, which sends out its thievish people with orders to plunder. And any women they capture they give as food to a voracious beast which comes in daily to the shore and finds each time a new woman or maiden to devour. / For merchants and pirates go about bringing them in, and the more beautiful the better— and counting one a day, you can readily imagine how many women and maidens have died. But if you have room for pity, and are not entirely closed to Love, be glad to be numbered with this host who will be setting forth on so bounteous an errand." /

Orlando could scarcely wait for the end of the story before he swore he would be the first at that enterprise, like a person who cannot endure to listen to an account of some wicked, loathsome deed. And he found himself thinking, then fearing, that those people had taken Angelica, for he had been seeking her high and low and still had found no trace of her. / This idea so perturbed him, quite sweeping out of his mind any previous plan, that without waiting a moment he decided to set sail for that evil land.

* * *

Summary   Searching for Angelica, Orlando meets and aids Olimpia, whose lover has been captured by Cimosco, a neighboring king whose son had loved Olimpia and been killed by her on their wedding night. Orlando reunites Olimpia with her beloved Bireno, defeats Cimosco, and casts his magical fire-spitting tube (the first gun) to the bottom of the ocean.

FROM CANTOS 10 AND 11

[Ruggiero Learns from Logistilla and Takes a Grand Tour]

I want to take up Ruggiero's story: he was riding along the shore, weary and exhausted under the intense midday heat. The sun beat down on the hill and reverberated off it, while under foot the fine white sand smoldered. The armor he wore was well nigh glowing red-hot, as at its first making. / Thirst, the exhaustion of plodding through the deep sand, and the solitude of his journey kept him tedious, unwelcome company as he rode along the sun-blinded beach.[7] After a while he came to an old tower which stood out of the water at the beach's edge, and in its shadow he discovered three ladies from Alcina's court: he recognized them by their dress and manner. / Reclining on Egyptian rugs, they were enjoying the fresh shade and a wide choice of wines in various jugs and all sorts of delicacies to eat. They had a little boat waiting off the beach; it was playing with the rippling waves until a helpful breeze should spring up and fill its sails, for at the moment the air was utterly still. / The ladies saw Ruggiero pursuing his way along the shifting dunes. They noticed how thirst had left its imprint on his lips, and how his worn face was bathed in sweat, and they invited him, bidding him not to be so set upon his journey, but to relent awhile and seek the fresh, sweet shade and give solace to his weary body. /

One of them approached his horse to hold his stirrup and invite him to dismount; another came with a crystal goblet of sparkling wine, which only

---

7. Ariosto elaborates the idea of the desert as a middle ground between captivity (on Alcina's island) and understanding (under Logistilla's tutelage).

excited his thirst. But Ruggiero was not going to dance to their tune: any delay would favor Alcina, giving her time to catch him up—she was now close behind him. / Imagine fine saltpeter and pure sulphur touched with a flame and igniting; or the sea boiling up when a dark whirlwind descends upon it. Far worse was the anger, the rage into which the third damsel flared when she saw Ruggiero calmly trudging on across the sand, ignoring them—and they fancied themselves as beauties! /

"A fine gentleman you are!" she shrieked at him. "Those arms of yours—you stole them! And that horse would in no other wise be yours. I know what I'm talking about, which is why I'd like to see you properly punished—with death! You ought to be quartered, set on fire, hanged, you hideous thief, you scurvy, arrogant knave!" / The insolent woman heaped abuse on him, but Ruggiero answered her not a word, for he could expect little honor from so paltry a quarrel. With her sisters she straightway put out in the boat which awaited them on the water, and rowing frantically, they followed him along the shore, keeping him in view. / She kept intensifying her stream of abuse, ceaselessly inventive in finding new epithets.

Meanwhile Ruggiero came to the channel separating him from the land of Logistilla, the more engaging sorceress. Here he noticed an old boatman casting off from the further shore, as though he had already been told and was there ready waiting for Ruggiero's arrival. / On sight of him the boatman cast off and came gladly to fetch him over to a happier shore. If the face gives a true warrant for the heart, he was a kindly man, the soul of discretion. Ruggiero set foot upon the little skiff thanking God. He set forth across the tranquil reach, and enjoyed some conversation with the ferryman, a wise and experienced man, / who praised him for having contrived to tear himself free of Alcina in time, before she gave him the enchanted cup which she ultimately presented to all her lovers.[8] And as he was conveying him to Logistilla's, where he would be able to witness virtuous behavior, perennial beauty, and infinite grace, which / nourishes but never cloys the heart, "At first sight," he explained, "wonder and reverence are the emotions that Logistilla excites; on further contemplation of her fathomless presence, all other good dwindles to little value. Her love is different to others': normally, hope or fear erodes the heart of a man in love. Now in her love, desire craves no more, but rests content on sight of her. / She will teach you more alluring preoccupations than music and dancing, perfumes, baths, and fine fare: rather, how your mind, better informed, can soar to the heights, loftier than the kite: and how the glory of the blessed can in part permeate the bodies of mortals." As he spoke the boatman made great progress towards the safer shore. /

Now he noticed a fleet of ships out at sea all heading in their direction: they were bearing the slighted Alcina and the host she had assembled to bring ruin upon herself and her realm, or else to recapture her ravished treasure. Love played no small part in her motives, but an equal part was taken by injured pride. / Never since she was born had she been eaten by so intense an anger. She so urged the oars through the water that they threw up great plumes of spray to either side of the bows. So great was the noise, both sea and shore echoed with it.

"Bring out your shield, Ruggiero, now you must: else you are a dead man,

---

8. On the model of Homer's Circe, Alcina presents an enchanted cup to her former lovers that transforms them into beasts and plants; Alcina, however, is herself enchanted by Atlas so that she will always adore Ruggiero.

or shamefully captured." / So urged Logistilla's boatman; and, acting on his own words, he himself grasped the sheath, drew it off the shield and disclosed its light for all to see. The magic radiance it gave off so dazzled the eyes of the enemy that they were struck blind on the instant; some of them fell overboard from the stern, others from the bows. / A man keeping watch from the castle saw Alcina's fleet approaching and raised the alarm, hammering on the bell to summon the defenders to the harbor. The artillery rained missiles against the intruders who were contriving harm against good Ruggiero. So he received support from every side and was able to save his life and liberty. / Four ladies now came down to the beach, sent hither by Logistilla: stout-hearted Andronica, prudent Fronesia, Dicilla the just, and chaste Sophrosina[9] who, having more to do here than the others, blazed and sparkled. And the army, which was unrivaled throughout the world, sallied forth from the castle and spread out along the shore. / Beneath the castle in the quiet estuary rode many a large vessel—a whole fleet of them—ready at the trumpet's shrill, ready day or night at a spoken command to issue forth to battle. Thus by the sea and land the battle was engaged, fierce and terrible; and because of it the realm which Alcina had earlier seized from her sister was thrown into turmoil. / How many battles have ended in a way never predicted for them! Not only did Alcina fail to retrieve, as she expected, her fugitive lover; but her ships, which had been so numerous that the sea could barely find room for them all, were all consumed by the fires which broke out, till but one remained to her in which to make her sorry escape. /

Alcina fled, leaving her wretched followers in disarray, some burnt, others drowned or captured. Ruggiero's loss stung her far worse than any other of her afflictions. Night and day she would be given over to bitter lament and to abundant tears because of him, and often she regretted that she was unable to die and thus put an end to her cruel agony. / No fairy may ever die so long as the sun holds his course and the Heavens remain unchanged. Were it otherwise, Alcina's grief was such that Clotho might have spun out her life-thread faster: or she herself might, as Dido, have ended her misery with a dagger; she might have followed the majestic queen of the Nile[1] into a mortal sleep. But fairies never can die. /

Let us return to Ruggiero, the knight worthy of eternal glory, and leave Alcina to her sorrow. He stepped out of the boat and onto the safer shore, thanking God for the happy outcome of his enterprise. Then, turning his back to the sea, he hastened across the dry land up to the castle. / Never before or since has mortal eye beheld a mightier nor a more beautiful castle. Its walls could not have been more precious had they been made of diamond or garnet. Jewels such as those to be found in it are never spoken of here below: whoever would hear tell of them needs must make the journey there himself—I don't believe that he would come across them anywhere else, except perhaps in Paradise. / What in particular gives these jewels their supremacy over every other is this: on looking at them, a man sees right into his own soul; he sees there reflected his vices and virtues, so that he no longer believes in the compliments he is paid, nor does he heed blame when he is charged unfairly. Looking into these bright mirrors, he discovers himself, and learns wisdom. / They give off a light, too, brilliant as the sun and

---

9. Their names mean strength, prudence, justice, and temperance.   1. Cleopatra, who killed herself by applying asps to her breasts. *Clotho*: one of the fates. *Dido*: Virgil's queen, who committed suicide when Aeneas abandoned her.

so abundant that whoever possesses one of them may, wherever he be, make broad daylight at will, in spite of Phoebus. Nor are the walls remarkable only for their gems: the materials and the refinement of construction vie with each other, so that between the two there is no deciding which perfection is the greater. / Above the soaring arches, which looked as though they supported the very dome of Heaven, gardens extended which were so spacious and magnificent that even at ground-level they would be hard to lay out. Through the luminous crenellations could be seen the verdure of the fragrant trees, which were a delight in the summer, and in winter remained a mass of blossom and ripe fruit. / Trees as noble do not grow outside these lovely gardens, nor do such roses, violets and lilies, amarants and jasmine. You will observe, anywhere else, how all in one day a flower will be born, live out its term and die, drooping its head on its bereaved stalk, for it is subject to the changing seasons. / Here, though, every thing remained verdant green; the flowers bloomed in perpetual radiance, not through any beneficent working of Nature, but through the studious care of Logistilla: with no need to depend upon the climate (impossible though this would seem to anyone else), she maintained perennial spring in her garden. /

Logistilla was visibly pleased that so worthy a knight should have come to her, and she gave orders that everyone should make much of him and study to do him reverence. Astolfo had arrived some time earlier, and Ruggiero was delighted to see him. A few days later all the others arrived whom Melissa had restored to their proper selves. /

After a day or two in which to rest, Ruggiero went to the wise enchantress accompanied by Astolfo who, no less than he, was anxious to see the West again. Melissa spoke to her on behalf of them both, humbly entreating her to give them counsel and assistance in making good their return to whence they came. / "I shall give the matter thought," replied Logistilla, "and two days hence I shall let you know what I have devised." She took counsel with herself how best to help Ruggiero and, after him, the duke. Her conclusion was that the winged horse would have to return the former to the shores of Aquitania; but first the beast would have to be fitted with a special bridle wherewith Ruggiero could turn him in flight and rein him in. / She showed him what to do if he wanted the steed to climb, what to do to make him descend, how to make him wheel in a circle, or go fast, or simply hover. And whatever the knight was accustomed to performing on a good earth-bound horse he soon became adept at achieving in the air on the feathered steed. / When Ruggiero was fully prepared he took leave of the kind enchantress, to whom he remained attached ever after by a strong bond of affection, and departed from that country. He set off, and first I shall tell of his adventures. Afterwards I shall relate how the English knight, on a longer and more arduous journey, made his way back to Charlemagne, and to the court where his friends were. /

Ruggiero departed, but did not retrace the path he had earlier taken against his will, when the hippogryph kept course out over the sea and he scarcely sighted land. This time, as he could make the beast fly hither and yon at his own whim, he chose to take a different way back, like the Wise Men when they avoided Herod.[2] / Coming hither, he had left Spain behind and made a direct line for India, where it is washed by the Eastern Sea—

2. Biblical tyrant.

where Alcina was entertaining a quarrel with her fellow-sorceress. This time he was disposed to see other lands than those where Aeolus incites the winds, and to complete the circle[3] he had started, so as to girdle the earth, like the sun. / On his journey he saw Cathay to one side and to the other Mangiana, as he passed over great Quinsai. He flew over the Himavian range, and skirted Sericana to his right. From the hyperborean land of the Scythians, he turned in towards the Hyrcanian sea and reached Sarmatia; then, arriving at the point where Europe and Asia meet, he beheld the lands of the Russians and Prussians, and came to Pomerania. / For all his pressing desire to return to Bradamant, Ruggiero was unwilling to forgo the pleasure of discovering the world, but had perforce to pass by way of the Poles, Hungarians, and Germans and the rest of those bleak northern lands. Finally he arrived in far-off England. / You must not imagine, my Lord, that he was constantly on the wing; every evening he put up at some hostelry, avoiding poor accommodation as best he could. Days and months went by as he pursued his way, so eager was he to visit lands and seas. Then, arriving one morning at London, the hippogryph swooped down over the Thames.

* * *

After this he turned his steed South towards the sea that washes the Breton coast, and looking down, he espied Angelica chained to the bare rock. / Chained to the bare rock, she was, on the Isle of Tears—for this was the name given to the island inhabited by those cruel savages, those barbarous folk who, as I related in a previous canto, went marauding along many a shore abducting every comely damsel in order to feed her infamously to a monster. / That very morning she was chained there for the huge sea-monster, the orc, to come and swallow her alive; for this, horrible to relate, was how he fed. I explained earlier that she was the prize of the corsairs who found her on the beach asleep beside the old hermit who had lured her there by magic. / The brutal, ruthless savages left the exquisitely beautiful damsel exposed on the shore to the cruel monster, and as naked as when Nature first fashioned her; not even a veil did she have to cover the lily-white, the rose-red, unfading in December as in July, which colored her lustrous limbs. / Ruggiero would have taken her for a statue fashioned in alabaster or some lambent marble, and tethered thus to the rock by some diligent sculptor's artifice, were it not that he distinctly saw tears coursing down her rose-fresh, lily-white cheeks and bedewing her unripe apple-breasts, and her golden tresses flowing in the wind. /

As he looked into her lovely eyes Ruggiero was reminded of his Bradamant; he was pricked with compassion and love, and could scarcely refrain from weeping. Tenderly he addressed the maiden, after reining in his charger. "Gentle lady, the only fetter you merit is that with which love binds his votaries: / quite undeserving must you be of this plight or of any other. Who is the miscreant so perverted as to blemish the smooth ivory of your delicate hands with unwelcome bruising?" On hearing him speak she perforce became like white ivory sprinkled with carmine, seeing those parts of her exposed to view which, for all their beauty, modesty would conceal. / She would have covered her face with her hands were they not tied to the hard

---

3. Ruggiero takes a world tour to complete his humanist education.

rock. But she bathed it in tears—this at least she was free to do—and tried to keep it bowed. After sobbing a little, she prepared to speak, in a sad, small voice; but the words did not come—they were thwarted by the loud noise now to be heard from the sea. /

The colossal monster now appeared, half submerged; like a long ship making port, driven before the wind from North or South, so was the terrible orc as it approached the morsel shown to it. Now the monster had almost reached her. The damsel was half-dead with fright—she was past comforting. / Ruggiero was holding his lance not in rest, but in free play, and he struck at the orc, a beast I can only describe as a great coiling, twisting mass, quite unlike an animal in shape, except for its head, with protruding eyes and teeth like a boar's. Ruggiero struck at it between the eyes, but he might as well have been striking at solid iron or stone. / His first thrust proving ineffectual, he returned to do better the second time. The orc, seeing the shadow cast by the spreading wings flitting here and there across the water, left its certain prey awaiting it on shore and started a furious chase, curving and coiling, after the elusive one instead. Ruggiero dropped down and struck many a blow, / like an eagle dropping from the sky when it has spotted a snake weaving through the grass, or lying on a bare stone in the sun, smoothing and titivating its golden scales: it does not attack so as to meet the hissing, venomous jaws head-on, but endeavors rather to sink its talons into the serpent's back, and aims its flight so as to avoid the snake's turning and biting it. / So Ruggiero wielded his sword and lance so as to avoid the monster's snout bristling with teeth, but aimed blows between its ears, on its back and at its tail.

If the beast turned, he swerved aside, choosing the right moment to descend and to gain height. But as what he struck was always adamantine he could not penetrate the rock-hard carapace. / Such a battle will be fought between an impudent fly and a mastiff in dusty August, or the months before and after—from the corn harvest to that of the grape. The fly will infest him and buzz around him, stinging him now on the eye, now on the snapping muzzle. And frequently the mastiff will snap his jaws shut on nothing—but the moment he catches the fly, that moment makes up for everything. / So powerfully did the orc thrash the water with its tail that the seas surged up to the skies, and Ruggiero could not tell whether his mount was beating the air with its wings or swimming in the waves. Many times he wished himself safely on dry land, fearing that if the hippogryph continued having to endure the flying spray, his wings would be so sodden that he would vainly wish for something floatable, be it only a cockle-shell. /

He hit on a new and better plan: to overcome the cruel monster with other weapons. He would dazzle it with the flash of the enchanted shield still in its cover. He flew to the shore and, as a precaution, took the ring which defied all magic and slipped it onto the little finger of the damsel chained to the bare rock. / This was the ring which Bradamant, to effect Ruggiero's release, had seized from Brunello,[4] and subsequently sent to him in India by Melissa, to rescue him from wicked Alcina's hands. Melissa, as I described to you earlier, had used the ring to the advantage of many; then she had returned it to Ruggiero, who thereafter had always worn it on his finger. /

4. A clever thief.

He gave it now to Angelica, lest she be harmed by the glint of the shield, and to protect her eyes, which had already ensnared him. The monstrous sea-beast was approaching the shore, his belly displacing half the ocean. Ruggiero took up his station and lifted the veil: and it was as though another sun had entered the sky. / The enchanted light struck the monster's eyes and wrought its wonted effect.[5] As a trout or perch floats down a river made turbid with lime by some hill-dweller, thus was the monster, a ghastly sight as it lay upturned in the foaming sea. Ruggiero thrust at it all over but could find no way to penetrate its hide. /

All this while the beautiful damsel besought him not to continue his vain onslaught against the horny scales. "Come back good sir, for God's sake," she begged, weeping; "unchain me before the orc revives. Take me with you, drown me in the depths of the sea, but let me not end in the belly of the ghastly fish." Moved by this just entreaty, Ruggiero untied the damsel and carried her away from the shore. / Spurred, the steed thrust off the beach and launched into the air and galloped through the sky. On his back he carried the knight, with the damsel mounted right behind him. Thus did he deprive the monster of a feast which was far too dainty and delicious for it. He kept turning round, and in his breast, and in his lively eyes a thousand kisses were a-smoldering. / Instead of circling Spain, as he had earlier planned,[6] he put down at a neighboring shore, where Brittany juts furthest out to sea.

By the shore there was a shady oak-wood, which forever resounded with Philomena's[7] lament; in the middle was a grassy clearing with a spring, and to either side, a solitary hill. / Here the eager knight drew rein and set foot in the clearing; he had his charger fold his wings, (leaving at liberty, however, another steed, who had now spread his even wider). He dismounted, but could scarcely restrain himself from climbing onto a different mount; but his gear delayed him: it delayed him, for he had to pull it off; it obstructed the impetus of his desire. / With hasty fingers he fumbled confusedly at his armor, now this side, now the other. Never before had it seemed such a long business—for every thong unlaced, two seemed to become entangled. But this canto has gone on too long, my Lord, and perhaps you are growing a-weary with listening to it: I shall defer my story to another time when it may prove more welcome.

. . .

A mettlesome charger will often suffer himself to be reined in from a full gallop, however gentle the hand on the rein. Seldom, however, will the bridle of Reason check rabid Lust once it scents its quarry. It is like a bear: there is no distracting him from the honey once he has sniffed at it or tasted a drop left in the jar. /

What argument can there be to stop Ruggiero and change his mind about taking his pleasure with lovely Angelica, whom he holds naked there in the convenient solitude of the glade? Bradamant he has quite forgotten, though

---

5. Compare Perseus's use of Medusa's head, the sight of which turns men to stone, to conquer the sea monster and save Andromeda; the story is told in Ovid, *Metamorphoses* 4.663–803, where Perseus, unlike Ruggiero, kills the stunned orc.   6. Ruggiero breaks off his educational world tour just short of a perfect circle.   7. The nightingale, named after a mythical young woman who was raped by her brother-in-law, Tereus; Ovid tells the tale in *Metamorphoses* 6.424–674.

she had always reigned in his heart. Or, if her memory was indeed fresh as ever, well—he would still be a fool not to make the most of the maiden present. / In this situation Xenocrates[8] himself, that austere paragon, would have yielded to lechery. Ruggiero had thrown down his lance and shield and was feverishly pulling off his armor. The damsel had modestly lowered her eyes to her exquisite body when she noticed on her finger the precious ring which Brunello had earlier stolen from her at Albracca. / This was the ring she took with her to France the first time she made the journey with her brother, who brought the lance which passed to the paladin Astolfo. With this ring she neutralized the spells Maugis[9] cast on her at Merlin's tomb. With it she helped Orlando and others to escape one morning from Dragontina;[1] / with this ring she made herself invisible and escaped from the dungeon where a wicked old man had imprisoned her. But why should I enumerate all the instances when it had proved its virtues? You know them as well as I do. Brunello found his way into her castle and stole the ring from her, for Agramant wanted it. Ever since that moment Fortune had frowned upon her until she lost her kingdom. /

Noticing the ring on her finger, as I said, she was so stunned with joy and amazement, she thought she must be dreaming, and could scarcely believe her eyes. She slipped it off her finger and straight into her mouth, and in less than a twinkling had vanished from Ruggiero's sight as completely as the sun behind a cloud. / Ruggiero looked in every direction and searched frantically all over the place, until he remembered the ring. He stopped, thunderstruck, thwarted. Cursing himself for his carelessness, he inveighed against Angelica for her discourtesy, her ingratitude—a fine way to thank him for his help! / "Heartless damsel," he complained, "is this how you reward me? You would snatch the ring from me rather than allow me to offer it to you. Why will you not accept it from me? Not only the ring, but the shield, too, and the fleet-footed horse, and myself I would give to you, to use me as you will—only hide not your lovely face from me. I know, heartless one, that you hear me but will not answer." / As he spoke, he went groping round the spring like a blind man; many a time he hugged the empty air, hoping to clasp the damsel in the same embrace.

She meanwhile was already well on her way, and kept on walking until she came to a spacious cave beneath a hill; here she found some food. / This was the abode of an old herdsman with a large herd of mares, which were browsing on the tender grass along the fresh streams down in the valley. On either side of the cave there were stables where they could take refuge from the midday sun. That day Angelica stopped here at leisure, unseen by anybody. / When evening came and she felt sufficiently restored, she dressed herself in rustic garments, all too different from her normal gay apparel, made after every conceivable fashion and hue—in shades of green, yellow, purple, blue, and red. Even so humble attire, however, could not disguise her natural beauty and nobility. / You who praise Phyllis, Neiera, Amaryllis, or elusive Galatea, be silent! For beauty none of them can touch Angelica— saving your presence, Tityrus, and yours, Meliboeus.[2] The beautiful damsel selected from the herd of mares one which pleased her well, and the idea

8. Plato's unseducible disciple.   9. Christian wizard.   1. Boiardo's witch.   2. Pastoral shepherds and their shepherdesses.

came to her there and then to make away back to the Orient. /

Ruggiero waited a long time to see if she would discover herself, but to no purpose; once it was clear to him that he was wasting his time and she was no longer there to listen to him, he turned back to remount the horse which was at home in the air as well as on the ground. But he saw that the hippogryph had worked free of the bit and was climbing unimpeded through the sky. / It was a sorry blow, coming on top of the last, to find himself deprived of the flying horse. The loss weighed heavily upon him, no less than the damsel's trick. But what hurt more than either was the loss of the precious ring—this grieved him most especially, less for its magical properties than for the fact that it had been a gift from his lady. / Utterly dejected, he put on his armor, slung his shield on his shoulder, turned his back to the sea and set off through the grassy glades towards a broad valley. Here, amid the deep shady woods he came upon a wider, more frequented path, which he pursued only a short way when to his right, where the forest was thicker, he heard a great din. /

A great din he heard, and the shock of arms, a terrifying sound. He hastened in amid the trees and came upon two antagonists hemmed in a narrow glade and locked in battle. I know not what their quarrel was, but they were exchanging savage blows without mercy. One of them was a fierce-looking giant; the other a bold, valiant knight. / The knight was defending himself with sword and shield, and side-stepping deftly to avoid being laid out by the club which the giant was wielding two-handed. The knight's steed lay dead on the path. Ruggiero stopped to watch the battle, and soon reached the conclusion that he would prefer to see the knight win, / though he did not interfere, but stood out of the way and continued to watch. Now the giant raised his massy club over the knight's helmet and brought it down with both hands. Under the impact the knight fell. The other saw him lying dazed and, in order to put an end to him, unloosed his helmet. This enabled Ruggiero to see the knight's face. / The face he set eyes on was that of sweet, lovely Bradamant, his heart's delight; and here was the wicked giant making ready to slay her. Ruggiero challenged him to battle and advanced with drawn sword, but the giant, not prepared for another combat, took the stunned woman in his arms, / and threw her over his shoulder and carried her off as a wolf seizes a lamb, or an eagle seizes in its hooked talons a dove or some such bird. Ruggiero could see how urgently his help was needed and ran after the giant as fast as he could; but the giant strode away so fast that Ruggiero could scarcely follow him with his eyes. / The giant ran off and Ruggiero pursued him down a path through the deep shade; the path gradually broadened out until it took them clear of the wood into a broad meadow.

Summary   Orlando, still searching for Angelica, kills the orc and liberates his beautiful and naked victim, who turns out to be none other than Olimpia. Embarrassed by her nakedness, Orlando finds clothes for her and learns how she was deserted by Bireno. In the meantime, a young knight, Uberto, gazes his fill at the naked Olimpia and falls in love with her. After uniting them, Orlando continues his search.

FROM CANTOS 12 AND 22

[*Orlando Finds an Enchanted Castle, and Ruggiero and Bradamant Unite*]

When Ceres,[3] after visiting her mother on Mount Ida, sped back to the secluded valley where Mount Etna straddles the shoulders of Encelades,[4] the stricken giant, she did not find her daughter where she had left her, away from the trodden paths. After her cheeks and eyes, her hair and breast had borne the brunt of her grief, she uprooted two pines; / she lit them in Vulcan's[5] fire, enduing them with a flame which could never be quenched; and taking one in each hand, she entered her chariot, drawn by a pair of dragons. Thus she set off to search woods, fields, hills and plains, valleys, streams, pools and torrents, the land and sea: when she had scoured all the daylight world, she plunged down into the infernal regions. / Had Orlando possessed not only the zeal but also the powers of the Eleusinian goddess,[6] he would not have left a single wood, field, pond, stream, valley, hill, plain, land, or sea unsearched, nor even the heavens or the pit of eternal oblivion, in his quest for Angelica. But since he did not have the chariot with the dragons, he sought her as best he could. / He had sought her throughout France; now he was preparing to search for her through Italy and Germany, through new and old Castille, and thence across the Spanish sea to Libya.

While he was thus deciding, a voice came to his ear, and what sounded like weeping. He darted forward, and saw a knight approaching at a trot upon a great charger; / seated in front of him on the saddle and pinioned forcibly by his arm was a damsel in deepest distress. She wept and fought and gave evidence of utter sorrow, and she kept crying out, invoking the help of Orlando, the valiant Prince of Anglant; as his gaze rested upon the beautiful maiden, she looked just like the very one whom he had been seeking night and day through the length and breadth of France. / I do not say that she *was* sweet Angelica, his well-beloved—but she looked like her. Seeing his lady, his goddess being carried off in such a wretched, pitiful state, he was possessed by a frenzy of black rage, and with a terrible roar he hailed the knight; full of menace he hailed him, and drove Brigliador forward at full tilt. / The villain, wholly intent upon his prize, his booty, did not wait for him or answer, but shot away so swiftly through the trees that even the wind could scarcely have followed him. One fled, the other pursued, and a high lament could be heard sounding through the deep forest. They came galloping out into a broad meadow, in the middle of which stood a magnificent great palace. /

The stately edifice was built of many kinds of marble, a work of intricate design. In through the gate, wrought in gold, ran the knight with the lady in his arms, followed shortly after by Brigliador carrying fierce Orlando, fuming with indignation. Once inside, Orlando looked about him, but saw no sign of the knight nor of the damsel. / He jumped from his horse and stormed through into the living quarters. He dashed hither and thither, never stopping until he had looked into every room, every gallery; after vainly probing

---

3. Goddess of the harvest, she goes into mourning and blights the Earth when Pluto, god of the underworld, abducts her daughter, Proserpine. **4.** Giant struck by Jupiter's thunderbolt and buried under the volcanic Mount Etna. **5.** God of fire. **6.** Ceres.

the secrets of all the ground-floor rooms, he climbed the stairs and wasted no less time and effort searching upstairs. / The beds, he noticed, were all adorned with silk and thread of gold; not a wall was to be seen, for they, and the floors were covered with tapestries and carpets. Upstairs and downstairs and all over again Orlando hunted, but there was no joy for him: never did he set eyes upon Angelica or the thief who had wafted her sweet delicate face away from his sight. / And while vainly pursuing his quest hither and thither, full of care and anxiety, he came across Ferraù, Brandimart, King Gradasso, and King Sacripant[7] and other knights who were also searching high and low, pursuing a quest as fruitless as his own. They all complained about the malicious invisible lord of that palace— / the invisible lord for whom they were all searching. All accused him of one theft or another; one was grieving over the loss of his horse, another was raging over the loss of his lady; others had other thefts to charge him with, and none of them could tear themselves away from this cage—some there were, the victims of his deception, who had been there for whole weeks and months. /

After combing through the weird palace five and six times, Orlando said to himself: "I could stay here wasting time and effort to no purpose; the thief could have borne her out through another gate and now be far away." Thus thinking, he sallied out into the green meadow in the middle of which the palace stood. / As he skirted the outside of the woodland abode, his eyes fixed on the ground in case he caught sight of fresh footprints to right or left, he heard his name called from a window, and raised his eyes; and he imagined he heard that divine voice, thought he beheld the very face which had so transformed him. / He thought he heard Angelica addressing him in tearful entreaty: "Help! Help! I commend my virginity to you more than my soul, more than my life. Am I to be ravished by this brigand in the presence of my dearest Orlando? Rather slay me by your own hand than let me come to so sorry a pass." / These words set Orlando on a diligent search of every room, over and over, in desperation but with hope renewed. Now and then he would stop, and he would hear a voice which sounded like Angelica's, begging for help. But wherever he was, it always came from somewhere else and he could never locate it. /

But to go back to Ruggiero: I left him pursuing his lady, borne off by a giant along a densely shaded path which emerged from the wood into a broad meadow. He came to this very spot where Orlando arrived earlier, if I recognize the place aright. The giant disappeared in through the door with Ruggiero on his heels in tireless pursuit. / As he set foot inside the threshold he looked round the great courtyard and loggias, but could not espy the giant or the lady; in vain did he turn his gaze this way and that; he looked upstairs and down many a time but all to no avail—nor could he imagine where the villain could so quickly have found a hiding-place with the damsel. / When he had gone through the bedrooms, galleries, and public rooms, upstairs and down four or five times, he searched yet again and did not give up before searching even beneath the stairs. Finally, in the hope that they might be in the neighboring woods, he left; but a voice recalled him, just as it had recalled Orlando, and made him, too, return inside the palace. / The same voice, the same person whom Orlando took for Angelica, Ruggiero took for Bradamant,

---

7. Christian and Islamic knights all wandering in circles after their desires: the enchanted castle is one of Ariosto's figures for romance.

on whose account he was beside himself. Whether the voice spoke to Gradasso or to any other of those wandering about the palace, each one identified it with the object of his search. / This was a new and unusual piece of magic devised by the wizard Atlas, who meant thus to keep Ruggiero so preoccupied with this bitter-sweet love-quest of his that the evil influence would pass him by—the influence appointing him to an early death. The steel-girt castle had proved useless, so had Alcina; here he was, trying something else. / It was not only Ruggiero whom Atlas plotted to draw into this magic trap, but anyone else in France who enjoyed the highest reputation for valor—these he lured in lest Ruggiero die at their hands. And while he condemned them to this enforced residence, he had left the palace so abundantly provided that knights and ladies could dwell there in comfort and eat their fill. /

* * *

Summary   Orlando rescues Isabel from brigands. Rodomont, the strongest of the Islamic knights, storms Paris. Meanwhile, Mandricard abducts Doralice, who is betrothed to Rodomont. In the great battle at Paris, Cloridan and Medor try to rescue the body of their captain, killed by Rinaldo. Cloridan dies trying to save Medor, who refuses to leave the body; Medor, left for dead, is found by Angelica, who cures and falls in love with him. In one of the many episodes to follow, Astolfo destroys Atlas's enchanted castle by using his magical horn, which emits a noise so terrifyingly disgusting that all who hear it run for their lives. After all the captives flee in terror, Astolfo is left in custody of the hippogryph.

* * *

But if I'm to tell you the rest of the story, I must first go after Ruggiero and Bradamant. When the horn fell silent and the handsome couple were well away from this place, Ruggiero was quick to recognize at a glance what Atlas had concealed from him: Atlas had seen to it that until this moment the pair had not recognized each other. / Ruggiero looked at Bradamant and she at him in utter amazement, for their mind and vision had been clouded for so many days by the magic illusion. Ruggiero embraced his fair one who blushed redder than a rose; then he culled from her lips the first blooms of their blissful love. / A thousand times the two happy lovers renewed their embraces and hugged each other; they were so blissful, their breasts could scarcely contain their joy. They were grieved beyond measure that the magic spell had prevented their recognizing each other while they were in that restless palace, and so had made them lose so many days of happiness. / Bradamant was ready to concede all the pleasures that an honest virgin may give to a lover in order to keep him from sadness without hurting her own honor. Now she suggested to Ruggiero that if he was not to find her forever restive and stubborn about giving him the ultimate fruits, he should ask her father Aymon, in due form, for her hand—after accepting baptism. / Ruggiero would have submitted not merely to turning Christian for love of her (like her father and grandfather and all her noble house), but would there and then have given her what life remained to him, to please her. "It would be a small thing," he told her, "to place my head in fire, let alone in water,[8]

8. Fire and water are the two forms of baptism.

for love of you." / To receive baptism, and then to have Bradamant to wife, Ruggiero set out to escort the damsel to Vallombrosa—a fair, rich monastery, devout and hospitable to all comers.

On emerging from the forest they came upon a woman whose face betrayed deep sorrow. / Ruggiero, kind and courteous with everyone, but especially with women, was moved at the sight of the lovely tears streaking her delicate face, and burned to know the cause of her grief. He turned to her and, after greeting her politely, enquired why her face was thus wet with tears. / She raised her beautiful, brimming eyes and answered him with good grace, giving him a full account of the reason for her sadness, as he had asked her: "Gentle sir," she said, "these cheeks are thus tear-streaked out of pity for a young man who is to die in a castle here today. / He loves a beautiful maiden, gently born, daughter of Marsilius, the Spanish king; and, concealed beneath a white veil and in a woman's skirts, disguising his voice and countenance, without raising the suspicions of the household, every night he has been sleeping with her. But there is no secret but must eventually come to another's attention. / One man found out and told two others who related it to others still, until it came to the ears of the king. One of the king's henchmen came two days ago and had the pair seized in bed. They have both been shut in separate dungeon cells, and I don't believe that the young man will see today through before he dies under torture. / I have escaped to avoid witnessing such cruelty, for they will burn him alive; nothing can distress me more than the suffering to be inflicted upon so fine a young man. There is no pleasure so great but my enjoyment of it must turn at once to grief when I think of the cruel flames which have scorched those handsome and delicate limbs." /

As Bradamant listened she appeared to be much disturbed by this story, and greatly upset; she seemed as concerned over the condemned man's fate as if he were a brother of hers—and her fear was not wholly unfounded, as I shall explain. She turned to Ruggiero and, "It seems to me," she observed, "that our arms should favor this man." / And to the grieving woman she said: "Take heart, and see to introducing us into the castle; if they have not yet slain the youth, they shall not, take my word!" Ruggiero, noticing his lady's kindly disposition, her pity and concern, was fired with eagerness to prevent the youth from dying. /

* * *

Summary   Ruggiero and Bradamant are separated when she recognizes and chases Pinabello, the enemy who tried to kill her by pushing her into a cavern. When she catches and kills him (her only victim in the entire poem), she gets lost in the woods and then finds herself back at the home of her parents. There she is trapped in the role of dutiful daughter. Meanwhile, Orlando rescues Zerbin, the beloved of Isabel, and continues his search for Angelica.

FROM CANTOS 23 AND 24

[Orlando's Great Madness]

* * *

He came to a stream which looked like crystal; a pleasant meadow bloomed on its banks, picked out with lovely pure colors and adorned with many beautiful trees.[9] / A welcome breeze tempered the noontide for the rugged flock and naked shepherd, and Orlando felt no discomfort, for all that he was wearing breastplate, helmet, and shield. Here he stopped, then, to rest— but his welcome proved to be harsh and painful, indeed quite unspeakably cruel, on this unhappy, ill-starred day. / Looking about him, he saw inscriptions on many of the trees by the shady bank; he had only to look closely at the letters to be sure that they were formed by the hand of his goddess. This was one of the spots described earlier, to which the beautiful damsel, Queen of Cathay, often resorted with Medor, from the shepherd's house close by. / He saw "Angelica" and "Medor" in a hundred places, united by a hundred love-knots. The letters were so many nails with which Love pierced and wounded his heart. He searched in his mind for any number of excuses to reject what he could not help believing; he tried to persuade himself that it was some other Angelica who had written her name on the bark. / "But I recognize these characters," he told himself; "I've seen and read so many just like them. Can she perhaps be inventing this Medor? Perhaps by this name she means me." Thus deceiving himself with far-fetched notions, disconsolate Orlando clung to hopes which he knew he was stretching out to grasp. / But the more he tried to smother his dark suspicions the more they flared up with new vigor: he was like an unwary bird caught in a web or in birdlime—the more he beats his wings and tries to free himself, the worse ensnared he becomes.

Orlando came to where a bow-shaped curve in the hillside made a cave overlooking the clear spring. / Twisting on their stems, ivy and rambling vines adorned the entrance. Here during the heat of the day the two happy lovers used to lie in each other's arms. Their names figured here more than elsewhere; they were inscribed within and without, sometimes in charcoal, sometimes in chalk, or scratched with the point of a knife. / The dejected count approached on foot. At the entrance he saw many words which Medor had written in his own hand; they seem to have been freshly inscribed. The inscription was written in verse and spoke of the great pleasure he had enjoyed in this cave. I believe it was written in his native tongue; in ours this is how it reads: / "Happy plants, verdant grass, limpid waters, dark, shadowy cave, pleasant and cool, where fair Angelica, born of Galafron, and loved in vain by many, often lay naked in my arms. I, poor Medor, cannot repay you for your indulgence otherwise than by ever praising you, / and by entreating every lover, knight, or maiden, every person, native or alien, who happens upon this spot by accident or by design, to say to the grass, the shadows, the cave, stream, and plants: 'May sun and moon be kind to you, and the chorus of the nymphs, and may they see that shepherds never lead their flocks to you.'" / It was written in Arabic, which the count knew as well as he knew Latin. He knew many and many a tongue, but Arabic is one with which he was most familiar: his grasp of it had saved him on more than one occasion from injury and insult when he was among the Saracens. But he was not to boast if formerly his knowledge had helped him—the pain it now brought him quite discounted every former advantage. /

Five and six times the unfortunate man re-read the inscription, trying in vain to wish it away, but it was more plain and clear each time he read it.

9. The scene resembles Orlando's dream.

And each time, he felt a cold hand clutch his heart in his afflicted breast. Finally he fell to gazing fixedly at the stone—stonelike himself. / He was ready to go out of his mind, so complete was his surrender to grief. Believe one who has experienced it—this is a sorrow to surpass all others. His chin had dropped onto his chest, his head was bowed, his brow had lost its boldness. So possessed was he by sorrow that he had no voice for laments, no moisture for tears. / His impetuous grief, set upon erupting all too quickly, remained within. A broad-bellied, narrow-necked vase full of water has the same effect, as can be observed: when the vase is inverted, the liquid so surges to the neck that it blocks its own egress, and can scarcely do more than come out drop by drop. / Returning to himself a little, he considered how he might yet be mistaken about it: he hoped against hope that it might simply be someone trying to besmirch his lady's name this way, or to charge him with a burden of jealousy so unendurable that he would die of it; and that whoever it was who had done this had copied her hand most skilfully. / With such meager, such puny hopes he roused his spirits and found a little courage.

He mounted Brigliador, now that the sun was giving place to his sister in the sky. Before he had gone far he saw smoke issuing from the housetops, and heard dogs barking and cows lowing; he came to a farmhouse and found lodging. / Listlessly he dismounted, and left Brigliador to the care of a discreet stable-boy. Others there were to help him off with his armor and his golden spurs, and to refurbish them. This was the house where Medor lay wounded, and met with his great good fortune. Orlando did not ask for supper but for a bed: he was replete with sadness, not with other fare. / The harder he sought for rest, the worse the misery and affliction he procured himself—every wall, every door, every window was covered with the hateful inscriptions. He wanted to make enquiries there, but chose to keep his lips sealed: he was afraid to establish too clearly the very question he wanted to cloud with mist so as to dull the pain. / Little good did it do him to deceive himself; somebody there was to speak of the matter unasked. The herdsman, who saw him so downcast and sad and wanted to cheer him up, embarked, without asking leave, upon the story of those two lovers: he knew it well, and often repeated it to those who would listen. There were many who enjoyed hearing it. / He told how at the prayer of beautiful Angelica he had brought Medor back to his house. Medor was gravely wounded, and she tended his wound, and in a few days had healed it—but Love inflicted upon her heart a wound far worse than his, and from a small spark kindled so blazing a fire that she was all aflame and quite beside herself; / and, forgetting that she was daughter of the greatest monarch of the East, driven by excessive passion, she chose to become wife to a poor simple soldier. The herdsman ended his story by having the bracelet brought in—the one Angelica had given him on her departure as a token of thanks for his hospitality. /

This evidence shown in conclusion proved to be the axe which took his head off his shoulders at one stroke, now that Love, that tormentor, was tired of raining blows upon him. Orlando tried to conceal his grief, but it so pressed him, he could not succeed: willy nilly the sighs and tears had to find a vent through his eyes and lips. / When he was free to give rein to his sorrow, once he was alone without others to consider, tears began to stream from his eyes and furrow his cheeks, running down onto his breast. He sighed and moaned, and made great circular sweeps of the bed with his arms: it felt harder than rock; it stung worse than a bed of nettles. / Amid such bitter anguish the thought occurred to him that on this very bed in which he was lying the thankless damsel must have lain down many a time with her lover. The downy bed sent a shudder through him and he leapt off it with all the alacrity of a yokel who has lain down in the grass for a nap and spies a snake aclose by. /

The bed, the house, the herdsman filled him on a sudden with such revulsion that, without waiting for moonrise, or for the first light preceding the new day, he fetched his arms and his steed and went out into the darkest, most tangled depths of the wood; when he felt he was quite alone, he gave vent to his grief with cries and howls. / There was no checking his cries and tears; night and day he allowed himself no respite. Towns and villages he avoided, and lay out in the open on the hard forest-floor. He wondered that his head could hold such an unquenchable source of water, and that he could sigh so much. Frequently as he wept he said to himself: / "These are no longer tears that drop from my eyes so copiously. The tears were not enough for my grief: they came to an end before my grief was half expressed. Urged by fire, my vital spirit is now escaping by the ducts which lead to the eyes: this is what is now spilling out, and with it my sorrow and my life will flow out at its last hour. / These sighs, which are a token of my anguish, are not truly sighs: sighs are not like this—now and then they will cease, but never do I feel a relaxing of my pain as my breast exhales it. Love, which burns my heart, makes this wind, beating his wings about the flames. By what miracle, Love, do you keep my heart ever burning but never consumed by fire? / I am not who my face proclaims me; the man who was Orlando is dead and buried, slain by his most thankless lady who assailed him by her betrayal. I am his spirit sundered from him, and wandering tormented in its own hell, so that his shade, all that remains of him, should serve as an example to any who place hope in Love." /

All night the count wandered in the wood; at sunrise, Fate brought him back to the spring where Medor had carved his inscription. To see his calamity written there in the hillside so inflamed him that he was drained of every drop that was not pure hate, fury, wrath, and violence. On impulse he drew his sword, / and slashed at the words and the rock-face, sending tiny splinters shooting skywards. Alas for the cave, and for every trunk on which the names of Medor and Angelica were written! They were left, that day, in such a state that never more would they afford cool shade to shepherd or flock. The spring, too, which had been so clear and pure, was scarcely safer from wrath such as his; / branches, stumps and boughs, stones and clods he kept hurling into the lovely waters until he so clouded them from surface to bottom that they were clear and pure never again. In the end, exhausted and sweat-soaked, his stamina given out and no longer answering to his deep, bitter hate, his burning wrath, he dropped onto the grass and sighed up at the heavens. / Weary and heart-stricken, he dropped onto the grass and gazed mutely up at the sky. Thus he remained, without food or sleep while the sun three times rose and set. His bitter agony grew and grew until it drove him out of his mind.

On the fourth day, worked into a great frenzy, he stripped off his armor and chain-mail. / The helmet landed here, the shield there, more pieces of armor further off, the breastplate further still: arms and armor all found their resting-place here and there about the wood. Then he tore off his clothes and exposed his hairy belly and all his chest and back.

Now began the great madness, so horrifying that none will ever know a worse instance. / He fell into a frenzy so violent that his every sense was darkened. He did not think to draw his sword, with which I expect he would have performed marvels. But in view of his colossal strength he had no need of it, nor of any hatchet or battle-axe. He now performed some truly astonishing feats: at one jerk he rooted up a tall pine, / after which he tore up several more as though they were so many celery-stalks. He did the same to oaks and ancient elms, to beech and ash-trees, to ilexes and firs. What a birdcatcher does when clearing the ground before he lays nets—rooting up rushes, brushwood, and nettles—Orlando did to oaks and other age-old timber. / The shepherds who heard the din left their flocks scattered through the woodland and hastened from all parts to this spot to see what was happening. But I have reached a point which I must not overstep for fear of boring you with my story; I should rather postpone it than annoy you by making it too long.

. . .

If you have put your foot in the birdlime spread by Cupid, try to pull it out, and take care not to catch your wing in it too: love, in the universal opinion of wise men, is nothing but madness. Though not everyone goes raving mad like Orlando, Love's folly shows itself in other ways; what clearer sign of lunacy than to lose your own self through pining for another? / The effects vary, but the madness which promotes them is always the same. It is like a great forest into which those who venture must perforce lose their way: one here, another there, one and all go off the track. Let me tell you this, to conclude: whoever grows old in love ought, in addition to Cupid's torments, to be chained and fettered. / "You, my friend, are preaching to others," someone will tell me, "but you overlook your own failing." The answer is that now, in an interval of lucidity, I understand a great deal. And I am taking pains (with imminent success, I hope) to find peace and withdraw from the dance—though I cannot do so as quickly as I should wish, for the disease has eaten me to the bone. /

In the last canto I was telling you, my Lord, how Orlando, crazed and demented, had torn off arms and armor and scattered them everywhere, ripped his clothes, tossed away his sword, rooted up trees, and made the hollow caves and deep woods re-echo. And some shepherds were attracted to the noise, whether by their stars, or for some wicked misdeed of theirs. / When they had a closer sight of the madman's incredible feats and his prodigious strength, they turned to flee, but without direction, as people do when suddenly scared. The madman was after them at once; he grabbed one and took off his head with all the ease of a person plucking an apple from a tree or a dainty bloom from a briar. / He picked up the heavy carcass by one leg and used it to club the rest; he laid out two, leaving them in a sleep from which perhaps they would awake on Judgment Day. The others cleared off at once: they were quickfooted and had their wits about them. The madman would not have been slow to pursue them, but he had now turned upon their flocks. /

In the fields the laborers, wise from the shepherds' example, left their ploughs, hoes, and sickles and scrambled onto the housetops or onto the church roofs—there being no safety up elm or willow tree. From here they contemplated the fearsome frenzy unleashed upon horse and oxen: they were shattered, battered, and destroyed by dint of punches, thumps, and bites, kicks and scratches. It was a fast mover who could escape him. / Now you could have heard the neighboring farms resound with shouts, the shrill of horns, and rustic trumpets and, most persistently, the peal of clarions; you could have seen a thousand men streaming down from the hills, armed with pikes and bows, spears, and slings; as many more came up from the plain, ready to wage a peasant war against the madman. / Imagine waves, driven by the South Wind which earlier had been playful, breaking on the shore; the second wave is higher than the first, the third follows with greater force; and, each time, the water builds up more and seethes more widely across the beach. Thus did the pitiless mob increase, coming down from the hills and out of the valleys against Orlando. / Out of that disorderly throng ten he killed who came within his reach, and then another ten. This experiment made it clear that it was far safer to stand well away. No one was able to draw blood from his body; steel was powerless to strike and wound it—the King of Heaven had given him this endowment so as to make him guardian of His holy faith. / Had he been capable of dying, his life would have been in danger; he might have learned what it was to throw aside his sword and, unarmed, to overreach himself.[1]

Now having seen their every blow prove ineffective, the throng began to ebb. With no one left to confront him, Orlando made off and came to a hamlet. / Here he found not a soul, man or child, for everyone had abandoned the place in terror. There was plenty of food set out, humble fare of which shepherds partake. Spurred by hunger and frenzy, he made no distinction between bread and acorns but set to with his hands and teeth and devoured whatever came first within reach, whether raw or cooked. / After this he roamed about the countryside, preying upon men and wild beasts. He would range through the woods catching fleet-footed goats and nimble fawns. Often he would fight with bears and boars, wrestling them to the ground bare-handed; often he filled his ravenous belly with their meat, carcass and all. / He roamed across the length and breadth of France, until one day he came to a bridge. Beneath it a broad, full river flowed between steep, craggy banks. Beside it there stood a tower commanding a sweeping view in all directions. What he did here you shall learn later on.

Summary   Zerbin and Isabel find Orlando's armor. Zerbin dies trying to protect the armor for Orlando when Mandricard appears and claims the helmet (Mambrino's helmet), which once belonged to Hector of Troy. Isabel meets a hermit, who teaches her Christian consolation and converts her. Zerbin's death marks the beginning of tragedy's influence over the world of the *Furioso*.

1. Orlando's frenzy resembles that of Hercules, the strongest man in classical mythology.

FROM CANTO 25

[Fiordispina's Love for Bradamant]

Oh what conflict there can be in a young man's mind between a thirst for glory and the impulses of Love! There is no telling which of the two motives is the stronger when now one, now the other predominates. * * * / He had not traveled a mile beyond the well before he saw a messenger approaching at a gallop; he was one of those sent by Agramant to the warriors from whom he was expecting help. He learnt that the Saracens were in such danger from Charlemagne's blockade that, short of immediate assistance, degradation or even death would be their lot. / Ruggiero was perplexed by many thoughts which all assailed him at once; but this was not the time or the place to decide on his best course. He let the messenger go, then turned his steed to follow the damsel who was guiding him; he kept urging her to hasten, as there was no time to lose. / They continued along their way until, as the sun was setting, they came to a stronghold of Marsilius in the middle of France, one which he had seized from Charlemagne in the course of the war. They did not stop at the drawbridge nor at the gate—nobody blocked or obstructed their entry, even though the palisade and fosse were thronged with armed men. / As the damsel accompanying him was recognized by the bystanders, they were allowed through unhindered without even being asked from where they had come. They reached the square which they found aglow with flames and teeming with a malicious throng.

In the middle he saw the young man condemned to death. His face was white; / it was tearful and downcast, and when Ruggiero looked up at it he imagined he was looking at Bradamant, so closely did the youth resemble her. The more he gazed at his face and figure the more the likeness struck him. "Either this is Bradamant," he told himself, "or else I'm no longer Ruggiero. / Perhaps she was over-hasty in taking up the condemned boy's defence: her intervention must have miscarried and she has been captured, as I see. Oh why such haste, why could I not have been with her on this venture? But I have arrived, thank God, and there's still time for me to save her." / And without further delay he grasped his sword—he had broken his lance at Pinabello's castle—and drove his steed into the unarmed throng, assailing them in the chest, sides, and belly. He whirled his sword, catching one man on the brow, the next at the throat, another on the cheek. The rabble fled screaming: the entire throng was left maimed, if not with cracked skulls. / Imagine a flock of birds by a lake, flitting about confidently as they grub for food, when suddenly a hawk plummets down upon them from the sky and strikes or snatches one of their number; the rest scatter, each deserting his companion to attend to his own escape. Thus you would have seen the crowd behave the moment Ruggiero drove into them. / Some half dozen who were slow in leaving had their heads lopped off clean; as many more he split down to the chest, while a countless number were cleft down to the eyes or the jaw.

I'll grant you that they were not wearing helmets, but merely head-pieces of shining metal; had they been properly helmeted, though, he would have slashed them with almost as much ease. / No knight of the present day could match him for sheer strength—nor could any bear or lion or more ferocious beast, whether native or foreign to our shores. An earthquake might have equaled him, or the mighty Devil: not the one in hell—it's my Lord's Devil[2] I mean, the one which spits fire and forces its way everywhere, by land, sea, and air. / At every stroke at least one man fell, and more often two; he killed four and even five at a stroke, which soon brought the total to a hundred. The sword he had unsheathed could cut through steel as though it were soft whey. Falerina the sorceress[3] had made this cruel sword in the garden of Orgagna, for the purpose of slaying Orlando; / much did she regret having made it when she saw it used to destroy her garden. Imagine, then, the havoc and devastation wrought by it in the hands of a champion such as Ruggiero! If ever he manifested his rage, his strength, his supreme valor it was here and now as he strove to rescue his lady. /

The mob stood up to him as well as hare to unleashed hounds. A good number were killed; those who fled were legion. Meanwhile the damsel guiding Ruggiero had released the youth from the bonds tying his wrists, and procured him arms as best she could, a sword for his hand, a shield to sling from his neck. / He now did his utmost to avenge himself on these folk who had done him grievous wrong; he laid about him to such effect that he left a reputation for prowess and valor. The sun had dipped his golden rays into the Western sea when victorious Ruggiero and the young man set out from the castle. /

When the youth was outside the gates with Ruggiero, he thanked him profusely and most gracefully: his benefactor had, after all, risked his life to save him without knowing who he was. He asked Ruggiero to divulge his name, as he wanted to know who it was to whom he owed such a debt of gratitude. / "I am looking at the comely face and beautiful figure of my Bradamant," Ruggiero mused, "but I do not hear the dulcet tones of her voice. And her words are not appropriate to thanking a faithful lover. If she really is Bradamant, how is it that she has so soon forgotten my name?" / To establish who it was, Ruggiero employed subtlety. "I have seen you somewhere before," he remarked, "but though I have pondered and racked my brains I cannot remember where it was. Will you remind me, then, if you can recollect? And do me the pleasure of telling me your name, so that I may know who it was whom I saved today from the pyre." /

"It could be that you have seen me before," replied the other, "but I cannot say where or when. I too wander about the world seeking high adventure. Perhaps it was a sister of mine you saw, one who wears armor and carries a sword at her side; we are twins from birth and look so alike that even our family cannot tell us apart. / You are not the first, nor the second, nor even the fourth to have mistaken us; neither our father, nor our brothers, nor even our mother who bore us at one birth is able to tell us apart. True, our hair used to mark a sharp difference between us when I wore my hair short and loose in the male fashion, while she wore hers long and coiled in a plait. / But one day she was wounded in the head (it would take too long to tell the story) and to heal her a servant of God cut her hair till it only half covered her ears. After that there was nothing to distinguish us beyond our sex and name: mine is Richardet, hers is Bradamant; we are brother and sister to Rinaldo. / And if it would not bore you to listen, I would tell you a story to

---

2. Duke Alfonso's great cannon.   3. Boiardo's sorceress, who created the sword Balisardo to kill Orlando.

amuse you—something that happened to me on account of my resemblance to her: at first it was rapture, but it ended in agony." Ruggiero, in whose ears no song was sweeter, no story dearer than one in which his lady featured, begged him to tell his story. /

"My sister had been wounded by a party of Saracens who had come upon her without a helmet, so she had been obliged to cut her long tresses if her dangerous head-wound was to heal. Now recently she happened to be traveling through these woods, her head shorn as I have said. / On her way she came to a shady spring and, being weary and dejected, she dismounted, took off her helmet and fell asleep in the tender grass. (I don't believe there can be a story more beautiful than this one.) Who should come upon her but the Spanish Princess Fiordispina, who had come into the woods to hunt. / When she saw my sister clad in armor all except for her face, and with a sword in place of a distaff, she imagined she was looking at a knight. After gazing awhile at her face and her manly build she felt her heart stolen. So she invited my sister to join the hunt, and ended by eluding her retinue and disappearing with her among the shady boughs. /

"Once she had brought her into a solitary place where she felt unlikely to be disturbed, little by little, by words and gestures she revealed that she was love-struck. With burning looks and fiery sighs she showed how consumed she was with desire. She paled and blushed and, summoning her courage, gave her a kiss. / It was clear to my sister that the damsel had illusions about her; my sister could never have satisfied her need and was quite perplexed as to what to do. 'My best course is to undeceive her,' she decided, 'and to reveal myself as a member of the gentle sex rather than to have myself reckoned an ignoble man.' / And she was right. It would have been a sheer disgrace, the conduct of a man made of plaster, if he had kept up a conversation with a damsel as fair as Fiordispina, sweet as nectar, who had set her cap at him, while like a cuckoo, he just trailed his wings. So Bradamant tactfully had her know that she was a maiden. / She was in quest of glory at arms, like Hippolyta and Camilla[4] of old. Born in Africa, in the seaside city of Arzilla, she was accustomed from childhood to the use of lance and shield. These revelations did not abate love-struck Fiordispina's passion one jot; Cupid had thrust in his dart to make so deep a gash that this remedy was now too late. / To Fiordispina my sister's face seemed no less beautiful for this, her eyes, her movements no less graceful; she did not on this account retrieve mastery over her heart, which had gone out to Bradamant to bask in her adorable eyes. Seeing her accoutred as a man, she had imagined that there would be no need for her passion to remain unassuaged; but now the thought that her beloved was also a woman made her sigh and weep and betray boundless sorrow. /

"Anyone who heard her tears and grieving that day would have wept with her. 'Never was any torment so cruel,' she lamented, 'but mine is crueler. Were it a question of any other love, evil or virtuous, I could hope to see it consummated, and I should know how to cull the rose from the briar. My desire alone can have no fulfilment. / If you wanted to torment me, Love, because my happy state offended you, why could you not rest content with those torments which other lovers experience? Neither among humans nor

---

4. Virgil's Amazon warrior; *Hippolyta*: queen of the Amazons.

among beasts have I ever come across a woman loving a woman; to a woman another woman does not seem beautiful, nor does a hind to a hind, a ewe to a ewe. / By land, sea, and air I alone suffer thus cruelly at your hands—you have done this to make an example of my aberration, the ultimate one in your power. King Ninus's wife was evil and profane in her love for her son; so was Myrrha, in love with her father, and Pasiphae with the bull. But my love is greater folly than any of theirs. / These females made designs upon the males and achieved the desired consummation, so I am told. Pasiphae went inside the wooden cow, the others achieved their end by other means. But even if Daedalus came flying to me with every artifice at his command, he would be unable to untie the knot made by that all-too-diligent Maker, Nature, who is all-powerful.'[5] /

"Thus the fair damsel grieved and fretted and would not be assuaged. She struck her face and tore her hair and sought to vent her feelings against her own person. My sister wept for pity and felt embarrassed[6] as she listened to her grieving. She tried to deflect her from this insane and profitless craving, but her words were in vain and to no effect. / It was help, not consolation, that she required and her grief only continued to increase. The day was now drawing to a close and the sun was reddening in the West; rather than spending the night in the woods it was time now to withdraw to some lodging. So the damsel invited Bradamant to this castle of hers not far away. / My sister was unable to refuse, so they came to the very spot where the wicked mob would have burned me to death had you not appeared. Here Fiordispina made much of my sister; she dressed her once more in feminine attire and made it plain to one and all that her guest was a woman. / Realizing how little benefit she derived from Bradamant's apparent masculinity, Fiordispina did not want any blame to attach to herself on her guest's account. In addition, she nurtured the hope that the sickness already implanted in her as a result of Bradamant's male aspect might be dispelled by a dose of femininity to show how matters really stood. /

"That night they shared a bed but they did not rest equally well. The one slept, the other wept and moaned, her desire ever mounting. And if sleep did occasionally press upon her eyelids, it was but a brief sleep charged with dreams in which it seemed to her that Heaven had allotted to her a Bradamant transformed into a preferable sex. / If a thirst-tormented invalid goes to sleep craving for water, in his turbid, fitful rest he calls to mind every drop of water he ever saw. Likewise her dreaming mind threw up images to requite her desires. Then she would wake and reach out, only to find that what she had seen was but an empty dream. / How many prayers and vows did she not offer that night to Mahomet and all the gods, asking them to change Bradamant's sex for the better by a clear and self-evident miracle! But she saw that all her prayers were vain; perhaps Heaven even mocked her. The night ended and Phoebus lifted his fair head out of the sea and gave light to the world. / With the new day they left their bed, and Fiordispina's pain was aggravated when Bradamant, anxious to be clear of her predicament, men-

---

5. The entire speech is based on the soliloquy of Ovid's Myrrha, who loved her father (*Metamorphoses* 10). *King Ninus's wife:* Semiramis, Syrian queen who married her son. *Pasiphae:* wife of King Minos, who loved a bull. *Daedalus:* created the labyrinth in which Minos kept the Minotaur, the monstrous offspring of Pasiphae.   6. The Italian verb for Bradamant's emotional response, *è costretta*, indicates that she feels obliged or compelled to help Fiordispina rather than "embarrassed," as the translator puts it.

tioned that she was leaving. As a parting gift, Fiordispina presented her with an excellent jennet, caparisoned in gold; also with a costly surcoat woven by her own hand. / Fiordispina accompanied her a step of the way then returned, weeping, to her castle, while my sister pressed on so hastily that she reached Montauban the same day. Our poor mother and we, her brothers, crowded round her, rejoicing—for lack of news of her, we had been gravely anxious for fear she were dead. /

"When she removed her helmet we all stared at her cropped hair which previously had fallen about her neck; and the new surcoat she was wearing also caught our attention. And she told us all that had befallen her, from start to finish just as I've told you: how after she was wounded in the wood she cut off her fair tresses in order to be healed; / and how the beautiful huntress came upon her as she was by the spring; and how she took to her deceptive appearance and segregated her from her party. She did not pass in silence over Fiordispina's grief, and we were all filled with pity at it. She described how she lodged with her, and all she did until her return to our castle. /

"Now I had heard a great deal about Fiordispina, whom I had seen in Saragossa and in France. I had been much allured by her lovely eyes and smooth cheeks, but had not let my thoughts dwell upon her; to love without hope is idle dreaming. But, brought again so fully to the fore, she reawakened my passion at once. / Out of this hope, Love prepared bonds for me, having no other cord with which to capture me. He showed me how to set about obtaining what I wanted of this damsel. A little deception would procure an easy success: the similarity between my sister and myself had often deceived others, so perhaps it would deceive her too. / Shall I, shan't I? My conclusion was that it is always good to go in pursuit of one's pleasure. I did not divulge my thought to a soul, nor seek anyone's advice on the matter. When it was night, I went to where my sister had left her armor; I put it on and away I went on her horse without waiting for dawn to break. / I set off by night, with Cupid for guide, to be with lovely Fiordispina, and I arrived before the Sun had hidden his radiance in the sea. Happy the man who outstripped his fellows in bringing the news to the princess: as bearer of good tidings he could expect thanks and a reward from her. /

"They all of them took me for Bradamant—just as you did—the more so in that I had both the attire and the horse with which she had left the previous day. Fiordispina lost no time in coming out to meet me; she was so jubilant and affectionate, she could not possibly have shown greater pleasure and joy. / Throwing her graceful arms around my neck, she softly hugged me and kissed me on the lips. You can imagine after this how Love guided his dart to pierce me at the heart of my heart! She took me by the hand and quickly led me into her bedroom; here she would suffer none but herself to undo my armor, from helmet to spurs; no one else was to take a hand. / Next she sent for a dress of hers, richly ornate, which she herself spread out and put on me as though I were a woman; and she caught my hair in a golden net. I studied modesty in my glances, and none of my gestures betrayed my not being a woman. My voice might have betrayed me, but I controlled it so well that it aroused no suspicions. / Then we went into a hall crowded with knights and ladies who received us with the sort of honor paid to queens and great ladies. Here several times I was amused when certain men, unaware that my skirts concealed something sturdy and robust, kept making eyes at me. / When the evening was further advanced and the meal had been over for some while—the fare had been an excellent choice of what was then in season—Fiordispina did not wait for me to ask the favor which was the object of my visit, but invited me hospitably to share her bed for the night. /

"When the waiting-women and maidens, the pages, and attendants had withdrawn, and we were both changed and in bed, while the flaming sconces left the room bright as day, I said to her: 'Do not be surprised, my lady, at my returning to you so soon—perhaps you thought that you would not see me again for God knows how long. / First I shall tell you why I left, then why I have returned. Had I been able to abate your ardor by staying, I should have wanted to live and die in your service, and never for an hour be without you. But seeing how much pain my presence occasioned you, as I could do you no better service, I chose to leave. / Fate drew me off my path into the thick of a tangled wood, where I heard a cry sound close by, as of a damsel calling for help. I came running and found myself at the edge of a crystal lake where a faun had hooked a naked maiden in the water and was cruelly preparing to eat her raw. / I went over, sword in hand—only this way could I help her—and slew the boorish fisherman. Straight away she dived into the water and said: "It is not for nothing that you have saved me. You shall be richly rewarded and given as much as you ask for: I am a nymph and I live in this limpid lake. / I have the power to perform miracles, to coerce nature and the elements. Ask to the limits of my capabilities, then just leave it to me: at my singing the moon comes down from the sky, fire turns to ice, the air turns brittle, and with mere words I have moved the earth and stopped the sun." /

" 'I did not ask her for a hoard of treasure, or for power over nations, or for greater valor or might, or for honorable victory in every war. My only request was that she would show me some way I could fulfil your desire; I did not ask to achieve this in one way or in another, but left the method up to her own discretion. / Scarcely had I disclosed my wish than I saw her dive a second time, and for all reply to my request she splashed the enchanted water at me. The moment it touched my face I was quite transformed, I know not how. I could see, I could feel—though I could scarcely believe my senses—that I was changing from woman to man.[7] / You would never believe me, except that now, right away, you shall be able to see for yourself. In my new sex as in my old, my desire is to give you ready service. Command my faculties, then, and you shall find them now and ever more alert and bestirred for you.' Thus I spoke to her, and I guided her hand to test the truth for herself. /

"Imagine the case of a person who has given up hope of having something for which he craves; the more he bemoans his deprivation, the more he works himself into a state of despair; and if later he acquires it, he is so vexed over the time wasted sowing seed in the sand, and despair has so eroded him that he is dumbfounded and cannot believe his luck. / So it was with Fiordispina: she saw and touched the object she had so craved for, but she could not

---

7. Richardet invents a fictional metamorphosis, which he bases generally on Ovid's tales, with specific allusions to the famous tales of Actaeon (who sees the goddess Diana naked and is metamorphosed into a stag when she sprinkles him with water) and Salmacis and Hermaphroditus (who together become the hermaphrodite).

believe her eyes or her fingers or herself, and kept wondering whether she
were awake or asleep. She needed solid proof to convince her that she was
actually feeling what she thought she felt. 'O God, if this is a dream,' she
cried, 'keep me asleep for good, and never wake me again!' /

"There was no roll of drums, no peal of trumpets to herald the amorous
assault: but caresses like those of billing doves gave the signal to advance or
to stand firm. We used arms other than arrows and slingstones; and I, without a ladder, leapt onto the battlements and planted my standard there at
one jab, and thrust my enemy beneath me. / If on the previous night that
bed had been laden with heavy sighs and laments, this night made up for it
with as much laughter and merriment, pleasure and gentle playfulness.
Never did twisting acanthus entwine pillars and beams with more knots than
those which bound us together, our necks and sides, our arms, legs, and
breasts in a close embrace. / It remained a secret between us, so our pleasure
continued for a few months. But eventually someone found us out, so the
matter became known to the king—to my undoing. You, who rescued me
from his people who had lit the pyre in the square, you can understand the
rest: but God knows what an ache I am left with." /

*　*　*

Summary   When Doralice chooses to stay with Mandricard, Rodomont leaves the
Saracen camp in a furious gloom, complaining of the fickleness of women. He is
consoled by a spectacularly misogynistic tale, which Ariosto recommends that his
readers disregard. Continuing in his journey, he comes across Isabel, who is mourning
for Zerbin, and instantly feels the flame of lust kindle in his breast.

FROM CANTOS 29 AND 30

[*Isabel Outwits Rodomont, and Angelica Encounters Orlando*]

Oh the weak, inconstant minds of men! How ready we are to vacillate,
how ready to change our ideas, especially those born of lovers' spite. I had
just seen Rodomont so incensed against women that he broke all bounds: I
could never imagine him cooling his passion, let alone quenching it. / Gentle
ladies, I am so offended by what he said against you without cause that until
I have shown him, to his chagrin, just how wrong he has been I shall not
forgive him. I shall so exert myself, with pen and ink, that it will be plain to
everyone how much better he would have done to have remained silent, even
to have bitten his tongue sooner than slander you. /

Now experience clearly reveals the crass ignorance of his speech. He brandished the dagger of his wrath against the whole sex indiscriminately: then
one glance of Isabel's so touched him that he changed his mind on the spot—
he wanted her, now, instead of Doralice, though he had scarcely set eyes on
her and did not yet know who she was. / Hot and tingling with this new love,
he reasoned with her (to little purpose) to break her total, steadfast dedication to the Creator of all things. But the hermit acted as her buckler, her
plate-armor; lest her chaste decision be destroyed, he shielded her as best
he could with the surest, most valid arguments. / After enduring a great deal
of tedious discourse from the valiant monk and vainly inviting him to take
himself off to his desert without the damsel, and after seeing himself brazenly
flouted by the uncompromising fellow, the Saracen angrily grasped him by

the beard and pulled out a whole fistful of hair. / Then, his rage redoubled, he closed his fingers round the other's neck like pincers and, whirling him about a couple of times, tossed him up into the sky, towards the sea. What became of the monk I cannot tell—I do not know. Various and conflicting stories exist: one claims that he was so shattered against a rock that there was no telling his head from his foot; / another, that he landed in the sea, three miles away, and died for not being able to swim, having vainly offered up many a prayer and supplication; another, that a saint came to his aid, carrying him ashore with visible hand. One of these may be the truth—at any rate my story says no more about him. /

Once rid of the garrulous monk, cruel Rodomont turned back to the distressed, bewildered damsel with greater composure and, using the terms employed between lovers, told her that she was his heart, his life, his consolation, his dearest hope, and all the rest of it. / He behaved towards her most gallantly, without the slightest display of force: her gentle look which captured his heart quenched and stifled his customary arrogance. And although he might simply have seized the fruit, he chose not to attack the bark, deeming that the fruit could not be good unless he received it from her as a gift. / In this way he expected little by little to win Isabel to do his pleasure. But she, finding herself in this strange, solitary place, like a mouse at the feet of a cat, would sooner have found herself in the midst of a fire. She kept pondering what to do, what path to take in order to escape unblemished and intact. / She was resolved to slay herself before the cruel savage had his way with her and forced her to so grave a sin against Zerbin, the knight whom harsh and pitiless Fate had allowed to expire in her arms: to him she had privately vowed her chastity for all time. / She saw the pagan king's blind appetite ever growing and could not think what to do, well realizing that his ultimate aim was the squalid act to which her opposition would have scant effect. But as she considered one thing and another, she hit upon a way to protect herself and save her chastity, as I shall relate to her enduring fame. /

As the evil Saracen was now accosting her with language and actions quite devoid of the courtesy he had originally shown, "If you leave my honor safe," she told him, "and I need not fear for it in your company, I, for my part, shall give you something of far greater value to you than the depriving me of it. / Do not despise a lasting contentment, a true joy second to none, for the sake of a trifling pleasure so easily available the world over: you can find a hundred, a thousand comely women any time, but no one in the world, or very few, can give you what I can. / I know of an herb—I've seen it on my way here and know where to find it—which, boiled with ivy and rue over a fire of cypress-wood, and then pressed out between innocent hands, produces a juice: and whoever bathes himself with this juice three times so hardens his body that he becomes proof against fire and steel. / Truly, whoever applies the liquid three times is invulnerable for a month—every month it must be re-applied, for its virtue lasts no longer. I know how to make it and today I shall do so, and today you shall feel its effect: and, if I am not mistaken, you will be better pleased than by the conquest this day of all Europe. / In reward for this, here is what I ask of you: swear on your honor neither in word nor deed ever more to threaten my chastity."

With these words she recalled Rodomont to his honor, for he conceived such a craving to be invulnerable that he promised her even more than she asked. / He would keep his oath until he had tried the remarkable juice for himself; meanwhile he would refrain from any act or show of violence. Later, he decided, he would not keep his word, for he neither feared nor respected God and the saints—when it came to breaking faith, the whole of deceitful Africa yielded to him. / Rodomont swore a thousand oaths to Isabel not to molest her provided that she prepared the juice that could render him invulnerable as Cygnus and Achilles.[8]

Up cliffs and down dark ravines, remote from towns and villages, she went gathering herbs; the Saracen never left her side but stayed close to her. / After gathering here and there as many herbs (with and without roots) as were needed, they returned home late; here Isabel, that paragon of chastity, spent the rest of the night boiling the herbs most expertly. Throughout the whole mysterious operation Rodomont was present. / Now as he passed the night in games with his few attendants, the heat from the fire in that confined place produced in him such a thirst that, with a sip here, a gulp there, he emptied two whole casks of Greek wine which a day or two earlier his pages had taken from some travelers. / But Rodomont was unaccustomed to wine, which Moslem law forbids and condemns. And it tasted to him like the liquor of the gods, better than nectar or manna; so, repudiating Saracen custom, he drank it by the bumper-full, flasks at a time. The excellent wine was passed round many a time till all their heads were spinning like lathes. /

Meanwhile the damsel took off the boil the cauldron in which the herbs were cooking and said to Rodomont: "Lest you should think my words are just air, I shall give you what it takes to distinguish truth from deceit and convince the dullest mind—I shall give you proof, here and now, and on my own person, not upon another's. / I want to be the first to try the potency of the benignant juice in case you imagine it contains a deadly poison. I shall bathe myself with it from the crown of my head down my neck and over my breast. Then turn your might and your sword upon me to try the juice's power, the sword's sharpness." / She bathed herself as she said, then joyfully offered her bare neck to the unwary pagan: he was all unwary and perhaps befuddled by the wine, against which helmet and shield are unavailing. The brute believed her and used his hand and his cruel sword to such effect that he lopped her fair head, once the abode of love, clean from her shoulders. /

Her head bounced thrice: from it a voice could be clearly heard pronouncing the name of Zerbin, to follow whom she had found so novel a way to escape from the Saracen. Depart in peace, then, beautiful, blessed spirit, who preferred fidelity and a name for chastity (virtually alien and unknown in our day) to your life, your green years! / If only my verses had the power, how hard I should work to the limit of my poet's art, which so refines and enhances speech, so that for a thousand years and more the world would have knowledge of your illustrious name. Go in peace to the supernal seat, and leave to other women an example of your faith. / At this incomparable, this amazing act, the Creator looked down from Heaven and said: "I commend you more than Lucretia, whose death deprived Tarquin[9] of his realm. For this cause I mean to make a law, one such that time may never dissolve,

8. Both invulnerable to the sword.   9. The Roman king who raped Lucretia, a chaste Roman matron who committed suicide rather than live with the shame.

and I swear by the inviolable waters of Styx that no future age shall alter it: / in future every woman bearing your name shall be sublime of spirit, beautiful, noble, kind, and wise; she shall achieve the mark of true virtue, and afford writers cause to celebrate the praiseworthy, illustrious name, so that Parnassus, Pindus, and Helicon[1] shall ever ring with the name of Isabel." / God spoke thus, and made the air serener, the sea calmer than ever before. The chaste soul returned to the third heaven, back into the arms of her Zerbin.

Shamed and flouted, merciless Rodomont, a second Brehus, remained on earth. Once he had digested his excess of wine, he cursed his mistake and regretted it, / and considered how to placate or in part to satisfy Isabel's blessed soul: though he had slain her body, at least he could give life to her memory. To this end he converted the chapel in which he was living—the site of her death—into a tomb for her. This is how he did it. / He assembled masons from the whole vicinity, some with blandishments, others with threats; when he had a good six thousand men, he alleviated the neighboring hills of many a heavy rock and had these compacted as a great mound, ninety yards from top to bottom, which encased the chapel containing the pair of lovers. / It almost copied the imposing mound thrown up by Hadrian[2] on the Tiber's bank. Beside the tomb he had a tall tower built in which he planned to live awhile.

Over the nearby river he built a narrow bridge, but two yards wide. The bridge was long, but so narrow that it scarcely allowed room for two horses, / whether approaching it abreast or arriving from opposite ends. The bridge had no parapet of any kind: it was possible to fall off either side. He meant to exact a high toll from every knight who crossed the bridge, whether pagan or Christian—he promised their spoils as trophies for the couple's tomb. /

In less than ten days the bridge across the river was completed. The tomb was not so quickly built, nor was the tower yet carried to its summit, though it was raised high enough for a sentry to take up his post on it and alert Rodomont with his horn each time a knight approached the bridge. / Rodomont would arm and go to challenge him from whichever bank served his purpose—if the passing knight arrived from the tower-side, Rodomont would cross to the further bank. The bridge was the jousting-place, and any charger veering at all off centre would fall into the river, which was deep—there was no danger in the world to match it. / The Saracen imagined that by frequently incurring the risk of falling from the bridge headfirst into the river, where he would be bound to drink a great deal of water, he would be cleansed of the fault to which he was induced by too much wine—as though the water would dilute not merely the wine he had drunk but also the evil which the wine had made his hand or tongue commit. / Many knights passed this way within a few days. Some arrived in the course of their journey, for this was the most frequented road leading to Italy and Spain. Others were attracted hither by adventure and by honor (dearer than life itself) to try their mettle. One and all, confident of winning the palm, forfeited their arms and many their life as well. / If those he overthrew were pagans, he contented himself with despoiling them and taking their arms on which, before hanging them

---

1. Sites sacred to the Muses and therefore popular topics in poetry.   2. *Mound . . . Hadrian:* Castel Sant' Angelo. Originally the mausoleum of the Roman emperor Hadrian.

on the marble of the tomb, he clearly inscribed the name of their erstwhile owner. The Christians he held prisoner, and I believe he later sent them all to Algiers. The building-work was not yet completed when who should arrive but mad Orlando. /

The raving count chanced to arrive at the wide river where Rodomont, as I've said, was urgently building the tower and the tomb; these were still unfinished, and the bridge barely completed. Except for his visor the pagan was fully armed at the moment when Orlando came to the river and the bridge. / Impelled by his madness, Orlando jumped over the barrier and ran onto the bridge. Rodomont glowered as he waited on foot in front of the great tower, and yelled threats at him from a distance: he would not deign to use his sword against him. "Stop, you rash, reckless peasant, you impudent, meddlesome oaf: / this bridge is for lords and knights, not for the like of you!" Now Orlando, who was in a day-dream, did not listen but simply kept on. "I'll have to punish the idiot," thought the pagan and, nothing loth, made to hurl him into the water, never imagining he would meet resistance. / At this point a gentle maiden arrived at the bridge to cross the river. She was dainty in her dress, her face comely and her manner studiedly modest. She was Fiordiligi, the damsel (you may remember, my Lord) who was looking for the traces of her lover Brandimart, in every place except where he actually was, in Paris. / She reached the bridge at the moment when Orlando came to grips with Rodomont, who wanted to throw him into the river.

Now she was well acquainted with the count and recognized him at once. She was astonished at the folly that possessed him to go about naked. / She stopped to see what would result from the fury of two men as strong as these. Each was intent on putting all his might into heaving the other off the bridge. "How can a madman be so strong?" the pagan muttered between his teeth as he twisted and turned this way and that, full of bile, contempt, and rage. / He tried out new holds with either hand, looking for the best grip, and skilfully advanced his right foot or his left, now between the other's legs, now outside them. Rodomont at grips with Orlando looked like a sturdy bear expecting to uproot the tree out of which he has fallen—as though the tree were wholly to blame and he were furious with it. / Orlando, whose wits had foundered, I know not where, and who was relying solely on his brawn (which few, if any, could match), dropped backwards off the bridge still clasping the pagan. They fell into the river with a mighty splash and sank to the bottom together, while the banks groaned. / The water parted them at once. Orlando, who was naked and swam like a fish, struck out with his arms and legs and reached the bank; as soon as he was out of the river he ran off without waiting to consider whether what he had done redounded to his credit or not. The pagan, however, was hampered by his armor and made a slower, more labored return to the shore. / Meanwhile Fiordiligi, having safely crossed the bridge and the river, explored the tomb in search of her Brandimart's insignia; finding here neither his arms nor his surcoat, she hoped to find him elsewhere.

But let us return to Orlando, who left the tower, river, and bridge behind him. / I should be mad if I undertook to relate each and every folly of Orlando, for they were so many, I wouldn't know when I should finish. But I shall select a few important ones, fit to be sung in verse and appropriate to my story. And I shall not pass in silence over his prodigious feat in the

Pyrenees above Toulouse. / He had traveled a long way, prompted by his dire insanity; eventually he came up into the mountains which divide France from Spain. As he proceeded in the direction of the setting sun he came onto a narrow path overhanging a deep valley. / Here two young woodcutters found him on their path. They were driving before them a donkey laden with wood; one look at him told them that there were no brains in his head, so they shouted at him threateningly to go back or move aside and clear out of their way. / For all reply Orlando gave the donkey a petulant kick in the chest: there was nothing like it for sheer drive, and the beast rose into the air, so that to an observer he looked like a little bird on the wing, and landed on the top of a hill rearing up across the valley a mile or so away. Then he fell upon the two young men. /

One of them had better luck than sense: in a panic he hurled himself into the precipice which fell away twice a hundred feet. Half-way down he hit a soft, pliant, leafy bush, which, apart from some scratches to his face from its thorns, let him go safe and sound. / The other grasped a spur jutting from the rockface to scramble up it; he hoped, if he gained the top, to find safety from the madman—who did not, however, intend that he survive: he grabbed the fugitive by the feet as he was trying to climb up, and, extending his hands to arm's length, tore him in two, / the way one may see a man tear a heron or chicken apart to feed its warm entrails to a falcon or goshawk. How fortunate it was that the one who risked breaking his neck was not killed! He related this prodigy to others so that Turpin[3] came to hear of it and wrote it down for us. / This and many other fantastic feats he accomplished as he crossed the mountains.

After much wandering he finally descended Southwards towards Spain. He took his way along the sea-shore in the region of Tarragona and, as his compelling madness dictated, he chose to make his home on the beach; / to afford himself some protection from the sun he dug into the fine, dry sand. While he was here, fair Angelica and her husband chanced upon him. (As I told you earlier, they had come down to the Spanish shore from the mountains.) Now she came within an arm's length of him, not having yet noticed his presence. / It never crossed her mind that he might be Orlando: he had changed too much.

From the moment he was possessed by madness he had always gone naked, in the shade as in the sun. Had he been born in sunny Assuan or where the Libyan Garamants worship Ammon, or in the mountains at the source of the Nile his skin could not have been more deeply tanned. / His eyes were almost hidden in his face, which was lean and wizened; his hair was a matted, bristling mass, his bushy beard looked appalling and hideous. Angelica had no sooner set eyes on him than she turned back, quaking; quaking, she filled heaven with shrieks and turned to her escort for help. / When crazed Orlando noticed her he started to his feet to grab her—he took a liking to her delicate face and immediately wanted her. That he had once so loved and worshipped her was a memory now totally destroyed in him. He ran after her the way a hound pursues game. / Young Medor, seeing the madman in pursuit of his lady, charged at him on horseback and struck at him, finding his back turned. He expected to strike the head off his shoulders but found his skin as hard

3. Ariosto's fictional source.

as bone, indeed harder than steel—Orlando was born under a spell of invulnerability. /

As he felt himself struck from behind, Orlando turned, clenching his fist, and, with a force beyond measure, punched the Saracen's horse. The blow landed on the steed's head, smashing it like glass, and killing him. On the instant, he turned away and chased after the fleeing Angelica, / who was frantically whipping and spurring on her mare—even had she flown faster than an arrow from a bow, the beast would have seemed slow for her present need. Then she remembered the ring on her finger: this could save her, and she thrust it into her mouth. The ring, which had not lost its virtue, made her vanish like a flame puffed out. / Whether it was fright, or that she lost her seat while transferring the ring, or that the mare stumbled—I cannot say which was the reason—the moment that she put the ring into her mouth and hid her lovely face she pitched out of the saddle and landed on her back in the sand. / Had her fall landed her two inches closer, she would have collided with the madman and been slain by the impact alone. Great good fortune helped her at this point: as to the horse, she needs would have to help herself to another horse as she had done before—she was never to recover this one who was trampling the beach ahead of the paladin. / Do not fear: she will secure another.

Let us follow Orlando now, whose frenzied impetus was no whit dispelled with the vanishing of Angelica. He followed the steed across the bare sand, constantly gaining on her; now he could touch her . . . he had her by the mane . . . now by the bridle . . . at last he held her. / He seized her as gleefully as another man would a maiden. He adjusted the reins and headstall then gained the saddle in one leap, only to drive her many a mile at a gallop restlessly hither and yon, never unharnessing her, never letting her taste grass or hay. / Wanting to jump a ditch, he landed in it upside down with the mare. He was unscathed—never felt a jolt—but the wretched beast threw out her shoulder. Seeing no way of pulling her out, he finally loaded her onto his shoulder, climbed out of the ditch and walked with his burden the length of three arrows' flights and more. / When she grew too heavy he set her down in order to lead her; she limped slowly after him. "Come on," he urged her, but he urged in vain: had the mare followed him at a gallop she would not have satisfied his crazy whim. In the end he slipped the halter from her head and tied it above her right hind hoof. / Thus he dragged her along, assuring her that this way she would be able to follow him more comfortably. The road was rough: one stone tore at her coat, the next at her skin, and finally the ill-used beast died from her lacerations and sufferings. Orlando spared her not a glance, not a thought: he pressed on at a run. /

Even when she was dead he did not stop dragging her as he continued his way Westward, sacking farms and houses as he went, whenever he felt the need for food. He seized fruit, meat, and bread which he guzzled, and overpowered everybody: some he left dead, others, maimed; he tarried little and kept pressing onward. / He would have dealt scarcely more tenderly with his lady had she not hidden herself: he could not tell black from white and believed that his inflictions were a kindness.

A curse upon the ring, and upon the knight who gave it her—were it not for that, Orlando would at a stroke have been avenged on his own and on many another's account! / Would that not she alone but the whole surviving sex had fallen into Orlando's hands: they're a nasty tribe and not an ounce of good is to be found in any of them! But before my slackened strings produce a discordant note in this canto, I should do well to continue it later, lest it prove irksome to my listeners.

• • •

Allow your reason to be mastered by sheer pique, put up no defence against it, leave blind rage to force your hand (or tongue) into offending your friends: then well may you weep for it—the wrong is not so easily righted! Alas, in vain I regret and curse myself for what I said in anger at the end of the last canto. / But I am like a sick man who has endured all too much pain and, at the end of his tether, gives way to passion and starts to curse. This relieves the pain, and with it the impulse which has allowed his tongue such freedom. Then he comes to his senses and regrets his impulse: but what has been said cannot be unsaid. / I crave pardon, ladies, which I hope your kindness shall afford me. You must excuse me if, overwhelmed as I am by a strong passion, I babble deliriously. Blame it on my enemy—a lady[4] who has reduced me to the most abject condition, making me say things I regret. That she's at fault, God knows: that I love her, she knows. / I am no less divorced from myself than was Orlando. I have no worse an excuse than he does, as he wanders over hill and over dale, scouring great tracts of Marsilius's kingdom.

For many a day he dragged the dead mare after him without let or hindrance, until he came to where a broad river flowed into the sea: here he had to abandon the carcass. / As he swam like an otter, he entered the river and emerged on the further shore, where he met a shepherd riding his horse down to the river to water him. The shepherd did not avoid Orlando as he approached, seeing that he was naked and alone. "I should like to swap my mare for that jade of yours," the madman told him. / "I'll point her out from here, if you like: there she is, lying dead on the other shore. You can have her seen to by a doctor—that apart, I find no fault in her. Let's have your nag, then, with some makeweight. Come now, dismount please: I want him." The shepherd laughed and, without a word, drew away and made for the ford. / "Hey, can't you hear? I want your horse!" cried Orlando, going after him in a temper. Now the shepherd had a staff with good solid knots to it, which he used against the paladin, sending him into a blind fury—more savage than he had ever looked before. He let fly with a punch at the shepherd's head, smashing his skull and knocking him dead to the ground. / He jumped onto the hack and dashed off at a venture, robbing many a man. The horse never tasted hay nor oats, so in a few days he collapsed. Did Orlando continue on foot? No—he meant to have horses a-plenty: as many as he found he purloined to his own use, after slaying their owners. /

Finally he came to Malaga, where he wrought greater havoc than anywhere previously. Not only did the fearsome lunatic rob everybody, leaving them in such straits that neither this year nor next would they have made up for their losses, but also he killed so many people and razed and burned so many houses that he laid waste more than a third of the city. / After this he came to a town called Algeciras, on the straits of Gibraltar (or Hibraltar as it is also called). Here he noticed a boat casting off. It was full of merrymakers

---

4. Alessandra Benucci, Ariosto's great love.

setting off across the glassy-smooth waters for a pleasant sail in the morning breeze. / The madman started yelling: "Stop!" for he had a sudden urge to ride in a boat. But his shouts and yells were all in vain, for he was not a cargo they were ready to embark. Their vessel drove through the water as swiftly as a migrant swallow through the air. Orlando beat and belabored his mount and forced him into the water with his crop, / until the beast had no choice but to plunge in, for all his efforts to resist were in vain. He went in up to his knees, to his belly and rump, so far that barely his head emerged from the water. He could not hope to turn back, for the crop kept drumming him between the ears. Poor wretch, he would have to make the crossing to Africa or else drown on the way. /

The boat that had put out from dry land was meanwhile lost to view: Orlando could not descry its hull from any angle—it was too far off and the billowing waves concealed it from his low vantage-point. He kept urging the horse through the waves, his mind made up on crossing the sea, until the steed, waterlogged and breathless, reached the end of his swim—and of his life: / he sank to the bottom, and would have taken his burden with him, but Orlando used his arms to stay afloat. He bestirred his legs and the palms of his hands as he blew the water from his face. The day was serene, the water calm; and he certainly needed the fairest weather, for with any sea running, he would have been left dead in the water. / But Fortune, who takes care of the insane, pulled him from the sea onto a beach at Ceuta, about two arrows' flights from the town walls. For many days he pursued his course at a venture, hastening Eastward along the shore, until he came upon a countless horde of black soldiers camped by the sea. / Now let us leave the paladin to his travels: we shall revert to him when the time comes. As to what became of Angelica, my Lord, after her narrow escape from the madman, and how she found a good ship and better weather to return to her own country, and how she gave Medor the scepter of the Indies: perhaps another will sing to a better accompaniment. / I have so many things I want to relate that I do not care to pursue her adventures any further.[5]

* * *

FROM CANTOS 34 AND 35

[Astolfo's Voyage to the Moon][6]

* * *

* * * / Then he mounted his flying horse and rose into the air to reach the summit of the mountain, for it was generally believed that the orb of the moon stood not far from its highest peak. His urge to explore directed his aspirations heavenward, spurning the earth. More and more height he gained until he reached the summit. /

The flowers which the breeze had painted on these smiling slopes looked like so many colored gems—sapphires, rubies, gold, topaz, and pearls, diamonds, chrysolites, and jacinth. And the grass was so green that were it to grow down here it would outdo emeralds. No less beautiful were the boughs

5. Angelica's last appearance in the poem.   6. Astolfo mounts the hippogryph and travels to the moon to recover Orlando's wits.

of the trees, permanently in fruit and in blossom. / In the branches lovely little birds sang; they were of many hues, white, blue and green, red and yellow. The murmuring brooks and quiet lakes were more limpid than crystal. A soft breeze, which seemed never to falter or fail, kept the air constantly astir so as to temper the heat of the day. / And as it blew, it ravished each blossom, fruit, and leaf of its particular odor, blending them all into a sweetness which nourished the spirit. In the middle of the plain stood a palace which seemed to be ablaze with a living flame, it radiated such splendor and light, beyond all mortal experience. / The palace had a perimeter of over thirty miles. Astolfo on his steed ambled slowly towards it, admiring the beautiful scene on every side. As he compared what he saw with this rank world we live in, he dismissed our world as ugly and evil and loathed by Heaven and nature in comparison with the sweetness, light, and happiness up there. /

When he was close to the gleaming edifice he was stunned with amazement: its smooth wall was fashioned from a single stone which shone redder than a carbuncle. What a stupendous work, what ingenious architect! What structure in our world resembles it? Let him be silent who proposes any of our Seven Wonders[7] for such glory. / In the luminous vestibule of that house of bliss Astolfo was approached by an old man in a carmine robe and milk-white cloak. He was white-haired and a thick white beard mantled his chin and fell to his chest. His face was so venerable, he looked like one of the elect of Paradise. / With a cheerful smile he addressed the paladin, who had respectfully dismounted: "O baron," he said, "who by God's will have ascended to the earthly paradise: as the cause of your journey and the object of your desire are equally hidden from you, your arrival here from the Northern hemisphere is, believe me, not without highly placed help. / It is to discover how you are to help Charlemagne and rescue the Holy Faith from peril that you have made so long a journey to come, all unawares, to consult me. You are not to attribute your coming here to your intelligence or courage, my son: neither your horn nor the winged horse would be of any use to you had not God given them to you. / Later we shall converse at greater leisure and I shall tell you how you are to proceed. But first come in and restore yourself—you must feel by now you have fasted long enough."

The old man had more to say, and much surprised Astolfo when he revealed himself as the Evangelist: / it was John, beloved of the Redeemer, on whose account the word went around the disciples that he was destined not to end his years in death.[8] The Son of God was induced, therefore, to tell Peter: "If I have him remain thus till I come, what is it to you?" Now although he did not say, "he is not to die," it is clear that this is what he meant. / John, upon his assumption here, found company, for the patriarch Enoch had arrived already, and also the great prophet Elias:[9] they were yet to see their last evening, and they are to enjoy eternal spring outside the foul, pestilential air until the angels' trumpets give the signal that Christ is returning on the white clouds. /

The saints gave the knight a good welcome and allotted him a room. In

7. The Pyramids, the gardens of Babylon, the statue of Jove at Olympia, the Colossus of Rhodes, the temple of Diana at Ephesus, the mausoleum at Halicarnassus, and the palace of Cyrus.   8. Christians thought that John, author of Revelation, would remain alive until the Second Coming of Christ for the universal judgment.   9. Enoch and Elias, or Elijah, ascended to the heavens.

another his steed was provided with good forage a-plenty. They gave Astolfo some of the fruits of paradise; in view of their flavor he was inclined to think that Man's first parents might well have been excused if this is what made them fail in obedience. / The adventurous duke had partaken of food and sleep enough to give Nature her due, for every conceivable amenity was here available, and Aurora had left her aged consort (of whom she never tired, for all his years) when he too left his bed—to find that the disciple so beloved of God had come to fetch him. / He took him by the hand and told him many things which need to remain unspoken.

Then he said: "Perhaps you don't know what is happening in France, my son, though you've come from there. Your Orlando has misappropriated the standards committed to him, and God is punishing him—for He is harshest against those He most loves, when they offend Him. / At his birth God endowed him with strength and courage to the highest degree and—what was quite abnormal—made him invulnerable to steel of any sort, in order thus to constitute him defender of His holy Faith, just as He made Samson defender of the Hebrews against the Philistines. / But your Orlando has given his Lord a poor return for such great benefits: for the greater duty he had to foster the Faithful the worse has been his desertion of them; so blinded has he been by his lustful passion for a pagan woman, the Faithful have suffered twice and more from his ruthless attempts to slay Rinaldo, his faithful cousin. / Therefore God has sent him mad, to go about with bared chest and belly, and has so clouded his reason that he cannot recognize anyone, still less himself. We read that in this fashion God also punished Nebuchadnezzar,[1] driving him to folly for seven years, when he cropped grass and hay like an ox. / But since the paladin's wrongdoing has been far less serious than Nebuchadnezzar's, the divine will has imposed a period of only three months to purge his sin. And if our Redeemer has permitted you to arrive up here after so long a journey, it is quite simply so that you may learn from us the way to bring Orlando to his senses. / You shall, in fact, have to make a further journey with me and leave the earth altogether: I have to take you to the orb of the moon, this being the planet that travels closest to us, for the medicine to restore Orlando's sanity is kept there. Tonight when the moon arrives over us we shall set out." /

The apostle discoursed about this and that for the rest of the day. But when the sun had plunged into the sea and the sickle-moon had risen above them, a chariot was made ready, designed for traveling about those skies— it had once lifted Elias from mortal gaze in the mountains of Judaea.[2] / The holy Evangelist harnessed four horses (of the most fiery red) to the shafts, and when he and Astolfo were settled in the chariot he took the reins and urged the steeds skywards. The chariot made a circle before lifting into the air, and soon arrived in the midst of the eternal fire, but the old man wrought a miracle whereby it gave no heat. / They crossed the whole sphere of fire and thence continued to the realm of the moon, which looked to them for the most part like untarnished steel. They found it equal in size (or nearly) to this ultimate sphere of ours, the earth, including the ocean that girdles it. /

Here Astolfo had a double surprise: what a big place the moon was from

1. Wicked Babylonian king.　2. Elijah was borne to heaven in a flaming chariot.

close up, when to us, who look at it from down here, it seems but a little sphere! And how he had to screw up his eyes if from up there he wanted to descry the earth and the sea spread over it; the earth being unilluminated, its features can span but a short distance. / The rivers, lakes, and fields up there were not as they are down here. The plains, valleys, mountains, cities, and castles were different, and there were houses the like of which for sheer size the paladin had never seen before or since. And there were spacious, empty forests where nymphs were forever hunting game. /

Astolfo did not stop to explore everything, for that was not the object of his coming. He was led by the holy apostle into a valley shut in between two hills, where everything that is lost on earth (be the fault ours or that of time or fate) fetches up miraculously. What is lost here collects up there. / I do not mean only dominion and wealth, subject to the vagaries of fickle Fortune. I mean also what is beyond Fortune's power to give or take: there is many a reputation up there which, little by little, time has consumed down here like a moth. There, too, are countless prayers and vows made to God by us sinners. / The tears and sighs of lovers, the useless time lost in gaming, the chronic idleness of ignorant men, the empty plans which know no rest, the vain desires are in such numbers that they clutter almost the whole place. In short, no matter what you ever lost here you would find if you went up there. /

As Astolfo passed among these mounds he asked his guide about various of them. Noticing a lofty pile of tumid bladders from which seemed to emanate a hubbub of cries, he was told that these were the ancient crowns of the Assyrians and of Lydia, of the Persians and Greeks—once so illustrious, now forgotten almost to their very names. / Next he saw a heap of gold and silver hooks: gifts made in hope of reward to kings, to greedy princes, to patrons. He asked about garlands he saw which concealed a noose: all flattery, he was told. Verses written in praise of patrons wore the guise of exploded crickets. / Love affairs pursued to little purpose had the shape of gilded bonds, jewel-studded shackles. There were eagles' talons—and these were, I am told, the authority which lords vest in their servants. The bellows littering the hillside all around denoted the praise given by princes and the favors conferred upon their favorites, all wafted away with the flower of their years. /

Cities and castles and immense treasures lay here in a confused jumble of ruins. They were treaties, he was told, and ill-concealed plots. He saw snakes with maidens' faces: the works of coiners and thieves. Then he noticed an assortment of broken phials: service as wretched courtiers. / He came upon a great mess of pottage and asked his mentor about it. "That," he explained, "is the charity left by a person after his death." Then he skirted a great mound of sundry flowers once sweet-smelling but now reeking. This (begging your pardons) was the Donation of Constantine to good Sylvester.[3] He saw great quantities of bird-lime for ensnaring: your charms, good ladies. It would take an age if I were to describe in verse each thing that was pointed out to him—after countless thousands I should still not be finished, for every one of our needs is to be found up there. Folly, however, whatever its degree,

---

3. Deed of Rome to the popes, discredited by the humanist scholar Lorenza Valla, who proved on linguistic grounds that the deed was a forgery.

is missing from there: it stays down here and never leaves us. / Astolfo had some lost days and other oddments of his own to look for; without his guide, he would never have recognized them in their different transformations.

Next he came upon the substance which, it seems, is so innate in us that never were prayers offered to God for its possession: I mean brains. There was a mountain of them here, only a far bigger one than of anything previously mentioned. / They took the form of a soft, tenuous liquid, apt to vaporize if not kept tightly sealed. It could be seen collected in various phials of greater or lesser size adapted for this purpose. The one containing the mighty brain of mad Orlando was the biggest of them all. It was also distinguished from the others by the inscription upon it: "The wits of Orlando." / All the rest were similarly inscribed with the name of the person to whom the wits belonged. The valiant duke discovered a good portion of his own; but what surprised him far more was how many belonged to people he had credited with having all their wits about them—there was abundant evidence of how witless they really were, to judge by the amount that was here to hand. / Some lose their wits in loving, some in seeking honors, some in scouring the seas in search of wealth, some in hopes placed in princes, some in cultivating magical baubles; some lose them over jewels, some over paintings, and some over other objects which they value above all else. Here the wits of sophists, astrologers, and poets abound. /

Astolfo collected his, for the author of the mysterious Apocalypse permitted him. He held to his nose the phial containing his wits and they just seemed to make their way back into place. Turpin asserts, it seems, that from there on Astolfo lived sensibly for a long time, until a subsequent caprice of his lost him his wits a second time. / Astolfo took the fullest, most capacious phial which contained the wherewithal to restore Orlando to his senses. It was not as light as he had imagined when it lay on the pile with the others.

Before he returned down to the lower spheres from this radiant one, he was led by the holy apostle into a palace built beside a river. / Each room was full of lengths of spun flax, silk, cotton, and wool, dyed in various colors, some pleasing, others hideous. In the first courtyard a white-haired woman was winding them onto reels—the way in summer one sees peasant women drawing the moist cocoons off the silkworms as they harvest the new silk. / When one skein was finished, another was brought in its place, the first taken away; another woman would sort out the attractive from the ugly threads which the first left all in confusion. "What is going on here? I can't make it out," asked Astolfo. "The old women are the Fates," replied John; "with these threads they spin lives for you mortals. / As long as one of these threads is spun out, so long does a human life last, and not a moment longer. Here Death and Nature keep watch to know the hour when a person is to die. The other Fate is responsible for selecting the beautiful strands to be woven into an adornment for paradise; out of the ugliest ones tough bonds are fashioned for the damned." / The skeins already wound and requisitioned for further use were all given little plaques stamped with the relevant name, some in iron, others in silver or gold. / Then they were disposed in thick piles from which a tireless old man was seen taking them away with never a moment's pause, always returning for more. / The old man was so swift and expeditious, he seemed to have been born to run. He kept leaving that hillside with a load of these name-plates gathered in his lap. Where he went and why he did this will be explained to you in the next canto, if you signify with your usual kind attention that this would be agreeable to you.

. . .

Who will ascend to heaven, mistress mine, to fetch me back my lost wits? They have been ebbing away ever since my heart was transfixed by the arrows shot from your fair eyes—not that I complain of my misfortune so long as it grows no worse than it is now: I fear that any further depletion of my wits shall reduce me to the very condition I have described in Orlando. / I do not imagine, however, that there is any need for me to take flight through the air to the orb of the moon or into paradise in order to recover my wits. I don't believe they inhabit those heights. Their haunts are your beautiful eyes, your radiant face, your ivory breasts, those alabastrine hillocks; and I shall sip them up with my lips if that proves the way to recover them.[4] /

Astolfo went through the spacious palace gazing at all those lives-to-be, after seeing those already spun reeled onto the fateful spools. And he noticed one life-thread which seemed to glitter more than fine gold. If jewels could be skilfully powdered and then spun out in a thread, such a thread[5] would not be remotely as splendid as this one. / The gorgeous thread delighted him beyond measure—it was unique—and there came to him a strong desire to know when this life was to be lived and whose it was to be. The Evangelist made no secret of it: its first year was to be twenty years before the ciphers M and D marked the interval since the birth of the Word Incarnate.[6] / And as this thread was resplendent and beautiful beyond compare, so also would be the uniquely fortunate era which was then to begin: it would derive as a perpetual and unfailing inheritance every one of those rare and eminent graces which man acquires by Nature's or Fortune's kindness, or by his own efforts. /

"Between the mighty branches of the king of rivers," he continued, "there now nestles a humble little village; before it flows the Po; behind it spreads a misty vortex of deep marsh. I see it becoming, with the passage of time, the fairest of all the cities[7] of Italy, not only for its walls and great regal piles, but also for the quality of its learning and manners. / Such high and sudden eminence will not result from random chance: Heaven has ordained it, so that the city may be a fitting birthplace for the man of whom I speak. A branch is grafted, and its growth carefully fostered when it is expected to fruit; and the jeweller refines his gold if he intends it as a setting for precious gems. / No soul in the realm of Earth was ever clothed in such beauty. Rare has been—and shall be—the spirit descending from these higher spheres who can match the excellence that the Eternal Mind intends to bestow upon Hippolytus of Este. Hippolytus of Este is the name of the one whom God has chosen to inherit so rich a gift. / Those accomplishments which, shared among many, would shed sufficient luster on them all, will be all concentrated upon the adornment of the man of whom you have asked me to speak. He shall foster the pursuit of every virtue. Were I to give a full description of his eminent merits, I should be carried so far that Orlando would wait in vain for his lost wits." /

Thus did Christ's imitator[8] talk to Astolfo. And when they had seen every room in the great building from which human lives emanated, they emerged

---

4. Another joking reference to the influence of Alessandra Benucci on the poet.   5. Woven by the Parcae, the Roman fates.   6. Ariosto's hyperbolic and Dantesque announcement of the birth of Ippolito d'Este in 1479.   7. Ferrara.   8. The apostle John.

beside the river, whose sand-clouded waters ran turbid and repellent. Here they found the old man who kept coming to the river-bank with the name-plates. / I don't know if you remember—the old man we left at the end of the last canto (old in his features, that is, but so sprightly in his movements that he was faster than any deer). He kept endlessly reducing the pile of name-plates, filling his lap with them and dropping—or rather dispersing—his precious burden into the river, known as Lethe.[9] / When the old prodigal came to the river-bank, he shook out his brimming lap and tipped all his plaques into the turbid waters. A countless number sank to the bottom without any use being derived from them; and of the myriad sunk in the sand of the river-bed, scarcely one was preserved. / Crows of every species, greedy vultures and various other birds wheeled and scudded along that river in a strident discord of cries. They all fell on this plentiful bounty when they saw it being scattered; some grasped the plaques in their beaks, others in their hooked talons, but they carried them no distance: / when they tried to take wing, they lacked the strength to lift their burden, so that these magnificent names, too, were robbed by Lethe of their renown. Among so many birds there was but a pair of swans, as white, my Lord,[1] as your device; they, with serene assurance, brought back in their beaks the plaques which fell to them. / In this way those beneficent creatures recovered a few despite the evil designs of the mischievous old man, who would have consigned them all to the river; oblivion consumed the rest. Now swimming, now winging their way through the air, the sacred swans reached a hill beside the cruel river, and on the hill-top, a shrine. / The place was sacred to Immortality. Here a beautiful nymph[2] came down from the hill to the shore of Lethe's stream and took the names from the swans' beaks. And she affixed the names round a statue set upon a pillar in the middle of the shrine. Here she consecrated them and took such care of them that they remained on view for all time. /

Who was the old man, and why did he so fruitlessly impart all those fine names to the river? And what of the birds, and the holy shrine from which the fair nymph came down to the river's edge? Astolfo wanted to know the latent meaning, to penetrate the mystery of all these things. He asked the man of God about them, and here was his reply: / "Understand that not a bough moves down on earth but its motion is remarked up here. There must be a correspondence, albeit under differing guise, between every effect on earth and in heaven. The old man, whose beard flows down his chest and who is so swift-footed that nothing ever stops him, achieves up here the same effects, the same work, that Time does on earth. / When the threads are fully wound upon the reel, human life comes to an end, down below. Down there fame would persist, up here the echo of it—immortality and divinity subsisting in both spheres—were it not for the bearded one here, and down there for Time constantly at work, ravaging. Our old man, as you can see, throws the names into the river; Time immerses them in eternal oblivion. / And just as up here the crows of various sorts, the vultures and other kinds of birds all strive to pick out of the water the names which catch their eye, so down on earth the same is done by the panders, sycophants, buffoons, pretty-boys, tale-bearers, those who infest the courts and are better welcomed there than men of integrity and worth, / those who are reputed gentlemen at court because they can emulate the donkey, the scavenging hog. Now

9. The river of oblivion separating the world of the living from that of the dead. 1. Ippolito. 2. Fame.

when just Fate (or rather Venus and Bacchus) have wound up their master's life-thread, all these folk I mention, supine cravens that they are, born only to feed their bellies, carry his name on their lips for a day or two, only to let the burden fall into oblivion. / But as the swans with their glad song convey the plaques safely to the shrine, so it is that men of worth are rescued from oblivion—crueler than death—by poets. O shrewd and sagacious princes, if you follow Caesar's example and make writers your friends you need have no fear of Lethe's waters![3] /

"Poets too are rare as swans—poets worthy of the name—partly because God will not permit too many men of eminence to reign at a time, and partly through the fault of niggardly lords who leave the heaven-sent geniuses to beg. Suppressing good and exalting evil, they banish the fair arts. / Believe me, God has robbed these simpletons of their wits and clouded their judgment, making them shun Poetry so that death should consume them whole and entire. They would otherwise emerge living from the grave even if their lives had been a disgrace: had they only known how to cultivate her friendship, they would give off a fragrance better than spikenard or myrrh. / Aeneas was not as devoted, nor Achilles as strong, nor Hector as ferocious as their reputations suggest.[4] There have existed men in their thousands who could claim preference over them. What has brought them their sublime renown have been the writers honored with gifts of palaces and great estates donated by these heroes' descendants. / Augustus was not as august and beneficent as Virgil makes him out in clarion tones—but his good taste in poetry compensates for the evil of his proscriptions. And no one would know whether Nero had been wicked—he might even, for all his enemies on earth and in heaven, have left a better name—had he known how to keep friendly with writers. / Homer made Agamemnon appear the victor and the Trojans mere poltroons; he made Penelope faithful to her husband, and victim of a thousand slights from her suitors. But if you want to know what really happened, invert the story: Greece was vanquished, Troy triumphant, and Penelope a whore. / Listen on the other hand to what reputation Dido left behind, whose heart was so chaste: she was reputed a strumpet purely because Virgil was no friend of hers.

"Don't be surprised if this embitters me and if I talk about it at some length—I like writers and am doing my duty by them, for in your world I was a writer too. / And I, above all others, acquired something which neither Time nor Death can take from me: I praised Christ and merited from Him the reward of so great a good fortune. I am sorry for those who live in an evil day when Courtesy has shut her door: pallid, lean, and wizened, they beat at it day and night in vain. / So, as I was saying, poets and scholars are few and far between. Where they are offered neither board nor lodging even the wild beasts desert the place." As the saintly old man said this his eyes blazed like two flames. Then he turned to Astolfo with a gentle smile and his overwrought face became once more serene. /

But let us leave Astolfo with the Gospel-maker, for I want to leap the distance between heaven and earth—my wings can no longer support me at such heights.

---

3. Augustus Caesar was patron of the poets Virgil and Horace, whose verse immortalized the Roman emperor.   4. Aeneas is the epic hero of Virgil's *Aeneid*, and Achilles and Hector are the chief warriors of Homer's *Iliad*.

* * *

FROM CANTO 39

[Orlando Regains His Wits]

The fleet was still waiting off the Moorish coast for a more favorable wind when a ship put in there, laden with captive warriors.[5] / It was carrying those whom bold Rodomont had captured at the perilous bridge where the tilting-ground was so restricted, as I have several times mentioned earlier. Among these were Oliver (brother of Orlando's wife), loyal Brandimart, Samsonet, and others whom I need not name—Germans, Italians, and Gascons. / Here the master, unaware of the enemy's presence, brought in his galley, leaving the port of Algiers, his intended goal, many miles astern, for a strong wind had got up and driven him beyond it. Now he imagined he was putting into a safe refuge, like Procne[6] returning to her twittering nest. / But when he noticed the Imperial Eagle, the Golden Lilies, and the Leopards[7] close by, he blanched like a man suddenly aware that his incautious foot has trodden upon a horrid poisonous snake which has been slumbering torpidly in the grass: he recoils in a fright and flees from the angry, venomous reptile. / But the master could not escape, nor conceal his prisoners. With Brandimart, Oliver, Samsonet, and many others he was brought before Astolfo and Dudone, who showed delight on seeing their friends. These requested that their warder, to requite him for bringing them here, be condemned to the galley-benches. / The Christian knights, as I said, were welcomed by Astolfo, in whose pavilion a banquet was given in their honor, and they were provided with arms and all else of which they stood in need. For their sakes Dudone postponed his departure: no less was to be gained, he felt, from conversing with barons such as these than from setting out a day or two earlier. / He received reliable information about France and Charlemagne—how they were faring—and about where a landing would be safest and most effective.

While he was listening to them, they became aware of a growing pandemonium, and the alarm was raised so frantically that they all fell to wondering. / Astolfo and his goodly company, all in a group conversing, were armed and mounted in a trice and hastened towards the centre of the commotion, questioning everyone along the way. And they reached a spot where they beheld a man so ferocious that, though naked and alone, he was ravaging the whole army. / He had a wooden staff which he swung before him, and it was so solid and heavy and so firmly clenched that at every swing a man fell to the ground in not the best of health. Already he had dispatched more than a hundred, and no one any longer tried to resist him unless by shooting arrows from a distance—certainly no one ventured to await his approach. / Dudone, Astolfo, and Brandimart and Oliver, who had hastened toward the noise, were still marveling at the savage's great strength and remarkable spirit when they saw a damsel dressed in black come galloping up on a palfrey; she greeted Brandimart and threw her arms about his neck. /

It was Fiordiligi, who was so inflamed with love for Brandimart that, when she left him captive at the narrow bridge, she almost went crazy with sorrow. She had crossed the sea after learning from Rodomont, his captor, that he

---

had been sent prisoner to Algiers with many knights. / On the point of embarking at Marseilles, she had found a Levantine ship which had brought an old retainer of King Monodant, Brandimart's father. He had scoured many a province, wandering over land and sea in search of Brandimart; on the way he had received news that he was to be found in France. / Now she recognized him for Bardino, the man who had abducted Brandimart as a little boy from his father and taken him to be brought up at Rocca Silvana. When she learned the reason for his journey, she had induced him to set sail with her, telling him how Brandimart had come to cross over to Africa. / On landing, they heard that Bizerta was besieged by Astolfo, and it was rumored that Brandimart was with him. At sight of him, Fiordiligi sped towards him, giving clear evidence of the joy which was all the greater for the sorrows that had preceded it. / The courteous knight was no less pleased to see his loyal true-love whom he adored above all else; he embraced and hugged her in a gentle welcome, and the first kiss did not sate his inflamed desire, nor did the second or third.

He looked up, however, and noticed Bardino, her companion. / He reached out, meaning to embrace him and ask what brought him here, but there was no time: the army was fleeing in disorder before the staff with which the naked madman was clearing himself a path. Fiordiligi scrutinized the naked man's face and cried to Brandimart, "It's the count!" / At the same time Astolfo, who was present, recognized him for Orlando by certain signs he had been advised of by the holy ancients in the Earthly Paradise. Otherwise they should none of them have recognized in him the noble baron: after so long disdaining his own body, in his folly, his face resembled a beast's more than a man's. / Stabbed to the heart with pity, Astolfo turned, weeping, to Dudone, who stood beside him, and then to Oliver: "Look!" he cried. "That's Orlando!" And they all gazed at him intently, wide-eyed; to find him thus reduced filled them with wonder and compassion. / Most of those lords were moved to tears of distress.

"Now is the time to discover the art of healing him," observed Astolfo, "not to weep over him." With this he jumped from his horse, and so did Brandimart, Samsonet, Oliver, and saintly Dudone, and all together they fell upon Charlemagne's nephew, to capture him. / Seeing himself encircled, Orlando swung his staff in frantic desperation, and taught Dudone the serious consequences of his rashness when he tried to venture within arm's length, his head protected by his shield. Were it not for Oliver absorbing part of the blow with his sword, Orlando's injudicious staff would have shattered Dudone's shield, helmet, head, and torso. / It broke only his shield, though landing such a thump on his helmet that he fell to the ground.

Meanwhile Samsonet swung his sword with such vigor that it caught the staff two arms' lengths from the top and cut it clean in two, while Brandimart grabbed him from behind, clinching him with both arms as tightly as he could, and Astolfo seized him round the legs. / Orlando gave a jerk which sent Astolfo flying off to land on his back ten feet away. But Brandimart, who had a tighter hold, he could not shake off. Oliver ventured too close and received a clout so severe that it felled him: he turned ashy pale and the blood gushed from his nose and eyes. / Had his helmet been less than perfect, Oliver would have been killed by that clout; as it was, he fell like one who has rendered up his soul to paradise. Back on their feet, Astolfo, Dudone (the latter's face swollen), and Samsonet, who had delivered the deft stroke, all jumped on Orlando together. / Dudone clasped him forcefully from behind and tried tripping him up. Astolfo and the rest clung onto his arms, but even so, their combined efforts could not hold him. Anyone who has seen a bull being baited—savage jaws snap at his ears, and as he runs off, bellowing, he drags the hounds along with him but cannot shake free of them— / may imagine Orlando dragging all those warriors with him.

At this point Oliver got up from the ground where the great blow had felled him; and seeing that this was no way to achieve what Astolfo intended, he hit upon a plan to bring down Orlando, and put it into effect—successfully. / He called for ropes, quickly made a slipknot in one end of each, had some of them secured to the Count's arms and legs, the rest round his body. Then he distributed the other rope-ends to those present, and thus brought down Orlando, the way a farrier will bring down a horse or ox. / Once down, they were all on top of him, and bound his hands and feet yet more securely. Orlando jerked this way and that, but his efforts were all in vain. Astolfo now ordered him to be removed, saying that he was going to heal him. Dudone, a giant, loaded him onto his back and carried him down the beach to the water's edge. / Astolfo had him washed seven times, and seven times had him plunged beneath the water so as to cleanse his face and brutish limbs of the unsightly layers of grime. Then, with certain herbs gathered to this end, he had his mouth sealed, as it puffed and huffed, for he was not to draw breath other than through his nose. / Astolfo had prepared the phial which contained Orlando's wits. This he applied to the count's nose to such effect that, as he inhaled, he sucked it dry.

O wonder of wonders! He recovered his wits in their pristine condition—and intellect, brighter and more lucid than ever, once more informed his graceful speech. / As one who, in a heavy, oppressive sleep, has been seeing horrible shapes of monsters who do not and cannot exist, or has dreamt of having committed some gross enormity, lingers in wonderment when sleep is ended and he is once more master of his senses: so Orlando, recovered from his ravings, remained bemused and stupefied. / He stared at Brandi-mart, at Oliver (fair Aude's brother[8]), and at Astolfo who had restored his senses to him; and, as he looked at them in utter silence, he mused on how and since when he came to be here. He turned his gaze this way and that but could not conceive where he was. He wondered at finding himself naked, and bound with so many ropes from shoulders to feet. / Then, choosing the words uttered by sobered Silenus to those who had trussed him up in the cave, "Solvite me,"[9] he said; and his face was so serene, his eyes so much less crazy than before, that he was untied; and they supplied him with clothing which they had sent for. Bitterly he regretted his aberration, and they all consoled him. /

His old self once more, a paragon of wisdom and manliness, Orlando also found himself cured of love: the damsel who had seemed hitherto so beautiful and good in his eyes, and whom he had so adored, he now dismissed as utterly worthless. His only concern, his only wish now was to recover all that Love had stolen from him.

* * *

8. First allusion to the fact that Orlando is married, to Aude (or Alda).   9. "Release me," the words spoken by Virgil's Silenus, father of the satyrs, when he awakens from a drunken stupor in eclogue 8.

Lyric Poetry: Carpe Diem Poems

"Come live with me and be my love, / And we will all the pleasures prove." "Gather ye rosebuds while ye may." "Had we but world enough, and time, / This coyness, Lady, were no crime." These are some of the best-known and best-loved lines in all lyric poetry. They derive from two famous words in a Latin poem by Horace: *carpe diem* ("seize the day"), the poet wrote, urging his lady to give up her reservations and give in to love. Horace does not indicate whether his lyrical persuasions succeeded with the woman in question, but they have certainly prevailed with many generations of poets and readers. The unbroken line of lyric adaption from the Renaissance to modern poetry and popular songs illustrates the success of this poetic genre. The carpe diem poem, or lyric invitation to love, has long stood for the sweetest temptation that poetry can offer. It is "ear candy," in the words of a recent American poet laureate, Robert Pinsky (in reference to sixteenth-century English verse), and the "finest of all human makings."

The carpe diem poem's charm comes from the contrast between the speaker's bold and passionate desires and the sweet and simple qualities of his language, song-like meter, and imagery from the world of nature (springtime and countryside settings are common). Lovemaking is the speaker's immediate or short-term goal: he aims to convince a woman to put aside her doubts, give in to passion, and surrender her body to him. Yet erotic desire is generally not his only motive for persuading his lady to throw caution to the wind. On a social level, he aims to defy the moral conventions and censures associated with an older generation. On a psychological level, he longs to unite spiritually as well as physically with another human being and thus overcome the solitary aspects of human existence—what John Donne calls "the defects of loneliness." On a philosophical or spiritual level, he uses the vitality and sweetness of poetry to cope with the bitter fact of his own mortality. Through the ferocity of his passion, as embodied in love-making and in immortal verse, he denies the inevitability of death.

Renaissance poets are not, of course, identical with their speakers. The poets presented here, such as Leonardo da Vinci and Torquato Tasso in Italian and Christopher Marlowe and Andrew Marvell in English, address themselves to a wide readership of friends and literary connoisseurs. They draw on the traditions of amorous poetry, for example, to sustain intimacies with friends and patrons; in this sense, poetry is a kind of correspondence (and, as John Donne wrote, "more than kisses, letters mingle souls"). They use poetry also to establish relationships with other poets, living or dead. One reason that poets contribute to an established poetic tradition is to converse (or compete) with other writers, regardless of linguistic, national, or historical differences. The carpe diem tradition brings poets together to join in a conversation about erotic persuasion and, above all, about the persuasive nature of love poetry itself. Just as the speakers within the love poems aim to break the rules of moral propriety, the poets seek to challenge the oldest rule governing poetic composition, which is that it must teach as well as please. The carpe diem poem utterly disregards the traditional responsibility of poetry to serve a moral purpose. It invites readers to enjoy poetry based wholly on the sensual pleasures of meter and language. Its views on the nature of poetry are summed up by the twentieth-century poet Archibald MacLeish, who proclaimed, "A poem should not mean / But be."

LORENZO DE' MEDICI
1449–1492

Triumph of Bacchus and Ariadne[1]

How beautiful youth is
Though ever fleeing!
Let him be happy who wants to be:
There's no certainty of tomorrow.

Here are Bacchus and Ariadne,[2]   5
Handsome, and burning for each other:
Because time flies and beguiles,
They remain ever happy together.
These nymphs and these others
Are always merry.   10
Let him be happy who wants to be:
There's no certainty of tomorrow.

These happy little satyrs[3]
Enamored of the nymphs
In caves and groves   15
Have set a hundred traps for them:
Now warmed by Bacchus,
They're always dancing and leaping.
Let him be happy who wants to be:
There's no certainty of tomorrow.   20

These nymphs in turn are glad
To be beguiled by them;
No one can shield himself from Love
Except crude and ungrateful people:
Now mingling together   25
They play instruments and sing always.
Let him be happy who wants to be:
There's no certainty of tomorrow.

This load coming behind
Upon the ass, is Silenus:[4]   30
Old as he is, he's drunk and happy,
Already full of flesh and years;
If he can't hold himself straight, at least
He laughs and revels always.
Let him be happy who wants to be: 35
There's no certainty of tomorrow.

---

1. Translated by Luciano Rebay.   2. A mythological nymph loved and wed by Bacchus, god of wine, fertility, and revelry.   3. Creatures who were half-men, half-goats.   4. Oldest of the satyrs and tutor of Bacchus, Silenus was always drunk. The wisdom of Silenus lay in his knowledge that humans are happiest if unborn and, if born, happiest if they die young.

Midas[5] comes after these:
Whatever he touches turns to gold.
And what's the good of having treasure,
If one then is not satisfied?   40
What sweet pleasure do you think he feels—
One who is always thirsty?
Let him be happy who wants to be:
There's no certainty of tomorrow.

Let every one open his ears well: 45
Let no one feed on tomorrow;
Today, young and old, let's be
Happy, everybody, women and men:
May every sad thought fall away;
Let's be celebrating always.   50
Let him be happy who wants to be:
There's no certainty of tomorrow.

Ladies and young men in love,
Long live Bacchus and long live Love!
Let every one make music, dance, and sing!   55
Let hearts be fired with sweetness!
No straining, no grieving!
Whatever has to be, must be.
Let him be happy who wants to be:
There's no certainty of tomorrow.   60

How beautiful youth is
Though ever fleeing!

5. According to myth, King Midas was so hospitable to Silenus that Bacchus granted him any wish; Midas wished for the golden touch.

ANGELO POLIZIANO
1454–1494

Welcome to May[6]

Welcome to May
And its wild banner:[7]

Welcome to spring
Which wants one to fall in love.
And you, young girls, in a group   5

6. Translated by Luciano Rebay.   7. A branch that a young man cut from a tree to attach to the door of his sweetheart's home on May Day.

With your sweethearts,
You who with roses and flowers
Make yourselves pretty in May,

Come to the cool shade
Of the green young trees.   10
Every pretty maiden is safe
Among so many youths;
For beasts and birds
Burn with love in May.

She who is young and beautiful,   15
Pray that she not be bitter,
For it does not renew itself,
Age—as does the grass:
Let no one remain proud
With her sweetheart in May.   20

Let each girl dance and sing
In this group of ours.
Behold your sweet lovers
Going, my pretty ones, to joust for you:
She who shows herself harsh to them   25
Will cause the withering of May.

To capture the young girls
Their lovers have armed themselves.
Surrender, my pretty ones,
To those in love with you;   30
Give back the hearts you have thieved,
Do not wage war in May.

Let her who has stolen someone's heart
Give her own heart in return.
But who is that one flying?   35
It's the young angel of Love,
Who is coming to do honor
With you, young girls, to May.

Love comes forth laughing
With roses and lilies on his head,   40
And he comes looking for you.
Greet him with joy, my pretty ones.
Which of you will be the first
To give him the flower of May?

Welcome to the pilgrim.   45
Love, what is your command?
That for her lover's hair
Each pretty one weave a garland;
For young girls and grown women
Fall in love in May.   50

TORQUATO TASSO
1544–1595

[What dew or what weeping][8]

What dew or what weeping,
What tears were those
I saw scattered from night's mantle
And from the pale face of the stars?
And why did the white moon sow   5
A pure cloud of crystalline stars
In the lap of the fresh grass?
Why in the dark air
Could one hear, almost lamenting, around and around
The breezes roaming till daybreak?   10
Were they perhaps signs of your departure,
Life of my life?

[The woods and the rivers are silent][9]

The woods and the rivers are silent,
And the waveless sea is at rest;
In their caves the winds are at truce and peace,
And in the dark night
The white moon creates lofty silence;   5
And we keep hidden
The sweetnesses of love:
Let love not speak or breathe,
Let kisses be soundless, and soundless my sighs.

[I'd like to be a bee][1]

I'd like to be a bee,
O beautiful cruel lady,
Who, murmuring, would suck the honey in you,
And, being unable [to sting] your heart, could at least
Sting your white breast   5
And in so sweet a wound
Leave its own life, avenged.

8. Translated by Luciano Rebay.   9. Translated by Luciano Rebay.   1. Translated by Luciano Rebay.

CHRISTOPHER MARLOWE
1564–1593

The Passionate Shepherd to His Love

Come live with me and be my love,
And we will all the pleasures prove
That valleys, groves, hills, and fields,
Woods or steepy mountain yields.

And we will sit upon the rocks,   5
Seeing the shepherds feed their flocks,
By shallow rivers to whose falls
Melodious birds sing madrigals.

And I will make thee beds of roses
And a thousand fragrant posies,   10
A cap of flowers, and a kirtle[2]
Embroidered all with leaves of myrtle;[3]

A gown made of the finest wool
Which from our pretty lambs we pull;
Fair lined slippers for the cold,   15
With buckles of the purest gold;

A belt of straw and ivy buds,
With coral clasps and amber studs:
And if these pleasures may thee move,
Come live with me and be my love.   20

The shepherds' swains shall dance and sing
For thy delight each May morning:
If these delights thy mind may move,
Then live with me and be my love.

---

2. Light garment worn beneath the outer skirts.   3. Tree sacred to Venus, goddess of love.

SIR WALTER RALEGH
1552–1618

The Nymph's Reply to the Shepherd

If all the world and love were young,
And truth in every shepherd's tongue,
These pretty pleasures might me move
To live with thee and be thy love.

Time drives the flocks from field to fold,   5
When rivers rage and rocks grow cold,
And Philomel[4] becometh dumb;
The rest complains of cares to come.

The flowers do fade, and wanton fields
To wayward winter reckoning yields;   10
A honey tongue, a heart of gall,
Is fancy's spring, but sorrow's fall.

Thy gowns, thy shoes, thy beds of roses,
Thy cap, they kirtle, and they posies
Soon break, soon wither, soon forgotten—   15
In folly ripe, in reason rotten.

Thy belt of straw and ivy buds,
The coral clasps and amber studs,
All these in me no means can move
To come to thee and be thy love.   20

But could youth last and love still breed,
Had joys no date nor age no need,
Then these delights my mind might move
To live with thee and be thy love.

---

4. The nightingale, who, as legend has it, sings despite her pain at betrayal.

EDMUND SPENSER
1552–1599

From Amoretti

54

Of this world's Theatre in which we stay,
My love like the Spectator idly sits
Beholding me that all the pageants play,
Disguising diversely my troubled wits.
Sometimes I joy when glad occasion fits,   5
And mask in mirth like to a Comedy:
Soon after when my joy to sorrow flits,
I wail and make my woes a Tragedy.
Yet she beholding me with constant eye,
Delights not in my mirth nor rues my smart: 10
But when I laugh she mocks, and when I cry
She laughs, and hardens evermore her heart.
What then can move her? if nor mirth, nor moan,
She is no woman, but a senseless stone.

67

Like as a huntsman after weary chase,
Seeing the game from him escap'd away,
Sits down to rest him in some shady place,
With panting hounds beguiled of their prey:
So after long pursuit and vain assay,   5
When I all weary had the chase forsook,
The gentle deer return'd the self-same way,
Thinking to quench her thirst at the next brook.
There she beholding me with milder look,
Sought not to fly, but fearless still did bide: 10
Till I in hand her yet half trembling took,
And with her own goodwill her firmly tied.
Strange thing, me seem'd, to see a beast so wild,
So goodly won, with her own will beguil'd.

SIR PHILIP SIDNEY
1554–1586

From Astrophil and Stella

71

Who will in fairest book of nature know
How virtue may best lodg'd in beauty be,
Let him but learn of love to read in thee,
Stella,[5] those fair lines which true goodness show.
There shall he find all vices' overthrow,   5
Not by rude force, but sweetest sovereignty
Of reason, from whose light those night-birds fly;
That inward sun in thine eyes shineth so.
And, not content to be perfection's heir
Thyself, dost strive all minds that way to move,   10
Who mark in thee what is in thee most fair.
So while thy beauty draws they heart to love,
As fast thy virtue bends that love to good:
But "Ah," Desire still cries, "Give me some food!"

5. Penelope Rich, beloved of Sidney, called Stella ("star") in his poetry.

JOHN DONNE
1572–1631

Elegy 19

To His Mistress, Going to Bed

Come, madam, come, all rest my powers defy;
Until I labor, I in labor lie.
The foe ofttimes, having the foe in sight,
Is tired with standing, though he never fight.
Off with that girdle, like heaven's zone[6] glittering   5
But a far fairer world encompassing.
Unpin that spangled breast-plate, which you wear,
That th' eyes of busy fools may be stopp'd there.
Unlace yourself, for that harmonious chime
Tells me from you that now it is bed-time.   10
Off with that happy busk,[7] which I envy,
That still can be, and still can stand so nigh.
Your gown going off such beauteous state reveals,
As when from flowery meads th' hill's shadow steals.
Off with your wiry coronet, and show   15

6. The constellation of Orion.   7. Corset.

The hairy diadems which on you do grow.
Off with your hose and shoes; then softly tread
In this love's hallow'd temple, this soft bed.
In such white robes heaven's angels used to be
Revealed to men; thou, angel, bring'st with thee   20
A heaven-like Mahomet's paradise;[8] and though
Ill spirits walk in white, we easily know
By this these angels from an evil sprite;
Those set our hairs, but these our flesh upright.
License my roving hands, and let them go   25
Before, behind, between, above, below.
O, my America, my New-found-land,[9]
My kingdom, safest when with one man mann'd,
My mine of precious stones, my empery;[1]
How am I blest in thus discovering thee!   30
To enter in these bonds, is to be free;
Then, where my hand is set, my soul shall be.
Full nakedness! All joys are due to thee;
As souls unbodied, bodies unclothed must be
To taste whole joys. Gems which you women use   35
Are like Atlanta's balls[2] cast in men's views;
That, when a fool's eye lighteth on a gem,
His earthly soul might court that, not them.
Like pictures, or like books' gay coverings made
For laymen, are all women thus array'd.   40
Themselves are only mystic books, which we
—Whom their imputed grace will dignify—
Must see reveal'd. Then, since that I may know,
As liberally as to thy midwife show
Thyself; cast all, yea, this white linen hence;   45
There is no penance due to innocence:
To teach thee, I am naked first; why then,
What needst thou have more covering than a man?

The Flea

Mark but this flea, and mark in this,
How little that which thou deniest me is;
It suck'd me first, and now sucks thee,
And in this flea our two bloods mingled be.
Thou know'st that this cannot be said   5
A sin, nor shame, nor loss of maidenhead;[3]
Yet this enjoys before it woo,
And pamper'd swells with one blood made of two;
And this, alas! is more than we would do.
O stay, three lives in one flea spare,   10

8. A proverbial garden of pleasures.   9. Note the images of world travel and conquest.   1. Empire, region ruled by an emperor (*with one man mann'd*).   2. Atlanta (i.e., Atalanta) competed with, and defeated, all her suitors in a footrace. One suitor, Hippomanes, tossed golden balls to distract her and thus won the race and the woman.   3. Virginity, as represented by the unbroken hymen.

Where we almost, yea, more than married are.
This flea is you and I, and this
Our marriage bed, and marriage temple is.
Though parents grudge, and you, we're met,
And cloister'd in these living walls of jet.[4]   15
Though use make you apt to kill me,
Let not to that self-murder added be,
And sacrilege, three sins in killing three.
Cruel and sudden, hast thou since
Purpled thy nail in blood of innocence?   20
Wherein could this flea guilty be,
Except in that drop which it suck'd from thee?
Yet thou triumph'st, and say'st that thou
Find'st not thyself nor me the weaker now.
'Tis true; then learn how false fears be;   25
Just so much honor, when thou yield'st to me,
Will waste, as this flea's death took life from thee.

4. Jet black.

BEN JONSON
1572–1637

[Come my Celia, let us prove][5]

Come my Celia, let us prove,[6]
While we can, the sports of love;
Time will not be ours forever;
He at length, our good will sever.
Spend not then his gifts in vain.   5
Suns that set, may rise again;
But, if once wee lose this light,
'Tis, with us, perpetual night.
Why should we defer our joys?
Fame, and rumor are but toys.   10
Cannot we delude the eyes
Of a few poor household spies?
Or his[7] easier ears beguile,
So removed by our wile?
'Tis no sin, love's fruits to steal,   15
But the sweet theft to reveal,
To be taken, to be seen,
These have crimes accounted been.

5. From Jonson's play *Volpone, or the Fox*. Celia is the virtuous wife whom Volpone unsuccessfully tries
to seduce.   6. Test, try.   7. Celia's husband.

[Drink to me, only, with thine eyes]

Drink to me, only, with thine eyes,
  And I will pledge with mine;
Or leave a kiss but in the cup,
  And I'll not look for wine.
The thirst that from the soul doth rise,   5
  Doth ask a drink divine;
But might I of Jove's nectar sup,
  I would not change for thine.

I sent thee, late, a rosy wreath,
  Not so much honoring thee,   10
As giving it a hope, that there
  It could not withered be.
But thou thereon did'st only breathe,
  And sent'st it back to me;
Since when it grows, and smells, I swear,   15
  Not of itself, but thee.

Inviting a Friend to Supper[8]

Tonight, grave sir, both my poor house, and I
Do equally desire your company;
Not that we think us worthy such a guest,
But that your worth will dignify our feast,
With those that come, whose grace may make that seem   5
Something, which else could hope for no esteem.
It is the fair acceptance, Sir, creates
The entertainment perfect: not the cates.[9]
Yet shall you have, to rectify your palate,
An olive, capers, or some better salad   10
Ushering the mutton; with a short-legged hen,
If we can get her, full of eggs, and then,
Lemons, and wine for sauce; to these, a cony[1]
Is not to be despaired of, for our money;
And, though fowl, now, be scarce, yet there are clerks,[2]   15
The sky not falling, think we may have larks.
I'll tell you of more, and lie, so you will come:
Of partridge, pheasant, wood-cock, of which some
May yet be there; and godwit,[3] if we can;
Knat, rail, and ruff[4] too. Howsoe'er, my man   20
Shall read a piece of Virgil, Tacitus,
Livy,[5] or of some better book to us,

---

8. Not all poems of invitation aim to seduce a woman to enjoy sexual liberties; this one invites a friend to enjoy dinner and conversational liberties.   9. Delicacies.   1. Rabbit.   2. Scholars.   3. A wading bird.   4. A freshwater fish; *knat* is a sandpiper; *rail* is a marsh bird. The poetic effect of these obscure monosyllabic words is to display both erudition and modesty.   5. All Roman authors, Jonson refers to *Livy*, historian of the Roman Republic; *Virgil*, poet of Rome's imperial origins in the *Aeneid*; and *Tacitus*, historian of the Roman Empire.

Of which we'll speak our minds, amidst our meat;
And I'll profess no verses to repeat:
To this, if ought appear, which I not know of,   25
That will the pastry, not my paper, show of.
Digestive cheese, and fruit there sure will be;
But that, which most doth take my Muse, and me,
Is a pure cup of rich Canary wine,
Which is the Mermaid's,[6] now, but shall be mine;   30
Of which had Horace, or Anacreon[7] tasted,
Their lives, as doe their lines, till now had lasted.
Tobacco, nectar, or the Thespian spring,[8]
Are all but Luther's beer,[9] to this I sing.
Of this we will sup free, but moderately,   35
And we will have no Pooley, or Parrot[1] by,
Nor shall our cups make any guilty men;
But, at our parting, we will be, as when
We innocently met. No simple word
That shall be uttered at our mirthful board   40
Shall make us sad next morning or affright
The liberty, that we'll enjoy tonight.

6. A famous London tavern.   7. Greek lyric poet; *Horace* was a Roman lyric poet.   8. Thespis was the Greek originator of drama; *tobacco* was the sensational new stimulant from the New World; *nectar* is the drink of the gods.   9. German beer was weaker than English beer; the reference to Martin Luther may suggest that the Reformation marks the historical distance of Christians from the spiritual inspiration of the Apostles. (It was commonplace to observe that "the age of miracles" was over.)   1. Henry Parrot and Robert Pooley were government spies.

ROBERT HERRICK
1591–1674

To the Virgins, to Make Much of Time

Gather ye rosebuds while ye may,
    Old Time is still a-flying;
And this same flower that smiles today,
    To-morrow will be dying.

The glorious lamp of heaven, the Sun,   5
    The higher he's a-getting;
The sooner will his race be run,
    And nearer he's to setting.

That age is best, which is the first,
    When youth and blood are warmer;   10
But being spent, the worse, and worst
    Times still succeed the former.

Then be not coy, but use your time,
And while ye may, go marry;
For having lost but once your prime,   15
You may for ever tarry.

Delight in Disorder

A sweet disorder in the dress
Kindles in clothes a wantonness;
A lawn about the shoulders thrown
Into a fine distraction;
An erring lace, which here and there   5
Enthralls the crimson stomacher;[2]
A cuff neglectful, and thereby
Ribbons to flow confusedly;
A winning wave, deserving note,
In the tempestuous petticoat;   10
A careless shoe-string, in whose tie
I see a wild civility:
Do more bewitch me, than when art
Is too precise in every part.

2. Decorative garment, embroidered or bejeweled, worn over the stomach and chest.

MARTIN OPITZ
1597–1639

[Ah, Dearest, let us haste us][3]

Ah Dearest, let us haste us,
    While we have time;
Delaying doth but waste us
    And lose our prime.

The gifts that beauty nourish   5
    Fly with the year,
And everything we cherish
    Must disappear.

The cheeks so fair turn pallid,
    And grey the hair,   10
The flashing eyes turn gelid,
    And ice, desire.

3. Translated by Frank J. Warnke.

From coral lips must flee then
  The outline bold;
The snowy hands decay then,   15
  And thou art old.

So therefore let us swallow
  Youth's precious fruit,
E'er we are forc'd to follow
  The years in flight.   20

As thou thyself then lovest,
  Love also me;
Give me, that when thou givest
  I lose to thee.

ANDREW MARVELL
1621–1678

To His Coy Mistress

Had we but world enough, and time,
This coyness,[4] Lady, were no crime.
We would sit down and think which way
To walk and pass our long love's day.
Thou by the Indian Ganges' side   5
Shouldst rubies find: I by the tide
Of Humber would complain. I would
Love you ten years before the Flood,
And you should, if you please, refuse
Till the conversion of the Jews.   10
My vegetable love should grow
Vaster than empires, and more slow;
An hundred years should go to praise
Thine eyes and on thy forehead gaze;
Two hundred to adore each breast;   15
But thirty thousand to the rest;
An age at least to every part,
And the last age should show your heart;
For, Lady, you deserve this state,[5]
Nor would I love at lower rate.   20
  But at my back I always hear
Time's wingèd chariot hurrying near;
And yonder all before us lie
Deserts of vast eternity.
Thy beauty shall no more be found,   25
Nor, in thy marble vault, shall sound

---

4. Reticence, modesty.   **5.** Ceremony.

My echoing song: then worms shall try
That long preserved virginity,
And your quaint[6] honor turn to dust,
And into ashes all my lust: 30
The grave's a fine and private place,
But none, I think, do there embrace.
  Now therefore, while the youthful hue
Sits on thy skin like morning dew,
And while thy willing soul transpires   35
At every pore with instant fires,
Now let us sport us while we may,
And now, like amorous birds of prey,
Rather at once our time devour
Than languish in this slow-chapt[7] power.   40
Let us roll all our strength and all
Our sweetness up into one ball,
And tear our pleasures with rough strife
Through the iron gates of life:
Thus, though we cannot make our sun   45
Stand still,[8] yet we will make him run.

6. Elegant, unusual, prim; with a pun on slang for women's genitalia. 7. Slow-moving jaws. 8. Gods (Jupiter in his seduction of Alcmene) and prophets (Joshua) can make the sun stand still.

BALDASSARE CASTIGLIONE
1478–1529

Of the many arts cultivated in the brilliant courts of sixteenth-century Europe—including those of warfare, politics, poetry, painting, and architecture—the art of social conduct ranked among the most popular. No book shaped the ideal formulation of manners more than Castiglione's *The Book of the Courtier* (1528), a handbook on the qualities of the perfect courtier. Although Castiglione originally intended to celebrate one particular court—that of Urbino, Italy—the *Courtier* quickly became a European phenomenon, reaching audiences across the boundaries of class, sex, and nation. The emperor Charles V considered it one of his favorite books, and Henry VIII, Mary Queen of Scots, Catherine de Medici, and Francis I owned copies in the original Italian. The *Courtier* soon moved from the courts of kings to the studies of the learned elite when it was translated into Latin, then the universal language of diplomacy in Europe. Castiglione's book had achieved the broadest possible appeal as a truly cosmopolitan statement on style. Aspiring European nations and social classes sought to display familiarity with the *Courtier*'s views on good dress, horsemanship, dance, conversation, and habits of love. In his 1561 English translation, Sir Thomas Hoby remarked that Castiglione's courtier "has a long time haunted all the courts of Christendom," and has now "become an Englishman . . . and willing to dwell in the Court of England." The year 1566 saw the appearance of a *Polish Courtier*, which carefully revised the Italian text to suit the customs of its new country. Long enjoyed by aristocrats and the educated elite (from John Locke in England to the Inca Garcilaso in Peru), Castiglione's manual on stylish behavior came, by the end of the century, to be owned, read, and loved by lawyers, physicians, merchants, and their wives.

Baldassare Castiglione, a nobleman from the region of Mantua in Northern Italy, was born in Casanatico in 1478. His parents—his father was a courtier and mother a Gonzaga, related to the powerful Mantuan lords—sent him to Milan to be brought up in the spectacular court of Ludovico Sforza, who compensated for his upstart status by flamboyantly displaying his wealth and power. Castiglione served Francesco Gonzaga, marquis of Mantua, from 1499 until 1503, when he requested a transfer to the service of Guidobaldo daMontelfetro, duke of Urbino. Infuriated by the request, Francesco Gonzaga barred Castiglione from entering Mantuan territory, even to visit his mother; he did not forgive Castiglione until 1516, when he once again employed him in diplomatic services, and even arranged Castiglione's marriage. In the court of Urbino, Castiglione served as a diplomat for Guidobaldo and later for his adopted heir, Francesco Maria della Rovere, commander of the pope's army. In 1506 he traveled to England to accept the Order of the Garter from Henry VII on behalf of Duke Guidobaldo. He later fought in the siege of Mirandola under Pope Julius II (1511) and, in reward for this and other services, was given the title of count. During the time he lived in Rome, as the Gonzaga's family's ambassador to Pope Leo X, Castiglione made many friends, including the artists Michelangelo and Raphael, who painted a splendid portrait of Castiglione for his wedding.

Castiglione worked on the first draft of his *Courtier*, a dialogue on courtly ideals set in Urbino, during the years 1513–18. His tasks was complicated when the grasping Pope Leo X excommunicated Francesco Maria della Rovere in 1516 and appropriated the dukedom of Urbino for his nephew. More trials beset Castiglione when he worked on the second draft of the *Courtier* in the early 1520s; he experienced a series of losses, including the deaths of his friend Raphael in April of 1520 and of his wife, who died in childbirth in August of the same year. In 1524 Pope Clement VII sent him to Spain as papal ambassador or *nuncio* to the court of the emperor Charles V. Castiglione was still jointly serving the pope and Charles V three years later when Charles marched through Italy and attacked and plundered Rome, to the horror of Europeans who venerated Rome as the eternal, unconquerable city. The shock and embarrassment to Castiglione, put in an impossible position between the pope and the emperor, cost him his health: despite receiving continued approval from both of his masters—he was even elected bishop of Avila in Spain—Castiglione died in Toledo in 1529, one year after the *Courtier* appeared and two years after the Sack of Rome. At his funeral, the emperor Charles V famously declared, "I tell you that one of the best knights (*caballeros*) of the world is dead."

The inspiration for *The Book of the Courtier*, as Castiglione explains in his introductory letter (addressed to the Bishop of Viseu), was his sense of emotional debt to Duke Guidobaldo, whose death stirred Castiglione's nostalgia for the graceful and distinguished court that had once flourished at Urbino. To commemorate the duke and his court, Castiglione recalled a brilliant and stimulating conversation that had taken place at Urbino at a time when many illustrious courtiers and statesmen had gathered at the tiny court (the occasion was a visit by the pope). The subject of discussion was the ideal courtier. What social and moral qualities should he possess? How should he dress or dance? How should he converse or jest with his equals, his prince, or women? How should he experience and express love? What are the ideal manners of the courtier's female counterpart, the court lady? Castiglione divides his text into four parts, each devoted to one evening's conversation, and each led by a new speaker. Although the company is mixed, the speakers are all men, as stipulated by the Guidobaldo's duchess, Elisabetta Gonzaga. It is evidently her choice to spur the competition among the male courtiers by requiring the silence of all women present except Emilia Pia, whom she places in charge of directing the conversation.

The vital spark of Castiglione's book comes largely from the animated disagreements that the group at Urbino have over fine points of style, for no detail of social performance is too small for lively consideration. The various speakers have strongly held opinions on many topics, beginning with the question of whether the ideal courtier should have aristocratic blood (the answer then, as today, is that pedigree is not strictly necessary but it helps). The hallmark of excellence among Castiglione's courtiers is the ability to express opinions freely but without violating the almost magical atmosphere of social harmony. This task has its difficulties, since the community gathered at Urbino must constantly negotiate its social differences in order to sustain the conversation and the spirit of affection. The speakers generally succeed, despite the natural tensions of class (the count differs with his social inferior on the importance of nobility), sex (the women at one point laughingly assault the group's most outspoken misogynist), and geography (natives of Florence, Venice, Naples, and Milan, for example, have many historical rivalries). When the spirit of competition occasionally goes too far, Emilia Pia intervenes to tease the tactless speaker and guide the conversation back from dangerous extremes.

A point on which all speakers agree is that the courtier has attained such prominence in the courts of princes that a new and specialized vocabulary is required to describe his role and social arts. (The phenomenon continues today with the coinage of time-stamped words from "hip" or "cool" to "metrosexual"). Grace and ease are the skills that the perfect courtier must display without a trace of affectation or obvious premeditation. He must perform his courtly duties with a display of moderation, or heightened show of control over himself and his surroundings. The Italian word, *mediocrità*, evokes the classical ideal of the "golden mean" and suggests that the Renaissance courtier makes an art of avoiding behavioral extremes (taciturn and flamboyant men, for example, are equally ridiculous). There is no adequate translation for the word, *sprezzatura*, invented by Castiglione to sum up the courtier's most distinctive art (although "nonchalance" comes close). *Sprezzatura* may be defined as the fine art of performing without apparent effort. Etymologically related to the verbs "disdain" and "deprecate" or "appraise at a low value," it suggests that the most effective way to make an awe-inspiring impression is to appear utterly unconcerned about one's performance and its effect on beholders. One of Castiglione's characters, Unico Aretino, provides an example of *sprezzatura* when, challenged to speak by another character, he pauses a moment to reflect and then utters a complete sonnet in praise of the duchess. He gains a thrilling moment of social victory when everyone begins to wonder: was his performance spontaneous or carefully planned? *Sprezzatura* aims to keep them guessing and wanting more.

When the ideal courtier has mastered music, arms, horsemanship, poetry, and the art of love, what does he do with his skills? Although this is the larger question of Castiglione's handbook, it is in many ways hard for Castiglione's speakers to answer with certainty. They all agree that the courtier cultivates his skills in order to ingratiate himself to a prince, who might offer him employment. Like modern job seekers trying to break into a prestigious business, Castiglione's courtiers know the importance of clothes, conversation, style, and even reading habits (Shakespeare and Nietzsche on a discreet shelf to be noticed by the connoisseur, the *New Yorker* and *GQ* on the coffee table to be noted by all). Then, as now, it is entirely up to the prince (or CEO) to decide whether a talented individual is to play a significant role on the local and international scene or whether he is to spend his days as an idle hanger-on, a courtly ornament. In Castiglione's world, the most cherished hope is the one articulated by his final speaker, Signor Ottaviano: the successful courtier may gain and use his influence over the prince to guide him in political ethics. The classical model invoked throughout the book is that of Alexander the Great, the world-conqueror, whose tutor was none other than the philosopher Aristotle. Italian history gave Castiglione good reason to wish for the kind of moral and political influence that Aristotle had over his royal pupil, for the princes of Renaissance Italy could be brutal in their exercise of power. (Francesco Maria della Rovere, for example, murdered his sister's lover and ordered his men to assassinate a cardinal over a minor annoyance.) Overshadowing the idealized and gorgeous dreams of courtly grace laid out in the pages of the pages of the *Courtier*, as Castiglione knew, was the growing power of Machiavelli's pragmatic and ruthless prince.

The following list uses common English syllables and stress accents to provide rough equivalents of selected words whose pronunciation may be unfamiliar to the general reader.

Cesare Gonzaga: *chay'-zah-ray gon-zah'gah*

Giuliano de' Medici: *juh-lee-ah'noh day may'dee-chee*

disinvoltura: *dees-een-vol-tuh'rah*

roegarze: *roh-ay-gahr'tzay*

Gaspar Pallavicino: *gahs-pahr' pahl-lah-vee-chee'noh*

The Book of the Courtier[1]

[From *The Dedication*]

The Reverend and Illustrious Signor Don Michel de Silva, Bishop of Viseu[2]

[1]

When signor Guidobaldo of Montefeltro, Duke of Urbino, departed this life, I, together with several other gentlemen who had served him, remained in the service of Duke Francesco Maria della Rovere,[3] his heir and successor in the state. And, as the savor of Duke Guido's virtues was fresh in my mind, and the delight that in those years I had felt in the loving company of such excellent persons as then frequented the Court of Urbino, I was moved by the memory thereof to write these books of the Courtier: which I did in but a few days, meaning in time to correct those errors which had resulted from my desire to pay this debt quickly. But Fortune for many years now has kept me ever oppressed by such constant travail that I could never find the leisure to bring these books to a point where my weak judgment was satisfied with them.

Now being in Spain, and being informed from Italy that signora Vittoria della Colonna, Marchioness of Pescara,[4] to whom I had already given a copy of the book, had, contrary to her promise, caused a large part of it to be transcribed, I could not but feel a certain annoyance, fearing the considerable mischief that can arise in such cases.[5] Nevertheless, I trusted that the wisdom and prudence of that lady (whose virtue I have always held in veneration as something divine) would avail to prevent any wrong from befalling me for having obeyed her commands. In the end I learned that that part of the book was in Naples, in the hands of many persons; and, as men are always avid of new things, it appeared that certain of these persons were trying to have it printed. Wherefore, alarmed at this danger, I decided to revise at once such small part of the book as time would permit, with the intention of publishing it, thinking it better to let it be seen even slightly corrected by my own hand than much mutilated by the hands of others.

And so, to carry out this thought, I started to reread it; and immediately,

1. Translated by Charles S. Singleton. 2. Dom Miguel de Silva (d. 1556), ambassador to Popes Leo X, Adrian VI, and Clement VII. 3. Nephew and heir (1490–1538) of Guidobaldo of Montefeltro (1472–1508), duke of Urbino. 4. Renowned poet (1492–1547) and wife of the marquess of Pescara. 5. Publication was considered undignified for gentlemen.

at the very outset, by reason of the dedication, I was seized by no little sadness (which greatly grew as I proceeded), when I remembered that the greater part of those persons who are introduced in the conversations were already dead; for, besides those who are mentioned in the proem of the last Book, even messer Alfonso Ariosto, to whom the book is dedicated, is dead: an affable youth, prudent, abounding in the gentlest manners, and apt in everything befitting a man who lives at court. Likewise Duke Giuliano de' Medici, whose goodness and noble courtesy deserved to be enjoyed longer by the world. Messer Bernardo, Cardinal of Santa Maria in Pòrtico, who for his keen and entertaining readiness of wit was the delight of all who knew him, he too is dead. Dead also is signor Ottaviano Fregoso,[6] a most rare man in our times: magnanimous, devout, full of goodness, talent, prudence, and courtesy, and truly a lover of honor and worth, and so deserving of praise that his very enemies were always obliged to praise him; and those misfortunes which he so firmly endured were indeed enough to prove that fortune, as she ever was, is, even in these days, the enemy of virtue. Dead, too, are many others named in the book, to whom nature seemed to promise very long life.

But what should not be told without tears is that the Duchess,[7] too, is dead. And if my mind is troubled at the loss of so many friends and lords, who have left me in this life as in a desert full of woes, it is understandable that I should feel sorrow far more bitter for the death of the Duchess than for any of the others, because she was worth more than the others, and I was much more bound to her than to all the rest. Therefore, in order not to delay paying what I owe to the memory of so excellent a lady, and to that of the others who are no more, and moved too by the threat to my book, I have had it printed and published in such form as the brevity of time permitted.

And since, while they lived, you did not know the Duchess or the others who are dead (except Duke Giuliano and the Cardinal of Santa Maria in Pòrtico), in order to make you acquainted with them, in so far as I can, after their death, I send you this book as a portrait of the Court of Urbino, not by the hand of Raphael or Michelangelo,[8] but by that of a lowly painter and one who only knows how to draw the main lines, without adorning the truth with pretty colors or making, by perspective art,[9] that which is not seem to be. And, although I have endeavored to show in these conversations the qualities and conditions of those who are named therein, I confess that I have not even suggested, let alone expressed, the virtues of the Duchess, because not only is my style incapable of expressing them, but my mind cannot even conceive them; and if I be censured for this or for any other thing deserving of censure (and well do I know that such things are not wanting in the book), I shall not be gainsaying the truth.

* * *

6. Nephew (d. 1524) of Duke Guidobaldo and older brother of Federico (1480–1541). Alfonso Ariosto (1475–1525), distant cousin of the poet Ludovico Ariosto; he urged Castiglione to write the *Courtier* on the suggestion of Francis I of France. Giuliano de' Medici (1479–1516), youngest son of Lorenzo de' Medici Il Magnifico and brother of Pope Leo X. Messer Bernardo Dovizi da Bibbiena (1470–1520), a Tuscan, author of the comedy *The Foolish Woman*, friend of the Medici, made cardinal by Pope Leo X. 7. Elisabetta Gonzaga (1471–1526), daughter of the Marquess Federico Gonzaga of Mantua, married Duke Guidobaldo in 1489; due to the frequent illness and retired life of her husband, the duchess was the central and presiding figure in the life of the court [Translator's note]. 8. Michelangelo Buonarroti (1475–1564), sculptor, painter, architect, and poet. Raffaello Sanzio (1483–1520), painter and native of Urbino. 9. Illusion of three-dimensional space in artwork.

[3]

Others say that since it is so difficult, and well-nigh impossible, to find a man as perfect as I wish the Courtier to be, it was wasted effort to write of him, because it is useless to try to teach what cannot be learned. To such as these I answer (without wishing to get into any dispute about the Intelligible World or the Ideas) that I am content to have erred with Plato, Xenophon, and Marcus Tullius;[1] and just as, according to these authors, there is the Idea of the perfect Republic, the perfect King, and the perfect Orator, so likewise there is that of the perfect Courtier. And if I have been unable to approach the image of the latter, in my style, then courtiers will find it so much the easier to approach in their deeds the end and goal which my writing sets before them. And if, for all that, they are unable to attain to that perfection, such as it is, that I have tried to express, the one who comes the nearest to it will be the most perfect; as when many archers shoot at a target and none of them hits the bull's eye, the one who comes the closest is surely better than all the rest.

Still others say I have thought to take myself as a model, on the persuasion that the qualities which I attribute to the Courtier are all in me. To these persons I will not deny having tried to set down everything that I could wish the Courtier to know; and I think that anyone who did not have some knowledge of the things that are spoken of in the book, however erudite he might be, could not well have written of them; but I am not so wanting in judgment and self-knowledge as to presume to know all that I could wish to know.

Thus all defense against these charges, and perhaps many others, I leave for the present to the tribunal of public opinion; because more often than not the many, even without perfect knowledge, know by natural instinct the certain savor of good and bad, and, without being able to give any reason for it, enjoy and love one thing and reject and detest another. Hence, if my book pleases in a general way, I shall take it to be good, and I shall think that it is to survive. If, instead, it should not please, I shall take it to be bad and shall at once believe that the memory of it must needs be lost. And if my censors be not yet satisfied with this verdict of public opinion, then let them be content at least with that of time, which reveals the hidden defects of all things, and, being the father of truth and a judge without passion, is wont to pronounce always, on all writing, a just sentence of life or death.

BALDASSARE CASTIGLIONE

From *Book 1*

To Messer *Alfonso Ariosto*

[1]

I have long wondered, dearest messer Alfonso, which of two things was the more difficult for me: to deny you what you have repeatedly and so insistently asked of me, or to do it. For, on the one hand, it seemed very hard for me to deny a thing—especially when it was something praiseworthy—to

---

1. Plato's *Republic*, Xenophon's *Education of Cyrus*, and Cicero's *Orator*.

one whom I love most dearly and by whom I feel I am most dearly loved; yet, on the other hand, to undertake a thing which I was not sure I could finish seemed unbecoming to one who esteems just censure as much as it ought to be esteemed. Finally, after much thought, I have resolved that I would try in this to see how much aid to diligence might be had from affection and the intense desire that I have to please, which, in things generally, is so wont to increase men's industry.

Now, you have asked me to write my opinion as to what form of Courtiership most befits a gentleman living at the courts of princes, by which he can have both the knowledge and the ability to serve them in every reasonable thing, thereby winning favor from them and praise from others: in short, what manner of man he must be who deserves the name of perfect Courtier, without defect of any kind. Wherefore, considering this request, I say that, had it not seemed to me more blameworthy to be judged by you to be wanting in love than by others to be wanting in prudence, I should have eschewed this labor, out of fear of being thought rash by all who know what a difficult thing it is to choose, from among so great a variety of customs as are followed at the courts of Christendom, the most perfect form and, as it were, the flower of Courtiership. For custom often makes the same things pleasing and displeasing to us; whence it comes about sometimes that the customs, dress, ceremonies, and fashions that were once prized become despised; and, contrariwise, the despised become prized. Hence, it is clearly seen that usage is more powerful than reason in introducing new things among us and in blotting out old things; and anyone who tries to judge of perfection in such matters is often deceived. For which reason, since I am well aware of this and of many another difficulty in the matter whereof it is proposed that I should write, I am forced to excuse myself somewhat and to submit evidence that this is an error (if indeed it can be called error) which I share with you, so that, if I am to be blamed for it, that blame will be shared by you, because your having put upon me a burden beyond my powers must not be deemed a lesser fault than my own acceptance of it.

So let us now make a beginning of our subject, and, if that be possible, let us form such a Courtier that any prince worthy of being served by him, even though he have but small dominion, may still be called a very great lord.

In these books we shall not follow any set order or rule of distinct precepts, as is most often the custom in teaching anything whatever, but, following the manner of many ancient writers, and to revive a pleasant memory, we shall rehearse some discussions which took place among men singularly qualified in such matters. And even though I was not present and did not take part in them, being in England at the time when they occurred, I learned of them shortly thereafter from a person who gave me a faithful report of them;[2] and I shall attempt to recall them accurately, in so far as my memory permits, so that you may know what was judged and thought in this matter by men worthy of the highest praise, and in whose judgment on all things one may have unquestioned faith. Nor will it be beside the purpose to give some account of the occasion of the discussions that took place, so that in due order we may come to the end at which our discourse aims.

---

2. Castiglione, who did not travel to England until after the events described, removes himself from the dialogue for modesty's sake.

[2]

On the slopes of the Apennines toward the Adriatic, at almost the center of Italy, is situated, as everyone knows, the little city of Urbino. And although it sits among hills that are perhaps not as pleasant as those we see in many other places, still it has been blessed by Heaven with a most fertile and bountiful countryside, so that, besides the wholesomeness of the air, it abounds in all the necessities of life. But among the greater blessings that can be claimed for it, this I believe to be the chief, that for a long time now it has been ruled by excellent lords (even though, in the universal calamity of the wars of Italy, it was deprived of them for a time).[3] But, to look no further, we can cite good proof thereof in the glorious memory of Duke Federico,[4] who in his day was the light of Italy. Nor are there wanting many true witnesses still living who can testify to his prudence, humanity, justice, generosity, undaunted spirit, to his military prowess, signally attested by his many victories, the capture of impregnable places, the sudden readiness of his expeditions, the many times when with but small forces he routed large and very powerful armies, and the fact that he never lost a single battle; so that not without reason may we compare him to many famous men among the ancients.

Among his other laudable deeds, he built on the rugged site of Urbino a palace thought by many the most beautiful to be found anywhere in all Italy and he furnished it so well with every suitable thing that it seemed not a palace but a city in the form of a palace; and furnished it not only with what is customary, such as silver vases, wall hangings of the richest cloth of gold, silk, and other like things, but for ornament he added countless ancient statues of marble and bronze, rare paintings, and musical instruments of every sort; nor did he wish to have anything there that was not most rare and excellent. Then, at great expense, he collected many very excellent and rare books in Greek, Latin, and Hebrew, all of which he adorned with gold and silver, deeming these to be the supreme excellence of his great palace.

[3]

Following then the course of nature and being already sixty-five years old,[5] he died as gloriously as he had lived, leaving as his successor his only son, a child ten years of age and motherless, named Guidobaldo. This boy, even as he was heir to the state, seemed to be heir to all his father's virtues as well, and in his remarkable nature began at once to promise more than it seemed right to expect of a mortal; so that men judged none of the notable deeds of Duke Federico to be greater than his begetting such a son. But Fortune, envious of so great a worth, set herself against this glorious beginning with all her might, so that, before Duke Guido had reached the age of twenty, he fell sick of the gout, which grew upon him with grievous pain, and in a short time so crippled all his members that he could not stand upon his feet or move. Thus, one of the fairest and ablest persons in the world was deformed and marred at a tender age.

3. For a certain period of time, Duke Guidobaldo had to relinquish the duchy of Urbino to Cesare Borgia, who occupied it by force.   4. Federico II (1422–1482), of the house of Montefeltro, duke of Urbino. 5. Actually only sixty.

And not even content with this, Fortune opposed him so in his every undertaking that he rarely brought to a successful issue anything he tried to do; and, although he was very wise in counsel and undaunted in spirit, it seemed that whatever he undertook always succeeded ill with him whether in arms or in anything, great or small; all of which is attested by his many and diverse calamities, which he always bore with such strength of spirit that his virtue was never overcome by Fortune; nay, despising her storms with stanch heart, he lived in sickness as if in health, and in adversity as if most fortunate, with the greatest dignity and esteemed by all. So that, although he was infirm of body in this way, he campaigned with a most honorable rank[6] in the service of their Serene Highnesses Kings Alfonso and Ferdinand the Younger of Naples;[7] and later with Pope Alexander VI,[8] as well as the signories of Venice and Florence.

Then when Julius II became Pope,[9] the Duke was made Captain of the Church;[1] during which time, and following his usual style, he saw to it that his household was filled with very noble and worthy gentlemen, with whom he lived on the most familiar terms, delighting in their company; in which the pleasure he gave others was not less than that which he had from them, being well versed in both Latin and Greek and combining affability and wit with the knowledge of an infinitude of things. Besides this, so much did the greatness of his spirit spur him on that, even though he could not engage personally in chivalric activities as he had once done, he still took the greatest pleasure in seeing others so engaged; and by his words, now criticizing and now praising each man according to his deserts, he showed clearly how much judgment he had in such matters. Wherefore, in jousts and tournaments, in riding, in the handling of every sort of weapon, as well as in revelries, in games, in musical performances, in short, in all exercises befitting noble cavaliers, everyone strove to show himself such as to deserve to be thought worthy of his noble company.

[4]

Thus, all the hours of the day were given over to honorable and pleasant exercises both of the body and of the mind; but because, owing to his infirmity, the Duke always retired to sleep very early after supper, everyone usually repaired to the rooms of the Duchess, Elisabetta Gonzaga, at that hour; where also signora Emilia Pia[2] was always to be found, who being gifted with such a lively wit and judgment, as you know, seemed the mistress of all, and all appeared to take on wisdom and worth from her. Here, then, gentle discussions and innocent pleasantries were heard, and on everyone's face a jocund gaiety could be seen depicted, so much so that this house could be called the very abode of joyfulness. Nor do I believe that the sweetness that is had from a beloved company was ever savored in any other place as it once was there. For, not to speak of the great honor it was for each of us to serve such a lord as I have described above, we all felt a supreme happiness arise within us whenever we came into the presence of the Duchess. And it

6. As a mercenary captain, or *condottiere*.   7. Alfonso II and Ferdinand II (both of the house of Aragon), kings of Naples in the late 15th century.   8. Rodrigo Borgia, pope from 1492 to 1503.   9. In 1503. 1. Captain in the pontiff's army.   2. Sister-in-law and companion of the duchess, she wittily directs much of the conversation.

seemed that this was a chain that bound us all together in love, in such wise that never was there concord of will or cordial love between brothers greater than that which was there among us all.

The same was among the ladies, with whom one had very free and most honorable association, for to each it was permitted to speak, sit, jest, and laugh with whom he pleased; but the reverence that was paid to the wishes of the Duchess was such that this same liberty was a very great check; nor was there anyone who did not esteem it the greatest pleasure in the world to please her and the greatest grief to displease her. For which reason most decorous customs were there joined with the greatest liberty, and games and laughter in her presence were seasoned not only with witty jests but with a gracious and sober dignity; for that modesty and grandeur which ruled over all the acts, words, and gestures of the Duchess, in jest and laughter, caused anyone seeing her for the first time to recognize her as a very great lady. And, in impressing herself thus upon those about her, it seemed that she tempered us all to her own quality and fashion, wherefore each one strove to imitate her style, deriving, as it were, a rule of fine manners from the presence of so great and virtuous a lady; whose high qualities I do not now intend to recount, this being not to my purpose, because they are well known to all the world, and much more than I could express either with tongue or pen; and those which might have remained somewhat hidden, Fortune, as if admiring such rare virtues, chose to reveal through many adversities and stings of calamity, in order to prove that in the tender breast of a woman, and accompanied by singular beauty, there may dwell prudence and strength of spirit, and all those virtues which are very rare even in austere men.

[5]

But, passing over this, I say that the custom of all the gentlemen of the house was to betake themselves immediately after supper to the Duchess; where, amidst the pleasant pastimes, the music and dancing which were continually enjoyed, fine questions would sometimes be proposed, and some-times ingenious games, now at the behest of one person and now of another, in which, under various concealments, those present revealed their thoughts allegorically to whomever they chose. Sometimes other discussions would turn on a variety of subjects, or there would be a sharp exchange of quick retorts; often "emblems,"[3] as we nowadays call them, were devised; in which discussions a marvelous pleasure was had, the house (as I have said) being full of very noble talents. * * * So that poets, musicians, and all sorts of buffoons, and the most excellent of every kind of talent that could be found in Italy, were always gathered there.

[6]

Now Pope Julius II,[4] having, by his presence and with the help of the French, brought Bologna under the rule of the Apostolic See in the year 1506, and being on his way back to Rome, passed through Urbino, where he was received with all possible honor and with as magnificent and splendid

---

3. Figure ("body") and motto or verse ("soul").   4. Giuliano della Rovere (1443–1513), elected pope in 1503, famous as a patron of arts and letters.

a welcome as could have been offered in any of the noble cities of Italy: so that, besides the Pope, all the cardinals and other courtiers were highly gratified. And there were some who were so captivated by the charm of the company they found here that when the Pope and his court had departed, they stayed on for many days in Urbino; during which time not only was the usual style of festivities and ordinary diversions kept up, but every man endeavored to contribute something more, and especially in the games that were played almost every evening. And the order of these was such that, as soon as anyone came into the presence of the Duchess, he would take a seat in a circle wherever he pleased or where chance would have it; and so seated, all were arranged alternately, a man, then a woman, as long as there were women (for almost always the number of men was much the larger); then, the company was governed as it pleased the Duchess, who most of the time left this charge to signora Emilia.

So, the day following the departure of the Pope, when the company had gathered at the usual hour and place, after many pleasant discussions, it was the Duchess's wish that signora Emilia should begin the games; and she, after having declined the task for a time, spoke thus: "Madam, since it is your pleasure that I should be the one to begin the games this evening, and since I cannot in reason fail to obey you, I will propose a game for which I think I can have little blame and even less labor: and this shall be that each propose some game after his own liking that we have never played; then we shall choose the one which seems the worthiest of being played in this company."

And, so saying, she turned to signor Gaspar Pallavicino,[5] bidding him to tell his choice; and he replied at once: "It is for you, Madam, to tell yours first."

"But I have already told it," said signora Emilia; "now do you, Duchess, bid him obey."

To this the Duchess said, laughing: "So that all shall be bound to obey you, I make you my deputy, and give you all my authority."

[7]

"It is indeed a remarkable thing," replied signor Gasparo, "that women are always permitted such exemption from labor, and it is only right to wish to understand why; but, in order not to be the first to disobey, I will leave that for another time, and will speak now as required"; and he began: "It seems to me that in love, as in everything else, our minds judge differently; and so it often happens that what is most pleasing to one is most odious to another; but, for all that, our minds do, however, agree in prizing highly what is loved; so that often the excessive affection of lovers beguiles their judgment, causing them to think that the person whom they love is the only one in the world who is adorned with every excellent quality and is wholly without defect. But, since human nature does not admit of such complete perfection, nor is anyone to be found in whom something is not wanting, it cannot be said that these lovers are not deceived, or that the lover is not blinded respecting the beloved. I would therefore have our game this evening be so:

5. A Lombard (1486–1511) and friend of Castiglione.

let each one say which virtue above all others he would wish the one he loves to be adorned with; and, since it is inevitable that everyone have some defect, let him say also which fault he would desire in the beloved: so that we may see who can think of the most praiseworthy and useful virtues and of the faults which are the most excusable and least harmful either to the lover or to the beloved."

When signor Gasparo had spoken thus, signora Emilia made a sign to madam Costanza Fregosa,[6] as she sat next in order, that she should speak; and she was making ready to do so, when suddenly the Duchess said: "Since signora Emilia does not choose to go to the trouble of devising a game, it would be quite right for the other ladies to share in this ease, and thus be exempt from such a burden this evening, especially since there are so many men here that we risk no lack of games."

"So be it," replied signora Emilia; and, imposing silence on madam Costanza, she turned to messer Cesare Gonzaga[7] who sat next, and bade him speak; and he began thus:

[8]

"Whoever considers carefully all our actions will always find various defects in them; the reason being that, in this, nature is variable, as in other things, bestowing the light of reason on one man in one respect and on another man in another: wherefore it happens that as one man knows what another does not know, and is ignorant of what the other knows, each easily perceives his neighbor's error and not his own; and we all think that we are very wise and perhaps the more so in that wherein we are most foolish. Thus, we have seen it happen in this house that many who were at first held to be very wise have been known, in the course of time, to be full of folly, and this came about through nothing save the attention we gave to it. For, even as they say that in Apulia many musical instruments are used for those who are bitten by the tarantula, and various tunes are tried until the humor which is causing the malady is (through a certain affinity which it has with some one of those tunes) suddenly stirred by the sound of it and so agitates the sick man that he is restored to health by that agitation: so we, whenever we have detected some hidden trace of folly, have stimulated it so artfully and with such a variety of inducements and in so many different ways that finally we have understood what its tendency was; then, having recognized the humor, we agitated it so thoroughly that it was always brought to the perfection of an open folly. Thus, one turned out to be foolish in verse, another in music, another in love, another in dancing, another in morrises, another in riding, another in fencing—each one according to the native quality of his metal; wherein, as you know, we have had some wonderful entertainment. I hold this, then, to be certain: that in each of us there is some seed of folly which, once awakened, can grow almost without limitation.

"Hence, I wish that for this evening our game might be a discussion of this matter, and that each would say: 'In case I should openly reveal my folly, what sort mine would be and about what, judging such an eventuality by the sparks of folly which are seen to come forth from me every day'; and let the

6. Sister of Ottaviano and Federico, companion of the duchess. 7. Cousin (1475–1512) and friend of Castiglione, a great warrior, a diplomat, and a pastoral poet.

same be said of all the others, keeping to the order of our games, and let each one seek to base his opinion on some real sign and evidence. Thus, each of us will profit from this game of ours by knowing his faults, the better thereby to guard against them. And if the vein of folly which we discover chances to be so abundant that it seems beyond repair, we will encourage it and, according to the doctrine of fra Mariano,[8] we shall have saved a soul, which will be no small gain."

There was much laughter about this game, nor was there anyone who could keep from talking. One said: "My folly would be in thinking"; another "in looking"; and another said: "I am already a fool in love," and the like.

[9]

Then fra Serafino[9] said, laughing as usual: "That would take too long; but if you want a good game, let everyone say why he thinks it is that nearly all women hate rats and love snakes; and you will see that no one will hit upon the reason except myself, for I know this secret by a strange way." And already he was starting his usual stories. But signora Emilia bade him keep quiet, and, passing over the lady who sat next, she made a sign to the Unico Aretino,[1] whose turn it was. And he, without awaiting further bidding, said: "Would that I were a judge with the authority to use any sort of torture to extract the truth from criminals; and this in order to uncover the deceits of a certain ingrate who, with an angel's eyes and a serpent's heart, never speaks as she thinks, and with a deceitful, feigned compassion attends to nothing but dissecting hearts. Nor is there in sandy Libya a snake so venomous, so avid of human blood, as this false one; who not only with the sweetness of her voice and her honeyed words, but also with her eyes, her smiles, her looks, and in all her ways, is a veritable Siren.[2] However, since I am not allowed (as I could wish I were) to make use of chains, rope, or fire, in order to learn a certain truth, I wish to learn it with a game, which is this: let each one say what he thinks that letter *s* means that the Duchess is wearing on her forehead; because, though this is certainly but another artful veil to make deception possible, perchance some interpretation will be given of it such as she would not have expected; and it will be found that Fortune, compassionate spectator of the sufferings of men, has led her to reveal by this little sign, and in spite of herself, her secret desire to kill and bury alive in calamities anyone who looks upon her or serves her."

The Duchess laughed, and Aretino, seeing that she wished to exonerate herself from this imputation, said: "Nay, Madam, it is not now your turn to speak."

Then signora Emilia turned to him and said: "Signor Unico, there is no one among us here who does not yield to you in all things, but most of all in your knowledge of our Duchess's mind. And just as you know it better than the rest, even so do you love it more than the rest, who are like those weak-sighted birds that fix not their eyes upon the orb of the sun and thus cannot

---

8. Fra Mariano (1460–1531), a Dominican friar and renowned buffoon who lived under the protection of Lorenzo, then at the papal court [Translator's note]. 9. A Mantuan, servant of the Gonzagas, organizer of festivals [Translator's note]. 1. Bernardo Accolti (1458–1535), known as the Unico Aretino because born in Arezzo and "unique" as an improviser of verse [Translator's note]. 2. Songs of the Sirens lured sailors to their deaths.

well know how perfect it is. Hence, any attempt to clear up this doubt would be in vain, save by your own judgment. Therefore, let this task be left to you alone, as to the only one who can perform it."

Aretino remained silent for a while; then, being urged to speak, he at last recited a sonnet[3] on the aforesaid subject, declaring what was meant by that letter s; which sonnet was thought by many to have been improvised; but because it was more ingenious and polished than the brevity of time would seem to have allowed, some thought that it had been prepared.

[10]

Then, when the sonnet had been praised with merry applause, and after some further talk, signor Ottaviano Fregoso,[4] whose turn it was, began laughingly as follows: "Gentlemen, if I should affirm that I have never felt any passion of love, I am sure that the Duchess and signora Emilia, even if they did not believe it, would make a show of believing it, and would say that this is because I have mistrusted my own ability to induce any woman ever to love me: wherein, to speak the truth, up to now I have not made any such persistent effort as to have reason to despair of being able to succeed some day. Nor certainly have I refrained from making that effort because I esteem myself so much, or women so little, as to think that many are not worthy of being loved and served by me. But I have rather been frightened away by the continual laments of certain lovers who, pale, sad, and taciturn, seem always to wear their unhappiness depicted in their eyes; and whenever they speak, they accompany every word with tripled sighs and talk of nothing but tears, torments, despairs, and longings for death. So that even if at times any spark of love did kindle my heart, I have immediately made every effort to extinguish it, not out of any hate that I feel towards women, as these ladies may think, but for my own good.

"And then I have known other lovers utterly different from such lamenters, who not only take joy and satisfaction in the kind looks and tender words and gentle mien of their ladies, but flavor all woes with sweetness, so that they say that their ladies' quarrels, wrath, and scorn are things most sweet: wherefore such lovers as these strike me as being exceedingly happy. For if they find such sweetness in those amorous fits of temper which the others hold to be more bitter than death, I think that in the manifestations of love they must experience that final beatitude which we seek in vain in this world. I wish therefore that our game this evening might be that each one should say, in case she whom he loves must be angry with him, what he would wish the cause of that anger to be. For if there be some here who have experienced such sweet outbursts of anger, I am sure that out of courtesy they will elect one of those causes that make these so sweet; and perhaps I shall find the courage to venture a little further in love, in the hope that I too may find this sweetness where some find bitterness; and thus these ladies will no longer be able to defame me for not loving."

3. Not included in Castiglione's text.   4. Ottaviano Fregoso (d. 1524), Genoese nobleman, nephew of Duke Guidobaldo, elected doge of Genoa in 1513 and later appointed governor of the city by Francis I [Translator's note].

[11]

All liked this game and were already preparing to speak on such a topic; but, as signora Emilia said nothing about it, messer Pietro Bembo,[5] who sat next in order, spoke thus: "Gentlemen, the game proposed by signor Ottaviano has brought no little doubt to my mind, since he has spoken of the angers of love, which, even though they have variety, yet have always been most bitter to me, nor do I think that there could be learned from me any flavoring sufficient to sweeten them; but it may be that they are more or less bitter according to the cause whereby they arise. For I remember having seen the lady whom I was serving angry with me, either out of an idle doubt as to my faithfulness which she herself had conceived, or out of some other false notion awakened in her by what someone had said to my detriment; so that I judged no suffering could be compared to mine, and it seemed to me that the greatest pain that I felt was in having to suffer when I had not deserved it and in having this affliction through no fault of mine but through her lack of love. At other times I saw her angry at some error of mine, and recognized that her wrath was caused by my fault; and at such a point I would judge that my former woe was light indeed compared with what I now felt. And it seemed to me that the fact of having displeased (and through my own fault) the sole person whom I desired and sought so to please was the torment that surpassed all others. I wish therefore that our game might be that each should tell, if she whom he loves must be angry with him, where he would wish the cause of her anger to lie, in her or in himself, so that we may know which is the greater suffering, to give displeasure to one's beloved, or to receive the same from her."

[12]

Everyone was awaiting signora Emilia's reply; but she, saying nothing more to Bembo, turned to messer Federico Fregoso[6] and signified that he should tell his game; and he began at once as follows: "Madam, I wish that, as sometimes happens, I might be allowed to defer to someone else's judgment, since I, for one, would gladly approve any of the games proposed by these gentlemen, because truly it seems to me that they would all be amusing. Still, so as not to upset our order, I will say that if anyone should wish to praise our court—apart from the merits of our Duchess which, together with her divine virtue, would suffice to uplift from earth to heaven the meanest souls of this world—he might well say, without suspicion of flattery, that in all Italy it would perhaps be hard to find an equal number of cavaliers as outstanding and as excellent in different things, quite beyond their principal profession of chivalry, as are found here: wherefore, if there are anywhere men who deserve to be called good courtiers and who can judge of what belongs to the perfection of Courtiership, we must rightfully think that they are here present. So, in order to put down the many fools who in their presumption and ineptitude think to gain the name of good courtiers, I would

---

5. Pietro Bembo (1470–1547), a Venetian nobleman, a famous man of letters of the Italian Renaissance, later papal secretary to Leo X; he corrected the proofs of *The Courtier* [Translator's note].   6. Federico Fregoso (1480–1541), younger brother of Ottaviano, nephew of Duke Guidobaldo, made archbishop of Salerno by Julius II in 1507 [Translator's note].

have our game this evening be this, that one of this company be chosen and given the task of forming in words a perfect Courtier, setting forth all the conditions and particular qualities that are required of anyone who deserves this name; and that everyone be allowed to speak out against those things which seem not right, as in the schools of the philosophers it is permitted to offer objections to anyone maintaining a thesis."

Messer Federico was going on in his discourse when signora Emilia interrupted him, saying: "This, should it please the Duchess, shall be our game for the present."

"It does please me," the Duchess replied.

Whereupon nearly all of those present began to say, both to the Duchess and among themselves, that this was the finest game that could possibly be played. And no one waited for the other's answer, but all urged signora Emilia to decide who should begin. And she, turning to the Duchess, said: "Madam, will you command him who it most pleases you should have this task, for I do not wish, in choosing one rather than another, to appear to decide which I judge to be more capable than the others in this matter, and so offend anyone."

The Duchess replied: "Nay, make the choice yourself, and take care lest you set others an example of not obeying, prompting them to refuse obedience in their turn."

[13]

Then signora Emilia laughed and said to Count Ludovico da Canossa:[7] "So, in order not to lose more time, you, Count, shall be the one to undertake this task in the way messer Federico has said; not indeed because we think you so good a Courtier that you know what befits one, but because if you say everything contrariwise, as we hope you will do, the game will be the livelier since everyone will have something to answer you; whereas, if another with more knowledge than you had this task, nothing could be objected to him because he would speak the truth, and so the game would be tedious."

The Count answered at once: "Madam, there could be no danger that anyone who speaks the truth would lack someone to gainsay him, so long as you are present." And when the company had laughed a while at this retort, he went on: "But truly I should be very glad to escape from this labor, since it seems too difficult for me; and I recognize as true in myself what you have affirmed in jest, namely, that I do not know what befits a good Courtier. Nor do I seek to prove this by any other witness than by the fact that since I do not perform the deeds of one such, it can be concluded that I do not have the knowledge. I believe that I may be blamed less in this, for it is surely worse not to wish to perform well than not to know how. Still, since it is your pleasure that I should have this charge, I cannot and will not refuse it, for I would not contravene our rule and your judgment, which I esteem far more than my own."

Then messer Cesare Gonzaga said: "As it is already rather late in the evening and we have many other kinds of entertainment ready at hand, perhaps it may be well to postpone this discussion until tomorrow; and this will give

---

7. A relative (1476–1532) of Castiglione and friend of the painter Raphael, he was later a bishop and papal ambassador to England.

the Count time to think about what he is going to say, for truly it is a difficult thing to improvise on such a subject."

The Count replied: "I do not wish to be like the man who stripped to his doublet and jumped less far than he had done in his greatcoat; wherefore it seems to me fortunate that the hour is late, for by the brevity of the time I shall be forced to say very little, and shall be excused by the fact that I have given no thought to this matter and so, free of censure, I shall be permitted to say whatever comes first to my lips. Therefore, in order not to bear this burden of obligation longer upon my shoulders, I will say that in all things it is so difficult to know what true perfection is that it is well-nigh impossible; and this is due to the diversity of our judgments. Thus, there are many who will welcome a man who talks a great deal, and will call him pleasing. Others will prefer a modest man; others, an active and restless man; still others, someone who shows calm and deliberation in all things. And so everyone praises or blames according to his own opinion, always hiding a vice under the name of the corresponding virtue, or a virtue under the name of the corresponding vice: for example, calling a presumptuous man, frank; a modest man, dull; a simpleton, good; a rascal, discreet; and likewise throughout. Still I do think that there is a perfection for everything, even though it be hidden; and that this perfection can be determined by someone reasoning about it who has knowledge of the subject. And because, as I have said, the truth is often hidden, and I do not claim to have this knowledge, I can only praise the manner of Courtier that I most esteem, and can approve of what seems to me to be nearest the right, according to my poor judgment: which you may follow if it seems good to you; or you may hold to your own, should it differ from mine. Certainly I will not protest that mine is better than yours, for not only can you think one thing and I another, but I myself may sometimes think one thing and sometimes another.

[14]

"Thus, I would have our Courtier born of a noble and genteel family; because it is far less becoming for one of low birth to fail to do virtuous things than for one of noble birth, who, should he stray from the path of his forebears, stains the family name, and not only fails to achieve anything but loses what has been achieved already. For noble birth is like a bright lamp that makes manifest and visible deeds both good and bad, kindling and spurring on to virtue as much for fear of dishonor as for hope of praise. And since this luster of nobility does not shine forth in the deeds of the lowly born, they lack that spur, as well as that fear of dishonor, nor do they think themselves obliged to go beyond what was done by their forebears; whereas to the wellborn it seems a reproach not to attain at least to the mark set them by their ancestors. Hence, it almost always happens that, in the profession of arms as well as in other worthy pursuits, those who are most distinguished are men of noble birth, because nature has implanted in everything that hidden seed which gives a certain force and quality of its own essence to all that springs from it, making it like itself: as we can see not only in breeds of horses and other animals, but in trees as well, the shoots of which nearly always resemble the trunk; and if they sometimes degenerate, the fault lies with the husbandman. And so it happens with men, who, if they are tended in the right way, are almost always like those from whom they spring, and often are better; but if they lack someone to tend them properly, they grow wild and never attain their full growth.

"It is true that, whether favored by the stars or by nature, some men are born endowed with such graces that they seem not to have been born, but to have been fashioned by the hands of some god, and adorned with every excellence of mind and body; even as there are many others so inept and uncouth that we cannot but think that nature brought them into the world out of spite and mockery. And just as the latter, for the most part, yield little fruit even with constant diligence and good care, so the former with little labor attain to the summit of the highest excellence. And take, as an example, Don Ippolito d'Este, Cardinal of Ferrara,[8] who enjoyed such a happy birth that his person, his appearance, his words, and all his actions are so imbued and ruled by this grace that, although he is young, he evinces among the most aged prelates so grave an authority that he seems more fit to teach than to be taught. Similarly, in conversing with men and women of every station, in play, in laughter, in jest, he shows a special sweetness and such gracious manners that no one who speaks with him or even sees him can do otherwise than feel an enduring affection for him.

"But, to return to our subject, I say that there is a mean to be found between such supreme grace on the one hand and such stupid ineptitude on the other, and that those who are not so perfectly endowed by nature can, with care and effort, polish and in great part correct their natural defects. Therefore, besides his noble birth, I would wish the Courtier favored in this other respect, and endowed by nature not only with talent and with beauty of countenance and person, but with that certain grace which we call an 'air,' which shall make him at first sight pleasing and lovable to all who see him; and let this be an adornment informing and attending all his actions, giving the promise outwardly that such a one is worthy of the company and the favor of every great lord."

[15]

At this point, without waiting any longer, signor Gaspar Pallavicino said: "So that our game may have the form prescribed and that we may not appear to esteem little that privilege of opposing which has been allowed us, I say that to me this nobility of birth does not seem so essential. And if I thought I was uttering anything not already known to us all, I would adduce many instances of persons born of the noblest blood who have been ridden by vices; and, on the contrary, many persons of humble birth who, through their virtue, have made their posterity illustrious. And if what you said just now is true, that there is in all things that hidden force of the first seed, then we should all be of the same condition through having the same source, nor would one man be more noble than another. But I believe that there are many other causes of the differences and the various degrees of elevation and lowliness among us. Among which causes I judge Fortune to be foremost; because we see her hold sway over all the things of this world and, as it seems, amuse herself often in uplifting to the skies whom she pleases and

8. Ippolito d'Este (1479–1520), patron of Ludovico Ariosto, friend of Leonardo da Vinci, made a cardinal by Pope Alexander VI.

in burying in the depths those most worthy of being exalted.

"I quite agree with what you call the good fortune of those who are endowed at birth with all goodness of mind and body; but this is seen to happen with those of humble as well as with those of noble birth, because nature observes no such subtle distinctions as these. Nay, as I said, the greatest gifts of nature are often to be seen in persons of the humblest origin. Hence, since this nobility of birth is not gained either by talents or by force or skill, and is rather due to the merit of one's ancestors than to one's own, I deem it passing strange to hold that if the parents of our Courtier be of humble birth, all his good qualities are ruined, and that those other qualities which you have named would not suffice to bring him to the height of perfection; that is, talent, beauty of countenance, comeliness of person, and that grace which will make him at first sight lovable to all."

[16]

Then Count Ludovico replied: "I do not deny that the same virtues can rule in the lowborn as in the wellborn: but (in order not to repeat what we have said already, along with many further reasons which might be adduced in praise of noble birth, which is always honored by everyone, because it stands to reason that good should beget good), since it is our task to form a Courtier free of any defect whatsoever, and endowed with all that is praiseworthy, I deem it necessary to have him be of noble birth, not only for many other reasons, but also because of that public opinion which immediately sides with nobility. For, in the case of two courtiers who have not yet given any impression of themselves either through good or bad deeds, immediately when the one is known to be of gentle birth and the other not, the one who is lowborn will be held in far less esteem than the one who is of noble birth, and will need much time and effort in order to give to others that good impression of himself which the other will give in an instant and merely by being a gentleman. And everyone knows the importance of these impressions, for, to speak of ourselves, we have seen men come to this house who, though dull-witted and maladroit, had yet the reputation throughout Italy of being very great courtiers; and, even though they were at last discovered and known, still they fooled us for many days and maintained in our minds that opinion of themselves which they found already impressed thereon, even though their conduct was in keeping with their little worth. Others we have seen who at first enjoyed little esteem and who, in the end, achieved a great success.

"And there are various causes of such errors, one being the judgment of princes who, thinking to work miracles, sometimes decide to show favor to one who seems to them to deserve disfavor. And they too are often deceived; but, because they always have countless imitators, their favor engenders a great fame which on the whole our judgments will follow. And if we notice anything which seems contrary to the prevailing opinion, we suspect that we must be mistaken, and we continue to look for something hidden: because we think that such universal opinions must after all be founded on the truth and arise from reasonable causes. And also because our minds are quick to love and hate, as is seen in spectacles of combats and of games and in every sort of contest, where the spectators often side with one of the parties without any evident reason, showing the greatest desire that this one should win and the other should lose. Moreover, as for the general opinion concerning a man's qualities, it is good or ill repute that sways our minds at the outset to one of these two passions. Hence, it happens that, for the most part, we judge from love or hate. Consider, then, how important that first impression is, and how anyone who aspires to have the rank and name of good Courtier must strive from the beginning to make a good impression.

[17]

"But to come to some particulars: I hold that the principal and true profession of the Courtier must be that of arms; which I wish him to exercise with vigor; and let him be known among the others as bold, energetic, and faithful to whomever he serves. And the repute of these good qualities will be earned by exercising them in every time and place, inasmuch as one may not ever fail therein without great blame. And, just as among women the name of purity, once stained, is never restored, so the reputation of a gentleman whose profession is arms, if ever in the least way he sullies himself through cowardice or other disgrace, always remains defiled before the world and covered with ignominy. Therefore, the more our Courtier excels in this art, the more will he merit praise; although I do not deem it necessary that he have the perfect knowledge of things and other qualities that befit a commander, for since this would launch us on too great a sea, we shall be satisfied, as we have said, if he have complete loyalty and an undaunted spirit, and be always seen to have them. For oftentimes men are known for their courage in small things rather than in great. And often in important perils and where there are many witnesses, some men are found who, although their hearts sink within them, still, spurred on by fear of shame or by the company of those present, press forward with eyes shut, as it were, and do their duty, God knows how; and in things of little importance and when they think they can avoid the risk of danger, they are glad to play safe. But those men who, even when they think they will not be observed or seen or recognized by anyone, show courage and are not careless of anything, however slight, for which they could be blamed, such have the quality of spirit we are seeking in our Courtier.

"However, we do not wish him to make a show of being so fierce that he is forever swaggering in his speech, declaring that he has wedded his cuirass, and glowering with such dour looks as we have often seen Berto[9] do; for to such as these one may rightly say what in polite society a worthy lady jestingly said to a certain man (whom I do not now wish to name) whom she sought to honor by inviting him to dance, and who not only declined this but would not listen to music or take any part in the other entertainments offered him, but kept saying that such trifles were not his business. And when finally the lady said to him: 'What then is your business?' he answered with a scowl: 'Fighting.' Whereupon the lady replied at once: 'I should think it a good thing, now that you are not away at war or engaged in fighting, for you to have yourself greased all over and stowed away in a closet along with all your battle harness, so that you won't grow any rustier than you already are'; and

---

9. An otherwise unidentified character.

so, amid much laughter from those present, she ridiculed him in his stupid presumption. Therefore, let the man we are seeking be exceedingly fierce, harsh, and always among the first, wherever the enemy is; and in every other place, humane, modest, reserved, avoiding ostentation above all things as well as that impudent praise of himself by which a man always arouses hatred and disgust in all who hear him."

[18]

Then signor Gasparo replied: "As for me, I have known few men excellent in anything whatsoever who did not praise themselves; and it seems to me that this can well be permitted them, because he who feels himself to be of some worth, and sees that his works are ignored, is indignant that his own worth should lie buried; and he must make it known to someone, in order not to be cheated of the honor that is the true reward of all virtuous toil. Thus, among the ancients, seldom does anyone of any worth refrain from praising himself. To be sure, those persons who are of no merit, and yet praise themselves, are insufferable; but we do not assume that our Courtier will be of that sort."

Then the Count said: "If you took notice, I blamed impudent and indiscriminate praise of one's self: and truly, as you say, one must not conceive a bad opinion of a worthy man who praises himself modestly; nay, one must take that as surer evidence than if it came from another's mouth. I do say that whoever does not fall into error in praising himself and does not cause annoyance or envy in the person who listens to him is indeed a discreet man and, besides the praises he gives himself, deserves praises from others; for that is a very difficult thing."

Then signor Gasparo said: "This you must teach us."

The Count answered: "Among the ancients there is no lack of those who have taught this; but, in my opinion, the whole art consists in saying things in such a way that they do not appear to be spoken to that end, but are so very apropos that one cannot help saying them; and to seem always to avoid praising one's self, yet do so; but not in the manner of those boasters who open their mouths and let their words come out haphazardly. As one of our friends the other day who, when he had had his thigh run through by a spear at Pisa, said that he thought a fly had stung him; and another who said that he did not keep a mirror in his room because when he was angry he became so fearful of countenance that if he were to see himself, he would frighten himself too much."

Everyone laughed at this, but messer Cesare Gonzaga added: "What are you laughing at? Do you not know that Alexander the Great, upon hearing that in the opinion of one philosopher there were countless other worlds, began to weep, and when asked why, replied: 'Because I have not yet conquered one'—as if he felt able to conquer them all? Does that not seem to you a greater boast than that of the fly sting?"

Then said the Count: "And Alexander was a greater man than the one who spoke so. But truly one has to excuse excellent men when they presume much of themselves, because anyone who has great things to accomplish must have the daring to do those things, and confidence in himself. And let him not be abject and base, but modest rather in his words, making it clear that he presumes less of himself than he accomplishes, provided such presumption does not turn to rashness."

[19]

When the Count paused here briefly, messer Bernardo Bibbiena said, laughing: "I remember you said before that this Courtier of ours should be naturally endowed with beauty of countenance and person, and with a grace that would make him lovable. Now this grace and beauty of countenance I do believe that I have myself, wherefore it happens that so many ladies, as you know, are ardently in love with me; but, as to the beauty of my person, I am rather doubtful, and especially as to these legs of mine which in truth do not seem to me as well disposed as I could wish; as to my chest and the rest, I am quite well enough satisfied. Now do determine a little more in detail what this beauty of body should be, so that I can extricate myself from doubt and put my mind at ease."

After some laughter at this, the Count added: "Certainly such grace of countenance you can truly be said to have; nor will I adduce any other example in order to make clear what that grace is; because we do see beyond any doubt that your aspect is very agreeable and pleasant to all, although the features of it are not very delicate: it has something manly about it, and yet is full of grace. And this is a quality found in many different types of faces. I would have our Courtier's face be such, not so soft and feminine as many attempt to have who not only curl their hair and pluck their eyebrows, but preen themselves in all those ways that the most wanton and dissolute women in the world adopt; and in walking, in posture, and in every act, appear so tender and languid that their limbs seem to be on the verge of falling apart; and utter their words so limply that it seems they are about to expire on the spot; and the more they find themselves in the company of men of rank, the more they make a show of such manners. These, since nature did not make them women as they clearly wish to appear and be, should be treated not as good women, but as public harlots, and driven not only from the courts of great lords but from the society of all noble men.

[20]

"Then, coming to bodily frame, I say it is enough that it be neither extremely small nor big, because either of these conditions causes a certain contemptuous wonder, and men of either sort are gazed at in much the same way that we gaze at monstrous things. And yet, if one must sin in one or the other of these two extremes, it is less bad to be on the small side than to be excessively big; because men who are so huge of body are often not only obtuse of spirit, but are also unfit for every agile exercise, which is something I very much desire in the Courtier. And hence I would have him well built and shapely of limb, and would have him show strength and lightness and suppleness, and know all the bodily exercises that befit a warrior. And in this I judge it his first duty to know how to handle every kind of weapon, both on foot and on horse, and know the advantages of each kind; and be especially acquainted with those arms that are ordinarily used among gentlemen, because, apart from using them in war (where perhaps so many fine points are not necessary), there often arise differences between one gentleman and another, resulting in duels, and quite often those weapons are used which happen to be at hand. Hence, knowledge of them is a very safe thing. Nor am I one of those who say that skill is forgotten in the hour of need; for he who loses his skill at such times shows that out of fear he has already lost his heart and head.

[21]

"I deem it highly important, moreover, to know how to wrestle, because this frequently accompanies the use of weapons on foot. Then, both for his own sake and for his friends', he must understand the quarrels and differences that can arise, and must be alert to seize an advantage, and must show courage and prudence in all things. Nor should he be quick to enter into a fight, except in so far as his honor demands it of him; for, besides the great danger that an uncertain fate can bring, he who rushes into such things precipitately and without urgent cause deserves greatly to be censured, even though he should meet with success. But when he finds that he is so far involved that he cannot withdraw without approach, he must be very deliberate both in the preliminaries to the duel and in the duel itself, and always show readiness and daring. Nor must he do as some who spend their time in wrangling and arguing over points of honor; and, when they have the choice of weapons, select those which neither cut nor prick, and arm themselves as if they were expecting to stand against cannonades; and, thinking it enough not to be defeated, stand always on the defensive and give ground to such a degree that they show extreme cowardice. And so they make themselves the laughingstock of children, like those two men from Ancona who fought at Perugia recently and made everyone laugh who saw them."

"And who were they?" asked signor Gaspar Pallavicino.

"Two cousins," replied messer Cesare.

Then the Count said: "In their fighting they seemed true brothers." Then he went on: "Weapons are also often used in various exercises in time of peace, and gentlemen are seen in public spectacles before the people and before ladies and great lords. Therefore I wish our Courtier to be a perfect horseman in every kind of saddle; and, in addition to having a knowledge of horses and what pertains to riding, let him put every effort and diligence into outstripping others in everything a little, so that he may be always recognized as better than the rest. And even as we read that Alcibiades[1] surpassed all those peoples among whom he lived, and each in the respect wherein it claimed greatest excellence, so would I have this Courtier of ours excel all others in what is the special profession of each. And as it is the peculiar excellence of the Italians to ride well with the rein, to manage wild horses especially with great skill, to tilt and joust, let him be among the best of the Italians in this. In tourneys, in holding a pass, in attacking a fortified position, let him be among the best of the French. In stick-throwing, bull-fighting, in casting spears and darts, let him be outstanding among the Spaniards. But, above all, let him temper his every action with a certain good judgment and grace, if he would deserve that universal favor which is so greatly prized.

1. Athenian general and follower of Socrates.

[22]

"There are also other exercises which, although not immediately depend-ent upon arms, still have much in common therewith and demand much manly vigor; and chief among these is the hunt, it seems to me, because it has a certain resemblance to war. It is a true pastime for great lords, it befits a Courtier, and one understands why it was so much practiced among the ancients. He should also know how to swim, jump, run, throw stones; for, besides their usefulness in war, it is frequently necessary to show one's prow-ess in such things, whereby a good name is to be won, especially with the crowd (with whom one must reckon after all). Another noble exercise and most suitable for a man at court is the game of tennis which shows off the disposition of body, the quickness and litheness of every member, and all the qualities that are brought out by almost every other exercise. Nor do I deem vaulting on horseback to be less worthy, which, though it is tiring and difficult, serves more than anything else to make a man agile and dextrous; and besides its usefulness, if such agility is accompanied by grace, in my opinion it makes a finer show than any other.

"If, then, our Courtier is more than fairly expert in such exercises, I think he ought to put aside all others, such as vaulting on the ground, rope-walking, and the like, which smack of the juggler's trade and little befit a gentleman.

"But since one cannot always engage in such strenuous activities (more-over, persistence causes satiety, and drives away the admiration we have for rare things), we must always give variety to our lives by changing our activ-ities. Hence, I would have our Courtier descend sometimes to quieter and more peaceful exercises. And, in order to escape envy and to enter agreeably into the company of others, let him do all that others do, yet never depart from comely conduct, but behave himself with that good judgment which will not allow him to engage in any folly; let him laugh, jest, banter, frolic, and dance, yet in such a manner as to show always that he is genial and discreet; and let him be full of grace in all that he does or says."

[23]

Then messer Cesare Gonzaga said: "Certainly no one ought to interrupt the course of this discussion; but if I were to remain silent, I should neither be exercising the privilege I have of speaking nor satisfying the desire I have of learning something. And I may be pardoned if I ask a question when I ought to be speaking in opposition; for I think this can be allowed me, after the example set by our messer Bernardo who, in his excessive desire to be thought handsome, has violated the laws of our game by asking instead of gainsaying."

Then the Duchess said: "You see how from a single error a host of others can come. Therefore, he who transgresses and sets a bad example, as messer Bernardo has done, deserves to be punished not only for his own transgres-sion but for that of the others as well."

To this messer Cesare replied: "And so, Madam, I shall be exempt from penalty, since messer Bernardo is to be punished both for his own error and for mine."

"Nay," said the Duchess, "you both must be doubly punished: he for his own transgression and for having brought you to yours, you for your transgression and for having imitated him."

"Madam," answered messer Cesare, "I have not transgressed as yet; however, in order to leave all this punishment to messer Bernardo alone, I will keep quiet."

And he was already silent, when signora Emilia laughed and said: "Say what you will, for, with the permission of the Duchess, I pardon both the one that has transgressed and the one that is about to do so ever so little."

"So be it," the Duchess went on, "but take care lest you make the mistake of thinking it more commendable to be clement than to be just; for the excessive pardon of a transgressor does wrong to those who do not transgress. Still, at the moment, I would not have my austerity in reproaching your indulgence cause us not to hear messer Cesare's question."

And so, at a sign from the Duchess and from signora Emilia, he began forthwith:

[24]

"If I well remember, Count, it seems to me you have repeated several times this evening that the Courtier must accompany his actions, his gestures, his habits, in short, his every movement, with grace. And it strikes me that you require this in everything as that seasoning without which all the other properties and good qualities would be of little worth. And truly I believe that everyone would easily let himself be persuaded of this, because, by the very meaning of the word, it can be said that he who has grace finds grace. But since you have said that this is often a gift of nature and the heavens, and that, even if it is not quite perfect, it can be much increased by care and industry, those men who are born as fortunate and as rich in such treasure as some we know have little need, it seems to be, of any teacher in this, because such benign favor from heaven lifts them, almost in spite of themselves, higher than they themselves had desired, and makes them not only pleasing but admirable to everyone. Therefore I do not discuss this, it not being in our power to acquire it of ourselves. But as for those who are less endowed by nature and are capable of acquiring grace only if they put forth labor, industry, and care, I would wish to know by what art, by what discipline, by what method, they can gain this grace, both in bodily exercises, in which you deem it to be so necessary, and in every other thing they do or say. Therefore, since by praising this quality so highly you have, as I believe, aroused in all of us an ardent desire, according to the task given you by signora Emilia, you are still bound to satisfy it."

[25]

"I am not bound," said the Count, "to teach you how to acquire grace or anything else, but only to show you what a perfect Courtier ought to be. Nor would I undertake to teach you such a perfection; especially when I have just now said that the Courtier must know how to wrestle, vault, and so many other things which, since I never learned them myself, you all know well enough how I should be able to teach them. Let it suffice that just as a good soldier knows how to tell the smith what shape, style, and quality his armor must have, and yet is not able to teach him to make it, nor how to hammer or temper it; just so I, perhaps, shall be able to tell you what a perfect Courtier should be, but not to teach you what you must do to become one. Still, in order to answer your question in so far as I can (although it is almost proverbial that grace is not learned), I say that if anyone is to acquire grace in bodily exercises (granting first of all that he is not by nature incapable), he must begin early and learn the principles from the best of teachers. And how important this seemed to King Philip of Macedon can be seen by the fact that he wished Aristotle, the famous philosopher and perhaps the greatest the world has ever known, to be the one who should teach his son Alexander the first elements of letters. And among men whom we know today, consider how well and gracefully signor Galeazzo Sanseverino, Grand Equerry of France,[2] performs all bodily exercises; and this because, besides the natural aptitude of person that he possesses, he has taken the greatest care to study with good masters and to have about him men who excel, taking from each the best of what they know. For just as in wrestling, vaulting, and in the handling of many kinds of weapons, he took our messer Pietro Monte[3] as his guide, who is (as you know) the only true master of every kind of acquired strength and agility—so in riding, jousting, and the rest he has ever had before his eyes those men who are known to be most perfect in these matters.

[26]

"Therefore, whoever would be a good pupil must not only do things well, but must always make every effort to resemble and, if that be possible, to transform himself into his master. And when he feels that he has made some progress, it is very profitable to observe different men of that profession; and, conducting himself with that good judgment which must always be his guide, go about choosing now this thing from one and that from another. And even as in green meadows the bee flits about among the grasses robbing the flowers, so our Courtier must steal this grace from those who seem to him to have it, taking from each the part that seems most worthy of praise; not doing as a friend of ours whom you all know, who thought he greatly resembled King Ferdinand the Younger of Aragon, but had not tried to imitate him in anything save in the way he had of raising his head and twisting one side of his mouth, which manner the King had contracted through some malady. And there are many such, who think they are doing a great thing if only they can resemble some great man in something; and often they seize upon that which is his only bad point.

"But, having thought many times already about how this grace is acquired (leaving aside those who have it from the stars), I have found quite a universal rule which in this matter seems to me valid above all others, and in all human affairs whether in word or deed: and that is to avoid affectation in every way possible as though it were some very rough and dangerous reef; and (to pronounce a new word perhaps) to practice in all things a certain *sprezzatura* [nonchalance], so as to conceal all art and make whatever is done or said appear to be without effort and almost without any thought about it. And I

---

2. Of a famous Neapolitan family, he fought for Louis XII and Francis I of France and died at the battle of Pavia (1525). 3. Fencing master at the court of Urbino.

believe much grace comes of this: because everyone knows the difficulty of things that are rare and well done; wherefore facility in such things causes the greatest wonder; whereas, on the other hand, to labor and, as we say, drag forth by the hair of the head, shows an extreme want of grace, and causes everything, no matter how great it may be, to be held in little account.

"Therefore we may call that art true art which does not seem to be art; nor must one be more careful of anything than of concealing it, because if it is discovered, this robs a man of all credit and causes him to be held in slight esteem. And I remember having read of certain most excellent orators in ancient times who, among the other things they did, tried to make everyone believe that they had no knowledge whatever of letters; and, dissembling their knowledge, they made their orations appear to be composed in the simplest manner and according to the dictates of nature and truth rather than of effort and art; which fact, had it been known, would have inspired in the minds of the people the fear that they could be duped by it.

"So you see how art, or any intent effort, if it is disclosed, deprives everything of grace. Who among you fails to laugh when our messer Pierpaolo[4] dances after his own fashion, with those capers of his, his legs stiff on tiptoe, never moving his head, as if he were a stick of wood, and all this so studied that he really seems to be counting his steps? What eye is so blind as not to see in this the ungainliness of affectation; and not to see the grace of that cool *disinvoltura* [ease] (for when it is a matter of bodily movements many call it that) in many of the men and women here present, who seem in words, in laughter, in posture not to care; or seem to be thinking more of everything than of that, so as to cause all who are watching them to believe that they are almost incapable of making a mistake?"

[27]

Here messer Bernardo Bibbiena said, without waiting: "Now you see that our messer Roberto[5] has at last found someone to praise his style of dancing, as it seems that none of the rest of you esteem it at all. For if this excellence consists in nonchalance, in showing no concern, and in seeming to have one's thoughts elsewhere rather than on what one is doing, then in dancing messer Roberto has no peer on earth, because to make it quite plain that he is giving no thought to what he is doing, he lets his clothes fall from his back and his slippers from his feet, and goes right on dancing without picking them up."

Then the Count replied: "Since you are determined that I shall go on talking, I will say something more of our faults. Do you not see that what you are calling nonchalance in messer Roberto is really affectation, because we clearly see him making every effort to show that he takes no thought of what he is about, which means taking too much thought; and because it exceeds certain limits of moderation, such nonchalance is affected, is unbecoming, and results in the opposite of the desired effect, which is to conceal the art. Hence, I do not believe that the vice of affectation is any less present in a nonchalance (in itself a praiseworthy thing) wherein one lets his clothes fall off than in a studied concern for one's personal appearance (also, in

---

4. Unidentified.   5. Young gentleman of the court of Urbino and close friend of Castiglione.

itself, a praiseworthy thing), bearing the head so stiff for fear of spoiling one's coiffure, or carrying a mirror in the fold of one's cap and a comb in one's sleeve, and having one's page follow about through the streets with a sponge and brush; because such care for personal appearance and such nonchalance both tend too much to extremes, which is always a fault, and is contrary to that pure and charming simplicity which is so appealing to all. Consider how ungraceful that rider is who tries to sit so very stiff in his saddle (in the Venetian style, as we are wont to say), compared with one who appears to give no thought to the matter and sits his horse as free and easy as if he were on foot. How much more pleasing and how much more praised is a gentleman whose profession is arms, and who is modest, speaking little and boasting little, than another who is forever praising himself, swearing and blustering about as if to defy the whole world—which is simply the affectation of wanting to cut a bold figure. And the same holds true in every practice, indeed in everything that is said or done."

[28]

Then the Magnifico Giuliano said: "It holds true as well in music, wherein it is a great mistake to place two perfect consonances one after the other, for our sense of hearing abhors this, whereas it often enjoys a second or a seventh which in itself is a harsh and unbearable discord. And this is due to the fact that to continue in perfect consonances generates satiety and gives evidence of a too affected harmony, which is avoided when imperfect consonances are mixed in, establishing a kind of comparison, by which our ears are held in greater suspense, and more avidly wait upon and enjoy the perfect consonances, delighting in that discord of the second or seventh as in something that shows nonchalance."

"So, you see," replied the Count, "that affectation is detrimental in this as in other things. Moreover, it is said to have been proverbial with certain most excellent painters of antiquity that excessive care is harmful, and Protogenes is said to have been censured by Apelles[6] for not knowing when to take his hands from the board."

Then messer Cesare said: "It seems to me that our fra Serafino has this same fault of not knowing when to take his hands from the board, at least not before all of the food has been taken from it too."

The Count laughed and added: "Apelles meant that Protogenes did not know when to stop in painting, which was nothing if not a kind of reproach for his being affected in his work. Thus, this excellence (which is opposed to affectation, and which, at the moment, we are calling *nonchalance*), besides being the real source from which grace springs, brings with it another adornment which, when it accompanies any human action however small, not only reveals at once how much the person knows who does it, but often causes it to be judged much greater than it actually is, since it impresses upon the minds of the onlookers the opinion that he who performs well with so much facility must possess even greater skill than this, and that, if he were to devote care and effort to what he does, he could do it far better.

"And, to multiply such examples, take a man who is handling weapons and

6. Both legendary Greek painters.

is about to throw a dart or is holding a sword or other weapon in his hand:
if immediately he takes a position of readiness, with ease, and without thinking, with such facility that his body and all his members fall into that posture
naturally and without any effort, then, even if he does nothing more, he
shows himself to be perfectly accomplished in that exercise. Likewise in
dancing, a single step, a single movement of the body that is graceful and
not forced, reveals at once the skill of the dancer. A singer who utters a
single word ending in a group of four notes with a sweet cadence, and with
such facility that he appears to do it quite by chance, shows with that touch
alone that he can do much more than he is doing. Often too in painting, a
single line which is not labored, a single brush stroke made with ease and in
such a manner that the hand seems of itself to complete the line desired by
the painter, without being directed by care or skill of any kind, clearly reveals
that excellence of craftsmanship, which people will then proceed to judge,
each by his own lights. And the same happens in almost every other thing.

"Therefore our Courtier will be judged excellent, and will show grace in
all things and particularly in his speech, if he avoids affectation." * * *

[40]

"Madam," replied the Count,[7] "I think the thread is broken. Still, if I am
not mistaken, I believe we were saying that the bane of affectation always
produces extreme gracelessness in all things and that, on the other hand,
the greatest grace is produced by simplicity and nonchalance: in praise of
which, and in blame of affectation, many other things could be said; but I
wish to add only one thing more. All women have a great desire to be—and
when they cannot be, at least to seem—beautiful. Therefore, wherever
nature has failed in this regard, they try to remedy it with artifice: whence
that embellishing of the face with so much care and sometimes with pain,
that plucking of the eyebrows and the forehead, and the use of all those
methods and the enduring of those nuisances which you ladies think are
hidden to men, but which are well known."

Here madam Costanza Fregosa laughed and said: "It would be much more
courteous of you to go on with your discussion, and tell us what the source
of grace is, and speak of Courtiership, instead of trying to uncover the defects
of women, which is not to the purpose."

"On the contrary, it is much to the purpose," replied the Count, "for the
defects that I am speaking of deprive you ladies of grace, since they are
caused by nothing but affectation, through which you openly let everyone
know your inordinate desire to be beautiful. Do you not see how much more
grace a woman has who paints (if at all) so sparingly and so little that whoever
sees her is uncertain whether she is painted or not; than another woman so
plastered with it that she seems to have put a mask on her face and dares
not laugh so as not to cause it to crack, and never changes color except in
the morning when she dresses; and, then, for the rest of the entire day
remains motionless like a wooden statue and shows herself only by torchlight, like wily merchants who display their cloth in a dark place. And how

---

7. The speaker is Count Ludovico da Canossa, who picks up his thread after a long digression on the purity
of the Italian dialect that comes from Tuscany.

much more attractive than all the others is one (not ugly, I mean) who is plainly seen to have nothing on her face, it being neither too white nor too red, but has her own natural color, a bit pale, and tinged at times with an open blush from shame or other cause, with her hair artlessly unadorned and in disarray, with gestures simple and natural, without showing effort or care to be beautiful. Such is that careless purity which is so pleasing to the eyes and minds of men who are ever fearful of being deceived by art.

"Beautiful teeth are very attractive in a woman, for since they do not show as openly as the face, not being visible most of the time, we may believe that less care has been taken to make them beautiful than with the face: and yet whoever laughs without cause and solely to display the teeth would betray his art, and, no matter how beautiful they are, would seem most ungraceful to all, like Catullus's Egnatius.[8] The same is true of the hands which, if they are delicate and beautiful, and are uncovered at the proper time, when there is need to use them and not merely to make a show of their beauty, leave one with a great desire to see them more and especially when they are covered with gloves again; for whoever covers them seems to have little care or concern whether they are seen or not, and to have beautiful hands more by nature than by any effort or design.

"Have you ever noticed when a woman, in passing along the street to church or elsewhere, unwittingly happens (in play or through whatever cause) to raise just enough of her dress to show her foot and often a little of her leg? Does this not strike you as something full of grace, if she is seen in that moment, charmingly feminine, dressed in velvet shoes and dainty stockings. Certainly to me it is a pleasing sight, as I believe it is to all of you, because everyone thinks that such elegance of dress, when it is where it would be hidden and rarely seen, must be natural and instinctive with the lady rather than calculated, and that she has no thought of gaining any praise thereby.

[41]

"In such a way one avoids or hides affectation, and you may now see how opposed the latter is to grace, how it deprives of grace every act of the body and the soul: of which so far we have spoken but little, and yet this is not to be neglected; for, as the soul is far more worthy than the body, it deserves to be more cultivated and adorned. And as to what ought to be done in the case of our Courtier, we will lay aside the precepts of the many wise philosophers who have written on this subject to define the virtues of the soul and who discuss their worth with such subtlety; and, holding to our purpose, we will declare in a few words that it suffices if he is, as we say, a man of honor and integrity: for included in this are prudence, goodness, fortitude, and temperance of soul, and all the other qualities proper to such an honored name. And I maintain that he alone is a true moral philosopher who wishes to be good; and for this he has need of few precepts beyond that wish. Socrates was right, therefore, in saying that all his teachings seemed to him to bear good fruit when anyone was incited by them to wish to know and under-

8. Catullus's poem 39 makes fun of the ever-smiling, white-toothed Egnatius, who brushes his teeth with urine.

stand virtue: for those persons who have reached the point of desiring nothing more ardently than to be good manage easily to learn all that is needed for that. Hence, we will discuss this no further.

[42]

"But, besides goodness, for everyone the true and principal adornment of the mind is, I think, letters; although the French recognize only the nobility of arms and reckon all the rest as nought; and thus not only do they not esteem, but they abhor letters, and consider all men of letters to be very base; and they think that it is a great insult to call anyone a clerk."

Then the Magnifico Giuliano replied: "What you say is true; this error has prevailed among the French for a long time now. But if kind fate will have it that Monseigneur d'Angoulême[9] succeed to the crown, as is hoped, then I think that just as the glory of arms flourishes and shines in France, so must that of letters flourish there also with the greatest splendor. Because, when I was at that court not so long ago, I saw this prince; and, besides the disposition of his body and the beauty of his countenance, he appeared to me to have in his aspect such greatness (yet joined with a certain gracious humanity) that the realm of France must always seem a petty realm to him. Then later, from many gentlemen, both French and Italian, I heard much about his noble manners, the greatness of his spirit, his valor and liberality; and I was told, among other things, how he loved and esteemed letters and how he held all men of letters in the greatest honor; and how he condemned the French themselves for being so hostile to this profession, especially as they have in their midst a university such as that of Paris, frequented by the whole world."

Then the Count said: "It is a great wonder that, at such a tender age, and solely by natural instinct and against the custom of his country, he should of himself have chosen so worthy a path; and, since subjects always imitate the ways of their superiors, it could be, as you say, that the French will yet come to esteem letters at their true worth: which they can easily be persuaded to do if they will but listen to reason, since nothing is more naturally desired by men or more proper to them than knowledge, and it is great folly to say or believe that knowledge is not always a good thing.

[43]

"And if I could speak with them or with others who hold an opinion contrary to mine, I would try to show them how useful and necessary to our life and dignity letters are, being truly bestowed upon men by God as a crowning gift; nor should I lack instances of many excellent commanders in antiquity, who all added the ornament of letters to valor in arms. For, as you know, Alexander venerated Homer so much that he always kept the *Iliad* by his bed. And he gave the greatest attention not only to these studies but to philosophical speculations as well, under Aristotle's guidance. Alcibiades increased his own good qualities and made them greater through letters and the teachings of Socrates. Also the effort that Caesar[1] devoted to study is witnessed by the surviving works he so divinely wrote. Scipio Africanus, it is

9. Francis I, who succeeded Louis XII in 1515. 1. Julius Caesar, author of *The Gallic Wars*.

said, always kept in his hand the works of Xenophon, wherein, under the name of Cyrus, a perfect king is imagined. I could tell you of Lucullus, Sulla, Pompey, Brutus,[2] and many other Romans and Greeks; but I will only remind you that Hannibal,[3] so excellent a military commander, and yet fierce by nature and a stranger to all humanity, faithless and a despiser of men and the gods—had nonetheless some knowledge of letters and was conversant with Greek. And, if I am not mistaken, I think I once read that he even left a book written by him in Greek.

"But there is no need to tell you this, for I am sure you all know how mistaken the French are in thinking that letters are detrimental to arms. You know that the true stimulus to great and daring deeds in war is glory, and whosoever is moved thereto for gain or any other motive, apart from the fact that he never does anything good, deserves to be called not a gentleman, but a base merchant. And it is true glory that is entrusted to the sacred treasury of letters, as all may understand except those unhappy ones who have never tasted them.

"What soul is so abject, timid, and humble that when he reads of the great deeds of Caesar, Alexander, Scipio, Hannibal, and many others, does not burn with a most ardent desire to resemble them, and does not reckon this transitory life of a few days' span as less important, in order to win to an almost eternal life of fame which, in spite of death, makes him live on in far greater glory than before. But he who does not taste the sweetness of letters cannot know how great the glory is that letters so long preserve, and measures it only by the life of one or two men, because his own memory extends no further. Hence, he cannot value so brief a glory as he would one that is almost eternal (if, to his misfortune, he were not denied knowledge of it); and since he does not much esteem it, we may with reason think that he will not risk such danger to win it as one would who knows of it.

"But I should not want some objector to cite me instances to the contrary in order to refute my opinion, alleging that for all their knowledge of letters the Italians have shown little worth in arms for some time now—which, alas, is only too true. But it must be said that the fault of a few men has brought not only serious harm but eternal blame upon all the rest, and that they have been the true cause of our ruin and of the prostrate (if not dead) virtue of our spirits. Yet it would be a greater shame if we made this fact public than it is to the French to be ignorant of letters. Hence, it is better to pass over in silence what cannot be remembered without pain: and, leaving this subject, upon which I entered against my will, to return to our Courtier.

[44]

"I would have him more than passably learned in letters, at least in those studies which we call the humanities. Let him be conversant not only with the Latin language, but with Greek as well, because of the abundance and variety of things that are so divinely written therein. Let him be versed in the poets, as well as in the orators and historians, and let him be practiced also in writing verse and prose, especially in our own vernacular; for, besides the personal satisfaction he will take in this, in this way he will never want

---

2. Ambitious Roman politicians.   3. Great Carthaginian general who crossed the Alps to fight Rome.

for pleasant entertainment with the ladies, who are usually fond of such things. And if, because of other occupations or lack of study, he does not attain to such a perfection that his writings should merit great praise, let him take care to keep them under cover so that others will not laugh at him, and let him show them only to a friend who can be trusted; because at least they will be of profit to him in that, through such exercise, he will be capable of judging the writing of others. For it very rarely happens that a man who is unpracticed in writing, however learned he may be, can ever wholly understand the toils and industry of writers, or taste the sweetness and excellence of styles, and those intrinsic niceties that are often found in the ancients.

These studies, moreover, will make him fluent, and (as Aristippus[4] said to the tyrant) bold and self-confident in speaking with everyone. However, I would have our Courtier keep one precept firmly in mind, namely, in this as in everything else, to be cautious and reserved rather than forward, and take care not to get the mistaken notion that he knows something he does not know. For we are all by nature more avid of praise than we ought to be and, more than any other sweet song or sound, our ears love the melody of words that praise us; and thus, like Sirens' voices, they are the cause of shipwreck to him who does not stop his ears to such beguiling harmony. This danger was recognized by the ancients, and books were written to show how the true friend is to be distinguished from the flatterer.[5] But to what avail is this, if many, indeed countless persons know full well when they are being flattered, yet love the one who flatters them and hate the one who tells them the truth? And finding him who praises them to be too sparing in his words, they even help him and proceed to say such things of themselves that they make the impudent flatterer himself feel ashamed.

"Let us leave these blind ones to their error, and let us have our Courtier be of such good judgment that he will not let himself be persuaded that black is white, or presume of himself more than he clearly knows to be true; and especially in those points which (if your memory serves you) messer Cesare said we had often used as the means of bringing to light the folly of many persons. Indeed, even if he knows that the praises bestowed upon him are true, let him avoid error by not assenting too openly to them, nor concede them without some protest; but let him rather disclaim them modestly, always showing and really esteeming arms as his chief profession, and the other good accomplishments as ornaments thereto; and do this especially when among soldiers, in order not to act like those who in studies wish to appear as soldiers, and, when in the company of warriors, wish to appear as men of letters. In this way, for the reasons we have stated, he will avoid affectation and even the ordinary things he does will appear to be very great things."

[45]

Messer Pietro Bembo replied: "Count, I do not see why you insist that this Courtier, who is lettered and who has so many other worthy qualities, should regard everything as an ornament of arms, and not regard arms and the rest as an ornament of letters; which, without any other accompaniment, are as

---

4. Companion of Socrates.   5. Plutarch's *Moralia* addresses the topic.

superior to arms in worth as the soul is to the body, because the practice of them pertains properly to the soul, even as that of arms does to the body."

Then the Count replied: "Nay, the practice of arms pertains to both the soul and the body. But I would not have you be a judge in such a case, messer Pietro, because you would be too much suspected of bias by one of the parties. And as this is a debate that has long been waged by very wise men, there is no need to renew it; but I consider it decided in favor of arms; and since I may form our Courtier as I please, I would have him be of the same opinion. And if you are contrary-minded, wait until you can hear of a contest wherein the one who defends the cause of arms is permitted to use arms, just as those who defend letters make use of letters in defending their own cause; for if everyone avails himself of his own weapons, you will see that the men of letters will lose."

"Ah," said messer Pietro, "a while ago you damned the French for their slight appreciation of letters, and you spoke of what a light of glory letters shed on a man, how they make him immortal; and now it appears that you have changed your mind. Do you not remember that

> Giunto Alessandro alla famosa tomba
> del fero Achille, sospirando disse:
> "O fortunato, che sì chiara tromba
> trovasti, e chi di te sì alto scrisse!"

When Alexander had come to the famous tomb of Achilles,[6] sighing, he said: "O fortunate man, to find so clear a trumpet and someone to write of you so loftily!"

And if Alexander envied Achilles, not for his exploits, but for the fortune which had granted him the blessing of having his deeds celebrated by Homer, we see that the esteemed Homer's letters above Achilles's arms. What other judge would you have, or what other sentence on the worthiness of arms and of letters than what has been pronounced by one of the greatest commanders that have ever been?"

[46]

Then the Count replied: "I blame the French for thinking that letters are detrimental to the profession of arms, and I hold that to no one is learning more suited than to a warrior; and I would have these two accomplishments conjoined in our Courtier, each an aid to the other, as is most fitting: nor do I think I have changed my opinion in this. But, as I said, I do not wish to argue as to which of the two is more deserving of praise. Let it suffice to say that men of letters almost never choose to praise any save great men and glorious deeds, which in themselves deserve praise because of the essential worthiness from which they derive; besides this, such men and deeds are very noble material for writers, and are in themselves a great ornament and partly the reason why such writing is perpetuated, which perhaps would not be so much read or prized if it lacked a noble subject, but would be empty and of little moment.

"And if Alexander envied Achilles for being praised by Homer, this does

6. The great warrior of Homer's *Iliad*.

not prove that he esteemed letters more than arms; wherein if he had thought himself to be as far beneath Achilles as he deemed all those who were to write of him to be beneath Homer, I am certain that he would have much preferred fine deeds on his own part to fine talk on the part of others. Hence, I believe that what he said was tacit praise of himself, expressing a desire for what he thought he lacked, namely, the supreme excellence of some writer, and not for what he believed he had already attained, namely, prowess in arms, wherein he did not at all take Achilles to be his superior. Wherefore he called him fortunate, as though to suggest that if his own fame had hitherto not been so celebrated in the world as Achilles's had (which was made bright and illustrious by a poem so divine), this was not because his valor and merits were fewer or less deserving of praise, but because Fortune had granted Achilles such a miracle of nature to be the glorious trumpet for his deeds. Perhaps he wished also to incite some noble talent to write about him, thereby showing that his pleasure in this would be as great as his love and veneration for the sacred monuments of letters: about which by now we have said quite enough."

"Nay, too much," replied signor Ludovico Pio,[7] "for I believe it is not possible in all the world to find a vessel large enough to contain all the things you would have be in our Courtier."

Then the Count said: "Wait a little, for there are yet many more to come."

"In that case," replied Pietro da Napoli, "Grasso de' Medici[8] will have much the advantage over Pietro Bembo!"

[47]

Here everyone laughed, and the Count began again: "Gentlemen, you must know that I am not satisfied with our Courtier unless he be also a musician, and unless, besides understanding and being able to read music, he can play various instruments. For, if we rightly consider, no rest from toil and no medicine for ailing spirits can be found more decorous or praiseworthy in time of leisure than this; and especially in courts where, besides the release from vexations which music gives to all, many things are done to please the ladies, whose tender and delicate spirits are readily penetrated with harmony and filled with sweetness. Hence, it is no wonder that in both ancient and modern times they have always been particularly fond of musicians, finding music a most welcome food for the spirit."

Then signor Gasparo said: "I think that music, along with many other vanities, is indeed well suited to women, and perhaps also to others who have the appearance of men, but not to real men; for the latter ought not to render their minds effeminate and afraid of death."

"Say not so," replied the Count, "or I shall launch upon a great sea of praise for music, reminding you how greatly music was always celebrated by the ancients and held to be a sacred thing; and how it was the opinion of very wise philosophers that the world is made up of music, that the heavens in their motion make harmony, and that even the human soul was formed on the same principle, and is therefore awakened and has its virtues brought to life, as it were, through music. Wherefore it is recorded that Alexander was sometimes so passionately excited by music that, almost in spite of him-

---

7. Brave military captain and distant cousin of Emilia Pia.   8. Nickname of a fat (*grasso*) servant of the Medici. Nothing is known of Pietro da Napoli.

self, he was obliged to quit the banquet table and rush off to arms; whereupon the musician would change the kind of music, and he would then grow calm and return from arms to the banquet. And, I tell you, grave Socrates learned to play the cithara when he was very old. I remember also having heard once that both Plato and Aristotle wish a man who is well constituted to be a musician; and with innumerable reasons they show that music's power over us is very great; and (for many reasons which would be too long to tell now) that music must of necessity be learned from childhood, not so much for the sake of that outward melody which is heard, but because of the power it has to induce a good new habit of mind and an inclination to virtue, rendering the soul more capable of happiness, just as corporal exercise makes the body more robust; and that not only is music not harmful to the pursuits of peace and of war, but greatly to their advantage.

"Moreover, Lycurgus[9] approved of music in his harsh laws. And we read that the bellicose Lacedemonians and the Cretans used citharas and other delicate instruments in battle; that many very excellent commanders of antiquity, like Epaminondas, practiced music, and that those who were igno-rant of it, like Themistocles,[1] were far less esteemed. Have you not read that music was among the first disciplines that the worthy old Chiron[2] taught the boy Achilles, whom he reared from the age of nurse and cradle; and that such a wise preceptor wished the hands that were to shed so much Trojan blood to busy themselves often at playing the cithara? Where, then, is the soldier who would be ashamed to imitate Achilles, not to speak of many another famous commander that I could cite? Therefore, do not wish to deprive our Courtier of music, which not only makes gentle the soul of man, but often tames wild beasts; and he who does not take pleasure in it can be sure that his spirit lacks harmony among its parts.

"Consider that its power is such that it once caused a fish to let itself be ridden by a man over the stormy sea. You find it used in sacred temples to give praise and thanks to God, and we must believe that it is pleasing to Him, and that He has given it to us as a sweet respite from our toils and vexations. Wherefrom rude laborers in the fields under the burning sun will often beguile their heavy time with crude and rustic song. With it the simple peas-ant lass, rising before dawn to spin or weave, wards off sleep and makes pleasant her toil. This is the happy pastime of poor sailors after the rains and the winds and the storms. This is the consolation of tired pilgrims in their long and weary journeys, and oftentimes of miserable prisoners in their chains and fetters.

"Thus, as stronger evidence that even rude melody provides the greatest relief from every human toil and care, nature seems to have taught it to the nurse as the chief remedy for the continual crying of tender babes who by the sound of her voice are lulled to restful and placid sleep, forgetting the tears which are so much their lot and at that age are given us by nature as a presage of our later life."

[48]

As the Count now remained silent for a little, the Magnifico Giuliano said: "I am not at all of signor Gasparo's opinion. Indeed I think, for the reasons

9. Traditional founder of the Spartan constitution.   1. Athenian democratic statesman. Epaminondas of Thebes was famous for a crushing defeat of Sparta.   2. Teacher of Achilles.

given by you and for many others, that music is not only an ornament but a necessity to the Courtier. Yet I would have you state how this and the other accomplishments which you assign to him are to be practiced, and at what times and in what manner. For many things which are praiseworthy in themselves often become most unseemly when practiced at the wrong times; and, on the contrary, others which appear to be quite trivial are much prized when done in a proper way."

[49]

Then the Count said: "Before we enter upon that subject, I would discuss another matter which I consider to be of great importance and which I think must therefore in no way be neglected by our Courtier: and this is a knowledge of how to draw and an acquaintance with the art of painting itself.

"And do not marvel if I require this accomplishment, which perhaps nowadays may seem mechanical and ill-suited to a gentleman; for I recall reading that the ancients, especially throughout Greece, required boys of gentle birth to learn painting in school, as a decorous and necessary thing, and admitted it to first rank among the liberal arts; then by public edict they prohibited the teaching of it to slaves. Among the Romans, too, it was held in highest honor and from it the very noble house of the Fabii took its name; for the first Fabius was called *Pictor*; and he was in fact a most excellent painter, and so devoted to painting that, when he painted the walls of the Temple of Salus,[3] he inscribed his name thereon; for, even though he was born of a family illustrious and honored by so many consular titles, triumphs, and other dignities, and even though he was a man of letters and learned in law, and was numbered among the orators, still it seemed to him that he could add splendor and ornament to his fame by leaving a memorial that he had been a painter. Nor was there any lack of others too who were born of illustrious families and were celebrated in this art; which, besides being most noble and worthy in itself, proves useful in many ways, and especially in warfare, in drawing towns, sites, rivers, bridges, citadels, fortresses, and the like; for, however well they may be stored away in the memory (which is something that is very hard to do), we cannot show them to others so.

"And truly he who does not esteem this art strikes me as being quite lacking in reason; for this universal fabric which we behold, with its vast heaven so resplendent with bright stars, with the earth at the center girdled by the seas, varied with mountains, valleys, rivers, adorned with such a variety of trees, pretty flowers, and grasses—can be said to be a great and noble picture painted by nature's hand and God's; and whoever can imitate it deserves great praise, in my opinion: nor is such imitation achieved without the knowledge of many things, as anyone knows who attempts it. For this reason the ancients held art and artists in the greatest esteem, wherefore art attained to the pinnacle of the highest excellence, very sure proof of which is to be found in the antique statues of marble and bronze that can still be seen. And, although painting differs from sculpture, both spring from the same source, namely, good design. Therefore, since those statues are divine, we can believe that the paintings were divine too; and the more so in being susceptible of greater artistry."

---

3. Temple of an old Roman goddess associated with hygiene and medicine.

[50]

Then signora Emilia turned to Giancristoforo Romano[4] who was sitting there with the others, and said: "What do you think of this opinion? Do you agree that painting is susceptible of greater artistry than sculpture?"

Giancristoforo replied: "I think, Madam, that sculpture requires more labor and more skill and is of greater dignity than painting."

The Count rejoined: "Because statues are more durable, one might perhaps say they have a greater dignity; for, since they are made as memorials, they serve better than painting the purpose for which they are made. But, apart from this service to memory, both painting and sculpture are made to adorn, and in this painting is much superior; for if it is not so diuturnal, so to say, as sculpture, still it lasts a long time: and the while it lasts, it is much more beautiful."

Then Giancristoforo replied: "I truly believe that you are speaking contrary to your own persuasion, and that you do this entirely for your Raphael's sake; and you may also be thinking that the excellence in painting which you find in him is so supreme that sculpture in marble cannot attain to such a mark. But, take care, this is to praise an artist and not an art."

Then he went on: "I do indeed think that both the one and the other are artful imitations of nature; but I do not know how you can say that that which is real and is nature's own work is any less imitated by a marble or bronze figure, in which all the members are round, fashioned and proportioned just as nature makes them, than on a panel where one sees only a surface and colors that deceive the eyes; nor will you tell me, surely, that being is not nearer truth than seeming. Besides, I consider sculpture to be more difficult because, if you happen to make a mistake, you cannot correct it, since marble cannot be patched up again, but you have to execute another figure; which does not happen in painting wherein you can make a thousand changes, adding and taking away, improving it all the while."

[51]

The Count said, laughing: "I am not speaking for Raphael's sake, nor must you think me so ignorant as not to know Michelangelo's excellence in sculpture, your own, and that of others. But I am speaking of the art and not of the artists.

"What you say is quite true, that both the one and the other are imitations of nature; but it is not a matter of painting seeming and of sculpture being. For, although statues are in the round as in life and painting is seen only no the surface, statues lack many things which paintings do not lack, and especially light and shade (for the color of flesh is one thing and that of marble another). And this the painter imitates in a natural manner, with light and dark, less or more, according to the need—which the sculptor in marble cannot do. And even though the painter does not fashion his figure in the round, he does make muscles and members rounded in such a manner as to join up with the parts which are not so seen, whereby we see clearly that the painter knows and understands those parts as well. And in this an even

---

4. Renowned sculptor (1465–1512), goldsmith, and architect, was at the court of Urbino at the time of the dialogue of the *Courtier*.

greater skill is needed to depict those members that are foreshortened and that diminish in proportion to the distance, on the principle of perspective; which, by means of proportioned lines, colors, light, and shade, gives you foreground and distance on the surface of an upright wall, and as bold or as faint as he chooses. And do you think it a trifle to imitate nature's colors in doing flesh, clothing, and all the other things that have color? This the sculptor cannot do; neither can he render the grace of black eyes or blue eyes, shining with amorous rays. He cannot render the color of blond hair or the gleam of weapons, or the dark of night, or a storm at sea, or lightnings and thunderbolts, or the burning of a city, or the birth of rosy dawn with its rays of gold and red. In short, he cannot do sky, sea, land, mountains, woods, meadows, gardens, rivers, cities, or houses—all of which the painter can do.

[52]

"Therefore I deem painting more noble and more susceptible of artistry than sculpture, and I think that among the ancients it must have had that excellence which other things had; and this we can still see from certain slight remains, particularly in the grottoes of Rome;[5] but we can know it much more clearly from the writings of the ancients in which there is such frequent and honored mention both of the works and of the masters, from which we learn how much the latter were always honored by great lords and republics.

"So we read that Alexander loved Apelles of Ephesus dearly—so much so that once, when he had him paint one of his favorite women and heard that the worthy painter had conceived a most passionate love for her because of her great beauty, he made him an outright gift of her: a generosity truly worthy of Alexander, to give away not only treasures and states, but his own affections and desires; and a sign of a very great love for Apelles to care nothing if, in pleasing the artist, he displeased that woman whom he so dearly loved—whereas we may believe that the woman was sorely grieved to exchange so great a king for a painter. Many other instances are cited of Alexander's kindness to Apelles; but he showed his esteem for him most clearly in giving order by public edict that no other painter should be so bold as to paint his portrait.

"Here I could tell of the rivalry of many noble painters who were the praise and wonder of nearly the whole world; I could tell you with what majesty the ancient emperors adorned their triumphs with paintings, dedicated them in public places, bought them as cherished objects; how some painters have been known to make a gift of their works, deeming gold and silver insufficient to pay for them; and how a painting by Protogenes was so highly prized that when Demetrius[6] was laying siege to Rhodes and could have entered the city and set fire to the quarter where he knew the painting was, he refrained from giving battle and so did not take the city; how Metrodorus, a philosopher and very excellent painter, was sent by the Athenians to Lucius Paulus[7] to teach his children and to decorate the triumph which he had to make ready. And many noble authors have also written about this art, which is a great sign of

5. Famous caves. 6. Famous Macedonian general. 7. Roman general, defeated King Perseus of Macedon.

the esteem it enjoyed: but I would not have us discuss it any further.

"So let it be enough simply to say that it is fitting for our Courtier to have knowledge of painting also, since it is decorous and useful and was prized in those times when men were of greater worth than now. And even if no other utility or pleasure were had from it, it helps in judging the excellence of statues both ancient and modern, vases, buildings, medallions, cameos, intaglios, and the like, and it also brings one to know the beauty of living bodies, not only in the delicacy of the face but in the proportions of the other parts, both in man and in all other creatures. And so you see how a knowledge of painting is the source of very great pleasure. And let those consider this who are so enraptured when they contemplate a woman's beauty that they believe themselves to be in paradise, and yet cannot paint; but if they could, they would gain much greater pleasure because they would more perfectly discern the beauty that engenders so much satisfaction in their hearts."

[53]

Here messer Cesare Gonzaga laughed and said: "I, of course, am no painter; still I am sure I take much greater pleasure in looking at a certain woman than would that most worthy Apelles whom you mentioned a moment ago, were he to return to life now."

The Count replied: "This pleasure of yours does not derive entirely from her beauty but from the affection that you perchance feel for her; and if you were to tell the truth, the first time you beheld that woman, you did not feel a thousandth part of the pleasure that you later felt, even though her beauty was the same. Thus, you can see how much greater a part affection had in your pleasure than did beauty."

"That I do not deny," said messer Cesare; "but just as my pleasure arises from affection, so my affection arises from beauty; hence, we can still say that beauty is the cause of my pleasure."

The Count replied: "Many other causes besides beauty inflame our souls: such as manners, knowledge, speech, gestures, and a thousand other things (which might, however, in some way be called beauties too); but, above all, the feeling that one is loved. Thus, it is possible to love most ardently even in the absence of that beauty of which you speak; but the love which arises solely from the outward beauty we see in bodies will surely give far greater pleasure to him who discerns that beauty more than to him who discerns it less. Therefore, to return to our subject, I think Apelles must have taken more pleasure in contemplating the beauty of Campaspe[8] than did Alexander, because we can readily believe that both men's love sprang solely from her beauty, and that for this reason, perhaps, Alexander decided to give her to Apelles who appeared to have the ability to discern it more perfectly.

"Have you not read that those five girls of Crotone, whom the painter Zeuxis chose from among the others of that city for the purpose of forming from all five a single figure of surpassing beauty, were celebrated by many poets for having been judged beautiful by one who must have been a consummate judge of beauty?"

---

8. Beautiful slave given by Alexander to Apelles.

[54]

Messer Cesare seemed not to be satisfied with this, and would not at all grant that anyone except himself could experience the pleasure he felt in contemplating a certain woman's beauty, and was starting to speak again. But in that moment a great tramping of feet was heard and the noise of loud talking; whereupon everyone turned to see a great light from torches appear at the door of the room; and immediately following there arrived, with a numerous and noble company, the Prefect,[9] who was just coming back from accompanying the Pope part of his way. On entering the palace he had at once asked what the Duchess was doing and had learned what kind of game was being played that evening and the charge given to Count Ludovico to speak of Courtiership. Hence, he was hurrying as fast as he could in order to arrive in time to hear something. Thus, when he had at once made his reverence to the Duchess and had urged the others to be seated (all had stood when he came in), he too sat down in the circle along with some of his gentlemen, among whom were the Marquess Febus da Ceva and his brother Ghirardino, messer Ettore Romano, Vincenzo Calmeta, Orazio Florido,[1] and many others; and, as everyone remained silent, the Prefect said: "Gentlemen, my coming here would indeed do great harm if I were thus to put an obstacle in the way of such fine discussions as I believe those are that were taking place among you just now. But do not do me the wrong of depriving yourselves and me of such pleasure."

Then Count Ludovico said: "Nay, Sir, I think we all must find it far more pleasant to keep silent than to talk; for since this labor has fallen more to me this evening than to the others, I am weary now of speaking, as I think all the others must be of listening; for my talk was not worthy of this company nor equal to the great matter I was charged with; in which, having little satisfied myself, I think I have satisfied the others even less. Hence, you, Sir, were fortunate to come in at the end. And it is well now to give the charge of what remains to someone else who can take my place, because whoever he may be, I know he will do much better than I should if I tried to go on, tired as I now am."

[55]

"Certainly I," replied the Magnifico Giuliano, "shall in no way allow myself to be cheated of the promise you made me; and I am sure that the Prefect will not be displeased to hear this part of it."

"And what was the promise?" asked the Count.

"To tell us how the Courtier should put into effect those good qualities which you have said befit him," replied the Magnifico.

The Prefect, although a mere boy, was more wise and discreet than it seemed could be in such tender years, and in his every movement showed a greatness of spirit together with a certain vivacity of temper that gave true presage of the high mark of virtue to which he would attain. Wherefore he said quickly: "If all this is still to be told, it seems to me that I have arrived

9. Maria Francesco della Rovere.   1. Attendants of the Prefect.

in very good time; for in hearing how the Courtier must put into effect those good qualities, I shall also hear what they are, and in this way I shall come to know all that has been said up to now. Therefore, do not refuse, Count, to pay the debt, a part of which you have already settled."

"I should not have such a heavy debt to pay," replied the Count, "if labors were more equally distributed; but the mistake was in giving the authority of command to a lady who is too partial." And thus, laughing, he turned to signora Emilia, who quickly said: "It is not you who should complain of my partiality; but since you do so without reason, we will give someone else a portion of this honor which you call a labor," and, turning to messer Federico Fregoso, she said: "It was you who proposed this game of the Courtier; therefore it is only right that it should fall to you to carry on with part of it; and that part shall be to satisfy the request of the Magnifico Giuliano, declaring in what way, manner, and time, the Courtier is put into effect his good qualities and practice those things which the Count said befitted him."

Then messer Federico said: "Madam, you are trying to separate what cannot be separated, for these are the very things that make his qualities good and his practice good. Therefore, since the Count has spoken so long and so well, and has also said something of such matters as these and has prepared in his mind the remainder of what he has to say, it was only right that he should continue up to the end."

"Consider yourself to be the Count," signora Emilia replied, "and say what you think he would say; and in this way all satisfaction will be done."

[56]

Then Calmeta[2] said: "Gentlemen, since the hour is late and in order that messer Federico may have no excuse for not telling what he knows, I think it would be well to put off the rest of this discussion until tomorrow, and let the brief time that remains be spent in some other more modest entertainment."

When everyone agreed, the Duchess desired that madonna Margherita[3] and madonna Costanza Fregosa should dance. Whereupon Barletta, a delightful musician and an excellent dancer, who always kept the court amused, began to play upon his instruments; and the two ladies, joining hands, danced first a *bassa*, and then a *roegarze*[4] with extreme grace, much to the delight of those who watched. Then, the night being already far spent, the Duchess rose to her feet, whereupon everyone reverently took leave and retired to sleep.

From *Book 4*

[5]

"Therefore,[5] I think that the aim of the perfect Courtier, which we have not spoken of up to now, is so to win for himself, by means of the accom-

---

2. Poet, improviser of verses, and prose writer.   3. Attendant on the duchess.   4. French dance, sometimes danced by four or eight persons. *Bassa:* a popular Spanish dance, often danced by two or three persons.
5. The speaker is Ottaviano Fregoso of the Genoese Republic.

plishments ascribed to him by these gentlemen, the favor and mind of the prince whom he serves that he may be able to tell him, and always will tell him, the truth about everything he needs to know, without fear or risk of displeasing him; and that when he sees the mind of his prince inclined to a wrong action, he may dare to oppose him and in a gentle manner avail himself of the favor acquired by his good accomplishments, so as to dissuade him of every evil intent and bring him to the path of virtue. And thus, having in himself the goodness which these gentlemen attributed to him, together with readiness of wit, charm, prudence, knowledge of letters and of many other things—the Courtier will in every instance be able adroitly to show the prince how much honor and profit will come to him and to his from justice, liberality, magnanimity, gentleness, and the other virtues that befit a good prince; and, on the other hand, how much infamy and harm result from the vices opposed to these virtues. Hence, I think that even as music, festivals, games, and the other pleasant accomplishments are, as it were, the flower; so to bring or help one's prince toward what is right and to frighten him away from what is wrong are the true fruit of Courtiership. And because the real merit of good deeds consists chiefly in two things, one of which is to choose a truly good end to aim at, and the other is to know how to find means timely and fitting to attain that good end—it is certain that a man aims at the best end when he sees to it that his prince is deceived by no one, listens to no flatterers or slanderers or liars, and distinguishes good from evil, loving the one and hating the other.

[6]

"I think too that the accomplishments attributed to the Courtier by these gentlemen may be a good means of attaining that end—and this because, among the many faults that we see in many of our princes nowadays, the greatest are ignorance and self-conceit. And the root of these two evils is none other than falsehood: which vice is deservedly odious to God and to men, and more harmful to princes than any other; because they have the greatest lack of what they would most need to have in abundance—I mean, someone to tell them the truth and make them mindful of what is right: because their enemies are not moved by love to perform these offices, but are well pleased to have them live wickedly and never correct themselves; and, on the other hand, their enemies do not dare to speak ill of them in public for fear of being punished. Then among their friends there are few who have free access to them, and those few are wary of reprehending them for their faults as freely as they would private persons, and, in order to win grace and favor, often think of nothing save how to suggest things that can delight and please their fancy, although these things be evil and dishonorable; thus, from friends these men become flatterers, and, to gain profit from their close association, always speak and act in order to please, and for the most part make their way by dint of lies that beget ignorance in the prince's mind, not only of outward things but of himself; and this may be said to be the greatest and most monstrous falsehood of all, for an ignorant mind deceives itself and inwardly lies to itself.

[7]

"From this it results that, besides never hearing the truth about anything at all, princes are made drunk by the great license that rule gives; and by a profusion of delights are submerged in pleasures, and deceive themselves so and have their minds so corrupted—seeing themselves always obeyed and almost adored with so much reverence and praise, without ever the least contradiction, let alone censure—that from this ignorance they pass to an extreme self-conceit, so that then they become intolerant of any advice or opinion from others. And since they think that to know how to rule is a very easy thing, and that to succeed therein they need no other art or discipline save sheer force, they give their mind and all their thoughts to maintaining the power they have, deeming true happiness to lie in being able to do what one wishes. Therefore some princes hate reason or justice, thinking it would be a kind of bridle and a way of reducing them to servitude, and of lessening the pleasure and satisfaction they have in ruling if they chose to follow it, and that their rule would be neither perfect nor complete if they were obliged to obey duty and honor, because they think that one who obeys is not a true ruler.

"Therefore, following these principles and allowing themselves to be transported by self-conceit, they become arrogant, and with imperious countenance and stern manner, with pompous dress, gold, and gems, and by letting themselves be seen almost never in public, they think to gain authority among men and to be held almost as gods. And to my mind these princes are like the colossi that were made last year at Rome on the day of the festival in Piazza d'Agone,[6] which outwardly had the appearance of great men and horses in a triumph, and which within were full of tow and rags. But princes of this kind are much worse in that these colossi were held upright by their own great weight, whereas these princes, since they are ill-balanced within and are heedlessly placed on uneven bases, fall to their ruin by reason of their own weight, and pass from one error to a great many: for their ignorance, together with the false belief that they cannot make a mistake and that the power they have comes from their own wisdom, brings them to seize states boldly, by fair means or foul, whenever the possibility presents itself.

[8]

"But if they would take it upon themselves to know and do what they ought, they would then strive not to rule as they now strive to rule, because they would see how monstrous and pernicious a thing it is when subjects, who have to be governed, are wiser than the princes who have to govern. Take note that ignorance of music, of dancing, of horsemanship, does not harm to anyone; nevertheless, one who is not a musician is ashamed and dares not sing in the presence of others, or dance if he does not know how, or ride if he does not sit his horse well. But from not knowing how to govern peoples there come so many woes, deaths, destructions, burnings, ruins, that it may be said to be the deadliest plague that exists on earth. And yet some princes who are so very ignorant of government are not ashamed to attempt

6. Modern Piazza Navono.

to govern, I will not say in the presence of four or six men, but before the whole world, for they hold such a high rank that all eyes gaze upon them and hence not only their great but their least defects are always seen. Thus, it is recorded that Cimon was blamed for loving wine, Scipio for loving sleep, Lucullus for loving feasts. But would to God that the princes of our day might accompany their sins with as many virtues as did those ancients; who, even though they erred in some things, yet did not flee from the promptings and teachings of anyone who seemed to them able to correct those errors; nay, they made every effort to order their lives on the model of excellent men: as Epaminondas on that of Lysias the Pythagorean, Agesilaus on that of Xenophon, Scipio on that of Panaetius,[7] and countless others. But if some of our princes should happen upon a strict philosopher, or anyone at all who might try openly and artlessly to reveal to them the harsh face of true virtue, and teach them what good conduct is and what a good prince's life ought to be, I am certain they would abhor him as they would an asp, or indeed would deride him as a thing most vile.

[9]

"I say, then, that, since the princes of today are so corrupted by evil customs and by ignorance and a false esteem of themselves, and since it is so difficult to show them the truth and lead them to virtue, and since men seek to gain their favor by means of lies and flatteries and such vicious ways— the Courtier, through those fair qualities that Count Ludovico and messer Federico have given him, can easily, and must, seek to gain the good will and captivate the mind of his prince that he may have free and sure access to speak to him of anything whatever without giving annoyance. And if he is such as he has been said to be, he will have little trouble in succeeding in this, and will thus be able always adroitly to tell him the truth about all things; and also, little by little, to inform his prince's mind with goodness, and teach him continence, fortitude, justice, and temperance, bringing him to taste how much sweetness lies hidden beneath the slight bitterness that is at first tasted by anyone who struggles against his vices; which are always noxious and offensive and attended by infamy and blame, just as the virtues are beneficial, smiling, and full of praise. And he will be able to incite his prince to these by the example of the famous captains and other excellent men to whom the ancients were wont to make statues of bronze, of marble, and sometimes of gold, and to erect these in public places, both to honor these men and to encourage others, so that through worthy emulation they may be led to strive to attain that glory too.

[10]

"In this way the Courtier will be able to lead his prince by the austere path of virtue, adorning it with shady fronds and strewing it with pretty flowers to lessen the tedium of the toilsome journey for one whose strength is slight; and now with music, now with arms and horses, now with verses, now with discourse of love, and with all those means whereof these gentlemen have

---

7. Greek Stoic philosopher of the 2nd century B.C.E. *Lysias*: Athenian general. *Agesilaus*: king of Sparta and noted general.

spoken, to keep his mind continually occupied in worthy pleasures, yet always impressing upon him also some virtuous habit along with these enticements, as I have said, beguiling him with salutary deception; like shrewd doctors who often spread the edge of the cup with some sweet cordial when they wish to give a bitter-tasting medicine to sick and overdelicate children.

"Thus, by using the veil of pleasure to such an end, the Courtier will reach his aim in every time and place and activity, and for this will deserve much greater praise and reward than for any other good work that he could do in the world. For there is no good more universally beneficial than a good prince, nor any evil more universally pernicious than a bad prince: likewise, there is no punishment atrocious and cruel enough for those wicked courtiers who direct gentle and charming manners and good qualities of character to an evil end, namely to their own profit, and who thereby seek their prince's favor in order to corrupt him, turn him from the path of virtue, and bring him to vice; for such as these may be said to contaminate with a deadly poison, not a single cup from which one man alone must drink, but the public fountain that is used by all the people."

MARGUERITE DE NAVARRE
1492–1549

The French "discovered" Italy in the latter part of the fifteenth century, both through travel and, starting with the expedition of 1494 under King Charles VIII, through military invasions. Covetous of the fame and distinction enjoyed by the smaller and more sophisticated Italian city-states (such as Castiglione's Urbino), French rulers and aristocrats adapted Italian artistic, literary, and social values to their own culture. Marguerite de Navarre, one of the most influential members of French courtly society, played a significant part in bringing about this transformation of court culture. As a writer and a patron of artists, she also responded seriously to the spiritual and intellectual challenge to Christian faith brought about by the Reformation movements, including the Christian humanism associated with Erasmus.

Marguerite was born at Angoulême on April 11, 1492, the daughter of Charles of Orléans, count of Angoulême, and of Louise of Savoy. Her brother, the future King Francis I, was born two years later. From her earliest years, Marguerite received an exceptionally good education, including instruction in Latin, Italian, Spanish, and German; later in life she also studied Greek and Hebrew. Marriages in her class were at the time arrangements between ruling houses, dictated by political and social convenience; thus at seventeen she was married to Charles, duke of Alençon, a feudal lord who was culturally not her match. When her brother succeeded Louis XII to the French throne in 1515, Marguerite became one of the most influential women at the royal court, where she advised the king and received dignitaries and ambassadors as well as eminent men of letters. Under Francis I, the French court flourished culturally, bringing artists as famous as Leonardo da Vinci (1452–1519) and Benvenuto Cellini (1500–1571) to work in the court.

Francis I also inherited the military tradition of his predecessors in carrying on the Italian wars, the complicated conflicts fought on Italian soil between his forces and those of the Holy Roman Emperor, Charles V. His defeat in the crucial battle of Pavia in 1525 was a double blow for Marguerite: her brother was taken to Madrid as a prisoner and her husband, thought to be in part responsible for the defeat, died upon his return to France that same year. Marguerite went to Madrid to assist her sick brother and helped negotiate with Charles V for his release, which was sanctioned by the Treaty of Madrid in 1526.

The year following her husband's death, Marguerite became "Queen of Navarre" when she married Henri d'Albret, the king of Navarre in title only, since most of that domain had been annexed by Spain in 1516, limiting the possessions of the d'Albret dynasty to the lower, French section. This region contained important castles at such places as Pau and Nérac, where Marguerite held court and received visiting intellectuals and reformist religious thinkers. Eleven years younger than Marguerite, Henri d'Albret was a dashing, flighty, and intellectually disappointing husband—and is thought to be the prototype for the philandering and misogynistic character of Hircan in the *Heptameron*. Their only daughter, Jeanne, born in 1527, was the mother of the future King Henry IV of France.

Marguerite continued to be involved in her royal brother's activities: in 1529 she took part in the negotiations that led to the Treaty of Cambrai and she participated in diplomacy and peace talks in the years 1536–38. Her interest, however, was increasingly focused on intellectual and literary pursuits and on religious meditation and debate. Erasmus, John Calvin, and Pope Paul III were among her numerous correspondents. Throughout her life she was a protector of writers and thinkers accused or suspected of Protestant leanings, including Rabelais, who dedicated the third book of *Gargantua and Pantagruel* to her. Her first published work, *The Mirror of the Sinful Soul* (1531), was found by the theologians of the Sorbonne to contain elements of Protestant "heresy"; the edition of 1533, containing an additional "Dialogue in the Form of a Night Vision" written earlier and dealing with the theological problem of salvation, was condemned. The king had to intervene on behalf of his sister and her chaplain. Later it became more difficult for Francis I to maintain a lenient and conciliatory stance in the rivalry between Catholics and Protestants, which was a political and military matter as much as it was a religious dispute. Protestants and their sympathizers were persecuted, and several prominent intellectuals went into prudent exile or were burned at the stake. Marguerite, who had an intellectual and mystical faith, appears never to have abandoned Catholicism but to have hoped for internal reform.

During the last part of her life, Marguerite took several retreats to the convent at Tusson in the French region of Poitou. There in April of 1547 she received news of her brother's death. In the same year she published her *Marguerite de la Marguerite des Princesses* (with a play on the word *marguerite*, which in French means both "pearl" and "daisy"), a collection including long devotional poems and theatrical pieces ranging from allegory to farce. Both in the collection and in later poems she returns to the theme of her sorrow at her brother's death, tempered by the solace of religious faith. During the following year Marguerite returned only for short periods to the French court, where her relations with her nephew, the new king, Henry II, were uneasy. In 1549 she retired to Navarre and died in the castle of Odos on December 21.

Marguerite's greatest literary achievement is the *Heptameron*, a collection of seventy stories organized into a series of ten tales told over seven days and framed by a larger narrative that reveals the storytellers' characters and relationships with each other. In the prologue, five men and five women are brought together in the Pyrenees, when natural and criminal forces—including a flood, bandits, a bear, and murderers—prevent them from returning home. They arrive independently at an abbey, where, at the suggestion of Parlamente, thought to represent Marguerite herself, they agree to tell stories each day until they are able to return home. Within the fiction, the stories are presented as a collective enterprise by courtly storytellers.

The stories largely deal with love, sexuality, clerical abuse in the Church, moderate struggles between social classes, and above all, the antagonism between the sexes, particularly concerning issues of marital fidelity and the status of women. The *Heptameron* pays considerable attention to ideas of masculinity and to ideals and stereotypes about women. Class tensions are somewhat more muted, but the conflicts between social superiors and inferiors are the same as those that emerge from the war between the sexes: the prerogative of powerful lords and husbands to dominance in social and marital contracts is set in conflict with the rights of those victimized to avenge their compromised honor, usually by cleverness. On these subjects, the men and women who narrate and hear the stories are, to say the least, unafraid to disagree with each other about the tales' significances, both in the dialogues of the frame and in their stories, which implicitly debate such issues as the appropriate evaluation of the philandering husband or the clever wife.

The *Heptameron* belongs to a tradition of storytelling that includes the *Arabian Nights*, Chaucer's *Canterbury Tales*, and Boccaccio's *Decameron*. In the prologue, Parlamente overtly ties the storytelling game to the *Decameron* and a recent translation into French (commissioned by Marguerite) that drew, she says, the admiration of the French court, including Francis I, the Dauphin (heir to the throne), Queen Catherine de Médicis, and Marguerite. When the two women, along with other members of the court, propose to write a French *Decameron,* they agree to one difference from Boccaccio's precedent: "they should not write any story that was not truthful." The Dauphin (the future Henry II), moreover, rules out literary scholars on the grounds that "rhetorical ornament would in part falsify the truth of the account." The stories are, in fact, mysterious in origin, and with one exception, which the group approves after debate, none is drawn from a literary source.

The stipulation to relate only truthful stories identifies a dominant thematic concern of the *Heptameron*: the relationship between language and truth. For this overarching concern, there are two broad and largely irreconcilable frames of reference— one religious and the other social. In the prologue, when the travelers are considering how they should pass the time until they may safely return home, they acknowledge that the only means to calm their restless and dissatisfied souls is to devote themselves to the holy word of God as the only source of truth and consolation. Even Hircan, who places the most faith in his social position and manly self-assertion, indicates that he finds moments of solace in reading God's word, although he goes on to hint that he would choose the temporary solace of an adulterous conquest (like Petrarch, he "sees the better but chooses the worst"). Conversely, Oisille, the oldest and most evangelical of the group, chooses her strict regimen of religious study and devotion as the one "remedy"—of the many she has tried—for "boredom and . . . sorrow." Unable to "become so mortified in the flesh" as Oisille, however, the group desires a "pastime, which, while not being prejudicial to the soul, will be agreeable to the body." The conversation between Oisille and Hircan darkly suggests that to devote oneself entirely to spiritual contemplation is threatening to the young because it is tantamount to preparing oneself for death. Storytelling, then, is the group's concession to their social and physical needs: it is a middle ground between physical pleasures such as the adulterous liaison that Hircan contemplates and the worldly renunciation recommended by Oisille. The choice of strictly "truthful" stories emphasizes the group's compromise.

Yet the "truthfulness" of stories has little to do with the transcendent truth of God: as nonfiction, the tales instead heighten the social tensions that are frequently the themes of the characters' narratives. When the characters comment—in the frame and in their own stories—on each others' tales and motives for particular narrative choices, they reveal how social factors influence the ways in which they evaluate and interpret the world. Divine "truth" gives way to individual and social perspective: age, gender, social standing, education, marital status, and religious disposition form the grounds for rivalry and dispute among the group members. In this way, the *Hepta-*

meron philosophically explores the relationship between fiction-making and spiritual knowledge at the same time that it presents a lively and complex portrait of the broad social and religious concerns entertained by the brilliant, aristocratic court to which Marguerite de Navarre belonged.

PRONOUNCING GLOSSARY

The following list uses common English syllables and stress accents to provide rough equivalents of selected words whose pronunciation may be unfamiliar to the general reader.

Alençon: *ah-lon-sohnh′*

Angoulême: *ahn-goo-lem′*

Cordeliers: *cohr-del-yay′*

Coucer: *coo-say′*

Dagoucin: *da-goo-sanh′*

d'Albret: *dahl-bray*

Ennasuite: *en-nah-sweet′*

Gave de Pau: *gav deu poh*

Geburon: *zhay-byew-ronh′*

Grand-Maître de Chaumont: *grahn— etr′ deu shoh-mon′*

Hircan: *eer′-canh*

lever: *leu-vay′*

Longarine: *lohn-gah-reen′*

Monseigneur the Dauphin: *mohnh-sen- yeur′ leu doh-fanh′*

de Navarre: *deu na-vahr′*

Nomerfide: *noh-mehr-feed′*

Oisille: *wah-zee′*

Parlamente: *pahr-lah-mawnt′*

Sendras: *sawnh-dra′*

serviteur: *sehr-vee-teur′*

Simontaut: *see-mohn-toh′*

The Heptameron[1]

From Prologue

* * *

* * * Parlamente, the wife of Hircan,[2] was not one to let herself become idle or melancholy, and having asked her husband for permission, she spoke to the old Lady Oisille.[3]

"Madame," she said, "you have had much experience of life, and you now occupy the position of mother in regard to the rest of us women, and it surprises me that you do not consider some pastime to alleviate the boredom and distress that we shall have to bear during our long stay here. Unless we have some amusing and virtuous way of occupying ourselves, we run the risk of [falling][4] sick."

Longarine,[5] the young widow, added, "What is worse, we'll all become miserable and disagreeable—and that's an incurable disease. There isn't a man or woman amongst us who hasn't every cause to sink into despair, if we consider all that we have lost."

1. Translated by P. A. Chilton. 2. Hircan is variously described, in the book itself and by its commentators, as brilliant, flighty, sensual, capable of sarcasm and grossness. The name is related to Hircania, an imaginary and proverbially wild region in classical literature; the root is that of *hircus*, Latin for "goat" (cf. English *hircine*: libidinous). Parlamente probably represents Marguerite, whose name can be construed as *perle amante*, "loving pearl," or as *parlementer*, which refers to eloquent speaking. 3. The oldest, most authoritative, and most evangelical of the storytellers; she seems to be named for Louise—either Louise of Savoy, Marguerite's mother, or her lady-in-waiting, Louise de Daillon. 4. Brackets indicate translator's interpolations. 5. A young and wisely talkative widow, often identified with one of Marguerite's ladies-in-waiting, who among her titles had that of lady of Langrai (hence her name, which is also interpreted as a play on *langue orine*, meaning "tongue of gold").

Ennasuite[6] laughed and rejoined, "Not everyone's lost a husband, like you, you know. And as for losing servants, no need to despair about that—there are plenty of men ready to do service! All the same, I do agree that we ought to have something to amuse us, so that we can pass the time as pleasantly as we can."

Her companion Nomerfide[7] said that this was a very good idea, and that if she had to spend a single day without some entertainment, she would be sure to die the next.

All the men supported this, and asked the Lady Oisille if she would kindly organize what they should do.

"My children," replied Oisille, "when you ask me to show you a pastime that is capable of delivering you from your boredom and your sorrow, you are asking me to do something that I find very difficult. All my life I have searched for a remedy, and I have found only one—the reading of holy Scripture, in which one may find true and perfect spiritual joy, from which proceed health and bodily repose. And if you ask what the prescription is that keeps me happy and healthy in my old age, I will tell you. As soon as I rise in the morning I take the Scriptures and read them. I see and contemplate the goodness of God, who for our sakes has sent His son to earth to declare the holy word and the good news by which He grants remission of all our sins, and payment of all our debts, through His gift to us of His love, His passion and His merits. And my contemplations give me such joy, that I take my psalter, and with the utmost humility, sing the beautiful psalms and hymns that the Holy Spirit has composed in the heart of David and the other authors. The contentment this affords me fills me with such well-being that whatever the evils of the day, they are to me so many blessings, for in my heart I have by faith Him who has borne these evils for me. Likewise, before supper, I withdraw to nourish my soul with readings and meditations. In the evening I ponder in my mind everything I have done during the day, so that I may ask God forgiveness of my sins, and give thanks to Him for His mercies. And so I lay myself to rest in His love, fear and peace, assured against all evils. And this, my children, is the pastime that long ago I adopted. All other ways have I tried, but none has given me spiritual contentment. I believe that if, each morning, you give one hour to reading, and then, during mass, say your prayers devoutly, you will find even in this wilderness all the beauty a city could afford. For, a person who knows God will find all things beautiful in Him, and without Him all things will seem ugly. So I say to you, if you would live in happiness, heed my advice."

Then Hircan spoke: "Madame, anyone who has read the holy Scriptures— as indeed I think we all have here—will readily agree that what you have said is true. However, you must bear in mind that we have not yet become so mortified in the flesh that we are not in need of some sort of amusement and physical exercise in order to pass the time. After all, when we're at home, we've got our hunting and hawking to distract us from the thousand and one foolish thoughts that pass through one's mind. The ladies have their house-work and their needlework. They have their dances, too, which provide a respectable way for them to get some exercise. All this leads me to suggest,

6. *Enna* may stand for "Anne," and *suite* means "retinue"; so the character is identifiable with Anne de Vivonne, one of the ladies in Marguerite's entourage who collaborated on the *Heptameron* project at court. Her attitude toward men can be bitter and sharply ironical.   7. The youngest member of the group, who generally views life with joyful optimism.

on behalf of the men here, that you, Madame, since you are the oldest among us, should read to us every morning about the life of our Lord Jesus Christ, and the great and wonderful things He has done for us. Between dinner and vespers I think we should choose some pastime, which, while not being prejudicial to the soul, will be agreeable to the body. In that way we shall spend a very pleasant day."

Lady Oisille replied that she herself found it so difficult to put behind her the vanities of life, that she was afraid the pastime suggested by Hircan might not be a good choice. However, the question should, she thought, be judged after an open discussion, and she asked Hircan to put his point of view first.

"Well, my point of view wouldn't take long to give," he began, "if I thought that the pastime I would really like were as agreeable to a certain lady among us as it would be to me. So I'll keep quiet for now, and abide by what the others say."

Thinking he was intending this for her, his wife, Parlamente, began to blush. "It may be, Hircan," she said, half angrily and half laughing, "that the lady you think ought to be the most annoyed at what you say would have ways and means of getting her own back, if she so desired. But let's leave on one side all pastimes that require only two participants, and concentrate on those which everybody can join in."

Hircan turned to the ladies. "Since my wife has managed to put the right interpretation on my words," he said, "and since private pastimes don't appeal to her, I think she's in a better position than anyone to know which pastime all of us will be able to enjoy. Let me say right now that I accept her opinion as if it were my own."

They all concurred in this, and Parlamente, seeing that it had fallen to her to make the choice, addressed them all as follows.

"If I felt myself to be as capable as the ancients, by whom the arts were discovered, then I would invent some pastime myself that would meet the requirements you have laid down for me. However, I know what lies within the scope of my own knowledge and ability—I can hardly even remember the clever things other people have invented, let alone invent new things myself. So I shall be quite content to follow closely in the footsteps of other people who have already provided for your needs. For example, I don't think there's one of us who hasn't read the hundred tales by Boccaccio,[8] which have recently been translated from Italian into French, and which are so highly thought of by the [most Christian] King Francis I, by Monseigneur the Dauphin, Madame the Dauphine[9] and Madame Marguerite. If Boccaccio could have heard how highly these illustrious people praised him, it would have been enough to raise him from the grave. As a matter of fact, the two ladies I've mentioned, along with other people at the court, made up their minds to do the same as Boccaccio. There was to be one difference—that they should not write any story that was not truthful. Together with Monseigneur the Dauphin the ladies promised to produce ten stories each, and to get together a party of ten people who were qualified to contribute something, excluding those who studied and were men of letters. Monseigneur the Dauphin didn't want their art brought in, and he was afraid that rhetor-

8. The *Decameron*. 9. The future queen Catherine de Médicis. The Dauphin is the future Henry II, nephew of Marguerite.

ical ornament would in part falsify the truth of the account. A number of things led to the project being completely forgotten—the major affairs of state that subsequently overtook the King, the peace treaty between him and the King of England, the confinement of Madame the Dauphine and several other events of sufficient importance to keep the court otherwise occupied. However, it can now be completed in the ten days of leisure we have before us, while we wait for our bridge to be finished. If you so wished, we could go each afternoon between midday and four o'clock to the lovely meadow that borders the Gave de Pau, where the leaves on the trees are so thick that the hot sun cannot penetrate the shade and the cool beneath. There we can sit and rest, and each of us will tell a story which he has either witnessed himself, or which he has heard from somebody worthy of belief. At the end of our ten days we will have completed the whole hundred. And if, God willing, the lords and ladies I've mentioned find our endeavors worthy of their attention, we shall make them a present of them when we get back, instead of the usual statuettes and beads. I'm sure they would find that preferable. In spite of all this, if any of you is able to think of something more agreeable, I shall gladly bow to his or her opinion."

But every one of them replied that it would be impossible to think of anything better, and that they could hardly wait for the morrow. So the day came happily to a close with reminiscences of things they had all experienced in their time.

As soon as morning came they all went into Madame Oisille's room, where she was already at her prayers. When they had listened for a good hour to the lesson she had to read them, and then devoutly heard mass, they went, at ten o'clock, to dine, after which they retired to their separate rooms to attend to what they had to do. At midday they all went back as arranged to the meadow, which was looking so beautiful and fair that it would take a Boccaccio to describe it as it really was. Enough for us to say that a more beautiful meadow there never was seen. When they were all seated on the grass, so green and soft that there was no need for carpets or cushions, Simontaut[1] said: "Which of us shall be [the one in charge]?"

* * *

Story 3

I've often wished, Ladies, that I'd been able to share the good fortune of the man in the story I'm about to tell you.[2]

So here it is. In the town of Naples in the time of King Alfonso[3] (whose well-known lasciviousness was, one might say, the very scepter by which he ruled) there lived a nobleman—a handsome, upright and likeable man, a

1. Identified with François de Bourdeille, the husband of Anne of Vivonne. He is the long-standing *serviteur* to Parlamente: "According to the *serviteur*'s practice, as the *Heptameron* presents it, a married aristocratic woman has the right to maintain several devoted knights in her service. . . . Since it is supposed to be chaste, the *serviteur*'s relationship, this remnant of courtly and chivalrous love, can coexist with faithful marriage. . . . Nevertheless, there is evidently considerable anxiety about the institution as such" [From the translator's introduction]. His name punningly alludes to masculinity (*monte haut*: rises high). 2. The narrator is Saffredent, one of the younger members of the party, fond of company and pleasure, and a devoted admirer of Parlamente. He is often identified with an Admiral Bonnivet, whom Marguerite knew well and some of whose amorous adventures are the subject of other stories in the *Heptameron*. 3. Alfonso V of Aragon (1396–1458), the cultivated and unfaithful husband of Maria, daughter of King Henry III of Castile.

man indeed whose qualities were so excellent that a certain old gentleman granted him the hand of his daughter. In beauty and charm she was in every way her husband's equal, and they lived in deep mutual affection until a carnival, in the course of which the King disguised himself and went round all the houses in the town, where the people vied with one another to give him a good reception. When he came to the house of the gentleman I have referred to, he was entertained more lavishly than in any of the other houses. Preserves, minstrels, music—all were laid before him, but above all there was the presence of the most beautiful lady that the King had ever seen. At the end of the banquet, the lady sang for the King with her husband, and so sweetly did she sing that her beauty was more than ever enhanced. Seeing such physical perfection, the King took less delight in contemplating the gentle harmony that existed between the lady and her husband, than he did in speculating as to how he might go about spoiling it. The great obstacle to his desires was the evident deep mutual love between them, and so, for the time being, he kept his passion hidden and as secret as he could. But in order to obtain at least some relief for his feelings, he held a series of banquets for the lords and ladies of Naples, to which he did not, of course, omit to invite the gentleman and his fair wife.

As everyone knows, men see and believe just what they want to, and the King thought he caught something in the lady's eyes which augured well— if only the husband were not in the way. To find out if his surmise was correct, therefore, he sent the husband off for two or three weeks to attend to some business in Rome. Up till then the wife had never had him out of her sight, and she was heartbroken the moment he walked out of the door. The King took the opportunity to console her as often as possible, showering blandishments and gifts of all kinds upon her, with the result that in the end she felt not only consoled, but even content in her husband's absence. Before the three weeks were up she had fallen so much in love with the King that she was every bit as upset about her husband's imminent return as she had been about his departure. So, in order that she should not be deprived of the King after her husband's return, it was agreed that she would let her royal lover know whenever her husband was going to his estates in the country. He could then come to see her without running any risks, and in complete secrecy, so that her honor and reputation—which gave her more concern than her conscience—could not possibly be damaged in any way.

Dwelling on the prospect of the King's visits with considerable pleasure, the lady gave her husband such an affectionate reception that, although he had heard during his absence that the King had been paying her a lot of attention, he had not the slightest suspicion of how far things had gone. However, the fire of passion cannot be concealed for long, and as time went by its flames began to be somewhat obvious. He naturally began to guess at the truth, and kept a close watch on his wife until there was no longer any room for doubt. But he decided to keep quiet about it, because he was afraid that if he let on that he knew, he might suffer even worse things at the hands of the King than he had already. He considered, in short, that it was better to put up with the affront, than to risk his life for the sake of a woman who apparently no longer loved him. He was, all the same, angry and bitter, and determined to get his own back if at all possible.

Now he was well aware of the fact that bitterness and jealousy can drive women to do things that love alone will never make them do, and that this is particularly true of women with strong feelings and high principles of honor. So one day, while he was conversing with the Queen, he made so bold as to say that he felt very sorry for her when he saw how little the King really loved her. The Queen had heard all about the affair between the King and the gentleman's wife, and merely replied:

"I do not expect to be able to combine both honor and pleasure in my position. I am perfectly well aware that while I receive honor and respect, it is *she* who has all the pleasure. But then, I know too that while she may have the pleasure, she does not receive the honor and respect."

He knew, of course, to whom she was referring, and this was his reply. "Madame, you were born to honor and respect. You are after all of such high birth that, being queen or being empress could scarcely add to your nobility. But you are also beautiful, charming, and refined, and you deserve to have your pleasures as well. The woman who is depriving you of those pleasures which are yours by right, is in fact doing herself more harm—because her moment of glory will eventually turn to shame and she will forfeit as much pleasure as she, you or any woman in the Kingdom of Naples could ever have. And if I may say so, Madame, if the King didn't have a crown on his head, he wouldn't have the slightest advantage over me as far as giving pleasure to ladies is concerned. What is more, I'm quite sure that in order to satisfy a refined person such as yourself, he really ought to be wishing he could exchange his constitution for one more like my own!"

The Queen laughed, and said: "The King may have a more delicate constitution than your own. Even so, the love which he bears me gives me so much satisfaction that I prefer it to all else."

"Madame, if that were the case, then I would not feel so sorry for you, because I know that you would derive great happiness from the pure love you feel within you, if it were matched by an equally pure love on the part of the King. But God has denied you this, in order that you should not find in this man the answer to all your wants and so make him your god on earth."

"I admit," said the Queen, "that my love for him is so deep that you will never find its like, wherever you may look."

"Forgive me," said the gentlemen, "but there are hearts whose love you've never sounded. May I be so bold as to tell you that there is a certain person who loves you, and loves you so deeply and so desperately, that in comparison your love for the King is as nothing? And his love grows and goes on growing in proportion as he sees the King's love for you diminishing. So, if it were, Madame, to please you, and you were to receive his love, you would be more than compensated for all that you have lost."

The Queen began to realize, both from what he was saying, and from the expression on his face, that he was speaking from the depths of his heart. She remembered that he had some time ago sought to do her service,[4] and that he had felt so deeply about it that he had become quite melancholy. At the time she had assumed the cause of his mood lay with his wife, but she was now quite convinced that the real reason was his love for her. Love is a powerful force, and will make itself felt whenever it is more than mere pretense, and it was this powerful force that now made her certain of what

---

4. I.e., become her *serviteur*. See n. 1, p. 2107.

remained hidden from the rest of the world. She looked at him again. He was certainly more attractive than her husband. He had been left by his wife, too, just as she had been left by the King. Tormented by jealousy and bitterness, allured by the gentleman's passion, she sighed, tears came to her eyes, and she began: "Oh God! Must it take the desire for revenge to drive me to do what love alone would never have driven me to?"

Her words were not lost on the gentleman who replied: "Madame, vengeance is sweet indeed, when instead of taking one's enemy's life, one gives life to a lover who is true. It is time, I think, that the truth freed you from this foolish love for a man who certainly has no love for you. It is time that a just and reasonable love banished from you these fears that so ill become one whose spirit is so strong and so virtuous. Why hesitate, Madame? Let us set aside rank and station. Let us look upon ourselves as a man and a woman, as the two most wronged people in the world, as two people who have been betrayed and mocked by those whom we loved with all our hearts. Let us, Madame, take our revenge, not in order to punish them as they deserve, but in order to do justice to our love. My love for you is unbearable. If it is not requited I shall die. Unless your heart is as hard as diamond or as stone, it is impossible that you should not feel some spark from this fire that burns the more fiercely within me the more I try to stifle it. I am dying for love of you! And if that cannot move you to take pity on me and grant me your love, then at least your own love for yourself must surely force you to do so. For you, who are so perfect that you merit the devotion of all the honorable and worthy men in all the world, have been despised and deserted by the very man for whose sake you have disdained all others!"

At this speech the Queen was quite beside herself. Lest her face betray the turmoil of her mind, she took his arm and led him into the garden adjoining her room. For a long time she walked up and down with him saying nothing. But he knew that the conquest was almost complete, and when they reached the end of the path, where no one could see them, he expressed in the clearest possible way the love that for so long he had kept concealed. At last they were of one mind. And so it was, one might say, that together they enacted a Vengeance, having found the Passion too much to bear.[5]

Before they parted they arranged that whenever the husband made his trips to his village, he would, if the King had gone off to the town, go straight to the castle to see the Queen. Thus they would fool the very people who were trying to fool them. Moreover, there would now be four people joining in the fun, instead of just two thinking they had it all to themselves. Once this was settled, the Queen retired to her room and the gentleman went home, both of them now sufficiently cheered up to forget all their previous troubles. No longer did the King's visits to the gentleman's lady distress either of them. Dread had now turned to desire, and the gentleman started to make trips to his village rather more often than he had in the past. It was, after all, only half a league[6] out of the town. Whenever the King heard that the gentleman had gone to the country, he would make his way straight to his lady. Similarly, whenever the gentleman heard that the King had left his castle, he would wait till nightfall and then go straight to the Queen—to act,

---

5. An allusion to medieval mystery plays: after the Passion and Resurrection, the mystery of Vengeance depicted the punishment of Christ's slayers [Translator's note].   6. Three miles.

so to speak, as the King's viceroy. He managed to do this in such secrecy that no one had the slightest inkling of what was going on. They proceeded in this fashion for quite a while, but the King, being a public person, had much greater difficulty concealing his love-affair sufficiently to prevent anyone at all getting wind of it. In fact, there were a few unpleasant wags who started to make fun of the gentleman, saying he was a cuckold, and putting up their fingers like cuckold's horns whenever his back was turned. Anyone with any decency felt very sorry for the man. He knew what they were saying, of course, but derived a good deal of amusement from it, and reckoned his horns were surely as good as the King's crown.

One day when the King was visiting the gentleman and his wife at their home, he noticed a set of antlers mounted on the wall. He burst out laughing, and could not resist the temptation to remark that the horns went very well with the house. The gentleman was a match for the King, however. He had an inscription placed on the antlers which read as follows:

> *Io porto le corna, ciascun lo vede,*
> *Ma tal le porta, che no lo crede.*[7]

Next time the king was in the house, he saw the inscription, and asked what it meant.

The gentleman simply said: "If the King doesn't tell his secrets to his subjects, then there's no reason why his subjects should tell their secrets to the King. And so far as horns are concerned, you should bear in mind that they don't always stick up and push their wearers' hats off. Sometimes they're so soft that you can wear a hat on top of them, without being troubled by them, and even without knowing they're there at all!"

From these words the King realized that the gentleman knew about his affair with his wife. But he never suspected that the gentleman was having an affair with *his* wife. For her part, the Queen was careful to feign displeasure at her husband's behavior, though secretly she was pleased, and the more she was pleased, the more displeasure she affected. This amicable arrangement permitted the continuation of their amours for many years to come, until at length old age brought them to order.

"Well, Ladies," concluded Saffredent, "let that story be a lesson to you. When your husbands give you little roe-deer horns, make sure that you give them great big stag's antlers!"

"Saffredent," said Ennasuite, laughing, "I'm quite sure that if you were still such an ardent lover as you used to be, you wouldn't mind putting up with horns as big as oaks, as long as you could give a pair back when the fancy took you. But you're starting to go grey, you know, and it really is time you began to give your appetites a rest!"

"Mademoiselle," he replied, "even if the lady I love gives me no hope, and even if age has dampened my ardor somewhat, my desires are as strong as ever. But seeing that you object to my harboring such noble desires, let me invite you to tell the fourth story, and let's see if you can produce an example to refute what I say."

During this exchange one of the ladies had started to laugh. She knew

7. "I am wearing horns, everyone sees that, / But there is one who wears them who doesn't know it."

that the lady who had just taken Saffredent's words to be aimed at her was not in fact so much the object of his affections that he would put up with cuckoldry, disgrace or injury of any kind for her sake. When Saffredent saw that she was laughing and that she had understood him, he was [highly] pleased, and let Ennasuite go on. This is what she said:

"I have a story to tell, Ladies, which will show Saffredent and everyone else here that not *all* women are like the Queen he has told us about, and that not all men who are rash enough to try their tricks get what they want. It's a story that ought not to be kept back, and it tells of a lady in whose eyes failure in love was worse than death itself. I shan't mention the real names of the people involved, because it's not long since it all happened, and I should be afraid of giving offense to their close relatives."

Story 8

In the county of Alès there was once a man by the name of Bornet, who had married a very decent and respectable woman. He held her honor and reputation very dear, as I am sure all husbands here hold the honor and reputation of *their* wives dear. He wanted her to be faithful to him, but was not so keen on having the rule applied to them both equally. He had become enamored of his chambermaid, though the only benefit he got from transferring his affections in this way was the sort of pleasure one gets from varying one's diet. He had a neighbor called Sendras, who was of similar station and temperament to himself—he was a tailor and a drummer. These two were such close friends that, with the exception of the wife, there was nothing that they did not share between them. Naturally he told him that he had designs on the chambermaid.

Not only did his friend wholeheartedly approve of this, but did his best to help him, in the hope that he too might get a share in the spoils.

The chambermaid herself refused to have anything to do with him, although he was constantly pestering her and in the end she went to tell her mistress about it. She told her that she could not stand being badgered by him any longer, and asked permission to go home to her parents. Now the good lady of the house, who was really very much in love with her husband, had often had occasion to suspect him, and was therefore rather pleased to be one up on him, and to be able to show him that she had found out what he was up to. So she said to her maid: "Be nice to him dear, encourage him a little bit, and then make a date to go to bed with him in my dressing-room. Don't forget to tell me which night he's supposed to be coming, and make sure you don't tell anyone else."

The maid did exactly as her mistress had instructed. As for her master, he was so pleased with himself that he went off to tell his friend about his stroke of luck, whereupon the friend insisted on taking his share afterwards, since he had been in on the business from the beginning. When the appointed time came, off went the master, as had been agreed, to get into bed, as he thought, with his little chambermaid. But his wife, having abandoned her position of authority in order to serve in a more pleasurable one, had taken her maid's place in the bed. When he got in with her, she did not act like a wife, but like a bashful young girl, and he was not in the slightest suspicious. It would be impossible to say which of them enjoyed themselves more—the wife deceiving her husband, or the husband who thought he was deceiving his wife. He stayed in bed with her for some time, not as long as he might have wished (many years of marriage were beginning to tell on him), but as long as he could manage. Then he went out to rejoin his accomplice, and tell him what a good time he had had. The lustiest piece of goods he had ever come across, he declared. His friend, who was younger and more active than he was, said: "Remember what you promised?"

"Hurry up, then," replied the master, "in case she gets up, or my wife wants her for something."

Off he went and climbed into bed with the supposed chambermaid his friend had just failed to recognize as his wife. *She* thought it was her husband again, and did not refuse anything he asked for (I say "asked," but "took" would be nearer the mark, because he did not dare open his mouth). He made a much longer business of it than the husband, to the surprise of the wife, who was not used to these long nights of pleasure. However, she did not complain, and looked forward to what she was planning to say to him in the morning, and the fun she would have teasing him. When dawn came, the man got up, and fondling her as he got out of bed, pulled off a ring she wore on her finger, a ring that her husband had given her at their marriage. Now the women in this part of the world are very superstitious about such things. They have great respect for women who hang on to their wedding rings till the day they die, and if a woman loses her ring, she is dishonored, and is looked upon as having given her faith to another man. But she did not mind him taking it, because she thought it would be sure evidence against her husband of the way she had hoodwinked him.

The husband was waiting outside for his friend, and asked him how he had got on. The man said he shared the husband's opinion, and added that he would have stayed longer, had he not been afraid of getting caught by the daylight. The pair of them then went off to get as much sleep as they could. When morning came, and they were getting dressed together, the husband noticed that his friend had on his finger a ring that was identical to the one he had given his wife on their wedding day. He asked him where he had got it, and when he was told it had come from the chambermaid the night before, he was aghast. He began banging his head against the wall, and shouted: "Oh my God! Have I gone and made myself a cuckold without my wife even knowing about it?"

His friend tried to calm him down. "Perhaps your wife had given the ring to the girl to look after before going to bed?" he suggested. The husband made no reply, but marched straight out and went back to his house.

There he found his wife looking unusually gay and attractive. Had she not saved her chambermaid from staining her conscience, and had she not put her husband to the ultimate test, without any more cost to herself than a night's sleep? Seeing her in such good spirits, the husband thought to himself: "She wouldn't be greeting me so cheerfully if she knew what I'd been up to."

As they chatted, he took hold of her hand and saw that the ring, which normally never left her finger, had disappeared. Horrified, he stammered: "What have you done with your ring?"

She was pleased that he was giving her the opportunity to say what she had to say.

"Oh! You're the most dreadful man I ever met! Who do you think you got it from? You think you got it from the chambermaid, don't you? You think you got it from that girl you're so much in love with, the girl who gets more out of you than I've ever had! The first time you got into bed you were so passionate that I thought you must be about as madly in love with her as it was possible for any man to be! But when you came back the *second* time, after getting up, you were an absolute devil! Completely uncontrolled you were, didn't know when to stop! You miserable man! You must have been blinded by desire to pay such tribute to my body—after all you've had me long enough without showing much appreciation for my figure. So it wasn't because that young girl is so pretty and so shapely that you were enjoying yourself so much. Oh no! You enjoyed it so much because you were seething with some depraved pent-up lust—in short the sin of concupiscence was raging within you, and your senses were dulled as a result. In fact you'd worked yourself up into such a state that I think any old nanny-goat would have done for you, pretty or otherwise! Well, my dear, it's time you mended your ways. It's high time you were content with me for what I am—your own wife and an honest woman, and it's high time that you found *that* just as satisfying as when you thought I was a poor little erring chambermaid. I did what I did in order to save you from your wicked ways, so that when you get old, we can live happily and peacefully together without anything on our consciences. Because if you go on in the way you have been, I'd rather leave you altogether than see you destroying your soul day by day, and at the same time destroying your physical health and squandering everything you have before my very eyes! But if you will acknowledge that you've been in the wrong, and make up your mind to live according to the ways of God and His commandments, then I'll overlook all your past misbehavior, even as I hope God will forgive me *my* ingratitude to Him, and failure to love Him as I ought."

If there was ever a man who was dumbfounded and despairing, it was this poor husband. There was his wife, looking so pretty, and yet so sensible and so chaste, and he had gone and left her for a girl who did not love him. What was worse, he had had the misfortune to have gone and made her do something wicked without her even realizing what was happening. He had gone and let another man share pleasures which, rightly, were his alone to enjoy. He had gone and given himself cuckold's horns and made himself look ridiculous for evermore. But he could see she was already angry enough about the chambermaid, and he did not dare tell her about the other dirty trick he had played. So he promised that he would leave his wicked ways behind him, asked her to forgive him and gave her the ring back. He told his friend not to breathe a word to anybody, but secrets of this sort nearly always end up being proclaimed from the [roof-tops], and it was not long before the facts became public knowledge. The husband was branded as a cuckold without his wife having done a single thing to disgrace herself.

"Ladies, it strikes me that if all the men who offend their wives like that got a punishment like that, then Hircan and Saffredent ought to be feeling a bit nervous."

"Come now, Longarine," said Saffredent, "Hircan and I aren't the only married men here, you know."

"True," she replied, "but you're the only two who'd play a trick like that."

"And just when have you heard of us chasing our wives' maids?" he retorted.

"If the ladies in question were to tell us the facts," Longarine said, "then you'd soon find plenty of maids who'd been dismissed before their pay-day!"

"Really," intervened Geburon, "a fine one you are! You promise to make us all laugh, and you end up making these two gentlemen annoyed."

"It comes to the same thing," said Longarine. "As long as they don't get their swords out, their getting angry makes it all the more amusing."

"But the fact remains," said Hircan, "that if our wives were to listen to what this lady here has to say, she'd make trouble for every married couple here!"

"I know what I'm saying, and who I'm saying it to," Longarine replied. "Your wives are so good, and they love you so much, that even if you gave them horns like a stag's, they'd still convince themselves, and everybody else, that they were garlands of roses!"

Everyone found this remark highly amusing, even the people it was aimed at, and the subject was brought to a close. Dagoucin,[8] however, who had not yet said a word, could not resist saying: "When a man already has everything he needs in order to be contented, it is very unreasonable of him to go off and seek satisfaction elsewhere. It has often struck me that when people are not satisfied with what they already have, and think they can find something better, then they only make themselves worse off. And they do not get any sympathy, because inconstancy is one thing that is universally condemned."

"But what about people who have not yet found their other half?" asked Simontaut. "Would you still say it was inconstancy if they seek her wherever she may be found?"

"No man can know," replied Dagoucin, "where his other half is to be found, this other half with whom he may find a union so equal that between [the parts] there is no difference; which being so, a man must hold fast where Love constrains him and, whatever may befall him, he must remain steadfast in heart and will. For if she whom you love is your true likeness, if she is of the same will, then it will be your own self that you love, and not her alone."

"Dagoucin, I think you're adopting a position that is completely wrong," said Hircan. "You make it sound as if we ought to love women without being loved in return!"

"What I mean, Hircan, is this. If love is based on a woman's beauty, charm and favors, and if our aim is merely pleasure, ambition, or profit, then such love can never last. For if the whole foundation on which our love is based should collapse, then love will fly from us and there will be no love left in us. But I am utterly convinced that if a man loves with no other aim, no other desire, than to love truly, he will abandon his soul in death rather than allow his love to abandon his heart."

"Quite honestly, Dagoucin, I don't think you've ever really been in love," said Simontaut, "because if you had felt the fire of passion, as the rest of us have, you wouldn't have been doing what you've just been doing—describing Plato's republic, which sounds all very fine in writing, but is hardly true to experience."

"If I have loved," he replied, "I love still, and shall love till the day I die.

---

8. The most philosophical member of the group, described elsewhere (story 11) as "so wise that he would rather die than say something foolish." He is also the saintliest; our translator indicates that his name is "a fairly obvious pun: *de goûts saints* (of saintly tastes)."

But my love is a perfect love, and I fear lest showing it openly should betray it. So greatly do I fear this, that I shrink to make it known to the lady whose love and friendship I cannot but desire to be equal to my own. I scarcely dare think my own thoughts, lest something should be revealed in my eyes, for the longer I conceal the fire of my love, the stronger grows the pleasure in knowing that it is indeed a perfect love."

"Ah, but all the same," said Geburon, "I don't think you'd be sorry if she did return your love!"

"I do not deny it. But even if I were loved as deeply as I myself love, my love could not possibly increase, just as it could not possibly decrease if I were loved less deeply than I love."

At this point, Parlamente, who was suspicious of these flights of fancy, said: "Watch your step, Dagoucin. I've seen plenty of men who've died rather than speak what's in their minds."

"Such men as those," he replied, "I would count happy indeed."

"Indeed," said Saffredent, "and worthy to be placed among the ranks of the Innocents—of whom the Church chants 'Non loquendo, sed moriendo confessi sunt'![9] I've heard a lot of talk about these languishing lovers, but I've never seen a single one actually die. I've suffered enough from such torture, but I got over it in the end, and that's why I've always assumed that nobody else ever really dies from it either."

"Ah! Saffredent, the trouble is that you desire your love to be returned," Dagoucin replied, "and men of your opinions never die for love. But I know of many who *have* died, and died for no other cause than that they have loved, and loved perfectly."

Story 10

In Aragon, in the province of Aranda, there once lived a lady. She was the widow of the Count of Aranda, who had died while she was still very young, and left her with a son and a daughter, who was called Florida. As was right and proper for the children of a noble lord, they were brought up by her according to the strictest codes of virtue and honor. So carefully did she school them that her house was known far and wide as the most honorable in the whole of Spain. She would often go to Toledo, which was then the seat of the King of Spain,[1] and when she visited Saragossa, which was not far from the family home, she would spend her time at the Queen's court, where she was as highly esteemed as any lady could be.

One day, when the King was in residence at his castle in Saragossa, the Castillo de la Aljaferia, the Countess, on her way to pay her respects as was her wont, was passing through a little village that belonged to the Viceroy of Catalonia.[2] Normally the Viceroy never moved from the border at Perpignan, where he was in command during the war between France and Spain, but peace[3] had just been declared, and he returned with his officers in order to do homage to his King. He knew that the Countess would be passing through his lands, and went to meet her, not only to do her the honor that was her due as the King's kinswoman, but also because of the goodwill that he had

9. "Not by speaking but by dying they confessed," a line recited during the Feast of the Holy Innocents.
1. Ferdinand V of Spain (1452–1516). 2. Don Henri of Aragon. 3. Treaty of Blois (1505).

long borne her. Now in the Viceroy's entourage there were not a few noble-men of outstanding valor, courageous men, who, after long service in the wars had earned such heroic reputations that there was no one in the land who was not anxious to meet them and be seen in their company. Amongst these men there was one by the name of Amador. Although he was only eighteen or nineteen years of age, he had such confidence, and such sound judgment, that you could not have failed to regard him as one of those rare men fit to govern any state. Not only was he a man of sound judgment, he was also endowed with an appearance so handsome, so open and natural, that he was a delight for all to behold. This was not all, for his handsome looks were equally matched by the fairness of his speech. Poise, good looks, eloquence—it was impossible to say with which gift he was more richly blessed. But what gained him even higher esteem was his fearlessness, which, despite his youth, was famed throughout all lands. For he had already in many different places given evidence of his great abilities. Not only throughout the kingdoms of Spain, but also in France and Italy people looked upon him with admiration. Not once during the recent wars had he shrunk from battle, and when his country had been at peace, he had gone to seek action in foreign parts, and there too had been loved and admired by friend and foe alike.

This young nobleman had devotedly followed his commander back home, to meet the Countess of Aranda. He could not fail to notice her daughter, Florida, who was then but twelve years of age. Never, he thought to himself, as he contemplated her grace and beauty, had he beheld so fair and noble a creature. If only she might look with favor upon him, that alone would give him more happiness than anything any other woman in the world could ever give him. For a long while he gazed at her. His mind was made up. He would love her. The promptings of reason were in vain. He would love her even though she was of far higher birth than he. He would love her, even though she was not yet of an age to hear and understand the words of love. But his misgivings were as nothing against the firm hope that grew within him, as he promised himself that time and patient waiting would in the end bring his toils to a happy conclusion. Noble Love, through the power that is its own, and for no other cause, had entered Amador's breast and now held out to him the promise of a happy end, and the means of attaining it.

The greatest obstacle was the distance that separated his own homeland from that of Florida, and the lack of opportunity to see her. To [overcome] this problem he decided, contrary to his previous intentions, to marry some lady from Barcelona or Perpignan. His reputation stood so high there that there was little or nothing anyone would refuse him. Moreover, he had spent so long on the frontier during the wars, that although he came from the region of Toledo, he was more like a Catalan than a Castilian.[4] His family was rich and distinguished, but he was the youngest son, and possessed little in the way of inheritance. But Love and Fortune, seeing him ill-provided for by his parents, and resolving to make him their paragon, bestowed upon him through the gift of virtue and valor that which the laws of the land denied him. He was experienced in matters of war, and much sought after by noble

---

4. Although a native of Castile, Amador has lived with, and fought alongside of, the Catalans and Arago-nese—i.e., although a foreigner, he looks like a native.

lords and princes. He did not have to go out of his way to ask for rewards. More often than not he had to refuse them.

The Countess meanwhile continued on her way, and arrived at Saragossa, where she was well received by the King and the whole court. The Viceroy of Catalonia visited her frequently, and Amador took the opportunity of accompanying him. In this way he might at least have the chance of looking at Florida, for there was no way in which he might be able to speak to her. In order to introduce himself into the society of the Countess, he approached the daughter of an old knight, who came from his home town. Her name was Avanturada, and she [had been brought up alongside] Florida, so that she knew the innermost secrets of her heart. Since she was a good, respectable girl, and expected to receive three thousand ducats a year by way of dowry, Amador made up his mind to address himself to her as a suitor, and seek her hand in marriage. She was only too willing to listen. But her father was a rich man, and she felt that he would never consent to her marriage with a man as poor as Amador unless she enlisted the aid of the Countess. So she first approached Florida.

"My lady, you have seen the Castilian gentleman, who often talks to me," she said. "I believe that it is his intention to ask my hand in marriage. But you know what my father is like. You know that he will never consent, unless the Countess and yourself persuade him."

Florida, who loved the young lady dearly, assured her that she would do everything she could for her, just as if her own interests were at stake. Then Avanturada presented Amador to Florida. As he kissed her hand, he almost fainted in rapture. He, the most eloquent man in Spain, was speechless as he stood before her. This somewhat surprised Florida, for, although she was only twelve years of age, she knew well enough that there was not a man in Spain who could express his mind more eloquently than Amador. He stood there in silence, so she said to him:

"Señor Amador, your reputation has spread through all the kingdoms of Spain, and it would be surprising indeed if you were not known to us also. All of us who have heard about you are anxious to find some way in which we can be of service. So if there is anything I can do, I hope you will not be afraid to ask."

Amador stood gazing at his lady's beauty. He was transported with joy, and was only just able to utter a few words of grateful thanks. Florida was astonished to see that he was still incapable of making any kind of reply, but she attributed it to some momentary whim, completely failing to see that the true cause of his behavior lay in the violence of his love. She ignored his silence, and said no more.

Amador, for his part, had perceived what great virtue was beginning to appear in Florida, young as she was, and later he said to the lady he was planning to marry:

"Avanturada, do not be surprised that I couldn't speak a word in front of Lady Florida. She is so young, yet she speaks so well and so wisely, and behind her tender years there clearly lie hidden such virtues, that I was overcome with admiration and didn't know what to say to her. Tell me, Avanturada, since you are her friend and must know her closest secrets, how is it possible that she hasn't stolen the heart of every single man at court? Any man who has met her, and hasn't fallen in love with her, must be a dumb beast or made of stone!"

Avanturada, who by now was much in love with Amador, could keep nothing from him. She told him that the Lady Florida was indeed greatly loved by everyone, but that very few people actually spoke with her, that being the custom in that part of the land. There were only two men who seemed to show any inclination—Don Alfonso, son of Henry of Aragon, otherwise known as the Infante of Fortune,[5] and the young Duke of Cardona.

"Tell me," said Amador, "which of the two do you think she likes the best?"

"She is so good and wise," replied Avanturada, "that she would never confess to anything that was not in accordance with the wishes of her mother. But, as far as we can judge, she prefers the son of the Infante of Fortune to the Duke of Cardona, although it is the Duke of Cardona her mother prefers, because with him she would stay closer to home. But you are a man of perception and sound judgment, so perhaps you would help us decide what the truth of the matter is. It's like this. The son of the Infante of Fortune was brought up at this court, and he is one of the most handsome and most accomplished young princes in Christendom. What I and the other girls think is that he is the one she should marry—they'd make the loveliest couple in the whole of Spain. And I ought to tell you as well that although they're both very young—she's only twelve and he's fifteen—they've been in love for three years already. If you want to get in her good books you ought to make a friend of him and enter into his service."

Amador was relieved to hear that his lady was capable of love at all. One day, he hoped, he might win the right to become her true and devoted servant, even though he might never become her husband. Of her virtue he was not afraid. His sole anxiety had been that she might reject love completely. From this conversation onward, Amador made friends with the son of the Infante of Fortune. He had little difficulty in gaining his goodwill, for he was versed in all the sports and diversions that the young prince enjoyed, being an excellent horseman, skilled in the use of arms and indeed good at everything that a young man ought to be able to do.

War broke out again in Languedoc, and Amador was obliged to return with the governor. His sorrow was great, the more so as he had no means of ensuring that he would return to a post where he would still be able to see his Florida. So before his departure, he spoke to a brother of his, who was major-domo[6] in the household of the Queen. He told him what an excellent match he had found in the Lady Avanturada while in the Countess's household, and asked him to do everything in his power during his absence to bring the marriage about, by drawing on the influence of the Queen, the King and all his other friends. The brother, who was very fond of Amador, not only because of their common blood, but because he admired his prowess, promised to do as he was bidden. He was as good as his word. The Countess of Aranda, the young Count, who was growing to appreciate virtue and valor, and above all the the beautiful Florida, joined in singing the praises of Amador. The result was that Avanturada's miserly old father put aside his grasping habits for once and was brought to recognize Amador's excellent qualities. The marriage was duly agreed upon by the parents of the couple, and, during the truce that had been declared by the two warring kings, Amador was summoned home by his brother.

It was at that time that the King of Spain withdrew to Madrid, where he was safe from the unhealthy air that was affecting a number of places throughout the country. Acting on the advice of his Council, but also at the request of the Countess, he had arranged a marriage between her son, the little Count, and a rich heiress, the Duchess of Medinaceli, in order to bring the two families together in an advantageous union and to please the Countess herself, whose interests were very dear to his heart. In accordance with his wishes the marriage was celebrated in the King's palace at Madrid. Amador was present, and was able to pursue his own matrimonial plans so successfully that he too was married—to Avanturada, in whom he inspired a good deal more love than he returned. His marriage was no more than a cover, no more than a convenient excuse to enable him to visit her on whom his mind constantly dwelled.

After his marriage he made himself so familiar in the Countess's household that no one took any more notice of him than if he had been a woman. He was only twenty-two at this time, but had such good sense that the Countess used to keep him informed of all her business affairs. She even instructed her son and her daughter to listen carefully to his conversation, and heed any advice he might give. Having reached these heights in the Countess's esteem, he behaved in such a sensible, such a restrained manner, that even the lady whom he loved so dearly failed to perceive his feelings. In fact, being so fond of Amador's wife, she hid nothing from Amador himself, not even her most intimate thoughts, [and went so far as] to tell him about her love for the son of the Infante of Fortune. Amador's sole concern was to win her completely, and he talked to her constantly about the Infante's son. Provided he was able to converse with her, he did not care what was the topic of their conversation. However, he had been there hardly a month after his marriage when he was obliged to go back to the wars. Not once, during the two years that followed, did he return to see his wife, who waited for him, living as she always had done in the household of the Countess. Throughout this time Amador would write to his wife, but his letters consisted principally of messages for Florida. She for her part would reply, and even insert something amusing in her own hand in Avanturada's letters—which alone was enough to make Amador very conscientious in writing to his wife. But throughout all this Florida was aware of nothing, except perhaps that she was as fond of Amador as if he had been her own brother.

Several times Amador came and went, but for five whole years he never saw Florida for two months together. Yet in spite of these long absences, and the long distances that separated them, his love grew. At last he was able to travel to see his wife. He found the Countess far from the court, for the King had gone into Andalusia, taking with him the young Count of Aranda, who had already started to bear arms. The Countess had moved to a country house she owned on the borders of Aragon and Navarre. She was delighted to see Amador, who had been away now for three years, and commanded that he was to be treated like a son. There was nobody who did not make him welcome. During his stay, the Countess told him all her domestic business, and asked his advice on almost every aspect of it. The family's regard for him was unbounded. Wherever he went, there was always an open door. He was looked upon as a man of such integrity that he was trusted in everything. Had he been a saint or an angel, he could hardly have been trusted more. Florida, fond as she was of Avanturada, went straight to Amador whenever she saw him. Having not the slightest suspicion as to his true intentions, she was quite unreserved in her behavior toward him. There was not a trace of passion in her heart, unless it was a feeling of contentment at being by his side. Nothing else occurred to her. But there are people who can guess from the expression in a man's eyes whether that man is in love or not, and Amador was constantly anxious lest he be thus found out. When Florida came to speak to him alone, in complete innocence, the fire that burned in his breast would flare up so violently that, do what he might, the color would mount to his cheeks and the flames of passion would gleam in his eyes.

In order that no one should guess from his intimacy with Florida that he was in love with her, he began to make approaches to an extremely attractive lady called Paulina, whose charms were highly celebrated in her day, and from whose snares few men managed to escape. She had heard how Amador had been successful with the ladies in Barcelona and Perpignan, and how he had won the hearts of the most beautiful and most noble ladies in the land; in particular she had heard how a certain Countess of Palamos, who was regarded as the most beautiful woman in Spain, had lost her heart to him. So she told him how deeply she pitied him for having married such an ugly wife, after all his past good fortunes in love. Amador realized from what she said that she was ready to provide him with any consolation he might require, and replied with as encouraging words as he was able, thinking that it would be possible to cover up the truth of his real feelings by making her believe a lie. But she was shrewd, experienced in the ways of love, and not a woman to make do with mere words. She sensed that his heart was not entirely taken up with love for her, and suspected that he wanted to use her as a cover. She watched him so closely that not a single glance escaped her. Amador's eyes were well-practiced in the art of dissembling, however, and Paulina could get no further than her vague suspicions. But it was only with extreme difficulty that he was able to hide his feelings, especially when Florida, who had not the slightest idea of the game he was playing, talked to him with her customary intimacy in front of Paulina herself. It was only by making the most painful effort that on such occasions he was able to control the expression in his eyes, and prevent them reflecting the feelings in his heart. So to forestall any unfortunate consequences in the future, he said to her one day as he leaned against the window where they had been chatting: "Tell me, [my Lady], is it better to speak or to die?"

"I would always advise my friends to speak," she replied quickly, "because there are very few words that can't be remedied, but once you've lost your life, there's no way of getting it back."

"So will you promise that you will not only not be angry at what I am going to say, but also, if you are shocked, that you will not say anything until I have finished?"

"Say whatever you please," she said, "because if *you* shock me, then there's no one in the world who could reassure me."

So he began.

"My Lady, there are two reasons why I have not yet told you of the feelings I have for you. One reason is that I hoped to give you proof of my love through long and devoted service. The other is that I feared that you would consider it [overweening presumption] that I, an ordinary nobleman, should dare to aspire to the love of a lady of birth so high. Even if I were, like you, my Lady, of princely estate, a heart so true and loyal as your own would not suffer such talk of love from anyone but the son of the Infante of Fortune, who has taken possession of your heart. Yet, my Lady, just as in the hardships of war one may be compelled to destroy one's own land, to lay waste one's rising crops, in order to prevent the enemy taking advantage of them, even so do I now seek to anticipate the fruit that I had hoped to reap only in the fullness of time, in order to prevent our enemies from taking advantage of it to your loss. I must tell you, my Lady, that from the time I first saw you, when you were still so young, I have wholly consecrated myself to your service. I have never ceased to seek the means to obtain your good grace, and it was for this reason alone that I married the very lady who is your own dearest friend. Knowing, too, that you loved the son of the Infante, I did my utmost to serve him, to become his friend. In short, I have striven to do everything that I thought would give you pleasure. You have seen how the Countess, your mother, has looked favorably upon me, as has the Count your brother, and all those of whom you are fond, with the result that I am treated in this house, not as a man serving his superiors, but as a son. All the efforts that I made five years ago were for no other end than to live my whole life by you. But you must believe me, my Lady, when I tell you that I am not one of those men who would exploit this advantage. I desire no favor, nor pleasure, from you, except what is in accordance with the dictates of virtue. I know that I cannot marry you. And even if I could, I should not seek to do so, for your love is given to another, and it is he whom I long to see your husband. Nor is my love a base love. I am not one of those men who hope that if they serve their lady long enough they will be rewarded with her dishonor. Such intentions could not be further from my heart, for I would rather see you dead, than have to admit that my own gratification had sullied your virtue, had, in a word, made you less worthy to be loved. I ask but one thing in recompense of my devotion and my service. I ask only that you might be my true and faithful Lady, so true, so faithful, that you will never cast me from your good grace, that you will allow me to continue in my present estate, and that you will place your trust in me above all others. And if your honor, or any cause close to your heart, should demand that a noble gentleman lay down his life, then mine will I gladly lay down for your sake. On this you may depend. Know, too, that whatsoever deeds of mine may be counted noble, good or brave, these deeds will be performed for love of you alone. Yes, and if for ladies less exalted my deeds have met acclaim, then be you assured that for a lady such as you I shall perform such deeds of greatness, that acts which once I deemed impossible I shall now perform with ease. But if you will not accept me as wholly yours, my Lady, then I shall make up my mind to abandon my career at arms. I shall renounce the valor and the virtue that were mine, for they will have availed me nought. Wherefore, my Lady, I do humbly beseech that my just demand might be granted, since your honor and your conscience cannot refuse it."

The young Lady Florida changed color at this speech, the like of which she had never heard before. Then she lowered her gaze, like a mature woman, her modesty shocked. Then, with all the virtue and good sense that was hers, she said:

"If, as seems to be the case, Amador, you're only asking me for something that you already have, then why do you insist on making such a long, highflown speech about it? I am rather afraid that there is some evil intent hidden away underneath all these fine words, and that you're trying to beguile me because I'm young and innocent. It makes me very uncertain as to how I should reply to you. If I were to reject the noble love that you offer me, I would only be contradicting the way I've behaved toward you up till now, because in you I've placed more trust than in any other man in the world. Neither my honor nor my conscience stand in the way of your request. Nor does the love I bear the son of the Infante of Fortune, for my love for him is founded on marriage, to which you lay no claim. In fact I can think of no reason why I should not grant your wishes, except perhaps for one anxiety that troubles my mind. You have no reason to address me in the way you do. If you already have what you desire, what can it be that now makes you tell me about it in such an emotional manner?"

Amador was ready with his reply.

"My Lady, you speak most prudently," he said, "and do me great honor to place in me such trust as you declare. If I were not happy to receive this blessing from you, I should be unworthy indeed to receive any other. But let me explain, my Lady, that the man who desires to build an edifice that will endure throughout eternity should take the utmost care to lay a safe and sure foundation. So it is that I, who desire most earnestly to serve you through all eternity, should take the greatest care that I have the means to ensure not only that I shall remain always by you, but that I shall be able to prevent all others from knowing of the great love I bear you. For, though my love is pure and noble enough to be announced to the whole world, yet there are people who will never understand a lover's soul, and whose pronouncements will always belie the truth. The rumors that result are none the less unpleasant for being untrue. The reason why I have made so bold as to say all this to you, is that Paulina has become very suspicious. She senses in her heart that I am unable to give her my love, and she is constantly on the watch for me to give myself away. And when you come to talk to me alone in your affectionate way, I am so nervous lest she discern something in my expression to confirm her suspicions that I find myself in just the awkward situation that I am most anxious to avoid. So I made up my mind to beg you not to take me unawares when Paulina is present, or anyone else whom you know to have an equally malicious disposition. For I would die rather than let any living creature know of my feelings. Were it not that your honor is so dear to me, I should never have entertained the idea of speaking to you in the way I have spoken. For I feel myself so content in the love that you have for me, that there is nothing further that I desire, unless it be that you should continue in the same for ever."

At these words Florida was filled with delight beyond bounds. Deep within her heart she began to feel stirrings that she had never felt before. And as she could see that the arguments he brought forth were honorable and good, she was able to grant his request, saying that virtue and honor answered for her. Amador was transported with joy, as anyone who has ever truly loved will understand.

However, Florida took his advice too seriously. She became nervous, not only in the presence of Paulina, but in other circumstances too, until she began not to seek Amador's company at all in the way she had in the past. Moreover, she took it badly that he spent so much time with Paulina, who seemed so attractive that she felt it impossible for Amador not to be in love with her. To relieve her distress she would talk at great length with Avanturada, who was herself beginning to be jealous of her husband and Paulina, and often bemoaned her lot to her friend. Florida, suffering from the same affliction, would offer what consolation she was able. It was not long before Amador noticed Florida's strange behavior, and concluded that she was keeping away from him, not just as a result of his advice, but because she was displeased with him. One day, as they were returning from vespers at a monastery, he said to her: "My Lady, why do you treat me the way you do?"

"Because that is the way I thought you wanted it," she replied.

Then, suspecting the truth of the matter, and wishing to know whether he was right, Amador said: "My Lady, because of the time I have spent with her, Paulina no longer suspects you."

"Then you couldn't have done better, either for yourself or for me," she answered, "for in giving yourself a little pleasure, you are acting in the interests of my honor."

Amador understood from these words that she thought he derived pleasure from talking with Paulina. So hurt was he that he could not restrain his anger:

"Ah! My Lady, so you're starting already to torment your servant, by hurling abuse at him for [acting in your interests]! There's nothing more irksome and distressing than being obliged to spend one's time with a woman one isn't even in love with! Since you take exception to tasks I undertake solely in your service, I'll never speak to her again. And let the consequences take care of themselves! To cover up my anger, just as in the past I've hidden my joy, I shall go away to a place not far from here, and wait until your mood has passed. But I hope that when I get there I shall receive orders from my commanding officer to return to the wars, where I shall stay long enough to prove to you that nothing keeps me here but you, my Lady."

So saying, he went, without even waiting for her reply. Florida was left utterly dejected and downcast. Love, having been thwarted, was aroused now, and began to demonstrate its power. She acknowledged that she had wronged Amador, and wrote to him over and over again, beseeching him to come back to her—as indeed he did several days later, once his anger had subsided. I could not begin to tell you in detail what they said to one another to resolve their jealousies. To cut a long story short, he won the day. She promised that she would never again suspect him of being in love with Paulina. More than that, she swore she was and would remain convinced that it was for Amador almost unbearable to have to speak with Paulina or any other woman, nay that it was a martyrdom suffered for no other reason than to render service to his lady.

No sooner had Love overcome these first suspicions and jealousies, no sooner had the two lovers begun to take more pleasure than ever from talking together, than word came that the King of Spain was sending the entire army to Salces. Amador, who was accustomed to be the first to join the royal standards, was as eager as ever to follow the path of honor and glory. Yet this time it was with particular regret, a regret deeper than that which he had experienced before, for not only was he relinquishing the one pleasure of his life, but he now feared that Florida might change during his absence. She had already reached the age of fifteen or sixteen, and was wooed by lords and princes from far and wide. He feared that she might be married while he was away, and that he might never see her again. He had one safeguard, however—that the Countess should make his wife the special companion to Florida. Accordingly, he employed his influence to obtain promises both from the Countess and from Florida herself that wherever she should go after her marriage Avanturada should go with her. And so, in spite of the fact that the talk at that time was of a marriage in Portugal, Amador was certain in his mind that she would never abandon him. With this assurance, yet none the less filled with sorrow beyond words, he departed for the wars, leaving his wife with the Countess.

After her faithful servant had left, Florida found herself quite alone. She set herself to perform all manner of good and virtuous deeds, hoping thereby to acquire the reputation of being the most perfect lady in the land, and worthy to have a man such as Amador devoted to her service. As for Amador himself, when he arrived at Barcelona, he was, as he had been in the past, greeted with delight by all the ladies. But they found him a changed man. They would never have thought that marriage had such a hold over a man, for he now seemed to have nothing but distaste for all the things that before he had pursued. Even the Countess of Palamos, of whom he had once been so enamored, could no longer find a way of luring him even as far as the door of her residence. Anxious to be away to the scene of battle [where glory was to be won], Amador spent as little time as possible in Barcelona. No sooner had he arrived at Salces, than war did indeed break out between the two kings.[7] It was a great and merciless war. I have no intention of relating the course of events in detail, or even of recounting the many heroic deeds accomplished by Amador, for to tell you all this I should need a whole day. Suffice it to say that Amador won renown above all his comrades in arms. The Duke of Nájera arrived at Perpignan in charge of two thousand men, and invited Amador to be his second-in-command. He answered the call of duty, and led his men with such success that in every skirmish the air rang with shouts of "Nájera! Nájera!"

Now it came to the ears of the King of Tunis that the kings of Spain and France were waging war on the border between Perpignan and Narbonne. He had long been at war himself with the King of Spain, and he now saw that he could not wish for a better opportunity to harass him more. So he sent a large fleet of galleys and other vessels to pillage and lay waste every inch of unguarded territory that he could find along the Spanish coasts. When the inhabitants of Barcelona saw the vast number of sailing ships looming on the horizon, they immediately sent word to their Viceroy at Salces, who reacted by sending the Duke of Nájera to Palamos without delay. The Moors[8] arrived to find the coasts well garrisoned and acted as if they were sailing on. But toward midnight they returned, and put large numbers of men ashore. The Duke was taken completely by surprise, and was in fact taken prisoner. Amador, vigilant as ever, had heard the noise, marshaled as many of his men as he could and defended himself so effectively that it was a long time before the stronger forces of the enemy were able to make any inroads. In the end, however, realizing that the Duke of Nájera had been

7. When the Treaty of Blois failed, the wars between Spain and France resumed at the border of the two countries (Perpignan).   8. Moslems from North Africa.

captured, and that the Turks were determined to set fire to the whole of Palamos, and destroy the building which he had defended against them, he thought it better to surrender than to be the cause of the annihilation of his valiant comrades. It was also in his mind that if he were held to ransom, there would be some hope of seeing Florida again. Without more ado, he gave himself up to the Turkish chief-in-command, a man called Dorlin, who took Amador before the King of Tunis himself. He was received respectfully and treated well. He was guarded well, too, for the Turkish King was aware that the man he had in his hands was the veritable Achilles of Spain.

For two years Amador remained the prisoner of the King of Tunis. When the news reached Spain, the family of the Duke of Nájera was stricken with grief, but people who held the honor of their country dear judged the capture of Amador an even greater loss. It was broken to the Countess of Aranda and her household at a time when the poor Avanturada lay seriously ill. The Countess (who had guessed how Amador felt about her daughter, and had kept quiet, raising no objections, because she appreciated the young man's qualities) called Florida to one side to tell her the distressing news. But Florida knew how to hide her true feelings, and merely said that it was a great loss for all the family, and that she felt especially sorry for Amador's poor wife lying sick in bed. But seeing her mother weeping bitterly, she shed a few tears with her, lest her secret be discovered by being too well disguised. From this time on the Countess often spoke to Florida about Amador, but never once was she able to draw from her any reaction that would confirm her thoughts. I shall leave aside for now the pilgrimages, the prayers, the devotions, the fasts, which Florida began regularly to offer for Amador's salvation. As for Amador himself, as soon as he reached Tunis, he lost no time in sending messengers to his friends. To Florida he naturally sent the most trustworthy man he could find, to let her know that he was well and living in the hope of seeing her again. This was all she had to sustain her in her distress, but you may be sure that since she was allowed to write to him, she assiduously performed this task, and Amador did not go without the consolation of her letters.

The Countess of Aranda was summoned to Saragossa, where the King had taken up residence. There she found the young Duke of Cardona, who had been actively seeking the support of the King and Queen in his suit for the hand of Florida. Pressed by the King to agree to the marriage, the Countess, as a loyal subject, could not refuse his request. She was sure that her daughter, still so young in years, could have no other will than that of her mother, and, once the agreement was concluded, she took her on one side to explain how she had chosen for her the match which was most fitting. Florida knew that the matter was already settled and that further deliberation was useless. "May the Lord be praised in everything," was all she could bring herself to say, for her mother looked so stern, and she judged it preferable to obey rather than indulge in self-pity. To crown all her sorrows, she then heard that the son of the Infante of Fortune had fallen sick and was close to death. But never once in the presence of her mother, or of anyone else, did she show any sign of how she felt. So hard indeed did she repress her feelings that her tears, having been held back in her heart by force, caused violent bleeding from the nose which threatened her life. And all the cure she got was marriage to a man she would gladly have exchanged for death. After the

marriage was over she went to the Duchy of Cardona. With her went Avanturada, to whom she was able to unburden herself, bemoaning the harsh
treatment she had received from her mother and the sorrow she nursed in
her heart at the loss of the son of the Infante. But never once did she mention
the fact that she missed Amador, except by way of consoling Avanturada
herself. In short, the young Lady Florida resolved to have God and honor
constantly before her eyes, and she so carefully hid her troubles, that no one
had the slightest suspicion that her husband gave her no pleasure.

For a long time Florida lived this life, a life that seemed to her little better
than death. She wrote of her woe to her servant Amador, who, knowing how
great and noble was his lady's heart, and how deep was her love for the son
of the Infante, could only think her end was nigh. This new anguish heightened his affliction, and he grieved bitterly, for Florida's plight seemed already
worse than death. Yet he knew what torment his beloved must be suffering,
and his own paled into insignificance. Gladly would he have stayed a slave
to the end of his days, if only that might have ensured Florida the husband
of her desires. One day he learned from a friend he had made at the court
of Tunis that the King, who would have liked to keep Amador in his service,
provided he could make a good Turk of him, was planning to threaten him
with impalement if he did not renounce his faith. To forestall this move,
therefore, he prevailed upon the man who had captured him and had become
his master to let him go on parole, without informing the King. The ransom
was set so high that the Turk reckoned no one as poor as Amador could ever
possibly find the money to pay it.

So, having been allowed to depart, he went to the court of the King of
Spain, from where, as soon as he was able, he set off again to seek his ransom
among his friends. He went straight to Barcelona, where the young Duke of
Cardona, his mother and Florida were staying on account of some family
business. As soon as Amador's wife, Avanturada, heard the news, she told
Florida, who, as if for Avanturada's sake, expressed her joy. But she was afraid
lest the joy she felt at seeing him again should show in her face, and lest
people who did not know her well should put a bad interpretation on it. So
instead of going to meet him, she stood at a window to watch his arrival from
afar. Immediately he came into sight she went down by way of a staircase,
which was dark enough to prevent anybody seeing whether her cheeks
changed color. She embraced Amador, took him to her room, and then to
meet her husband's mother, who had not yet made his acquaintance. Needless to say, he had not been there two days before he had endeared himself
to the whole household, exactly as he had in the house of the Countess of
Aranda. I shall leave you to imagine the words that passed between him and
Florida, and how Florida sorrowfully told of all that she had been through
during his absence. She wept bitterly at having had to marry against her
inclinations, and at having lost the man whom she loved so dearly, without
hope of ever seeing him again. Then she made up her mind to take consolation in her love for Amador and the sense of security it afforded her, though
she never once dared declare to him her intent. Amador guessed, however,
and never lost an opportunity to make known to her how great was his love
for her.

Florida was almost won. She was almost at the point where she was ready
not merely to accept Amador as a devoted servant, but to admit him as a

sure and perfect lover. But it was then that a most unhappy accident occurred. Amador had received word from the King to go to him immediately on urgent business. Avanturada was very upset at the news, and fainted. Unfortunately she happened to be standing at the top of a flight of stairs. She fell, and injured herself so badly that she never recovered. Florida was deeply affected by Avanturada's death. There could be no consolation for her now. It was as if she felt herself bereft of all relatives and friends. She went into deep mourning for her loss. To Amador the blow was even more overwhelming, for not only had he lost one of the most virtuous wives who ever lived, but he had also lost all hope now of continuing to be near Florida. He sank into a state of such dejection, that he thought he himself had not long to live. The old Duchess of Cardona visited him at frequent intervals, and quoted the sayings of the philosophers, in the hope of inducing him to bear the death of his wife with fortitude. But to no avail. The specter of death tormented him from one side. From the other, his martyrdom was made more painful by the force of his love. His wife was dead and buried. His sovereign lord had called him. What further reason could he have for staying where he was? In his heart was such despair that he thought he would lose his reason. Florida sought to give consolation, but desolation was all she brought him. One whole afternoon she spent in an attempt to console him with gentle words, doing all she would to lessen the pain of his grief, and assuring him that she would find a way of seeing him far more often than he supposed. Since he was due to depart the following morning, and since he was so weak that he was unable to move from his bed, he begged her to come and visit him again that same evening, when everyone else had gone. This she promised to do, not realizing that such extremity of love as Amador's knew no rational bounds. He had served her long and well, without any reward other than what I have described in my story. Now he despaired of ever being able to return to see her again, and, racked by a love that had been hidden away within him, he made up his mind to make one last desperate gamble—to risk losing all, or to gain everything and treat himself to one short hour of the bliss that he considered he had earned. He had his bed hung with heavy curtains, so that it was impossible for anyone in the room to see in, and when his visitors came he moaned even more than before, so that people thought that he must surely die before another day passed.

In the evening, when all the visitors had gone, Florida came, with the full approval of her husband, who had encouraged her to tend the sick man. She hoped to give him consolation by declaring her feelings and her desire to love him within the limits permitted by honor. She sat down on a chair at the head of his bed, and began, as she thought, to comfort him, by joining her tears to his. Seeing her so overcome with sorrow and regret, Amador judged that it was now, while she was in this state of torment, that his intentions would most easily be accomplished. He rose from his bed. Florida, thinking he was too weak for such exertions, tried to stop him. But he fell on his knees in front of her, saying, "Must I lose you for ever from my sight?" Whereupon he collapsed into her arms, as if all his strength had suddenly drained from him. The poor Florida put her arms around him and supported him for a while, doing her utmost to console him. He said not a word, and pretending still that he was at the brink of death, began to pursue the path that leads to the forbidden goal of a lady's honor. When Florida realized that his intentions were not pure, she found it beyond belief. Had not his conversation in the past always been pure and good? She asked him what he was trying to do. Amador still said nothing. He did not want to receive a reply that could not but be virtuous and chaste. He struggled with all the strength in his body to have his way. Florida, terrified, thought he must be out of his mind. Rather that, than have to admit he had desired to stain her honor. She called out to a gentleman who she knew would be in the room. Amador, now utterly despairing, threw himself back on the bed with such violence that the other man thought he had breathed his last. Florida, who had now got up from her chair, said: "Quick, go and fetch some fresh vinegar!"

While the gentleman was doing as he had been bidden, she turned to Amador.

"What kind of madness is this, Amador? Are you beginning to lose your mind? What did you think you were trying to do?"

"What cruelty!" exclaimed Amador, now bereft of all reason through the violence of love. "Is this the only reward I deserve after serving you so long?"

"And what," she replied, "has become of the honor you preached about so often?"

"Ah! my Lady," he said, "no one in the world could possibly hold your honor as dear as I do! Before you were married I was able to overcome the desires of my heart so successfully that you knew nothing at all of my feelings. But now you are a married woman. You have a cover and your honor is safe. So what wrong can I possibly be doing you in asking for what is truly mine? It is I who have really won you, through the power of my love. The man who first won your heart so irresolutely pursued your body that he well deserved to lose both. As for the man who now possesses your body—he's not worthy of the smallest corner in your heart. So you do not really belong to him, even in body. But consider, my Lady, what trials and tribulations I have gone through in the last five or six years for your sake. Surely you cannot fail to realize that it is to me alone that you belong, body and heart, for is it not for you that I have refused to give thought to my own body and my own heart? And if you are thinking that you can justify yourself on grounds of conscience, bear in mind that no sin may be imputed when the heart and the body are constrained by the power of love. When men kill themselves in a violent fit of madness, in no way do they commit a sin. For passion leaves no room for reason. And if it is the case that the passion of love is the most difficult to bear of all, if it is—as indeed it is—the passion that most completely blinds the senses, then what sin can you impute to a man who merely lets himself be swept along by an insuperable force? Now I must depart. All hope of seeing you again is gone. Had I but the guarantee that my great love deserves, I would have all the strength I need to endure in patience what will surely be a long and painful absence. If, however, you do not deign to grant me my request, then ere long you shall hear that your severity has brought me to a cruel and unhappy end!"

Florida was as distressed as she was taken aback to hear a speech like this from a man of whom she would never have expected anything of the kind, and her tears flowed.

"Alas! Amador," she began, "what has happened to all the virtuous things you used to say to me when I was young? Is this the honor, is this the conscience, for which you so often told me to die, rather than lose my soul? Have you forgotten all the lessons you taught me from examples of virtuous ladies who resisted senseless and wicked passion? Have you forgotten how you have always spoken with scorn of women who succumb to it? It is hard, Amador, to believe that you have left your former self so far behind that all regard for God, for your conscience, and for my honor is completely dead. But if it really is as you seem to say, then I thank God that in His goodness He has forewarned me of the disaster that was about to befall me. By the words you have uttered God has revealed to me what your heart is really like. How could I have remained ignorant for so long? I lost the son of the Infante of Fortune, not just because I was obliged to marry somebody else, but because I knew that he really loved another woman. Now I am married to a man whom I cannot love and cherish however hard I try. That is why I had made up my mind to give you all the love that is in me, to love you with my whole heart. And the foundation of this love was to have been virtue, that virtue which holds honor and conscience dearer than life itself, that virtue which I first found in you, and which, through you, I think I have now attained. Thus it was that I came to you, Amador, firmly resolved to build upon this rock of honor. But in this short space of time you have clearly demonstrated to me that I would have been building not upon the solid rock of purity, but upon the shifting sands, nay, upon a treacherous bog of vice. I had begun to build a dwelling in which I could live for evermore, but with a single blow you have razed it to the ground. So now you must abandon hope. You must be resolved never again, wherever it may be, to seek to speak to me or look into my eyes. Nor may you hope that one day I could change my mind, even should I so desire. My heart brims with sorrow for what might have been. But had it come to pass that I had sworn myself to you in the bond of perfect love, my poor heart would have been wounded unto death by what has transpired. To think that I have been so deceived! If it does not bring me to an early grave, I shall surely suffer for the rest of my days. This is my final word to you. Adieu. For ever more adieu!"

I shall not try to describe Amador's feelings as he listened to these words. It would be impossible to set such anguish down in writing. It is difficult even for anyone to imagine such anguish, unless they have experienced the same kind of suffering themselves. What a cruel end! Realizing that she was going to leave him on this note, and that he would lose her for ever if he did not clear his name, he seized her by the arm.

"My Lady," he said, putting on the most convincing expression he could manage, "for as long as I can remember I have longed to love a good and honorable woman. But I have found few who are truly virtuous, and that is why I wanted to test you out—to see if you were as worthy to be admired for your virtue, as you are to be loved for your other attributes. And now I know for certain that you are. For this I praise God, and give Him thanks that He has brought my heart to love such consummate perfection! So I beseech you, forgive this whim, pardon my rash behavior. For as you can see, all has turned out for the best. Your honor is vindicated, and I am happy indeed that this should be so!"

But Florida was beginning to understand the evil ways of men. If she had before found it hard to believe that Amador's intentions were bad, she now found it even harder to believe him when he said that in reality they were good.

"Would to God that you were speaking the truth!" she said. "But I am a married woman, and I am not so ignorant that I do not clearly realize that it was violent passion that drove you to do what you did. If God had not stood by me, and my hold on the reins had slackened, I am not at all convinced that you would have been the one to tighten the bridle. Those who truly seek virtue do not take the route that you took. But enough has been said. I was too ready to believe you were a good man. It is time that I recognized the truth, for it is by truth that now I am delivered from your clutches."

With these words, Florida left the room. The whole night long she wept. This sudden change caused her such pain that her heart was hard pressed to withstand the assaults of bitter regret which love hurled against it. For, while in accordance with reason she was determined to love him no more, the heart, over which none of us has control, would never yield. Thus, unable to love him less than before, she resolved to propitiate love, since love it was that was the cause. She resolved, in short, to go on loving Amador with all her heart, but, in order to obey the dictates of honor, never to let it be known, either to him or to anyone.

The next morning Amador departed in a state of mind which I leave to your imagination. But no one in the world had a more valiant heart than he, and, instead of sinking into despair, he began to seek new ways of seeing Florida again, and winning her. So, being due to present himself to the King of Spain, who at that time was in residence at Toledo, he went by way of the County of Aranda. He arrived late one night at the castle of the Countess, and found her ailing, and pining for her daughter. When she saw Amador she put her arms around him and kissed him, as if he were her own son, for she loved him dearly, and had guessed that he was in love with Florida. She pressed him for news, and he told her as much as he could without telling the whole truth. Then he told her what her daughter had always concealed, and confessed their love, begging the Countess to help him have news of Florida, and to bring her soon to live with her.

The next morning he left, and continued on his journey. When his business with the King had been dispatched, he went off to join the army on active service. He was downcast and so changed in every respect that the ladies and officers whose company he had always kept no longer recognized him. He continually dressed himself in clothes of coarse black cloth, much more austere than was called for by the death of his wife. But the death of his wife served merely as a cover for a much deeper grief. Three or four years went by, and Amador never once returned to court. The Countess meanwhile had word that such a change had come over her daughter that she was piteous to behold. She summoned Florida to her, in the hope that she might want to come back and live with her permanently. But Florida would not hear of it. When she heard that Amador had told her mother about their love, and that her mother, good and wise as she was, had confided in Amador and told him she approved, her consternation was great indeed. On the one hand, she could see that her mother had considerable admiration for Amador, and that if she had the truth told to her, it might bring him harm. That was the last thing she wanted, and in any case, she felt quite well able to punish him for his outrageous behavior without help from her family. On the other hand, she could see that if she concealed the bad things she knew about him, she would be obliged by her mother and all her friends to talk with him and receive him favorably. That, she feared, could only strengthen him in his base intentions. However, he was in distant parts, so she made little fuss, and wrote him letters whenever the Countess asked her to do so. But when she did write, she made sure that he would realize that they were written out of obedience, and not from any inclination of her own. There had once been a time when her letters had brought him transports of joy. Now he felt nothing but sorrow as he read them.

Three years went by, during which time Amador performed so many glorious deeds that no writer could ever hope to set them all down, even if he had all the paper in Spain. It was now that he devised his grand scheme—not a scheme to win back Florida's heart, for he deemed her lost for ever, but a scheme to score a victory over her as his mortal enemy, for that was how she now appeared. Throwing all reason to the winds, and setting aside all fear of death, he took the greatest risk of his life. His mind was made up. He was not to be deterred from his aim. Since his credit stood high with the governor, he was able to get himself appointed to a mission to the King for the purpose of discussing some secret campaign directed against the town of Leucate. He also managed to get himself issued with orders to inform the Countess of Aranda of the plan, and to take her advice before meeting the King. Knowing that Florida was there, he went post-haste into Aranda, and on his arrival sent a friend in secrecy to tell the Countess that he wished to see her, and that they must meet only at dead of night, without anyone else knowing about it. Overjoyed to hear that Amador was in the neighborhood, the Countess told Florida, and sent her to undress in her husband's room, so that she should be ready to be called once everyone had retired. Florida made no objection. But she had not yet recovered from her earlier terrifying experience, and, instead of doing as she was bidden, went straight to an oratory to commend herself to our Lord, and to pray to Him that He might preserve her heart from all base affections. Remembering that Amador had often praised her beauty, which in spite of long sickness had in no way diminished, she could not bear the thought that this beauty of hers should kindle so base a fire in the heart of a man who was so worthy and so good. Rather than that she would disfigure herself, impair her beauty. She seized a stone that lay on the chapel floor, and struck herself in the face with great force, severely injuring her mouth, nose and eyes. Then, so that no one would suspect her when she was summoned, she deliberately threw herself against a [large piece of stone] as she left the chapel. She lay with her face to the ground, screaming, and was found in this appalling state by the Countess, who immediately had her wounds dressed and her face swathed in bandages.

Once she had been made comfortable, the Countess took her into her chamber and told her that she wanted her to go and talk to Amador in her private room till she had dismissed her attendants. Thinking that Amador would not be unaccompanied, Florida obeyed, but, once the door closed behind her, she was horrified to find herself completely alone with him. Amador, for his part, was not at all displeased, for now, he thought, he would by fair means or foul surely get what he had so long desired. A few words were sufficient to tell him that her attitude was the same as when he had last seen her, and that she would die rather than change her mind. In a state of utter desperation he said:

"Almighty God, Florida, I'm not going to have the just deserts of all my efforts frustrated by your scruples! Seeing that all my love, all my patient waiting, all my begging and praying are useless, I shall use every ounce of strength in my body to get the one thing that will make life worth living! Without it I shall die!"

His whole expression, his face, his eyes, had changed as he spoke. The fair complexion was flushed with fiery red. The kind, gentle face was contorted with a terrifying violence, as if there was some raging inferno belching fire in his heart and behind his eyes. One powerful fist roughly seized hold of her two weak and delicate hands. Her feet were held in a vice-like grip. There was nothing she could do to save herself. She could neither fight back, nor could she fight free. She had no other recourse than to see if there might not yet be some trace of his former love, for the sake of which he might relent and have mercy.

"Amador," she gasped, "even if you think I'm your enemy now, I beg you, in the name of that pure love which I used to think you felt for me in your heart, please listen to me, before you torture me!"

Seeing that he was prepared to hear her out, she continued: "Alas, Amador! What is it that drives you to seek that which can give you no satisfaction, and to cause me the greatest sorrow anyone could ever cause me? You came to know my feelings so well in the days when I was young, when my beauty was at its most fresh, and when your passion might have had some excuse, that I marvel now that at the age I am, ugly as I am, ravaged by deepest sorrow as I am, you should seek that which you know you cannot find. I am certain that you can have no doubt but that my feelings remain as they have always been, and that [only by use of force therefore can you obtain that which you ask]. If you will look at the way my face is now adorned, you will lose all memory of the delights that once you found there, you will lose all your desire to approach it nearer! If there is the slightest trace in you of the love you used to bear me, you must surely have pity on me and overcome this violent madness. In the name of all the [pity and noble virtue] that I have known in you in the past, I plead with you, and beg you for mercy. Just let me live in peace! Let me live the life of honor and virtue to which, as you yourself once urged me, I have committed myself. And if your former love for me really has turned to hatred, and if, more out of a desire for revenge than some form of love, your intention is to make me the most wretched woman on earth, then I tell you plainly that you will not have your way. I shall be forced, against all my previous intentions, to make known your vicious designs to the very lady, who hitherto has held you in the highest esteem. You will realize that if I take this action, you will be in danger of your life . . ."

"If I am to die anyway," Amador broke in, "then the agony will be over all the sooner! Nor am I going to be deterred because you've disfigured your face! I'm quite sure you did it yourself, of your own volition. No! If all I could get were your bare bones, still I should want to hold them close!"

Florida could see that neither tears, nor entreaties, nor reasoning were to any avail. She could see that he was going to act out his evil desires, unmoved and merciless. Exhausted and unable to struggle any more, there was only one thing left she could do to save herself, the one thing that she had shrunk from as from death itself. With a heart-rending cry, she shouted out to her mother with all the strength that was in her. There was something in Florida's voice that made the Countess go cold with horror. Suspecting what had happened, she flew to the room with all possible haste. Amador, not quite so ready to die as he had just declared, had had enough time to gather himself together. When the Countess entered, there he was standing by the door, with Florida at a distance.

"Amador, what's the matter?" she demanded, "Tell me the truth!"

Amador was never at loss when it came to finding his way out of a difficult situation. Looking shocked and pale, he gave his answer.

"Alas! Madame, what has come over Florida? I've never been so astonished as I am at this moment. I used to think, as you know, that I had some share in her goodwill. But now I see that I have none at all. I do not think that she was any less modest, any less virtuous in the days when she was living in your household than she is now, but she used not to have such scruples about seeing men and talking to them. I only have to look at her now, and she can't bear it! I thought it was a dream or a trance, when I saw her acting like that, and I asked her if I could kiss her hand, which after all is quite normal in this part of the world, but she completely refused! I am prepared to admit that I was in the wrong over one thing, Madame, and for this I do ask your forgiveness: I'm afraid I did hold her hand as you might say by force, and kissed it. But that was the only thing I asked of her. But she seems to be so determined that I should die, that she called out to you, as you must have heard. I can't understand why she did it, unless she was afraid that I had other intentions. Anyway, whatever the reason, Madame, I take the blame for it. She really ought to show affection for all your loyal servants. But such is fate! I happen to be the one who's in love, and yet I'm the only one who loses favor! Of course, I'll always feel the same way about you, Madame, and about your daughter, as I have in the past, and I hope and pray that I shan't lose your good opinion, even if, through no fault of my own, I have lost hers."

The Countess, who half believed, half doubted these words, turned to Florida. "Why did you call out for me like that?" she asked.

Florida replied that she had been afraid, and, in spite of her mother's insistent and repeated questions, she refused ever to give more details. It was enough for her that she had been delivered from the hands of her enemy, and as far as she was concerned Amador had been quite sufficiently punished by being thwarted in his attempt. The Countess had a long talk with Amador, and then let him speak again to Florida, though she stayed in the room while he did so, in order to observe from a distance how he would comport himself. He had little to say, though he did thank Florida for not telling her mother the whole truth, and he did ask her that since he was banished from her heart for ever, she would at least not admit a successor.

"If I had had any other way of protecting myself," came her reply, "I would not have shouted out, and no one would have heard anything about what happened. Provided that you don't drive me to it, that is the worst you will have from me. And you need have no fear that I shall give my love to some other man. For since I have not found that which I desired in the heart which I regarded as the most virtuous in the world, I shall never believe it is to be found in any man. Thanks to what has happened I shall be free for ever more from the passions that can arise from love."

So saying, she bade Amador farewell. The Countess had been watching closely, but she could come to no conclusion, except that her daughter plainly no longer felt any affection for Amador. She was convinced that Florida was just being perverse, and had taken it into her head to dislike anyone that her mother was fond of. From that time on, the Countess became so hostile toward her daughter, that for seven whole years she did not speak to her except in anger—and all this for the sake of Amador.

Up till this time Florida had had a horror of being with her husband, but during this period her attitude changed, and, in order to [escape] the harshness of her mother, she refused to move from his side. But this did not help her in her plight, so she conceived a plan which involved deceiving Amador. Dropping for a day or two her hostile air, she advised Amador to make amorous overtures to a certain woman, who, she said, had spoken of their love. The woman in question was a lady by the name of Loretta, who was attached to the household of the Queen. Amador believed Florida, and in the hope of eventually regaining her favor, he made advances to Loretta, who was only too pleased to have such an eminently desirable servant. Indeed she made it so obvious by her simperings, that the whole court soon got to hear of it. The Countess herself was at court at this time, and when she heard the rumors, she began to be less severe than she had been with her daughter. One day, however, it came to Florida's ears that Loretta's husband, who was a high-ranking officer in the army, and one of the King of Spain's highest governors, had become so jealous, that he had sworn to stop at nothing to kill Amador. Now Florida was incapable of wishing harm on Amador, however harsh a mask she might wear, and she informed him immediately of the danger he was in. Amador, anxious to return to her, replied that he would never again speak a word to Loretta, provided that Florida would agree to see him for three hours each day. To that she could not give her consent.

"Then why," said Amador to her, "if you do not wish to give me life, do you wish to save me from death? There can only be one reason—that you want to keep me alive in order to torture me, and hope thereby to cause me greater pain than a thousand deaths could ever do. Death may shun me, yet I shall seek it out, and I shall find it, for only in death shall I have repose!"

Even as they spoke, news arrived that the King of Granada had declared war on the King of Spain, and had attacked so fiercely that the King had had to send his son, the Prince, to the front, together with two old and experienced lords, the Constable of Castile and the Duke of Alba. The Duke of Cardona, too, and the Count of Aranda, were anxious to join the campaign, and petitioned the King for a commission. His majesty granted their requests, appointing each to the command appropriate to his birth. Amador was appointed to lead them. His exploits during that campaign were so extraordinary that they had more the appearance of acts of desperation than acts of bravery. Indeed, to bring my story to its conclusion, this bravery, going beyond all bounds, was demonstrated at the last in death.

The Moors had indicated that they were about to join battle. Then, seeing the size of the Christian forces, they had staged a sham retreat. The Spaniards had been about to follow in hot pursuit. But the old Constable and the Duke of Alba, realizing that it was a trap, had managed to restrain the Prince from crossing the river. The Count of Aranda and the Duke of Cardona, however, had defied orders. The Moors, seeing their pursuers were reduced in number, had wheeled round. Cardona had been killed, cut down by thrusts from Moorish scimitars. Aranda had been left gravely wounded, and as good as dead. In the midst of the carnage Amador arrived, riding furiously, and forcing his way like a madman through the thick of the battle. He had the two bodies transported back to the Prince's encampment. The Prince was as overcome as if they had been his own brothers. When the wounds were examined, however, it was found that the Count of Aranda was still alive, so he was carried back in a litter[9] to the family home, where he lay ill for a very long time. The Duke's corpse was sent back to Cardona. Amador, having rescued the two bodies, was so heedless of his own safety that he found himself surrounded by vast numbers of Moors. He made up his mind what he should do. His enemies would not enjoy the glory either of capturing him alive or of slaying him. Even as he had failed to take his lady, so now his enemies would be frustrated in taking him. His faith to her he had broken. His faith to God he would not break. He knew, too, that if he was taken before the King of Granada, he would have to abjure Christianity, or die a horrible death. Commending body and soul to God, he kissed the cross of his sword, and plunged it with such force into his body that he killed himself in one fell blow.

Thus died poor Amador, his loss bemoaned as his virtue and prowess deserved. The news of his death spread throughout Spain, and eventually reached Florida, who was at Barcelona, where her husband had expressed his wish to be buried. She conducted the obsequies with due honor. Then, saying not a word either to her own mother or to the mother of her dead husband, she entered the Convent of Jesus. Thus she took Him as lover and as spouse who had delivered her from the violent love of Amador and from the misery of her life with her earthly husband. All her affections henceforth were bent on the perfect love of God. As a nun she lived for many long years, until at last she commended her soul to God with the joy of the bride who goes to meet her bridegroom.

"I'm afraid, Ladies, that this story has been rather long, and that some of you might have found it somewhat tedious—but it would have been even longer if I'd done justice to the person who originally told it to me. I hope you will take Florida's example to heart, but at the same time I would beg you to be less harsh, and not to have so much faith in men that you end up being disappointed when you learn the truth, drive them to a horrible death and give yourselves a miserable life."

Parlamente had had a patient and attentive audience. She now turned to Hircan, and said: "Don't you think that this woman was tried to the limits of her endurance, and that she put up a virtuous resistance in the face of it all?"

"No," replied Hircan, "for screaming is the least resistance a woman can offer. If she'd been somewhere where nobody could have heard her, I don't know what she'd have done. And as for Amador, if he'd been more of a lover and less of a coward, he wouldn't have been quite so easily put off. The example of Florida is not going to make me change my opinion on this matter. I still maintain that no man who loved perfectly, or who was loved by a lady, could fail in his designs, provided he went about things in a proper manner. All the same, I must applaud Amador for at least partly fulfilling his duty."

9. A stretcher.

"What duty?" demanded Oisille. "Do you call it duty when a man who devotes himself to a lady's service tries to take her by force, when what he owes to her is obedience and reverence?"

"Madame," replied Saffredent, "when our ladies are holding court and sit in state like judges, then we men bend our knees before them, we timidly invite them to dance, we serve them so devotedly that we anticipate their every wish. Indeed, we have the appearance of being so terrified of offending them, so anxious to serve their every whim, that anybody else observing us would think we must be either out of our minds, or struck dumb, so idiotic is our animal-like devotion. Then all the credit goes to the ladies, because they put on such haughty expressions and adopt such refined ways of speaking, that people who see nothing but their external appearance go in awe of them, and feel obliged to admire and love them. However, in private it is quite another matter. Then Love is the only judge of the way we behave, and we soon find out that they are just women, and we are just men. The title 'lady' is soon exchanged for 'mistress,' and her 'devoted servant' soon becomes her 'lover.' Hence the well-known proverb: 'loyal service makes the servant master.'"

"They have honor, just as men, who can give it to them or take it away, have honor; and they see the things we patiently endure; but it is therefore only right that our long-suffering should be rewarded when honor cannot be injured."

"But you are not talking about true honor," intervened Longarine, "true honor which alone gives true contentment in this world. Suppose that everybody said I was a decent woman, while I knew that the opposite was true—then their praise would only increase my dishonor and make me feel inwardly ashamed. Equally, if everybody criticized me, while I knew that I was completely innocent, I would only derive contentment from their criticism. For no one is truly contented, unless he is contented within himself."

"Well, whatever you all might say," said Geburon, "in my opinion Amador was the most noble and valiant knight that ever lived. I think I recognize him beneath his fictitious name, but since Parlamente has preferred not to disclose the identities of her characters, I shall not disclose them either. Suffice it to say that if it's the man I think it is, then he's a man who never experienced fear in his life, a man whose heart was never devoid of love or the desire for courageous action."

Then Oisille turned to them all and said: "I think it has been a delightful day, and if the remaining days are equally enjoyable, then we shall have seen how swiftly the time can be made to pass in refined conversation. See how low the sun is already. And listen to the Abbey bell calling us to vespers! It started ringing a while ago, but I didn't draw your attention to it because your desire to hear the end of the story was more devout than your desire to hear vespers!"

Upon these words they all got up and made their way to the Abbey, where they found the monks had been waiting for them for a good hour. After hearing vespers, they had their supper, and spent the evening discussing the stories they had heard that day and racking their brains for new stories to make the next day as enjoyable as the first. Then, after playing not a few games in the meadow, they retired to bed, thus bringing the first day to a happy and contented close.

FRANÇOIS RABELAIS
1495?–1553

François Rabelais created a distinctive blend of broad, lusty, and unsqueamish humor so influential that it took its creator's name: to this day, humor that blends the lofty and low, elegant and grotesque, erudite and physical is called *Rabelaisian*. Rabelais displays great artistic control over his work, which never shies away from the body: without breaking decorum, he introduces elements that elsewhere might seem crude or obscene (even a hiccup is inconceivable in Castiglione's Urbino). He creates a capacious narrative in which one character (the giant Gargantua) uses his dandruff for cannonballs, another (Panurge) proposes to rebuild the city walls of Paris out of women's genitals, and yet another (Alcofribas Nasier, the narrator) ventures into the mouth of the giant Pantagruel, wherein he discovers another world and converses with a farmer who is planting cabbages in the giant's tongue. Although irreverent, these scenarios allude to the epic tasks of founding city walls and colonizing new worlds. With bawdy humor, Rabelais both imitates and parodies the grandest of all literary genres, the imperial epic.

Rabelais, the son of a successful lawyer, was in all likelihood born around 1495 in the province of Touraine. He trained as a Franciscan monk and priest, gained proficiency in Greek, and came to the attention of Guillaume Budé, secretary to the king of France, as a promising young scholar. Rabelais experienced in 1523 the first of many dispiriting brushes with the Sorbonne, the college of powerful and conservative theologians at the University of Paris, when it banned the study of Greek in France and his books were confiscated. Disturbed at these antihumanist actions, he sought and gained authorization from Pope Clement VII to transfer to the less strict Benedictine order. He immortalized his hatred of the Sorbonne, which in future years would condemn with depressing regularity each of his books as they appeared, in his grotesque inventory of "sophistes, Sorbillans, Sorbonagres, Sorbonigènes, Sorbonicoles, Sorboniformes, Sorbonisecques, Niborcisans, Borsonisans, Saniborsans. . . ." Around 1527 he decided to pursue a career in medicine and gave up the monk's habit, an act for which he was not to receive papal absolution until 1536. Rabelais received the degree of bachelor of medicine from the University of Montpellier in 1530 and was by 1532 a successful physician at the important hospital of the Pont-du-Rhône at Lyon.

Under the pseudonym Alcofribas Nasier, an anagram for François Rabelais, he published a book about Pantagruel, the son he created for Gargantua, a gigantic folk hero of French oral tradition. He seems to have published his *Gargantua* just before a political nightmare, called the Affair of the Placards, in 1534. In this event, Reformers plastered antipapal posters in the main squares of Paris and even on the door of the king's bedchamber, alienating King Francis I from all reformers, even the peaceful Evangelicals associated with Rabelais and Francis's sister, Marguerite de Navarre. The king had previously been sympathetic to reform and had taken the unprecedented step of founding a nontheological university in France (the College of Royal Lecturers) where scholars taught Hebrew and Greek. After the affair, Francis I retaliated with persecutions of French Protestants. Rabelais felt threatened enough to leave his post at the hospital and disappear until the persecutions eased (due to interventions by the German princes and Pope Paul III). In 1537 Rabelais received his doctorate of medicine at Montpellier, where he later gave lectures, using the original texts of ancient Greek physicians such as Hippocrates. In the following years he traveled widely as doctor to Jean du Bellay, bishop of Paris, and his important brother, Seigneur de Langey. Rabelais even came to hold a minor post in the retinue of Francis I, and in 1538 he attended the meeting between Francis I and Charles V, the Holy Roman Emperor, that led to increased persecution of Reformers. Prepared to hold his religious opinions "up to but excluding the stake," Rabelais conformed.

In his definitive edition of *Gargantua and Pantagruel* of 1541, Rabelais toned down his lampoons of the Sorbonne, which nonetheless condemned the book, preventing its sale or possession. In 1544 he gained Francis I's permission to publish his third book, less flamboyant and optimistic than the first two. His efforts to appease the Sorbonne were unsuccessful, and when the third book appeared two years later, it too was condemned; at the time, Rabelais himself was in flight at Metz in Alsace (or on a secret mission—we do not know which). Encouraged by Chastillon, his last great patron and protector, and by the new king, Henry II, Rabelais published his fourth book in 1551; all too predictably it was condemned by the Sorbonne until the king lifted the ban. A fifth book, attributed to Rabelais but of unknown authorship, appeared in 1562–64. Tradition has it that in 1553 Rabelais died in Paris, in the Rue de Jardins.

As inspiration for his giant humanist, the title hero of *Pantagruel*, Rabelais chose a little devil from a medieval mystery play who provoked thirst wherever he went and liked to pour salt down the throats of drunkards. Pantagruel's father, Gargantua, explains that his son was born in a drought and that his name means "dominator of thirsts." Although Pantagruel loves good wine, his chief thirsts are intellectual. In the book's first chapters, Pantagruel completes his prodigious education along the lines recommended by his father and is well on his way to becoming an ideal humanist prince. Once educated and matured into a rational and generous-minded young prince, however, Pantagruel becomes less suited for the adventurous and mischievous middle of Rabelais's narrative than for its comparatively high-minded and educational beginning and conclusion. *Gargantua and Pantagruel* follows other Renaissance epics, using its middle chapters to test, question, and toy with the ideals of heroism and civility that epic narratives ultimately sanctify in a final battle and the founding of a new imperial city.

The playful and exploratory character at the center of *Pantagruel* is Panurge (Greek *pan + ourgos*, "he who will do all things"), a trickster, bad boy, and shadow version of Pantagruel. Panurge knows much, invents more, and stops at nothing. When Pantagruel first spies the noble but bedraggled figure, Panurge inspires the young giant's compassionate interest. He and his companions offer their help, and Panurge answers in no fewer than thirteen languages—three imaginary, three ancient, and seven modern. In pompous German, the language of the Antipodes (who dwell at the opposite side of the world), Italian, Scottish, vulgar Basque, "Lanternese," Dutch, Spanish, Danish, Hebrew, ancient Greek, "Utopian," and Latin, Panurge repeatedly laments that Pantagruel and his friends cannot understand him and begs for the food and drink they wish to give him (although the idiom of the Antipodes implies a threat to sodomize Pantagruel if he does not comply). When his would-be benefactors finally ask if he knows any French, Panurge delightedly reveals that he is a native, "born and brought up in the garden of France, that is Touraine"—precisely the birthplace of Rabelais himself.

Although not exactly a double for Rabelais, Panurge vibrantly embodies his author's intellectual and narrative tactics. He is an inventive and imitative trickster, an extroverted entertainer, and a multilingual scholar. He loves games and practical jokes that create an expansive sense of community (for all except the butts of his jokes). Eloquence of word and gesture comes easily to him. His rhetorical virtuosity is akin to that of Erasmus's Folly, although he takes far greater liberties in diction, ascending to high Ciceronian expression or descending to earthy obscenity at will. He achieves similar feats in the language of bodily gesture, notably in his sign-language debate with the daunting English scholar Thaumaste: by making liberal use of his enormous codpiece, which ornaments and enlarges the appearance of his penis, Panurge vanquishes his opponent. Farts, displays of incontinence, and phallic play are as expressive to Panurge as a classical or biblical allusion, a neologism (made-up word), or a cheerful obscenity.

Like Panurge, Rabelais mingles the earthy and grotesque with the lofty and elegant in *Gargantua and Pantagruel*: he chooses Virgil's *Aeneid* and Old Testament stories as his dominant models. Both of Rabelais's books juxtapose and mingle the erudite and bawdy, classical and folk, and high and low ("head" and "bottom" better suit the books' corporeal spirit). As the Russian critic Mikhail Bakhtin noted, Rabelais's epic seriousness cannot be properly understood apart from his presentation of the body, marked by its yawning mouth, flared nostrils, and anus. The lower regions of the Rabelaisian body—belly, buttocks, and genitals—prevail over the head or reason. Eating, drinking, defecating, farting, sweating, and nose-blowing pervade Rabelais's narratives. The gaping orifices mark the grotesque body's openness to sexual, economic, and emotional exchange and its stark contrast with the classical body, which is well-proportioned, closed, and upwardly focused. To an extent, Rabelais compares the classical body with classical epic and contrasts them with the grotesque body and the vital folk traditions that broaden the scope of his text.

The episodes from *Gargantua and Pantagruel* represented in this anthology include the bawdy and the epic: they begin with the education of the gigantic heroes in the humanistic arts and conclude with the ethical, learned giants' battle against tyrannical forces that threaten their fathers' kingdoms. When Pantagruel learns that a nation called the Dipsodes has invaded Gargantua's kingdom, he is forced to leave his "Dido" (a Parisian lady) and, like Virgil's Aeneas, choose the fatherland over love. Giant though he is, Pantagruel becomes a second David set in unequal battle with a new Goliath, the gigantic Werewolf who captains King Anarchy's army. Pantagruel's enemies represent terrifying worldly evils: anarchy means lawlessness, and the werewolf is a traditional figure for a tyrant. Rabelais uses the biblical story of David and Goliath (1 Samuel 17.4–51) to celebrate the fight of humanist enlightenment against menacing political abuses.

Gargantua, too, has an epic destiny in the first book (composed second and in many ways a revision of the first): his father's lands are under attack by a former ally, King Picrochole (Greek for "bitter bile"), and Gargantua returns home to defend them. Bad counselors have turned Picrochole from a friendly neighbor into an imperial marauder bent on conquering the world. They urge him to sail through the straits of Gibraltar and—in a Renaissance image of transgressive audacity—to "erect two columns more magnificent than those of Hercules in perpetual memory of [his] name." The Strait of Gibraltar, they promise him, "shall be called the Picrocholine Sea." The columns that these warmongering counselors have in mind were erected by Hercules, the legendary Greco-Roman demigod, to mark the ends of the Western world, beyond which no man should go (although Dante's bold Ulysses did). These pillars were also the emblem of the Holy Roman Emperor, Charles V, with whom Rabelais implicitly compares Picrochole. In *Gargantua*, Rabelais compares recent European history with an imperial epic in which Charles V and Francis I struggle for dominion in Europe and the title of emperor.

Yet Rabelais does not celebrate imperial expansion: Gargantua and his friends resist the would-be conquerors of their books, which form an anti-imperialistic epic. In his commitment to pacifism, Rabelais does not follow Virgil, who accepts the sacrifices of empire, but instead Erasmus, who believes that the only wars Christians should fight are defensive, a position that leaves out crusades and conquests.

After Gargantua and his friends defeat Picrochole's armies, they found a city that will cultivate the values for which they fought. They establish a community that affirms pacifist, liberal, humanistic values and name it the Abbey of Thélème, derived from the Greek word for "will" or "desire." The abbey's rules forbid men to live without women, and vice versa; ban clocks; and decree that all entrances and exits be voluntary (monks needed a papal dispensation to leave the monastery). Moreover, since monks and nuns usually took vows of chastity, poverty, and obedience, it was decided that in Thélème all inhabitants could marry with honor, be rich, and live wherever they wanted. On the great gate of Thélème, the architects inscribed a poem about Christian life, restored to its pristine state: hypocrites, bigots, liars, frauds, lawyers, and judges are cordially asked to stay away: they are dogs, frogs, fleas, and plague sores! "Sportsmen, lovers, friends," on the other hand, know and love the holy Word of God and are joyfully welcomed within the abbey's walls. Like the idealized court of Castiglione's Urbino, the abbey is populated with beautiful, intelligent, and learned youths who dress, converse, play games, value communal harmony, and relish the goal of married, sexual love. Designed to promote the simultaneous fulfillment of individual and communal will, Rabelais's abbey cultivates marriages that are free from conflicts of will and then releases the couples into the larger community, where the blissful unions lay the foundation of an equally harmonious society—one based on consent and the exercise of liberties.

Rabelais's abbey is not, however, a completely imagined world. It begins as a fantasy *negating* undesirable aspects of social reality in Europe rather than *creating* an independent social model. As Rabelais describes the abbey, he grows increasingly interested in the material conditions that produce the splendor of his fantasy world. His utopia, for example, follows the laws of supply and demand: as it turns out, there is a wing of low-lying buildings outside the abbey walls, where craftsmen import the wealth of the West Indies and set about their bourgeois trade of manufacturing luxuries for the wealthy. The more interested Rabelais grows in his abbey, the more it develops into an alluring paradox, beginning and ending in criticism of imperialism and colonization.

Few works in the Renaissance are as artistically and intellectually expansive as Rabelais's *Gargantua and Pantagruel*. The books are outrageous and serious, entertaining and thought-provoking. Rabelais's work takes the idea of "serious play" to such extremes that readers caught up in its rollicking humor may enter fully into the hedonistic escape that a brilliantly conceived fiction can offer. The same readers, drawn into its weighty artistic, intellectual, and sociopolitical thought, may at other times "forget" to laugh. Both are appropriate responses to Rabelais's extraordinary books.

PRONOUNCING GLOSSARY

The following list uses common English syllables and stress accents to provide rough equivalents of selected words whose pronunciation may be unfamiliar to the general reader.

Alcofribas Nasier: *ahl-coh-free-bahs'*
 nah-zyay'

Almain: *ahl-manh'*

Anatole: *ahn-ah-tohl'*

Artice: *ahr-tees*

Basché: *bah-shay'*

Beauce: *bohs*

Bonnivet: *bon-ee-vay'*

Boulogne: *boo-lun'*

Calaer: *cah-lah-ehr'*

Chantilly: *shawn-tee-yee'*

Chastillon: *shah-tee-yohnh'*

Chinon: *shee-nohn'*

Cryere: *cree-yehr'*

Fontainebleau: *fohn-ten-bloh'*

Gentilly: *zhawn-tee-yee'*

Grandgousier: *grawn-goo-zyay'*

Jean Thenaud: *zhawn tay-noh'*

Langeais: *lawnh-zhay'*

Languedoc: *lawnh-ge-dawk'*

Mesembriné: *may-zawn-bree-nay'*

Nantes: *nawnt*

Papeligosse: *pah-plee-gaws'*

Philippe des Marais: *fee-leep' day*
 mahr-ay'

Picrochole: *pee-craw-shol'*

Port-Huault: *por—yew-oh'*

rondelle: *rohn-del'*

Rouen: *roo-awnh'*

Rue de Jardins: *rew deu zhahr-danh'*

Saint Denis: *sanh deu-nee'*

Saint-Cloud: *sanh—cloo'*

Saint-Mars: *sanh–mahr'*

Saint-Martin d'Ainay: *sanh–mahr-tanh'
den-ay'*

Seine: *sen*

Thaumaste: *toh-mahst'*

Thélème: *tay-lem'*

Touraine: *too-ren'*

Vanves: *vahnv*

FROM GARGANTUA AND PANTAGRUEL[1]

From Book I

[*Education of a Giant Humanist*]

CHAPTER 14

How Gargantua Was Taught Latin by a Terribly Learned Philosopher

This subject disposed of, that good man Grandgousier was ravished with admiration, thinking about the good sense and marvelous comprehension of his son Gargantua. And so he said to his governesses:

"Philip, king of Macedonia, understood the good sense of his son Alexander by his skill in handling a certain horse, which was so terrible, so completely wild, that no one could even get up on its back. He bucked and threw everyone who tried to ride him, breaking the neck of one, the legs of another, cracking one man's skull and shattering another's jawbone. When Alexander went down into the Hippodrome (which was where they trained and exercised their horses) and analyzed the problem, he saw that the horse's desperate fury came, simply enough, from being afraid of his own shadow. Having come to this understanding, he jumped up on the horse's back and forced him to run straight toward the sun, so that his shadow fell behind him, and by this procedure turned the horse gentle and obedient. And that showed his father what divine understanding his son possessed, and he arranged that the boy be thoroughly trained by Aristotle, who was at that time considered the best philosopher in Greece.

"But I tell you that from this one discussion, which my son and I have just had, right here in front of you, I too understand that his understanding has something divine about it—so acute, subtle, profound, and yet serene—and will attain to a singularly lofty degree of wisdom, provided he is well taught. Accordingly, I wish to put him in the hands of some scholarly man who will teach him everything he is capable of learning. And to this end I propose to open my purse as freely as need be."

So they sent for a great philosopher, Maître Tubalcain Holofernes, who taught him the alphabet so well that he could say it backward, by heart, at which point he was five years and three months old. Then he read with the boy a Latin grammar by Donatus, plus a dull and well-meaning treatise on courtesy, and a long book by Bishop Theodulus, in which he proves that ancient mythology is all a heap of nonsense, and finally an exceedingly long

1. Translated by Burton Raffel.

poem in dreadfully moral quatrains.[2] All this took thirteen years, six months, and two weeks to accomplish.

Of course, it's also true that he learned to write in Gothic letters, and wrote out all his own books that way, since this was before the art of printing had been invented.

Most of the time he carried a large writing desk, weighing more than thirty tons, with a pencil box as big and heavy as the four great pillars of Saint-Martin d'Ainay, the old church in Lyons. And the inkpot hung down on huge iron chains, capable of supporting barrels and barrels of merchandise.

And then they read *De modis significandi,* "The Methods of Reasoned Analysis," with the commentaries of Broken Biscuithead, Bouncing Rock, Talktoomuch, Galahad, John the Fatted Calf, Balogny, Cuntprober, and a pile of others. And this took more than eighteen years and six months. And by then Gargantua knew it all so well that, if you asked him, he could recite every single line, backward, proving to his mother that he had the whole thing at his fingertips and, most important of all, that *de modis significandi non erat scientia,* the methods of reasoned analysis were neither reasonable nor a science.

Then they read that great book *Calculation,* surely the longest almanac ever compiled: this took another sixteen years and two months. And then, suddenly, his teacher died, being four hundred and twenty years old: it was the pox that carried him off.

So they brought in another old cougher, Maître Blowhard Birdbrain, with whom he read Bishop Huguito of Ferrara, Eberhard de Bethune's *Greekish-nessisms,* Alexander de Villedieu's barbarous Latin grammar, Remigius's *Petty Doctrines* and also his *What's What,* a charming discourse set in question-and-answer form, the *Supplement to All Supplements,* a fat glossary of saints' lives and the like, Sulpicius's long, long poem on the psalms and death, Seneca's *De quatuor virtutibus cardinalibus,* The Four Cardinal Virtues (which wasn't by Seneca at all), Passavantus's *Mirror of True Penitence,* and the same author's *Sleep in Peace,* a collection of sermons chosen to make happy days still happier—and he also read other tough birds of the same feather. And in reading all this he became quite as wise as any blackbird ever baked in a pie.

CHAPTER 15

How Gargantua Got to Study with Other Teachers

By that point his father could see that although he was studying as hard as he could, and spending all his time at it, he didn't seem to be learning much and, what's worse, he was becoming distinctly stupid, a real simpleton, all wishy-washy and driveling.

When he complained of this to Don Philippe des Marais, viceroy of Pape-ligosse,[3] he was told that it would be better for Gargantua to learn nothing at all than to study such books with such teachers, whose learning was noth-

---

2. The books mentioned in this chapter were actually part of the educational curriculum that Rabelais is here satirizing.   3. Probably an allusion to a real person. Rabelais's method is to take real people and introduce them into his fantastic world; he also mentions real places and draws on local lore.

ing but stupidity and whose wisdom was nothing but gloves with no hands in them—empty. They were specialists in ruining good and noble spirits and nipping the flowering of youth in the bud.

"To show you what I mean," he said, "take some modern youngster, who has only been studying for two years. If he doesn't show better judgment, better use of words, better ability to analyze and discuss than your son, as well as greater ease and courtesy in dealing with the world, then call me a fat-head from Brenne."

Grandgousier was delighted and told him to do exactly that.

That night, at supper, des Marais introduced one of his young pages, a young fellow named Rightway (in Greek, Eudemon), who was from Ville-gongis, near Saint-Genou. And he was so well-groomed, so beautifully dressed, so clean and neat in every respect, so courteous in his bearing, that he more nearly resembled a little angel than a human being. And des Marais said to Grandgousier:

"See this child? He's only twelve years old. Shall we see, if you care to, what a difference there is between the learning of your bird-chirping old philosophers and modern youngsters like this?"

Grandgousier liked the idea, and told the page to give them a demonstration of what he knew. Then Rightway, after asking his master's permission to proceed, stood on his feet, his hat in his hands, his face open, his lips red, his eyes confident, his glance fixed on Gargantua with a modesty appropriate to his age, and began both to praise and to glorify Grandgousier's son, first for his virtue and his good manners, second for his knowledge, third for his nobility, fourth for his physical beauty, and then, fifth, sweetly urged him always to honor his father, who had taken such pains to have him well brought up, finally begging Gargantua to consider Master Rightway the most insignificant of his servants, for the boy asked no other gift from the heavens but the grace of pleasing Gargantua by some cheerfully rendered service. And all of this was spoken with such extraordinarily tactful gestures, with a pronunciation so clear, a voice so eloquent, and in language so elegant and such good Latin, that he more nearly resembled a kind of ancient Gracchus, or Cicero, or Ennius than a young person of his own time.

But all Gargantua could do was weep like a cow. He hid his face behind his hat, and it was no more possible to draw a word from him than to get a fart from a dead donkey.

All of which made his father so furious that he wanted to kill Maître Blowhard Birdbrain. But des Marais checked him with a well-turned word of warning, so neatly administered that it cooled his anger. But he ordered that Blowhard Birdbrain be paid what he was owed and allowed to guzzle like a philosopher. And when he'd drunk to his heart's content, he was to be told to go to the devil.

"It won't cost me a thing," he said, "not today at least, if he gets so drunk that he dies of it, like an Englishman."

Maître Blowhard Birdbrain left the house. Grandgousier sought des Marais's advice about who might be available to be Gargantua's new teacher, and the two of them decided that Powerbrain (in Greek, Ponocrates), Rightway's teacher, would be the best man for the job. The three of them would then travel to Paris, the better to understand how the young men of France were pursuing their studies.

CHAPTER 16

How Gargantua Was Sent to Paris, Riding an Enormous Brood Mare,
Which Waged War against the Cow Flies of Beauce

Now, at this same time Fayoles, fourth king of Numidia, happened to send Grandgousier, all the way from Africa, the biggest, tallest brood mare anyone had ever seen. And the most monstrous, too (it being well known that Africa always brings forth new things), for it was the size of six elephants and it had toes, like Julius Caesar's horse; its ears hung down like a Languedoc goat, and it had a horn sticking out of its ass. For the rest, it had a kind of burned chestnut hide, mottled with gray. Most impressive of all was its ghastly tail, because—give a pound, take a pound—it was as big as the old ruin of Saint-Mars, near Langeais (which is forty feet high), and every bit as wide, with hair as closely woven as the tassels on an ear of corn.

And if that strikes you as astonishing, what do you think of those amazing Scythian rams, weighing in at more than thirty pounds apiece, and those Syrian sheep, which (if Jean Thenaud is telling the truth) have an ass so heavy, so long and massive, that they have to tie a supporting cart to its rear end so it can get about at all. You haven't got anything like it, you lowland ass bangers!

It came by sea, in three Genoan schooners and a man-of-war, to the port of Les Sables-d'Olonne, in Talmont.

When Grandgousier saw it:

"This is exactly the right thing," he said, "to carry my son to Paris. Now, God be thanked, everything will turn out all right. Someday he'll surely be a great scholar. If it weren't for our friends the animals, we'd all have to live like philosophers."

The next day, but of course only after having drunk their fill, Gargantua, his new teacher Powerbrain, and all his attendants, together with the young page Rightway, took to the road. And because the weather was calm and moderate, his father had them make soft laced boots for Gargantua. (That great bootmaker Babin tells me they go by the name of buskins.)

So they went merrily down the highway, laughing and singing, until they had almost reached Orleáns. There they entered a large forest, ninety miles long and forty miles wide. The place swarmed with horrible cow flies, millions of them, and wasps and hornets, too, the sort that were true highway robbers for all poor mares and mules and horses. But Gargantua's mare took an appropriate revenge for all the outrages her species had suffered, playing a trick that those insects had never expected. Suddenly, as they entered the wood and the flies and wasps began their assault, she whipped out her tail and swatted them so vigorously that in fact she knocked down the entire forest. Left, right, here, there, length and width, over and under, she smashed those trees like a mower cutting grass, until finally there were neither any trees nor any insects, but just a nice flat stretch of land, which is all you can see to this day.

Gargantua watched this performance with immense delight. But he didn't want to sound vainglorious, so all he said to his companions was, "This is fine, but I don't want to boast." And ever since that part of the country has been known as Beauce. But all they got to put in their open mouths was their own yawns—in memory of which the gentlemen of Beauce (and everyone knows how poor they've always been) still dine by yawning and opening and closing their empty mouths, which they've grown to like, especially since it helps them spit.

When at last they reached Paris, Gargantua spent two or three days resting and recovering from their journey, drinking and chatting with the townsfolk and asking what scholars happened to be in the city at that time and what wine Parisians liked to drink.

* * *

CHAPTER 21

[*Gargantua's Studies, and His Way of Life, according to His Philosophical Teachers*]

Some days after the bells had been put back, and in recognition of Gargantua's courtesy in thus restoring them, the citizens of Paris offered to feed and maintain his mare for as long as he might like, an offer which Gargantua found most acceptable. So the mare was put to pasture in Fontainebleau Forest. I don't think she is still there.

Gargantua was absolutely determined to study under Powerbrain. To begin with, however, Powerbrain directed his new pupil to proceed exactly as he always had, the better to understand how, over such a long period of time, his former teachers had turned him into such a fop, such a fool and ignoramus.

Accordingly, Gargantua lived just as he usually did, waking up between eight and nine (whether it was daylight or not), exactly as his old teachers had prescribed. And they cited the words of King David: *Vanum est vobis ante lucem surgere,* It does you no good to wake before day begins.[4]

So he fooled about, swaggering, wallowing away the time in his bed (the better to enliven his animal spirits), and then dressed himself as the season dictated. But what he really liked to put on was a great long gown of heavy wool, lined with fox fur. And then he combed his hair as that great Ockhamist philosopher Jacob Almain always did—that is, with four fingers and a thumb, because his teachers used to say that, in this world of ours, to pay any more attention than that to your hair—or to washing and keeping yourself clean— was simply a waste of time.

Then he shat, pissed, vomited, belched, farted, yawned, spat, coughed, sighed, sneezed, and blew his nose abundantly. Then he put away a good breakfast, the better to protect himself against the dew and the bad morning air: good fried tripe, some nice broiled steak, several cheerful hams, some good grilled beef, and several platters of bread soaked in bouillon.

Powerbrain objected, observing that, fresh out of bed and before he'd been exercising, he hardly needed to take in so much refreshment. Gargantua replied:

"What! Haven't I already done enough exercise? I turned over in bed six or seven times before I got up. Isn't that enough? That's exactly what Pope Alexander used to do, and he was following the advice of his great Jewish

4. Psalm 127.2: "It is vain for you to rise up early, to sit up late, to eat the bread of sorrows: for so he giveth his beloved sleep."

doctor and astrologer, Bonnet de Lates. And he lived until he died, too, in spite of those who did not wish him well. This is what my prior teachers got me used to doing, saying that breakfast helped you develop your memory: that was why they started drinking at breakfast, too. I think it's marvelous—and it starts me off so well that I eat an even better supper. And Maître Tubalcain Holofernes (who was right at the head of his class, here in Paris) used to say there was no point at all just to running well: the idea was to leave early enough. So true good health for all of us doesn't require, does it, that we gulp it down, cup after cup after cup, like ducks, but certainly that we start to drink in the morning—*unde versus,* as the little poem says:

> To wake up early in the morning isn't the point:
> You've got to wet your whistle and bend that joint."

And so, after a hearty breakfast, he went to church, where they brought him, in a huge basket, a great fat prayer book, all wrapped in velvet, so heavily oiled, with such heavy clasps, and on such luxurious parchment that it must have weighed at least twenty-five hundred pounds. And then they heard twenty-six or maybe thirty masses. And then his private chaplain would come, dressed like a society swell, and with his breath nicely fortified by wine. He and Gargantua would mumble through the litany, thumbing the rosary so carefully that not a single bead ever fell to the ground.

As he walked out of church, they brought in a heavy-wheeled log carrier and delivered for his personal use an entire cask of carved-wood rosaries, each of them as round around as the rim of a man's hat. And as he and his chaplain strolled through the cloister of the church, and its galleries and gardens, they worked at their beads, saying more prayers than sixteen hermits.

Then he put in a scant half-hour of studying, keeping his eyes on his book. But, like the character in Terence's play, his soul was in the kitchen.[5]

Then he pissed his urinal full, sat down to table, and—being naturally of a calm and imperturbable disposition—began his meal with several dozen hams, smoked beef tongues, caviar, fried tripe, and assorted other appetizers.

Meanwhile, four of his servants began to toss into his mouth, one after the other—but never stopping—shovelfuls of mustard, after which he drank an incredibly long draft of white wine, to make things easier for his kidneys. And then, eating whatever happened to be in season and he happened to like, he stopped only when his belly began to hang down.

His drinking was totally unregulated, without any limits or decorum. As he said, the time to restrict your drinking was only when the cork soles of your slippers absorb enough so they swell half a foot thick.

* * *

CHAPTER 23

How Gargantua Was So Well Taught by Powerbrain That He Never Wasted a Single Hour of the Day

Once Powerbrain understood Gargantua's vicious way of life, he began to reflect on other—and better—ways of instructing him in humanistic matters.

5. *The Eunuch,* line 816.

But for the first few days he did not make any changes, realizing that nature would not allow abrupt shifts without cataclysmic violence.

Accordingly, to begin his work in the best way possible, he sought the advice of a wise physician, Holygift, with whom he discussed how to set Gargantua on a better path. The learned doctor, proceeding according to his profession's canonical rules, first purged the young man with a sovereign remedy for madness, Anticyrian hellebore, which powerful herb quickly cleaned away all the deterioration and perverse habits to which his brain had succumbed. This procedure had the advantage, also, of making Gargantua forget everything he had learned from his early teachers, just as in ancient times Timotheus[6] did with disciples who'd studied under other musicians.

To help in the good work, Powerbrain introduced Gargantua to some of Paris's truly learned scholars. In trying to be like them, he came to understand their spirit, wanting to acquire knowledge and to make something of himself.

And then he got him into such a way of studying that no hour in the day was wasted: all his time was spent in pursuit of humanistic learning and honest knowledge.

Accordingly, Gargantua now woke up at four in the morning. He would be given a massage, while a portion of the holy Scriptures was read aloud to him, in a high, clear voice, with precise and accurate pronunciation. A young page named Reader, a native of Basché, was given this task. The subject, and also the argument, of this lesson often led Gargantua into reverence and adoration of God, the majesty and marvelous wisdom of whom had thus been exhibited to him, and into prayer and supplication.

Then he would go off and, in some private place, permit the natural result of his digestive process to be excreted. While he was thus occupied, his teacher would repeat what had been read to him, clarifying and explaining the more obscure and difficult points.

Coming back, they would examine and reflect on the state of the heavens: was everything as it had been when they'd seen the sky the night before? into what constellations had the sun newly entered, and likewise the moon?

And then he was dressed and combed, his hair was properly done, and he was equipped and perfumed, while all the time the lessons he'd been given the day before were repeated for him. He recited them by heart, showing by some practical and compassionate illustrations that he understood their meaning. This often lasted two or three hours, though ordinarily they stopped when he was fully dressed.

Then he was read to for three solid hours.

After which they went outdoors, always discussing the meaning of what had been read, and went to the park or somewhere near it, where they played various games, especially three-handed palm ball, giving their bodies the same elegant exercise they had earlier given their souls.

Their games were entirely free: they stopped whenever they felt like stopping—usually when they'd worked up a sweat or when they grew tired. Then they had a vigorous massage, and were wiped clean; they'd change their shirts and, walking quietly, would go to see if dinner was ready. And as they waited they'd recite, clearly and eloquently, remembered portions of the lesson.

6. Of Miletus, famous musician of the time of Alexander the Great (356–323 B.C.E.).

However, Sir Appetite arrived, and when they could they seated themselves at the table.

Some entertaining story of ancient heroism was read to them, at the start of the meal, until wine was poured in Gargantua's cup.

Then, if they liked the idea, the reading was resumed, or else they'd begin to chat happily. At the beginning of this new regime, they talked about virtue, proper behavior, the nature and effect of everything placed on their table that day: bread, wine, water, salt, meat, fish, fruit, herbs, roots, and about the preparation of these things. In so doing, Gargantua soon learned all the appropriate passages from Pliny, Athenaeus, Dioscorides, Julius Pollux, Galen, Porphyry, Oppian, Polybius, Heliodorus, Aristotle, Claudius Aelian,[7] and others. In order to be sure they had their authorities right, they'd often have the books brought right to the table. And what was said became so clearly and entirely fixed in Gargantua's memory that no doctor alive understood anything like as much as he did.

Then, talking about the lessons read that morning, and finishing their meal with some quinced sweet, Gargantua would clean his teeth with a bit of fresh green mastic twig. He'd wash his hands and his eyes with good fresh water, and give thanks to God with sweet hymns of praise for His munificence and divine kindness. And cards were brought, not for playing games of chance, but to learn a thousand gracious things and new inventions, all founded in arithmetic.

And in this way Gargantua developed a genuine liking for the numerical science. Every day, after both dinner and supper, he passed his time in arithmetical games just as pleasantly as when he'd been in the habit of playing at dice or cards. Indeed, he came to understand both the theory and the practice of arithmetic so well that Cuthbert Tunstal,[8] the Englishman who had written so much on the subject, was obliged to admit that, truly, in comparison to Gargantua, all he understood was a pack of nonsense.

But arithmetic wasn't the end of it, for they went on to other mathematical sciences, like geometry, astronomy, and music. While waiting for their meal to be digested and properly absorbed, they worked out a thousand pleasant geometrical figures, and shaped appropriate instruments, and practiced astronomical laws in the same way.

Later, they had a wonderful good time, singing four- and five-part rounds, and sometimes singing variations on some melody that was a delight to their throats.

As for musical instruments, Gargantua learned to play the lute, the clavier, the harp, the transverse flute as well as the recorder, the viol, and also the trombone.

As this hour passed, digestion was indeed accomplished, and so he proceeded to purge himself of his natural excrement. Then he at once returned to his main studies for three hours or even more, in order to repeat the morning's lesson and also to continue with whatever book had been set for him. And he practiced writing in the Italian and the Gothic alphabets, and also drawing.

And then they'd go back to their rooms, and along with them went a young

---

7. Some of the most famous scientific authors of antiquity. The new curriculum, exacting as it is, reflects a less "medieval" type of learning than was embodied in his earlier course of study. See also the enumeration of authors in chap. 14. 8. Author of the treatise *The Art of Computation* (*De arte supputandi*, 1522).

gentleman from Touraine, Squire Gymnast by name, who was teaching Gargantua the arts of knighthood.

After changing his clothes, Gargantua would mount a battle horse, a traveling steed, a Spanish stallion, an Arabian racehorse, and a light, quick horse, and ride a hundred laps, making his mount fairly fly through the air, jump ditches, leap over fences, make quick circular turns, both to the right and to the left.

Nor did he break his lance, for it is sheer nonsense to say, "I broke ten lances in battle." Any carpenter could do as much. Real glory comes from breaking ten of your enemies' with one of your own. So, with his steel-tipped, solid, firm lance he learned to break down a door, crack open a suit of armor, uproot a tree, strike right through the center of a hoop, knock a knight's saddle right off his horse, and carry away a coat of mail or a pair of armored gloves. And all the time he was himself in armor, from his head right down to his toes.

When it came to marching his horse in rhythm, or making the animal obey his commands, there was simply no one better. Even Cesare Fieschi, the famous equestrian acrobat, seemed no better than a monkey on horseback, in comparison. He was especially good at leaping from one horse to another, without ever setting foot on the ground—the horses were known as leapers—and he could do this from either side, lance erect, without stirrups. Without any reins or bridle he could make a horse do anything he wanted it to do. In short, he was accomplished at everything useful in military matters.

Some days he exercised with the battle-ax, which he could wield like a razor, swinging it so powerfully, slicing it around in a circle so deftly, that he was ranked a knight at arms, passing every sort of trial and declared fit for any battle.

And then he'd practice with the pickax, or at wielding the two-handed sword, or with the short sword (so perfect for thrusting and parrying), and the dagger—sometimes wearing armor, sometimes not, or using a shield, or wearing a cape, or carrying a small wrist shield, known as a *rondelle*.

He hunted deer—stag and doe and fallow buck—bears, wild boar, hares, partridge, pheasant, buzzards. He played with the big kickball, making it bound high in the air, sometimes with his foot, sometimes with his fist. He fought and ran and leaped and jumped—but not a mere three-foot hop and leap, or a high jump in the German style—because, as Gymnast said, jumps of that sort were useless and of no good whatever, when it came to real war—but he'd jump great wide ditches, go flying over a hedgerow, climb six paces up a wall, and thus get in through a window as high off the ground as a lance.

He swam in deep water, breaststroke, backstroke, sidestroke, using his entire body or only his legs, or with one hand high in the air and holding a book, crossing the Seine River without getting a page wet. He swam with his cloak in his teeth, as Julius Caesar did (says Plutarch). Then, pulling himself right into a boat with just one hand, he'd throw himself back into the water, head first, going all the way down to the bottom, sinking among the rocks and swimming to great depths, plunging down to all sorts of chasms and deep abysses. Then he'd turn the boat, and steer it, sometimes quickly, sometimes slowly, now downstream, now upstream, sometimes bringing it to a halt by pressing it against a milldam, guiding it with one hand, his other wielding a great oar or raising the sail. He'd climb up the guide ropes, right to the top of the mast, and run out along the spars. He'd adjust the compass, brace the bowlines, tighten the helm.

Leaving the water, he'd go directly up a mountain and then come right down again. He'd climb trees like a cat, jumping from one to the other like a squirrel, tearing down thick branches as if he were another Milo of Croton. With a pair of sharp-pointed daggers and a couple of good marlinespikes, he'd climb to the top of a house exactly like a rat, then leap down so expertly that the drop wouldn't cause him so much as a twinge.

He threw the javelin, and the iron bar, the millstone, the boar spear, the hunting spear, the spiked halberd. He drew the longbow like an archer, pulled crossbows taut (though this was usually done with a winch), sighted a rifle right against his eye (though usually it had to be rested against the shoulder), set up and mounted cannon, centering them right in on target, aimed them so they could knock a stuffed parrot off a pole, pointing them straight up a mountain or right down into a valley, directing their fire up ahead or to the side or, like the ancient Parthians, back behind him.

They would attach a rope cable to some high tower, hanging down to the ground, and he would climb this, hand over hand, then come down so strongly and with such confidence that he might just as well have been strolling along some nice, flat meadow.

They would rig up a long pole, supported on each side by a tree, and he'd hang from it by his hands, going this way and that without his feet ever touching the ground—and at such a speed that, even running on flat ground, it would have been impossible to catch him.

And in order to exercise his chest and lungs, he would shout like all the devils in hell. Once, I heard him call to Rightway, from the Saint Victor Gate all the way across Paris to Montmartre. Even bull-throated Stentor,[9] at the battle of Troy, could not shout so loud.

To toughen his nerves, they made him two huge molded lead weights, cast in the shape of salmon, each just over eighty thousand pounds: he called them his dumbbells. He'd lift one in each hand, starting from the ground, and hold them both high up over his head—and then he'd keep them there, not moving a muscle, for three-quarters of an hour or even more. This was literally unmatchable strength!

No one was stronger, not in barriers or tug-of-war or any of the games. When it was his turn, he stood his ground so firmly that he could afford to let the most adventurous try to move him a single inch from his place, exactly as Milo of Croton used to do—and in imitation of whom he would clasp a pomegranate in his hand and offer it to anyone who could take it from him. Nor would he permit the fruit to be damaged in the attempt.

Having thus spent his time, he'd have another massage, then clean himself and change his clothes, returning with a smile and, strolling through meadows and other grassy spots, he'd turn his attention to trees and plants, examining them in the light of what the ancients wrote—Theophrastus, Dioscorides, Marinus, Pliny, Nicander, Aemilius Macer, and Galen.[1] He and his companions would fill their hands with herbs and roots and flowers, then bring it all back to their lodgings, where a young page, Rootgatherer, was in

9. The loud-voiced herald in the *Iliad* 5.   1. Greek and Roman scientists.

charge of all such matters, including care of the hoes, picks, rakes, spades, shovels, and everything else needed for the proper care of growing things.

And once they were back at their lodgings, and while waiting for their supper, they would repeat selected passages from what they had read, earlier, and also what they had discussed at table.

Note, please, that although dinner was a sober and even frugal meal, at which Gargantua would eat only just enough to control the growling in his stomach, supper was a great abundant affair. He would consume everything he needed to sustain and properly nourish himself, which is exactly the sort of diet prescribed by any good, knowing doctor, though there are plenty of medical hacks (in constant dispute, of course, with learned academic philosophers) who advise exactly the opposite.

Gargantua continued his lessons all during supper, or for as long as he felt in the mood. And then he would turn to good solid discussion, literate, informed, useful.

After a final grace had been said, they would turn to music, singing, the harmonious playing of various instruments, or to pleasant card and dice games. And there they would stay, having a fine time, often amusing themselves until it was time to go to bed. And sometimes they would go visiting the houses of learned people, or perhaps those newly returned from foreign countries.

When night had truly arrived, but before they climbed into bed, they would stand in their lodgings, in the spot from which the sky could be most closely observed, and compare notes about any comets they might see, and the configuration of the stars, their location and aspect, their oppositions and conjunctions.

And then Gargantua and Powerbrain would briefly recapitulate, according to the Pythagorean fashion, everything Gargantua had read and seen and understood, everything he had done and heard, all day long.

They would both pray to God their Creator, worshiping, reaffirming their faith, glorifying Him for His immense goodness and thanking Him for all they had been given, and forever placing themselves in His hands.

And then they would go to sleep.

CHAPTER 24

[What Gargantua Did When It Was Rainy]

When the weather turned rainy and bad, the time before dinner went exactly as usual, except that Gargantua had a good bright fire lit, to help moderate the intemperate air. But after dinner, in place of exercise, they would stay indoors and, according to the best therapeutic approach, amuse themselves by baling hay, sawing and splitting wood, and threshing the grain stored in the barn. Then they would study the art of painting and sculpture, or else (following ancient custom) play knucklebones, an entertainment about which Leonicus Thomaeus has written so well—and a game which Andreas Lascaris,[2] teacher and friend of Erasmus, and my good friend too, has played with such pleasure. And while they played they turned over in

---

2. André-Jean de Lascaris (ca. 1445–ca. 1535), librarian to King Francis I and a friend of Rabelais's. Leonicus Thomaeus (d. 1531), a Venetian and professor at Padua.

their mind all the passages from classical authors in which the game is either mentioned or used as a metaphor.

In the same way, they would either go to watch the work at metal foundries, or the casting of cannon, or go to observe jewelers, goldsmiths, and those who cut precious stones, or else alchemists and coin makers, or tapestry weavers, silk weavers, velvet makers, watchmakers, mirror makers, printers, organ manufacturers, dyers, and other craftsmen of that sort. And treating all of them to wine, they learned from the mouths of these masters what their various trades and inventions were all about.

They would go to hear public lectures, solemn convocations, and the careful orations, declamations, and pleadings of wellborn lawyers, or the sermons of evangelical preachers.

He went to all the places where swordsmanship was practiced and taught, and tested himself against those who taught it, in every aspect of fencing and with all the sorts of swords and foils known. And he demonstrated to them that he knew as much as they did, and more.

Instead of going off to collect herbs and examine plants and flowers, they would go to drugstores, herb sellers, and other apothecaries, and contemplate with great care the fruits, roots, leaves, gums, seeds, and all the exotic unguents, and then how they were prepared and diluted for more effective use.

He went to see the jugglers and clowns, the magicians and those who peddled wonderful, half-magical remedies, and contemplated their games and tricks, their somersaults and smooth patter, especially those famous mountebanks from Chauny, in Picardy—born with a silver tongue, every one of them, able to sell water to people swimming in a lake or firewood to those who live inside a volcano.

They would return for supper, and eat more sparingly than on other days— in particular, meats that tend to dry and tame the body. This was made necessary by the excessive humidity in the air, which under the circumstances there was no way to avoid. These simple dietary measures corrected that natural imbalance and saved them from being bothered by the loss of their usual exercise.

And this was how Gargantua's life was regulated. He kept to these rules every day, and he benefited—to be sure!—as a young man of his years can, a youth with good sense. All regular exercise, no matter how hard it may at first seem, becomes pleasant and easy and finally great good fun, more like a royal pastime than a scholar's plodding.

In spite of which, and in order to allow him some relief from such a whirlwind way of life, Powerbrain made sure that Gargantua took off at least one day a month, some day of great clarity and calm brightness. They would leave Paris early in the morning and go to one of the pleasant villages beloved of all Parisian students—Gentilly, perhaps, or Boulogne on the Seine, or Montrouge, or Pont-Charenton, or Vanves, or Saint-Cloud. And they would spend the entire day there, just as happily as they could manage, laughing, telling jokes, drinking gaily, playing, singing, dancing, lying on their backs in beautiful meadows, hunting for sparrows' nests, catching quail, and fishing for frogs and crayfish.

But even on this day spent without books and reading, they didn't completely neglect higher matters, because even lying there in the lovely meadows they would recite from memory cheerful verses from Virgil's *Georgics*, from Hesiod, from Politian's *Rusticus* (Farming), or some pleasant Latin epigrams, which they'd then turn into equally pleasant poems in their own language.

And when they feasted they would not simply mix their wine and water. Instead, as Cato advises in his *Country Matters*, and Pliny too, they would use a cup of ivy wood and wash the wine in a full basin of water, then pour it back out with a funnel.[3] And they would pour the water from one glass to another and construct tiny automatic engines that seemed to work of their own accord, like automatons.

[The Abbey of Thélème]

CHAPTER 52

How Gargantua Built the Abbey of Desire (Thélème) for Brother John

The only one still left to be provided for was the monk.[4] Gargantua wanted to make him abbot of Seuilly, but the monk refused. Gargantua also offered him the abbey of Bourgueil or that of Saint-Florent, whichever best pleased him—and said he could have both those rich, old Benedictine cloisters, if he preferred that.[5] But the monk answered him in no uncertain terms: he wanted neither to govern nor to be in charge of other monks:

"And how," he asked, "should I govern others, when I don't know how to govern myself? If you really think I've done something for you, and I might in the future do something to please you, grant me this: establish an abbey according to my plan."

The request pleased Gargantua, so he offered him the whole land of Thélème, alongside the river Loire, two leagues from the great forest of Port-Huault. And the monk then asked Gargantua to establish this abbey's rules and regulations completely differently from all the others.

"Obviously," said Gargantua, "it won't be necessary to build walls all around it, because all the other abbeys are brutally closed in."

"Indeed," said the monk, "and for good reason. Whenever you've got a whole load of stones in front and a whole load of stones in back, you've got a whole lot of grumbling and complaining, and jealousy, and all kinds of conspiracies."

Moreover, since some of the cloisters already built in this world are in the habit, whenever any woman enters them (I speak only of modest, virtuous women), of washing the ground where she walked, it was decreed that if either a monk or a nun happened to enter the abbey of Thélème, they would scrub the blazes out of the places where they'd been. And since everything is completely regulated, in all the other cloistered houses, tied in and bound down, hour by hour, according to a fierce schedule, it was decreed that in Thélème there would not be a single clock, or even a sundial, and that work would be distributed strictly according to what was needed and who was available to do it—because (said Gargantua) the worst waste of time he knew

3. Both Cato's *On Farming (De re rustica)* 109 and Pliny's *Natural History* 16.63 suggest an ivy-wood cup as a means to detect water in wine.   4. Brother John of the Funnels, the muscular and highly unconventional monk who has had a major part in helping the party of Gargantua's father win the mock-heroic war against the arrogant Picrochole.   5. A satiric allusion to the custom of accumulating church livings.

of was counting the hours—what good could possibly come of it?—and the biggest, fattest nonsense in the whole world was to be ruled by the tolling of a bell rather than by the dictates of common sense and understanding.

Item: because in these times of ours women don't go into convents unless they're blind in one eye, lame, humpbacked, ugly, misshapen, crazy, stupid, deformed, or pox-ridden, and men only if they're tubercular, low born, blessed with an ugly nose, simpletons, or a burden on their parents . . .

("Oh yes," said the monk, "speaking of which: if a woman isn't pretty and she isn't good, what sort of path can she cut for herself?"

"Straight into a convent," said Gargantua.

"To be sure," said the monk, "especially with a scissors and a needle.")

. . . it was decreed that, in Thélème, women would be allowed only if they were beautiful, well formed, and cheerful, and men only if they were handsome, well formed, and cheerful.

Item: since men were not allowed in convents, unless they sneaked in under cover of darkness, it was decreed that in Thélème there would never be any women unless there were men, nor any men unless there were women.

Item: because both men and women, after they'd entered a cloister and served their probationary year, were obliged to spend the entire rest of their lives there, it was decided that men and women who came to Thélème could leave whenever they wanted to, freely and without restriction.

Item: because monks and nuns usually took three vows—chastity, poverty, and obedience—it was decided that in Thélème one could perfectly honorably be married, that anyone could be rich, and that they could all live wherever they wanted to.

As an age limitation, women should be allowed in at any time from ten to fifteen, and men from twelve to eighteen.

CHAPTER 53

How the Abbey of Desire (Thélème) Was Built and Endowed

In order to build and equip the abbey, Gargantua gave two million seven hundred thousand eight hundred and thirty-one gold pieces. Further, until everything had been completed, he assigned the yearly sum of one million six hundred and sixty thousand gold pieces, from the tolls on the river Dive, payable in funds of an unimaginable astrological purity. To endow and perpetually maintain the abbey he gave two million three hundred thousand and sixty-nine English pounds in property rentals, tax-free, fully secured, and payable yearly at the abbey gate, to which effect he had written out all the appropriate deeds and grants.

The building was hexagonal, constructed so that at each angle there was a great round tower sixty feet in diameter, and each of the towers was exactly like all the others. The river Loire was on the north side. One of the towers, called Artice (meaning "Arctic," or "Northern"), ran down almost to the riverbank; another, called Calaer (meaning "Lovely Air"), was just to the east. Then came Anatole (meaning "Oriental," or "Eastern"), and Mesembriné (meaning "Southern"), and then Hesperia (meaning "Occidental," or "Western"), and finally Cryere (meaning "Glacial"). The distance between each of the towers was three hundred and twelve feet. The building had six floors, counting the subterranean cellars as the first. The second or ground floor had a high vault, shaped like a basket handle. The other floors were stuccoed in a circular pattern, the way they do such things in Flanders; the roof was of fine slate, the coping being lead-decorated with small figurines and animals, handsomely colored and gilded; and there were rainspouts jutting out from the walls, between the casement windows, painted all the way to the ground with blue and gold stripes and ending in great pipes which led down to the river, below the building.

This was all a hundred times more magnificent than the grand chateau at Bonnivet, or that at Chambord, or that at Chantilly,[6] because it had nine thousand three hundred and thirty-two suites, each furnished with an antechamber, a private reading room, a dressing room, and a small personal chapel, and also because each and every room adjoined its own huge hall. Between each tower, in the middle of the main building, was a spiral staircase, its stairs made of crystal porphyry and red Numidian marble and green marble struck through with red and white, all exactly twenty-two feet wide and three fingers thick, there being twelve stairs between each landing. Further: each landing had a beautiful double arch, in Greek style, thus allowing light to flood through and also framing an entryway into overhanging private rooms, each of them just as broad as the stairway itself. The stair wound all the way to the roof, ending there in a pavilion. Off the stair, on each side, one could come to a great hall; the stair also led the way to the private suites and rooms.

Between the tower called Artice and that called Cryere were great beautiful reading rooms, well stocked with books in Greek, Latin, Hebrew, French, Italian, and Spanish, carefully divided according to the languages in which they had been written.

In the center of the main building, entered through an arch thirty-six yards across, stood a marvelous circular ramp. It was fashioned so harmoniously, and built so large, that six men-at-arms, their lances at the ready, could ride clear up to the top of the building, side by side.

Between the tower called Anatole and that called Mesembriné were beautiful galleries, large and open, painted with scenes of ancient heroism, episodes drawn from history, and strange and fascinating plants and animals. Here, too, just as on the side facing the river, were a ramp and a gate. And on this gate was written, in large antique letters, the poem which follows:

CHAPTER 54

[The Inscription on the Great Gate of Thélème]

Hypocrites, bigots, stay away!
Old humbugs, puffed-up liars, playful
Religious frauds, worse than Goths
Or Ostrogoths (or other sloths):
No hairshirts, here, no sexy monks,   5
No healthy beggars, no preaching skunks,
No cynics, bombasts ripe with abuse:
Go peddle them elsewhere, your filthy views.

6. Châteaux built in the early and middle years of the 16th century. Rabelais is again mixing realism with fantasy.

Your wicked talk
Would clutter our walks
Like clustering flies: 10
But flies or lies,
We've no room for your cries,
Your wicked talk.

Hungry lawyers, stay away!   15
People eaters, who grab while praying,
Scribes and assessors, and gouty judges
Who beat good men with the law's thick cudgels
And tie old pots to their tails, like dogs,
We'll hop you up and down like frogs,   20
We'll hang you high from the nearest tree:
We're decent men, not legal fleas.

    Summons and complaints
    Don't strike us as quaint,
    And we haven't got time   25
    For your legal whine
    As you hang from the line
    Of your summons and complaints.

Money suckers, stay away!
Greedy gougers, spending your days   30
Gobbling up men, stuffing your guts
With gold, you black-faced crows, busting
Your butts for another load of change,
Though your cellar's bursting with rotten exchange.
O lazy scum, you'll pile up more,   35
Till smiling death knocks at your door.

    Inhuman faces
    With ghastly spaces
    That no heart can see,
    Find other places: 40
    Here you can't be,
    You inhuman faces.

Slobbering old dogs, stay away!
Old bitter faces, old sour ways,
We want you elsewhere—the jealous, the traitors,   45
The slime who live as danger creators,
Wherever you come from, you're worse than wolves:
Shove it, you mangy, scabby oafs!
None of your stinking, ugly sores:
We've seen enough, we want no more.   50

    Honor and praise
    Fill all our days:
    We sing delight
    All day, all night:

These are our ways: 55
Honor and praise.

But you, you, you can always come,
Noble knights and gentlemen,
For this is where you belong: there's money
Enough, and pleasure enough: honey   60
And milk for all, and all as one:
Come be my friends, come join our fun,
O gallants, sportsmen, lovers, friends,
Or better still: come, gentlemen.

    Gentle, noble,   65
    Serene and subtle,
    Eternally calm;
    Civility's balm
    To live without trouble,
    Gentle, noble.   70

And welcome, you who know the Word
And preach it wherever the Word should be heard:
Make this place your holy castle
Against the false religious rascals
Who poison the world with filthy lies: 75
Welcome, you with your eyes on the skies
And faith in your hearts: we can fight to the death
For truth, fight with our every breath.

    For the holy Word
    Can still be heard,   80
    That Word is not dead:
    It rings in our heads,
    And we rise from our beds
    For that holy Word.

And welcome, ladies of noble birth,   85
Live freely here, like nowhere on earth!
Flowers of loveliness, with heaven in your faces,
Who walk like angels, the wisdom of ages
In your hearts: welcome, live here in honor,
As the lord who made this refuge wanted: 90
He built it for you, he gave it gold
To keep it free: Enter, be bold!

    Money's a gift
    To give, to lift
    The souls of others: 95
    It makes men brothers
    In eternal bliss:
    For money's a gift.

CHAPTER 55

How They Lived at Thélème

In the middle of the inner court was a magnificent fountain of beautiful alabaster. Above it stood the three Graces, holding the symbolic horns of abundance: water gushed from their breasts, mouths, ears, eyes, and every other body opening.

The building which rose above this fountain stood on giant pillars of translucent quartz and porphyry, joined by archways of sweeping classical proportions. And inside there were handsome galleries, long and large, decorated with paintings and hung with antlers and the horns of the unicorn, rhinoceros, hippopotamus, as well as elephant teeth and tusks and other spectacular objects.

The women's quarters ran from the tower called Artice all the way to the gates of the tower called Mesembriné. The rest was for men. Right in front of the women's quarters was a kind of playing field, an arena-like space set just between the two first towers, on the outer side. Here too were the horse-riding circle, a theater, and the swimming pools, with attached baths at three different levels, all provided with everything one could need, as well as with an endless supply of myrtle water.

Next to the river was a beautiful pleasure garden, and in the middle of it stood a handsome labyrinth. Between the other two towers were fields for playing palm ball and tennis. Alongside the tower called Cryere were the orchards, full of fruit trees of every description, carefully arranged in groups of five, staggered by rows of three. At the end was a great stretch of pastures and forest, well stocked with all kinds of wild animals.

Between the third pair of towers were the target ranges for muskets, bows, and crossbows. The offices were in a separate building, only one story high, which stood just beside the tower called Hesperia, and the stables were just beyond there. The falcon house was situated in front of the offices, staffed with thoroughly expert falconers and hawk trainers: every year supplies of every sort of bird imaginable, all perfect specimens of their breed, were sent by the Cretans, the Venetians, and the Sarmatian-Poles: eagles, great falcons, goshawks, herons and cranes and wild geese, partridge, gyrfalcons, sparrow hawks, tiny but fierce merlins, and others, so well trained and domesticated that, when they left the chateau to fly about in the fields, they would catch everything they found and bring everything to their handlers. The kennels were a bit farther away, in the direction of the woods and pastures.

All the rooms in all the suites, as well as all the smaller private rooms, were hung with a wide variety of tapestries, which were regularly changed to suit the changing seasons. The floors were covered with green cloth; the beds with embroidery. Every dressing room had a mirror of Venetian crystal, framed in fine gold, decorated around with pearls, and so exceedingly large that one could in truth see oneself in it, complete and entire. Just outside the doorways, in the ladies' quarters, were perfumers and hairdressers, who also attended to the men who visited. Every morning, too, they brought rose-water to each of the ladies' rooms, and also orange and myrtle water—and brought each lady a stick of precious incense, saturated with all manner of aromatic balms.

CHAPTER 56

How the Men and Women Who Dwelled at Thélème Were Dressed

In the beginning, the ladies dressed themselves as they pleased. Later, of their own free will, they changed and styled themselves all as one, in the following way:

They wore scarlet or yellow stockings, bordered with pretty embroidery and fretwork, which reached exactly three fingers above the knee. Their garters were colored like their bracelets (gold, enameled with black, green, red, and white), fastened both above and below the knee. Their shoes, dancing pumps, and slippers were red or purple velvet, with edges jagged like lobsters' claws.

Over the chemise they wore a handsome corset, woven of rich silk shot through with goat hair. Over this they wore taffeta petticoats, in white, red, tan, gray, and so on, and on top of this petticoat a tunic of silver taffeta embroidered with gold thread, sewn in tight spirals—or if they were in the mood and the weather was right, their tunics might be of satin, or damask, or orange-colored velvet, or perhaps tan, green, mustard gray, blue, clear yellow, red, scarlet, white, gold, or silvered linen, with bordered spirals, or embroidery, according to what holiday was being celebrated.

Their dresses, again according to the season, were of golden linen waved with silver, or red satin decorated with gold thread, or taffeta in white, blue, black, or tan, or silk serge, or that same rich silk shot through with goat hair, or velvet slashed with silver, or silvered linen, or golden, or else velvet or satin laced with gold in a variety of patterns.

Sometimes, in the summer, they wore shorter gowns, more like cloaks, ornamented in the ways I have described, or else full-length capes in the Moorish style, of purple velvet waved with gold and embroidered with thin spirals of silver, or else with heavier gold thread, decorated at the seams with small pearls from India. They were never without beautiful feathers in their hair, colored to match the sleeves of their gowns and always spangled in gold. In the winter they wore taffeta dresses, colored as I have described, lined with lynx fur, or black skunk, or Calabrian marten, or sable, or some other precious pelt.

Their prayer beads, rings, neck chains, and collar pieces were made of fine gems—red garnets, rubies, orange-red spinels, diamonds, sapphires, emeralds, turquoises, garnets, agates, green beryls, pearls, and fat onion pearls of a rare excellence.

They covered their heads, once again, as the season demanded: in winter, in the French style, with a velvet hood hanging down in the back like a pigtail; in spring, in the Spanish style, with a lace veil; in summer, in the Italian mode, with bare ringed hair studded with jewels, except on Sundays and holidays, when they used the French fashion, which seemed to them both more appropriate and more modest.

And the men wore their fashions, too: their stockings were of light linen or serge, colored scarlet, yellow, white, or black; their breeches were velvet, in the same colors (or very nearly), embroidered and patterned however they pleased. Their jackets were of gold or silver cloth, in velvet, satin, damask, taffeta, once again in the same colors, impeccably patterned and decorated and worn. Their shoes were laced to the breeches with silken thread, colored as before, each lace closed with an enameled gold tip. Their undervests and cloaks were of golden cloth or linen, or silver cloth, or velvet embroidered however they liked. Their gowns were as costly and beautiful as the women's, with silk belts, colored to match their breeches. Each of them wore a handsome sword, with a decorated hilt, the scabbard of velvet (the color matching their stockings), its endpiece of gold and heavily worked jewelry—and their daggers were exactly the same. Their hats were of black velvet, thickly garnished with golden berries and buttons, and the feathered plumes were white, delicately spangled in gold rows and fringed with rubies, emeralds, and the like.

But there was such a close fellowship between the men and the women that they were dressed almost exactly alike, day after day. And to make sure that this happened, certain gentlemen were delegated to inform the others, each and every morning, what sort of clothing the women had chosen to wear that day—because of course the real decisions, in this matter, were made by the women.

Although they wore such well-chosen and rich clothing, don't think these women wasted a great deal of time on their gowns and cloaks and jewelry. There were wardrobe men who, each day, had everything prepared in advance, and their ladies' maids were so perfectly trained that everyone could be dressed from head to toe, and beautifully, in the twinkling of an eye. And to make sure that all of this was perpetually in good order, the wood of Thélème was surrounded by a vast block of houses, perhaps half a league long, good bright buildings well stocked and supplied, and here lived goldsmiths, jewelers, embroiderers, tailors, specialists in hammering and filamenting gold and silver, velvet makers, tapestry weavers, and upholsterers, and they all worked at their trades right there alongside Thélème, and only for the men and women who dwelled in that abbey. All their supplies, metals and minerals and cloths, came to them courtesy My Lord Shipmaster (Nausiclète, in Greek), who each year brought in seven boats from the Little Antilles, the Pearl and Cannibal islands, loaded down with gold ingots, raw silk, pearls, and all sorts of gemstones. And any of the fat pearls which began to lose their sparkle and their natural whiteness were restored by feeding them to handsome roosters (as Avicenna recommends), just as we give laxatives to hawks and falcons.

CHAPTER 57

How the Men and Women of Thélème Governed Their Lives

Their lives were not ordered and governed by laws and statutes and rules, but according to their own free will. They rose from their beds when it seemed to them the right time, drank, ate, worked, and slept when they felt like it. No one woke them or obliged them to drink, or to eat, or to do anything whatever. This was exactly how Gargantua had ordained it. The constitution of this abbey had only a single clause:

DO WHAT YOU WILL

—because free men and women, wellborn, well taught, finding themselves joined with other respectable people, are instinctively impelled to do virtuous things and avoid vice. They draw this instinct from nature itself, and they name it "honor." Such people, if they are subjected to vile constraints, brought down to a lower moral level, oppressed and enslaved and turned away from that noble passion toward which virtue pulls them, find themselves led by that same passion to throw off and break any such bondage, just as we always seek out forbidden things and long for whatever is denied us.

And their complete freedom set them nobly in competition, all of them seeking to do whatever they saw pleased any one among them. If he or she said, "Let's drink," everyone drank. If he or she said, "Let's play," they all played. If he or she said, "Let's go and have fun in the meadows," there they all went. If they were engaged in falconry or hunting, the women joined in, mounted on their good tame horses, light but proud, delicately sporting heavy leather gloves, a sparrow hawk perched on their wrists, or a small falcon, or a tiny but fierce merlin. (The other birds were carried by men.)

All of them had been so well educated that there wasn't one among them who could not read, write, sing, play on harmonious instruments, speak five or six languages, and write easy poetry and clear prose in any and all of them. There were never knights so courageous, so gallant, so light on their feet, and so easy on their horses, knights more vigorous, agile, or better able to handle any kind of weapon. There were never ladies so well bred, so delicate, less irritable, or better trained with their hands, sewing and doing anything that any free and worthy woman might be asked to do.

And for this reason, when the time came for anyone to leave the abbey, whether because his parents had summoned him or on any other account, he took one of the ladies with him, she having accepted him, and then they were married. And whatever devotion and friendship they had shown one another, when they lived at Thélème, they continued and even exceeded in their marriage, loving each other to the end of their days just as much as they did on the first day after their wedding. . . .

From Book II

[Pantagruel: Birth and Education]

CHAPTER 2

The Birth of the Very Formidable Pantagruel

When he was four hundred and ninety-four, plus four more, Gargantua begat his son Pantagruel on his wife, the daughter of the king of the Amaurotes, in Utopia. Her name was Bigmouth, or Babedec,[1] as we say in the provinces, and she died giving birth to the baby: he was so immensely big, and weighed so incredibly much, that it was impossible for him to see the light without snuffing out his mother.

Now, to truly understand how he got his name, which was bestowed on him at the baptismal font, you must be aware that in the year of his birth

---

1. Names taken from Sir Thomas More's *Utopia*. Literally, "no place," the word *utopia* has become synonymous with "ideal country."

there had been such a fearful drought, all across the continent of Africa, that it had not rained for more than thirty-six months, three weeks, four days, thirteen hours, and a little bit over, and the sun had been so hot, and so fierce, that the whole earth had dried up. It wasn't any hotter even in the days of the prophet Elijah than in that year, for not a tree on earth had a leaf or a bud. Grass never turned green, rivers dried up, fountains went dry; the poor fish, deprived of their proper element, flopped about on the ground, crying horribly; since there was no dew to make the air dense enough, the birds could not fly; dead animals lay all over the fields and meadows, their mouths gaping wide—wolves, foxes, stags, wild boars, fallow does, hares, rabbits, weasels, martens, badgers, and many, many others. And it was no better for human beings, whose lives became pitiful things. You could see them with their tongues hanging out, like hares that have been running for six solid hours. Some of them threw themselves down into wells; others crawled into a cow's belly, to stay in the shade (Homer calls them *Alibantes*, desiccated people[2]). Everything everywhere stood still, like a ship at anchor. It was painful to see how hard men worked to protect themselves from this ghastly change in nature: it wasn't easy to keep even the holy water in churches from being used up, though the pope and the College of Cardinals expressly ordered that no one should dare to dip from these blessed basins more than once. All the same, when a priest entered his church you'd see dozens and dozens of these poor parched people come crowding around behind him, and if he blessed anyone the mouths would all gape open to snatch up every single drop, letting nothing fall wasted to the ground—just like the tormented rich man in Luke, who begged for the relief of cool water.[3] Oh, the fortunate ones, in that burning year, whose vaults were cool and well stocked!

The Philosopher tells us, asking why seawater is salty, that once, when Phoebus Apollo let his son Phaeton drive his gleaming chariot,[4] the boy had no idea how to manage it, nor any notion how to follow the sun's proper orbit from tropic to tropic, and drove off the right road and came so close to the earth that he dried up all the countries over which he passed, and burned a great swath through heaven, called by the philosophers *Via Lactea*, the Milky Way, but known to drunkards and lazy louts as Saint John's Road. But the fancy-pants poets say it's really where Juno's milk fell, when she suckled Hercules. Then the earth got so hot that it developed an enormous sweat, which proceeded to sweat away the entire ocean, which thus became salty, because sweat is always salty. And you can see for yourself that this is perfectly true, because all you have to do is taste it—or the sweat of pox-ridden people when they're put in steam baths and work up a great sweat. Try whichever you like: it doesn't matter to me.

It was almost exactly like that, in this year of which I write. One Friday, when everyone was saying prayers and making a beautiful procession, and litanies were being said, and psalms chanted, and they were begging omnipotent God to look mercifully down on them in their desolation, they could suddenly see great drops of water coming out of the earth, exactly as if some-

---

2. The allusion to Homer is apparently mistaken, but *Alibantes*—possibly derived from Alibas, a dry river in hell—is used by other ancient writers with reference to the dead or the very old.   **3.** Luke 16.24: "And he cried and said, Father Abraham, have mercy on me, and send Lazarus, that he may dip the tip of his finger in water, and cool my tongue; for I am tormented in this flame."   **4.** The chariot of the sun.

one were sweating profusely. And the poor people began to rejoice, as if this were something truly useful, some of them saying that since there wasn't a drop of liquid in the air from which one could have expected rain, the very ground itself was making up for what they lacked. Others, more scholarly, said that this was rain from the opposite side of the earth, as Seneca explains in the fourth book of *Questionum naturalium*, in which he speaks of the source and origin of the river Nile. But they were deceived: once the procession was over, and they went back to collect this precious dew and drink down a full glass, they found that it was just pickle brine, even worse to drink, and even saltier, than seawater.

And it was precisely because Pantagruel was born that very day that his father named him as he did: *Panta* in Greek means "all," and *Gruel* in Arabic means "thirsty," thus indicating that at the hour of his birth the whole world was thirsty—and he saw, prophetically, that someday his son would be lord of the thirsty, for this was shown to him at that same time and by a sign even more obvious. For when the child's mother was in labor, and all the midwives were waiting to receive him, the first thing that came out of her womb was sixty-eight mule drivers, each one leading a pack mule loaded with salt by its halter, after which came nine one-humped camels loaded with hams and smoked beef tongue, and then seven two-humped camels loaded with pickled eels, followed by twenty-five carts all loaded with onions, garlic, leeks, and spring onions. The midwives were frightened out of their wits. But some of them said to the others:

"Here's God's plenty. It signifies that we shouldn't either hold back, when we drink, or, on the other hand, pour it down the way the Swiss do. It's a good sign: these are truly wining signs."

And while they were gabbling and cackling about such trivialities, out popped Pantagruel, as hairy as a bear, at which one of them pronounced prophetically:

"He's been born all covered with fur, so he'll do wonderful things, and if he lives he'll live to an immense age."

[Father's Letter from Home]

CHAPTER 8

How Pantagruel, at Paris, Received a Letter from His Father, Gargantua, with a Copy of That Letter

Pantagruel studied hard, of course, and learned a great deal, because his brain was twice normal size and his memory was as capacious as a dozen kegs of olive oil. While he was thus occupied in Paris,[5] one day he received a letter from his father, which read as follows:

"My very dear son,

"Among the gifts, the graces and the prerogatives with which from the very beginning our sovereign Creator and God has blessed and endowed

---

5. Like his father before him, Pantagruel has been sent to Paris to study. The letter, patterned after Ciceronian models of eloquence, summarizes Rabelais's view of an ideal education, and generally illustrates the attitude of the Renaissance intellectual elite toward culture.

human nature, that which seems to me uniquely wonderful is the power to acquire a kind of immortality while still in this our mortal state—that is, while passing through this transitory life a man may perpetuate both his name and his race, and this we accomplish through the legitimate issue of holy wedlock. And by that means we partially reestablish that which we lost through the sin of our first parents, Adam and Eve, to whom it was declared that, because they had not obeyed the commands of God their Creator, they would know death and in dying would utterly destroy the magnificent form in which mankind had been shaped.

"But this seminal propagation permits what the parents lose to live on in their children, and what dies in the children to live on in the grandchildren, and so it will continue until the hour of the Last Judgment, when Jesus Christ will return to the hands of God the Father His purified and peaceful kingdom, now utterly beyond any possibility or danger of being soiled by sin. And then all the generations and all the corruptions will come to an end, and all the elements will be taken from their endless cycle of transformations, for the peace so devoutly desired will be achieved, and will be perfect, and all things will be brought to their fit and proper ending.

"So I have very fair and just cause to be thankful to God, my preserver, for having permitted me to see my hoary old age blossoming once again in your youth. Whenever, at His pleasure, He who rules and governs all things, my soul leaves this human dwelling place, I will not consider myself entirely dead, but simply transported from one place to another, for in you, and by you, my visible image lives in in this world, wholly alive, able to see and speak to all honorable men, and all my friends, just as I myself was able to do. I confess that my life on this earth, though I have had divine help and divine grace to show me the way, has not been sinless (for indeed we are all sinners and continually beg God to wash away our sins), and yet it has been beyond reproach.

"Just as the image of my flesh lives on in you, so too shine on the ways of my soul, or else no one would think you the true keeper and treasure of our immortal name, and I would take little pleasure in seeing that, because in that case the least part of me, my body, would live on, and the best part, my soul, in which our name lives and is blessed among men, would be decayed and debased. Nor do I say this because I have any doubt about your virtue, which I have long since tested and approved, but simply to encourage you to proceed from good to still better. And the reason I write to you now is not so much to ensure that you follow the pathways of virtue, but rather that you rejoice in thus living and having lived, and find new joys and fresh courage for the future.

"To consummate and perfect that task, it should be enough for you to remember that I have held back nothing, but have given help and assistance as if I had no other treasure in the world but to someday see you, while I still lived, accomplished and established in virtue, integrity, and wisdom, perfected in all noble and honorable learning, and to be able to thus leave you, after my death, as a mirror representing me, your father—perhaps in actual practice not so perfect an image as I might have wished, but certainly exactly that in both intention and desire.

"But though my late father of worthy memory, Grandgousier, devoted all his energy to those things of which I might take the fullest advantage, and from which I might acquire the most sensible knowledge, and though my own effort matched his—or even surpassed it—still, as you know very well, it was neither so fit nor so right a time for learning as exists today, nor was there an abundance of such teachers as you have had. It was still a murky, dark time, oppressed by the misery, unhappiness, and disasters of the Goths, who destroyed all worthwhile literature of every sort. But divine goodness has let me live to see light and dignity returned to humanistic studies, and to see such an improvement, indeed, that it would be hard for me to qualify for the very first class of little schoolboys—I who, in my prime, had the reputation (and not in error) of the most learned man of my day. Nor do I say this as an empty boast, though indeed I could honorably do so in writing to you—for which you have the authority of Cicero in his book *On Old Age,* and also the judgment of Plutarch, in his book *How a Man May Praise Himself without Fear of Reproach.* No, I say these things to make you wish to surpass me.

"For now all courses of study have been restored, and the acquisition of languages has become supremely honorable: Greek, without which it is shameful for any man to be called a scholar; Hebrew; Chaldean; Latin.[6] And in my time we have learned how to produce wonderfully elegant and accurate printed books,[7] just as, on the other hand, we have also learned (by diabolic suggestion) how to make cannon and other such fearful weapons. The world is full of scholars, of learned teachers, of well-stocked libraries, so that in my opinion study has never been easier, not in Plato's time, or Cicero's, or Papinian's.[8] From this day forward no one will dare to appear anywhere, or in any company, who has not been well and properly taught in the wisdom of Minerva. Thieves and highwaymen, hangmen and executioners, common foot soldiers, grooms and stableboys, are now more learned than the scholars and preachers of my day. What should I say? Even women and girls have come to aspire to this marvelous, this heavenly manna of solid learning. Old as I am, I have felt obliged to learn Greek, though I had not despised it, as Cato[9] did: I simply had no leisure for it, when I was young. And how exceedingly glad I am, as I await the hour when it may please God, my Creator, to call me to leave this earth, to read Plutarch's *Morals,* Plato's beautiful *Dialogues,* Pausanias's *Monuments,* and Athenaeus's *Antiquities.*[1]

"Which is why, my son, I strongly advise you not to waste your youth, but to make full use of it for the acquisition of knowledge and virtue. You are in Paris, you have your tutor, Epistemon: you can learn from them, by listening and speaking, by all the noble examples held up in front of your eyes.

"It is my clear desire that you learn languages perfectly, first Greek,

---

6. The languages that are the instruments of classical learning are listed along with those useful for the study of the Old Testament of the Bible.   7. Printing from movable type was invented in Europe about the middle of the fifteenth century.   8. Jurisconsult of the time of Emperor Septimius Severus (reigned 193–211 C.E.).   9. Plutarch's life of Cato is the source of the notion that he despised Greek.   1. The works of Pausanias and Athenaeus were standard sources of information on ancient geography, art, and everyday life.

as Quintilian decreed, and then Latin.[2] And after that Hebrew, for the Holy Bible, and similarly Chaldean and Arabic. I wish you to form your literary style both on the Greek, following Plato, and on the Latin, following Cicero. Let there be nothing in all of history that is not clear and vivid in your mind, a task in which geographical tltxs will be of much assistance.

"I gave you some awareness of the liberal arts—geometry, arithmetic, and music—when you were still a child of five and six. Follow them further, and learn all the rules of astronomy. Ignore astrology and its prophecies, and all the hunt for the philosopher's stone which occupied Ramon Lully[3]—leave all those errors and vanities alone.

"As for the civil law, I wish you to know by heart all the worthy texts: deal with them and philosophy side by side.

"I wish you to carefully devote yourself to the natural world. Let there be no sea, river, or brook whose fish you do not know. Nothing should be unknown to you—all the birds of the air, each and every tree and bush and shrub in the forests, every plant that grows from the earth, all the metals hidden deep in the abyss, all the gems of the Orient and the Middle East—nothing.

"Then carefully reread all the books of the Greek physicians, and the Arabs and Romans, without turning your back on the talmudic scholars or those who have written on the Cabala. Make free use of anatomical dissection and acquire a perfect knowledge of that other world which is man himself. Spend several hours each day considering the holy Gospels, first the New Testament and the Apostles' letters, in Greek, and then the Old Testament, in Hebrew.

"In short, plumb all knowledge to the very depths, because when you are a grown man you will be obliged to leave the peace and tranquillity of learning, and acquire the arts of chivalry and warfare, in order to defend my house and lands and come to the aid of our friends if in any way they are attacked by evildoers.

"And soon I shall ask you to demonstrate just how much you have learned, which you can do in no better way than by publicly defending, in front of the entire world and against all who may come to question you, a thesis of your own devising. And continue, as you have been doing, to frequent the company of those leaned men who are so numerous in Paris.

"But since, as the wise Solomon says, wisdom can find no way into a malicious heart, and knowledge without self-awareness is nothing but the soul's ruin, you should serve, and love, and fear God. Put all your thought in Him, and all your hopes, and by faith which has been shaped by love unite yourself with Him so firmly that sin will never separate you away. Be ever watchful of the world's wicked ways. Never put your heart in vanity, for ours is a transitory existence and the Word of God lives forever. Help your neighbors and love them as you love yourself. Honor your teachers. Avoid the company of those you do not desire to imitate;

2. In his *Institutio oratoria* 1.1.12 he recommends studying Greek before Latin. 3. Raymond Lully (13th century), Spanish philosopher who dabbled in magic.

do not take in vain the blessings God has given you. And when, finally, you know that you have learned all that Paris can teach you, return to me, so that I may look on you and, before I die, give you my blessing.

"My son, may the peace and grace of our Lord be with you. *Amen.*

"Written from Utopia, this seventeenth day of the month of March.

Your father,
GARGANTUA"

After receiving and reading this letter, Pantagruel was filled with new zeal, positively on fire to learn more than ever before—so much so that, had you seen him at his studies, and observed how much he learned, you would have declared that he was to his books like a fire in dry grass, burning with such an intense and consuming flame.

[The World in Pantagruel's Mouth]

CHAPTER 18

How a Great English Scholar Wanted to Dispute with Pantagruel, But Was Beaten by Panurge

At about the same time, a scholar named Thaumaste (in Greek, "Wonderful"), hearing all the fuss over Pantagruel's incomparable learning, and seeing how famous he'd become, came from England with the sole intention of meeting Pantagruel and finding out if his knowledge matched his reputation. Arriving in Paris, he immediately went to Pantagruel's lodgings, which were at the abbey of Saint Denis.[4] At that moment, Pantagruel was in the garden with Panurge, walking up and down and philosophizing after the fashion of the ancient Peripatetics.[5] Thaumaste quivered with fear, seeing how huge Pantagruel was, but then he greeted him in customary style and said, with great courtesy:

"How true it is, as Plato, prince of philosophers, says, that if the image of wisdom and learning is a physical matter, visible to human eyes, it excites the whole world with admiration. The very word of such accomplishments, spread through the air and received by the ears of those who study and love philosophy, prevents them from taking any further rest, stirring them, urging them to hurry to where they may find and see the person in whom knowledge has erected its temple and given forth its oracles. Which was clearly demonstrated for us by the queen of Sheba, who traveled from the farthest reaches of the Orient and the Persian Sea to visit the house of the wise Solomon and hear his sage words;[6]

"and by Anacharsis,[7] who came from Scythia only to see Solon;

"and by Pythagoras, who journeyed to the prophets of Memphis;[8]

"and by Plato, who visited the Egyptian magi, and also Archytas of Tarentum;[9]

---

4. A college for Benedictines.   5. Followers of the Greek philosopher Aristotle, who wandered about in the Lyceum of ancient Athens while lecturing.   6. 2 Chronicles 9.1–12; the Queen of Sheba came from southern Arabia to test Solomon's legendary wisdom.   7. Scythian prince, renowned for his travels and wisdom (6th century B.C.E.).   8. Capital of ancient Egypt. *Pythagoras:* Greek philosopher of the 6th century B.C.E.   9. Said to be the founder of mathematics (4th century B.C.E.).

"and by Apollonius of Tyana,[1] who went to the Caucasian mountains, who journeyed among the Scythians, the Massagetae, and the Indians, who sailed down the great river Physon, all the way to the land of the Brahmans, to see Hiarchos, and who traveled in Babylonia, Chaldea, the land of the Medes, Assyria, Parthia, Syria, Phoenicia, Arabia, Palestine, and Alexandria, and in Ethiopia, too, to see the Gymnosophists.[2]

"We have another example in Livy,[3] to see and hear whom certain studious folk came to Rome from the farthest boundaries of France and Spain.

"I am not so presumptuous as to include myself among the ranks of such illustrious men. But I deeply desire to be thought of as a student and lover not only of humanistic learning but also of men of such learning.

"And, in fact, hearing of your priceless learning, I have left my country, my parents, and my home and come here, indifferent to the weariness of the journey, the anxiety of a voyage by sea, the strangeness of different lands, solely for the purpose of seeing and conferring with you about certain passages of philosophy, and geometrical divination, and also of cabalistic knowledge,[4] passages of which I am myself unsure and, about which I cannot rest content. If you can resolve these difficulties for me, I will be your servant from this day forth, and not only me but all my posterity, for I command no other gifts sufficient to repay you.

"I will put all of this in writing, and tomorrow I shall notify all the learned men of this city, so that we can discuss these matters publicly and in their presence.

"But I intend that our discussions, and any disputes in which we may engage, shall be conducted as follows. I do not wish to argue any bare-bones *for* and *against*, as do the besotted sophistical minds[5] of this and other cities. Nor do I wish to dispute after the fashion of academics, by declamation, or by the use of numbers, as Pythagoras did and as Picodella Mirandola,[6] at Rome, wished to do. I wish to dispute simply by signs, without a word being spoken, for these are matters so intricate and difficult that, as far as I am concerned, mere human speech will not be adequate to deal with them.

"May it please Your Magnificence to accept my invitation and join me, at seven in the morning, in the great hall of the College of Navarre."

When he had finished, Pantagruel said to him, courteously:

"My dear sir, how could I deny anyone the right to share in whatever blessings God has given me? All good things come from Him, and surely He wishes us to spread the celestial manna we have from Him among men both worthy and capable of receiving true learning—among whose number in our time, as I know very well, you belong in the very first rank. Let me say to you, therefore, that you will find me ready at any time to accede to any of your requests, to the extent that my poor powers may enable me, and well aware as I am that it is I who should be learning from you. And so, as you have declared, we will discuss these doubts of yours together, and hunt as hard as we can for their resolution, diving even as far as the bottom of that

---

1. An ascetic wandering teacher of the early Christian period.   2. Ancient sect of Hindu ascetics.
3. Titus Livius (59 B.C.E.–17 C.E. or 64 B.C.E.–12 C.E.), Roman historian.   4. Lore from an occult system of mystical speculation of rabbinical origin.   5. Sophists, for Thaumaste, are specious, overly subtle rhetoricians.   6. Pico della Mirandola (1463–1494), Italian humanist scholar. Pythagoras (6th century B.C.E.) discovered the mathematical basis of the musical intervals.

bottomless well in which, according to Heraclitus,[7] the truth is said to be hidden.

"And I highly commend the style of argument you have proposed, that is to say, by using signs, without any words, for thus you and I will truly understand one another, free from the sort of hand clapping and applause produced during their discussions by these puerile sophists, whenever one party has the better of the argument.

"So, then, tomorrow I shall appear without fail at the time and place you have requested. I ask of you only that, as between us, there may be no contentiousness and fuss, and that we seek neither honor nor men's applause, but only the truth."

To which Thaumaste replied:

"Sir, may God keep you in His grace. I thank Your High Magnificence for being so willing to condescend to my humble talents. Until tomorrow, I leave you in His hands."

"Farewell," said Pantagruel.

Gentlemen, you who may read this book, please don't imagine that anyone was ever more exalted, more transported, that whole night long, than Thaumaste and Pantagruel. Thaumaste told the concierge at his lodgings, in the abbey of Cluny, that in his entire life he had never been so incredibly thirsty:

"It feels to me," he said, "as if Pantagruel has me by the throat. Order me wine, if you please, and make sure that there's enough fresh water so I can lubricate the roof of my mouth."

And for his part, Pantagruel felt himself carried away, so that all that night he did nothing but tear through:

The Venerable Bede's *De numeris et signis,* Numbers and Signs;
Plotinus's *De inenarrabilibus,* Inexpressible Things;
Proclus's *De sacrificio et magia,* Sacrifices and Magic;
Artemidorus's *Per onirocriticon,* On the Interpretation of Dreams;
Anaxagoras's *Peri semion,* On Signs;
Dinarius's *Peri aphaton,* Unknowable Things;
Philistion's books;
Hipponax's *Peri anecphoneton,* Things Better Left Undiscussed;

And many, many others, so that finally Panurge said to him:

"My lord, stop all this intellectual groping and go to bed, for I can see you're far too agitated—indeed, such an extravagance of thinking and straining may well make you feverish. But first, have twenty-five or thirty good drinks, then go to bed and sleep comfortably—for tomorrow I will answer our English friend, I will argue with him, and if I don't get him *ad metam non loqui,*[8] to the point where he can't say a word, well, then you can say anything you like about me."

"All right," said Pantagruel, "but Panurge, my good friend, he's a deeply learned man. How will you deal with him?"

"Very easily," said Panurge. "Please: don't even speak about it. Just leave

7. Greek philosopher of the 6th century B.C.E.   8. Translated in the next phrase, "to the point where he can't say a word."

the whole thing to me. Do you know any man as learned as the devils in hell?"

"Not really," said Pantagruel, "unless blessed by some special divine grace."

"You see?" said Panurge. "I've had many arguments with devils, and I've made them look like idiots, I've knocked them on their asses. So tomorrow you can be sure I'll make this glorious Englishman shit vinegar, right out in public."

Then Panurge spent the night boozing with the servants and playing games, at which he lost all the roses and ribbons from his breeches. And then, when the agreed-upon hour came, he conducted his master Pantagruel to the assigned meeting place, where as you can easily understand everyone in Paris, from the most important to the least, had assembled, all of them thinking:

"This devil of a Pantagruel, he's beaten all our clever fellows, and all those naive theologians and philosophers. But now he'll get what's coming to him, because this Englishman is a regular devil. We'll see who beats whom today."

Everyone was assembled; Thaumaste was waiting for them. And when Pantagruel and Panurge arrived in the hall, all the students—elementary, high school, and college—began to applaud, in their usual ridiculous way. But Pantagruel shouted at them, his voice as loud as the sound of a double cannon:

"Quiet! In the name of the devil, quiet! By God, you rascals, bother me and I'll cut the heads off every last one of you!"

Which announcement struck them as dumb as ducks: they were afraid even to cough, no matter if they'd swallowed fifteen pounds of feathers. And the very sound of his voice left them so parched and dry that their tongues hung half a foot out of their mouths, as if Pantagruel had roasted their throats.

Then Panurge began to speak, saying to the Englishman:

"Sir, have you come here seeking a debate, a contest, about these propositions which you have posted, or are you here to learn, to honestly understand the truth?"

To which Thaumaste answered:

"Sir, the only thing which has brought me here is my deep desire to understand that which I have struggled all my life to understand, and which neither books nor men have ever been able to resolve for me. As far as disputing and arguing is concerned, I have no interest whatever in that. That is a vulgar affair, and I leave it to villainous sophists, who never truly seek for truth when they argue, but only contradict each other and emptily debate."

"And so," said Panurge, "if I, who am no more than a minor disciple of my master Pantagruel, am able to satisfy you in all these matters, it would be an indignity and an imposition to trouble my master. Accordingly, it would be better if for now he simply presided over this discussion, judging what we say—and I need hardly say that he will himself satisfy you, should I be unable to fully quench your scholarly thirst."

"Indeed," said Thaumaste, "that's perfectly true."

"Then let us begin."

But note, please, that Panurge had hung a handsome tassel of red, white, green, and blue silk at the end of his long codpiece,[9] and inside it he had stuffed a fat, juicy orange.

CHAPTER 19

How Panurge Made the Englishman Who Argued by Signs Look Like an Idiot

Then, with everyone watching and listening in absolute silence, the Englishman raised his hands high in the air, first one and then the other, holding his fingertips in the shape called, in Chinon, the hen's asshole. He struck the nails of one hand against the nails of the other four times in a row, then opened his hands and slapped his palms together with a sharp crack. Joining his hands once again, as he had done at the start, he clapped them twice, then opened them out and clapped them four times more. Then he clasped them and extended one right over the other, as if praying devoutly to God.

Suddenly Panurge raised his right hand and stuck his thumb into his nose, keeping the other four fingers extended in a row straight out from the tip of his nose. He closed his left eye and winked the right one, making a deep hollow between eyebrow and eyelid. Then he lifted his left hand, the four fingers held rigidly extended, the thumb raised, and lined it up precisely with his right hand, keeping it perhaps half again the width of his nose distant. Then he lowered both hands, keeping them just as they were, and ended by raising them halfway and holding them there, as if aiming at the Englishman's nose.

"And yet if Mercury[1]—" the Englishman began.

But Panurge interrupted him:

"You have spoken. Be silent."

Then the Englishman made the following sign: With palm open, he raised his left hand high in the air, then closed its four fingers in a tight fist, with the thumb lying across the bridge of his nose. And then, suddenly, he raised his right hand, palm out, and lowered it again, placing the thumb against the little finger of his left hand, the four fingers of which he moved slowly up and down. Then, in reverse, he repeated with his right hand what he had just done with his left and with his left hand what he had done with his right.

Not a bit surprised, Panurge lifted his immense codpiece with his left hand, and with his right pulled from it a piece of white ox rib and two bits of wood in the same shape, one of black ebony, the other of rose-colored brazilwood. Arranging these objects symmetrically, in the fingers of his right hand, he clapped them together, making a sound exactly like that produced by the lepers in Brittany, to warn people off—but a sound infinitely more resonant and harmonious. And then, pulling his tongue slowly back into his mouth, he stood there, humming happily, staring at the Englishman.

The theologians, physicians, and surgeons thought this sign meant that the Englishman was a leper.

The counselors, jurists, and canon lawyers, however, thought his meaning was that being a leper brought with it a certain sort of happiness, as once our Lord had declared.

9. Ornamental pouch at the crotch of tightly fitting breeches, worn by men of the 15th and 16th centuries.
1. Thaumaste may be referring to the messenger god or to quicksilver, used in alchemy. Panurge reminds him of the rule of silent, gestural communication.

Not at all frightened, the Englishman raised both hands, holding them with the three largest fingers balled into a fist, then placed both thumbs between the index and middle fingers, with the little fingers sticking straight out. He presented his hands to Panurge, then rearranged them so that the right thumb touched the left one, and his little fingers, too, were pressed against each other.

At this, without a word, Panurge raised his hands and made the following sign: he put the nail of his right index finger against the thumbnail, shaping a loop. He bent all the fingers of his right hand into a fist, except for the index finger, which he jabbed in and out of the space framed by his other hand. Then he extended both the index and the middle fingers of his right hand, separating them as widely as he possibly could and pointing them at Thaumaste. Then placing his left thumb in the corner of his left eye, he extended his entire hand like a bird's wing or a fish's backbone, and waved it very delicately up and down. Then he did the same thing with his right hand and his right eye.

Thaumaste began to turn pale and tremble, then made the following sign: he struck the middle finger of his right hand against the muscle of his palm, just below the thumb, then inserted the index finger of his right hand into a loop shaped exactly like that Panurge had made, except that Thaumaste inserted it from below, not from above.

Accordingly, Panurge clapped his hands together and breathed into his palms. Then, once again, he shaped a loop with his left hand and, over and over, inserted into it the index finger of his right hand. Then he thrust his chin forward and stood staring at Thaumaste.

And though no one there understood what these signs meant, they understood perfectly well that he was asking Thaumaste, without a word being spoken:

"Hey, what do you make of that, eh?"

And indeed Thaumaste began to sweat heavily, looking like a man swept away by high contemplation. Then he stared back at Panurge and put the nails of his left hand against those of his right, opening all the fingers into semicircles, then raised his hands as high as he could, exhibiting this sign.

At which Panurge suddenly put his right thumb under his jaw, and stuck the little finger into the loop fashioned by his left hand, and proceeded to vigorously snap his jaw, making his teeth crash harmoniously together.

In great anguish, Thaumaste stood up, but as he rose let fly a fat baker's fart, with the dung right after it. He pissed a good dose of vinegar, and stank like the devils in hell. All those in the hall began to hold their noses, because, clearly, it was anxiety that was obliging him to beshit himself. Then he raised his right hand, the ends of all the fingers clutched together, and spread out his left hand, flat against his chest.

At which Panurge pulled out his long codpiece with its waving tassel, stretching it a good foot and a half or more, holding it in the air with his left hand and with his right, taking the ripe orange, he threw it in the air seven times, the eighth time catching it in his right fist and then holding it quietly, calmly high in the air. Then he began to shake his handsome codpiece, as if displaying it to Thaumaste.

After this, Thaumaste began to puff out his cheeks like a bagpipe musician, blowing as hard as if he were inflating a pig's bladder.

At which Panurge stuck one finger of his left hand right up his ass, sucking in air with his mouth, as if eating oysters in the shell or inhaling soup. Then he opened his mouth a bit and slapped himself with the palm of his right hand, making an immensely loud sound which seemed to work its way up from the very depths of his diaphragm all along the trachial artery. And he did this sixteen times.

But all Thaumaste could do was snuffle like a goose.

So Panurge next stuck his right index finger into his mouth, clamping down hard on it. Then he pulled it out and, as he did so, made a loud noise, like little boys firing turnips from an elderwood cannon. And he did this nine times.

And Thaumaste cried:

"Ah ha, gentlemen! The great secret! He's got his hand in there up to the elbow."

And he pulled out a dagger, holding it with the point facing down.

At which Panurge grabbed his great codpiece and shook it against his breeches as hard as he could. Then he joined his hands like a comb and put them on top of his head, sticking out his tongue as far as he could and rolling his eyes like a dying goat.

"Ah ha, I understand," said Thaumaste. "But what?" And he set the handle of his dagger against his chest, and put his palm over the point, letting his fingertips turn lightly against it.

At which Panurge bent his head to the left and put his middle finger in his left ear, raising his thumb. Then he crossed his arms on his chest, coughed five times, and the fifth time banged his right foot on the ground. Then he raised his left arm and, tightening his fingers into a fist, held the thumb against his forehead, and with his right hand clapped himself six times on the chest.

But Thaumaste, as though still unsatisfied, put his left thumb to the end of his nose and closed the rest of that hand.

So Panurge put his forefingers on each side of his mouth, pulling back as hard as he could and showing all his teeth. His thumbs drew his lower eyelids as far down as they would go, making an exceedingly ugly face, or so it seemed to everyone watching.

CHAPTER 20

What Thaumaste Said about Panurge's Virtues and His Learning

Then Thaumaste stood up and, removing his hat, thanked Panurge graciously, then turned to the audience and said in a loud voice:

"Gentlemen, now I can truly speak the biblical words: *Et ecce plus quam Solomon hic,* And here is one who is greater than Solomon.[2] You see in front of you an incomparable treasure: and that is Monsieur Pantagruel, whose fame drew me from the farthest reaches of England in order to discuss with him certain insoluble problems, involving not only magic, academy, cabalistic learning, geometrical divination, and astrology but philosophy as well, which had long been troubling me. But now his fame bothers me, because

---

2. Matthew 12.42 and Luke 11.31.

it seems to be afflicted with jealousy—certainly, it hasn't granted him a thousandth part of what he deserves.

"You have seen for yourselves how his only disciple has satisfied my questions—has even told me more than I'd asked. Moreover, he has first shown and then solved for me other problems of inexpressible difficulty and importance, and in so doing he has opened for me, I can assure you, the deepest, purest well of encyclopedic learning, and in a fashion, indeed, that I had never thought any man could accomplish—not even begin to accomplish. I refer to our disputation by signs alone, without a word being spoken. But in due time I will record everything he has said and shown me, so no one will think that this has been more tomfoolery in which we have been engaged, and I will have that record put into print so others can learn from it as I have. Then you will be able to judge how little the master is truly esteemed, when the mere disciple can demonstrate such ability, for as it is written, *Non est discipulus super magistrum*, The disciple is not superior to his master.[3]

"And now let praise be given to God, and let me humbly thank you all for the honor you have shown us. May the good Lord repay you through all the eternity."

Pantagruel said similarly courteous things to all who were gathered there, and as he left took Thaumaste with him, to dine—and you will believe they drank until they had to open their breeches to let their bellies breathe. (In those days men buttoned up their bellies, the way they buttoned up their collars today.) They drank, indeed, until all they could say was, "Where do *you* come from?"

Holy Mother of God, how they guzzled, and how many bottles of wine they put away:

"Over here!"

"More, more!"

"Waiter, wine!"

"Pour it, in the name of the devil, pour it!"

No one drank fewer than twenty-five or thirty jugs, and do you know how? *Sicut terra sine aqua*, Like a dry land with no water—for it was warm weather and, besides, they were good and thirsty.

But as for Thaumaste's explanation of the signs they used, in their disputation, well, I'd be glad to explain them all myself, but I'm told that Thaumaste in fact wrote a huge book, printed in London, in which he sets out everything, omitting not a single item. In consideration of which, for now at least I'll just leave the subject.

CHAPTER 32

How Pantagruel Shielded an Entire Army with His Tongue, and What the Author Saw in His Mouth

As Pantagruel and all his people entered the land of the Dipsodes,[4] the inhabitants were delighted and immediately surrendered to him, bringing him of their own free will the keys to every city to which he journeyed—all except the Almyrods, who intended to resist him and told his heralds that they refused to surrender, except on good terms.

---

3. Matthew 10.24. 4. Fictive peoples, led by King Anarche (Unrule), who invade Pantagruel's kingdom.

"What!" said Pantagruel. "They want more than their hand in the pot and a cup in their fist? Let's go, so you can knock down their walls for me."

So they got themselves ready, as if about to launch their attack.

But as they marched past a huge field, they were struck by a huge downpour, which began to knock their lines about and break up their formation. Seeing this, Pantagruel ordered the captains to assure them that this was nothing and he could see, past the clouds, that it was only a bit of dew. Whatever happened, however, they should maintain military discipline and he would provide them with cover. And when they had restored good marching order, Pantagruel stuck out his tongue, but just barely halfway, and shielded them as a mother hen protects her chicks.

Now I,[5] who report these totally true tales to you, had hidden myself under the leaf of a burdock weed, which was at least as big as the Mantrible Bridge. But when I saw how well they had been shielded, I went to take cover alongside them, but I couldn't, since there were so many of them and (as they say) "all things come to an end." So I climbed up as best I could and walked along his tongue for a good six miles, until I got into his mouth.

But, O you gods and goddesses, what did I see there? May Jupiter blow me away with his three-pointed lightning if I tell you a lie. I walked along in there, as you might promenade around Saint Sophia's Cathedral in Constantinople, and I saw immense boulders, just like the mountains of Denmark (I think they were his teeth), and great meadows, and huge forests, with castles and large cities, no smaller than Lyons or Poitiers.

The first person I met was an old man planting cabbage. And quite astonished I asked him:

"My friend, what are you doing here?"

"I," he said, "am planting cabbage."

"But why, and how?" I said.

"Oh ho, sir," said he, "we can't all walk around with our balls hanging down like mortars, and we can't all be rich. This is how I earn my living. They take this to the city you see over there, and sell them."

"Jesus!" I said. "Is this a whole new world in here?"

"Not at all," he said, "it isn't completely new, no. But I've heard that there is a new world outside of here, and that there's a sun and a moon out there, and all kinds of things going on. But this world is older."

"Well, my friend," I said, "what's the name of that city where they sell your cabbage?"

"It's called Throattown," he said, "and the people are good Christians, and will be pleased to see you."

So, in a word, I decided to go there.

Now, as I walked I found a fellow setting pigeon snares, and I asked him:

"My friend, where do these pigeons of yours come from?"

"Sir," he said, "they come from the other world."

And then I realized that, when Pantagruel yawned, pigeons with fully extended wings flew right down his throat, thinking it was a great bird house.

Then I came to the city, which seemed extremely pleasant, well fortified, and nicely located, with a good climate. But at the gates the porters asked

---

5. Alcofribas Nasier, the narrator.

for my passport and my certificate of good health, which truly astonished me, so I said to them:

"Gentlemen, is there any danger of plague here?"

"Oh, sir," they said, "they're dying of it so rapidly, not very far from here, that the body wagon is always rattling through the streets."

"Good God!" I said. "And just where is this?"

So they informed me that it was in Larynx and Pharynx, which were two cities as big as Rouen and Nantes, rich and doing a fine business, and that the plague was due to a stinking, infectious odor recently flowing up to them from the abysses below. More than twenty-two hundred and seventy-six people had died of it in the last week. So I thought about this, and added up the days, and realized that this was a foul breath from Pantagruel's stomach, which had begun after he'd eaten so much garlic (at Anarch's wedding feast), as I've already explained.

Leaving there, I walked between the great boulders that were his teeth, and climbed up on one, and found it one of the loveliest places in the whole world, with fine tennis courts, handsome galleries, beautiful meadows, and many vineyards. And these delightful fields were dotted with more Italian-style summerhouses than I could count, so I stayed on there for four months and have never been happier.

Then I climbed down the back teeth, in order to get to his lips, but as I journeyed I was robbed by a band of highwaymen in the middle of a huge forest, somewhere in the neighborhood of his ears.

Then I found a little village on the slope (I forget its name), where I was happier than ever, and worked happily for my supper. Can you guess what I did? I slept: they hire day laborers to sleep, down there, and you can make five or six dollars a day. But those who snore really loud can make seven or even seven and a half. And I told the senators how I'd been robbed in the valley, and they told me that, truthfully, the people in that neighborhood were naturally bad, and thieves to boot, which made me realize that, just as we have the Right Side of the Alps and the Wrong Side of the Alps, so they have the Right Side of the Teeth and the Wrong Side of the Teeth, but it was better on the Right Side, and the air was better, too.

And I began to think how true it was that half the world has no idea how the other half lives, seeing that no one has ever written a thing about that world down there, although it's inhabited by more than twenty-five kingdoms, not to mention the deserts and a great bay. Indeed, I have written a fat book entitled *History of an Elegant Throat Land*, which is what I called that country, since they lived in the throat of my master Pantagruel.

Finally, I decided to go back, and going past his beard I dropped onto his shoulders, and from there I got down to the ground and fell right in front of him.

And seeing me, he asked:

"Where are you coming from, Alcofribas?"

And I answered him:

"From your throat, sir."

"And how long have you been down there?" he said.

"Since you marched against the Almyrods," I said.

"But that," he said, "is more than six months. How did you live? What did you drink?"

I answered:

"My lord, just as you did, and I took a tax of the freshest morsels that came down your throat."

"Indeed," he said. "But where did you shit?"

"In your throat, sir," I said.

"Ha, ha, but you're a fine fellow!" he said. "Now, with God's help, we've conquered the entire land of the Dipsodes. And you shall have the castle of Salmagundi."

"Many thanks, sir," I said. "You're far more generous than I deserve."

MICHEL DE MONTAIGNE
1533–1592

The stylistically rich and thematically varied essays of Michel Eyquem de Montaigne offer an unparalleled view into a single Renaissance mind exploring its own workings. The first writer to ask "Who am I?" and pursue the question with extraordinary honesty and rigor, Montaigne presents himself, in his essays, as an explorer of existential dilemmas and of cultural and psychological identity crises. If at times he appears surprisingly modern in his outlook, his habits of thought, and his theories of selfhood, he is, in fact, best viewed as at once a precursor of modernity, a representative of his time, and an avid student of the classical past. The ease with which his thought turns from classical antiquity to the emerging modern world underscores Montaigne's awareness of his own position in history: he knew the world he inhabited was undergoing dramatic cultural and geopolitical changes, and he understood that the idea of the self was transforming along with it.

Montaigne was born on February 28, 1533, in the castle of Montaigne, to a Catholic father and a Protestant mother of Spanish-Jewish descent. His father, Pierre Eyquem, was for two terms mayor of Bordeaux and had fought in Italy under Francis I. Though no man of learning, Pierre had unconventional ideas of upbringing: Michel was awakened in the morning by the sound of music and had Latin taught him as his mother tongue. At six Michel went to the famous Collège de Guienne at Bordeaux; later he studied law, probably at Toulouse; and in 1557 he was a member of the Bordeaux parliament. In 1565 he married Françoise de la Chassaigne, daughter of a man who, as one of Montaigne's colleagues in the Bordeaux parliament, was a member of the new legal nobility (noblesse de robe). Perhaps because of disappointed political ambitions, Montaigne retired from politics in 1570 at the age of thirty-eight: he sold his post as magistrate and retreated to his castle of Montaigne, which he had inherited two years earlier. There in his country estate, he devoted himself to meditation and writing. His famous Essays, which began as a collection of interesting quotations, observations, and recordings of remarkable events, slowly developed into its final form of three large books. Although Montaigne spent, as he put it, "most of his days, and most hours of the day" in his library on the third floor of a round tower, the demands of his health and France's tumultuous politics often drew him out of retirement. For the sake of his health (he suffered from gallstones), in 1580 he took a journey through Switzerland, Germany, and Italy. While in Italy he received news that he had been appointed mayor of Bordeaux, an office he held for two terms (1581–85).

His greatest political distractions, however, concerned the Catholic and Protestant factions that violently divided the court and France itself. French politics profoundly influenced the attitudes toward warfare, political resistance, and clemency expressed in Montaigne's *Essays*. When Henry II died in a jousting accident in 1559 and left the fifteen-year-old Francis II to succeed him, the Huguenots (French Reformers in the tradition of John Calvin), recognized the opportunity to influence the weakened royal government. Catherine de Médicis, the queen mother, seized power when Francis II died in 1560 (his successor, Charles IX, was only ten years old). Her policy of limited religious toleration satisfied neither the Catholic nor the Huguenot factions, and from 1562 to 1568 France fell into civil war three times. Struggles among France, Spain, and England over territorial rights in the Netherlands led to the dangerous possibility of a French war with Spain, which Catherine tried to avoid by planning the assassination of its most influential supporter, the Huguenot Coligny. When her plot failed, she persuaded the young Charles IX that the Huguenots were planning a coup. He is said to have shouted "Then kill them all," sanctioning the St. Bartholomew's Day Massacre of August 24, 1572: noblemen, municipal authorities, and the Parisian mobs indiscriminately slaughtered the Protestants in Paris. The slaughter was imitated in other French cities, and the civil wars once again broke out, with the house of Guise leading the Catholic party and the Bourbons leading the Huguenots.

A third party of *politiques*, including Montaigne, the political theorist Jean Bodin, and the duke of Alençon (Catherine's youngest son), arose. This party favored religious tolerance and sought a compromise to the old saying that had facilitated so much carnage in France on religious grounds: "one faith, one law, one king." Throughout his country's political struggles, Montaigne sympathized with the unfanatical Henry of Navarre, leader of the Protestants, but his attitude was neutral and conservative. He expressed his joy when Henry of Navarre became King Henry IV and turned Catholic to do so: "Paris," Henry memorably observed, "is well worth a Mass." Montaigne, who died on September 13, 1592, did not live to see Henry's triumphal entrance into Paris.

Montaigne's essays are at once highly personal and outward-looking; they present a curious mind in acts of investigating history, the complex and changing sociopolitical world, and the mind's own slightly mysterious workings. "I am a man," he says, quoting the Roman playwright Terence, and "I consider nothing human to be alien to me." As an ethnographer and historian, he studies the characteristics of geographically and historically distant cultures and insists that cultural norms are relative and should be free from judgment by sixteenth-century European standards. As a psychologist, he is drawn to the "alien" or disowned thoughts and experiences of himself and his countrymen. His method is not didactic, and his criticism, which he reserves for fellow Europeans, emerges largely through subtle ironies that he leaves readers to detect. He moves suddenly, for example, from introspection to an ethical challenge. "Authors communicate themselves to the world by some special and extrinsic mark," he comments in the essay *Of Repentance*, but "I am the first to do so by my general being, as Michel de Montaigne, not as a grammarian or a poet or a lawyer. If the world finds fault with me for speaking too much of myself, I find fault with the world for not even thinking of itself."

When Montaigne thinks of himself, he seeks to enlarge knowledge of how the mind works. Far from prizing his capacity for reason and judgment, for example, he neutrally observes, "My judgment floats, it wanders." Montaigne is disarmingly modest: "Reader, I am myself the subject of my book; it is not reasonable to expect you to waste your leisure on a matter so frivolous and empty." Although massively learned, he emphasizes not what he knows but rather, like Plato's Socrates, the ways that knowledge reveals how little he truly knows. Ultimately, his essays lead readers away from character study toward philosophical questions about the grounds for knowledge itself (the branch of philosophy called *epistemology*).

Montaigne's assertions of doubt and consciousness of human vanity have little to do with gloomy despair: his stance is skeptical, not cynical. Thus if he "essays" or probes the human capacity to act purposefully and coherently—as he does in the essay *Of the Inconsistency of Our Actions*—his implicit verdict is not that our action is absolutely futile. Instead, he refuses to attribute to the human mind a coherence it does not possess; to Montaigne, if a man were able to achieve the Stoic ideal of the "constant man," unmoved by circumstance or emotion (the butt of Folly's jokes in Erasmus), the result would be impoverishing. "Our actions are nothing but a patch-work," he remarks, and the insight into the fragmentary, inconsistent pattern of our personal lives leads him to a dramatic perception of the strangeness and instability of the self: "There is as much difference between us and ourselves as between us and others." This idea became highly influential in Renaissance thinking and shaped such haunting insights as John Donne's observation that "ourselves are what we know not." For Renaissance thinkers who embraced Montaigne's perception of psychological mysteriousness, the difficult philosophical imperative of Socrates, "know thyself," seemed endlessly intriguing but doomed.

Montaigne pursues his arguments about the elusive and unstable character of the "self" by considering a wide range of anecdotes, both contemporary and classical. A slippery or undefinable historical character intrigues him far more than a monolithic or single-minded one. Alexander the Great—the legendary warrior who also haunts the pages of Castiglione's *Courtier*—is rendered frighteningly transparent by his obsession with power and conquest: he wants nothing less than to be a god. Emperor Augustus, on the other hand, rewards study precisely because his character has "escaped" the willful reductions of historians bent on "fashioning a consistent and solid fabric" of his character. As Montaigne admiringly puts it in *Of the Inconsistency of Our Actions*, there is in the life of Augustus "such an obvious, abrupt, and continual variety of actions that even the boldest judges have had to let him go, intact and unsolved."

Why was Montaigne so unusually able to suspend the self-interest and bias he considered ingrained in human nature in order to analyze himself, his culture, and the place of humankind in the cosmos? As his life in politics indicates, the violent instability of French history taught him tolerance, skepticism about human self-interest, and hatred of dogmatic positions:

> It demands a great deal of self-love and presumption, to take one's own opinions so seriously as to disrupt the peace in order to establish them, introducing so many inevitable evils, and so terrible a corruption of manners as civil wars and political revolutions with them.

His hatred of political radicalism influenced much of what he saw in ancient history and in contemporary accounts of New World discovery and conquest. This alienation from his own political context suggests one cause of his celebrated doubleness of perspective, which is at once ethnographic (outward-looking and impartial) and self-critical (introspective and moral). As he reflects on the ancient and new worlds, he pays special attention to how human beings respond to adversity, oppression, and physical torture. If we keep in mind his impatience with the political and religious ideologues of his own country, we may understand why the heroic self-assertions of Alexander the Great or Hernán Cortés fail to sway his imagination and sympathies. Violent repression and implacable resistance alike repel Montaigne, who keenly scrutinizes displays of courage that camouflage less-than-noble motives.

In the most famous essay, *Of Cannibals* (which influenced Shakespeare's reflections in *The Tempest* on the ideal commonwealth, colonialism, and the nature of savages), Montaigne compares the behavioral codes of Brazilian cannibals and those of "ourselves" (Europeans) and concludes that "each man calls barbarism whatever is not his own practice." Once he has asserted the relativity of customs, Montaigne is able to praise elements of the savages' culture that he regards as superior to Europe's. He admires the savages' courage, for instance, in which "the honor of valor consists in combating, not in beating." Moreover, he finds in the positive example of the Brazilian cannibals an implicit criticism of violence by Europeans both at home and in the New World. Montaigne remarks, "I am not sorry that we notice the barbarous horror" of cannibal culture, and then continues,

> but I am heartily sorry that judging their faults rightly, we should be so blind to our own. I think there is more barbarity in eating a man alive than in eating him dead; and in tearing by tortures and the rack a body still full of feeling, in roasting a man bit by bit, in having him bitten and mangled by dogs and swine (as we have not only read but seen within fresh memory, not among ancient enemies, but among neighbors and fellow citizens and what is worse, on the pretext of piety and religion), than in roasting and eating him after he is dead.

As an ethnographer, Montaigne grapples with the distinct and alien culture of the savages without passing judgment; but when he reflects on France, he becomes a moralist. Central to the entire essay is the invocation of the Catholics' torture and burning of fellow citizens (Huguenots) that Montaigne ironically tucks in parentheses. Montaigne here juxtaposes two kinds of savagery: that which appears foreign (cannibalism) and that which has grown too familiar (religious persecution).

Montaigne shows as much interest in the behavior of Brazilian and European victims as he does in their torturers. Montaigne writes of paintings that show a Brazilian prisoner-of-war "spitting in the face of his slayers and scowling at them. Indeed, to the last gasp they never stop braving and defying their enemies by word and look." He continues, "Truly, here are real savages by our standards; for either they must be thoroughly so, or we must be; there is an amazing distance between their character and ours." What Montaigne's example suggests is an unnerving *identity* between the defiant Brazilian natives and the Huguenots of France, who have become inured to the ideas of violent resistance and martyrdom. Like the Brazilian victims of cannibalism, the Huguenots are unwilling, even in the face of death, to moderate their dealings with their torturers, the Catholics who dominate French politics. Montaigne's cannibals, then, help make the entrenched behavior of France's religious factions seem foreign, strange, and savage: both sides are guilty (if not equally so) of "so terrible a corruption of manners as civil wars and political revolutions." His own country's civil strife inspires in Montaigne an unusual ability to transcend smug cultural bias, making him a powerful critic of European culture and an ethnographer able to imagine and study communities other than his own. Like the world of antiquity, which also riveted his imagination, the idea of America allowed Montaigne to explore alternate worlds for their own sake and for their illumination of his own.

PRONOUNCING GLOSSARY

The following list uses common English syllables and stress accents to provide rough equivalents of selected words whose pronunciation may be unfamiliar to the general reader.

de la Chassaigne: *deu lah shah-sen'*

Dordogne: *dor-don'*

Guise: *geez*

Jacques Peletier: *zhahk pel-tyay'*

Montaigne: *mon-ten'*

Soissons: *swah-sohnh'*

Suidas: *soo'-ee-dahs*

Valois: *val-wah'*

Villegaignon: *veel-gahn-yonh'*

Vitry-le-François: *vee-tree—leu—frahn-swah'*

FROM ESSAYS[1]

To the Reader

This book was written in good faith, reader. It warns you from the outset that in it I have set myself no goal but a domestic and private one. I have had no thought of serving either you or my own glory. My powers are inadequate for such a purpose. I have dedicated it to the private convenience of my relatives and friends, so that when they have lost me (as soon they must), they may recover here some features of my habits and temperament, and by this means keep the knowledge they have had of me more complete and alive.

If I had written to seek the world's favor, I should have bedecked myself better, and should present myself in a studied posture. I want to be seen here in my simple, natural, ordinary fashion, without straining or artifice; for it is myself that I portray. My defects will here be read to the life, and also my natural form, as far as respect for the public has allowed. Had I been placed among those nations which are said to live still in the sweet freedom of nature's first laws, I assure you I should very gladly have portrayed myself here entire and wholly naked.

Thus, reader, I am myself the matter of my book; you would be unreasonable to spend your leisure on so frivolous and vain a subject.

So farewell. Montaigne, this first day of March, fifteen hundred and eighty.

Of the Power of the Imagination

A strong imagination creates the event, say the scholars. I am one of those who are very much influenced by the imagination. Everyone feels its impact, but some are overthrown by it. Its impression on me is piercing. And my art is to escape it, not to resist it. I would live solely in the presence of gay, healthy people. The sight of other people's anguish causes very real anguish to me, and my feelings have often usurped the feelings of others. A continual cougher irritates my lungs and throat. I visit less willingly the sick toward whom duty directs me than those toward whom I am less attentive and concerned. I catch the disease that I study, and lodge it in me. I do not find it strange that imagination brings fevers and death to those who give it a free hand and encourage it.

Simon Thomas was a great doctor in his time. I remember that one day, when he met me at the house of a rich old consumptive with whom he was discussing ways to cure his illness, he told him that one of these would be to give me occasion to enjoy his company; and that by fixing his eyes on the freshness of my face and his thoughts on the blitheness and overflowing vigor of my youth, and filling all his senses with my flourishing condition, he might improve his constitution. But he forgot to say that mine might get worse at the same time.

1. Translated by Donald Frame.

Gallus Vibius[2] strained his mind so hard to understand the essence and impulses of insanity that he dragged his judgment off its seat and never could get it back again; and he could boast of having become mad through wisdom. There are some who through fear anticipate the hand of the executioner. And one man who was being unbound to have his pardon read him dropped stone dead on the scaffold, struck down by his mere imagination. We drip with sweat, we tremble, we turn pale and turn red at the blows of our imagination; reclining in our feather beds we feel our bodies agitated by their impact, sometimes to the point of expiring. And boiling youth, fast asleep, grows so hot in the harness that in dreams it satisfies its amorous desires:

> So that as though it were an actual affair,
> They pour out mighty streams, and stain the clothes they wear.
>   LUCRETIUS[3]

And although it is nothing new to see horns grow overnight on someone who did not have them when he went to bed, nevertheless what happened to Cippus,[4] king of Italy, is memorable; having been in the daytime a very excited spectator at a bullfight and having all night in his dreams had horns on his head, he grew actual horns on his forehead by the power of his imagination. Passion gave the son of Croesus the voice that nature had refused him. And Antiochus took fever from the beauty of Stratonice too vividly imprinted in his soul. Pliny says he saw Lucius Cossitius changed from a woman into a man on his wedding day. Pontanus[5] and others report similar metamorphoses as having happened in Italy in these later ages. And through his and his mother's vehement desire,

> Iphis the man fulfilled vows made when he was a girl.
>   OVID[6]

Passing through Vitry-le-François, I might have seen a man whom the bishop of Soissons had named Germain at confirmation, but whom all the inhabitants of that place had seen and known as a girl named Marie until the age of twenty-two. He was now heavily bearded, and old, and not married. Straining himself in some way in jumping, he says, his masculine organs came forth; and among the girls there a song is still current by which they warn each other not to take big strides for fear of becoming boys, like Marie Germain. It is not so great a marvel that this sort of accident is frequently met with. For if the imagination has power in such things, it is so continually and vigorously fixed on this subject that in order not to have to relapse so often into the same thought and sharpness of desire, it is better off if once and for all it incorporates this masculine member in girls.

Some attribute to the power of imagination the scars of King Dagobert and of Saint Francis. It is said that thereby bodies are sometimes removed from their places. And Celsus tells of a priest who used to fly with his soul

---

2. Roman orator. Montaigne illustrates his points with many examples from both antiquity and contemporary Europe; it is less important to know who these historical persons were than to follow Montaigne's presentation of telling moments of their lives. 3. Titus Lucretius Caro (94–55 b.c.e.), Roman poet and Epicurean philosopher; *On the Nature of Things* 4.1035–36. 4. The story of Cippus is told by Pliny (23/24–79 c.e.). 5. Johannes Pontanus (1426–1503), Renaissance scholar and philosopher. Croesus, last king of Lydia (ca. 560–546 b.c.e.). Antiochus I (324–261 b.c.e.), who ruled the eastern Seleucid territories from 293/2 b.c.e., took Seleucus's wife, Stratonice. 6. *Metamorphoses* 9.793.

into such ecstasy that his body would remain a long time without breath and without sensation. Saint Augustine[7] names another who whenever he heard lamentable and plaintive cries would suddenly go into a trance and get so carried away that it was no use to shake him and shout at him, to pinch him and burn him, until he had come to; then he would say that he had heard voices, but as if coming from afar, and he would notice his burns and bruises. And that this was no feigned resistance to his senses was shown by the fact that while in this state he had neither pulse nor breath.

It is probable that the principal credit of miracles, visions, enchantments, and such extraordinary occurrences comes from the power of imagination, acting principally upon the minds of the common people, which are softer. Their belief has been so strongly seized that they think they see what they do not see.

I am still of this opinion, that those comical inhibitions by which our society is so fettered that people talk of nothing else are for the most part the effects of apprehension and fear. For I know by experience that one man,[8] whom I can answer for as for myself, on whom there could fall no suspicion whatever of impotence and just as little of being enchanted, having heard a friend of his tell the story of an extraordinary impotence into which he had fallen at the moment when he needed it least, and finding himself in a similar situation, was all at once so struck in his imagination by the horror of this story that he incurred the same fate. And from then on he was subject to relapse, for the ugly memory of his mishap checked him and tyrannized him. He found some remedy for this fancy by another fancy: which was that by admitting this weakness and speaking about it in advance, he relieved the tension of his soul, for when the trouble had been presented as one to be expected, his sense of responsibility diminished and weighed upon him less. When he had a chance of his own choosing, with his mind unembroiled and relaxed and his body in good shape, to have his bodily powers first tested, then seized and taken by surprise, with the other party's full knowledge of his problem, he was completely cured in this respect. A man is never after incapable, unless from genuine impotence, with a woman with whom he has once been capable.

This mishap is to be feared only in enterprises where our soul is immoderately tense with desire and respect, and especially if the opportunity is unexpected and pressing; there is no way of recovering from this trouble. I know one man who found it helpful to bring to it a body that had already begun to be sated elsewhere, so as to lull his frenzied ardor, and who with age finds himself less impotent through being less potent. And I know another who was helped when a friend assured him that he was supplied with a counterbattery of enchantments that were certain to save him. I had better tell how this happened.

A count, a member of a very distinguished family, with whom I was quite intimate, upon getting married to a beautiful lady who had been courted by a man who was present at the wedding feast, had his friends very worried and especially an old lady, a relative of his, who was presiding at the wedding and holding it at her house. She was fearful of these sorceries, and gave me to understand this. I asked her to rely on me. I had by chance in my coffers

---

7. Early Christian Church father (354–430 c.e.).   8. Possibly Montaigne himself.

a certain little flat piece of gold on which were engraved some celestial figures, to protect against sunstroke and take away a headache by placing it precisely on the suture of the skull; and, to keep it there, it was sewed to a ribbon intended to be tied under the chin: a kindred fancy to the one we are speaking of. Jacques Peletier[9] had given me this singular present. I thought of making some use of it, and said to the count that he might incur the same fate as others, there being men present who would like to bring this about; but that he should boldly go to bed and I would do him a friendly turn and would not, if he needed it, spare a miracle which was in my power, provided that he promised me on his honor to keep it most faithfully secret; he was only to make a given signal to me, when they came to bring him the midnight meal, if things had gone badly with him. He had had his soul and his ears so battered that he did find himself fettered by the trouble of his imagination, and gave me his signal. I told him then that he should get up on the pretext of chasing us out, and playfully take the bathrobe that I had on (we were very close in height) and put it on him until he had carried out my prescription, which was this: when we had left, he should withdraw to pass water, say certain prayers three times and go through certain motions; each of these three times he should tie the ribbon I was putting in his hand around him and very carefully lay the medal that was attached to it on his kidneys, with the figure in such and such a position; this done, having tied this ribbon firmly so that it could neither come untied nor slip from its place, he should return to his business with complete assurance and not forget to spread my robe over his bed so that it should cover them both. These monkey tricks are the main part of the business, our mind being unable to get free of the idea that such strange means must come from some abstruse science. Their inanity gives them weight and reverence. All in all, it is certain that the characters on my medal proved themselves more venereal than solar, more useful for action than for prevention. It was a sudden and curious whim that led me to do such a thing, which was alien to my nature. I am an enemy of subtle and dissimulated acts and hate trickery in myself, not only for sport but also for someone's profit. If the action is not vicious, the road to it is.

Amasis,[1] king of Egypt, married Laodice, a very beautiful Greek girl; and he, who showed himself a gay companion everywhere else, fell short when it came to enjoying her, and threatened to kill her, thinking it was some sort of sorcery. As is usual in matters of fancy, she referred him to religion; and having made his vows and promises to Venus, he found himself divinely restored from the first night after his oblations and sacrifices.

Now women are wrong to greet us with those threatening, quarrelsome, and coy countenances, which put out our fires even as they light them. The daughter-in-law of Pythagoras used to say that the woman who goes to bed with a man should put off her modesty with her skirt and put it on again with her petticoat. The soul of the assailant, when troubled with many various alarms, is easily discouraged; and when imagination has once made a man suffer this shame—and it does so only at the first encounters, inasmuch as these are more boiling and violent, and also because in this first intimacy a man is much more afraid of failing—having begun badly, he gets from this

---

9. Renaissance mathematician (1517–1582).   **1.** Pharaoh ca. 569 B.C.E., known for his great public works and unconventional life.

accident a feverishness and vexation which lasts into subsequent occasions.

Married people, whose time is all their own, should neither press their undertaking nor even attempt it if they are not ready; it is better to fail unbecomingly to handsel the nuptial couch,[2] which is full of agitation and feverishness, and wait for some other more private and less tense opportunity, than to fall into perpetual misery for having been stunned and made desperate by a first refusal. Before taking possession, the patient should try himself out and offer himself, lightly, by sallies at different times, without priding himself and obstinately insisting on convincing himself definitively. Those who know that their members are naturally obedient, let them take care only to counteract the tricks of their fancies.

People are right to notice the unruly liberty of this member, obtruding so importunately when we have no use for it, and failing so importunately when we have the most use for it, and struggling for mastery so imperiously with our will, refusing with so much pride and obstinacy our solicitations, both mental and manual.

If, however, in the matter of his rebellion being blamed and used as proof to condemn him, he had paid me to plead his cause, I should perhaps place our other members, his fellows, under suspicion of having framed this trumped-up charge out of sheer envy of the importance and pleasure of the use of him, and of having armed everyone against him by a conspiracy, malignantly charging him alone with their common fault. For I ask you to think whether there is a single one of the parts of our body that does not often refuse its function to our will and exercise it against our will. They each have passions of their own which rouse them and put them to sleep without our leave. How many times do the forced movements of our face bear witness to the thoughts that we were holding secret, and betray us to those present. The same cause that animates this member also animates, without our knowledge, the heart, the lungs, and the pulse; the sight of a pleasing object spreading in us imperceptibly the flame of a feverish emotion. Are there only these muscles and these veins that stand up and lie down without the consent, not only of our will, but even of our thoughts? We do not command our hair to stand on end or our skin to shiver with desire or fear. The hand often moves itself to where we do not send it. The tongue is paralyzed, and the voice congealed, at their own time. Even when, having nothing to put in to fry, we should like to forbid it, the appetite for eating and drinking does not fail to stir the parts that are subject to it, no more nor less than that other appetite; and it likewise abandons us inopportunely when it sees fit. The organs that serve to discharge the stomach have their own dilatations and compressions, beyond and against our plans, just like those that are destined to discharge the kidneys. To vindicate the omnipotence of our will, Saint Augustine alleges that he knew a man who commanded his behind to produce as many farts as he wanted, and his commentator Vives[3] goes him one better with another example of his own time, of farts arranged to suit the tone of verses pronounced to their accompaniment; but all this does not really argue any pure obedience in this organ; for is there any that is ordinarily more indiscreet or tumultuous? Besides, I know one so turbulent and

---

2. To consummate the marriage on one's wedding night. 3. Juan Luis Vives (1492–1540), Renaissance philosopher and scholar.

unruly, that for forty years it has kept its master farting with a constant and unremitting wind and compulsion, and is thus taking him to his death.

But as for our will, on behalf of whose rights we set forth this complaint, how much more plausibly may we charge it with rebellion and sedition for its disorderliness and disobedience! Does it always will what we would will it to will? Doesn't it often will what we forbid it to will, and that to our evident disadvantage? Is it any more amenable than our other parts to the decisions of our reason?

To conclude, I would say this in defense of the honorable member whom I represent: May it please the court to take into consideration that in this matter, although my client's case is inseparably and indistinguishably linked with that of an accessory, nevertheless he alone has been brought to trial; and that the arguments and charges against him are such as cannot—in view of the status of the parties—be in any manner pertinent or relevant to the aforesaid accessory. Whereby is revealed his accusers' manifest animosity and disrespect for law. However that may be, Nature will meanwhile go her way, protesting that the lawyers and judges quarrel and pass sentence in vain. Indeed, she would have done no more than is right if she had endowed with some particular privilege this member, author of the sole immortal work of mortals. Wherefore to Socrates generation is a divine act; and love, a desire for immortality and itself an immortal daemon.[4]

Perhaps it is by this effect of the imagination that one man here gets rid of the scrofula which his companion carries back to Spain.[5] This effect is the reason why, in such matters, it is customary to demand that the mind be prepared. Why do the doctors work on the credulity of their patient beforehand with so many false promises of a cure, if not so that the effect of the imagination may make up for the imposture of their decoction? They know that one of the masters of the trade left them this in writing, that there have been men for whom the mere sight of medicine did the job.

And this whole caprice[6] has just come to hand apropos of the story that an apothecary, a servant of my late father, used to tell me, a simple man and Swiss, of a nation little addicted to vanity and lying. He had long known a merchant at Toulouse,[7] sickly and subject to the stone, who often needed enemas, and ordered various kinds from his doctors according to the circumstances of his illness. Once they were brought to him, nothing was omitted of the accustomed formalities; often he tested them by hand to make sure they were not too hot. There he was, lying on his stomach, and all the motions were gone through—except that no injection was made. After this ceremony, the apothecary having retired and the patient being accommodated as if he had really taken the enema, he felt the same effect from it as those who do take them. And if the doctor did not find its operation sufficient, he would give him two or three more, of the same sort. My witness swears that when to save the expense (for he paid for them as if he had taken them) this sick man's wife sometimes tried to have just warm water used, the effect revealed the fraud; and having found that kind useless, they were obliged to return to the first method.

4. Socrates (ca. 470–399 B.C.E.) describes love as a *daemon* in Plato's *Symposium*.   5. Scrofula, or king's evil, was supposed to be curable by the touch of the kings of France. In Montaigne's time great numbers of Spaniards came to France for this purpose [Translator's note].   6. Montaigne's "cure" for his impotent friend.   7. City of southwestern France.

A woman, thinking she had swallowed a pin with her bread, was screaming in agony as though she had an unbearable pain in her throat, where she thought she felt it stuck; but because externally there was neither swelling nor alteration, a smart man, judging that it was only a fancy and notion derived from some bit of bread that had scratched her as it went down, made her vomit, and, on the sly, tossed a crooked pin into what she threw up. The woman, thinking she had thrown it up, felt herself suddenly relieved of her pain. I know that one gentleman, having entertained a goodly company at his house, three or four days later boasted, as a sort of joke (for there was nothing in it), that he had made them eat cat in a pie; at which one lady in the party was so horrified that she fell into a violent stomach disorder and fever, and it was impossible to save her. Even animals are subject like ourselves to the power of imagination. Witness dogs, who let themselves die out of grief for the loss of their masters. We also see them yap and twitch in their dreams, and horses whinny and writhe.

But all this may be attributed to the narrow seam between the soul and body, through which the experience of the one is communicated to the other. Sometimes, however, one's imagination acts not only against one's own body, but against someone else's. And just as a body passes on its sickness to its neighbor, as is seen in the plague, the pox, and soreness of the eyes, which are transmitted from one body to the other—

> By looking at sore eyes, eyes become sore:
> From body into body ills pass o'er
> > OVID[8]

—likewise the imagination, when vehemently stirred, launches darts that can injure an external object. The ancients maintained that certain women of Scythia,[9] when animated and enraged against anyone, would kill him with their mere glance. Tortoises and ostriches hatch their eggs just by looking at them, a sign that their sight has some ejaculative virtue. And as for sorcerers, they are said to have baleful and harmful eyes:

> some evil eye bewitched my tender lambs.
> > VIRGIL[1]

To me, magicians are poor authorities. Nevertheless, we know by experience that women transmit marks of their fancies to the bodies of the children they carry in their womb; witness the one who gave birth to the Moor.[2] And there was presented to Charles, king of Bohemia and Emperor, a girl from near Pisa, all hairy and bristly, who her mother said had been thus conceived because of a picture of Saint John the Baptist hanging by her bed.

With animals it is the same: witness Jacob's sheep,[3] and the partridges and hares that the snow turns white in the mountains. Recently at my house a cat was seen watching a bird on a treetop, and, after they had locked gazes

---

8. *The Cure for Love*, lines 615–16.   9. Scythians, the Greek name for Asian tribes who lived in what are now parts of Iran and Turkey, were legendary in the Renaissance for their "barbarity."   1. *Eclogue* 3.103.   2. Saint Jerome tells of a woman who, accused of adultery for giving birth to a black child, was absolved when Hippocrates explained that she had a picture of a dark man hanging in her room by her bed [Translator's note].   3. Genesis 30.37–42. After Laban agreed to give Jacob the striped sheep from his flocks, Jacob bred the sheep in front of rods (the visual stimulation was thought to cause the females to produce striped offspring).

for some time, the bird let itself fall as if dead between the cat's paws, either intoxicated by its own imagination or drawn by some attracting power of the cat. Those who like falconry have heard the story of the falconer who, setting his gaze obstinately upon a kite in the air, wagered that by the sole power of his gaze he would bring it down, and did. At least, so they say—for I refer the stories that I borrow to the conscience of those from whom I take them. The reflections are my own, and depend on the proofs of reason, not of experience; everyone can add his own examples to them; and he who has none, let him not fail to believe that there are plenty, in view of the number and variety of occurrences. If I do not apply them well, let another apply them for me.

So in the study that I am making of our behavior and motives, fabulous testimonies, provided they are possible, serve like true ones. Whether they have happened or no, in Paris or Rome, to John or Peter, they exemplify, at all events, some human potentiality, and thus their telling imparts useful information to me. I see it and profit from it just as well in shadow as in substance. And of the different readings that histories often give, I take for my use the one that is most rare and memorable. There are authors whose end is to tell what has happened. Mine, if I could attain it, would be to talk about what can happen. The schools are justly permitted to suppose similitudes when they have none at hand. I do not do so, however, and in that respect I surpass all historical fidelity, being scrupulous to the point of superstition. In the examples that I bring in here of what I have heard, done, or said, I have forbidden myself to dare to alter even the slightest and most inconsequential circumstances. My conscience does not falsify one iota; my knowledge, I don't know.

In this connection, I sometimes fall to thinking whether it befits a theologian, a philosopher, and such people of exquisite and exact conscience and prudence, to write history. How can they stake their fidelity on the fidelity of an ordinary person? How be responsible for the thoughts of persons unknown and give their conjectures as coin of the realm? Of complicated actions that happen in their presence they would refuse to give testimony if placed under oath by a judge; and they know no man so intimately that they would undertake to answer fully for his intentions. I consider it less hazardous to write of things past than present, inasmuch as the writer has only to give an account of a borrowed truth.

Some urge me to write the events of my time, believing that I see them with a view less distorted by passion than another man's, and from closer, because of the access that fortune has given me to the heads of different parties.[4] What they forget is that even for all the glory of Sallust,[5] I would not take the trouble, being a sworn enemy of obligation, assiduity, perseverance; and that there is nothing so contrary to my style as an extended narration. I cut myself off so often for lack of breath; I have neither composition nor development that is worth anything; I am more ignorant than a child of the phrases and terms that serve for the commonest things. And so I have chosen to say what I know how to say, accommodating the matter to my

---

4. A centrist, Montaigne knew leaders of the rivaling factions in France.   5. Roman historian (probably 86–35 B.C.E.).

power. If I took a subject that would lead me along, I might not be able to measure up to it; and with my freedom being so very free, I might publish judgments which, even according to my own opinion and to reason, would be illegitimate and punishable. Plutarch[6] might well say to us, concerning his accomplishments in this line, that the credit belongs to others if his examples are wholly and everywhere true; but that their being useful to posterity, and presented with a luster which lights our way to virtue, that is his work. There is no danger—as there is in a medicinal drug—in an old story being this way or that.

Of Cannibals

When King Pyrrhus[7] passed over into Italy, after he had reconnoitered the formation of the army that the Romans were sending to meet him, he said: "I do not know what barbarians these are" (for so the Greeks called all foreign nations), "but the formation of this army that I see is not at all barbarous." The Greeks said as much of the army that Flaminius brought into their country, and so did Philip, seeing from a knoll the order and distribution of the Roman camp, in his kingdom, under Publius Sulpicius Galba.[8] Thus we should beware of clinging to vulgar opinions, and judge things by reason's way, not by popular say.

I had with me for a long time a man who had lived for ten or twelve years in that other world which has been discovered in our century, in the place where Villegaignon landed, and which he called Antarctic France.[9] This discovery of a boundless country seems worthy of consideration. I don't know if I can guarantee that some other such discovery will not be made in the future, so many personages greater than ourselves having been mistaken about this one. I am afraid we have eyes bigger than our stomachs, and more curiosity than capacity. We embrace everything, but we clasp only wind.

Plato brings in Solon,[1] telling how he had learned from the priests of the city of Saïs in Egypt that in days of old, before the Flood, there was a great island named Atlantis, right at the mouth of the Strait of Gibraltar, which contained more land than Africa and Asia put together, and that the kings of that country, who not only possessed that island but had stretched out so far on the mainland that they held the breadth of Africa as far as Egypt, and the length of Europe as far as Tuscany, undertook to step over into Asia and subjugate all the nations that border on the Mediterranean, as far as the Black Sea; and for this purpose crossed the Spains, Gaul, Italy, as far as Greece, where the Athenians checked them; but that some time after, both the Athenians and themselves and their island were swallowed up by the Flood.

It is quite likely that that extreme devastation of waters made amazing changes in the habitations of the earth, as people maintain that the sea cut off Sicily from Italy—

---

6. Philosopher and biographer (ca. 50–120 C.E.).   7. King of Epirus (in Greece) who fought the Romans in Italy in 280 B.C.E.   8. Both Titus Quinctius Flaminius and Publius Sulpicius Galba were Roman statesmen and generals who fought Philip V of Macedon in the early years of the 2nd century B.C.E.   9. In Brazil. Villegaignon landed there in 1557.   1. In his *Timaeus*.

> 'Tis said an earthquake once asunder tore
> These lands with dreadful havoc, which before
> Formed but one land, one coast
>
> VIRGIL[2]

—Cyprus from Syria, the island of Euboea from the mainland of Boeotia;
and elsewhere joined lands that were divided, filling the channels between
them with sand and mud:

> A sterile marsh, long fit for rowing, now
> Feeds neighbor towns, and feels the heavy plow.
>
> HORACE[3]

But there is no great likelihood that that island was the new world which we
have just discovered; for it almost touched Spain, and it would be an incredible result of a flood to have forced it away as far as it is, more than twelve
hundred leagues; besides, the travels of the moderns have already almost
revealed that it is not an island, but a mainland connected with the East
Indies on one side, and elsewhere with the lands under the two poles; or, if
it is separated from them, it is by so narrow a strait and interval that it does
not deserve to be called an island on that account.

It seems that there are movements, some natural, others feverish, in these
great bodies, just as in our own. When I consider the inroads that my river,
the Dordogne, is making in my lifetime into the right bank in its descent,
and that in twenty years it has gained so much ground and stolen away the
foundations of several buildings, I clearly see that this is an extraordinary
disturbance; for if it had always gone at this rate, or was to do so in the
future, the face of the world would be turned topsy-turvy. But rivers are
subject to changes: now they overflow in one direction, now in another, now
they keep to their course. I am not speaking of the sudden inundations whose
causes are manifest. In Médoc, along the seashore, my brother, the sieur
d'Arsac, can see an estate of his buried under the sands that the sea spews
forth; the tops of some buildings are still visible; his farms and domains have
changed into very thin pasturage. The inhabitants say that for some time the
sea has been pushing toward them so hard that they have lost four leagues
of land. These sands are its harbingers; and we see great dunes of moving
sand that march half a league ahead of it and keep conquering land.

The other testimony of antiquity with which some would connect this
discovery is in Aristotle, at least if that little book *Of Unheard-of Wonders* is
by him. He there relates that certain Carthaginians, after setting out upon
the Atlantic Ocean from the Strait of Gibraltar and sailing a long time, at
last discovered a great fertile island, all clothed in woods and watered by
great deep rivers, far remote from any mainland; and that they, and others
since, attracted by the goodness and fertility of the soil, went there with their
wives and children, and began to settle there. The lords of Carthage, seeing
that their country was gradually becoming depopulated, expressly forbade
anyone to go there any more, on pain of death, and drove out these new
inhabitants, fearing, it is said, that in course of time they might come to
multiply so greatly as to supplant their former masters and ruin their state.

---

2. *Aeneid* 3.414–15.   3. Horatius Flaccus (65–68 B.C.E.), great poet of Augustan Rome; *Art of Poetry*,
lines 65–66.

This story of Aristotle does not fit our new lands any better than the other.

This man I had was a simple, crude fellow—a character fit to bear true witness; for clever people observe more things and more curiously, but they interpret them; and to lend weight and conviction to their interpretation, they cannot help altering history a little. They never show you things as they are, but bend and disguise them according to the way they have seen them; and to give credence to their judgment and attract you to it, they are prone to add something to their matter, to stretch it out and amplify it. We need a man either very honest, or so simple that he has not the stuff to build up false inventions and give them plausibility; and wedded to no theory. Such was my man; and besides this, he at various times brought sailors and merchants, whom he had known on that trip, to see me. So I content myself with his information, without inquiring what the cosmographers say about it.

We ought to have topographers who would give us an exact account of the places where they have been. But because they have over us the advantage of having seen Palestine, they want to enjoy the privilege of telling us news about all the rest of the world. I would like everyone to write what he knows, and as much as he knows, not only in this, but in all other subjects; for a man may have some special knowledge and experience of the nature of a river or a fountain, who in other matters knows only what everybody knows. However, to circulate this little scrap of knowledge, he will undertake to write the whole of physics. From this vice spring many great abuses.

Now, to return to my subject, I think there is nothing barbarous and savage in that nation, from what I have been told, except that each man calls barbarism whatever is not his own practice; for indeed it seems we have no other test of truth and reason than the example and pattern of the opinions and customs of the country we live in. *There* is always the perfect religion, the perfect government, the perfect and accomplished manners in all things. Those people are wild, just as we call wild the fruits that Nature has produced by herself and in her normal course; whereas really it is those that we have changed artificially and led astray from the common order, that we should rather call wild. The former retain alive and vigorous their genuine, their most useful and natural, virtues and properties, which we have debased in the latter in adapting them to gratify our corrupted taste. And yet for all that, the savor and delicacy of some uncultivated fruits of those countries is quite as excellent, even to our taste, as that of our own. It is not reasonable that art should win the place of honor over our great and powerful mother Nature. We have so overloaded the beauty and richness of her works by our inventions that we have quite smothered her. Yet wherever her purity shines forth, she wonderfully puts to shame our vain and frivolous attempts:

> Ivy comes readier without our care;
> In lonely caves the arbutus grows more fair;
> No art with artless bird song can compare.
> PROPERTIUS[4]

All our efforts cannot even succeed in reproducing the nest of the tiniest little bird, its contexture, its beauty and convenience; or even the web of the

4. *Elegies* 1.2.10–12.

puny spider. All things, says Plato,[5] are produced by nature, by fortune, or by art; the greatest and most beautiful by one or the other of the first two, the least and most imperfect by the last.

These nations, then, seem to me barbarous in this sense, that they have been fashioned very little by the human mind, and are still very close to their original naturalness. The laws of nature still rule them, very little corrupted by ours; and they are in such a state of purity that I am sometimes vexed that they were unknown earlier, in the days when there were men able to judge them better than we. I am sorry that Lycurgus[6] and Plato did not know of them; for it seems to me that what we actually see in these nations surpasses not only all the pictures in which poets have idealized the golden age and all their inventions in imagining a happy state of man, but also the conceptions and the very desire of philosophy. They could not imagine a naturalness so pure and simple as we see by experience; nor could they believe that our society could be maintained with so little artifice and human solder. This is a nation, I should say to Plato, in which there is no sort of traffic, no knowledge of letters, no science of numbers, no name for a magistrate or for political superiority, no custom of servitude, no riches or poverty, no contracts, no successions, no partitions, no occupations but leisure ones, no care for any but common kinship, no clothes, no agriculture, no metal, no use of wine or wheat.[7] The very words that signify lying, treachery, dissimulation, avarice, envy, belittling, pardon—unheard of. How far from this perfection would he find the republic that he imagined: *Men fresh sprung from the gods* [Seneca].[8]

> These manners nature first ordained.
>   VIRGIL[9]

For the rest, they live in a country with a very pleasant and temperate climate, so that according to my witnesses it is rare to see a sick man there; and they have assured me that they never saw one palsied, bleary-eyed, toothless, or bent with age. They are settled along the sea and shut in on the land side by great high mountains, with a stretch about a hundred leagues wide in between. They have a great abundance of fish and flesh which bear no resemblance to ours, and they eat them with no other artifice than cooking. The first man who rode a horse there, though he had had dealings with them on several other trips, so horrified them in this posture that they shot him dead with arrows before they could recognize him.

Their buildings are very long, with a capacity of two or three hundred souls; they are covered with the bark of great trees, the strips reaching to the ground at one end and supporting and leaning on one another at the top, in the manner of some of our barns, whose covering hangs down to the ground and acts as a side. They have wood so hard that they cut with it and make of it their swords and grills to cook their food. Their beds are of a cotton weave, hung from the roof like those in our ships, each man having his own; for the wives sleep apart from their husbands.

They get up with the sun, and eat immediately upon rising, to last them through the day; for they take no other meal than that one. Like some other

5. See his *Laws*. 6. The half-legendary Spartan lawgiver (9th century B.C.E.). 7. This passage is always compared with Shakespeare's *The Tempest* 2.1.147 ff. 8. Roman tragedian (4? B.C.E.–65 C.E.), philosopher, and political leader; *Epistles* 90. 9. *Georgics* 2.20.

Eastern peoples, of whom Suidas[1] tells us, who drank apart from meals, they do not drink then; but they drink several times a day, and to capacity. Their drink is made of some root, and is of the color of our claret wines. They drink it only lukewarm. This beverage keeps only two or three days; it has a slightly sharp taste, is not at all heady, is good for the stomach, and has a laxative effect upon those who are not used to it; it is a very pleasant drink for anyone who is accustomed to it. In place of bread they use a certain white substance like preserved coriander. I have tried it; it tastes sweet and a little flat.

The whole day is spent in dancing. The younger men go to hunt animals with bows. Some of the women busy themselves meanwhile with warming their drink, which is their chief duty. Some one of the old men, in the morning before they begin to eat, preaches to the whole barnful in common, walking from one end to the other, and repeating one single sentence several times until he has completed the circuit (for the buildings are fully a hundred paces long). He recommends to them only two things: valor against the enemy and love for their wives. And they never fail to point out this obligation, as their refrain, that it is their wives who keep their drink warm and seasoned.

There may be seen in several places, including my own house, specimens of their beds, of their ropes, of their wooden swords and the bracelets with which they cover their wrists in combats, and of the big canes, open at one end, by whose sound they keep time in their dances. They are close shaven all over, and shave themselves much more cleanly than we, with nothing but a wooden or stone razor. They believe that souls are immortal, and that those who have deserved well of the gods are lodged in that part of heaven where the sun rises, and the damned in the west.

They have some sort of priests and prophets, but they rarely appear before the people, having their home in the mountains. On their arrival there is a great feast and solemn assembly of several villages—each barn, as I have described it, makes up a village, and they are about one French league[2] from each other. The prophet speaks to them in public, exhorting them to virtue and their duty; but their whole ethical science contains only these two articles: resoluteness in war and affection for their wives. He prophesies to them things to come and the results they are to expect from their undertakings, and urges them to war or holds them back from it; but this is on the condition that when he fails to prophesy correctly, and if things turn out otherwise than he has predicted, he is cut into a thousand pieces if they catch him, and condemned as a false prophet. For this reason, the prophet who has once been mistaken is never seen again.

Divination is a gift of God; that is why its abuse should be punished as imposture. Among the Scythians, when the soothsayers failed to hit the mark, they were laid, chained hand and foot, on carts full of heather and drawn by oxen, on which they were burned. Those who handle matters subject to the control of human capacity are excusable if they do the best they can. But these others who come and trick us with assurances of an extraordinary faculty that is beyond our ken, should they not be punished for not making good their promise, and for the temerity of their imposture?

They have their wars with the nations beyond the mountains, further

1. A Byzantine lexicographer.   2. About 2.49 miles.

inland, to which they go quite naked, with no other arms than bows or wooden swords ending in a sharp point, in the manner of the tongues of our boar spears. It is astonishing what firmness they show in their combats, which never end but in slaughter and bloodshed; for as to routs and terror, they know nothing of either.

Each man brings back his trophy the head of the enemy he has killed, and sets it up at the entrance to his dwelling. After they have treated their prisoners well for a long time with all the hospitality they can think of, each man who has a prisoner calls a great assembly of his acquaintances. He ties a rope to one of the prisoner's arms, by the end of which he holds him, a few steps away, for fear of being hurt, and gives his dearest friend the other arm to hold in the same way; and these two, in the presence of the whole assembly, kill him with their swords. This done, they roast him and eat him in common and send some pieces to their absent friends. This is not, as people think, for nourishment, as of old the Scythians used to do; it is to betoken an extreme revenge. And the proof of this came when they saw the Portuguese, who had joined forces with their adversaries, inflict a different kind of death on them when they took them prisoner, which was to bury them up to the waist, shoot the rest of their body full of arrows, and afterward hang them. They thought that these people from the other world, being men who had sown the knowledge of many vices among their neighbors and were much greater masters than themselves in every sort of wickedness, did not adopt this sort of vengeance without some reason, and that it must be more painful than their own; so they began to give up their old method and to follow this one.

I am not sorry that we notice the barbarous horror of such acts, but I am heartily sorry that, judging their faults rightly, we should be so blind to our own. I think there is more barbarity in eating a man alive than in eating him dead; and in tearing by tortures and the rack a body still full of feeling, in roasting a man bit by bit, in having him bitten and mangled by dogs and swine (as we have not only read but seen within fresh memory, not among ancient enemies, but among neighbors and fellow citizens, and what is worse, on the pretext of piety and religion),[3] than in roasting and eating him after he is dead.

Indeed, Chrysippus and Zeno, heads of the Stoic sect, thought there was nothing wrong in using our carcasses for any purpose in case of need, and getting nourishment from them; just as our ancestors,[4] when besieged by Caesar in the city of Alesia, resolved to relieve their famine by eating old men, women, and other people useless for fighting.

> The Gascons once, 'tis said, their life renewed
> By eating of such food.
>
> JUVENAL[5]

And physicians do not fear to use human flesh in all sorts of ways for our health, applying it either inwardly or outwardly. But there never was any opinion so disordered as to excuse treachery, disloyalty, tyranny, and cruelty, which are our ordinary vices.

So we may well call these people barbarians, in respect to the rules of

---

3. The allusion is to the spectacles of religious warfare that Montaigne himself had witnessed in his time and country. 4. The Gauls. 5. Decimus Junius Juvenal (fl. early 2nd century C.E.), last great Roman satirist; *Satires* 15.93–94.

reason, but not in respect to ourselves, who surpass them in every kind of barbarity.

Their warfare is wholly noble and generous, and as excusable and beautiful as this human disease can be; its only basis among them is their rivalry in valor. They are not fighting for the conquest of new lands, for they still enjoy that natural abundance that provides them without toil and trouble with all necessary things in such profusion that they have no wish to enlarge their boundaries. They are still in that happy state of desiring only as much as their natural needs demand; anything beyond that is superfluous to them.

They generally call those of the same age, brothers; those who are younger, children; and the old men are fathers to all the others. These leave to their heirs in common the full possession of their property, without division or any other title at all than just the one that Nature gives to her creatures in bringing them into the world.

If their neighbors cross the mountains to attack them and win a victory, the gain of the victor is glory, and the advantage of having proved the master in valor and virtue; for apart from this they have no use for the goods of the vanquished, and they return to their own country, where they lack neither anything necessary nor that great thing, the knowledge of how to enjoy their condition happily and be content with it. These men of ours do the same in their turn. They demand of their prisoners no other ransom than that they confess and acknowledge their defeat. But there is not one in a whole century who does not choose to die rather than to relax a single bit, by word or look, from the grandeur of an invincible courage; not one who would not rather be killed and eaten than so much as ask not to be. They treat them very freely, so that life may be all the dearer to them, and usually entertain them with threats of their coming death, of the torments they will have to suffer, the preparations that are being made for the purpose, the cutting up of their limbs, and the feast that will be made at their expense. All this is done for the sole purpose of extorting from their lips some weak or base word, or making them want to flee, so as to gain the advantage of having terrified them and broken down their firmness. For indeed, if you take it the right way, it is in this point alone that true victory lies:

> It is no victory
> Unless the vanquished foe admits your mastery.
> CLAUDIAN[6]

The Hungarians, very bellicose fighters, did not in olden times pursue their advantage beyond putting the enemy at their mercy. For having wrung a confession from him to this effect, they let him go unharmed and unransomed, except, at most, for exacting his promise never again to take up arms against them.

We win enough advantages over our enemies that are borrowed advantages, not really our own. It is the quality of a porter, not of valor, to have sturdier arms and legs; agility is a dead and corporeal quality; it is a stroke of luck to make our enemy stumble, or dazzle his eyes by the sunlight; it is a trick of art and technique, which may be found in a worthless coward, to be an able fencer. The worth and value of a man is in his heart and his will;

---

6. *Of the Sixth Consulate of Honorius,* lines 248–49.

there lies his real honor. Valor is the strength, not of legs and arms, but of heart and soul; it consists not in the worth of our horse or our weapons, but in our own. He who falls obstinate in his courage, *if he has fallen, he fights on his knees* [Seneca].[7] He who relaxes none of his assurance, no matter how great the danger of imminent death; who, giving up his soul, still looks firmly and scornfully at his enemy—he is beaten not by us, but by fortune; he is killed, not conquered.

The most valiant are sometimes the most unfortunate. Thus there are triumphant defeats that rival victories. Nor did those four sister victories, the fairest that the sun ever set eyes on—Salamis, Plataea, Mycale, and Sicily[8]—ever dare match all their combined glory against the glory of the annihilation of King Leonidas and his men at the pass of Thermopylae.[9]

Who ever hastened with more glorious and ambitious desire to win a battle than Captain Ischolas to lose one? Who ever secured his safety more ingeniously and painstakingly than he did his destruction? He was charged to defend a certain pass in the Peloponnesus against the Arcadians. Finding himself wholly incapable of doing this, in view of the nature of the place and the inequality of the forces, he made up his mind that all who confronted the enemy would necessarily have to remain on the field. On the other hand, deeming it unworthy both of his own virtue and magnanimity and of the Lacedaemonian name to fail in his charge, he took a middle course between these two extremes, in this way. The youngest and fittest of his band he preserved for the defense and service of their country, and sent them home; and with those whose loss was less important, he determined to hold this pass, and by their death to make the enemy buy their entry as dearly as he could. And so it turned out. For he was presently surrounded on all sides by the Arcadians, and after slaughtering a large number of them, he and his men were all put to the sword. Is there a trophy dedicated to victors that would not be more due to these vanquished? The role of true victory is in fighting, not in coming off safely; and the honor of valor consists in combating, not in beating.

To return to our story. These prisoners are so far from giving in, in spite of all that is done to them, that on the contrary, during the two or three months that they are kept, they wear a gay expression; they urge their captors to hurry and put them to the test; they defy them, insult them, reproach them with their cowardice and the number of battles they have lost to the prisoners' own people.

I have a song composed by a prisoner which contains this challenge, that they should all come boldly and gather to dine off him, for they will be eating at the same time their own fathers and grandfathers, who have served to feed and nourish his body. "These muscles," he says, "this flesh and these veins are your own, poor fools that you are. You do not recognize that the substance of your ancestors' limbs is still contained in them. Savor them well; you will find in them the taste of your own flesh." An idea that certainly does not smack of barbarity. Those that paint these people dying, and who show the execution, portray the prisoner spitting in the face of his slayers and scowling at them. Indeed, to the last gasp they never stop braving and defying their

7. *Of Providence* 2.   8. References to the famous Greek victories against the Persians and (at Himera, Sicily) against the Carthaginians in or about 480 B.C.E.   9. The Spartan king Leonidas's defense here also took place in 480 B.C.E., during the war against the Persians.

enemies by word and look. Truly here are real savages by our standards; for either they must be thoroughly so, or we must be; there is an amazing distance between their character and ours.

The men there have several wives, and the higher their reputation for valor the more wives they have. It is a remarkably beautiful thing about their marriages that the same jealousy our wives have to keep us from the affection and kindness of other women, theirs have to win this for them. Being more concerned for their husbands' honor than for anything else, they strive and scheme to have as many companions as they can, since that is a sign of their husbands' valor.

Our wives will cry "Miracle!" but it is no miracle. It is a properly matrimonial virtue, but one of the highest order. In the Bible, Leah, Rachel, Sarah, and Jacob's wives gave their beautiful handmaids to their husbands; and Livia seconded the appetites of Augustus to her own disadvantage; and Stratonice, the wife of King Deiotarus,[1] not only lent her husband for his use a very beautiful young chambermaid in her service, but carefully brought up her children, and backed them up to succeed to their father's estates.

And lest it be thought that all this is done through a simple and servile bondage to usage and through the pressure of the authority of their ancient customs, without reasoning or judgment, and because their minds are so stupid that they cannot take any other course, I must cite some examples of their capacity. Besides the warlike song I have just quoted, I have another, a love song, which begins in this vein: "Adder, stay; stay, adder, that from the pattern of your coloring my sister may draw the fashion and the workmanship of a rich girdle that I may give to my love; so may your beauty and your pattern be forever preferred to all other serpents." This first couplet is the refrain of the song. Now I am familiar enough with poetry to be a judge of this: not only is there nothing barbarous in this fancy, but it is altogether Anacreontic.[2] Their language, moreover, is a soft language, with an agreeable sound, somewhat like Greek in its endings.

Three of these men, ignorant of the price they will pay some day, in loss of repose and happiness, for gaining knowledge of the corruptions of this side of the ocean; ignorant also of the fact that of this intercourse will come their ruin (which I suppose is already well advanced: poor wretches, to let themselves be tricked by the desire for new things, and to have left the serenity of their own sky to come and see ours!)—three of these men were at Rouen, at the time the late King Charles IX was there. The king talked to them for a long time; they were shown our ways, our splendor, the aspect of a fine city. After that, someone asked their opinion, and wanted to know what they had found most amazing. They mentioned three things, of which I have forgotten the third, and I am very sorry for it; but I still remember two of them. They said that in the first place they thought it very strange that so many grown men, bearded, strong, and armed, who were around the king (it is likely that they were talking about the Swiss of his guard) should submit to obey a child, and that one of them was not chosen to command instead. Second (they have a way in their language of speaking of men as halves of one another), they had noticed that there were among us men full and gorged

---

1. Tetrarch of Galatia, in Asia Minor.   2. Worthy of Anacreon (572?–488? B.C.E.), major Greek writer of amatory lyrics.

with all sorts of good things, and that their other halves were beggars at their doors, emaciated with hunger and poverty; and they thought it strange that these needy halves could endure such an injustice, and did not take the others by the throat, or set fire to their houses.

I had a very long talk with one of them; but I had an interpreter who followed my meaning so badly, and who was so hindered by his stupidity in taking in my ideas, that I could get hardly any satisfaction from the man. When I asked him what profit he gained from his superior position among his people (for he was a captain, and our sailors called him king), he told me that it was to march foremost in war. How many men followed him? He pointed to a piece of ground, to signify as many as such a space could hold; it might have been four or five thousand men. Did all this authority expire with the war? He said that this much remained, that when he visited the villages dependent on him, they made paths for him through the underbrush by which he might pass quite comfortably.

All this is not too bad—but what's the use? They don't wear breeches.

Of the Inconsistency of Our Actions

Those who make a practice of comparing human actions are never so perplexed as when they try to see them as a whole and in the same light; for they commonly contradict each other so strangely that it seems impossible that they have come from the same shop. One moment young Marius is a son of Mars, another moment a son of Venus.[3] Pope Boniface VIII, they say, entered office like a fox, behaved in it like a lion, and died like a dog. And who would believe that it was Nero, that living image of cruelty, who said, when they brought him in customary fashion the sentence of a condemned criminal to sign: "Would to God I had never learned to write!" So much his heart was wrung at condemning a man to death!

Everything is so full of such examples—each man, in fact, can supply himself with so many—that I find it strange to see intelligent men sometimes going to great pains to match these pieces; seeing that irresolution seems to me the most common and apparent defect of our nature, as witness that famous line of Publilius, the farce writer:

> Bad is the plan that never can be changed.
> PUBLILIUS SYRUS[4]

There is some justification for basing a judgment of a man on the most ordinary acts of his life; but in view of the natural instability of our conduct and opinions, it has often seemed to me that even good authors are wrong to insist on fashioning a consistent and solid fabric out of us. They choose one general characteristic, and go and arrange and interpret all a man's actions to fit their picture; and if they cannot twist them enough, they go and set them down to dissimulation. Augustus has escaped them; for there is in this man throughout the course of his life such an obvious, abrupt, and

---

3. Goddess of love. *Marius* was the nephew of the older and better-known Marius. Montaigne's source is Plutarch's *Life of Marius*. Mars was the god of war.   4. *Apothegms (Sententiae)*, line 362.

continual variety of actions that even the boldest judges have had to let him go, intact and unsolved. Nothing is harder for me than to believe in men's consistency, nothing easier than to believe in their inconsistency. He who would judge them in detail and distinctly, bit by bit, would more often hit upon the truth.

In all antiquity it is hard to pick out a dozen men who set their lives to a certain and constant course, which is the principal goal of wisdom. For, to comprise all wisdom in a word, says an ancient [Seneca], and to embrace all the rules of our life in one, it is "always to will the same things, and always to oppose the same things."[5] I would not deign, he says, to add "provided the will is just"; for if it is not just, it cannot always be whole.

In truth, I once learned that vice is only unruliness and lack of moderation, and that consequently consistency cannot be attributed to it. It is a maxim of Demosthenes, they say, that the beginning of all virtue is consultation and deliberation; and the end and perfection, consistency. If it were by reasoning that we settled on a particular course of action, we would choose the fairest course—but no one has thought of that:

> He spurns the thing he sought, and seeks anew
> What he just spurned; he seethes, his life's askew.
> HORACE[6]

Our ordinary practice is to follow the inclinations of our appetite, to the left, to the right, uphill and down, as the wind of circumstance carries us. We think of what we want only at the moment we want it, and we change like that animal which takes the color of the place you set it on. What we have just now planned, we presently change, and presently again we retrace our steps: nothing but oscillation and inconsistency:

> Like puppets we are moved by outside strings.
> HORACE[7]

We do not go; we are carried away, like floating objects, now gently, now violently, according as the water is angry or calm:

> Do we not see all humans unaware
> Of what they want, and always searching everywhere,
> And changing place, as if to drop the load they bear?
> LUCRETIUS[8]

Every day a new fancy, and our humors shift with the shifts in the weather:

> Such are the minds of men, as is the fertile light
> That Father Jove himself sends down to make earth bright.
> HOMER[9]

We float between different states of mind; we wish nothing freely, nothing absolutely, nothing constantly. If any man could prescribe and establish definite laws and a definite organization in his head, we should see shining throughout his life an evenness of habits, an order, and an infallible relation between his principles and his practice.

Empedocles noticed this inconsistency in the Agrigentines, that they aban-

5. Epistles 20.   6. Epistles 1.1.98–99.   7. Satires 2.7.82.   8. On the Nature of Things 3.1057–59.
9. Odyssey 18.135–36, 152–53 in the Fitzgerald translation.

doned themselves to pleasures as if they were to die on the morrow, and built as if they were never to die.[1]

This man would be easy to understand, as is shown by the example of the younger Cato[2]: he who has touched one chord of him has touched all; he is a harmony of perfectly concordant sounds, which cannot conflict. With us, it is the opposite: for so many actions, we need so many individual judgments. The surest thing, in my opinion, would be to trace our actions to the neighboring circumstances, without getting into any further research and without drawing from them any other conclusions.

During the disorders of our poor country,[3] I was told that a girl, living near where I then was, had thrown herself out of a high window to avoid the violence of a knavish soldier quartered in her house. Not killed by the fall, she reasserted her purpose by trying to cut her throat with a knife. From this she was prevented, but only after wounding herself gravely. She herself confessed that the soldier had as yet pressed her only with requests, solicitations, and gifts; but she had been afraid, she said, that he would finally resort to force. And all this with such words, such expressions, not to mention the blood that testified to her virtue, as would have become another Lucrece.[4] Now, I learned that as a matter of fact, both before and since, she was a wench not so hard to come to terms with. As the story[5] says: Handsome and gentlemanly as you may be, when you have had no luck, do not promptly conclude that your mistress is inviolably chaste; for all you know, the mule driver may get his will with her.

Antigonus,[6] having taken a liking to one of his soldiers for his virtue and valor, ordered his physicians to treat the man for a persistent internal malady that had long tormented him. After his cure, his master noticed that he was going about his business much less warmly, and asked him what had changed him so and made him such a coward. "You yourself, Sire," he answered, "by delivering me from the ills that made my life indifferent to me." A soldier of Lucullus[7] who had been robbed of everything by the enemy made a bold attack on them to get revenge. When he had retrieved his loss, Lucullus, having formed a good opinion of him, urged him to some dangerous exploit with all the fine expostulations he could think of,

> With words that might have stirred a coward's heart.
>
> HORACE[8]

"Urge some poor soldier who has been robbed to do it," he replied;

> Though but a rustic lout,
> "That man will go who's lost his money," he called out;
>
> HORACE[9]

and resolutely refused to go.

We read that Sultan Mohammed outrageously berated Hassan, leader of his Janissaries, because he saw his troops giving way to the Hungarians and

---

1. From Diogenes Laertius's life of the Greek philosopher Empedocles (fifth century).   2. Cato Uticensis (1st century B.C.E.), a philosopher. He is traditionally considered the epitome of moral and intellectual integrity.   3. See n. 3, p. 2195.   4. The legendary virtuous Roman who stabbed herself after being raped by King Tarquinius Superbus's son.   5. A common folktale.   6. Macedonian king (382–301 B.C.E.).   7. Roman general (1st century B.C.E.).   8. *Epistles* 2.2.36.   9. *Epistles* 2.2.39–40.

Hassan himself behaving like a coward in the fight. Hassan's only reply was to go and hurl himself furiously—alone, just as he was, arms in hand—into the first body of enemies that he met, by whom he was promptly swallowed up; this was perhaps not so much self-justification as a change of mood, nor so much his natural valor as fresh spite.

That man whom you saw so adventurous yesterday, do not think it strange to find him just as cowardly today: either anger, or necessity, or company, or wine, or the sound of a trumpet, had put his heart in his belly. His was a courage formed not by reason, but by one of these circumstances; it is no wonder if he has now been made different by other, contrary circumstances.

These supple variations and contradictions that are seen in us have made some imagine that we have two souls, and others that two powers accompany us and drive us, each in its own way, one toward good, the other toward evil; for such sudden diversity cannot well be reconciled with a simple subject.

Not only does the wind of accident move me at will, but, besides, I am moved and disturbed as a result merely of my own unstable posture; and anyone who observes carefully can hardly find himself twice in the same state. I give my soul now one face, now another, according to which direction I turn it. If I speak of myself in different ways, that is because I look at myself in different ways. All contradictions may be found in me by some twist and in some fashion. Bashful, insolent; chaste, lascivious; talkative, taciturn; tough, delicate; clever, stupid; surly, affable; lying, truthful; learned, ignorant; liberal, miserly, and prodigal: all this I see in myself to some extent according to how I turn; and whoever studies himself really attentively finds in himself, yes, even in his judgment, this gyration and discord. I have nothing to say about myself absolutely, simply, and solidly, without confusion and without mixture, or in one word. *Distinguo*[1] is the most universal member of my logic.

Although I am always minded to say good of what is good, and inclined to interpret favorably anything that can be so interpreted, still it is true that the strangeness of our condition makes it happen that we are often driven to do good by vice itself—were it not that doing good is judged by intention alone.

Therefore one courageous deed must not be taken to prove a man valiant; a man who was really valiant would be so always and on all occasions. If valor were a habit of virtue, and not a sally, it would make a man equally resolute in any contingency, the same alone as in company, the same in single combat as in battle; for, whatever they say, there is not one valor for the pavement and another for the camp. As bravely would he bear an illness in his bed as a wound in camp, and he would fear death no more in his home than in an assault. We would not see the same man charging into the breach with brave assurance, and later tormenting himself, like a woman, over the loss of a lawsuit or a son. When, though a coward against infamy, he is firm against poverty; when, though weak against the surgeons' knives, he is steadfast against the enemy's swords, the action is praiseworthy, not the man.

Many Greeks, says Cicero, cannot look at the enemy, and are brave in sickness; the Cimbrians and Celtiberians, just the opposite; *for nothing can be uniform that does not spring from a firm principle* [Cicero].[2]

---

1. I distinguish (Latin)—that is, I separate into its components.   2. Marcus Tullius Cicero (106–43 B.C.E.), Roman orator; *Tusculan Disputations* 2.27.

There is no more extreme valor of its kind than Alexander's; but it is only of one kind, and not complete and universal enough. Incomparable though it is, it still has its blemishes; which is why we see him worry so frantically when he conceives the slightest suspicion that his men are plotting against his life, and why he behaves in such matters with such violent and indiscriminate injustice and with a fear that subverts his natural reason. Also superstition, with which he was so strongly tainted, bears some stamp of pusillanimity. And the excessiveness of the penance he did for the murder of Clytus[3] is also evidence of the unevenness of his temper.

Our actions are nothing but a patchwork—*they despise pleasure, but are too cowardly in pain; they are indifferent to glory, but infamy breaks their spirit* [Cicero][4]—and we want to gain honor under false colors. Virtue will not be followed except for her own sake; and if we sometimes borrow her mask for some other purpose, she promptly snatches it from our face. It is a strong and vivid dye, once the soul is steeped in it, and will not go without taking the fabric with it. That is why, to judge a man, we must follow his traces long and carefully. If he does not maintain consistency for its own sake, *with a way of life that has been well considered and preconcerted* [Cicero][5]; if changing circumstances makes him change his pace (I mean his path, for his pace may be hastened or slowed), let him go: that man goes before the wind, as the motto of our Talbot[6] says.

It is no wonder, says an ancient [Seneca], that chance has so much power over us, since we live by chance.[7] A man who has not directed his life as a whole toward a definite goal cannot possibly set his particular actions in order. A man who does not have a picture of the whole in his head cannot possibly arrange the pieces. What good does it do a man to lay in a supply of paints if he does not know what he is to paint? No one makes a definite plan of his life; we think about it only piecemeal. The archer must first know what he is aiming at, and then set his hand, his bow, his string, his arrow, and his movements for that goal. Our plans go astray because they have no direction and no aim. No wind works for the man who has no port of destination.

I do not agree with the judgment given in favor of Sophocles, on the strength of seeing one of his tragedies, that it proved him competent to manage his domestic affairs, against the accusation of his son. Nor do I think that the conjecture of the Parians sent to reform the Milesians was sufficient ground for the conclusion they drew. Visiting the island, they noticed the best-cultivated lands and the best-run country houses, and noted down the names of their owners. Then they assembled the citizens in the town and appointed these owners the new governors and magistrates, judging that they, who were careful of their private affairs, would be careful of those of the public.

We are all patchwork, and so shapeless and diverse in composition that each bit, each moment, plays its own game. And there is as much difference between us and ourselves as between us and others. *Consider it a great thing to play the part of one single man* [Seneca].[8] Ambition can teach men valor,

3. A commander in Alexander's army who was killed by him during an argument, an act Alexander immediately and bitterly regretted, as related by Plutarch in his *Life of Alexander*, chaps. 50–52.   4. *On Duties (De officiis)* 1.21.   5. *Paradoxes* 5.   6. An English captain who fought in France and died there in 1453.   7. *Epistles* 71.   8. *Epistles* 120.

and temperance, and liberality, and even justice. Greed can implant in the heart of a shop apprentice, brought up in obscurity and idleness, the confidence to cast himself far from hearth and home, in a frail boat at the mercy of the waves and angry Neptune; it also teaches discretion and wisdom. Venus herself supplies resolution and boldness to boys still subject to discipline and the rod, and arms the tender hearts of virgins who are still in their mothers' laps:

> Furtively passing sleeping guards, with Love as guide,
> Alone by night the girl comes to the young man's side.
>   TIBULLUS[9]

In view of this, a sound intellect will refuse to judge men simply by their outward actions; we must probe the inside and discover what springs set men in motion. But since this is an arduous and hazardous undertaking, I wish fewer people would meddle with it.

Of Coaches

It is very easy to demonstrate that great authors, when they write about causes, adduce not only those they think are true but also those they do not believe in, provided they have some originality and beauty. They speak truly and usefully enough if they speak ingeniously. We cannot make sure of the master cause; we pile up several of them, to see if by chance it will be found among them,

> For one cause will not do;
> We must state many, one of which is true.
>   LUCRETIUS[1]

Do you ask me whence comes this custom of blessing those who sneeze? We produce three sorts of wind. That which issues from below is too foul; that which issues from the mouth carries some reproach of gluttony; the third is sneezing. And because it comes from the head and is blameless, we give it this civil reception. Do not laugh at this piece of subtlety; it is, they say, from Aristotle.

It seems to me I have read in Plutarch (who, of all the authors I know, is the one who best combined art with nature and judgment with knowledge) that he gives the reason for the heaving of the stomach that afflicts those who travel by sea, as fear, having found some reason by which he proves that fear can produce such an effect. I, who am very subject to seasickness, know very well that this cause does not affect me, and I know it, not by reasoning, but by necessary experience. Not to mention what I have been told, that the same thing often happens to animals, and especially to pigs, without any apprehension of danger; and what an acquaintance of mine has told me about himself, that though he was very subject to it, the desire to vomit had left him two or three times when he found himself oppressed with fright in a big storm. And hear this ancient: *I was too sick to think about the danger*

---

9. *Elegies* 2.1.75–76. 1. *On the Nature of Things* 6.704–705.

[Seneca].[2] I was never afraid on the water, nor indeed anywhere else (and I have often enough had just occasions, if death is one), at least not to the point of being confused or bewildered.

Fear sometimes arises from want of judgment as well as from want of courage. All the dangers I have seen, I have seen with open eyes, with my sight free, sound, and entire; besides, it takes courage to be afraid. It once served me in good stead, compared with others, so to conduct my flight and keep it orderly, that it was carried out, if not without fear, at all events without terror and without dismay; it was excited, but not dazed or distracted.

Great souls go much further yet and offer us examples of flights not merely composed and healthy, but proud. Let us tell of the one that Alcibiades reports of Socrates, his comrade in arms:[3] "I found him," he says, "after the rout of our army, him and Laches, among the last of the fugitives; and I observed him at my leisure and in safety, for I was on a good horse and he on foot, and we had fought that way. I noticed first how much presence of mind and resolution he showed compared with Laches; and then the boldness of his walk, no different from his ordinary one, his firm and steady gaze, considering and judging what was going on around him, looking now at one side, now the other, friends and enemies, in a way that encouraged the former and signified to the latter that he was a man to sell his blood and his life very dear to anyone who should try to take them away. And thus they made their escape; for people are not inclined to attack such men; they run after the frightened ones." That is the testimony of that great captain, which teaches us what we experience every day, that there is nothing that throws us so much into dangers as an unthinking eagerness to get clear of them. *Where there is less fear, there is generally less danger* [Livy].[4]

Our common people are wrong to say that such-and-such a man fears death, when they mean to say that he thinks about it and foresees it. Foresight is equally suitable in whatever concerns us, whether for good or ill. To consider and judge the danger is in a way the opposite of being stunned by it.

I do not feel myself strong enough to sustain the impact and impetuosity of this passion of fear, or of any other vehement passion. If I were once conquered and thrown by it, I would never get up again quite intact. If anything made my soul lose its footing, it would never set it back upright in its place; it probes and searches itself too keenly and deeply, and therefore would never let the wound that had pierced it close up and heal. It has been well for me that no illness has yet laid it low. Each attack made on me I meet and fight off in my full armor; thus the first one that swept me off my feet would leave me without resources. I have no secondary defense: no matter where the torrent should break my dike, I would be helpless and be drowned for good.

Epicurus[5] says that the wise man can never pass into a contrary state. I have an opinion about the converse of this saying: that anyone who has once been very foolish will never at any other time be very wise.

God tempers the cold according to the cloak, and gives me passions according to my means of withstanding them. Nature, having uncovered me

2. *Moral Epistles* 53.3.   3. Plato, *Symposium*.   4. Titus Livius (59 B.C.E.–17 C.E. or 64 B.C.E.–12 C.E.), Roman historian; *On the Founding of Rome* 22.5.   5. Greek moral and natural philosopher (341–270 B.C.E.)

on one side, has covered me up on the other; having disarmed me of strength, she has armed me with insensibility and a controlled, or dull, apprehensiveness.

Now I cannot long endure (and I could endure them less easily in my youth) either coach, or litter, or boat; and I hate any other transportation than horseback, both in town and in the country. But I can endure a litter less than a coach, and for the same reason I can more easily bear a rough tossing on the water, whereby fear is produced, than the movement felt in calm weather. By that slight jolt given by the oars, stealing the vessel from under us, I somehow feel my head and stomach troubled, as I cannot bear a shaky seat under me. When the sail or the current carries us along evenly or when we are towed, this uniform movement does not bother me at all. It is an interrupted motion that annoys me, and most of all when it is languid. I cannot otherwise describe its nature. The doctors have ordered me to bind and swathe my abdomen with a towel to remedy this trouble; which I have not tried, being accustomed to wrestle with the weaknesses that are in me and overcome them by myself.

If my memory were sufficiently stored with them, I should not begrudge my time to tell here the infinite variety of examples that histories offer us of the use of coaches in the service of war, varying according to the nations and according to the age; of great effect, it seems to me, and very necessary, so that it is a wonder that we have lost all knowledge of them. I will say only this, that quite recently, in our fathers' time, the Hungarians put coaches very usefully to work against the Turks, there being in each one a targeteer and a musketeer and a number of harquebuses lined up, loaded and ready, the whole thing covered with a wall of shields, like a galiot. They formed their battlefront of three thousand such coaches, and after the cannon had played, had them advance and made the enemy swallow this salvo before tasting the rest; which was no slight advantage. Or they launched them into the enemy squadrons to break them and open them up; not to mention the advantage they could derive from them by flanking enemy troops on their march through open country where they were vulnerable, or by covering a camp in haste and fortifying it.

In my time a gentleman on one of our frontiers, who was unwieldy of person and found no horse capable of bearing his weight, having a feud on his hands, went about the country in a coach of this very description, and made out very well. But let us leave these war coaches. The kings of our first dynasty went about the country in a chariot drawn by four oxen.

Mark Antony[6] was the first who had himself drawn in Rome—and a minstrel girl beside him—by lions harnessed to a chariot. Heliogabalus did as much later, calling himself Cybele, the mother of the gods; and also by tigers, imitating the god Bacchus; he also sometimes harnessed two stags to his coach, and another time four dogs, and yet again four naked wenches, having himself, starked naked too, drawn by them in pomp. The Emperor Firmus had his chariot drawn by ostriches of marvelous size, so that it seemed rather to fly than to roll.

The strangeness of these inventions puts into my head this other notion:

6. Marcus Antonius (83–31 B.C.E.), Roman general, libertine, and triumvir, whose associations with Eastern luxury and religious cults are invoked here.

that it is a sort of pusillanimity in monarchs, and evidence of not sufficiently feeling what they are, to labor at showing off and making a display by excessive expense. It would be excusable in a foreign country; but among his own subjects, where he is all-powerful, he derives from his dignity the highest degree of honor he can attain. Just as, it seems to me, for a gentleman it is superfluous to dress with studied care at home: his house, his retinue, his cuisine, answer for him sufficiently.

The advice that Isocrates[7] gives his king seems to me not without reason: that he be splendid in furniture and plate, since that is a lasting investment which passes on to his successors; and that he avoid all magnificences that flow away immediately out of use and memory.

I liked to adorn myself when I was a youth, for lack of other adornments, and it was becoming to me; there are those on whom fine clothes weep. We have marvelous stories of the frugality of our kings about their own persons and in their gifts—kings great in prestige, in valor, and in fortune. Demosthenes[8] fights tooth and nail against the law of his city that allotted public monies to lavish games and feasts; he wants the greatness of the city to be manifest in its quantity of well-equipped ships and of good, well-supplied armies.

And Theophrastus[9] is rightly blamed for setting forth a contrary opinion in his book on riches, and maintaining that lavish expenditure was the true fruit of opulence. These are pleasures, says Aristotle, that touch only the lowest of the people, that vanish from memory as soon as people are sated with them, and that no judicious and serious man can esteem. The outlay would seem to me much more royal as well as more useful, just, and durable, if it were spent on ports, harbors, fortifications, and walls, on sumptuous buildings, churches, hospitals, colleges, and the improvement of streets and roads, for which Pope Gregory XIII is gratefully remembered in my time, and in which our Queen Catherine[1] would leave evidence for many years of her natural liberality and munificence, if her means were equal to her wish. Fortune has given me great displeasure by interrupting the construction of the handsome new bridge[2] of our great city, and depriving me of the hope of seeing it in full use before I die.

Besides, it seems to the subjects, spectators of these triumphs, that they are given a display of their own riches, and entertained at their own expense. For peoples are apt to assume about kings, as we do about our servants, that they should take care to prepare for us in abundance all we need, but that they should not touch it at all for their own part. And therefore the Emperor Galba,[3] having taken pleasure in a musician's playing during his supper, sent for his money box and gave into his hand a handful of crowns that he fished out of it, with these words: "This is not the public money, this is my own." At all events, it most often happens that the people are right, and that their eyes are feasted with what should go to feed their bellies.

Liberality itself is not in its proper light in the hands of a sovereign; private people have more right to exercise it. For, to be precise about it, a king has nothing that is properly his own; he owes his very self to others.

---

7. Athenian orator (436–338 B.C.E.).   8. Greatest Athenian orator (384–322 B.C.E.).   9. Greek philosopher and botanist, follower of Aristotle (ca. 370–288 B.C.E.).   1. Catherine de Médicis (1519–1589). 2. The Pont Neuf, as it is still called, was completed in 1604 [Translator's note].   3. Roman emperor (ca. 3 B.C.E.–69 C.E.) after Nero.

The authority to judge is not given for the sake of the judge, but for the sake of the person judged. A superior is never appointed for his own benefit, but for the benefit of the inferior, and a doctor for the sick, not for himself. All authority, like all art, has its end outside of itself: *no art is directed to itself* [Cicero].[4]

Wherefore the tutors of young princes who make it a point to impress on them this virtue of liberality and preach to them not to know how to refuse anything, and to think nothing so well spent as what they give away (a lesson that I have seen in great favor in my time), either look more to their own profit than to their master's, or do not well understand to whom they speak. It is all too easy to impress liberality on a man who has the means to practice it all he wants at the expense of others. And since its value is reckoned not by the measure of the gift, but by the measure of the giver's means, it amounts to nothing in such powerful hands. They find themselves prodigal before they are liberal. Therefore liberality is little to be commended compared with other royal virtues, and it is the only one, as the tyrant Dionysius said, that goes with tyranny itself. I would rather teach him this verse of the ancient farmer: that whoever wants to reap a good crop must sow with the hand, not pour out of the sack; he must scatter the seed, not spill it; and that since he has to give, or, to put it better, pay and restore to so many people according to their deserts, he should be a fair and wise distributor. If the liberality of a prince is without discretion and without measure, I would rather he were a miser.

Royal virtue seems to consist most of all in justice; and of all the parts of justice, that one best marks kings which accompanies liberality; for they have particularly reserved it as their function, whereas they are prone to exercise all other justice through the intermediary of others. Immoderate largesse is a feeble means for them to acquire good will; for it alienates more people than it wins over: *The more you have already practiced it on, the fewer you will be able to practice it on. What is more foolish than to take pains so that you can no longer do what you enjoy doing?* [Cicero.][5] And if it is exercised without regard to merit, it puts to shame him who receives it, and is received ungraciously. Tyrants have been sacrificed to the hatred of the people by the hands of the very ones whom they have unjustly advanced; for such men think to assure their possession of undeserved goods by showing contempt and hatred for the man from whom they received them, and rallying to the judgment and opinion of the people in that respect.

The subjects of a prince who is excessive in gifts become excessive in requests; they adjust themselves not to reason but to example. Surely we often have reason to blush for our impudence; we are overpaid according to justice when the recompense equals our service; for do we owe no service to our prince by natural obligation? If he bears our expenses, he does too much; it is enough that he helps out. The surplus is called benefit, and it cannot be exacted, for the very name of liberality rings of liberty. By our method, it is never done; the receipts are no longer taken into account; people love only the future liberality. Wherefore the more a prince exhausts himself in giving, the poorer he makes himself in friends. How could he assuage desires that grow the more they are fulfilled? He who has his mind on taking, no longer

4. *De finibus* 5.6.16.   5. *On Duties* 2.15.52–54.

has it on what he has taken. Covetousness has nothing so characteristic about it as ingratitude.

The example of Cyrus[6] will not be amiss here to serve the kings of our time as a touchstone for ascertaining whether their gifts are well or ill bestowed, and to make them see how much more happily that emperor dealt them out than they do. Whereby they are reduced to doing their borrowing from unknown subjects, and rather from those they have wronged than from those they have benefited; and from them they receive no aid that is gratuitous in anything but the name.

Croesus reproached Cyrus for his extravagance and calculated how much his treasure would amount to if he had been more close-fisted. Cyrus, wanting to justify his liberality, sent dispatches in all directions to the grandees of his state whose career he had particularly advanced, and asked each one to help him out with as much money as he could for an urgent need of his, and to send him a declaration of the amount. When all these statements were brought to him, since each of his friends, thinking it was not enough to offer him merely as much as he had received from his munificence, added much that was more properly his own, it turned out that the total amounted to much more than the savings estimated by Croesus. Whereupon Cyrus said to him: "I am no less in love with riches than other princes, and am rather a more careful manager of them. You see at how small a cost I have acquired the inestimable treasure of so many friends, and how much more faithful treasurers they are to me than mercenary men without obligation, without affection, would be; and how much better my wealth is lodged than in coffers, where it would call down upon me the hatred, envy, and contempt of other princes."

The emperors derived an excuse for the superfluity of their public games and spectacles from the fact that their authority depended somewhat (at least in appearance) on the will of the Roman people, who from time immemorial had been accustomed to being flattered by that sort of spectacle and extravagance. But it was private citizens who had nourished this custom of gratifying their fellow citizens and companions, chiefly out of their own purse, by such profusion and magnificence; this had an altogether different flavor when it was the masters who came to imitate it *The transfer of money from its rightful owners to strangers should not be regarded as liberality* [Cicero].[7]

Philip, because his son was trying to win the good will of the Macedonians by presents, scolded him for it in a letter in this manner: "What, do you want your subjects to regard you as their purser, not as their king? Do you want to win them over? Win them over with the benefits of your virtue, not the benefits of your coffers."[8]

It was, however, a fine thing to bring and plant in the amphitheater a great quantity of big trees, all branching and green, representing a great shady forest, arranged in beautiful symmetry, and on the first day to cast into it a thousand ostriches, a thousand stags, a thousand wild boars, and a thousand fallow deer, leaving them to be hunted down by the people; on the next day to have a hundred big lions, a hundred leopards, and three hundred bears slaughtered in their presence; and for the third day, to have three hundred

---

6. Ideal prince of Xenophon's *Education of Cyrus.*   7. *On Duties* 1.14.43.   8. *On Duties* 2.15.53–54; Philip of Macedon was the father of Alexander the Great.

pairs of gladiators fight it out to the death, as the Emperor Probus[9] did.

It was also a fine thing to see those great amphitheaters faced with marble on the outside, wrought with ornaments and statues, the inside sparkling with many rare enrichments—

> Here is the diamond circle, the golden portico
>
> CALPURNIUS[1]

—all the sides of this vast space filled and surrounded from top to bottom with three or four score tiers of seats, also of marble, covered with cushions—

> "Let him begone," he says,
> "And leave the cushioned seats of knights, seeing he pays
> None of the lawful tax"
>
> JUVENAL[2]

—where a hundred thousand men could sit at their ease. Also, first of all, to have the place at the bottom, where the games were played, open artificially and split into crevasses representing caverns that vomited forth the beasts destined for the spectacle; and then, second, to flood it with a deep sea, full of sea monsters and laden with armed vessels to represent a naval battle; and third, to level it and dry it off again for the combat of the gladiators; and for the fourth show to strew it with vermilion and storax instead of sand, in order to set up a stately banquet there for all that huge number of people—the final act of a single day:

> How often have we seen
> Part of the sandy floor sink down, wild beasts emerge
> Out of the open chasm, and from its depths upsurge
> Forests of golden growing trees with yellow bark.
> Not only forest monsters were for us to mark,
> But I saw sea-calves mingled in with fighting bears,
> And hippopotami, the shapeless herd that wears
> The name of river-horse.
>
> CALPURNIUS[3]

Sometimes they created a high mountain there, full of fruit trees and other trees in leaf, spouting a stream of water from its top as from the mouth of a living spring. Sometimes they brought in a great ship which opened and came apart of itself and, after having spewed forth from its belly four or five hundred fighting beasts, closed up again and vanished without assistance. At other times, from the floor of the place, they made spouts and jets of water spring forth which shot upward to an infinite height, then sprinkled and perfumed that infinite multitude. To protect themselves against damage from the weather, they had that immense space hung with awnings, sometimes made of purple worked with the needle, sometimes of silk of one color or another, and they drew them forward or back in a moment, as they had a mind to:

> The awnings, though the sun scorches the skin,
> Are, when Hermogenes appears, drawn in.
>
> MARTIAL[4]

---

9. Marcus Aurelius Probus (232–282 C.E.), a stern disciplinarian, eventually killed by his own troops. 1. Calpurnius Siculus (1st century C.E.), pastoral poet; *Bucolics* 7.47. 2. *Satires* 3.153–55. 3. *Bucolics* 7.64–75. 4. Marcus Valerius Martial (ca. 40–ca. 104 C.E.), famous for his witty epigrams; *Epigrams* 12.29.15–16.

The nets, too, which they put in front of the people to protect them from the violence of the loosened beasts, were woven of gold:

> Even the woven nets
> Glitter with gold.
> CALPURNIUS[5]

If there is anything excusable in such extravagances, it is when the inventiveness and the novelty of them, not the expense, provide amazement.

Even in these vanities we discover how fertile those ages were in minds different from ours. It is with this sort of fertility as with all other productions of Nature. This is not to say that she then put forth her utmost effort. We do not go in a straight line; we rather ramble, and turn this way and that. We retrace our steps. I fear that our knowledge is weak in every direction; we do not see very far ahead or very far behind. It embraces little and has a short life, short in both extent of time and extent of matter:

> Ere Agamemnon, heroes were the same;
> Many there were, but no one knows their name;
> They all are hurried on unwept
> Into unending night.
> HORACE

> Before the Trojan War, before Troy fell,
> Were other bards with other tales to tell.
> LUCRETIUS[6]

And Solon's story of what he had heard from the priests of Egypt about the long life of their state, and their manner of learning and preserving the histories of other countries, does not seem to me a testimony to be rejected in this consideration. *If we could view that expanse of countries and ages, boundless in every direction, into which the mind, plunging and spreading itself, travels so far and wide that it can find no limit where it can stop, there would appear in that immensity an infinite capacity to produce innumerable forms* [adapted from Cicero].[7]

Even if all that has come down to us by report from the past should be true and known by someone, it would be less than nothing compared with what is unknown. And of this very image of the world which glides along while we live on it, how puny and limited is the knowledge of even the most curious! Not only of particular events which fortune often renders exemplary and weighty, but of the state of great governments and nations, there escapes us a hundred times more than comes to our knowledge. We exclaim at the miracle of the invention of our artillery, of our printing; other men in another corner of the world, in China, enjoyed these a thousand years earlier. If we saw as much of the world as we do not see, we would perceive, it is likely, a perpetual multiplication and vicissitude of forms.

There is nothing unique and rare as regards nature, but there certainly is as regards our knowledge, which is a miserable foundation for our rules and which is apt to represent to us a very false picture of things. As vainly as we today infer the decline and decrepitude of the world from the arguments we draw from our own weakness and decay—

5. *Bucolics* 7.53–54. 6. *On the Nature of Things* 5.327–28. Above, *Odes* 4.9.25–28. 7. *On the Nature of the Gods* 1.20.54. Solon (ca. 200 C.E.), geographer.

> This age is broken down, and broken down the earth
> LUCRETIUS[8]

—so vainly did this poet infer the world's birth and youth from the vigor he saw in the minds of his time, abounding in novelties and inventions in various arts:

> The universe, I think, is very new,
> The world is young, its birth not far behind;
> Hence certain arts grow more and more refined
> Even today; the naval art is one.
> LUCRETIUS[9]

Our world has just discovered another world (and who will guarantee us that it is the last of its brothers, since the daemons, the Sibyls,[1] and we ourselves have up to now been ignorant of this one?) no less great, full, and well-limbed than itself, yet so new and so infantile that it is still being taught its A B C; not fifty years ago it knew neither letters, nor weights and measures, nor clothes, nor wheat, nor vines. It was still quite naked at the breast, and lived only on what its nursing mother provided. If we are right to infer the end of our world, and that poet is right about the youth of his own age, this other world will only be coming into the light when ours is leaving it. The universe will fall into paralysis; one member will be crippled, the other in full vigor.

I am much afraid that we shall have very greatly hastened the decline and ruin of this new world by our contagion, and that we will have sold it our opinions and our arts very dear. It was an infant world; yet we have not whipped it and subjected it to our discipline by the advantage of our natural valor and strength, nor won it over by our justice and goodness, nor subjugated it by our magnanimity. Most of the responses of these people and most of our dealings with them show that they were not at all behind us in natural brightness of mind and pertinence.

The awesome magnificence of the cities of Cuzco[2] and Mexico (and, among many similar things, the garden of that king in which all the trees, the fruits, and all the herbs were excellently fashioned in gold, and of such size and so arranged as they might be in an ordinary garden; and in his curio room were gold replicas of all the living creatures native to his country and its waters), and the beauty of their workmanship in jewelry, feathers, cotton, and painting, show that they were not behind us in industry either. But as for devoutness, observance of the laws, goodness, liberality, loyalty, and frankness, it served us well not to have as much as they: by their advantage in this they lost, sold, and betrayed themselves.

As for boldness and courage, as for firmness, constancy, resoluteness against pains and hunger and death, I would not fear to oppose the examples I could find among them to the most famous ancient examples that we have in the memories of our world on this side of the ocean. For as regards the men who subjugated them, take away the ruses and tricks that they used to deceive them, and the people's natural astonishment at seeing the unexpected arrival of bearded men, different in language, religion, shape, and

---

8. *On the Nature of Things* 2.1136.   9. *On the Nature of Things* 5.331–35.   1. Female prophets.
2. Former capital of the Inca Empire in southeastern Peru.

countenance, from a part of the world so remote, where they had never imagined there was any sort of human habitation, mounted on great unknown monsters, opposed to men who had never seen not only a horse, but any sort of animal trained to carry and endure a man or any other burden; men equipped with a hard and shiny skin and a sharp and glittering weapon, against men who, for the miracle of a mirror or a knife, would exchange a great treasure in gold and pearls, and who had neither the knowledge nor the material by which, even in full leisure, they could pierce our steel; add to this the lightning and thunder of our cannon and harquebuses—capable of disturbing Caesar[3] himself, if he had been surprised by them with as little experience and in his time—against people who were naked (except in some regions where the invention of some cotton fabric had reached them), without other arms at the most than bows, stones, sticks, and wooden bucklers; people taken by surprise, under color of friendship and good faith, by curiosity to see strange and unknown things: eliminate this disparity, I say, and you take from the conquerors the whole basis of so many victories.

When I consider that indomitable ardor with which so many thousands of men, women, and children came forth and hurled themselves so many times into inevitable dangers for the defense of their gods and of their liberty, and that noble, stubborn readiness to suffer all extremities and hardships, even death, rather than submit to the domination of those by whom they had been so shamefully deceived (for some of them when captured chose rather to let themselves perish of hunger and fasting than to accept food from the hands of such basely victorious enemies), I conclude that if anyone had attacked them on equal terms, with equal arms, experience, and numbers, it would have been just as dangerous for him as in any other war we know of, and more so.

Why did not such a noble conquest fall to Alexander or to those ancient Greeks and Romans? Why did not such a great change and alteration of so many empires and peoples fall into hands that would have gently polished and cleared away whatever was barbarous in them, and would have strengthened and fostered the good seeds that nature had produced in them, not only adding to the cultivation of the earth and the adornment of cities the arts of our side of the ocean, in so far as they would have been necessary, but also adding the Greek and Roman virtues to those originally in that region? What an improvement that would have been, and what an amelioration for the entire globe, if the first examples of our conduct that were offered over there had called those peoples to the admiration and imitation of virtue and had set up between them and us a brotherly fellowship and understanding! How easy it would have been to make good use of souls so fresh, so famished to learn, and having, for the most part, such fine natural beginnings! On the contrary, we took advantage of their ignorance and inexperience to incline them the more easily toward treachery, lewdness, avarice, and every sort of inhumanity and cruelty, after the example and pattern of our ways. Who ever set the utility of commerce and trading at such a price? So many cities razed, so many nations exterminated, so many millions of people put to the sword, and the richest and most beautiful part of the world turned upside down, for the traffic in pearls and pepper! Base and mechan-

---

3. Julius Caesar (100–44 B.C.E.), the great Roman general and conqueror.

ical victories! Never did ambition, never did public enmities, drivemen against one another to such horrible hostilities and such miserable calamities.

Coasting the sea in quest of their mines, certain Spaniards landed in a fertile, pleasant, well-populated country, and made their usual declarations to its people: that they were peaceable men, coming from distant voyages, sent on behalf of the king of Castile, the greatest prince of the habitable world, to whom the Pope, representing God on earth, had given the principality of all the Indies; that if these people would be tributaries to him, they would be very kindly treated. They demanded of them food to eat and gold to be used in a certain medicine, and expounded to them the belief in one single God and the truth of our religion, which they advised them to accept, adding a few threats.

The answer was this: As for being peaceable, they did not look like it, if they were. As for their king, since he was begging, he must be indigent and needy; and he who had awarded their country to him must be a man fond of dissension, to go and give another person something that was not his and thus set him at strife with its ancient possessors. As for food, they would supply them. Gold they had little of, and it was a thing they held in no esteem, since it was useless to the service of their life, their sole concern being with passing life happily and pleasantly; however, they might boldly take any they could find, except what was employed in the service of their gods. As for one single God, the account had pleased them, but they did not want to change their religion, having followed it so advantageously for so long, and they were not accustomed to take counsel except of their friends and acquaintances. As for the threats, it was a sign of lack of judgment to threaten people whose nature and means were unknown to them. Thus they should promptly hurry up and vacate their land, for they were not accustomed to take in good part the civilities and declarations of armed strangers; otherwise they would do to them as they had done to these others—showing them the heads of some executed men around their city.

There we have an example of the babbling of this infancy. But at all events, neither in that place nor in several others where the Spaniards did not find the merchandise they were looking for, did they make any stay or any attack, whatever other advantages there might be; witness my Cannibals.[4]

Of the two most powerful monarchs of that world, and perhaps of this as well, kings of so many kings, the last two that they drove out, one, the king of Peru, was taken in a battle and put to so excessive a ransom that it surpasses all belief; and when this had been faithfully paid, and the king in his dealings had given signs of a frank, liberal, and steadfast spirit and a clear and well-ordered understanding, the conquerors, after having extracted from him one million three hundred and twenty-five thousand five hundred ounces of gold, besides silver and other things that amounted to no less, so that their horses thenceforth went shod with solid gold, were seized with the desire to see also, at the price of whatever treachery, what could be the remainder of this king's treasures, and to enjoy freely what he had reserved. They trumped up against him a false accusation and false evidence that he was planning to rouse his provinces in order to regain his freedom.

---

4. Of Cannibals.

Whereupon, in a beautiful sentence pronounced by those very men who had set afoot this treachery against him, he was condemned to be publicly hanged and strangled, after being permitted to buy his way out of the torment of being burned alive by submitting to baptism at the moment of the execution. A horrible and unheard-of calamity, which nevertheless he bore without belying himself either by look or word, with a truly royal bearing and gravity. And then, to lull the people, stunned and dazed by such a strange thing, they counterfeited great mourning over his death and ordered a sumptuous funeral for him.

The other one, the king of Mexico, had long defended his besieged city and shown in this siege all that endurance and perseverance can do, if ever prince and people did so, when his bad fortune put him in his enemies' hands alive, on their promise that they would treat him as a king; nor did he in his captivity show anything unworthy of this title. After this victory, his enemies, not finding all the gold they had promised themselves, first ransacked and searched everything, and then set about seeking information by inflicting the cruelest tortures they could think up on the prisoners they held. But having gained nothing by this, and finding their prisoners' courage stronger than their torments, they finally flew into such a rage that, against their word and against all law of nations, they condemned the king himself and one of the principal lords of his court to the torture in each other's presence. This lord, finding himself overcome with the pain, surrounded with burning braziers, in the end turned his gaze piteously toward his master, as if to ask his pardon because he could hold out no longer. The king, fixing his eyes proudly and severely on him in reproach for his cowardice and pusillanimity, said to him only these words, in a stern, firm voice: "And I, am I in a bath? Am I more comfortable than you?" The other immediately after succumbed to the pain and died on the spot. The king, half roasted, was carried away from there, not so much out of pity (for what pity ever touched souls who, for dubious information about some gold vase to pillage, had a man grilled before their eyes, and what is more, a king so great in fortune and merit?), but because his fortitude made their cruelty more and more shameful. They hanged him later for having courageously attempted to deliver himself by arms from such a long captivity and subjection, and he made an end worthy of a great-souled prince.

Another time they burned alive, all at once and in the same fire, four hundred and sixty men, the four hundred being of the common people, the sixty from among the chief lords of a province, all merely prisoners of war.

We have these narrations from themselves, for they not only admit them but boast of them and preach them. Would it be as a testimonial to their justice or their zeal for religion? Truly, those are ways too contrary and hostile to so holy an end. If they had proposed to extend our faith, they would have reflected that faith is not spread by possession of territory but by possession of men, and they would have been more than satisfied with the murders brought about by the necessity of war, without adding to these an indiscriminate butchery, as of wild animals, as universal as fire and sword could make it, after purposely sparing only as many as they wanted to make into miserable slaves for the working and service of their mines: with the result that many of the leaders were punished with death by order of the kings of Castile, who were justly shocked by the horror of their conduct; and almost all were disesteemed and loathed. God deservedly allowed this great plunder to be swallowed up by the sea in transit, or by the intestine wars in which they devoured one another; and most of them were buried on the spot without any profit from their victory.

As for the fact that the revenue from this, even in the hands of a thrifty and prudent prince,[5] corresponds so little to the expectation of it given to his predecessors and to the abundance of riches that was first encountered in these new lands (for although much is being gotten out, we see that it is nothing compared with what was to be expected), the reason is that the use of money was entirely unknown, and that consequently their gold was found all collected together, being of no other use than for show and parade, like a chattel preserved from father to son by many powerful kings who were constantly exhausting their mines to make that great heap of vases and statues for the adornment of their palaces and their temples; whereas our gold is all in circulation and in trade. We cut it up small and change it into a thousand forms; we scatter and disperse it. Imagine it if our kings thus accumulated all the gold they could find for many centuries and kept it idle.

The people of the kingdom of Mexico were somewhat more civilized and skilled in the arts than the other nations over there. Thus they judged, as we do, that the universe was near its end, and they took as a sign of this the desolation that we brought upon them. They believed that the existence of the world was divided into five ages and into the life of five successive suns, of which four had already run their time, and that the one which gave them light was the fifth. The first perished with all other creatures by a universal flood of water. The second, by the heavens falling on us, which suffocated every living thing; to which age they assign the giants, and they showed the Spaniards some of their bones, judging by the size of which these men must have stood twenty hands high. The third, by fire, which burned and consumed everything. The fourth, by a turbulence of air and wind which beat down even many mountains; the men did not die, but they were changed into baboons (to what notions will the laxness of human credulity not submit!). After the death of this fourth sun, the world was twenty-five years in perpetual darkness, in the fifteenth of which a man and a woman were created who remade the human race; ten years later, on a certain day of their calendar, the sun appeared newly created, and since then they reckon their years from that day. The third day after its creation the old gods died; the new ones have been born since little by little. What they think about the manner in which this last sun will perish, my author[6] did not learn. But their calculation of this fourth change coincides with that great conjunction of stars which produced, some eight hundred years ago, according to the reckoning of the astrologers, many great alterations and innovations in the world.

As for pomp and magnificence, whereby I entered upon this subject, neither Greece nor Rome nor Egypt can compare any of its works, whether in utility or difficulty or nobility, with the road which is seen in Peru, laid out by the kings of the country, from the city of Quito as far as Cuzco (a distance of three hundred leagues), straight, even, twenty-five paces wide, paved, lined on both sides with fine high walls, and along these, on the inside, two

---

5. Philip II of Spain (1527–1598).   6. Lopez de Gomara (1511–1564), a Spanish contemporary of Montaigne; Montaigne read his histories of Cortez and the West Indies in translation [Translator's note].

ever-flowing streams, bordered by beautiful trees, which they call *molly*. Wherever they encountered mountains and rocks, they cut through and leveled them, and filled the hollows with stone and lime. At the end of each day's journey there are fine palaces furnished with provisions, clothes, and arms, for travelers as well as for the armies that have to pass that way.

In my estimate of this work I have counted the difficulty, which is particularly considerable in that place. They did not build with any stones less than ten feet square; they had no other means of carrying than by strength of arm, dragging their load along; and they had not even the art of scaffolding, knowing no other device than to raise an equal height of earth against their building as it rose, and remove it afterward.

Let us fall back to our coaches. Instead of these or any other form of transport, they had themselves carried by men, and on their shoulders. That last king of Peru, the day that he was taken, was thus carried on shafts of gold, seated in a chair of gold, in the midst of his army. As many of these carriers as they killed to make him fall—for they wanted to take him alive—so many others vied to take the place of the dead ones, so that they never could bring him down, however great a slaughter they made of those people, until a horseman seized him around the body and pulled him to the ground.

MIGUEL DE CERVANTES
1547–1616

The author of Don Quixote's extravagant adventures himself had a most unusual and adventurous life. The son of an apothecary, Miguel de Cervantes Saavedra was born in Alcalá de Henares, a university town near Madrid. Almost nothing is known of his childhood and early education. Only in 1569 is he mentioned as a favorite pupil by a Madrid humanist, Juan López. Records indicate that by the end of that year he had left Spain and was living in Rome, for a time in the service of Giulio Acquaviva, who later became a cardinal. We know that he enlisted in the Spanish fleet under the command of Don John of Austria and that he took part in the struggle of the allied forces of Christendom against the Turks. He was at the crucial Battle of Lepanto (1571), where in spite of fever he fought valiantly and received three gunshot wounds, one of which permanently impaired the use of his left hand, "for the greater glory of the right." After further military action and garrison duty at Palermo and Naples, he and his brother Rodrigo, bearing testimonials from Don John and from the viceroy of Sicily, began the journey back to Spain, where Miguel hoped to obtain a captaincy. In September 1575 their ship was captured near the Marseille coast by Barbary pirates, and the two brothers were taken as prisoners to Algiers. Cervantes's captors, considering him a person of some consequence, held him as a slave for a high ransom. He repeatedly attempted to escape, and his daring and fortitude excited the admiration of Hassan Pasha, the viceroy of Algiers, who bought him for five hundred crowns after five years of captivity.

Cervantes was freed on September 15, 1580, and reached Madrid in December of that year. There his literary career began rather inauspiciously; he wrote twenty to thirty plays, with little success, and in 1585 published a pastoral romance, *Galatea*. At about this time he had a daughter with Ana Franca de Rojas, and during the same period married Catalina de Salazar, who was eighteen years his junior. Seeking nonliterary employment, he obtained a position in the navy, requisitioning and collecting supplies for the "Invincible Armada." Irregularities in his administration, for which he was held responsible if not directly guilty, caused him to spend more time in prison. In 1590 he tried unsuccessfully to obtain colonial employment in the New World. Later he served as tax collector in the province of Granada but was dismissed from government service in 1597.

The following years of Cervantes's life are the most obscure; there is a legend that *Don Quixote* was first conceived and planned while its author was in prison in Seville. In 1604 he was in Valladolid, then the temporary capital of Spain, living in sordid surroundings with the numerous women of his family (his wife, daughter, niece, and two sisters). It was in Valladolid, in late 1604, that he obtained the official license for the publication of *Don Quixote* (Part I). The book appeared in 1605 and was a popular success. Cervantes followed the Spanish court when it returned to Madrid, where he continued to live poorly in spite of a popularity with readers that quickly made proverbial figures of his heroes. A false sequel to his book appeared, prompting him to write his own continuation, *Don Quixote*, Part II, published in 1615. His *Exemplary Tales* had appeared in 1613. He died on April 23, 1616, and was buried in the convent of the Barefooted Trinitarian nuns. *Persiles and Sigismunda*, his last novel, was published posthumously in 1617.

Although, as we have indicated, *The Ingenious Gentleman Don Quixote de la Mancha* was a popular success from the time Part I was published in 1605, it was only later recognized as an important work of literature. This delay was due partly to the fact that in a period of established and well-defined literary genres such as the epic, the tragedy, and the pastoral romance (Cervantes himself had tried his hand at some of these forms), the unconventional combination of elements in *Don Quixote* resulted in a work of considerable novelty, with the serious aspects hidden under a mocking surface.

The initial and overt purpose of the book was to satirize the romances of chivalry. In those long yarns—which had to do with the Carolingian and Arthurian legends and which were full of supernatural deeds of valor, implausible and complicated adventures, duels, and enchantments—the literature that had expressed the medieval spirit of chivalry and romance had degenerated to the same extent to which, in our day, certain conventions of romantic literature have degenerated in "pulp" fiction and film melodrama. Up to a point, then, what Cervantes set out to do was to produce a parody, a caricature of a literary type. But neither the nature of his genius nor the particular method he chose allowed him to limit himself to such a relatively simple and direct undertaking. The actual method he followed to expose the silliness of the romances of chivalry was to show to what extraordinary consequences they would lead a man insanely infatuated with them, once this man set out to live "now" according to their patterns of action and belief.

So what we have is not mere parody or caricature; for there is a great deal of difference between presenting a remote and more or less imaginary world and presenting an individual deciding to live by the standards of that world in a modern and realistic context. The first consequence is a mingling of genres. On the one hand much of the book has the color and intonation of the world of medieval chivalry as its poets had portrayed it. The fact that that vision and that tone depend for their existence in the book on the self-deception of the hero makes them no less operative artistically and adds, in fact, an important element of idealization. On the other hand the chivalric world is continuously jostled by elements of contemporary life evoked by the narrator—the realities of landscape and speech, peasants and nobles, inns and highways. So the author can draw on two sources, roughly the realistic and the romantic, truth and vision, practical facts and lofty values. In this respect—having found a way to bring together concrete actuality and highly ideal values—Cervantes can be said to have created the modern novel.

The consequences of Cervantes's invention are more apparent when we begin to analyze a little more closely the nature of these worlds, romantic and realistic, and the kind of impact the first exerts on the second. The hero embodying the world of the romances is not, as we know, a cavalier; he is an impoverished country gentleman who embraces that code in the "modern" world. Chivalry is not directly satirized; it is simply placed in a context different from its native one. The result of that new association is a new whole, a new unity. The "code" is renovated; it is put into a different perspective, given another chance.

We should remember at this point that in the process of deterioration that the romances of chivalry had undergone, certain basically attractive ideals had become empty conventions—for instance, the ideal of love as devoted "service." In this connection, it may be especially interesting to observe that the treatment of love and Don Quixote's conception of it are not limited to his well-known admiration for his purely fantastic lady Dulcinea but are also dealt with from a feminine point of view. See, as illustration, Marcela's elaborate, logical, and poetic speech (Part I, chapter 14, printed here) that Don Quixote warmly admires; in it the noble shepherdess defends herself against the accusation of being "a wild beast and a basilisk" for having caused Grisóstomo's death and proclaims her right to choose her particular kind of freedom in nature, where "these mountain trees are my company, the clear running waters in these brooks are my mirror."

No less relevant are Quixote's ideals of adventurousness, of loyalty to high concepts of valor and generosity. In the new context those values are reexamined. Cervantes may well have gained a practical sense of them in his own life while still a youth, for instance at the Battle of Lepanto (the great victory of the European coalition against the "infidels") and as a pirate's captive. Because he began writing *Don Quixote* in his late fifties, a vantage point from which the adventures of his youth must have appeared impossibly remote, a factor of nostalgia—which could hardly have been present in a pure satire—may well have entered into his work. Furthermore, had he undertaken a direct caricature of the romance genre, the serious and noble values of chivalry could not have been made apparent except negatively, whereas in the context devised by him in *Don Quixote* they find a way to assert themselves positively as well.

The book in its development is, to a considerable extent, the story of that assertion—of the impact that Don Quixote's revitalization of the chivalric code has on a contemporary world. We must remember, of course, that there is ambiguity in the way the assertion is made; it works slowly on the reader, as his or her own discovery rather than as the narrator's overt suggestion. Actually, whatever attraction the chivalric world of his hero's vision may have had for Cervantes, he does not openly support Don Quixote at all. He even seems at times to go further in repudiating him than he needs to, for the hero is officially insane, and the narrator never tires of reminding us of this. One critic has described the attitude Cervantes affects toward his creature as "animosity." Nevertheless, by the very magniloquence and, often, the extraordinary coherence and beauty that the narrator allows his hero to display in his speeches in defense of his vision and his code, we are gradually led to discover for ourselves the serious and important elements these contain. For instance, Don Quixote's speech evoking the lost Golden Age and justifying the institution of knight-errantry (in Part I, chapter 11, printed here) is described by the narrator—after Don Quixote has delivered it—as a "futile harangue" that "might very well have been dispensed with"; but there it is, in all of its fervor and effectiveness. Thus the narrator's so-called animosity ultimately does nothing but intensify our interest in Don Quixote and our sympathy for him. And in that process we are, as audience, simply repeating the experience many characters have on the "stage" of the book, in their relationships with him.

Generally speaking, the encounters between the ordinary world and Don Quixote are encounters between the world of reality and that of illusion, between reason and imagination, and ultimately between the world in which action is prompted by material considerations and interests and a world in which action is prompted by ideal motives. The selections printed here illustrate these aspects of the experience. Among the first adventures are some that have most contributed to the popularity of the Don Quixote legend: he sees windmills and decides they are giants, country inns become castles, and flocks of sheep become armies. Though the conclusions of such episodes often have the ludicrousness of slapstick comedy, there is a powerfully imposing quality about Don Quixote's insanity; his madness always has method, a commanding persistence and coherence. And there is perhaps an inevitable sense of moral grandeur in the spectacle of anyone remaining so unflinchingly faithful to his or her own vision. The world of "reason" may win in point of fact, but we come to wonder whether from a moral point of view Quixote is not the victor.

Furthermore, we increasingly realize that Quixote's own manner of action has greatness in itself, and not only the greatness of persistence: his purpose is to redress wrongs, to come to the aid of the afflicted, to offer generous help, to challenge danger, and to practice valor. And we finally feel the impact of the arguments that sustain his action—for example, in the episode of the lions in which he expounds "the meaning of valor." The ridiculousness of the situation is counterbalanced by the basic seriousness of Quixote's motives; his notion of courage for its own sake appears, and is recognized, as singularly noble, a sort of generous display of integrity in a world usually ruled by lower standards. Thus the distinction between reason and madness, truth and illusion, becomes, to say the least, ambiguous. The hero's delusions are indeed exposed when they come up against hard facts, but the authority of such facts is seen to be morally questionable.

The effectiveness of Don Quixote's conduct and vision is seen most clearly in his relationship with his "squire," Sancho Panza. It would be a crude oversimplification to say that Don Quixote and Sancho represent illusion and reality, the insane code of knight-errantry versus down-to-earth practicalities. Actually Sancho—though his nature is strongly defined by such elements as his common sense, his earthy speech, his simple phrases studded with proverbs set against the hero's magniloquence—is mainly characterized in his development by the degree to which he believes in his master. He is caught in the snare of Don Quixote's vision; the seeds of the imaginative life are successfully implanted in him.

The impact of Quixote's view of life on Sancho serves, therefore, to illustrate one of the important qualities of the protagonist and, we may finally say, one of the important aspects of Renaissance literature: the attempt, ultimately frustrated but extremely attractive as long as it lasts, of the individual mind to produce a vision and a system of its own in a world that often seems to have lost a universal frame of reference and a fully satisfactory sense of the value and meaning of action. What Don Quixote presents is a vision of a world that, for all its aberrant qualities, appears generally to be more colorful and more thrilling and also, incidentally, to be inspired by more honorable rules of conduct than the world of ordinary people, "realism," current affairs, private interests, easy jibes, and petty pranks. It is a world in which actions are performed out of a sense of their beauty and excitement, not for the sake of their usefulness. It is, again, the world as stage, animated by "folly"; in this case the lights go out at the end, an end that is "reasonable" and, therefore, gloomy. Sancho provides the main example of one who is exposed to that vision and absorbs that light while it lasts. How successfully he has done so is seen during Don Quixote's death scene, in which Sancho begs his master not to die but to continue the play, as has been suggested, in a new costume—that of shepherds in an Arcadian setting. But at that final point the hero is "cured" and killed, and Sancho is restored to the petty interests of the world as he can see it by his own lights, after the cord connecting him to his imaginative master is cut by the latter's "repentance" and death.

The following list uses common English syllables and stress accents to provide rough equivalents of selected words whose pronunciation may be unfamiliar to the general reader.

Acquaviva: *ahk-wah-vee'-vah*

Benengeli: *ben-en-hel'-ee*

Boiardo: *boy-ar'-doh*

Eugenio: *yoo-hen'-yoh*

Fonseca: *fon-say'-kah*

Mondoñedo: *mon-don-yay'-thoh*

Orbaneja: *or-bah-nay'-hah*

Periquillo: *pehr-i-kee'-yoh*

Quejana: *kay-hah'-nah*

Quesada: *kay-sah'-dah*

Quijada: *kee-hah'-dah*

Quintanar: *kin-ta-nar'*

real: *ray-al'*

Requesenses: *re-ke-sen'-ses*

Roque: *ro'-kay*

Tordesillas: *tor-thay-see'-yas*

From Don Quixote[1]

From Part I

Prologue

Idling reader, you may believe me when I tell you that I should have liked this book, which is the child of my brain, to be the fairest, the sprightliest, and the cleverest that could be imagined; but I have not been able to contravene the law of nature which would have it that like begets like. And so, what was to be expected of a sterile and uncultivated wit such as that which I possess if not an offspring that was dried up, shriveled, and eccentric: a story filled with thoughts that never occurred to anyone else, of a sort that might be engendered in a prison where every annoyance has its home and every mournful sound its habitation?[2] Peace and tranquility, the pleasures of the countryside, the serenity of the heavens, the murmur of fountains, and ease of mind can do much toward causing the most unproductive of muses to become fecund and bring forth progeny that will be the marvel and delight of mankind.

It sometimes happens that a father has an ugly son with no redeeming grace whatever, yet love will draw a veil over the parental eyes which then behold only cleverness and beauty in place of defects, and in speaking to his friends he will make those defects out to be the signs of comeliness and intellect. I, however, who am but Don Quixote's stepfather, have no desire to go with the current of custom, nor would I, dearest reader, beseech you with tears in my eyes as others do to pardon or overlook the faults you discover in this book; you are neither relative nor friend but may call your soul your own and exercise your free judgment. You are in your own house where you are master as the king is of his taxes, for you are familiar with the saying,

1. Translated by Samuel Putnam. 2. Cervantes was imprisoned in Seville in 1597 and 1602.

"Under my cloak I kill the king."[3] All of which exempts and frees you from any kind of respect or obligation; you may say of this story whatever you choose without fear of being slandered for an ill opinion any more than you will be rewarded for a good one.

I should like to bring you the tale unadulterated and unadorned, stripped of the usual prologue and the endless string of sonnets, epigrams, and eulogies such as are commonly found at the beginning of books. For I may tell you that, although I expended no little labor upon the work itself, I have found no task more difficult than the composition of this preface which you are now reading. Many times I took up my pen and many times I laid it down again, not knowing what to write. On one occasion when I was thus in suspense, paper before me, pen over my ear, elbow on the table, and chin in hand, a very clever friend of mine came in. Seeing me lost in thought, he inquired as to the reason, and I made no effort to conceal from him the fact that my mind was on the preface which I had to write for the story of Don Quixote, and that it was giving me so much trouble that I had about decided not to write any at all and to abandon entirely the idea of publishing the exploits of so noble a knight.

"How," I said to him, "can you expect me not to be concerned over what that venerable legislator, the Public, will say when it sees me, at my age, after all these years of silent slumber, coming out with a tale that is as dried as a rush, a stranger to invention, paltry in style, impoverished in content, and wholly lacking in learning and wisdom, without marginal citations or notes at the end of the book when other works of this sort, even though they be fabulous and profane, are so packed with maxims from Aristotle and Plato and the whole crowd of philosophers as to fill the reader with admiration and lead him to regard the author as a well read, learned, and eloquent individual? Not to speak of the citations from Holy Writ! You would think they were at the very least so many St. Thomases[4] and other doctors of the Church; for they are so adroit at maintaining a solemn face that, having portrayed in one line a distracted lover, in the next they will give you a nice little Christian sermon that is a joy and a privilege to hear and read.

"All this my book will lack, for I have no citations for the margins, no notes for the end. To tell the truth, I do not even know who the authors are to whom I am indebted, and so am unable to follow the example of all the others by listing them alphabetically at the beginning, starting with Aristotle and closing with Xenophon, or, perhaps, with Zoilus or Zeuxis, notwithstanding the fact that the former was a snarling critic, the latter a painter. This work will also be found lacking in prefatory sonnets by dukes, marquises, counts, bishops, ladies, and poets of great renown; although if I were to ask two or three colleagues of mine, they would supply the deficiency by furnishing me with productions that could not be equaled by the authors of most repute in all Spain.

"In short, my friend," I went on, "I am resolved that Señor Don Quixote shall remain buried in the archives of La Mancha until Heaven shall provide him with someone to deck him out with all the ornaments that he lacks; for I find myself incapable of remedying the situation, being possessed of little

---

3. I.e., the king does not own your body. 4. Thomas Aquinas (1225–1274), Italian philosopher and theologian.

learning or aptitude, and I am, moreover, extremely lazy when it comes to hunting up authors who will say for me what I am unable to say for myself. And if I am in a state of suspense and my thoughts are woolgathering, you will find a sufficient explanation in what I have just told you."

Hearing this, my friend struck his forehead with the palm of his hand and burst into a loud laugh.

"In the name of God, brother," he said, "you have just deprived me of an illusion. I have known you for a long time, and I have always taken you to be clever and prudent in all your actions; but I now perceive that you are as far from all that as Heaven from the earth. How is it that things of so little moment and so easily remedied can worry and perplex a mind as mature as yours and ordinarily so well adapted to break down and trample underfoot far greater obstacles? I give you my word, this does not come from any lack of cleverness on your part, but rather from excessive indolence and a lack of experience. Do you ask for proof of what I say? Then pay attention closely and in the blink of an eye you shall see how I am going to solve all your difficulties and supply all those things the want of which, so you tell me, is keeping you in suspense, as a result of which you hesitate to publish the history of that famous Don Quixote of yours, the light and mirror of all knight-errantry."

"Tell me, then," I replied, "how you propose to go about curing my diffidence and bringing clarity out of the chaos and confusion of my mind?"

"Take that first matter," he continued, "of the sonnets, epigrams, or eulogies, which should bear the names of grave and titled personages: you can remedy that by taking a little trouble and composing the pieces yourself, and afterward you can baptize them with any name you see fit, fathering them on Prester John of the Indies or the Emperor of Trebizond, for I have heard tell that they were famous poets; and supposing they were not and that a few pedants and bachelors of arts should go around muttering behind your back that it is not so, you should not give so much as a pair of maravedis[5] for all their carping, since even though they make you out to be a liar, they are not going to cut off the hand that put these things on paper.

"As for marginal citations and authors in whom you may find maxims and sayings that you may put in your story, you have but to make use of those scraps of Latin that you know by heart or can look up without too much bother. Thus, when you come to treat of liberty and slavery, jot down:

Non bene pro toto libertas venditur auro.[6]

And then in the margin you will cite Horace or whoever it was that said it. If the subject is death, come up with:

Pallida mors aequo pulsat pede pauperum tabernas
Regumque turres.[7]

If it is friendship or the love that God commands us to show our enemies, then is the time to fall back on the Scriptures, which you can do by putting yourself out very little; you have but to quote the words of God himself:

---

5. Coin worth a thirty-fourth of a *real*; that is, even two *maravedis* were worth very little.   6. Freedom is not bought by gold (Latin); from the anonymous *Aesopian Fables* 3.14.   7. Pale death knocks at the cottages of the poor and the palaces of kings with equal foot (Latin); Horace, *Odes* 1.4.13–14.

Ego autem dico vobis: diligite inimicos vestros.[8]

If it is evil thoughts, lose no time in turning to the Gospels:

De corde exeunt cogitationes malae.[9]

If it is the instability of friends, here is Cato for you with a distich:

Donec eris felix multos numerabis amicos;
Tempora si fuerint nubila, solus eris.[1]

With these odds and ends of Latin and others of the same sort, you can cause yourself to be taken for a grammarian, although I must say that is no great honor or advantage these days.

"So far as notes at the end of the book are concerned, you may safely go about it in this manner: let us suppose that you mentioned some giant, Goliath let us say; with this one allusion which costs you little or nothing, you have a fine note which you may set down as follows: *The giant Golias or Goliath. This was a Philistine whom the shepherd David slew with a mighty cast from his slingshot in the valley of Terebinth,*[2] according to what we read in the Book of Kings, chapter so-and-so where you find it written.

"In addition to this, by way of showing that you are a learned humanist and a cosmographer, contrive to bring into your story the name of the River Tagus, and there you are with another great little note: *The River Tagus was so called after a king of Spain; it rises in such and such a place and empties into the ocean, washing the walls of the famous city of Lisbon; it is supposed to have golden sands,* etc. If it is robbers, I will let you have the story of Cacus,[3] which I know by heart. If it is loose women, there is the Bishop of Mondoñedo,[4] who will lend you Lamia, Laïs, and Flora, an allusion that will do you great credit. If the subject is cruelty, Ovid will supply you with Medea; or if it is enchantresses and witches, Homer has Calypso and Vergil Circe. If it is valorous captains, Julius Caesar will lend you himself, in his *Commentaries*, and Plutarch will furnish a thousand Alexanders. If it is loves, with the ounce or two of Tuscan that you know you may make the acquaintance of Leon the Hebrew,[5] who will satisfy you to your heart's content. And in case you do not care to go abroad, here in your own house you have Fonseca's *Of the Love of God*,[6] where you will encounter in condensed form all that the most imaginative person could wish upon this subject. The short of the matter is, you have but to allude to these names or touch upon those stories that I have mentioned and leave to me the business of the notes and citations; I will guarantee you enough to fill the margins and four whole sheets at the back.

"And now we come to the list of authors cited, such as other works contain but in which your own is lacking. Here again the remedy is an easy one; you have but to look up some book that has them all, from A to Z as you were saying, and transfer the entire list as it stands. What if the imposition is plain for all to see? You have little need to refer to them, and so it does not matter; and some may be so simple-minded as to believe that you have drawn upon

---

8. But I say unto you, love your enemies (Latin); Matthew 5.44.   9. For out of the heart proceed evil thoughts (Latin); Matthew 15.19.   1. As long as you are happy, you will count many friends, but if times become clouded, you will be alone (Latin); Ovid, *Sorrows* 1.9.5–6.   2. 1 Samuel 17.48–49.   3. Gigantic thief in *Aeneid* 8, defeated by Hercules.   4. Father Anthony of Guevara.   5. Leone Ebreo, Neoplatonic author of the *Dialogues of Love* (1535).   6. Cristóbal de Fonseca, *Treatise of the Love of God* (1592).

them all in your simple unpretentious little story. If it serves no other purpose, this imposing list of authors will at least give your book an unlooked-for air of authority. What is more, no one is going to put himself to the trouble of verifying your references to see whether or not you have followed all these authors, since it will not be worth his pains to do so.

"This is especially true in view of the fact that your book stands in no need of all these things whose absence you lament; for the entire work is an attack upon the books of chivalry of which Aristotle never dreamed, of which St. Basil has nothing to say, and of which Cicero had no knowledge; nor do the fine points of truth or the observations of astrology have anything to do with its fanciful absurdities; geometrical measurements, likewise, and rhetorical argumentations serve for nothing here; you have no sermon to preach to anyone by mingling the human with the divine, a kind of motley in which no Christian intellect should be willing to clothe itself.

"All that you have to do is to make proper use of imitation in what you write, and the more perfect the imitation the better will your writing be. Inasmuch as you have no other object in view than that of overthrowing the authority and prestige which books of chivalry enjoy in the world at large and among the vulgar, there is no reason why you should go begging maxims of the philosophers, counsels of Holy Writ, fables of the poets, orations of the rhetoricians, or miracles of the saints; see to it, rather, that your style flows along smoothly, pleasingly, and sonorously, and that your words are the proper ones, meaningful and well placed, expressive of your intention in setting them down and of what you wish to say, without any intricacy or obscurity.

"Let it be your aim that, by reading your story, the melancholy may be moved to laughter and the cheerful man made merrier still; let the simple not be bored, but may the clever admire your originality; let the grave ones not despise you, but let the prudent praise you. And keep in mind, above all, your purpose, which is that of undermining the ill-founded edifice that is constituted by those books of chivalry, so abhorred by many but admired by many more; if you succeed in attaining it, you will have accomplished no little."

Listening in profound silence to what my friend had to say, I was so impressed by his reasoning that, with no thought of questioning them, I decided to make use of his arguments in composing this prologue. Here, gentle reader, you will perceive my friend's cleverness, my own good fortune in coming upon such a counselor at a time when I needed him so badly, and the profit which you yourselves are to have in finding so sincere and straightforward an account of the famous Don Quixote de la Mancha, who is held by the inhabitants of the Campo de Montiel region to have been the most chaste lover and the most valiant knight that had been seen in those parts for many a year. I have no desire to enlarge upon the service I am rendering you in bringing you the story of so notable and honored a gentleman; I merely would have you thank me for having made you acquainted with the famous Sancho Panza, his squire, in whom, to my mind, is to be found an epitome of all the squires and their drolleries scattered here and there throughout the pages of those vain and empty books of chivalry. And with this, may God give you health, and may He be not unmindful of me as well. VALE.[7]

7. Farewell (Latin).

["I Know Who I Am, and Who I May Be, If I Choose"]

CHAPTER 1

Which treats of the station in life and the pursuits of the famous gentleman, Don Quixote de la Mancha.

In a village of La Mancha[1] the name of which I have no desire to recall, there lived not so long ago one of those gentlemen who always have a lance in the rack, an ancient buckler, a skinny nag, and a greyhound for the chase. A stew with more beef than mutton in it, chopped meat for his evening meal, scraps for a Saturday, lentils on Friday, and a young pigeon as a special delicacy for Sunday, went to account for three-quarters of his income. The rest of it he laid out on a broadcloth greatcoat and velvet stockings for feast days, with slippers to match, while the other days of the week he cut a figure in a suit of the finest homespun. Living with him were a housekeeper in her forties, a niece who was not yet twenty, and a lad of the field and market place who saddled his horse for him and wielded the pruning knife.

This gentleman of ours was close on to fifty, of a robust constitution but with little flesh on his bones and a face that was lean and gaunt. He was noted for his early rising, being very fond of the hunt. They will try to tell you that his surname was Quijada or Quesada—there is some difference of opinion among those who have written on the subject—but according to the most likely conjectures we are to understand that it was really Quejana. But all this means very little so far as our story is concerned, providing that in the telling of it we do not depart one iota from the truth.

You may know, then, that the aforesaid gentleman, on those occasions when he was at leisure, which was most of the year around, was in the habit of reading books of chivalry with such pleasure and devotion as to lead him almost wholly to forget the life of a hunter and even the administration of his estate. So great was his curiosity and infatuation in this regard that he even sold many acres of tillable land in order to be able to buy and read the books that he loved, and he would carry home with him as many of them as he could obtain.

Of all those that he thus devoured none pleased him so well as the ones that had been composed by the famous Feliciano de Silva,[2] whose lucid prose style and involved conceits were as precious to him as pearls; especially when he came to read those tales of love and amorous challenges that are to be met with in many places, such a passage as the following, for example: "The reason of the unreason that afflicts my reason, in such a manner weakens my reason that I with reason lament me of your comeliness." And he was similarly affected when his eyes fell upon such lines as these: ". . . the high Heaven of your divinity divinely fortifies you with the stars and renders you deserving of that desert your greatness doth deserve."

The poor fellow used to lie awake nights in an effort to disentangle the meaning and make sense out of passages such as these, although Aristotle himself would not have been able to understand them, even if he had been resurrected for that sole purpose. He was not at ease in his mind over those

---

1. Efforts at identifying the village have proved inconclusive. La Mancha is a section of Spain south of Madrid.   2. Author of romances (16th century); the lines that follow are from his *Don Florisel de Niguea*.

wounds that Don Belianís[3] gave and received; for no matter how great the surgeons who treated him, the poor fellow must have been left with his face and his entire body covered with marks and scars. Nevertheless, he was grateful to the author for closing the book with the promise of an interminable adventure to come; many a time he was tempted to take up his pen and literally finish the tale as had been promised, and he undoubtedly would have done so, and would have succeeded at it very well, if his thoughts had not been constantly occupied with other things of greater moment.

He often talked it over with the village curate, who was a learned man, a graduate of Sigüenza,[4] and they would hold long discussions as to who had been the better knight, Palmerin of England or Amadis of Gaul; but Master Nicholas, the barber of the same village, was in the habit of saying that no one could come up to the Knight of Phoebus,[5] and that if anyone *could* compare with him it was Don Galaor, brother of Amadis of Gaul, for Galaor was ready for anything—he was none of your finical knights, who went around whimpering as his brother did, and in point of valor he did not lag behind him.

In short, our gentleman became so immersed in his reading that he spent whole nights from sundown to sunup and his days from dawn to dusk in poring over his books, until, finally, from so little sleeping and so much reading, his brain dried up and he went completely out of his mind. He had filled his imagination with everything that he had read, with enchantments, knightly encounters, battles, challenges, wounds, with tales of love and its torments, and all sorts of impossible things, and as a result had come to believe that all these fictitious happenings were true; they were more real to him than anything else in the world. He would remark that the Cid Ruy Díaz had been a very good knight, but there was no comparison between him and the Knight of the Flaming Sword, who with a single backward stroke had cut in half two fierce and monstrous giants. He preferred Bernardo del Carpio, who at Roncesvalles had slain Roland despite the charm the latter bore, availing himself of the stratagem which Hercules employed when he strangled Antaeus,[6] the son of Earth, in his arms.

He had much good to say for Morgante;[7] who, though he belonged to the haughty, overbearing race of giants, was of an affable disposition and well brought up. But, above all, he cherished an admiration for Rinaldo of Montalbán,[8] especially as he beheld him sallying forth from his castle to rob all those that crossed his path, or when he thought of him overseas stealing the image of Mohammed which, so the story has it, was all of gold. And he would have liked very well to have had his fill of kicking that traitor Galalón,[9] a privilege for which he would have given his housekeeper with his niece thrown into the bargain.

At last, when his wits were gone beyond repair, he came to conceive the strangest idea that ever occurred to any madman in this world. It now

3. The allusion is to a romance by Jerónimo Fernández.   4. Ironical, for Sigüenza was the seat of a minor and discredited university.   5. Or Knight of Sun. Heroes of romances customarily adopted emblematic names and also changed them according to circumstances. *Palmerin . . . Amadis:* each a hero of a very famous romance of chivalry.   6. The mythological Antaeus was invulnerable as long as he maintained contact with his mother, Earth. Hercules killed him while holding him raised in his arms. *Charm:* the magic gift of invulnerability.   7. In Pulci's *Morgante maggiore*, a comic-epic poem of the Italian Renaissance. 8. Roland's cousin. In Boiardo's *Roland in Love* (*Orlando Innamorato*) and Ariosto's *Roland Mad* (*Orlando Furioso*), romantic and comic-epic poems of the Italian Renaissance.   9. Ganelón, the villain in the Charlemagne legend who betrayed the French at Roncesvalles.

appeared to him fitting and necessary, in order to win a greater amount of honor for himself and serve his country at the same time, to become a knight-errant and roam the world on horseback, in a suit of armor; he would go in quest of adventures, by way of putting into practice all that he had read in his books; he would right every manner of wrong, placing himself in situations of the greatest peril such as would redound to the eternal glory of his name. As a reward for his valor and the might of his arm, the poor fellow could already see himself crowned Emperor of Trebizond at the very least; and so, carried away by the strange pleasure that he found in such thoughts as these, he at once set about putting his plan into effect.

The first thing he did was to burnish up some old pieces of armor, left him by his great-grandfather, which for ages had lain in a corner, moldering and forgotten. He polished and adjusted them as best he could, and then he noticed that one very important thing was lacking: there was no closed helmet, but only a morion, or visorless headpiece, with turned up brim of the kind foot soldiers wore. His ingenuity, however, enabled him to remedy this, and he proceeded to fashion out of cardboard a kind of half-helmet, which, when attached to the morion, gave the appearance of a whole one. True, when he went to see if it was strong enough to withstand a good slashing blow, he was somewhat disappointed; for when he drew his sword and gave it a couple of thrusts, he succeeded only in undoing a whole week's labor. The ease with which he had hewed it to bits disturbed him no little, and he decided to make it over. This time he placed a few strips of iron on the inside, and then, convinced that it was strong enough, refrained from putting it to any further test; instead, he adopted it then and there as the finest helmet ever made.

After this, he went out to have a look at his nag; and although the animal had more *cuartos*, or cracks, in its hoof than there are quarters in a real,[1] and more blemishes than Gonela's steed which *tantum pellis et ossa fuit*,[2] it nonetheless looked to its master like a far better horse than Alexander's Bucephalus or the Babieca of the Cid.[3] He spent all of four days in trying to think up a name for his mount; for—so he told himself—seeing that it belonged to so famous and worthy a knight, there was no reason why it should not have a name of equal renown. The kind of name he wanted was one that would at once indicate what the nag had been before it came to belong to a knight-errant and what its present status was; for it stood to reason that, when the master's worldly condition changed, his horse also ought to have a famous, high-sounding appellation, one suited to the new order of things and the new profession that it was to follow.

After he in his memory and imagination had made up, struck out, and discarded many names, now adding to and now subtracting from the list, he finally hit upon "Rocinante," a name that impressed him as being sonorous and at the same time indicative of what the steed had been when it was but a hack, whereas now it was nothing other than the first and foremost of all the hacks[4] in the world.

Having found a name for his horse that pleased his fancy, he then desired to do as much for himself, and this required another week, and by the end

---

1. A coin (about five cents). *Cuarto*: one-eighth of a *real*.   2. Was so much skin and bones (Latin).
3. The chief (Spanish)—that is, Ruy Díaz, celebrated hero of *Poema del Cid* (12th century).   4. In Spanish, *rocín*.

of that period he had made up his mind that he was henceforth to be known as Don Quixote, which, as has been stated, has led the authors of this veracious history to assume that his real name must undoubtedly have been Quijada, and not Quesada as others would have it. But remembering that the valiant Amadis was not content to call himself that and nothing more, but added the name of his kingdom and fatherland that he might make it famous also, and thus came to take the name Amadis of Gaul, so our good knight chose to add his place of origin and become "Don Quixote de la Mancha"; for by this means, as he saw it, he was making very plain his lineage and was conferring honor upon his country by taking its name as his own.

And so, having polished up his armor and made the morion over into a closed helmet, and having given himself and his horse a name, he naturally found but one thing lacking still: he must seek out a lady of whom he could become enamored; for a knight-errant without a lady-love was like a tree without leaves or fruit, a body without a soul.

"If," he said to himself, "as a punishment for my sins or by a stroke of fortune I should come upon some giant hereabouts, a thing that very commonly happens to knights-errant, and if I should slay him in a hand-to-hand encounter or perhaps cut him in two, or, finally, if I should vanquish and subdue him, would it not be well to have someone to whom I may send him as a present, in order that he, if he is living, may come in, fall upon his knees in front of my sweet lady, and say in a humble and submissive tone of voice, 'I, lady, am the giant Caraculiambro, lord of the island Malindrania, who has been overcome in single combat by that knight who never can be praised enough, Don Quixote de la Mancha, the same who sent me to present myself before your Grace that your Highness may dispose of me as you see fit'?"

Oh, how our good knight reveled in this speech, and more than ever when he came to think of the name that he should give his lady! As the story goes, there was a very good-looking farm girl who lived near by, with whom he had once been smitten, although it is generally believed that she never knew or suspected it. Her name was Aldonza Lorenzo, and it seemed to him that she was the one upon whom he should bestow the title of mistress of his thoughts. For her he wished a name that should not be incongruous with his own and that would convey the suggestion of a princess or a great lady; and, accordingly, he resolved to call her "Dulcinea del Toboso," she being a native of that place. A musical name to his ears, out of the ordinary and significant, like the others he had chosen for himself and his appurtenances.

CHAPTER 2

Which treats of the first sally that the ingenious Don Quixote made from his native heath.

Having, then, made all these preparations, he did not wish to lose any time in putting his plan into effect, for he could not but blame himself for what the world was losing by his delay, so many were the wrongs that were to be righted, the grievances to be redressed, the abuses to be done away with, and the duties to be performed. Accordingly, without informing anyone of his intention and without letting anyone see him, he set out one morning before daybreak on one of those very hot days in July. Donning all his armor, mounting Rocinante, adjusting his ill-contrived helmet, bracing his shield on his arm, and taking up his lance, he sallied forth by the back gate of his stable yard into the open countryside. It was with great contentment and joy that he saw how easily he had made a beginning toward the fulfillment of his desire.

No sooner was he out on the plain, however, than a terrible thought assailed him, one that all but caused him to abandon the enterprise he had undertaken. This occurred when he suddenly remembered that he had never formally been dubbed a knight, and so, in accordance with the law of knighthood, was not permitted to bear arms against one who had a right to that title. And even if he had been, as a novice knight he would have had to wear white armor, without any device on his shield, until he should have earned one by his exploits. These thoughts led him to waver in his purpose, but, madness prevailing over reason, he resolved to have himself knighted by the first person he met, as many others had done if what he had read in those books that he had at home was true. And so far as white armor was concerned, he would scour his own the first chance that offered until it shone whiter than any ermine. With this he became more tranquil and continued on his way, letting his horse take whatever path it chose, for he believed that therein lay the very essence of adventures.

And so we find our newly fledged adventurer jogging along and talking to himself. "Undoubtedly," he is saying, "in the days to come, when the true history of my famous deeds is published, the learned chronicler who records them, when he comes to describe my first sally so early in the morning, will put down something like this: 'No sooner had the rubicund Apollo spread over the face of the broad and spacious earth the gilded filaments of his beauteous locks, and no sooner had the little singing birds of painted plumage greeted with their sweet and mellifluous harmony the coming of the Dawn, who, leaving the soft couch of her jealous spouse, now showed herself to mortals at all the doors and balconies of the horizon that bounds La Mancha—no sooner had this happened than the famous knight, Don Quixote de la Mancha, forsaking his own downy bed and mounting his famous steed, Rocinante, fared forth and began riding over the ancient and famous Campo de Montiel.'"[5]

And this was the truth, for he was indeed riding over that stretch of plain.

"O happy age and happy century," he went on, "in which my famous exploits shall be published, exploits worthy of being engraved in bronze, sculptured in marble, and depicted in paintings for the benefit of posterity. O wise magician, whoever you be, to whom shall fall the task of chronicling this extraordinary history of mine! I beg of you not to forget my good Rocinante, eternal companion of my wayfarings and my wanderings."

Then, as though he really had been in love: "O Princess Dulcinea, lady of this captive heart! Much wrong have you done me in thus sending me forth with your reproaches and sternly commanding me not to appear in your beauteous presence. O lady, deign to be mindful of this your subject who endures so many woes for the love of you."

And so he went on, stringing together absurdities, all of a kind that his books had taught him, imitating insofar as he was able the language of their authors. He rode slowly, and the sun came up so swiftly and with so much heat that it would have been sufficient to melt his brains if he had had any.

5. The scene of a battle in 1369.

He had been on the road almost the entire day without anything happening that is worthy of being set down here; and he was on the verge of despair, for he wished to meet someone at once with whom he might try the valor of his good right arm. Certain authors say that his first adventure was that of Puerto Lápice, while others state that it was that of the windmills; but in this particular instance I am in a position to affirm what I have read in the annals of La Mancha; and that is to the effect that he went all that day until nightfall, when he and his hack found themselves tired to death and famished. Gazing all around him to see if he could discover some castle or shepherd's hut where he might take shelter and attend to his pressing needs, he caught sight of an inn not far off the road along which they were traveling, and this to him was like a star guiding him not merely to the gates, but rather, let us say, to the palace of redemption. Quickening his pace, he came up to it just as night was falling.

By chance there stood in the doorway two lasses of the sort known as "of the district"; they were on their way to Seville in the company of some mule drivers who were spending the night in the inn. Now, everything that this adventurer of ours thought, saw, or imagined seemed to him to be directly out of one of the storybooks he had read, and so, when he caught sight of the inn, it at once became a castle with its four turrets and its pinnacles of gleaming silver, not to speak of the drawbridge and moat and all the other things that are commonly supposed to go with a castle. As he rode up to it, he accordingly reined in Rocinante and sat there waiting for a dwarf to appear upon the battlements and blow his trumpet by way of announcing the arrival of a knight. The dwarf, however, was slow in coming, and as Rocinante was anxious to reach the stable, Don Quixote drew up to the door of the hostelry and surveyed the two merry maidens, who to him were a pair of beauteous damsels or gracious ladies taking their ease at the castle gate.

And then a swineherd came along, engaged in rounding up his drove of hogs—for, without any apology, that is what they were. He gave a blast on his horn to bring them together, and this at once became for Don Quixote just what he wished it to be: some dwarf who was heralding his coming; and so it was with a vast deal of satisfaction that he presented himself before the ladies in question, who, upon beholding a man in full armor like this, with lance and buckler, were filled with fright and made as if to flee indoors. Realizing that they were afraid, Don Quixote raised his pasteboard visor and revealed his withered, dust-covered face.

"Do not flee, your Ladyships," he said to them in a courteous manner and gentle voice. "You need not fear that any wrong will be done you, for it is not in accordance with the order of knighthood which I profess to wrong anyone, much less such highborn damsels as your appearance shows you to be."

The girls looked at him, endeavoring to scan his face, which was half hidden by his ill-made visor. Never having heard women of their profession called damsels before, they were unable to restrain their laughter, at which Don Quixote took offense.

"Modesty," he observed, "well becomes those with the dower of beauty, and, moreover, laughter that has not good cause is a very foolish thing. But I do not say this to be discourteous or to hurt your feelings; my only desire is to serve you."

The ladies did not understand what he was talking about, but felt more than ever like laughing at our knight's unprepossessing figure. This increased his annoyance, and there is no telling what would have happened if at that moment the innkeeper had not come out. He was very fat and very peaceably inclined; but upon sighting this grotesque personage clad in bits of armor that were quite as oddly matched as were his bridle, lance, buckler, and corselet, mine host was not at all indisposed to join the lasses in their merriment. He was suspicious, however, of all this paraphernalia and decided that it would be better to keep a civil tongue in his head.

"If, Sir Knight," he said, "your Grace desires a lodging, aside from a bed—for there is none to be had in this inn—you will find all else that you may want in great abundance."

When Don Quixote saw how humble the governor of the castle was—for he took the innkeeper and his inn to be no less than that—he replied, "For me, Sir Castellan,[6] anything will do, since

> Arms are my only ornament,
> My only rest the fight, etc."

The landlord thought that the knight had called him a castellan because he took him for one of those worthies of Castile, whereas the truth was, he was an Andalusian from the beach of Sanlúcar, no less a thief than Cacus[7] himself, and as full of tricks as a student or a page boy.

"In that case," he said,

> "Your bed will be the solid rock,
> Your sleep: to watch all night.

This being so, you may be assured of finding beneath this roof enough to keep you awake for a whole year, to say nothing of a single night."

With this, he went up to hold the stirrup for Don Quixote, who encountered much difficulty in dismounting, not having broken his fast all day long. The knight then directed his host to take good care of his steed, as it was the best piece of horseflesh in all the world. The innkeeper looked it over, and it did not impress him as being half as good as Don Quixote had said it was. Having stabled the animal, he came back to see what his guest would have and found the latter being relieved of his armor by the damsels, who by now had made their peace with the new arrival. They had already removed his breastplate and backpiece but had no idea how they were going to open his gorget or get his improvised helmet off. That piece of armor had been tied on with green ribbons which it would be necessary to cut, since the knots could not be undone, but he would not hear of this, and so spent all the rest of that night with his headpiece in place, which gave him the weirdest, most laughable appearance that could be imagined.

Don Quixote fancied that these wenches who were assisting him must surely be the chatelaine and other ladies of the castle, and so proceeded to address them very gracefully and with much wit:

> Never was knight so served
> By any noble dame

---

6. The Spanish, *castellano*, means both "castellan" and "Castilian."   7. In Roman mythology he stole some of Hercules's cattle, concealing the theft by having them walk backward into his cave; Cacus was finally discovered and slain.

As was Don Quixote
When from his village he came,
With damsels to wait on his every need
While princesses cared for his hack . . .

"By hack," he explained, "is meant my steed Rocinante, for that is his name, and mine is Don Quixote de la Mancha. I had no intention of revealing my identity until my exploits done in your service should have made me known to you; but the necessity of adapting to present circumstances that old ballad of Lancelot has led to your becoming acquainted with it prematurely. However, the time will come when your Ladyships shall command and I will obey and with the valor of my good right arm show you how eager I am to serve you."

The young women were not used to listening to speeches like this and had not a word to say, but merely asked him if he desired to eat anything.

"I could eat a bite of something, yes," replied Don Quixote. "Indeed, I feel that a little food would go very nicely just now."

He thereupon learned that, since it was Friday, there was nothing to be had in all the inn except a few portions of codfish, which in Castile is called *abadejo*, in Andalusia *bacalao*, in some places *curadillo*, and elsewhere *truchuella* or small trout. Would his Grace, then, have some small trout, seeing that was all there was that they could offer him?

"If there are enough of them," said Don Quixote, "they will take the place of a trout, for it is all one to me whether I am given in change eight reales or one piece of eight. What is more, those small trout may be like veal, which is better than beef, or like kid, which is better than goat. But however that may be, bring them on at once, for the weight and burden of arms is not to be borne without inner sustenance."

Placing the table at the door of the hostelry, in the open air, they brought the guest a portion of badly soaked and worse cooked codfish and a piece of bread as black and moldy as the suit of armor that he wore. It was a mirth-provoking sight to see him eat, for he still had his helmet on with his visor fastened, which made it impossible for him to put anything into his mouth with his hands, and so it was necessary for one of the girls to feed him. As for giving him anything to drink, that would have been out of the question if the innkeeper had not hollowed out a reed, placing one end in Don Quixote's mouth while through the other end he poured the wine. All this the knight bore very patiently rather than have them cut the ribbons of his helmet.

At this point a gelder of pigs approached the inn, announcing his arrival with four or five blasts on his horn, all of which confirmed Don Quixote in the belief that this was indeed a famous castle, for what was this if not music that they were playing for him? The fish was trout, the bread was the finest, the wenches were ladies, and the innkeeper was the castellan. He was convinced that he had been right in his resolve to sally forth and roam the world at large, but there was one thing that still distressed him greatly, and that was the fact that he had not as yet been dubbed a knight; as he saw it, he could not legitimately engage in any adventure until he had received the order of knighthood.

CHAPTER 3

CHAPTER 3

Of the amusing manner in which Don Quixote had himself dubbed a knight.

Wearied of his thoughts, Don Quixote lost no time over the scanty repast which the inn afforded him. When he had finished, he summoned the landlord and, taking him out to the stable, closed the doors and fell on his knees in front of him.

"Never, valiant knight," he said, "shall I arise from here until you have courteously granted me the boon I seek, one which will redound to your praise and to the good of the human race."

Seeing his guest at his feet and hearing him utter such words as these, the innkeeper could only stare at him in bewilderment, not knowing what to say or do. It was in vain that he entreated him to rise, for Don Quixote refused to do so until his request had been granted.

"I expected nothing less of your great magnificence, my lord," the latter then continued, "and so I may tell you that the boon I asked and which you have so generously conceded me is that tomorrow morning you dub me a knight. Until that time, in the chapel of this your castle, I will watch over my armor, and when morning comes, as I have said, that which I so desire shall then be done, in order that I may lawfully go to the four corners of the earth in quest of adventures and to succor the needy, which is the chivalrous duty of all knights-errant such as I who long to engage in deeds of high emprise."

The innkeeper, as we have said, was a sharp fellow. He already had a suspicion that his guest was not quite right in the head, and he was now convinced of it as he listened to such remarks as these. However, just for the sport of it, he determined to humor him; and so he went on to assure Don Quixote that he was fully justified in his request and that such a desire and purpose was only natural on the part of so distinguished a knight as his gallant bearing plainly showed him to be.

He himself, the landlord added, when he was a young man, had followed the same honorable calling. He had gone through various parts of the world seeking adventures, among the places he had visited being the Percheles of Málaga, the Isles of Riarán, the District of Seville, the Little Market Place of Segovia, the Olivera of Valencia, the Rondilla of Granada, the beach of Sanlúcar, the Horse Fountain of Cordova, the Small Taverns of Toledo,[8] and numerous other localities where his nimble feet and light fingers had found much exercise. He had done many wrongs, cheated many widows, ruined many maidens, and swindled not a few minors until he had finally come to be known in almost all the courts and tribunals that are to be found in the whole of Spain.

At last he had retired to his castle here, where he lived upon his own income and the property of others; and here it was that he received all knights-errant of whatever quality and condition, simply out of the great affection that he bore them and that they might share with him their possessions in payment of his good will. Unfortunately, in this castle there was

---

8. All reputed to be haunts of robbers and rogues.

no chapel where Don Quixote might keep watch over his arms, for the old chapel had been torn down to make way for a new one; but in case of necessity, he felt quite sure that such a vigil could be maintained anywhere, and for the present occasion the courtyard of the castle would do; and then in the morning, please God, the requisite ceremony could be performed and his guest be duly dubbed a knight, as much a knight as anyone ever was.

He then inquired if Don Quixote had any money on his person, and the latter replied that he had not a cent, for in all the storybooks he had never read of knights-errant carrying any. But the innkeeper told him he was mistaken on this point: supposing the authors of those stories had not set down the fact in black and white, that was because they did not deem it necessary to speak of things as indispensable as money and a clean shirt, and one was not to assume for that reason that those knights-errant of whom the books were so full did not have any. He looked upon it as an absolute certainty that they all had well-stuffed purses, that they might be prepared for any emergency; and they also carried shirts and a little box of ointment for healing the wounds that they received.

For when they had been wounded in combat on the plains and in desert places, there was not always someone at hand to treat them, unless they had some skilled enchanter for a friend who then would succor them, bringing to them through the air, upon a cloud, some damsel or dwarf bearing a vial of water of such virtue that one had but to taste a drop of it and at once his wounds were healed and he was as sound as if he had never received any.

But even if this was not the case, knights in times past saw to it that their squires were well provided with money and other necessities, such as lint and ointment for healing purposes; and if they had no squires—which happened very rarely—they themselves carried these objects in a pair of saddlebags very cleverly attached to their horses' croups in such a manner as to be scarcely noticeable, as if they held something of greater importance than that, for among the knights-errant saddlebags as a rule were not favored. Accordingly, he would advise the novice before him, and inasmuch as the latter was soon to be his godson, he might even command him, that henceforth he should not go without money and a supply of those things that have been mentioned, as he would find that they came in useful at a time when he least expected it.

Don Quixote promised to follow his host's advice punctiliously; and so it was arranged that he should watch his armor in a large barnyard at one side of the inn. He gathered up all the pieces, placed them in a horse trough that stood near the well, and, bracing his shield on his arm, took up his lance and with stately demeanor began pacing up and down in front of the trough even as night was closing in.

The innkeeper informed his other guests of what was going on, of Don Quixote's vigil and his expectation of being dubbed a knight; and, marveling greatly at so extraordinary a variety of madness, they all went out to see for themselves and stood there watching from a distance. For a while the knight-to-be, with tranquil mien, would merely walk up and down; then, leaning on his lance, he would pause to survey his armor, gazing fixedly at it for a considerable length of time. As has been said, it was night now, but the brightness of the moon, which well might rival that of Him who lent it, was such that everything the novice knight did was plainly visible to all.

At this point one of the mule drivers who were stopping at the inn came out to water his drove, and in order to do this it was necessary to remove the armor from the trough.

As he saw the man approaching, Don Quixote cried out to him, "O bold knight, whoever you may be, who thus would dare to lay hands upon the accouterments of the most valiant man of arms that ever girded on a sword, look well what you do and desist if you do not wish to pay with your life for your insolence!"

The muleteer gave no heed to these words—it would have been better for his own sake had he done so—but, taking it up by the straps, tossed the armor some distance from him. When he beheld this, Don Quixote rolled his eyes heavenward and with his thoughts apparently upon his Dulcinea exclaimed, "Succor, O lady mine, this vassal heart in this my first encounter; let not your favor and protection fail me in the peril in which for the first time I now find myself."

With these and other similar words, he loosed his buckler, grasped his lance in both his hands, and let the mule driver have such a blow on the head that the man fell to the ground stunned; and had it been followed by another one, he would have had no need of a surgeon to treat him. Having done this, Don Quixote gathered up his armor and resumed his pacing up and down with the same calm manner as before. Not long afterward, without knowing what had happened—for the first muleteer was still lying there unconscious—another came out with the same intention of watering his mules, and he too was about to remove the armor from the trough when the knight, without saying a word or asking favor of anyone, once more adjusted his buckler and raised his lance, and if he did not break the second mule driver's head to bits, he made more than three pieces of it by dividing it into quarters. At the sound of the fracas everybody in the inn came running out, among them the innkeeper; whereupon Don Quixote again lifted his buckler and laid his hand on his sword.

"O lady of beauty," he said, "strength and vigor of this fainting heart of mine! Now is the time to turn the eyes of your greatness upon this captive knight of yours who must face so formidable an adventure."

By this time he had worked himself up to such a pitch of anger that if all the mule drivers in the world had attacked him he would not have taken one step backward. The comrades of the wounded men, seeing the plight those two were in, now began showering stones on Don Quixote, who shielded himself as best he could with his buckler, although he did not dare stir from the trough for fear of leaving his armor unprotected. The landlord, meanwhile, kept calling for them to stop, for he had told them that this was a madman who would be sure to go free even though he killed them all. The knight was shouting louder than ever, calling them knaves and traitors. As for the lord of the castle, who allowed knights-errant to be treated in this fashion, he was a lowborn villain, and if he, Don Quixote, had but received the order of knighthood, he would make him pay for his treachery.

"As for you others, vile and filthy rabble, I take no account of you; you may stone me or come forward and attack me all you like; you shall see what the reward of your folly and insolence will be."

He spoke so vigorously and was so undaunted in bearing as to strike terror in those who would assail him; and for this reason, and owing also to the persuasions of the innkeeper, they ceased stoning him. He then permitted them to carry away the wounded, and went back to watching his armor with the same tranquil, unconcerned air that he had previously displayed.

The landlord was none too well pleased with these mad pranks on the part of his guest and determined to confer upon him that accursed order of knighthood before something else happened. Going up to him, he begged Don Quixote's pardon for the insolence which, without his knowledge, had been shown the knight by those of low degree. They, however, had been well punished for their impudence. As he had said, there was no chapel in this castle, but for that which remained to be done there was no need of any. According to what he had read of the ceremonial of the order, there was nothing to this business of being dubbed a knight except a slap on the neck and one across the shoulder, and that could be performed in the middle of a field as well as anywhere else. All that was required was for the knight-to-be to keep watch over his armor for a couple of hours, and Don Quixote had been at it more than four. The latter believed all this and announced that he was ready to obey and get the matter over with as speedily as possible. Once dubbed a knight, if he were attacked one more time, he did not think that he would leave a single person in the castle alive, save such as he might command be spared, at the bidding of his host and out of respect to him.

Thus warned, and fearful that it might occur, the castellan brought out the book in which he had jotted down the hay and barley for which the mule drivers owed him, and, accompanied by a lad bearing the butt of a candle and the two aforesaid damsels, he came up to where Don Quixote stood and commanded him to kneel. Reading from the account book—as if he had been saying a prayer—he raised his hand and, with the knight's own sword, gave him a good thwack upon the neck and another lusty one upon the shoulder, muttering all the while between his teeth. He then directed one of the ladies to gird on Don Quixote's sword, which she did with much gravity and composure; for it was all they could do to keep from laughing at every point of the ceremony, but the thought of the knight's prowess which they had already witnessed was sufficient to restrain their mirth.

"May God give your Grace much good fortune," said the worthy lady as she attached the blade, "and prosper you in battle."

Don Quixote thereupon inquired her name, for he desired to know to whom it was he was indebted for the favor he had just received, that he might share with her some of the honor which his strong right arm was sure to bring him. She replied very humbly that her name was Tolosa and that she was the daughter of a shoemaker, a native of Toledo who lived in the stalls of Sancho Bicnaya.[9] To this the knight replied that she would do him a very great favor if from then on she would call herself Doña Tolosa, and she promised to do so. The other girl then helped him on with his spurs, and practically the same conversation was repeated. When asked her name, she stated that it was La Molinera and added that she was the daughter of a respectable miller of Antequera. Don Quixote likewise requested her to assume the "don" and become Doña Molinera and offered to render her further services and favors.

These unheard-of ceremonies having been dispatched in great haste, Don

9. An old square in Toledo.

Quixote could scarcely wait to be astride his horse and sally forth on his quest for adventures. Saddling and mounting Rocinante, he embraced his host, thanking him for the favor of having dubbed him a knight and saying such strange things that it would be quite impossible to record them here. The innkeeper, who was only too glad to be rid of him, answered with a speech that was no less flowery, though somewhat shorter, and he did not so much as ask him for the price of a lodging, so glad was he to see him go.

CHAPTER 4

Of what happened to our knight when he sallied forth from the inn.

Day was dawning when Don Quixote left the inn, so well satisfied with himself, so gay, so exhilarated, that the very girths of his steed all but burst with joy. But remembering the advice which his host had given him concerning the stock of necessary provisions that he should carry with him, especially money and shirts, he decided to turn back home and supply himself with whatever he needed, and with a squire as well; he had in mind a farmer who was a neighbor of his, a poor man and the father of a family but very well suited to fulfill the duties of squire to a man of arms. With this thought in mind he guided Rocinante toward the village once more, and that animal, realizing that he was homeward bound, began stepping out at so lively a gait that it seemed as if his feet barely touched the ground.

The knight had not gone far when from a hedge on his right hand he heard the sound of faint moans as of someone in distress.

"Thanks be to Heaven," he at once exclaimed, "for the favor it has shown me by providing me so soon with an opportunity to fulfill the obligations that I owe to my profession, a chance to pluck the fruit of my worthy desires. Those, undoubtedly, are the cries of someone in distress, who stands in need of my favor and assistance."

Turning Rocinante's head, he rode back to the place from which the cries appeared to be coming. Entering the wood, he had gone but a few paces when he saw a mare attached to an oak, while bound to another tree was a lad of fifteen or thereabouts, naked from the waist up. It was he who was uttering the cries, and not without reason, for there in front of him was a lusty farmer with a girdle who was giving him many lashes, each one accompanied by a reproof and a command, "Hold your tongue and keep your eyes open"; and the lad was saying, "I won't do it again, sir; by God's Passion, I won't do it again. I promise you that after this I'll take better care of the flock."

When he saw what was going on, Don Quixote was very angry. "Discourteous knight," he said, "it ill becomes you to strike one who is powerless to defend himself. Mount your steed and take your lance in hand"—for there was a lance leaning against the oak to which the mare was tied—"and I will show you what a coward you are."

The farmer, seeing before him this figure all clad in armor and brandishing a lance, decided that he was as good as done for. "Sir Knight," he said, speaking very mildly, "this lad that I am punishing here is my servant; he tends a flock of sheep which I have in these parts and he is so careless that every day one of them shows up missing. And when I punish him for his carelessness or his roguery, he says it is just because I am a miser and do not want to pay him the wages that I owe him, but I swear to God and upon my soul that he lies."

"It is you who lie, base lout," said Don Quixote, "and in my presence; and by the sun that gives us light, I am minded to run you through with this lance. Pay him and say no more about it, or else, by the God who rules us, I will make an end of you and annihilate you here and now. Release him at once."

The farmer hung his head and without a word untied his servant. Don Quixote then asked the boy how much has master owed him. For nine months' work, the lad told him, at seven reales the month. The knight did a little reckoning and found that this came to sixty-three reales; whereupon he ordered the farmer to pay over the money immediately, as he valued his life. The cowardly bumpkin replied that, facing death as he was and by the oath that he had sworn—he had not sworn any oath as yet—it did not amount to as much as that; for there were three pairs of shoes which he had given the lad that were to be deducted and taken into account, and a real for two blood-lettings when his servant was ill.

"That," said Don Quixote, "is all very well; but let the shoes and the blood-lettings go for the undeserved lashings which you have given him; if he has worn out the leather of the shoes that you paid for, you have taken the hide off his body, and if the barber let a little blood for him when he was sick,[1] you have done the same when he was well; and so far as that goes, he owes you nothing."

"But the trouble is, Sir Knight, that I have no money with me. Come along home with me, Andrés, and I will pay you real for real."

"I go home with him!" cried the lad. "Never in the world! No, sir, I would not even think of it; for once he has me alone he'll flay me like a St. Bartholomew."

"He will do nothing of the sort," said Don Quixote. "It is sufficient for me to command, and he out of respect will obey. Since he has sworn to me by the order of knighthood which he has received, I shall let him go free and I will guarantee that you will be paid."

"But look, your Grace," the lad remonstrated, "my master is no knight; he has never received any order of knighthood whatsoever. He is Juan Haldudo, a rich man and a resident of Quintanar."

"That makes little difference," declared Don Quixote, "for there may well be knights among the Haldudos, all the more so in view of the fact that every man is the son of his works."

"That is true enough," said Andrés, "but this master of mine—of what works is he the son, seeing that he refuses me the pay for my sweat and labor?"

"I do not refuse you, brother Andrés," said the farmer. "Do me the favor of coming with me, and I swear to you by all the orders of knighthood that there are in this world to pay you, as I have said, real for real, and perfumed at that."

"You can dispense with the perfume," said Don Quixote; "just give him the reales and I shall be satisfied. And see to it that you keep your oath, or by the one that I myself have sworn I shall return to seek you out and chastise

1. Barbers were also surgeons.

you, and I shall find you though you be as well hidden as a lizard. In case you would like to know who it is that is giving you this command in order that you may feel the more obliged to comply with it, I may tell you that I am the valorous Don Quixote de la Mancha, righter of wrongs and injustices; and so, God be with you, and do not fail to do as you have promised, under that penalty that I have pronounced."

As he said this, he put spurs to Rocinante and was off. The farmer watched him go, and when he saw that Don Quixote was out of the wood and out of sight, he turned to his servant, Andrés.

"Come here, my son," he said. "I want to pay you what I owe you as that righter of wrongs has commanded me."

"Take my word for it," replied Andrés, "your Grace would do well to observe the command of that good knight—may he live a thousand years; for as he is valorous and a righteous judge, if you don't pay me then, by Rocque,[2] he will come back and do just what he said!"

"And I will give you my word as well," said the farmer; "but seeing that I am so fond of you, I wish to increase the debt, that I may owe you all the more." And with this he seized the lad's arm and bound him to the tree again and flogged him within an inch of his life. "There, Master Andrés, you may call on that righter of wrongs if you like and you will see whether or not he rights this one. I do not think I have quite finished with you yet, for I have a good mind to flay you alive as you feared."

Finally, however, he unbound him and told him he might go look for that judge of his to carry out the sentence that had been pronounced. Andrés left, rather down in the mouth, swearing that he would indeed go look for the brave Don Quixote de la Mancha; he would relate to him everything that had happened, point by point, and the farmer would have to pay for it seven times over. But for all that, he went away weeping, and his master stood laughing at him.

Such was the manner in which the valorous knight righted this particular wrong. Don Quixote was quite content with the way everything had turned out; it seemed to him that he had made a very fortunate and noble beginning with his deeds of chivalry, and he was very well satisfied with himself as he jogged along in the direction of his native village, talking to himself in a low voice all the while.

"Well may'st thou call thyself fortunate today, above all other women on earth, O fairest of the fair, Dulcinea del Toboso! Seeing that it has fallen to thy lot to hold subject and submissive to thine every wish and pleasure so valiant and renowned a knight as Don Quixote de la Mancha is and shall be, who, as everyone knows, yesterday received the order of knighthood and this day has righted the greatest wrong and grievance that injustice ever conceived or cruelty ever perpetrated, by snatching the lash from the hand of the merciless foeman who was so unreasonably flogging that tender child."

At this point he came to a road that forked off in four directions, and at once he thought of those crossroads where knights-errant would pause to consider which path they should take. By way of imitating them, he halted there for a while; and when he had given the subject much thought, he slackened Rocinante's rein and let the hack follow its inclination. The ani-

---

2. The origin of this oath is unknown.

mal's first impulse was to make straight for its own stable. After they had gone a couple of miles or so Don Quixote caught sight of what appeared to be a great throng of people, who, as was afterward learned, were certain merchants of Toledo on their way to purchase silk at Murcia. There were six of them altogether with their sunshades, accompanied by four attendants on horseback and three mule drivers on foot.

No sooner had he sighted them than Don Quixote imagined that he was on the brink of some fresh adventure. He was eager to imitate those passages at arms of which he had read in his books, and here, so it seemed to him, was one made to order. And so, with bold and knightly bearing, he settled himself firmly in the stirrups, couched his lance, covered himself with his shield, and took up a position in the middle of the road, where he paused to wait for those other knights-errant (for such he took them to be) to come up to him. When they were near enough to see and hear plainly, Don Quixote raised his voice and made a haughty gesture.

"Let everyone," he cried, "stand where he is, unless everyone will confess that there is not in all the world a more beauteous damsel than the Empress of La Mancha, the peerless Dulcinea del Toboso."

Upon hearing these words and beholding the weird figure who uttered them, the merchants stopped short. From the knight's appearance and his speech they knew at once that they had to deal with a madman; but they were curious to know what was meant by that confession that was demanded of them, and one of their number who was somewhat of a jester and a very clever fellow raised his voice.

"Sir Knight," he said, "we do not know who this beauteous lady is of whom you speak. Show her to us, and if she is as beautiful as you say, then we will right willingly and without any compulsion confess the truth as you have asked of us."

"If I were to show her to you," replied Don Quixote, "what merit would there be in your confessing a truth so self-evident? The important thing is for you, without seeing her, to believe, confess, affirm, swear, and defend that truth. Otherwise, monstrous and arrogant creatures that you are, you shall do battle with me. Come on, then, one by one, as the order of knighthood prescribes; or all of you together, if you will have it so, as is the sorry custom of those of your breed. Come on, and I will await you here, for I am confident that my cause is just."

"Sir Knight," responded the merchant, "I beg your Grace, in the name of all the princes here present, in order that we may not have upon our consciences the burden of confessing a thing which we have never seen nor heard, and one, moreover, so prejudicial to the empresses and queens of Alcarria and Estremadura,[3] that your Grace will show us some portrait of this lady, even though it be no larger than a grain of wheat, for by the thread one comes to the ball of yarn; and with this we shall remain satisfied and assured, and your Grace will likewise be content and satisfied. The truth is, I believe that we are already so much of your way of thinking that though it should show her to be blind of one eye and distilling vermilion and brimstone from the other, nevertheless, to please your Grace, we would say in her behalf all that you desire.'

---

3. Ironical, because both were known as particularly backward regions.

"She distills nothing of the sort, infamous rabble!" shouted Don Quixote, for his wrath was kindling now. "I tell you, she does not distill what you say at all, but amber and civet[4] wrapped in cotton; and she is neither one-eyed nor hunchbacked but straighter than a spindle that comes from Guadarrama. You shall pay for the great blasphemy which you have uttered against such a beauty as is my lady!"

Saying this, he came on with lowered lance against the one who had spoken, charging with such wrath and fury that if fortune had not caused Rocinante to stumble and fall in mid-career, things would have gone badly with the merchant and he would have paid for his insolent gibe. As it was, Don Quixote went rolling over the plain for some little distance, and when he tried to get to his feet, found that he was unable to do so, being too encumbered with his lance, shield, spurs, helmet, and the weight of that ancient suit of armor.

"Do not flee, cowardly ones," he cried even as he struggled to rise. "Stay, cravens, for it is not my fault but that of my steed that I am stretched out here."

One of the muleteers, who must have been an ill-natured lad, upon hearing the poor fallen knight speak so arrogantly, could not refrain from giving him an answer in the ribs. Going up to him, he took the knight's lance and broke it into bits, and then with a companion proceeded to belabor him so mercilessly that in spite of his armor they milled him like a hopper[5] of wheat. The merchants called to them not to lay on so hard, saying that was enough and they should desist, but the mule driver by this time had warmed up to the sport and would not stop until he had vented his wrath, and, snatching up the broken pieces of the lance, he began hurling them at the wretched victim as he lay there on the ground. And through all this tempest of sticks that rained upon him Don Quixote never once closed his mouth nor ceased threatening Heaven and earth and these ruffians, for such he took them to be, who were thus mishandling him.

Finally the lad grew tired, and the merchants went their way with a good story to tell about the poor fellow who had had such a cudgeling. Finding himself alone, the knight endeavored to see if he could rise; but if this was a feat that he could not accomplish when he was sound and whole, how was he to achieve it when he had been thrashed and pounded to a pulp? Yet nonetheless he considered himself fortunate; for as he saw it, misfortunes such as this were common to knights-errant, and he put all the blame upon his horse; and if he was unable to rise, that was because his body was so bruised and battered all over.

CHAPTER 5

In which is continued the narrative of the misfortune that befell our knight.

Seeing, then, that he was indeed unable to stir, he decided to fall back upon a favorite remedy of his, which was to think of some passage or other in his books; and as it happened, the one that he in his madness now recalled

4. A musky substance used in perfume, imported from Africa in cotton packings. 5. Funnel-shaped container for grain.

was the story of Baldwin and the Marquis of Mantua, when Carloto left the former wounded upon the mountainside,[6] a tale that is known to children, not unknown to young men, celebrated and believed in by the old, and, for all of that, not any truer than the miracles of Mohammed. Moreover, it impressed him as being especially suited to the straits in which he found himself; and, accordingly, with a great show of feeling, he began rolling and tossing on the ground as he feebly gasped out the lines which the wounded knight of the wood is supposed to have uttered:

> "Where art thou, lady mine,
> That thou dost not grieve for my woe?
> Either thou art disloyal,
> Or my grief thou dost not know."

He went on reciting the old ballad until he came to the following verses:

> "O noble Marquis of Mantua,
> My uncle and liege lord true!"

He had reached this point when down the road came a farmer of the same village, a neighbor of his, who had been to the mill with a load of wheat. Seeing a man lying there stretched out like that, he went up to him and inquired who he was and what was the trouble that caused him to utter such mournful complaints. Thinking that this must undoubtedly be his uncle, the Marquis of Mantua, Don Quixote did not answer but went on with his recitation of the ballad, giving an account of the Marquis' misfortunes and the amours of his wife and the emperor's son, exactly as the ballad has it.

The farmer was astounded at hearing all these absurdities, and after removing the knight's visor which had been battered to pieces by the blows it had received, the good man bathed the victim's face, only to discover, once the dust was off, that he knew him very well.

"Señor Quejana," he said (for such must have been Don Quixote's real name when he was in his right senses and before he had given up the life of a quiet country gentleman to become a knight-errant), "who is responsible for your Grace's being in such a plight as this?"

But the knight merely went on with his ballad in response to all the questions asked of him. Perceiving that it was impossible to obtain any information from him, the farmer as best he could relieved him of his breastplate and backpiece to see if he had any wounds, but there was no blood and no mark of any sort. He then tried to lift him from the ground, and with a great deal of effort finally managed to get him astride the ass, which appeared to be the easier mount for him. Gathering up the armor, including even the splinters from the lance, he made a bundle and tied it on Rocinante's back, and, taking the horse by the reins and the ass by the halter, he started out for the village. He was worried in his mind at hearing all the foolish things that Don Quixote said, and that individual himself was far from being at ease. Unable by reason of his bruises and his soreness to sit upright on the donkey, our knight-errant kept sighing to Heaven, which led the farmer to ask him once more what it was that ailed him.

---

6. The allusion is to an old ballad about Charlemagne's son Charlot (Carloto) wounding Baldwin, nephew of the marquis of Mantua.

It must have been the devil himself who caused him to remember those tales that seemed to fit his own case; for at this point he forgot all about Baldwin and recalled Abindarráez, and how the governor of Antequera, Rodrigo de Narváez, had taken him prisoner and carried him off captive to his castle. Accordingly, when the countryman turned to inquire how he was and what was troubling him, Don Quixote replied with the very same words and phrases that the captive Abindarráez used in answering Rodrigo, just as he had read in the story *Diana* of Jorge de Montemayor,[7] where it is all written down, applying them very aptly to the present circumstances as the farmer went along cursing his luck for having to listen to such a lot of nonsense. Realizing that his neighbor was quite mad, he made haste to reach the village that he might not have to be annoyed any longer by Don Quixote's tiresome harangue.

"Señor Don Rodrigo de Narváez," the knight was saying, "I may inform your Grace that this beautiful Jarifa of whom I speak is not the lovely Dulcinea del Toboso, in whose behalf I have done, am doing, and shall do the most famous deeds of chivalry that ever have been or will be seen in all the world."

"But, sir," replied the farmer, "sinner that I am, cannot your Grace see that I am not Don Rodrigo de Narváez nor the Marquis of Mantua, but Pedro Alonso, your neighbor? And your Grace is neither Baldwin nor Abindarráez but a respectable gentleman by the name of Señor Quijana."

"I know who I am," said Don Quixote, "and who I may be, if I choose: not only those I have mentioned but all the Twelve Peers of France and the Nine Worthies[8] as well; for the exploits of all of them together, or separately, cannot compare with mine."

With such talk as this they reached their destination just as night was falling; but the farmer decided to wait until it was a little darker in order that the badly battered gentleman might not be seen arriving in such a condition and mounted on an ass. When he thought the proper time had come, they entered the village and proceeded to Don Quixote's house, where they found everything in confusion. The curate and the barber were there, for they were great friends of the knight, and the housekeeper was speaking to them.

"Señor Licentiate Pero Pérez," she was saying, for that was the manner in which she addressed the curate, "what does your Grace think could have happened to my master? Three days now, and not a word of him, nor the hack, nor the buckler, nor the lance, nor the suit of armor. Ah, poor me! I am as certain as I am that I was born to die that it is those cursed books of chivalry he is always reading that have turned his head; for now that I recall, I have often heard him muttering to himself that he must become a knighterrant and go through the world in search of adventures. May such books as those be consigned to Satan and Barabbas,[9] for they have sent to perdition the finest mind in all La Mancha."

---

7. The reference is to the tale of the love of Abindarráez, a captive Moor, for the beautiful Jarifa, included in the second edition of Jorge de Montemayor's *Diana,* a pastoral romance. 8. In a tradition originating in France, the Nine Worthies consisted of three biblical, three classical, and three Christian figures (David, Hector, Alexander, Charlemagne, and so on). In French medieval epics, the Twelve Peers (Roland, Oliver, and so on) were warriors all equal in rank, forming a kind of guard of honor around Charlemagne. 9. The thief whose release, rather than that of Jesus, the crowd requested when Pilate, conforming to Passover custom, was ready to have one prisoner set free.

The niece was of the same opinion. "I may tell you, Señor Master Nicholas," she said, for that was the barber's name, "that many times my uncle would sit reading those impious tales of misadventure for two whole days and nights at a stretch; and when he was through, he would toss the book aside, lay his hand on his sword, and begin slashing at the walls. When he was completely exhausted, he would tell us that he had just killed four giants as big as castle towers, while the sweat that poured off him was blood from the wounds that he had received in battle. He would then drink a big jug of cold water, after which he would be very calm and peaceful, saying that the water was the most precious liquid which the wise Esquife, a great magician and his friend, had brought to him. But I blame myself for everything. I should have advised your Worships of my uncle's nonsensical actions so that you could have done something about it by burning those damnable books of his before things came to such a pass; for he has many that ought to be burned as if they were heretics."

"I agree with you," said the curate, "and before tomorrow's sun has set there shall be a public *auto da fé,* and those works shall be condemned to the flames that they may not lead some other who reads them to follow the example of my good friend."

Don Quixote and the farmer overheard all this, and it was then that the latter came to understand the nature of his neighbor's affliction.

"Open the door, your Worships," the good man cried. "Open for Sir Baldwin and the Marquis of Mantua, who comes badly wounded, and for Señor Abindarráez the Moor whom the valiant Rodrigo de Narváez, governor of Antequera, brings captive."

At the sound of his voice they all ran out, recognizing at once friend, master, and uncle, who as yet was unable to get down off the donkey's back. They all ran up to embrace him.

"Wait, all of you," said Don Quixote, "for I am sorely wounded through fault of my steed. Bear me to my couch and summon, if it be possible, the wise Urganda to treat and care for my wounds."

"There!" exclaimed the housekeeper. "Plague take it! Did not my heart tell me right as to which foot my master limped on? To bed with your Grace at once, and we will take care of you without sending for that Urganda of yours. A curse, I say, and a hundred other curses, on those books of chivalry that have brought your Grace to this."

And so they carried him off to bed, but when they went to look for his wounds, they found none at all. He told them it was all the result of a great fall he had taken with Rocinante, his horse, while engaged in combating ten giants, the hugest and most insolent that were ever heard of in all the world.

"Tut, tut," said the curate. "So there are giants in the dance now, are there? Then, by the sign of the cross, I'll have them burned before nightfall tomorrow."

They had a thousand questions to put to Don Quixote, but his only answer was that they should give him something to eat and let him sleep, for that was the most important thing of all; so they humored him in this. The curate then interrogated the farmer at great length concerning the conversation he had had with his neighbor. The peasant told him everything, all the absurd things their friend had said when he found him lying there and afterward on the way home, all of which made the licentiate more anxious than ever to do what he did the following day,[1] when he summoned Master Nicholas and went with him to Don Quixote's house.

[Fighting the Windmills and a Choleric Biscayan]

CHAPTER 7

Of the second sally of our good knight, Don Quixote de la Mancha.

* * * After that he remained at home very tranquilly for a couple of weeks, without giving sign of any desire to repeat his former madness. During that time he had the most pleasant conversations with his two old friends, the curate and the barber, on the point he had raised to the effect that what the world needed most was knights-errant and a revival of chivalry. The curate would occasionally contradict him and again would give in, for it was only by means of this artifice that he could carry on a conversation with him at all.

In the meanwhile Don Quixote was bringing his powers of persuasion to bear upon a farmer who lived near by, a good man—if this title may be applied to one who is poor—but with very few wits in his head. The short of it is, by pleas and promises, he got the hapless rustic to agree to ride forth with him and serve him as his squire. Among other things, Don Quixote told him that he ought to be more than willing to go, because no telling what adventure might occur which would win them an island, and then he (the farmer) would be left to be the governor of it. As a result of these and other similar assurances, Sancho Panza forsook his wife and children and consented to take upon himself the duties of squire to his neighbor.

Next, Don Quixote set out to raise some money, and by selling this thing and pawning that and getting the worst of the bargain always, he finally scraped together a reasonable amount. He also asked a friend of his for the loan of a buckler and patched up his broken helmet as well as he could. He advised his squire, Sancho, of the day and hour when they were to take to the road and told him to see to laying in a supply of those things that were most necessary, and, above all, not to forget the saddlebags. Sancho replied that he would see to all this and added that he was also thinking of taking along with him a very good ass that he had, as he was not much used to going on foot.

With regard to the ass, Don Quixote had to do a little thinking, trying to recall if any knight-errant had ever had a squire thus asininely mounted. He could not think of any, but nevertheless he decided to take Sancho with the intention of providing him with a nobler steed as soon as occasion offered; he had but to appropriate the horse of the first discourteous knight he met. Having furnished himself with shirts and all the other things that the inn-keeper had recommended, he and Panza rode forth one night unseen by anyone and without taking leave of wife and children, housekeeper or niece. They went so far that by the time morning came they were safe from discovery had a hunt been started for them.

Mounted on his ass, Sancho Panza rode along like a patriarch, with saddle-

1. He and the barber burned most of Don Quixote's library.

bags and flask, his mind set upon becoming governor of that island that his master had promised him. Don Quixote determined to take the same route and road over the Campo de Montiel that he had followed on his first journey; but he was not so uncomfortable this time, for it was early morning and the sun's rays fell upon them slantingly and accordingly did not tire them too much.

"Look, Sir Knight-errant," said Sancho, "your Grace should not forget that island you promised me; for no matter how big it is, I'll be able to govern it right enough."

"I would have you know, friend Sancho Panza," replied Don Quixote, "that among the knights-errant of old it was a very common custom to make their squires governors of the islands or the kingdoms that they won, and I am resolved that in my case so pleasing a usage shall not fall into desuetude. I even mean to go them one better; for they very often, perhaps most of the time, waited until their squires were old men who had had their fill of serving their masters during bad days and worse nights, whereupon they would give them the title of count, or marquis at most, of some valley or province more or less. But if you live and I live, it well may be that within a week I shall win some kingdom with others dependent upon it, and it will be the easiest thing in the world to crown you king of one of them. You need not marvel at this, for all sorts of unforeseen things happen to knights like me, and I may readily be able to give you even more than I have promised."

"In that case," said Sancho Panza, "if by one of those miracles of which your Grace was speaking I should become king, I would certainly send for Juana Gutiérrez, my old lady, to come and be my queen, and the young ones could be infantes."

"There is no doubt about it," Don Quixote assured him.

"Well, I doubt it," said Sancho, "for I think that even if God were to rain kingdoms upon the earth, no crown would sit well on the head of Mari Gutiérrez,[2] for I am telling you, sir, as a queen she is not worth two maravedis. She would do better as a countess, God help her."

"Leave everything to God, Sancho," said Don Quixote, "and he will give you whatever is most fitting; but I trust you will not be so pusillanimous as to be content with anything less than the title of viceroy."

"That I will not," said Sancho Panza, "especially seeing that I have in your Grace so illustrious a master who can give me all that is suitable to me and all that I can manage."

CHAPTER 8

Of the good fortune which the valorous Don Quixote had in the terrifying and never-before-imagined adventure of the windmills, along with other events that deserve to be suitably recorded.

At this point they caught sight of thirty or forty windmills which were standing on the plain there, and no sooner had Don Quixote laid eyes upon them than he turned to his squire and said, "Fortune is guiding our affairs better than we could have wished; for you see there before you, friend Sancho Panza, some thirty or more lawless giants with whom I mean to do battle.

2. Sancho's wife, Juana Gutiérrez.

I shall deprive them of their lives, and with the spoils from this encounter we shall begin to enrich ourselves; for this is righteous warfare, and it is a great service to God to remove so accursed a breed from the face of the earth."

"What giants?" said Sancho Panza.

"Those that you see there," replied his master, "those with the long arms some of which are as much as two leagues in length."

"But look, your Grace, those are not giants but windmills, and what appear to be arms are their wings which, when whirled in the breeze, cause the millstone to go."

"It is plain to be seen," said Don Quixote, "that you have had little experience in this matter of adventures. If you are afraid, go off to one side and say your prayers while I am engaging them in fierce, unequal combat."

Saying this, he gave spurs to his steed Rocinante, without paying any heed to Sancho's warning that these were truly windmills and not giants that he was riding forth to attack. Nor even when he was close upon them did he perceive what they really were, but shouted at the top of his lungs, "Do not seek to flee, cowards and vile creatures that you are, for it is but a single knight with whom you have to deal!"

At that moment a little wind came up and the big wings began turning.

"Though you flourish as many arms as did the giant Briareus,"[3] said Don Quixote when he perceived this, "you still shall have to answer to me."

He thereupon commended himself with all his heart to his lady Dulcinea, beseeching her to succor him in this peril; and, being well covered with his shield and with his lance at rest, he bore down upon them at a full gallop and fell upon the first mill that stood in his way, giving a thrust at the wing, which was whirling at such a speed that his lance was broken into bits and both horse and horseman went rolling over the plain, very much battered indeed. Sancho upon his donkey came hurrying to his master's assistance as fast as he could, but when he reached the spot, the knight was unable to move, so great was the shock with which he and Rocinante had hit the ground.

"God help us!" exclaimed Sancho, "did I not tell your Grace to look well, that those were nothing but windmills, a fact which no one could fail to see unless he had other mills of the same sort in his head?"

"Be quiet, friend Sancho," said Don Quixote. "Such are the fortunes of war, which more than any other are subject to constant change. What is more, when I come to think of it, I am sure that this must be the work of that magician Frestón, the one who robbed me of my study and my books,[4] and who has thus changed the giants into windmills in order to deprive me of the glory of overcoming them, so great is the enmity that he bears me; but in the end his evil arts shall not prevail against this trusty sword of mine."

"May God's will be done," was Sancho Panza's response. And with the aid of his squire the knight was once more mounted on Rocinante, who stood there with one shoulder half out of joint. And so, speaking of the adventure that had just befallen them, they continued along the Puerto Lápice highway; for there, Don Quixote said, they could not fail to find many and varied

---

3. Mythological giant with a hundred arms.   4. Don Quixote had promptly attributed the ruin of his library to magical intervention (see n. 1, p. 2246).

adventures, this being a much traveled thoroughfare. The only thing was, the knight was exceedingly downcast over the loss of his lance.

"I remember," he said to his squire, "having read of a Spanish knight by the name of Diego Pérez de Vargas, who, having broken his sword in battle, tore from an oak a heavy bough or branch and with it did such feats of valor that day, and pounded so many Moors, that he came to be known as Machuca,[5] and he and his descendants from that day forth have been called Vargas y Machuca. I tell you this because I too intend to provide myself with just such a bough as the one he wielded, and with it I propose to do such exploits that you shall deem yourself fortunate to have been found worthy to come with me and behold and witness things that are almost beyond belief."

"God's will be done," said Sancho. "I believe everything that your Grace says; but straighten yourself up in the saddle a little, for you seem to be slipping down on one side, owing, no doubt, to the shaking-up that you received in your fall."

"Ah, that is the truth," replied Don Quixote, "and if I do not speak of my sufferings, it is for the reason that it is not permitted knights-errant to complain of any wound whatsoever, even though their bowels may be dropping out."

"If that is the way it is," said Sancho, "I have nothing more to say; but, God knows, it would suit me better if your Grace did complain when something hurts him. I can assure you that I mean to do so, over the least little thing that ails me—that is, unless the same rule applies to squires as well."

Don Quixote laughed long and heartily over Sancho's simplicity, telling him that he might complain as much as he liked and where and when he liked, whether he had good cause or not; for he had read nothing to the contrary in the ordinances of chivalry. Sancho then called his master's attention to the fact that it was time to eat. The knight replied that he himself had no need of food at the moment, but his squire might eat whenever he chose. Having been granted this permission, Sancho seated himself as best he could upon his beast, and, taking out from his saddlebags the provisions that he had stored there, he rode along leisurely behind his master, munching his victuals and taking a good, hearty swig now and then at the leather flask in a manner that might well have caused the biggest-bellied tavern-keeper of Málaga to envy him. Between draughts he gave not so much as a thought to any promise that his master might have made him, nor did he look upon it as any hardship, but rather as good sport, to go in quest of adventures however hazardous they might be.

The short of the matter is, they spent the night under some trees, from one of which Don Quixote tore off a withered bough to serve him as a lance, placing it in the lance head from which he had removed the broken one. He did not sleep all night long for thinking of his lady Dulcinea; for this was in accordance with what he had read in his books, of men of arms in the forest or desert places who kept a wakeful vigil, sustained by the memory of their ladies fair. Not so with Sancho, whose stomach was full, and not with chicory water. He fell into a dreamless slumber, and had not his master called him, he would not have been awakened either by the rays of the sun in his face

5. "The Crusher," the hero of a folk ballad.

or by the many birds who greeted the coming of the new day with their merry song.

Upon arising, he had another go at the flask, finding it somewhat more flaccid then it had been the night before, a circumstance which grieved his heart, for he could not see that they were on the way to remedying the deficiency within any very short space of time. Don Quixote did not wish any breakfast; for, as has been said, he was in the habit of nourishing himself on savorous memories. They then set out once more along the road to Puerto Lápice, and around three in the afternoon they came in sight of the pass that bears that name.

"There," said Don Quixote as his eyes fell upon it, "we may plunge our arms up to the elbow in what are known as adventures. But I must warn you that even though you see me in the greatest peril in the world, you are not to lay hand upon your sword to defend me, unless it be that those who attack me are rabble and men of low degree, in which case you may very well come to my aid; but if they be gentlemen, it is in no wise permitted by the laws of chivalry that you should assist me until you yourself shall have been dubbed a knight."

"Most certainly, sir," replied Sancho, "your Grace shall be very well obeyed in this; all the more so for the reason that I myself am of a peaceful disposition and not fond of meddling in the quarrels and feuds of others. However, when it comes to protecting my own person, I shall not take account of those laws of which you speak, seeing that all laws, human and divine, permit each one to defend himself whenever he is attacked."

"I am willing to grant you that," assented Don Quixote, "but in this matter of defending me against gentlemen you must restrain your natural impulses."

"I promise you I shall do so," said Sancho. "I will observe this precept as I would the Sabbath day."

As they were conversing in this manner, there appeared in the road in front of them two friars of the Order of St. Benedict, mounted upon dromedaries—for the she-mules they rode were certainly no smaller than that. The friars wore travelers' spectacles and carried sunshades, and behind them came a coach accompanied by four or five men on horseback and a couple of muleteers on foot. In the coach, as was afterwards learned, was a lady of Biscay, on her way to Seville to bid farewell to her husband, who had been appointed to some high post in the Indies. The religious were not of her company although they were going by the same road.

The instant Don Quixote laid eyes upon them he turned to his squire. "Either I am mistaken or this is going to be the most famous adventure that ever was seen; for those black-clad figures that you behold must be, and without any doubt are, certain enchanters who are bearing with them a captive princess in that coach, and I must do all I can to right this wrong."

"It will be worse than the windmills," declared Sancho. "Look you, sir, those are Benedictine friars and the coach must be that of some travelers. Mark well what I say and what you do, lest the devil lead you astray."

"I have already told you, Sancho," replied Don Quixote, "that you know little where the subject of adventures is concerned. What I am saying to you is the truth, as you shall now see."

With this, he rode forward and took up a position in the middle of the road along which the friars were coming, and as soon as they appeared to be within earshot he cried out to them in a loud voice, "O devilish and monstrous beings, set free at once the highborn princesses whom you bear captive in that coach, or else prepare at once to meet your death as the just punishment of your evil deeds."

The friars drew rein and sat there in astonishment, marveling as much at Don Quixote's appearance as at the words he spoke. "Sir Knight," they answered him, "we are neither devilish nor monstrous but religious of the Order of St. Benedict who are merely going our way. We know nothing of those who are in that coach, nor of any captive princesses either."

"Soft words," said Don Quixote, "have no effect on me. I know you for what you are, lying rabble!" And without waiting for any further parley he gave spur to Rocinante and, with lowered lance, bore down upon the first friar with such fury and intrepidity that, had not the fellow tumbled from his mule of his own accord, he would have been hurled to the ground and either killed or badly wounded. The second religious, seeing how his companion had been treated, dug his legs into his she-mule's flanks and scurried away over the countryside faster than the wind.

Seeing the friar upon the ground, Sancho Panza slipped lightly from his mount and, falling upon him, began stripping him of his habit. The two mule drivers accompanying the religious thereupon came running up and asked Sancho why he was doing this. The latter replied that the friar's garments belonged to him as legitimate spoils of the battle that his master Don Quixote had just won. The muleteers, however, were lads with no sense of humor, nor did they know what all this talk of spoils and battles was about; but, perceiving that Don Quixote had ridden off to one side to converse with those inside the coach, they pounced upon Sancho, threw him to the ground, and proceeded to pull out the hair of his beard and kick him to a pulp, after which they went off and left him stretched out there, bereft at once of breath and sense.

Without losing any time, they then assisted the friar to remount. The good brother was trembling all over from fright, and there was not a speck of color in his face, but when he found himself in the saddle once more, he quickly spurred his beast to where his companion, at some little distance, sat watching and waiting to see what the result of the encounter would be. Having no curiosity as to the final outcome of the fray, the two of them now resumed their journey, making more signs of the cross than the devil would be able to carry upon his back.

Meanwhile Don Quixote, as we have said, was speaking to the lady in the coach.

"Your beauty, my lady, may now dispose of your person as best may please you, for the arrogance of your abductors lies upon the ground, overthrown by this good arm of mine; and in order that you may not pine to know the name of your liberator, I may inform you that I am Don Quixote de la Mancha, knight-errant and adventurer and captive of the peerless and beauteous Doña Dulcinea del Toboso. In payment of the favor which you have received from me, I ask nothing other than that you return to El Toboso and on my behalf pay your respects to this lady, telling her that it was I who set you free."

One of the squires accompanying those in the coach, a Biscayan,[6] was listening to Don Quixote's words, and when he saw that the knight did not propose to let the coach proceed upon its way but was bent upon having it turn back to El Toboso, he promptly went up to him, seized his lance, and said to him in bad Castilian and worse Biscayan, "Go, *caballero,* and bad luck go with you; for by the God that created me, if you do not let this coach pass, me kill you or me no Biscayan."

Don Quixote heard him attentively enough and answered him very mildly, "If you were a *caballero,*[7] which you are not, I should already have chastised you, wretched creature, for your foolhardiness and your impudence."

"Me no *caballero,*" cried the Biscayan. "Me swear to God, you lie like a Christian. If you will but lay aside your lance and unsheath your sword, you will soon see that you are carrying water to the cat![8] Biscayan on land, gentleman at sea, but a gentleman in spite of the devil, and you lie if you say otherwise."

" 'You shall see as to that presently,' said Agrajes,"[9] Don Quixote quoted. He cast his lance to the earth, drew his sword, and, taking his buckler on his arm, attacked the Biscayan with intent to slay him. The latter, when he saw his adversary approaching, would have liked to dismount from his mule, for she was one of the worthless sort that are let for hire and he had no confidence in her; but there was no time for this, and so he had no choice but to draw his own sword in turn and make the best of it. However, he was near enough to the coach to be able to snatch a cushion from it to serve him as a shield; and then they fell upon each other as though they were mortal enemies. The rest of those present sought to make peace between them but did not succeed, for the Biscayan with his disjointed phrases kept muttering that if they did not let him finish the battle then he himself would have to kill his mistress and anyone else who tried to stop him.

The lady inside the carriage, amazed by it all and trembling at what she saw, directed her coachman to drive on a little way; and there from a distance she watched the deadly combat, in the course of which the Biscayan came down with a great blow on Don Quixote's shoulder, over the top of the latter's shield, and had not the knight been clad in armor, it would have split him to the waist.

Feeling the weight of this blow, Don Quixote cried out, "O lady of my soul, Dulcinea, flower of beauty, succor this your champion who out of gratitude for your many favors finds himself in so perilous a plight!" To utter these words, lay hold of his sword, cover himself with his buckler, and attack the Biscayan was but the work of a moment; for he was now resolved to risk everything upon a single stroke.

As he saw Don Quixote approaching with so dauntless a bearing, the Biscayan was well aware of his adversary's courage and forthwith determined to imitate the example thus set him. He kept himself protected with his cushion, but he was unable to get his she-mule to budge to one side or the other, for the beast, out of sheer exhaustion and being, moreover, unused to such childish play, was incapable of taking a single step. And so, then, as has been stated, Don Quixote was approaching the wary Biscayan, his sword raised

---

6. From the Basque region.   7. Knight, gentleman (Spanish).   8. An inversion of a proverbial phrase: "carrying the cat to the water."   9. A violent character in the romance *Amadis de Gaul.* His challenging phrase is the conventional opener of a fight.

on high and with the firm resolve of cleaving his enemy in two; and the Biscayan was awaiting the knight in the same posture, cushion in front of him and with uplifted sword. All the bystanders were trembling with suspense at what would happen as a result of the terrible blows that were threatened, and the lady in the coach and her maids were making a thousand vows and offerings to all the images and shrines in Spain, praying that God would save them all and the lady's squire from this great peril that confronted them.

But the unfortunate part of the matter is that at this very point the author of the history breaks off and leaves the battle pending, excusing himself upon the ground that he has been unable to find anything else in writing concerning the exploits of Don Quixote beyond those already set forth. It is true, on the other hand, that the second author[1] of this work could not bring himself to believe that so unusual a chronicle would have been consigned to oblivion, nor that the learned ones of La Mancha were possessed of so little curiosity as not to be able to discover in their archives or registry offices certain papers that have to do with this famous knight. Being convinced of this, he did not despair of coming upon the end of this pleasing story. * * *

CHAPTER 9

In which is concluded and brought to an end the stupendous battle between the gallant Biscayan and the valiant Knight of La Mancha.

* * * We left the valorous Biscayan and the famous Don Quixote with swords unsheathed and raised aloft, about to let fall furious slashing blows which, had they been delivered fairly and squarely, would at the very least have split them in two and laid them wide open from top to bottom like a pomegranate; and it was at this doubtful point that the pleasing chronicle came to a halt and broke off, without the author's informing us as to where the rest of it might be found.

I was deeply grieved by such a circumstance, and the pleasure I had had in reading so slight a portion was turned into annoyance as I thought of how difficult it would be to come upon the greater part which it seemed to me must still be missing. It appeared impossible and contrary to all good precedent that so worthy a knight should not have had some scribe to take upon himself the task of writing an account of these unheard-of exploits; for that was something that had happened to none of the knights-errant who, as the saying has it, had gone forth in quest of adventures, seeing that each of them had one or two chroniclers, as if ready at hand, who not only had set down their deeds, but had depicted their most trivial thoughts and amiable weaknesses, however well concealed they might be. The good knight of La Mancha surely could not have been so unfortunate as to have lacked what Platir and others like him had in abundance. And so I could not bring myself to believe that this gallant history could have remained thus lopped off and mutilated, and I could not but lay the blame upon the malignity of time, that devourer and consumer of all things, which must either have consumed it or kept it hidden.

On the other hand, I reflected that inasmuch as among the knight's books

---

1. Cervantes himself, adopting here—with tongue in cheek—a device used in the romances of chivalry to create suspense.

had been found such modern works as *The Disenchantments of Jealousy* and *The Nymphs and Shepherds of Henares*, his story likewise must be modern, and that even though it might not have been written down, it must remain in the memory of the good folk of his village and the surrounding ones. This thought left me somewhat confused and more than ever desirous of knowing the real and true story, the whole story, of the life and wondrous deeds of our famous Spaniard, Don Quixote, light and mirror of the chivalry of La Mancha, the first in our age and in these calamitous times to devote himself to the hardships and exercises of knight-errantry and to go about righting wrongs, succoring widows, and protecting damsels—damsels such as those who, mounted upon their palfreys and with riding-whip in hand, in full possession of their virginity, were in the habit of going from mountain to mountain and from valley to valley; for unless there were some villain, some rustic with an ax and hood, or some monstrous giant to force them, there were in times past maiden ladies who at the end of eighty years, during all which time they had not slept for a single day beneath a roof, would go to their graves as virginal as when their mothers had borne them.

If I speak of these things, it is for the reason that in this and in all other respects our gallant Quixote is deserving of constant memory and praise, and even I am not to be denied my share of it for my diligence and the labor to which I put myself in searching out the conclusion of this agreeable narrative; although if heaven, luck, and circumstance had not aided me, the world would have had to do without the pleasure and the pastime which anyone may enjoy who will read this work attentively for an hour or two. The manner in which it came about was as follows:

I was standing one day in the Alcaná, or market place, of Toledo when a lad came up to sell some old notebooks and other papers to a silk weaver who was there. As I am extremely fond of reading anything, even though it be but the scraps of paper in the streets, I followed my natural inclination and took one of the books, whereupon I at once perceived that it was written in characters which I recognized as Arabic. I recognized them, but reading them was another thing; and so I began looking around to see if there was any Spanish-speaking Moor near by who would be able to read them for me. It was not very hard to find such an interpreter, nor would it have been even if the tongue in question had been an older and a better one.[2] To make a long story short, chance brought a fellow my way; and when I told him what it was I wished and placed the book in his hands, he opened it in the middle and began reading and at once fell to laughing. When I asked him what the cause of his laughter was, he replied that it was a note which had been written in the margin.

I besought him to tell me the content of the note, and he, laughing still, went on, "As I told you, it is something in the margin here: 'This Dulcinea del Toboso, so often referred to, is said to have been the best hand at salting pigs of any woman in all La Mancha.' "

No sooner had I heard the name Dulcinea del Toboso than I was astonished and held in suspense, for at once the thought occurred to me that those notebooks must contain the history of Don Quixote. With this in mind I urged him to read me the title, and he proceeded to do so, turning the

---

2. I.e., Hebrew.

Arabic into Castilian upon the spot: *History of Don Quixote de la Mancha, Written by Cid Hamete Benengeli*[3] Arabic Historian. It was all I could do to conceal my satisfaction and, snatching them from the silk weaver, I bought from the lad all the papers and notebooks that he had for half a real; but if he had known or suspected how very much I wanted them, he might well have had more than six reales for them.

The Moor and I then betook ourselves to the cathedral cloister, where I requested him to translate for me into the Castilian tongue all the books that had to do with Don Quixote, adding nothing and subtracting nothing; and I offered him whatever payment he desired. He was content with two arrobas of raisins and two fanegas[4] of wheat and promised to translate them well and faithfully and with all dispatch. However, in order to facilitate matters, and also because I did not wish to let such a find as this out of my hands, I took the fellow home with me, where in a little more than a month and a half he translated the whole of the work just as you will find it set down here.

In the first of the books there was a very lifelike picture of the battle between Don Quixote and the Biscayan, the two being in precisely the same posture as described in the history, their swords upraised, the one covered by his buckler, the other with his cushion. As for the Biscayan's mule, you could see at the distance of a crossbow shot that it was one for hire. Beneath the Biscayan there was a rubric which read: "Don Sancho de Azpeitia," which must undoubtedly have been his name; while beneath the feet of Rocinante was another inscription: "Don Quixote." Rocinante was marvelously portrayed: so long and lank, so lean and flabby, so extremely consumptive-looking that one could well understand the justness and propriety with which the name of "hack" had been bestowed upon him.

Alongside Rocinante stood Sancho Panza, holding the halter of his ass, and below was the legend: "Sancho Zancas." The picture showed him with a big belly, a short body and long shanks, and that must have been where he got the names of Panza y Zancas[5] by which he is a number of times called in the course of the history. There are other small details that might be mentioned, but they are of little importance and have nothing to do with the truth of the story—and no story is bad so long as it is true.

If there is any objection to be raised against the veracity of the present one, it can be only that the author was an Arab, and that nation is known for its lying propensities; but even though they be our enemies, it may readily be understood that they would more likely have detracted from, rather than added to, the chronicle. So it seems to me, at any rate; for whenever he might and should deploy the resources of his pen in praise of so worthy a knight, the author appears to take pains to pass over the matter in silence; all of which in my opinion is ill done and ill conceived, for it should be the duty of historians to be exact, truthful, and dispassionate, and neither interest nor fear nor rancor nor affection should swerve them from the path of truth, whose mother is history, rival of time, depository of deeds, witness of the past, exemplar and adviser to the present, and the future's councilor. In this work, I am sure, will be found all that could be desired in the way of pleasant reading; and if it is lacking in any way, I maintain that this is the

---

3. Citing some ancient chronicle as the author's source and authority is very much in the tradition of the romances. *Benengeli:* eggplant (Arabic).   4. About fifty pounds. *Two arrobas:* three bushels.
5. Paunch and Shanks (Spanish).

fault of that hound of an author rather than of the subject.

But to come to the point, the second part, according to the translation, began as follows:

As the two valorous and enraged combatants stood there, swords upraised and poised on high, it seemed from their bold mien as if they must surely be threatening heaven, earth, and hell itself. The first to let fall a blow was the choleric Biscayan, and he came down with such force and fury that, had not his sword been deflected in mid-air, that single stroke would have sufficed to put an end to this fearful combat and to all our knight's adventures at the same time; but fortune, which was reserving him for greater things, turned aside his adversary's blade in such a manner that, even though it fell upon his left shoulder, it did him no other damage than to strip him completely of his armor on that side, carrying with it a good part of his helmet along with half an ear, the headpiece clattering to the ground with a dreadful din, leaving its wearer in a sorry state.

Heaven help me! Who could properly describe the rage that now entered the heart of our hero of La Mancha as he saw himself treated in this fashion? It may merely be said that he once more reared himself in the stirrups, laid hold of his sword with both hands, and dealt the Biscayan such a blow, over the cushion and upon the head, that, even so good a defense proving useless, it was as if a mountain had fallen upon his enemy. The latter now began bleeding through the mouth, nose, and ears; he seemed about to fall from his mule, and would have fallen, no doubt, if he had not grasped the beast about the neck, but at that moment his feet slipped from the stirrups and his arms let go, and the mule, frightened by the terrible blow, began running across the plain, hurling its rider to the earth with a few quick plunges.

Don Quixote stood watching all this very calmly. When he saw his enemy fall, he leaped from his horse, ran over very nimbly, and thrust the point of his sword into the Biscayan's eyes, calling upon him at the same time to surrender or otherwise he would cut off his head. The Biscayan was so bewildered that he was unable to utter a single word in reply, and things would have gone badly with him, so blind was Don Quixote in his rage, if the ladies of the coach, who up to then had watched the struggle in dismay, had not come up to him at this point and begged him with many blandishments to do them the very great favor of sparing their squire's life.

To which Don Quixote replied with much haughtiness and dignity, "Most certainly, lovely ladies, I shall be very happy to do that which you ask of me, but upon one conditon and understanding, and that is that this knight promise me that he will go to El Toboso and present himself in my behalf before Doña Dulcinea, in order that she may do with him as she may see fit."

Trembling and disconsolate, the ladies did not pause to discuss Don Quixote's request, but without so much as inquiring who Dulcinea might be they promised him that the squire would fulfill that which was commanded of him.

"Very well, then, trusting in your word, I will do him no further harm, even though he has well deserved it."

CHAPTER 10

*Of the pleasing conversation that took place between Don Quixote and
Sancho Panza, his squire.*

By this time Sancho Panza had got to his feet, somewhat the worse for
wear as the result of the treatment he had received from the friars' lads. He
had been watching the battle attentively and praying God in his heart to give
the victory to his master, Don Quixote, in order that he, Sancho, might gain
some island where he could go to be governor as had been promised him.
Seeing now that the combat was over and the knight was returning to mount
Rocinante once more, he went up to hold the stirrup for him; but first he
fell on his knees in front of him and, taking his hand, kissed it and said,
"May your Grace be pleased, Señor Don Quixote, to grant me the governorship of that island which you have won in this deadly affray; for however
large it may be, I feel that I am indeed capable of governing it as well as any
man in this world has ever done."

To which Don Quixote replied, "Be advised, brother Sancho, that this
adventure and other similar ones have nothing to do with islands; they are
affairs of the crossroads in which one gains nothing more than a broken head
or an ear the less. Be patient, for there will be others which will not only
make you a governor, but more than that."

Sancho thanked him very much and, kissing his hand again and the skirt
of his cuirass, he assisted him up on Rocinante's back, after which the squire
bestraddled his own mount and started jogging along behind his master, who
was now going at a good clip. Without pausing for any further converse with
those in the coach, the knight made for a near-by wood, with Sancho following as fast as his beast could trot; but Rocinante was making such speed that
the ass and its rider were left behind, and it was necessary to call out to Don
Quixote to pull up and wait for them. He did so, reining in Rocinante until
the weary Sancho had drawn abreast of him.

"It strikes me, sir," said the squire as he reached his master's side, "that it
would be better for us to take refuge in some church; for in view of the way
you have treated that one with whom you were fighting, it would be small
wonder if they did not lay the matter before the Holy Brotherhood[6] and have
us arrested; and faith, if they do that, we shall have to sweat a-plenty before
we come out of jail."

"Be quiet," said Don Quixote. "And where have you ever seen, or read of,
a knight being brought to justice no matter how many homicides he might
have committed?"

"I know nothing about omecils,"[7] replied Sancho, "nor ever in my life did
I bear one to anybody; all I know is that the Holy Brotherhood has something
to say about those who go around fighting on the highway, and I want nothing
of it."

"Do not let it worry you," said Don Quixote, "for I will rescue you from
the hands of the Chaldeans, not to speak of the Brotherhood. But answer
me upon your life: have you ever seen a more valorous knight than I on all

6. A tribunal instituted by Ferdinand and Isabella at the end of the 15th century to punish highway robbers.
7. In Spanish a wordplay on *homecidio-omecillo*. Not to bear an *omecillo* to anybody means not to bear a
grudge, and good-natured Sancho does not.

the known face of the earth? Have you ever read in the histories of any other who had more mettle in the attack, more perseverance in sustaining it, more dexterity in wounding his enemy, or more skill in overthrowing him?"

"The truth is," said Sancho, "I have never read any history whatsoever, for I do not know how to read or write; but what I would wager is that in all the days of my life I have never served a more courageous master than your Grace; I only hope your courage is not paid for in the place that I have mentioned. What I would suggest is that your Grace allow me to do something for that ear, for there is much blood coming from it, and I have here in my saddlebags some lint and a little white ointment."

"We could well dispense with all that," said Don Quixote, "if only I had remembered to bring along a vial of Fierabrás's[8] balm, a single drop of which saves time and medicines."

"What vial and what balm is that?" inquired Sancho Panza.

"It is a balm the receipt[9] for which I know by heart; with it one need have no fear of death nor think of dying from any wound. I shall make some of it and give it to you; and thereafter, whenever in any battle you see my body cut in two—as very often happens—all that is necessary is for you to take the part that lies on the ground, before the blood has congealed, and fit it very neatly and with great nicety upon the other part that remains in the saddle, taking care to adjust it evenly and exactly. Then you will give me but a couple of swallows of the balm of which I have told you, and you will see me sounder than an apple in no time at all."

"If that is so," said Panza, "I herewith renounce the governorship of the island you promised me and ask nothing other in payment of my many and faithful services than that your Grace give me the receipt for this wonderful potion, for I am sure that it would be worth more than two reales the ounce anywhere, and that is all I need for a life of ease and honor. But may I be so bold as to ask how much it costs to make it?"

"For less than three reales you can make something like six quarts," Don Quixote told him.

"Sinner that I am!" exclaimed Sancho. "Then why does your Grace not make some at once and teach me also?"

"Hush, my friend," said the knight, "I mean to teach you greater secrets than that and do you greater favors; but, for the present, let us look after this ear of mine, for it is hurting me more than I like."

Sancho thereupon took the lint and the ointment from his saddlebags; but when Don Quixote caught a glimpse of his helmet, he almost went out of his mind and, laying his hand upon his sword and lifting his eyes heavenward, he cried, "I make a vow to the Creator of all things and to the four holy Gospels in all their fullness of meaning that I will lead from now on the life that the great Marquis of Mantua did after he had sworn to avenge the death of his nephew Baldwin: not to eat bread of a tablecloth, not to embrace his wife, and other things which, although I am unable to recall them, we will look upon as understood—all this until I shall have wreaked an utter vengeance upon the one who has perpetrated such an outrage upon me."

"But let me remind your Grace," said Sancho when he heard these words, "that if the knight fulfills that which was commanded of him, by going to

---

8. A giant Saracen healer in the medieval epics of the Twelve Peers (see n. 8, p. 2244).　　9. Recipe.

present himself before my lady Dulcinea del Toboso, then he will have paid his debt to you and merits no further punishment at your hands, unless it be for some fresh offense."

"You have spoken very well and to the point," said Don Quixote, "and so I annul the vow I have just made insofar as it has to do with any further vengeance, but I make it and confirm it anew so far as leading the life of which I have spoken is concerned, until such time as I shall have obtained by force of arms from some other knight another headpiece as good as this. And do not think, Sancho, that I am making smoke out of straw; there is one whom I well may imitate in this matter, for the same thing happened in all literalness in the case of Mambrino's helmet[1] which cost Sacripante so dear."

"I wish," said Sancho, "that your Grace would send all such oaths to the devil, for they are very bad for the health and harmful for the conscience as well. Tell me, please; supposing that for many days to come we meet no man wearing a helmet, then what are we to do? Must you still keep your vow in spite of all the inconveniences and discomforts, such as sleeping with your clothes on, not sleeping in any town, and a thousand other penances contained in the oath of that old madman of a Marquis of Mantua, an oath which you would now revive? Mark you, sir, along all these roads you meet no men of arms but only muleteers and carters, who not only do not wear helmets but quite likely have never heard tell of them in all their livelong days."

"In that you are wrong," said Don Quixote, "for we shall not be at these crossroads for the space of two hours before we shall see more men of arms than came to Albraca to win the fair Angélica."[2] "Very well, then," said Sancho, "so be it, and pray God that all turns out for the best so that I may at last win that island that is costing me so dearly, and then let me die."

"I have already told you, Sancho, that you are to give no thought to that; should the island fail, there is the kingdom of Denmark or that of Sobradisa, which would fit you like a ring on your finger, and you ought, moreover, to be happy to be on *terra firma*.[3] But let us leave all this for some other time, while you look and see if you have something in those saddlebags for us to eat, after which we will go in search of some castle where we may lodge for the night and prepare that balm of which I was telling you, for I swear to God that my ear is paining me greatly."

"I have here an onion, a little cheese, and a few crusts of bread," said Sancho, "but they are not victuals fit for a valiant knight like your grace."

"How little you know about it!" replied Don Quixote. "I would inform you, Sancho, that it is a point of honor with knights-errant to go for a month at a time without eating, and when they do eat, it is whatever may be at hand. You would certainly know that if you had read the histories as I have. There are many of them, and in none have I found any mention of knights eating unless it was by chance or at some sumptuous banquet that was tendered them; on other days they fasted. And even though it is well understood that, being men like us, they could not go without food entirely, any more than they could fail to satisfy the other necessities of nature, nevertheless, since they spent the greater part of their lives in forest and desert places without

---

1. The enchanted helmet of Mambrino, a Moorish king, is stolen by Rinaldo in Boiardo's *Roland in Love*. 2. Another allusion to *Roland in Love*. 3. Solid earth (Latin, literal trans.), here Firm Island, an imaginary final destination for the squires of knights-errant. Sobradisa is an imaginary realm.

any cook to prepare their meals, their diet ordinarily consisted of rustic viands such as those that you now offer me. And so, Sancho my friend, do not be grieved at that which pleases me, nor seek to make the world over, nor to unhinge the institution of knight-errantry."

"Pardon me, your Grace," said Sancho, "but seeing that, as I have told you I do not know how to read or write, I am consequently not familiar with the rules of the knightly calling. Hereafter, I will stuff my saddlebags with all manner of dried fruit for your Grace, but inasmuch as I am not a knight, I shall lay in for myself a stock of fowls and other more substantial fare."

"I am not saying, Sancho, that it is incumbent upon knights-errant to eat only those fruits of which you speak; what I am saying is that their ordinary sustenance should consist of fruit and a few herbs such as are to be found in the fields and with which they are well acquainted, as am I myself."

"It is a good thing," said Sancho, "to know those herbs, for, so far as I can see, we are going to have need of that knowledge one of these days."

With this, he brought out the articles he had mentioned, and the two of them ate in peace, and most companionably. Being desirous, however, of seeking a lodging for the night, they did not tarry long over their humble and unsavory repast. They then mounted and made what haste they could that they might arrive at a shelter before nightfall but the sun failed them, and with it went the hope of attaining their wish. As the day ended they found themselves beside some goatherds' huts, and they accordingly decided to spend the night there. Sancho was as much disappointed at their not having reached a town as his master was content with sleeping under the open sky; for it seemed to Don Quixote that every time this happened it merely provided him with yet another opportunity to establish his claim to the title of knight-errant.

[Of Goatherds, Roaming Shepherdesses, and Unrequited Loves]

CHAPTER 11

Of what happened to Don Quixote in the company of certain goatherds.

He was received by the herders with good grace, and Sancho having looked after Rocinante and the ass to the best of his ability, the knight, drawn by the aroma, went up to where some pieces of goat's meat were simmering in a pot over the fire. He would have liked then and there to see if they were done well enough to be transferred from pot to stomach, but he refrained in view of the fact that his hosts were already taking them off the fire. Spreading a few sheepskins on the ground, they hastily laid their rustic board and invited the strangers to share what there was of it. There were six of them altogether who belonged to that fold, and after they had urged Don Quixote, with rude politeness, to seat himself upon a small trough which they had turned upside down for the purpose, they took their own places upon the sheep hides round about. While his master sat there, Sancho remained standing to serve him the cup, which was made of horn. When the knight perceived this, he addressed his squire as follows.

"In order, Sancho, that you may see the good that there is in knight-errantry and how speedily those who follow the profession, no matter what the nature of their service may be, come to be honored and esteemed in the eyes of the world, I would have you here in the company of these good folk seat yourself at my side, that you may be even as I who am your master and natural lord, and eat from my plate and drink from where I drink; for of knight-errantry one may say the same as of love that it makes all things equal."

"Many thanks!" said Sancho, "but if it is all the same to your Grace, providing there is enough to go around, I can eat just as well, or better, standing up and alone as I can seated beside an emperor. And if the truth must be told, I enjoy much more that which I eat in my own corner without any bowings and scrapings, even though it be only bread and onions, that I do a meal of roast turkey where I have to chew slowly, drink little, be always wiping my mouth, and can neither sneeze nor cough if I feel like it, nor do any of those other things that you can when you are free and alone.

"And so, my master," he went on, "these honors that your Grace would confer upon me as your servant and a follower of knight-errantry—which I am, being your Grace's squire—I would have you convert, if you will, into other things that will be of more profit and advantage to me; for though I hereby acknowledge them as duly received, I renounce them from this time forth to the end of the world."

"But for all that," said Don Quixote, "you must sit down, for whosoever humbleth himself, him God will exalt." And, laying hold of his squire's arm, he compelled him to take a seat beside him.

The goatherds did not understand all this jargon about squires and knights-errant; they did nothing but eat, keep silent, and study their guests, who very dexterously and with much appetite were stowing away chunks of meat as big as your fist. When the meat course was finished, they laid out upon the sheepskins a great quantity of dried acorns and half a cheese, which was harder than if it had been made of mortar. The drinking horn all this while was not idle but went the rounds so often—now full, now empty, like the bucket of a water wheel—that they soon drained one of the two wine bags that were on hand. After Don Quixote had well satisfied his stomach, he took up a handful of acorns and, gazing at them attentively, fell into a soliloquy.

"Happy the age and happy those centuries to which the ancients gave the name of golden, and not because gold, which is so esteemed in this iron age of ours, was then to be had without toil, but because those who lived in that time did not know the meaning of the words 'thine' and 'mine.' In that blessed year all things were held in common, and to gain his daily sustenance no labor was required of any man save to reach forth his hand and take it from the sturdy oaks that stood liberally inviting him with their sweet and seasoned fruit. The clear-running fountains and rivers in magnificent abundance offered him palatable and transparent water for his thirst; while in the clefts of the rocks and the hollows of the trees the wise and busy honey-makers set up their republic so that any hand whatever might avail itself, fully and freely, of the fertile harvest which their fragrant toil had produced. The vigorous cork trees of their own free will and grace, without the asking, shed their broad, light bark with which men began to cover their dwellings, erected upon rude stakes merely as a protection against the inclemency of the heavens.

"All then was peace, all was concord and friendship; the crooked plowshare had not as yet grievously laid open and pried into the merciful bowels of our first mother, who without any forcing on man's part yielded her spacious fertile bosom on every hand for the satisfaction, sustenance, and delight of her first sons. Then it was that lovely and unspoiled young shepherdesses, with locks that were sometimes braided, sometimes flowing, went roaming from valley to valley and hillock to hillock with no more garments than were needed to cover decently that which modesty requires and always had required should remain covered. Nor were their adornments such as those in use today—of Tyrian purple and silk worked up in tortured patterns; a few green leaves of burdock or of ivy, and they were as splendidly and as becomingly clad as our ladies of the court with all the rare and exotic tricks of fashion that idle curiosity has taught them.

"Thoughts of love, also, in those days were set forth as simply as the simple hearts that conceived them, without any roundabout and artificial play of words by way of ornament. Fraud, deceit, and malice had not yet come to mingle with truth and plain-speaking. Justice kept its own domain, where favor and self-interest dared not trespass, dared not impair her rights, becloud, and persecute her as they now do. There was no such thing then as arbitrary judgments, for the reason that there was no one to judge or be judged. Maidens in all their modesty, as I have said, went where they would and unattended; whereas in this hateful age of ours none is safe, even though she go to hide and shut herself up in some new labyrinth like that of Crete; for in spite of all her seclusion, through chinks and crevices or borne upon the air, the amorous plague with all its cursed importunities will find her out and lead her to her ruin.

"It was for the safety of such as these, as time went on and depravity increased, that the order of knights-errant was instituted, for the protection of damsels, the aid of widows and orphans, and the succoring of the needy. It is to this order that I belong, my brothers, and I thank you for the welcome and the kindly treatment that you have accorded to me and my squire. By natural law, all living men are obliged to show favor to knights-errant, yet without being aware of this you have received and entertained me; and so it is with all possible good will that I acknowledge your own good will to me."

This long harangue on the part of our knight—it might very well have been dispensed with—was all due to the acorns they had given him, which had brought back to memory the age of gold; whereupon the whim had seized him to indulge in this futile harangue with the goatherds as his auditors. They listened in open-mouthed wonderment, saying not a word, and Sancho himself kept quiet and went on munching acorns, taking occasion very frequently to pay a visit to the second wine bag, which they had suspended from a cork tree to keep it cool.

It took Don Quixote much longer to finish his speech than it did to put away his supper; and when he was through, one of the goatherds addressed him.

"In order that your Grace may say with more truth that we have received you with readiness and good will, we desire to give you solace and contentment by having one of our comrades, who will be here soon, sing for you. He is a very bright young fellow and deeply in love, and what is more, you could not ask for anything better than to hear him play the three-stringed lute."

Scarcely had he done saying this when the sound of a rebec was heard, and shortly afterward the one who played it appeared. He was a goodlooking youth, around twenty-two years of age. His companions asked him if he had had his supper, and when he replied that he had, the one who had spoken to Don Quixote said to him, "Well, then, Antonio, you can give us the pleasure of hearing you sing, in order that this gentleman whom we have as our guest may see that we of the woods and mountains also know something about music. We have been telling him how clever you are, and now we want you to show him that we were speaking the truth. And so I beg you by all means to sit down and sing us that lovesong of yours that your uncle the prebendary composed for you and which the villagers liked so well."

"With great pleasure," the lad replied, and without any urging he seated himself on the stump of an oak that had been felled and, tuning up his rebec, soon began singing, very prettily, the following ballad:

The Ballad That Antonio Sang

I know well that thou dost love me,
My Olalla, even though
Eyes of thine have never spoken—
Love's mute tongues—to tell me so.
    Since I know thou knowest my passion,   5
Of thy love I am more sure:
No love ever was unhappy
When it was both frank and pure.
· True it is, Olalla, sometimes
Thou a heart of bronze hast shown,   10
And it seemed to me that bosom,
White and fair, was made of stone.
    Yet in spite of all repulses
And a chastity so cold,
It appeared that I Hope's garment   15
By the hem did clutch and hold.
    For my faith I ever cherished;
It would rise to meet the bait;
Spurned, it never did diminish;
Favored, it preferred to wait.   20
    Love, they say, hath gentle manners:
Thus it is it shows its face;
Then may I take hope, Olalla,
Trust to win a longed for grace.
    If devotion hath the power   25
Hearts to move and make them kind,
Let the loyalty I've shown thee
Plead my cause, be kept in mind.
    For if thou didst note my costume,
More than once thou must have seen,   30
Worn upon a simple Monday
Sunday's garb so bright and clean.
    Love and brightness go together.
Dost thou ask the reason why

I thus deck myself on Monday? 35
It is but to catch thine eye.
    I say nothing of the dances
I have danced for thy sweet sake;
Nor the serenades I've sung thee
Till the first cock did awake. 40
    Nor will I repeat my praises
Of that beauty all can see;
True my words but oft unwelcome—
Certain lasses hated me.
    One girl there is, I well remember— 45
She's Teresa on the hill—
Said, "You think you love an angel,
But she is a monkey still.
    "Thanks to all her many trinkets
And her artificial hair 50
And her many aids to beauty,
Love's own self she would ensnare."
    She was lying, I was angry,
And her cousin, very bold,
Challenged me upon my honor; 55
What ensued need not be told.
    Highflown words do not become me;
I'm a plain and simple man.
Pure the love that I would offer,
Serving thee as best I can. 60
    Silken are the bonds of marriage,
When two hearts do intertwine;
Mother Church the yoke will fasten;
Bow your neck and I'll bow mine.
    Or if not, my word I'll give thee, 65
From these mountains I'll come down—
Saint most holy be my witness—
Wearing a Capuchin gown.

With this the goatherd brought his song to a close, and although Don Quixote begged him to sing some more, Sancho Panza would not hear of this as he was too sleepy for any more ballads.

"Your Grace," he said to his master, "would do well to find out at once where his bed is to be, for the labor that these good men have to perform all day long does not permit them to stay up all night singing."

"I understand, Sancho," replied Don Quixote. "I perceive that those visits to the wine bag call for sleep rather than music as a recompense."

"It tastes well enough to all of us, God be praised," said Sancho.

"I am not denying that," said his master; "but go ahead and settle yourself down wherever you like. As for men of my profession, they prefer to keep vigil. But all the same, Sancho, perhaps you had better look after this ear, for it is paining me more than I like."

Sancho started to do as he was commanded, but one of the goatherds, when he saw the wound, told him not to bother, that he would place a remedy upon it that would heal it in no time. Taking a few leaves of rosemary, of which there was a great deal growing thereabouts, he mashed them in his mouth and, mixing them with a little salt, laid them on the ear, with the assurance that no other medicine was needed; and this proved to be the truth.

CHAPTER 12

Of the story that one of the goatherds told to Don Quixote and the others.

Just then, another lad came up, one of those who brought the goatherds their provisions from the village.

"Do you know what's happening down there, my friends?" he said.

"How should we know?" one of the men answered him.

"In that case," the lad went on, "I must tell you that the famous student and shepherd known as Grisóstomo died this morning, muttering that the cause of his death was the love he had for that bewitched lass of a Marcela, daughter of the wealthy Guillermo—you know, the one who's been going around in these parts dressed like a shepherdess."

"For love of Marcela, you say?" one of the herders spoke up.

"That is what I'm telling you," replied the other lad. "And the best part of it is that he left directions in his will that he was to be buried in the field, as if he were a Moor, and that his grave was to be at the foot of the cliff where the Cork Tree Spring is; for, according to report, and he is supposed to have said so himself, that is the place where he saw her for the first time. There were other provisions, which the clergy of the village say cannot be carried out, nor would it be proper to fulfill them, seeing that they savor of heathen practices. But Grisóstomo's good friend, the student Ambrosio, who also dresses like a shepherd, insists that everything must be done to the letter, and as a result there is great excitement in the village.

"Nevertheless, from all I can hear, they will end by doing as Ambrosio and Grisóstomo's other friends desire, and tomorrow they will bury him with great ceremony in the place that I have mentioned. I believe it is going to be something worth seeing; at any rate, I mean to see it, even though it is too far for me to be able to return to the village before nightfall."

"We will all do the same," said the other goatherds. "We will cast lots to see who stays to watch the goats."

"That is right, Pedro," said one of their number, "but it will not be necessary to go to the trouble of casting lots. I will take care of the flocks for all of us; and do not think that I am being generous or that I am not as curious as the rest of you; it is simply that I cannot walk on account of the splinter I picked up in this foot the other day."

"Well, we thank you just the same," said Pedro.

Don Quixote then asked Pedro to tell him more about the dead man and the shepherd lass; to which the latter replied that all he knew was that Grisóstomo was a rich gentleman who had lived in a near-by village. He had been a student for many years at Salamanca and then had returned to his birthplace with the reputation of being very learned and well read; he was especially noted for his knowledge of the science of the stars and what the sun and moon were doing up there in the heavens, "for he would promptly tell us when their clips was to come."

"*Eclipse*, my friend, not *clips*," said Don Quixote, "is the name applied to the darkening-over of those major luminaries."

But Pedro, not pausing for any trifles, went on with his story. "He could also tell when the year was going to be plentiful or estil—"

"*Sterile*, you mean to say, friend—"

"*Sterile* or *estil*," said Pedro, "it all comes out the same in the end. But I can tell you one thing, that his father and his friends, who believed in him, did just as he advised them and they became rich; for he would say to them, 'This year, sow barley and not wheat'; and again, 'Sow chickpeas and not barley'; or, 'This season there will be a good crop of oil[4] but the three following ones you will not get a drop.' "

"That science," Don Quixote explained, "is known as astrology."

"I don't know what it's called," said Pedro, "but he knew all this and more yet. Finally, not many months after he returned from Salamanca, he appeared one day dressed like a shepherd with crook and sheepskin jacket; for he had resolved to lay aside the long gown that he wore as a scholar, and in this he was joined by Ambrosio, a dear friend of his and the companion of his studies. I forgot to tell you that Grisóstomo was a great one for composing verses; he even wrote the carols for Christmas Eve and the plays that were performed at Corpus Christi by the lads of our village, and everyone said that they were the best ever.

"When the villagers saw the two scholars coming out dressed like shepherds, they were amazed and could not imagine what was the reason for such strange conduct on their part. It was about that time that Grisóstomo's father died and left him the heir to a large fortune, consisting of land and chattels, no small quantity of cattle, and a considerable sum of money, of all of which the young man was absolute master; and, to tell the truth, he deserved it, for he was very sociable and charitably inclined, a friend to all worthy folk, and he had a face that was like a benediction. Afterward it was learned that if he had changed his garments like this, it was only that he might be able to wander over the wastelands on the trail of that shepherdess Marcela of whom our friend was speaking, for the poor fellow had fallen in love with her. And now I should like to tell you, for it is well that you should know, just who this lass is; for it may be—indeed, there is no maybe about it—you will never hear the like in all the days of your life, though you live to be older than Sarna."

"You should say *Sarah*," Don Quixote corrected him; for he could not bear hearing the goatherd using the wrong words all the time.[5]

"The itch," said Pedro, "lives long enough; and if, sir, you go on interrupting me at every word, we'll never be through in a year."

"Pardon me, friend," said Don Quixote, "it was only because there is so great a difference between Sarna and Sarah that I pointed it out to you; but you have given me a very good answer, for the itch does live longer than Sarah; and so go on with your story, and I will not contradict you any more."

"I was about to say, then, my dear sir," the goatherd went on, "that in our village there was a farmer who was richer still than Grisóstomo's father. His name was Guillermo, and, over and above his great wealth, God gave him a daughter whose mother, the most highly respected woman in these parts, died in bearing her. It seems to me I can see the good lady now, with that face that rivaled the sun and moon; and I remember, above all, what a friend

---

4. Olive oil.   5. Actually in this case the goatherd is not really wrong, for *sarna* means "itch" and "older than the itch" was a proverbial expression.

she was to the poor, for which reason I believe that her soul at this very moment must be enjoying God's presence in the other world.

"Grieving for the loss of so excellent a wife, Guillermo himself died, leaving his daughter Marcela, now a rich young woman, in the custody of one of her uncles, a priest who holds a benefice in our village. The girl grew up with such beauty as to remind us of her mother, beautiful as that lady had been. By the time she was fourteen or fifteen no one looked at her without giving thanks to God who had created such comeliness, and almost all were hopelessly in love with her. Her uncle kept her very closely shut up, but, for all of that, word of her great beauty spread to such an extent that by reason of it, as much as on account of the girl's wealth, her uncle found himself besought and importuned not only by the young men of our village, but by those for leagues around who desired to have her for a wife.

"But he, an upright Christian, although he wished to marry her off as soon as she was of age, had no desire to do so without her consent, not that he had any eye to the gain and profit which the custody of his niece's property brought him while her marriage was deferred. Indeed, this much was said in praise of the good priest in more than one circle of the village; for I would have you know, Sir Knight, that in these little places everything is discussed and becomes a subject of gossip; and you may rest assured, as I am for my part, that a priest must be more than ordinarily good if his parishioners feel bound to speak well of him, especially in the small towns."

"That is true," said Don Quixote, "but go on. I like your story very much, and you, good Pedro, tell it with very good grace."

"May the Lord's grace never fail me, for that is what counts. But to go on: Although the uncle set forth to his niece the qualities of each one in particular of the many who sought her hand, begging her to choose and marry whichever one she pleased, she never gave him any answer other than this: that she did not wish to marry at all, since being but a young girl she did not feel that she was equal to bearing the burdens of matrimony. As her reasons appeared to be proper and just, the uncle did not insist but thought he would wait until she was a little older, when she would be capable of selecting someone to her taste. For, he said, and quite right he was, parents ought not to impose a way of life upon their children against the latters' will. And then, one fine day, lo and behold, there was the finical Marcela turned shepherdess; and without paying any attention to her uncle or all those of the village who advised against it, she set out to wander through the fields with the other lasses, guarding flocks as they did.

"Well, the moment she appeared in public and her beauty was uncovered for all to see, I really cannot tell you how many rich young bachelors, gentlemen, and farmers proceeded to don a shepherd's garb and go to make love to her in the meadows. One of her suitors, as I have told you, was our deceased friend, and it is said that he did not love but adored her. But you must not think that because Marcela chose so free and easy a life, and one that offers little or no privacy, that she was thereby giving the faintest semblance of encouragement to those who would disparage her modesty and prudence; rather, so great was the vigilance with which she looked after her honor that of all those who waited upon her and solicited her favors, none could truly say that she had given him the slightest hope of attaining his desire.

"For although she does not flee nor shun the company and conversation of the shepherds, treating them in courteous and friendly fashion, the moment she discovers any intentions on their part, even though it be the just and holy one of matrimony, she hurls them from her like a catapult. As a result, she is doing more damage in this land than if a plague had fallen upon it; for her beauty and graciousness win the hearts of all who would serve her, but her disdain and the disillusionment it brings lead them in the end to despair, and then they can only call her cruel and ungrateful, along with other similar epithets that reveal all too plainly the state of mind that prompts them. If you were to stay here some time, sir, you would hear these uplands and valleys echo with the laments of those who have followed her only to be deceived.

"Not far from here is a place where there are a couple of dozen tall beeches, and there is not a one of them on whose smooth bark Marcela's name has not been engraved; and above some of these inscriptions you will find a crown, as if by this her lover meant to indicate that she deserved to wear the garland of beauty above all the women on the earth. Here a shepherd sighs and there another voices his lament. Now are to be heard amorous ballads, and again despairing ditties. One will spend all the hours of the night seated at the foot of some oak or rock without once closing his tearful eyes, and the morning sun will find him there, stupefied and lost in thought. Another, without giving truce or respite to his sights, will lie stretched upon the burning sands in the full heat of the most exhausting summer noontide, sending up his complaint to merciful Heaven.

"And, meanwhile, over this one and that one, over one and all, the beauteous Marcela triumphs and goes her own way, free and unconcerned. All those of us who know her are waiting to see how far her pride will carry her, and who will be the fortunate man who will succeed in taming this terrible creature and thus come into possession of a beauty so matchless as hers. Knowing all this that I have told you to be undoubtedly true, I can readily believe this lad's story about the cause of Grisóstomo's death. And so I advise you, sir, not to fail to be present tomorrow at his burial; it will be well worth seeing, for he has many friends, and the place is not half a league from here."

"I will make a point of it," said Don Quixote, "and I thank you for the pleasure you have given me by telling me so delightful a tale."

"Oh," said the goatherd, "I do not know the half of the things that have happened to Marcela's lovers; but it is possible that tomorrow we may meet along the way some shepherd who will tell us more. And now it would be well for you to go and sleep under cover, for the night air may not be good for your wound, though with the remedy that has been put on it there is not much to fear."

Sancho Panza, who had been sending the goatherd to the devil for talking so much, now put in a word with his master, urging him to come and sleep in Pedro's hut. Don Quixote did so; and all the rest of the night was spent by him in thinking of his lady Dulcinea, in imitation of Marcela's lovers. As for Sancho, he made himself comfortable between Rocinante and the ass and at once dropped off to sleep, not like a lovelorn swain but, rather, like a man who has had a sound kicking that day.

CHAPTER 13

In which is brought to a close the story of the shepherdess Marcela, along with other events.

Day had barely begun to appear upon the balconies of the east when five or six goatherds arose and went to awaken Don Quixote and tell him that if he was still of a mind to go see Grisóstomo's famous burial they would keep him company. The knight, desiring nothing better, ordered Sancho to saddle at once, which was done with much dispatch, and then they all set out forthwith.

They had not gone more than a quarter of a league when, upon crossing a footpath, they saw coming toward them six shepherds clad in black sheep-skins and with garlands of cypress and bitter rosebay on their heads. Each of them carried a thick staff made of the wood of the holly, and with them came two gentlemen on horseback in handsome traveling attire, accompanied by three lads on foot. As the two parties met they greeted each other courteously, each inquiring as to the other's destination, where upon they learned that they were all going to the burial, and so continued to ride along together.

Speaking to his companion, one of them said, "I think, Señor Vivaldo, that we are going to be well repaid for the delay it will cost us to see this famous funeral; for famous it must surely be, judging by the strange things that these shepherds have told us of the dead man and the homicidal shepherdess."

"I think so too," agreed Vivaldo. "I should be willing to delay our journey not one day, but four, for the sake of seeing it."

Don Quixote then asked them what it was they had heard of Marcela and Grisóstomo. The traveler replied that on that very morning they had fallen in with those shepherds and, seeing them so mournfully trigged out, had asked them what the occasion for it was. One of the fellows had then told them of the beauty and strange demeanor of a shepherdess by the name of Marcela, her many suitors, and the death of this Grisóstomo, to whose funeral they were bound. He related, in short, the entire story as Don Quixote had heard it from Pedro.

Changing the subject, the gentleman called Vivaldo inquired of Don Quixote what it was that led him to go armed in that manner in a land that was so peaceful.

"The calling that I profess," replied Don Quixote, "does not permit me to do otherwise. An easy pace, pleasure, and repose—those things were invented for delicate courtiers; but toil, anxiety, and arms—they are for those whom the world knows as knights-errant, of whom I, though unworthy, am the very least."

No sooner had they heard this than all of them immediately took him for a madman. By way of assuring himself further and seeing what kind of madness it was of which Don Quixote was possessed, Vivaldo now asked him what was meant by the term knights-errant.

"Have not your Worships read the annals and the histories of England that treat of the famous exploits of King Arthur, who in our Castilian balladry is always called King Artús? According to a very old tradition that is common throughout the entire realm of Great Britain, this king did not die, but by an act of enchantment was changed into a raven; and in due course of time he is to return and reign once more, recovering his kingdom and his scepter; for which reason, from that day to this, no Englishman is known to have killed one of those birds. It was, moreover, in the time of that good king that the famous order of the Knights of the Round Table was instituted; and as for the love of Sir Lancelot of the Lake and Queen Guinevere, everything took place exactly as the story has it, their confidante and go-between being the honored matron Quintañona; whence comes that charming ballad that is such a favorite with us Spaniards:

> Never was there a knight
> So served by maid and dame
> As the one they call Sir Lancelot
> When from Britain he came—

to carry on the gentle, pleasing course of his loves and noble deeds.

"From that time forth, the order of chivalry was passed on and propagated from one individual to another until it had spread through many and various parts of the world. Among those famed for their exploits was the valiant Amadis of Gaul, with all his sons and grandsons to the fifth generation; and there was also the brave Felixmarte of Hircania, and the never sufficiently praised Tirant lo Blanch; and in view of the fact that he lived in our own day, almost, we came near to seeing, hearing, and conversing with that other courageous knight, Don Belianís of Greece.

"And that, gentlemen, is what it means to be a knight-errant, and what I have been telling you of is the order of chivalry which such a knight professes, an order to which, as I have already informed you, I, although a sinner, have the honor of belonging; for I have made the same profession as have those other knights. That is why it is you find me in these wild and lonely places, riding in quest of adventure, being resolved to offer my arm and my person in the most dangerous undertaking fate may have in store for me, that I may be of aid to the weak and needy."

Listening to this speech, the travelers had some while since come to the conclusion that Don Quixote was out of his mind, and were likewise able to perceive the peculiar nature of his madness, and they wondered at it quite as much as did all those who encountered it for the first time. Being endowed with a ready wit and a merry disposition and thinking to pass the time until they reached the end of the short journey which, so he was told, awaited them before they should arrive at the mountain where the burial was to take place, Vivaldo decided to give him a further opportunity of displaying his absurdities.

"It strikes me, Sir Knight-errant," he said, "that your Grace has espoused one of the most austere professions to be found anywhere on earth—even more austere, if I am not mistaken, than that of the Carthusian monks."

"Theirs may be as austere as ours," Don Quixote replied, "but that it is as necessary I am very much inclined to doubt. For if the truth be told, the soldier who carries out his captain's order does no less than the captain who gives the order. By that I mean to say that the religious, in all peace and tranquility, pray to Heaven for earth's good, but we soldiers and knights put their prayers into execution by defending with the might of our good right arms and at the edge of the sword those things for which they pray; and we

do this not under cover of a roof but under the open sky, beneath the insufferable rays of the summer sun and the biting cold of winter. Thus we
become the ministers of God on earth, and our arms the means by which
He executes His decrees. And just as war and all the things that have to do
with it are impossible without toil, sweat, and anxiety, it follows that those
who have taken upon themselves such a profession must unquestionably
labor harder than do those who in peace and tranquility and at their ease
pray God to favor the ones who can do little in their own behalf.

"I do not mean to say—I should not think of saying—that the state of
knight-errant is as holy as that of the cloistered monk; I merely would imply,
from what I myself endure, that ours is beyond a doubt the more laborious
and arduous calling, more beset by hunger and thirst, more wretched, ragged,
and ridden with lice. It is an absolute certainty that the knights-errant of old
experienced much misfortune in the course of their lives; and if some by
their might and valor came to be emperors, you may take my word for it, it
cost them dearly in blood and sweat, and if those who rose to such a rank
had lacked enchanters and magicians to aid them, they surely would have
been cheated of their desires, deceived in their hopes and expectations."

"I agree with you on that," said the traveler, "but there is one thing among
others that gives me a very bad impression of the knights-errant, and that is
the fact that when they are about to enter upon some great and perilous
adventure in which they are in danger of losing their lives, they never at that
moment think of commending themselves to God as every good Christian is
obliged to do under similar circumstances, but, rather, commend themselves
to their ladies with as much fervor and devotion as if their mistresses were
God himself; all of which to me smacks somewhat of paganism."

"Sir," Don Quixote answered him, "it could not by any means be otherwise;
the knight-errant who did not do so would fall into disgrace, for it is the
usage and custom of chivalry that the knight, before engaging in some great
feat of arms, shall behold his lady in front of him and shall turn his eyes
toward her, gently and lovingly, as if beseeching her favor and protection in
the hazardous encounter that awaits him, and even though no one hears
him, he is obliged to utter certain words between his teeth, commending
himself to her with all his heart; and of this we have numerous examples in
the histories. Nor is it to be assumed that he does not commend himself to
God also, but the time and place for that is in the course of the undertaking."

"All the same," said the traveler, "I am not wholly clear in this matter; for
I have often read of two knights-errant exchanging words until, one word
leading to another, their wrath is kindled; whereupon, turning their steeds
and taking a good run up the field, they whirl about and bear down upon
each other at full speed, commending themselves to their ladies in the midst
of it all. What commonly happens then is that one of the two topples from
his horse's flanks and is run through and through with the other's lance; and
his adversary would also fall to the ground if he did not cling to his horse's
mane. What I do not understand is how the dead man would have had time
to commend himself to God in the course of this accelerated combat. It
would be better if the words he wasted in calling upon his lady as he ran
toward the other knight had been spent in paying the debt that he owed as
a Christian. Moreover, it is my personal opinion that not all knights-errant
have ladies to whom to commend themselves; for not all of them are in love."

"That" said Don Quixote, "is impossible. I assert there can be no knight-errant without a lady; for it is as natural and proper for them to be in love as it is for the heavens to have stars, and I am quite sure that no one ever read a story in which a loveless man of arms was to be met with, for the simple reason that such a one would not be looked upon as a legitimate knight but as a bastard one who had entered the fortress of chivalry not by the main gate, but over the walls, like a robber and a thief."

"Nevertheless," said the traveler, "if my memory serves me right, I have read that Don Galaor, brother of the valorous Amadis of Gaul, never had a special lady to whom he prayed, yet he was not held in any the less esteem for that but was a very brave and famous knight."

Once again, our Don Quixote had an answer. "Sir, one swallow does not make a summer. And in any event, I happen to know that this knight was secretly very much in love. As for his habit of paying court to all the ladies that caught his fancy, that was a natural propensity on his part and one that he was unable to resist. There was, however, one particular lady whom he had made the mistress of his will and to whom he did commend himself very frequently and privately; for he prided himself upon being a reticent knight."

"Well, then," said the traveler, "if it is essential that every knight-errant be in love, it is to be presumed that your Grace is also, since you are of the profession. And unless it be that you pride yourself upon your reticence as much as did Don Galaor, then I truly, on my own behalf and in the name of all this company, beseech your Grace to tell us your lady's name, the name of the country where she resides, what her rank is, and something of the beauty of her person, that she may esteem herself fortunate in having all the world know that she is loved and served by such a knight as your Grace appears to me to be."

At this, Don Quixote heaved a deep sigh. "I cannot say," he began, "as to whether or not my sweet enemy would be pleased that all the world should know I serve her. I can only tell you, in response to the question which you have so politely put to me, that her name is Dulcinea, her place of residence El Toboso, a village of La Mancha. As to her rank, she should be at the very least a princess, seeing that she is my lady and my queen. Her beauty is superhuman, for in it are realized all the impossible and chimerical attributes that poets are accustomed to give their fair ones. Her locks are golden, her brow the Elysian Fields, her eyebrows rainbows, her eyes suns, her cheeks roses, her lips coral, her teeth pearls, her neck alabaster, her bosom marble, her hands ivory, her complexion snow-white. As for those parts which modesty keeps covered from the human sight, it is my opinion that, discreetly considered, they are only to be extolled and not compared to any other."

"We should like," said Vivaldo, "to know something as well of her lineage, her race and ancestry."

"She is not," said Don Quixote, "of the ancient Roman Curtii, Caii, or Scipios, nor of the modern Colonnas and Orsini, nor of the Moncades and Requesenses of Catalonia, nor is she of the Rebellas and Villanovas of Valencia, or the Palafoxes, Nuzas, Rocabertis, Corellas, Lunas, Alagones, Urreas, or Gurreas of Aragon, the Cerdas, Manriques, Mendozas, or Guzmanes of Castile, the Alencastros, Pallas, or Menezes of Portugal; but she is of the Tobosos of La Mancha, and although the line is a modern one, it well may give rise to the most illustrious families of the centuries to come. And let none dispute this with me, unless it be under the conditions which Zerbino has set forth in the inscription beneath Orlando's arms:

> These let none move
> Who dares not with Orlando his valor prove."[6]

"Although my own line," replied the traveler, "is that of the Gachupins of Laredo, I should not venture to compare it with the Tobosos of La Mancha, in view of the fact that, to tell you the truth, I have never heard the name before."

"How does it come that you have never heard it!" exclaimed Don Quixote.

The others were listening most attentively to the conversation of these two, and even the goatherds and shepherds were by now aware that our knight of La Mancha was more than a little insane. Sancho Panza alone thought that all his master said was the truth, for he was well acquainted with him, having known him since birth. The only doubt in his mind had to do with the beauteous Dulcinea del Toboso, for he knew of no such princess and the name was strange to his ears, although he lived not far from that place.

They were continuing on their way, conversing in this manner, when they caught sight of some twenty shepherds coming through the gap between two high mountains, all of them clad in black woolen garments and with wreaths on their heads, some of the garlands, as was afterward learned, being of cypress, others of yew. Six of them were carrying a bier covered with a great variety of flowers and boughs.

"There they come with Grisóstomo's body," said one of the goatherds, "and the foot of the mountain yonder is where he wished to be buried."

They accordingly quickened their pace and arrived just as those carrying the bier had set it down on the ground. Four of the shepherds with sharpened picks were engaged in digging a grave alongside the barren rock. After a courteous exchange of greetings, Don Quixote and his companions turned to look at the bier. Upon it lay a corpse covered with flowers, the body of a man dressed like a shepherd and around thirty years of age. Even in death it could be seen that he had had a handsome face and had been of a jovial disposition. Round about him upon the bier were a number of books and many papers, open and folded.

Meanwhile, those who stood gazing at the dead man and those who were digging the grave—everyone present, in fact—preserved an awed silence, until one of the pallbearers said to another, "Look well, Ambrosio, and make sure that this is the place that Grisóstomo had in mind, since you are bent upon carrying out to the letter the provisions of his will."

"This is it," replied Ambrosio; "for many times my unfortunate friend told me the story of his misadventure. He told me that it was here that he first laid eyes upon that mortal enemy of the human race, and it was here, also, that he first revealed to her his passion, for he was as honorable as he was lovelorn; and it was here, finally, at their last meeting, that she shattered his illusions and showed him her disdain, thus bringing to an end the tragedy of his wretched life. And here, in memory of his great misfortune, he wished to be laid in the bowels of eternal oblivion."

---

6. From Ludovico Ariosto's *Orlando Furioso*, canto XXIV, stanza 57.

Then, turning to Don Quixote and the travelers, he went on, "This body, gentlemen, on which you now look with pitying eyes was the depository of a soul which heaven had endowed with a vast share of its riches. This is the body of Grisóstomo, who was unrivaled in wit, unequaled in courtesy, supreme in gentleness of bearing, a model of friendship, generous without stint, grave without conceit, merry without being vulgar—in short, first in all that is good and second to none in the matter of misfortunes. He loved well and was hated, he adored and was disdained; he wooed a wild beast, importuned a piece of marble, ran after the wind, cried out to loneliness, waited upon ingratitude, and his reward was to be the spoils of death midway in his life's course—a life that was brought to an end by a shepherdess whom he sought to immortalize that she might live on in the memory of mankind, as those papers that you see there would very plainly show if he had not commanded me to consign them to the flames even as his body is given to the earth."

"You," said Vivaldo, "would treat them with greater harshness and cruelty than their owner himself, for it is neither just nor fitting to carry out the will of one who commands what is contrary to all reason. It would not have been a good thing for Augustus Caesar to consent to have them execute the behests of the divine Mantuan in his last testament.[7] And so, Señor Ambrosio, while you may give the body of your friend to the earth, you ought not to give his writings to oblivion. If out of bitterness he left such an order, that does not mean that you are to obey it without using your own discretion. Rather, by granting life to these papers, you permit Marcela's cruelheartedness to live forever and serve as an example to the others in the days that are to come in order that they may flee and avoid such pitfalls as these.

"I and those that have come with me know the story of this lovesick and despairing friend of yours; we know the affection that was between you, and what the occasion of his death was, and the things that he commanded be done as his life drew to a close. And from this lamentable tale anyone may see how great was Marcela's cruelty; they may behold Grisóstomo's love, the loyalty that lay in your friendship, and the end that awaits those who run headlong, with unbridled passion, down the path that doting love opens before their gaze. Last night we heard of your friend's death and learned that he was to be buried here, and out of pity and curiosity we turned aside from our journey and resolved to come see with our own eyes that which had aroused so much compassion when it was told to us. And in requital of that compassion, and the desire that has been born in us to prevent if we can a recurrence of such tragic circumstances, we beg you, O prudent Ambrosio!— or, at least, I for my part implore you—to give up your intention of burning these papers and let me carry some of them away with me."

Without waiting for the shepherd to reply he put out his hand and took a few of those that were nearest him.

"Out of courtesy, sir," said Ambrosio when he saw this, "I will consent for you to keep those that you have taken; but it is vain to think that I will refrain from burning the others."

Vivaldo, who was anxious to find out what was in the papers, opened one of them and perceived that it bore the title "Song of Despair."

---

7. Virgil (born near Mantua) had left instructions that his Roman epic, the *Aeneid*, should be burned.

Hearing this, Ambrosio said, "That is the last thing the poor fellow wrote; and in order, sir, that you may see the end to which his misfortunes brought him, read it aloud if you will, for we shall have time for it while they are digging the grave."

"That I will very willingly do," said Vivaldo.

And since all the bystanders had the same desire, they gathered around as he in a loud clear voice read the following poem.

CHAPTER 14

In which are set down the despairing verses of the deceased shepherd, with other unlooked-for happenings.

Grisóstomo's Song

Since thou desirest that thy cruelty
Be spread from tongue to tongue and land to land,
The unrelenting sternness of thy heart
Shall turn my bosom's hell to minstrelsy
That all men everywhere may understand   5
The nature of my grief and what thou art.
And as I seek my sorrows to impart,
Telling of all the things that thou hast done,
My very entrails shall speak out to brand
Thy heartlessness, thy soul to reprimand,   10
Where no compassion ever have I won.
Then listen well, lend an attentive ear;
This ballad that thou art about to hear
Is not contrived by art; 'tis a simple song
Such as shepherds sing each day throughout the year—   15
Surcease of pain for me, for thee a prong.

Then let the roar of lion, fierce wolf's cry,
The horrid hissing of the scaly snake,
The terrifying sound of monsters strange,
Ill-omened call of crow against the sky,   20
The howling of the wind as it doth shake
The tossing sea where all is constant change,
Bellow of vanquished bull that cannot range
As it was wont to do, the piteous sob
Of the widowed dove as if its heart would break,   25
Hoot of the envied owl,[8] ever awake,
From hell's own choir the deep and mournful throb—
Let all these sounds come forth and mingle now.
For if I'm to tell my woes, why then, I vow,
I must new measures find, new modes invent,   30
With sound confusing sense, I may somehow
Portray the inferno where my days are spent.

The mournful echoes of my murmurous plaint
Father Tagus[9] shall not hear as he rolls his sand,

---

8. Envied by other birds as the only one that witnessed the Crucifixion.   9. The river Tagus. *Betis:* the Guadalquivir.

Nor olive-bordered Betis; my lament shall be   35
To the tall and barren rock as I acquaint
The caves with my sorrow; the far and lonely strand
No human foot has trod shall hear from me
The story of thine inhumanity
As told with lifeless tongue but living word.   40
I'll tell it to the valleys near at hand
Where never shines the sun upon the land;
By venomous serpents shall my tale be heard
On the low-lying, marshy river plain.
And yet, the telling will not be in vain;   45
For the reverberations of my plight,
Thy matchless austerity and this my pain,
Through the wide world shall go, thee to indict.
    Didsain may kill; suspicion false or true
May slay all patience; deadliest of all   50
Is jealousy; while absence renders life
Worse than a void; Hope lends no roseate hue
Against forgetfulness or the dread call
Of death inevitable, the end of strife.
Yet—unheard miracle!—with sorrows rife,   55
My own existence somehow still goes on;
The flame of life with me doth rise and fall.
Jealous I am, disdained; I know the gall
Of those suspicions that will not be gone,
Which leave me not the shadow of a hope,   60
And, desperate, I will not even grope
But rather will endure until the end,
And with despair eternally I'll cope,
Knowing that things for me will never mend.
    Can one both hope and fear at the same season?   65
Would it be well to do so in any case,
Seeing that fear, by far, hath the better excuse?
Confronting jealousy, is there any reason
For me to close my eyes to its stern face,
Pretend to see it not? What is the use,   70
When its dread presence I can still deduce
From countless gaping wounds deep in my heart?
When suspicion—bitter change!—to truth gives place,
And truth itself, losing its virgin grace,
Becomes a lie, is it not wisdom's part   75
To open wide the door to frank mistrust?
When disdain's unveiled, to doubt is only just.
O ye fierce tyrants of Love's empery!
Shackle these hands with stout cord, if ye must.
My pain shall drown your triumph—woe is me!   80
    I die, in short, and since nor life nor death
Yields any hope, to my fancy will I cling.
That man is freest who is Love's bond slave:
I'll say this with my living-dying breath,
And the ancient tyrant's praises I will sing.   85
Love is the greatest blessing Heaven e'er gave.

What greater beauty could a lover crave
Than that which my fair enemy doth show
In soul and body and in everything?
E'en her forgetfulness of me doth spring   90
From my own lack of grace, that I well know.
In spite of all the wrongs that he has wrought,
Love rules his empire justly as he ought.
Throw all to the winds and speed life's wretched span
By feeding on his self-deluding thought.   95
No blessing holds the future that I scan.
    Thou whose unreasonableness reason doth give
For putting an end to this tired life of mine,
From the deep heart wounds which thou mayest plainly see,
Judge if the better course be to die or live.   100
Gladly did I surrender my will to thine,
Gladly I suffered all thou didst to me;
And now that I'm dying, should it seem to thee
My death is worth a tear from thy bright eyes,
Pray hold it back, fair one, do not repine,   105
For I would have from thee no faintest sign
Of penitence, e'en though my soul thy prize.
Rather, I'd have thee laugh, be very gay,
And let my funeral be a festive day—
But I am very simple! knowing full well   110
That thou art bound to go thy blithesome way,
And my untimely end thy fame shall swell.
    Come, thirsting Tantalus from out Hell's pit;
Come, Sisyphus with the terrifying weight
Of that stone thou rollest; Tityus, bring   115
Thy vulture and thine anguish infinite;
Ixion[1] with thy wheel, be thou not late;
Come, too, ye sisters ever laboring;[2]
Come all, your griefs into my bosom fling,
And then, with lowered voices, intone a dirge,   120
If dirge be fitting for one so desperate,
A body without a shroud, unhappy fate!
And Hell's three-headed gateman,[3] do thou emerge
With a myriad other phantoms, monstrous swarm,
Beings infernal of fantastic form,   125
Raising their voices for the uncomforted
In a counterpoint of grief, harmonious storm.
What better burial for a lover dead?
    Despairing song of mine, do not complain,
Nor let our parting cause thee any pain,   130
For my misfortune is not wholly bad,
Seeing her fortune's bettered by my demise.
Then, even in the grave, be thou not sad.

---

1. In Greek myth, all four are proverbial images of mortals punished by the Gods with different forms of torture: *Tantalus*, craving water and fruit which he always fails to reach; *Sisyphus*, forever vainly trying to roll a stone upward to the top of a hill; *Tityus*, having his liver devoured by a vulture; and *Ixion*, being bound to a revolving wheel.   **2.** In classical mythology the three Fates (Moerae to the Greeks, Parcae to the Romans), spinners of man's destiny.   **3.** Cerberus, a dog-like three-headed monster, the mythological guardian of Hell.

Those who had listened to Grisóstomo's poem liked it well enough, but the one who read it remarked that it did not appear to him to conform to what had been told him of Marcela's modesty and virtue, seeing that in it the author complains of jealousy, suspicion, and absence, all to the prejudice of her good name. To this Ambrosio, as one who had known his friend's most deeply hidden thoughts, replied as follows:

"By way of satisfying, sir, the doubt that you entertain, it is well for you to know that when the unfortunate man wrote that poem, he was by his own volition absent from Marcela, to see if this would work a cure; but when the enamored one is away from his love, there is nothing that does not inspire in him fear and torment, and such was the case with Grisóstomo, for whom jealous imaginings, fears, and suspicions became a seeming reality. And so, in this respect, Marcela's reputation for virtue remains unimpaired; beyond being cruel and somewhat arrogant, and exceedingly disdainful, she could not be accused by the most envious of any other fault."

"Yes, that is so," said Vivaldo.

He was about to read another of the papers he had saved from the fire when he was stopped by a marvelous vision—for such it appeared—that suddenly met his sight; for there atop the rock beside which the grave was being hollowed out stood the shepherdess Marcela herself, more beautiful even than she was reputed to be. Those who up to then had never seen her looked on in silent admiration, while those who were accustomed to beholding her were held in as great a suspense as the ones who were gazing upon her for the first time.

No sooner had Ambrosio glimpsed her than, with a show of indignation, he called out to her, "So, fierce basilisk[4] of these mountains, have you perchance come to see if in your presence blood will flow from the wounds of this poor wretch whom you by your cruelty have deprived of life?[5] Have you come to gloat over your inhuman exploits, or would you from that height look down like another pitiless Nero upon your Rome in flames and ashes?[6] Or perhaps you would arrogantly tread under foot this poor corpse, as an ungrateful daughter did that of her father Tarquinius?[7] Tell us quickly why you have come and what it is that you want most; for I know that Grisóstomo thoughts never failed to obey you in life, and though he is dead now, I will see that all those who call themselves his friends obey you likewise."

"I do not come, O Ambrosio, for any of the reasons that you have mentioned," replied Marcela. "I come to defend myself and to demonstrate how unreasonable all those persons are who blame me for their sufferings and for Grisóstomo's death. I therefore ask all present to hear me attentively. It will not take long and I shall not have to spend many words in persuading those of you who are sensible that I speak the truth.

"Heaven made me beautiful, you say, so beautiful that you are compelled to love me whether you will or no; and in return for the love that you show me, you would have it that I am obliged to love you in return. I know, with that natural understanding that God has given me, that everything beautiful

---

4. A mythical lizard-like creature whose look and breath were supposed to be lethal.   5. According to folklore, the corpse of a murdered person was supposed to bleed in the presence of the murderer.   6. The Roman emperor Nero is supposed, in tale and proverb, to have been singing while from a tower he observed the burning of Rome in 64 C.E.   7. The inaccurate allusion is to Tullia, actually the wife of the last of the legendary kings of early Rome, Tarquinius; she let the wheel of her carriage trample over the body of her father—the previous king Servius Tullius—whom her husband Tarquinius had liquidated.

is lovable; but I cannot see that it follows that the object that is loved for its beauty must love the one who loves it. Let us suppose that the lover of the beautiful were ugly and, being ugly, deserved to be shunned; it would then be highly absurd for him to say, 'I love you because you are beautiful; you must love me because I am ugly.'

"But assuming that two individuals are equally beautiful, it does not mean that their desires are the same; for not all beauty inspires love, but may sometimes merely delight the eye and leave the will intact. If it were otherwise, no one would know what he wanted, but all would wander vaguely and aimlessly with nothing upon which to settle their affections; for the number of beautiful objects being infinite, desires similarly would be boundless. I have heard it said that true love knows no division and must be voluntary and not forced. This being so, as I believe it is, then why would you compel me to surrender my will for no other reason than that you say you love me? But tell me: supposing that Heaven which made me beautiful had made me ugly instead, should I have any right to complain because you did not love me? You must remember, moreover, that I did not choose this beauty that is mine; such as it is, Heaven gave it to me of its grace, without any choice or asking on my part. As the viper is not to be blamed for the deadly poison that it bears, since that is a gift of nature, so I do not deserve to be reprehended for my comeliness of form.

"Beauty in a modest woman is like a distant fire or a sharp-edged sword: the one does not burn, the other does not cut, those who do not come near it. Honor and virtue are the adornments of the soul, without which the body is not beautiful though it may appear to be. If modesty is one of the virtues that most adorn and beautiful body and soul, why should she who is loved for her beauty part with that virtue merely to satisfy the whim of one who solely for his own pleasure strives with all his force and energy to cause her to lose it? I was born a free being, and in order to live freely I chose the solitude of the fields; these mountain trees are my company, the clear-running waters in these brooks are my mirror, and to the trees and waters I communicate my thoughts and lend them of my beauty.

"In short, I am that distant fire, that sharp-edged sword, that does not burn or cut. Those who have been enamored by the sight of me I have disillusioned with my words; and if desire is sustained by hope, I gave none to Grisóstomo or any other, and of none of them can it be said that I killed them with my cruelty, for it was rather their own obstinacy that was to blame. And if you reproach me with the fact that his intentions were honorable and that I ought for that reason to have complied with them, I will tell you that when, on this very spot where his grave is now being dug, he revealed them to me, I replied that it was my own intention to live in perpetual solitude and that only the earth should enjoy the fruit of my retirement and the spoils of my beauty; and if he with all this plain-speaking was still stubbornly bent upon hoping against hope and sailing against the wind, is it to be wondered at if he drowned in the gulf of his own folly?

"Had I led him on, it would have been falsely; had I gratified his passion, it would have been against my own best judgment and intentions; but, though I had disillusioned him, he persisted, and though I did not hate him, he was driven to despair. Ask yourselves, then, if it is reasonable to blame me for his woes! Let him who has been truly deceived complain; let him despair who has been cheated of his promised hopes; if I have enticed any, let him speak up; if I have accepted the attentions of any, let him boast of it; but let not him to whom I have promised nothing, whom I have neither enticed nor accepted, apply to me such terms as cruel and homicidal. It has not as yet been Heaven's will to destine me to love any man, and there is no use expecting me to love of my own free choice.

"Let what I am saying now apply to each and every one of those who would have me for their own, and let it be understood from now on that if any die on account of me, he is not to be regarded as an unfortunate victim of jealousy, since she that cares for none can give to none the occasion for being jealous; nor is my plain-speaking to be taken as disdain. He who calls me a wild beast and a basilisk, let him leave me alone as something that is evil and harmful; let him who calls me ungrateful cease to wait upon me; let him who finds me strange shun my acquaintance; if I am cruel, do not run after me; in which case this wild beast, this basilisk, this strange, cruel, ungrateful creature will not run after them, seek them, out, wait upon them, nor endeavor to know them in any way.

"The thing that killed Grisóstomo was his impatience and the impetuosity of his desire; so why blame my modest conduct and retiring life? If I choose to preserve my purity here in the company of the trees, how can he complain of my unwillingness to lose it who would have me keep it with other men? I, as you know, have a worldly fortune of my own and do not covet that of others. My life is a free one, and I do not wish to be subject to another in any way. I neither love nor hate anyone; I do not repel this one and allure that one; I do not play fast and loose with any. The modest conversation of these village lasses and the care of my goats is sufficient to occupy me. Those mountains there represent the bounds of my desire, and should my wishes go beyond them, it is but to contemplate the beauty of the heavens, that pathway by which the soul travels to its first dwelling place."

Saying this and without waiting for any reply, she turned her back and entered the thickest part of a near-by wood, leaving all present lost in admiration of her wit as well as her beauty. A few—those who had felt the powerful dart of her glances and bore the wounds inflicted by her lovely eyes—were of a mind to follow her, taking no heed of the plainly worded warning they had just had from her lips; whereupon Don Quixote, seeing this and thinking to himself that here was an opportunity to display his chivalry by succoring a damsel in distress, laid his hand upon the hilt of his sword and cried out, loudly and distinctly, "Let no person of whatever state or condition he may be dare to follow the beauteous Marcela under pain of incurring my furious wrath. She has shown with clear and sufficient reasons that little or no blame for Grisóstomo's death is to be attached to her; she has likewise shown how far she is from acceding to the desires of any of her suitors, and it is accordingly only just that in place of being hounded and persecuted she should be honored and esteemed by all good people in this world as the only woman in it who lives with such modesty and good intentions."

Whether it was due to Don Quixote's threats or because Ambrosio now told them that they should finish doing the things which his good friend had desired should be done, no one stirred from the spot until the burial was over and Grisóstomo's papers had been burned. As the body was laid in the grave, many tears were shed by the bystanders. Then they placed a heavy stone upon it until the slab which Ambrosio was thinking of having made should be ready, with an epitaph that was to read:

> Here lies a shepherd by love betrayed,
> His body cold in death,
> Who with his last and faltering breath
> Spoke of a faithless maid.
> He died by the cruel, heartless hand
> Of a coy and lovely lass,
> Who by bringing men to so sorry a pass
> Love's tyranny doth expand.

They then scattered many flowers and boughs over the top of the grave, and, expressing their condolences to the dead man's friend, Ambrosio, they all took their leave, including Vivaldo and his companions. Don Quixote now said good-by to the travelers as well, although they urged him to come with them to Seville, assuring him that he would find in every street and at every corner of that city more adventures than are to be met with anywhere else. He thanked them for the invitation and the courtesy they had shown him in offering it, but added that for the present he had no desire to visit Seville, not until he should have rid these mountains of the robbers and bandits of which they were said to be full.

Seeing that his mind was made up, the travelers did not urge him further but, bidding him another farewell, left him and continued on their way; and the reader may be sure that in the course of their journey they did not fail to discuss the story of Marcela and Grisóstomo as well as Don Quixote's madness. As for the good knight himself, he was resolved to go seek the shepherdess and offer her any service that lay in his power; but things did not turn out the way he expected. . . .

[Fighting the Sheep]

CHAPTER 18

In which is set forth the conversation that Sancho Panza had with his master, Don Quixote, along with other adventures deserving of record.

* * * Don Quixote caught sight down the road of a large cloud of dust that was drawing nearer.

"This, O Sancho," he said, turning to his squire, "is the day when you shall see the boon that fate has in store for me; this, I repeat, is the day when, as well as on any other, shall be displayed the valor of my good right arm. On this day I shall perform deeds that will be written down in the book of fame for all centuries to come. Do you see that dust cloud rising there, Sancho? That is the dust stirred up by a vast army marching in this direction and composed of many nations."

"At that rate," said Sancho, "there must be two of them, for there is another one just like it on the other side."

Don Quixote turned to look and saw that this was so. He was overjoyed by the thought that these were indeed two armies about to meet and clash in the middle of the broad plain; for at every hour and every moment his imagination was filled with battles, enchantments, nonsensical adventures, tales of love, amorous challenges, and the like, such as he had read of in the books of chivalry, and every word he uttered, every thought that crossed his mind, every act he performed, had to do with such things as these. The dust clouds he had sighted were raised by two large droves of sheep coming along the road in opposite directions, which by reason of the dust were not visible until they were close at hand, but Don Quixote insisted so earnestly that they were armies that Sancho came to believe it.

"Sir," he said, "what are we to do?"

"What are we to do?" echoed his master. "Favor and aid the weak and needy. I would inform you, Sancho, that the one coming toward us is led and commanded by the great emperor Alifanfarón, lord of the great isle of Trapobana. This other one at my back is that of his enemy, the king of the Garamantas, Pentapolín of the Rolled-up Sleeve, for he always goes into battle with his right arm bare."

"But why are they such enemies?" Sancho asked.

"Because," said Don Quixote, "this Alifanfarón is a terrible pagan and in love with Pentapolín's daughter, who is a very beautiful and gracious lady and a Christian, for which reason her father does not wish to give her to the pagan king unless the latter first abjures the law of the false prophet, Mohammed, and adopts the faith that is Pentapolín's own."

"Then, by my beard," said Sancho, "if Pentapolín isn't right, and I am going to aid him all I can."

"In that," said Don Quixote, "you will only be doing your duty; for to engage in battles of this sort you need not have been dubbed a knight."

"I can understand that," said Sancho, "but where are we going to put this ass so that we will be certain of finding him after the fray is over? As for going into battle on such a mount, I do not think that has been done up to now."

"That is true enough," said Don Quixote. "What you had best do with him is to turn him loose and run the risk of losing him; for after we emerge the victors we shall have so many horses that even Rocinante will be in danger of being exchanged for another. But listen closely to what I am about to tell you, for I wish to give you an account of the principal knights that are accompanying these two armies; and in order that you may be the better able to see and take note of them, let us retire to that hillock over there which will afford us a very good view."

They then stationed themselves upon a slight elevation from which they would have been able to see very well the two droves of sheep that Don Quixote took to be armies if it had not been for the blinding clouds of dust. In spite of this, however, the worthy gentleman contrived to behold in his imagination what he did not see and what did not exist in reality.

Raising his voice, he went on to explain, "That knight in the gilded armor that you see there, bearing upon his shield a crowned lion crouched at the feet of a damsel, is the valiant Laurcalco, lord of the Silver Bridge; the other with the golden flowers on his armor, and on his shield three crowns argent on an azure field, is the dread Micocolembo, grand duke of Quirocia. And that one on Micocolembo's right hand, with the limbs of a giant, is the ever undaunted Brandabarbarán de Boliche, lord of the three Arabias. He goes armored in a serpent's skin and has for shield a door which, so report has it, is one of those from the temple that Samson pulled down, that time when he avenged himself on his enemies with his own death.

"But turn your eyes in this direction, and you will behold at the head of the other army the ever victorious, never vanquished Timonel de Carcajona, prince of New Biscay, who comes with quartered arms—azure, vert, argent, and or—and who has upon his shield a cat or on a field tawny, with the inscription *Miau*, which is the beginning of his lady's name; for she, so it is said, is the peerless Miulina, daughter of Alfeñquén, duke of Algarve. And that one over there, who weights down and presses the loins of that powerful charger, in a suit of snow-white armor with a white shield that bears no device whatever—he is a novice knight of the French nation, called Pierres Papin, lord of the baronies of Utrique. As for him you see digging his iron spurs into the flanks of that fleet-footed zebra courser and whose arms are vairs azure, he is the mighty duke of Nervia, Espartafilardo of the Wood, who has for device upon his shield an asparagus plant with a motto in Castilian that says 'Rastrea mi suerte.'"[8]

In this manner he went on naming any number of imaginary knights on either side, describing on the spur of the moment their arms, colors, devices, and mottoes; for he was completely carried away by his imagination and by this unheard-of madness that had laid hold of him.

Without pausing, he went on, "This squadron in front of us is composed of men of various nations. There are those who drink the sweet waters of the famous Xanthus; woodsmen who tread the Massilian plain; those that sift the fine gold nuggets of Arabia Felix; those that are so fortunate as to dwell on the banks of the clear-running Thermodon, famed for their coolness; those who in many and diverse ways drain the golden Pactolus; Numidians, whose word is never to be trusted; Persians, with their famous bows and arrows; Medes and Parthians, who fight as they flee; Scythians, as cruel as they are fair of skin; Ethiopians, with their pierced lips; and an infinite number of other nationalities whose visages I see and recognize although I cannot recall their names.

"In this other squadron come those that drink from the crystal currents of the olive-bearing Betis; those that smooth and polish their faces with the liquid of the ever rich and gilded Tagus; those that enjoy the beneficial waters of the divine Genil; those that roam the Tartessian plains with their abundant pasturage; those that disport themselves in the Elysian meadows of Jerez; the men of La Mancha, rich and crowned with golden ears of corn; others clad in iron garments, ancient relics of the Gothic race; those that bathe in the Pisuerga, noted for the mildness of its current; those that feed their herds in the wide-spreading pasture lands along the banks of the winding Guadiana, celebrated for its underground course;[9] those that shiver from the cold of the wooded Pyrenees or dwell amid the white peaks of the lofty Apennines—in short, all those whom Europe holds within its girth."

So help me God! How many provinces, how many nations did he not mention by name, giving to each one with marvelous readiness its proper attributes; for he was wholly absorbed and filled to the brim with what he had read in those lying books of his! Sancho Panza hung on his words, saying nothing, merely turning his head from time to time to have a look at those knights and giants that his master was pointing out to him; but he was unable to discover any of them.

8. Probably a pun on *rastrear*. The meaning of the motto may be either "On Fortune's track" or "My Fortune creeps."   9. The Guadiana does run underground part of the way through La Mancha.

"Sir," he said, "may I go to the devil if I see a single man, giant, or knight of all those that your Grace is talking about. Who knows? Maybe it is another spell, like last night."[1]

"How can you say that?" replied Don Quixote. "Can you not hear the neighing of the horses, the sound of trumpets, the roll of drums?"

"I hear nothing," said Sancho, "except the bleating of sheep."

And this, of course, was the truth; for the flocks were drawing near.

"The trouble is, Sancho," said Don Quixote, "you are so afraid that you cannot see or hear properly; for one of the effects of fear is to disturb the senses and cause things to appear other than what they are. If you are so craven as all that, go off to one side and leave me alone, and I without your help will assure the victory to that side to which I lend my aid."

Saying this, he put spurs to Rocinante and, with his lance at rest, darted down the hillside like a flash of lightning.

As he did so, Sancho called after him, "Come back, your Grace, Señor Don Quixote; I vow to God those are sheep that you are charging. Come back! O wretched father that bore me! What madness is this? Look you, there are no giants, nor knights, nor cats, nor shields either quartered or whole, nor vairs azure or bedeviled. What is this you are doing, O sinner that I am in God's sight?"

But all this did not cause Don Quixote to turn back. Instead, he rode on, crying out at the top of his voice, "Ho, knights, those of you who follow and fight under the banners of the valiant Pentapolín of the Rolled-up Sleeve; follow me, all of you, and you shall see how easily I give you revenge on your enemy, Alifanfarón of Trapobana."

With these words he charged into the middle of the flock of sheep and began spearing at them with as much courage and boldness as if they had been his mortal enemies. The shepherds and herdsmen who were with the animals called to him to stop; but seeing it was no use, they unloosed their slings and saluted his ears with stones as big as your fist.

Don Quixote paid no attention to the missiles and, dashing about here and there, kept crying, "Where are you, haughty Alifanfarón? Come out to me; for here is a solitary knight who desires in single combat to test your strength and deprive you of your life, as a punishment for that which you have done to the valorous Pentapolín Garamanta."

At that instant a pebble from the brook struck him in the side and buried a couple of ribs in his body. Believing himself dead or badly wounded, and remembering his potion, he took out his vial, placed it to his mouth, and began to swallow the balm; but before he had had what he thought was enough, there came another almond, which struck him in the hand, crushing the tin vial and carrying away with it a couple of grinders from his mouth, as well as badly mashing two of his fingers. As a result of these blows the poor knight tumbled from his horse. Believing that they had killed him, the shepherds hastily collected their flock and, picking up the dead beasts, of which there were more than seven, they went off down the road without more ado.

Sancho all this time was standing on the slope observing the insane things

---

1. The inn where they had spent the previous night had been pronounced by Don Quixote to be an enchanted castle.

that his master was doing; and as he plucked savagely at his beard he cursed the hour and minute when luck had brought them together. But when he saw him lying there on the ground and perceived that the shepherds were gone, he went down the hill and came up to him, finding him in very bad shape though not unconscious.

"Didn't I tell you, Señor Don Quixote," he said, "that you should come back, that those were not armies you were charging but flocks of sheep?"

"This," said Don Quixote, "is the work of that thieving magician, my enemy, who thus counterfeits things and causes them to disappear. You must know, Sancho, that it is very easy for them to make us assume any appearance that they choose; and so it is that malign one who persecutes me, envious of the glory he saw me about to achieve in this battle, changed the squadrons of the foe into flocks of sheep. If you do not believe me, I beseech you on my life to do one thing for me, that you may be undeceived and discover for yourself that what I say is true. Mount your ass and follow them quietly, and when you have gone a short way from here, you will see them become their former selves once more; they will no longer be sheep but men exactly as I described them to you in the first place. But do not go now, for I need your kind assistance; come over here and have a look and tell me how many grinders are missing, for it feels as if I did not have a single one left."

["To Right Wrongs and Come to the Aid of the Wretched"]

CHAPTER 22

Of how Don Quixote freed many unfortunate ones who, much against their will, were being taken where they did not wish to go.

Cid Hamete Benengeli, the Arabic and Manchegan;[2] author, in the course of this most grave, high-sounding, minute, delightful, and imaginative history, informs us that, following the remarks that were exchanged between Don Quixote de la Mancha and Sancho Panza, his squire, . . . the knight looked up and saw coming toward them down the road which they were following a dozen or so men on foot, strung together by their necks like beads on an iron chain and all of them wearing handcuffs. They were accompanied by two men on horseback and two on foot, the former carrying wheel-lock muskets while the other two were armed with swords and javelins.

"That," said Sancho as soon as he saw them, "is a chain of galley slaves, people on their way to the galleys where by order of the king they are forced to labor."

"What do you mean by 'forced'?" asked Don Quixote. "Is it possible that the king uses force on anyone?"

"I did not say that," replied Sancho. "What I did say was that these are folks who have been condemned for their crimes to forced labor in the galleys for his Majesty the King."

"The short of it is," said the knight, "whichever way you put it, these people are being taken there by force and not of their own free will."

"That is the way it is," said Sancho.

"Well, in that case," said his master, "now is the time for me to fulfill the

2. Of La Mancha.

duties of my calling, which is to right wrongs and come to the aid of the wretched."

"But take note, your Grace," said Sancho, "that justice, that is to say, the king himself, is not using any force upon, or doing any wrong to, people like these, but is merely punishing them for the crimes they have committed."

The chain of galley slaves had come up to them by this time, whereupon Don Quixote very courteously requested the guards to inform him of the reason or reasons why they were conducting these people in such a manner as this. One of the men on horseback then replied that the men were prisoners who had been condemned by his Majesty to serve in the galleys, whither they were bound, and that was all there was to be said about it and all that he, Don Quixote, need know.

"Nevertheless," said the latter, "I should like to inquire of each one of them, individually, the cause of his misfortune." And he went on speaking so very politely in an effort to persuade them to tell him what he wanted to know that the other mounted guard finally said, "Although we have here the record and certificate of sentence of each one of these wretches, we have not the time to get them out and read them to you; and so your Grace may come over and ask the prisoners themselves, and they will tell you if they choose, and you may be sure that they will, for these fellows take a delight in their knavish exploits and in boasting of them afterward."

With this permission, even though he would have done so if it had not been granted him, Don Quixote went up to the chain of prisoners and asked the first whom he encountered what sins had brought him to so sorry a plight. The man replied that it was for being a lover that he found himself in that line.

"For that and nothing more?" said Don Quixote. "And do they, then, send lovers to the galleys? If so, I should have been rowing there long ago."

"But it was not the kind of love that your Grace has in mind," the prisoner went on. "I loved a wash basket full of white linen so well and hugged it so tightly that, if they had not taken it away from me by force, I would never of my own choice have let go of it to this very minute. I was caught in the act, there was no need to torture me, the case was soon disposed of, and they supplied me with a hundred lashes across the shoulders and, in addition, a three-year stretch in the *gurapas*, and that's all there is to tell."

"What are *gurapas*?" asked Don Quixote.

"*Gurapas* are the galleys," replied the prisoner. He was a lad of around twenty-four and stated that he was a native of Piedrahita.

The knight then put the same question to a second man, who appeared to be very downcast and melancholy and did not have a word to say. The first man answered for him.

"This one, sir," he said, "is going as a canary—I mean, as a musician and singer."

"How is that?" Don Quixote wanted to know. "Do musicians and singers go to the galleys too?"

"Yes, sir; and there is nothing worse than singing when you're in trouble."

"On the contrary," said Don Quixote, "I have heard it said that he who sings frightens away his sorrows."

"It is just the opposite," said the prisoner; "for he who sings once weeps all his life long."

"I do not understand," said the knight.

One of the guards then explained. "Sir Knight, with this *non sancta*[3] tribe, to sing when you're in trouble means to confess under torture. This singer was put to the torture and confessed his crime, which was that of being a *cuatrero,* or cattle thief, and as a result of his confession he was condemned to six years in the galleys in addition to two hundred lashes which he took on his shoulders; and so it is he is always downcast and moody, for the other thieves, those back where he came from and the ones here, mistreat, snub, ridicule, and despise him for having confessed and for not having had the courage to deny his guilt. They are in the habit of saying that the word *no* has the same number of letters as the word *sí,* and that a culprit is in luck when his life or death depends on his own tongue and not that of witnesses or upon evidence; and, in my opinion, they are not very far wrong."

"And I," said Don Quixote, "feel the same way about it." He then went on to a third prisoner and repeated his question.

The fellow answered at once, quite unconcernedly. "I'm going to my ladies, the *gurapas,* for five years, for the lack of five ducats."

"I would gladly give twenty," said Don Quixote, "to get you out of this."

"That," said the prisoner, "reminds me of the man in the middle of the ocean who has money and is dying of hunger because there is no place to buy what he needs. I say this for the reason that if I had had, at the right time, those twenty ducats your Grace is now offering me, I'd have greased the notary's quill and freshened up the attorney's wit with them, and I'd now be living in the middle of Zocodover Square in Toledo instead of being here on this highway coupled like a greyhound. But God is great; patience, and that's enough of it."

Don Quixote went on to a fourth prisoner, a venerable-looking old fellow with a white beard that fell over his bosom. When asked how he came to be there, this one began weeping and made no reply, but a fifth comrade spoke up in his behalf.

"This worthy man," he said, "is on his way to the galleys after having made the usual rounds clad in a robe of state and on horseback."[4]

"That means, I take it," said Sancho, "that he has been put to shame in public."

"That is it," said the prisoner, "and the offense for which he is being punished is that of having been an ear broker, or, better, a body broker. By that I mean to say, in short, that the gentleman is a pimp, and besides, he has his points as a sorcerer."

"If that point had not been thrown in," said Don Quixote, "he would not deserve, for merely being a pimp, to have to row in the galleys, but rather should be the general and give orders there. For the office of pimp is not an indifferent one; it is a function to be performed by persons of discretion and is most necessary in a well-ordered state; it is a profession that should be followed only by the wellborn, and there should, moreover, be a supervisor or examiner as in the case of other offices, and the number of practitioners should be fixed by law as is done with brokers on the exchange. In that way many evils would be averted that arise when this office is filled and this

---

3. Unholy (Latin).   4. After having been flogged in public, with all the ceremony that accompanied that punishment.

calling practiced by stupid folk and those with little sense, such as silly women and pages or mountebanks with few years and less experience to their credit, who, on the most pressing occasions, when it is necessary to use one's wits, let the crumbs freeze between their hand and their mouth and do not know which is their right hand and which is the left.

"I would go on and give reasons why it is fitting to choose carefully those who are to fulfill so necessary a state function, but this is not the place for it. One of these days I will speak of the matter to someone who is able to do something about it. I will say here only that the pain I felt at seeing those white hairs and this venerable countenance in such a plight, and all for his having been a pimp, has been offset for me by the additional information you have given me, to the effect that he is a sorcerer as well; for I am convinced that there are no sorcerers in the world who can move and compel the will, as some simple-minded persons think, but that our will is free and no herb or charm can force it.[5] All that certain foolish women and cunning tricksters do is to compound a few mixtures and poisons with which they deprive men of their senses while pretending that they have the power to make them loved, although, as I have just said, one cannot affect another's will in that manner."

"That is so," said the worthy old man; "but the truth is, sir, I am not guilty on the sorcery charge. As for being a pimp, that is something I cannot deny. I never thought there was any harm in it, however, my only desire being that everyone should enjoy himself and live in peace and quiet, without any quarrels or troubles. But these good intentions on my part cannot prevent me from going where I do not want to go, to a place from which I do not expect to return; for my years are heavy upon me and an affection of the urine that I have will not give me a moment's rest."

With this, he began weeping once more, and Sancho was so touched by it that he took a four-real piece from his bosom and gave it to him as an act of charity.

Don Quixote then went on and asked another what his offense was. The fellow answered him, not with less, but with much more, briskness than the preceding one had shown.

"I am here," he said, "for the reason that I carried a joke too far with a couple of cousins-german of mine and a couple of others who were not mine, and I ended by jesting with all of them to such an extent that the devil himself would never be able to straighten out the relationship. They proved everything on me, there was no one to show me favor, I had no money, I came near swinging for it, they sentenced me to the galleys for six years, and I accepted the sentence as the punishment that was due me. I am young yet, and if I live long enough, everything will come out all right. If, Sir Knight, your Grace has anything with which to aid these poor creatures that you see before you, God will reward you in Heaven, and we here on earth will make it a point to ask God in our prayers to grant you long life and good health, as long and as good as your amiable presence deserves."

This man was dressed as a student, and one of the guards told Don Quixote that he was a great talker and a very fine Latinist.

---

5. Here Don Quixote despises charms and love potions, although often elsewhere, in his own vision of himself as a knight-errant, he accepts enchantments and spells as part of his world of fantasy.

Back of these came a man around thirty years of age and of very good appearance, except that when he looked at you his eyes were seen to be a little crossed. He was shackled in a different manner from the others, for he dragged behind a chain so huge that it was wrapped all around his body, with two rings at the throat, one of which was attached to the chain while the other was fastened to what is known as a keep-friend or friend's foot, from which two irons hung down to his waist, ending in handcuffs secured by a heavy padlock in such a manner that he could neither raise his hands to his mouth nor lower his head to reach his hands.

When Don Quixote asked why this man was so much more heavily chained than the others, the guard replied that it was because he had more crimes against him than all the others put together, and he was so bold and cunning that, even though they had him chained like this, they were by no means sure of him but feared that he might escape from them.

"What crimes could he have committed," asked the knight, "if he has merited a punishment no greater than that of being sent to the galleys?"

"He is being sent there for ten years," replied the guard, "and that is equivalent to civil death. I need tell you no more than that this good man is the famous Ginés de Pasamonte, otherwise known as Ginesillo de Parapilla."

"Señor Commissary," spoke up the prisoner at this point, "go easy there and let us not be so free with names and surnames. My just name is Ginés and not Ginesillo; and Pasamonte, not Parapilla as you make it out to be, is my family name. Let each one mind his own affairs and he will have his hands full."

"Speak a little more respectfully, you big thief, you," said the commissary, "unless you want me to make you be quiet in a way you won't like."

"Man goes as God pleases, that is plain to be seen," replied the galley slave, "but someday someone will know whether my name is Ginesillo de Parapilla or not."

"But, you liar, isn't that what they call you?"

"Yes," said Ginés, "they do call me that; but I'll put a stop to it, or else I'll skin their you-know-what. And you, sir, if you have anything to give us, give it and may God go with you, for I am tired of all this prying into other people's lives. If you want to know anything about my life, know that I am Ginés de Pasamonte whose life story has been written down by these fingers that you see here."

"He speaks the truth," said the commissary, "for he has himself written his story, as big as you please, and has left the book in the prison, having pawned it for two hundred reales."

"And I mean to redeem it," said Ginés, "even if it costs me two hundred ducats."

"Is it as good as that?" inquired Don Quixote.

"It is so good," replied Ginés, "that it will cast into the shade *Lazarillo de Tormes*[6] and all others of that sort that have been or will be written. What I would tell you is that it deals with facts, and facts so interesting and amusing that no lies could equal them."

"And what is the title of the book?" asked Don Quixote.

"The Life of Ginés de Pasamonte."

___

6. A picaresque or rogue novel, published anonymously about the middle of the 15th century.

"Is it finished?"

"How could it be finished," said Ginés, "when my life is not finished as yet? What I have written thus far is an account of what happened to me from the time I was born up to the last time that they sent me to the galleys."

"Then you have been there before?"

"In the service of God and the king I was there four years, and I know what the biscuit and the cowhide are like. I don't mind going very much, for there I will have a chance to finish my book. I still have many things to say, and in the Spanish galleys I shall have all the leisure that I need, though I don't need much, since I know by heart what it is I want to write."

"You seem to be a clever fellow," said Don Quixote.

"And an unfortunate one," said Ginés; "for misfortunes always pursue men of genius."

"They pursue rogues," said the commissary.

"I have told you to go easy, Señor Commissary," said Pasamonte, "for their Lordships did not give you that staff in order that you might mistreat us poor devils with it, but they intended that you should guide and conduct us in accordance with his Majesty's command. Otherwise, by the life of— But enough. It may be that someday the stains made in the inn will come out in the wash. Meanwhile, let everyone hold his tongue, behave well, and speak better, and let us be on our way. We've had enough of this foolishness."

At this point the commissary raised his staff as if to let Pasamonte have it in answer to his threats, but Don Quixote placed himself between them and begged the officer not to abuse the man; for it was not to be wondered at if one who had his hands so bound should be a trifle free with his tongue. With this, he turned and addressed them all.

"From all that you have told me, my dearest brothers," he said, "one thing stands out clearly for me, and that is the fact that, even though it is a punishment for offenses which you have committed, the penalty you are about to pay is not greatly to your liking and you are going to the galleys very much against your own will and desire. It may be that the lack of spirit which one of you displayed under torture, the lack of money on the part of another, the lack of influential friends, or, finally, warped judgment on the part of the magistrate, was the thing that led to your downfall; and, as a result, justice was not done you. All of which presents itself to my mind in such a fashion that I am at this moment engaged in trying to persuade and even force myself to show you what the purpose was for which Heaven sent me into this world, why it was it led me to adopt the calling of knighthood which I profess and take the knightly vow to favor the needy and aid those who are oppressed by the powerful.

"However, knowing as I do that it is not the part of prudence to do by foul means what can be accomplished by fair ones, I propose to ask these gentlemen, your guards, and the commissary to be so good as to unshackle you and permit you to go in peace. There will be no dearth of others to serve his Majesty under more propitious circumstances; and it does not appear to me to be just to make slaves of those whom God created as free men. What is more, gentlemen of the guard, these poor fellows have committed no offense against you. Up there, each of us will have to answer for his own sins; for God in Heaven will not fail to punish the evil and reward the good; and it is not good for self-respecting men to be executioners of their fellow-men in something that does not concern them. And so, I ask this of you, gently and quietly, in order that, if you comply with my request, I shall have reason to thank you; and if you do not do so of your own accord, then this lance and this sword and the valor of my arm shall compel you to do it by force."

"A fine lot of foolishness!" exclaimed the commissary. "So he comes out at last with this nonsense! He would have us let the prisoners of the king go free, as if we had any authority to do so or he any right to command it! Be on your way, sir, at once; straighten that basin that you have on your head, and do not go looking for three feet on a cat."[7]

"You," replied Don Quixote, "are the cat and the rat and the rascal!" And, saying this, he charged the commissary so quickly that the latter had no chance to defend himself but fell to the ground badly wounded by the lance blow. The other guards were astounded by this unexpected occurrence; but, recovering their self-possession, those on horseback drew their swords, those on foot leveled their javelins, and all bore down on Don Quixote, who stood waiting for them very calmly. Things undoubtedly would have gone badly for him if the galley slaves, seeing an opportunity to gain their freedom, had not succeeded in breaking the chain that linked them together. Such was the confusion that the guards, now running to fall upon the prisoners and now attacking Don Quixote, who in turn was attacking them, accomplished nothing that was of any use.

Sancho for his part aided Ginés de Pasamonte to free himself, and that individual was the first to drop his chains and leap out onto the field, where, attacking the fallen commissary, he took away that officer's sword and musket; and as he stood there, aiming first at one and then at another, though without firing, the plain was soon cleared of guards, for they had taken to their heels, fleeing at once Pasamonte's weapon and the stones which the galley slaves, freed now, were hurling at them. Sancho, meanwhile, was very much disturbed over this unfortunate event, as he felt sure that the fugitives would report the matter to the Holy Brotherhood, which, to the ringing of the alarm bell, would come out to search for the guilty parties. He said as much to his master, telling him that they should leave at once and go into hiding in the near-by mountains.

"That is all very well," said Don Quixote, "but I know what had best be done now." He then summoned all the prisoners, who, running riot, had by this time despoiled the commissary of everything that he had, down to his skin, and as they gathered around to hear what he had to say, he addressed them as follows:

"It is fitting that those who are wellborn should give thanks for the benefits they have received, and one of the sins with which God is most offended is that of ingratitude. I say this, gentlemen, for the reason that you have seen and had manifest proof of what you owe to me; and now that you are free of the yoke which I have removed from about your necks, it is my will and desire that you should set out and proceed to the city of El Toboso and there present yourselves before the lady Dulcinea del Toboso and say to her that her champion, the Knight of the Mournful Countenance, has sent you; and then you will relate to her, point by point, the whole of this famous adventure which has won you your longed-for freedom. Having done that, you may go where you like, and may good luck go with you."

To this Ginés de Pasamonte replied in behalf of all of them, "It is abso-

---

7. Looking for the impossible ("five feet" is the more usual form of the proverb).

lutely impossible, your Grace, our liberator, for us to do what you have commanded. We cannot go down the highway all together but must separate and go singly, each in his own direction, endeavoring to hide ourselves in the bowels of the earth in order not to be found by the Holy Brotherhood, which undoubtedly will come out to search for us. What your Grace can do, and it is right that you should do so, is to change this service and toll that you require of us in connection with the lady Dulcinea del Toboso into a certain number of Credos and Hail Marys which we will say for your Grace's intention, as this is something that can be accomplished by day or night, fleeing or resting, in peace or in war. To imagine, on the other hand, that we are going to return to the fleshpots of Egypt, by which I mean, take up our chains again by setting out along the highway for El Toboso, is to believe that it is night now instead of ten o'clock in the morning and is to ask of us something that is the same as asking pears of the elm tree."

"Then by all that's holy!" exclaimed Don Quixote, whose wrath was now aroused, "you, Don Son of a Whore, Don Ginesillo de Parapilla, or whatever your name is, you shall go alone, your tail between your legs and the whole chain on your back."

Pasamonte, who was by no means a long-suffering individual, was by this time convinced that Don Quixote was not quite right in the head, seeing that he had been guilty of such a folly as that of desiring to free them; and so, when he heard himself insulted in this manner, he merely gave the wink to his companions and, going off to one side, began raining so many stones upon the knight that the latter was wholly unable to protect himself with his buckler, while poor Rocinante paid no more attention to the spur than if he had been made of brass. As for Sancho, he took refuge behind his donkey as a protection against the cloud and shower of rocks that was falling on both of them, but Don Quixote was not able to shield himself so well, and there is no telling how many struck his body, with such force as to unhorse and bring him to the ground.

No sooner had he fallen than the student was upon him. Seizing the basin from the knight's head, he struck him three or four blows with it across the shoulders and banged it against the ground an equal number of times until it was fairly shattered to bits. They then stripped Don Quixote of the doublet which he wore over his armor, and would have taken his hose as well, if his greaves had not prevented them from doing so, and made off with Sancho's greatcoat, leaving him naked; after which, dividing the rest of the battle spoils amongst themselves, each of them went his own way, being a good deal more concerned with eluding the dreaded Holy Brotherhood than they were with burdening themselves with a chain or going to present themselves before the lady Dulcinea del Toboso.

They were left alone now—the ass and Rocinante, Sancho and Don Quixote: the ass, crestfallen and pensive, wagging its ears now and then, being under the impression that the hurricane of stones that had raged about them was not yet over; Rocinante, stretched alongside his master, for the hack also had been felled by a stone; Sancho, naked and fearful of the Holy Brotherhood; and Don Quixote, making wry faces at seeing himself so mishandled by those to whom he had done so much good.

["Set Free at Once That Lovely Lady"]

CHAPTER 52

Of the quarrel that Don Quixote had with the goatherd, together with the rare adventure of the penitents, which the knight by the sweat of his brow brought to a happy conclusion.[8]

All those who had listened to it were greatly pleased with the goatherd's story, especially the canon,[9] who was more than usually interested in noting the manner in which it had been told. Far from being a mere rustic herdsman, the narrator seemed rather a cultured city dweller; and the canon accordingly remarked that the curate had been quite right in saying that the mountain groves bred men of learning. They all now offered their services to Eugenio, and Don Quixote was the most generous of any in this regard.

"Most assuredly, brother goatherd," he said, "if it were possible for me to undertake any adventure just now, I would set out at once to aid you and would take Leandra out of that convent, where she is undoubtedly being held against her will, in spite of the abbess and all the others who might try to prevent me, after which I would place her in your hands to do with as you liked, with due respect, however, for the laws of chivalry, which command that no violence be offered to any damsel. But I trust in God, Our Lord, that the power of one malicious enchanter is not so great that another magician may not prove still more powerful, and then I promise you my favor and my aid, as my calling obliges me to do, since it is none other than that of succoring the weak and those who are in distress."

The goatherd stared at him, observing in some astonishment the knight's unprepossessing appearance.

"Sir," he said, turning to the barber who sat beside him, "who is this man who looks so strange and talks in this way?"

"Who should it be," the barber replied, "if not the famous Don Quixote de la Mancha, righter of wrongs, avenger of injustices, protector of damsels, terror of giants, and champion of battles?"

"That," said the goatherd, "sounds to me like the sort of thing you read of in books of chivalry, where they do all those things that your Grace has mentioned in connection with this man. But if you ask me, either your Grace is joking or this worthy gentleman must have a number of rooms to let inside his head."

"You are the greatest villain that ever was!" cried Don Quixote when he heard this. "It is you who are the empty one; I am fuller than the bitch that bore you ever was." Saying this, he snatched up a loaf of bread that was lying beside him and hurled it straight in the goatherd's face with such force as to flatten the man's nose. Upon finding himself thus mistreated in earnest, Eugenio, who did not understand this kind of joke, forgot all about the carpet, the tablecloth, and the other diners and leaped upon Don Quixote.

8. Last chapter of Part I. Through various devices, including the use of Don Quixote's own belief in enchantments and spells, the curate and the barber have persuaded the knight to let himself be taken home in an ox cart.   9. A canon from Toledo who has joined Don Quixote and his guardians on the way; conversing about chivalry with the knight, he has had cause to be "astonished at Don Quixote's well-reasoned nonsense." Eugenio, a very literate goatherd met on the way, has just told them the story of his unhappy love for Leandra. The girl, instead of choosing one of her local suitors, had eloped with a flashy and crooked soldier; robbed and abandoned by him, she had been put by her father in a convent.

Seizing him by the throat with both hands, he would no doubt have strangled him if Sancho Panza, who now came running up, had not grasped him by the shoulders and flung him backward over the table, smashing plates and cups and spilling and scattering all the food and drink that was there. Thus freed of his assailant, Don Quixote then threw himself upon the shepherd, who, with bleeding face and very much battered by Sancho's feet, was creeping about on his hands and knees in search of a table knife with which to exact a sanguinary vengeance, a purpose which the canon and the curate prevented him from carrying out. The barber, however, so contrived it that the goatherd came down on top of his opponent, upon whom he now showered so many blows that the poor knight's countenance was soon as bloody as his own.

As all this went on, the canon and the curate were laughing fit to burst, the troopers[1] were dancing with glee, and they all hissed on the pair as men do at a dog fight. Sancho Panza alone was in despair, being unable to free himself of one of the canon's servants who held him back from going to his master's aid. And then, just as they were all enjoying themselves hugely, with the exception of the two who were mauling each other, the note of a trumpet fell upon their ears, a sound so mournful that it caused them all to turn their heads in the direction from which it came. The one who was most excited by it was Don Quixote; who, very much against his will and more than a little bruised, was lying pinned beneath the goatherd.

"Brother Demon," he now said to the shepherd, "for you could not possibly be anything but a demon, seeing that you have shown a strength and valor greater than mine, I request you to call a truce for no more than an hour; for the doleful sound of that trumpet that we hear seems to me to be some new adventure that is calling me."

Tired of mauling and being mauled, the goatherd let him up at once. As he rose to his feet and turned his head in the direction of the sound, Don Quixote then saw, coming down the slope of a hill, a large number of persons clad in white after the fashion of penitents; for, as it happened, the clouds that year had denied their moisture to the earth, and in all the villages of that district processions for prayer and penance were being organized with the purpose of beseeching God to have mercy and send rain. With this object in view, the good folk from a near-by town were making a pilgrimage to a devout hermit who dwelt on these slopes. Upon beholding the strange costumes that the penitents wore, without pausing to think how many times he had seen them before, Don Quixote imagined that this must be some adventure or other, and that it was for him alone as a knight-errant to undertake it. He was strengthened in this belief by the sight of a covered image that they bore, as it seemed to him this must be some highborn lady whom these scoundrelly and discourteous brigands were forcibly carrying off; and no sooner did this idea occur to him than he made for Rocinante, who was grazing not far away.

Taking the bridle and his buckler from off the saddletree, he had the bridle adjusted in no time, and then, asking Sancho for his sword, he climbed into the saddle, braced his shield upon his arm, and cried out to those present,

---

1. Law officers from the Holy Brotherhood. They had wanted to arrest Don Quixote for his attempt to liberate the galley slaves, but had been persuaded not to do so because of the knight's insanity.

"And now, valorous company, you shall see how important it is to have in the world those who follow the profession of knight-errantry. You have but to watch how I shall set at liberty that worthy lady who there goes captive, and then you may tell me whether or not such knights are to be esteemed."

As he said this, he dug his legs into Rocinante's flanks, since he had no spurs, and at a fast trot (for nowhere in this veracious history are we ever told that the hack ran full speed) he bore down on the penitents in spite of all that the canon, the curate, and the barber could do to restrain him—their efforts were as vain as were the pleadings of his squire.

"Where are you bound for, Señor Don Quixote?" Sancho called after him. "What evil spirits in your bosom spur you on to go against our Catholic faith? Plague take me, can't you see that's a procession of penitents and that lady they're carrying on the litter is the most blessed image of the Immaculate Virgin? Look well what you're doing, my master, for this time it may be said that you really do not know."

His exertions were in vain, however, for his master was so bent upon having it out with the sheeted figures and freeing the lady clad in mourning that he did not hear a word, nor would he have turned back if he had, though the king himself might have commanded it. Having reached the procession, he reined in Rocinante, who by this time was wanting a little rest, and in a hoarse, excited voice he shouted, "You who go there with your faces covered, out of shame, it may be, listen well to what I have to say to you."

The first to come to a halt were those who carried the image; and then one of the four clerics who were intoning the litanies, upon beholding Don Quixote's weird figure, his bony nag, and other amusing appurtenances, spoke up in reply.

"Brother, if you have something to say to us, say it quickly, for these brethren are engaged in macerating their flesh, and we cannot stop to hear any thing, nor is it fitting that we should, unless it is capable of being said in a couple of words."

"I will say it to you in one word," Don Quixote answered, "and that word is the following: 'Set free at once that lovely lady whose tears and mournful countenance show plainly that you are carrying her away against her will and that you have done her some shameful wrong. I will not consent to your going one step farther until you shall have given her the freedom that should be hers.'"

Hearing these words, they all thought that Don Quixote must be some madman or other and began laughing heartily; but their laughter proved to be gunpowder to his wrath, and without saying another word he drew his sword and fell upon the litter. One of those who bore the image, leaving his share of the burden to his companions, then sallied forth to meet the knight, flourishing a forked stick that he used to support the Virgin while he was resting; and upon this stick he now received a mighty slash that Don Quixote dealt him, one that shattered it in two, but with the piece about a third long that remained in his hand he came down on the shoulder of his opponent's sword arm, left unprotected by the buckler, with so much force that the poor fellow sank to the ground sorely battered and bruised.

Sancho Panza, who was puffing along close behind his master, upon seeing him fall cried out to the attacker not to deal another blow, as this was an unfortunate knight who was under a magic spell but who had never in all the days of his life done any harm to anyone. But the thing that stopped the rustic was not Sancho's words; it was, rather, the sight of Don Quixote lying there without moving hand or foot. And so, thinking that he had killed him, he hastily girded up his tunic and took to his heels across the countryside like a deer.

By this time all of Don Quixote's companions had come running up to where he lay; and the penitents, when they observed this, and especially when they caught sight of the officers of the Brotherhood with their crossbows, at once rallied around the image, where they raised their hoods and grasped their whips as the priests raised their tapers aloft in expectations of an assault; for they were resolved to defend themselves and even, if possible, to take the offensive against their assailants, but, as luck would have it, things turned out better than they had hoped. Sancho, meanwhile, believing Don Quixote to be dead, had flung himself across his master's body and was weeping and wailing in the most lugubrious and, at the same time, the most laughable fashion that could be imagined; and the curate had discovered among those who marched in the procession another curate whom he knew, their recognition of each other serving to allay the fears of all parties concerned. The first curate then gave the second a very brief account of who Don Quixote was, whereupon all the penitents came up to see if the poor knight was dead. And as they did do, they heard Sancho Panza speaking with tears in his eyes.

"O flower of chivalry,[2] he was saying, "the course of whose well-spent years has been brought to an end by a single blow of a club! O honor of your line, honor and glory of all La Mancha and of all the world, which, with you absent from it, will be full of evil-doers who will not fear being punished for their deeds! O master more generous than all the Alexanders, who after only eight months of service presented me with the best island that the sea washes and surrounds! Humble with the proud, haughty with the humble, brave in facing dangers, long-suffering under outrages, in love without reason, imitator of the good, scourge of the wicked, enemy of the mean—in a word, a knight-errant, which is all there is to say."

At the sound of Sancho's cries and moans, Don Quixote revived, and the first thing he said was, "He who lives apart from thee, O fairest Dulcinea, is subject to greater woes than those I now endure. Friend Sancho, help me onto that enchanted cart, as I am in no condition to sit in Rocinante's saddle with this shoulder of mine knocked to pieces the way it is."

"That I will gladly do, my master," replied Sancho, "and we will go back to my village in the company of these gentlemen who are concerned for your welfare, and there we will arrange for another sally and one, let us hope, that will bring us more profit and fame than this one has."

"Well spoken, Sancho," said Don Quixote, "for it will be an act of great prudence to wait until the present evil influence of the stars has passed."

The canon, the curate, and the barber all assured him that he would be wise in doing this; and so, much amused by Sancho Panza's simplicity, they placed Don Quixote upon the cart as before, while the procession of penitents re-formed and continued on its way. The goatherd took leave of all of them, and the curate paid the troopers what was coming to them, since they

2. Note how Sancho has absorbed some of his master's speech mannerisms.

did not wish to go any farther. The canon requested the priest to inform him of the outcome of Don Quixote's madness, as to whether it yielded to treatment or not; and with this he begged permission to resume his journey. In short, the party broke up and separated, leaving only the curate and the barber, Don Quixote and Panza, and the good Rocinante, who looked upon everything that he had seen with the same resignation as his master. Yoking his oxen, the carter made the knight comfortable upon a bale of hay, and then at his customary slow pace proceeded to follow the road that the curate directed him to take. At the end of the six days they reached Don Quixote's village, making their entrance at noon of a Sunday, when the square was filled with a crowd of people through which the cart had to pass.

They all came running to see who it was, and when they recognized their townsman, they were vastly astonished. One lad sped to bring the news to the knight's housekeeper and his niece, telling them that their master had returned lean and jaundiced and lying stretched out upon a bale of hay on an ox-cart. It was pitiful to hear the good ladies' screams, to behold the way in which they beat their breasts, and to listen to the curses which they once more heaped upon those damnable books of chivalry, and this demonstration increased as they saw Don Quixote coming through the doorway.

At news of the knight's return, Sancho Panza's wife had hurried to the scene, for she had some while since learned that her husband had accompanied him as his squire; and now, as soon as she laid eyes upon her man, the first question she asked was if all was well with the ass, to which Sancho replied that the beast was better off than his master.

"Thank God," she exclaimed, "for all his blessings! But tell me now, my dear, what have you brought me from all your squirings? A new cloak to wear? Or shoes for the young ones?"

"I've brought you nothing of the sort, good wife," said Sancho, "but other things of greater value and importance."

"I'm glad to hear that," she replied. "Show me those things of greater value and importance, my dear. I'd like a sight of them just to cheer this heart of mine which has been so sad and unhappy all the centuries that you've been gone."

"I will show them to you at home, wife," said Sancho. "For the present be satisfied that if, God willing, we set out on another journey in search of adventures, you will see me in no time a count or the governor of an island, and not one of those around here, but the best that is to be had."

"I hope to Heaven it's true, my husband, for we certainly need it. But tell me, what is all this about islands? I don't understand."

"Honey," replied Sancho, "is not for the mouth of an ass. You will find out in good time, woman; and you're going to be surprised to hear yourself called 'my Ladyship' by all your vassals."

"What's this you are saying, Sancho, about ladyships, islands, and vassals?" Juana Panza insisted on knowing—for such was the name of Sancho's wife, although they were not blood relatives, it being the custom in La Mancha for wives to take their husbands' surnames.

"Do not be in such a hurry to know all this, Juana," he said. "It is enough that I am telling you the truth. Sew up your mouth, then; for all I will say, in passing, is that there is nothing in the world that is more pleasant than being a respected man, squire to a knight-errant who goes in search of adventures. It is true that most of the adventures you meet with do not come out the way you'd like them to, for ninety-nine out of a hundred will prove to be all twisted and crosswise. I know that from experience, for I've come out of some of them blanketed and out of others beaten to a pulp. But, all the same, it's a fine thing to go along waiting for what will happen next, crossing mountains, making your way through woods, climbing over cliffs, visiting castles, and putting up at inns free of charge, and the devil take the maravedi that is to pay."

Such was the conversation that took place between Sancho Panza and Juana Panza, his wife, as Don Quixote's housekeeper and niece were taking him in, stripping him, and stretching him out on his old-time bed. He gazed at them blankly, being unable to make out where he was. The curate charged the niece to take great care to see that her uncle was comfortable and to keep close watch over him so that he would not slip away from them another time. He then told them of what it had been necessary to do in order to get him home, at which they once more screamed to Heaven and began cursing the books of chivalry all over again, praying God to plunge the authors of such lying nonsense into the center of the bottomless pit. In short, they scarcely knew what to do, for they were very much afraid that their master and uncle would give them the slip once more, the moment he was a little better, and it turned out just the way they feared it might.

From Part II

Prologue

TO THE READER

God bless me, gentle or, it may be, plebeian reader, how eagerly you must be awaiting this prologue, thinking to find in it vengeful scoldings and vituperations directed against the author of the second Don Quixote—I mean the one who, so it is said, was begotten in Tordesillas and born in Tarragona.[1] The truth is, however, that I am not going to be able to satisfy you in this regard; for granting that injuries are capable of awakening wrath in the humblest of bosoms, my own must be an exception to the rule. You would, perhaps, have me call him an ass, a crackbrain, and an upstart, but it is not my intention so to chastise him for his sin. Let him eat it with his bread and have done with it.

What I cannot but resent is the fact that he describes me as being old and one-handed, as if it were in my power to make time stand still for me, or as if I had lost my hand in some tavern instead of upon the greatest occasion that the past or present has ever known or the future may ever hope to see.[2] If my wounds are not resplendent in the eyes of the chance beholder, they are at least highly thought of by those who know where they were received. The soldier who lies dead in battle has a more impressive mien than the one who by flight attains his liberty. So strongly do I feel about this that even if

---

1. A continuation of *Don Quixote* was published by a writer who gave himself the name of Avellaneda and claimed to come from Tordesillas. The mood of the second prologue is grim in comparison to the optimistic and witty prologue to Part I.   2. The Battle of Lepanto in 1571.

it were possible to work a miracle in my case, I still would rather have taken part in that prodigious battle than be today free of my wounds without having been there. The scars that the soldier has to show on face and breast are stars that guide others to the Heaven of honor, inspiring them with a longing for well-merited praise. What is more, it may be noted that one does not write with gray hairs but with his understanding, which usually grows better with the years.

I likewise resent his calling me envious; and as though I were some ignorant person, he goes on to explain to me what is meant by envy; when the truth of the matter is that of the two kinds, I am acquainted only with that which is holy, noble, and right-intentioned.[3] And this being so, as indeed it is, it is not likely that I should attack any priest, above all, one that is a familiar of the Holy Office.[4] If he made this statement, as it appears that he did, on behalf of a certain person, then he is utterly mistaken; for the person in question is one whose genius I hold in veneration and whose works I admire, as well as his constant industry and powers of application. But when all is said, I wish to thank this gentlemanly author for observing that my Novels[5] are more satirical than exemplary, while admitting at the same time that they are good; for they could not be good unless they had in them a little of everything.

You will likely tell me that I am being too restrained and overmodest, but it is my belief that affliction is not to be heaped upon the afflicted, and this gentleman must be suffering greatly, seeing that he does not dare to come out into the open and show himself by the light of day, but must conceal his name and dissemble his place of origin, as if he had been guilty of some treason or act of lese majesty. If you by chance should come to know him, tell him on my behalf that I do not hold it against him; for I know what temptations the devil has to offer, one of the greatest of which consists in putting it into a man's head that he can write a book and have it printed and thereby achieve as much fame as he does money and acquire as much money as he does fame; in confirmation of which I would have you, in your own witty and charming manner, tell him this tale.

There was in Seville a certain madman whose madness assumed one of the drollest forms that ever was seen in this world. Taking a hollow reed sharpened at one end, he would catch a dog in the street or somewhere else; and, holding one of the animal's legs with his foot and raising the other with his hand, he would fix his reed as best he could in a certain part, after which he would blow the dog up, round as a ball. When he had it in this condition he would give it a couple of slaps on the belly and let it go, remarking to the bystanders, of whom there were always plenty, "Do your Worships think, then, that it is so easy a thing to inflate a dog?" So you might ask, "Does your Grace think that it is so easy a thing to write a book?" And if this story does not set well with him, here is another one, dear reader, that you may tell him. This one, also, is about a madman and a dog.

The madman in this instance lived in Cordova. He was in the habit of carrying on his head a marble slab or stone of considerable weight, and when he met some stray cur he would go up alongside it and drop the weight full

3. *Jealousy* and *zealousness* are etymologically related. 4. An allusion to the Spanish playwright Lope de Vega (see p. 2350), who had been made a priest and appointed an official of the Spanish Inquisition. Avellaneda accused Cervantes of envying Lope's enormous popularity. 5. *Exemplary Tales.*

upon it, and the dog in a rage, barking and howling, would then scurry off down three whole streets without stopping. Now, it happened that among the dogs that he treated in this fashion was one belonging to a capmaker, who was very fond of the beast. Going up to it as usual, the madman let the stone fall on its head, whereupon the animal set up a great yowling, and its owner, hearing its moans and seeing what had been done to it, promptly snatched up a measuring rod and fell upon the dog's assailant, flaying him until there was not a sound bone left in the fellow's body; and with each blow that he gave him he cried, "You dog! You thief! Treat my greyhound like that, would you? You brute, couldn't you see it was a greyhound?" And repeating the word "greyhound" over and over, he sent the madman away beaten to a pulp.

Profiting by the lesson that had been taught him, the fellow disappeared and was not seen in public for more than a month, at the end of which time he returned, up to his old tricks and with a heavier stone than ever on his head. He would go up to a dog and stare at it, long and hard, and without daring to drop his stone, would say, "This is a greyhound; beware." And so with all the dogs that he encountered: whether they were mastiffs or curs, he would assert that they were greyhounds and let them go unharmed.

The same thing possibly may happen to our historian; it may be that he will not again venture to let fall the weight of his wit in the form of books which, being bad ones, are harder than rocks.

As for the threat he has made to the effect that through his book he will deprive me of the profits on my own,[6] you may tell him that I do not give a rap. Quoting from the famous interlude, *La Perendenga*,[7] I will say to him in reply, "Long live my master, the Four-and-twenty,[8] and Christ be with us all." Long live the great Count of Lemos, whose Christian spirit and well-known liberality have kept me on my feet despite all the blows an unkind fate has dealt me. Long life to his Eminence of Toledo, the supremely charitable Don Bernardo de Sandoval y Rojas.[9] Even though there were no printing presses in all the world, or such as there are should print more books directed against me than there are letters in the verses of *Mingo Revulgo*,[1] what would it matter to me? These two princes, without any cringing flattery or adulation on my part but solely out of their own goodness of heart, have taken it upon themselves to grant me their favor and protection, in which respect I consider myself richer and more fortunate than if by ordinary means I had attained the peak of prosperity. The poor man may keep his honor, but not the vicious one. Poverty may cast a cloud over nobility but cannot wholly obscure it. Virtue of itself gives off a certain light, even though it be through the chinks and crevices and despite the obstacles of adversity, and so comes to be esteemed and as a consequence favored by high and noble minds.

Tell him no more than this, nor do I have anything more to say to you, except to ask you to bear in mind that this *Second Part of Don Quixote*, which I herewith present to you, is cut from the same cloth and by the same craftsman as Part I. In this book I give you Don Quixote continued and, finally, dead and buried, in order that no one may dare testify any further concerning

---

6. Avellaneda asserted that his second part would earn the profits Cervantes might have expected from a continuation of his own.   7. No interlude by this name has survived.   8. Council of the town hall at Andalucía.   9. Archbishop of Toledo, uncle of the duke of Lerma, and patron of Cervantes.   1. Long verse satire.

him, for there has been quite enough evidence as it is. It is sufficient that a reputable individual should have chronicled these ingenious acts of madness once and for all, without going into the matter again; for an abundance even of good things causes them to be little esteemed, while scarcity may lend a certain worth to those that are bad.

I almost forgot to tell you that you may look forward to the *Persiles*, on which I am now putting the finishing touches, as well as Part Second of the *Galatea*.[2]

["Put into a Book"]

CHAPTER 3

Of the laughable conversation that took place between Don Quixote, Sancho Panza, and the bachelor Sansón Carrasco.

Don Quixote remained in a thoughtful mood as he waited for the bachelor Carrasco,[1] from whom he hoped to hear the news as to how he had been put into a book, as Sancho had said. He could not bring himself to believe that any such history existed, since the blood of the enemies he had slain was not yet dry on the blade of his sword; and here they were trying to tell him that his high deeds of chivalry were already circulating in printed form. But, for that matter, he imagined that some sage, either friend or enemy, must have seen to the printing of them through the art of magic. If the chronicler was a friend, he must have undertaken the task in order to magnify and exalt Don Quixote's exploits above the most notable ones achieved by knights-errant of old. If an enemy, his purpose would have been to make them out as nothing at all, by debasing them below the meanest acts ever recorded of any mean squire. The only thing was, the knight reflected, the exploits of squires never were set down in writing. If it was true that such a history existed, being about a knight-errant, then it must be eloquent and lofty in tone, a splendid and distinguished piece of work and veracious in its details.

This consoled him somewhat, although he was a bit put out at the thought that the author was a Moor, if the appellation "Cid" was to be taken as an indication,[2] and from the Moors you could never hope for any word of truth, seeing that they are all of them cheats, forgers, and schemers. He feared lest his love should not have been treated with becoming modesty but rather in a way that would reflect upon the virtue of his lady Dulcinea del Toboso. He hoped that his fidelity had been made clear, and the respect he had always shown her, and that something had been said as to how he had spurned queens, empresses, and damsels of every rank while keeping a rein upon those impulses that are natural to a man. He was still wrapped up in these and many other similar thoughts when Sancho returned with Carrasco.

Don Quixote received the bachelor very amiably. The latter, although his name was Sansón, or Samson, was not very big so far as bodily size went, but he was a great joker, with a sallow complexion and a ready wit. He was

---

2. Never published.   1. The bachelor of arts Sansón Carrasco, an important new character who appears at the beginning of Part II and will play a considerable role in the story with his attempts at "curing" Don Quixote. Just now he has been telling Sancho about a book relating the adventures of Don Quixote and his squire, by which the two have been made famous; the book is, of course, *Don Quixote*, Part I.   2. The allusion is to Cid Hamete Benengeli (see n. 3, p. 2255). The word *cid* is of Arabic derivation.

going on twenty-four and had a round face, a snub nose, and a large mouth, all of which showed him to be of a mischievous disposition and fond of jests and witticisms. This became apparent when, as soon as he saw Don Quixote, he fell upon his knees and addressed the knight as follows:

"O mighty Don Quixote de la Mancha, give me your hands; for by the habit of St. Peter that I wear[3]—though I have received but the first four orders—your Grace is one of the most famous knights-errant that ever have been or ever will be anywhere on this earth. Blessings upon Cid Hamete Benengeli who wrote down the history of your great achievements, and upon that curious-minded one who was at pains to have it translated from the Arabic into our Castilian vulgate for the universal entertainment of the people."

Don Quixote bade him rise. "Is it true, then," he asked, "that there is a book about me and that it was some Moorish sage who composed it?"

"By way of showing you how true it is," replied Sansón, "I may tell you that it is my belief that there are in existence today more than twelve thousand copies of that history. If you do not believe me, you have but to make inquiries in Portugal, Barcelona, and Valencia, where editions have been brought out, and there is even a report to the effect that one edition was printed at Antwerp. In short, I feel certain that there will soon not be a nation that does not know it or a language into which it has not been translated."

"One of the things," remarked Don Quixote, "that should give most satisfaction to a virtuous and eminent man is to see his good name spread abroad during his own lifetime, by means of the printing press, through translations into the languages of the various peoples. I have said 'good name,' for if he has any other kind, his fate is worse than death."

"If it is a matter of good name and good reputation," said the bachelor, "your Grace bears off the palm from all the knights-errant in the world; for the Moor in his tongue and the Christian in his have most vividly depicted your Grace's gallantry, your courage in facing dangers, your patience in adversity and suffering, whether the suffering be due to wounds or to misfortunes of another sort, and your virtue and continence in love, in connection with that platonic relationship that exists between your Grace and my lady Doña Dulcinea del Toboso."

At this point Sancho spoke up. "Never in my life," he said, "have I heard my lady Dulcinea called 'Doña,' but only 'la Señora Dulcinea del Toboso'; so on that point, already, the history is wrong."

"That is not important," said Carrasco.

"No, certainly not," Don Quixote agreed. "But tell me, Señor Bachelor, what adventures of mine as set down in this book have made the deepest impression?"

"As to that," the bachelor answered, "opinions differ, for it is a matter of individual taste. There are some who are very fond of the adventure of the windmills—those windmills which to your Grace appeared to be so many Briareuses and giants. Others like the episode at the fulling mill. One relishes the story of the two armies which took on the appearance of droves of sheep, while another fancies the tale of the dead man whom they were taking to

---

3. The dress of one of the minor clerical orders.

Segovia for burial. One will assert that the freeing of the galley slaves is the best of all, and yet another will maintain that nothing can come up to the Benedictine giants and the encounter with the valiant Biscayan."

Again Sancho interrupted him. "Tell me, Señor Bachelor," he said, "does the book say anything about the adventure with the Yanguesans, that time our good Rocinante took it into his head to go looking for tidbits in the sea?"

"The sage," replied Sansón, "has left nothing in the inkwell. He has told everything and to the point, even to the capers which the worthy Sancho cut as they tossed him in the blanket."

"I cut no capers in the blanket," objected Sancho, "but I did in the air, and more than I liked."

"I imagine," said Don Quixote, "that there is no history in the world, dealing with humankind, that does not have its ups and downs, and this is particularly true of those that have to do with deeds of chivalry, for they can never be filled with happy incidents alone."

"Nevertheless," the bachelor went on, "there are some who have read the book who say that they would have been glad if the authors had forgotten a few of the innumerable cudgelings which Señor Don Quixote received in the course of his various encounters."

"But that is where the truth of the story comes in," Sancho protested.

"For all of that," observed Don Quixote, "they might well have said nothing about them; for there is no need of recording those events that do not alter the veracity of the chronicle, when they tend only to lessen the reader's respect for the hero. You may be sure that Aeneas was not as pious as Vergil would have us believe, nor was Ulysses as wise as Homer depicts him."

"That is true enough," replied Sansón, "but it is one thing to write as a poet and another as a historian. The former may narrate or sing of things not as they were but as they should have been; the latter must describe them not as they should have been but as they were, without adding to or detracting from the truth in any degree whatsoever."

"Well," said Sancho, "if this Moorish gentleman is bent upon telling the truth, I have no doubt that among my master's thrashings my own will be found; for they never took the measure of his Grace's shoulders without measuring my whole body. But I don't wonder at that; for as my master himself says, when there's an ache in the head the members have to share it."

"You are a sly fox, Sancho," said Don Quixote. "My word, but you can remember things well enough when you choose to do so!"

"Even if I wanted to forget the whacks they gave me," Sancho answered him, "the welts on my ribs wouldn't let me, for they are still fresh."

"Be quiet, Sancho," his master admonished him, "and do not interrupt the bachelor. I beg him to go on and tell me what is said of me in this book."

"And what it says about me, too," put in Sancho, "for I have heard that I am one of the main presonages in it—"

"*Personages*, not *presonages*, Sancho my friend," said Sansón.

"So we have another one who catches you up on everything you say," was Sancho's retort. "If we go on at this rate, we'll never be through in a lifetime."

"May God put a curse on *my* life," the bachelor told him, "if you are not the second most important person in the story; and there are some who would rather listen to you talk than to anyone else in the book. It is true, there are those who say that you are too gullible in believing it to be the truth that you could become the governor of that island that was offered you by Señor Don Quixote, here present."

"There is still sun on the top of the wall," said Don Quixote, "and when Sancho is a little older, with the experience that the years bring, he will be wiser and better fitted to be a governor than he is at the present time."

"By God, master," said Sancho, "the island that I couldn't govern right now I'd never be able to govern if I lived to be as old as Methuselah. The trouble is, I don't know where that island we are talking about is located; it is not due to any lack of noddle on my part."

"Leave it to God, Sancho," was Don Quixote's advice, "and everything will come out all right, perhaps even better than you think; for not a leaf on the tree stirs except by His will."

"Yes," said Sansón, "if it be God's will, Sancho will not lack a thousand islands to govern, not to speak of one island alone."

"I have seen governors around here," said Sancho, "that are not to be compared to the sole of my shoe, and yet they call them 'your Lordship' and serve them on silver plate."

"Those are not the same kind of governors," Sansón informed him. "Their task is a good deal easier. The ones that govern islands must at least know grammar."

"I could make out well enough with the *gram*," replied Sancho, "but with the *mar* I want nothing to do, for I don't understand it at all. But leaving this business of the governorship in God's hands—for He will send me wherever I can best serve Him—I will tell you, Señor Bachelor Sansón Carrasco, that I am very much pleased that the author of the history should have spoken of me in such a way as does not offend me; for, upon the word of a faithful squire, if he had said anything about me that was not becoming to an old Christian, the deaf would have heard of it."

"That would be to work miracles," said Sansón.

"Miracles or no miracles," was the answer, "let everyone take care as to what he says or writes about people and not be setting down the first thing that pops into his head."

"One of the faults that is found with the book," continued the bachelor, "is that the author has inserted in it a story entitled *The One Who Was Too Curious for His Own Good*. It is not that the story in itself is a bad one or badly written; it is simply that it is out of place there, having nothing to do with the story of his Grace, Señor Don Quixote."[4]

"I will bet you," said Sancho, "that the son of a dog has mixed the cabbages with the baskets."[5]

"And I will say right now," declared Don Quixote, "that the author of this book was not a sage but some ignorant prattler who at haphazard and without any method set about the writing of it, being content to let things turn out as they might. In the same manner, Orbaneja,[6] the painter of Ubeda, when

---

4. The story, a tragic tale about a jealousy-ridden husband, occupies several chapters of Part I. Here, as elsewhere in this chapter, Cervantes echoes criticism currently aimed at his book.　5. Has jumbled together things of different kinds.　6. Unidentified.

asked what he was painting would reply, 'Whatever it turns out to be.' Sometimes it would be a cock, in which case he would have to write alongside it,
in Gothic letters, 'This is a cock.' And so it must be with my story, which will
need a commentary to make it understandable."

"No," replied Sansón, "that it will not; for it is so clearly written that none
can fail to understand it. Little children leaf through it, young people read
it, adults appreciate it, and the aged sing its praises. In short, it is so thumbed
and read and so well known to persons of every walk in life that no sooner
do folks see some skinny nag than they at once cry, 'There goes Rocinante!'
Those that like it best of all are the pages; for there is no lord's antechamber
where a *Don Quixote* is not to be found. If one lays it down, another will
pick it up; one will pounce upon it, and another will beg for it. It affords the
pleasantest and least harmful reading of any book that has been published
up to now. In the whole of it there is not to be found an indecent word or a
thought that is other than Catholic."

"To write in any other manner," observed Don Quixote, "would be to write
lies and not the truth. Those historians who make use of falsehoods ought
to be burned like the makers of counterfeit money. I do not know what could
have led the author to introduce stories and episodes that are foreign to the
subject matter when he had so much to write about in describing my adventures. He must, undoubtedly, have been inspired by the old saying, 'With
straw or with hay[7] . . .' For, in truth, all he had to do was to record my
thoughts, my sighs, my tears, my lofty purposes, and my undertakings, and
he would have had a volume bigger or at least as big as that which the works
of El Tostado[8] would make. To sum the matter up, Señor Bachelor, it is my
opinion that, in composing histories or books of any sort, a great deal of
judgment and ripe understanding is called for. To say and write witty and
amusing things is the mark of great genius. The cleverest character in a
comedy is the clown, since he who would make himself out to be a simpleton
cannot be one. History is a near-sacred thing, for it must be true, and where
the truth is, there is God. And yet there are those who compose books and
toss them out into the world as if they were no more than fritters."

"There is no book so bad," opined the bachelor, "that there is not some
good in it."

"Doubtless that is so," replied Don Quixote, "but it very often happens
that those who have won in advance a great and well-deserved reputation for
their writings, lose it in whole or in part when they give their works to the
printer."

"The reason for it," said Sansón, "is that, printed works being read at
leisure, their faults are the more readily apparent, and the greater the reputation of the author the more closely are they scrutinized. Men famous for
their genius, great poets, illustrious historians, are almost always envied by
those who take a special delight in criticizing the writings of others without
having produced anything of their own."

"That is not to be wondered at," said Don Quixote, "for there are many
theologians who are not good enough for the pulpit but who are very good

---

7. The proverb concludes either "the mattress is filled" or "I fill my belly."   8. Alonso de Madrigal, bishop
of Ávila, a prolific author of devotional works.

indeed when it comes to detecting the faults or excesses of those who preach."

"All of this is very true, Señor Don Quixote," replied Carrasco, "but, all the same, I could wish that these self-appointed censors were a bit more forbearing and less hypercritical; I wish they would pay a little less attention to the spots on the bright sun of the work that occasions their fault-finding. For if *aliquando bonus dormitat Homerus*,[9] let them consider how much of his time he spent awake, shedding the light of his genius with a minimum of shade. It well may be that what to them seems a flaw is but one of those moles which sometimes add to the beauty of a face. In any event, I insist that he who has a book printed runs a very great risk, inasmuch as it is an utter impossibility to write it in such a manner that it will please all who read it."

"This book about me must have pleased very few," remarked Don Quixote.

"Quite the contrary," said Sansón, "for just as *stultorum infinitus est numerus*,[1] so the number of those who have enjoyed this history is likewise infinite. Some, to be sure, have complained of the author's forgetfulness, seeing that he neglected to make it plain who the thief was who stole Sancho's gray;[2] for it is not stated there, but merely implied, that the ass was stolen; and, a little further on, we find the knight mounted on the same beast, although it has not made its reappearance in the story. They also say that the author forgot to tell us what Sancho did with those hundred crowns that he found in the valise on the Sierra Morena, as nothing more is said of them and there are many who would like to know how he disposed of the money or how he spent it. This is one of the serious omissions to be found in the work."

To this Sancho replied, "I, Señor Sansón, do not feel like giving any account or accounting just now; for I feel a little weak in my stomach, and if I don't do something about it by taking a few swigs of the old stuff, I'll be sitting on St. Lucy's thorn.[3] I have some of it at home, and my old woman is waiting for me. After I've had my dinner, I'll come back and answer any questions your Grace or anybody else wants to ask me, whether it's about the loss of the ass or the spending of the hundred crowns."

And without waiting for a reply or saying another word, he went on home. Don Quixote urged the bachelor to stay and take potluck with him, and Sansón accepted the invitation and remained. In addition to the knight's ordinary fare, they had a couple of pigeons, and at table their talk was of chivalry and feats of arms.

---

9. Good Homer sometimes nods too (Latin); Horace, *Art of Poetry*, line 359. 1. Infinite is the number of fools (Latin). 2. In Part I, chap. 23. 3. I shall be weak and exhausted.

[*A Victorious Duel*]

CHAPTER 12

Of the strange adventure that befell the valiant Don Quixote with the fearless Knight of the Mirrors.[4]

The night following the encounter with Death was spent by Don Quixote and his squire beneath some tall and shady trees,[5] the knight having been persuaded to eat a little from the stock of provisions carried by the gray.

"Sir," said Sancho, in the course of their repast, "how foolish I'd have been if I had chosen the spoils from your Grace's first adventure rather than the foals from the three mares.[6] Truly, truly, a sparrow in the hand is worth more than a vulture on the wing."[7]

"And yet, Sancho," replied Don Quixote, "if you had but let me attack them as I wished to do, you would at least have had as spoils the Empress's gold crown and Cupid's painted wings;[8] for I should have taken them whether or no and placed them in your hands."

"The crowns and scepters of stage emperors," remarked Sancho, "were never known to be of pure gold; they are always of tinsel or tinplate."

"That is the truth," said Don Quixote, "for it is only right that the accessories of a drama should be fictitious and not real, like the play itself. Speaking of that, Sancho, I would have you look kindly upon the art of the theater and, as a consequence, upon those who write the pieces and perform in them, for they all render a service of great value to the State by holding up a mirror for us at each step that we take, wherein we may observe, vividly depicted, all the varied aspects of human life; and I may add that there is nothing that shows us more clearly, by similitude, what we are and what we ought to be than do plays and players.

"Tell me, have you not seen some comedy in which kings, emperors, pontiffs, knights, ladies, and numerous other characters are introduced? One plays the ruffian, another the cheat, this one a merchant and that one a soldier, while yet another is the fool who is not so foolish as he appears, and still another the one of whom love has made a fool. Yet when the play is over and they have taken off their players' garments, all the actors are once more equal."

"Yes," replied Sancho, "I have seen all that."

"Well," continued Don Quixote, "the same thing happens in the comedy that we call life, where some play the part of emperors, others that of pontiffs—in short, all the characters that a drama may have—but when it is all over, that is to say, when life is done, death takes from each the garb that differentiates him, and all at last are equal in the grave."

"It is a fine comparison," Sancho admitted, "though not so new but that I

---

4. Until he earns this title (in chap. 15), he will be referred to as the Knight of the Wood.   5. Don Quixote and his squire are now in the woody region around El Toboso, Dulcinea's town. Sancho has been sent to look for his knight's lady and has saved the day by pretending to see the beautiful damsel in a "village wench, and not a pretty one at that, for she was round-faced and snub-nosed." But by his imaginative lie he has succeeded, as he had planned, in setting in motion Don Quixote's belief in spells and enchantments: enemy magicians, envious of him, have hidden his lady's splendor only from his sight. While the knight was still under the shock of this experience, farther along their way he and his squire have met a group of itinerant players dressed in their proper costumes for a religious play, *The Parliament of Death.*   6. Don Quixote has promised them to Sancho as a reward for bringing news of Dulcinea.   7. I.e., a bird in the hand is worth two in the bush.   8. The Empress and Cupid were characters in *The Parliament of Death.*

have heard it many times before. It reminds me of that other one, about the game of chess. So long as the game lasts, each piece has its special qualities, but when it is over they are all mixed and jumbled together and put into a bag, which is to the chess pieces what the grave is to life."

"Every day, Sancho," said Don Quixote, "you are becoming less stupid and more sensible."

"It must be that some of your Grace's good sense is sticking to me," was Sancho's answer. "I am like a piece of land that of itself is dry and barren, but if you scatter manure over it and cultivate it, it will bear good fruit. By this I mean to say that your Grace's conversation is the manure that has been cast upon the barren land of my dry wit; the time that I spend in your service, associating with you, does the cultivating; and as a result of it all, I hope to bring forth blessed fruits by not departing, slipping, or sliding, from those paths of good breeding which your Grace has marked out for me in my parched understanding."

Don Quixote had to laugh at this affected speech of Sancho's, but he could not help perceiving that what the squire had said about his improvement was true enough; for every now and then the servant would speak in a manner that astonished his master. It must be admitted, however, that most of the time when he tried to use fine language, he would tumble from the mountain of his simple-mindedness into the abyss of his ignorance. It was when he was quoting old saws and sayings, whether or not they had anything to do with the subject under discussion, that he was at his best, displaying upon such occasions a prodigious memory, as will already have been seen and noted in the course of this history.

With such talk as this they spent a good part of the night. Then Sancho felt a desire to draw down the curtains of his eyes, as he was in the habit of saying when he wished to sleep, and, unsaddling his mount, he turned him loose to graze at will on the abundant grass. If he did not remove Rocinante's saddle, this was due to his master's express command; for when they had taken the field and were not sleeping under a roof, the hack was under no circumstances to be stripped. This was in accordance with an old and established custom which knights-errant faithfully observed: the bridle and saddlebow might be removed, but beware of touching the saddle itself! Guided by this precept, Sancho now gave Rocinante the same freedom that the ass enjoyed.

The close friendship that existed between the two animals was a most unusual one, so remarkable indeed that it has become a tradition handed down from father to son, and the author of this veracious chronicle even wrote a number of special chapters on the subject, although, in order to preserve the decency and decorum that are fitting in so heroic an account, he chose to omit them in the final version. But he forgets himself once in a while and goes on to tell us how the two beasts when they were together would hasten to scratch each other, and how, when they were tired and their bellies were full, Rocinante would lay his long neck over that of the ass—it extended more than a half a yard on the other side—and the pair would then stand there gazing pensively at the ground for as much as three whole days at a time, or at least until someone came for them or hunger compelled them to seek nourishment.

I may tell you that I have heard it said that the author of this history, in one of his writings, has compared the friendship of Rocinante and the gray to that of Nisus and Euryalus and that of Pylades and Orestes;[9] and if this be true, it shows for the edification of all what great friends these two peace-loving animals were, and should be enough to make men ashamed, who are so inept at preserving friendship with one another. For this reason it has been said:

> There is no friend for friend,
> Reeds to lances turn[1] . . .

And there was the other poet who sang:

> Between friend and friend the bug[2] . . .

Let no one think that the author has gone out of his way in comparing the friendship of animals with that of men; for human beings have received valuable lessons from the beasts and have learned many important things from them. From the stork they have learned the use of clysters; the dog has taught them the salutary effects of vomiting as well as a lesson in gratitude; the cranes have taught them vigilance, the ants foresight, the elephants modesty, and the horse loyalty.[3]

Sancho had at last fallen asleep at the foot of a cork tree, while Don Quixote was slumbering beneath a sturdy oak. Very little time had passed when the knight was awakened by a noise behind him, and, starting up, he began looking about him and listening to see if he could make out where it came from. Then he caught sight of two men on horseback, one of whom, slipping down from the saddle, said to the other, "Dismount, my friend, and unbridle the horses; for there seems to be plenty of grass around here for them and sufficient silence and solitude for my amorous thoughts."

Saying this, he stretched himself out on the ground, and as he flung himself down the armor that he wore made such a noise that Don Quixote knew at once, for a certainty, that he must be a knight-errant. Going over to Sancho, who was still sleeping, he shook him by the arm and with no little effort managed to get him awake.

"Brother Sancho," he said to him in a low voice, "we have an adventure on our hands."

"God give us a good one," said Sancho. "And where, my master, may her Ladyship, Mistress Adventure, be?"

"Where, Sancho?" replied Don Quixote. "Turn your eyes and look, and you will see stretched out over there a knight-errant who, so far as I can make out, is not any too happy; for I saw him fling himself from his horse to the ground with a certain show of despondency, and as he fell his armor rattled."

"Well," said Sancho, "and how does your Grace make this out to be an adventure?"

"I would not say," the knight answered him, "that this is an adventure in itself, but rather the beginning of one, for that is the way they start. But listen; he seems to be tuning a lute or guitar, and from the way he is spitting and clearing his throat he must be getting ready to sing something."

9. Famous examples of friendship in Virgil's *Aeneid* and in Greek tradition and drama.   1. From a popular ballad.   2. The Spanish "a bug in the eye" implies keeping a watchful eye on somebody.   3. All folkloristic beliefs about the virtues of animals.

"Faith, so he is," said Sancho. "He must be some lovesick knight."

"There are no knights-errant that are not lovesick," Don Quixote informed him. "Let us listen to him, and the thread of his song will lead us to the yarn-ball of his thoughts; for out of the abundance of the heart the mouth speaketh."

Sancho would have liked to reply to his master, but the voice of the Knight of the Wood, which was neither very good nor very bad, kept him from it; and as the two of them listened attentively, they heard the following:

Sonnet

Show me, O lady, the pattern of thy will,
That mine may take that very form and shape;
For my will in thine own I fain would drape,
Each slightest wish of thine I would fulfill.
If thou wouldst have me silence this dead ill   5
Of which I'm dying now, prepare the crape!
Or if I must another manner ape,
Then let Love's self display his rhyming skill.
Of opposites I am made, that's manifest:
In part soft wax, in part hard-diamond fire;   10
Yet to Love's laws my heart I do adjust,
And, hard or soft, I offer thee this breast:
Print or engrave there what thou may'st desire,
And I'll preserve it in eternal trust.[4]

With an *Ay!* that appeared to be wrung from the very depths of his heart, the Knight of the Wood brought his song to a close, and then after a brief pause began speaking in a grief-stricken voice that was piteous to hear.

"O most beautiful and most ungrateful woman in all the world!" he cried, "how is it possible, O most serene Casildea de Vandalia,[5] for you to permit this captive knight of yours to waste away and perish in constant wanderings, amid rude toils and bitter hardships? Is it not enough that I have compelled all the knights of Navarre, all those of León, all the Tartessians and Castilians, and, finally, all those of La Mancha, to confess that there is no beauty anywhere that can rival yours?"

"That is not so!" cried Don Quixote at this point. "I am of La Mancha, and I have never confessed, I never could nor would confess a thing so prejudicial to the beauty of my lady. The knight whom you see there, Sancho, is raving; but let us listen and perhaps he will tell us more."

"That he will," replied Sancho, "for at the rate he is carrying on, he is good for a month at a stretch."

This did not prove to be the case, however; for when the Knight of the Wood heard voices near him, he cut short his lamentations and rose to his feet.

"Who goes there?" he called in a loud but courteous tone. "What kind of people are you? Are you, perchance, numbered among the happy or among the afflicted?"

---

4. The poem intentionally follows affected conventions of the time.   5. The Knight of the Wood's counterpart to Don Quixote's Dulcinea del Toboso.

"Among the afflicted," was Don Quixote's response.

"Then come to me," said the one of the Wood, "and, in doing so, know that you come to sorrow's self and the very essence of affliction."

Upon receiving so gentle and courteous an answer, Don Quixote and Sancho as well went over to him, whereupon the sorrowing one took the Manchegan's arm.

"Sit down here, Sir Knight," he continued, "for in order to know that you are one of those who follow the profession of knight-errantry, it is enough for me to have found you in this place where solitude and serenity keep you company, such a spot being the natural bed and proper dwelling of wandering men of arms."

"A knight I am," replied Don Quixote, "and of the profession that you mention; and though sorrows, troubles, and misfortunes have made my heart their abode, this does not mean that compassion for the woes of others has been banished from it. From your song a while ago I gather that your misfortunes are due to love—the love you bear that ungrateful fair one whom you named in your lamentations."

As they conversed in this manner, they sat together upon the hard earth, very peaceably and companionably, as if at daybreak they were not going to break each other's heads.

"Sir Knight," inquired the one of the Wood, "are you by any chance in love?"

"By mischance I am," said Don Quixote, "although the ills that come from well-placed affection should be looked upon as favors rather than as misfortunes."

"That is the truth," the Knight of the Wood agreed, "if it were not that the loved one's scorn disturbs our reason and understanding; for when it is excessive scorn appears as vengeance."

"I was never scorned by my lady," said Don Quixote.

"No, certainly not," said Sancho, who was standing near by, "for my lady is gentle as a ewe lamb and soft as butter."

"Is he your squire?" asked the one of the Wood.

"He is," replied Don Quixote.

"I never saw a squire," said the one of the Wood, "who dared to speak while his master was talking. At least, there is mine over there; he is as big as your father, and it cannot be proved that he has ever opened his lips while I was conversing."

"Well, upon my word," said Sancho, "I have spoken, and I will speak in front of any other as good—but never mind; it only makes it worse to stir it."

The Knight of the Wood's squire now seized Sancho's arm. "Come along," he said, "let the two of us go where we can talk all we like, squire fashion, and leave these gentlemen our masters to come to lance blows as they tell each other the story of their loves; for you may rest assured, daybreak will find them still at it."

"Let us, by all means," said Sancho, "and I will tell your Grace who I am, so that you may be able to see for yourself whether or not I am to be numbered among the dozen most talkative squires."

With this, the pair went off to one side, and there then took place between them a conversation that was as droll as the one between their masters was solemn.

CHAPTER 13

*In which is continued the adventure of the Knight of the Wood, together
with the shrewd, highly original, and amicable conversation that took
place between the two squires.*

The knights and the squires had now separated, the latter to tell their life
stories, the former to talk of their loves; but the history first relates the
conversation of the servants and then goes on to report that of the masters.
We are told that, after they had gone some little distance from where the
others were, the one who served the Knight of the Wood began speaking to
Sancho as follows:

"It is a hard life that we lead and live, *Señor mio,* those of us who are
squires to knights-errant. It is certainly true that we eat our bread in the
sweat of our faces, which is one of the curses that God put upon our first
parents."[6]

"It might also be said," added Sancho, "that we eat it in the chill of our
bodies, for who endures more heat and cold than we wretched ones who
wait upon these wandering men of arms? It would not be so bad if we did
eat once in a while, for troubles are less where there is bread; but as it is,
we sometimes go for a day or two without breaking our fast, unless we feed
on the wind that blows."

"But all this," said the other, "may very well be put up with, by reason of
the hope we have of being rewarded; for if a knight is not too unlucky, his
squire after a little while will find himself the governor of some fine island
or prosperous earldom."

"I," replied Sancho, "have told my master that I would be satisfied with
the governorship of an island, and he is so noble and so generous that he
has promised it to me on many different occasions."

"In return for my services," said the Squire of the Wood, "I'd be content
with a canonry. My master has already appointed me to one—and what a
canonry!"

"Then he must be a churchly knight," said Sancho, "and in a position to
grant favors of that sort to his faithful squire; but mine is a layman, pure and
simple, although, as I recall, certain shrewd and, as I see it, scheming persons
did advise him to try to become an archbishop. However, he did not want to
be anything but an emperor. And there I was, all the time trembling for fear
he would take it into his head to enter the Church, since I was not educated
enough to hold any benefices. For I may as well tell your Grace that, though
I look like a man, I am no more than a beast where holy orders are concerned."

"That is where you are making a mistake," the Squire of the Wood assured
him. "Not all island governments are desirable. Some of them are misshapen
bits of land, some are poor, others are gloomy, and, in short, the best of them
lays a heavy burden of care and trouble upon the shoulders of the unfortunate one to whose lot it falls. It would be far better if we who follow this
cursed trade were to go back to our homes and there engage in pleasanter
occupations, such as hunting or fishing, for example; for where is there in

---

6. Cf. Genesis 3.19. "In the sweat of thy face shalt thou eat bread, till thou return unto the ground."

this world a squire so poor that he does not have a hack, a couple of grey-hounds, and a fishing rod to provide him with sport in his own village?"

"I don't lack any of those," replied Sancho. "It is true, I have no hack, but I do have an ass that is worth twice as much as my master's horse. God send me a bad Easter, and let it be the next one that comes, if I would make a trade, even though he gave me four fanegas[7] of barley to boot. Your Grace will laugh at the price I put on my gray—for that is the color of the beast. As to greyhounds, I shan't want for them, as there are plenty and to spare in my village. And, anyway, there is more pleasure in hunting when someone else pays for it."

"Really and truly, Sir Squire," said the one of the Wood, "I have made up my mind and resolved to have no more to do with the mad whims of these knights; I intend to retire to my village and bring up my little ones—I have three of them, and they are like oriental pearls."

"I have two of them," said Sancho, "that might be presented to the Pope in person, especially one of my girls that I am bringing up to be a countess, God willing, in spite of what her mother says."

"And how old is this young lady that is destined to be a countess?"

"Fifteen," replied Sancho, "or a couple of years more or less. But she is tall as a lance, fresh as an April morning, and strong as a porter."

"Those," remarked the one of the Wood, "are qualifications that fit her to be not merely a countess but a nymph of the verdant wildwood. O whore's daughter of a whore! What strength the she-rogue must have!"

Sancho was a bit put out by this. "She is not a whore," he said, "nor was her mother before her, nor will either of them ever be, please God, so long as I live. And you might speak more courteously. For one who has been brought up among knights-errant, who are the soul of courtesy, those words are not very becoming."

"Oh, how little your Grace knows about compliments, Sir Squire!" the one of the Wood exclaimed. "Are you not aware that when some knight gives a good lance thrust to the bull in the plaza, or when a person does anything remarkably well, it is the custom for the crowd to cry out, 'Well done, whore-son rascal!' and that what appears to be vituperation in such a case is in reality high praise? Sir, I would bid you disown those sons or daughters who do nothing to cause such praise to be bestowed upon their parents."

"I would indeed disown them if they didn't," replied Sancho, "and so your Grace may go ahead and call me, my children, and my wife all the whores in the world if you like, for everything that they say and do deserves the very highest praise. And in order that I may see them all again, I pray God to deliver me from mortal sin, or, what amounts to the same thing, from this dangerous calling of squire, seeing that I have fallen into it a second time, decoyed and deceived by a purse of a hundred ducats that I found one day in the heart of the Sierra Morena.[8] The devil is always holding up a bag full of doubloons in front of my eyes, here, there—no, not here, but there—everywhere, until it seems to me at every step I take that I am touching it with my hand, hugging it, carrying it off home with me, investing it, drawing an income from it, and living on it like a prince. And while I am thinking such thoughts, all the hardships I have to put up with serving this crack-

7. About 1.6 bushels.   8. When Don Quixote retired there in Part I, chap. 23.

brained master of mine, who is more of a madman than a knight, seem to me light and easy to bear."

"That," observed the Squire of the Wood, "is why it is they say that avarice bursts the bag. But, speaking of madmen, there is no greater one in all this world than my master; for he is one of those of whom it is said, 'The cares of others kill the ass.' Because another knight has lost his senses, he has to play mad too[9] and go hunting for that which, when he finds it, may fly up in his snout."

"Is he in love, maybe?"

"Yes, with a certain Casildea de Vandalia, the rawest[1] and best-roasted lady to be found anywhere on earth; but her rawness is not the foot he limps on, for he has other and greater schemes rumbling in his bowels, as you will hear tell before many hours have gone by."

"There is no road so smooth," said Sancho, "that it does not have some hole or rut to make you stumble. In other houses they cook horse beans, in mine they boil them by the kettleful.[2] Madness has more companions and attendants than good sense does. But if it is true what they say, that company in trouble brings relief, I may take comfort from your Grace, since you serve a master as foolish as my own."

"Foolish but brave," the one of the Wood corrected him, "and more of a rogue than anything else."

"That is not true of my master," replied Sancho. "I can assure you there is nothing of the rogue about him; he is as open and aboveboard as a wine pitcher and would not harm anyone but does good to all. There is no malice in his make-up, and a child could make him believe it was night at midday. For that very reason I love him with all my heart and cannot bring myself to leave him, no matter how many foolish things he does."

"But, nevertheless, good sir and brother," said the Squire of the Wood, "with the blind leading the blind, both are in danger of falling into the pit. It would be better for us to get out of all this as quickly as we can and return to our old haunts; for those that go seeking adventures do not always find good ones."

Sancho kept clearing his throat from time to time, and his saliva seemed rather viscous and dry; seeing which, the woodland squire said to him, "It looks to me as if we have been talking so much that our tongues are cleaving to our palates, but I have a loosener over there, hanging from the bow of my saddle, and a pretty good one it is." With this, he got up and went over to his horse and came back a moment later with a big flask of wine and a meat pie half a yard in diameter. This is no exaggeration, for the pasty in question was made of a hutch-rabbit of such a size that Sancho took it to be a goat, or at the very least a kid.

"And are you in the habit of carrying this with you, Señor?" he asked.

"What do you think?" replied the other. "Am I by any chance one of your wood-and-water[3] squires? I carry better rations on the flanks of my horse than a general does when he takes the field."

Sancho ate without any urging, gulping down mouthfuls that were like the knots on a tether, as they sat there in the dark.

9. In the Sierra Morena, Don Quixote had decided to imitate Amadis de Gaul and Ariosto's Roland "by playing the part of a desperate and raving madman" as a consequence of love. 1. The Spanish has a pun on *crudo*, meaning both "raw" and "cruel." 2. Meaning that his misfortunes always come in large quantities. 3. Of low quality.

"You are a squire of the right sort," he said, "loyal and true, and you live in grand style as shown by this feast, which I would almost say was produced by magic. You are not like me, poor wretch, who have in my saddlebags only a morsel of cheese so hard you could crack a giant's skull with it, three or four dozen carob beans, and a few nuts. For this I have my master to thank, who believes in observing the rule that knights-errant should nourish and sustain themselves on nothing but dried fruits and the herbs of the field."

"Upon my word, brother," said the other squire, "my stomach was not made for thistles, wild pears, and woodland herbs. Let our masters observe those knightly laws and traditions and eat what their rules prescribe; I carry a hamper of food and a flask on my saddlebow, whether they like it or not. And speaking of that flask, how I love it! There is scarcely a minute in the day that I'm not hugging and kissing it, over and over again."

As he said this, he placed the wine bag in Sancho's hands, who put it to his mouth, threw his head back, and sat there gazing up at the stars for a quarter of an hour. Then, when he had finished drinking, he let his head loll on one side and heaved a deep sigh.

"The whoreson rascal!" he exclaimed, "that's a fine vintage for you!"

"There!" cried the Squire of the Wood, as he heard the epithet Sancho had used, "do you see how you have praised this wine by calling it 'whoreson'?"

"I grant you," replied Sancho, "that it is no insult to call anyone a son of a whore so long as you really do mean to praise him. But tell me, sir, in the name of what you love most, is this the wine of Ciudad Real?"[4]

"What a winetaster you are! It comes from nowhere else, and it's a few years old, at that."

"Leave it to me," said Sancho, "and never fear, I'll show you how much I know about it. Would you believe me, Sir Squire, I have such a great natural instinct in this matter of wines that I have but to smell a vintage and I will tell you the country where it was grown, from what kind of grapes, what it tastes like, and how good it is, and everything that has to do with it. There is nothing so unusual about this, however, seeing that on my father's side were two of the best winetasters La Mancha has known in many a year, in proof of which, listen to the story of what happened to them.

"The two were given a sample of wine from a certain vat and asked to state its condition and quality and determine whether it was good or bad. One of them tasted it with the tip of his tongue while the other merely brought it up to his nose. The first man said that it tasted of iron, the second that it smelled of Cordovan leather. The owner insisted that the vat was clean and that there could be nothing in the wine to give it a flavor of leather or of iron, but, nevertheless, the two famous winetasters stood their ground. Time went by, and when they came to clean out the vat they found in it a small key attached to a leather strap. And so your Grace may see for yourself whether or not one who comes of that kind of stock has a right to give his opinion in such cases."

"And for that very reason," said the Squire of the Wood, "I maintain that we ought to stop going about in search of adventures. Seeing that we have loaves, let us not go looking for cakes, but return to our cottages, for God will find us there if He so wills."

4. The main town in La Mancha and the center of a wine region.

"I mean to stay with my master," Sancho replied, "until he reaches Saragossa, but after that we will come to an understanding."

The short of the matter is, the two worthy squires talked so much and drank so much that sleep had to tie their tongues and moderate their thirst, since to quench the latter was impossible. Clinging to the wine flask, which was almost empty by now, and with half-chewed morsels of food in their mouths, they both slept peacefully; and we shall leave them there as we go on to relate what took place between the Knight of the Wood and the Knight of the Mournful Countenance.

CHAPTER 14

Wherein is continued the adventure of the Knight of the Wood.

In the course of the long conversation that took place between Don Quixote and the Knight of the Wood, the history informs us that the latter addressed the following remarks to the Manchegan:

"In short, Sir Knight, I would have you know that my destiny, or, more properly speaking, my own free choice, has led me to fall in love with the peerless Casildea de Vandalia. I call her peerless for the reason that she has no equal as regards either her bodily proportions or her very great beauty. This Casildea, then, of whom I am telling you, repaid my worthy affections and honorable intentions by forcing me, as Hercules[5] was forced by his stepmother, to incur many and diverse perils; and each time as I overcame one of them she would promise me that with the next one I should have that which I desired; but instead my labors have continued, forming a chain whose links I am no longer able to count, nor can I say which will be the last one, that shall mark the beginning of the realization of my hopes.

"One time she sent me forth to challenge that famous giantess of Seville, known as La Giralda,[6] who is as strong and brave as if made of brass, and who without moving from the spot where she stands is the most changeable and fickle woman in the world. I came, I saw, I conquered her, I made her stand still and point in one direction only, and for more than a week nothing but north winds blew. Then, there was that other time when Casildea sent me to lift those ancient stones, the mighty Bulls of Guisando,[7] an enterprise that had better have been entrusted to porters than to knights. On another occasion she commanded me to hurl myself down into the Cabra chasm[8]—an unheard-of and terribly dangerous undertaking—and bring her back a detailed account of what lay concealed in that deep and gloomy pit. I rendered La Giralda motionless, I lifted the Bulls of Guisando, and I threw myself into the abyss and brought to light what was hidden in its depths; yet my hopes are dead—how dead!—while her commands and her scorn are as lively as can be.

"Finally, she commanded me to ride through all the provinces of Spain and compel all the knights-errant whom I met with to confess that she is the most beautiful woman now living and that I am the most enamored man of arms that is to be found anywhere in the world. In fulfillment of this behest

5. Son of Zeus and Alcmena; he was persecuted by Zeus's wife, Hera.   6. Actually a statue on the Moorish belfry of the cathedral at Seville.   7. Statues representing animals and supposedly marking a place where Caesar defeated Pompey.   8. Possibly an ancient mine in the Sierra de Cabra near Cordova.

I have already traveled over the greater part of these realms and have vanquished many knights who have dared to contradict me. But the one whom I am proudest to have overcome in single combat is that famous gentleman, Don Quixote de la Mancha; for I made him confess that my Casildea is more beautiful than his Dulcinea, and by achieving such a conquest I reckon that I have conquered all the others on the face of the earth, seeing that this same Don Quixote had himself routed them. Accordingly, when I vanquished him, his fame, glory, and honor passed over and were transferred to my person.

> The brighter is the conquered one's lost crown,
> The greater is the conqueror's renown.[9]

Thus, the innumerable exploits of the said Don Quixote are now set down to my account and are indeed my own."

Don Quixote was astounded as he listened to the Knight of the Wood, and was about to tell him any number of times that he lied; the words were on the tip of his tongue, but he held them back as best he could, thinking that he would bring the other to confess with his own lips that what he had said was a lie. And so it was quite calmly that he now replied to him.

"Sir Knight," he began, "as to the assertion that your Grace has conquered most of the knights-errant in Spain and even in all the world, I have nothing to say, but that you have vanquished Don Quixote de la Mancha, I am inclined to doubt. It may be that it was someone else who resembled him, although there are very few that do."

"What do you mean?" replied the one of the Wood. "I swear by the heavens above that I did fight with Don Quixote and that I overcame him and forced him to yield. He is a tall man, with a dried-up face, long, lean legs, graying hair, an eagle-like nose somewhat hooked, and a big, black, drooping mustache. He takes the field under the name of the Knight of the Mournful Countenance, he has for squire a peasant named Sancho Panza, and he rides a famous steed called Rocinante. Lastly, the lady of his heart is a certain Dulcinea del Toboso, once upon a time known as Aldonza Lorenzo, just as my own lady, whose name is Casildea and who is an Andalusian by birth, is called by me Casildea de Vandalia. If all this is not sufficient to show that I speak the truth, here is my sword which shall make incredulity itself believe."

"Calm yourself, Sir Knight," replied Don Quixote, "and listen to what I have to say to you. You must know that this Don Quixote of whom you speak is the best friend that I have in the world, so great a friend that I may say that I feel toward him as I do toward my own self; and from all that you have told me, the very definite and accurate details that you have given me, I cannot doubt that he is the one whom you have conquered. On the other hand, the sight of my eyes and the touch of my hands assure me that he could not possibly be the one, unless some enchanter who is his enemy— for he has many, and one in particular who delights in persecuting him— may have assumed the knight's form and then permitted himself to be routed, by way of defrauding Don Quixote of the fame which his high deeds of chivalry have earned for him throughout the known world. To show you how

---

9. From Alonso de Ercilla y Zúñiga's *Araucana,* a poem about the Spanish struggle against the Araucanian Indians of Chile.

true this may be, I will inform you that not more than a couple of days ago those same enemy magicians transformed the figure and person of the beauteous Dulcinea del Toboso into a low and mean village lass, and it is possible that they have done something of the same sort to the knight who is her lover. And if all this does not suffice to convince you of the truth of what I say, here is Don Quixote himself who will maintain it by force of arms, on foot or on horseback, or in any way you like."

Saying this, he rose and laid hold of his sword, and waited to see what the Knight of the Wood's decision would be. That worthy now replied in a voice as calm as the one Don Quixote had used.

"Pledges," he said, "do not distress one who is sure of his ability to pay. He who was able to overcome you when you were transformed, Señor Don Quixote, may hope to bring you to your knees when you are your own proper self. But inasmuch as it is not fitting that knights should perform their feats of arms in the darkness, like ruffians and highwaymen, let us wait until it is day in order that the sun may behold what we do. And the condition governing our encounter shall be that the one who is vanquished must submit to the will of his conqueror and perform all those things that are commanded of him, provided they are such as are in keeping with the state of knighthood."

"With that condition and understanding," said Don Quixote, "I shall be satisfied."

With this, they went off to where their squires were, only to find them snoring away as hard as when sleep had first overtaken them. Awakening the pair, they ordered them to look to the horses; for as soon as the sun was up the two knights meant to stage an arduous and bloody single-handed combat. At this news Sancho was astonished and terrified, since, as a result of what the other squire had told him of the Knight of the Wood's prowess, he was led to fear for his master's safety. Nevertheless, he and his friend now went to seek the mounts without saying a word, and they found the animals all together, for by this time the two horses and the ass had smelled one another out. On the way the Squire of the Wood turned to Sancho and addressed him as follows:

"I must inform you, brother, that it is the custom of the fighters of Andalusia, when they are godfathers in any combat, not to remain idly by, with folded hands, while their godsons fight it out. I tell you this by way of warning you that while our masters are settling matters, we, too, shall have to come to blows and hack each other to bits."

"The custom, Sir Squire," replied Sancho, "may be all very well among the fighters and ruffians that you mention, but with the squires of knights-errant it is not to be thought of. At least, I have never heard my master speak of any such custom, and he knows all the laws of chivalry by heart. But granting that it is true and that there is a law which states in so many words that squires must fight while their masters do, I have no intention of obeying it but rather will pay whatever penalty is laid on peaceable-minded ones like myself, for I am sure it cannot be more than a couple of pounds of wax,[1] and that would be less expensive than the lint which it would take to heal my head—I can already see it split in two. What's more, it's out of the question

1. In some confraternities, penalties were paid in wax, presumably to make church candles.

for me to fight since I have no sword nor did I ever in my life carry one."

"That," said the one of the Wood, "is something that is easily remedied. I have here two linen bags of the same size. You take one and I'll take the other and we will fight that way, on equal terms."

"So be it, by all means," said Sancho, "for that will simply knock the dust out of us without wounding us."

"But that's not the way it's to be," said the other squire. "Inside the bags, to keep the wind from blowing them away, we will put a half-dozen nice smooth pebbles of the same weight, and so we'll be able to give each other a good pounding without doing ourselves any real harm or damage."

"Body of my father!" cried Sancho, "just look, will you, at the marten and sable and wads of carded cotton that he's stuffing into those bags so that we won't get our heads cracked or our bones crushed to a pulp. But I am telling you, Señor mio, that even though you fill them with silken pellets, I don't mean to fight. Let our masters fight and make the best of it, but as for us, let us drink and live; for time will see to ending our lives without any help on our part by way of bringing them to a close before they have reached their proper season and fall from ripeness."

"Nevertheless," replied the Squire of the Wood, "fight we must, if only for half an hour."

"No," Sancho insisted, "that I will not do. I will not be so impolite or so ungrateful as to pick any quarrel however slight with one whose food and drink I've shared. And, moreover, who in the devil could bring himself to fight in cold blood, when he's not angry or vexed in any way?"

"I can take care of that, right enough," said the one of the Wood. "Before we begin, I will come up to your Grace as nicely as you please and give you three or four punches that will stretch you out at my feet; and that will surely be enough to awaken your anger, even though it's sleeping sounder than a dormouse."

"And I," said Sancho, "have another idea that's every bit as good as yours. I will take a big club, and before your Grace has had a chance to awaken my anger I will put yours to sleep with such mighty whacks that if it wakes at all it will be in the other world; for it is known there that I am not the man to let my face be mussed by anyone, and let each look out for the arrow.[2] But the best thing to do would be to leave one's anger to its slumbers, for no one knows the heart of any other, he who comes for wool may go back shorn, and God bless peace and curse all strife. If a hunted cat when surrounded and cornered turns into a lion, God knows what I who am a man might not become. And so from this time forth I am warning you, Sir Squire, that all the harm and damage that may result from our quarrel will be upon your head."

"Very well," the one of the Wood replied, "God will send the dawn and we shall make out somehow."

At that moment gay-colored birds of all sorts began warbling in the trees and with their merry and varied songs appeared to be greeting and welcoming the fresh-dawning day, which already at the gates and on the balconies of the east was revealing its beautiful face as it shook out from its hair an infinite

---

2. A proverbial expression from archery: let each one take care of his or her own arrow. Other obviously proverbial expressions follow, as is typical of Sancho's speech.

number of liquid pearls. Bathed in this gentle moisture, the grass seemed to shed a pearly spray, the willows distilled a savory manna, the fountains laughed, the brooks murmured, the woods were glad, and the meadows put on their finest raiment. The first thing that Sancho Panza beheld, as soon as it was light enough to tell one object from another, was the Squire of the Wood's nose, which was so big as to cast into the shade all the rest of his body. In addition to being of enormous size, it is said to have been hooked in the middle and all covered with warts of a mulberry hue, like eggplant; it hung down for a couple of inches below his mouth, and the size, color, warts, and shape of this organ gave his face so ugly an appearance that Sancho began trembling hand and foot like a child with convulsions and made up his mind then and there that he would take a couple of hundred punches before he would let his anger be awakened to a point where he would fight with this monster.

Don Quixote in the meanwhile was surveying his opponent, who had already adjusted and closed his helmet so that it was impossible to make out what he looked like. It was apparent, however, that he was not very tall and was stockily built. Over his armor he wore a coat of some kind or other made of what appeared to be the finest cloth of gold, all bespangled with glittering mirrors that resembled little moons and that gave him a most gallant and festive air, while above his helmet were a large number of waving plumes, green, white, and yellow in color. His lance, which was leaning against a tree, was very long and stout and had a steel point of more than a palm in length. Don Quixote took all this in, and from what he observed concluded that his opponent must be of tremendous strength, but he was not for this reason filled with fear as Sancho Panza was. Rather, he proceeded to address the Knight of the Mirrors, quite boldly and in a highbred manner.

"Sir Knight," he said, "if in your eagerness to fight you have not lost your courtesy, I would beg you to be so good as to raise your visor a little in order that I may see if your face is as handsome as your trappings."

"Whether you come out of this emprise the victor or the vanquished, Sir Knight," he of the Mirrors replied, "there will be ample time and opportunity for you to have a sight of me. If I do not now gratify your desire, it is because it seems to me that I should be doing a very great wrong to the beauteous Casildea de Vandalia by wasting the time it would take me to raise my visor before having forced you to confess that I am right in my contention, with which you are well acquainted."

"Well, then," said Don Quixote, "while we are mounting our steeds you might at least inform me if I am that knight of La Mancha whom you say you conquered."

"To that our[3] answer," said he of the Mirrors, "is that you are as like the knight I overcame as one egg is like another; but since you assert that you are persecuted by enchanters, I should not venture to state positively that you are the one in question."

"All of which," said Don Quixote, "is sufficient to convince me that you are laboring under a misapprehension; but in order to relieve you of it once and for all, let them bring our steeds, and in less time than you would spend in lifting your visor, if God, my lady, and my arm give me strength, I will see

---

3. Note the dignified, "majestic" plural form.

your face and you shall see that I am not the vanquished knight you take me to be."

With this, they cut short their conversation and mounted, and, turning Rocinante around, Don Quixote began measuring off the proper length of field for a run against his opponent as he of the Mirrors did the same. But the Knight of La Mancha had not gone twenty paces when he heard his adversary calling to him, whereupon each of them turned halfway and he of the Mirrors spoke.

"I must remind you, Sir Knight," he said, "of the condition under which we fight, which is that the vanquished, as I have said before, shall place himself wholly at the disposition of the victor."

"I am aware of that," replied Don Quixote, "not forgetting the provision that the behest laid upon the vanquished shall not exceed the bounds of chivalry."

"Agreed," said the Knight of the Mirrors.

At that moment Don Quixote caught sight of the other squire's weird nose and was as greatly astonished by it as Sancho had been. Indeed, he took the fellow for some monster, or some new kind of human being wholly unlike those that people this world. As he saw his master riding away down the field preparatory to the tilt, Sancho was alarmed; for he did not like to be left alone with the big-nosed individual, fearing that one powerful swipe of that protuberance against his own nose would end the battle so far as he was concerned and he would be lying stretched out on the ground, from fear if not from the force of the blow.

He accordingly ran after the knight, clinging to one of Rocinante's stirrup straps, and when he thought it was time for Don Quixote to whirl about and bear down upon his opponent, he called to him and said, "Señor mio, I beg your Grace, before you turn for the charge, to help me up into that cork tree yonder where I can watch the encounter which your Grace is going to have with this knight better than I can from the ground and in a way that is much more to my liking."

"I rather think, Sancho," said Don Quixote, "that what you wish to do is to mount a platform where you can see the bulls without any danger to yourself."

"The truth of the matter is," Sancho admitted, "the monstrous nose on that squire has given me such a fright that I don't dare stay near him."

"It is indeed of such a sort," his master assured him, "that if I were not the person I am, I myself should be frightened. And so, come, I will help you up."

While Don Quixote tarried to see Sancho ensconced in the cork tree, the Knight of the Mirrors measured as much ground as seemed to him necessary and then, assuming that his adversary had done the same, without waiting for sound of trumpet or any other signal, he wheeled his horse, which was no swifter nor any more impressive-looking than Rocinante, and bore down upon his enemy at a mild trot; but when he saw that the Manchegan was busy helping his squire, he reined in his mount and came to a stop midway in his course, for which his horse was extremely grateful, being no longer able to stir a single step. To Don Quixote, on the other hand, it seemed as if his enemy was flying, and digging his spurs with all his might into Rocinante's lean flanks he caused that animal to run a bit for the first and only time, according to the history, for on all other occasions a simple trot had represented his utmost speed. And so it was that, with an unheard-of fury, the Knight of the Mournful Countenance came down upon the Knight of the Mirrors as the latter sat there sinking his spurs all the way up to the buttons without being able to persuade his horse to budge a single inch from the spot where he had come to a sudden standstill.

It was at this fortunate moment, while his adversary was in such a predicament, that Don Quixote fell upon him, quite unmindful of the fact that the other knight was having trouble with his mount and either was unable or did not have time to put his lance at rest. The upshot of it was, he encountered him with such force that, much against his will, the Knight of the Mirrors went rolling over his horse's flanks and tumbled to the ground, where as a result of his terrific fall he lay as if dead, without moving hand or foot.

No sooner did Sancho perceive what had happened than he slipped down from the cork tree and ran up as fast as he could to where his master was. Dismounting from Rocinante, Don Quixote now stood over the Knight of the Mirrors, and undoing the helmet straps to see if the man was dead, or to give him air in case he was alive, he beheld—who can say what he beheld without creating astonishment, wonder, and amazement in those who hear the tale? The history tells us that it was the very countenance, form, aspect, physiognomy, effigy, and image of the bachelor Sansón Carrasco!

"Come, Sancho," he cried in a loud voice, "and see what is to be seen but is not to be believed. Hasten, my son, and learn what magic can do and how great is the power of wizards and enchanters."

Sancho came, and the moment his eyes fell on the bachelor Carrasco's face he began crossing and blessing himself a countless number of times. Meanwhile, the overthrown knight gave no signs of life.

"If you ask me, master," said Sancho, "I would say that the best thing for your Grace to do is to run his sword down the mouth of this one who appears to be the bachelor Carrasco; maybe by so doing you would be killing one of your enemies, the enchanters."

"That is not a bad idea," replied Don Quixote, "for the fewer enemies the better." And, drawing his sword, he was about to act upon Sancho's advice and counsel when the Knight of the Mirrors' squire came up to them, now minus the nose which had made him so ugly.

"Look well what you are doing, Don Quixote!" he cried. "The one who lies there at your feet is your Grace's friend, the bachelor Sansón Carrasco, and I am his squire."

"And where is your nose?" inquired Sancho, who was surprised to see him without that deformity.

"Here in my pocket," was the reply. And, thrusting his hand into his coat, he drew out a nose of varnished pasteboard of the make that has been described. Studying him more and more closely, Sancho finally exclaimed, in a voice that was filled with amazement, "Holy Mary preserve me! And is this not my neighbor and crony, Tomé Cecial?"

"That is who I am!" replied the de-nosed squire, "your good friend Tomé Cecial, Sancho Panza. I will tell you presently of the means and snares and falsehoods that brought me here. But, for the present, I beg and entreat your master not to lay hands on, mistreat, wound, or slay the Knight of the Mirrors whom he now has at his feet; for without any doubt it is the rash and ill-advised bachelor Sansón Carrasco, our fellow villager."

The Knight of the Mirrors now recovered consciousness, and, seeing this, Don Quixote at once placed the naked point of his sword above the face of the vanquished one.

"Dead you are, knight," he said, "unless you confess that the peerless Dulcinea del Toboso is more beautiful than your Casildea de Vandalia. And what is more, you will have to promise that, should you survive this encounter and the fall you have had, you will go to the city of El Toboso and present yourself to her in my behalf, that she may do with you as she may see fit. And in case she leaves you free to follow your own will, you are to return to seek me out—the trail of my exploits will serve as a guide to bring you wherever I may be—and tell me all that has taken place between you and her. These conditions are in conformity with those that we arranged before our combat and they do not go beyond the bounds of knight-errantry."

"I confess," said the fallen knight, "that the tattered and filthy shoe of the lady Dulcinea del Toboso is of greater worth than the badly combed if clean beard of Casildea, and I promise to go to her presence and return to yours and to give you a complete and detailed account concerning anything you may wish to know."

"Another thing," added Don Quixote, "that you will have to confess and believe is that the knight you conquered was not and could not have been Don Quixote de la Mancha, but was some other that resembled him, just as I am convinced that you, though you appear to be the bachelor Sansón Carrasco, are another person in his form and likeness who has been put here by my enemies to induce me to restrain and moderate the impetuosity of my wrath and make a gentle use of my glorious victory."

"I confess, think, and feel as you feel, think, and believe," replied the lamed knight. "Permit me to rise, I beg of you, if the jolt I received in my fall will let me do so, for I am in very bad shape."

Don Quixote and Tomé Cecial the squire now helped him to his feet. As for Sancho, he could not take his eyes off Tomé but kept asking him one question after another, and although the answers he received afforded clear enough proof that the man was really his fellow townsman, the fear that had been aroused in him by his master's words—about the enchanters' having transformed the Knight of the Mirrors into the bachelor Sansón Carrasco—prevented him from believing the truth that was apparent to his eyes. The short of it is, both master and servant were left with this delusion as the other ill-errant knight and his squire, in no pleasant state of mind, took their departure with the object of looking for some village where they might be able to apply poultices and splints to the bachelor's battered ribs.

Don Quixote and Sancho then resumed their journey along the road to Saragossa, and here for the time being the history leaves them in order to give an account of who the Knight of the Mirrors and his long-nosed squire really were.

CHAPTER 15

Wherein is told and revealed who the Knight of the Mirrors and his squire were.

Don Quixote went off very happy, self-satisfied, and vainglorious at having achieved a victory over so valiant a knight as he imagined the one of the Mirrors to be, from whose knightly word he hoped to learn whether or not the spell which had been put upon his lady was still in effect; for, unless he chose to forfeit his honor, the vanquished contender must of necessity return and give an account of what had happened in the course of his interview with her. But Don Quixote was of one mind, the Knight of the Mirrors of another, for, as has been stated, the latter's only thought at the moment was to find some village where plasters were available.

The history goes on to state that when the bachelor Sansón Carrasco advised Don Quixote to resume his feats of chivalry, after having desisted from them for a while, this action was taken as the result of a conference which he had held with the curate and the barber as to the means to be adopted in persuading the knight to remain quietly at home and cease agitating himself over his unfortunate adventures. It had been Carrasco's suggestion, to which they had unanimously agreed, that they let Don Quixote sally forth, since it appeared to be impossible to prevent his doing so, and that Sansón should then take to the road as a knight-errant and pick a quarrel and do battle with him. There would be no difficulty about finding a pretext, and then the bachelor knight would overcome him (which was looked upon as easy of accomplishment), having first entered into a pact to the effect that the vanquished should remain at the mercy and bidding of his conqueror. The behest in this case was to be that the fallen one should return to his village and home and not leave it for the space of two years or until further orders were given him, it being a certainty that, once having been overcome, Don Quixote would fulfill the agreement, in order not to contravene or fail to obey the laws of chivalry. And it was possible that in the course of his seclusion he would forget his fancies, or they would at least have an opportunity to seek some suitable cure for his madness.

Sansón agreed to undertake this, and Tomé Cecial, Sancho's friend and neighbor, a merry but featherbrained chap, offered to go along as squire. Sansón then proceeded to arm himself in the manner that has been described, while Tomé disguised his nose with the aforementioned mask so that his crony would not recognize him when they met. Thus equipped, they followed the same route as Don Quixote and had almost caught up with him by the time he had the adventure with the Cart of Death. They finally overtook him in the wood, where those events occurred with which the attentive reader is already familiar; and if it had not been for the knight's extraordinary fancies, which led him to believe that the bachelor was not the bachelor, the said bachelor might have been prevented from ever attaining his degree of licentiate, as a result of having found no nests where he thought to find birds.

Seeing how ill they had succeeded in their undertaking and what an end they had reached, Tomé Cecial now addressed his master.

"Surely, Señor Sansón Carrasco," he said, "we have had our deserts. It is easy enough to plan and embark upon an enterprise, but most of the time it's hard to get out of it. Don Quixote is a madman and we are sane, yet he goes away sound and laughing while your Grace is left here, battered and sorrowful. I wish you would tell me now who is the crazier: the one who is so because he cannot help it, or he who turns crazy of his own free will?"

"The difference between the two," replied Sansón, "lies in this: that the one who cannot help being crazy will be so always, whereas the one who is a madman by choice can leave off being one whenever he so desires."

"Well," said Tomé Cecial, "since that is the way it is, and since I chose to be crazy when I became your Grace's squire, by the same reasoning I now choose to stop being insane and to return to my home."

"That is your affair," said Sansón, "but to imagine that I am going back before I have given Don Quixote a good thrashing is senseless; and what will urge me on now is not any desire to see him recover his wits, but rather a thirst for vengeance; for with the terrible pain that I have in my ribs, you can't expect me to feel very charitable."

Conversing in this manner they kept on until they reached a village where it was their luck to find a bonesetter to take care of poor Sansón. Tomé Cecial then left him and returned home, while the bachelor meditated plans for revenge. The history has more to say of him in due time, but for the present it goes on to make merry with Don Quixote.

CHAPTER 16

Of what happened to Don Quixote upon his meeting with a prudent gentleman of La Mancha.

With that feeling of happiness and vainglorious self-satisfaction that has been mentioned, Don Quixote continued on his way, imagining himself to be, as a result of the victory he had just achieved, the most valiant knight-errant of the age. Whatever adventures might befall him from then on he regarded as already accomplished and brought to a fortunate conclusion. He thought little now of enchanters and enchantments and was unmindful of the innumerable beatings he had received in the course of his knightly wanderings, of the volley of pebbles that had knocked out half his teeth, of the ungratefulness of the galley slaves and the audacity of the Yanguesans whose poles had fallen upon his body like rain. In short, he told himself, if he could but find the means, manner, or way of freeing his lady Dulcinea of the spell that had been put upon her, he would not envy the greatest good fortune that the most fortunate of knights-errant in ages past had ever by any possibility attained.

He was still wholly wrapped up in these thoughts when Sancho spoke to him.

"Isn't it strange, sir, that I can still see in front of my eyes the huge and monstrous nose of my old crony, Tomé Cecial?"

"And do you by any chance believe, Sancho, that the Knight of the Mirrors was the bachelor Sansón Carrasco and that his squire was your friend Tomé?"

"I don't know what to say to that," replied Sancho. "All I know is that the things he told me about my home, my wife and young ones, could not have come from anybody else; and the face, too, once you took the nose away, was the same as Tomé Cecial's, which I have seen many times in our village, right next door to my own house, and the tone of voice was the same also."

"Let us reason the matter out, Sancho," said Don Quixote. "Look at it this way: how can it be thought that the bachelor Sansón Carrasco would come as a knight-errant, equipped with offensive and defensive armor, to contend with me? Am I, perchance, his enemy? Have I given him any occasion to cherish a grudge against me? Am I a rival of his? Or can it be jealousy of the fame I have acquired that has led him to take up the profession of arms?"

"Well, then, sir," Sancho answered him, "how are we to explain the fact that the knight was so like the bachelor and his squire like my friend? And if this was a magic spell, as your Grace has said, was there no other pair in the world whose likeness they might have taken?"

"It is all a scheme and a plot," replied Don Quixote, "on the part of those wicked magicians who are persecuting me and who, foreseeing that I would be the victor in the combat, saw to it that the conquered knight should display the face of my friend the bachelor, so that the affection which I bear him would come between my fallen enemy and the edge of my sword and might of my arm, to temper the righteous indignation of my heart. In that way, he who had sought by falsehood and deceits to take my life, would be left to go on living. As proof of all this, Sancho, experience, which neither lies nor deceives, has already taught you how easy it is for enchanters to change one countenance into another, making the beautiful ugly and the ugly beautiful. It was not two days ago that you beheld the peerless Dulcinea's beauty and elegance in its entirety and natural form, while I saw only the repulsive features of a low and ignorant peasant girl with cataracts over her eyes and a foul smell in her mouth. And if the perverse enchanter was bold enough to effect so vile a transformation as this, there is certainly no cause for wonderment at what he has done in the case of Sansón Carrasco and your friend, all by way of snatching my glorious victory out of my hands. But in spite of it all, I find consolation in the fact that, whatever the shape he may have chosen to assume, I have laid my enemy low."

"God knows what the truth of it all may be," was Sancho's comment. Knowing as he did that Dulcinea's transformation had been due to his own scheming and plotting, he was not taken in by his master's delusions. He was at a loss for a reply, however, lest he say something that would reveal his own trickery.

As they were carrying on this conversation, they were overtaken by a man who, following the same road, was coming along behind them. He was mounted on a handsome flea-bitten mare and wore a hooded greatcoat of fine green cloth trimmed in tawny velvet and a cap of the same material, while the trappings of his steed, which was accoutered for the field, were green and mulberry in hue, his saddle being of the *jineta*[4] mode. From his broad green and gold shoulder strap there dangled a Moorish cutlass, and his half-boots were of the same make as the baldric. His spurs were not gilded but were covered with highly polished green lacquer, so that harmonizing as they did with the rest of his apparel, they seemed more appropriate than if they had been of purest gold. As he came up, he greeted the pair courteously and, spurring his mare, was about to ride on past when Don Quixote called to him.

"Gallant sir," he said, "If your Grace is going our way and is not in a hurry, it would be a favor to us if we might travel together."

"The truth is," replied the stranger, "I should not have ridden past you if I had not been afraid that the company of my mare would excite your horse."

"In that case, sir," Sancho spoke up, "you may as well rein in, for this horse of ours is the most virtuous and well mannered of any that there is. Never on such an occasion has he done anything that was not right—the only time

4. It has a high pommel and short stirrups.

he did misbehave, my master and I suffered for it aplenty. And so, I say again, your Grace may slow up if you like; for even if you offered him your mare on a couple of platters, he'd never try to mount her."

With this, the other traveler drew rein, being greatly astonished at Don Quixote's face and figure. For the knight was now riding along without his helmet, which was carried by Sancho like a piece of luggage on the back of his gray, in front of the packsaddle. If the green-clad gentleman stared hard at his new-found companion, the latter returned his gaze with an even greater intensity. He impressed Don Quixote as being a man of good judgment, around fifty years of age, with hair that was slightly graying and an aquiline nose, while the expression of his countenance was half humorous, half serious. In short, both his person and his accoutrements indicated that he was an individual of some worth.

As for the man in green's impression of Don Quixote de la Mancha, he was thinking that he had never before seen any human being that resembled this one. He could not but marvel at the knight's long neck, his tall frame, and the leanness and the sallowness of his face, as well as his armor and his grave bearing, the whole constituting a sight such as had not been seen for many a day in those parts. Don Quixote in turn was quite conscious of the attentiveness with which the traveler was studying him and could tell from the man's astonished look how curious he was; and so, being very courteous and fond of pleasing everyone, he proceeded to anticipate any questions that might be asked him.

"I am aware," he said, "that my appearance must strike your Grace as being very strange and out of the ordinary, and for that reason I am not surprised at your wonderment. But your Grace will cease to wonder when I tell you, as I am telling you now, that I am a knight, one of those

> Of whom it is folks say,
> They to adventures go.

I have left my native health, mortgaged my estate, given up my comfortable life, and cast myself into fortune's arms for her to do with me what she will. It has been my desire to revive a knight-errantry that is now dead, and for some time past, stumbling here and falling there, now throwing myself down headlong and then rising up once more, I have been able in good part to carry out my design by succoring widows, protecting damsels, and aiding the fallen, the orphans, and the young, all of which is the proper and natural duty of knights-errant. As a result, owing to my many valiant and Christian exploits, I have been deemed worthy of visiting in printed form nearly all the nations of the world. Thirty thousand copies of my history have been published, and, unless Heaven forbid, they will print thirty million of them.

"In short, to put it all into a few words, or even one, I will tell you that I am Don Quixote de la Mancha, otherwise known as the Knight of the Mournful Countenance. Granted that self-praise is degrading, there still are times when I must praise myself, that is to say, when there is no one else present to speak in my behalf. And so, good sir, neither this steed nor this lance nor this buckler nor this squire of mine, nor all the armor that I wear and arms I carry, nor the sallowness of my complexion, nor my leanness and gauntness, should any longer astonish you, now that you know who I am and what the profession is that I follow."

Having thus spoken, Don Quixote fell silent, and the man in green was so slow in replying that it seemed as if he was at a loss for words. Finally, however, after a considerable while, he brought himself to the point of speaking.

"You were correct, Sir Knight," he said, "about my astonishment and my curiosity, but you have not succeeded in removing the wonderment that the sight of you has aroused in me. You say that, knowing who you are, I should not wonder any more, but such is not the case, for I am now more amazed than ever. How can it be that there are knights-errant in the world today and that histories of them are actually printed? I find it hard to convince myself that at the present time there is anyone on earth who goes about aiding widows, protecting damsels, defending the honor of wives, and succoring orphans, and I should never have believed it had I not beheld your Grace with my own eyes. Thank Heaven for that book that your Grace tells me has been published concerning your true and exalted deeds of chivalry, as it should cast into oblivion all the innumerable stories of fictitious knights-errant with which the world is filled, greatly to the detriment of good morals and the prejudice and discredit of legitimate histories."

"As to whether the stories of knights-errant are fictitious or not," observed Don Quixote, "there is much that remains to be said."

"Why," replied the gentleman in green, "is there anyone who can doubt that such tales are false?"

"I doubt it," was the knight's answer, "but let the matter rest there. If our journey lasts long enough, I trust with God's help to be able to show your Grace that you are wrong in going along with those who hold it to be a certainty that they are not true."

From this last remark the traveler was led to suspect that Don Quixote must be some kind of crackbrain, and he was waiting for him to confirm the impression by further observations of the same sort; but before they could get off on another subject, the knight, seeing that he had given an account of his own station in life, turned to the stranger and politely inquired who his companion might be.

"I, Sir Knight of the Mournful Countenance," replied the one in the green-colored greatcoat, "am a gentleman, and a native of the village where, please God, we are going to dine today. I am more than moderately rich, and my name is Don Diego de Miranda. I spend my life with my wife and children and with my friends. My occupations are hunting and fishing, though I keep neither falcon nor hounds but only a tame partridge[5] and a bold ferret or two. I am the owner of about six dozen books, some of them in Spanish, others in Latin, including both histories and devotional works. As for books of chivalry, they have not as yet crossed the threshold of my door. My own preference is for profane rather than devotional writings, such as afford an innocent amusement, charming us by their style and arousing and holding our interest by their inventiveness, although I must say there are very few of that sort to be found in Spain.

"Sometimes," the man in green continued, "I dine with my friends and neighbors, and I often invite them to my house. My meals are wholesome and well prepared and there is always plenty to eat. I do not care for gossip,

5. Used as a decoy.

nor will I permit it in my presence. I am not lynx-eyed and do not pry into the lives and doings of others. I hear mass every day and share my substance with the poor, but make no parade of my good works lest hypocrisy and vainglory, those enemies that so imperceptibly take possession of the most modest heart, should find their way into mine. I try to make peace between those who are at strife. I am the devoted servant of Our Lady, and my trust is in the infinite mercy of God Our Savior."

Sancho had listened most attentively to the gentleman's account of his mode of life, and inasmuch as it seemed to him that this was a good and holy way to live and that the one who followed such a pattern ought to be able to work miracles, he now jumped down from his gray's back and, running over to seize the stranger's right stirrup, began kissing the feet of the man in green with a show of devotion that bordered on tears.

"Why are you doing that, brother?" the gentleman asked him. "What is the meaning of these kisses?"

"Let me kiss your feet," Sancho insisted, "for if I am not mistaken, your Grace is the first saint riding *jineta* fashion that I have seen in all the days of my life."

"I am not a saint," the gentleman assured him, "but a great sinner. It is you, brother, who are the saint; for you must be a good man, judging by the simplicity of heart that you show."

Sancho then went back to his packsaddle, having evoked a laugh from the depths of his master's melancholy and given Don Diego fresh cause for astonishment.

Don Quixote thereupon inquired of the newcomer how many children he had, remarking as he did so that the ancient philosophers, who were without a true knowledge of God, believed that mankind's greatest good lay in the gifts of nature, in those of fortune, and in having many friends and many and worthy sons.

"I, Señor Don Quixote," replied the gentleman, "have a son without whom I should, perhaps, be happier than I am. It is not that he is bad, but rather that he is not as good as I should like him to be. He is eighteen years old, and for six of those years he has been at Salamanca studying the Greek and Latin languages. When I desired him to pass on to other branches of learning, I found him so immersed in the science of Poetry (if it can be called such) that it was not possible to interest him in the Law, which I wanted him to study, nor in Theology, the queen of them all. My wish was that he might be an honor to his family; for in this age in which we are living our monarchs are in the habit of highly rewarding those forms of learning that are good and virtuous, since learning without virtue is like pearls on a dunghill. But he spends the whole day trying to decide whether such and such a verse of Homer's *Iliad* is well conceived or not, whether or not Martial is immodest in a certain epigram, whether certain lines of Vergil are to be understood in this way or in that. In short, he spends all of his time with the books written by those poets whom I have mentioned and with those of Horace, Persius, Juvenal, and Tibullus. As for our own moderns, he sets little store by them, and yet, for all his disdain of Spanish poetry, he is at this moment racking his brains in an effort to compose a gloss on a quatrain that was sent him from Salamanca and which, I fancy, is for some literary tournament."

To all this Don Quixote made the following answer:

"Children, sir, are out of their parents' bowels and so are to be loved whether they be good or bad, just as we love those that gave us life. It is for parents to bring up their offspring, from the time they are infants, in the paths of virtue, good breeding, proper conduct, and Christian morality, in order that, when they are grown, they may be a staff to the old age of the ones that bore them and an honor to their own posterity. As to compelling them to study a particular branch of learning, I am not so sure as to that, though there may be no harm in trying to persuade them to do so. But where there is no need to study *pane lucrando*[6]—where Heaven has provided them with parents that can supply their daily bread—I should be in favor of permitting them to follow that course to which they are most inclined; and although poetry may be more pleasurable than useful, it is not one of those pursuits that bring dishonor upon those who engage in them.

"Poetry in my opinion, my dear sir," he went on, "is a young and tender maid of surpassing beauty, who has many other damsels (that is to say, the other disciplines) whose duty it is to bedeck, embellish, and adorn her. She may call upon all of them for service, and all of them in turn depend upon her nod. She is not one to be rudely handled, nor dragged through the streets, nor exposed at street corners, in the market place, or in the private nooks of palaces. She is fashioned through an alchemy of such power that he who knows how to make use of it will be able to convert her into the purest gold of inestimable price. Possessing her, he must keep her within bounds and not permit her to run wild in bawdy satires or soulless sonnets. She is not to be put up for sale in any manner, unless it be in the form of heroic poems, pity-inspiring tragedies, or pleasing and ingenious comedies. Let mountebanks keep hands off her, and the ignorant mob as well, which is incapable of recognizing or appreciating the treasures that are locked within her. And do not think, sir, that I apply that term 'mob' solely to plebeians and those of low estate; for anyone who is ignorant, whether he be lord or prince, may, and should, be included in the vulgar herd.

"But," Don Quixote continued, "he who possesses the gift of poetry and who makes the use of it that I have indicated, shall become famous and his name shall be honored among all the civilized nations of the world. You have stated, sir, that your son does not greatly care for poetry written in our Spanish tongue, and in that I am inclined to think he is somewhat mistaken. My reason for saying so is this: the great Homer did not write in Latin, for the reason that he was a Greek, and Vergil did not write in Greek since he was a Latin. In a word, all the poets of antiquity wrote in the language which they had imbibed with their mother's milk and did not go searching after foreign ones to express their loftiest conceptions. This being so, it would be well if the same custom were to be adopted by all nations, the German poet being no longer looked down upon because he writes in German, nor the Castilian or the Basque for employing his native speech.

"As for your son, I fancy, sir, that his quarrel is not so much with Spanish poetry as with those poets who have no other tongue or discipline at their command such as would help to awaken their natural gift; and yet, here, too,

6. Earning one's bread (Latin).

he may be wrong. There is an opinion, and a true one, to the effect that 'the poet is born,' that is to say, it is as a poet that he comes forth from his mother's womb, and with the propensity that has been bestowed upon him by Heaven, without study or artifice, he produces those compositions that attest the truth of the line: *'Est deus in nobis,'*[7] etc. I further maintain that the born poet who is aided by art will have a great advantage over the one who by art alone would become a poet, the reason being that art does not go beyond, but merely perfects, nature; and so it is that, by combining nature with art and art with nature, the finished poet is produced.

"In conclusion, then, my dear sir, my advice to you would be to let your son go where his star beckons him; for being a good student as he must be, and having already successfully mounted the first step on the stairway of learning, which is that of languages, he will be able to continue of his own accord to the very peak of humane letters, an accomplishment that is altogether becoming in a gentleman, one that adorns, honors, and distinguishes him as much as the miter does the bishop or his flowing robe the learned jurisconsult. Your Grace well may reprove your son, should he compose satires that reflect upon the honor of other persons; in that case, punish him and tear them up. But should he compose discourses in the manner of Horace, in which he reprehends vice in general as that poet so elegantly does, then praise him by all means; for it is permitted the poet to write verses in which he inveighs against envy and the other vices as well, and to lash out at the vicious without, however, designating any particular individual. On the other hand, there are poets who for the sake of uttering something malicious would run the risk of being banished to the shores of Pontus.[8]

"If the poet be chaste where his own manners are concerned, he would likewise be modest in his verses, for the pen is the tongue of the mind, and whatever thoughts are engendered there are bound to appear in his writings. When kings and princes behold the marvelous art of poetry as practiced by prudent, virtuous, and serious-minded subjects of their realm, they honor, esteem, and reward those persons and crown them with the leaves of the tree that is never struck by lightning[9]—as if to show that those who are crowned and adorned with such wreaths are not to be assailed by anyone."

The gentleman in the green-colored greatcoat was vastly astonished by this speech of Don Quixote's and was rapidly altering the opinion he had previously held, to the effect that his companion was but a crackbrain. In the middle of the long discourse, which was not greatly to his liking, Sancho had left the highway to go seek a little milk from some shepherds who were draining the udders of their ewes near by. Extremely well pleased with the knight's sound sense and excellent reasoning, the gentleman was about to resume the conversation when, raising his head, Don Quixote caught sight of a cart flying royal flags that was coming toward them down the road and, thinking it must be a fresh adventure, began calling to Sancho in a loud voice to bring him his helmet. Whereupon Sancho hastily left the shepherds and spurred his gray until he was once more alongside his master, who was now about to encounter a dreadful and bewildering ordeal.

---

7. There is a god in us (Latin); Ovid's *Fasti* 6.5.   8. As Ovid was by Augustus in 8 C.E.   9. The laurel.

[*"For I Well Know the Meaning of Valor"*]

CHAPTER 17

Wherein Don Quixote's unimaginable courage reaches its highest point, together with the adventure of the lions and its happy ending.

The history relates that, when Don Quixote called to Sancho to bring him his helmet, the squire was busy buying some curds from the shepherds and, flustered by his master's great haste, did not know what to do with them or how to carry them. Having already paid for the curds, he did not care to lose them, and so he decided to put them into the headpiece, and, acting upon this happy inspiration, he returned to see what was wanted of him.

"Give me that helmet," said the knight; "for either I know little about adventures or here is one where I am going to need my armor."

Upon hearing this, the gentleman in the green-colored greatcoat looked around in all directions but could see nothing except the cart that was approaching them, decked out with two or three flags which indicated that the vehicle in question must be conveying his Majesty's property. He remarked as much to Don Quixote, but the latter paid no attention, for he was always convinced that whatever happened to him meant adventures and more adventures.

"Forewarned is forearmed," he said. "I lose nothing by being prepared, knowing as I do that I have enemies both visible and invisible and cannot tell when or where or in what form they will attack me."

Turning to Sancho, he asked for his helmet again, and as there was no time to shake out the curds, the squire had to hand it to him as it was. Don Quixote took it and, without noticing what was in it, hastily clapped it on his head; and forthwith, as a result of the pressure on the curds, the whey began running down all over his face and beard, at which he was very much startled.

"What is this, Sancho?" he cried. "I think my head must be softening or my brains melting, or else I am sweating from head to foot. If sweat it be, I assure you it is not from fear, though I can well believe that the adventure which now awaits me is a terrible one indeed. Give me something with which to wipe my face, if you have anything, for this perspiration is so abundant that it blinds me."

Sancho said nothing but gave him a cloth and at the same time gave thanks to God that his master had not discovered what the trouble was. Don Quixote wiped his face and then took off his helmet to see what it was that made his head feel so cool. Catching sight of that watery white mass, he lifted it to his nose and smelled it.

"By the life of my lady Dulcinea del Toboso!" he exclaimed. "Those are curds that you have put there, you treacherous, brazen, ill-mannered squire!"

To this Sancho replied, very calmly and with a straight face, "If they are curds, give them to me, your Grace, so that I can eat them. But no, let the devil eat them, for he must be the one who did it. Do you think I would be so bold as to soil your Grace's helmet? Upon my word, master, by the understanding that God has given me, I, too, must have enchanters who are persecuting me as your Grace's creature and one of his members, and they are the ones who put that filthy mess there to make you lose your patience and your temper and cause you to whack my ribs as you are in the habit of doing. Well, this time, I must say, they have missed the mark; for I trust my master's good sense to tell him that I have neither curds nor milk nor anything of the kind, and if I did have, I'd put it in my stomach and not in that helmet."

"That may very well be," said Don Quixote.

Don Diego was observing all this and was more astonished than ever, especially when, after he had wiped his head, face, beard, and helmet, Don Quixote once more donned the piece of armor and, settling himself in the stirrups, proceeded to adjust his sword and fix his lance.

"Come what may, here I stand, ready to take on Satan himself in person!" shouted the knight.

The cart with the flags had come up to them by this time, accompanied only by a driver riding one of the mules and a man seated up in front.

"Where are you going, brothers?" Don Quixote called out as he placed himself in the path of the cart. "What conveyance is this, what do you carry in it, and what is the meaning of those flags?"

"The cart is mine," replied the driver, "and in it are two fierce lions in cages which the governor of Oran is sending to court as a present for his Majesty. The flags are those of our lord the King, as a sign that his property goes here."

"And are the lions large?" inquired Don Quixote.

It was the man sitting at the door of the cage who answered him. "The largest," he said, "that ever were sent from Africa to Spain. I am the lion-keeper and I have brought back others, but never any like these. They are male and female. The male is in this first cage, the female in the one behind. They are hungry right now, for they have had nothing to eat today; and so we'd be obliged if your Grace would get out of the way, for we must hasten on to the place where we are to feed them."

"Lion whelps against me?" said Don Quixote with a slight smile. "Lion whelps against me? And at such an hour? Then, by God, those gentlemen who sent them shall see whether I am the man to be frightened by lions. Get down, my good fellow, and since you are the lionkeeper, open the cages and turn those beasts out for me; and in the middle of this plain I will teach them who Don Quixote de la Mancha is, notwithstanding and in spite of the enchanters who are responsible for their being here."

"So," said the gentleman to himself as he heard this, "our worthy knight has revealed himself. It must indeed be true that the curds have softened his skull and mellowed his brains."

At this point Sancho approached him. "For God's sake, sir," he said, "do something to keep my master from fighting those lions. For if he does, they're going to tear us all to bits."

"Is your master, then, so insane," the gentleman asked, "that you fear and believe he means to tackle those fierce animals?"

"It is not that he is insane," replied Sancho, "but, rather, foolhardy."

"Very well," said the gentleman, "I will put a stop to it." And going up to Don Quixote, who was still urging the lionkeeper to open the cages, he said, "Sir Knight, knights-errant should undertake only those adventures that afford some hope of a successful outcome, not those that are utterly hopeless to begin with; for valor when it turns to temerity has in it more of madness than of bravery. Moreover, these lions have no thought of attacking your

Grace but are a present to his Majesty, and it would not be well to detain them or interfere with their journey."

"My dear sir," answered Don Quixote, "you had best go mind your tame partridge and that bold ferret of yours and let each one attend to his own business. This is my affair, and I know whether these gentlemen, the lions, have come to attack me or not." He then turned to the lionkeeper. "I swear, Sir Rascal, if you do not open those cages at once, I'll pin you to the cart with this lance!"

Perceiving how determined the armed phantom was, the driver now spoke up. "Good sir," he said, "will your Grace please be so kind as to let me unhitch the mules and take them to a safe place before you turn those lions loose? For if they kill them for me, I am ruined for life, since the mules and cart are all the property I own."

"O man of little faith!" said Don Quixote. "Get down and unhitch your mules if you like, but you will soon see that it was quite unnecessary and that you might have spared yourself the trouble."

The driver did so, in great haste, as the lionkeeper began shouting, "I want you all to witness that I am being compelled against my will to open the cages and turn the lions out, and I further warn this gentleman that he will be responsible for all the harm and damage the beasts may do, plus my wages and my fees. You other gentlemen take cover before I open the doors; I am sure they will not do any harm to me."

Once more Don Diego sought to persuade his companion not to commit such an act of madness, as it was tempting God to undertake anything so foolish as that; but Don Quixote's only answer was that he knew what he was doing. And when the gentleman in green insisted that he was sure the knight was laboring under a delusion and ought to consider the matter well, the latter cut him short.

"Well, then, sir," he said, "if your Grace does not care to be a spectator at what you believe is going to turn out to be a tragedy, all you have to do is to spur your flea-bitten mare and seek safety."

Hearing this, Sancho with tears in his eyes again begged him to give up the undertaking, in comparison with which the adventure of the windmills and the dreadful one at the fulling mills—indeed, all the exploits his master had ever in the course of his life undertaken—were but bread and cakes.

"Look, sir," Sancho went on, "there is no enchantment here nor anything of the sort. Through the bars and chinks of that cage I have seen a real lion's claw, and judging by the size of it, the lion that it belongs to is bigger than a mountain."

"Fear, at any rate," said Don Quixote, "will make him look bigger to you than half the world. Retire, Sancho, and leave me, and if I die here, you know our ancient pact: you are to repair to Dulcinea—I say no more."

To this he added other remarks that took away any hope they had that he might not go through with his insane plan. The gentleman in the green-colored greatcoat was of a mind to resist him but saw that he was no match for the knight in the matter of arms. Then, too, it did not seem to him the part of wisdom to fight it out with a madman; for Don Quixote now impressed him as being quite mad in every way. Accordingly, while the knight was repeating his threats to the lionkeeper, Don Diego spurred his mare, Sancho his gray, and the driver his mules, all of them seeking to put as great a distance as possible between themselves and the cart before the lions broke loose.

Sancho already was bewailing his master's death, which he was convinced was bound to come from the lions' claws, and at the same time he cursed his fate and called it an unlucky hour in which he had taken it into his head to serve such a one. But despite his tears and lamentations, he did not leave off thrashing his gray in an effort to leave the cart behind them. When the lionkeeper saw that those who had fled were a good distance away, he once more entreated and warned Don Quixote as he had warned and entreated him before, but the answer he received was that he might save his breath as it would do him no good and he had best hurry and obey. In the space of time that it took the keeper to open the first cage, Don Quixote considered the question as to whether it would be well to give battle on foot or on horseback. He finally decided that he would do better on foot, as he feared that Rocinante would become frightened at sight of the lions; and so, leaping down from his horse, he fixed his lance, braced his buckler, and drew his sword, and then advanced with marvelous daring and great resoluteness until he stood directly in front of the cart, meanwhile commending himself to God with all his heart and then to his lady Dulcinea.

Upon reaching this point, the reader should know, the author of our veracious history indulges in the following exclamatory passage:

"O great-souled Don Quixote de la Mancha, thou whose courage is beyond all praise, mirror wherein all the valiant of the world may behold themselves, a new and second Don Manuel de León,[1] once the glory and the honor of Spanish knighthood! With what words shall I relate thy terrifying exploit, how render it credible to the ages that are to come? What eulogies do not belong to thee of right, even though they consist of hyperbole piled upon hyperbole? On foot and singlehanded, intrepid and with greathearted valor, armed but with a sword, and not one of the keen-edged Little Dog[2] make, and with a shield that was not of gleaming and polished steel, thou didst stand and wait for the two fiercest lions that ever the African forests bred! Thy deeds shall be thy praise, O valorous Manchegan; I leave them to speak for thee, since words fail me with which to extol them."

Here the author leaves off his exclamations and resumes the thread of the story.

Seeing Don Quixote posed there before him and perceiving that, unless he wished to incur the bold knight's indignation there was nothing for him to do but release the male lion, the keeper now opened the first cage, and it could be seen at once how extraordinarily big and horribly ugly the beast was. The first thing the recumbent animal did was to turn round, put out a claw, and stretch himself all over. Then he opened his mouth and yawned very slowly, after which he put out a tongue that was nearly two palms in length and with it licked the dust out of his eyes and washed his face. Having done this, he stuck his head outside the cage and gazed about him in all directions. His eyes were now like live coals and his appearance and demeanor were such as to strike terror in temerity itself. But Don Quixote merely stared at him attentively, waiting for him to descend from the cart so

---

1. Don Manuel Ponce de León, a paragon of gallantry and courtesy, from the time of Ferdinand and Isabella.   2. The trademark of a famous armorer of Toledo and Saragossa.

that they could come to grips, for the knight was determined to hack the brute to pieces, such was the extent of his unheard-of madness.

The lion, however, proved to be courteous rather than arrogant and was in no mood for childish bravado. After having gazed first in one direction and then in another, as has been said, he turned his back and presented his hind parts to Don Quixote and then very calmly and peaceably lay down and stretched himself out once more in his cage. At this, Don Quixote ordered the keeper to stir him up with a stick in order to irritate him and drive him out.

"That I will not do," the keeper replied, "for if I stir him, I will be the first one he will tear to bits. Be satisfied with what you have already accomplished, Sir Knight, which leaves nothing more to be said on the score of valor, and do not go tempting your fortune a second time. The door was open and the lion could have gone out if he had chosen; since he has not done so up to now, that means he will stay where he is all day long. Your Grace's stout-heartedness has been well established; for no brave fighter, as I see it, is obliged to do more than challenge his enemy and wait for him in the field; his adversary, if he does not come, is the one who is disgraced and the one who awaits him gains the crown of victory."

"That is the truth," said Don Quixote. "Shut the door, my friend, and bear me witness as best you can with regard to what you have seen me do here. I would have you certify: that you opened the door for the lion, that I waited for him and he did not come out, that I continued to wait and still he stayed there, and finally went back and lay down. I am under no further obligation. Away with enchantments, and God uphold the right, the truth, and true chivalry! So close the door, as I have told you, while I signal to the fugitives in order that they who were not present may hear of this exploit from your lips."

The keeper did as he was commanded, and Don Quixote, taking the cloth with which he had dried his face after the rain of curds, fastened it to the point of his lance and began summoning the runaways, who, all in a body with the gentleman in green bringing up the rear, were still fleeing and turning around to look back at every step. Sancho was the first to see the white cloth.

"May they slay me," he said, "if my master hasn't conquered those fierce beasts, for he's calling to us."

They all stopped and made sure that the one who was doing the signaling was indeed Don Quixote, and then, losing some of their fear, they little by little made their way back to a point where they could distinctly hear what the knight was saying. At last they returned to the cart, and as they drew near Don Quixote spoke to the driver.

"You may come back, brother, hitch your mules, and continue your journey. And you, Sancho, may give each of them two gold crowns to recompense them for the delay they have suffered on my account."

"That I will, right enough," said Sancho. "But what has become of the lions? Are they dead or alive?"

The keeper thereupon, in leisurely fashion and in full detail, proceeded to tell them how the encounter had ended, taking pains to stress to the best of his ability the valor displayed by Don Quixote, at sight of whom the lion had been so cowed that he was unwilling to leave his cage, though the door had been left open quite a while. The fellow went on to state that the knight had wanted him to stir the lion up and force him out, but had finally been convinced that this would be tempting God and so, much to his displeasure and against his will, had permitted the door to be closed.

"What do you think of that, Sancho?" asked Don Quixote. "Are there any spells that can withstand true gallantry? The enchanters may take my luck away, but to deprive me of my strength and courage is an impossibility."

Sancho then bestowed the crowns, the driver hitched his mules, and the lionkeeper kissed Don Quixote's hands for the favor received, promising that, when he reached the court, he would relate this brave exploit to the king himself.

"In that case," replied Don Quixote, "if his Majesty by any chance should inquire who it was that performed it, you are to say that it was the Knight of the Lions; for that is the name by which I wish to be known from now on, thus changing, exchanging, altering, and converting the one I have previously borne, that of Knight of the Mournful Countenance; in which respect I am but following the old custom of knights-errant, who changed their names whenever they liked or found it convenient to do so."

With this, the cart continued on its way, and Don Quixote, Sancho, and the gentleman in the green-colored greatcoat likewise resumed their journey. During all this time Don Diego de Miranda had not uttered a word but was wholly taken up with observing what Don Quixote did and listening to what he had to say. The knight impressed him as being a crazy sane man and an insane one on the verge of sanity. The gentleman did not happen to be familiar with the first part of our history, but if he had read it he would have ceased to wonder at such talk and conduct, for he would then have known what kind of madness this was. Remaining as he did in ignorance of his companion's malady, he took him now for a sensible individual and now for a madman, since what Don Quixote said was coherent, elegantly phrased, and to the point, whereas his actions were nonsensical, foolhardy, and downright silly. What greater madness could there be, Don Diego asked himself, than to don a helmet filled with curds and then persuade oneself that enchanters were softening one's cranium? What could be more rashly absurd than to wish to fight lions by sheer strength alone? He was roused from these thoughts, this inward soliloquy, by the sound of Don Quixote's voice.

"Undoubtedly, Señor Don Diego de Miranda, your Grace must take me for a fool and a madman, am I not right? And it would be small wonder if such were the case, seeing that my deeds give evidence of nothing else. But, nevertheless, I would advise your Grace that I am neither so mad nor so lacking in wit as I must appear to you to be. A gaily caparisoned knight giving a fortunate lance thrust to a fierce bull in the middle of a great square makes a pleasing appearance in the eyes of his king. The same is true of a knight clad in shining armor as he paces the lists in front of the ladies in some joyous tournament. It is true of all those knights who, by means of military exercises or what appear to be such, divert and entertain and, if one may say so, honor the courts of princes. But the best showing of all is made by a knight-errant who, traversing deserts and solitudes, crossroads, forests, and mountains, goes seeking dangerous adventures with the intention of bringing them to a happy and successful conclusion, and solely for the purpose of winning a glorious and enduring renown.

"More impressive, I repeat, is the knight-errant succoring a widow in some unpopulated place than a courtly man of arms making love to a damsel in the city. All knights have their special callings: let the courtier wait upon the ladies and lend luster by his liveries to his sovereign's palace; let him nourish impoverished gentlemen with the splendid fare of his table; let him give tourneys and show himself truly great, generous, and magnificent and a good Christian above all, thus fulfilling his particular obligations. But the knight-errant's case is different.

"Let the latter seek out the nooks and corners of the world; let him enter into the most intricate of labyrinths; let him attempt the impossible at every step; let him endure on desolate highlands the burning rays of the midsummer sun and in winter the harsh inclemencies of wind and frost; let no lions inspire him with fear, no monsters frighten him, no dragons terrify him, for to seek them out, attack them, and conquer them all is his chief and legitimate occupation. Accordingly, I whose lot it is to be numbered among the knights-errant cannot fail to attempt anything that appears to me to fall within the scope of my duties, just as I attacked those lions a while ago even though I knew it to be an exceedingly rash thing to do, for that was a matter that directly concerned me.

"For I well know the meaning of valor: namely, a virtue that lies between the two extremes of cowardice on the one hand and temerity on the other. It is, nonetheless, better for the brave man to carry his bravery to the point of rashness than for him to sink into cowardice. Even as it is easier for the prodigal to become a generous man than it is for the miser, so is it easier for the foolhardy to become truly brave than it is for the coward to attain valor. And in this matter of adventures, you may believe me, Señor Don Diego, it is better to lose by a card too many than a card too few, and 'Such and such a knight is temerarious and overbold' sounds better to the ear than 'That knight is timid and a coward.'"

"I must assure you, Señor Don Quixote," replied Don Diego, "that everything your Grace has said and done will stand the test of reason; and it is my opinion that if the laws and ordinances of knight-errantry were to be lost, they would be found again in your Grace's bosom, which is their depository and storehouse. But it is growing late; let us hasten to my village and my home, where your Grace shall rest from your recent exertions; for if the body is not tired the spirit may be, and that sometimes results in bodily fatigue."

"I accept your offer as a great favor and an honor, Señor Don Diego," was the knight's reply. And, by spurring their mounts more than they had up to then, they arrived at the village around two in the afternoon and came to the house that was occupied by Don Diego, whom Don Quixote had dubbed the Knight of the Green-colored Greatcoat.

[Last Duel]

CHAPTER 64

Which treats of the adventure that caused Don Quixote the most sorrow of all those that have thus far befallen him.

* * * One morning, as Don Quixote went for a ride along the beach,[3] clad in full armor—for, as he was fond of saying, that was his only ornament, his only rest the fight, and, accordingly, he was never without it for a moment— he saw approaching him a horseman similarly arrayed from head to foot and with a brightly shining moon blazoned upon his shield.

As soon as he had come within earshot the stranger cried out to Don Quixote in a loud voice. "O illustrious knight, the never to be sufficiently praised Don Quixote de la Mancha, I am the Knight of the White Moon whose incomparable exploits you will perhaps recall. I come to contend with you and try the might of my arm, with the purpose of having you acknowledge and confess that my lady, whoever she may be, is beyond comparison more beautiful than your own Dulcinea del Toboso. If you will admit the truth of this fully and freely, you will escape death and I shall be spared the trouble of inflicting it upon you. On the other hand, if you choose to fight and I should overcome you, I ask no other satisfaction than that, laying down your arms and seeking no further adventures, you retire to your own village for the space of a year, during which time you are not to lay hand to sword but are to dwell peacefully and tranquilly, enjoying a beneficial rest that shall redound to the betterment of your worldly fortunes and the salvation of your soul. But if you are the victor, then my head shall be at your disposal, my arms and steed shall be the spoils, and the fame of my exploits shall go to increase your own renown. Consider well which is the better course and let me have your answer at once, for today is all the time I have for the dispatching of this business."

Don Quixote was amazed at the knight's arrogance as well as at the nature of the challenge, but it was with a calm and stern demeanor that he replied to him.

"Knight of the White Moon," he said, "of whose exploits up to now I have never heard, I will venture to take an oath that you have not once laid eyes upon the illustrious Dulcinea; for I am quite certain that if you had beheld her you would not be staking your all upon such an issue, since the sight of her would have convinced you that there never has been, and never can be, any beauty to compare with hers. I do not say that you lie, I simply say that you are mistaken; and so I accept your challenge with the conditions you have laid down, and at once, before this day you have fixed upon shall have ended. The only exception I make is with regard to the fame of your deeds being added to my renown, since I do not know what the character of your exploits has been and am quite content with my own, such as they are. Take, then, whichever side of the field you like, and I will take up my position, and may St. Peter bless what God may give."

3. Don Quixote and Sancho, after numberless encounters and experiences (of which the most prominent have been Don Quixote's descent into the cave of Montesinos and their residence at the castle of the playful ducal couple who give Sancho the "governorship of an island" for ten days), are now in Barcelona. Famous as they are, they meet the viceroy and the nobles; their host is Don Antonio Moreno, "a gentleman of wealth and discernment who was fond of amusing himself in an innocent and kindly way."

Now, as it happened, the Knight of the White Moon was seen by some of the townspeople, who informed the viceroy that he was there, talking to Don Quixote de la Mancha. Believing this to be a new adventure arranged by Don Antonio Moreno or some other gentleman of the place, the viceroy at once hastened down to the beach, accompanied by a large retinue, including Don Antonio, and they arrived just as Don Quixote was wheeling Rocinante to measure off the necessary stretch of field. When the viceroy perceived that they were about to engage in combat, he at once interposed and inquired of them what it was that impelled them thus to do battle all of a sudden.

The Knight of the White Moon replied that it was a matter of beauty and precedence and briefly repeated what he had said to Don Quixote, explaining the terms to which both parties had agreed. The viceroy then went up to Don Antonio and asked him if he knew any such knight as this or if it was some joke that they were playing, but the answer that he received left him more puzzled than ever; for Don Antonio did not know who the knight was, nor could he say as to whether this was a real encounter or not. The viceroy, accordingly, was doubtful about letting them proceed, but inasmuch as he could not bring himself to believe that it was anything more than a jest, he withdrew to one side, saying, "Sir Knights, if there is nothing for it but to confess or die, and if Señor Don Quixote's mind is made up and your Grace, the Knight of the White Moon, is even more firmly resolved, then fall to it in the name of God and may He bestow the victory."

The Knight of the White Moon thanked the viceroy most courteously and in well-chosen words for the permission which had been granted them, and Don Quixote did the same, whereupon the latter, commending himself with all his heart to Heaven and to his lady Dulcinea, as was his custom at the beginning of a fray, fell back a little farther down the field as he saw his adversary doing the same. And then, without blare of trumpet or other warlike instrument to give them the signal for the attack, both at the same instant wheeled their steeds about and returned for the charge. Being mounted upon the swifter horse, the Knight of the White Moon met Don Quixote two-thirds of the way and with such tremendous force that, without touching his opponent with his lance (which, it seemed, he deliberately held aloft) he brought both Rocinante and his rider to the ground in an exceedingly perilous fall. At once the victor leaped down and placed his lance at Don Quixote's visor.

"You are vanquished, O knight! Nay, more, you are dead unless you make confession in accordance with the conditions governing our encounter."

Stunned and battered, Don Quixote did not so much as raise his visor but in a faint, wan voice, as if speaking from the grave, he said, "Dulcinea del Toboso is the most beautiful woman in the world and I the most unhappy knight upon the face of this earth. It is not right that my weakness should serve to defraud the truth. Drive home your lance, O knight, and take my life since you already have deprived me of my honor."

"That I most certainly shall not do," said the one of the White Moon. "Let the fame of my lady Dulcinea del Toboso's beauty live on undiminished. As for me, I shall be content if the great Don Quixote will retire to his village for a year or until such a time as I may specify, as was agreed upon between us before joining battle."

The viceroy, Don Antonio, and all the many others who were present heard this, and they also heard Don Quixote's response, which was to the effect that, seeing nothing was asked of him that was prejudicial to Dulcinea, he would fulfill all the other conditions like a true and punctilious knight. The one of the White Moon thereupon turned and with a bow to the viceroy rode back to the city at a mild canter. The viceroy promptly dispatched Don Antonio to follow him and make every effort to find out who he was; and, in the meanwhile, they lifted Don Quixote up and uncovered his face, which held no sign of color and was bathed in perspiration. Rocinante, however, was in so sorry a state that he was unable to stir for the present.

Brokenhearted over the turn that events had taken, Sancho did not know what to say or do. It seemed to him that all this was something that was happening in a dream and that everything was the result of magic. He saw his master surrender, heard him consent not to take up arms again for a year to come as the light of his glorious exploits faded into darkness. At the same time his own hopes, based upon the fresh promises that had been made him, were whirled away like smoke before the wind. He feared that Rocinante was maimed for life, his master's bones permanently dislocated—it would have been a bit of luck if his madness also had been jolted out of him.[4]

Finally, in a hand litter which the viceroy had them bring, they bore the knight back to town. The viceroy himself then returned, for he was very anxious to ascertain who the Knight of the White Moon was who had left Don Quixote in so lamentable a condition.

CHAPTER 65

Wherein is revealed who the Knight of the White Moon was.

The Knight of the White Moon was followed not only by Don Antonio Moreno, but by a throng of small boys as well, who kept after him until the doors of one of the city's hostelries had closed behind him. A squire came out to meet him and remove his armor, for which purpose the victor proceeded to shut himself up in a lower room, in the company of Don Antonio, who had also entered the inn and whose bread would not bake until he had learned the knight's identity. Perceiving that the gentleman had no intention of leaving him, he of the White Moon then spoke.

"Sir," he said, "I am well aware that you have come to find out who I am; and, seeing that there is no denying you the information that you seek, while my servant here is removing my armor I will tell you the exact truth of the matter. I would have you know, sir, that I am the bachelor Sansón Carrasco from the same village as Don Quixote de la Mancha, whose madness and absurdities inspire pity in all of us who know him and in none more than me. And so, being convinced that his salvation lay in his returning home for a period of rest in his own house, I formed a plan for bringing him back.

"It was three months ago that I took to the road as a knight-errant, calling myself the Knight of the Mirrors, with the object of fighting and overcoming him without doing him any harm, intending first to lay down the condition that the vanquished was to yield to the victor's will. What I meant to ask of him—for I looked upon him as conquered from the start—was that he should return to his village and not leave it for a whole year, in the course of which

---

4. The Spanish has an untranslatable pun on *deslocado,* which means "out of joint" ("dislocated") and also "cured of madness" (from *loco,* "mad").

time he might be cured. Fate, however, ordained things otherwise; for he was the one who conquered me and overthrew me from my horse, and thus my plan came to naught. He continued on his wanderings, and I went home, defeated, humiliated, and bruised from my fall, which was quite a dangerous one. But I did not for this reason give up the idea of hunting him up once more and vanquishing him as you have seen me do today.

"Since he is the soul of honor when it comes to observing the ordinances of knight-errantry, there is not the slightest doubt that he will keep the promise he has given me and fulfill his obligations. And that, sir, is all that I need to tell you concerning what has happened. I beg you not to disclose my secret or reveal my identity to Don Quixote, in order that my well-intentioned scheme may be carried out and a man of excellent judgment be brought back to his senses—for a sensible man he would be, once rid of the follies of chivalry."

"My dear sir," exclaimed Don Antonio, "may God forgive you for the wrong you have done the world by seeking to deprive it of its most charming madman! Do you not see that the benefit accomplished by restoring Don Quixote to his senses can never equal the pleasure which others derive from his vagaries? But it is my opinion that all the trouble to which the Señor Bachelor has put himself will not suffice to cure a man who is so hopelessly insane; and if it were not uncharitable, I would say let Don Quixote never be cured, since with his return to health we lose not only his own drolleries but also those of his squire, Sancho Panza, for either of the two is capable of turning melancholy itself into joy and merriment. Nevertheless, I will keep silent and tell him nothing, that I may see whether or not I am right in my suspicion that Señor Carrasco's efforts will prove to have been of no avail."

The bachelor replied that, all in all, things looked very favorable and he hoped for a fortunate outcome. With this, he took his leave of Don Antonio, after offering to render him any service that he could; and, having had his armor tied up and placed upon a mule's back, he rode out of the city that same day on the same horse on which he had gone into battle, returning to his native province without anything happening to him that is worthy of being set down in this veracious chronicle.

[Homecoming and Death]

CHAPTER 73

Of the omens that Don Quixote encountered upon entering his village, with other incidents that embellish and lend credence to this great history.

As they entered the village, Cid Hamete informs us, Don Quixote caught sight of two lads on the communal threshing floor who were engaged in a dispute.

"Don't let it worry you, Periquillo," one of them was saying to the other; "you'll never lay eyes on it again as long as you live."

Hearing this, Don Quixote turned to Sancho. "Did you mark what that boy said, my friend?" he asked. " 'You'll never lay eyes on it[5] again . . .' "

"Well," replied Sancho, "what difference does it make what he said?"

---

5. The same as *her* in the Spanish, because the reference is to a cricket cage, which is a feminine noun. Hence Don Quixote's inference concerning Dulcinea.

"What difference?" said Don Quixote. "Don't you see that, applied to the one I love, it means I shall never again see Dulcinea."

Sancho was about to answer him when his attention was distracted by a hare that came flying across the fields pursued by a large number of hunters with their greyhounds. The frightened animal took refuge by huddling down beneath the donkey, whereupon Sancho reached out his hand and caught it and presented it to his master.

"*Malum signum, malum signum,*"[6] the knight was muttering to himself. "A hare flees, the hounds pursue it, Dulcinea appears not."

"It is very strange to hear your Grace talk like that," said Sancho. "Let us suppose that this hare *is* Dulcinea del Toboso and the hounds pursuing it are those wicked enchanters that transformed her into a peasant lass; she flees, I catch her and turn her over to your Grace, you hold her in your arms and caress her. Is that a bad sign? What ill omen can you find in it?"

The two lads who had been quarreling now came up to have a look at the hare, and Sancho asked them what their dispute was about. To this the one who had uttered the words "You'll never lay eyes on it again as long as you live," replied that he had taken a cricket cage from the other boy and had no intention of returning it ever. Sancho then brought out from his pocket four cuartos and gave them to the lad in exchange for the cage, which he placed in Don Quixote's hands.

"There, master," he said, "these omens are broken and destroyed, and to my way of thinking, even though I may be a dunce, they have no more to do with what is going to happen to us than the clouds of yesteryear. If I am not mistaken, I have heard our curate say that sensible persons of the Christian faith should pay no heed to such foolish things, and you yourself in the past have given me to understand that all those Christians who are guided by omens are fools. But there is no need to waste a lot of words on the subject; come, let us go on and enter our village."

The hunters at this point came up and asked for the hare, and Don Quixote gave it to them. Continuing on their way, the returning pair encountered the curate and the bachelor Carrrasco, who were strolling in a small meadow on the outskirts of the town as they read their breviaries. And here it should be mentioned that Sancho Panza, by way of sumpter cloth, had thrown over his gray and the bundle of armor it bore the flame-covered buckram robe in which they had dressed the squire at the duke's castle, on the night that witnessed Altisidora's[7] resurrection; and he had also fitted the miter over the donkey's head, the result being the weirdest transformation and the most bizarrely appareled ass that ever were seen in this world. The curate and the bachelor recognized the pair at once and came forward to receive them with open arms. Don Quixote dismounted and gave them both a warm embrace; meanwhile, the small boys (boys are like lynxes in that nothing escapes them), having spied the ass's miter, ran up for a closer view.

"Come, lads," they cried, "and see Sancho Panza's ass trigged out finer than Mingo,[8] and Don Quixote's beast is skinnier than ever!"

Finally, surrounded by the urchins and accompanied by the curate and the bachelor, they entered the village and made their way to Don Quixote's

6. Meeting a hare is considered an ill omen (Latin)—that is, a bad sign.   7. A girl in the duke's castle, where Don Quixote and Sancho were guests for a time. She dramatically pretended to be in love with Don Quixote.   8. The allusion is to the opening lines of *Mingo Revulgo* (15th century), a satire.

house, where they found the housekeeper and the niece standing in the doorway, for the news of their return had preceded them. Teresa Panza, Sancho's wife, had also heard of it, and, half naked and disheveled, dragging her daughter Sanchica by the hand, she hastened to greet her husband and was disappointed when she saw him, for he did not look to her as well fitted out as a governor ought to be.

"How does it come, my husband," she said, "that you return like this, tramping and footsore? You look more like a vagabond than you do like a governor."

"Be quiet, Teresa," Sancho admonished her, "for very often there are stakes where there is no bacon. Come on home with me and you will hear marvels. I am bringing money with me, which is the thing that matters, money earned by my own efforts and without harm to anyone."

"You just bring along the money, my good husband," said Teresa, "and whether you got it here or there, or by whatever means, you will not be introducing any new custom into the world."

Sanchica then embraced her father and asked him if he had brought her anything, for she had been looking forward to his coming as to the showers in May. And so, with his wife holding him by the hand while his daughter kept one arm about his waist and at the same time led the gray, Sancho went home, leaving Don Quixote under his own roof in the company of niece and housekeeper, the curate and the barber.

Without regard to time or season, the knight at once drew his guests to one side and in a few words informed them of how he had been overcome in battle and had given his promise not to leave his village for a year, a promise that he meant to observe most scrupulously, without violating it in the slightest degree, as every knight-errant was obliged to do by the laws of chivalry. He accordingly meant to spend that year as a shepherd,[9] he said, amid the solitude of the fields, where he might give free rein to his amorous fancies as he practiced the virtues of the pastoral life; and he further begged them, if they were not too greatly occupied and more urgent matters did not prevent their doing so, to consent to be his companions. He would purchase a flock sufficiently large to justify their calling themselves shepherds; and, moreover, he would have them know, the most important thing of all had been taken care of, for he had hit upon names that would suit them marvelously well. When the curate asked him what these names were, Don Quixote replied that he himself would be known as "the shepherd Quixotiz," the bachelor as "the shepherd Carrascón," the curate as "the shepherd Curiambro," and Sancho Panza as "the shepherd Pancino."

Both his listeners were dismayed at the new form which his madness had assumed. However, in order that he might not go faring forth from the village on another of his expeditions (for they hoped that in the course of the year he would be cured), they decided to fall in with his new plan and approve it as being a wise one, and they even agreed to be his companions in the calling he proposed to adopt.

"What's more," remarked Sansón Carrasco, "I am a very famous poet, as everyone knows, and at every turn I will be composing pastoral or courtly verses or whatever may come to mind, by way of a diversion for us as we

9. Because the knight-errant's life has been forbidden him by his defeat, Don Quixote for a time plans to live according to another and no less "literary" code, that of the pastoral. The following paragraphs, especially through the bachelor Carrasco, refer humorously to some of the conventions of pastoral literature.

wander in those lonely places; but what is most necessary of all, my dear sirs, is that each one of us should choose the name of the shepherd lass to whom he means to dedicate his songs, so that we may not leave a tree, however hard its bark may be, where their names are not inscribed and engraved as is the custom with lovelorn shepherds."

"That is exactly what we should do," replied Don Quixote, "although, for my part, I am relieved of the necessity of looking for an imaginary shepherdess, seeing that I have the peerless Dulcinea del Toboso, glory of these brookside regions, adornment of these meadows, beauty's mainstay, cream of the Graces—in short, one to whom all praise is well becoming however hyperbolical it may be."

"That is right," said the curate, "but we will seek out some shepherd maids that are easily handled, who if they do not square with us will fit in the corners."

"And," added Sansón Carrasco, "if we run out of names we will give them those that we find printed in books the world over: such as Fílida, Amarilis, Diana, Flérida, Galatea, and Belisarda; for since these are for sale in the market place, we can buy them and make them our own. If my lady, or, rather, my shepherdess, should be chance be called Ana, I will celebrate her charms under the name of Anarda; if she is Francisca, she will become Francenia; if Lucía, Luscinda; for it all amounts to the same thing. And Sancho Panza, if he enters this confraternity, may compose verses to his wife, Teresa Panza, under the name of Teresaina."

Don Quixote had to laugh at this, and the curate then went on to heap extravagant praise upon him for his noble resolution which did him so much credit, and once again he offered to keep the knight company whenever he could spare the time from the duties of his office. With this, they took their leave of him, advising and beseeching him to take care of his health and to eat plentifully of the proper food.

As fate would have it, the niece and the housekeeper had overheard the conversation of the three men, and as soon as the visitors had left they both descended upon Don Quixote.

"What is the meaning of this, my uncle? Here we were thinking your Grace had come home to lead a quiet and respectable life, and do you mean to tell us you are going to get yourself involved in fresh complications—

> Young shepherd, thou who comest here,
> Young shepherd, thou who goest there . . . [1]

For, to tell the truth, the barley is too hard now to make shepherds' pipes of it."[2]

"And how," said the housekeeper, "is your Grace going to stand the midday heat in summer, the winter cold, the howling of the wolves out there in the fields? You certainly cannot endure it. That is an occupation for robust men, cut out and bred for such a calling almost from their swaddling clothes. Setting one evil over against another, it is better to be a knight-errant than a shepherd. Look, sir, take my advice, for I am not stuffed with bread and wine when I give it to you but am fasting and am going on fifty years of age: stay at home, attend to your affairs, go often to confession, be charitable to the poor, and let it be upon my soul if any harm comes to you as a result of it."

1. From a ballad. 2. A proverb.

"Be quiet, daughters," said Don Quixote. "I know very well what I must do. Take me up to bed, for I do not feel very well; and you may be sure of one thing: whether I am a knight-errant now or a shepherd to be, I never will fail to look after your needs as you will see when the time comes."

And good daughters that they unquestionably were, the housekeeper and the niece helped him up to bed, where they gave him something to eat and made him as comfortable as they could.

CHAPTER 74

Of how Don Quixote fell sick, of the will that he made, and of the manner of his death.

Inasmuch as nothing that is human is eternal but is ever declining from its beginning to its close, this being especially true of the lives of men, and since Don Quixote was not endowed by Heaven with the privilege of staying the downward course of things, his own end came when he was least expecting it. Whether it was owing to melancholy occasioned by the defeat he had suffered, or was, simply, the will of Heaven which had so ordained it, he was taken with a fever that kept him in bed for a week, during which time his friends, the curate, the bachelor, and the barber, visited him frequently, while Sancho Panza, his faithful squire, never left his bedside.

Believing that the knight's condition was due to sorrow over his downfall and disappointment at not having been able to accomplish the disenchantment and liberation of Dulcinea, Sancho and the others endeavored to cheer him up in every possible way. The bachelor urged him to take heart and get up from bed that he might begin his pastoral life, adding that he himself had already composed an eclogue that would cast in the shade all that Sannazaro[3] had ever written, and had purchased with his own money from a herdsman of Quintanar two fine dogs to guard the flock, one of them named Barcino and the other Butrón. All this, however, did not serve to relieve Don Quixote's sadness; whereupon his friends called in the doctor, who took his pulse and was not very well satisfied with it. In any case, the physician told them, they should attend to the health of his soul as that of his body was in grave danger.

Don Quixote received this news calmly enough, but not so his housekeeper, niece, and squire, who began weeping bitterly, as if he were already lying dead in front of them. It was the doctor's opinion that melancholy and depression were putting an end to his patient's life. The knight then requested them to leave him alone as he wished to sleep a little, and they complied. He slept for more than six hours at a stretch, as the saying is, and so soundly that the housekeeper and niece thought he would never wake.

At last he did, however, and at once cried out in a loud voice, "Blessed be Almighty God who has given me so many blessings! Truly His mercy is boundless and is not limited or restrained by the sins of men."

The niece listened carefully to what her uncle said, and it seemed to her that he was speaking more rationally than was his wont, at least during his illness.

"Sir," she said to him, "what does your Grace mean? Has something occurred that we know nothing about? What is this talk of mercy and sins?"

---

3. Jacopo Sannazaro (1456–1530), Italian poet, whose *Arcadia* is one of the milestones in the pastoral tradition.

"The mercy that I speak of," replied Don Quixote, "is that which God is showing me at this moment—in spite of my sins, as I have said. My mind now is clear, unencumbered by those misty shadows of ignorance that were cast over it by my bitter and continual reading of those hateful books of chivalry. I see through all the nonsense and fraud contained in them, and my only regret is that my disillusionment has come so late, leaving me no time to make any sort of amends by reading those that are the light of the soul. I find myself, niece, at the point of death, and I would die in such a way as not to leave the impression of a life so bad that I shall be remembered as a madman; for even though I have been one, I do not wish to confirm it on my deathbed. And so, my dear, call in my good friends: the curate, the bachelor Sansón Carrasco, and Master Nicholas the barber; for I want to confess my sins and make my last will and testament."

The niece, however, was relieved of this errand, for the three of them came in just then.

"I have good news for you, kind sirs," said Don Quixote the moment he saw them. "I am no longer Don Quixote de la Mancha but Alonso Quijano, whose mode of life won for him the name of 'Good.' I am the enemy of Amadis of Gaul and all his innumerable progeny; for those profane stories dealing with knight-errantry are odious to me, and I realize how foolish I was and the danger I courted in reading them; but I am in my right senses now and I abominate them."

Hearing this, they all three were convinced that some new kind of madness must have laid hold of him.

"Why, Señor Don Quixote!" exclaimed Sansón. "What makes you talk like that, just when we have received news that my lady Dulcinea is disenchanted? And just when we are on the verge of becoming shepherds so that we may spend the rest of our lives in singing like a lot of princes, why does your Grace choose to turn hermit? Say no more, in Heaven's name, but be sensible and forget these idle tales."

"Tales of that kind," said Don Quixote, "have been the truth for me in the past, and to my detriment, but with Heaven's aid I trust to turn them to my profit now that I am dying. For I feel, gentlemen, that death is very near; so, leave all jesting aside and bring me a confessor for my sins and a notary to draw up my will. In such straits as these a man cannot trifle with his soul. Accordingly, while the Señor Curate is hearing my confession, let the notary be summoned."

Amazed at his words, they gazed at one another in some perplexity, yet they could not but believe him. One of the signs that led them to think he was dying was this quick return from madness to sanity and all the additional things he had to say, so well reasoned and well put and so becoming in a Christian that none of them could any longer doubt that he was in full possession of his faculties. Sending the others out of the room, the curate stayed behind to confess him, and before long the bachelor returned with the notary and Sancho Panza, who had been informed of his master's condition, and who, finding the housekeeper and the niece in tears, began weeping with them. When the confession was over, the curate came out.

"It is true enough," he said, "that Alonso Quijano the Good is dying, and it is also true that he is a sane man. It would be well for us to go in now while he makes his will."

At this news the housekeeper, niece, and the good squire Sancho Panza were so overcome with emotion that the tears burst forth from their eyes and their bosoms heaved with sobs; for, as has been stated more than once, whether Don Quixote was plain Alonso Quijano the Good or Don Quixote de la Mancha, he was always of a kindly and pleasant disposition and for this reason was beloved not only by the members of his household but by all who knew him.

The notary had entered along with the others, and as soon as the preamble had been attended to and the dying man had commended his soul to his Maker with all those Christian formalities that are called for in such a case, they came to the matter of bequests, with Don Quixote dictating as follows:

"ITEM. With regard to Sancho Panza, whom, in my madness, I appointed to be my squire, and who has in his possession a certain sum of money belonging to me: inasmuch as there has been a standing account between us, of debits and credits, it is my will that he shall not be asked to give any accounting whatsoever of this sum, but if any be left over after he has had payment for what I owe him, the balance, which will amount to very little, shall be his, and much good may it do him. If when I was mad I was responsible for his being given the governorship of an island, now that I am of sound mind I would present him with a kingdom if it were in my power, for his simplicity of mind and loyal conduct merit no less."

At this point he turned to Sancho. "Forgive me, my friend," he said, "for having caused you to appear as mad as I by leading you to fall into the same error, that of believing that there are still knights-errant in the world."

"Ah, master," cried Sancho through his tears, "don't die, your Grace, but take my advice and go on living for many years to come; for the greatest madness that a man can be guilty of in this life is to die without good reason, without anyone's killing him, slain only by the hands of melancholy. Look you, don't be lazy but get up from this bed and let us go out into the fields clad as shepherds as we agreed to do. Who knows but behind some bush we may come upon the lady Dulcinea, as disenchanted as you could wish. If it is because of worry over your defeat that you are dying, put the blame on me by saying that the reason for your being overthrown was that I had not properly fastened Rocinante's girth. For the matter of that, your Grace knows from reading your books of chivalry that it is a common thing for certain knights to overthrow others, and he who is vanquished today will be the victor tomorrow."

"That is right," said Sansón, "the worthy Sancho speaks the truth."

"Not so fast, gentlemen," said Don Quixote. "In last year's nests there are no birds this year. I was mad and now I am sane; I was Don Quixote de la Mancha, and now I am, as I have said, Alonso Quijano the Good. May my repentance and the truth I now speak restore to me the place I once held in your esteem. And now, let the notary proceed:

"ITEM. I bequeath my entire estate, without reservation, to my niece Antonia Quijana, here present, after the necessary deductions shall have been made from the most available portion of it to satisfy the bequests that I have stipulated. The first payment shall be to my housekeeper for the wages due her, with twenty ducats over to buy her a dress. And I hereby appoint the Señor Curate and the Señor Bachelor Sansón Carrasco to be my executors.

"ITEM. It is my will that if my niece Antonia Quijana should see fit to marry, it shall be to a man who does not know what books of chivalry are; and if it shall be established that he is acquainted with such books and my niece still insists on marrying him, then she shall lose all that I have bequeathed her and my executors shall apply her portion to works of charity as they may see fit.

"ITEM. I entreat the aforementioned gentlemen, my executors, if by good fortune they should come to know the author who is said to have composed a history now going the rounds under the title of *Second Part of the Exploits of Don Quixote de la Mancha,* to beg his forgiveness in my behalf, as earnestly as they can, since it was I who unthinkingly led him to set down so many and such great absurdities as are to be found in it; for I leave this life with a feeling of remorse at having provided him with the occasion for putting them into writing."

The will ended here, and Don Quixote, stretching himself at length in the bed, fainted away. They all were alarmed at this and hastened to aid him. The same thing happened very frequently in the course of the three days of life that remained to him after he had made his will. The household was in a state of excitement, but with it all the niece continued to eat her meals, the housekeeper had her drink, and Sancho Panza was in good spirits; for this business of inheriting property effaces or mitigates the sorrow which the heir ought to feel and causes him to forget.

Death came at last for Don Quixote, after he had received all the sacraments and once more, with many forceful arguments, had expressed his abomination of books of chivalry. The notary who was present remarked that in none of those books had he read of any knight-errant dying in his own bed so peacefully and in so Christian a manner. And thus, amid the tears and lamentations of those present, he gave up the ghost; that is to say, he died. Perceiving that their friend was no more, the curate asked the notary to be a witness to the fact that Alonso Quijano the Good, commonly known as Don Quixote, was truly dead, this being necessary in order that some author other than Cid Hamete Benengeli might not have the opportunity of falsely resurrecting him and writing endless histories of his exploits.

Such was the end of the Ingenious Gentleman of La Mancha, whose birthplace Cid Hamete was unwilling to designate exactly in order that all the towns and villages of La Mancha might contend among themselves for the right to adopt him and claim him as their own, just as the seven cities of Greece did in the case of Homer. The lamentations of Sancho and those of Don Quixote's niece and his housekeeper, as well as the original epitaphs that were composed for his tomb, will not be recorded here, but mention may be made of the verses by Sansón Carrasco:

> Here lies a gentleman bold
> Who was so very brave
> He went to lengths untold,
> And on the brink of the grave
> Death had on him no hold. 5
> By the world he set small store—
> He frightened it to the core—
> Yet somehow, by Fate's plan,
> Though he'd lived a crazy man,
> When he died he was sane once more. 10

LOPE DE VEGA
1562–1635

One of the great dramatists of the Spanish golden age, Lope Félix de Vega Carpio achieved such enormous popularity and admiration that his very name became a synonym for excellence. The impact of his art on drama was no less impressive: his method of composing three-act plays with comic or serious subplots came to dominate Spanish drama well into the eighteenth century. The importance of his dramatic legacy far exceeded his own estimation of it: Lope did not consider plays to be serious art and openly admitted that he wrote for money and for the pleasure of the people. He claimed to have composed some fifteen hundred plays (an early biographer puts the figure at eighteen hundred), and many of the thousands of characters he created were based on favorite types he frequently recycled.

Born in Madrid, Lope led a life spectacularly complicated by his three passionate loves: women, religion, and Spain, which was emerging as a nation. Married twice, Lope had at least sixteen children (six in wedlock) and affairs so numerous that some biographical sketches arrange his life by his serial (and overlapping) cohabitation with the women he celebrated in verse. Religious faith played a serious role in his private and public lives: Lope took holy orders in 1614, was elected a judge by the Spanish Inquisition, and served as an official censor. In 1622 Pope Urban VIII made him a member of the Order of St. John of Jerusalem and an honorary doctor of theology. His career in the Church and participation in the Inquisition suggest how intimately tied religious and national feeling were in Lope's mind. His devotion to Spain also led him to fight in two battles, one of them against England with the Spanish Armada. When he died in 1635, the nation mourned him with a nine-day funeral in Madrid.

Lope's dramatic art reflects his various passions. He wrote brilliant sacred plays in addition to his comedies. He created strong female characters, such as Laurencia, the heroine of the play presented in this anthology: she not only makes the most influential speech in a town council but also, when she turns from politics to romance, speaks a complete sonnet (she is the only female character in the history of Spanish drama to do so). Lope's efforts to link his plays to the idea of Spain as a nation are, perhaps, the clearest evidence of a consistent dramatic project in his many plays. He believed that plays should deal with historically important issues, such as "the events, wars, peace, counsels, fortune, change, prosperity, the decline of kingdoms and epochs of great empires and monarchies" (*The Bell of Aragon*). In his mock-epic, *The Cat-fight,* he associates his subjects more specifically with the land and institutions of Spain: her woods, fields, trees, and flowers and "the arms and laws that maintain kingdoms and kings."

Lope's *Fuente Ovejuna* (Sheepwell) is a comedy. Charm and humor characterize its scenes, peasant characters, and dialogue, and the play ends in a jubilant affirmation of community and social order. It also has serious political dimensions and stages a daring foray into questions about law and government. Rape is the crime that finally drives the long-suffering people of Fuente Ovejuna to rise up and kill the abusive Comendador, Fernán Gómez de Guzmán, who lives in (and off) their small pastoral village. As the aristocratic Guzmán mistreats Fuente Ovejuna's councilmen, seduces and harasses its women, and imposes burdensome taxes, the villagers' thoughts turn to social contracts, law, and justice. They finally take action when the Comendador interrupts the wedding of a young couple, Frondoso and Laurencia, strips the mayor of his office, seizes Laurencia, and arrests Frondoso: they attack his household and throw the Comendador from a window to land upon the swords and spears of the women below. While the villagers celebrate by composing songs and parading raucously with Guzmán's head on a pole, word of the bloody rebellion reaches the Spanish kings, who send a judge to interrogate the villagers and administer justice. Aware of the legal consequences of their actions, the community resolves to stand by each other: even under torture, the men, women, and children of Fuente Ovejuna have one answer to the zealous judge's demand to learn the names of those responsible: "Everyone—Fuente Ovejuna did it." Left with the options of destroying the entire village or issuing a general pardon, the king chooses clemency. In the play's final scene, the villagers joyfully submit themselves to the rule of the Catholic kings—none other than the historical Ferdinand and Isabella, who completed the Reconquest of Spain, sent Christopher Columbus to America in 1492, and launched Spain's reputation as the most powerful empire of the sixteenth century.

Lope did not invent the subject of *Fuente Ovejuna*: he drew on historical events that took place in the small pastoral village in the province of Córdoba. His principal source, the chronicle history of Fray Francisco de Rades y Andrada, records that the Comendador "committed great injuries and dishonors to the people of the village, taking their daughters and wives by force, and robbing their households to maintain his soldiers." At length the villagers, calling out "long live Kings Ferdinand and Isabel, and death to traitors and bad Christians," rebelled, refused to hear the Comendador's promises of restitution, and killed him along with fourteen of his men. After his death, according to the chronicle, "they pulled his beard out by the roots with great cruelty, and broke his teeth with the pommels of their swords," mutilated the body, carried his head on a pole, refused him a Christian burial, and robbed his household. Had a single villager collapsed under torture and identified the ringleaders in order to save his or her own skin, the events at Fuente Ovejuna would be chronicled as a lurid and bloody uprising during a period of widespread cultural upheaval in Spanish history. But since each was willing to die for the others, they left a memorable and even proverbial example of resistance and solidarity. The phrase "Fuente Ovejuna lo hizo" ("Sheepwell did it") became proverbial for a dedication to community and democratic process.

Lope shows considerable sympathy for his peasants, who are goaded into their seditious frenzy. Left to their own devices, the villagers are law-abiding and peaceable: even the names of the lead characters, Frondoso ("leafy") and Laurencia ("laurel"), associate them with the most nonviolent aspects of nature. Lope's spotlight shines on the Comendador's abuses—including reports of a gang rape, brutal beatings, and the administration of an ink enema to a hapless peasant (a bizarre punishment, perhaps suggesting the censorship of writing). The attempted rape of Laurencia, the play's most dynamic and articulate character, is Lope's invention, and it plays a decisive role in defining the nature of the political violence that Guzmán perpetrates on the entire village: first, rape was an inalterable dishonor to a woman and to her father and husband, and second, it represents, in a most visceral way, Guzmán's violent disregard for consent, the key term in all social contracts. The assault shocks Laurencia into a hair-raising harangue at the town council, where she spurs the dishonored villagers to revenge. The murder scene, which follows, is fast-paced, giddy, and carnivalesque. Questions of moral interpretation are left to performance, which might emphasize either the spirit of liberation or the spirit of dangerous transgression. Lope acknowledges the more ghoulish details from the chronicle, but places them in the biased report that Flores, the Comendador's bully and pimp, makes to the Catholic kings. What compels Lope's imagination is the villagers' redemptive commitment to community. Lope uses the historical event and example to raise fundamental questions of political philosophy: does authority come from above (God) or below (the people)? is government based on a social contract? do laborers have the right to honor? are the people, if governed cruelly, entitled to revoke their consent or to resist by violence? Lope, who was no political radical, suggests that government without popular consent and mutual respect is morally bankrupt.

The rebellion of Fuente Ovejuna took place in 1476, seven years after Ferdinand and Isabella secretly married in hopes of uniting the Crowns of Aragon and Castile and two years after Isabella declared herself queen of Castile, following the death of her half brother, Henry IV. At the time of the villagers' uprising, the security of the Catholic kings and the political destiny of Spain itself hung in the balance, in part because Isabella's was not the only (or even the best) claim to the Crown of Castile. In 1476 Ferdinand and Isabella were at war with Alfonso V of Portugal and his wife, Juana, alleged to be the daughter of Henry IV. Moreover, it was by no means clear how the Crowns of Castile and Aragon would reconcile the radically opposed forms of government that each province traditionally upheld. Castile espoused monarchical absolutism, a theory of power holding that the king is above the law and that "what pleases the king *is* law." The Castilian monarchy was locked in a struggle with its most powerful aristocratic families, the dynasties of Mendoza, Enríquez, and Guzmán (from which the Comendador comes). Aragon, on the other hand, rejoiced in its constitutional government, which strongly emphasized the reciprocal obligations of the monarch and his subjects. The Aragonese oath of allegiance ran "We who are as good as you swear to you, who are no better than we, to accept you as our king and sovereign lord, provided that you observe all our liberties and laws; but if not, not." To the Aragonese the liberties of subjects outstripped the prerogatives of the monarch. The events at Fuente Ovejuna coincided with the rise to power of the Catholic kings, giving Lope an opportunity to explore both the ideal form of government and Spain's future as a powerful empire. Controversy never hurt the box office, Lope knew, and so he brought to the stage political debates over dominion by consent, divine right, and force.

Lope dedicates his play's subplot to Ferdinand and Isabella. Fuente Ovejuna is under siege, and so is the Royal City (*Ciudad Real*) of Castile; Laurencia's honor is under assault, and so is Isabella's authority. Until the end of the play, when the villagers meet the Catholic kings, the sole figure to pass between the two plots is Fernán Gómez de Guzmán: when the Comendador is not brutalizing the villagers of Fuente Ovejuna, he is on the battlefield fighting against Ferdinand and Isabella. Guzmán belongs to the chivalric order of Calatrava, one of the three great military and religious orders established in the twelfth century to bring about the Reconquest of Spain, following the Arab invasion of 711. Lope's Guzmán perfectly embodies the ethos of the aristocratic *hidalgo*: "a man who lived for war, who could do the impossible through sheer physical courage and a constant effort of the will, who conducted his relations with others according to a strictly regulated code of honor, and who reserved his respect for the man who had won riches by force of arms rather than by the sweat of manual labor," as one historian puts it.

The rapacious and arrogant style of dominion exemplified by Lope's Guzmán contrasts with the military and judicial policies of the Catholic kings, whom Lope celebrates as prudent, just, and respectful of law. Guzmán abuses the idea, central to the theory of monarchical absolutism, that "what pleases the king is law." He speaks of ownership of his subjects, seduces and rapes his female subjects, and attempts to dissolve the local administration of law when he strips the mayor of office and orders the villagers to vacate the central plaza. In the play's very first scene, Guzmán greets the young Master of the chivalric Order of Calatrava with the blunt assertion "You are right to honor me," and proceeds to manipulate the youth into attacking the Royal City. Guzmán violates the reciprocal obligations governing the relationship of the good king and his subjects: he contemptuously rejects the suggestion that he owes anything to the villagers of Fuente Ovejuna, and it is in the role of bad counselor that he coerces the powerful but impressionable Master of the Order of Calatrava. The Catholic kings, on the other hand, later exemplify the magnanimous and prudential nature of good kings: they pardon the Master for his assault on the Royal City and direct his aggression toward wars beneficial to Spain and befitting the traditions of his Order, crusades against the Arabs. Guzmán's moral and military opposition to the idealized Catholic kings suggests that the villagers of Fuente Ovejuna are justified in their cry "Death to bad Christians and traitors."

Guzmán is not the only figure in Lope's play to wed dramatic stereotype to controversial concepts in political theory. So do the young lovers, Laurencia and Frondoso, who are both stock types from comedy and initially act like the intelligent, beautiful, unattainable young woman and the good-hearted, callow, fashion-happy young man who adores her. The characters soon reveal how they vary from their stereotypes, however. Because she has known only the Comendador's attempts to entrap her, Laurencia at first disdains love. She understandably insists that love is merely self-interest, while Frondoso, who views her coldness in purely conventional terms, seems oddly unaware that he inhabits a politically mired world and not a standard comedy. Frondoso soon learns what love requires of him: while he and Laurencia are in the woods debating about love, the Comendador, who has been out hunting deer, appears and decides to "hunt" Laurencia instead. If he is to prevent her rape, Frondoso must come out from his hiding place, pick up the Comendador's discarded crossbow, and threaten his life. Heroic and ethical but illegal, Frondoso's act wins Laurencia's love and the Comendador's murderous enmity. The Comendador's abuses habitually force peasants—and otherwise typical comic characters—to think strenuously about the nature of social contracts. The peasants conclude that those who govern owe a debt to those who serve and that communal bonds are formed by love: the willingness to enter into a social relationship and to treat the interest of others as one's own. This is the lesson that gives the villagers the courage to protect their community despite torture. In Lope's play, love is both the erotic mainstay of comedy and the harmonizing principle of government: in matters of the heart and of law, the subject must have the right to consent.

PRONOUNCING GLOSSARY

The following list uses common English syllables and stress accents to provide rough equivalents of selected words whose pronunciation may be unfamiliar to the general reader. Note that in Castilian Spanish, as opposed to the Spanish spoken in the Americas, *d* is pronounced as *th*.

Calatrava: *cah-lah-trah'-vah*

Cimbranos: *seem-brah'-nos*

Ciudad Real: *see-oo-dthahth' ray-ahl'*

Comendador: *koh-men-da-thor'*

Cuadrado: *kwah-drah'-thoh*

Fernán Gómez de Guzman: *fer-nahn' goh'-mez day gus'-mahn*

Frondoso: *frohn-doh'-so*

Fuente Ovejuna: *fu-en'-tay o-vay-hu'-nah*

Jacinta: *ha-seen'-tah*

Juan Chamorro: *hwan cha-mor'-roh*

Juan Rojo: *hwan ro'-hoh*

Laurencia: *lau-ren'-see-ah*

Leon: *lay-own'*

Lope de Vega: *loh'-pay duh vay'-gah*

Manrique: *man-ree'-kay*

maravedíes: *mah-rah-vay-dee'-es*

Ortuño: *or-tun'-yoh*

Pascuala: *pas-kwah'-lah*

Rodrigo Téllez Girón: *ro-dree'-goh tay'-yez hi-rohn'*

Villena: *vi-yay'-nah*

Fuente Ovejuna[1]

CHARACTERS

FERNÁN GÓMEZ, *the Grand Com-*
  mander of Calatrava
ORTUÑO ⎫
         ⎬ *his servants*
FLORES   ⎭
THE MASTER OF CALATRAVA, *Rodrigo*
  Téllez Girón
PASCUALA ⎫
           ⎬ *peasant women*
LAURENCIA ⎭
LEONELO, *a graduate*
MENGO   ⎫
BARRILDO ⎬ *peasants*
FRONDOSO ⎭
JUAN ROJO, *alderman, Laurencia's*
  uncle

ESTEBAN, *magistrate, Laurencia's*
  father
ALONSO, *magistrate*
KING FERNANDO *of Aragón*
QUEEN ISABEL *of Castile*
MANRIQUE, *Master of Santiago*
TWO ALDERMEN
CIMBRANOS, *a soldier*
JACINTA, *a peasant woman*
BOY
PEASANTS
JUDGE
MUSICIANS

Act One

[*Enter the* COMMANDER, *with his servants* FLORES, *and* ORTUÑO.]

COMMANDER Doesn't the Master[2] know I'm here?

FLORES He does.

ORTUÑO   Now that he's older, he's much
More high and mighty.

COMMANDER   But he surely knows
That I am Fernán Gómez de Guzmán?

FLORES He's still a boy. It's not surprising.   5

COMMANDER But if not my name, my rank of Grand
Commander.

ORTUÑO   There are those who advise
Him not to show respect.

COMMANDER   Then he'll not
Win much affection. Respect's the key
To men's good will; discourtesy merely   10
Makes enemies.

ORTUÑO   If such men knew
How everyone detests them and longs
To see them grovel, they'd sooner die.

FLORES Such people are so hard to take!
Such surliness and lack of manners.   15
Amongst equals it's pure folly;
Towards inferiors sheer tyranny.
But you shouldn't take it to heart, sir.
He's still too young to know what it means
To be loved by others.

COMMANDER   The day

---

1. Translated by Gwynne Edwards. 2. The Grand Master of the Order of Calatrava, one of three military and religious orders founded in the 12th century in order to defend the Christian states of Spain against the Muslims.

20

The sword was placed around his waist,
The cross of Calatrava on
His breast, it should have been enough
To teach him due respect.
FLORES   You'll soon know
If they've turned him against you.
ORTUÑO   Look   25
This way. Find out for yourself.
COMMANDER   Let's hear
What he has to say.
         [*The* MASTER *enters with his attendants.*]
MASTER   Forgive me, Fernán Gómez de Guzmán!
   I've only just been told
   Of your arrival.
COMMANDER   I have good reason to   30
   Complain. My love and background led
   Me to expect much more respect
   From you, Master of Calatrava,
   Toward your most obedient servant and
   Commander.
MASTER   I was expecting the warmest   35
   Of welcomes, Fernando. Let me
   Embrace you.
COMMANDER   You are right to honor me.
   How often have I risked my life
   On your account, before the Pope
   Acknowledged you had come of age![3]   40
MASTER   Of course! And I swear by the cross
   Displayed on your breast and mine
   That I am grateful, and honor you
   As much as my own father.
COMMANDER   Then I
   Am happy.
MASTER   What news of the war?   45
COMMANDER   Hear my account and you shall learn
   Where your duty lies.
MASTER   Proceed, then. I
   Am listening.
COMMANDER   Rodrigo Téllez
   Girón, Master of Calatrava,
   You owe your high position to
   Your brave and famous father. When you   50
   Were only eight, he stepped
   Aside, granting you his great authority,
   Which was then ratified by kings
   And great commanders too, as well   55
   As papal bulls, first from Pius, then

---

3. Pope Pius II increased the age of the eight-year-old Rodrigo Téllez Girón in 1466 so that he might inherit his father's position as the Grand Master.

From Paul, but on condition that Juan
Pacheco, Master of Santiago, shared
Your rule. Now that he's dead and you,
Though still so young, govern alone,   60
Do not forget that you are duty bound
To carry out the wishes of
Your family. They insist that, after
The death of King Henry the Fourth,
His subjects swear allegiance to   65
Alonso King of Portugal,
Who, through his wife and consort, Juana,
The child of Henry, rightly claims
Castile. And though Fernando, Prince
Of Aragon, contests that claim,   70
And seeks the kingdom for his wife,
And Henry's sister, Isabel,[4]
Your family favours Juana, at present in
Your cousin's power, denying that
Her claims are false. So I am here   75
To urge you call upon the Knights
Of Calatrava, assemble them in
Almagro, and take Ciudad Real,[5]
A town that, placed between Castile
And Andalusia, faces both.   80
We'll not need many men. The soldiers who
Protect it are its own inhabitants,
Together with some minor nobles,
Who both defend the name of Isabel
And call Fernando their king.   85
You would do well, Rodrigo, to astonish those
Who think you are too young and that
Great Cross too much for you to bear.
Remember your ancestors,
The Counts of Urueña, and take   90
As your example their great deeds.
Villena's Marquesses[6] as well,
And other captains too whose feats
The wings of Fame can scarcely bear.
Take your sword, so far unstained   95
By blood, and turn it red as the Cross
Upon your breast. How else can I
Address you as Master of the Cross
If the one is red and not the other?
Let both of them be crimson, and you,   100
Worthy Girón, crown the immortal temple of

---

4. The Commander lectures his youthful superior on the rival claims for sovereignty in Castile by Juana and Alfonso V of Portugal and by Ferdinand of Aragon and Isabella of Castile, the monarchs who prevail historically and appear at the end of the play. **5.** The capital of New Castile. **6.** One of *Villena's Marquesses* was Juan Pacheco, the uncle of Rodrigo (the Grand Master). Don Pedro Girón, Rodrigo's father, became Count of Urueña in 1464.

Your famous ancestors.

MASTER   Fernán Gómez,
You may be sure that in this conflict I
Support my family, for their cause
Is just. If you want proof, you'll see   105
Me march upon Ciudad Real,
And like a bolt from heaven, destroy
Its walls. My uncle may be dead,
But no one should assume, because
I'm still so young, that with his death   110
My courage vanished too. I'll take
My sword and make the brightness of
Its blade the colour of this Cross,
Bathed in blood. From where you govern, can
You provide some soldiers?

COMMANDER   Not many;   115
In fact my vassals. But if they are obliged,
They'll fight as fiercely as lions.
In Fuente Ovejuna[7] they
Are humble people, more used to fields
And ploughshares than battles.

MASTER   Is that
Where you live?   120

COMMANDER   In times as dangerous
As these, it's where I chose to live. Summon
Your men. No one shall remain behind.

MASTER   You shall see me ride out, my lance
At the ready.   125
        [*They exit and* PASCUALA *and* LAURENCIA *enter.*]

LAURENCIA   Let's hope he never comes back!

PASCUALA   Well, I'm damned!
I thought you'd be broken-hearted at
The news.

LAURENCIA   Heaven forbid! I'd rather not
See him again in Fuente Ovejuna!

PASCUALA   Believe me, Laurencia, I've seen others   130
As fierce as you, some fiercer still,
And underneath a heart as soft
As butter.

LAURENCIA   Have you seen an oak
As dry and hard as myself?

PASCUALA   Oh, get
Away with you! No one should say   135
"I'll never drink that water!"

LAURENCIA   Well I
Shan't, though others may say differently.
What good would it do me to fall

---

7. The town is situated in the province of Córdoba; at the historical time of the play's events, Córdoba's
population was less than one thousand. Until 1468 its citizens owed allegiance to the city of Córdoba, but
in that year it was seized by Fernán Gómez, the speaker.

For Fernando? Do you think he'd marry me?
PASCUALA No.
LAURENCIA   Then I'll have nothing to do   140
With him. How many girls in our village
Have put their trust in the Commander,
And seen their reputation shot
To pieces?
PASCUALA   I'll be amazed if you
Escape his clutches.
LAURENCIA   You shouldn't believe   145
Everything you see. He's chased me for
A month, Pascuala, and still got nowhere.
Flores, his pimp, and that scoundrel, Ortuño,
They showed me a bodice, a necklace, and
A bonnet, and said so many things   150
About their master, Fernando,
They frightened me really, but they won't
Persuade me.
PASCUALA   So where did this take place?
LAURENCIA There by the stream. Six days ago.
PASCUALA Well, I fancy they'll change your mind,   155
Laurencia.
LAURENCIA What, me?
PASCUALA   I don't mean the priest,
Now do I?
LAURENCIA I'm a young bird, true, but far
Too tough for his holiness. Believe me,
Pascuala, for breakfast I'd much
Rather have a nice slice of bacon,   160
With a piece of bread from a loaf
I've baked myself, and pinch a glass
Of wine from my mother's jar. At noon
I'd rather see beef and cabbage
Dancing to a merry, bubbling tune,   165
And when I'm tired from traveling,
A slice of bacon wedded to
An aubergine. Then later on,
While supper's cooking, a bunch of grapes
(God protect the vines from hailstones!),   170
And, when it's ready, a tasty fry
Of chopped-up meat with oil and peppers.
And so at last happily to bed,
To say my prayers, including "lead
Me not into temptation!" I much   175
Prefer all this to the tricks and lies
Of rogues with all their talk and promises
Of love. Their only aim's to leave
Us in the lurch. They take us to bed
For their pleasure; when morning comes,   180
It's "Goodbye, treasure!"

PASQUALA   Quite right, Laurencia.
When they stop loving, men are more
Ungrateful than the sparrows. In winter,
When the fields are frozen, they come down
From the rooftops—"chirp, chirp"—and eat   185
The crumbs from your kitchen table.
But once the cold of winter's passed,
And they see the fields grow green at last,
It's not "chirp, chirp" any longer; more
"Twerp, twerp," from the safety of the rooftops,   190
All the farmer's kindness quite forgotten.
Such are men! Whenever they need us, we
Are their lives, their entire being;
Because of us their life has meaning.
But once their fire starts to cool,   195
They act just like those sparrows.[8] Never again
Will you hear "sweetheart." Suddenly,
You become just a tart!
LAURENCIA   Never trust
A man!
PASCUALA   Oh, I agree, Laurencia!
     [*Enter* MENGO, BARRILDO, *and* FRONDOSO.]
FRONDOSO   Your argument's ridiculous,   200
Barrildo.
BARRILDO   At least there's someone here
Who'll settle it.
MENGO   Before you ask,
Let's come to an agreement. If they
Decide I'm right you both pay up
The prize for winning.
BARRILDO   Fair enough.   205
But if you lose, you'll give us something.
MENGO   You can have this fiddle. It's worth
A granary, and to me much more
Than that.
BARRILDO   Agreed then.
FRONDOSO   Let's do it!
God be with you, lovely ladies!   210
LAURENCIA   Since when, Frondoso, do you call us ladies?
FRONDOSO   We are followers of fashion.
Nowadays your schoolboy's called a graduate,
Your blind as a bat, myopic;
Your cross-eyed man has just a squint,   215
And your totally lame's arthritic.
The couldn't-care-less are upright chaps,
The stupid are called clever;
A pig of a man's described as bold,
And a big mouth an entertainer.   220

---

8. *Sparrows* were traditionally associated with lechery.

A beady eye is said to be sharp,
Argumentative people try hard;
A silly ass is amusing,
And a chatterbox is a card.
A common upstart, oh, he's brave,   225
A coward lacks initiative;
Your hothead, well, he's really dashing,
And your dolt is someone well worth knowing.
If you're off your head, you're free as air,
If down in the dumps, just full of care;   230
If you're bald, you have authority,
If you're stupid, oh, so very witty.
Big feet are the sign of a solid man,
The pox is only a runny nose,
Arrogance is but reserve,   235
And a hunchback wears bad-fitting clothes.
This is why, you see, I call you ladies.
I shan't say more or I might go on
Forever.
LAURENCIA   That's city talk when they want
To be polite. But take my word   240
For it, they use a different style
When they insult you.
FRONDOSO   How exactly?
LAURENCIA   Everything's just the opposite.
They call a serious man a bore,
You speak your mind and you are rash;   245
A thoughtful person's melancholic,
You criticize, and you are brash.
You give advice, it's pure cheek,
Be generous, you stick your nose in;
If you are just, you're seen as cruel,   250
Show mercy and you're just a weakling.
Be constant and they call you boring,
Polite and you're a flatterer;
Be kind and you're a hypocrite,
A Christian's someone seeking favor.   255
If you've got talent, that's just lucky,
You tell the truth, that's impudence;
Put up with things and you're a coward,
When things go wrong, it's your come-uppance.
A modest woman is a fool,   260
Pretty but chaste, she's into seduction;
If she's virtuous, she's . . . no, no,
That's it, end of demonstration!
MENGO   I swear you are a little devil.
BARRILDO   In the name of God, that wasn't bad!   265
MENGO   You must have been christened with something
Much saltier than water.[9]

9. Since "salt" was another word for "wit" or "ingenuity," Mengo is remarking on Laurencia's quick wits.

LAURENCIA   Anyway,
  What were you arguing about?
FRONDOSO   I'll tell you.
LAURENCIA   Right.
FRONDOSO   Pay attention.
LAURENCIA   You have it, for nothing. I'm all ears.   270
FRONDOSO   I put my faith in your judgment.
LAURENCIA   So what's the argument?
FRONDOSO   It's me
  And Barrildo against Mengo.
LAURENCIA   About what?
BARRILDO   Something that, though obviously true, he
  Denies.
MENGO   Only because I know I'm right.   275
LAURENCIA   So what's he say?
BARRILDO   That love does not
  Exist.
LAURENCIA   That's very sweeping.
BARRILDO   As well
  As stupid. If love did not exist,
  Neither would this world of ours.
MENGO   I'm no philosopher and, more's   280
  The pity, I can't read. But if
  The elements are always in
  A state of war, and our bodies—blood,
  Phlegm, melancholy, choler[1]—draw
  Their sustenance from them—where   285
  Is love?
BARRILDO   In this world and the next,
  My friend, there's perfect harmony.
  And harmony is love, since love's
  Harmonious.
MENGO   Oh, I don't deny
  That love is natural and has   290
  Great power. It governs everything,
  And everything we see it keeps
  In balance. Nor have I ever said
  That love does not exist in every man,
  According to his humor, and that's   295
  What helps him to survive. If someone aims
  A punch at me, my hand protects
  My face. If danger comes, my feet
  Will help me to escape it; if something
  Approaches my eyes, my lids close sharpish.   300
  That's natural love.
PASCUALA   So what's the point
  You want to make?
MENGO   That we love ourselves

---

1. The four bodily humors associated with Galenic physiology were blood, phlegm, melancholy, and choler. For good health, one needed a balance of these elements.

And no one else.

PASCUALA Excuse me, Mengo,
But that's plain daft. The proof lies in
The fact that men and women love   305
Each other passionately, as does
An animal its mate.

MENGO That's still
Self-love, not love. Tell me what love is.

LAURENCIA A desire for beauty.

MENGO And why
Does love desire it?

LAURENCIA To enjoy it.   310

MENGO Right. And doesn't it want that pleasure for
Itself?

LAURENCIA Well, yes.

MENGO In other words, because
It loves itself, it seeks enjoyment for
Itself?

LAURENCIA I suppose so.

MENGO Well, there you have it.
Self-love's the only kind of love.   315
I seek it just for my own pleasure.
I'm the object of the whole endeavor.

BARRILDO But I remember the village priest
Once talked in his sermon about
A certain Plato[2] and what he said   320
On love, which was that we should love
Only the soul and virtue of
The one we love.

PASCUALA Such topics frazzle
The brains of wise professors in
Our colleges and great academies.   325

LAURENCIA She's right. So don't get tangled up
Yourself, supporting their idiocies.
Be thankful, Mengo, you weren't made
To love.

MENGO So who do you love?

LAURENCIA Only
My honor

FRONDOSO Then may God punish you   330
And make you jealous!

BARRILDO So who's the winner?

PASCUALA You'd best go to the sacristan.
He or the priest are bound to have
An answer. As for the two of us,
Laurencia's not in love and I've   335
Got no experience. We can't judge.

FRONDOSO Her coldness is my answer!

2. Lope's villagers allude to the theories of love developed by the 15th-century philosophers, or Neopla-
tonists, who followed the Greek philosopher Plato. Marsilio Ficino and Leone Ebreo were particularly
known for their writings on Neoplatonic love.

[*Enter* FLORES.]

FLORES   May God be with you, good people!

PASCUALA   It's the Commander's lackey.

LAURENCIA   Such a fine falcon![3] So where have you come   340
    From, friend?

FLORES   Can't you tell by my uniform?

LAURENCIA   Is Don Fernando here as well?

FLORES   The battle's finished. It's cost us friends
    And no little blood.

FRONDOSO   So give us an account
    Of it.

FLORES   Who better if my eyes   345
    Were witness to it all? In order to
    Prepare for that campaign against the town,
    Ciudad Real, the gallant Master chose
    From all his valiant followers
    Two thousand infantry, supported by   350
    Three hundred men on horseback, secular
    And clerical—for if they wear
    The Cross upon their breast, they are
    Obliged, though they be friars, to take
    Up arms against the Moorish infidel.   355
    The young man was a splendid sight,
    His doublet green with gold embroidery,
    Revealing at the sleeves armlets held
    In place by six bright fastenings
    He sat astride a mighty stallion,   360
    In color dapple-grey, which drank
    From the Guadalquivir[4] and grazed
    Upon the fertile pasture of its banks.
    Its tail was bound by strips of leather,
    Its name adorned by bows that in   365
    Their whiteness matched the dappled pattern of
    Its skin. And at the Master's side
    Fernán Gómez, your overlord, upon
    A strong and honey-colored steed,
    Its hooves black, its mouth white. Over   370
    A coat of mail in Turkish style,
    Brightest armor front and back,
    And an orange doublet, and set atop
    All this a helmet whose white plumes
    Seemed, against that orange, more   375
    Like blossoms. About his arm a band
    Of red and white, couching a lance
    Which seemed a mighty oak before
    Which all Granada[5] trembles. Ciudad Real
    Then took to arms, its people claiming they   380

3. Laurencia sees Flores, the Commander's lackey, as a bird of prey.   4. A large and important river about sixty miles south of Ciudad Real.   5. By 1476, the historical time of the play, the Moorish domination of Spain was virtually over and only the kingdom of Granada remained in the Moors' power. The city itself surrendered to the Catholic kings, Ferdinand and Isabella, in 1492.

Were loyal to the Crown and would
Defend their rights to so remain.
Despite all this, the Master seized
The town, and those who had offended his
Good name soon had their heads cut off,   385
While those of lesser worth were gagged
And flogged in public view. He is
So feared there and yet so loved,
They all believe that one who, though
So young, can fight and overwhelm   390
His enemies, will one day be
The scourge of Moorish Africa, forcing
Those blue and crescent moons to yield
To his red Cross. He has displayed
Such generosity to all—   395
To our Commander too—the sacking of
The town seems more the plunder of
His own estate. But now the music sounds.
Receive him joyfully! Goodwill
Is easily the best reward   400
For such a triumph.

     [*Enter the* COMMANDER *and* ORTUÑO; MUSICIANS; JUAN ROJO;
     and ESTEBAN *and* ALONSO, *magistrates.*]

MUSICIANS [*sing*]   All hail our great Commander,
    We welcome him most warmly;
    He conquers foreign lands for us,
    And overcomes our enemy.   405
    Long live all the Guzmanes!
    Long live all the Girones!
    In peace he is so gentle,
    He speaks his words so sweetly;
    But when it comes to killing Moors,   410
    As strong as any oak-tree!
    He comes now from Ciudad Real,
    The great and glorious victor;
    He brings his banners with him
    To Fuente Ovejuna!   415
    May he enjoy long life!
    All hail Fernán Gómez!
COMMANDER   People of this town, I duly thank
  You for this demonstration of
  Your love.
ALONSO   It is but part of what   420
  We feel. But since you are deserving of
  Our love, why be surprised by it?
ESTEBAN   Fuente Ovejuna and its councilors,
  Whom you so honor, now request
  That you receive the humble offerings   425
  Brought by these carts in all due modesty,
  For they, adorned by leafy boughs,

Contain not costly gifts but much
Goodwill. First, two baskets filled
With polished pots of clay. And then   430
An entire flock of geese who stretch
Their necks through nets, eager to sing
Of your warlike deeds. Ten salted hogs,
Choice animals, as well as other kinds
Of cured meats whose skins are sweet   435
As amber-scented gloves. A hundred pairs
Of hens and capons, whose widowed spouses can
Be found in all our neighboring villages.
They cannot offer arms or horses,
Or bridles edged with pure gold,   440
And yet your vassals' love is in
Itself the purest gold. And since
I mention "pure," I promise you that these
Twelve wineskins would, if your troops
But drank from them, give them such strength   445
That they, though naked in the midst
Of winter, could defend a battlement
Much better than the hardest steel.
For wine can truly give a man
The extra steel he needs. As for   450
The cheeses and the other smaller gifts,
I'll not describe them; merely say
They are the offerings of all
The love that you deserve. And so,
May they provide good cheer for   455
Your household and yourself!
COMMANDER   My heartfelt thanks! Good concilors,
   You may depart!
ALONSO   And you, my lord,
   May take your ease. You are most welcome.
   If it were possible, we'd turn   460
   The reeds and rushes at your door
   To purest pearl, though you deserve
   Much better still.
COMMANDER   I really do
   Believe you, gentlemen. God be with you.
ESTEBAN   Singers, come! The song again!   465
MUSICIANS [sing]   All hail our great Commander,
      We welcome him most warmly,
      He conquers foreign lands for us,
      And overcomes our enemies . . .
      [They leave.]
COMMANDER   You two, stay!
LAURENCIA   What's your lordship want   470
   Of us?
COMMANDER   You were quite cool the other day,
   And toward me!

LAURENCIA   Does he mean you, Pascuala?

PASCUALA   Me? Oh, don't be silly!

COMMANDER   I'm talking to you, my pretty creature,
   And to your friend. You belong to me,   475
   Do you not?

PASCUALA   We do, my lord, but not
   In the way you mean.

COMMANDER   Step inside.
   My men are there. Don't be afraid.

LAURENCIA   I shall if the magistrates come too.
   One of them's my father, but otherwise   480

COMMANDER   Flores!

FLORES   Yes, sir?

COMMANDER   Why aren't they doing what
   I say?

FLORES   Get in there!

LAURENCIA   Get your hands
   Off us!

FLORES   Come on, you stupid girls!

PASCUALA   Whoa now! For you to lock the stable-door?

FLORES   Inside! He wants to show you all   485
   The spoils of war.

COMMANDER [*aside, as he exits*]   Ortuño, once
   Inside, you'll lock them in.

LAURENCIA   Flores,
   Get out of our way!

ORTUÑO   But you are part
   Of all his presents.

PASCUALA   I don't believe it!
   Move yourself, or you'll get it!

FLORES   Alright,   490
   They are too excitable.

LAURENCIA   Your master's had
   Enough flesh for today!

ORTUÑO   It's yours
   He fancies most!

LAURENCIA   Let's hope he chokes!

                                      [*They leave.*]

FLORES   Wait till we give him this good news!
   Imagine what he'll say when we   495
   Turn up without them!

ORTUÑO   That's the way
   Things are for those who serve. If you want
   To get on, put up with it; otherwise,
   Best out of it, and quick!

                                       [*They leave.*]

   [*Enter* KING FERNANDO, QUEEN ISABEL, MANRIQUE, *and* ATTENDANTS.]

ISABEL   My lord, there must be no delay   500
   In this. Alfonso is well placed
   And even now prepares his troops.

Before he strikes at us, it's best
We strike at him. If we do not,
The risk is clear.
KING   We can rely   505
On both Navarre and Aragon for our
Support. When I have managed to control
Castile, our victory will be
Assured.
ISABEL   I know, my lord, all this
Will guarantee our triumph.
MANRIQUE   Your Majesty,   510
Two aldermen who represent
Ciudad Real. Will you see them?
KING   Of course. You'll show them in.
        [*Enter two* ALDERMEN *from Ciudad Real.*]
FIRST ALDERMAN   Most Catholic King Fernando,
Whom Heaven has sent from Aragon   515
To be our help and savior in
Castile, we come as spokesmen from
Ciudad Real to seek in all
Humility your royal favour.
To be your subjects was for us   520
The greatest happiness, but now
We are deprived of that by cruel fate.
Rodrigo Téllez Girón, renowned,
Though still so young, for such great bravery,
And seeking to enhance his name   525
As Master of Calatrava, attacked
Our city. We fought as best we could;
Resisted him till all our streams
Ran red with our blood. At last
He seized the town, but would have failed   530
Without the help and good advice
Of Fernán Gómez. And so he has
Possession of the town and we
Will be his vassals soon unless
Your majesty decides to help us.   535
KING   Where is Fernán Gómez?
FIRST ALDERMAN   I think
In Fuente Ovejuna. He is
Its overlord and has his house
And seat of power there. He rules
The place just as he wishes, denying   540
His subjects any kind of happiness.
KING   Do you have a leader?
SECOND ALDERMAN   We do not,
Your Majesty. Every nobleman
Was captured, hurt, or killed.
ISABEL   Then we
Should not delay. To do so is   545

To give the enemy encouragment
And greater heart. Extremadura[6] is
The door whereby the King of Portugal
Can now advance and damage us.
KING   Don Manrique, prepare to leave.   550
You'll take two companies and curb
The enemy's excesses. Not
A moment's respite, understand?
The Count of Cabra goes with you.
A man of valor, Córdoba.   555
The whole world knows how brave he is.
In the circumstances, this is the best
Way forward.
MANRIQUE   A bold decision, my lord.
I'll put an end to their arrogance,
As long as I have breath in me.   560
ISABEL   Your presence there will guarantee
Our triumph.
          [*Exit all. Enter* LAURENCIA *and* FRONDOSO.]
LAURENCIA   I had to leave the stream,
My clothes half done, because of you!
You are too bold, Frondoso, yet well
You know how people love to talk.   565
"She fancies him," "He fancies her,"
All over town, their eyes on stalks
To see if it is true or not.
And since you are . . . well . . . better looking than
The rest, and dress more smartly, there's not   570
A single person in the place
Who doesn't think we're as good as spliced
Already, and waiting for the day
When Juan Chamorro, our sacristan,
Stops playing his bassoon to announce   575
Instead our marriage-bans. But they,
As far as I'm concerned, would be
Much better occupied in stocking up
Their barns with golden grain, their vats
With wine, than harboring such wild   580
Imaginings. To tell the truth,
I never gave this marriage thing
A second thought.
FRONDOSO   This coldness does
Me such an injury, Laurencia,
I risk my life each time I look   585
At you. If you already know
I want to marry you, does my
Good faith deserve such scant reward?

6. The region between Portugal and Spain.

LAURENCIA   There is no other I can give.

FRONDOSO   Does not the state I'm in succeed   590
  In moving you at all? Or knowing that,
  Because of you, I cannot eat
  Or drink or sleep? How can an angel's face
  Contain such coldness? By God, I shall
  Go mad!

LAURENCIA   Then see a doctor.

FRONDOSO   But you,   595
  Laurencia, are my cure. When we
  Get married, we'll be like turtle-doves,
  Our little beaks together, making sweet
  And soothing music.

LAURENCIA   Go tell it to
  My uncle John! You know full well   600
  I'm not in love with you, but maybe there's . . .
  Well . . . just a little spark . . .

FRONDOSO   Look there!
  The Commander!

LAURENCIA   He must be hunting deer.
  Hide in the trees!

FRONDOSO   I shall, and burn
  With jealousy!

      [*The* COMMANDER *enters.*]

COMMANDER   Well who'd have thought   605
  That, in pursuit of frightened deer,
  I'd come across much prettier game?

LAURENCIA   I'm having a break from washing clothes.
  I'll get back to the stream if you
  Don't mind, sir.

COMMANDER   Such coldness, my sweet   610
  Laurencia, offends the beauty God
  Has given you. It makes of you
  A real monster. But if at other times
  You've managed to escape my amorous
  Requests, this place shall now become   615
  Their silent witness. I cannot think
  That, since we are alone, you are
  So proud as to reject your lord
  And master, turning away from me!
  Sebastiana, Pedro Redondo's wife,   620
  Surrendered willingly, as did
  Martin del Pozo's after just
  Two days of marriage.

LAURENCIA   Both of them
  Had been along that road before,
  My lord. They knew exactly how   625
  To please you. So God go with you
  In the hunt, sir . . . I mean for deer.
  If it weren't for that cross upon

Your chest, I'd take you for the devil, such
  Is your pursuit of me!
COMMANDER   Such language is   630
  Offensive! I'll put my bow aside
  And let my hands overcome those airs
  And graces!
LAURENCIA   What are you doing? Have you
  Gone mad?
        [Enter FRONDOSO, picking up the crossbow.]
COMMANDER   Stop struggling!
FRONDOSO   The bow!
  Please God I shan't be forced to use it!   635
COMMANDER   Come on! No point resisting!
LAURENCIA   Oh, God,
  Please help me!
COMMANDER   We're all alone. No need
  To be afraid!
FRONDOSO   Noble Commander, leave her!
  Despite my reverence for the Cross,
  My anger will not hesitate   640
  To make your breast the arrow's target.
COMMANDER   You peasant dog!
FRONDOSO   I don't see any dog, sir.
  Laurencia, run!
LAURENCIA   Frondoso, be careful!
FRONDOSO   Go!
                   [She leaves.]
COMMANDER   The man's a fool who leaves his sword
  Behind. I left it, thinking it   645
  Would scare my quarry.
FRONDOSO   I only need
  To press the trigger and it's your feet
  They'll be tying together.
COMMANDER   She's gone,
  You fool! Give me the bow! Release it!
FRONDOSO   Why?
  So you can kill me? Have you forgotten love 650
  Is deaf? Where it rules it doesn't listen.
COMMANDER   Am I, a man of worth, to turn
  My back upon a peasant? I shall not break
  The rules of chivalry!
FRONDOSO   I don't
  Intend to kill you. I know my place.   655
  But since I need to stay alive,
  I'll keep the crossbow.
                [Exit FRONDOSO.]
COMMANDER   That was, indeed,
  A close-run thing! But I shall take
  Revenge on him for this, both for

The insult and the interruption.   660
I should have tackled him! That I
Did not adds further to my sense of shame!

                                        [*Exit the* COMMANDER.]

                        Act Two

        [*Enter* ESTEBAN *and* FIRST ALDERMAN.]
ESTEBAN   I think it wiser if we do
   Not draw upon our stocks of grain.
   The year bodes ill, the weather worsens.
   Although the others don't agree,
   We need to keep the grain we have.   5
FIRST ALDERMAN   That's always been my policy
   In seeking to govern properly.
ESTEBAN   Then let's approach Fernán Gómez.
   I cannot stand these forecasters
   Who, knowing nothing, claim that they   10
   Can tell the future, making us
   Believe that they alone have access to
   God's secrets. They carry on like theologians,
   Debating what has and will occur,
   But, as for the present, which is   15
   What matters most to us, the one who seems
   The wisest is the greatest fool.
   You'd think the clouds and all the movements of
   The stars are their property!
   How can they know what's happening   20
   Above to worry us to death
   With their prophecies? They tell
   Us what and when we ought to sow:
   Your wheat here, your barley there; your veg,
   Your mustard, cucumbers, pumpkins.   25
   Ask me, it's them that are pumpkins!
   They forecast the death of some great leader;
   It happens, yes, but in Transylvania.
   As for wine, they tell us there won't be any,
   But the beer's alright—in Germany!   30
   In Gascony all the cherries will freeze,
   In Hircania[7] tigers will grow on trees!
   But sow or not, does it really matter
   If we know every year ends in December?
        [*Enter* LEONELO, *a graduate, and* BARRILDO.]
LEONELO   No way you'll be teacher's pet today.   35
   The others have got there before us.
BARRILDO   How was it in Salamanca?[8]
LEONELO   So, so.

---

7. Part of ancient Persia, famous for its tigers since Antiquity.   8. The University of Salamanca, established in the 13th century, was one of the most famous in Europe.

BARRILDO   You'll know as much as Bartolo,[9] then.

LEONELO   But not as much as your local barber.
Everything I told you's known   40
To everyone.

BARRILDO   But even so,
You've come back educated.

LEONELO   I've tried
To learn the things that matter.

BARRILDO   There's such
A lot of books these days, everyone thinks
He's an expert.

LEONELO   Which is why I think   45
They know far less. It's not condensed
Enough, you see. Instead of summaries,
It's all long-winded stuff, all froth
That only leads to more confusion.
The experienced reader sees so many books,   50
He ends up driven to distraction.
I don't deny, of course, that printing has
Allowed true genius to emerge,
And furthermore protects great works
Against the ruthless march of time,   55
Making them known throughout the world.
It was invented by a German,
A certain Gutenberg from Mainz,[1]
Whose place in history is thus
Assured. But many men, who were   60
Regarded as important, lost
Their reputation when their works
Appeared in print. As well as this,
There are those so-called experts who
Have published pure rubbish in   65
The guise of wisdom, and those who,
Driven by envy, publish in the name
Of someone else they hate, merely to harm
His reputation.

BARRILDO   I disagree
With you.

LEONELO   You think it right that fools   70
Should take revenge on men of talent?

BARRILDO   But Leonelo, printing is progress.

LEONELO   For centuries we've done without it.
What's more, this century of ours,
It hasn't given us another Saint Jerome   75
Or an Augustine!

BARRILDO   Let's leave it! Take
A seat! No point in arguing.

---

9. Bartolus of Sassoferrato, an Italian jurist of the 14th century,
regarded as the European inventor of printing from movable types.

1. Johann Gutenberg of Mainz,

[*Enter* JUAN ROJO *and another* PEASANT.]

JUAN ROJO Believe me, nowadays you'd need
  To sell four farms to give a girl
  A proper dowry. The people here   80
  Can criticize, but really they
  Have no idea.

PEASANT   Any news
  Of the Commander? Did I say something
  I shouldn't?

JUAN ROJO   You heard how he treated
  Laurencia!

PEASANT   The man's a beast!   85
  I'd have him swing from that olive-tree!

    [*Enter the* COMMANDER, ORTUÑO, *and* FLORES.]

COMMANDER   God be with you all!

ALDERMAN   My good lord!

COMMANDER   I beg you, do not rise!

ALDERMAN   But let
  Your lordship sit as usual.
  The rest of us are better standing.   90

COMMANDER   I insist, you must be seated.

ESTEBAN   It falls
  To noblemen to grant true honor. Those
  Who have no honor cannot grant it.

COMMANDER   Come now, sit! There are matters to discuss.

ESTEBAN   Did your lordship see the greyhound?   95

COMMANDER   My men were quite amazed to see
  How fleet of foot it was.

ESTEBAN   In truth,
  An amazing creature. As fast
  As any runaway thief or coward's tongue.

COMMANDER   I'd like to have you set it on   100
  A hare that keeps escaping me.

ESTEBAN   It shall be done. Where is it?

COMMANDER   There!
  Your daughter!

ESTEBAN   My daughter? You think
  She merits being chased by you?

COMMANDER   She needs a talking to!

ESTEBAN   But why?   105

COMMANDER   She persists in annoying me.
  One of the other women here,
  The wife of someone in this square,
  And quite important, saw how taken I was
  With her and let herself be taken.   110

ESTEBAN   Then she did wrong. And you, my lord,
  Do wrong in speaking quite so freely.

COMMANDER   Oh, what an eloquent peasant you are!
  Flores! Arrange for him to have
  A copy of Aristotle's *Politics*.   115

He has to read it.
ESTEBAN   This town, my lord,
    Is happy to be governed by you.
    But there are people of great worth
    In Fuente Ovejuna.
LEONELO   Was there ever
    Such scant respect?
COMMANDER   Alderman, have I   120
    Said something to upset you?
ALDERMAN   You speak
    Unjustly. To speak of us like that
    Is to deny us honor.
COMMANDER   You believe
    You have honor? You'll be claiming next
    You are knights of Calatrava!   125
ALDERMAN   There are doubtless some who wear the Cross
    You place upon their breast whose blood
    Is far less pure than ours.[2]
COMMANDER   You think
    My blood makes yours more impure?
ALDERMAN   Bad deeds have never cleansed, my lord.   130
    They merely stain.
COMMANDER   At all events,
    I honor your women.
MAGISTRATE   Your words
    Dishonor them, your actions even more.
COMMANDER   Such tedious peasant values! Thank God
    For cities! There at least a man   135
    Of quality enjoys himself
    Without hindrance. Why, married men
    Are glad to see their wives favored.
ESTEBAN   I'm sure they aren't. You are saying this
    To put us off our guard. God lives   140
    In cities too, and punishment
    Can come with even greater speed.
COMMANDER   Away with you!
MAGISTRATE   How dare he speak to us
    Like this!
COMMANDER   Get out of the square! All of you!
ESTEBAN   We are going.
COMMANDER   And show more respect!   145
FLORES   Please, sir, calm down!
COMMANDER   They intend to hatch
    Some plot behind my back!
ORTUÑO   Patience, sir!
COMMANDER   I can't believe I *am* so patient!
    Go back to your houses . . . separately!

2. Renaissance Spain, where Muslims and Jews lived alongside of Christians, was preoccupied with the
purity of Christian blood. Esteban uses the theme to allude to the Commander's impurity of sexual intention
toward Laurencia and his political abuse of all the peasants of Fuente Ovejuna.

LEONELO   Heavens, can you endure this? 150
ESTEBAN   I'm going this way.

[*Exit* PEASANTS.]

COMMANDER   What can one say
  Of such people?
ORTUÑO   You never hide
  The fact you can't be bothered listening
  When they complain.
COMMANDER   Are they my equals?
FLORES   It's not a question of being equal, sir. 155
COMMANDER   And the peasant who stole my bow!
  Is he to go unpunished?
FLORES   I think
  I saw him at Laurencia's door
  Last night, or at the very least
  Someone whose cloak looked just like his. 160
  I gave him a present—from ear
  To ear—to mark the occasion.
COMMANDER   Where is the fellow now?
FLORES   I'm told
  He's around, sir.
COMMANDER   He has a nerve!
  Still here after trying to kill me! 165
FLORES   We'll get him soon, like a bird in a snare
  Or a fish on a hook.
COMMANDER   Before my sword
  Granada and Córdoba both tremble,
  Yet this boy, this peasant, dares point
  An arrow at my breast! The world 170
  Has gone mad, Flores.
FLORES   The power of love,
  My lord. But since he let you live,
  You're in his debt.
COMMANDER   I've controlled myself,
  Ortuño. If I had not, this town
  In two short hours would have been 175
  Reduced to ashes. Until the time
  Is ripe, I shall rein in my longing for
  Revenge. What did Pascuala have
  To say?
FLORES   She says she's soon to be married.
COMMANDER   And does she plan to settle her account? 180
FLORES   She says you can have it in cash, sir.
COMMANDER   And Olalla?
ORTUÑO   An amusing answer.
COMMANDER   She's a spirited creature.
ORTUÑO   She says
  Her fiancé's on his guard, because
  You send her messages and visit her 185
  So often with your servants. But when

He's looking the other way, she'll let
You enter.

COMMANDER   Excellent! But the yokel's careful?

ORTUÑO   He is, but his head's in the clouds.

COMMANDER   And what about Inés?

FLORES   Which one?   190

COMMANDER   Antón's wife.

FLORES   You can have her any time.
I spoke to her in the stable-yard.
It's the back way in with her!

COMMANDER   I love
These easy women well and pay them ill.
Ah, Flores, if they only knew   195
Their true worth!

FLORES   A woman's coolness makes
For better satisfaction. She yields
Too soon, it spoils anticipation.
There are some, as Aristotle says,
Who long for men as matter longs   200
For form.[3] But where's the surprise
In that?

COMMANDER   A man who's driven mad
By passion cannot complain if she
Yields quickly, even though he then
Has little time for her. The things   205
We long for, easily obtained,
Are easily forgotten.

          [Enter CIMBRANOS, a soldier.]

CIMBRANOS   Is
The Commander here?

ORTUÑO   He stands before you.

CIMBRANOS   Fernán Gómez, bravest of men.
Remove at once this cap of green,   210
This cloak, and in their place put on
Your shining helmet, your suit of armor.
The Master of Santiago, aided by
The Count of Cabra, both of them
Supporting Isabella's cause,[4]   215
Surround Ciudad Real and thus
Girón. We run the risk of losing what
For Calatrava has cost us so
Much blood. From high upon the battlements
Torchlights illuminate the lions   220
And castles of Castile, the bars
Of Aragon. And though the King
Of Portugal supports Girón,
He will do well if he survives

---

3. An Aristotelian idea popularized in the Renaissance held that "female" matter longs for "male" form;
Flores reduces and sexualizes the idea.   4. The Grand Master of the Order of Santiago, the most powerful
of the three orders, supported the cause of Isabella of Castile.

To see Almagro. Ride out, my Lord. 225
The very sight of you will make
Them turn and seek the safety of Castile.
COMMANDER   We'll hear no more. Ortuño, let
The trumpet sound in the square at once.
What soldiers do we have?
ORTUÑO   Some fifty, sir. 230
COMMANDER   Let all of them be mounted.
CIMBRANOS   Unless
You hurry, Castile will take Ciudad Real.
COMMANDER   I promise you, it will not fall!
          [*Exit all. Enter* MENGO, *and* LAURENCIA *and* PASCUALA *running.*]
PASCUALA   Mengo, stay with us!
MENGO   But why so frightened here?
LAURENCIA   It's safest if we go to town 235
Together, when there aren't any men,
In case we meet him.
MENGO   The devil's[5] ruining
Our lives!
LAURENCIA   He gives us no peace by night
Or day.
MENGO   If only a bolt from Heaven
Would strike this madman!
LAURENCIA   More beast 240
Than madman! Foul pestilence poisoning
Our village.
MENGO   I'm told Frondoso, in this
Meadow, to save you from him, aimed
An arrow at his black heart.
LAURENCIA   I hated men,
As you well know, but since that day 245
I see them differently. Frondoso was
So brave. And yet he could pay dearly
For that.
MENGO   It's best he gets away
From here.
LAURENCIA   I've told him so, as fond
Of him as I've become. But when 250
I try to speak to him, it puts
Him in a furious temper, even though
The Commander's sworn to hang him upside down.
PASCUALA   Let's hope that someone strangles him!
MENGO   I'd rather see him stoned to death. 255
I swear to God, if I let loose
The stone I carry in my sling,
You'd hear the crack as it split his skull
In two. That Roman Sabalus
Wasn't half as vicious.

---

5. The Commander, Fernán Gómez.

LAURENCIA   I think you must   260
   Mean Heliogabalus.[6] He was a real beast.

MENGO   Sabalus, Gabalus, whatever!
   I'm no historian. But he was nothing
   Compared with this one. Nothing in
   The whole of Nature can compare   265
   With Fernán Gómez.

PASCUALA   True enough.
   He has the nature of a tigress.
       [Enter JACINTA.]

JACINTA   My friends, you have to help me, please!

LAURENCIA   Jacinta, what's the matter?

PASCUALA   You know
   We are your friends.

JACINTA   The Commander's servants . . .   270
   They're on their way to Ciudad Real.
   Armed less with noble steel than with
   Their vile and sordid wickedness,
   They plan to take me to him!

LAURENCIA   In that
   Case, God be with you! If he's going   275
   To take advantage of you, I dread
   To think what he'd do to me!

                          [She leaves.]

PASCUALA   And since
   I'm not a man, Jacinta, I
   Can't help you, either.

                          [She leaves.]

MENGO   But I am,
   And I will. Come here, stand close to me!   280

JACINTA   Do you have any weapons to defend us?

MENGO   The first God made

JACINTA   You mean you don't?

MENGO   These stones, Jacinta. Lots of them!
       [Enter FLORES and ORTUÑO.]

FLORES   Did you think you could run away
   From us?

JACINTA   Mengo, I'm done for!

MENGO   Gentlemen,   285
   We are poor peasants!

ORTUÑO   Are you
   Intending to defend the girl?

MENGO   I'm asking you to leave her be.
   She's a relative. It's my duty to
   Protect her.

FLORES   Kill him!

MENGO   I swear to God,   290
   Provoke me and I'll use my sling!

---

6. Roman emperor from 218–222 C.E.

It's your life that will be lost!
    [*Enter the* COMMANDER *and* CIMBRANOS.]
COMMANDER   What's going on? You get me to dismount
  For this?
FLORES   These village scum defy us!
  You'd do well to raze their village to   295
  The ground. They are nothing but trouble.
MENGO   My lord, I beg you. Punish these men
  For what they try to do to us.
  In your name they would take this girl
  Away with them, despite the fact   300
  She's married and has honorable parents.
  I ask for leave to take her home.
COMMANDER   I give them leave to take revenge
  On you. Hand over the sling at once!
MENGO   My lord!
COMMANDER   Flores, Ortuño, Cimbranos,   305
  Use it to tie his hands.
MENGO   Is this
  How you defend her honor?
COMMANDER   Who
  Does Fuente Ovejuna and its rabble think
  I am?
MENGO   But how have I or any of
  The villagers offended you?   310
FLORES   Is he to die?
COMMANDER   Don't tarnish your swords
  On him! They'll find more honorable tasks
  Ahead.
ORTUÑO   What, then?
COMMANDER   He shall be flogged!
  That oak tree there! Tie him fast, remove
  His clothes, and use these reins!
MENGO   My lord,   315
  Have pity! You are a noble man.
COMMANDER   Beat him, until the studs fly free
  From their stitching!
MENGO   Oh, Heavens, will you
  Allow such cruel deeds to go
  Unpunished?
        [*Exit* MENGO *and the* SERVANTS.]
COMMANDER   Well now, my pretty peasant,   320
  Why run away? Would you prefer
  A yokel to a man of my
  Great rank?
JACINTA   They offended my honor.
  To take me for yourself is not.
  The way to give it back to me.   325
COMMANDER   To take you for myself?
JACINTA   My father is

An honorable man. Not of
Such noble birth as you, my lord,
But nobler in his deeds and actions.
COMMANDER You think these peasant insults will   330
Dispel my anger? Come!
JACINTA   Come where?
COMMANDER With me!
JACINTA   Consider this well, my lord.
COMMANDER I consider it ill for you, my dear.
You shan't be mine. You shall become
My soldiers' baggage.
JACINTA   As long as I   335
Have life, there's no one in the world
Can do me wrong.
COMMANDER   Get moving!
JACINTA   Have pity!
COMMANDER You'll find none here!
JACINTA   I call on Heaven
To punish your cruelty!

                                [*They carry her off. All exit.*]

        [*Enter* LAURENCIA *and* FRONDOSO.]
LAURENCIA You know how dangerous it is,   340
And yet you dare to come here.
FRONDOSO   Which goes
To show how fond of you I am.
I was up there on the hill. I saw
The Commander leave. My faith in you
Got rid of all my fear. Let's hope   345
He never comes back and rots in Hell!
LAURENCIA No point in cursing him. They say
The one you want to die lives longest.
FRONDOSO Then let him live a thousand years
And die the quickest! Laurencia, I want   350
To know if you care for me at all;
If the loyalty I've shown has made
Me in the least deserving. The town
Already sees the two of us as one
And cannot understand why we   355
Are not. Why not forget all past
Disdain? I'm asking you to marry me.
LAURENCIA Then you and all the village too
Had better know . . . that I agree.
FRONDOSO I kiss your feet for such a favor.   360
I promise you it gives my life
New meaning.
LAURENCIA   All right, enough of that.
The thing you have to do is ask
My father. Oh, look! He's coming with
My uncle. Don't worry, Frondoso!   365
I'll be your wife, no problem.

FRONDOSO   I place my trust in God.
> [*She hides. Enter* ESTEBAN *the magistrate and the* ALDERMAN.]

ESTEBAN   The way that he behaved upset
  The entire crowd. His actions were
  Outrageous. No one is surprised   370
  By his excesses. And now Jacinta's made
  To suffer for it.

ALDERMAN   The Catholic kings[7]—
  The people call them that already—
  Will soon have Spain obedient to their laws.
  Santiago, their Captain-General,   375
  Already rides against Girón,
  Who holds Ciudad Real. But yes,
  Jacinta is a decent girl.
  I do feel sorry for her.

ESTEBAN   And Mengo too
  Was flogged?

ALDERMAN   His body the color of   380
  The blackest cloth or ink.

ESTEBAN   I'll hear
  No more. It makes me boil to see
  Such wickedness. Everyone speaks ill
  Of him. As for myself, what use
  Is this rod of office?

ALDERMAN   But if   385
  His servants were to blame, why be
  Upset?

ESTEBAN   You'd like to hear more? I'm told
  The other day they came across
  Pedro Redondo's wife, down in
  The valley, and when he'd had his way   390
  With her, he gave her to his servants.

ALDERMAN   There's someone there! Who is it?

FRONDOSO   It's me,
  Frondoso. I'd like permission to speak
  With you.

ESTEBAN   Since when do family
  Require permission? Your father gave   395
  You life and I much love. I've seen
  You grow. To me you are a son.

FRONDOSO   Then, trusting in your love, I'd ask
  Of you the greatest favor. You know
  My father . . .

ESTEBAN   Has this Fernán Gómez wronged you?   400

FRONDOSO   He has.

ESTEBAN   I thought as much.

FRONDOSO   The fact is, sir,

---

7. Ferdinand and Isabella, whose rise to absolute sovereignty holds out the promise of political reform to the peasants of Fuente Ovejuna.

That knowledge of your love for me
Makes me so bold as to declare
I love Laurencia and wish
To marry her. Forgive me if,   405
In asking for her hand, my tongue
Has run away with me or my
Request seems over-bold.
ESTEBAN   No, not
At all, Frondoso. You give me another lease
Of life, allaying my greatest fear.   410
I thank the heavens that you do me
This honor; am grateful to your love
That you have shown such honesty.
But now it's only right, of course,
Your father is informed. If he   415
Does not object, I am agreed.
That being so, you have my blessing.
ALDERMAN   Should not the girl be asked, before
You agree to anything?
ESTEBAN   Oh, don't
You worry, they'll have seen to that,   420
Agreed between themselves before
It's gone this far. We could discuss
The dowry if you want. I'd like
To give you money.
FRONDOSO   But I don't need
A dowry, sir. It's not important.   425
ALDERMAN   Be thankful, Esteban, he'll take
Her as God made her.
ESTEBAN   I think it best
I ask her what she thinks.
FRONDOSO   Of course.
No point in going against a person's wishes.
ESTEBAN   Daughter! Laurencia!
LAURENCIA   Yes, father?   430
ESTEBAN   You see how she always obeys me?
Laurencia, my dear, there's something I'd like
To ask you . . . (come over here a moment) . . .
How do you feel about your friend, Gila,
Taking Frondoso as a husband?   435
He's an honorable boy, as good
As any in Fuente Ovejuna.
LAURENCIA   Gila . . . ?
ESTEBAN   A deserving girl, a match
For him in every respect.
LAURENCIA   Well, yes, father,
I have to agree.
ESTEBAN   But even so,   440
As ugly as sin! Frondoso's far
Better off with you.

LAURENCIA   Father, that's such
   A rotten trick, and at your age!
ESTEBAN   You love him?
LAURENCIA   I'm very fond of him
   And have grown fonder still. But as   445
   You know . . .
ESTEBAN   You want me to say "yes?"
LAURENCIA   On my behalf.
ESTEBAN   It's in my hands?
   All right, that's settled. Come on, we'll find
   My old friend in the square.
ALDERMAN   Let's go.
ESTEBAN   My boy, the question of the dowry.   450
   What shall we say to him? I'm quite prepared
   To give you four thousand maravedis.[8]
FRONDOSO   But, sir, to accept it would offend me.
ESTEBAN   Oh, come along. Such things are soon
   Forgotten. If there's no dowry, I tell   455
   You you'll regret it afterward.
         [*Exit* ESTEBAN *and the* ALDERMAN. FRONDOSO *and* LAURENCIA *remain.*]
LAURENCIA   Are you happy, Frondoso?
FRONDOSO   Why would
   I not be? I'm head over heels with joy!
   My eyes reveal the feelings of
   My heart when they see you are mine,   460
   My sweet Laurencia!
         [*They leave. Enter the* MASTER, *the* COMMANDER, FLORES, *and* ORTUÑO.]
COMMANDER   You must escape. There's nothing else
   To do.
MASTER   The wall was weak, the enemy
   Immensely powerful.
COMMANDER   Even so,
   They paid for it in blood and lives.   465
MASTER   Nor can they boast that their spoils
   Include the flag of Calatrava.
   That would have crowned their enterprise
   And been their greatest victory.
COMMANDER   But still, Girón, your hopes now lie   470
   In ruins.
MASTER   What can I do if Fortune is
   So blind that he who tastes success
   Today, must see it snatched away
   Tomorrow?
VOICES [*off*]   All hail Castile's great victory!
MASTER   Their torches crown the battlements.   475
   The flags of victory adorn
   The windows of the highest towers.
COMMANDER   They could as easily adorn

8. A Spanish coin.

Them with their blood. This is more tragedy
 Than celebration.
MASTER   I shall return   480
 To Calatrava.
COMMANDER   And I to Fuente Ovejuna.
 You must decide if you'll pursue
 Your kinsman's cause or now accept
 The Catholic Kings.
MASTER   I'll write and let
 You know.
COMMANDER   Time will help you make the right   485
 Decision.
MASTER   Unless, as often happens in
 Our youth, it proves the agent of deception.
    [*They leave. Enter the wedding party:* MUSICIANS, MENGO, FRONDOSO,
    LAURENCIA, PASCUALA, BARRILDO, ESTEBAN, MAGISTRATE, *and* JUAN ROJO.]
MUSICIANS Long life to them,
     The newly-weds!
     Long life!   490
MENGO   Come on, you lot! It's the song that needs
 More life.
BARRILDO   No doubt you think you could write
 A better one!
FRONDOSO   Mengo knows more
 Of whipping than composing.
MENGO   That's true,
 But there down in the valley there's   495
 A chap the Commander . . .
BARRILDO   No! Say
 No more! The man's an animal,
 Dishonors all of us!
MENGO   He had
 A hundred soldiers beat me! I had
 A sling, that's all. It was terrible!   500
 But not as bad as this other fellow, who shall
 Be nameless. They pumped black ink
 And stones right up his backside. Can you
 Imagine?
BARRILDO   It must have been a joke!
MENGO   Since when are enemas a joke!   505
 They may be good for you, but I think
 It would kill me.
FRONDOSO   Anyway, let's hear
 The song now, let's see how good it is.
BARRILDO [*sings*] I pray to God that their life
    Be long and always happy;   510
    That they will never come to blows
    On account of jealousy.
    Oh, let them go to their graves,
    Worn out by being carefree.

I pray to God that their life   515
  Be long and always happy.
MENGO   And the devil take the author of
  Such dreadful poetry!
BARRILDO   I had to get
  It written quickly!
MENGO   I'll tell you what
  I think of such poets. You must   520
  Have seen a fellow making fritters.
  He throws great lumps of dough into
  A pan of boiling oil until it's full.
  Some come out swollen, some deformed,
  Some totally misshapen, some   525
  Are fine, others not, some burnt to death,
  Some soggy. And that's your poetry too.
  The subject matter is the poet's dough.
  He throws it in the pan, which is
  His paper, and after it spoonfuls   530
  Of honey to cover up the taste
  And make it sweeter. Trouble is,
  There's no one wants to try it when
  It's done. So he's the one who's left
  With indigestion.
BARRILDO   Stop fooling about.   535
  Let the young lovers speak.
LAURENCIA   Let me kiss
  Your hand.
JUAN ROJO   My hand? But why, Laurencia?
  You should kiss your father's hand,
  In gratitude for what he's done
  For you and for Frondoso.
ESTEBAN   My friend,   540
  I pray that Heaven will offer them
  Its hand and constant blessing.
FRONDOSO   Why don't
  The two of you bless both of us?
JUAN ROJO   Come on! Let's have some music. Sing!
  They are as one!   545
MUSICIANS [*sing*]   The village-girl came down the path
  From Fuente Ovejuna.
  She was soon followed by the knight
  Who came from Calatrava.
  She hid amongst the branches there,   550
  She felt such shame and fear;
  Pretending she had not seen him,
  She drew the leaves around her.
  "Why try to hide yourself away?
  You really are quite pretty.   555
  My eyes can see through walls of stone
  When someone takes my fancy."

And so the knight went up to her,
And she grew still more terrified;
She used the trees to form a screen,   560
Behind which she could safely hide.
But, as you know, a man in love
Can conquer any mountain;
There's nothing can keep him at bay,
And so he spoke to her again: 565
"Why try to hide yourself away?
You really are quite pretty;
My eyes can see through walls of stone
When someone takes my fancy."

[*Enter the* COMMANDER, FLORES, ORTUÑO, *and* CIMBRANOS.]

COMMANDER   Stop these celebrations now!   570
Let no one cause any trouble here.
JUAN ROJO   This is a serious business, sir,
But if that's what you want. Perhaps
You'd like to join us? But why this show
Of arms? I take it you have been   575
Victorious.
FRONDOSO   Heaven help me! I'm as good
As dead!
LAURENCIA   That way, Frondoso! Run!
COMMANDER   Get hold of him and tie him up!
JUAN ROJO   Best give yourself up, lad!
FRONDOSO   You mean
You'll let them kill me?
JUAN ROJO   Why should they   580
Do that?
COMMANDER   I'm not the kind of man
To kill someone who's innocent.
In any case, if he were guilty,
My men would have put an end to him.
Take him away and lock him up!   585
His father shall be his judge and so
Pass sentence.
PASCUALA   But can't you see, my lord,
He's getting married?
COMMANDER   You think that matters?
There must be someone else to take
His place.
PASCUALA   If he's offended you,   590
You should forgive him, being the man
You are.
COMMANDER   Pascuala, I've no authority
In this. His crime has been against
Téllez Girón, the Master; against
The Order and its sacred honor.   595
The punishment must serve as an
Example, just in case others in

The future choose to rise against him.
You know already that he aimed
The crossbow at myself, the Grand   600
Commander—proof enough, I think,
Of his true loyalty!
ESTEBAN   I am
His father-in-law and therefore speak
On his behalf. Are you surprised
That someone so in love should act   605
As he has done? If you attempted to
Abduct his wife, it's natural
That he should want to save her.
COMMANDER   You are
An idiot, magistrate.
ESTEBAN   I appeal
To your virtuous nature, sir.
COMMANDER   I did   610
Not try to take his wife. She wasn't his wife.
ESTEBAN   Of course you did! There's nothing more
To say. There are new rulers in
Castile who'll introduce such laws
And orders as will put an end   615
To all disorder. When they have ceased
To be engaged in war, they would
Do well to rid their villages
And towns of men whose power comes
From wearing crosses. The King alone   620
Should be allowed to wear the cross.[9]
COMMANDER   Seize his rod of office!
ESTEBAN   My lord,
You are most welcome.
COMMANDER   Just the thing
To beat him with, as if he were
Some over-frisky horse!
ESTEBAN   Then beat me!   625
I bow to you as overlord.
PASCUALA   You'd make an old man suffer?
LAURENCIA   You do
This now because he is my father.
What wrong have I done you that you
Must punish him?
COMMANDER   Take her away!   630
And let ten soldiers guard her!

                                    [*He and his men exit.*]

ESTEBAN   Let Heaven administer its justice!

                                            [*He exits.*]

PASCUALA   The wedding's become a wake.

9. One of the first tasks confronted by Isabella when she became ruler of Castile was the government of
the three orders; by 1499, her husband Ferdinand had become Grand Master of all three orders, and in
1523 they were incorporated into the crown of Castile by papal edict.

BARRILDO   Will no
  One here speak out?
MENGO   Exactly what
  I did. I've got the marks to prove it.   635
  Someone else can test his anger.
JUAN ROJO   We need
  To talk, all of us.
MENGO   Much better bite
  Your tongue. My kettle-drums¹ ache,
  And both as red as salmon steaks.

Act Three

[*Enter* ESTEBAN, ALONSO, *and* BARRILDO.]

ESTEBAN Haven't they come yet?
BARRILDO   No, not yet.
ESTEBAN Everything goes from bad to worse.
BARRILDO Most of them know about the meeting.
ESTEBAN Frondoso locked up in the tower,
  Laurencia in such terrible danger . . .   5
  We need God's help in this!

    [*Enter* JUAN ROJO *and the* ALDERMAN.]

JUAN ROJO   Esteban, keep
  Your voice down! This meeting must be secret,
  For all our sakes!
ESTEBAN   The wonder is
  I do not shout much louder.

    [*Enter* MENGO.]

MENGO   Alright,
  I'm here. Let the meeting begin.   10
ESTEBAN Honorable friends, I speak to you
  As someone whose grey beard is bathed
  In tears, and ask what final rites
  We can perform in honor of
  This town, so damaged and destroyed.   15
  What honorable rites indeed,
  If there is not a single one
  Of us whose life that criminal
  Has not dishonored? Tell me now if there
  Is someone here whose honor is   20
  Unscathed. You are as one, I think,
  In your complaints. And so I say
  To you: if you have common cause,
  What are you waiting for? Is not
  What has befallen us the greatest of   25
  Misfortunes?
JUAN ROJO   The greatest the world
  Has ever seen. But now, we have

---

1. The two cheeks of his bottom.

Been told, the King and Queen bring peace
To all Castile. Soon they will be
In Córdoba, so why not send   30
Two aldermen to state our case
And beg them to put right these wrongs?
BARRILDO   But Fernando is still at war
With many enemies. He won't
Have time for our complaints. It's best   35
We think of something else.
ALDERMAN   If you
Ask me, I think we should evacuate
The town.
JUAN ROJO   There isn't time.
MENGO   And once
He gets to know our plans, it's going
To cost a good few lives.
ALDERMAN   The mast   40
Of our ship is broken, all
Of us are overcome by panic.
They violently seize the daughter of
An honorable man, the man
Who justly rules this town of ours, and on   45
His head unjustly break the very rod
Of justice. When was any slave
So vilely treated?
JUAN ROJO   So what do you think
The town should do?
ALDERMAN   The town should die,
Or kill these tyrants. We are many, they   50
Are few.
BARRILDO   Take arms against our overlord?
ESTEBAN   In the eyes of God the King alone
Is our lord, not men like these;
No better than wild animals.
If God is on our side, why should we be   55
Afraid?
MENGO   Listen to me, my friends.
I beg of you, take care. I speak
For all the common peasants. They
Are the ones who suffer most, and so,
Although I know how fearful   60
They are, I also know that they
Are sensible.
JUAN ROJO   If all of us
Are made to suffer equally,
What are we waiting for? They burn
Our houses and our vineyards. I say   65
We take revenge!
          [Enter LAURENCIA, disheveled.]
LAURENCIA   Let me in! This meeting is for men,

I know, but if a woman has no vote,
  She has a voice! Don't you know me?
ESTEBAN Are you my daughter?
JUAN ROJO   Who else is it
  But your Laurencia?
LAURENCIA   You see? I am   70
  So changed, you even wonder who I am.
ESTEBAN My dear daughter!
LAURENCIA   No, not your daughter!
ESTEBAN Why not, why not, Laurencia?
LAURENCIA   For many reasons.
  The first is that you let them take
  Me off and did not seek revenge   75
  For it, did not attempt to make
  Those traitors pay. I'm not Frondoso's wife
  As yet, which means I have no husband to
  Avenge my name. You are responsible
  For that. Until the marriage-night,   80
  That obligation is a father's, not
  A husband's; it's like a precious stone:
  I'm not responsible for seeing that
  It's safe from thieves until it's in
  My hands. When Fernán Gómez took   85
  Me off, you let him do it, just
  As shepherds stand and watch the wolf
  Which steals their sheep! They threatened me
  With knives, abused me with their words,
  Did everything they could to force   90
  My chastity to their foul desires!
  You see my hair? You see these marks,
  These cuts and bruises? These stains of blood?
  Do you believe that you are men
  Of honor? Do you believe you are   95
  True fathers? How can you see me here
  And not feel all the pain I feel pierce
  Your very souls? You are like sheep,
  The name of our town well chosen.
  I'll take up arms, pursue my cause   100
  Myself. You are like stones, unfeeling bronze
  Or jasper . . . tigresses . . . But no,
  Not tigresses! For when the hunters steal
  Their cubs, they chase and kill them in
  Their rage, then plunge into the sea   105
  Until they drown. But you are more
  Like timid hares. True Spaniards, no!
  Barbarians, yes! Or clucking hens!
  You allow others to carry off
  Your wives! You should bear distaffs!²   110

2. Used in spinning, normally the task of women.

Your swords are ornaments that serve
No purpose! I swear to God above
That women alone shall be responsible
For their honor, for their blood,
And make these traitors, these tyrants pay.   115
As for yourselves, you should be stoned
For what you are: housewives, men who are
Not men, effeminate cowards who would
Look better dressed in our skirts
And bonnets, rouge upon your cheeks   120
And lipstick on your lips! No doubt
You know our great Commander plans
To have Frondoso hanged upon
The battlements, without a charge
Or trial. He'll do the same to all   125
Of you. And I'll rejoice in that,
You men who are not men, for then
This town will have more dignity,
And once again we'll see that age
Return when there were women who   130
Were strong, true Amazons,[3] whose deeds
Amazed the world.
ESTEBAN   Listen, daughter. I will
Not take these insults lying down!
I'll go alone, no matter who
The enemy.
JUAN ROJO   Me too, no matter what   135
His strength and number.
ALDERMAN   All of us
Shall die together.
BARRILDO   A pole shall bear
Our banner on the wind. We'll put
An end to all these monsters!
JUAN ROJO   What order shall
We march in?
MENGO   We'll keep no order. We are   140
As one, a single voice. We're all
Agreed. The tyrants have to die!
ESTEBAN   Take bows, lances, staves, sticks!
MENGO   Long live
The King and Queen!
ALL   Long may they live!
MENGO   And all the traitors die!
                                    [*Exit the men.*]
LAURENCIA   Go now,   145
And may God guide you! Women of
This town, come quickly! Restore your honor!
     [*Enter* PASCUALA, JACINTA, *and others.*]

---

3. The legendary civilization of women warriors in Scythia.

PASCUALA   What is it? Why this shouting?
LAURENCIA   See there!
LAURENCIA   They go to kill Fernán Gómez,
    Our men, both young and old, as well   150
    As boys, all joined in common cause.
    But do you think that they alone
    Deserve the praise for this, that they
    Have suffered more than us?
JACINTA   So what do you have
    In mind?
LAURENCIA   We should arrange ourselves   155
    In ordered ranks to undertake
    A task which will amaze the world.
    Jacinta, the wrong you suffered means
    That you should be the corporal in
    Our women's regiment.
JACINTA   But yours   160
    Was just as great.
LAURENCIA   Pascuala, our ensign.
PASCUALA   I'll find a flagpole for our flag.
    I'll show you I deserve to be
    Our standard-bearer.
LAURENCIA   No time for that.
    Since fortune favors us, our shawls   165
    Shall be our flags.
PASCUALA   Let's choose a captain.
LAURENCIA   No.
PASCUALA   Why not?
LAURENCIA   Because no hero from the past,
    No Cid or Rodomonte[4] is
    My match in bravery!
        [*Exit the women. Enter* FRONDOSO *with his hands ties;* FLORES, ORTUÑO,
        CIMBRANOS, *and the* COMMANDER.]
COMMANDER   The rope you've used to tie his hands . . .   170
    There's some left over. Use it to string
    Him up. Make him suffer even more.
FRONDOSO   You do your name much good by this,
    My lord!
COMMANDER   Hang him from the battlements.
FRONDOSO   But I'd no intention of killing you.   175
                                        [*Noise off.*]

FLORES   Listen! That noise!
COMMANDER   What is it?
FLORES   They want
    To stop the judgment, sir.
                                        [*Noise.*]

ORTUÑO   They try

---

4. Rodomonte is the anti-hero of Ariosto's *Orlando Furioso*, whereas the Cid is the hero of the medieval
Spanish epic, *The Poem of My Cid*.

To break the doors down!

COMMANDER   The doors of this house,
The residence of our sacred Order?

FLORES The entire town is there!

JUAN ROJO [*off*]   Come! Break   180
It down, smash everything! We'll burn
It to the ground!

ORTUÑO   The people rise against us.
We'll never stop them.

COMMANDER   Against me?

ORTUÑO Such is the fury of the crowd,
They've smashed the doors down.

COMMANDER   Untie him! 185
Frondoso, calm the magistrate.

FRONDOSO I'll try, my lord. Their love for me
Inspires them.

                [*Exits.*]

MENGO [*off*]   Long live the King
And Queen! The traitors have to die!

FLORES My lord, they must not find you here.   190

COMMANDER What they will find is that this room
Is strong and well protected. They'll soon
Turn back.

FLORES   When people rise against
The wrongs that have been done to them,
They never stop until they've tasted blood
Or been avenged.   195

COMMANDER   This door will serve
As our portcullis, these swords as our
Defence.

FRONDOSO [*off*] Long live Fuente Ovejuna!

COMMANDER Oh, what a leader! Let's meet them face
To face, show them how rash they are!   200

FLORES My lord, it's you who might be rash.

ESTEBAN [*off*] We have the tyrant and his vile
Accomplices. Fuente Ovejuna! They
Must die!

    [*Enter* VILLAGERS.]

COMMANDER Wait, all of you!

VILLAGERS   Injustice does
Not wait!

COMMANDER You have to tell me what   205
Injustices they are. I'll put them right,
I swear.

VILLAGERS Fuente Ovejuna! Long
Live King Fernando! Death to all
False Christians and foul traitors!

COMMANDER   Listen!
I am your lord and master.

VILLAGERS   The Catholic Kings 210

Are our lords and masters!
COMMANDER   Wait!
    [*Exit the* COMMANDER.]
VILLAGERS   Fuente Ovejuna! Death to Fernán Gómez!
    [*The men of the village leave. The women enter, armed.*]
LAURENCIA   Halt! Women—no, brave soldiers! This
  Is where our hopes will be fulfilled.
PASCUALA   He'll see what women are when they   215
  Want vengeance. We'll drink his blood!
JACINTA   Stick
  His body on our lances!
PASCUALA   We're all agreed!
ESTEBAN [*off*]   See how the treacherous Commander dies!
COMMANDER [*off*]   Please God, have pity! Help me!
BARRILDO [*off*]   There's Flores!
MENGO [*off*]   Get him! He's the one who flogged me!
FRONDOSO [*off*]   I'm not   220
  Avenged until I've ripped his soul out!
LAURENCIA   We should go in.
PASCUALA   Don't get so worked up!
  Just watch the door.
BARRILDO [*off*]   I'll not be moved
  By your tears, you puffed-up marquesses!
LAURENCIA   Pascuala, I'm going in. What use   225
  Is any sword still in its scabbard?
                             [*Exit* LAURENCIA.]
BARRILDO [*off*]   Why, here's Ortuño.
FRONDOSO [*off*]   Slash his face!
    [FLORES *enters running, pursued by* MENGO.]
FLORES   Mengo, spare me! I'm not to blame.
MENGO   It wasn't enough to be a pimp,
  You went and whipped my arse as well!   230
PASCUALA   Hey, give him to us women, Mengo!
  Leave him to us! We'll see to him!
MENGO   He's yours. I know you'll do your best!
PASCUALA   Tit for tat for your flogging.
MENGO   See
  To it!
JACINTA   Come on, the traitor dies!   235
FLORES   At the hands of women?
JACINTA   You think
  It's not appropriate?
PASCUALA   Is that
  Why you are crying?
JACINTA   You organized
  His pleasures. Now you die.
PASCUALA   Let's kill
  The traitor.
FLORES   Please! Have pity!   240
    [*Enter* ORTUÑO, *pursued by* LAURENCIA.]

ORTUÑO   I swear it wasn't me . . .

LAURENCIA   I know

It was! Come! Stain your weapons with
The blood of these vile men!

PASCUALA   I'll kill

Until I have no strength for more!

ALL   Fuente Ovejuna! Long live Fernando,[5]   245
Our King!

> [*Exit all. Enter* KING FERNANDO *and* QUEEN ISABEL, *and* DON MANRIQUE,
> *Master of Santiago.*]

MANRIQUE   Our plan worked well and our hopes
Were quickly realized. Our troops
Faced little opposition, and if
They had, I doubt it would have caused   250
Us problems. Cabra holds the town
And will remain there just in case
Our enemies should try to take
It once again.

KING   A wise decision.

It's best he stays and that his troops   255
Be reinforced so their control
Is even more assured. If we
Do this, Alonso cannot do
Us harm, however many men
He seeks in Portugal. Cabra is well   260
Advised to stay and demonstrate
His bravery. By doing so
He guarantees our safety here,
And like a loyal sentinel
Protects the needs of our kingdom.   265

> [*Enter* FLORES, *wounded.*]

FLORES   Oh, noble King Fernando, whom
The heavens have chosen to become
The ruler of Castile: I beg
You let me speak and tell you of
The foulest deed the world has seen   270
From where the sun begins and ends
Its daily course.

KING   Control yourself.

FLORES   Oh, sovereign King, my injuries
Are such, my time so short, I must
Inform you of these terrible   275
Events without delay. I come
From Fuente Ovejuna. The people there
Have mercilessly killed their lord
And master: Fernán Gómez murdered by
His faithless subjects, vassals who   280
Believing they'd been wronged, rose up

---

5. The Spanish name of Ferdinand of Aragon.

Without good cause. These people called
Him tyrant, and on the strength of that
Committed this foul deed. They broke into
His house, and though he offered, as   285
An honorable man, to see
To their complaints, not only did
They fail to heed his words but rained
Upon the Cross upon his breast
A thousand cruel blows. And then   290
They threw him from the window to
The ground where all the women caught
Him on their pikes and swords.
They dragged his body to a house
And there, in competition with   295
Each other, tore his beard and hair,
And cut his face to shreds. Such was
The fury of the mob, that of
His mutilated flesh his ears
Remained the largest pieces. They smashed   300
His coat of arms with pikes and shouted that
Your coat of arms should take their place,
For his offended them. They then
Ransacked his house, as if he was
Some enemy they'd overcome,   305
And, having triumphed, shared the spoils
Among themselves. I saw all this
From where I chose to hide, for my
Unhappy fate declared that I,
Despite this tragedy, should live.   310
I did not move the whole day long,
But when night came I managed to escape
Unseen and bring you this account
Of what occurred. You are renowned
For being just, your Majesty,   315
And so I ask of you that for
Their evil deeds these criminals
Be made to pay.
KING   I promise you
They shall be punished. What you describe
Is so incredible, I shall   320
At once dispatch a magistrate
With orders to investigate
The case and punish those who are
To blame, so everyone may see
Crime does not pay. He'll have a captain for   325
Protection, for wrongs as great as these
Demand a punishment that is
Exemplary. See to this soldier's wounds . . .

    [*Exit all. Enter the* PEASANTS, *men and women, with* FERNÁN GÓMEZ's
    head fixed on a lance.]

MUSICIANS   Long life to King Fernando,
    Long life to Isabel;
    A cruel death to tyrants,   330
    And let them rot in Hell.
BARRILDO   Let's hear your song, Frondoso.
FRONDOSO   It goes
Like this. If someone thinks he can
Improve on it, then he can try.   335
    Long life to lovely Isabel
    And our King Fernando,
    They suit each other very well,
    Their love is strong, their love is true;
    One day Saint Michael at the gates,   340
    Will welcome them and let them in;
    Till then long life to both of them,
    And punish tyrants for their sins!
LAURENCIA   Barrildo, your turn.
BARRILDO   Alright,
Here goes. I've put some effort into this.   345
PASCUALA   Just sing it clearly. It'll be fine.
BARRILDO   Long life to both the Catholic kings,
    For theirs is the victory;
    We welcome them as our Lords
    To rule our lands successfully.   350
    Whatever battles lie ahead,
    We know they'll be triumphant,
    Their enemies both great and small,
    And down with cruel tyrants!
MUSICIANS   Long life to King Fernando,   355
    Long life to Isabel;
    A cruel death to tyrants,
    And let them rot in Hell.
LAURENCIA   Now Mengo!
FRONDOSO   Yes, come on! Let's hear you!
MENGO   You know I've a gift for poetry.   360
PASCUALA   Let's hear about the other gift,
  On the backside of your belly!
MENGO   One Sunday morning recently,
    He ordered me a whipping;
    I promise you it really hurt,   365
    My backside's still complaining.
    But then we put them on our spit
    And gave them all a roasting.
    Long life to both our Catholic kings,
    An end to the tyrants' boasting.   370
MUSICIANS   Long life to King Fernando,
    Long life to Isabel;
    A cruel death to tyrants,
    And let them rot in Hell.
ESTEBAN   Take the head down now.

MENGO   He looks as if   375
He's just been hanged.
    [*Enter* JUAN ROJO *with the royal coat of arms.*]
ALDERMAN   He's brought the coat
Of arms.
ESTEBAN   Let's see.
JUAN ROJO   Where shall I put it?
ALDERMAN   Why, there, outside the Council Chamber.
ESTEBAN   It looks magnificent!
BARRILDO   A joy
To behold!
FRONDOSO   As bright as any sun,   380
It marks the dawn of our new day!
ESTEBAN   Long live León and old Castile,
The bars of Aragón, and death
To tyranny! But listen now,
People of Fuente Ovejuna.   385
I may be old but my advice
Can do no harm. The King and Queen
Will want to know what's happened here,
Not least because our town is on
The route they take. You'd best
Agree on what you are to say to them.   390
FRONDOSO   So what is your advice?
ESTEBAN   On pain
Of death you all say "Fuente Ovejuna,"
And stick to it.
FRONDOSO   I think you're right.
Fuente Ovejuna did it!
ESTEBAN   Are you all   395
Agreed?
ALL   Agreed!
ESTEBAN   Imagine, then, that I'm
The judge. We'd best rehearse what we
Must do. Mengo's to be tortured first.
MENGO   There must be someone less strong-willed
Than me!
ESTEBAN   We're only pretending, Mengo!   400
MENGO   All right, get on with it!
ESTEBAN   Who killed
The Commander?
MENGO   Fuente Ovejuna!
ESTEBAN   You dog, you shall be tortured!
MENGO   Ahhhhh!
You can kill me! I'll not confess!
ESTEBAN   Confess, you wretch!
MENGO   All right, all right!   405
ESTEBAN   Who killed him, then?
MENGO   Fuente Ovejuna!
ESTEBAN   Turn

The screw![6]

MENGO   I shan't confess!

ESTEBAN   To hell
With the trial!
        [Enter the ALDERMAN.]

ALDERMAN   What are you doing here?

FRONDOSO What's happened, Cuadrado?

ALDERMAN   A judge
Has just arrived.

ESTEBAN   Let's go! The other way!   410

ALDERMAN He's brought a captain with him.

ESTEBAN   Who cares

ESTEBAN If he's brought the devil himself!
All of you know what you have to say.

ALDERMAN They're arresting everyone.

ESTEBAN   No need
To be afraid. Mengo, who killed   415
The Commander?

MENGO   Fuente Ovejuna!
        [*All exit. Enter the* MASTER OF CALATRAVA *and a* SOLDIER.]

MASTER You mean this really happened? I can't
Believe it. The poor man! For news
Like this you could be put to death!

SOLDIER My lord, I'm just the messenger.   420
I didn't mean to make you angry.

MASTER How can a mere village, though
Incensed, commit this dreadful crime?
I'll take five hundred men and raze
It to the ground. I shall obliterate   425
The memory of their names.

SOLDIER It's best you calm yourself, my lord.
They now obey the King. It would
Not do to anger him.

MASTER   How can
They serve the King when they have sworn   430
Allegiance to the Order?

SOLDIER   The courts
Would have to settle it.

MASTER   No court
Will give to me what was initially
Within his power. The King is sovereign,
I must accept it. And if they swear   435
Their loyalty to him, I must
Control my rage and now submit
To his authority. If I
Have made mistakes, my youth will be
My saviour and salvation. I feel   440
A sense of shame, but even so

6. Either thumbscrews or the rack, on which prisoners were tied and stretched out by tightening screws.

My honor is what matters most.
I know full well my obligations.
    [*They leave. Enter* LAURENCIA.]
LAURENCIA When we're in love, our fear for
  The one we love becomes true anguish,   445
  And adds to love a greater care
  When it concerns the one we cherish.
  Although our love be strong and true,
  Our fears affect our sense of trust,
  And haunt us with the dreadful thought   450
  The one we love may be lost to us.
  I worship my beloved husband.
  I know my life will be as nothing
  If fortune does not favor him.
  I only think of his well-being;   455
  His presence here adds to my worry,
  And yet I die when he's not with me.
    [*Enter* FRONDOSO.]
FRONDOSO Laurencia!
LAURENCIA   My dearest husband!
  It isn't safe. You shouldn't be here!
FRONDOSO Am I to think my love for you   460
  Deserves such coolness?
LAURENCIA   Your life's at risk.
  You must stay hidden.
FRONDOSO   Heaven forbid
  I ever give you cause to grieve.
LAURENCIA You've seen how cruelly the rest
  Are treated, how furiously this judge   465
  Proceeds to punish them. You have
  To save yourself, avoid the risk,
  Not seek it out.
FRONDOSO   You think I could
  Behave like that? Turn my back on all
  My friends when they most need me? Leave   470
  You here to face the danger? No!
  Don't ask me to! It isn't right
  For me to save my skin and not
  Concern myself with all of you
  At such a time.
                                        [*Cries off-stage.*]
                Listen! Someone   475
  Is being tortured. Listen!
JUDGE [*off*]   Speak!
  Old man, I want the truth!
FRONDOSO   Laurencia,
  They are torturing one of the old men!
LAURENCIA They show no mercy.
ESTEBAN [*off*]   All right! All right!
JUDGE [*off*] So let him speak! Who killed Fernando?   480

ESTEBAN [*off*] Feunte Ovejuna!
LAURENCIA   Such a noble father!
FRONDOSO The bravest of men!
JUDGE [*off*]   The boy!
  Still tighter! I know you know.
  Say who it was. Why won't you speak?
  Pull tighter still!
BOY [*off*]   Fuente Ovejuna!   485
JUDGE [*off*] In the King's name, I'll hang you all
  With my own hands. Who killed the Commander?
FRONDOSO They torture a mere boy and still
  He will not tell them!
LAURENCIA   Such brave people!
FRONDOSO Each one courageous!
JUDGE [*off*]   Bring the girl! Stretch   490
  Her on the rack! Tighten the screw!
LAURENCIA He's blind with anger!
JUDGE [*off*]   Believe me, the rack
  Will see to all of you! Who killed
  The Commander?
PASCUALA [*off*]   Fuente Ovejuna!
JUDGE [*off*] Once more. Tighten!
FRONDOSO   He's wasting his time.   495
LAURENCIA Pascuala refuses to tell him.
FRONDOSO Why be surprised? The children do
  So too.
JUDGE [*off*] You're only tickling them!
  Much harder!
PASCUALA [*off*] Oh, God, have mercy!
JUDGE [*off*]   Again!
  Are you deaf?
PASCUALA [*off*] Fuente Ovejuna!   500
JUDGE [*off*] The fat one there, the one half-naked.
  On the rack with him!
LAURENCIA   It must be Mengo!
FRONDOSO I'm afraid he'll tell them!
MENGO [*off*]   No! No!
JUDGE [*off*] Now tighter!
MENGO [*off*]   No!
JUDGE [*off*]   Do you need assistance?
MENGO [*off*] No, please!
JUDGE [*off*]   Then tell me, peasant! Who killed   505
  The Commander?
MENGO [*off*]   All right, I'll tell you.
JUDGE [*off*] Ease off a little.
FRONDOSO [*off*]   He's going to tell him!
JUDGE [*off*] Apply more pressure!
MENGO [*off*]   No more, no more!
  I'll tell you.
JUDGE [*off*] Who killed the Commander?

MENGO Fuente Ovejuna! Our little town!   510
JUDGE Who ever saw such scoundrels? They mock
  Their pain. The very one I thought
  Would crack is most defiant. Release them!
  This has become most tiresome.
FRONDOSO God bless you, Mengo! I was scared   515
  Beyond belief, but you have overcome
  My fear!
          [*Enter* MENGO, BARRILDO, *and the* ALDERMAN.]
BARRILDO You were brilliant, Mengo!
ALDERMAN Oh, very good indeed!
BARRILDO   A star!
MENGO Oh, ah!
BARRILDO   Here, have a drink! Take this!
MENGO Oh, ah! What is it?
BARRILDO   Lemon curd.   520
MENGO Aaahh!
FRONDOSO   Get it down you!
BARRILDO   That's the way.
FRONDOSO He's drunk it all. Now he'll be fine.
LAURENCIA Give him some food.
MENGO   Oh, ah!
BARRILDO   Have this
  On me!
LAURENCIA He only wants the wine!
FRONDOSO A man who's said "no" should have some, yes?   525
BARRILDO Do you want another?
MENGO   Ah, no, yes, yes!
FRONDOSO And you deserve it, Mengo!
LAURENCIA   Just look
  At him knocking them back!
FRONDOSO   Give him
  Some clothes. He must be freezing.
BARRILDO   Do you want
  Some more?
MENGO   Three or four? Fine, fine!   530
FRONDOSO He really means "wine, wine."
BARRILDO   Here, drink
  It down. A man who's said "no" deserves
  His wine. What's wrong with it?
MENGO   It's rough,
  That's what. And it's gone to my head.
FRONDOSO The best place for you is in your bed!   535
  Who was it killed the Commander?
MENGO Fuente Ovejuna! Our little town!
          [*Exit all, except* FRONDOSO *and* LAURENCIA.]
FRONDOSO They do right to praise him. So tell me,
  My sweet, who killed the Commander?
LAURENCIA Why, Fuente Ovejuna!
FRONDOSO   The truth!   540

Who killed him?

LAURENCIA   Oh, my sweet, you don't
  Half scare me! Fuente Ovejuna!

FRONDOSO   Then tell me! How did I kill you?

LAURENCIA   By making me love you to death, that's how!
      [*Exit both. Enter the* KING *and* QUEEN.]

ISABEL   This is a true surprise, my lord.   545
  I wasn't expecting you.

KING   And such
  A joy to see you once again!
  I was on my way to Portugal.
  I couldn't resist breaking my journey.

ISABEL   I trust you will never resist, my lord,   550
  Such welcome opportunities.

KING   What news of Castile?

ISABEL   At last it is
  At peace. Everything seems calm enough.

KING   I'm not surprised. You are the one
  Who fought to bring that peace.   555
      [*Enter* MANRIQUE.]

MANRIQUE   The Master of Calatrava attends you.
  He is outside and seeks an audience.

ISABEL   Then show him in, I wish to speak with him.

MANRIQUE   I would point out that though he's young
  In years, he is a valiant soldier.   560
      [*Enter the* MASTER OF CALATRAVA.]

MASTER   Rodrigo Téllez Girón, Master
  Of Calatrava. I come to seek
  Forgiveness, knowing that I was
  Deceived and ill-advised in causing you
  Displeasure. I was misled both by   565
  Fernán Gómez and my self-interest.
  I humbly beg that you forgive me.
  If I am worthy of such favor,
  I swear that from this moment on
  I am your loyal and obedient servant.   570
  The great campaign you plan against
  Granada . . . I promise you you'll see
  The valor of my sword. Before
  It's even drawn, the Moors shall know
  What fear is and see my crimson cross   575
  Fly from their battlements.
  Five hundred soldiers now in my
  Command shall fight on your behalf.
  You have my word that I shall not
  Offend again.

KING   Rise, Master. You are   580
  Most welcome here and always shall be.

MASTER   Your words, your Majesty, provide
  True comfort to the penitent.

ISABEL Young man, you show true spirit. In that
    Respect, your deeds are equalled by   585
    Your speech.
MASTER   Your majesties, you are
    The lovely Esther, the mighty Xerxes.[7]
    [*Enter* MANRIQUE.]
MANRIQUE The judge who went to Fuente Ovejuna . . .
    He has returned and wishes to report,
    Your Majesty.
KING   You shall decide what's to   590
    Be done with these assassins.
MASTER   If it
    Were up to me, your Majesty,
    They'd get what they deserve. How dare
    They murder the Commander!
KING   The matter is
    No longer in your hands.
ISABEL   But soon   595
    Will be in yours, my lord, God willing.
    [*Enter the* JUDGE.]
JUDGE I went, as you instructed me,
    To Fuente Ovejuna, and there
    Made every effort to investigate
    The crime. I could not find a scrap   600
    Of proof as to the murder; the evidence
    Is not enough to fill a single page.
    The citizens are all of one accord,
    United in their fortitude.
    For when I asked who was to blame,   605
    They all replied: "Fuente Ovejuna."
    I tortured them, three hundred on
    The rack, including boys of ten
    Years old, but none would tell me more.
    Whatever method I employed,   610
    From force to flattery, had no
    Effect. And so, your Majesty, all
    Of them must now be pardoned or
    Be put to death. They come before you.
    They wish to state their case and let   615
    You question them.
KING   Then let them enter.
    [*Enter the two* MAGISTRATES, FRONDOSO, *the* WOMEN, *and a group of*
    PEASANTS.]
LAURENCIA Is that the King and Queen?
FRONDOSO   Rulers
    Of all Castile.
LAURENCIA I swear they are

---

7. Xerxes was the king of Persia from 485–465 B.C.E. Esther was the favorite wife of Ahasuerus, king of
Persia, and noted for her compassion.

The finest couple. Saint Anthony bless them!
ISABEL Are these the villains?
ESTEBAN   Fuente Ovejuna,   620
Your Majesty: your humble and
Obedient servants. The tyranny,
The cruelty, the insults of
The dead Commander, they were the cause
Of all the trouble. He robbed us of   625
Our own possessions, raped our women,
And showed us not the slightest mercy.
FRONDOSO This girl . . . Heaven favored me with her,
So making me the happiest of men . . .
Was seized and carried off by him   630
On our wedding-night, as if
She were his property. What would
Have happened is quite plain if she'd
Not fought him off and showed how virtuous
She is.
MENGO If I may have my say, now.   635
I doubt you'll credit what he did
To me. I tried to save a girl
His men abused and would have raped.
For that this wicked Nero[8] had
My backside beaten, red as salmon steaks.   640
I have the marks still plain to see,
So savagely did three of them
Complete the task. To tell the truth,
I've spent more money than my farm
Would cost on every ointment you   645
Can think of.
ESTEBAN   Your Majesty, we wish
To be your loyal vassals. You are
Our rightful King, and so we have displayed
Your coat of arms in our town.
We pray you will be merciful,   650
Accepting our innocence as our defence.
KING There is no written evidence
As proof of your guilt, and so,
Although this was a serious crime,
You must be pardoned. Since you have sworn   655
Your loyalty, I shall assume
Responsibility for your town,
Until a new Commander can
Be found.
FRONDOSO Your Majesty has shown
Himself to be in this the wisest ruler.   660
And so, my friends, we end *Fuente Ovejuna*.

---

8. Roman emperor from 54–68 C.E., Nero became the byword for the cruel tyrant.

WILLIAM SHAKESPEARE
1564–1616

William Shakespeare was born in the rural community of Stratford-upon-Avon in Warwickshire. His father, John Shakespeare, was a glover and, when William was born, prominent in the town's government. Little is known of Shakespeare's early life, although it is likely that he received an education at the good local grammar school and certain that he married Anne Hathaway, about seven years his senior, when he was eighteen. The couple had three children, Susanna (1583) and the twins Judith and Hamnet (1585). By 1592 Shakespeare was in London, rapidly becoming the "greatest shake-scene" around, in the irritated words of a rival who envied Shakespeare's ability to impress audiences despite his lack of a university education. Shakespeare soon became a shareholder in a prominent players' company that claimed the Lord Chamberlain as patron and the tragic actor Richard Burbage and the comedian Will Kempe as members. Composing dramas that drew on the strengths of his repertory company, Shakespeare brought to the English stage such famous characters as Falstaff and Prince Hal, Hamlet and Ophelia, Othello and Desdemona, and King Lear.

The company originally performed at the Theatre, north of the city of London, where its actor-owner, James Burbage, faced steady opposition from the puritanical city officials who sought to close the theaters, which they considered to be hotbeds of immorality. Burbage conceived of a means to escape civic legislation against theatrical performances, and secretly moved the boards of his playhouse across the river Thames to the south bank; with these planks he constructed the Globe, the theater most often associated with Shakespeare's name. The Globe was open to all social classes: anyone who wished could enter the theater by paying a penny, and at the cost of another, get a bench, cushion, and protection (in the boxes) from bad weather. Shakespeare, who began his career as a player, found his calling as a playwright and his fortune as a shareholder in his company. His financial successes enabled him to purchase the title of gentleman for his father, a purchase that made Shakespeare himself officially a "gentleman born."

The influence of Shakespeare's plays on the course of English literature is matched only by the King James translation of the Bible. In his time, Shakespeare gained the interest of two British monarchs (Elizabeth I and James I), the love of popular audiences, and the respect of such tough critics as the poet and playwright Ben Jonson. After Shakespeare's death in 1616, when his friends and colleagues John Heminges and Henry Condell collected his plays into one volume (the *First Folio*), Ben Jonson wrote a magnificent verse memorial to the rival whose wit had seemed almost too fertile for the good of his art. In a poem that introduces the collected plays, Jonson praises Shakespeare as a poet who was "the Soule of the Age" and "Not of an age, but for all time!" Jonson's insistence that Shakespeare transcended the age he simultaneously embodied is paradoxical. For Jonson, however, great artists immortalize their nations and eras. In his view, the publication of Shakespeare's plays in the form of a book meant that the entire age of "Eliza, and our James" would enter triumphantly into world history: "Triumph, my Britain, thou hast one to show, / To whom all scenes of Europe homage owe." Shakespeare himself may have suspected that his dramatic works would one day count as cultural arts, but he also kept his eye on more humble and material successes. When he retired to Stratford-upon-Avon in 1612, he lived a quiet life in the house he had built (New House) from the savings he had accumulated while working in London's premiere playhouse.

Shakespeare's plays constitute the most important body of dramatic work in the modern world, and no character in literature is more familiar to audiences around the globe than Hamlet. The unparalleled reputation of the work may also have certain nonliterary causes. For instance, it is a play whose central role is singularly cherished by actors in all languages as the test of their skill, and conversely, audiences some-times content themselves with a rather vague notion of the work as a whole and concentrate on the attractively problematical and eloquent hero and on the actor impersonating him, waiting for his performance of his famous soliloquies rather than following the action and interpretation of the play. But along with the impact of the protagonist, there are other and deeper reasons why *Hamlet* has commanded a leading place in our literary heritage. Though it is a drama that concerns persons of superior station and the conflicts and problems associated with men and women of high degree, it reveals these problems in terms of a particular family, presenting an indi-vidual and domestic dimension along with a public one—the pattern of family conflict within the larger pattern of the *polis*—like the plays of antiquity that deal with the Theban myth, such as *Oedipus* and *Antigone*.

This public dimension of *Hamlet* helps us see it, for our present purposes, in rela-tion to the literature of the Renaissance—for the framework within which the char-acters are presented and come into conflict is a court. In spite of the Danish locale and the relatively remote period of the action, it is plainly a Renaissance court exhib-iting the structure of interests to which Machiavelli's *Prince* has potently drawn our attention. There is a ruler holding power, and much of the action is related to ques-tions concerning the nature of that power—the way in which he had acquired it and the ways in which it can be preserved. Moreover, there is a courtly structure: the king has several courtiers around him, among whom Hamlet, the heir apparent, is only the most prominent.

We have seen some of the forms of the Renaissance court pattern in earlier selec-tions in this anthology—in Castiglione, Rabelais, and Machiavelli. The court, the ruling nucleus of the community, was also an arena for conflicts of interest and of wit, a setting for the cultivation and codification of aristocratic virtues (valor, physical and intellectual brilliance, "courtesy"). The positive view of human achievement on earth, so prominent in the Renaissance, was given in courtly life its characteristic setting and testing ground. And as we have observed, the negative view (melancholy, sense of void and purposelessness) also emerged there.

Examining *Hamlet*, we soon realize that its temper belongs more to the negative than to the positive Renaissance outlook. Certain outstanding forms of human endeavor (the establishment of earthly power, the display of gallantry, the confident attempt of the mind to acquire knowledge and to inspire purposeful action), which elsewhere are presented as highly worthwhile, or are at least soberly discussed in terms of their value and limits, seem to be caught here in a condition of disorder and imbued with a sense of vanity and emptiness.

The way in which the state and the court of Denmark are presented in *Hamlet* is significant: they are shown in images of disease and rottenness. And here again, excessive stress on the protagonist himself must be avoided. His position as denouncer of the prevailing decadence, and the major basis for his denunciation—the murder of his father, which leads to his desire to obtain revenge and purify the court by destroying the present king—are central elements in the play, but they are not the *whole* play. The public situation is indicated, and Marcellus has pronounced his famous "Something is rotten" before Hamlet has talked to the Ghost and learned the Ghost's version of events. Moreover, the sense of outside dangers and internal dis-ruption everywhere transcends the personal story of Hamlet, of his revenge, of Clau-dius's crime; these are rather the signs of the breakdown, portents of a general situation. In this sense, we may tentatively say that the general theme of the play has to do with a kingdom, a society, a *polis*, going to pieces—or even more, with its realization that it has already gone to pieces. Concomitant with this is a sense of the vanity of those forms of human endeavor and power of which the kingdom and the court are symbols.

The tone Shakespeare wants to establish is evident from the opening scenes: the night air is full of dread premonitions; sentinels turn their eyes toward the threatening outside world; meanwhile, the Ghost has already made his appearance, a sinister omen. The kingdom, as we proceed, is presented in terms that are an almost point by point reversal of the ideal. Claudius, the *pater patriae* and *pater familias,* whether we believe the Ghost's indictment or not (Hamlet does not necessarily, and some of his famous indecision has been attributed to his seeking evidence of the Ghost's truthfulness before acting), has by marrying the queen committed an act that by Elizabethan standards is incestuous. There is an overwhelming sense of disintegration in the body of the state, evident in the first court assembly and in all subsequent ones. In their various ways the two courtiers, Hamlet and Laertes, are strangers, contemplating departure; they offer, around their king, a picture quite unlike that of the conventional paladins, supports of the throne, in a well-manned and well-mannered court. (In Rabelais's "kingdom," when Grangousier is ruler, the pattern is also a courtly and knightly one, but the young heir, Gargantua, who is like Hamlet a university student, readily abandons his studies to answer the fatherland's call; here the direction is reversed.)

On the other hand, as in all late and decadent phases of a social or artistic structure (the court in a sense is both), we have semblance instead of substance, ornate and empty facades, of which the more enlightened members of the group are mockingly aware. Thus Polonius, who after Hamlet is the major figure in the king's retinue, is presented satirically in his empty formalities of speech and conventional patterns of behavior. And there are numerous instances (e.g., Osric) of manners being replaced by mannerisms. Hence the way courtly life is depicted in the play suggests always the hollow, the fractured, and the crooked. The traditional forms and institutions of gentle living and all the pomp and solemnity are marred by corruption and distortion. Courtship and love are reduced to Hamlet's mockery of a "civil conversation" in the play scene, his phrases presenting not Castiglione's Platonic loftiness and the repartee of "gentilesse" but punning undercurrents of bawdiness. The theater, a traditional institution of court life, is "politically" used by the hero as a device to expose the king's crime. There are elements of macabre caricature in Shakespeare's treatment of the solemn theme of death (see, for instance, the manner of Polonius's death, which is a sort of sarcastic version of a cloak-and-dagger scene, or the effect of the clownish gravediggers' talk). Finally, the arms tournament, the typical occasion for the display of courtiers' gallantry in front of their king, is here turned by the scheming of the king himself into the play's conclusive scene of carnage. And the person who, on the king's behalf, invites Hamlet to that feast is Osric, the "waterfly," the caricature of the hollow courtier.

This sense of corruption and decadence dominates the temper of the play and obviously qualifies the character of Hamlet, his indecision, and his sense of vanity and disenchantment with the world in which he lives. In Hamlet the relation between thought and deed, intent and realization, is confused in the same way the norms and institutions that would regulate the life of a well-ordered court have been deprived of their original purpose and beauty. He and the king are "mighty opposites," and it can be argued that against Hamlet's indecision and negativism the king presents a more positive scheme of action, at least in the purely Machiavellian sense, at the level of practical power politics. But even this conclusion will prove only partly true. There are indeed moments in which all that the king seems to wish for himself is to forget the past and rule honorably. He advises Hamlet not to mourn his father excessively, for melancholy is not in accord with "nature." On various occasions the king shows a high and competent conception of his office: a culminating instance is the courageous and cunning way in which he confronts and handles Laertes's wrath. The point can be made that since his life is obviously threatened by Hamlet (who was seeking to kill him when by mistake he killed Polonius instead), the king acts within a legitimate pattern of politics in wanting to have Hamlet liquidated. But this argument cannot be carried so far as to demonstrate that he represents a fully positive attitude toward life and the world, even in the strictly amoral terms of political technique. For in fact his action is corroded by an element alien to that technique—the vexations of his own conscience. Despite his energy and his extrovert qualities, he too becomes part of the negative picture of disruption and lacks concentration of purpose. The images of decay and putrescence that characterize his court extend to his own speech: his "offense," in his own words, "smells to heaven."

Hamlet as a Renaissance tragedy presents a world particularly "out of joint," a world that, having long ago lost the sense of a grand extratemporal design that was so important in medieval times (to Hamlet the thought of the afterlife is even more puzzling and dark than that of this life), looks with an even greater sense of disenchantment at the circle of temporal action symbolized by the kingdom and the court. These structures could have offered certain codes of conduct and objects of allegiance that would have given individual action a purposeful meaning. But now their order has been destroyed. Ideals that once had power and freshness have lost their vigor under the impact of satiety, doubt, and melancholy.

Because communal values are so degraded, it is natural to ask in the end whether some alternative attempt at a settlement could be imagined, with Hamlet—like other Renaissance heroes—adopting an individual code of conduct, however extravagant. On the whole, Hamlet seems too steeped in his own hopelessness and in the courtly mechanism to which he inevitably belongs to be able to find personal intellectual and moral compromise or his own version of total escape or total dream; for his "antic disposition" is a strategy, his "folly" is politically motivated. Still, the tone of his brooding and often moralizing speech, his melancholy and dissatisfaction, his very desire for revenge imply a nostalgia for a world—associated with his father—of loyal allegiances and ideals of honor. Yet in *Hamlet* the political world turns out to offer no protection for the values—friendship, loyalty, and honesty—that Hamlet himself most cherishes. These virtues belong only to intimate relationships, such as that between Hamlet and Horatio, and to the world of story, such as the one Horatio will tell of Hamlet after his death.

Hamlet, Prince of Denmark

CHARACTERS

CLAUDIUS, *king of Denmark*
HAMLET, *son to the late, and nephew*
   to the present king
POLONIUS, *lord chamberlain*
HORATIO, *friend to Hamlet*
LAERTES, *son of Polonius*
PRIEST
MARCELLUS, } *officers*
BERNARDO, }
FRANCISCO, *a soldier*
REYNALDO, *servant to Polonius*
PLAYERS
TWO CLOWNS, *grave-diggers*
FORTINBRAS, *prince of Norway*
CAPTAIN

VOLTIMAND,
CORNELIUS,
ROSENCRANTZ,
GUILDENSTERN, } *courtiers*
OSRIC,
GENTLEMAN,
ENGLISH AMBASSADORS
GERTRUDE, *queen of Denmark, and*
   mother to Hamlet
OPHELIA, *daughter of Polonius*
LORDS, LADIES, OFFICERS, SOLDIERS,
   SAILORS, MESSENGERS, *and*
   OTHER ATTENDANTS
GHOST OF HAMLET'S FATHER

[SCENE: *Denmark.*]

Act I

SCENE 1

[SCENE: *Elsinore. A platform before the castle.*]

[FRANCISCO *at his post. Enter to him* BERNARDO.]

BERNARDO Who's there?

FRANCISCO Nay, answer me: stand, and unfold yourself.

BERNARDO Long live the king!

FRANCISCO Bernardo?

BERNARDO He.   5

FRANCISCO You come most carefully upon your hour.

BERNARDO 'Tis now struck twelve; get thee to bed, Francisco.

FRANCISCO For this relief much thanks: 'tis bitter cold,
And I am sick at heart.

BERNARDO Have you had quiet guard?

FRANCISCO   Not a mouse stirring.   10

BERNARDO Well, good night.
If you do meet Horatio and Marcellus,
The rivals[1] of my watch, bid them make haste.

FRANCISCO I think I hear them. Stand, ho! Who is there?

[*Enter* HORATIO *and* MARCELLUS.]

HORATIO Friends to this ground.

MARCELLUS   And liegemen to the Dane.[2]   15

FRANCISCO Give you good night.

MARCELLUS   O, farewell, honest soldier:
Who hath relieved you?

FRANCISCO   Bernardo hath my place.
Give you good night.

[*Exit.*]

MARCELLUS   Holla! Bernardo!

BERNARDO   Say,
What, is Horatio there?

HORATIO   A piece of him.

BERNARDO Welcome, Horatio; welcome, good Marcellus.   20

MARCELLUS What, has this thing appeared again to-night?

BERNARDO I have seen nothing.

MARCELLUS Horatio says 'tis but our fantasy,
And will not let belief take hold of him
Touching this dreaded sight, twice seen of us: 25
Therefore I have entreated him along
With us to watch the minutes of this night,
That if again this apparition come,
He may approve our eyes[3] and speak to it.

HORATIO Tush, tush, 'twill not appear.

BERNARDO   Sit down a while;   30
And let us once again assail your ears,

---

1. Partners.   2. The king of Denmark.   3. Confirm what we saw.

That are so fortified against our story,
What we have two nights seen.
HORATIO   Well, sit we down,
And let us hear Bernardo speak of this.
BERNARDO   Last night of all,   35
When yond same star that's westward from the pole
Had made his course to illume that part of heaven
Where now it burns, Marcellus and myself,
The bell then beating one,—
        [*Enter* GHOST.]
MARCELLUS   Peace, break thee off; look, where it comes again!   40
BERNARDO   In the same figure, like the king that's dead.
MARCELLUS   Thou art a scholar; speak to it, Horatio.
BERNARDO   Looks it not like the king? mark it, Horatio.
HORATIO   Most like it: it harrows me with fear and wonder.
BERNARDO   It would be spoke to.
MARCELLUS   Question it, Horatio.   45
HORATIO   What art thou, that usurp'st this time of night,
Together with that fair and warlike form
In which the majesty of buried Denmark
Did sometimes[4] march? by heaven I charge thee, speak!
MARCELLUS   It is offended.
BERNARDO   See, it stalks away!   50
HORATIO   Stay! speak, speak! I charge thee, speak!
        [*Exit* GHOST.]
MARCELLUS   'Tis gone, and will not answer.
BERNARDO   How now, Horatio! you tremble and look pale:
Is not this something more than fantasy?
What think you on't?   55
HORATIO   Before my God, I might not this believe
Without the sensible and true avouch
Of mine own eyes.
MARCELLUS   Is it not like the king?
HORATIO   As thou art to thyself:
Such was the very armor he had on   60
When he the ambitious Norway[5] combated;
So frown'd he once, when, in an angry parle,
He smote the sledded[6] Polacks on the ice.
'Tis strange.
MARCELLUS   Thus twice before, and jump[7] at this dead hour,   65
With martial stalk hath he gone by our watch.
HORATIO   In what particular thought to work I know not;
But, in the gross and scope of my opinion,[8]
This bodes some strange eruption to our state.
MARCELLUS   Good now, sit down, and tell me, he that knows,   70
Why this same strict and most observant watch
So nightly toils the subject[9] of the land,

4. Formerly. *Denmark:* the king of Denmark.   5. The king of Norway (the elder Fortinbras).   6. They travel in sledges. *Parle:* parley.   7. Just.   8. Taking a general view.   9. The people.

And why such daily cast of brazen cannon,
And foreign mart for implements of war;
Why such impress of shipwrights,[1] whose sore task   75
Does not divide the Sunday from the week;
What might be toward,[2] that this sweaty haste
Doth make the night joint-laborer with the day:
Who is't that can inform me?

HORATIO   That can I;
At least the whisper goes so. Our last king,   80
Whose image even but now appear'd to us,
Was, as you know, by Fortinbras of Norway,
Thereto pricked on by a most emulate pride,
Dared to the combat; in which our valiant Hamlet—
For so this side of our known world esteem'd him—   85
Did slay this Fortinbras; who by a seal'd compact
Well ratified by law and heraldry,[3]
Did forfeit, with his life, all those his lands
Which he stood seized of, to the conqueror:
Against the which, a moiety competent   90
Was gagèd[4] by our king; which had returned
To the inheritance of Fortinbras,
Had he been vanquisher; as, by the same covenant
And carriage[5] of the article design'd,
His fell to Hamlet. Now, sir, young Fortinbras,   95
Of unimprovèd metal hot and full,
Hath in the skirts[6] of Norway here and there
Shark'd up a list of lawless resolutes,
For food and diet, to some enterprise
That hath a stomach in't:[7] which is no other—   100
As it doth well appear unto our state—
But to recover of us, by strong hand
And terms compulsatory, those foresaid lands
So by his father lost: and this, I take it,
Is the main motive of our preparations,   105
The source of this our watch and the chief head
Of this post-haste and romage[8] in the land.

BERNARDO   I think it be no other but e'en so:
Well may it sort,[9] that this portentous figure
Comes armèd through our watch, so like the king   110
That was and is the question of these wars.

HORATIO   A mote it is to trouble the mind's eye.
In the most high and palmy state of Rome,
A little ere the mightiest Julius fell,
The graves stood tenantless, and the sheeted dead   115
Did squeak and gibber in the Roman streets:
As stars with trains of fire and dews of blood,

1. Ship carpenters. *Mart:* trading. *Impress:* pressing into service.   2. Impending.   3. Duly ratified and
proclaimed through heralds.   4. Pledged. *Seized:* possessed. *Moiety competent:* equal share.   5. Purport.   6. Outskirts, border regions. *Unimprovèd:* untested.   7. Calls for courage.   8. Bustle. *Head:*
origin, cause.   9. Fit with the other signs of war.

Disasters in the sun; and the moist star,
Upon whose influence Neptune's empire stands,[1]
Was sick almost to doomsday with eclipse: 120
And even the like precurse[2] of fierce events,
As harbingers preceding still the fates
And prologue to the omen coming on,
Have heaven and earth together demonstrated
Unto our climatures[3] and countrymen.   125
      [Re-enter GHOST.]
But soft, behold! lo, where it comes again!
I'll cross it, though it blast me. Stay, illusion!
If thou hast any sound, or use of voice,
Speak to me:
If there be any good thing to be done,   130
That may to thee do ease and grace to me,
Speak to me:
If thou art privy to thy country's fate,
Which, happily, foreknowing may avoid,
O, speak!   135
Or if thou hast uphoarded in thy life
Extorted treasure in the womb of earth,
For which, they say, you spirits oft walk in death,
Speak of it: stay, and speak! [*The cock crows.*] Stop it, Marcellus.
MARCELLUS   Shall I strike at it with my partisan?   140
HORATIO   Do, if it will not stand.
BERNARDO   'Tis here!
HORATIO   'Tis here!
      [Exit GHOST.]
MARCELLUS   'Tis gone!
We do it wrong, being so majestical,
To offer it the show of violence;
For it is, as the air, invulnerable,   145
And our vain blows malicious mockery.
BERNARDO   It was about to speak, when the cock crew.
HORATIO   And then it started like a guilty thing
Upon a fearful summons. I have heard
The cock, that is the trumpet to the morn,   150
Doth with his lofty and shrill-sounding throat
Awake the god of day, and at his warning,
Whether in sea or fire, in earth or air,
The extravagant[4] and erring spirit hies
To his confine: and of the truth herein   155
This present object made probation.[5]
MARCELLUS   It faded on the crowing of the cock.
Some say that ever 'gainst[6] that season comes
Wherein our Saviour's birth is celebrated,
The bird of dawning singeth all night long: 160

---

1. The moon (*moist star*) regulates the sea's tides. *Disasters:* Ill omens.   2. Foreboding.   3. Regions.
4. Wandering out of its confines.   5. Gave proof.   6. Just before.

And then, they say, no spirit dare stir abroad,
The nights are wholesome, then no planets strike,
No fairy takes nor witch hath power to charm,
So hallowed and so gracious[7] is the time.
HORATIO   So have I heard and do in part believe it.   165
But look, the morn, in russet mantle clad,
Walks o'er the dew of yon high eastward hill:
Break we our watch up; and by my advice,
Let us impart what we have seen to-night
Unto young Hamlet; for, upon my life,   170
This spirit, dumb to us, will speak to him:
Do you consent we shall acquaint him with it,
As needful in our loves, fitting our duty?
MARCELLUS   Let's do't, I pray; and I this morning know
Where we shall find him most conveniently.   175
      [Exeunt.]

SCENE 2

[SCENE: A room of state in the castle.]

[Flourish. Enter the KING, QUEEN, HAMLET, POLONIUS, LAERTES,
   VOLTIMAND, CORNELIUS, LORDS, and ATTENDANTS.]
KING   Though yet of Hamlet our dear brother's death
The memory be green, and that it us befitted
To bear our hearts in grief and our whole kingdom
To be contracted in one brow of woe,
Yet so far hath discretion[8] fought with nature   5
That we with wisest sorrow think on him,
Together with remembrance of ourselves.
Therefore our sometime sister, now our queen,
The imperial jointress to this warlike state,
Have we, as 'twere with a defeated joy,—   10
With an auspicious and a dropping eye,
With mirth in funeral and with dirge in marriage,
In equal scale weighing delight and dole,—
Taken to wife: nor have we herein barr'd[9]
Your better wisdoms, which have freely gone   15
With this affair along. For all, our thanks.
Now follows, that[1] you know, young Fortinbras,
Holding a weak supposal of our worth,
Or thinking by our late dear brother's death
Our state to be disjoint and out of frame,   20
Colleaguèd with this dream[2] of his advantage,
He hath not failed to pester us with message,
Importing the surrender of those lands
Lost by his father, with all bonds of law,
To our most valiant brother. So much for him.

7. Full of blessing. Strike: exercise evil influence (compare "moonstruck"). Fairy takes: bewitches.
8. Restraint (on grief).   9. Ignored. Dole: grief.   1. What.   2. Combined with this fantastic notion.

Now for ourself, and for this time of meeting: 25
Thus much the business is: we have here writ
To Norway, uncle of young Fortinbras,—
Who, impotent and bed-rid, scarcely hears
Of this his nephew's purpose,—to suppress   30
His further gait herein; in that the levies,
The lists and full proportions,[3] are all made
Out of his subject: and we here dispatch
You, good Cornelius, and you, Voltimand,
For bearers of this greeting to old Norway,   35
Giving to you no further personal power
To business with the king more than the scope
Of these delated[4] articles allow.
Farewell, and let your haste commend your duty.   40
CORNELIUS }
VOLTIMAND }   In that and all things will we show our duty.
KING   We doubt it nothing: heartily farewell.
      [Exeunt VOLTIMAND and CORNELIUS.]
And now, Laertes, what's the news with you?
You told us of some suit; what is't, Laertes?
You cannot speak of reason to the Dane,
And lose your voice: what wouldst thou beg, Laertes,   45
That shall not be my offer, not thy asking?
The head is not more native to[5] the heart,
The hand more instrumental to the mouth,
Than is the throne of Denmark to thy father.
What wouldst thou have, Laertes?
LAERTES   My dread lord,   50
Your leave and favor to return to France,
From whence though willingly I came to Denmark,
To show my duty in your coronation,
Yet now, I must confess, that duty done,
My thoughts and wishes bend again toward France   55
And bow them to your gracious leave and pardon.
KING   Have you your father's leave? What says Polonius?
POLONIUS   He hath, my lord, wrung from me my slow leave
By laborsome petition, and at last
Upon his will I sealed my hard consent: 60
I do beseech you, give him leave to go.
KING   Take thy fair hour, Laertes; time be thine,
And thy best graces spend it at thy will!
But now, my cousin Hamlet, and my son,—
HAMLET [Aside.]   A little more than kin, and less than kind.   65
KING   How is it that the clouds still hang on you?
HAMLET   Not so, my lord; I am too much i' the sun.[6]
QUEEN   Good Hamlet, cast thy nighted color off,
And let thine eye look like a friend on Denmark.

---

3. Amounts of forces and supplies. *Gait:* proceeding.   **4.** Detailed.   **5.** Naturally bound to.   **6.** The cue to Hamlet's irony is given by the King's "my cousin . . . my son" (line 64). Hamlet is punning on *son.*

Do not for ever with thy vailèd[7] lids   70
Seek for thy noble father in the dust:
Thou know'st 'tis common; all that lives must die,
Passing through nature to eternity.

HAMLET   Aye, madam, it is common.

QUEEN   If it be,
Why seems it so particular with thee?   75

HAMLET   Seems, madam! nay, it is; I know not "seems."
'Tis not alone my inky cloak, good mother,
Nor customary suits of solemn black,
Nor windy suspiration of forced breath,
No, nor the fruitful river in the eye,   80
Nor the dejected havior of the visage,
Together with all forms, moods, shapes of grief,
That can denote me truly: these indeed seem,
For they are actions that a man might play:
But I have that within which passeth show;   85
These but the trappings and the suits of woe.

KING   'Tis sweet and cómmendàble in your nature, Hamlet,
To give these mourning duties to your father:
But, you must know, your father lost a father,
That father lost, lost his, and the survivor bound   90
In filial obligation for some term
To do obsequious[8] sorrow: but to persevere
In obstinate condolement is a course
Of impious stubborness; 'tis unmanly grief:
It shows a will most incorrect[9] to heaven,   95
A heart unfortified, a mind impatient,
An understanding simple and unschool'd:
For what we know must be and is as common
As any the most vulgar thing to sense,
Why should we in our peevish opposition   100
Take it to heart? Fie! 'tis a fault to heaven,
A fault against the dead, a fault to nature,
To reason most absurd, whose common theme
Is death of fathers, and who still hath cried,
From the first corse till he that died to-day,   105
"This must be so." We pray you, throw to earth
This unprevailing[1] woe, and think of us
As of a father: for let the world take note,
You are the most immediate to our throne,
And with no less nobility of love   110
Than that which dearest father bears his son
Do I impart toward you. For your intent
In going back to school in Wittenberg,
It is most retrograde[2] to our desire:
And we beseech you, bend you to remain   115

---

7. Downcast.   8. Dutiful, especially concerning funeral rites (obsequies).   9. Not subdued.
1. Useless.   2. Opposed. *Wittenberg*: the seat of a university; at the peak of fame in Shakespeare's time because of its connection with Martin Luther.

Here in the cheer and comfort of our eye,
Our chiefest courtier, cousin and our son.
QUEEN Let not thy mother lose her prayers, Hamlet:
  I pray thee, stay with us; go not to Wittenberg.
HAMLET I shall in all my best obey you, madam.   120
KING Why, 'tis a loving and a fair reply:
  Be as ourself in Denmark. Madam, come;
  This gentle and unforced accord of Hamlet
  Sits smiling to my heart: in grace whereof,
  No jocund health that Denmark drinks to-day,   125
  But the great cannon to the clouds shall tell,
  And the king's rouse the heaven shall bruit[3] again,
  Re-speaking earthly thunder. Come away.
     [*Flourish. Exeunt all but* HAMLET.]
HAMLET O, that this too too sullied flesh would melt,
  Thaw and resolve itself into a dew!   130
  Or that the Everlasting had not fixed
  His canon[4] 'gainst self-slaughter! O God! God!
  How weary, stale, flat and unprofitable
  Seem to me all the uses of this world!
  Fie on't! ah fie! 'tis an unweeded garden,   135
  That grows to seed; things rank and gross in nature
  Possess it merely. That it should come to this!
  But two months dead! nay, not so much, not two:
  So excellent a king; that was, to this,
  Hyperion to a satyr: so loving to my mother,   140
  That he might not beteem[5] the winds of heaven
  Visit her face too roughly. Heaven and earth!
  Must I remember? why, she would hang on him,
  As if increase of appetite had grown
  By what it fed on: and yet, within a month—   145
  Let me not think on't—Frailty, thy name is woman!—
  A little month, or ere those shoes were old
  With which she followed my poor father's body,
  Like Niobe,[6] all tears:—why she, even she,—
  O God! a beast that wants discourse[7] of reason   150
  Would have mourned longer,—married with my uncle,
  My father's brother, but no more like my father
  Than I to Hercules: within a month;
  Ere yet the salt of most unrighteous tears
  Had left the flushing in her gallèd[8] eyes,   155
  She married. O, most wicked speed, to post
  With such dexterity to incestuous sheets![9]
  It is not, nor it cannot come to good:
  But break, my heart, for I must hold my tongue!

---

3. Proclaim, echo. *Rouse:* carousal, revel. 4. Law. 5. Allow. *Hyperion* is the sun god. 6. A proud mother who boasted of having more children than Leto; her seven sons and seven daughters were slain by Apollo and Artemis, children of Leto. The grieving Niobe was changed by Zeus into a continually weeping stone. 7. Lacks the faculty. 8. Inflamed. 9. According to principles that Hamlet accepts, marrying one's brother's widow is incest.

[*Enter* HORATIO, MARCELLUS, *and* BERNARDO.]

HORATIO   Hail to your lordship!

HAMLET   I am glad to see you well: 160
   Horatio,—or I do forget myself.

HORATIO   The same, my lord, and your poor servant ever.

HAMLET   Sir, my good friend; I'll change[1] that name with you:
   And what make you from Wittenberg, Horatio?
   Marcellus?   165

MARCELLUS   My good lord?

HAMLET   I am very glad to see you. [*To* BERNARDO.] Good even, sir.
   But what, in faith, make you from Wittenberg?

HORATIO   A truant disposition, good my lord.

HAMLET   I would not hear your enemy say so,   170
   Nor shall you do my ear that violence,
   To make it truster of your own report
   Against yourself: I know you are no truant.
   But what is your affair in Elsinore?
   We'll teach you to drink deep ere you depart.   175

HORATIO   My lord, I came to see your father's funeral.

HAMLET   I pray thee, do not mock me, fellow-student;
   I think it was to see my mother's wedding.

HORATIO   Indeed, my lord, it followed hard upon.

HAMLET   Thrift, thrift, Horatio! the funeral baked-meats   180
   Did coldly furnish forth the marriage tables.
   Would I had met my dearest[2] foe in heaven
   Or ever I had seen that day, Horatio!
   My father!—methinks I see my father.

HORATIO   O where, my lord?

HAMLET   In my mind's eye, Horatio.   185

HORATIO   I saw him once; he was a goodly king.

HAMLET   He was a man, take him for all in all,
   I shall not look upon his like again.

HORATIO   My lord, I think I saw him yesternight.

HAMLET   Saw? who?   190

HORATIO   My lord, the king your father.

HAMLET   The king my father!

HORATIO   Season your admiration[3] for a while
   With an attent ear, till I may deliver,
   Upon the witness of these gentlemen,
   This marvel to you.

HAMLET   For God's love, let me hear.   195

HORATIO   Two nights together had these gentlemen,
   Marcellus and Bernardo, on their watch,
   In the dead vast and middle of the night,
   Been thus encountered. A figure like your father,
   Armed at point exactly, cap-a-pe,[4]   200
   Appears before them, and with solemn march
   Goes slow and stately by them: thrice he walked

1. Exchange.   2. Bitterest.   3. Restrain your astonishment.   4. From head to foot. *At point:* completely.

By their oppressed and fear-surprisèd eyes,
Within his truncheon's length; whilst they, distilled
Almost to jelly with the act of fear,   205
Stand dumb, and speak not to him. This to me
In dreadful secrecy impart they did;
And I with them the third night kept the watch:
Where, as they had delivered, both in time,
Form of the thing, each word made true and good,   210
The apparition comes: I knew your father;
These hands were not more like.

HAMLET   But where was this?
MARCELLUS   My lord, upon the platform where we watched.
HAMLET   Did you not speak to it?
HORATIO   My lord, I did.
But answer made it none: yet once methought   215
It lifted up its head and did address
Itself to motion, like as it would speak:
But even then the morning cock crew loud,
And at the sound it shrunk in haste away
And vanished from our sight.

HAMLET   'Tis very strange.   220
HORATIO   As I do live, my honored lord, 'tis true,
And we did think it writ down in our duty
To let you know of it.

HAMLET   Indeed, indeed, sirs, but this troubles me.
Hold you the watch to-night?   225
MARCELLUS ⎱
BERNARDO ⎰   We do, my lord.
HAMLET   Armed, say you?
MARCELLUS ⎱
BERNARDO ⎰   Armed, my lord.
HAMLET   From top to toe?
MARCELLUS ⎱
BERNARDO ⎰   My lord, from head to foot.
HAMLET   Then saw you not his face?
HORATIO   O, yes, my lord; he wore his beaver⁵ up.
HAMLET   What, looked he frowningly?   230
HORATIO   A countenance more in sorrow than in anger.
HAMLET   Pale, or red?
HORATIO   Nay, very pale.
HAMLET   And fixed his eyes upon you?
HORATIO   Most constantly.
HAMLET   I would I had been there.
HORATIO   It would have much amazed you.   235
HAMLET   Very like, very like. Stayed it long?
HORATIO   While one with moderate haste might tell⁶ a hundred.
MARCELLUS ⎱
BERNARDO ⎰   Longer, longer.
HORATIO   Not when I saw't.

5. Visor.   6. Count.

HAMLET His beard was grizzled?[7] no?
HORATIO It was, as I have seen it in his life,   240
  A sable silvered.[8]
HAMLET I will watch to-night;
  Perchance 'twill walk again.
HORATIO I warrant it will.
HAMLET If it assume my noble father's person,
  I'll speak to it, though hell itself should gape
  And bid me hold my peace. I pray you all,   245
  If you have hitherto concealed this sight,
  Let it be tenable in your silence still,[9]
  And whatsoever else shall hap to-night,
  Give it an understanding, but no tongue:
  I will requite your loves. So fare you well: 250
  Upon the platform, 'twixt eleven and twelve,
  I'll visit you.
ALL Our duty to your honor.
HAMLET Your loves, as mine to you: farewell.
  [_Exeunt all but_ HAMLET.]
  My father's spirit in arms! all is not well;
  I doubt[1] some foul play: would the night were come!   255
  Till then sit still, my soul: foul deeds will rise,
  Though all the earth o'erwhelm them, to men's eyes.
  [_Exit._]

SCENE 3

[SCENE: _A room in Polonius's house._]

[_Enter_ LAERTES _and_ OPHELIA.]
LAERTES My necessaries are embarked: farewell:
  And, sister, as the winds give benefit
  And convoy[2] is assistant, do not sleep,
  But let me hear from you.
OPHELIA Do you doubt that?
LAERTES For Hamlet, and the trifling of his favor,   5
  Hold it a fashion, and a toy in blood,
  A violet in the youth of primy nature,
  Forward,[3] not permanent, sweet, not lasting,
  The perfume and suppliance of a minute;
  No more.   10
OPHELIA No more but so?
LAERTES Think it no more:
  For nature crescent does not grow alone
  In thews and bulk; but, as this temple[4] waxes,
  The inward service of the mind and soul   15
  Grows wide withal. Perhaps he loves you now;

---

7. Gray. 8. Black and white. 9. Consider it still a secret. 1. Suspect. 2. Conveyance, means
of transport. 3. Early. _Fashion:_ passing mood. _Primy:_ early, young. 4. The body. _Crescent:_ growing.

And now no soil nor cautel[5] doth besmirch
The virtue of his will: but you must fear,
His greatness weighed,[6] his will is not his own;
For he himself is subject to his birth: 20
He may not, as unvalued persons do,
Carve for himself, for on his choice depends
The safety and health of this whole state,
And therefore must his choice be circumscribed
Unto the voice and yielding[7] of that body   25
Whereof he is the head. Then if he says he loves you,
It fits your wisdom so far to believe it
As he in his particular act and place
May give his saying deed; which is no further
Than the main voice of Denmark goes withal.[8]   30
Then weigh what loss your honor may sustain,
If with too credent ear you list his songs,
Or lose your heart, or your chaste treasure open
To his unmastered importunity.
Fear it, Ophelia, fear it, my dear sister,   35
And keep you in the rear of your affection,
Out of the shot and danger of desire.
The chariest maid is prodigal enough
If she unmask her beauty to the moon:
Virtue itself 'scapes not calumnious strokes: 40
The canker galls the infants of the spring
Too oft before their buttons be disclosed,
And in the morn and liquid dew of youth
Contagious blastments[9] are most imminent.
Be wary then; best safety lies in fear: 45
Youth to itself[1] rebels, though none else near.
OPHELIA   I shall the effect of this good lesson keep,
  As watchman to my heart. But, good my brother,
  Do not, as some ungracious pastors do,
  Show me the steep and thorny way to heaven,   50
  Whilst, like a puffed and reckless libertine,
  Himself the primrose path of dalliance treads
  And recks not his own rede.[2]
LAERTES   O, fear me not.
  I stay too long; but here my father comes.
      [Enter POLONIUS.]
  A double blessing is a double grace;   55
  Occasion smiles upon a second leave.
POLONIUS   Yet here, Laertes! Aboard, aboard, for shame!
  The wind sits in the shoulder of your sail,
  And you are stayed for. There; my blessing with thee!
  And these few precepts in thy memory   60
  See thou chárácter.[3] Give thy thoughts no tongue,

---

5. No foul or deceitful thoughts.   **6.** When you consider his rank. *Will:* desire.   **7.** Assent.   **8.** Goes along with, agrees. *Main:* powerful.   **9.** Blights.   **1.** Against its better self.   **2.** Does not follow his own advice.   **3.** Engrave in your memory.

Nor any unproportioned[4] thought his act.
Be thou familiar, but by no means vulgar.
Those friends thou hast, and their adoption tried,
Grapple them to thy soul with hoops of steel,   65
But do not dull thy palm[5] with entertainment
Of each new-hatched unfledged comrade. Beware
Of entrance to a quarrel; but being in,
Bear't, that the opposèd may beware of thee.
Give every man thy ear, but few thy voice: 70
Take each man's censure,[6] but reserve thy judgment.
Costly thy habit as thy purse can buy,
But not expressed in fancy; rich, not gaudy:
For the apparel oft proclaims the man;
And they in France of the best rank and station   75
Are of a most select and generous chief[7] in that.
Neither a borrower nor a lender be:
For loan oft loses both itself and friend,
And borrowing dulls the edge of husbandry.[8]
This above all: to thine own self be true,   80
And it must follow, as the night the day,
Thou canst not then be false to any man.
Farewell: my blessing season[9] this in thee!
LAERTES   Most humbly do I take my leave, my lord.
POLONIUS   The time invites you; go, your servants tend.[1]   85
LAERTES   Farewell, Ophelia, and remember well
    What I have said to you.
OPHELIA   'Tis in my memory locked,
    And you yourself shall keep the key of it.
LAERTES   Farewell.
        [Exit.]
POLONIUS   What is't, Ophelia, he hath said to you?
OPHELIA   So please you, something touching the Lord Hamlet.   90
POLONIUS   Marry, well bethought:
    'Tis told me, he hath very oft of late
    Given private time to you, and you yourself
    Have of your audience been most free and bounteous:
    If it be so—as so 'tis put on me,   95
    And that in way of caution—I must tell you,
    You do not understand yourself so clearly
    As it behoves my daughter and your honor.
    What is between you? give me up the truth.
OPHELIA   He hath, my lord, of late made many tenders   100
    Of his affection to me.
POLONIUS   Affection! pooh! you speak like a green girl,
    Unsifted[2] in such perilous circumstance.
    Do you believe his tenders, as you call them?
OPHELIA   I do not know, my lord, what I should think.   105

---

4. Unsuitable.   5. Make the palm of your hand callous (by the indiscriminate shaking of hands).
6. Opinion.   7. Preeminence.   8. Thriftiness.   9. Ripen.   1. Wait.   2. Untested.

POLONIUS   Marry, I'll teach you: think yourself a baby,
That you have ta'en these tenders for true pay,
Which are not sterling. Tender[3] yourself more dearly;
Or—not to crack the wind of the poor phrase,
Running it thus—you'll tender me a fool.[4]   110
OPHELIA   My lord, he hath importuned me with love
In honorable fashion.
POLONIUS   Aye, fashion you may call it; go to, go to.
OPHELIA   And hath given countenance[5] to his speech, my lord,
With almost all the holy vows of heaven.   115
POLONIUS   Aye, springes to catch woodcocks. I do know,
When the blood burns, how prodigal the soul
Lends the tongue vows: these blazes, daughter,
Giving more light than heat, extinct in both,
Even in their promise, as it is a-making,   120
You must not take for fire. From this time
Be something scanter of your maiden presence;
Set your entreatments[6] at a higher rate
Than a command to parley. For Lord Hamlet,
Believe so much in him, that he is young,   125
And with a larger tether may he walk
Than may be given you: in few, Ophelia,
Do not believe his vows; for they are brokers,
Not of that dye which their investments[7] show,
But mere implorators of unholy suits,   130
Breathing like sanctified and pious bawds,
The better to beguile. This is for all:
I would not, in plain terms, from this time forth,
Have you so slander any moment[8] leisure,
As to give words or talk with the Lord Hamlet.   135
Look to't, I charge you: come your ways.
OPHELIA   I shall obey, my lord.
        [*Exeunt.*]

SCENE 4

[SCENE: *The platform.*]

[*Enter* HAMLET, HORATIO, *and* MARCELLUS.]
HAMLET   The air bites shrewdly; it is very cold.
HORATIO   It is a nipping and an eager[9] air.
HAMLET   What hour now?
HORATIO   I think it lacks of twelve.
MARCELLUS   No, it is struck.
HORATIO   Indeed? I heard it not: it then draws near the season   5
Wherein the spirit held his wont to walk.
        [*A flourish of trumpets, and ordnance shot off within.*]

3. Regard.   4. You'll furnish me with a fool (a foolish daughter).   5. Authority.   6. Conversation,
company.   7. Clothes. *Brokers:* procurers, panders.   8. Use badly any momentary.   9. Sharp.

What doth this mean, my lord?

HAMLET   The king doth wake to-night, and takes his rouse,
Keeps wassail, and the swaggering up-spring reels;
And as he drains his draughts of Rhenish[1] down,   10
The kettle-drum and trumpet thus bray out
The triumph of his pledge.[2]

HORATIO   Is it a custom?

HAMLET   Aye, marry, is't:
But to my mind, though I am native here
And to the manner born, it is a custom   15
More honored[3] in the breach than the observance.
This heavy-headed revel east and west
Makes us traduced and taxed of other nations:
They clepe us drunkards, and with swinish phrase
Soil our addition;[4] and indeed it takes   20
From our achievements, though performed at height,[5]
The pith and marrow of our attribute.[6]
So, oft it chances in particular men,
That for some vicious mole of nature in them,
As, in their birth,—wherein they are not guilty,   25
Since nature cannot choose his origin,—
By the o'ergrowth of some complexion,[7]
Oft breaking down the pales and forts of reason,
Or by some habit that too much o'er-leavens[8]
The form of plausive[9] manners, that these men,—   30
Carrying, I say, the stamp of one defect,
Being nature's livery, or fortune's star,—
Their virtues else[1]—be they as pure as grace,
As infinite as man may undergo—
Shall in the general censure take corruption   35
From that particular fault: the dram of evil
Doth all the noble substance often dout
To his own scandal.[2]

[*Enter* GHOST.]

HORATIO   Look, my lord it comes!

HAMLET   Angels and ministers of grace defend us!
Be thou a spirit of health or goblin damned,   40
Bring with thee airs from heaven or blasts from hell,
Be thy intents wicked or charitable,
Thou comest in such a questionable shape
That I will speak to thee: I'll call thee Hamlet,
King, father, royal Dane: O, answer me!   45
Let me not burst in ignorance; but tell
Why thy canónized bones, hearsèd in death,
Have burst their cerements; why the sepulchre,
Wherein we saw thee quietly inurned,

---

1. Rhine wine. *Up-spring reels*: wild dances.   2. In downing the cup in one draught.   3. Honorable.
4. Reputation. *Taxed*: blamed. *Clepe*: call.   5. Done in the best possible manner.   6. Reputation.
7. Excess in one side of their temperament.   8. Modifies, as yeast changes dough.   9. Agreeable.
1. The rest of their qualities.   2. To its own harm. *Dout*: extinguish, nullify.

Hath oped his ponderous and marble jaws,   50
To cast thee up again. What may this mean,
That thou, dead corse, again, in complete steel,
Revisit'st thus the glimpses of the moon,
Making night hideous; and we fools of nature
So horridly to shake our disposition   55
With thoughts beyond the reaches of our souls?
Say, why is this? Wherefore? what should we do?
    [GHOST *beckons* HAMLET.]

HORATIO   It beckons you to go away with it,
    As if it some impartment did desire
    To you alone.   60

MARCELLUS   Look, with what courteous action
    It waves you to a more removèd ground:
    But do not go with it.

HORATIO   No, by no means.

HAMLET   It will not speak; then I will follow it.

HORATIO   Do not, my lord.

HAMLET   Why, what should be the fear?   65
    I do not set my life at a pin's fee;
    And for my soul, what can it do to that,
    Being a thing immortal as itself?
    It waves me forth again: I'll follow it.

HORATIO   What if it tempt you toward the flood, my lord,   70
    Or to the dreadful summit of the cliff
    That beetles o'er[3] his base into the sea,
    And there assume some other horrible form,
    Which might deprive your sovereignty of reason
    And draw you into madness? think of it: 75
    The very place puts toys[4] of desperation,
    Without more motive, into every brain
    That looks so many fathoms to the sea
    And hears it roar beneath.

HAMLET   It waves me still.
    Go on; I'll follow thee.   80

MARCELLUS   You shall not go, my lord.

HAMLET   Hold off your hands.

HORATIO   Be ruled; you shall not go.

HAMLET   My fate cries out,
    And makes each petty artery in this body
    As hardy as the Nemean lion's nerve.[5]
    Still am I called, unhand me, gentlemen;   85
    By heaven, I'll make a ghost of him that lets[6] me:
    I say, away! Go on; I'll follow thee.
        [*Exeunt* GHOST *and* HAMLET.]

HORATIO   He waxes desperate with imagination.

MARCELLUS   Let's follow; 'tis not fit thus to obey him.

3. Juts over.   4. Fancies.   5. Sinew, muscle. The *Nemean lion* was slain by Hercules as one of his
twelve labors.   6. Hinders.

HORATIO   Have after. To what issue will this come?   90
MARCELLUS   Something is rotten in the state of Denmark.
HORATIO   Heaven will direct it.
MARCELLUS   Nay, let's follow him.
          [*Exeunt.*]

SCENE 5

[SCENE: *Another part of the platform.*]

[*Enter* GHOST *and* HAMLET.]
HAMLET   Whither wilt thou lead me? speak; I'll go no further.
GHOST   Mark me.
HAMLET   I will.
GHOST   My hour is almost come,
     When I to sulphurous and tormenting flames[7]
     Must render up myself.
HAMLET   Alas, poor ghost!
GHOST   Pity me not, but lend thy serious hearing   5
     To what I shall unfold.
HAMLET   Speak; I am bound to hear.
GHOST   So art thou to revenge, when thou shalt hear.
HAMLET   What?
GHOST   I am thy father's spirit;
     Doomed for a certain term to walk the night,   10
     And for the day confined to fast in fires,
     Till the foul crimes done in my days of nature
     Are burnt and purged away. But that I am forbid
     To tell the secrets of my prison-house,
     I could a tale unfold whose lightest word   15
     Would harrow up thy soul, freeze thy young blood,
     Make thy two eyes, like stars, start from their spheres,[8]
     Thy knotted and combinèd locks to part
     And each particular hair to stand on end,
     Like quills upon the fretful porpentine: 20
     But this eternal blazon[9] must not be
     To ears of flesh and blood. List, list, O, list!
     If thou didst ever thy dear father love—
HAMLET   O God!
GHOST   Revenge his foul and most unnatural murder.   25
HAMLET   Murder!
GHOST   Murder most foul, as in the best it is,
     But this most foul, strange, and unnatural.
HAMLET   Haste me to know't, that I, with wings as swift
     As meditation or the thoughts of love,   30
     May sweep to my revenge.

---

7. Of purgatory.   8. Transparent revolving shells in each of which, according to Ptolemaic astronomy,
a planet or other heavenly body was placed.   9. Publication of the secrets of the other world (of eternity).
Porpentine: porcupine.

GHOST   I find thee apt;
And duller shouldst thou be than the fat weed
That roots itself in ease on Lethe[1] wharf,
Wouldst thou not stir in this. Now, Hamlet, hear:
'Tis given out that, sleeping in my orchard,   35
A serpent stung me; so the whole ear of Denmark
Is by a forgèd process of my death
Rankly abused: but know, thou noble youth,
The serpent that did sting thy father's life
Now wears his crown.

HAMLET   O my prophetic soul!   40
My uncle!

GHOST   Aye, that incestuous, that adulterate beast,
With witchcraft of his wit, with traitorous gifts,—
O wicked wit and gifts, that have the power
So to seduce!—won to his shameful lust   45
The will of my most seeming-virtuous queen:
O Hamlet, what a falling-off was there!
From me, whose love was of that dignity
That it went hand in hand even with the vow
I made to her in marriage; and to decline   50
Upon a wretch, whose natural gifts were poor
To those of mine!
But virtue, as it never will be moved,
Though lewdness court it in a shape of heaven,[2]
So lust, though to a radiant angel linked,   55
Will sate itself in a celestial bed
And prey on garbage.
But, soft! methinks I scent the morning air;
Brief let me be. Sleeping within my orchard,
My custom always of the afternoon,   60
Upon my secure hour thy uncle stole,
With juice of cursed hebenon[3] in a vial,
And in the porches of my ears did pour
The leperous distilment; whose effect
Holds such an enmity with blood of man   65
That swift as quicksilver it courses through
The natural gates and alleys of the body;
And with a sudden vigor it doth posset
And curd, like eager[4] droppings into milk,
The thin and wholesome blood: so did it mine;   70
And a most instant tetter barked about,[5]
Most lazar-like,[6] with vile and loathsome crust,
All my smooth body.
Thus was I, sleeping, by a brother's hand
Of life, of crown, of queen, at once dispatched: 75
Cut off even in the blossoms of my sin,

1. The river of forgetfulness in Hades.   2. A heavenly, angelic form.   3. Henbane, a poisonous herb.
4. Sour. *Posset:* coagulate.   5. The skin immediately became thick like the bark of a tree.   6. Leper-
like (from the beggar Lazarus, "full of sores," in Luke 16.20).

Unhouseled, disappointed, unaneled;[7]
No reckoning made, but sent to my account
With all my imperfections on my head:
O, horrible! O, horrible! most horrible!   80
If thou hast nature in thee, bear it not;
Let not the royal bed of Denmark be
A couch for luxury and damned incest.
But, howsoever thou pursuest this act,
Taint not thy mind, nor let thy soul contrive   85
Against thy mother aught: leave her to heaven,
And to those thorns that in her bosom lodge,
To prick and sting her. Fare thee well at once!
The glow-worm shows the matin to be near,
And 'gins to pale his uneffectual fire: 90
Adieu, adieu, adieu! remember me.
          [Exit.]
HAMLET   O all you host of heaven! O earth! what else?
And shall I couple hell? O, fie! Hold, hold, my heart;
And you, my sinews, grow not instant old,
But bear me stiffly up. Remember thee!   95
Aye, thou poor ghost, while memory holds a seat
In this distracted globe. Remember thee!
Yea, from the table[8] of my memory
I'll wipe away all trivial fond records,
All saws of books, all forms, all pressures past,   100
That youth and observation copied there:
And thy commandment all alone shall live
Within the book and volume of my brain,
Unmixed with baser matter: yes, by heaven!
O most pernicious woman!   105
O villain, villain, smiling, damnèd villain!
My tables,—meet it is I set it down,
That one may smile, and smile, and be a villain;
At least I'm sure it may be so in Denmark.
          [Writing.]
So, uncle, there you are. Now to my word;   110
It is "Adieu, adieu! remember me."
I have sworn't.

HORATIO   ⎱
               ⎰ [Within.] My lord, my lord!
MARCELLUS

          [Enter HORATIO and MARCELLUS.]

MARCELLUS   Lord Hamlet!
HORATIO   Heaven
                                                     secure him!

HAMLET   So be it!
MARCELLUS   Illo,[9] ho, ho, my lord!   115
HAMLET   Hillo, ho, ho, boy! come, bird, come.

---

7. Without sacrament, unprepared, without extreme unction.   8. Writing tablet; used in the same sense
in line 107. Globe: head.   9. A falconer's call.

MARCELLUS   How is't, my noble lord?
HORATIO   What news, my lord?
HAMLET   O, wonderful!
HORATIO   Good my lord, tell it.
HAMLET   No; you will reveal it.
HORATIO   Not I, my lord, by heaven.
MARCELLUS   Nor I, my lord.   120
HAMLET   How say you, then; would heart of man once think it?
    But you'll be secret?
HORATIO   }
MARCELLUS   }   Aye, by heaven, my lord.
HAMLET   There's ne'er a villain dwelling in all Denmark
    But he's an arrant knave.
HORATIO   There needs no ghost, my lord, come from the grave   125
    To tell us this.
HAMLET   Why, right; you are i' the right;
    And so, without more circumstance[1] at all,
    I hold it fit that we shake hands and part:
    You, as your business and desire shall point you;
    For every man hath business and desire,   130
    Such as it is; and for my own poor part,
    Look you, I'll go pray.
HORATIO   These are but wild and whirling words, my lord.
HAMLET   I'm sorry they offend you, heartily;
    Yes, faith, heartily.
HORATIO   There's no offense, my lord.   135
HAMLET   Yes, by Saint Patrick, but there is, Horatio,
    And much offense too. Touching this vision here,
    It is an honest[2] ghost, that let me tell you:
    For your desire to know what is between us,
    O'ermaster't as you may. And now, good friends,   140
    As you are friends, scholars and soldiers,
    Give me one poor request.
HORATIO   What is't, my lord? we will.
HAMLET   Never make known what you have seen tonight.
MARCELLUS   }
HORATIO   }   My lord, we will not.
HAMLET   Nay, but swear't.
HORATIO   In faith,
    My lord, not I.
MARCELLUS   Nor I, my lord, in faith.   145
HAMLET   Upon my sword.
MARCELLUS   We have sworn, my lord, already.
HAMLET   Indeed, upon my sword, indeed.
GHOST [Beneath.]   Swear.
HAMLET   Ah, ha, boy! say'st thou so? art thou there, true-penny?[3]
    Come on: you hear this fellow in the cellarage:
    Consent to swear.

1. Ceremony.   2. Genuine.   3. Honest fellow.

HORATIO   Propose the oath, my lord.   150
HAMLET   Never to speak of this that you have seen,
    Swear by my sword.
GHOST [*Beneath.*]   Swear.
HAMLET   Hic et ubique?⁴ then we'll shift our ground.
    Come hither, gentlemen,   155
    And lay your hands again upon my sword:
    Never to speak of this that you have heard,
    Swear by my sword.
GHOST [*Beneath.*]   Swear.
HAMLET   Well said, old mole! canst work i' the earth so fast?   160
    A worthy pioner!⁵ Once more remove, good friends.
HORATIO   O day and night, but this is wondrous strange!
HAMLET   And therefore as a stranger give it welcome.
    There are more things in heaven and earth, Horatio,
    Than are dreamt of in your philosophy.   165
    But come;
    Here, as before, never, so help you mercy,
    How strange or odd soe'er I bear myself,
    As I perchance hereafter shall think meet
    To put an antic⁶ disposition on,   170
    That you, at such times seeing me, never shall,
    With arms encumbered⁷ thus, or this head-shake,
    Or by pronouncing of some doubtful phrase,
    As "Well, well, we know," or "We could, an if we would,"
    Or "If we list to speak," or "There be, an if they might,"   175
    Or such ambiguous giving out, to note
    That you know aught of me: this not to do,
    So grace and mercy at your most need help you,
    Swear.
GHOST [*Beneath.*]   Swear.   180
HAMLET   Rest, rest, perturbèd spirit!
        [*They swear.*]
    So, gentlemen,
    With all my love I do commend⁸ me to you:
    And what so poor a man as Hamlet is
    May do, to express his love and friending to you,   185
    God willing, shall not lack. Let us go in together;
    And still your fingers on your lips, I pray.
    The time is out of joint: O cursèd spite,
    That ever I was born to set it right!
    Nay, come, let's go together.   190
        [*Exeunt.*]

---

4. Here and everywhere (Latin).   5. Miner.   6. Odd, fantastic.   7. Folded.   8. Entrust.

Act II

SCENE 1

[SCENE: *A room in Polonius's house.*]

[*Enter* POLONIUS *and* REYNALDO.]

POLONIUS Give him this money and these notes, Reynaldo.
REYNALDO I will, my lord.
POLONIUS You shall do marvelous wisely, good Reynaldo,
  Before you visit him, to make inquire
  Of his behavior.
REYNALDO   My lord, I did intend it.   5
POLONIUS Marry, well said, very well said. Look you, sir,
  Inquire me first what Danskers are in Paris,
  And how, and who, what means, and where they keep,[9]
  What company, at what expense, and finding
  By this encompassment[1] and drift of question   10
  That they do know my son, come you more nearer
  Than your particular demands will touch it:
  Take you, as 'twere, some distant knowledge of him,
  As thus, "I know his father and his friends,
  And in part him": do you mark this, Reynaldo?   15
REYNALDO Aye, very well, my lord.
POLONIUS "And in part him; but," you may say, "not well:
  But if 't be he I mean, he's very wild,
  Addicted so and so"; and there put on him
  What forgeries you please; marry, none so rank   20
  As may dishonor him; take heed of that;
  But, sir, such wanton, wild and usual slips
  As are companions noted and most known
  To youth and liberty.
REYNALDO   As gaming, my lord.
POLONIUS Aye, or drinking, fencing, swearing, quarreling,   25
  Drabbing:[2] you may go so far.
REYNALDO My lord, that would dishonor him.
POLONIUS Faith, no; as you may season it in the charge.[3]
  You must not put another scandal on him,
  That he is open to incontinency;   30
  That's not my meaning: but breathe his faults so quaintly[4]
  That they may seem the taints of liberty,
  The flash and outbreak of a fiery mind,
  A savageness in unreclaimèd blood,
  Of general assault.[5]
REYNALDO   But, my good lord,—   35
POLONIUS Wherefore should you do this?
REYNALDO   Aye, my lord,

---

9. Dwell. *Danskers*: Danes.   1. Roundabout way.   2. Whoring.   3. Qualify it in making the accusation.   4. Delicately, skillfully. *Incontinency*: extreme sensuality.   5. Assailing all. *Unreclaimèd*: untamed.

I would know that.
POLONIUS   Marry, sir, here's my drift,
And I believe it is a fetch of warrant:[6]
You laying these slight sullies on my son,
As 'twere a thing a little soiled i' the working,   40
Mark you,
Your party in converse, him you would sound,
Having ever seen in the prenominate[7] crimes
The youth you breathe of guilty, be assured
He closes with you in this consequence;[8]   45
"Good sir," or so, or "friend," or "gentleman,"
According to the phrase or the addition[9]
Of man and country.
REYNALDO   Very good, my lord.
POLONIUS And then, sir, does he this—he does—what was I about to
say? By the mass, I was about to say something: where did I leave?   50
REYNALDO At "closes in the consequence," at "friend or so," and "gen-
tleman."
POLONIUS At "closes in the consequence," aye, marry;
He closes with you thus: "I know the gentleman;
I saw him yesterday, or t' other day,   55
Or then, or then, with such, or such, and, as you say,
There was a' gaming, there o'ertook in 's rouse,[1]
There falling out at tennis": or perchance,
"I saw him enter such a house of sale,"
Videlicet,[2] a brothel, or so forth.   60
See you now;
Your bait of falsehood takes this carp of truth:
And thus do we of wisdom and of reach,[3]
With windlasses and with assays of bias,[4]
By indirections find directions out: 65
So, by my former lecture and advice,
Shall you my son. You have me, have you not?
REYNALDO My lord, I have.
POLONIUS   God be wi' ye; fare ye well.
REYNALDO Good my lord!
POLONIUS Observe his inclination in yourself.[5]   70
REYNALDO I shall, my lord.
POLONIUS And let him ply his music.
REYNALDO   Well, my lord.
POLONIUS Farewell!
          [*Exit* REYNALDO.—*Enter* OPHELIA.]
How now, Ophelia! what's the matter?
OPHELIA O, my lord, I have been so affrighted!   75
POLONIUS With what, i' the name of God?
OPHELIA My lord, as I was sewing in my closet,

6. Allowable stratagem.   7. Aforementioned. *Having ever:* if he has ever.   8. You may be sure he will
agree in this conclusion.   9. Title.   1. Intoxicated in his reveling.   2. Namely.   3. Wise and far-
sighted.   4. Sending the ball indirectly (in bowling), devious attacks. *Windlasses:* winding ways, roundabout courses.   5. Ways of procedure by yourself.

Lord Hamlet, with his doublet[6] all unbraced,
No hat upon his head, his stockings fouled,
Ungartered and down-gyvèd[7] to his ankle;   80
Pale as his shirt, his knees knocking each other,
And with a look so piteous in purport
As if he had been loosèd out of hell
To speak of horrors, he comes before me.
POLONIUS   Mad for thy love?
OPHELIA   My lord, I do not know,   85
But truly I do fear it.
POLONIUS   What said he?
OPHELIA   He took me by the wrist and held me hard;
Then goes he to the length of all his arm,
And with his other hand thus o'er his brow,
He falls to such perusal of my face   90
As he would draw it. Long stayed he so;
At last, a little shaking of mine arm,
And thrice his head thus waving up and down,
He raised a sigh so piteous and profound
As it did seem to shatter all his bulk   95
And end his being: that done, he lets me go:
And with his head over his shoulder turned,
He seemed to find his way without his eyes;
For out o' doors he went without their help,
And to the last bended their light on me.   100
POLONIUS   Come, go with me: I will go seek the king.
This is the very ecstasy of love;
Whose violent property fordoes itself[8]
And leads the will to desperate undertakings
As oft as any passion under heaven   105
That does afflict our natures. I am sorry.
What, have you given him any hard words of late?
OPHELIA   No, my good lord, but, as you did command,
I did repel his letters and denied
His access to me.
POLONIUS   That hath made him mad.   110
I am sorry that with better heed and judgment
I had not quoted him: I fear'd he did but trifle
And meant to wreck thee; but beshrew my jealousy![9]
By heaven, it is as proper to our age
To cast beyond ourselves[1] in our opinions   115
As it is common for the younger sort
To lack discretion. Come, go we to the king:
This must be known; which, being kept close, might move
More grief to hide than hate to utter love.[2]
Come.   120
        [Exeunt.]

---

6. Jacket. *Closet:* private room.   7. Pulled down like fetters on a prisoner's leg.   8. Which, when violent, destroys itself. *Ecstasy:* madness.   9. Curse my suspicion. *Quoted:* noted.   1. Overshoot, go too far.   2. If Hamlet's love is revealed. *To hide:* if kept hidden.

SCENE 2

[SCENE: *A room in the castle.*]

[*Flourish. Enter* KING, QUEEN, ROSENCRANTZ, GUILDENSTERN, *and* ATTENDANTS.]

KING Welcome, dear Rosencrantz and Guildenstern!
Moreover that we much did long to see you,
The need we have to use you did provoke
Our hasty sending. Something have you heard
Of Hamlet's transformation; so call it,   5
Sith³ nor the exterior nor the inward man
Resembles that it was. What it should be,
More than his father's death, that thus hath put him
So much from the understanding of himself,
I cannot dream of: I entreat you both,   10
That, being of so young days brought up with him
And sith so neighbored to his youth and behavior,
That you vouchsafe your rest⁴ here in our court
Some little time: so by your companies
To draw him on to pleasures, and to gather   15
So much as from occasion you may glean,
Whether aught to us unknown afflicts him thus,
That opened⁵ lies within our remedy.
QUEEN Good gentlemen, he hath much talked of you,
And sure I am two men there are not living   20
To whom he more adheres.⁶ If it will please you
To show us so much gentry⁷ and good will
As to expend your time with us awhile
For the supply and profit of our hope,
Your visitation shall receive such thanks   25
As fits a king's remembrance.
ROSENCRANTZ   Both your majesties
Might, by the sovereign power you have of us,
Put your dread pleasures more into⁸ command
Than to entreaty.
GUILDENSTERN   But we both obey,
And here give up ourselves, in the full bent⁹   30
To lay our service freely at your feet,
To be commanded.
KING Thanks, Rosencrantz and gentle Guildenstern.
QUEEN Thanks, Guildenstern and gentle Rosencrantz:
And I beseech you instantly to visit   35
My too much changéd son. Go, some of you,
And bring these gentlemen where Hamlet is.
GUILDENSTERN Heavens make our presence and our practices
Pleasant and helpful to him!

---

3. Since.   4. Consent to stay.   5. Once revealed.   6. Is more attached.   7. Courtesy.   8. Give
your sovereign wishes the form of.   9. Bent (as a bow) to the limit.

QUEEN   Aye, amen!

[*Exeunt* ROSENCRANTZ, GUILDENSTERN, *and some* ATTENDANTS.—*Enter*
POLONIUS.]

POLONIUS   The ambassadors from Norway, my good lord,   40
  Are joyfully returned.
KING   Thou still[1] hast been the father of good news.
POLONIUS   Have I, my lord? I assure my good liege,
  I hold my duty as I hold my soul,
  Both to my God and to my gracious king: 45
  And I do think, or else this brain of mine
  Hunts not the trail of policy so sure
  As it hath used to do, that I have found
  The very cause of Hamlet's lunacy.
KING   O, speak of that; that do I long to hear.   50
POLONIUS   Give first admittance to the ambassadors;
  My news shall be the fruit to that great feast.
KING   Thyself do grace[2] to them, and bring them in.
      [*Exit* POLONIUS.]
  He tells me, my dear Gertrude, he hath found
  The head and source of all your son's distemper.   55
QUEEN   I doubt it is no other but the main;
  His father's death and our o'erhasty marriage.
KING   Well, we shall sift him.
      [*Re-enter* POLONIUS, *with* VOLTIMAND *and* CORNELIUS.]
                        Welcome, my good friends!
  Say, Voltimand, what from our brother Norway?
VOLTIMAND   Most fair return of greetings and desires.   60
  Upon our first,[3] he sent out to suppress
  His nephew's levies, which to him appeared
  To be a preparation 'gainst the Polack,
  But better looked into, he truly found
  It was against your highness: whereat grieved,   65
  That so his sickness, age and impotence
  Was falsely borne in hand,[4] sends out arrests
  On Fortinbras; which he, in brief, obeys,
  Receives rebuke from Norway, and in fine[5]
  Makes vow before his uncle never more   70
  To give the assay[6] of arms against your majesty.
  Whereon old Norway, overcome with joy,
  Gives him three thousand crowns in annual fee
  And his commission to employ those soldiers,
  So levied as before, against the Polack: 75
  With an entreaty, herein further shown,
      [*Giving a paper.*]
  That it might please you to give quiet pass
  Through your dominions for this enterprise,
  On such regards of safety and allowance

---

1. Always.   2. Honor. *Fruit:* dessert.   3. As soon as we made the request.   4. Deceived, deluded.
5. Finally.   6. Test.

As therein are set down.

KING   It likes us well,   80
And at our more considered time we'll read,
Answer, and think upon this business.
Meantime we thank you for your well-took labor:
Go to your rest; at night we'll feast together:
Most welcome home!
        [*Exeunt* VOLTIMAND *and* CORNELIUS.]
POLONIUS   This business is well ended.   85
My liege, and madam, to expostulate
What majesty should be, what duty is,
Why day is day, night night, and time is time,
Were nothing but to waste night, day and time.
Therefore, since brevity is the soul of wit   90
And tediousness the limbs and outward flourishes,
I will be brief. Your noble son is mad:
Mad call I it; for, to define true madness,
What is 't but to be nothing else but mad?
But let that go.
QUEEN   More matter, with less art.   95
POLONIUS   Madam, I swear I use no art at all.
That he is mad, 'tis true: 'tis true 'tis pity,
And pity 'tis 'tis true: a foolish figure;[7]
But farewell it, for I will use no art.
Mad let us grant him then: and now remains   100
That we find out the cause of this effect,
Or rather say, the cause of this defect,
For this effect defective comes by cause:
Thus it remains and the remainder thus.
Perpend.[8]   105
I have a daughter,—have while she is mine,—
Who in her duty and obedience, mark,
Hath given me this: now gather and surmise.
[*Reads.*] "To the celestial, and my soul's idol, the most beautified
Ophelia,"—That's an ill phrase, a vile phrase; "beautified" is a vile   110
phrase; but you shall hear. Thus:
    [*Reads.*] "In her excellent white bosom, these," &c.
QUEEN   Came this from Hamlet to her?
POLONIUS   Good madam, stay awhile; I will be faithful.   115
        [*Reads.*]   "Doubt thou the stars are fire;
                Doubt that the sun doth move;
                Doubt truth to be a liar;
                But never doubt I love.
"O dear Ophelia, I am ill at these numbers;[9] I have not art to reckon
my groans: but that I love thee best, O most best, believe it. Adieu.   120
            "Thine evermore, most dear lady, whilst this
                machine is to him,[1] HAMLET."
This in obedience hath my daughter shown me;

7. Of speech.   8. Consider.   9. Verses.   1. Body is attached.

And more above,[2] hath his solicitings,
As they fell out by time, by means and place,   125
All given to mine ear.
KING   But how hath she
Received his love?
POLONIUS   What do you think of me?
KING   As of a man faithful and honorable.
POLONIUS   I would fain prove so. But what might you think,
When I had seen this hot love on the wing,—   130
As I perceived it, I must tell you that,
Before my daughter told me,—what might you,
Or my dear majesty your queen here, think,
If I had played the desk or table-book,[3]
Or given my heart a winking,[4] mute and dumb,   135
Or looked upon this love with idle sight;
What might you think? No, I went round[5] to work,
And my young mistress thus I did bespeak:
"Lord Hamlet is a prince, out of thy star;[6]
This must not be:" and then I prescripts gave her,   140
That she should lock herself from his resort,
Admit no messengers, receive no tokens.
Which done, she took the fruits of my advice;
And he repulsed, a short tale to make,
Fell into a sadness, then into a fast,   145
Thence to a watch, thence into a weakness,
Thence to a lightness,[7] and by this declension
Into the madness wherein now he raves
And all we mourn for.
KING   Do you think this?
QUEEN   It may be, very like.   150
POLONIUS   Hath there been such a time, I'd fain know that,
That I have positively said " 'tis so,"
When it proved otherwise?
KING   Not that I know.
POLONIUS [*Pointing to his head and shoulder.*]   Take this, from this,
   if this be otherwise: 155
If circumstances lead me, I will find
Where truth is hid, though it were hid indeed
Within the center.[8]
KING   How may we try it further?
POLONIUS   You know, sometimes he walks for hours together
Here in the lobby.
QUEEN   So he does, indeed.   160
POLONIUS   At such a time I'll loose my daughter to him:
Be you and I behind an arras then;
Mark the encounter: if he love her not,
And be not from his reason fall'n thereon,[9]

2. Moreover.   3. If I had acted as a desk or notebook (in keeping the matter secret).   4. Shut my heart's eye.   5. Straight.   6. Sphere.   7. Light-headedness. *Watch:* insomnia.   8. Of the earth.
9. For that reason.

Let me be no assistant for a state, 165
But keep a farm and carters.

KING   We will try it.

QUEEN   But look where sadly the poor wretch comes reading.

POLONIUS   Away, I do beseech you, both away:
I'll board him presently.[1]

[*Exeunt* KING, QUEEN, *and* ATTENDANTS.—*Enter* HAMLET, *reading.*]

O, give me leave: how does my good Lord Hamlet? 170

HAMLET   Well, God-a-mercy.

POLONIUS   Do you know me, my lord?

HAMLET   Excellent well; you are a fishmonger.[2]

POLONIUS   Not I, my lord.

HAMLET   Then I would you were so honest a man. 175

POLONIUS: Honest, my lord!

HAMLET   Aye, sir; to be honest, as this world goes, is to be one man
picked out of ten thousand.

POLONIUS   That's very true, my lord.

HAMLET   For if the sun breed maggots in a dead dog, being a good 180
kissing carrion[3]—Have you a daughter?

POLONIUS   I have, my lord.

HAMLET   Let her not walk i' the sun: conception is a blessing; but as
your daughter may conceive,—friend, look to 't.

POLONIUS [*Aside.*]   How say you by that? Still harping on my daughter: 185
yet he knew me not at first; he said I was a fishmonger: he is far
gone: and truly in my youth I suffered much extremity for love; very
near this. I'll speak to him again.—What do you read, my lord?

HAMLET   Words, words, words.

POLONIUS   What is the matter,[4] my lord? 190

HAMLET   Between who?

POLONIUS   I mean, the matter that you read, my lord.

HAMLET   Slanders, sir: for the satirical rogue says here that old men
have gray beards, that their faces are wrinkled, their eyes purging
thick amber and plum-tree gum, and that they have a plentiful lack 195
of wit, together with most weak hams: all which, sir, though I most
powerfully and potently believe, yet I hold it not honesty to have it
thus set down; for yourself, sir, shall grow old as I am, if like a crab
you could go backward.

POLONIUS [*Aside.*]   Though this be madness, yet there is method in 200
't.—Will you walk out of the air, my lord?

HAMLET   Into my grave.

POLONIUS   Indeed, that's out of the air.
[*Aside.*]
How pregnant sometimes his replies are! a happiness[5] that often
madness hits on, which reason and sanity could not so prosperously 205
be delivered of. I will leave him, and suddenly contrive the means of
meeting between him and my daughter.—My honorable lord, I will
most humbly take my leave of you.

1. Approach him at once.   2. Fish seller but also slang for procurer.   3. Good bit of flesh for kissing.
4. The subject matter of the book. Hamlet responds as if he referred to the subject of a quarrel.   5. Apt-
ness of expression.

HAMLET You cannot, sir, take from me any thing that I will more
willingly part withal: except my life, except my life, except my life. 210
POLONIUS Fare you well, my lord.
HAMLET These tedious old fools.
    [*Re-enter* ROSENCRANTZ *and* GUILDENSTERN.]
POLONIUS You go to seek the Lord Hamlet; there he is.
ROSENCRANTZ [*To* POLONIUS.] God save you, sir!
    [*Exit* POLONIUS.]
GUILDENSTERN My honored lord! 215
ROSENCRANTZ My most dear lord!
HAMLET My excellent good friends! How dost thou, Guildenstern? Ah,
Rosencrantz! Good lads, how do you both?
ROSENCRANTZ As the indifferent[6] children of the earth.
GUILDENSTERN Happy, in that we are not over-happy; 220
On Fortune's cap we are not the very button.[7]
HAMLET Nor the soles of her shoe?
ROSENCRANTZ Neither, my lord.
HAMLET Then you live about her waist, or in the middle of her
favors?
GUILDENSTERN Faith, her privates[8] we. 225
HAMLET In the secret parts of Fortune? O, most true; she is a strum-
pet. What's the news?
ROSENCRANTZ None, my lord, but that the world's grown honest.
HAMLET Then is doomsday near: but your news is not true. Let
me question more in particular: what have you, my good friends, 230
deserved at the hands of Fortune, that she sends you to prison
hither?
GUILDENSTERN Prison, my lord!
HAMLET Denmark's a prison.
ROSENCRANTZ Then is the world one. 235
HAMLET A goodly one; in which there are many confines, wards[9] and
dungeons, Denmark being one o' the worst.
ROSENCRANTZ We think not so, my lord.
HAMLET Why, then, 'tis none to you; for there is nothing either good
or bad, but thinking makes it so: to me it is a prison. 240
ROSENCRANTZ Why, then your ambition makes it one; 'tis too narrow
for your mind.
HAMLET O God, I could be bounded in a nut-shell and count myself
a king of infinite space, were it not that I have bad dreams.
GUILDENSTERN Which dreams indeed are ambition; for the very sub- 245
stance of the ambitious is merely the shadow of a dream.
HAMLET A dream itself is but a shadow.
ROSENCRANTZ Truly, and I hold ambition of so airy and light a quality
that it is but a shadow's shadow.
HAMLET Then are our beggars bodies, and our monarchs and out- 250
stretched heroes the beggars' shadows. Shall we to the court? for, by
my fay, I cannot reason.

---

6. Average. 7. Top. 8. Ordinary men (with obvious play on the sexual term *private parts*).
9. Cells. *Confines:* places of confinement.

ROSENCRANTZ
GUILDENSTERN } We'll wait upon you.

HAMLET No such matter: I will not sort you[1] with the rest of my servants; for, to speak to you like an honest man, I am most dreadfully 255
attended. But, in the beaten way of friendship, what make you at
Elsinore?

ROSENCRANTZ To visit you, my lord; no other occasion.

HAMLET Beggar that I am, I am even poor in thanks; but I thank you:
and sure, dear friends, my thanks are too dear a halfpenny.[2] Were 260
you not sent for? Is it your own inclining? Is it a free visitation?
Come, deal justly[3] with me: come, come; nay, speak.

GUILDENSTERN What should we say, my lord?

HAMLET Why, any thing, but to the purpose. You were sent for; and
there is a kind of confession in your looks, which your modesties 265
have not craft enough to color: I know the good king and queen have
sent for you.

ROSENCRANTZ To what end, my lord?

HAMLET That you must teach me. But let me conjure you, by the
rights of our fellowship, by the consonancy of our youth, by the obli- 270
gation of our ever-preserved love, and by what more dear a better
proposer[4] could charge you withal, be even and direct with me,
whether you were sent for, or no.

ROSENCRANTZ [Aside to GUILDENSTERN.] What say you?

HAMLET [Aside.] Nay then, I have an eye of[5] you.—If you love me, 275
hold not off.

GUILDENSTERN My lord, we were sent for.

HAMLET I will tell you why; so shall my anticipation prevent your discovery,[6] and your secrecy to the king and queen moult no feather. I
have of late—but wherefore I know not—lost all my mirth, forgone 280
all custom of exercises; and indeed it goes so heavily with my disposition that this goodly frame, the earth, seems to me a sterile promontory; this most excellent canopy, the air, look you, this brave
o'erhanging firmament, this majestical roof fretted[7] with golden fire,
why, it appears no other thing to me than a foul and pestilent con- 285
gregation of vapors. What a piece of work is a man! how noble in
reason! how infinite in faculty! in form and moving how express[8] and
admirable! in action how like an angel! in apprehension how like a
god! the beauty of the world! the paragon of animals! And yet, to me,
what is this quintessence of dust? man delights not me; no, nor 290
woman neither, though by your smiling you seem to say so.

ROSENCRANTZ My lord, there was no such stuff in my thoughts.

HAMLET Why did you laugh then, when I said "man delights not me"?

ROSENCRANTZ To think, my lord, if you delight not in man, what 295
lenten entertainment the players shall receive from you: we coted[9]
them on the way; and hither are they coming, to offer you service.

HAMLET He that plays the king shall be welcome; his majesty shall
have tribute of me; the adventurous knight shall use his foil and

---

1. Put you together. 2. If priced at a halfpenny. 3. Honestly. 4. Speaker. 5. On. 6. Precede your disclosure. 7. Adorned. 8. Precise. 9. Overtook.

target; the lover shall not sigh gratis; the humorous[1] man shall end   300
his part in peace; the clown shall make those laugh whose lungs are
tickle o' the sere,[2] and the lady shall say her mind freely, or the blank
verse shall halt for 't. What players are they?

ROSENCRANTZ   Even those you were wont to take such delight in, the
tragedians of the city.   305

HAMLET   How chances it they travel? their residence, both in reputation and profit, was better both ways.

ROSENCRANTZ   I think their inhibition comes by means of the late
innovation.[3]

HAMLET   Do they hold the same estimation they did when I was in the   310
city? are they so followed?

ROSENCRANTZ   No, indeed, are they not.

HAMLET   How comes it? do they grow rusty?

ROSENCRANTZ   Nay, their endeavor keeps in the wonted pace: but
there is, sir, an eyrie of children, little eyases,[4] that cry out on the   315
top of question[5] and are most tyrannically clapped for 't: these are
now the fashion, and so berattle[6] the common stages—so they call
them—that many wearing rapiers are afraid of goose-quills,[7] and
dare scarce come thither.

HAMLET   What, are they children? who maintains 'em? how are they   320
escoted? Will they pursue the quality[8] no longer than they can sing?
will they not say afterwards, if they should grow themselves to common players—as it is most like, if their means are no better,—their
writers do them wrong, to make them exclaim against their own
succession?[9]   325

ROSENCRANTZ   Faith, there has been much to-do on both sides, and
the nation holds it no sin to tarre[1] them to controversy: there was
for a while no money bid for argument unless the poet and the player
went to cuffs in the question.[2]

HAMLET   Is 't possible?   330

GUILDENSTERN   O, there has been much throwing about of brains.

HAMLET   Do the boys carry it away?[3]

ROSENCRANTZ   Aye, that they do, my lord; Hercules and his load too.[4]

HAMLET   It is not very strange; for my uncle is king of Denmark, and
those that would make mows[5] at him while my father lived, give   335
twenty, forty, fifty, a hundred ducats a-piece, for his picture in little.
'Sblood, there is something in this more than natural, if philosophy
could find it out.

   [Flourish of trumpets within.]

GUILDENSTERN   There are the players.

HAMLET   Gentlemen, you are welcome to Elsinore. Your hands, come   340
then: the appurtenance of welcome is fashion and ceremony: let me

---

1. Eccentric, whimsical.   2. Ready to shoot off at a touch.   3. The introduction of the children (line
314), as Rosencrantz explains in his subsequent replies to Hamlet. *Inhibition:* prohibition.   4. Nestling
hawks. *Eyrie:* nest.   5. Above others on matter of dispute.   6. Berate.   7. Gentlemen are afraid of
pens (that is, of poets satirizing the "common stages").   8. Profession of acting. *Escoted:* financially supported.   9. Recite satiric pieces against what they are themselves likely to become, common players.
1. Incite.   2. No offer to buy a plot for a play if it did not contain a quarrel between poet and player on
that subject.   3. Win out.   4. The sign in front of the Globe theater showed Hercules bearing the
world on his shoulders.   5. Faces, grimaces.

comply with you in this garb, lest my extent[6] to the players, which,
I tell you, must show fairly outwards, should more appear like entertainment[7] than yours. You are welcome: but my uncle-father and
aunt-mother are deceived.

GUILDENSTERN In what, my dear lord?   345

HAMLET I am but mad north-north-west: when the wind is southerly
I know a hawk from a handsaw.[8]

      [Re-enter POLONIUS.]

POLONIUS Well be with you, gentlemen!

HAMLET Hark you, Guildenstern; and you too: at each ear a hearer: 350
that great baby you see there is not yet out of his swaddling clouts.[9]

ROSENCRANTZ Happily he's the second time come to them; for they
say an old man is twice a child.

HAMLET I will prophesy he comes to tell me of the players; mark it.
You say right, sir: o' Monday morning; 'twas so, indeed.[1]   355

POLONIUS My lord, I have news to tell you.

HAMLET My lord, I have news to tell you. When Roscius[2] was an actor
in Rome,—

POLONIUS The actors are come hither, my lord.

HAMLET Buz, buz![3]   360

POLONIUS Upon my honor,—

HAMLET Then came each actor on his ass,—

POLONIUS The best actors in the world, either for tragedy, comedy,
history, pastoral, pastoral-comical, historical-pastoral, tragical-
historical, tragical-comical-historical-pastoral, scene individable, or 365
poem unlimited:[4] Seneca cannot be too heavy, nor Plautus too light.
For the law of writ and the liberty,[5] these are the only men.

HAMLET O Jephthah,[6] judge of Israel, what a treasure hadst thou!

POLONIUS What a treasure had he, my lord?

HAMLET Why,   370
    "One fair daughter, and no more,
      The which he lovèd passing well."[7]

POLONIUS *[Aside.]* Still on my daughter.

HAMLET Am I not i' the right, old Jephthah?

POLONIUS If you call me Jephthah, my lord, I have a daughter that I   375
love passing well.

HAMLET Nay, that follows not.

POLONIUS What follows, then, my lord?

HAMLET Why,
      "As by lot, God wot."
and then you know,   380
      "It came to pass, as most like it was,"—
the first row of the pious chanson will show you more; for look, where
my abridgment[8] comes.

---

6. Welcoming behavior. *Garb:* style.   7. Welcome.   8. A hawk from a heron as well as a kind of ax
from a handsaw.   9. Clothes.   1. Hamlet, for Polonius's sake, pretends he is deep in talk with Rosencrantz.   2. A famous Roman comic actor (126?–62? B.C.E.).   3. An expression used to stop the teller
of a stale story.   4. For plays governed and those not governed by classical rules.   5. Possibly, for both
written and extemporized plays. Seneca (after 4 B.C.E.–65 C.E.) was a Roman who wrote tragedies. Plautus
(254?–184? B.C.E.) was a Roman who wrote comedies.   6. Who was compelled to sacrifice a dearly
beloved daughter (Judges 11).   7. From an old ballad about Jephthah.   8. That is, the players interrupting him. *Row:* stanza. *Chanson:* song.

[*Enter four or five* PLAYERS.]

You are welcome, masters; welcome, all. I am glad to see thee well.
Welcome, good friends. O, my old friend! Why thy face is valanced⁹   385
since I saw thee last; comest thou to beard me in Denmark? What,
my young lady and mistress! By'r lady, your ladyship is nearer to
heaven than when I saw you last, by the altitude of a chopine. Pray
God, your voice, like a piece of uncurrent gold, be not cracked within
the ring.¹ Masters, you are all welcome. We'll e'en to 't like French   390
falconers, fly at any thing we see: we'll have a speech straight: come,
give us a taste of your quality; come, a passionate speech.

FIRST PLAYER   What speech, my good lord?

HAMLET   I heard thee speak me a speech once, but it was never acted;
or, if it was, not above once; for the play, I remember, pleased not   395
the million; 'twas caviare to the general:² but it was—as I received
it, and others, whose judgments in such matters cried in the top of
mine³—an excellent play, well digested in the scenes, set down with
as much modesty as cunning. I remember, one said there were no
sallets in the lines to make the matter savory, nor no matter in the   400
phrase that might indict the author of affection;⁴ but called it an
honest method, as wholesome as sweet, and by very much more
handsome than fine.⁵ One speech in it I chiefly loved: 'twas Æneas'
tale to Dido; and thereabout of it especially, where he speaks of
Priam's slaughter:⁶ it live in your memory, begin at this line; let me   405
see, let me see;
"The rugged Pyrrhus, like th' Hyrcanian beast,"⁷—
It is not so: it begins with "Pyrrhus."
"The rugged Pyrrhus, he whose sable arms,
Black as his purpose, did the night resemble   410
When he lay couchèd in the ominous horse,⁸
Hath now this dread and black complexion smeared
With heraldry more dismal: head to foot
Now is he total gules; horridly tricked⁹
With the blood of fathers, mothers, daughters, sons,   415
Baked and impasted with the parching streets,
That lend a tyrannous¹ and a damnèd light
To their lord's murder: roasted in wrath and fire,
And thus o'er-sizèd² with coagulate gore,
With eyes like carbuncles, the hellish Pyrrhus   420
Old grandsire Priam seeks."
So, proceed you.

POLONIUS   'Fore God, my lord, well spoken, with good accent and good
discretion.

FIRST PLAYER   'Anon he finds him   425
Striking too short at Greeks; his antique sword,
Rebellious to his arm, lies where it falls,

---

9. Draped (with a beard).   1. A pun on the *ring* of the voice and the *ring* around the king's head on a
coin. *Chopine:* a thick-soled shoe. *Uncurrent:* unfit for currency.   2. A delicacy wasted on the general
public.   3. Were louder (more authoritative than) mine.   4. Affectation. *Sallets:* salads (that is, relish,
spicy passages).   5. More elegant than showy.   6. The story of the fall of Troy, told by Aeneas to Queen
Dido. Priam was the king of Troy.   7. Tiger. Pyrrhus was Achilles's son (also called Neoptolemus).
8. The wooden horse in which Greek warriors were smuggled into Troy.   9. Adorned. *Gules:* heraldic
term for red.   1. Savage.   2. Glued over.

Repugnant to command: unequal matched,
Pyrrhus at Priam drives; in rage strikes wide;
But with the whiff and wind of his fell sword   430
The unnervèd father falls. Then senseless Ilium,[3]
Seeming to feel this blow, with flaming top
Stoops to his base, and with a hideous crash
Takes prisoner Pyrrhus's ear: for, lo! his sword,
Which was declining on the milky[4] head   435
Of reverend Priam seemed i' the air to stick:
So, as a painted tyrant, Pyrrhus stood,
And like a neutral to his will and matter,
Did nothing.
But as we often see, against some storm,   440
A silence in the heavens, the rack[5] stand still,
The bold winds speechless and the orb below
As hush as death, anon the dreadful thunder
Doth rend the region, so after Pyrrhus's pause
Aroused vengeance sets him new a-work;   445
And never did the Cyclops'[6] hammers fall
On Mars's armor, forged for proof[7] eterne,
With less remorse than Pyrrhus's bleeding sword
Now falls on Priam.
Out, thou strumpet, Fortune! All you gods,   450
In general synod take away her power,
Break all the spokes and fellies from her wheel,
And bowl the round nave[8] down the hill of heaven
As low as to the fiends!

POLONIUS This is too long.   455
HAMLET It shall to the barber's, with your beard. Prithee, say on: he's
    for a jig[9] or a tale of bawdry, or he sleeps: say on: come to Hecuba.
FIRST PLAYER "But who, O, who had seen the mobled[1] queen—"
HAMLET "The mobled queen?"
POLONIUS That's good; "mobled queen" is good.   460
FIRST PLAYER "Run barefoot up and down, threatening the flames
    With bisson rheum; a clout[2] upon that head
    Where late the diadem stood; and for a robe,
    About her lank and all o'er-teemèd loins,[3]
    A blanket, in the alarm of fear caught up: 465
    Who this had seen, with tongue in venom steeped
    'Gainst Fortune's state[4] would treason have pronounced:
    But if the gods themselves did see her then,
    When she saw Pyrrhus make malicious sport
    In mincing with his sword her husband's limbs,   470
    The instant burst of clamor that she made,
    Unless things mortal move them[5] not at all,

---

3. Troy's citadel.   4. White-haired.   5. Clouds. *Against:* just before.   6. The gigantic workmen of
Hephaestus (Vulcan), god of blacksmiths and fire.   7. Protection.   8. Hub. *Fellies:* rims.   9. Ludi-
crous sung dialogue, short farce.   1. Muffled.   2. Cloth. *Bisson rheum:* blinding moisture, tears.
3. Worn out by childbearing.   4. Government.   5. The gods.

Would have made milch the burning eyes of heaven[6]
And passion in the gods."

POLONIUS Look, whether he has not turned his color and has tears in   475
's eyes. Prithee, no more.

HAMLET 'Tis well; I'll have thee speak out the rest of this soon. Good
my lord, will you see the players well bestowed?[7] Do you hear, let
them be well used, for they are the abstracts and brief chronicles of
the time: after your death you were better have a bad epitaph than   480
their ill report while you live.

POLONIUS My lord, I will use them according to their desert.

HAMLET God's bodykins,[8] man, much better: use every man after his
desert, and who shall 'scape whipping? Use them after your own
honor and dignity: the less they deserve, the more merit is in your   485
bounty. Take them in.

POLONIUS Come, sirs.

HAMLET Follow him, friends: we'll hear a play to-morrow. [Exit
POLONIUS with all the PLAYERS but the first.] Dost thou hear me, old
friend; can you play the Murder of Gonzago?   490

FIRST PLAYER Aye, my lord.

HAMLET We'll ha 't to-morrow night. You could, for a need, study a
speech of some dozen or sixteen lines, which I would set down and
insert in 't, could you not?

FIRST PLAYER Aye, my lord.   495

HAMLET Very well. Follow that lord; and look you mock him not.
[Exit FIRST PLAYER.] My good friends, I'll leave you till night: you are
welcome to Elsinore.

ROSENCRANTZ Good my lord!

HAMLET Aye, so, God be wi' ye! [Exeunt ROSENCRANTZ and GUILDEN-   500
STERN.] Now I am alone.
O, what a rogue and peasant slave am I!
Is it not monstrous that this player here,
But in a fiction, in a dream of passion,
Could force his soul so to his own conceit   505
That from her[9] working all his visage wanned;
Tears in his eyes, distraction in 's aspect,
A broken voice, and his whole function[1] suiting
With forms to his conceit? and all for nothing!
For Hecuba![2]   510
What's Hecuba to him, or he to Hecuba,
That he should weep for her? What would he do,
Had he the motive and the cue for passion
That I have? He would drown the stage with tears
And cleave the general air with horrid speech,   515
Make mad the guilty and appal the free,
Confound the ignorant, and amaze indeed
The very faculties of eyes and ears.
Yet I,

6. The stars. *Milch:* moist (milk-giving).   7. Taken care of, lodged.   8. By God's little body.   9. His
soul's.   1. Bodily action.   2. Queen of Troy, Priam's wife. *Conceit:* imagination, conception of the role
played.

A dull and muddy-mettled rascal, peak,[3]   520
Like John-a-dreams, unpregnant of my cause,[4]
And can say nothing; no, not for a king,
Upon whose property and most dear life
A damn'd defeat was made. Am I a coward?
Who calls me villain? breaks my pate across?   525
Plucks off my beard, and blows it in my face?
Tweaks me by the nose? gives me the lie i' the throat,
As deep as to the lungs? who does me this?
Ha!
'Swounds, I should take it: for it cannot be   530
But I am pigeon-livered and lack gall
To make oppression bitter, or ere this
I should have fatted all the region kites[5]
With this slave's offal: bloody, bawdy villain!
Remorseless, treacherous, lecherous, kindless[6] villain!   535
O, vengeance!
Why, what an ass am I! This is most brave,
That I, the son of a dear father murdered,
Prompted to my revenge by heaven and hell,
Must, like a whore, unpack my heart with words,   540
And fall a-cursing, like a very drab,
A scullion!
Fie upon 't! About,[7] my brain! Hum, I have heard
That guilty creatures, sitting at a play,
Have by the very cunning of the scene   545
Been struck so to the soul that presently
They have proclaimed their malefactions;
For murder, though it have no tongue, will speak
With most miraculous organ. I'll have these players
Play something like the murder of my father   550
Before mine uncle: I'll observe his looks;
I'll tent him to the quick: if he but blench,[8]
I know my course. The spirit that I have seen
May be the devil; and the devil hath power
To assume a pleasing shape; yea, and perhaps   555
Out of my weakness and my melancholy,
As he is very potent with such spirits,
Abuses me to damn me. I'll have grounds
More relative[9] than this. The play's the thing
Wherein I'll catch the conscience of the king.   560
     [Exit.]

---

3. Mope. *Muddy-mettled:* of poor metal (spirit, temper), dull-spirited.   4. Not really conscious of my cause, unquickened by it. *John-a-dreams:* a dreamy, absentminded character.   5. Kites (hawks) of the air.   6. Unnatural.   7. To work!   8. Flinch. *Tent:* probe.   9. Relevant.

Act III

SCENE 1

[SCENE: *A room in the castle.*]

[*Enter* KING, QUEEN, POLONIUS, OPHELIA, ROSENCRANTZ, *and*
GUILDENSTERN.]

KING   And can you, by no drift of circumstance,[1]
Get from him why he puts on this confusion,
Grating so harshly all his days of quiet
With turbulent and dangerous lunacy?
ROSENCRANTZ   He does confess he feels himself distracted,   5
But from what cause he will by no means speak.
GUILDENSTERN   Nor do we find him forward to be sounded;
But, with a crafty madness, keeps aloof,
When we would bring him on to some confession
Of his true state.
QUEEN   Did he receive you well?   10
ROSENCRANTZ   Most like a gentleman.
GUILDENSTERN   But with much forcing of his disposition.
ROSENCRANTZ   Niggard of question, but of our demands
Most free in his reply.
QUEEN   Did you assay[2] him
To any pastime?   15
ROSENCRANTZ   Madam, it so fell out that certain players
We o'er-raught[3] on the way: of these we told him,
And there did seem in him a kind of joy
To hear of it: they are about the court,
And, as I think, they have already order   20
This night to play before him.
POLONIUS   'Tis most true:
And he beseeched me to entreat your majesties
To hear and see the matter.
KING   With all my heart; and it doth much content me
To hear him so inclined.   25
Good gentlemen, give him a further edge,[4]
And drive his purpose on to these delights.
ROSENCRANTZ   We shall, my lord.
[*Exeunt* ROSENCRANTZ *and* GUILDENSTERN.]
KING   Sweet Gertrude, leave us too;
For we have closely[5] sent for Hamlet hither,
That he, as 'twere by accident, may here   30
Affront Ophelia:
Her father and myself, lawful espials,
Will so bestow[6] ourselves that, seeing unseen,
We may of their encounter frankly judge,
And gather by him, as he is behaved,   35

1. Turn of talk, or roundabout way.   2. Try to attract him.   3. Overtook.   4. Incitement.   5. Privately.   6. Place. *Affront:* confront. *Espials:* spies.

If 't be the affliction of his love or no
That thus he suffers for.

QUEEN   I shall obey you:
And for your part, Ophelia, I do wish
That your good beauties be the happy cause
Of Hamlet's wildness: so shall I hope your virtues   40
Will bring him to his wonted way again,
To both your honors.

OPHELIA   Madam, I wish it may.

     [Exit QUEEN.]

POLONIUS   Ophelia, walk you here. Gracious, so please you,
We will bestow ourselves. [To OPHELIA.] Read on this book;
That show of such an exercise may color[7]   45
Your loneliness. We are oft to blame in this,—
'Tis too much proved—that with devotion's visage
And pious action we do sugar o'er
The devil himself.

KING [Aside.]   O, 'tis too true!
How smart a lash that speech doth give my conscience!   50
The harlot's cheek, beautied with plastering art,
Is not more ugly to the thing that helps it
Than is my deed to my most painted word:
O heavy burthen!

POLONIUS   I hear him coming: let's withdraw, my lord.   55

     [Exeunt KING and POLONIUS.—Enter HAMLET.]

HAMLET   To be, or not to be: that is the question:
Whether 'tis nobler in the mind to suffer
The slings and arrows of outrageous fortune,
Or to take arms against a sea of troubles,
And by opposing end them. To die: to sleep;   60
No more; and by a sleep to say we end
The heart-ache, and the thousand natural shocks
That flesh is heir to, 'tis a consummation[8]
Devoutly to be wished. To die, to sleep;
To sleep: perchance to dream: aye, there's the rub;[9]   65
For in that sleep of death what dreams may come,
When we have shuffled off this mortal coil,[1]
Must give us pause: there's the respect
That makes calamity of so long life;[2]
For who would bear the whips and scorns of time,   70
The oppressor's wrong, the proud man's contumely,
The pangs of despisèd love, the law's delay,
The insolence of office, and the spurns
That patient merit of the unworthy takes,
When he himself might his quietus make   75
With a bare bodkin? who would fardels[3] bear,
To grunt and sweat under a weary life,

---

7. Excuse.   8. Final settlement.   9. The impediment (a bowling term).   1. Have rid ourselves of the turmoil of mortal life.   2. So long-lived. *Respect:* consideration.   3. Burdens. *Bodkin:* poniard, dagger.

But that the dread of something after death,
The undiscovered country from whose bourn[4]
No traveler returns, puzzles the will,   80
And makes us rather bear those ills we have
Than fly to others that we know not of?
Thus conscience does make cowards of us all,
And thus the native hue of resolution
Is sicklied o'er with the pale cast of thought,   85
And enterprises of great pitch[5] and moment
With this regard their currents turn awry
And lose the name of action. Soft you now!
The fair Ophelia! Nymph, in thy orisons[6]
Be all my sins remembered.

OPHELIA   Good my lord,   90
How does your honor for this many a day?

HAMLET   I humbly thank you: well, well, well.

OPHELIA   My lord, I have remembrances of yours,
That I have longed to re-deliver;
I pray you, now receive them.

HAMLET   No, not I;   95
I never gave you aught.

OPHELIA   My honored lord, you know right well you did;
And with them words of so sweet breath composed
As made the things more rich: their perfume lost,
Take these again; for to the noble mind   100
Rich gifts wax poor when givers prove unkind.
There, my lord.

HAMLET   Ha, ha! are you honest?

OPHELIA   My lord?   105

HAMLET   Are you fair?

OPHELIA   What means your lordship?

HAMLET   That if you be honest and fair, your honesty should admit no
discourse to your beauty.

OPHELIA   Could beauty, my lord, have better commerce[7] than with
honesty?   110

HAMLET   Aye, truly; for the power of beauty will sooner transform honesty from what it is to a bawd than the force of honesty can translate
beauty into his[8] likeness: this was sometime a paradox, but now the
time gives it proof.[9] I did love you once.

OPHELIA   Indeed, my lord, you made me believe so.   115

HAMLET   You should not have believed me; for virtue cannot so inoculate our old stock, but we shall relish[1] of it: I loved you not.

OPHELIA   I was the more deceived.

HAMLET   Get thee to a nunnery: why wouldst thou be a breeder of
sinners? I am myself indifferent honest; but yet I could accuse me   120
of such things that it were better my mother had not borne me: I am
very proud, revengeful, ambitious; with more offenses at my beck

4. Boundary. 5. Height. 6. Prayers. 7. Intercourse. 8. Its. 9. In his mother's adultery.
1. Retain the flavor of. *Inoculate:* graft itself onto.

than I have thoughts to put them in, imagination to give them shape,
or time to act them in. What should such fellows as I do crawling
between heaven and earth! We are arrant knaves all; believe none   125
of us. Go thy ways to a nunnery. Where's your father?

OPHELIA At home, my lord.

HAMLET Let the doors be shut upon him, that he may play the fool
no where but in 's own house. Farewell.

OPHELIA O, help him, you sweet heavens!   130

HAMLET If thou dost marry, I'll give thee this plague for thy dowry: be
thou as chaste as ice, as pure as snow, thou shalt not escape cal-
umny. Get thee to a nunnery, go: farewell. Or, if thou wilt needs
marry, marry a fool; for wise men know well enough what monsters[2]
you make of them. To a nunnery, go; and quickly too. Farewell.   135

OPHELIA O heavenly powers, restore him!

HAMLET I have heard of your paintings too, well enough; God hath
given you one face, and you make yourselves another: you jig, you
amble, and you lisp, and nick-name God's creatures, and make your
wantonness your ignorance.[3] Go to, I'll no more on 't; it hath made   140
me mad. I say, we will have no more marriages: those that are married already, all but one, shall live; the rest shall keep as they are.
To a nunnery, go.
    [Exit.]

OPHELIA O, what a noble mind is here o'erthrown!
The courtier's, soldier's, scholar's, eye, tongue, sword: 145
The expectancy and rose of the fair state,
The glass of fashion and the mould of form,[4]
The observed of all observers, quite, quite down!
And I, of ladies most deject and wretched,
That sucked the honey of his music vows,   150
Now see that noble and most sovereign reason,
Like sweet bells jangled, out of tune and harsh;
That unmatched form and feature of blown[5] youth
Blasted with ecstasy: O, woe is me,
To have seen what I have seen, see what I see!   155
    [Re-enter KING and POLONIUS.]

KING Love! his affections do not that way tend;
Nor what he spake, though it lacked form a little,
Was not like madness. There's something in his soul
O'er which his melancholy sits on brood,
And I do doubt[6] the hatch and the disclose   160
Will be some danger: which for to prevent,
I have in quick determination
Thus set it down:—he shall with speed to England,
For the demand of our neglected tribute:
Haply the seas and countries different   165
With variable objects shall expel
This something-settled matter in his heart,

---

2. Cuckolds bear imaginary horns and "a horned man's a monster" (*Othello* 4.1).   3. Misname (out of
affectation) the most natural things, and pretend that this is due to ignorance instead of affectation.
4. The mirror of fashion and the model of behavior.   5. In full bloom.   6. Fear.

Whereon his brains still beating puts him thus
From fashion of himself.[7] What think you on 't?
POLONIUS   It shall do well: but yet do I believe   170
    The origin and commencement of his grief
    Sprung from neglected love. How now, Ophelia!
    You need not tell us what Lord Hamlet said;
    We heard it all. My lord, do as you please;
    But, if you hold it fit, after the play,   175
    Let his queen mother all alone entreat him
    To show his grief: let her be round[8] with him;
    And I'll be placed, so please you, in the ear
    Of all their conference. If she find him not,
    To England send him, or confine him where   180
    Your wisdom best shall think.
KING   It shall be so:
    Madness in great ones must not unwatched go.
        [Exeunt.]

SCENE 2

[SCENE: A hall in the castle.]

[Enter HAMLET and PLAYERS.]
HAMLET   Speak the speech, I pray you, as I pronounced it to you,
trippingly on the tongue: but if you mouth it, as many of your players do, I had as lief the town-crier spoke my lines. Nor do not saw
the air too much with your hand, thus; but use all gently: for in the
very torrent, tempest, and, as I may say, whirlwind of your passion,   5
you must acquire and beget a temperance that may give it smooth-
ness. O, it offends me to the soul to hear a robustious periwig-pated
fellow tear a passion to tatters, to very rags, to split the ears of the
groundlings,[9] who, for the most part, are capable of nothing but
inexplicable dumb-shows and noise: I would have such a fellow   10
whipped for o'er doing Termagant;[1] it out-herods Herod: pray you,
avoid it.
FIRST PLAYER   I warrant your honor.
HAMLET   Be not too tame neither, but let your own discretion be your
tutor: suit the action to the word, the word to the action; with this   15
special observance, that you o'erstep not the modesty[2] of nature: for
anything so overdone is from the purpose of playing, whose end, both
at the first and now, was and is, to hold, as 'twere, the mirror up to
nature; to show virtue her own feature, scorn her own image, and
the very age and body of the time his form and pressure.[3] Now this   20
overdone or come tardy off, though it make the unskillful laugh,
cannot but make the judicious grieve; the censure of the which one
must in your allowance o'erweigh a whole theater of others. O, there

7. Makes him behave unusually.   8. Direct.   9. Spectators in the pit, where admission was cheapest.
1. God of the Mohammedans in old romances and morality plays; he was portrayed as being noisy and
excitable.   2. Moderation.   3. Impress, shape. Feature: form. His: its.

be players that I have seen play, and heard others praise, and that
highly, not to speak it profanely,[4] that neither having the accent of   25
Christians nor the gait of Christian, pagan, nor man, have so strutted
and bellowed, that I have thought some of nature's journeymen had
made men, and not made them well, they imitated humanity so
abominably.

FIRST PLAYER   I hope we have reformed that indifferently[5] with us, sir.   30
HAMLET   O, reform it altogether. And let those that play your clowns
speak no more than is set down for them: for there be of them that
will themselves laugh, to set on some quantity of barren[6] spectators
to laugh too, though in the mean time some necessary question of
the play be then to be considered: that's villainous, and shows a most   35
pitiful ambition in the fool that uses it. Go, make you ready.

[*Exeunt* PLAYERS. —*Enter* POLONIUS, ROSENCRANTZ, *and* GUILDEN-
STERN.]

How now, my lord! will the king hear this piece of work?
POLONIUS   And the queen too, and that presently.
HAMLET   Bid the players make haste.

[*Exit* POLONIUS.]

Will you two help to hasten them?   40
ROSENCRANTZ
GUILDENSTERN   } We will, my lord.

[*Exeunt* ROSENCRANTZ *and* GUILDENSTERN.]

HAMLET   What ho! Horatio!

[*Enter* HORATIO.]

HORATIO   Here, sweet lord, at your service.
HAMLET   Horatio, thou art e'en as just a man
As e'er my conversation coped withal.[7]   45
HORATIO   O, my dear lord,—
HAMLET   Nay, do not think I flatter;
For what advancement may I hope from thee,
That no revenue hast but thy good spirits,
To feed and clothe thee? Why should the poor be flattered?
No, let the candied tongue lick absurd pomp,   50
And crook the pregnant hinges of the knee
Where thrift may follow fawning.[8] Dost thou hear?
Since my dear soul was mistress of her choice,
And could of men distinguish, her election
Hath sealed thee for herself: for thou hast been   55
As one, in suffering all, that suffers nothing;
A man that fortune's buffets and rewards
Hast ta'en with equal thanks: and blest are those
Whose blood and judgment[9] are so well commingled
That they are not a pipe for fortune's finger   60
To sound what stop she please.[1] Give me that man
That is not passion's slave, and I will wear him

---

4. Hamlet apologizes for the profane implication that there could be men not of God's making.   5. Pretty
well.   6. Silly.   7. As I ever associated with.   8. Material profit may be derived from cringing. *Preg-*
nant hinges: supple joints.   9. Passion and reason.   1. For Fortune to put her finger on any windhole
of the pipe she wants.

In my heart's core, ay, in my heart of heart,
As I do thee. Something too much of this.
There is a play to-night before the king;   65
One scene of it comes near the circumstance
Which I have told thee of my father's death:
I prithee, when thou sees that act a-foot,
Even with the very comment of thy soul[2]
Observe my uncle: if his occulted guilt   70
Do not itself unkennel in one speech
It is a damned ghost that we have seen,
And my imaginations are as foul
As Vulcan's stithy.[3] Give him heedful note;
For I mine eyes will rivet to his face,   75
And after we will both our judgments join
In censure of his seeming.[4]

HORATIO   Well, my lord:
If he steal aught the whilst this play is playing,
And 'scape detecting, I will pay the theft.

HAMLET   They are coming to the play: I must be idle:[5]   80
Get you a place.

     [Danish march. A flourish. Enter KING, QUEEN, POLONIUS, OPHELIA,
       ROSENCRANTZ, GUILDENSTERN, and other LORDS attendant, with the
       GUARD carrying torches.]

KING   How fares our cousin Hamlet?

HAMLET   Excellent, i' faith; of the chameleon's dish: I eat the air,[6]
promise-crammed: you cannot feed capons so.

KING   I have nothing with this answer, Hamlet; these words are not   85
mine.[7]

HAMLET   No, nor mine now. [To POLONIUS.] My lord, you played once
i' the university, you say?

POLONIUS   That did I, my lord, and was accounted a good actor.

HAMLET   What did you enact?   90

POLONIUS   I did enact Julius Caesar: I was killed i' the Capitol; Brutus
killed me.

HAMLET   It was a brute part of him to kill so capital a calf there. Be
the players ready?

ROSENCRANTZ   Aye, my lord; they stay upon your patience.   95

QUEEN   Come hither, my dear Hamlet, sit by me.

HAMLET   No, good mother, here's metal more attractive.

POLONIUS [To the KING.]   O, ho! do you mark that?

HAMLET   Lady, shall I lie in your lap? [Lying down at OPHELIA's feet.]

OPHELIA   No, my lord.   100

HAMLET   I mean, my head upon your lap?

OPHELIA   Aye, my lord.

HAMLET   Do you think I meant country matters?

OPHELIA   I think nothing, my lord.

HAMLET   That's a fair thought to lie between maids' legs.   105

---

2. With all your powers of observation.   3. Smithy.   4. To judge his behavior.   5. Crazy.   6. The
chameleon was supposed to feed on air.   7. Have nothing to do with my question.

OPHELIA What is, my lord?

HAMLET Nothing.[8]

OPHELIA You are merry, my lord.

HAMLET Who, I?

OPHELIA Aye, my lord.   110

HAMLET O God, your only jig-maker.[9] What should a man do but be
merry? for, look you, how cheerfully my mother looks, and my father
died within 's two hours.

OPHELIA Nay, 'tis twice two months, my lord.

HAMLET So long? Nay then, let the devil wear black, for I'll have a   115
suit of sables.[1] O heavens! die two months ago, and not forgotten
yet? Then there's hope a great man's memory may outlive his life
half a year: but, by 'r lady, he must build churches then; or else shall
he suffer not thinking on, with the hobby-horse,[2] whose epitaph is,
"For, O, for, O, the hobby-horse is forgot."   120

[*Hautboys play. The dumb-show enters. —Enter a King and a Queen
very lovingly; the Queen embracing him and he her. She kneels, and
makes show of protestation unto him. He takes her up, and declines his
head upon her neck; lays him down upon a bank of flowers: she, seeing
him asleep, leaves him. Anon comes in a fellow, takes off his crown,
kisses it, and pours poison in the King's ears, and exits. The Queen
returns; finds the King dead, and makes passionate action. The Poisoner,
with some two or three Mutes comes in again, seeming to lament with
her. The dead body is carried away. The Poisoner woos the Queen with
gifts: she seems loath and unwilling awhile, but in the end accepts his
love. —Exeunt.*]

OPHELIA What means this, my lord?

HAMLET Marry, this is miching mallecho;[3] it means mischief.

OPHELIA Belike this show imports the argument of the play.

[*Enter* PROLOGUE.]

HAMLET We shall know by this fellow: the players cannot keep coun-
sel;[4] they'll tell all.   125

OPHELIA Will he tell us what this show meant?

HAMLET Aye, or any show that you'll show him: be not you ashamed
to show, he'll not shame to tell you what it means.

OPHELIA You are naught,[5] you are naught: I'll mark the play.

PROLOGUE For us, and for our tragedy,   130
          Here stooping to your clemency,
          We beg your hearing patiently.

HAMLET Is this a prologue, or the posy[6] of a ring?

OPHELIA 'Tis brief, my lord.

HAMLET As woman's love.   135

[*Enter two* PLAYERS, KING *and* QUEEN.]

PLAYER KING Full thirty times hath Phœbus's cart[7] gone round
          Neptune's salt wash and Tellus's orbed ground,
          And thirty dozen moons with borrowed sheen

---

8. A sexual pun: no thing.   9. Maker of comic songs.   1. Hamlet notes sarcastically the lack of mourning for his father in the fancy dress of court and king.   2. A figure in the old May Day games and Morris
dances.   3. Sneaking misdeed.   4. A secret.   5. Naughty, improper.   6. Motto, inscription.
7. The chariot of the sun.

About the world have times twelve thirties been,
Since love our hearts and Hymen did our hands   140
Unite commutual in most sacred bands.
PLAYER QUEEN   So many journeys may the sun and moon
Make us again count o'er ere love be done!
But, woe is me, you are so sick of late,
So far from cheer and from your former state,   145
That I distrust you.[8] Yet, though I distrust,
Discomfort you, my lord, it nothing must:
For women's fear and love holds quantity,[9]
In neither aught, or in extremity.
Now, what my love is, proof hath made you know,   150
And as my love is sized, my fear is so:
Where love is great, the littlest doubts are fear,
Where little fears grow great, great love grows there.
PLAYER KING   Faith, I must leave thee, love, and shortly too;
My operant powers their functions leave[1] to do: 155
And thou shalt live in this fair world behind,
Honored, beloved; and haply one as kind
For husband shalt thou—
PLAYER QUEEN   O, confound the rest!
Such love must needs be treason in my breast:
In second husband let me be accurst!   160
None wed the second but who killed the first.
HAMLET [Aside.]   Wormwood, wormwood.
PLAYER QUEEN   The instances that second marriage move
Are base respects of thrift,[2] but none of love:
A second time I kill my husband dead,   165
When second husband kisses me in bed.
PLAYER KING   I do believe you think what now you speak,
But what we do determine oft we break.
Purpose is but the slave to memory,
Of violent birth but poor validity: 170
Which now, like fruit unripe, sticks on the tree,
But fall unshaken when they mellow be.
Most necessary 'tis that we forget
To pay ourselves what to ourselves is debt:
What to ourselves in passion we propose,   175
The passion ending, both the purpose lose.
The violence of either grief or joy
Their own enactures[3] with themselves destroy:
Where joy most revels, grief doth most lament;
Grief joys, joy grieves, on slender accident.   180
This world is not for aye, nor 'tis not strange
That even our loves should with our fortunes change,
For 'tis a question left us yet to prove,
Whether love lead fortune or else fortune love.

---

8. I am worried about you.   9. Maintain mutual balance.   1. Cease.   2. Considerations of material
profit. *Instances*: motives.   3. Their own fulfillment in action.

The great man down, you mark his favorite flies; 185
The poor advanced makes friends of enemies:
And hitherto doth love on fortune tend;
For who not needs shall never lack a friend,
And who in want a hollow friend doth try
Directly seasons[4] him his enemy. 190
But, orderly to end where I begun,
Our wills and fates do so contrary run,
That our devices still are overthrown,
Our thoughts are ours, their ends none of our own:
So think thou wilt no second husband wed, 195
But die thy thoughts when thy first lord is dead.

PLAYER QUEEN   Nor earth to me give food nor heaven light!
Sport and repose lock from me day and night!
To desperation turn my trust and hope!
An anchor's cheer in prison be my scope! 200
Each opposite, that blanks[5] the face of joy,
Meet what I would have well and it destroy!
Both here and hence pursue me lasting strife,
If, once a widow, ever I be wife!

HAMLET   If she should break it now! 205

PLAYER KING   'Tis deeply sworn. Sweet, leave me here a while;
My spirits grow dull, and fain I would beguile
The tedious day with sleep.
                    [Sleeps.]

PLAYER QUEEN   Sleep rock thy brain;
And never come mischance between us twain!
                    [Exit.]

HAMLET   Madam, how like you this play? 210

QUEEN   The lady doth protest[6] too much, methinks.

HAMLET   O, but she'll keep her word.

KING   Have you heard the argument?[7] Is there no offense in 't?

HAMLET   No, no, they do but jest, poison in jest; no offense i' the 215
world.

KING   What do you call the play?

HAMLET   The Mouse-Trap. Marry, how? Tropically.[8] This play is the
image of a murder done in Vienna: Gonzago is the duke's name; his
wife, Baptista: you shall see anon; 'tis a knavish piece of work; but 220
what o' that? your majesty, and we that have free souls, it touches
us not: let the galled jade wince, our withers are unwrung.[9]
                    [Enter LUCIANUS.]
This is one Lucianus, nephew to the king.

OPHELIA   You are as good as a chorus, my lord.

HAMLET   I could interpret[1] between you and your love, if I could see 225
the puppets dallying.

OPHELIA   You are keen,[2] my lord, you are keen.

HAMLET   It would cost you a groaning to take off my edge.

---

4. Matures.   5. Makes pale. *Anchor's cheer:* hermit's, or anchorite's, fare.   6. Promise.   7. Plot of
the play in outline.   8. By a trope, figuratively.   9. Not wrenched. *Galled jade:* injured horse. *Withers:*
the area between a horse's shoulders.   1. Act as interpreter (regular feature in puppet shows).   2. Bitter, but Hamlet chooses to take the word sexually.

OPHELIA   Still better and worse.

HAMLET   So you must take[3] your husbands. Begin, murderer; pox,   230
leave thy damnable faces, and begin. Come: the croaking raven doth
bellow for revenge.

LUCIANUS   Thoughts black, hands apt, drugs fit, and time agreeing;
Confederate season, else no creature seeing;
Thou mixture rank, of midnight weeds collected,   235
With Hecate's ban[4] thrice blasted, thrice infected,
Thy natural magic and dire property,
On wholesome life usurp immediately.

    [*Pours the poison into the sleeper's ear.*]

HAMLET   He poisons him i' the garden for his estate. His name's Gonzago: the story is extant, and written in very choice Italian: you shall   240
see anon how the murderer gets the love of Gonzago's wife.

OPHELIA   The king rises.

HAMLET   What, frighted with false fire![5]

QUEEN   How fares my lord?

POLONIUS   Give o'er the play.   245

KING   Give me some light. Away!

POLONIUS   Lights, lights, lights!

    [*Exeunt all but* HAMLET *and* HORATIO.]

HAMLET   Why, let the stricken deer go weep,
    The hart ungallèd play;
For some must watch, while some must sleep: 250
    Thus runs the world away.
Would not this, sir, and a forest of feathers—if the rest of my fortunes turn Turk with me—with two Provincial roses on my razed
shoes, get me a fellowship in a cry[6] of players, sir?

HORATIO   Half a share.   255

HAMLET   A whole one, I.
    For thou dost know, O Damon dear,
      This realm dismantled was
    Of Jove himself; and now reigns here
      A very, very—pajock.   260

HORATIO   You might have rhymed.[7]

HAMLET   O good Horatio, I'll take the ghost's word for a thousand
pound. Didst perceive?

HORATIO   Very well, my lord.

HAMLET   Upon the talk of the poisoning?   265

HORATIO   I did very well note him.

HAMLET   Ah, ha! Come, some music! come, the recorders!
    For if the king like not the comedy,
    Why then, belike, he likes it not, perdy.[8]
Come, some music!

    [*Re-enter* ROSENCRANTZ *and* GUILDENSTERN.]   270

GUILDENSTERN   Good my lord, vouchsafe me a word with you.

HAMLET   Sir, a whole history.

---

3. That is, for better or for worse, as in the marriage service—but in fact you "mis-take," deceive them.
4. Goddess of witchcraft's curse. *Confederate:* favorable.   5. Blank shot.   6. Company; a term generally used with hounds. *Turk with:* betray. *Razed shoes:* sometimes worn by actors.   7. *Ass* would have
rhymed. *Pajock:* peacock.   8. By God (*per Dieu*).

GUILDENSTERN   The king, sir—

HAMLET   Aye, sir, what of him?

GUILDENSTERN   Is in his retirement marvelous distempered.   275

HAMLET   With drink, sir?

GUILDENSTERN   No, my lord, rather with choler.[9]

HAMLET   Your wisdom should show itself more richer to signify this to
the doctor; for, for me to put him to his purgation would perhaps
plunge him into far more choler.   280

GUILDENSTERN   Good my lord, put your discourse into some frame,
and start not so wildly from my affair.

HAMLET   I am tame, sir: pronounce.

GUILDENSTERN   The queen, your mother, in most great affliction of
spirit, hath sent me to you.   285

HAMLET   You are welcome.

GUILDENSTERN   Nay, good my lord, this courtesy is not of the right
breed. If it shall please you to make me a wholesome[1] answer, I will
do your mother's commandment: if not, your pardon and my return
shall be the end of my business.   290

HAMLET   Sir, I cannot.

GUILDENSTERN   What, my lord?

HAMLET   Make you a wholesome answer; my wit's diseased: but, sir,
such answer as I can make, you shall command; or rather, as you
say, my mother: therefore no more, but to the matter: my mother,   295
you say,—

ROSENCRANTZ   Then thus she says; your behavior hath struck her into
amazement and admiration.[2]

HAMLET   O wonderful son, that can so astonish a mother! But is there
no sequel at the heels of this mother's admiration? Impart.   300

ROSENCRANTZ   She desires to speak with you in her closet, ere you go
to bed.

HAMLET   We shall obey, were she ten times our mother. Have you any
further trade with us?

ROSENCRANTZ   My lord, you once did love me.   305

HAMLET   So I do still, by these pickers and stealers.[3]

ROSENCRANTZ   Good my lord, what is your cause of distemper? you do
surely bar the door upon your own liberty, if you deny your griefs to
your friend.

HAMLET   Sir, I lack advancement.[4]   310

ROSENCRANTZ   How can that be, when you have the voice of the king
himself for your succession in Denmark?

HAMLET   Aye, sir, but "while the grass grows,"[5]—the proverb is something musty.

   [Re-enter PLAYERS with recorders.]

O, the recorders! let me see one. To withdraw with you:—why do   315
you go about to recover the wind of me, as if you would drive me
into a toil?[6]

GUILDENSTERN   O, my lord, if my duty be too bold, my love is too
unmannerly.

9. Bile, anger.   1. Sensible.   2. Confusion and surprise.   3. The hands.   4. Hamlet pretends
that the cause of his "distemper" is frustrated ambition.   5. The proverb ends: "oft starves the silly steed."
6. Snare. *Withdraw*: retire, talk in private. *Recover the wind of*: get to the windward.

HAMLET   I do not well understand that. Will you play upon this pipe? 320
GUILDENSTERN   My lord, I cannot.
HAMLET   I pray you.
GUILDENSTERN   Believe me, I cannot.
HAMLET   I do beseech you.
GUILDENSTERN   I know no touch of it, my lord.   325
HAMLET   It is as easy as lying: govern these ventages[7] with your fingers
   and thumb, give it breath with your mouth, and it will discourse most
   eloquent music. Look you, these are the stops.
GUILDENSTERN   But these cannot I command to any utterance of har-
   mony; I have not the skill.   330
HAMLET   Why, look you now, how unworthy a thing you make of me!
   You would play upon me; you would seem to know my stops; you
   would pluck out the heart of my mystery; you would sound me from
   my lowest note to the top of my compass: and there is much music,
   excellent voice, in this little organ; yet cannot you make it speak.   335
   'Sblood, do you think I am easier to be played on than a pipe? Call
   me what instrument you will, though you can fret[8] me, yet you can-
   not play upon me.
      [Re-enter POLONIUS.]
   God bless you, sir!
POLONIUS   My lord, the queen would speak with you, and presently.   340
HAMLET   Do you see yonder cloud that's almost in shape of a camel?
POLONIUS   By the mass, and 'tis like a camel, indeed.
HAMLET   Methinks it is like a weasel.
POLONIUS   It is backed like a weasel.
HAMLET   Or like a whale?   345
POLONIUS   Very like a whale.
HAMLET   Then I will come to my mother by and by. They fool me to
   the top of my bent. I will come by and by.
POLONIUS   I will say so.
      [Exit POLONIUS.]
HAMLET   "By and by" is easily said. Leave me, friends.   350
      [Exeunt all but HAMLET.]
   'Tis now the very witching time of night,
   When churchyards yawn, and hell itself breathes out
   Contagion to this world: now could I drink hot blood,
   And do such bitter business as the day
   Would quake to look on. Soft! now to my mother.   355
   O heart, lose not thy nature; let not ever
   The soul of Nero[9] enter this firm bosom:
   Let me be cruel, not unnatural:
   I will speak daggers to her, but use none;
   My tongue and soul in this be hypocrites;   360
   How in my words soever she be shent,
   To give them seals[1] never, my soul, consent!
      [Exit.]

---

7. Windholes.   8. Vex, with a pun on *frets*, meaning the ridges placed across the finger board of a guitar
to regulate the fingering.   9. A Roman emperor (37–68 C.E.) who murdered his mother.   1. Ratify
them by action. *Shent*: reproached.

SCENE 3

[SCENE: *A room in the castle.*]

[*Enter* KING, ROSENCRANTZ, *and* GUILDENSTERN.]

KING   I like him not, nor stands it safe with us
    To let his madness range. Therefore prepare you;
    I your commission will forthwith dispatch,
    And he to England shall along with you:
    The terms of our estate² may not endure   5
    Hazard so near us as doth hourly grow
    Out of his lunacies.
GUILDENSTERN   We will ourselves provide:
    Most holy and religious fear it is
    To keep those many many bodies safe
    That live and feed upon your majesty.   10
ROSENCRANTZ   The single and peculiar³ life is bound
    With all the strength and armor of the mind
    To keep itself from noyance; but much more
    That spirit upon whose weal depends and rests
    The lives of many. The cease⁴ of majesty   15
    Dies not alone, but like a gulf doth draw
    What 's near it with it; it is a massy wheel,
    Fixed on the summit of the highest mount,
    To whose huge spokes ten thousand lesser things
    Are mortised⁵ and adjoined; which, when it falls,   20
    Each small annexment, petty consequence,
    Attends the boisterous ruin. Never alone
    Did the king sigh, but with a general groan.
KING   Arm you, I pray you, to this speedy voyage,
    For we will fetters put about this fear,   25
    Which now goes too free-footed.
ROSENCRANTZ   }
GUILDENSTERN   }   We will haste us.

[*Exeunt* ROSENCRANTZ *and* GUILDENSTERN.—*Enter* POLONIUS.]

POLONIUS   My lord, he's going to his mother's closet:
    Behind the arras I'll convey myself,
    To hear the process: I'll warrant she'll tax him home:⁶   30
    And, as you said, and wisely was it said
    'Tis meet that some more audience than a mother,
    Since nature makes them partial, should o'erhear
    The speech, of vantage.⁷ Fare you well, my liege:
    I'll call upon you ere you go to bed,   35
    And tell you what I know.
KING   Thanks, dear my lord.

[*Exit* POLONIUS.]

    O, my offense is rank, it smells to heaven;

---

2. My position as king.   3. Individual.   4. Decease, extinction.   5. Fastened.   6. Take him to
task thoroughly.   7. From a vantage point.

It hath the primal eldest curse[8] upon 't,
A brother's murder. Pray can I not,
Though inclination be as sharp as will: 40
My stronger guilt defeats my strong intent,
And like a man to double business bound,
I stand in pause where I shall first begin,
And both neglect. What if this cursed hand
Were thicker than itself with brother's blood, 45
Is there not rain enough in the sweet heavens
To wash it white as snow? Whereto serves mercy
But to confront the visage of offense?[9]
And what's in prayer but this twofold force,
To be forestalled ere we come to fall, 50
Or pardoned being down? Then I'll look up;
My fault is past. But O, what form of prayer
Can serve my turn? "Forgive me my foul murder?"
That cannot be, since I am still possessed
Of those effects for which I did the murder, 55
My crown, mine own ambition and my queen.
May one be pardoned and retain the offense?[1]
In the corrupted currents of this world
Offense's gilded hand may shove by justice,
And oft 'tis seen the wicked prize itself 60
Buys out the law:[2] but 'tis not so above;
There is no shuffling, there the action lies
In his[3] true nature, and we ourselves compelled
Even to the teeth and forehead of our faults
To give in evidence. What then? what rests?[4] 65
Try what repentance can: what can it not?
Yet what can it when one can not repent?
O wretched state! O bosom black as death!
O limèd soul, that struggling to be free
Art more engaged! Help, angels! make assay![5] 70
Bow, stubborn knees, and, heart with strings of steel,
Be soft as sinews of the new-born babe!
All may be well.
      [*Retires and kneels.—Enter* HAMLET.]
HAMLET Now might I do it pat,[6] now he is praying
And now I'll do 't: and so he goes to heaven: 75
And so am I revenged. That would be scanned:[7]
A villain kills my father; and for that,
I, his sole son, do this same villain send
To heaven.
O, this is hire and salary, not revenge. 80
He took my father grossly, full of bread,
With all his crimes broad blown, as flush as May;

---

8. The curse of Cain.   9. Guilt.   1. The things obtained through the offense.   2. The wealth unduly acquired is used for bribery.   3. Its.   4. What remains?   5. Make the attempt! *Limèd:* caught as with birdlime.   6. Conveniently.   7. Would have to be considered carefully.

And how his audit[8] stands who knows save heaven?
But in our circumstance and course of thought,
'Tis heavy with him: and am I then revenged,   85
To take him in the purging of his soul,
When he is fit and seasoned[9] for his passage?
No.
Up, sword, and know thou a more horrid hent:[1]
When he is drunk asleep, or in his rage,   90
Or, in the incestuous pleasure of his bed;
At game, a-swearing, or about some act
That has no relish of salvation in 't;
Then trip him, that his heels may kick at heaven
And that his soul may be as damned and black   95
As hell, whereto it goes. My mother stays:
This physic but prolongs thy sickly days.
      [Exit.]
KING [Rising.]   My words fly up, my thoughts remain below:
Words without thoughts never to heaven go.
      [Exit.]

SCENE 4

[SCENE: The Queen's closet.]

[Enter QUEEN and POLONIUS.]
POLONIUS He will come straight. Look you lay home to him:
Tell him his pranks have been too broad[2] to bear with,
And that your grace hath screen'd and stood between
Much heat and him. I'll sconce me even here.
Pray you, be round[3] with him.
HAMLET [Within.]   Mother, mother, mother!   5
QUEEN I'll warrant you; fear me not. Withdraw,
I hear him coming.
    [POLONIUS hides behind the arras.—Enter HAMLET.]
HAMLET Now, mother, what's the matter?
QUEEN Hamlet, thou hast thy father much offended.
HAMLET Mother, you have my father much offended.   10
QUEEN Come, come, you answer with an idle tongue.
HAMLET Go, go, you question with a wicked tongue.
QUEEN Why, how now, Hamlet!
HAMLET   What's the matter now?
QUEEN Have you forgot me?
HAMLET   No, by the rood,[4] not so:
You are the queen, your husband's brother's wife;   15
And—would it were not so!—you are my mother.
QUEEN Nay, then, I'll set those to you that can speak.
HAMLET Come, come, and sit you down; you shall not budge:

8. Account. Broad blown: in full bloom.   9. Ripe, ready.   1. Grip.   2. Unrestrained. Lay home: give
him a stern lesson.   3. Straightforward.   4. Cross.

You go not till I set you up a glass⁵
Where you may see the inmost part of you.   20
QUEEN   What wilt thou do? thou wilt not murder me?
  Help, help, ho!
POLONIUS [*Behind.*]   What, ho! help, help, help!
HAMLET [*Drawing.*]   How now! a rat? Dead, for a ducat, dead!
        [*Makes a pass through the arras.*]
POLONIUS [*Behind.*]   O, I am slain!
        [*Falls and dies.*]
QUEEN   O me, what hast thou done?   25
HAMLET   Nay, I know not: is it the king?
QUEEN   O, what a rash and bloody deed is this!
HAMLET   A bloody deed! almost as bad, good mother,
  As kill a king, and marry with his brother.
QUEEN   As kill a king!
HAMLET   Aye, lady, 'twas my word.   30
        [*Lifts up the arras and discovers* POLONIUS.]
  Thou wretched, rash, intruding fool, farewell!
  I took thee for thy better: take thy fortune;
  Thou find'st to be too busy⁶ is some danger.
  Leave wringing of your hands: peace! sit you down,
  And let me wring your heart: for so I shall,   35
  If it be made of penetrable stuff;
  If damned custom have not brassed it so,
  That it be proof and bulwark against sense.⁷
QUEEN   What have I done, that thou darest wag thy tongue
  In noise so rude against me?
HAMLET   Such an act   40
  That blurs the grace and blush of modesty,
  Calls virtue hypocrite, takes off the rose
  From the fair forehead of an innocent love,
  And sets a blister there; makes marriage vows
  As false as dicers' oaths: O, such a deed   45
  As from the body of contraction⁸ plucks
  The very soul, and sweet religion makes
  A rhapsody of words: heaven's face doth glow;⁹
  Yea, this solidity and compound mass,
  With tristful visage, as against the doom,¹   50
  Is thought-sick at the act.
QUEEN   Aye me, what act,
  That roars so loud and thunders in the index?²
HAMLET   Look here, upon this picture, and on this,
  The counterfeit presentment³ of two brothers.   55
  See what a grace was seated on this brow;
  Hyperion's curls, the front of Jove himself,
  An eye like Mars, to threaten and command;
  A station⁴ like the herald Mercury

---

5. Mirror. 6. Too much of a busybody. 7. Feeling. 8. Duty to the marriage contract. 9. Blush
with shame. 1. Doomsday. *Tristful:* sad. 2. Prologue, table of contents. 3. Portrait. 4. Posture.

New-lighted on a heaven-kissing hill; 60
A combination and a form indeed,
Where every god did seem to set his seal
To give the world assurance of a man:
This was your husband. Look you now, what follows:
Here is your husband; like a mildewed ear,[5] 65
Blasting his wholesome brother. Have you eyes?
Could you on this fair mountain leave to feed,
And batten[6] on this moor? Ha! have you eyes?
You cannot call it love, for at your age
The hey-day in the blood is tame, it's humble, 70
And waits upon[7] the judgment: and what judgment
Would step from this to this? Sense sure you have,
Else could you not have motion: but sure that sense
Is apoplexed: for madness would not err,
Nor sense to ecstasy was ne'er so thralled 75
But it reserved some quantity of choice,
To serve in such a difference. What devil was 't
That thus hath cozened you at hoodman-blind?[8]
Eyes without feeling, feeling without sight,
Ears without hands or eyes, smelling sans[9] all, 80
Or but a sickly part of one true sense
Could not so mope.[1]
O shame! where is thy blush? Rebellious hell,
If thou canst mutine in a matron's bones,
To flaming youth let virtue be as wax 85
And melt in her own fire: proclaim no shame
When the compulsive ardor gives the charge,[2]
Since frost itself as actively doth burn,
And reason panders[3] will.

QUEEN   O Hamlet, speak no more:
Thou turn'st mine eyes into my very soul, 90
And there I see such black and grained spots
As will not leave their tinct.[4]

HAMLET   Nay, but to live
In the rank sweat of an enseamèd[5] bed,
Stew'd in corruption, honeying and making love
Over the nasty sty,—

QUEEN   O, speak to me no more; 95
These words like daggers enter in my ears;
No more, sweet Hamlet!

HAMLET   A murderer and a villain;
A slave that is not twentieth part the tithe[6]
Of your precédent lord; a vice of kings;
A cutpurse[7] of the empire and the rule, 100

---

5. Of corn.   6. Gorge, fatten. *Leave:* cease.   7. Is subordinated to.   8. Blindman's buff. *Cozened:*
tricked.   9. Without.   1. Be stupid.   2. Attack.   3. Becomes subservient to.   4. Lose their
color. *Grained:* dyed in.   5. Greasy.   6. Tenth.   7. Pickpocket. *Vice:* clown, from the custom in the
old morality plays of having a buffoon take the part of Vice or of a particular vice.

That from a shelf the precious diadem stole
And put it in his pocket!
QUEEN   No more!
HAMLET A king of shreds and patches—
        [Enter GHOST.]
  Save me, and hover o'er me with your wings,
  You heavenly guards! What would your gracious figure? 105
QUEEN Alas, he's mad!
HAMLET Do you not come your tardy son to chide,
  That, lapsed in time and passion, lets go by
  The important acting of your dread command?
  O, say!
GHOST   Do not forget: this visitation 110
  Is but to whet thy almost blunted purpose.
  But look, amazement on thy mother sits:
  O, step between her and her fighting soul:
  Conceit[8] in weakest bodies strongest works:
  Speak to her, Hamlet.
HAMLET   How is it with you, lady? 115
QUEEN Alas, how is 't with you,
  That you do bend your eye on vacancy
  And with the incorporal air do hold discourse?
  Forth at your eyes your spirits wildly peep;
  And, as the sleeping soldiers in the alarm, 120
  Your bedded hairs, like life in excrements,[9]
  Start up and stand on end. O gentle son,
  Upon the heat and flame of thy distemper
  Sprinkle cool patience. Whereon do you look?
HAMLET On him, on him! Look you how pale he glares! 125
  His form and cause conjoined, preaching to stones,
  Would make them capable.[1] Do not look upon me,
  Lest with this piteous action you convert
  My stern effects:[2] then what I have to do
  Will want true color; tears perchance for[3] blood. 130
QUEEN To whom do you speak this?
HAMLET   Do you see nothing there?
QUEEN Nothing at all; yet all that is I see.
HAMLET Nor did you nothing hear?
QUEEN   No, nothing but ourselves.
HAMLET Why, look you there! look, how it steals away!
  My father, in his habit as he lived! 135
  Look, where he goes, even now, out at the portal!
        [Exit GHOST.]
QUEEN This is the very coinage of your brain:
  This bodiless creation ecstasy
  Is very cunning in.
HAMLET   Ecstasy!

---

8. Imagination.   9. Outgrowths. *Alarm:* call to arms.   1. Of feeling.   2. You make me change my
purpose.   3. Instead of.

My pulse, as yours, doth temperately keep time,   140
And makes as healthful music: it is not madness
That I have uttered: bring me to the test,
And I the matter will re-word, which madness
Would gambol from. Mother, for love of grace,
Lay not that flattering unction to your soul,   145
That not your trespass but my madness speaks:
It will but skin and film the ulcerous place,
Whiles rank corruption, mining all within,
Infects unseen. Confess yourself to heaven;
Repent what's past, avoid what is to come,   150
And do not spread the compost on the weeds,
To make them ranker. Forgive me this my virtue,
For in the fatness of these pursy⁴ times
Virtue itself of vice must pardon beg.
Yea, curb⁵ and woo for leave to do him good.   155
QUEEN   O Hamlet, thou hast cleft my heart in twain.
HAMLET   O, throw away the worser part of it,
And live the purer with the other half.
Good night: but go not to my uncle's bed;
Assume a virtue, if you have it not.   160
That monster, custom, who all sense doth eat,
Of habits devil, is angel yet in this,
That to the use of actions fair and good
He likewise gives a frock or livery,
That aptly is put on.⁶ Refrain to-night,   165
And that shall lend a kind of easiness
To the next abstinence; the next more easy;
For use almost can change the stamp⁷ of nature,
And either curb the devil, or throw him out
With wondrous potency. Once more, good night: 170
And when you are desirous to be blest,
I'll blessing beg of you. For this same lord,
      [Pointing to POLONIUS.]
I do repent: but heaven hath pleased it so,
To punish me with this, and this with me,
That I must be their scourge and minister.   175
I will bestow⁸ him, and will answer well
The death I gave him. So, again, good night.
I must be cruel, only to be kind:
Thus bad begins, and worse remains behind.
One word more, good lady.
QUEEN   What shall I do?   180
HAMLET   Not this, by no means, that I bid you do:
Let the bloat⁹ king tempt you again to bed;

4. Swollen from pampering.   5. Bow.   6. I.e., habit, although like a devil establishing evil ways in
us, is like an angel in doing the same for virtues. *Aptly:* easily.   7. Cast, form. *Use:* habit.   8. Stow
away. *Minister:* agent of punishment.   9. Bloated with drink.

Pinch wanton on your cheek, call you his mouse;
And let him, for a pair of reechy[1] kisses,
Or paddling in your neck with his damned fingers,   185
Make you to ravel all this matter out,
That I essentially am not in madness,
But mad in craft.[2] 'Twere good you let him know;
For who, that's but a queen, fair, sober, wise,
Would from a paddock, from a bat, a gib,   190
Such dear concernings[3] hide? who would do so?
No, in despite of sense and secrecy,
Unpeg the basket on the house's top,
Let the birds fly, and like the famous ape,[4]
To try conclusions, in the basket creep   195
And break your own neck down.
QUEEN   Be thou assured, if words be made of breath
And breath of life, I have no life to breathe
What thou hast said to me.
HAMLET   I must to England; you know that?
QUEEN   Alack,   200
I had forgot: 'tis so concluded on.
HAMLET   There's letters sealed: and my two schoolfellows,
Whom I will trust as I will adders fanged,
They bear the mandate; they must sweep my way,
And marshal me to knavery. Let it work;   205
For 'tis the sport to have the enginer
Hoist with his own petar:[5] and 't shall go hard
But I will delve one yard below their mines,
And blow them at the moon: I, 'tis most sweet
When in one line two crafts directly meet.   210
This man shall set me packing:
I'll lug the guts into the neighbor room.
Mother, good night. Indeed this councillor
Is now most still, most secret and most grave,[6]
Who was in life a foolish prating knave.   215
Come, sir, to draw toward an end with you.
Good night, mother.
    [*Exeunt severally*; HAMLET *dragging in* POLONIUS.]

---

1. Fetid.   2. Simulation.   3. Matters with which one is closely concerned. *Paddock*: toad. *Gib*: tom-cat.   4. The ape in the unidentified animal fable to which Hamlet alludes; apparently the animal saw birds fly out of a basket and drew the conclusion that by placing himself in a basket he could fly, too. 5. Petard, a variety of bomb. *Marshal*: lead. *Enginer*: military engineer. *Hoist*: blow up.   6. Hamlet is punning on the word.

Act IV

SCENE 1

[SCENE: *A room in the castle.*]

[*Enter* KING, QUEEN, ROSENCRANTZ, *and* GUILDENSTERN.]

KING   There's matter in these sighs, these profound heaves:
You must translate: 'tis fit we understand them.
Where is your son?

QUEEN   Bestow this place on us[7] a little while.

[*Exeunt* ROSENCRANTZ *and* GUILDENSTERN.]

Ah, mine own lord, what have I seen to-night!   5

KING   What, Gertrude? How does Hamlet?

QUEEN   Mad as the sea and wind, when both contend
Which is the mightier: in his lawless fit,
Behind the arras hearing something stir,
Whips out his rapier, cries "A rat, a rat!"   10
And in this brainish apprehension[8] kills
The unseen good old man.

KING   O heavy deed!
It had been so with us, had we been there:
His liberty is full of threats to all,
To you yourself, to us, to every one.   15
Alas, how shall this bloody deed be answered?
It will be laid to us, whose providence
Should have kept short,[9] restrained and out of haunt,
This mad young man: but so much was our love,
We would not understand what was most fit,   20
But, like the owner of a foul disease,
To keep it from divulging, let it feed
Even on the pith of life. Where is he gone?

QUEEN   To draw apart the body he hath killed:
O'er whom his very madness, like some ore   25
Among a mineral[1] of metals base,
Shows itself pure; he weeps for what is done.

KING   O Gertrude, come away!
The sun no sooner shall the mountains touch,
But we will ship him hence: and this vile deed   30
We must, with all our majesty and skill,
Both countenance[2] and excuse. Ho, Guildenstern!

[*Re-enter* ROSENCRANTZ *and* GUILDENSTERN.]

Friends both, go join you with some further aid:
Hamlet in madness hath Polonius slain,
And from his mother's closet hath he dragged him: 35
Go seek him out; speak fair, and bring the body
Into the chapel. I pray you, haste in this.

[*Exeunt* ROSENCRANTZ *and* GUILDENSTERN.]

7. Leave us alone.   8. Imaginary notion.   9. Under close watch.   1. Mine. *Ore:* gold.   2. Recognize.

Come, Gertrude, we'll call up our wisest friends;
And let them know, both what we mean to do,
And what's untimely done. . . . [3]   40
Whose whisper o'er the world's diameter
As level as the cannon to his blank[4]
Transports his poisoned shot, may miss our name
And hit the woundless air. O, come away!
My soul is full of discord and dismay.   45
    [*Exeunt.*]

SCENE 2

[SCENE: *Another room in the castle.*]

    [*Enter* HAMLET.]
HAMLET Safely stowed.
ROSENCRANTZ } [*Within.*] Hamlet! Lord Hamlet!
GUILDENSTERN
HAMLET But soft, what noise? who calls on Hamlet?
  O, here they come.
    [*Enter* ROSENCRANTZ *and* GUILDENSTERN.]   5
ROSENCRANTZ What have you done, my lord, with the dead body?
HAMLET Compounded[5] it with dust, whereto 'tis kin.
ROSENCRANTZ Tell us where 'tis, that we may take it thence
  And bear it to the chapel.
HAMLET Do not believe it.   10
ROSENCRANTZ Believe what?
HAMLET That I can keep your counsel and not mine own. Besides, to
  be demanded of a sponge! what replication[6] should be made by the
  son of a king?
ROSENCRANTZ Take you me for a sponge, my lord?
HAMLET Aye, sir; that soaks up the king's countenance,[7] his rewards,   15
  his authorities. But such officers do the king best service in the end:
  he keeps them, like an ape, in the corner of his jaw; first mouthed,
  to be last swallowed: when he needs what you have gleaned, it is but
  squeezing you, and sponge, you shall be dry again.
ROSENCRANTZ I understand you not, my lord.   20
HAMLET I am glad of it: a knavish speech sleeps in a foolish ear.
ROSENCRANTZ My lord, you must tell us where the body is, and go
  with us to the king.
HAMLET The body is with the king, but the king is not with the body.
  The king is a thing—   25
GUILDENSTERN A thing, my lord?
HAMLET Of nothing: bring me to him. Hide fox, and all after.[8]
    [*Exeunt.*]

---

3. This gap in the text has been guessingly filled in with "So envious slander."   4. His target.
5. Mixed.   6. Formal reply. *Demanded:* questioned by.   7. Favor.   8. A children's game.

SCENE 3

[SCENE: *Another room in the castle.*]

[*Enter* KING, *attended.*]

KING I have sent to seek him, and to find the body.
How dangerous is it that this man goes loose!
Yet must not we put the strong law on him:
He's loved of the distracted multitude,
Who like not in their judgment, but their eyes;   5
And where 'tis so, the offender's scourge is weighed,
But never the offense. To bear⁹ all smooth and even,
This sudden sending away must seem
Deliberate pause: diseases desperate grown
By desperate appliance¹ are relieved,   10
Or not at all.
     [*Enter* ROSENCRANTZ.]
             How now! what hath befall'n?
ROSENCRANTZ Where the dead body is bestowed, my lord,
We cannot get from him.
KING   But where is he?
ROSENCRANTZ Without, my lord; guarded, to know your pleasure.
KING Bring him before us.   15
ROSENCRANTZ Ho, Guildenstern! bring in my lord.
     [*Enter* HAMLET *and* GUILDENSTERN.]
KING Now, Hamlet, where's Polonius?
HAMLET At supper.
KING At supper! where?
HAMLET Not where he eats, but where he is eaten: a certain convo-   20
cation of public worms are e'en at him. Your worm is your only
emperor for diet:² we fat all creatures else to fat us, and we fat our-
selves for maggots: your fat king and your lean beggar is but variable
service,³ two dishes, but to one table: that's the end.
KING Alas, alas!   25
HAMLET A man may fish with the worm that hath eat of a king, and
eat of the fish that hath fed of that worm.
KING What dost thou mean by this?
HAMLET Nothing but to show you how a king may go a progress⁴
through the guts of a beggar.   30
KING Where is Polonius?
HAMLET In heaven; send thither to see: if your messenger find him
not there, seek him i' the other place yourself. But indeed, if you
find him not within this month, you shall nose⁵ him as you go up
the stairs into the lobby.   35
KING [*To some* ATTENDANTS.] Go seek him there.
HAMLET He will stay till you come.

---

9. Conduct. *Scourge:* punishment.   1. Treatment. *Deliberate pause:* the result of careful argument.
2. Possibly a punning reference to the Diet (assembly) of the Holy Roman Empire at Worms.   3. That
is, the service varies, not the food.   4. Royal state journey.   5. Smell.

[*Exeunt* ATTENDANTS.]

KING Hamlet, this deed, for thine especial safety,
Which we do tender,[6] as we dearly grieve
For that which thou hast done, must send thee hence 40
With fiery quickness: therefore prepare thyself;
The bark is ready and the wind at help,
The associates tend, and every thing is bent
For England.

HAMLET   For England?

KING   Aye, Hamlet.

HAMLET   Good.

KING So is it, if thou knew'st our purposes. 45

HAMLET I see a cherub that sees them. But, come; for England!
Farewell, dear mother.

KING Thy loving father, Hamlet.

HAMLET My mother: father and mother is man and wife; man and
wife is one flesh, and so, my mother. Come, for England! 50
[*Exit.*]

KING Follow him at foot;[7] tempt him with speed aboard;
Delay it not; I'll have him hence to-night:
Away! for every thing is sealed and done
That else leans on[8] the affair: pray you, make haste.
[*Exeunt* ROSENCRANTZ *and* GUILDENSTERN.]
And, England,[9] if my love thou hold'st at aught— 55
As my great power thereof may give thee sense,
Since yet thy cicatrice looks raw and red
After the Danish sword, and thy free awe
Pays homage to us—thou mayst not coldly set[1]
Our sovereign process; which imports at full, 60
By letters conjuring[2] to that effect,
The present death of Hamlet. Do it, England;
For like the hectic[3] in my blood he rages,
And thou must cure me; till I know 'tis done,
Howe'er my haps, my joys were ne'er begun. 65
[*Exit.*]

SCENE 4

[SCENE: *A plain in Denmark.*]

[*Enter* FORTINBRAS, *a* CAPTAIN *and* SOLDIERS, *marching.*]

FORTINBRAS Go, captain, from me greet the Danish king;
Tell him that by his license Fortinbras
Craves the conveyance[4] of a promised march
Over his kingdom. You know the rendezvous.
If that his majesty would aught with us, 5
We shall express our duty in his eye;[5]

6. Care for.   7. At his heels.   8. Pertains to.   9. The king of England.   1. Regard with indifference.   2. Enjoining.   3. Fever.   4. Convoy.   5. Presence.

And let him know so.
CAPTAIN   I will do 't, my lord.
FORTINBRAS   Go softly on.
    [*Exeunt* FORTINBRAS *and* SOLDIERS.—*Enter* HAMLET, ROSENCRANTZ,
    GUILDENSTERN, *and others.*]
HAMLET   Good sir, whose powers[6] are these?
CAPTAIN   They are of Norway, sir.   10
HAMLET   How purposed, sir, I pray you?
CAPTAIN   Against some part of Poland.
HAMLET   Who commands them, sir?
CAPTAIN   The nephew to Old Norway, Fortinbras.
HAMLET   Goes it against the main[7] of Poland, sir,   15
  Or for some frontier?
CAPTAIN   Truly to speak, and with no addition,
  We go to gain a little patch of ground
  That hath in it no profit but the name.
  To pay five ducats, five, I would not farm it;   20
  Nor will it yield to Norway or the Pole
  A ranker rate, should it be sold in fee.[8]
HAMLET   Why, then the Polack never will defend it.
CAPTAIN   Yes, it is already garrisoned.
HAMLET   Two thousand souls and twenty thousand ducats   25
  Will not debate the question of this straw!
  This is the imposthume[9] of much wealth and peace,
  That inward breaks, and shows no cause without
  Why the man dies. I humbly thank you, sir.
CAPTAIN   God be wi' you, sir.
    [*Exit.*]
ROSENCRANTZ   Will 't please you go, my lord?   30
HAMLET   I'll be with you straight. Go a little before.
    [*Exeunt all but* HAMLET.]
  How all occasions do inform against[1] me,
  And spur my dull revenge! What is a man,
  If his chief good and market[2] of his time
  Be but to sleep and feed? a beast, no more.   35
  Sure, he that made us with such large discourse,[3]
  Looking before and after, gave us not
  That capability and god-like reason
  To fust[4] in us unused. Now, whether it be
  Bestial oblivion, or some craven scruple   40
  Of thinking too precisely on the event,[5]—
  A thought which, quartered, hath but one part wisdom
  And ever three parts coward,—I do not know
  Why yet I live to say "this thing's to do,"
  Sith I have cause, and will, and strength, and means,   45
  To do 't. Examples gross as earth exhort me:

6. Armed forces.   7. The whole of.   8. For absolute possession. *Ranker:* higher.   9. Ulcer.
1. Denounce.   2. Payment for, reward.   3. Reasoning power.   4. Become moldy, taste of the cask.
5. Outcome.

Witness this army, of such mass and charge,[6]
Led by a delicate and tender prince,
Whose spirit with divine ambition puffed
Makes mouths[7] at the invisible event,   50
Exposing what is mortal and unsure
To all that fortune, death, and danger dare,
Even for an egg-shell. Rightly to be great
Is not to stir without great argument,
But greatly to find quarrel in a straw   55
When honor's at the stake. How stand I then,
That have a father killed, a mother stained,
Excitements of my reason and my blood,
And let all sleep, while to my shame I see
The imminent death of twenty thousand men,   60
That for a fantasy and trick[8] of fame
Go to their graves like beds, fight for a plot
Whereon the numbers cannot try the cause,[9]
Which is not tomb enough and continent[1]
To hide the slain? O, from this time forth,   65
My thoughts be bloody, or be nothing worth!
　　　[*Exit.*]

SCENE 5

[SCENE: *Elsinore. A room in the castle.*]

　　[*Enter* QUEEN, HORATIO, *and a* GENTLEMAN.]
QUEEN　I will not speak with her.
GENTLEMAN　She is importunate, indeed distract:
　Her mood will needs be pitied.
QUEEN　　　　　　　　　　　What would she have?
GENTLEMAN　She speaks much of her father, says she hears
　There's tricks i' the world, and hems and beats her heart,   5
　Spurns enviously at straws;[2] speaks things in doubt,
　That carry but half sense: her speech is nothing,
　Yet the unshapèd use of it doth move
　The hearers to collection; they aim[3] at it,
　And botch[4] the words up fit to their own thoughts;   10
　Which, as her winks and nods and gestures yield them,
　Indeed would make one think there might be thought,
　Though nothing sure, yet much unhappily.
HORATIO　'Twere good she were spoken with, for she may strew
　Dangerous conjectures in ill-breeding minds.[5]   15
QUEEN　Let her come in.
　　　[*Exit* GENTLEMAN.]

---

6. Cost.　7. Laughs at.　8. Trifle.　9. So small that it cannot hold the men who fight for it.
1. Container.　2. Gets angry at trifles.　3. Guess. *Collection:* gathering up her words and trying to
make sense of them.　4. Patch.　5. Minds breeding evil thoughts.

[*Aside.*] To my sick soul, as sin's true nature is,
Each toy seems prologue to some great amiss:
So full of artless jealousy⁶ is guilt,
It spills itself in fearing to be spilt.   20

[*Re-enter* GENTLEMAN, *with* OPHELIA.]

OPHELIA   Where is the beauteous majesty of Denmark?
QUEEN   How now, Ophelia!
OPHELIA [*Sings.*]   How should I your true love know
                              From another one?
                              By his cockle hat and staff   25
                              And his sandal shoon.⁷
QUEEN   Alas, sweet lady, what imports this song?
OPHELIA   Say you? nay, pray you, mark.
[*Sings.*]   He is dead and gone, lady,
                              He is dead and gone;   30
                              At his head a grass-green turf,
                              At his heels a stone.
Oh, oh!
QUEEN   Nay, but Ophelia,—
OPHELIA   Pray you, mark.
[*Sings.*]   White his shroud as the mountain snow,—
[*Enter* KING.]
QUEEN   Alas, look here, my lord.   35
OPHELIA [*Sings.*]   Larded⁸ with sweet flowers;
                              Which bewept to the grave did—not—go
                              With true-love showers.
KING   How do you, pretty lady?   40
OPHELIA   Well, God 'ild⁹ you! They say the owl was a baker's daughter.
   Lord, we know what we are, but know not what we may be.¹ God be
   at your table!
KING   Conceit upon her father.
OPHELIA   Pray you, let's have no words of this; but when they ask
   you what it means, say you this: 45
[*Sings.*]   To-morrow is Saint Valentine's day
                              All in the morning betime,
                              And I a maid at your window,
                              To be your Valentine.
                              Then up he rose, and donned his clothes,   50
                              And dupped² the chamber-door;
                              Let in the maid, that out a maid
                              Never departed more.
KING   Pretty Ophelia!
OPHELIA   Indeed, la, without an oath, I'll make an end on 't: 55
[*Sings.*]   By Gis³ and by Saint Charity,
                              Alack, and fie for shame!
                              Young men will do 't, if they come to 't;

---

6. Uncontrolled suspicion. *Toy:* trifle. *Amiss:* misfortune.   7. Shoes. These are all typical signs of pilgrims
traveling to places of devotion.   8. Garnished.   9. Yield—that is, repay.   1. An allusion to a folk tale
about a baker's daughter changed into an owl for having shown no charity to those in need.   2. Opened.
3. By Jesus.

By Cock,[4] they are to blame.
Quoth she, before you tumbled me,   60
You promised me to wed.
He answers:
So would I ha' done, by yonder sun,
An thou hadst not come to my bed.

KING   How long hath she been thus?   65

OPHELIA   I hope all will be well. We must be patient: but I cannot
choose but weep, to think they should lay him i' the cold ground.
My brother shall know of it: and so I thank you for your good counsel.
Come, my coach! Good night, ladies; good night, sweet ladies; good
night, good night.   70
    [*Exit.*]

KING   Follow her close; give her good watch, I pray you.
    [*Exit* HORATIO.]
O, this is the poison of deep grief; it springs
All from her father's death. O Gertrude, Gertrude,
When sorrows come, they come not single spies,
But in battalions! First, her father slain: 75
Next, your son gone; and he most violent author
Of his own just remove: the people muddied,[5]
Thick and unwholesome in their thoughts and whispers,
For good Polonius' death; and we have done but greenly
In hugger-mugger[6] to inter him: poor Ophelia   80
Divided from herself and her fair judgment,
Without the which we are pictures, or mere beasts:
Last, and as much containing as all these,
Her brother is in secret come from France,
Feeds on his wonder,[7] keeps himself in clouds,   85
And wants not buzzers[8] to infect his ear
With pestilent speeches of his father's death;
Wherein necessity, of matter beggared,[9]
Will nothing stick our person to arraign[1]
In ear and ear. O my dear Gertrude, this,   90
Like to a murdering-piece,[2] in many places
Gives me superfluous death.
    [*A noise within.*]

QUEEN   Alack, what noise is this?

KING   Where are my Switzers?[3] Let them guard the door.
    [*Enter another* GENTLEMAN.]
What is the matter?

GENTLEMAN   Save yourself, my lord:
The ocean, overpeering of his list,[4]   95
Eats not the flats with more impetuous haste
Than young Laertes, in a riotous head,[5]

4. Corruption of *God*, but with a sexual undermeaning.   5. Confused, their thoughts made turbid (as water by mud).   6. Hasty secrecy. *Greenly*: foolishly.   7. Broods, keeps wondering.   8. Lacks not tale-bearers.   9. The necessity to build up a story without the materials for doing so.   1. Will not hesitate to accuse me.   2. A variety of cannon that scattered its shot in many directions.   3. Swiss guards.   4. Overflowing above the high-water mark.   5. Group of rebels.

O'erbears your officers. The rabble call him lord;
And, as the world were now but to begin,
Antiquity forgot, custom not known,   100
The ratifiers and props of every word,
They cry "Choose we; Laertes shall be king!"
Caps, hands and tongues applaud it to the clouds,
"Laertes shall be king, Laertes king!"
QUEEN   How cheerfully on the false trail they cry!   105
  O, this is counter,[6] you false Danish dogs!
          [Noise within.]
KING   The doors are broke.
          [Enter LAERTES, armed; DANES following.]
LAERTES   Where is this king? Sirs, stand you all without.
DANES   No, let's come in.
LAERTES   I pray you, give me leave.
DANES   We will, we will.   110
          [They retire without the door.]
LAERTES   I thank you: keep the door. O thou vile king,
  Give me my father!
QUEEN   Calmly, good Laertes.
LAERTES   That drop of blood that's calm proclaims me bastard;
  Cries cuckold to my father; brands the harlot
  Even here, between the chaste unsmirchèd brows   115
  Of my true mother.
KING   What is the cause, Laertes,
  That thy rebellion looks so giant-like?
  Let him go, Gertrude; do not fear[7] our person
  There's such divinity doth hedge a king,
  That treason can but peep to what it would,[8]   120
  Acts little of his[9] will. Tell me, Laertes,
  Why thou art thus incensed: let him go, Gertrude
  Speak, man.
LAERTES   Where is my father?
KING   Dead.
QUEEN   But not by him.
KING   Let him demand his fill.   125
LAERTES   How came he dead? I'll not be juggled with
  To hell, allegiance! vows, to the blackest devil!
  Conscience and grace, to the profoundest pit
  I dare damnation: to this point I stand,
  That both the worlds I give to negligence,[1]   130
  Let come what comes; only I'll be revenged
  Most thoroughly for my father.
KING   Who shall stay you?
LAERTES   My will, not all the world
  And for my means, I'll husband them so well,
  They shall go far with little.

---

6. Following the scent in the wrong direction.   7. Fear for.   8. Look from a distance at what it desires.
9. Its.   1. I don't care what may happen to me in either this world or the next.

KING   Good Laertes,   135
  If you desire to know the certainty
  Of your dear father's death, is 't writ in your revenge
  That, swoopstake,² you will draw both friend and foe,
  Winner and loser?
LAERTES   None but his enemies.
KING   Will you know them then?   140
LAERTES   To his good friends thus wide I'll ope my arms;
  And, like the kind life-rendering pelican,³
  Repast them with my blood.
KING   Why, now you speak
  Like a good child and a true gentleman.
  That I am guiltless of your father's death,   145
  And am most sensibly in grief for it,
  It shall as level to your judgment pierce
  As day does to your eye.
DANES [Within.]   Let her come in.
LAERTES   How now! what noise is that?
    [Re-enter OPHELIA.]
  O heat, dry up my brains! tears seven times salt,   150
  Burn out the sense and virtue⁴ of mine eye!
  By heaven, thy madness shall be paid with weight,
  Till our scale turn the beam. O rose of May!
  Dear maid, kind sister, sweet Ophelia!
  O heavens! is 't possible a young maid's wits   155
  Should be as mortal as an old man's life?
  Nature is fine in love, and where 'tis fine
  It sends some precious instance⁵ of itself
  After the thing it loves.
OPHELIA [Sings.]   They bore him barefaced on the bier   160
       Hey non nonny, nonny, hey nonny
       And in his grave rained many a tear,—
  Fare you well, my dove!
LAERTES   Hadst thou thy wits, and didst persuade revenge,
  It could not move thus.   165
OPHELIA [Sings.]   You must sing down a-down,
       An you call him a-down-a.
  O, how the wheel becomes it! It is the false steward,⁶ that stole his
  master's daughter.
LAERTES   This nothing's more than matter.⁷   170
OPHELIA   There's rosemary, that's for remembrance: pray you, love,
  remember: and there is pansies, that's for thoughts.
LAERTES   A document⁸ in madness; thoughts and remembrance fitted.
OPHELIA   There's fennel for you, and columbines: there's rue for you:
  and here's some for me: we may call it herbs of grace o' Sundays: O,   175

2. Without making any distinction, as the winner takes the whole stake in a card game.   3. In myth, the pelican is supposed to feed its young with its own blood.   4. Power, faculty.   5. Sample, token. *Fine*: refined.   6. An allusion (probably to a lost ballad) further expressing Ophelia's preoccupation with betrayal, lost love, and death. *How the wheel becomes it*: that is, how well the refrain fits.   7. This nonsense is more indicative than sane speech.   8. Lesson. Traditionally, flowers and herbs have symbolic meanings. Here rosemary is the symbol for remembrance and pansies symbolize thoughts.

you must wear your rue with a difference. There's a daisy: I would
give you some violets,[9] but they withered all when my father died:
they say he made a good end,—

[*Sings.*]   For bonnie sweet Robin is all my joy.

LAERTES   Thought and affliction, passion, hell itself,   180
She turns to favor[1] and to prettiness.

OPHELIA [*Sings.*]   And will he not come again?
                              And will he not come again?
                                    No, no, he is dead,
                                    Go to thy death-bed,   185
                              He never will come again.

                              His beard was as white as snow,
                              All flaxen was his poll
                                    He is gone, he is gone,
                                    And we cast away moan   190
                              God ha' mercy on his soul!

And of all Christian souls, I pray God. God be wi' you.

         [*Exit.*]

LAERTES   Do you see this, O God?

KING   Laertes, I must commune with your grief,
Or you deny me right. Go but apart,   195
Make choice of whom your wisest friends you will,
And they shall hear and judge 'twixt you and me:
If by direct or by collateral hand
They find us touched,[2] we will our kingdom give,
Our crown, our life, and all that we call ours,   200
To you in satisfaction; but if not,
Be you content to lend your patience to us,
And we shall jointly labor with your soul
To give it due content.

LAERTES   Let this be so;
His means of death, his obscure funeral,   205
No trophy, sword, nor hatchment[3] o'er his bones,
No noble rite nor formal ostentation,
Cry to be heard, as 'twere from heaven to earth,
That I must call 't in question.

KING   So you shall;
And where the offense is let the great axe fall.   210
I pray you, go with me.

         [*Exeunt.*]

                         SCENE 6

              [SCENE: *Another room in the castle.*]

              [*Enter* HORATIO *and a* SERVANT.]

HORATIO   What are they that would speak with me?

SERVANT   Sea-faring men, sir: they say they have letters for you.

---

9. Violets symbolize faithfulness. Fennel stands for flattery, columbines for cuckoldom, and rue for sorrow
and repentance (compare the verb *rue*).   1. Charm.   2. Involved (in the murder). *Collateral:* indirect.
3. Coat of arms.

HORATIO   Let them come in.
          [*Exit* SERVANT.]
    I do not know from what part of the world
    I should be greeted, if not from Lord Hamlet.   5
          [*Enter* SAILORS.]
FIRST SAILOR   God bless you, sir.
HORATIO   Let him bless thee too.
FIRST SAILOR   He shall, sir, an 't please him.
    There's a letter for you, sir; it comes from the ambassador that was
    bound for England; if your name be Horatio, as I am let to know it   10
    is.
HORATIO [*Reads.*]   "Horatio, when thou shalt have overlooked[4] this,
    give these fellows some means to the king: they have letters for him.
    Ere we were two days old at sea, a pirate of very warlike appointment
    gave us chase. Finding ourselves too slow of sail, we put on a com-   15
    pelled valor, and in the grapple I boarded them: on the instant they
    got clear of our ship; so I alone became their prisoner. They have
    dealt with me like thieves of mercy:[5] but they knew what they did; I
    am to do a good turn for them. Let the king have the letters I have
    sent; and repair thou to me with as much speed as thou wouldst fly   20
    death. I have words to speak in thine ear will make thee dumb; yet
    are they much too light for the bore[6] of the matter. These good
    fellows will bring thee where I am. Rosencrantz and Guildenstern
    hold their course for England: of them I have much to tell thee.
    Farewell.   25
          "He that thou knowest thine, HAMLET."
    Come, I will make you way for these your letters;
    And do 't the speedier, that you may direct me
    To him from whom you brought them.
          [*Exeunt.*]

                          SCENE 7

               [SCENE: *Another room in the castle.*]

          [*Enter* KING *and* LAERTES.]
KING   Now must your conscience my acquittance seal,
    And you must put me in your heart for friend,
    Sith you have heard, and with a knowing ear,
    That he which hath your noble father slain
    Pursued my life.
LAERTES   It well appears: but tell me   5
    Why you proceeded not against these feats,
    So crimeful and so capital in nature,
    As by your safety, wisdom, all things else,
    You mainly[7] were stirred up.
KING   O, for two special reasons,
    Which may to you perhaps seem much unsinewed,[8]   10
    But yet to me they're strong. The queen his mother

---

4. Read over.   5. Merciful.   6. Caliber, that is, importance.   7. Powerfully.   8. Weak.

Lives almost by his looks; and for myself—
My virtue or my plague, be it either which—
She's so conjunctive[9] to my life and soul,
That, as the star moves not but in his sphere,   15
I could not but by her. The other motive,
Why to a public count I might not go,
Is the great love the general gender[1] bear him;
Who, dipping all his faults in their affection,
Would, like the spring that turneth wood to stone,   20
Convert his gyves[2] to graces; so that my arrows,
Too slightly timber'd for so loud a wind,
Would have reverted to my bow again
And not where I had aim'd them.

LAERTES   And so have I a noble father lost;   25
A sister driven into desperate terms,
Whose worth, if praises may go back again,
Stood challenger on mount of[3] all the age
For her perfections: but my revenge will come.

KING   Break not your sleeps for that: you must not think   30
That we are made of stuff so flat and dull
That we can let our beard be shook with danger
And think it pastime. You shortly shall hear more:
I loved your father, and we love ourself;
And that, I hope, will teach you to imagine—   35
      [Enter a MESSENGER, with letters.]
How now! what news?

MESSENGER   Letters, my lord, from Hamlet:
This to your majesty; this to the queen.

KING   From Hamlet! who brought them?

MESSENGER   Sailors, my lord, they say; I saw them not:
They were given me by Claudio; he received them   40
Of him that brought them.

KING   Laertes, you shall hear them.
Leave us.
      [Exit MESSENGER.]
[Reads.] "High and mighty, you shall know I am set naked on your
kingdom. To-morrow shall I beg leave to see your kingly eyes: when
I shall, first asking your pardon thereunto, recount the occasion of   45
my sudden and more strange return.   HAMLET.
What should this mean? Are all the rest come back?
Or is it some abuse, and no such thing?[4]

LAERTES   Know you the hand?

KING   'Tis Hamlet's character.[5] "Naked!"   50
And in a postscript here, he says "alone."
Can you advise me?

LAERTES   I'm lost in it, my lord. But let him come;
It warms the very sickness in my heart,

---

9. Closely joined.   1. Common people. *Count*: accounting, trial.   2. Leg irons (shames).   3. Above.
Go back: to what she was before her madness.   4. A delusion, not a reality.   5. Handwriting.

That I shall live and tell him to his teeth,   55
"Thus diddest thou."
KING   If it be so, Laertes,—
  As how should it be so? how otherwise?—
  Will you be ruled by me?
LAERTES   Aye, my lord;
  So you will not o'errule me to a peace.
KING   To thine own peace. If he be now returned,   60
  As checking[6] at his voyage, and that he means
  No more to undertake it, I will work him
  To an exploit now ripe in my device,
  Under the which he shall not choose but fall:
  And for his death no wind of blame shall breathe;
  But even his mother shall uncharge the practice,[7]   65
  call it accident.
LAERTES   My lord, I will be ruled;
  The rather, if you could devise it so
  That I might be the organ.[8]
KING   It falls right.
  You have been talked of since your travel much,   70
  And that in Hamlet's hearing, for a quality
  Wherein, they say, you shine; your sum of parts[9]
  Did not together pluck such envy from him,
  As did that one, and that in my regard
  Of the unworthiest siege.[1]
LAERTES   What part is that, my lord?   75
KING   A very riband in the cap of youth,
  Yet needful too; for youth no less becomes[2]
  The light and careless livery that it wears
  Than settled age his sables and his weeds,[3]
  Importing health and graveness. Two months since   80
  Here was a gentleman of Normandy:—
  I've seen myself, and served against, the French,
  And they can well on horseback: but this gallant
  Had witchcraft in 't; he grew unto his seat,
  And to such wondrous doing brought his horse   85
  As had he been incorpsed and demi-natured[4]
  With the brave beast: so far he topped my thought
  That I, in forgery of shapes and tricks,[5]
  Come short of what he did.
LAERTES   A Norman was 't?
KING   A Norman.   90
LAERTES   Upon my life, Lamord.
KING   The very same.
LAERTES   I know him well: he is the brooch[6] indeed
  And gem of all the nation.

6. Changing the course of, refusing to continue.   7. Not recognize it as a plot.   8. Instrument.
9. The sum of your gifts.   1. Seat, that is, rank.   2. Is the appropriate age for. *Riband:* ribbon, ornament.   3. Furs (also meaning "blacks," dark colors) and robes.   4. Incorporated and split his nature
in two.   5. In imagining methods and skills of horsemanship.   6. Ornament.

KING   He made confession of you,
　　And gave you such a masterly report,　　　　　　　　　95
　　For art and exercise in your defense,[7]
　　And for your rapier most especial,
　　That he cried out, 'twould be a sight indeed
　　If one could match you: the scrimers[8] of their nation,
　　He swore, had neither motion, guard, nor eye,　　　　100
　　If you opposed them. Sir, this report of his
　　Did Hamlet so envenom with his envy
　　That he could nothing do but wish and beg
　　Your sudden coming o'er, to play with him.
　　Now, out of this—
LAERTES　　　　　　　　What out of this, my lord?　　　105
KING   Laertes, was your father dear to you?
　　Or are you like the painting of a sorrow,
　　A face without a heart?
LAERTES　　　　　　　　Why ask you this?
KING   Not that I think you did not love your father,
　　But that I know love is begun by time,　　　　　　　110
　　And that I see, in passages of proof,[9]
　　Time qualifies[1] the spark and fire of it.
　　There lives within the very flame of love
　　A kind of wick or snuff[2] that will abate it;
　　And nothing is at a like goodness still,　　　　　　　115
　　For goodness, growing to a plurisy,[3]
　　Dies in his own too much: that we would do
　　We should do when we would; for this "would" changes
　　And hath abatements and delays as many
　　As there are tongues, are hands, are accidents,　　　120
　　And then this "should" is like a spendthrift sigh,
　　That hurts by easing.[4] But, to the quick o' the ulcer:
　　Hamlet comes back: what would you undertake,
　　To show yourself your father's son in deed
　　More than in words?
LAERTES　　　　　　　　To cut his throat i' the church.　125
KING   No place indeed should murder sanctuarize;
　　Revenge should have no bounds. But, good Laertes,
　　Will you do this, keep close within your chamber.
　　Hamlet returned shall know you are come home:
　　We'll put on[5] those shall praise your excellence　　130
　　And set a double varnish on the fame
　　The Frenchman gave you; bring you in fine together
　　And wager on your heads: he, being remiss,[6]
　　Most generous and free from all contriving,
　　Will not peruse[7] the foils, so that with ease,　　　135
　　Or with a little shuffling, you may choose

---

7. Report of your mastery in the theory and practice of fencing.　8. Fencers.　9. Instances that prove
it.　1. Weakens.　2. Charred part of the wick.　3. Excess. *Still:* constantly.　4. A sigh that gives
relief but is harmful (according to an old notion that it draws blood from the heart).　5. Instigate.
6. Careless. *In fine:* finally.　7. Examine closely.

A sword unbated, and in a pass of practice[8]
Requite him for your father.
LAERTES   I will do 't;
And for that purpose I'll anoint my sword.
I bought an unction of a mountebank,[9]   140
So mortal that but dip a knife in it,
Where it draws blood no cataplasm so rare,
Collected from all simples[1] that have virtue
Under the moon, can save the thing from death
That is but scratched withal: I'll touch my point   145
With this contagion, that, if I gall[2] him slightly,
It may be death.
KING   Let's further think of this;
Weigh what convenience both of time and means
May fit us to our shape: if this should fail,
And that our drift look through[3] our bad performance,   150
'Twere better not assayed: therefore this project
Should have a back or second, that might hold
If this did blast in proof.[4] Soft! let me see:
We'll make a solemn wager on your cunnings:
I ha 't: 155
When in your motion you are hot and dry—
As make your bouts more violent to that end—
And that he calls for drink, I'll have prepared him
A chalice for the nonce;[5] whereon but sipping,
If he by chance escape your venomed stuck,[6]   160
Our purpose may hold there. But stay, what noise?
        [Enter QUEEN.]
How now, sweet queen!
QUEEN   One woe doth tread upon another's heel,
So fast they follow: your sister's drowned, Laertes.
LAERTES   Drowned! O, where?   165
QUEEN   There is a willow grows aslant[7] a brook,
That shows his hoar leaves in the glassy stream;
There with fantastic garlands did she come
Of crow-flowers, nettles, daisies, and long purples,
That liberal shepherds give a grosser name,   170
But our cold maids do dead men's fingers call them:
There, on the pendent boughs her coronet weeds
Clambering to hang, an envious sliver[8] broke;
When down her weedy trophies and herself
Fell in the weeping brook. Her clothes spread wide,   175
And mermaid-like a while they bore her up:
Which time she chanted snatches of old tunes,
As one incapable of[9] her own distress,

---

8. Treacherous thrust. *Unbated:* not blunted (as a rapier for exercise ordinarily would be).   9. Ointment
of a peddler of quack medicines.   1. Healing herbs. *Cataplasm:* plaster.   2. Scratch.   3. Our design
should show through. *Shape:* plan.   4. Burst (like a new firearm) once it is put to the test.   5. For that
particular occasion.   6. Thrust.   7. Across.   8. Malicious bough.   9. Insensitive to.

Or like a creature native and indued[1]
Unto that element: but long it could not be   180
Till that her garments, heavy with their drink,
Pulled the poor wretch from her melodious lay
To muddy death.
LAERTES   Alas, then she is drowned!
QUEEN   Drowned, drowned.
LAERTES   Too much of water hast thou, poor Ophelia,   185
And therefore I forbid my tears: but yet
It is our trick;[2] nature her custom holds,
Let shame say what it will: when these are gone,
The woman[3] will be out. Adieu, my lord:
I have a speech of fire that fain would blaze,   190
But that this folly douts[4] it.
     [Exit.]
KING   Let's follow, Gertrude:
How much I had to do to calm his rage!
Now fear I this will give it start again;
Therefore let's follow.
     [Exeunt.]

Act V

SCENE 1

[SCENE: *A churchyard.*]

[*Enter two* CLOWNS, *with spades, etc.*]
FIRST CLOWN   Is she to be buried in Christian burial that willfully seeks
   her own salvation?
SECOND CLOWN   I tell thee she is; and therefore make her grave
   straight: the crowner[5] hath sat on her, and finds it Christian burial.
FIRST CLOWN   How can that be, unless she drowned herself in her own   5
   defense?
SECOND CLOWN   Why, 'tis found so.
FIRST CLOWN   It must be "se offendendo";[6] it cannot be else. For here
   lies the point: if I drown myself wittingly, it argues an act: and an
   act hath three branches; it is, to act, to do, to perform: argal,[7] she   10
   drowned herself wittingly.
SECOND CLOWN   Nay, but hear you, goodman delver.
FIRST CLOWN   Give me leave. Here lies the water; good: here stands
   the man; good: if the man go to this water and drown himself, it is,
   will he, nill he,[8] he goes; mark you that; but if the water come to   15
   him and drown him, he drowns not himself: argal, he that is not
   guilty of his own death shortens not his own life.
SECOND CLOWN   But is this law?
FIRST CLOWN   Aye, marry, is 't; crowner's quest[9] law.

---

1. Adapted, in harmony with.   2. Peculiar trait.   3. The softer qualities, the woman in me.
4. Extinguishes.   5. Coroner. *Straight*: right away.   6. The Clown's blunder for *se defendendo*: "in self-
defense" (Latin).   7. Blunder for *ergo*: "therefore" (Latin).   8. Willy-nilly.   9. Inquest.

SECOND CLOWN   Will you ha' the truth on 't? If this had not been a   20
gentlewoman, she should have been buried out o' Christian burial.
FIRST CLOWN   Why, there thou say'st: and the more pity that great folk
should have countenance[1] in this world to drown or hang themselves, more than their even[2] Christian. Come, my spade. There is
no ancient gentlemen but gardeners, ditchers and gravemakers: they   25
hold up Adam's profession.
SECOND CLOWN   Was he a gentleman?
FIRST CLOWN   A' was the first that ever bore arms.
SECOND CLOWN   Why, he had none.
FIRST CLOWN   What, art a heathen? How dost thou understand the   30
Scripture? The Scripture says Adam digged: could he dig without
arms? I'll put another question to thee: if thou answerest me not to
the purpose, confess thyself—
SECOND CLOWN   Go to.
FIRST CLOWN   What is he that builds stronger than either the mason,   35
the shipwright, or the carpenter?
SECOND CLOWN   The gallows-maker; for that frame outlives a thou-
sand tenants.
FIRST CLOWN   I like thy wit well, in good faith: the gallows does well;
but how does it well? it does well to those that do ill: now, thou dost   40
ill to say the gallows is built stronger than the church: argal, the
gallows may do well to thee. To 't again, come.
SECOND CLOWN   "Who builds stronger than a mason, a shipwright, or
a carpenter?"
FIRST CLOWN   Aye, tell me that, and unyoke.[3]
SECOND CLOWN   Marry, now I can tell.   45
FIRST CLOWN   To 't.
SECOND CLOWN   Mass, I cannot tell.
   [Enter HAMLET and HORATIO, afar off.]
FIRST CLOWN   Cudgel thy brains no more about it, for your dull ass
will not mend his pace with beating, and when you are asked this   50
question next, say "a grave-maker": the houses that he makes last till
doomsday. Go, get thee to Yaughan; fetch me a stoup[4] of liquor.
   [Exit SECOND CLOWN.—FIRST CLOWN digs and sings.]
      In youth, when I did love, did love,
         Methought it was very sweet,
      To contract, O, the time, for-a my behove,   55
         O, methought, there-a was nothing-a meet.[5]
HAMLET   Has this fellow no feeling of his business that he sings at
grave-making?
HORATIO   Custom hath made it in him a property of easiness.[6]
HAMLET   'Tis e'en so: the hand of little employment hath the daintier[7]   60
sense.
FIRST CLOWN [Sings.]   But age, with his stealing steps,
         Hath clowed me in his clutch,
      And hath shipped me intil[8] the land,
         As if I had never been such.   65

1. Sanction.   2. Fellow.   3. Call it a day.   4. Mug. *Yaughan:* apparently a tavern keeper's name.
5. Fitting. *Contract:* shorten. *Behove:* profit.   6. Has made it a matter of indifference to him.   7. Finer
sensitivity. *Of little employment:* that does little labor.   8. Into.

[*Throws up a skull.*]

HAMLET   That skull had a tongue in it, and could sing once: how the
knave jowls it to the ground, as if it were Cain's jaw-bone, that did
the first murder! It might be the pate of a politician,[9] which this ass
now o'er-reaches;[1] one that would circumvent God, might it not?

HORATIO   It might, my lord.   70

HAMLET   Or of a courtier, which could say, "Good morrow, sweet lord!
How dost thou, sweet lord?" This might be my lord such-a-one, that
praised my lord such-a-one's horse, when he meant to beg it; might
it not?

HORATIO   Aye, my lord.   75

HAMLET   Why, e'en so: and now my Lady Worm's; chapless, and
knocked about the mazzard[2] with a sexton's spade: here's fine revolution, an we had the trick to see 't. Did these bones cost no more
the breeding, but to play at loggats[3] with 'em? mine ache to think
on 't.   80

FIRST CLOWN [*Sings.*]   A pick-axe, and a spade, a spade,
                        For a shrouding sheet:
                      O, a pit of clay for to be made
                        For such a guest is meet.

[*Throws up another skull.*]

HAMLET   There's another: why may not that be the skull of a lawyer?   85
Where be his quiddities now, his quillets, his cases, his tenures,[4] and
his tricks? why does he suffer this rude knave now to knock him
about the sconce with a dirty shovel, and will not tell him of his
action of battery?[5] Hum! This fellow might be in 's time a great buyer
of land, with his statutes, his recognizances,[6] his fines, his double   90
vouchers, his recoveries: is this the fine[7] of his fines and the recovery
of his recoveries, to have his fine pate full of fine dirt? will his vouchers vouch him no more of his purchases, and double ones too, than
the length and breadth of a pair of indentures? The very convey-
ances[8] of his lands will hardly lie in this box; and must the inheritor   95
himself have no more, ha?

HORATIO   Not a jot more, my lord.

HAMLET   Is not parchment made of sheep-skins?

HORATIO   Aye, my lord, and of calf-skins too.

HAMLET   They are sheep and calves which seek out assurance[9] in that.   100
I will speak to this fellow. Whose grave's this, sirrah?

FIRST CLOWN   Mine, sir.

[*Sings.*]   O, a pit of clay for to be made
                        For such a guest is meet.

HAMLET   I think it be thine indeed, for thou liest in 't.   105

FIRST CLOWN   You lie out on 't, sir, and therefore 'tis not yours: for my
part, I do not lie in 't, and yet it is mine.

---

9. In a pejorative sense. *Jowls*: knocks. *First murder*: possibly an allusion to the legend that Cain slew Abel
with an ass's jawbone.   1. Outwits.   2. Pate. *Chapless*: the lower jawbone missing.   3. A game
resembling bowls. *Trick*: faculty.   4. Real estate holdings. *Quiddities*: subtle definitions. *Quillets*: quib-
bles.   5. Assault. *Sconce*: head.   6. Varieties of bonds. This passage contains legal terms relating to
the transfer of estates.   7. End. Hamlet is punning on the legal and nonlegal meanings of the word.
8. Deeds. *Indentures*: contracts drawn in duplicate on the same piece of parchment; the two copies were
separated by an indented line.   9. Security; another pun, because the word is also a legal term.

HAMLET   Thou dost lie in 't, to be in 't and say it is thine: 'tis for the
dead, not for the quick;[1] therefore thou liest.

FIRST CLOWN   'Tis a quick lie, sir; 'twill away again, from me to you.   110

HAMLET   What man dost thou dig it for?

FIRST CLOWN   For no man, sir.

HAMLET   What woman then?

FIRST CLOWN   For none neither.

HAMLET   Who is to be buried in 't?   115

FIRST CLOWN   One that was a woman, sir; but, rest her soul, she's dead.

HAMLET   How absolute the knave is! we must speak by the card,[2] or
equivocation will undo us. By the Lord, Horatio, these three years I
have taken note of it; the age is grown so picked[3] that the toe of the
peasant comes so near the heel of the courtier, he galls his kibe.[4]   120
How long hast thou been a grave-maker?

FIRST CLOWN   Of all the days i' the year, I came to 't that day that our
last King Hamlet o'ercame Fortinbras.

HAMLET   How long is that since?

FIRST CLOWN   Cannot you tell that? every fool can tell that: it was that   125
very day that young Hamlet was born: he that is mad, and sent into
England.

HAMLET   Aye, marry, why was he sent into England?

FIRST CLOWN   Why, because a' was mad; a' shall recover his wits there:
or, if a' do not, 'tis no great matter there.   130

HAMLET   Why?

FIRST CLOWN   'Twill not be seen in him there; there the men are as
mad as he.

HAMLET   How came he mad?

FIRST CLOWN   Very strangely, they say.   135

HAMLET   How "strangely?"

FIRST CLOWN   Faith, e'en with losing his wits.

HAMLET   Upon what ground?

FIRST CLOWN   Why, here in Denmark: I have been sexton here, man
and boy, thirty years.   140

HAMLET   How long will a man lie i' the earth ere he rot?

FIRST CLOWN   I' faith, if a' be not rotten before a' die—as we have
many pocky corses now-a-days, that will scarce hold the laying in[5]—
a' will last you some eight year or nine year: a tanner will last you
nine year.   145

HAMLET   Why he more than another?

FIRST CLOWN   Why, sir, his hide is so tanned with his trade that a' will
keep out water a great while; and your water is a sore decayer of
your whoreson dead body. Here's a skull now: this skull has lain in
the earth three and twenty years.   150

HAMLET   Whose was it?

FIRST CLOWN   A whoreson mad fellow's it was: whose do you think it
was?

HAMLET   Nay, I know not.

---

1. Living.   2. By the chart, that is, exactness. *Absolute:* positive.   3. Choice, fastidious.   4. Hurts
the chilblain on the courtier's heel.   5. Hold together till they are buried. *Pocky:* with marks of disease
(from "pox").

FIRST CLOWN   A pestilence on him for a mad rogue! a' poured a flagon   155
of Rhenish on my head once. This same skull, sir, was Yorick's skull,
the king's jester.

HAMLET   This?

FIRST CLOWN   E'en that.

HAMLET   Let me see. [*Takes the skull.*] Alas, poor Yorick! I knew him,   160
Horatio: a fellow of infinite jest, of most excellent fancy: he hath
borne me on his back a thousand times; and now how abhorred in
my imagination it is! my gorge rises at it. Here hung those lips that
I have kissed I know not how oft. Where be your gibes now? your
gambols? your songs? your flashes of merriment, that were wont to   165
set the table on a roar? Not one now, to mock your own grinning?
quite chop-fallen?[6] Now get you to my lady's chamber, and tell her,
let her paint an inch thick, to this favor[7] she must come; make her
laugh at that. Prithee, Horatio, tell me one thing.

HORATIO   What's that, my lord?   170

HAMLET   Dost thou think Alexander looked o' this fashion i' the earth?

HORATIO   E'en so.

HAMLET   And smelt so? pah!
            [*Puts down the skull.*]

HORATIO   E'en so, my lord.

HAMLET   To what base uses we may return, Horatio! Why may not   175
imagination trace the noble dust of Alexander, till he find it stopping
a bung-hole?

HORATIO   'Twere to consider too curiously, to consider so.

HAMLET   No, faith, not a jot; but to follow him thither with modesty
enough[8] and likelihood to lead it: as thus: Alexander died, Alexander   180
was buried, Alexander returneth into dust; the dust is earth; of earth
we make loam; and why of that loam, whereto he was converted,
might they not stop a beer-barrel?
            Imperious Caesar, dead and turned to clay,
            Might stop a hole to keep the wind away: 185
            O, that that earth, which kept the world in awe,
            Should patch a wall to expel the winter's flaw!
But soft! but soft! aside: here comes the king.
            [*Enter* PRIESTS *etc., in procession; the Corpse of Ophelia,* LAERTES *and*
            MOURNERS *following;* KING, QUEEN, *their trains, etc.*]
The queen, the courtiers: who is this they follow?
And with such maimèd rites?[9] This doth betoken   190
The corse they follow did with desperate hand
Fordo its own life: 'twas of some estate.[1]
Couch we awhile, and mark.
            [*Retiring with* HORATIO.]

LAERTES   What ceremony else?

HAMLET   That is Laertes, a very noble youth: mark.   195

LAERTES   What ceremony else?

FIRST PRIEST   Her obsequies have been as far enlarged

6. The lower jaw fallen down, hence dejected.   7. Appearance.   8. Without exaggeration.
9. Incomplete, mutilated ritual.   1. Rank. *Fordo:* destroy.

As we have warranty: her death was doubtful;
And, but that great command o'ersways the order[2]
She should in ground unsanctified have lodged   200
Till the last trumpet; for[3] charitable prayers,
Shards, flints and pebbles should be thrown on her:
Yet here she is allowed her virgin crants,
Her maiden strewments and the bringing home[4]
Of bell and burial.   205

LAERTES   Must there no more be done?

FIRST PRIEST   No more be done:
We should profane the service of the dead
To sing a requiem and such rest to her
As to peace-parted souls.

LAERTES   Lay her i' the earth:
And from her fair and unpolluted flesh   210
May violets spring! I tell thee, churlish priest,
A ministering angel shall my sister be,
When thou liest howling.

HAMLET   What, the fair Ophelia!

QUEEN [Scattering flowers.]   Sweets to the sweet: farewell!
I hoped thou shouldst have been my Hamlet's wife;   215
I thought thy bride-bed to have decked, sweet maid,
And not have strewed thy grave.

LAERTES   O, treble woe
Fall ten times treble on that cursed head
Whose wicked deed thy most ingenious sense
Deprived thee of! Hold off the earth a while,   220
Till I have caught her once more in mine arms.
          [Leaps into the grave.]
Now pile your dust upon the quick and dead,
Till of this flat a mountain you have made
To o'ertop old Pelion[5] or the skyish head
Of blue Olympus.   225

HAMLET [Advancing.]   What is he whose grief
Bears such an emphasis? whose phrase of sorrow
Conjures the wandering stars and makes them stand
Like wonder-wounded hearers? This is I,
Hamlet the Dane.   230
          [Leaps into the grave.]

LAERTES   The devil take thy soul!
          [Grappling with him.]

HAMLET   Thou pray'st not well.
I prithee, take thy fingers from my throat;
For, though I am not splenitive[6] and rash,
Yet have I in me something dangerous,
Which let thy wisdom fear. Hold off thy hand.   235

2. The king's command prevails against ordinary rules. *Doubtful:* of uncertain cause (that is, accident or suicide).   3. Instead of.   4. Laying to rest. *Crants:* garlands. *Strewments:* strews the grave with flowers.
5. The mountain on which the Aloadae, two rebellious giants in Greek mythology, piled up Mount Ossa in their attempt to reach Olympus.   6. Easily moved to anger.

KING Pluck them asunder.

QUEEN   Hamlet, Hamlet!

ALL   Gentlemen,—

HORATIO Good my lord, be quiet.

      [*The* ATTENDANTS *part them, and they come out of the grave.*]

HAMLET Why, I will fight with him upon this theme

  Until my eyelids will no longer wag.

QUEEN O my son, what theme?   240

HAMLET I loved Ophelia: forty thousand brothers

  Could not, with all their quantity of love,

  Make up my sum. What wilt thou do for her?

KING O, he is mad, Laertes.

QUEEN For love of God, forbear him.   245

HAMLET 'Swounds, show me what thou 'lt do:

  Woo't weep? woo't fight? woo't fast? woo't tear thyself?

  Woo't drink up eisel?[7] eat a crocodile?

  I'll do't. Dost thou come here to whine?

  To outface me with leaping in her grave?   250

  Be buried quick with her, and so will I:

  And, if thou prate of mountains, let them throw

  Millions of acres on us, till our ground,

  Singeing his pate against the burning zone,

  Make Ossa like a wart! Nay, an thou 'lt mouth,   255

  I'll rant as well as thou.

QUEEN   This is mere madness:

  And thus a while the fit will work on him;

  Anon, as patient as the female dove

  When that her golden couplets are disclosed,[8]

  His silence will sit drooping.

HAMLET   Hear you, sir;   260

  What is the reason that you use me thus?

  I loved you ever: but it is no matter;

  Let Hercules himself do what he may,

  The cat will mew, and dog will have his day.

      [*Exit.*]

KING I pray thee, good Horatio, wait upon him.   265

      [*Exit* HORATIO.]

  [*To* LAERTES.] Strengthen your patience in our last night's speech;

  We'll put the matter to the present push.[9]

  Good Gertrude, set some watch over your son.

  This grave shall have a living monument:

  An hour of quiet shortly shall we see;   270

  Till then, in patience our proceeding be.

      [*Exeunt.*]

---

7. Vinegar (the bitter drink given to Christ). *Woo't:* wilt thou.   8. Twins are hatched.   9. We'll push the matter on immediately.

SCENE 2

[SCENE: *A hall in the castle.*]

[*Enter* HAMLET *and* HORATIO.]

HAMLET   So much for this, sir: now shall you see the other;
  You do remember all the circumstance?
HORATIO   Remember it, my lord?
HAMLET   Sir, in my heart there was a kind of fighting,
  That would not let me sleep: methought I lay   5
  Worse than the mutines in the bilboes.[1] Rashly,
  And praised be rashness for it, let us know,
  Our indiscretion sometime serves us well
  When our deep plots do pall;[2] and that should learn us
  There's a divinity that shapes our ends,   10
  Rough-hew them how we will.
HORATIO   That is most certain.
HAMLET   Up from my cabin,
  My sea-gown scarfed about me, in the dark
  Groped I to find out them; had my desire,
  Fingered their packet, and in fine withdrew   15
  To mine own room again; making so bold,
  My fears forgetting manners, to unseal
  Their grand commission; where I found, Horatio,—
  O royal knavery!—an exact command,
  Larded with many several sorts of reasons,   20
  Importing[3] Denmark's health and England's too,
  With, ho! such bugs and goblins in my life,
  That, on the supervise, no leisure bated,[4]
  No, not to stay the grinding of the axe,
  My head should be struck off.
HORATIO   Is't possible?   25
HAMLET   Here's the commission: read it at more leisure.
  But wilt thou hear now how I did proceed?
HORATIO   I beseech you.
HAMLET   Being thus be-netted round with villainies,—
  Ere I could make a prologue to my brains,   30
  They had begun the play,—I sat me down;
  Devised a new commission; wrote it fair:
  I once did hold it, as our statists[5] do,
  A baseness to write fair, and labored much
  How to forget that learning; but, sir, now   35
  It did me yeoman's service:[6] wilt thou know
  The effect of what I wrote?
HORATIO   Aye, good my lord.
HAMLET   An earnest conjuration from the king,

---

1. Mutineers in iron fetters. 2. Become useless. 3. Concerning. 4. As soon as the message was read, with no time subtracted for leisure. *Bugs:* imaginary horrors to be expected if I lived. 5. Statesmen. 6. Excellent service.

As England was his faithful tributary,
As love between them like the palm might flourish,   40
As peace should still her wheaten garland wear
And stand a comma[7] 'tween their amities,
And many such-like "As"es of great charge,[8]
That, on the view and knowing of these contents,
Without debatement further, more or less,   45
He should the bearers put to sudden death,
Not shriving-time[9] allowed.

HORATIO   How was this sealed?

HAMLET   Why, even in that was heaven ordinant.[1]
I had my father's signet in my purse,
Which was the model of that Danish seal: 50
Folded the writ up in the form of the other;
Subscribed it; gave 't the impression;[2] placed it safely,
The changeling never known. Now, the next day
Was our sea-fight; and what to this was sequent
Thou know'st already.   55

HORATIO   So Guildenstern and Rosencrantz go to 't.

HAMLET   Why, man, they did make love to this employment;
They are not near my conscience; their defeat
Does by their own insinuation[3] grow:
'Tis dangerous when the baser nature comes   60
Between the pass and fell[4]-incensèd points
Of mighty opposites.

HORATIO   Why, what a king is this!

HAMLET   Does it not, think'st thee, stand me now upon[5]—
He that hath killed my king, and whored my mother;
Popped in between the election and my hopes;   65
Thrown out his angle for my proper life,[6]
And with such cozenage—is't not perfect conscience,
To quit[7] him with this arm? and is't not to be damned,
To let this canker of our nature come
In further evil?   70

HORATIO   It must be shortly known to him from England
What is the issue of the business there.

HAMLET   It will be short: the interim is mine;
And a man's life's no more than to say "One."
But I am very sorry, good Horatio,   75
That to Laertes I forgot myself;
For, by the image of my cause, I see
The portraiture of his: I'll court his favors:
But, sure, the bravery[8] of his grief did put me
Into a towering passion.

HORATIO   Peace! who comes here?   80

7. Connecting element. 8. "As"es: a pun on as and ass, which extends to of great charge, signifying both
"moral weight" and "ass's burden." 9. Time for confession and absolution. 1. Ordaining. 2. Of
the seal. 3. Meddling. Defeat: destruction. 4. Fiercely. Baser: lower in rank than the king and Prince
Hamlet. Pass: thrust. 5. Is it not my duty now? 6. An angling line for my own life. 7. Pay back.
8. Ostentation, bravado.

[*Enter* OSRIC.]

OSRIC   Your lordship is right welcome back to Denmark.

HAMLET   I humbly thank you, sir. Dost know this waterfly?

HORATIO   No, my good lord.

HAMLET   Thy state is the more gracious, for 'tis a vice to know him.
He hath much land, and fertile: let a beast be lord of beasts, and his   85
crib shall stand at the king's mess: 'tis a chough,⁹ but, as I say, spacious in the possession of dirt.

OSRIC   Sweet lord, if your lordship were at leisure, I should impart a
thing to you from his majesty.

HAMLET   I will receive it, sir, with all diligence of spirit. Put your   90
bonnet to his right use; 'tis for the head.

OSRIC   I thank your lordship, it is very hot.

HAMLET   No, believe me, 'tis very cold; the wind is northerly.

OSRIC   It is indifferent¹ cold, my lord, indeed.

HAMLET   But yet methinks it is very sultry and hot, or my complex-   95
ion—

OSRIC   Exceedingly, my lord; it is very sultry, as 'twere,—I cannot tell
how. But, my lord, his majesty bade me signify to you that he has
laid a great wager on your head: sir, this is the matter—

HAMLET   I beseech you, remember—   100
[HAMLET *moves him to put on his hat.*]

OSRIC   Nay, good my lord; for mine ease, in good faith. Sir, here is
newly come to court Laertes; believe me, an absolute gentleman, full
of most excellent differences, of very soft society and great showing:²
indeed, to speak feelingly of him, he is the card or calendar of gentry,³ for you shall find in him the continent of what part⁴   105
a gentleman would see.

HAMLET   Sir, his definement suffers no perdition in you; though, I
know, to divide him inventorially would dizzy the arithmetic⁵ of
memory, and yet but yaw neither, in respect of his quick sail.⁶ But
in the verity of extolment, I take him to be a soul of great article,   110
and his infusion⁷ of such dearth and rareness, as, to make true diction of him, his semblable is his mirror, and who else would trace
him, his umbrage,⁸ nothing more.

OSRIC   Your lordship speaks most infallibly of him.

HAMLET   The concernancy, sir? why do we wrap the gentleman⁹ in   115
our more rawer breath?

OSRIC   Sir?

HORATIO   Is 't not possible to understand in another tongue?¹ You will
do 't, sir, really.

HAMLET   What imports the nomination of this gentleman?   120

OSRIC   Of Laertes?

HORATIO   His purse is empty already; all's golden words are spent.

---

9. Jackdaw. *Mess:* table.   1. Fairly.   2. Agreeable company, handsome in appearance. *Differences:* distinctions.   3. Chart and model of gentlemanly manners.   4. Whatever quality. *Continent:* container.
5. Arithmetical power. *Definement:* definition. *Perdition:* loss. *Inventorially:* make an inventory of his virtues.   6. And yet would only be able to steer unsteadily (unable to catch up with the *sail* of Laertes's
virtues).   7. The virtues infused into him. *Verify of extolment:* to prize Laertes truthfully. *Article:* importance.   8. Keep pace with him, his shadow.   9. Lartes. *Concernancy:* meaning.   1. In a less affected
jargon or in the same jargon when spoken by another (that is, Hamlet's) tongue.

HAMLET Of him, sir.

OSRIC I know you are not ignorant—

HAMLET I would you did, sir; yet, in faith, if you did, it would not 125
much approve me.[2] Well, sir?

OSRIC You are not ignorant of what excellence Laertes is—

HAMLET I dare not confess that, lest I should compare with him in
excellence; but, to know a man well, were to know himself.[3]

OSRIC I mean, sir, for his weapon; but in the imputation laid on him 130
by them, in his meed he's unfellowed.[4]

HAMLET What's his weapon?

OSRIC Rapier and dagger.

HAMLET That's two of his weapons: but, well.

OSRIC The king, sir, hath wagered with him six Barbary horses: 135
against the which he has imponed, as I take it, six French rapiers
and poniards, with their assigns,[5] as girdle, hanger, and so: three of
the carriages, in faith, are very dear to fancy, very responsive[6] to the
hilts, most delicate carriages, and of very liberal conceit.[7]

HAMLET What call you the carriages? 140

HORATIO I knew you must be edified by the margent[8] ere you had
done.

OSRIC The carriages, sir, are the hangers.

HAMLET The phrase would be more germane to the matter if we could
carry a cannon by our sides:[9] I would it might be hangers till then. 145
But, on: six Barbary horses against six French swords, their assigns,
and three liberal-conceited carriages; that's the French bet against
the Danish. Why is this "imponed," as you call it?

OSRIC The king, sir, hath laid, sir, that in a dozen passes between
yourself and him, he shall not exceed you three hits: he hath laid 150
on twelve for nine; and it would come to immediate trial, if your
lordship would vouchsafe the answer.[1]

HAMLET How if I answer "no"?

OSRIC I mean, my lord, the opposition of your person in trial.

HAMLET Sir, I will walk here in the hall: if it please his majesty, it is 155
the breathing time[2] of day with me; let the foils be brought, the
gentleman willing, and the king hold his purpose, I will win for him
an I can; if not, I will gain nothing but my shame and the odd hits.

OSRIC Shall I redeliver you e'en so?[3]

HAMLET To this effect, sir, after what flourish your nature will. 160

OSRIC I commend my duty to your lordship.

HAMLET Yours, yours. [Exit OSRIC] He does well to commend it himself; there are no tongues else for's turn.

HORATIO This lapwing[4] runs away with the shell on his head.

HAMLET He did comply with his dug before he sucked it. Thus has 165
he—and many more of the same breed that I know the drossy[5] age

---

2. Be to my credit.   3. To know others one has to know oneself.   4. In the reputation given him by
his weapons, his merit is unparalleled.   5. Appendages. *Imponed*: wagered.   6. Closely matched. *Carriages*: ornamented straps by which the rapiers hung from the belt. *Very dear to fancy*: agreeable to the taste.
7. Elegant design.   8. Instructed by the marginal note.   9. Hamlet is playfully criticizing Osric's
affected application of the term *carriage*, more properly used to mean "gun carriage."   1. The terms of
this wager have never been satisfactorily clarified.   2. Time for exercise.   3. Is that the reply you want
me to carry back?   4. A bird supposedly able to run as soon as it is out of its shell.   5. Degenerate.
Comply: use ceremony.

dotes on—only got the tune of the time and outward habit of
encounter; a kind of yesty[6] collection, which carries them through
and through the most fond and winnowed opinions;[7] and do but blow
them to their trial, the bubbles are out.   170
            [*Enter a* LORD.]
LORD   My lord, his majesty commended him[8] to you by young Osric,
     who brings back to him, that you attend him in the hall: he sends to
     know if your pleasure hold to play with Laertes, or that you will take
     longer time.
HAMLET   I am constant to my purposes; they follow the king's pleasure: 175
     if his fitness speaks, mine is ready; now or whensoever, provided I
     be so able as now.
LORD   The king and queen and all are coming down.
HAMLET   In happy time.
LORD   The queen desires you to use some gentle entertainment[9] to   180
     Laertes before you fall to play.
HAMLET   She well instructs me.
            [*Exit* LORD.]
HORATIO   You will lose this wager, my lord.
HAMLET   I do not think so; since he went into France, I have been in
     continual practice; I shall win at the odds. But thou wouldst not   185
     think how ill all's here about my heart: but it is no matter.
HORATIO   Nay, good my lord,—
HAMLET   It is but foolery; but it is such a kind of gaingiving[1] as would
     perhaps trouble a woman.
HORATIO   If your mind dislike anything, obey it. I will forestall their   190
     repair[2] hither, and say you are not fit.
HAMLET   Not a whit; we defy augury: there is special providence in
     the fall of a sparrow. If it be now, 'tis not to come; if it be not to
     come, it will be now; if it be not now, yet it will come: the readiness
     is all; since no man has aught of what he leaves, what is't to leave   195
     betimes?[3] Let be.
            [*Enter* KING, QUEEN, LAERTES, *and* LORDS, OSRIC *and other* ATTENDANTS
            with foils and gauntlets; a table and flagons of wine on it.]
KING   Come, Hamlet, come, and take this hand from me.
            [*The* KING *puts* LAERTES's *hand into* HAMLET's.]
HAMLET   Give me your pardon, sir: I've done you wrong;
     But pardon't, as you are a gentleman.
     This presence[4] knows,   200
     And you must needs have heard, how I am punished
     With sore distraction. What I have done,
     That might your nature, honor and exception[5]
     Roughly awake, I here proclaim was madness.
     Was't Hamlet wronged Laertes? Never Hamlet: 205
     If Hamlet from himself be ta'en away,
     And when he's not himself does wrong Laertes,
     Then Hamlet does it not, Hamlet denies it.
     Who does it then? His madness: if't be so,

---

6. Frothy.   7. Makes them pass the test of the most refined judgment.   8. Sent his regards.
9. Kind word of greeting.   1. Misgiving.   2. Coming.   3. What is wrong with dying early (leaving
betimes), because man knows nothing of life (*what he leaves*)?   4. Audience.   5. Objection.

Hamlet is of the faction that is wronged; 210
His madness is poor Hamlet's enemy.
Sir, in this audience,
Let my disclaiming from a purposed evil
Free me so far in your most generous thoughts,
That I have shot mine arrow o'er the house, 215
And hurt my brother.

LAERTES   I am satisfied in nature,
Whose motive, in this case, should stir me most
To my revenge: but in my terms of honor[6]
I stand aloof, and will no reconcilement,
Till by some elder masters of known honor 220
I have a voice and precedent of peace,
To keep my name ungored.[7] But till that time
I do receive your offered love like love
And will not wrong it.

HAMLET   I embrace it freely,
And will this brother's wager frankly play. 225
Give us the foils. Come on.

LAERTES   Come, one for me.

HAMLET I'll be your foil,[8] Laertes: in mine ignorance
Your skill shall, like a star i' the darkest night,
Stick fiery off[9] indeed.

LAERTES   You mock me, sir.

HAMLET No, by this hand.

KING Give them the foils, young Osric. Cousin Hamlet, 230
You know the wager?

HAMLET   Very well, my lord;
Your grace has laid the odds o' the weaker side.

KING I do not fear it; I have seen you both:
But since he is bettered, we have therefore odds. 235

LAERTES This is too heavy; let me see another.

HAMLET This likes me well. These foils have all a length?
   [*They prepare to play.*]

OSRIC Aye, my good lord.

KING Set me the stoups[1] of wine upon that table.
If Hamlet give the first or second hit, 240
Or quit in answer of the third exchange,[2]
Let all the battlements their ordnance fire;
The king shall drink to Hamlet's better breath;
And in the cup an union[3] shall he throw,
Richer than that which four successive kings 245
In Denmark's crown have worn. Give me the cups;
And let the kettle[4] to the trumpet speak,
The trumpet to the cannoneer without,

---

6. Laertes answers separately each of the two points brought up by Hamlet in line 86. *Nature* is Laertes's natural feeling toward his father. *Honor* is the code of honor with its conventional rules. 7. Unwounded. *A voice and:* an opinion based on. 8. A pun, because *foil* means both "rapier" and "a thing that sets off another to advantage" (as gold leaf under a jewel). 9. Stand out brilliantly. 1. Cups. 2. Requite, or repay (by scoring a hit) on the third bout. 3. A large pearl. 4. Kettledrum.

The cannons to the heavens, the heaven to earth,
"Now the king drinks to Hamlet." Come, begin;   250
And you, the judges, bear a wary eye.
HAMLET   Come on, sir.
LAERTES   Come, my lord.
          [*They play.*]
HAMLET   One.
LAERTES   No.
HAMLET   Judgment.
OSRIC   A hit, a very palpable hit.
LAERTES   Well; again.
KING   Stay; give me drink. Hamlet, this pearl is thine;
  Here's to thy health.   255
          [*Trumpets sound, and cannon shot off within.*]
                        Give him the cup.
HAMLET   I'll play this bout first; set it by awhile.
  Come. [*They play.*] Another hit; what say you?
LAERTES   A touch, a touch, I do confess.
KING   Our son shall win.
QUEEN   He's fat and scant of breath.
  Here, Hamlet, take my napkin,[5] rub thy brows: 260
  The queen carouses to thy fortune, Hamlet.
HAMLET   Good madam!
KING   Gertrude, do not drink.
QUEEN   I will, my lord; I pray you, pardon me.
KING [*Aside.*]   It is the poisoned cup; it is too late.
QUEEN   Come, let me wipe thy face.   265
LAERTES   My lord, I'll hit him now.
KING   I do not think't.
LAERTES [*Aside.*]   And yet it is almost against my conscience.
HAMLET   Come, for the third, Laertes: you but dally;
  I pray you, pass with your best violence;
  I am afeard you make a wanton[6] of me.   270
LAERTES   Say you so? come on.
          [*They play.*]
OSRIC   Nothing, neither way.
LAERTES   Have at you now!
          [LAERTES *wounds* HAMLET; *then, in scuffling, they change rapiers, and*
          HAMLET *wounds* LAERTES.]
KING   Part them; they are incensed.
HAMLET   Nay, come, again.
          [*The* QUEEN *falls.*]
OSRIC   Look to the queen there, ho!
HORATIO   They bleed on both sides. How is it, my lord?   275
OSRIC   How is't, Laertes?
LAERTES   Why, as a woodcock to mine own springe,[7] Osric;
  I am justly killed with mine own treachery.
HAMLET   How does the queen?

---

5. Handkerchief. *Fat:* sweaty, or soft, because out of training.   6. Weakling, spoiled child.   7. Snare.

KING   She swounds to see them bleed.   280

QUEEN   No, no, the drink, the drink,—O my dear Hamlet,—
    The drink, the drink! I am poisoned.
        [*Dies.*]

HAMLET   O villainy! Ho! let the door be locked:
    Treachery! seek it out.
        [LAERTES *falls.*]

LAERTES   It is here, Hamlet: Hamlet, thou art slain;   285
    No medicine in the world can do thee good,
    In thee there is not half an hour of life;
    The treacherous instrument is in thy hand,
    Unbated and envenomed: the foul practice[8]
    Hath turned itself on me; lo, here I lie,   290
    Never to rise again: thy mother's poisoned:
    I can no more: the king, the king's to blame.

HAMLET   The point envenomed too!
    Then, venom, to thy work.
        [*Stabs the* KING.]

ALL   Treason! treason!   295

KING   O, yet defend me, friends; I am but hurt.

HAMLET   Here, thou incestuous, murderous, damnèd Dane,
    Drink off this potion: is thy union here?
    Follow my mother.
        [KING *dies.*]

LAERTES   He is justly served;
    It is a poison tempered[9] by himself.   300
    Exchange forgiveness with me, noble Hamlet:
    Mine and my father's death come not upon thee,
    Nor thine on me!
        [*Dies.*]

HAMLET   Heaven make thee free of it! I follow thee.
    I am dead, Horatio. Wretched queen, adieu!   305
    You that look pale and tremble at this chance,
    That are but mutes or audience to this act,
    Had I but time—as this fell sergeant, death,
    Is strict in his arrest—O, I could tell you—
    But let it be. Horatio, I am dead;   310
    Thou livest; report me and my cause aright
    To the unsatisfied.

HORATIO   Never believe it:
    I am more an antique Roman than a Dane:
    Here's yet some liquor left.

HAMLET   As thou'rt a man,
    Give me the cup: let go; by heaven, I'll have 't.   315
    O good Horatio, what a wounded name,
    Things standing thus unknown, shall live behind me!
    If thou didst ever hold me in thy heart,
    Absent thee from felicity a while,

---

8. Plot.   9. Compounded.

And in this harsh world draw thy breath in pain, 320
To tell my story.
　　　[*March afar off, and shot within.*]
　　　　　What warlike noise is this?
OSRIC　Young Fortinbras, with conquest come from Poland,
　To the ambassadors of England gives
　This warlike volley.
HAMLET　　　　　　O, I die, Horatio;
　The potent poison quite o'er-crows[1] my spirit: 325
　I cannot live to hear the news from England;
　But I do prophesy the election lights
　On Fortinbras: he has my dying voice;
　So tell him, with the occurrents, more and less,
　Which have solicited.[2] The rest is silence. 330
　　　[*Dies.*]
HORATIO　Now cracks a noble heart. Good night sweet prince,
　And flights of angels sing thee to thy rest;
　　　[*March within.*]
　Why does the drum come hither?
　　　[*Enter* FORTINBRAS, *and the* ENGLISH AMBASSADORS, *with drum, colors,*
　　　and ATTENDANTS.]
FORTINBRAS　Where is this sight?
HORATIO　　　　　　　　What is it you would see?
　If aught of woe or wonder, cease your search. 335
FORTINBRAS　This quarry cries on havoc.[3] O proud death,
　What feast is toward[4] in thine eternal cell,
　That thou so many princes at a shot
　So bloodily hast struck?
FIRST AMBASSADOR　　　　The sight is dismal;
　And our affairs from England come too late: 340
　The ears are senseless that should give us hearing,
　To tell him his commandment is fulfilled,
　That Rosencrantz and Guildenstern are dead:
　Where should we have our thanks?
HORATIO　　　　　　　　Not from his mouth
　Had it the ability of life to thank you: 345
　He never gave commandment for their death.
　But since, so jump upon[5] this bloody question,
　You from the Polack wars, and you from England
　Are here arrived, give order that these bodies
　High on a stage be placèd to the view; 350
　And let me speak to the yet unknowing world
　How these things came about; so shall you hear
　Of carnal, bloody and unnatural acts,
　Of accidental judgments, casual slaughters,
　Of deaths put on[6] by cunning and forced cause, 355
　And, in this upshot, purposes mistook

---

1. Overcomes. 　2. Which have brought all this about. *Occurrents:* occurrences. 　3. This heap of
corpses proclaims a carnage. 　4. Imminent. 　5. So immediately on. 　6. Prompted. *Casual:* chance.

Fall'n on the inventors' heads: all this can I
Truly deliver.
FORTINBRAS   Let us haste to hear it,
And call the noblest to the audience.
For me, with sorrow I embrace my fortune: 360
I have some rights of memory in this kingdom,
Which now to claim my vantage[7] doth invite me.
HORATIO   Of that I shall have also cause to speak,
And from his mouth whose voice will draw on more:[8]
But let this same be presently performed,   365
Even while men's minds are wild; lest more mischance
On[9] plots and errors happen.
FORTINBRAS   Let four captains
Bear Hamlet, like a soldier, to the stage;
For he was likely, had he been put on,[1]   370
To have proved most royal: and, for his passage,[2]
The soldiers' music and the rites of war
Speak loudly for him.
Take up the bodies: such a sight as this
Becomes the field, but here shows much amiss.   375
Go, bid the soldiers shoot.
        [*A dead march. Exeunt, bearing off the bodies: after which a peal of
        ordnance is shot off.*]

---

7. Advantageous position, opportunity. *Have some rights of memory:* am still remembered.   8. More
voices.   9. Following on.   1. Tried (as a king).   2. Death.

TRAVEL AND DISCOVERY

The Renaissance idea of travel in many ways begins in fiction and moves toward fact, both in the realm of geography and in that of narrative. The first text presented here is the late-medieval *Travels of Sir John Mandeville*, a fanciful narrative filled with curiosities on the order of *Ripley's Believe It or Not!* Medieval Europeans had a passion for pilgrimage to holy sites that developed into a profound curiosity about foreign peoples and places—the more exotic, the better. In this anonymously written book the elaborate inventory of people with strange bodies and customs creates, by implication, a strong sense of European norms. Running alongside the delight taken in novelty is a deep certainty about the proper and normal orientation of the world.

The travel narratives describing actual encounters with new people and places, however, suggest an experience of admiration and wonder of another order. Christopher Columbus's account of his first voyage to the Indies, for example, describes Hispaniola (modern-day Haiti and the Dominican Republic) as "a marvel." Its physical beauty is astonishing and thus counts as an appropriate staging ground of the first, equally astonishing, meeting between the natives and the explorers traveling under Columbus's command. Both the "brave new world" (in Shakespeare's phrase) and the people in it produce in the European explorers a sense that reality has been decisively altered and can never revert to older, familiar ways. Europe, with its traditions rooted in the medieval and ancient eras, seems almost magically transformed into the Old

World by its encounter with the New World. The mood of Columbus's letter on his first voyage is infused with wonder, admiration, and doubt: the new world's beauty and difference inspire awe in the European sailors as well as uncertainty about its significance. Is there any just comparison of the Western Hemisphere and the Eastern one? The line between the familiar and the foreign emerges, in Columbus's account, as excitingly blurry.

The conquest narratives of Hernán Cortés and Bernal Díaz del Castillo contain little, if any, of the marvel experienced and described by the fictional traveler, Mandeville, or the historical explorer, Columbus. Their accounts of reconnaissance missions, marches, councils, and armed conflict are rooted less in travel literature than in military history and epic poetry. The eye that the soldiers turn on the artifacts and buildings of Mexico is that of the experienced merchant (who can evaluate at a glance the European monetary equivalent of a piece of golden artwork) and conqueror (who assesses the prize and its worth, once divided among the various claimants). There is, to be sure, a sense of strong admiration for the city and institutions of the Aztecs; but unlike Columbus, both Cortés and Díaz del Castillo are obligated to moderate their aesthetic and spiritual engagement with the civilization they must be prepared to destroy. One can sense, beneath the flat surface of the conquest narratives, the constant moral and economic accounting that goes on in the minds of the conquerors. It is harder, for example, for Díaz del Castillo to admire the city and people he helped to conquer than "our Cortés," who single-handedly recovered a fortress from the attacking Aztecs, or the "Hectors" and "Rolands" among the common soldiers from Spain.

The moral question hovering over the conquest of the New World becomes paramount with Bartholomé de las Casas, who composed his histories to shock Europe and spur the Spanish king to implementing reforms in the colonizing mission. For las Casas, the marvels of the New World have been utterly destroyed by the colonists, who have forfeited spiritual wonder of the sort felt by Columbus for land, gold, and slaves. Inspired by a biblical text, he writes as a "voice from the wilderness," but a wilderness created, not found, by the Spanish. The idea of liberation theology in many ways goes as far back as the discovery of the New World.

In all modes of exploration—discovery, conquest, and defense or self-critique—Renaissance Europeans staged an encounter with their own ethical convictions about what it means to be human in an ever-changing world.

SIR JOHN MANDEVILLE
flourished 1356

The *Travels of Sir John Mandeville* are both anonymously written and fictitious. Yet the book was enormously influential on the early European conception of the world and especially the East. First printed in England in 1499, the book was soon translated into many European languages, including Czech, Danish, Dutch, French, German, Italian, and Spanish, as well as Latin. Mandeville's *Travels*, in fact, set the template for the first-hand and supposedly authentic accounts of travel in Asia, Africa, and the New World. It has consequently achieved the status of the "father of lies," or the authority on fabulous narration in geography and ethnography.

From The Travels of Sir John Mandeville

* * *

Beside the land of Chaldea is the land of Amazonia, that is the land of Feminye. And in that realm is all women and no man; not, as some men say, that men may not live there, but for because that the women will not suffer no men among them to be their sovereigns.

For sometime there was a king in that country. And men married, as in other countries. And so befell that the king had war with them of Scythia, the which king hight Colopeus, that was slain in battle, and all the good blood of his realm. And when the queen and all the other noble ladies saw that they were all widows, and that all the royal blood was lost, they armed them and, as creatures out of wit, they slew all the men of the country that were left; for they would that all the women were widows as the queen and they were. And from that time hitherward they never would suffer man to dwell among them longer than seven days and seven nights; ne[1] that no child that were male should dwell among them longer than he were nourished; and then sent to his father. And when they will have any company of man then they draw them toward the lands marching next to them. And then they have loves that use them; and they dwell with them an eight days or ten, and then go home again. And if they have any knave[2] child they keep it a certain time, and then send it to the father when he can go alone and eat by himself; or else they slay it. And if it be a female they do away that one pap[3] with an hot iron. And if it be a woman of great lineage they do away the left pap that they may the better bear a shield. And if it be a woman on foot they do away the right pap, for to shoot with bow turkeys: for they shoot well with bows.

In that land they have a queen that governeth all that land, and all they be obeissant to her. And always they make her queen by election that is most worthy in arms; for they be right good warriors and orped,[4] and wise, noble, and worthy. And they go oftentime in solde[5] to help of other kings in their wars, for gold and silver as other soldiers do; and they maintain themselves right vigorously. This land of Amazonia is an isle, all environed with the sea save in two places, where be two entries. And beyond that water dwell the men that be their paramours and their loves, where they go to solace them when they will.

Beside Amazonia is the land of Tarmegyte that is a great country and a full delectable. And for the goodness of the country King Alexander let first make there the city of Alexandria, and yet he made twelve cities of the same name; but that city is now clept[6] Celsite.

And from that other coast of Chaldea, toward the south, is Ethiopia, a great country that stretcheth to the end of Egypt. Ethiopia is departed in two parts principal, and that is in the east part and in the meridional part; the which part meridional is clept Mauritania; and the folk of that country be black enough and more black than in the tother part, and they be clept Moors. In that part is a well, that in the day it is so cold, that no man may drink thereof; and in the night it is so hot, that no man may suffer his hand therein. And beyond that part, toward the south, to pass by the sea Ocean, is a great land and a great country; but men may not dwell there for

---

1. Nor.   2. Male.   3. Breast.   4. Valiant, bold.   5. Pay.   6. Called, named.

the fervent burning of the sun, so is it passing hot in that country.

In Ethiopia all the rivers and all the waters be trouble,[7] and they be some-deal[8] salt for the great heat that is there. And the folk of that country be lightly drunken and have but little appetite to meat. And they have commonly the flux of the womb. And they live not long. In Ethiopia be many diverse folk; and Ethiope is clept Cusis. In that country be folk that have but one foot, and they go so blyve[9] that it is marvel. And the foot is so large, that it shadoweth all the body against the sun, when they will lie and rest them. In Ethiopia, when the children be young and little, they be all yellow; and, when that they wax of age, that yellowness turneth to be all black. In Ethiopia is the city of Saba, and the land of the which one of the three kings that presented our Lord in Bethlehem, was king of.

*   *   *

In that isle [of Dondun] be folk of diverse kinds, so that the father eateth the son, the son the father, the husband the wife, and the wife the husband. And if it so befall, that the father or mother or any of their friends be sick, anon the son goeth to the priest of their law and prayeth him to ask the idol if his father or mother or friend shall die on that evil or not. And then the priest and the son go together before the idol and kneel full devoutly and ask of the idol their demand. And if the devil that is within answer that he shall live, they keep him well; and if he say that he shall die, then the priest goeth with the son, with the wife of him that is sick, and they put their hands upon his mouth and stop his breath, and so they slay him. And after that, they chop all the body in small pieces, and pray all his friends to come and eat of him that is dead. And they send for all the minstrels of the country and make a solemn feast. And when they have eaten the flesh, they take the bones and bury them, and sing and make great melody. And all those that be of his kin or pretend them to be his friends, an they come not to that feast, they be reproved for evermore and shamed, and make great dole,[1] for never after shall they be holden as friends. And they say also, that men eat their flesh for to deliver them out of pain; for if the worms of the earth eat them the soul should suffer great pain, as they say. And namely when the flesh is tender and meager, then say their friends, that they do great sin to let them have so long langor to suffer so much pain without reason. And when they find the flesh fat, then they say, that it is well done to send them soon to Paradise, and that they have not suffered him too long to endure in pain.

The king of this isle is a full great lord and a mighty, and hath under him fifty-four great isles that give tribute to him. And in everych;[2] of these isles is a king crowned; and all be obeissant to that king. And he hath in those isles many diverse folk.

In one of these isles be folk of great stature, as giants. And they be hideous for to look upon. And they have but one eye, and that is in the middle of the front. And they eat nothing but raw flesh and raw fish.

And in another isle toward the south dwell folk of foul stature and of cursed kind that have no heads. And their eyen[3] be in their shoulders.

And in another isle be folk that have the face all flat, all plain, without nose and without mouth. But they have two small holes, all round, instead of their eyes, and their mouth is plat also without lips.

7. Troublesome. 8. Somewhat. 9. Swift. 1. Sorrow. 2. Everyone. 3. Eyes.

And in another isle be folk of foul fashion and shape that have the lip above the mouth so great, that when they sleep in the sun they cover all the face with that lip.

And in another isle there be little folk, as dwarfs. And they be two so much as the pigmies. And they have no mouth; but instead of their mouth they have a little round hole, and when they shall eat or drink, they take through a pipe or a pen or such a thing, and suck it in, for they have no tongue; and therefore they speak not, but they make a manner of hissing as an adder doth, and they make signs one to another as monks do, by the which every of them understandeth other.

And in another isle be folk that have great ears and long, that hang down to their knees.

And in another isle be folk that have horses' feet. And they be strong and mighty, and swift runners; for they take wild beasts with running, and eat them.

And in another isle be folk that go upon their hands and their feet as beasts. And they be all skinned and feathered, and they will leap as lightly into trees, and from tree to tree, as it were squirrels or apes.

And in another isle be folk that be both man and woman, and they have kind of that one and of that other. And they have but one pap on the one side, and on that other none. And they have members of generation of man and woman, and they use both when they list, once that one, and another time that other. And they get children, when they use the member of man; and they bear children, when they use the member of woman.

And in another isle be folk that go always upon their knees full marvelously. And at every pace that they go, it seemeth that they would fall. And they have in every foot eight toes.

Many other diverse folk of diverse natures be there in other isles about, of the which it were too long to tell, and therefore I pass over shortly.

* * *

CHRISTOPHER COLUMBUS
ca. 1450–1506

Of the discovery of America, a sixteenth-century historian (Francisco Lopez de Gomara) famously declared it was the greatest event since the creation of the world other than the incarnation and death of God, who created it. Although earlier navigators and geographers of the Renaissance speculated on the probability of land in the Western Hemisphere, it was Christopher Columbus who transformed the theory into established fact. Born in Italy and most likely in Genoa, Columbus became a sailor and, after considerable experience on the Mediterranean and Atlantic oceans, he established himself also as a navigator and map-maker. While most thinkers of his day agreed that the earth was spherical, there was considerable disagreement over the globe's size and the habitability of its various zones. Columbus used his own geographical theories, along with his conviction that he was led by providence to persuade the Spanish king Ferdinand and Queen Isabella to fund his expedition to the Indies in 1492.

In Hispaniola (present-day Haiti and the Dominican Republic), he found what seemed to him an earthly paradise, filled with an inexhaustible variety of flowering and fruit-bearing trees, large tracts of arable land, and honey, along with gentle and welcoming natives, who denied him nothing. Hispaniola, he wrote in his record of his first voyage, "is a marvel." His later voyages proved less idyllic, due to hostilities of some native tribes and increasing opposition from rivals in Spain, who sought to alienate the affections of the Spanish kings from Columbus, whom they portrayed as an inept administrator. The exact significance of his legacy was questioned in his own day and has been debated ever since. What follows is the letter he wrote to an unknown recipient about his first voyage.

[Letter Concerning the First Voyage][1]

Sir: As I know that you will have pleasure from the great victory which our Lord hath given me in my voyage, I write you this, by which you shall know that in thirty-three days I passed over to the Indies with the fleet which the most illustrious King and Queen, our Lords, gave me; where I found very many islands peopled with inhabitants beyond number. And, of them all, I have taken possession for their Highnesses, with proclamation and the royal standard displayed; and I was not gainsaid. To the first which I found, I gave the name Sant Salvador, in commemoration of His High Majesty, who marvellously hath given all this: the Indians call it Guanaham. The second I named the Island of Santa Maria de Concepcion, the third Ferrandina, the fourth, Fair Island, the fifth La Isla Juana; and so for each one a new name. When I reached Juana, I followed its coast westwardly, and found it so large that I thought it might be mainland, the province of Cathay. And as I did not thus find any towns and villages on the sea-coast, save small hamlets with the people whereof I could not get speech, because they all fled away forthwith, I went on further in the same direction, thinking I should not miss of great cities or towns. And at the end of many leagues, seeing that there was no change, and that the coast was bearing me northwards, whereunto my desire was contrary, since the winter was already confronting us, I formed the purpose of making from thence to the South, and as the wind also blew against me, I determined not to wait for other weather and turned back as far as a port agreed upon; from which I sent two men into the country to learn if there were a king, or any great cities. They traveled for three days, and found innumerable small villages and a numberless population, but nought of ruling authority; wherefore they returned. I understood sufficiently from other Indians whom I had already taken, that this land, in its continuousness, was an island; and so I followed its coast eastwardly for a hundred and seven leagues as far as where it terminated; from which headland I saw another island to the east, eighteen leagues distant from this, to which I at once gave the name La Spañola. And I proceeded thither, and followed the northern coast, as with La Juana, eastwardly for a hundred and eighty-eight great leagues in a direct easterly course, as with La Juana. The which, and all the others, are most fertile to an excessive degree, and this extremely so. In it, there are many havens on the sea-coast, incomparable with any others

1. Translated by Sir Clements R. Markham.

that I know in Christendom, and plenty of rivers so good and great that it is a marvel. The lands thereof are high, and in it are very many ranges of hills, and most lofty mountains incomparably beyond the island of Tenerife, all most beautiful in a thousand shapes, and all accessible, and full of trees of a thousand kinds, so lofty that they seem to reach the sky. And I am assured that they never lose their foliage; as may be imagined, since I saw them as green and as beautiful as they are in Spain during May. And some of them were in flower, some in fruit, some in another stage according to their kind. And the nightingale was singing, and other birds of a thousand sorts, in the month of November, there where I was going. There are palm-trees of six or eight species, wondrous to see for their beautiful variety; but so are the other trees, and fruits, and plants therein. There are wonderful pine-groves, and very large plains of verdure, and there is honey, and many kinds of birds, and many various fruits. In the earth there are many mines of metals; and there is a population of incalculable number. Española is a marvel; the mountains and hills, and plains, and fields, and the soil, so beautiful and rich for planting and sowing, for breeding cattle of all sorts, for building of towns and villages. There could be no believing, without seeing, such harbors as are here, as well as the many and great rivers, and excellent waters, most of which contain gold. In the trees and fruits and plants, there are great diversities from those of Juana. In this, there are many spiceries, and great mines of gold and other metals. The people of this island, and of all the others that I have found and seen, or not seen, all go naked, men and women, just as their mothers bring them forth; although some women cover a single place with the leaf of a plant, or a cotton something which they make for that purpose. They have no iron or steel, nor any weapons; nor are they fit thereunto; not because they be not a well-formed people and of fair stature, but that they are most wondrously timorous. They have no other weapons than the stems of reeds in their seeding state, on the end of which they fix little sharpened stakes. Even these, they dare not use; for many times has it happened that I sent two or three men ashore to some village to parley, and countless numbers of them sallied forth, but as soon as they saw those approach, they fled away in such wise that even a father would not wait for his son. And this was not because any hurt had ever been done to any of them:—on the contrary, at every headland where I have gone and been able to hold speech with them, I gave them of everything which I had, as well cloth as many other things, without accepting aught therefore;—but such they are, incurably timid. It is true that since they have become more assured, and are losing that terror, they are artless and generous with what they have, to such a degree as no one would believe but him who had seen it. Of anything they have, if it be asked for, they never say no, but do rather invite the person to accept it, and show as much lovingness as though they would give their hearts. And whether it be a thing of value, or one of little worth, they are straightway content with whatsoever trifle of whatsoever kind may be given them in return for it. I forbade that anything so worthless as fragments of broken platters, and pieces of broken glass, and strap buckles, should be given them; although when they were able to get such things, they seemed to think they had the best jewel in the world, for it was the hap of a sailor to get, in exchange for a strap, gold to the weight of two and a half castellanos, and others much more for other things of far less value; while for new blancas they gave everything they had, even though it were [the worth of] two or three gold castellanos, or one or two arrobas of spun cotton. They took even pieces of broken barrel-hoops, and gave whatever they had, like senseless brutes; insomuch that it seemed to me bad. I forbade it, and I gave gratuitously a thousand useful things that I carried, in order that they may conceive affection, and furthermore may become Christians; for they are inclined to the love and service of their Highnesses and of all the Castilian nation, and they strive to combine in giving us things which they have in abundance, and of which we are in need. And they knew no sect, nor idolatry; save that they all believe that power and goodness are in the sky, and they believed very firmly that I, with these ships and crews, came from the sky; and in such opinion, they received me at every place where I landed, after they had lost their terror. And this comes not because they are ignorant: on the contrary, they are men of very subtle wit, who navigate all those seas, and who give a marvelously good account of everything, but because they never saw men wearing clothes nor the like of our ships. And as soon as I arrived in the Indies, in the first island that I found, I took some of them by force, to the intent that they should learn [our speech] and give me information of what there was in those parts. And so it was, that very soon they understood [us] and we them, what by speech or what by signs; and those [Indians] have been of much service. To this day I carry them [with me] who are still of the opinion that I come from Heaven [as appears] from much conversation which they have had with me. And they were the first to proclaim it wherever I arrived; and the others went running from house to house and to the neighboring villages, with loud cries of "Come! come to see the people from Heaven!" Then, as soon as their minds were reassured about us, every one came, men as well as women, so that there remained none behind, big or little; and they all brought something to eat and drink, which they gave with wondrous lovingness. They have in all the islands very many *canoas*, after the manner of rowing-galleys, some larger, some smaller; and a good many are larger than a galley of eighteen benches. They are not so wide, because they are made of a single log of timber, but a galley could not keep up with them in rowing, for their motion is a thing beyond belief. And with these, they navigate through all those islands, which are numberless, and ply their traffic. I have seen some of those *canoas* with seventy and eighty men in them, each one with his oar. In all those islands, I saw not much diversity in the looks of the people, nor in their manners and language; but they all understand each other, which is a thing of singular advantage for what I hope their Highnesses will decide upon for converting them to our holy faith, unto which they are well disposed. I have already told how I had gone a hundred and seven leagues, in a straight line from West to East, along the sea-coast of the Island of Juana; according to which itinerary, I can declare that that island is larger than England and Scotland combined; as, over and above those hundred and seven leagues, there remain for me, on the western side, two provinces whereto I did not go—one of which they call Avan, where the people are born with tails—which provinces cannot be less in length than fifty or sixty leagues, according to what may be understood from the Indians with me, who know all the islands. This other, Española, has a greater circumference than the whole of Spain from Col[ibre in Catal]unya, by the sea-coast, as far as Fuente Ravia in Biscay; since, along one of its four sides, I went for a hundred and eighty-eight great leagues in a straight line from west to east. This is [a land] to be desired,—and once seen, never to be relinquished—in which (although, indeed, I have taken possession of them all for their Highnesses, and all are more richly endowed than I have skill and power to say, and I hold them all in the name of their Highnesses who can dispose thereof as much and as completely as of the kingdoms of Castile) in this Española, in the place most suitable and best for its proximity to the gold mines, and for traffic with the mainland both on this side and with that over there belonging to the Great Can, where there will be great commerce and profit, I took possession of a large town which I named the city of Navidad. And I have made fortification there, and a fort (which by this time will have been completely finished) and I have left therein men enough for such a purpose, with arms and artillery, and provisions for more than a year, and a boat, and a [man who is] master of all seacraft for making others; and great friendship with the king of that land, to such a degree that he prided himself on calling and holding me as his brother. And even though his mind might change towards attacking those men, neither he nor his people know what arms are, and go naked. As I have already said, they are the most timorous creatures there are in the world, so that the men who remain there are alone sufficient to destroy all that land, and the island is without personal danger for them if they know how to behave themselves. It seems to me that in all those islands, the men are all content with a single wife; and to their chief or king they give as many as twenty. The women, it appears to me, do more work than the men. Nor have I been able to learn whether they held personal property, for it seemed to me that whatever one had, they all took share of, especially of eatable things. Down to the present, I have not found in those islands any monstrous men, as many expected, but on the contrary all the people are very comely; nor are they black like those in Guinea, but have flowing hair; and they are not begotten where there is an excessive violence of the rays of the sun. It is true that the sun is there very strong, although it is twenty-six degrees distant from the equinoctial line. In those islands, where there are lofty mountains, the cold was very keen there, this winter; but they endure it by being accustomed thereto, and by the help of the meats which they eat with many and inordinately hot spices. Thus I have not found, nor had any information of monsters, except of an island which is here the second in the approach to the Indies, which is inhabited by a people whom, in all the islands, they regard as very ferocious, who eat human flesh. These have many canoes with which they run through all the islands of India, and plunder and take as much as they can. They are no more ill-shapen than the others, but have the custom of wearing their hair long, like women; and they use bows and arrows of the same reed stems, with a point of wood at the top, for lack of iron which they have not. Among those other tribes who are excessively cowardly, these are ferocious; but I hold them as nothing more than the others. These are they who have to do with the women of Matinino—which is the first island that is encountered in the passage from Spain to the Indies—in which there are no men. Those women practise no female usages, but have bows and arrows of reed such as above mentioned; and they arm and cover themselves with plates of copper of which they have much. In another island, which they assure me is larger than Española, the people have no hair. In this there is incalculable gold; and concerning these and the rest I bring Indians with me as witnesses. And in conclusion, to speak only of what has been done in this voyage, which has been so hastily performed, their Highnesses may see that I shall give them as much gold as they may need, with very little aid which their Highnesses will give me; spices and cotton at once, as much as their Highnesses will order to be shipped, and as much as they shall order to be shipped of mastic,—which till now has never been found except in Greece, in the island of Xio, and the Seignory sells it for what it likes; and aloe-wood as much as they shall order to be shipped; and slaves as many as they shall order to be shipped,—and these shall be from idolators. And I believe that I have discovered rhubarb and cinnamon, and I shall find that the men whom I am leaving there will have discovered a thousand other things of value; as I made no delay at any point, so long as the wind gave me an opportunity of sailing, except only in the town of Navidad till I had left things safely arranged and well established. And in truth I should have done much more if the ships had served me as well as might reasonably have been expected. This is enough; and [thanks to] Eternal God our Lord who gives to all those who walk His way, victory over things which seem impossible; and this was signally one such, for although men have talked or written of those lands, it was all by conjecture, without confirmation from eyesight, amounting only to this much that the hearers for the most part listened and judged that there was more fable in it than anything actual, however trifling. Since thus our Redeemer has given to our most illustrious King and Queen, and to their famous kingdoms, this victory in so high a matter, Christendom should have rejoicing therein and make great festivals, and give solemn thanks to the Holy Trinity for the great exaltation they shall have by the conversion of so many peoples to our holy faith; and next for the temporal benefit which will bring hither refreshment and profit, not only to Spain, but to all Christians. This briefly, in accordance with the facts. Dated, on the caravel, off the Canary Islands, the 15 February of the year 1493.

> At your command,
>
> THE ADMIRAL.

HERNÁN CORTÉS
1485–1547

The heroism and brutality of conquest are the main themes of the life of Hernán Cortés. From his early years, he had determined to make his fortune in the New World and set sail for the West Indies at the age of nineteen. Once there, he attracted the notice of Governor Diego Velasquez, who gave Cortés a military command in his push to conquer Cuba. Velasquez again considered Cortés for the command of an expedition to Yucatán and, according to one account, Cortés secretly loaded the ships and debarked before the governor could change his mind about sending so ambitious and independent a man on a trading mission. Cortés certainly regarded this expedition as an opportunity to break away from the authority of Velasquez, redefine his mission from trade to conquest, and place himself directly under the Spanish king. He arranged for his own election as chief administrative officer, made plans to conquer and settle Mexico, and ordered his ships burned so that no early return was possible.

In five letters written to Charles V, Cortés provides accounts of his diplomatic and military encounters with native tribes together with inventories of the wealth he accrued for the Crown. His most memorable records concern his extensive negotiations with the Aztecs, which concluded in the death of their king, Moctezuma, and the destruction of their chief city, Tenochtitlán. Other accounts of the conquest of Mexico differ in emphasis, detail, and especially the distribution of credit for the astonishing success of Cortés's slender military resources against the massive and well-organized Aztec Empire. The soldier Bernal Díaz del Castillo, for example, emphasizes the role played by the officers in making important decisions and the strategic advice given by their interpreters, Aguilar and the native woman called La Malinche by the natives and Doña Marina by the Spanish Christians. By contrast, Cortés's letters to the king place the focus on himself as a wise leader and military hero. Yet he carefully avoids any hint of bravado or dramatic flourish, preferring instead to let his shrewd judgment and personal bravery emerge from an understated narrative of events.

Religion, too, plays a powerful and complex role in Cortés's effort to legitimize his military actions and the authority he had already claimed for himself in Mexico. He emphasizes his efforts to convert the natives to Christianity and suggests to both Moctezuma and Charles V that the Aztecs met their downfall because they refused to give up their devotion to their local gods. In Cortés's account, certain religious and sexual practices (human sacrifice and sodomy) of the Aztecs become mandates for the conquest. Finally, the Aztecs' belief that the Spanish conquerors were their ancestral gods proves useful to Cortés in more ways than one. Cortés neither accepts nor denies the position of the white or light-complexioned god who was expected, according to Aztec prophecy, to return to Mexico from the east. The prophecy acts, in his narrative account of the events, both as proof of the Aztecs' idolatry and as sanction for the Spanish conquest of Mexico.

From The Second Letter[1]

On the following day I set out again and after half a mile entered upon a causeway which crosses the middle of the lake arriving finally at the great city of Tenochtitlan[2] which is situated at its center. This causeway was as broad as two lances and very stoutly made such that eight horsemen could ride along it abreast, and in these two leagues either on the one hand or the other we met with three cities all containing very fine buildings and towers, especially the houses of the chief men and the mosques and little temples in which they keep their idols. In these towns there is quite a brisk trade in salt which they make from the water of the lake and what is cast up on the land that borders it; this they cook in a certain manner and make the salt into cakes which they sell to the inhabitants and neighboring tribes. I accordingly proceeded along this causeway and half a league from the city of Tenochtitlan itself, at the point where another causeway from the mainland joins it, I came upon an extremely powerful fort with two towers, surrounded by a six foot wall with a battlement running round the whole of the side abutting on the two causeways, and having two gates and no more for going in and out. Here nearly a thousand of the chief citizens came out to greet me, all dressed alike and, as their custom is, very richly; on coming to speak with me each performed a ceremony very common among them, to wit, placing his hand on the ground and then kissing it, so that for nearly an hour I stood while they performed this ceremony. Now quite close to the city there is a

---

1. Translated by J. Bayard Morris.   2. The capital of the Aztec Empire, site of present-day Mexico City.

wooden bridge some ten paces broad, which cuts the causeway and under which the water can flow freely, for its level in the two parts of the lake is constantly changing: moreover it serves as a fortification to the city, for they can remove certain very long and heavy beams which form the bridge whenever they so desire; and there are many such bridges throughout the city as your Majesty will see from that which I shall presently relate.

When we had passed this bridge Muteczuma himself came out to meet us with some two hundred nobles, all barefoot and dressed in some kind of uniform also very rich, in fact more so than the others. They came forward in two long lines keeping close to the walls of the street, which is very broad and fine and so straight that one can see from one end of it to the other, though it is some two-thirds of a league in length and lined on both sides with very beautiful, large houses, both private dwellings and temples. Muteczuma himself was borne along in the middle of the street with two lords one on his right hand and one on his left. * * * All three were dressed in similar fashion except that Muteczuma wore shoes whereas the others were barefoot. The two lords bore him along each by an arm, and as he drew near I dismounted and advanced alone to embrace, but the two lords prevented me from touching him, and they themselves made me the same obeisance as did their comrades, kissing the earth. * * * After he had spoken to me all the other lords who were in the two long lines came up likewise in order one after the other, and then re-formed in line again. And while speaking to Muteczuma I took off a necklace of pearls which I was wearing and threw it round his neck; whereupon having proceeded some little way up the street a servant of his came back to me with two necklaces wrapped up in a napkin, made from the shells of sea snails, which are much prized by them; and from each necklace hung eight prawns fashioned very beautifully in gold some six inches in length. The messenger who brought them put them round my neck and we then continued up the street in the manner described until we came to a large and very handsome house which Muteczuma had prepared for our lodging. There he took me by the hand and led me to a large room opposite the patio by which we had entered, and seating me on a daïs very richly worked, for it was intended for royal use, he bade me await him there, and took his departure. After a short time, when all my company had found lodging, he returned with many various ornaments of gold, silver and featherwork, and some five or six thousand cotton clothes, richly dyed and embroidered in various ways, and having made me a present of them he seated himself on another low bench which was placed next to mine, and addressed me in this manner:

"Long time have we been informed by the writings of our ancestors that neither myself nor any of those who inhabit this land are natives of it, but rather strangers who have come to it from foreign parts. We likewise know that from those parts our nation was led by a certain lord (to whom all were subject), and who then went back to his native land, where he remained so long delaying his return that at his coming those whom he had left had married the women of the land and had many children by them and had built themselves cities in which they lived, so that they would in no wise return to their own land nor acknowledge him as lord; upon which he left them. And we have always believed that among his descendants one would surely come to subject this land and us as rightful vassals. Now seeing the regions from which you say you come, which is from where the sun rises, and the news you tell of this great king and ruler who sent you hither, we believe and hold it certain that he is our natural lord: especially in that you say he has long had knowledge of us. Wherefore be certain that we will obey you and hold you as lord in place of that great lord of whom you speak, in which service there shall be neither slackness nor deceit: and throughout all the land, that is to say all that I rule, you may command anything you desire, and it shall be obeyed and done, and all that we have is at your will and pleasure. And since you are in your own land and house, rejoice and take your leisure from the fatigues of your journey and the battles you have fought; for I am well informed of all those that you have been forced to engage in on your way here from Potonchan, as also that the natives of Cempoal and Tlascala have told you many evil things of me; but believe no more than what you see with your own eyes, and especially not words from the lips of those who are my enemies, who were formerly my vassals and on your coming rebelled against me and said these things in order to find favor with you: I am aware, moreover, that they have told you that the walls of my houses were of gold as was the matting on my floors and other household articles, even that I was a god and claimed to be so, and other like matters. As for the houses, you see that they are of wood, stones and earth." Upon this he lifted his clothes showing me his body, and said: "and you see that I am of flesh and blood like yourself and everyone else, mortal and tangible."

Grasping with his hands his arms and other parts of his body, he continued: "You see plainly how they have lied. True I have a few articles of gold which have remained to me from my forefathers, and all that I have is yours at any time that you may desire it. I am now going to my palace where I live. Here you will be provided with all things necessary for you and your men, and let nothing be done amiss seeing that you are in your own house and land."

I replied to all that he said, satisfying him in those things which seemed expedient, especially in having him believe that your Majesty was he whom they had long expected, and with that he bade farewell. On his departure we were very well regaled with great store of chickens, bread, fruit, and other necessities, particularly household ones. And in this wise I continued six days very well provided with all that was necessary and visited by many of the principal men of the city.

I have already related, most catholic Lord, how at the time when I departed from the town of Vera Cruz in search of this ruler Muteczuma, I left in it a hundred and fifty men to finish the fortress which I had already begun: likewise how that I had left many neighboring towns and strongholds under the dominion of your royal Majesty, and the natives very peaceably disposed and loyal subjects of your Majesty. Being in the city of Cholula I received letters from the officer whom I left in Vera Cruz, by which I learnt that Qualpopoca, the native ruler of Almería, had sent in messengers to say that he desired to become a vassal of your Majesty, the reason for his delay being that enemy country lay between him and Vera Cruz and he had been chary of passing through it, but that if four Spaniards would return to his land, the enemies through whose country they would have to pass would refrain from molesting them and he would come forthwith to make his submission. The officer, thinking the message to have been sent in good faith, for many others had done the same, sent four Spaniards as requested. But Qualpopoca having once received them into his house ordered them to be killed . . . and two of them thus died.

* * *

Having passed six days, then, in the great city of Tenochtitlan, invincible Prince, and having seen something of its marvels, though little in comparison with what there was to be seen and examined, I considered it essential both from my observation of the city and the rest of the land that its ruler should be in my power and no longer entirely free; to the end that he might in nowise change his will and intent to serve your Majesty, more especially as we Spaniards are somewhat intolerant and stiff-necked, and should he get across with us he would be powerful enough to do us great damage, even to blot out all memory of us in the land; and in the second place, could I once get him in my power all the other provinces subject to him would come more promptly to the knowledge and service of your Majesty, as indeed afterward happened. I decided to capture him and place him in the lodging where I was, which was extremely strong. * * *

* * *

But before beginning to relate the wonders of this city and people, their rights and government, I should perhaps for a better understanding say something of the state of Mexico itself which contains this city and the others of which I have spoken, and is the principal seat of Muteczuma. The province is roughly circular in shape and entirely surrounded by very lofty and rocky mountains, the level part in the middle being some seventy leagues[3] in circumference and containing two lakes which occupy it almost entirely, for canoes travel over fifty leagues in making a circuit of them. One of the lakes is of fresh water, the other and larger one of salt. A narrow but very lofty range of mountains cuts across the valley and divides the lakes almost completely save for the western end where they are joined by a narrow strait no wider than a sling's throw which runs between the mountains. Commerce is carried on between the two lakes and the cities on their banks by means of canoes, so that land traffic is avoided. Moreover, since the salt lake rises and falls with the tide sea water pours from it at high tide into the fresh water lake with the rapidity of a mountain torrent, and likewise at low tide flows back from the fresh to the salt.

The great city of Tenochtitlan is built in the midst of this salt lake, and it is two leagues from the heart of the city to any point on the mainland. Four causeways lead to it, all made by hand and some twelve feet wide. The city itself is as large as Seville or Córdova. The principal streets are very broad and straight, the majority of them being of beaten earth, but a few and at least half the smaller thoroughfares are waterways along which they pass in their canoes. Moreover, even the principal streets have openings at regular distances so that the water can freely pass from one to another, and these openings which are very broad are spanned by great bridges of huge beams, very stoutly put together, so firm indeed that over many of them ten horsemen can ride at once. Seeing that if the natives intended any treachery against us they would have every opportunity from the way in which the city is built, for by

---

3. Cortés's estimations of distance are approximate; a Spanish league is about three to four miles.

removing the bridges from the entrances and exits they could leave us to die
of hunger with no possibility of getting to the mainland, I immediately set to
work as soon as we entered the city on the building of four brigs, and in a
short space of time had them finished, so that we could ship three hundred
men and the horses to the mainland whenever we so desired.

The city has many open squares in which markets are continuously held
and the general business of buying and selling proceeds. One square in particular is twice as big as that of Salamanca and completely surrounded by
arcades where there are daily more than sixty thousand folk buying and selling. Every kind of merchandise such as may be met with in every land is for
sale there, whether of food and victuals, or ornaments of gold and silver, or
lead, brass, copper, tin, precious stones, bones, shells, snails and feathers;
limestone for building is likewise sold there, stone both rough and polished,
bricks burnt and unburnt, wood of all kinds and in all stages of preparation.
There is a street of game where they sell all manner of birds that are to be
found in their country, including hens, partridges, quails, wild duck, fly-
catchers, widgeon, turtle doves, pigeons, little birds in round nests made of
grass, parrots, owls, eagles, vulcans, sparrow-hawks and kestrels; and of some
of these birds of prey they sell the skins complete with feathers, head, bill
and claws. They also sell rabbits, hares, deer and small dogs which they breed
especially for eating. There is a street of herb-sellers where there are all
manner of roots and medicinal plants that are found in the land. There are
houses as it were of apothecaries where they sell medicines made from these
herbs, both for drinking and for use as ointments and salves. There are barbers' shops where you may have your hair washed and cut. There are other
shops where you may obtain food and drink. There are street porters such
as we have in Spain to carry packages. There is a great quantity of wood,
charcoal, braziers made of clay and mats of all sorts, some for beds and others
more finely woven for seats, still others for furnishing halls and private apartments. All kinds of vegetables may be found there, in particular onions, leeks,
garlic, cresses, watercress, borage, sorrel, artichokes, and golden thistles.
There are many different sorts of fruits including cherries and plums very
similar to those found in Spain. They sell honey obtained from bees, as also
the honeycomb and that obtained from maize plants which are as sweet as
sugar canes; they also obtain honey from plants which are known both here
and in other parts as *maguey*,[4] which is preferable to grape juice; from *maguey*
in addition they make both sugar and a kind of wine, which are sold in their
markets. All kinds of cotton thread in various colors may be bought in skeins,
very much in the same way as in the great silk exchange of Granada, except
that the quantities are far less. They have colors for painting of as good
quality as any in Spain, and of as pure shades as may be found anywhere.
There are leathers of deer both skinned and in their natural state, and either
bleached or dyed in various colors. A great deal of chinaware is sold of very
good quality and including earthen jars of all sizes for holding liquids, pitchers, pots, tiles and an infinite variety of earthenware all made of very special
clay and almost all decorated and painted in some way. Maize is sold both
as grain and in the form of bread and is vastly superior both in the size of
the ear and in taste to that of all the other islands or the mainland. Pasties
made from game and fish pies may be seen on sale, and there are large

---

4. Mexican aloe.

quantities of fresh and salt water fish both in their natural state and cooked ready for eating. Eggs from fowls, geese and all the other birds I have described may be had, and likewise omelettes ready made. There is nothing to be found in all the land which is not sold in these markets, for over and above what I have mentioned there are so many and such various other things that on account of their very number and the fact that I do not know their names, I cannot now detail them. Each kind of merchandise is sold in its own particular street and no other kind may be sold there: this rule is very well enforced. All is sold by number and measure, but up till now no weighing by balance has been observed. A very fine building in the great square serves as a kind of audience chamber where ten or a dozen persons are always seated, as judges, who deliberate on all cases arising in the market and pass sentence on evildoers. In the square itself there are officials who continually walk among the people inspecting goods exposed for sale and the measures by which they are sold, and on certain occasions I have seen them destroy measures which were false.

There are a very large number of mosques or dwelling places for their idols throughout the various districts of this great city, all fine buildings, in the chief of which their priests live continuously, so that in addition to the actual temples containing idols there are sumptuous lodgings. These pagan priests are all dressed in black and go habitually with their hair uncut; they do not even comb it from the day they enter the order to that on which they leave. Chief men's sons, both nobles and distinguished citizens, enter these orders at the age of six or seven and only leave when they are of an age to marry, and this occurs more frequently to the first-born who will inherit their fathers' estates than to others. They are denied all access to women, and no woman is ever allowed to enter one of the religious houses. Certain foods they abstain from and more so at certain periods of the year than at others. Among these temples there is one chief one in particular whose size and magnificence no human tongue could describe. For it is so big that within the lofty wall which entirely circles it one could set a town of fifteen thousand inhabitants.

Immediately inside this wall and throughout its entire length are some admirable buildings containing large halls and corridors where the priests who live in this temple are housed. There are forty towers at the least, all of stout construction and very lofty, the largest of which has fifty steps leading up to its base: this chief one is indeed higher than the great church of Seville. The workmanship both in wood and stone could not be bettered anywhere, for all the stonework within the actual temples where they keep their idols is cut into ornamental borders of flowers, birds, fishes and the like, or trellis-work, and the woodwork is likewise all in relief highly decorated with monsters of very various device. The towers all serve as burying places for their nobles, and the little temples which they contain are all dedicated to a different idol to whom they pay their devotions.

There are three large halls in the great mosque where the principal idols are to be found, all of immense size and height and richly decorated with sculptured figures both in wood and stone, and within these halls are other smaller temples branching off from them and entered by doors so small that no daylight ever reaches them. Certain of the priests but not all are permitted to enter, and within are the great heads and figures of idols, although as I have said there are also many outside. The greatest of these idols and those in which they placed most faith and trust I ordered to be dragged from their places and flung down the stairs, which done I had the temples which they occupy cleansed for they were full of the blood of human victims who had been sacrificed, and placed in them the image of Our Lady and other saints, all of which made no small impression upon Muteczuma and the inhabitants. They at first remonstrated with me, for should it be known, they said, by the people of the country they would rise against me, believing as they did that to these idols were due all temporal goods, and that should they allow them to be ill used they would be wroth against them and would give them nothing, denying them the fruits of the earth, and thus the people would die of starvation. I instructed them by my interpreters how mistaken they were in putting their trust in idols made by their own hands from unclean things, and that they must know that there was but one God, Lord of all, Who created the sky, the earth and all things, Who made both them and ourselves, Who was without beginning and immortal, Whom alone they had to adore and to believe in, and not in any created thing whatsoever: I told them moreover all things else that I knew of touching this matter in order to lead them from their idolatry and bring them to the knowledge of Our Lord: and all, especially Muteczuma, replied that they had already told me that they were not natives of this land but had come to it long time since, and that therefore they were well prepared to believe that they had erred somewhat from the true faith during the long time since they had left their native land, and I as more lately come would know more surely the things that it was right for them to hold and believe than they themselves: and that hence if I would instruct them they would do whatever I declared to be best. Upon this Muteczuma and many of the chief men of the city went with me to remove the idols, cleanse the chapels, and place images of the saints therein, and all with cheerful faces. I forbade them moreover to make human sacrifice to the idols as was their wont, because besides being an abomination in the sight of God it is prohibited by your Majesty's laws which declare that he who kills shall be killed. From this time henceforth they departed from it, and during the whole time that I was in the city not a single living soul was known to be killed and sacrificed.

* * *

Finally, to avoid prolixity in telling all the wonders of this city, I will simply say that the manner of living among the people is very similar to that in Spain, and considering that this is a barbarous nation shut off from a knowledge of the true God or communication with enlightened nations, one may well marvel at the orderliness and good government which is everywhere maintained.

* * *

On the day of Saint John after having heard mass I entered the city about midday, seeing few people about, and certain doors at the crossroads and turnings taken down, which appeared to be a bad sign, although I considered that it was done out of fright for what had already occurred and that my entrance would serve to calm them. I went straight to the fortress and the great temple next to it in which my men had taken up their quarters, and where they received us with such joy as if we had given them back their lives which they counted already lost: and so we remained there very much at ease throughout the rest of that day and night, thinking that all disturbance had settled down. Next day after hearing mass I despatched a messenger to Vera Cruz giving them the good news that I had entered the city to find the Christians alive and the city now quiet. But in half an hour he returned all covered with bruises and wounds, crying that the whole populace of the city was advancing in war dress and all the bridges were raised. And immediately behind him came a multitude of people from all parts so that the streets and house-roofs were black with natives; all of whom came on with the most frightful yells and shouts it is possible to imagine.

The stones from their slings came down on us within the fortress as if they were raining from the sky; the arrows and darts fell so thickly that the walls and courtyards were full of them and one could hardly move without treading on them. I made sallies in one or two parts and they fought against us with tremendous fury; one of my officers led two hundred men out by another door and before he could retire they had killed four of them and wounded both him and many others. I myself and many of my men were also wounded. We killed but few of them for they were waiting for us on the other side of the bridges, and did us much damage from the flat housetops with stones: some of these flat roofs we gained possession of and burnt the houses. But there were so many and so strongly fortified, being held by such numbers of natives and all so well provided with stones and other missiles, that we were not numerous enough to take all of them nor to hold what we had taken, for they could attack us at their pleasure.

The fight went on so fiercely in the fortress itself that they succeeded in setting fire to it in many parts, and actually burnt a large portion, without our being able to stop the flames until at last we broke down a stretch of wall and thus prevented it from spreading further. Indeed, had it not been for the strong guard I placed there of musketeers, crossbowmen and guns they would have entered under our eyes without our being able to stop them. We continued thus fighting all day until night was well come, though even then the yelling and commotion did not cease. During the night I ordered the doorways which had suffered by the fire to be repaired and all other places of the fortress which seemed to me weak. I decided upon the squads that were to defend the various parts of the fortress on the morrow and also the one that was to sally out with me to attack the Indians outside: I also ordered the wounded to be looked to, who numbered more than eighty.

As soon as it was day the enemy began to attack us with greater fury even than the day before: they came on in such numbers that the gunners had no need to take aim but simply poured their shot into the mass. Yet in spite of the damage done by the guns, for there were three arquebuses[5] without counting muskets and crossbows, they made so little impression that their effect could hardly be perceived, for wherever a shot carried away ten or a dozen men, the gap closed up with others so that it seemed as if no damage had been done. Upon this, leaving such suitable guard as I could in the fortress I sallied out and got possession of a few houses, killing many of those who were defending them: but their numbers were so great that although we had done still greater damage it would have had but slight effect. Moreover, whereas we had to continue fighting all the day they could fight for several hours and then give way to others, for their forces were amply sufficient. They again wounded as many as fifty to seventy Spaniards that day,

5. A heavy but portable gun of the 15th century.

although no one was killed, and so we fought on till nightfall when we had to retire worn out to the fortress.

Seeing then the great damage that our enemies did us, and that they could wound and kill us almost unhurt themselves, we spent the whole of that night and next day in making three wooden engines, each one of which would protect twenty men when they had got inside it: the engines were covered with boards to protect the men from the stones which were thrown from the housetops; and those chosen to go inside were crossbowmen and musketeers together with others provided with pickaxes, hoes and iron bars to burrow under the houses and tear down the barricades which they had erected in the streets. All the while these wooden affairs were being made fighting did not cease for a moment, in such wise that as we prepared to make a sally[6] out of the fortress they attempted to force an entrance, and it was as much as we could do to resist them. Muteczuma, who was still a prisoner together with his son and many other nobles who had been taken on our first entering the city, requested to be taken out on to the flat roof of the fortress, where he would speak to the leaders of the people and make them stop fighting. I ordered him to be brought forth and as he mounted a breast-work that extended beyond the fortress, wishing to speak to the people who were fighting there, a stone from one of their slings struck him on the head so severely that he died three days later: when this happened I ordered two of the other Indian prisoners to take out his dead body on their shields to the people, and I know not what became of it; save only this that the fighting did not cease but rather increased in intensity every day.

The day that Muteczuma was wounded they called out to me from the place where he had been struck down saying that some of the native captains wished to speak to me; and thither I went and spent much time talking with them, begging them to cease fighting against me, for they had no reason to do so, and should consider that I had always treated them very well. They replied that I should depart and abandon their land when they would immediately stop fighting; but otherwise they were of a mind to kill us, or die themselves to a man. This they said, as it appeared, in order to persuade me to leave the fortress, when they would fall upon us at their pleasure between the bridges as we left the city. I replied that they were not to think that I besought them for peace because I feared them in any way, but because I was grieved at the damage I was doing them and should have to do them, and in order not to destroy so fine a city: to which they still replied that they would not cease fighting until I should leave the city.

* * *

* * * They forced their way almost to the inner towers and succeeded in taking the temple, the chief tower of which was quickly filled with as many as five hundred Indians, all seemingly of high rank. Forthwith they proceeded to carry up large stores of bread, water and other food, together with plentiful supplies of stones. Most of them, moreover, were armed with long lances with heads of flint broader but no whit less sharp than our own; and from their position they did great damage to my men within the fortress for they were very close. The Spaniards two or three times attacked this tower and attempted to mount it, but as it was very tall and steep, having more than a

---

6. A rush made by the defense on an attacking army.

hundred steps, and those above were well provided with stones and arms and moreover protected to a certain extent since we had been unable to take the neighboring roofs, they were forced to descend every time they attempted, and suffered many casualties; whereupon the natives in other parts of the city were so encouraged as to rush on the fortress without any signs of fear. Seeing that if our enemies were allowed to hold the tower they would not only do us much damage but would encourage the rest, I sallied out from the fortress, though disabled in the left hand from a wound received in the first day's fighting. Tying my shield on to my arm, however, I made for the tower followed by certain others and we surrounded it entirely at its base; this was done with no great difficulty, although not without danger, since my men had to deal with the enemy who were rushing up on all sides to support their comrades. I myself with a few behind me began to mount the staircase of the tower. And although they defended themselves very furiously, so much so that three or four Spaniards were knocked spinning downstairs, nevertheless with the help of God and our Gracious Mother, to whose honor the building had been dedicated and crowned with her statue, we finally got up the tower, and fought with them on top so fiercely that they were forced to leap down on to certain flat roofs, between which and the tower there was a gap of about a yard. There were about three or four of these all about eighteen feet below the top of the tower. Some fell right to the ground and were either broken by the fall or dispatched by the Spaniards who were below. Those who escaped on to the flat roofs continued to fight with extreme bravery so that it was more than three hours before we finished with them, and then there was not a man left alive. And your Majesty may well believe that had not God broken their ranks twenty of them might have stopped a thousand men from mounting the tower. Nevertheless those who died fought very valiantly. When it was all over I set fire to this tower and the other towers of the temple, having already abandoned them and removed all the images of the saints which we had placed there.

They lost somewhat of their pride on our taking this stronghold from them; so much so that on all sides their attack slackened, on which I returned to the housetop and spoke to the captains with whom I had already held speech and who were somewhat dismayed by what they had seen. On their approach I bade them note that they could not help themselves, that each day we should do them great hurt and kill many of them; already we were burning and destroying their city and would have to continue so to do until nothing of it or of them remained. To which they replied that they plainly perceived this but were determined to die to a man, if need be, to finish with us. And they bade me observe that the streets, squares and rooftops were all packed full of people, and that they had reckoned that if twenty-five thousand of them were to die for every one of us yet we should perish sooner, for we were few and they were many; and they gave me to know that all the bridges in the streets had been removed, as was indeed the case excepting a single one. We had therefore no way of escape except by water. Moreover, they knew well that we had but slight store of food and drinking water so that we could not hold out long without dying of hunger, even if they should not kill us themselves. And in truth they were perfectly right: for had we no other foes than hunger and general shortness of provisions, we were like to die in a short time. Many other arguments were put forward each supporting his own position.

After nightfall I went out with a few Spaniards and taking them off their guard succeeded in capturing a whole street in which we burnt more than three hundred houses. So soon as the natives had rushed there I returned by another street where I likewise set fire to many houses, especially to certain ones with low flat roofs lying close to the fortress from which they had inflicted great damage upon us. What was done that night inspired them with great terror.* * *

BERNAL DÍAZ DEL CASTILLO
1492–1580

Bernal Díaz del Castillo was an experienced Spanish soldier, who participated in two explorations of the Mexican coast before joining in the conquest of Mexico under Hernán Cortés. He was, as he repeatedly asserts in his *True History of the Conquest of New Spain*, a soldier and not a writer. Nonetheless, he had strong views of what made for good history: *accuracy* in the reporting of the lands, people and customs, and military actions. He was spurred in old age to write an account of the historical events by the appearance of a flood of misleading histories written by contemporaries who had no first-hand knowledge of the march on Mexico and fall of Tenochtitlán. As the last surviving conquistador, he wrote to set the record straight. What he provided is the compelling perspective of a soldier who saw himself as one of a group of brave and daring men. His account offers striking differences from that of Cortés himself, mainly in his portrayal of the many personalities it took to make Cortés the hero he wished to be. In Díaz's story, the Spanish soldiers and officers play a dynamic role in many key decisions. What is more, he offers a riveting account of the interdependence of the Spanish on many of the natives, including the king Moctezuma as well as many humble persons. Among the quick-witted and brave figures that share the limelight with Cortés are the translators, Jeronimo de Aguilar and the native woman, Doña Marina (in her Christian name) or Malintzin, called La Malinche by Díaz. These translators, as Díaz knew, were the ones to advise Cortés to find allies among the natives hostile to the Aztecs.

From The True History of the Conquest of New Spain[1]

As we had determined the day before to seize Montezuma, we were praying to God all that night that it would turn out in a manner redounding to His Holy service, and the next morning the way it should be done was settled.

Cortés took with him five captains who were Pedro de Alvarado, Gonzalo de Sandoval, Juan Velásquez de Leon, Francisco de Lugo and Alonzo de Ávila, and he took me and our interpreters Doña Marina and Aguilar, and he told us all to keep on the alert, and the horsemen to have their horses saddled and bridled. As for our arms I need not call them to mind, for by day or night we always went armed and with our sandals on our feet, for at that time such was our footgear, and Montezuma had always seen us armed

1. Translated by Alfred Percival Maudslay.

in that way when we went to speak to him. I mention this because although Cortés and those who went with him to seize Montezuma were all armed, Montezuma did not take it as anything new, nor was he disturbed at all.

When we were all ready, our captain sent to tell Montezuma that we were coming to his palace, for this had always been our custom, and so that he should not be alarmed by our arriving suddenly.

* * *

When Cortés entered, after having made his usual salutations, he said to him through our interpreters, "Señor Montezuma, I am very much astonished that you, who are such a valiant prince, after having declared that you are our friend, should order your captains, whom you have stationed on the coast near to Tuxpan, to take arms against my Spaniards, and that they should dare to rob the towns which are in the keeping and under the protection of our king and master and to demand of them Indian men and women for sacrifice, and should kill a Spaniard, one of my brothers, and a horse." (He did not wish to speak of the captain nor of the six soldiers who died as soon as they arrived at Villa Rica, for Montezuma did not know about it, nor did the Indian captains who had attacked them), and Cortés went on to say, "being such a friend of yours I ordered my captains to do all that was possible to help and serve you, and you have done exactly the contrary to us. Also in the affair at Cholula your captains and a large force of warriors had received your own commands to kill us. I forgave it at the time out of my great regard for you, and now again your vassals and captains have become insolent, and hold secret consultations stating that you wish us to be killed. I do not wish to begin a war on this account nor to destroy this city, I am willing to forgive it all, if silently and without raising any disturbance you will come with us to our quarters where you will be as well served and attended to as though you were in your own house, but if you cry out or make any disturbance you will immediately be killed by these my captains, whom I brought solely for the purpose." When Montezuma heard this he was terrified and dumfounded, and replied that he had never ordered his people to take arms against us, and that he would at once send to summon his captains so that the truth should be known, and he would chastise them and at that very moment he took from his arm and wrist the sign and seal of Huichilobos, which was only done when he gave an important and weighty command which was to be carried out at once. With regard to being taken prisoner and leaving his palace against his will, he said that he was not the person to whom such an order could be given, and that it was not his wish to go. Cortés replied to him with very good arguments and Montezuma answered him with even better, showing that he ought not to leave his house. In this way more than half an hour was spent over talk, and when Juan Velásquez de Leon and the other captains saw that they were wasting time over it and could not longer await the moment when they should remove him from his house and hold him a prisoner, they spoke to Cortés somewhat angrily and said, "what is the good of your making so many words, let us either take him prisoner, or stab him, tell him once more that if he cries out or makes an uproar we will kill him, for it is better at once to save our lives or to lose them," and as Juan Velásquez said this with a loud and rather terrifying voice, for such was his way of speaking, Montezuma, who saw that our captains were angered, asked Doña Marina what they were saying in such loud tones. As Doña Marina was very clever, she said, "Señor Montezuma, what I counsel you, is to go at once to their quarters without any disturbance at all, for I know that they will pay you much honor as a great prince such as you are, otherwise you will remain here a dead man, but in their quarters you will learn the truth." Then Montezuma said to Cortés, "Señor Malinche, if this is what you desire, I have a son and two legitimate daughters, take them as hostages, and do not put this affront on me, what will my chieftains say if they see me taken off as a prisoner?" Cortés replied to him that he must come with them himself, and there was no alternative. At the end of much more discussion that took place, Montezuma said that he would go willingly, and then Cortés and our captains bestowed many caresses on him and told him that they begged him not to be annoyed, and to tell his captains and the men of his guard that he was going of his own free will, because he had spoken to his Idol Huichilobos and the priests who attended him, and that it was beneficial for his health and the safety of his life that he should be with us. His rich litter, in which he was used to go out with all the captains who accompanied him was promptly brought, and he went to our quarters where we placed guards and watchmen over him.

* * *

I will not say anything more at present about this imprisonment, and will relate how the messengers whom Montezuma sent with his sign and seal to summon the captains who had killed our soldiers, brought them before him as prisoners, and what he said to them I do not know, but he sent them on to Cortés, so that he might do justice to them, and their confession was taken when Montezuma was not present and they confessed that what I have already stated was true, that their prince had ordered them to wage war and to extract tribute, and that if any Teules should appear in defence of the towns, they too should be attacked or killed. When Cortés heard this confession he sent to inform Montezuma how it implicated him in the affair, and Montezuma made all the excuses he could, and our captain sent him word that he believed it [the confession] himself, but that although he [Montezuma] deserved punishment in conformity with the ordinances of our King, to the effect that any person causing others, whether guilty or innocent, to be killed, shall die for it, yet he was so fond of him and wished him so well, that even if that crime lay at his door, he, Cortés, would pay the penalty with his own life sooner than allow Montezuma's to pass away. With all this that he [Cortés] sent to tell him, he [Montezuma] felt anxious, and without any further discussion Cortés sentenced those captains to death and to be burned in front of Montezuma's palace. This sentence was promptly carried out, and, so that there could be no obstruction while they were being burned, Cortés ordered shackles to be put on Montezuma himself, and when this was done Montezuma roared [with rage], and if before this he was scared, he was then much more so. After the burning was over our Cortés with five of our captains went to Montezuma's apartment and Cortés himself took off the fetters, and he spoke such loving words to him that his anger soon passed off, for our Cortés told him that he not only regarded him as a brother, but much more, and that, as he was already lord and king of so many towns and provinces, if it were possible he would make him lord of many more countries as time went on, such as he had not been able to subdue, and which did not now obey him, and he told him that if he now wished to go to his palace, that he would give him leave to go. Cortés told him this through our interpreters and while Cortés was saying it the tears apparently sprang to Montezuma's eyes. He answered with great courtesy, that he thanked him for it, (but he well knew that Cortés's speech was mere words,) and that now at present it was better for him to stay there a prisoner, for there was danger, as his chieftains were numerous, and his nephews and relations came every day to him to say that it would be a good thing to attack us and free him from prison, that as soon as they saw him outside they might drive him to it [to attack us]. He did not wish to see revolutions in his city, but if he did not comply with their wishes possibly they would want to set up another Prince in his place, and so he was putting those thoughts out of their heads by saying that Huichilobos had sent him word that he should remain a prisoner. (From what we understood, and there is no doubt about it, Cortés had told Aguilar to tell Montezuma secretly, that although Malinche wished to release him from his imprisonment, that the rest of our captains and soldiers would not agree to it.) When he heard this reply, Cortés threw his arms round him and embraced him and said, "It is not in vain Señor Montezuma that I care for you as I care for myself." Then Montezuma asked Cortés that a Spanish page named Orteguilla who already knew something of his language might attend on him, and this was very advantageous both for Montezuma and for us, for through this page Montezuma asked and learned many things about Spain, and we learned what his captains said to him, and in truth this page was so serviceable that Montezuma got to like him very much.

* * *

[Diaz describes the armed conflict with the Aztecs. See Cortés, pp. 2516 ff.]

Here Cortés showed himself very much of a man, as he always was. Oh! what a fight and what a fierce battle it was that took place; it was a memorable thing to see us all streaming with blood, and covered with wounds and others slain. It pleased our lord that we reached the place where we used to keep the image of Our Lady, and we did not find it, and it appears, as we came to know, that the great Montezuma paid devotion to Her, and ordered it [the image] to be preserved in safety.

We set fire to their Idols and a good part of the chamber with the Idols Huichilobos and Tezcatepuca[2] was burned. On that occasion the Tlaxcalans helped us very greatly. After this was accomplished, while some of us were fighting and others kindling the fire, as I have related, oh! to see the priests who were stationed on this great Cue, and the three or four thousand Indians, all men of importance. While we descended, oh! how they made us tumble down six or even ten steps at a time! And so much more there is to tell of the other squadrons posted on the battlements and recesses of the great Cue discharging so many darts and arrows that we could face neither one group of squadrons nor the other. We resolved to return, with much toil and risk to ourselves, to our quarters, our castles being destroyed, all of us wounded and sixteen slain, with the Indians constantly pressing on us and other squadrons on our flanks.

---

2. These are the Aztec gods, repeatedly consulted by Montezuma as he struggled with his decision about handling the Spaniards. The oracle associated with Huichilobos consistently told the Aztec king to kill the Spaniards once they entered the city.

However clearly I may tell all this, I can never [fully] explain it to any one who did not see us. So far, I have not spoken of what the Mexican squadrons did who kept on attacking our quarters while we were marching outside, and the great obstinacy and tenacity they displayed in forcing their way in.

In this battle, we captured two of the chief priests, whom Cortés ordered us to convey with great care.

Many times I have seen among the Mexicans and Tlaxcalans, paintings of this battle, and the ascent that we made of the great Cue, as they look upon it as a very heroic deed. And although in the pictures that they have made of it, they depict all of us as badly wounded and streaming with blood and many of us dead they considered it a great feat, this setting fire to the Cue, when so many warriors were guarding it both on the battlements and recesses, and many more Indians were below on the ground and the courts were full of them and there were many more on the sides; and with our towers destroyed, how was it possible to scale it?

* * *

Let us go back to our story. It was decided to sue for peace so that we could leave Mexico, and as soon as it was dawn many more squadrons of Mexicans arrived and very effectually surrounded our quarters on all sides, and if they had discharged many stones and arrows before, they came much thicker and with louder howls and whistles on this day, and other squadrons endeavored to force an entrance in other parts, and cannon and muskets availed nothing, although we did them damage enough.

When Cortés saw all this, he decided that the great Montezuma should speak to them from the roof and tell them that the war must cease, and that we wished to leave this city. When they went to give this message from Cortés to the great Montezuma, it is reported that he said with great grief, "What more does Malinche[3] want from me? I neither wish to live nor to listen to him, to such a pass has my fate brought me because of him." And he did not wish to come, and it is even reported that he said he neither wished to see nor hear him, nor listen to his false words, promises or lies. Then the Padre de la Merced and Cristóbal de Olid went and spoke to him with much reverence and in very affectionate terms, and Montezuma said, "I believe that I shall not obtain any result towards ending this war, for they have already raised up another lord and have made up their minds not to let you leave this place alive, therefore I believe that all of you will have to die."

Let us return to the great attacks they made on us; Montezuma was placed by a battlement of the roof with many of us soldiers guarding him, and he began to speak to them [his people], with very affectionate expressions [telling them] to desist from the war, and that we would leave Mexico. Many of the Mexican chieftains and captains knew him well and at once ordered their people to be silent and not to discharge darts, stones or arrows, and four of them reached a spot where Montezuma could speak to them, and they to him, and with tears they said to him: "Oh! Señor, and our great lord, how all your misfortune and injury and that of your children and relations afflicts us, we make known to you that we have already raised one of your kinsmen

---

3. Montezuma calls Cortés "Malinche," since he regards the Spanish commander as the consort of La Malinche, or Doña Marina (who had a son by Cortés).

to be our lord," and there he stated his name, that he was called Cuitlahuac, the Lord of Ixtapalapa, (for it was not Guatemoc, he who was Lord soon after,) and moreover they said that the war must be carried through, and that they had vowed to their Idols not to relax it until we were all dead, and that they prayed every day to their Huichilobos and Texcatepuca to guard him free and safe from our power, and that should it end as they desired, they would not fail to hold him in higher regard as their Lord than they did before, and they begged him to forgive them. They had hardly finished this speech when suddenly such a shower of stones and darts was discharged that (our men who were shielding him having neglected their duty [to shield him] for a moment, because they saw how the attack ceased while he spoke to them) he was hit by three stones, one on the head, another on the arm and another on the leg, and although they begged him to have the wounds dressed and to take food, and spoke kind words to him about it, he would not. Indeed, when we least expected it, they came to say that he was dead. Cortés wept for him, and all of us captains and soldiers, and there was no man among us who knew him and was intimate with him, who did not bemoan him as though he were our father, and it is not to be wondered at, considering how good he was. It was stated that he had reigned for seventeen years and that he was the best king there had ever been in Mexico, and that he had conquered in person, in three wars which he had carried on in the countries he had subjugated.

* * *

HANS STADEN
ca. 1525–1558

Hans Staden was a German gunner. On the second of the two expeditions that he made to Brazil between 1548 and 1555, he was captured by the cannibalistic Tupinamba Indians. Held captive for over nine months, he expected at any moment to be eaten. Yet he suffered no lasting harm from his captors, and survived to provide an illuminating and often comic account of his life and conversation with the Tupinamba. His captors appeared to take their meat with humor, in one case tying Staden's legs together and then joking, "Here comes our meat, hopping along." Staden responded in kind to this kind of irony, memorably asserting, when he was delivered to his captors, "Here I am, your food!"

Also fascinating is the record of relations between rival European explorers: the Portuguese had discovered and explored Brazil well before the arrival of any French or Germans, and it is a Portuguese prisoner—far more than the cannibals—that plays the villain's role in Staden's story.

The best-known account in English of Staden's captivity is that of Sir Richard Burton, the nineteenth-century explorer. He commissioned the first English translation and provided a brief prefatory essay.

From The Captivity of Hans Staden[1]

How I was captured by the savages, and the way in which this happened.

I had a savage man, of a tribe called Carios; he was my slave, who caught game for me, and with him I also went occasionally into the forest.

Now it happened once upon a time, that a Spaniard from the island of Sancte Vincente came to me in the island of Sancte Maro, which is five miles (leagues) therefrom, and remained in the fort wherein I lived, and also a German by name Heliodorus, from Hesse, son of the late Eoban of Hesse, the same who was in the island of Sanct Vincente at an ingenio, where sugar is made, and the ingenio belonged to a Genoese named Josepe Ornio. This Heliodorus was the clerk and manager of the merchants to whom the ingenio belonged. (Ingenio are called houses in which sugar is made). With the said Heliodorus I had before had some acquaintance, for when I was shipwrecked with the Spaniards in that country, I found him in the island of Sancte Vincente, and he showed me friendship. He came again to me, wanting to see how I got on, for he had perhaps heard that I was sick.

Having sent my slave the day before into the wood to catch game, I purposed going the next day to fetch it, so that we might have something to eat. For in that country one has little else beyond what comes from the forests.

Now as I with this purpose walked through the woods, there arose on both sides of the path loud yells such as the savages are accustomed to make, and they came running toward me; I knew them, and found that they had all surrounded me, and levelling their bows with arrows, they shot in upon me. Then I cried, "Now God help my soul"; I had scarcely finished saying these words when they struck me to the ground and shot (arrows) and stabbed at me. So far they had not (thank God!) wounded me further than in one leg, and torn my clothes off my body; one the jerkin, the other the hat, the third the shirt and so forth. Then they began to quarrel about me, one said he was the first who came up to me, the other said that he had captured me. Meanwhile the others struck me with their bows. But at last two of them raised me from the ground where I lay naked, one took me by one arm, another by the other, and some went behind me, and others before. They ran in this manner quickly with me through the wood towards the sea, where they had their canoes. When they had taken me to the shore, I sighted their canoes which they had drawn up from the sea on to the land under a hedge, at the distance of a stone's-throw or two, and also a great number more of them who had remained with the canoes. When they, ornamented with feathers according to their custom, saw me being led along they ran towards me, and pretended to bite into their arms, and threatened as though they would eat me. And a king paraded before me with a club wherewith they despatched the prisoners. He harangued and said how they had captured me their slave from the Perot[2] (so they call the Portuguese), and they would now thoroughly revenge on me the death of their friends. And when they brought me to the canoes, several of them struck me with their fists. Then they made haste among one another, to shove their canoes back into the water, for they feared that an alarm would be made at Brikioka, as also happened.

---

1. Translated by Albert Tootal. 2. It is unknown why the Brazilians called the Portuguese "the Perot."

Now before they launched the canoes, they tied my hands together, and not being all from the same dwelling-place, those of each village were loath to go home empty-handed, and disputed with those who held me. Some said that they been just as near me as the others, and that they would also have their share of me, and they wanted to kill me at once on that very spot.

Then I stood and prayed, looking round for the blow. But at last the king, who desired to keep me, began and said they would take me living homeward, so that their wives might also see me alive, and make their feast upon me. For they purposed killing me "Kawewi Pepicke," that is, they would brew drinks and assemble together, to make a feast, and then they would eat me among them. At these words they left off disputing, and tied four ropes round my neck, and I had to get into a canoe, whilst they still stood on the shore, and bound the ends of the ropes to the boats and pushed them off into the sea, in order to sail home again.

How they behaved to me on the day when they brought me to their habitations.

On that same day about vesper time, reckoning by the sun, we beheld their habitations, having therefore been three days on the return voyage. For the place I was led to was thirty miles (leagues) distant from Brikioka.

Now when we arrived close to their dwellings, these proved to be a village which had seven huts, and they called it Uwattibi. We ran up on a beach which borders the sea, and close to it were their women in the plantations of the root which they call Mandioka. In this said plantation walked many of their women pulling up the roots; to these I was made to call out in their language: "A junesche been ermi vramme," that is: "I, your food, have come."

Now when we landed, all young and old ran out of their huts (which lay on a hill), to look at me. And the men with their bows and arrows entered their huts, and left me in the custody of their women, who took me between them and went along, some before me and others behind, singing and dancing in unison, with the songs which they are accustomed to sing to their own people when they are about to eat them.

Now they brought me before the Iwara huts, that is the fort which they make round about their huts with great long rails, like the fence of a garden. This they do on account of their enemies.

As I entered, the women ran to me, and struck me with their fists, and pulled my beard, and spoke in their language: "Sche innamme pepicke a e." That is as much as to say: "with this blow I revenge my friend, him whom those among whom thou hast been, have killed."

Thereupon they led me into the huts, where I had to lie in a hammock, whilst the women came and struck and pulled me before and behind, and threatened me how they would eat me.

And the men were together in a hut, and drank the beverage which they call Kawi, and had with them their gods, called Tammerka,[3] and they sang in praise of them, for their having so well prophesied that I should be captured by them.

This song I heard, and for half an hour none of the men came near me, but only women and children.

3. Maracá is the modern term.

BARTOLOMÉ DE LAS CASAS
1484–1566

A Spanish priest and colonist, Bartolomé de las Casas experienced firsthand the brutality of Spain's conquest of the New World and became a passionate and energetic defender of the rights of native populations. Nothing of his early life suggested a future in humanitarian activism: his father (Pedro de las Casas) made his fortune as a soldier serving under Christopher Columbus in his first voyage, and las Casas himself participated in the conquests of Hispaniola and Cuba. Yet the violence of the Spanish colonists shocked las Casas, spurring him to spiritual conversion (he became the first priest ordained in the New World) and political activism. He used the resources of law, the Church, and the press to sway the Spanish Crown and public sentiment; most effective were his published exposés of the practices—including slavery, torture, and mass murder—used by the colonists to subjugate the Indians.

Las Casas's conversion was in part prompted by a sermon he heard delivered in 1511 by a Dominican priest, Antonio de Montesinos, who used the biblical text, "I am a voice crying in the wilderness" to call for reforms in Spain's treatment of the Indians. Las Casas was moved to take up the cause: he renounced his claim to his own Indian serfs and committed his energies to informing Spain and all of Europe of the Indians' plight. He worked especially hard to reform the *requerimiento* (requirement) and the *encomienda*, two practices officially used to cast a moral legitimacy upon the Spanish conquest but actually used to disenfranchise and enslave the natives. The *requerimiento* was a document that the Spanish colonists were obligated by law to read to the Indians prior to a military attack. According to las Casas, the colonists usually read to the natives in a foreign language or out of their hearing. The *encomienda*, a policy instituted by Ferdinand and Isabella, was designed to offer legal protection, religious instruction, and a small wage to the natives, who were expected in return to work the land for the Spanish Crown. In his major publications, such as *A Short Account of the Destruction of the Indies*, las Casas exposed the grim reality of the colonists' efforts to secure the land for their own use and profit. Much of his writing elaborates the torture, starvation, massacre, and enslavement that had become routine practice.

In his writings, las Casas addressed the Church and the Spanish Crown in particular and the European community in general. His reports of Christian conduct in the New World shocked the Old World with the spectacle of its own brutality in relation to the supposedly barbarian natives. They also inspired meditation on the spiritual, moral, and rational equality of races foreign to European education and institutions. Las Casas may, for example, have influenced Montaigne in the writing of his essay "On Cannibals."

From A Short Account of the Destruction of the Indies[1]

PROLOGUE

of Bishop Brother Bartolomé de las Casas, or Casaus, to the most high and most mighty Prince of Spain, our Lord the Prince Philip

Most high and most mighty Lord:

As Divine Providence has ordained that the world shall, for the benefit and proper government of the human race, be divided into kingdoms and peoples

---

1. Translated by Nigel Griffin.

and that these shall be ruled by kings, who are (as Homer has it) fathers and shepherds to their people and are, accordingly, the noblest and most virtuous of beings, there is no doubt, nor could there in all reason be any such doubt, but that these kings entertain nothing save that which is morally unimpeachable. It follows that if the commonwealth suffers from some defect, or shortcoming, or evil, the reason can only be that the ruler is unaware of it; once the matter is brought to his notice, he will work with the utmost diligence to set matters right and will not rest content until the evil has been eradicated. This would appear to be the sense of the words of Solomon in the Bible: "A king that sitteth in the throne of judgment scattereth away all evil with his eyes."[2] For, granted the innate and natural virtue of the ruler, it follows that the simple knowledge that something is wrong in his kingdom is quite sufficient to ensure that he will see that it is corrected, for he will not tolerate any such evil for a moment longer than it takes him to right it.

Contemplating, therefore (most mighty Lord), as a man with more than fifty years' experience of seeing at first hand the evil and the harm, the losses and diminutions suffered by those great kingdoms, each so vast and so wonderful that it would be more appropriate to refer to them as the New World of the Americas—kingdoms granted and entrusted by God and His Church to the Spanish Crown so that they might be properly ruled and governed, converted to the Faith, and tenderly nurtured to full material and spiritual prosperity—[3] I am persuaded that, if Your Highness had been informed of even a few of the excesses which this New World has witnessed, all of them surpassing anything that men hitherto have imagined even in their wildest dreams, Your Highness would not have delayed for even one moment before entreating His Majesty to prevent any repetition of the atrocities which go under the name of "conquests," excesses which, if no move is made to stop them, will be committed time and again, and which (given that the indigenous peoples of the region are naturally so gentle, so peace-loving, so humble and so docile) are of themselves iniquitous, tyrannical, contrary to natural, canon, and civil law, and are deemed wicked and are condemned and proscribed by all such legal codes. I therefore concluded that it would constitute a criminal neglect of my duty to remain silent about the enormous loss of life as well as the infinite number of human souls despatched to Hell in the course of such "conquests," and so resolved to publish an account of a few such outrages (and they can be only a few out of the countless number of such incidents that I could relate) in order to make that account the more accessible to Your Highness.

* * *

[PREFACE]

The Americas were discovered in 1492, and the first Christian settlements established by the Spanish the following year. It is accordingly forty-nine years now since Spaniards began arriving in numbers in this part of the world. They first settled the large and fertile island of Hispaniola,[4] which boasts six

---

2. Proverbs 20.8.   3. Pope Alexander VI granted sovereignty over the Americas to Ferdinand and Isabella in 1493 and required the Spanish kings to convert the natives to Christianity.   4. Present-day Haiti and the Dominican Republic.

hundred leagues of coastline and is surrounded by a great many other large islands, all of them, as I saw for myself, with as high a native population as anywhere on earth. Of the coast of the mainland, which, at its nearest point, is a little over two hundred and fifty leagues from Hispaniola, more than ten thousand leagues had been explored by 1541, and more are being discovered every day. This coastline, too, was swarming with people and it would seem, if we are to judge by those areas so far explored, that the Almighty selected this part of the world as home to the greater part of the human race.

God made all the peoples of this area, many and varied as they are, as open and as innocent as can be imagined. The simplest people in the world—unassuming, long-suffering, unassertive, and submissive—they are without malice or guile, and are utterly faithful and obedient both to their own native lords and to the Spaniards in whose service they now find themselves. Never quarrelsome or belligerent or boisterous, they harbor no grudges and do not seek to settle old scores; indeed, the notions of revenge, rancor, and hatred are quite foreign to them. At the same time, they are among the least robust of human beings: their delicate constitutions make them unable to withstand hard work or suffering and render them liable to succumb to almost any illness, no matter how mild. Even the common people are no tougher than princes or than other Europeans born with a silver spoon in their mouths and who spend their lives shielded from the rigors of the outside world. They are also among the poorest people on the face of the earth; they own next to nothing and have no urge to acquire material possessions. As a result they are neither ambitious nor greedy, and are totally uninterested in worldly power. Their diet is every bit as poor and as monotonous, in quantity and in kind, as that enjoyed by the Desert Fathers. Most of them go naked, save for a loincloth to cover their modesty; at best they may wrap themselves in a piece of cotton material a yard or two square. Most sleep on matting, although a few possess a kind of hanging net, known in the language of Hispaniola as a hammock. They are innocent and pure in mind and have a lively intelligence, all of which makes them particularly receptive to learning and understanding the truths of our Catholic faith and to being instructed in virtue; indeed, God has invested them with fewer impediments in this regard than any other people on earth. Once they begin to learn of the Christian faith they become so keen to know more, to receive the Sacraments, and to worship God, that the missionaries who instruct them do truly have to be men of exceptional patience and forbearance; and over the years I have time and again met Spanish laymen who have been so struck by the natural goodness that shines through these people that they frequently can be heard to exclaim: "These would be the most blessed people on earth if only they were given the chance to convert to Christianity."

It was upon these gentle lambs, imbued by the Creator with all the qualities we have mentioned, that from the very first day they clapped eyes on them the Spanish fell like ravening wolves upon the fold, or like tigers and savage lions who have not eaten meat for days. The pattern established at the outset has remained unchanged to this day, and the Spaniards still do nothing save tear the natives to shreds, murder them and inflict upon them untold misery, suffering and distress, tormenting, harrying and persecuting them mercilessly. * * *

* * *

The reason the Christians have murdered on such a vast scale and killed anyone and everyone in their way is purely and simply greed. They have set out to line their pockets with gold and to amass private fortunes as quickly as possible so that they can then assume a status quite at odds with that into which they were born. Their insatiable greed and overweening ambition know no bounds; the land is fertile and rich, the inhabitants simple, forbearing, and submissive. The Spaniards have shown not the slightest consideration for these people, treating them (and I speak from first-hand experience, having been there from the outset) not as brute animals—indeed, I would to God they had done and had shown them the consideration they afford their animals—so much as piles of dung in the middle of the road. They have had as little concern for their souls as for their bodies, all the millions that have perished having gone to their deaths with no knowledge of God and without the benefit of the Sacraments. One fact in all this is widely known and beyond dispute, for even the tyrannical murderers themselves acknowledge the truth of it: the indigenous peoples never did the Europeans any harm whatever; on the contrary, they believed them to have descended from the heavens, at least until they or their fellow-citizens had tasted, at the hands of these oppressors, a diet of robbery, murder, violence, and all other manner of trials and tribulations.

HISPANIOLA

As we have said, the island of Hispaniola was the first to witness the arrival of Europeans and the first to suffer the wholesale slaughter of its people and the devastation and depopulation of the land. It all began with the Europeans taking native women and children both as servants and to satisfy their own base appetites; then, not content with what the local people offered them of their own free will (and all offered as much as they could spare), they started taking for themselves the food the natives contrived to produce by the sweat of their brows, which was in all honesty little enough. Since what a European will consume in a single day normally supports three native households of ten persons each for a whole month, and since the newcomers began to subject the locals to other vexations, assaults, and iniquities, the people began to realize that these men could not, in truth, have descended from the heavens. Some of them started to conceal what food they had, others decided to send their women and children into hiding, and yet others took to the hills to get away from the brutal and ruthless cruelty that was being inflicted on them. The Christians punched them, boxed their ears and flogged them in order to track down the local leaders, and the whole shameful process came to a head when one of the European commanders raped the wife of the paramount chief of the entire island. It was then that the locals began to think up ways of driving the Europeans out of their lands and to take up arms against them. Their weapons, however, were flimsy and ineffective both in attack and in defence (and, indeed, war in the Americas is no more deadly than our jousting, or than many European children's games) and, with their horses and swords and lances, the Spaniards easily fended them off, killing them and committing all kind of atrocities against them.

They forced their way into native settlements, slaughtering everyone they found there, including small children, old men, pregnant women, and even women who had just given birth. They hacked them to pieces, slicing open their bellies with their swords as though they were so many sheep herded into a pen. They even laid wagers on whether they could manage to slice a man in two at a stroke, or cut an individual's head from his body, or disembowel him with a single blow of their axes. They grabbed suckling infants by the feet and, ripping them from their mothers' breasts, dashed them headlong against the rocks. Others, laughing and joking all the while, threw them over their shoulders into a river, shouting: "Wriggle, you little perisher." They slaughtered anyone and everyone in their path, on occasion running through a mother and her baby with a single thrust of their swords. They spared no one, erecting especially wide gibbets on which they could string their victims up with their feet just off the ground and then burn them alive thirteen at a time, in honor of our Savior and the twelve Apostles, or tie dry straw to their bodies and set fire to it. Some they chose to keep alive and simply cut their wrists, leaving their hands dangling, saying to them: "Take this letter"— meaning that their sorry condition would act as a warning to those hiding in the hills. The way they normally dealt with the native leaders and nobles was to tie them to a kind of griddle consisting of sticks resting on pitchforks driven into the ground and then grill them over a slow fire, with the result that they howled in agony and despair as they died a lingering death.

* * *

After the fighting was over and all the men had been killed, the surviving natives—usually, that is, the young boys, the women, and the children— were shared out between the victors. One got thirty, another forty, a third as many as a hundred or even twice that number; everything depended on how far one was in the good books of the despot who went by the title of governor. The pretext under which the victims were parceled out in this way was that their new masters would then be in a position to teach them the truths of the Christian faith; and thus it came about that a host of cruel, grasping and wicked men, almost all of them pig-ignorant, were put in charge of these poor souls. And they discharged this duty by sending the men down the mines, where working conditions were appalling, to dig for gold, and putting the women to labor in the fields and on their master's estates, to till the soil and raise the crops, properly a task only for the toughest and strongest of men. Both women and men were given only wild grasses to eat and other unnutritious foodstuffs. The mothers of young children promptly saw their milk dry up and their babies die; and, with the women and the men separated and never seeing each other, no new children were born. The men died down the mines from overwork and starvation, and the same was true of the women who perished out on the estates. The islanders, previously so numerous, began to die out as would any nation subjected to such appalling treatment. For example, they were made to carry burdens of three and four arrobas[5] for distances of up to a hundred or even two hundred leagues, and were forced to carry their Christian masters in hammocks, which are like nets slung from the shoulders of the bearers. In short, they were treated as

5. A unit of weight about 25 pounds.

beasts of burden and developed huge sores on their shoulders and backs as happens with animals made to carry excessive loads. And this is not to mention the floggings, beatings, thrashings, punches, curses and countless other vexations and cruelties to which they were routinely subjected and to which no chronicle could ever do justice nor any reader respond save with horror and disbelief.

It is of note that all these island territories began to go to the dogs once news arrived of the death of our most gracious Queen Isabella, who departed this life in 1504. Up to then, only a small number of provinces had been destroyed through unjust military action, not the whole area, and news of even this partial destruction had by and large been kept from the queen, because, she—may her soul rest in peace—took a close personal interest in the physical and spiritual welfare of the native peoples, as those of us who lived through those years and saw examples of it with our own eyes can attest. There is one other general rule in all this, and it is that, wherever the Spaniards set foot, right throughout the Americas, they subjected the native inhabitants to the cruelties of which we have spoken, killing these poor and innocent people, tyrannizing them, and oppressing them in the most abominable fashion. The longer they spent in the region the more ingenious were the torments, each crueler than the last, that they inflicted on their victims, as God finally abandoned them and left them to plummet headlong into a life of full-time crime and wickedness.

CAPTAIN JOHN SMITH
1580–1631

Captain John Smith was a traveler, colonist, and historian of New England. His published writings include *The Generall Historie of Virginia* (1624), *A Description of New England* (1625), and *The True Travels, Adventures and Observations of Captaine John Smith in Europe, Asia, Africa and America* (1630). What he is most famous for, however, is his encounter with Chief Powhatan and his daughter, Pocahontas. In 1607, when Smith was leader of the Jamestown colony in the Chesapeake Bay, he was captured by local natives under the leadership of Powhatan, who was on the verge of executing his captive when his daughter, Pocahontas, successfully pled for the white man's life. This is the stuff of legend as well as history. In popular fantasy, such as the Disney film of 1995, the Indian princess and the English colonist fall in love and marry, adding both romance and legitimacy to the story of English conquest in the New World. The story distills the most cherished myth of English settlers, which is that the natives—especially those who suffered under the rapacious Spanish conquerors—wanted and consented to English rule. In reality, Pocahontas married John Rolfe, a friend of Smith's; traveled to England, where she met King James I and Queen Anne; and died there in 1617 at the age of twenty-two.

The Story of Pocahontas

To the most high and vertuous Princesse Queene Anne of Great Brittanie.

Most admired Queene,

The love I beare my God, my King and Countrie, hath so oft emboldened mee in the worst of extreme dangers, that now honestie doth constraine mee presume thus farre beyond my selfe, to present your Majestie this short discourse: if ingratitude be a deadly poyson to all honest vertues, I must bee guiltie of that crime if I should omit any meanes to bee thankfull. So it is,

That some ten yeeres agoe being in Virginia, and taken prisoner by the power of Powhatan their chiefe King, I received from this great Salvage exceeding great courtesie, especially from his sonne Nantaquaus, the most manliest, comeliest, boldest spirit, I ever saw in a Salvage, and his sister Pocahontas, the Kings most deare and well-beloved daughter, being but a childe of twelve or thirteene yeeres of age, whose compassionate pitifull heart, of my desperate estate, gave me much cause to respect her: I being the first Christian this proud King and his grim attendants ever saw: and thus inthralled in their barbarous power, I cannot say I felt the least occasion of want that was in the power of those my mortall foes to prevent, notwith-standing al their threats. After some six weeks fatting amongst those Salvage Courtiers, at the minute of my execution, she hazarded the beating out of her owne braines to save mine, and not onely that, but so prevailed with her father, that I was safely conducted to James towne, where I found about eight and thirtie miserable poore and sicke creatures, to keepe possession of all those large territories of Virginia, such was the weakenesse of this poore Common-wealth, as had the Salvages not fed us, we directly had starved.

And this reliefe, most gracious Queene, was commonly brought us by this Lady Pocahontas, notwithstanding all these passages when inconstant For-tune turned our peace to warre, this tender Virgin would still not spare to dare to visit us, and by her our jarres have beene oft appeased, and our wants still supplyed; were it the policie of her father thus to imploy her, or the ordi-nance of God thus to make her his instrument, or her extraordinarie affection to our Nation, I know not: but of this I am sure; when her father with the utmost of his police and power, sought to surprize mee, having but eighteene with mee, the darke night could not affright her from comming through the irkesome woods, and with watered eies gave me intelligence, with her best advice to escape his furie; which had hee knowne, hee had surely slaine her. James towne with her wild traine[1] she as freely frequented, as her fathers habitation; and during the time of two or three yeeres, she next under God, was still the instrument to preserve this Colonie from death, famine, and utter confusion, which if in those times had once beene dissolved, Virginia might have line[2] as it was at our first arrivall to this day. Since then, this bus-inesse having beene turned and varied by many accidents from that I left it at: it is most certaine, after a long and troublesome warre after my departure, betwixt her father and our Colonie, all which time shee was not heard of,

---

1. Group of followers.   2. Remained.

about two yeeres after she her selfe was taken prisoner, being so detained neere two yeeres longer, the Colonie by that meanes was relieved, peace concluded, and at last rejecting her barbarous condition, was maried to an English Gentleman, with whom at this present she is in England; the first Christian ever of that Nation, the first Virginian ever spake English, or had a childe in mariage by an Englishman, a matter surely, if my meaning bee truly considered and well understood, worthy a Princes understanding.

Thus most gracious Lady, I have related to your Majestie, what at your best leasure our approved Histories will account you at large, and done in the time of your Majesties life, and however this might bee presented you from a more worthy pen, it cannot from a more honest heart, as yet I never begged any thing of the state, or any, and it is my want of abilitie and her exceeding desert, your birth, meanes and authoritie, hir birth, vertue, want and simplicitie, doth make mee thus bold, humbly to beseech your Majestie to take this knowledge of her, though it be from one so unworthy to be the reporter, as my selfe, her husbands estate not being able to make her fit to attend your Majestie: the most and least I can doe, is to tell you this, because none so oft hath tried it as my selfe, and the rather being of so great a spirit, how ever her stature: if she should not be well received, seeing this Kingdome may rightly have a Kingdome by her meanes; her present love to us and Christianitie, might turne to such scorne and furie, as to divert all this good to the worst of evill, where finding so great a Queene should doe her some honour more than she can imagine, for being so kinde to your servants and subjects, would so ravish her with content, as endeare her dearest bloud to effect that, your Majestie and all the Kings honest subjects most earnestly desire: And so I humbly kisse your gracious hands.

Being about this time preparing to set saile for New-England, I could not stay to doe her that service I desired, and she well deserved; but hearing shee was at Branford[3] with divers of my friends, I went to see her: After a modest salutation, without any word, she turned about, obscured her face, as not seeming well contented; and in that humor her husband, with divers others, we all left her two or three houres, repenting my selfe to have writ she could speake English. But not long after, she began to talke, and remembred mee well what courtesies shee had done: saying, You did promise Powhatan what was yours should bee his, and he the like to you; you called him father being in his land a stranger, and by the same reason so must I doe you: which though I would have excused, I durst not allow of that title, because she was a Kings daughter;[4] with a well set countenance she said, Were you not afraid to come into my fathers Countrie, and caused feare in him and all his people (but mee) and feare you here I should call you father; I tell you then I will, and you shall call mee childe, and so I will bee for ever and ever your Countrieman. They did tell us alwaies you were dead, and I knew no other till I came to Plimoth; yet Powhatan did command Uttamatomakkin[5] to seeke you, and know the truth, because your Countriemen will lie much.

This Salvage, one of Powhatans Councell, being amongst them held an understanding fellow; the King purposely sent him, as they say, to number the people here, and informe him well what wee were and our state. Arriving

---

3. Brentford in Middlesex. **4.** Smith fears the disapproval of the English court if he is viewed as the equal of the Indian royalty. **5.** Identified below as one of Powhattan's council.

at Plimoth, according to his directions, he got a long sticke, whereon by notches hee did thinke to have kept the number of all the men hee could see, but he was quickly wearie of that taske: Comming to London, where by chance I met him, having renewed our acquaintance, where many were desirous to heare and see his behaviour, hee told me Powhatan did bid him to finde me out, to shew him our God, the King, Queene, and Prince, I so much had told them of: Concerning God, I told him the best I could, the King I heard he had seene, and the rest hee should see when he would; he denied ever to have seene the King, till by circumstances he was satisfied he had: Then he replyed very sadly, You gave Powhatan a white Dog, which Powhatan fed as himselfe, but your King gave me nothing, and I am better than your white Dog.

The small time I staid in London, divers Courtiers and others, my acquaintances, hath gone with mee to see her, that generally concluded, they did thinke God had a great hand in her conversion, and they have seene many English Ladies worse favoured, proportioned and behavioured, and as since I have heard, it pleased both the King and Queenes Majestie honorably to esteeme her, accompanied with that honorable Lady the Lady De la Ware, and that honorable Lord her husband, and divers other persons of good qualities, both publikely at the maskes[6] and otherwise, to her great satisfaction and content, which doubtlesse she would have deserved[7] had she lived to arrive in Virginia.

6. Theatrical entertainments at court.   7. Returned in kind; reciprocated.

JOHN DONNE
1572–1631

Of all English Renaissance poets, John Donne was the most fascinated by the capacity of poetic language to transform the ways in which human beings understand their minds and the world around them. The idea that rhetoric—the use of ornamented language to sway audiences—conferred authority on gifted speakers was not new in Donne's era any more than it is in ours. But Donne's use of it was so startlingly original that literary criticism was unable or unwilling to assimilate his poetry into the poetic canon until the twentieth century. The major reason for the delay in reaching a consensus on Donne's talent is that Donne refused to submit his poetic voice to past traditions and therefore had no obvious poetic lineage. He characteristically aimed for more power over his readers than they were accustomed to give. In his own words, he wished for nothing less than "to trouble the understanding, to displace, and discompose, and disorder the judgment or, to empty it of former apprehensions, and to shake beliefs, with which it had possessed itself before; and then when it is thus melted, to pour it into new molds, when it is thus mollified, to stamp and imprint new forms, new images, new opinions in it." How, one wonders, did one man come to have such ambition to recreate the world of the mind and to trust in his own ability to accomplish such mental change?

Donne was born in London in 1572 to a Catholic family and attended Oxford, Cambridge, and Lincoln's Inn (law school) without obtaining degrees or becoming a lawyer. He considered his intellectual energy, his voracious reading, and his travels (including expeditions to Cadiz and to the Azores with Raleigh and Essex) as preparations for a brilliant career at court. His talents were considerable, and in 1598 he was appointed private secretary to Sir Thomas Egerton, Lord Keeper of England, who presided over the House of Lords. But Donne sabotaged his prospects by a single momentous act: he secretly married Ann More, the sixteen-year-old niece of Lady Egerton. Donne was imprisoned in the Fleet until the marriage was judged to be legal and was also, predictably, dismissed from Egerton's service. Although it took him years of frustration to accept it, he had permanently disqualified himself from public office. It is a stunning irony of his life that Donne, following his conversion from Catholicism, was pressed into entering the Church because he was considered unfit for public service. At the repeated insistence of King James, Donne was ordained deacon of St. Paul's Cathedral. Donne brought the same passion and intelligence to his ecclesiastical and pastoral charge that startled and swayed the readers of his poetry.

In part because he long held out hopes for advancement, Donne never sought to publish his poetry. There was a social stigma attached to print that kept gentlemen from publishing their poetry, and Donne, especially when he had taken religious orders, was not about to jeopardize his reputation further. When one of his patrons asked for a collection of his lyrics, Donne had to write to various friends and ask if they would send any poems they happened to have on hand. He referred slightingly to his poems as "light flashes" and "evaporations," characteristically strong terms for the way that other poets, such as Christopher Marlowe, would refer to their poems as idle "toys" or "games." Yet poets who offered to insult their own poetry before anyone else had the chance often loved their poems with the ardent possessiveness that a child has for a favorite toy or game, and Donne was no different. He was fascinated by all things subtle, evanescent, and illuminating, which are the most obvious properties of light flashes and evaporations. It is through such figures that he was able to communicate his most elusive and cherished emotions and ideas.

John Donne's readers must prepare themselves for his extensive use of complex metaphors designed to arrest the readers' attention and drive a wedge, in effect, between the intellect and the senses. This technique inspired the label of "metaphysical" that has come to be associated with the poetry of Donne and his followers. One of the earliest critics of poetry, John Dryden, remarked that Donne "affects the metaphysics not only in his satires, but in his amorous verses, where nature only should reign, and perplexes the minds of the fair sex with nice speculations of philosophy." Samuel Johnson followed up the thought when he memorably wrote that in Donne's poetry, "the most heterogeneous ideas are yoked by violence together." What they have in mind is that the foundation of many of Donne's poems exists in a paradox, oxymoron, or demanding intellectual idea.

For example, when Donne takes up the familiar idea of the "flame of love," usually invoked to establish a bond with the reader through sensual appeal, he uses a series of increasingly intellectual images that finally make the commonplace notion of the erotic flame seem strange and novel. In "The Canonization," he asserts that he and his lover (his wife, Ann More) are like moths to the flame; then candles burning their own resources; and finally the phoenix, the Arabian bird of myth that rises afresh out of its own ashes. Donne never allows his readers entirely to forget that he is pinning his unusual images to the ordinary scene of lovemaking. Yet he insists on characterizations of love and sexuality that momentarily bewilder and then stimulate the reader to work through the logic of his paradoxes. If the reader chooses to believe in the power of the complex metaphors, then Donne has successfully transformed a cliché ("love is a flame") into a mystery revealed. In his erotic and religious poetry alike, Donne forces his readers to move along a polar continuum between cynicism and awe or wonder (i.e., tightly closed or widely open states of mind). Perhaps the most most extraordinary accomplishment of his poetry is, in the end, its ability to change readers' minds from certainty to doubt and from cynicism to wonder.

The Good-Morrow

I wonder, by my troth, what thou and I
    Did, till we loved? were we not weaned till then?
But sucked on country pleasures, childishly?
    Or snorted we in the Seven Sleepers' den?[1]
'Twas so; but[2] this, all pleasures fancies be.   5
If ever any beauty I did see,
Which I desired, and got, twas but a dream of thee.

And now good-morrow to our waking souls,
    Which watch not one another out of fear;
For love, all love of other sights controls,   10
    And makes one little room an everywhere.
Let sea-discoverers to new worlds have gone,
Let maps to other; worlds on worlds have shown,[3]
Let us possess one world, each hath one, and is one.

My face in thine eye, thine in mine appears,   15
    And true plain hearts do in the faces rest;
Where can we find two better hemispheres,
    Without sharp north, without declining west?
Whatever dies was not mixed equally,[4]
If our two loves be one, or, thou and I   20
Love so alike that none do slacken, none can die.

The Sun Rising

Busy old fool, unruly Sun,
    Why dost thou thus,
Through windows, and through curtains, call on us?
Must to thy motions lovers' seasons run?
    Saucy pedantic wretch, go chide   5
    Late schoolboys, and sour prentices,
Go tell court-huntsmen that the king will ride,
Call country ants to harvest offices,
Love, all alike,[5] no season knows, nor clime,
Nor hours, days, months, which are the rags of time.   10

Thy beams, so reverend and strong
    Why shouldst thou think?
I could eclipse and cloud them with a wink,
But that I would not lose her sight so long:
    If her eyes have not blinded thine,   15

1. Both Christian and Islamic authors recite the legend of seven Christian youths of Ephesus who hid in a cave for 187 years to escape Roman persecution.   2. Except.   3. I.e., let us concede that maps to other investigators have shown, etc.   4. Scholastic philosophy taught that when the elements were imperfectly ("not equally") mixed, matter was mortal and mutable; but when they were perfectly mixed, it was undying and unchanging.   5. Love, which never changes.

Look, and tomorrow late, tell me
    Whether both th' Indias[6] of spice and mine
    Be where thou leftst them, or lie here with me.
Ask for those kings whom thou saw'st yesterday,
And thou shalt hear, All here in one bed lay.   20

    She's all states, and all princes I,
        Nothing else is.
Princes do but play us; compared to this,
All honor's mimic, all wealth alchemy.[7]
    Thou, sun, art half as happy as we,   25
        In that the world's contracted thus.
    Thine age asks ease, and since thy duties be
    To warm the world, that's done in warming us.
Shine here to us, and thou art everywhere;
This bed thy center is, these walls, thy sphere.[8]   30

The Canonization

For God's sake hold your tongue and let me love!
    Or chide my palsy or my gout,
My five gray hairs or ruined fortune flout;
With wealth your state, your mind with arts improve,
    Take you a course,[9] get you a place,[1]   5
    Observe[2] his Honor or his Grace,
Or the king's real or his stampéd face[3]
    Contemplate; what you will, approve,
        So you will let me love.

Alas, alas, who's injured by my love?   10
    What merchant's ships have my sighs drowned?
Who says my tears have overflowed his ground?
When did my colds a forward spring remove?
    When did the heats which my veins fill
    Add one man to the plaguy bill?[4]   15
Soldiers find wars, and lawyers find out still
    Litigious men which quarrels move,
        Though she and I do love.

Call us what you will, we are made such by love.
    Call her one, me another fly,   20
We're tapers[5] too, and at our own cost die;
And we in us find th' eagle and the dove.[6]
    The phoenix riddle hath more wit

---

6. The East and West Indies.   7. Base metal that imitates gold.   8. According to Ptolemaic astronomy, the sun orbits in its sphere around the earth, which occupies the center.   9. A direction (in life).
1. An appointment at court or elsewhere.   2. Pay court to.   3. On coins.   4. List of the dead from
bubonic plague, always worst in summer.   5. Candles.   6. Representing meekness and purity, as the
eagle represents strength and wisdom.

By us; we two, being one, are it.
So to one neutral thing both sexes fit,   25
    We die and rise the same,[7] and prove
        Mysterious by this love.

We can die by it, if not live by love;
    And if unfit for tombs and hearse
Our legend be, it will be fit for verse;   30
And if no piece of chronicle we prove,
    We'll build in sonnets pretty rooms[8]
    (As well a well-wrought urn becomes
The greatest ashes, as half-acre tombs),
    And by these hymns all shall approve   35
        Us canonized[9] for love.

And thus invoke us: "You whom reverent love
    Made one another's hermitage,
You to whom love was peace, that now is rage,
Who did the whole world's soul extract, and drove   40
    Into the glasses of your eyes
    (So made such mirrors and such spies
That they did all to you epitomize)
    Countries, towns, courts; beg from above
        A pattern of your love!"   45

The Ecstasy[1]

Where, like a pillow on a bed
    A pregnant bank swelled up to rest
The violet's reclining head,
    Sat we two, one another's best.
Our hands were firmly cemented   5
    With a fast balm, which thence did spring;
Our eye-beams[2] twisted, and did thread
    Our eyes upon one double string;
So to'intergraft our hands, as yet
    Was all the means to make us one,   10
And pictures in our eyes to get
    Was all our propagation.
As 'twixt two equal armies fate
    Suspends uncertain victory,
Our souls (which to advance their state   15
    Were gone out) hung 'twixt her and me.

---

7. Like flies we burn up in the candle flame; like candles we are consumed as we burn; like the phoenix we are reborn from the ashes. (A fabulous Arabian bird, the phoenix was alleged to make its own pyre, die in song, and arise from its own ashes.) 8. Sonnets are composed of stanzas, the Italian word for "rooms." 9. Made saints, whose aid other lovers will invoke. 1. A mystical state in which the soul leaves the body. 2. According to Renaissance theory, eyes emitted a beam that grasped objects of sight.

And whilst our souls negotiate there,
    We like sepulchral statues lay;
All day, the same our postures were,
    And we said nothing, all the day.   20
If any,[3] so by love refined
    That he soul's language understood,
And by good love were grown all mind,
    Within convenient distance stood,
He (though he knew not which soul spake,   25
    Because both meant, both spake the same)
Might thence a new concoction[4] take
    And part far purer than he came.
This ecstasy doth unperplex,
    We said, and tell us what we love;   30
We see by this it was not sex,
    We see we saw not what did move;
But as all several souls contain
    Mixture of things, they know not what,
Love these mixed souls doth mix again   35
    And makes both one, each this and that.
A single violet transplant,
    The strength, the color, and the size,
(All which before was poor and scant)
    Redoubles still, and multiplies.   40
When love with one another so
    Interinanimates two souls,
That abler soul, which thence doth flow,
    Defects of loneliness controls.
We then, who are this new soul, know   45
    Of what we are composed and made,
For, th' atomies[5] of which we grow
    Are souls, whom no change can invade.
But O alas, so long, so far,
    Our bodies why do we forbear?   50
They're ours, though they're not we; we are
    The intelligences, they the spheres.[6]
We owe them thanks, because they thus
    Did us, to us at first convey,
Yielded their forces, sense to us,   55
    Nor are dross to us, but allay.[7]
On man heaven's influence works not so,
    But that it first imprints the air;
So soul into the soul may flow,
    Though it to body first repair.   60
As our blood labors to beget
    Spirits,[8] as like souls as it can,
Because such fingers need to knit

---

3. An imagined spectator, trained in Neoplatonic theories of love.   4. In alchemy, base metals were purified or concocted by heat.   5. Atoms.   6. Heavenly bodies moved by angelic spirits or intelligences. 7. Alloy.   8. Vapors thought to rise from the blood.

That subtle knot which makes us man,
So must pure lovers' souls descend 65
To affections, and to faculties,
Which sense may reach and apprehend,
Else a great prince in prison lies.[9]
To our bodies turn we then, that so
Weak men on love revealed may look; 70
Love's mysteries in souls do grow,
But yet the body is his book.
And if some lover, such as we,
Have heard this dialogue of one,
Let him still mark us, he shall see 75
Small change, when we're to bodies gone.

The Relic

When my grave is broke up again
Some second guest to entertain,
(For graves have learned that woman head,[1]
To be to more than one a bed)
And he that digs it, spies 5
A bracelet of bright hair about the bone,
Will he not let us alone,
And think that there a loving couple lies,
Who thought that this device might be some way 10
To make their souls, at the last busy day,[2]
Meet at this grave, and make a little stay?

If this fall in a time, or land,
Where mis-devotion doth command,
Then he, that digs us up, will bring
Us to the bishop, and the king, 15
To make us relics; then
Thou shalt be a Mary Magdalen,[3] and I
A something else thereby;[4]
All women shall adore us, and some men;
And since at such time miracles are sought, 20
I would have that age by this paper taught
What miracles we harmless lovers wrought.

First, we loved well and faithfully,
Yet knew not what we loved, nor why;
Difference of sex no more we knew 25
Than our guardian angels do;
Coming and going, we

9. Alchemical emblems represent the gold thought to be inside base metal as a prince in captivity.
1. Natural characteristic of women. 2. Judgment Day. 3. Sexual penitent and devoted follower of Jesus. 4. I.e., if she is taken to be Mary Magdalen, he will be taken for another saint.

Perchance might kiss, but not between those meals;
  Our hands ne'er touched the seals[5]
Which nature, injured by late law, sets free;   30
These miracles we did, but now alas,
All measure, and all language, I should pass,
Should I tell what a miracle she was.

Holy Sonnet 14

Batter[6] my heart, three-personed God, for you
As yet but knock, breathe, shine, and seek to mend;
That I may rise and stand, o'erthrow me, and bend
Your force to break, blow, burn, and make me new.
I, like an usurped town to another due,   5
Labor to admit to you, but oh, to no end;
Reason, your viceroy in me, me should defend,
But is captived, and proves weak or untrue.
Yet dearly I love you, and would be lovéd fain[7]
But am betrothed unto your enemy;   10
Divorce me, untie or break that knot again;
Take me to you, imprison me, for I,
Except you enthrall me, never shall be free,
Nor ever chaste, except you ravish me.

5. Sexual organs.   6. Puff up with pride.   7. I.e., he desires to be loved.

LYRIC POETRY: OTHER METAPHYSICALS

For all of his self-representation as a phoenix or an original, Donne had the company of sympathetic spirits, both in England and on the Continent. Poets such as San Juan de la Cruz, Constantijn Huygens, George Herbert, and Robert Herrick continued and developed Donne's poetry of paradox and wonder. Spiritual, erotic, and intellectual conflicts are the major theme of the poetry that is variously called "metaphysical" and "baroque," and these themes are rooted in historical conflict. The sixteenth and seventeenth centuries saw revolutions in the religious, political, and scientific understanding of the world. Lyric poets responded to these crises with stylistic and conceptual changes in their own medium.

Lyric poetry, which characteristically places a strong focus on the speaker's inward thoughts, was particularly well adapted to exploring the effects of intellectual and spiritual change on the lyric "I" and, by extension, the human subject. Central to European metaphysical poetry is the conviction that little can be taken for granted: who we are and what the nature of the world might be are under constant review. The poets presented here require a skeptical focus on the place of humankind in a universe of mystery and, simultaneously, an act of faith. What holds the complex and even chaotic world together at moments of duress is an intent gaze at what the poets, as devout Christians, recognize as the anchoring event in human history: the Crucifixion, or sacrifice made by a loving God to heal a breach in human relations with the divine. The idea of spiritual meditation could not rest on convention and cliché: the upheavals in the scientific and religious understanding of the physical and spiritual world saw to it that old and familiar modes of devotion no longer sufficed. For this reason, the poets' intellectualism is ferocious, their passions vehement, and their style hard.

Metaphysical verse, with its passionate and intellectual conflicts, has an afterlife in modern lyric traditions, particularly in geopolitical sites where political and religious strife continue to put pressure on what it means to live in a Christian state. A good example is the musical output of the Irish rock-and-roll band U2, which fuses spiritual devotion and erotic feeling in the lyrics and rhythms of such songs as "Gloria," "Sunday, Bloody Sunday," and "I Will Follow."

GUY LE FÈVRE DE LA BODERIE
1541–1590

To Materialists and Unbelievers[1]

Just as the beauteous Sun with constant ray
Doth subtly through a window pierce and pass,
But neither cracks nor breaks the pane of glass
Nor is itself divided any way;

Just so did God the eternal Father send   5
His word in splendor to us in the Maid,[2]
But did not break her crystal nor divide
Her barrier, nor his unity suspend.

You who believe not in the holy Book,
At Nature's mysteries cast a single look,   10
Open your Souls' eyes that you may perceive
The Sun of Suns,[3] which in our hearts would shine.
No more to servant than to lord assign:
Mighty is he in whom all power doth live.

---

1. Translated by Frank J. Warnke.   2. Mary, mother of Jesus.   3. Jesus Christ.

SAN JUAN DE LA CRUZ
1542–1591

Song of the Soul in Union with God[4]

Oh living flame of love
Which tenderly doth wound
My soul within its secret deepest center!
Since not averse you prove,
Oh end what you do sound,   5
And tear the fabric of this sweet encounter.

Oh cautery so smooth!
Oh so desired pain!
Oh gentle hand! Oh touch most delicate,
Which eternal life endueth,   10
And doth all debts unchain!
In killing, you do life perpetuate.

Oh lamps of fire pure,
In whose resplendent blaze
The caverns of my senses most profound,   15
Just now blind and obscure,
Find strangely lovely rays,
And give their love the heat and light now found.

How amorous and mild
The thoughts you give my breast,   20
Where secretly in solitude you dwell:
By your sweet breath beguil'd,
In grace and glory best,
How delicately you do love compel!

4. Translated by Frank J. Warnke.

THÉODORE-AGRIPPA D'AUBIGNÉ
1552–1630

Stanzas to Diane[5]

I open here my breast, a bloody tomb
Of lurid woes: for God's sake, turn your eyes,
Diane, and see my cleft heart where it lies
And see my lungs engrav'd with passion's doom.

5. Translated by Frank J. Warnke.

My frothing blood all blacken'd with the flame,   5
My wretched bones dried out with my despair;
But also what invisibly is there:
The torments which ransack my spirit's frame.

You burn me, and at the furnace of desire
You warm your icy hands; in careful wise   10
You stir my coals, and your inhuman eyes
Weep not with pity but with burning ire.

In the fire of the fury I provoke
Your eyes swell up with pain and overflow,
But 'tis not the unhappiness I owe—   15
Your eyes are troubled by my bitter smoke.

At least my death may please your greedy soul,
Burning the heart and body of your slave;
May then my spirit sweeter torture have,
In dying thus your rage exhausting whole.   20

FRANCISCO DE QUEVEDO
1580–1634

A Love Constant beyond Death[6]

The last shade that takes from me white day
May close my eyes and may release my soul
At once, and may with flattery fulfill
The spirit's eager urge to be away.

But my soul shall not the memory forsake   5
Of where it burn'd there on the other shore;
My passion swims in waters cold and, more,
The rigid law of nature still doth break.

A soul which has a god entire confin'd,
Veins which have given fuel to such a fire,   10
A marrow which so gloriously has burn'd,
Shall from their body, not their care, remove,
Shall turn to ash, but ash which knows desire,
Dust they shall be, but always dust in love.

6. Translated by Frank J. Warnke.

GEORGE HERBERT
1593–1633

Easter Wings[7]

Lord, who createdst man in wealth and store,
    Though foolishly he lost the same,
        Decaying more and more
           Till he became
             Most poor: 5
             With thee
           O let me rise
        As larks, harmoniously,
    And sing this day thy victories:
Then shall the fall further the flight in me.   10

My tender age in sorrow did begin;
    And still with sicknesses and shame
        Thou didst so punish sin,
           That I became
             Most thin.   15
             With thee
           Let me combine,
        And feel this day thy victory;
    For, if I imp my wing on thine,
Affliction shall advance the flight in me.   20

Prayer (1)

Prayer the church's banquet, angel's age,
    God's breath in man returning to his birth,
    The soul in paraphrase, heart in pilgrimage,
The Christian plummet sounding heaven and earth;

Engine against th' Almighty, sinner's tower,   5
    Reversed thunder, Christ-side-piercing spear,
    The six-days world transposing in an hour,
A kind of tune, which all things hear and fear;

Softness, and peace, and joy, and love, and bliss,
    Exalted manna, gladness of the best,   10
    Heaven in ordinary,[8] man well dressed,
The milky way, the bird of Paradise,

Church-bells beyond the stars heard, the soul's blood,
The land of spices; something understood.

---

7. An emblem or picture poem, whose stanzas imitate wings.   8. The part of the Mass that remains unchanged from day to day.

Virtue

Sweet day, so cool, so calm, so bright,
The bridal of the earth and sky;
The dew shall weep thy fall to-night,
        For thou must die.

Sweet rose, whose hue angry and brave   5
Bids the rash gazer wipe his eye;
Thy root is ever in its grave,
        And thou must die.

Sweet spring, full of sweet days and roses,
A box where sweets compacted lie;   10
My music shows ye have your closes,[9]
        And all must die.

Only a sweet and virtuous soul,
Like seasoned timber, never gives;
But though the whole world turn to coal,   15
        Then chiefly lives.

The Collar[1]

I struck the board,[2] and cried, "No more!
        I will abroad!
What! shall I ever sigh and pine?
My lines and life are free; free as the road,
Loose as the wind, as large as store.   5
        Shall I be still in suit?[3]
Have I no harvest but a thorn
To let me blood, and not restore
What I have lost with cordial[4] fruit?
        Sure there was wine   10
Before my sighs did dry it; there was corn
Before my tears did drown it.
Is the year only lost to me?
        Have I no bays[5] to crown it?
No flowers, no garlands gay? all blasted?   15
        All wasted?
Not so, my heart; but there is fruit,
        And thou hast hands.
Recover all thy sigh-blown age
On double pleasures; leave thy cold dispute   20

9. Cadences that bring musical phrases to conclusion.   1. The priest's collar, but also choler (anger), and caller (one who calls) are relevant.   2. Table.   3. In secular terms, in court as a servant of a powerful lord (with a pun on livery); in legal terms, in a court of law attempting to claim a lost right or entitlement.   4. Liqueur, or distilled fruit, with pun on the heart (cor).   5. Crowns made of the bay laurel signified triumph.

Of what is fit and not; forsake thy cage,
    Thy rope of sands,
Which petty thoughts have made, and made to thee
Good cable, to enforce and draw,
    And be thy law,   25
While thou didst wink and wouldst not see.
    Away! Take heed;
    I will abroad.
Call in thy death's-head there; tie up thy fears;
    He that forbears   30
    To suit and serve his need
    Deserves his load."
But as I raved, and grew more fierce and wild
    At every word,
Me thoughts[6] heard one calling, "Child!"   35
    And I replied, "My Lord."

Love (3)

Love bade me welcome, yet my soul drew back,
    Guilty of dust[7] and sin.
But quick-eyed Love, observing me grow slack
    From my first entrance in,
Drew nearer to me, sweetly questioning   5
    If I lacked anything.

"A guest," I answered, "worthy to be here";
    Love said, "You shall be he."
"I, the unkind, the ungrateful? ah my dear,
    I cannot look on thee."   10
Love took my hand and smiling did reply,
    "Who made the eyes but I?"

"Truth, Lord, but I have marred them; let my shame
    Go where it doth deserve."
"And know you not," says Love, "who bore the blame?"   15
    "My dear, then I will serve."
"You must sit down," says Love, "and taste my meat."
    So I did sit and eat.

6. An older form of English, intensifying the passive sense of "it occurred to me."   7. As if from the road. Also relevant is the creation of Adam from dust, to which all Christians return in penalty for the Fall.

CONSTANTIJN HUYGENS
1596–1687

Good Friday[8]

What ails the midday sun? Why shines it not?
Is night at noon then come? Tell me, thou moon,
With thy starry train, why sinkest thou so soon?
Must ye sea-water drink e'er half your route?

Nay, nay, now I perceive your strength abated   5
At the shameful Cross, where Zion's daughters stand
And drown in tears upon the barren land
At those awesome holy words, " 'Tis consummated."[9]

My consummating God, may I presume?
This consummation doth me not consume,   10
Unless thou dost me kill, and soften so
My harden'd soul it may its duty know
And humbly do, so that I hearth and house,
And body, will and time hang on this Cross.

8. Translated by Frank J. Warnke.   9. Christ's words on the cross at the moment of his death [Editor's note]. The full complexity of the original cannot be caught in translation. Actually, in place of the biblical " 'Tis volmaekt" ("It is consummated"), Huygens writes " 'Tis voldaen" ("It is paid for"). The verb "voldoen," however, may mean "to satisfy" as well as "to pay for," and consequently line 10 may have the readings "This payment does not satisfy me" and "This payment does not pay for me" in addition to the implied meaning which I have chosen to render [Translator's note].

JOHN MILTON
1608–1674

The poetic achievement of John Milton is generally regarded as the last flourishing of Christian humanism in Renaissance England; in his poetic work, the Renaissance commitment to classical revival and the Reformation emphasis on the Bible came together. Milton's late position allowed him both to "outdo" the grand epic tradition on its own terms and to criticize its pagan roots. As he well knew, Renaissance epic poets, like Christian humanists, struggled in varying degrees with their mixed allegiances to classical learning and to Christianity. To Christian scholars, the strain of serving the two masters of secular knowledge and religious faith could be distracting: even the Church father Saint Jerome (ca. 347–419 or 420) had a dream in which God denounced him with the charge "You are not a Christian: you are a Ciceronian." In *Paradise Lost*, Milton attempts to resolve the conflict between the seductions of the classics and the imperatives of Christianity: he tells the biblical story of the Fall, and to this authoritative plot he subordinates the classical materials of the epic tradition. What is more, when he wishes to "body forth" the material, tactile richness of beauty—in, for example, the Garden of Eden, Eve, and the snake—he heightens the classicism of his verse. Concentrating classical allusions on the physically sensuous and psychologically disruptive elements of his poem, he allows his classical material to appear in sumptuous glory and, simultaneously, under restraint by the highest authority, the Bible. To an extent, the curbs Milton imposes on his classical sources distract attention from his equally assertive handling of the Bible; yet he does not shy away from telling a highly individual version of the story of "man's first disobedience." The story of Genesis, in which Adam and Eve broke God's prohibition and ate from the tree of knowledge, suggested to Milton an opportunity to expound his own ideas about liberty, knowledge, doubt, sexuality, and marriage.

Milton's life divides conveniently into three stages: a period of long study, which culminated in the great pastoral elegy Lycidas (1637) and his travels on the Continent (1638–39), where he met important literary figures in addition to the astronomer Galileo; his long involvement in doctrinal and political controversy and his service as Latin secretary to Oliver Cromwell's Council of State (1640–60); and, after the restoration of the English monarchy and his banishment from politics, the more solitary and disillusioned years in which Milton (totally blind since 1651) produced his major poetic works, Paradise Lost (1667), Paradise Regained (1671), and Samson Agonistes (1671).

Born in London on December 9, 1608, he received an excellent education at St. Paul's in London and Christ's College, Cambridge, where he prepared for a career in the ministry. He received his B.A. in 1629 and his M.A. in 1632, but did not take holy orders (due to his growing dissatisfaction with Church of England hierarchy). Instead, he lived reclusively at his father's estate at Horton, near Windsor, where he continued his studies and followed his dream curriculum of science and the new discoveries, mathematics, Greek and Latin authors, music, the systematic research of world history, and volumes upon volumes of poetry. In his view, his intensive studies were preparing him for the poet's role as moral leader: whoever hopes to write well, he wrote in an autobiographical sketch, "ought himself to be a true poem, that is, a composition and pattern of the best and honorablest things; not presuming to sing high praises of heroic men or famous Cities, unless he have in himself the experience and the practice of all that is praiseworthy." The complete identification of poet and poem, reading and experience, indicates how important it was to Milton to be morally "fit," not just technically skilled, to compose epic verse.

Politics and not poems were on Milton's mind, however, when he returned from his travels in Italy. Word had reached him that political trouble was brewing at home (the beginnings of the Puritan Revolt), and he returned to London, where he inserted himself into the political controversies by writing pamphlets that he hoped would inspire debate. Some of his political arguments shaped the concepts of religious, civil, and domestic liberties that he explores in Paradise Lost (1667). His most notable tract, Areopagitica (1644), opposed censorship of the press and took to task the parliamentary government (his own party) for trying to restrict the opposition: Parliament was historically bound to defend the liberties of the people, and Milton could not abide its lapse in principle. Throughout his public career he forcefully insisted on popular liberty from arbitrary rule, and he had gone so far as to defend, in print, the execution of his king (Charles I was executed in 1641). How could he justify regicide? Law, he felt, should arise from the reasoning conscience of the individual Christian; to deprive individuals of the free exercise of their reason called for violent resistance.

His most notorious prose writings, however, were directly inspired by his failed marriage and earned him the epithet "the Divorcer": at thirty-two he married the seventeen-year-old Mary Powell, who left him after six weeks. In the argumentative Milton, this event inspired considerable thought and print concerning the grounds of marriage. He complained bitterly of the English law that permitted divorce only to those who had not consummated their marriages and protested that the law left unhappy couples to "grind in the mill of an undelighted and servile copulation" (anything worth saying is worth saying grandly). Without depth of conversation, he argued, men and women were not joined in a genuine marriage. God, he claimed, meant spouses to be spiritual helpmeets and partners in "civil fellowship." In *Paradise Lost*, where Adam and Eve make love without shame and converse with delight, he illustrates his ideal of marriage. Conversation and the "sweet intercourse / Of looks and smiles" turn out to be the essential ingredients of a successful marriage. They are, Milton's Adam says, the way that human beings cope with their fundamental loneliness. When Adam asks God for a companion, he claims that man needs "conversation with his like to help / Or solace his defects" (his lonely distance from God). This loneliness is so intense that even after Eve falls, Adam affirms his need for her (although it means severing himself from God): "with thee / Certain my resolution is to die; / How can I live without thee, how forgo / Thy sweet converse and love so dearly joined?"

Milton's chief source for *Paradise Lost* is the biblical account of Creation, Eden, the Fall, and the expulsion of Adam and Eve from paradise. From the first three chapters of Genesis, he forged twelve capacious books of epic verse, which he fleshed out with his vast knowledge of the classics, history, theology, and science. He had long wanted to write something lasting and once considered composing an epic on King Arthur. Had he written a chivalric romance, he would have inserted himself directly into Virgil's imperial tradition. He began his work on *Paradise Lost*, however, after his banishment from public life: Restoration England had "fallen on evil days," and to his mind no longer had political glory to celebrate. Politically disappointed in the failure of republican government and the reinstatement of monarchy in England, he had reason to look skeptically on the imperial and romance epic tradition he once loved. In fact, he casts Satan as his empire-builder, colonizer, and merchant-adventurer, the positions that Aeneas holds in Virgil's epic. More generally, he asserts the superiority of his own subject over the epic tradition stemming from Homer and Virgil: it is, he declares, "Not less but more heroic than the wrath / Of stern Achilles" or "rage / of Turnus," the Latin warrior Aeneas must defeat in order to found Rome. He goes on to scorn the kind of medieval romance that he once planned to compose: "with long and tedious havoc" these tales have merely "*fabled* knights / In battles *feigned*." His own tale, by implicit contrast, is genuinely historical and heroic. While epic poets assert their continuity with cultural origins, Milton characteristically insists that his own poem disrupts the heroic tradition. *Paradise Lost* alone, he implies, is genuinely concerned with historical origins and is wholly original as creative verse.

Milton's attitude toward the recovery of truth, as his confidence in his poem suggests, is paradoxically traditional and radical. The poet is at once committed to the recovery of biblical truth and determined to smash the trite conventions through which truths have passed to successive generations. When his poem first appeared, it scandalized and bewildered the reading public. Even his verse style was shocking evidence of his radicalism: the rhyming couplets and stanzas that defined English verse for many readers were nowhere to be found, and in their place were rolling periodic sentences of unrhymed verse (iambic pentameter). His rejection of rhyme so upset his contemporaries that he added a brief note explaining and defending his practice: "This neglect then of Rime so little is to be taken for a defect, though it may seem so perhaps to vulgar Readers, that it rather is to be esteem'd an example set, the first in *English*, of ancient liberty recover'd to Heroic Poem from the troublesome and modern bondage of Riming." Milton proclaimed his heroic break from literary tradition and his victorious recovery of an ancient poetic practice. More momentously, he described his poetic innovation as a politically significant act: he was liberating the intellect from bondage and restoring ancient liberties. He had destroyed the shackles of convention (rhymes) and rescued intellectual freedom, and he did it for his reader. And since liberty is meaningless unless exercised vigorously, he intended every sentence and verse line of his poem to be challenging.

Since Milton set out to innovate in verse, revolutionize interpretation, and liberate the intellect, we might suspect that he chose the wrong text: the choice of Adam and Eve to seek knowledge at the cost of their obedience to God. In fact, the status of knowledge is a central, and not fully resolved, problem in *Paradise Lost*. In *Areopagitica*, Milton argued that virtue is meaningful only when gained and tested by experience. Goodness based on mere ignorance of evil, for him, seems inferior to the reasoned choice of the good over a known and alluring evil. He speculated that the Fall caused a change in the way that human beings gained knowledge. In Eden humanity knew only good; after the Fall, humanity knew good by distinguishing it from evil. "What wisdom can there be to choose, what continence to forbear without the knowledge of evil?" he asked. "I cannot praise a fugitive and cloistered virtue, unexercised and unbreathed, that never sallies out and sees her adversary."

This is the position that the more cautious Milton of *Paradise Lost* places in the mouth of his "Adventurous" Eve just before the Fall. Eve, always more independent than Adam, wants to work alone in another part of the Garden, and when she suspects that her husband mistrusts her ability to withstand the temptations of Satan by herself, she grows adamant about facing a trial, should Satan come her way: "what is Faith, Love, Virtue unassay'd / Alone, without exterior help sustain'd?" Like the younger and rasher Milton, she considers such virtue "but a name" or an abstraction rather than an inner quality; she rejects the idea that her obedience has any significance if it is maintained only by "exterior help." If she is to enjoy a reputation for virtue, she wants it to arise from a personal history of her experiences and trials.

Adam, by contrast, seems curious and anxious about his relationship to knowledge. In his conversations with God and with the angel Raphael, he reveals how inquisitive he is about himself, Eve, the world around him, and above all, the mysterious heavens. To Raphael he expresses doubts about the excesses of God's Creation: why are there so many superior heavenly bodies revolving about the earth? The "needless" superfluity and abundance of Creation indicate mysterious purposes that make Adam question his centrality to the cosmos. When Raphael warns him that "Heav'n is for thee too high / To know what passes there; be lowly wise; / Think only what concerns thee and thy being; / Dream not of other Worlds," Adam declares himself "cleared of doubt." He assures the angel (or himself) that it is better to be "freed from intricacies" and "perplexing" and "wand'ring" thoughts that "rove" endlessly until "warn'd, or by experience taught," the imagination learns to "not to know." Although the difference between receiving a warning and learning by experience is great, Adam falls back on the traditionalist position about knowledge, summed up in the caution to "be lowly wise": don't analyze (etymologically, to "break things apart" logically) or use empirical observation to make inquiries that can lead only to hypothesis and speculation. Expound what you know to be true; do not theorize about "high" matters from "low" or material observation (i.e., use inductive reasoning): receive, do not create your own body of wisdom.

It is a truism of the classical tradition that the beauty of temptresses (like Homer's Circe and Ariosto's Alcina) has a disruptive power over epic heroes who otherwise display Stoic constancy and integrity (literally, "wholeness"). To a limited extent, this model of heroic manhood threatened by female corruption applies to *Paradise Lost*. The telling difference is that for Milton, the "kindly rupture" of sexual experience relates to the acquisition of knowledge and can therefore be rejected only at great personal cost to the hero. After Adam has agreed to be "lowly wise," he admits to Raphael that sexual passion, like the superabundant universe, troubles him because it is overwhelming. When he approaches his wife's "loveliness," he says,

> so absolute she seems
> And in herself complete, so well to know
> Her own, that what she wills to do or say,
> Seems wisest, virtuousest, discreetest, best . . .

Adam repeats his error of inductive reasoning: based on the empirical evidence of sight and touch, he wonders if Eve is in fact "one intended first, not after made / Occasionally." Although no less an authority than God tells him that Eve is "inferior" and "subject" to him, Adam cannot ignore his own experience. His social and spiritual interactions with Eve "subject not," he notes, but passion does, and Adam wants to know what to make of this unorthodox fact.

Through Adam's appealing inquisitiveness, Milton's readers learn an answer to a further question about sex that they might have been afraid to ask: do angels make love? Raphael, who has just reproached Adam for his own "vehement" response to sexuality, blushes and admits that they do. His blush is as revealing as his affirmation: do heavenly beings, as much as earthly ones, experience a "kindly rupture" of passion? A blush, after all, is an involuntary sign of a powerful internal fluctuation. If angels make love and blush about their rapture, then sexuality is not an evil in *Paradise Lost*—and indeed Milton has no patience for the patristic tradition that condemns sexuality as degrading. For Milton, sexuality is instead a powerful testimony to the *unfallen*, if ambiguous, quest for knowledge through experience.

And what of Milton the epic poet: does he, too, experience ruptures in his self-assertiveness? Freeing the individual believer from received wisdom is an anxious, as well as heroic, activity for Milton. In his invocations to his heavenly muse, he raises the awkward question of the source of his poetic inspiration: in book 9, for example, he mentions his "Celestial Patroness, who deigns / Her nightly visitation unimplor'd, / And dictates to me slumb'ring, or inspires / Easy my unpremeditated Verse." From her, he hopes to gain what he calls "answerable style"—poetic expression that echoes the revelation he has received. He boasts that he does not have to ask for his inspiration (as Homer and Virgil did), yet he does not assert its legitimacy. At the end of this invocation, in fact, Milton acknowledges his doubts and fears that "all be mine, / Not Hers who brings it nightly to my Ear." If he is to retell the story of the Bible in what he calls "answerable style," his imagination must be guided by heavenly authority. If his personal revelation is false, perhaps Milton will have to "answer" to his God. His style must be innovative, or it will merely recycle flawed and human-generated conventions; but it must not be "invented" by the poet himself. When Milton reflects on the ambiguous source of his inspiration, he acknowledges the anxiety of a radical Protestant who believes in the principle of personal revelation but cannot confirm it outside his own experience. He fascinatingly returns, in effect, to the basic tension that Christian humanists experienced between recovering truth (through scholarly discoveries) and revolutionizing it (by breaking with tradition).

Milton's achievements in *Paradise Lost* include his powerful rendering of human spiritual need and its relationship to domestic life. His poem might be considered "adventurous" in its explorations of the rational, sexual, and emotional psychologies that lead his Adam and Eve to fall, although it is also uncompromising about the fatal error of the Fall. Milton committed himself intellectually to disrupting the received wisdom of the classics and the Church in order to discover truths verifiable by experience. In the story of Genesis he discovers questions central to the Renaissance and Reformation: how do we know things? to what extent should "external help" such as warnings govern us? how much more rewarding—and dangerous—is the wisdom of experience? can we learn from vicarious experiences, such as sympathy and interpretation (a possibility that enlarges the moral role of art)? Milton, who wished to break the bonds constraining the intellectual and imaginative possibilities of his readers, bestowed on them what must be regarded, paradoxically, as the burden of interpretive liberty: Milton works to make the reading of *Paradise Lost* a simultaneously demanding and highly personal experience.

Paradise Lost

FROM BOOK 1

The Argument[1]

This first book proposes, first in brief, the whole subject, man's disobedience, and the loss thereupon of Paradise wherein he was placed: then touches the prime cause of his fall, the Serpent, or rather Satan in the Serpent; who revolting from God, and drawing to his side many legions of angels, was by the command of God driven out of Heaven with all his crew into the great deep. Which action passed over, the poem hastes into the midst of things,[2] presenting Satan with his angels now fallen into Hell, described here, not in the center[3] (for Heaven and Earth may be supposed as yet not made, certainly not yet accursed) but in a place of utter darkness, fitliest called Chaos: here Satan with his angels lying on the burning lake, thunderstruck and astonished, after a certain space recovers, as from confusion, calls up him who next in order and dignity lay by him; they confer of their miserable fall. Satan awakens all his legions, who lay till then in the same manner confounded; they rise, their numbers, array of battle, their chief leaders named, according to the idols known afterwards in Canaan and the countries adjoining. To these Satan directs his speech, comforts them with hope yet of regaining Heaven, but tells them lastly of a new world and new kind of creature to be created, according to an ancient prophecy or report in Heaven; for that angels were long before this visible creation, was the opinion of many ancient Fathers.[4] To find out the truth of this prophecy, and what to determine[5] thereon he refers to a full council. What his associates thence attempt. Pandemonium the palace of Satan rises, suddenly built out of the deep: the infernal peers there sit in council.

["This Great Argument"]

Of man's first disobedience, and the fruit[6]
Of that forbidden tree, whose mortal taste[7]
Brought death into the world, and all our woe,
With loss of Eden, till one greater Man[8]
Restore us, and regain the blissful seat,   5
Sing Heav'nly Muse,[9] that on the secret top
Of Oreb, or of Sinai, didst inspire
That shepherd, who first taught the chosen seed,[1]

---

1. *Paradise Lost* appeared originally without any sort of prose aid to the reader, but the printer asked Milton for some "Arguments," or summary explanations of the action in the various books, and these were prefixed to later issues of the poem.   2. According to Horace, the epic poet should begin, *"in medias res."*   3. I.e., of the earth.   4. Church Fathers, the Christian writers of the first century.   5. I.e., what action to take.   6. The apple itself, and also the consequences of Adam and Eve's disobedience.   7. The tasting of which brought mortality into the world.   8. Christ.   9. The opening invocation to the muse who will inspire (*sing* to) the poet is a regular feature of epic poems. Milton's heavenly muse elsewhere in the poem (7.1) is given the name of the mythological Urania; in another passage (9.21) she is given the adjective *celestial*. Both words—of Greek and Latin derivation, respectively—mean "heavenly." Clearly and typically, in Milton's heavenly muse pagan elements and images are adopted and given new substance within the framework of Judeo-Christian culture and beliefs.   1. The Hebrew people. Oreb and Sinai designate the mountain where God spoke to Moses (*that shepherd*), who in Genesis taught the Hebrew people the story of the Creation.

In the beginning how the Heavens and earth
Rose out of Chaos: or if Sion hill   10
Delight thee more, and Siloa's brook that flowed
Fast by the oracle of God,[2] I thence
Invoke thy aid to my adventurous song,
That with no middle flight intends to soar
Above th' Aonian mount,[3] while it pursues   15
Things unattempted yet in prose or rhyme.
And chiefly thou O Spirit,[4] that dost prefer
Before all temples th' upright heart and pure,
Instruct me,[5] for thou know'st; thou from the first
Wast present, and, with mighty wings outspread,   20
Dove-like sat'st brooding[6] on the vast abyss,
And mad'st it pregnant: what in me is dark
Illumine, what is, low raise and support;
That, to the height of this great argument,[7]
I may assert Eternal Providence,   25
And justify the ways of God[8] to men.

[Satan on the Fiery Lake]

Say first, for Heav'n hides nothing from thy view
Nor the deep tract of Hell, say first what cause[9]
Moved our grand parents in that happy state,
Favored of Heav'n so highly, to fall off   30
From their Creator, and transgress his will
For one restraint, lords of the world besides?
Who first seduced them to that foul revolt?
Th' infernal Serpent; he it was, whose guile
Stirred up with envy and revenge, deceived   35
The mother of mankind, what time his pride
Had cast him out from Heav'n, with all his host
Of rebel angels, by whose aid aspiring
To set himself in glory above his peers,
He trusted to have equaled the Most High,   40
If he opposed; and with ambitious aim
Against the throne and monarchy of God
Raised impious war in Heav'n and battle proud
With vain attempt. Him the Almighty Power
Hurled headlong flaming from th' ethereal sky   45
With hideous ruin and combustion down

2. The Temple. The biblical localities suggested here as haunts for Milton's muse are emblematic of his certainty about the higher nature of his theme compared with the epic subjects of pagan antiquity. The fact that *Siloa's brook* is flowing by the Temple suggests the holy nature of Milton's subject. Adventurous (line 13): perilous, as the poet is daring something new (see line 16).   3. Helicon, the Greek mountain that was the seat of the Nine Muses. The spring Aganippe, which gives poetic power, and an altar of Zeus were part of that landscape (compare the location of Siloa's brook, lines 11–12).   4. Described in Milton's Latin treatise on Christian doctrine as "that impulse or voice of God by which the prophets were inspired," the *Spirit* is a further source of inspiration over and above the heavenly muse.   5. The poet asks not for song but for knowledge (*instruct me*) and identifies the Spirit with the Spirit of God that "moved upon the face of the waters" (Genesis 1.2).   6. As a bird hatching eggs. The image is pursued in line 22 with *pregnant. Dovelike*: the traditional figuration of the Holy Spirit (for example, Luke 3.22: "the Holy Ghost descended in a bodily shape like a dove").   7. Subject, theme. "*Assert* (line 25): champion, vindicate. 8. Demonstrate the justice of the course of God's providence.   9. An opening question like this is an epic convention.

To bottomless perdition, there to dwell
In adamantine chains and penal fire,
Who durst defy th' Omnipotent to arms.
Nine times the space that measures day and night   50
To mortal men, he with his horrid crew
Lay vanquished, rolling in the fiery gulf
Confounded though immortal: but his doom
Reserved him to more wrath; for now the thought
Both of lost happiness and lasting pain   55
Torments him; round he throws his baleful eyes
That witnessed huge affliction and dismay
Mixed with obdúrate pride and steadfast hate:
At once as far as angels ken[1] he views
The dismal situation waste and wild,   60
A dungeon horrible, on all sides round
As one great furnace flamed, yet from those flames
No light, but rather darkness visible
Served only to discover sights of woe,
Regions of sorrow, doleful shades, where peace   65
And rest can never dwell, hope never comes
That comes to all; but torture without end
Still urges, and a fiery deluge, fed
With ever-burning sulphur unconsumed:
Such place Eternal Justice had prepared   70
For those rebellious, here their prison ordained
In utter darkness, and their portion set
As far removed from God and light of Heav'n
As from the center thrice to th' utmost pole.[2]
O how unlike the place from whence they fell!   75
There the companions of his fall, o'erwhelmed
With floods and whirlwinds of tempestuous fire,
He soon discerns, and welt'ring by his side
One next himself in power, and next in crime,
Long after known in Palestine, and named   80
Beëlzebub.[3] To whom th' Arch-Enemy,
And thence in Heav'n called Satan,[4] with bold words
Breaking the horrid silence thus began.
    "If thou beest he; but O how fall'n! how changed
From him, who in the happy realms of light   85
Clothed with transcendent brightness didst outshine
Myriads though bright: if he whom mutual league,
United thoughts and counsels, equal hope
And hazard in the glorious enterprise,
Joined with me once, now misery hath joined   90
In equal ruin: into what pit thou seest
From what height fall'n, so much the stronger proved
He with his thunder: and till then who knew
The force of those dire arms? Yet not for those,

1. Range of sight.　　2. According to the Ptolemaic conception of the universe, the earth is the center of
the cosmos of ten concentric spheres; the fall from Heaven to Hell is thrice as far as the distance from the
center (earth) to the outermost sphere.　　3. A Phoenician deity, or Baal, he is called the prince of devils
in Matthew 12.24.　　4. In Hebrew the name means "adversary."

Nor what the potent victor in his rage   95
Can else inflict, do I repent or change,
Though changed in outward luster, that fixed mind
And high disdain, from sense of injured merit,
That with the mightiest raised me to contend,
And to the fierce contention brought along   100
Innumerable force of Spirits armed
That durst dislike his reign, and me preferring,
His utmost power with adverse power opposed
In dubious battle on the plains of Heav'n,
And shook his throne. What though the field be lost?   105
All is not lost; the unconquerable will,
And study of revenge, immortal hate,
And courage never to submit or yield:
And what is else not to be overcome?
That glory never shall his wrath or might   110
Extort from me. To bow and sue for grace
With suppliant knee, and deify his power
Who from the terror of this arm so late
Doubted his empire, that were low indeed,
That were an ignominy and shame beneath   115
This downfall; since by fate the strength of gods
And this empyreal⁵ substance cannot fail,
Since through experience of this great event
In arms not worse, in foresight much advanced,
We may with more successful hope resolve   120
To wage by force or guile eternal war
Irreconcilable, to our grand foe,
Who now triúmphs, and in th' excess of joy
Sole reigning holds the tyranny of Heav'n."
        So spake th' apostate angel, though in pain,   125
Vaunting aloud, but racked with deep despair:
And him thus answered soon his bold compeer.
    "O Prince, O Chief of many thronéd Powers,
That led th' embattled Seraphim⁶ to war
Under thy conduct, and in dreadful deeds   130
Fearless, endangered Heav'ns perpetual King;
And put to proof his high supremacy,
Whether upheld by strength, or chance, or fate;
Too well I see and rue the dire event,
That with sad overthrow and foul defeat   135
Hath lost us Heav'n, and all this mighty host
In horrible destruction laid thus low,
As far as gods and heav'nly essences
Can perish: for the mind and spirit remains
Invincible, and vigor soon returns,   140
Though all our glory extinct, and happy state
Here swallowed up in endless misery.

5. Divine element.   6. One of nine orders of angels, including the cherubim, thrones, dominions, virtues, powers, principalities, archangels, and angels.

But what if he our conqueror (whom I now
Of force believe almighty, since no less
Than such could have o'erpow'red such force as ours)   145
Have left us this our spirit and strength entire
Strongly to suffer and support our pains,
That we may so suffice his vengeful ire,
Or do him mightier service as his thralls
By right of war, whate'er his business be   150
Here in the heart of Hell to work in fire,
Or do his errands in the gloomy deep;
What can it then avail though yet we feel
Strength undiminished, or eternal being
To undergo eternal punishment?"   155
Whereto with speedy words th' Arch-Fiend replied.
  "Fall'n Cherub, to be weak is miserable
Doing or suffering: but of this be sure,
To do aught good never will be our task,
But ever to do ill our sole delight,   160
As being the contrary to his high will
Whom we resist. If then his providence
Out of our evil seek to bring forth good,
Our labor must be to pervert that end,
And out of good still to find means of evil;   165
Which ofttimes may succeed, so as perhaps
Shall grieve him, if I fail not, and disturb
His inmost counsels from their destined aim.
But see the angry victor hath recalled
is ministers of vengeance and pursuit   170
Back to the gates of Heav'n: the sulphurous hail
Shot after us in storm, o'erblown hath laid
The fiery surge, that from the precipice
Of Heav'n received us falling, and the thunder,
Winged with red lightning and impetuous rage,   175
Perhaps hath spent his shafts, and ceases now
To bellow through the vast and boundless deep.
Let us not slip th' occasion, whether scorn,
Or satiate fury yield it from our foe.
Seest thou yon dreary plain, forlorn and wild,   180
The seat of desolation, void of light,
Save what the glimmering of these livid flames
Casts pale and dreadful? Thither let us tend
From off the tossing of these fiery waves,
There rest, if any rest can harbor there,   185
And reassembling our afflicted powers,[7]
Consult how we may henceforth most offend
Our enemy, our own loss how repair,
How overcome this dire calamity,
What reinforcement we may gain from hope,   190
If not what resolution from despair."

7. Military forces.

[Satan summons his army of fallen angels, who rise from the Fiery lake to attend their commander.]

* * * he above the rest
In shape and gesture proudly eminent   590
Stood like a tow'r; his form had yet not lost
All her[8] original brightness, nor appeared
Less than Archangel ruined, and th' excess
Of glory obscured: as when the sun new-ris'n
Looks through the horizontal misty air   595
Shorn of his beams, or from behind the moon
In dim eclipse disastrous twilight sheds
On half the nations, and with fear of change
Perplexes monarchs. Darkened so, yet shone
Above them all th' Archangel: but his face   600
Deep scars of thunder had intrenched, and care
Sat on his faded cheek, but under brows
Of dauntless courage, and considerate pride
Waiting revenge: cruel his eye, but cast
Signs of remorse and passion to behold   605
The fellows of his crime, the followers rather
(Far other once beheld in bliss) condemned
For ever now to have their lot in pain,
Millions of Spirits for his fault amerced[9]
Of Heav'n, and from eternal splendors flung   610
For his revolt, yet faithful how they stood,
Their glory withered: as when Heaven's fire
Hath scathed the forest oaks, or mountain pines,
With singèd top their stately growth though bare
Stands on the blasted heath. He now prepared   615
To speak; whereat their doubled ranks they bend
From wing to wing, and half enclose him round
With all his peers: attention held them mute.
Thrice he essayed, and thrice, in spite of scorn,
Tears such as angels weep burst forth: at last   620
Words interwove with sighs found out their way.
    "O myriads of immortal Spirits, O Powers
Matchless, but with th' Almighty, and that strife
Was not inglorious, though th' event[1] was dire,
As this place testifies, and this dire change   625
Hateful to utter: but what power of mind
Foreseeing or presaging, from the depth
Of knowledge past or present, could have feared,
How such united force of gods, how such
As stood like these, could ever know repulse?   630
For who can yet believe, though after loss,
That all these puissant[2] legions, whose exile
Hath emptied Heav'n, shall fail to reascend
Self-raised, and repossess their native seat?
For me, be witness all the host of Heav'n,   635

---

8. "Forma" in Latin is feminine.   9. Deprived.   1. Outcome.   2. Powerful.

If counsels different, or danger shunned
By me, have lost our hopes. But he who reigns
Monarch in Heav'n, till then as one secure
Sat on his throne, upheld by old repute,
Consent or custom, and his regal state   640
Put forth at full, but still his strength concealed,
Which tempted our attempt, and wrought our fall.
Henceforth his might we know, and know our own
So as not either to provoke, or dread
New war, provoked; our better part remains   645
To work in close design, by fraud or guile
What force effected not: that he no less
At length from us may find, who overcomes
By force, hath overcome but half his foe.
Space may produce new worlds; whereof so rife³   650
There went a fame⁴ in Heav'n that he ere long
Intended to create, and therein plant
A generation, whom his choice regard
Should favor equal to the sons of Heaven:
Thither, if but to pry, shall be perhaps   655
Our first eruption, thither or elsewhere:
For this infernal pit shall never hold
Celestial Spirits in bondage, not th' abyss
Long under darkness cover. But these thoughts
Full counsel must mature: peace is despaired,   660
For who can think submission? War then, war
Open or understood must be resolved."
    He spake: and to confirm his words, out flew
Millions of flaming swords, drawn from the thighs
Of mighty Cherubim; the sudden blaze   665
Far round illumined Hell: highly they raged
Against the Highest, and fierce with grasp'ed arms
Clashed on their sounding shields the din of war,
Hurling defiance toward the vault of Heav'n.

FROM BOOK 2

The Argument

    The consultation begun, Satan debates whether another battle be to be
hazarded for the recovery of heaven: some advise it, others dissuade: a third
proposal is preferred, mentioned before by Satan, to search the truth of that
prophecy or tradition in heaven concerning another world, and another kind
of creature equal or not much inferior to themselves, about this time to be
created: their doubt who shall be sent on this difficult search: Satan their
chief undertakes alone the voyage, is honored and applauded. The council
thus ended, the rest betake them several ways and to several employments,
as their inclinations lead them, to entertain the time till Satan return. He
passes on his journey to hell gates, finds them shut, and who sat there to
guard them, by whom at length they are opened, and discover to him the

---

3. Common.   4. Rumor.

great gulf between hell and heaven; with what difficulty he passes through,
directed by Chaos, the power of that place, to the sight of this new world
which he sought.

[The Devil's Consult]

High on a throne of royal state, which far
Outshone the wealth of Ormus and of Ind,[5]
Or where the gorgeous East with richest hand
Show'rs on her kings barbaric pearl and gold,
Satan exalted sat, by merit raised   5
To that bad eminence; and from despair
Thus high uplifted beyond hope, aspires
Beyond thus high, insatiate to pursue
Vain war with Heav'n, and by success untaught
His proud imaginations[6] thus displayed.   10
    "Powers and Dominions, deities of Heaven,
For since no deep within her gulf can hold
Immortal vigor, though oppressed and fall'n,
I give not Heav'n for lost. From this descent
Celestial Virtues rising, will appear   15
More glorious and more dread than from no fall,
And trust themselves to fear no second fate.
Me though just right, and the fixed laws of Heav'n
Did first create your leader, next, free choice,
With what besides, in counsel or in fight,   20
Hath been achieved of merit, yet this loss
Thus far at least recovered, hath much more
Established in a safe unenvied throne
Yielded with full consent. The happier state
In Heaven, which follows dignity, might draw   25
Envy from each inferior; but who here
Will envy whom the highest place exposes
Foremost to stand against the Thunderer's aim
Your bulwark, and condemns to greatest share
Of endless pain? Where there is then no good   30
For which to strive, no strife can grow up there
From faction; for none sure will claim in Hell
Precédence, none, whose portion is so small
Of present pain, that with ambitious mind
Will covet more. With this advantage then   35
To union, and firm faith, and firm accord,
More than can be in Heav'n, we now return
To claim our just inheritance of old,
Surer to prosper than prosperity
Could have assured us; and by what best way,   40
Whether of open war or covert guile,
We now debate; who can advise, may speak."
    He ceas'd, and next him Moloch, sceptered king
Stood up, the strongest and the fiercest Spirit

---

5. India. *Ormus:* an island in the Persian Gulf, modern Hormuz, famous for pearls.   6. Plans or schemes.

That fought in Heav'n; now fiercer by despair: 45
His trust was with th' Eternal to be deemed
Equal in strength, and rather than be less
Cared not to be at all; with that care lost
Went all his fear: of God, or Hell, or worse
He recked[7] not, and these words thereafter spake. 50
   "My sentence[8] is for open war: of wiles,
More unexpert, I boast not: them let those
Contrive who need, or when they need, not now.
For while they sit contriving, shall the rest,
Millions that stand in arms, and longing wait 55
The signal to ascend, sit lingering here
Heav'n's fugitives, and for their dwelling-place
Accept this dark opprobrious den of shame,
The prison of his tyranny who reigns
By our delay? No, let us rather choose 60
Armed with Hell flames and fury all at once
O'er Heav'n's high tow'rs to force resistless way,
Turning our tortures into horrid[9] arms
Against the Torturer; when to meet the noise
Of his almighty engine[1] he shall hear 65
Infernal thunder, and for lightning see
Black fire and horror shot with equal rage
Among his angels; and his throne itself
Mixed with Tartarean[2] sulfur, and strange fire,
His own invented torments. But perhaps 70
The way seems difficult and steep to scale
With upright wing against a higher foe.
Let such bethink them, if the sleepy drench
Of that forgetful lake benumb not still,
That in our proper motion we ascend 75
Up to our native seat: descent and fall
To us is adverse. Who but felt of late
When the fierce foe hung on our broken rear
Insulting, and pursued us through the deep,
With what compulsion and laborious flight 80
We sunk thus low? Th' ascent is easy then;
Th' event is feared; should we again provoke
Our stronger, some worse way his wrath may find
To our destruction: if there be in Hell
Fear to be worse destroyed: what can be worse 85
Than to dwell here, driven out from bliss, condemned
In this abhorrèd deep to utter woe;
Where pain of unextinguishable fire
Must exercise us without hope of end
The vassals of his anger, when the scourge 90
Inexorably, and the torturing hour
Calls us to penance? More destroyed than thus
We should be quite abolished and expire.

7. Cared.   8. Judgment.   9. Bristling, terrible.   1. The thunderbolt.   2. Tartarus is a classical
name for Hell.

What fear we then? What[3] doubt we to incense
His utmost ire? which to the high enraged, 95
Will either quite consume us, and reduce
To nothing this essential,[4] happier far
Than miserable to have eternal being:
Or if our substance be indeed divine,
And cannot cease to be, we are at worst 100
On this side nothing;[5] and by proof we feel
Our power sufficient to disturb his Heav'n,
And with perpetual inroads to alarm,
Though inaccessible, his fatal[6] throne:
Which if not victory is yet revenge." 105
    He ended frowning, and his look, denounced
Desperate revenge, and battle dangerous
To less than gods. On th' other side up rose
Belial, in act more graceful and humane;
A fairer person lost not Heav'n; he seemed 110
For dignity composed and high exploit:
But all was false and hollow; though his tongue
Dropped manna, and could make the worse appear
The better reason, to perplex and dash
Maturest counsels: for his thoughts were low; 115
To vice industrious, but to nobler deeds
Timorous and slothful: yet he pleased the ear,
And with persuasive accent thus began.
    "I should be much for open war, O Peers,
As not behind in hate; if what was urged 120
Main reason to persuade immediate war,
Did not dissuade me most, and seem to cast
Ominous conjecture on the whole success:
When he who most excells in fact of arms,
In what he counsels and in what excels 125
Mistrustful, grounds his courage on despair
And utter dissolution, as the scope
Of all his aim, after some dire revenge.
First, what revenge? The tow'rs of Heav'n are filled
With armèd watch, that render all access 130
Impregnable; oft on the bordering deep
Encamp their legions, or with óbscure wing
Scout far and wide into the realm of Night,
Scorning surprise. Or could we break our way
By force, and at our heels all Hell should rise 135
With blackest insurrection, to confound
Heav'n's purest light, yet our great enemy
All incorruptible would on his throne
Sit unpolluted, and th' ethereal mold[7]
Incapable of stain would soon expel 140
Her mischief, and purge off the baser fire

---

3. Why.   4. Essence.   5. I.e., we are already experiencing the worst possible form of existence.
6. Established by Fate, deadly to challenge.   7. "Ether" is the purest of the elements.

Victorious. Thus repulsed, our final hope
Is flat despair: we must exasperate
Th' almighty victor to spend all his rage,
And that must end us, that must be our cure,   145
To be no more; sad cure; for who would lose,
Though full of pain, this intellectual being,
Those thoughts that wander through eternity,
To perish rather, swallowed up and lost
In the wide womb of uncreated night,   150
Devoid of sense and motion? And who knows,
Let this be good, whether our angry foe
Can give it, or will ever? How he can
Is doubtful; that he never will is sure.
Will he, so wise, let loose at once his ire,   155
Belike[8] through impotence, or unaware,
To give his enemies their wish, and end
Them in his anger, whom his anger saves
To punish endless? 'Wherefore cease we then?'
Say they who counsel war, 'We are decreed,   160
Reserved and destined to eternal woe;
Whatever doing, what can we suffer more,
What can we suffer worse?' Is this then worst,
Thus sitting, thus consulting, thus in arms?
What when we fled amain, pursued and strook[9]   165
With Heav'n's afflicting thunder, and besought
The deep to shelter us? This Hell then seemed
A refuge from those wounds. Or when we lay
Chained on the burning lake? That sure was worse.
What if the breath that kindled those grim fires   170
Awaked should blow them into sevenfold rage
And plunge us in the flames? Or from above
Should intermitted vengeance[1] arm again
His red right hand to plague us? What if all
Her[2] stores were opened, and this firmament   175
Of Hell should spout her cataracts of fire,
Impendent[3] horrors, threat'ning hideous fall
One day upon our heads; while we perhaps
Designing or exhorting glorious war,
Caught in a fiery tempest shall be hurled   180
Each on his rock transfixed, the sport and prey
Of racking whirlwinds, or for ever sunk
Under yon boiling ocean, wrapped in chains;
There to converse with everlasting groans,
Unrespited, unpitied, unreprieved,   185
Ages of hopeless end; this would be worse.
War therefore, open or concealed, alike
My voice dissuades; for what can force or guile[4]
With him, or who deceive his mind, whose eye
Views all things at one view? He from Heav'n's high   190

8. Perhaps.   9. Struck.   1. Revenge temporarily suspended.   2. Hell's.   3. Looming, overhanging.   4. The verb "achieve" is understood.

All these our motions⁵ vain, sees and derides;
Not more almighty to resist our might
Than wise to frustrate all our plots and wiles.
Shall we then live thus vile, the race of Heav'n
Thus trampled, thus expelled to suffer here   195
Chains and these torments? Better these than worse
By my advice; since fate inevitable
Subdues us, and omnipotent decree,
The victor's will. To suffer, as to do,
Our strength is equal, nor the law unjust   200
That so ordains: this was at first resolved,
If we were wise, against so great a foe
Contending, and so doubtful what might fall.
I laugh, when those who at the spear are bold
And vent'rous, if that fail them, shrink and fear   205
What yet they know must follow, to endure
Exile, or ignominy, or bonds, or pain,
The sentence of their conqueror: This is now
Our doom; which if we can sustain and bear,
Our Súpreme Foe in time may much remit   210
His anger, and perhaps thus far removed
Not mind us not offending, satisfied
With what is punished; whence these raging fires
Will slacken, if his breath stir not their flames.
Our purer essence then will overcome   215
Their noxious vapor, or inured not feel,
Or changed at length, and to the place conformed
In temper and in nature, will receive
Familiar the fierce heat, and void of pain;
This horror will grow mild, this darkness light,   220
Besides what hope the never-ending flight
Of future days may bring, what chance, what change
Worth waiting, since our present lot appears
For happy though but ill, for ill not worst,⁶
If we procure not to ourselves more woe."   225
    Thus Belial, with words clothed in reason's garb,
Counseled ignoble ease and peaceful sloth,
Not peace: and after him thus Mammon spake.
    "Either to disenthrone the King of Heav'n
We war, if war be best, or to regain   230
Our own right lost: him to unthrone we then
May hope when everlasting fate shall yield
To fickle chance, and Chaos judge the strife:
The former vain to hope argues as vain
The latter: for what place can be for us   235
Within Heav'n's bound, unless Heav'n's Lord supreme
We overpower? Suppose he should relent
And publish grace to all, on promise made
Of new subjection; with what eyes could we
Stand in his presence humble, and receive   240

5. Proposals.   6. I.e., although happiness is not possible, our state could be worse.

Strict laws imposed, to celebrate his throne
With warbled hymns, and to his Godhead sing
Forced hallelujahs; while he lordly sits
Our envied Sovran,[7] and his altar breathes
Ambrosial[8] odors and ambrosial flowers,   245
Our servile offerings. This must be our task
In Heav'n, this our delight; how wearisome
Eternity so spent in worship paid
To whom we hate. Let us not then pursue
By force impossible, by leave obtained   250
Unácceptable, though in Heav'n, our state
Of splendid vassalage,[9] but rather seek
Our own good from ourselves, and from our own
Live to ourselves, though in this vast recess,
Free, and to none accountable, preferring   255
Hard liberty before the easy yoke
Of servile pomp. Our greatness will appear
Then most conspicuous, when great things of small,
Useful of hurtful, prosperous of adverse
We can create, and in what place soe'er   260
Thrive under evil, and work ease out of pain
Through labor and endurance. This deep world
Of darkness do we dread? How oft amidst
Thick clouds and dark doth Heav'n's all-ruling Sire
Choose to reside, his glory unobscured,   265
And with the majesty of darkness round
Covers his throne; from whence deep thunders roar
Must'ring their rage, and Heav'n resembles Hell?
As he our darkness, cannot we his light
Imitate when we please? This desert soil   270
Wants[1] not her hidden luster, gems and gold;
Nor want we skill or art, from whence to raise
Magnificence; and what can Heav'n show more?
Our torments also may in length of time
Become our elements, these piercing fires   275
As soft as now severe, our temper[2] changed
Into their temper; which must needs remove
The sensible of pain.[3] All things invite
To peaceful counsels, and the settled state
Of order, how in safety best we may   280
Compose our present evils, with regard
Of what we are and where, dismissing quite
All thoughts of war: ye have what I advise."
       He scarce had finished, when such murmur filled
Th' assembly, as when hollow rocks retain   285
The sound of blust'ring winds, which all night long
Had roused the sea, now with hoarse cadence lull
Seafaring men o'erwatched, whose bark by chance
Or pinnace anchors in a craggy bay

7. Sovereign, lord.   8. Divinely aromatic.   9. Servitude.   1. Lacks.   2. Constitution.   3. Pain
felt by the senses.

After the tempest: such applause was heard   290
As Mammon ended, and his sentence pleased,
Advising peace: for such another field
They dreaded worse than Hell: so much the fear
Of thunder and the sword of Michaël⁴
Wrought still within them; and no less desire   295
To found this nether empire, which might rise
By policy, and long process of time,
In emulation opposite to Heav'n.
Which then Beëlzebub perceived, than whom,
Satan except, none higher sat, with grave   300
Aspect he rose, and in his rising seemed
A pillar of state; deep on his front engraven
Deliberation sat and public care;
And princely counsel in his face yet shone,
Majestic though in ruin: sage he stood   305
With Atlantean⁵ shoulders fit to bear
The weight of mightiest monarchies; his look
Drew audience and attention still as night
Or summer's noontide air, while thus he spake.
  "Thrones and imperial Powers, offspring of Heav'n   310
Ethereal Virtues; or these titles⁶ now
Must we renounce, and changing style be called
Princes of Hell? for so the popular vote
Inclines, here to continue, and build up here
A growing empire. Doubtless! while we dream,   315
And know not that the King of Heav'n hath doomed
This place our dungeon, not our safe retreat
Beyond his potent arm, to live exempt
From Heav'n's high jurisdiction, in new league
Banded against his throne, but to remain   320
In strictest bondage, though thus far removed,
Under th' inevitable curb, reserved
His captive multitude: for he, be sure,
In height or depth, still first and last will reign
Sole King, and of his kingdom lose no part   325
By our revolt, but over Hell extend
His empire, and with iron scepter rule
Us here, as with his golden those in Heav'n.
What sit we then projecting peace and war?
War hath determined us, and foiled with loss   330
Irreparable; terms of peace yet none
Vouchsafed or sought; for what peace will be giv'n
To us enslaved, but custody severe,
And stripes, and arbitrary punishment
Inflicted? And what peace can we return,   335
But, to our power,⁷ hostility and hate,
Untamed reluctance,⁸ and revenge though slow,
Yet ever plotting how the conqueror least

---

4. The warrior angel, chief of the angelic armies.   5. Atlas, the Titan who held up the heavens on his
shoulders.   6. The official titles of angelic orders.   7. I.e., to the best of our ability.   8. Resistance.

May reap his conquest, and may least rejoice
In doing what we most in suffering feel?   340
Nor will occasion want, nor shall we need
With dangerous expedition to invade
Heav'n, whose high walls fear no assault or siege,
Or ambush from the deep. What if we find
Some easier enterprise? There is a place   345
(If ancient and prophetic fame in Heav'n
Err not) another world, the happy seat
Of some new race called Man, about this time
To be created like to us, though less
In power and excellence, but favored more   350
Of him who rules above; so was his will
Pronounced among the gods, and by an oath,
That shook Heav'n's whole circumference, confirmed.
Thither let us bend all our thoughts, to learn
What creatures there inhabit, of what mold,   355
Or substance, how endued, and what their power,
And where their weakness, how attempted best,
By force or subtlety. Though Heav'n be shut,
And Heav'n's high arbitrator sit secure
In his own strength, this place may lie exposed,   360
The utmost border of his kingdom, left
To their defense who hold it:⁹ here perhaps
Some advantageous act may be achieved
By sudden onset, either with Hell fire
To waste his whole creation, or possess   365
All as our own, and drive as we were driven,
The puny habitants, or if not drive,
Seduce them to our party, that their God
May prove their foe, and with repenting hand
Abolish his own works. This would surpass   370
Common revenge, and interrupt his joy
In our confusion, and our joy upraise
In his disturbance; when his darling sons
Hurled headlong to partake with us, shall curse
Their frail original,¹ and faded bliss,   375
Faded so soon. Advise² if this be worth
Attempting, or to sit in darkness here
Hatching vain empires." Thus Beëlzebub
Pleaded his devilish counsel, first devised
By Satan, and in part proposed: for whence,   380
But from the author of all ill could spring
So deep a malice, to confound the race
Of mankind in one root,³ and earth with Hell
To mingle and involve, done all to spite
The great Creator? But their spite still serves   385
His glory to augment. The bold design
Pleased highly those infernal States, and joy

---

9. To be defended by the occupants.   1. Original or first parent.   2. Consider.   3. Adam, the first
man, is the "root" of the human race.

Sparkled in all their eyes; with full assent
They vote: whereat his speech he thus renews.
    "Well have ye judged, well ended long debate,   390
Synod of gods, and like to what ye are,
Great things resolved, which from the lowest deep
Will once more lift us up, in spite of fate,
Nearer our ancient seat; perhaps in view
Of those bright confines, whence with neighboring arms   395
And opportune excursion we may chance
Re-enter Heav'n; or else in some mild zone
Dwell not unvisited of Heav'n's fair light
Secure, and at the bright'ning orient beam
Purge off this gloom; the soft delicious air,   400
To heal the scar of these corrosive fires
Shall breathe her balm. But first whom shall we send
In search of this new world, whom shall we find
Sufficient? Who shall tempt with wand'ring feet
The dark unbottomed infinite abyss   405
And through the palpable obscure⁴ find out
His uncouth⁵ way, or spread his aery flight
Upborne with indefatigable wings
Over the vast abrupt,⁶ ere he arrive
The happy isle? what strength, what art can then   410
Suffice, or what evasion bear him safe
Through the strict senteries⁷ and stations thick
Of angels watching round? Here he had need
All circumspection, and we now no less
Choice in our suffrage; for on whom we send,   415
The weight of all and our last hope relies."
    This said, he sat; and expectation held
His look suspense, awaiting who appeared
To second, or oppose, or undertake
The perilous attempt: but all sat mute,   420
Pondering the danger with deep thoughts; and each
In other's count'nance read his own dismay
Astonished. None among the choice and prime
Of those Heav'n-warring champions could be found
So hardy as to proffer or accept   425
Alone the dreadful voyage; till at last
Satan, whom now transcendent glory raised
Above his fellows, with monarchal pride
Conscious of highest worth, unmoved thus spake.
    "O progeny of Heav'n, empyreal Thrones,   430
With reason hath deep silence and demur⁸
Seized us, though undismayed: long is the way
And hard, that out of Hell leads up to light;
Our prison strong, this huge convex of fire,
Outrageous to devour, immures us round   435
Ninefold,⁹ and gates of burning adamant

---

4. Darkness so heavy it oppresses the senses.   5. Unfamiliar.   6. Chaos.   7. Sentries.   8. Hesitation.   9. Hell's walls have nine thicknesses.

Barred over us prohibit all egress.
These passed, if any pass, the void profound
Of unessential Night receives him next
Wide gaping, and with utter loss of being   440
Threatens him, plunged in that abortive gulf.
If thence he scape into whatever world,
Or unknown region, what remains him less
Than unknown dangers and as hard escape?
But I should ill become this throne, O Peers,   445
And this imperial sovranty, adorned
With splendor, armed with power, if aught proposed
And judged of public moment, in the shape
Of difficulty or danger could deter
Me from attempting. Wherefore do I assume   450
These royalties, and not refuse to reign,
Refusing to accept as great a share
Of hazard as of honor, due alike
To him who reigns, and so much to him due
Of hazard more, as he above the rest   455
High honored sits? Go therefore mighty Powers,
Terror of Heav'n, though fall'n; intend[1] at home,
While here shall be our home, what best may ease
The present misery, and render Hell
More tolerable; if there be cure or charm   460
To respite or deceive, or slack the pain
Of this ill mansion: intermit no watch
Against a wakeful foe, while I abroad
Through all the coasts of dark destruction seek
Deliverance for us all: this enterprise   465
None shall partake with me." Thus saying rose
The monarch, and prevented all reply,
Prudent, lest from his resolution raised
Others among the chief might offer now
(Certain to be refused) what erst they feared;   470
And so refused might in opinion stand
His rivals, winning cheap the high repute
Which he through hazard huge must earn. But they
Dreaded not more th' adventure than his voice
Forbidding; and at once with him they rose;   475
Their rising all at once was as the sound
Of thunder heard remote. Towards him they bend
With awful reverence prone; and as a god
Extol him equal to the Highest in Heav'n:
Nor failed they to express how much they praised,   480
That for the general safety he despised
His own: for neither do the Spirits damned
Lose all their virtue; lest bad men should boast
Their specious deeds on earth, which glory excites,
Or close ambition varnished o'er with zeal.   485
    Thus they their doubtful consultations dark

1. Consider.

Ended rejoicing in their matchless chief:
As when from mountain tops the dusky clouds
Ascending, while the north wind sleeps, o'erspread
Heav'n's cheerful face, the louring element   490
Scowls o'er the darkened landscape snow, or show'r;
If chance the radiant sun with farewell sweet
Extend his evening beam, the fields revive,
The birds their notes renew, and bleating herds
Attest their joy, that hill and valley rings.   495
O shame to men! Devil with devil damned
Firm concord holds, men only disagree
Of creatures rational, though under hope
Of heavenly grace: and God proclaiming peace,
Yet live in hatred, enmity, and strife   500
Among themselves, and levy cruel wars,
Wasting the earth, each other to destroy:
As if (which might induce us to accord)
Man had not hellish foes enow besides,
That day and night for his destruction wait.   505

[Satan leaves Hell to find and destroy Eden.]

* * *

FROM BOOK 4

The Argument

Satan now in prospect of Eden, and nigh the place where he must now attempt the bold enterprise which he undertook alone against God and man, falls into many doubts with himself, and many passions, fear, envy, and despair; but at length confirms himself in evil, journeys on to Paradise, whose outward prospect and situation is described, overleaps the bounds, sits in the shape of a cormorant on the Tree of Life, as highest in the Garden to look about him. The Garden described; Satan's first sight of Adam and Eve; his wonder at their excellent form and happy state, but with resolution to work their fall; overhears their discourse, thence gathers that the Tree of Knowledge was forbidden them to eat of, under penalty of death; and thereon intends to found his temptation, by seducing them to transgress: then leaves them a while, to know further of their state by some other means. Meanwhile Uriel descending on a sunbeam warns Gabriel, who had in charge the gate of Paradise, that some evil Spirit had escaped the deep, and passed at noon by his sphere in the shape of a good angel down to Paradise, discovered after by his furious gestures in the mount. Gabriel promises to find him ere morning. Night coming on, Adam and Eve discourse of going to their rest: their bower described; their evening worship. Gabriel drawing forth his bands of nightwatch to walk the round of Paradise, appoints two strong angels to Adam's bower, lest the evil Spirit should be there doing some harm to Adam or Eve sleeping; there they find him at the ear of Eve, tempting her in a dream, and bring him, though unwilling, to Gabriel; by whom questioned, he scornfully answers, prepares resistance, but hindered by a sign from heaven, flies out of Paradise.

[Satan's Entry into Paradise; Adam and Eve in Their Bower]

O for that warning voice which he[2] who saw
Th' Apocalypse heard cry in Heaven aloud,
Then when the dragon, put to second rout,
Came furious down to be revenged on men,
Woe to the inhabitants on Earth! that now, 5
While time was, our first parents had been warned
The coming of their secret foe, and scaped,
Haply so scaped, his mortal snare! For now
Satan, now first inflamed with rage, came down,
The tempter ere th' accuser of mankind, 10
To wreak on innocent frail man his loss
Of that first battle, and his flight to Hell.
Yet not rejoicing in his speed though bold
Far off and fearless, nor with cause to boast,
Begins his dire attempt; which nigh the birth 15
Now rolling, boils in his tumultuous breast,
And like a devilish engine[3] back recoils
Upon himself. Horror and doubt distract
His troubled thoughts, and from the bottom stir
The Hell within him; for within him Hell 20
He brings, and round about him, nor from Hell
One step no more than from himself can fly
By change of place. Now conscience wakes despair
That slumbered, wakes the bitter memory
Of what he was, what is, and what must be 25
Worse; of worse deeds worse sufferings must ensue.
Sometimes towards Eden, which now in his view
Lay pleasant, his grieved look he fixes sad;
Sometimes towards heaven and the full-blazing sun,
Which now sat high in his meridian tower; 30
Then, much revolving, thus in sighs began:
"O thou that with surpassing glory crowned
Look'st from thy sole dominion like the god
Of this new world—at whose sight all the stars
Hide their diminished heads—to thee I call, 35
But with no friendly voice, and add thy name,
O sun, to tell thee how I hate thy beams,
That bring to my remembrance from what state
I fell, how glorious once above thy sphere,
Till pride and worse ambition threw me down, 40
Warring in Heaven against Heaven's matchless King!
Ah, wherefore? He deserved no such return
From me, whom he created what I was
In that bright eminence, and with his good
Upbraided none; nor was his service hard.
What could be less than to afford him praise, 45
The easiest recompense, and pay him thanks,
How due! Yet all his good proved ill in me,

---

2. St. John, author of Revelation.　　3. A cannon.

And wrought but malice. Lifted up so high,
I'sdained[4] subjection, and thought one step higher   50
Would set me highest, and in a moment quit
The debt immense of endless gratitude,
So burdensome, still paying, still to owe,
Forgetful what from him I still received;
And understood not that a grateful mind   55
By owing owes not, but still pays, at once
Indebted and discharged—what burden then?
O had his powerful destiny ordained
Me some inferior angel, I had stood
Then happy; no unbounded hope had raised   60
Ambition. Yet why not? Some other power
As great might have aspired, and me, though mean,
Drawn to his part. But other powers as great
Fell not, but stand unshaken, from within
Or from without to all temptations armed!   65
Hadst thou the same free will and power to stand?
Thou hadst. Whom hast thou then, or what, to accuse,
But Heaven's free love dealt equally to all?
Be then his love accursed, since, love or hate,
To me alike it deals eternal woe.   70
Nay, cursed be thou; since against his thy will
Chose freely what it now so justly rues.
Me miserable! which way shall I fly
Infinite wrath and infinite despair?
Which way I fly is Hell; myself am Hell;   75
And in the lowest deep a lower deep
Still threatening to devour me opens wide,
To which the Hell I suffer seems a Heaven.
O then at last relent! Is there no place
Left for repentance, none for pardon left?   80
None left but by submission; and that word
Disdain forbids me, and my dread of shame
Among the spirits beneath, whom I seduced
With other promises and other vaunts
Than to submit, boasting I could subdue   85
Th' omnipotent. Ay me! they little know
How dearly I abide that boast so vain,
Under what torments inwardly I groan.
While they adore me on the throne of Hell,
With diadem and scepter high advanced,   90
The lower still I fall, only supreme
In misery: such joy ambition finds!
But say I could repent and could obtain
By act of grace my former state, how soon
Would height recall high thoughts, how soon unsay   95
What feigned submission swore! Ease would recant
Vows made in pain, as violent and void.
For never can true reconcilement grow

4. Disdained.

Where wounds of deadly hate have pierced so deep;
Which would but lead me to a worse relapse   100
And heavier fall: so should I purchase dear
Short intermission, bought with double smart.
This knows my punisher; therefore as far
From granting he, as I from begging, peace.
All hope excluded thus, behold, instead   105
Of us outcast, exiled, his new delight,
Mankind created, and for him this world!
So farewell hope, and with hope farewell fear,
Farewell remorse! All good to me is lost;
Evil, be thou my good: by thee at least   110
Divided empire with Heaven's king I hold,
By thee, and more than half perhaps will reign;
As man ere long, and this new world, shall know."
    Thus while he spake, each passion dimmed his face,
Thrice changed with pale—ire, envy, and despair;   115
Which marred his borrowed visage, and betrayed
Him counterfeit, if any eye beheld:
For heavenly minds from such distempers foul
Are ever clear. Whereof he soon aware
Each perturbation smoothed with outward calm,   120
Artificer of fraud; and was the first
That practiced falsehood under saintly show,
Deep malice to conceal, couched with revenge:
Yet not enough had practiced to deceive
Uriel,[5] once warned; whose eye pursued him down   125
The way he went, and on th' Assyrian mount[6]
Saw him disfigured, more than could befall
Spirit of happy sort: his gestures fierce
He marked and mad demeanor, then alone,
As he supposed, all unobserved, unseen.   130
    So on he fares, and to the border comes
Of Eden, where delicious Paradise,
Now nearer, crowns with her enclosure green
As with a rural mound the champaign head
Of a steep wilderness, whose hairy sides   135
With thicket overgrown, grotesque and wild,
Access denied; and overhead up grew
Insuperable height of loftiest shade,
Cedar, and pine, and fir, and branching palm,
A sylvan scene, and as the ranks ascend   140
Shade above shade, a woody theater
Of stateliest view. Yet higher than their tops
The verdurous wall of Paradise up sprung;
Which to our general sire gave prospect large
Into his nether empire neighboring round.   145
And higher than that wall a circling row
Of goodliest trees loaden with fairest fruit,

---

5. An angel set to guard Eden from Satan's assault.   6. Niphates, a mountain on the border of Armenia and Assyria.

Blossoms and fruits at once of golden hue,
Appeared, with gay enameled colors mixed;
On which the sun more glad impressed his beams 150
Than in fair evening cloud, or humid bow,
When God hath showered the earth: so lovely seemed
That landscape. And of pure now purer air
Meets his approach, and to the heart inspires
Vernal delight and joy, able to drive[7] 155
All sadness but despair. Now gentle gales,
Fanning their odoriferous wings, dispense
Native perfumes, and whisper whence they stole
Those balmy spoils. As when to them who sail
Beyond the Cape of Hope, and now are past 160
Mozambic, off at sea northeast winds blow
Sabean[8] odors from the spicy shore
Of Araby the Blest, with such delay
Well pleased they slack their course, and many a league
Cheered with the grateful smell old Ocean smiles; 165
So entertained those odorous sweets the fiend
Who came their bane, though with them better pleased
Than Asmodëus[9] with the fishy fume
That drove him, though enamored, from the spouse
Of Tobit's son,[1] and with a vengeance sent 170
From Media post to Egypt, there fast bound.
    Now to th' ascent of that steep savage hill
Satan had journeyed on, pensive and slow;
But further way found none; so thick entwined,
As one continued brake, the undergrowth 175
Of shrubs and tangling bushes had perplexed
All path of man or beast that passed that way.
One gate there only was, and that looked east
On th' other side; which when th' arch-felon saw,
Due entrance he disdained, and in contempt 180
At one slight bound high overleaped all bound
Of hill or highest wall, and sheer within
Lights on his feet. As when a prowling wolf,
Whom hunger drives to seek new haunt for prey,
Watching where shepherds pen their flocks at eve 185
In hurdled cotes amid the field secure,
Leaps o'er the fence with ease into the fold;
Or as a thief, bent to unhoard the cash
Of some rich burgher, whose substantial doors,
Cross-barred and bolted fast, fear no assault, 190
In at the window climbs, or o'er the tiles;
So clomb this first grand thief into God's fold:
So since into his church lewd hirelings climb.
Thence up he flew, and on the Tree of Life,
The middle tree and highest there that grew, 195
Sat like a cormorant; yet not true life

7. Drive out.   8. Sheba of the Bible. Mozambique was an important Portuguese province in the trade route. Milton joins biblical, classical, and modern sources to describe the exotic pleasures of Eden. 9. Demon lover of Sara in the Apocryphal Book of Tobit.   1. Tobias.

Thereby regained, but sat devising death
To them who lived; nor on the virtue thought
Of that life-giving plant, but only used
For prospect, what, well used, had been the pledge   200
Of immortality. So little knows
Any, but God alone, to value right
The good before him, but perverts best things
To worst abuse, or to their meanest use.
  Beneath him with new wonder now he views   205
To all delight of human sense exposed
In narrow room Nature's whole wealth; yea more,
A Heaven on Earth; for blissful Paradise
Of God the garden was, by him in the east
Of Eden planted. Eden stretched her line   210
From Auran eastward to the royal towers
Of great Seleucia, built by Grecian kings,
Or where the sons of Eden long before
Dwelt in Telassar.[2] In this pleasant soil
His far more pleasant garden God ordained.   215
Out of the fertile ground he caused to grow
All trees of noblest kind for sight, smell, taste;
And all amid them stood the Tree of Life,
High eminent, blooming ambrosial fruit
Of vegetable gold; and next to life,   220
Our death, the Tree of Knowledge, grew fast by—
Knowledge of good bought dear by knowing ill.
Southward through Eden went a river large,
Nor changed his course, but through the shaggy hill
Passed underneath engulfed; for God had thrown   225
That mountain, as his garden-mold, high raised
Upon the rapid current, which, through veins
Of porous earth with kindly thirst up drawn,
Rose a fresh fountain, and with many a rill
Watered the garden; thence united fell   230
Down the steep glade, and met the nether flood,
Which from his darksome passage now appears,
And now, divided into four main streams,
Runs diverse, wandering many a famous realm
And country, whereof here needs no account;   235
But rather to tell how, if art could tell,
How from that sapphire fount the crispèd brooks,
Rolling on orient pearl and sands of gold,
With mazy error under pendant shades
Ran nectar, visiting each plant, and fed   240
Flowers worthy of Paradise; which not nice art
In beds and curious knots, but Nature boon
Poured forth profuse on hill and dale and plain,
Both where the morning sun first warmly smote
The open field, and where the unpierced shade   245
Embrowned the noontide bowers. Thus was this place,

2. City in Eden.

A happy rural seat of various view:
Groves whose rich trees wept odorous gums and balm;
Others whose fruit, burnished with golden rind,
Hung amiable—Hesperian fables[3] true,   250
If true, here only—and of delicious taste.
Betwixt them lawns, or level downs, and flocks
Grazing the tender herb, were interposed,
Or palmy hillock; or the flowery lap
Of some irriguous valley spread her store,   255
Flowers of all hue, and without thorn the rose.
Another side, umbrageous grots and caves
Of cool recess, o'er which the mantling vine
Lays forth her purple grape, and gently creeps
Luxuriant; meanwhile murmuring waters fall   260
Down the slope hills dispersed, or in a lake,
That to the fringèd bank with myrtle crowned
Her crystal mirror holds, unite their streams.
The birds their choir apply; airs, vernal airs,
Breathing the smell of field and grove, attune   265
The trembling leaves, while universal Pan,[4]
Knit with the Graces and the Hours in dance,
Led on th' eternal spring. Not that fair field
Of Enna, where Proserpin gathering flowers,
Herself a fairer flower, by gloomy Dis   270
Was gathered, which cost Ceres all that pain
To seek her through the world;[5] nor that sweet grove
Of Daphne, by Orontes and th' inspired
Castalian spring,[6] might with this Paradise
Of Eden strive; nor that Nyseian isle,   275
Girt with the river Triton, where old Cham,
Whom Gentiles Ammon call and Libyan Jove,
Hid Amalthea and her florid son
Young Bacchus from his stepdame Rhea's eye;[7]
Nor where Abassin kings their issue guard,   280
Mount Amara (though this by some supposed
True Paradise), under the Ethiop line[8]
By Nilus's head, enclosed with shining rock,
A whole day's journey high, but wide remote
From this Assyrian[9] garden, where the fiend   285
Saw undelighted all delight, all kind
Of living creatures, new to sight and strange.
Two of far nobler shape, erect and tall,
Godlike erect, with native honor clad

3. In Ovid's *Metamorphoses* 10, a dragon guarded the golden apples on the islands known as the Hesperides.
4. A pastoral god whose name Renaissance mythographers took from the Greek *pas* or *pan*, meaning "all"
(or "universal"). 5. In Ovid's *Fasti* 4, Dis, the god of the underworld, abducts Proserpine, daughter of
Ceres (the goddess of the Earth's natural fecundity). Because she eats seven seeds of a pomegranate in the
underworld, Proserpine must remain there seven months of each year, during which time Ceres mourns
and blights the Earth. 6. The groves of Daphne by the river Orontes in Syria had a temple to Apollo
and a spring named after the Castalian spring of Parnassus. 7. Ammon, king of Libya, had an affair
with the nymph Amalthea, who bore the god Bacchus; Ammon hid the child from his jealous wife, Rhea,
on the island of Nysa. Ammon was identified with the Libyan Jove and with Ham, or Cham, son of Noah.
8. I.e., on the equator in Abyssinia. 9. The Garden was near the Euphrates in Assyria.

In naked majesty, seemed lords of all, 290
And worthy seemed; for in their looks divine
The image of their glorious Maker shone,
Truth, wisdom, sanctitude severe and pure—
Severe, but in true filial freedom placed,
Whence true authority in men; though both 295
Not equal, as their sex not equal seemed;[1]
For contemplation he and valor formed,
For softness she and sweet attractive grace;
He for God only, she for God in him.[2]
His fair large front and eye sublime declared 300
Absolute rule;[3] and hyacinthine locks
Round from his parted forelock manly hung
Clustering, but not beneath his shoulders broad:
She, as a veil down to the slender waist,
Her unadornèd golden tresses wore 305
Disheveled, but in wanton ringlets waved
As the vine curls her tendrils, which implied
Subjection,[4] but required with gentle sway,
And by her yielded, by him best received,
Yielded with coy submission, modest pride, 310
And sweet, reluctant, amorous delay.
Nor those mysterious parts were then concealed;
Then was not guilty shame. Dishonest shame
Of Nature's works, honor dishonorable,
Sin-bred, how have ye troubled all mankind 315
With shows instead, mere shows of seeming pure,
And banished from man's life his happiest life,
Simplicity and spotless innocence!
So passed they naked on, nor shunned the sight
Of God or angel, for they thought no ill; 320
So hand in hand they passed, the loveliest pair
That ever since in love's embraces met:
Adam the goodliest man of men since born
His sons; the fairest of her daughters Eve.
Under a tuft of shade that on a green 325
Stood whispering soft, by a fresh fountain-side,
They sat them down; and after no more toil
Of their sweet gardening labor than sufficed
To recommend cool Zephyr,[5] and made ease
More easy, wholesome thirst and appetite 330
More grateful, to their supper fruits they fell,
Nectarine fruits which the compliant boughs
Yielded them, sidelong as they sat recline
On the soft downy bank damasked[6] with flowers.

---

1. Milton includes both biblical accounts of creation, beginning with Genesis 1.27: "So God created man in his own image, in the image of God created he him; male and female created he them." He next uses the account of creating Eve from Adam's rib.   2. "The head of every man is Christ; and the head of the woman is the man" (1 Corinthians 11.3).   3. Adam's body "declares" the political theory associated with monarchical absolutism.   4. Eve's body "implies" the subjection that fulfills Adam's "Absolute rule," but negotiates the distribution of "Authority in men." In *Tetrachordon*, Milton writes of the "golden dependence of [male] headship and [female] subjection" in marriage.   5. West wind.   6. Richly patterned.

The savory pulp they chew, and in the rind
Still as they thirsted scoop the brimming stream;
Nor gentle purpose, nor endearing smiles
Wanted, nor youthful dalliance, as beseems
Fair couple linked in happy nuptial league,
Alone as they. About them frisking played   340
All beasts of th' earth, since wild, and of all chase
In wood or wilderness, forest or den.
Sporting the lion ramped, and in his paw
Dandled the kid; bears, tigers, ounces, pards,[7]
Gamboled before them; th' unwieldy elephant   345
To make them mirth used all his might, and wreathed
His lithe proboscis;[8] close the serpent sly,
Insinuating, wove with Gordian twine
His braided train, and of his fatal guile
Gave proof unheeded. Others on the grass   350
Couched, and now filled with pasture gazing sat,
Or bedward ruminating; for the sun,
Declined, was hasting now with prone career
To th' ocean isles, and in th' ascending scale
Of heaven the stars that usher evening rose: 355
When Satan, still in gaze as first he stood,
Scarce thus at length failed speech recovered sad:
    "O Hell! what do mine eyes with grief behold?
Into our room of bliss thus high advanced
Creatures of other mold, Earth-born perhaps,   360
Not spirits, yet to heavenly spirits bright
Little inferior; whom my thoughts pursue
With wonder, and could love; so lively shines
In them divine resemblance, and such grace
The hand that formed them on their shape hath poured.   365
Ah! gentle pair, ye little think how nigh
Your change approaches, when all these delights
Will vanish, and deliver ye to woe,
More woe, the more your taste is now of joy:
Happy, but for so happy ill secured   370
Long to continue, and this high seat, your Heaven,
Ill fenced for Heaven to keep out such a foe
As now is entered; yet no purposed foe
To you, whom I could pity thus forlorn,
Though I unpitied. League with you I seek,   375
And mutual amity so strait, so close,
That I with you must dwell, or you with me,
Henceforth. My dwelling, haply, may not please,
Like this fair Paradise, your sense; yet such
Accept your Maker's work; he gave it me,   380
Which I as freely give. Hell shall unfold,
To entertain you two, her widest gates,
And send forth all her kings; there will be room,
Not like these narrow limits, to receive

7. Lynxes and leopards.   8. Trunk.

Your numerous offspring; if no better place,   385
Thank him who puts me, loath, to this revenge
On you, who wrong me not, for him who wronged.
And should I at your harmless innocence
Melt, as I do, yet public reason just—
Honor and empire with revenge enlarged   390
By conquering this new world—compels me now
To do what else, though damned, I should abhor."
    So spake the fiend, and with necessity,
The tyrant's plea, excused his devilish deeds.
Then from his lofty stand on that high tree   395
Down he alights among the sportful herd
Of those four-footed kinds, himself now one,
Now other, as their shape served best his end
Nearer to view his prey, and unespied
To mark what of their state he more might learn   400
By word or action marked. About them round
A lion now he stalks with fiery glare;
Then as a tiger, who by chance hath spied
In some purlieu⁹ two gentle fawns at play,
Straight couches close; then, rising, changes oft   405
His couchant¹ watch, as one who chose his ground,
Whence rushing he might surest seize them both
Gripped in each paw; when Adam first of men
To first of women Eve thus moving speech,
Turned him all ear to hear new utterance flow.   410
    "Sole partner and sole part of all these joys,
Dearer thyself than all; needs must the power
That made us, and for us this ample world,
Be infinitely good, and of his good
As liberal and free as infinite,   415
That raised us from the dust and placed us here
In all this happiness, who at his hand
Have nothing merited, nor can perform
Aught of which he hath need; he who requires
From us no other service than to keep   420
This one, this easy charge, of all the trees
In Paradise that bear delicious fruit
So various, not to taste that only Tree
Of Knowledge, planted by the Tree of Life,
So near grows death to life, whate'er death is,   425
Some dreadful thing, no doubt; for well thou know'st
God hath pronounced it death to taste that tree,
The only sign of our obedience left
Among so many signs of power and rule
Conferred upon us, and dominion given   430
Over all other creatures that possess
Earth, air, and sea. Then let us not think hard
One easy prohibition, who enjoy
Free leave so large to all things else, and choice

9. Region on the outskirts of a given area.   1. From heraldry: lying down with the head raised.

Unlimited of manifold delights; 435
But let us ever praise him, and extol
His bounty, following our delightful task
To prune these growing plants and tend these flowers,
Which were it toilsome, yet with thee were sweet."
    To whom thus Eve replied: "O thou for whom 440
And from whom I was formed flesh of thy flesh,
And without whom am to no end, my guide
And head, what thou hast said is just and right.
For we to him indeed all praises owe
And daily thanks, I chiefly who enjoy 445
So far the happier lot, enjoying thee
Preeminent by so much odds, while thou
Like consort to thyself canst nowhere find.
That day I oft remember, when from sleep
I first awaked, and found myself reposed 450
Under a shade on flowers, much wondering where
And what I was, whence thither brought, and how.
Not distant far from thence a murmuring sound
Of waters issued from a cave and spread
Into a liquid plain, then stood unmoved, 455
Pure as th' expanse of heaven; I thither went
With unexperienced thought, and laid me down
On the green bank, to look into the clear
Smooth lake that to me seemed another sky.
As I bent down to look, just opposite, 460
A shape within the wat'ry gleam appeared,
Bending to look on me. I started back,
It started back; but pleased I soon returned,
Pleased it returned as soon with answering looks
Of sympathy and love. There I had fixed 465
Mine eyes till now, and pined with vain desire,[2]
Had not a voice thus warned me: 'What thou seest,
What there thou seest, fair creature, is thyself;
With thee it came and goes. But follow me,
And I will bring thee where no shadow stays 470
Thy coming, and thy soft embraces, he
Whose image thou art, him thou shalt enjoy
Inseparably thine, to him shalt bear
Multitudes like thyself, and thence be called
Mother of human race.'[3] What could I do 475
But follow straight, invisibly thus led?
Till I espied thee, fair indeed and tall
Under a platan, yet methought[4] less fair,
Less winning soft, less amiably mild
Than that smooth wat'ry image. Back I turned; 480
Thou following cried'st aloud, 'Return, fair Eve,
Whom fli'st thou? whom thou fli'st, of him thou art,
His flesh, his bone; to give thee being I lent

---

2. Like Ovid's Narcissus in *Metamorphoses* 3.339–510, Eve falls in love with her image; unlike Narcissus, she is led by God's voice to Adam, whose image she is.   3. Eve means "Mother of all things living" (11.159).   4. It seemed to me. A *platan* is a plane tree.

Out of my side to thee, nearest my heart,
Substantial life, to have thee by my side 485
Henceforth an individual solace dear.
Part of my soul I seek thee, and thee claim
My other half.' With that, thy gentle hand
Seized mine, I yielded, and from that time see
How beauty is excelled by manly grace 490
And wisdom, which alone is truly fair."
    So spake our general mother, and with eyes
Of conjugal attraction unreproved
And meek surrender, half embracing leaned
On our first father; half her swelling breast 495
Naked met his under the flowing gold
Of her loose tresses hid. He in delight
Both of her beauty and submissive charms
Smiled with superior love, as Jupiter
On Juno smiles,[5] when he impregns the clouds 500
That shed May flowers, and pressed her matron lip
With kisses pure. Aside the Devil turned
For envy, yet with jealous leer malign
Eyed them askance, and to himself thus plained:
    "Sight hateful, sight tormenting! thus these two 505
Imparadised in one another's arms,
The happier Eden, shall enjoy their fill
Of bliss on bliss, while I to Hell am thrust,
Where neither joy nor love, but fierce desire,
Among our other torments not the least, 510
Still unfulfilled with pain of longing pines.
Yet let me not forget what I have gained
From their own mouths: all is not theirs, it seems.
One fatal tree there stands, of knowledge called,
Forbidden them to taste. Knowledge forbidden? 515
Suspicious, reasonless. Why should their lord
Envy them that? Can it be sin to know,
Can it be death? and do they only stand
By ignorance, is that their happy state,
The proof of their obedience and their faith? 520
O fair foundation laid whereon to build
Their ruin! Hence I will excite their minds
With more desire to know, and to reject
Envious commands, invented with design
To keep them low whom knowledge might exalt 525
Equal with gods. Aspiring to be such,
They taste and die; what likelier can ensue?
But first with narrow search I must walk round
This garden, and no corner leave unspied;
A chance but chance may lead where I may meet 530
Some wandering spirit of Heaven, by fountain side
Or in thick shade retired, from him to draw

5. In Greco-Roman mythology, Jupiter is king of the gods and Juno is his sister and wife. The marital hierarchies of the pagan gods and of the human couple differ. While Jupiter reigns (and rains) supreme, Adam and Eve enjoy "give and take." Adam smiles *with superior love*, yet Eve is physically "on top."

What further would be learnt. Live while ye may,
Yet happy pair; enjoy, till I return,
Short pleasures, for long woes are to succeed."   535

* * *

FROM BOOK 8

The Argument

Adam inquires concerning celestial motions, is doubtfully answered, and
exhorted to search rather things more worthy of knowledge: Adam assents,
and still desirous to detain Raphael, relates to him what he remembered
since his own creation, his placing in Paradise, his talk with God concerning
solitude and fit society, his first meeting and nuptials with Eve, his discourse
with the angel thereupon; who after admonitions repeated departs.

[Adam Describes His Own Creation and That of Eve; The Angel Repeats His Warning and Departs]

* * *

"Solicit not thy thoughts with matters hid,[6]
Leave them to God above, him serve and fear;
Of other creatures, as him pleases best,
Wherever placed, let him dispose: joy thou   170
In what he gives thee, this Paradise
And thy fair Eve; heaven is for thee too high
To know what passes there; be lowly wise:
Think only what concerns thee and thy being;
Dream not of other worlds, what creatures there   175
Live, in what state, condition or degree,
Contented that thus far hath been revealed
Not of earth only but of highest heaven."
    To whom thus Adam cleared of doubt, replied.
"How fully hast thou satisfied me, pure   180
Intelligence of heaven, angel serene,
And freed from intricacies, taught to live,
The easiest way, nor with perplexing thoughts
To interrupt the sweet of life, from which
God hath bid dwell far off all anxious cares,   185
And not molest us, unless we ourselves
Seek them with wandering thoughts, and notions vain.
But apt the mind or fancy is to rove
Unchecked, and of her roving is no end;
Till warned, or by experience taught, she learn,   190
That not to know at large of things remote
From use, obscure and subtle, but to know
That which before us lies in daily life,
Is the prime wisdom, what is more is fume,
Or emptiness, or find impertinence,   195

6. In conversation with the angel Raphael, Adam has asked questions about astronomy and expressed
uncertainty about divine intention.

And renders us in things that most concern
Unpracticed, unprepared, and still to seek.
Therefore from this high pitch let us descend
A lower flight, and speak of things at hand
Useful, whence haply mention may arise   200
Of something not unseasonable to ask
By sufferance, and they wonted favor deigned.
Thee I have heard relating what was done
Ere my remembrance: now hear me relate
My story, which perhaps thou hast not heard;   205
And Day is yet not spent; till then thou seest
How subtly to detain thee I devise,
Inviting thee to hear while I relate,
Fond, were it not in hope of thy reply:
For while I sit with thee, I seem in heaven,   210
And sweeter thy discourse is to my ear
Then fruits of palm-tree pleasantest to thirst
And hunger both, from labor, at the hour
Of sweet repast; they satiate, and soon fill,
Though pleasant, but thy words with grace divine   215
Imbued, bring to their sweetness no satiety."
    To whom thus Raphael answered heavenly meek.
"Nor are thy lips ungraceful, sire of men,
Nor tongue ineloquent; for God on thee
Abundantly his gifts hath also poured   220
Inward and outward both, his image fair:
Speaking or mute all comeliness and grace
Attends thee, and each word, each motion forms.
Nor less think we in heaven of thee on earth
Than of our fellow servant, and inquire   225
Gladly into the ways of God with man:
For God we see hath honored thee, and set
On man his equal love: say therefore on;
For I that day was absent, as befell,
Bound on a voyage uncouth and obscure,   230
Far on excursion toward the gates of hell;[7]
Squared in full legion (such command we had)
To see that none thence issued forth a spy,
Or enemy, while God was in his work,
Lest he incensed at such eruption bold,   235
Destruction with creation might have mixed.
Nor that they durst without his leave attempt,
But us he sends upon his high behests
For state, as sovereign king, and to inure
Our prompt obedience. Fast we found, fast shut   240
The dismal gates, and barricadoed strong;
But long ere our approaching heard within
Noise, other then the sound of dance or song,
Torment, and loud lament, and furious rage.

---

7. God sent Raphael to watch the gates of hell and prevent Satan from disturbing Him during the Creation of the world.

Glad we returned up to the coasts of light   245
Ere Sabbath evening: so we had in charge.
But thy relation now; for I attend,
Pleased with thy words no less than thou with mine."
    So spake the godlike power, and thus our sire:
"For man to tell how human life began   250
Is hard; for who himself beginning knew?
Desire with thee still longer to converse
Induced me. As new waked from soundest sleep,
Soft on the flowery herb I found me laid
In balmy sweat, which with his beams the sun   255
Soon dried, and on the reeking[8] moisture fed.
Straight toward heaven my wondering eyes I turned,
And gazed a while the ample sky, till raised
By quick instinctive motion up I sprung
As thitherward endeavoring, and upright   260
Stood on my feet; about me round I saw
Hill, dale, and shady woods, and sunny plains
And liquid lapse of murmuring streams; by these,
Creatures that lived and moved, and walked or flew,
Birds on the branches warbling. All things smiled;   265
With fragrance and with joy my heart o'erflowed.
Myself I then perused, and limb by limb
Surveyed, and sometimes went and sometimes ran
With supple joints as lively vigor led:
But who I was, or where, or from what cause,   270
Knew not. To speak I tried, and forthwith spake,
My tongue obeyed, and readily could name
Whate'er I saw. 'Thou sun,' said I, 'fair light,
And thou enlightened earth, so fresh and gay,
Ye hills and dales, ye rivers, woods, and plains,   275
And ye that live and move, fair creatures, tell,
Tell, if ye saw, how came I thus, how here?
Not of myself; by some great maker, then,
In goodness and in power preëminent.
Tell me how may I know him, how adore,   280
From whom I have that thus I move and live,
And feel that I am happier than I know.'
    "While thus I called, and strayed I knew not whither
From where I first drew air and first beheld
This happy light, when answer none returned,   285
On a green shady bank profuse of flowers
Pensive I sat me down; there gentle sleep
First found me and with soft oppression seized
My drowsèd sense—untroubled, though I thought
I then was passing to my former state   290
Insensible, and forthwith to dissolve;
When suddenly stood at my head a dream,
Whose inward apparition gently moved
My fancy to believe I yet had being

8. Steaming.

And lived. One came, methought, of shape divine,   295
And said, 'Thy mansion wants thee, Adam, rise,
First man, of men innumerable ordained
First father; called by thee I come thy guide
To the garden of bliss, thy seat prepared.'
So saying, by the hand he took me raised,   300
And over fields and waters, as in air
Smooth sliding without step, last led me up
A woody mountain whose high top was plain,
A circuit wide, enclosed, with goodliest trees
Planted, with walks and bowers, that what I saw   305
Of earth before scarce pleasant seemed. Each tree
Loaden with fairest fruit that hung to the eye
Tempting, stirred in me sudden appetite
To pluck and eat; whereat I waked, and found
Before mine eyes all real, as the dream   310
Had lively shadowed. Here had new begun
My wandering, had not he who was my guide
Up hither, from among the trees appeared,
Presence divine. Rejoicing, but with awe,
In adoration at his feet I fell   315
Submiss: he reared me, and, 'Whom thou soughtest I am,'
Said mildly, 'author⁹ of all this thou seest
Above or round about thee or beneath.
This Paradise I give thee, count it thine
To till and keep, and of the fruit to eat.   320
Of every tree that in the garden grows
Eat freely with glad heart; fear here no dearth.
But of the tree whose operation brings
Knowledge of good and ill, which I have set
The pledge of thy obedience and thy faith   325
Amid the garden by the Tree of Life,
Remember what I warn thee, shun to taste
And shun the bitter consequence: for know
The day thou eat'st thereof, my sole command
Transgressed, inevitably thou shalt die,   330
From that day mortal, and this happy state
Shalt lose, expelled from hence into a world
Of woe and sorrow.' Sternly he pronounced
The rigid interdiction, which resounds
Yet dreadful in mine ear, though in my choice   335
Not to incur; but soon his clear aspèct
Returned, and gracious purpose thus renewed:
'Not only these fair bounds, but all the Earth
To thee and to thy race I give; as lords
Possess it, and all things that therein live,   340
Or live in sea or air, beast, fish, and fowl.
In sign whereof each bird and beast behold
After their kinds; I bring them to receive
From thee their names, and pay thee fealty

9. Creator, augmenter.

With low subjection; understand the same   345
Of fish within their watery residence,
Not hither summoned, since they cannot change
Their element to draw the thinner air.'
As thus he spake, each bird and beast behold
Approaching two and two, these cowering low   350
With blandishment, each bird stooped on his wing.
I named them as they passed, and understood
Their nature, with such knowledge God endued
My sudden apprehension. But in these
I found not what methought I wanted[1] still,   355
And to the heavenly vision thus presumed:
    " 'O by what name, for thou above all these,
Above mankind, or aught than mankind higher,
Surpassest far my naming, how may I
Adore thee, author of this universe   360
And all this good to man, for whose well-being
So amply and with hands so liberal
Thou hast provided all things? But with me
I see not who partakes. In solitude
What happiness? Who can enjoy alone,   365
Or all enjoying, what contentment find?'
Thus I presumptuous; and the vision bright,
As with a smile more brightened, thus replied:
    " 'What callest thou solitude? Is not the earth
With various living creatures, and the air,   370
Replenished, and all these at thy command
To come and play before thee? Knowest thou not
Their language and their ways? They also know
And reason not contemptibly; with these
Find pastime and bear rule; thy realm is large.'   375
So spake the universal Lord, and seemed
So ordering. I with leave of speech implored
And humble deprecation, thus replied:
    " 'Let not my words offend thee, heavenly power,
My maker; be propitious while I speak.   380
Hast thou not made me here thy substitute,
And these inferior far beneath me set?
Among unequals what society
Can sort, what harmony or true delight?
Which must be mutual, in proportion due   385
Given and received. But in disparity,
The one intense, the other still remiss,
Cannot well suit with either, but soon prove
Tedious alike. Of fellowship I speak
Such as I seek, fit to participate   390
All rational delight, wherein the brute
Cannot be human consort. They rejoice
Each with their kind, lion with lioness,
So fitly them in pairs thou hast combined:

1. Desired, lacked.

Much less can bird with beast, or fish with fowl   395
So well converse, nor with the ox the ape;
Worse then can man with beast, and least of all.'
   "Whereto the Almighty answered, not displeased:
'A nice and subtle happiness I see
Thou to thyself proposest, in the choice   400
Of thy associates, Adam, and wilt taste
No pleasure, though in pleasure, solitary.
What thinkest thou then of me and this my state?
Seem I to thee sufficiently possessed
Of happiness or not? who am alone   405
From all eternity, for none I know
Second to me or like, equal much less.
How have I then with whom to hold converse
Save with the creatures which I made, and those
To me inferior, infinite descents   410
Beneath what other creatures are to thee?'
   "He ceased, I lowly answered: 'To attain
The height and depth of thy eternal ways
All human thoughts come short, supreme of things.
Thou in thyself art perfect, and in thee   415
Is no deficience found; not so is man,
But in degree, the cause of his desire
By conversation with his like to help
Or solace his defects. No need that thou
Shouldst propagate, already infinite,   420
And through all number absolute, though one.
But man by number is to manifest
His single imperfection, and beget
Like of his like, his image multiplied,
In unity defective, which requires   425
Collateral[2] love and dearest amity.
Thou in thy secrecy although alone,
Best with thyself accompanied, seekest not
Social communication; yet, so pleased,
Canst raise thy creature to what height thou wilt   430
Of union or communion, deified;
I by conversing cannot these erect
From prone, nor in their ways complacence find.'
Thus I emboldened spake, and freedom used
Permissive, and acceptance found, which gained   435
This answer from the gracious voice divine:
   " 'Thus far to try thee, Adam, I was pleased,
And find thee knowing, not of beasts alone
Which thou hast rightly named, but of thyself,
Expressing well the spirit within thee free,   440
My image, not imparted to the brute,
Whose fellowship, therefore unmeet for thee,
Good reason was thou freely shouldst dislike;
And be so minded still. I, ere thou spak'st,

---

2. Equal, with a pun on Latin *latus, lateris,* the "side" from which Eve will be formed.

Knew it not good for man to be alone,   445
And no such company as then thou sawest
Intended thee, for trial only brought,
To see how thou couldst judge of fit and meet.
What next I bring shall please thee, be assured:
Thy likeness, thy fit help, thy other self,   450
Thy wish exactly to thy heart's desire.'
    "He ended, or I heard no more, for now,
My earthly by his heavenly overpowered
Which it had long stood under, strained to the height
In that celestial colloquy sublime,   455
As with an object that excels the sense
Dazzled and spent, sunk down and sought repair
Of sleep, which instantly fell on me, called
By nature as in aid, and closed mine eyes.
Mine eyes he closed, but open left the cell   460
Of fancy,[3] my internal sight, by which
Abstract as in a trance methought I saw,
Though sleeping, where I lay, and saw the shape
Still glorious before whom awake I stood;
Who stooping opened my left side, and took   465
From thence a rib, with cordial[4] spirits warm
And life-blood streaming fresh. Wide was the wound,
But suddenly with flesh filled up and healed.
The rib he formed and fashioned with his hands;
Under his forming hands a creature grew,   470
Manlike, but different sex, so lovely fair
That what seemed fair in all the world seemed now
Mean, or in her summed up, in her contained,
And in her looks, which from that time infused
Sweetness into my heart, unfelt before,   475
And into all things from her air inspired
The spirit of love and amorous delight.
She disappeared, and left me dark; I waked
To find her or forever to deplore
Her loss, and other pleasures all abjure;   480
When out of hope, behold her, not far off,
Such as I saw her in my dream, adorned
With what all Earth or Heaven could bestow
To make her amiable. On she came,
Led by her heavenly maker, though unseen,   485
And guided by his voice, nor uninformed
Of nuptial sanctity and marriage rites.
Grace was in all her steps, heaven in her eye,
In every gesture dignity and love.
I overjoyed could not forbear aloud: 490
    " 'This turn hath made amends; thou hast fulfilled
Thy words, Creator bounteous and benign,
Giver of all things fair, but fairest this
Of all thy gifts; nor enviest. I now see

---

3. Imagination.   4. From the Latin *cors, cordis*, relating to the heart.

Bone of my bone, flesh of my flesh, my self   495
Before me; woman is her name, of man
Extracted; for this cause he shall forego
Father and mother, and to his wife adhere,
And they shall be one flesh, one heart, one soul.'
    "She heard me thus, and though divinely brought,   500
Yet innocence and virgin modesty,
Her virtue and the conscience of her worth
That would be wooed and not unsought be won,
Not obvious, not obtrusive, but retired,
The more desirable—or, to say all,   505
Nature herself, though pure of sinful thought,
Wrought in her so that, seeing me, she turned.
I followed her; she what was honor knew,
And with obsequious[5] majesty approved
My pleaded reason. To the nuptial bower   510
I led her blushing like the morn. All heaven
And happy constellations on that hour
Shed their selectest influence; the earth
Gave sign of gratulation,[6] and each hill;
Joyous the birds; fresh gales and gentle airs   515
Whispered it to the woods, and from their wings
Flung rose, flung odors from the spicy shrub,
Disporting, till the amorous bird of night
Sung spousal, and bid haste the evening star
On his hill-top, to light the bridal lamp.   520
    "Thus have I told thee all my state, and brought
My story to the sum of earthly bliss
Which I enjoy, and must confess to find
In all things else delight indeed, but such
As, used or not, works in the mind no change,   525
Nor vehement[7] desire—these delicacies
I mean of taste, sight, smell, herbs, fruits, and flowers,
Walks and the melody of birds. But here,
Far otherwise, transported I behold,
Transported touch; here passion first I felt,   530
Commotion strange, in all enjoyments else
Superior and unmoved, here only weak
Against the charm of beauty's powerful glance.
Or nature failed in me and left some part
Not proof enough such object to sustain,   535
Or from my side subducting[8] took perhaps
More than enough; at least on her bestowed
Too much of ornament, in outward show
Elaborate, of inward less exact.
For well I understand in the prime end   540
Of nature her th' inferior, in the mind
And inward faculties which most excel,
In outward also her resembling less

5. Obedient ("following," literally), displaying the essential virtue of the wife.   6. Congratulation.
7. Overpowering, distracting.   8. Taking away.

His image who made both, and less expressing
The character of that dominion given
O'er other creatures. Yet when I approach
Her loveliness, so absolute she seems
And in herself complete, so well to know
Her own, that what she wills to do or say
Seems wisest, virtuousest, discreetest, best.   550
All higher knowledge in her presence falls
Degraded; wisdom in discourse with her
Loses discountenanced, and like folly shows;
Authority and reason on her wait
As one intended first, not after made   555
Occasionally;⁹ and to consùmmate all,
Greatness of mind and nobleness their seat
Build in her loveliest, and create an awe
About her as a guard angelic placed."
    To whom the Angel with contracted brow: 560
"Accuse not nature, she hath done her part;
Do thou but thine, and be not diffident
Of wisdom; she deserts thee not if thou
Dismiss not her when most thou need'st her nigh
By àttributing overmuch to things   565
Less excellent, as thou thyself perceiv'st.
For what admir'st thou, what transports thee so?
An outside? Fair no doubt, and worthy well
Thy cherishing, thy honoring, and thy love;
Not thy subjection. Weigh her with thyself,   570
Then value. Ofttimes nothing profits more
Then self-esteem, grounded on just and right
Well managed. Of that skill the more thou know'st,
The more she will acknowledge thee her head,
And to realities yield all her shows—   575
Made so adorn for thy delight the more,
So aweful¹ that with honor thou may'st love
Thy mate, who sees when thou art seen least wise.
But if the sense of touch whereby mankind
Is propagated seem such dear delight   580
Beyond all other, think the same vouchsafed
To cattle and each beast; which would not be
To them made common and divulged if aught
Therein enjoyed were worthy to subdue
The soul of man, or passion in him move.   585
What higher in her society thou find'st
Attractive, human, rational—love still;
In loving thou dost well, in passion not,
Wherein true love consists not. Love refines
The thoughts, and heart enlarges, hath his seat   590
In reason, and is judicious, is the scale
By which to heavenly love thou may'st ascend,
Not sunk in carnal pleasure, for which cause

9. For a particular purpose or occasion, i.e., Adam's request for a companion.   1. Awe-inspiring.

Among the beasts no mate for thee was found."
    To whom thus half abashed Adam replied: 595
"Neither her outside formed so fair, nor aught
In procreation common to all kinds
(Though higher of the genial[2] bed by far
And with mysterious reverence I deem)
So much delights me as those graceful acts,   600
Those thousand decencies that daily flow
From all her words and actions, mixed with love
And sweet compliance, which declare unfeigned
Union of mind, or in us both one soul,
Harmony to behold in wedded pair   605
More grateful than harmonious sound to the ear.
Yet these subject not; I to thee disclose
What inward thence I feel, not therefore foiled,
Who meet with various objects from the sense
Variously representing; yet still free   610
Approve the best, and follow what I approve.
    "To love thou balm'st me not, for love thou say'st
Leads up to Heaven, is both the way and guide;
Bear with me then, if lawful what I ask:
Love not the heavenly spirits, and how their love   615
Express they, by looks only, or do they mix
Irradiance, virtual or immediate touch?"
    To whom the Angel with a smile that glowed
Celestial rosy red, love's proper hue,
Answered: "Let it suffice thee that thou know'st   620
Us happy, and without love no happiness.
Whatever pure thou in the body enjoy'st
(And pure thou wert created), we enjoy
In eminence, and obstacle find none
Of membrane, joint, or limb, exclusive bars.   625
Easier than air with air, if spirits embrace,
Total they mix, union of pure with pure
Desiring; nor restrained conveyance need
As flesh to mix with flesh, or soul with soul.
But I can now no more; the parting sun   630
Beyond the earth's green cape and verdant isles
Hesperian sets, my signal to depart.
Be strong, live happy, and love, but first of all
His whom to love is to obey, and keep
His great command; take heed lest passion sway   635
Thy judgment to do aught which else free will
Would not admit; thine and of all thy sons
The weal or woe in thee is placed: beware.
I in thy persevering shall rejoice,
And all the blest. Stand fast; to stand or fall   640
Free in thine own arbitrement[3] it lies.
Perfect within, no outward aid require;
And all temptation to transgress repel."

2. Procreative.   3. Judgment.

So saying, he arose; whom Adam thus
Followed with benediction: "Since to part,   645
Go, heavenly guest, ethereal messenger,
Sent from whose sovereign goodness I adore.
Gentle to me and affable⁴ hath been
Thy condescension, and shall be honored ever
With grateful memory. Thou to mankind   650
Be good and friendly still, and oft return."
   So parted they, the Angel up to Heaven
From the thick shade, and Adam to his bower.

BOOK 9

The Argument

   Satan, having compassed the Earth, with meditated guile returns as a mist
by night into Paradise; enters into the serpent sleeping. Adam and Eve in
the morning go forth to their labors, which Eve proposes to divide in several
places, each laboring apart: Adam consents not, alleging the danger lest that
enemy of whom they were forewarned should attempt her found alone. Eve,
loath to be thought not circumspect or firm enough, urges her going apart,
the rather desirous to make trial of her strength; Adam at last yields. The
serpent finds her alone: his subtle approach, first gazing, then speaking, with
much flattery extolling Eve above all other creatures. Eve, wondering to hear
the serpent speak, asks how he attained to human speech and such understanding not till now; the serpent answers that by tasting of a certain tree in
the garden he attained both to speech and reason, till then void of both. Eve
requires him to bring her to that tree, and finds it to be the Tree of Knowledge
forbidden: the serpent, now grown bolder, with many wiles and arguments
induces her at length to eat. She, pleased with the taste, deliberates a while
whether to impart thereof to Adam or not; at last brings him of the fruit;
relates what persuaded her to eat thereof. Adam, at first amazed, but perceiving her lost, resolves, through vehemence of love, to perish with her,
and, extenuating the trespass, eats also of the fruit. The effects thereof in
them both; they seek to cover their nakedness; then fall to variance and
accusation of one another.

[Temptation and Fall]

No more of talk where God or angel guest⁵
With man, as with his friend, familiar used
To sit indulgent, and with him partake
Rural repast, permitting him the while
Venial⁶ discourse unblamed. I now must change   5
Those notes to tragic; foul distrust, and breach
Disloyal, on the part of man, revolt
And disobedience; on the part of Heaven,
Now alienated, distance and distaste,

---

4. Easy to converse with.   5. Raphael, the "affable archangel," who in preceding books (5–8) has sat
with Adam sharing "rural repast" and discoursing on such highly relevant matters as Lucifer's fall, the
Creation, the structure of the universe. To him, Adam has told of the warning he has received from God
not to touch the Tree of Knowledge.   6. Unblemished.

Anger and just rebuke, and judgment given, 10
That brought into this world a world of woe,
Sin and her shadow Death, and Misery,
Death's harbinger. Sad task! yet argument
Not less but more heroic than the wrath
Of stern Achilles on his foe pursued 15
Thrice fugitive about Troy wall;[7] or rage
Of Turnus for Lavinia disespoused;[8]
Or Neptune's ire, or Juno's, that so long
Perplexed the Greek, and Cytherea's son:[9]
If answerable style I can obtain 20
Of my celestial Patroness,[1] who deigns
Her nightly visitation unimplored,
And dictates to me slumbering, or inspires
Easy my unpremeditated[2] verse,
Since first this subject for heroic song 25
Pleased me,[3] long choosing and beginning late,
Not sedulous by nature to indite
War, hitherto the only argument
Heroic deemed, chief mastery to dissect[4]
With long and tedious havoc fabled knights 30
In battles feigned (the better fortitude
Of patience and heroic martyrdom
Unsung), or to describe races and games,[5]
Or tilting furniture, emblazoned shields,
Impresses quaint, caparisons and steeds, 35
Bases[6] and tinsel trappings, gorgeous knights
At joust and tournament; then marshaled feast
Served up in hall with sewers and seneschals:[7]
The skill of artifice or office mean;
Not that which justly gives heroic name 40
To person or to poem. Me,[8] of these
Nor skilled nor studious, higher argument
Remains, sufficient of itself to raise
That name, unless an age too late, or cold
Climate, or years, damp my intended wing[9] 45
Depressed; and much they may if all be mine,
Not hers who brings it nightly to my ear.
    The sun was sunk, and after him the star
Of Hesperus, whose office is to bring

---

7. At the end of the *Iliad* Achilles, whose *wrath* is the subject announced in the first line of the epic, will chase his enemy, the Trojan Hector, three times around the walls of Troy before killing him.   8. In Virgil's *Aeneid*, Lavinia, fated to be Aeneas's wife, had earlier been promised to King Turnus.   9. In the *Odyssey* Neptune (Poseidon) is the god hostile to Odysseus (*the Greek*). In the *Aeneid* the hero is persecuted by the wrath of the goddess Juno, who had quarreled with Aeneas's mother, Cytherea (Venus).   1. Urania, originally the Muse of astronomy. To Milton she is the source of *celestial* inspiration. *Answerable*: suitable.   2. In other passages of the poem, Milton refers to inspiration coming to him at night or at early dawn, with spontaneous (*unpremeditated*) ease.   3. The choice of his present heroic theme had occurred early, as had the rejection of the kind of subject matter described in the following lines.   4. To analyze but also to cut up; a possible allusion to the abundance of bloody battle wounds described in classical epics.   5. There are long descriptions of games in the *Iliad* (23) and in the *Aeneid* (10).   6. Skirtlike housings for warhorses. *Tilting furniture*: the paraphernalia of arms tournaments. *Impresses*: fancy emblems on shields.   7. Attendants at meals and stewards in noble households.   8. To me.   9. The notion that nordic climates *damp* (benumb) human wit was accepted by Milton and is as old as Aristotle. *That name*: that of epic poet. *An age too late*: a time no longer fit for epic poetry.

Twilight upon the Earth, short arbiter   50
'Twixt day and night, and now from end to end
Night's hemisphere had veiled the horizon round,
When Satan, who late fled before the threats
Of Gabriel out of Eden,[1] now improved
In meditated fraud and malice, bent   55
On man's destruction, mauger[2] what might hap
Of heavier on himself, fearless returned.
By night he fled, and at midnight returned
From compassing the Earth—cautious of day
Since Uriel, regent of the sun, descried   60
His entrance, and forewarned the Cherubim[3]
That kept their watch. Thence, full of anguish, driven,
The space of seven continued nights he rode
With darkness; thrice the equinoctial line
He circled, four times crossed the car of Night   65
From pole to pole, traversing each colure;[4]
On the eighth returned, and on the coast averse[5]
From entrance or cherubic watch by stealth
Found unsuspected way. There was a place
(Now not, though sin, not time, first wrought the change)   70
Where Tigris, at the foot of Paradise,[6]
Into a gulf shot under ground, till part
Rose up a fountain by the Tree of Life.
In with the river sunk, and with it rose,
Satan, involved in rising mist; then sought   75
Where to lie hid. Sea he had searched and land
From Eden over Pontus, and the pool
Maeotis, up beyond the river Ob;[7]
Downward as far antarctic; and, in length,
West from Orontes to the ocean barred   80
At Darien,[8] thence to the land where flows
Ganges and Indus.[9] Thus the orb he roamed
With narrow search, and with inspection deep
Considered every creature, which of all
Most opportune might serve his wiles, and found   85
The serpent subtlest beast of all the field.[1]
Him, after long debate, irresolute
Of thoughts revolved, his final sentence chose
Fit vessel, fittest imp[2] of fraud, in whom
To enter, and his dark suggestions hide   90
From sharpest sight; for in the wily snake
Whatever sleights none would suspicious mark,
As from his wit and native subtlety
Proceeding, which, in other beasts observed,

---

1. As described in the conclusion of book 4.   2. In spite of.   3. Gabriel's troops. Uriel (whose name means "fire of God") is, according to Milton, *regent of the sun* and heat. In book 4, he warns Gabriel and his troops against Satan entering Eden.   4. A celestial circle that crosses the poles. Satan manages always to stay on the dark side of the Earth by circling it three times along the equator (*the equinoctial line*) and twice on each of the two colures.   5. The side opposite the gate guarded by Gabriel.   6. Cf. Genesis 2.10: "And a river went out of Eden to water the garden."   7. Siberian river flowing into the Arctic Ocean. *Pontus*: the Black Sea. *Maeotis*: the Sea of Azov.   8. The Isthmus of Panama. *Orontes*: a river in Syria. 9. Rivers in India.   1. Cf. Genesis 3.1: "Now the serpent was more subtil than any beast of the field." 2. Offspring, with a devilish connotation. *Sentence*: decision.

Doubt[3] might beget of diabolic power 95
Active within beyond the sense of brute.
Thus he resolved, but first from inward grief
His bursting passion into plaints thus poured:
    "O Earth, how like to Heaven, if not preferred
More justly, seat worthier of Gods, as built 100
With second thought, reforming what was old!
For what God, after better, worse would build?
Terrestrial Heaven, danced round by other Heavens,
That shine, yet bear their bright officious[4] lamps,
Light above light, for thee alone, as seems, 105
In thee concent'ring all their precious beams
Of sacred influence! As God in Heaven
Is center, yet extends to all, so thou
Cent'ring receiv'st from all those orbs; in thee,
Not in themselves, all their known virtue appears, 110
Productive in herb, plant, and nobler birth
Of creatures animate with gradual life
Of growth, sense, reason, all summed up in man.[5]
With what delight could I have walked thee round,
If I could joy in aught; sweet interchange 115
Of hill and valley, rivers, woods, and plains,
Now land, now sea, and shores with forest crowned,
Rocks, dens, and caves! But I in none of these
Find place or refuge; and the more I see
Pleasures about me, so much more I feel 120
Torment within me, as from the hateful siege[6]
Of contraries; all good to me becomes
Bane,[7] and in Heaven much worse would be my state.
But neither here seek I, no, nor in Heaven,
To dwell, unless by mastering Heaven's Supreme; 125
Nor hope to be myself less miserable
By what I seek, but others to make such
As I, though thereby worse to me redound.
For only in destroying I find ease
To my relentless thoughts, and him[8] destroyed, 130
Or won to what may work his utter loss,
For whom all this was made, all this[9] will soon
Follow, as to him linked in weal or woe:
In woe then, that destruction wide may range!
To me shall be the glory sole among 135
The infernal Powers, in one day to have marred
What he, Almighty styled, six nights and days
Continued making, and who knows how long
Before had been contriving? though perhaps
Not longer than since I in one night freed 140
From servitude in glorious well-nigh half
Th' angelic name,[1] and thinner left the throng
Of his adorers. He, to be avenged,

---

3. Suspicion.   4. Performing their function.   5. What Adam called (5.509) "the scale of Nature"
ascends from the vegetable order (pure growth), to the animal (sensation), to the human (the two plus
reason).   6. Seat, place.   7. Poison.   8. Man.   9. All of created nature.   1. Family, clan.

And to repair his numbers thus impaired,
Whether such virtue,[2] spent of old, now failed   145
More angels to create (if they at least
Are his created),[3] or to spite us more,
Determined to advance into our room
A creature formed of earth, and him endow,
Exalted from so base original,   150
With heavenly spoils, our spoils. What he decreed
He effected; man he made, and for him built
Magnificent this World, and Earth his seat,
Him lord pronounced, and, O indignity!
Subjected to his service angel-wings   155
And flaming ministers, to watch and tend
Their earthy charge. Of these the vigilance
I dread, and to elude, thus wrapt in mist
Of midnight vapor, glide obscure, and pry
In every bush and brake, where hap may find   160
The serpent sleeping, in whose mazy folds
To hide me, and the dark intent I bring.
O foul descent! that I, who erst contended
With Gods to sit the highest, am now constrained
Into a beast, and, mixed with bestial slime,   165
This essence[4] to incarnate and imbrute,
That to the height of deity aspired!
But what will not ambition and revenge
Descend to? Who aspires must down as low
As high he soared, obnoxious,[5] first or last,   170
To basest things. Revenge, at first though sweet,
Bitter ere long back on itself recoils.
Let it; I reck not, so it light well aimed,
Since higher[6] I fall short, on him who next
Provokes my envy, this new favorite   175
Of Heaven, this man of clay, son of despite,
Whom, us the more to spite, his Maker raised
From dust: spite then with spite is best repaid."
    So saying, through each thicket, dank or dry,
Like a black mist low-creeping, he held on   180
His midnight search, where soonest he might find
The serpent. Him fast sleeping soon he found,
In labyrinth of many a round self-rolled,
His head the midst, well stored with subtle wiles:
Not yet in horrid shade or dismal den,   185
Nor nocent[7] yet, but on the grassy herb,
Fearless, unfeared, he slept. In at his mouth
The devil entered, and his brutal sense,
In heart or head, possessing soon inspired
With act intelligential; but his sleep   190
Disturbed not, waiting close[8] th' approach of morn.

---

2. Power, force.   3. Inciting the angels to rebellion, Satan pretended that they were not God's creation, but "self-begot" (5.860).   4. The supernatural substance of which he considers himself to be made. 5. Exposed to.   6. Against God. *I reck not:* I don't mind.   7. Harmful.   8. Hidden. *Act intelligental:* intellectual activity.

Now, whenas sacred light began to dawn
In Eden on the humid flowers, that breathed
Their morning incense, when all things that breathe
From th' Earth's great altar send up silent praise   195
To the Creator, and his nostrils fill
With grateful smell, forth came the human pair,
And joined their vocal worship to the choir
Of creatures wanting[9] voice; that done, partake
The season, prime for sweetest scents and airs;   200
Then còmmune how that day they best may ply
Their growing work; for much their work outgrew
The hands' dispatch of two gardening so wide:
And Eve first to her husband thus began:
     "Adam, well may we labor still[1] to dress   205
This garden, still to tend plant, herb, and flower,
Our pleasant task enjoined; but, till more hands
Aid us, the work under our labor grows,
Luxurious by restraint: what we by day
Lop overgrown, or prune, or prop, or bind,   210
One night or two with wanton growth derides,
Tending to wild. Thou, therefore, now advise,
Or hear what to my mind first thoughts present.
Let us divide our labors; thou where choice
Leads thee, or where most needs, whether to wind   215
The woodbine round this arbor, or direct
The clasping ivy where to climb; while I
In yonder spring[2] of roses intermixed
With myrtle find what to redress till noon.
For, while so near each other thus all day   220
Our task we choose, what wonder if so near
Looks intervene and smiles, or objects new
Casual discourse draw on, which intermits
Our day's work, brought to little, though begun
Early, and th' hour of supper comes unearned!"   225
To whom mild answer Adam thus returned:
"Sole Eve, associate sole, to me beyond
Compare above all living creatures dear!
Well hast thou motioned,[3] well thy thoughts employed
How we might best fulfil the work which here   230
God hath assigned us, nor of me shalt pass
Unpraised; for nothing lovelier can be found
In woman than to study household good,
And good works in her husband to promote.
Yet not so strictly hath our Lord imposed   235
Labor as to debar us when we need
Refreshment, whether food or talk between,
Food of the mind, or this sweet intercourse
Of looks and smiles; for smiles from reason flow,
To brute denied, and are of love the food,   240
Love, not the lowest end[4] of human life.

---

9. Lacking.   1. Constantly.   2. Thicket, grove.   3. Suggested.   4. Object.

For not to irksome toil, but to delight,
He made us, and delight to reason joined.
These paths and bowers doubt not but our joint hands
Will keep from wilderness[5] with ease, as wide   245
As we need walk, till younger hands ere long
Assist us. But, if much converse perhaps
Thee satiate, to short absence I could yield;
For solitude sometimes is best society,
And short retirement urges sweet return.   250
But other doubt possesses me, lest harm
Befall thee, severed from me; for thou know'st
What hath been warned us, what malicious foe,
Envying our happiness, and of his own
Despairing, seeks to work us woe and shame   255
By sly assault, and somewhere nigh at hand
Watches, no doubt, with greedy hope to find
His wish and best advantage, us asunder,
Hopeless to circumvent us joined, where each
To other speedy aid might lend at need.   260
Whether his first design be to withdraw
Our fealty from God, or to disturb
Conjugal love, than which perhaps no bliss
Enjoyed by us excites his envy more;
Or this, or worse,[6] leave not the faithful side   265
That gave thee being, still shades thee and protects.
The wife, where danger or dishonor lurks,
Safest and seemliest by her husband stays,
Who guards her, or with her the worst endures."
    To whom the virgin[7] majesty of Eve,   270
As one who loves, and some unkindness meets,
With sweet austere composure thus replied:
    "Offspring of Heaven and Earth, and all Earth's lord!
That such an enemy we have, who seeks
Our ruin, both by thee informed I learn,   275
And from the parting angel[8] overheard,
As in a shady nook I stood behind,
Just then returned at shut of evening flowers.
But that thou shouldst my firmness therefore doubt
To God or thee, because we have a foe   280
May tempt it, I expected not to hear.
His violence thou fear'st not, being such
As we, not capable of death or pain,
Can either not receive, or can repel.
His fraud is, then, thy fear; which plain infers   285
Thy equal fear that my firm faith and love
Can by his fraud be shaken or seduced:
Thoughts, which how found they harbor in thy breast,
Adam, misthought of her to thee so dear?"[9]
    To whom, with healing words, Adam replied: 290

---

5. Wildness.   6. Whether his design be this or something even worse.   7. Pure, sinless.   8. Raphael.   9. A misjudgment (*misthought*) of me.

"Daughter of God and man, immortal Eve,
For such thou art, from sin and blame entire;[1]
Not diffident of thee do I dissuade
Thy absence from my sight, but to avoid
Th' attempt itself, intended by our foe.   295
For he who tempts, though in vain, at least asperses[2]
The tempted with dishonor foul, supposed
Not incorruptible of faith,[3] not proof
Against temptation. Thou thyself with scorn
And anger wouldst resent the offered wrong,   300
Though ineffectual found; misdeem not, then,
If such affront I labor to avert
From thee alone, which on us both at once
The enemy, though bold, will hardly dare;
Or, daring, first on me th' assault shall light.   305
Nor thou his malice and false guile contemn—
Subtle he needs must be who could seduce
Angels—nor think superfluous others' aid.
I from the influence of thy looks receive
Access in every virtue;[4] in thy sight   310
More wise, more watchful, stronger, if need were
Of outward strength; while shame, thou looking on,
Shame to be overcome or overreached,[5]
Would utmost vigor raise, and raised unite.
Why shouldst not thou like sense[6] within thee feel   315
When I am present, and thy trial choose
With me, best witness of thy virtue tried?"
    So spake domestic Adam in his care
And matrimonial love; but Eve, who thought
Less[7] àttributed to her faith sincere,   320
Thus her reply with accent sweet renewed:
    "If this be our condition, thus to dwell
In narrow circuit straitened by a foe,
Subtle or violent, we not endued[8]
Single with like defence wherever met,   325
How are we happy, still in fear of harm?
But harm precedes not sin: only our foe
Tempting affronts us with his foul esteem
Of our integrity: his foul esteem
Sticks no dishonor on our front,[9] but turns   330
Foul on himself; then wherefore shunned or feared
By us, who rather double honor gain
From his surmise proved false, find peace within,
Favor from Heaven, our witness, from th' event?
And what is faith, love, virtue, unassayed   335
Alone, without exterior help sustained?[1]
Let us not then suspect our happy state
Left so imperfect by the Maker wise
As not secure to single or combined.

1. Intact.   2. Literally, sprinkles.   3. Faithfulness, loyalty.   4. Increased strength.   5. Outdone.
6. Sensation.   7. Less than she deserves.   8. Endowed.   Straitened: confined.   9. Brow.
1. Without being put to test by outside forces.

Frail is our happiness, if this be so; 340
And Eden were no Eden, thus exposed."
    To whom thus Adam fervently replied:
"O woman, best are all things as the will
Of God ordained them; his creating hand
Nothing imperfect or deficient left 345
Of all that he created, much less man,
Or aught that might his happy state secure,
Secure from outward force. Within himself
The danger lies, yet lies within his power;
Against his will he can receive no harm. 350
But God left free the will; for what obeys
Reason is free; and reason he made right,
But bid her well beware, and still erect,[2]
Lest, by some fair appearing good surprised,
She dictate false, and misinform the will 355
To do what God expressly hath forbid.
Not then mistrust, but tender love, enjoins
That I should mind[3] thee oft; and mind thou me.
Firm we subsist, yet possible to swerve,
Since reason not impossibly may meet 360
Some specious object by the foe suborned,[4]
And fall into deception unaware,
Not keeping strictest watch, as she was warned.
Seek not temptation, then, which to avoid
Were better, and most likely if from me 365
Thou sever not: trial will come unsought.
Wouldst thou approve[5] thy constancy, approve
First thy obedience; th' other who can know,
Not seeing thee attempted, who attest?
But if thou think trial unsought may find 370
Us both securer[6] than thus warned thou seem'st,
Go; for thy stay, not free, absents thee more.
Go in thy native innocence; rely
On what thou hast of virtue; summon all;
For God towards thee hath done his part: do thine." 375
    So spake the patriarch of mankind; but Eve
Persisted; yet submiss,[7] though last, replied:
    "With thy permission, then, and thus forewarned,
Chiefly by what thy own last reasoning words
Touched only, that our trial, when least sought, 380
May find us both perhaps far less prepared,
The willinger I go, nor much expect
A foe so proud will first the weaker seek;
So bent, the more shall shame him his repulse."
Thus saying, from her husband's hand her hand 385
Soft she withdrew, and like a wood nymph light,

---

2. On the alert against temptation, because God has "created Man free and able enough to have withstood his Tempter" (3.Argument).   3. Remind.   4. Procured for treacherous purposes.   5. Give proof, test.   6. Less careful, less alert to danger.   7. Submissive. Eve's submissiveness, however, is qualified by Adam's reluctant tone as he agrees to let her go and by the fact that it is she who speaks the final words of their dialogue.

Oread or dryad, or of Delia's train,[8]
Betook her to the groves, but Delia's self
In gait surpassed and goddesslike deport,
Though not as she with bow and quiver armed,						390
But with such gardening tools as art yet rude,
Guiltless of fire[9] had formed, or angels brought.
To Pales, or Pomona, thus adorned,
Likest she seemed, Pomona when she fled
Vertumnus, or to Ceres in her prime,						395
Yet virgin of Proserpina from Jove.[1]
Her long with ardent look his eye pursued
Delighted, but desiring more her stay.
Oft he to her his charge of quick return
Repeated; she to him as oft engaged						400
To be returned by noon amid the bower,
And all things in best order to invite
Noontide repast, or afternoon's repose.
O much deceived, much failing, hapless Eve,
Of[2] thy presumed return! Event perverse!						405
Thou never from that hour in Paradise
Found'st either sweet repast, or sound repose;
Such ambush hid among sweet flowers and shades
Waited with hellish rancor imminent[3]
To intercept thy way, or send thee back						410
Despoiled of innocence, of faith, of bliss.
For now, and since first break of dawn, the fiend,
Mere serpent in appearance, forth was come,
And on his quest, where likeliest he might find
The only two of mankind, but in them						415
The whole included race, his purposed prey.
In bower and field he sought, where any tuft
Of grove or garden-plot more[4] pleasant lay,
Their tendance[5] or plantation for delight;
By fountain or by shady rivulet						420
He sought them both, but wished his hap might find
Eve separate; he wished, but not with hope
Of what so seldom chanced; when to his wish,
Beyond his hope, Eve separate he spies,
Veiled in a cloud of fragrance, where she stood,						425
Half spied, so thick the roses bushing round
About her glowed, oft stooping to support
Each flower of slender stalk, whose head though gay
Carnation, purple, azure, or specked with gold,
Hung drooping unsustained, them she upstays						430
Gently with myrtle band, mindless the while

---

8. Delia (born on the island of Delos) is the goddess Diana (Artemis), the huntress, with her train of nymphs. In Greek mythology the oreads were mountain nymphs and the dryads were wood nymphs. 9. The ability to produce fire will become necessary only after the Fall (cf. 10.1070–82).   1. In practical-minded Roman mythology, Pales and Pomona are deities who preside over flocks and fruit, respectively. Ceres is the goddess of agriculture in general. Both Pomona and Ceres are presented here in virginal youth: Pomona fleeing from her suitor Vertumnus (another agriculture deity), and Ceres before the time when Jove (Jupiter) made her the mother of Proserpina.   2. About.   3. Ominously ready.   4. Particularly. 5. A spot that they tended.

Herself, though fairest unsupported flower,
From her best prop so far, and storm so nigh.
Nearer he drew, and many a walk traversed
Of stateliest covert, cedar, pine, or palm;   435
Then voluble and bold, now hid, now seen
Among thick-woven arborets and flowers
Embordered on each bank, the hand[6] of Eve:
Spot more delicious than those gardens feigned[7]
Or of revived Adonis, or renowned   440
Alcinous, host of old Laertes's son,[8]
Or that, not mystic, where the sapient king
Held dalliance with his fair Egyptian spouse.[9]
Much he the place admired, the person more.
As one who long in populous city pent,   445
Where houses thick and sewers annoy[1] the air,
Forth issuing on a summer's morn to breathe
Among the pleasant villages and farms
Adjoined, from each thing met conceives delight,
The smell of grain, or tedded[2] grass, or kine,   450
Or dairy, each rural sight, each rural sound:
If chance with nymphlike step fair virgin pass,
What pleasing seemed, for her[3] now pleases more,
She most, and in her look sums[4] all delight.
Such pleasure took the serpent to behold   455
This flowery plat,[5] the sweet recess of Eve
Thus early, thus alone; her heavenly form
Angelic, but more soft, and feminine,
Her graceful innocence, her every air
Of gesture or least action overawed   460
His malice, and with rapine[6] sweet bereaved
His fierceness of the fierce intent it brought:
That space the evil one abstracted[7] stood
From his own evil, and for the time remained
Stupidly good, of enmity disarmed,   465
Of guile, of hate, of envy, of revenge.
But the hot Hell that always in him burns,
Though in mid Heaven, soon ended his delight,
And tortures him now more, the more he sees
Of pleasure not for him ordained: then soon   470
Fierce hate he recollects, and all his thoughts
Of mischief, gratulating,[8] thus excites:
    "Thoughts, whither have ye led me? with what sweet
Compulsion thus transported to forget
What hither brought us? hate, not love, nor hope   475
Of Paradise for Hell, hope here to taste

---

6. Handiwork. *Voluble:* rolling. *Arborets:* shrubs. *Embordered on each bank:* bordering a walk.   7. Imagined by the poets (cf. 9.31).   8. Odysseus. Alcinous was the king of the Phaeacians. His perpetually flowering garden is described in the *Odyssey.* (7). *Of revived Adonis:* the mythical garden where Aphrodite (Venus) nursed her lover Adonis, wounded by a boar. The most famous description of the garden, certainly known to Milton, is in Spenser's *Faerie Queene* 3.   9. Pharaoh's daughter (see 1 Kings 3.1). *Not mystic:* not mythical like the previous "feigned" gardens of pagan antiquity. *Sapient king:* Solomon.   1. Make noisome, pollute.   2. Spread out for drying.   3. Because of her. *If chance:* if it should happen that.   4. Rounds out and brings to perfection.   5. Plot.   6. Theft.   7. Drawn off, separated.   8. Rejoicing.

Of pleasure, but all pleasure to destroy,
Save what⁹ is in destroying; other joy
To me is lost. Then let me not let pass
Occasion which now smiles; behold alone   480
The woman, opportune to all attempts,¹
Her husband, for I view far round, not nigh,
Whose higher intellectual more I shun,
And strength, of courage haughty, and of limb
Heroic built, though of terrestrial mold.²   485
Foe not informidable, exempt from wound,
I not; so much hath Hell debased, and pain
Enfeebled me, to what I was in Heaven.
She fair, divinely fair, fit love for gods,
Not terrible, though terror be in love   490
And beauty, not approached by stronger hate,³
Hate stronger, under show of love well feigned,
The way which to her ruin now I tend."
   So spake the enemy of mankind, enclosed
In serpent, inmate bad, and toward Eve   495
Addressed his way, not with indented wave,⁴
Prone on the ground, as since, but on his rear,
Circular base of rising folds, that towered
Fold above fold a surging maze; his head
Crested aloft, and carbuncle⁵ his eyes;   500
With burnished neck of verdant gold, erect
Amidst his circling spires, that on the grass
Floated redundant.⁶ Pleasing was his shape,
And lovely; never since of serpent kind
Lovelier, not those that in Illyria changed   505
Hermione and Cadmus,⁷ or the god
In Epidaurus;⁸ nor to which transformed
Ammonian Jove, or Capitoline was seen,
He with Olympias, this with her who bore
Scipio, the height of Rome.⁹ With tract oblique   510
At first, as one who sought access, but feared
To interrupt, sidelong he works his way.
As when a ship by skillful steersman wrought
Nigh river's mouth or foreland, where the wind
Veers oft, as oft so steers, and shifts her sail: 515
So varied he, and of his tortuous train
Curled many a wanton wreath in sight of Eve,
To lure her eye: she busied heard the sound
Of rustling leaves, but minded not, as used

9. Whatever pleasure.   1. In the appropriate situation for Satan's attempts on her.   2. Formed of earth.   3. If not approached, and counteracted, by hate.   4. Zigzagging.   5. Fiery red.   6. In great abundance. *Spires:* coils, loops.   7. Those that Hermione and Cadmus were turned into. Cadmus, the founder of Thebes, and his wife Hermione (Harmonia), according to their story as told by Ovid (*Metamorphoses* 4.562–602), were transformed into snakes when they retired to Illyria after much family tragedy. 8. The place in Greece where Aesculapius, the god of medicine, had his major temple and appeared to worshipers in the form of an erect, flashy-eyed serpent (Ovid's *Metamorphoses* 15.622–744).   9. According to hero-deifying legends, Jove, in his personification as Jupiter Ammon (a mingling of Greco-Roman and Egyptian cults), loved Princess Olympias and became the father of Alexander the Great. As the Capitoline Jupiter (worshiped in the major Roman temple on the Capitol), he fathered Scipio, the supreme hero (*the height*) of Rome's African wars. In both cases, the father god appeared in the form of a snake.

To such disport before her through the field,   520
From every beast, more duteous at her call,
Than at Circean call the herd disguised.[1]
He bolder now, uncalled before her stood:
But as in gaze admiring; oft he bowed
His turret[2] crest, and sleek enameled neck,   525
Fawning, and licked the ground whereon she trod.
His gentle dumb expression turned at length
The eye of Eve to mark his play: he, glad
Of her attention gained, with serpent tongue
Organic, or impulse of vocal air,[3]   530
His fraudulent temptation thus began.
    "Wonder not, sovereign mistress, if perhaps
Thou canst, who art sole wonder; much less arm
Thy looks, the heaven of mildness, with disdain,
Displeased that I approach thee thus, and gaze   535
Insatiate, I thus single, nor have feared
Thy awful brow, more awful thus retired.
Fairest resemblance of thy Maker fair,
Thee all things living gaze on, all things thine
By gift, and thy celestial beauty adore   540
With ravishment beheld, there best beheld
Where universally admired: but here
In this enclosure wild, these beasts among,
Beholders rude, and shallow[4] to discern
Half what in thee is fair, one man except,   545
Who sees thee? (and what is one?) who shouldst be seen
A goddess among gods, adored and served
By angels numberless, thy daily train."
    So glozed the tempter, and his proem[5] tuned;
Into the heart of Eve his words made way,   550
Though at the voice much marveling: at length,
Not unamazed, she thus in answer spake.
"What may this mean? Language of man pronounced
By tongue of brute, and human sense expressed?
The first at least of these I thought denied   555
To beasts, whom God on their creation-day
Created mute to all articulate sound;
The latter I demur, for in their looks
Much reason,[6] and in their actions oft appears.
Thee, serpent, subtlest beast of all the field   560
I knew, but not with human voice endued:
Redouble then this miracle, and say,
How cam'st thou speakable of mute,[7] and how
To me so friendly grown above the rest
Of brutal kind, that daily are in sight?   565
Say, for such wonder claims attention due."

---

1. The enchantress Circe, in the *Odyssey* (10), is surrounded by subjected beasts and transforms some of the hero's companions into swine.   **2.** Towering.   **3.** Producing a voice either by using his serpent's (*organic*) tongue or by some more direct impulse on the air.   **4.** Mentally inadequate.   **5.** Preamble, introduction. *Glozed:* flattered.   **6.** Eve, well acquainted with animals, which are *duteous at her call* (line 521), questions the notion (*I demur*) that they are wholly deprived of *human sense and reason.*   **7.** How did you acquire speech after being dumb?

To whom the guileful tempter thus replied:
"Empress of this fair world, resplendent Eve!
Easy to me it is to tell thee all
What thou command'st and right thou shouldst be obeyed: 570
I was at first as other beasts that graze
The trodden herb, of abject thoughts and low,
As was my food, nor aught but food discerned
Or sex, and apprehended nothing high:
Till on a day, roving the field, I chanced   575
A goodly tree far distant to behold
Loaden with fruit of fairest colors mixed,
Ruddy and gold; I nearer drew to gaze;
When from the boughs a savory odor blown,
Grateful to appetite, more pleased my sense   580
Than smell of sweetest fennel, or the teats
Of ewe or goat dropping with milk⁸ at even,
Unsucked of lamb or kid, that tend their play.
To satisfy the sharp desire I had
Of tasting those fair apples, I resolved   585
Not to defer: hunger and thirst at once,
Powerful persuaders, quickened at the scent
Of that alluring fruit, urged me so keen.
About the mossy trunk I wound me soon,
For, high from ground, the branches would require   590
Thy utmost reach, or Adam's: round the tree
All other beasts that saw, with like desire
Longing and envying stood, but could not reach.
Amid the tree now got, where plenty hung
Tempting so nigh, to pluck and eat my fill   595
I spared not; for such pleasure till that hour
At feed or fountain never had I found.
Sated at length, ere long I might perceive
Strange alteration in me, to degree
Of reason⁹ in my inward powers, and speech   600
Wanted not long, though to this shape retained.¹
Thenceforth to speculations high or deep
I turned my thoughts, and with capacious mind
Considered all things visible in Heaven,
Or Earth, or middle, all things fair and good: 605
But all that fair² and good in thy divine
Semblance, and in thy beauty's heavenly ray
United I beheld: no fair to thine
Equivalent or second, which compelled
Me thus, though importune perhaps, to come   610
And gaze, and worship thee of right declared
Sovereign of creatures, universal dame."³
    So talked the spirited⁴ sly snake: and Eve
Yet more amazed, unwary thus replied:

---

8. According to old folklore, snakes were fond of fennel, which was supposed to sharpen their eyesight, and of goat's milk.   9. To the point of acquiring the faculty of reason.   1. Restrained, kept to his outward appearance. *Wanted not long:* the faculty of speech soon followed.   2. Fairness, beauty. *Middle:* the air.   3. Mistress of this world.   4. Possessed by an evil spirit.

"Serpent, thy overpraising leaves in doubt   615
The virtue of that fruit, in thee first proved.
But say, where grows the tree, from hence how far?
For many are the trees of God that grow
In Paradise, and various, yet unknown
To us; in such abundance lies our choice,   620
As leaves a greater store of fruit untouched,
Still hanging incorruptible, till men
Grow up to their provision, and more hands
Help to disburden Nature of her bearth."⁵
    To whom the wily adder, blithe and glad: 625
"Empress, the way is ready, and not long,
Beyond a row of myrtles, on a flat,
Fast by a fountain, one small thicket past
Of blowing⁶ myrrh and balm: if thou accept
My conduct, I can bring thee thither soon."   630
    "Lead then," said Eve. He leading swiftly rolled
In tangles, and made intricate seem straight,
To mischief swift. Hope elevates, and joy
Brightens his crest; as when a wandering fire
Compact of unctuous vapor,⁷ which the night   635
Condenses, and the cold environs round,
Kindled through agitation to a flame
(Which oft, they say, some evil spirit attends),
Hovering and blazing with delusive light,
Misleads th' amazed night-wanderer from his way   640
To bogs and mires, and oft through pond or pool,
There swallowed up and lost, from succor far:
So glistered the dire snake, and into fraud
Led Eve our credulous mother, to the tree
Of prohibition,⁸ root of all our woe: 645
Which when she saw, thus to her guide she spake:
    "Serpent, we might have spared our coming hither,
Fruitless to me, though fruit be here to excess,
The credit of whose virtue rest with thee;⁹
Wondrous indeed, if cause of such effects!   650
But of this tree we may not taste nor touch:
God so commanded, and left that command
Sole daughter of his voice; the rest,¹ we live
Law to ourselves; our reason is our law."
    To whom the tempter guilefully replied: 655
"Indeed? Hath God then said that of the fruit
Of all these garden trees ye shall not eat,
Yet lords declared of all in Earth or air?"
To whom thus Eve, yet sinless: "Of the fruit
Of each tree in the garden we may eat,   660
But of the fruit of this fair tree amidst

---

5. Products.   6. Blossoming.   7. Composed of greasy vapor. *Wandering fire:* will-o'-the-wisp, a light
attributed to marsh gas.   8. The forbidden Tree of Knowledge.   9. Because the forbidden tree is as
good as fruitless to Eve, the only proof of its power (*virtue*) will remain with the Serpent.   1. For the
rest. *Sole daughter of his voice:* translation from the Hebrew of God's command, described as "one easy
prohibition" (4.433).

The garden, God hath said, 'Ye shall not eat
Thereof, nor shall yet touch it, lest ye die.' "
　　She scarce had said, though brief, when now more bold,
The tempter, but with show of zeal and love　　　　　　　665
To man, and indignation at his wrong,
New part puts on, and as to passion moved,
Fluctuates disturbed, yet comely, and in act
Raised,[2] as of some great matter to begin.
As when of old some orator renowned　　　　　　　　670
In Athens or free Rome, where eloquence
Flourished, since mute, to some great cause addressed,
Stood in himself collected, while each part,[3]
Motion, each act, won audience ere the tongue,
Sometimes in height began, as no delay　　　　　　　675
Of preface brooking,[4] through his zeal of right.
So standing, moving, or to height upgrown
The tempter all impassioned thus began:
　　"O sacred, wise, and wisdom-giving plant,
Mother of science![5] now I feel thy power　　　　　　680
Within me clear, not only to discern
Things in their causes, but to trace the ways
Of highest agents, deemed however wise.
Queen of this universe! do not believe
Those rigid threats of death. Ye shall not die;　　　　685
How should ye? By the fruit? it gives you life
To[6] knowledge; by the Threatener? look on me,
Me who have touched and tasted, yet both live,
And life more perfect have attained than Fate
Meant me, by venturing higher than my lot.　　　　　690
Shall that be shut to man, which to the beast
Is open? Or will God incense his ire
For such a petty trespass, and not praise
Rather your dauntless virtue, whom the pain
Of death denounced, whatever thing death be,　　　　695
Deterred not from achieving what might lead
To happier life, knowledge of good and evil?
Of good, how just! Of evil, if what is evil
Be real, why not known, since easier shunned?
God therefore cannot hurt ye, and be just;　　　　　700
Not just, not God; not feared then, nor obeyed:
Your fear itself of death removes the fear.[7]
Why then was this forbid? Why but to awe,
Why but to keep ye low and ignorant,
His worshipers? He knows that in the day　　　　　705
Ye eat thereof, your eyes that seem so clear,
Yet are but dim, shall perfectly be then
Opened and cleared, and ye shall be as gods,

---

2. Assuming the orator's posture. *New part:* new role, as of an actor in drama. *Fluctuates:* undulates his
body.　　3. Of the body.　　4. Plunging into the middle of the subject (*in medias res*), without any preamble.　　5. Knowledge.　　6. As well as.　　7. The Serpent's captious argument is that God is by definition just, but because a death-giving God would not be just, he would not be God; consequently, he
would not have to be feared and obeyed.

Knowing both good and evil, as they know.
That ye should be as gods, since I as man, 710
Internal man,[8] is but proportion meet,
I, of brute, human; ye, of human, gods.
So ye shall die perhaps, by putting off
Human, to put on gods:[9] death to be wished,
Though threatened, which no worse than this can bring. 715
And what are gods that man may not become
As they, participating godlike food?
The gods are first, and that advantage use
On our belief, that all from them proceeds.
I question it; for this fair Earth I see, 720
Warmed by the sun, producing every kind,
Them nothing: If they[1] all things, who enclosed
Knowledge of good and evil in this tree,
That whoso eats thereof forthwith attains
Wisdom without their leave? And wherein lies 725
Th' offense, that man should thus attain to know?
What can your knowledge hurt him, or this tree
Impart against his will if all be his?
Or is it envy, and can envy dwell
In heavenly breasts? These, these, and many more 730
Causes import[2] your need of this fair fruit.
Goddess humane, reach then, and freely taste!"
    He ended, and his words, replete with guile,
Into her heart too easy entrance won:
Fixed on the fruit she gazed, which to behold 735
Might tempt alone, and in her ears the sound
Yet rung of his persuasive words, impregned[3]
With reason, to her seeming, and with truth;
Meanwhile the hour of noon drew on, and waked
An eager appetite, raised by the smell 740
So savory of that fruit, which with desire,
Inclinable[4] now grown to touch or taste,
Solicited her longing eye; yet first
Pausing a while, thus to herself she mused:
    "Great are thy virtues, doubtless, best of fruits, 745
Though kept from man, and worthy to be admired,
Whose taste, too long forborne, at first assay
Gave elocution to the mute, and taught
The tongue not made for speech to speak thy praise:
Thy praise he also who forbids they use, 750
Conceals not from us, naming thee the Tree
Of Knowledge, knowledge both of good and evil;
Forbids us then to taste; but his forbidding
Commends thee more, while it infers[5] the good
By thee communicated, and our want: 755
For good unknown, sure is not had, or had
And yet unknown, is as not had at all.

8. The Serpent has acquired human faculties although his outer form has remained unchanged (compare *inward,* line 600).   9. Divinity. *Human:* humanity.   1. If they produced.   2. Imply, indicate.
3. Impregnated, filled.   4. Favorably disposed.   5. Implies.

In plain[6] then, what forbids he but to know?
Forbids us good, forbids us to be wise!
Such prohibitions bind not.[7] But if Death   760
Bind us with after-bands, what profits then
Our inward freedom?[8] In the day we eat
Of this fair fruit, our doom is, we shall die.
How dies the serpent? He hath eaten and lives,
And knows, and speaks, and reasons, and discerns,   765
Irrational till then. For us alone
Was death invented? Or to us denied
This intellectual food, for beasts reserved?
For beasts it seems: yet that one beast which first
Hath tasted, envies not, but brings with joy   770
The good befallen him, author unsuspect,[9]
Friendly to man, far from deceit or guile.
What fear I then, rather what know to fear
Under this ignorance of good and evil,[1]
Of God or death, of law or penalty?   775
Here grows the cure of all, this fruit divine,
Fair to the eye, inviting to the taste,
Of virtue[2] to make wise: what hinders then
To reach, and feed at once both body and mind?"
    So saying, her rash hand in evil hour,   780
Forth reaching to the fruit, she plucked, she eat.[3]
Earth felt the wound, and Nature from her seat
Sighing through all her works gave signs[4] of woe,
That all was lost. Back to the thicket slunk
The guilty serpent, and well might, for Eve   785
Intent now wholly on her taste, naught else
Regarded; such delight till then, as seemed,
In fruit she never tasted, whether true
Or fancied so, through expectation high
Of knowledge; nor was godhead from her thought.[5]   790
Greedily she engorged without restraint,
And knew not eating[6] death: satiate at length,
And heightened as with wine, jocund and boon,[7]
Thus to herself she pleasingly began:
    "O sovereign, virtuous, precious of all trees   795
In Paradise! of operation blest
To sapience, hitherto obscured, infamed,[8]
And thy fair fruit let hang, as to no end
Created; but henceforth my early care,
Not without song each morning, and due praise   800
Shall tend thee, and the fertile burden ease
Of thy full branches offered free to all;

---

6. In plain words.   7. Eve, who has learned from the Serpent the art of sophistical argument, claims
that God himself, by naming the tree, has indicated the *good* in it, but a *good unknown* is as nothing.
Besides, forbidding the experience of the Tree of Knowledge is forbidding humanity *to be wise*; hence the
prohibition is not binding.   8. Death would constitute a later bond (*after-bands*), after God has granted
free will (*inward freedom*).   9. An unsuspectable authority on the subject.   1. Having no knowledge
of good and evil, Eve doesn't know what is to be feared.   2. With the power.   3. Ate.   4. Omens,
metaphorically given as—and punning with—the sighs of Nature; forebodings of disaster.   5. She
thought of acquiring divinity.   6. That she was eating.   7. Cheerful.   8. Made famous. *Blest to sapience*: endowed with the power to give wisdom.

2612 / JOHN MILTON

Till dieted by thee I grow mature
In knowledge, as the gods who all things know;
Though others envy what they cannot give: 805
For had the gift been theirs, it had not here
Thus grown.[9] Experience, next to thee I owe,
Best guide; not following thee I had remained
In ignorance; thou open'st Wisdom's way,
And giv'st access, though secret she retire.   810
And I perhaps am secret; Heaven is high,
High and remote to see from thence distinct
Each thing on Earth; and other care perhaps
May have diverted from continual watch
Our great Forbidder, safe[1] with all his spies   815
About him. But to Adam in what sort[2]
Shall I appear? Shall I to him make known
As yet my change, and give him to partake
Full happiness with me, or rather not,
But keep the odds[3] of knowledge in my power   820
Without copartner? so to add what wants
In female sex, the more to draw his love,
And render me more equal, and perhaps,
A thing not undesirable, sometime
Superior: for, inferior, who is free?   825
This may be well: but what if God have seen
And death ensue? Then I shall be no more,
And Adam, wedded to another Eve,
Shall live with her enjoying, I extinct;
A death to think. Confirmed then I resolve,   830
Adam shall share with me in bliss or woe:
So dear I love him, that with him all deaths
I could endure, without him live no life."[4]
    So saying, from the tree her step she turned,
But first low reverence done, as to the power   835
That dwelt within, whose presence had infused
Into the plant sciential[5] sap, derived
From nectar, drink of gods. Adam the while
Waiting desirous her return, had wove
Of choicest flowers a garland to adorn   840
Her tresses, and her rural labors crown,
As reapers oft are wont their harvest queen.
Great joy he promised to his thoughts, and new
Solace in her return, so long delayed:
Yet oft his heart, divine of[6] something ill,   845
Misgave him; he the faltering measure[7] felt;
And forth to meet her went, the way she took

---

9. Eve has adopted the Serpent's argument (cf. lines 720–30).   1. Not dangerous.   2. Manner.
3. Advantage.   4. In these crucial lines Eve's thoughts are shown moving through three stages: first, the
idea of not sharing her knowledge with Adam, so as to enhance her own power, with the gratuitous notion
that lesser power brings no freedom at all; then jealousy at the thought of her own possible death and
Adam *wedded to another Eve*; finally, with an opportune resurgence of *love*, the resolve to be with Adam *in
bliss or woe*, i.e., to make him her partner in sin. Thus the passage is centrally representative of Milton's
characterization of Eve in her relation to Adam and possibly of some of the poet's own conceptions of
women in general (cf. lines 377–84, 869–85, and 1155–61).   5. Infusing knowledge.   6. *Divine of*:
divining, foreseeing.   7. Irregularity of heartbeats.

That morn when first they parted. By the Tree
Of Knowledge he must pass; there he her met,
Scarce from the tree returning; in her hand   850
A bough of fairest fruit that downy smiled,
New gathered, and ambrosial smell diffused.
To him she hastened, in her face excuse
Came prologue, and apology to prompt,[8]
Which with bland words at will she thus addressed: 855
    "Hast thou not wondered, Adam, at my stay?
Thee I have missed, and thought it long, deprived
Thy presence, agony of love till now
Not felt, nor shall be twice; for never more
Mean I to try, what rash untried I sought,   860
The pain of absence from thy sight. But strange
Hath been the cause, and wonderful to hear:
This tree is not as we are told, a tree
Of danger tasted,[9] nor to evil unknown
Opening the way, but of divine effect   865
To open eyes, and make them gods who taste;
And hath been tasted such.[1] The serpent wise,
Or not restrained as we, or not obeying,
Hath eaten of the fruit, and is become,
Not dead, as we are threatened, but thenceforth   870
Endued with human voice and human sense,
Reasoning to admiration,[2] and with me
Persuasively hath so prevailed, that I
Have also tasted, and have also found
Th' effects to correspond, opener mine eyes,   875
Dim erst, dilated spirits, ampler heart,
And growing up to godhead; which for thee
Chiefly I sought, without thee can despise.
For bliss, as thou hast part, to me is bliss,
Tedious, unshared with thee, and odious soon.   880
Thou therefore also taste, that equal lot
May join us, equal joy, as equal love;
Lest, thou not tasting, different degree[3]
Disjoin us, and I then too late renounce
Deity for thee, when Fate will not permit."[4]   885
    Thus Eve with countenance blithe her story told;
But in her cheek distemper[5] flushing glowed.
On th' other side, Adam, soon as he heard
The fatal trespass done by Eve, amazed,
Astonied stood and blank, while horror chill   890
Ran through his veins, and all his joints relaxed;[6]
From his slack hand the garland wreathed for Eve
Down dropped, and all the faded roses shed.
Speechless he stood and pale, till thus at length
First to himself he inward silence broke: 895

8. A pleading expression on her face came as an introduction (the *prologue* to a play) to prepare for (*prompt*)
the formal *apology*.   9. When tasted.   1. Has been proved by tasting.   2. Admirably.   3. A difference in rank between us.   4. Cf. lines 825–33.   5. Disharmony in the body's humors, disease.
6. Slackened. *Astonied*: stunned.

"O fairest of creation, last and best
Of all God's works, creature in whom excelled
Whatever can to sight or thought be formed,
Holy, divine, good, amiable, or sweet!
How art thou lost, how on a sudden lost,   900
Defaced, deflowered, and now to death devote?[7]
Rather how hast thou yielded to transgress
The strict forbiddance, how to violate
The sacred fruit forbidden! Some cursèd fraud
Of enemy hath beguiled thee, yet unknown,[8]   905
And me with thee hath ruined, for with thee
Certain my resolution is to die.
How can I live without thee, how forgo
Thy sweet converse and love so dearly joined,
To live again in these wild woods forlorn?   910
Should God create another Eve, and I
Another rib afford, yet loss of thee
Would never from my heart; no, no! I feel
The link of nature draw me: flesh of flesh,
Bone of my bone thou art, and from thy state   915
Mine never shall be parted, bliss or woe."
    So having said, as one from sad dismay
Recomforted, and after thoughts disturbed
Submitting to what seemed remediless,
Thus in calm mood his words to Eve he turned: 920
    "Bold deed thou hast presumed, adventurous Eve
And peril great provoked, who thus hath dared
Had it been only coveting to eye
That sacred fruit, sacred to abstinence,
Much more to taste it, under ban to touch.   925
But past who can recall, or done undo?
Not God omnipotent, nor Fate! Yet so
Perhaps thou shalt not die, perhaps the fact
Is not so heinous now, foretasted fruit,
Profaned first by the serpent, by him first   930
Made common and unhallowed ere our taste,
Nor yet on him found deadly; he yet lives,
Lives, as thou saidst, and gains to live as man
Higher degree of life: inducement strong
To us, as likely, tasting, to attain   935
Proportional[9] ascent, which cannot be
But to be gods, or angels, demigods.
Nor can I think that God, Creator wise,
Though threatening, will in earnest so destroy
Us his prime creatures, dignified so high,   940
Set over all his works, which in our fall,
For us created, needs with us must fail,
Dependent made; so God shall uncreate,
Be frustrate, do, undo, and labor lose;

7. Doomed.   8. Unknown enemy.   9. Proportionate to our human status (compare the Serpent's argument, lines 710–12).

Not well conceived of God,[1] who, though his power   945
Creation could repeat, yet would be loath
Us to abolish, lest the adversary
Triùmph and say: 'Fickle their state whom God
Most favors; who can please him long? Me first
He ruined, now mankind; whom will he next?'
Matter of scorn, not to be given the foe.   950
However, I with thee have fixed my lot.
Certain[2] to undergo like doom: if death
Consort with thee, death is to me as life;
So forcible within my heart I feel
The bond of nature draw me to my own,   955
My own in thee, for what thou art is mine;
Our state cannot be severed; we are one,
One flesh; to lose thee were to lose myself."
    So Adam, and thus Eve to him replied:
"O glorious trial of exceeding love,   960
Illustrious evidence, example high!
Engaging me to emulate; but short
Of thy perfection, how shall I attain,
Adam? from whose dear side I boast me sprung,
And gladly of our union hear thee speak,   965
One heart, one soul in both; whereof good proof
This day affords, declaring thee resolved,
Rather than death or aught than death more dread
Shall separate us, linked in love so dear,
To undergo with me one guilt, one crime,   970
If any be, of tasting this fair fruit;
Whose virtue (for of good still good proceeds,
Direct, or by occasion)[3] hath presented
This happy trial of thy love, which else
So eminently never had been known.   975
Were it[4] I thought death menaced would ensue
This my attempt, I would sustain alone
The worst, and not persuade thee, rather die
Deserted, than oblige[5] thee with a fact
Pernicious to thy peace, chiefly assured   980
Remarkably so late of thy so true,
So faithful love unequaled; but I feel
Far otherwise th' event;[6] not death, but life
Augmented, opened eyes, new hopes, new joys,
Taste so divine, that what of sweet before   985
Hath touched my sense, flat seems to this, and harsh.
On my experience, Adam, freely taste,
And fear of death deliver to the winds."
    So saying, she embraced him, and for joy
Tenderly wept, much won that he his love   990
Had so ennobled, as of choice to incur
Divine displeasure for her sake, or death.

---

1. That would be a wrong conception of God.   2. Resolved.   3. Indirectly.   4. If.   5. Involve
Adam in her guilty action.   6. The eventual consequence of her transgression.

In recompense (for such compliance bad
Such recompense best merits), from the bough
She gave him of that fair enticing fruit   995
With liberal hand; he scrupled not to eat,
Against his better knowledge, not deceived,[7]
But fondly overcome with female charm.
Earth trembled from her entrails, as again
In pangs, and Nature gave a second groan.   1000
Sky lowered, and muttering thunder, some sad drops
Wept at completing of the mortal sin
Original; while Adam took no thought,
Eating his fill, nor Eve to iterate
Her former trespass feared, the more to soothe   1005
Him with her loved society; that now
As with new wine intoxicated both,
They swim in mirth, and fancy that they feel
Divinity within them breeding wings
Wherewith to scorn the Earth. But that false fruit   1010
Far other operation first displayed,
Carnal desire inflaming; he on Eve
Began to cast lascivious eyes, she him
As wantonly repaid; in lust they burn,
Till Adam thus 'gan Eve to dalliance move: 1015
    "Eve, now I see thou art exact of taste,
And elegant, of sapience[8] no small part,
Since to each meaning savor we apply,
And palate call judicious. I the praise
Yield thee, so well this day thou hast purveyed.   1020
Much pleasure we have lost, while we abstained
From this delightful fruit, nor known till now
True relish, tasting; if such pleasure be
In things to us forbidden, it might be wished,
For[9] this one tree had been forbidden ten.   1025
But come; so well refreshed, now let us play,
As meet is, after such delicious fare;
For never did thy beauty, since the day
I saw thee first and wedded thee, adorned
With all perfections, so enflame my sense   1030
With ardor to enjoy thee, fairer now
Than ever, bounty of this virtuous[1] tree."
    So said he, and forbore not glance or toy
Of[2] amorous intent, well understood
Of Eve, whose eye darted contagious fire.   1035
Her hand he seized, and to a shady bank,
Thick overhead with verdant roof embowered
He led her, nothing loath; flowers were the couch,
Pansies, and violets, and asphodel,
And hyacinth, Earth's freshest, softest lap.   1040

---

7. Adam, unlike Eve, acts in full consciousness, not having been *deceived* by the Serpent.   8. In both meanings—"wisdom" and "taste." Both *sapience* and *savor* (line 1019) are from the Latin *sapere. Elegant:* choosy, refined.   9. Instead of.   1. Endowed with special power (compare lines 649 and 778).   2. With. *Toy:* toying, playing.

There they their fill of love and love's disport
Took largely, of their mutual guilt the seal,
The solace of their sin, till dewy sleep
Oppressed them, wearied with their amorous play.
    Soon as the force of that fallacious fruit, 1045
That with exhilarating vapor bland
About their spirits had played, and inmost powers
Made err, was now exhaled, and grosser sleep
Bred of unkindly fumes,[3] with conscious dreams
Encumbered, now had left them, up they rose 1050
As from unrest, and each the other viewing,
Soon found their eyes how opened, and their minds
How darkened. Innocence, that as a veil
Had shadowed them from knowing ill, was gone;
Just confidence, and native righteousness, 1055
And honor from about them, naked left
To guilty Shame; he covered, but his robe
Uncovered more. So rose the Danite[4] strong,
Herculean Samson, from the harlot-lap
Of Philistean Dàlilàh, and waked 1060
Shorn of his strength;[5] they destitute and bare
Of all their virtue. Silent, and in face
Confounded, long they sat, as strucken mute;
Till Adam, though not less than Eve abashed,
At length gave utterance to these words constrained: 1065
    "O Eve, in evil hour thou didst give ear
To that false worm,[6] of whomsoever taught
To counterfeit man's voice, true in our fall,
False in our promised rising; since our eyes
Opened we find indeed, and find we know 1070
Both good and evil, good lost, and evil got:
Bad fruit of knowledge, if this be to know,
Which leaves us naked thus, of honor void,
Of innocence, of faith, of purity,
Our wonted ornaments now soiled and stained, 1075
And in our faces evident the signs
Of foul concupiscence; whence evil store,
Even shame, the last[7] of evils; of the first
Be sure then. How shall I behold the face
Henceforth of God or angel, erst with joy 1080
And rapture so oft beheld? Those heavenly shapes
Will dazzle now this earthly[8] with their blaze
Insufferably bright. O might I here
In solitude live savage, in some glade
Obscured, where highest woods, impenetrable 1085
To star or sunlight, spread their umbrage broad,
And brown[9] as evening! Cover me, ye pines,
Ye cedars, with innumerable boughs

---

3. Unnatural exhalations.   4. Of the tribe of Dan. Shame (personified) covered them, but his cover
(*robe*) only made them aware of their nakedness (*uncovered more*).   5. See Judges 16.4–20.   6. I. e.,
the Serpent, now disparaged.   7. Extreme, ultimate. *Evil store*: an abundance of evils.   8. Adam's now
earthly nature and sense.   9. Dark.

Hide me, where I may never see them[1] more!
But let us now, as in[2] bad plight, devise   1090
What best may for the present serve to hide
The parts of each from other, that seem most
To shame obnoxious,[3] and unseemliest seen;
Some tree whose broad smooth leaves together sewed,
And girded on our loins, may cover round   1095
Those middle parts, that this newcomer, Shame,
There sit not, and reproach us as unclean."
     So counseled he, and both together went
Into the thickest wood; there soon they chose
The figtree, not that kind for fruit renowned   1100
But such as at this day, to Indians known,
In Malabar or Deccan[4] spreads her arms
Branching so broad and long, that in the ground
The bended twigs take root, and daughters grow
About the mother tree, a pillared shade   1105
High overarched, and echoing walks between;
There oft the Indian herdsman, shunning heat,
Shelters in cool, and tends his pasturing herds
At loopholes cut through thickest shade. Those leaves
They gathered, broad as Amazonian targe,[5]   1110
And with what skill they had, together sewed,
To gird their waist; vain covering, if to hide
Their guilt and dreaded shame! O how unlike
To that first naked glory! Such of late
Columbus found th' American, so girt   1115
With feathered cincture,[6] naked else and wild
Among the trees on isles and woody shores.
Thus fenced, and, as they thought, their shame in part
Covered, but not at rest or ease of mind,
They sat them down to weep; nor only tears   1120
Rained at their eyes, but high winds worse within
Began to rise, high passions, anger, hate,
Mistrust, suspicion, discord, and shook sore
Their inward state of mind, calm region once
And full of peace, now tossed and turbulent: 1125
For Understanding ruled not, and the Will
Heard not her lore, both in subjection now
To sensual Appetite, who, from beneath
Usurping over sovereign Reason, claimed
Superior sway.[7] From thus distempered breast,   1130
Adam, estranged in look and altered style,
Speech intermitted thus to Eve renewed:
     "Would thou hadst hearkened to my words, and stayed
With me, as I besought thee, when that strange
Desire of wandering, this unhappy morn,   1135

1. The *heavenly shapes* (line 1082).   2. As we are in.   3. Exposed to.   4. In southern India. *Figtree:*
identified as the banyan or Indian fig tree, also classified in botany as *Ficus religiosa.*   5. Shield. The
Amazons were women warriors in Greco-Roman myth (and in Virgil's *Aeneid*). Actually the tree's leaf is
small; Milton's inaccurate notion comes from contemporary sources and goes back to antiquity.   6. Belt.
7. The victory of *Sensual Appetite* over *Reason* (cf. line 113 and n. 5, p. 2597) and over humankind's free
will (compare lines 351 ff.)—humanity's distinguishing traits—summarizes the history of the Fall.

I know not whence possessed thee! we had then
Remained still happy, not as now, despoiled
Of all our good, shamed, naked, miserable.
Let none henceforth seek needless cause to approve
The faith they owe;[8] when earnestly they seek   1140
Such proof, conclude, they then begin to fail."
   To whom, soon moved with touch of blame, thus Eve:
"What words have passed thy lips, Adam severe?
Imput'st thou that to my default, or will   1145
Of wandering, as thou call'st it, which who knows
But might as ill have happened, thou being by,
Or to thyself perhaps? Hadst thou been there,
Or here th' attempt, thou couldst not have discerned
Fraud in the serpent, speaking as he spake;
No ground of enmity between us known,   1150
Why he should mean me ill, or seek to harm?
Was I to have never parted from thy side?
As good have grown there still a lifeless rib.
Being as I am, why didst not thou, the head,
Command me absolutely not to go,   1155
Going into such danger, as thou saidst?
Too facile then, thou didst not much gainsay,
Nay, didst permit, approve, and fair dismiss.
Hadst thou been firm and fixed in thy dissent,
Neither had I transgressed, nor thou with me."[9]   1160
   To whom, then first incensed, Adam replied:
"Is this the love, is this the recompense
Of mine to thee, ingrateful Eve, expressed[1]
Immutable when thou were lost, not I,
Who might have lived and joyed immortal bliss,   1165
Yet willingly chose rather death with thee?
And am I now upbraided as the cause
Of thy transgressing? not enough severe,
It seems, in thy restraint![2] What could I more?
I warned thee, I admonished thee, foretold   1170
The danger, and the lurking enemy
That lay in wait; beyond this had been force,
And force upon free will hath here no place.
But confidence then bore thee on, secure
Either to meet no danger, or to find   1175
Matter of glorious trial and perhaps
I also erred in overmuch admiring
What seemed in thee so perfect, that I thought
No evil durst attempt thee! but I rue
That error now, which is become my crime,   1180
And thou th' accuser. Thus it shall befall
Him who, to worth in women overtrusting,

---

8. Own. *Approve:* prove by testing.   9. The notion of man's authority over woman—recognized by Milton's Eve (e.g., in 4.442–43: "my guide / and head") and echoing St. Paul (1 Corinthians 11.3: "the head of the woman is the man") is here used by her to make Adam her equal in guilt, accusing him of indulgence in letting her go (*too facile*).   1. Demonstrated, proved.   2. In restraining Eve.

Lets her will rule; restraint she will not brook,[3]
And, left to herself, if evil thence ensue,
She first his weak indulgence will accuse."   1185
    Thus they in mutual accusation spent
The fruitless hours, but neither self-condemning;
And of their vain contést appeared no end.

FROM BOOK 10

The Argument

    Man's transgression known, the guardian Angels forsake Paradise, and
return up to Heaven to approve their vigilance, and are approved; God declaring that the entrance of Satan could not be by them prevented. He sends his
Son to judge the transgressors; who descends, and gives sentence accordingly; then, in pity, clothes them both, and reascends. Sin and Death, sitting
till then at the gates of Hell, by wondrous sympathy feeling the success of
Satan in this new World, and the sin by Man there committed, resolve to sit
no longer confined in Hell, but to follow Satan, their sire, up to the place of
Man: to make the way easier from Hell to this World to and fro, they pave
a broad highway or bridge over Chaos, according to the track that Satan first
made; then, preparing for Earth, they meet him, proud of his success, returning to Hell; their mutual gratulation. Satan arrives at Pandemonium; in full
assembly relates, with boasting, his success against Man; instead of applause
is entertained with a general hiss by all his audience, transformed, with himself also, suddenly into Serpents, according to his doom given in Paradise;
then, deluded with a show of the Forbidden Tree springing up before them,
they, greedily reaching to take of the fruit, chew dust and bitter ashes. The
proceedings of Sin and Death: God foretells the final victory of his Son over
them, and the renewing of all things; but, for the present, commands his
Angels to make several alterations in the Heavens and Elements. Adam, more
and more perceiving his fallen condition, heavily bewails,[4] rejects the condolement of Eve; she persists, and at length appeases him: then, to evade
the curse likely to fall on their offspring, proposes to Adam violent ways;
which he approves not, but, conceiving better hope, puts her in mind of the
late promise made them, that her seed should be revenged on the Serpent,
and exhorts her, with him, to seek peace of the offended Deity by repentance
and supplication.

[Acceptance, Reconciliation, Hope]

                    * * * Thus began
    Outrage from lifeless things; but Discord first,
Daughter of Sin, among th' irrational
Death introduced through fierce antipathy:[5]
Beast now with beast 'gan war, and fowl with fowl,   710
And fish with fish: to graze the herb all leaving,
Devoured each other; nor stood much in awe

---

3. Put up with.   4. The selection printed here starts toward the end of Adam's long lamentation.
5. I.e., Discord introduced death to the irrational (beasts) through antipathy; Milton paves the way for the
role of sympathy in reconciling Adam to Eve.

Of man, but fled him, or with countenance grim
Glared on him passing. These were from without
The growing miseries, which Adam saw   715
Already in part, though hid in gloomiest shade,
To sorrow abandoned, but worse felt within,
And in a troubled sea of passion tossed,
Thus to disburden sought with sad complaint:
    "O miserable of happy! Is this the end   720
Of this new glorious world, and me so late
The glory of that glory? who now, become
Accursed of blessèd, hide me from the face
Of God, whom to behold was then my height
Of happiness! Yet well, if here would end   725
The misery; I deserved it, and would bear
My own deservings; but this will not serve.
All that I eat or drink, or shall beget,
Is propagated curse.⁶ O voice, once heard
Delightfully, 'Increase and multiply,'   730
Now death to hear! for what can I increase
Or multiply, but curses on my head?
Who of all ages to succeed, but, feeling
The evil on him brought by me, will curse
My head: 'Ill fare our ancestor impure!   735
For this we may thank Adam!' but his thanks
Shall be the execration;⁷ so besides
Mine own that bide upon me, all from me
Shall with a fierce reflux on me redound,
On me, as on their natural center, light   740
Heavy, though in their place. O fleeting joys
Of Paradise, dear bought with lasting woes!
Did I request thee, Maker, from my clay
To mold me man? Did I solicit thee
From darkness to promote me, or here place   745
In this delicious garden? As my will
Concurred not to my being, it were but right
And equal to reduce me to my dust,
Desirous to resign and render back
All I received, unable to perform   750
Thy terms too hard, by which I was to hold
The good I sought not. To the loss of that,
Sufficient penalty, why hast thou added
The sense of endless woes? Inexplicable
Thy justice seems; yet to say truth, too late   755
I thus contèst; then should have been refused
Those terms whatever, when they were proposed.
Thou didst accept them; wilt thou enjoy the good,
Then cavil⁸ the conditions? And though God
Made thee without thy leave, what if thy son   760
Prove disobedient, and reproved, retort,

6. Eating, drinking, and procreating all increase or extend God's curse.   7. I.e., posterity's curses on
Adam.   8. Raise petty objections.

'Wherefore didst thou beget me? I sought it not.'
Wouldst thou admit for his contempt of thee
That proud excuse? Yet him not thy election,
But natural necessity begot.   765
God made thee of choice his own, and of his own
To serve him; thy reward was of his grace;
Thy punishment then justly is at his will.
Be it so, for I submit; his doom is fair,⁹
That dust I am and shall to dust return.   770
O welcome hour whenever! Why delays
His hand to execute what his decree
Fixed on this day? Why do I overlive?
Why am I mocked with death, and lengthened out
To deathless pain? How gladly would I meet   775
Mortality, my sentence, and be earth
Insensible! how glad would lay me down
As in my mother's lap!¹ here I should rest
And sleep secure; his dreadful voice no more
Would thunder in my ears; no fear of worse   780
To me and to my offspring would torment me
With cruel expectation. Yet one doubt
Pursues me still, lest all I cannot die;
Lest that pure breath of life, the spirit of man
Which God inspired, cannot together perish   785
With this corporeal clod; then, in the grave,
Or in some other dismal place, who knows
But I shall die a living death? O thought
Horrid, if true!² Yet why? It was but breath
Of life that sinned; what dies but what had life   790
And sin? the body properly hath neither.
All of me then shall die: let this appease
The doubt, since human reach no further knows.
For though the Lord of all be infinite,
Is his wrath also? Be it, man is not so,   795
But mortal doomed. How can he exercise
Wrath without end on man whom death must end?
Can he make deathless death? That were to make
Strange contradiction, which to God himself
Impossible is held, as argument   800
Of weakness, not of power.³ Will he draw out,
For anger's sake, finite to infinite
In punished man, to satisfy his rigor
Satisfied never? That were to extend
His sentence beyond dust and Nature's law;   805
By which all causes else according still

9. In his inner debate, Adam has just been arguing to himself that God created us "of choice his own, / and of his own to serve him." Hence in the same way as reward "was of his [God's] grace," so punishment "justly is at his will" and, therefore, acceptable.   1. I.e., the earth (in 11.536, Michael, addressing Adam, calls the Earth "thy mother's lap"), probably an echo of Job 3.   2. Adam fears that the soul, breathed (inspired) into the corporeal clod at Creation, may be immortal and so suffer a living death in the grave. 3. Adam corrects himself, arguing (as Milton did in his theological writings) that because only the spirit (breath of life, line 784) sinned it shall die with the body (and, implicitly, await resurrection). Otherwise, according to the same theological line of thinking, there would be strange contradiction, an inadmissable sign of weakness in God.

To the reception of their matter act,
Not to th' extent of their own sphere.[4] But say
That death be not one stroke, as I supposed,
Bereaving sense, but endless misery   810
From this day onward, which I feel begun
Both in me and without[5] me, and so last
To perpetuity—Ay me! that fear
Comes thundering back with dreadful revolution
On my defenseless head! Both death and I   815
Am found eternal, and incorporate both:[6]
Nor I on my part single; in me all
Posterity stands cursed. Fair patrimony
That I must leave ye, sons! O, were I able
To waste it all myself, and leave ye none!   820
So disinherited, how would ye bless
Me, now your curse! Ah, why should all mankind
For one man's fault thus guiltless be condemned,
If guiltless? But from me what can proceed,
But all corrupt, both mind and will depraved,   825
Not to do only, but to will the same
With me? How can they then acquitted stand
In sight of God?[7] Him, after all disputes,
Forced I absolve. All my evasions vain
And reasonings, though through mazes, lead me still   830
But to my own conviction: first and last
On me, me only, as the source and spring
Of all corruption, all the blame lights due;
So might the wrath! Fond[8] wish! Couldst thou support
That burden, heavier than the earth to bear;   835
Than all the world much heavier, though divided
With that bad woman? Thus, what thou desir'st,
And what thou fear'st, alike destroys all hope[9]
Of refuge, and concludes thee miserable
Beyond all past example[1] and future;   840
To Satan only like, both crime and doom.[2]
O Conscience! into what abyss of fears
And horrors hast thou driven me; out of which
I find no way, from deep to deeper plunged!"
    Thus Adam to himself lamented loud   845
Through the still night, not now, as ere man fell,
Wholesome and cool and mild, but with black air
Accompanied, with damps and dreadful gloom;
Which to his evil conscience represented

---

4. Once body and spirit die, further punishment is impossible. According to *Nature's law* the power of all
agents, God excepted (*all causes else*), cannot be exercised to its utmost (the *extent of their own sphere*) but
is limited by the capacity for *reception* that the object of that power possesses.   5. Outside. *Bereaving
sense:* removing all sensory powers.   6. The use of *am*, the singular form, stresses Adam's concentration
on himself and on the fact that he and death are now united in one body (*incorporate*).   7. Inheriting
Adam's original sin, his descendants, like him (*with me*), are going to act sinfully by their own free will.
8. Foolish.   9. Actually, by his desperate self-accusation and by wanting to assume, alone, the burden
of guilt, Adam is shown to be already on the way to full repentance and to his own regeneration.   1. That
of the fallen angels. *Concludes thee:* demonstrates that you are.   2. The comparison is clearly invalid,
Adam's remorse and repentant despair being opposite to Satan's choice, as seen, for example, in 4.109–10:
"Farewell remorse! All good to me is lost; / Evil, be thou my good."

All things with double terror. On the ground   850
Outstretched he lay, on the cold ground, and oft
Cursed his creation; Death as oft accused
Of tardy execution, since denounced
The day of his offense. "Why comes not Death,"
Said he, "with one thrice-àcceptàble stroke   855
To end me? Shall Truth fail to keep her word,
Justice divine not hasten to be just?
But Death comes not at call; Justice divine
Mends not her slowest pace for prayers or cries.
O woods, O fountains, hillocks, dales, and bowers!   860
With other echo late I taught your shades
To answer, and resound far other song."
Whom thus afflicted when sad Eve beheld,
Desolate where she sat, approaching nigh,
Soft words to his fierce passion she essayed;   865
But her with stern regard he thus repelled:
    "Out of my sight, thou serpent! that name best
Befits thee, with him leagued, thyself as false
And hateful: nothing wants, but that thy shape,
Like his, and color serpentine, may show   870
Thy inward fraud, to warn all creatures from thee
Henceforth; lest that too heavenly form, pretended[3]
To hellish falsehood, snare them. But for thee
I had persisted happy, had not thy pride
And wandering vanity, when least was safe,   875
Rejected my forewarning, and disdained
Not to be trusted, longing to be seen
Though by the devil himself, him overweening
To overreach,[4] but, with the serpent meeting,
Fooled and beguiled; by him thou, I by thee,   880
To trust thee from my side, imagined wise,
Constant, mature, proof against all assaults;
And understood not all was but a show
Rather than solid virtue, all but a rib
Crooked by nature—bent, as now appears,   885
More to the part sinìster—from me drawn;
Well if thrown out, as supernumerary
To my just number found![5] Oh, why did God,
Creator wise, that peopled highest Heaven
With spirits masculine, create at last   890
This novelty on earth, this fair defect
Of nature, and not fill the world at once
With men, as angels, without feminine;
Or find some other way to generate
Mankind?[6] This mischief had not then befallen,   895
And more that shall befall—innumerable

---

3. Put up as a screen.   4. Overestimating your power to outwit him.   5. Folklore has it that the rib
from which Eve was created was an extra rib on Adam's left (Latin: *sinister*) side. Note double meaning of
sinister.   6. Adam's frenzied speech belongs to a tradition of misogynistic rhetoric that goes back to
antiquity. These lines, in particular, seem to echo Euripides' *Hippolytus*, lines 617–20 (Euripides was one
of Milton's favorite writers).

Disturbances on earth through female snares,
And strait conjunction with this sex. For either
He never shall find out fit mate, but such
As some misfortune brings him, or mistake;   900
Or whom he wishes most shall seldom gain,
Through her perverseness, but shall see her gained
By a far worse, or, if she love, withheld
By parents, or his happiest choice too late
Shall meet, already linked and wedlock-bound   905
To a fell⁷ adversary, his hate or shame:
Which infinite calamity shall cause
To human life, and household peace confound."
    He added not, and from her turned; but Eve,
Not so repulsed, with tears that ceased not flowing,   910
And tresses all disordered, at his feet
Fell humble, and, embracing them, besought
His peace, and thus proceeded in her plaint:
    "Forsake me not thus, Adam! witness Heaven
What love sincere and reverence in my heart   915
I bear thee, and unweeting have offended,
Unhappily deceived! Thy suppliant⁸
I beg, and clasp thy knees; bereave me not,
Whereon I live, thy gentle looks, thy aid,
Thy counsel in this uttermost distress,   920
My only strength and stay: forlorn of thee,
Whither shall I betake me, where subsist?
While yet we live, scarce one short hour perhaps,
Between us two let there be peace; both joining,
As joined in injuries, one enmity   925
Against a foe by doom express assigned us,
That cruel serpent. On me exercise not
Thy hatred for this misery befallen;
On me already lost, me than thyself
More miserable. Both have sinned, but thou   930
Against God only; I against God and thee,
And to the place of judgment will return,
There with my cries importune Heaven, that all
The sentence, from thy head removed, may light
On me, sole cause to thee of all this woe,   935
Me, me only, just object of his ire."
    She ended weeping; and her lowly plight,
Immovable⁹ till peace obtained from fault
Acknowledged and deplored, in Adam wrought
Commiseration. Soon his heart relented   940
Towards her, his life so late and sole delight,
Now at his feet submissive in distress,
Creature so fair his reconcilement seeking,
His counsel, whom she had displeased, his aid;
As one disarmed, his anger all he lost,   945

---

7. Fierce, bitter. *Already linked:* i.e., when he is already linked.   8. As thy suppliant. *Unweeting:* unknowingly.   9. Modifies both Eve in her lowly posture of repentance and Adam in his first reluctance to forgive.

And thus with peaceful words upraised her soon:
    "Unwary, and too desirous, as before,
So now, of what thou know'st not,[1] who desir'st
The punishment all on thyself! Alas!
Bear thine own first, ill able to sustain   950
His full wrath, whose thou feel'st as yet least part,[2]
And my displeasure bear'st so ill. If prayers
Could alter high decrees, I to that place
Would speed before thee, and be louder heard,
That on my head all might be visited,   955
Thy frailty and infirmer sex forgiven,
To me committed, and by me exposed.[3]
But rise; let us no more contend, nor blame
Each other, blamed enough elsewhere,[4] but strive
In offices of love, how we may lighten   960
Each other's burden in our share of woe;
Since this day's death denounced, if aught I see,
Will prove no sudden, but a slow-paced evil,
A long day's dying to augment our pain,
And to our seed (O hapless seed!) derived."[5]   965
    To whom thus Eve, recovering heart, replied:—
"Adam, by sad experiment I know
How little weight my words with thee can find,
Found so erroneous, thence by just event
Found so unfortunate. Nevertheless,   970
Restored by thee, vile as I am, to place
Of new acceptance, hopeful to regain
Thy love, the sole contentment of my heart,
Living or dying from thee I will not hide
What thoughts in my unquiet breast are risen,   975
Tending to some relief of our extremes,
Or end, though sharp and sad, yet tolerable,
As in our evils,[6] and of easier choice.
If care of our descent[7] perplex us most,
Which must be born to certain woe, devoured   980
By Death at last (and miserable it is
To be to others cause of misery,
Our own begotten, and of our loins to bring
Into this cursed world a woeful race,
That, after wretched life, must be at last   985
Food for so foul a monster), in thy power
It lies, yet ere conception, to prevent
The race unblest, to being yet unbegot.[8]
Childless thou art; childless remain. So Death
Shall be deceived his glut,[9] and with us two   990
Be forced to satisfy his ravenous maw.

---

1. Once more Eve is *too desirous* of the unknown, but her situation and her tone are now totally different—as are those of Adam, whose *counsel* and *aid* she has sought.   **2.** Eve would not be able to bear the weight of God's full wrath, of which she has until now experienced only the smallest part.   **3.** In the present atmosphere of reconciliation, Adam seems to accept Eve's earlier charge (see n. 9, p. 2619); now he blames himself for having exposed her to temptation.   **4.** I.e., at the place of judgment (see also lines 932, 953, and 1098–99).   **5.** Transmitted.   **6.** We being in such evils.   **7.** Descendants, lineage.   **8.** To forestall, by abstinence, the birth of descendants.   **9.** Shall be cheated of its fill.

But, if thou judge it hard and difficult,
Conversing, looking, loving, to abstain
From love's due rites, nuptial embraces sweet,
And with desire to languish without hope   995
Before the present object[1] languishing
With like desire—which would be misery
And torment less than none of what we dread—
Then, both our selves and seed at once to free
From what we fear for both, let us make short;   1000
Let us seek Death, or, he not found, supply
With our own hands his office on ourselves.
Why stand we longer shivering under fears
That show no end but death, and have the power,
Of many ways to die the shortest choosing   1005
Destruction with destruction to destroy?"[2]
    She ended here, or vehement despair
Broke off the rest; so much of death her thoughts
Had entertained as dyed her cheeks with pale.
But Adam, with such counsel nothing swayed,   1010
To better hopes his more attentive mind
Laboring had raised, and thus to Eve replied:—
    "Eve, thy contempt of life and pleasure seems
To argue in thee something more sublime
And excellent than what thy mind contemns: 1015
But self-destruction therefore sought refutes
That excellence thought in thee, and implies
Not thy contempt, but anguish and regret
For loss of life and pleasure overloved.[3]
Or, if thou covet death, as utmost end   1020
Of misery, so thinking to evade
The penalty pronounced, doubt not but God
Hath wiselier armed his vengeful ire than so
To be forestalled. Much more I fear lest death
So snatched will not exempt us from the pain   1025
We are by doom to pay; rather such acts
Of contumacy will provoke the Highest
To make death in us live. Then let us seek
Some safer resolution—which methinks
I have in view, calling to mind with heed   1030
Part of our sentence,[4] that thy seed shall bruise
The Serpent's head. Piteous amends! unless
Be meant whom I conjecture,[5] our grand foe,
Satan, who in the Serpent hath contrived
Against us this deceit. To crush his head   1035

1. Eve herself, object of Adam's love, and now in his presence.   2. Destroy destruction (Death's power
to destroy future mankind) by destroying ourselves now.   3. The suicide project excludes (refutes) the
idea that Eve be contemptuous of life and pleasure in view of something more sublime; it rather implies
anguish and regret at the thought of losing those goods.   4. Earlier in this book (the Argument and lines
163–208) the Lord gives sentence on the Serpent and the transgressors. The references here are to that
passage, which is quite literally based on Genesis 30 (esp. lines 179–81; "Between thee and the Woman I
will put / Enmity, and between thine and her seed; / Her seed shall bruise thy head, thou bruise his heel").
5. The notion that Satan spoke through the Serpent was not at first given to humanity (lines 170–71:
"Concerned not Man. . . . / Nor altered his offense"). Adam is late in coming to that conclusion (I conjecture), and on it he bases the following eloquent argument in favor of survival, hope, procreation, and activity.

Would be revenge indeed—which will be lost
By death brought on ourselves, or childless days
Resolved as thou proposest; so our foe
Shall scape his punishment ordained, and we
Instead shall double ours upon our heads.   1040
No more be mentioned, then, of violence
Against ourselves, and wilful barrenness
That cuts us off from hope, and savors only
Rancor and pride, impatience and despite,
Reluctance[6] against God and his just yoke   1045
Laid on our necks. Remember with what mild
And gracious temper he both heard and judged,
Without wrath or reviling. We expected
Immediate dissolution, which we thought
Was meant by death that day; when, lo! to thee   1050
Pains only in child-bearing were foretold,
And bringing forth, soon recompensed with joy,
Fruit of thy womb. On me the curse aslope
Glanced on the ground.[7] With labor I must earn
My bread; what harm: Idleness had been worse;   1055
My labor will sustain me; and, lest cold
Or heat should injure us, his timely care
Hath, unbesought, provided, and his hands
Clothed us unworthy, pitying while he judged.
How much more, if we pray him, will his ear   1060
Be open, and his heart to pity incline,
And teach us further by what means to shun
The inclement seasons, rain, ice, hail, and snow!
Which now the sky, with various face, begins
To show us in this mountain,[8] while the winds   1065
Blow moist and keen, shattering the graceful locks
Of these fair spreading trees; which bids us seek
Some better shroud, some better warmth to cherish
Our limbs benumbed—ere this diurnal star
Leave cold the night, how we his gathered beams   1070
Reflected may with matter sere foment,[9]
Or by collision of two bodies grind
The air attrite to fire;[1] as late the clouds,
Justling, or pushed with winds, rude in their shock,
Tine the slant lightning, whose thwart[2] flame, driven down,   1075

6. Resistance, opposition.   7. The curse descending (aslope) on Adam took an oblique course (glanced) toward the ground. Thus Adam is not only accepting the Lord's sentence (in lines 201–02 and 205; "Curs'd is the ground for thy sake; thou in sorrow / Shalt eat thereof all the days of thy life; / . . . In the sweat of thy face thou shalt eat bread") but turning it into a project for an active life after the Fall.   8. In his description of delicious Paradise (4.132–58), Milton situates it on a high plateau at the top of a "steep wilderness" that denies access to the "enclosure green" and its "Insuperable height of loftiest shade, / Cedar, and pine, and fir, and branching palm, / A sylvan scene, and as the ranks ascend / Shade above shade, a woody theater / Of stateliest view" where "gentle gales / . . . dispense / Native perfumes, and whisper whence they stole / Those balmy spoils." That stately and blissful order is now disrupted, and after the radical alterations in the heavens and in the elements that God has commanded, Adam is preparing to cope with the hardships and challenges of his mortal state in a time-conditioned universe of seasonal changes, dawns and sunset, heat and ice, and shattering winds.   9. Heat, warm. Diurnal star: day star, the sun. How: seek how.   1. The implied belief is that rubbing two bodies (as two flints) against each other, the air thus ground down by the attrition (attrite) turns into fire.   2. Passing across the sky. Tine: kindle; that fire was produced by lightning is one of the ancient theories about its origin on earth.

Kindles the gummy bark of fir or pine,
And sends a comfortable heat from far,
Which might supply the Sun. Such fire to use,
And what may else be remedy or cure
To evils which our own misdeeds have wrought,   1080
He will instruct us praying,[3] and of grace
Beseeching him; so as we need not fear
To pass commodiously this life, sustained
By him with many comforts, till we end
In dust, our final rest and native home.   1085
What better can we do, than to the place
Repairing where he judged us, prostrate fall
Before him reverent, and there confess
Humbly our faults, and pardon beg, with tears
Watering the ground, and with our sighs the air   1090
Frequenting,[4] sent from hearts contrite, in sign
Of sorrow unfeigned and humiliation meek?
Undoubtedly he will relent, and turn
From his displeasure, in whose look serene,
When angry most he seemed and most severe,   1095
What else but favor, grace, and mercy shone?"
    So spake our Father penitent; nor Eve
Felt less remorse. They, forthwith to the place
Repairing where he judged them, prostrate fell
Before him reverent, and both confessed   1100
Humbly their faults, and pardon begged, with tears
Watering the ground, and with their sighs the air
Frequenting, sent from hearts contrite, in sign
Of sorrow unfeigned and humiliation meek.

FROM BOOK 12

After God's acceptance of the transgressors' prayers and the decree that "they
must no longer abide in Paradise" (11, "The Argument"), Michael the archangel, with a band of cherubim, has been sent "to dispossess them." After
Eve's lamentation and his own pleading, Adam has submitted; Michael has
led him up to a high hill where, in a mixture of prophecy and instruction, he
has set "before him in vision" the future of humankind, from Cain and Abel
through Noah (11) and the prophets, thus coming "by degrees to explain
who that Seed of Woman shall be which was promised Adam and Eve in the
Fall: his incarnation, death, resurrection, and ascension; the state of the
Church till his second coming" (12, "The Argument"). Toward the close of
his speech, Michael has recommended the exercise of the basic Christian
virtues, culminating in love, "By name to come called Charity, the soul / Of
all the rest: then will thou not be loath / To leave this Paradise, but shalt
possess / A Paradise within thee, happier far" (12.584–87). Michael has just
ended his long speech.

3. If we pray to him.   4. Filling.

["The World Was All before Them"]

* * *

He ended, and they both descend the hill.
Descended, Adam to the bower where Eve
Lay sleeping[5] ran before, but found her waked;
And thus with words not sad she him received:
    "Whence thou return'st and whither went'st, I know;   610
For God is also in sleep, and dreams[6] advise,
Which he hath sent propitious, some great good
Presaging, since, with sorrow and heart's distress
Wearied, I fell asleep. But now lead on;
In me is no delay; with thee to go   615
Is to stay here; without thee here to stay
Is to go hence unwilling; thou to me
Art all things under Heaven, all places thou,
Who for my willful crime art banished hence.
This further consolation yet secure   620
I carry hence: though all by me is lost,
Such favor I unworthy am vouchsafed,
By me the Promised Seed shall all restore."
    So spake our mother Eve; and Adam heard
Well pleased, but answered not; for now too nigh   625
Th' archangel stood, and from the other hill[7]
To their fixed station, all in bright array,
The cherubim descended; on the ground
Gliding meteorous, as evening mist
Risen from a river o'er the marish[8] glides,   630
And gathers ground fast at the laborer's heel
Homeward returning. High in front advanced,[9]
The brandished sword of God before them blazed,
Fierce as a comet; which with torrid heat,
And vapor as the Libyan air adust,[1]   635
Began to parch that temperate clime; whereat
In either hand the hastening angel caught
Our lingering parents, and to th' eastern gate[2]
Led them direct, and down the cliff as fast
To the subjected[3] plain; then disappeared.   640
They, looking back, all th' eastern side beheld
Of Paradise, so late their happy seat,
Waved over by that flaming brand;[4] the gate
With dreadful faces thronged and fiery arms.

5. Michael has just said to Adam (lines 594–97): "Go, waken Eve; / Her also I with gentle dreams have calmed, / Portending good, and all her spirits composed / To meek submission."   6. The fact that Adam was granted a vision and Eve a dream may symbolize a difference in the mode of perception between man and woman; at any rate, both are God's revelations.   7. The hill that Michael had pointed out to Adam in lines 590–93: "and, see! the guards, / By me encamped on yonder hill, expect / Their motion, at whose front a flaming sword, / In signal of remove, waves fiercely round."   8. Marsh.   9. Raised high, carried like a banner.   1. Burned up, as the air of the Sahara Desert in Libya.   2. The eastern gate of Eden, guarded by Gabriel, was described earlier (4. 543–47): "It was a rock / Of alabaster, piled up to the clouds, / Conspicuous far, winding with one ascent / Accessible from earth, one entrance high; / The rest was craggy cliff."   3. Lying below.   4. Here meaning sword, but also conveying the image of burning (flaming). Seat: abode.

Some natural tears they dropped, but wiped them soon;   645
The world was all before them, where to choose
Their place of rest,[5] and Providence their guide.
They, hand in hand, with wandering steps and slow,
Through Eden took their solitary way.

5. Not, of course, a place of repose, but their new, earthly abode.

A Note on Translation

Reading literature in translation is a pleasure on which it is fruitless to frown. The purist may insist that we ought always read in the original languages, and we know ideally that this is true. But it is a counsel of perfection, quite impractical even for the purist, since no one in a lifetime can master all the languages whose literatures it would be a joy to explore. Master languages as fast as we may, we shall always have to read to some extent in translation, and this means we must be alert to what we are about: if in reading a work of literature in translation we are not reading the "original," what precisely are we reading? This is a question of great complexity, to which justice cannot be done in a brief note, but the following sketch of some of the considerations may be helpful.

One of the memorable scenes of ancient literature is the meeting of Hector and Andromache in book 6 of Homer's *Iliad*. Hector, leader and mainstay of the armies defending Troy, is implored by his wife, Andromache, to withdraw within the city walls and carry on the defense from there, where his life will not be constantly at hazard. In Homer's text her opening words to him are these: δαιμόνιε, φθίσει σε τὸ σὸν μένος (daimonie, phthisei se to son menos). How should they be translated into English?

Here is how they have actually been translated into English by capable translators, at various periods, in verse and prose:

1. George Chapman, 1598:

> O noblest in desire,
> Thy mind, inflamed with others' good, will set thy self on fire.

2. John Dryden, 1693:

> Thy dauntless heart (which I foresee too late),
> Too daring man, will urge thee to thy fate.

3. Alexander Pope, 1715:

> Too daring Prince! . . .
> For sure such courage length of life denies,
> And thou must fall, thy virtue's sacrifice.

4. William Cowper, 1791:

> Thy own great courage will cut short thy days,
> My noble Hector . . .

5. Lang, Leaf, and Myers, 1883 (prose):

Dear my lord, this thy hardihood will undo thee. . . .

6. A. T. Murray, 1924 (prose):

Ah, my husband, this prowess of thine will be thy doom. . . .

7. E. V. Rieu, 1950 (prose):

"Hector," she said, "you are possessed. This bravery of yours will be your end."

8. I. A. Richards, 1950 (prose):

"Strange man," she said, "your courage will be your destruction."

9. Richmond Lattimore, 1951:

> Dearest,
> Your own great strength will be your death. . . .

10. Robert Fitzgerald, 1979:

> O my wild one, your bravery will be
> Your own undoing!

11. Robert Fagles, 1990:

> reckless one,
> Your own fiery courage will destroy you!

From these strikingly different renderings of the same six words, certain facts about the nature of translation begin to emerge. We notice, for one thing, that Homer's word μένος (menos) is diversified by the translators into "mind," "dauntless heart," "such courage," "great courage," "hardihood," "prowess," "bravery," "courage," "great strength," "bravery," and "fiery courage." The word has in fact all these possibilities. Used of things, it normally means "force"; of animals, "fierceness" or "brute strength" or (in the case of horses) "mettle"; of men and women, "passion" or "spirit" or even "purpose." Homer's application of it in the present case points our attention equally— whatever particular sense we may imagine Andromache to have uppermost—to Hector's force, strength, fierceness in battle, spirited heart and mind. But since English has no matching term of like inclusiveness, the passage as the translators give it to us reflects this lack and we find one attribute singled out to the exclusion of the rest.

Here then is the first and most crucial fact about any work of literature read in translation. It cannot escape the linguistic characteristics of the language into which it is turned: the grammatical, syntactical, lexical, and phonetic boundaries that constitute collectively the individuality or "genius" of that language. A Greek play or a Russian novel in English will be governed first of all by the resources of the English language, resources that are certain to be in every instance very different, as the efforts with μένος show, from those of the original.

Turning from μένος to δαιμόνιε (daimonie) in Homer's clause, we encounter a second crucial fact about translations. Nobody knows exactly what shade of meaning δαιμόνιε had for Homer. In later writers the word normally suggests divinity, something miraculous, wondrous; but in Homer it appears as a vocative of address for both chieftain and commoner, man and wife. The coloring one gives it must, therefore, be determined either by the way one thinks a Greek wife of Homer's era might actually address her husband (a subject on which we have no information whatever) or in the way one thinks it suitable for a hero's wife to address her husband in an epic poem, that is to say, a highly stylized and formal work. In general, the translators of our century have abandoned formality to stress the intimacy; the wifeliness; and, especially in Lattimore's case, a certain chiding tenderness, in Andromache's appeal: (6) "Ah, my husband," (7) "Hector" (with perhaps a hint, in "you are possessed," of the alarmed distaste with which wives have so often viewed their husbands' bellicose moods), (8) "Strange man," (9) "Dearest," (10) "O my wild one" (mixing an almost motherly admiration with reproach and concern), and (11) "reckless one." On the other hand, the older translators have obviously removed Andromache to an epic or heroic distance from her beloved, whence she sees and kindles to his selfless courage, acknowledging, even in the moment of pleading with him to be otherwise, his moral grandeur and the tragic destiny this too certainly implies: (1) "O noblest in desire, . . . inflamed by others' good"; (2) "Thy dauntless heart (which I foresee too late), / Too daring man"; (3) "Too daring Prince! . . . / And thou must fall, thy virtue's sacrifice"; (4) "My noble Hector." Even the less specific "Dear my lord" of Lang, Leaf, and Myers looks in the same direction because of its echo of the speech of countless Shakespearean men and women who have shared this powerful moral sense: "Dear my lord, make me acquainted with your cause of grief"; "Perseverance, dear my lord, keeps honor bright"; etc.

The fact about translation that emerges from all this is that just as the translated work reflects the individuality of the language it is turned into, so it reflects the individuality of the age in which it is made, and the age will permeate it everywhere like yeast in dough. We think of one kind of permeation when we think of the governing verse forms and attitudes toward verse at a given epoch. In Chapman's time, experiments seeking an "heroic" verse form for English were widespread, and accordingly he tries a "fourteener" couplet (two rhymed lines of seven stresses each) in his *Iliad* and a pentameter couplet in his *Odyssey.* When Dryden and Pope wrote, a closed pentameter couplet had become established as the heroic form par excellence. By Cowper's day, thanks largely to the prestige of *Paradise Lost,* the couplet had gone out of fashion for narrative poetry in favor of blank verse. Our age, inclining to prose and in verse to proselike informalities and relaxations, has, predictably, produced half a dozen excellent prose translations of the *Iliad* but only three in verse (by Fagles, Lattimore, and Fitzgerald), all relying on rhythms that are much of the time closer to the verse of William Carlos Williams and some of the prose of novelists like Faulkner than to the swift firm tread of Homer's Greek. For if it is true that what we translate from a given work is what, wearing the spectacles of our time, we see in it, it is also true that we see in it what we have the power to translate.

Of course, there are other effects of the translator's epoch on a translation besides those exercised by contemporary taste in verse and verse forms. Chapman writes in a great age of poetic metaphor and, therefore, almost instinctively translates his understanding of Homer's verb φθίσει (phthisei, "to cause to wane, consume, waste, pine") into metaphorical terms of flame, presenting his Hector to us as a man of burning generosity who will be consumed by his very ardor. This is a conception rooted in large part in the psychology of the Elizabethans, who had the habit of speaking of the soul as "fire," of one of the four temperaments as "fiery," of even the more material bodily processes, like digestion, as if they were carried on by the heat of fire ("concoction," "decoction"). It is rooted too in that characteristic Renaissance élan so unforgettably expressed in characters such as Tamburlaine and Dr. Faustus, the former of whom exclaims to the stars above:

> . . . I, the chiefest lamp of all the earth,
> First rising in the East with mild aspect,
> But fixèd now in the meridian line,
> Will send up fire to your turning spheres,
> And cause the sun to borrow light of you. . . .

Pope and Dryden, by contrast, write to audiences for whom strong metaphor has become suspect. They, therefore, reject the fire image (which we must recall is not present in the Greek) in favor of a form of speech more congenial to their age, the *sententia* or aphorism, and give it extra vitality by making it the scene of a miniature drama: in Dryden's case, the hero's dauntless heart "urges" him (in the double sense of physical as well as moral pressure) to his fate; in Pope's, the hero's courage, like a judge, "denies" continuance of life, with the consequence that he "falls"—and here Pope's second line suggests analogy to the sacrificial animal—the victim of his own essential nature, of what he is.

To pose even more graphically the pressures that a translator's period brings, consider the following lines from Hector's reply to Andromache's appeal that he withdraw, first in Chapman's Elizabethan version, then in Lattimore's twentieth-century one:

Chapman, 1598:

> The spirit I did first breathe
> Did never teach me that—much less since the contempt of death
> Was settled in me, and my mind knew what a Worthy was,
> Whose office is to lead in fight and give no danger pass
> Without improvement. In this fire must Hector's trial shine.
> Here must his country, father, friends be in him made divine.

Lattimore, 1951:

> and the spirit will not let me, since I have learned to be valiant
> and to fight always among the foremost ranks of the Trojans,
> winning for my own self great glory, and for my father.

If one may exaggerate to make a necessary point, the world of Henry V and Othello suddenly gives way here to our own, a world whose discomfort with any form of heroic self-assertion is remarkably mirrored in the burial of Homer's key terms (*spirit, valiant, fight, foremost, glory*)—five out of twenty-two words in the original, five out of thirty-six in the translation—in a cushioning huddle of harmless sounds.

Besides the two factors so far mentioned (language and period) as affecting the character of a translation, there is inevitably a third—the translator, with a particular degree of talent; a personal way of regarding the work to be translated; a special hierarchy of values, moral, aesthetic, metaphysical (which may or may not be summed up in a "worldview"); and a unique style or lack of it. But this influence all readers are likely to bear in mind, and it needs no laboring here. That, for example, two translators of Hamlet, one a Freudian, the other a Jungian, will produce impressively different translations is obvious from the fact that when Freudian and Jungian argue about the play in English they often seem to have different plays in mind.

We can now return to the question from which we started. After all allowances have been made for language, age, and individual translator, is anything of the original left? What, in short, does the reader of translations read? Let it be said at once that in utility prose—prose whose function is mainly referential—the reader who reads a translation reads everything that matters. "Nicht Rauchen," "Défense de Fumer," and "No Smoking," posted in a railway car, make their point, and the differences between them in sound and form have no significance for us in that context. Since the prose of a treatise and of most fiction is preponderantly referential, we rightly feel, when we have paid close attention to Cervantes or Montaigne or Machiavelli or Tolstoy in a good English translation, that we have had roughly the same experience as a native Spaniard, Frenchman, Italian, or Russian. But *roughly* is the correct word; for good prose points iconically to itself as well as referentially beyond itself, and everything that it points to in itself in the original (rhythms, sounds, idioms, wordplay, etc.) must alter radically in being translated. The best analogy is to imagine a van Gogh painting reproduced in the medium of tempera, etching, or engraving: the "picture" remains, but the intricate interanimation of volumes with colorings with brushstrokes has disappeared.

When we move on to poetry, even in its longer narrative and dramatic forms— plays like *Oedipus*, poems like the *Iliad* or *The Divine Comedy*—our situation as English readers worsens appreciably, as the many unlike versions of Andromache's appeal to Hector make very clear. But, again, only appreciably. True, this is the point at which the fact that a translation is *always* an interpretation explodes irresistibly on our attention; but if it is the best translation of its time, like Robert Fagles's translation of the *Iliad* for our time, the result will be not only a sensitive interpretation but also a work with intrinsic interest in its own right—at very best, a true work of art, a new poem. In these longer works, moreover, even if the translation is uninspired, many distinctive structural features—plot, setting, characters, meetings, partings, confrontations, and specific episodes generally—survive virtually unchanged. It is only when the shorter, primarily lyrical forms of poetry are presented that the reader of translations faces insuperable disadvantage. In these forms, the referential aspect of language has a tendency to disappear into, or, more often, draw its real meaning and accreditation from, the iconic aspect. Let us look for just a moment at a brief poem by Federico García Lorca and its English translation (by Stephen Spender and J. L. Gili):

> ¡Alto pinar!
> Cuatro palomas por el aire van.
>
> Cuatro palomas
> vuelan y tornan.
> Llevan heridas
> sus cuatro sombras.
>
> ¡Bajo pinar!
> Cuatro palomas en la tierra están.
>
> the pine trees:
> Four pigeons go through the air.
>
> Four pigeons
> fly and turn round.
> They carry wounded
> their four shadows.
>
> Below the pine trees:
> Four pigeons lie on the earth.

In this translation the referential sense of the English words follows with remarkable exactness the referential sense of the Spanish words they replace. But the life of Lorca's poem does not lie in that sense. It lies in such matters as the abruptness, like an intake of breath at a sudden revelation, of the two exclamatory lines (1 and 7), which then exhale musically in images of flight and death; or as the echoings of *palomas* in *heridas* and *sombras*, bringing together (as in fact the hunter's gun has done) these unrelated nouns and the unrelated experiences they stand for in a sequence that seems, momentarily, to have all the logic of a tragic action, in which *doves* become *wounds* become *shadows*, or as the external and internal rhyming among the five verbs, as though all motion must (as in fact it must) end with *están*.

Since none of this can be brought over into another tongue (least of all Lorca's rhythms), the translator must decide between leaving a reader to wonder why Lorca is a poet to be bothered about at all and making a new but true poem, whose merit will almost certainly be in inverse ratio to its likeness to the original. Samuel Johnson made such a poem in translating Horace's famous *Diffugere nives*, and so did A. E. Housman. If we juxtapose the last two stanzas of each translation, and the corresponding Latin, we can see at a glance that each has the consistency and inner life of a genuine poem and that neither of them (even if we consider only what is obvious to the eye, the line-lengths) is very close to Horace:

> Cum semel occideris, et de te splendida Minos
>   fecerit arbitria,
> non, Torquate, genus, non te facundia, non te
>   restituet pietas.

Infernis neque enim tenebris Diana pudicum
    liberat Hippolytum
nec Lethaea valet Theseus abrumpere caro
    vincula Pirithoo.

Johnson:

Not you, Torquatus, boast of Rome,
When Minos once has fixed your doom,
Or eloquence, or splendid birth,
Or virtue, shall restore to earth.
Hippolytus, unjustly slain,
Diana calls to life in vain;
Nor can the might of Theseus rend
The chains of hell that hold his friend.

Housman:

When thou descendest once the shades among,
    The stern assize and equal judgment o'er,
Not thy long lineage nor thy golden tongue,
    No, nor thy righteousness, shall friend thee more.

Night holds Hippolytus the pure of stain,
    Diana steads him nothing, he must stay;
And Theseus leaves Pirithous in the chain
    The love of comrades cannot take away.

    The truth of the matter is that when the translator of short poems chooses to be literal, most or all of the poetry is lost; and when the translator succeeds in forging a new poetry, most or all of the original author is lost.

    The best practical advice for those of us who must read poems in English translations is to focus intently on the images and dramatic scenes these poems evoke and ask ourselves what there is in them or in their effect on each other that produces each poem's particular electricity. To that extent, we can compensate for a part of our losses, learn something positive about the immense explosive powers of imagery, and rest easy in the secure knowledge that translation even in the mode of the short poem brings us (despite losses) closer to the work itself than not reading it at all. "To a thousand cavils," said Samuel Johnson, "one answer is sufficient; the purpose of a writer is to be read, and the criticism which would destroy the power of pleasing must be blown aside." Johnson was defending Pope's Homer for those marks of its own time and place that make it the great interpretation it is, but Johnson's exhilarating common sense applies equally to the problem we are considering here. Literature is to be read, and the criticism that would destroy the reader's power to make some form of contact with much of the world's great writing must indeed be blown aside.

Maynard Mack

Selected Bibliography

THE ANCIENT WORLD

H. M. Orlinsky, *Ancient Israel*, 2nd ed. (1960), is a short but clearly written outline of the history of Israel up to the return from Babylonian exile. John Boardman, Jasper Griffin, and Oswyn Murray, eds., *The Oxford History of the Classical World* (1986), is a handsomely illustrated survey, by many different specialists, of the whole sweep of classical culture—social, political, literary, artistic, and religious. For the history of Greece, see J. B. Bury, *A History of Greece to the Death of Alexander the Great*, 4th ed., revised by Russell Meiggs (1975), and Thomas R. Martin, *Ancient Greece* (1996)—the latter clearly written especially for the nonspecialist reader. Michael Grant, *History of Rome* (1978), presents a well-illustrated, eminently readable survey. For surveys of Greek and Roman civilization organized according to different types of people and their social experiences, see Jean-Pierre Vernant, ed., *The Greeks* (1995), and Andrea Giardina, ed., *The Romans* (1993). A rich and beautifully illustrated survey of women in Greece and Rome is Elaine Fantham, Helene Foley, Natalie Kampen, Sarah Pomeroy, and Alan Shapiro, eds., *Women in the Classical World* (1994). *Perseus* is a superb interactive CD-ROM program on Greek civilization, with a huge database of texts (in Greek and English), maps, images of sites and artifacts, and a short version of Martin's historical outline (above). Much of what is on the CD-ROM can be found at the excellent Perseus Web site. For a wealth of links to other Web sites on the ancient world, see the University of Michigan's Classics and Mediterranean Archaeology Home Page (this and the Perseus site can easily be located with standard Web search engines).

Aeschylus

D. J. Conacher, *Aeschylus' Oresteia: A Literary Commentary* (1987), is a scene-by-scene (and sometimes line-by-line) commentary addressed as much to Greekless readers as to classical scholars. James Hogan, *A Commentary on the Complete Greek Tragedies: Aeschylus* (1987), contains a line-by-line commentary on Richmond Lattimore's translation of the *Oresteia* (1953). John Herington, *Aeschylus* (1986), deals with the political and religious background of the tragedies and provides a perceptive discussion of the plays (*Oresteia*, pp. 111–56). Oliver Taplin, *Greek Tragedy in Action* (1978), gives a sensitive scene-by-scene discussion of the significance of stage action and spectacle in all three plays. Simon Goldhill, *Aeschylus: The Oresteia* (1992; 2nd ed., 2004), includes a chapter on the trilogy's historical and cultural context and is an excellent guide through the complexities of each play. Froma Zeitlin's *Playing the Other: Gender and Society in Classical Greek Literature* (1996) includes (pp. 87–119) her outstanding essay on the *Oresteia*, "The Dynamics of Misogyny."

Aristophanes

K. J. Dover, *Aristophanic Comedy* (1972), is a general survey of the whole range of Aristophanic comedy. Helpful introductions to the *Lysistrata* are given by Jeffrey Henderson, *Aristophanes' Lysistrata* (1987), pp. xv–xli, and Douglas M. MacDowell, *Aristophanes and Athens: An Introduction to the Plays* (1996), pp. 229–50. Erich Segal, *Oxford Readings in Aristophanes* (1996), includes an excellent selection of essays on various aspects of Aristophanes' drama. See also Kenneth J. Reckford, *Aristophanes' Old-and-New Comedy* (1987), pp. 301–11, and Rosemary M. Harriott, *Aristophanes, Poet and Dramatist* (1986). On gender in the play, see A. M. Bowie, *Aristophanes: Myth, Ritual and Comedy* (1993), pp. 178–204, and Lauren Taaffe, *Aristophanes and Women* (1993), pp. 48–73.

Aristotle

Kenneth McLeish, *Poetics/Aristotle* (1999), is a succinct guide to the argument and its implications. Stephen Halliwell, *The Poetics of Aristotle* (1987), gives a translation and detailed commentary.

Augustine

Peter Brown, *Augustine of Hippo* (1967), is an authoritative and engrossing account of Augustine's career and major works. Warren Thomas Smith, *Augustine, His Life and Thought* (1980), gives a brief and readable overview of his biography, his times, and his intellectual development. Another introduction to Augustine's life and thought, with a substantial discussion of the *Confessions*, is James J. O'Donnell, *Augustine* (1985). Gillian Clark, *Augustine, the Confessions*

(1993), is an excellent short guide to this work, with discussions of various literary and intellectual issues that it raises and particular attention to the historical context. See also Colin Stearnes, *Augustine's Conversion: A Guide to the Argument of Confessions I–IX* (1990); Gary Wills, *Saint Augustine* (1999); and Eleanor Stump and Norman Kretzmann, eds., *The Cambridge Companion to Augustine* (2001).

Catullus
The best general introduction to Catullus, with essential background and perceptive discussion of the poetry, is Charles Martin, *Catullus* (1992). For more detailed but highly readable discussions of contemporary culture and society, Clodia and her circle, and the poems' relation to this context, T. P. Wiseman, *Catullus and His World: A Reappraisal* (1985), is excellent. Two older books are still valuable: A. L. Wheeler, *Catullus and the Traditions of Ancient Poetry* (1934), and E. A. Havelock, *The Lyric Genius of Catullus* (1964). The first puts Catullus in his cultural and literary context; the second translates selected poems and offers a sensitive appreciation of them. Kenneth Quinn, *Catullus: An Interpretation* (1973), gives an interesting if idiosyncratic view of the poetry. An excellent newer discussion is William Fitzgerald, *Catullan Provocations: Lyric Poetry and the Drama of Position* (1995). For a depiction of Catullus as well as Lesbia/Clodia and her circle in a carefully researched historical detective novel, see Steven Saylor, *The Venus Throw* (1995).

The Christian Bible
Recommended reading is Bruce M. Metzger, *The New Testament: Its Background, Growth, and Content* (1965), and the relevant chapters in Robert Alter and Frank Kermode, eds., *The Literary Guide to the Bible* (1987). For a translation with commentary, see *The New Oxford Annotated Bible* (1975), edited by Herbert E. May and Bruce Metzger. *The Oxford Companion to the Bible* (1993), edited by Bruce Metzger and Michael Coogan, is a mine of information on almost any Biblical topic.

Euripides
For a short, general survey of Euripidean drama, see B. M. W. Knox in *The Cambridge History of Classical Literature* (1985), pp. 316–39. Perceptive analyses of *Medea* can be found in Emily A. McDermott, *Euripides' Medea: The Incarnation of Disorder* (1989), and E. Segal, ed., *Euripides: A Collection of Critical Essays* (1968). William Allen, *Euripides: Medea* (2001), is a helpful short guide to the context of the play and to such issues as gender, the relation between Greek and non-Greek in the play, and revenge. Knox, "The *Medea* of Euripides," and P. E. Easterling, "The Infanticide in Euripides' *Medea*," both in *Yale Classical Studies* 24 (1977), will also be helpful to students, as will the introduction to

Donald Mastronarde's edition of the Greek text, *Euripides/Medea* (2002). Helene Foley, *Female Acts in Greek Tragedy* (2001), contains her essay "Tragic Wives: Medea's Divided Self" (pp. 243–71). For essays on Medea in ancient myth, literature, and art and on the modern stage, see James J. Clauss and Sarah Iles Johnston, eds., *Medea* (1997).

Gilgamesh
Andrew George's two-volume *The Babylonian Gilgamesh Epic: Introduction, Critical Edition, and Cuneiform Texts* (2003) is an authoritative new edition and discussion of ancient texts. Jeffrey Tigay, *The Evolution of the Gilgamesh Epic* (1982), examines differences among successive versions of the epic. Benjamin Foster's critical edition, *The Epic of Gilgamesh* (2001), includes a helpful brief introduction, translations of analogous Sumerian and Hittite *Gilgamesh* texts and a Mesopotamian parody of Tablet VIII, four valuable critical essays, and a glossary. More essays and a large bibliography are available in John Maier, ed., *Gilgamesh: A Reader* (1997). Alexander Heidel addresses the importance of *Gilgamesh* for biblical studies in *The Gilgamesh Epic and Old Testament Parallels* (1963), and Malcolm C. Lyons, *The Arabian Epic: Heroic and Oral Story-Telling* (1995), includes references to *Gilgamesh* in his copious notes on shared epic motifs. Useful studies of ancient Near Eastern civilization include Amélie Kuhrt, *The Ancient Near East, c. 3000–330 BC* (1995); Thorkild Jacobsen, *The Treasures of Darkness: A History of Mesopotamian Religion* (1976); and Rivkah Harris, *Gender and Aging in Mesopotamia: The Gilgamesh Epic and Other Ancient Literature* (2000).

The Hebrew Bible
The student will find good background in R. R. Ackroyd and C. F. Evans, eds., *The Cambridge History of the Bible* (1970), vol. 1. The various volumes of *The Anchor Bible* contain modern translations and informative introductions and notes. The volume on the Song of Songs by Marvin Pope (1977) is especially helpful. Full and helpful articles on a great variety of topics can be found in Bruce M. Metzger and Michael D. Coogan, eds., *The Oxford Companion to the Bible* (1993). For Job, see P. Sanders, ed., *Twentieth-Century Interpretations of the Book of Job* (1968), and Harold Bloom, ed., *Modern Critical Interpretations: The Book of Job* (1988). See also Robert Alter and Frank Kermode, eds., *The Literary Guide to the Bible* (1987), and Leland Ryken and Tremper Longman III, eds., *A Complete Literary Guide to the Bible* (1993).

Homer
A sensitive exploration of Homer's vision of human life and the nature of the gods is Jasper Griffin, *Homer on Life and Death* (1980). Mark W. Edwards, *Homer: Poet of the Iliad* (1987),

discusses the oral style and gives a detailed commentary on selected books of the poem, including all of those printed here. Martin Mueller, *The Iliad* (1984), is a highly readable discussion of almost every aspect of the poem, and Seth Schein, *The Mortal Hero: An Introduction to Homer's Iliad* (1987), is an eloquent reading. The psychiatrist Jonathan Shay, in *Achilles in Vietnam: Combat Trauma and the Undoing of Character* (1994), gives a highly interesting discussion of violence and its effects in Homer and in modern warfare, drawing on his work with Vietnam veterans. Basic introductions to the *Odyssey* are Jasper Griffin, *Homer: The Odyssey* (1987), and W. G. Thalmann, *The Odyssey: An Epic of Return* (1992). An excellent companion to the poem is Ralph Hexter, *A Guide to the Odyssey: A Companion to the Translation by Robert Fitzgerald* (1993). Essays covering various aspects of the poem may be found in Charles Segal, *Singers, Heroes, and Gods in the Odyssey* (1994); Seth Schein, *Reading the Odyssey: Selected Interpretive Essays* (1996); and (on women) Beth Cohen, *The Distaff Side: Representing the Female in Homer's Odyssey* (1995). An excellent discussion of gender in the poem is Nancy Felson, *Regarding Penelope: From Character to Poetics* (1994), with further bibliography.

Lucian

An excellent discussion of Lucian's satire and his relation to tradition is R. Bracht Branham, *Unruly Eloquence: Lucian and the Comedy of Traditions* (1989). Aristoula Georgiadou and David Larmour, eds., *Lucian's Science Fiction Novel, True Histories* (1998), gives a detailed commentary on the Greek text; the student will find the introduction especially useful. C. P. Jones, *Culture and Society in Lucian* (1986), examines the question of whether Lucian's art is connected to its surrounding culture or only to the Greek past, and Christopher Robinson, *Lucian and His Influence in Europe* (1979), surveys his effects on later European literature and thought. On the complexities of Lucian's cultural identity, see Simon Swain, *Hellenism and Empire: Language, Classicism, and Power in the Greek World, AD 50–250* (1996), pp. 298–329. On Lucian and cultural identity under the Roman empire, and on his role in controversies involving Erasmus in the Renaissance, see the first two chapters of Simon Goldhill, *Who Needs Greek? Contests in the Cultural History of Hellenism* (2002).

Ovid

Sara Mack, *Ovid* (1988), provides an excellent introduction to all of Ovid's poems for the general reader, with a long chapter on the *Metamorphoses*. A classic treatment of this poem is Brooks Otis, *Ovid as an Epic Poet* (1966; 2nd ed. 1970). G. K. Galinsky, *Ovid's Metamorphoses: An Introduction to the Basic Aspects,*

is also a useful guide. L. P. Wilkinson, *Ovid Recalled* (1955), abridged as *Ovid Surveyed* (1962), gives a comprehensive overview of various aspects of Ovid's poetry. See also Niklas Holzberg, *Ovid: The Poet and His Work* (1997; trans. 2002). For later poets' and artists' uses of Ovid, see the essays collected in Charles Martindale, *Ovid Renewed: Ovidian Influences on Literature and Art from the Middle Ages to the Twentieth Century* (1988). An excellent collection of essays on Ovid's poetry, its historical context, and its reception is Philip Hardie, ed., *The Cambridge Companion to Ovid* (2002).

Petronius

The introduction to *Petronius: The Satyricon* (1977), translated by J. P. Sullivan, will be helpful to the student, as will William Arrowsmith's introduction to his *The Satyricon of Petronius* (1959) and the introduction and notes to *Satyrica* (1996), translated by R. Bracht Branham and Daniel Kinney. J. P. Sullivan, *The Satyricon of Petronius: A Literary Study* (1968), and Niall Slater, *Reading Petronius* (1990), are full-length critical discussions of the work.

Plato

A. E. Taylor, *Plato, the Man and His Work* (1927), is a detailed analysis of the whole corpus of Platonic dialogues. Excellent succinct discussions of various aspects of Plato's writings and thought may be found in Bernard Williams, *Plato* (1999), and Julia Annas, *Plato: A Very Short Introduction* (2003). For an introduction to Socrates' life and thought, see W. K. C. Guthrie, *Socrates* (1971). C. D. C. Reeve, *Socrates in the Apology* (1989), offers a detailed interpretation of the *Apology* and an assessment of Socrates as he is presented there. Thomas G. West, in *Plato's Apology of Socrates* (1979), accompanies his translations with detailed interpretive essays. On Socrates' condemnation and death, see I. F. Stone, *The Trial of Socrates* (1989).

Plautus

George Duckworth, *The Nature of Roman Comedy: A Study in Popular Entertainment* (1952), is a mine of information about the origins, conventions, style, and influence of Roman comedy. The performance and social context of Roman comedy are well discussed by Richard Beacham, *The Roman Theatre and Its Audience* (1992). A good general introduction to Plautus is W. S. Anderson, *Barbarian Play: Plautus' Roman Comedy* (1993). Erich Segal, *Roman Laughter: The Comedy of Plautus*, 2nd ed. (1987), is a classic interpretation with particular reference to the festival setting. David Konstan, *Roman Comedy* (1983), discusses the ideology of the city-state in various plays by Plautus and Terence. On metatheater in Plautus, see Niall Slater, *Plautus in Performance: The Theatre of the Mind* (1985), and Timothy Moore, *The Theater of Plautus: Playing to the Audience* (1998). On slavery in Plautus, see Kathleen McCarthy,

Slaves, Masters and the Art of Authority in Plautine Comedy (2000).

Sappho

Another recent translation of Sappho's poetry, with excellent introduction and notes, is given in Diane Rayor, *Sappho's Lyre: Archaic Lyric and Women Poets of Ancient Greece* (1991). Margaret Williamson, *Sappho's Immortal Daughters* (1995), is a comprehensive introduction to various aspects of the poetry. Accessible surveys from varying points of view may be found in Jane M. Snyder, *The Woman and the Lyre: Women Writers in Classical Greece and Rome* (1989), Richard Jenkyns, *Three Classical Poets: Sappho, Catullus, and Juvenal* (1982), and Anne Burnett, *Three Archaic Poets: Archilochus, Alcaeus, Sappho* (1983). An outstanding assessment of Sappho's position as a woman in Greek society is John J. Winkler, "Double Consciousness in Sappho's Lyrics," in his *The Constraints of Desire: The Anthropology of Sex and Gender in Ancient Greece* (1990). Page duBois, *Sappho Is Burning* (1995), is a challenging discussion of Sappho's poetry as resisting the categories of Western thought. Two collections of essays edited by Ellen Greene, *Reading Sappho: Contemporary Approaches* (1996) and *Re-reading Sappho: Reception and Transmission* (1996), offer a generous sampling of approaches to Sappho's poetry and its later reception.

Sophocles

For a short, general survey of Sophoclean drama, see P. E. Easterling in *The Cambridge History of Classical Literature* (1985), pp. 295–316. B. M. W. Knox, *Oedipus at Thebes* (1957), is a detailed examination of the play in the context of its age; Knox's *The Heroic Temper* (1964) concentrates on the characters of Oedipus, Antigone, Electra, and Philoctetes. Harold Bloom, *Sophocles's Oedipus Rex* (1988), is a well-chosen collection of essays on the play, and Charles Segal, *Oedipus Tyrannus: Tragic Heroism and the Limits of Knowledge* (1993; 2nd, expanded ed., 2001), is an outstanding full-length treatment. Helene Foley, *Female Acts in Greek Tragedy* (2001), contains an essay on Antigone as a moral agent (pp. 172–200). Jean-Pierre Vernant and Pierre Vidal-Naquet, *Myth*

and Tragedy in Ancient Greece (1972; English trans. 1988) contains Vernant's influential essays "Oedipus without the Complex," a critical engagement with Freudian readings, and "Ambiguity and Reversal: On the Enigmatic Structure of *Oedipus Rex*." Mark Griffith's *Antigone/Sophocles* (1999), although an edition meant to guide a reading of the Greek text, contains an excellent and accessible introduction, including a survey of various critical approaches to the play. See also R. P. Winnington-Ingram, *Sophocles: An Interpretation* (1980), pp. 91–149 (*Antigone*) and 150–204 (*Oedipus the King*), and Charles Segal, *Tragedy and Civilization: An Interpretation of Sophocles* (1981), pp. 152–206 (*Antigone*) and 207–48 (*Oedipus the King*). David Seale, *Vision and Stagecraft in Sophocles* (1982), is a stimulating discussion of the themes of sight, blindness, and knowledge in relation to the experience of watching a play.

Virgil

Useful and accessible discussions of basic aspects of the *Aeneid* and of its historical and literary context are W. A. Camps, *An Introduction to Virgil's Aeneid* (1969); Jasper Griffin, *Virgil* (1986); and K. W. Gransden, *Virgil, the Aeneid* (1990; 2nd ed., 2004). Articles on individual books of the poem, and on general topics, may be found in Christine Perkell, ed., *Reading Vergil's Aeneid: An Interpretive Guide* (1999). Peter Levi, *Virgil: His Life and Times* (1998), surveys all of Virgil's poetry with particular attention to contemporary historical events and the poems' relation to Italy (chapters 5–8 are on the *Aeneid*). W. S. Anderson, *The Art of the Aeneid* (1969), is a sensible book-by-book reading of the poem. Brooks Otis, *Virgil: A Study in Civilized Poetry* (1963), and R. O. A. M. Lyne, *Further Voices in Virgil's Aeneid* (1987), are more detailed but readable and influential works of criticism. Valuable collections of essays by various authors are Steele Commager, ed., *Virgil: A Collection of Critical Essays* (1966); Harold Bloom, ed., *Virgil* (1986); and Harold Bloom, ed., *Virgil's Aeneid* (1987). Charles Martindale, ed., *The Cambridge Companion to Virgil* (1997), contains essays on various aspects of Virgil's life and works, including the later reception of the poetry.

THE MIDDLE AGES

An excellent reference work that contains articles on virtually all medieval topics, with bibliographies, is *The Dictionary of the Middle Ages*, 13 vols. (1987). Specific questions about medieval Christian doctrines can be answered by consulting Jaroslav Pelikan, *The Christian Tradition: A History of the Development of Doctrine*, vols. 1–4 (1971–84). C. W. Previté-Orton,

Shorter Cambridge Medieval History, 2 vols. (1952), provides useful information on the relevant historical context of each literary work. An authoritative and readable introduction to social and economic conditions is M. M. Postan, *The Medieval Economy and Society* (1975). Two classic accounts well worth reading are R. W. Southern, *The Making of the Middle Ages*

(1953), and J. W. Huizinga, *The Autumn of the Middle Ages* (first published in 1919, newly translated in 1996).

Beowulf
A good introduction to the Anglo-Saxon period, and to the techniques of Anglo-Saxon poetry, can be found in the essays collected by Malcolm Godden and Michael Lapidge, eds., *The Cambridge Companion to Old English Literature* (1991). *A Beowulf Handbook* (1997), ed. Robert E. Bjork and John D. Niles, provides useful essays about the poem, its context, and its criticism. Other useful collections of essays are R. D. Fulk, ed., *Interpretations of Beowulf* (1991), and Peter S. Baker, ed., *Beowulf: Basic Readings* (1995). An excellent account of the relation of pagan to Christian in the poem is Fred C. Robinson, *Beowulf and the Appositive Style* (1985), and a good treatment of other issues is Edward B. Irving, *Rereading Beowulf* (1989).

Giovanni Boccaccio
Vittore Branca, *Boccaccio: The Man and His Works* (1975), is the standard biography with useful literary commentary; for guides to the *Decameron*, see Giuseppe Mazzotta, *The World at Play in Boccaccio's Decameron* (1986), and David Wallace, *Giovanni Boccaccio: Decameron* (1991).

Geoffrey Chaucer
The standard edition of Chaucer's works is Larry Benson, ed., *The Riverside Chaucer*, 3rd ed. (1987), which provides a fully annotated text in Middle English with a glossary and full introductions and notes. Useful guides to *The Canterbury Tales* are provided in accessible books by Derek A. Pearsall (1985) and Winthrop Wetherbee (1989). More detailed analyses of the three tales selected here may be found in Lee Patterson, *Chaucer and the Subject of History* (1991).

Chrétien de Troyes
A complete translation of *The Story of the Grail*, and of Chrétien's four other romances, can be found in Chrétien de Troyes, *Arthurian Romances*, trans. William W. Kibler and Carleton W. Carroll (1991). Useful criticism on *The Story of the Grail* is provided by Keith Busby, *Chrétien de Troyes, Perceval (Le conte du Grail)* (1993) and Joseph J. Duggan, *Romances of Chrétien de Troyes* (2001). Good introductions to medieval Arthurian literature are W.R.J. Barron, ed., *Arthur of the English* (1999), E. D. Kennedy, ed., *King Arthur: A Casebook* (1996), and Richard Barber, *King Arthur: Hero and Legend* (1986).

Dante Alighieri
Of the many excellent commentaries in English, one of the most complete is in the edition and translation by Charles S. Singleton (1970–75). An excellent commentary on the *Inferno* can be found in the edition and translation by Robert M. Durling and Ronald L. Martinez (1996), who are preparing similar volumes for the rest of the poem. Useful commentaries on individual cantos can also be found in Ricardo Quinones, *Dante* (1979). A rightly celebrated essay on *Inferno* 10, with important comments on the *Comedy* as a whole, is by Erich Auerbach in his *Mimesis*, and illuminating and learned essays by one of the leading English-speaking Dantists are in John Freccero, *Dante: The Poetics of Conversion* (1986). *Dante Studies* is published annually and includes an annotated bibliography.

Everyman
A good collection of medieval English plays, with commentary, is David Bevington, ed., *Medieval Drama* (1975). For discussions of *Everyman*, see Robert Potter, *The English Morality Play* (1975), and the edition, with bibliography, by A. C. Cawley, ed., *Everyman and Medieval Miracle Plays*, revised by Anne Rooney (1993). Guides to drama in the Middle Ages generally are provided by Glynne Wickham, *The Medieval Theatre*, 3rd ed. (1987), and John W. Harris, *Medieval Theatre in Context* (1992).

The Koran
The most informative general introduction to the Koran is the revised edition of *Bell's Introduction to the Qur'ân* (1970). Michael Cook, *Muhammad* (1983), is an excellent brief biography of the Prophet of Islam. Fazlur Rahman, *Major Themes of the Qur'ân* (1980), is a lucid presentation by a Muslim scholar who has taught in the United States for many years of the principal beliefs of Islam as they appear in the Koran. Marilyn R. Waldman, "New Approaches to 'Biblical' Materials in the Qur'ân," *The Muslim World* 75.1 (January 1985): 1–16, gives a good comparison of Joseph in the Koran and the Bible.

Marie de France
A complete translation of the *Lais*, with a helpful introduction and full bibliography, can be found in Glyn S. Burgess and Keith Busby, trans., *The Lais of Marie de France* (1986). A verse translation with commentary is provided by Robert Hanning and Joan Ferrante, *The Lais of Marie de France* (1978).

Medieval Lyrics
Accessible guides to the individual poets and to the development of the lyric within the various languages of medieval Europe can be found in the relevant articles in *The Dictionary of the Middle Ages*, 13 vols., ed. J. P. Strayer (1987). An excellent introduction, with commentary on a number of the poems printed here, is Peter

Dronke, *The Medieval Lyric*, 3rd ed. (1996). Both these works contain suggestions for further reading. A brilliant study that locates Rabbi Ephraim's poem in the context of both Jewish tradition and the Christian massacres of Jews in the eleventh and twelfth centuries is Shalom Spiegel, *The Last Trial* (1979).

Medieval Tales
A good discussion of the *exempla* as a form can be found in F. A. C. Martello and A. G. Rigg, *Medieval Latin: An Introduction and Bibliographical Guide* (1996). Charles Muscatine, *The Old French Fabliaux* (1986), is an informative account.

Sir Gawain and the Green Knight
An accessible edition of the original poem is by J. A. Burrow (1972). Helpful articles, and a full bibliography, are available in Derek Brewer and Jonathan Gibson, eds., *A Companion to the Gawain-Poet* (1997).

The Song of Roland
A scholarly edition, with translation and commentary, is Gerald S. Brault, *The Song of Roland: An Analytical Edition*, 2 vols. (1978). Useful critical discussions are Eugene Vance, *Reading the Song of Roland* (1970), and Robert Francis Cook, *The Sense of the Song of Roland* (1987).

Thorstein the Staff-Struck
A concise general account of the family sagas is Peter Hallberg, trans. Paul Schach, *The Icelandic Saga* (1962). A critical study of structure and organization, with plot summaries, is Theodore M. Andersson, *The Icelandic Family Saga* (1967). Admirable translations of several of the principal sagas are available in the Penguin paperback series.

The Thousand and One Nights
Husain Haddawy, *The Arabian Nights* (1990), is a complete translation of the text of Muhsin Mahdi's critical edition of the Syrian manuscript (1984), and his *Arabian Nights II: Sindbad and Other Popular Stories* (1995) is a selection of tales that were added to it by later authors. The earliest English version of the *Nights*, made from the French of Antoine Galland by an anonymous English translator, has been published in paperback by R. L. Mack as *Arabian Nights' Entertainments* (1995). The nineteenth-century translations by Edward William Lane (1838–42) and Richard Burton (1885–68) were made directly from Arabic but were based on late, heterogeneous manuscripts. Burton's is the better known, but Lane's is closer to the original although it bowdlerizes the erotic scenes. Muhsin Mahdi has published an introduction to his edition entitled simply *The Thousand and One Nights* (1995). Mia Gerhardt's *The Art of Storytelling: A Literary Study of the Thousand and One Nights* (1963) is virtually the only interpretive study of the whole of the *Thousand and One Nights* in English. It contains an excellent discussion of European interest in the work but is less satisfactory for individual stories. Ferial Jabouri Ghazoul, *The Arabian Nights: A Structural Analysis* (1980), focuses on several stories and groups of stories, among them the *Prologue*. She also argues the central importance of the feminine in the *Nights*. Bruno Bettelheim, *The Uses of Enchantment: The Meaning and Importance of Fairy Tales* (1976), includes a brief discussion of Shahrazad in his study of the therapeutic role of fairy tales. Jerome W. Clinton gives a more detailed discussion of this same question in "Madness and Cure in the 1001 Nights," in *Fairy Tales and Society: Illusion, Allusion, Paradigm*, edited by Ruth B. Bottigheimer (1986).

THE RENAISSANCE

Richard L. DeMolen, ed., *The Meaning of Renaissance and Reformation* (1974), is a collection of essays by experts on the Renaissance and Reformation, with maps and illustrations. Eugene Rice with Anthony Grafton, *The Foundations of Early Modern Europe*, 2nd ed. (1994), is the finest introduction to the contexts in which Renaissance or early modern literature was produced. Theodore K. Rabb, *Renaissance Lives: Portrait of au Age* (2000), offers an illuminating perspective on key figures in the period. William Bouwsma, *A Usable Past: Essays in European Cultural History* (1990), especially the chapter "Anxiety and the Formation of Early Modern Culture," also offers illuminating perspectives on the intellectual character of the period. Constance Jordan, *Renaissance Feminism: Literary Texts and Political Models* (1990), is a recommended study of the place of women in history and political thought. William Kerrigan and Gordon Braden, *The Idea of the Renaissance* (1989), offers a helpful and direct analysis of the critical construction of the Renaissance as a concept. Harry Berger Jr., *Second World and Green World: Studies in Renaissance Fiction-Making* (1988), especially the title essay, is a dense but recommended study of the aims of fiction-making.

Ludovico Ariosto
Important work on Ariosto includes Patricia Parker, *Inescapable Romance* (1970), A. Bartlett

Giamatti, *The Earthly Paradise and the Renaissance Epic* (1966), and Robert M. Durling, *The Figure of the Poet in Renaissance Epic* (1965). A more specialized study can be found in Elizabeth J. Bellamy, *Translations of Power* (1992). Edmund Gardner, *Arioso: King of Court Poets* (1906), remains the indispensable work on Ariosto's life and the Ferrarese court. Other useful readings are Elizabeth Chesney, *The Counter-Voyage of Rabelais and Ariosto* (1982), and Robert Griffin, *Ludovico Ariosto* (1974).

Baldassare Castiglione
Students will find valuable and accessible studies of Castiglione in Peter Burke, *The Fortunes of the Courtier: The European Reception of Castiglione's Cortegiano* (1995), and the essays in R. W. Hanning and David Rosand, eds, *Castiglione: The Ideal and the Real in Renaissance Culture* (1983). Of more specialized interest are Harry Berger, Jr., *The Absence of Grace: Sprezzatura and Suspicion in Two Renaissance Courtesy Books* (2000); Virginia Cox, *The Renaissance Dialogue: Literary Dialogue in Its Social and Political Contexts, Castiglione to Galileo* (1992); and Wayne A. Rebhorn, *Courtly Performances* (1978). For an exciting, thorough discussion of Castiglione's broad historical context, see Lauro Martines, *Power and Imagination: City-States in Renaissance Italy* (1979).

Miguel de Cervantes
William Byron, *Cervantes: A Biography* (1978), is thorough. Anthony J. Cascard, *The Cambridge Companion to Cervantes* (2002), is an indispensible guide to Cervantes and his works. Ruth El Saffar, ed., *Critical Essays on Cervantes* (1986), offers interesting essays by eminent scholars. Vladimir Nabokov, *Lectures on Don Quixote* (1983), presents an elegant engagement with Cervantes's fiction. More-technical studies can be found in Henry Higuera, *Eros and Empire: Politics and Christianity in Don Quijote* (1995); Thomas R. Hart, *Cervantes and Ariosto: Renewing Fiction* (1989); Howard Mancing, *The Chivalric World of Don Quijote: Style, Structure, and Narrative Techniques* (1982); Stephen Gilman, *The Novel According to Cervantes* (1980); and Ruth El Saffar, *Distance and Control: A Study in Narrative Technique* (1975).

John Donne
Arthur F. Marotti, *John Donne: Coterie Poet* (1986), and, as editor, *Critical Essays on John Donne* (1994), are recommended. Also helpful are Helen Gardner, ed., *John Donne: A Collection of Critical Essays* (1985), and Pieter Amadeus Fiore, ed., *Just So Much Honor: Essays Commemorating the Four-Hundredth Anniversary of the Birth of John Donne* (1970).

Desiderius Erasmus
Lisa Jardine's *Erasmus, Man of Letters: The Construction of Charisma in Print* (1993) offers a stimulating analysis of Erasmus's career and scholarly image. Cornelius Augustijn, trans. J. C. Grayson, *Erasmus: His Life, Works, and Influence* (1991), is recommended, as is Arthur F. Kinney, *Continental Humanist Poetics* (1989), ch. 2. Johan Huizinga, *Erasmus and the Age of Reformation* (1984), is an informative and interesting biography. Richard DeMolen, *Erasmus of Rotterdam: A Quintennial Symposium* (1971), and Kathleen Williams, eds., *Twentieth-Century Interpretations of "The Praise of Folly"* (1969), contain useful essays. More specialized but valuable is J. M. Coetzee, "Erasmus' Praise of Folly: Rivalry and Madness," *Neophilologus* 76. 1 (Jan. 1992): 1–18.

Lope de Vega
Walter Cohen, *Drama of a Nation: Public Theater and Renaissance England and Spain* (1985), Donald R. Larson, *The Honor Plays of Lope de Vega* (1977), Robert L. Fiore, *Drama and Ethos: Natural-Law Ethics in Spanish Golden Age Theater* (1975), and Edward M. Wilson and Duncan Moir, *The Golden Age: Drama 1492–1700* (1971), present useful and illuminating studies of Lope de Vega's work and its relation to Spanish theater in general. J. B. Hall, *Lope de Vega: Fuenteovejuna* (1985), presents a detailed study of the play. J. H. Elliott's *Imperial Spain 1469–1716* (1963), is an indispensable study of Spanish history and politics.

Niccolò Machiavelli
Peter E. Bondanella focuses on the literary aspects of Machiavelli's works in *Machiavelli and the Art of Renaissance History* (1973). Sebastian De Grazia, *Machiavelli in Hell* (1989), on politics in *The Prince*, contains indexes and a bibliography. J. R. Hale's biography, *Machiavelli and Renaissance Italy* (1972), places Machiavelli in a historical perspective. A political analysis is provided by Anthony Parel in *The Political Calculus: Essays on Machiavelli's Political Philosophy* (1972). Roberto Ridolfi, *The Life of Niccolò Machiavelli* (1963), is still considered the best and most accurate biography. Silvia Ruffo-Fiore, *Niccolò Machiavelli* (1982), is a useful comprehensive guide for the beginning student. Victoria Kahn, *Machiavellian Rhetoric: From the Counter-Reformation to Milton* (1994), and Wayne A. Rebhorn, *Foxes and Lions: Machiavelli's Confidence Men* (1988), are recommended.

John Milton
The standard biography is William Riley Parker, *Milton: A Biography*, 2 vols. (1981). See also Barbara Lewalski, *The Life of John Milton: A Critical Biography* (2001). Annabel Patterson, ed., *John Milton* (1992), and David Quint, *Epic and Empire: Politics and Generic Form from Virgil to Milton* (1993), offer useful studies of Milton. Rewarding essays can also be found in

Re-membering Milton: Essays on the Texts and Traditions (1987), edited by Mary Nyquist and Margaret W. Ferguson. Barbara Kiefer Lewalski, *Paradise Lost and the Rhetoric of Literary Forms* (1985), offers a lucid and comprehensive study of Milton's uses of literary genre. Patricia Parker discusses Milton's suggestive linkage of doubt, the romance form, and Eve in a chapter of *Inescapable Romance* (1975). Stanley Fish directs attention to the role of readers' responses in determining or creating meaning in *Surprised by Sin: The Reader in Paradise Lost* (1967). A. Bartlett Giamatti, *The Earthly Paradise and the Renaissance Epic* (1966), analyzes the "coalescence of classical and Christian material" in the poem. Robert Crosman, *Reading Paradise Lost* (1980), is a helpful introduction for first-time readers of Milton's poem.

Michel de Montaigne
Hugo Friedrich, *Montaigne* (1991), is a careful historical study of the author. David Quint, *Montaigne and the Quality of Mercy* (1999) analyzes the rhetorical structure and political implications of Montaigne's famous essay on the Cannibals. Judith Shklar, *Ordinary Vices* (1984), and Edwin Duval, "Lessons of the New World: Design and Meaning in Montaigne's 'Des Cannibales' (I:31) and 'Des coches' (III:6)," in *Montaigne: Essays in Reading*, ed. Gerard Defaux, *Yale French Studies* 64 (1983): 95–112, provide excellent studies of Montaigne that include, but are not limited to, his New World contexts. Marcel Tetel, *Montaigne*, updated ed. (1990), and Richard Sayce, *The Essays of Montaigne: A Critical Exploration* (1972), are excellent introductions designed for the general reader.

Marguerite de Navarre
P. A. Chilton's justly praised translation of the *Heptameron* (1984) has an excellent introduction. John D. Lyons and Mary B. McKinley, eds., *Critical Tales: New Studies of the Heptameron and Early Modern Culture* (1993), contains useful essays on the *Heptameron*. B. J. Davis, *The Storytellers in Marguerite de Navarre's Heptameron* (1978), presents detailed discussions of the narrators, and Glyn P. Norton, "Narrative Function in the *Heptaméron* Frame-Story," in *La Nouvelle française à la Renaissance* (1981), analyzes the framing narrative. Marcel Tetel, *Marguerite de Navarre's Heptameron: Themes, Language, and Structure* (1973), is meant for the advanced student. Samuel Putnam, *Marguerite de Navarre* (1935), is an informative and readable biography.

Francis Petrarch
Ernest Hatch Wilkins's biography, *Life of Petrarch* (1961), is informative, but tends to take Petrarch's autobiographical writings at face value. In *The Poet as Philosopher* and *In Our*

Image and Likeness (1970), Charles Trinkaus provides general studies of Petrarch and humanism. Robert Durling's introduction to *Petrarch's Lyric Poems* (1976) and Leonard Forster's essays in *The Icy Fire: Five Studies in European Petrarchism* (1969) are outstanding introductions to Petrarch's lyric poetry. Indispensable, if specialized, are Giuseppe Mazzotta, *The Worlds of Petrarch* (1993); Leonard Barkan, *The Gods Made Flesh: Metamorphosis and the Pursuit of Paganism* (1986); Thomas M. Greene, *The Light in Troy: Imitation and Discovery in Renaissance Poetry* (1982); Nancy Vickers, "Diana Described: Scattered Woman and Scattered Rhyme," in *Writing and Sexual Difference*, ed. Elizabeth Abel (1982): 65–79; and John Freccero, "The Fig Tree and the Laurel: Petrarch's Poetics," *Literary Theory / Renaissance Texts*, eds. Patricia Parker and David Quint (1986): 20–32.

François Rabelais
Donald M. Frame, *François Rabelais: A Study* (1977), provides an overview of Rabelais's life, narrative techniques, and themes. Mikhail Bakhtin, *Rabelais and His World* (1968, 1984), is a groundbreaking analysis of the popular festivities that Rabelais draws on in his work. Thomas M. Greene, *Rabelais: A Study in Comic Courage* (1970), provides a concise overview and introduction. Although not meant for the general reader, Edwin M. Duval, *The Design of Rabelais's Pantagruel* (1991), Carla Freccero, *Father Figures: Genealogy and Narrative Structure in Rabelais* (1991), and Walter Stephens, *Giants in Those Days: Folklore, Ancient History, and Nationalism* (1989), are rewarding studies. Elizabeth Chesney Zegura and Marcel Tetel, *Rabelais Revisited* (1990), offers a good general introduction.

William Shakespeare
Anthony Burgess, *Shakespeare* (1970), is an informed and imaginative biography. William Schoenbaum, *William Shakespeare: A Compact Documentary Life* (1977), is the standard reference. On the theatrical companies and players, Muriel Bradbrook, *The Rise of the Common Player* (1964), and Andrew Gurr, *The Shakespearean Stage, 1574–1642*, 3rd ed. (1992), are recommended. *William Shakespeare's "Hamlet"* (1986), ed. Harold Bloom, contains some unconventional critical approaches. A biography placing Shakespeare in his social context is M. C. Bradbrook, *Shakespeare the Poet in His World* (1978), while E. K. Chambers, *William Shakespeare, A Study of Facts and Problems*, 2 vols. (1930), is considered the most fully documented biography. Paul Arthur Cantor, *Shakespeare, "Hamlet"* (1989), is an in-depth study of the tragedy. Arthur F. Kinney, *Hamlet: New Critical Essays* (2002), offers a useful guide.

Valuable studies are to be found in Maynard Mack, "The World of *Hamlet*," *Yale Review* 41 (1952); Harry Levin, *The Question of "Hamlet"* (1959); and Janet Adelman, *Suffocating Mothers* (1992).

Travel and Discovery
The bibliography on European travel and encounters with the New World is extensive and varied. Good starting points include Rebecca Ann Bach, *Colonial Transformations: The Cultural Production of the New Atlantic World, 1580–1640* (2001); Nicholas Canny, *The Origins of Empire* (1998); Carlo M. Cipollo, *Sails and Empires: Technological Innovation and the Early Phases of European Expansion, 1400–1700* (1965); Philip D. Curtin, *Cross-Cultural Trade in World History* (1984); J. H. Elliott, *The Old World and the New, 1492–1650* (1970); Jack Goody, *The East in the West* (1996); Stephen Greenblatt, *Marvellous Possessions* (1991); Anthony Pagden, *European Encounters with the New World* (1992); John Thornton, *Africa and Africans in the Making of the Atlantic World, 1400–1680* (1992); and Tzvetan Todorov, *The Conquest of America* (1984).

Beowulf: From BEOWULF: A NEW PROSE TRANSLATION, translated by E. Talbot Donaldson. Translation copyright © 1966 by W. W. Norton & Company, Inc. Reprinted by permission of W. W. Norton & Company, Inc.

Francesco Berni: From INTRODUCTION TO ITALIAN POETRY, edited by Luciano Rebay. Copyright © 1969 by Dover Publications, Inc. Used by permission of Dover Publications, Inc.

Bertran de Born: *In Praise of War* ("I love the joyful time of Easter") from THE LYRICS OF THE TROUBADOURS AND TROUVÈRES by Frederick Goldin. Copyright © 1973 by Frederick Goldin. Reprinted by permission of Doubleday, a division of Bantam Doubleday Dell Publishing Group, Inc.

Giovanni Boccaccio: Selections from THE DECAMERON by Giovanni Boccaccio, translated by G. H. McWilliam (Penguin Classics 1972, Second Edition 1995). Copyright © 1972, 1995 by G. H. McWilliam. Reproduced by permission of Penguin Books, Ltd.

Bartolomé de las Casas: From A SHORT ACCOUNT OF THE DESTRUCTION OF THE INDIES, edited by Nigel Griffin, introduction by Anthony Pagden (Penguin Classics, 1992). The translation and notes copyright © 1992 by Nigel Griffin. Introduction copyright © 1992 by Anthony Pagden. Used by permission of Penguin Group (UK).

Baldessare Castiglione: Excerpt from THE BOOK OF THE COURTIER by Baldesar Castiglione, illus., edited by Edgar Mayhew. Copyright © 1959 by Charles S. Singleton and Edgar de N. Mayhew. Used by permission of Doubleday, a division of Bantam Doubleday Dell Publishing Group, Inc.

Catullus: Selections from POEMS OF CATULLUS, translated by Charles Martin (pp. 4, 7, 10, 14, 51, 59, 107, 109, 112–13, 120, 122–24, 146). Copyright © 1990. Reprinted by permission of Johns Hopkins University Press.

Guido Cavalcanti: *An Encounter* ("Once within a little grove a shepherdess I spied") from LYRICS OF THE MIDDLE AGES: AN ANTHOLOGY, translated by James J. Wilhelm. Reprinted by permission of Garland Press.

Miguel de Cervantes: Excerpts from DON QUIXOTE by Miguel de Cervantes Saavedra, translated by Samuel Putnam. Translation copyright © 1949 by The Viking Press, Inc. Used by permission of Viking Penguin, a division of Penguin Putnam, Inc.

Charles d'Orléans: *Balade* ("If you wish to sell your kisses") from THE FRENCH CHANSONS OF CHARLES D'ORLÉANS, edited and translated by Sarah Spence. Reprinted by permission of Garland Press.

Geoffrey Chaucer: *Prologue, The Prologue to the Miller's Tale, The Miller's Tale, The Prologue to the Pardoner's Tale, The Pardoner's Tale, The Prologue to the Wife of Bath's Tale, The Wife of Bath's Tale* from THE PORTABLE CHAUCER by Theodore Morrison. Copyright © 1949, 1975, renewed © 1977 by Theodore Morrison. Reprinted by permission of Viking Penguin, a division of Penguin Putnam, Inc.

Chrétien de Troyes: *Perceval, or the Story of the Grail*, translation copyright © 1957 by Random House, Inc. from MEDIEVAL ROMANCES, translated and edited by Roger S. Loomis and Laura H. Loomis. Used by permission of Modern Library, a division of Random House, Inc.

The Christian Bible: The New Testament: From Luke 2, Luke 15, Matthew 5–7, Matthew 13, and Matthew 26–28, from THE FOUR GOSPELS AND THE REVELATION by Richard Lattimore. Copyright © 1979 by Richard Lattimore. Reprinted by permission of Farrar, Straus, and Giroux, LLC.

Christine de Pizan: From SELECTED WRITINGS OF CHRISTINE DE PIZAN, A NORTON CRITICAL EDITION, edited and translated by Renate Blumenfeld-Kosinski. Copyright © 1997 by W. W. Norton & Company, Inc. Used by permission of W. W. Norton & Company, Inc.

Hernán Cortés: From HERNANDO CORTÉS: FIVE LETTERS, 1519–1526, translated by J. Bayard Morris. Copyright © 1969, 1991. All rights reserved. Used by permission of W. W. Norton & Company, Inc.

Dafydd ap Gwilym: *The Fox* ("Yesterday was I, sure of purpose") from DAFYDD AP GWILYM: THE POEMS. Translation and commentary by Richard Morgan Loomis. Reprinted by permission of the publisher, the Center for Medieval and Early Renaissance Studies, SUNY Binghamton.

Dante Alighieri: *Love and Poetry* ("Guido, I wish that you and Lapo and I") from LYRICS OF THE MIDDLE AGES: AN ANTHOLOGY, translated by James J. Wilhelm. Reprinted by permission of Garland Press. *Sonnet* ("Love and the gentle heart are one thing") from DANTE ALIGHIERI/VITA NUOVA, Italian text with facing English translation by Dino S. Cervigni and Edward Vasta. Copyright © 1995 by University of Notre Dame Press. Used by permission of the publisher. From THE DIVINE COMEDY OF DANTE ALIGHIERI: INFERNO, PURGATORIO, PARADISO, translated by Mark Musa: Copyright © 1971 by Indiana University Press. Used by permission of Indiana University Press: Bloomington and Indianapolis.

Théodore-Agrippa d'Aubigné: From EUROPEAN METAPHYSICAL POETRY, edited by Frank J. Warnke. Copyright © 1961 by Yale University Press. Copyright © 1974 by Frank J. Warnke. Used by permission of Yale University Press.

Rabbi Ephraim ben Jacob: *The Sacrifice of Issac*, excerpt from THE LAST TRIAL: ON THE LEGENDS AND LORE OF THE COMMAND TO ABRAHAM TO OFFER ISAAC AS A SACRIFICE by Shalom Spiegel, translated with an introduction by Judah Goldin (Woodstock, VT: Jewish Lights Publishing, 1993). Permission granted by Jewish Lights Publishing, P.O. Box 237, Woodstock, VT 05091.

Desiderius Erasmus: *The Praise of Folly* from DESIDERIUS ERASMUS: THE PRAISE OF FOLLY, translated by Clarence H. Miller. Reprinted by permission of the publisher, Yale University Press.

Euripides: *Medea* from THREE GREAT PLAYS OF EURIPIDES by Euripides and Rex Warner, translated by Rex Warner. Translation copyright © 1958, renewed 1986 by Rex Warner. First published by Chatto & Windus. Used by permission of Dutton Signet, a division of Penguin Putnam, Inc., and Random House UK Ltd.

Everyman: Modernized text by E. Talbot Donaldson. Copyright © 1962 by W. W. Norton & Company, Inc. and renewed 1990 by W. W. Norton & Company, Inc. Reprinted by permission of W. W. Norton & Company, Inc.

Four Fabliaux: Translations of *The Butcher of Abbeville*, *The Three Hunchbacks*, *The Wild Dream*, and *The Ring That Controlled Erections* by Ned Dubin. Copyright by Ned Dubin. Reprinted by permission of the translator.

Veronica Franco: *Capitolo 13 [A challenge to a lover who has offended her]* from POEMS AND SELECTED LETTERS BY VERONICA FRANCO, edited and translated by A. R. Jones and M. F. Rosenthal. Copyright © 1998. Used by permission of the University of Chicago Press.

Gilgamesh: From THE EPIC OF GILGAMESH, translated by Benjamin R. Foster. Copyright © 2001 by W. W. Norton & Company, Inc. Reprinted by permission of W. W. Norton & Company, Inc. GILGAMESH: A NEW ENGLISH VERSION by Stephen Mitchell. Copyright © 2004 by Stephen Mitchell. Reprinted by permission of The Free Press, a division of Simon and Schuster Adult Publishing Group. All rights reserved.

Guillaume de Mailly: From MEDIEVAL MARRIAGE SERMONS: MASS COMMUNICATION IN A CULTURE WITHOUT PRINT, edited by D. L. D'Avray. Copyright © 2001. Used by permission of Oxford University Press.

Guido Guinizzelli: *Love and Nobility* ("Love always repairs to the noble heart") from LYRICS OF THE MIDDLE AGES: AN ANTHOLOGY, translated by James J. Wilhelm. Reprinted by permission of Garland Press.

Hadewijch of Brabant: *The Cult of Love* ("The birds have long been silent") from THE MEDIEVAL LYRIC, THIRD EDITION, by Peter Dronke (Cambridge: D. S. Brewer, 1996). Reprinted by permission of the publisher.

The Hebrew Bible: From GENESIS: TRANSLATION AND COMMENTARY, translated by Robert Alter. Copyright © 1996 by Robert Alter. From *Exodus*, from THE FIVE BOOKS OF MOSES: A TRANSLATION WITH COMMENTARY by Robert Alter. Copyright © 2004 by Robert Alter. From THE BOOK OF JOB, translated by Raymond P. Scheindlin. Copyright © 1998 Raymond P. Scheindlin. Used by permission of W. W. Norton & Company, Inc.

Heinrich von Morungen: *The Wound of Love* ("She has wounded me") from THE MEDIEVAL LYRIC, THIRD EDITION, by Peter Dronke (Cambridge: D. S. Brewer, 1996). Reprinted by permission of the publisher.

Heloise: From THE LETTERS OF ABELARD AND HELOISE, translated by Betty Radice. Copyright © 1974 by Betty Radice. Used by permission of Penguin Group (UK).

Herodotus: From HERODOTUS: THE HISTORIES, A NORTON CRITICAL EDITION, edited by Walter Blanco and Jennifer T. Roberts, translated by Walter Blanco. Copyright © 1992 by W. W. Norton & Company, Inc. Used by permission of W. W. Norton & Company, Inc.

Index